# BOOKS FOR COLLEGE LIBRARIES

# BOOKS
# FOR COLLEGE
# LIBRARIES

A CORE COLLECTION OF 50,000 TITLES

*Third edition*

A project of the Association of College and Research Libraries

Volume 4
Social Sciences

American Library Association
*Chicago and London 1988*

Preliminary pages composed by Impressions, Inc.,
in Times Roman on a Penta-driven
Autologic APS-$\mu$5
Phototypesetting system

Text pages composed by Logidec, Inc., in Times Roman on an
APS-5 digital typesetter

Printed on 50 lb. Glatfelter B-16, a pH neutral stock,
and bound in Roxite B-grade cloth by
Edwards Brothers.

The paper used in this publication meets the minimum
requirements of American National Standard for Information
Sciences—Permanence of Paper for Printed Library Materials,
ANSI Z39.48-1984.

**Library of Congress Cataloging-in-Publication Data**

Books for college libraries.

"A project of the Association of College and Research
Libraries."

Contents: v. 1. Humanities—v. 2. Language
and literature—v. 3. History—[etc.]
1. Libraries, University and college—Book
lists. 2. Bibliography—Best books. I. Association of
College and Research Libraries.
Z1039.C65B67   1988        025.2′1877        88-16714
ISBN 0-8389-3357-2 (v. 1)
ISBN 0-8389-3356-4 (v. 2)
ISBN 0-8389-3355-6 (v. 3)
ISBN 0-8389-3354-8 (v. 4)
ISBN 0-8389-3358-0 (v. 5)
ISBN 0-8389-3359-9 (v. 6)

# BOOKS FOR COLLEGE LIBRARIES

# Volumes 1–6    Contents

**Vol. 1    HUMANITIES**

A   General Works
B–BD, BH–BJ   Philosophy
BL–BX   Religion. Mythology
M–MT   Music
N–NX   Fine Arts

**Vol. 2    LANGUAGE AND LITERATURE**

P   Language and Literature: General
PA   Classical Languages and Literatures
PB–PH   Modern European Languages. Slavic Languages and Literatures
PJ–PL   Oriental Languages and Literatures
PN   Literature: General and Comparative
PQ   Romance Literatures: French, Italian, Spanish, Portuguese
PR   English Literature
PS   American Literature
PT   German, Dutch, and Scandinavian Literatures

**Vol. 3    HISTORY**

C   Auxiliary Sciences of History
CB   History of Civilization and Culture
CC–CN   Archaeology. Minor Historical Sciences
CR–CT   Heraldry. Genealogy. General Biography
D   History: General. Historiography
DA–DR   Europe
DS   Asia
DT   Africa
DU–DX   Australia. New Zealand. Oceania
E–F   The Americas

**Vol. 4    SOCIAL SCIENCES**

G–GF   Geography. Oceanography. Human Ecology
GN   Anthropology. Ethnology. Archaeology

GR–GT   Folklore. Customs. Costume
GV   Recreation. Physical Training. Sports. Dance
H–HA   Social Sciences: General. Statistics
HB–HJ   Economics. Population
HM–HV   Sociology. Social History. Social Pathology
HX   Socialism. Communism. Anarchism
J   Political Science
K   Law
L   Education

**Vol. 5    PSYCHOLOGY. SCIENCE. TECHNOLOGY. BIBLIOGRAPHY**

BF   Psychology
Q–QA   Science. Mathematics. Computer Science
QB–QE   Physical Sciences: Astronomy, Physics, Meteorology, Chemistry, Geology
QH–QR   Natural Sciences: Biology, Botany, Zoology, Anatomy, Physiology, Bacteriology
R   Medicine. Psychiatry. Nursing
S   Agriculture. Conservation
T   Technology. Engineering
TR   Photography
TS–TX   Manufactures. Crafts. Home Economics
U–V   Military Science. Naval Science
Z   Book Industries. Bibliography. Library Science

**Vol. 6    INDEXES**

Author
Title
Subject

# Volume 4 Contents


Introduction vii
Acknowledgments xi

**G–GF GEOGRAPHY. OCEANOGRAPHY. HUMAN ECOLOGY 1**
- G–GA Geography: General. Mathematical Geography. Cartography 1
- GB–GC Physical Geography. Oceanography 13
- GF Human Ecology. Anthropogeography 18

**GN ANTHROPOLOGY. ETHNOLOGY. ARCHAEOLOGY 21**

**GR–GT FOLKLORE. CUSTOMS. COSTUME 38**

**GV RECREATION. PHYSICAL TRAINING. SPORTS. GAMES. DANCE 45**

**H–HA SOCIAL SCIENCES: GENERAL. STATISTICS 61**

**HB–HJ ECONOMICS 65**
- HB Economic Theory 65
- HB849–3700 Population. Demography 79
- HB3711–3840 Business Cycles. Economic Fluctuations. Forecasting 86
- HC Economic History and Conditions 86
- HC95–407 Economic History: North America. Latin America. Europe 93
- HC410–1085 Economic History: Asia. Arab Countries. Africa. Australia. Oceania 121
- HD19–91 Production 131
- HD101–2210 Land. Agriculture 139
- HD2321–4730 Industry 149
- HD4801–6940 Labor: Unions 153
- HD6951–8943 Labor: Sociology 170
- HD9000–9999 Special Industries and Trades 184
- HE Transportation. Communication 194
- HF1–4040 Commerce 205
- HF5000–6191 Business 213
- HG Finance 222
- HJ Public Finance 232

**HM–HV SOCIOLOGY 237**
- HM Sociology: Theory. Social Psychology 237
- HN Social History and Conditions. Problems. Reform 252
- HQ Family. Marriage. Children. Women 272
- HS Associations. Societies 306
- HT Communities. Classes. Races 316
- HV1–5840 Social Pathology. Social Welfare 320
- HV6001–9920 Criminology 331

**HX SOCIALISM. COMMUNISM. ANARCHISM 344**

**J POLITICAL SCIENCE 357**
- JC Political Theory. The State 362
- JF Constitutional History and Administration: General. Comparative 379
- JK United States 383
- JK511–1599 Branches of Government 390
- JK1711–2246 Politics. Civil Rights 396
- JK2251–2391 Political Parties 400
- JK2403–9600 State Government 404
- JL Canada. Latin America 406
- JN Europe 410
- JQ Asia. Africa. Australia. New Zealand. Oceania 426
- JS Local Government 433
- JV Colonies. Imperialism. Emigration. Immigration 436
- JX International Law. International Relations. International Organization 439

**K LAW 458**
- KB Ancient Law. Theocratic Systems 460
- KD–KE United Kingdom. Anglo-American Law. Common Law. Canada 460

| | | |
|---|---|---|
| KF | United States | 462 |
| KF4501–5130 | Constitutional Law | 471 |
| KF8700–9075 | Courts. Procedure | 480 |
| KF9201–9760 | Criminal Law. Criminal Procedure | 483 |
| KJ–KT | Law of Other Countries | 486 |
| KJ–KM | Europe | 486 |
| KP–KQ | Asia | 487 |
| KR | Africa | 487 |

## L   EDUCATION   488

| | | |
|---|---|---|
| LA | History of Education | 488 |
| LB | Theory and Practice of Education. Teaching | 499 |
| LB1051–1139 | Educational Psychology. Child Study | 507 |
| LB1140–1695 | Preschool, Elementary, Secondary Education | 510 |
| LB1705–2278 | Teacher Education and Training | 515 |
| LB2300–2411 | Higher Education | 517 |
| LB2801–3095 | School Administration. Organization | 521 |
| LC | Special Aspects of Education | 526 |
| LC1390–5163 | Education of Special Classes of Persons | 531 |
| LD–LT | Individual Institutions. Textbooks | 539 |

# Introduction

BOOKS FOR COLLEGE LIBRARIES (BCL3) presents a third recommended core collection for undergraduate libraries in full awareness of the tensions and paradoxes implicit in such list making. There is the pull between ideals of excellence and sufficient coverage of all subjects. There is the balance to be weighed among subjects. There are the rival temptations to identify the basic with the time tested and to equate the important with the new. There is the risk of ranking with the obsolete the merely temporary victims of scholarly fashion. There is the certainty that new definitive works will be published just as the selection closes.

That BCL3 exists supposes some resolution of these problems. A final paradox remains: BCL3 can fully succeed only by failing. It would be disastrous should the collection it suggests serve perfectly to ratify the finished work of the book selection in any library. Some inclusions and some omissions should displease everyone; for on-going professional questioning and the search for individual library answers remain as basic to collection development as basic book lists.

In overall plan and appearance, BCL3 is much the same as BCL2 (1975). The division into five volumes takes the same liberties with Library of Congress classification to provide coherent subject groups and volumes similar in size. Individual entries contain the same elements of full cataloging and classification information; and within volumes, entries are arranged in exact call number order.

BCL3 also exists as a database to allow further development of formats alternative to print. An electronic tape version will be made available. Since BCL2, online catalogs and reference databases have become familiar library tools. The provision of BCL3 in searchable form is thus important; and it may add possible uses of the list within larger libraries—easy identification of key titles in very large online catalogs, for instance.

## HISTORY

The first bibliography to bear this title was published in 1967 as a replacement for Charles B. Shaw's *List of Books for College Libraries* (1931). The origin of BCL1 was in the University of California's New Campuses Program (1961–1964), which also made use of other compilations such as the published catalog of Harvard's Lamont Library (1953) and the shelflist of the undergraduate library of the University of Michigan. The 1963 cut-off date for BCL1 titles deliberately coincided with the 1964 beginning of *Choice*, whose current reviews for academic libraries were foreseen as a complementary, on-going revision and supplement. Such a role proved impossible, however, even for so comprehensive a journal as *Choice* with its 6,600 reviews a year and its retrospective evaluation of perhaps another 1,000 titles in topical monthly bibliographic essays. Periodic reassessments that could include categories of material not usually reviewed by *Choice* (revisions, fiction, works published abroad, for instance) seemed still an essential aid in college library collection development. BCL2 appeared in 1975; work on BCL3 began in late 1985.

## SIZE AND SCOPE: STANDARDS, LIBRARIES AND BOOK LISTS

The number of books of which college libraries need potentially to be aware continues its relentless growth. In the years from the Shaw list to BCL1, total annual United States book output averaged slightly more than 11,500 volumes. Between the cut-off dates for BCL1 and BCL2, that figure (revised to show titles, a lesser number) was just under 32,000. Since the 1973 BCL2 cut-off, the annual average has been 41,000.[1] Given such increase, the task of book selectors would be challenging enough, even had the growth of buildings and book budgets characteristic of the late 1960s and early 1970s continued. By the time BCL2 was published, however, the rate of academic library book acquisitions had begun to fall. This downward trend continues, and it makes careful title selection ever more vital, especially for the small library.[2]

When BCL1 was published, the already outdated 1959 standards for college libraries called for a minimum undergraduate collection of only 50,000 titles; BCL1 recommended 53,400. BCL2 and the 1975 revision of those standards appeared in the same year. The new standards set out a formula whose add-on stipulations plus a starting figure of 85,000 raised basic requirements for even very small institutions to 100,000. The 1970 proposal for BCL2 called for a list of 40,000 titles. The thinking behind this lower figure may be explained by a published study of 1977 library

[1] *Bowker Annual of Library & Book Trade Information.* New York: Bowker. 26th ed., 1981; 32nd ed., 1987.

[2] "Three Years of Change in College and University Libraries, Prepared by the National Center for Education Statistics, Washington, D.C." *College & Research Libraries News* 45 (July/August 1984): 359–361.

statistics against the 1975 standards. This analysis found that 52 percent of all undergraduate libraries still reported fewer than 100,000 volumes and that 55 percent of private undergraduate libraries held even fewer than the "starter" figure of 85,000.[3] A very brief basic list might thus serve rather than intimidate the many libraries still far below standard.

The college library standards were revised again in 1985, just as work on BCL3 began.[4] The same formula (Standard 2.2, Formula A) was recommended. Applying it to a very small hypothetical college of 100 faculty and 1,000 students pursuing majors in only 10 fields of study yields a basic book requirement of 104,000 volumes. BCL3 suggests about half that number, hoping again to pause somewhere between usefulness and utopia. Very recent figures show that the average book expenditures for academic libraries in 26 U.S. states fall below the figure that would be necessary to meet the median annual growth rate of our hypothetical library, also set by the 1985 standards.[5]

In scope, the focus of BCL3 remains the traditionally book-using disciplines. Contributors were asked to keep in mind an imaginary college or small university that concentrates on the customary liberal arts and sciences curriculum but also offers work at the undergraduate level in business, computer science, engineering, and the health sciences. The proportions of the broad subject groupings by volume have remained roughly constant through the three BCL editions. (See Table 1.) There have been steady decreases in the humanities and literature allocations, however, very slightly offset by increased use of single-entry "complete works" citations that include large numbers of titles.

These changes have come about despite editorial quotas candidly designed to minimize them. Sharp

[3]Ray L. Carpenter, "College Libraries: A Comparative Analysis in Terms of the ACRL Standards," *College and Research Libraries* 42 (January 1981): 7–18.

[4]"Standards for College Libraries, 1986, Prepared by the College Library Standards Committee, Jacquelyn M. Morris, chair," *College & Research Libraries News* 47 (March 1986): 189–200.

[5]*Bowker Annual of Library & Book Trade Information.* 32nd ed. New York: Bowker, 1987. The preceding calculation by the BCL editor is based on figures given in the *Bowker Annual* using the formula in the standards cited in note 4.

difficulties confront both BCL editors and librarians juggling hopes for lasting value, necessities for current coverage, and the certainties of obsolescence. Some of the growth in Volume 5 is attributable to a marked increase in its bibliography component, which serves all subjects; but it may be well to repeat, with reference both to Volume 4 and to Volume 5, a statement from my BCL2 introduction that "Perhaps only those works already sufficiently outdated to be ranked as history may safely be included in a 'basic' collection." Despite their increases, both volumes remain brief in comparison with the volume of publication.

As to those titles constituting the rest of the minimal 104,000 requirement but not named in BCL3, much of any collection must respond uniquely to the demands of individual and current curricula. But some, it is to be hoped, will continue to consist of those works, especially belles lettres, not subject to cumulation and replacement by current scholarship. These are often difficult to continue to justify in lists which though "basic" cannot remain immune to shifts in academic enthusiasms.

Across these proportionate subject representations, the focus remains the undergraduate user of the undergraduate library. Both are protean concepts, but they permit some limitation, for instance almost wholly to works in English except for dictionaries and editions chosen to support foreign-language study. With the exception of some of the more basic surveys among "annual reviews" and some serial reference works, the limitation is not only to print but, further, to monographs. There is a need for college-level model collections of periodicals and of nonprint material, but this project does not address it. Still further to define the print universe, BCL3 contributors were asked not to recommend classroom texts unless exceptional, especially for their bibliographies. Volumes of previously published works are seldom listed except for literary anthologies which, together with their indexes, received special consideration in this edition. In-print availability was not considered an important factor.

## CONTRIBUTORS AND WORKING MATERIALS

BCL3 was from the beginning designed as a two-stage selection process and there were two distinct sets

Table 1. Distribution of Titles by Volume. (In percentages.)

| Volumes & Subjects | BCL1 | BCL2 | BCL3 |
|---|---|---|---|
| v. 1 (Humanities) | 16.4 | 15.1 | 13.6 |
| v. 2 (Language & Literature) | 32.2 | 30.0 | 28.4 |
| v. 3 (History) | 18.7 | 19.7 | 18.8 |
| v. 4 (Social Sciences) | 20.8 | 21.2 | 22.2 |
| v. 5 (Psychology, Science, Technology, Bibliography) | 11.9 | 14.0 | 17.0 |

of contributors. The first-round team numbered more than 400 college faculty members and about 50 academic reference librarians who made the reference selections. The second group consisted of 64 academic librarian referees, picked for their combination of subject specialization and collection development skills. The librarian referees were asked to review broader subject areas than their faculty counterparts with the intent of adding a wider perspective to help assure the overall coverage and balance to the collection.

Virtually all of the first-round contributors and about half of the second-round referees are *Choice* reviewers. They were selected for excellence, needed subject coverage, altruism (all served unpaid), and availability at the crucial time. (A few sabbaticals were much regretted in the BCL office.) Contributors were not selected with statistical games in mind, but it is an interesting if incidental function of the nature of the *Choice* reviewer pool that they prove a nationally representative lot. They come from 265 institutions in 44 states. The 10 states with the most academic institutions provide 8 of the 10 largest contributor groups. Institutions are divided between public, including federal (145) and private (120), with a mix of small and large from each sector. There are 10 representatives of 2-year campuses. There are 134 women. There are 15 Canadian and 2 British contributors.

As working materials, the round-one contributors received pages from BCL2 (latest titles 1973) and selected *Choice* review cards (1972 through 1985). Approximately 60,000 of some 85,000 reviews published in those years were distributed. Contributors were asked to assign one of four rankings to each title; they were also urged to recommend any other titles they felt essential to undergraduate work in their fields. Many did so. Assignments, some of which overlapped, ranged from 25 to 600 titles.

Preparation of 450 packets of working lists involved the fascinating task of reconciling various assumptions about the organization of knowledge. It was necessary to "deconstruct" and rearrange the LC-classed BCL2 and the subject organization of *Choice* to match the convictions of academics as to just what constituted the definitions and boundaries of their subjects.

## COMPILATION AND REVIEW

Working list packets came back displaying varying neatness, erudition, zeal, and attention to editorial instructions and deadlines. A very few were reassigned; most were extremely well done and miraculously on time. All titles rated "essential" (and some lesser ratings, depending on subject coverage and the rigor of contributor selectivity) were requested, by LC card number if possible, from the Utlas database. (Utlas, the Canadian bibliographic utility, had previously been

selected as the vendor to house the BCL3 database while the collection was being compiled.)

As lists came in and major blocks of LC classification were judged to be reasonably complete, Utlas was asked to produce provisional catalogs in LC class order, showing complete catalog records. These catalogs, after review by the editor, were divided among the second-round referees, whose assignments typically included the work of several first-round contributors. Referees were asked to assess overall quality and suitability of the selections, coverage of the various aspects of a field, and compliance with numerical quotas. The editor's review included the making and insertion of page headings and further observations of (and occasional interventions in) rival views of knowledge as the academic visions of round one were once more refracted through the prism, the worldview of LC classification. A second set of provisional catalogs, reviewed by the editor's assistant, incorporated referee suggestions and the page headings for a final check before typesetting.

## PRESENTATION: HEADINGS, ENTRIES, AND ARRANGEMENT

Page headings are phrased to outline LC classification, to gloss the sometimes very miscellaneous contents of the sections they head, and to indicate the method of arrangement of some special sequences. The printed BCL3 entries contain conventionally complete cataloging and classification information, but not every element of a full LC MARC record. Among notes, only the general (MARC tag 500) are printed; cross-reference and authority information tagged in the 800s is omitted. Those entries for items retained from BCL2 in exactly the same version carry a special symbol, a heavy dot (.) preceding the item number. Entries are sequentially numbered within each volume. The cataloging in some of the entries made by contributors to the Utlas database is less full than the original LC cataloging; some entries vary in other ways.

Database response to titles requested for the collection displayed significant changes since the compilation of BCL2. During that project, both LC MARC and electronic cataloging and bibliographic utilities were new. Nearly two-thirds of BCL2 entries had to be converted especially for that project. BCL3 is in some ways the victim of the success of such cataloging enterprises. There are now many versions of catalog records, especially for pre-1968 titles. These offer varying degrees of adoption of AACR2 and equally various and often unsignalled states of adherence to LC classification, to say nothing of the range of simple cataloging and typing skills. It is therefore impossible to repeat here the certainties of the BCL2 Introduction about the use of LC cataloging and classification, although preference was certainly for LC records. Call numbers completed or assigned by BCL are identified with "x" as the final character, but there are numbers not so flagged that are not LC assignments. BCL3 is designed as a book selection guide, however, not as an exemplar of either cataloging or classification.

Arrangement has been stated to be by LC call number; but some catalog records carry more than one number, some sections of LC classification are being redeveloped, and some allow alternate treatments. BCL3's editor, therefore, had decisions to make. In all volumes, the existence of new LC sequences is signposted with cross-references. Individual subject classification of titles published in series was preferred to numerical gatherings within series. For Volume 2, alternate national literature numbers were selected or created in preference to PZ3 and PZ4 for fiction. Works by and about individual Canadian, Caribbean, African, South Asian, and Australasian authors writing in English have been pulled from the PR4000–6076 sequence and united with the general historical and critical material on those literatures in the PR9000s. Volume 5 displays the decision to keep most subject bibliography in class Z.

## INDEXES

The computer-made Author Index lists personal and institutional names of writers, editors, compilers, translators, sponsoring bodies, and others identified in the numbered "tracings" that bear roman numerals at the ends of entries. The Title Index, also machine generated, lists both uniform and title page titles from the printed entries, including nondistinctive titles and adding variant titles if traced. Because of the use of many "complete works" entries, many famous and highly recommended titles, especially novels, are absent from this index though present by implication in the list. References in the Author and Title indexes are to the sequential numbers, within volume, as-

signed to each entry. The Subject Index is a handmade guide to classification. It has its own brief explanatory introduction.

## LACUNAE, ERRORS AND REVISIONS

The virtual absence of serials and the exclusion of formats other than print have been noted under Size and Scope. Additionally, although undergraduate study ranges ever wider, student information needs outside fairly "academic" disciplines and some traditional sporting activities are not fulfilled here; users are referred to college bookstores and recommended lists for public libraries for titles in many craft, technical, and recreational subjects.

Errors of cataloging and questionable classifications will, as it has been stated, be noted. They are present in the database used and though many were corrected, others as surely remain. Reports of errors, expressions of opinion about favorite titles missing and abhorrences present, and general suggestions for future revisions are sincerely sought. They may be addressed to: Editor, Books for College Libraries, c/o *Choice*, 100 Riverview Center, Middletown, CT 06457–3467.

With the breakup of BCL1 into the individual volumes of BCL2, separate revision in an on-going project was predicted. That did not happen, and it would offer some difficulties in indexing and the handling of subjects split among volumes. It is a challenge to assemble the mix of organization to command the seemingly more and more specialized contributors required, the technology to facilitate presentation, and the finance to enable the whole. But it is to be hoped that the even greater challenges college libraries face in collection development will continue to find *Choice* and its reviewers, ACRL, and ALA ready with the help future circumstances require.

Virginia Clark, *Editor*

# Acknowledgments

Without the contributors and referees of the many subject lists, BCL3 would not exist. They are named in the appropriate volumes and identified by academic or other professional institution and by subject field. To enable the calling together of this team, however, and the presentation of its work took vision, planning, determination, and much help from many groups and individuals.

Both the users and the editorial staff of BCL3 owe thanks to the staff and two successive Executive Directors of the Association of College and Research Libraries (ACRL). Julie Virgo and JoAn S. Segal convened a preliminary investigative committee and commissioned a request for proposal (RFP) that established the first outline of the project for the revised edition. Patricia Sabosik, newly appointed Editor and Publisher of *Choice*, encompassed in her initial plans for the magazine the BCL project. Her response to ACRL's RFP involved the *Choice* staff in the editorial work and the Canadian bibliographic utility Utlas in the technical construction of the database. The staffs of *Choice* and BCL3 are grateful to ACRL for accepting this proposal and to Publishing Services of the American Library Association for co-funding the project with ACRL. Patricia Sabosik served as Project Manager. Liaison with ALA Books was Managing Editor Helen Cline.

An editorial advisory committee, chaired by Richard D. Johnson, SUNY College at Oneonta, was selected to allow the BCL3 Editor to draw advice from representatives of academic libraries of different types, sizes, and locales. Stephen L. Gerhardt, Cerritos College; Michael Haeuser, Gustavus Adolphus College; Barbara M. Hirsh, formerly Marist College; Thomas Kirk, Berea College; Craig S. Likness, Trinity University; and Mary K. Sellen, Spring Valley College, served the project well. Special thanks are due Richard D. Johnson and Craig S. Likness, each of whom also contributed subject lists, and Michael Haeuser, who spent several days as a volunteer in the BCL office and served as committee secretary.

The BCL project was housed in space in the *Choice* office and enjoyed a unique member/guest relationship that involved virtually every member of the *Choice* staff in some work for BCL. The subject editors—Robert Balay, Claire C. Dudley, Ronald H. Epp, Francine Graf, Helen MacLam, and Kenneth McLintock—suggested from their reviewer lists most of the BCL contributors and several referees. Claire C. Dudley and Helen MacLam served as referees; Claire C. Dudley and Francine Graf gave much other valuable help. Library Technical Assistant Nancy Sbona, Systems Manager Lisa Gross, Office Assistant Mary Brooks, and Administrative Assistant Lucille Calarco deserve special mention for extraordinary assistance.

In addition to using the bibliographic and personnel resources of *Choice*, the Editor of BCL relied for vital support on the collections, equipment, and staffs of five very gracious institutions. Particular thanks go to the libraries of Kenyon College, Wesleyan University, and the Library Association, London, for use of behind-the-scenes cataloging and classification tools in addition to reference sources publicly available; to Trinity University, San Antonio, for tapes of BCL2; and to Trinity College, Hartford, for outstanding help from George R. Graf on preliminary aspects of the project in addition to those for which he is named in the contributor lists.

For work without regard for office hours or job description the Editor would particularly like to thank Judith Douville. She edited the science sections of Volume 5 in addition to assisting the Editor with some parts of Volume 4. She coordinated the corrections to the BCL3 computer file and reviewed the final page proofs. Her enthusiasm and dedication were vital in bringing the project to completion.

BCL3 secretary Anna Barron worked throughout the project. Special thanks are also owed to short-term staff members Alison Johnson and Virginia Carrington.

## CONTRIBUTORS

Title selection for BCL3 reflects three types of expert opinion: from scholars teaching in the field, from reference librarians, and from special referees chosen for their combination of subject and collection-development knowledge. Names appear in the approximate order of contributions in the volume, but Library of Congress classification will have scattered many titles selected by those named here into other sections of the list. The topical labels try to suggest both the depth of specialization required of some contributors and the broad knowledge and responsibility demanded of others; but no list such as this can do more than hint at the nature and amount of work for which these contributors are most gratefully thanked. Some regional and country experts are specified within the

Economics and Politics acknowledgments. The historians thanked in Volume 3 also participated in making such selections in this volume.

GEOGRAPHY: Chauncy D. Harris, University of Chicago; W. A. Douglas Jackson, University of Washington; Peter O. Muller, University of Miami. *Reference & Referees*: Marie Dvorzak, University of Wisconsin–Madison; Mary L. Larsgaard, Colorado School of Mines.

ANTHROPOLOGY: William Arens, SUNY at Stony Brook; Daniel G. Bates, Hunter College, CUNY; Riva Berleant-Schiller, University of Connecticut; Keith A. Dixon, California State University, Long Beach; Gretchen Gwynne, SUNY at Stony Brook; Sue-Ellen Jacobs, University of Washington; Robert F. Maher, Western Michigan University; Maria Messina, SUNY at Stony Brook; Lynn R. Metzger, University of Akron; Charles Morrison, Michigan State University. *Referee*: Christopher J. Busick, University of Colorado at Boulder.

FOLKLORE: John Miles Foley, University of Missouri–Columbia.

CLOTHING & DRESS: Barbara Schreier, University of Massachusetts at Amherst.

SPORTS & RECREATION: Joseph F. Barresi, College of Staten Island, CUNY; Joe R. Feagin, University of Texas at Austin; Mary L. Frye, Oklahoma State University; Herbert F. Kenny, Jr., Wesleyan University; Harold VanderZwaag, University of Massachusetts at Amherst. *Reference*: Thomas A. Tollman, University of Nebraska at Omaha. *Referee*: Wayne Wilson, formerly Chapman College.

DANCE: Lana Kay Rosenberg, Miami University, Ohio. *Reference & Referee*: Lynn Magdol, University of Wisconsin–Madison.

SOCIAL SCIENCES: *General*: see Sociology listings.

STATISTICS: see Sociology Reference listings; see Mathematics, v. 5.

ECONOMICS: *General & Economic History*: Robert T. Averitt, Smith College; Susan Kyle Howson, University of Toronto; John L. Mikesell, Indiana University; Richard A. Miller, Wesleyan University; Donald E. Moggridge, University of Toronto; John C. Murdock, University of Missouri–Columbia, emeritus; James W. Nordyke, New Mexico State University; Morton Rothstein, University of California, Davis (Agriculture); C. Glyn Williams, University of South Carolina (Labor). *Economic History & Development for Special Regions*: Robert J. Alexander, Rutgers University; Robert A. Battis, Trinity College, Conn.; Robert P. Gardella, U.S. Merchant Marine Academy; Bogdan Mieczkowski, Ithaca College; George L. Montagno, Mount Union College; E. Wayne Nafziger, Kansas State University; J. S. Uppal, SUNY at Albany. *Special Fields*: Daniel A. Brand, Harvard University (Transportation); Emily P. Hoffman, Western Michigan University (Women); Robert Kelly, Fairfield University (Housing); Wallace S. Reed, Maine Maritime Acad-

emy (Maritime Economics & Law); Gaston Rimlinger, Rice University (Social Insurance, Pensions); Donald B. Stafford, Clemson University (Transportation); Thomas H. Tietenberg, Colby College (Energy & Environmental Economics); Dorothy Wigmore, Manitoba Federation of Labor (Occupational Health & Safety). *Reference*: Peter W. Wood, Boston University. *Referee*: Diane K. Harvey, Johns Hopkins University.

BUSINESS: Robert Foster, University of Texas at El Paso; Thomas Gutteridge, Southern Illinois University at Carbondale; Sanford R. Kahn, University of Cincinnati; Francis A. Marino, Assumption College; Mildred S. Myers, Carnegie-Mellon University; Eugene Owens, Western Washington University; Alfred E. Pierce, Lafayette College; William C. Struning, Seton Hall University; Jesse S. Tarleton, College of William and Mary; Edward A. Tomeski, Barry University. *Reference*: Peter W. Wood, Boston University.

DEMOGRAPHY: Donald W. Hastings, University of Tennessee; Brenda Seals, University of Tennessee.

SOCIOLOGY & SOCIAL PSYCHOLOGY: *General*: Wayne P. Anderson, University of Missouri-Columbia; Robert W. Avery, University of Pittsburgh; Ernest J. Green, Prince George's Community College; Karen L. Hartlep, California State University, Bakersfield; Harjinder Singh Jassal, SUNY College at Cortland; E. D. Lawson, SUNY College at Fredonia; Aldora Lee, formerly Washington State University; William P. Nye, Hollins College. *Social Work*: Anthony N. Maluccio, University of Connecticut. *Social Pathology*: Norman Bell, University of Toronto; Joe R. Feagin, University of Texas at Austin; David J. Hanson, SUNY College at Potsdam; Sharon Herzberger, Trinity College, Conn.; John Lynxwiler, University of Alabama. *Criminology*: Peter Wickman, SUNY College at Potsdam; Alvin J. T. Zumbrun, Catonsville Community College. *Reference*: Beth J. Shapiro, Michigan State University; Kris Salomon, Oakland University. *Referees*: Shari T. Grove, Boston College; Karin Sandvik, University of Wisconsin–La Crosse; Gary B. Thompson, Hobart and William Smith Colleges.

SOCIAL HISTORY: see the History listings, v. 3.

WOMEN'S STUDIES: *General*: Myra Marx Ferree, University of Connecticut. Other contributors are listed with subjects. *Reference*: Beth Stafford, University of Illinois at Urbana-Champaign. *Referee*: Susan E. Searing, University of Wisconsin–Madison.

POLITICS & LAW: *General*: Charles E. Butterworth, University of Maryland at College Park; Thomas P. Campbell, Jr., Northeastern University; Edwin M. Coulter, Clemson University; Diane L. Fowlkes, Georgia State University; Charles T. Goodsell, Virginia Polytechnic Institute and State University; Frank W. Neuber, Western Kentucky University; Nelson W. Polsby, University of California, Berkeley; Sanford R. Silverburg, Catawba College; Leo Weinstein, Smith College. *Special Regions*: Robert J. Alexander, Rutgers University; Cecil Carter Brett, Monmouth College;

Jeffrey B. Freyman, Transylvania University; Melville T. Kennedy, Jr., Bryn Mawr College, emeritus; Richard H. Leach, Duke University; Vincent E. McHale, Case Western Reserve University; George L. Montagno, Mount Union College; Joseph R. Smaldone, University of Maryland at College Park; Alan J. Ward, College of William and Mary; Jane Shapiro Zacek, SUNY Rockefeller Institute. *Special Topics*: A. B. Cochran, Agnes Scott College (Socialism, Marxism); Leslie C. Duly, Bemidji State University (Imperialism); Diane L. Fowlkes, Georgia State University (Women); Richard H. Leach, Duke University (State & Local Government); Peter A. Lupsha, University of New Mexico (Terrorism); Barbara S. Roberts, formerly University of Connecticut (Diplomatic History; Peace & Pacifism); Alan J. Ward, College of William and Mary (Imperialism). *Reference*: George R. Graf, Trinity College, Conn; Helen Q. Schroyer, Purdue University. *Referees*: Patricio Aranda-Coddou, International Monetary Fund; George R. Graf, Trinity College, Conn; Diane K. Harvey, Johns Hopkins University.

EDUCATION: Jane M. Bingham, Oakland University; George E. Hein, Lesley College; Faustine C. Jones-Wilson, Howard University; Kathleen Kennedy, Glassboro State College; George P. McMeen, University of Nevada–Reno; Robert M. Porter, SUNY College at Oneonta; Sanford W. Reitman, California State University, Fresno; Francis X. Russo, University of Rhode Island; Mary Kay Smith, Bemidji State University; Sally Sugarman, Bennington College; Elizabeth Sherman Swing, St. Joseph's University; Conrad F. Toepfer, Jr., SUNY at Buffalo; Eli Velder, Goucher College; L. Steven Zwerling, New York University. *Reference*: Thomas A. Tollman, University of Nebraska at Omaha. *Referees*: Kathleen Kennedy, Glassboro State College; Richard H. Quay, Miami University, Ohio; Mary Kay Smith, Bemidji State University.

## G GEOGRAPHY: GENERAL

**Wright, John Kirtland, 1891-1969.** • 4.1
Geography in the making: the American Geographical Society, 1851–1951 / by John Kirtland Wright; foreword by Richard Upjohn Light. — New York: Published by the Society, 1952. xxi,437 p.: ill., ports., maps; 26 cm. Includes index. 1. American Geographical Society of New York. I. T.
G3.A56 W7     910.6273     LC 52-11527

**International Symposium on Man's Role in Changing the Face** • 4.2
**of the Earth, Princeton, N.J., 1955.**
Man's role in changing the face of the earth / Edited by William L. Thomas, with the collaboration of Carl O. Sauer, Marston Bates [and] Lewis Mumford. — Chicago: Published for the Wenner-Gren Foundation for Anthropological Research and the National Science Foundation by the University of Chicago Press, [1956] xxxviii, 1193 p.: ill., maps (part fold. col. on lining papers); 25 cm. 1. Anthropo-geography — Congresses. I. Thomas, William Leroy, 1920- ed. II. T.
G56.I63 1955     910 572.9*     LC 56-5865

**Davis, William Morris, 1850-1934.** • 4.3
Geographical essays / edited by Douglas Wilson Johnson. — New York: Dover Publications, 1954. 777 p.: illus; 21 cm. 1. Geography — Addresses, essays, lectures. 2. Geography — Study and teaching 3. Physical geography I. T.
G59.D3 1954     LC 54-11800

**United States. Dept. of State. Office of Media Services.** 4.4
Background notes. [Washington: For sale by the Superintendent of Documents, U. S. Govt. Print. Off., 1964-. v.: maps; 27 cm. 1. Geography — Collected works. I. T.
G59.U5     LC 65-60213

**Clark, Audrey N.** 4.5
Longman dictionary of geography: human and physical / Audrey N. Clark. — Harlow, Essex, UK: Longman, 1985. ix, 724 p.; 23 cm. 1. Geography — Dictionaries I. T.
G63.C56 1985     910/.3/21 19     LC 85-4290     ISBN 0582352614

**Lock, Clara Beatrice Muriel, 1914-.** 4.6
Geography and cartography: a reference handbook / C. B. Muriel Lock. 3rd ed. rev. and enl. — London: C. Bingley: Hamden, Conn.: Linnet Books, 1976. 762 p.; 23 cm. Combined and rev. ed. of Geography: a reference handbook, first published in 1968, and of Modern maps and atlases, first published in 1969. Includes index. 1. Geography — Dictionaries 2. Cartography I. T.
G63.L6 1976     910/.3     LC 76-8273     ISBN 0208015221

**Worldmark encyclopedia of the nations.** 4.7
6th ed. — New York: Worldmark Press: J. Wiley, exclusive world distributor, c1984. 5 v.: maps; 29 cm. 1. United Nations. 2. History — Dictionaries 3. Economics — Dictionaries. 4. Geography — Dictionaries 5. Political science — Dictionaries.
G63.W67 1984     910/.3/21 19     LC 83-26013     ISBN 047188622X

**Directory of applied geographers.** 4.8
Washington, D.C.: Association of American Geographers, 1986. 1 v. 1. Geographers — United States — Directories. 2. Geographers — Canada — Directories. I. Association of American Geographers.
G64.D57     910/.25/73 19     LC 84-21519

**Parks, George Bruner, 1890-.** • 4.9
Richard Hakluyt and the English voyages. Edited, with an introd., by James A. Williamson. — 2d ed. — New York: F. Ungar Pub. Co., [1961] xix, 288 p.: illus., ports., maps (part fold.) facsims.; 26 cm. 1. Hakluyt, Richard, 1552?-1616. 2. Hakluyt, Richard, d. 1591. 3. Discoveries (in geography) — English. I. T.
G69.H2 P3 1961     910.82     LC 61-13628

**Wanklyn, Harriet Grace.** • 4.10
Friedrich Ratzel: a biographical memoir and bibliography. Cambridge [Eng.]: University Press, 1961. ix, 96 p.; 20 cm. 1. Ratzel, Friedrich, 1844-1904. I. T.
G69.R28 W3     923.943     LC 61-65229

## G70–71 Philosophy. Relation to Other Topics. Methodology

**Ackerman, Edward Augustus, 1911-.** • 4.11
Geography as a fundamental research discipline. Chicago, 1958. 37 p. 23 cm. (The University of Chicago. Dept. of Geography. Research paper no. 53.) 1. Geography — Research I. T.
G70.A3x     910.72     LC 58-14934

**Bowman, Isaiah, 1878-1950.** • 4.12
Geography in relation to the social sciences / by Isaiah Bowman. Geography in the schools of Europe / by Rose B. Clark. — New York: Scribner's, c1934. xxii, 382 p.: ill., maps; 21 cm. — (Report of the Commission on the social studies [American Historical Association].; pt. v) Includes index. 1. Geography 2. Anthropo-geography 3. Geography — Study and teaching I. Clark, Rose Bertha. Geography in the schools of Europe. II. T. III. Title: Geography in the schools of Europe.
G70.B6     H62.A55 pt.5.     LC 34-27078

**Estes, John E.** 4.13
Remote sensing: techniques for environmental analysis / edited by John E. Estes and Leslie W. Senger. — Santa Barbara, Calif.: Hamilton Pub. Co., 1974. 340 p.: ill.; 28 cm. 1. Geography — Methodology 2. Astronautics in geographical research 3. Remote sensing I. Senger, Leslie W., joint author. II. T.
G70.E84     910/.02/028     LC 73-8601     ISBN 047124595X

**Hartshorne, Richard, 1899-.** • 4.14
The nature of geography: a critical survey of current thought in the light of the past / by Richard Hartshorne. — Lancaster, Pa.: The Association of American Geographers, 1939 [i.e. 1949] xv, 21, xvii-lii, 22-482, [13] p.; 23 cm. 1. Geography I. Association of American Geographers. II. T.
G70.H3 1949     LC 49-3072

**Hartshorne, Richard, 1899-.** • 4.15
Perspective on the nature of geography / Richard Hartshorne. — Chicago: Published for the Association of American Geographers by Rand McNally, 1959. 201 p. — (Association of American Geographers. Monograph series; 1) 1. Geography I. T. II. Title: Nature of geography. III. Series.
G70.H32     910     LC 59-7032

**Huggett, Richard J.** 4.16
Systems analysis in geography / Richard Huggett. — Oxford: Clarendon Press; New York: Oxford University Press, 1980. ix, 208 p.: ill.; 24 cm. (Contemporary problems in geography) Includes index. 1. Geography — Methodology 2. System analysis I. T.
G70.H8     910/.01/8     LC 79-41097     ISBN 0198740816

**Themes in geographic thought / edited by Milton E. Harvey** 4.17
**and Brian P. Holly.**
New York: St. Martin's Press, 1981. 224 p.: ill.; 22 cm. Includes index. 1. Geography — Philosophy — Addresses, essays, lectures. I. Harvey, Milton. II. Holly, Brian P.
G70.T44 1981     910/.01 19     LC 80-28423     ISBN 0312795300

**Hammond, Robert.** 4.18
Quantitative techniques in geography: an introduction / by Robert Hammond and Patrick McCullagh. — 2d ed. — Oxford: Clarendon Press; New York: Oxford University Press, 1978. xx, 364 p.: ill.; 24 cm. Includes index. 1. Geography — Statistical methods I. McCullagh, Patrick. joint author. II. T.
G70.3.H35 1978     910/.01/82     LC 79-308406     ISBN 0198740662

**Barrett, E. C. (Eric Charles)** 4.19
Introduction to environmental remote sensing / E. C. Barrett and L. F. Curtis. — London: Chapman and Hall; New York: Wiley, c1976. ix, 336 p., [4] leaves of plates: ill.; 26 cm. 'A Halsted Press book.' 1. Geography — Remote sensing. 2. Remote sensing I. Curtis, L. F. (Leonard Frank) joint author. II. T.
G70.4.B37 1976     621.36/7     LC 76-40968     ISBN 0470989599

**Digital image processing for remote sensing / edited by Ralph** 4.20
**Bernstein, associate editors, Paul E. Anuta... [et al.].**
New York: IEEE Press: sole worldwide distributor (exclusive of the IEEE), Wiley, c1978. vi, 473 p.: ill.; 28 cm. — (IEEE Press selected reprint series)

Errata slip inserted. Includes indexes. 1. Remote sensing — Data processing — Addresses, essays, lectures. I. Bernstein, Ralph, 1933-
G70.4.D53    621.36/7    LC 77-94520    ISBN 0879421053

**Introduction to remote sensing of the environment / edited by**    **4.21**
**Benjamin F. Richason, Jr.**
2nd ed. — Dubuque, Iowa, USA: Kendall/Hunt Pub. Co., c1983. xii, 582 p.: ill. (some col.); 24 cm. — (A National Council for Geographic Education pacesetter book) Includes index. 1. Remote sensing I. Richason, Benjamin F.
G70.4.I59 1983    621.36/78 19    LC 82-83014    ISBN 0840328346

**Lillesand, Thomas M.**    **4.22**
Remote sensing and image interpretation / Thomas M. Lillesand, Ralph W. Kiefer. — 2nd ed. — New York: Wiley, c1987. 1 v. 1. Remote sensing I. Kiefer, Ralph W. II. T.
G70.4.L54 1987    621.36/78 19    LC 86-26804    ISBN 0471845175

**Manual of remote sensing.**    **4.23**
2nd ed. / editor in chief, Robert N. Colwell. — Falls Church, Va.: American Society of Photogrammetry, c1983. 2 v. (2440 p., [214] p. of plates): ill. (some col.); 26 cm. 1. Remote sensing I. Colwell, Robert N. II. American Society of Photogrammetry.
G70.4.M36 1983    621.36/78 19    LC 83-6055    ISBN 0937294411

**Multilingual dictionary of remote sensing and photogrammetry:**    **4.24**
**English glossary and dictionary / George A. Rabchevsky,**
**editor–in–chief; editors/translators, Pierre–Marie Adrien ... [et**
**al.].**
Falls Church, Va.: American Society of Photogrammetry, c1984. xxi, 343 p.; 29 cm. Includes indexes. 1. Remote sensing — Dictionaries — Polyglot. 2. Photogrammetry — Dictionaries — Polyglot. 3. Dictionaries, Polyglot I. Rabchevsky, George A., 1936- II. American Society of Photogrammetry.
G70.4.M84 1984    621.36/78 19    LC 82-20609    ISBN 0937294462

**Sabins, Floyd F.**    **4.25**
Remote sensing: principles and interpretation / Floyd F. Sabins, Jr. — 2nd ed. — New York: Freeman, c1987. x, 449 p., [16] p. of plates: ill. (some col.); 29 cm. 1. Remote sensing I. T.
G70.4.S15 1987    621.36/78 19    LC 86-2144    ISBN 071671793X

**Short, Nicholas M.**    **4.26**
The Landsat tutorial workbook: basics of satellite remote sensing / Nicholas M. Short; prepared under the auspices of the Eastern Regional Remote Sensing Applications Center, with sections contributed by W. Campbell ... [et al.]. — Washington, D.C.: National Aeronautics and Space Administration, Scientific and Technical Information Branch: For sale by the Supt. of Docs., U.S. G.P.O., 1982. viii, 553 p.: ill.; 28 cm. + visual aids (11 plates and 3 overlays). — (NASA reference publication. 1078) 'Goddard Space Flight Center.' SN/033-000-00845-7 Item 830-H-11 1. Remote sensing 2. Landsat satellites I. Eastern Regional Remote Sensing Applications Center (U.S.) II. United States. National Aeronautics and Space Administration. Scientific and Technical Information Branch. III. Goddard Space Flight Center. IV. T. V. Series.
G70.4.S526 1982    526.9/823 19    LC 81-600117

**Slater, Philip N.**    **4.27**
Remote sensing, optics and optical systems / Philip N. Slater. — Reading, Mass.: Addison-Wesley Pub. Co., 1980. xvi, 575 p., [1] leaf of plates: ill.; 24 cm. — (Remote sensing; [no. 1]) 1. Remote sensing 2. Remote sensing — Equipment and supplies I. T. II. Series.
G70.4.S6    621.36/78    LC 80-13224    ISBN 0201072505

**The surveillant science: remote sensing of the environment /**    **4.28**
**[edited by] Robert K. Holz.**
2nd ed. — New York: Wiley, c1985. xvi, 413 p., [4] p. of plates: ill. (some col.); 28 cm. 1. Geography — Remote sensing. 2. Astronautics in geographical research 3. Aerial photography in geography I. Holz, Robert K., 1930-
G70.4.S87 1985    621.36/7 19    LC 84-7508    ISBN 047108638X

**Ulaby, Fawwaz T. (Fawwaz Tayssir), 1943-.**    **4.29**
Microwave remote sensing: active and passive / Fawwaz T. Ulaby, Richard K. Moore, Adrian K. Fung. — Reading, Mass.: Addison-Wesley Pub. Co., Advanced Book Program/World Science Division, 1981-c1986. 3 v. (xvii, 2162 p.): ill.; 24 cm. (Remote sensing; no. 2-[4]) 1. Remote sensing — Equipment and supplies 2. Microwave devices I. Moore, Richard K. II. Fung, Adrian K. III. T. IV. Series.
G70.6.U4    621.36/78 19    LC 81-17643

**Environmental perception and behavior: an inventory and**    **4.30**
**prospect / Thomas F. Saarinen, David Seamon, and James L.**
**Sell, editors.**
Chicago, Ill.: University of Chicago, Dept. of Geography, 1984. x, 263 p.; 23 cm. — (Research papers / University of Chicago, Dept. of Geography; no. 209) 1. Geographical perception I. Saarinen, Thomas F. (Thomas Frederick) II. Seamon, David. III. Sell, James L., 1947-
G71.5.E7x    910 s 912/.01/4 19    LC 84-2492    ISBN 0890651140

**Gould, Peter R.**    **4.31**
Mental maps / Peter Gould and Rodney White. — 2nd ed. — Boston: Allen & Unwin, 1986. xii, 172 p.: ill.; 23 cm. Includes index. 1. Geographical perception I. White, Rodney. II. T.
G71.5.G68 1986    304.2 19    LC 85-15742    ISBN 004526001X

# G72–77 Study. Teaching

**Chorley, Richard J.**    **4.32**
Frontiers in geographical teaching; edited by Richard J. Chorley & Peter Haggett. — 2nd ed. — London: Methuen, 1970. xii, 385 p.: illus., maps.; 22 cm. 1. Geography — Study and teaching — Addresses, essays, lectures. 2. Geography — Addresses, essays, lectures. I. Haggett, Peter. joint ed. II. T.
G73.C53 1970    910/.007    LC 76-503388    ISBN 041616840X

**University of London. Institute of Education.**    **4.33**
Handbook for geography teachers / editor, M. Long. — 6th ed. — London: Metheun, 1974. xii, 724 p.: maps; 23 cm. 1. Geography — Study and teaching 2. Geography — Bibliography. I. Long, Iris L. M. II. T.
G73.L74 1974    910/.7/1041    LC 75-312586    ISBN 0423888307

**National Research Council. Ad Hoc Committee on Geography.**    **• 4.34**
The science of geography; report. Washington, National Academy of Sciences-National Research Council, 1965. viii,80 p. 23 cm. (Publication (National Research Council (U.S.)) 1277.) 1. Geography — Research I. T. II. Series.
G73.N33    910    LC 65-60052

**New perspectives on geographic education: putting theory into**    **4.35**
**practice / edited by Gary A. Manson and Merrill K. Ridd.**
Dubuque, Iowa: Kendall/Hunt Pub. Co., c1977. x, 214 p.: ill.; 24 cm. — (NCGE pacesetters in geography; no. 3) 1. Geography — Study and teaching I. Manson, Gary. II. Ridd, Merrill K.
G73.N56    910/.7    LC 77-82146    ISBN 0840317824

**New Unesco source book for geography teaching / edited by**    **4.36**
**Norman J. Graves (Commission on Geographical Education of**
**the International Geographical Union).**
Harlow, Essex: Longman; Paris, France: Unesco Press, 1982. xxii, 394 p.: ill.; 22 cm. Errata slip inserted. Includes index. 1. Geography — Study and teaching I. Graves, Norman John. II. Unesco. III. International Geographical Union. Commission on Geographical Education.
G73.N57 1982    910/.7 19    LC 83-169878    ISBN 0582361222

**The Study and teaching of geography / Jan O.M. Broek ... [et**    **4.37**
**al.].**
Columbus: C.E. Merrill Pub. Co., c1980. xi, 108 p.: ill.; 25 cm. — (Study and teaching of social science series.) 1. Geography — Study and teaching I. Broek, Jan Otto Marius, 1904-1974. II. Series.
G73.S776    910/.01 19    LC 80-80723    ISBN 0675081637

**James, Preston Everett, 1899-.**    **• 4.38**
American geography: inventory & prospect / Preston E. James & Clarence F. Jones, editors. Syracuse, N.Y.: Published for the Association of American Geographers by Syracuse University Press, 1954. 590 p.,: ill., maps. 1. Geography — Study and teaching 2. Geographers, American. I. Jones, Clarence Fielden, 1893- II. T.
G73.3.U5 J3    910.7    LC 54-9225

**Association of American Geographers. Geography in Liberal**    **• 4.39**
**Education Project.**
Geography in undergraduate liberal education: a report of the Geography in Liberal Education Project. — Washington: Association of American Geographers, 1965. v, 66 p.; 23 cm. — Cover title. 1. Geography — Study and teaching (Higher) I. T.
G74.A78    910.711    LC 65-19784

**Geographers abroad; essays on the problems and prospects of**    **4.40**
**research in foreign areas [by] H. C. Brookfield [and others]**
**Marvin W. Mikesell, editor.**
[Chicago] University of Chicago, Dept. of Geography, 1973. ix, 296 p. 23 cm. (University of Chicago. Dept. of Geography. Research paper no. 152) Based on a conference held at the University of Chicago in November 1972. 1. Geography — Research — Congresses. 2. Area studies — Congresses. I. Brookfield, H. C. II. Mikesell, Marvin W. ed.
G74.G4x    910 s 910/.7/2    LC 73-87829

**Gregory, S. (Stanley)**                                                  **4.41**
Statistical methods and the geographer / S. Gregory. — 4th ed. — London;
New York: Longman, 1978. xv, 240 p.: graphs; 22 cm. — (Geographies for
advanced study.) 1. Geography — Statistical methods I. T. II. Series.
G70.3.G74 1978      G74.G78 1978.      519.5/02/491      LC 77-7025
　　ISBN 0582481864

**New approaches in introductory college geography courses.**           **• 4.42**
Washington: Association of American Geographers, Commission on College
Geography, [1967] viii, 174 p.: illus., maps.; 23 cm. — (Association of
American Geographers. Commission on College Geography. Publication no. 4)
Contains course outline syllabi by R. B. McNee, A. L. Kolars (signed: Ann E.
Larimore), K. W. Rumage, L. P. Cummings, and W. C. Calef. 1. Geography —
Study and teaching (Higher) — United States. I. Series.
G74.N48      LC 67-26421

**New directions in geography teaching; papers from the 1970**           **4.43**
**Charney Manor conference, edited by Rex Walford.**
[London] Longman [1973] 197 p. illus. 22 cm. 1. Geography — Study and
teaching (Secondary) — Great Britain. I. Walford, Rex. ed.
G76.5.G7 N48 1973      910/.7/1241 19      LC 73-166670      ISBN
0582312418 ISBN 058231240X

**Guide to departments of geography in the United States and**           **4.44**
**Canada.**
1984-1985-. Washington, D.C.: Association of American Geographers, c1984-.
v.; 23 cm. Annual. 1. Geography — Study and teaching (Higher) — United
States — Directories. 2. Geography — Study and Teaching (Higher) —
Canada — Directories. I. Association of American Geographers.
G76.5.U5 G8      910/.7/1173 19      LC 85-641423

# G80–99 History of Geography

**Baker, John Norman Leonard.**                                          **4.45**
A history of geographical discovery and exploration, by J. N. L. Baker. New ed.
rev. New York, Cooper Square Publishers, 1967. 552 p. maps, 24 cm.
1. Discoveries (in geography) I. T.
G80.B3 1967      910.09      LC 66-30785

**Debenham, Frank, 1883-1965.**                                          **• 4.46**
Discovery and exploration: an atlas–history of man's journeys into the
unknown / introduction by Edward Shackleton. — 2nd ed. — London:
Hamlyn, 1968. 272 p.: ill. (some col.), facsims. (some col.), maps (some col.),
ports. (some col.); 29 cm. Col. maps on lining papers. 1. Discoveries (in
geography) — History. I. T.
G80.D4 1968      910.09      LC 68-117130

**Dickinson, Robert Eric, 1905-.**                                       **• 4.47**
The making of geography / by R.E. Dickinson and O.J.R. Howarth. Oxford:
Clarendon Press, 1933. 264 p.: ill., plates, maps; 21 cm. Includes index.
1. Geography — History I. Howarth, Osbert John Radcliffe, 1877- II. T.
G80.D5      LC 33-30104

**James, Preston Everett, 1899-.**                                       **4.48**
All possible worlds: a history of geographical ideas / Preston E. James and
Geoffrey J. Martin; maps and ill. by Eileen W. James. — 2d ed. — New York:
Wiley, c1981. xvii, 508 p.: ill.; 24 cm. Includes indexes. 1. Geography —
History I. Martin, Geoffrey J. joint author. II. T.
G80.J34 1981      910/.9 19      LC 80-25021      ISBN 0471061212

**Newby, Eric.**                                                         **4.49**
[World atlas of exploration] The Rand McNally world atlas of exploration / by
Eric Newby; introd. by Sir Vivian Fuchs. — Chicago: Rand McNally, c1975.
288 p.: ill.; 30 cm. Australian ed. published under title: World atlas of
exploration. Includes index. 1. Discoveries (in geography) — History.
2. Explorers I. T. II. Title: World atlas of exploration.
G80.N43 1975      910/.9      LC 74-27897      ISBN 0528830155

**Parry, J. H. (John Horace), 1914-.**                                   **4.50**
The age of reconnaissance / J.H. Parry. — Berkeley: University of California
Press, c1981. vii, 365 p., [10] p. of plates: ill.; 24 cm. Includes index.
1. Discoveries (in geography) 2. Colonization — History. I. T.
G80.P36 1981      910/.94 19      LC 81-51175      ISBN 0520042344

**Parry, J. H. (John Horace), 1914-.**                                   **4.51**
The discovery of the sea [by] J. H. Parry. New York, Dial Press, 1974. xv, 302 p.
illus. 26 x 29 cm. 1. Discoveries (in geography) — History. 2. Ocean travel —
History. I. T.
G80.P37      910/.45      LC 74-8966      ISBN 080372019X

**Sauer, Carl Ortwin, 1889-.**                                           **• 4.52**
Northern mists [by] Carl O. Sauer. — Berkeley: University of California Press,
[1968] 204 p.: ill., maps.; 23 cm. 1. Discoveries (in geography) I. T.
G80.S35      973.1      LC 68-16757

**A Source book in geography / edited by George Kish.**                  **4.53**
Cambridge: Harvard University Press, 1978. xvi, 453 p.: ill.; 24 cm. — (Source
books in the history of the sciences.) 1. Geography — History — Sources.
I. Kish, George, 1914- II. Series.
G80.S63      910/.9      LC 77-25972      ISBN 0674822706

**Stefansson, Vilhjalmur, 1879-1962.**                                   **• 4.54**
Great adventures and explorations from the earliest times to the present / as
told by the explorers themselves. Edited with an introd. and comments by
Vilhjalmur Stefansson, with the collaboration of Olive Rathbun Wilcox. Maps
designed by Richard Edes Harrison. New rev. ed. New York, Dial Press, 1952,
c1947. 788 p. illus. 22 cm. 1. Discoveries (in geography) 2. Explorers I. T.
G80.S78 1952      LC 52-13350

**Sykes, Percy Molesworth, Sir, 1867-1945.**                             **• 4.55**
A history of exploration from the earliest times to the present day / by Sir Percy
Sykes. — 3d ed. (with appendix). — London: Routledge & K. Paul, 1950. —
xiv, 426 p., [23] leaves of plates (some fold.): ill. (1 col.), maps, ports.; 26 cm.
Includes index. 1. Discoveries (in geography) 2. Explorers I. T.
G80.S9

## G82–88 Ancient

**Cary, M. (Max), 1881-1958.**                                           **4.56**
The ancient explorers / M. Cary, E.H. Warmington. — Harmondsworth,
Middlesex: Penguin Books, 1963. 319 p.: 15 maps. — (Pelican books; A 420)
1. Explorers 2. Discoveries (in geography) I. Warmington, E. H. (Eric
Herbert), 1898- II. T.
G82.C3 1963      G200.G3 1963.

**Bunbury, Edward Herbert, Sir, bart., 1811-1895.**                      **• 4.57**
The history of ancient geography among the Greeks and Romans, from the
earliest ages till the fall of the Roman Empire / by E.H. Bunbury; with a new
introduction by W. H. Stahl.— 2d ed. — New York: Dover Publications,
[1959]. 2 v.: maps (part fold.); 21 cm. 1. Geography, Ancient — History
2. Classical geography I. T.
G84.B95 1959      911.3      LC 60-749

**Thomson, James Oliver.**                                               **4.58**
History of ancient geography / by J. Oliver Thomson. — New York: Biblo and
Tannen, 1965. x, 427 p., 2 leaves of plates: ill., maps (some col.); 24 cm.
1. Geography, Ancient — History. I. T.
G84.T5 1965      LC 64-23024

**Warmington, E. H. (Eric Herbert), 1898-.**                             **4.59**
Greek geography, by E. H. Warmington. London, J. M. Dent; New York,
Dutton. [New York, AMS Press, 1973] xlviii, 269 p. 23 cm. A compilation of
extracts in English from Greek authors. Reprint of the 1934 ed., which was
issued as no. 7 of the Library of Greek thought. 1. Classical geography
2. Cosmology 3. Greek literature — Translations into English. 4. English
literature — Translations from Greek. I. T.
G87.A3 W3 1973      910/.938      LC 70-177849      ISBN 0404078052

## G89–99 Medieval. Modern

**Beazley, Charles Raymond, Sir, 1868-1955.**                            **• 4.60**
The dawn of modern geography ...: A history of exploration and geographical
science ... New York: P. Smith, 1949. 3 v.: ill., maps (part fold.); 24 cm.
1. Geography — History 2. Discoveries (in geography) I. T.
G89.B38 1949      LC a 51-8933

**Kimble, George Herbert Tinley, 1908-.**                                **• 4.61**
Geography in the Middle Ages, by George H. T. Kimble. — New York: Russell
& Russell, [1968] 272 p.: illus., facsims.; 22 cm. Reissue of the 1938 ed.
1. Geography, Medieval I. T.
G89.K5 1968      910/.9/02      LC 68-10930

**Newton, Arthur Percival, 1873-1942. ed.**                             **• 4.62**
Travel and travellers of the Middle Ages. — New York: Barnes & Noble, [1968]
vi, 223 p.: illus., col. map.; 25 cm. — (The History of civilization) 1. Travel,
Medieval 2. Voyages and travels I. T.
G89.N4 1968      910.4      LC 68-5572

**Wright, John Kirtland, 1891-1969.** • **4.63**
The geographical lore of the time of the Crusades; a study in the history of medieval science and tradition in Western Europe. With a new introd. by Clarence J. Glacken. — New York, Dover Publications [1965] xxxii, 563 p. illus., maps. 21 cm. 'T1376.' 'Unabridged and corrected republication of the work first published ... in 1925.' Bibliographical notes: p. [490]-502. Bibliography: p. [503]-543. 1. Geography — Hist. 2. Geography, Medieval I. T.
G89.W7 1965      910.902      *LC* 65-12262

**Ahmad, Nafis, 1911-.** **4.64**
Muslim contribution to geography / Nafis Ahmad. Lahore: Sh. Muhammad Ashraf, 1972. x, 178 p., [4] leaves of plates: ill.; 21 cm. Reprint of the 1965 ed. Includes index. 1. Geography, Arabic I. T.
G93.A43 1972      910/.9      *LC* 75-930835

**Penrose, Boies.** • **4.65**
Travel and discovery in the Renaissance, 1420–1620. — Cambridge, Mass.: Harvard UP, 1955. xvi, 377 p.: maps . 1. Discoveries (in geography) 2. Geography — 15th-16th century. I. T.
G95 P45 1962      G95.P45 1955.      *LC* 55-2546

**Taylor, E. G. R. (Eva Germaine Rimington), 1879-.** **4.66**
Late Tudor and early Stuart geography, 1583–1650; a sequel to Tudor geography, 1485–1583, by E. G. R. Taylor. New York, Octagon Books, 1968. ix, 322 p. illus., ports. 24 cm. Reprint of the 1934 ed. 1. Geography — Great Britain. 2. Geography — Bibliography. I. T.
G95.T29 1968      910.09/42      *LC* 68-21958

**Taylor, E. G. R. (Eva Germaine Rimington), 1879-.** **4.67**
Tudor geography, 1485–1583, by E. G. R. Taylor. New York, Octagon Books, 1968. ix, 290 p. illus., facsims., maps. 24 cm. Reprint of the 1930 ed. 1. Geography — Great Britain. 2. Geography — Bibliography. 3. Maps, Early I. T.
G95.T3 1968      910.09      *LC* 68-21957

**Freeman, Thomas Walter.** • **4.68**
A hundred years of geography. — Chicago: Aldine Pub. Co., [1963, c1961] 334 p.; 23 cm. 1. Geography — History I. T.
G99.F7 1963      910.9      *LC* 62-14753

# G103 Dictionaries. Gazetteers

**The Columbia Lippincott gazetteer of the world. Edited by Leon** • **4.69**
**E. Seltzer with the geographical research staff of Columbia University Press and with the cooperation of the American Geographical Society. With 1961 supplement.**
Morningside Heights, New York: Columbia University Press, [1962] x, 2148, 22 p.; 31 cm. Based on the 1905 edition of Lippincott's new gazetteer which was published in 1855 under title: Lippincott's pronouncing gazetteer. 1. Geography — Dictionaries I. Seltzer, Leon E. ed. II. Columbia University. Press. III. Title: Lippincott's pronouncing gazetteer.
G103.L7 1962      910.3      *LC* 62-4711

**Times (London, England)** • **4.70**
Index–gazetteer of the world. — London: Times Publishing, 1965. xxxi, 964 p. Includes map references to The Times Atlas of the world, Midcentury ed. 1. Times (London, England) Times atlas of the world — Indexes. 2. Atlases, British — Indexes. 3. Geography — Dictionaries I. T.
G103.T5      910.003      *LC* 66-70286

**Webster's new geographical dictionary.** **4.71**
Springfield, Mass.: Merriam-Webster, c1984. xxix, 1376 p., [2] p. of plates: maps; 25 cm. 1. Geography — Dictionaries I. Merriam-Webster, Inc.
G103.5.W42 1984      910/.3/21 19      *LC* 83-22019      *ISBN* 0877794464

# G104–110 Geographic Names and Terms. Tables. Distances

**United States. Board on Geographic Names.** **4.72**
Gazetteer: official standard names approved by the United States Board on Geographic Names. — 1955-. Washington: U.S. Dept. of Defense, Defense Mapping Agency Topographic Center, Geographic Names Division. v.: maps; 21 cm. Gazetteers have been published for all countries other than the continental United States. Item 617 Issued 1955-May 1971 as no. 1-116, June 1971- without numbering. 1. Gazetteers 2. Geography — Dictionaries

3. Names, Geographical I. United States. Geographic Names Division. II. United States. Office of Geography. III. T.
G105.U5x      *LC* gp 77-732

**Taylor, Isaac, 1829-1901.** **4.73**
Words and places: illustrations of history, ethnology & geography. London & Toronto, J. M. Dent & sons, ltd.; New York, E. P. Dutton & co. [1927] xx, 467 p. maps. 18 cm. 1. Names — Etymology. 2. Names, Geographical I. T.
AC1.E8 no. 517      G106.T26x.      *LC* 36-37641

**British Association for the Advancement of Science. Research** **4.74**
**Committee.**
A glossary of geographical terms: based on a list prepared by a committee of the British Association for the Advancement of Science / edited by Dudley Stamp and Audrey N. Clark. — 3d ed. — London; New York: Longman, 1979. xxix, 571 p.; 23 cm. 1. Geography — Terminology I. Stamp, L. Dudley (Laurence Dudley), 1898-1966. II. Clark, Audrey N. III. T.
G107.9.B74 1979      910/.3      *LC* 79-40238      *ISBN* 0582352584

**Multilingual dictionary of technical terms in cartography.** **4.75**
**Dictionnaire multilingue de termes techniques cartographiqes.**
**Diccionario multilingüe de términos técnicos cartográficos.**
**[Mnogoiazychnyĭslovar' tekhnicheskikh terminov kartografii (romanized form)]. Mehrsprachiges Wörterbuch kartographischer Fachbegriffe.**
Wiesbaden: F. Steiner, 1973. lxxxiii, 573 p.; 29 cm. At head of title: International Cartographic Association. Commission II. Sample map-sheets: 3 fold. in pocket. English, French, German, Russian and Spanish. 1. Maps — Terminology I. International Cartographic Association. Commission II: Definition, Classification and Standardization of Technical Terms in Cartography. II. Title: Dictionnaire multilingue de termes techniques cartographiques. III. Title: Diccionario multilingüe de términos técnicos cartográficos. IV. Title: Mnogoiazychnyĭ slovar' tekhnicheskikh terminov kartografii. V. Title: Mehrsprachiges Wörterbuch kartographischer Fachbegriffe.
G108.A2 M84      526/.03      *LC* 74-154516

**Swayne, James Colin.** **4.76**
A concise glossary of geographical terms, by J. C. Swayne. — 3rd ed. — London: G. Philip, 1968. 164 p.; 19 cm. 1. Geography — Terminology I. T.
G108.A2 S9 1968      910/.003      *LC* 75-382759      *ISBN* 0540000159

**Monkhouse, Francis John.** • **4.77**
A dictionary of geography, by F. J. Monkhouse. — 2d ed. — Chicago: Aldine Pub. Co., [1970] v, 378 p.: illus., maps.; 23 cm. 1. Geography — Dictionaries I. T.
G108.E5 M6 1970b      910/.003      *LC* 76-115941

**United States. Dept. of the Army.** **4.78**
Official table of distances: continental United States, Alaska, Hawaii, Canada, Canal Zone, Central America, Mexico, and Puerto Rico. — [Washington]: Depts. of the Army, the Navy, and the Air Force, 19-. v. (loose-leaf); 27 cm. (1976- : Air Force manual) At head of title: Transportation and travel. 1. United States — Distances, etc. 2. North America — Distances, etc. I. United States. Navy Dept. Transportation and travel: official table of distances continental United States, Alaska, Hawaii, Canada, Canal Zone, Central America, Mexico, and Puerto Rico. II. United States. Dept. of the Air Force. Transportation and travel: official table of distances continental United States, Alaska, Hawaii, Canada, Canal Zone, Central America, Mexico, and Puerto Rico. III. T.
UG633.A3763 subser G110.U5      G110.A5 U5x.      358.4 s 917/.002/12
     *LC* 76-649823

# G112–142 General Works

**Vidal de La Blache, Paul Marie Joseph, 1845-1918, ed.** **4.79**
Géographie universelle, publié sous la direction de P. Vidal de La Blache et L. Gallois. Paris, A. Colin, 1927-48. 15 v. in 23. illus., maps (part fold., part col.) 29 cm. Vol. 6, pts. 2-3 also published separately under title: Géographie économique et humaine de la France. 1. Geography I. Gallois, Lucien Louis Joseph, 1857- joint author. II. T.
G115.V55      *LC* 28-3786

**Ullman, Edward Louis, 1912-1976.** **4.80**
Geography as spatial interaction / Edward L. Ullman; ed. by Ronald R. Boyce; foreword by Chauncy D. Harris. — Seattle: University of Washington Press, c1980. xix, 231 p.: ill.; 25 cm. Includes index. 1. Geography I. Boyce, Ronald R. II. T.
G116.U44      910      *LC* 79-6759      *ISBN* 0295957115

**World factbook (Washington, D.C.)**    **4.81**
The world factbook. — 1981-    . — Washington, D.C.: Central Intelligence Agency: Supt. of Docs., U.S. G.P.O., [distributor], 1981-. v.: maps (some col.); 28 cm. Annual. 1. Geography — Periodicals. I. United States. Central Intelligence Agency. II. National Foreign Assessment Center (U.S.) III. T.
G122.U56a    910/.5    *LC* 81-641760

**Broek, Jan Otto Marius, 1904-1974.**    **4.82**
A geography of mankind / Jan O. M. Broek, John W. Webb. — 3d ed. — New York: McGraw-Hill, c1978. xvi, 494 p.: ill.; 25 cm. — (McGraw-Hill series in geography) 1. Geography — Text-books — 1945- I. Webb, John Winter. joint author. II. T.
G128.B73 1978    910/.7    *LC* 77-12586    *ISBN* 0070080127

**Haggett, Peter.**    **4.83**
Geography: a modern synthesis / Peter Haggett. — Rev. 3rd ed. — New York: Harper & Row, c1983. xxii, 644 p.: ill.; 24 cm. — (Harper & Row series in geography.) 1. Geography — Text-books — 1945- I. T. II. Series.
G128.H3 1983    910 19    *LC* 82-23282    *ISBN* 0060425792

**Murphey, Rhoads, 1919-.**    **4.84**
Patterns on the earth: an introduction to geography / Rhoads Murphey. — 4th ed. — Chicago: Rand McNally College Pub. Co., c1978. xviii, 544 p.: ill.; 24 cm. Third ed. published in 1971 under title: An introduction to geography. Includes index. 1. Geography — Text-books — 1945- I. T.
G128.M86 1978    910    *LC* 77-77728    *ISBN* 0528630008

# G149–503 Voyages and Travels. Discovery and Exploration

**Hosts and guests: the anthropology of tourism / Valene L.**    **4.85**
**Smith, editor.**
Philadelphia: University of Pennsylvania Press, 1977. vi, 254 p.: ill.; 24 cm. Includes index. 1. Tourist trade I. Smith, Valene L.
G155.A1 H67    338.4/7/91    *LC* 77-81447    *ISBN* 0812277287

**Bernard, Paul P.**    **4.86**
Rush to the Alps: the evolution of vacationing in Switzerland / Paul P. Bernard. — Boulder [Colo.]: East European Quarterly; New York: distributed by Columbia University Press, 1978. ix, 228 p., [4] leaves of plates: ill.; 23 cm. — (East European monographs. no. 37) 1. Tourist trade — Switzerland. I. T. II. Series.
G155.S8 B46    338.4/7/91494    *LC* 77-82391    *ISBN* 0914710303

**Works issued by the Hakluyt Society.**    • **4.87**
[Vol. 1]-100; 2d ser., no. 1-    . — [London: The Society], 1847-. v.: ill. (some col.) ports., maps, facsims. (some col.) plans; 23 cm. Vols. 1-50 issued without numbering. Annual reports appended to many volumes. 1. Voyages and travels — Collected works I. Hakluyt Society.
G161.H2    910.4 19    *LC* 06-6987

**Crone, G. R. (Gerald Roe) ed.**    **4.88**
The explorers: great adventurers tell their own stories of discovery. Compiled and edited by G.R. Crone. Introd. by Serge A. Korff. New York, Crowell [c1962] 361 p. illus. 22 cm. 1. Explorers 2. Discoveries (in geography) I. T.
G200.C7 1962a    910.82    *LC* 63-13306

**Beaglehole, J. C. (John Cawte)**    **4.89**
The life of Captain James Cook. Stanford, Calif., Stanford University Press [1974] xi, 760 p. illus. 25 cm. 1. Cook, James, 1728-1779. I. T.
G246.C7 B38    910/.92/4 B    *LC* 73-87124    *ISBN* 0804708487

**Burney, James, 1750-1821.**    **4.90**
With Captain James Cook in the Antarctic and Pacific: the private journal of James Burney, second lieutenant of the 'Adventure' on Cook's second voyage, 1772-1773 / edited and with an introduction by Beverley Hooper. — Canberra: National Library of Australia, 1975. xi, 112 p., 8 p. of plates: diagr., maps; 25 cm. Includes index. 1. Cook, James, 1728-1779. 2. Burney, James, 1750-1821. 3. Adventure (Ship) 4. Explorers — England — Biography. I. Hooper, Beverley. II. T.
G246.C7 B8 1975    910/.92/4    *LC* 79-302159    *ISBN* 0642990387

**Captain James Cook and his times / edited by Robin Fisher &**    **4.91**
**Hugh Johnston.**
Vancouver, B.C.: Douglas & McIntyre, c1979. 278 p.: ill., maps; 24 cm. Twelve papers from a conference on Captain Cook's explorations held at Simon Fraser University in 1978. 1. Cook, James, 1728-1779 — Congresses. 2. Explorers —

England — Biography — Congresses. I. Fisher, Robin, 1946- II. Johnston, Hugh J. M., 1939-
G246.C7 C33    G246C7 C28.    910/.92/4 B    *LC* 78-73989
*ISBN* 0888942303

**Moorehead, Alan, 1910-.**    • **4.92**
The fatal impact; an account of the invasion of the South Pacific, 1767–1840. — [1st ed.]. — New York, Harper & Row [1966] xiv, 230 p. illus., maps (1 fold. col.) plates, ports. 22 cm. Bibliography: p. 221-222. 1. Cook, James, 1728-1779. 2. Australia — Disc. & explor. 3. Antarctic regions 4. Tahiti — Disc. & explor. I. T.
G246.C7M6 1966a    910.0916654    *LC* 66-11888

**Bell, Christopher Richard Vincent, 1911-.**    **4.93**
Portugal and the quest for the Indies / Christopher Bell. — New York: Barnes & Noble, 1974. 247 p., [5] leaves of plates: ill.; 23 cm. Includes index. 1. Discoveries (in geography) — Portuguese. 2. Portugal — History — Period of discoveries, 1385-1580 3. East Indies — Discovery and exploration — Portuguese. I. T.
G282.B36 1974b    910/.9469    *LC* 74-2862    *ISBN* 0064903524

**Spate, O. H. K. (Oskar Hermann Khristian), 1911-.**    **4.94**
The Spanish lake / O. H. K. Spate. — Minneapolis: University of Minnesota Press, 1979. xxiv, 372 p.: ill.; 26 cm. ([His The Pacific since Magellan; v. 1]) 1. Discoveries (in geography) — Spanish. 2. Pacific Ocean 3. Oceania — History. I. T.
G288.S68 1979    910/.09/164    *LC* 78-23614    *ISBN* 0816608822

**Fisher, Raymond Henry, 1907-.**    **4.95**
Bering's voyages: whither and why / Raymond H. Fisher. — Seattle: University of Washington Press, 1978 (c1977). xiii, 217 p.: maps; 25 cm. Includes index. 1. Bering, Vitus Jonassen, 1681-1741. 2. Kamchatskaia ėkspeditsiia. 3. Kamchatskaia ėkspeditsiia. 2nd, 1733-1743. I. T.
G296.B4 F57    910/.92/4 B    *LC* 77-73307    *ISBN* 0295955627

**Rachewiltz, Igor de.**    **4.96**
Papal envoys to the great khans, by I. de Rachewiltz. Stanford, Calif., Stanford University Press, 1971. 230 p. illus. 21 cm. 1. Catholic Church — Missions — Asia. 2. Voyages and travels 3. Mongols — History I. T.
G370.A2 R3 1971    950/.2    *LC* 77-150327    *ISBN* 0804707707

**Wilson, Derek A.**    **4.97**
The world encompassed: Francis Drake and his great voyage / by Derek Wilson. — 1st U.S. ed. — New York: Harper & Row, c1977. xiii, 240 p.: ill.; 24 cm. Includes index. 1. Drake, Francis, Sir, 1540?-1596. 2. Voyages around the world I. T.
G420.D7 W53 1977b    910/.41/0924    *LC* 77-3782    *ISBN* 0060146796

**Golovnin, Vasiliĭ Mikhaĭlovich, 1776-1831.**    **4.98**
[Puteshestvīe vokrug sveta. English] Around the world on the Kamchatka, 1817–1819 / V. M. Golovnin; translated, with an introd. and notes, by Ella Lury Wiswell; foreword by John J. Stephan. — Honolulu: Hawaiian Historical Society, c1979. xxxix, 353 p.: ill.; 25 cm. Translation of Puteshestvīe vokrug svieta. Includes index. 1. Golovnin, Vasiliĭ Mikhaĭlovich, 1776-1831. 2. Kamchatka (Sloop of war) 3. Voyages around the world 4. Explorers — Russia — Biography. I. Wiswell, Ella Lury, 1909- II. T.
G420.G64 G6413    910/.41    *LC* 79-15230    *ISBN* 0824806409

**Magnificent voyagers: the U.S. exploring expedition, 1838–1842**    **4.99**
**/ Herman J. Viola and Carolyn Margolis, editors; with the**
**assistance of Jan S. Danis and Sharon D. Galperin.**
Washington, D.C.: Smithsonian Institution Press, 1985. 303 p.: ill. (some col.), maps; 29 cm. Maps on lining papers. Includes index. 1. United States Exploring Expedition (1838-1842) I. Viola, Herman J. II. Margolis, Carolyn.
G420.U55 M34 1985    973.5/7 19    *LC* 85-40192    *ISBN* 0874749468

**Stafford, Barbara Maria, 1941-.**    **4.100**
Voyage into substance: art, science, nature, and the illustrated travel account, 1760–1840 / Barbara Maria Stafford. — Cambridge, Mass.: MIT Press, c1984. xxiii, 645 p.: ill.; 29 cm. Includes index. 1. Voyages and travels — Pictorial works. 2. Landscape in art 3. Illustration of books I. T.
G468.S73 1984    910/.9/033 19    *LC* 83-18802    *ISBN* 0262192233

# G535–550 Seafaring Life. Pirates

**Defoe, Daniel, 1661?-1731.**    **4.101**
[General history of the robberies and murders of the most notorious pyrates] A general history of the pyrates. Edited by Manuel Schonhorn. Columbia, University of South Carolina Press [1972] xlviii, 717 p. illus. 24 cm. Originally published under title: A general history of the robberies and murders of the most notorious pyrates ... by Captain Charles Johnson. 1. Pirates I. Johnson,

Charles, fl. 1724-1736. A general history of the robberies and murders of the most notorious pyrates. II. Schonhorn, Manuel, ed. III. T.
G535.D43 1972b    910/.453    *LC* 72-5341    *ISBN* 0872492702

**Masefield, John, 1878-1967.**    **4.102**
Sea life in Nelson's time. With an introd. by C. C. Lloyd. 3d ed. [Annapolis, Md.] United States Naval Institute, 1971. xii, 108 p. 38 illus. 26 cm. 1. Great Britain. Royal Navy. 2. Seamen I. T.
G549.M3 1971    359.1/0942    *LC* 77-175637    *ISBN* 0870218697

## G575–890 Arctic and Antarctic Regions

**Victor, Paul Emile.**    • **4.103**
Man and the conquest of the poles. Translation by Scott Sullivan. — New York: Simon and Schuster, 1963. 320 p.: illus.; 24 cm. 1. Polar regions — History. I. T.
G580.V513    998    *LC* 63-12568

**Sugden, David E.**    **4.104**
Arctic and Antarctic: a modern geographical synthesis / David Sugden. — Totowa, N.J.: Barnes & Noble, 1982. viii, 472 p.: ill.; 25 cm. Includes index. 1. Polar regions I. T.
G587.S93 1982    G587 S93 1982.    919.8 19    *LC* 82-13788    *ISBN* 0389202983

**Hood, Robert, 1797-1821.**    **4.105**
To the Arctic by canoe, 1819–1821: the journal and paintings of Robert Hood, midshipman with Franklin / edited by C. Stuart Houston. — Montreal: McGill-Queen's, Artic Institute of North America, 1974. xxxv, 217 p., [25] leaves of plates: col. ill.; 29 cm. Includes index. 1. Franklin, John, Sir, 1786-1847. 2. Natural history — Arctic regions. 3. Northwest Passage 4. Northwest, Canadian — Description and travel — To 1821 I. Houston, Charles S. II. T.
G650 1819.H66 1974    919.8    *LC* 74-77504    *ISBN* 0773501924

**Amundsen, Roald, 1872-1928.**    **4.106**
[Sydpolen. English] The South Pole: an account of the Norwegian Antarctic expedition in the 'Fram', 1910–1912 / by Roald Amundsen; translated from the Norwegian by A. G. Chater. — New York: Barnes & Noble, 1976. xxxv, 392, x, 449 p., [105] leaves of plates (2 fold.): ill.; 23 cm. Translation of Sydpolen. First published in 1912 in 2 v. by J. Murray, London. Includes index. 1. South Pole 2. Antarctic regions I. T.
G850 1910.A5213 1976    919.8/9    *LC* 75-41594    *ISBN* 0064910661

**Ponting, Herbert George.**    **4.107**
Scott's last voyage, through the Antarctic camera of Herbert Ponting. Edited by Ann Savours. Introduced by Sir Peter Scott. — New York: Praeger Publishers, [1975, c1974] 160 p.: illus.; 26 cm. 1. Scott, Robert Falcon, 1868-1912. 2. British Antarctic ('Terra Nova') Expedition, 1910-1913. I. Savours, Ann. II. T.
G850 1910.S658 1975    919.8/9    *LC* 74-13507    *ISBN* 0275526704

**Wilson, Edward Adrian, 1872-1912.**    **4.108**
Diary of the Terra Nova Expedition to the Antarctic, 1910–1912. An account of Scott's last expedition edited from the original mss. in the Scott Polar Research Institute and the British Museum by H. G. R. King. — New York: Humanities Press, [1972] xxiii, 279 p.: illus. (part col.); 25 cm. 1. Wilson, Edward Adrian, 1872-1912. 2. British Antarctic ('Terra Nova') Expedition, 1910-1913. I. King, H. G. R. ed. II. T.
G850 1910.S95    919.89/04    *LC* 72-76897

## G905–922 Tropics

**Bates, Marston, 1906-1974.**    **4.109**
Where winter never comes; a study of man and nature in the Tropics. New York, Scribner, 1952. 310 p. illus. 22 cm. 1. Tropics I. T.
G905.B3x    *LC* 52-6464

**Gourou, Pierre, 1900-.**    **4.110**
[Pays tropicaux. English] The tropical world: its social and economic conditions and its future status / Pierre Gourou; translated by S. H. Beaver. — 5th ed. — London; New York: Longman, 1980. 190 p.: ill.; 24 cm. — (Geographies for advanced study) Translation of Les pays tropicaux. Includes index. 1. Tropics I. T.
G905.G6813 1980    910/.09/13    *LC* 79-41083    *ISBN* 0582300126

# G1001–2799 Atlases

## G1001–1025 WORLD ATLASES

**Encyclopaedia Britannica.**    • **4.111**
Britannica world atlas international. — Chicago, [1968] 367 p.: col. maps (part fold.); 41 cm. 'Political-physical maps' (p. 1-117) by Istituto geografico De Agostini, Novara. 1. Atlases 2. Commerical statistics. I. Istituto geografico DeAgostini, Novara. II. T.
G1019.E58 1968    *LC* map68-873

**Goode, J. Paul, 1862-1932.**    **4.112**
Goode's World atlas / Edward B. Espenshade, Jr., editor; Joel L. Morrison, senior consultant. — 16th ed., 4th print., rev. — Chicago: Rand McNally, 1983, c1982. 1 atlas (xvi, 368 p.): col. ill., col. maps; 29 cm. At head of title: Rand McNally. 'Formerly Goode's School Atlas.' Includes indexes. 1. Atlases I. Espenshade, Edward Bowman, 1910- II. T. III. Title: World Atlas. IV. Title: Rand McNally Goode's World atlas.
G1021.G6 1983    912 19    *LC* 81-51412    *ISBN* 0528831259

**Mitchell Beazley Ltd.**    **4.113**
The great geographical atlas. — London: M. Beazley in association with Istituto geografico de Agostini and Rand McNally, c1982. 1 atlas (xvi, 256, 144 p.): col. ill., col. maps; 38 cm. Includes index. 1. Atlases, British I. Istituto geografico De Agostini. II. Rand McNally and Company. III. T.
G1021.M5 1982    912 19    *LC* 83-118754    *ISBN* 0855333863

**National Geographic Society (U.S.). Cartographic Division.**    **4.114**
National Geographic atlas of the world. — 5th ed. — Washington, D.C.: National Geographic Society, 1981. 1 atlas (383 p.): col. ill., col. maps; 47 cm. Includes glossary and index. 1. Atlases I. T.
G1021.N38 1981    912 19    *LC* 81-675324    *ISBN* 087044347X

**Rand McNally and Company.**    **4.115**
The new international atlas = Der neue internationale Atlas = El nuevo atlas internacional = Le nouvel atlas international = O nôvo atlas internacional. — Chicago: Rand McNally, c1980. 1 atlas (xvi, 320, 232 p.): col. ill., col. maps; 39 cm. English, French, German, Portuguese, and Spanish. Cover title: Rand McNally, the new international atlas. Editorial and cartographic direction, Russell L. Voisin, Jon M. Leverenz; art and design direction, Chris Arvetis, Gordon Hartshorne ... et al. Includes indexes. 1. Atlases I. Voisin, Russell L., 1932- II. T. III. Title: Neue internationale Atlas. IV. Title: Nuevo atlas internacional. V. Title: Nouvel atlas international. VI. Title: Nôvo atlas internacional. VII. Title: Rand McNally, the new international atlas.
G1021.R23 1980    912 19    *LC* 80-51969

**The Times atlas of the world / Times Books in collaboration**    **4.116**
**with John Bartholomew & Son Limited.**
7th comprehensive ed. — New York: Times Books, 1985. xlviii, [245], 227 p.: col. maps. Published simultaneously in Great Britain by Times Books Limited, London. Includes index. 1. Atlases I. John Bartholomew and Son. II. Times Books (Firm) III. Title: Atlas of the world.
G1021.T55 1985    912 19    *LC* 85-675126    *ISBN* 0812912985

**Touring club italiano.**    **4.117**
Atlante internazionale: del Touring club italiano. — 8. ed., ristampa aggiornata 1977. — Milano: the Club, 1978. ca 300 p.: chiefly col. maps.; 50 cm. & index (1032 p.; 25 cm.) 1. Atlases, Italian I. T.
G1021.T6 1978    912    *LC* 79-383311

**Nordenskiöld, A. E. (Adolf Erik), 1832-1901.**    **4.118**
Facsimile–atlas to the early history of cartography with reproductions of the most important maps printed in the XV and XVI centuries [by] A. E. Nordenskiöld. Translated from the Swedish original by Johan Adolf Ekelöf and Clements R. Markham. With a new introd. by J. B. Post. New York, Dover Publications [1973] x, 141 p. 51 plates, maps. 41 cm. 1. Maps, Early — Facsimiles. 2. Maps, Early 3. Cartography — History I. T.
G1025.N72 1973    912/.1/526    *LC* 72-83741    *ISBN* 0486229645

## G1030–1038 HISTORICAL ATLASES

**Banks, Arthur.**    **4.119**
A world atlas of military history, 1861–1945 / by Arthur Banks. — New York: Hippocrene Books, 1978. 160 p.: maps. 1. Geography, Historical — Maps

2. Military history — Maps. I. Hartman, Tom, 1935- World atlas of military history, 1945-1984. II. T.
G1030.B29      *ISBN* 0882544543

**Gilbert, Martin, 1936-.**                                    **4.120**
Jewish history atlas. Cartography by Arthur Banks. [1st American ed. New York] Macmillan [1969] 112 p. of maps., [14] p. 24 cm. 1. Jews — History — Maps. 2. Israel — Historical geography — Maps. I. Banks, Arthur. II. T.
G1030.G5 1969a      *LC* 74-653401

**Hartman, Tom, 1935-.**                                    **4.121**
A world atlas of military history, 1945–1984 / by Tom Hartman; maps by John Mitchell; introduction by J.D. Lunt. — New York: Hippocrene Books, 1985 (c1984). xi, 108 p.: maps; 31 cm. Includes index. Continues: A world atlas of military history, 1861-1945 / by Arthur Banks. 1. Geography, Historical — Maps 2. Military history — Maps I. Mitchell, John, cartographer. II. Banks, Arthur. World atlas of military history, 1861-1945. III. T.
G1030.H38 1984      911      *ISBN* 0870520008

**Muir, Ramsay, 1872-1941.**                              • **4.122**
[Philips' new historical atlas for students] Muir's historical atlas: medieval and modern. 11th ed.; edited by the late R. F. Treharne and Harold Fullard. London, G. Philip, 1969. xvi, 96 p. of col. maps, 24 p. 29 cm. First ed. published in 1911 under title: Philips' new historical atlas for students. 1. Geography, Historical — Maps I. Treharne, R. F. (Reginald Francis), 1901-1967. ed. II. Fullard, Harold. ed. III. T. IV. Title: Historical atlas, medieval and modern.
G1030.M84 1969      911      *LC* 75-476122

**Rand McNally and Company.**                              • **4.123**
Rand McNally atlas of world history. Chicago [1965] 216 p. (Rand McNally history series) 1. Geography, Historical — Maps I. Palmer, R. R. (Robert Roswell), 1909- ed. II. T. III. Title: Atlas of world history.
G1030.R3 1965      *LC* map65-4

**Shepherd, William R. (William Robert), 1871-1934.**        • **4.124**
Shepherds historical atlas. [1st]- ed.; 1911-. New York, Barnes & Noble, 1911-. v. col. maps. Imprint varies: 1911-29, New York, H. Holt. - 1956-57, Pikesville, Md., Colonial Offset Co. Vols. published 1956- include maps for period since 1929 prepared by C. S. Hammond and Co. 1. Geography, Historical — Maps I. C.S. Hammond & Company. II. T. III. Title: Historical atlas.
G1030.S4      *LC* map64-26

**The Times atlas of world history / edited by Geoffrey**        **4.125**
**Barraclough.**
Rev. ed. — Maplewood, N.J.: Hammond, 1984. 1 atlas (360 p.): col. ill., col. maps; 37 cm. Copyright Times Books Ltd., London. Published simultaneously: London: Times Newspapers Ltd. Includes index and glossary. Includes index and glossary. 1. Geography, Historical — Maps I. Barraclough, Geoffrey, 1908- II. Times Books (Firm) III. Title: Atlas of world history.
G1030.T54 1984      911 19      *LC* 84-675088      *ISBN* 0843711299

**Atlas of the Greek and Roman world in antiquity / Nicholas**    **4.126**
**G.L. Hammond, editor-in-chief.**
Park Ridge, N.J.: Noyes Press, 1981. viii, [30], 56 p.: 46 col. maps; 41 cm. Includes gazetteer and index. 1. Civilization, Greco-Roman — Maps. 2. Classical geography — Maps 3. Geography, Ancient — Maps 4. History, Ancient 5. Greece — History 6. Greece — Antiquities — Maps. 7. Rome — Antiquities — Maps. 8. Rome — History I. Hammond, N. G. L. (Nicholas Geoffrey Lemprière), 1907-
G1033.A84 1981      912/.38 19      *LC* 81-675203      *ISBN* 081555060X

**Young, Peter, 1915-.**                                    **4.127**
Atlas of the Second World War / edited by Peter Young; cartography by Richard Natkiel. — [1st American ed.]. — New York: G. P. Putnam's Sons, [1974, c1973] 288 p.: ill., maps. (part col.); 29 cm. 1. World War, 1939-1945 — Maps I. Natkiel, Richard. II. T.
G1038.Y6 1974      911      *LC* 73-78626      *ISBN* 0399111824

## G1046 SUBJECT ATLASES

**United States Military Academy. Dept. of Geography and**        **4.128**
**Computer Science.**
Atlas of landforms / H. Allen Curran ... [et al.]. — 3rd ed. — New York: Wiley, c1984. 1 atlas (165 p.): ill. (some col., maps (some col.): 32 x 38 cm. Includes index. 1. Landforms — Maps. I. Curran, H. Allen (Harold Allen), 1940- II. T.
G1046.C2 A8 1984      912/.15514 19      *LC* 83-675974      *ISBN* 0471874345

**Nouvel atlas des formes du relief = New atlas of relief forms.**    **4.129**
[Paris]: Nathan, c1985. 1 atlas (viii, 216 p.): ill. (some col.), col. maps; 33 cm. English and French. 'En collaboration avec l'Institut Géographique National.'

Rev. ed. of: Atlas des formes du relief. 1956. 1. Geomorphology — Maps 2. Landforms — Maps. I. Fernand Nathan (Firm) II. Institut géographique national (France) III. Atlas des formes du relief. IV. Title: New atlas of relief forms.
G1046.C2 N6 1985      912/.15514 19      *LC* 86-119230      *ISBN* 209178320X

**Snead, Rodman E.**                                    **4.130**
World atlas of geomorphic features / Rodman E. Snead. — Huntington, N.Y.: R.E. Krieger Pub. Co., c1980. ix, 301 p.: col. ill., col. maps; 29 cm. Includes index. 1. Geomorphology — Maps 2. Landforms — Maps. I. T.
G1046.C2 S6 1980      912/1/5514      *LC* 77-28009      *ISBN* 0882752723

**Rodenwaldt, E. (Ernst), 1878- ed.**                        **4.131**
World maps of climatology. 2d ed. Berlin, New York, Springer, 1965. 28 p. illus., 5 fold. col. maps (in pocket) 30 cm. 1. Climatology — Charts, diagrams, etc. 2. Solar radiation I. Landsberg, Helmut Erich, 1906- II. Troll, Carl, 1890-III. Jusatz, Helmut J. (Helmut Joachim), 1907- joint ed. IV. T. V. Title: Weltkarten zur Klimakunde.
G1046.C8 R6 1965 (Map)      *LC* map65-10

**Littell, Franklin Hamlin.**                                **4.132**
The Macmillan atlas history of Christianity / by Franklin H. Littell; cartography by E. Hausman; prepared by Carta, Jerusalem. — New York: Macmillan, c1976. 176 p.: ill., col. maps; 30 cm. Includes index. 1. Ecclesiastical geography — Maps 2. Geography, Historical — Maps 3. Church history 4. Civilization, Christian I. Hausman, E. II. Karta (Firm) III. T.
G1046.E4 L5 1976      912/.1/2      *LC* 75-22113      *ISBN* 0025731408

**Meer, Frederik van der, 1904-.**                          • **4.133**
Atlas of the early Christian world [by] F. van der Meer [and] Christine Mohrmann. Translated and edited by Mary F. Hedlund and H.H. Rowley. [London] Nelson, 1958. 215 p. illus., 42 col. maps. 36 cm. Translation of Atlas van de oudchristelijke wereld. 1. Ecclesiastical geography — Maps 2. Church history — Primitive and early church, ca. 30-600 3. Christian antiquities I. Mohrmann, Christine. joint author. II. T.
G1046.E42 M4 1958      *LC* map58-7

**Ginsburg, Norton Sydney.**                                • **4.134**
Atlas of economic development. With a foreword by Bert F. Hoselitz, and pt. 8, a statistical analysis by Brian J. L. Berry. — [Chicago] University of Chicago Press [1961] vii, 119 p. maps (1 fold., part col.) diagrs., tables. 25x36 cm. Includes bibliographical references. 1. Geography, Economic — Maps I. T.
G1046.G1G53 1961      330.84      *LC* Map61-6

**Oxford University Press.**                                **4.135**
Oxford economic atlas of the world; prepared by the Cartographic Department of the Clarendon Press. 4th ed.; advisory editor D. B. Jones. London, Oxford University Press, 1972. viii, 239 p. col. maps. 39 cm. Previous editions prepared by the Economist Intelligence Unit. 1. Geography, Economic — Maps I. Jones, David Brian, ed. II. Economist Intelligence Unit (Great Britain) Oxford economic atlas of the world. III. T.
G1046.G1 O92 1972      912/.1/33      *LC* 72-169337      *ISBN* 0198941064

**World atlas of agriculture: under the aegis of the International**    **4.136**
**Association of Agricultural Economists / monographs edited by**
**the Committee for the World Atlas of Agriculture.**
Novara: Instituto Geografico De Agostini, 1973. v.: ill.; 36 cm.; and portfolios (1-17, plates) 49 cm. 'Land utilization maps and relief maps prepared by the Committee for the World Atlas of Agriculture.' 1. Agriculture 2. Agriculture — Maps 3. Land use — Classification — Maps. I. International Association of Agricultural Economists. II. Committee for the World Atlas of Agriculture. III. Istituto geografico De Agostini.
G1046.J1 W6      912.16/3      *LC* 77-653907

**Lloyd, Christopher, 1906-.**                              **4.137**
Atlas of maritime history / Christopher Lloyd. New York: Arco Pub. Co., c1975. 144 p.: ill. (some col.), maps; 34 cm. Includes indexes. 1. Naval history — Maps. 2. Naval battles — Maps. I. T.
G1060.L65 1975      911      *LC* 74-32634      *ISBN* 0668037792

## G1100–3102 Special Regions. Countries

## G1100–1779 Canada. United States. Mexico

**Modelski, Andrew M., 1929-.**     **4.138**
Railroad maps of North America: the first hundred years / by Andrew M. Modelski. — Washington: Library of Congress: For sale by the Supt. of Docs., U.S. G.P.O., 1984. 1 atlas (xxi, 186 p.): ill., maps (some col.); 29 x 37 cm. Includes index. 1. Railroads — North America — Maps. 2. Cartography — North America. 3. North America — Maps. I. Library of Congress. II. T.
G1106.P3 M6 1984    912/.1385/097 19    LC 82-675134    ISBN 0844403962

**Canada. Geography Division.**     **4.139**
The national atlas of Canada. — 5th ed. — Ottawa: Energy, Mines and Resources, 1985-. v.    : fold. col. maps.; 38 cm. Cover title. Issued in parts. Issued also in sheets. First-3d eds. published under title: Atlas of Canada; 1st-2d eds. issued by the Dept. of the Interior; 3d ed. issued by the Geographical Branch. 'The 5th Edition of the National Atlas is a serial publication the first map of which was published in 1978. Maps will be published over the next several years and may be accumulated in special containers first produced in 1985.' The National Atlas of Canada is also published in French under the title L'Atlas National du Canada. 1. Canada — Maps. I. Canada. Geographical Branch. Atlas of Canada. II. T. III. Title: Atlas of Canada.
G1115.C55 1985    912.71

**Canada gazetteer atlas.**     **4.140**
[Montreal?]: Macmillan of Canada, 1980. 1 atlas ([9], 164 p.): 48 col. maps; 46 cm. Issued also under title: Canada atlas toponymique. 'Published by Macmillan of Canada—a Division of Maclean-Hunter Limited, in co-operation with Energy, Mines and Resources Canada and the Canadian Government Publishing Centre, Supply and Services Canada.' Includes gazetteer and index. 1. Canada — Maps.
G1115.C6313 1980    912/.71 19    LC 81-675339    ISBN 0770518737

**Kerr, Donald Gordon Grady, 1913-.**     **4.141**
Historical atlas of Canada / D. G. G. Kerr; [cartography preparation by C. C. J. Bond; drawing by Ellsworth Walsh ... et al.]. 3d rev. ed. — Don Mills, Ont.: T. Nelson & Sons (Canada), 1975. iii, 100 p.: col. ill., col. maps; 32 cm. Includes index. 1. Canada — Historical geography — Maps. I. Bond, Courtney C. J. II. T.
G1116.S1 K4 1975    911/.71    LC 77-356671    ISBN 0176004092

**Gentilcore, R. Louis, 1924-.**     **4.142**
Ontario's history in maps / R. Louis Gentilcore, C. Grant Head; with a cartobibliographical essay by Joan Winearls. — Toronto; Buffalo: University of Toronto Press, c1984. 1 atlas (xvii, 284 p.): maps (some col.); 32 x 42 cm. (Ontario historical studies series.) Includes reproductions of maps, charts, plans, and views produced from the 17th through the 20th centuries. 1. Cartography — Ontario — History. 2. Ontario — Historical geography — Maps. 3. Ontario — History I. Head, C. Grant, 1939- II. Winearls, Joan. III. T. IV. Series.
G1146.S1 G46 1984    911/.713 19    LC 84-193884    ISBN 0802034004

**Geological Survey (U.S.)**     • **4.143**
The national atlas of the United States of America. [Arch C. Gerlach, editor] Washington, 1970. xiii, 417 p. col. maps. 49 cm. Six transparent overlays in envelope inserted. 1. United States — Maps I. Gerlach, Arch C. ed. II. T.
G1200.U57 1970    912.73    LC 79-654043

**Water atlas of the United States [by] Geraghty [and others].**     **4.144**
Port Washington: Water Information Center, [1973] 1 v. (unpaged): 122 col. maps.; 24 x 36 cm. Text on verso of maps. Previous edition (1962) by D. W. Miller. 1. Water-supply — United States — Maps. I. Geraghty, James J. II. Miller, David William, 1929- Water atlas of the United States. III. Water Information Center, inc.
G1201.C3 W3 1973    912/.1/3339100973    LC 73-76649    ISBN 091239403X

**United States. Environmental Data Service.**     **4.145**
[Climatic atlas of the United States] Weather atlas of the United States = originally titled Climatic atlas of the United States / U.S. Dept. of Commerce, Environmental Science Services Administration, Environmental Data Service. — Detroit: Gale Research Co., 1975. 262 p.: chiefly maps; 28 cm. 'The climatic maps in this atlas were prepared primarily by John L. Baldwin.' Reprint of the 1968 ed. published by the Service and sold by the Supt. of Docs., U.S. Govt. Print. Off. 1. United States — Climate — Maps. I. Baldwin, John L. II. T.
G1201.C8 U55 1975    912/.1/5516973    LC 74-11931    ISBN 0810310481

**This remarkable continent: an atlas of United States and**     **4.146**
**Canadian society and culture** / general editors, John F. Rooney, Jr., Wilbur Zelinsky, and Dean R. Louder; cartographic editor, John D. Vitek; coordinating editor, Campbell W. Pennington; associate editors, James P. Allen ... [et al.].
1st ed. — College Station [Tex.]: Published for The Society for the North American Cultural Survey by Texas A & M University Press, c1982. 1 atlas (viii, 316 p.): ill., maps; 24 x 32 cm. Includes index. 1. Land settlement patterns — Canada — Maps. 2. Land settlement patterns — United States — Maps. 3. United States — Social life and customs — Maps. 4. Canada — Social life and customs — Maps. I. Rooney, John F. II. Zelinsky, Wilbur, 1921- III. Louder, Dean R., 1943- IV. Vitek, John D. V. Society for the North American Cultural Survey.
G1201.E1 T5 1982    912/.1306/0973 19    LC 80-6113    ISBN 0890961115

**Infomap, Inc.**     **4.147**
Atlas of demographics: U.S. by county: from the 1980 census. — Boulder, Colo.: Infomap, c1982. 1 atlas (60 p.): col. maps; 44 cm. 'Companion products to this Atlas are laminated, large-scale wall maps, transparent overlays, and 35mm slides of all 16 maps'—Cover p. [4] 1. United States — Population — Maps. 2. United States — Statistics, Vital I. T.
G1201.E2 I5 1982    912/.13173 19    LC 82-83101    ISBN 0910471002

**Gaustad, Edwin Scott.**     **4.148**
Historical atlas of religion in America / Edwin Scott Gaustad. Rev. ed. — New York: Harper & Row, c1976. xii, 189 p.: ill., maps (1 fold. col. in pocket); 32 cm. 1. Ecclesiastical geography — United States — Maps. 2. United States — Church history I. T. II. Title: Religion in America.
G1201.E4 G3 1976    912/.1/200973    LC 76-25947    ISBN 0060630892

**Parsons, Stanley B.**     **4.149**
United States congressional districts, 1788–1841 / Stanley B. Parsons, William W. Beach, Dan Hermann. — Westport, Conn.: Greenwood Press, 1978. xvi, 416 p.: maps; 29 cm. Includes index. 1. United States. Congress. House — Election districts — History. I. Beach, William W. joint author. II. Hermann, Dan. joint author. III. T.
G1201.F7 P3 1978    328.73/07/345    LC 77-83897    ISBN 0837198283

**United States. Bureau of the Census.**     **4.150**
Congressional district atlas of the United States. — 86th Congress, Apr. 1, 1960-. — Washington, D.C.: U.S. Dept. of Commerce, Bureau of the Census: For sale by the Supt. of Docs., U.S. G.P.O., [1960]. v.: maps; 29 cm. 1. United States. Congress. House — Election districts — Maps. I. T.
G1201.F7 U45    912/.132873/07345 19    LC 84-643169

**Martis, Kenneth C.**     **4.151**
The historical atlas of United States Congressional districts, 1789–1983 / author and editor, Kenneth C. Martis; cartographer and assistant editor, Ruth Anderson Rowles; compilation draftsmen, David Durham, Brian Raber, Thomas Kokernak; research assistants, Rowland Dent ... [et al.]. — New York: Free Press; London: Collier Macmillan, c1982. 1 atlas (xiii, 302 p.): maps (some col.); 35 x 47 cm. Based on: The Atlas of congressional roll calls / prepared by the Historical Records Survey in New York City, 1938-39 and New Jersey, 1940-42. Foreword by Clifford Lee Lord. 1. United States. Congress — Voting — Maps. 2. United States. Congress — Election districts — Maps. 3. United States. Congress — History. 4. Legislation — United States I. Lord, Clifford Lee, 1912- II. Rowles, Ruth Anderson. III. Historical Records Survey (New York, N.Y.) IV. T.
G1201.F9 M3 1982    912/.132873/0775 19    LC 82-70583    ISBN 0029201500

**Oxford University Press.**     **4.152**
The United States and Canada / prepared by the Cartographic Department of Oxford University Press; advisory editors John D. Chapman, John C. Sherman. — 2nd ed. / prepared with the assistance of Quentin H. Stanford. — London: Oxford University Press, 1975. [12], 128 p.: chiefly col. maps; 27 cm. (Oxford regional economic atlas) Includes index 1. United States — Economic conditions — Maps. 2. Canada — Economic conditions — Maps. I. Chapman, John D. (John Doneric), 1923- ed. II. Sherman, John Clinton. ed. III. Stanford, Quentin H. IV. T.
G1201.G1 O9 1975    912/.1/330973092    LC 76-362820

**United States. Dept. of Agriculture.**     • **4.153**
Atlas of American agriculture: physical basis, including land relief, climate, soils, and natural vegetation of the United States / United States Dept. of Agriculture; prepared under the supervision of O.E. Baker. — Washington, D.C.: U.S. Govt. Print. Off., 1936. 4 v. in 1: ill. (some col.), maps (some col.); 49 cm. Each part has separate title page and pagination. The three last parts have previously been issued as advance sheets. 1. Agriculture — United States — Maps 2. Physical geography — United States — Maps 3. United States — Agriculture — Maps 4. United States — Physical geography — Maps 5. United States — Maps I. Baker, Oliver Edwin, 1883-1949. II. T.
G1201.J1 U55

**United States. Forest Service.**     • **4.154**
Atlas of United States trees. Washington: [For sale by the Supt. of Docs., U.S. Govt. Print. Off.] 1971-. v.: maps (part fold. in pocket); 36 cm. (United States. Dept. of Agriculture. Miscellaneous publication no. 1146, [etc.]) 1. Trees — United States — Maps. I. Little, Elbert Luther, 1907- II. Viereck, Leslie A. III. T.
G1201.K1U5x S21.A46 no. 1146, etc    630/.8 s 582.16/0973    *LC* 79-653298

**Rand McNally and Company.**     • **4.155**
Commercial atlas and marketing guide. Chicago. maps. 36-54 cm. Commercial atlas and marketing guide. The [42d-46th] ed., 1911-1915, called 1st-5th ed. Road atlas of the United States, Canada and Mexico issued in pocket accompanying the Commercial atlas and also issued and catalogued separately 1953- to date. 1. Marketing — Atlases. 2. United States — Commerce — Atlases. I. T.
G 1201.Q1 R35    *LC* Map06-9

**Paullin, Charles Oscar, 1868 or 9-1944.**     • **4.156**
Atlas of the historical geography of the United States, by Charles O. Paulin, edited by John K. Wright. [Washington, D.C., New York] Pub. jointly by Carnegie institution of Washington and the American geographical society of New York, 1932. 2 p. *β*., iii-xv p., 1 *β*., 162 p., 1 *β*., 688 maps (part col.) on 166 pl. (part double) 37 cm. (Carnegie Institution of Washington publication. no. 401]) A collection of maps, cartograms, and reproductions of early maps on many different scales, illustrating the natural environment of the United States and its demographic, economic, political, and military history. The text explains the maps and lists the sources from which they compiled. 1. Atlases 2. Geography, Historical 3. Cartography — America. 4. United States — Historical geography — Maps I. Wright, John Kirtland, 1891-1969. ed. II. American Geographical Society of New York. III. Carnegie Institution of Washington. Division of Historical Research. IV. T. V. Series.
G1201.S1 P3 1932    *LC* map32-54

**United States Military Academy. Dept. of Military Art and**     • **4.157**
**Engineering.**
The West Point atlas of American Wars / chief editor: Vincent J. Esposito; with an introductory letter by Dwight D. Eisenhower. — New York: Praeger [1959] 2 v.: col. maps; 27 x 37 cm. (Books that matter) 1. United States — History, Military — Maps. I. Esposito, Vincent Joseph, 1900- ed. II. T.
G1201.S1 U5 1959    912.73    *LC* 59-7452

**Atlas of early American history: the Revolutionary era,**     **4.158**
**1760–1790 / Lester J. Cappon, editor–in–chief; Barbara Bartz**
**Petchenik, cartographic editor; John Hamilton Long, assistant**
**editor; William B. Bedford ... [et al.], research associates; Nancy**
**K. Morbeck, cartographic assistant; Gretchen M. Oberfranc,**
**editorial assistant.**
[Princeton, N.J.]: Published for the Newberry Library and the Institute of Early American History and Culture by the Princeton University Press, 1976. 157 p.: col. maps; 47 cm. 1. United States — History — Revolution, 1775-1783 — Maps 2. United States — History — Revolution, 1775-1783 I. Cappon, Lester Jesse, 1900- II. Petchenik, Barbara Bartz. III. Long, John Hamilton.
G1201.S3 A8 1976    911/.73    *LC* 75-2982

**Nebenzahl, Kenneth, 1927-.**     **4.159**
Atlas of the American Revolution / map selection and commentary by Kenneth Nebenzahl; narrative text by Don Higginbotham. — Chicago: Rand McNally, 1974. 218 p.: col. ill., col. maps; 39 cm. Includes index. 1. United States — History — Revolution, 1775-1783 — Maps I. Higginbotham, Don. II. Rand McNally and Company. III. T.
G1201.S3 N4 1974    911/.73    *LC* 74-6976

**Adams, John S., 1938-.**     **4.160**
A comparative atlas of America's great cities: twenty metropolitan regions / [editor, Ronald Abler; text, John S. Adams and Ronald Abler; chief cartographer, Ki-Suk Lee]. — [Minneapolis]: University of Minnesota Press, c1976. xxii, 503 p.: ill.; 34 cm. 'One of three products of the Comparative Metropolitan Analysis Project.' 1. Metropolitan areas — United States — Maps. 2. Regional planning — Environmental aspects — United States. 3. Municipal powers and service beyond corporate limits — United States. 4. United States — Population — Maps. 5. United States — Economic conditions — 1971-1981 — Maps. 6. United States — Social conditions — 1960- — Maps. I. Abler, Ronald. joint author. II. Lee, Ki-Suk. III. Association of American Geographers. Comparative Metropolitan Analysis Project. IV. T. V. Title: America's great cities.
G1204.A1 A3 1976    912/.73    *LC* 76-14268    *ISBN* 0816607532

**Hilliard, Sam Bowers.**     **4.161**
Atlas of antebellum southern agriculture / Sam Bowers Hilliard; cartography by Clifford P. Duplechin, Mary Lee Eggart. — Baton Rouge: Louisiana State University Press, 1985 (c1984). 1 atlas (77 p.): 111 col. maps; 29 cm. 1. Agriculture — Southern States — Maps. 2. Slavery — United States — Southern States — Maps. 3. Southern States — Population — Maps. I. T.
G1281.J1 H5    912/.13381/0975 19    *LC* 84-675089    *ISBN* 0807111821

**Miller, John Frederick, 1928-.**     **4.162**
Precipitation–frequency atlas of the Western United States / J. F. Miller, R. H. Frederick, and R. J. Tracey; prepared for U.S Dept. of Agriculture, Soil Conservation Service, Engineering Division. — Silver Spring, Md.: U.S. Dept. of Commerce, National Oceanic and Atmospheric Administration, National Weather Service: for sale by the Supt. of Docs., U.S. Govt. Print. Off., Washington, 1973. 11 v.: ill., maps (some col.); 40 x 55 cm. (NOAA Atlas; 2) Scale of maps 1:2,000,000. 1. Precipitation (Meteorology) — West (U.S.) — Charts, diagrams, etc. I. Frederick, Ralph H. joint author. II. Tracey, R. J., joint author. III. T.
G1461.C88 M5 1973    912/.1/551577278    *LC* 74-603349

**Oregon State University.**     **4.163**
Atlas of the Pacific Northwest / edited by A. Jon Kimmerling and Philip L. Jackson; contributing authors, Robert E. Frenkel ... [et al.]. — 7th ed. — Corvalis, Or.: Oregon State University Press, c1985. 1 atlas (136 p.): ill. (some col.), col. maps; 29 cm. Scale of principal maps ca. 1:750,000. 1. Natural resources — Northwest, Pacific — Maps. 2. Northwest, Pacific — Economic conditions — Maps. I. Kimerling, A. Jon. II. Jackson, Philip L. III. T.
G1466.G3 O7 1985    912/.13337/09795 19    *LC* 86-107258    *ISBN* 0870714147

## G1785–1787 Islamic World. Near East

**An Historical atlas of Islam / edited by William C. Brice under**     **4.164**
**the patronage of the Encyclopaedia of Islam.**
Leiden: Brill, 1981. 1 atlas (viii, 71 p.): col. maps; 42 cm. 1. Islamic countries — Historical geography — Maps. 2. Islamic countries — Civilization — Maps. I. Brice, William Charles.
G1786.S1 H6 1981    911/.17671 19    *LC* 81-212100    *ISBN* 9004061169

**Roolvink, Roelof.**     • **4.165**
Historical atlas of the Muslim peoples / [compiled by R. Roolvink; with the collaboration of Saleh A. El Ali, Hussain Monés, and Mohd. Salim; with a foreword by H.A. R. Gibb]. — Cambridge: Harvard University Press, 1957. x p., 40 p.: col. maps. 1. Muslims — History — Maps. 2. Muslims — Maps. I. T.
G1786.S1 R    *LC* a 59-4149

## G1791–2193 Europe

**Esposito, Vincent Joseph, 1900-1965.**     • **4.166**
A military history and atlas of the Napoleonic Wars / compiled by the Department of Military Art and Engineering, prepared by Vincent J. Esposito, John Robert Elting. — New York: Praeger [1964] 1 v. (unpaged): ill., 169 col. maps.; 27 x 37 cm. 1. Napoleon I, Emperor of the French, 1769-1821. 2. Military history, Modern 3. Europe — History — 1789-1815 — Maps. I. Elting, John Robert. joint author. II. United States Military Academy. Dept. of Military Art and Engineering. III. T.
G1796.S62 E8    911/.4    *LC* 77-14708    *ISBN* 0404169503

**Gilbert, Martin, 1936-.**     **4.167**
The Macmillan atlas of the Holocaust / Martin Gilbert. — New York: Macmillan Pub. Co., c1982. 1 atlas (256 p.): ill., maps; 26 cm. Includes index. 1. Holocaust, Jewish (1939-1945) — Maps. I. T.
G1797.21.E29 G48 1982    940.53/15/039240222 19    *LC* 81-675599    *ISBN* 0025433806

**Oxford University Press.**     • **4.168**
Western Europe, prepared by the Cartographic Department of the Clarendon Press; advisory editors: K. M. Clayton, I. B. F. Kormoss. — London: Oxford University Press, 1971. xix p., 96 p. of col. maps, [42] p.; 27 cm. — (Oxford regional economic atlas) 1. Europe — Economic conditions — Maps. I. Clayton, Keith M. ed. II. Kormoss, I. B. F. ed. III. T.
G1801.G1 O8 1971    912.1/33094    *LC* 74-654598    *ISBN* 0198943067

**Oxford University Press.**     **4.169**
The atlas of Britain and Northern Ireland / Planned and directed by D.P. Bickmore and M.A. Shaw. Editorial committee: G. E. Blackman [and others]. Executed by the Cartographic Dept. of the Clarendon Press. Oxford: Clarendon, 1963. xii p., 200 p. of col. maps; 53 cm. "Most of the maps are at one of two scales,1:2,000,000 and 1:1,000,000." "Transparent reference overlay" inserted. Erratum slip inserted at p. 114. 1. Great Britain — Maps. 2. Great Britain — Economic conditions — Maps. — 1945- . 3. Northern Ireland — Maps. I. Bickmore, D. P. II. Shaw, Mary Alison, 1932- III. Blackman, Geoffrey Emett. IV. T.
G1810.O85 1963    *LC* MAP63-436

**Historical atlas of Britain** / Malcolm Falkus, John Gillingham    **4.170**
[general editors].
New York, N.Y.: Continuum, 1981. 1 atlas (223 p.): ill. (some col.), col. maps;
30 cm. Includes index. 1. Great Britain — Historical geography — Maps.
2. Great Britain — History I. Falkus, Malcolm E. II. Gillingham, John.
G1812.21.S1 H5 1981    911/.41 19    *LC* 81-675330    *ISBN*
0826401791

**Historic towns; maps and plans of towns and cities in the**    **4.171**
**British Isles, with historical commentaries, from earliest times**
**to 1800.** General editor: M. D. Lobel. [Topographical mapping
editor: W. H. Johns]
Baltimore, Johns Hopkins Press [1969?-. v. maps (part col.) 42 cm. A project of
the International Commission for the History of Towns and the British
Committee of Historic Towns. 1. Cities and towns — British Isles — Maps.
2. Cities and towns — British Isles — History. 3. Cities and towns, Medieval
— British Isles. I. Lobel, Mary Doreen, 1900- ed. II. Johns, William Henry.
ed. III. British Committee of Historic Towns. IV. International Commission
for the History of Towns.
G1814.A1 H5 1969a    912.42    *LC* 72-131565    *ISBN* 0801812437

**Edwards, Ruth Dudley.**    **4.172**
An atlas of Irish history / Ruth Dudley Edwards. — 2nd ed. — London; New
York: Methuen, 1981. 1 atlas (286 p.): maps; 24 cm. Includes index. 1. Ireland
— Historical geography — Maps. 2. Ireland — History I. T.
G1831.S1 E3 1981    911/.415 19    *LC* 80-41921    *ISBN* 0416748201

**Comité national français de géographie.**    • **4.173**
Atlas de France (Métropole) [2. éd.] Paris, Éditions géographiques de France
[1951-. pts.: Col. maps; 50 cm. 1. France — Maps I. T.
f G 1840 C73 1951    G1840.C6 1951.    *LC* 54-1163

**C. Bertelsmann Verlag.**    • **4.174**
Atlas of Central Europe. [Prepared by Kartographisches Institut Bertelsmann
under the direction of W. Bormann. London] J. Murray [1963] 101-120 p. of
col. maps, A4, 52 p. 33 cm. 1. Central Europe — Maps. I. Bormann, Werner,
1915- ed. II. T.
G1880.B4 1963    912.43    *LC* map64-539

**Dewdney, John C.**    **4.175**
The U.S.S.R. in maps / J.C. Dewdney. — New York: Holmes & Meier, 1982. 1
atlas (vi, 117 p.): maps; 24 x 27 cm. Includes index. 1. Soviet Union — Maps.
2. Soviet Union — Economic conditions — Maps. 3. Soviet Union —
Population — Maps. I. T.
G2110.D5 1982    912/.47 19    *LC* 82-675000    *ISBN* 0841907609

**Chew, Allen F.**    • **4.176**
An atlas of Russian history; eleven centuries of changing borders, by Allen F.
Chew. — Rev. ed. — New Haven: Yale University Press, 1970. xi, 127 p.:
maps.; 28 cm. 1. Soviet Union — Historical geography — Maps. I. T.
G2111.S1 C5 1970    911.47    *LC* 78-653611    *ISBN* 0300014457 Pbk

**Gilbert, Martin, 1936-.**    **4.177**
Russian history atlas; cartographic consultant: Arthur Banks. [1st American
ed.] New York, Macmillan Co. [1972] [13], 146, [29] p. maps. 25 cm. 1. Soviet
Union — Historical geography — Maps. I. Banks, Arthur. II. T.
G2111.S1 G52 1972    911.47    *LC* 72-80174

# G2200–2799 Asia. Africa. Oceania

**Djambatan (Firm: Amsterdam, Netherlands)**    • **4.178**
Atlas of the Arab world and the Middle East. With an introd. by C. F.
Beckingham. London, Macmillan; New York, St. Martin's Press, 1960. 55,
[17] p. illus., maps (part col.) 35 cm. 1. Islamic countries — Maps. 2. Islamic
countries — Economic conditions — Maps. I. T.
G2205.D4 1960a    912.56    *LC* map60-313

**Aharoni, Yohanan, 1919-1976.**    **4.179**
The Macmillan Bible atlas / by Yohanan Aharoni and Michael Avi–Yonah;
prepared by Carta, Ltd. — Rev. ed. — New York: Macmillan, c1977. 184 p.: ill.
(some col.), col. maps; 30 cm. Includes index. 1. Bible — Geography — Maps
I. Avi-Yonah, Michael, 1904-1974. joint author. II. Karta (Firm) III. T.
G2230.A2 1977    912/.56    *LC* 77-4313    *ISBN* 0025005901

**A Historical atlas of South Asia** / edited by Joseph E.    **4.180**
**Schwartzberg, with the collaboration of Shiva G. Bajpai ... [et**
**al.]; final map drafts by the American Geographical Society of**
**New York; principal sponsors, Charles Lesley Ames ... [et al.].**
Chicago: University of Chicago Press, 1978. xxv, 352 p.: ill., col. maps; 42 cm.
— (Reference series - the Association for Asian Studies; no. 2) 2 map overlays
and 3 charts in pocket. Includes index. 1. South Asia — Historical geography
— Maps. 2. South Asia — History. I. Schwartzberg, Joseph E. II. Bajpai,
Shiva G.
G2261.S1 H5 1978    911/.54    *LC* 77-81713    *ISBN* 0226742210

**George Philip & Son.**    **4.181**
China in maps. Edited by Harold Fullard. — London, 1968. 25 p. col. maps 22
x 28 cm. 1. China — Maps. I. Fullard, Harold. ed. II. T.
G2305.P5 1968    *LC* Map68-975    *ISBN* 540050415

**Herrmann, Albert, 1886-1945.**    • **4.182**
An historical atlas of China / by Albert Herrmann; General editor, Norton
Ginsburg; prefatory essay by Paul Wheatley. — New ed. — Chicago: Aldine
Pub. Co., [1966] xxxii, 88 p.: col. maps; 30 cm. Based on the author's Historical
and commercial atlas of China. 1. China — Historical geography — Maps.
2. Asia — Historical geography — Maps. 3. China — Economic conditions —
1949- — Maps. I. Ginsburg, Norton Sydney. ed. II. Wheatley, Paul.
III. Herrmann, Albert, 1886-1945. Historical and commercial atlas of China.
IV. T.
G2306.S1 H4 1966    912.51    *LC* map65-13

**Kokusai Kyōiku Jōhō Sentā.**    **4.183**
Atlas of Japan: physical, economic, and social. — 2d [rev.] ed. — Tokyo:
International Society for Educational Information, 1974. viii, 64, 64 p.: col.
maps; 37 cm. Second ed. prepared under the joint guidance of A. Ebato and K.
Watanabe. Text in English, French, and Spanish. Part of illustrative matter in
pocket. 1. Japan — Maps. I. Ebato, Akira, 1932- II. Watanabe, Kazuo, 1921-
III. T.
G2355.K65 1974    912/.52    *LC* 75-314450

**Fund for Assistance to Private Education.**    **4.184**
The Philippine atlas / Fund for Assistance to Private Education. — Manila:
The Fund, c1975. 2 v.: col. ill., col. maps; 39 cm. Includes indexes.
Accompanied by 18 map overlays. 1. Education — Philippine Islands —
Statistics. 2. Philippines — Economic conditions — Maps. 3. Philippines —
Social conditions — Maps. I. T.
G2391.G1 F8 1975    912/.599    *LC* 75-23840

**Conklin, Harold C.**    **4.185**
Ethnographic atlas of Ifugao: a study of environment, culture, and society in
Northern Luzon / Harold C. Conklin; with the special assistance of Puggũwon
Lupãih; and Miklos Pinther, cartographer. — New Haven: Yale University
Press, 1980. vii, 116 p.: ill. (some col.) col. maps; 42 x 47 cm. Published with the
cooperation of The American Geographical Society of New York. Includes
index. 1. Ethnology — Philippine Islands — Ifugao — Maps. 2. Agriculture
— Philippine Islands — Ifugao — Maps. 3. Ifugao (Philippines) — Philippine
Islands — Agriculture — Maps. I. Lupãih, Puggũwon. II. Pinther, Miklos.
III. American Geographical Society of New York. IV. T.
G2393.I35E6 C6 1980    959.9/1    *LC* 79-689774    *ISBN* 0300025297

**Clark, J. Desmond (John Desmond), 1916-.**    • **4.186**
Atlas of African prehistory / compiled by J. Desmond Clark. — Chicago:
University of Chicago Press, c1967. 62 p.: 50 maps (part col.) In portfolio. Maps
printed on transparent overlays. Scale of maps 1: 20,000,000 and 1: 38,000,000.
1. Man, Prehistoric — Africa — Maps. 2. Africa — Antiquities — Maps. I. T.
G2446.E1 C5 1967    *LC* Map 66-22

**African history in maps** / Michael Kwamena–Poh ... [et al.].    **4.187**
New York, N.Y.: Longman, 1982. 1 atlas (76 p.): maps; 28 cm. Includes index.
1. Africa — Historical geography. I. Kwamena-Poh, M. A. II. Longman
Group Ltd.
G2446.S1 A4 1982    911/.6 19    *LC* 81-675343    *ISBN* 0582603315

**Fage, J. D.**    **4.188**
An atlas of African history / J. D. Fage. — 2d ed. — New York: African
Publishing Company, 1978. [84] p.: 71 maps; 29 cm. Includes index. 1. Africa
— Historical geography — Maps. I. T.
G2446.S1 F3 1978    911/.6    *LC* 78-16131    *ISBN* 0841904294 cloth

**Historical atlas of Africa** / general editors, J.F. Ade Ajayi &    **4.189**
**Michael Crowder; geographical editor, Paul Richards; linguistic**
**editor, Elizabeth Dunstan, cartographic designer, Alick**
**Newman.**
Cambridge; New York: Cambridge University Press, 1985. 1 atlas ([167] p.):
ill., col. maps; 41 cm. 1. Africa — Historical geography — Maps. 2. Africa —
Maps I. Ajayi, J. F. Ade. II. Crowder, Michael, 1934- III. Richards, Paul.
IV. Dunstan, Elizabeth. V. Newman, Alick.
G2446.S1 H5 1985    911/.6 19    *LC* 83-675975    *ISBN* 0521253535

**Talbot, A. M.**    **4.190**
Atlas of the Union of South Africa, by A. M. Talbot and W. J. Talbot; prepared
in collaboration with the Trigonometrical Survey Office, and under the aegis of
the National Council for Social Research. Pretoria, Govt. Printer, 1960. lxiv,
178 p. maps (part col.) diagrs., tables. 45 x 58 cm. English and Afrikaans; added
t.p. in Afrikaans. Includes colored transparent overlay. Errata slip inserted.
1. South Africa — Economic conditions — Maps. I. Talbot, William John,
joint author. II. T. III. Title: Union of South Africa.
G2566.G1 T3 1960    *LC* map61-153

Nigeria in maps / edited by K.M. Barbour ... [et al.].                    **4.191**
New York: Africana Pub. Co., 1982. 1 atlas (vii, 148 p.): ill., maps; 27 x 28 cm.
1. Nigeria — Maps. 2. Nigeria — Economic conditions — Maps. 3. Nigeria
— Social conditions — Maps. I. Barbour, Kenneth Michael.
G2695.N6 1982       912/.669 19       *LC* 82-675001       *ISBN* 0841907633

New Zealand atlas / edited by Ian Wards.                    **4.192**
Wellington: A. R. Shearer, Govt. Printer, 1976. xv, 291 p.: ill. (some col.), col.
maps; 32 cm. Includes index. 1. New Zealand — Maps. I. Wards, Ian
McLean.
G2795.N4 1976       912/.931       *LC* 76-381751       *ISBN* 0477010008

## G2800–3102 Oceans

The Rand McNally atlas of the oceans / [editor, Martyn                    **4.193**
Bramwell].
New York: Rand McNally, c1977. 208 p.: ill. (some col.), col. maps; 38 cm.
Simultaneously published in London by Mitchell Beazley under title: Mitchell
Beazley atlas of the oceans; also simultaneously published in South Melbourne,
Victoria by Macmillan under title: The Macmillan atlas of the oceans. Includes
index. 1. Oceanography — Charts, diagrams, etc. I. Bramwell, Martyn.
II. Title: Atlas of the oceans.
G2800.R3 1977       912/.1/55146       *LC* 77-73772       *ISBN* 0528830821

The Times atlas of the oceans / editor, Alastair Couper.                    **4.194**
New York: Van Nostrand Reinhold Co., [1983] 1 atlas (272 p.): col. ill., col.
maps; 37 cm. 1. Oceanography — Charts, diagrams, etc. 2. Marine resources
3. Shipping I. Couper, A. D.
G2800.T5 1983       912/.155146 19       *LC* 82-675461       *ISBN*
0442216610

New Zealand. Dept. of Lands and Survey.                    **4.195**
Islands of the South Pacific. 2d ed. [Wellington] 1976. col. map 71 x 107 cm.
(NZMS. 275) Relief shown by shading and spot heights. Depths shown by
gradient tints. 'Lambert conformal conic projection, standard parallels at 0$sS
and 45$sS.' Scale 1:10,000,000. 1. Oceania — Maps. I. T. II. Series.
G9250 1976.N4       *LC* 78-691553

# GA MATHEMATICAL GEOGRAPHY. CARTOGRAPHY

Berry, Brian Joe Lobley, 1934- comp.                    • **4.196**
Spatial analysis: a reader in statistical geography / [by] Brian J. L. Berry [and]
Duane F. Marble. — Englewood Cliffs, N.J.: Prentice-Hall, [1968] xi, 512 p.:
ill., maps; 26 cm. 1. Geography, Mathematical 2. Spatial analysis (Statistics)
I. Marble, Duane Francis, 1931- joint comp. II. T.
GA9.B53       910/.001/82       *LC* 68-10856

Birch, Thomas William.                    • **4.197**
Maps, topographical and statistical, by T.W. Birch. 2d ed. Oxford, Clarendon
Press, 1964. xiv, 240 p. ill., maps. 1. Cartography I. T.
GA9 B56 1964       *LC* 65-3116

Bunge, William Wheeler, 1928-.                    • **4.198**
Theoretical geography / by William Bunge. — 2., rev. and enl. ed. — Lund:
Royal University of Lund, Dept. of Geography; Gleerup, 1966. xvii, 289 p.: ill.
— (Lund studies in geography: Ser. C, General and mathematical geography;
no. 1) 1. Geography — Methodology I. T. II. Series.
GA9.L8 no.1 1966       910/.001/8       *LC* 67-97303

Chorley, Richard J.                    • **4.199**
Models in geography; edited by Richard J. Chorley [and] Peter Haggett. —
London: Methuen; distributed in the U.S.A. by Barnes & Noble, 1967. 816 p.:
illus., 12 plates, maps, tables, diagrs.; 25 cm. — (Madingley lectures 2)
1. Geography — Mathematical models I. Haggett, Peter. joint author. II. T.
III. Series.
GA23.C46 1967       910/.001/82       *LC* 68-71825

United States. Defense Mapping Agency. Hydrographic/                    **4.200**
Topographic Center.
Glossary of mapping, charting, and geodetic terms / prepared for Dept. of
Defense by Defense Mapping Agency, Hydrographic/Topographic Center. —
4th ed. — Washington: The Agency, 1981. 204 p.; 26 cm. Second ed. prepared
by the agency under its earlier name: United States Army Topographic
Command; and 3rd ed. by Defense Mapping Agency, Topographic Center.
1. Cartography — Dictionaries. 2. Geodesy — Dictionaries. I. United States.
Dept. of Defense. II. T.
GA102.D43 1973       526/.03

MacDougall, E. Bruce (Edward Bruce), 1939-.                    **4.201**
Computer programming for spatial problems / E. Bruce MacDougall. — New
York: Wiley, 1976. vii, 158 p.: ill.; 26 cm. 'A Halsted Press book.' Includes
index. 1. Cartography — Data processing 2. Programming (Electronic
computers) I. T.
GA102.4.E4 M3 1976       526/.028/5424       *LC* 76-46976       *ISBN*
0470990112

Monmonier, Mark S.                    **4.202**
Computer-assisted cartography: principles and prospects / Mark S.
Monmonier. — Englewood Cliffs, N.J.: Prentice-Hall, c1982. x, 214 p.: ill.; 25
cm. Includes index. 1. Digital mapping I. T.
GA102.4.E4 M66       526/.028/54 19       *LC* 81-14380       *ISBN*
0131653083

Keates, J. S.                    **4.203**
Cartographic design and production [by] J. S. Keates. — New York: Wiley,
[1973] xvi, 240 p.: illus.; 26 cm. 'A Halsted Press book.' 1. Cartography I. T.
GA105.K42       526       *LC* 72-9251       *ISBN* 0470462353

Monkhouse, Francis John.                    • **4.204**
Maps and diagrams: their compilation and construction [by] F. J. Monkhouse
and H. R. Wilkinson. 3rd ed. revised and enlarged. London, Methuen, 1971.
xxii, 522 p., 7 plates (2 fold.) illus., maps (some col.) 22 cm. (University
paperbacks, UP75) 'Distributed in the U.S.A. by Barnes & Noble Inc.'
1. Cartography I. Wilkinson, Henry Robert. joint author. II. T.
GA105.M64 1971       526.8/6       *LC* 70-578537       *ISBN* 0416074502

Raisz, Erwin Josephus, 1893-.                    • **4.205**
General cartography. — 2d ed. — New York: McGraw-Hill, 1948. xiii, 354 p.:
ill., maps. — (McGraw-Hill series in geography) 1. Cartography I. T.
GA105.R3 1948       526.98       *LC* 48-9621

United States Coast and Geodetic Survey.                    **4.206**
Cartography / by H. Deetz. — U.S. Govt. Print. Off., 1936. 83p. (Its Special
publication, no. 205) 1. Cartography I. Deetz, Charles Henry, 1864- II. T.
GA105 U48 1936

Elements of cartography / Arthur H. Robinson ... [et al.].                    **4.207**
5th ed. — New York: Wiley, c1984. 544 p.: ill. (some col.), maps; 25 cm.
Revision of: Robinson, A.H. Elements of cartography. 4th ed. c1978.
1. Cartography I. Robinson, Arthur Howard, 1915-
GA105.3.E43 1984       526 19       *LC* 84-11860       *ISBN* 0471098779

Muehrcke, Phillip.                    **4.208**
Map use: reading, analysis, and interpretation / Phillip C. Muehrcke, with
Juliana O. Muehrcke. — 2nd ed. — Madison, WI: JP Publications, c1986. —
xi, 512 p.: ill.; 26 cm. 1. Maps I. Muehrcke, Juliana O. joint author. II. T.
GA105.3.M83 1986       912/.014       *LC* 85-82616       *ISBN* 0960297820

Robinson, Arthur Howard, 1915-.                    **4.209**
The nature of maps: essays toward understanding maps and mapping / Arthur
H. Robinson and Barbara Bartz Petchenik. Chicago: University of Chicago
Press, 1976. xi, 138 p.: ill.; 23 cm. Includes index. 1. Cartography 2. Maps
I. Petchenik, Barbara Bartz, joint author. II. T.
GA105.3.R62       526       *LC* 75-36401       *ISBN* 0226722813

Wilford, John Noble.                    **4.210**
The mapmakers / by John Noble Wilford. — 1st ed. — New York: Knopf,
1981. xi, 414 p.: ill.; 25 cm. Includes bibliographical references and index.
1. Cartography — History I. T.
GA105.3.W49 1981       912/.09 19       *LC* 80-2716       *ISBN* 0394461940

Dickinson, Gordon Cawood.                    **4.211**
Statistical mapping and the presentation of statistics [by] G. C. Dickinson. —
2d ed. — London: Edward Arnold, 1973. 195, [1] p.: illus., maps (1 col.); 26 cm.
Includes index. 1. Maps, Statistical 2. Statistics — Graphic methods I. T.
GA109.8.D5 1973       001.4/226       *LC* 72-91355       *ISBN* 0713156414

Deetz, Charles Henry, 1864-1946.                    • **4.212**
Elements of map projection with applications to map and chart construction /
Charles H. Deetz and Oscar S. Adams. — 5th ed., rev. — Washington, D.C.:
U.S. Govt. Print.Off., 1945. 226 p.: diagrs., maps. (Special publication (U.S.
Coast and Geodetic Survey) no. 68) At head of title: U.S. Dept of
Commerce...Coast and geodetic survey. 1. Map-projection I. Adams, Oscar
Sherman, 1874-      . II. T. III. Series.
GA110.D45 1945       *LC* 45-35996

McDonnell, Porter W., 1929-.                    **4.213**
Introduction to map projections / Porter W. McDonnell, Jr. — New York: M.
Dekker, c1979. vii, 174 p.: ill.; 28 cm. 1. Map-projection I. T.
GA110.M25       526.8       *LC* 79-13560       *ISBN* 0824768302

Pearson, Frederick, 1936-.                    **4.214**
Map projection equations / by Frederick Pearson II. — Dahlgren, Va.: Naval
Surface Weapons Center, Dahlgren Laboratory, 1977. ix, 329 p.: ill.; 28 cm. —

(NSWC/DL TR; 3624) Cover title. 1. Map-projection I. Dahlgren Laboratory. II. T.
VF7.U64 no. 3624 GA110.G4x　　623.4/08 s 526.8　　*LC* 77-602944

**Steers, J. A. (James Alfred), 1899-.**　　　　　　　　　　**4.215**
An introduction to the study of map projections, by J. A. Steers. With a foreword by F. Debenham. [13th ed.] London, University of London Press [1962] 288 p. illus. 23 cm. 1. Map-projection I. T.
GA110.S85 1962　　*LC* 65-4022

**Larsgaard, Mary Lynette, 1946-.**　　　　　　　　　　**4.216**
Topographic mapping of the Americas, Australia, and New Zealand / Mary Lynette Larsgaard. — Littleton, Colo.: Libraries Unlimited, 1984. xii, 180 p.; 25 cm. 1. Topographic maps 2. North America — Maps, Topographic. 3. Latin America — Maps, Topographic. 4. Australia — Maps, Topographic. 5. New Zealand — Maps, Topographic. I. T.
GA125.L37 1984　　912 19　　*LC* 84-3874　　*ISBN* 0872872769

**Lobeck, A. K. (Armin Kohl), 1886-1958.**　　　　　　　● **4.217**
Block diagrams and other graphic methods used in geology and geography. 2d ed. Amherst, Mass., Emerson-Trussell Book Co., 1958. 212 p. illus. 21 x 28 cm. 1. Block diagrams I. T.
GA140.L6 1958　　550.84　　*LC* 58-1245

**Foreign maps.**　　　　　　　　　　　　　　　　　　**4.218**
[Washington, D.C.]: Headquarters, Dept. of the Army, 1963. i, 286 p., [46] leaves of plates: ill. (some col.); 27 cm. — (Department of the Army technical manual. TM 5-248) Cover title. 'Figure 151, Natural scale indicator' ([2] p.) folded in pocket. 'Supersedes TM 5-248, 12 June 1956'—P. 1. 'October 1963.' Includes index. 1. Maps I. Series.
GA151.F64 1964　　912 19　　*LC* 85-151735

**Microcartography, applications for archives and libraries /**　　**4.219**
**edited by Larry Cruse with the assistance of Sylvia B. Warren.**
Santa Cruz, CA: Western Association of Map Libraries, 1981, c1982. 200 p.: ill.; 23 cm. — (Occasional paper / Western Association of Map Libraries; no. 6) 'Outgrowth of a meeting held by the Western Association of Map Libraries ... at the University of California, San Diego ... October 6-7, 1977'—Introd. Accompanied by microfiche entitled: Microchart navigation systems; in pocket. Includes index. 1. Map collections — Congresses. 2. Microphotography — Congresses. I. Cruse, Larry, 1944- II. Warren, Sylvia B., 1949- III. Western Association of Map Libraries.
GA192.M52　　025.1/29 19　　*LC* 81-19718　　*ISBN* 0939112078

**Cobb, David A., 1945-.**　　　　　　　　　　　　　**4.220**
Guide to U.S. map resources / compiled by David. Cobb. — Chicago, Ill.: American Library Association, 1986. xvi, 196 p. Includes index. 1. Map collections — United States — Directories. I. T.
GA193.U5 C62 1985　　026/.912/0973 19　　*LC* 85-22958　　*ISBN* 0838904394

**Map collections in the United States and Canada: a directory /**　　**4.221**
**David K. Carrington and Richard W. Stephenson, editors.**
4th ed. — New York: Special Libraries Association, c1985. 178 p.; 28 cm. Includes index. 1. Map collections — United States — Directories. 2. Map collections — Canada — Directories. I. Carrington, David K., 1938- II. Stephenson, Richard W., 1930-
GA193.U5 M36 1985　　026/.912/02573 19　　*LC* 84-27571　　*ISBN* 0871113066

**Skelton, Raleigh Ashlin.**　　　　　　　　　　　　**4.222**
Maps: a historical survey of their study and collecting / [by] R. A. Skelton. — Chicago: University of Chicago Press, [1972] xvii, 138 p.: port.; 21 cm. — (The Kenneth Nebenzahl, Jr., lectures in the history of cartography at the Newberry Library) 'Published for the Hermon Dunlap Smith Center for the History of Cartography; the Newberry Library.' 1. Maps, Early — Collectors and collecting. 2. Cartography — History I. Hermon Dunlap Smith Center for the History of Cartography. II. T. III. Series.
GA197.3.S55　　912/.075　　*LC* 72-650049　　*ISBN* 0226761649

**Tooley, R. V. (Ronald Vere), 1898-.**　　　　　　　　**4.223**
[Dictionary of mapmakers] Tooley's Dictionary of mapmakers / compiled by Ronald Vere Tooley; with a pref. by Helen Wallis. — New York: A. R. Liss,; Amsterdam, Netherlands: Meridian Pub. Co., c1979. xii, 684 p.: ill.; 26 cm. First half of work originally appeared in parts in the Map collectors' series published by the Map Collectors' Circle. 1. Cartographers — Biography. I. T. II. Title: Dictionary of mapmakers.
GA198.T66　　526/.092/2 B　　*LC* 79-1936　　*ISBN* 0845117017

**Bagrow, Leo.**　　　　　　　　　　　　　　　　　**4.224**
[Geschichte der Kartographie. English] History of cartography / Leo Bagrow. — 2nd. ed., enl. with additional maps and ill. / rev. and enl. by R.A. Skelton. — Chicago, Ill.: Precedent Pub.; New Brunswick, USA; Oxford, UK: Distributed by Transaction Books, 1985. 312 p., [168] p. of plates: ill. (some col.); 28 cm.

Translation of: Geschichte der Kartographie. Includes index. 1. Cartography — History 2. Maps I. Skelton, R. A. (Raleigh Ashlin), 1906-1970. II. T.
GA201.B313 1985　　526/.09 19　　*LC* 85-16958

**Brown, Lloyd Arnold, 1907-.**　　　　　　　　　　　● **4.225**
The story of maps. — [1st ed.]. — Boston: Little, Brown, 1949. xix, 397 p.: illus., ports., maps.; 27 cm. 1. Cartography — History I. T.
GA201.B76 1949　　526.9809　　*LC* 49-9542

**Crone, G. R. (Gerald Roe)**　　　　　　　　　　　● **4.226**
Maps and their makers: an introduction to the history of cartography [by] G.R. Crone. 3rd ed. London, Hutchinson, 1966. xiv, 15-192 p. col. front., maps. 1. Cartography — History I. T.
GA201 C7 1966　　*LC* 66-2401

**Robinson, Arthur Howard, 1915-.**　　　　　　　　　**4.227**
Early thematic mapping in the history of cartography / Arthur H. Robinson. — Chicago: University of Chicago Press, c1982. xiv, 266 p.: ill.; 25 cm. Includes index. 1. Cartography — History I. T.
GA201.R63 1982　　912 19　　*LC* 81-11516　　*ISBN* 0226722856

**Thrower, Norman Joseph William.**　　　　　　　　　**4.228**
Maps & man; an examination of cartography in relation to culture and civilization [by] Norman J. W. Thrower. — Englewood Cliffs, N.J.: Prentice-Hall, [1972] vii, 184 p.; 23 cm. 1. Cartography — History I. T. II. Title: An examination of cartography in relation to culture and civilization.
GA201.T47 1972　　526/.09　　*LC* 70-166141　　*ISBN* 0135559618

**Tooley, R. V. (Ronald Vere), 1898-.**　　　　　　　　**4.229**
Maps and map–makers / by R. V. Tooley. — 6th ed. — London: B. T. Batsford, 1978. xv, 140 p., [4] leaves of plates: ill. (some col.); 26 cm. 1. Cartography — History I. T.
GA201.T6 1978b　　912/.09　　*LC* 78-318874　　*ISBN* 0713413956

**Skelton, R. A. (Raleigh Ashlin), 1906-1970.**　　　　　● **4.230**
Explorers' maps: chapters in the cartographic record of geographical discovery / by R. A. Skelton. — New York: F. A. Praeger, 1958. xi, 337 p., plate: ill. (1 col.), charts, maps, plans; 29 cm. 1. Cartography — History 2. Discoveries (in geography) I. T.
GA203.S55　　910.9　　*LC* 58-8182

**Dilke, Oswald Ashton Wentworth.**　　　　　　　　　**4.231**
Greek and Roman maps / O.A.W. Dilke with 62 illustrations. — Ithaca, N.Y.: Cornell University Press, 1985. 224 p., [16] p. of plates: ill.; 23 cm. (Aspects of Greek and Roman life) Includes index. 1. Classical geography — Maps 2. Maps, Early I. T.
GA213.D44 1985　　526/.093 19　　*LC* 84-72221　　*ISBN* 0801418011

**Lock, Clara Beatrice Muriel, 1914-.**　　　　　　　　**4.232**
Modern maps and atlases: an outline to twentieth century production / [by] C. B. Muriel Lock. — [Hamden, Conn.]: Archon Books, [1969] 619 p.: front.; 23 cm. 1. Cartography I. T.
GA246.L6 1969　　912　　*LC* 70-6153　　*ISBN* 0208008691

**Langeraar, W., 1915-.**　　　　　　　　　　　　　**4.233**
Surveying and charting of the seas / W. Langeraar. — Amsterdam; New York: Elsevier, 1984. xvii, 612 p.: ill.; 26 cm. — (Elsevier oceanography series. 37) Includes index. 1. Nautical charts 2. Cartography I. T. II. Series.
GA359.L36 1984　　623.89/2/0222 19　　*LC* 83-25286　　*ISBN* 0444422781

**Moffat, Riley Moore, 1947-.**　　　　　　　　　　　**4.234**
Map index to topographic quadrangles of the United States, 1882–1940 / by Riley Moore Moffat; foreword by Mary Larsgaard. — Santa Cruz, CA: Western Association of Map Libraries, c1985. xv, 1 v. (various pagings): ill., col. maps; 21 x 28 cm. — (Occasional paper / Western Association of Map Libraries; no. 10) 1. United States — Maps, Topographic — Indexes. I. T.
GA405.M64 1985　　016.912/73 19　　*LC* 84-21984　　*ISBN* 0939112124

**Harley, J. B. (John Brian)**　　　　　　　　　　　**4.235**
Mapping the American Revolutionary War / J. B. Harley, Barbara Bartz Petchenik, and Lawrence W. Towner. — Chicago: University of Chicago Press, 1978, c1977. viii, 187 p., [14] leaves of plates: ill.; 29 cm. — (The Kenneth Nebenzahl, Jr., lectures in the history of cartography at the Newberry Library) 'Lectures were given 11-14 November 1974.' Includes index. 1. United States — History — Revolution, 1775-1783 — Cartography — Addresses, essays, lectures. I. Petchenik, Barbara Bartz, joint author. II. Towner, Lawrence W. joint author. III. T. IV. Series.
GA405.5.H37　　911/.73　　*LC* 77-8023　　*ISBN* 0226316319

**Nicholson, N. L. (Norman Leon)**　　　　　　　　　**4.236**
The maps of Canada: a guide to official Canadian maps, charts, atlases, and gazetteers / N.L. Nicholson, L.M. Sebert. — Folkestone, Kent, England: Wm. Dawson; Hamden, Conn., USA: Archon Books, 1982. x, 251 p., [1] leaf of

plates: ill., maps; 26 cm. 1. Cartography — Canada — History. 2. Canada — Surveys — History. 3. Canada — Maps. I. Sebert, L. M. II. T.
GA471.N52    912/.71 19    *LC* 79-41118    *ISBN* 0208017828

# GB PHYSICAL GEOGRAPHY

**The Encyclopaedic dictionary of physical geography** / edited by    **4.237**
Andrew Goudie ... [et al.].
Oxford, OX, England; New York, NY, USA: Blackwell, 1985. xvi, 528 p.: ill.; 25 cm. (Blackwell reference) 1. Physical geography — Dictionaries. I. Goudie, Andrew.
GB10.E53 1985    910/.02/0321 19    *LC* 85-6190    *ISBN* 0631132929

**Fairbridge, Rhodes Whitmore, 1914-.**    • **4.238**
The encyclopedia of geomorphology / edited by Rhodes W. Fairbridge. — New York: Reinhold Book Corp., [c1968] xvi, 1295 p.: illus.; 27 cm. — (Encyclopedia of earth sciences. v. 3) 1. Geomorphology — Dictionaries. I. T. II. Series.
GB10.F3    551.4/03    *LC* 68-58342

**Whittow, John Byron.**    **4.239**
The Penguin dictionary of physical geography / John B. Whittow. — Harmondsworth: Penguin, 1984. — 591 p.: ill., maps; 20 cm. — (Penguin reference books) 1. Physical geography — Dictionaries. I. T. II. Title: Dictionary of physical geography.
GB10.W48    910/.02/0321 19    *ISBN* 014051094X

**Sauer, Carl Ortwin, 1889-.**    • **4.240**
The morphology of landscape. — Berkeley, Calif.: University of California Press, [1925] [19]-53 p. (University of California publications in geography, 2:2) 1. Landscape 2. Geography I. T.
GB23.S3

**King, Cuchlaine A. M.**    **4.241**
Physical geography / Cuchlaine A. M. King. — Totowa, N.J.: Barnes and Noble Books, 1980. 332 p.: ill.; 26 cm. 1. Physical geography I. T.
GB54.5.K56 1980b    910/.02 19    *LC* 80-134479    *ISBN* 0389200891

**Strahler, Arthur Newell, 1918-.**    **4.242**
Elements of physical geography / Arthur N. Strahler, Alan H. Strahler. — 3rd ed. — New York: Wiley, c1984. xiv, 538 p.: col. ill.; 29 cm. Includes index. 1. Physical geography I. Strahler, Alan H. II. T.
GB54.5.S79 1984    910/.02 19    *LC* 83-7005    *ISBN* 0471889733

**Strahler, Arthur Newell, 1918-.**    **4.243**
Modern physical geography / Arthur N. Strahler, Alan H. Strahler. — 3rd ed. — New York: J. Wiley, c1987. xii, 544 p., [64] p. of plates: ill. (some col.); 29 cm. Includes index. 1. Physical geography — Text-books — 1945- I. Strahler, Alan H. II. T.
GB54.5.S8 1987    551 19    *LC* 86-24662    *ISBN* 0471850640

**Leopold, Luna Bergere, 1915-.**    • **4.244**
Fluvial processes in geomorphology [by] Luna B. Leopold, M. Gordon Wolman [and] John P. Miller. San Francisco, W.H. Freeman [1964] xiii, 522 p. ill., maps. (A Series of books in geology) 1. Rivers 2. Physical geography I. T.
GB55 L4    *LC* 64-10919

**Thornbury, William D. (William David), 1900-.**    • **4.245**
Principles of geomorphology [by] William D. Thornbury. 2d ed. New York, Wiley [1968, c1969] xi, 594 p. illus., maps. 23 cm. 1. Geomorphology I. T.
GB55.T49 1969    551.4    *LC* 68-8323    *ISBN* 0471861979

**Lobeck, A. K. (Armin Kohl), 1886-1958.**    • **4.246**
Things maps don't tell us; an adventure into map interpretation. New York, Macmillan, 1957. x, 159 p. maps, profiles. 28 cm. 1. Physical geography 2. Geophysics I. T.
GB59.L6    551    *LC* 56-10626

**White, Gilbert Fowler, 1911-.**    **4.247**
Natural hazards, local, national, global / edited by Gilbert F. White. — New York: Oxford University Press, 1974. xvi, 288 p.: ill.; 28 cm. 1. Natural disasters 2. Disaster relief I. T.
GB70.W45    363.3/4    *LC* 73-90368    *ISBN* 0195017579 pbk

# GB111–398 By Region or Country

**Hunt, Charles Butler, 1906-.**    **4.248**
Natural regions of the United States and Canada [by] Charles B. Hunt. — San Francisco: W. H. Freeman, [1973, c1974] xii, 725 p.: illus.; 26 cm. — (A series of books in geology) 1. Physical geography — United States. I. T.
GB121.H79    917/.02    *LC* 73-12030    *ISBN* 071670255X

**Fenneman, Nevin Melancthon, 1865-1945.**    **4.249**
Physiography of eastern United States / by Nevin M. Fenneman. — New York and London: McGraw-Hill book company, inc., 1938. xiii, 714 p.: ill., maps. 1. Physical geography — United States. 2. Geology — United States I. T.
GB124A113 F    *LC* 38-9303

**Fenneman, Nevin Melancthon, 1865-.**    • **4.250**
Physiography of western United States / by Nevin M. Fenneman. — 1st ed. New York: McGraw-Hill book company, inc., 1931. xiii, 534 p.: ill., maps (1 fold. in pocket) diagrs. 1. Physical geography — The West 2. Geology — The West I. T.
GB124 W4 F4    *LC* 31-4608

**Houston, J. M. (James Macintosh), 1922-.**    • **4.251**
The western Mediterranean world; an introduction to its regional landscapes [by] J. M. Houston. With contributions by J. Roglić and J. I. Clarke. New York, Praeger [1967] xxxii, 800 p. illus., maps, plates. 23 cm. (Praeger advanced geographies) 1. Physical geography — Western Mediterranean. 2. Landscape — Western Mediterranean. I. T.
GB178.H6 1967    910.09/18/22    *LC* 67-25037

**Martonne, Emmanuel de, 1873-1955.**    • **4.252**
Geographical regions of France. Translated from the latest ed. by H. C. Brentnall. — 2d ed. — London, Heinemann [1950] 224 p. illus. 20 cm. 1. Physical geography — France. 2. Geology — France. I. T.
GB206.M32 1950    914.4    *LC* 52-16016

**Berg, L. S. (Lev Semenovich), 1876-1950.**    • **4.253**
Natural regions of the U.S.S.R. Translated from the Russian by Olga Adler Titelbaum. Edited by John A. Morrison and C. C. Nikiforoff. — New York, Macmillan, 1950. xxxi, 436 p. illus., maps. 25 cm. — ([American Council of Learned Societies Devoted to Humanistic Studies. Russian Translation Project. Series, 6]) Translated from Cyrillic (or Arabic, Japanese, Chinese, Hebrew, etc.) (transliterated: Priroda SSSR) Bibliography: p. 363-365. 1. Physical geography — Russia. 2. Botany — Russia. 3. Zoology — Russia. I. T. II. Series.
GB236.B433    551    *LC* 50-7599

**Suslov, S. P. (Sergeĭ Petrovich)**    • **4.254**
[Fizicheskaia geografiia SSSR:Aziatskaia chast'. English] Physical geography of Asiatic Russia. Translated from the Russian by Noah D. Gershevsky and edited by Joseph E. Williams. San Francisco, W. H. Freeman [1961] xiv, 594 p. illus., maps. 26 cm. 1. Physical geography — Russia, Asiatic. I. T.
GB325.S813    551.40957    *LC* 61-5762

**Taylor, Thomas Griffith, 1880-.**    • **4.255**
Australia; a study of warm environments and their effect on British settlement. 7th ed. London, Methuen, 1959, c1958. xv, 490 p. illus., maps, charts. 23 cm. 1. Physical geography — Australia. 2. Anthropo-geography — Australia. I. T.
GB381.T3 1959    551.40994    *LC* 60-51380

**White, Gilbert Fowler, 1911-.**    **4.256**
Science and the future of arid lands / Gilbert F. White. — Westport, Conn.: Greenwood Press, 1976, c1960. 95 p., [8] leaves of plates: ill.; 23 cm. Reprint of the ed. published by Unesco, Paris. 1. Arid regions I. T.
GB398.W45 1976    333.7/3    *LC* 76-4551    *ISBN* 0837187869

# GB400–648 Geomorphology. Landforms

**Thornes, John B.**    **4.257**
Geomorphology and time / J. B. Thornes and D. Brunsden. New York: Wiley, 1977. xvi, 208 p.: ill.; 24 cm. 'A Halsted Press book.' Includes index. 1. Geomorphology — Methodology. 2. Geological time I. Brunsden, Denys. joint author. II. T.
GB400.4.T46 1977    551.4    *LC* 76-30862    *ISBN* 0470990708

**Garner, H. F.**      **4.258**
The origin of landscapes: a synthesis of geomorphology / [by] H. F. Garner; with drawings by Mary Craig Garner. — New York: Oxford University Press, 1974. xx, 734 p.: ill.; 26 cm. 1. Geomorphology I. T.
GB401.G37      551.4      *LC* 73-90377

**Small, R. J. (Ronald John)**      **4.259**
The study of landforms: a textbook of geomorphology / R. J. Small. — 2d ed. — Cambridge; New York: Cambridge University Press, 1978. viii, 502 p.: ill.; 24 cm. Includes indexes. 1. Geomorphology I. T.
GB401.S6 1978      551.4      *LC* 77-71427      *ISBN* 0521216346

**Bloom, Arthur L. (Arthur Leroy), 1928-.**      **4.260**
Geomorphology: a systematic analysis of Late Cenozoic landforms / Arthur L. Bloom. — Englewood Cliffs, N.J.: Prentice-Hall, c1978. xvii, 510 p.: ill.; 24 cm. 1. Geomorphology 2. Geology, Stratigraphic — Quaternary I. T.
GB401.5.B55      551.4      *LC* 77-25816      *ISBN* 0133530868

**Chorley, Richard J.**      **4.261**
Geomorphology / Richard J. Chorley, Stanley A. Schumm, David E. Sugden. — London; New York: Methuen, 1985, c1984. xxiii, 605 p., [20] p. of plates: ill.; 26 cm. 1. Geomorphology I. Schumm, Stanley Alfred, 1927- II. Sugden, David E. III. T.
GB401.5.C5 1985      551.4 19      *LC* 84-14709      *ISBN* 0416325904

**Coates, Donald Robert, 1922- comp.**      **4.262**
Environmental geomorphology and landscape conservation, edited by Donald R. Coates. — Stroudsburg, Pa.: Dowden, Hutchinson & Ross, 1972. 485 p.: ill., map. (Benchmark papers in geology) 1. Geomorphology — Addresses, essays, lectures. 2. Human ecology — Addresses, essays, lectures. 3. Conservation of natural resources — Addresses, essays, lectures. I. T.
GB406.C62      333.7/2/08      *LC* 72-77882      *ISBN* 0879330058

**Ollier, Cliff.**      **4.263**
Tectonics and landforms / Cliff Ollier; edited by K. M. Clayton. — London; New York: Longman, 1981. 324 p.: ill.; 26 cm. — (Geomorphology texts. 6) Includes index. 1. Geomorphology 2. Plate tectonics 3. Geology, Structural I. Clayton, Keith M. II. T. III. Series.
GB406.O44      551.4      *LC* 79-41722      *ISBN* 0582300320

**Thomas, Michael Frederic.**      **4.264**
Tropical geomorphology; a study of weathering and landform development in warm climates [by] Michael F. Thomas. — New York: Wiley, [1974] xii, 332 p.: illus.; 23 cm. 'A Halsted Press book.' 1. Geomorphology — Tropics. I. T.
GB406.T47 1974      551.4/0913      *LC* 73-13428      *ISBN* 0470858974

**Tricart, Jean.**      **4.265**
[Précis de géomorphologie. v. 1. Géomorphologie structurale. English] Structural geomorphology [by] J. Tricart; translated by S. H. Beaver and E. Derbyshire. [London, New York] Longman [1974] xiii, 305 p. illus. 24 cm. (Geographies for advanced studies) Translation of Géomorphologie structurale which is v. 1 of the author's Précis de géomorphologie. 1. Geomorphology 2. Geology, Structural I. T.
GB406.T7613 1974      551.4      *LC* 73-86130      *ISBN* 0582484626

**Way, Douglas S.**      **4.266**
Terrain analysis: a guide to site selection using aerial photographic interpretation / Douglas S. Way. — 2d ed. — Stroudsburg, Pa.: Dowden, Hutchinson & Ross, 1978. x, 438 p.: ill.; 22 x 29 cm. — (Community development series) 1. Landforms 2. Petrology 3. Building sites 4. Aerial photography in geomorphology I. T.
GB406.W39 1978      551.4/028      *LC* 77-20240      *ISBN* 0070686416

**Douglas, Ian.**      **4.267**
Humid landforms / Ian Douglas. — Cambridge, Mass.: MIT Press, 1977. xvi, 288 p.: ill.; 22 cm. — (An introduction to systematic geomorphology; v. 1) Includes index. 1. Landforms — Tropics. 2. Landforms 3. Erosion 4. Hydrology I. T. II. Series.
GB446.D68 1977      551.3/5/0913      *LC* 77-76682      *ISBN* 0262040549

**Selby, Michael John.**      **4.268**
Hillslope materials and processes / M.J. Selby. — Oxford [Oxfordshire]; New York: Oxford University Press, 1983 (c1982). ix, 264 p.: ill.; 25 cm. Includes index. 1. Slopes (Physical geography) 2. Weathering I. T.
GB448.S44 1982      551.4/36 19      *LC* 81-22458      *ISBN* 019874126X

**The Encyclopedia of beaches and coastal environments / edited**      **4.269**
**by Maurice L. Schwartz.**
Stroudsburg, Pa.: Hutchinson Ross Pub. Co., c1982. xx, 940 p.: ill.; 27 cm. — (Encyclopedia of earth sciences. v. 15) 1. Coasts — Dictionaries. 2. Beaches — Dictionaries. 3. Coastal ecology — Dictionaries. I. Schwartz, Maurice L. II. Series.
GB450.4.E53 1982      551.4/57/0321 19      *LC* 81-7250      *ISBN* 0879332131

**Johnson, Douglas Wilson, 1878-1944.**      **4.270**
Shore processes and shoreline development. Facsimile of the ed. of 1919. New York, Hafner Pub. Co., 1965, [c1919] xvii, 584 p. illus., charts, maps 24 cm. 1. Shore-lines 2. Coasts I. T.
GB451.J6 1919a      *LC* 64-66007

**King, Cuchlaine A. M.**      **4.271**
Beaches and coasts [by] Cuchlaine A. M. King. — 2d ed. — New York: St. Martin's Press, [1972] x, 570 p.: illus.; 26 cm. 1. Beaches 2. Coasts 3. Ocean waves I. T.
GB451.K5 1972b      551.4/5      *LC* 74-187106

**Bird, E. C. F. (Eric Charles Frederick), 1930-.**      **4.272**
Coasts: an introduction to coastal geomorphology / Eric C. F. Bird. — 3rd ed. — Oxford, England; New York, NY, USA: B. Blackwell, 1984. xv, 320 p.: ill.; 22 cm. Includes indexes. 1. Coasts I. T.
GB451.2.B57 1984      551.4/5 19      *LC* 83-72678      *ISBN* 0631135677

**Snead, Rodman E.**      **4.273**
Coastal landforms and surface features: a photographic atlas and glossary / Rodman E. Snead. — Stroudsburg, Pa.: Hutchinson Ross, c1982. xx, 247 p.: ill.; 29 cm. Includes index. 1. Coasts — Pictorial works. 2. Coasts — Dictionaries. I. T.
GB452.S64      551.4/57 19      *LC* 81-2949      *ISBN* 087933052X

**Huxley, Anthony Julian, 1920- ed.**      • **4.274**
Standard encyclopedia of the world's oceans and islands. London: Weidenfeld & Nicolson [1963, c1962] 383 p.: ill. (part col.) col. maps; 25 cm. 1. Ocean 2. Islands I. T.
GB471.H9 1963      *LC* 63-276

**Huxley, Anthony Julian, 1920- ed.**      • **4.275**
Standard encyclopedia of the world's mountains. [1st ed.] New York: Putnam [1962] 383 p.: ill., col. plates, col. maps; 25 cm. 1. Mountains 2. Mountaineering I. T.
GB501 H8      *LC* 62-7984

**Haan, C. T. (Charles Thomas), 1941-.**      **4.276**
Statistical methods in hydrology / Charles T. Haan. — 1st ed. — Ames: Iowa State University Press, 1977. xv, 378 p.: ill.; 24 cm. Includes index. 1. Hydrology — Statistical methods. I. T.
GB656.2.S7 H3      551.4/8/0182      *LC* 77-11734      *ISBN* 081381510X

**Embleton, Clifford.**      **4.277**
Glacial geomorphology / Clifford Embleton, Cuchlaine A. M. King. — 2d ed. — New York: Wiley, 1975. vi, 573 p.: ill.; 24 cm. (Their Glacial and periglacial geomorphology; v. 1) 'A Halsted Press Book.' 1. Glacial landforms I. King, Cuchlaine A. M. joint author. II. T.
GB581.E452 1975 vol. 1      551.3/1/08 s 551.3/1      *LC* 75-14188
     *ISBN* 0470238925

**Embleton, Clifford.**      **4.278**
Periglacial geomorphology / Clifford Embleton, Cuchlaine A. M. King. — 2d ed. — New York: Wiley, 1975. vi, 203 p.: ill.; 24 cm. (Their Glacial and periglacial geomorphology; v.2) 'A Halsted Press Book.' 1. Glacial landforms I. King, Cuchlaine A. M. joint author. II. T. III. Series.
GB581.E452 1975 vol. 2      551.3/1/08 s 551.3/1      *LC* 75-14187
     *ISBN* 0470238941

**Jennings, J. N. (Joseph Newell)**      **4.279**
Karst geomorphology / J.N. Jennings. — [2nd ed.]. — Oxford, UK; New York: B. Blackwell, 1985. x, 293 p.: ill.; 24 cm. Rev. ed. of: Karst. c1971. Includes indexes. 1. Karst I. Jennings, J. N. (Joseph Newell) Karst. II. T.
GB600.J46 1985      551.4/47 19      *LC* 84-21589      *ISBN* 063114031X

**The Science of speleology / edited by T. D. Ford and C. H. D.**      **4.280**
**Cullingford.**
London; New York: Academic Press, 1976. xiv, 593 p., fold. plate: ill., maps, 2 ports.; 24 cm. 1. Speleology 2. Hydrology, Karst 3. Cave ecology I. Ford, Trevor David. II. Cullingford, Cecil Howard Dunstan.
GB601.S38      551.4/4      *LC* 75-46330      *ISBN* 0122625501

**Cooke, Ronald U.**      **4.281**
Geomorphology in deserts [by] Ronald U. Cooke and Andrew Warren. — Berkeley: University of California Press, 1973. 374 p.: illus.; 24 cm. 1. Deserts 2. Geomorphology I. Warren, Andrew. joint author. II. T.
GB611.C66 1973      551.4/0915/4      *LC* 72-82230      *ISBN* 0520022807

**Hills, E. Sherbon (Edwin Sherbon) ed.**      • **4.282**
Arid lands: a geographical appraisal, edited by E. S. Hills. — London, Methuen; Paris, Unesco, 1966. xviii, 461 p. front., illus., maps, tables, diagrs. 24 1/2 cm. Includes bibliographies. 1. Arid regions I. T.
GB611.H5      910.09154      *LC* 67-72563

**Reference handbook on the deserts of North America / edited**   **4.283**
**by Gordon L. Bender.**
Westport, Conn.: Greenwood Press, 1982. xi, 594 p.: ill.; 29 cm. 1. Deserts — North America — Handbooks, manuals, etc. I. Bender, Gordon Lawrence, 1918-
GB612.R43 1982   917.3/0954 19   *LC* 80-24791   *ISBN* 0313213070

**Moore, Peter D.**   **4.284**
Peatlands / [by] P. D. Moore [and] D. J. Bellamy. — New York: Springer-Verlag [c1974] vi, 221 p.: ill.; 23 cm. Includes bibliographical references. 1. Peat bogs 2. Peat industry I. Bellamy, David J. joint author. II. T.
GB621.M66 1974   574.5/2632   *LC* 74-165364

**Tricart, Jean.**   • **4.285**
[Géomorphologie des régions froides. English] Geomorphology of cold environments / translated [from the French] by Edward Watson. — London: Macmillan, 1970. xvi, 320 p.: 12 plates, ill., maps; 24 cm. Originally published as Géomorphologie des régions froides. Paris, Presses Universitaires de France, 1963. 1. Geomorphology — Cold regions. I. T.
GB641.T6813   551.4/0911   *LC* 77-84839   *ISBN* 0333086848

**Washburn, Albert Lincoln, 1911-.**   **4.286**
Geocryology: a survey of periglacial processes and environments / A. L. Washburn. — New York: Wiley, c1980. vi, 406 p.: ill.; 26 cm. Edition for 1973 published under title: Periglacial processes and environments. 'A Halsted Press book.' Includes index. 1. Frozen ground 2. Erosion I. T.
GB641.W37 1980   551.3/8   *LC* 78-22026   *ISBN* 0470265825

# GB651–2398 Water. Hydrology

**Pinder, George Francis, 1942-.**   **4.287**
Finite element simulation in surface and subsurface hydrology / George F. Pinder, William G. Gray. — New York: Academic Press, 1977. xii, 295 p.: ill.; 24 cm. 1. Hydrology — Mathematical models. 2. Hydrology — Data processing 3. Finite element method I. Gray, William G. (William Gurin), 1948- joint author. II. T.
GB656.2.M33 P56   551.4/8/018   *LC* 76-42977   *ISBN* 0125569505

**Chow, Ven Te, 1919- ed.**   • **4.288**
Handbook of applied hydrology; a compendium of water–resources technology. — New York: McGraw-Hill, [1964] 1 v. (various pagings): illus. maps.; 23 cm. 1. Hydrology I. T.
GB661.C56   551.49   *LC* 63-13931

**Van der Leeden, Frits.**   **4.289**
Water resources of the world: selected statistics / compiled and edited by Frits van der Leeden. — Port Washington, N.Y.: Water Information Center, c1975. xi, 568 p.: ill.; 27 cm. 1. Hydrology — Statistics. 2. Water-supply — Statistics. I. Water Information Center, inc. II. T.
GB661.V34   333.9/1/00212   *LC* 75-20952   *ISBN* 0912394145

**Knapp, Brian J.**   **4.290**
Elements of geographical hydrology / Brian Knapp. — London; Boston: Allen & Unwin, 1979. 85 p.: ill.; 25 cm. Includes index. 1. Hydrology I. T.
GB661.2.K55   551.4/8   *LC* 78-40373   *ISBN* 004551030X

**Linsley, Ray K.**   **4.291**
Hydrology for engineers / Ray K. Linsley, Jr., Max A. Kohler, Joseph L.H. Paulhus. — 3rd ed. — New York: McGraw-Hill, c1982. xx, 508 p.: ill.; 25 cm. — (McGraw-Hill series in water resources and environmental engineering.) 1. Hydrology I. Kohler, Max Adam, 1915- II. Paulhus, Joseph L. H. III. T. IV. Series.
GB661.2.L56 1982   551.48 19   *LC* 81-3689   *ISBN* 0070379564

**Miller, David Hewitt, 1918-.**   **4.292**
Water at the surface of the earth: an introduction to ecosystem hydrodynamics / David H. Miller. New York: Academic Press, 1977. xii, 557 p.: ill.; 24 cm. (International geophysics series. v. 21) 1. Hydrology 2. Ecology I. T. II. Series.
GB661.2.M53   551.4/8   *LC* 76-13947   *ISBN* 0124967507

**American Association for the Advancement of Science.**   • **4.293**
The future of arid lands; papers and recommendations from the international arid lands meetings. Edited by Gilbert F. White. Washington, 1956. ix, 453 p. ill., maps, charts. (Its Publication no. 43) 1. Arid regions I. White, Gilbert Fowler, 1911- ed. II. T. III. Title: International arid lands meetings IV. Series.
GB665 A55   *LC* 56-6107

**Fleming, George.**   **4.294**
Computer simulation techniques in hydrology / George Fleming. — New York: Elsevier, c1975. ix, 333 p.: ill.; 27 cm. (Environmental science series) 1. Hydrology — Simulation methods. 2. Water-supply — Simulation methods. I. T.
GB665.F54   551.4/8/0184   *LC* 74-21788   *ISBN* 0444001573

**Flow through porous media. Edited by Roger J. M. De Wiest.**   **4.295**
**Contributors: Jacob Bear [and others].**
New York: Academic Press, 1969. xiii, 530 p.: illus., port.; 24 cm. Based on the lectures presented at the Institute in Hydrology for College Teachers held at Princeton University in 1965. 1. Ground water flow. I. De Wiest, Roger J. M. ed. II. Bear, Jacob. III. Institute in Hydrology for College Teachers, Princeton University, 1965.
GB665.F55   551.4/9   *LC* 68-59161   *ISBN* 0122142500

**Symposium on World Water Balance, University of Reading,**   **4.296**
**1970.**
World water balance; proceedings of the Reading symposium, July 1970. Bilan hydrique mondial; actes du colloque de Reading, juillet 1970. A contribution to the International Hydrological Decade. Gentbrugge [Belgium] IASH, 1972. 3 v. (xiii, 706 p.) illus. 25 cm. (Studies and reports in hydrology. 11) 'SC.71/XX,11/AF.' Text in English and/or French; abstracts in English, French, Russian and Spanish. Convened by Unesco; United Kingdom National Commission for Unesco and the World Meteorological Organization collaborated in the organization of the Symposium. 1. Water balance (Hydrology) — Congresses. I. Unesco. II. Great Britain. United Kingdom National Commission for U.N.E.S.C.O. III. World Meteorological Organization. IV. T. V. Title: Bilan hydrique mondial. VI. Series.
GB665.S98 1970   551.4/8   *LC* 74-150569

**White, Gilbert Fowler, 1911-.**   • **4.297**
Choice of adjustment to floods / by Gilbert F. White; with an appendix by John Eric Edinger. — Chicago: Dept. of Geography, University of Chicago, 1964. xii, 150 p.: ill., maps. — (University of Chicago. Department of Geography. Research paper; no.93) 1. Flood damage prevention — United States I. T. II. Series.
GB665.W5x H31.C514 no. 93   *LC* 64-25664

**Leopold, Luna Bergere, 1915-.**   **4.298**
Water; a primer [by] Luna B. Leopold. — San Francisco: W. H. Freeman, [1974] xvi, 172 p.: ill.; 24 cm. — (A Series of books in geology) An expansion of the work, A primer on water, published in 1960, prepared by the author and W. B. Langbein. 1. Water I. T.
GB671.L39 1974   551.4/8   *LC* 73-19844   *ISBN* 0716702649

**Lee, Richard, 1926-.**   **4.299**
Forest hydrology / Richard Lee. — New York: Columbia University Press, 1980. xv, 349 p.: ill.; 24 cm. 1. Hydrology, Forest I. T.
GB842.L43   551.4/8/09152   *LC* 79-19542   *ISBN* 0231047185

**Milanović, Petar T.**   **4.300**
[Hidrogeologija karsta i metode istraživanja. English] Karst hydrogeology / by Petar T. Milanović; [translated by J.J. Buhac]. — Littleton, Colo.: Water Resources Publications, c1981. x, 434 p.: ill.; 24 cm. Translation of: Hidrogeologija Karsta i metode istraživanja. Errata slip inserted. Includes indexes. 1. Hydrology, Karst I. T.
GB843.M5413 1981   551.4/47 19   *LC* 80-54287   *ISBN* 0918334365

**Hydrological forecasting / edited by M.G. Anderson and T.P.**   **4.301**
**Burt.**
Chichester [West Sussex]; New York: Wiley, c1985. xii, 604 p.: ill.; 24 cm. (Landscape systems.) 'A Wiley-Interscience publication.' 1. Hydrological forecasting I. Anderson, M. G. II. Burt, T. P. III. Series.
GB845.H93 1985   551.48 19   *LC* 84-17364   *ISBN* 047190614X

**Stumm, Werner, 1924-.**   **4.302**
Aquatic chemistry: an introduction emphasizing chemical equilibria in natural waters / Werner Stumm, James J. Morgan. — [2d ed.]. — New York: Wiley, c1981. xiv, 780 p.: ill.; 24 cm. 'A Wiley-Interscience publication.' 1. Water chemistry I. Morgan, James J., 1932- joint author. II. T.
GB855.S78 1981   551.4 19   *LC* 80-25333   *ISBN* 0471048313

**Walton, William Clarence.**   **4.303**
Practical aspects of groundwater modeling: flow, mass and heat transport, and subsidence: analytical and computer models / by William C. Walton. — 2nd ed. — Worthington, Ohio: National Water Well Association, c1985. vi, 587 p.: ill.; 28 cm. Reprint. Originally published: Worthington, Ohio: National Water Well Association, c1984. Includes index. 1. Water, Underground — Mathematical models. 2. Water, Underground — Data processing. I. T.
GB1001.72.M35 W35 1985   551.49/0724 19   *LC* 85-29755

**Walton, William Clarence.**   **4.304**
Groundwater resource evaluation [by] William C. Walton. — New York: McGraw-Hill, [1970] vi, 664 p.: illus., maps.; 23 cm. — (McGraw-Hill series in

Descriptive physical oceanography: an introduction / by George L. Pickard and William J. Emery. — 4th enl. ed.

**Pickard, George L.**    **4.345**
Descriptive physical oceanography: an introduction / by George L. Pickard and William J. Emery. — 4th enl. ed. (in SI units). — Oxford, [Oxfordshire]; New York: Pergamon Press, 1982. xiv, 249 p., [4] p. of plates: ill.; 24 cm. Includes index. 1. Oceanography I. Emery, William J. II. T.
GC150.5.P52 1982   551.46 19   LC 81-20967   ISBN 0080262805

**Jerlov, Nils Gunnar.**    **4.346**
Marine optics / by N.G. Jerlov. 2nd revised and enlarged ed. Amsterdam; Oxford [etc.]: Elsevier, 1976. xiv, 231 p.: ill., maps; 25 cm. (Elsevier oceanography series. 14) Index. 1. Optical oceanography I. T. II. Title: Optical oceanography. III. Series.
GC178.J4x   551.4/601   ISBN 0444414908

**Air–sea interaction: instruments and methods / edited by F.**    **4.347**
**Dobson, L. Hasse, and R. Davis.**
New York: Plenum Press, c1980. xii, 801 p.: ill.; 26 cm. 1. Ocean-atmosphere interaction — Instruments. 2. Ocean-atmosphere interaction — Methodology. I. Dobson, F. II. Hasse, L. III. Davis, R. (Russ E.)
GC190.5.A37   551.47   LC 80-17895   ISBN 0306405431

# GC201–399 Ocean Dynamics. Waves. Currents

**Bascom, Willard.**    **4.348**
Waves and beaches: the dynamics of the ocean surface / Willard Bascom; ill. by the author. Rev. and updated. Garden City, N.Y.: Anchor Press/Doubleday, c1980. 366 p. ill., maps, diagrs. 22 cm. Includes index. 1. Ocean waves 2. Beaches I. T.
GC211.2.B37 1980   551.4/7022   LC 79-7038   ISBN 0385148453

**Stommel, Henry M., 1920-.**    • **4.349**
The Gulf Stream: a physical and dynamical description. — 2d ed. Berkeley: University of California Press, 1965. xiii, 248 p.: ill., charts; 24 cm. 1. Gulf Stream I. T.
GC296.G9 S7 1965   551.471   LC 64-23710

**Symposium on the Mediterranean Sea, Heidelberg, 1971.**    **4.350**
The Mediterranean Sea; a natural sedimentation laboratory. Edited by Daniel J. Stanley. Assisted by Gilbert Kelling and Yehezkiel Weiler. — Stroudsburg, Pa.: Dowden, Hutchinson & Ross, [1973, c1972] xvi, 765 p.: illus., col. map (fold. in pocket); 29 cm. English or French; each paper with English and French résumés. The majority of the papers were presented at the Symposium on the Mediterranean Sea, held Aug. 30-Sept. 1, 1971, during the 8th International Sedimentological Congress. 1. Marine sediments — Mediterranean Sea — Congresses. 2. Geology — Mediterranean Sea — Congresses. I. Stanley, Daniel J. ed. II. International Sedimentological Congress. 8th, Heidelberg, 1971. III. T.
GC389.S95 1971   551.4/62   LC 72-88984   ISBN 0879330104

**Coachman, Lawrence K., 1926-.**    **4.351**
Bering Strait: the regional physical oceanography / L. K. Coachman, K. Aagaard, R. B. Tripp. — Seattle: University of Washington Press, c1975. 172 p.: ill.; 24 cm. Includes index. 1. Oceanography — Bering Strait. I. Aagaard, Knut, 1939- joint author. II. Tripp, Richard B., joint author. III. T.
GC411.C62   551.4/65/51   LC 75-40881   ISBN 0295954426

# GC1000–1572 Marine Resources. Marine Pollution

**Managing the ocean: resources, research, law / Jacques G.**    **4.352**
**Richardson, editor.**
Mt. Airy, Md.: Lomond Publications, 1985. xv, 407 p., [2] folded p. of plates: ill; 24 cm. Includes index. 1. Marine resources 2. Oceanography — Research 3. Marine pollution 4. Submarine geology 5. Oceanography and state 6. Marine resources conservation — Law and legislation I. Richardson, Jacques.
GC1015.2.M35 1985   333.91/64 19   LC 85-50823   ISBN 0912338490

**Ross, David A., 1936-.**    **4.353**
Opportunities and uses of the ocean / David A. Ross. — New York: Springer Verlag, 1980, c1978. xi, 320 p.: ill.; 25 cm. 1. Marine resources I. T.
GC1015.2.R67 1980   333.9/1   LC 79-12694   ISBN 0387904484

**Impact of marine pollution on society / Virginia K. Tippie,**    **4.354**
**Dana R. Kester, editors.**
New York, N.Y.: Praeger; South Hadley, Mass.: Bergin, 1982. vi, 313 p.: ill.; 24 cm. 'Papers presented at the fourth annual conference organized by the Center for Ocean Management Studies, University of Rhode Island'—Introd. 1. Marine pollution — Social aspects — Congresses. I. Tippie, Virginia K. II. Kester, Dana R. III. University of Rhode Island. Center for Ocean Management Studies.
GC1081.I48 1982   363.7/394 19   LC 81-12270   ISBN 0030597323

**Hood, D. W. (Donald Wilbur), 1918-.**    **4.355**
Impingement of man on the oceans. Edited by Donald W. Hood. New York, Wiley-Interscience [1971] x, 738 p. illus., maps. 23 cm. 1. Marine pollution 2. Oceanography and state I. T.
GC1085.H66   628/.168/09162   LC 74-151728   ISBN 0471408700

# GF Human Ecology. Anthropogeography

**The Dictionary of human geography / edited by R.J. Johnston,**    **4.356**
**Derek Gregory, David M. Smith; consultant editors, Peter Haggett, D. R. Stoddart.**
2nd ed. — Oxford: Blackwell Reference, 1986. xv, 576 p.: ill.; 23 cm. 1. Anthropo-geography — Dictionaries. I. Johnston, R. J. (Ronald John) II. Gregory, Derek. III. Smith, David M.
GF4.D52 1986   304.2/03/21 19   ISBN 0631146563

**Larkin, Robert P.**    **4.357**
Dictionary of concepts in human geography / Robert P. Larkin and Gary L. Peters; foreword by Elizabeth Frick. — Westport, Conn.: Greenwood Press, 1983. viii, 286 p.; 25 cm. — (Reference sources for the social sciences and humanities. 0730-3335; no. 2) 1. Anthropo-geography — Dictionaries. I. Peters, Gary L. II. T. III. Series.
GF4.L37 1983   304.2/03/21 19   LC 82-24258   ISBN 0313227292

**Wagner, Philip Laurence, 1921-.**    • **4.358**
Readings in cultural geography / edited with introductions and translations by Philip L. Wagner and Marvin W. Mikesell. — [Chicago]: University of Chicago Press, [1962] xii, 589 p.: ill.; 25 cm. 1. Anthropo-geography — Collected works. 2. Human ecology I. Mikesell, Marvin W. II. T.
GF7.W3   LC 62-9740

**Johnston, R. J. (Ronald John)**    **4.359**
Geography and geographers: Anglo–American human geography since 1945 / R.J. Johnston. — 2nd ed. — London: E. Arnold, 1983. vi, 264 p.: ill.; 22 cm. Includes index. 1. Anthropo-geography — United States — History. 2. Anthropo-geography — Great Britain — History. I. T.
GF13.J63 1983   304/.2/0973 19   LC 83-126365   ISBN 0713163879

**Chisholm, Michael, 1931-.**    **4.360**
Human geography: evolution or revolution? / [by] Michael Chisholm. — Harmondsworth; Baltimore [etc.]: Penguin, 1975. 207 p.: ill., maps; 20 cm. — (Pelican geography and environmental studies) (Pelican books) Includes indexes. 1. Anthropo-geography — Methodology 2. Geography — Methodology 3. Geography — Research I. T.
GF21.C48   901/.8   LC 76-357706   ISBN 0140218831

**Smith, David Marshall, 1936-.**    **4.361**
Patterns in human geography: an introduction to numerical methods / David M. Smith. — Newton Abbot [Eng.]: David & Charles; New York: Crane Russak & Co., 1975. 373 p.: ill., maps; 23 cm. Includes index. 1. Anthropo-geography — Mathematics I. T.
GF23.M35 S64 1975   901/.8   LC 75-21520   ISBN 0844807648

**Brown, Harrison, 1917-1986.**    • **4.362**
The challenge of man's future: an inquiry concerning the condition of man during the years that lie ahead / by Harrison Brown. — New York: Viking Press, 1954. xii, 290 p.: illus.; 22 cm. 1. Natural resources I. T.
GF31.B68   333.7 19   LC 54-6422

**Brunhes, Jean, 1869-1930.**    • **4.363**
Human geography, an attempt at a positive classification, principles and examples, by Jean Brunhes ... translated by T. C. Le Compte ... edited by Isaiah Bowman ... and Richard Elwood Dodge ... Illustrated with 77 maps and diagrams and 146 half-tones. Chicago; New York,: Rand, McNally & company, c1929. xvi, 648 p. ill., maps; 22 cm. 1. Geography, Economic 2. Ethnology I. Lecompte, Irvill Charles, 1872- II. Bowman, Isaiah, 1878-1950. III. Dodge, Richard Elwood, 1868-. IV. T.
GF31.B73   LC 20-7929

**Glacken, Clarence J.**     **4.364**
Traces on the Rhodian shore; nature and culture in Western thought from ancient times to the end of the eighteenth century [by] Clarence J. Glacken. Berkeley, University of California Press [1973, c1967] xxviii, 763 p. illus. 26 cm. (California library reprint series.) 1. Nature — Religious aspects — History of doctrines. I. T. II. Series.
GF31.G6 1973     301.31     *LC* 72-95298     *ISBN* 0520023676

**Huntington, Ellsworth, 1876-1947.**     ● **4.365**
Mainsprings of civilization [by] Ellsworth Huntington ... New York, J. Wiley and sons, inc.; London, Chapman and Hall, limited [1947] xii, 660 p. illus. (maps) diagrs. 22 cm. Bibliography: p. 613-629. 1. Man — Influence of environment 2. Heredity 3. Evolution I. T.
GF31.H818 1947     573.4     *LC* 45-5027

**Marsh, George Perkins, 1801-1882.**     **4.366**
Man and nature / Edited by David Lowenthal. — New ed. — Cambridge.: Belknap Press of Harvard University Press, 1970. xxix, 472 p.; 24 cm. — (John Harvard library.) 'The text...is the first edition, as published in New York by Charles Scribner in 1864.' 1. Man — Influence on nature 2. Conservation of natural resources I. T. II. Series.
GF31.M35 1970     910

**Semple, Ellen Churchill, 1863-1932.**     ● **4.367**
Influences of geographic environment, on the basis of Ratzel's system of anthropo–geography. — New York: Russell & Russell, [1968, c1911] xvi, 637 p.: maps.; 23 cm. 1. Anthropo-geography 2. Man — Influence of environment I. Ratzel, Friedrich, 1844-1904. Anthropogeographie. II. T.
GF31.S5 1968     910.03     *LC* 68-27087

**Sorre, Maximilien, 1880-1962.**     ● **4.368**
Les fondements biologiques de la géographie humaine / Max. Sorre. — Paris: A. Colin, 1948-1952. 3 v. in 4: ill., maps. Vols. 2-3 have title: Les fondements de la géographie humaine. 1. Anthropo-geography 2. Man — Influence of environment 3. Food supply 4. Medical geography I. T. II. Title: Les fondements de la géographie humaine.
GF31.S6     910     *LC* 46-13843

**Vidal de La Blache, Paul Marie Joseph, 1845-1918.**     ● **4.369**
Principles of human geography, by P. Vidal de La Blache, edited by Emmanuel de Martonne, translated from the French by Millicent Todd Bingham, PH. D. New York, H. Holt and company [c1926] xv, 511 p. double maps. 23 cm. 1. Anthropo-geography 2. Man — Influence of environment I. Martonne, Emmanuel de, 1873-1955. II. Bingham, Millicent (Todd) 1880- III. T. IV. Title: Human geography.
GF31.V53     *LC* 26-14572

**Fairgrieve, James, 1870-1953.**     **4.370**
Geography and world power. [8th ed. rev.] London, University of London Press, 1948. 376 p. ill. 1. Anthropo-geography 2. Civilization — History I. T.
GF33 F3 1948     *LC* 52-20163

**Spencer, J. E. (Joseph Earle), 1907-.**     ● **4.371**
Cultural geography; an evolutionary introduction to our humanized earth [by] J. E. Spencer [and] William L. Thomas. Cartography by Robert E. Winter. — New York: Wiley, [1969] xv, 591 p.: illus. (part col.), maps (part col.); 27 cm. 1. Anthropo-geography I. Thomas, William Leroy, 1920- joint author. II. T.
GF33.S64     301.2/4     *LC* 67-28950     *ISBN* 0471815500

**Gutkind, Erwin Anton, 1886-.**     ● **4.372**
Our world from the air, an international survey of man and his environment. With a foreword by G.P. Gooch and an introd. by E.G.R. Taylor. Garden City, N.Y.: Doubleday, 1952. 1 v. (chiefly maps, photos) 1. Anthropo-geography 2. Geography, Aerial I. T.
GF37 G85

**Sauer, Carl Ortwin, 1889-.**     ● **4.373**
Land and life; a selection from the writings of Carl Ortwin Sauer. Edited by John Leighly. Berkeley, University of California Press, 1963. vi, 435 p. port., 2 maps ( 1 fold.) profile. 24 cm. 1. Anthropo-geography — Collected works. I. Leighly, John, 1895- ed. II. T.
GF37.S3 1963     *LC* 63-21069

# GF41–75 Human Ecology

**Ward, Barbara, 1914-.**     ● **4.374**
Only one earth: the care and maintenance of a small planet / by Barbara Ward and René Dubos. — [1st ed.] New York: Norton [1972] xxv, 225 p.; 21 cm. 'An unofficial report commissioned by the Secretary-General of the United Nations Conference on the Human Environment, prepared with the assistance of a 152-member committee of corresponding consultants in 58 countries.'

1. Human ecology I. Dubos, René J. (René Jules), 1901- joint author. II. United Nations Conference on the Human Environment (1972: Stockholm, Sweden) III. T.
GF41.J3     301.31     *LC* 72-447     *ISBN* 0393063917

**Jordan, Terry G.**     **4.375**
The human mosaic: a thematic introduction to cultural geography / Terry G. Jordan, Lester Rowntree. — 3rd ed. — New York: Harper & Row, c1982. xv, 444 p.: ill.; 29 cm. 1. Anthropo-geography 2. Ethnology I. Rowntree, Lester, 1938- II. T.
GF41.J67 1982     900 19     *LC* 81-6968     *ISBN* 0060434619

**Humanistic geography: prospects and problems / edited by**     **4.376**
**David Ley and Marwyn S. Samuels.**
Chicago: Maaroufa Press, c1978. viii, 337 p.: ill.; 24 cm. 1. Anthropo-geography — Addresses, essays, lectures. 2. Anthropo-geography — Methodology — Addresses, essays, lectures. I. Ley, David. II. Samuels, Marwyn S.
GF49.H86     910     *LC* 78-52408     *ISBN* 088425013X

**Haggett, Peter.**     **4.377**
Locational analysis in human geography / Peter Haggett, Andrew D. Cliff, Allan Frey. — 2d ed. — New York: Wiley, 1977. xiv, 605 p.: ill.; 25 cm. 'A Halsted Press book.' Includes indexes. 1. Anthropo-geography 2. Geography, Economic I. Cliff, Andrew David. joint author. II. Frey, Allan E. joint author. III. T.
GF50.H33 1977     301.3     *LC* 77-8967     *ISBN* 0470992077

**Bowman, Isaiah, 1878-1950.**     ● **4.378**
The pioneer fringe / by Isaiah Bowman. — New York: American Geographical Society, 1931. ix, 361 p.: ill., maps. (Special publication - American Geographical Society; no.13) 1. Frontier and pioneer life 2. Pioneers I. T.
GF51.B6     910.03     *LC* 32-1721

**Moran, Emilio F.**     **4.379**
Human adaptability: an introduction to ecological anthropology / Emilio F. Moran. — Boulder, Colo.: Westview Press, 1982. xii, 404 p.: ill.; 24 cm. Includes indexes. 1. Man — Influence of environment 2. Adaptation (Physiology) I. T.
GF51.M58 1982     304.2 19     *LC* 82-8605     *ISBN* 0865314306

**Vayda, Andrew Peter. comp.**     ● **4.380**
Environment and cultural behavior; ecological studies in cultural anthropology. Edited by Andrew P. Vayda. [1st ed.] Garden City, N.Y., Published for American Museum of Natural History [by] Natural History Press, 1969. xvi, 485 p. illus., maps. 22 cm. (American Museum sourcebooks in anthropology) 1. Human ecology — Addresses, essays, lectures. 2. Man — Influence of environment — Addresses, essays, lectures. 3. Ethnology — Addresses, essays, lectures. I. American Museum of Natural History. II. T. III. Series.
GF51.V35     301.31     *LC* 69-10994

**Goudie, Andrew.**     **4.381**
The human impact: man's role in environmental change / Andrew Goudie. — 1st MIT Press ed. — Cambridge, Mass.: MIT Press, 1982, c1981. x, 316 p.: ill.; 25 cm. Includes index. 1. Man — Influence on nature I. T.
GF75.G68 1982     304.2 19     *LC* 81-15643     *ISBN* 0262070863

# GF90–95 Landscape Assessment. Spatial Studies

**The Interpretation of ordinary landscapes: geographical essays /**     **4.382**
**D. W. Meinig, editor; J. B. Jackson ... [et al.].**
New York: Oxford University Press, 1979. viii, 255 p.: ill.; 23 cm. Seven of the nine essays derive from a special series of lectures presented at Syracuse University. Includes index. 1. Landscape assessment — Addresses, essays, lectures. I. Meinig, D. W. (Donald William), 1924- II. Jackson, John Brinckerhoff, 1909-
GF90.I57     301.31     *LC* 78-23182     *ISBN* 0195025369

**Behavioral problems in geography revisited / edited by Kevin R.**     **4.383**
**Cox and Reginald G. Golledge.**
New York: Methuen, c1981. xxix, 290 p.: ill.; 23 cm. 1. Anthropo-geography — Addresses, essays, lectures. 2. Anthropo-geography — Methodology — Addresses, essays, lectures. I. Cox, Kevin R., 1939- II. Golledge, Reginald G., 1937-
GF95.B43 1981     304 19     *LC* 82-176781     *ISBN* 0416724302

**Jackson, Peter, 1955-.**     **4.384**
Exploring social geography / Peter Jackson, Susan J. Smith. — London; Boston: G. Allen & Unwin, 1984. xii, 239 p.; 22 cm. Includes index.

1. Anthropo-geography 2. Social interaction 3. Sociology, Urban I. Smith, Susan, 1956- II. T.
GF95.J33 1984     301 19     *LC* 83-25732     *ISBN* 0043011705

# GF500–895 Anthropogeography, by Region

**Sears, Paul Bigelow, 1891-.**                    **4.385**
Deserts on the march / Paul B. Sears. — 4th ed. — Norman: University of Oklahoma Press, c1980. viii, 264 p.: ill.; 22 cm. Includes index. 1. Man — Influence on nature — United States. 2. Desertification — United States. 3. Agricultural ecology — United States. 4. Conservation of natural resources — United States I. T.
GF503.S42 1980     333.7/2/0973     *LC* 79-6721     *ISBN* 0806116676

**Cronon, William.**                    **4.386**
Changes in the land: Indians, colonists, and the ecology of New England / William Cronon. — 1st ed. — New York: Hill and Wang, 1983. x, 241 p.; 22 cm. Includes index. 1. Man — Influence on nature — New England — History. 2. New England — History — Colonial period, ca. 1600-1775 I. T.
GF504.N45 C76 1983     974/.02 19     *LC* 83-7899     *ISBN* 0809034050

**Malin, James Claude, 1893-.**                    **4.387**
History & ecology: studies of the Grassland / James C. Malin; edited by Robert P. Swierenga. — Lincoln: University of Nebraska Press, c1984. xxix, 376 p.; 23 cm. Includes index. 1. Man — Influence of environment — West (U.S.) 2. Grasslands — West (U.S.) 3. Agriculture — Kansas — History. 4. West (U.S.) — Description and travel 5. West (U.S.) — History 6. Kansas — Rural conditions. I. Swierenga, Robert P. II. T. III. Title: History and ecology.
GF504.W35 M34 1984     333.74/0978 19     *LC* 83-16951     *ISBN* 0803241445

**Social fabric and spatial structure in colonial Latin America /**                    **4.388**
**edited by David J. Robinson.**
Ann Arbor, MI: Published for Dept. of Geography, Syracuse University by University Microfilms International, 1979. xviii, 478 p.: ill.; 23 cm. (Dellplain Latin American studies. 1) (Monograph publishing: Sponsor series) 1. Anthropo-geography — Latin America — Addresses, essays, lectures. 2. Land settlement patterns — Latin America — Addresses, essays, lectures. 3. Latin America — Social conditions — Addresses, essays, lectures. 4. Latin America — Economic conditions — Addresses, essays, lectures. I. Robinson, D. J. (David James), 1939- II. Syracuse University. Dept. of Geography. III. Series.
GF514.S63     309.1/8/01     *LC* 79-15744     *ISBN* 083570419X

**McBryde, F. Webster (Felix Webster), 1908-.**                    • **4.389**
Cultural and historical geography of Southwest Guatemala. Westport, Conn., Greenwood Press [1971] xv, 184 p. illus., fold. maps. 29 cm. Reprint of the 1947 ed. Based on the author's thesis, University of California, 1940. 'Prepared in cooperation with the United States Department of State as a project of the Interdepartmental Committee on Scientific and Cultural Cooperation.' 1. Anthropo-geography — Guatemala. 2. Ethnology — Guatemala. I. T.
GF522.G9 M3 1971     917.281     *LC* 74-89017     *ISBN* 0837131235

**Fleure, H. J. (Herbert John), 1877-1969.**                    • **4.390**
A natural history of man in Britain: conceived as a study of changing relations between men and environments [by] H. J. Fleure. — London: Collins, 1951. xviii, 349 p.: illus. (some col.), maps, plans, ports.; 23 cm. — (New naturalist.) 1. Human ecology — Great Britain. 2. Great Britain — History I. T. II. Series.
GF551.F48 1970     914.2/03     *LC* 52-17011     *ISBN* 0002131536

**Fox, Cyril, Sir, 1882-1967.**                    • **4.391**
The personality of Britain, its influence on inhabitant and invader ... — 4th ed. — Cardiff: National Museum of Wales, 1947. 99 p. + maps. 1. Anthropogeography — Gt. Brit. 2. Great Britain — Antiquities I. T.
GF551 F6 1947

**Taylor, Christopher, 1935-.**                    **4.392**
Village and farmstead: a history of rural settlement in England / Christopher Taylor. — London: G. Philip, 1983. 254 p.: ill.; 26 cm. Includes index. 1. Land settlement patterns — England — History. 2. Villages — England — History. 3. England — Rural conditions. I. T.
GF551.T39 1983     307.7/2/0942 19     *LC* 83-157398     *ISBN* 0540010715

## GN4–11 Collections. Dictionaries

**Haring, Douglas Gilbert, 1894-.**    • **4.393**
Personal character and cultural milieu: a collection of readings. 3d rev. ed. — [Syracuse, N.Y.] Syracuse University Press [1956] 834 p. ill. 1. Anthropology — Collected works. I. T.
GN4.H37 M56    *LC* 56-14435

**International Symposium on Anthropology, New York, 1952.**    • **4.394**
Anthropology today: an encyclopedic inventory, prepared under the chairmanship of A.L. Kroeber. Chicago, University of Chicago Press [1953] xv, 966 p. diagrs. 1. Anthropology — Collections I. Kroeber, A. L. (Alfred Louis), 1876-1960. II. T.
GN4 I52    *LC* 53-6171

**Current anthropology: a supplement to Anthropology today /**    • **4.395**
**edited by William L. Thomas.**
Chicago: University of Chicago Press, 1956. xii, 377 p.; 25 cm. 'Consists of the first three parts of the Yearbook of anthropology, 1955.'—Pref. 1. Anthropology — Collected works I. Thomas, William L., 1920- II. International Symposium on Anthropology (1952: New York). Anthropology today III. Yearbook of anthropology
GN4.I52 1952 Suppl    *LC* 56-7961

**Manners, Robert Alan, 1913- comp.**    • **4.396**
Theory in anthropology, a source–book, edited by Robert A. Manners and David Kaplan. — Chicago: Aldine Pub. Co., [1968] xii, 578 p.; 26 cm. 1. Anthropology — Collected works. I. Kaplan, David, 1929- joint comp. II. T.
GN4.M32    390    *LC* 67-17606

**Benedict, Ruth, 1887-1948.**    • **4.397**
An anthropologist at work; writings of Ruth Benedict, by Margaret Mead. Boston, Houghton Mifflin, 1959. xxii, 583 p. illus., ports. 22 cm. 1. Anthropology — Collected works. I. Mead, Margaret, 1901-1978. ed. II. T.
GN6.B4    572.081    *LC* 58-9071

**Boas, Franz, 1858-1942.**    **4.398**
The shaping of American anthropology, 1883–1911; a Franz Boas reader. Edited by George W. Stocking, Jr. — New York: Basic Books, [1974] xi, 354 p.: port.; 24 cm. 1. Boas, Franz, 1858-1942. 2. Anthropology — Addresses, essays, lectures. I. Stocking, George W., 1928- ed. II. T.
GN6.B57 1974    301.2    *LC* 73-81727    *ISBN* 0465077676

**Hallowell, A. Irving (Alfred Irving), 1892-1974.**    • **4.399**
Culture and experience, by A. Irving Hallowell. New York, Schocken Books [1967, c1955] xiv, 434 p. map. 23 cm. 1. Anthropology — Collected works. 2. Chippewa Indians 3. Indians of North America 4. Indians of North America — Psychology I. T.
GN6.H3 1967    390    *LC* 67-26989

**Kroeber, A. L. (Alfred Louis), 1876-1960.**    • **4.400**
The nature of culture. Chicago, University of Chicago Press [1952] 437 p. ill. 1. Anthropology — Addresses, essays, lectures 2. Culture I. T.
GN6 K7    *LC* 52-12545

**Leach, Edmund Ronald.**    • **4.401**
Rethinking anthropology, by E. R. Leach. — London: Athlone P.; New York: Humanities P., 1966. 143 p.: tables, diagrs.; 21 1/2 cm. — (Monographs on social anthropology. no. 22) 1. Kinship 2. Marriage customs and rites 3. Anthropology — Addresses, essays, lectures. I. T. II. Series.
GN6.L4 1966    301.42    *LC* 66-19115

**Redfield, Robert, 1897-.**    • **4.402**
Papers. Edited by Margaret Park Redfield. [Chicago] University Press [1962-63] 2 v.: illus.; 25cm. 1. Anthropology—Collected works I. T. II. Title: Human nature and the study of society III. Title: The social uses of social science
GN6 R4 A25

**Boas, Franz, 1858-1942.**    • **4.403**
Race, language and culture, by Franz Boas ... New York, The Macmillan company, 1940. xx, 647 p. incl. ill., tables, diagrs. 1. Anthropology

2. Ethnology 3. Indians of North America — Languages 4. Race 5. Indians of North America I. T.
GN8 B68    *LC* 40-4051

**Firth, Raymond William, 1901- ed.**    **4.404**
Man and culture: an evaluation of the work of Bronislaw Malinowski. — London: Routledge & K. Paul [1957] 292 p.: ill. 1. Malinowski, Bronislaw, 1884-1942. 2. Ethnology — Addresses, essays, lectures I. T.
GN8 F5    *LC* 57-4671

**Malinowski, Bronislaw, 1884-1942.**    • **4.405**
Magic, science and religion, and other essays. With an introd. by Robert Redfield. Garden City, N.Y., Doubleday, 1954 [c1948] 274 p. 18 cm. (Doubleday anchor books, A23) 1. Ethnology — Addresses, essays, lectures. 2. Religion, Primitive — Addresses, essays, lectures. I. T.
GN8.M286 1954    306 19    *LC* 54-4389

**Shapiro, Harry Lionel, 1902- ed.**    **4.406**
Man, culture, and society; edited by Harry L. Shapiro. — Rev. ed. — London; New York: Oxford University Press, 1971. v, 456 p.: illus.; 21 cm. — (A Galaxy book, GB 32) 1. Anthropology — Addresses, essays, lectures. I. T.
GN8.S5 1971    301.2/08    *LC* 79-146443    *ISBN* 0195013921

**Dictionary of anthropology / [edited by] Charlotte Seymour–**    **4.407**
**Smith.**
Boston, Mass.: G.K. Hall, 1986. p. cm. 1. Anthropology — Dictionaries. I. Seymour-Smith, Charlotte.
GN11.D48 1986    306/.03/21 19    *LC* 86-214    *ISBN* 0816188173

**Encyclopedia of anthropology / edited by David E. Hunter,**    **4.408**
**Phillip Whitten.**
New York: Harper & Row, c1976. 411 p.: ill.; 24 cm. 1. Anthropology — Dictionaries. I. Hunter, David E. II. Whitten, Phillip.
GN11.E52    301.2/03    *LC* 75-41386    *ISBN* 0060470941

**Pearson, Roger, 1927-.**    **4.409**
Anthropological glossary / Roger Pearson. — Original ed. — Malabar, Fla.: R.E. Krieger Pub. Co., 1985. vi, 282 p.; 24 cm. 1. Anthropology — Dictionaries. I. T.
GN11.P43 1985    306/.03/21 19    *LC* 85-195    *ISBN* 0898745101

**Winick, Charles, 1922-.**    • **4.410**
Dictionary of anthropology. New York: Philosophical Library [1956] vii, 579 p.; 22 cm. (Midcentury reference library) 1. Anthropology — Dictionaries I. T.
GN11 W5    *LC* 56-14738

## GN17–21 History. Biography

**Anthropology & the colonial encounter. Edited by Talal Asad.**    **4.411**
[London]: Ithaca Press, [1973] 281 p.; 23 cm. Papers presented at a seminar held in Hull in Sept. 1972. 1. Ethnology — History — Addresses, essays, lectures. 2. Applied anthropology — Addresses, essays, lectures. 3. Great Britain — Colonies — Addresses, essays, lectures. I. Asad, Talal. ed.
GN17.A57 1973b    301.2    *LC* 73-180718    *ISBN* 0903729008

**Lowie, Robert Harry, 1883-1957.**    • **4.412**
The history of ethnological theory, by Robert H. Lowie ... London, Farrar & Rinehart, inc. [c1937] xiii, 296 p. 1. Ethnology — History I. T. II. Title: Ethnological theory
GN17 L6    *LC* 38-2861

**Penniman, T. K. (Thomas Kenneth), 1895-.**    • **4.413**
A hundred years of anthropology, by T. K. Penniman. With contributions by Beatrice Blackwood and J. S. Weiner. 3d ed., rev. London: G. Duckworth, [1965] 397 p. 23 cm. 1. Anthropology — History. I. T.
GN17.P4 1970    *LC* 65-4600

**Slotkin, James Sydney, 1913-1958, comp.**    • **4.414**
Readings in early anthropology, edited by J. S. Slotkin. Chicago, Aldine Pub. Co. [1965] xvii, 530 p. 27 cm. (Viking Fund publications in anthropology. no. 40) 1. Anthropology — History — Collections. I. T. II. Series.
GN17.S46    573.09    *LC* 65-16645

**Totems and teachers: perspectives on the history of**     **4.415**
**anthropology** / Sydel Silverman, editor.
New York: Columbia University Press, 1981. xv, 322 p.; 24 cm. Includes index.
1. Anthropology — History — Addresses, essays, lectures. 2. Anthropologists
— Addresses, essays, lectures. I. Silverman, Sydel.
GN17.T69          301/.092/2          LC 80-18457          *ISBN* 0231050860

*GN 17 V63*

**Voget, Fred W.**     **4.416**
A history of ethnology / Fred W. Voget. — New York: Holt, Rinehart and
Winston, [1975] ix, 879 p.: port.; 25 cm. Includes index. 1. Ethnology —
History. I. T.
GN17.V63          301.2/09          LC 75-6576          *ISBN* 0030796652

**Mead, Margaret, 1901-1978.**     **4.417**
Ruth Benedict. New York, Columbia University Press, 1974. viii, 180 p. illus.
23 cm. (Leaders of modern anthropology series) 1. Benedict, Ruth, 1887-1948.
2. Ethnology I. T.
GN21.B45 M42 1974          301.2/092/4 B          LC 74-6400          *ISBN*
0231035195 *ISBN* 0231035209

**Modell, Judith Schachter, 1941-.**     **4.418**
Ruth Benedict, patterns of a life / Judith Schachter Modell. — Philadelphia:
University of Pennsylvania Press, 1983. x, 355, [8] p. of plates: ports.; 24 cm.
Includes index. 1. Benedict, Ruth, 1887-1948. 2. Anthropologists — United
States — Biography. I. T.
GN21.B45 M63 1983          306/.092/4 B 19          LC 82-21989          *ISBN*
0812278747

**Herskovits, Melville J. (Melville Jean), 1895-1963.**     **4.419**
Franz Boas: the science of man in the making / Melville J. Herskovits. — New
York: Scribner, 1953. 131 p.; 21 cm. — (Twentieth century library.) 1. Boas,
Franz, 1858-1942. I. T.
GN21.B56 H4          925.72          LC 53-2397

**Woodbury, Richard Benjamin, 1917-.**     **4.420**
Alfred V. Kidder / by Richard B. Woodbury. — New York: Columbia
University Press, 1973. viii, 199 [1] p.: ill.; 23 cm. — (Leaders of modern
anthropology series) Part II contains excerpts from Kidder's professional
writings, 1910-1961. 1. Kidder, Alfred Vincent, 1885-1963. I. T. II. Series.
GN21.K5 W66          917.2/03/50924 B          LC 72-10082          *ISBN*
0231034849

**Steward, Julian Haynes, 1902-1972.**     **4.421**
Alfred Kroeber. New York, Columbia University Press, 1973. xii, 137 p. 23 cm.
(Leaders of modern anthropology series) 1. Kroeber, A. L. (Alfred Louis),
1876-1960. I. Kroeber, A. L. (Alfred Louis), 1876-1960. Selections. 1973.
II. T. III. Series.
GN21.K7 S84          301.2/092/4 B          LC 72-8973          *ISBN* 023103489X
*ISBN* 0231034903

**Leakey, Mary D. (Mary Douglas), 1913-.**     **4.422**
Disclosing the past / Mary Leakey. — Garden City, N.Y.: Doubleday, 1984.
224 p., [16] p. of plates: ill. (some col.); 25 cm. Includes index. 1. Leakey, Mary
D. (Mary Douglas), 1913- 2. Anthropologists — Africa — Biography.
3. Fossil man — Africa. I. T.
GN21.L372 A33 1984          306/.092/4 B 19          LC 84-10189          *ISBN*
0385189613

**Leach, Edmund Ronald.**     **4.423**
Claude Lévi-Strauss / Edmund Leach. — Rev. ed. — New York: Viking Press,
1974. xi, 146 p.: ill.; 20 cm. — (Modern masters) Includes index. 1. Lévi-
Strauss, Claude. I. T.
GN21.L4 L38 1974          GN21L4 L38 1974.          301.2/092/4          LC
74-1122          *ISBN* 0670225150

**Mead, Margaret, 1901-1978.**     •**4.424**
Blackberry winter; my earlier years. New York, Morrow, 1972. 305 p. illus. 24
cm. 1. Mead, Margaret, 1901-1978. 2. Anthropologists — United States —
Biography. I. T.
GN21.M36 A32          301.2/092/4 B          LC 72-7187          *ISBN* 0688000517
*ISBN* 0688050514

*GN 21 M36 B37 1984*

**Bateson, Mary Catherine.**     **4.425**
With a daughter's eye: a memoir of Margaret Mead and Gregory Bateson /
Mary Catherine Bateson. — 1st U.S. ed. — New York: W. Morrow, c1984.
242 p., [24] p. of plates: ill.; 24 cm. 1. Mead, Margaret, 1901-1978. 2. Bateson,
Gregory. 3. Bateson, Mary Catherine. 4. Anthropologists — United States —
Biography. I. T.
GN21.M36 B38 1984          306/.092/2 19          LC 84-60564          *ISBN*
0688039626

## GN23–32 General Works

**General anthropology** / edited by Franz Boas; with     •**4.426**
contributions by Ruth Benedict and others.
New York: Johnson Reprint Corp., 1965,c1938. 718p. ill., map, bibl. —
(Landmarks in anthropology.) 1. Anthropology I. Boas, Franz, 1858-1942.
II. Benedict, Ruth Fulton.
GN24.B63 1965          572.08          LC 66-5417

**Firth, Raymond William, 1901-.**     •**4.427**
Human types: an introduction to social anthropology / Raymond Firth. —
Rev. ed. — London; Toronto: T. Nelson, [1956]. 224 p., [8] leaves of plates: ill.,
maps. 1. Ethnology 2. Society, Primitive 3. Race I. T.
GN24.F5 1956          LC 57-4417

**Foster, George McClelland, 1913-.**     •**4.428**
Applied anthropology [by] George M. Foster. — Boston: Little, Brown, [1969]
xiv, 238 p.; 22 cm. — ([The Little, Brown series in anthropology]) 1. Applied
anthropology I. T.
GN24.F6          301.2          LC 69-20322

**Kroeber, A. L. (Alfred Louis), 1876-1960.**     •**4.429**
Anthropology: race, language, culture, psychology, pre–history. [New ed., rev.]
New York, Harcourt, Brace [1948] xii, 856, xxxix p. ill., maps.
1. Anthropology I. T.
GN24 K7 1948          LC 48-6956

**Montagu, Ashley, 1905-.**     •**4.430**
Man: his first two million years; a brief introduction to anthropology. — New
York: Columbia University Press, 1969. vi, 262 p.: illus., maps.; 22 cm. First ed.
published in 1957 under title: Man: his first million years. 1. Anthropology
I. T.
GN24.M58 1969          573          LC 69-16956

**Tylor, Edward Burnett, Sir, 1832-1917.**     •**4.431**
Anthropology. Abridged and with a foreword by Leslie A. White. — [Ann
Arbor] University of Michigan Press [1960] 275 p. illus. 21 cm. — (Ann Arbor
paperbacks, AA44) 1. Anthropology 2. Civilization I. T.
GN24.T9 1960          572          LC 60-64263 rev

**Greenwood, Davydd J.**     **4.432**
Nature, culture, and human history: a bio–cultural introduction to
anthropology / Davydd J. Greenwood, William A. Stini. — New York: Harper
& Row, c1977. ix, 531 p.: ill.; 25 cm. 1. Anthropology 2. Sociobiology I. Stini,
William A. joint author. II. T.
GN25.G73          301.2          LC 77-9425          *ISBN* 0060425059

**Boas, Franz, 1858-1942.**     •**4.433**
Anthropology and modern life, by Franz Boas ... New York, W.W. Northon &
company, inc. [c1928] vii p., 1 l., 11-246 p. 1. Anthropology 2. Social problems
3. Civilization I. T.
GN27 B6          LC 28-29158

**Dubos, René J. (René Jules), 1901-.**     **4.434**
Celebrations of life / by René Dubos. — New York: McGraw-Hill, c1981. xi,
260 p.; 25 cm. Includes index. 1. Man 2. Human ecology I. T.
GN27.D8          302 19          LC 81-3764          *ISBN* 0070178933

**Kluckhohn, Clyde, 1905-1960.**     •**4.435**
Mirror for man; the relation of anthropology to modern life. New York,
Whittlesey House [1949] xi, 313 p. 1. Anthropology 2. United States —
Civilization I. T.
GN27 K6          LC 49-7012

**Linton, Ralph, 1893-1953.**     •**4.436**
The tree of culture. [1st ed.] New York, Knopf, 1955. 692 p. illus. 24 cm.
1. Anthropology 2. Civilization — History I. T.
GN27.L5          572          LC 55-5173

**Malinowski, Bronislaw, 1884-1942.**     •**4.437**
A scientific theory of culture, and other essays by Bronislaw Malinowski; with a
preface by Huntington Cairns. — Chapel Hill: The University of North
Carolina press, 1944. ix, 228 p.; 21 cm. 1. Frazer, James George, Sir,
1854-1941. 2. Culture 3. Anthropology I. T.
GN27.M34          LC 44-8385

**Murdock, George Peter, 1897-.**     •**4.438**
Social structure. New York, Macmillan Co., 1949. xvii, 387 p. 1. Anthropology
2. Family 3. Marriage I. T.
GN27 M95          LC 49-9317

**Frantz, Charles.**      4.439
The student anthropologist's handbook; a guide to research, training, and career. — Cambridge, Mass.: Schenkman Pub. Co.; distributed by General Learning Press, [Morristown, N.J., 1972] xi, 228 p.; 21 cm. 1. Anthropology — Study and teaching. 2. Anthropology — Bibliography. I. T.
GN42.F7      301.2      *LC* 77-170649

# GN49–294 Physical Anthropology

**Molnar, Stephen, 1931-.**      4.440
Races, types, and ethnic groups: the problem of human variation / Stephen Molnar. — Englewood Cliffs, N.J.: Prentice-Hall, [1975] xiv, 193 p.: ill.; 23 cm. — (The Prentice-Hall series in anthropology) Rev. ed. published as: Human variation. 2nd ed. c1983. 1. Physical anthropology 2. Race I. T.
GN62.8.M64      573      *LC* 74-23935      *ISBN* 0137502575. *ISBN* 0137502400 pbk

**Physiological anthropology / edited by Albert Damon.**      4.441
New York: Oxford University Press, 1975. xiii, 367 p.: ill.; 23 cm. 1. Physical anthropology 2. Physiology I. Damon, Albert, 1918-1973.
GN221.P45      573      *LC* 75-4349      *ISBN* 0195018877

**Hsu, Francis L. K., 1909- ed.**      • 4.442
Psychological anthropology / Edited by Francis L. K. Hsu. — New ed. — Cambridge, Mass.: Schenkman Pub. Co.; distributed by General Learning Press [Morristown, N.J., 1972] x, 623 p.; 24 cm. 1. Ethnopsychology 2. Personality and culture I. T.
GN270.H75 1972      155.8      *LC* 75-170651

**Alland, Alexander, 1931-.**      4.443
The human imperative. — New York: Columbia University Press, 1972. viii, 185 p.; 21 cm. 1. Human behavior 2. Ethnopsychology 3. Aggressiveness (Psychology) I. T.
GN273.A4      155.7      *LC* 77-183227      *ISBN* 0231032285

**Montagu, Ashley, 1905-.**      • 4.444
Statement on race; an annotated elaboration and exposition of the four statements on race issued by the United Nations Educational, Scientific, and Cultural Organization. — 3d ed. — New York: Oxford University Press, 1972. xii, 278 p.; 21 cm. 1. Unesco. 2. Race I. T.
GN280.M6 1972      572      *LC* 76-177994      *ISBN* 0195015304

**Morris, Desmond.**      • 4.445
The naked ape; a zoologist's study of the human animal. [1st American ed.] New York, McGraw-Hill [1967] 252 p. 22 cm. 1. Man — Animal nature 2. Human behavior 3. Primates — Behavior I. T.
GN280.7.M675 1967      599.9      *LC* 67-29198

## GN281–289 Human Evolution

**Birx, H. James.**      4.446
Theories of evolution / by H. James Birx. — Springfield, Ill., U.S.A.: Thomas, c1984. xiv, 417 p.: port.; 24 cm. Includes index. 1. Human evolution — Philosophy. I. T.
GN281.B59 1984      573.2 19      *LC* 83-12046      *ISBN* 0398049025

**Campbell, Bernard Grant.**      4.447
Human evolution; an introduction to man's adaptations, by Bernard G. Campbell. — 2d ed. — Chicago: Aldine Pub. Co., [1974] xiv, 469 p.: illus.; 25 cm. 1. Human evolution I. T.
GN281.C35 1974      573.2      *LC* 72-140006      *ISBN* 0202020126

**The Emergence of man: a joint symposium of the Royal Society and the British Academy / organized by J.Z. Young, E.M. Jope, and K.P. Oakley.**      4.448
London: The Society and the Academy, 1981. 216 p., [8] p. of plates: ill.; 31 cm. 'First published in Philosophical transactions of the Royal Society of London, series B, volume 292 (no. 1057).' 1. Human evolution — Congresses. I. Young, J. Z. (John Zachary) II. Jope, E. M. (Edward Martyn) III. Oakley, Kenneth Page, 1911- IV. Royal Society (Great Britain) V. British Academy.
GN281.E47 1981      573.2 19      *LC* 81-670182      *ISBN* 0854031529

**The Origins of modern humans: a world survey of the fossil evidence / editors, Fred H. Smith, Frank Spencer.**      4.449
New York: A.R. Liss, c1984. xxii, 590 p.: ill.; 24 cm. 1. Human evolution — Addresses, essays, lectures. I. Smith, Fred H. II. Spencer, Frank.
GN281.O75 1984      573.2 19      *LC* 84-859      *ISBN* 0845102338

**Pfeiffer, John E., 1915-.**      4.450
The emergence of humankind / John E. Pfeiffer. — 4th ed. — New York: Harper & Row, c1985. xxiv, 440 p.: ill.; 24 cm. Rev. ed. of: The emergence of man. 3rd ed. c1978. Includes index. 1. Human evolution 2. Man, Prehistoric 3. Society, Primitive I. Pfeiffer, John E., 1915- Emergence of man. II. T.
GN281.P45 1985      573.2 19      *LC* 84-15784      *ISBN* 0060452013

**Itzkoff, Seymour W.**      4.451
Triumph of the intelligent: the creation of Homo sapiens sapiens / by Seymour W. Itzkoff. — Ashfield, Mass.: Paideia, c1985. 210 p.; 22 cm. (The Evolution of human intelligence; 2) Includes index. 1. Human evolution 2. Intellect 3. Genetic psychology 4. Social evolution I. T.
GN281.4.I894 1985      573.2 19      *LC* 84-19110      *ISBN* 0913993018

**Tanner, Nancy Makepeace.**      4.452      — 0 —
On becoming human / Nancy Makepeace Tanner. — Cambridge; New York: Cambridge University Press, 1981. xviii, 373 p.: ill.; 24 cm. Includes index. 1. Human evolution 2. Social evolution I. T.
GN281.4.T36      573.2 19      *LC* 80-21526      *ISBN* 0521235545

**Day, Michael H.**      4.453
Guide to fossil man / Michael H. Day. — 4th ed., completely rev. and enl. — Chicago: University of Chicago Press, 1986. xv, 432 p.: ill.; 26 cm. 1. Fossil man I. T.
GN282.D39 1986      569/.9 19      *LC* 86-5548      *ISBN* 0226138895

**Millar, Ronald William, 1928-.**      4.454
The Piltdown men, by Ronald Millar. — New York: St. Martin's Press, [c1972] 264 p.: illus.; 22 cm. 1. Piltdown forgery I. T.
GN282.5.M54 1972b      001.9/5      *LC* 72-94380

**Johanson, Donald C.**      4.455
Lucy, the beginnings of humankind / Donald C. Johnson and Maitland A. Edey. — New York: Simon and Schuster, c1981. 409 p. [8] p. of plates: ill. Includes index. 1. Australopithecus afarensis 2. Fossil man — Africa. 3. Fossil man — Ethiopia I. Edey, Maitland Armstrong, 1910- joint author. II. T.
GN283.25.J63      GN283.25 J63.      569/.9 19      *LC* 80-21759      *ISBN* 0671250361

**Trinkaus, Erik.**      4.456
The Shanidar Neandertals / Erik Trinkaus. — New York: Academic Press, 1983. xxiv, 502 p.: ill.; 24 cm. Includes index. 1. Neanderthal race 2. Shanidar Cave (Iraq) I. T.
GN285.T74 1983      573.3 19      *LC* 83-2488      *ISBN* 0127005501

**Bajema, Carl Jay, 1937- comp.**      4.457
Natural selection in human populations; the measurement of ongoing genetic evolution in contemporary societies. New York: Wiley, [1971] viii, 406 p.: illus.; 24 cm. 1. Human evolution — Addresses, essays, lectures. 2. Natural selection — Addresses, essays, lectures. 3. Human population genetics — Addresses, essays, lectures. I. T.
GN289.B33 1971      573.2/1/08      *LC* 72-154322      *ISBN* 047104380X

**Current developments in anthropological genetics / edited by James H. Mielke and Michael H. Crawford.**      4.458
New York: Plenum Press, c1980-c1982. 2 v.: ill.; 24 cm. 1. Human population genetics — Addresses, essays, lectures. 2. Human evolution — Addresses, essays, lectures. 3. Human genetics — Addresses, essays, lectures. I. Mielke, James H. II. Crawford, Michael H., 1939-
GN289.C87      573.2      *LC* 79-24900      *ISBN* 0306403900

**Underwood, Jane Hainline.**      4.459
Human variation and human microevolution / Jane H. Underwood. — Englewood Cliffs, N.J.: Prentice-Hall, c1979. viii, 245 p.: ill.; 23 cm. 1. Human population genetics 2. Human evolution 3. Human genetics I. T.
GN289.U5      573.2      *LC* 78-15301      *ISBN* 0134475739

## GN294 Women

**Martin, M. Kay, 1942-.**      4.460
Female of the species / M. Kay Martin, Barbara Voorhies. — New York: Columbia University Press, 1975. x, 432 p.: ill.; 23 cm. Includes index. 1. Women 2. Sex role I. Voorhies, Barbara, 1939- joint author. II. T.
GN294.M37      301.41/2      *LC* 74-23965      *ISBN* 0231038755

**Toward an anthropology of women / edited by Rayna R. Reiter.**      4.461
New York: Monthly Review Press, [1975] 416 p.; 21 cm. 1. Women — Addresses, essays, lectures. 2. Sex role — Addresses, essays, lectures. I. Reiter, Rayna R.
GN294.T68      301.41/2      *LC* 74-21476      *ISBN* 0853453721

## GN296–298 MEDICAL ANTHROPOLOGY. SOCIAL ASPECTS OF HUMAN BODY

**Culture and curing: anthropological perspectives on traditional medical beliefs and practices** / edited by Peter Morley and Roy Wallis.   **4.462**
[Pittsburgh]: University of Pittsburgh Press, 1979, c1978. vii, 190 p.; 23 cm. — (Contemporary community health series.) 1. Medical anthropology — Addresses, essays, lectures. 2. Medicine, Primitive — Addresses, essays, lectures. 3. Folk medicine — Addresses, essays, lectures. I. Morley, Peter. II. Wallis, Roy. III. Series.
GN296.C83 1979     362.1     *LC* 78-62194     *ISBN* 0822911361

**Foster, George McClelland, 1913-.**   **4.463**
Medical anthropology / George M. Foster, Barbara Gallatin Anderson. — New York: Wiley, c1978. x, 354 p.; 24 cm. Includes index. 1. Medical anthropology I. Anderson, Barbara Gallatin. joint author. II. T.
GN296.F67     362.1     *LC* 78-18449     *ISBN* 0471043427

**Health and the human condition: perspectives on medical anthropology** / Michael H. Logan, Edward E. Hunt, Jr.   **4.464**
North Scituate, Mass.: Duxbury Press, c1978. xvii, 443 p.; 24 cm. 1. Medical anthropology — Addresses, essays, lectures. 2. Folk medicine — Cross-cultural studies — Addresses, essays, lectures. 3. Medicine, Primitive — Addresses, essays, lectures. I. Logan, Michael H. II. Hunt, Edward E.
GN296.H42     362.1     *LC* 77-22936     *ISBN* 0878721401

**Murdock, George Peter, 1897-.**   **4.465**
Theories of illness: a world survey / George Peter Murdock. — Pittsburgh: University of Pittsburgh Press, c1980. xv, 127 p.; 22 cm. 1. Medical anthropology 2. Diseases — Causes and theories of causation 3. Medicine, Primitive I. T.
GN296.M87     362.1     *LC* 80-5257     *ISBN* 0822934280

**Social anthropology and medicine** / edited by J. B. Loudon.   **4.466**
London; New York: Academic Press, 1976. xxv, 600 p.: ill.; 24 cm. — (A.S.A. monograph; 13) 1. Medical anthropology — Addresses, essays, lectures. 2. Medicine, Primitive — Addresses, essays, lectures. 3. Folk medicine — Addresses, essays, lectures. I. Loudon, Joseph Buist. II. Association of Social Anthropologists of the Commonwealth.
GN296.S62     362.1     *LC* 76-10489     *ISBN* 0124563503

**Wood, Corinne Shear.**   **4.467**
Human sickness and health: a biocultural view / Corinne Shear Wood. — 1st ed. — Palo Alto, Calif.: Mayfield Pub. Co., 1979. xviii, 376 p.: ill.; 23 cm. Includes index. 1. Medical anthropology I. T.
GN296.W66     362.1     *LC* 78-71608     *ISBN* 0874844185

**O'Neill, John, 1933-.**   **4.468**
Five bodies: the human shape of modern society / John O'Neill. — Ithaca: Cornell University Press, 1985. 181 p.: ill.; 24 cm. Includes index. 1. Body, Human — Social aspects 2. Civilization, Modern — 1950- 3. Religion and sociology 4. Social problems I. T.
GN298.O54 1985     573/.6 19     *LC* 84-22947     *ISBN* 0801417279

## GN301–686 Ethnology. Social and Cultural Anthropology

**Beattie, J. H. M. (John H. M.)**   **4.469**
Studies in social anthropology: essays in memory of E.E. Evans–Pritchard / by his former Oxford colleagues; edited by J.H.M. Beattie and R.G. Lienhardt. — Oxford [Eng.]: Clarendon Press, 1975. x, 394 p., [5] leaves of plates: ill.; 23 cm. 1. Evans-Pritchard, E. E. (Edward Evan), 1902-1973. 2. Ethnology — Addresses, essays, lectures. I. Evans-Pritchard, E. E. (Edward Evan), 1902-1973. II. Lienhardt, Godfrey. III. T.
GN303.S88     301.2     *LC* 75-324498     *ISBN* 0198231830

**Barth, Fredrik, 1928-.**   **4.470**
Selected essays of Fredrik Barth. — London: Routledge & Kegan Paul, 1981. 2 v.: ill., map. (International library of anthropology.) 1. Ethnology — Collected works I. T. II. Series.
GN304.B377     GN304 B377.     306     *LC* 80-41283 (v. 1)     *ISBN* 9710007205

**International dictionary of regional European ethnology and folklore.** [Editorial committee: Sigurd Erixon, chairman, and others. Chief editor: Åke Hultkrantz] Under the auspices of the International Council for Philosophy and Humanistic Studies and with the support of UNESCO; published by CIAP (International Commission on Folk Arts and Folklore)   **4.471**
Copenhagen, Rosenkilde and Bagger, 1960-. v. 22 cm. Vols. 1- have also special t. p. 1. Ethnology — Dictionaries. 2. Folklore — Dictionaries. I. Erixon, Sigurd Emanuel, 1888-1968. II. Hultkrantz, Åke. III. International Commission of Folk Arts and Folklore.
GN307.I5     *LC* 67-121536

**Hays, H. R. (Hoffman Reynolds), 1904-.**   ● **4.472**
From ape to angel: an informal history of social anthropology / drawings by Sue Allen. — [1st ed.] New York: Knopf, 1958. xxii, 440, xv p.: ill.; 25 cm. 1. Ethnology — History. I. T.
GN308.H37 1958     572.09 19     *LC* 58-7713

**Kuper, Adam.**   **4.473**
Anthropology and anthropologists: the modern British school / Adam Kuper. — Rev. ed. — London; Boston: Routledge & Kegan Paul, 1983. x, 228 p.; 22 cm. 1. Ethnology — Great Britain — History. 2. Ethnologists — Great Britain. I. T.
GN308.3.G7 K86 1983     306/.0941 19     *LC* 82-20530     *ISBN* 0710094094

## GN310–340 GENERAL WORKS

**Beattie, John.**   ● **4.474**
Other cultures; aims, methods and achievements in social anthropology. — New York: Free Press of Glencoe, 1964. xii, 283 p.; 23 cm. 1. Ethnology I. T. II. Title: Aims, methods and achievements in social anthropology.
GN315.B37     572     *LC* 64-16952

**Geertz, Clifford.**   **4.475**
The interpretation of cultures; selected essays. — New York: Basic Books, [1973] ix, 470 p.; 25 cm. 1. Ethnology 2. Culture I. T.
GN315.G36     301.2     *LC* 73-81196     *ISBN* 046503425X

**Hatch, Elvin.**   **4.476**
Theories of man and culture [by] Elvin Hatch. — New York: Columbia University Press, 1973. viii, 384 p.; 23 cm. 1. Ethnology 2. Anthropologists I. T.
GN315.H36     301.2     *LC* 73-1250     *ISBN* 0231036388

**Honigmann, John Joseph.**   **4.477**
Handbook of social and cultural anthropology. Edited by John J. Honigmann. Contributors: Alexander Alland, Jr. [and others]. — Chicago: Rand McNally Co., [c1973] 1295 p.: illus.; 25 cm. — (Rand McNally anthropology series) 1. Ethnology I. Alland, Alexander, 1931- II. T.
GN315.H642     301.2     *LC* 72-184062     *ISBN* 0528699962

**Honigmann, John Joseph.**   ● **4.478**
Understanding culture. — New York: Harper & Row, [1963] 468 p.: illus.; 25 cm. 1. Culture 2. Ethnology I. T.
GN315.H643 1963     301.2     *LC* 63-7293

**Montagu, Ashley, 1905-.**   ● **4.479**
Man's most dangerous myth: the fallacy of race. 4th ed., rev. and enl. Cleveland, World Pub. Co. [1964] 499 p. tables. 22 cm. 1. Race 2. Race relations I. T.
GN315.M55 1964     572 19     *LC* 64-12067

**Barrett, Richard A.**   **4.480**
Culture and conduct: an excursion in anthropology / Richard A. Barrett. — Belmont, Calif.: Wadsworth Pub. Co., c1984. viii, 240 p.; 19 cm. Includes index. 1. Ethnology 2. Culture I. T.
GN316.B377 1984     306 19     *LC* 83-14836     *ISBN* 0534030343

**Leach, Edmund Ronald.**   **4.481**
Social anthropology / Edmund Leach. — New York: Oxford University Press, 1982. 254 p.: ill.; 22 cm. Includes index. 1. Ethnology I. T.
GN316.L4 1982     306 19     *LC* 81-85134     *ISBN* 0195203712

**Lewis, Ioan M.**   **4.482**
Social anthropology in perspective: the relevance of social anthropology / [by] I. M. Lewis. Harmondsworth; New York: Penguin, 1976. 386 p.; 18 cm. Includes index. 1. Ethnology I. T.
GN316.L49     301.2     *LC* 76-374994     *ISBN* 0140219153

**Pocock, David Francis.**     **4.483**
Understanding social anthropology / [by] David Pocock. London: Hodder & Stoughton, 1975. x, 255 p.: ill.; 18 cm. (Teach yourself books) 1. Ethnology I. T.
GN316.P62     301.2     *LC* 76-364827     *ISBN* 0340203765

**Diamond, Stanley, 1922-.**     **4.484**
In search of the primitive; a critique of civilization. Foreword [by] Eric R. Wolf. — New Brunswick, N.J.: Transaction Books; distributed by E. P. Dutton [New York, 1974] xvi, 387 p.; 23 cm. 1. Ethnology — Addresses, essays, lectures. 2. Society, Primitive — Addresses, essays, lectures. I. T.
GN320.D5     301.2     *LC* 72-82195     *ISBN* 0878550453

**Harris, Marvin, 1927-.**     **4.485**
Cows, pigs, wars & witches; the riddles of culture. — [1st ed.]. — New York: Random House, [1974] viii, 276 p.; 22 cm. 1. Ethnology — Miscellanea. 2. Witchcraft I. T.
GN320.H328     392     *LC* 73-20268     *ISBN* 0394483383

**Harris, Marvin, 1927-.**     **• 4.486**
The rise of anthropological theory; a history of theories of culture. — New York: Crowell, [1968] 806 p.; 24 cm. 1. Ethnology — History. I. T.
GN320.H33     572/.09     *LC* 68-17392

**Kardiner, Abram, 1891-.**     **• 4.487**
The individual and his society: the psychodynamics of primitive social organization / by Abram Kardiner; with a foreword and two ethnological reports by Ralph Linton. — New York: Columbia university press, 1939. xxvi p., 2 l., 503 p.: incl. tables; 24 cm. 1. Ethnopsychology 2. Society, Primitive 3. Social psychology 4. Ethnology — Marquesas Islands 5. Ethnology — Madagascar 6. Tanalas I. Linton, Ralph, 1893-1953. II. T.
GN320.K3     136.4     *LC* 40-322

**Freilich, Morris, 1928-.**     **• 4.488**
Marginal natives; anthropologists at work. Contributors: Morris Freilich [and others] Morris Freilich, editor. — New York: Harper & Row, [c1970] xi, 624 p.; 25 cm. 1. Ethnology — Field work — Addresses, essays, lectures. I. T.
GN325.F7     527/.07/2     *LC* 76-91252

**Kluckhohn, Clyde, 1905-1960.**     **• 4.489**
Culture and behavior; collected essays. Edited by Richard Kluckhohn. — [New York]: Free Press of Glencoe, [1962] 402 p.; 22 cm. 1. Ethnology — Addresses, essays, lectures. I. T.
GN325.K6     572     *LC* 61-14108

**Radcliffe-Brown, A. R. (Alfred Reginald), 1881-1955.**     **• 4.490**
Method in social anthropology: selected essays / edited by M. N. Srinivas. — Chicago: University of Chicago Press, 1958. 188 p.; 22 cm. 1. Ethnology — Methodology 2. Social sciences — Methodology I. T.
GN325.R2     *LC* 58-11954

**Mair, Lucy Philip, 1901-.**     **• 4.491**
An introduction to social anthropology [by] Lucy Mair. — Oxford: Clarendon Press, 1965. 283 p.; 23 cm. 1. Ethnology I. T. II. Title: Social anthropology.
GN330.M3     301     *LC* 66-2864

## GN345–347 PHILOSOPHY. METHODOLOGY

**A Crack in the mirror: reflexive perspectives in anthropology /**     **4.492**
**Jay Ruby, editor.**
Philadelphia: University of Pennsylvania Press, 1982. vi, 299 p.; 24 cm. Includes index. 1. Ethnology — Methodology — Addresses, essays, lectures. 2. Ethnology — Philosophy — Addresses, essays, lectures. I. Ruby, Jay.
GN345.C73 1982     306 19     *LC* 81-51147     *ISBN* 0812278151

**Naroll, Raoul.**     **• 4.493**
A handbook of method in cultural anthropology. Edited by Raoul Naroll and Ronald Cohen. [1st ed.] Garden City, N.Y., Published for the American Museum of Natural History [by] the Natural History Press, 1970. xxi, 1017 p. illus. 27 cm. 'Published under the auspices of the Council for Intersocietal Studies, Northwestern University.' 1. Ethnology — Methodology I. Cohen, Ronald. joint author. II. American Museum of Natural History. III. T.
GN345.N37     301.2     *LC* 78-123703

**Sahlins, Marshall David, 1930-.**     **4.494**
Culture and practical reason / Marshall Sahlins. Chicago: University of Chicago Press, 1976. xi, 252 p.: ill.; 23 cm. Includes index. 1. Ethnology 2. Dialectical materialism 3. Structural anthropology I. T.
GN345.S24     301.2     *LC* 75-27899

**Levinson, David, 1947-.**     **4.495**
Toward explaining human culture: a critical review of the findings of worldwide cross–cultural research / David Levinson and Martin J. Malone; with an appendix, Language universals by Cecil H. Brown and Stanley R. Witkowski. — [New Haven, Conn.]: HRAF Press, 1981 (c1980). xiv, 397 p.: ill.; 23 cm. 1. Cross-cultural studies 2. Ethnology I. Malone, Martin J. II. Brown, Cecil H., 1944- Language universals. 1980. III. T.
GN345.7.L48     306 19     *LC* 80-83324     *ISBN* 0875363393

**Agar, Michael.**     **4.496**
The professional stranger: an informal introduction to ethnography / Michael H. Agar. — New York: Academic Press, c1980. xi, 227 p.; 23 cm. — (Studies in anthropology) Includes index. 1. Ethnology — Field work. 2. Ethnology — Methodology I. T.
GN346.A42     301/.01/8     *LC* 79-8870     *ISBN* 012043850X

**Stocking, George W., 1928-.**     **4.497**
Observers observed: essays on ethnographic fieldwork / edited by George W. Stocking, Jr. — Madison, Wis.: University of Wisconsin Press, 1983. vi, 242 p.: ill.; 24 cm. — (History of anthropology. v. 1) 1. Ethnology — Field work — Addresses, essays, lectures. 2. Participant observation — Addresses, essays, lectures. 3. Ethnology — History — Addresses, essays, lectures. I. T. II. Series.
GN346.O27 1983     306/.0723 19     *LC* 83-47771     *ISBN* 0299094502

**Collier, John, 1913-.**     **4.498**
Visual anthropology: photography as a research method / John Collier, Jr., and Malcolm Collier. — Rev. and expanded ed. — Albuquerque: University of New Mexico Press, c1986. p. cm. Includes index. 1. Photography in ethnology 2. Motion pictures in ethnology I. Collier, Malcolm, 1948- II. T.
GN347.C64 1986     306/.0208 19     *LC* 86-6926     *ISBN* 0826308988

## GN357–367 CULTURE AND CULTURAL PROCESSES

**Lamberg-Karlovsky, C. C., 1937-.**     **4.499**
Ancient civilizations: the Near East and Mesoamerica / C. C. Lamberg–Karlovsky, and Jeremy A. Sabloff. — Menlo Park, Calif.: Benjamin/Cummings Pub. Co., c1979. xvii, 350 p.: ill.; 24 cm. Includes index. 1. Culture 2. Social evolution 3. Middle East — Civilization 4. Central America — Civilization. I. Sabloff, Jeremy A. joint author. II. T.
GN357.L35     930/.1     *LC* 78-72309     *ISBN* 080535672X

**Partridge, Colin.**     **4.500**
The making of new cultures: a literary perspective / by Colin Partridge. — Amsterdam: Rodopi, 1982. 131 p. — (Costerus. new series, v. 34) 1. Culture 2. Social change I. T. II. Series.
GN357.M34     *ISBN* 9062036449

**White, Leslie A., 1900-1975.**     **4.501**
The concept of cultural systems: a key to understanding tribes and nations / Leslie A. White. — New York: Columbia University Press, 1975. xiii, 192 p.; 22 cm. 1. Culture 2. Ethnology I. T.
GN357.W47     301.2     *LC* 75-33003     *ISBN* 0231039611

**Bodley, John H.**     **4.502**
Victims of progress / John H. Bodley. — 2nd ed. — Menlo Park, Calif.: Benjamin/Cummings Pub. Co., 1982. 264 p.: ill. Includes index. 1. Social change 2. Culture conflict 3. Man, Primitive 4. Acculturation I. T.
GN358.B63 1981     306 19     *LC* 81-8087     *ISBN* 0805309500

**Harris, Marvin, 1927-.**     **4.503**
Cannibals and kings: the origins of cultures / Marvin Harris. — 1st ed. — New York: Random House, c1977. xii, 239 p.; 25 cm. Includes index. 1. Social evolution 2. Culture — Origin 3. Man — Influence of environment 4. Food supply I. T.
GN358.H37     301.2     *LC* 77-5977     *ISBN* 0394407652

**Steward, Julian Haynes, 1902-1972.**     **4.504**
Evolution and ecology: essays on social transformation / by Julian H. Steward; edited by Jane C. Steward and Robert F. Murphy. Urbana: University of Illinois Press, c1977. 406 p.: ill.; 24 cm. 1. Steward, Julian Haynes, 1902-1972. 2. Social evolution — Addresses, essays, lectures. 3. Social change — Addresses, essays, lectures. 4. Indians — Addresses, essays, lectures. I. T.
GN360.4.S73 1977     301.24     *LC* 76-46341     *ISBN* 0252006127

**Leach, Edmund Ronald.**     **4.505**
Culture & communication: the logic by which symbols are connected: an introduction to the use of structuralist analysis in social anthropology / by Edmund Leach. — Cambridge [Eng.]; New York: Cambridge University Press, 1976. 105 p.: ill.; 24 cm. (Themes in the social sciences.) Includes index. 1. Structural anthropology 2. Semiotics I. T. II. Series.
GN362.L42     301.2     *LC* 75-30439     *ISBN* 052121131X

**Lévi-Strauss, Claude.** • 4.506
Structural anthropology / Claude Lévi–Strauss; translated from the French by Claire Jacobson and Brooke Grundfest Schoepf. — New York: Basic Books, c1963. xvi, 410 p.: illus., diagrs., plan.; 25 cm. Includes index. 1. Structural anthropology I. T.
GN362.L4813 1963b      301.2      *LC* 63-17344      *ISBN* 0465082297

**Stocking, George W., 1928-.** 4.507
Functionalism historicized: essays on British social anthropology / edited by George W. Stocking, Jr. — Madison, Wis.: University of Wisconsin Press, 1984. 244 p.: ports. — (History of anthropology. v. 2) 1. Functionalism (Social sciences) — History — Addresses, essays, lectures. 2. Ethnology — Great Britain — History — Addresses, essays, lectures. I. T. II. Series.
GN363.F86 1984      306/.0941 19      *LC* 84-40160      *ISBN* 0299099008

**Current problems in sociobiology / edited by King's College** 4.508
**sociobiology group.**
Cambridge [Cambridgeshire]; New York: Cambridge University Press, 1982. xi, 394 p.: Ill.; 24 cm. 'Originally presented at a conference held at King's College, Cambridge on 4-6 July 1980'—Pref. 1. Sociobiology — Congresses. 2. Human evolution — Congresses. I. King's College (University of Cambridge)
GN365.9.C84 1982      304.5 19      *LC* 81-10129      *ISBN* 0521242037

**Evolutionary biology and human social behavior: an** 4.509
**anthropological perspective / edited by Napoleon A. Chagnon,**
**William Irons.**
North Scituate, Mass.: Duxbury Press, c1979. xvi, 623 p.: graphs; 25 cm. Based on papers presented at two symposia organized for the American Anthropological Association's 1976 annual meeting. Includes index. 1. Sociobiology — Congresses. 2. Social structure — Congresses. I. Chagnon, Napoleon A., 1938- II. Irons, William. III. American Anthropological Association.
GN365.9.E96      301.2      *LC* 78-14564      *ISBN* 0878721932

**Kitcher, Philip, 1947-.** 4.510
Vaulting ambition: sociobiology and the quest for human nature / Philip Kitcher. — Cambridge, Mass.: MIT Press, c1985. xi, 456 p.; 24 cm. Includes index. 1. Sociobiology I. T.
GN365.9.K58 1985      *LC* 85-7229      *ISBN* 0262111098

**Wilson, Edward Osborne, 1929-.** 4.511
On human nature / Edward O. Wilson. — Cambridge: Harvard University Press, 1978. xii, 260 p.; 25 cm. 1. Sociobiology 2. Social Darwinism I. T.
GN365.9.W54      301.2      *LC* 78-17675      *ISBN* 0674634411

## GN378–395 SPECIAL CATEGORIES OF PEOPLES

**Atlas of man / [editor, John Gaisford].** 4.512
New York: St. Martin's Press, 1978. 272 p.: ill.; 31 cm. Includes index. 1. Ethnology I. Gaisford, John, 1949-
GN378.A84      909      *LC* 78-4364      *ISBN* 0312059914

**Politics and history in band societies / edited by Eleanor** 4.513
**Leacock, Richard Lee.**
Cambridge [Cambridgeshire]; New York: Cambridge University Press; Paris: Editions de la Maison des Sciences de l'Homme, 1982. xiv, 500 p.; ill.; 24 cm. 1. Hunting and gathering societies — Addresses, essays, lectures. 2. Political anthropology — Addresses, essays, lectures. 3. Native races — Addresses, essays, lectures. I. Leacock, Eleanor Burke, 1922- II. Lee, Richard B.
GN388.P64 1982      909.82 19      *LC* 81-18043      *ISBN* 0521240638

**Hannerz, Ulf.** 4.514
Exploring the city: inquiries toward an urban anthropology / Ulf Hannerz. — New York: Columbia University Press, 1980. x, 378 p.; 24 cm. Includes index. 1. Urban anthropology 2. Cities and towns I. T.
GN395.H36      307.7/6      *LC* 79-29707      *ISBN* 0231039824

**Southall, Aidan William. ed.** 4.515
Urban anthropology: cross–cultural studies of urbanization / edited by Aidan Southall. — New York: Oxford University Press, 1973. vi, 489 p.: maps; 23 cm. Chiefly papers resulting from a seminar held at Burg Wartenstein, Austria, Sept. 1964; sponsored by the Wenner-Gren Foundation for Anthropological Research. 1. Urban anthropology — Congresses. 2. Urbanization — Congresses. I. Wenner-Gren Foundation for Anthropological Research. II. T.
GN395.U72      301.36/1      *LC* 73-76911      *ISBN* 0195016912

## GN397 APPLIED ANTHROPOLOGY

**Development from below: anthropologists and development** 4.516
**situations / editor, David C. Pitt.**
The Hague: Mouton; Chicago: distributed in the USA and Canada by Aldine, [1976] x, 277 p.; 24 cm. (World anthropology.) Papers prepared for the 9th International Congress of Anthropological and Ethnological Sciences held in Chicago, 1973. 1. Applied anthropology — Congresses. 2. Economic development — Social aspects — Congresses. 3. Community development — Congresses. I. Pitt, David C. II. International Congress of Anthropological and Ethnological Sciences. 9th, Chicago, 1973. III. Series.
GN397.5.D48      309.2/12      *LC* 76-379453      *ISBN* 0202900371

**Social anthropology and development policy / edited by Ralph** 4.517
**Grillo and Alan Rew.**
London; New York: Tavistock Publications, 1985. vi, 208 p.; 25 cm. (ASA monographs; 23) 1. Applied anthropology — Congresses. 2. Economic development — Social aspects — Congresses. 3. Developing countries — Economic policy — Congresses. I. Grillo, R. D. II. Rew, Alan, 1942-
GN397.5.S65 1985      306 19      *LC* 84-26821      *ISBN* 0422797901

# GN400–499 Cultural Traits, Customs, and Institutions

**Benedict, Ruth, 1887-1948.** • 4.518
Patterns of culture. With a new pref. by Margaret Mead. Boston, Houghton Mifflin, 1961 [c1959] 290 p. 21 cm. (Sentry edition, 8) 1. Society, Primitive 2. Zuñi Indians 3. Kwakiutl Indians 4. Anthropology 5. Dobu Island. I. T.
GN400.B4 1961      572      *LC* 61-19375

**Bohannan, Paul.** • 4.519
Social anthropology. — New York: Holt, Rinehart and Winston, [1963] 421 p.: illus.; 24 cm. 1. Ethnology I. T.
GN400.B64      572      *LC* 63-13322

**Evans-Pritchard, E. E. (Edward Evan), 1902-1973.** • 4.520
Social anthropology / by E.E. Evans–Pritchard. Glencoe, Ill.: Free Press, 1952. vii, 134 p.; 22 cm. 1. Ethnology — Addresses, essays, lectures. I. T.
GN400.E8x

**Firth, Raymond William, 1901-.** • 4.521
Elements of social organization, by Raymond Firth. — [3d ed.]. — Boston, Beacon Press [1963] xi, 260 p. illus. 21 cm. — (Josiah Mason lectures, 1947) First published 1951.Beacon paperback, no.153. 1. Society, Primitive I. T. II. Series.
GN400.F5x 1951      *LC* 66-3650

**Tylor, Edward Burnett, Sir, 1832-1917.** • 4.522
Primitive culture. — [New York: Harper, 1958] 2 v.; 21 cm. — (The Library of religion and culture) Harper torchbooks, TB33-34. 1. Ethnology 2. Religion, Primitive 3. Social evolution 4. Animism I. T. II. Title: The origins of culture. III. Title: Religion in primitive culture.
GN400.T8 1958      572      *LC* 58-7113

**Gluckman, Max, 1911-1975. ed.** • 4.523
Essays on the ritual of social relations. Manchester, Eng. Manchester University Press [1963, c1962] vii, 190 p. 21 cm. 1. Society, Primitive 2. Rites and ceremonies I. Forde, Cyril Daryll, 1902- II. T. III. Title: The ritual of social relations.
GN405.G55 1963      *LC* 63-1735

**Herskovits, Melville J. (Melville Jean), 1895-1963.** 4.524
Cultural relativism; perspectives in cultural pluralism. Edited by Frances Herskovits. [1st ed.] New York, Random House [1972] xxvi, 293 p. 22 cm. 1. Cultural relativism — Addresses, essays, lectures. I. T.
GN405.H4      301.2      *LC* 72-6102      *ISBN* 0394481542

**Kardiner, Abram, 1891-.** • 4.525
They studied man [by] Abram Kardiner and Edward Preble. — [1st ed.]. — Cleveland: World Pub. Co., [1961] 287 p.: illus.; 22 cm. 1. Culture — Addresses, essays, lectures. I. Preble, Edward, 1922- joint author. II. T.
GN405.K3      572      *LC* 61-5808

**Murdock, George Peter, 1897-.** • 4.526
Ethnographic atlas. — [Pittsburgh]: University of Pittsburgh Press, [1967] 128 p.; 24 cm. 1. Ethnology — Classification. I. T.
GN405.M8      301.2/01/2      *LC* 67-21648

**Murdock, George Peter, 1897-.**       • **4.527**
Outline of world cultures. 3d ed., rev. New Haven, Human Relations Area Files, 1963. xi, 222 p. 28 cm. (Behavior science outlines; 3) 'Addenda' slip inserted. 1. Classification — Books — Culture I. T. II. Series.
H62.B36 vol.3 1963 GN405.M8x     *LC* 64-2981

**Sahlins, Marshall David, 1930- ed.**       **4.528**
Evolution and culture, by Thomas G. Harding [and others] Edited by Marshall D. Sahlins & Elman R. Service. Foreword by Leslie A. White. Ann Arbor, University of Michigan Press [1960] 131 p. ill. 1. Social change I. Service, Elman Rogers, 1915- jt. ed. II. Harding, Thomas G. III. T.
GN405 S25     *LC* 60-7930

## GN407-448 TECHNOLOGY. MATERIAL CULTURE

**Nutrition and anthropology in action / editor, Thomas K.**    **4.529**
**Fitzgerald.**
Assen: Van Gorcum, 1977 (c1976). xi, 155 p., [1] leaf of plates: ill.; 24 cm. — (Studies of developing countries. 21) 1. Food habits — Addresses, essays, lectures. 2. Man, Primitive — Food — Addresses, essays, lectures. 3. Nutrition — Addresses, essays, lectures. 4. Applied anthropology — Addresses, essays, lectures. I. Fitzgerald, Thomas K. II. Series.
GN407.N87    641.1    *LC* 78-342540    *ISBN* 9023214471

**Herskovits, Melville J. (Melville Jean), 1895-1963.**     • **4.530**
Economic anthropology; a study in comparative economics. [2d ed., rev., enl., rewritten] New York, Knopf, 1952. xiii, 547, xxiii p. illus., maps. 22 cm. 'Originally published in 1940 as The economic life of primitive peoples.' 1. Economic anthropology 2. Industries, Primitive I. T.
GN420.H4 1952    572 572.7*    *LC* 52-5074

**Symposium on Man the Hunter (1966: University of Chicago)**    • **4.531**
Man the hunter. Edited by Richard B. Lee and Irven DeVore, with the assistance of Jill Nash. Chicago, Aldine Pub. Co. [1969, c1968] xvi, 415 p. illus., maps. 26 cm. Sponsored by the Wenner-Gren Foundation For Anthropological Research. 1. Hunting and gathering societies — Congresses. I. Lee, Richard B. ed. II. DeVore, Irven. ed. III. Wenner-Gren Foundation for Anthropological Research. IV. T.
GN422.S9 1966    390    *LC* 67-17603

**Waddell, Eric.**       **4.532**
The mound builders: agricultural practices, environment, and society in the central highlands of New Guinea / [by] Eric Waddell. — Seattle: University of Washington Press [1972] xvi, 253 p.: ill.; 23 cm. (American Ethnological Society. Monograph; 53) A revision of the author's thesis, Australian National University, 1969. 1. Enga (New Guinea people) 2. Agriculture, Primitive 3. Anthropo-geography — New Guinea (Ter.) I. T.
GN425.W33 1972    309.1/95/5    *LC* 70-159437    *ISBN* 0295951699

**Gulliver, P. H.**       • **4.533**
The family herds: a study of two pastoral tribes in East Africa, the Jie and Turkana / P. H. gulliver. — London: Routledge & K. Paul, [1955] xv, 271 p.: ill., maps; 23 cm.— (International library of sociology and social reconstruction) 1. Cattle — Uganda. 2. Jie (African people) 3. Turkana (African people) I. T.
GN426 G8 1955    *LC* 55-4622

**Douglas, Mary.**       **4.534**
In the active voice / Mary Douglas. — London; Boston: Routledge & K. Paul, 1982. xi, 306 p.; 22 cm. 1. Economic anthropology — Addresses, essays, lectures. 2. Food habits — Addresses, essays, lectures. 3. Ethnology — Addresses, essays, lectures. I. T.
GN448.D68 1982    306/.3 19    *LC* 81-18263    *ISBN* 071009065X

## GN451-452.5 INTELLECTUAL LIFE

**Belo, Jane.**       • **4.535**
Trance in Bali. New York, Columbia University Press, 1960. xiii, 284 p. illus. 27 cm. 1. Trance 2. Bali (Island) I. T.
GN451.B4 1960    *LC* 60-6545

**Boas, Franz, 1858-1942.**       • **4.536**
The mind of primitive man. With a new foreword by Melville J. Herskovits. Rev. ed. New York, Collier Books [1963] 254 p. 18 cm. 'AS557.' 1. Ethnopsychology 2. Race I. T.
GN451.B7 1963    136.41    *LC* 63-9984

**Lévi-Strauss, Claude.**       • **4.537**
[Pensée sauvage. English] The savage mind. [Chicago] University of Chicago Press [1966] xii, 290 p. illus., port. 23 cm. (The Nature of human society series) 1. Ethnopsychology I. T.
GN451.L3813    155.81    *LC* 66-28197

**Lévy-Bruhl, Lucien, 1857-1939.**       • **4.538**
Primitive mentality, by Lucien Lévy-Bruhl ... Authorized translation by Lilian A. Clare. — London: George Allen & Unwin ltd.; New York: The Macmillan company, [1923] 458 p., 1 l.; 22 cm. 1. Society, Primitive 2. Ethnopsychology I. Clare, Lilian Ada (Long) Mrs. 1865- tr. II. T.
GN451.L55    *LC* 23-17174

**Turner, Victor Witter.**       **4.539**
Dramas, fields, and metaphors: symbolic action in human society / [by] Victor Turner. — Ithaca [N.Y.]: Cornell University Press, [1974] 309 p.; 22 cm. — (Symbol, myth, and ritual) 1. Symbolism — Addresses, essays, lectures. 2. Rites and ceremonies — Addresses, essays, lectures. 3. Metaphor — Addresses, essays, lectures. I. T.
GN451.T87    GN451 T87.    301.2/1    *LC* 73-16968    *ISBN* 0801408164

**Singer, Milton B.**       **4.540**
Man's glassy essence: explorations in semiotic anthropology / Milton Singer. — Bloomington: Indiana University Press, c1984. xiv, 222 p.; 25 cm. — (Advances in semiotics.) Includes index. 1. Ethnology — Philosophy 2. Symbolism 3. Semiotics I. T. II. Series.
GN452.5.S56 1984    306/.01 19    *LC* 83-48108    *ISBN* 0253336759

**Blanchard, Kendall, 1942-.**       **4.541**
The anthropology of sport: an introduction / Kendall Blanchard and Alyce Taylor Cheska; introduction by Edward Norbeck. — S. Hadley, Mass.: Bergin & Garvey, 1985. xii, 306 p.: ill.; 24 cm. Includes index. 1. Games, Primitive 2. Sports — History I. Cheska, Alyce Taylor. II. T.
GN454.B56 1985    306/.483 19    *LC* 84-12395    *ISBN* 089789040X

## GN470-474 RELIGION. RITUAL

**De Waal Malefijt, Annemarie, 1914-.**       • **4.542**
Religion and culture; an introduction to anthropology of religion. — New York: Macmillan, [1968] vii, 407 p.: illus., map.; 21 cm. 1. Religion, Primitive I. T.
GN470.D4    290    *LC* 68-12717

**Durkheim, Emile, 1858-1917.**       • **4.543**
[Formes élémentaires de la vie religieuse. English] The elementary forms of the religious life. Translated from the French by Joseph Ward Swain. New York, Free Press [1965, c1915] 507 p. 21 cm. (Free Press paperbacks) 1. Religion, Primitive 2. Totemism I. T.
GN470.D8 1965    291    *LC* 65-1903

**Evans-Pritchard, E. E. (Edward Evan), 1902-1973.**       • **4.544**
Theories of primitive religion, by E. E. Evans-Pritchard. Oxford, Clarendon Press, 1965. 132 p. 23 cm. (Sir D. Owen Evans lectures, 1962) 1. Religion, Primitive I. T. II. Series.
GN470.E9    *LC* 65-29790

**Gill, Sam D., 1943-.**       **4.545**
Beyond the primitive: the religions of nonliterate peoples / Sam D. Gill. — Englewood Cliffs, N.J.: Prentice-Hall, c1982. xvii, 120 p.: ill.; 23 cm. — (Prentice-Hall series in world religions.) Includes index. 1. Religion, Primitive I. T. II. Series.
GN470.G5    306/.6 19    *LC* 81-5913    *ISBN* 013076034X

**Howells, William White, 1908-.**       • **4.546**
The heathens, primitive man and his religions. [1st ed.] Garden City, N. Y.: Doubleday, 1948. 306 p.: ill., map (on lining-papers); 22 cm. Bibliographical footnotes. 1. Religion, Primitive I. T.
GN470.H6    290    *LC* 48-5578 *

**Leslie, Charles M., 1923- ed.**       • **4.547**
Anthropology of folk religion. — [1st ed.]. — New York, Vintage Books, 1960. xviii, 453 p. illus. 19 cm. — (A Vintage original, V-105) 1. Religion, Primitive I. T.
GN470.L45    572.082    *LC* 60-15525

**Lowie, Robert Harry, 1883-1957.**       • **4.548**
Primitive religion. — New York: Liveright, [1970, c1948] xxii, 388 p.; 21 cm. — (Black and gold library) 1. Religion, Primitive I. T.
GN470.L6 1970    291    *LC* 75-114373

**Middleton, John, 1921- comp.**    ● **4.549**
Gods and rituals: readings in religious beliefs and practices. — [1st ed.] Garden City, N.Y.: Published for the American Museum of Natural History [New York, by] the Natural History Press, 1967. x, 468 p.: ill.; 22 cm. (American Museum sourcebooks in anthropology) 1. Religion, Primitive — Addresses, essays, lectures. I. American Museum of Natural History. II. T. III. Series.
GN470.M48    291    LC 67-12870

**Middleton, John.**    ● **4.550**
Lugbara religion; ritual and authority among an East African people. London; New York: Published for the International African Institute, by the Oxford U.P. 1960. 275p.illus.,map. 1. Lugbara (African people) 2. Religion, Primitive I. T.
GN470.M5    572.96761    LC 60-51074

**Needham, Rodney. comp.**    **4.551**
Right & left: essays on dual symbolic classification / edited and with an introd. by Rodney Needham; foreword by E. E. Evans–Pritchard. — Chicago: University of Chicago Press, 1974 (c1973) xxxix, 449 p.: ill.; 24 cm. Essays by Hertz, Granet and Kruyt translated by R. Needham; one by Chelhod translated by J. J. Fox. 1. Left and right (Symbolism) — Addresses, essays, lectures. 2. Folk classification — Addresses, essays, lectures. I. T.
GN470.N43    301.2/1    LC 73-82982    ISBN 0226569950

**Radin, Paul, 1883-1959.**    ● **4.552**
Primitive religion: its nature and origin. — New York: Dover Publications, 1957. 322 p.; 21 cm. 'An unabridged republication of the first edition [published in 1937] with a new preface by the author.' 1. Religion, Primitive I. T.
GN470.R3 1957    291    LC 57-4452

**Dobkin de Rios, Marlene.**    **4.553**
Hallucinogens, cross–cultural perspectives / Marlene Dobkin de Rios. — 1st ed. — Albuquerque: University of New Mexico Press, 1984. x, 255 p.: ill.; 24 cm. Includes index. 1. Hallucinogenic plants — Cross-cultural studies 2. Hallucinogenic drugs and religious experience — Cross-cultural studies I. T.
GN472.4.D625 1984    394 19    LC 84-7244    ISBN 082630737X

## GN473 Rites. Ceremonies

**Curley, Richard T.**    **4.554**
Elders, shades, and women: ceremonial change in Lango, Uganda / [by] Richard T. Curley. — Berkeley: University of California Press, [1973] x, 223 p.: ill.; 24 cm. 1. Lango (African tribe) — Rites and ceremonies. 2. Women, Lango (African people) 3. Social change I. T.
GN473.C87    301.29/676/1    LC 70-634788    ISBN 0520021495

**Firth, Raymond William, 1901-.**    ● **4.555**
The work of the gods in Tikopia / by Raymond Firth. — 2nd ed., with new introd. and epilogue. — London: Athlone, 1967. viii, 492 p., [4] feuillets de planches: diagr., plans, portr.; 23 cm. — (Monographs on social anthropology; no. 1-2) 1. Tikopians 2. Rites and ceremonies — Polynesia. I. T. II. Series.
GN473 F5 1967    299/.9    LC 67-10515

**Fried, Martha Nemes.**    **4.556**
Transitions: four rituals in eight cultures / Martha Nemes Fried and Morton H. Fried. — 1st ed. — New York: Norton, c1980. 306 p.; 22 cm. Includes index. 1. Rites and ceremonies 2. Initiation rites 3. Ethnology I. Fried, Morton H. (Morton Herbert), 1923-1986. joint author. II. T.
GN473.F68 1980    301.2/1    LC 79-24473    ISBN 0393013502

**Gennep, Arnold van, 1873-1957.**    ● **4.557**
[Rites de passage. English] The rites of passage. Translated by Monika B. Vizedom and Gabrielle L. Caffee. Introd. by Solon T. Kimball. [Chicago] University of Chicago Press [1960] 198 p. 23 cm. 1. Rites and ceremonies I. T.
GN473.G513 1960a    392    LC 59-14321

**Secular ritual / edited by Sally F. Moore, Barbara G. Myerhoff.**    **4.558**
Assen: Van Gorcum, 1977. x, 293 p.; 24 cm. Papers originally presented at a conference entitled Secular rituals considered, Aug. 24-Sept. 1, 1974 at Burg Wartenstein, Austria. 1. Rites and ceremonies — Congresses. 2. Associations, institutions, etc — Congresses. I. Moore, Sally Falk, 1924- II. Myerhoff, Barbara G.
GN473.S43    392    LC 77-379589    ISBN 9023214579

**Turner, Victor Witter.**    **4.559**
The ritual process: structure and anti–structure [by] Victor W. Turner. — Chicago: Aldine Pub. Co., [1969] viii, 213 p.: illus.; 22 cm. — (The Lewis Henry Morgan lectures, 1966) 1. Rites and ceremonies I. T. II. Series.
GN473.T82    301.2    LC 67-17612

## GN475 Magic. Witchcraft

**Middleton, John, 1921- comp.**    ● **4.560**
Magic, witchcraft, and curing. Garden City, N.Y., Published for the American Museum of Natural History [New York, by] the Natural History Press, 1967. x, 346 p. illus. 21 cm. (American Museum sourcebooks in anthropology) 1. Magic — Addresses, essays, lectures. 2. Witchcraft — Addresses, essays, lectures. I. American Museum of Natural History. II. T. III. Series.
GN475.M47    133.4    LC 67-12895

**The Evil eye / Clarence Maloney, editor.**    **4.561**
New York: Columbia University Press, 1976. xix, 335 p.: ill.; 24 cm. Outgrowth of a symposium on the evil eye belief held at the 1972 meeting of the American Anthropological Association. 1. Evil eye — Congresses. I. Maloney, Clarence.
GN475.6.E94    133.4/25    LC 76-16861    ISBN 0231040067

**Evans-Pritchard, E. E. (Edward Evan), 1902-1973.**    ● **4.562**
Witchcraft, oracles and magic among the Azande, by E. E. Evans–Pritchard ... with a foreword by Professor C. G. Seligman ... Oxford, The Clarendon Press, 1937. xxv, 1, 558 p., 1 l., illus. (incl. maps) XXXIV pl. (incl. front.) 23 cm. 1. Azande. 2. Witchcraft — Africa, Central. 3. Oracles 4. Medicine, Magic, mystic, and spagiric 5. Magic I. T.
GN475.8.E9    LC 38-5545    ISBN 0198231032

## GN478–491 Social Organization

**Heusch, Luc de.**    **4.563**
Why marry her?: society and symbolic structures / Luc de Heusch; translated by Janet Lloyd. — Cambridge; New York: Cambridge University Press, 1981. vi, 218 p.; 24 cm. — (Cambridge studies in social anthropology. 33) 'The main body of this volume is composed of four of twelve studies published by Gallimard under the title Pourquoi l'épouser? et autres essais (1971)'—Pref. Includes index. 1. Social structure — Addresses, essays, lectures. 2. Religion, Primitive — Addresses, essays, lectures. 3. Structural anthropology — Addresses, essays, lectures. I. Heusch, Luc de. Pourquoi l'épouser? II. T. III. Series.
GN478.H4713 1981    305 19    LC 80-41710    ISBN 0521224608

**Morgan, Lewis Henry, 1818-1881.**    **4.564**
Ancient society / Lewis Henry Morgan; foreword by Elisabeth Tooker. — Tucson, Ariz.: University of Arizona Press, 1985. xxxii, 560 p.; 22 cm. (Classics of anthropology) Reprint. Originally published: New York: H. Holt, 1878, c1877. Includes index. 1. Social structure 2. Social evolution 3. Political anthropology I. T.
GN478.M67 1985    301 19    LC 85-1121    ISBN 0816509247

**Schapera, Isaac, 1905-.**    ● **4.565**
Married life in an African tribe, by I. Schapera. — [Evanston, Ill.]: Northwestern University Press, 1966. 364 p.: illus., maps.; 23 cm. 1. Marriage — Bechuanaland. 2. Family — Bechuanaland. 3. Society, Primitive 4. Kgatla (African tribe) 5. Ethnology — Bechuanaland. I. T.
GN478.S35 1966    392.509681    LC 65-24633

**Malinowski, Bronislaw, 1884-1942.**    ● **4.566**
The father in primitive psychology / by Bronislaw Malinowski. — New York: W.W. Norton, c1927. 93 p. — (New science series) 1. Ethnology — Papua New Guinea — Trobriand Islands 2. Family — Papua New Guinea — Trobriand Islands. 3. Matriarchy — Papua New Guinea — Trobriand Islands. I. T. II. Title: Primitive psychology.
GN479 M3 1927    LC 27-7009

**Montagu, Ashley, 1905-.**    ● **4.567**
Coming into being among the Australian aborigines; a study of the procreative beliefs of the native tribes of Australia / by M. F. Ashley Montagu; with a foreword by B. Malinowski. — London: G. Routledge, [1937] xxxv, 364 p.: ill. (incl. maps) 1. Birth (in religion, folk-lore, etc.) 2. Ethnology — Australia I. T.
GN479 M6 1937    LC 38-17469

**Social inequality: comparative and developmental approaches / edited by Gerald D. Berreman, with the assistance of Kathleen M. Zaretsky.**    **4.568**
New York: Academic Press, c1981. xvii, 361 p.: ill.; 24 cm. (Studies in anthropology.) Papers presented at the Burg Wartenstein Symposium no. 80 sponsored by the Wenner-Gren Foundation for Anthropological Research, and held Aug. 25-Sept. 3, 1978. 1. Equality — Congresses. 2. Social status — Congresses. 3. Society, Primitive — Congresses. I. Berreman, Gerald Duane, 1930- II. Zaretsky, Kathleen M. III. Wenner-Gren Foundation for Anthropological Research.
GN479.S6    305.5 19    LC 80-685550    ISBN 0120931605

**Sexual meanings, the cultural construction of gender and**    **4.569**
**sexuality / edited by Sherry B. Ortner and Harriet Whitehead.**
Cambridge; New York: Cambridge University Press, 1981. x, 435 p.; 24 cm.
1. Sex role — Addresses, essays, lectures. 2. Sex symbolism — Addresses,
essays, lectures. I. Ortner, Sherry B., 1941- II. Whitehead, Harriet.
GN479.65.S49    305.3 19    *LC* 80-26655    *ISBN* 0521239656

**In her prime: a new view of middle–aged women / Judith K.**    **4.570**
**Brown, Virginia Kerns, and contributors; foreword by Beatrice**
**Blyth Whiting.**
S. Hadley, Mass.: Bergin & Garvey Publishers, 1985. xii, 217 p.: ill.; 24 cm.
1. Middle aged women — Cross-cultural studies. I. Brown, Judith K.
II. Kerns, Virginia, 1948-
GN479.7.I5 1985    305.2/44 19    *LC* 84-14671    *ISBN* 0897890566

**International Congress of Anthropological and Ethnological**    **4.571**
**Sciences. 9th, Chicago, 1973.**
Being female: reproduction, power, and change / editor, Dana Raphael. — The
Hague: Mouton; Chicago: distributed by Aldine, c1975. xiii, 293 p.; 24 cm. —
(World anthropology.) 1. Women — Congresses 2. Women — Social
conditions — Congresses. 3. Pregnancy — Congresses. I. Raphael, Dana,
1926- II. T. III. Series.
GN479.7.I57 1973    301.41/2    *LC* 75-331375    *ISBN* 0202011518

**Leacock, Eleanor Burke, 1922-.**    **4.572**
Myths of male dominance: collected articles on women cross–culturally /
Eleanor Burke Leacock. — New York: Monthly Review Press, c1981. viii,
344 p.: ill.; 21 cm. Includes index. 1. Women — Social conditions — Collected
works. 2. Sex role — Collected works. I. T.
GN479.7.L4    305.4/2 19    *LC* 79-3870    *ISBN* 0853455376

**Sexual stratification: a cross–cultural view / Alice Schlegel,**    **4.573**
**editor.**
New York: Columbia University Press, 1977. xix, 371 p.; 24 cm. 1. Sex role
2. Women — Social conditions I. Schlegel, Alice.
GN479.7.S48    301.41    *LC* 77-2742    *ISBN* 0231042140

## GN480–487 Family. Kinship. Life Cycle

**Barnes, J. A. (John Arundel), 1918-.**    **4.574**
Three styles in the study of kinship / [by] J. A. Barnes. — [London]: Tavistock,
[1971] xxiv, 318 p.; 23 cm. 1. Kinship 2. Ethnology — Methodology I. T.
GN480.B32 1971    301.42/1    *LC* 70-889483    *ISBN* 0422738204

**Evans-Pritchard, E. E. (Edward Evan), 1902-1973.**    • **4.575**
Kinship and marriage among the Nuer. Oxford, Clarendon Press, 1951. xi,
183 p. ill. 1. Marriage customs and rites — Sudan, Egyptian 2. Kinship
3. Nuer (African tribe) I. T.
GN480 E78    *LC* 51-6828

**Firth, Raymond William, 1901-.**    • **4.576**
We, the Tikopia; a sociological study of kinship in primitive Polynesia. With a
pref. by Bronislaw Malinowski. [2d ed.] London, Allen & Unwin [1961, c1957]
xxvi, 605 p. illus., maps, geneal. tables. 23 cm. Imprint covered by label: New
York, Barnes & Noble. Bibliography: p. 282-283. 1. Tikopians 2. Kinship
I. T.
GN480.F5 1961    572.9935    *LC* 63-25918

**Fortes, Meyer. ed.**    • **4.577**
Marriage in tribal societies. Cambridge [Eng.] Published for the Dept. of
Archaeology and Anthropology at the University Press, 1962. vii, 157 p. ill.
(Cambridge papers in social anthropology. no. 3) 1. Marriage 2. Kinship
3. Society, Primitive I. T. II. Series.
GN480 F6    *LC* 62-51026

**Fox, Robin, 1934-.**    **4.578**
Kinship and marriage: an anthropological perspective. — [Harmondsworth]
Penguin [1974, c1967] 271 p. diagrs. 18 cm. — (Pelican anthropology library)
Pelican books. A884. Bibliography: p. [263]-266. 1. Kinship 2. Marriage
customs and rites I. T.
GN480.F68    392/.32    *LC* 67-114065

**Geertz, Hildred.**    • **4.579**
The Javanese family; a study of kinship and socialization. New York, Free Press
of Glencoe [1961] 176 p. ill. 1. Kinship 2. Ethnology — Java I. T.
GN480 G4    *LC* 61-9166

**Homans, George Caspar, 1910-.**    • **4.580**
Marriage, authority, and final causes: a study of unilateral cross-cousin
marriage / by George C. Homans and David M. Schneider. — Glencoe, Ill.:
Free Press, 1955. 64 p.: ill.; 23 cm. 1. Consanguinity 2. Kinship I. Schneider,
David Moses, 1899- joint author. II. T.
GN480.H63    *LC* 55-11001

**Lévi-Strauss, Claude.**    • **4.581**
[Structures élémentaires de la parenté. English] The elementary structures of
kinship. Translated from the French by James Harle Bell, John Richard von
Sturmer, and Rodney Needham, editor. Rev. ed. Boston, Beacon Press [1969]
xlii, 541 p. illus. 25 cm. Translation of Les structures élémentaires de la parenté.
1. Marriage 2. Society, Primitive I. T.
GN480.L413 1969b    392/.32    *LC* 68-12840

**Radcliffe-Brown, A. R. (Alfred Reginald), 1881-1955. ed.**    • **4.582**
African systems of kinship and marriage, edited by A. R. Radcliffe–Brown and
Daryll Forde. — London; New York: Published for the International African
Institute by the Oxford University Press, 1950. viii, 399 p.: illus., maps.; 23 cm.
1. Kinship — Africa. 2. Marriage customs and rites — Africa. I. Forde, Cyril
Daryll, 1902- joint ed. II. T.
GN480.R3    392    *LC* 51-10699

**Van den Berghe, Pierre L.**    **4.583**
Human family systems: an evolutionary view / Pierre L. van den Berghe. —
New York: Elsevier, c1979. viii, 254 p. Includes index. 1. Family 2. Kinship
3. Social evolution 4. Sociobiology I. T.
GN480.V18    GN480 V18.    301.42/1    *LC* 79-10528    *ISBN*
0444990615

**Schlegel, Alice.**    **4.584**
Male dominance and female autonomy: domestic authority in matrilineal
societies / with a foreword by Raoul Naroll. — [New Haven, Conn.]: HRAF
Press, 1972. xiv, 206 p.; 22 cm. 1. Matrilineal kinship 2. Authority I. T.
GN480.4.S33    301.42    *LC* 72-78401

**Schneider, David Murray, 1918- ed.**    • **4.585**
Matrilineal kinship, edited by David M. Schneider and Kathleen Gough.
Berkeley, University of California Press, 1961. xx, 761 p. ill., map.
1. Matrilineal kinship I. Gough, Kathleen, 1925- II. T.
GN480.4 S37    *LC* 61-7523

**Goodale, Jane Carter, 1926-.**    **4.586**
Tiwi wives; a study of the women of Melville Island, North Australia [by] Jane
C. Goodale. Seattle, University of Washington Press [1971] xxiv, 368 p. illus. 23
cm. (American Ethnological Society. Monograph 51) 1. Women, Tiwi
(Australian people) 2. Tiwi (Melville Island people) — Social life and customs.
I. T.
GN481.G6    301.41/2/099429    *LC* 72-117728

**Frayser, Suzanne G.**    **4.587**
Varieties of sexual experience: an anthropological perspective on human
sexuality / Suzanne G. Frayser. — New Haven, Conn.: HRAF Press, 1985. xii,
546 p.; 23 cm. 'Ethnographic bibliography': p. 495-510. Includes index. 1. Sex
customs — Cross-cultural studies. 2. Sex (Biology) I. T.
GN484.3.F73 1985    *LC* 85-60217    *ISBN* 0875363423

**Age and anthropological theory / edited by David I. Kertzer**    **4.588**
**and Jennie Keith; with a foreword by Matilda White Riley.**
Ithaca, N.Y.: Cornell University Press, 1984. 344 p.: ill.; 24 cm. — (Cornell
paperbacks) Cover title: Age & anthropological theory. 1. Aged — Addresses,
essays, lectures. 2. Aging — Addresses, essays, lectures. 3. Anthropology —
Philosophy — Addresses, essays, lectures. I. Kertzer, David I., 1948-
II. Keith, Jennie. III. Title: Age & anthropological theory.
GN485.A33 1984    305.2/6 19    *LC* 83-21060    *ISBN* 0801415675

**Fry, Christine L.**    **4.589**
Dimensions: aging, culture, and health / Christine L. Fry and contributors. —
New York: Praeger, 1981. vi, 345 p.: ill.; 24 cm. 'A J.F. Bergin Publishers book.'
Includes indexes. 1. Aging — Cross-cultural studies — Addresses, essays,
lectures. 2. Aged — Care and hygiene — Addresses, essays, lectures. I. T.
GN485.D55 1981    305.2/6 19    *LC* 80-28607    *ISBN* 0030529719

**Huntington, Richard.**    **4.590**
Celebrations of death: the anthropology of mortuary ritual / Richard
Huntington, Peter Metcalf. — Cambridge [Eng.]; New York: Cambridge
University Press, 1979. xv, 230 p.: ill.; 24 cm. Includes index. 1. Funeral rites
and ceremonies 2. Death I. Metcalf, Peter. joint author. II. T.
GN486.H84    393    *LC* 79-478    *ISBN* 0521225310

**Schneider, David Murray, 1918-.**    **4.591**
A critique of the study of kinship / David M. Schneider. — Ann Arbor:
University of Michigan Press, c1984. ix, 208 p.; 23 cm. 1. Kinship I. T.
GN487.S36 1984    306.8/3 19    *LC* 84-5246    *ISBN* 0472080512

## GN488–491 Other Topics

**Lowie, Robert Harry, 1883-1957.**    • **4.592**
Primitive society. — New York: Liveright Pub. Corp., [1947] xii, 463 p.; 22 cm.
'Black and gold edition.' 1. Society, Primitive I. T.
GN488.L6 1947    572    *LC* 47-6946

**Whiting, John Wesley Mayhew.**     • **4.593**
Becoming a Kwoma: a teaching and learning in a New Guinea tribe / by John W. M. Whiting; with a foreword by John Dollard. — London: H. Milford, Oxford University Press, 1941. xix, 226 p., 1 l.: incl. ill., geneal. tables, plates, ports.; 24 cm. 1. Kwoma (Papua New Guinea people) I. Yale university. Institute of human relations. II. T.
GN488.5.W5     *LC* 42-14232

**Clark, Grahame, 1907-.**     • **4.594**
Prehistoric Europe; the economic basis, by J. G. D. Clark. Stanford, Calif., Stanford University Press, 1966, c1952. xix, 349 p. illus., maps (1 col.) plates. 27cm. 1. Economic anthropology 2. Europe — Antiquities I. T.
GN489.C6 1966     338/.0936     *LC* 66-16986

**Forde, Cyril Daryll, 1902-.**     • **4.595**
Habitat, economy and society; a geographical introduction to ethnology. [8th ed.] London, Methuen; New York, Dutton [1950] xv, 500 p. illus., maps. 22 cm. 1. Society, Primitive 2. Ethnology 3. Anthropo-geography I. T.
GN489.F6 1950     *LC* 51-1952

**Schneider, Harold K.**     **4.596**
Economic man; the anthropology of economics [by] Harold K. Schneider. — New York: Free Press, [1974] x, 278 p.: illus.; 22 cm. 1. Economic anthropology 2. Microeconomics I. T.
GN489.S36     330     *LC* 73-8493

**Leach, Edmund Ronald.**     • **4.597**
Pul Eliya, a village in Ceylon; a study of land tenure and kinship. Cambridge, University Press, 1961. xiv, 343 p. ill., maps, diagrs., tables. 1. Land tenure — Pul Eliya, Ceylon 2. Kinship I. T.
GN489.1 L4     *LC* 61-1517

**Adams, Robert McCormick, 1926-.**     • **4.598**
The evolution of urban society: early Mesopotamia and prehispanic Mexico, by Robert McC. Adams. Chicago, Aldine Pub. Co. [1966] ix, 191 p. maps. 22 cm. (Lewis Henry Morgan lectures. 1965) 1. Society, Primitive 2. Ethnology — Iraq 3. Indians of Mexico — History. I. T. II. Series.
GN490.A4     301.364     *LC* 66-15195

**Berndt, Ronald Murray, 1916-.**     **4.599**
Politics in New Guinea: traditional and in the context of change, some anthropological perspectives / editors: Ronald M. Berndt [and] Peter Lawrence. — [Seattle]: University of Washington Press, [1973, c1971] xviii, 430 p.: illus.; 25 cm. 1. Tribal government — Papua New Guinea. 2. Political anthropology — Papua New Guinea. 3. Papua New Guinea — Politics and government I. Lawrence, Peter. II. T.
GN490.B43 1973     301.4/00995/5     *LC* 73-161356     *ISBN* 0295952350

**Colson, Elizabeth, 1917-.**     **4.600**
Tradition and contract: the problem of order / Elizabeth Colson. — Chicago: Aldine Pub. Co., 1974. xi, 140 p.; 22 cm. (Lewis Henry Morgan lectures. 1973) Includes index. 1. Morgan, Lewis Henry, 1818-1881. 2. Political anthropology 3. Social structure I. T. II. Series.
GN490.C62     301.15     *LC* 74-82603     *ISBN* 0202011313

**Durkheim, Emile, 1858-1917.**     • **4.601**
[De quelques formes primitives de classification. English] Primitive classification, by Émile Durkheim and Marcel Mauss. Translated from the French and edited with an introd. by Rodney Needham. [Chicago] University of Chicago Press [1963] xlviii, 96 p. 23 cm. Translation of De quelques formes primitives de classification published in 1903 in Année sociologique, 1901-2. 1. Society, Primitive 2. Folk classification I. Mauss, Marcel, 1872-1950. joint author. II. T.
GN490.D813 1963     572.012     *LC* 63-9737

**Fortes, Meyer. ed.**     • **4.602**
African political systems, edited by M. Fortes and E. E. Evans–Pritchard. London, Pub. for the International Institute of African Languages & Cultures by the Oxford University Press, H. Milford, 1940. xxiii, 301 p., 1 l. incl. maps, geneal. tab., diagrs. 22 cm. 1. Society, Primitive 2. Tribes — Africa. 3. Africa — Native races. I. Evans-Pritchard, E. E. (Edward Evan), 1902-1973. joint ed. II. International Institute of African languages and cultures. III. T.
GN490.F6     572.96     *LC* 41-6881

**Hammel, Eugene A.**     • **4.603**
Alternative social structures and ritual relations in the Balkans [by] Eugene A. Hammel. — Englewood Cliffs, N.J.: Prentice-Hall, [1968] xv, 110 p.: illus., maps.; 23 cm. — (Anthropology of modern societies series) 1. Ethnology — Balkan Peninsula I. T.
GN490.H3     392/.09496     *LC* 68-28875

**Middleton, John, 1921- ed.**     • **4.604**
Tribes without rulers; studies in African segmentary systems [by] Laura Bohannan [and others] Edited by John Middleton and David Tait. Pref. by E.E. Evans–Pritchard. London, Routledge & Paul [1958] xi, 234 p. ill. 1. Political anthropology 2. Africa — Native races I. Tait, David. jt. ed. II. Bohannan, Laura. III. T.
GN490 M5     *LC* 59-418

**Park, George K., 1925-.**     **4.605**
The idea of social structure [by] George Park. — [1st ed.]. — Garden City, N.Y.: Anchor Books, 1974. viii, 392 p.; 18 cm. 1. Social structure 2. Ethnology I. T.
GN490.P37     301.4     *LC* 73-9043     *ISBN* 038501158X

**Radcliffe-Brown, A. R. (Alfred Reginald), 1881-1955.**     • **4.606**
Structure and function in primitive society, essays and addresses; with a foreword by E. E. Evans–Pritchard and Fred Eggan. Glencoe, Ill., The Free Press, 1952. vii, 219 p. 22 cm. 1. Society, Primitive — Addresses, essays, lectures. I. T.
GN490.R3 1952     *LC* A 54-3649

**Service, Elman Rogers, 1915-.**     **4.607**
Origins of the state and civilization: the process of cultural evolution / Elman R. Service. — 1st ed. — New York: Norton, [1975] xix, 361 p.: map; 21 cm. Includes index. 1. Political anthropology 2. Social evolution 3. Civilization — History I. T.
GN490.S44 1975     321.1/2     *LC* 75-1494     *ISBN* 0393055477. *ISBN* 0393092240 pbk

**Wilson, Monica Hunter.**     • **4.608**
Good company: a study of Nyakyusa age–villages. — London; New York: Published for the International African Institute by the Oxford University Press, 1951. xii, 278 p.: ill., ports., fold. maps; 23 cm. 1. Nyakyusa (African tribe) 2. Society, Primitive I. T.
GN490.W3     572.9678     *LC* 51-14867

# GN492–498 POLITICAL ORGANIZATION. ETHNICITY

**Lewellen, Ted C., 1940-.**     **4.609**
Political anthropology: an introduction / Ted C. Lewellen. — South Hadley, Mass.: Bergin & Garvey, 1983. xii, 148 p.: ill.; 24 cm. Includes index. 1. Political anthropology I. T.
GN492.L48 1983     306/.2 19     *LC* 82-22778     *ISBN* 0897890280

**Origins of the state: the anthropology of political evolution / edited by Ronald Cohen and Elman R. Service.**     **4.610**
Philadelphia: Institute for the Study of Human Issues, c1978. 233 p.; 25 cm. 1. Political anthropology — Addresses, essays, lectures. 2. State, The — Addresses, essays, lectures. I. Cohen, Ronald. II. Service, Elman Rogers, 1915-
GN492.6.O7     320.1/1     *LC* 77-19091     *ISBN* 0915980681. *ISBN* 0915980843 pbk

**Malinowski, Bronislaw, 1884-1942.**     • **4.611**
Crime and custom in savage society / by Bronislaw Malinowski. — New York: Harcourt, Brace & company, inc., 1932. xii, 132 p.: VI pl. (incl. front.); 22 cm. 1. Law, Primitive 2. Society, Primitive 3. Ethnology — Melanesia I. T.
GN493.M3     *LC* 31-12921

**Gluckman, Max, 1911-1975.**     • **4.612**
The ideas in Barotse jurisprudence. New Haven, Yale University Press, 1965. xix, 301 p. ill., map. (Storrs lectures on jurisprudence, Yale Law School, 1963) 1. Lozi (African tribe) 2. Law, Lozi I. T.
GN493.4 B3 G5     *LC* 65-11179

**Douglas, Mary.**     • **4.613**
Purity and danger: an analysis of concepts of pollution and taboo / by Mary Douglas. New York: Praeger, 1966. viii, 188 p. 23 cm. 1. Taboo 2. Purity, Ritual I. T.
GN494.D6 1966a     390     *LC* 66-23887

**Kuper, Hilda.**     • **4.614**
An African aristocracy; rank among the Swazi of Bechuanaland. London, New York, Pub. for the International African Institute by the Oxford Univ. Press, 1947. 251 p. 16 plates, fold. map. 23 cm. Subtitle covered by label: Rank among the Swazi. 1. Kings and rulers, Primitive 2. Swazi (African tribe) I. T.
GN495.5.K8     *LC* 48-743

**Epstein, A. L. (Arnold Leonard)**     **4.615**
Ethos and identity: three studies in ethnicity / A. L. Epstein. — London: Tavistock Publications; Chicago: Aldine Pub. Co., 1978. xvi, 181 p.; 23 cm. Includes indexes. 1. Ethnicity — Addresses, essays, lectures. I. T.
GN495.6.E67     301.45/1     *LC* 78-314380     *ISBN* 0202011658

**Ethnic change / edited by Charles F. Keyes.**    **4.616**
Seattle: University of Washington Press, c1981. xii, 331 p.: ill.; 24 cm. (Publications on ethnicity and nationality of the School of International Studies, University of Washington,; v. 2) 1. Ethnicity — Addresses, essays, lectures. 2. Ethnology — Addresses, essays, lectures. 3. Cross-cultural studies — Addresses, essays, lectures. I. Keyes, Charles F.
GN495.6.E86    305.8 19    *LC* 80-54426    *ISBN* 029595812X

**Patterson, Orlando, 1940-.**    **4.617**
Ethnic chauvinism: the reactionary impulse / Orlando Patterson. — New York: Stein and Day, 1977. 347 p.; 24 cm. 1. Chauvinism and jingoism 2. Social groups 3. Conformity 4. Universals (Philosophy) 5. Fascism and culture I. T.
GN495.6.P37    301.45/1    *LC* 76-54912    *ISBN* 081282180X

**Royce, Anya Peterson.**    **4.618**
Ethnic identity: strategies of diversity / Anya Peterson Royce. — Bloomington: Indiana University Press, c1982. viii, 247 p.; 24 cm. Includes index. 1. Ethnicity I. T.
GN495.6.R68    305.8 19    *LC* 81-47168    *ISBN* 0253310350

**Cultures in contact: studies in cross–cultural interaction / edited**    **4.619**
**by Stephen Bochner.**
1st ed. — Oxford [Oxfordshire]; New York: Pergamon Press, 1982. xiv, 232 p.: ill.; 24 cm. — (International series in experimental social psychology. v. 1) 1. Intercultural communication — Addresses, essays, lectures. 2. Ethnic relations — Addresses, essays, lectures. I. Bochner, Stephen. II. Series.
GN496.C84 1982    306 19    *LC* 82-3852    *ISBN* 0080258050

**Francis, Emerich K., 1906-.**    **4.620**
Interethnic relations: an essay in sociological theory / by E. K. Francis. — New York: Elsevier, [1976] xx, 432 p.; 26 cm. 1. Ethnic relations 2. Race relations 3. Ethnicity I. T.
GN496.F7    301.45/1    *LC* 75-8271    *ISBN* 0444990119

# GN502–517 Psychological Anthropology

**Bock, Philip K.**    **4.621**
Continuities in psychological anthropology: a historical introduction / Philip K. Bock. — San Francisco: W. H. Freeman, c1980. xii, 288 p.: ill.; 21 cm. Includes index. 1. Ethnopsychology I. T.
GN502.B62    155.8    *LC* 79-23200    *ISBN* 0716711362

**Handbook of cross–cultural psychology.**    **4.622**
Boston: Allyn and Bacon, c1980-c1981. 6 v.: ill.; 24 cm. 1. Ethnopsychology — Collected works. I. Triandis, Harry Charalambos, 1926-
GN502.H36    155.8    *LC* 79-15905    *ISBN* 0205064973

**Jahoda, Gustav.**    **4.623**
Psychology and anthropology: a psychological perspective / Gustav Jahoda. — London; New York: Academic Press, 1982. xi, 305 p.: ill.; 24 cm. Includes indexes. 1. Ethnopsychology 2. Psychology — Methodology 3. Anthropology — Methodology I. T.
GN502.J33 1982    301 19    *LC* 82-71239    *ISBN* 0123798205

**Perspectives on cross–cultural psychology / edited by Anthony**    **4.624**
**J. Marsella, Roland G. Tharp, Thomas J. Ciborowski.**
New York: Academic Press, 1979. xv, 413 p.; 24 cm. 1. Ethnopsychology 2. Personality and culture — Cross-cultural studies I. Marsella, Anthony J. II. Tharp, Roland G., 1930- III. Ciborowski, Thomas J.
GN502.P47    155.8    *LC* 79-6950    *ISBN* 0124735509

**Urban ethnicity / edited by Abner Cohen.**    **4.625**
London; New York: Tavistock Publications [Distributed in the USA by Harper & Row Publishers, Barnes & Noble Import Division, 1974] xxiv, 391 p.: ill.; 23 cm. — (A.S.A. monographs. 12) 'Derives from material presented at a conference on urban ethnicity, sponsored by the Association of Social Anthropologists of the Commonwealth, held in London, 31 March to 3 April 1971.' 1. Urban anthropology — Congresses. 2. Ethnicity — Congresses. I. Cohen, Abner. ed. II. Association of Social Anthropologists of the Commonwealth. III. Series.
GN505.U72    301.45/1/091732    *LC* 74-165226    *ISBN* 0422740802

# GN537–673 Ethnic Groups, by Region

(see also: area listings D-F, v. 3)

## GN575–585 Europe

**Arensberg, Conrad Maynadier.**    ● **4.626**
Family and community in Ireland / [by] Conrad M. Arensberg [and] Solon T. Kimball. 2d ed. Cambridge: Harvard University Press, 1968. xxxiii, 417 p.: ill.; maps, plans; 25 cm. 1. Family — Ireland. 2. Community life 3. Social psychology 4. Ireland — Social life and customs — 20th century 5. Ireland — Social conditions. I. Kimball, Solon Toothaker. joint author. II. T.
GN585.I7 A69 1968    301.3/5/09415    *LC* 68-14251

**Arensberg, Conrad Maynadier.**    ● **4.627**
The Irish countryman: an anthropological study / [by] Conrad M. Arensberg. — Garden City, N.Y.: published for the American Museum of Natural History [by] Natural History Press, 1968. 197 p.; 18 cm. (American Museum science books, B18) Originally published in 1937. 1. Ireland — Social life and customs — 20th century I. T.
GN585.I7 A7 1968    914.15    *LC* 68-13630

**Family and kinship in the Soviet Union: field studies / edited by**    **4.628**
**Tamara Dragadze.**
London; Boston: Routledge & Kegan Paul, 1984. 269 p.: ill. 1. Kinship — Soviet Union — Addresses, essays, lectures. 2. Family — Soviet Union — Addresses, essays, lectures. 3. Ethnology — Soviet Union — Addresses, essays, lectures. 4. Soviet Union — Social life and customs — 1917- — Addresses, essays, lectures. I. Dragadze, Tamara.
GN585.S65 F36 1984    306.8/3/0947 19    *LC* 83-24607    *ISBN* 071000995X

**Weinberg, Daniela.**    **4.629**
Peasant wisdom: cultural adaptation in a Swiss village / Daniela Weinberg. — Berkeley: University of California Press, c1975. xii, 214 p.: map; 24 cm. Includes index. 1. Ethnology — Switzerland — Bruson. 2. Bruson, Switzerland — Social life and customs. I. T.
GN585.S9 W47    301.35/2/094947    *LC* 74-79776    *ISBN* 0520027892

## GN625–635 Asia

**Wallace, Ben J., 1937-.**    ● **4.630**
Village life in insular Southeast Asia [by] Ben J. Wallace. — Boston: Little, Brown, [1971] xi, 146 p.: illus., map.; 21 cm. — (The Little, Brown series in anthropology) 1. Ethnology — Asia, Southeastern 2. Villages — Asia, Southeastern. I. T.
GN635.A75 W3    301.3/5/0959    *LC* 71-155319

**Inden, Ronald B.**    **4.631**
Kinship in Bengali culture / Ronald B. Inden and Ralph W. Nicholas. — Chicago: University of Chicago Press, 1977. xvii, 139 p.: diagr.; 23 cm. Includes index. 1. Kinship — Bengal. 2. Bengal (India) — Social life and customs. I. Nicholas, Ralph W., joint author. II. T.
GN635.B46 I53    301.42/1/095492    *LC* 76-25639    *ISBN* 0226378357

**Du Bois, Cora Alice, 1903-.**    ● **4.632**
The people of Alor: a social–psychological study of an East Indian island / with analyses by Abram Kardiner and Emil Oberholzer. — Cambridge: Harvard University Press, 1960. 2 v. (xxxvi, 654 p.) in 1: ill., maps, diagrs.; 22 cm. 1. Ethnology — Alor (Island) 2. Society, Primitive 3. Ethnopsychology I. T.
GN635.D9 D8 1960    136.49923    *LC* 60-16359

**Dumont, Louis, 1911-.**    **4.633**
Affinity as a value: marriage alliance in South India, with comparative essays on Australia / Louis Dumont. — Chicago: University of Chicago Press, 1983. x, 230 p.: ill.; 22 cm. Includes index. 1. Kinship — India, South — Addresses, essays, lectures. 2. Australian aborigines — Kinship — Addresses, essays, lectures. 3. Marriage — India, South — Addresses, essays, lectures. I. T.
GN635.I4 D85 1983    306.8/3/0954 19    *LC* 82-13468    *ISBN* 0226169642

**Fürer-Haimendorf, Christoph von, 1909-.**      **4.634**
Tribes of India: the struggle for survival / Christoph von Fürer–Haimendorf; with contributions by Michael Yorke and Jayaprakash Rao. — Berkeley: University of California Press, c1982. xiii, 342 p.: ill.; 24 cm. Includes index. 1. Ethnology — India 2. India — Social conditions — 1947- I. T.
GN635.I4 F83 1982     954 19     LC 80-28647     *ISBN* 0520043154

**Gittinger, Mattiebelle.**      **4.635**
Splendid symbols: textiles and tradition in Indonesia / Mattiebelle Gittinger; [edited by Nancy Donovan Segal]. — [S.l.]: Oxford University Press, 1983. 240 p.: ill., maps (on lining paper); 28 cm. 1. Textile fabrics — Indonesia. 2. Costume — Indonesia. 3. Indonesia — Social life and customs. I. Textile Museum (Washington, D.C.) II. T.
GN635.I65 G57     746/.09598     LC 79-50373

**Watson, Patty Jo, 1932-.**      **4.636**
Archaeological ethnography in western Iran / Patty Jo Watson. — Tucson: University of Arizona Press, c1979. xv, 327 p.: ill.; 28 cm. (Viking Fund publications in anthropology. no. 57) 'Published for the Wenner-Gren Foundation for Anthropological Research, inc.' Includes index. 1. Ethnology — Iran 2. Man, Prehistoric — Iran. 3. Archaeology — Methodology 4. Iran — Antiquities I. Wenner-Gren Foundation for Anthropological Research. II. T. III. Series.
GN635.I7 W37     955     LC 78-5853     *ISBN* 0816505772

**Embree, John Fee, 1908-.**      • **4.637**
Suye mura, a Japanese village by John Fee Embree. Chicago, Ill.: The University of Chicago press, c1939, 1964. xxvii, 354 p.: ill.; 20 1/2 cm. (The University of Chicago publications in anthropology.Ethnological series.) Published also without thesis note. 'The present study is part of a larger research on types of society in eastern Asia beingmade by the Social science division of the University of Chicago under the direction of Professor A. R. Radcliffe- Brown.'—Pref. 1. Suye mura, Japan. 2. Japan — Social life and customs 3. Japan — Civilization I. T. II. Series.
GN635.J2 E5 1937     LC 40-7437

**Carey, Iskandar, 1924-.**      **4.638**
Orang Asli: the aboriginal tribes of peninsular Malaysia / Iskandar Carey. Kuala Lumpur; New York: Oxford University Press, 1976. x, 376 p., [7] leaves of plates: ill.; 23 cm. Includes index. 1. Ethnology — Malaysia I. T.
GN635.M4 C37     959.5/1     LC 76-378135     *ISBN* 0195802705

**Eickelman, Dale F., 1942-.**      **4.639**
The Middle East: an anthropological approach / Dale F. Eickelman. — Englewood Cliffs, N.J.: Prentice-Hall, c1981. xiv, 336 p.: ill.; 23 cm. — (Prentice-Hall series in anthropology) 1. Ethnology — Middle East 2. Ethnology — Africa, North. 3. Middle East — Social life and customs. 4. Africa, North — Social life and customs. I. T.
GN635.N42 E38     956 19     LC 80-19547     *ISBN* 0135816297

**Economic exchange and social interaction in Southeast Asia:**      **4.640**
**perspectives from prehistory, history, and ethnography / edited by Karl L. Hutterer.**
Ann Arbor: Center for South and Southeast Asian Studies, University of Michigan, 1977, c1978. vi, 318 p., [1] leaf of plates: ill.; 23 cm. (Michigan papers on South and Southeast Asia. 13) 1. Economic anthropology — Asia, Southeastern — Congresses. 2. Economics, Prehistoric — Asia, Southeastern — Congresses. 3. Asia, Southeastern — Economic conditions — Congresses. I. Hutterer, Karl L. II. Series.
GN635.S58 E27     380.1/0959     LC 77-95147     *ISBN* 0891480137

**LeBar, Frank M.**      **4.641**
Ethnic groups of insular Southeast Asia. Frank M. LeBar, editor and compiler. Contributing authors: George N. Appell [and others] New Haven, Human Relations Area Files Press [c1972-75] 2 v. maps. 29 cm. 1. Ethnology — Asia, Southeastern I. Appell, George N. II. T.
GN635.S58 L42     301.45/0959     LC 72-90940     *ISBN* 0875364039

**The Anthropology of Taiwanese society / edited by Emily**      **4.642**
**Martin Ahern and Hill Gates; contributors, Emily Martin Ahern ... [et al.]; sponsored by the Joint Committee on Contemporary China of the American Council of Learned Societies and the Social Science Research Council.**
Stanford, Calif.: Stanford University Press, 1981. xi, 491 p., [1] leaf of plates: map; 24 cm. 1. Ethnology — Taiwan 2. Taiwan — Social life and customs — 1945- I. Ahern, Emily M. II. Gates, Hill. III. Joint Committee on Contemporary China.
GN635.T28 A57     951/.249 19     LC 79-64212     *ISBN* 0804710430

**Cohen, Myron L., 1937-.**      **4.643**
House united, house divided: the Chinese family in Taiwan / Myron L. Cohen. — New York: Columbia University Press, 1976. xvi, 267 p.: ill.; 24 cm. (Studies of the East Asian Institute, Columbia University) Includes index. 1. Ethnology — Taiwan 2. Family — Taiwan. 3. Taiwan — Social life and customs — 1945- I. T.
GN635.T28 C63     301.42/1     LC 75-28473     *ISBN* 0231038496

**Highlanders of Thailand / edited by John McKinnon, Wanat**      **4.644**
**Bhruksasri.**
Kuala Lumpur; New York: Oxford University Press, 1983. xx, 358 p., 35 p. of plates: ill., col. map; 26 cm. Folded map in pocket. 1. Ethnology — Thailand 2. Thailand — Social life and customs. 3. Thailand — Social conditions. I. McKinnon, John. II. Wanat Bhruksasri.
GN635.T4 H53 1983     306/.09593 19     LC 83-232171     *ISBN* 0195804724

**Potter, Jack M.**      **4.645**
Thai peasant social structure / Jack M. Potter. — Chicago: University of Chicago Press, c1976. xi, 249 p., [4] leaves of plates: ill.; 24 cm. Includes index. 1. Ethnology — Thailand — Chiang Mai (Province) 2. Villages — Thailand — Chiang Mai (Province) 3. Chiang Mai (Thailand: Province) — Social life and customs. I. T.
GN635.T4 P67     301.35/2/09593     LC 75-43237     *ISBN* 0226676358

# GN643-661 AFRICA

**The African diaspora: interpretive essays / edited by Martin L.**      **4.646**
**Kilson, Robert I. Rotberg.**
Cambridge, Mass.: Harvard University Press, 1976. xiii, 510 p.; 25 cm. 1. Blacks — Addresses, essays, lectures. 2. Slave-trade — Addresses, essays, lectures. I. Kilson, Martin. II. Rotberg, Robert I.
GN645.A36     909/.04/96     LC 75-30643     *ISBN* 0674007794

**Erny, Pierre.**      **4.647**
[Enfant et son milieu en Afrique noire. English] The child and his environment in Black Africa: an essay on traditional education / Pierre Erny; translated, abridged, and adapted by G.J. Wanjohi. — Nairobi; New York: Oxford University Press, 1981. xxii, 230 p.; 23 cm. Rev. translation of: L'enfant et son milieu en Afrique noire. Includes indexes. 1. Education, Primitive — Africa, Sub-Saharan. 2. Socialization 3. Education — Africa, Sub-Saharan. I. Wanjohi, G. J. II. T.
GN645.E7613 1981     303.3/2/0967 19     LC 83-122735     *ISBN* 0195725093

**Explorations in African systems of thought / edited by Ivan**      **4.648**
**Karp & Charles S. Bird.**
Bloomington: Indiana University Press, c1980. vi, 337 p.; 24 cm. — (African systems of thought.) Papers given at a seminar organized for the African Studies Program at Indiana University in 1977. 1. Ethnophilosophy — Africa. 2. Cognition and culture — Africa. 3. Religion, Primitive — Africa. I. Karp, Ivan. II. Bird, Charles S. (Charles Stephen), 1935- III. Indiana University, Bloomington. African Studies Program. IV. Series.
GN645.E92     960     LC 80-7492     *ISBN* 0253195233

**Gluckman, Max, 1911-1975.**      • **4.649**
Custom and conflict in Africa / by Max Gluckman. Glencoe, Ill.: Free Press, 1955 [i.e. 1956]. ix, 173 p.; 19 cm. These are six lectures given on the Third Programme of the British Broadcasting Corporation, 1955. 1. Social conflict 2. Social problems 3. Africa — Social life and customs. I. T.
GN645.G55

**Gluckman, Max, 1911-1975.**      • **4.650**
Order and rebellion in tribal Africa: collected essays: with an autobiographical introd. / Max Gluckman. — New York: Free Press of Glencoe [1963] 273 p.; 22 cm. 1. Malinowski, Bronislaw, 1884-1942. 2. Society, Primitive 3. Tribes 4. Ethnology — Africa, Sub-Saharan. I. T.
GN645.G56 1963     572     LC 63-4522

**Herbert, Eugenia W.**      **4.651**
Red gold of Africa: copper in precolonial history and culture / Eugenia W. Herbert. — Madison, Wis.: University of Wisconsin Press, 1984. xxiii, 413 p., [4] p. of plates: ill. (some col.); 24 cm. Includes index. 1. Industries, Primitive — Africa, Sub-Saharan. 2. Copper industry and trade — Africa, Sub-Saharan. 3. Copper mines and mining — Africa, Sub-Saharan. 4. Copper — Folklore. 5. Africa, Sub-Saharan — Industries. I. T.
GN645.H44 1984     669/.3/0967 19     LC 83-40264     *ISBN* 0299096009

**Hiernaux, Jean.**      **4.652**
The people of Africa / Jean Hiernaux. — New York: Scribner, [1975] xii, 217 p., [11] leaves of plates: ill., maps; 21 cm. (Peoples of the world series) Includes index. 1. Ethnology — Africa 2. Anthropometry — Africa. 3. Man, Prehistoric — Africa. 4. Africa — Antiquities. I. T.
GN645.H53 1975     572.9/6     LC 74-26003     *ISBN* 0684140403

**July, Robert William.**      **4.653**
Precolonial Africa: an economic and social history / Robert W. July. — New York: Scribner, [1975] xii, 304 p.: ill.; 24 cm. 1. Ethnology — Africa 2. Economic anthropology — Africa. 3. Africa — Economic conditions — To 1918 I. T.
GN645.J84     330.9/39/7     LC 75-6920     *ISBN* 0684143186

**Mair, Lucy Philip, 1901-.**     **4.654**
African kingdoms / Lucy Mair. — Oxford [Eng.]: Clarendon Press, 1977. 151 p.: map; 22 cm. Includes index. 1. Ethnology — Africa, Sub-Saharan. 2. Africa, Sub-Saharan — Kings and rulers. 3. Africa, Sub-Saharan — Politics and government I. T.
GN645.M26    301.5/92    *LC* 77-4861    *ISBN* 019821698X

**Mair, Lucy Philip, 1901-.**     **4.655**
African societies [by] Lucy Mair. — [London; New York]: Cambridge University Press, [1974] v, 251 p.: maps.; 22 cm. 1. Ethnology — Africa, Sub-Saharan. I. T.
GN645.M27    301.29/6    *LC* 73-93398    *ISBN* 0521204429

**Ottenberg, Simon. ed.**     • **4.656**
Cultures and societies of Africa / Edited, with a general introd., commentaries, and notes, by Simon and Phoebe Ottenberg. — New York: Random House, [1960] 614 p.: plates, col. map (on lining papers); 24 cm. 1. Ethnology — Africa I. Ottenberg, Phoebe, joint ed. II. T.
GN645.O75    572.96    *LC* 60-6194

**Schneider, Harold K.**     **4.657**
The Africans: an ethnological account / Harold K. Schneider. — Englewood Cliffs, N.J.: Prentice-Hall, c1981. x, 278 p.: ill.; 23 cm. — (Prentice-Hall series in anthropology) Includes index. 1. Ethnology — Africa, Sub-Saharan. 2. Africa, Sub-Saharan — Social life and customs. I. T.
GN645.S28    967    *LC* 80-11485    *ISBN* 0130186481

**Evans-Pritchard, E. E. (Edward Evan), 1902-1973.**     • **4.658**
Essays in social anthropology. — New York: Free Press of Glencoe, 1963 (c1962) 233 p.; 23 cm. Includes bibliography. 1. Shilluks 2. Azande. 3. Ethnology — Addresses, essays, lectures. I. T. II. Title: Social anthropology.
GN651.E9    572.9624    *LC* 63-669

**Kuper, Adam.**     **4.659**
Wives for cattle: bridewealth and marriage in Southern Africa / Adam Kuper. — London; Boston: Routledge & Kegan Paul, 1982. xiii, 202, 14 p.: ill.; 22 cm. — (International library of anthropology.) Includes index. 1. Bride price — Africa, Southern. 2. Marriage customs and rites — Africa, Southern. 3. Africa, Southern — Social life and customs. I. T. II. Series.
GN656.K86 1982    392/.5/0968 19    *LC* 81-17872    *ISBN* 0710009895

**Mair, Lucy Philip, 1901-.**     **4.660**
Primitive government: a study of traditional political systems in eastern Africa / Lucy Mair. — Rev. ed. — Bloomington: Indiana University Press, 1978 (c1977). 244 p.: maps; 20 cm. Includes index. 1. Political anthropology — Africa, East. 2. Africa, East — Politics and government. I. T.
GN658.M34 1977    321.1/2    *LC* 77-6963    *ISBN* 0253346037

**Robertson, A. F.**     **4.661**
Community of strangers: a journal of discovery in Uganda / A. F. Robertson. — London: Scolar Press, 1978. xv, 252 p.: ill.; 22 cm. 1. Robertson, A. F. 2. Ethnology — Uganda — Ntenjeru County. 3. Ethnologists — Great Britain — Biography. 4. Ntenjeru County, Uganda — Ethnic relations. I. T.
GN659.U3 R6    301.29/676/1    *LC* 79-313760    *ISBN* 0859674096

# GN662–671 AUSTRALIA. PACIFIC ISLANDS

**Furnas, J. C. (Joseph Chamberlain), 1905-.**     **4.662**
Anatomy of paradise: Hawaii and the islands of the South seas / issued in cooperation with the American Institute of Pacific Relations. — New York: W. Sloane Associates [1948] 542 p.: ill., ports., maps (on lining-papers) 1. Oceania — Native races I. T.
GN662 F8    *LC* 48-8518

**Howells, William White, 1908-.**     **4.663**
The Pacific islanders [by] William Howells. — New York: Scribner, [1974, c1973] xvi, 299 p.: illus.; 21 cm. — (Peoples of the world series) 1. Oceanians 2. Australian aborigines I. T.
GN662.H68 1974    301.29/9    *LC* 73-19277    *ISBN* 0684137852

**Kaeppler, Adrienne Lois.**     **4.664**
'Artificial curiosities': being an exposition of native manufactures collected on the three Pacific voyages of Captain James Cook, R. N., at the Bernice Pauahi Bishop Museum, January 18, 1978–August 31, 1978, on the occasion of the bicentennial of the European discovery of the Hawaiian Islands by Captain Cook, January 18, 1778 / by Adrienne L. Kaeppler. — Honolulu: Bishop Museum Press, c1978. xvi, 293 p.: ill. (some col.); 31 cm. (Bernice P. Bishop Museum special publication; 65 0067-6179) 1. Cook, James, 1728-1779 — Exhibitions. 2. Ethnology — Pacific Area — Exhibitions. 3. Material culture

— Pacific Area — Exhibitions. 4. Pacific Area — Industries — Exhibitions. 5. Pacific Area — Discovery and exploration — Exhibitions. I. T.
GN663.K33    996    *LC* 77-91442    *ISBN* 0910240248

**Broome, Richard, 1948-.**     **4.665**
Aboriginal Australians: black response to white dominance, 1788–1980 / Richard Broome. — Sydney; Boston: Allen & Unwin, 1982. 227 p.: ill.; 22 cm. — (Australian experience. no. 4) Includes index. 1. Australian aborigines — History. 2. Australia — Native races I. T. II. Series.
GN665.B76 1982    994/.0049915 19    *LC* 81-40687    *ISBN* 0868610437

**Róheim, Géza, 1891-1953.**     **4.666**
The children of the desert; the Western tribes of central Australia. Edited and with an introd. by Werner [i.e. Warner] Muensterberger. — New York: Basic Books, [1974-. v.    : illus.; 22 cm. 1. Australian aborigines — Social life and customs. 2. Australian aborigines — Psychology. I. Muensterberger, Warner, 1913- ed. II. T.
GN665.R59    301.29/942    *LC* 73-91079    *ISBN* 0465010423

**Tindale, Norman Barnett, 1900-.**     **4.667**
Aboriginal tribes of Australia: their terrain, environmental controls, distribution, limits, and proper names / by Norman B. Tindale; with an appendix on Tasmanian tribes by Rhys Jones. — Berkeley: University of California Press, 1974. xii, 404 p., [27] leaves of plates: ill. (some col.), maps (4 fold. col. in case); 29 cm. Includes indexes. 1. Australian aborigines I. T.
GN665.T56    994/.004/991    *LC* 72-89583    *ISBN* 0520020057

**Biskup, Peter.**     **4.668**
Not slaves, not citizens; the aboriginal problem in Western Australia, 1898–1954. — St. Lucia: University of Queensland Press; New York: Crane, Russak, [1973] 342 p.: illus.; 23 cm. 1. Australian aborigines — Australia — Western Australia 2. Western Australia — Native races. I. T.
GN666.B57    301.45/19/910941    *LC* 72-90072    *ISBN* 0884801224

*[handwritten: GN 666 B57]*

**Elkin, A. P. (Adolphus Peter), 1891-1979.**     **4.669**
Aboriginal men of high degree / A. P. Elkin. — 2d ed. — New York: St. Martin's Press, 1978, c1977. xxii, 185 p., [1] leaf of plates: maps; 23 cm. 1. Australian aborigines — Medicine 2. Shamans — Australia. 3. Australian aborigines — Religion. I. T.
GN666.E43 1978    615/.899/0994    *LC* 77-87170    *ISBN* 0312001673

**Montagu, Ashley, 1905-.**     **4.670**
Coming into being among the Australian Aborigines: a study of the procreative beliefs of the native tribes of Australia / Ashley Montagu; with a foreword by Bronislaw Malinowski. — Fully rev. and expanded 2nd ed. — London; Boston: Routledge and Kegan Paul, 1974. x1, 426 p.: ill., 2 maps; 23 cm. Includes index. 1. Australian aborigines — Social life and customs. 2. Australian aborigines — Religion. 3. Childbirth — Religious aspects I. T.
GN666.M58 1974    299/.9    *LC* 74-80751    *ISBN* 0710079338

**Ritualized homosexuality in Melanesia / edited by Gilbert H. Herdt.**     **4.671**
Berkeley: University of California Press, c1984. xvii, 409 p.: maps; 24 cm. Includes index. 1. Melanesians — Rites and ceremonies — Addresses, essays, lectures. 2. Melanesians — Social life and customs — Addresses, essays, lectures. 3. Homosexuality, Male — Melanesia — Addresses, essays, lectures. 4. Sex customs — Melanesia — Addresses, essays, lectures. I. Herdt, Gilbert H., 1949-
GN668.R54 1984    306.7/662/0993 19    *LC* 83-18015    *ISBN* 0520050371

**Bellwood, Peter S.**     **4.672**
The Polynesians: prehistory of an island people / [by] Peter Bellwood. — London: Thames and Hudson, 1978. 180 p.: ill., maps, plans, port.; 25 cm. — (Ancient peoples and places) Includes index. 1. Ethnology — Polynesia 2. Polynesians I. T.
GN670.B36    996    *LC* 78-55086    *ISBN* 0500020930

**Kirch, Patrick Vinton.**     **4.673**
The evolution of the Polynesian chiefdoms / Patrick Vinton Kirch. — Cambridge [Cambridgeshire]; New York: Cambridge University Press, 1984. xii, 314 p.: ill.; 24 cm. (New studies in archaeology.) Includes index. 1. Political anthropology — Polynesia. 2. Polynesia — Politics and government. 3. Polynesia — Antiquities. I. T. II. Series.
GN670.K56 1984    306/.2/0996 19    *LC* 84-3249    *ISBN* 0521253322

**The Prehistory of Polynesia / Jesse D. Jennings, editor.**     **4.674**
Cambridge, Mass.: Harvard University Press, 1979. 399 p.: ill.; 27 cm. 1. Man, Prehistoric — Polynesia. 2. Polynesians — Origin. I. Jennings, Jesse David, 1909-
GN670.P7    996    *LC* 79-1055    *ISBN* 0674700600

**Williamson, Robert Wood, 1856-1932.** • **4.675**
The social and political systems of central Polynesia / by Robert W. Williamson. — Oosterhout: Anthropological Publications, 1967. 3 v.: maps (part fold.); 24 cm. Reprint of 1924 edition. Distributed in the U.S.A. by Humanities Press, New York. 1. Polynesians I. T.
GN670.W54 1967      309.1/96      *LC* 68-97999

**Smith, DeVerne Reed, 1936-.** **4.676**
Palauan social structure / DeVerne Reed Smith. — New Brunswick, N.J.: Rutgers University Press, c1983. xx, 348 p.: ill.; 24 cm. Includes index. 1. Kinship — Palau. 2. Palau — Social life and customs. I. T.
GN671.C3 S64 1983      306.8/3/09966 19      *LC* 81-19987      *ISBN* 081350953X

**Berndt, Ronald Murray, 1916-.** • **4.677**
Excess and restraint; social control among a New Guinea mountain people. Chicago, University of Chicago Press [1962] xxii, 474 p. ill., maps. 1. Ethnology — New Guinea 2. Social control I. T.
GN671 N5 B47      *LC* 62-10996

**Brown, Paula, 1925-.** **4.678**
Highland peoples of New Guinea / Paula Brown. — Cambridge; New York: Cambridge University Press, 1978. xiv, 258 p.: ill.; 22 cm. Includes index. 1. Ethnology — Papua New Guinea 2. Chimbu (New Guinea people) I. T.
GN671.N5 B73      301.29/95      *LC* 77-80830      *ISBN* 0521217482

**Herdt, Gilbert H., 1949-.** **4.679**
Guardians of the flutes: idioms of masculinity / Gilbert H. Herdt. — New York: McGraw-Hill, c1980. xviii, 382 p.: map (on lining papers); 24 cm. 'The editors of this book were Lawrence B. Apple and Suzette H. Annin.' Includes indexes. 1. Sex customs — Papua New Guinea. 2. Initiation rites — Papua New Guinea. 3. Homosexuality, Male — Papua New Guinea. 4. Masculinity (Psychology) — Papua New Guinea. 5. Sex symbolism — Case studies. I. Apple, Lawrence B. II. Annin, Suzette H. III. T.
GN671.N5 H44      301.2/1      *LC* 79-23417      *ISBN* 007028315X

**Malinowski, Bronislaw, 1884-1942.** • **4.680**
Argonauts of the Western Pacific: an account of native enterprise and adventure in the archipelagoes of Melanesian New Guinea / by Bronislaw Malinowski; with a preface by Sir James G. Fraser. — London: G. Routledge, 1922. xxxi, [1] 527 p., lxv pl. on 31 l.: ill., front., (maps), diagrs. — (Studies in economics and political science; no.65) 1. Trobriand Islands. 2. Anthropology — New Guinea. 3. Folklore — New Guinea. 4. Ethnology — New Guinea 5. Magic 6. Barter I. T.
GN671.N5 M3      *ISBN* 0710017855

**Mead, Margaret, 1901-1978.** • **4.681**
Growing up in New Guinea: a comparative study of primitive education / with a new pref. by the author. — [New York]: New American Library [1953, c1930] 223 p.: maps; 18 cm. — (A Mentor book, M91) 1. Manus tribe. 2. Children — New Guinea I. T.
GN671.N5M4 1953      572.995      *LC* 53-2526

**Rituals of manhood: male initiation in Papua New Guinea /** **4.682**
**edited by Gilbert H. Herdt; with an introduction by Roger M. Keesing.**
Berkeley: University of California Press, c1982. xxvi, 365 p.: ill.; 24 cm. 1. Puberty rites — Papua New Guinea — Addresses, essays, lectures. 2. Papua New Guinea — Social life and customs — Addresses, essays, lectures. I. Herdt, Gilbert H., 1949-
GN671.N5 R55 1982      392/.14 19      *LC* 81-1807      *ISBN* 0520044487

**Weiner, Annette B., 1933-.** **4.683**
Women of value, men of renown: new perspectives in Trobriand exchange / Annette B. Weiner. — Austin, Tex.: University of Texas Press, c1976. xxi, 299 p.: ill.; 24 cm. Includes index. 1. Ethnology — Papua New Guinea — Trobriand Islands. 2. Women — Papua New Guinea — Trobriand Islands. I. T.
GN671.N5 W44      392/.09953      *LC* 76-14847      *ISBN* 029279004X

**Hart, Donn Vorhis, 1918-.** **4.684**
Compadrinazgo: ritual kinship in the Philippines / by Donn V. Hart. — De Kalb: Northern Illinois University Press, c1977. xvi, 256 p.: ill.; 24 cm. Includes index. 1. Sponsors — Philippine Islands. 2. Kinship — Philippine Islands. 3. Philippines — Social life and customs. I. T.
GN671.P5 H37      301.42/1/09599      *LC* 75-15015      *ISBN* 0875800629

**Freeman, Derek.** **4.685**
Margaret Mead and Samoa: the making and unmaking of an anthropological myth / Derek Freeman. — Cambridge, Mass.: Harvard University Press, 1983. xvii, 379 p., [6] p. of plates: ill.; 24 cm. 1. Mead, Margaret, 1901-1978. 2. Ethnology — Samoan Islands 3. Adolescence 4. Nature and nurture I. T.
GN671.S2 F73 1983      306/.0996 19      *LC* 82-15620      *ISBN* 0674548302

**Shore, Bradd, 1945-.** **4.686**
Sala'ilua, a Samoan mystery / Bradd Shore. — New York: Columbia University Press, 1982. xvii, 338 p.: ill.; 24 cm. Includes index. 1. Ethnology — Western Samoa — Sala'ilua. 2. Sala'ilua (Western Samoa) — Social life and customs. I. T.
GN671.S2 S54 1982      306/.0996/14 19      *LC* 81-24188      *ISBN* 0231053827

**Oliver, Douglas L.** **4.687**
Two Tahitian villages: a study in comparisons / Douglas Oliver. — Laie, Hawaii: Institute for Polynesian Studies, c1981. xiv, 557 p.: ill.; 24 cm. Maps on lining papers. 1. Ethnology — Society Islands. 2. Economic anthropology — Society Islands. 3. Society Islands — Economic conditions. 4. Society Islands — Social life and customs. I. T.
GN671.S55 O45 1981      306/.0996/21 19      *LC* 83-186110      *ISBN* 0939154226

**Haddon, Alfred C. (Alfred Cort), 1855-1940.** **4.688**
Reports of the Cambridge anthropological expedition to Torres Straits. Cambridge, University Press [1901–]1935. New York, Johnson Reprint Corp., 1971. 6 v. illus. 27 cm. 1. Ethnology — Australia — Torres Strait Islands (Qld.) 2. Papuans I. T.
GN671.T6 H2 1971      301.29/93/4      *LC* 70-171628

## GN673 ARCTIC REGIONS

**Graburn, Nelson H. H.** **4.689**
Circumpolar peoples: an anthropological perspective / [by] Nelson H. H. Graburn [and] B. Stephen Strong.— Pacific Palisades, Calif.: Goodyear Pub. Co., [c1973] 236 p.: ill.; 25 cm. — (Goodyear regional anthropology series) 1. Arctic races I. Strong, B. Stephen, joint author. II. T.
GN673.G72 1973      301.29/11      *LC* 72-91155      *ISBN* 0876201842

# GN700–875 Prehistoric Archaeology

**Research Seminar in Archaeology and Related Subjects.** **4.690**
**University of Sheffield, 1971.**
The explanation of culture change: models in prehistory; proceedings. Edited by Colin Renfrew. — [Pittsburgh]: University of Pittsburgh Press, [1973] xv, 788 p.: illus.; 26 cm. 1. Man, Prehistoric — Congresses. 2. Social change — Congresses. 3. Archaeology — Methodology — Congresses. I. Renfrew, Colin, 1937- ed. II. T.
GN700.R47 1971a      913/.031/028      *LC* 73-10034      *ISBN* 0822911116

**Daniel, Glyn Edmund.** • **4.691**
A hundred years of archaeology. London, Duckworth [1950] 343 p. ill., maps. ([The Hundred years series]) 1. Archaeology — History I. T.
GN720 D3      *LC* 50-3526

**Grayson, Donald K.** **4.692**
The establishment of human antiquity / Donald K. Grayson. — New York: Academic Press, 1983. xii, 262 p.: ill.; 24 cm. Includes index. 1. Anthropology, Prehistoric — History — 18th century. 2. Anthropology, Prehistoric — History — 19th century. 3. Archaeology — History — 18th century. 4. Archaeology — History — 19th century. 5. Man — Origin I. T.
GN720.G73 1983      930.1 19      *LC* 82-11571      *ISBN* 0122972503

**Childe, V. Gordon (Vere Gordon), 1892-1957.** • **4.693**
Social evolution. London, Watts [1951] viii, 184 p. (The Josiah Mason lectures, 1947-8) 1. Man, Prehistoric I. T. II. Series.
GN738 C45      *LC* 51-3788

**Hawkes, Jacquetta Hopkins, 1910- ed.** • **4.694**
The world of the past. — [1st ed.]. — New York: Knopf, 1963. 2 v.: illus., maps.; 25 cm. 1. Archaeology — History. 2. Man, Prehistoric I. T.
GN738.H39      913.082      *LC* 63-12396

**Clark, Grahame, 1907-.** • **4.695**
World prehistory: a new outline, by Grahame Clark. 2nd ed. London, Cambridge U.P., 1969. xvi, 331 p. 17 plates, illus., maps. 23 cm. 1. Man, Prehistoric I. T.
GN739.C55 1969      913.03/1      *LC* 69-19374      *ISBN* 0521073340

**Leone, Mark P.** **4.696**
Contemporary archaeology; a guide to theory and contributions. Edited by Mark P. Leone. — Carbondale: Southern Illinois University Press, [1972] xv,

460 p.: illus.; 28 cm. 1. Archaeology — Addresses, essays, lectures. 2. Indians — Antiquities — Addresses, essays, lectures. 3. America — Antiquities — Addresses, essays, lectures. I. T.
GN739.L46        913/.031        *LC* 79-156779        *ISBN* 0809305135

**Willey, Gordon Randolph, 1913-.**                                          **4.697**
Archaeological researches in retrospect, edited by Gordon R. Willey. — Cambridge, Mass.: Winthrop Publishers, [1974] xix, 296 p.: illus.; 24 cm. 1. Man, Prehistoric — Addresses, essays, lectures. 2. Indians — Antiquities — Addresses, essays, lectures. 3. Archaeology — Addresses, essays, lectures. 4. America — Antiquities — Addresses, essays, lectures. I. T.
GN739.W54        913/.031        *LC* 73-20134        *ISBN* 087626044X

**Daniel, Glyn, 1914-.**                                          **4.698**
The idea of prehistory / Glyn Daniel and Colin Renfrew. — New ed. — Edinburgh: Edinburgh University Press, 1987. [228] p.: ill.; 20 cm. 1. Anthropology, Prehistoric I. Renfrew, Colin. II. T.
GN740.Dx        930 19        *ISBN* 0852245327

**Butzer, Karl W.**                                          • **4.699**
Environment and archeology; an ecological approach to prehistory [by] Karl W. Butzer. 2d ed. — Chicago: Aldine-Atherton, [1971] xxvi, 703 p.: illus., maps.; 25 cm. 1. Man, Prehistoric 2. Paleoclimatology 3. Geology, Stratigraphic — Pleistocene 4. Paleontology — Pleistocene I. T.
GN741.B8 1971        551.7/92        *LC* 74-115938        *ISBN* 0202330231

**Pfeiffer, John E., 1915-.**                                          **4.700**
The emergence of society: a pre-history of the establishment / by John E. Pfeiffer. New York: McGraw-Hill, c1977. 512 p.: ill.; 23 cm. Includes index. 1. Man, Prehistoric 2. Social evolution 3. Society, Primitive I. T.
GN741.P33        301.2        *LC* 76-27308        *ISBN* 0070497591

## GN768–776 Stone Age

**Brain, C. K. (Charles Kimberlin)**                                          **4.701**
The hunters or the hunted?: An introduction to African cave taphonomy / C. K. Brain. — Chicago: University of Chicago Press, 1981. x, 365 p.: ill.; 31 cm. Includes index. 1. Australopithecines 2. Animal remains (Archaeology) — Africa, Southern. 3. Caves — Africa, Southern. I. T.
GN772.22.S6 B7        573        *LC* 79-28104        *ISBN* 0226070891

**Coon, Carleton Stevens, 1904-.**                                          • **4.702**
The seven caves; archaeological explorations in the Middle East. [1st ed.] New York, Knopf, 1957 [c1956] 338 p. illus. 22 cm. 1. Coon, Carleton Stevens, 1904- 2. Paleolithic period — Middle East. 3. Caves — Middle East. 4. Excavations (Archaeology) — Middle East. 5. Middle East — Antiquities. I. T.
GN772.32.N4 C66 1957        939/.4 19        *LC* 56-8918

**Washburn, S. L. (Sherwood Larned), 1911- ed.**                                          • **4.703**
Social life of early man. Subscribers ed. [New York] Distributed through Current anthropology for the Wenner-Gren Foundation for Anthropological Research, 1961. vii, 299 p. illus. 26 cm. (Viking Fund publications in anthropology. no. 31) 1. Man, Prehistoric 2. Primates — Behavior I. Wenner-Gren Foundation for Anthropological Research. II. T. III. Series.
GN773.W3        573.3        *LC* 62-10630

**Breuil, Henri, 1877-1961.**                                          • **4.704**
The men of the old stone age (palaeolithic & mesolithic) [by] Henri Breuil and Raymond Lantier. Translated by B.B. Rafter. New York, St. Martin's Press [1965] 272 p. ill. 1. Stone age I. Lantier, Raymond, 1886-, joint author II. T.
GN775 B833        *LC* 65-10190

**Clark, J. Desmond (John Desmond), 1916-.**                                          • **4.705**
The prehistory of Africa [by] J. Desmond Clark. New York, Praeger [1970] 302 p. 120 illus., 10 maps. 21 cm. (Ancient peoples and places, v. 72) (Praeger paperbacks, P-265.) 1. Man, Prehistoric — Africa. 2. Africa — Antiquities. I. T.
GN776.A15 C55 1970        573/.3/096        *LC* 77-108243

**Clark, Grahame, 1907-.**                                          **4.706**
Excavations at Star Carr; an early Mesolithic site at Seamer near Scarborough, Yorkshire, by J.G.D. Clark. With chapters by D. Walker [and others] and with an appendix by John W. Moore. Cambridge, University Press, 1972 (c1971). xxiii, 200 p. illus., maps, profiles, tables 29 cm. First published 1954; reprinted with a new preface 1971. 1. Stone age — England 2. Scarborough (North Yorkshire) — Antiquities I. T.
GN776.G7 C47        571.1        *LC* 75-172830

**Piggott, Stuart.**                                          • **4.707**
The neolithic cultures of the British Isles: a study of the stone–using agricultural communities of Britain in the second millennium B.C. / by Stuart

Piggott. — Cambridge: University Press, 1954. xix, 420 p.: ill., maps. 1. Stone age — Great Britain. I. T.
GN776.G7 P5        913.3/62        *LC* 54-2828

**Whittle, A. W. R.**                                          **4.708**
Neolithic Europe: a survey / Alasdair Whittle. -- Cambridge [Cambridgeshire]; New York: University of Cambridge Press, 1985. xiv, 363 p.: ill.; 26 cm. (Cambridge world archaeology.) Includes index. 1. Neolithic period — Europe 2. Man, Prehistoric — Europe. 3. Europe — Antiquities I. T. II. Series.
GN776.2.A1 W45 1985        936 19        *LC* 84-23844        *ISBN* 0521247993

**Tringham, Ruth.**                                          **4.709**
Hunters, fishers and farmers of Eastern Europe, 6000–3000 B.C. — London: (3 Fitzroy Sq., W. 1), Hutchinson and Co. (Publishers) Ltd, 1971. 240 p., 9 plates (1 fold.);: illus., maps, plans.; 23 cm. 1. Neolithic period — Europe, Eastern 2. Copper age — Europe, Eastern. I. T.
GN776.22.E8 T7        913.39/8/03        *LC* 72-181580        *ISBN* 0091087902

**Ancient France: Neolithic societies and their landscapes,**          **4.710**
**6000–2000 BC / edited by Christopher Scarre; with a preface by**
**Glyn Daniel.**
Edinburgh: University Press, 1984. viii, 390 p.: ill.; 24 cm. Includes index. 1. Neolithic period — France — Addresses, essays, lectures. 2. France — Antiquities — Addresses, essays, lectures. I. Scarre, Christopher.
GN776.22.F7 A53 1983        936.4 19        *LC* 84-112334

**Mellaart, James.**                                          **4.711**
The Neolithic of the Near East / James Mellaart. — New York: Scribner, c1975. 300 p.: ill.; 25 cm. — (The World of archaeology). 1. Neolithic period — Middle East. 2. Neolithic period — Balkan Peninsula. 3. Neolithic period — Asia, Central. 4. Middle East — Antiquities. 5. Balkan Peninsula — Antiquities. 6. Asia, Central — Antiquities. I. T.
GN776.32.N4 M44 1975b        939        *LC* 75-15209        *ISBN* 0684144832

## GN777–780 Copper, Bronze, Iron Ages

**Mellaart, James.**                                          • **4.712**
The chalcolithic and early bronze ages in the Near East and Anatolia. — Beirut: Khayats, 1966. viii, 212 p.: illus., maps.; 23 cm. 1. Bronze age I. T.
GN777.M4        913.39/03        *LC* 67-4304

**Coles, J. M. (John M.)**                                          **4.713**
The bronze age in Europe: an introduction to the prehistory of Europe c. 2000–700 BC / J. M. Coles & A. F. Harding. — New York: St. Martin's Press, 1979. xviii, 581 p., [12] leaves of plates: ill.; 24 cm. Includes index. 1. Bronze age — Europe 2. Europe — Antiquities I. Harding, A. F. joint author. II. T.
GN778.2.A1 C64 1979        940        *LC* 79-14507        *ISBN* 0312105975

**Glob, Peter Vilhelm, 1911-.**                                          • **4.714**
[Mosefolket. English] The bog people; Iron Age man preserved [by] P. V. Glob. Translated from the Danish by Rupert Bruce–Mitford. Ithaca, N.Y., Cornell University Press [1969] 200 p. illus., maps. 26 cm. Translation of Mosefolket. 1. Iron age — Denmark. 2. Man, Prehistoric — Denmark. I. T.
GN780.D4 G53 1969b        913.3/6        *LC* 69-20391

**Wells, Peter S.**                                          **4.715**
Farms, villages, and cities: commerce and urban origins in late prehistoric Europe / Peter S. Wells. — Ithaca: Cornell University Press, 1984. 270 p.: ill.; 24 cm. Includes index. 1. Iron age — Europe. 2. Commerce, Prehistoric — Europe. 3. Urbanization — Europe. 4. Europe — Antiquities I. T.
GN780.2.A1 W45 1984        936 19        *LC* 84-45142        *ISBN* 0801415543

**Oliver, Roland Anthony.**                                          **4.716**
Africa in the Iron Age, c500 B.C. to A.D. 1400 / Roland Oliver, Brian M. Fagan. Cambridge; New York: Cambridge University Press, 1975. xi, 228 p.: ill.; 22 cm. Includes index. 1. Iron age — Africa. 2. Africa — Antiquities. 3. Africa — History I. Fagan, Brian M. joint author. II. T.
GN780.4.A1 O44        960        *LC* 74-25639        *ISBN* 0521205980

## GN799 Special Topics, A–Z

**Bender, Barbara.**                                          **4.717**
Farming in prehistory: from hunter–gatherer to food–producer / Barbara Bender; ill. by Annabel Rowe and Jan Farquharson. — New York: St. Martin's Press, 1975. xi, 268 p.: ill.; 25 cm. Includes indexes. 1. Agriculture — History 2. Man, Prehistoric 3. Agriculture, Prehistoric I. T.
GN799.A4 B46 1975b        630/.9/01        *LC* 75-13899

**Reed, Charles A.** 4.718
Origins of agriculture / ed. Charles A. Reed. — The Hague: Mouton, 1978
(c1977). xvi, 1017 p.: ill.; 24 cm. (World anthropology.) 'Distributed in the USA
and Canada by Aldine, Chicago.' Papers prepared for the 9th. International
Congress of Anthropological and Ethnological Sciences, Chicago, 1973.
1. Agriculture — Origin — Congresses. 2. Man, Prehistoric — Congresses.
3. Agriculture, Prehistoric — Congresses. I. International Congress of
Anthropological and Ethnological Sciences. 9th, Chicago, 1973. II. T.
III. Series.
GN799.A4 O74      630/.9      LC 79-300652      ISBN 0202900436

**Exchange systems in prehistory / edited by Timothy K. Earle,** 4.719
**Jonathon E. Ericson.**
New York: Academic Press, c1977. xiii, 274 p.: ill.; 25 cm. — (Studies in
archeology) 1. Commerce, Prehistoric — Addresses, essays, lectures. I. Earle,
Timothy K. II. Ericson, Jonathon E.
GN799.C45 E95      380.1/09/01      LC 76-13933      ISBN 0122276507

**Jochim, Michael A.** 4.720
Hunter–gatherer subsistence and settlement: a predictive model / Michael A.
Jochim. — New York: Academic Press, c1976. xvii, 206 p.: ill.; 24 cm. —
(Studies in archeology) Includes index. 1. Economics, Prehistoric —
Mathematical models. 2. Economics, Prehistoric — Data processing.
3. Economic anthropology — Mathematical models. 4. Economic
anthropology — Data processing. I. T.
GN799.E4 J62      330/.9/01      LC 75-40609      ISBN 0123854504

**Cohen, Mark Nathan.** 4.721
The food crisis in prehistory: overpopulation and the origins of agriculture /
Mark Nathan Cohen. New Haven [Conn.]: Yale University Press, 1977. x,
341 p.; 22 cm. Includes index. 1. Man, Prehistoric — Food 2. Man, Prehistoric
— Population 3. Agriculture — Origin 4. Food supply — History. I. T.
GN799.F6 C64      338.1/9/3      LC 76-41858      ISBN 0300020163

**Renfrew, Jane M.** 4.722
Palaeoethnobotany: the prehistoric food plants of the Near East and Europe
[by] Jane M. Renfrew. Figures drawn by Alan Eade. — New York: Columbia
University Press, 1973. xviii, 248 p.: illus.; 26 cm. 1. Man, Prehistoric — Food
2. Ethnobotany 3. Plant remains (Archaeology) I. T.
GN799.F6 R46      581.6/32/093      LC 72-12752      ISBN 0231037457

## GN800–875 PREHISTORIC REMAINS

## GN803–841 Europe

**Bibby, Geoffrey.** • 4.723
The testimony of the spade. — [1st ed.]. — New York: Knopf, 1956. xviii, 414,
x p.: illus., 32 plates, maps.; 25 cm. 'Some remarks on reading': p. 412-414.
1. Man, Prehistoric — Europe. 2. Europe — Antiquities I. T.
GN803.B5      913.4 940*      LC 56-8916

**Childe, V. Gordon (Vere Gordon), 1892-1957.** 4.724
The Danube in prehistory, by V. Gordon Childe. Oxford, Clarendon Press,
1929. xix, 479 p. illus. 26 cm. 1. Man, Prehistoric — Europe. 2. Danube River
3. Hungary — Antiquities. 4. Danube River Valley — Antiquities. I. T.
GN803.C5      LC 30-8886

**Daniel, Glyn Edmund.** • 4.725
The megalith builders of Western Europe. Baltimore, Penguin Books [1963,
c1962] 155 p. illus., maps. 18 cm. (Pelican books, A633) 1. Megalithic
monuments — Europe 2. Europe — Antiquities I. T.
GN803.D36 1963      571.9      LC 63-24739

**Milisauskas, Sarunas.** 4.726
European prehistory / Sarunas Milisauskas. — New York: Academic Press,
c1978. xii, 333 p.: ill.; 24 cm. — (Studies in archeology) Includes index. 1. Man,
Prehistoric — Europe. I. T.
GN803.M49      936      LC 78-212      ISBN 0124979505

**Phillips, Patricia (Ann Patricia)** 4.727
The prehistory of Europe / Patricia Phillips. — Bloomington: Indiana
University Press, c1980. 314 p., [8] leaves of plates: ill.; 25 cm. Includes index.
1. Man, Prehistoric — Europe. 2. Europe — Antiquities I. T.
GN803.P45      936      LC 79-3787      ISBN 0253119561

**Piggott, Stuart.** 4.728
The earliest wheeled transport: from the Atlantic Coast to the Caspian Sea /
Stuart Piggott. — Ithaca, N.Y.: Cornell University Press, 1983. 272 p.: ill.; 27
cm. Includes index. 1. Man, Prehistoric — Europe. 2. Man, Prehistoric —

Middle East. 3. Wheels — History. 4. Vehicles — History. 5. Middle East —
Antiquities. 6. Europe — Antiquities I. T.
GN803.P53 1983      688.6/094 19      LC 82-73810      ISBN 0801416043

**Renfrew, Colin, 1937-.** 4.729
Before civilization: the radiocarbon revolution and prehistoric Europe. [1st
American ed.] New York, Knopf; [distributed by Random House] 1973. 292,
viii, p. illus. 25 cm. 1. Man, Prehistoric — Europe. 2. Megalithic monuments
— Europe 3. Radiocarbon dating 4. Europe — Antiquities I. T.
GN803.R46 1973      913.36/03      LC 73-6552      ISBN 0394481933

**Burl, Aubrey.** 4.730
The stone circles of the British Isles / Aubrey Burl. New Haven: Yale
University Press, 1976. xxi, 410 p.: ill.; 26 cm. Includes index. 1. Megalithic
monuments — Great Britain. 2. Great Britain — Antiquities I. T.
GN805.B87      936.2      LC 75-43311      ISBN 0300019726

**Evans, John G.** 4.731
The environment of early man in the British Isles / John G. Evans. — Berkeley:
University of California Press, 1975. xiv, 216 p.: ill.; 25 cm. Includes index.
1. Man, Prehistoric — Great Britain. 2. Geology, Stratigraphic — Quaternary
3. Human ecology — Great Britain. 4. Geology — Great Britain. 5. Great
Britain — Antiquities I. T.
GN805.E9 1975b      301.31/09361      LC 74-29803      ISBN 0520029739

**Forde-Johnston, James L.** 4.732
Prehistoric Britain and Ireland / J. Forde–Johnston. 1st American ed. — New
York: Norton, 1976. 208 p.: ill.; 25 cm. Includes index. 1. Man, Prehistoric —
Great Britain. 2. Man, Prehistoric — Ireland. 3. Great Britain — Antiquities
4. Ireland — Antiquities I. T.
GN805.F67 1976      936.1      LC 76-20287      ISBN 0393056058

**Renfrew, Colin, 1937-.** 4.733
British prehistory: a new outline / edited by Colin Renfrew. — Park Ridge,
N.J.: Noyes Press, [1975] c1974. xiv, 348 p.: ill.; 22 cm. Includes index. 1. Man,
Prehistoric — Great Britain. 2. Great Britain — Antiquities I. T.
GN805.R46 1975      936.2      LC 74-83800      ISBN 0815550324

**Piggott, Stuart. ed.** • 4.734
The prehistoric peoples of Scotland. — London: Routledge and Paul, [1962] ix,
165 p.: illus., maps, diagr.; 24 cm. — (Studies in ancient history and
archaeology) Imprint covered by label: New York, Humanities Press. 1. Man,
Prehistoric — Scotland. 2. Scotland — Antiquities 3. Scotland — History —
To 1057 I. T.
GN806.S4 P47 1962      936.1/1 19      LC 63-3786

**Herity, Michael.** 4.735
Ireland in prehistory / Michael Herity and George Eogan. — London; Boston:
Routledge & K. Paul, 1977. xvi, 302 p., [8] leaves of plates: ill.; 25 cm. Includes
index. 1. Man, Prehistoric — Ireland. 2. Ireland — Antiquities I. Eogan,
George. joint author. II. T.
GN806.5.H47      936.1/5/01      LC 77-372869      ISBN 0710084137

**Sulimirski, Tadeusz, 1898-.** • 4.736
Prehistoric Russia: an outline. — London: J. Baker; New York: Humanities
Press, 1970. xxiii, 449 p., 38 plates.: illus., 32 maps.; 26 cm. 1. Russia —
Antiquities. I. T.
GN823.S9      914.7/03/1      LC 74-468067      ISBN 0212998315

**Jensen, Jørgen, 1936 July 30-.** 4.737
[Dansk socialhistorie. Volume 1. English] The prehistory of Denmark / Jørgen
Jensen. — London; New York: Methuen, 1983. xviii, 331 p.: ill.; 25 cm.
Translation of: Dansk socialhistorie. v. 1. Includes index. 1. Man, Prehistoric
— Denmark. 2. Denmark — Antiquities I. T.
GN826.J4613 1982      948.9/01 19      LC 82-24885      ISBN 041634190X

**Gilman, Antonio.** 4.738
Land–use and prehistory in south–east Spain / Antonio Gilman and John B.
Thornes, with Stephen Wise. — London; Boston: Allen & Unwin, 1985. xii,
217 p.: ill.; 24 cm. (London research series in geography. 0261-0485; 8) Includes
indexes. 1. Economics, Prehistoric — Spain. 2. Copper age — Spain.
3. Bronze age — Spain 4. Land settlement patterns, Prehistoric — Spain.
5. Land use — Spain — Social aspects. 6. Spain — Antiquities I. Thornes,
John B. II. Wise, Stephen. III. T. IV. Series.
GN835.G55 1985      936.6 19      LC 84-9363      ISBN 0049130226

**Sauter, Marc Rodolphe, 1914-.** 4.739
Switzerland, from earliest times to the Roman conquest / Marc–R. Sauter. —
Boulder, Colo.: Westview Press, 1976. 208 p.: ill.; 21 cm. (Ancient peoples and
places; v. 86) Includes index. 1. Man, Prehistoric — Switzerland.
2. Switzerland — Antiquities I. T.
GN841.S27      936.3      LC 76-977      ISBN 0891585435

## GN851–865 Asia. Africa

**Frankfort, Henri, 1897-1954.**      • **4.740**
The birth of civilization in the Near East. 5th impression. London, Ernest Benn; New York, Barnes & Noble, 1968. 116 p. illus., maps. 26 cm. 'Expanded versions of lectures delivered at Indiana University in the winter of 1948-9 on the Patten foundation.' 1. Egypt — Antiquities 2. Iraq — Antiquities 3. Middle East — Civilization — To 622 I. T.
GN851.F7 1968      913.3      *LC* 76-362953      *ISBN* 0510268013

**Masson, V. M. (Vadim Mikhaĭlovich), 1929-.**      **4.741**
Central Asia: Turkmenia before the Achaemenids [by] V. M. Masson and V. I. Sarianidi. Translated and edited with a pref. by Ruth Tringham. [New York, Praeger [1972] 219 p. illus. 21 cm. (Ancient peoples and places, v. 79) 1. Man, Prehistoric — Asia, Central. 2. Asia, Central — Antiquities. I. Sarianidi, V. I. (Viktor Ivanovich) joint author. II. T. III. Title: Turkmenia before the Achaemenids.
GN855.C4 M3 1972b      913.39/6/03      *LC* 70-131350

**Aikens, C. Melvin.**      **4.742**
Prehistory of Japan / C. Melvin Aikens, Takayasu Higuchi. — New York: Academic Press, c1982. xv, 354 p.: ill.; 24 cm. — (Studies in archaeology.) Includes index. 1. Man, Prehistoric — Japan. 2. Japan — Antiquities I. Higuchi, Takayasu. II. T. III. Series.
GN855.J2 A36      952/.01 19      *LC* 81-12850      *ISBN* 0120452804

**Chernetsov, Valeriĭ Nikolaevich, 1905-1970.**      **4.743**
Prehistory of western Siberia / V. N. Chernetsov and W. Moszyńska; edited by Henry N. Michael. — Montreal: [Published for] Arctic Institute of North America [by] McGill-Queen's University Press, 1974. xxv, 377 p.: ill.; 26 cm. (Anthropology of the North: Translations from Russian sources; no. 9) 1. Man, Prehistoric — Russian S.F.S.R. — Siberia, Western. 2. Siberia, Western (R.S.F.S.R.) — Antiquities. I. Moszyńska, W., joint author. II. Arctic Institute of North America. III. T. IV. Series.
GN4.A65 no. 9 GN855.R9      930/.1 s 957/.3      *LC* 73-79092      *ISBN* 0773590749

**From hunters to farmers: the causes and consequences of food**      **4.744**
**production in Africa / edited by J. Desmond Clark and Steven A. Brandt.**
Berkeley: University of California Press, c1984. xi, 433 p.: ill.; 27 cm. Includes index. 1. Agriculture, Prehistoric — Africa — Addresses, essays, lectures. 2. Agriculture — Origin — Addresses, essays, lectures. 3. Neolithic period — Africa — Addresses, essays, lectures. 4. Africa — Antiquities — Addresses, essays, lectures. I. Clark, J. Desmond (John Desmond), 1916- II. Brandt, Steven A.
GN861.F73 1984      307.7/2/096 19      *LC* 82-20004      *ISBN* 0520045742

**Phillipson, D. W.**      **4.745**
African archaeology / David W. Phillipson. — Cambridge [Cambridgeshire]; New York: Cambridge University Press, 1985. ix, 234 p.: ill.; 26 cm. (Cambridge world archaeology.) Includes index. 1. Man, Prehistoric — Africa. 2. Africa — Antiquities. I. T. II. Series.
GN861.P47 1985      960/.1 19      *LC* 83-25235      *ISBN* 0521252342

**Hoffman, Michael A., 1944-.**      **4.746**
Egypt before the pharaohs: the prehistoric foundations of Egyptian civilization / Michael A. Hoffman. — 1st ed. — New York: Knopf, 1979. xxi, 391 p.: ill.; 25 cm. Includes index. 1. Man, Prehistoric — Egypt. 2. Egypt — Antiquities I. T.
GN865.E3 H63 1979      932      *LC* 78-20371      *ISBN* 0394410491

**Clark, J. Desmond (John Desmond), 1916-.**      • **4.747**
Kalambo Falls prehistoric site [by] J. D. Clark; with contributions by C. H. Cole [and others] London, Cambridge U.P., 1969-. v. plates, illus., maps, plans. 26 cm. 1. Kalambo Falls site. I. T.
GN865.T33 C55      916.78/2      *LC* 68-25084      *ISBN* 0521069629

## GN871 Oceania. Australia

**Bellwood, Peter S.**      **4.748**
Man's conquest of the Pacific: the prehistory of Southeast Asia and Oceania / Peter Bellwood. — New York: Oxford University Press, 1979, c1978. 462 p., [4] leaves of plates: ill.; 27 cm. Includes index. 1. Man, Prehistoric — Oceania. 2. Man, Prehistoric — Asia, Southeastern. 3. Oceania — Antiquities. 4. Asia, Southeastern — Antiquities. I. T.
GN871.B44 1979      959      *LC* 78-59765      *ISBN* 0195201035

**Mulvaney, Derek John.**      **4.749**
The prehistory of Australia / [by] D. J. Mulvaney. Rev. ed. — Ringwood, Vic.; Harmondsworth, Eng.: Penguin Books, 1975. 327 p.: ill., diagrs., maps; 20 cm. (Pelican books) Includes index. 1. Australian aborigines — Antiquities 2. Australia — Antiquities I. T.
GN871.M8 1975      994.01      *LC* 76-364607      *ISBN* 0140217738

**White, J. Peter (John Peter), 1937-.**      **4.750**
A prehistory of Australia, New Guinea, and Sahul / J. Peter White, with James F. O'Connell; illustrations by Margrit Koettig. — Sydney; New York: Academic Press, c1983. xiii, 286 p.: ill.; 24 cm. Includes indexes. 1. Man, Prehistoric — Australia. 2. Man, Prehistoric — Papua New Guinea. 3. Australia — Antiquities 4. Papua New Guinea — Antiquities I. O'Connell, James F. II. Koettig, Margrit. III. T.
GN875.A8 W55 1983      994.01 19      *LC* 81-71781      *ISBN* 0127467505

# GR FOLKLORE

**Dorson, Richard Mercer, 1916-.**    **4.751**
Folklore and fakelore: essays toward a discipline of folk studies / Richard M. Dorson. — Cambridge, Mass.: Harvard University Press, 1976. x, 391 p.; 24 cm. Includes index. 1. Folklore — Addresses, essays, lectures. 2. Folklore and history — Addresses, essays, lectures. 3. Oral tradition — Addresses, essays, lectures. I. T.
GR20.D67    398/.042    *LC* 75-30734    *ISBN* 0674307151

**Thompson, Stith, 1885- comp.**    • **4.752**
One hundred favorite folktales. Drawings by Franz Altschuler. — Bloomington: Indiana University Press, [1968] xii, 439 p.: illus.; 24 cm. 1. Tales I. T.
GR25.T5    398.2    *LC* 68-27355

**Funk & Wagnalls standard dictionary of folklore, mythology**    • **4.753**
**and legend / Maria Leach, editor; Jerome Fried, associate**
**editor.**
New York: Funk & Wagnalls Co., 1949. v.; 26 cm. 1. Folklore — Dictionaries. I. Leach, Maria. ed. II. Fried, Jerome. ed. III. Funk and Wagnalls standard dictionary of folklore, mythology, and legend.
GR35.F8    398.03    *LC* 49-48675

**Jobes, Gertrude.**    • **4.754**
Dictionary of mythology, folklore and symbols. New York, Scarecrow Press, 1961. 2 v. (1759 p.) 1. Mythology — Dictionaries 2. Folklore — Dictionaries 3. Signs and symbols I. T.
GR35 J6    *LC* 61-860

**Goldstein, Kenneth S.**    • **4.755**
A guide for field workers in folklore, by Kenneth S. Goldstein. Pref. by Hamish Henderson. Hatboro, Pa., Folklore Associates, 1964. xviii, 199 p. 23 cm. 1. Folklore — Methodology I. T.
GR40.G6    *LC* 64-24801

**Toelken, Barre.**    **4.756**
The dynamics of folklore / Barre Toelken. — Boston: Houghton Mifflin, c1979. xiii, 395 p., [32] leaves of plates: ill.; 25 cm. 1. Folklore — Methodology 2. Folklore — United States 3. United States — Social life and customs I. T.
GR40.T63    390/.01    *LC* 78-69536    *ISBN* 0395270685

**Foley, John Miles.**    **4.757**
Oral–formulaic theory and research: an introduction and annotated bibliography / John Miles Foley. — New York: Garland Pub., 1985. xvi, 718 p.; 23 cm. (Garland folklore bibliographies; vol. 6) (Garland reference library of the humanities; v. 400) Includes index. 1. Oral-formulaic analysis — Bibliography. I. T.
GR44.O72 F65 1985    016.398/042 19    *LC* 84-49146    *ISBN* 0824091485

**Dundes, Alan.**    • **4.758**
The study of folklore. Englewood Cliffs, N.J. Prentice Hall [c1965] xi, 481 p. ill. 24 cm. 1. Folklore — Study and teaching I. T.
GR45 D8    *LC* 65-22195

**Dorson, Richard Mercer, 1916-.**    • **4.759**
Folklore and folklife, an introduction. Edited by Richard M. Dorson. Chicago, University of Chicago Press [1972] x, 561 p. illus. 24 cm. 1. Folklore — Addresses, essays, lectures. 2. Ethnology — Addresses, essays, lectures. I. T.
GR65.D57    398/.042    *LC* 77-189038    *ISBN* 0226158705

**Thompson, Stith, 1885-.**    • **4.760**
Motif–index of folk–literature; a classification of narrative elements in folktales, ballads, myths, fables, mediaeval romances, exempla, fabliaux, jest–books, and local legends. — Rev. and enl. ed. — Bloomington: Indiana University Press, [1955-58] 6 v.; 26 cm. 1. Folklore — Classification 2. Folk literature — Classification. 3. Folk literature — Themes, motives 4. Folk literature — Bibliography. I. T.
GR67.T52    398.012    *LC* 55-8085

**Dorson, Richard Mercer, 1916-.**    **4.761**
Folklore: selected essays [by] Richard M. Dorson. — Bloomington: Indiana University Press, [1972] 311 p.; 25 cm. 1. Folklore — Addresses, essays, lectures. 2. Folklore — Methodology — Addresses, essays, lectures. I. T.
GR71.D67    398/.042    *LC* 72-76944    *ISBN* 0253323207

**Oral traditional literature: a Festschrift for Albert Bates Lord /**    **4.762**
**John Miles Foley, editor.**
Columbus, Ohio: Slavica Publishers, 1981. 461 p.: port.; 24 cm. 1. Lord, Albert Bates — Bibliography. 2. Lord, Albert Bates. 3. Folk literature — Addresses, essays, lectures. 4. Oral tradition — Addresses, essays, lectures. 5. Oral-formulaic analysis — Addresses, essays, lectures. I. Lord, Albert Bates. II. Foley, John Miles.
GR72.O7    398/.094 19    *LC* 81-210308    *ISBN* 0893570737

**Bynum, David E.**    **4.763**
The dæmon in the wood: a study of oral narrative patterns / by David E. Bynum; with a foreword by Albert B. Lord. — Cambridge, Mass.: Center for Study of Oral Literature, Harvard University, 1978. xviii, 454 p.: ill.; 25 cm. — (Publications of the Milman Parry Collection: Monograph series; no. 1) 1. Parry, Milman. 2. Oral tradition 3. Folk literature — Themes, motives 4. Oral-formulaic analysis I. T.
GR74.4.B96    398/.042    *LC* 78-20294    *ISBN* 0674180313

**MacDonald, Margaret Read.**    **4.764**
The storyteller's sourcebook: a subject, title, and motif index to folklore collections for children / by Margaret Read MacDonald. — 1st ed. — Detroit, Mich.: Neal-Schuman Publishers in association with Gale Research, c1982. xviii, 818 p.; 29 cm. A portion of this work is based on part of the author's thesis (doctoral)—Indiana University, 1979. 1. Folklore — Juvenile literature — Classification. 2. Folk literature — Themes, motives 3. Tales — Indexes. 4. Tales — Bibliography. I. T.
GR74.6.M3 1982    016.3982/088054 19    *LC* 82-954    *ISBN* 0810304716

**Cinderella, a folklore casebook / [edited by] Alan Dundes.**    **4.765**
New York: Garland Pub., 1982. xix, 311 p.: maps; 23 cm. — (Garland folklore casebooks. v. 3) 1. Cinderella (Tale) — History and criticism — Addresses, essays, lectures. I. Dundes, Alan. II. Series.
GR75.C4 C4 1982    398.2/1 19    *LC* 81-43334    *ISBN* 0824092953

**Oedipus, a folklore casebook / [edited by] Lowell Edmunds,**    **4.766**
**Alan Dundes.**
New York: Garland, 1983. xv, 266 p.: ill.; 23 cm. — (Garland folklore casebooks. v. 4) 1. Oedipus (Tale) — History and criticism — Addresses, essays, lectures. I. Edmunds, Lowell. II. Dundes, Alan. III. Series.
GR75.O3 O3 1983    398.2/2 19    *LC* 82-48286    *ISBN* 0824092422

# GR100–385 By Country

## GR100–113 UNITED STATES

**Abrahams, Roger D.**    • **4.767**
Deep down in the jungle ...; Negro narrative folklore from the streets of Philadelphia [by] Roger D. Abrahams. — 1st rev. ed. — Chicago: Aldine Pub. Co., [1970] ix, 278 p.; 22 cm. — (Aldine folklore series) 1. Afro-Americans — Pennsylvania — Folklore. 2. Afro-Americans — Pennsylvania — Philadelphia 3. Toasts (Afro-American folk poetry) 4. Philadelphia (Pa.) — Social life and customs I. T.
GR103.A2 1970    917.48/11/097496    *LC* 78-124404    *ISBN* 0202010911

**Dundes, Alan. comp.**    **4.768**
Mother wit from the laughing barrel: readings in the interpretation of Afro–American folklore. — Englewood Cliffs, N.J.: Prentice-Hall, 1973 (c1972) xiv, 673 p.; 24 cm. 1. Afro-Americans — Folklore 2. Folklore — United States I. T.
GR103.D86 1973    917.3/06/96073    *LC* 72-171619    *ISBN* 013603019X *ISBN* 0136030017

**Hughes, Langston, 1902-1967.**                                   • **4.769**
The book of Negro folklore / edited by Langston Hughes and Arna Bontemps. — New York: Dodd, Mead, 1958. 624 p.: ill.; 22 cm. 1. Folk-lore, Negro. I. Bontemps, Arna Wendell, 1902-1973. joint ed. II. T.
GR103.H74        *LC* 58-13097

**Hurston, Zora Neale.**                                            **4.770**
Mules and men. — Philadelphia, Pa.: Lippincott, 1935. 342 p.: ill.; 22 cm. 1. Afro-American tales. 2. Voodooism — Louisiana. 3. Afro-Americans — Florida 4. Afro-Americans — Louisiana 5. Afro-American songs. I. T.
GR103.H8 1978        398.2/09759

**Levine, Lawrence W.**                                             **4.771**
Black culture and black consciousness: Afro–American folk thought from slavery to freedom / Lawrence W. Levine. — New York: Oxford University Press, 1977. xx, 522 p.; 24 cm. 1. Afro-Americans — Folklore 2. Folklore — United States I. T.
GR103.L48        398.2      *LC* 76-9223        *ISBN* 019502088X

**Brunvand, Jan Harold.**                                          • **4.772**
The study of American folklore: an introduction / Jan Harold Brunvand. — 2d ed. — New York: Norton, c1978. xiv, 460 p.; 22 cm. 1. Folklore — United States 2. United States — Social life and customs I. T.
GR105.B7 1978        398/.07      *LC* 77-13707        *ISBN* 0393090485

**Brunvand, Jan Harold.**                                          **4.773**
The vanishing hitchhiker: American urban legends and their meanings / Jan Harold Brunvand. — 1st ed. — New York: Norton, c1981. xiv, 208 p.; 22 cm. 1. Urban folklore — United States. 2. Legends — United States. 3. Legends — United States — History and criticism. I. T.
GR105.B72 1981        398.2/09173/2 19      *LC* 81-4744        *ISBN* 0393014738

**A Celebration of American family folklore: tales and traditions**        **4.774**
**from the Smithsonian collection / Steven J. Zeitlin, Amy J.**
**Kotkin, Holly Cutting Baker.**
1st ed. — New York: Pantheon Books, c1982. xii, 291 p.: ill.; 24 cm. Collected from the Family Folklore Program of the Smithsonian's Festival of American Folklife. 1. Family — United States — Folklore. 2. United States — Social life and customs I. Zeitlin, Steven J. II. Kotkin, Amy. III. Baker, Holly Cutting, 1949- IV. Festival of American Folklife. Family Folklore Program.
GR105.C34 1982        398.2/7/0973 19      *LC* 82-47873        *ISBN* 0394520955

**Dorson, Richard Mercer, 1916-.**                                 **4.775**
American folklore: with revised bibliographical notes, 1977 / Richard M. Dorson. — Chicago: University of Chicago Press, c1977. xi, 338 p.; 21 cm. — (Chicago history of American civilization. 4) Includes index. 1. Folklore — United States 2. United States — Social life and customs I. T. II. Series.
GR105.D65 1977        398/.0973      *LC* 77-77491        *ISBN* 0226158594

**Handbook of American folklore / edited by Richard M. Dorson;**        **4.776**
**Inta Gale Carpenter, associate editor; Elizabeth Peterson,**
**Angela Maniak, assistant editors; with an introduction by W.**
**Edson Richmond.**
Bloomington: Indiana University Press, c1983. xix, 584 p.: ill.; 24 cm. Includes index. 1. Folklore — United States — Addresses, essays, lectures. 2. United States — Social life and customs — Addresses, essays, lectures. I. Dorson, Richard Mercer, 1916-
GR105.H36 1983        398/.0973 19      *LC* 82-47574        *ISBN* 0253327067

**The Parade of heroes: legendary figures in American lore /**        **4.777**
**selected and edited by Tristram Potter Coffin and Hennig Cohen**
**from journals and archives of American folklore and culture.**
1st ed. — Garden City, N.Y.: Anchor Press/Doubleday, 1978. xxxviii, 630 p.: music; 22 cm. 1. Folklore — United States 2. Legends — United States. 3. Heroes — United States. I. Coffin, Tristram Potter, 1922- II. Cohen, Hennig.
GR105.P37        398.2/0973      *LC* 77-80881        *ISBN* 0385097115

**Randolph, Vance, 1892- ed.**                                     • **4.778**
Who blowed up the church house? and other Ozark folk tales. New York, Columbia University Press, 1952. 232 p. illus. 23 cm. 1. Tales, American — Ozark Mountains. I. T.
GR110.M77 E3        *LC* 52-4469

**Pissing in the snow and other Ozark folktales / [compiled by]**        **4.779**
**Vance Randolph; introd. by Rayna Green; annotations by Frank**
**A. Hoffmann.**
Urbana: University of Illinois Press, c1976. xxxiii, 153 p.; 21 cm. 1. Tales — Ozark Mountains. 2. Erotic stories, American — Ozark Mountains. I. Randolph, Vance, 1892-
GR110.M77 P57        398.2/097/1      *LC* 76-18181        *ISBN* 0252006186

**Goehring, Eleanor, 1904-.**                                      **4.780**
Tennessee folk culture: an annotated bibliography / by Eleanor E. Goehring. — 1st ed. — Knoxville: University of Tennessee Press, c1982. xviii, 133 p.; 24 cm. Includes indexes. 1. Folklore — Tennessee — Bibliography. 2. Tennessee — Social life and customs — Bibliography. I. T.
GR110.T4 G63 1982        016.390/09768 19      *LC* 81-16036        *ISBN* 0870493442

**Afro–American folktales: stories from Black traditions in the**        **4.781**
**New World / selected and edited by Roger D. Abrahams.**
1st ed. — New York: Pantheon Books, c1985. xxii, 327 p.: ill.; 25 cm. 1. Afro-Americans — Folklore 2. Tales — United States 3. Blacks — Caribbean — Folklore. 4. Tales — Caribbean. I. Abrahams, Roger D.
GR111.A47 A38 1985        398.2/08907 19      *LC* 84-16601        *ISBN* 0394527550

**Trotter, Robert T.**                                             **4.782**
Curanderismo, Mexican American folk healing / Robert T. Trotter II and Juan Antonio Chavira. — Athens: University of Georgia Press, c1981. xi, 204 p.: ill.; 22 cm. Includes index. 1. Mexican Americans — Folklore 2. Folk medicine — United States 3. Healing — United States — Folklore. I. Chavira, Juan Antonio. II. T.
GR111.M49 T76        398/.353 19      *LC* 81-602        *ISBN* 0820305561

**Espinosa, Aurelio Macedonio, 1880-1958.**                        **4.783**
The folklore of Spain in the American Southwest: traditional Spanish folk literature in northern New Mexico and southern Colorado / by Aurelio M. Espinosa; edited by J. Manuel Espinosa. — Norman: University of Oklahoma Press, c1985. xiii, 310 p.: ill., map, ports.; 25 cm. Includes index. 1. Espinosa, Aurelio Macedonio, 1880-1958. 2. Latin Americans — Colorado — Folklore. 3. Latin Americans — New Mexico — Folklore. 4. Folk literature, Spanish — Colorado — History and criticism. 5. Folk literature, Spanish — New Mexico — History and criticism. I. Espinosa, J. Manuel (José Manuel), 1909- II. T.
GR111.S65 E87 1985        398/.09788 19      *LC* 85-40473        *ISBN* 080611942X

## GR114–133 LATIN AMERICA

**Paredes, Américo. comp.**                                        • **4.784**
Folktales of Mexico. Edited and translated by Américo Paredes. Foreword by Richard M. Dorson. Chicago, University of Chicago Press [1970] lxxxiii, 282 p. 23 cm. (Folktales of the world) 1. Tales — Mexico I. T.
GR115.P36        398.2/0972      *LC* 79-107225        *ISBN* 0226645711

**Courlander, Harold, 1908-.**                                     • **4.785**
The drum and the hoe; life and lore of the Haitian people. Berkeley, University of California Press, 1960. xv, 371 p. illus. 27 cm. 'The music: musical notations by Mieczyslaw Kolinski of 186 songs and drum rhythms': p. [203]-313. 1. Folklore — Haiti. 2. Folk-songs — Haiti. 3. Haiti — Social life and customs. I. T.
GR121.H3 C65 1960        398.097294      *LC* 60-8760

**Price-Mars, Jean, 1876-1969.**                                   **4.786**
[Ainsi parla l'oncle. English] So spoke the uncle — Ainsi parla l'oncle / by Jean Price-Mars; translation and introduction by Magdaline W. Shannon. — Washington, D.C.: Three Continents Press, c1983. xxviii, 252 p.; 23 cm. Translation of: Ainsi parla l'oncle. 1. Folklore — Haiti. 2. Ethnology — Africa 3. Voodooism — Haiti. 4. Haiti — Social life and customs. I. T. II. Title: Ainsi parla l'oncle.
GR121.H3 P713 1983        398/.097294 19      *LC* 82-74251        *ISBN* 0894103903

## GR135–263 EUROPE

**Lüthi, Max, 1909-.**                                             **4.787**
[Europäische Volksmärchen. English] The European folktale: form and nature / Max Lüthi; John D. Niles, translator. — Philadelphia: Institute for the Study of Human Issues, c1982. xxv, 173 p.; 22 cm. — (Translations in folklore studies.) Translation of: Das europäische Volksmärchen. 1. Tales — Europe — History and criticism. I. T. II. Series.
GR135.L8313 1982        398.2/094 19      *LC* 81-6891        *ISBN* 089727024X

**Briggs, Katharine Mary.**                                        • **4.788**
A dictionary of British folk–tales in the English language, incorporating the F. J. Norton collection [by] Katharine M. Briggs. — Bloomington: Indiana University Press, [1970]- v. ; 26 cm. 1. Tales, British. I. Norton, F. J. II. T.
GR141.B69        398.2/0942      *LC* 70-97241        *ISBN* 0253317150

**Marshall, Sybil.** 4.789
Everyman's book of English folk tales / Sybil Marshall; illustrated with wood engravings by John Lawrence. — London: Dent, 1981. 384 p.: ill.; 25 cm. 1. Tales — England 2. Legends — England. I. T.
GR141.M34 398.2/1/0942 19 *LC* 81-170596 *ISBN* 0460044729

**Palmer, Roy, 1932-.** 4.790
The folklore of Warwickshire / Roy Palmer; drawings by Gay John Galsworthy. — Totowa, N.J.: Rowman and Littlefield, 1976. 208 p.: ill.; 23 cm. — (The Folklore of the British Isles) Includes indexes. 1. Folklore — England — Warwickshire. 2. Warwickshire — Social life and customs. I. T.
GR142.W3 P34 1976 398.2/09424/8 *LC* 76-375220 *ISBN* 0874718384

**Yeats, W. B. (William Butler), 1865-1939. ed.** • 4.791
Irish fairy and folk tales, ed. by W.B. Yeats. New York, Modern Library [n.d.] xviii, 351 p. illus. (music) 17 cm. (The modern library [of the world's best books]) 1. Fairy tales 2. Folklore — Ireland I. T.
GR147.Y4x *LC* 18-22751

**Dégh, Linda.** • 4.792
[Märchen, Erzähler, und Erzählgemeinschaft. English] Folktales and society; story-telling in a Hungarian peasant community. Translated by Emily M. Schossberger. Bloomington, Indiana University Press [1969] xi, 430 p. illus., map. 25 cm. Revision and translation of Märchen, Erzähler, und Erzählgemeinschaft. 1. Folklore — Hungary. 2. Tales — Hungary — History and criticism. 3. Storytelling — Hungary. 4. Szeklers — Hungary — Folklore. I. T.
GR158.D4253 398/.09439/1 *LC* 69-15994

**Dundes, Alan.** 4.793
Life is like a chicken coop ladder: a portrait of German culture through folklore / Alan Dundes. — New York: Columbia University Press, 1984. xi, 174 p.: ill.; 22 cm. Includes index. 1. Folklore — Germany 2. Excretion — Folklore 3. Anus (Psychology) — Folklore. 4. Toilet training — Germany — Folklore. 5. Feces — Folklore. 6. National characteristics, German I. T.
GR166.D86 1984 398/.0943 19 *LC* 83-7540 *ISBN* 0231054947

**Herzfeld, Michael, 1947-.** 4.794
Ours once more: folklore, ideology, and the making of modern Greece / by Michael Herzfeld. — 1st ed. — Austin: University of Texas Press, 1982. x, 197 p.: 1 map; 24 cm. — (The Dan Danciger publication series) Includes index. 1. Folklore and nationalism — Greece. 2. National characteristics, Greek I. T.
GR170.H47 1982 398/.09495 19 *LC* 81-10398 *ISBN* 0292760183

**Calvino, Italo. comp.** 4.795
[Fiabe italiane. English] Italian folktales / selected and retold by Italo Calvino; translated by George Martin. — 1st ed. — New York: Harcourt Brace Jovanovich, c1980. xxxii, 763 p.: ill.; 24 cm. Translation of Fiabe italiane. 'A Helen and Kurt Wolff book.' 1. Tales — Italy I. T.
GR176.C3413 398.2/1/0945 *LC* 80-11879 *ISBN* 0151457700

**Oinas, Felix J. comp.** 4.796
The study of Russian folklore, edited and translated by Felix J. Oinas and Stephen Soudakoff. — [2nd ed.] The Hague: Mouton, 1975. 341 p. (Indiana University. Folklore Institute. Monograph series; 25.) (Slavistic printings and reprintings. Textbook series, 4.) 1. Folk-lore, Russian — Addresses, essays, lectures. I. Soudakoff, Stephen, joint comp. II. T. III. Series.
GR202.O35 398/.0947 *LC* 76-173045

**Propp, V. IA. (Vladimir IAkovlevich), 1895-1970.** 4.797
Theory and history of folklore / Vladimir Propp; translation from the Russian by Ariadna Y. and Richard P. Martin; edited, with an introduction and notes by Anatoly Liberman. — Minneapolis: University of Minnesota Press, 1984. p. cm. — (Theory and history of literature. v. 5) Includes indexes. 1. Folk literature, Russian — History and criticism — Addresses, essays, lectures. 2. Tales — Soviet Union — History and criticism — Addresses, essays, lectures. 3. Tales — History and criticism — Addresses, essays, lectures. 4. Folklore — Methodology — Addresses, essays, lectures. I. Liberman, Anatoly. II. T. III. Series.
GR202.P7513 1984 398.2/0947 19 *LC* 83-14840 *ISBN* 0816611807

**Russian folklore: an anthology in English translation / by Alex** 4.798
**E. Alexander; foreword by William E. Harkins.**
Belmont, Mass.: Nordland Pub. Co., [1975] 400 p.; 23 cm. 1. Folklore — Soviet Union 2. Folk literature — Soviet Union. I. Alexander, Alex E.
GR202.R78 398.2/0947 *LC* 74-22860

**Christiansen, Reidar Thoralf, 1886- ed.** 4.799
Folktales of Norway. edited by Reidar Thorwald Christiansen. Translated by Pat Shaw Iversen. [Chicago] University of Chicago Press [1964] xlix, 284 p. (Folktales of the world) 1. Tales, Norwegian I. T.
GR221 C5 *LC* 64-15830

**Brandes, Stanley H.** 4.800
Metaphors of masculinity: sex and status in Andalusian folklore / Stanley Brandes. — [Philadelphia]: University of Pennsylvania Press, 1980. 236 p.: ill.; 24 cm. (Publications of the American Folklore Society: New Series; v. 1) Includes index. 1. Folklore — Spain — Andalusia. 2. Men — Spain — Andalusia — Folklore. 3. Sex customs — Spain — Andalusia — Folklore. 4. Masculinity (Psychology) — Folklore. 5. Andalusia (Spain) — Social life and customs. I. T.
GR237.A52 B7 398/.353/09468 *LC* 79-5258 *ISBN* 0812277767

**Walker, Warren S.** • 4.801
Tales alive in Turkey [by] Warren S. Walker & Ahmet E. Uysal. — Cambridge: Harvard University Press, 1966. xii, 310 p.: map.; 24 cm. 1. Tales — Turkey I. Uysal, Ahmet E., joint author. II. T.
GR245.W3 398.2 *LC* 66-21348

**Bulgarian folktales / edited and translated by Assen Nicoloff.** 4.802
Cleveland: Nicoloff, 1979. xxxiv, 296 p.; 22 cm. Most of the tales taken from Bŭlgarsko narodno tvorchestvo. Includes indexes. 1. Tales — Bulgaria 2. Legends — Bulgaria. I. Nicoloff, Assen.
GR253.B83 398.2/094977 *LC* 79-113484

# GR265-385 ASIA. AFRICA. OCEANIA

**Buitenen, J. A. B. van (Johannes Adrianus Bernardus van)** • 4.803
Tales of ancient India / translated from the Sanskit by J. A. B. Van Buitenen. — Chicago: University of Chicago Press, 1959. 260 p.: ill. 1. Tales, Indic. I. T.
GR305.B813 398.20934 *LC* 59-10430

**Dimock, Edward C. ed.and tr.** • 4.804
The thief of love: Bengali tales from court and village / translated by Edward C. Dimock. — Chicago: University of Chicago Press, c1963. xi, 305 p. 1. Bengalis — Folklore I. T.
GR305.D5 398.2 *LC* 63-11396

**Thompson, Stith, 1885-.** • 4.805
The oral tales of India, by Stith Thompson and Jonas Balys. Bloomington, Indiana University Press, 1958. xxvi, 448 p. map. (Indiana University publications. Folklore series, no. 10) 1. Folklore — India — Indexes 2. Folk literature, Indic — Themes, motives 3. Folk literature, Indic — Bibliography I. Balys, Jonas, 1909- jt. author II. T.
GR305 T48 *LC* 58-62883

**Sĕjarah Melayu, or, Malay annals / an annotated translation by** 4.806
**C.C. Brown; with a new introduction by R. Roolvink.**
Rev. and reset. ed. — Kuala Lumpur; Oxford: Oxford University Press, 1970 (1983 [printing]) xxxv, 273 p.: 2 maps; 22 cm. — (Oxford in Asia paperbacks) 1. Legends — Malaysia — Malaya. I. Brown, C. C. (Charles Cuthbert)
GR316.M3 398.2/095951 19 *ISBN* 0195803566

**Eberhard, Wolfram, 1909- ed. and tr.** • 4.807
[Chinese fairy tales and folk tales] Folktales of China. [Rev. ed. Chicago] University of Chicago Press [1965] xiii, 267 p. 23 cm. (Folktales of the world) First published in 1937 under title: Chinese fairy tales and folk tales. 1. Tales — China 2. Fairy tales — China. I. T.
GR335.E4 1965 398.20951 *LC* 65-25440

**Ancient tales in modern Japan: an anthology of Japanese folk** 4.808
**tales / selected and translated by Fanny Hagin Mayer.**
Bloomington: Indiana University Press, [1985?] xxi, 360 p.: ill.; 24 cm. Includes index. 1. Tales — Japan I. Mayer, Fanny Hagin, 1899-
GR340.A5 1985 398.2/0952 19 *LC* 84-47746 *ISBN* 0253307104

**Seki, Keigo, 1899- ed.** • 4.809
Folktales of Japan. Translated by Robert J. Adams. [Chicago] University of Chicago Press [1963] 221 p. 23 cm. (Folktales of the world) 1. Tales — Japan I. T.
GR340.S383 398.2 *LC* 63-13071

**African dilemma tales / [compiled by] William R. Bascom.** 4.810
The Hague: Mouton; Chicago: distributed by Aldine, c1975. xiii, 162 p.; 24 cm. — (World anthropology.) Presented at the 9th International Congress of Anthropological and Ethnological Sciences. Includes index. 1. Tales — Africa I. Bascom, William Russell, 1912- II. Series.
GR350.A34 398.2/096 *LC* 75-332990 *ISBN* 0202011402

**Diop, Birago.** 4.811
Les nouveaux contes d'Amadou Koumba. Préf. de Léopold Sédar Senghor. 3. Ed. Paris Présence Africaine [1967] 188p. (Collection 'Contes africains') 1. Tales, African I. Amadou-Koumba II. T.
GR350 D54 1967

GR
353
D89

**Dwyer, Daisy Hilse.**   **4.812**
Images and self–images: male and female in Morocco / Daisy Hilse Dwyer. — New York: Columbia University Press, 1978. xvii, 194 p.; 22 cm. Includes index. 1. Women — Morocco — Folklore. 2. Women — Morocco — Taroudant. 3. Women, Muslim — Morocco — Taroudant. 4. Tales — Morocco I. T.
GR353.3.D89    392/.6/0964    *LC* 77-27835    *ISBN* 0231043023. *ISBN* 0231043031 pbk

**Seitel, Peter.**   **4.813**
See so that we may see: performances and interpretations of traditional tales from Tanzania / Peter Seitel; from performances tape–recorded by Sheila Dauer and Peter Seitel. — Bloomington: Indiana University Press, c1980. viii, 307 p.; 24 cm. 1. Tales — Tanzania 2. Tales — Tanzania — History and criticism. 3. Haya (African people) — Folklore 4. Oral tradition — Tanzania. I. Dauer, Sheila. II. T.
GR356.72.H38 S44    398.2/09678    *LC* 79-3036    *ISBN* 0253159172

**Scheub, Harold.**   **4.814**
The Xhosa Ntsomi / Harold Scheub. — Oxford [Eng.]: Clarendon Press, 1975. x, 446 p., [2] leaves of plates: ill.; 22 cm. (Oxford library of African literature) Includes indexes. 1. Storytelling — South Africa — Transkei. 2. Storytelling — South Africa — Zululand. 3. Drama, Primitive. 4. Xosa — Folklore. 5. Tales — South Africa — Transkei. 6. Tales — South Africa — Zululand. I. T.
GR359.2.X64 S33    398/.042/0968    *LC* 76-353769    *ISBN* 0198151403

**Herskovits, Melville J. (Melville Jean), 1895-1963.**   ● **4.815**
Dahomean narrative; a cross–cultural analysis, by Melville J. and Frances S. Herskovits. Evanston [Ill.] Northwestern University Press [1958] xvi, 490 p. 24 cm. (Northwestern University (Evanston, Ill.) African studies, no. 1) 1. Fon (African people) — Folklore I. Herskovits, Frances (Shapiro), 1897- joint author. II. T. III. Series.
GR360.D3H4    398.2    *LC* 58-7312 rev

**Finnegan, Ruth H. comp.**   ● **4.816**
Limba stories and story–telling; [compiled and translated by] Ruth Finnegan. Oxford, Clarendon P., 1967. xii, 352 p. 22 1/2 cm. (Oxford library of African literature) 1. Limba (African people) — Folklore 2. Tales — Sierra Leone 3. Storytelling — Sierra Leone. I. T.
GR360.L6 F5    398.2/0966/4    *LC* 67-85735

# GR440–950 Folklore of Special Subjects

**Opie, Iona Archibald.**   ● **4.817**
The lore and language of schoolchildren / by Iona and Peter Opie. — Oxford: Clarendon Press, [1960, c1959] xviii, 417 p.: ill., maps; 25 cm. Prose and verse. 1. Children — Folklore I. Opie, Peter. joint author II. T.
GR475.O67    GR475.O6 1977.    *LC* 60-905    *ISBN* 0586083111

**Aarne, Antti Amatus, 1867-1925.**   ● **4.818**
The types of the folktale; a classification and bibliography. Antti Aarne's Verzeichnis der Märchentypen (FF communications no. 3) translated and enl. by Stith Thompson. 2d revision. Helsinki, Suomalainen Tiedeakatemia, 1961. 588 p. 25 cm. (FF communications, v. 75, n:o 184) 1. Fairy tales — Classification 2. Fairy tales — Bibliography. 3. Tales — Bibliography. I. Thompson, Stith, 1885- II. T.
GR550.Ax    016.3982    *LC* 62-5252

**Bettelheim, Bruno.**   **4.819**
The uses of enchantment: the meaning and importance of fairy tales / Bruno Bettelheim. — 1st ed. — New York: Knopf: distributed by Random House, 1976. vi, 328, xi p.; 24 cm. Includes index. 1. Fairy tales — History and criticism. 2. Psychoanalysis and folklore 3. Folklore and children 4. Children's stories — Psychological aspects. I. T.
GR550.B47 1976    398/.45    *LC* 75-36795    *ISBN* 0394497716

**Haughton, Rosemary.**   **4.820**
Tales from eternity; the world of fairytales and the spiritual search. — New York: Seabury Press, [1973] 190, [1] p.; 22 cm. — (A Continuum book) 1. Fairy tales — Moral and religious aspects. I. T.
GR550.H36    398.2    *LC* 73-6416    *ISBN* 0816491615

**Propp, V. IA. (Vladimir IAkovlevich), 1895-1970.**   ● **4.821**
[Morfologiia skazki. English] Morphology of the folktale, by V. Propp. Translated by Laurence Scott [and] with an introd. by Svatava Pirkova–Jakobson. 2d ed., rev. and edited with a pref. by Louis A. Wagner [and a] new introd. by Alan Dundes. Austin, University of Texas Press [1968] xxvi, 158 p. 24 cm. (Publications of the American Folklore Society. Bibliographical and

special series. v. 9) 'Published for the American Folklore Society and the Indiana University Research Center for Language Sciences.' Translation of Morfologiia skazki. 1. Afanas'ev, A. N. (Aleksandr Nikolaevich), 1826-1871. Narodnyia russkiia skazki. 2. Fairy tales — Classification 3. Fairy tales — Soviet Union — Classification. 4. Tales — Structural analysis 5. Tales — Soviet Union — Structural analysis. I. T. II. Series.
GR550.P7613 1968    398.21/0947    *LC* 68-65567    *ISBN* 0292783760

**Fontenrose, Joseph Eddy, 1903-.**   ● **4.822**
Python; a study of Delphic myth and its origins. Berkeley, University of California Press, 1959. xvii, 616 p. illus., plates, maps, tables. 25 cm. 1. Dragons 2. Good and evil I. T. II. Title: A study of Delphic myth and its origins.
GR830.D7F6    *LC* 59-5144

**Hand, Wayland Debs, 1907-.**   **4.823**
Magical medicine: the folkloric component of medicine in the folk belief, custom, and ritual of the peoples of Europe and America: selected essays of Wayland D. Hand / foreword by Lloyd G. Stevenson. — Berkeley: University of California Press, c1980. xxvii, 345 p.: ill.; 24 cm. 1. Folk medicine — Addresses, essays, lectures. 2. Medicine, Magic, mystic, and spagiric — Addresses, essays, lectures. 3. Folk medicine — United States — Addresses, essays, lectures. 4. Folk medicine — Europe — Addresses, essays, lectures. I. T.
GR880.H35    398/.353    *LC* 80-51238    *ISBN* 0520041291

# GT Customs. Costume

**The Invention of tradition / edited by Eric Hobsbawm and Terence Ranger.**   **4.824**
Cambridge [Cambridgeshire]; New York: Cambridge University Press, 1983. vi, 320 p.; 23 cm. (Past and present publications) 1. Manners and customs — Origin — Addresses, essays, lectures. 2. Rites and ceremonies — Origin — Addresses, essays, lectures. 3. Folklore — Addresses, essays, lectures. I. Hobsbawm, E. J. (Eric J.), 1917- II. Ranger, T. O. (Terence O.) III. Title: Tradition.
GT95.I58 1983    390 19    *LC* 82-14711    *ISBN* 0521246458

**Holmes, Urban Tigner, 1900-.**   ● **4.825**
Daily living in the twelfth century, based on the observations of Alexander Neckam in London and Paris. Madison, University of Wisconsin Press, 1952. 337 p. illus. 22 cm. 1. Neckam, Alexander, 1157-1217. 2. Civilization, Medieval — 12th century 3. London (England) — Social life and customs 4. Paris (France) — Social life and customs 5. France — Social life and customs I. T.
GT120.H64 1952    940.1/82 19    *LC* 52-62000

**Shelter, sign & symbol / edited by Paul Oliver.**   **4.826**
Woodstock: Overlook Press, 1977. 228 p.: ill., plans; 25 cm. 1. Dwellings 2. Symbolism in architecture 3. Architecture, Primitive I. Oliver, Paul, 1927-
GT170.S44    *LC* 77-77809    *ISBN* 0879510684

# GT500–2370 Dress. Costume

**Yarwood, Doreen.**   **4.827**
Encyclopedia of world costume / by Doreen Yarwood. — New York: Scribner, 1979, c1978. 471 p., [4] leaves of plates: ill. (some col.); 28 cm. Includes index. 1. Costume — Dictionaries. I. T.
GT507.Y37    391/.003    *LC* 78-3726    *ISBN* 0684158051

**Arnold, Janet.**   **4.828**
A handbook of costume. — [London]: Macmillan, [1973] 336 p.: illus.; 24 cm. 1. Costume I. T.
GT510.A75    391/.002/02    *LC* 74-154619    *ISBN* 0333124812

**Boucher, François León Louis, 1885-.**   ● **4.829**
[Histoire du costume en Occident. English] 20,000 years of fashion; the history of costume and personal adornment [by] François Boucher. New York, H. N. Abrams [1967] 441 p. illus. (part col.) fold. maps. 29 cm. Translation of Histoire du costume en Occident. 1. Costume — History I. T.
GT510.B6713 1967a    746.9/09    *LC* 66-12103

GT→
511
L39
1980

**Laver, James, 1899-.**    **4.830**
The concise history of costume and fashion. New York, H. N. Abrams [1969] 288 p. 315 illus. (58 col.) 22 cm. 1. Costume — History 2. Fashion — History. I. T.
GT510.L286 1969b    391/.009    *LC* 79-92258

**Yarwood, Doreen.**    **4.831**
Costume of the western world: pictorial guide and glossary / Doreen Yarwood. — New York: St. Martin's Press, 1980. 192 p.: ill. (some col.) 1. Costume — History I. T.
GT510.Y37    391    *LC* 80-53011    *ISBN* 0312170130

**Davenport, Millia.**    **4.832**
The book of costume. — New York: Crown Publishers, [1948] 2 v. (xii, 958 p.): illus. (part col.); 29 cm. 1. Costume — History I. T.
GT513.D38    391.09    *LC* 48-9980

**Bell, Quentin.**    **4.833**
On human finery / Quentin Bell. — 2d ed., rev. and enl. — New York: Schocken Books, 1976. 239 p., [2] col. plates: ill. 1. Costume 2. Fashion I. T.
GT521.B4 1976    GT521 B4 1976.    391    *LC* 76-9129    *ISBN* 0805236295

**Rubens, Alfred, 1903-.**    **4.834**
A history of Jewish costume. Foreword by James Laver. — New York: Crown, [1973] xvi, 221 p.: illus. (part col.); 33 cm. 1. Costume, Jewish I. T.
GT540.R73 1973    391    *LC* 73-75286    *ISBN* 0517503921

**Los Angeles County Museum of Art.**    **4.835**
An elegant art: fashion & fantasy in the eighteenth century: Los Angeles County Museum of Art collection of costumes and textiles / organized by Edward Maeder; essays by Edward Maeder ... [et al.]. — Los Angeles: Los Angeles County Museum of Art; New York: H.N. Abrams, c1983. 255 p.: ill. (some col.); 27 cm. 1. Costume — History — 18th century — Exhibitions. 2. Fashion — History — 18th century — Exhibitions. 3. Fashion and art — History — 18th century — Exhibitions. I. Maeder, Edward. II. T.
GT585.L64 1983    391/.009/033074019494 19    *LC* 82-11531    *ISBN* 0875871119

# GT601–1605 BY REGION

## GT607–625 The Americas

**McClellan, Elisabeth, 1851-1920.**    • **4.836**
[Historic dress in America] History of American costume, 1607–1870. Illustrated by Sophie B. Steel and Cecil W. Trout. With a new introd. by Robert Riley. New York: Tudor Pub. Co. [c1969] 655 p.: ill.; 25 cm. Running title: Historic dress in America. First published separately in 1904 and 1910 under title: Historic dress in America, 1607-1800 and Historic dress in America, 1800-1870, respectively. 1. Costume — United States I. T.
GT607.M22 1969    391/.00973    *LC* 68-58934

**Sayer, Chloë.**    **4.837**
Costumes of Mexico / Chloë Sayer. — 1st ed. — Austin: University of Texas Press, 1985. 240 p.: ill. (some col.); 29 cm. 'Published in co-operation with British Museum Publications.' Includes index. 1. Costume — Mexico — History. 2. Decoration and ornament — Mexico — History. 3. Textile fabrics — Mexico — History. I. T.
GT625.S29 1985    391/.00972 19    *LC* 84-51016    *ISBN* 0292710992

## GT720–737 Europe

**Squire, Geoffrey.**    **4.838**
[Dress, art, and society, 1560-1970] Dress and society, 1560–1970. New York: Viking Press [1974] 176 p. illus. (part col.) 29 cm. (A Studio book) 'Originally published in England under the title: Dress, art, and society, 1560-1970.' 1. Costume — Europe — History. I. T.
GT720.S6 1974    391/.009/03    *LC* 73-11542    *ISBN* 067028484X

**Cunnington, C. Willett (Cecil Willett), 1878-1961.**    • **4.839**
A dictionary of English costume, by C. Willett Cunnington, Phillis Cunnington and Charles Beard. With colour frontispiece and 303 line illus. by Cecil Everitt and Phillis Cunnington. New York, Barnes & Noble [1968, c1960] vi, 281 p. illus., col. port. 25 cm. 1. Costume — Great Britain — Dictionaries. I. Cunnington, Phillis Emily, 1887- joint author. II. Beard, Charles Relly, 1891-1958. joint author. III. T.
GT730.C86 1968    391/.00942    *LC* 72-28853    *ISBN* 0389041904

**Cunnington, C. Willett (Cecil Willett), 1878-1961.**    • **4.840**
Handbook of English costume in the sixteenth century, by C. Willett & Phillis Cunnington. Illus. by Barbara Phillipson. [Rev. ed.] Boston, Plays, inc. [1970] 244 p. illus. (part col.) 23 cm. 'First American edition.' 1. Costume — Great Britain. I. Cunnington, Phillis Emily, 1887- joint author. II. T.
GT730.C872 1970b    391/.00942    *LC* 78-113741    *ISBN* 0823800814

**Kelly, Francis Michael, 1879-1945.**    **4.841**
A short history of costume and armor ... / Francis M. Kelly and Randolph Schwabe. — New York: Arco, 1973. 2 v. in 1: ill.; 24 cm. Reprint of the 1931 ed. published in 2 v. by B.T. Batsford, London. 1. Costume — Great Britain — History. 2. Arms and armor, English — History. 3. Arms and armor — History. 4. Costume — History I. Schwabe, Randolph, 1885-1948. joint author. II. T.
GT730.K4 1973    391/.00942    *LC* 72-92287    *ISBN* 0668029064

**Cunnington, C. Willett (Cecil Willett), 1878-1961.**    • **4.842**
Handbook of English mediaeval costume, by C. Willett Cunnington and Phillis Cunnington. With illus. by Barbara Phillipson and Catherine Lucas. [1st American ed.] Boston, Plays, inc. [1969] 210 p. illus. (part col.) 23 cm. 1. Costume — Great Britain. 2. Costume — History — Medieval, 500-1500 I. Cunnington, Phillis Emily, 1887- joint author. II. T.
GT732.C84 1969    391    *LC* 79-78804

**Cunnington, Phillis Emily, 1887-.**    **4.843**
Charity costumes of children, scholars, almsfolk, pensioners / Phillis Cunnington, Catherine Lucas. — New York: Barnes & Noble Books, 1978. x, 331 p.: ill.; 24 cm. 1. Costume — England — History. 2. Uniforms — England. 3. Charities — England. 4. School children — England — Clothing. I. Lucas, Catherine. joint author. II. T.
GT733.C78 1978b    391/.01    *LC* 77-8742    *ISBN* 0064913465

**Cunnington, Phillis Emily, 1887-.**    **4.844**
Costume for births, marriages & deaths [by] Phillis Cunnington & Catherine Lucas. New York, Barnes & Noble [1972] 331 p. illus. 24 cm. 1. Costume — England — History. 2. Funeral rites and ceremonies — England. 3. Marriage customs and rites — England. 4. Childbirth — England — Folklore. 5. Birth customs — England. I. Lucas, Catherine. joint author. II. T.
GT733.C86 1972    391/.8    *LC* 72-190906    *ISBN* 0064913376

**Ashelford, Jane.**    **4.845**
A visual history of costume: the sixteenth century / Jane Ashelford. — London: Batsford; New York: Drama Book Publishers, 1983. 144 p.: ill.; 26 cm. Includes index. 1. Costume — England — History — 16th century. I. T.
GT733.V57 1983    391/.009 19

**Cunnington, C. Willett (Cecil Willett), 1878-1961.**    • **4.846**
Handbook of English costume in the seventeenth century, by C. Willett & Phillis Cunnington; with illustrations by Barbara Phillipson and Phillis Cunnington. 2nd ed. London, Faber, 1967. 3-222 p. col. front., illus. 23 cm. 1. Costume — Great Britain — History. 2. Costume — History — 17th century I. Cunnington, Phillis Emily, 1887- joint author. II. T.
GT735.C8 1967    391/.00942    *LC* 67-77817

**Cunnington, C. Willett (Cecil Willett), 1878-1961.**    • **4.847**
Handbook of English costume in the eighteenth century, by C. Willett Cunnington & Phillis Cunnington. With illus. by Barbara Phillipson and Phillis Cunnington. Boston, Plays [1972] 453 p. illus. 23 cm. 1. Costume — Great Britain — History. 2. Costume — History — 18th century I. Cunnington, Phillis Emily, 1887- joint author. II. T.
GT736.C8 1972    391/.00942    *LC* 72-166009    *ISBN* 0823801284

**Ribeiro, Aileen.**    **4.848**
The eighteenth century / Aieen Ribeiro. — London: Batsford; New York: Drama Book Publishers, 1983. 144 p., [8] p. of plates: ill. (some col.), ports. (some col.); 26 cm. — (A Visual history of costume) Includes index. 1. Costume — England — History — 18th century. I. T. II. Series.
GT736.R5x    391/.00942 19    *ISBN* 0713440910

**Cunnington, C. Willett (Cecil Willett), 1878-1961.**    • **4.849**
Handbook of English costume in the nineteenth century, by C. Willett Cunnington & Phillis Cunnington. Illus. by Phillis Cunnington, Cecil Everitt, and Catherine Lucas. [1st American ed.] Boston, Plays, inc. [1971, c1970] 617 p. illus. (part col.) 23 cm. 1. Costume — Great Britain. 2. Costume — History — 19th century I. Cunnington, Phillis Emily, 1887- joint author. II. T.
GT737.C814 1971    391/.00942    *LC* 72-78805    *ISBN* 0823800806

## GT1370–1580 Asia. Africa

**Fairservis, Walter Ashlin, 1921-.**    • **4.850**
Costumes of the East [by] Walter A. Fairservis, Jr. Costumes photographed by Thomas Beiswenger. Drawings by Jan Fairservis. — Riverside, Conn.:

Chatham Press; [distributed by Viking Press, New York, 1971] 160 p.: illus.; 27 cm. 1. Costume, Oriental. I. T.
GT1370.F3    391/.0095    *LC* 77-159783    *ISBN* 0856990290

**Vollmer, John E.**      **4.851**
Decoding dragons: status garments in Ch'ing Dynasty China / John E. Vollmer. — Eugene, Or.: Museum of Art, University of Oregon, 1983.— 224 p.: ill. (some col.); 26 cm. 1. Costume — China I. University of Oregon. Museum of Art. II. T.
GT1555 V64

**Fisher, Angela.**      **4.852**
Africa adorned / by Angela Fisher. — New York: Abrams, 1984. 304 p.: ill. (some col.); 37 cm. Includes index. 1. Jewelry — Africa. 2. Body-marking — Africa. I. T.
GT1580.F57 1984    391/.7/096 19    *LC* 84-6461    *ISBN* 0810918234

**Ewing, Elizabeth.**      **4.853**
History of children's costume / Elizabeth Ewing. — New York: Scribner, 1978. 191 p., [2] leaves of plates: ill. (some col.); 26 cm. Includes index. 1. Children — Costume 2. Costume — Great Britain — History. I. T.
GT1730.E88 1978    391/.07/309    *LC* 77-79905    *ISBN* 0684153572

## GT1770–2220 SPECIAL GROUPS. SPECIAL ARTICLES OF CLOTHING

**Ewing, Elizabeth.**      **4.854**
Dress and undress: a history of women's underwear / Elizabeth Ewing. — New York: Drama Book Specialists, 1978. 191 p.: ill.; 25 cm. Includes index. 1. Underwear — History. 2. Lingerie — History. I. T.
GT2073.E89    391/.42    *LC* 78-16819    *ISBN* 0896760006

**Clark, Fiona.**      **4.855**
Hats / Fiona Clark. — London: Batsford, 1982. 96 p., [4] p. of plates: ill. (some col.), ports. (some col.); 26 cm. — (Costume accessories series.) 1. Hats — History. I. T. II. Series.
GT2110    GT2110 C43.    391/.43/09 19    *ISBN* 071343774X

**Swann, June.**      **4.856**
Shoes / June Swann. — London: B. T. Batsford; New York: Drama Book [distributors], 1982. 96 p. , [4] p. of plates: ill. (some col.), ports.; 26 cm. (Costume accessories series.) Includes index. 1. Boots and shoes — History. I. T. II. Series.
GT2130.S8x    *ISBN* 0713409428

**Cumming, Valerie.**      **4.857**
Gloves / Valerie Cumming. — London: Batsford, 1982. 96 p., [4] p. of plates: ill. (soem col.), ports.; 26 cm. — (Costume accessories series.) 1. Gloves — History. I. T. II. Series.
GT2170.C8x    391/.412/09 19    *ISBN* 0713410086

**Foster, Vanda.**      **4.858**
Bags and purses / Vanda Foster. — London: B.T. Batsford: New York: distributed by Drama Book, 1982. 96 p.: ill. (some col.). — (Costume accessories series.) 1. Handbags — History. I. T. II. Series.
GT2180.F6    685.51    *ISBN* 0713437723

## GT2400–7070 Customs

**McLaren, Angus.**      **4.859**
Reproductive rituals: the perception of fertility in England from the sixteenth to the nineteenth century / Angus McLaren. — London; New York, NY: Methuen, 1985 (c1984). viii, 206 p.; 23 cm. Includes index. 1. Fertility, Human — England — History. 2. Fertility, Human — England — Folklore — History. 3. Birth control — England — History. 4. Birth control — England — Folklore — History. 5. Conception — Folklore. I. T.
GT2465.G7 M35    392/.6 19    *LC* 84-1068    *ISBN* 0416374506

**Glasse, Robert M.**      • **4.860**
Pigs, pearlshells, and women: marriage in the New Guinea highlands: a symposium / edited by R. M. Glasse and M. J. Meggitt. — Englewood Cliffs, N.J.: Prentice-Hall [1969] vii, 246 p.: ill., maps; 21 cm. 1. Marriage customs and rites — New Guinea. I. Meggitt, Mervyn J., 1924- joint author. II. T.
GT2796.N4 G55    392/.5/0995    *LC* 70-79453    *ISBN* 0136764940

**Tannahill, Reay.**      **4.861**
Food in history. — New York: Stein and Day, [1973] 448 p.: illus.; 24 cm. 1. Food — History. 2. Dinners and dining I. T.
GT2850.T34    641.3/009    *LC* 75-160342    *ISBN* 0812814371

**Food in Chinese culture: anthropological and historical perspectives** / edited by K.C. Chang; contributors, Eugene N. Anderson ... [et al.].      **4.862**
New Haven: Yale University Press, 1977. 429 p.: ill.; 24 cm. Includes index. 1. Food habits — China — History. 2. Dinners and dining — History. 3. Cookery, Chinese — History. I. Chang, Kwang-chih. II. Anderson, Eugene Newton, 1941-
GT2853.C6 F66    394.1/2/0951    *LC* 75-43312    *ISBN* 0300019386

**The Sociology of food and eating: essays on the sociological significance of food** / edited by Anne Murcott.      **4.863**
Aldershot, Hants, England: Gower, 1983. viii, 195 p.; 23 cm. — (Gower international library of research and practice.) Includes index. 1. Food habits — Great Britain — Addresses, essays, lectures. 2. Food — Social aspects — Great Britain — Addresses, essays, lectures. 3. Great Britain — Social life and customs — Addresses, essays, lectures. I. Murcott, Anne. II. Series.
GT2853.G7 S62 1983    394.1/2/0941 19    *LC* 83-123810    *ISBN* 0566005808

**Food in the social order: studies of food and festivities in three American communities** / Mary Douglas, editor.      **4.864**
New York: Russell Sage Foundation, c1984. xi, 292 p.: ill.; 24 cm. 1. Food habits — United States — Addresses, essays, lectures. I. Douglas, Mary.
GT2853.U5 F66 1984    394.1/2/0973 19    *LC* 84-60262    *ISBN* 0871542102

**Okakura, Kakuzo.**      **4.865**
The book of tea / Kakuzo Okakura; with foreword & biographical sketch by Elise Grilli. — Rutland, Vt.: Tuttle Co., 1956. 133 p.: ill. 1. Tea 2. Japan — Social life and customs I. T.
GT2910.O6 1956    394.1    *LC* 56-13134

**Mauss, Marcel, 1872-1950.**      **4.866**
The gift; forms and functions of exchange in archaic societies. Translated by Ian Cunnison. With an introduction by E. E. Evans–Pritchard. Glencoe, Ill., Free Press, 1954. xiv, 130 p. 23 cm. Translation of Essai sur le don. 1. Gifts I. T.
GT3050.M313    *LC* 54-12872

**Mitford, Jessica, 1917-.**      **4.867**
The American way of death. New York, Simon and Schuster, 1963. 333 p. 22 cm. 1. Funeral rites and ceremonies — Economic aspects — United States. 2. Undertakers and undertaking — United States. I. T.
GT3203.M5    393.0973    *LC* 63-12575

**Pine, Vanderlyn R.**      **4.868**
Caretaker of the dead: the American funeral director / by Vanderlyn R. Pine. — New York: Irvington Publishers: distributed by Halsted Press, [1975] x, 219 p.; 24 cm. Includes index. 1. Funeral rites and ceremonies — United States. 2. Undertakers and undertaking — United States. I. T.
GT3203.P56    393.1/023    *LC* 75-8687    *ISBN* 0470689927

**Danforth, Loring M., 1949-.**      **4.869**
The death rituals of rural Greece / by Loring M. Danforth; photography by Alexander Tsiaras. — Princeton, N.J.: Princeton University Press, c1982. ix, 169 p., [31] p. of plates: ill.; 24 cm. Includes index. 1. Funeral rites and ceremonies — Greece. 2. Death — Social aspects — Greece. 3. Laments — Greece. 4. Greece — Rural conditions. 5. Greece — Social life and customs I. Tsiaras, Alexander. II. T.
GT3251.A2 D36 1982    393/.09495 19    *LC* 82-47589    *ISBN* 0691031320

**Billington, Sandra.**      **4.870**
A social history of the fool / Sandra Billington. — Brighton, Sussex: Harvester Press; New York: St. Martin's Press, 1984. x, 150 p.; 23 cm. Includes index. 1. Fools and jesters — England — History. 2. Fools and jesters in literature I. T.
GT3670.B45 1984    306/.48 19    *LC* 83-40624    *ISBN* 0312732937

**Rice, Kym S.**      **4.871**
Early American taverns: for the entertainment of friends and strangers / by Kym S. Rice for Fraunces Tavern Museums. — Chicago: Regnery Gateway, c1983. xviii, 168 p.: ill.; 28 cm. 'Published in association with Fraunces Tavern Museum.' Includes index. 1. Hotels, taverns, etc — United States — History. 2. Amusements — United States — History. 3. United States — Social life and customs — Colonial period, ca. 1600-1775 4. United States — Popular culture — History. I. Fraunces Tavern Museum. II. T.
GT3803.R5 1983    647/.9573 19    *LC* 82-42786    *ISBN* 0895268426

**Gregory, Ruth W. (Ruth Wilhelme), 1910-.**      **4.872**
Anniversaries and holidays / by Ruth W. Gregory. — 4th ed. — Chicago: American Library Association, c1983. xiii, 262 p.; 27 cm. Includes index.

1. Holidays 2. Anniversaries 3. Fasts and feasts 4. Holidays — Bibliography. 5. Anniversaries — Bibliography. 6. Fasts and feasts — Bibliography. I. T.
GT3930.G74 1983      394.2/6 19      *LC* 83-3784      *ISBN* 0838903894

**Hatch, Jane M.**          **4.873**
The American book of days / compiled and edited by Jane M. Hatch. — 3d ed. — New York: Wilson, 1978. xxvi, 1214 p.; 26 cm. Based on the earlier editions by G. W. Douglas. Includes index. 1. Holidays — United States 2. Fasts and feasts — United States. 3. Festivals — United States I. Douglas, George William, 1863-1945. The American book of days. II. T.
GT4803.D6 1978      394.2/6973      *LC* 78-16239      *ISBN* 0824205936

**Scullard, H. H. (Howard Hayes), 1903-.**      **4.874**
Festivals and ceremonies of the Roman Republic / H.H. Scullard. — Ithaca, N.Y.: Cornell University Press, 1981. 288 p.: ill.; 23 cm. — (Aspects of Greek and Roman life) 1. Festivals — Rome. 2. Rites and ceremonies — Rome. 3. Games — Rome. 4. Rome — Religious life and customs. 5. Rome — Social life and customs. I. T.
GT4852.R6 S35      394.2/6937 19      *LC* 80-70447      *ISBN* 0801414024

**Redfield, Robert, 1897-.**      • **4.875**
Peasant society and culture; an anthropological approach to civilization. — [Chicago] University of Chicago Press [1956] 162 p. 20 cm. 1. Peasantry I. T.
GT5650.R4      323.33      *LC* 56-6644 rev

HM
131
R31

# GV Recreation. Physical Training. Sports. Games. Dancing

## GV1–191 RECREATION. LEISURE

**Cheek, Neil H.** 4.876
The social organization of leisure in human society / Neil H. Cheek, Jr., William R. Burch, Jr. New York: Harper & Row, c1976. xx, 283 p.; 24 cm. Includes index. 1. Leisure 2. Recreation I. Burch, William R., 1933- joint author. II. T.
GV14.C47    301.5/7    *LC* 76-20582    *ISBN* 006041037X

**Nash, Jay Bryan, 1886-.** • 4.877
Philosophy of recreation and leisure / Jay B. Nash. — Dubuque, Iowa: W.C. Brown, [1960]. 222 p.: ill.; 24 cm. 1. Recreation I. T.
GV14.N25 1960    *LC* 60-16532

**Falkener, Edward, 1814-1896.** • 4.878
Games ancient and oriental: and how to play them; being the games of the ancient Egyptians, the hiera gramme of the Greeks, the ludus iatrunculorum of the Romans, and the oriental games of chess, draughts, backgrammon and magic squares / by Edward Falkener. — New York: Dover, 1961. 366 p.: ill.; 21 cm. "Unabridged and corrected republication of the work first published in 1892." 1. Games, Oriental. 2. Games — Greece 3. Chess 4. Magic squares I. T.
GV15.F2 1961    794.093    *LC* 61-1636    *ISBN* 0486207390

**Harris, Harold Arthur.** • 4.879
Greek athletes and athletics [by] H. A. Harris. With an introd. by the Marquess of Exeter. — Bloomington: Indiana University Press, [1966, c1964] 244 p.: illus., maps.; 24 cm. 1. Athletics — Greece. 2. Athletes — Greece. I. T.
GV21.H3 1966    796.0938    *LC* 66-22440

**Kieran, John, 1892-.** 4.880
The story of the Olympic games: 776 B.C. to 1976 / by John Kieran, Arthur Daley, and Pat Jordan. Rev. ed. — Philadelphia: Lippincott, 1977. 575 p., [20] leaves of plates: ill.; 22 cm. Includes index. 1. Olympic games. I. Daley, Arthur. joint author. II. Jordan, Pat. joint author. III. T.
GV23.K5 1977    796.4/8/09    *LC* 76-56106    *ISBN* 0397011687

**Denney, Reuel, 1913-.** • 4.881
The astonished muse. — [Chicago]: University of Chicago Press, [1957] 264 p.; 23 cm. 1. Recreation 2. Leisure I. T.
GV45.D4    790    *LC* 57-6985

**Edwards, Harry, 1942-.** 4.882
The revolt of the black athlete. With a foreword by Samuel J. Skinner, Jr. New York, Free Press [1969] xx, 202 p. illus., ports. 22 cm. 1. Afro-American athletes I. T.
GV53.E34    796/.09174/96    *LC* 70-85475

**Where does the time go?: the United Media Enterprises report** 4.883
**on leisure in America / conducted by Research & Forecasts, Inc.**
New York: Newspaper Enterprise Association, 1983. viii, 182 p. Sponsored by United Media Enterprises, a Scripps-Howard Company On spine: The United Media Enterprises report on leisure in America. 1. Leisure — United States. I. United Media Enterprises II. Research & Forecasts, Inc. III. Title: The United Media Enterprises report on leisure in America
GV53.W44    *LC* 83-60420    *ISBN* 091510623X

**Bailey, Peter, 1937-.** 4.884
Leisure and class in Victorian England: rational recreation and the contest for control, 1830–1885 / Peter Bailey. — London: Routledge & K. Paul; Buffalo: University of Toronto Press, 1978. x, 260 p.; 22 cm. — (Studies in social history) Revision of the author's thesis, University of British Columbia, 1974. Includes index. 1. Recreation — Great Britain — History — 19th century. 2. Labor and laboring classes — Great Britain — Recreation — History — 19th century. 3. Middle classes — Great Britain — Recreation — History — 19th century. I. T.
GV75.B33 1978    301.5/7/0941    *LC* 78-40390    *ISBN* 0802022588

**Sutton-Smith, Brian.** 4.885
A history of children's play: New Zealand, 1840–1950 / Brian Sutton–Smith. — Philadelphia: University of Pennsylvania Press, 1981. xvi, 331 p.: ill.; 24 cm. Includes index. 1. Play — New Zealand — History. I. T.
GV149.S87 1981    790.1/922/09931 19    *LC* 81-51140    *ISBN* 0812278089

**Butler, George D. (George Daniel), 1893-.** 4.886
Introduction to community recreation: prepared for the National Recreation and Park Association / George D. Butler. — 5th ed. — New York: McGraw-Hill, [1976] xiv, 538 p.: ill.; 24 cm. Includes index. 1. Recreation — United States 2. Playgrounds — United States. I. National Recreation and Park Association. II. T.
GV171.B85 1976    790/.0973    *LC* 75-9650    *ISBN* 007009361X

**Niepoth, E. William, 1928-.** 4.887
Leisure leadership: working with people in recreation and park settings / E. William Niepoth. — Englewood Cliffs, N.J.: Prentice-Hall, c1983. xv, 380 p.; 24 cm. 1. Recreation leadership I. T.
GV181.4.N53 1983    790/.023 19    *LC* 82-18118    *ISBN* 0135300711

**Shivers, Jay Sanford, 1930-.** 4.888
Recreational leadership: group dynamics and interpersonal behavior / Jay S. Shivers. — Princeton, N.J.: Princeton Book Co., c1980. ix, 268 p.; 25 cm. 1. Recreation leadership I. T.
GV181.4.S54    790 19    *LC* 79-92381    *ISBN* 0916622177

**Recreation planning and management / edited by Stanley R.** 4.889
**Lieber and Daniel R. Fesenmaier.**
State College, Pa.: Venture Pub., c1983. viii, 396 p.: ill.; 23 cm. 1. Recreation — Management — Addresses, essays, lectures. 2. Leisure — Planning — Addresses, essays, lectures. 3. Outdoor recreation — Addresses, essays, lectures. 4. Recreation — United States — Planning — Addresses, essays, lectures. I. Lieber, Stanley R. II. Fesenmaier, Daniel R.
GV181.5.R43 1983    333.78/0973 19    *LC* 82-50955    *ISBN* 0910251037

**Bannon, Joseph J.** 4.890
Leisure resources, its comprehensive planning / Joseph J. Bannon. — Englewood Cliffs, N.J.: Prentice-Hall, c1976. xxii, 454 p.: ill.; 24 cm. 1. Recreation — Management 2. City planning I. T.
GV182.15.B36    711/.4    *LC* 75-30512    *ISBN* 013528208X

**Wurman, Richard Saul, 1935-.** 4.891
The nature of recreation; a handbook in honor of Frederick Law Olmsted, using examples from his work [by] Richard Saul Wurman, Alan Levy [and] Joel Katz, with Jean McClintock and Howard Brunner. Cambridge, Mass., MIT Press for the American Federation of Arts, 1972. 76 p. illus. 24 x 31 cm. 1. Olmsted, Frederick Law, 1822-1903. 2. Outdoor recreation 3. Outdoor life 4. Parks I. Levy, Alan, 1932 Feb. 21- joint author. II. Katz, Joel, 1943- joint author. III. T.
GV182.2.W87    790/.013    *LC* 72-8898    *ISBN* 0262230631 *ISBN* 0262730340

## GV191.2–200.5 OUTDOOR LIFE. OUTDOOR RECREATION

**Jensen, Clayne R.** 4.892
Outdoor recreation in America / Clayne R. Jensen. — 4th ed. — Minneapolis, Minn.: Burgess Pub. Co., c1985. vi, 412 p.: ill.; 25 cm. 1. Outdoor recreation — United States. 2. Outdoor recreation — United States — Management. 3. Outdoor recreation — Government policy — United States. 4. Natural resources — United States I. T.
GV191.4.J46 1985    790/.0973 19    *LC* 84-7709    *ISBN* 0808710826

**Brockman, C. Frank (Christian Frank), 1902-.** 4.893
Recreational use of wild lands / C. Frank Brockman, Lawrence C. Merriam, Jr., with two specially prepared chapters by William R. Catton, Jr., Barney Dowdle. — 3d ed. — New York: McGraw-Hill, c1979. xiv, 337 p.: ill.; 24 cm. (McGraw-Hill series in forest resources) 1. Wilderness areas — Recreational

use 2. Recreation areas — Management. 3. Recreation leadership 4. National parks and reserves I. Merriam, Lawrence C. joint author. II. T.
GV191.67.W5 B76 1979    333.7/8    *LC* 78-15712    *ISBN*
007007982X

**Jones, Chris, 1939-.**                                                                  **4.894**
Climbing in North America / Chris Jones. Berkeley: Published for the American Alpine Club by the University of California Press, c1976. x, 392 p.: ill.; 23 cm. 1. Mountaineering — North America — History. 2. Rock climbing — North America — History. I. T.
GV199.44.N67 J66    796.5/22/097    *LC* 75-3771    *ISBN* 0520029763

**Fletcher, Colin.**                                                                      **4.895**
The complete walker III: the joys and techniques of hiking and backpacking / Colin Fletcher; illustrations by Vanna Prince. — 3rd ed., rev., enl., and updated. — New York: Knopf, 1984. xiv, 668 p.: ill.; 24 cm. Rev. ed. of: The new complete walker. 2nd ed., rev., enl., and updated. 1974. Includes index. 1. Backpacking 2. Hiking I. Fletcher, Colin. New complete walker. II. T. III. Title: Complete walker 3.
GV199.6.F53 1984    796.5/1 19    *LC* 83-48870    *ISBN* 0394722647

**Hart, John, 1948-.**                                                                    **4.896**
Walking softly in the wilderness: the Sierra Club guide to backpacking / John Hart. — San Francisco: Sierra Club Books, 1977. 436 p.: ill.; 21 cm. Includes index. 1. Backpacking I. Sierra Club. II. T.
GV199.6.H37    796.5    *LC* 76-21620    *ISBN* 0871561913

**Loughman, Michael, 1938-.**                                                             **4.897**
Learning to rock climb / by Michael Loughman; photos. by the author; drawings by Rose Craig. — San Francisco: Sierra Club Books, c1981. ix, 141 p.: ill.; 30 cm. Includes index. 1. Rock climbing I. T.
GV200.2.L68    796.5/223 19    *LC* 80-28639    *ISBN* 0871562790

---

# GV201–555 PHYSICAL TRAINING

---

**Van Dalen, Deobold B., 1911-.**                                                         **4.898**
A world history of physical education: cultural, philosophical, comparative [by] Deobold B. Van Dalen [and] Bruce L. Bennett. — 2d ed. — Englewood Cliffs, N.J.: Prentice Hall, [1971] x, 694 p.; 25 cm. 1. Physical education and training — History. I. Bennett, Bruce Lanyon, 1917- joint author. II. T.
GV211.V35 1971    613.7    *LC* 71-128341    *ISBN* 0139679197

**Lee, Mabel, 1886-.**                                                                    **4.899**
A history of physical education and sports in the U.S.A. / Mabel Lee. — New York: Wiley, c1983. xiv, 399 p.: ill.; 24 cm. 1. Physical education and training — United States — History. 2. School sports — United States — History. 3. Physical education teachers — United States — Biography. 4. Physical education for women — United States — History. 5. Sports for women — United States — History. I. T.
GV223.L43 1983    613.7/0973 19    *LC* 82-24746    *ISBN* 0471863157

**Bucher, Charles Augustus, 1912-.**                                                      **4.900**
Foundations of physical education and sport / Charles A. Bucher, Deborah A. Wuest. — 10th ed. — St. Louis: Times Mirror/Mosby College Pub., 1987. xiii, 385 ill.; 165 ill.; 24 cm. 1. Physical education and training 2. Sports 3. Physical education and training — Vocational guidance. 4. Sports — Vocational guidance. I. Wuest, Deborah A. II. T.
GV341.B86 1987    613.7 19    *LC* 86-12875    *ISBN* 0801608856

**Education in the 80's—physical education / Celeste Ulrich,**                            **4.901**
**editor; classroom teacher consultant, Jeffrey L. McCarley.**
Washington, D.C.: National Education Association, c1982. 103 p.; 23 cm. — (Education in the 80's.) 1. Physical education and training — Addresses, essays, lectures. I. Ulrich, Celeste. II. Title: Education in the eighties— physical education. III. Series.
GV341.E36 1982    613.7/07 19    *LC* 81-22296    *ISBN* 0810631601

**Wilmore, Jack H., 1938-.**                                                              **4.902**
Athletic training and physical fitness: physiological principles and practices of the conditioning process / Jack H. Wilmore. — Boston: Allyn and Bacon, 1977 (c1976). iv, 266 p.: ill.; 25 cm. Rev. ed. published as: Training for sport and activity. 1. Physical education and training I. T.
GV341.W577    613.7/1    *LC* 76-50449    *ISBN* 020505630X

**International Congress of Sport Psychology, 2d, Washington,**                           **• 4.903**
**D.C., 1968.**
Contemporary psychology of sport. Gerald S. Kenyon, editor. Tom M. Grogg, associate editor. — [Rome?]: International Society of Sport Psychology; [sold by Athletic Institute, Chicago, 1970] xix, 878 p.: illus.; 23 cm. 'Proceedings of the Second International Congress of Sport Psychology held in Washington,

D.C., Oct. 29-Nov. 2, 1968.' 1. Physical education and training — Philosophy — Congresses. 2. Sports — Psychological aspects — Congresses. I. Kenyon, Gerald S. ed. II. Grogg, Tom M., ed. III. T.
GV342.I57 1968    796/.01    *LC* 78-116420    *ISBN* 0876708602

**Martens, Rainer, 1942-.**                                                               **4.904**
Social psychology and physical activity. — New York: Harper & Row, [1975] xi, 180 p.: illus.; 21 cm. — (Harper's series on scientific perspectives of physical education) 1. Physical education and training — Psychological aspects. 2. Sports — Social aspects. 3. Socialization 4. Social interaction I. T.
GV342.M258    613.7/01/9    *LC* 74-7674    *ISBN* 006044231X

**The Organization and administration of physical education /**                          **4.905**
**Edward F. Voltmer ... [et al.].**
5th ed. — Englewood Cliffs, N.J.: Prentice-Hall, c1979. xii, 480 p.: ill.; 24 cm. First-4th ed., by E. F. Voltmer and A. A. Esslinger. 1. Physical education and training — Administration. I. Voltmer, Edward Frank. Organization and administration of physical education.
GV343.5.V67 1979    375/.6137 19    *LC* 78-18724    *ISBN*
0136411002

**Sports safety: accident prevention and injury control in physical**                    **• 4.906**
**education, athletics, and recreation.**
[Washington: Division of Safety Education, American Association for Health, Physical Education, and Recreation, 1971] xiii, 322 p.: ill.; 27 cm. 'Prepared under contract PH 86-67-260 Department of Health, Education, and Welfare, Public Health Service, Bureau of Community Environmental Management (Injury Control)' 1. Sports — Safety measures I. Yost, Charles Peter, 1922- ed. II. American Association for Health, Physical Education, and Recreation. Division of Safety Education.
GV344.S65    614.8/77    *LC* 74-30228

**Fuoss, Donald E.**                                                                      **4.907**
Creative management techniques in interscholastic athletics / Donald E. Fuoss, Robert J. Troppmann. New York: Wiley, c1977. xviii, 494 p.; 24 cm. 1. School sports — Management. I. Troppmann, Robert. joint author. II. T.
GV346.F86    375/.6137    *LC* 76-46500    *ISBN* 0471288152

**Mangan, J. A.**                                                                         **4.908**
Athleticism in the Victorian and Edwardian public school: the emergence and consolidation of an educational ideology / J. A. Mangan. — Cambridge [Eng.]; New York: Cambridge University Press, 1981. xv, 345 p.: ill.; 24 cm. Includes index. 1. School sports — Great Britain — History. 2. Public schools, Endowed (Great Britain) — History. I. T.
GV346.M36    796/.07/1242 19    *LC* 80-41516    *ISBN* 0521233887

**VanderZwaag, Harold J.**                                                                **4.909**
Sport management in schools and colleges / Harold J. VanderZwaag. — New York; Toronto: Wiley, c1984. xviii, 265 p.: ill.; 24 cm. 1. School sports — Management. 2. Sports — Organization and administration 3. School sports — United States — Management. 4. Sports — Organization and administration — United States. I. T.
GV346.V36 1984    796/.07/1173 19    *LC* 83-14763    *ISBN*
0471871354

**Sport and higher education / Donald Chu, Jeffrey O. Segrave &**                         **4.910**
**Beverly J. Becker, editors.**
Champaign, IL: Human Kinetics Publishers, c1985. xv, 423 p.; 24 cm. 1. College sports — United States — Addresses, essays, lectures. I. Chu, Donald. II. Segrave, Jeffrey. III. Becker, Beverly J., 1930-
GV351.S66 1985    796/.07/1173 19    *LC* 85-143    *ISBN* 0087322005

**Bucher, Charles Augustus, 1912-.**                                                      **4.911**
Methods and materials for secondary school physical education / Charles A. Bucher, Constance R. Koenig. — 6th ed. — St. Louis: Mosby, 1983. vii, 454 p.: ill.; 25 cm. 1. Physical education and training — Teacher training 2. Physical education and training — Study and teaching (Secondary) I. Koenig, Constance R. II. T.
GV363.B73 1983    613.7/07/12 19    *LC* 82-2243    *ISBN* 0801608740

**Bengtsson, Arvid.**                                                                     **4.912**
Adventure playgrounds / edited by Arvid Bengtsson. — New York: Praeger Publishers, [1972] 167 p.: ill.; 25 cm. 1. Playgrounds I. T.
GV424.B4    796/.068    *LC* 76-186478

**Mathews, Donald K.**                                                                    **4.913**
Measurement in physical education / Donald K. Mathews; ill. by Nancy Allison Close. — 5th ed. — Philadelphia: Saunders, 1978. x, 495 p.: ill.; 25 cm. 1. Physical fitness — Testing 2. Physical education and training I. T.
GV436.M37 1978    613.7    *LC* 77-24002    *ISBN* 0721661785

**Dauer, Victor Paul, 1909-.**                                                            **4.914**
Dynamic physical education for elementary school children / Victor P. Dauer, Robert P. Pangrazi. — 8th ed. — Edina, MN: Burgess Pub., c1986. xiii, 600 p.: ill.; 29 cm. 1. Physical education for children — United States. 2. Physical education for children — United States — Curricula. 3. Physical education for

children — Study and teaching — United States. 4. Child development — United States. I. Pangrazi, Robert P. II. T.
GV443.D32 1986    372.8/6/0973 19    *LC* 85-29071    *ISBN* 0808744445

**Daniels, Arthur Simpson.**      **4.915**
Adapted physical education / Arthur S. Daniels, Evelyn A. Davies. 3d ed. — New York: Harper & Row, [1975] xiii, 443 p.; 24 cm. (Harper's series in school and public health education, physical education, and recreation) 1. Physical education for handicapped persons I. Davies, Evelyn A., joint author. II. T.
GV445.D3 1975    371.9/044    *LC* 74-15933    *ISBN* 0060414928

**Masters, Lowell F.**      **4.916**
Adapted physical education: a practitioner's guide / Lowell F. Masters, Allen A. Mori, Ernest K. Lange. — Rockville, Md.: Aspen Systems Corp., 1983. xi, 387 p.: ill.; 24 cm. Includes index. 1. Physical education for handicapped persons I. Mori, Allen A. II. Lange, Ernest K. III. T.
GV445.M28 1983    371.9/044 19    *LC* 82-20672    *ISBN* 0894436694

**Fowler, John Stuart.**      **4.917**
Movement education / John S. Fowler. — Philadelphia: Saunders College Pub., c1981. ix, 341 p.: ill.; 25 cm. — (Saunders series in physical education.) 1. Movement education — Curricula. I. T. II. Series.
GV452.F68    372.8/6044 19    *LC* 80-53928    *ISBN* 0030578817

# GV460–555 Gymnastics. Exercises

**Boone, William T., 1944-.**      **4.918**
Better gymnastics: how to spot the performer / William T. Boone. — Mountain View, Calif.: World Publications, c1979. 221 p.: ill.; 28 cm. 1. Gymnastics — Safety measures. 2. Gymnastics — Study and teaching. I. T.
GV461.B63    796.4/1    *LC* 78-368    *ISBN* 089037127X

**Gymnastics guide / edited by Hal Straus.**      **4.919**
Mountain View, Calif.: World Publications, c1978. xiii, 384 p.: ill.; 22 cm. Includes index. 1. Gymnastics — Addresses, essays, lectures. 2. Gymnastics — Biography — Addresses, essays, lectures. I. Straus, Hal.
GV461.G9    796.4/1/0922 B    *LC* 78-55790    *ISBN* 0890371393

**Mauldon, Elizabeth.**      **4.920**
[Teaching gymnastics] Teaching gymnastics and body control [by] E. Mauldon [and] J. Layson. [1st American ed.] Boston, Plays, inc. [1975, c1965] xiv, 192 p. illus. 23 cm. First published in 1965 under title: Teaching gymnastics. 1. Gymnastics — Study and teaching. I. Layson, June. joint author. II. T.
GV461.M39 1975    796.4/1    *LC* 74-13397    *ISBN* 0823801764

**United States Gymnastics Safety Association.**      **4.921**
Gymnastics safety manual: the official manual of the United States Gymnastics Safety Association / [et al.]; contributors to text, Norman Barnes ... Eugene Wettstone, editor, with the assistance of Raleigh DeGeer Amyx ... [et al.]; drawings in text by C. K. Bingham]. — 2d ed. — University Park: Pennsylvania State University Press, 1979. 147 p.: ill.; 23 cm. 1. Gymnastics 2. Gymnastics — Safety measures. I. Barnes, Norman. II. Wettstone, Eugene. III. Amyx, Raleigh DeGeer. IV. T.
GV461.U53 1979    796.4/1/0289    *LC* 80-105595    *ISBN* 0271002425

**George, Gerald S.**      **4.922**
Biomechanics of women's gymnastics / Gerald S. George. — Englewood Cliffs, N.J.: Prentice-Hall, c1980. xv, 221 p.: ill.; 25 cm. Includes index. 1. Gymnastics for women — Physiological aspects. I. T.
GV464.G46    796.4/1    *LC* 79-18854    *ISBN* 0130774618

**Murray, Mimi.**      **4.923**
Women's gymnastics: coach, participant, spectator / Mimi Murray. — Boston: Allyn and Bacon, c1979. xiv, 289 p.: ill.; 24 cm. Includes index. 1. Gymnastics for women I. T.
GV464.M87    796.4/1    *LC* 78-11569    *ISBN* 0205061621

**Schmid, Andrea Bodó.**      **4.924**
Modern rhythmic gymnastics / Andrea Bodo Schmid. 1st ed. — Palo Alto, Calif.: Mayfield Pub. Co., 1976. ix, 379 p.: ill.; 23 cm. 1. Gymnastics for women I. T.
GV464.S32    796.4/1    *LC* 75-21074    *ISBN* 0874842816

**Reid, J. Gavin.**      **4.925**
Exercise prescription for fitness / J. Gavin Reid, John M. Thomson. — Englewood Cliffs, N.J.: Prentice-Hall, c1985. xii, 255 p.: ill.; 24 cm. 1. Exercise 2. Exercise — Physiological aspects 3. Physical fitness I. Thomson, John M., 1937- II. T.
GV481.R44 1985    613.7/1 19    *LC* 84-18084    *ISBN* 0132946386

# GV561–1195 Sports

**Encyclopedia of physical education, fitness, and sports / Thomas**      **4.926**
**K. Cureton, Jr., series editor; sponsored by the American**
**Alliance for Health, Physical Education, and Recreation.**
Salt Lake City, Utah: Brighton Pub. Co., 1981. 721 p.: ill.; 25 cm. 1. Sports — Dictionaries. 2. Physical education and training — Dictionaries. I. Cureton, Thomas Kirk, 1901-
GV567.E49    796/.03    *LC* 76-46608    *ISBN* 0201010771

**Menke, Frank Grant, 1885-1954.**      **4.927**
The encyclopedia of sports / Frank G. Menke. — 6th rev. ed. / revisions by Pete Palmer. — South Brunswick [N.J.]: A. S. Barnes, 1978, c1977. 1132 p.: ill.; 25 cm. Includes index. 1. Sports — Dictionaries. I. Palmer, Pete. II. T.
GV567.M46 1978    796/.03    *LC* 76-58581    *ISBN* 0498021149

**Webster's sports dictionary.**      **4.928**
Springfield, Mass.: G. & C. Merriam, c1976. 8, 503 p.: ill.; 25 cm. 1. Sports — Dictionaries. I. Title: Sports dictionary.
GV567.W37    796/.03    *LC* 75-42076    *ISBN* 0877790671

**Baker, William J. (William Joseph), 1938-.**      **4.929**
Sports in the Western world / William J. Baker. — Totowa, N.J.: Rowman and Littlefield, 1982. viii, 360 p.: ill.; 25 cm. Includes index. 1. Sports — History I. T.
GV571.B25 1982    796/.09 19    *LC* 82-3669    *ISBN* 0847670759

**Harris, Harold Arthur.**      **4.930**
Sport in Greece and Rome [by] H. A. Harris. — Ithaca, N.Y.: Cornell University Press, [1972] 288 p.: ill.; 23 cm. — (Aspects of Greek and Roman life) 1. Sports — Greece. 2. Sports — Rome. I. T. II. Series.
GV573.H3    796/.0938    *LC* 77-39824    *ISBN* 0801407184

**Berry, Robert C.**      **4.931**
Labor relations in professional sports / Robert C. Berry, William B. Gould IV, Paul D. Staudohar. — Dover, Mass.: Auburn House Pub. Co., c1986. xii, 289 p.; 25 cm. 1. Professional sports — Economic aspects — United States. 2. Professional sports — United States — Contracts. 3. Professional sports — Law and legislation — United States. 4. Collective bargaining — Sports — United States. I. Gould, William B. II. Staudohar, Paul D. III. T.
GV583.B46 1986    331.88/11796/0973 19    *LC* 85-26806    *ISBN* 0865691371

**Betts, John Rickards, 1917-1971.**      **4.932**
America's sporting heritage, 1850–1950 / John Rickards Betts. — Reading, Mass.: Addison-Wesley Pub. Co., [1974] xv, 428 p.: ill.; 25 cm. (Addison-Wesley series in social significance of sports) Includes index. 1. Sports — United States — History. I. T.
GV583.B47    796/.0973    *LC* 73-10590    *ISBN* 0201005573

**Cozens, Frederick Warren, 1890-.**      **• 4.933**
Sports in American life / by Frederick W. Cozens and Florence Scovil Stumpf. — Chicago: University of Chicago Press, 1953. 366 p.; 22 cm. 1. Sports — United States. I. Stumpf, Florence Scovil. II. T.
GV583.C68    *LC* 53-12897

**Government and the sports business; papers prepared for a**      **4.934**
**conference of experts, with an introduction and summary. Roger**
**G. Noll, editor.**
Washington, D.C.: Brookings Institution, [1974] xiv, 445 p.: illus.; 24 cm. — (Studies in the regulation of economic activity) 1. Sports and state — United States — Congresses. 2. Sports — United States — Congresses. I. Noll, Roger G. ed. II. Series.
GV583.G68 1974    338.4/7/7960973    *LC* 74-4371    *ISBN* 0815761066

**Michener, James A. (James Albert), 1907-.**      **4.935**
Sports in America / James A. Michener. — 1st ed. — New York: Random House, c1976. 466 p.; 24 cm. Includes index. 1. Sports — United States. 2. Physical education and training — United States. I. T.
GV583.M5    796/.0973    *LC* 75-40549    *ISBN* 039440646X

**Mrozek, Donald J.**      **4.936**
Sport and American mentality, 1880–1910 / Donald J. Mrozek. — Knoxville: University of Tennessee Press, c1983. xx, 284 p.: ill.; 22 cm. Includes index. 1. Sports — United States — History. 2. Sports — Social aspects — United States. 3. National characteristics, American — History. 4. Social values — History. I. T.
GV583.M76 1983    796/.0973 19    *LC* 83-3667    *ISBN* 0870493949

# GV742 Mass Media and Sports

**Rader, Benjamin G.**      **4.981**
In its own image: how television has transformed sports / Benjamin G. Rader. — New York: Free Press; London: Collier Macmillan, c1984. ix, 228 p.; 24 cm. Includes index. 1. Television broadcasting of sports — United States — History. 2. Sports — United States — History. I. T.
GV742.3.R33 1984    070.4/49796/0973 19    *LC* 84-47856    *ISBN* 002925700X

**Killanin, Michael Morris, Baron, 1914-.**      **4.982**
My Olympic years / by Lord Killanin. — 1st U.S. ed. — New York: Morrow, 1983. 240 p.: ill.; 25 cm. Includes index. 1. Killanin, Michael Morris, Baron, 1914- 2. International Olympic Committee — Presidents — Biography. 3. Olympic Games — History. 4. Sports promoters — Ireland — Biography. I. T.
GV742.42.K54 A35 1983    796.4/8/0924 B 19    *LC* 83-61562    *ISBN* 068802209X

# GV750–1195 Particular Sports

## GV770.3–840 Water Sports

**Bridge, Raymond.**      **4.983**
The complete canoeist's guide / Raymond Bridge. — New York: Scribner, c1978. 301 p.: ill.; 21 cm. Includes index. 1. Canoes and canoeing 2. Whitewater canoeing I. T.
GV783.B65    797.1/22    *LC* 77-27865    *ISBN* 0684153696

**Sandreuter, William O.**      **4.984**
Whitewater canoeing / William O. Sandreuter. — New York: Winchester Press, c1976. xiii, 208 p.: ill.; 24 cm. Includes index. 1. White-water canoeing I. T.
GV788.S26    797.1/22    *LC* 75-34448    *ISBN* 0876912234

**Kiesling, Stephen.**      **4.985**
The shell game: reflections on rowing and the pursuit of excellence / Stephen Kiesling. — 1st ed. — New York: Morrow, 1982. 200 p.; 22 cm. 1. Kiesling, Stephen. 2. Yale University — Rowing. 3. Rowers — United States — Biography. I. T.
GV790.92.K53 A37    797.1/23/0924 B 19    *LC* 81-14187    *ISBN* 0688009581

**Shields, Cornelius, 1895-.**      **4.986**
Racing with Cornelius Shields and the masters. — Rev. ed. — Englewood Cliffs, N.J.: Prentice-Hall, [1974] xvi, 352 p.: ill.; 25 cm. 'Revision of Cornelius Shields On sailing.' 1. Yacht racing 2. Sailing I. T.
GV826.5.S53 1974    797.1/4    *LC* 74-9744    *ISBN* 0137502249

**Armbruster, David Alvin, 1890-.**      • **4.987**
[Competitive swimming and diving] Swimming and diving [by] David A. Armbruster, Robert H. Allen [and] Hobert Sherwood Billingsley. 5th ed. St. Louis, Mosby, 1968. ix, 372 p. illus., plans. 25 cm. First ed. published in 1942 under title: Competitive swimming and diving. 1. Swimming 2. Diving I. Allen, Robert H., joint author. II. Billingsley, Hobert Sherwood. joint author. III. T.
GV837.A65 1968    797.2    *LC* 68-11233

**Besford, Pat.**      **4.988**
Encyclopaedia of swimming / compiled by Pat Besford. — 2d ed. — London: R. Hale; New York: St. Martin's Press, 1976. 302 p., [8] leaves of plates: ill.; 23 cm. Includes index. 1. Swimming — Dictionaries. I. T.
GV837.B44 1976    797.2/1/03    *LC* 76-16687    *ISBN* 0709150636

**Counsilman, James E.**      **4.989**
The complete book of swimming / James E. Counsilman. 1st ed. — New York: Atheneum, 1977. ix, 178 p.: ill.; 22 cm. 1. Swimming I. T.
GV837.C79 1977    797.2/1    *LC* 72-82682    *ISBN* 0689105304

**Maglischo, Ernest W.**      **4.990**
Swimming faster: a comprehensive guide to the science of swimming / Ernest W. Maglischo. — 1st ed. — Palo Alto, Calif.: Mayfield Pub. Co., 1982. xxi, 472 p.: ill.; 25 cm. 1. Swimming — Training 2. Swimming — Physiological aspects. I. T.
GV838.67.M33 1982    797.2/1 19    *LC* 81-81278    *ISBN* 0874845483

**Ketels, Henry.**      **4.991**
Safe skin and scuba diving: adventure in the underwater world / by Henry Ketels and Jack McDowell; foreword, Glen Egstrom; ill., Joseph P. McLelland. — Boston: Educational Associates, [1975] vi, 234 p.: ill.; 24 cm. Includes index. 1. Skin diving 2. Scuba diving I. McDowell, Jack. joint author. II. T.
GV840.S78 K47    797.2/3    *LC* 74-31973

## GV841–857 Winter Sports

**Fischler, Stan, 1932-.**      **4.992**
Everybody's hockey book / Stan & Shirley Fischler. — 1st Charles Scribner's Sons pbk. ed. — New York: Scribner, 1985, c1983. xvi, 384 p.: ill., ports. Includes index. 1. Hockey I. Fischler, Shirley. II. T.
GV847.F458 1983    796.9622 19    *LC* 83-16411    *ISBN* 0684185075

**Watt, Tom.**      **4.993**
How to play hockey: a guide for players and their coaches / illustrated by Bob Berger; foreword by Dave Keon. — Toronto: Doubleday Canada Ltd.; Garden City, N.Y.: Doubleday, 1971. 176 p.: ill.; 22 cm. 1. Hockey I. T.
GV847.W38    796.9/62/028    *LC* 78-157635

**The complete encyclopedia of hockey / edited by Zander**      **4.994**
**Hollander and Hal Bock.**
3rd ed., rev. and updated. — New York: New American Library, c1983. xiii, 466 p., [8] p. of plates: ill. (some col.); 25 cm. Rev. and updated ed. of: The complete encyclopedia of ice hockey. 1974. 'An Associated Features book.' Includes index. 1. National Hockey League — History. 2. Hockey players — Biography. 3. Hockey — Records. I. Hollander, Zander. II. Bock, Hal. III. Hollander, Zander. Complete encyclopedia of ice hockey.
GV847.8.N3 C64 1983    796.96/2/09 19    *LC* 83-62080    *ISBN* 0453004490

**McFarlane, Brian.**      **4.995**
60 years of hockey: the intimate story behind North America's fastest, most exciting sport: complete statistics and records / Brian McFarlane. Toronto: Pagurian Press; New York: distributed by Publishers Marketing Group, c1976. 269 p.: ill.; 24 cm. 'A Christopher Ondaatje publication.' 1. National Hockey League — History. 2. Stanley Cup (Hockey) — History. I. T.
GV847.8.N3 M317    796.9/62    *LC* 77-359637    *ISBN* 0889320373

**Abraham, Horst, 1941-.**      **4.996**
Skiing right / by Horst Abraham; with a collection of assorted essays and observations by Phil Brittin ... [et al.]. — 1st ed. — Boulder, Colo.: Johnson Books, c1983. 237 p.: ill. (some col.); 28 cm. At head of title: The Professional Ski Instructors of America present. 1. Skis and skiing 2. Skis and skiing — United States — Directories. 3. Skis and skiing — Canada — Directories. I. Professional Ski Instructors of America. II. T.
GV854.A29 1983b    796.93/025/7 19    *LC* 82-84105    *ISBN* 0933472749

**Berry, I. William.**      **4.997**
The great North American ski book / I. William Berry. — A completely rev. and updated 3rd ed. of America's ski book. — New York: Scribner, c1982. xxxvi, 471 p.: ill.; 24 cm. Rev. and updated ed. of: America's ski book / by the editors of Ski magazine. Rev. ed. 1973. Includes index. 1. Skis and skiing 2. Skis and skiing — United States. I. America's ski book. II. T.
GV854.B377 1982    796.93/0973 19    *LC* 82-6029    *ISBN* 0684176548

**Scharff, Robert. comp.**      • **4.998**
Ski magazine's encyclopedia of skiing / Edited by Robert Scharff and the editors of Ski Magazine. — [1st ed.]. — New York: Harper & Row, [1970] 427 p.: ill.; 27 cm. 1. Skis and skiing I. Ski magazine. II. T. III. Title: Encyclopedia of skiing.
GV854.S237 1970    796.9/3    *LC* 78-123963

**Caldwell, John H., 1928-.**      **4.999**
The cross–country ski book / John Caldwell. — 7th ed. — Brattleboro, Vt.: S. Greene Press, c1984. x, 180 p.: ill.; 23 cm. Includes index. 1. Cross-country skiing I. T.
GV855.3.C34 1984    796.93 19    *LC* 84-13588    *ISBN* 0828905444

## GV862–881 Baseball

**James, Bill, 1949-.**      **4.1000**
The Bill James historical baseball abstract / Bill James; [text designed and illustrated by Mary A. Wirth]. — 1st ed. — New York: Villard Books, 1986, c1985. xii, 721 p.: ill.; 24 cm. Includes index. 1. Baseball — United States — History. 2. Baseball — United States — Records. I. T.
GV863.A1 J36 1986    796.357/0973 19    *LC* 84-40603    *ISBN* 0394537130

**Riess, Steven A.**    **4.1001**
Touching base: professional baseball and American culture in the Progressive Era / Steven A. Riess. — Westport, Conn.: Greenwood Press, 1980. xiv, 268 p.; 22 cm. — (Contributions in American studies; no. 48 0084-9227) Includes index. 1. Baseball — Social aspects — United States. 2. Baseball — United States — History. 3. United States — Social conditions I. T.
GV863.A1 R53    796.357/0973    LC 79-6570    ISBN 0313206716

**Voigt, David Quentin.**    **4.1002**
American baseball / David Quentin Voigt. — University Park: Pennsylvania State University Press, c1983. 3 v.: ill., ports.; 24 cm. Vol. 1 foreword by Allan Nevins; v. 2 foreword by Ronald A. Smith; v. 3 foreword by Clifford Kachline. Vols. 1-2 are reprints. Originally published: Norman: University of Oklahoma Press, 1966-1970. 1. Baseball — United States — History — Collected works. I. T.
GV863.A1 V65 1983    796.357/64/0973 19    LC 83-2300    ISBN 0271003316

**Robinson, Jackie, 1919-1972.**    **4.1003**
I never had it made / by Jackie Robinson as told to Alfred Duckett. — New York: Putnam [1972] 287 p.; 22 cm. 1. Robinson, Jackie, 1919-1972. 2. Afro-Americans I. Duckett, Alfred. II. T.
GV865.R6 A29 1972    796.357/092/4    LC 75-175272    ISBN 0399110100

**Tygiel, Jules.**    **4.1004**
Baseball's great experiment: Jackie Robinson and his legacy / Jules Tygiel. — New York: Oxford University Press, 1983. xii, 392 p., [12] p. of plates: ill.; 24 cm. 1. Robinson, Jackie, 1919-1972. 2. Baseball players — United States — Biography. 3. Baseball — United States — History. 4. United States — Race relations I. T.
GV865.R6 T93 1983    796.357/092/4 B 19    LC 83-4042    ISBN 0195033000

**Kindall, Jerry.**    **4.1005**
Sports illustrated baseball / by Jerry Kindall; photography by Heinz Kluetmeier; illustrations by Don Tonry. — 1st ed. — New York: Harper & Row, c1983. 256 p.: ill.; 23 cm. — (Sports illustrated library.) 1. Baseball I. T. II. Series.
GV867.K56 1983    796.357/2 19    LC 82-48670    ISBN 0060150793

**Kahn, Roger.**    **4.1006**
The boys of summer. [1st ed.] New York, Harper & Row [1972] xxii, 442 p. illus. 22 cm. 1. Brooklyn Dodgers (Baseball team) 2. Baseball — United States — History. I. T.
GV875.B7 K3 1972    796.357/64/0974723 19    LC 76-144179    ISBN 0060122390

**The Baseball encyclopedia: the complete and official record of**    **4.1007**
**major league baseball / Joseph L. Reichler, editor.**
6th ed., rev., updated, and expanded. — New York: Macmillan; London: Collier Macmillan, 1985. 2733 p.; 25 cm. 1. Baseball — United States — Statistics. I. Reichler, Joe.
GV877.B27 1985    796.357/0973/021 19    LC 85-306    ISBN 0026019302

**Markham, Jesse William, 1916-.**    **4.1008**
Baseball economics and public policy / Jesse W. Markham, Paul V. Teplitz. — Lexington, Mass.: Lexington Books, c1981. xiv, 179 p.; 24 cm. Includes index. 1. Baseball — Economic aspects — United States. 2. Baseball — Law and legislation — United States. 3. Antitrust law — United States. I. Teplitz, Paul V. joint author. II. T.
GV880.M37    338.4/7/7796357/0973 19    LC 79-6032    ISBN 0669036072

## GV882-888 Basketball

**Isaacs, Neil David, 1931-.**    **4.1009**
All the moves: a history of college basketball / Neil D. Isaacs. — 1st ed. — Philadelphia: Lippincott, c1975. 319 p.: ill.; 26 cm. Includes index. 1. Basketball — History 2. Basketball — United States — History. I. T. II. Title: College basketball.
GV883.I82    796.32/363/0973    LC 75-6574    ISBN 0397010451

**Webb, Bernice Larson.**    **4.1010**
The basketball man, James Naismith. — Lawrence: University Press of Kansas, [1973] xi, 381 p.: illus.; 24 cm. 1. Naismith, James, 1861-1939. I. T.
GV884.N34 W42    796.32/3/0924 B    LC 72-87821    ISBN 0700600981

**Hollander, Zander.**    **4.1011**
The modern encyclopedia of basketball / edited by Zander Hollander. — 2d rev. ed. — Garden City, N.Y.: Dolphin Books, 1979. xvi, 624 p.: ill.; 26 cm. 'An Associated features book.' Includes index. 1. Basketball — Dictionaries. I. T.
GV885.H587 1979    796.32/3/0973    LC 78-22636    ISBN 0385143818

**Holzman, Red.**    **4.1012**
Holzman's basketball: winning strategy and tactics [by] Red Holzman and Leonard Lewin. — New York: Macmillan, [c1973] x, 242 p.: illus.; 24 cm. 1. Basketball I. Lewin, Leonard. joint author. II. T.
GV885.H64    796.32/3    LC 72-90551

**Wooden, John R.**    • **4.1013**
Practical modern basketball / [by] John R. Wooden. — New York: Ronald Press Co. [1966] vi, 418 p.: ill., group port.; 24 cm. 1. Basketball — Coaching I. T.
GV885.W64    796.323077    LC 66-16855

**The NBA's official encyclopedia of pro basketball / edited by**    **4.1014**
**Zander Hollander; foreword by Lawrence F. O'Brien.**
New York: New American Library, c1981. xi, 532 p., [16] p. of plates: ill. (some col.); 24 cm. 'An Associated Features book.' Rev. ed. of: The Pro basketball encyclopedia. c1977. Includes index. 1. Basketball — United States — History. I. Hollander, Zander. II. National Basketball Association. III. Pro basketball encyclopedia. IV. Title: N.B.A.'s official encyclopedia of pro basketball.
GV885.7.N37 1981    796.32/364/0973 19    LC 81-82815    ISBN 0453004075

## GV937-959 Soccer. Football

**Brondfield, Jerry, 1913-.**    **4.1015**
Rockne, the coach, the man, the legend / by Jerry Brondfield. — 1st ed. — New York: Random House, c1976. viii, 271 p., [8] leaves of plates: ill.; 22 cm. 1. Rockne, Knute, 1888-1931. 2. Football — Coaches — Biography I. T.
GV939.R6 B67    796.33/2/0924 B    LC 76-14175    ISBN 039440145X

**Gardner, Paul, 1930-.**    **4.1016**
The simplest game: the intelligent American's guide to the world of soccer / Paul Gardner; with a foreword by Pelé. — 1st ed. — Boston: Little, Brown, c1976. 291 p.: ill.; 22 cm. 'A Sports illustrated book.' Includes index. 1. Soccer 2. Soccer — United States. I. T.
GV943.G29    796.33/4/0973    LC 76-24861    ISBN 0316303763

**Henshaw, Richard, 1945-.**    **4.1017**
The encyclopedia of world soccer / by Richard Henshaw; foreword by Sir Stanley Rous. — Washington: New Republic Books, 1979. xix, 828 p.: ill.; 26 cm. 1. Soccer — Dictionaries I. T.
GV943.H367    796.33/4/03    LC 78-26570    ISBN 0915220342

**Widdows, Richard.**    **4.1018**
The Arco book of soccer techniques and tactics / Richard Widdows; illustrated by Paul Buckle. — New York: Arco Pub., 1983, c1982. 192 p.: ill. (some col.); 31 cm. Includes index. 1. Soccer 2. Soccer — Coaching 3. Soccer — Goalkeeping I. Arco Publishing II. T. III. Title: Soccer techniques and tactics.
GV943.W54 1983    796.334/2 19    LC 83-9967    ISBN 0668058889

**Lover, Stanley F.**    • **4.1019**
Association football laws illustrated / officially approved and recommended by the Referees' Committee of F.I.F.A.; with the laws of the game and decisions of the International Football Association Board, revised June 1971. — [London]: Pelham Books, [1971, c1970] 128 p.: ill.; 22 cm. 1. Soccer — Rules I. International Football Association Board. II. T.
GV943.4.L68 1971    796.33/4    LC 72-193498    ISBN 0722156480

**Sellin, Eric, 1933-.**    **4.1020**
The inner game of soccer / by Eric Sellin; cover and drawings by Micá. — Mountain View, CA: World Publications, c1976. 343 p.: ill.; 23 cm. 1. Soccer — Refereeing I. T.
GV943.9.R43 S44    796.33/4/077    LC 75-21407    ISBN 0890371075

**Tischler, Steven.**    **4.1021**
Footballers and businessmen: the origins of professional soccer in England / Steven Tischler. — New York: Holmes & Meier Publishers, 1982 (c1981). x, 154 p., [2] leaves of plates: ill.; 24 cm. Includes index. 1. Soccer — England — History. 2. Soccer — Social aspects — England. 3. Soccer — Economic aspects — England. 4. Professional sports — England. I. T.
GV944.G7 T57 1981    796.334/0942 19    LC 80-26656    ISBN 0841906580

**The American encyclopedia of soccer / edited by Zander**     **4.1022**
**Hollander.**
1st ed. — New York: Everest House Publishers, c1980. 544 p.: ill., ports.; 26
cm. 'An Associated Features book.' Includes index. 1. Soccer — United States
— History. 2. Soccer — United States — Records. I. Hollander, Zander.
GV944.U5 A42 1980     796.334/0973 19     *LC* 79-51205     *ISBN*
0896960579

**Powell, John T.**     **4.1023**
Inside rugby: the team game / John T. Powell. Chicago: Regnery, c1976. vii,
102 p.: ill.; 29 cm. Includes index. 1. Rugby football I. T.
GV945.P66 1976     796.33/32     *LC* 76-6281     *ISBN* 0809280809

**DeLuca, Sam.**     **4.1024**
The football handbook / by Sam DeLuca. — Middle Village, N.Y.: Jonathan
David Publishers, c1978. 416 p.: ill.; 24 cm. 1. Football I. T.
GV951.D358    .796.33/22     *LC* 78-18764     *ISBN* 0824602315

**DeLuca, Sam.**     **4.1025**
The football playbook. — Middle Village, N.Y.: Jonathan David Publishers,
[1972] xi, 385 p.: illus.; 26 cm. 1. Football I. T.
GV951.D36     796.33/2     *LC* 74-188241     *ISBN* 0824601432

**Lombardi, Vince.**     **4.1026**
Vince Lombardi on football. Edited by George L. Flynn. Introd. by Red Smith.
— [Greenwich, Conn.]: New York Graphic Society, [1973] 2 v.: illus. (part
col.); 29 cm. Issued in a case. 1. Football I. T.
GV951.L74     796.33/22     *LC* 73-79992     *ISBN* 0821205404

**Parseghian, Ara, 1923-.**     **4.1027**
Parseghian and Notre Dame football [by] Ara Parseghian and Tom Pagna.
Garden City, N.Y., Doubleday [1973, c1971] xv, 319 p. illus. 25 cm.
1. University of Notre Dame — Football. 2. Football I. Pagna, Tom, joint
author. II. T.
GV951.P3 1973     796.33/2/0924     *LC* 73-79700     *ISBN* 0385068913

**Anderson, Ken, 1949-.**     **4.1028**
The art of quarterbacking / by Ken Anderson, with Jack Clary; foreword by
Paul Brown; photographs by Jon Naso ... [et al.]. — New York: Linden Press,
c1984. 220 p.: ill.; 28 cm. 'A Mountain Lion book.' Includes index.
1. Quarterback (Football) I. Clary, Jack T. II. T.
GV951.3.A6 1984     796.332/25 19     *LC* 84-7193     *ISBN* 0671476513

**National Football League Properties, inc. Creative Services**     **4.1029**
**Division.**
The NFL's official encyclopedic history of professional football / prepared by
the Creative Services Division, National Football League Properties, inc.;
produced by Rutledge Books; edited, written, and compiled by Tom Bennett ...
[et al.]. — 2d ed. — New York: Macmillan, c1977. 512 p.: ill.; 27 cm. 'A
National Football League book.' 1. Football — United States I. Bennett, Tom,
1944- II. Rutledge Books, inc. III. T.
GV954.N37 1977     796.33/2/0973     *LC* 76-30547     *ISBN*
0025890107

**Football coaching / compiled by the American Football Coaches**     **4.1030**
**Association; edited by Dick Herbert.**
New York: Scribner, c1981. ix, 278 p.: ill.; 28 cm. 1. Football — Coaching —
Addresses, essays, lectures. I. American Football Coaches Association.
GV956.6.F66     796.332/07/7 19     *LC* 81-9056     *ISBN* 068417149X

**Bergin, Thomas Goddard, 1904-.**     **4.1031**
The Game: the Harvard–Yale football rivalry, 1875–1983 / Thomas G. Bergin;
foreword by Will Cloney. — New Haven: Yale University Press, c1984. xiii,
367 p.: ill.; 24 cm. 1. Harvard University — Football — History. 2. Yale
University — Football — History. I. T.
GV958.H3 B47 1984     796.332/72 19     *LC* 84-40189     *ISBN*
0300032676

## GV961–987 Golf

**Golf magazine's encyclopedia of golf / edited by John M. Ross**     **4.1032**
**and the editors of Golf magazine.**
Updated and rev. — New York: Harper & Row, c1979. vi, 439 p.: ill.; 27 cm.
Includes index. 1. Golf I. Ross, John M. II. Golf magazine. III. Title:
Encyclopedia of golf.
GV965.G5455 1979     796.352     *LC* 77-11818     *ISBN* 0060115521

**Hay, Alex.**     **4.1033**
The handbook of golf / Alex Hay; foreword by Peter Alliss. — Salem, New
Hampshire: Salem House, 1985. 223 p.: ill. (certaines en coul.) I. T. II. Title:
Golf
GV965.H3x     823/.912 19     *LC* 84-51780     *ISBN* 0881620254

**Nicklaus, Jack.**     **4.1034**
Golf my way, by Jack Nicklaus with Ken Bowden. Illus. by Jim McQueen. —
New York: Simon and Schuster, [1974] 264 p.: illus.; 25 cm. 1. Golf
I. Bowden, Ken. joint author. II. T.
GV965.N494     796.352/3     *LC* 73-14090     *ISBN* 067121702X

## GV989 Lacrosse

**Scott, Bob.**     **4.1035**
Lacrosse: technique and tradition / Bob Scott. Baltimore: Johns Hopkins
University Press, c1976. x, 219 p.: ill.; 26 cm. Includes index. 1. Lacrosse I. T.
GV989.S36     796.34/7     *LC* 76-17223     *ISBN* 0801818737

## GV990–1007 Tennis and Related Games

**United States Lawn Tennis Association.**     • **4.1036**
Official encyclopedia of tennis / edited by the staff of the U.S.L.T.A. — [1st ed.].
— New York: Harper & Row, [1972] viii, 472 p.: ill.; 27 cm. 1. Tennis —
Dictionaries. I. T.
GV990.U5 1972     796.34/2/03     *LC* 71-181644     *ISBN* 0060144793

**Scott, Eugene L., 1937-.**     **4.1037**
Tennis: game of motion. New York, Crown Publishers [1973] 256 p. illus. 29
cm. 'A Rutledge book.' 1. Tennis — History. I. T.
GV993.S36     796.34/2/09     *LC* 72-82972     *ISBN* 0517503913

**Faulkner, Edwin J.**     • **4.1038**
Ed Faulkner's tennis: how to play it, how to teach it / [by] Edwin J. Faulkner
and Frederick Weymuller; pref. by Arthur Ashe. — New York: Dial Press,
1970. 294 p.: ill., ports.; 26 cm. 1. Tennis I. Weymuller, Frederick, joint
author. II. T.
GV995.F3     796.34/2     *LC* 70-76967

**Tennis, a professional guide / by United States Professional**     **4.1039**
**Tennis Association.**
1st ed. — Tokyo; New York: Kodansha International; New York, N.Y.:
Distributed by Harper & Row, 1984. 326 p.: ill. (some col.); 25 cm. Includes
index. 1. Tennis — Addresses, essays, lectures. 2. Tennis — Study and
teaching — Addresses, essays, lectures. I. United States Professional Tennis
Association.
GV995.T413 1984     796.342/07 19     *LC* 84-846     *ISBN* 0870116827

**Barnaby, John M.**     **4.1040**
Winning squash racquets / Jack Barnaby. — Boston: Allyn and Bacon, c1979.
xv, 286 p.: ill.; 24 cm. Includes index. 1. Squash rackets (Game) I. T.
GV1004.B32     796.34/3     *LC* 78-25730     *ISBN* 0205061753

**Hashman, Judy Devlin.**     **4.1041**
Beginning badminton / Judy Hashman and C. M. Jones. — New York: Arco
Pub. Co., c1977. 96 p.: ill.; 21 cm. 1. Badminton (Game) I. Jones, Clarence
Medlycott, 1912- joint author. II. T.
GV1007.H33 1977     796.34/5     *LC* 77-5535     *ISBN* 0668042656 lib.
bdg

## GV1015–1017 Other Ball Games

**Slaymaker, Thomas.**     **4.1042**
Power volleyball / Thomas Slaymaker, Virginia H. Brown; illustrated by
Vernon Hüppi. — 3rd ed. — Philadelphia: Saunders College Pub., c1983. x,
109 p.: ill.; 24 cm. — (Saunders physical activities series.) 1. Volleyball
I. Brown, Virginia H. II. T. III. Series.
GV1015.3.S58 1983     796.32/5 19     *LC* 82-61058     *ISBN* 0030628377

**Flint, Rachael Heyhoe.**     **4.1043**
Field hockey / Rachael Heyhoe Flint; photos. by Gordon Jones. — Woodbury,
N.Y.: Barron's, 1978. 64 p.: ill.; 27 cm. — (Barron's pictorial sports instruction
series) (Barron's sports books) Published in 1976 under title: Women's hockey.
1. Field hockey I. T.
GV1017.H7 W6 1978     796.35/5     *LC* 78-103697     *ISBN* 0812051580

**Scates, Allen E.**     • **4.1044**
Winning volleyball: fundamentals, tactics and strategy [by] Allen E. Scates. —
Boston: Allyn and Bacon, [1972] vii, 261 p.: illus.; 24 cm. 1. Volleyball I. T.
GV1017.V6 S28     796.32/5     *LC* 70-162880

## GV1040–1059 Cycling
(see also: TL410)

**Sloane, Eugene A.**　　　　**4.1045**
The all new complete book of bicycling / by Eugene A. Sloane. — 3d totally rev. and updated ed. — New York: Simon & Schuster, c1980. 736 p.: ill.; 24 cm. Published in 1974 under title: The new complete book of bicycling. Includes index. 1. Cycling 2. Bicycles I. T.
GV1041.S55 1980　　629.2/272 19　　*LC* 80-20298　　*ISBN* 0671249673

**Borysewicz, Edward, 1939-.**　　　　**4.1046**
Bicycle road racing: complete program for training and competition / by Edward Borysewicz with Ed Pavelka. — Brattleboro, Vt.: Velo-News, c1985 (1986 printing) 276 p.: ill.; 28 cm. 1. Bicycle racing 2. Bicycle racing — Training I. Pavelka, Ed. II. T.
GV1049.B595 1986　　796.6/2 19　　*LC* 84-52282　　*ISBN* 0941950077

**Smith, Robert A., 1918-.**　　　　**4.1047**
A social history of the bicycle: its early life and times in America / by Robert A. Smith. — New York: McGraw-Hill, [1972] xii, 269 p.: illus.; 24 cm. 1. Cycling — United States — History. I. T.
GV1052.U6 S6　　796.6　　*LC* 72-3733　　*ISBN* 0070584575

## GV1060.5–1097 Track Athletics

**Encyclopedia of track and field athletics / compiled by Mel Watman.**　　　　**4.1048**
2nd. ed. — New York: St. Martin's Press; London: R. Hale, 1981. 240 p., [8] leaves of plates: ill.; 23 cm. Previously published as: The encyclopaedia of athletics. Includes index. 1. Track-athletics — Dictionaries. I. Watman, Melvyn Francis.
GV1060.5.E53 1981　　796.4/2/03 19　　*LC* 81-52468　　*ISBN* 0312250673

**Jacoby, Ed.**　　　　**4.1049**
Applied techniques in track & field / Ed Jacoby. — New York: Leisure Press, c1983. 256 p.: ill.; 23 cm. 1. Track-athletics 2. Track-athletics — Training I. T. II. Title: Applied techniques in track and field.
GV1060.5.J33 1983　　796.4/2 19　　*LC* 82-81819　　*ISBN* 0880110503

**Championship track and field for women / edited by Fred Wilt, Tom Ecker and Jim Hay.**　　　　**4.1050**
West Nyack, N.Y.: Parker Pub. Co., c1978. 270 p.: ill.; 26 cm. 1. Track-athletics 2. Track-athletics — Coaching 3. Sports — Physiological aspects 4. Sports — Psychological aspects I. Wilt, Fred, 1920- II. Ecker, Tom. III. Hay, James G., 1936-
GV1060.8.C4　　796.4/2　　*LC* 77-10520　　*ISBN* 0131278452

**Fixx, James F.**　　　　**4.1051**
The complete book of running / James F. Fixx. — 1st ed. — New York: Random House, c1977. xx, 314 p.: ill.; 25 cm. Includes index. 1. Running 2. Jogging 3. Sports — Psychological aspects I. T.
GV1061.F55　　796.4/26　　*LC* 77-5984　　*ISBN* 0394411595

**Ullyot, Joan, 1940-.**　　　　**4.1052**
Women's running / by Joan Ullyot. — Mountain View, CA: World Publications, c1976. 153, [2] p.: ill.; 22 cm. 1. Running for women 2. Track-athletics for women I. T.
GV1061.U43　　796.4/26　　*LC* 75-20962　　*ISBN* 0890371008. *ISBN* 0890370737 pbk

## GV1107–1108 Bullfighting

**Hemingway, Ernest, 1899-1961.**　　　　**4.1053**
Death in the afternoon. New York, Scribner, 1932. 517 p. illus. 24 cm. A description of Spanish bull-fights. 1. Bullfights. I. T.
GV1107.H4　　791.8　　*LC* 32-29071

## GV1111–1198 Boxing. Shooting. Wrestling

**Wise, Arthur, 1923-.**　　　　**4.1054**
The art and history of personal combat. — New York: Graphic, 1972 (c1971) 256 p.: illus.; 29 cm. 1. Hand-to-hand fighting — History. I. T.
GV1111.W76 1972　　355.8/2　　*LC* 70-179957　　*ISBN* 0821204459

**Gilmore, Al-Tony.**　　　　**4.1055**
Bad Nigger! The national impact of Jack Johnson. Port Washington, N.Y., Kennikat Press, 1975. 162 p. illus. 23 cm. (Kennikat Press national university publications. Series in American studies) 1. Johnson, Jack, 1878-1946. 2. Boxing I. T.
GV1132.J7 G54　　796.8/3/0924 B　　*LC* 74-80590　　*ISBN* 0804690618

**Mead, Chris, 1959-.**　　　　**4.1056**
Champion—Joe Louis, Black hero in white America / Chris Mead. — New York, NY: Penguin Books, 1986, c1985. xii, 330 p., [16] p. of plates: ill.; 20 cm. — (Penguin sports library.) Reprint. Originally published: New York: Scribner, c1985. 1. Louis, Joe, 1914- 2. Boxers (Sports) — United States — Biography. I. T. II. Series.
GV1132.L6 M4 1986　　796.8/3/0924 B 19　　*LC* 86-5047　　*ISBN* 0140092854

**Oates, Joyce Carol, 1938-.**　　　　**4.1057**
On boxing / Joyce Carol Oates; with photographs by John Ranard. — 1st ed. — Garden City, N.Y.: Dolphin/Doubleday, 1987. 118 p.: ill. 1. Boxing I. T.
GV1133.O2 1987　　796.8/3 19　　*LC* 86-19710　　*ISBN* 0385239424

**The Ring ... record book and boxing encyclopedia.**　　　　**4.1058**
1941- . — [New York]: Ring Pub. Co., 1941-. v.: ill.; 24 cm. Annual. Title varies. 1. Boxing — Statistics — Periodicals.
GV1137.R5　　796.8/3/0212　　*LC* 81-66027

**The Book of shooting for sport and skill / edited by Frederick Wilkinson.**　　　　**4.1059**
New York: Crown Publishers, 1980. 351 p.: ill. (some col.); 25 cm. 'A Herbert Michelman book.' Includes index. 1. Shooting I. Wilkinson, Frederick, 1922-
GV1153.B65 1980　　799.3/12 19　　*LC* 80-50322　　*ISBN* 0517541777

**Clayton, Thompson.**　　　　**• 4.1060**
A handbook of wrestling terms and holds / compiled by Thompson Clayton with the help of Doug Parker [and others]. — South Brunswick [N.J.]: A. S. Barnes, [1968] 142 p.: ill.; 26 cm. 1. Wrestling 2. Wrestling holds I. T. II. Title: Wrestling terms and holds.
GV1195.C55　　796.8/12　　*LC* 68-11460

## GV1200–1561 GAMES

**Avedon, Elliott M.**　　　　**4.1061**
The study of games / Elliott M. Avedon and Brian Sutton-Smith. — Huntington, N.Y.: R. E. Krieger Pub. Co., 1979, c1971. xiv, 530 p.; 24 cm. Reprint of the ed. published by J. Wiley, New York. 1. Games — Addresses, essays, lectures. 2. Games — Bibliography. 3. Game theory I. Sutton-Smith, Brian. joint author. II. T.
GV1200.A9 1979　　793　　*LC* 79-21194　　*ISBN* 0898740452

**Hindman, Darwin Alexander.**　　　　**4.1062**
[Handbook of active games] Kick the can, and over 800 other active games and sports for all ages / Darwin A. Hindman. — Englewood Cliffs, N.J.: Prentice-Hall, [1978] c1951. 415 p.; 21 cm. Originally published under title: Handbook of active games. Includes index. 1. Games I. T.
GV1201.H63 1978　　790　　*LC* 77-14156　　*ISBN* 0135151635

**Opie, Iona Archibald.**　　　　**4.1063**
Children's games in street and playground: chasing, catching, seeking, hunting, racing, duelling, exerting, daring, guessing, acting, pretending / by Iona and Peter Opie. — Oxford; New York: Oxford University Press, 1984. xxvi, 371 p., [2] p. of plates: ill., maps; 20 cm. (Oxford paperbacks) Includes index. 1. Games — Great Britain. 2. Games — Great Britain — History. 3. Games — History. I. Opie, Peter. II. T.
GV1204.43.O65 1984　　796/.0941 19　　*LC* 84-3919　　*ISBN* 0192814893

**Opie, Iona Archibald.**　　　　**4.1064**
The singing game / by Iona and Peter Opie. — Oxford; New York: Oxford University Press, 1985. xxii, 521 p.: ill.; music; 24 cm. Includes indexes. 1. Singing games — Great Britain. I. Opie, Peter. II. T.
GV1215.O65 1985　　796.1/3 19　　*LC* 85-193118　　*ISBN* 0192115626

**Ainslie, Tom.**　　　　**4.1065**
Ainslie's complete Hoyle / by Tom Ainslie; ill. by Jill Schwartz. — New York: Simon and Schuster, [1975] xvii, 526 p.: ill.; 24 cm. 1. Cards 2. Games 3. Indoor games I. T.
GV1243.A34　　795　　*LC* 74-32023　　*ISBN* 0671219677

# GV1282–1561 Particular Games

## GV1282 Bridge

**American Contract Bridge League.**      • **4.1066**
The official encyclopedia of bridge / authorized by the American Contract Bridge League and prepared by its editorial staff; Richard L. Frey, editor–in–chief; Alan F. Truscott, executive editor; Thomas M. Smith, managing editor. — New, rev. and expanded ed. — New York: Crown Publishers, [1971] 793 p.; 25 cm. 1. Contract bridge — Dictionaries. I. Frey, Richard L. ed. II. Truscott, Alan F. ed. III. Smith, Thomas M., ed. IV. T.
GV1282.3.A44 1971      795.4/15/03      *LC* 73-108084

**Goren, Charles Henry, 1901-.**      **4.1067**
[Bridge complete] Goren's Bridge complete / Chas H. Goren, with Omar Sharif. — Updated and rev. ed. of the standard work for all bridge players, to include a chapter on five-card major openings. — New York: Doubleday, c1980. xv, 705 p.: ill.; 24 cm. 'A Chancellor Hall book.' Includes index. 1. Contract bridge I. Sharif, Omar, 1932- II. T. III. Title: Bridge complete.
GV1282.3.G6532 1980      795.41/5 19      *LC* 80-155021      *ISBN* 0385043554

## GV1301–1311 Games of Chance. Probabilities

**Levinson, Horace C. (Horace Clifford)**      **4.1068**
[Your chance to win] Chance, luck and statistics; the science of chance. [Rev. and enl.] New York, Dover Publications [1963] 357 p. illus. 21 cm. First published in 1939 under title: Your chance to win. 'T1007.' 1. Probabilities 2. Statistics I. T.
GV1302.L4 1963      519.1      *LC* 63-3453

## GV1313–1458 Chess

**The encyclopaedia of chess / compiled by Anne Sunnucks.**      **4.1069**
2d ed. / with contributions from M. Euwe ... [et al.]. — London: Hale; New York: St. Martin's Press, 1977. 587 p., [8] leaves of plates: ill., facsims., ports.; 24 cm. Includes index. 1. Chess — Dictionaries. 2. Chess I. Sunnucks, Anne, 1927-
GV1314.5.S93 1976      794.1/03      *LC* 76-21149      *ISBN* 0709146973

**Golombek, Harry, 1911-.**      **4.1070**
Chess: a history / Harry Golombek. New York: Putnam, c1976. 256 p.: ill.; 27 cm. Includes indexes. 1. Chess — History. I. T.
GV1317.G64      794.1/09      *LC* 76-6033      *ISBN* 0399115757

**Harkness, Kenneth.**      • **4.1071**
Official chess handbook. — New York: D. McKay Co., [1967] xi, 304 p.: illus.; 22 cm. 1956 ed. published under title: The official blue book and encyclopedia of chess. 'Approved by the United States Chess Federation.' 1. Chess — Dictionaries. I. United States Chess Federation. II. T.
GV1445.H27 1967      794.1/02/02      *LC* 66-13085

**Gligorić, Svetozar.**      **4.1072**
Fischer vs. Spassky; world chess championship match, 1972 [by] Svetozar Gligoric. New York, Simon and Schuster [c1972] 127 p. illus. 21 cm. 1. Fischer, Bobby, 1943- 2. Spassky, Boris Vasilyevich, 1937- 3. Chess — Tournaments, 1972. I. T.
GV1455.G54      794.1/57      *LC* 72-83892      *ISBN* 0671213989 *ISBN* 0671213970

**Gligorić, Svetozar.**      **4.1073**
The world chess championship / [by] S. Gligorić; match scores edited by R. G. Wade; pt. 1 translated by Lovett F. Edwards. — Updated. — New York: Harper & Row, [c1972] 221 p.: il.; 22 cm. 1. Chess — Tournaments I. Wade, Robert Graham. II. T.
GV1455.G5513 1972c      794.1/57      *LC* 72-10681      *ISBN* 0060115718

**Kasparov, G. K. (Garri Kimovich)**      **4.1074**
New world chess champion: all the championship games with annotations / by Garry Kasparov; translated by Kenneth P. Neat. — 1st ed. — Oxford; New York: Pergamon Press, 1986. ix, 117 p.: ill.; 25 cm. — (Pergamon Russian chess series.) Translated from Russian. Includes index. 1. Chess — Tournaments —

Russian S.F.S.R. — Moscow. I. Kasparov, G. K. (Garri Kimovich) II. Karpov, Anatoly, 1951- III. T. IV. Series.
GV1455.K263 1986      794.1/54 19      *LC* 86-4988      *ISBN* 008034044X

**Keene, Raymond D.**      **4.1075**
The world chess championship: Korchnoi vs. Karpov: the inside story of the match / by Raymond Keene. — New York: Simon & Schuster, 1978. 159 p.: ill.; 20 cm. 1. Korchnoĭ, Viktor, 1931- 2. Karpov, Anatoly, 1951- 3. Chess — Tournaments I. T.
GV1455.K388      794.1/57      *LC* 78-16067      *ISBN* 067124647X. *ISBN* 0671246488 pbk

## GV1470–1561 Other Games. Puzzles

**Hindman, Darwin Alexander.**      **4.1076**
Handbook of indoor games and contests [by] Darwin A. Hindman; edited by D. Cyril Joynson. — 2nd cheap ed. — London: Kaye & Ward, 1972, c1955. 299 p.: illus.; 20 cm. 1. Indoor games I. T.
GV1471.H55 1967      793      *ISBN* 0718205812

### GV1541–1561 PARLOR MAGIC AND TRICKS

**Christopher, Milbourne.**      **4.1077**
The illustrated history of magic. — New York: Crowell, [1973] 452 p.: illus.; 26 cm. 1. Conjuring — History. I. T.
GV1543.C45      793.8      *LC* 73-10390      *ISBN* 0690431651

# GV1580–1799 DANCING

**Dance index. v. 1–7, no. 7/8; Jan. 1942–[July/Aug.] 1948.**      • **4.1078**
New York, Arno Press [1970] 7 v. illus., ports. 26 cm. (Arno series of contemporary art, no. 32) Reprint, with an introduction and index added, of a periodical published monthly (irregular) in New York by Ballet Caravan, inc. 1. Dancing — Periodicals. I. Ballet Caravan, inc., New York.
GV1580.D242      793.3/05      *LC* 73-96916

**The Director.**      **4.1079**
v. 1; Dec. 1897-Oct./Nov. 1898. [Brooklyn, Dance Horizons, 1976?] 306 p. ill. 29 cm. 'Dancing, deportment, etiquette, aesthetics, physical training.' 1. Dancing — Periodicals. I. Gilbert, Melvin Ballou.
GV1580.D57      793.3/1973      *LC* 75-9159

**Chujoy, Anatole, 1894- ed.**      • **4.1080**
The dance encyclopedia / compiled and edited by Anatole Chujoy and P. W. Manchester. — Rev. and enl. ed. — New York: Simon and Schuster, [1967] xii, 992 p.: ill., facsims, ports.; 24 cm. 1. Dancing — Dictionaries. I. Manchester, Phyllis Winifred, joint ed. II. T.
GV1585.C5 1967      793.3/03      *LC* 67-28038

**The Concise Oxford dictionary of ballet / [compiled by] Horst**      **4.1081**
**Koegler.**
London; New York: Oxford University Press, 1977. viii, 583 p.; 21 cm. Originally published in German under title: Friedrichs Ballettlexikon von A-Z. 1. Ballet — Dictionaries. I. Koegler, Horst.
GV1585.C73 1977      792.8/0321 19      *LC* 77-355620      *ISBN* 0193113147

**Wilson, George Buckley Laird.**      **4.1082**
A dictionary of ballet / G. B. L. Wilson. — 3d ed. — New York: Theatre Arts Books, 1974. xi, 539 p., [4] leaves of plates: ill.; 23 cm. 1. Ballet — Dictionaries. I. T.
GV1585.W5 1974      792.8/03      *LC* 73-88212      *ISBN* 0878300392

**Guest, Ann Hutchinson.**      **4.1083**
Dance notation: the process of recording movement on paper / Ann Hutchinson Guest. — New York: Dance Horizons, 1984. xiv, 226 p.: ill., music; 24 cm. Includes index. 1. Movement notation 2. Dance notation I. T.
GV1587.G83 1984      793.3 19      *LC* 84-70511      *ISBN* 0871271419

**Guest, Ann Hutchinson.**      • **4.1084**
Labanotation: or, Kinetography Laban: the system of analyzing and recording movement / Ann Hutchinson; illustrated by Doug Anderson. — 3d ed., rev. — New York: Theatre Arts Books, 1977, c1970. xvi, 528 p.: ill.; 21 cm. — (TAB paperback; no. 27) Includes index. 1. Dance notation I. T.
GV1587.H8 1977      793.3/01/48      *LC* 78-102498      *ISBN* 0878305270

**Laban, Rudolf von, 1879-1958.**        **4.1085**
Laban's principles of dance and movement notation / by Rudolf Laban; with 114 basic movement graphs and their explanation. — 2d ed. / annotated and edited by Roderyk Lange; art work by Diana Baddeley. — Boston: Plays, inc., 1975. xv, 61 p.: ill.; 25 cm. Published in 1956 and 1970 under title: Principles of dance and movement notation. Includes indexes. 1. Dance notation 2. Movement notation I. T. II. Title: Principles of dance and movement notation.
GV1587.L26 1975        793.3/2        LC 75-11503        ISBN 082380187X

**Dance directory: programs of professional preparation in        4.1086
American colleges and universities / edited by Vera Lundahl.**
Reston, Va. (1900 Association Dr., Reston 22091): National Dance Association, c1986. xiii, 126 p.; 28 cm. 1. Dancing — Study and teaching (Higher) — United States — Directories. 2. Dancing — United States — Curricula. 3. Universities and colleges — United States — Directories. I. Lundahl, Vera. II. National Dance Association.
GV1589.D36 1986        793.3/07/1173 19        LC 86-217876        ISBN 0883143321

**Blasis, Carlo, 1803-1878.**        **4.1087**
[Code complet de la danse. English] The code of Terpsichore: a practical and historical treatise, on the ballet, dancing, and pantomime: with a complete theory of the art of dancing: intended as well for the instruction of amateurs as the use of professional persons / by C. Blasis; translated under the author's immediate inspection by R. Barton. — Brooklyn, N.Y.: Dance Horizons, [1976]. 548, 22 p. of music, [9] leaves of plates: ill.; 21 cm. Translation of Code complet de la danse. 'Unabridged republication of the first edition published for James Bulcock, London, in 1828.' Includes t.p. for the 2d ed. published in 1831 under title: The art of dancing. 1. Dancing 2. Dancing — History. I. T.
GV1590.B5713 1976        793.3        LC 75-9166        ISBN 0871270552

**Feuillet, Raoul-Auger, 1659 or 60-1710.**        • **4.1088**
[Chorégraphie. English] Orchesography; translated from the French of Feuillet [by] John Weaver; and, A small treatise of time and cadence in dancing, [by] John Weaver. Farnborough, Gregg, 1971. [12], 59, 13 p., 42 plates; illus., music. 21 cm. Facsimile reprints of the London, 1706 eds. 1. Dancing — Early works to 1800. I. Weaver, John, 1673-1760. A small treatise of time and cadence in dancing. 1971. II. T.
GV1590.F613 1971        793.3        LC 71-875887        ISBN 0576282014

**Rameau, Pierre.**        • **4.1089**
[Maître à danser. English] The dancing master. Translated by Cyrill W. Beaumont. [Brooklyn] Dance Horizons [1970] xx, 150 p. illus. 21 cm. (A Dance horizons republication, 29) Translation of Le maître à danser. 1. Dancing — Early works to 1800. I. T.
GV1590.R413 1970        793.3/19/033        LC 75-77183        ISBN 0871270293

**Arbeau, Thoinot, 1519-1595.**        • **4.1090**
[Orchesographie. English] Orchesography [by] Thoinot Arbeau. Translated by Mary Stewart Evans. With a new introd. and notes by Julia Sutton and a new Labanotation section by Mireille Backer and Julia Sutton. New York, Dover Publications [1967] 266 p. illus. 24 cm. (American Musicological Society. Reprint series) 'Unabridged and corrected republication of the English translation ... first published in 1948.' Includes music. 1. Dancing — Early works to 1800. I. T. II. Series.
GV1590.T32 1967        793.3        LC 65-26021

**H'Doubler, Margaret Newell, 1889-.**        • **4.1091**
Dance: a creative art experience, by Margaret N. H'Doubler; with dance sketches by Wayne LM. Claxton. — New York: F. S. Crofts and company, 1940. xviii, 200 p.: front., plates, diagrs.; 23 cm. 1. Dancing I. T.
GV1593.H39        793.3        LC 40-11519

**Martin, John Joseph, 1893-.**        • **4.1092**
Introduction to the dance, by John Martin. — Brooklyn: Dance Horizons, [1965] 363 p.: illus., ports.; 21 cm. 'Unabridged republication of the original edition, first published in 1939.' 1. Dancing I. T.
GV1593.M3 1965        793.3        LC 65-24217

**The dance catalog / edited by Nancy Reynolds; designed by        4.1093
Joan Peckolick.**
New York: Harmony Books, c1979. 256 p.: ill.; 31 cm. 1. Dancing — Addresses, essays, lectures. 2. Dancing — Study and teaching — United States — Directories. 3. Dance companies — United States — Directories. I. Reynolds, Nancy, 1938-
GV1594.D36 1979        793.3        LC 78-25553        ISBN 0517536420

**Dance Film Association.**        **4.1094**
Dance and mime film and videotape catalog / compiled by Susan Braun, Jessie Kitching. — 2d ed. of Catalog of dance films. — New York, N.Y.: Dance Films Association, 1980. v, 146 p.; 28 cm. Includes index. 1. Dancing — Film catalogs. 2. Mime — Film catalogs. I. Braun, Susan. II. Kitching, Jessie Beatrice, 1919- III. T.
GV1594.D364 1980        793.3 19        LC 80-138843

**Jacob, Ellen.**        **4.1095**
Dancing, a guide for the dancer you can be / Ellen Jacob. — Reading, Mass.: Addison-Wesley Pub. Co., c1981. 350 p.: ill.; 26 cm. — (Danceways book.) Includes index. 1. Dancing — Addresses, essays, lectures. 2. Dancing — United States — Addresses, essays, lectures. I. T. II. Series.
GV1594.J33        793.3/2 19        LC 80-66832        ISBN 0201049562

**Moore, Lillian.**        • **4.1096**
Images of the dance; historical treasures of the Dance Collection, 1581-1861. — New York: New York Public Library, [1965] 86 p.: illus., ports. (part col.); 29 cm. 1. Dancing — Pictorial works. I. New York Public Library. Dance Collection. II. T.
GV1595.M6        793.30222        LC 65-18552

**Mueller, John E.**        **4.1097**
Dance film directory: an annotated and evaluative guide to films on ballet and modern dance / John Mueller. — Princeton, N.J.: Princeton Book Co., c1979. 97 p.: ill.; 28 cm. Includes indexes. 1. Ballet — Film catalogs. 2. Modern dance — Film catalogs. I. T.
GV1595.M89        016.79143/0909/31        LC 78-70263        ISBN 0916622088

**Nadel, Myron Howard, comp.**        • **4.1098**
The dance experience; readings in dance appreciation. Edited by Myron Howard Nadel and Constance Gwen Nadel. — New York: Praeger, [1970] xii, 388 p.; 25 cm. 1. Dancing — Philosophy — Addresses, essays, lectures. I. Nadel, Constance Gwen, joint comp. II. T.
GV1595.N3 1970        793.3/08        LC 75-101673

**Wigman, Mary, 1886-1973.**        • **4.1099**
The language of dance. Translated from the German by Walter Sorell. [1st ed.] Middletown, Conn., Wesleyan University Press [1966] 118 p. illus. (part col.) port. 24 x 30 cm. 1. Dancing I. T.
GV1595.W453        793.30924        LC 66-18118

**Cohen, Selma Jeanne, 1920-.**        **4.1100**
Next week, Swan Lake: reflections on dance and dances / Selma Jeanne Cohen. — 1st ed. — Middletown, Conn.: Wesleyan University Press, c1982. xii, 193 p.: ill.; 23 cm. Includes index. 1. Dancing — Addresses, essays, lectures. 2. Dancing — Philosophy — Addresses, essays, lectures. I. T.
GV1599.C64 1982        793.3 19        LC 82-2614        ISBN 0819550620

**Noverre, Jean Georges, 1727-1810.**        • **4.1101**
[Lettres sur la danse et sur les ballets. English] Letters on dancing and ballets. Translated by Cyril W. Beaumont from the rev. and enl. ed. published at St. Petersburg, 1803. Brooklyn, N.Y., Dance Horizons [1966] xiii, 169 p. illus. 21 cm. 1. Dancing 2. Ballet I. Beaumont, Cyril W. (Cyril William), 1891-1976. tr. II. T.
GV1599.N613 1966        793.32        LC 66-22779

---

# GV1601–1728 History

**Sachs, Curt, 1881-1959.**        • **4.1102**
[Weltgeschichte des tanzes] World history of the dance, by Curt Sachs, translated by Bessie Schönberg. New York, W. W. Norton & company, inc. [c1937] xii, 469 p. illus. (music) 32 pl. on 16 l. 27 cm. 'Published in Germany under the title: 'Eine weltgeschichte des tanzes'.' 'First edition.' 1. Dancing — History. I. Schönberg, Bessie, tr. II. T.
GV1601.S27        793.309        LC 38-27011

**Marks, Joseph E.**        **4.1103**
America learns to dance: a historical study of dance education in America before 1900 / by Joseph E. Marks. — New York: Dance Horizons, [1976], c1957. 133 p. Réimpression de l'édition de 1957 publiée à New York par Exposition Press. 1. Dancing — Study and teaching — History. 2. Dancing — United States — History. I. T.
GV1623.Mx        LC 75-9162        ISBN 0871270811

**Siegel, Marcia B.**        • **4.1104**
At the vanishing point; a critic looks at dance [by] Marcia B. Siegel. — New York: Saturday Review Press, [1972] ix, 320 p.: illus.; 25 cm. 1. Dancing — United States — Addresses, essays, lectures. 2. Dancing — Addresses, essays, lectures. I. T.
GV1623.S53        793.3/08        LC 72-79040        ISBN 0841501742

**Siegel, Marcia B.**        **4.1105**
Watching the dance go by / Marcia B. Siegel. — Boston: Houghton Mifflin, 1977. xvii, 345 p., [8] leaves of plates: ill.; 24 cm. Includes index. 1. Dancing — United States — Reviews. I. T.
GV1623.S54        793.3/2        LC 76-58029        ISBN 0395251737

**Croce, Arlene.**     **4.1106**
Afterimages / Arlene Croce. — 1st ed. — New York: Knopf, 1977. 466 p.; 25 cm. Includes index. 1. Dancing — New York (City) — Reviews. I. T.
GV1624.5.N4 C76 1977    793.3'2    *LC* 77-74992    *ISBN* 0394410939

**Emery, Lynne Fauley.**     • **4.1107**
Black dance in the United States from 1619 to 1970. With a foreword by Katherine Dunham. [1st ed. Palo Alto, Calif.] National Press Books [1972] x, 370 p. illus. 23 cm. 1. Afro-Americans — Dancing I. T.
GV1624.7.N4 E44 1972    793.3/1973    *LC* 79-187213    *ISBN* 0874842034 *ISBN* 0874842026

**Lawson, Joan.**     • **4.1108**
European folk dance, its national and musical characteristics. With illus. by Iris Brooke. — [Rev. and reprinted]. — London: I. Pitman, [1955] xii, 244 p.: illus., maps (2 fold.) music.; 25 cm. Includes directions for dancing and tunes. 1. Dancing — Europe. I. T.
GV1643.L3 1955    793.31    *LC* 56-34417

**Bowers, Faubion, 1917-.**     • **4.1109**
Theatre in the East; a survey of Asian dance and drama. — New York: Grove Press, [1969, c1956] x, 374 p.: illus.; 26 cm. 1. Dancing — Asia. 2. Theater — Asia. I. T.
GV1689.B6 1969    791/.095    *LC* 76-84879

**Bhavnani, Enakshi.**     • **4.1110**
The dance in India: the origin and history, foundations, the art, and science of the dance in India, classical, folk, and tribal. Foreword by Kamaladevi Chattopadhyaya. — [1st ed.]. — Bombay: D. B. Taraporevala Sons, [1965] xxvi, 261 p.: illus. (part col.); 29 cm. — (Taraporevala's treasure house of books) 1. Dancing — India I. T.
GV1693.B57    *LC* sa 65-9231

**Huet, Michel, 1917-.**     **4.1111**
[Danses d'Afrique. English] The dance, art, and ritual of Africa / Michel Huet; introd. by Jean Laude; text by Jean–Louis Paudrat; translated from the French. — 1st American ed. — New York: Pantheon Books, c1978. 241 p.: chiefly ill.; 32 cm. Translation of Danses d'Afrique. 1. Dancing — Africa. 2. Africa — Social life and customs. I. Paudrat, Jean Louis. II. T.
GV1705.H8313 1978    793.3/196    *LC* 78-7248    *ISBN* 0394502728

**Parker, David L.**     **4.1112**
Guide to dance in film: a catalog of U.S. productions including dance sequences, with names of dancers, choreographers, directors, and other details / David L. Parker and Esther Siegel. — Detroit: Gale Research, c1978. xix, 220 p.; 22 cm. (Performing arts information guide series; v. 3) (Gale information guide library) Includes indexes. 1. Dancing in motion pictures, television, etc — United States — Film catalogs. 2. Dancing — United States — Film catalogs. I. Siegel, Esther. joint author. II. T.
GV1779.P37    011/.37 19    *LC* 76-20339    *ISBN* 0810313774

# GV1781–1796 Theatrical Dancing. Ballet

**Martin, John Joseph, 1893-.**     • **4.1113**
Book of the dance. — New York: Tudor Pub. Co., [1963] 192 p.: illus., ports.; 27 cm. Published in 1947 under title: The dance. 1. Dancing 2. Dancers I. T. II. Title: The dance.
GV1781.M33 1963    793.32    *LC* 63-20408

**Sorell, Walter, 1905- ed.**     • **4.1114**
The dance has many faces. — 2d ed. — New York: Columbia University Press, 1966. x, 276 p.: illus., ports.; 23 cm. 1. Dancing I. T.
GV1781.S6 1966    793.3    *LC* 66-25457

**Sorell, Walter, 1905-.**     • **4.1115**
The dancer's image: points & counterpoints. — New York: Columbia University Press, 1971. 469 p.: illus.; 23 cm. 1. Dancing I. T.
GV1781.S62    793.3    *LC* 75-170923    *ISBN* 0231032498

**Van Vechten, Carl, 1880-1964.**     **4.1116**
The dance writings of Carl Van Vechten / edited, and with an introd. by Paul Padgette. — New York: Dance Horizons, c1974. xxi, 182 p., [8] leaves of plates: ill.; 21 cm. 1. Dancing — Addresses, essays, lectures. 2. Ballet — Addresses, essays, lectures. I. T.
GV1781.V32 1974    792.8/4    *LC* 74-81412    *ISBN* 0871270528

**Beaumont, Cyril W. (Cyril William), 1891-1976.**     **4.1117**
A manual of the theory and practice of classical theatrical dancing (méthode Cecchetti) / by Cyril W. Beaumont and Stanislas Idzikowski; with a pref. by Enrico Cecchetti; and ill. by Randolph Schwabe. — New York: Dover Publications, 1975. 201 p., [22] leaves of plates: ill.; 22 cm. Reprint of the 1922 ed. published in London. 1. Modern dance I. Idzikowski, Stanislas, joint author. II. T.
GV1783.B4 1975    793.3/2    *LC* 75-17363    *ISBN* 0486232239

**Cohen, Selma Jeanne, 1920- ed.**     • **4.1118**
The modern dance; seven statements of belief. — [1st ed.]. — Middletown, Conn.: Wesleyan University Press, [1966] 106 p.: illus., ports.; 21 cm. Statements by José Limón, Anna Sokolow, Erick Hawkins, Donald McKayle, Alwin Nikolais, Pauline Koner, and Paul Taylor. 1. Modern dance I. T.
GV1783.C6    793.32    *LC* 66-14663

**Duncan, Isadora, 1878-1927.**     • **4.1119**
The art of the dance. Edited, with an introd. by Sheldon Cheney. — New York: Theatre Arts Books, [1970, c1928] 147 p.: illus.; 28 cm. A memorial volume consisting of essays by Isadora Duncan, forewords by R. Duncan, Margherita Duncan, Mary F. Roberts, and others; with reproductions of original drawings by L. Bakst, A. Bourdelle, J. Clará, and others, and with photographs by A. Genthe and E. Steichen. 1. Dancing I. Cheney, Sheldon, 1886- ed. II. T.
GV1783.D78 1970    793.3/2    *LC* 71-85671

**Hodgson, Moira.**     **4.1120**
Quintet: five American dance companies / text by Moira Hodgson; photos. by Thomas Victor; pref. by Richard Howard. — New York: Morrow, 1976. 161 p., [15] leaves of plates: ill.; 29 cm. 1. Modern dance — United States — History. 2. Dancing — United States — History. I. Victor, Thomas. II. T.
GV1783.H62    793.3/2/09    *LC* 76-26881    *ISBN* 0688030955

**Humphrey, Doris, 1895-1958.**     • **4.1121**
The art of making dances. Edited by Barbara Pollack. — New York: Rinehart, [1959] 189 p.: illus.; 26 cm. 1. Choreography I. T.
GV1783.H83    792.82    *LC* 59-6573

**McDonagh, Don.**     **4.1122**
The complete guide to modern dance / Don McDonagh. — 1st ed. — Garden City, N.Y.: Doubleday, 1976. x, 534 p., [8] leaves of plates: ill.; 24 cm. Includes index. 1. Modern dance I. T.
GV1783.M26    793.3/2    *LC* 75-21235    *ISBN* 0385050550

**McDonagh, Don.**     • **4.1123**
The rise and fall and rise of modern dance. — New York: Outerbridge & Dienstfrey; distributed by Dutton, [1970] viii, 344 p.: illus. 1. Modern dance I. T.
GV1783.M27 1970    793.3/2    *LC* 74-102217    *ISBN* 0876900139

**Mazo, Joseph H.**     **4.1124**
Prime movers: the makers of modern dance in America / Joseph H. Mazo. — New York: Morrow, c1977. 322 p.: ill.; 25 cm. Includes index. 1. Modern dance — History. 2. Dancing — United States — History. I. T.
GV1783.M347 1977    793.3/2/09    *LC* 76-15375    *ISBN* 0688030785

# GV1785 Biography

## GV1785 A–F

**Cohen-Stratyner, Barbara Naomi.**     **4.1125**
Biographical dictionary of dance / Barbara Naomi Cohen–Stratyner. — New York: Schirmer Books; London: Collier Macmillan, c1982. vi, 970 p.; 24 cm. 'A Dance Horizons book.' 1. Dancing — Biography I. T.
GV1785.A1 C58 1982    793.3/092/2 B 19    *LC* 81-86153    *ISBN* 0028702603

**Lloyd, Margaret.**     • **4.1126**
The Borzoi book of modern dance, by Margaret Lloyd. — [New York: Dance Horizons, 1969?, c1949] xxiii, 356, xxvi, p.: illus.; 21 cm. — (A Republication by Dance Horizons 23) 1. Dancers 2. Dancing — History. I. T.
GV1785.A1 L6 1969    793.3/2    *LC* 78-77181    *ISBN* 0872170234

**Rogosin, Elinor.**     **4.1127**
The dance makers: conversations with American choreographers / Elinor Rogosin. — New York: Walker, 1980. 186 p.: ports.; 26 cm. Includes index. 1. Choreographers — United States — Interviews. 2. Choreography 3. Modern dance I. T.
GV1785.A1 R62 1980    792.8/092/2 19    *LC* 79-56003    *ISBN* 0802706487

**Vaughan, David, 1924-.**     **4.1128**
Frederick Ashton and his ballets / David Vaughan. 1st American ed. — New York: Knopf: distributed by Random House, 1977. xx, 522 p.: ill.; 26 cm.

Chronology: p. 451-494. Includes index. 1. Ashton, Frederick, Sir, 1906-2. Choreographers — Great Britain — Biography. I. T.
GV1785.A8 V38 1977    792.8/092/4 B    *LC* 76-47939    *ISBN* 0394410858

**Croce, Arlene.**        • **4.1129**
The Fred Astaire & Ginger Rogers book. — New York: Outerbridge & Lazard; distributed by Dutton, [1972] 191 p.: illus.; 22 cm. 1. Astaire, Fred. 2. Rogers, Ginger, 1911- 3. Dancing I. T.
GV1785.A83 C76    791.43/028/0922    *LC* 72-83107    *ISBN* 0876900279

**Taper, Bernard.**        **4.1130**
Balanchine, a biography / Bernard Taper. — New York, N.Y.: Times Books, c1984. x, 438 p.: ill.; 24 cm. Includes index. 1. Balanchine, George. 2. Choreographers — United States — Biography. I. T.
GV1785.B32 T3 1984    792.8/2/0924 B 19    *LC* 84-40107    *ISBN* 0812911369

**De Mille, Agnes.**        • **4.1131**
Dance to the piper. — [1st American ed.]. — Boston: Little, Brown, 1952. 342 p.: illus.; 22 cm. 'An Atlantic Monthly Press book.' 1. Dancing 2. Ballet I. T.
GV1785.D36 A3 1952    927.933    *LC* 52-119

**Buckle, Richard.**        **4.1132**
Diaghilev / Richard Buckle. — 1st American ed. — New York: Atheneum, 1979. xxiv, 616 p., [12] leaves of plates: ill.; 25 cm. Includes index. 1. Diaghilev, Serge, 1872-1929. 2. Impresarios — Russia — Biography. I. T.
GV1785.D5 B79 1979b    792.8/092/4 B 19    *LC* 78-73084    *ISBN* 0689109520

**Duncan, Isadora, 1878-1927.**        **4.1133**
[Selections. 1981] Isadora speaks / Isadora Duncan; edited and introduced by Franklin Rosemont. — San Francisco: City Lights Books, c1981. xviii, 147 p.: ill.; 21 cm. 1. Duncan, Isadora, 1878-1927 — Addresses, essays, lectures. 2. Dancers — United States — Biography — Addresses, essays, lectures. I. Rosemont, Franklin. II. T.
GV1785.D8 A25 1981    793.3/2/0924 B 19    *LC* 81-21692    *ISBN* 0872861333

**Duncan, Isadora, 1878-1927.**        • **4.1134**
My life, by Isadora Duncan ... — New York: Boni and Liveright, 1927. 4 p.l., 359 p. front., plates, ports.; 23 cm. 'This work ends with Isadora Duncan's departure for Russia in 1921.'—Publisher's foreword. I. T.
GV1785.D8 A3    *LC* 28-577

**Seroff, Victor Ilyitch, 1902-.**        • **4.1135**
The real Isadora. — New York: Dial Press, 1971. 441 p.: illus., ports.; 24 cm. 1. Duncan, Isadora, 1878-1927. I. T.
GV1785.D8 S47    793.3/2/0924 B    *LC* 75-144385

**Dunham, Katherine.**        • **4.1136**
A touch of innocence. — [1st ed.]. — New York: Harcourt, Brace, [1959] 312 p.; 22 cm. Autobiographical. I. T.
GV1785.D82 A3    927.933    *LC* 59-10256

**Fanny Elssler in America: comprising seven facsimilies of rare**    **4.1137**
**Americana—never before offered the public—depicting her astounding conquest of America in 1840–42, a memoir, a libretto, two verses, a penny–terrible blast, letters and journal, and an early comic strip—the sad tale of her impresario's courtship** / [edited] with an introd. and notes by Allison Delarue.
Brooklyn: Dance Horizons, 1976. 219 p.: ill.; 26 cm. 1. Elssler, Fanny, 1810-1884. I. Delarue, Allison.
GV1785.E4 F36    792.8/092/4 B    *LC* 75-37381    *ISBN* 0871270846

**Fokine, Michel, 1880-1942.**        • **4.1138**
Fokine: memoirs of a ballet master. Translated by Vitale Fokine. Edited by Anatole Chujoy. — [1st ed.]. — Boston: Little, Brown, [1961] 318 p.: illus.; 24 cm. 1. Ballet — History. I. T.
GV1785.F6 A3    792.809    *LC* 61-5754

## GV1785 G–I

**Geva, Tamara.**        **4.1139**
Split seconds; a remembrance. — [1st ed.]. — New York: Harper & Row, [1972] 358 p.; 22 cm. — 1. Geva, Tamara. I. T.
GV1785.G44 A37 1972    792.8/2/0924    *LC* 72-79666    *ISBN* 0060115122

**Armitage, Merle, 1893-1975. ed.**        • **4.1140**
Martha Graham, edited and with a foreword by Merle Armitage. Articles by John Martin [and others]. — New York: Dance Horizons, 1966] 132 p.: illus.,

music, ports.; 21 cm. 1. Graham, Martha — Addresses, essays, lectures. I. Martin, John Joseph, 1893- II. T.
GV1785.G7 A7 1966    793.30924    *LC* 66-26859

**Leatherman, Le Roy.**        • **4.1141**
Martha Graham; portrait of the lady as an artist. Photos. by Martha Swope. — [1st ed.]. — New York: Knopf, 1966. 178 p.: illus., ports.; 29 cm. 1. Graham, Martha. I. T.
GV1785.G7 L43    793.30924    *LC* 66-19377

**McDonagh, Don.**        **4.1142**
Martha Graham: a biography. — New York: Praeger, [1973] x, 341 p.: illus.; 24 cm. 1. Graham, Martha. I. T.
GV1785.G7 M32    793.3/092/4 B    *LC* 72-87297

**Morgan, Barbara Brooks, 1900-.**        **4.1143**
Martha Graham, sixteen dances in photographs / by Barbara Morgan. — 1st rev. ed. — Dobbs Ferry, N.Y.: Morgan & Morgan, c1980. 144 p.: chiefly ill.; 30 cm. Originally published: New York: Duell, Sloan & Pearce, 1941. 1. Graham, Martha. 2. Modern dance I. T.
GV1785.G7 M6 1980    793.3/2/0924 B 19    *LC* 80-81766    *ISBN* 0871001764

**Stodelle, Ernestine.**        **4.1144**
Deep song: the dance story of Martha Graham / Ernestine Stodelle. — New York: Schirmer Books; London: Collier Macmillan, c1984. xxi, 329 p., 48 [p.] of plates: ill., ports.; 25 cm. 'A Dance Horizons book.' Includes index. 1. Graham, Martha. 2. Choreographers — United States — Biography. 3. Choreography I. T.
GV1785.G7 S86 1984    793.3/092/4 B 19    *LC* 84-1261    *ISBN* 0028725204

**Warren, Larry.**        **4.1145**
Lester Horton, modern dance pioneer / Larry Warren. — New York: M. Dekker, c1977. xvi, 265 p.: ill.; 24 cm. — ([The Dance program; v. 3]) 1. Horton, Lester, 1906-1953. 2. Choreographers — United States — Biography. 3. Modern dance I. T. II. Series.
GV1785.H64 W37    793.3/2/0924 B    *LC* 76-23364    *ISBN* 0824765036

**Hughes, Russell Meriwether, 1898-.**        **4.1146**
Dance out the answer: an autobiography / La Meri (Russell Meriwether Hughes); foreword by John Martin. — New York: M. Dekker, c1977. xi, 194 p., [6] leaves of plates: ill.; 23 cm. — (The Dance program; v. 7) Includes index. 1. Hughes, Russell Meriwether, 1898- 2. Dancers — Biography. 3. Folk dancing I. T. II. Series.
GV1785.H77 A33    793.3/092/4 B    *LC* 77-20139    *ISBN* 0824766334

**Humphrey, Doris, 1895-1958.**        • **4.1147**
[Artist first] Doris Humphrey: an artist first. An autobiography, edited and completed by Selma Jeanne Cohen. Introd. by John Martin; foreword by Charles Humphrey Woodford; chronology by Christena L. Schlundt. [1st ed.] Middletown, Conn.: Wesleyan University Press [1972] xiv, 305 p. illus. 23 cm. 1. Humphrey, Doris, 1895-1958. I. Cohen, Selma Jeanne, 1920- ed. II. T.
GV1785.H8 A3    793.3/2 B    *LC* 72-3695    *ISBN* 0819540544

**Stodelle, Ernestine.**        **4.1148**
The dance technique of Doris Humphrey and its creative potential / Ernestine Stodelle; line drawings by Teri Loren. — Princeton, N.J.: Princeton Book Co., 1978. xiii, 264 p., [1] leaf of plates: ill.; 24 cm. 1. Humphrey, Doris, 1895-1958. 2. Modern dance I. T.
GV1785.H8 S75    793.3/2 19    *LC* 78-107197    *ISBN* 091662207X

**Caldwell, Helen.**        **4.1149**
Michio Ito: the dancer and his dances / Helen Caldwell. — Berkeley: University of California Press, c1977. xi, 184 p.: ill.; 25 cm. 1. Itō, Michio, 1934- I. T.
GV1785.I86 C34    792.8/0924/ B    *LC* 76-7756    *ISBN* 0520032195

## GV1785 K–Z

**Karsavina, Tamara.**        **4.1150**
Theatre Street; the reminiscences of Tamara Karsavina. — [Brooklyn, N.Y.]: Dance Horizons, [1973? c1950] xi, 301 p.: illus.; 21 cm. — (A Dance horizons republication 43) Reprint of the ed. published by Dutton, New York. 1. Karsavina, Tamara. 2. Ballet I. T.
GV1785.K3 A3 1973    792.8/092/4 B    *LC* 73-77506    *ISBN* 0871270439

**Nijinsky, Waslaw, 1890-1950.**        • **4.1151**
The diary of Vaslav Nijinsky. Edited by Romola Nijinsky. — Berkeley: University of California Press, 1968 [c1936] xvi, 187 p.: illus., ports.; 21 cm. 1. Nijinsky, Waslaw, 1890-1950. I. Nijinsky, Romola de Pulszky. ed. II. T.
GV1785.N6 A3 1968    792.8/0924    *LC* 68-12426

**Buckle, Richard.** • **4.1152**
Nijinsky. New York: Simon and Schuster, [c1971] xiv, 482 p.: illus.; 25 cm. 1. Nijinsky, Waslaw, 1890-1950. 2. Dancers — Biography. I. T.
GV1785.N6 B8 1971b 792.8/2/0924 B *LC* 78-180717 *ISBN* 0671211692

**Nijinska, Bronislava, 1891-1972.** **4.1153**
Bronislava Nijinska—early memoirs / translated and edited by Irina Nijinska and Jean Rawlinson; with an introd. and in consultation with Anna Kisselgoff. — 1st ed. — New York: Holt, Rinehart and Winston, c1981. xxv, 546 p., [32] leaves of plates: ill.; 24 cm. Includes index. 1. Nijinsky, Waslaw, 1890-1950. 2. Ballet dancers — Russia — Biography. I. Nijinska, Irina. II. Rawlinson, Jean. III. Kisselgoff, Anna. IV. T.
GV1785.N6 N5713 792.8/092/4 B 19 *LC* 80-21825 *ISBN* 003020951X

**Ivchenko, Valerian IAkovlevich, 1860-1935.** **4.1154**
Anna Pavlova / V. Svetloff [i.e. V. I. Ivchenko]; translated from the Russian by A. Grey. — New York: Dover Publications, 1974. 194 p., [15] leaves of plates: ill. (some col.); 28 cm. 1. Pavlova, Anna, 1881-1931. 2. Ballet I. T.
GV1785.P3 I8 1974 792.8/092/4 *LC* 74-75707 *ISBN* 0486230473

**Lazzarini, John.** **4.1155**
Pavlova: repertoire of a legend / John and Roberta Lazzarini. — New York: Schirmer Books; London: Collier Macmillan, c1980. 224 p.: ill.; 32 cm. 'A Dance Horizons book.' Includes index. 1. Pavlova, Anna, 1881-1931. 2. Ballet dancers — Russia — Biography. I. Lazzarini, Roberta. joint author. II. T.
GV1785.P3 L39 792.8/092/4 B 19 *LC* 80-5560 *ISBN* 0028719700

**Rambert, Marie.** • **4.1156**
Quicksilver: the autobiography of Marie Rambert. — London: Macmillan; New York: St. Martin's Press, 1972. 231, [29] p.: illus., facsim., music, ports.; 24 cm. 1. Rambert, Marie. 2. Marie Rambert Ballet. I. T.
GV1785.R36 A36 792.8/2/0924 *LC* 72-83628 *ISBN* 0333089421

**St. Denis, Ruth, 1880-1968.** • **4.1157**
Ruth St. Denis, an unfinished life; an autobiography. — New York and London: Harper & brothers, 1939. x p., 2 l., 391, [1] p.: front., plates, ports.; 25 cm. 'First edition.' I. T.
GV1785.S3 A3 927.933 *LC* 39-6663

**Shelton, Suzanne.** **4.1158**
Divine dancer: a biography of Ruth St. Denis / by Suzanne Shelton. — 1st ed. — Garden City, N.Y.: Doubleday, 1981. xvi, 338 p., [24] leaves of plates: ill.; 24 cm. Includes index. 1. St. Denis, Ruth, 1880-1968. 2. Dancers — United States — Biography. 3. Modern dance I. T.
GV1785.S3 S53 793.3/2/0924 B 19 *LC* 80-2442 *ISBN* 0385141599

**Terry, Walter.** **4.1159**
Ted Shawn, father of American dance: a biography / by Walter Terry. — New York: Dial Press, 1976. 186 p., [8] leaves of plates: ill.; 24 cm. Includes index. 1. Shawn, Ted, 1891-1972. 2. Dancing I. T.
GV1785.S5 T47 793.3/2/0924 B *LC* 76-13200 *ISBN* 0803785577

**Sherman, Jane, 1908-.** **4.1160**
Soaring: the diary and letters of a Denishawn dancer in the Far East, 1925-1926. / by Jane Sherman. — 1st ed. — Middletown, Conn.: Wesleyan University Press, c1976. 278 p.: ill.; 22 cm. 'The De la Torre Bueno prize/1975.' Includes index. 1. Sherman, Jane, 1908- 2. St. Denis, Ruth, 1880-1968. 3. Shawn, Ted, 1891-1972. 4. Dancing I. T.
GV1785.S553 A37 793.3/2/0924 B *LC* 75-34445 *ISBN* 0819540935

**Wigman, Mary, 1886-1973.** **4.1161**
The Mary Wigman book: her writings / edited and translated by Walter Sorell. — 1st ed. — Middletown, Conn.: Wesleyan University Press, [1975] 214 p.: ill.; 21 cm. Includes index. 1. Wigman, Mary, 1886-1973. 2. Dancing I. T.
GV1785.W5 A35 793.3/092/4 *LC* 74-23113 *ISBN* 081954079X

## GV1786 SPECIAL GROUPS OR COMPANIES

**Payne, Charles.** **4.1162**
American Ballet Theatre / text & commentary by Charles Payne; with essays by Alicia Alonso ... [et al.]. — 1st ed. — New York: Knopf, 1978, c1977. 380 p.: ill.; 31 cm. 'Ballet Theatre productions, 1940-1977': p. [357]-368. Includes index. 1. American Ballet Theatre. I. Alonso, Alicia. II. T.
GV1786.A43 A44 792.8/4 *LC* 77-75002 *ISBN* 0394498356

**Kriegsman, Sali Ann.** **4.1163**
Modern dance in America—the Bennington years / Sali Ann Kriegsman. — Boston, Mass.: G.K. Hall, c1981. xiv, 357 p.: ill.; 29 cm. Includes indexes. 1. Bennington School of the Dance — History. 2. Modern dance — United States — History. I. T.
GV1786.B38 K74 793.3/2/097438 19 *LC* 81-13332 *ISBN* 081618528X

**Sherman, Jane, 1908-.** **4.1164**
Denishawn, the enduring influence / Jane Sherman. — [Boston, Mass.]: Twayne Publishers, [1983] 167 p.: ill.; 23 cm. — (Twayne's dance series.) Includes index. 1. Denishawn School of Dancing — History. I. T. II. Series.
GV1786.D43 S528 1983 793.3/2/0973 19 *LC* 83-6099 *ISBN* 0805796029

**Sherman, Jane, 1908-.** **4.1165**
The drama of Denishawn dance / by Jane Sherman. — 1st ed. — Middletown, Conn.: Wesleyan University Press, c1979. xi, 185 p.: ill.; 26 cm. Includes index. 1. St. Denis, Ruth, 1880-1968. 2. Shawn, Ted, 1891-1972. 3. Humphrey, Doris, 1895-1958. 4. Denishawn School of Dancing. I. T.
GV1786.D43 S53 793.3 *LC* 77-14846 *ISBN* 0819550337

**Banes, Sally.** **4.1166**
Democracy's body: Judson Dance Theater, 1962–1964 / by Sally Banes. — Ann Arbor, Mich.: UMI Research Press, c1983. xviii, 270 p., [9] p. of plates: ill.; 24 cm. — (Studies in the fine arts. The Avant-garde; no. 43) Includes index. 1. Judson Dance Theater — History. I. T.
GV1786.J82 B36 1983 793.3/2 19 *LC* 83-15920 *ISBN* 0835714810

**Cameron, Judy.** **4.1167**
The Bolshoi Ballet / photos. by Judy Cameron; introd. and notes by Walter Terry. — 1st ed. — New York: Harper & Row, [1975] 178 p.: chiefly ill.; 25 cm. (Icon editions) 'A Helene Obolensky Enterprises, inc., book.' 1. Bol'shoĭ teatr SSSR. Balet — Pictorial works. 2. Ballet — Pictorial works. I. Terry, Walter. II. T.
GV1786.M6 C35 792.8/0947/31 *LC* 75-322984 *ISBN* 0064306003. *ISBN* 0064300633 pbk

**Kirstein, Lincoln, 1907-.** **4.1168**
The New York City Ballet. Text by Lincoln Kirstein. Photos. by Martha Swope and George Platt Lynes. — [1st ed.]. — New York: Knopf; [distributed by Random House], 1973. 261 p.: illus.; 32 cm. 1. Kirstein, Lincoln, 1907- 2. New York City Ballet. I. Swope, Martha. II. T.
GV1786.N4 K57 792.8/09747/1 *LC* 70-79331 *ISBN* 0394466527

**Kirstein, Lincoln, 1907-.** **4.1169**
Thirty years: Lincoln Kirstein's The New York City Ballet: expanded to include the years 1973–1978, in celebration of the company's thirtieth anniversary. — 1st ed. — New York: Knopf, 1978. p. cm. Includes index. 1. New York City Ballet. I. Kirstein, Lincoln, 1907- The New York City Ballet. II. T.
GV1786.N4 K58 792.8/09747/1 *LC* 78-7132 *ISBN* 0394502574

## GV1787–1790 BALLET

**Beaumont, Cyril W. (Cyril William), 1891-1976.** • **4.1170**
Complete book of ballets: a guide to the principal ballets of the nineteenth and twentieth centuries / by Cyril W. Beaumont. — New York: G. P. Putnam's sons, 1938. xxiv p., 1 l., 900 p.: front., plates, ports.; 22 cm. 1. Ballet — Stories, plots, etc. I. T.
GV1787.B35 1938 792.8 *LC* 38-8995

**Denby, Edwin, 1903-.** • **4.1171**
Dancers, buildings and people in the streets. With an introd. by Frank O'Hara. — New York: Horizon Press, [1965] 287 p.; 21 cm. 1. Ballet I. T.
GV1787.D429 792.8 *LC* 65-22559

**Denby, Edwin, 1903-.** • **4.1172**
Looking at the dance. Introd. by B. H. Haggin. — New York: Horizon Press, [1968, c1949] xx, 432 p.; 22 cm. 1. Ballet I. T.
GV1787.D43 1968 792.8 *LC* 68-54187

**Gautier, Théophile, 1811-1872.** • **4.1173**
The romantic ballet as seen by Théophile Gautier, being his notices of all the principal performances fo ballet given at Paris during the years 1837–1848; now first translated from the French by Cyril W. Beaumont. London, C. W. Beaumont, 1932. 93 p. front., pl., ports. 23 cm. 'The edition of this book is limited to 250 copies, of which 25 are not for sale. This is no. 81.' 1. Ballet I. Beaumont, Cyril W. (Cyril William), 1891-1976. tr. II. T.
GV1787.G35 792.8 *LC* 33-22427

**Grant, Gail.** 4.1174
Technical manual and dictionary of classical ballet. Illustrated by the author. —
2d rev. ed. — New York: Dover Publications, [1967] xiv, 127 p.: illus.; 22 cm.
1. Ballet — Terminology. I. T. II. Title: Dictionary of classical ballet.
GV1787.G68 1967          792.8/01/4          LC 67-26481

**Kirstein, Lincoln, 1907-.** 4.1175
Ballet, bias and belief: Three pamphlets collected and other dance writings of
Lincoln Kirstein / with an introduction and comments by Nancy Reynolds. —
New York: Dance Horizons, c1983. xviii, 458 p.: ill.; 24 cm. Includes index.
1. Ballet — Addresses, essays, lectures. 2. Dancing — Addresses, essays,
lectures. I. Reynolds, Nancy, 1938- II. T.
GV1787.K474 1983          792.8/2 19          LC 82-83628          ISBN 0871271338

**Kirstein, Lincoln, 1907-.** • 4.1176
Movement & metaphor; four centuries of ballet. — New York: Praeger, [1970]
viii, 290 p.: illus., ports.; 28 cm. 1. Ballet — History. I. T.
GV1787.K513          792.8/09          LC 75-95677

**Buckle, Richard.** 4.1177
Buckle at the ballet / selected criticism by Richard Buckle. — 1st American ed.
— New York: Atheneum, 1980. 416 p.: ill.; 25 cm. Includes index. 1. Ballet —
Addresses, essays, lectures. I. T.
GV1787.6.B82 1980          792.8/4 19          LC 80-66015          ISBN 0689110855

**Bruhn, Erik.** • 4.1178
Bournonville and ballet technique; studies and comments on August
Bournonville's Études chorégraphiques, by Erik Bruhn and Lillian Moore.
London, A. & C. Black [1961] 70 p. illus. 26 cm. 1. Bournonville, August,
1805-1879. Études chorégraphiques. 2. Ballet I. Moore, Lillian. joint author.
II. T.
GV1788.B63 B7 1961          LC 61-66774

**Lewis, Daniel.** 4.1179
The illustrated dance technique of José Limón / by Daniel Lewis; descriptive
text written in collaboration with Lesley Farlow; labanotation by Mary Corey;
drawings by Edward C. Scattergood. — 1st ed. — New York: Harper & Row,
c1984. 208 p.: ill.; 27 cm. 1. Limón, José. 2. Ballet dancing 3. Choreography
I. Farlow, Lesley. II. T.
GV1788.L46 1984          792.8/2/0924 B 19          LC 83-48365          ISBN
0060151854

**Vaganova, A. IA. (Agrippina IAkovlevna), 1879-1951.** • 4.1180
[Osnovy klassicheskogo tantsa English] Basic principles of classical ballet;
Russian ballet technique, by Agrippina Vaganova. Translated from the Russian
by Anatole Chujoy. Incorporating all the material from the 4th Russian ed.
Including Vaganova's Sample lesson with musical accompaniment, translated
by John Barker. New York, Dover Publications [1969] xiv, 171 p. illus., music,
port. 22 cm. Translation of Osnovy klassicheskogo tantsa (romanized form)
1. Ballet dancing I. T.
GV1788.V27 1969          792.82          LC 68-17402

## GV1790 Ballets

**Terry, Walter.** 4.1181
Ballet guide: background, listings, credits, and descriptions of more than five
hundred of the world's major ballets / by Walter Terry. — New York: Dodd,
Mead, c1976. xx, 388 p., [16] leaves of plates: ill.; 24 cm. Includes index.
1. Ballet — Dictionaries. 2. Ballets — Stories, plots, etc. — Dictionaries. I. T.
GV1790.A1 T47          792.8/4          LC 75-20240          ISBN 0396070248

**L'Après-midi d'un faune: Vaslav Nijinsky, 1912 / thirty-three** 4.1182
**photographs by Baron Adolf de Meyer; with an essay by**
**Jennifer Dunning and contributions by Richard Buckle and Ann**
**Hutchinson Guest.**
New York: Dance Horizons, c1983. 130 p.: ill.; 32 cm. 1. Nijinsky, Waslaw,
1890-1950 — Addresses, essays, lectures. 2. Mallarmé, Stéphane, 1842-1898.
Après-midi d'un faune. 3. Afternoon of a faun (Ballet) — Addresses, essays,
lectures. 4. Choreography — Addresses, essays, lectures. I. De Meyer, Adolf,
Baron, 1868-1949.
GV1790.A38 A67 1983          792.8/42 19          LC 82-83627          ISBN
0871271362

## GV1799 Children's Dances

**Murray, Ruth Lovell.** 4.1183
Dance in elementary education, a program for boys and girls. — 3d ed. — New
York: Harper & Row, [1975] xv, 446 p.: illus.; 24 cm. — (Harper's school and
public health education, physical education, and recreation series) 1. Dancing
— Children's dances I. T.
GV1799.M85 1975          372.8/7          LC 74-11386          ISBN 0060446811

## GV1800–1853 Circuses. Spectacles. Outdoor Amusements

**Croft-Cooke, Rupert, 1903-.** 4.1184
Circus: a world history / Rupert Croft-Cooke & Peter Cotes. 1st American ed.
New York: Macmillan, 1977, c1976. 192 p.: ill.; 31 cm. Includes index.
1. Circus — History. I. Cotes, Peter, 1912- joint author. II. T.
GV1801.C698 1976          791.3/09          LC 76-25319

**Hippisley Coxe, Antony.** 4.1185
A seat at the circus / by Antony Hippisley Coxe; with special ill. by John
Skeaping. — Rev. ed. — Hamden, Conn.: Archon Books, 1980. 258 p.: ill.; 24
cm. — (An Archon book on popular entertainments) Includes index. 1. Circus
— History. I. T.
GV1801.H5 1980          791.3          LC 79-19155          ISBN 0208017666

**May, Earl Chapin, 1873-1960.** 4.1186
The Circus from Rome to Ringling / by Earl Chapin May. — [s.l.]: Duffield and
Green, 1932. xxii, 332 p.: ill.; 22 cm. 'T103' 1. Circus I. T.
GV1801.M3 1963          791.3          LC 32-9230

**Saxon, A. H.** 4.1187
Enter foot and horse; a history of hippodrama in England and France, by A. H.
Saxon. — New Haven: Yale University Press, 1968. — xiv, 249 p.: illus.; 23 cm.
1. Hippodrome I. T. II. Title: Hippodrama in England and France.
GV1801.S37          791.3/2          LC 68-27764

**Speaight, George.** 4.1188
A history of the circus / by George Speaight. — London: Tantivy Press; San
Diego: A.S. Barnes, c1980. 216 p., [4] leaves of plates: ill.; 29 cm. 1. Circus —
History. I. T.
GV1801.S6          791.309          LC 80-17376          ISBN 0498024709

**Chindahl, George Leonard.** 4.1189
A history of the circus in America. — Caldwell, Idaho: Caxton Printers, 1959.
279 p.: illus.; 22 cm. 1. Circus — United States — History. I. T.
GV1803.C47          791.30973          LC 58-5336

**McNamara, Brooks.** 4.1190
Step right up / Brooks McNamara. — [1st ed.]. — Garden City, N.Y.:
Doubleday, 1976. xviii, 233 p.: illus.; 27 cm. 1. Medicine shows — History.
I. T.
GV1803.M32          GV1803 M32.          791.1          LC 73-20522          ISBN
0385029594

**Slout, William L. (William Lawrence)** 4.1191
Theatre in a tent, the development of a provincial entertainment. — Bowling
Green, Ohio: Bowling Green University Popular Press, [1972] xi, 153 p.: illus.;
24 cm. 1. Circus — United States — History. 2. Theater — United States —
History. 3. Medicine shows — United States. 4. Chautauquas I. T.
GV1803.S55          791/.0973          LC 72-186635          ISBN 087972028X

**Harris, Neil, 1938-.** 4.1192
Humbug; the art of P. T. Barnum. [1st ed.] Boston, Little, Brown [1973] xiv,
337 p. illus. 25 cm. 1. Barnum, P. T. (Phineas Taylor), 1810-1891. I. T.
GV1811.B3 H37          791.3/.092/4 B          LC 73-9743          ISBN 0316348236

**Saxon, A. H.** 4.1193
The life and art of Andrew Ducrow & the romantic age of the English circus /
by A. H. Saxon. — Hamden, Conn.: Archon Books, 1978. 511 p., [4] leaves of
plates: ill. (some col.); 24 cm. Includes indexes. 1. Ducrow, Andrew,
1793-1842. 2. Circus — England — History. 3. Horsemanship 4. Performing
arts — England — History. 5. Entertainers — England — Biography. I. T.
GV1811.D78 S39          791.3/092/4 B          LC 77-13010          ISBN
0208016511

**Towsen, John H.** 4.1194
Clowns / John H. Towsen. — New York: Hawthorn Books, c1976. xiii, 400 p.,
[8] leaves of plates: ill.; 24 cm. Includes index. 1. Clowns I. T.
GV1828.T68 1976          791.3/3          LC 75-41793          ISBN 0801539625

**McKennon, Joe.** 4.1195
A pictorial history of the American carnival. — Sarasota, Fla.: Carnival
Publishers of Sarasota, [1972]-. v. in: illus.; 29 cm. 1. Amusement parks —
History. I. T. II. Title: American carnival.
GV1835.M26          GV1835 M26.          791.1          LC 72-85200

**Wilmeth, Don B.**      **4.1196**
Variety entertainment and outdoor amusements: a reference guide / Don B. Wilmeth. — Westport, Conn.: Greenwood Press, 1982. xiii, 242 p.; 24 cm. — (American popular culture. 0193-6859) 1. Amusements — United States — History. 2. Music-halls (Variety-theaters, cabarets, etc.) — United States — History. 3. United States — Popular culture I. T. II. Series.
GV1853.2.W54 1982      790/.0973 19      *LC* 81-13417      *ISBN* 0313214557

# H SOCIAL SCIENCES

## H31–59 Collections. Dictionaries. Encyclopedias. History

**Weber, Max, 1864-1920.** • 4.1197
[Selected works. English] From Max Weber: essays in sociology / translated, edited, and with an introduction, by H. H. Gerth and C. Wright Mills. — New York: Oxford University Press, 1946. xi, 490 p.: front. (port.); 25 cm. 1. Social sciences — Addresses, essays, lectures. I. Gerth, Hans Heinrich, 1908- ed. and tr. II. Mills, C. Wright (Charles Wright), 1916-1962. III. T.
H33.W36    LC 46-5298

**International encyclopedia of the social sciences / David L.** • 4.1198
**Sills, editor.**
[New York]: Macmillan, 1968. 17 v.: ill.; 29 cm. 1. Social sciences — Dictionaries. I. Sills, David L. ed.
H40.A2 I5    300/.3/21 19    LC 68-10023

**Encyclopaedia of the social sciences, editor–in–chief, Edwin R.** • 4.1199
**A. Seligman; associate editor, Alvin Johnson ...**
New York, The Macmillan company, 1937. 15 v. in 8. 28 cm. 'Published January, 1930[-June 1935] ... Reissued ... November 1937.' 1. Social sciences — Dictionaries. I. Seligman, Edwin Robert Anderson, 1861-1939. ed. II. Johnson, Alvin Saunders, 1874- ed.
H41.E6 1937    303    LC 37-28589

**Miller, P. McC.** 4.1200
A dictionary of social science methods / P. McC. Miller and M.J. Wilson. — Chichester [West Sussex]; New York: Wiley, c1983. viii, 124 p.: ill.; 24 cm. 1. Social sciences — Methodology — Dictionaries. I. Wilson, M. J. (Michael John), 1939- II. T.
H41.M54 1983    300/.1/8 19    LC 82-13681    ISBN 0471900354

**Gutek, Gerald Lee.** 4.1201
George S. Counts and American civilization: the educator as social theorist / by Gerald L. Gutek. — [Macon, GA]: Mercer University Press, c1984. 174 p.; 24 cm. Includes index. 1. Counts, George S. (George Sylvester), 1889-1974. 2. Social scientists — United States — Biography. 3. United States — Civilization 4. United States — Social conditions I. T.
H59.C68 G87 1984    300/.92/4 B 19    LC 83-23762    ISBN 0865540918

## H61 Methodology

**Bartholomew, David J.** 4.1202
Stochastic models for social processes / D.J. Bartholomew. — 3rd ed. — Chichester; New York: Wiley, c1982. xii, 365 p.; 24 cm. — (Wiley series in probability and mathematical statistics.) Includes indexes. 1. Social sciences — Mathematical models. 2. Stochastic processes I. T. II. Series.
H61.B26 1982    300/.724 19    LC 82-117228    ISBN 0471280402

**Bernstein, Richard J.** 4.1203
The restructuring of social and political theory / Richard J. Bernstein. 1st ed. — New York: Harcourt Brace Jovanovich, c1976. xxiv, 286 p.; 24 cm. Includes index. 1. Social sciences 2. Political science I. T.
H61.B472    300/.1    LC 76-12544    ISBN 0151769400

**Blalock, Hubert M.** 4.1204
Conceptualization and measurement in the social sciences / Hubert M. Blalock, Jr. — Beverly Hills: Sage Publications, c1982. 285 p.: ill.; 22 cm. Includes index. 1. Social sciences — Methodology 2. Social sciences — Statistical methods I. T.
H61.B4823 1982    300/.724 19    LC 81-23269    ISBN 0803918046

**Dunn, William N.** 4.1205
Public policy analysis: an introduction / William N. Dunn. — Englewood Cliffs, N.J.: Prentice-Hall, c1981. xii, 388 p.: graphs; 24 cm. 1. Policy sciences I. T.
H61.D882    H61 D882.    361.6/1 19    LC 80-19571    ISBN 0137379579

**Kaplan, Abraham, 1918-.** • 4.1206
The conduct of inquiry; methodology for behavioral science. — San Francisco: Chandler Pub. Co., [1964] xix, 428 p.; 24 cm. — (Chandler publications in anthropology and sociology) 1. Social sciences — Methodology I. T.
H61.K24    301.018    LC 64-13470

**Kaufmann, Félix.** • 4.1207
Methodology of the social sciences. New York: Humanities P., 1958. 272 p. 1. Social sciences — Methodology I. T.
H61.K3 1958    LC 60-774

**Lazarsfeld, Paul Felix. ed.** • 4.1208
The language of social research: a reader in the methodology of social research / edited by Paul F. Lazarsfeld and Morris Rosenberg. — Glencoe, Ill.: Free Press, [1955] 590 p.: ill.; 25 cm. Published in 1972 under title: Continuities in the language of social research. 1. Social sciences — Methodology I. Rosenberg, Morris. joint ed. II. T.
H61.L346    301.8 301.01*    LC 55-7342

**Schoolman, Morton.** 4.1209
The imaginary witness: the critical theory of Herbert Marcuse / Morton Schoolman. — New York: Free Press; London: Collier Macmillan, c1980. xv, 399 p.; 25 cm. Includes index. 1. Marcuse, Herbert, 1898- 2. Marcuse, Herbert, 1898- — Bibliography. 3. Social sciences — Philosophy 4. Political science 5. Civilization, Modern I. T.
H61.M4234 S36    300/.1    LC 80-640    ISBN 0029280400

**Mills, C. Wright (Charles Wright), 1916-1962.** • 4.1210
The sociological imagination. New York: Oxford University Press, 1959. 234 p.; 22 cm. 1. Social sciences 2. Sociology I. T.
H61.M5    301    LC 59-7506

**O'Neill, John, 1933- comp.** 4.1211
Modes of individualism and collectivism. — New York: St. Martin's Press, [1973] x, 358 p.; 23 cm. 1. Social sciences — Methodology — Addresses, essays, lectures. 2. Individualism — Addresses, essays, lectures. 3. Collectivism — Addresses, essays, lectures. I. T.
H61.O53 1973b    300/.1/8    LC 73-86363

**Outhwaite, William.** 4.1212
Understanding social life: the method called Verstehen / by William Outhwaite. New York: Holmes & Meier, 1976, c1975. 127 p.; 23 cm. (Controversies in sociology; 2) Includes index. 1. Social sciences — Methodology 2. Knowledge, Sociology of 3. Hermeneutics I. T.
H61.O9 1976    300/.1/8    LC 75-28500    ISBN 0841902399

**Rosnay, Joël de.** 4.1213
[Macroscope. English] The macroscope: a new world scientific system / by Joël de Rosnay; translated from the French by Robert Edwards. — 1st ed. — New York: Harper & Row, c1979. xix, 247 p.: ill.; 24 cm. Translation of Le macroscope. Includes index. 1. Social systems 2. System theory 3. Energy policy 4. Communication 5. Time I. T.
H61.R6813    301.1    LC 76-5122    ISBN 0060110295

**Runciman, W. G. (Walter Garrison), 1934-.** • 4.1214
Social science and political theory / by W. G. Runciman. — 1st ed. — Cambridge [Eng.] University Press, 1963. vii, 200 p. 1. Political science I. T.
H61.R8    LC 63-4170

**Schutz, Alfred, 1899-1959.** • 4.1215
Collected papers / Alfred Schutz; edited and introduced by Maurice Natanson; with a preface by H.L. van Breda. — The Hague: M. Nijhoff, 1962-66. 3 v.: port. (Phaenomenologica. 11, 15, 22) Preface in French and English. Vol. 2 edited and introduced by A. Brodersen; v.3 edited by I. Schutz, with an introd. by Aron Gurwitsch. 1. Phenomenology 2. Social sciences — Methodology I. T. II. Series.
H61.S44 197-    300.1    LC 63-39472 rev.

**Weber, Max, 1864-1920.** • 4.1216
The methodology of the social sciences / translated and edited by Edward A. Shils, and Henry A. Finch; with a foreword by Edward A. Shils. — [1st ed.]. —

Glencoe, Ill.: Free Press, 1949. xvii, 188 p. 1. Social sciences — Methodology I. Shils, Edward Albert, 1911- II. T.
H61.W4     *LC* 49-9843

**Weber, Max, 1864-1920.**     **4.1217**
[Roscher und Knies und die logischen Probleme der historischen Nationalökonomie. English] Roscher and Knies: the logical problems of historical economics / Max Weber; translated with an introd. by Guy Oakes. — New York: Free Press, [1975] vii, 294 p.; 22 cm. Translation of Roscher und Knies und die logischen Probleme der historischen Nationalökonomie. 1. Roscher, Wilhelm, 1817-1894. 2. Knies, Karl, 1821-1898. 3. Social sciences — Methodology I. T.
H61.W4213 1975     300/.7     *LC* 75-6315     *ISBN* 0029340500

**Wildavsky, Aaron B.**     **4.1218**
Speaking truth to power: the art and craft of policy analysis / Aaron Wildavsky. — Boston: Little, Brown, c1979. xiv, 431 p.; 24 cm. 1. Policy sciences I. T.
H61.W554     309.1     *LC* 78-61738

**Winch, Peter.**     **4.1219**
The idea of a social science and its relation to philosophy. — London: Routledge & Kegan Paul; New York: Humanities Press, [1967, c1958] 143 p.; 19 cm. — (Studies in philosophical psychology.) 1. Social sciences — Philosophy I. T. II. Series.
H61.W56 1967     300/.1     *LC* 77-112410

**Shubik, Martin.**     **4.1220**
Game theory in the social sciences: concepts and solutions / Martin Shubik. — Cambridge, Mass.: MIT Press, c1982. 514 p.: ill.; 24 cm. Includes index. 1. Social sciences — Mathematical models. 2. Game theory I. T.
H61.25.S49 1982     300/.1/5193 19     *LC* 82-63     *ISBN* 0262191954

**Ayres, Robert U.**     **4.1221**
Uncertain futures: challenges for decision–makers / Robert U. Ayres. — New York: Wiley, c1979. xviii, 429 p.; 24 cm. 'A Wiley-Interscience publication.' 1. Forecasting 2. Economic forecasting 3. Technological forecasting I. T.
H61.4.A9     338.5/44     *LC* 78-10252     *ISBN* 0471042501

# H62–67 Teaching. Research

**National Council for the Social Studies.**     • **4.1222**
Yearbook – National Council for the Social Studies. 1st- 1931-. [Arlington, Va., etc., National Council for the Social Sciences, etc.] v. ill., maps 24 cm. Annual. Two yearbooks issued in 1937. 1. Social sciences — Yearbooks. I. T.
H62.A1 N3     307     *LC* 31-6192

**Diener, Edward, 1946-.**     **4.1223**
Ethics in social and behavioral research / Edward Diener and Rick Crandall. — Chicago: University of Chicago Press, 1978. x, 266 p.; 22 cm. Includes indexes. 1. Social sciences — Research — United States. 2. Ethical problems I. Crandall, Rick. joint author. II. T.
H62.D53     174/.9/301     *LC* 78-8881     *ISBN* 0226148238 pbk

**Ivey, Allen E.**     **4.1224**
Microcounseling: innovations in interviewing, counseling, psychotherapy, and psychoeducation / by Allen E. Ivey and Jerry Authier; foreword by Bernard G. Guerney, Jr.; introd. by Dwight W. Allen; with contributions by Norma B. Gluckstern, Kay Gustafson, Jerry A. Kasdorf. — 2d ed. — Springfield, Ill.: Thomas, c1978. xxxii, 584 p.; 24 cm. Includes indexes. 1. Interviewing — Study and teaching. 2. Counseling — Study and teaching. I. Authier, Jerry, joint author. II. T.
H62.I85 1978     658.3/112 19     *LC* 77-21556     *ISBN* 0398037124

**Jay, Martin, 1944-.**     **4.1225**
The dialectical imagination; a history of the Frankfurt School and the Institute of Social Research, 1923–1950. — [1st ed.]. — Boston: Little, Brown, [1973] xxi, 382 p.; 25 cm. 1. Institut für Sozialforschung (Frankfurt am Main, Germany) — History. 2. Frankfurt school of sociology 3. Social science research — United States. I. T.
H62.J37     300/.7/204341     *LC* 72-10119     *ISBN* 0316460494

**Kenworthy, Leonard Stout, 1912-.**     **4.1226**
Guide to social studies teaching in secondary schools [by] Leonard S. Kenworthy. — 4th ed. — Belmont, Calif.: Wadsworth Pub. Co., [1973] vi, 414 p.: illus.; 28 cm. 1. Social sciences — Study and teaching (Secondary) I. T.
H62.K42 1973     300/.7/1273     *LC* 73-78388     *ISBN* 0534003052

**Miller, Delbert Charles, 1913-.**     **4.1227**
Handbook of research design and social measurement / Delbert C. Miller. — 3d ed. — New York: D. McKay, 1977. x, 518 p.; 26 cm. 1. Social sciences — Research 2. Sociometry I. T.
H62.M44 1977     302/.072 19     *LC* 77-128     *ISBN* 067930312X

**Rothman, Jack.**     **4.1228**
Promoting innovation and change in organizations and communities: a planning manual / Jack Rothman, John L. Erlich, Joseph G. Teresa. — New York: Wiley, [1976] ix, 309 p.; 24 cm. Abridged and rev. ed. published as: Changing organizations and community programs. c1981. 1. Community organization — Handbooks, manuals, etc. 2. Community development — Handbooks, manuals, etc. 3. Diffusion of innovations — Handbooks, manuals, etc. 4. Evaluation research (Social action programs) — United States — Handbooks, manuals, etc. I. Erlich, John. joint author. II. Teresa, Joseph G., 1941- joint author. III. T.
H62.R675     361.6/1/068 19     *LC* 75-19454     *ISBN* 0471739677

**Schuman, Howard.**     **4.1229**
Questions and answers in attitude surveys: experiments on question form, wording, and context / Howard Schuman, Stanley Presser. — New York: Academic Press, c1981. xii, 370 p.; 24 cm. — (Quantitative studies in social relations.) Includes index. 1. Social sciences — Research 2. Social surveys 3. Interviewing I. Presser, Stanley, 1950- II. T. III. Series.
H62.S349     300/.723 19     *LC* 81-10991     *ISBN* 0126313504

**Sudman, Seymour.**     **4.1230**
Asking questions / Seymour Sudman, Norman M. Bradburn. — 1st ed. — San Francisco: Jossey-Bass, 1982. xvi, 397 p.; 24 cm. — (Jossey-Bass series in social and behavioral sciences) Includes index. 1. Social sciences — Research 2. Questionnaires I. Bradburn, Norman M. II. T. III. Series.
H62.S7968 1982     300/.723 19     *LC* 82-48065     *ISBN* 0875895468

**Sudman, Seymour.**     **4.1231**
Response effects in surveys; a review and synthesis, by Seymour Sudman and Norman M. Bradburn. — Chicago: Aldine Pub. Co., [1974] xvii, 257 p.; 23 cm. — (National Opinion Research Center. Monographs in social research, 16) 1. Interviewing 2. Social surveys I. Bradburn, Norman M. joint author. II. T. III. Series.
H62.S797     001.4/33     *LC* 73-89510     *ISBN* 0202302709

**Clark, Terry N.**     **4.1232**
Prophets and patrons: the French university and the emergence of the social sciences [by] Terry Nichols Clark. — Cambridge, Mass.: Harvard University Press, 1973. x, 282 p.; 25 cm. 1. Social sciences — Study and teaching — France — History. 2. Social sciences — Research — France — History. 3. Universities and colleges — France — History. I. T.
H62.5.F7 C5     300.7/1144     *LC* 72-93947     *ISBN* 0674715802

**Kuznets, Simon.**     **4.1233**
Quantitative economic research: trends and problems, by Simon Kuznets. New York, National Bureau of Economic Research; distributed by Columbia University Press, 1972. xxii, 93 p. 24 cm. (Economic research: retrospect and prospect, v. 7) (National Bureau of Economic Research. General series, 96) (Fiftieth Anniversary Colloquium series) 1. Economics — Research — United States — Congresses. 2. Econometrics — Congresses. I. Kuznets, Simon Smith, 1901- II. T. III. Series.
H62.5.U5 K8x     330.9/73/092 s 330/.01/8     *LC* 77-187321     *ISBN* 0870142569 *ISBN* 087014281X

**Chase, Stuart, 1888-.**     • **4.1234**
The proper study of mankind / by Stuart Chase in consultation with Edmund deS. Brunner. — [2d rev. ed.]. — New York: Harper & Row, [1962, c1956] xiv, 327 p.; 22 cm. 1. Social sciences 2. Anthropology 3. Social problems I. T.
H91.C5 1962     301     *LC* 63-12603

**Mullins, Carolyn J.**     **4.1235**
A guide to writing and publishing in the social and behavioral sciences / Carolyn J. Mullins. — New York: Wiley, c1977. xvi, 431 p.; 22 cm. 'A Wiley-Interscience publication.' Includes index. 1. Social sciences — Authorship. 2. English language — Technical English I. T.
H91.M8     808/.0663021 19     *LC* 77-1153     *ISBN* 0471624209. *ISBN* 0471027081 pbk

**Pitfalls of analysis / edited by Giandomenico Majone, Edward**     **4.1236**
**S. Quade.**
Chichester [W. Sussex]; New York: Wiley, c1980. viii, 213 p.; 24 cm. (International series on applied systems analysis. 8) 'A Wiley—Interscience publication.' 1. Policy sciences — Addresses, essays, lectures. 2. System analysis — Addresses, essays, lectures. I. Majone, Giandomenico. II. Quade, E. S. (Edward S.) III. Series.
H97.P57 1980     003 19     *LC* 79-41700     *ISBN* 0471277460

# HA STATISTICS

**United Nations. Statistical Office.**    • **4.1237**
Statistical yearbook. Annuaire statistique. 1st- issue; 1948-. New York [etc.]
United Nations. v. 30 cm. Annual. 1. Statistics — Periodicals. I. United
Nations. Statistical Office. Annuaire statistique. II. T.
HA12.5.U63     310/.5     *LC* 50-2746

**Demographic yearbook. Annuaire démographique.**    • **4.1238**
[1st]- 1948-. New York [etc.] Dept. of Economic and Social Affairs, Statistical
Office, United Nations. v. 30 cm. (< 1974- >: [Document] - United Nations,
ST/ESA/STAT/ser. R) Annual. Yearbooks for 1948- issued with the United
Nations publications sales no.: 1949.XIII.1. Issue no. 2 covers 2 years, 1949-50.
Issue for 1978 has: Historical supplement. 1. Population — Statistics —
Periodicals. I. United Nations. Statistical Office. II. United Nations. Dept. of
Social Affairs. III. United Nations. Dept. of Economic Affairs. IV. United
Nations. Dept. of Economic and Social Affairs. V. United Nations. Dept. of
International Economic and Social Affairs.
HA17.D45     312.058     *LC* 50-641

# HA29–48 Theory. Method. Statistical Services

**Federer, Walter Theodore, 1915-.**    **4.1239**
Statistics and society; data collection and interpretation [by] Walter T. Federer.
New York, M. Dekker, 1973. ix, 399 p. illus. 26 cm. (Statistics: textbooks and
monographs, v. 3) 1. Statistics I. T.
HA29.F34     001.4/22     *LC* 73-79457     *ISBN* 0824760832

**Hoel, Paul Gerhard, 1905-.**    **4.1240**
Elementary statistics / Paul G. Hoel. — 4th ed. — New York: Wiley, c1976. xi,
361 p.: ill.; 24 cm. (Wiley series in probability and mathematical statistics)
Includes index. 1. Statistics I. T.
HA29.H662 1976     519.5     *LC* 75-33400     *ISBN* 0471403024

**Wallis, W. Allen (Wilson Allen), 1912-.**    • **4.1241**
Statistics, a new approach, by W. Allen Wallis and Harry V. Roberts. Glencoe,
Ill., Free Press [1956] 646 p. illus. 25 cm. 1. Statistics I. Roberts, Harry V.
joint author. II. T.
HA29.W3354     311.2     *LC* 56-8453

**The Forecasting accuracy of major time series methods / S.**    **4.1242**
**Makridakis ... [et al.].**
Chichester; New York: Wiley, c1984. viii, 301 p.: ill.; 24 cm. 1. Time-series
analysis 2. Economic forecasting — Statistical methods. 3. Business
forecasting — Statistical methods. I. Makridakis, Spyros G.
HA30.3.F67 1984     338.5/442/0151955 19     *LC* 83-17055     *ISBN*
0471903272

**Jessen, Raymond James, 1910-.**    **4.1243**
Statistical survey techniques / Raymond J. Jessen. — New York: Wiley, c1978.
vi, 520 p.: ill.; 24 cm. — (Wiley series in probability and mathematical statistics)
(A Wiley publication in applied statistics) 1. Sampling (Statistics) 2. Statistics
I. T.
HA31.2.J48     519.5     *LC* 77-21476     *ISBN* 0471442607

**Lorr, Maurice, 1911-.**    **4.1244**
Cluster analysis for social scientists / Maurice Lorr. — 1st ed. — San
Francisco: Jossey-Bass, 1983. xvi, 233 p.: ill.; 24 cm. — (Jossey-Bass social and
behavioral science series.) Includes index. 1. Cluster analysis 2. Social sciences
— Statistical methods I. T. II. Series.
HA31.3.L67 1983     519.5/3 19     *LC* 82-49283     *ISBN* 0875895662

**Deming, W. Edwards (William Edwards), 1900-.**    **4.1245**
Sample design in business research. New York, Wiley [1960] 517 p. ill. (A Wiley
publication in applied statistics) 1. Sampling (Statistics) I. T.
HA33 D39     *LC* 60-6451

**Kurian, George Thomas.**    **4.1246**
The new book of world rankings / by George Thomas Kurian. — New York,
N.Y.: Facts on File, c1984. xxiv, 490 p.; 27 cm. Updated, rev., and expanded ed.
of: The book of world rankings. 1st ed. 1979. Includes index. 1. Statistics
2. Social indicators 3. Economic indicators 4. Quality of life — Statistics.
I. Kurian, George Thomas. Book of world rankings. II. T.
HA155.K87 1984     310 19     *LC* 82-7380     *ISBN* 087196743X

**The World in figures / editorial information compiled by the**    **4.1247**
**Economist.**
4th ed. — New York: Rand McNally, 1984. 294 p.: ill. (some col.); 27 cm.
Includes indexes. 1. Statistics I. Economist (London, England)
HA155.W66 1984     310 19     *LC* 84-42956     *ISBN* 0528810499

# HA175–4026 Statistics by Country

**Mitroff, Ian I.**    **4.1248**
The 1980 census, policymaking amid turbulence / Ian I. Mitroff, Richard O.
Mason, Vincent P. Barabba. — Lexington, Mass.: LexingtonBooks, c1983. xxv,
255 p.; 24 cm. Includes index. 1. United States. Bureau of the Census.
2. Census undercounts — United States. 3. United States — Census, 20th,
1980. I. Mason, Richard O. II. Barabba, Vincent P., 1934- III. T.
HA201 1980f     304.6/0723 19     *LC* 81-47992     *ISBN* 0669052248

**Andriot, John L.**    **4.1249**
Population abstract of the United States / compiled and edited by John L.
Andriot. — McLean, Va. (Box 195, McLean 22101): Andriot Associates,
c1983. 2 v.: maps; 29 cm. Companion publication to: Township atlas of the
United States. 1979. 'Enlarged and revised edition'-Foreword. 1. United States
— Population — Statistics. I. T.
HA202.A686 1983     312/.0973 19     *LC* 83-196909

**United States. Bureau of the Census.**    **4.1250**
Historical statistics of the United States, colonial times to 1970. — Bicentennial
ed. — Washington: U.S. Dept. of Commerce, Bureau of the Census: for sale by
the Supt. of Docs., U.S. Govt. Print. Off., 1975. 2 v. (xvi, 1200, 32 p.); 30 cm.
(House document - 93d Congress, 1st session; no. 93-78) 1. United States —
Statistics I. T.
HA202.B87 1975     317.3     *LC* 75-38832

**McClelland, Peter D.**    **4.1251**
Demographic dimensions of the New Republic: American interregional
migration, vital statistics, and manumissions, 1800–1860 / Peter D. McClelland
and Richard J. Zeckhauser. — Cambridge [Cambridgeshire]; New York:
Cambridge University Press, 1982. xiv, 222 p.: map; 24 cm. Includes index.
1. Migration, Internal — United States — Statistics — History — 19th
century. 2. Slavery — United States — Emancipation — Statistics — History
— 19th century. 3. United States — Population — Statistics — History — 19th
century. 4. United States — Statistics, Vital — History — 19th century.
5. United States — Census — History — 19th century. I. Zeckhauser,
Richard. II. T.
HA214.M38 1982     312/.0973 19     *LC* 82-9648     *ISBN* 0521243092

**Canada year book.**    • **4.1252**
1905-. Ottawa: Statistics Canada. v.: ill. (some fold., some col.), maps (some
fold., some col.); 26 cm. Annual. Subtitle varies. — Includes indexes. —
1. Canada — Statistics — Yearbooks. I. Statistics Canada. II. Canada.
Dominion Bureau of Statistics.
HA744.S81     F5003.C3 A3.     317.1     *LC* 73-640929

**Historical statistics of Canada.**    **4.1253**
2nd ed. / F.H. Leacy, editor. — [Ottawa]: Statistics Canada, c1983. ca. 900 p.;
30 cm. 'M.C. Urquhart, editor and K.A.H. Buckley, assistant editor, 1st ed.'
'Published by Statistics Canada in joint sponsorship with the Social Science
Federation of Canada.' Includes index. 1. Canada — Statistics — History.
I. Leacy, F. H. II. Statistics Canada. III. Social Science Federation of
Canada.
HA745.H57 1983     317.1 19     *LC* 83-173149     *ISBN* 0660112590

**Mitchell, B. R. (Brian R.)**    **4.1254**
European historical statistics, 1750–1975 / B.R. Mitchell. — 2nd rev. ed. —
New York, N.Y.: Facts on File, 1980. xx, 868 p.; 28 cm. Rev. ed. of: European
historical statistics, 1750-1970 / B.R. Mitchell. 1975. 1. Europe — Statistics —
History. I. T. II. Title: European historical statistics, seventeen fifty-nineteen
seventy-five.
HA1107.M5 1980     314 19     *LC* 80-67014     *ISBN* 0871963299

**Shoup, Paul.**    **4.1255**
The East European and Soviet data handbook: political, social, and
developmental indicators, 1945–1975 / Paul S. Shoup. — New York: Columbia
University Press; Stanford, Calif.: Hoover Institution Press, 1981. xv, 482 p.; 31
cm. 1. Russia — Statistics. 2. Europe, Eastern — Statistics. I. T.
HA1446.S53     314.7 19     *LC* 80-25682     *ISBN* 0231042523

**United Nations. Secretariat.**    • **4.1256**
Population growth and manpower in the Philippines / joint study by the United
Nations [Secretariat] and the Government of the Philippines National
Economic Council. — New York: United Natiosn, Dept. of Economic and
Social Affairs, 1960. v, 66 p.: ill. (Population studies, no. 32) United Nations.

[Document] ST/SOA/ser.A/32. 'United Nations publication. Sales no.: 61.XIII.2. 1. Philippines — Population. I. Philippines (Republic). National Economic Council. II. T.
HA1825.U55 1960

**Japan statistical yearbook.**                                    • **4.1257**
1st- 1949-. [Tokyo?]: Nihon Statistical Association. v. 27 cm. Annual. Title and text also in Japanese. 1. Japan — Statistics.
HA1832.J36      315.2      LC 52-30656

**Nihon Ginkō. Tōkeikyoku.**                                    • **4.1258**
Meiji ikō hompō shuyō keizai tōkei = Hundred–year statistics of the Japanese economy. Tokyo: Statistics Dept., Bank of Japan, 1966. 616 p. 27 cm. 1. Japan — Statistics. I. T. II. Title: Hundred-year statistics of the Japanese economy.
HA1835.N5      LC j 68-2071

**Peebles, Patrick.**                                             **4.1259**
Sri Lanka: a handbook of historical statistics / Patrick Peebles. — Boston, Mass.: G.K. Hall, c1982. xxvi, 357 p.; 29 cm. — (Reference publication in international historical statistics.) 1. Sri Lanka — Statistics. I. T. II. Series.
HA4570.8.P43 1982      315.49/3 19      LC 81-20210      ISBN 0816181608

**Mitchell, B. R. (Brian R.)**                                    **4.1260**
International historical statistics: Africa and Asia / B.R. Mitchell. — New York: New York University Press, 1982. xx, 761 p.; 28 cm. Companion vol. to: European historical statistics, 1750-1975 / B.R. Mitchell. 2nd rev. ed. 1980. 1. Africa — Statistics — History. 2. Asia — Statistics — History. I. T.
HA4675.M55 1982      315 19      LC 81-18905      ISBN 081475385X

# HB ECONOMIC THEORY

## HB31–55 Collections

**Edgeworth, Francis Ysidro, 1845-1926.** • 4.1261
Papers relating to political economy. — New York, B. Franklin [1963-. v. illus. 24 cm. 'Articles and reviews which appeared in the Economic journal ... (1891-1921 inclusive)' Includes bibliography. 1. Economics — Addresses, essays, lectures. I. T.
HB33.E32    330.82    *LC* 63-12656

**Friedman, Milton, 1912-.** • 4.1262
Essays in positive economics. [Chicago] University of Chicago Press [1953] 328 p. ill. 1. Economics — Addresses, essays, lectures I. T.
HB33 F7    *LC* 53-3533

**Robinson, Joan, 1903-.** • 4.1263
Collected economic papers / Joan Robinson. — Oxford: B. Blackwell, 1951-1980. 5 v: ill. and index. 1. Economics — Addresses, essays, lectures. I. T.
HB33.R6    *LC* 52-995    *ISBN* 0391002414

**Robertson, Dennis Holme, Sir, 1890-1963.** • 4.1264
Lectures on economic principles / Sir Dennis H. Robertson. — London: Staples Press, 1957-. v.; 21 cm. 1. Economics — Addresses, essays, lectures I. T.
HB33 R6 1957b    *LC* A 58-2335

**Samuelson, Paul Anthony, 1915-.** 4.1265
The collected scientific papers of Paul A. Samuelson. Edited by Joseph E. Stiglitz. — Cambridge, Mass.: M.I.T. Press, 1966-. 3 v.: illus.; 25 cm. Vol. 3 edited by R. C. Merton. 1. Economics — Collected works. I. T.
HB33.S2    330/.08    *LC* 65-28408

**Smith, Adam, 1723-1790.** 4.1266
The Glasgow edition of the works ... — See full entry at AC7.S59 1986. I. T.

**Wicksell, Knut, 1851-1926.** • 4.1267
Selected papers on economic theory. Edited with an introd. by Erik Lindahl. — New York: A. M. Kelley, 1969. 292 p.: port.; 22 cm. — (Reprints of economic classics) Reprint of the 1958 ed. 1. Economics — Addresses, essays, lectures. I. T.
HB33.W5 1969    330/.08    *LC* 68-58667

**American Economic Association.** • 4.1268
Surveys of economic theory. Prepared for the American Economic Association and the Royal Economic Society. London, Macmillan; New York, St Martin's Press, 1965-66. 3 v. illus. 26 cm. 'First published in the American economic review and the Economic journal.' 1. Economics — Addresses, essays, lectures. I. Royal Economic Society (Great Britain) II. T.
HB34.A48    330    *LC* 65-26933

**Hayek, Friedrich A. von (Friedrich August), 1899-.** • 4.1269
Individualism and economic order, by Friedrich A. Hayek. — [1st Gateway ed.]. — Chicago: H. Regnery Co., [1972, c1948] vi, 271 p.; 21 cm. 'A Gateway edition.' 1. Economics — Addresses, essays, lectures. I. T.
HB34.H3 1972    330    *LC* 74-183821

**Spengler, Joseph John, 1902- ed.** • 4.1270
Essays in economic thought: Aristotle to Marshall, edited by Joseph J. Spengler and William R. Allen. Chicago, Rand McNally [1960] 800 p. ill. (Rand McNally economics series) 1. Economics — Collections I. Allen, William Richard, 1924- jt. ed. II. T.
HB34 S66    *LC* 60-8991

**Veblen, Thorstein, 1857-1929.** • 4.1271
Essays in our changing order, by Thorstein Veblen; edited by Leon Ardzrooni ... New York, The Viking press, 1934. xviii, 472 p.: front. (port.); 20 cm. 'A list of book reviews, written for 'The Journal of political economy' by Thorstein Veblen': p. 471-472. 1. Economics — Addresses, essays, lectures. 2. World War, 1914-1918 — Addresses, sermons, etc. I. Ardzrooni, Leon. II. T. III. Title: Our changing order.
HB34.V38    330.4    *LC* 34-27284

**Veblen, Thorstein, 1857-1929.** • 4.1272
The place of science in modern civilisation, and other essays. — New York, Russell & Russell, 1961. 509 p. 22 cm. 1. Economics — Addresses, essays, lectures. 2. Science — Addresses, essays, lectures. I. T.
HB34.V4 1961    330.8    *LC* 60-10709

## HB61 Dictionaries

**Encyclopedia of economics / Douglas Greenwald, editor–in–chief.** 4.1273
New York: McGraw-Hill, c1982. xxxiii, 1070 p.; 24 cm. 1. Economics — Dictionaries. I. Greenwald, Douglas.
HB61.E55    330/.03/21 19    *LC* 81-4969    *ISBN* 0070243670

**The McGraw–Hill dictionary of modern economics: a handbook of terms and organizations / [edited by] Douglas Greenwald in collaboration with Henry C.F. Arnold ... [et al.].** 4.1274
3rd ed. — New York: McGraw-Hill, c1983. xiii, 632 p.; 21 cm. 1. Economics — Dictionaries. I. Greenwald, Douglas.
HB61.M3 1983    330/.03/21 19    *LC* 82-17243    *ISBN* 007024376X

**Palgrave, Robert Harry Inglis, Sir, 1827-1919.** • 4.1275
Palgrave's Dictionary of political economy / edited by Henry Higgs. — New York: A. M. Kelly, 1963. 3 v.: ill. — (Reprints of economic classics) 1. Economics — Dictionaries. I. Higgs, Henry, 1864-1940, ed. II. T. III. Title: Dictionary of political economy.
HB61.P17 1963    330.3    *LC* 63-22261

## HB71–74 Economics: General. Methodology

**Dorfman, Robert.** • 4.1276
Linear programming and economic analysis [by] Robert Dorfman, Paul A. Samuelson [and] Robert M. Solow. New York, McGraw-Hill, 1958. 527 p. illus. 24 cm. (The Rand series) 1. Input-output analysis 2. Economics — Mathematical models I. T.
HB71.D6    330.182    *LC* 57-7999

**Hutchison, T. W. (Terence Wilmot)** 4.1277
Knowledge and ignorance in economics / T. W. Hutchison. — Chicago: University of Chicago Press, 1977. 186 p.; 23 cm. 1. Economics 2. Economics — Methodology I. T.
HB71.H799 1977    330    *LC* 76-54771    *ISBN* 0226362361

**Information sources in economics / editor, John Fletcher.** 4.1278
2nd ed. — London; Boston: Butterworths, 1984. xii, 339 p.; 23 cm. — (Butterworths guides to information sources.) Rev. ed. of: The Use of economics literature. 1971. Includes index. 1. Economics literature — Addresses, essays, lectures. I. Fletcher, John, 1931- II. Use of economics literature. III. Series.
HB71.I53 1984    016.33 19    *LC* 83-25230    *ISBN* 0408114711

**Miernyk, William H.** 4.1279
The elements of input–output analysis / by William H. Miernyk. — New York: Random House [1965] xi, 156 p.: ill.; 21 cm. 1. Input-output analysis I. T.
HB71.M62    339.23    *LC* 65-23339

**Nelson, Richard R.** 4.1280
An evolutionary theory of economic change / Richard R. Nelson and Sidney G. Winter. — Cambridge, Mass.: Belknap Press of Harvard University Press, 1982. xi, 437 p.: ill.; 24 cm. Includes index. 1. Economics 2. Economic development 3. Organizational change I. Winter, Sidney G. II. T. III. Title: Economic change.
HB71.N44 1982    338.9/001 19    *LC* 81-13455    *ISBN* 0674272277

**Parsons, Talcott, 1902-.**      • **4.1281**
Economy and society; a study in the integration of economic and social theory, by Talcott Parsons and Neil J. Smelser. — Glencoe, Ill.: Free Press, [1956] 322 p.: illus.; 23 cm. 1. Economics I. Smelser, Neil J. joint author. II. T.
HB71.P18      330.1      *LC* 57-3481

**Robinson, Joan, 1903-.**      • **4.1282**
Economic philosophy. — Chicago, Aldine Pub. Co. [1962] 150 p. 22 cm. Includes bibliography. 1. Economics I. T.
HB71.R6      330.1      *LC* 62-15526

**Thurow, Lester C.**      **4.1283**
Dangerous currents: the state of economics / Lester C. Thurow. — 1st ed. — New York: Random House, 1983. xix, 247 p.: ill.; 24 cm. 1. Economics 2. United States — Economic policy — 1981- I. T.
HB71.T475 1983      338.973 19      *LC* 83-42824      *ISBN* 0394531507

**Tinbergen, Jan, 1903-.**      • **4.1284**
Mathematical models of economic growth [by] Jan Tinbergen [and] Hendricus C. Bos. New York, McGraw-Hill, 1962. 131 p. ill. (Economics handbook series) 1. Economics — Mathematical models I. Bos, Hendricus Cornelis, 1926- jt. author II. T.
HB71 T5      *LC* 61-13760

**Weintraub, E. Roy.**      **4.1285**
Microfoundations: the compatibility of microeconomics and macroeconomics / E. Roy Weintraub. — Cambridge [Eng.]; New York: Cambridge University Press, 1979. viii, 175 p.; 22 cm. — (Cambridge surveys of economic literature) Includes indexes. 1. Microeconomics 2. Macroeconomics 3. Equilibrium (Economics) 4. Economics — Mathematical models I. T.
HB71.W397      330.1      *LC* 78-16551      *ISBN* 0521223059

**Alt, James E.**      **4.1286**
Political economics / James E. Alt and K. Alec Chrystal. — Berkeley: University of California Press, c1983. xii, 275 p.; 22 cm. — (California series on social choice and political economy.) Includes index. 1. Economics 2. Political science 3. Economic policy I. Chrystal, K. Alec, 1946- II. T. III. Series.
HB73.A42 1983      330 19      *LC* 82-23721      *ISBN* 0520049349

**Carnoy, Martin.**      **4.1287**
Economic democracy: the challenge of the 1980's / Martin Carnoy and Derek Shearer. — White Plains, N.Y.: M.E. Sharpe, 1980. 436 p. Includes index. 1. Economics 2. Democracy I. Shearer, Derek. II. T.
HB74.D4 C37      HB74D4 C37.      *LC* 79-55934      *ISBN* 0394738896

## HB74.M3 MATHEMATICAL ECONOMICS.
### ECONOMETRICS
(see also: HB135-145)

**Allen, R. G. D. (Roy George Douglas).**      • **4.1288**
Macro–economic theory: a mathematical treatment, by R. G. D. Allen. London: Macmillan; New York: St. Martin's P., 1967. xii, 420 p.: tables, diagrs.; 23 cm. 1. Economics, Mathematical 2. Macroeconomics I. T.
HB74.M3 A36      330.1/84      *LC* 67-86310

**Allen, Roy George Douglas.**      • **4.1289**
Mathematical analysis for economists / by R.G.D. Allen. — London: Macmillan; New York: St. Martin's Press, 1964. xv, 548 p.: ill. 1. Mathematical analysis 2. Economics, Mathematical I. T.
HB74.M3 A38 1964      *LC* 66-5641

**Arrow, Kenneth Joseph, 1921-.**      **4.1290**
General competitive analysis [by] Kenneth J. Arrow [and] F. H. Hahn. San Francisco, Holden-Day [1971] xii, 452 p. illus. 24 cm. (Mathematical economics texts, 6) 1. Economics, Mathematical 2. Microeconomics I. Hahn, Frank. joint author. II. T. III. Series.
HB74.M3 A75      330/.01/82      *LC* 72-170637      *ISBN* 0816202753

**Bowley, A. L. (Arthur Lyon) Sir, 1869-1957.**      • **4.1291**
The mathematical groundwork of economics: an introductory treatise / by A. L. Bowley. — New York: A. M. Kelley, 1965. viii, 98 p.: ill. — (Reprints of economic classics) 1. Economics, Mathematical I. T.
HB74.M3 B6 1965      330.182      *LC* 65-16995

**Christ, Carl F.**      • **4.1292**
Econometric models and methods [by] Carl F. Christ. — New York: Wiley, [1966] xxiii, 705 p.: illus.; 24 cm. 1. Econometrics I. T.
HB74.M3 C56      *LC* 66-21050

**Cournot, A. A. (Antoine Augustin), 1801-1877.**      • **4.1293**
Researches into the mathematical principles of the theory of wealth, 1838. Translated by Nathaniel T. Bacon. With an essay on Cournot and mathematical

economics and a bibliography of mathematical economics by Irving Fisher. — New York, A. M. Kelley, 1960. xxiv, 213 p. illus. 18 cm. — (Reprints of economic classics) 'Bibliography of mathematical economics': p. 173-209. 1. Economics, Mathematical I. Fisher, Irving, 1867-1947. II. T.
HB74.M3C653 1960      *LC* 64-7663

**Edgeworth, Francis Ysidro, 1845-1926.**      • **4.1294**
Mathematical physics; an essay on the application of mathematics to the moral sciences. London, Kegan Paul, 1881. [New York, A. M. Kelley, 1961] 150 p. illus. 22 cm. 1. Economics, Mathematical 2. Utilitarianism I. T.
HB74.M3 E3 1961      *LC* 63-5313

**Fisher, Irving, 1867-1947.**      • **4.1295**
Mathematical investigations in the theory of value and price, 1892. Appreciation and interest, 1896. New York, A.M. Kelley, 1965. 126, x, 100 p. illus. 24 cm. (Reprints of economic classics) 1. Economics, Mathematical 2. Value 3. Prices 4. Interest 5. Bimetallism I. Fisher, Irving, 1867-1947. Appreciation and interest. II. T. III. Title: Appreciation and interest.
HB74.M3 F53 1965      330.162      *LC* 65-19655

**Fox, Karl August, 1917-.**      • **4.1296**
Intermediate economic statistics [by] Karl A. Fox. New York, Wiley [1968] x, 568 p. illus. 24 cm. 1. Econometrics 2. Economics — Statistical methods I. T.
HB74.M3 F67      330/.01/82      *LC* 67-27273

**Goldfeld, Stephen M.**      **4.1297**
Nonlinear methods in econometrics. [By] Stephen M. Goldfeld and Richard E. Quandt. With a contribution by Dennis E. Smallwood. — Amsterdam: North-Holland Pub. Co., 1972. xi, 280 p.; 23 cm. — (Contributions to economic analysis. v. 77) 1. Econometrics I. Quandt, Richard E. joint author. II. T. III. Series.
HB74.M3 G62      330/.01/82      *LC* 77-157013      *ISBN* 0720431778

**Hansen, Bent, 1920-.**      • **4.1298**
A survey of general equilibrium systems. — New York: McGraw-Hill, [1970] xiii, 238 p.: illus.; 23 cm. — (Economics handbook series) 1. Economics, Mathematical 2. Statics and dynamics (Social sciences) I. T. II. Title: General equilibrium systems.
HB74.M3 H325      339.5 19      *LC* 74-115142

**Johnston, J. (John), 1923-.**      **4.1299**
Econometric methods [by] J. Johnston. 2d ed. New York, McGraw-Hill [1971, c1972] x, 437 p. illus. 24 cm. 1. Econometrics 2. Mathematical statistics I. T.
HB74.M3 J577 1972      330/.01/82      *LC* 79-142968      *ISBN* 0070326797

**Kalecki, Michał.**      • **4.1300**
Theory of economic dynamics; an essay on cyclical and long–run changes in capitalist economy, by M. Kalecki. — New York: A. M. Kelley, 1969 [c1965] 178 p.: illus.; 23 cm. 1. Economics, Mathematical 2. Business cycles — Mathematical models. I. T.
HB74.M3 K32 1969      330/.01/82      *LC* 79-86244      *ISBN* 0678060010

**Malinvaud, Edmond.**      • **4.1301**
[Méthodes statistiques de l'économétrie. English] Statistical methods of econometrics [by] E. Malinvaud. Translation by A. Silvey. 2d rev. ed. Amsterdam, North-Holland Pub. Co; New York, American Elsevier Pub. Co., 1970. xv, 744 p. 23 cm. (Studies in mathematical and managerial economics. v. 6) Translation of Méthodes statistiques de l'économétrie. 1. Econometrics I. T. II. Series.
HB74.M3 M253 1970      330/.01/82      *LC* 78-126504      *ISBN* 0444100482

**Morgenstern, Oskar, 1902-.**      • **4.1302**
On the accuracy of economic observations. 2d ed., completely rev. Princeton, N.J., Princeton University Press, 1963. xiv, 322 p. diagrs., tables. 1. Economics, Mathematical I. T.
HB74 M3 M63 1963      *LC* 63-15358

**Zellner, Arnold.**      **4.1303**
An introduction to Bayesian inference in econometrics. — New York: J. Wiley, [1971] xv, 431 p.; 24 cm. — (Wiley series in probability and mathematical statistics) 1. Econometrics 2. Bayesian statistical decision theory I. T.
HB74.M3 Z44      330/.01/82      *LC* 70-156329      *ISBN* 0471981656

# HB75–129 History of Economic Theory

## HB75–87 GENERAL WORKS

**Blaug, Mark.**      **4.1304**
Economic theory in retrospect / Mark Blaug. — 4th ed. — Cambridge; New York: Cambridge University Press, 1985. xxvii, 737 p.: ill.; 24 cm. 1. Economics — History I. T.
HB75.B664 1985    330.1/09 19    *LC* 84-19994    *ISBN* 0521303540

**Commons, John Rogers, 1862-1945.**      • **4.1305**
Institutional economics, its place in political economy. — Madison, University of Wisconsin Press, 1961 [c1934] 2 v. (xiii, 921 p.) illus. 21 cm. Includes bibliography. 1. Economics — Hist. 2. Political science — Hist. I. T.
HB75.C7 1959    330.1    *LC* 59-9716 rev

**Galbraith, John Kenneth, 1908-.**      **4.1306**
The age of uncertainty / John Kenneth Galbraith. Boston: Houghton Mifflin, 1977. 365 p.: ill.; 26 cm. Based on a BBC television series scheduled for release in 1977. 1. Economics — History 2. Economic history I. T.
HB75.G27    330/.09    *LC* 76-26965    *ISBN* 0395249007

**Hutchison, T. W. (Terence Wilmot)**      **4.1307**
On revolutions and progress in economic knowledge / T. W. Hutchison. — Cambridge; New York: Cambridge University Press, 1978. xiv, 349 p.; 24 cm. Includes indexes. 1. Economics — History 2. Economics — Methodology I. T.
HB75.H79    330/.09    *LC* 77-82498    *ISBN* 0521218055

**Hutchison, Terence Wilmot.**      **4.1308**
The politics and philosophy of economics: Marxians, Keynesians, and Austrians / T.W. Hutchison. — New York: New York University Press, 1981. x, 310 p.; 24 cm. 1. Economics 2. Marxian economics 3. Keynesian economics 4. Austrian school of economists I. T.
HB75.H792    330.1 19    *LC* 81-11239    *ISBN* 0814734162

**Knight, Frank Hyneman, 1885-.**      • **4.1309**
On the history and method of economics; selected essays. [Chicago] University of Chicago Press [1956] 308 p. 1. Economics — History 2. Economics — Methodology I. T.
HB75 K55    *LC* 56-6632

**Myrdal, Gunnar, 1898-.**      • **4.1310**
The political element in the development of economic theory. Translated from the German by Paul Streeten. — Cambridge: Harvard University Press, 1954. xvii, 248 p.; 23 cm. Title of original Swedish ed.: Vetenskap och politik i nationalekonomien. 'Appendix: Recent controversies, by Paul Streeten': p. 208-217. 'Notes': p. 218-241. 1. Economics — History 2. Economic policy I. T.
HB75.M97    *LC* A 54-6170

**Polanyi, Karl, 1886-1964.**      **4.1311**
Primitive, archaic, and modern economies; essays of Karl Polanyi. Edited by George Dalton. [1st ed.] Garden City, N.Y., Anchor Books, 1968. liv, 346 p. port. 18 cm. 1. Economics 2. Economic anthropology I. T.
HB75.P67    330.1    *LC* 68-10606

**Schumpeter, Joseph Alois, 1883-1950.**      • **4.1312**
History of economic analysis; edited from manuscript by Elizabeth Boody Schumpeter. New York, Oxford University Press, 1954. xxv, 1260 p. illus. 24 cm. 1. Economics — History I. T. II. Title: Economic analysis.
HB75.S456    330/.09 19    *LC* 52-9434

**Stigler, George J. 1911-.**      • **4.1313**
Production and distribution theories, 1870 to 1895 the formative period [by] George J. Stigler. — New York, The Macmillan company, 1941. vii, 392 p. diagrs. 21 cm. 'This work was first completed in 1937 as a doctoral dissertation, which was submitted early in 1938 to the University of Chicago. It has since been revised and a chapter on John Bates Clark has been added.'—Pref. 1. Economics — Hist. I. T.
HB75.S77 1941    338    *LC* 41-6430

**Williams, Philip L., 1949-.**      **4.1314**
The emergence of the theory of the firm. from Adam Smith to Alfred Marshall / Philip L. Williams. — New York: St. Martin's Press, 1979, c1978. vii, 207 p.: ill.; 23 cm. 1. Microeconomics — History. I. T.
HB75.W6 1979    338.5    *LC* 78-13349    *ISBN* 0312243871

**Heilbroner, Robert L.**      **4.1315**
The worldly philosophers: the lives, times, and ideas of the great economic thinkers / Robert L. Heilbroner. — 5th ed., completely rev. for the 1980's. — New York: Simon and Schuster, c1980. 347 p.; 22 cm. — (A Touchstone book) Includes index. 1. Economists — Biography. 2. Economics — History I. T.
HB76.H4 1980    330.1/092/2    *LC* 79-10331    *ISBN* 0671255959

**Berg, Maxine, 1950-.**      **4.1316**
The machinery question and the making of political economy, 1815–1848 / Maxine Berg. — Cambridge [Eng.]; New York: Cambridge University Press, 1980. 379 p.: ill.; 24 cm. Revision of the author's thesis, Oxford, 1976. Includes index. 1. Economics — History — 19th century 2. Machinery in industry — History — 19th century. 3. Technological innovations — History — 19th century. I. T.
HB85.B35 1980    338/.06/09034    *LC* 79-15271    *ISBN* 0521227828

**O'Brien, D. P. (Denis Patrick), 1939-.**      **4.1317**
The classical economists / by D. P. O'Brien. — [S.l.]: Oxford, 1975. xiii, 306 p.: graphs; 24 cm. 1. Economics — History — 19th century I. T.
HB85.O27    330.15/3    *LC* 75-308578    *ISBN* 0198770154

**Schumpeter, Joseph Alois, 1883-1950.**      • **4.1318**
Ten great economists, from Marx to Keynes. New York, Oxford University Press, 1951. xiv, 305 p. 1. Economists 2. Economics — History I. T.
HB85 S35    *LC* 51-3200

**Supply–side economics: a critical appraisal / edited by Richard H. Fink.**      **4.1319**
[S.l.]: University Publications of America, 1982. xxiv, 488 p.; 24 cm. 1. Supply-side economics 2. United States — Economic policy — 1971- I. Fink, Richard H.
HB87.S85 1982    *ISBN* 0890934606

**Twelve contemporary economists / edited by J.R. Shackleton and Gareth Locksley.**      **4.1320**
New York: Wiley, 1981. ix, 263 p.: ill.; 23 cm. 'A Halsted Press book.' 1. Economics — History — 20th century — Addresses, essays, lectures. 2. Economists — Addresses, essays, lectures. I. Shackleton, J. R. II. Locksley, Gareth.
HB87.T93 1981    330/.092/2 19    *LC* 81-2403    *ISBN* 047027168X

## HB90–99 SPECIAL SCHOOLS

### HB90 Comparative Economics

**Bornstein, Morris, 1927-.**      **4.1321**
Comparative economic systems: models and cases / edited by Morris Bornstein. — 5th ed. — Homewood, Ill.: R.D. Irwin, 1985. x, 386 p.; 24 cm. (Irwin publications in economics.) 1. Comparative economics — Addresses, essays, lectures. I. T. II. Series.
HB90.C654 1985    330.1 19    *LC* 84-82488    *ISBN* 0256032157

**Okun, Arthur M.**      **4.1322**
Equality and efficiency, the big tradeoff / Arthur M. Okun. — Washington: The Brookings Institution, [1975] xi, 124 p.; 22 cm. 'Revised and expanded version of material presented in the Godkin lectures at the John F. Kennedy School of Government of Harvard University in April 1974.' 1. Comparative economics 2. Equality I. T.
HB90.O38 1975    330.12    *LC* 75-5162    *ISBN* 0815764766

### HB91 Mercantile School

**Heckscher, Eli F. (Eli Filip), 1879-1952.**      • **4.1323**
Mercantilism. Authorized translation by Mendel Shapiro. — Rev. [2d] ed. edited by E. F. Sörderlund. — London, Allen & Unwin; New York, Macmillan [1955, c1935] 2 v. 23 cm. 1. Mercantile system 2. Economics — Hist. I. T.
HB91.H42 1955    330.151    *LC* 56-4993

### HB97.5 Marxian Economics

**Brunhoff, Suzanne de.**      **4.1324**
[Monnaie chez Marx. English] Marx on money / by Suzanne de Brunhoff; translated by Maurice J. Goldbloom; pref. by Duncan K. Foley. — New York: Urizen Books, c1976. 139 p.; 23 cm. Translation of La monnaie chez Marx. 1. Marxian economics 2. Money I. T.
HB97.5.B6713    335.4/12    *LC* 76-8249    *ISBN* 0916354431

**Horvat, Branko.**                                                                                      **4.1325**
The political economy of socialism: a Marxist social theory / Branko Horvat. —
Armonk, N.Y.: M.E. Sharpe, c1982. xx, 671 p.: ill.; 24 cm. 1. Marxian
economics 2. Communism and society I. T.
HB97.5.H653        335.4 19        *LC* 81-9430        *ISBN* 0873321847

**Howard, Michael Charles, 1945-.**                                                                      **4.1326**
The political economy of Marx / M.C. Howard and J.E. King. — 2nd ed. —
London; New York: Longman, 1985. x, 269 p.: ill.; 24 cm. — (Modern
economics.) Includes index. 1. Marxian economics I. King, J. E. (John
Edward) II. T. III. Series.
HB97.5.H66 1985        335.4 19        *LC* 84-3953        *ISBN* 0582296277

**Prybyla, Jan S.**                                                                                      **4.1327**
Issues in Socialist economic modernization / Jan S. Prybyla. — New York,
N.Y.: Praeger, 1980. xiii, 121 p.; 25 cm. Includes index. 1. Marxian economics
2. Communist countries — Economic policy. I. T.
HB97.5.P895        335.4/13        *LC* 80-18647        *ISBN* 0030579627

**Roemer, John E.**                                                                                      **4.1328**
Analytical foundations of Marxian economic theory / John E. Roemer. —
Cambridge; New York: Cambridge University Press, 1981. xi, 220 p.: ill.; 24
cm. Includes index. 1. Marxian economics I. T.
HB97.5.R616        335.4 19        *LC* 80-22646        *ISBN* 0521230470

**Ward, Benjamin Needham.**                                                                              **4.1329**
The socialist economy; a study of organizational alternatives, by Benjamin N.
Ward. New York, Random House [1967] ix, 272 p. ill. 1. Marxian economics
2. Socialism I. T.
HB97.5 W3        *LC* 67-15465

## HB98 Austrian School

**Kirzner, Israel M.**                                                                                   **4.1330**
Perception, opportunity, and profit: studies in the theory of entrepreneurship /
Israel M. Kirzner. — Chicago: University of Chicago Press, 1979. xiv, 274 p.;
23 cm. 1. Entrepreneurship 2. Austrian school of economists I. T.
HB98.K57        338.5/2/01        *LC* 79-11765        *ISBN* 0226437736

**The Marginal revolution in economics; interpretation and**                                             **4.1331**
**evaluation. Edited by R. D. Collison Black, A. W. Coats [and]**
**Craufurd D. W. Goodwin.**
Durham, N.C., Duke University Press, 1973. viii, 367 p. 24 cm. 'Papers
presented at a conference held at the Villa Serbelloni, Bellagio, Italy, August
22-28, 1971.' 1. Marginal utility — Congresses. 2. Economics — History —
Congresses. I. Black, R. D. Collison. ed. II. Coats, A. W. (Alfred William),
1924- ed. III. Goodwin, Craufurd D. W. ed.
HB98.M25        330.15/7        *LC* 72-91850        *ISBN* 0822302780

## HB98.2 Neoclassical School

**Ferguson, C. E. (Charles E.)**                                                                       • **4.1332**
The neoclassical theory of production and distribution [by] C. E. Ferguson.
London, Cambridge U.P., 1969. xviii, 384 p. illus. 24 cm. 1. Neoclassical
school of economics 2. Economics — Mathematical models I. T.
HB98.2.F47        330.15/3        *LC* 71-92248        *ISBN* 0521074533

**Marshall, Alfred.**                                                                                    **4.1333**
The early economic writings of Alfred Marshall, 1867–1890 / edited and
introduced by J. K. Whitaker. — New York: Free Press, 1975. 2 v.: ill., graph.;
23 cm. I. Whitaker, John King. II. Marshall, Alfred, 1842-1924. III. T.
HB98.2.M37 1975        *LC* 74-29102

## HB99.3 Welfare Economics

**Lerner, Abba Ptachya, 1903-.**                                                                       • **4.1334**
The economics of control; principles of welfare economics, by Abba P. Lerner.
— New York: A. M. Kelley, 1970. xxii, 428 p.; 22 cm. — (Reprints of economic
classics) Reprint of the 1944 ed. 1. Welfare economics I. T.
HB99.3.L4 1970        320.12        *LC* 75-107922        *ISBN* 0678006180

**Mishan, E. J. (Edward J.), 1917-.**                                                                    **4.1335**
Cost–benefit analysis; an introduction [by] E. J. Mishan. New York, Praeger
[1971] 364 p. illus. 22 cm. (New directions in management and economics)
1. Welfare economics 2. Cost effectiveness 3. Expenditures, Public I. T.
HB99.3.M55        658.1/554 19        *LC* 70-150700

**Scitovsky, Tibor.**                                                                                  • **4.1336**
Welfare and competition. — Rev ed. — Homewood, Ill.: R. D. Irwin, 1971.
xvii, 492 p.: illus.; 24 cm. — (The Irwin series in economics) 1. Welfare
economics 2. Microeconomics I. T.
HB99.3.S33 1971        338        *LC* 73-141396

## HB99.5 Institutional Economics

**Gambs, John Saké, 1899-.**                                                                           • **4.1337**
Beyond supply and demand: a reappraisal of institutional economics / by John
S. Gambs. — New York: Columbia Univ. Press, 1946. 105 p.; 23 cm. 1. Veblen,
Thorstein, 1857-1929. 2. Institutional economics I. T.
HB99.5.V4 G35        330.1        *LC* 46-2666

## HB99.7 Keynesian Economics

**Collins, Robert M.**                                                                                   **4.1338**
The business response to Keynes, 1929–1964 / Robert M. Collins. — New
York: Columbia University Press, 1981. xii, 293 p.; 24 cm. — (Contemporary
American history series.) Includes index. 1. Keynesian economics — History.
2. Industry and state — United States — History. 3. United States —
Economic policy I. T. II. Series.
HB99.7.C63        338.973 19        *LC* 81-3898        *ISBN* 0231044860

**Johnson, Elizabeth S.**                                                                                **4.1339**
The shadow of Keynes: understanding Keynes, Cambridge, and Keynesian
economics / Elizabeth S. Johnson, Harry G. Johnson. — Chicago: University of
Chicago Press, 1979 (c1978). xiv, 253 p.; 23 cm. 1. Keynes, John Maynard,
1883-1946. 2. Keynesian economics I. Johnson, Harry G. (Harry Gordon),
1923-1977. II. T.
HB99.7.J64        330.15/6        *LC* 78-56338        *ISBN* 0226401480

**Keynes, Cambridge, and The general theory: the process of**                                            **4.1340**
**criticism and discussion connected with the development of The**
**general theory: proceedings of a conference held at the**
**University of Western Ontario / sponsored by the University of**
**Western Ontario, the Hebrew University of Jerusalem, the**
**Canada Council; edited by Don Patinkin and J. Clark Leith.**
Toronto; Buffalo: University of Toronto Press, 1978. xii, 182 p.: ill.; 23 cm.
Includes indexes. 1. Keynes, John Maynard, 1883-1946. General theory of
employment, interest and money. 2. Keynesian economics I. Patinkin, Don.
II. Leith, J. Clark. III. University of Western Ontario. IV. Universitah ha-
'Ivrit bi-Yerushalayim.
HB99.7.K3817 1978        330.15/6        *LC* 78-320853        *ISBN* 0802022960

**Leijonhufvud, Axel.**                                                                                • **4.1341**
On Keynesian economics and the economics of Keynes; a study in monetary
theory. — New York: Oxford University Press, 1968. xiv, 431 p.; 24 cm.
1. Keynesian economics I. T.
HB99.7.L38        330.15/6/0924        *LC* 68-29721

**Patinkin, Don.**                                                                                       **4.1342**
Anticipations of The general theory? and other essays on Keynes / Don
Patinkin. — Chicago: University of Chicago Press, 1982. xxiv, 283 p.; 24 cm.
1. Keynes, John Maynard, 1883-1946. The general theory of employment,
interest, and money. 2. Kalecki, Michał. 3. Keynesian economics
4. Economics — Sweden. I. T.
HB99.7.P26 1982        330.15/6 19        *LC* 81-21929        *ISBN* 0226648737

**Patinkin, Don.**                                                                                       **4.1343**
Keynes' monetary thought: a study of its development / Don Patinkin. —
Durham, N.C.: Duke University Press, 1976. 163 p.: graphs; 25 cm. Includes
index. 1. Keynes, John Maynard, 1883-1946. 2. Keynesian economics I. T.
HB99.7.P27        332.4/01        *LC* 75-40630        *ISBN* 0822303604

## HB101–129 ECONOMIC THEORY, BY COUNTRY

## HB101 Austria

**Gray, John, 1948-.**                                                                                   **4.1344**
Hayek on liberty / John Gray. — Oxford; New York, N.Y., U.S.A.: B.
Blackwell, 1984. x, 230 p.; 23 cm. 1. Hayek, Friedrich A. von (Friedrich
August), 1899- 2. Liberty. I. T.
HB101.H39 G73 1984        323.44 19        *LC* 84-146568        *ISBN*
0855207108

## HB103 Britain

**Cannan, Edwin, 1861-1935.**                                                                          • **4.1345**
A history of the theories of production & distribution in English political
economy, from 1776 to 1848. — New York: A. M. Kelley, 1967. xi, 336 p.; 22

cm. — (Reprints of economic classics) Reprint of the 3d ed., 1917. 1. Economics — Great Britain — History. I. T. HB103.A2 C2 1967     330.942     *LC* 66-22618

**Wealth and virtue: the shaping of political economy in the**    **4.1346** **Scottish enlightenment / edited by Istvan Hont and Michael Ignatieff.** Cambridge [Cambridgeshire]; New York: Cambridge University Press, 1983. viii, 371 p.: ill.; 24 cm. 1. Economics — Scotland — History — Addresses, essays, lectures. 2. Philosophy, Scottish — Addresses, essays, lectures. 3. Enlightenment — History — Addresses, essays, lectures. 4. Scotland — Intellectual life — History — Addresses, essays, lectures. I. Hont, Istvan, 1947- II. Ignatieff, Michael. HB103.A2 W4 1983    330/.09411 19    *LC* 83-1898    *ISBN* 0521233976

**Pioneers of modern economics in Britain / edited by D.P.**    **4.1347** **O'Brien and John R. Presley.** Totowa, N.J.: Barnes & Noble Books, 1981. xix, 272 p.: ill.; 23 cm. 1. Economists — Great Britain — Biography — Addresses, essays, lectures. I. O'Brien, D. P. (Denis Patrick), 1939- II. Presley, John R. HB103.A3 P56 1981    330/.092/2 B 19    *LC* 81-178128    *ISBN* 0389201812

**Jevons, William Stanley, 1835-1882.**    **4.1348** Papers and correspondence of William Stanley Jevons: vol. 1: Biography and personal journal / ed. by R.D. Collison Black and Rosamond Könekamp. — Clifton [N.J.]: A. M. Kelley, 1972. 243 p.: ill. 1. Jevons, William Stanley, 1835-1882. 2. Economists — Correspondence. 3. Economics — Collections. HB103.J5 A4 1972    330/.08    *LC* 72-77230

**Harrod, Roy Forbes, Sir, 1900-.**    • **4.1349** The life of John Maynard Keynes, by R. F. Harrod. — New York: A. M. Kelley, 1969. xvi, 674 p.: illus., ports.; 23 cm. — (Reprints of economic classics) Reprint of the 1951 ed. 1. Keynes, John Maynard, 1883-1946. 2. Keynesian economics I. T. HB103.K47 H28 1969    330.15/6/0924 B    *LC* 68-30524

**Moggridge, D. E. (Donald Edward), 1943-.**    **4.1350** John Maynard Keynes / D. E. Moggridge. — New York: Penguin Books 1976. xii, 190 p.; 18 cm. (Penguin modern masters) Includes index. 1. Keynes, John Maynard, 1883-1946. 2. Keynesian economics I. T. HB103.K47 M55 1976    330.15/6 B    *LC* 76-21630    *ISBN* 0140043195 pbk

**Skidelsky, Robert Jacob Alexander, 1939-.**    **4.1351** John Maynard Keynes: a biography / Robert Skidelsky. — New York: Viking, 1986. v. < 1 > ; 24 cm. 'Elisabeth Sifton books.' Includes index. 1. Keynes, John Maynard, 1883-1946. 2. Economists — Great Britain — Biography. I. T. HB103.K47 S57 1986    330.15/6 B 19    *LC* 86-1514    *ISBN* 0670408107

**Blaug, Mark.**    • **4.1352** Ricardian economics; a historical study. New Haven: Yale University Press, 1958. x, 269 p.: diagrs.; 25 cm. (Yale studies in economics. 8) 1. Ricardo, David, 1772-1823. 2. Economics — History — Great Britain I. T. II. Series. HB103 R5 B6    *LC* 58-7187

**Hollander, Samuel.**    **4.1353** The economics of David Ricardo / Samuel Hollander. — Toronto; Buffalo: University of Toronto Press, c1979. xiv, 759 p.; 25 cm. — (His Studies in classical political economy; 2) Includes index. 1. Ricardo, David, 1772-1823. 2. Economics — Great Britain — History. I. T. II. Series. HB103.R5 H72    330.15/3    *LC* 79-4392    *ISBN* 0802054382

**Bowley, Marian, 1911-.**    • **4.1354** Nassau Senior and classical ecnomics. — New York, Octagon Books, 1967. 358 p. 24 cm. Reprint of the 1937 ed. 'Bibliography of Senior's writings, etc., published and unpublished': p. [340]-351. Bibliographical footnotes. 1. Senior, Nassau William, 1790-1864. 2. Economics — Hist. I. T. HB103.S4B6 1967    330.15/3/0924    *LC* 67-18754

**Campbell, R. H. (Roy Hutcheson)**    **4.1355** Adam Smith / R.H. Campbell and A.S. Skinner. — New York: St. Martin's Press, 1982. 231 p.; 23 cm. 1. Smith, Adam, 1723-1790. 2. Economists — Great Britain — Biography. I. Skinner, Andrew S. II. T. HB103.S6 C35 1982    330.15/3/0924 B 19    *LC* 82-3308    *ISBN* 0312004230

**Hollander, Samuel.**    **4.1356** The economics of Adam Smith. — [Toronto; Buffalo]: University of Toronto Press, [1973] x, 351 p.; 25 cm. — (His Studies in classical political economy, 1) 1. Smith, Adam, 1723-1790. 2. Economics I. T. II. Series. HB103.S6 H65    330.15/3    *LC* 72-185717    *ISBN* 0802018114

**Raphael, D. D. (David Daiches), 1916-.**    **4.1357** Adam Smith / D.D. Raphael. — Oxford [Oxfordshire]; New York: Oxford University Press, 1985. viii, 120 p.; 23 cm. (Past masters.) 1. Smith, Adam, 1723-1790. I. T. II. Series. HB103.S6 R27 1985    330.15/3/0924 19    *LC* 84-20629    *ISBN* 0192875590

**Skinner, Andrew S.**    **4.1358** A system of social science papers relating to Adam Smith / by Andrew S. Skinner. — Oxford: Clarendon Press; New York: Oxford University Press, 1979. x, 278 p.; 23 cm. 1. Smith, Adam, 1723-1790. I. T. HB103.S6 S56    300/.92/4    *LC* 79-40343    *ISBN* 0198284225

**Robbins, Lionel Charles, 1898-.**    • **4.1359** Robert Torrens and the evolution of classical economics. — London: Macmillan; New York: St. Martin's Press, 1958. xiii, 366 p.; 23 cm. 1. Torrens, R. (Robert), 1780-1864. 2. Economics I. T. HB103.T55R6

# HB105–118 Other European Countries

**Cole, Charles Woolsey, 1906-.**    • **4.1360** Colbert and a century of French mercantilism [by] Charles Woolsey Cole ... New York, Columbia university press, 1939. 2 v. fronts. (ports.) 1. Colbert, Jean Baptiste, 1619-1683. 2. Mercantile system — France 3. France — Economic policy I. T. HB105 C6 C6    *LC* 39-11008

**Woodcock, George, 1912-.**    **4.1361** Pierre Joseph Proudhon: his life and work / [by] George Woodcock. — New York: Schocken Books [1972] 295 p.: port.; 21 cm. (Studies in the libertarian and utopian tradition) (Schocken paperbacks) Originally published in 1956 under title: Pierre-Joseph Proudhon, a biography. 1. Proudhon, P.-J. (Pierre-Joseph), 1809-1865. I. T. HB105.P8 W6 1972    301/.092/4 B    *LC* 72-80045    *ISBN* 0805203729

**Henderson, W. O. (William Otto), 1904-.**    **4.1362** Friedrich List, economist and visionary, 1789–1846 / W.O. Henderson. — London, England; Totowa, N.J.: F. Cass, 1983. viii, 288 p., [5] p. of plates: ill.; 23 cm. Includes index. 1. List, Friedrich, 1789-1846. 2. Economists — Germany — Biography. I. T. HB107.L6 H26 1983    330/.092/4 B 19    *LC* 83-217276    *ISBN* 0714631612

**Weber, Marianne, 1870-1954.**    **4.1363** [Max Weber. English] Max Weber: a biography / Marianne Weber; translated from the German and edited by Harry Zohn. — New York: Wiley, [1975] xiv, 719 p.: ill.; 23 cm. 'A Wiley-Interscience publication.' 1. Weber, Max, 1864-1920. I. T. HB107.W4 W413 1975    301/.092/4 B    *LC* 74-23904    *ISBN* 0471923338

**Cirillo, Renato.**    **4.1364** The economics of Vilfredo Pareto / R. Cirillo; preface by F. Oulès. — London; Totowa, N.J.: Cass, 1979. ix, 148 p.; 23 cm. Includes index. 1. Pareto, Vilfredo, 1848-1923. I. T. HB109.P3 C57 1979    330.15/43    *LC* 79-313800    *ISBN* 0714631086

**Zauberman, Alfred.**    **4.1365** The mathematical revolution in Soviet economics / Alfred Zauberman. — London; New York: Published for the Royal Institute of International Affairs by Oxford University Press, 1975. xiii, 62 p.; 22 cm. 1. Economics — History — Russia. 2. Economics, Mathematical I. T. HB113.A2 Z38    330/.0947    *LC* 75-315679    *ISBN* 0192183036

**Feiwel, George R.**    **4.1366** The intellectual capital of Michał Kalecki: a study in economic theory and policy / by George R. Feiwel; foreword by Laurence R. Klein. — Knoxville: University of Tennessee Press, [1975] xxii, 583 p.; 24 cm. Includes index. 1. Kalecki, Michał. 2. Economics I. T. HB113.K28 F43    330.15/6    *LC* 74-22487    *ISBN* 087049161X

**Jaffé, William.**    **4.1367** [Essays on Walras] William Jaffé's Essays on Walras / edited by Donald A. Walker. — Cambridge [Cambridgeshire]; New York: Cambridge University Press, 1983. xiv, 377 p.; 24 cm. 1. Walras, Léon, 1834-1910 — Addresses, essays, lectures. 2. Economists — Switzerland — Biography — Addresses, essays, lectures. I. Walker, Donald A. (Donald Anthony), 1934- II. T. III. Title: Essays on Walras. HB118.W34 J33 1983    330/.092/4 B 19    *LC* 82-22001    *ISBN* 0521251427

## HB119 United States

**Dorfman, Joseph, 1905-.**    • **4.1368**
The economic mind in American civilization. New York, Viking Press, 1946-1959. 5 v. 22 cm. 'Bibliographic notes' at end of each volume. 1. Economics — United States — History. 2. United States — Economic conditions — To 1865 I. T.
HB119.A2 D6    330.973    *LC* 45-11318

**Veblen, Thorstein, 1857-1929.**    **4.1369**
Essays, reviews, and reports; previously uncollected writings. Edited and with an introd., New light on Veblen, by Joseph Dorfman. — Clifton [N.J.]: A. M. Kelley, 1973. viii, 690 p.: illus.; 22 cm. Most of the writings originally published in the Journal of political economy. 1. Economics — Addresses, essays, lectures. I. Dorfman, Joseph, 1905- New light on Veblen. 1973. II. T.
HB119.A2 V42 1973    330    *LC* 72-13590    *ISBN* 0678009600

**Commons, John Rogers, 1862-1945.**    • **4.1370**
Myself, the autobiography of John R. Commons. Madison: University of Wisconsin Press, 1963. 201 p.: ill.; 21 cm. I. T.
HB119 C58 A3    *LC* 63-15619

**Rader, Benjamin G.**    • **4.1371**
The academic mind and reform; the influence of Richard T. Ely in American life [by] Benjamin G. Rader. — [Lexington]: University of Kentucky Press, [1966] 276 p.; 23 cm. 1. Ely, Richard Theodore, 1854-1943. I. T.
HB119.E5 R3    330.0924    *LC* 66-26694

**Galbraith, John Kenneth, 1908-.**    **4.1372**
A life in our times: memoirs / John Kenneth Galbraith. — Boston: Houghton Mifflin, 1981. x, 563 p.; 24 cm. Includes index. 1. Galbraith, John Kenneth, 1908- 2. Economists — United States — Biography. 3. United States — Politics and government — 1945- I. T.
HB119.G33 A34    330/.092/4 B 19    *LC* 80-27373    *ISBN* 0395305098

**De Mille, Anna Angela (George) 1877-.**    • **4.1373**
Henry George, citizen of the world; edited by Don C. Shoemaker, with an introd. by Agnes de Mille. Chapel Hill, University of North Carolina Press [1950] xv, 276 p. illus., ports. 1. George, Henry, 1839-1897. I. T.
HB119.G4 D4

**George, Henry, 1862-1916.**    • **4.1374**
The life of Henry George / by his son Henry George, jr. — New York: Doubleday and McClure Co., 1900. 2 v. (634 p.): ill.; 23 cm. — (Memorial edition of the writings of Henry George) 1. George, Henry, 1839-1897. I. T.
HB119.G4 G4 1900    330/.092/4 B

**Fox, Daniel M.**    • **4.1375**
The discovery of abundance: Simon N. Patten and the transformation of social theory, by Daniel M. Fox. — Ithaca, N.Y.: Published for the American Historical Association [by] Cornell University Press, [1967] xiii, 259 p.; 24 cm. 1. Patten, Simon Nelson, 1852-1922. 2. Wealth 3. Social problems I. American Historical Association. II. T.
HB119.P35 F6    330.1/61/0924    *LC* 67-22192

**Paul Samuelson and modern economic theory / edited by E.**    **4.1376**
**Cary Brown, Robert M. Solow.**
New York: McGraw-Hill, c1983. xiii, 210 p.; 25 cm. 1. Samuelson, Paul Anthony, 1915- — Addresses, essays, lectures. 2. Economics — Addresses, essays, lectures. I. Brown, E. Cary (Edgar Cary) II. Solow, Robert M.
HB119.S25 P38 1983    330 19    *LC* 82-20343    *ISBN* 0070596670

**Clemence, Richard Vernon, 1910-.**    • **4.1377**
The Schumpeterian system / by Richard V. Clemence and Francis S. Doody. — Cambridge, Mass.: Addison-Wesley Press, 1950. 117 p. Includes index. 1. Schumpeter, Joseph Alois, 1883-1950. 2. Business cycles I. Doody, Francis S 1917- II. T.
HB119.S35 C55    *LC* 50-4879

**Harris, Seymour Edwin, 1897-.**    • **4.1378**
Schumpeter, social scientist. — Freeport, N.Y.: Books for Libraries Press, [1969, c1951] x, 142 p.: ports.; 29 cm. — (Essay index reprint series) I. Schumpeter, Joseph Alois, 1883-1950. II. T.
HB119.S35 H3 1969    330/.0924    *LC* 71-80387    *ISBN* 0836911385

**Dorfman, Joseph, 1905-.**    • **4.1379**
Thorstein Veblen and his America, with new appendices. — [Corr. imp. — Clifton, N. J., A. M. Kelley, 1966. 572 p. port. 24 cm. — (Reprints of economic classics) 'Original edition 1934 ... Published in Reprints of economic classics ... 1961 with new appendices and 1966 with some corrections and new material.' 'Bibliography of Thorstein Veblen': p. 519-524. 'References': p. 525-539. 1. Veblen, Thorstein, 1857-1929. 2. Economics — Hist. — United States. 3. Socialism — United States I. T.
HB119.V4D6 1972    330.0924 (b)    *LC* 64-7662

**Riesman, David, 1909-.**    • **4.1380**
Thorstein Veblen, a critical interpretation. New York, Scribner, 1953. xv, 221 p. (Twentieth century library) 1. Veblen, Thorstein, 1857-1929. I. T.
HB119 V4 R5    *LC* 53-12337

## HB121–129 Canada. Australia

**Goodwin, Craufurd David Wycliffe, 1934-.**    • **4.1381**
Canadian economic thought; the political economy of a developing nation, 1814-1914. Durham, N.C., Published for the Duke University Commonwealth-Studies Center [by] Duke University Press, 1961. xvi, 214 p. diagrs. (Publication (Duke University. Commonwealth-Studies Center) no. 15) 1. Economics — History — Canada I. T. II. Series.
HB121 A2 G6    *LC* 61-6223

**Goodwin, Craufurd David Wycliffe, 1934-.**    • **4.1382**
Economic enquiry in Australia [by] Craufurd D.W. Goodwin. Durham, N.C., Duke University Press, 1966. xv, 659 p. (Duke University Commonwealth-Studies Center. Publication no. 24) 1. Economics — History — Australia 2. Australia — Economic conditions I. T.
HB129 A2 G6    *LC* 65-27768

## HB131–145 METHODOLOGY. MATHEMATICAL ECONOMICS
(see also: HB74.M3)

**Blaug, Mark.**    **4.1383**
The methodology of economics: or, How economists explain / Mark Blaug. — Cambridge [Eng.]; New York: Cambridge University Press, 1980. xiv, 296 p.; 22 cm. — (Cambridge surveys of economic literature) Includes indexes. 1. Economics — Methodology I. T.
HB131.B56    330/.01/8    *LC* 80-13802    *ISBN* 0521222885

**Caldwell, Bruce J.**    **4.1384**
Beyond positivism: economic methodology in the twentieth century / Bruce J. Caldwell. — London; Boston: Allen & Unwin, 1982. x, 277 p.; 23 cm. 1. Economics — Methodology 2. Positivism I. T.
HB131.C37 1982    330/.01/8 19    *LC* 82-11494    *ISBN* 0043303277

**Baumol, William J.**    **4.1385**
Economic theory and operations analysis / William J. Baumol. 4th ed. — Englewood Cliffs, N.J.: Prentice-Hall, c1977. xxi, 695 p.: ill.; 24 cm. (Prentice-Hall international series in management) 1. Microeconomics 2. Economics, Mathematical 3. Operations research 4. Mathematical analysis I. T.
HB135.B38 1977    330/.01/84    *LC* 76-46591    *ISBN* 013227132X

**Bressler, Barry.**    **4.1386**
A unified introduction to mathematical economics / Barry Bressler. — New York: Harper & Row, [1975] xviii, 667 p.: ill.; 24 cm. Includes index. 1. Economics, Mathematical I. T.
HB135.B74    330/.01/51    *LC* 75-5689    *ISBN* 0060409525

**Burrows, Paul.**    **4.1387**
Macroeconomic theory: a mathematical introduction / [by] Paul Burrows and Theodore Hitiris. — London; New York: Wiley, 1974. xiii, 210 p.: ill.; 24 cm. Includes indexes. 1. Economics, Mathematical 2. Macroeconomics — Mathematical models. I. Hitiris, Theodore, joint author. II. T.
HB135.B87    339/.01/82    *LC* 73-2779    *ISBN* 0471125253

**Dixit, Avinash K.**    **4.1388**
Optimization in economic theory / by A. K. Dixit. — London; New York: Oxford University Press, 1976. vi, 134 p.: ill.; 21 cm. 1. Economics, Mathematical 2. Mathematical optimization I. T.
HB135.D58    330/.01/51    *LC* 76-379483    *ISBN* 0198770820

**Eastman, Byron D.**    **4.1389**
Interpreting mathematical economics and econometrics / Byron D. Eastman. — New York: St. Martin's Press, 1984. ix, 110 p.: ill.; 23 cm. Includes index. 1. Economics, Mathematical 2. Econometrics 3. Economics — Mathematical models I. T.
HB135.E27 1984    330/.028 19    *LC* 84-8303    *ISBN* 0312424779

**Kennedy, Gavin.**    **4.1390**
Mathematics for innumerate economists / Gavin Kennedy. — New York: Holmes & Meier, 1982. vii, 134 p.: ill.; 24 cm. Includes index. 1. Economics, Mathematical 2. Mathematics I. T.
HB135.K47 1982    510/.24339 19    *LC* 81-13337    *ISBN* 0841907773

**Mathematical methods in economics** / edited by Frederick van der Ploeg.     **4.1391**
Chichester; New York: Wiley, c1984. xix, 580 p.: ill.; 24 cm. (Handbook of applicable mathematics. Guidebook. 6) 'A Wiley Interscience publication.'
1. Economics, Mathematical I. Ploeg, Frederick van der, 1956- II. Series.
HB135.M366 1984     330/.01/51 19     *LC* 84-2327     *ISBN* 0471904228

**New quantitative techniques for economic analysis** / edited by Giorgio P. Szegö.     **4.1392**
New York: Academic Press, 1982. xiv, 319 p.: ill.; 24 cm. — (Economic theory, econometrics, and mathematical economics.) 1. Economics, Mathematical — Addresses, essays, lectures. 2. Economics — Mathematical models — Addresses, essays, lectures. I. Szegö, G. P. II. Series.
HB135.N48     330/.0724 19     *LC* 81-17576     *ISBN* 0126807604

**Samuelson, Paul Anthony, 1915-.**     **4.1393**
Foundations of economic analysis / Paul A. Samuelson. — Enl. ed. — Cambridge, Mass.; London, England: Harvard University Press, 1983. xxvi, 604 p.; 22 cm. — (Harvard economic studies. v. 80) Includes index. 1. Economics, Mathematical I. T. II. Series.
HB135.S24 1983     330/.01/51 19     *LC* 82-21304     *ISBN* 0674313011

**Bowden, Roger J. (Roger John), 1943-.**     **4.1394**
Instrumental variables / Roger J. Bowden and Darrell A. Turkington. — Cambridge [Cambridgeshire]; New York: Cambridge University Press, 1984. viii, 227 p.: ill.; 24 cm. (Econometric Society monographs in quantitative economics. no. 6) 1. Instrumental variables (Statistics) I. Turkington, Darrell A. II. T. III. Series.
HB139.B69 1984     519.5/35 19     *LC* 84-7802     *ISBN* 0521262410

**Kennedy, Peter, 1943-.**     **4.1395**
A guide to econometrics / Peter Kennedy. — 1st MIT Press ed. — Cambridge, Mass.: MIT Press, 1979. xi, 175 p.: graphs; 22 cm. Includes index. 1. Econometrics I. T.
HB139.K45 1979     330/.01/51     *LC* 79-63894     *ISBN* 0262110733

**Maddala, G. S.**     **4.1396**
Limited–dependent and qualitative variables in econometrics / by G.S. Maddala. — Cambridge [Cambridgeshire]; New York: Cambridge University Press, 1983. xi, 401 p.; 24 cm. — (Econometric Society monographs in quantitative economics. 3) Includes index. 1. Econometrics I. T. II. Title: Qualitative variables in econometrics. III. Series.
HB139.M355 1983     330/.028 19     *LC* 82-9554     *ISBN* 052124143X

**Phillips, P. C. B.**     **4.1397**
Exercises in econometrics / P. C. B. Phillips, M. R. Wickens. — Oxford: P. Allan; Cambridge, Mass.: Ballinger Pub. Co., 1978. 2 v. (xvii, 493, xxxvi p.); 24 cm. 1. Econometrics — Problems, exercises, etc. I. Wickens, M. R. joint author. II. T.
HB139.P53     330/.076     *LC* 79-304172     *ISBN* 0860030067

**Stewart, Mark B.**     **4.1398**
Introductory econometrics / Mark B. Stewart and Kenneth F. Wallis. — 2nd ed. — New York: Halsted Press, 1981. 337 p. 1. Econometrics I. Wallis, Kenneth Frank. II. T.
HB139.S78 1981     *ISBN* 0470271329

**Wonnacott, Ronald J.**     **4.1399**
Econometrics / Ronald J. Wonnacott, Thomas H. Wonnacott. — 2d ed. — New York: Wiley, c1979. xxiii, 580 p.: ill.; 24 cm. — (Wiley series in probability and mathematical statistics) Includes index. 1. Econometrics I. Wonnacott, Thomas H., 1935- joint author. II. T.
HB139.W66 1979     330/.01/8     *LC* 78-31257     *ISBN* 0471959812

**Contemporary macroeconomic modelling** / edited by Pierre Malgrange and Pierre–Alain Muet.     **4.1400**
Oxford [Oxfordshire]; New York, NY: Blackwell, 1984. x, 319 p.: ill.; 24 cm. 1. Economics — Mathematical models — Addresses, essays, lectures. 2. Macroeconomics — Mathematical models — Addresses, essays, lectures. I. Malgrange, Pierre. II. Muet, Pierre-Alain.
HB141.C659 1984     339/.0724 19     *LC* 84-16722     *ISBN* 0631134719

**Kravis, Irving B.**     **4.1401**
World product and income: international comparisons of real gross product / produced by the Statistical Office of the United Nations and the World Bank; Irving B. Kravis, Alan Heston, Robert Summers, in collaboration with Alicia R. Civitello ... [et al.]. — Baltimore: Published for the World Bank [by] the Johns Hopkins University Press, c1982. x, 388 p.; 29 cm. Half title: United Nations International Comparison Project, phase III. Includes index.
1. National income 2. Gross national product 3. Comparative economics I. Heston, Alan W. II. Summers, Robert, 1922- III. United Nations. Statistical Office. IV. International Bank for Reconstruction and Development. V. United Nations International Comparison Project. VI. T.
HB141.5.K72 1982     339.3 19     *LC* 81-15569     *ISBN* 0801823595

**Miller, Ronald E.**     **4.1402**
Input–output analysis: foundations and extensions / Ronald E. Miller, Peter D. Blair. — Englewood Cliffs, N.J.: Prentice-Hall, c1985. xii, 464 p.; 24 cm. 1. Input-output analysis I. Blair, Peter D. II. T.
HB142.M55 1985     339.2/3 19     *LC* 84-17975     *ISBN* 0134667158

**Mills, Gordon.**     **4.1403**
Optimisation in economic analysis / Gordon Mills. — London; Boston: Allen & Unwin, c1984. ix, 195 p.: ill.; 25 cm. 1. Mathematical optimization 2. Economics, Mathematical I. T.
HB143.7.M54 1984     330/.01/51 19     *LC* 84-359     *ISBN* 0043110010

**Case, James H., 1940-.**     **4.1404**
Economics and the competitive process / by James H. Case. — New York: New York University Press, 1979. xiii, 295 p.: ill.; 24 cm. — (Studies in game theory and mathematical economics.) 1. Game theory 2. Competition I. T. II. Series.
HB144.C37     *LC* 78-376     *ISBN* 0814713734

**Walsh, Vivian Charles.**     **4.1405**
Classical and neoclassical theories of general equilibrium: historical origins and mathematical structure / Vivian Walsh, Harvey Gram. — New York: Oxford University Press, 1980. xvi, 426 p.: graphs; 24 cm. 1. Equilibrium (Economics) 2. Economics — Mathematical models 3. Economics — History I. Gram, Harvey, 1946- joint author. II. T.
HB145.W34     330/.01/8     *LC* 78-31129     *ISBN* 0195026748

---

# HB151–846 Economic Theory: General Works. Treatises

## HB151–181 BY PERIOD

### HB151–159 Before Adam Smith (to 1776/1789)

**Cantillon, Richard, d. 1734.**     • **4.1406**
Essai sur la nature du commerce en général / by Richard Cantillon; edited with an English translation and other material by Henry Higgs. — London: Macmillan, 1931. viii, 394 p.: ports. — Facsim. of original t. p. in French. French and English on opposite pages. 1. Commerce 2. Economics I. Higgs, Henry, 1864-1940. II. T.
HB153.C3 1931     *LC* 32-15071

**Quesnay, François, 1694-1774.**     **4.1407**
[Tableau economique. English and French] Quesnay's Tableau économique. Edited, with new material, translations and notes by Marguerite Kuczynski & Ronald L. Meek. London, Macmillan; New York, A. M. Kelley for the Royal Economic Society and the American Economic Association [1972] 1 v. (various pagings) 26 cm. Parallel French text and English translation; introd. and notes in English. 'Enlarged and revised with added material from the German edition.' 1. Economics 2. Physiocrats I. Kuczynski, Marguerite (Steinfeld), ed. II. Meek, Ronald L. ed. III. T. IV. Title: Tableau économique.
HB153.Q55713     330.15/2     *LC* 78-157694     *ISBN* 0333111737 *ISBN* 0678070075

### HB161–169 Classical Period (1776/1789–1843/1876)

**Bentham, Jeremy, 1748-1832.**     • **4.1408**
Jeremy Bentham's economic writings. — Critical ed. based on his printed works and unprinted mss., by W. Stark. — London: Published for the Royal Economic Society by Allen & Unwin, [1952-54] 3 v.; 22 cm. 1. Economics I. T.
HB161.B45     330.1     *LC* a 52-8753

**Cardozo, Jacob N. (Jacob Newton), 1786-1873.**     **4.1409**
Notes on political economy, by Jacob N. Cardozo. With an introductory essay: J. N. Cardozo and American economic thought, by Joseph Dorfman. And with selections from Cardozo's other economic writings. Clifton [N.J.] A. M. Kelley, 1972 [c1826] xiv, 273 p. 22 cm. (Reprints of economic classics) Reprint of the 1960 ed., with additional writings of Cardozo. 1. Economics. I. T.
HB161.C2 1972     330/.08     *LC* 72-187225     *ISBN* 0678008604

**Carey, Henry Charles, 1793-1879.** • 4.1410
Principles of political economy. New York, A.M. Kelley, bookseller, 1965. 4 pts. in 3 v. (Reprints of economic classics) 1. Economics 2. Social sciences I. T.
HB161 C25 1837A     *LC* 65-16983

**Carey, Henry Charles, 1793-1879.** • 4.1411
Principles of social science (1858–1859). — New York, A. M. Kelley, 1963. 3 v. diagrs. 23 cm. — (Reprints of economic classics) Bibliographical footnotes. 1. Social sciences 2. Economics I. T.
HB161.C26 1963     330.1     *LC* 63-22257

**Hollander, Samuel, 1937-.** 4.1412
The economics of John Stuart Mill / Samuel Hollander. — Toronto: University of Toronto Press, 1985. 2 v.; 25 cm. (Hollander, Samuel. Studies in classical political economy 3) Includes index (v. 2). 1. Mill, John Stuart, 1806-1873. 2. Mill, John Stuart, 1806-1873. Principles of political economy. 3. Economics I. T. II. Series.
HB161.H54 1985     330.15/3/0924 19     *ISBN* 0802056717

**Hume, David, 1711-1776.** • 4.1413
Writings on economics. Edited and introduced by Eugene Rotwein. Madison, University of Wisconsin Press, 1955. cxi, 224 p. port. 1. Economics I. Rotwein, Eugene. II. T.
HB161.H84     *LC* 55-12064

**Lauderdale, James Maitland, 8th earl of, 1759-1839.** • 4.1414
An inquiry into the nature and origin of public wealth and into the means and causes of its increase, 1804. Edited, with an introd. and revisions appearing in the 2d ed., 1819, by Morton Paglin. New York, A. M. Kelly, 1966 [i.e. 1967] x, 482 p. 23 cm. 1. Economics I. Paglin, Morton. ed. II. T.
HB161.L39 1967     *LC* 66-24414

**Malthus, T. R. (Thomas Robert), 1766-1834.** • 4.1415
Occasional papers of T.R. Malthus on Ireland, population, and political economy, from contemporary journals, written anonymously and hitherto uncollected. Edited and with an introductory essay by Bernard Semmel. New York, B. Franklin, 1963. 281 p. (Burt Franklin essays in history & social science 1) 1. Economics — Addresses, essays, lectures 2. Population — Addresses, essays, lectures 3. Ireland — Economic conditions — Addresses, essays, lectures I. Semmel, Bernard. ed. II. T.
HB161 M23     *LC* 63-12661

**Malthus, T. R. (Thomas Robert), 1766-1834.** • 4.1416
Definitions in political economy. Preceded by an inquiry into the rules which ought to guide political economists in the definition and use of their terms, with remarks on the deviation from these rules in their writings. London, J. Murray, 1827. viii, 261 p. 1. Economics 2. Economics — Terminology I. T.
HB161 M29

**Ricardo, David, 1772-1823.** • 4.1417
Works and correspondence; edited by Piero Sraffa, with the collaboration of M.H. Dobb. Cambridge, Eng., At the University Press for the Royal Economic Society, 1951-. v.: ill., ports., facsims.; 24 cm. 1. Malthus, T. R. (Thomas Robert), 1766-1834. Principles of political economy 2. Economics I. T.
HB161 R4812     *LC* 51-12245

**Ruskin, John, 1819-1900.** • 4.1418
Munera pulveris; six essays on the elements of political economy. With an introd. by Charles Eliot Norton. — Brantwood ed. — New York: Greenwood Press, [1969] xl, 218 p.; 18 cm. Reprint of the 1891 ed. 1. Economics I. T.
HB161.R93 1969     330.15/3     *LC* 69-14065

**Senior, Nassau William, 1790-1864.** • 4.1419
An outline of the science of political economy. — New York, A. M. Kelley, 1965. xii, 249 p. 23 cm. — (Reprints of economic classics) First published in 1836. 'On certain terms which are peculiarly liable to be used ambiguously in political economy, from Elements of logic,' by R. Whately: p. [227]-239. 1. Economics I. Whately, Richard, 1787-1863. II. T.
HB161.S46 1965     330     *LC* 65-16991

**Smith, Adam, 1723-1790.** 4.1420
The Glasgow edition of the works and correspondence of Adam Smith. — Oxford: Clarendon Press, 198-. See LC class AC7.S59 1986. I. T.

**Torrens, R. (Robert), 1780-1864.** • 4.1421
An essay on the production of wealth. 1821. With an introductory essay, Robert Torrens and American economic thought, by Joseph Dorfman. New York, A.M. Kelley, 1965. 17, xvi, 430 p. (Reprints of economic classics) Original t.p. reads: An essay on the production of wealth; with an appendix in which the principles of political economy are applied to the actual circumstances of this country. By R. Torrens, Esq. London, Printed for Longman, Hurst, Rees, Orme, and Brown, 1821. 1. Economics I. T.
HB161 T69 1821A     *LC* 64-7670

**Marx, Karl, 1818-1883.** • 4.1422
The poverty of philosophy. With an introd. by Frederick Engels. New York, International Publishers [1963] 233 p. 21 cm. 1. Marxian economics I. T.
HB163.P97 M282 1963     330.1     *LC* 63-10632

# HB171–180 1843/1876–

## HB171–172 ENGLISH AND AMERICAN ECONOMISTS, A–Z

### HB171 A–G

**Buchanan, James M.** • 4.1423
Fiscal theory and political economy; selected essays. Chapel Hill, University of North Carolina Press [1960] 197 p. 1. Economics — Addresses, essays, lectures 2. Finance, Public — Addresses, essays, lectures I. T.
HB171 B86     *LC* 60-50887

**Clark, John Bates, 1847-1938.** • 4.1424
Essentials of economic theory, as applied to modern problems of industry and public policy. — New York: A. M. Kelley, 1968. xiv, 566 p.: illus.; 22 cm. — (Reprints of economic classics) Reprint of the 1907 ed. 1. Economics I. T.
HB171.C57 1968     330.1     *LC* 68-8972

**Clark, John Bates, 1847-1938.** • 4.1425
The philosophy of wealth; economic principles newly formulated. New York, A. M. Kelley Publishers, 1967. xv, 236 p. 21 cm. (Reprints of economic classics) Reprint of the 1887 ed. 1. Economics I. T.
HB171.C59 1967     330.15/5     *LC* 67-25955

**Commons, John Rogers, 1862-1945.** • 4.1426
The economics of collective action [by] John R. Commons. Edited with introd. and supplementary essay by Kenneth H. Parsons. With a biographical sketch by Selig Perlman. — Madison: University of Wisconsin Press, 1970 [c1950] xxi, 382 p.; 23 cm. 1. Economics 2. Economic policy I. Parsons. Kenneth H., ed. II. T.
HB171.C77 1970     330.1     *LC* 69-17328     *ISBN* 0299053601

**Dobb, Maurice Herbert, 1900-.** • 4.1427
On economic theory and socialism; collected papers. — New York: International Publishers, [1955] 293 p.: ill.; 23 cm. 1. Economics — Addresses, essays, lectures. 2. Socialism — Addresses, essays, lectures. I. T. II. Title: Economic theory and socialism.
HB171.D695 1955a     330.4     *LC* 55-13844

**George, Henry, 1839-1897.** • 4.1428
The science of political economy, by Henry George ... New York, Robert Schalkenbach Foundation, 1938. xxxix, 545 p.; 20 cm. 'First American printing since 1898.' The work, though not quite complete at the author's death, is presented here as it was left by him, except for necessary corrections, summaries and index. cf.Prefatory note, signed: Henry George, jr. 1. Economics I. George, Henry, 1862-1916. ed. II. T.
HB171.G33 1938     *LC* 39-14683

**George, Henry, 1839-1897.** • 4.1429
Social problems, by Henry George. New York, Robert Schalkenbach Foundation, 1934. 256 p. 20 cm. 1. Economics — Addresses, essays, lectures. 2. Social sciences — Addresses, essays, lectures. 3. Single tax I. T.
HB171.G37 1934     304     *LC* 34-32078

**Lawrence, Elwood Parsons.** • 4.1430
Henry George in the British Isles / by Elwood P. Lawrence. — East Lansing: Michigan State University Press, 1957. 203 p.; 22 cm. 1. George, Henry, 1839-1897. I. T.
HB171.G4 L3

**George, Henry, 1839-1897.** • 4.1431
Progress and poverty; an inquiry into the cause of industrial depressions and of increase of want with increase of wealth ... the remedy. [75th anniversary ed.] New York, Robert Schalkenbach Foundation, 1955. xxix, 599 p. 22 cm. Includes bibliographies. 1. Economics 2. Single tax I. T.
HB171.G46 1955     *LC* A 56-949

**Graaff, J. de V.** • 4.1432
Theoretical welfare economics. Cambridge [Eng.] University Press, 1957. 178 p. illus. 22 cm. 1. Economics I. T.
HB171.G66     330.1     *LC* 57-2863

**George, Henry, 1839-1897.** • 4.1433
The land question. Property in land. The condition of labor. New York, Robert Schalkenbach Foundation, 1935. 109, 74, 151 p. 1. Rome, Church of. Pope, 1878-1903 (Leo XIII) Rerum novarum (May 15, 1891) 2. Single tax 3. Labour

and labouring classes 4. Social problems 5. Sociology, Christian 6. Ireland — Land I. Argyll, George Douglas Campbell, 8th Duke of, 1823-1900 II. Rome, Church of. Pope, 1878-1903 (Leo XIII) Rerum novarum (May 15, 1891) III. T.
HB171.Gx

## HB171 H–L

**Henderson, James Mitchell, 1929-.**                    • **4.1434**
Microeconomic theory: a mathematical approach [by] James M. Henderson [and] Richard E. Quandt. — New York: McGraw-Hill, 1958. 291 p.: illus.; 24 cm. — (Economics handbook series) 1. Microeconomics 2. Economics, Mathematical I. Quandt, Richard E. joint author. II. T.
HB171.H52     330.182     *LC* 58-8844

**Hicks, John Richard, Sir, 1904-.**                    • **4.1435**
Capital and growth, by John Hicks. — New York, Oxford University Press, 1965. xii, 339 p. illus. 22 cm. Bibliographical footnotes. 1. Economics I. T.
HB171.H634     330.1     *LC* 65-25577

**Hicks, John Richard, Sir, 1904-.**                    **4.1436**
Economic perspectives: further essays on money and growth / by John Hicks. — [S.l.]: Oxford, 1977. xviii, 199 p.: ill.; 20 cm. 1. Economics — Addresses, essays, lectures. 2. Money — Addresses, essays, lectures. 3. Economic development — Addresses, essays, lectures. I. T.
HB171.H6343     330     *LC* 77-5770     *ISBN* 0198284071

**Hicks, John Richard, Sir, 1904-.**                    • **4.1437**
Value and capital; an inquiry into some fundamental principles of economic theory. — 2d ed. — Oxford: Clarendon Press, 1946. xi, 340 p.: diagrs.; 23 cm. 1. Economics I. T.
IIB171.H635 1946     330.1     *LC* 47-5770

**Jevons, William Stanley, 1835-1882.**                    • **4.1438**
The theory of political economy. With pref. and notes and an extension of the bibliography of mathematical economic writings by H. Stanley Jevons. 5th ed. New York, A.M. Kelley, 1965. lxiv, 343 p. (Reprints of economic classics) 1. Economics 2. Economics, Mathematical I. Jevons, Herbert Stanley, 1875-, ed. II. T.
HB171 J57 1965     *LC* 65-18334

**Kaldor, Nicholas, 1908-1986.**                    **4.1439**
Essays on economic stability and growth / Nicholas Kaldor. — 2d ed. — New York: Holmes & Meier Publishers, 1980. 312 p.: ill.; 23 cm. — (His Collected economic essays; 2) 1. Macroeconomics — Addresses, essays, lectures. 2. Economic stabilization — Addresses, essays, lectures. 3. Business cycles — Addresses, essays, lectures. 4. Economic development — Addresses, essays, lectures. I. T. II. Series.
HB171.K28 1980     339.5     *LC* 80-18145     *ISBN* 0841904529

**Kaldor, Nicholas, 1908-1986.**                    • **4.1440**
[Essays. Selections] Essays on value and distribution / Nicholas Kaldor. — 2nd ed. — New York: Holmes & Meier Publishers, 1981, c1980. xxxi, 238 p.; 23 cm. — (Collected economic essays; 1) 1. Value — Addresses, essays, lectures. 2. Equilibrium (Economics) — Addresses, essays, lectures. 3. Competition, Imperfect — Addresses, essays, lectures. 4. Welfare economics — Addresses, essays, lectures. 5. Capital — Addresses, essays, lectures. 6. Distribution (Economic theory) — Addresses, essays, lectures. 7. Competition, Imperfect — Addresses, essays, lectures. I. T.
HB171.K2852 1981     330 19     *LC* 81-6523     *ISBN* 0841904510

**Keynes, John Maynard, 1883-1946.**                    **4.1441**
The collected writings of John Maynard Keynes. [London]: Macmillan; [New York]: St. Martin's Press, for the Royal Economic Society, [1971-. v.; 24 cm. Vol. 8 has imprint: New York, St. Martin's Press, for the Royal Economic Society. 1. Economics — Collected works. I. Royal Economic Society (Great Britain) II. T.
HB171.K44     330.15/6/08     *LC* 74-13349     *ISBN* 0333107381

**Pigou, A. C. (Arthur Cecil), 1877-1959.**                    • **4.1442**
Keynes's 'General theory'; a retrospective view. London, Macmillan, 1950. viii, 68 p. 'Comprises two lectures given in Cambridge in November 1949.' 1. Keynes, John Maynard, 1883-1946. General theory of employment, interest and money I. T.
HB171 K46 P5     *LC* 51-9572

**Koopmans, Tjalling Charles, 1910-.**                    • **4.1443**
Three essays on the state of economic science. New York, McGraw-Hill, 1957. 231 p. ill. 1. Economics 2. Economics, Mathematical I. T. II. Title: The state of economic science
HB171 K69     *LC* 57-8008

**Kuenne, Robert E.**                    • **4.1444**
The theory of general economic equilibrium. — Princeton, N.J.: Princeton University Press, 1963. xv, 590 p.: illus.; 24 cm. 1. Economics I. T.
HB171.K73     330.182     *LC* 62-21105

**Little, Ian Malcolm David.**                    • **4.1445**
A critique of welfare economics. 2d ed. Oxford: Clarendon Press, 1957. vi, 302 p.: diagrs., tables; 23 cm. 1. Economics I. T.
HB171 L73 1957

## HB171 M–Z

**Marshall, Alfred, 1842-1924.**                    • **4.1446**
Memorials of Alfred Marshall, edited by A. C. Pigou. — New York, Kelley & Millman, 1956. ix, 518 p. ports., diagrs. 23 cm. — ([Reprints of economic classics]) 1. Economics — Collected works. I. Pigou, A. C. (Arthur Cecil), 1877-1959. ed. II. T.
HB171.M335 1956     330.81     *LC* 56-4978

**Marshall, Alfred, 1842-1924.**                    • **4.1447**
Official papers, by Alfred Marshall ... Published for the Royal economic society. — London, Macmillan and co., limited, 1926. vii, 428 p. 22 cm. Editor's preface signed: J. M. Keynes. 1. Currency question — Gt. Brit. 2. Gt. Brit. — Econ. condit. 3. Tariff — Gt. Brit. 4. Gt. Brit. — Commercial policy. I. Keynes, John Maynard, 1883-1946. ed. II. Royal Economic Society (Great Britain) III. T.
HB171.M354     *LC* 27-15292

**Marshall, Alfred, 1842-1924.**                    • **4.1448**
Principles of economics. 9th (variorum) ed., with annotations by C. W. Guillebaud. London, New York, Macmillan for the Royal Economic Society, 1961. 2 v. port., diagrs. 25 cm. 1. Economics I. Guillebaud, Claude William, 1890- ed. II. Royal Economic Society (Great Britain) III. T.
HB171.M355 1961     330     *LC* 61-65917

**Meade, J. E. (James Edward), 1907-.**                    • **4.1449**
The growing economy, by J. E. Meade. Chicago, Aldine Pub. Co. [1968] 512 p. illus. 22 cm. (His Principles of political economy, v. 2) 1. Economics I. T.
HB171.M478 vol. 2     330     *LC* 79-6047

**Modigliani, Franco.**                    **4.1450**
The collected papers of Franco Modigliani / edited by Andrew Abel. — Cambridge, Mass.: MIT Press, c1980. 3 v.: ill.; 24 cm. 1. Economics — Addresses, essays, lectures. I. Abel, Andrew B., 1952- II. T.
HB171.M557     330 19     *LC* 78-21041     *ISBN* 0262131501

**Pigou, A. C. (Arthur Cecil), 1877-1959.**                    • **4.1451**
Employment & equilibrium; a theoretical discussion. London, Macmillan, 1941. 283 p. 1. Economics 2. Money 3. Unemployed I. T.
HB171 P58

**Robbins, Lionel Charles, 1898-.**                    • **4.1452**
An essay on the nature & significance of economic science, by Lionel Robbins. — 2d ed., rev. and extended. — London, Macmillan and co., limited, 1935. xviii, 160 p. 23 cm. 1. Economics I. T. II. Title: Nature & significance of economic science, An essay on the.
HB171.R6 1935     *LC* 36-10554

**Schumacher, E. F. (Ernst Friedrich), 1911-1977.**                    **4.1453**
Small is beautiful; economics as if people mattered [by] E. F. Schumacher. New York, Harper & Row [1973] 290 p. 21 cm. (Harper torchbooks, TB 1778) 1. Economics I. T.
HB171.S384     330     *LC* 73-180875     *ISBN* 0061361224 *ISBN* 0061317880

*HB 171 S38*

**Veblen, Thorstein, 1857-1929.**                    • **4.1454**
The portable Veblen; edited, and with an introd., by Max Lerner. — New York: Viking Press, 1948. vii, 632 p.; 18 cm. — (The Viking portable library) 1. Economics — Collections. I. Lerner, Max, 1902- ed. II. T.
HB171.V4     330.1     *LC* 48-6993

**Wanniski, Jude, 1936-.**                    **4.1455**
The way the world works: how economies fail—and succeed / Jude Wanniski. — New York: Basic Books, c1978. xiii, 319 p.; 24 cm. 1. Economics I. T.
HB171.W22     330     *LC* 77-20412     *ISBN* 0465090958

**Wicksteed, Philip Henry, 1844-1927.**                    • **4.1456**
The common sense of political economy, and selected papers and reviews on economic theory. Edited with an introd. by Lionel Robbins. [Rev. and enl. ed.] London, G. Routledge, 1933. 2 v. (871 p.) ill. 1. Economics I. Robbins, Lionel Charles, 1898-, ed. II. T.
HB171 W45 1933

## HB171.5 Textbooks

**Friedman, Milton, 1912-.** • **4.1457**
Price theory, a provisional text. Chicago: Aldine Pub. Co., [1962] 285 p.: illus.; 27 cm. 1. Microeconomics I. T.
HB171.5.F75 1962      338.52      LC 62-18607

**Samuelson, Paul Anthony, 1915-.** **4.1458**
Economics / Paul A. Samuelson, William D. Nordhaus. — 12th ed. — New York: McGraw-Hill, c1985. xxxv, 950 p.: col. ill.; 25 cm. 1. Economics I. Nordhaus, William D. II. T.
HB171.5.S25 1985      330 19      LC 84-19407      ISBN 0070546851

**Theil, Henri.** **4.1459**
The system–wide approach to microeconomics / Henri Theil. — Chicago: University of Chicago Press, 1980. xii, 260 p.; 24 cm. Includes index. 1. Microeconomics 2. Consumption (Economics) I. T.
HB171.5.T26      338.5      LC 78-31999      ISBN 0226794377

## HB172.5 Macroeconomics

**Begg, David K. H.** **4.1460**
The rational expectations revolution in macroeconomics: theories and evidence / David K.H. Begg. — Baltimore, Md.: Johns Hopkins University Press, 1982. xii, 291 p.: ill.; 23 cm. Includes indexes. 1. Rational expectations (Economic theory) 2. Macroeconomics I. T.
HB172.5.B43 1982      339/.0724 19      LC 82-47785      ISBN 0801828813

**Chick, Victoria.** **4.1461**
Macroeconomics after Keynes: a reconsideration of the General theory / Victoria Chick. — 1st MIT Press ed. — Cambridge, Mass.: MIT Press, 1983. x, 374 p.; 24 cm. Includes index. Originally published: London: P. Allan, 1983. 1. Keynes, John Maynard, 1883-1946. General theory of employment, interest and money. 2. Macroeconomics I. T.
HB172.5.C455 1983      339 19      LC 83-844      ISBN 0262030950

**Conversations with economists: new classical economists and** **4.1462**
**opponents speak out on the current controversy in**
**macroeconomics / [compiled by] Arjo Klamer.**
Totowa, N.J.: Rowman & Allanheld, 1984 (c1983). xii, 265 p.; 22 cm. 1. Macroeconomics 2. Economics 3. Economic policy I. Klamer, Arjo.
HB172.5.C66 1984      339 19      LC 83-17765      ISBN 0865981469

**Moss, Scott J.** **4.1463**
Markets and macroeconomics: macroeconomic implications of rational individual behaviour / Scott Moss. — Oxford, OX; New York, NY, USA: B. Blackwell, 1985 (c1984). xi, 344 p.: ill.; 24 cm. Spine title: Markets & macroeconomics. Bibliography: p. [334]-338. 1. Macroeconomics I. T. II. Title: Markets & macroeconomics.
HB172.5.M683      339 19      LC 84-147330      ISBN 0855207566

**Okun, Arthur M.** **4.1464**
Prices and quantities: a macroeconomic analysis / Arthur M. Okun. — Washington, D.C.: Brookings Institution, c1981. xiii, 367 p.; 24 cm. 1. Macroeconomics 2. Inflation (Finance) I. Brookings Institution. II. T.
HB172.5.O38      339 19      LC 80-70076      ISBN 0815764804

**Sheffrin, Steven M.** • **4.1465**
Rational expectations / Steven M. Sheffrin. — Cambridge [Cambridgeshire]; New York: Cambridge University Press, 1983. x, 203 p.: ill.; 22 cm. — (Cambridge surveys of economic literature.) Includes index. 1. Rational expectations (Economic theory) 2. Macroeconomics I. T. II. Series.
HB172.5.S523 1983      339 19      LC 82-19747      ISBN 0521243106

## HB173–179 European Economists, By Country

**Walras, Léon, 1834-1910.** • **4.1466**
[Éléments d'économie politique pure. English] Elements of pure economics; or, The theory of social wealth. Translated by William Jaffé. New York, A. M. Kelley, 1969 [c1954] 620 p. illus., facsims. 23 cm. (Reprints of economic classics) Original imprint covered by label, as above. Translation of Éléments d'économie politique pure. 1. Economics 2. Economics, Mathematical I. T.
HB173.W2213 1969      330      LC 70-7658

**Cassel, Gustav, 1866-1945.** • **4.1467**
The theory of social economy. Translated by S. L. Barron. — New rev. ed. — New York, A. M. Kelley, 1967. viii, 708 p. illus. 22 cm. — (Reprints of economic classics) Reprint of the 1932 ed., which was translated from the MS. of the 5th German ed. of Theoretische Sozialökonomie. 1. Economics I. Barron, Samuel Landon, 1910- tr. II. T. III. Title: Social economy.
HB175.C3513 1967      330/.01      LC 67-19584

**Menger, Carl, 1840-1921.** • **4.1468**
Principles of economics / trans. and ed. by James Dingwall and Bert F. Hoselitz; with an introd. by Frank H. Knight. Glencoe: Free Press, 1950. 328 p. 1. Economics I. T.
HB175.M4812      LC 51-9720

**Menger, Carl, 1840-1921.** • **4.1469**
Problems of economics and sociology (Untersuchungen über die Methode der Socialwissenschaften und der politischen Oekonomie insbesondere) Edited and with an introd. by Louis Schneider. Translated by Francis J. Nock. — Urbana, University of Illinois Press, 1963. 237 p. 24 cm. Includes bibliography. 1. Economics 2. Social sciences I. T.
HB175.M48153      330.18      LC 63-10318

**Schumpeter, Joseph Alois, 1883-1950.** • **4.1470**
The theory of economic development; an inquiry into profits, capital, credit, interest, and the business cycle, by Joseph A. Schumpeter ... translated from the German by Redvers Opie ... Cambridge, Mass., Harvard university press, 1934. xii, 255 p. (Harvard economic studies. vol. XLVI) 1. Economics 2. Economic history I. T.
HB175 S462      LC 34-38868

**Von Mises, Ludwig, 1881-1973.** • **4.1471**
Epistemological problems of economics; translated by George Reisman. — Princeton, N. J., Van Nostrand [1960] 239 p. 24 cm. — (The William Volker Fund series in the humane studies) Translation of Grundprobleme der Nationalökonomie. 1. Economics 2. Value I. T.
HB175.V643      330.18      LC 60-11061

**Von Mises, Ludwig, 1881-1973.** • **4.1472**
Human action; a treatise on economics. — 3d rev. ed. — Chicago: H. Regnery Co., [1966, c1963] xvii, 907 p.; 24 cm. 1. Economics 2. Commerce I. T.
HB175.V65 1966      330      LC 67-3943

**Weber, Max, 1864-1920.** • **4.1473**
The theory of social and economic organization, tr. by A.M. Henderson and Talcott Parsons, ed. with an introd. by Talcott Parsons. [1st American ed.] New York, Oxford Univ. Press, 1947. x, 436 p. 1. Economics 2. Sociology I. Henderson, Alexander Morell, 1914-, tr. II. Parsons, Talcott, 1902- ed. and tr. III. T.
HB175 W364      LC 47-5841

**Pantaleoni, Maffeo, 1857-1924.** • **4.1474**
Pure economics. Translated by T. Boston Bruce. London, Macmillan, 1898. xiii, 315 p. ill. 1. Economics 2. Economics, Mathematical I. T.
HB177 P253

**Pareto, Vilfredo, 1848-1923.** • **4.1475**
[Manuale di economia politica. English] Manual of political economy. Translated by Ann S. Schwier. Edited by Ann S. Schwier and Alfred N. Page. New York, A. M. Kelley, 1971. xii, 504 p. illus. 24 cm. Translation of Manuale di economia politica. 1. Economics I. T.
HB177.P2913      330      LC 71-179960      ISBN 0678008817

**Lundberg, Erik, 1907-.** • **4.1476**
Studies in the theory of economic expansion. — New York: Kelley & Millman, 1955. 265 p.: ill.; 22 cm. ([Reprints of economic classics]) 1. Economics 2. Economics, Mathematical 3. Money 4. Business cycles I. T.
HB179.L83      330.1      LC 56-4963

**Wicksell, Knut, 1851-1926.** • **4.1477**
[Föreläsingar i nationalekonomi. English] Lectures on political economy. Translated from the Swedish by E. Classen, and edited, with an introd., by Lionel Robbins. New York, A. M. Kelley, 1967. 2 v. illus. 23 cm. (Reprints of economic classics) Translation of Föreläsingar i nationalekonomi. Reprint of the 1934-35 ed. 1. Economics 2. Money I. T.
HB179.S95 W53 1967      330      LC 67-28341

## HB199–846 Special Aspects. Special Topics

**Baumol, William J.** • **4.1478**
Economic dynamics; an introduction [by] William J. Baumol. With a contribution by Ralph Turvey. — 3d ed. — [New York]: Macmillan, [1970] xix, 472 p.: illus.; 21 cm. 1. Economics 2. Statics and dynamics (Social sciences) I. T.
HB199.B33 1970      330/.01      LC 76-84434

**Buchanan, James M.** • **4.1479**
Cost and choice; an inquiry in economic theory, by James M. Buchanan. — Chicago: Markham Pub. Co., [1969] xv, 104 p.: illus.; 23 cm. — (Markham

economics series) 1. Cost 2. Economics — History 3. Welfare economics 4. Social choice I. T.
HB199.B82     338/.013     LC 70-85975

**Clark, John Maurice, 1884-.**     • 4.1480
Studies in the economics of overhead costs, by J. Maurice Clark ... — Chicago, Ill., The University of Chicago press [1965,c1923] xiii, 502 p. diagrs. 21.5 cm. — (Half-title: Materials for the study of business) 1. Cost 2. Supply and demand I. T. II. Title: Economics of overhead costs. III. Title: Overhead costs.
HB199.C6     LC 24-2488

**Kirby, Andrew.**     4.1481
The politics of location: an introduction / Andrew Kirby. — London; New York: Methuen, 1982. xvii, 199 p.: ill.; 23 cm. 1. Space in economics 2. Geography, Political 3. Anthropo-geography 4. City planning — Great Britain. I. T.
HB199.K424 1982     304.2 19     LC 82-8132     ISBN 041633900X

**Noyes, Charles Reinold, 1884-.**     • 4.1482
Economic man in relation to his natural environment. New York, Columbia University Press, 1948. 2 v. (xiv, 1443 p.) 25 cm. 1. Economics 2. Man I. T.
HB199.N6     330.16     LC 48-7550

**Olsson, Gunnar, 1935-.**     • 4.1483
Distance and human interaction; a review and bibliography. Philadelphia, Regional Science Research Institute [c1965] vi, 112 p. 22 cm. (Regional Science Research Institute. Bibliography series, no. 2) 1. Space in economics 2. Industry — Location I. T. II. Series.
HB199.O46     338/.09     LC 68-6340

**Rostow, W. W. (Walt Whitman), 1916-.**     • 4.1484
The economics of take–off into sustained growth: proceedings of a Conference held by the International Economic Association / edited by W.W. Rostow. — New York: St. Martin's Press, 1963 [i.e. 1964] xxvi, 481 p.: ill.; 23 cm. 1. Economic development — Addresses, essays, lectures. 2. Industrialization — Addresses, essays, lectures. I. International Economic Association. II. T.
HB199.R64     HB199.E386 1964.

**Rostow, W. W. (Walt Whitman), 1916-.**     • 4.1485
The stages of economic growth; a non–communist manifesto [by] W. W. Rostow. 2d ed. Cambridge [Eng.] University Press, 1971. 253 p. 21 cm. 1. Economic development I. T.
HB199.R66 1971     338.9     LC 70-152634     ISBN 0521081009

**Tawney, R. H. (Richard Henry), 1880-1962.**     • 4.1486
The acquisitive society, by R. H. Tawney ... — New York, Harcourt, Brace and Howe, 1920. 2 p. l., 188 p. 20 cm. 1. Economics 2. Industry 3. Social problems I. T.
HB199.T35     LC 20-21421

**Von Mises, Ludwig, 1881-1973.**     • 4.1487
The ultimate foundation of economic science; an essay on method. Princeton, N.J., Van Nostrand [1962] 148 p. (The William Volker Fund series in the humane studies) 1. Economics 2. Dialectical materialism I. T. II. Series.
HB199 V6     LC 62-4930

## HB201–205 Value

**Chamberlin, Edward, 1899-1967.**     • 4.1488
The theory of monopolistic competition; a re–orientation of the theory of value. 8th ed. Cambridge, Harvard University Press, 1962. 396 p. illus. 22 cm. (Harvard economic studies, v. 38) 1. Value 2. Monopolistic competition 3. Prices 4. Economics, Mathematical I. T.
HB201.C5 1962     330.162     LC 63-649

**Graham, Frank Dunstone, 1890-1949.**     • 4.1489
The theory of international values. — New York: Greenwood Press, [1969, c1948] vii, 349 p.; 23 cm. 1. Value 2. Commerce I. T.
HB201.G68 1969     338.52/1     LC 69-13918     ISBN 0837119871

**Hicks, John Richard, Sir, 1904-.**     • 4.1490
A revision of demand theory. — Oxford, Clarendon Press, 1956. 196 p. illus. 19 cm. 1. Supply and demand I. T.
HB201.H63     330.162     LC 56-14058

**Kirzner, Israel M.**     4.1491
Competition and entrepreneurship [by] Israel M. Kirzner. — Chicago: University of Chicago Press, [1973] x, 246 p.; 22 cm. 1. Prices 2. Competition 3. Entrepreneurship I. T.
HB201.K49     338.5/2/01     LC 72-95424     ISBN 0226437752

**Machlup, Fritz, 1902-.**     • 4.1492
The economics of sellers' competition; model analysis of sellers' conduct. Baltimore, Johns Hopkins Press, 1952. 582 p. ill. 1. Competition I. T.
HB201 M285     LC 53-6339

**Malthus, T. R. (Thomas Robert), 1766-1834.**     • 4.1493
The measure of value stated and illustrated, with an application of it to the alterations in the value of the English currency since 1790. — New York: Kelley & Millman, 1957. v, 81 p.; 22 cm. — (Reprints of economic classics) 1. Value 2. Money — Great Britain. I. T.
HB201.M3 1957     HB201.M25.     LC 63-23988

**Robinson, Joan, 1903-.**     • 4.1494
The economics of imperfect competition, by Joan Robinson. — London, Macmillan, 1965 [c1933] xii, 352 p. diagrs. 22 cm. 'First edition 1933. Reprinted ... 1961.' 1. Value 2. Monopolies 3. Competition 4. Prices 5. Economics, Mathematical I. T.
HB201.R6 1965     330.1     LC 33-30842

**Schultz, Henry, 1893-1938.**     • 4.1495
The theory and measurement of demand. Chicago, University of Chicago Press [1938] xxxi, 817 p. ill. Half-title: Social science studies, directed by the Social science research committee of the University of Chicago. No. XXXVI. 1. Economics, Mathematical 2. Supply and demand I. T.
HB201 S43     LC 38-19565

**Wicksell, Knut, 1851-1926.**     • 4.1496
[Über Wert, Kapital und Rente. English] Value, capital and rent. [Translated by S. H. Frowein] New York, A.M. Kelley, 1970. 180 p. 22 cm. (Reprints of economic classics) Reprint of the 1954 London ed. Translation of Über Wert, Kapital und Rente. 1. Value 2. Capital 3. Interest 4. Economics, Mathematical I. T.
HB201.W6313 1970     330.1     LC 68-58668     ISBN 0678006520

**Wicksteed, Philip Henry, 1844-1927.**     • 4.1497
The alphabet of economic science; elements of the theory of value or worth. — New York, Kelley & Millman, 1955. 142 p. illus. 18 cm. — ([Reprints of economic classics]) 1. Value I. T.
HB201.W634     330.162     LC 56-1926

**Wieser, Friedrich, Freiherr von, 1851-1926.**     • 4.1498
Natural value. Edited with a pref. and analysis by William Smart; the translation by Christian A. Malloch. — New York, Kelley & Millman, 1956. xiv, 243 p. 22 cm. — ([Reprints of economic classics]) 1. Value I. T.
HB201.W65 1956     330.162     LC 56-4895

**Commons, John Rogers, 1862-1945.**     • 4.1499
Legal foundations of capitalism. — Madison: University of Wisconsin Press, 1968, c[1957] x, 394 p.; 20 cm. 1. Value 2. Property — United States. I. T.
HB203.C6

**Marx, Karl, 1818-1883.**     • 4.1500
A history of economic theories / edited with a pref., by Karl Kautsky; translated from the French with an introd. and notes, by Terence McCarthy. — 1st ed. New York: Langland Press, 1952-. v.; 23 cm. 1. Value 2. Economics — History I. T.
HB203.M315     LC 52-8392

**Marx, Karl, 1818-1883.**     • 4.1501
[Theorien uber den Mehrwert. English. 1952] Theories of surplus value; selections, translated from the German by G. A. Bonner and Emile Burns. New York, International Publishers [1952] 432 p. 23 cm. 1. Surplus value — History. 2. Economics — History I. T.
HB203.M32     330.1     LC 52-9527

## HB221–236 Prices

**American Economic Association.**     • 4.1502
Readings in price theory, selected by a committee of the American Economic Association. — Chicago: Published for the Association by R. D. Irwin, 1952. x, 568 p.: diagrs.; 24 cm. — (The Series of republished articles on economics, v. 6) 'Selection committee ... George J. Stigler, Kenneth E. Boulding.' 1. Prices 2. Value 3. Cost I. Stigler, George Joseph, 1911- ed. II. T.
HB221.A45     338.5082     LC 52-2167

**Bosworth, Barry, 1942-.**     4.1503
Commodity prices and the new inflation / Barry P. Bosworth, Robert Z. Lawrence. — Washington, D.C.: Brookings Institution, c1982. xiii, 215 p.: ill.; 24 cm. 1. Prices 2. Raw materials — Prices. 3. Commodity control 4. Inflation (Finance) I. Lawrence, Robert Z., 1949- II. T.
HB221.B593     338.5/2 19     LC 81-70467     ISBN 0815710348

**Debreu, Gerard.**      • **4.1504**
Theory of value; an axiomatic analysis of economic equilibrium. New York, Wiley [1959] 114 p. ill. (Cowles Foundation for Research in Economics at Yale University. Monograph 17) 1. Prices I. T.
HB221 D38     *LC* 59-11812

**Beveridge, William Henry Beveridge, baron, 1879-1963.**      • **4.1505**
Prices and wages in England from the twelfth to the nineteenth century / with the collaboration of L. Liepmann [et al.]. — N.Y., Kelley, 1966-. v.: facsims., tables (folded in pocket of vol. 1) (Publications of the International scientific committee on price history) (Reprints of economic classics) 1. Prices — Great Britain — History. I. T.
HB235.G7 B4 1966     *LC* 66-6227

**Hamilton, Earl J. (Earl Jefferson), 1899-.**      • **4.1506**
American treasure and the price revolution in Spain, 1501–1650. New York: Octagon Books, 1965 [c1934] xxxv, 428 p.: ill.; 24 cm. (Harvard economic studies. v. 43) 1. Prices — History 2. Prices — Spain 3. Precious metals 4. Spain — Economic conditions I. T. II. Series.
HB235 S7 H3 1965     *LC* 65-25882

**Hamilton, Earl J. (Earl Jefferson), 1899-.**      • **4.1507**
War and prices in Spain, 1651–1800, by Earl J. Hamilton. — New York: Russell & Russell, [1969, c1947] xxvi, 295 p.: illus., facsim., map.; 23 cm. — (Harvard economic studies. v. 81) 1. Prices — Spain — History. 2. Currency question — Spain — History. I. T. II. Series.
HB235.S75 H35 1969     338.52/0946     *LC* 68-27062

**Stigler, George Joseph, 1911-.**      • **4.1508**
The behavior of industrial prices [by] George J. Stigler & James K. Kindahl. — New York: National Bureau of Economic Research; distributed by Columbia University Press, 1970. xiv, 202 p.: illus.; 23 cm. — (National Bureau of Economic Research. General series, no. 90) 1. Prices — U.S. 2. Price indexes I. Kindahl, James Keith, 1931- joint author. II. T. III. Series.
HB235.U6 S7     338.52/0973     *LC* 79-121003     *ISBN* 087014216X

## HB301 Labor. Wages

**Marx, Karl, 1818-1883.**      • **4.1509**
Wage–labour and capital: Value, price and profit / by Karl Marx. — New York: International Pub., [1935]. 48, 62 p. — (Marxist library; v. 37) Each part has also special t.p. 'Value, price and profit is here published in the original version as delivered by Marx in English and edited by his daughter, Eleanor Marz Aveling.'—Publisher's note. 1. Wages 2. Capital 3. Economics I. Aveling, Eleanor Marx, 1855-1898. II. T. III. Title: Value, price and profit.
HB301.M4     *LC* 37-13364

**Microeconomic foundations of employment and inflation theory**    • **4.1510**
**[by] Edmund S. Phelps [and others.**
1st ed.]. — New York: Norton, [1970] viii, 434 p.: illus.; 25 cm. 1. Employment (Economic theory) — Addresses, essays, lectures. 2. Inflation (Finance) — Addresses, essays, lectures. I. Phelps, Edmund S.
HB301.M57     330.1/63     *LC* 75-80022

**Senior, Nassau William, 1790-1864.**      • **4.1511**
Three lectures on the rate of wages. 2d ed. New York: A.M. Kelley, 1966. xix, 57 p.; 22 cm. (Reprints of economic classics.) Reprint of the 2d ed., 1831. 1. Wages — Great Britain. 2. Labor and laboring classes — Great Britain I. T.
HB301.S6 1966     *LC* 65-25863

## HB401 Rent. Land

**Jones, Richard, 1790-1855.**      • **4.1512**
An essay on the distribution of wealth and on the sources of taxation. London J. Murray 1831. 329;49p. 1. Rent I. T.
HB401 J8 1831

**Malthus, T. R. (Thomas Robert), 1766-1834.**      • **4.1513**
An inquiry into the nature and progress of rent, and the principles by which it is regulated. New York, Greenwood Press [1969] 61 p. 23 cm. Reprint of the 1815 ed. 1. Rent I. T.
HB401.M19 1969     333.5     *LC* 69-13984     *ISBN* 0837123623

**Toward a theory of the rent–seeking society / edited by James**    **4.1514**
**M. Buchanan, Robert D. Tollison, and Gordon Tullock.**
College Station: Texas A & M University, 1981 (c1980). xi, 367 p.: graphs; 24 cm. (Texas A & M University economics series; no. 4) 1. Rent (Economic theory) — Addresses, essays, lectures. 2. Transfer payments — Addresses, essays, lectures. 3. Industry and state — Addresses, essays, lectures.

I. Buchanan, James M. II. Tollison, Robert D. III. Tullock, Gordon. IV. Title: Rent-seeking society.
HB401.T68     333/.012 19     *LC* 79-5276     *ISBN* 0890960909

## HB501 Capital. Capitalism

### HB501 A–L

**Althusser, Louis.**      **4.1515**
[Lire Le capital. Selections. English] Reading 'Capital' / by Louis Althusser [and] Etienne Balibar; translated [from the French] by Ben Brewster. — London: NLB, 1970. 340 p.; 24 cm. Consists of two essays, one by Althusser, the other by Balibar which were presented as papers at a seminar on Marx's 'Capital' at the Ecole Normale Supérieure in 1905, and included along with a number of other contributions in the original edition, Lire Le Capital, vols. I and II, Maspero, Paris, 1965. 1. Marx, Karl, 1818-1883. Das Kapital. I. Balibar, Etienne, 1942- II. T.
HB501.A5613     335.41/2     *LC* 70-576019     *ISBN* 0902308807

**Amin, Samir.**      **4.1516**
[Développement inégal. English] Unequal development: an essay on the social formations of peripheral capitalism / by Samir Amin; translated by Brian Pearce. — New York: Monthly Review Press, c1976. 440 p.; 21 cm. Translation of Le développement inégal. Includes index. 1. Capitalism 2. Socialism 3. Economic history 4. Developing countries — Economic conditions I. T.
HB501.A5913     330.9/172/4     *LC* 75-15364     *ISBN* 0853453802

**Arnold, Thurman Wesley, 1891-1969.**      • **4.1517**
The folklore of capitalism, by Thurman W. Arnold. — New Haven: Yale University press; London: H. Milford, Oxford University press, 1937. vii, 400 p.: diagrs.; 21 cm. 1. Political science 2. Capitalism 3. Economics 4. Social psychology I. T.
HB501.A73     330.15     *LC* 37-32402

**Baran, Paul A.**      • **4.1518**
Monopoly capital: an essay on the American economic and social order / Paul A. Baran and Paul M. Sweezy. — New York: Monthly Review Press, 1966. ix, 402 p.: ill. 1. Monopolies — United States. 2. Marxian economics 3. Capital I. Sweezy, Paul Marlor, 1910- II. T.
HB501.B244     *LC* 65-15269

**Barratt Brown, Michael.**      **4.1519**
The economics of imperialism / Michael Barratt Brown. — Harmondsworth: Penguin Education, 1974. 380 p.; 18 cm. (Penguin modern economics texts: political economy) (Penguin education) Includes index. 1. Capitalism 2. Imperialism 3. Marxian economics I. T.
HB501.B354     338.91     *LC* 75-308955     *ISBN* 0140809074

**Böhm-Bawerk, Eugen von, 1851-1914.**      • **4.1520**
Capital and interest. Translated by George D. Huncke and Hans F. Sennholz. South Holland, Ill., Libertarian Press [1959] 3 v. ill. Vol. 2: Translated by George D. Huncke; Hans F. Sennholz, consulting economist; v. 3: Translated by Hans F. Sennholz. 1. Capital 2. Interest and usury I. T.
HB501 B665     *LC* 58-5555

**Bukharin, Nikolaĭ Ivanovich, 1888-1938.**      • **4.1521**
[Mirovoe khoziaĭstvo i imperializm. English] Imperialism and world economy. With an introd. by V. I. Lenin. [1st Modern Reader paperback ed.] New York, Monthly Review Press [1973, c1929] 173 p. 21 cm. (Modern reader, PB-290) Translation of Mirovoe khoziaĭstvo i imperializm. 1. Capitalism 2. Imperialism 3. Economics I. T.
HB501.B84613 1973     330.1     *LC* 72-93461     *ISBN* 0853452903

**Burmeister, Edwin.**      **4.1522**
Capital theory and dynamics / Edwin Burmeister. — Cambridge [Eng.]; New York: Cambridge University Press, 1980. xii, 330 p.: ill.; 22 cm. — (Cambridge surveys of economic literature) Includes index. 1. Capital — Mathematical models 2. Saving and investment — Mathematical models. 3. Economic development — Mathematical models. 4. Statics and dynamics (Social sciences) I. T.
HB501.B8469     332/.041     *LC* 79-28412     *ISBN* 0521228891

**Friedman, Milton, 1912-.**      • **4.1523**
Capitalism and freedom. With the assistance of Rose D. Friedman. [Chicago] University of Chicago Press [1962] 202 p. 23 cm. 1. Capitalism 2. State, The 3. Liberty. 4. United States — Economic policy I. T.
HB501.F7     330.15     *LC* 62-19619

**Galbraith, John Kenneth, 1908-.**      • **4.1524**
American capitalism; the concept of countervailing power. Rev. ed. Boston, Houghton Mifflin, 1956. 208 p. 21 cm. 1. Capitalism — United States.

2. Countervailing power — United States. 3. United States — Economic conditions — 1918- I. T.
HB501.G3 1956   330.15   *LC* 56-4515

**Gilder, George F., 1939-.**   **4.1525**
Wealth and poverty / George Gilder. — New York: Basic Books, c1981. xii, 306 p.; 24 cm. Includes index. 1. Capitalism 2. Wealth 3. United States — Economic conditions — 1945- 4. United States — Economic policy I. T.
HB501.G46   330.12/2 19   *LC* 80-50556   *ISBN* 0465091059

**Harcourt, Geoffrey Colin.**   **4.1526**
Some Cambridge controversies in the theory of capital [by] G. C. Harcourt. — Cambridge [Eng.]: University Press, 1972. x, 272 p.: illus.; 22 cm. 1. Capital 2. Capital — Mathematical models I. T.
HB501.H349   332/.041   *LC* 71-161294   *ISBN* 0521082943

**Harvey, David, 1935-.**   **4.1527**
The limits to capital / David Harvey. — Chicago: University of Chicago Press, 1982. xviii, 478 p.: ill.; 24 cm. Includes indexes. 1. Capitalism 2. Marxian economics I. T.
HB501.H3597 1982   335.4 19   *LC* 82-40322   *ISBN* 0226319520

**Heilbroner, Robert L.**   **4.1528**
Business civilization in decline / Robert L. Heilbroner. — 1st ed. — New York: Norton, c1976. 127 p. 1. Capitalism 2. Industry — Social aspects 3. Civilization, Modern — 1950- 4. Economic forecasting I. T.
HB501.H397   HB501 H397.   330.9/04   *LC* 75-33367   *ISBN* 039305571X

**Heilbroner, Robert L.**   **4.1529**
The nature and logic of capitalism / Robert L. Heilbroner. — 1st ed. — New York: Norton, c1985. 225 p.; 22 cm. Includes index. 1. Capitalism I. T.
HB501.H398 1985   330.12/2 19   *LC* 85-5656   *ISBN* 0393022277

**Hicks, John Richard, Sir, 1904-.**   **4.1530**
Capital and time; a neo–Austrian theory, by John Hicks. — [S.l.]: Oxford, 1973. xi, 213 p.: illus.; 23 cm. 1. Capital — Mathematical models 2. Austrian school of economists I. T.
HB501.H48   332/.041   *LC* 73-161959   *ISBN* 019828179X

**Hilferding, Rudolf, 1877-1941.**   **4.1531**
[Finanzkapital. English]. Finance capital: a study of the latest phase of capitalist development / Rudolf Hilferding; edited with an introduction by Tom Bottomore; from translations by Morris Watnick and Sam Gordon. — London; Boston: Routledge & Kegan Paul, 1981. vi, 466 p.; 25 cm. Translation of: Das Finanzkapital. Includes index. 1. Capitalism 2. Finance I. Bottomore, T. B. II. T.
HB501.H51513   330.12/2 19   *LC* 80-41226   *ISBN* 0710006187

**Lenin, Vladimir Il'ich, 1870-1924.**   • **4.1532**
Imperialism, the highest stage of capitalism, a popular outline [by] V. I. Lenin. — 1st ed. — Moscow: Foreign Languages Press, [19—] 226, [1] p.; 17 cm. Translation of Imperializm, kak noveĭshiĭ ėtap kapitalizma. 1. Capitalism 2. Imperialism I. T.
HB501.L332   330.12/2

**Lenin, Vladimir Il'ich, 1870-1924.**   • **4.1533**
[Novye materialy k rabote V. I. Lenina. English] New data for V. I. Lenin's 'Imperialism, the highest stage of capitalism.' Edited by E. Varga [and] L. Mendelsohn. New York: AMS Press [1970] vii, 322 p.: ill.; 24 cm. Reprint of the 1938 ed. Translation of Novye materialy k rabote V. I. Lenina: Imperializm, kak vysshaia stadiia kapitalizma. 1. Capitalism 2. Imperialism 3. Economic history — 20th century I. Lenin, Vladimir Il'ich, 1870-1924. Imperializm, kak vysshaia stadiia kapitalizma. II. Varga, Eugen, 1879-1964. ed. III. Mendel'son, Lev Abramovich, ed. IV. T.
HB501.L372 1970   330.12/2   *LC* 71-121288   *ISBN* 0404039650

## HB501 M–Z

**Marx, Karl, 1818-1883.**   • **4.1534**
Pre–capitalist economic formations / Karl Marx; translated by Jack Cohen; edited and with an introd. by E. J. Hobsbawm. — 1st U. S. ed. — New York: International Publishers, [1965, c1964] 153 p.; 21 cm. Translation of Formen, die der kapitalistischen Produktion vorhergehen, originally published as a part of the author's Grundrisse der Kritik der politischen Ökonomie and later published separately. 1. Capital 2. Economics I. Hobsbawm, E. J. (Eric J.), 1917- II. T.
HB501.M3393   *LC* 65-16393   *ISBN* 0717801667

**Marx, Karl, 1818-1883.**   • **4.1535**
[Kapital. English] Capital; a critique of political economy. Edited by Frederick Engels. New York, International Publishers [1967] 3 v. facsims. 21 cm. (New World paperbacks) 1. Capital 2. Economics I. Engels, Friedrich, 1820-1895. ed. II. T.
HB501.M3633   335.4/1   *LC* 67-19754

**Brewer, Anthony, 1942-.**   **4.1536**
A guide to Marx's Capital / Anthony Brewer. — Cambridge [Cambridgeshire]; New York: Cambridge University Press, 1984. xiv, 211 p.; 22 cm. Includes index. 1. Marx, Karl, 1818-1883. Kapital I. Marx, Karl, 1818-1883. Kapital II. T.
HB501.M37 B73 1984   335.4/1 19   *LC* 83-14329   *ISBN* 0521257301

**Engels, Friedrich, 1820-1895.**   • **4.1537**
Engels on Capital; synopsis, reviews, letters and supplementary material. New York, International publishers [c1937] ix, 147 p. 22 cm. 'Translated and edited by Leonard E. Mins.' 1. Marx, Karl, 1818-1883. Das Kapital. 2. Capital 3. Economics I. Mins, Leonard E., ed. and tr. II. T.
HB501.M5E48   331   *LC* 38-1498

**Kautsky, Karl, 1854-1938.**   • **4.1538**
The economic doctrines of Karl Marx, by Karl Kautsky, translated by H. J. Stenning. London, A. & C. Black, ltd., 1925. vi, 248 p. 20 cm. 1. Marx, Karl, 1818-1883. 2. Capital 3. Value 4. Capitalism I. Stenning, Henry James, 1889- tr. II. T.
HB501.M5K23   *LC* 26-5573

**Sweezy, Paul Marlor, 1910-.**   • **4.1539**
The theory of capitalist development; principles of Marxian political economy [by] Paul M. Sweezy ... New York, Oxford university press, 1942. xiv, 398 p.: diagrs.; 22 cm. 1. Marx, Karl, 1818-1883. 2. Economics 3. Socialism 4. Capitalism I. T.
HB501 M5 S9   *LC* 42-25876

**Webb, Sidney, 1859-1947.**   • **4.1540**
The decay of capitalist civilization, by Sidney and Beatrice Webb. New York, Greenwood Press [1969, c1923] xvii, 242 p. 23 cm. 1. Capitalism 2. Great Britain — Economic conditions — 1918-1945 I. Webb, Beatrice Potter, 1858-1943. joint author. II. T.
HB501.P35 1969   330.12/2   *LC* 69-14030   *ISBN* 0837120373

**Schumpeter's vision: capitalism, socialism and democracy after 40 years / edited by Arnold Heertje.**   **4.1541**
Eastbourne [England]: Praeger, 1981. xvi, 208 p. (Praeger special studies.) (Praeger scientific.) 1. Schumpeter, Joseph Alois, 1883-1950 — Addresses, essays, lectures 2. Capitalism — History — Addresses, essays, lectures I. Heertje, Arnold, 1934- II. Series. III. Series: Praeger scientific.
HB501.S315   *ISBN* 0030602769

**Scott, John, 1949-.**   **4.1542**
Corporations, classes, and capitalism / John Scott. — New York: St. Martin's Press, 1980, c1979. 219 p.; 23 cm. Includes index. 1. Capitalism 2. Corporations 3. International business enterprises 4. Industry and state I. T.
HB501.S47 1980   338.7/4/01   *LC* 80-5097   *ISBN* 0312170114

**Sombart, Werner, 1863-1941.**   • **4.1543**
[Bourgeois. English] The quintessence of capitalism: a study of the history and psychology of the modern business man. Translated and edited by M. Epstein. New York, H. Fertig, 1967. 400 p. 24 cm. First published in English in 1915. Translation of Der Bourgeois. 1. Capitalism 2. Middle classes I. Epstein, Mortimer, 1880-1946. ed. and tr. II. T.
HB501.S673 1967   330.1   *LC* 67-13645

**Sombart, Werner, 1863-1941.**   • **4.1544**
[Luxus und Kapitalismus. English.] Luxury and capitalism. Introd. by Philip Siegelman. [Translated by W. R. Dittmar] Ann Arbor, University of Michigan Press [1967] xxxii, 200 p. 22 cm. 1. Luxury 2. Capital 3. Capitalism I. T.
HB501.S682 1967   330.12/2   *LC* 67-11982

**Sweezy, Paul Marlor, 1910-.**   **4.1545**
The transition from feudalism to capitalism / Paul Sweezy ... [et al.]; introd. by Rodney Hilton. — [Rev. ed.]. — London: NLB; Atlantic Highlands [N.J.]: Humanities Press, 1976. 195 p.; 21 cm. (Foundations of history library) 1. Capitalism — History — Addresses, essays, lectures. I. T.
HB501.S98 1976   330.12/2   *LC* 76-361182   *ISBN* 0902308211

**Universities—National Bureau Committee for Economic Research.**   • **4.1546**
Capital formation and economic growth: a conference of the Universities–National Bureau Committee for Economic Research. — Princeton: Princeton University Press, 1955. xiii, 677 p.: tables; 24 cm. — (National Bureau of Economic Research. Special conference series, 6) 'A report of the National Bureau of Economic Research, New York.' Bibliographical footnotes. 1. Saving and investment 2. Economic policy I. T. II. Series.
HB501.U57   332   *LC* 55-6699

**Kiker, B. F. comp.**                                                    **4.1547**
Investment in human capital, edited by B. F. Kiker. — [1st ed.]. — Columbia:
University of South Carolina Press, [1971] xii, 608 p.: illus.; 24 cm. 1. Human
capital — Addresses, essays, lectures. I. T.
HB501.5.K54      331      *LC* 70-120581      *ISBN* 0872491897

**Schultz, Theodore William, 1902-.**                                    • **4.1548**
Investment in human capital; the role of education and of research [by]
Theodore W. Schultz. — New York: Free Press, [1970, c1971] xii, 272 p.; 21
cm. 1. Human capital 2. Education — Economic aspects I. T. II. Title:
Human capital.
HB501.5.S3      331      *LC* 77-122273

## HB531–549 Interest

**Cassel, Gustav, 1866-1945.**                                          • **4.1549**
The nature and necessity of interest. New York, A. M. Kelley, 1971. xii, 188 p.
illus. 22 cm. (Reprints of economic classics) Reprint of the 1903 ed. 1. Interest
I. T.
HB539.C33 1971      332.8      *LC* 77-147898      *ISBN* 0678008485

**Fisher, Irving, 1867-1947.**                                          • **4.1550**
The theory of interest as determined by impatience to spend income and
opportunity to invest it. New York: Kelley & Millman, 1954. 566 p.: ill.; 23 cm.
([Reprints of economic classics]) 1. Interest and usury 2. Economics,
Mathematical I. T.
HB539 F54 1954

**Lutz, Friedrich A. (Friedrich August), 1901-.**                      • **4.1551**
[Zinstheorie. English] The theory of interest. [By] Friedrich A. Lutz.
[Translated fron the German by Claus Wittich] Dordrecht, D. Reidel [1968] ix,
339 p. 22 cm. Translation of Zinstheorie. 1. Interest I. T.
HB539.L813      332.8      *LC* 68-81397

## HB601–615 Profit. Entrepreneurship. Risk

**Kilby, Peter. comp.**                                                  **4.1552**
Entrepreneurship and economic development. — New York, Free Press [1971]
viii, 384 p. 24 cm. Includes bibliographical references. 1. Entrepreneurship —
Addresses, essays, lectures. 2. Economic development — Addresses, essays,
lectures. I. T.
HB601.K53      338/.04      *LC* 79-122279

**Knight, Frank Hyneman, 1885-.**                                        • **4.1553**
Risk, uncertainty and profit [by] Frank H. Knight. With an introd. by George J.
Stigler. — Chicago: University of Chicago Press, [1971] xiv, 381 p.; 21 cm. —
(A Phoenix book, P396) Reprint of the 1921 ed. 1. Risk 2. Profit I. T.
HB601.K7 1971      338.5      *LC* 76-149593      *ISBN* 0226446905

**Measuring profitability and capital costs: an international study**      **4.1554**
**/ edited by Daniel M. Holland.**
Lexington, Mass.: Lexington Books, c1984. viii, 494 p.: ill.; 24 cm. 1. Profit —
Statistical methods. 2. Corporate profits — Statistical methods. I. Holland,
Daniel M. (Daniel Mark), 1920-
HB601.M387 1984      658.1/5 19      *LC* 82-48491      *ISBN* 066906159X

**Encyclopedia of entrepreneurship / edited by Calvin A. Kent,**          **4.1555**
**Donald L. Sexton, Karl H. Vesper.**
Englewood Cliffs, NJ: Prentice-Hall, c1982. xxxviii, 425 p.: ill.; 24 cm.
1. Entrepreneurship 2. Small business — Technological innovations I. Kent,
Calvin A. II. Sexton, Donald L. III. Vesper, Karl H.
HB615.E59      338/.04 19      *LC* 81-10602      *ISBN* 0132758261

**Entrepreneurs in cultural context / edited by Sidney M.**               **4.1556**
**Greenfield, Arnold Strickon, and Robert T. Aubey.**
1st ed. — Albuquerque: University of New Mexico Press, c1979. xiv, 373 p.; 24
cm. (School of American Research, advanced seminar series) 'A School of
American Research book.' Includes index. 1. Entrepreneurship — Addresses,
essays, lectures. I. Greenfield, Sidney M. II. Strickon, Arnold. III. Aubey,
Robert T.
HB615.E6      301.18/32      *LC* 78-21433      *ISBN* 0826305040

**The Environment for entrepreneurship / edited by Calvin A.**            **4.1557**
**Kent.**
Lexington, Mass.: Lexington Books, c1984. xi, 191 p.; 24 cm. Includes
expanded versions of a series of lectures given during 1982-83 at the Center for
Private Enterprise and Entrepreneurship, Baylor University.
1. Entrepreneurship — Addresses, essays, lectures. I. Kent, Calvin A.

II. Hankamer School of Business. Center for Private Enterprise and
Entrepreneurship.
HB615.E65 1984      338/.04 19      *LC* 83-48736      *ISBN* 0669075078

**Hébert, Robert F.**                                                    **4.1558**
The entrepreneur: mainstream views and radical critiques / Robert F. Hébert,
Albert N. Link; foreword by G.L.S. Shackle. — New York, N.Y.: Praeger,
1982. xiii, 128 p.; 25 cm. Includes index. 1. Entrepreneurship — History.
I. Link, Albert N. II. T.
HB615.H34 1982      338/.04/09 19      *LC* 81-21134      *ISBN* 0030595894

## HB701–751 Property

**Godwin, William, 1756-1836.**                                          • **4.1559**
[Enquiry concerning political justice. Of property] Godwin's 'Political justice.'
A reprint of the essay on 'Property,' from the original edition. Edited by H. S.
Salt. London, S. Sonnenschein, 1890. St. Clair Shores, Mich., Scholarly Press
[1969?] 155 p. 22 cm. First published in the author's An enquiry concerning
political justice, 1793. 1. Property I. Salt, Henry Stephens, 1851-1939. ed.
II. T.
HB701.G45 1969      330.1/7      *LC* 78-8160

**Proudhon, P.-J. (Pierre-Joseph), 1809-1865.**                          • **4.1560**
[Qu'est-ce que la propriété? English] What is property? An inquiry into the
principle of right and of government. Translated from the French by Benj. R.
Tucker. With a new introd. by George Woodcock. New York, Dover
Publications [1970] liii, 457 p. 22 cm. (The Dover anarchy library) Translation
of Qu'est-ce que la propriété? 'Unabridged and unaltered republication of the
English translation originally published ... c. 1890.' 1. Property 2. Economics
I. T.
HB701.P78 1970      335/.83      *LC* 72-124179      *ISBN* 0486224864

**Ryan, Alan.**                                                          **4.1561**
Property and political theory / Alan Ryan. — Oxford, England; New York,
N.Y.: B. Blackwell, 1984. 198 p.; 24 cm. 1. Property — History. I. T.
HB701.R9 1984      330/.17/09 19      *LC* 84-11126      *ISBN* 0631136916

## HB771 Competition. Income Distribution. Wealth

**Bain, Joe Staten, 1912-.**                                            • **4.1562**
Barriers to new competition; their character and consequences in
manufacturing industries / Joe S. Bain. — Cambridge: Harvard University
Press, c1956. x, 329 p.; 25 cm. — (Harvard University series on competition in
American industry; 3) 1. Competition 2. United States — Manufactures I. T.
II. Series.
HB771.B23      *LC* 56-11278

**Bronfenbrenner, Martin, 1914-.**                                      • **4.1563**
Income distribution theory. — Chicago: AldineAtherton, [1971] xiii, 487 p.; 25
cm. — (Aldine treatises in modern economics) 1. Income distribution
2. Wealth I. T.
HB771.B74      339.2      *LC* 77-131045      *ISBN* 0202060373

**Clark, John Bates, 1847-1938.**                                        • **4.1564**
The distribution of wealth; a theory of wages, interest, and profits. New York,
Kelley & Millman, 1956. 445 p. ill. (Reprints of economic classics) 1. Wealth
I. T.
HB771 C6 1956      *LC* 57-2998

**Clark, John Maurice, 1884-.**                                          • **4.1565**
Competition as a dynamic process. Washington, Brookings Institution [1961]
501 p.; 24 cm. 1. Competition I. T.
HB771 C65      *LC* 61-18475

**Commons, John Rogers, 1862-1945.**                                     • **4.1566**
The distribution of wealth (1893) With an introductory essay, The foundations
of Commons' economics / by Joseph Dorfman. — New York: A. M. Kelley,
1963. xv, x, 258 p.: ill. (1 fold.); 22 cm. — (Reprints of economic classics) With
reproduction of the t. p. of the 1893 ed. published by Macmillan. Includes
bibliographical references. 1. Wealth I. T.
HB771.C73 1963      330.16      *LC* 64-54864

**Fouraker, Lawrence E.**                                                • **4.1567**
Bargaining behavior / [by] Lawrence E. Fouraker [and] Sidney Siegel. — New
York: McGraw-Hill [1963] ix, 309 p.: diagrs., tables; 22 cm. Bibliography: p.
211-214. 1. Monopolies 2. Oligopolies I. Siegel, Sidney, 1916-1961. joint
author. II. T.
HB771.F6      338.5018      *LC* 63-17337

**Pigou, A. C. (Arthur Cecil), 1877-1959.**   • **4.1568**
The economics of welfare, by A. C. Pigou. 4th ed. London, Macmillan and co., limited, 1932. xxxi, 837 p. diagrs. 23 cm. 1. Welfare economics 2. Wealth 3. Labor and laboring classes — 1914- 4. Finance I. T.
HB771.P6 1932    330.1    *LC* 33-22321

**Shubik, Martin.**   • **4.1569**
Strategy and market structure; competition, oligopoly, and the theory of games. New York, Wiley [1959] 387 p. ill. 1. Competition 2. Oligopolies 3. Marketing 4. Game theory I. T.
HB771 S5    *LC* 58-14221

## HB801–843 Consumption

**Duesenberry, James Stemble, 1918-.**   • **4.1570**
Income, saving, and the theory of consumer behavior. — Cambridge, Harvard University Press, 1949. 128 p. diagrs. 23 cm. — (Harvard economic studies. v. 87) 'Under the title 'The consumption function' the original version of this book was submitted as a doctoral dissertation at the University of Michigan in February 1948.' Bibliography: p. [117]-124. 1. Income 2. Consumption (Economics) I. T. II. Series.
HB801.D8 1949    339.4    *LC* 49-50134 *

**Friedman, Milton, 1912-.**   • **4.1571**
A theory of the consumption function. A study by the National Bureau of Economic Research, New York. — Princeton: Princeton University Press, 1957. 243 p.: illus.; 24 cm. — (National Bureau of Economic Research. General series, no. 63) 1. Consumption (Economics) I. National Bureau of Economic Research. II. T.
HB801.F7    339.4    *LC* 57-5454

**Veblen, Thorstein, 1857-1929.**   • **4.1572**
The theory of the leisure class. 1899. With the addition of a review by William Dean Howells. — New York: A. M. Kelley, bookseller, 1965. 400 p.: facsim.; 21 cm. — (His Writings) Reprints of economic classics. 1. Leisure class I. T.
HB831.V4 1965    301.44    *LC* 65-15958

**Carnegie, Andrew, 1835-1919.**   • **4.1573**
The gospel of wealth, and other timely essays. Edited by Edward C. Kirkland. — Cambridge: Belknap Press of Harvard University Press, 1962. xx, 239 p.; 22 cm. — (John Harvard library.) 1. Wealth — Addresses, essays, lectures. 2. Economics — Addresses, essays, lectures. 3. United States — Politics and government — Addresses, essays, lectures. I. T. II. Series.
HB835.C3 1962    308.1    *LC* 62-11395

**Rescher, Nicholas.**   • **4.1574**
Distributive justice; a constructive critique of the utilitarian theory of distribution. Indianapolis, Bobbs-Merrill [1967, c1966] xvi, 166 p. illus. 22 cm. 1. Distributive justice 2. Wealth, Ethics of 3. Utilitarianism I. T.
HB835.R45    330.15/3    *LC* 66-29532

## HB846 Welfare Theory

**Cummings, Ronald G.**   **4.1575**
Valuing environmental goods: an assessment of the contingent valuation method / R.G. Cummings, D.S. Brookshire, W.D. Schulze; contributors, Richard Bishop ... [et al.]; commentators, Kenneth Arrow ... [et al.]. — Totowa, N.J.: Rowman & Allanheld, 1986. xiii, 270 p.; 25 cm. Includes index. 1. Public goods — Cost effectiveness. 2. Public goods — Valuation. I. Brookshire, David S. II. Schulze, William D. III. Bishop, Richard C. IV. Arrow, Kenneth Joseph, 1921- V. T.
HB846.5.C86 1986    363 19    *LC* 85-14298    *ISBN* 0847674487

## HB849–3700 Demography. Vital Events. Population

### HB849 COLLECTED WORKS. REFERENCE WORKS. THEORY

**Population growth: anthropological implications / edited by**   **4.1576**
**Brian Spooner.**
Cambridge, Mass.: MIT Press [1972] xxvii, 425 p.: ill.; 23 cm. 'Proceedings of a colloquium in general anthropology entitled 'Population, resources, and technology,' held at the University of Pennsylvania, March 11-14, 1970, under the combined auspices of the Near East Center, the University Museum, and the Department of Anthropology of the University of Pennsylvania, in association with the Wenner-Gren Foundation for Anthropological Research, Incorporated.' 1. Population — Congresses. 2. Social change — Congresses. 3. Technological innovations — Congresses. I. Spooner, Brian. ed. II. University of Pennsylvania. Near East Center. III. University of Pennsylvania. University Museum. IV. Pennsylvania. University. Dept. of Anthropology.
HB849.P67    301.32    *LC* 72-4209    *ISBN* 0262191024

**Social demography / edited by Karl E. Taeuber, Larry L.**   **4.1577**
**Bumpass, James A. Sweet; Center for Demography and Ecology, University of Wisconsin—Madison.**
New York: Academic Press, c1978. xv, 336 p.: ill.; 24 cm. (Studies in population.) Proceedings of a conference held by the Center for Population Research at the University of Wisconsin, Madison, June 15-16, 1975. 1. Fertility, Human — Congresses. 2. Population density — Congresses. 3. Social mobility — Congresses. 4. Population research — Congresses. I. Taeuber, Karl E. II. Bumpass, Larry L. III. Sweet, James A. IV. University of Wisconsin—Madison. Center for Demography and Ecology. V. Center for Population Research (National Institute of Child Health and Human Development) VI. Series.
HB849.S62    301.32    *LC* 78-606153    *ISBN* 0126826501

**World Population Conference (2nd: 1965: Belgrade)**   • **4.1578**
Proceedings. New York, United Nations, 1966-. v. map. 26 cm. ([Document] (United Nations) E/Conf.41/2) 'United Nations publication. Sales no.: 66.XIII.5.' At head of title: Department of Economic and Social Affairs. 1. Population — Congresses. I. United Nations. Dept. of Economic and Social Affairs. II. T. III. Series.
HB849.W6    301.3/2/0631    *LC* 67-3159

**International encyclopedia of population / editor in chief, John**   **4.1579**
**A. Ross (Center for Population and Family Health, International Institute for the Study of Human Reproduction, Faculty of Medicine, Columbia University).**
New York: Free Press, c1982. 2 v. (xxiii, 750 p.): ill.; 29 cm. 1. Population — Dictionaries. I. Ross, John A., 1934- II. International Institute for the Study of Human Reproduction. Center for Population and Family Health.
HB849.2.I55 1982    304.6/03/21 19    *LC* 82-2326    *ISBN* 0029274303

**Willigan, J. Dennis.**   **4.1580**
Sources and methods of historical demography / J. Dennis Willigan, Katherine A Lynch. — New York, N.Y.: Academic Press, c1982. xv, 505 p.: ill.; 23 cm. — (Studies in social discontinuity.) Includes indexes. 1. Population — History — Methodology. 2. Demography I. Lynch, Katherine A. II. T. III. Title: Historical demography. IV. Series.
HB849.4.W54 1982    304.6/09 19    *LC* 82-8819    *ISBN* 0127570225

**Population estimates: methods for small area analysis / edited**   **4.1581**
**by Everett S. Lee, Harold F. Goldsmith.**
Beverly Hills: Sage Publications, c1982. 248 p.; 23 cm. 'Results of the Small Area Estimation Conference sponsored by the National Institute of Mental Health (NIMH) and held in Annapolis, Maryland in November, 1978'— Introd. 1. Population forecasting — Congresses. I. Lee, Everett Spurgeon. II. Goldsmith, Harold F. III. National Institute of Mental Health (U.S.) IV. Small Area Estimation Conference (1978: Annapolis, Md.)
HB849.53.P66 1982    304.6/2/028 19    *LC* 82-648    *ISBN* 0803918127

### HB851–875 HISTORY OF DEMOGRAPHY

**McEvedy, Colin.**   **4.1582**
Atlas of world population history / Colin McEvedy and Richard Jones. — New York: Facts on File, c1978. 368 p.: ill.; 21 cm. Includes index. 1. Population — History 2. Population — Statistics 3. Population — Charts, diagrams, etc. I. Jones, Richard, 1947- joint author. II. T.
HB851.M32    301.32/9    *LC* 78-16954    *ISBN* 0871964023

**Osborn, Fairfield, 1887-1969. ed.**   • **4.1583**
Our crowded planet: essays on the pressures of population / sponsored by the Conservation Foundation. [1st ed.]. Garden City, N.Y.: Doubleday, 1962. 240 p.; 22 cm. 1. Population — Addresses, essays, lectures. I. T.
HB851.O8    301.32    *LC* 62-11378

**Petersen, William.**   **4.1584**
Population. — 3d ed. — New York: Macmillan, [1975] xi, 784 p.: illus.; 23 cm. 1. Population I. T.
HB851.P46 1975    301.32    *LC* 73-18768    *ISBN* 0023948809

**Pollard, J. H.**      **4.1585**
Mathematical models for the growth of human populations [by] J. H. Pollard. — Cambridge [Eng.]: University Press, [1973] xii, 186 p.; 24 cm. 1. Population — Mathematical models. I. T.
HB851.P54     301.32     *LC* 72-91957     *ISBN* 052120111X

## HB861–863 Malthus

**Malthus, T. R. (Thomas Robert), 1776-1834.**     • **4.1586**
[Essay on the principle of population] Population: the first essay. With a foreword by Kenneth E. Boulding. [Ann Arbor] University of Michigan Press [1959] xix, 139 p. 21 cm. (Ann Arbor paperbacks, AA31) First published in 1798 under title: An essay on the principle of population. 1. Population I. T.
HB861.E7 1959     301.32     *LC* 59-63526

**Malthus, T. R. (Thomas Robert), 1766-1834.**     **4.1587**
An essay on the principle of population: text, sources and background, criticism / Thomas Robert Malthus; edited by Philip Appleman. — 1st ed. — New York: Norton, c1976. xxvii, 260 p.; 22 cm. (A Norton critical edition) The text of the 1798 ed. together with commentaries from the 19th and 20th centuries. 1. Population I. Appleman, Philip, 1926- II. T.
HB861.E7 1976     301.32     *LC* 75-26853     *ISBN* 039304419X. *ISBN* 039309202X pbk

**James, Patricia D.**     **4.1588**
Population Malthus, his life and times / Patricia James. — London; Boston: Routledge & Kegan Paul, 1979. xv, 524 p., [4] leaves of plates: ill.; 24 cm. 1. Malthus, T. R. (Thomas Robert), 1766-1834. 2. Demographers — Great Britain — Biography. 3. Economists — Great Britain — Biography. I. T.
HB863.M23 J35 1979     304.6/092/4 B     *LC* 79-40584     *ISBN* 0710002661

**Marx, Karl, 1818-1883.**     • **4.1589**
[Selections. English] Marx and Engels on the population bomb; selections from the writings of Marx and Engels dealing with the theories of Thomas Robert Malthus. Edited by Ronald L. Meek. Translations from the German by Dorothea L. Meek and Ronald L. Meek. [2d ed. Berkeley, Calif.] Ramparts Press [1971] xxii, 215 p. 21 cm. First published in 1953 under title: Marx and Engels on Malthus. 1. Malthus, T. R. (Thomas Robert), 1766-1834. 2. Malthusianism I. Engels, Friedrich, 1820-1895. II. Meek, Ronald L. ed. and tr. III. T.
HB863.M253 197/1     301.3/1     *LC* 71-132220     *ISBN* 0878670025

**Petersen, William.**     **4.1590**
Malthus / William Petersen. — Cambridge, Mass.: Harvard University Press, 1979. vi, 302 p.; 24 cm. Includes index. 1. Malthus, T. R. (Thomas Robert), 1766-1834. 2. Demographers — Great Britain — Biography. 3. Economists — Great Britain — Biography. I. T.
HB863.P47     301.32/092/4 B     *LC* 78-31479     *ISBN* 0674544250

## HB871–875 Later Works

**Boserup, Ester.**     **4.1591**
Population and technological change: a study of long–term trends / Ester Boserup. — Chicago: University of Chicago Press, 1981. xi, 255 p.; 24 cm. Includes index. 1. Population 2. Technological innovations I. T.
HB871.B587     304.6/2 19     *LC* 80-21116     *ISBN* 0226066738

**Brown, Lester Russell, 1934-.**     **4.1592**
In the human interest: a strategy to stabilize world population / [by] Lester R. Brown. — [1st ed.]. — New York: Norton, [1974] 190 p.; 21 cm. Sponsored by Aspen Institute for Humanistic Studies and Overseas Development Council. 1. Population I. Aspen Institute for Humanistic Studies. II. Overseas Development Council. III. T.
HB871.B74     301.32     *LC* 74-6339     *ISBN* 0393055264

**Ehrlich, Paul R.**     • **4.1593**
Population, resources, environment: issues in human ecology / [by] Paul R. Ehrlich [and] Anne H. Ehrlich. — 2d ed. — San Francisco: W. H. Freeman, [1972] xiv, 509 p.: ill.; 27 cm. — (A Series of books in biology) Third ed. published in 1977 under title: Ecoscience. 1. Population 2. Pollution 3. Human ecology I. Ehrlich, Anne H. joint author. II. T.
HB871.E35 1972     301.3     *LC* 70-179799     *ISBN* 0716706954

**Food and Agriculture Organization of the United Nations. Development Research and Training Service. Policy Analysis Division.**     **4.1594**
Population and agricultural development: selected relationships and possible planning uses. — Rome: Development Research and Training Service, Policy Analysis Division, Food and Agriculture Organization of the United Nations, 1977. vi, 130 p.: diagr.; 28 cm. 'M-04.' 1. Demography 2. Agriculture and state I. T.
HB871.F64 1977     304.6 19     *LC* 81-454399     *ISBN* 9251004900

**Hauser, Philip Morris, 1909- ed.**     • **4.1595**
The study of population: an inventory and appraisal, edited by Philip M. Hauser and Otis Dudley Duncan. [Chicago] University of Chicago Press [1959] 864 p. ill. 1. Demography 2. Population I. Duncan, Otis Dudley. jt. ed. II. T.
HB871 H37     *LC* 58-11949

**Kleinman, David S., 1920-.**     **4.1596**
Human adaptation and population growth: a non–Malthusian perspective / David S. Kleinman. — Montclair, N.J.: Allanheld, Osmun, 1980. xiii, 281 p.; 24 cm. 1. Population 2. Fertility, Human 3. Human ecology I. T.
HB871.K59     301.32     *LC* 78-59176     *ISBN* 0916672182

**The More developed realm: a geography of its population / general editor, Glenn T. Trewartha.**     **4.1597**
1st ed. — Oxford; New York: Pergamon Press, 1978. viii, 275 p.: ill.; 25 cm. — (Pergamon Oxford geography series) (Pergamon international library of science, technology, engineering, and social studies) 1. Population — Addresses, essays, lectures. I. Trewartha, Glenn Thomas, 1896-
HB871.M8 1978     301.32     *LC* 76-39897     *ISBN* 008020631X

**Political and Economic Planning.**     • **4.1598**
World population and resources: a report / by PEP. — London: PEP (Political and Economic Planning), 1955. xxxvii, 339 p.: ill., maps. 1. Population 2. Natural resources I. T.
HB871.P627     *LC* 56-1234

**Sauvy, Alfred, 1898-.**     • **4.1599**
[Théorie générale de la population. English] General theory of population / with a foreword by E. A. Wrigley; translated by Christophe Campos. — New York: Basic Books [1970, c1969] x, 550 p.: ill.; 25 cm. Translation of Théorie générale de la population. 1. Population I. T.
HB871.S25213 1970     301.3/2     *LC* 69-16315

**Simon, Julian Lincoln, 1932-.**     **4.1600**
The economics of population growth / Julian L. Simon. — Princeton, N.J.: Princeton University Press, c1977. xxx, 555 p.: ill.; 24 cm. Includes index. 1. Population 2. Fertility, Human — Economic aspects. 3. Birth control I. T.
HB871.S57     301.32     *LC* 75-15278     *ISBN* 0691100535

**Simon, Julian Lincoln, 1932-.**     **4.1601**
The ultimate resource / by Julian L. Simon. — Princeton, N.J.: Princeton University Press, c1981. x, 415 p.: ill.; 24 cm. Includes index. 1. Population 2. Natural resources 3. Economic policy I. T.
HB871.S573     333.7 19     *LC* 80-8575     *ISBN* 069109389X

**Spengler, Joseph John, 1902-.**     • **4.1602**
Declining population growth revisited [by] Joseph J. Spengler. — [Chapel Hill]: Carolina Population Center, 1971. 60 p.; 23 cm. — (Carolina Population Center. Monograph, 14) 1. Population 2. Economic development I. T. II. Series.
HB871.S65     301.3/2     *LC* 70-26877

**Spengler, Joseph John, 1902-.**     **4.1603**
Facing zero population growth: reactions and interpretations, past and present / Joseph J. Spengler. — Durham, N.C.: Duke University Press, 1978. xiv, 288 p.; 25 cm. — (Studies in social and economic demography, 1) Includes indexes. 1. Population 2. Stable population model 3. Stagnation (Economics) 4. United States — Population I. T. II. Series.
HB871.S6514     301.32/1     *LC* 78-52031     *ISBN* 0822304120

**Thomlinson, Ralph.**     **4.1604**
Population dynamics: causes and consequences of world demographic change / Ralph Thomlinson. — 2d ed. — New York: Random House, c1976. xvii, 653 p.: ill.; 24 cm. 1. Population 2. Demography I. T.
HB871.T38 1976     301.32     *LC* 75-29037     *ISBN* 0394301056

**World population and development: challenges and prospects / edited by Philip M. Hauser.**     **4.1605**
1st ed. — Syracuse, N.Y.: Syracuse University Press, 1979. xxii, 683 p.: ill.; 24 cm. 1. Population — Addresses, essays, lectures. 2. Economic development — Addresses, essays, lectures. I. Hauser, Philip Morris, 1909-
HB871.W75     301.32     *LC* 79-15471     *ISBN* 0815622163

**Zelinsky, Wilbur, 1921-.**     • **4.1606**
A prologue to population geography. Englewood Cliffs, N.J., Prentice-Hall [1966] ix, 150 p. ill., maps (part fold.) (Prentice-Hall foundations of economic geography series) 1. Population I. T.
HB871 Z45     *LC* 66-10948

**Ehrlich, Paul R.**     • **4.1607**
The population bomb [by] Paul R. Ehrlich. — Rev. [& expanded ed.]. — New York: [Ballantine Books, 1971] xiv, 201 p.; 18 cm. 'A Sierra Club/Ballantine book.' 1. Population I. T.
HB875.E35 1971    301.3/2    *LC* 78-22647    *ISBN* 0345021711

**Llewellyn-Jones, Derek.**     **4.1608**
People populating / Derek Llewellyn–Jones; ill. by Audrey Besterman. — London: Faber & Faber, 1976 (c1975). 368 p.: ill.; 23 cm. Includes index. 1. Population 2. Birth control I. T.
HB875.L53    301.32    *LC* 75-315639    *ISBN* 0571099432

## HB881 General Works

**Bates, Marston, 1906-1974.**     • **4.1609**
The prevalence of people. New York, Scribner, 1955. 283 p. illus. 22 cm. 1. Population 2. Public health 3. Birth control I. T.
HB881.B34    312 301.32*    *LC* 55-7190

**Bogue, Donald Joseph, 1918-.**     • **4.1610**
Principles of demography [by] Donald J. Bogue. — New York: Wiley, [1969] xiii, 917 p.: ill., maps.; 26 cm. 1. Demography I. T.
HB881.B564    312    *LC* 68-26847    *ISBN* 0471086207

**Carr-Saunders, A. M. (Alexander Morris), Sir, 1886-1966.**     • **4.1611**
World population, past growth and present trends. New York, Barnes & Noble [1965] xv, 336 p. illus. 23 cm. 1. Population I. T.
HB881.C3 1965    *LC* 65-3121

**Chicago. University. Norman Wait Harris Memorial Foundation. 30th Institute, 1954.**     • **4.1612**
Population and world politics, edited by Philip M. Hauser. Glencoe, Ill., Free Press [1958] 297 p. 22 cm. 1. Population — Congresses. 2. Social history — Congresses. I. Hauser, Philip Morris, 1909- ed. II. T.
HB881.C54 1954    312.082 301.32*    *LC* 58-9400

**Cox, Peter R.**     • **4.1613**
Demography / by Peter R. Cox. 4th ed. Cambridge [Eng.]: Published for the Institute of Actuaries and the Faculty of Actuaries at the University Press, 1970. viii, 470 p.: ill.; 22 cm. 1. Demography I. T.
HB881.C783 1970    312    *LC* 70-92245    *ISBN* 0521076968

**Glass, D. V. (David Victor), 1911-.**     • **4.1614**
Population in history: essays in historical demography / edited by D.V. Glass and D.E.C. Eversley. — London: E. Arnold, 1965. ix, 692 p.: graphs; 24 cm. 1. Population — Addresses, essays, lectures. I. Eversley, David Edward Charles. II. T.
HB881.G59 1965a    *ISBN* 0713151609

**Henry, Louis, writer on demography.**     **4.1615**
[Démographie. English] Population: analysis and models / Louis Henry; translated by Etienne van de Walle and Elise F. Jones. — New York: Academic Press, c1976. xiii, 301 p.: ill.; 24 cm. Translation of Démographie. Includes index. 1. Demography 2. Demography — Mathematical models. I. T.
HB881.H41913    301.32    *LC* 76-43172    *ISBN* 0123412501

**Hollingsworth, Thomas Henry.**     • **4.1616**
Historical demography, by T. H. Hollingsworth. — Ithaca, N.Y.: Cornell University Press, [1969] 448 p.; 23 cm. — (The Sources of history: studies in the uses of historical evidence) 1. Demography I. T.
HB881.H625    312    *LC* 71-79388    *ISBN* 0801404975

**Keyfitz, Nathan, 1913-.**     **4.1617**
Applied mathematical demography / Nathan Keyfitz. New York: Wiley, c1977. xxiv, 388 p.: ill.; 24 cm. 'A Wiley-Interscience publication.' Includes index. 1. Demography I. T.
HB881.K473    301.32/01/51    *LC* 77-1360    *ISBN* 0471473502

**Keyfitz, Nathan, 1913-.**     • **4.1618**
World population; an analysis of vital data [by] Nathan Keyfitz and Wilhelm Flieger. — Chicago: University of Chicago Press, [1968] xi, 672 p.; 29 cm. 1. Population — Statistics I. Flieger, Wilhelm. joint author. II. T.
HB881.K48    312    *LC* 68-14010

**Ohlin, Göran, 1925-.**     • **4.1619**
Population control and economic development. Paris: Development Centre of the Organisation for Economic Co-operation and Development, 1967. 138 p.: ill., tables; 24 cm. (Development Centre studies) 1. Population 2. Birth control I. T.
HB881.O4    301.3/2    *LC* 68-70137

**Pressat, Roland.**     **4.1620**
[Analyse démographique. English] Demographic analysis: methods, results, applications / translated by Judah Matras; with a foreword by Nathan Keyfitz. — Chicago: Aldine-Atherton [1972] xx, 498 p.: ill.; 24 cm. 1. Demography I. T.
HB881.P7413    301.32/07/2    *LC* 69-11228    *ISBN* 0202300935

**Sax, Karl, 1892-.**     • **4.1621**
[Standing room only: the challenge of overpopulation] Standing room only: the world's exploding population. New ed. Boston, Beacon Press [1960] 206 p. illus. 21 cm. (Beacon BP101) First published in 1955 under title: Standing room only: the challenge of overpopulation. 1. Population 2. Food supply 3. Natural resources I. T.
HB881.S33 1960    301.32    *LC* 60-2042

**Shryock, Henry S.**     **4.1622**
The methods and materials of demography / Henry S. Shryock, Jacob S. Siegel, and associates. — Condensed ed. / by Edward G. Stockwell. — New York: Academic Press, c1976. ix, 577 p.: ill.; 29 cm. — (Studies in population.) 1. Demography I. Siegel, Jacob S. II. Stockwell, Edward G. III. T. IV. Series.
HB881.S526 1976    301.32/01/82    *LC* 76-18312    *ISBN* 0126411506

**Spengler, Joseph John, 1902- ed.**     • **4.1623**
Demographic analysis: selected readings / edited by Joseph J. Spengler and Otis Dudley Duncan. — Glencoe, Ill.: Free Press, [c1956] xiii, 819 p.: maps, diagrs., tables.; 25 cm. 1. Population — Collections. I. Duncan, Otis Dudley. joint ed. II. T.
HB881.S66    312.082    *LC* 56-10585

**Spiegelman, Mortimer.**     • **4.1624**
Introduction to demography. — Rev. ed. — Cambridge: Harvard University Press, 1968. xix, 514 p.: illus.; 25 cm. 1. Demography I. T.
HB881.S68 1968    312    *LC* 68-21984

**Trewartha, Glenn Thomas, 1896-.**     **4.1625**
The less developed realm: a geography of its population [by] Glenn T. Trewartha. Cartography by Randall B. Sale. New York, Wiley [1972] xi, 449 p. illus. 24 cm. 1. Developing countries — Population. I. T.
HB881.T74    301.32/9/1724    *LC* 76-173680    *ISBN* 0471887943
*ISBN* 0471887951

**International Review Group of Social Science Research on Population and Development.**     **4.1626**
Population policy: research priorities in the developing world: report of the International Review Group of Social Science Research on Population and Development / prepared by Carmen A. Miró and Joseph E. Potter. — New York: St. Martin's Press, 1981 (c1980). xi, 197 p.; 22 cm. 1. Developing countries — Population policy. 2. Developing countries — Population. I. Miró, Carmen A. II. Potter, Joseph E. III. T.
HB884.I57 1980    304.6/6/091724 19    *LC* 80-18671    *ISBN* 0312631588

## HB885 Special Aspects

**Bayles, Michael D.**     **4.1627**
Morality and population policy / Michael D. Bayles. — University: University of Alabama Press, c1980. 143 p.; 24 cm. Includes index. 1. Population — Moral and religious aspects. 2. Population policy — Moral and ethical aspects. I. T.
HB885.B333    176    *LC* 79-23965    *ISBN* 0817300333

**Coale, Ansley J.**     **4.1628**
The growth and structure of human populations: a mathematical investigation [by] Ansley J. Coale. — Princeton, N.J.: Princeton University Press, 1972. xvii, 227 p.: illus.; 25 cm. 1. Demography — Mathematical models. I. T.
HB885.C54    301.32/01/51    *LC* 76-166365    *ISBN* 0691093571

**Coontz, Sydney H.**     • **4.1629**
Population theories and the economic interpretation. London: Routledge & Paul, 1957. 200 p.; 22 cm. 1. Population 2. Family 3. Fertility, Human I. T.
HB885.C6    *LC* 58-1138

**Ford, Thomas R., comp.**     • **4.1630**
Social demography. Edited by Thomas R. Ford [and] Gordon F. De Jong. — Englewood Cliffs, N.J.: Prentice-Hall, [1970] x, 690 p.: illus.; 25 cm. — (Prentice-Hall sociology series) 1. Demography — Addresses, essays, lectures. 2. Sociology — Addresses, essays, lectures. I. De Jong, Gordon F. joint comp. II. T.
HB885.F58    301.3/2/08    *LC* 69-14426    *ISBN* 0138155550

**Goldscheider, Calvin.**    • **4.1631**
Population, modernization, and social structure. — Boston: Little, Brown, [1971] xiii, 345 p.; 24 cm. 1. Demography 2. Population I. T.
HB885.G63     301.3/2     *LC* 74-165756

**Keyfitz, Nathan, 1913-.**    • **4.1632**
Introduction to the mathematics of population. — Reading, Mass.: Addison-Wesley Pub. Co., [1968] xiv, 450 p.: illus.; 25 cm. — (Addison-Wesley series in behavioral science: quantitative methods) 1. Demography — Mathematical models. I. T. II. Title: Mathematics of population.
HB885.K4     312/.01/84     *LC* 68-25926

**Leibenstein, Harvey.**    • **4.1633**
A theory of economic–demographic development. Foreword by Frank Notestein. — New York: Greenwood Press, [1969, c1954] xi, 204 p.: illus.; 27 cm. 1. Population 2. Economic development I. T.
HB885.L36 1969     301.3/2     *LC* 69-13971     *ISBN* 0837110467

**Miller, Warren B., 1935-.**    **4.1634**
Psyche and demos: individual psychology and the issues of population / Warren B. Miller and R. Kenneth Godwin. — New York: Oxford University Press, 1977. xv, 332 p.; 22 cm. — (Reconstruction of society series) Includes indexes. 1. Population 2. Population policy I. Godwin, R. Kenneth. joint author. II. T. III. Series.
HB885.M53     301.32     *LC* 76-42618     *ISBN* 0195022009. *ISBN* 0195021991 pbk

**Ng, Larry K. Y., ed.**    • **4.1635**
The population crisis; implications and plans for action. Edited by Larry K. Y. Ng. Stuart Mudd, co–editor. Associate editors: Hugo Boyko [and others]. — Bloomington, Indiana University Press, 1965. xi, 364 p. illus., maps. 21 cm. — (Midland book, MB75) At head of title: World Academy of Art and Science. 'Abridged and revised from The population crisis and the use of world resources ... edited by Stuart Mudd, published in 1964.' Bibliography: p. 347-350. 1. Population — Addresses, essays, lectures. 2. Natural resources — Addresses, essays, lectures. I. Mudd, Stuart, 1893- ed. The population crisis and the use of world resources. II. World Academy of Art and Science. III. T.
HB885.N5 1965     301.32082     *LC* 65-11796

**Universities—National Bureau Committee for Economic**    • **4.1636**
**Research.**
Demographic and economic change in developed countries: a conference of the Universities–National Bureau Committee for Economic Research. Princeton: Princeton University Press, 1960. xi, 536 p.: ill., maps; 24 cm. (National Bureau of Economic Research. Special conference series, 11) 1. Population 2. Economic history — 20th century I. T. II. Series.
HB885 U58     *LC* 60-5753

## HB891–1947 FERTILITY. MARRIAGES. MORTALITY

**Eversley, David Edward Charles.**    • **4.1637**
Social theories of fertility and the Malthusian debate. Oxford, Clarendon Press, 1959. 313 p. ill. 1. Fertility, Human 2. Demography I. T.
HB891 E85     *LC* 59-3491

**Lorimer, Frank, 1894-.**    • **4.1638**
Culture and human fertility; a study of the relation of cultural conditions to fertility in non–industrial and transitional societies. With special contributions by Meyer Fortes [and others] Foreword by Frank W. Notestein. New York, Greenwood Press [1969, c1958] 510 p. illus. 23 cm. (Population and culture [1]) 1. Fertility, Human 2. Social history I. T.
HB891.L6 1969     301.3/2     *LC* 78-90549     *ISBN* 0837121523

**Westoff, Charles F.**    • **4.1639**
The third child; a study in the prediction of fertility by Charles F. Westoff, Robert G. Potter, Jr., and Philip C. Sagi. Princeton, N.J., Princeton University Press, 1963. xxiii, 293 p. tables. 1. Fertility, Human 2. Family size I. Princeton University. Office of Population Research. II. National Analysts, inc. III. T.
HB891 W47     *LC* 63-12672

**Determinants of fertility in developing countries / Panel on**    **4.1640**
**Fertility Determinants, Committee on Population and**
**Demography, Commission on Behavioral and Social Sciences**
**and Education, National Research Council; edited by Rodolfo A.**
**Bulatao, Ronald D. Lee with Paula E. Hollerbach, John**
**Bongaarts.**
New York: Academic Press, 1983-. v. < 1-2 >; 23 cm. (Studies in population.) 1. Fertility, Human — Developing countries. 2. Family size — Developing countries 3. Birth control — Developing countries I. Bulatao, Rodolfo A., 1944- II. Lee, Ronald Demos, 1941- III. National Research Council (U.S.).

**Committee on Population and Demography. Panel on Fertility Determinants.**
IV. Series.
HB901.D48 1983     304.6/32/091724 19     *LC* 83-17135     *ISBN* 012140501X

**United Nations. Dept. of Economic and Social Affairs.**    • **4.1641**
Human fertility and national development: a challenge to science and technology. — New York: United Nations, 1971. x, 140 p.: ill. fold. map.; 23 cm. — ([Document] (United Nations) ST/ECA/138) 'United Nations publication. Sales no.: E.71.II:A.12.' 1. Population 2. Fertility, Human 3. Birth control I. T. II. Series.
HB901.U6x     *LC* 77-26170

**Working women in socialist countries: the fertility connection /**    **4.1642**
**edited by Valentina Bodrova and Richard Anker.**
Geneva: International Labour Office, 1985. xvi, 234 p.: ill.; 25 cm. (WEP study.) 1. Fertility, Human — Communist countries — Case studies. 2. Women — Employment — Communist countries — Case studies. 3. Women — Employment — Government policy — Communist countries — Case studies. 4. Maternal and infant welfare — Government policy — Communist countries — Case studies. 5. Communist countries — Population policy — Case studies. I. Bodrova, Valentina. II. Anker, Richard, 1943- III. Series.
HB901.W657 1985     304.6/32/091717 19     *LC* 85-181464     *ISBN* 9221039102

**Kiser, Clyde Vernon, 1904-.**    • **4.1643**
Trends and variations in fertility in the United States [by] Clyde V. Kiser, Wilson H. Grabill [and] Arthur A. Campbell. — Cambridge: Harvard University Press, 1968. xxx, 338 p.: illus., map.; 25 cm. — (Vital and health statistics monographs) 1. Fertility, Human — United States. 2. United States — Statistics, Vital I. Grabill, Wilson H., joint author. II. Campbell, Arthur A. joint author. III. T. IV. Series.
HB903.F4 K57     312/.1/73     *LC* 68-25613

**Lindert, Peter H.**    **4.1644**
Fertility and scarcity in America / Peter H. Lindert. — Princeton, N.J.: Princeton University Press, c1978. xi, 395 p.: ill.; 24 cm. 1. Family size — Economic aspects — United States. 2. Fertility, Human — Economic aspects — United States. 3. Income distribution — United States. I. T.
HB915.L56     301.32/1/0973     *LC* 77-71992     *ISBN* 0691042179

**Rindfuss, Ronald R., 1946-.**    **4.1645**
Postwar fertility trends and differentials in the United States / Ronald R. Rindfuss, James A. Sweet. — New York: Academic Press, c1977. x, 225 p.: graph; 24 cm. — (Studies in population.) Includes index. 1. Fertility, Human — United States. 2. United States — Statistics, Vital I. Sweet, James A. joint author. II. T. III. Series.
HB915.R56     301.32/1/0973     *LC* 76-50403     *ISBN* 0125892500

**Gittins, Diana.**    **4.1646**
Fair sex, family size and structure in Britain, 1900–39 / Diana Gittins. — New York: St. Martin's Press, 1982. 240 p.: ill.; 23 cm. Includes index. 1. Fertility, Human — Great Britain — History — 20th century. 2. Family size — Great Britain — History — 20th century. 3. Women — Employment — Great Britain — History — 20th century. 4. Family — Great Britain — History — 20th century. I. T.
HB995.G55 1982     304.6/3/0941 19     *LC* 81-21248     *ISBN* 0312279620

**Fertility in developing countries: an economic perspective on**    **4.1647**
**research and policy issues / edited by Ghazi M. Farooq and**
**George B. Simmons; foreword by Rafael M. Salas.**
New York: St. Martin's Press, 1985. xxiv, 533 p.: ill.; 23 cm. Includes index. 1. Fertility, Human — Developing countries — Addresses, essays, lectures. I. Farooq, Ghazi Mumtaz. II. Simmons, George B., 1940-
HB1108.F46 1985     304.6/32/091724 19     *LC* 83-40609     *ISBN* 0312287526

**Carter, Hugh, 1895-.**    • **4.1648**
Marriage and divorce: a social and economic study [by] Hugh Carter and Paul C. Glick. — Cambridge, Mass.: Harvard University Press, 1970. xxix, 451 p.: ill.; 24 cm. — (Vital and health statistics monographs) 1. Marriage — U.S. — Statistics. 2. Divorce — U.S. — Statistics. I. Glick, Paul C. joint author. II. T. III. Series.
HB1125.C33     301.42     *LC* 79-105369     *ISBN* 0674550757

**Preston, Samuel H.**    **4.1649**
Causes of death: life tables for national population [by] Samuel H. Preston, Nathan Keyfitz [and] Robert Schoen. With the collaboration of Verne E. Nelson. — New York: Seminar Press, 1972. xi, 787 p.; 21 x 27 cm. — (Studies in population.) 1. Mortality I. Keyfitz, Nathan, 1913- joint author. II. Schoen, Robert. joint author. III. T. IV. Series.
HB1321.P73     312/.2     *LC* 72-80305

**Diaz-Briquets, Sergio.**     **4.1650**
The health revolution in Cuba / by Sergio Díaz–Briquets. — 1st ed. — Austin: University of Texas Press, 1983. xvii, 227 p.: ill.; 24 cm. — (Special publication / Institute of Latin American Studies, University of Texas at Austin) Includes index. 1. Mortality — Cuba — History. 2. Public health — Cuba — History. 3. Cuba — Statistics, Vital — History. I. T.
HB1379.D52 1983     304.6/4/097291 19     *LC* 82-10865     *ISBN* 0292750714

# HB1951–2577 POPULATION GEOGRAPHY.
## MIGRATION

**Beaujeu-Garnier, Jacqueline.**     **4.1651**
[Géographie de la population. English] Geography of population / by J. Beaujeu–Garnier; translated by S. H. Beaver. — 2d ed. — London; New York: Longman, 1978. xii, 400 p.: ill.; 22 cm. — (Geographies for advanced study) Includes index. 1. Population geography I. T.
HB1951.B3813 1978     301.32     *LC* 77-30726     *ISBN* 058248569X.
*ISBN* 0582485703 pbk

**Human migration: patterns and policies / edited by William H.**     **4.1652**
**McNeill and Ruth S. Adams.**
Bloomington, Ind.: Indiana University Press, c1978. xviii, 442 p.: ill.; 24 cm. Papers presented at a conference sponsored by the Midwest center of the American Academy of Arts and Sciences and Indiana University; held in New Harmony, Ind., Apr. 1976. 1. Migration, Internal — Congresses. 2. Emigration and immigration — Congresses. I. McNeill, William Hardy, 1917- II. Adams, Ruth, 1923- III. American Academy of Arts and Sciences. IV. Indiana University.
HB1951.H84 1978     301.32     *LC* 77-23685     *ISBN* 0253328756

**Jones, Huw Roland.**     **4.1653**
A population geography / Huw R. Jones. — London; San Francisco: Harper & Row, 1981. 330 p.: ill.; 25 cm. Includes indexes. 1. Population geography I. T.
HB1951.J66 1981b     304.2 19     *LC* 83-118273     *ISBN* 0063181886

**People on the move: studies on internal migration / edited by**     **4.1654**
**Leszek A. Kosiński & R. Mansell Prothero.**
London: Methuen; [New York]: distributed by Harper & Row, Barnes and Noble Import Division, 1975, c1974. 393 p.: ill.; 24 cm. (University paperbacks; UP 554) 'Based on papers submitted to and discussions held during a Symposium on Internal Migration organized by the International Geographical Union Commission on Population Geography in 1972.' Includes index. 1. Migration, Internal — Congresses. I. Kosiński, Leszek A. II. Prothero, R. Mansell. III. Symposium on Internal Migration, University of Alberta, 1972.
HB1951.P45 1975     301.32/6     *LC* 75-312011     *ISBN* 0416784100

**Lewis, G. J.**     **4.1655**
Human migration: a geographical perspective / G.J. Lewis. — New York: St. Martin's Press, 1982. 220 p.: ill.; 23 cm. Includes index. 1. Migration, Internal I. T.
HB1952.L48 1982     304.8/2 19     *LC* 81-21300     *ISBN* 0312399553

**Kuznets, Simon Smith, 1901- ed.**     • **4.1656**
Population redistribution and economic growth: United States, 1870–1950 / Prepared under the direction of Simon Kuznets and Dorothy Swaine Thomas. — Philadelphia, The American Philosophical Society, 1957-64. 3 v. map, diagrs., tables. 31 cm. — (Memoirs of the American Philosophical Society, v. 45, 51, 61) 1. Migration, Internal — United States. 2. Labor supply — United States. 3. Industry — Location — United States. I. Thomas, Dorothy Swaine Thomas, 1899- II. T.
HB1965.K8     312.8     *LC* 57-10071 rev

**Oosterbaan, John.**     **4.1657**
Population dispersal: a national imperative / John Oosterbaan. — Lexington, Mass.: Lexington Books, c1980. xix, 136 p.; 24 cm. 1. Migration, Internal — United States. 2. United States — Population density. I. T.
HB1965.O57     304.8/2/0973     *LC* 79-9672     *ISBN* 0669036153

**Migration in post–war Europe: geographical essays / edited by**     **4.1658**
**John Salt and Hugh Clout.**
London; New York: Oxford University Press, 1976. 228 p.: ill.; 24 cm. 1. Migration, Internal — Europe — Addresses, essays, lectures. 2. Rural-urban migration — Europe — Addresses, essays, lectures. 3. Migrant labor — Europe — Addresses, essays, lectures. I. Salt, John. II. Clout, Hugh D.
HB2041.M53     301.32/6/0941     *LC* 77-352366     *ISBN* 0198740271

**Weiner, Myron.**     **4.1659**
Sons of the soil: migration and ethnic conflict in India / Myron Weiner. — Princeton, N.J.: Princeton University Press, c1978. xviii, 383 p.: ill.; 22 cm. 1. Migration, Internal — India. 2. Social mobility — India. 3. Ethnology — India 4. India — Population. I. T.
HB2099.W44     301/32/6/0954     *LC* 78-51202     *ISBN* 0691093792

**Chao, Kang, 1929-.**     **4.1660**
Man and land in Chinese history: an economic analysis / Kang Chao. — Stanford, Calif.: Stanford University Press, 1986. xii, 268 p.: ill.; 24 cm. Includes index. 1. Land use — China — History. 2. China — Population density — History. I. T.
HB2114.A3 C45 1986     304.6/1 19     *LC* 84-51715     *ISBN* 0804712719

**Redistribution of population in Africa / edited by John I.**     **4.1661**
**Clarke and Leszek A. Kosiński.**
London; Exeter, N.H.: Heinemann Educational, 1982. x, 212 p.: ill.; 29 cm. Errata slip inserted. 1. Migration, Internal — Africa — Addresses, essays, lectures. 2. Africa — Population density — Addresses, essays, lectures. I. Clarke, John Innes. II. Kosiński, Leszek A.
HB2121.A3 R42 1982     304.8/096 19     *LC* 81-170774     *ISBN* 0435950304

**Weber, Adna Ferrin, 1870-1968.**     **4.1662**
The growth of cities in the nineteenth century; a study in statistics. Ithaca, N.Y., Cornell University Press [1963] xxvi, 495 p. fold. map, diagrs., tables. (Cornell reprints in urban studies) 1. Cities and towns — Growth 2. Population I. T. II. Series.
HB2161 W37 1963     *LC* 62-22217

**Freeman, Thomas Walter.**     • **4.1663**
The conurbations of Great Britain, by T.W. Freeman, with a chapter on the Scottish conurbations by Catherine P. Snodgrass. 2nd revised ed. Manchester, Manchester U.P., 1966. xiv, 402 p. plate, maps, tables. 1. Metropolitan areas — Great Britain 2. Great Britain — Social conditions 3. Great Britain — Population I. T.
HB2253 F7 1966     *LC* 66-75199

# HB2581–2787 PROFESSIONS.
## OCCUPATIONS

**Dictionary of occupational titles / U.S. Department of Labor,**     **4.1664**
**Employment and Training Administration, U.S. Employment**
**Service.**
4th ed. — [Washington]: The Administration: for sale by the Supt. of Docs., U.S. Govt. Print. Off., 1977. xli, 1371 p.; 28 cm. Supplement (xiii, 36 p.; 28 cm) published 1982. Includes indexes. 1. Occupations — Dictionaries. 2. Occupations — Classification 3. United States — Occupations I. United States Employment Service.
HB2595.U543 1977     331.7/003     *LC* 78-601723

# HB3501–3700 POPULATION, BY REGION
## OR COUNTRY

**Wells, Robert V., 1943-.**     **4.1665**
The population of the British colonies in America before 1776: a survey of census data / Robert V. Wells. — Princeton, N.J.: Princeton University Press, [1975] xii, 342 p.; 25 cm. 1. America — Population — History. 2. Great Britain — Colonies — America I. T.
HB3501.W45     301.32/9/73     *LC* 75-4976     *ISBN* 0691046166

# HB3505–3527 United States

**United States. Commission on Population Growth and the**     • **4.1666**
**American Future.**
Population and the American future: the report. — Washington: for sale by the Supt. of Docs., U.S. Govt. Print. Off., [1972] 186 p.: ill.; 30 cm. 1. United States — Population I. T.
HB3505.A525     301.32/9/73     *LC* 72-77389

**Bachrach, Peter.**     **4.1667**
Power and choice: the formulation of American population policy / [by] Peter Bachrach and Elihu Bergman. — Lexington, Mass.: Lexington Books, [1973] xi, 120 p.: ill.; 24 cm. 1. United States — Population policy I. Bergman, Elihu, joint author. II. T.
HB3505.B29     301.32/9/73     *LC* 72-3545     *ISBN* 0669842931

**Bogue, Donald Joseph, 1918-.**     **4.1668**
The population of the United States: historical trends and future projections / Donald J. Bogue; assisted by George W. Rumsey ... [et al.]. — New York: Free

Press, c1985. viii, 728 p.: ill.; 29 cm. 1. United States — Population 2. United States — Census, 20th, 1980. I. T.
HB3505.B63 1985        304.6/2/0973 19        *LC* 84-18688        *ISBN* 0029047005

**Cohen, Wilbur J. (Wilbur Joseph), 1913-1987.                    4.1669**
Demographic dynamics in America / Wilbur J. Cohen, Charles F. Westoff. — New York: The Free Press, c1977. 110 p.: graphs; 22 cm. — (Charles C. Moskowitz memorial lectures. no. 18) 1. Fertility, Human — United States — Addresses, essays, lectures. 2. Age distribution (Demography) — United States. 3. United States — Population — Addresses, essays, lectures. I. Westoff, Charles F. joint author. II. T. III. Series.
HB3505.C64        301.32/9/73        *LC* 77-80227

**Conference on Population and Intergroup Relations, New York,        4.1670
N.Y., 1975.**
Zero population growth—for whom?: Differential fertility and minority group survival / edited by Milton Himmelfarb and Victor Baras. — Westport, Conn.: Greenwood Press, 1978. viii, 213 p.: ill.; 25 cm. (Contributions in sociology; no. 30 0084-9278) Sponsored by the American Jewish Committee. 1. Fertility, Human — United States — Congresses. 2. Jews — United States — Congresses. 3. Minorities — United States — Congresses. 4. United States — Population — Congresses. I. Himmelfarb, Milton. II. Baras, Victor. III. American Jewish Committee. IV. T.
HB3505.C66 1975        301.32/9/73        *LC* 77-87966        *ISBN* 0313200416

**Driver, Edwin D.                                        4.1671**
Essays on population policy [by] Edwin D. Driver. — Lexington, Mass.: Lexington Books, [1972] xv, 202 p.; 23 cm. 1. Population policy — Addresses, essays, lectures. 2. United States — Population policy — Addresses, essays, lectures. I. T.
HB3505.D7        301.32/08        *LC* 75-183248        *ISBN* 0669816469

**Easterlin, Richard Ainley, 1926-.                        4.1672**
Birth and fortune: the impact of numbers on personal welfare / Richard A. Easterlin. — New York: Basic Books, c1980. xi, 205 p.: ill.; 22 cm. 1. Fertility, Human — United States. 2. United States — Population 3. United States — Economic conditions — 1945- 4. United States — Social conditions — 1945- I. T.
HB3505.E247        304.6        *LC* 79-56369        *ISBN* 0465006884

**The Economic consequences of slowing population growth /        4.1673
edited by Thomas J. Espenshade, William J. Serow.**
New York: Academic Press, 1978. xx, 288 p.: ill.; 24 cm. — (Studies in population) Includes index. 1. United States — Population — Economic aspects — Addresses, essays, lectures. I. Espenshade, Thomas J. II. Serow, William J.
HB3505.E35        330.9/73/092        *LC* 78-3334        *ISBN* 0122424506

**Kahn, E. J. (Ely Jacques), 1916-.                        4.1674**
The American people; the findings of the 1970 census [by] E. J. Kahn, Jr. New York, Weybright and Talley [c1974] viii, 340 p. 22 cm. 1. United States. Bureau of the Census. Population. 1970. 2. United States — Population I. T.
HB3505.K28        301.32/9/73        *LC* 73-84073        *ISBN* 0679400036

**Population policymaking in the American States; issues and        4.1675
processes. Edited by Elihu Bergman [and others].**
Lexington, Mass.: Lexington Books, [1974] ix, 318 p.: illus.; 23 cm. 1. United States — Population policy — Addresses, essays, lectures. I. Bergman, Elihu.
HB3505.P66        301.31        *LC* 73-22248        *ISBN* 0669929735

**Robey, Bryant.                                        4.1676**
The American people: a timely exploration of a changing America and the important new demographic trends around us / Bryant Robey. — 1st ed. — New York: Dutton, c1985. 287 p. 'A Truman Talley book.' Includes index. 1. United States — Population I. T.
HB3505.R63 1985        304.6/0973 19        *LC* 85-1481        *ISBN* 0525242961

**Spengler, Joseph John, 1902-.                        4.1677**
Population and America's future / Joseph J. Spengler. — San Francisco: W. H. Freeman, [1975] xi, 260 p.: graphs; 25 cm. Includes indexes. 1. United States — Population 2. United States — Population policy I. T.
HB3505.S65        301.31        *LC* 75-14031        *ISBN* 0716707454

**Sternlieb, George.                                        4.1678**
Demographic trends and economic reality: planning and markets in the '80s / George Sternlieb, James W. Hughes, and Connie O. Hughes. — New Brunswick, N.J.: Center for Urban Policy Research, c1982. xix, 154 p.; 23 cm. 1. United States — Population — Economic aspects. 2. United States — Economic conditions — 1971-1981 3. United States — Economic conditions — 1981- I. Hughes, James W. II. Hughes, Connie O. III. T.
HB3505.S733 1982        330.973/0927 19        *LC* 82-12876        *ISBN* 0882850814

**Taeuber, Conrad, 1906-.                                • 4.1679**
The changing population of the United States, by Conrad Taeuber and Irene B. Taeuber for the Social Science Research Council in cooperation with the U.S. Dept. of Commerce, Bureau of the Census. New York, Wiley [1958] xi, 357 p. map, diagrs., tables. 24 cm. (Census monograph series) 1. United States — Population I. Taeuber, Irene Barnes, 1906- joint author. II. Social Science Research Council (U.S.). III. T. IV. Series.
HB3505.T3        312        *LC* 57-13451

**Lind, Andrew William, 1901-.                            • 4.1680**
Hawaii's people [by] Andrew W. Lind. — 3d ed. — Honolulu: University of Hawaii Press, 1967. ix, 121 p.: ill., maps.; 24 cm. 1. Hawaii — Population. 2. Hawaii — Social conditions. I. T.
HB3525.H3 L5 1967        301.3/29/969        *LC* 67-27053

**Nordyke, Eleanor C.                                        4.1681**
The peopling of Hawaii / Eleanor C. Nordyke; foreword by Robert C. Schmitt. — Honolulu: Published for the East-West Center by the University Press of Hawaii, c1977. xx, 221 p.: ill.; 22 cm. 'An East-West Center Book.' Includes index. 1. Hawaii — Populatio. I. T.
HB3525.H3 N67        301.32/9/969        *LC* 77-8842        *ISBN* 0824805348

**Schmitt, Robert C.                                        • 4.1682**
Demographic statistics of Hawaii, 1778–1965 [by] Robert C. Schmitt. — Honolulu: University of Hawaii Press, 1968. xii, 271 p.; 21 cm. 1. Hawaii — Population. I. T.
HB3525.H3 S3        312/.09969        *LC* 67-30840

**Knights, Peter R.                                        4.1683**
The plain people of Boston, 1830–1860: a study in city growth / [by] Peter R. Knights. — New York: Oxford University Press, 1971. xx, 204 p.: ill.; 22 cm. (The Urban life in America series) 1. Boston (Mass.) — Population — History. I. T.
HB3527.B7 K6        301.3/29/74461        *LC* 74-159647        *ISBN* 019501488X

**Rosenwaike, Ira, 1936-.                                4.1684**
Population history of New York City. [Syracuse, N.Y.] Syracuse University Press, 1972. xvii, 224 p. map. 24 cm. 1. New York (N.Y.) — Population — History. I. T.
HB3527.N7 R66        301.32/9/7471        *LC* 75-39829        *ISBN* 0815621558

# HB3530.5–3579 Latin America

**Sánchez-Albornoz, Nicolás.                                4.1685**
[Población de América latina. English] The population of Latin America; a history. Translated by W. A. R. Richardson. Berkeley, University of California Press [1974] xv, 299 p. illus. 24 cm. Translation of La población de América latina. 1. Latin America — Population — History. I. T.
HB3530.5.S2613        301.32/9/8        *LC* 77-123621        *ISBN* 0520017668

**Cook, Sherburne Friend, 1896-1974.                        • 4.1686**
The population of central Mexico in the sixteenth century by Sherburne F. Cook and Lesley Byrd Simpson. Berkeley Univ. of California Press 1948. 241p. (Ibero-Americana; 31) 1. Mexico — Population I. Simpson, Lesley Byrd, 1891- jt. author II. T. III. Series.
HB3531 C6

**Pan-American Assembly on Population, Cali, Colombia, 1965.        • 4.1687**
Population dilemma in Latin America / [Ed. by J. Mayone Stycos and Jorge Arias] — Washington: Potomac Books, 1966. xiii, 249 p.: ill., maps; 21 cm. Sponsored by Universidad del Valle, the Association of Colombia Medical Schools, and the American Assembly of Columbia University, with the cooperation and financial support of the Population Council, inc. I. Stycos, J. Mayone. II. American Assembly. III. Universidad del Valle. IV. T.
HB3558.P187p 1965        *LC* 66-18575

**Lombardi, John V.                                        4.1688**
People and places in Colonial Venezuela / John V. Lombardi; maps and figures by Cathryn L. Lombardi. — Bloomington: Indiana University Press, c1976. xiv, 484 p.: ill.; 28 cm. 1. Catholic Church. Archdiocese of Caracas (Venezuela) — Population — History. I. T.
HB3580.C3 L65 1976        301.32/9/87        *LC* 75-25433        *ISBN* 0253343305

## HB3581–3632 Europe

**European demography and economic growth / edited by W. R.**                    **4.1689**
**Lee.**
New York: St. Martin's Press, 1979. 413 p.: ill.; 23 cm. 1. Europe —
Population — History — Addresses, essays, lectures. 2. Europe — Economic
conditions — Addresses, essays, lectures. I. Lee, W. Robert.
HB3581.E87 1979b          301.32/9/4      LC 77-26118      ISBN 0312269358

**Flinn, Michael W. (Michael Walter), 1917-.**                    **4.1690**
The European demographic system, 1500–1820 / Michael W. Flinn. —
Baltimore, Md.: Johns Hopkins University Press, c1981. 175 p.; 24 cm. (Johns
Hopkins symposia in comparative history. 12th) Based on the 1979 Schouler
lectures. Includes index. 1. Europe — Population — History. I. T. II. Series.
HB3581.F54          304.6/094 19      LC 80-19574      ISBN 0801824265

**McIntosh, C. Alison.**                    **4.1691**
Population policy in western Europe: responses to low fertility in France,
Sweden, and West Germany / C. Alison McIntosh. — Armonk, N.Y.: M.E.
Sharpe, c1983. viii, 286 p.: ill.; 24 cm. Includes index. 1. Fertility, Human —
Europe. 2. Europe — Population policy. I. T.
HB3581.M37 1983          363.9/1/094 19      LC 82-5840      ISBN
0873322266

**Möller, Herbert. ed.**                    **• 4.1692**
Population movements in modern European history. New York, Macmillan
[1964] vi, 138 p. (Main themes in European history) 1. Europe — Population
— Addresses, essays, lectures. 2. Europe — Emigration nd immigration —
Addresses, essays, lectures I. T.
HB3581 M58      LC 64-17604

**Hatcher, John.**                    **4.1693**
Plague, population, and the English economy, 1348–1530 / prepared by John
Hatcher. London: Macmillan, 1978 (c1977). 95 p.: graphs; 21 cm. (Studies in
economic and social history) Prepared for the Economic History Society.
Includes index. 1. Plague — Great Britain — History. 2. Great Britain —
Population — History. 3. Great Britain — Economic conditions I. Economic
History Society. II. T.
HB3585.H37          301.32/9/42      LC 77-364449      ISBN 0333212932

**Wrigley, E. A. (Edward Anthony), 1931-.**                    **4.1694**
The population history of England, 1541–1871: a reconstruction / E.A. Wrigley
and R.S. Schofield; with contributions by Ronald Lee and Jim Oeppen. —
Cambridge, Mass.: Harvard Univ. Press, 1982 (c1981). xv, 779 p., [1] fold. leaf
of plates: ill.; 24 cm. — (Studies in social and demographic history.) Includes
index. 1. England — Population — History. I. Schofield, R. S. II. T.
III. Series.
HB3585.W74          304.6/0942 19      LC 81-5010      ISBN 0674690079

**Scottish population history: from the 17th century to the 1930s**                    **4.1695**
**/ Michael Flinn ... [et al.], with contributions from Duncan**
**Adamson and Robin Lobban; edited by Michael Flinn.**
Cambridge; New York: Cambridge University Press, 1977. xxiii, 547 p.: ill.; 24
cm. Includes index. 1. Scotland — Population — History. I. Flinn, Michael
W. (Michael Walter), 1917-
HB3587.S36          301.32/9/411      LC 76-11060      ISBN 0521211735

**Connell, K. H. (Kenneth Hugh), 1917-1973.**                    **• 4.1696**
The population of Ireland, 1750–1845. Oxford, Clarendon Press, 1950. xi,
293 p. 23 cm. 1. Ireland — Population. 2. Ireland — Social conditions. I. T.
HB3589.C6      LC 50-11531

**Kennedy, Robert Emmet, 1937-.**                    **4.1697**
The Irish; emigration, marriage, and fertility [by] Robert E. Kennedy, Jr. —
Berkeley: University of California Press, [1973] xvii, 236 p.; 24 cm. 1. Ireland
— Population. 2. Ireland — Emigration and immigration. I. T.
HB3589.K45          301.32/9/415      LC 70-187740      ISBN 0520019873

**Dyer, Colin L.**                    **4.1698**
Population and society in twentieth century France / Colin Dyer. — New
York: Holmes & Meier Publishers, 1978. 247 p., [8] leaves of plates: ill.; 25 cm.
Includes index. 1. France — Population 2. France — Social conditions I. T.
HB3593.D9 1978          301.32/9/44      LC 77-2908      ISBN 0841903085

**Spengler, Joseph John, 1902-.**                    **4.1699**
France faces depopulation: postlude edition, 1936–1976 / Joseph J. Spengler. —
Durham, N.C.: Duke University Press, 1979. xiii, 383 p.; 24 cm. — (Studies in
social and economic demography. 2) Includes index. 1. Fertility, Human —
France. 2. France — Population 3. France — Statistics, Vital I. T. II. Series.
HB3593.S7 1979          301.32/9/44      LC 78-73006      ISBN 0822304228

**Lorimer, Frank, 1894-.**                    **• 4.1700**
The population of the Soviet Union: history and prospects / by Frank Lorimer.
— Geneva: League of nations, 1946. xiv, 289 p.: incl. tables, diagrs., maps; 27
cm. ([League of nations. Series of publications. II. Economic and financial.

1946.II.A.3]) 'One of a series of demographic studies which Princeton
University's Office of Population Research ... is preparing for the League of
Nations.' 1. Russia — Population I. League of nations. Secretariat. Economic,
Financial and Transit dept. II. Princeton University. Office of Population
Research. III. T.
HB3607 L6 1946A      LC 46-7027

**Myrdal, Alva Reimer, 1902-.**                    **• 4.1701**
Nation and family: the Swedish experiment in democratic family and
population policy / by Alva Myrdal. — London: K. Paul, Trench, Trubner,
1945. xiv, 441 p. — (International library of sociology and social
reconstruction) 'Written anew for the public in English-speaking countries...to
be considered as a substitute for an English version of the Kris i
befolkningsfragan, Stockholm, 1934, by the present author in collaboration
with Dr. Gunnar Mydral' - pref. 1. Public welfare — Sweden. 2. Family
3. Sweden — Population. I. T.
HB3617.M82      LC 45-7805

## HB3633–3693 Asia. Africa. Oceania

**Ness, Gayl D.**                    **4.1702**
The land is shrinking: population planning in Asia / Gayl D. Ness and
Hirofumi Ando. — Baltimore: Johns Hopkins University Press, c1984. xxii,
225 p.: ill.; 24 cm. — (Johns Hopkins studies in development.) Includes index.
1. Birth control — Asia. 2. Asia — Population policy. I. Andō, Hirofumi.
II. T. III. Series.
HB3633.A3 N47 1984          304.6/6/095 19      LC 83-48048      ISBN
0801829828

**United Nations. Bureau of Social Affairs.**                    **• 4.1703**
The population of Asia and the Far East, 1950–1980. New York: United
Nations Dept. of Economic and Social Affairs, 1959. viii, 110 p.: ill. , 28 cm.
(Future population estimates by sex and age, report 4.) Population studies, no.
31. Document ST/SOA/ser A/31. 1. Asia — Population. I. T.
HB3635.U5x      LC 60-1676

**Aird, John Shields, 1919-.**                    **• 4.1704**
The size, composition, and growth of the population of mainland China / by
John S. Aird. — [Washington]: United States Dept. of Commerce, Bureau of
the Census, 1961. — vi, 100 p.: ill.; 29 cm. Reprint of the ed., which was issued
as International population statistics reports, Series P-90, no. 15. 1. China —
Population. I. T.
HB3637.A55 1961          301.32/9/51

**Ho, Ping-ti.**                    **• 4.1705**
Studies on the population of China, 1368–1953. Cambridge, Harvard
University Press, 1959. xviii, 341, xxxii p. tables. (Harvard East Asian studies,
4) 1. China — Population I. T. II. Series.
HB3637 H6      LC 59-12970

**Cassen, Robert.**                    **4.1706**
India, population, economy, society / R. H. Cassen. — New York: Holmes &
Meier, 1978. xiii, 419 p.: ill.; 23 cm. Includes index. 1. India — Population.
2. India — Economic conditions — 1947- 3. India — Social conditions —
1947- I. T.
HB3639.C37 1978          304.6/0954 19      LC 77-16217      ISBN
084190300X

**Taeuber, Irene Barnes, 1906-.**                    **• 4.1707**
The population of Japan. Princeton: Princeton University Press, 1958. xv,
461 p.: maps, diagrs., tables; 31 cm. '[Prepared] under the editorial sponsorship
of Office of Population Research, Princeton University.' 1. Japan —
Population I. T.
HB3651 T3      LC 58-7122

**Barbour, Kenneth Michael. ed.**                    **• 4.1708**
Essays on African population. Edited by K. M. Barbour and R. M. Prothero.
New York, Praeger [1962, c1961] x, 336 p. maps., tables. 23 cm. (Books that
matter) 1. Africa — Population. I. Prothero, R. Mansell. joint ed. II. T.
HB3661.B3      LC 62-13487

**Hance, William Adams, 1916-.**                    **• 4.1709**
Population, migration, and urbanization in Africa [by] William A. Hance. —
New York: Columbia University Press, 1970. xiv, 450 p.: illus., maps.; 24 cm.
1. Migration, Internal — Africa. 2. Urbanization — Africa. 3. Africa —
Population. I. T.
HB3661.H35          301.3/2/096      LC 75-116378

**Princeton University. Office of Population Research.**                    **4.1710**
The demography of tropical Africa [by] William Brass [and others]. —
Princeton, N.J.: Princeton University Press, 1968. xxix, 539 p.: illus., maps.; 25
cm. Papers resulting from a project of the Office of Population Research,

Princeton University. 1. Africa, Sub-Saharan — Population. I. Brass, William.
II. T.
HB3661.P7       312/.0967       LC 67-21018

**Population and development in Kenya** / edited by S.H. Ominde      **4.1711**
with Roushdi A. Henin, and David F. Sly.
Nairobi: Heinemann Educational Books, 1985 (c1984). viii, 129 p.: ill.; 31 cm.
1. Land use — Kenya. 2. Population forecasting — Kenya. 3. Kenya —
Population. 4. Kenya — Economic policy. I. Ominde, Simeon Hongo.
II. Henin, R. A. III. Sly, David.
HB3662.5.A3 P64 1984       304.6/09676/2 19       LC 85-230770       ISBN
0435957619

**Population growth and socio–economic change in West Africa.**      **4.1712**
Edited by John C. Caldwell. With the collaboration of N. O.
Addo [and others]
New York, Published for the Population Council [by] Columbia University
Press, 1975. xiii, 763 p. illus. 26 cm. 1. Africa, West — Population. 2. Africa,
French-speaking West — Population. I. Caldwell, John Charles. ed. II. Addo,
N. O. ed. III. Population Council.
HB3665.P66       301.32/9/66       LC 74-17409       ISBN 0231237325

# HB3711–3840 Business Cycles. Economic Fluctuations. Forecasting

**Kondrat'ev, N. D. (Nikolaĭ Dmitrievich), 1892-.**      **4.1713**
The long wave cycle / Nikolai Kondratieff; translated by Guy Daniels,
introdution by Julian M. Snyder. — New York: Richardson & Snyder, 1984.
138 p.: ill. 1. Business cycles I. T.
HB3711.K6713 1984       LC 83-62181       ISBN 0943940079

**Lucas, Robert E.**      **4.1714**
Studies in business–cycle theory / Robert E. Lucas, Jr. — Cambridge, Mass.:
MIT Press, c1981. x, 300 p.; 24 cm. 1. Business cycles — Addresses, essays,
lectures. I. T.
HB3711.L83       338.5/42 19       LC 81-692       ISBN 0262120895

**Kindleberger, Charles Poor, 1910-.**      **4.1715**
Manias, panics, and crashes: a history of financial crises / Charles P.
Kindleberger. — New York: Basic Books, c1978. xii, 271 p.; 22 cm. 1. Business
cycles 2. Depressions I. T. II. Title: Financial crises.
HB3716.K55       338.5/4/09       LC 77-20424       ISBN 0465043801

**Galbraith, John Kenneth, 1908-.**      • **4.1716**
The great crash, 1929. — Boston: Houghton Mifflin, 1955. 212 p.: illus.; 22 cm.
1. Depressions — 1929 — United States I. T.
HB3717 1929.G3       338.54       LC 55-7639

**Kindleberger, Charles Poor, 1910-.**      **4.1717**
The world in depression, 1929–1939 / Charles P. Kindleberger. — Rev. and
enl. ed. — Berkeley: University of California Press, c1986. 1 v. (History of the
world economy in the twentieth century. v. 4) Includes index. 1. Depressions
— 1929 2. Economic history — 1918-1945 I. T. II. Series.
HB3717 1929.K55 1986       338.5/42 19       LC 85-8662       ISBN
0520055918

**Temin, Peter.**      **4.1718**
Did monetary forces cause the Great Depression? / Peter Temin. — 1st ed. —
New York: Norton, c1976. xiii, 201 p.: graphs; 21 cm. Includes index.
1. Depressions — 1929 — United States 2. Money supply — United States.
3. Monetary policy — United States. I. T.
HB3717 1929.T45 1976       338.5/42       LC 75-28367       ISBN
0393055612

**Harman, Willis W.**      **4.1719**
An incomplete guide to the future / Willis W. Harman. San Francisco: San
Francisco Book Co.; New York: trade distribution by Simon and Schuster,
1976. xiii, 160 p.: ill.; 23 cm. (The Portable Stanford series) Includes index.
1. Economic forecasting 2. Forecasting I. T.
HB3730.H318 1976b       338.5/443       LC 76-26076       ISBN 0913374466

**Pindyck, Robert S.**      **4.1720**
Econometric models and economic forecasts / Robert S. Pindyck, Daniel L.
Rubinfeld. — 2d ed. — New York: McGraw-Hill, c1981. xxii, 630 p.: ill.; 24
cm. Includes indexes. 1. Economic forecasting — Mathematical models.
2. Econometrics I. Rubinfeld, Daniel L. joint author. II. T.
HB3730.P54 1981       338.5/44       LC 80-14427       ISBN 0070500967

**World index of economic forecasts: industrial tendency surveys**      **4.1721**
and development plans / edited by George Cyriax.
2nd ed. — New York, N.Y.: Facts on File, 1981. xvi, 378 p.; 30 cm.
1. Economic forecasting — Directories. I. Cyriax, George.
HB3730.W66 1981       338.5/443/025 19       LC 81-590       ISBN
0871965291

# HC ECONOMIC HISTORY AND CONDITIONS

# HC1–28 Collections. General Works. Research

**Economic handbook of the world.**      **4.1722**
1981-. New York: Published for the Center for Social Analysis of the State
University of New York at Binghamton by McGraw-Hill, c1981-. v.; 29 cm.
Annual. 1. Economic history — 1971- — Handbooks, manuals, etc. I. State
University of New York at Binghamton. Center for Social Analysis.
HC10.E375       330.9/005       LC 81-643338

**Carus-Wilson, E. M. (Eleanora Mary), 1897-1977. ed.**      • **4.1723**
Essays in economic history; reprints, edited for the Economic History Society
by E. M. Carus–Wilson. — New York: St. Martin's Press, 1966. 3 v.: illus.; 25
cm. 1. Economic history — Addresses, essays, lectures. 2. Great Britain —
Economic conditions — Addresses, essays, lectures. I. Economic History
Society. II. T.
HC12.C32       330.9       LC 67-220

**Hicks, John Richard, Sir, 1904-.**      • **4.1724**
A theory of economic history, by John Hicks. — Oxford: Clarendon P., 1969.
ix, 181 p.; 21 cm. 1. Economic history 2. Economics — History I. T.
HC26.H5       330/.09       LC 70-437823       ISBN 0198282478

**Kaye, Harvey J.**      **4.1725**
The British Marxist historians: an introductory analysis / Harvey J. Kaye. —
New York: Polity Press, 1984. xii, 316 p.; 23 cm. Includes index. 1. Economic
history — Historiography. 2. Historical materialism 3. Marxian
historiography — Great Britain. I. T. II. Title: Marxist historians.
HC26.K39 1984       335.4/072041 19       LC 84-26304       ISBN
0745600158

**Research in economic history: an annual compilation of research**      **4.1726**
/ ed. by Paul Uselding.
v. 1- 1976-. Greenwich, Conn.: Jai Press, c1976-. v.; 24 cm. Subtitle varies.
1. Economic history — Yearbooks. I. Uselding, Paul J.
HC28.R42       ISBN 089232001X

# HC30–59 By Period

# HC31–39 ANCIENT

**Finley, M. I. (Moses I.), 1912-.**      **4.1727**
The ancient economy / by M.I. Finley. — 2nd ed. — Berkeley: University of
California Press, 1985, c1973. 262 p.: map; 23 cm. (Sather classical lectures. v.
48) Includes index. 1. Economic history — To 500 I. T. II. Series.
HC31.F5x 1985       LC 86-672785       ISBN 0520054520

**Polanyi, Karl, 1886-1964. ed.**      • **4.1728**
Trade and market in the early empires; economies in history and theory, edited
by Karl Polanyi, Conrad M. Arensberg, and Harry W. Pearson. Glencoe, Ill.,
Free Press [1957] xviii, 382 p. maps. 22 cm. 1. Economic history 2. Economic
anthropology 3. Economics I. T.
HC31.P6       330.901       LC 57-6745

**Weber, Max, 1864-1920.**      **4.1729**
[Selected Works] The agrarian sociology of ancient civilizations / Max Weber;
translated by R. I. Frank. — London: NLB; Atlantic Highlands, [N.J.]:
Humanities Press, 1976. 421 p.; 22 cm. — (Foundations of history library)

'First published as Agrarverhältnisse im Altertum, in Handwörterbuch der Staatswissenschaften, 1909; and Die sozialen Gründe des Untergangs der antiken Kultur, in Die Wahrheit, May 1896.' Includes index. 1. Economic history — To 500 2. Agriculture — History 3. Social history — To 500 4. Civilization, Ancient 5. Middle East — Economic conditions. I. T.
HC31.W42 1976    330.9/01    *LC* 76-370998    *ISBN* 0902308084

**Austin, M. M.**    **4.1730**
[Économies et sociétés en Grèce ancienne. English] Economic and social history of ancient Greece: an introduction / M. M. Austin and P. Vidal–Naquet; translated and revised by M. M. Austin. — Berkeley: University of California Press, 1978 (c1977). xv, 397 p.: maps; 23 cm. Translation of Économies et sociétés en Grèce ancienne. Includes indexes. 1. Greece — Economic conditions — To 146 B.C. 2. Greece — Social conditions — To 146 B.C. 3. Greece — Colonies I. Vidal-Naquet, Pierre, 1930- joint author. II. T.
HC37.A8813 1977b    309.1/38    *LC* 73-90665    *ISBN* 0520026586

**Figueira, Thomas J.**    **4.1731**
Aegina, society and politics / Thomas J. Figueira. — New York: Arno Press, 1981. xii, 360 p.; 24 cm. — (Monographs in classical studies.) Revision of pt. 1 of the author's thesis (Ph.D.—University of Pennsylvania, 1977) originally presented under title: Aegina and Athens in the archaic and classical periods. 1. Aegina Island (Greece) — Economic conditions. 2. Aegina Island (Greece) — Social conditions. 3. Aegina Island (Greece) — Politics and government. I. T. II. Series.
HC37.F54    330.939/1 19    *LC* 80-2649    *ISBN* 0405140363

**Finley, M. I. (Moses I.), 1912-.**    **4.1732**
Economy and society in ancient Greece / by M.I. Finley; edited with an introduction by Brent D. Shaw and Richard P. Saller. — New York: Viking Press, 1982. xxvi, 326 p.; 23 cm. Consists of 14 Finley articles from the early 1950s to the late 1970s. Includes index. 1. Greece — Economic conditions — To 146 B.C. — Addresses, essays, lectures. 2. Greece — Social conditions — To 146 B.C. — Addresses, essays, lectures. 3. Greece — History — To 146 B.C. — Addresses, essays, lectures. I. Shaw, Brent D. II. Saller, Richard P. III. T.
HC37.F56    330.938 19    *LC* 81-51886    *ISBN* 0670288470

**French, A. (Alfred), 1916-.**    **4.1733**
The growth of the Athenian economy / by A. French. — Westport, Conn.: Greenwood Press, 1975, c1964. xii, 208 p.; 22 cm. Reprint of the ed. published by Routledge & Paul, London. Includes index. 1. Athens (Greece) — Economic conditions. I. T.
HC37.F7 1975    330.9/385    *LC* 75-31363    *ISBN* 0837185068

**Hopper, R. J. (Robert John), 1910-.**    **4.1734**
Trade and industry in classical Greece / R. J. Hopper. — London: Thames and Hudson, c1979. 240 p., [8] leaves of plates: ill.; 23 cm. — (Aspects of Greek and Roman life) Includes index. 1. Greece — Economic conditions I. T. II. Series.
HC37.H66    330.9/495/07    *LC* 79-307194    *ISBN* 0500400385

**Michell, H. (Humfrey), 1883-.**    • **4.1735**
The economics of ancient Greece. 2d ed. New York: Barnes and Noble, 1957. 427 p.; 23 cm. Includes bibliography. I. T.
HC37.M5 1957

**Starr, Chester G., 1914-.**    **4.1736**
The economic and social growth of early Greece, 800–500 B.C. / Chester G. Starr. — New York: Oxford University Press, 1977. 267 p., [4] leaves of plates: ill.; 22 cm. Includes index. 1. Greece — Economic conditions — To 146 B.C. 2. Greece — Social conditions I. T.
HC37.S7    330.9/38/02    *LC* 76-57265    *ISBN* 0195022238

**Badian, E.**    **4.1737**
Publicans and sinners; private enterprise in the service of the Roman Republic [by] E. Badian. — Ithaca, N.Y.: Cornell University Press, [1972] 170 p.; 23 cm. 1. Capitalists and financiers — Rome. 2. Tax collection — Rome. 3. Entrepreneurship I. T.
HC39.B33    338/.04/0937    *LC* 70-164712    *ISBN* 0801406765

**Cipolla, Carlo M. comp.**    • **4.1738**
The economic decline of empires; edited with an introd. by Carlo M. Cipolla. — London: Methuen, [1970] 280 p.; 22 cm. Distributed in the U.S.A. by Barnes & Noble. 1. Economic history — Addresses, essays, lectures. I. T.
HC39.C53    330/.09    *LC* 79-19611    *ISBN* 0416160905

**Frank, Tenncy, 1876-1939. ed.**    **4.1739**
An economic survey of ancient Rome / edited by Tenney Frank, in collaboration with T. R. S. Broughton, R. G. Collingwood, A. Grenier ... [and others] Baltimore: The Johns Hopkins Press, 1933-40. 6 v.; 25 cm. Each volume has special t.-p. 1. Rome — Economic conditions — Collected works. 2. Rome — Provinces — Collected works. I. Johnson, Allan Chester, 1881- II. T.
HC39.F72 1940    330.9/37/6    *LC* 33-17382

**Jones, A. H. M. (Arnold Hugh Martin), 1904-1970.**    **4.1740**
The Roman economy; studies in ancient economic and administrative history. Edited by P. A. Brunt. Totowa, N.J., Rowman and Littlefield [1974] xi, 450 p. 23 cm. 1. Rome — Economic conditions — Addresses, essays, lectures. 2. Rome — Politics and government — 284-476 — Addresses, essays, lectures. I. T.
HC39.J65 1974    330.9/37/6    *LC* 73-5960    *ISBN* 0874711940

## HC41–45 MEDIEVAL

**Fourquin, Guy.**    **4.1741**
[Seigneurie et féodalité au Moyen âge. English] Lordship and feudalism in the Middle Ages / by Guy Fourquin; translated by Iris and A. L. Lytton Sells. — New York: Pica Press, 1976. 253 p.; 23 cm. Translation of Seigneurie et féodalité au Moyen âge. 1. Economic history — Medieval, 500-1500 2. Feudalism I. T.
HC41.F6913 1976b    330.9/4/01    *LC* 75-11141    *ISBN* 0876637187

**Latouche, Robert, 1881-.**    • **4.1742**
The birth of Western economy; economic aspects of the Dark Ages. / With a foreword by Philip Grierson. Translated by E. M. Wilkinson. — 2d ed. London: Methuen, [1961]. xviii, 341 p.: ill., facsims., maps (2 fold.); 23 cm. Translation of Les origines de l'economie occidentale. 1. Economic history — Medieval, 500-1500 I. T.
HC 41.L313    *LC* 67-7037

**Pirenne, Henri, 1862-1935.**    • **4.1743**
Economic and social history of medieval Europe, by Henri Pirenne. New York, Harcourt, Brace and company [1937] xii, 243 p. 19 cm. 'First American edition.' 'Translated from the French by I. E. Clegg.' 'First appeared in Histoire du moyen âge, by Henri Pirenne, Gustave Cohen, and Henri Focillon.' 1. Middle Ages — History 2. Europe — Economic conditions — To 1492 3. Europe — Social conditions — To 1492 I. T.
HC41.P52 1937    330.902    *LC* 37-28587

**Braudel, Fernand.**    **4.1744**
Afterthoughts on material civilization and capitalism / Fernand Braudel; translated by Patricia M. Ranum. — Baltimore: Johns Hopkins University Press, c1977. xi, 120 p.: ill.; 21 cm. (Johns Hopkins symposia in comparative history. 7th) Lectures presented at Johns Hopkins University, Apr. 1976. 1. Economic history — Addresses, essays, lectures. 2. Capitalism — Addresses, essays, lectures. I. T. II. Title: Material civilization and capitalism. III. Series.
HC45.B6913    330.12/2/09    *LC* 76-47368    *ISBN* 0801819016

**Wallerstein, Immanuel Maurice, 1930-.**    **4.1745**
The modern world–system; capitalist agriculture and the origins of the European world–economy in the sixteenth century [by] Immanuel Wallerstein. New York, Academic Press [1974] xiv, 410 p. illus. 25 cm. (Studies in social discontinuity.) 1. Economic history — 16th century 2. Capitalism 3. Europe — Economic conditions — 16th century I. T. II. Series.
HC45.W35 1974    330.9/4/022    *LC* 73-5318    *ISBN* 0127859209

## HC51–59 MODERN

**Boulding, Kenneth Ewart, 1910- comp.**    **4.1746**
Economic imperialism; a book of readings. Edited by Kenneth E. Boulding and Tapan Mukerjee. — Ann Arbor: University of Michigan Press, [1972] xviii, 338 p.: illus.; 24 cm. 1. Economic history — Addresses, essays, lectures. 2. Imperialism — Addresses, essays, lectures. I. Mukerjee, Tapan, joint comp. II. T.
HC51.B65 1972    330.9    *LC* 74-146490    *ISBN* 0472168304

**Braudel, Fernand.**    **4.1747**
[Civilisation matérielle, économie et capitalisme. English] Civilization and capitalism, 15th–18th century / Fernand Braudel. — 1st U.S. ed. — New York: Harper & Row, 1982-1984. 3 v.: ill.; 24 cm. Rev. translation of: Civilisation matérielle, économie et capitalisme: XVe-XVIIIe siècle. Vol. 1: Translation from the French revised by Siân Reynolds; v. 2-3: Translation from the French by Siân Reynolds. 1. Economic history 2. Social history — Modern, 1500- 3. Civilization, Modern — History. I. T.
HC51.B67413 1982    909.08 19    *LC* 81-47653    *ISBN* 0060148454

**Bruchey, Stuart Weems.**    • **4.1748**
The roots of American economic growth, 1607–1861; an essay in social causation, by Stuart Bruchey. — [1st ed.] — New York: Harper & Row, [1965] xiii, 234 p.; 22 cm. 1. United States — Economic conditions — To 1865 I. T.
HC51.B7    338.0973    *LC* 64-25110

**Dobb, Maurice Herbert, 1900-.**        • **4.1749**
Studies in the development of capitalism, by Maurice Dobb. — [Rev. ed.]. — New York: International Publishers, [1964, c1963] iv, 402 p.; 22 cm. 1. Capitalism — History. 2. Economic history I. T.
HC51.D6 1964       LC 64-13744

**Frank, Andre Gunder, 1929-.**        **4.1750**
World accumulation, 1492–1789 / Andre Gunder Frank. — New York: Monthly Review Press, c1978. 303 p. Includes index. 1. Economic history 2. Capitalism — History. I. T.
HC51.F68      330.9     LC 78-7538     ISBN 0853454426

**Heilbroner, Robert L.**        **4.1751**
The making of economic society / Robert L. Heilbroner. — 7th ed., Rev. for the mid-1980s. — Englewood Cliffs, N.J.: Prentice-Hall, c1985. xvii, 268 p.: ill.; 24 cm. 1. Economic history I. T.
HC51.H44 1985     330.9 19     LC 84-15912     ISBN 0135462010

**Kuznets, Simon Smith, 1901-.**        • **4.1752**
Economic growth: Brazil, India, Japan / edited by Simon Kuznets, Wilbert E. Moore, and Joseph J. Spengler. — Durham, N.C.: Duke University Press, 1955. xi, 613 p.: maps; 24 cm. 'The product of a research conference planned by the Committee on Economic Growth of the Social Science Research Council ... and held under its auspices in the spring of 1952.' 1. Brazil — Economic conditions 2. India — Economic conditions 3. Japan — Economic conditions I. T.
HC51.K8     LC 55-9491

**Kuznets, Simon Smith, 1901-.**        **4.1753**
Economic growth of nations; total output and production structure [by] Simon Kuznets. — Cambridge, Mass.: Belknap Press of Harvard University Press, 1971. xii, 363 p.; 25 cm. 1. Economic history 2. Economic development I. T.
HC51.K82     339     LC 71-127876     ISBN 0674227808

**Maddison, Angus.**        **4.1754**
Phases of capitalist development / Angus Maddison. — Oxford; New York: Oxford University Press, 1982. xiv, 274 p.; 23 cm. 1. Economic history 2. Business cycles — History. 3. Economic policy — History. 4. Capitalism — History. I. T.
HC51.M26 1982     330.9172/2 19     LC 82-3558     ISBN 0198284500

**Mukerji, Chandra.**        **4.1755**
From graven images: patterns of modern materialism / Chandra Mukerji. — New York: Columbia University Press, 1983. xiv, 329 p.: ill.; 24 cm. Includes index. 1. Consumption (Economics) — History. 2. Popular culture — History. 3. Materialism — History. 4. Printing — History 5. Europe — Manufactures — History. I. T.
HC51.M77 1983     338.4/76862/09 19     LC 83-10148     ISBN 0231051662

**Conrad, Alfred H.**        • **4.1756**
The economics of slavery, and other studies in econometric history, by Alfred H. Conrad and John R. Meyer. Chicago, Aldine Pub. Co. [1964] ix, 241 p. illus. 22 cm. Includes bibliographical references. 1. Slavery 2. Econometrics — Case studies. 3. Great Britain — Industries. 4. United States — Economic conditions I. Meyer, John Robert. joint author. II. T.
HC53.C57     339.2     LC 64-15914

**Lewis, W. Arthur (William Arthur), 1915-.**        **4.1757**
Growth and fluctuations, 1870–1913 / W. Arthur Lewis. — London; Boston: G. Allen & Unwin, 1978. 333 p.: ill.; 24 cm. 1. Economic history — 1750-1918 2. Economic development — History. I. T.
HC53.L43     330.9/03/3     LC 78-314920     ISBN 004300072X

**Morazé, Charles, 1913-.**        • **4.1758**
The triumph of the middle classes; a study of European values in the nineteenth century. — Cleveland, World Pub. Co. [1967, c1966] xv, 414 p. 28 illus., maps. 25 cm. — (Studies in world history) Translation of Les bourgeois conquérants, XIX siecle. 1. Economic history — 1750-1918 2. Social history — 19th century 3. Middle classes — Europe. I. T.
HC53.M613 1967     901.9/34     LC 67-13834

**Polanyi, Karl, 1886-1964.**        • **4.1759**
The great transformation. Foreword by Robert M. MacIver. — [1st Beacon paperback ed.]. — Boston, Beacon Press [1957, c1944] 315 p. 21 cm. — (Beacon paperback no. 45) 1. Economic history — 1750-1918 2. Social history 3. Economics — Hist. I. T.
HC53.P6x     330.9     LC 57-9208

**Woolf, Leonard, 1880-1969.**        • **4.1760**
Economic imperialism. New York, H. Fertig, 1970. 111 p. 21 cm. Reprint of the 1920 ed. 1. Colonies — Economic conditions. 2. Imperialism 3. Competition, International 4. Africa — Economic conditions — 1918-1945 5. China — Economic conditions — 1644-1912 I. T.
HC53.W6 1970     330.9172/4     LC 68-9627

## HC54–59 20th Century

**Cipolla, Carlo M.**        • **4.1761**
The economic history of world population. Baltimore, Penguin Books [1962] 125 p. illus. 19 cm. (Pelican books, A537) 1. Economic history — 1750-1918 2. Economic history — 20th century I. T.
HC54.C5     LC 62-6257

**Foreman-Peck, James.**        **4.1762**
A history of the world economy: international economic relations since 1850 / James Foreman–Peck. — Totowa, N.J.: Barnes & Noble, 1983. xiii, 394 p.: ill.; 25 cm. 1. Economic history — 20th century 2. Economic history — 1750-1918 3. International economic relations — History. I. T.
HC54.F565 1983     337/.09 19     LC 82-24295     ISBN 0389203378

**Habermas, Jürgen.**        **4.1763**
[Legitimationsprobleme im Spätkapitalismus. English] Legitimation crisis / by Jürgen Habermas; translated by Thomas McCarthy. — Boston: Beacon Press, [1975] xxiv, 166 p.; 21 cm. Translation of Legitimationsprobleme im Spätkapitalismus. 1. Capitalism 2. Economic history — 1971- 3. Social history — 20th century I. T.
HC54.H213 1975     301/.045     LC 74-17586     ISBN 0807015202. ISBN 0807015210 pbk

**Alexandersson, Gunnar.**        **4.1764**
World resources: energy, metals, and minerals: studies in economic and political geography / Gunnar Alexandersson, Bjorn–Ivar Klevebring. — Berlin; New York: W. de Gruyter, 1978. vii, 248 p.: ill.; 24 cm. (GeoSpectrum) Includes index. 1. Natural resources 2. Power resources 3. Mineral industries 4. Geography, Economic 5. Geography, Political I. Klevebring, Bjorn-Ivar, 1943- joint author. II. T. III. Series.
HC55.A36     333.7     LC 77-27560     ISBN 3110065770

**Avery, Thomas Eugene.**        **4.1765**
Natural resources measurements. — 2d ed. — New York: McGraw-Hill, [c1975] xxiii, 339 p.: illus.; 24 cm. — (McGraw-Hill series in forest resources) First ed. published in 1967 under title: Forest measurements. 1. Natural resources — Measurement. 2. Forests and forestry — Mensuration I. T. II. Title: Forest measurements.
HC55.A93 1975     HC55 A93 1975.     333.7     LC 74-11346     ISBN 0070025029

**Banks, Ferdinand E.**        **4.1766**
The economics of natural resources / Ferdinand E. Banks. New York: Plenum Press, c1976. xiii, 267 p.: ill.; 24 cm. Includes index. 1. Natural resources 2. Raw materials 3. Economics I. T.
HC55.B25     333.7     LC 76-25583     ISBN 0306309262

**Barnett, Harold Joseph, 1917-.**        • **4.1767**
Scarcity and growth: the economics of natural resource availability / by Harold J. Barnett and Chandler Morse. [Washington]: Published for Resources for the Future by Johns Hopkins Press, Baltimore, [1963] xv, 288 p.: diagrs.; 24 cm. 1. Natural resources I. Morse, Chandler, 1906- II. T.
HC55.B3

**Clark, Colin, 1905-.**        • **4.1768**
The conditions of economic progress. — 3d ed., largely rewritten. — London: Macmillan; New York: St. Martin's Press, 1957. xv, 720 p.: diagrs., tables; 23 cm. Bibliography: p. 685-691. 1. Economic history 2. Income 3. Cost and standard of living I. T.
HC55.C55 1957     330.904     LC 57-13924

**Dasgupta, Partha.**        **4.1769**
Economic theory and exhaustible resources / by P. S. Dasgupta, G. M. Heal. — Welwyn [Eng.]: J. Nisbet; [Cambridge, Eng.]: Cambridge University Press, 1979. xiv, 501 p.: ill.; 22 cm. — (Cambridge economic handbooks.) Includes index. 1. Natural resources 2. Economics I. Heal, G. M. joint author. II. T. III. Series.
HC55.D27 1979     333.7 19     LC 80-502562     ISBN 0720203120

**Mikdashi, Zuhayr M.**        **4.1770**
The international politics of natural resources / Zuhayr Mikdashi. Ithaca, N.Y.: Cornell University Press, 1976. 214 p.; 22 cm. 'Written under the auspices of the Center for International Affairs, Harvard University.' 1. Natural resources 2. International economic relations 3. World politics — 1965- I. Harvard University. Center for International Affairs. II. T.
HC55.M54 1976     333.7     LC 75-38002     ISBN 0801410010

**Novick, David.**        **4.1771**
A world of scarcities: critical issues in public policy / David Novick, with Kurt Bleicken ... [et al.]. — New York: Wiley, 1976. x, 194 p.: graphs; 24 cm. 'A Halsted Press book.' 1. Natural resources 2. Energy policy 3. Economic policy I. T.
HC55.N68 1976     333.7     LC 75-42278     ISBN 0470150025

**Resources for an uncertain future: papers presented at a forum**    **4.1772**
**marking the 25th anniversary of Resources for the Future,**
**October 13, 1977, Washington, D.C. / Charles J. Hitch, editor;**
**Lewis M. Branscomb ... [et al.].**
Baltimore: Published for Resources for the Future by the Johns Hopkins
University Press, c1978. ix, 105 p.; 23 cm. 1. Natural resources — Congresses.
2. Environmental policy — Congresses. I. Hitch, Charles Johnston.
II. Branscomb, Lewis M., 1926- III. Resources for the Future.
HC55.R473      333.7      LC 77-18378      ISBN 0801821053

**Wisconsin Seminar on Natural Resource Policies in Relation to**    **4.1773**
**Economic Development and International Cooperation**
**(1977-1978: University of Wisconsin—Madison)**
Resources and development: natural resource policies and economic
development in an interdependent world / edited by Peter Dorner, Mahmoud
A. El-Shafie. — Madison: University of Wisconsin Press; London: Croom
Helm, c1980. xv, 500 p.; 24 cm. Co-sponsored by the University of Wisconsin—
Madison and others. 1. Natural resources — Congresses. 2. Economic
development — Congresses. 3. International economic relations —
Congresses. I. Dorner, Peter, 1925- II. Shafie, Mahmoud A. III. University of
Wisconsin—Madison. IV. T.
HC55.W57 1977a      333.7      LC 80-10577      ISBN 0299082504

**Hardach, Gerd, 1941-.**    **4.1774**
[Erste Weltkrieg. English] The First World War, 1914–1918 / Gerd Hardach.
— Berkeley: University of California Press, c1977. xvi, 328 p.: map; 23 cm. —
(History of the world economy in the twentieth century. 2) Translation of Der
Erste Weltkrieg: 1914-1918. Includes index. 1. World War, 1914-1918 —
Economic aspects I. T. II. Series.
HC56.H3713      940.3/113      LC 75-17142      ISBN 0520030605

**Davis, Joseph Stancliffe, 1885-.**    **4.1775**
The world between the wars, 1919–39: an economist's view / Joseph S. Davis.
— Baltimore: Johns Hopkins University Press, [1975] viii, 436 p.; 23 cm.
1. Economic history — 1918-1945 2. Depressions — 1929 3. Business cycles
I. T.
HC57.D36 1975      330.9/04      LC 74-6821      ISBN 0801814502

**Keynes, John Maynard, 1883-1946.**    • **4.1776**
Essays in persuasion. New York, Norton [1963] 376 p. 20 cm. (The Norton
library) 1. Treaty of Versailles (1919). 2. Economic history — 1918-1945
3. Currency question 4. Currency question — Great Britain. 5. Gold
6. Inflation (Finance) I. T.
HC57.K45 1963      330.9/04 19      LC 63-1357

**Pigou, A. C. (Arthur Cecil), 1877-1959.**    • **4.1777**
Economics in practice: six lectures on current issues / by A. C. Pigou. —
London, Macmillan, 1935. vii, 154 p.; 19 cm. 1. Economics — Addresses,
essays, lectures. 2. Economic policy I. T.
HC57.P48      LC 35-13262

**Robbins, Lionel Charles Robbins, Baron, 1898-.**    • **4.1778**
The great depression, by Lionel Robbins. — Freeport, N.Y.: Books for
Libraries Press, [1971] xiv, 238 p.: illus.; 23 cm. Reprint of the 1934 ed.
1. Economic history — 1918-1945 2. Currency question 3. Depressions —
1929 4. Currency question — Gt. Brit. 5. U.S. — Economic policy — To 1933.
I. T.
HC57.R57 1971      330.9/04      LC 75-150198      ISBN 0836957113

**Milward, Alan S.**    **4.1779**
War, economy, and society, 1939–1945 / Alan S. Milward. — Berkeley:
University of California Press, c1977. xiv, 395 p.; 23 cm. (History of the world
economy in the twentieth century. 5) German version published in 1977 under
title: Der Zweite Weltkrieg: Krieg, Wirtschaft u. Gesellschaft, 1939-1945.
Includes index. 1. World War, 1939-1945 — Economic aspects I. T. II. Series.
HC58.M53 1977      940.53/14      LC 76-40823      ISBN 0520033388

## HC59 1945-

**World economic survey.**    • **4.1780**
1945- . — New York: United Nations, Centre for Development Planning,
Projections and Policies, 1945-. v. Annual. Each vol. has distinctive title.
Supplements also issued. 1. Economic history — 1945- - Yearbooks.
I. United Nations. Centre for Development Planning, Projections, and
Policies. II. United Nations. Bureau of Economic Affairs. III. Title: World
economic report.
HC59.A169      330.9/047

**Aron, Raymond, 1905-.**    • **4.1781**
War and industrial society. — London: Oxford University Press, 1958. 63 p.; 23
cm. (Auguste Comte memorial trust lecture, 3) 1. War and society I. T.
HC59.A83

**Brown, Lester Russell, 1934-.**    **4.1782**
World without borders [by] Lester R. Brown. — New York: Random House,
[1972] xviii, 395 p.; 22 cm. 1. Economic history — 1945- 2. Social history —
1945- I. T.
HC59.B765 1972b      330.9/046      LC 72-5409      ISBN 0394482204

**Cornwall, John.**    **4.1783**
The conditions for economic recovery: a post–Keynesian analysis / John
Cornwall. — Armonk, N.Y.: M.E. Sharpe, 1984 (c1983). xvi, 361 p.: ill.; 24 cm.
Includes index. 1. Economic history — 1971- 2. Unemployment — Effect of
inflation on 3. Wage-price policy I. T.
HC59.C726      339.5 19      LC 83-12802      ISBN 0873322630

**Economics and world order from the 1970's to the 1990's.**    **4.1784**
**Edited by Jagdish N. Bhagwati.**
[New York] Macmillan [1972] xii, 365 p. 25 cm. Papers presented at the
Northfield conference of the World Order Models Project, June 18-25, 1969.
'Sponsored by the World Law Fund.' 1. Economic history — 1971- —
Congresses. 2. International agencies — Congresses. 3. Developing countries
— Economic conditions — Congresses. I. Bhagwati, Jagdish N., 1934- ed.
II. World Order Models Project. III. World Law Fund.
HC59.E38      330.9/04      LC 73-179966

**Fisher, Anthony C.**    **4.1785**
Resource and environmental economics / Anthony C. Fisher. — Cambridge
[Cambridgeshire]; New York: Cambridge University Press, 1981. xv, 284 p.:
ill.; 22 cm. — (Cambridge surveys of economic literature.) Includes indexes.
1. Natural resources 2. Environmental policy 3. Pollution — Economic
aspects I. T. II. Series.
HC59.F558      333.7 19      LC 81-9951      ISBN 0521243068

**Henderson, Hazel.**    **4.1786**
The politics of the solar age: alternatives to economics / Hazel Henderson. —
1st ed., Anchor Press ed. — Garden City, N.Y.: Anchor Press/Doubleday,
1981. xxii, 433 p., [20] leaves of plates: ill.; 21 cm. 1. Economic history — 1971-
I. T.
HC59.H383      330.9/048 19      LC 80-1723      ISBN 0385171501

**Hoover, Calvin Bryce, 1897-.**    • **4.1787**
The economy, liberty, and the state. New York: Twentieth Century Fund, 1959.
445 p.; 24 cm. 1. Capitalism 2. Socialism 3. Liberty. I. T.
HC59 H63      LC 59-8021

**The Limits to growth; a report for the Club of Rome's project**    • **4.1788**
**on the predicament of mankind [by] Donella H. Meadows [and**
**others].**
New York: Universe Books, [1972] 205 p.: illus.; 21 cm. 'A Potomac Associates
book.' 1. Economic history — 1971- 2. Economic development 3. Social
history — 1945- I. Meadows, Donella H. II. Club of Rome.
HC59.L54      330.9/04      LC 73-187907      ISBN 0876631650

**Lundberg, Erik, 1907-.**    • **4.1789**
Business cycles and economic policy. Translated by J. Potter. — Cambridge,
Harvard University Press, 1957. xx, 346 p. diagrs., tables. 22 cm. Translation,
with revisions, of Konjunkturer och ekonomisk politik. Bibliographical
footnotes. 1. Business cycles 2. Economic policy I. T.
HC59.L8x      LC A 57-7370

**Meadows, Donella H.**    **4.1790**
Groping in the dark: the first decade of global modelling / Donella Meadows,
John Richardson, Gerhart Bruckmann. — Chichester [West Sussex]; New
York: Wiley, c1982. xxvii, 311 p.: ill.; 24 cm. 1. Economic history —
Mathematical models. I. Richardson, John M. (John Martin), 1938-
II. Bruckmann, Gerhart. III. T.
HC59.M413 1982      330.9 19      LC 81-14713      ISBN 0471100277

**Mesarović, Mihajlo D.**    **4.1791**
Mankind at the turning point: the second report to the Club of Rome / Mihajlo
Mesarovic and Eduard Pestel. — 1st ed. — New York: Dutton, 1974. xiii,
210 p.: ill.; 25 cm. Includes index. 1. Economic history — 1971- 2. Food
supply 3. Population 4. Power resources I. Pestel, Eduard C. joint author.
II. Club of Rome. III. T.
HC59.M458 1974      330.9/04      LC 74-16787      ISBN 052515230X

**Shonfield, Andrew, 1917-.**    • **4.1792**
Modern capitalism; the changing balance of public and private power. —
London, New York, Oxford University Press, 1965 [i. e. 1966] xvi, 456 p. 25
cm. 1. Economic history — 1945- 2. Economic policy I. T.
HC59.S494      330.904      LC 65-28179

**State of the world: a Worldwatch Institute report on progress**    **4.1793**
**toward a sustainable society.**
1984- . — New York: Norton, c1984-. v.: ill.; 25 cm. Annual. 1. Economic
history — 1971- — Periodicals. 2. Economic policy — Periodicals.

3. Population policy — Periodicals. 4. Environmental policy — Periodicals. I. Worldwatch Institute.
HC59.S734    330.9/005 19    *LC* 85-643206

**World tables.**    **4.1794**
3rd ed. — Baltimore: Published for the World Bank [by] the Johns Hopkins University Press, 1984, c1983. 2 v.: ill.; 31 cm. 1. Economic history — 1971- 2. Social history — 1970- 3. Statistics I. International Bank for Reconstruction and Development.
HC59.W669 1984    330.9/048 19    *LC* 83-25609    *ISBN* 0801832632

**Woytinsky, Wladimir S., 1885-1960.**    • **4.1795**
World population and production: trends and outlook / [by] W. S. Woytinsky and E. S. Woytinsky. — New York: Twentieth Century Fund, 1953. lxxii, 1268 p.: ill., maps; 27 cm. 1. Economic history — 1945-1971 2. Population 3. Natural resources I. Woytinsky, Emma Shadkhan, 1893-1968. joint author. II. Twentieth Century Fund. III. T.
HC59.W68    330.904    *LC* 53-7171

**Young, Oran R.**    **4.1796**
Resource regimes: natural resources and social institutions / Oran R. Young. — Berkeley: University of California Press, c1982. x, 276 p.: ill.; 23 cm. — (Studies in international political economy) 1. Natural resources — Economic aspects — Decision making. 2. Environmental protection — Decision making. I. T. II. Series.
HC59.Y69 1982    333.7 19    *LC* 81-16108    *ISBN* 0520045734

# HC59.7-60 Underdeveloped Areas. Assistance

(see also: HD72-89)

**Bagchi, Amiya Kumar.**    **4.1797**
The political economy of underdevelopment / Amiya Kumar Bagchi. — Cambridge; New York: Cambridge University Press, 1982. viii, 280 p.; 22 cm. (Modern Cambridge economics). Includes index. 1. Developing countries — Economic conditions I. T. II. Series.
HC59.7.B24 1982    330.9172/4 19    *LC* 81-10237    *ISBN* 0521240247

**Bairoch, Paul.**    **4.1798**
[Diagnostic de l'évolution économique du Tiers-monde. English] The economic development of the Third World since 1900 / Paul Bairoch; translated by Cynthia Postan. — Berkeley: University of California Press, 1975. xii, 260 p.; 25 cm. Translation of Diagnostic de l'évolution économique du Tiers-monde, with revision and updating. Includes index. 1. Developing countries — Economic conditions I. T.
HC59.7.B2813    330.9/172/4    *LC* 74-16706    *ISBN* 0520028589

**Ballance, Robert H.**    **4.1799**
The international economy and industrial development: the impact of trade and investment on the Third World / Robert H. Ballance, Javed A. Ansari, Hans W. Singer. — Totowa, N.J.: Allanheld, Osmun Publishers, 1982. 326 p.; 23 cm. 1. Industrialization 2. Developing countries — Industries. 3. Developing countries — Commerce. I. Ansari, Javed A. II. Singer, Hans Wolfgang, 1910- III. T.
HC59.7.B297 1982    338.09172/4 19    *LC* 82-6651    *ISBN* 0865980861

**Colman, David.**    **4.1800**
Economics of change in less developed countries / David Colman and Frederick Nixson. — New York: Wiley, c1978. ix, 309 p.; 24 cm. 'A Halsted Press book.' 1. Underdeveloped areas. 2. Economic development I. Nixson, F. I. joint author. II. T.
HC59.7.C595 1978    330.9/172/4    *LC* 78-9708    *ISBN* 0470264349

**Dialectics of Third World development** / edited by Ingolf    **4.1801**
**Vogeler and Anthony R. de Souza.**
Montclair, NJ: Allanheld, Osmun, 1980. xii, 349 p.: ill.; 24 cm. 1. Developing countries — Economic conditions — Addresses, essays, lectures. I. Vogeler, Ingolf. II. De Souza, Anthony R.
HC59.7.D485    338.9/009172/4    *LC* 79-53704    *ISBN* 0916672336

**Economic development, poverty, and income distribution** /    **4.1802**
**edited by William Loehr and John P. Powelson.**
Boulder, Colo.: Westview Press, 1977. xii, 307 p.: ill.; 24 cm. (Westview special studies in social, political and economic development) 1. Income distribution — Developing countries — Addresses, essays, lectures. 2. Developing countries — Economic conditions — Addresses, essays, lectures. I. Loehr, William. II. Powelson, John P., 1920-
HC59.7.E28    330.9/172/4    *LC* 77-23270    *ISBN* 0891582487

**Economic stabilization in developing countries** / William R.    **4.1803**
**Cline and Sidney Weintraub, editors; [authors] William R. Cline**
**... [et al.].**
Washington, D.C.: Brookings Institution, c1981. xv, 517 p.: ill.; 24 cm. 1. Economic stabilization — Developing countries. 2. Developing countries — Economic policy. I. Cline, William R. II. Weintraub, Sidney, 1914-
HC59.7.E313    338.9/009172/4 19    *LC* 80-26363    *ISBN* 0815714661

**Haq, Mahbub ul, 1934-.**    **4.1804**
The poverty curtain: choices for the third world / Mahbub ul Haq. — New York: Columbia University Press, 1976. xvii, 247 p.; 29 cm. Includes index. 1. Poverty 2. Economic development 3. Developing countries — Economic conditions I. T.
HC59.7.H35    330.9/172/4    *LC* 76-7470    *ISBN* 0231040628. *ISBN* 0231040636 pbk

**Harrington, Michael, 1928-.**    **4.1805**
The vast majority: a journey to the world's poor / Michael Harrington. — New York: Simon and Schuster, c1977. 281 p.; 22 cm. Includes index. 1. Economic assistance, American 2. Poor 3. Developing countries — Economic conditions I. T.
HC59.7.H353    330.9/172/4    *LC* 77-9525    *ISBN* 0671225294

**Hermassi, Elbaki.**    **4.1806**
The Third World reassessed / Elbaki Hermassi. — Berkeley: University of Calif. Press, c1980. 223 p.; 22 cm. Includes index. 1. Civilization, Modern — 20th century 2. Developing countries — Civilization I. T.
HC59.7.H4295    909/.09/7240827    *LC* 78-62848    *ISBN* 0520037642

**Higgins, Benjamin Howard, 1912-.**    **4.1807**
Economic development of a small planet / Benjamin Higgins and Jean Downing Higgins. — 1st ed. — New York: Norton, c1979. x, 292 p.; 24 cm. 1. Economic development 2. Developing countries — Economic conditions I. Higgins, Jean. joint author. II. T.
HC59.7.H45 1979    330.9/172/4    *LC* 79-13316    *ISBN* 039305697X

**Income distribution and growth in the less-developed countries** /    **4.1808**
**Charles R. Frank, Jr., and Richard C. Webb, editors.**
Washington: Brookings Institution, c1977. xiv, 641 p.; 25 cm. Papers presented at a workshop held at Princeton University, Sept. 1974. 1. Income distribution — Developing countries — Congresses. 2. Developing countries — Economic policy — Congresses. I. Frank, Charles Raphael. II. Webb, Richard Charles, 1937-
HC59.7.I475    339.2/09172/4    *LC* 77-86494    *ISBN* 0815729154

**Johnson, Harry G. (Harry Gordon), 1923-1977.**    • **4.1809**
Economic policies toward less developed countries [by] Harry G. Johnson. — Washington, Brookings Institution [1967] xvi, 279 p. 24 cm. 'The first draft of this book formed the agenda for a conference of experts on international trade and development policy convened at Brookings on December 9 and 10, 1965.' Bibliographical footnotes. 1. International economic relations 2. Economic policy 3. Underdeveloped areas. I. Brookings Institution. II. T.
HC59.7.J6    338.911724    *LC* 67-14972

**Kalecki, Michał.**    **4.1810**
Essays on developing economies / Michal Kalecki; with an introd. by Joan Robinson. — Hassocks, Eng.: Harvester Press; Atlantic Highlands, N.J.: Humanities Press, 1976. 208 p.: ill.; 23 cm. 1. Economic development — Addresses, essays, lectures. 2. Developing countries — Economic policy — Addresses, essays, lectures. I. T.
HC59.7.K24 1976    338.91    *LC* 75-40308    *ISBN* 0391005243

**Latham, A. J. H.**    **4.1811**
The international economy and the undeveloped world 1865–1914 / A. J. H. Latham. — London: Croom Helm; Totowa, N.J.: Rowman and Littlefield, 1978. 217 p.: ill.; 23 cm. Includes index. 1. International economic relations 2. Developing countries — Economic conditions I. T.
HC59.7.L322 1978    330.9/172/4    *LC* 79-303582    *ISBN* 0847660885

**Making the most of the least: alternative ways to development** /    **4.1812**
**edited by Leonard Berry and Robert W. Kates.**
New York: Holmes & Meier, 1980. xiv, 282 p.: ill.; 24 cm. Includes index. 1. International economic relations — Addresses, essays, lectures. 2. Developing countries — Economic policy — Addresses, essays, lectures. I. Berry, Leonard, 1930- II. Kates, Robert William.
HC59.7.M254 1980    338.91/172/4    *LC* 79-11619    *ISBN* 0841904340

**Mehmet, Ozay.**    **4.1813**
Economic planning and social justice in developing countries / Ozay Mehmet. — New York: St. Martin's Press, 1978. 282 p.; 23 cm. 1. Economic

development — Social aspects 2. Developing countries — Economic policy. I. T.
HC59.7.M427 1978    338.9/009172/4    *LC* 78-18797    *ISBN* 0312234430

**Morawetz, David.**          **4.1814**
Twenty–five years of economic development, 1950 to 1975 / David Morawetz. — Washington: World Bank, c1977. xi, 125 p.; 23 cm. 1. Economic development — History. 2. Developing countries — Economic conditions I. World Bank. II. T.
HC59.7.M578 1977b    330.9/172/4    *LC* 78-100218

**Morris, Morris David.**          **4.1815**
Measuring the condition of the world's poor: the physical quality of life index / Morris David Morris. — New York: Published for the Overseas Development Council [by] Pergamon Press, c1979. xiv, 176 p.: ill.; 24 cm. (Pergamon policy studies) 1. Poor — Developing countries 2. Economic indicators — Developing countries. 3. Social indicators — Developing countries I. Overseas Development Council. II. T. III. Title: Physical quality of life index.
HC59.7.M592 1979    330.9172/4 19    *LC* 79-16613    *ISBN* 0080238904

**Myrdal, Gunnar, 1898-.**          • **4.1816**
The challenge of world poverty: a world anti–poverty program in outline / with a foreword by Francis O. Wilcox. — New York: Pantheon Books [1970] xviii, 518 p.; 22 cm. (The Christian A. Herter lecture series [1969]) An outgrowth of the author's three lectures delivered at the Johns Hopkins University School of Advanced International Studies in Mar. 1969, and a continuation of the author's 3-v. work entitled Asian drama. 1. Economic assistance — Developing countries. I. T. II. Series.
HC59.7.M926    338.91/172/4    *LC* 78-79797

**Nafziger, E. Wayne.**          **4.1817**
The economics of developing countries / E. Wayne Nafziger. — Belmont, Calif.: Wadsworth Pub. Co., c1984. xvi, 496 p.: ill.; 24 cm. 1. Developing countries — Economic conditions 2. Income distribution — Developing countries 3. Economic development I. T.
HC59.7.N23 1984    330.9172/4 19    *LC* 83-12425    *ISBN* 0534029612

**Pearson, Charles S.**          **4.1818**
Environment, North and South: an economic interpretation / Charles Pearson, Anthony Pryor. — New York: Wiley, c1978. xxi, 355 p.: ill.; 26 cm. 'A Wiley-Interscience publication.' Includes index. 1. Environmental policy — Developing countries 2. Environmental policy 3. Economic development 4. International economic relations I. Pryor, Anthony, 1951- joint author. II. T.
HC59.7.P394    301.31/09172/4    *LC* 77-11143    *ISBN* 0471027413

**Redistribution with growth: policies to improve income**    **4.1819**
**distribution in developing countries in the context of economic growth: a joint study [commissioned] by the World Bank's Development Research Center and the Institute of Development Studies, University of Sussex / by Hollis Chenery ... [et al.].**
London: Published for the World Bank and the Institute of Development Studies, University of Sussex [by] Oxford University Press, 1974. xx, 304 p.: ill.; 24 cm. Synthesis of papers discussed at a workshop convened at the Rockefeller Foundation Conference Center in Bellagio, April, 1973, and at the Conference on Redistribution with Growth at the Institute of Development Studies, Sept., 1973. 1. Income distribution — Developing countries 2. Income distribution — Mathematical models 3. Developing countries — Economic policy. I. Chenery, Hollis Burnley. II. World Bank. Development Research Center. III. University of Sussex. Institute of Development Studies.
HC59.7.R365    338.91/172/4    *LC* 75-306757    *ISBN* 0199200696. *ISBN* 019920070X pbk

**Reynolds, Lloyd George, 1910-.**          **4.1820**
Economic growth in the Third World, 1850–1980 / Lloyd G. Reynolds. — New Haven: Yale University Press, c1985. xii, 469 p.; 25 cm. (Publication of the Economic Growth Center, Yale University.) Includes index. 1. Economic history — 1750-1918 2. Economic history — 1918- 3. Developing countries — Economic conditions I. T. II. Series.
HC59.7.R475 1985    338.9/009172/4 19    *LC* 84-19542    *ISBN* 0300032552

**Robinson, Joan, 1903-.**          **4.1821**
Aspects of development and underdevelopment / Joan Robinson. — Cambridge [Eng.]; New York: Cambridge University Press, 1979. x, 146 p.; 23 cm. (Modern Cambridge economics) 1. Economic development 2. Developing countries — Economic conditions I. T.
HC59.7.R56    330.9/172/4    *LC* 78-25610    *ISBN* 0521226376

**Streeten, Paul.**          **4.1822**
First things first: meeting basic human needs in the developing countries / Paul Streeten with Shahid Javed Burki ... [et al.]. — New York: Published for the World Bank [by] Oxford University Press, 1982 (c1981). xii, 206 p.; 23 cm.

Includes index. 1. Economic assistance — Developing countries. 2. Basic needs — Developing countries. 3. Developing countries — Economic policy. I. World Bank. II. T.
HC59.7.S859 1981    338.9/009172/4 19    *LC* 81-16836    *ISBN* 0195203682

**Uri, Pierre.**          **4.1823**
[Développement sans dépendance. English] Development without dependence / Pierre Uri; foreword by William P. Bundy. — New York: Praeger Publishers, 1976. xiii, 166 p.; 24 cm. (Praeger special studies in international economics and development) Translation of Développement sans dépendance. 'Published for the Atlantic Institute for International Affairs.' Includes index. 1. Economic development 2. International finance 3. Developing countries — Economic conditions I. Atlantic Institute for International Affairs. II. T.
HC59.7.U7713    382.1    *LC* 75-19829    *ISBN* 0275558304. *ISBN* 0275894703 pbk

**Woddis, Jack.**          • **4.1824**
An introduction to neo–colonialism. London, Lawrence & Wishart, 1967. 133 p. 18 1/2 cm. 1. States, New 2. World politics — 1945- 3. Developing countries — Colonial influence. I. T.
HC59.7.W6    309    *LC* 68-71402

**World development report.**          **4.1825**
1978-. [New York] Oxford University Press. v. 27 cm. Annual. Published for the World Bank. 1. Economic development — Periodicals. 2. Developing countries — Economic conditions — Periodicals. I. World Bank.
HC59.7.W659    330.9/172/4

**Beckford, George L.**          **4.1826**
Persistent poverty: underdevelopment in plantation economies of the Third World / George L. Beckford. — London: Zed Books; Totowa, N.J.: U.S. distributor, Biblio Distribution Center, c1983. xxv, 244 p.: ill.; 22 cm. (Third World studies.) 1. Poor — Developing countries 2. Agricultural laborers — Developing countries 3. Plantations — Developing countries. I. T. II. Series.
HC59.72.P6 B43 1983    338.1/09172/4 19    *LC* 85-149825    *ISBN* 0862322073

**Fransman, Martin.**          **4.1827**
Technology and economic development / Martin Fransman. — Boulder, Colo.: Westview Press, 1986. xi, 161 p.: ill.; 23 cm. Includes index. 1. Technological innovations — Developing countries 2. Developing countries — Economic policy. I. T.
HC59.72.T4 F7 1986    338.9/27/091724 19    *LC* 86-50429    *ISBN* 0813304180

**The Assault on world poverty: problems of rural development,**    **4.1828**
**education, and health / with a pref. by Robert S. McNamara.**
Baltimore: Published for the World Bank by the Johns Hopkins University Press, [1975] xi, 425 p.; 23 cm. 1. Economic assistance — Addresses, essays, lectures. 2. Agriculture — Economic aspects — Developing countries — Addresses, essays, lectures. 3. Education, Rural — Developing countries — Addresses, essays, lectures. 4. Medical care — Developing countries — Addresses, essays, lectures. I. World Bank.
HC60.A835    338.91/172/4    *LC* 75-7912    *ISBN* 0801817455. *ISBN* 0801817463 pbk

**Gran, Guy.**          **4.1829**
Development by people: citizen construction of a just world / by Guy Gran; foreword by Mary Racelis Hollnsteiner. — New York, N.Y.: Praeger, 1983. xxiv, 480 p.; 24 cm. Includes index. 1. Economic assistance 2. Economic assistance, American 3. Economic development projects 4. Community development 5. Rural development I. T.
HC60.G645 1983    338.9/009172/4 19    *LC* 82-22442    *ISBN* 0030632943

**Hoselitz, Berthold Frank, 1913- ed.**          • **4.1830**
The progress of underdeveloped areas. Chicago, University of Chicago Press [1952] x, 296 p. 1. Industrialization 2. Technical assistance I. T.
HC60 H67    *LC* 52-14480

**Ward, Barbara, 1914-.**          • **4.1831**
The rich nations and the poor nations. [1st ed.] New York: Norton, [1962] 159 p.; 22 cm. 1. Economic history 2. Economic development 3. Developing countries — Economic conditions I. T.
HC60.J28 1962    338.91    *LC* 62-11387

**Leontief, Wassily W., 1906-.**          **4.1832**
The future of the world economy: a United Nations study / by Wassily Leontief, et al. New York: Oxford University Press, 1977. vii, 110 p.; 29 cm. 1. Economic assistance 2. Economic development 3. Economic forecasting I. United Nations. II. T.
HC60.L443    338/.09    *LC* 77-72024    *ISBN* 0195022327

**Tendler, Judith.**    4.1833
Inside foreign aid / Judith Tendler. — Baltimore: Johns Hopkins University Press, [1975] viii, 140 p.; 24 cm. Includes index. 1. Economic assistance, American I. T.
HC60.T47    338.91/172/4073    *LC* 75-11353    *ISBN* 0801817315

**Sewell, James Patrick.**    4.1834
Functionalism and world politics: a study based on United Nations programs financing economic development / by James Patrick Sewell. — Princeton [N.J.]: Princeton University Press, 1966. xii, 359 p.: ill. 1. United Nations — Economic assistance 2. Development banks 3. Underdeveloped areas — Finance I. T.
HC60.U43 S4    *LC* 63-18650    *ISBN* 0691075085

**U.S. foreign assistance: investment or folly? / edited by John**    4.1835
**Wilhelm and Gerry Feinstein.**
New York: Praeger, 1984. ix, 398 p.: ill.; 25 cm. 1. Economic assistance, American 2. Military assistance, American 3. United States — Foreign relations — 20th century I. Wilhelm, John. II. Feinstein, Gerry. III. Title: US foreign assistance.
HC60.U532 1984    327.73 19    *LC* 84-15896    *ISBN* 0030005345

---

# HC79 Special Topics, A–Z

## HC79.C63 Consumer Policy

**Analysis of consumer policy.**    4.1836
Philadelphia, Pa.: Wharton Applied Research Center, [1981?] iii, 149 p.: ill.; 22 cm. 'Papers presented at the conference Analysis of Consumer Policy, May 18-19, 1981, Philadelphia Pa.' 'A distinguished panel of experts in economics and the social sciences analyzes public policy issues affecting consumers in the 1980's.' 1. Consumer protection 2. Consumers I. Wharton Applied Research Center.
HC79.C63 A53

## HC79.E5 Environmental Policy

**Baumol, William J.**    4.1837
Economics, environmental policy, and the quality of life / William J. Baumol, Wallace E. Oates, with major contributions by Sue Anne Batey Blackman. — Englewood Cliffs, N.J.: Prentice-Hall, c1979. vi, 377 p.: ill.; 24 cm. 1. Environmental policy 2. Economic policy I. Oates, Wallace E. joint author. II. Blackman, Sue Anne Batey. joint author. III. T.
HC79.E5 B374    301.31    *LC* 78-17933    *ISBN* 0132313650

**Divesting nature's capital: the political economy of**    4.1838
**environmental abuse in the Third World / editd by H. Jeffrey Leonard.**
New York: Holmes & Meier, 1985. 299 p.; 23 cm. 1. Environmental policy — Developing countries — Addresses, essays, lectures. 2. Developing countries — Economic policy — Addresses, essays, lectures. 3. Conservation of natural resources — Developing countries — Addresses, essays, lectures. I. Leonard, H. Jeffrey.
HC79.E5 D58 1985    363.7/009172/4 19    *LC* 83-18534    *ISBN* 0841908974

**Economics of environmental and natural resources policy /**    4.1839
**edited by J.A. Butlin.**
Boulder, Colo.: Westview Press, 1981. 206 p.: ill.; 25 cm. 1. Environmental policy — Addresses, essays, lectures. 2. Economic policy — Addresses, essays, lectures. 3. Conservation of natural resources — Addresses, essays, lectures. 4. Renewable natural resources — Addresses, essays, lectures. I. Butlin, J. A.
HC79.E5 E279    333.7 19    *LC* 80-54333    0865311900

**Environment, natural systems, and development: an economic**    4.1840
**valuation guide / Maynard M. Hufschmidt ... [et al.].**
Baltimore: Johns Hopkins University Press, c1983. xxii, 338 p.: ill.; 24 cm. Prepared by a team of experts assembled at the East-West Environment and Policy Institute. 1. Environmental policy — Cost effectiveness — Addresses, essays, lectures. 2. Economic development projects — Cost effectiveness — Addresses, essays, lectures. I. Hufschmidt, Maynard M. II. East-West Environment and Policy Institute (Honolulu, Hawaii)
HC79.E5 E573 1983    363.7/05 19    *LC* 82-17237    *ISBN* 0801829305

**Environmental improvement through economic incentives /**    4.1841
**Frederick R. Anderson ... [et al.].**
Baltimore: Published for Resources for the Future by Johns Hopkins University Press, c1977. xi, 195 p.; 24 cm. 1. Environmental policy 2. Pollution — Costs.

3. Pollution — Economic aspects I. Anderson, Frederick R. II. Resources for the Future.
HC79.E5 E578    301.31    *LC* 76-47400    *ISBN* 0801820006

**Freeman, A. Myrick, 1936-.**    4.1842
Air and water pollution control: a benefit–cost assessment / A. Myrick Freeman III. — New York: J. Wiley, c1982. xii, 186 p.: ill.; 24 cm. — (Environmental science and technology. 0194-0827) 'A Wiley-Interscience publication.' 1. Environmental policy — Cost effectiveness. 2. Air quality management — Cost effectiveness. 3. Water quality management — Cost effectiveness. I. T. II. Series.
HC79.E5 F697 1982    338.4/3363736/0973 19    *LC* 82-8409    *ISBN* 0471089850

**Freeman, A. Myrick, 1936-.**    4.1843
The benefits of environmental improvement: theory and practice / A. Myrick Freeman III. — Baltimore: Published for Resources for the Future by Johns Hopkins University Press, c1979. xiv, 272 p.: ill.; 24 cm. 1. Environmental policy — Cost effectiveness. I. Resources for the Future. II. T.
HC79.E5 F7    338.4/3    *LC* 78-20532    *ISBN* 0801821630

**Incentives for environmental protection / edited by Thomas C.**    4.1844
**Schelling.**
Cambridge, Mass.: MIT Press, c1983. xix, 355 p.; 24 cm. — (MIT Press series on the regulation of economic activity. 5) Includes index. 1. Environmental policy — Case studies. 2. Environmental protection — Economic aspects — Case studies. I. Schelling, Thomas C., 1921- II. Series.
HC79.E5 I513 1983    363.7 19    *LC* 82-4631    *ISBN* 0262192136

**Kneese, Allen V.**    4.1845
Environmental quality and residuals management: report of a research program on economic, technological, and institutional aspects / by Allen V. Kneese and Blair T. Bower. — Baltimore: Published for Resources for the Future by the Johns Hopkins University Press, c1979. xiv, 337 p.: ill.; 24 cm. Includes index. 1. Environmental policy 2. Pollution — Economic aspects 3. Waste products I. Bower, Blair T. joint author. II. Resources for the Future. III. T.
HC79.E5 K576    301.31    *LC* 79-2181    *ISBN* 0801822459

**Kneese, Allen V.**    4.1846
Measuring the benefits of clean air and water / Allen V. Kneese. — Washington, D.C.: Resources for the Future; [Baltimore, Md.]: Distributed by the Johns Hopkins University Press, c1984. xii, 159 p.: ill.; 23 cm. Includes index. 1. Environmental policy — Cost effectiveness. 2. Environmental protection — Cost effectiveness. 3. Air — Pollution — Economic aspects. 4. Water — Pollution — Economic aspects. I. T.
HC79.E5 K578 1984    338.4/33637392 19    *LC* 84-17899    *ISBN* 0915707098

**Milbrath, Lester W.**    4.1847
Environmentalists, vanguard for a new society / Lester W. Milbrath; with the advice and assistance of Barbara V. Fisher. — Albany: State University of New York Press, c1984. xv, 180 p.: ill.; 26 cm. (SUNY series in envirnonmental public policy) Includes index. 1. Environmental policy 2. Social change I. Fisher, Barbara V. II. T. III. Series.
HC79.E5 M47 1984    363.7 19    *LC* 83-24250    *ISBN* 087395887X

**Nichols, Albert L.**    4.1848
Targeting economic incentives for environmental protection / Albert L. Nichols. — Cambridge, Mass.: MIT Press, c1984. xvi, 189 p.: ill.; 24 cm. (MIT Press series on the regulation of economic activity. 8) Based on the author's thesis (doctoral), 1981. Includes index. 1. Environmental policy — Cost effectiveness. I. T. II. Series.
HC79.E5 N47 1984    338.4/33637 19    *LC* 83-24883    *ISBN* 0262140365

**Schnaiberg, Allan.**    4.1849
The environment, from surplus to scarcity / Allan Schaiberg. — New York: Oxford University Press, 1980. xiii, 464 p.; 23 cm. 1. Environmental policy 2. Environmental protection 3. Man — Influence on nature I. T.
HC79.E5 S29    301.31    *LC* 79-12439    *ISBN* 0195026101

**Centre for Housing, Building, and Planning (United Nations)**    4.1850
Human setlements: the environmental challenge / a compendium of United Nations papers prepared for the Stockholm Conference on the Human Environment, 1972. — [London]: Macmillan [for the] Centre for Housing, Building and Planning, United Nations Department of Economic and Social Affairs [1974] xvi, 209 p.; 22 cm. 1. Environmental policy — Addresses, essays, lectures. 2. Human settlements — Planning — Addresses, essays, lectures. I. United Nations. Conference on the Human Environment, Stockholm, 1972. II. T.
HC79.E5 U4 1974    301.31    *LC* 74-164526    *ISBN* 0333140710

**Watt, Kenneth E. F., 1929-.**      4.1851
Understanding the environment / Kenneth E.F. Watt. — Boston: Allyn and Bacon, c1982. xv, 431 p.: ill.; 24 cm. 1. Environmental policy 2. Human ecology 3. International economic relations I. T.
HC79.E5 W38 1982     333.7 19     *LC* 81-8050     *ISBN* 0205072658

### HC79.I5 Income

**Goldsmith, Raymond William, 1904-.**      4.1852
Comparative national balance sheets: a study of twenty countries, 1688–1978 / Raymond W. Goldsmith. — Chicago: University of Chicago Press, 1985. xvii, 353 p.; 24 cm. Includes index. 1. National income — Accounting I. T.
HC79.I5 G64 1985     339.3 19     *LC* 84-16277     *ISBN* 0226301532

**Income distribution and economic development: an analytical**      4.1853
**survey / Jacques Lecaillon ... [et al.].**
Geneva: International Labour Office, 1984. ix, 212 p.: ill.; 24 cm. (WEP study.) Includes index. 1. Income distribution 2. Economic development I. Lecaillon, Jacques. II. Series.
HC79.I5 I47 1984     339.2 19     *LC* 84-224880     *ISBN* 922103366X

**Usher, Dan, 1934-.**      • 4.1854
The price mechanism and the meaning of national income statistics. — Oxford: Clarendon P., 1968. xxiii, 180 p.: illus.; 23 cm. 1. National income — Accounting 2. National income — Thailand — Accounting. I. T.
HC79.I5 U7     339.3/593     *LC* 73-371203     *ISBN* 0198281595

### HC79.P55 Pollution

**Burrows, Paul.**      4.1855
The economic theory of pollution control / Paul Burrows. — 1st MIT Press ed. — Cambridge, Mass.: MIT Press, 1980. vi, 192 p.: graphs; 23 cm. Includes indexes. 1. Pollution — Economic aspects I. T.
HC79.P55 B87 1980     363.7/36     *LC* 79-56534     *ISBN* 0262520567

**Walter, Ingo.**      4.1856
International economics of pollution / Ingo Walter. — New York: Wiley, 1976 (c1975). 208 p.: graphs; 24 cm. 'A Halsted Press book.' 1. Pollution — Economic aspects 2. International economic relations 3. Environmental policy I. T.
HC79.P55 W3     301.31     *LC* 75-28273     *ISBN* 0470919280

### HC79.P6 Poverty

**Allen, Vernon L., 1933- comp.**      • 4.1857
Psychological factors in poverty. Edited by Vernon L. Allen. Chicago, Markham Pub. Co. [1970] viii, 392 p. 24 cm. (Institute for Research on Poverty monograph series.) 1. Poverty — Psychological aspects — Addresses, essays, lectures. 2. Poverty — Addresses, essays, lectures. I. T. II. Series.
HC79.P6 A56     339.4/6/019     *LC* 70-111978     *ISBN* 0841050031

**Galbraith, John Kenneth, 1908-.**      4.1858
The nature of mass poverty / John Kenneth Galbraith. — Cambridge, Mass.: Harvard University Press, 1979. viii, 150 p.; 22 cm. Cover title. Originally given as lectures at the Graduate Institute of International Studies, University of Geneva and at the Radcliffe Institute. 1. Poverty 2. Poor — Developing countries 3. Rural poor 4. Developing countries — Rural conditions. I. T.
HC79.P6 G34     339.4/6     *LC* 78-11839     *ISBN* 0674605330

**Lipton, Michael.**      4.1859
Why poor people stay poor: urban bias in world development / Michael Lipton. — Cambridge: Harvard University Press, 1977, c1976. 467 p.; 24 cm. Includes index. 1. Poor 2. Rural poor 3. Economic assistance, Domestic 4. Developing countries — Economic conditions I. T.
HC79.P6 L56 1977b     301.44/1     *LC* 76-23584     *ISBN* 0674952383

### HC79.T4 Technological Innovations

**Brown, Lawrence A., 1935-.**      4.1860
Innovation diffusion: a new perspective / Lawrence A. Brown. — London; New York: Methuen, 1981. xx, 345 p.: ill.; 23 cm. Includes index. 1. Technological innovations 2. Diffusion of innovations 3. Economic development I. T.
HC79.T4 B74 1981     338/.06 19     *LC* 80-49706     *ISBN* 041674270X

**The Diffusion of new industrial processes; an international**      4.1861
**study. Edited by L. Nabseth and G. F. Ray.**
Cambridge [Eng.] University Press [1974] xvii, 324 p. illus. 24 cm. (National Institute of Economic and Social Research. Economic and social studies, 29) Based on an inquiry initiated by the National Institute of Economic and Social Research in 1967. 1. Technological innovations — Addresses, essays, lectures. 2. Economic development — Addresses, essays, lectures. 3. Diffusion of innovations — Addresses, essays, lectures. 4. Manufacturing processes —

Addresses, essays, lectures. I. Nabseth, Lars, ed. II. Ray, G. F. (George Frank), 1915- ed. III. National Institute of Economic and Social Research.
HC79.T4 D53     338.4/5     *LC* 73-88309     *ISBN* 0521204305

**Freeman, Christopher.**      4.1862
Unemployment and technical innovation: a study of long waves and economic development / Christopher Freeman, John Clark, Luc Soete. — Westport, Conn.: Greenwood Press, 1982. xiii, 214 p.: ill.; 24 cm. Includes index. 1. Technological innovations 2. Unemployment 3. Economic development 4. Long waves (Economics) I. Clark, John, 1946- II. Soete, Luc. III. T.
HC79.T4 F74 1982     331.13/7042 19     *LC* 82-1113     *ISBN* 0313236011

**Kamien, Morton I.**      • 4.1863
Market structure and innovation / Morton I. Kamien and Nancy L. Schwartz. — Cambridge; New York: Cambridge University Press, 1982. xi, 241 p.; 22 cm. — (Cambridge surveys of economic literature.) Includes indexes. 1. Technological innovations 2. Industrial organization (Economic theory) I. Schwartz, Nancy Lou. II. T. III. Series.
HC79.T4 K3     338 19     *LC* 81-12254     *ISBN* 0521293855

**Rosenberg, Nathan, 1927-.**      4.1864
Inside the black box: technology and economics / Nathan Rosenberg. — Cambridge [Cambridgeshire]; New York: Cambridge University Press, 1983 (c1982). xi, 304 p.; 24 cm. Includes index. 1. Technological innovations 2. Technology — Social aspects 3. Economic development I. T.
HC79.T4 R673     338/.06 19     *LC* 82-4563     *ISBN* 0521248086

# HC80–710 Economic History, By Country

## HC95–110 North America: General. United States

**Smith, Joseph Russell, 1874-.**      • 4.1865
North America, its people and the resources, development, and prospects of the continent as the home of man [by] J. Russell Smith...[and] M. Ogden Phillips... New York: Harcourt, Brace and company, [1942] xii p. 1., 1016 p.: incl. illus., tables, diagrs. maps (1 fold., in pocket); 24 cm. Map on lining-papers. 1. North America — Economic conditions. I. Phillips, Merton Ogden, 1900- II. T.
HC95.S5 1942     *LC* 42-10344

**The Economic almanac for 1940-.**      • 4.1866
A handbook of useful facts about business, labor and government in the United States and other areas. — New York city: The Conference board, National industrial conference board, [1940]-. v.    : tables.; 21 cm. On cover, 1940-: Conference board business fact book. 1. Economic history — Yearbooks. 2. Statistics — Yearbooks. 3. United States — Economic conditions — Yearbooks. I. National Industrial Conference Board. II. T. III. Title: The conference board business fact book.
HC101.E38     330.58     *LC* 40-30704

**Levinson, Harry.**      4.1867
CEO: corporate leadership in action / Harry Levinson and Stuart Rosenthal. — New York: Basic Books, c1984. viii, 308 p.; 24 cm. Includes index. 1. Executives — United States — Biography. 2. Leadership — United States — Case studies. I. Rosenthal, Stuart, 1934- II. T. III. Title: C.E.O.
HC102.5.A2 L48 1984     658.4/2/0926 19     *LC* 83-46085     *ISBN* 0465007902

## HC103 Comprehensive Works

### HC103 A–E

**Andreano, Ralph L., 1929- ed.**      • 4.1868
New views on American economic development; a selective anthology of recent work. Edited, compiled, and with introductions by Ralph L. Andreano. — Cambridge, Mass., Schenkman Pub. Co. [c1965] x, 434 p. illus. 24 cm. Bibliographical footnotes. 1. U.S. — Econ. condit. 2. Economics — Hist. — U.S. I. T.
HC103.A5     330.973     *LC* 65-20307

**Approaches to American economic history. Edited by George** • 4.1869
**Rogers Taylor and Lucius F. Ellsworth.**
Charlottesville: Published for the Eleutherian Mills-Hagley Foundation [by]
the University Press of Virginia, [1971] xiv, 135 p.; 24 cm. Revised papers of a
seminar sponsored by the History Dept. of the University of Delaware and the
Eleutherian Mills-Hagley Foundation, held in the autumn of 1968. 1. United
States — Economic conditions — Congresses. I. Taylor, George Rogers, 1895-
ed. II. Ellsworth, Lucius F. ed. III. Eleutherian Mills-Hagley Foundation.
IV. Delaware. University, Newark. Dept. of History.
HC103.A74    330.973    LC 74-158808

**Cochran, Thomas Childs, 1902-.** • 4.1870
The age of enterprise; a social history of industrial America, by Thomas C.
Cochran and William Miller. Rev. ed. New York, Harper [1961] 396 p. 21 cm.
(Harper torchbooks. The Academy library, TB1054) 1. United States —
Economic conditions 2. United States — Social conditions I. Miller, William,
1912- joint author. II. T.
HC103.C6 1961    330.973    LC 61-66444

**Davis, Lance Edwin.** • 4.1871
Institutional change and American economic growth, by Lance E. Davis and
Douglass C. North. With the assistance of Calla Smorodin. — Cambridge
[Eng.]: University Press, 1971. viii, 282 p.; 24 cm. 1. U.S. — Economic
conditions. 2. U.S. — Economic conditions — Mathematical models.
I. North, Douglass Cecil. joint author. II. Smorodin, Calla, joint author.
III. T.
HC103.D36    301.5/1    LC 70-155584    ISBN 0521081114

**A Documentary history of American industrial society, edited** • 4.1872
**by John R. Commons, Ulrich B. Phillips, Eugene A. Gilmore,**
**Helen L. Sumner, and John B. Andrews. With pref. by Richard**
**T. Ely and introd. by John B. Clark.**
New York: Russell & Russell, 1958. 10 v.: ports., diagr., facsims., tables.; 25 cm.
'Prepared under the auspices of the American Bureau of Industrial Research
with the co-operation of the Carnegie Institution of Washington.' 1. Labor and
laboring classes — United States 2. United States — Economic conditions
I. Commons, John Rogers, 1862-1945.
HC103.D63 1958    330.973    LC 58-7086

**Dowd, Douglas Fitzgerald, 1919-.** 4.1873
The twisted dream: capitalist development in the United States since 1776 [by]
Douglas F. Dowd. [Cambridge, Mass.: Winthrop Publishers, [1974] xvii,
315 p.; 23 cm. 1. United States — Economic conditions I. T.
HC103.D75 1974    330.9/73    LC 73-16418    ISBN 0876268823

**Nettels, Curtis Putnam.** 4.1874
The emergence of a national economy, 1775-1815. New York, Holt, Rinehart
and Winston [1962] xvi, 424 p. illus., ports., maps, tables. 24 cm. 1. United
States — Economic conditions. I. T.
HC103.E25 vol. 2    LC 62-9523

**Gates, Paul Wallace, 1901-.** • 4.1875
The farmer's age: agriculture, 1815–1860. — New York, Holt, Rinehart and
Winston [1960] xviii, 460 p. illus., maps, facsims., tables. 24 cm. — (The
Economic history of the United States, v. 3) Bibliography: p. 421-439.
1. Agriculture — Economic aspects — U.S. I. T. II. Series.
HC103.E25 vol. 3    338.10973    LC 60-5170

**Taylor, George Rogers, 1895-.** • 4.1876
The transportation revolution, 1815–1860. New York, Rinehart [1951] xvii,
490 p. illus., ports., maps. 24 cm. (The Economic history of the United States, v.
4) Bibliography: p. 390-438. 1. Transportation — United States — History.
2. United States — Economic conditions I. T. II. Series.
HC103.E25 vol. 4    385.09    LC 51-14038

**Shannon, Fred A.** 4.1877
Farmers' last frontier. — See full entry at HD1765 1860.S5 1977. I. T.

**Kirkland, Edward Chase, 1894-.** • 4.1878
Industry comes of age; business, labor, and public policy, 1860–1897. New
York, Holt, Rinehart and Winston [1961] xiv, 445 p. illus., ports. 24 cm. (The
Economic history of the United States, v. 6) 'Bibliographical notes': p. 410-436.
1. United States — Economic conditions I. T. II. Series.
HC103.E25 vol. 6    330.973    LC 61-9816

**Faulkner, Harold Underwood, 1890-1968.** • 4.1879
The decline of laissez faire, 1897–1917. New York, Rinehart [1951] xiv, 433 p.
illus., ports. 24 cm. (The Economic history of the United States, v. 7)
Bibliography: p. 383-411. 1. United States — Economic conditions I. T.
II. Series.
HC103.E25 vol. 7    330.973    LC 51-5244

**Soule, George Henry, 1887-1970.** • 4.1880
Prosperity decade; from war to depression: 1917–1929. New York, Rinehart
[1947] xiv, 365 p. plates, ports. 24 cm. (The economic history of the United

States, v. 8) 'For further reading': p. 336-352. 1. United States — Economic
conditions — 1918- I. T. II. Series.
HC103.E25 vol. 8    330.973    LC 47-5631 *

**Mitchell, Broadus, 1892-.** • 4.1881
Depression decade; from New Era through New Deal, 1929–1941. New York,
Rinehart [1947] xviii, 462 p. illus. 24 cm. (The Economic history of the United
States, v. 9) 1. Depression — 1929 — United States. 2. New Deal, 1933-1939
3. United States — Economic conditions — 1918-1945 I. T. II. Series.
HC103.E25 vol. 9    330.973    LC 47-12331

**Encyclopedia of American economic history: studies of the** 4.1882
**principal movements and ideas / Glenn Porter, editor.**
New York: Scribner, 1980 (c1979). 3 v. (xii, 1286 p.); 29 cm. 1. United States
— Economic conditions — Addresses, essays, lectures. I. Porter, Glenn.
HC103.E52    330.9/73    LC 79-4946    ISBN 0684162717

## HC103 F–Z

**Faulkner, Harold Underwood, 1890-1968.** 4.1883
American economic history: a comprehensive revision of the earlier work by
Harold Underwood Faulkner / Harry N. Scheiber, Harold G. Vatter, Harold
Underwood Faulkner. [9th ed.]. — New York: Harper & Row, c1976. viii,
514 p.: ill.; 27 cm. Includes index. 1. United States — Economic conditions
I. Scheiber, Harry N. II. Vatter, Harold G. III. T.
HC103.F3 1976    330.9/73    LC 76-16126    ISBN 0060420014

**Fogel, Robert William. comp.** • 4.1884
The reinterpretation of American economic history. Edited by Robert William
Fogel and Stanley L. Engerman. — [1st ed.]. — New York: Harper & Row,
[1971] xxiv, 494 p.: illus., maps.; 27 cm. 1. U.S. — Economic conditions —
Addresses, essays, lectures. I. Engerman, Stanley L. joint comp. II. T.
HC103.F58    330.973    LC 75-141166    ISBN 0060421096

**Groner, Alex.** 4.1885
The American heritage history of American business & industry, by Alex
Groner and the editors of American heritage and Business week. Introd. by
Paul A. Samuelson. — New York: American Heritage Pub. Co., [1972] 384 p.:
illus.; 29 cm. On spine: The history of American business & industry. 1. United
States — Industries — History 2. United States — Economic conditions
I. American heritage. II. Business week (New York) III. T. IV. Title: The
history of American business & industry.
HC103.G797    330.9/73    LC 72-80699    ISBN 0070011567

**Hacker, Louis Morton, 1899-.** • 4.1886
The course of American economic growth and development [by] Louis M.
Hacker. — New York: Wiley, [1970] xxvi, 382 p.; 23 cm. — (The Wiley series in
American economic history) 1. U.S. — Economic conditions. I. T.
HC103.H1455    330.973    LC 75-105384    ISBN 0471338400

**Hacker, Louis Morton, 1899-.** • 4.1887
The triumph of American capitalism: the development of forces in American
history to the end of the nineteenth century / by Louis M. Hacker. — New
York: Columbia University Press, 1946. x, 460 p.; 24 cm. 1. Capitalism
2. United States — History 3. United States — Economic policy 4. United
States — Industries I. T.
HC103.H146 1946    LC 47-3113

**Harris, Seymour Edwin, 1897-.** • 4.1888
American economic history. New York, McGraw-Hill, 1961. 560 p. illus. 24
cm. Includes bibliography. 1. United States — Economic conditions I. T.
HC103.H22    330.973    LC 60-11957

**Kirkland, Edward Chase, 1894-.** • 4.1889
A history of American economic life, [by] Edward C. Kirkland. — 4th ed. —
New York: Appleton-Century-Crofts, [1969] xii, 623 p.; 24 cm. 1. U.S. —
Economic conditions. I. T. II. Title: American economic life.
HC103.K5 1969    330.973    LC 69-13070    ISBN 0390513318

**Kuznets, Simon Smith, 1901-.** • 4.1890
Income & wealth of the United States: trends and structure / papers by Simon
Kuznets & Raymond Goldsmith; edited by Simon Kuznets. — Cambridge:
Bowes & Bowes, 1952. 328 p.: tables; 22 cm. — (International Association for
Research in Income and Wealth. Income and Wealth) 1. Income — United
States. 2. Wealth — United States. 3. United States — Economic conditions
I. T. II. Series.
HC103.K78    LC 53-2064

**Larsen, Henrietta Melia.** 4.1891
Guide to business history: materials for the study of American business history
and suggestions for their use / index by Elsie Hight Bishop. Boston: J.S.
Canner, 1964. xxvi, 1181 p. — (Harvard studies in business history. 12.)
1. United States — Industry — History. I. T. II. Series.
HC103.L3

**Letwin, William. ed.**    • **4.1892**
A documentary history of American economic policy since 1789. Edinburgh, University Press [1962, c1961] 406 p.; 22 cm. 1. United States — Economic policy — Collections 2. United States — Economic conditions — Collections I. T. II. Title: American economic policy since 1789
HC103 L37 1962    *LC* 63-1785

**McLaughlin, Glenn Everett.**    • **4.1893**
Growth of American manufacturing areas; a comparative analysis with special emphasis on trends in the Pittsburgh district, by Glenn E. McLaughlin. Westport, Conn., Greenwood Press [1970, c1938] xxvii, 358 p. illus., maps. 23 cm. 1. United States — Manufactures 2. United States — Industries 3. Pittsburgh (Pa.) — Industries. 4. United States — Population 5. Pittsburgh (Pa.) — Population. I. T.
HC103.M33 1970    338/.0973    *LC* 75-98853    *ISBN* 0837128951

**Myers, Gustavus, 1872-1942.**    • **4.1894**
History of the great American fortunes, by Gustavus Myers. New York, The Modern library [c1936] 2 p. l., 7-732 p. 21 cm. (Half-title: The Modern library of the world's best books) 'First Modern library edition, 1936.' 'This edition ... is ... an entirely new book.'—Publishers' note. Previously published in three volumes. 1. Wealth — United States. 2. United States — Economic conditions I. T.
HC103.M8 1936    339.2    *LC* 36-31209

**North, Douglass Cecil.**    • **4.1895**
Growth and welfare in the American past; a new economic history [by] Douglass C. North. — Englewood Cliffs, N.J.: Prentice-Hall, [1966] xiv, 199 p.: illus.; 21 cm. 1. United States — Economic conditions I. T.
HC103.N6    330.973    *LC* 66-17371

**Strassmann, W. Paul (Wolfgang Paul), 1926-.**    • **4.1896**
Risk and technological innovation; American manufacturing methods during the nineteenth century. Ithaca, N. Y., Cornell University Press [1959] 249 p. 23 cm. Issued also in microfilm form in 1956 as thesis, University of Maryland, under title: Risk and technological innovation in producers' goods. Includes bibliography. 1. Technological innovation. 2. Risk — United States. 3. United States — Industries I. T.
HC103.S85 1959    338.0183    *LC* 59-9831

## HC103.7 Natural Resources

**Ciriacy-Wantrup, S. V. (Siegfried V.), 1906-1980.**    • **4.1897**
Resource conservation: economics and policies. Rev. ed. [Berkeley] University of California, Division of Agricultural Sciences, Agricultural Experiment Station, 1963. 395 p.; 25 cm. 1. Natural resources — United States I. T.
HC103.7 C5 1963

**Current issues in natural resource policy / edited by Paul R.**    **4.1898**
**Portney with the assistance of Ruth B. Haas; contributors, Lee G. Anderson ... [et al.].**
Washington, D.C.: Resources for the Future; Baltimore: Distributed by the Johns Hopkins University Press, c1982. xiii, 300 p.; 24 cm. 1. Natural resources — Government policy — United States — Addresses, essays, lectures. I. Portney, Paul R. II. Haas, Ruth B. III. Anderson, Lee G. IV. Resources for the Future.
HC103.7.C87 1982    333.7/0973 19    *LC* 82-47982    *ISBN* 080182916X

**Hamrin, Robert D.**    **4.1899**
A renewable resource economy / by Robert D. Hamrin. — New York: Praeger, 1983. xi, 174 p.; 24 cm. 1. Renewable natural resources — Government policy — United States. 2. Conservation of natural resources — Government policy — United States. I. T.
HC103.7.H25 1983    333.7 19    *LC* 83-17820    *ISBN* 0030637538

**Hays, Samuel P.**    • **4.1900**
Conservation and the gospel of efficiency; the progressive conservation movement, 1890-1920. — Cambridge: Harvard University Press, 1959. 297 p.; 21 cm. — (Harvard historical monographs. 40) 1. Conservation of natural resources — United States — History. 2. Environmental policy — United States — History. I. T. II. Series.
HC103.7.H3    333.720973    *LC* 59-9274

**Highsmith, Richard Morgan, 1920-.**    • **4.1901**
Conservation in the United States / by Richard M. Highsmith, Jr., J. Granville Jensen [and] Robert D. Rudd. — Chicago, Rand McNally [1962] 322 p.: ill.; 26 cm. (Rand McNally geography series) 1. Natural resources — United States I. T. II. Series.
HC103.7.H5    *LC* 62-8299

**Krutilla, John V.**    **4.1902**
The economics of natural environments: studies in the valuation of commodity and amenity resources / John V. Krutilla, Anthony C. Fisher. — Baltimore:

Published for Resources for the Future, inc. by the Johns Hopkins University Press, [1975] xviii, 292 p.: ill.; 23 cm. 'Represents a synthesis of selected work undertaken in the Natural Environments Program at Resources for the Future.' 1. Natural resources — United States 2. Natural resources — Valuation — United States. 3. United States — Public lands I. Fisher, Anthony C. joint author. II. Resources for the Future. III. T.
HC103.7.K78    333.7    *LC* 74-24400    *ISBN* 0801816998

**Stroup, Richard.**    **4.1903**
Natural resources: bureaucratic myths and environmental management / by Richard L. Stroup and John A. Baden, with the assistance of David T. Fractor; foreword by William A. Niskanen. — San Francisco, Calif.: Pacific Institute for Public Policy Research; Cambridge, Mass.: Ballinger, c1983. xvi, 148 p.; 24 cm. — (Pacific studies in public policy.) Includes index. 1. Conservation of natural resources — United States — Decision making. 2. Conservation of natural resources — Government policy — United States. 3. Environmental protection — United States — Decision making. 4. Environmental policy — United States. I. Baden, John. II. Fractor, David T. III. T. IV. Series.
HC103.7.S84 1983    333.7/0973 19    *LC* 83-2607    *ISBN* 0884103803

# HC104–106.6 U.S. Economic History, by Period

## HC104–105 COLONIAL TO 1900

**Jones, Alice Hanson, 1904-.**    **4.1904**
Wealth of a nation to be: the American colonies on the eve of the Revolution / Alice Hanson Jones. — New York: Columbia University Press, 1980. xxxvi, 494 p.: ill.; 24 cm. Includes indexes. 1. Wealth — United States — History. 2. United States — Economic conditions — To 1865 I. T.
HC104.J67    330.973/027    *LC* 79-28543    *ISBN* 0231036590

**Perkins, Edwin J.**    **4.1905**
The economy of colonial America / Edwin J. Perkins. — New York: Columbia University Press, 1980. xii, 177 p.: map; 22 cm. 1. United States — Economic conditions — To 1865 I. T.
HC104.P47    330.973/02    *LC* 80-16478    *ISBN* 0231049587

**Cochran, Thomas Childs, 1902-.**    **4.1906**
Frontiers of change: early industrialism in America / Thomas C. Cochran. — New York: Oxford University Press, 1981. 179 p.; 22 cm. Includes index. 1. Technological innovations — United States — History. 2. United States — Economic conditions — To 1865 3. United States — Industries — History 4. United States — Social conditions — To 1865 I. T.
HC105.C64    338.0973 19    *LC* 80-20788    *ISBN* 0195028759

**East, Robert Abraham, 1909-.**    • **4.1907**
Business enterprise in the American Revolutionary Era. — New York: AMS Press, [1969] 387 p.; 23 cm. — (Columbia University studies in the social sciences, 439) Reprint of the 1938 ed. 1. United States — Economic conditions — To 1865 2. United States — Commerce — History 3. United States — History — Revolution, 1775-1783 I. T.
HC105.E24 1969    330.973    *LC* 78-94923

**Grant, H. Roger, 1943-.**    **4.1908**
Self-help in the 1890s depression / H. Roger Grant. — 1st ed. — Ames: Iowa State University Press, 1983. xii, 163 p.: ill.; 21 cm. 1. Depressions — 1893 — United States. 2. Self-help groups — United States — History. 3. United States — Economic conditions — 1865-1918 I. T.
HC105.G82 1983    973.8/7 19    *LC* 82-13054    *ISBN* 0813816343

**Hamilton, Alexander, 1757-1804.**    • **4.1909**
Papers on public credit, commerce and finance / edited by Samuel McKee, Jr.; with an introduction by J. Harvie Williams. — New York: Liberal Arts Press, c1957. xiv, 304 p.; 21 cm. — (The American heritage series; no. 18.) 1. Finance, Public — United States — 1789-1800 2. Debts, Public — United States. 3. Credit — United States. 4. United States — Manufactures 5. United States — Commerce 6. United States — Politics & government — 1783-1809. I. McKee, Samuel. II. T. III. Title: Papers on public credit, commerce and finance.
HC105.H18    *LC* 57-1957

**Hays, Samuel P.**    • **4.1910**
The response to industrialism, 1885–1914. — [Chicago]: University of Chicago Press, [1957] 210 p.; 21 cm. — (The Chicago history of American civilization) 1. United States — Economic conditions — 1865-1918 2. United States — Social conditions — 1865-1918 I. T.
HC105.H35    330.973    *LC* 57-6981

**Hoffmann, Charles, 1921-.**    • **4.1911**
The depression of the nineties; an economic history. — Westport, Conn.: Greenwood Pub. Corp., [1970] lvi, 326 p.; 22 cm. — (Contributions in economics and economic history, no. 2) Originally published as the author's

thesis—Columbia University, 1954. 1. Depressions — 1893. 2. United States — Economic conditions — 1865-1918 I. T.
HC105.H8 1970    338.54    *LC* 78-90790    *ISBN* 0837118557

**Kirkland, Edward Chase, 1894-.**                • **4.1912**
Dream and thought in the business community, 1860–1900. Ithaca, N. Y., Cornell University Press [1956] 175 p. 23 cm. 1. Businessmen — United States. 2. United States — Industries I. T.
HC105.K633    338    *LC* 56-14414

**North, Douglass Cecil.**                • **4.1913**
The economic growth of the United States, 1790–1860. — Englewood Cliffs, N.J.: Prentice-Hall, 1961. 304 p.: illus.; 22 cm. 1. United States — Economic conditions — To 1865 I. T.
HC105.N6    330.973    *LC* 61-6358

**Pred, Allan Richard, 1936-.**                • **4.1914**
The spatial dynamics of U.S. urban–industrial growth, 1800–1914; interpretive and theoretical essays [by] Allan R. Pred. Cambridge, Mass., M.I.T. Press [1966] x, 225 p. illus., maps. 25 cm. (The Regional science studies series 6) 1. Cities and towns — Growth 2. Cities and towns — United States. 3. United States — Industry — History. I. T. II. Series.
HC105.P94    301.364    *LC* 66-26016

**Smith, Walter Buckingham.**                • **4.1915**
Fluctuations in American business, 1790–1860, by Walter Buckingham Smith and Arthur Harrison Cole. — New York: Russell & Russell, [1969, c1935] xxix, 195 p.: illus.; 28 cm. — (Harvard economic studies. v. 50) 1. Prices — U.S. — History. 2. U.S. — Economic conditions — To 1865. I. Cole, Arthur Harrison, 1889- joint author. II. T. III. Series.
HC105.S65 1969    330.973    *LC* 68-27088

**Tarbell, Ida M. (Ida Minerva), 1857-1944.**                • **4.1916**
The nationalizing of business, 1878–1898, by Ida M. Tarbell. — New York: The Macmillan company, 1936. xvi p., 1 l., 313 p.: front., plates (1 double) ports.; 22 cm. — (A History of American life, vol. IX) Illustrated lining-papers. 'Critical essays on authorities': p. 278-293. 1. Trusts, Industrial — United States 2. Monopolies — United States. 3. United States — Industry — History. I. T.
HC105.T3x.1.H67 vol. 9    *LC* 36-28986

**Temin, Peter.**                • **4.1917**
The Jacksonian economy. [1st ed.] New York, Norton [1969] 208 p. 21 cm. (The Norton essays in American history) 1. Jackson, Andrew, 1767-1845. 2. Depressions — 1836-1837 — United States 3. United States — Economic conditions — To 1865 I. T.
HC105.T4    330.973    *LC* 69-18099

**Williams, William Appleman.**                • **4.1918**
The roots of the modern American empire; a study of the growth and shaping of social consciousness in a marketplace society. — New York: Random House, [1969] xxiv, 547 p.; 25 cm. 1. U.S. — Economic conditions — 1865-1918. 2. U.S. — History — 1865-1898. I. T.
HC105.W54    330.973    *LC* 77-85619

**Andreano, Ralph L., 1929- ed.**                • **4.1919**
The economic impact of the American Civil War, edited by Ralph Andreano. — Cambridge [Mass.] Schenkman Pub. Co., 1962. 203 p. illus. 22 cm. Includes bibliography. 1. United States — Hist. — Civil War — Economic aspects. I. T.
HC105.6.A5    330.973    *LC* 62-53140 rev 2

**Conference on American Economic Institutional Change, 1850-1873, and the Impact of the Civil War, Greenville, Del., 1964.**                • **4.1920**
Economic change in the Civil War era; proceedings. Edited by David T. Gilchrist & W. David Lewis. Greenville, Del., Eleutherian Mills-Hagley Foundation, 1965. ix, 180 p. fold. map. 24 cm. Sponsored by the Eleutherian Mills-Hagley Foundation. Bibliographical footnotes. 1. United States — Econ. condit. 2. United States — Hist. — 1849-1877. I. Gilchrist, David T., ed. II. Lewis, W. David (Walter David), 1931- ed. III. Eleutherian Mills-Hagley Foundation. IV. T.
HC105.6.C6 1964    330.973    *LC* 65-19018

**Fite, Emerson David, 1874-1953.**                • **4.1921**
Social and industrial conditions in the North during the Civil War. New York, Ungar [1963] 318 p. 22 cm. (American classics) 1. United States — Economic conditions — To 1865 2. United States — Social conditions — To 1865 3. United States — History — Civil War, 1861-1865 — Economic aspects. I. T.
HC105.6.F6 1963    330.973    *LC* 62-22259

**Gates, Paul Wallace, 1901-.**                • **4.1922**
Agriculture and the Civil War, by Paul W. Gates. — [1st ed.]. — New York, Knopf, 1965. x, 383, xiii p. illus., facsims., maps (1 fold.) ports. 25 cm. — (Impact of the Civil War.) Includes bibliographical references. 1. U.S. — Hist. — Civil War — Economic aspects. 2. Agriculture — Economic aspects — U.S. I. T. II. Series.
HC105.6.G3    973.71    *LC* 65-13461

**Higgs, Robert.**                • **4.1923**
The transformation of the American economy, 1865–1914; an essay in interpretation. — New York: Wiley, [1971] xv, 143 p.: illus.; 24 cm. — (The Wiley series in American economic history) 1. U.S. — Economic conditions — 1865-1918. I. T.
HC105.6.H53    330.973/08    *LC* 74-165949    *ISBN* 0471390038

**Nevins, Allan, 1890-1971.**                • **4.1924**
The emergence of modern America, 1865–1878. New York, Macmillan. — St. Clair Shores, Mich.: Scholarly Press, [1972? c1927] xix, 446 p.: illus.; 21 cm. — (History of American life. v. 8) 1. U.S. — Economic conditions — 1865-1918. 2. U.S. — Social conditions — 1865-1918. 3. U.S. — Civilization — 1865-1918. I. T. II. Series.
HC105.6.N45 1972    917.3/03/8    *LC* 77-145207    *ISBN* 0403011272

**Massey, Mary Elizabeth.**                • **4.1925**
Ersatz in the Confederacy. Columbia, University of South Carolina Press, 1952. xii, 233 p. illus. 24 cm. 1. Confederate States of America — Economic conditions I. T.
HC105.65.M3    *LC* 52-13204

**Seip, Terry L.**                **4.1926**
The South returns to Congress: men, economic measures, and intersectional relationships, 1868–1879 / Terry L. Seip. — Baton Rouge: Louisiana State University Press, c1983. xii, 322 p.; 24 cm. Includes index. 1. United States. Congress — History. 2. Legislators — Southern States — History. 3. Reconstruction 4. Sectionalism (United States) 5. United States — Economic policy — To 1933 6. United States — Politics and government — 1865-1877 I. T.
HC105.7.S44 1983    328.73/073/0975 19    *LC* 82-4654    *ISBN* 0807110523

## HC106–106.2 1901–1918

**Adams, Walter, 1922 Aug. 27- ed.**                • **4.1927**
The structure of American industry. 4th ed. New York, Macmillan [1971] viii, 502 p. illus. 24 cm. 1. United States — Industries — Addresses, essays, lectures. I. T.
HC106.A34 1971    338.6/0973    *LC* 79-130019

**Alexandersson, Gunnar.**                • **4.1928**
The industrial structure of American cities; a geographic study of urban economy in the United States. Lincoln, University of Nebraska Press [1956] 133 p. maps (part fold., part col.) diagrs., tables. 1. United States — Industries I. T.
HC106 A385    *LC* 56-7647

**Berle, Adolf Augustus, 1895-1971.**                • **4.1929**
Power without property; a new development in American political economy. — [1st ed.]. — New York: Harcourt, Brace, [1959] 184 p.; 22 cm. 1. United States — Economic conditions — 1918-1945 I. T.
HC106.B44    330.973    *LC* 59-11771

**Brandeis, Louis Dembitz, 1856-1941.**                • **4.1930**
Business: a profession. — New York: A. M. Kelley, 1971. lvi, 327 p.: port.; 22 cm. — (Reprints of economic classics) Reprint of the 1914 ed. 1. Business 2. U.S. — Economic conditions. I. T.
HC106.B7 1971    330.973/091    *LC* 68-55491    *ISBN* 0678008558

**Chamberlain, John, 1903-.**                **4.1931**
The enterprising Americans: a business history of the United States. — New and updated ed. — New York: Harper & Row, [1974] xix, 282 p.: illus.; 24 cm. 1. United States — Economic conditions I. T.
HC106.C52 1974    330.9/73    *LC* 73-4069    *ISBN* 0060107022

**Cochran, Thomas Childs, 1902-.**                • **4.1932**
American business in the twentieth century [by] Thomas C. Cochran. — Cambridge: Harvard University Press, 1972. vi, 259 p.; 22 cm. 1. United States — Economic conditions I. T.
HC106.C6315    330.9/73/09    *LC* 72-78424    *ISBN* 0674021010

**Cochran, Thomas Childs, 1902-.**                • **4.1933**
The American business system: a historical perspective, 1900–1955. — Cambridge: Harvard University Press, 1957. viii, 227 p.; 22 cm. — (The Library of Congress series in American civilization) 1. United States — Economic conditions I. T. II. Series.
HC106.C638    330.973    *LC* 57-12964

**Denison, Edward Fulton, 1915-.**                • **4.1934**
The sources of economic growth in the United States and the alternatives before us. — [New York]: Committee for Economic Development, [1962] 297 p.: diagrs., tables; 26 cm. — (Committee for Economic Development. Supplementary paper no. 13) 1. United States — Economic conditions 2. United States — Economic conditions — 1945- I. T.
HC106.D48    330.973    *LC* 61-18717

**Galbraith, John Kenneth, 1908-.** • **4.1935**
Economics & the art of controversy / John Kenneth Galbraith. — New Brunswick: Rutgers University Press, 1955. ix, 111 p.; 20 cm. — (Brown & Haley lectures; 1954.) 1. Economics 2. United States — Economic policy I. T. II. Series.
HC106.G28      *LC* 55-6103

**Glover, John Desmond.** • **4.1936**
The attack on big business. — Boston, Division of Research, Graduate School of Business Administration, Harvard University, 1954. 375 p. 22 cm. 1. Big business — United States. I. T.
HC106.G56      338.7      *LC* 54-11415

**Harvard University. Harvard Economic Research Project.** • **4.1937**
Studies in the structure of the American economy: theoretical and empirical explorations in input–output analysis / by Wassily Leontief ...[et al]. — New York: Oxford University Press, 1953. x, 561 p.: maps, diagrs., tables (4 fold. in pocket); 25 cm. 1. Input-output analysis 2. United States — Economic conditions — 1918-1945 3. United States — Industries I. Leontief, Wassily W., 1906- II. T.
HC106.H34      330.72      *LC* 52-6167

**Kolko, Gabriel.** • **4.1938**
The triumph of conservatism; a re–interpretation of American history, 1900–1916. — [New York]: Free Press of Glencoe, [c1963] 344 p.; 22 cm. 1. Business and politics — United States. 2. Progressivism (U.S. politics) 3. United States — Economic conditions — 1865-1918 I. T.
HC106.K77      338.973      *LC* 63-16588

**Stein, Herbert, 1916-.** **4.1939**
Presidential economics: the making of economic policy from Roosevelt to Reagan and beyond / Herbert Stein. — New York: Simon and Schuster, c1984. 414 p.: ill.; 23 cm. 1. Presidents — United States — History. 2. United States — Politics and government — 1933-1945 3. United States — Politics and government — 1945- 4. United States — Economic policy I. T.
HC106.S79 1984      338.973 19      *LC* 83-19618      *ISBN* 0671441272

**Sutton, Francis Xavier.** • **4.1940**
The American business creed [by] Francis X. Sutton [and others] Cambridge, Harvard University Press, 1956. 414 p. 1. Businessmen — United States 2. Industrial management — United States 3. United States — Industries I. T.
HC106 S88      *LC* 56-8553

**Veblen, Thorstein, 1857-1929.** • **4.1941**
Absentee ownership and business enterprise in recent times; the case of America. — New York, A. M. Kelley, bookseller, 1964 [c1923] 445 p. 21 cm. — (Reprints of economic classics) Cover title: The writings of Thorstein B. Veblen. 1. Economic history — 1918-1945 2. United States — Industries I. T.
HC106.V4 1964      338.01      *LC* 63-23516

**Weiss, Leonard W.** **4.1942**
Case studies in American industry / Leonard W. Weiss. — 3d ed. — New York: Wiley, c1980. xix, 396 p.: ill.; 22 cm. — (Introduction to economics series) 1. Industry and state — United States — Case studies. 2. Agriculture and state — United States — Case studies. 3. United States — Economic policy — Case studies. I. T.
HC106.W515 1980      338/.0973      *LC* 78-31149      *ISBN* 0471031593

**Cuff, Robert D., 1941-.** • **4.1943**
The War Industries Board; business–government relations during World War I [by] Robert D. Cuff. Baltimore, Johns Hopkins University Press [1973] x, 304 p. 27 cm. 1. United States. War Industries Board. 2. World War, 1914-1918 — Economic aspects — United States. I. T.
HC106.2.C8      338/.0973      *LC* 72-4022      *ISBN* 0801813603

## HC106.3 1919–1939

## HC106.3 A–C

**United States. National Resources Committee.** • **4.1944**
Regional planning: June 1938. — Washington, U.S. Govt. Print. Off., 1938. 28 p.: maps; 24 cm. Part 4 issued by the Maryland State Planning Commission as its Publication, no. 16. Part 6, v. 2 is a portfolio of folded maps. 1. Regional planning — United States I. Maryland. State Planning Commission.
HC106.3 A5

**United States. National Resources Planning Board.** • **4.1945**
Regional factors in national planning and development. December 1935. Washington, U.S. Govt. Print. Off., 1935. xviii, 223 p.: maps, diagrs.; 29 cm. 1. Natural resources 2. United States — Economic conditions — 1918- 3. United States — Economic policy I. T.
HC106.3 A5 1935A

**United States. National Resources Committee.** • **4.1946**
The structure of the American economy. New York, Da Capo Press, 1972. 2 v. in 1. illus. 28 cm. (Franklin D. Roosevelt and the era of the New Deal.) First published 1939-40. 1. Natural resources — United States 2. New Deal, 1933-1939 3. United States — Economic policy 4. United States — Economic conditions — 1918-1945 I. Means, Gardiner Colt, 1896- II. T. III. Series.
HC106.3.A5 1972      330.973/0917      *LC* 78-173418      *ISBN* 0306703882

**Handler, Milton, 1903-.** • **4.1947**
A study of the construction and enforcement of the federal anti–trust laws / Milton Handler. — Washington: U.S. Govt. Print. Off., 1941. vii, 106 p.: tables; 23 cm. — ([U.S.] Temporary national economic committee. Investigation of concentration of economic power ... Monograph; no. 38.) At head of title: 76th Congress/3d session Senate committee print. Running title: Concentration of economic power. 1. Trusts, Industrial — United States — Law 2. Monopolies — United States I. T.
HC106.3.A5127 no.38      *LC* 41-50308

**Beard, Charles Austin, 1874-1948.** • **4.1948**
The future comes; a study of the New Deal, by Charles A. Beard and George H. E. Smith. Westport, Conn., Greenwood Press [1972, c1933] xii, 178 p. 22 cm. 1. Industry and state — United States. 2. National Industrial Recovery Act, 1933. 3. New Deal, 1933-1939 4. United States — Politics and government — 1933-1945 5. United States — Economic policy — 1933-1945 I. Smith, George H. E. (George Howard Edward), 1898-1962. joint author. II. T.
HC106.3.B42 1972      330.9/73/0917      *LC* 73-143307      *ISBN* 0837158087

**Beard, Charles Austin, 1874-1948.** • **4.1949**
The open door at home; a trial philosophy of national interest, by Charles A. Beard, with the collaboration of G. H. E. Smith. New York, The Macmillan company, 1934. viii, 331 p.; 22 cm. 1. Economic policy 2. United States — Economic policy 3. United States — Foreign relations 4. United States — Commercial policy I. Smith, George H. E. (George Howard Edward), 1898-1962. joint author. II. T.
HC106.3.B43      330.973      *LC* 34-38709

**Studies in income and wealth.** **4.1950**
Vol. 1 (1937)-. New York: National Bureau of Economic Research, 1937-. v.: diagrs.: 24-28 cm. With supplements. 1. Income — United States — Collected works. 2. Wealth — United States — Collected works. 3. United States — Economic conditions — 1918- — Collected works. I. National Bureau of Economic Research. II. Conference on Research in Income and Wealth. III. Conference on Research in National Income and Wealth.
HC106.3.C714      330 19      *LC* 38-2909

**Conference on Research in Income and Wealth.** • **4.1951**
Trends in the American economy in the nineteenth century: a report of the National Bureau of Economic Research. — New York: Princeton, Princeton University Press, 1960. xi, 780 p.: ill.; 24 cm. — (Studies in income and wealth. v. 24) 'Contains most of the papers presented at the joint sessions of the Economic History Association and the Conference on Research in Income and Wealth held in Williamstown, Massachusetts, in September 1957.' 1. United States — Economic conditions 2. Canada — Economic conditions I. National Bureau of Economic Research. II. Economic History Association. III. T. IV. Series.
HC106.3.C714 v.24      *LC* 60-6680

**Conference on Research in Income and Wealth.** • **4.1952**
Output, employment, and productivity in the United States after 1800. — New York, National Bureau of Economic Research; distributed by Columbia University Press, 1966. xiv, 660 p. illus. 24 cm. — (International Teleconference Symposium (1984: Sydney, N.S.W., etc.) Studies in income and wealth, v. 30) 'Contains most of the papers presented at the joint sessions of the Economic History Association and the Conference on Research in Income and Wealth, held at Chapel Hill, North Carolina, in September 1963.' Includes bibliographical references. 1. U.S. — Econ. condit. — Addresses, essays, lectures. I. National Bureau of Economic Research. II. Economic History Association. III. T. IV. Series.
HC106.3.C714 vol. 30      330.973      *LC* 65-15964

**Conference on Production Relations, New York, 1965.** • **4.1953**
The theory and empirical analysis of production: [papers] / Murray Brown, editor. — New York: National Bureau of Economic Research; distributed by Columbia University Press, 1967. x, 515 p.: ill.; 23 cm. (Studies in income and wealth. v. 31) Includes bibliographies. 1. Economics — Mathematical models 2. Canada — Industries — Addresses, essays, lectures. 3. United States — Industries — Addresses, essays, lectures. I. Brown, Murray, 1929- ed. II. National Bureau of Economic Research. III. T. IV. Series.
HC106.3.C714 vol. 31      338/.001/51      *LC* 66-28827 rev

**Conference on the Industrial Composition of Income and Product, Brookings Institute, 1966.** • **4.1954**
The industrial composition of income and product; [papers] John W. Kendrick, editor. New York, National Bureau of Economic Research; distributed by

Columbia University Press, 1968. viii, 494 p. illus. 24 cm. (Studies in income and wealth, v. 32) 1. Costs, Industrial — United States — Addresses, essays, lectures. 2. United States — Industries — Addresses, essays, lectures. 3. Canada — Industries — Addresses, essays, lectures. I. Kendrick, John W. ed. II. National Bureau of Economic Research. III. Brookings Institution. IV. T.
HC106.3.C714 vol. 32    339.2/097    *LC* 67-29642

**Conference on Education and Income, University of Wisconsin,** • **4.1955**
**1968.**
Education, income, and human capital, edited by W. Lee Hansen. New York, National Bureau of Economic Research; distributed by Columbia University Press, 1970. x, 320 p. 23 cm. (Studies in income and wealth by the Conference on Research in Income and Wealth, v. 35) Jointly sponsored by Dept. of Economics, University of Wisconsin and the Conference on Research in Income and Wealth. 1. Education — Economic aspects I. Hansen, W. Lee. ed. II. University of Wisconsin. Dept. of Economics. III. Conference on Research in Income and Wealth. IV. T.
HC106.3.C714 vol. 35    331.2/01    *LC* 75-106811    *ISBN* 0870142186

## HC106.3 D–K

**Denison, Edward Fulton, 1915-.**          **4.1956**
Accounting for United States economic growth, 1929–1969 [by] Edward F. Denison. Washington, Brookings Institution [1974] xviii, 355 p. illus. 26 cm. 1. United States — Economic conditions — 1918-1945 2. United States — Economic conditions — 1945- I. Brookings Institution. II. T.
HC106.3.D3667    330.9/73/09    *LC* 74-1137    *ISBN* 0815718047 *ISBN* 0815718039

**Hacker, Louis Morton, 1899-.**          • **4.1957**
A short history of the New Deal, by Louis M. Hacker ... — New York, F. S. Crofts & co., 1934. 151 p. diagrs. 24 cm. Bibliography: p. 145-146. 1. United States — Pol. & govt. — 1933- 2. United States — Economic policy I. T. II. Title: The new deal.
HC106.3.H22    330.973    *LC* 34-27295

**Hansen, Alvin Harvey, 1887-.**          • **4.1958**
The American economy. — New York: McGraw-Hill, 1957. 199 p.; 24 cm. — (Economics handbook series) 1. Economics — United States — History. 2. United States — Economic conditions — 1918- I. T.
HC106.3.H252    330.973    *LC* 56-12533

**Hickok, Lorena A.**          **4.1959**
One third of a nation: Lorena Hickok reports on the Great Depression / edited by Richard Lowitt and Maurine Beasley. — Urbana: University of Illinois Press, c1981. xxxv, 378 p., [12] leaves of plates: ill.; 23 cm. 1. Depressions — 1933 — United States. 2. United States — Economic conditions — 1918-1945 I. Lowitt, Richard, 1922- II. Beasley, Maurine Hoffman. III. T.
HC106.3.H518 1981    338.5/42 19    *LC* 80-25905    *ISBN* 0252008499

**Hicks, John Donald, 1890-.**          • **4.1960**
Rehearsal for disaster; the boom and collapse of 1919–1920 ... Gainesville, University of Florida Press, 1961. 102 p. 21 cm. 1. United States — Economic conditions — 1918- I. T.
HC106.3.H52    *LC* 61-12136

**Hoover, Herbert, 1874-1964.**          • **4.1961**
American ideals versus the New Deal. St. Clair Shores, Mich., Scholarly Press, 1972. 96 p. 21 cm. Reprint of the 1936 ed. 1. New Deal, 1933-1939 — Addresses, essays, lectures. 2. United States — Economic policy — 1933-1945 — Addresses, essays, lectures. 3. United States — Politics and government — 1933-1945 — Addresses, essays, lectures. I. T.
HC106.3.H6149 1972    330.9/73/0917    *LC* 78-131746    *ISBN* 0403006333

**Klein, Lawrence Robert.**          • **4.1962**
An econometric model of the United States, 1929–1952, by L. R. Klein and A. S. Goldberger. Amsterdam, North-Holland Pub. Co. [c1955] xv, 165 p.: diagrs., tables.; 23 cm. — (Contributions to economic analysis, 9) 1. United States — Economic conditions — 1918- I. Goldberger, Arthur Stanley, 1930- joint author. II. T.
HC106.3.K56    *LC* 56-1278

**Kuznets, Simon Smith, 1901-.**          • **4.1963**
National income and its composition, 1919–1938, by Simon Kuznets, assisted by Lillian Epstein and Elizabeth Jenks ... New York, National bureau of economic research, 1941. 2 v.: tables; 24 cm. (Publications of the National bureau of economic research, inc.; no.40) Paged continuously. 1. Income 2. United States — Economic conditions — 1918- I. Epstein, Lillian. II. Jenks, Elizabeth. III. T.
HC106.3.K82    339.2    *LC* 42-3712

## HC106.3 L–Z

**Leontief, Wassily W., 1906-.**          • **4.1964**
The structure of American economy, 1919–1939; an empirical application of equilibrium analysis. [2d ed., enl.] New York, Oxford University Press, 1951. xvi, 264 p. diagrs., tables (3 fold. in pocket) 25 cm. Bibliographical references included in 'Statistical sources and methods of computation' (p. [223]-244) 1. Prices — United States. 2. United States — Industries 3. United States — Economic conditions — 1918- 4. United States — Statistics I. T. II. Title: Equilibrium analysis.
HC106.3.L3945 1951    330.973    *LC* 51-2557

**Leuchtenburg, William Edward, 1922-.**          • **4.1965**
The perils of prosperity, 1914–32. [Chicago] University of Chicago Press [1958] 313 p. 21 cm. (The Chicago history of American civilization) 1. World War, 1914-1918 — Economic aspects — United States. 2. United States — Economic conditions — 1918-1945 I. T.
HC106.3.L3957    330.973    *LC* 58-5680

**Lynch, David, 1902-.**          • **4.1966**
The concentration of economic power. New York, Columbia University Press, 1946. — New York: Johnson Reprint Corp., [1970] x, 423 p.; 23 cm. — (History of American economy) 1. U.S. Temporary National Economic Committee. 2. U.S. — Economic policy. 3. U.S. — Economic conditions — 1918-1945. I. T.
HC106.3.L89 1970    330.973    *LC* 70-18747

**Lyon, Leverett Samuel, 1885-.**          • **4.1967**
Government and economic life; development and current issues of American public policy ... Washington, D.C., The Brookings institution, 1939-40. 2 v. diagr. 24 cm. (The Institute of economics of the Brookings institution. Publication; no. 79, 83.) 1. Industry and state — United States. 2. United States — Economic policy 3. United States — Politics and government I. Watkins, Myron Webster, joint author. II. Abramson, Victor, 1906- joint author. III. T.
HC106.3.L9    *LC* 39-31511

**Norton, Hugh Stanton, 1921-.**          **4.1968**
The quest for economic stability: Roosevelt to Reagan / by Hugh S. Norton. — Columbia, S.C.: University of South Carolina Press, c1985. xvii, 329 p.; 24 cm. Includes index. 1. Economic stabilization — United States — History — 20th century. 2. United States — Economic policy — To 1933 3. United States — Economic policy — 1933-1945 I. T.
HC106.3.N59 1985    338.973 19    *LC* 85-14002    *ISBN* 087249456X

**Veblen, Thorstein, 1857-1929.**          • **4.1969**
The engineers and the price system / by Thorstein Veblen. — New York, N.Y.: A.M. Kelley, 1965. 169 p.; 21 cm. — (Reprints of economic classics) Reprint. Originally published: New York, N.Y.: B.W. Huebsch, 1921. 1. Industry 2. Capitalism 3. United States — Economic conditions — 1918-1945 I. T.
HC106.3.V4 1965    *LC* 65-15955

**Wilcox, Clair, 1898-.**          • **4.1970**
Competition and monopoly in American industry. — Westport, Conn.: Greenwood Press, [1970] xi, 344 p.; 34 cm. Reprint of the 1940 ed. 1. Competition — United States. 2. Monopolies — United States. 3. United States — Industries I. T.
HC106.3.W49 1970    338.8/2/0973    *LC* 69-14151    *ISBN* 0837131731

## HC106.4 1939–1945

**U.S. Civilian Production Administration.**          • **4.1971**
Industrial mobilization for war; history of the War Production Board and predecessor agencies, 1940–1945. Vol. I. Program and administration. — New York: Greenwood Press, [1969] xvii, 1010 p.; 24 cm. No more published. Reprint of the 1947 ed. 'War Production Board, General study no. 1.' 1. U.S. War Production Board. 2. World War, 1939-1945 — Economic aspects — U.S. I. T.
HC106.4.A29334 1969    355.2/6    *LC* 78-90715    *ISBN* 0837126991

**Catton, Bruce, 1899-.**          • **4.1972**
The war lords of Washington. — New York: Greenwood Press, [1969, c1948] 313 p.; 23 cm. 1. U.S. War Production Board. 2. World War, 1939-1945 — Economic aspects — U.S. I. T.
HC106.4.C345 1969    355.2/6/0973    *LC* 70-90481    *ISBN* 0837121493

**Chase, Stuart, 1888-.**          • **4.1973**
The road we are traveling, 1914–1942; guide lines to America's future as reported to the Twentieth Century Fund. — New York: Greenwood Press, 1968 [c1942] 106 p.; 23 cm. — (His When the war ends, 1) 1. Reconstruction (1939-1951) — United States. 2. United States — Economic policy I. Twentieth Century Fund. II. T.
HC106.4.C42 1968    330.973    *LC* 68-8057

**Janeway, Eliot.**     • **4.1974**
The struggle for survival. — New York: Weybright and Talley, [1968, c1951] 311 p.; 24 cm. — (Chronicles of America series. v. 53) Includes a new foreword and epilogue by the author. 1. World War, 1939-1945 — Economic aspects — United States. I. T. II. Series.
HC106.4.J33 1968x E173.C55 vol. 53, 1968    330.973    *LC* 68-31742
8.50

**Somers, Herman Miles, 1911-.**     **4.1975**
Presidential agency: OWMR, the Office of War Mobilization and Reconversion. — [S.l.]: Harvard, 1950. 1 v. 1. U.S. Office of War Mobilization and Reconversion. 2. Reconstruction (1939-1951) — U.S. I. T.
HC106.4.S66    338.973    *LC* 78-88944    *ISBN* 0837122570

## HC106.5 1945–1960

## HC106.5 A–E

**American Economic Association.**     • **4.1976**
Readings in industrial organization and public policy, selected by a committee of the American Economic Association. Selection Committee: Richard B. Heflebower [and] George W. Stocking. — Homewood, Ill.: Published for the association by R. D. Irwin, 1958. 426 p.: illus.; 24 cm. — (The Series of republished articles on economics, v. 8) 1. Industrial management — United States. 2. United States — Industries I. Heflebower, Richard Brooks, 1903- ed. II. T. III. Title: Industrial organization and public policy.
HC106.5.A5947    338.973    *LC* 58-11852

**The American economy in transition / edited by Martin**     **4.1977**
**Feldstein.**
Chicago: University of Chicago Press, 1980. viii, 696 p.: ill.; 24 cm. Papers of a conference held in January 1980 marking the 60th anniversary of the National Bureau of Economic Research. Includes indexes. 1. United States — Economic conditions — 1945- — Addresses, essays, lectures. I. Feldstein, Martin S. II. National Bureau of Economic Research.
HC106.5.A5948    330.973/092    *LC* 80-17450    *ISBN* 0226240819

**Bazelon, David T., 1923-.**     • **4.1978**
The paper economy. — New York: Random House [1963] 467 p.; 22 cm. 1. U.S. — Econ. condit. — 1945- I. T.
HC106.5.B38    330.973    *LC* 63-8339

**Benoit, Emile.**     • **4.1979**
Disarmament and the economy, edited by Emile Benoit & Kenneth E. Boulding. [1st ed.] New York, Harper & Row [1963] x, 310 p. 22 cm. 'A publication from the Center for Research in Conflict Resolution at the University of Michigan.' Bibliographical footnotes. 1. United States — Economic policy 2. United States — Military policy I. Boulding, Kenneth Ewart, 1910- II. T.
HC106.5.B42    338.973    *LC* 63-12052

**Bunting, John R.**     • **4.1980**
The hidden face of free enterprise: the strange economics of the American businessman. — New York: McGraw-Hill [1964] vii, 248 p.; 22 cm. 1. Corporations — United States 2. United States — Economic conditions — 1945- I. T.
HC106.5.B814    330.973    *LC* 64-16841

**Bunzel, John H., 1924-.**     • **4.1981**
The American small businessman. [1st ed.] New York, Knopf, 1962. 307 p. (Borzoi book) 1. Small business I. T.
HC106.5 B85    *LC* 62-11051

**Edwards, Corwin D., 1901-.**     • **4.1982**
Big business and the policy of competition. Cleveland, Press of Western Reserve University, 1956. 180 p. 23 cm. 1. Big business — United States. 2. Trusts, Industrial — United States 3. Industry and state — United States. I. T.
HC106.5.E38    338.8    *LC* 56-7229

**Evans, Michael K.**     • **4.1983**
Macroeconomic activity: theory, forecasting, and control; an econometric approach [by] Michael K. Evans. Foreword by L. R. Klein. New York, Harper & Row [1969] xviii, 627 p. illus. 25 cm. 1. Business cycles — Econometric models. 2. Economic forecasting — Econometric models. 3. Macroeconomics 4. United States — Economic conditions — Econometric models I. T.
HC106.5.E82    330.973    *LC* 69-11111

## HC106.5 F–L

**Fourastié, Jean, 1907-.**     • **4.1984**
Révolution à l'Ouest / Jean Fourastié et André Laleuf. — 1. éd. — Paris: Presses universitaires de France, 1957. 235 p.: ill.; 23 cm. 1. Industrial

management 2. United States — Industries 3. France — Industries. I. Laleuf, André. II. T.
HC106.5.F6x    *LC* a 57-7219

**Galbraith, John Kenneth, 1908-.**     **4.1985**
The affluent society / John Kenneth Galbraith. — 4th ed. — Boston: Houghton Mifflin, 1984. xxxvii, 291 p.; 22 cm. 1. Economics — United States 2. United States — Economic policy 3. United States — Economic conditions — 1945- I. T.
HC106.5.G32 1984    330.973 19    *LC* 84-12880    *ISBN* 0395366135

**Galbraith, John Kenneth, 1908-.**     **4.1986**
The new industrial state / John Kenneth Galbraith. — 3d ed., rev. — Boston: Houghton Mifflin, 1978. xxiv, 438 p.; 22 cm. 1. Industry and state — United States. 2. United States — Industries I. T.
HC106.6.G35 1978    338/.0973    *LC* 78-6310    *ISBN* 0395257123

**Harris, Seymour Edwin, 1897-.**     **4.1987**
Economics of the Kennedy years: and a look ahead / [by] Seymour E. Harris. — New York, Harper & Row [1964] xii, 273 p. 22 cm. 1. United States — Economic conditions — 1945- I. T.
HC106.5.H3186    330.973    *LC* 64-18104

**Kaplan, A. D. H. (Abraham David Hannath), 1893-.**     • **4.1988**
Big enterprise in a competitive system, by A.D.H. Kaplan. Rev. ed. Washington, Brookings Institution [1964] xv, 240 p. ill. 1. Big business — United States 2. United States — Economic conditions — 1945- I. Brookings Institution. II. T.
HC106.5 K36 1964    *LC* 64-8754

**Knorr, Klaus Eugen, 1911- ed.**     • **4.1989**
What price economic growth? Edited by Klaus Knorr and William J. Baumol. Contributors: William J. Baumol [and others]. — Englewood Cliffs, N. J., Prentice-Hall, 1961. 174 p. illus. 22 cm. 1. U.S. — Economic policy. 2. Economic development I. Baumol, William J. joint ed. II. T.
HC106.5.K52 1970    330.973    *LC* 61-13344    U

**Leontief, Wassily W., 1906-.**     • **4.1990**
Input–output economics [by] Wassily Leontief. — New York, Oxford University Press, 1966. viii, 257 p. illus. 24 cm. Part of illustrative matter fold. in pocket. 1. Input–output analysis 2. United States — Economic conditions — 1945- I. T.
HC106.5.L37    339.230973    *LC* 66-14482

## HC106.5 M–Z

**Melman, Seymour.**     **4.1991**
The permanent war economy: American capitalism in decline. — New York: Simon and Schuster, [1974] 384 p.; 23 cm. 1. Disarmament — Economic aspects — United States. 2. War — Economic aspects — United States. 3. United States — Economic conditions — 1945- I. T.
HC106.5.M434    338.4/76234/0973 19    *LC* 74-11035    *ISBN* 0671218115

**Myrdal, Gunnar, 1898-.**     • **4.1992**
Challenge to affluence. — New York: Pantheon Books, [1963] viii, 172 p.; 22 cm. 1. United States — Economic conditions — 1945- 2. United States — Foreign economic relations I. T.
HC106.5.M9    338.973    *LC* 63-19684

**Reagan, Michael D.**     • **4.1993**
The managed economy. — New York: Oxford University Press, 1963. ix, 288 p.; 21 cm. 1. Big business — United States 2. Industry and state — United States. 3. Laissez-faire 4. United States — Economic policy I. T.
HC106.5.R37    338.973    *LC* 63-19946

*[handwritten: HC 106.5 R28]*

**Resources for the Future.**     • **4.1994**
Resources in America's future: patterns of requirements and availabilities, 1960–2000 / by Hans H. Landsberg, Leonard L. Fischman, and Joseph L. Fisher. — [Baltimore]: Published for Resources for the Future by the Johns Hopkins Press, [1963] xx, 1017 p.: col. maps, diagrs. (part col.), tables; 26 cm. 1. Natural resources — United States I. Landsberg, Hans H. II. T.
HC106.5.R48    333.70973    *LC* 63-7233

**Sommers, Albert T.**     **4.1995**
The U.S. economy demystified: what the major economic statistics mean and their significance for business / Albert T. Sommers (the Conference Board). — Lexington, Mass.: Lexington Books, c1985. xvi, 134 p., [2] leaves of plates: ill.; 24 cm. 1. National income — United States — Accounting. 2. United States — Economic conditions — 1945- 3. United States — Economic policy I. Conference Board. II. T. III. Title: US economy demystified. IV. Title: United States economy demystified.
HC106.5.S64 1985    330.973/0927 19    *LC* 84-48451    *ISBN* 0669094277

**Vatter, Harold G.** • **4.1996**
The U.S. economy in the 1950's: an economic history. — [1st ed.] New York: Norton [1963] 308 p.: ill.; 21 cm. 1. United States — Economic conditions — 1945- I. T.
HC106.5 V33    *LC* 62-12291

## HC106.6 1961–1971

**Burns, Scott.** **4.1997**
Home, inc.: the hidden wealth and power of the American household / by Scott Burns. — 1st ed. — Garden City, N.Y.: Doubleday, 1975. x, 252 p.: ill.; 22 cm. 1. Home economics 2. Cost and standard of living — United States. 3. United States — Economic conditions — 1971-1981 I. T.
HC106.6.B813    338.4/7/640973    *LC* 73-11699    *ISBN* 0385067291

**Galbraith, John Kenneth, 1908-.** **4.1998**
Economics and the public purpose. Boston, Houghton Mifflin, 1973. xvi, 334 p. 24 cm. 1. Corporations — United States 2. Industry and state — United States. 3. United States — Economic conditions — 1961- 4. United States — Economic policy — 1971-1981 I. T.
HC106.6.G344    338.973    *LC* 73-8750    *ISBN* 0395172063 *ISBN* 0395178940

**Heller, Walter W.** • **4.1999**
New dimensions of political economy, by Walter W. Heller. Cambridge, Harvard University Press, 1966. viii, 203 p. 21 cm. (Godkin lectures at Harvard University, 1966) 'An expansion of the Godkin lectures ... [delivered] at Harvard University in March 1966.' 1. Fiscal policy — United States. 2. Intergovernmental fiscal relations — United States. 3. United States — Economic policy — 1961-1971 I. T.
HC106.6.H4    338.973    *LC* 66-23467

**Fortune.** • **4.2000**
America in the sixties: the economy and the society / by the editors of Fortune. — New York: Harper, 1960. xvi, 266 p.: ill.; 22 cm. — (Harper torchbooks; TB/1015) (The Academy library) 'Originally published under the title, Markets of the sixties.' 1. United States — Economic conditions — 1945- 2. United States — Social conditions I. T.
HC106.6.M372 1960b    *LC* 61-3045

**Okun, Arthur M.** • **4.2001**
The political economy of prosperity [by] Arthur M. Okun. Washington, Brookings Institution [1970] vi, 152 p. illus. 22 cm. 'The substance of this book was presented as the Crawley Memorial Lectures at the Wharton School of Finance and Commerce of the University of Pennsylvania in April 1969.' 1. Economic stabilization 2. United States — Economic policy — 1961-1971 I. T.
HC106.6.O46    338.973    *LC* 76-108835    *ISBN* 0815764782

## HC106.7 1971–1981

**Benefit–cost analyses of social regulation: case studies from the** **4.2002**
**Council on Wage and Price Stability / edited by James C.**
**Miller III and Bruce Yandle.**
Washington: American Enterprise Institute for Public Policy Research, c1979. 171 p.: graphs; 23 cm. (Studies in government regulation.) (AEI studies; 231) 1. Industry and state — United States — Cost effectiveness. 2. Consumer protection — United States — Cost effectiveness. 3. Environmental policy — United States — Cost effectiveness. I. Miller, James Clifford. II. Yandle, Bruce. III. Council on Wage and Price Stability (U.S.) IV. Series.
HC106.7.B46    338.0973 19    *LC* 79-876    *ISBN* 0844733342

**Ferber, Robert, 1922-.** **4.2003**
Social experimentation and economic policy / Robert Ferber, Werner Z. Hirsch. — Cambridge; New York: Cambridge University Press, 1982. xii, 251 p.: ill.; 22 cm. — (Cambridge surveys of economic literature.) Includes index. 1. Public welfare — United States — Evaluation. 2. United States — Social policy — Evaluation. 3. United States — Economic policy — 1971-1981 — Evaluation. I. Hirsch, Werner Zvi, 1920- II. T. III. Series.
HC106.7.F47    338.973 19    *LC* 81-6146    *ISBN* 0521241855

**Porter, Roger B.** **4.2004**
Presidential decision making: the Economic Policy Board / Roger B. Porter. — Cambridge; New York: Cambridge University Press, 1980. xii, 265 p.; 25 cm. Includes index. 1. United States. President's Economic Policy Board. 2. United States — Economic policy — 1971-1981 I. T.
HC106.7.P67    353.0082 19    *LC* 80-10165    *ISBN* 0521233372

**Regional diversity: growth in the United States, 1960–1990 /** **4.2005**
**Gregory Jackson ... [et al.]; with a foreword by David T.**
**Kresge.**
Boston, Mass.: Auburn House Pub. Co., c1981. xviii, 198 p.: ill.; 24 cm. (Joint Center outlook report.) 1. Economic forecasting — United States.

2. Population forecasting — United States. 3. United States — Economic conditions — 1971-1981 I. Jackson, Gregory, 1948- II. Series.
HC106.7.R346    338.5/443/0973 19    *LC* 81-12768    *ISBN* 086569107X

**The Reindustrialization of America / by the Business week** **4.2006**
**team, Seymour Zucker ... [et al.].**
New York: McGraw-Hill, c1982. v, 200 p.: ill.; 24 cm. Includes index. 1. United States — Industries 2. United States — Economic policy — 1981- I. Zucker, Seymour. II. Business week (New York)
HC106.7.R35    338.0973 19    *LC* 81-8360    *ISBN* 0070093245

**Solomon, Ezra.** **4.2007**
Beyond the turning point: the U.S. economy in the 1980s / Ezra Solomon. — San Francisco: W.H. Freeman, c1982. ix, 157 p.: ill.; 25 cm. Includes index. 1. United States — Economic conditions — 1971-1981 2. United States — Economic conditions — 1981- 3. United States — Economic policy — 1971- I. T.
HC106.7.S6    338.973 19    *LC* 81-19542    *ISBN* 071671390X

## HC106.8 1981–

**Alperovitz, Gar.** **4.2008**
Rebuilding America / Gar Alperovitz & Jeff Faux. — 1st ed. — New York: Pantheon Books, [1984] xi, 319 p.; 25 cm. Includes index. 1. United States — Economic policy — 1981- I. Faux, Geoffrey P. II. T.
HC106.8.A42 1984    338.973 19    *LC* 83-4206    *ISBN* 0394532007

**Bowles, Samuel.** **4.2009**
Free lunch: a democratic program for restructuring the slack U.S. economy / Samuel Bowles, David M. Gordon, Thomas E. Weisskopf. — 1st ed. — Garden City, N.Y.: Doubleday, 1982. 1 v. Includes index. 1. Economic policy 2. United States — Economic policy — 1981- 3. United States — Economic conditions — 1971- I. Gordon, David M. II. Weisskopf, Thomas E. III. T.
HC106.8.B68 1982    338.973 19    *LC* 82-18342    *ISBN* 0385183453

**Eckstein, Otto.** **4.2010**
The DRI model of the U.S. economy / by Otto Eckstein. — New York: McGraw-Hill, c1983. xiii, 253 p.: ill.; 24 cm. 1. Data Resources, inc. 2. United States — Economic conditions — 1971-1981 — Econometric models. 3. United States — Economic conditions — 1981- — Econometric models. I. T. II. Title: D.R.I. model of the U.S. economy.
HC106.8.E26 1983    330.973/00724 19    *LC* 83-13528    *ISBN* 0070189722

**Etzioni, Amitai.** **4.2011**
An immodest agenda: rebuilding America before the 21st century / Amitai Etzioni. — New York: McGraw-Hill, 1982. xiv, 418 p. 1. United States — Economic policy — 1981- I. T.
HC106.8 E89    HC106.8 E89.    338.0973 19    *LC* 82-7136    *ISBN* 0070197237

**Greider, William.** **4.2012**
The education of David Stockman and other Americans / William Greider. — 1st ed. — New York: Dutton, c1982. xxx, 159 p.; 20 cm. 1. Stockman, David Alan, 1946- 2. Budget — United States 3. Government spending policy — United States 4. United States — Economic policy — 1981- I. T.
HC106.8.G73 1982    338.973 19    *LC* 82-72489    *ISBN* 0525480102

**Kahn, Herman, 1922-.** **4.2013**
The coming boom: economic, political, and social / by Herman Kahn. — New York: Simon and Schuster, c1982. 237 p.: ill.; 25 cm. 1. Economic forecasting — United States. 2. United States — Economic conditions — 1971-1981 3. United States — Politics and government — 1981- I. T.
HC106.8.K33 1982    303.4/973 19    *LC* 82-5944    *ISBN* 0671442627

**Miller, S. M. (Seymour Michael), 1922-.** **4.2014**
Recapitalizing America: alternatives to the corporate distortion of national policy / S.M. Miller and Donald Tomaskovic–Devey. — Boston: Routledge & Kegan Paul, 1983. xii, 215 p.: ill.; 22 cm. Includes index. 1. United States — Economic policy — 1981- 2. Great Britain — Economic policy — 1945- I. Tomaskovic-Devey, Donald, 1957- II. T.
HC106.8.M54 1983    338.973 19    *LC* 83-6658    *ISBN* 071009941X

**O'Hara, Frederick M.** **4.2015**
Handbook of United States economic and financial indicators / Frederick M. O'Hara, Jr., and Robert Sicignano. — Westport, Conn.: Greenwood Press, 1985. x, 224 p.; 24 cm. Includes index. 1. Economic indicators — United States — Handbooks, manuals, etc. I. Sicignano, Robert. II. T.
HC106.8.O47 1985    330.973 19    *LC* 84-22469    *ISBN* 0313239541

**Roberts, Paul Craig, 1939-.** **4.2016**
The supply–side revolution: an insider's account of policymaking in Washington / Paul Craig Roberts. — Cambridge, Mass.: Harvard University

Press, 1984. 327 p.: ill.; 24 cm. 1. Supply-side economics 2. United States — Economic policy — 1981- I. T.
HC106.8.R6 1984     338.973 19     *LC* 83-18340     *ISBN* 0674856201

**Adams, Walter, 1922 Aug. 27-.**          **4.2017**
The Structure of American industry / Walter Adams, editor. — 7th ed. — New York: Macmillan; London: Collier Macmillan, 1985. ix, 438 p.: ill.; 24 cm. 1. United States — Industries — Addresses, essays, lectures. I. T.
HC106.8.S78 1986     338.6/0973 19     *LC* 85-11533     *ISBN* 0023007702

# HC107 Regions. States, A–Z

**Estall, R. C.**                 • **4.2018**
New England; a study in industrial adjustment [by] R. C. Estall. — London, Bell, 1966. xv, 296 p. illus., maps. 23 cm. — (Bell's economic geographies.) Includes bibliographies. 1. New England — Econ. condit. 2. New England — Indus. I. T.
HC107.A11E78 1966     330.974     *LC* 66-12483

**McManis, Douglas R.**              **4.2019**
Colonial New England: a historical geography / Douglas R. McManis; cartographer, Miklos Pinther. — New York: Oxford University Press, 1975. ix, 159 p.: ill.; 23 cm. (Historical geography of North America series) 1. New England — Economic conditions. 2. New England — Historical geography. I. T.
HC107.A11 M17     330.9/74/02     *LC* 74-21824     *ISBN* 0195019075

**Eller, Ronald D., 1948-.**             **4.2020**
Miners, millhands, and mountaineers: industrialization of the Appalachian South, 1880–1930 / by Ronald D. Eller. — 1st ed. — Knoxville: University of Tennessee Press, c1982. xxvi, 272 p.: ill.; 24 cm. (Twentieth-century America series.) Includes index. 1. Appalachian Region, Southern — Economic conditions. 2. Appalachian Region, Southern — Social conditions. 3. Appalachian Region, Southern — History. I. T. II. Series.
HC107.A127 E4 1982     330.975 19     *LC* 81-16020     *ISBN* 087049340X

**Gaventa, John, 1949-.**            **4.2021**
Power and powerlessness: quiescence and rebellion in an Appalachian valley / by John Gaventa. — Urbana: University of Illinois Press, c1980. xi, 267 p.; 21 cm. 1. Poor — Appalachian Region — Case studies. 2. Power (Social sciences) — Case studies. 3. Appalachian Region — Economic conditions — Case studies. 4. Appalachian Region — Social conditions — Case studies. I. T.
HC107.A127 G38     320.974 19     *LC* 80-12988     *ISBN* 0252007727

**Cobb, James C. (James Charles), 1947-.**        **4.2022**
The selling of the South: the Southern crusade for industrial development, 1936–1980 / James C. Cobb. — Baton Rouge: Louisiana State University Press, c1982. xii, 293 p.; 24 cm. Includes index. 1. Industrial promotion — Southern States. 2. Southern States — Economic conditions — 1918- I. T.
HC107.A13 C65 1982     338.975 19     *LC* 81-18594     *ISBN* 0807109940

**Flynt, J. Wayne, 1940-.**            **4.2023**
Dixie's forgotten people: the South's poor whites / J. Wayne Flynt. — Bloomington: Indiana University Press, c1979. xviii, 206 p.: ill.; 22 cm. — (Minorities in modern America.) Includes index. 1. Poor — Southern States. I. T. II. Series.
HC107.A13 F66     301.44/1     *LC* 78-20613     *ISBN* 0253197651

**Ransom, Roger L., 1938-.**           **4.2024**
One kind of freedom: the economic consequences of emancipation / Roger L. Ransom, Richard Sutch. — Cambridge [Eng.]; New York: Cambridge University Press, 1977. xix, 409 p.: ill.; 24 cm. Includes index. 1. Afro-Americans — Southern States — Economic conditions. 2. Southern States — Economic conditions 3. Southern States — History — 1865- I. Sutch, Richard. joint author. II. T.
HC107.A13 R28     330.9/76/04     *LC* 76-27909     *ISBN* 0521214505

**Vance, Rupert Bayless, 1899-.**         • **4.2025**
Human geography of the South; a study in regional resources and human adequacy, by Rupert B. Vance. — 2d ed. — New York: Russell & Russell, [1968, c1935] xviii, 596 p.: illus., maps.; 23 cm. 1. Southern States — Economic conditions — 1918- 2. Southern States — Social conditions 3. Southern States — Description and travel 4. Southern States — Industrial. I. T.
HC107.A13 V3 1968     330.975     *LC* 68-25051

**Wright, Gavin.**                **4.2026**
The political economy of the cotton South: households, markets, and wealth in the nineteenth century / Gavin Wright. — 1st ed. — New York: Norton, c1978.

xv, 205 p.: ill.; 22 cm. Includes index. 1. Cotton trade — Southern States — History. 2. Southern States — Economic conditions I. T.
HC107.A13 W68 1978     330.9/75/04     *LC* 77-26715     *ISBN* 0393056864

**Wiley, Peter.**               **4.2027**
Empires in the sun: the rise of the new American West / Peter Wiley & Robert Gottlieb. — New York: Putnam, c1982. xvi, 332 p.: map; 25 cm. Includes index. 1. Minorities — Southwest, New. 2. Southwest, New — Economic conditions. 3. Southwest, New — Politics and government. I. Gottlieb, Robert. II. T.
HC107.A165 W53     330.978/033 19     *LC* 81-13857     *ISBN* 039912635X

**Lowitt, Richard, 1922-.**           **4.2028**
The New Deal and the West / Richard Lowitt. — Bloomington: Indiana University Press, c1984. xviii, 283 p.: ill.; 25 cm. — (West in the twentieth century.) Includes index. 1. New Deal, 1933-1939 — West (U.S.) 2. West (U.S.) — Economic conditions 3. West (U.S.) — Economic policy. 4. United States — Economic policy — 1933-1945 I. T. II. Series.
HC107.A17 L68 1984     338.973 19     *LC* 83-48188     *ISBN* 0253340055

**Nash, Gerald D.**             **4.2029**
The American West transformed: the impact of the Second World War / Gerald D. Nash. — Bloomington: Indiana University Press, c1985. x, 304 p., [16] p. of plates: ill.; 25 cm. Includes index. 1. World War, 1939-1945 — Economic aspects — West (U.S.) 2. World War, 1939-1945 — Social aspects — West (U.S.) I. T.
HC107.A17 N37 1985     330.978/032 19     *LC* 83-49524     *ISBN* 0253306493

**Worster, Donald, 1941-.**           **4.2030**
Rivers of empire: water, aridity, and the growth of the American West / Donald Worster. — 1st ed. — New York: Pantheon Books, 1986, c1985. x, 402 p.; 24 cm. Includes index. 1. Water resources development — West (U.S.) — History. 2. Water-supply — West (U.S.) — History. 3. Hydrology — West (U.S.) 4. West (U.S.) — Economic conditions 5. West (U.S.) — History I. T.
HC107.A17 W67 1986     333.91/00978 19     *LC* 85-42890     *ISBN* 039451680X

**Main, Jackson Turner.**            **4.2031**
Society and economy in colonial Connecticut / Jackson Turner Main. — Princeton, N.J.: Princeton University Press, c1985. xv, 395 p.: ill.; 25 cm. Includes index. 1. Wealth — Connecticut — History — 17th century. 2. Wealth — Connecticut — History — 18th century. 3. Connecticut — Economic conditions. 4. Connecticut — History — Colonial period, ca. 1600-1775 I. T.
HC107.C8 M35 1985     330.9746/02 19     *LC* 84-42892     *ISBN* 069104726X

**Caudill, Harry M., 1922-.**          • **4.2032**
Night comes to the Cumberlands: a biography of a depressed area / with a foreword by Stewart L. Udall. — [1st ed.]. — Boston: Little, Brown, [1963] 394 p.: ill.; 22 cm. 1. Appalachian Plateau — Economic conditions. 2. Appalachian Plateau — Social conditions. I. T.
HC107.K4 C3     309.1769154     *LC* 63-13450

**Hoffman, Ronald, 1941-.**           **4.2033**
A spirit of dissension: economics, politics, and the Revolution in Maryland. — Baltimore: Johns Hopkins University Press, [1973] xiv, 280 p.: maps.; 23 cm. — (Maryland bicentennial studies) 1. Maryland — Economic conditions. 2. Maryland — Politics and government — Colonial period, ca. 1600-1775 3. Maryland — Politics and government — Revolution, 1775-1783 I. T. II. Series.
HC107.M3 H63     975.2/03     *LC* 73-8127     *ISBN* 0801815215

**Main, Gloria L. (Gloria Lund), 1933-.**        **4.2034**
Tobacco colony: life in early Maryland, 1650–1720 / Gloria L. Main. — Princeton, N.J.: Princeton University Press, c1982. xv, 326 p.: map; 24 cm. Includes index. 1. Cost and standard of living — Maryland — History. 2. Plantation life — Maryland — History. 3. Tobacco industry — Maryland — History. 4. Maryland — Economic conditions. 5. Maryland — History — Colonial period, ca. 1600-1775 I. T.
HC107.M3 M23 1982     338.1/7371/09752 19     *LC* 82-47603     *ISBN* 069104693X

**Clemens, Paul G. E., 1947-.**          **4.2035**
The Atlantic economy and colonial Maryland's Eastern Shore: From tobacco to grain / Paul G. E. Clemens. — Ithaca, N.Y.: Cornell University Press, 1980. 249 p.: ill.; 23 cm. Includes index. 1. Eastern Shore (Md. and Va.) — Economic conditions. 2. Maryland — Economic conditions. I. T.
HC107.M32 E323     330.9/752/1     *LC* 79-26181     *ISBN* 080141251X

**Prude, Jonathan.**     4.2036
The coming of industrial order: town and factory life in rural Massachusetts, 1810–1860 / Jonathan Prude. — Cambridge [Cambridgeshire]; New York: Cambridge University Press, 1983. xvii, 364 p.: ill.; 24 cm. Includes index. 1. Massachusetts — Industries — History — 19th century. I. T.
HC107.M4 P78 1983     307/.332/09744 19     *LC* 82-14599     *ISBN* 0521248248

**Thelen, David P. (David Paul)**     4.2037
Paths of resistance: tradition and dignity in industrializing Missouri / David Thelen. — New York: Oxford University Press, 1986. x, 321 p.; 25 cm. Includes index. 1. Missouri — Economic conditions. 2. Missouri — Social conditions. 3. Missouri — Politics and government — 1865-1950 I. T.
HC107.M8 T44 1986     330.9778/03 19     *LC* 85-7255     *ISBN* 0195036670

**Billings, Dwight B., 1948-.**     4.2038
Planters and the making of a 'new South': class, politics, and development in North Carolina, 1865–1900 / by Dwight B. Billings, Jr. — Chapel Hill: University of North Carolina Press, c1979. xiii, 284 p.: ill.; 22 cm. Includes index. 1. North Carolina — Industries — History. 2. North Carolina — Economic conditions. 3. North Carolina — Social conditions. I. T.
HC107.N8 B5     330.9/756/04     *LC* 78-25952     *ISBN* 080781315X

**Ekirch, A. Roger, 1950-.**     4.2039
'Poor Carolina': politics and society in colonial North Carolina, 1729–1776 / A. Roger Ekirch. — Chapel Hill: University of North Carolina Press, c1981. xix, 305 p.: maps; 24 cm. Includes index. 1. North Carolina — Economic conditions. 2. North Carolina — Social conditions. 3. North Carolina — Politics and government — Colonial period, ca. 1600-1775 I. T.
HC107.N8 E37     330.9756/02 19     *LC* 80-39889     *ISBN* 080781475X

**Arrington, Leonard J.**     • **4.2040**
Great Basin Kingdom; an economic history of the Latter–Day Saints, 1830–1900. Cambridge, Harvard University Press, 1958. xviii, 534 p. illus., ports., maps. 25 cm. 1. Church of Jesus Christ of Latter-Day Saints. 2. Utah — Economic conditions. I. T.
HC107.U8 A8     *LC* 58-12961

## HC108 Cities, A–Z

**Preston, Howard L.**     4.2041
Automobile age Atlanta: the making of a southern metropolis, 1900–1935 / Howard L. Preston. — Athens: University of Georgia Press, c1979. xix, 203 p.: ill.; 23 cm. Includes index. 1. Automobiles — Social aspects — Georgia — Atlanta — History. 2. Transportation — Georgia — Atlanta — History. 3. Atlanta (Ga.) — Economic conditions. I. T.
HC108.A75 P73     309.1/758/23104     *LC* 78-17088     *ISBN* 0820304638

**Olson, Sherry H.**     4.2042
Baltimore, the building of an American city / Sherry H. Olson. — Baltimore: Johns Hopkins University Press, c1980. ix, 432 p.: ill.; 29 cm. 1. Baltimore (Md.) — Economic conditions. 2. Baltimore (Md.) — Social conditions. 3. Baltimore (Md.) — History I. T.
HC108.B2 O47     975.2/6     *LC* 79-21950     *ISBN* 0801822246

**Ross, Steven Joseph.**     4.2043
Workers on the edge: work, leisure, and politics in industrializing Cincinnati, 1788–1890 / Steven J. Ross. — New York: Columbia University Press, 1985. xx, 406 p.: ill.; 24 cm. — (Columbia history of urban life.) Includes index. 1. Labor and laboring classes — Ohio — Cincinnati — History. 2. Industrial relations — Ohio — Cincinnati — History. 3. Cincinnati (Ohio) — Industries — History. I. T. II. Series.
HC108.C5 R67 1985     331/.09771/78 19     *LC* 84-21376     *ISBN* 023105520X

**Zunz, Olivier.**     4.2044
The changing face of inequality: urbanization, industrial development, and immigrants in Detroit, 1880–1920 / by Olivier Zunz. — Chicago: University of Chicago Press, 1982. xiii, 481 p.: ill.; 25 cm. 1. Alien labor — Michigan — Detroit — History. 2. Social classes — Michigan — Detroit — History. 3. Detroit (Mich.) — Industries — History. I. T.
HC108.D6 Z86 1982     307.7/64/0977434 19     *LC* 82-6986     *ISBN* 0226994570

**Hoover, Edgar Malone, 1907-.**     • **4.2045**
Anatomy of a metropolis: the changing distribution of people and jobs within the New York metropolitan region / by Edgar M. Hoover and Raymond Vernon, with the assistance of Milton Abelson...[et al.]. — Cambridge, Mass.: Harvard University Press, 1959. xvi, 345 p.: ill., maps (part col. on lining papers) diagrs., tables.; 22 cm. — (New York metropolitan region study)

1. Industry — Location — New York metropolitan area. 2. New York Metropolitan Area — Population. I. Vernon, Raymond, 1913- II. T.
HC108.N7 H6     338.097472     *LC* 59-12971

**Starr, Roger.**     4.2046
The rise and fall of New York City / Roger Starr. — New York: Basic Books, c1985. xii, 258 p.; 22 cm. Includes index. 1. New York (N.Y.) — Economic conditions. 2. New York (N.Y.) — Social conditions. 3. New York (N.Y.) — Politics and government — 1951- I. T.
HC108.N7 S75 1985     330.9747/1043 19     *LC* 83-46086     *ISBN* 0465070310

**Twentieth Century Fund. Task Force on the Future of New**     4.2047
**York City.**
New York—world city: report of the Twentieth Century Fund Task Force on the Future of New York City: background paper / by Masha Sinnreich. — Cambridge, Mass.: Oelgeschlager, Gunn & Hain, c1980. xv, 230 p.; 24 cm. 1. Fiscal policy — New York (City) 2. New York (N.Y.) — Economic policy. I. Sinnreich, Masha. II. T.
HC108.N7 T86 1980     330.9/747/1     *LC* 79-25129     *ISBN* 0899460097

**Vernon, Raymond, 1913-.**     • **4.2048**
Metropolis 1985; interpretation of the findings of the New York metropolitan region study. Cambridge, Mass., Harvard University Press, 1960. xiii, 242 p. maps, diagrs. 22 cm. (New York metropolitan region study 9) 1. New York Metropolitan Area I. T. II. Series.
HC108.N7 V4     301.36097472     *LC* 60-15243

**Cobb, Edwin L.**     4.2049
No cease fires: the war on poverty in Roanoke valley / Edwin L. Cobb. — Cabin John, Md.: Seven Locks Press, c1984. xvi, 176 p.; 23 cm. Includes index. 1. Economic assistance, Domestic — Virginia — Roanoke. I. T.
HC108.R52 C63 1984     362.5/58/09755791 19     *LC* 84-5515     *ISBN* 0932020283

**Howell, Joseph T.**     4.2050
Hard living on Clay Street; portraits of blue collar families [by] Joseph T. Howell. [1st ed.] Garden City, N.Y., Anchor Press, 1973. xvi, 381 p. 18 cm. 1. Poor — Washington (D.C.) — Case studies. 2. Labor and laboring classes — Washington (D.C.) — Case studies. I. T.
HC108.W3 H68 1973     301.44/1     *LC* 73-79736     *ISBN* 0385053177

## HC110 Special Topics, A–Z

### HC110.A4 Air Pollution

**Crandall, Robert W.**     4.2051
Controlling industrial pollution: the economics and politics of clean air / Robert W. Crandall. — Washington, D.C.: Brookings Institution, c1983. xiv, 199 p.: ill.; 24 cm. — (Studies in the regulation of economic activity.) 1. Air — Pollution — Government policy — United States — Cost effectiveness. 2. Air quality management — Government policy — United States — Cost effectiveness. I. Brookings Institution. II. T. III. Series.
HC110.A4 C7 1983     363.7/31 19     *LC* 82-45982     *ISBN* 0815716044

**Tietenberg, Thomas H.**     4.2052
Emissions trading, an exercise in reforming pollution policy / T.H. Tietenberg. — Washington, D.C.: Resources for the Future; Baltimore: Distributed by Johns Hopkins University Press, 1985. xiii, 222 p.; 24 cm. 1. Air — Pollution — Government policy — United States. I. T.
HC110.A4 T54 1985     363.7/39256/0973 19     *LC* 84-18335     *ISBN* 0915707128

### HC110.C3 Capital

**Goldsmith, Raymond William, 1904-.**     • **4.2053**
The national wealth of the United States in the postwar period. — Princeton [N.J.]: Princeton University Press, 1962. xxix, 434 p. (chiefly diagrs., tables); 24 cm. — (National Bureau of Economic Research. Studies in capital formation and financing, 10) 'A study by the National Bureau of Economic Research, New York.' 'A continuation of the estimates of national wealth in volume III of [the author's] A study of saving in the United States.' 1. Capital — United States. I. T. II. Series.
HC110.C3 G6     339.373     *LC* 62-11952

**Perspectives on urban infrastructure / Royce Hanson, editor.**     4.2054
Washington, D.C.: National Academy Press, 1984. v, 216 p.: ill.; 23 cm. Papers and discussions from a Symposium on the Adequacy and Maintenance of Urban Public Facilities, held by the National Research Council, at Airlie House, Warrenton, Va., Feb. 25-26, 1983. 1. Infrastructure (Economics) —

United States — Congresses. 2. Urban policy — United States — Congresses. I. Hanson, Royce. II. National Research Council (U.S.) III. Symposium on the Adequacy and Maintenance of Urban Public Facilities (1983: Airlie House) HC110.C3 P47 1984     363/.0973 19     *LC* 80-63272     *ISBN* 0309034396

## HC110.C6 Consumers

**Andreasen, Alan R., 1934-.**        **4.2055**
The disadvantaged consumer / Alan R. Andreasen; foreword by Mary Gardiner Jones. New York: Free Press, [1975] xiv, 366 p.; 24 cm. 1. Poor as consumers — United States. 2. Afro-Americans as consumers 3. Consumer protection — United States. I. T.
HC110.C6 A74     381/.3     *LC* 75-802805     *ISBN* 0029006902

**Gibson, D. Parke.**        **4.2056**
$70 billion in the Black: America's Black consumers / D. Parke Gibson. — A rev. and updated version of The $30 billion Negro. — New York: Macmillan, c1978. x, 230 p., [8] leaves of plates: ill.; 25 cm. Includes index. 1. Afro-Americans as consumers I. T.
HC110.C6 G5 1978     339.4     *LC* 78-2662     *ISBN* 0025431609

**Harberger, Arnold C. ed.**        • **4.2057**
The demand for durable goods. With essays by Arnold C. Harberger [and others.] [Chicago] University of Chicago Press [1960] vi, 274 p. diagrs., tables. (Studies in economics of the Economics Research Center of the University of Chicago) 'A publication of the Research Group in Public Finance.' 1. Consumption (Economics) — United States 2. Business cycles I. T.
HC110 C6 H3     *LC* 60-7236

**Horowitz, Daniel, 1938-.**        **4.2058**
The morality of spending: attitudes toward the consumer society in America, 1875–1940 / Daniel Horowitz. — Baltimore: Johns Hopkins University Press, c1985. xxxi, 254 p.; 24 cm. (New studies in American intellectual and cultural history.) 1. Consumption (Economics) — United States — History. 2. Consumers — United States — History. 3. Consumption (Economics) — United States — Moral and ethical aspects — History. 4. Intellectuals — United States — Attitudes — History. 5. Social reformers — United States — Attitudes — History. I. T. II. Series.
HC110.C6 H58 1985     339.4/7/0973 19     *LC* 84-27851     *ISBN* 080182530X

**Houthakker, Hendrik S.**        • **4.2059**
Consumer demand in the United States: analyses and projections / [by] H. S. Houthakker [and] Lester D. Taylor. — 2d and enl. ed. — Cambridge, Mass.: Harvard University Press, 1970. xii, 321 p.: ill.; 25 cm. — (Harvard economic studies. v. 126) 1. Consumption (Economics) — United States. 2. Economic forecasting — United States. I. Taylor, Lester D. joint author. II. T. III. Series.
HC110.C6 H6 1970     339.4/7/0973     *LC* 79-95915     *ISBN* 0674166019

**Katona, George, 1901-.**        • **4.2060**
Consumer response to income increases [by] George Katona [and] Eva Mueller. Washington: Brookings Institution, [1968] xviii, 244 p.: illus.; 24 cm. — (Studies of government finance) 1. Consumers — United States 2. Income — United States. 3. Income tax — United States I. Mueller, Eva, 1920- joint author. II. T. III. Series.
HC110.C6 K328     339.41/0973     *LC* 67-30597

**Schutz, Howard G.**        **4.2061**
Lifestyles and consumer behavior of older Americans / Howard G. Schutz, Pamela C. Baird, Glenn R. Hawkes. — New York: Praeger, 1979. xvi, 276 p.; 24 cm. Includes index. 1. Aged as consumers — United States. 2. Aged — United States I. Baird, Pamela C. joint author. II. Hawkes, Glenn Rogers, 1919- joint author. III. T.
HC110.C6 S33     658.8/34     *LC* 79-13212     *ISBN* 003049821X

**Best, Arthur.**        **4.2062**
When consumers complain / Arthur Best. — New York: Columbia University Press, 1981. xi, 232 p.; 24 cm. 1. Consumer protection — United States. I. T.
HC110.C63 B47     381/.34/0973 19     *LC* 80-21789     *ISBN* 0231051247

**Consumerism in the United States: an inter–industry analysis /**        **4.2063**
**edited by Joel R. Evans.**
New York: Praeger, c1980. xiii, 452 p.; 24 cm. 1. Consumer protection — United States. I. Evans, Joel R.
HC110.C63 C6435     381/.34/0973     *LC* 79-25341     *ISBN* 0030568463

**Creighton, Lucy Black.**        **4.2064**
Pretenders to the throne: the consumer movement in the United States / Lucy Black Creighton. — Lexington, Mass.: Lexington Books, c1976. ix, 142 p.; 24

cm. Includes index. 1. Consumer protection — United States. 2. Consumer education — United States. I. T.
HC110.C63 C73     381/.3     *LC* 75-17334     *ISBN* 066900085X

**Wasserman, Paul.**        **4.2065**
Consumer sourcebook: a directory and guide to government organizations: information centers, clearinghouses, and toll–free numbers, associations, centers, and institutes: media services, publications relating to consumer topics, sources of recourse and advisory information: and company and trade name information / Paul Wasserman, managing editor; Gita Siegman, associate editor. — 4th ed. — Detroit, Mich.: Gale Research Co., c1983. 2 v. (xv, 1427 p.); 29 cm. Includes indexes. 1. Consumer protection — Information services — United States — Directories. 2. Consumer education — Information services — United States — Directories. I. Siegman, Gita. II. T.
HC110.C63 W37 1983     381/.33/02573 19     *LC* 83-232435     *ISBN* 0810303841

## HC110.D4 Defense. Disarmament: Economic Aspects

**Koistinen, Paul A. C.**        **4.2066**
The military–industrial complex: a historical perspective / Paul A. C. Koistinen; foreword by Les Aspin; introd. by Robert K. Griffith, Jr. — New York: Praeger, 1980. xiv, 168 p.; 24 cm. Includes index. 1. War — Economic aspects — United States. 2. Industry and state — United States. I. T.
HC110.D4 K64     330.9/73/09     *LC* 79-20569     *ISBN* 0030557666

**Mosley, Hugh G.**        **4.2067**
The arms race: economic and social consequences / Hugh G. Mosley. — Lexington, Mass.: Lexington Books, c1985. xiv, 203 p.; 24 cm. Includes index. 1. Arms race — Economic aspects — United States. 2. Armaments — Economic aspects — United States. 3. Disarmament — Economic aspects — United States. I. T.
HC110.D4 M67 1985     338.4/76234/0973 19     *LC* 81-48005     *ISBN* 066905237X

## HC110.D5 Distribution of Industry

**Duerksen, Christopher J., 1948-.**        **4.2068**
Environmental regulation of industrial plant siting: how to make it work better / Christopher J. Duerksen. — Washington, D.C.: Conservation Foundation, c1983. xxviii, 232 p.: ill.; 23 cm. 1. Environmental policy — United States. 2. United States — Industries — Location — Environmental aspects. I. T.
HC110.D5 D83 1983     338.6/042/0973 19     *LC* 83-20901     *ISBN* 0891640789

**Fuchs, Victor R.**        • **4.2069**
Changes in the location of manufacturing in the United States since 1929. New Haven: Yale University Press, 1962. xx, 566 p.: maps, tables; 26 cm. (Economic census studies, 1) 1. Industry — Location — United States 2. United States — Manufactures I. T. II. Series.
HC110 D5 F8     *LC* 62-8244

**Harris, Curtis C.**        **4.2070**
The urban economies, 1985: a multiregional, multi–industry forecasting model [by] Curtis C. Harris, Jr. — Lexington, Mass.: Lexington Books, [1973] xvi, 230 p.; 23 cm. 1. Industry — Location — United States — Mathematical models. 2. Regional planning — Mathematical models. I. T.
HC110.D5 H37     338/.09     *LC* 73-6593     *ISBN* 0669869341

**Nonmetropolitan industrialization / [editors] Richard E.**        **4.2071**
**Lonsdale, H. L. Seyler.**
Washington: V. H. Winston; New York: distributed solely by Halsted Press, a division of Wiley, c1979. xii, 196 p.: ill.; 24 cm. (Scripta series in geography.) 1. Community development — United States. 2. United States — Industries — Location. 3. United States — Rural conditions I. Lonsdale, Richard E. II. Seyler, H. L. III. Series.
HC110.D5 N66     338/.0973     *LC* 78-20887     *ISBN* 0470266317

## HC110.D6 Diversification

**Gort, Michael, 1923-.**        • **4.2072**
Diversification and integration in American industry. A study by the National Bureau of Economic Research. Princeton, [N.J.] Princeton University Press, 1962. xxi, 238 p. diagrs., tables. (National Bureau of Economic Research. General series, no. 77) 1. Diversification in industry I. National Bureau of Economic Research. II. T. III. Series.
HC110 D6 G6     *LC* 62-11959

## HC110.E5 Environmental Policy

**Current issues in U.S. environmental policy / Paul R. Portney,**        **4.2073**
**editor; A. Myrick Freeman III ... [et al.].**
Baltimore: Published for Resources for the Future by the Johns Hopkins University Press, c1978. xv, 207 p.: ill.; 24 cm. 1. Environmental policy — United States — Addresses, essays, lectures. 2. Pollution — Economic aspects — United States — Addresses, essays, lectures. I. Freeman, A. Myrick, 1936- II. Portney, Paul R. III. Resources for the Future.
HC110.E5 C87        301.31/0973        LC 78-4328        ISBN 0801821185.
ISBN 0801821193 pbk

**Davies, J. Clarence.**        **4.2074**
The politics of pollution / J. Clarence Davies, III, and Barbara S. Davies. — 2d ed. — Indianapolis: Pegasus, 1975. x, 254 p.: ill.; 21 cm. 1. Environmental policy — United States. I. Davies, Barbara S., 1938- joint author. II. T.
HC110.E5 D35 1975        353.008/232        LC 74-20996        ISBN 0672537206

**Environmental policy under Reagan's executive order: the role**        **4.2075**
**of benefit–cost analysis / edited by V. Kerry Smith.**
Chapel Hill: University of North Carolina Press, c1984. xii, 266 p.: ill.; 24 cm. Includes index. 1. Environmental policy — United States — Cost effectiveness — Addresses, essays, lectures. 2. United States — Politics and government — 1981- — Addresses, essays, lectures. I. Smith, V. Kerry (Vincent Kerry), 1945-
HC110.E5 E49878 1984        363.7/056/0973 19        LC 83-23397        ISBN 0807816000

**Environmental regulation and the U.S. economy / edited by**        **4.2076**
**Henry M. Peskin, Paul R. Portney, and Allen V. Kneese; with**
**contributions by Barry P. Bosworth ... [et al.].**
Baltimore: Published for Resources for the Future by Johns Hopkins University Press, c1981. ix, 163 p.: ill.; 24 cm. 'Reprinted ... from the Natural resources journal, vol. 21, no. 3, July 1981'—T.p. verso. 1. Environmental policy — Economic aspects — United States — Addresses, essays, lectures. 2. Environmental law — Economic aspects — United States — Addresses, essays, lectures. 3. Environmental law — United States — Addresses, essays, lectures. I. Peskin, Henry M. II. Portney, Paul R. III. Kneese, Allen V. IV. Bosworth, Barry, 1942- V. Resources for the Future.
HC110.E5 E4989 1981        330.973/092 19        LC 81-47620        ISBN 0801827116

**Kneese, Allen V.**        **4.2077**
Pollution, prices, and public policy: a study sponsored jointly by Resources for the Future, inc. and the Brookings Institution / Allen V. Kneese, Charles L. Schultze. — Washington: Brookings Institution, [1975] x, 125 p.; 24 cm. 1. Environmental policy — United States. 2. Environmental policy — United States — Finance. 3. Environmental law — United States. I. Schultze, Charles L. joint author. II. T.
HC110.E5 K57        301.31/0973        LC 74-1432        ISBN 0815749945

**McHarg, Ian L.**        • **4.2078**
Design with nature / [by] Ian L. McHarg. [1st ed.] Garden City, N.Y.: published for the American Museum of Natural History [by] the Natural History Press, 1969. viii, 197 p.: ill. (part col.), maps (part col.); 29 cm. 1. Environmental policy — United States. 2. Human ecology 3. Man — Influence on nature I. American Museum of Natural History. II. T.
HC110.E5 M33        301.3        LC 76-77344

**Petulla, Joseph M.**        • **4.2079**
American environmental history: the exploitation and conservation of natural resources / Joseph M. Petulla. — San Francisco: Boyd & Fraser, 1977. 399 p.: ill., graphs, maps. 1. Environmental policy — United States — History. 2. Conservation of natural resources — United States — History. I. T.
HC110.E5 P48        HC110E5 P48.        ISBN 0878350586

## HC110.I5 Income

**United States. Office of Business Economics.**        • **4.2080**
Income distribution in the United States, by size / prepared in the Office of Busines Economics, National Income Division. — Washington: U.S. Govt. Print. Off., 1944/50-. v.: diagrs., tables; 29 cm. Issued 1944/50 as a supplement to the Survey of current business. 1950/53-        as a reprint from the Survey of current business. 1. Income — United States. I. T.
HC110.I5 A32

**United States. Office of Business Economics.**        • **4.2081**
U.S. income and output; a supplement to the Survey of current business / prepared in the Office of Business Economics under the supervision of Charles F. Schwartz and George Jaszi. — Washington: U.S. Dept.of Commerce, Office of Business Economics,[ 1958.] 241 p.: ill.; 29 cm. 1. Income — United States. 2. Gross national product — United States. I. Schwartz, Charles F. II. Jaszi, George. III. T. IV. Title: Survey of current business.
HC 110 I5 U582 1958        HC110.I5 A55.        LC 59-60144 rev

**United States. Office of Business Economics.**        • **4.2082**
Personal income, by States, since 1929; a supplement to the Survey of current business, by Charles F. Schwartz and Robert E. Graham, Jr., National Income Division. — New York: Greenwood Press, [1969] iv, 229 p.: illus.; 29 cm. Reprint of the 1956 ed. 1. Income — United States. I. Schwartz, Charles F. II. Graham, Alexander Steel. Robert E. III. Survey of current business. IV. T.
HC110.I5 A55 1969        339.41/0973        LC 79-92310        ISBN 0837124921

**Creamer, Daniel Barnett, 1909-.**        • **4.2083**
Personal income during business cycles / by Daniel Creamer, with the assistance of Martin Bernstein. — Princeton: Princeton University Press, 1956. xlii, 166 p.: ill.; 24 cm. — (Studies in business cycles. 6.) 1. Income — United States. 2. Business cycles I. National Bureau of Economic Research. II. T. III. Series.
HC110.I5 C7        LC 55-5003

**Income maintenance and labor supply; econometric studies.**        **4.2084**
**Edited by Glen G. Cain and Harold W. Watts.**
Chicago, Rand McNally College Pub. Co. [c1973] xxiv, 373 p. illus. 24 cm. (Institute for Research on Poverty monograph series.) 'A Markham book.' 1. Labor supply — United States — Effect of income maintenance programs on — Addresses, essays, lectures. I. Cain, Glen George. ed. II. Watts, Harold W. ed. III. Series.
HC110.I5 I48        331.1/26/0973        LC 72-95717        ISBN 0528670204

**Kolko, Gabriel.**        • **4.2085**
Wealth and power in America: an analysis of social class and income distribution. — New York: Praeger, [1962] xii, 178 p.: tables; 22 cm. (Books that matter) 1. Income — United States. 2. Wealth — United States. 3. United States — Economic conditions — 1945- 4. United States — Social conditions — 1945- I. T.
HC110.I5 K6        339.410973        LC 62-11584

**Lebergott, Stanley.**        **4.2086**
The American economy: income, wealth, and want / Stanley Lebergott. Princeton, N.J.: Princeton University Press, c1976. vi, 382 p.; 23 cm. 1. Income distribution — United States. 2. Wealth — United States. 3. Poor — United States. I. T.
HC110.I5 L38 1976        339.2/0973        LC 75-4461        ISBN 0691042101

**University of Michigan. Survey Research Center.**        • **4.2087**
Income and welfare in the United States: a study / [by] James N. Morgan [and others]; with the assistance of Norma Meyers and Barbara Baldwin. — New York: McGraw-Hill [1962] x, 531 p.: diagrs., forms, tables; 24 cm. 1. Income — United States 2. Public welfare — United States I. Morgan, James N. II. T.
HC110 I5 M47        LC 62-17030

**International Productivity Symposium. (1st: 1983: Tokyo,**        **4.2088**
**Japan)**
Measuring productivity: trends and comparisons from the First International Productivity Symposium / sponsored by the Japan Productivity Center. — New York: UNIPUB, c1984. xiv, 290 p.: ill.; 24 cm. 1. Industrial productivity — United States — Measurement — Congresses. 2. Industrial productivity — Japan — Measurement — Congresses. I. Nihon Seisansei Honbu. II. T.
HC110.I52 I57 1983        338/.06/0973 19        LC 84-51512        ISBN 0890590354

**Productivity growth and U.S. competitiveness / edited by**        **4.2089**
**William J. Baumol and Kenneth McLennan.**
New York: Oxford University Press, c1985. x, 228 p.; 25 cm. 'A Supplementary paper of the Committee for Economic Development.' 1. Industrial productivity — United States — Addresses, essays, lectures. 2. Industrial productivity — Japan — Addresses, essays, lectures. I. Baumol, William J. II. McLennan, Kenneth. III. Committee for Economic Development. IV. Title: Productivity growth and United States competitiveness.
HC110.I52 P756 1985        338/.06/0973 19        LC 84-29577        ISBN 0195035267

**Productivity prospects for growth / edited by Jerome M.**        **4.2090**
**Rosow.**
New York: Van Nostrand Reinhold Co., [1981] xxi, 340 p.; 24 cm. — (Van Nostrand Reinhold/Work in America Institute series.) Includes index. 1. Industrial productivity — United States — Addresses, essays, lectures. I. Rosow, Jerome M. II. Series.
HC110.I52 P76        338/.06/0973 19        LC 80-22096        ISBN 0442293267

## HC110.L3 Labor Productivity

**Kendrick, John W.**        **4.2091**
Postwar productivity trends in the United States, 1948–1969, by John W. Kendrick. Assisted by Maude R. Pech. — New York: National Bureau of Economic Research; distributed by Columbia University Press, 1974 (c1973).

xx, 369 p.: illus.; 24 cm. — (National Bureau of Economic Research, no. 98, general series) 1. Labor productivity — United States. I. T.
HC110.L3 K39    331.11/8/0973    LC 72-188341    ISBN 0870142402

## HC110.P6 Poverty

**Coles, Robert.**         • 4.2091a
Children of crisis; a study of courage and fear. [1st ed.] Boston, Little, Brown [1967] xiv, 401 p. ill. 'An Atlantic monthly press book.' 1. Afro-Americans — Segregation 2. Afro-American children 3. Fear in children I. T.
HC110.P6C56    LC 67-14450

**Coles, Robert.**         • 4.2092
Migrants, sharecroppers, mountaineers. — [1st ed.]. — Boston: Little, Brown, [1971] xviii, 653 p.: col. illus.; 22 cm. — (His Children of crisis, v. 2) 'An Atlantic Monthly Press book.' 1. Migrant labor — U.S. 2. Share-cropping 3. Poor — Southern States. I. T.
HC110.P6 C56 vol. 2 HD5856.U5    331.5/44/0973    LC 76-162331

**Coles, Robert.**         • 4.2093
The South goes North. — [1st ed.]. — Boston: Little, Brown, [1971] xv, 687 p.: ill. (part col.); 22 cm. — (His Children of crisis, v. 3) 'An Atlantic Monthly Press book.' 1. Rural-urban migration — U.S. 2. Migration, Internal — U.S. 3. Poor — U.S. I. T.
HC110.P6 C56 vol. 3 HB1965    301.3/63/0973    LC 70-162332

**Coles, Robert.**         4.2094
Eskimos, Chicanos, Indians / Robert Coles. — 1st ed. — Boston: Little, Brown, c1977. xx, 587 p., [16] leaves of plates: ill.; 22 cm. (His Children of crisis; v. 4) 'An Atlantic Monthly Press book.' Includes index. 1. Eskimos — Alaska — Children. 2. Indians of North America — Children. 3. Mexican American children. 4. Eskimos — Alaska — Social conditions. 5. Indians of North America — Social conditions. 6. Mexican Americans — Social conditions. I. T.
HC110.P6 C56 vol. 4 E99.E7    309.1/73/092 s 309.1/73/092    LC 77-21430    ISBN 0316151629

**Coles, Robert.**         4.2095
Privileged ones: the well-off and the rich in America / Robert Coles. — 1st ed. — Boston: Little, Brown, c1977. xviii, 583 p., [16] leaves of plates: ill.; 22 cm. (His Children of crisis; v. 5) 'An Atlantic Monthly Press book.' Includes index. 1. Children of the rich — United States. I. T.
HC110.P6 C56 vol. 5 HQ792.U5    309.1/73/092 s 301.43/14/0973    LC 77-10825    ISBN 0316151491

**Ferman, Louis A. ed.**         • 4.2096
Poverty in America: a book of readings / edited by Louis A. Ferman, Joyce L. Kornbluh, and Alan Haber; introd. by Michael Harrington. — Rev. ed. Ann Arbor: University of Michigan Press [1968] xxxiii, 669 p.: ill.; 23 cm. 1. Poverty 2. Poor — United States. I. Kornbluh, Joyce L. joint ed. II. T.
HC110.P6 F4 1968    301.45/23    LC 68-29261

**Harrington, Michael, 1928-.**         4.2097
The new American poverty / Michael Harrington. — 1st ed. — New York: Holt, Rinehart, and Winston, c1984. xii, 271 p.; 24 cm. Includes index. 1. Poor — United States. 2. Economic assistance, Domestic — United States I. T.
HC110.P6 H37 1984    305.5/69/0973 19    LC 84-3746    ISBN 0030621577

**On understanding poverty; perspectives from the social sciences.**         • 4.2098
**Edited by Daniel P. Moynihan, with the assistance of Corinne Saposs Schelling.**
New York, Basic Books [1969] xviii, 425 p. 25 cm. (Perspectives on poverty, 1) (American Academy of Arts and Sciences library.) Based on papers presented at a continuing seminar of the American Academy of Arts and Sciences on problems of race and poverty during the academic year 1966-67. 1. Poor — United States. 2. Poverty I. Moynihan, Daniel P. (Daniel Patrick), 1927- ed. II. American Academy of Arts and Sciences. III. Series.
HC110.P6 O5    301.45/23/0973    LC 71-78451

**Rodgers, Harrell R.**         4.2099
Poverty amid plenty: a political and economic analysis / Harrell R. Rodgers, Jr. — Reading, Mass.: Addison-Wesley Pub. Co., c1979. xv, 222 p.: ill.; 21 cm. 1. Poor — United States. 2. Poverty 3. Income distribution — United States. 4. Economic assistance, Domestic — United States I. T.
HC110.P6 R64    301.44/1    LC 78-18642    ISBN 0201064715

**Schiller, Bradley R., 1943-.**         4.2100
The economics of poverty and discrimination / Bradley R. Schiller. — 2d ed. — Englewood Cliffs, N.J.: Prentice-Hall, c1976. xi, 241 p.: ill.; 23 cm. 1. Poor — United States. 2. Poverty 3. Discrimination — United States. 4. Economic assistance, Domestic — United States I. T.
HC110.P6 S27 1976    305.5/69/0973 19    LC 75-37660    ISBN 0132320096

**Thurow, Lester C.**         4.2101
Poverty and discrimination [by] Lester C. Thurow. Washington, Brookings Institution [1969] viii, 214 p. illus. 24 cm. (Studies in social economics.) 'Bibliographical notes': p. 201-208. 1. Poor — United States. 2. Afro-Americans — Economic conditions 3. Race discrimination — United States I. T. II. Series.
HC110.P6 T5    301.44/1    LC 69-18825    ISBN 0815784449

**Tussing, A. Dale.**         4.2102
Poverty in a dual economy / A. Dale Tussing. — New York: St. Martin's Press, [1975] ix, 229 p.: ill.; 22 cm. 1. Poor — United States. 2. Public welfare — United States 3. Economic assistance, Domestic — United States 4. Poverty I. T.
HC110.P6 T92    362.5/0973    LC 73-91692

**United States. President's Commission on Income Maintenance**         • 4.2103
**Programs.**
Poverty amid plenty, the American paradox: the report of the President's Commission on Income Maintenance Programs. — [Washington: For sale by the Supt. of Docs., U.S. Govt. Print. Off.], 1969. ix, 155 p.: ill.; 25 cm. Commonly known as the Heineman report. 1. Economic assistance, Domestic — United States 2. Income — United States. 3. Poor — United States. I. T. II. Title: Heineman report on income maintenance.
HC110.P63 A59    362.5/0973    LC 71-605334

**A Decade of Federal antipoverty programs: achievements,**         4.2104
**failures, and lessons / edited by Robert H. Haveman.**
New York: Academic Press, c1977. x, 381 p.; 24 cm. (Poverty policy analysis series.) Papers from a conference sponsored by the Institute for Research on Poverty, University of Wisconsin, in 1974. 1. Economic assistance, Domestic — United States — Congresses. I. Haveman, Robert H. II. University of Wisconsin—Madison. Institute for Research on Poverty. III. Series.
HC110.P63 D42 1977    362.5/0973    LC 76-42969    ISBN 0123332508. ISBN 0123332567 pbk

**Moynihan, Daniel P. (Daniel Patrick), 1927-.**         • 4.2105
Maximum feasible misunderstanding; community action in the war on poverty [by] Daniel P. Moynihan. New York, Free Press [1969] xxi, 218 p. 22 cm. (The Clarke A. Sanford lectures on local government and community life, 1967.) (An Arkville Press book.) 1. Community Action Program (U.S.) I. T. II. Series.
HC110.P63 M6    362.5/0973    LC 69-18005

**On fighting poverty: perspectives from experience / edited by**         • 4.2106
**James L. Sundquist, with the assistance of Corinne Saposs Schelling.**
New York: Basic Books [1969] x, 256 p.; 25 cm. (Perspectives on poverty, 2) (American Academy of Arts and Sciences library.) Based on papers presented at a continuing seminar of the American Academy of Arts and Sciences on problems of race and poverty during the academic year 1966-67. 1. Economic assistance, Domestic — United States I. Sundquist, James L. ed. II. American Academy of Arts and Sciences. III. Series.
HC110.P63 O5    338.973    LC 75-78452

## HC110.T4 Technological Innovation

**David, Paul A.**         4.2107
Technical choice innovation and economic growth: essays on American and British experience in the nineteenth century / Paul A. David. — London: Cambridge University Press, 1975. x, 334 p.; 23 cm. Includes index. 1. Technological innovations — United States — History. 2. Technological innovations — Great Britain — History. 3. Economic development — Mathematical models. I. T.
HC110.T4 D38    338/.06/0973    LC 74-76583    ISBN 0521205182

**The Production and application of new industrial technology /**         4.2108
**Edwin Mansfield ... [et al.].**
1st ed. — New York: Norton, c1977. x, 220 p.: ill.; 24 cm. 1. Technological innovations — United States — Addresses, essays, lectures. 2. Research, Industrial — United States — Addresses, essays, lectures. I. Mansfield, Edwin.
HC110.T4 P76 1977    338/.06/0973    LC 77-9281    ISBN 0393091686

**Rosenberg, Nathan, 1927-.**         4.2109
Technology and American economic growth. — New York: Harper & Row, [1972] xi, 211 p.; 21 cm. — (Harper torchbooks, TB 1606) 1. Technological innovations — United States — History. I. T.
HC110.T4 R65    330.9/73    LC 77-146795    ISBN 0061316067

## HC110.W2 Wage–Price Policy

**Exhortation and controls: the search for a wage–price policy,    4.2110
1945–1971 / Craufurd D. Goodwin ... [et al.]; Craufurd D.
Goodwin, editor.**
Washington: Brookings Institution, [1975] xiii, 432 p.; 23 cm. (Studies in wage-price policy) Includes index. 1. Wage-price policy — United States — History — Congresses. I. Goodwin, Craufurd D. W. II. Series.
HC110.W24 F94        331.2/1/01       LC 75-23483       ISBN 0815732082

**Rockoff, Hugh.                                    4.2111**
Drastic measures: a history of wage and price controls in the United States / Hugh Rockoff. — Cambridge [Cambridgeshire]; New York: Cambridge University Press, 1984. xi, 289 p.: ill.; 24 cm. — (Studies in economic history and policy.) Includes indexes. 1. Wage-price policy — United States — History. I. T. II. Series.
HC110.W24 R6 1984        331.2/973 19       LC 83-21019       ISBN 052124496X

## HC110.W4 Wealth

**Pessen, Edward, 1920-.                                    4.2112**
Riches, class, and power before the Civil War. — Lexington, Mass.: D. C. Heath, [1973] 378 p.: ill.; 25 cm. 1. Wealth — United States. 2. Social mobility — United States. 3. Social classes — United States. I. T.
HC110.W4 P47        301.44/1       LC 72-12460       ISBN 0669844594

**Soltow, Lee.                                    4.2113**
Men and wealth in the United States, 1850–1870 / Lee Soltow. — New Haven: Yale University Press, 1975. xx, 206 p.: graphs; 23 cm. (Yale series in economic history) 1. Wealth — United States — History. I. T.
HC110.W4 S64        330.1/6       LC 74-29738       ISBN 0300018142

## HC110.Z Zoning

**Hansen, Niles M.                                    4.2114**
The future of nonmetropolitan America: studies in the reversal of rural and small town population decline / [by] Niles M. Hansen. — Lexington, Mass.: Lexington Books [1973] xvi, 187 p.: maps; 23 cm. 1. Economic zoning — United States. 2. United States — Industries — Location. 3. United States — Economic conditions — 1971-1981 — Case studies. I. T.
HC110.Z6 H35        330.9/73/092       LC 73-8515       ISBN 0669871060

## HC111–120 CANADA

**Easterbrook, W. T.                                    • 4.2115**
Canadian economic history, by W. T. Easterbrook and Hugh G. J. Aitken. — Toronto, Macmillan Co. of Canada, 1956. 606 p. illus. 25 cm. 1. Canada — Econ. condit. I. Aitken, Hugh G. J. joint author. II. T.
HC113.E2        330.971       LC 56-14769

**Innis, Harold Adams, 1894-1952.                                    • 4.2116**
Essays in Canadian economic history. Edited by Mary Q. Innis. — [Toronto] University of Toronto Press, 1956. 418 p. 24 cm. Bibliogr. footnotes 1. Canada — Econ. condit. — Addresses, essays, lectures. I. T.
HC113.I49        330.971       LC 57-1639

**Marr, William L., 1944-.                                    4.2117**
Canada, an economic history / William L. Marr, Donald G. Paterson. — Toronto: Macmillan of Canada, 1980. xx, 539 p.: ill.; 23 cm. Includes index. 1. Canada — Economic conditions I. Paterson, Donald G., 1942- joint author. II. T.
HC113.M37        330.971 19       LC 80-486658       ISBN 0770518451

**Innis, Harold A., 1894-1952.                                    • 4.2118**
Select documents in Canadian economic history, 1497–1783 / edited by H. A. Innis. — Toronto: University of Toronto Press, 1929. xxxiv, 581 p.; 24 cm. 1. Fisheries — Canada. 2. Fur trade — Canada. 3. Canada — Economic conditions 4. Canada — Industries — History. I. T.
HC114.I5        LC 30-11351

**Tucker, Gilbert Norman, 1898-1955.                                    • 4.2119**
The Canadian commercial revolution, 1845–1851. — [Hamden, Conn.]: Archon Books, 1971 [c1936] 258 p.: illus., map.; 23 cm. 'The present work ... in an earlier form was accepted as a doctoral dissertation by the University of Cambridge.' 1. Canada — Commerce 2. Canada — Economic conditions I. T.
HC114.T8 1971        330.971/04       LC 71-147378       ISBN 0208010262

**Caves, Richard E.                                    • 4.2120**
The Canadian economy; prospect and retrospect, by Richard E. Caves [and] Richard H. Holton. — Cambridge, Harvard University Press, 1959. xxii, 676 p. diagrs., tables. 22 cm. — (Harvard economic studies. v. 112) Bibliography: p. [647]-669. 1. Canada — Econ. condit. 2. Canada — Economic policy I. Holton, Richard Henry, 1926- joint author. II. T. III. Series.
HC115.C45        330.971       LC 59-14734

**Harris, Richard Colebrook.                                    4.2121**
Canada before Confederation; a study in historical geography [by] R. Cole Harris and John Warkentin. Cartographer: Miklos Pinther. — New York: Oxford University Press, 1974. xiv, 338 p.: illus.; 23 cm. — (Historical geography of North America series) 1. Land settlement — Canada. 2. Canada — Economic conditions 3. Canada — History I. Warkentin, John, 1928- joint author. II. T.
HC115.H33        330.9/71       LC 73-87622       ISBN 0195017919

**Innis, Harold Adams, 1894-1952. ed.                                    • 4.2122**
Select documents in Canadian economic history, 1783–1885, edited by H. A. Innis ... and A. R. M. Lower ... — Toronto, The University of Toronto press, 1933. viii, 846 p. 24 cm. Includes 'References'. 1. Canada — Econ. condit. 2. Canada — Indus. — Hist. I. Lower, A. R. M., ed. II. T.
HC115.I63        330.971       LC 33-32211

**Phidd, Richard W.                                    4.2123**
The politics and management of Canadian economic policy / Richard W. Phidd, G. Bruce Doern. — Toronto: Macmillan of Canada, c1978. 598 p.: ill.; 23 cm. Includes index. 1. Canada — Economic policy. I. Doern, G. Bruce. joint author. II. T.
HC115.P47        338.971       LC 78-321329       ISBN 0770516114

**Royal Commission on the Economic Union and Development      4.2124
Prospects for Canada.**
Report / Royal Commission on the Economic Union and Development Prospects for Canada. — Ottawa, Canada: Minister of Supply and Services Canada, c1985. 3 v.: ill.; 25 cm. Issued also in French. Title on half-title page: Report of the Royal Commission on the Economic Union and Development Prospects for Canada. 1. Federal government — Canada. 2. Canada — Economic conditions — 1945- 3. Canada — Economic policy. 4. Canada — Social conditions — 1945- 5. Canada — Foreign economic relations — United States. 6. United States — Foreign economic relations — Canada. I. T. II. Title: Report of the Royal Commission on the Economic Union and Development Prospects for Canada.
HC115.R67x 1985        LC 86-672099       ISBN 0660118505

**MacKay, Robert Alexander, 1894- ed.                                    • 4.2125**
Newfoundland; economic, diplomatic, and strategic studies, edited by R. A. MacKay ... with a foreword by Sir Campbell Stuart .... — Toronto: Oxford university press, 1946. xiv, 577 p.: illus. (maps) diagrs.; 24 cm. Issued under the auspices of the Royal institute of international affairs. 1. Fisheries — Newfoundland. 2. Newfoundland — Economic conditions. 3. Newfoundland — Politics and government. 4. Newfoundland — History. I. T.
HC117.N4 M28 1946        LC 46-5095

**Nelles, H. V.                                    4.2126**
The politics of development; forests, mines & hydro–electric power in Ontario, 1849–1941 [by] H. V. Nelles. — [Hamden, Conn.]: Archon Books, 1974. xiii, 514 p.: illus.; 25 cm. 1. Natural resources — Ontario — History. 2. Environmental policy — Ontario — History. 3. Conservation of natural resources — Ontario — History. I. T.
HC117.O6 N44        333.7/09713       LC 74-4038       ISBN 0208014500

**Ouellet, Fernand.                                    4.2127**
Economic and social history of Quebec, 1760–1850 / Fernand Ouellet; translated under the auspices of the Institute of Canadian Studies. — Toronto: Macmillan of Canada; [Ottawa]: Institute of Canadian Studies at Carleton University, c1980. 696 p. — (The Carleton library; no. 120) Translation of Histoire économique et sociale du Québec, 1760-1850. 1. Québec (Province) — Social conditions. I. Carleton University. Institute of Canadian Studies. II. T. III. Title: Histoire économique et sociale du Québec, 1760-1850.
HC117.Q8 O8x        330.9714/02       ISBN 0770518087 pa

**Economic Council of Canada.                                    4.2128**
Western transition. — [Ottawa, Ont.]: Economic Council of Canada: Canadian Govt. Pub. Centre [distributor], 1984. x, 260 p.: ill.; 27 cm. 1. Canada, Western — Economic conditions. 2. Canada, Western — Economic policy. 3. Canada — Economic conditions — 1945- 4. Canada — Economic policy. I. Economic Council of Canada. II. T.
HC117.W47 W47 1984        338.9712 19       LC 85-147766       ISBN 0660116936

**Stampede City: power and politics in the West / edited by      4.2129
Chuck Reasons.**
Toronto: Between the Lines, c1984. 216 p.: ill.; 24 cm. 1. Business and politics — Alberta — Calgary — Addresses, essays, lectures. 2. Petroleum industry and trade — Alberta — Calgary — Addresses, essays, lectures. 3. Calgary

(Alta.) — Economic conditions — Addresses, essays, lectures. 4. Calgary (Alta.) — Politics and government — Addresses, essays, lectures. I. Reasons, Charles E., 1945-
HC118.C29 S7 1984     330.97123/3 19     *LC* 85-128599     *ISBN* 0919946461

**Tulchinsky, Gerald J. J., 1933-.**           **4.2130**
The river barons: Montreal businessmen and the growth of industry and transportation, 1837–53 / Gerald J. J. Tulchinsky. — Toronto; Buffalo: University of Toronto Press, c1977. xiv, 310 p.; 24 cm. Includes index. 1. Businessmen — Québec (Province) — Montreal — History. 2. Railroads — Canada — History. 3. Shipping — Canada — History. 4. Montreal — Industries — History. I. T.
HC118.M6 T84     338/.09714/281     *LC* 76-26019     *ISBN* 0802053394

**Banting, Keith G.**           **4.2131**
The welfare state and Canadian federalism / Keith G. Banting. — Kingston: McGill-Queen's University Press: Institute of Intergovernmental Relations, Queen's University, 1982. xii, 226 p.: ill.; 23 cm. — (Queen's studies on the future of the Canadian communities. 3) Includes index. 1. Income maintenance programs — Canada. 2. Social security — Canada. 3. Federal government — Canada. I. T. II. Series.
HC120.I5 B36 1982     354.710082/56 19     *LC* 82-203732     *ISBN* 0773503803

**Dales, John Harkness, 1920-.**         • **4.2132**
Pollution, property and prices; an essay in policy–making and economics [by] J. H. Dales. — [Toronto]: University of Toronto Press, [1970, c1968] vii, 111 p.; 22 cm. 1. Pollution — Economic aspects — Canada. I. T.
HC120.P55 D3 1970     338.4/7/6281680971     *LC* 77-19675     *ISBN* 0802015662

**Grayson, L. M., comp.**           **4.2133**
The wretched of Canada; letters to R. B. Bennett, 1930–1935; edited, with an introd. by L. M. Grayson and Michael Bliss. — [Toronto; Buffalo]: University of Toronto Press, [1971] xxvii, 199 p.; 22 cm. — (Social history of Canada.) English or French. 1. Poor — Canada — History. 2. Canada — Social conditions I. Bennett, Richard Bedford Bennett, 1st Viscount, 1870-1947. II. Bliss, Michael. joint comp. III. T. IV. Series.
HC120.P6 G7     301.44/1     *LC* 73-163838     *ISBN* 0802061273

## HC121–125 Latin America: General
(see also: HC161-170)

**Randall, Laura Regina Rosenbaum.**          **4.2134**
A comparative economic history of Latin America: 1500–1914 / by Laura Randall. — Ann Arbor, Mich.: University Microfilms International, 1977. 4 v.; 26 cm. — (Monograph publishing on demand: sponsor series) 1. Comparative economics — Collected works. 2. Latin America — Economic conditions — Collected works. 3. Mexico — Economic conditions 4. Argentina — Economic conditions 5. Brazil — Economic conditions 6. Peru — Economic conditions I. T.
HC121.R36 1977     330.9/8     *LC* 77-81283     *ISBN* 0835702618

**Blakemore, Harold.**           **4.2135**
Latin America: geographical perspectives, edited by Harold Blakemore and Clifford T. Smith. London, Methuen, 1972 (c1971). viii, 598 p. maps. 24 cm. 'Distributed in the U.S.A. by Barnes and Noble, Inc.' 1. Latin America — Economic conditions — Addresses, essays, lectures. 2. Latin America — Social conditions — 1945- — Addresses, essays, lectures. I. Smith, Clifford T. (Clifford Thorpe), 1924- joint author. II. T.
HC125.B55     309.1/8/003     *LC* 72-175723     *ISBN* 0416108202

**Cardoso, Fernando Henrique.**          **4.2136**
Dependency and development in Latin America / Fernando Henrique Cardoso and Enzo Faletto; translated by Marjory Mattingly Urquidi. — Berkeley: University of California Press, 1979, c1978. xxv, 227 p.; 23 cm. Expanded and emended translation of Dependencia y desarrollo en América Latina. 1. Latin America — Economic conditions — 1945- 2. Latin America — Social conditions — 1945- 3. Latin America — Politics and government — 1948- 4. Latin America — Dependency on foreign countries. I. Faletto, Enzo. joint author. II. T.
HC125.C34153     309.1/8/003     *LC* 75-46033     *ISBN* 0520031938

**Cole, J. P. (John Peter), 1928-.**          **4.2137**
Latin America; an economic and social geography. [2d. ed.] London, Butterworths, 1975. 470 p. ill. 25 cm. 1. Latin America — Economic conditions — 1945- 2. Latin America — Social conditions — 1945- I. T.
HC 125 C68 1975     *LC* 75-328418     *ISBN* 0408706538

**Economic issues and political conflict: US–Latin American**     **4.2138**
**relations / edited by Jorge I. Dominguez.**
London: Butterworth Scientific, 1982. 246 p.; 24 cm. — (Butterworths studies in international political economy.) 1. Economic development — Political aspects 2. Latin America — Economic conditions — 1945- I. Domínguez, Jorge I., 1945- II. Series.
HC125 E38     HC125 E38.     *ISBN* 040810807X

**Farley, Rawle, 1922-.**           **4.2139**
The economics of Latin America; development problems in perspective. — New York: Harper & Row, [1972] x, 400 p.: illus.; 25 cm. 1. Latin America — Economic conditions — 1945- I. T.
HC125.F36     330.9/8/003     *LC* 76-190661     *ISBN* 0060419989

**Furtado, Celso.**          • **4.2140**
[Formação econômica da América Latina. English] Economic development of Latin America; a survey from colonial times to the Cuban revolution. Translated by Suzette Macedo. Cambridge [Eng.] University Press, 1970. xvi, 271 p. maps. 22 cm. (Cambridge Latin American studies. no. 8) Translation of Formação econômica da América Latina. 1. Latin America — Economic conditions — Social conditions I. T. II. Series.
HC125.F78     330.98     *LC* 74-121365     *ISBN* 0521078288

**Galeano, Eduardo H., 1940-.**          **4.2141**
[Venas abiertas de América Latina. English] Open veins of Latin America; five centuries of the pillage of a continent [by] Eduardo Galeano. Translated by Cedric Belfrage. New York, Monthly Review Press [1973] 313 p. 21 cm. Translation of Las venas abiertas de América Latina. 1. Latin America — Economic conditions I. T.
HC125.G25313     330.9/8     *LC* 72-92036     *ISBN* 0853452792

**Inflation and stabilisation in Latin America / edited by**     **4.2142**
**Rosemary Thorp and Laurence Whitehead.**
New York: Holmes & Meier Publishers, 1979. ix, 285 p.: ill.; 23 cm. 1. Economic stabilization — Addresses, essays, lectures. 2. Inflation (Finance) — Latin America — Addresses, essays, lectures. 3. Latin America — Economic policy — Addresses, essays, lectures. 4. Latin America — Economic conditions — 1945- — Addresses, essays, lectures. I. Thorp, Rosemary. II. Whitehead, Laurence.
HC125.I4 1979     330.9/8/003     *LC* 79-11887     *ISBN* 0841905126

**Inter-American Development Bank.**         **4.2143**
Economic and social progress in Latin America; annual report. 1972-. Washington. v. ill. 23 cm. Annual. 1. Latin America — Economic conditions — 1945- — Periodicals. 2. Latin America — Social conditions — 1945- — Periodicals. I. T.
HC125.I514     330.9/8/003     *LC* 74-648164

**Odell, Peter R.**           **4.2144**
Economies and societies in Latin America: a geographical interpretation / Peter R. Odell and David A. Preston. 2d ed. — Chichester, Eng.; New York: Wiley, c1978. p. cm. 1. Latin America — Economic conditions 2. Latin America — Social conditions I. Preston, David A. joint author. II. T.
HC125.O33 1978     330.9/8     *LC* 77-12400     *ISBN* 0471995886

**Stein, Stanley J.**          • **4.2145**
The colonial heritage of Latin America; essays on economic dependence in perspective [by] Stanley J. and Barbara H. Stein. — New York: Oxford University Press, 1970. viii, 222 p.; 21 cm. Cover title: Essays on economic dependence in perspective. 1. Latin America — Economic conditions I. Stein, Barbara H., joint author. II. T. III. Title: Essays on economic dependence in perspective.
HC125.S76     330.98     *LC* 73-83053

## HC131–140 Mexico

**Cockcroft, James D.**          **4.2146**
Mexico: class formation, capital accumulation, and the state / James D. Cockcroft. — New York: Monthly Review Press, c1983. viii, 384 p.: ill.; 22 cm. Includes index. 1. Social classes — Mexico — History. 2. Mexico — Politics and government 3. Mexico — Social conditions 4. Mexico — Economic conditions I. T.
HC133.C6 1983     330.972 19     *LC* 81-84748     *ISBN* 0853455600

**Vernon, Raymond, 1913-.**         • **4.2147**
The dilemma of Mexico's development: the roles of the private and public sectors. — Cambridge, Mass.: Harvard University Press, 1963. xi, 226 p.: map, diagrs., tables.; 22 cm. 1. Mexico — Economic policy 2. Mexico — Economic conditions — 1918- I. T.
HC135.V4 1963     338.972     *LC* 63-17214

**Rothstein, Frances.**          **4.2148**
Three different worlds: women, men, and children in an industrializing community / Frances Abrahamer Rothstein. — Westport, Conn.: Greenwood

Press, c1982. xii, 148 p.: ill., map, ports.; 22 cm. — (Contributions in family studies. 0147-1023; no. 7) Includes index. 1. Mazatecochco (Mexico) — Economic conditions. 2. Mazatecochco (Mexico) — Social conditions. I. T. II. Series.
HC138.M33 R67 1982     306/.3/097247 19     *LC* 82-6216     *ISBN* 031322594X

**Cancian, Frank.**        **4.2149**
Change and uncertainty in a peasant economy: the Maya corn farmers of Zinacantan. Stanford, Calif., Stanford University Press, 1972. xi, 208 p. illus. 23 cm. 1. Tzotzil Indians — Economic conditions. 2. Corn — Mexico — Zinacantán. 3. Zinacantán (Mexico) — Economic conditions. 4. Zinacantán (Mexico) — Social conditions. I. T.
HC138.Z5 C35     330.9/72/7     *LC* 72-153814     *ISBN* 0804707871

# HC141–160 Central America. West Indies

**MacLeod, Murdo J.**        **4.2150**
Spanish Central America; a socioeconomic history, 1520–1720 [by] Murdo J. MacLeod. — Berkeley: University of California Press, [1973] xvi, 554 p.: illus.; 24 cm. 1. Central America — Economic conditions 2. Central America — Social conditions I. T.
HC141.M36     330.9/728/05     *LC* 70-174456     *ISBN* 0520021371

**Dependency under challenge: the political economy of the**        **4.2151**
**Commonwealth Caribbean / edited by Anthony Payne and Paul Sutton.**
Manchester, UK; Dover, N.H., USA: Manchester University Press, c1984. xi, 295 p.: map; 23 cm. 1. Caribbean Area — Economic policy — Addresses, essays, lectures. 2. Caribbean Area — Politics and government — 1945- — Addresses, essays, lectures. 3. Caribbean Area — Foreign economic relations — Addresses, essays, lectures. 4. Caribbean Area — Dependency on foreign countries — Addresses, essays, lectures. I. Payne, Anthony, 1952- II. Sutton, Paul K.
HC151.D46 1984     337/.09182/1 19     *LC* 83-9841     *ISBN* 0719009707

**Brundenius, Claes, 1938-.**        **4.2152**
Revolutionary Cuba, the challenge of economic growth with equity / Claes Brundenius. — Boulder, Colo.: Westview Press, c1984. xvi, 224 p.: ill.; 24 cm. — (Westview special studies on Latin America and the Caribbean.) Includes index. 1. Income distribution — Cuba. 2. Labor and laboring classes — Cuba. 3. Cuba — Economic conditions — 1959- 4. Cuba — Economic conditions I. T. II. Series.
HC152.5.B79 1984     338.97291 19     *LC* 83-12432     *ISBN* 0865313555

**Mesa-Lago, Carmelo, 1934-.**        **4.2153**
The economy of socialist Cuba: a two–decade appraisal / Carmelo Mesa–Lago. — 1st ed. — Albuquerque: University of New Mexico Press, c1981. xvi, 235 p.; 25 cm. 1. Cuba — Economic conditions — 1959- I. T.
HC152.5.M47     330.97291/064 19     *LC* 80-54570     *ISBN* 0826305784

**Lundahl, Mats, 1946-.**        **4.2154**
The Haitian economy: man, land, and markets / Mats Lundahl. — New York: St. Martin's Press, 1983. 290 p.: ill.; 23 cm. Includes index. 1. Peasantry — Haiti. 2. Agriculture — Haiti. 3. Poor — Haiti. 4. Haiti — Economic conditions — 1971- I. T.
HC153.L86 1983     330.97294/06 19     *LC* 83-13852     *ISBN* 0312356617

**Chernick, S. E.**        **4.2155**
The Commonwealth Caribbean: the integration experience: report of a mission sent to the Commonwealth Caribbean by the World Bank / Sidney E. Chernick. — Baltimore: Published for the World Bank [by] Johns Hopkins University Press, c1978. xv, 521 p.: ill.; 26 cm. — (A World Bank country economic report) 1. Caribbean Community. 2. Caribbean Area — Economic integration. 3. Caribbean Area — Economic conditions — 1945- I. World Bank. II. T.
HC155.C53     330.9/729     *LC* 77-17246     *ISBN* 0801820898

**Payne, Anthony, 1952-.**        **4.2156**
The politics of the Caribbean community, 1961–79: regional integration among new states / Anthony Payne. — New York: St. Martin's Press, 1980. xi, 299 p.; 23 cm. Includes index. 1. Caribbean Area — Economic integration. 2. Caribbean Area — Politics and government I. T.
HC155.P39 1980     337.1/729 19     *LC* 80-10500     *ISBN* 0312628749

**Thorndike, Tony.**        **4.2157**
Grenada: politics, economics, and society / Tony Thorndike. — Boulder, Colo.: L. Rienner Publishers, 1985. xx, 206 p.: ill.; 23 cm. (Marxist regimes series.)
Includes index. 1. Grenada — Economic conditions. 2. Grenada — Social conditions. 3. Grenada — Politics and government I. T. II. Series.
HC156.5.Z7 G848 1985     972.98/45 19     *LC* 84-62665     *ISBN* 0931477093

**Green, William A., 1935-.**        **4.2158**
British slave emancipation: the sugar colonies and the great experiment 1830–1865 / William A. Green. Oxford [Eng.]: Clarendon Press, 1976. x, 449 p., [2] leaves of plates: maps; 23 cm. Includes index. 1. Slavery — West Indies, British — Emancipation. 2. West Indies, British — Economic conditions. 3. West Indies, British — Social conditions. 4. Great Britain — Colonies — Administration I. T.
HC157.B8 G74     301.44/93/09729     *LC* 76-361326     *ISBN* 0198224362

**Mesa-Lago, Carmelo, 1934-.**        **4.2159**
Revolutionary change in Cuba. Carmelo Mesa–Lago, editor. [Pittsburgh, Pa.] University of Pittsburgh Press [1971] 544p. 1. Cuba — Economic conditions — 1959- - Addresses, essays, lectures 2. Cuba — Politics and government — 1959- - Addresses, essays, lectures 3. Cuba — Social conditions — Addresses, essays, lectures I. University of Pittsburgh. II. T.
HC157 C9 R45

**Moore, O. Ernest.**        **4.2160**
Haiti: its stagnant society and shackled economy; a survey, by O. Ernest Moore. [1st ed.] New York, Exposition Press [1972] x, 281 p. 21 cm. (An Exposition-university book) 1. Haiti — Economic conditions — 1971- 2. Haiti — Social conditions — 1971- I. T.
HC157.H2 M58     309.1/7294/06     *LC* 78-187036     *ISBN* 0682474258

**Picó, Rafael.**        **4.2161**
The geography of Puerto Rico. — [1st ed.]. — Chicago: Aldine Pub. Co., [1974] xii, 439 p.: illus.; 25 cm. Based on the author's Nueva geografía de Puerto Rico (1969) and on his The geographic regions of Puerto Rico (1950) 1. Agriculture — Economic aspects — Puerto Rico. 2. Puerto Rico — Economic conditions — 1952- 3. Puerto Rico — Description and travel — 1951-1980 I. T.
HC157.P8 P495     330.9/7295/053     *LC* 72-182916     *ISBN* 0202100561

# HC161–170 Latin America: General
(see also: HC121-125)

**Foxley, Alejandro.**        **4.2162**
Latin American experiments in neoconservative economics / Alejandro Foxley. — Berkeley: University of California Press, c1983. xv, 213 p.; 22 cm. 1. Economic stabilization — Southern Cone of South America. 2. Monetary policy — Southern Cone of South America. 3. Chicago school of economics 4. Southern Cone of South America — Economic policy. 5. Chile — Economic policy. I. T.
HC165.F675 1983     338.98 19     *LC* 82-20252     *ISBN* 0520048075

**Puyana de Palacios, Alicia, 1941-.**        **4.2163**
Economic integration among unequal partners: the case of the Andean group / Alicia Puyana de Palacios. — New York: Pergamon Press, c1982. xxvi, 405 p.: ill.; 24 cm. — (Pergamon policy studies on international development.) Includes index. 1. Cartagena Agreement (1969) 2. Andes Region — Economic integration. I. T. II. Series.
HC165.P89 1982     337.1/8 19     *LC* 81-21005     *ISBN* 0080288227

**Weaver, Frederick Stirton, 1939-.**        **4.2164**
Class, state, and industrial structure: the historical process of South American industrial growth / Frederick Stirton Weaver. — Westport, Conn.: Greenwood Press, 1980. xiv, 247 p.: ill.; 24 cm. — (Contributions in economics and economic history; no. 32 0084-9235) Includes index. 1. South America — Industries — History. 2. South America — Economic conditions 3. South America — Commerce — History. I. T.
HC165.W35     338/.098     *LC* 79-6571     *ISBN* 0313221146

# HC171–195 Argentina. Brazil. Chile

**Brown, Jonathan C., 1942-.**        **4.2165**
A socioeconomic history of Argentina, 1776–1860 / Jonathan C. Brown. — Cambridge [Eng.]; New York: Cambridge University Press, 1979. xiv, 302 p.: ill.; 22 cm. — (Cambridge Latin American studies. 35) Includes index. 1. Argentina — Economic conditions 2. Argentina — Social conditions I. T. II. Series.
HC175.B77     330.9/82     *LC* 78-6800     *ISBN* 0521222192

**Ferns, H. S. (Henry Stanley), 1913-.**        **4.2166**
The Argentine Republic, 1516–1971 [by] H. S. Ferns. Newton Abbot [Eng.] David & Charles; New York, Barnes & Noble [1973] 212 p. map. 22 cm.

(National economic histories) 1. Argentina — Economic conditions 2. Argentina — Economic policy. I. T.
HC175.F39 1973     330.9/82     *LC* 73-176628

**Randall, Laura Regina Rosenbaum.**       **4.2167**
An economic history of Argentina in the twentieth century / Laura Randall. New York: Columbia University Press, 1978 (c1977). 322 p.; 23 cm. Includes index. 1. Argentina — Economic conditions I. T.
HC175.R353     330.9/82/06     *LC* 77-24388     *ISBN* 0231033583

**Frank, Andre Gunder, 1929-.**       **4.2168**
Capitalism and underdevelopment in Latin America: historical studies of Chile and Brazil. — [Revised ed.]. — Harmonsworth: Penguin, 1971. 368 p.; 18 cm. — (The Pelican Latin American library) Includes index. 1. Brazil — Economic conditions 2. Chile — Economic conditions I. T.
HC187.F733 1971     330.9/81/06     *LC* 73-174622     *ISBN* 0140213341

**Furtado, Celso.**       • **4.2169**
The economic growth of Brazil, a survey from colonial to modern times. Translated by Ricardo W. de Aguiar and Eric Charles Drysdale. Berkeley, University of California Press, 1963. 285 p. 1. Brazil — Economic conditions I. T.
HC187 F813     *LC* 63-12818

**Lang, James.**       **4.2170**
Portuguese Brazil: the king's plantation / James Lang. — New York: Academic Press, c1979. xiv, 266 p.: maps; 24 cm. — (Studies in social discontinuity.) Includes index. 1. Brazil — Economic conditions 2. Brazil — Commerce — History. 3. Brazil — Politics and government 4. Portugal — Colonies — America — Administration. I. T. II. Series.
HC187.L3355     380.1/0981     *LC* 79-21005     *ISBN* 0124364802

**Pereira, Luiz Carlos Bresser.**       **4.2171**
Development and crisis in Brazil, 1930–1983 / Luiz Bresser Pereira; with a foreword by Thomas C Bruneau; translated from the Portuguese by Marcia Van Dyke. — Boulder, Colo.: Westview Press, 1984. xiv, 241 p.: ill.; 24 cm. — (Westview special studies on Latin America and the Caribbean.) Includes index. 1. Industry and state — Brazil — History — 20th century. 2. Brazil — Economic policy. 3. Brazil — Economic conditions — 1918- 4. Brazil — Politics and government — 20th century I. T. II. Series.
HC187.P392213 1984     338.981 19     *LC* 83-10232     *ISBN* 0865315590

**Robock, Stefan Hyman, 1915-.**       **4.2172**
Brazil: a study in development progress / Stefan H. Robock. — Lexington, Mass.: Lexington Books, [1975] xv, 204 p.: ill.; 24 cm. 1. Brazil — Economic conditions — 1945-1964 2. Brazil — Social conditions — 1945-1964 3. Brazil — Politics and government — 1964-1985 4. Brazil — Economic conditions — 1964-1985 5. Brazil — Social conditions — 1964- I. T.
HC187.R612     330.9/81/06     *LC* 75-18348     *ISBN* 0669001341

**Wythe, George, 1893-.**       • **4.2173**
Brazil, an expanding economy, by George Wythe, with the assistance of Royce A. Wight and Harold M. Midkiff. — New York: Greenwood Press, 1968 [c1949] xix, 412 p.: illus., maps.; 23 cm. 1. Brazil — Economic conditions I. T.
HC187.W9 1968     330.981     *LC* 68-8076

**Dean, Warren.**       **4.2174**
The industrialization of São Paulo, 1880-1945. Austin, Published for the Institute of Latin American Studies by the University of Texas Press [1969] x, 263 p. 24 cm. (Latin American monographs, no. 17) 1. São Paulo (Brazil: State) — Industries — History. I. T.
HC188.S3 D4     338/.0981/6     *LC* 73-96435     *ISBN* 0292700040

**Stein, Stanley J.**       • **4.2175**
Vassouras, a Brazilian coffee county, 1850–1900. Cambridge Harvard University Press 1957. 316p. (Harvard historical studies. v. 69) 1. Coffee — Brazil — Vassouras 2. Coffee trade — Vassouras I. T. II. Series.
HC188 V3 S8

**Ellsworth, P. T. (Paul Theodore), 1897-.**       • **4.2176**
Chile, an economy in transition [by] P.T. Ellsworth ... New York, The Macmillan Company, 1945. xi p., 1 β., 183 p. front. (map) diagrs. 21 cm. 1. Chile — Economic conditions — 1918- I. T.
HC192.E47     *LC* 44-40395

**Mamalakis, Markos.**       **4.2177**
The growth and structure of the Chilean economy: from independence to Allende / Markos J. Mamalakis. — New Haven: Yale University Press, 1976. xx, 390 p.: ill.; 24 cm. (A Publication of the Economic Growth Center, Yale University) 1. Chile — Economic conditions I. T.
HC192.M29     330.9/83/064     *LC* 74-29729     *ISBN* 0300018606

## HC196–239 Colombia. Peru. Uruguay. Venezuela

**Twinam, Ann, 1946-.**       **4.2178**
Miners, merchants, and farmers in colonial Colombia / by Ann Twinam. — Austin, Tex.: University of Texas Press, 1982. xii, 193 p.: ill.; 24 cm. — (Latin American monographs; no. 57) Includes index. 1. Antioquia (Colombia: Dept.) — Economic conditions. 2. Antioquia (Colombia: Dept.) — Social conditions. 3. Antioquia (Colombia: Dept.) — Civilization. I. T.
HC198.A5 T9 1982     338/.04/0986126 19     *LC* 82-11054     *ISBN* 0292720343

**Adamson, Alan H.**       **4.2179**
Sugar without slaves; the political economy of British Guiana, 1838–1904, by Alan H. Adamson. — New Haven: Yale University Press, 1972. ix, 315 p.; 23 cm. — (Caribbean series, 13) 1. Sugar trade — Guyana. 2. Guyana — Economic conditions 3. Guyana — Social conditions I. T. II. Series.
HC207.A64     330.9/88/103     *LC* 72-75186     *ISBN* 0300015038

**Brush, Stephen B., 1943-.**       **4.2180**
Mountain, field, and family: the economy and human ecology of an Andean valley / Stephen B. Brush. — [Philadelphia]: University of Pennsylvania Press, 1977. xiv, 199 p., [5] leaves of plates: ill.; 24 cm. Includes index. 1. Indians of South America — Peru — Economic conditions. 2. Peasantry — Peru. 3. Peru — Economic conditions — 1968- I. T.
HC227.B79     330.9/85/063     *LC* 77-24364

**Finch, M. H. J. (Martin Henry John)**       **4.2181**
A political economy of Uruguay since 1870 / M. H. J. Finch. — New York: St. Martin's Press, 1982, c1981. xiii, 339 p.: map; 22 cm. Includes index. 1. Uruguay — Economic policy. 2. Uruguay — Economic conditions I. T.
HC232.F56 1982     330.9895/06 19     *LC* 80-21047     *ISBN* 0312622449

**Roseberry, William, 1950-.**       **4.2182**
Coffee and capitalism in the Venezuelan Andes / by William Roseberry. — 1st ed. — Austin: University of Texas Press, 1983. xv, 256 p.: ill.; 24 cm. — (Latin American monographs; no. 59) Revision of thesis (Ph. D.)—University of Connecticut, 1977, presented under title: Social class and social process in the Venezuelan Andes. Includes index. 1. Peasantry — Venezuela — Boconó (District) 2. Boconó (Venezuela: District) — Social conditions. 3. Andes Region — Economic conditions. 4. Andes Region — Social conditions. 5. Boconó (Venezuela: District) — Economic conditions. I. T.
HC238.B58 R67 1983     330.987/14 19     *LC* 83-1350     *ISBN* 0292715358

## HC240–244 EUROPE: GENERAL

### HC240 A–H

**Arkes, Hadley.**       • **4.2183**
Bureaucracy, the Marshall Plan, and the national interest. Princeton, N.J., Princeton University Press [1973, c1972] xiv, 395 p. 25 cm. 1. United States. Economic Cooperation Administration. 2. Marshall Plan. 3. Economic assistance, American I. T.
HC240.A832     338.91/73     *LC* 78-166360     *ISBN* 0691046077

**Bautier, Robert Henri.**       **4.2184**
The economic development of medieval Europe. [Translated from the French by Heather Karolyi. 1st American ed. New York] Harcourt Brace Jovanovich [1971] 286 p. illus. (part col.), facsims., maps. 22 cm. 1. Europe — Economic conditions — To 1492 I. T.
HC240.B3613 1971     330.9/4/01     *LC* 73-141798     *ISBN* 015127438X

**Blacksell, Mark, 1942-.**       **4.2185**
Post–war Europe: a political geography / Mark Blacksell. — Boulder, Colo.: Westview Press, 1978. 205 p.: ill.; 23 cm. Includes index. 1. Europe — Economic conditions — 1945- I. T.
HC240.B57     330.9/4/055     *LC* 77-82814     *ISBN* 0891588221

**Burke, Peter. comp.**       **4.2186**
Economy and society in early modern Europe; essays from Annales. — New York: Harper & Row, [1972] 169 p.: illus.; 23 cm. — (A Torchbook library edition) 1. Prices — Europe — Addresses, essays, lectures. 2. Europe — Economic conditions — Addresses, essays, lectures. 3. Europe — Social conditions — Addresses, essays, lectures. I. Annales; économies, sociétés civilisations. II. T.
HC240.B88     330.9/4/02     *LC* 79-184873     *ISBN* 0061360740

**The Cambridge economic history of Europe; general editors,** • **4.2187**
**M.M. Postan and H.J. Habakkuk.**
2nd ed. Cambridge, Cambridge U.P., 1966. v. < 1- > illus. 24 cm. 1. Europe — Economic conditions 2. Europe — History I. Postan, M. M. (Michael Moïssey), 1899-1981. ed. II. Habakkuk, H. J. ed.
HC240.C312     330.94 19     LC 66-66029

**Cameron, Rondo E.** • **4.2188**
France and the economic development of Europe, 1800–1914; conquests of peace and seeds of war. Princeton, N.J., Princeton University Press, 1961. xviii, 586 p. ill., maps (1 fold. col.) 1. Europe — Economic conditions 2. France — Foreign economic relations 3. France — Economic conditions I. T.
HC240 C32     LC 60-12229

**Church, R. J. Harrison (Ronald James Harrison)** **4.2189**
An advanced geography of northern and western Europe / [by] R. J. Harrison Church ... [et al.]. — 2nd ed. — London: Hulton, 1973. 480 p.: ill., maps; 25 cm. 1. Europe — Economic conditions — 1945- I. T.
HC240.C49 1973     914     LC 74-183177     ISBN 0717504131

**Cipolla, Carlo M.** **4.2190**
[Storia economica dell'Europa pre-industriale. English] Before the Industrial Revolution: European society and economy, 1000–1700 / Carlo M. Cipolla. — 1st ed. — New York: Norton, c1976. xiv, 326 p.: ill.; 22 cm. Translation of Storia economica dell'Europa pre-industriale. Includes index. 1. Europe — Economic conditions I. T.
HC240.C49513 1976     330.9/4/01     LC 75-19366     ISBN 0393055388. ISBN 0393092550 pbk

**Clough, Shepard Bancroft, 1901- comp.** • **4.2191**
Economic history of Europe, twentieth century. Edited by Shepard B. Clough, Thomas Moodie [and] Carol Moodie. Maps by Willow Roberts. — New York: Harper & Row, [1968] xv, 384 p.: maps.; 21 cm. — (Documentary history of Western civilization) (Harper torchbooks, TB1388.) 1. Europe — Economic conditions I. Moodie, Thomas, joint comp. II. Moodie, Carol Gayle, joint comp. III. T.
HC240.C552     330.94     LC 72-517

**Davis, Ralph, 1915-.** **4.2192**
The rise of the Atlantic economies. — Ithaca, N.Y.: Cornell University Press, [1973] xiv, 352 p.: maps.; 23 cm. — (World economic history) 1. Europe — Economic conditions 2. America — Economic conditions I. T.
HC240.D32     330.9/4     LC 73-77683     ISBN 0801408016

**Denison, Edward Fulton, 1915-.** • **4.2193**
Why growth rates differ; postwar experience in nine western countries [by] Edward F. Denison, assisted by Jean–Pierre Poullier. — Washington: Brookings Institution, [1967] xxi, 494 p.; 26 cm. 1. Europe — Economic conditions — 1945- 2. United States — Economic conditions — 1945- I. T.
HC240.D45     339.3     LC 67-27682

**De Vries, Jan, 1943-.** **4.2194**
Economy of Europe in an age of crisis, 1600–1750 / Jan de Vries. — Cambridge, [Eng.]; New York: Cambridge University Press, 1976. xi, 284 p.: ill.; 21 cm. 1. Europe — Economic conditions — 17th century 2. Europe — History — 17th century 3. Europe — History — 18th century I. T.
HC240.D48 1976     330.9/4/055     LC 75-30438     ISBN 0521211239. ISBN 0521290503 pbk

**The European economy: growth and crisis / edited by Andrea** **4.2195**
**Boltho.**
New York: Oxford University Press, 1983 (c1982). xvii, 668 p.: graphs; 24 cm. 1. Europe — Economic conditions — 1945- — Addresses, essays, lectures. 2. Europe — Economic policy — Addresses, essays, lectures. I. Boltho, Andrea.
HC240.E8363     330.94/055 19     LC 82-7909     ISBN 0198771185

**The Fontana economic history of Europe / ed. by Carlo M.** **4.2196**
**Cipolla.**
New York: Barnes & Noble, 1976-1977. 6 v. in 9: ill.,: maps, 18 cm. 1. Europe — Economic conditions — Collected works. I. Cipolla, Carlo M.
HC240.F583     330.9/4     LC 75-324062     ISBN 0006334717

**Gerschenkron, Alexander.** • **4.2197**
Continuity in history, and other essays. — Cambridge, Mass.: Belknap Press of Harvard University Press, 1968. x, 545 p.; 24 cm. 1. Economic history — Addresses, essays, lectures. 2. Europe — Industries — History — Addresses, essays, lectures. 3. Europe — Economic conditions — Addresses, essays, lectures. I. T.
HC240.G465     330.9     LC 68-14257

**Hamerow, Theodore S.** **4.2198**
The birth of a new Europe: state and society in the nineteenth century / Theodore S. Hamerow. — Chapel Hill: University of North Carolina Press, c1983. xii, 447 p.: graphs; 24 cm. 1. Europe — Economic conditions —

1789-1900 2. Europe — Social conditions — 1789-1900 3. Europe — Politics and government — 1789-1900 4. Europe — Foreign relations I. T.
HC240.H314 1983     940.2/8 19     LC 82-20162     ISBN 0807815489

**Hodgett, Gerald Augustus John.** **4.2199**
A social and economic history of medieval Europe, [by] Gerald A. J. Hodgett. London, Methuen, 1972. [10], 246 p. 22 cm. 1. Europe — Economic conditions — To 1492 2. Europe — Social conditions — To 1492 I. T.
HC240.H58     309.1/4/01     LC 72-170170     ISBN 0416757405 ISBN 0416757502

## HC240 J–Z

**Jones, E. L. (Eric Lionel).** **4.2200**
The European miracle: environments, economies, and geopolitics in the history of Europe and Asia / E.L. Jones. — 2nd ed. — Cambridge; New York: Cambridge University Press, 1987. p. cm. Includes index. 1. Europe — Economic conditions 2. Asia — Economic conditions I. T.
HC240.J57 1987     330.94/02 19     LC 87-8092     ISBN 0521334497

**Landes, David S.** **4.2201**
The unbound Prometheus: technological change and industrial development in Western Europe from 1750 to the present [by] David S. Landes. — London: Cambridge U.P., 1969. ix, 566 p.; 23 cm. 'Chapters 2-5 and the Conclusion are revised versions of material first published in chapter 5 of The Cambridge economic history of Europe, volume 6, part 1.' 1. Europe — Industries — History. 2. Europe — Economic conditions I. T.
HC240.L26     338/.094     LC 68-21194     ISBN 052107200X

**Milward, Alan S.** **4.2202**
The development of the economies of continental Europe, 1850–1914 / Alan S. Milward and S. B. Saul. — Cambridge, Mass.: Harvard University Press, 1977. 555 p.: maps; 23 cm. 1. Europe — Economic conditions I. Saul, S. B. joint author. II. T.
HC240.M645 1977b     330.9/4/028     LC 76-55137     ISBN 0674200233

**Milward, Alan S.** **4.2203**
The economic development of continental Europe: 1780–1870 / by Alan S. Milward and S.B. Saul. — Totowa, N.J.: Rowman and Littlefield, 1973. 548 p. 1. Europe — Economic conditions I. Saul, S. B. joint author. II. T.
HC240.M646     330.9/4     LC 73-5905     ISBN 0874711932

**Milward, Alan S.** **4.2204**
The reconstruction of western Europe, 1945–51 / Alan S. Milward. — Berkeley: University of California Press, 1984. xxi, 527 p.: ill.; 25 cm. Includes index. 1. Reconstruction (1939-1951) — Europe 2. Europe — Economic conditions — 1945- 3. Europe — Economic integration — History. I. T.
HC240.M64623 1984     330.94/055 19     LC 83-17931     ISBN 0520052064

**Miskimin, Harry A.** **4.2205**
The economy of later Renaissance Europe, 1460–1600 / Harry A. Miskimin. — Cambridge, [Eng.]; New York: Cambridge University Press, 1977. x, 222 p.; 21 cm. Includes index. 1. Europe — Economic conditions I. T.
HC240.M649     330.9/4/02     LC 75-17120     ISBN 0521216087

**Nef, John Ulric, 1899-.** • **4.2206**
The conquest of the material world [by] John Nef. Chicago, University of Chicago Press [1964] xii, 408 p. 25 cm. Bibliography: p. [373]-387. 1. Civilization, Modern 2. Europe — Industries — History. I. T.
HC240.N42     338.09     LC 64-15804

**North, Douglass Cecil.** **4.2207**
The rise of the Western world; a new economic history [by] Douglass C. North and Robert Paul Thomas. — Cambridge [Eng.]: University Press, 1973. viii, 170 p.: illus.; 24 cm. 1. Europe — Economic conditions I. Thomas, Robert Paul. joint author. II. T.
HC240.N66     330.9/4     LC 73-77258     ISBN 0521201713

**Pollard, Sidney. comp.** **4.2208**
Documents of European economic history / [by] S. Pollard [and] C. Holmes. — New York: St. Martin's Press, [1968] 2 v.; 24 cm. 1. Europe — Economic conditions — Sources. I. Holmes, Colin, 1938- joint comp. II. T.
HC240.P5952     330.9/4     LC 68-10751

**Pollard, Sidney.** **4.2209**
Peaceful conquest: the industrialization of Europe, 1760–1970 / by Sidney Pollard. — Oxford; New York: Oxford University Press, 1981. xii, 451 p.; 24 cm. Includes index. 1. Europe — Industries — History. I. T.
HC240.P596     338.094 19     LC 80-41061     ISBN 0198770936

**Scitovsky, Tibor.** • **4.2210**
Economic theory and western European integration. — Stanford, Calif.: Stanford University Press, 1958. 153 p. 23 cm. — (Stanford studies in history,

economics, and political science, 16) Essays. 1. European federation 2. Europe — Economic policy. I. T.
HC240.S388    338.94    *LC* 58-12305

**Svennilson, Ingvar, 1908-.**      • **4.2211**
Growth and stagnation in the European economy. Geneva: United Nations Economic Commission for Europe, 1954. xvi, 342 p.: diagrs., tables.; 28 cm. (United Nations Publications; sales no.: 1954. 2.E. 3) 1. Europe — Economic conditions I. T.
HC240 S85

**Trebilcock, Clive.**      **4.2212**
The industrialization of the continental powers, 1780–1914 / Clive Trebilcock. — London; New York: Longman, 1981. xvi, 495 p.: maps; 24 cm. Includes index. 1. Europe — Industries — History. I. T.
HC240.T69    338/.094    *LC* 79-41543    *ISBN* 0582491193

**Wexler, Imanuel.**      **4.2213**
The Marshall Plan revisited: the European recovery program in economic perspective / Imanuel Wexler. — Westport, Conn.: Greenwood Press, 1983. xi, 327 p.; 24 cm. (Contributions in economics and economic history. 0084-9235; no. 55) Includes index. 1. Marshall Plan. 2. Economic assistance, American — Europe — History. 3. Europe — Economic conditions — 1945- I. T. II. Series.
HC240.W44 1983    338.91/7304 19    *LC* 83-5694    *ISBN* 0313240116

**Ulman, Lloyd.**      **4.2214**
Wage restraint: a study of incomes policies in Western Europe / by Lloyd Ulman and Robert J. Flanagan. — Berkeley: University of California Press, 1971. x, 257 p.; 22 cm. 1. Wage-price policy — Europe. I. Flanagan, Robert J. joint author. II. T.
HC240.9.W24 U37    331.2/1/01    *LC* 70-153555    *ISBN* 0520020243

## HC241 European Economic Integration

**Underdeveloped Europe: studies in core–periphery relations /**      **4.2215**
**edited by Dudley Seers, Bernard Schaffer, Marja–Liisa Kiljunen.**
Atlantic Highlands, N.J.: Humanities Press, 1979. xxi, 325 p.; 24 cm. (Harvester studies in development.) 1. Regional economics — Case studies. 2. Europe — Economic integration — Case studies. 3. Europe — Economic conditions — Regional disparities — Case studies. 4. Europe — Industries — Case studies. I. Seers, Dudley. II. Schaffer, Benjamin Bernard. III. Kiljunen, Marja-Liisa. IV. Series.
HC241.U52 1979    338.91/4    *LC* 78-26518    *ISBN* 0391009621

### HC241.2 EUROPEAN ECONOMIC COMMUNITY

**Bamford, C. G. (Colin Grahame)**      **4.2216**
Geography of the EEC: a systematic economic approach / C.G. Bamford, H. Robinson. — Estover, Plymouth: Macdonald and Evans, 1983. xvii, 296 p.: ill., maps; 22 cm. ('Aspect' geographies) 1. European Economic Community. 2. European Economic Community countries — Economic conditions I. Robinson, H. (Harry), 1915- II. T. III. Title: Geography of the E.E.C.
HC241.2.B2835 1983    337.1/42 19    *LC* 83-233298    *ISBN* 0712107320

**Eurofutures: the challenges of innovation / the Commission of**      **4.2217**
**the European Communities, in association with the journal Futures.**
London: Butterworths, c1984. xiii, 199 p.: ill. At head of title: The FAST report. 1. Technological innovations — European Economic Community countries 2. European Economic Community countries — Economic policy I. Commission of the European Communities. II. FAST (Program)
HC241.2 E76 1984    *ISBN* 040801556X

**Hudson, Raymond.**      **4.2218**
An atlas of EEC affairs / Ray Hudson, David Rhind, and Helen Mounsey. — London; New York: Methuen, 1984. xiv, 158 p.: ill., maps; 31 cm. Includes indexes. 1. European Economic Community. 2. European Economic Community — Maps. I. Rhind, David. II. Mounsey, Helen. III. T. IV. Title: Atlas of E.E.C. affairs.
HC241.2.H83 1984    341.24/22 19    *LC* 84-501    *ISBN* 0416309100

**Minshull, G. N.**      **4.2219**
The new Europe, an economic geography of the EEC / G. N. Minshull. — New York: Holmes & Meier, 1978. 281 p.: ill.; 24 cm. Includes index. 1. European Economic Community countries I. T.
HC241.2.M49 1978    382/.9142    *LC* 78-6581    *ISBN* 0841903913

**Parker, Geoffrey, 1933-.**      **4.2220**
The logic of unity: a geography of the European Economic Community / Geoffrey Parker. — 3d ed. — London; New York: Longman, 1981. 208 p.: ill.; 24 cm. Includes index. 1. European Economic Community countries — Economic conditions I. T.
HC241.2.P35 1981    330.94/0557    *LC* 80-40154    *ISBN* 0582300312

**Ransom, Charles, 1911-.**      **4.2221**
The European Community and Eastern Europe. — Totowa, N.J.: Rowman and Littlefield, [1974, c1973] xi, 112 p.; 22 cm. — (European Community studies) Errata slip inserted. 1. European Economic Community — Europe, Eastern. I. T.
HC241.25.E35 R35 1974    382/.9142    *LC* 73-6819    *ISBN* 0874712009

**Britain in Europe / edited by William Wallace.**      **4.2222**
London: Heinemann Educational, 1980. x, 213 p.; 23 cm. (Joint studies in public policy; 1) 1. European Economic Community — Great Britain — Addresses, essays, lectures. I. Wallace, William, 1941-
HC241.25.G7 B684    341.24/22 19    *LC* 81-109370    *ISBN* 0435839195

**Butler, David E.**      **4.2223**
The 1975 referendum / by David Butler and Uwe Kitzinger. New York: St. Martin's Press, 1976. xi, 315 p.: ill.; 23 cm. 1. European Economic Community — Great Britain — Public opinion. 2. Public opinion — Great Britain. 3. Referendum — Great Britain. I. Kitzinger, Uwe W. joint author. II. T.
HC241.25.G7 B77 1976    382/.9142/041

**Gregory, Francis E. C. (Francis Edward Coulton)**      **4.2224**
Dilemmas of government: Britain and the European Community / F.E.C. Gregory. — Oxford: M. Robertson, c1983. 265 p.: ill.; 23 cm. Includes index. 1. European Economic Community — Great Britain I. T.
HC241.25.G7 G8 1983    337.1/42 19    *LC* 83-178893    *ISBN* 0855205881

**King, Anthony Stephen.**      **4.2225**
Britain says yes: the 1975 referendum on the Common Market / Anthony King. — Washington: American Enterprise Institute for Public Policy Research, c1977. 153 p.; 23 cm. — (Studies in political and social processes.) (AEI studies; 160) 1. European Economic Community — Great Britain I. T. II. Series.
HC241.25.G7 K5    382/.9142/0941    *LC* 77-83257    *ISBN* 0844732605

**Kitzinger, Uwe W.**      **4.2226**
Diplomacy and persuasion: how Britain joined the Common Market [by] Uwe Kitzinger. — London: Thames and Hudson, 1973. 432 p.: illus.; 23 cm. 1. European Economic Community — Great Britain I. T.
HC241.25.G7 K54    382/.9142/0942    *LC* 73-153742    *ISBN* 0300010803

## HC244 Eastern Europe: General

**Bornstein, Morris, 1927-.**      **4.2227**
Plan and market: economic reform in Eastern Europe / Edited and with an introd. by Morris Bornstein. — New Haven: Yale University Press, 1973. viii, 416 p.: ill.; 25 cm. — (Yale Russian and East European studies; 12) 1. Europe, Eastern — Economic policy — Addresses, essays, lectures. 2. Europe, Eastern — Economic conditions — Addresses, essays, lectures. I. T. II. Series.
HC244.B67    HC244 B7.    *LC* 72-91289    *ISBN* 0300015844

**Crisis in the East European economy: the spread of the Polish**      **4.2228**
**disease / edited by Jan Drewnowski.**
London: Croom Helm; New York: St. Martin's Press, c1982. 177 p.; 23 cm. 1. Europe, Eastern — Economic conditions — 1945- — Addresses, essays, lectures. 2. Europe, Eastern — Economic policy — Addresses, essays, lectures. I. Drewnowski, Jan F.
HC244.C74 1982    330.947 19    *LC* 82-42560    *ISBN* 0312173148

**Csikós Nagy, Béla.**      **4.2229**
Socialist economic policy. [Translated by Elek Helvei] New York, St. Martin's Press [1973] 238 p. 25 cm. 'Based on the author's ... Bevezetés a gazdaság-politikába.' 1. Economic policy 2. Comparative economics 3. Europe, Eastern — Economic policy. I. T.
HC244.C7813 1973    335    *LC* 72-90020

**East European economic handbook.**      **4.2230**
London: Euromonitor Publications, 1985. 325 p.: ill.; 26 cm. 1. Europe, Eastern — Economic conditions — 1945- 2. Europe, Eastern — Economic policy. I. Euromonitor Publications Limited.
HC244.E216 1985    330.947 19    *LC* 85-199691    *ISBN* 0863380298

**East European integration and East–West trade / edited by**    **4.2231**
**Paul Marer, John Michael Montias.**
Bloomington: Indiana University Press, c1980. xvi, 432 p.: ill.; 24 cm. (Studies in East European and Soviet planning, development, and trade. no. 28) (The Joint Committee on Eastern Europe publication series; no. 7) Based on a conference held at Indiana University/Bloomington in Oct. 1976, which was sponsored by the Joint Committee on Eastern Europe. 1. East-West trade (1945- ) — Congresses. 2. Europe, Eastern — Economic integration — Congresses. I. Marer, Paul. II. Montias, John Michael, 1928- III. Joint Committee on Eastern Europe. IV. Series.
HC244.E22     337.47     *LC* 79-3181     *ISBN* 0253168651

**Kaser, Michael Charles.**      • **4.2232**
Comecon, integration problems of the planned economies. London: Oxford University Press, 1965. vi, 215 p.: ill., map (on lining paper); 22 cm. 'Issued under the auspices of the Royal Institute of International Affairs.' 1. Council for Mutual Economic Assistance. 2. Europe, Eastern — Economic integration I. Royal Institute of International Affairs. II. T.
HC244 K3     *LC* 65-4263

**Lavigne, Marie, 1935-.**      **4.2233**
The Socialist economies of the Soviet Union and Europe / Marie Lavigne; translated by T. G. Waywell. — 1st U.S. ed. — White Plains, N.Y.: International Arts and Sciences Press, 1975 (c1974). xvii, 396 p.; 24 cm. A translation with revisions of Les économies socialistes soviétiques et européennes. Includes index. 1. Europe, Eastern — Economic conditions — 1945- 2. Europe, Eastern — Economic policy. I. T.
HC244.L37513 1974b     338.947     *LC* 74-83551     *ISBN* 0873320638

**Höhmann, Hans-Hermann.**      **4.2234**
The New economic systems of Eastern Europe / Hans–Hermann Höhmann, Michael Kaser, Karl C. Thalheim, editors. — Berkeley: University of California Press, c1975. xxi, 585 p.; 23 cm. Revised translation of Die Wirtschaftsordnungen Osteuropas im Wandel. 1. Industry and state — Europe, Eastern — Case studies. 2. Europe, Eastern — Economic policy — Case studies. I. Kaser, Michael Charles. II. Thalheim, Karl Christian. III. T.
HC244.N4713     338.947     *LC* 74-76386     *ISBN* 0520027329

**Nove, Alec. comp.**      **4.2235**
Socialist economics: selected readings; edited by Alec Nove and D. M. Nuti. — Harmondsworth: Penguin, 1972. 526 p.: illus.; 18 cm. — (Penguin education) (Penguin modern economics readings) 1. Marxian economics — Addresses, essays, lectures. 2. Europe, Eastern — Economic policy — Addresses, essays, lectures. 3. Communist countries — Economic policy — Addresses, essays, lectures. I. Nuti, D. M., joint comp. II. T.
HC244.N63     335/.008     *LC* 72-170831     *ISBN* 0140806229

**Osborne, Richard Horsley.**      • **4.2236**
East–Central Europe: a geographical introduction to seven socialist states / by R.H. Osborne. London: Chatto & Windus, 1967. 384 p.: maps, tables.; 23cm. (Geographies for advanced study.) 1. Europe, Eastern I. T. II. Series.
HC244.O67     *LC* 67-88612

**Pounds, Norman John Greville.**      • **4.2237**
Eastern Europe [by] Norman J. G. Pounds. — Chicago: Aldine Pub. Co., [1969] xx, 912 p.: illus., maps.; 23 cm. — (Geographies for advanced study) 1. Europe, Eastern I. T.
HC244.P68 1969b     914.7     *LC* 69-16902

**Ránki, György, 1930-.**      **4.2238**
Economy and foreign policy: the struggle of the great powers for hegemony in the Danube valley, 1919–1939 / György Ránki. — Boulder: East European Monographs; New York: Distributed by Columbia University Press, 1983. 224 p.; 22 cm. — (East European monographs. no. 141) 1. Danube River Valley — Economic conditions. 2. Danube River Valley — Foreign economic relations. 3. Europe — Politics and government — 1918-1945 I. T. II. Series.
HC244.R229 1983     327.1/11 19     *LC* 83-80482     *ISBN* 0880330325

**Selucký, Radoslav.**      **4.2239**
Economic reforms in Eastern Europe: political background and economic significance / translated by Zdenek Elias. — New York: Praeger Publishers [1972] x, 179 p.; 25 cm. (Praeger special studies in international economics and development) 1. Europe, Eastern — Economic policy. 2. Europe, Eastern — Politics and government — 1945- I. T.
HC244.S3713     330.9/47/085     *LC* 72-181698

**Smith, Alan H.**      **4.2240**
The planned economies of Eastern Europe / Alan H. Smith. — New York: Holmes & Meier, 1983. 249 p.; 23 cm. Includes index. 1. Monetary policy — Europe, Eastern. 2. Europe, Eastern — Economic policy. 3. Europe, Eastern — Foreign economic relations. I. T.
HC244.S553 1983     338.947 19     *LC* 83-10748     *ISBN* 0841908915

**Warriner, Doreen, 1904- ed.**      • **4.2241**
Contrasts in emerging societies; readings in the social and economic history of south–eastern Europe in the nineteenth century, selected and translated by G.

F. Cushing [and others]. — Bloomington, Indiana University Press, 1965. xix, 402 p.: maps.; 23 cm. Bibliographical footnotes. 1. Europe, Eastern — Econ. condit. 2. Europe, Eastern — Soc. condit. I. T.
HC244.W29     330.9496     *LC* 65-12770

**Wilczynski, J. (Jozef), 1922-.**      **4.2242**
The economics of socialism: principles governing the operation of the centrally planned economies in the USSR and Eastern Europe under the new system [by] J. Wilczynski. [1st U.S. ed.] Chicago, Aldine Pub. Co. [1971, c1970] 233 p. illus. 23 cm. (Studies in economics) 1. Europe, Eastern — Economic conditions — 1945- 2. Europe, Eastern — Economic policy. I. T.
HC244.W55 1971     330.947     *LC* 72-119643     *ISBN* 0202060365

**Wilczynski, J. (Jozef), 1922-.**      **4.2243**
Profit, risk, and incentives under Socialist economic planning / [by] J. Wilczynski. — New York: Barnes & Noble [1973] viii, 231 p.; 23 cm. 1. Profit — Europe, Eastern. 2. Risk — Europe, Eastern. 3. Incentives in industry — Europe, Eastern. I. T.
HC244.Z9 P76 1973     338.947     *LC* 73-163425     *ISBN* 0064976557

## HC251–407 INDIVIDUAL EUROPEAN COUNTRIES

## HC251–260 Britain

**Tawney, R. H. (Richard Henry), 1880-1962.**      • **4.2244**
Tudor economic documents: being select documents illustrating the economic and social history of Tudor England / edited by R.H. Tawney and Eileen Power. — New York: Barnes & Noble [1963, c1961] 3 v.; 20 cm. — (University of London. Historical series; no. 4) 1. Great Britain — Economic conditions 2. Great Britain — Industries — History. 3. Great Britain — History — Tudors, 1485-1603 — Sources. I. Power, Eileen Edna, 1889-1940. II. T. III. Series.
HC251.T3     *LC* 64-55563

**Clapham, John Harold, Sir, 1873-1946.**      • **4.2245**
A concise economic history of Britain: from the earliest times to 1750 / by Sir John Clapham. — Cambridge [Eng.]: University Press, 1949. — xv, 324 p.; 21 cm. 1. Great Britain — Economic conditions I. T.
HC253.C57     330.9/41     *LC* 50-1413

**Court, William Henry Bassano.**      • **4.2246**
A concise economic history of Britain, from 1750 to recent times. — Cambridge [Eng.] University Press, 1954. 368 p. 21 cm. A sequel to Sir John Clapham's A concise economic history of Britain from the earliest times to A.D. 1750. 1. Great Britain — Econ. condit. I. T.
HC253.C67     330.942     *LC* 55-142

**Deane, Phyllis.**      • **4.2247**
British economic growth, 1688–1959: trends and structure, by Phyllis Deane and W. A. Cole. Cambridge [Eng.] University Press, 1962. xvi, 348 p. diagrs., tables. 25 cm. (University of Cambridge. Dept. of Applied Economics. Monographs, 8) 1. Great Britain — Economic conditions I. Cole, William Alan, joint author. II. T.
HC253.D38     330.942     *LC* 62-53045

**Hobsbawm, E. J. (Eric J.), 1917-.**      • **4.2248**
Industry and empire; the making of modern English society, 1750 to the present day [by] E. J. Hobsbawm. [1st American ed.] New York, Pantheon Books [1968] 336 p. illus., maps. 22 cm. 'Vol. II.' 1. Great Britain — Economic conditions. 2. Great Britain — Industries — History. I. T. II. Title: The making of modern English society, 1750 to the present day.
HC253.H57 1968     330.942     *LC* 68-10699

**Holderness, B. A.**      **4.2249**
Pre–industrial England: economy and society, 1500–1750 / [by] B. A. Holderness. London: Dent; Totowa, N.J.: Rowman & Littlefield, 1976. x, 244 p.: 2 ill., maps; 24 cm. 1. England — Economic conditions 2. England — Social conditions I. T.
HC253.H625 1976     330.9/42     *LC* 77-356202     *ISBN* 0874719100

**Pressnell, L. S. ed.**      • **4.2250**
Studies in the industrial revolution, presented to T. S. Ashton. — [London] University of London, Athlone Press, 1960. 350 p. illus., port., maps. 23 cm. Label mounted on t.p.: Fair Lawn, N. J., Essential Books. 'Bibliography of academic writings of T. S. Ashton': p. 328-333. 1. Ashton, T. S. (Thomas Southcliffe) 2. Great Britain — Econ. condit. I. T.
HC253.P7     338.0942     *LC* 60-2104

**Stamp, L. Dudley (Laurence Dudley), 1898-1966.**          **4.2251**
The British Isles: a geographic and economic survey [by] L. Dudley Stamp and Stanley H. Beaver. 6th ed. London, Longman, 1971. ix, 881 p. illus., maps. 25 cm. (Geographies for advanced study) 1. Great Britain — Economic conditions 2. Great Britain — Economic conditions — 1945- I. Beaver, Stanley Henry. II. T.
HC253.S67 1971b        914.2        *LC* 72-170778        *ISBN* 0582481449

**Unwin, George, 1870-1925.**          • **4.2252**
Studies in economic history: the collected papers of George Unwin / edited with an introductory memoir by R.H. Tawney. 2d ed. London: F. Cass; New York: A.M. Kelley, 1966. lxxiv, 490 p.: port.; 21 cm. (Reprints of economic classics.) 1. Economic history — Study and teaching. 2. Great Britain — Economic conditions 3. Great Britain — Industries — History. I. Tawney, R. H. (Richard Henry), 1880-1962. II. T. III. Series.
HC253.U5 1966        *LC* 66-9002

## HC254–256.6 BY PERIOD

## HC254–254.5 Middle Ages, to 1800

**Clark, George Norman, 1890-.**          • **4.2253**
The wealth of England from 1496–1760 / G. N. Clark. — London: New York: Oxford University Press, 1946. 199 p.; 17 cm. — (The home university library of modern knowledge; 196.) 1. Great Britain — Economic conditions 2. Great Britain — Commerce — History. I. T.
HC254.C6        330.942        *LC* 47-5296

**Hill, Christopher, 1912-.**          • **4.2254**
Reformation to Industrial Revolution; the making of modern English society, 1530–1780 [by] Christopher Hill. [1st American ed.] New York, Pantheon Books [1968, c1967] 256 p. 22 cm. (Pantheon studies in social history) 'Vol. I.' 1. Great Britain — Economic conditions 2. Great Britain — Politics and government 3. Great Britain — Social conditions I. T. II. Title: The making of modern English society, 1530-1780.
HC254.H55 1968        309.142        *LC* 68-10698

**Loyn, H. R. (Henry Royston)**          • **4.2255**
Anglo–Saxon England and the Norman Conquest. New York, St. Martin's Press [1963, c1962] xii, 422 p. maps. 23 cm. (Social and economic history of England.) 1. Great Britain — Economic conditions 2. Great Britain — Social conditions 3. Great Britain — History — Anglo Saxon period, 449-1066 I. T. II. Series.
HC254.L6        309.142        *LC* 63-15857

**Postan, M. M. (Michael Moïssey), 1899-1981.**          **4.2256**
The medieval economy and society; an economic history of Britain, 1100–1500 [by] M. M. Postan. — Berkeley: University of California Press, [1973, c1972] viii, 261 p.; 23 cm. 1. Manors — Great Britain. 2. Great Britain — Economic conditions 3. Great Britain — Social conditions I. T.
HC254.P68        330.9/42        *LC* 72-87202        *ISBN* 0520023250

**Vinogradoff, Paul, Sir, 1854-1925.**          • **4.2257**
English society in the eleventh century; essays in English mediaeval history. — Oxford: Clarendon P., 1968. xii, 599 p.; 23 cm. 1. Land tenure — Great Britain — History. 2. Great Britain — Economic conditions 3. England — Social conditions — Medieval period, 1066-1485 4. Great Britain — History — Medieval period, 1066-1485 I. T.
HC254.V48 1968b        309.1/42        *LC* 71-429427        *ISBN* 0198213808

**Bennett, Henry Stanley.**          • **4.2258**
Life on the English manor; a study of peasant conditions, 1150–1400, by H. S. Bennett ... — Cambridge [Eng.] The University press, 1937. xviii, 364 p. illus., plates. 23 cm. — (Half-title: Cambridge studies in medieval life and thought, edited by G. G. Coulton ...) 'Abbreviations and authorities': p. [341]-351. 1. Manors — Gt. Brit. 2. Peasantry — England. 3. England — Soc. life & cust. I. T.
HC254.3.B4        323.330942        *LC* 38-861

**Clay, C. G. A., 1940-.**          **4.2259**
Economic expansion and social change: England 1500–1700 / C.G.A. Clay. — Cambridge [Cambridgeshire]; New York: Cambridge University Press, 1985 (c1984). 2 v.: ill.; 24 cm. 1. England — Economic conditions 2. England — Social conditions I. T.
HC254.4.C59        942.05 19        *LC* 83-23221        *ISBN* 0521259428

**Coleman, D. C. (Donald Cuthbert), 1920-.**          **4.2260**
The economy of England, 1450–1750 / D. C. Coleman. — London; New York: Oxford University Press, 1977. viii, 223 p.: graphs; 21 cm. Includes index. 1. Great Britain — Economic conditions I. T.
HC254.4.C64        330.9/42        *LC* 77-364391        *ISBN* 0192153552

**Gregg, Pauline.**          **4.2261**
Black death to Industrial Revolution: a social and economic history of England / Pauline Gregg. New York: Barnes & Noble Books, 1974 [i.e. 1976] 344 p.: ill.; 23 cm. Publication date from errata slip. Includes index. 1. Great Britain — Economic conditions 2. Great Britain — Social conditions I. T.
HC254.4.G73 1976        309.1/42        *LC* 76-3815        *ISBN* 0064925404

## HC254.5 1600–1800

**Ashton, T. S. (Thomas Southcliffe)**          • **4.2262**
An economic history of England: the 18th century / by T.S. Ashton. New York: Barnes & Noble, 1955. vi, 257 p.: tables; 23 cm. (An Economic history of England) 1. England — Economic conditions I. T. II. Series.
HC254.5.A7

**Crafts, N. F. R.**          **4.2263**
British economic growth during the industrial revolution / N.F.R. Crafts. — Oxford [Oxfordshire]: Clarendon Press; New York: Oxford University Press, 1985. 193 p.; 23 cm. Includes index. 1. Great Britain — Industries — History. 2. Great Britain — Economic conditions — 1760-1860 I. T.
HC254.5.C73 1985        338.941 19        *LC* 85-2926        *ISBN* 0198730667

**Deane, Phyllis.**          **4.2264**
The first industrial revolution / Phyllis Deane. — 2d ed. — Cambridge [Eng.]; New York: Cambridge University Press, 1979. ix, 318 p.; 23 cm. Includes indexes. 1. Great Britain — Industries. 2. Great Britain — Economic conditions — 1760-1860 I. T.
HC254.5.D3 1979        338/.0941        *LC* 78-26388        *ISBN* 0521226678

**The Economic history of Britain since 1700 / edited by**          **4.2265**
**Roderick Floud and Donald McCloskey.**
Cambridge [Eng.]; New York: Cambridge University Press, 1981. 2 v.; 24 cm. Includes indexes. 1. Great Britain — Economic conditions — Addresses, essays, lectures. I. Floud, Roderick. II. McCloskey, Donald N.
HC254.5.E27        330.941/07        *LC* 79-41645        *ISBN* 0521298423

**Fisher, Frederick Jack, ed.**          • **4.2266**
Essays in the economic and social history of Tudor and Stuart England, in honour of R. H. Tawney. Cambridge [Eng.] University Press, 1961. 235 p. port., tables. 23 cm. Bibliographical footnotes. 1. Tawney, R. H. (Richard Henry), 1880-1962. 2. Great Britain — Social conditions — Addresses, essays, lectures. 3. Great Britain — Economic conditions — Addresses, essays, lectures. I. T.
HC254.5.F5        330.942        *LC* 61-19669

**Mantoux, Paul, 1877-1956.**          • **4.2267**
The industrial revolution in the eighteenth century; an outline of the beginnings of the modern factory system in England. — [Translated from the French by Marjorie Vernon] New and rev. ed. with a pref. by T. S. Ashton. — New York, Macmillan, [1961] 528 p. illus. 23 cm. Includes bibliography. 1. Gt. Brit. — Indus. — Hist. 2. Gt. Brit. — Econ. condit. I. T.
HC254.5.M33        330.942        *LC* 62-404

**Thirsk, Joan. comp.**          **4.2268**
Seventeenth–century economic documents, edited by Joan Thirsk and J. P. Cooper. [S.l.]: Oxford, 1972. xvii, 849 p. 23 cm. 1. Great Britain — Economic conditions — Sources. I. Cooper, J. P. (John Phillips), 1920-1978. joint comp. II. T.
HC254.5.T48        330.9/42/06        *LC* 72-189410        *ISBN* 0198282567

**Toynbee, Arnold, 1852-1883.**          • **4.2269**
The industrial revolution / Arnold Toynbee; with a preface by Arnold J. Toynbee. — Boston: Beacon Press, 1956. 139 p.; 21 cm. (Beacon paperback, no.32) 1. Economics — History — Great Britain. 2. Labor and laboring classes — Great Britain 3. Great Britain — Economic conditions I. T.
HC254.5.T73 1956        330.942        *LC* 57-1485        *ISBN* 0807050997

**Williams, Eric Eustace, 1911-.**          • **4.2270**
Capitalism & slavery. — New York: Russell & Russell, 1961 [c1944] 285 p.; 22 cm. 'Based on a doctoral dissertation ... Oxford University ... 1938.' 1. Slave-trade — Great Britain. 2. Great Britain — Industries — History. I. T.
HC254.5.W5 1961        338.0942        *LC* 61-13088

## HC255 19th Century

**Ashton, T. S. (Thomas Southcliffe)**          • **4.2271**
The industrial revolution, 1760–1830. — [1st ed., rev.]. — New York: Oxford University Press, 1964. 119 p.; 21 cm. — (A Galaxy book) 'GB 109.' 1. Great Britain — Economic conditions — 1760-1860 I. T.
HC255.A8 1964        *LC* 64-1714

**Cain, P.J.**          **4.2272**
Economic foundations of British overseas expansion, 1815–1914 / prepared for the Economic History Society [by] P.J. Cain. — London: Macmillan Press,

1980. 85 p. — (Studies in economic and social history.) Includes index. 1. Great Britain — Economic conditions — 19th century 2. Great Britain — Economic conditions — 20th century 3. Great Britain — Colonies — History — Sources 4. Great Britain — Economic policy I. Economic History Society. II. T. III. Series.
HC255.C35    ISBN 0333232844

**Church, Roy A.**                                         **4.2273**
The great Victorian boom, 1850–1873 / prepared for the Economic History Society by R. A. Church. [S.l.]: Humanities, 1976 (c1975). 95 p.; 21 cm. (Studies in economic and social history) Includes index. 1. Great Britain — Economic conditions — 19th century 2. Great Britain — Social conditions — 19th century I. Economic History Society. II. T.
HC255.C53    330.9/41/081    LC 76-352972    ISBN 0333143507

**Clapham, John Harold, Sir, 1873-1946.**                 • **4.2274**
An economic history of modern Britain ... by J. H. Clapham ... — 2d ed. — Cambridge [Eng.] The University press, 1930-. 3 v. maps (part fold.) diagrs. 25 cm. 1. Gt. Brit. — Econ. condit. I. T.
HC255.C55 1930    330.942    LC 31-9724

**Coleman, D. C. (Donald Cuthbert), 1920-.**              **4.2275**
Industry in Tudor and Stuart England / prepared for the Economic History Society by D. C. Coleman. — London: Macmillan, 1975. 63 p.; 21 cm. — (Studies in economic and social history) Includes index. 1. Great Britain — Industries — History. I. Economic History Society. II. T.
HC255.C62 1975    338/.0942    LC 76-355319    ISBN 0333143515

**Crouzet, François, 1922-.**                             **4.2276**
[Economie de la Grand-Bretagne victorienne. English] The Victorian economy / François Crouzet; translated by Anthony Forster. — New York: Columbia University Press, 1982. xiii, 430 p.; 25 cm. Translation of: L'Economie de la Grande-Bretagne victorienne. Includes index. 1. Great Britain — Economic conditions — 19th century I. T.
HC255.C7313 1982    330.941/081 19    LC 82-1292    ISBN 0231055420

**Fay, C. R. (Charles Ryle), 1884-.**                     • **4.2277**
Great Britain from Adam Smith to the present day: an economic and social survey / by C.R. Fay. — 5th ed. — London: Longmans, 1962. 496 p.: ill.; 22 cm. 1. Great Britain — Economic conditions 2. Great Britain — Industries — History. 3. Great Britain — Social conditions I. T.
HC255.F3 1962

**Joyce, Patrick.**                                        **4.2278**
Work, society, and politics: the culture of the factory in later Victorian England / Patrick Joyce. — New Brunswick. N.J.: Rutgers University Press, c1980. xxv, 356 p., [2] leaves of plates: ill.; 22 cm. 1. Social classes — England. 2. England — Industries — History. 3. Great Britain — Politics and government I. T.
HC255.J69 1980b    306/.3 19    LC 79-93087    ISBN 0813508991

**O'Brien, Patrick Karl.**                                **4.2279**
Economic growth in Britain and France, 1780–1914: two paths to the twentieth century / Patrick O'Brien and Caglar Keyder. — London; Boston: G. Allen & Unwin, 1978. 205 p.: 1 ill.; 23 cm. 1. Great Britain — Economic conditions — 19th century 2. France — Economic conditions I. Keyder, Çağlar. joint author. II. T.
HC255.O27    339.5/0941    LC 78-323888    ISBN 0043302882

**Rostow, W. W. (Walt Whitman), 1916-.**                  • **4.2280**
British economy of the nineteenth century: essays / by W. W. Rostow. — Oxford: Clarendon P., 1948. 240 p.: ill.; 23 cm. 1. Great Britain — Economic conditions I. T.
HC255.R58    LC 48-10361

## HC256–256.6 20th Century

**Hutchison, Keith.**                                      • **4.2281**
The decline & fall of British capitalism / by Keith Hutchinson; with a new foreword by David Owen [and a new pref. by the author]. — Hamden, Conn.: Archon Books, 1966. xviii, 355 p.; 22 cm. 1. Great Britain — Economic conditions I. T.
HC256.H8 1966    LC 66-25189

**Matthews, R. C. O. (Robert Charles Oliver), 1927-.**    **4.2282**
British economic growth, 1856–1973 / R.C.O. Matthews, C.H. Feinstein, and J.C. Odling–Smee. — Stanford, Calif.: Stanford University Press, 1982. xxiv, 712 p.: ill.; 24 cm. — (Studies of economic growth in industrialized countries.) Includes index. 1. Great Britain — Economic conditions — 20th century 2. Great Britain — Economic conditions — 19th century I. Feinstein, C. H. II. Odling-Smee, J. C. (John C.) III. T. IV. Series.
HC256.M37 1982    338.941 19    LC 80-53222    ISBN 0804711100

**Pollard, Sidney.**                                      **4.2283**
The development of the British economy, 1914–1980 / Sidney Pollard. — 3rd ed. — London; Baltimore, Md.: E. Arnold, 1983. vi, 440 p.; 24 cm. Includes index. 1. Great Britain — Economic conditions — 20th century I. T.
HC256.P62 1983    330.941 19    LC 85-128828    ISBN 071316395X

**Durbin, Elizabeth F.**                                  **4.2284**
New Jerusalems: the Labour Party and the economics of democratic socialism / Elizabeth Durbin; foreword by Roy Hattersley. — London; Boston: Routledge & Kegan Paul, 1985. xvii, 341 p.; 23 cm. Includes index. 1. Labour Party (Great Britain) — History — 20th century. 2. Socialism — Great Britain — History — 20th century. 3. Great Britain — Economic policy — 1918-1945 I. T.
HC256.3.D79 1985    338.941 19    LC 84-13306    ISBN 071009650X

**Middleton, Roger.**                                     **4.2285**
Towards the managed economy: Keynes, the Treasury, and the fiscal policy debate of the 1930s / Roger Middleton. — London; New York: Methuen, 1985. ix, 244 p.: ill.; 24 cm. Includes index. 1. Great Britain. Treasury — History. 2. Fiscal policy — Great Britain — History. 3. Keynesian economics — History. 4. Great Britain — Economic policy — 1918-1945 I. T.
HC256.3.M418 1985    339.5/2/0941 19    LC 84-29607    ISBN 0416358306

**Cairncross, Alec, Sir, 1911-.**                         **4.2286**
Years of recovery: British economic policy 1945–51 / Alec Cairncross. — New York, NY: Methuen, 1985. xiv, 527 p.; 25 cm. Includes index. 1. Great Britain — Economic policy — 1945- I. T.
HC256.5.C26 1985    338.941 19    LC 84-29581    ISBN 0416379206

**Gough, Ian.**                                           **4.2287**
The political economy of the welfare state / Ian Gough. — London: Macmillan, 1979. xii, 196 p.; 23 cm. — (Critical texts in social work and the welfare state.) 1. Welfare state 2. Great Britain — Economic policy — 1945- I. T. II. Series.
HC256.5.G68    330.9/41/0857    LC 79-315902    ISBN 0333215826

**Gregg, Pauline.**                                       • **4.2288**
The welfare state; an economic and social history of Great Britain from 1945 to the present day. — Amherst: University of Massachusetts Press, 1969. xii, 388 p.; 23 cm. 1. Great Britain — Economic policy — 1945- 2. Great Britain — Social policy. I. T.
HC256.5.G73 1969    309.1/42    LC 69-13109

**Gamble, Andrew.**                                       **4.2289**
Britain in decline: economic policy, political strategy, and the British state / Andrew Gamble. — Boston: Beacon Press, 1982, c1981. xxix, 279 p.; 21 cm. 1. Great Britain — Economic policy — 1945- 2. Great Britain — Politics and government — 1945- I. T.
HC256.6.G35 1982    338.941 19    LC 81-683554    ISBN 0807047007

**Hatfield, Michael.**                                    **4.2290**
The house the Left built: inside Labour policy–making, 1970–75 / by Michael Hatfield. — London: Gollancz, 1978. 272 p.; 23 cm. Includes index. 1. Labour Party (Great Britain) 2. Great Britain — Economic policy — 1945- I. T.
HC256.6.H38    329.9/41    LC 78-323164    ISBN 0575024712

**Holmes, Martin.**                                       **4.2291**
Political pressure and economic policy: British government 1970–1974 / Martin Holmes. — London; Boston: Butterworth Scientific, 1982. 164 p.; 24 cm. Includes index. 1. Great Britain — Economic policy — 1945- 2. Great Britain — Politics and government — 1964-1979 I. T.
HC256.6.H54 1982    338.941 19    LC 82-170177    ISBN 0408108304

**Nossiter, Bernard D.**                                  **4.2292**
Britain: a future that works / Bernard D. Nossiter. — Boston: Houghton Mifflin, 1978. viii, 275 p.; 22 cm. 1. Great Britain — Economic conditions — 1945- 2. Great Britain — Politics and government — 1964-1979 I. T.
HC256.6.N67    309.1/41/0857    LC 78-16283    ISBN 0395270944

**Riddell, Peter.**                                       **4.2293**
The Thatcher government / Peter Riddell. — [Rev. ed.]. — New York, NY: B. Blackwell, c1985. p. cm. Includes index. 1. Great Britain — Economic policy — 1945- 2. Great Britain — Social policy. 3. Great Britain — Politics and government — 1979- I. T.
HC256.6.R53 1985    338.941 19    LC 85-15678    ISBN 0631145192

**Shanks, Michael, 1927-.**                               **4.2294**
Planning and politics: the British experience 1960–1976 / Michael Shanks. — London: Political and Economic Planning, 1977. 142 p.; 23 cm. Includes index. 1. Great Britain — Economic policy — 1945- I. T.
HC256.6.S46    338.941    LC 78-300921    ISBN 0043302831

## HC257 LOCAL

### HC257.E5 England

**McKendrick, Neil.**     **4.2295**
The birth of a consumer society: the commercialization of eighteenth–century England / Neil McKendrick, John Brewer, and J.H. Plumb. — Bloomington: Indiana University Press, c1982. viii, 345 p.; 25 cm. 1. Consumers — England — History — 18th century. 2. Consumption (Economics) — England — History — 18th century. 3. Leisure — England — History — 18th century. 4. England — Economic conditions — 18th century I. Brewer, John, 1947- II. Plumb, J. H. (John Harold), 1911- III. T.
HC257.E5 M37 1982    306/.3/0942 19    *LC* 82-47953    *ISBN* 0253312051

### HC257.S4 Scotland

**Campbell, R. H. (Roy Hutcheson)**    &bull; **4.2296**
Scotland since 1707: the rise of an industrial society [by] R.H. Campbell. New York: Barnes & Noble, 1965. xii, 354 p.: fold. col. map.; 23 cm. 1. Scotland — Economic conditions 2. Scotland — Industries I. T.
HC257 S4 C3

**Campbell, R. H. (Roy Hutcheson)**    &bull; **4.2297**
Source book of Scottish economic and social history, by R. H. Campbell and J. B. A. Dow. Oxford, Blackwell, 1968. xxiii, 280 p. 22 cm. 1. Scotland — Economic conditions — Sources. 2. Scotland — Social conditions. I. Dow, James B. A., joint author. II. T.
HC257.S4 C33 1968    330.941    *LC* 78-370399    *ISBN* 0631110801

**Hamilton, Henry, 1896-.**    &bull; **4.2298**
An economic history of Scotland in the eighteenth century. — Oxford, Clarendon Press, 1963. xviii, 452 p. fold. map. 23 cm. Bibliography: p. [421]-430. 1. Scotland — Econ. condit. I. T.
HC257.S4H28    330.941    *LC* 63-5936

**Lythe, S. G. E.**    &bull; **4.2299**
The economy of Scotland in its European setting, 1550–1625. Edinburgh, Oliver and Boyd, 1960. 277 p.; 23 cm. 1. Scotland — Economic conditions I. T.
HC257.S4 L9    *LC* 60-4232

**Understanding the Scottish economy / edited by Keith P.D.**    **4.2300**
**Ingham and James Love.**
Oxford: M. Robertson, 1984 (c1983). viii, 311 p.: ill.; 23 cm. Includes index. 1. Scotland — Economic conditions — 1973- — Addresses, essays, lectures. I. Ingham, Keith P. D. II. Love, James, 1948-
HC257.S4 U53 1983    330.9411/0858 19    *LC* 83-170305    *ISBN* 0855206764

### HC257.W3 Wales

**Dodd, Arthur Herbert.**    **4.2301**
The Industrial Revolution in North Wales, [by] A. H. Dodd. — 3rd ed. — Cardiff: University of Wales Press, 1971. xlv, 439 p., 5 plates (2 fold);: maps.; 23 cm. 1. Wales, North — Economic conditions. 2. Wales, North — Industries — History. 3. Wales, North — Social conditions. I. T.
HC257.W3 D6 1971    338/.09429    *LC* 78-872048    *ISBN* 0900768924

**John, Arthur Henry.**    **4.2302**
The industrial development of South Wales, 1750–1850: an essay. — Cardiff: University of Wales Press, 1950. x, 201 p. maps. 1. Wales, South — Industries I. T.
HC257 W3 J6

### HC258 London

**Brooke, Christopher Nugent Lawrence.**    **4.2303**
London, 800–1216: the shaping of a city / Christopher N. L. Brooke, assisted by Gillian Keir. — Berkeley: University of California Press, 1975. xxi, 424 p., [16] leaves of plates: ill.; 24 cm. (History of London) Includes index. 1. London (England) — Economic conditions. 2. London (England) — Social conditions. 3. London (England) — Politics and government. 4. London (England) — History I. Keir, Gillian. joint author. II. T. III. Series.
HC258.L6 B76    330.9/421/2    *LC* 73-92620    *ISBN* 0520026861

**Sheppard, F. H. W. (Francis Henry Wollaston), 1921-.**    &bull; **4.2304**
London, 1808–1870: the infernal wen [by] Francis Sheppard. Berkeley, University of California Press, 1971. xx, 427 p. illus. 24 cm. (History of London) 1. London (England) — Economic conditions. 2. London (England)

— Social conditions. 3. London (England) — History — 1800-1950 I. T. II. Series.
HC258.L6 S5 1971    309.1/421/07    *LC* 71-142067    *ISBN* 0520018478

## HC259 COLONIES

**Constantine, Stephen.**    **4.2305**
The making of British colonial development policy, 1914–1940 / Stephen Constantine. — London, England; Totowa, N.J.: F. Cass, 1984. xii, 326 p.; 23 cm. Includes index. 1. Great Britain — Colonies — Economic policy I. T.
HC259.C73 1984    338.91/41/01724 19    *LC* 85-122006    *ISBN* 071463204X

**Drummond, Ian M.**    **4.2306**
Imperial economic policy, 1917–1939: studies in expansion and protection / by Ian M. Drummond. — Toronto: University of Toronto Press, 1974. 496 p.: ill.; 22 cm. — 1. Great Britain — Colonies — Economic policy 2. Great Britain — Colonies — Commerce I. T.
HC259.D79    *ISBN* 0802021492

## HC260 SPECIAL TOPICS, A–Z

**Fraser, W. Hamish.**    **4.2307**
The coming of the mass market, 1850–1914 / W. Hamish Fraser. — Hamden, Conn.: Archon Books, 1981. x, 268 p., [16] p. of plates: ill.; 22 cm. Includes index. 1. Consumption (Economics) — Great Britain — History. 2. Retail trade — Great Britain — History. 3. Great Britain — Industries — History. I. T.
HC260.C6 F7 1981    381/.1/0941 19    *LC* 81-12687    *ISBN* 020801960X

**Thirsk, Joan.**    **4.2308**
Economic policy and projects: the development of a consumer society in early modern England / by Joan Thirsk. — Oxford: Clarendon Press, 1978. vi, 199 p.; 23 cm. 1. Industrial promotion — England — History. 2. England — Economic policy — History. 3. England — Economic conditions I. T.
HC260.I53 T48    338/.0941    *LC* 78-315763    *ISBN* 0198282745

**Townsend, Peter, 1928-.**    **4.2309**
Poverty in the United Kingdom: a survey of household resources and standards of living / Peter Townsend. — Berkeley: University of California Press, c1979. 1216 p.: ill.; 22 cm. Includes indexes. 1. Poor — Great Britain. 2. Great Britain — Economic conditions 3. Great Britain — Social conditions I. T.
HC260.P6 T65    339.2/2/0941    *LC* 78-66023    *ISBN* 0520038711

**Panitch, Leo.**    **4.2310**
Social democracy & industrial militancy: the Labour Party, the trade unions, and incomes policy, 1945–1974 / Leo Panitch. — Cambridge [Eng.]; New York: Cambridge University Press, 1976. x, 318 p.; 24 cm. 1. Labour Party (Great Britain) 2. Labor policy — Great Britain — History. 3. Wage-price policy — Great Britain — History. I. T.
HC260.W24 P35    330.9/41/0854    *LC* 75-16869    *ISBN* 0521207797

## HC260.5 Ireland

**Black, R. D. Collison.**    &bull; **4.2311**
Economic thought and the Irish question, 1817–1870. — Cambridge [Eng.] University Press, 1960. xiv, 298 p. 24 cm. Bibliography: p. 249-292. 1. Ireland — Economic policy. 2. Land tenure — Ireland 3. Economics — Hist. — Gt. Brit. I. T.
HC260.5.B5x    330.9415    *LC* 60-3918

**Cullen, L. M. (Louis M.)**    **4.2312**
An economic history of Ireland since 1660 [by] L. M. Cullen. — London, Batsford [1972] 208 p. 22 cm. — (Studies in economic and social history) 1. Ireland — Economic conditions I. T.
HC260.5.C8x    330.9/415    *LC* 72-184126    *ISBN* 0713413816

**Gillmor, Desmond.**    **4.2313**
Economic activities in the Republic of Ireland: a geographical perspective / Desmond A. Gillmor. — Dublin: Gill and Macmillan, c1985. 394 p.: ill., maps; 23 cm. 1. Ireland — Economic conditions — 1949- 2. Ireland — Economic policy. I. T.
HC260.5.G56    *ISBN* 0717113906

**Ireland and Scotland 1600–1850: parallels and contrasts in**    **4.2314**
**economic and social development / edited by T.M. Devine and**
**David Dickson.**
Edinburgh: John Donald, c1983. 283 p.: maps; 24 cm. 1. Ireland — Economic conditions 2. Ireland — Social conditions. 3. Scotland — Economic conditions

— History. 4. Scotland — Social conditions — History. I. Devine, T. M. (Thomas Martin) II. Dickson, David.
HC260.5.I7    941.1 941.5 19    *ISBN* 0859760898

**Kennedy, Kieran Anthony.**      4.2315
Economic growth in Ireland: the experience since 1947 / Kieran A. Kennedy and Brendan R. Dowling. — [S.l.]: Barnes & Noble, 1975. 350 p. Includes index. 1. Economic development 2. Ireland — Economic conditions — 1949- I. Dowling, Brendan B. (Brendan Robert), joint author. II. T.
HC260.5.K4x    338/.09417    *LC* 76-357776    *ISBN* 0717107442

**Mokyr, Joel.**      4.2316
Why Ireland starved: a quantitative and analytical history of the Irish economy, 1800–1850 / Joel Mokyr. — London; Boston: Allen & Unwin, 1983. x, 330 p.; 24 cm. Includes index. 1. Poor — Ireland — History. 2. Famines — Ireland 3. Ireland — Economic conditions 4. Ireland — Rural conditions. I. T.
HC260.5.M64 1983    330.9415/081 19    *LC* 82-24508    *ISBN* 0049410105

**Daly, Mary E.**      4.2317
Dublin, the deposed capital: a social and economic history, 1860–1914 / Mary E. Daly. — Cork [Cork] Ireland: Cork University Press, 1984. 373 p.: ill.; 22 cm. Includes index. 1. Dublin (Dublin) — Economic conditions. 2. Dublin (Dublin) — Industries — History — 19th century. 3. Dublin (Dublin) — Social conditions. 4. Dublin (Dublin) — Politics and government. 5. Dublin (Dublin) — History — 19th century. I. T.
HC260.5.Z7 D83 1984    941.8/35 19    *LC* 84-152499    *ISBN* 0902561278

**An Economic history of Ulster, 1820–1940 / edited by Liam**    4.2318
**Kennedy and Philip Ollerenshaw.**
Manchester [Greater Manchester]; Dover, N.H., U.S.A.: Manchester University Press, c1985. 248 p.: maps; 23 cm. Includes indexes. 1. Ulster (Northern Ireland and Ireland) — Economic conditions — Addresses, essays, lectures. 2. Northern Ireland — Economic conditions — Addresses, essays, lectures. I. Kennedy, Liam, 1946- II. Ollerenshaw, Philip, 1953-
HC260.5.Z7 U474 1985    330.9416 19    *LC* 84-26079    *ISBN* 0719017505

## HC267–270 Czechoslovakia

**Michal, Jan M.**      • 4.2319
Central planning in Czechoslovakia; organization for growth in a mature economy. — Stanford, Calif., Stanford University Press, 1960. xii, 274 p. tables. 24 cm. Bibliography: p. [265]-268. 1. Czechoslovak Republic — Economic policy — 1945- I. T.
HC267.B2M5    338.9437    *LC* 60-11630

## HC271–280 France

**Caron, François.**      4.2320
[Histoire économique de la France, XIXe-XXe siècles. English] An economic history of modern France / François Caron; translated from the French by Barbara Bray. — New York: Columbia University Press, 1979 (c1978). 384 p.: ill.; 24 cm. — (Columbia economic history of the modern world.) Translation of: Histoire économique de la France, XIXe-XXe siècles. 1. France — Economic conditions I. T. II. Series.
HC273.C28 1979    330.9/44    *LC* 78-15353    *ISBN* 0231038607

**Clapham, John Harold, Sir, 1873-1946.**      • 4.2321
The economic development of France and Germany, 1815–1914 / by J. H. Clapham. — 4th ed. — Cambridge [Eng.]: University Press, 1936. ix, 420 p.: maps. 1. France — Economic conditions 2. Germany — Economic conditions I. T.
HC275.C55 1936    330.9034    *LC* 37-10958    *ISBN* 0521046645

**Dunham, Arthur Louis.**      • 4.2322
The industrial revolution in France, 1815–1848. [1st ed.] New York, Exposition Press [1955] xii, 516 p. (Exposition - University book) 1. France — Industry 2. France — Economic conditions I. T.
HC275 D88    *LC* 55-5715

**Gille, Bertrand, 1920-.**      • 4.2323
Recherches sur la formation de la grande entreprise capitaliste (1815–1848). — Paris: S. E. V. P. E. N., 1959. 164 p.; 25 cm. (Affaires et gens d'affairs; 17) At head of title: École pratique des hautes études, VIe section. Centre de recherches historiques. 1. Capitalism 2. France — History 3. France — Economic policy I. T. II. Series.
HC275.G5

**Palmade, Guy P.**      4.2324
[Capitalisme et capitalistes français au XIXs siècle. English] French capitalism in the nineteenth century [by] Guy P. Palmade. Translated, with an introd. by Graeme M. Holmes. New York, Barnes & Noble [1972] 256 p. 23 cm. Translation of Capitalisme et capitalistes français au XIXs siècle. 1. Capital — France. 2. France — Economic conditions — 19th century I. T.
HC275.P3513 1972    330.9/44/06    *LC* 72-181632    *ISBN* 0389041661

**Baum, Warren Charles.**      • 4.2325
The French economy and the state. — Princeton, N. J., Princeton University Press, 1958. xvi, 391 p. tables. 25 cm. 'A Rand Corporation research study.' 'Bibliographical notes': p. 359-373. Bibliography: p. 375-384. 1. France — Economic policy I. T.
HC276.B32    338.944    *LC* 58-7120

**Fourastié, Jean, 1907-.**      • 4.2326
L'Économie française dans le monde, par Jean Fourastié et Jean–Paul Courtheoux. 8 édition mise à jour. Paris, Presses universitaires de France, 1967. 128 p. 18 cm. (Que sais-je? No. 191) Cover illustrated in color. 1. France — Economic conditions — 1918-1945 2. France — Economic conditions — 1945- I. Courthéoux, Jean Paul. joint author. II. T.
HC276.F65 1967    330.944

**Kindleberger, Charles Poor, 1910-.**      • 4.2327
Economic growth in France and Britain, 1851–1950. — Cambridge, Mass.: Harvard University Press, 1964. viii, 378 p.; 25 cm. 1. France — Economic conditions 2. Great Britain — Economic conditions I. T.
HC276.K55 1964    *LC* 64-13424

**Kuisel, Richard F.**      4.2328
Capitalism and the state in modern France: renovation and economic management in the twentieth century / Richard F. Kuisel. — Cambridge [Eng.]; New York: Cambridge University Press, 1981. xiv, 344 p.; 24 cm. Includes index. 1. France — Economic policy — 20th century 2. France — Economic conditions — 20th century I. T.
HC276.K94    338.944 19    *LC* 81-616    *ISBN* 0521234743

**Ormsby, Hilda Rodwell (Jones)**      • 4.2329
France; a regional and economic geography. — [2d ed., rev.]. — London, Methuen; New York, Dutton [1950] xiv, 525 p. illus., maps. 23 cm. — ([Dutton advanced geographies]) Includes bibliographies. 1. France — Econ. condit. — 1918-1945. 2. France — Descr. & trav. — 1919- I. T.
HC276.O7 1950    330.944    *LC* 50-12866

**Sauvy, Alfred, 1898-.**      • 4.2330
Histoire économique de la France entre les deux guerres. [Paris] Fayard [1965-. v.: ill., maps.; 22 cm. 1. France — Economic conditions — 1918-1945 I. T.
HC276.S3155    *LC* 66-44843

**Ardagh, John, 1928-.**      4.2331
France in the 1980s / John Ardagh. — London: Secker & Warburg, 1983 (c1982). 672 p.: map; 25 cm. Includes index. 1. France — Economic conditions — 1945- 2. France — Social conditions — 1945- 3. France — Civilization — 1901- I. T. II. Title: France in the nineteen eighties.
HC276.2.A72    944.083 19    *LC* 82-148666    *ISBN* 0436017474

**Ardagh, John, 1928-.**      4.2332
The new France / [by] John Ardagh. — 3rd ed. — Harmondsworth: Penguin, 1977. 733 p.: map; 18 cm. — (Pelican books) First ed. published in 1968 under title: The new French revolution. Includes index. 1. France — Economic conditions — 1945- 2. France — Social conditions — 1945- 3. France — Civilization — 1945- I. T.
HC276.2.A73 1977    944/.082    *LC* 78-301519    *ISBN* 0140211713

**Carré, Jean Jacques.**      4.2333
[Croissance française. English] French economic growth / J.-J. Carré, P. Dubois, and E. Malinvaud; translated from the French by John P. Hatfield. — Stanford, Calif.: Stanford University Press, 1975. xviii, 581 p.: graphs; 24 cm. — (Studies of economic growth in industrialized countries) Translation of La croissance française. 1. France — Economic conditions — 1945- I. Dubois, Paul, joint author. II. Malinvaud, Edmond. joint author. III. T.
HC276.2.C3513    330.9/44/083    *LC* 74-82775    *ISBN* 0804708789

**McArthur, John H.**      • 4.2334
Industrial planning in France [by] John H. McArthur and Bruce R. Scott. With the assistance of Audrey T. Sproat. — Boston: Division of Research, Graduate School of Business Administration, Harvard University, 1969. xxv, 592 p.: illus.; 22 cm. 1. Industry and state — France. 2. Industrial management — France. 3. France — Economic policy — 1945- I. Scott, Bruce R. joint author. II. T.
HC276.2.M32    338.944    *LC* 76-82318    *ISBN* 0875840779

**Hufton, Olwen H.**      • 4.2335
Bayeux in the late eighteenth century: a social study, by Olwen H. Hufton. — Oxford, Clarendon P., 1967. iii-xi, 317 p. front. (map), tables. 22 1/2 cm.

Bibliography: p. [299]-309. 1. Bayeux (France) — Soc. condit. 2. Bayeux (France) — Econ. condit. I. T.
HC278.B3H8          309.1/44/22          *LC* 67-109452

## HC281–290 Germany. East Germany

**Lütge, Friedrich Karl, 1901-.**                                        • **4.2336**
Deutsche Sozial– und Wirtschaftsgeschichte: ein Überblick. — 2. wesentlich verm. und verb. Aufl. Berlin, Springer, 1960. 552 p.; 24 cm. 1. Germany (East) — Economic conditions. 2. Germany (East) — Social conditions. I. T.
HC283.L8 1960          *LC* 60-3614

**Böhme, Helmut.**                                                      • **4.2337**
Deutschlands Weg zur Grossmacht. Studien zum Verhältnis von Wirtschaft und Staat während der Reichsgründungszeit 1848–1881. — Köln, Berlin, Kiepenheuer u. Witsch (1966) xviii, 723 p. 24 cm. Bibliography: p. 637-700. 1. Germany — Economic policy 2. Germany — Commercial policy. I. T.
HC285.B58

**Hamerow, Theodore S.**                                               • **4.2338**
Restoration, revolution, reaction; economics and politics in Germany, 1815–1871. Princeton, Princeton University Press, 1958. 347 p. 23 cm. 1. Germany — Economic conditions — 19th century 2. Germany — Politics and government — 19th century I. T.
HC285.H2          330.943          *LC* 58-7117

**Henderson, W. O. (William Otto), 1904-.**                            **4.2339**
The rise of German industrial power, 1834–1914 / W. O. Henderson. — Berkeley: University of California Press, 1976 (c1975). 264 p.: maps; 23 cm. Includes index. 1. Germany — Industries — History. I. T.
HC285.H442          338/.0943          *LC* 75-17293          *ISBN* 0520030737. *ISBN* 0520031202 pbk

**Stolper, Gustav, 1888-1947.**                                        • **4.2340**
The German economy, 1870 to the present, by Gustav Stolper, Karl Häuser [and] Knut Borchardt. Translated by Toni Stolper. — New York, Harcourt, Brace & World [1967] xiv, 353 p. 24 cm. First published in 1940 under title: German economy, 1870-1940: issues and trends. Bibliography: p. 331-338. 1. Germany — Econ. condit. 2. Germany — Economic policy I. Häuser, Karl, joint author. II. Borchardt, Knut. joint author. III. T.
HC285.S84 1967          330.943          *LC* 67-13682

**Hardach, Karl.**                                                      **4.2341**
[Wirtschaftsgeschichte Deutschlands im 20. Jahrhundert. English] The political economy of Germany in the twentieth century / Karl Hardach. — Berkeley: University of California Press, c1980. xii, 235 p.: ill.; 24 cm. Translation of Wirtschaftsgeschichte Deutschlands im 20. Jahrhundert. 1. Germany — Economic conditions — 20th century I. T.
HC286.H3613          330.943/08          *LC* 78-64754          *ISBN* 0520038096

**Feldman, Gerald D.**                                                  • **4.2342**
Army, industry, and labor in Germany, 1914–1918, by Gerald D. Feldman. Princeton, N. J., Princeton University Press, 1966. xvi, 572 p.: ill.; 22 cm. Revision of thesis, Harvard University. 'Bibliographical note': p. 543-546. 1. World War, 1914-1918 — Economic aspects — Germany. 2. Manpower — Germany. I. T.
HC286.2.F4          940.31          *LC* 66-10553

**Klein, Burton H.**                                                    • **4.2343**
Germany's economic preparations for war. — Cambridge, Harvard University Press, 1959. xi, 272 p. 22 cm. — (Harvard economic studies. v. 109) Bibliography: p. [259]-264. 1. Germany — Military policy. 2. Germany — Indus. 3. World War, 1939-1945 — Economic aspects — Germany. I. T. II. Series.
HC286.4.K5          330.943          *LC* 59-7655

**Wallich, Henry Christopher, 1914-.**                                 • **4.2344**
Mainsprings of the German revival. — New Haven, Yale University Press, 1955. xi, 401 p. tables. 23 cm. — (Yale studies in economics. 5) Bibliography: p. 388-393. 1. Germany (Federal Republic, 1949-     ) — Econ. condit. I. T. II. Series.
HC286.5.W32          330.943          *LC* 55-8708

**Stolper, Wolfgang F.**                                                • **4.2345**
The structure of the East German economy. With the assistance of Karl W. Roskamp. — Cambridge: Harvard University Press, 1960. xxv, 478 p.: tables; 25 cm. Bibliography: p. [445]-455. 1. Germany (Democratic Republic, 1949-     ) — Econ. condit. I. T.
HC287.A2S7          330.9431          *LC* 60-13295

**Handbook of the economy of the German Democratic Republic**          **4.2346**
/ prepared by Doris Cornelsen ... [et al.] a research team of the German Institute for Economic Research, West Berlin; edited by Reinhard Pohl; translated from the German by Lux Furtmüller.
Farnborough, Eng.: Saxon House, c1979. xxiv, 366 p.: ill.; 23 cm. Translation of Handbuch DDR-Wirtschaft. 1. Germany (East) — Economic policy. 2. Germany (East) — Economic conditions. I. Cornelsen, Doris. II. Pohl, Reinhard, Dr. III. Deutsches Institut für Wirtschaftsforschung.
HC290.78.H2913          330.9431/0877          *LC* 79-322686          *ISBN* 0566002566

**Leptin, Gert, 1929-.**                                               **4.2347**
Economic reform in East German industry / Gert Leptin and Manfred Melzer; translated from the German by Roger A. Clarke. — Oxford; New York: Oxford University Press, 1979 (c1978). xxv, 200 p.: ill.; 23 cm. — (Economic reforms in East European industry) At head of title: Institute of Soviet and East European Studies, University of Glasgow. 1. Germany (East) — Economic policy. 2. Germany (East) — Industries. I. Melzer, Manfred. II. University of Glasgow. Institute of Soviet and East European Studies. III. T. IV. Series.
HC290.78.L4613          338.943/1          *LC* 77-30589          *ISBN* 0192153463

**Gianaris, Nicholas V.**                                              **4.2348**
Greece and Yugoslavia: an economic comparison / Nicholas V. Gianaris. — New York: Praeger, 1984. xiv, 258 p.; 24 cm. — Includes indexes. 1. Greece — Economic conditions — 1974- 2. Yugoslavia — Economic conditions — 1945- I. T.
HC295.G52 1984          330.9495/076 19          *LC* 83-27010          *ISBN* 0030714664

## HC300.2 Hungary

**Berend, T. Iván (Tibor Iván), 1930-.**                               **4.2349**
Hungary: a century of economic development / [by] I.T. [i.e. T.I.] Berend and G. Ranki. — Newton Abbot: David & Charles; New York: Barnes & Noble, [1974] 263 p.: maps; 22 cm. (National economic histories) 1. Hungary — Economic conditions I. Ránki, György, 1930- joint author. II. T.
HC300.2.B47          330.9/439/04          *LC* 74-158570          *ISBN* 0064903710

**Berend, T. Iván (Tibor Iván), 1930-.**                               **4.2350**
The Hungarian economy in the twentieth century / Ivan T. Berend and György Ránki. — New York: St. Martin's Press, 1985. 316 p.; 22 cm. Includes index. 1. Hungary — Economic conditions I. Ránki, György, 1930- II. T.
HC300.24.B44 1985          330.9439/05 19          *LC* 84-17773          *ISBN* 0312401183

**Hare, P. G.**                                                        **4.2351**
Hungary, a decade of economic reform / edited by P.G. Hare, H.K. Radice, and N. Swain. — London; Boston: Allen & Unwin, 1981. xiv, 257 p.; 23 cm. 1. Hungary — Economic policy — 1968- — Addresses, essays, lectures. 2. Hungary — Economic conditions — 1968- — Addresses, essays, lectures. I. Radice, H. K. (Hugo K.) II. Swain, N. (Nigel) III. T.
HC300.28.H88          338.9439 19          *LC* 80-42124          *ISBN* 0043390218

## HC301–310 Italy

**Luzzatto, Gino, 1878-1964.**                                         • **4.2352**
An economic history of Italy; from the fall of the Roman Empire to the beginning of the sixteenth century. Translated from the Italian by Philip Jones. New York, Barnes & Noble [1961] vii, 180 p. 1. Italy — Economic conditions I. T.
HC303 L813 1961A

**Carlyle, Margaret.**                                                 • **4.2353**
The awakening of Southern Italy. London, Oxford University Press, 1962. 147 p. ill. 1. Italy, Southern — Economic conditions 2. Italy, Southern — Social conditions I. T.
HC305 C332          *LC* 62-5059

**Clough, Shepard Bancroft, 1901-.**                                   • **4.2354**
The economic history of modern Italy. — New York: Columbia University Press, 1964. xi, 458 p.: maps, diagrs.; 24 cm. 1. Italy — Economic conditions I. T.
HC305.C55          330.945          *LC* 63-18434

**Hildebrand, George Herbert.**                                        • **4.2355**
Growth and structure in the economy of modern Italy [by] George H. Hildebrand. Cambridge, Harvard University Press, 1965. xx, 475 p. 1. Italy — Economic conditions — 1945- I. T.
HC305 H47          *LC* 65-24450

**Lutz, Vera C.**    • **4.2356**
Italy, a study in economic development. With a foreword by Frederic Benham and Muriel Grindrod. Issued under the auspices of the Royal Institute of International Affairs. London, Oxford University Press, 1962. 342 p. ill. 1. Italy — Economic conditions — 1945- 2. Italy — Economic policy I. T.
HC305 L8    *LC* 63-189

**Templeman, Donald C.**    **4.2357**
The Italian economy / Donald C. Templeman. — New York, N.Y.: Praeger, 1981. xxiv, 360 p.; 24 cm. Includes index. 1. Italy — Economic conditions — 1976- 2. Italy — Economic policy. I. T.
HC305.T357    330.945/0927 19    *LC* 80-23478    *ISBN* 0030576121

**Schneider, Jane.**    **4.2358**
Culture and political economy in western Sicily / Jane Schneider, Peter Schneider. New York: Academic Press, c1976. xv, 256 p.: ill.; 24 cm. (Studies in social discontinuity series) Includes index. 1. Sicily — Economic conditions 2. Sicily — Social conditions. 3. Sicily — Social life and customs. I. Schneider, Peter, 1933- joint author. II. T.
HC307.S5 S33    309.1/458/209    *LC* 76-18286    *ISBN* 0126278504

**Herlihy, David.**    **4.2359**
[Toscans et leurs familles. English] Tuscans and their families: a study of the Florentine catasto of 1427 / David Herlihy and Christiane Klapisch–Zuber. — New Haven: Yale University Press, c1985. xxiv, 404 p.: ill., maps; 24 cm. (Yale series in economic history.) Abridged translation of: Les Toscans et leurs familles. Includes index. 1. Florence (Italy) — Economic conditions — Sources. 2. Florence (Italy) — Social conditions — Sources. 3. Florence (Italy) — History — 1421-1737 — Sources. 4. Florence (Italy) — Census, 1427. I. Klapisch-Zuber, Christiane. II. T. III. Series.
HC308.F6 H4713 1985    945/.51 19    *LC* 84-40195    *ISBN* 0300030568

**Brown, Judith C.**    **4.2360**
In the shadow of Florence: provincial society in Renaissance Pescia / Judith C. Brown. — New York: Oxford University Press, 1982. xxv, 244 p.: ill.; 23 cm. Errata slip inserted. Includes index. 1. Pescia (Italy) — Economic conditions. 2. Pescia (Italy) — Social conditions. I. T.
HC308.P43 B76    330.945/52 19    *LC* 81-38377    *ISBN* 0195029933

**Rapp, Richard T.**    **4.2361**
Industry and economic decline in seventeenth–century Venice / Richard Tilden Rapp. — Cambridge, Mass.: Harvard University Press, 1976. ix, 195 p.: ill.; 24 cm. (Harvard historical monographs. 69) Includes index. 1. Venice (Italy) — Economic conditions. I. T. II. Series.
HC308.V4 R36    330.9/45/31    *LC* 75-16149    *ISBN* 0674445457

## HC310.5–330 Netherlands

**Mokyr, Joel.**    **4.2362**
Industrialization in the Low Countries, 1795–1850 / Joel Mokyr. — New Haven: Yale University Press, 1977 (c1976). xviii, 295 p.: ill.; 25 cm. (Yale series in economic history.) Includes index. 1. Industrialization — Mathematical models. 2. Netherlands — Industries — History. 3. Belgium — Industries — History. I. T. II. Series.
HC310.5.M64    338/.09492    *LC* 75-43326    *ISBN* 0300018924

**Pinder, David.**    **4.2363**
The Netherlands / David Pinder. Boulder, CO: Westview Press, 1976. 194 p.: ill.; 23 cm. (Studies in industrial geography) Includes index. 1. Netherlands — Industries. 2. Netherlands — Manufactures. I. T. II. Series.
HC325.P54 1976    338/.09492    *LC* 76-18924    *ISBN* 0891586261

## HC331–340 Soviet Union. Poland

**Bal'zak, S.S.**    • **4.2364**
Economic geography of the USSR, ed. by S.S. Balzak, V.F. Vasyutin, and Ya.G. Feigin. American ed., edited by Chauncy D. Harris, tr. from the Russian by Robert M. Hankin and Olga Adler Titelbaum; pref. by John A. Morrison. New York, Macmillan Co., 1949. xiv, 620 p.: maps (part fold.); 22 cm. 'Translated under the Russian Translation Project of the American Council of Learned Societies.' 1. Russia — Economic conditions I. Harris, Chauncy Dennison, 1914- II. T.
HC333 B333    *LC* 49-10927

**Blackwell, William Leslie.**    **4.2365**
[Russian economic development from Peter the Great to] Stalin. Edited, with an introd., by William L. Blackwell. — New York: New Viewpoints, 1974. xxxiv, 459 p.: illus.; 21 cm. — (Modern scholarship on European history) 1. Russia — Economic conditions — Addresses, essays, lectures. 2. Russia —

Economic policy — Addresses, essays, lectures. 3. Russia — Industries — History — Addresses, essays, lectures. I. T.
HC333.B543    HC333 B543.    330.9/47    *LC* 73-11162    *ISBN* 0531063631

**Liashchenko, Petr I. (Petr Ivanovich), 1876-1955.**    • **4.2366**
History of the national economy of Russia, to the 1917 revolution; translated by L. M. Herman. Introd. by Calvin B. Hoover; maps redrawn under the supervision of Leonard H. Dykes. — New York, Macmillan, 1949. xiii, 880 p. maps (part fold.) 25 cm. — ([American Council of Learned Societies Devoted to Humanistic Studies. Russian Translation Project. Series 4]) 'Bibliographic index': p. 785-827. 1. Russia — Econ. condit. I. T. II. Series.
HC333.L455    330.947    *LC* 49-49384 *

**Mavor, James, 1854-1925.**    • **4.2367**
An economic history of Russia. 2nd ed., rev. and enl. New York, Russell & Russell, 1965. 2 v.; 22 cm. 'Reissued 1965 ... from the revised and corrected edition of 1925.' 1. Soviet Union — Economic conditions 2. Soviet Union — Social conditions 3. Soviet Union — Politics and government I. T.
HC333.M3 1965    *LC* 64-66397

**Institut geografii (Akademiia nauk SSSR)**    • **4.2368**
Natural resources of the Soviet Union: their use and renewal. Edited by I. P. Gerasimov, D. L. Armand, and K. M. Yefron. Translated from the Russian by Jacek I. Romanowski. — English ed. edited by W. A. Douglas Jackson. — San Francisco, W. H. Freeman [c1971] xiii, 349 p. illus. 25 cm. Translation of Prirodnye resursy Sovetskogo Soiuza. 1. Natural resources — Russia. I. Gerasimov, I. P. (Innokentiĭ Petrovich), 1905- ed. II. Armand, D. L. (David L'vovich) ed. III. Éfron, K. M., ed. IV. T.
HC333.5.A42913    333.7/.0947    *LC* 74-138667    *ISBN* 0716702487

**Soviet natural resources in the world economy / edited by Robert G. Jensen, Theodore Shabad, and Arthur W. Wright.**    **4.2369**
Chicago: University of Chicago Press, c1983. xviii, 700 p.: ill.; 29 cm. 1. Natural resources — Soviet Union. I. Jensen, Robert G. II. Shabad, Theodore. III. Wright, Arthur W., 1938-
HC333.5.S68 1983    333.7/0947 19    *LC* 82-17317    *ISBN* 0226398315

**Crisp, Olga.**    **4.2370**
Studies in the Russian economy before 1914 / Olga Crisp. — New York: Barnes & Noble Books, 1976. x, 278 p.; 23 cm. (Studies in Russian and East European history) Includes index. 1. Soviet Union — Economic conditions — 1861-1917 I. T.
HC334.5.C75    330.9/47    *LC* 75-39083    *ISBN* 0064913171

**Von Laue, Theodore H. (Theodore Hermann)**    • **4.2371**
Sergei Witte and the industrialization of Russia. — New York, Columbia University Press, 1963. 360 p. illus. 24 cm. — (Studies of the Russian Institute, Columbia University) Includes bibliography. 1. Witte, Sergeĭ IUl'evich, graf, 1849-1915. 2. Russia — Indus. I. T.
HC334.5.V58    338.947    *LC* 63-10520

**Baykov, Alexander, 1899-.**    • **4.2372**
The development of the Soviet economic system; an essay on the experience of planning in the U.S.S.R., by Alexander Baykov ... Cambridge [Eng.] University Press, 1946. xv, 514 p. 22 cm. — (Economic and social studies. 5) 1. Soviet Union — Economic policy — 1917- I. T. II. Series.
HC335.B357    *LC* 46-6158    *ISBN* 0521077699

**Bergson, Abram, 1914- ed.**    • **4.2373**
Economic trends in the Soviet Union. Edited by Abram Bergson and Simon Kuznets. — Cambridge, Harvard University Press, 1963. xiv, 392 p. diagr., tables. 25 cm. Outgrowth of a conference held at Princeton, N. J., on May 6-8, 1961; sponsored by the Committee on Economic Growth of the Social Science Research Council. Includes bibliographical references. 1. Russia — Econ. condit. — 1918- I. Kuznets, Simon Smith, 1901- joint editor. II. Social Science Research Council (U.S.). Committee on Economic Growth. III. T.
HC335.B365    330.947    *LC* 63-9548

**Campbell, Robert Wellington.**    • **4.2374**
Soviet economic power: its organization, growth, and challenge [by] Robert W. Campbell. 2d ed. Boston, Houghton Mifflin [1966] xii, 184 p. 21 cm. Third ed. published in 1973 under title: The Soviet-type economies. 1. Soviet Union — Economic conditions — 1918- I. T.
HC335.C28 1966    338.947    *LC* 66-3779

**Degras, Jane Tabrisky, 1905-.**    • **4.2375**
Soviet planning: essays in honour of Naum Jasny / edited by Jane Degras and Alec Nove. — Oxford: B. Blackwell, 1964. xi, 225 p.: ill.; 22 cm. 1. Soviet Union — Economic policy — 1917- I. Degras, Jane Tabrisky, 1905- II. Jasny, Naum, 1883-1967. III. Nove, Alec. IV. T.
HC335.S5945 1964a    HC335.D36.

**Dobb, Maurice Herbert, 1900-.**    • **4.2376**
Soviet economic development since 1917, by Maurice Dobb. [Rev. and enl. ed.]
New York, International Publishers [1967, c1966] viii, 515 p. illus. 21 cm.
1. Soviet Union — Economic conditions — 1918-1945 2. Soviet Union —
Economic conditions — 1945-1955 I. T.
HC335.D63 1966a     330.947     *LC* 67-911

**Dyker, David A.**    **4.2377**
The future of the Soviet economic planning system / David A. Dyker. —
Armonk, N.Y.: M.E. Sharpe, c1985. 172 p.: ill.; 23 cm. Includes index.
1. Central planning — Soviet Union. 2. Soviet Union — Economic policy —
1917- I. T.
HC335.D87 1985     338.947 19     *LC* 84-27594     *ISBN* 0873323246

**Erlich, Alexander.**    • **4.2378**
The Soviet industrialization debate, 1924–1928. — Cambridge, Harvard
University Press, 1960. xxiii, 214 p. diagrs. 22 cm. — (Russian Research Center
studies, 41) Based on thesis—New School for Social Research. Bibliography: p.
[195]-201. 1. Russia — Economic policy — 1917-1928. I. T.
HC335.E645     330.947     *LC* 60-13287

**Goldman, Marshall I.**    • **4.2379**
The Soviet economy: myth and reality [by] Marshall I. Goldman. Englewood
Cliffs, N.J., Prentice-Hall [1968] xiii, 176 p. 21 cm. (A Spectrum book)
1. Soviet Union — Economic conditions — 1918- I. T.
HC335.G565     330.947     *LC* 68-14467

**Granick, David.**    • **4.2380**
Management of the industrial firm in the USSR: a study in Soviet economic
planning. — New York: Columbia University Press, 1954. xiii, 346 p.; 24 cm.
(Studies of the Russian Institute, Columbia University) 1. Industrial
management — Russia 2. Russia — Industries I. T.
HC335 G66     *LC* 53-11451

**Gregory, Paul R.**    **4.2381**
Soviet economic structure and performance / Paul R. Gregory, Robert C.
Stuart. — 3rd ed — New York: Harper & Row, c1986. xiii, 447 p.; ill.; 24 cm.
1. Soviet Union — Economic conditions — 1918- 2. Soviet Union —
Economic policy — 1917- I. Stuart, Robert C., 1938- II. T.
HC335.G723 1986     330.947/0853 19     *LC* 85-31740     *ISBN*
0060425075

**Jasny, Naum, 1883-1967.**    • **4.2382**
Soviet industrialization, 1928–1952. — [Chicago] University of Chicago Press
[1961] xviii, 467 p. diagrs., tables. 25 cm. Bibliographical footnotes. 1. Russia
— Indus. I. T.
HC335.J384     338.0947     *LC* 61-5605

*O*

**Mellor, Roy E. H.**    **4.2383**
The Soviet Union and its geographical problems / Roy E.H. Mellor. —
London: Macmillan, 1982. xii, 207 p.: ill.; 25 cm. Includes index. 1. Soviet
Union — Economic conditions — 1918- 2. Soviet Union — Population. I. T.
HC335.M419 1982     947 19     *LC* 82-184376     *ISBN* 0333276620

**Munting, Roger, 1945-.**    **4.2384**
The economic development of the USSR / Roger Munting. — New York: St.
Martin's Press, 1982. 228 p.; 23 cm. Includes index. 1. Soviet Union —
Economic conditions — 1918- 2. Soviet Union — Economic policy — 1917-
I. T.
HC335.M86 1982     338.947 19     *LC* 82-42545     *ISBN* 0312228856

**Nove, Alec.**    **4.2385**
An economic history of the U.S.S.R. / Alec Nove. — Repr. with revisions. —
Harmondsworth, Middlesex, England; New York, N.Y., U.S.A.: Penguin
Books, 1982, c1969. 429 p.; 20 cm. — (Pelican books) Includes indexes.
1. Soviet Union — Economic conditions — 1918- 2. Soviet Union —
Economic policy — 1917- I. T. II. Title: Economic history of the USSR.
HC335.N68 1982     330.947/084 19     *LC* 83-134598     *ISBN*
0140214038

**Nove, Alec.**    **4.2386**
The Soviet economic system / Alec Nove. — 3rd ed. — Boston: Allen & Unwin,
c1986. xix, 425 p.; 23 cm. Includes index. 1. Soviet Union — Economic
conditions — 1918- 2. Soviet Union — Economic policy — 1917- I. T.
HC335.N692 1986     330.947/085 19     *LC* 86-13992     *ISBN*
0044970250

**Nutter, G. Warren.**    • **4.2387**
Growth of industrial production in the Soviet Union, by G. Warren Nutter,
assisted by Israel Borenstein and Adam Kaufman. A study by the National
Bureau of Economic Research. Princeton, N.J., Princeton University Press,
1962. xxvii, 706 p. diagrs., tables. 24 cm. (National Bureau of Economic
Research. General series, no. 75) 1. Soviet Union — Industries I. T. II. Series.
HC335.N8     338.947     *LC* 61-12101

**Spulber, Nicolas.**    **4.2388**
Soviet strategy for economic growth. Bloomington: Indiana University Press,
1964. 175 p. (Indiana. University. International studies) 1. Russia —
Economic policy — 1917- I. T.
HC335 S676     *LC* 64-10101

**Vucinich, Alexander, 1914-.**    • **4.2389**
Soviet economic institutions: the social structure of production units. Introd. by
Sergius Yakobson. [Stanford] Stanford University Press, 1952. x, 150 p. diagrs.
23 cm. (Hoover Institute studies. Series E: Institutions, no. 1) Bibliography: p.
138-150. 1. Russia — Industries. I. T. II. Series.
HC335.V885     338.947     *LC* 52-8306

**Zaleski, Eugène.**    • **4.2390**
[Planification de la croissance et fluctuations économiques en U.R.S.S.
1:1918-1932. English] Planning for economic growth in the Soviet Union,
1918–1932. Translated from the French and edited by Marie–Christine
MacAndrew and G. Warren Nutter. Chapel Hill, University of North Carolina
Press [1971] xxxviii, 425 p. 24 cm. Translation of Planification de la croissance
et fluctuations économiques en U.R.S.S., v. 1: 1918-1932. 1. Russia —
Economic policy — 1917- 2. Russia — Economic conditions — 1918. I. T.
HC335.Z4413     330.947/084     *LC* 78-97018     *ISBN* 0807811602

## HC336 1951–

**Lane, David Stuart.**    **4.2391**
Soviet economy and society / David Lane. — New York: New York University
Press, 1985. xiii, 342 p.: ill., map; 24 cm. 1. Soviet Union — Economic
conditions — 1918- 2. Soviet Union — Social conditions — 1917- I. T.
HC336.L29 1985     306/.0947 19     *LC* 84-16523     *ISBN* 081475015X

**Bergson, Abram, 1914-.**    • **4.2392**
The economics of Soviet planning. New Haven, Yale University Press, 1964.
xvii, 394 p. 21 cm. (Studies in comparative economics. 5) 1. Industrial
management — Russia. 2. Soviet Union — Economic policy — 1959-1965
I. T. II. Series.
HC336.2.B43     338.947     *LC* 64-20910

**Cole, J. P. (John Peter), 1928-.**    • **4.2393**
A geography of the U.S.S.R.: the background to a planned economy [by] J. P.
Cole and F. C. German. 2nd ed. London, Butterworths, 1970. 324 p. illus.,
maps. 26 cm. 1. Economic zoning — Soviet Union. 2. Soviet Union —
Economic conditions — 1955-1965 I. German, Frank Clifford, joint author.
II. T.
HC336.2.C63 1970     330.947/085     *LC* 73-563423     *ISBN*
0408497513

*HC*
*336.2*
*C68*
*1970*

**Miller, Margaret Stevenson.**    • **4.2394**
Rise of the Russian consumer / [by] Margaret Miller. — [London]: Institute of
Economic Affairs, 1965. 254 p.; 19 cm. 1. Consumers — Russia 2. Russia —
Economic policy — 1959- 3. Europe, Eastern — Economic conditions
I. Institute of Economic Affairs (Great Britain) II. T.
HC336.2 M52 1965     *LC* 66-31927

**Nove, Alec.**    • **4.2395**
The Soviet economy; an introduction. 2d rev. ed. New York, F. A. Praeger
[1969, c1968] xiii, 373 p. 22 cm. 1. Soviet Union — Economic conditions —
1955-1965 I. T.
HC336.2.N62 1969     330.947     *LC* 68-8136

**Zaleski, Eugène.**    **4.2396**
Planning reforms in the Soviet Union, 1962–1966; an analysis of recent trends
in economic organization and management. Translated by Marie–Christine
MacAndrew and G. Warren Nutter. Chapel Hill, University of North Carolina
Press [1967] viii, 203 p. illus. 23 cm. Translation of a French ms. based on a
series of 3 periodical articles published 1964-66, rev. and brought up-to-date as
of October 1966. 1. Soviet Union — Economic policy — 1959-1965 I. T.
HC336.2.Z327     *LC* 67-17035

**Demko, George J., 1933- comp.**    **4.2397**
Geographical perspectives in the Soviet Union; a selection of readings, edited
and translated by George J. Demko and Roland J. Fuchs. Columbus, Ohio
State University Press [1974] xiv, 742 p. illus. 25 cm. 1. Geography, Economic
— Addresses, essays, lectures. 2. Soviet Union — Economic conditions —
1965- — Addresses, essays, lectures. I. Fuchs, Roland J. joint author. II. T.
HC336.23.D3913     309.1/47/085     *LC* 74-9853     *ISBN* 0814201962

**Feiwel, George R.**    **4.2398**
The Soviet quest for economic efficiency: issues, controversies, and reforms [by]
George R. Feiwel. Expanded and updated ed. New York, Praeger [1972] xxiv,
790 p. 25 cm. (Praeger special studies in international economics and
development) 1. Soviet Union — Economic conditions — 1965-1975 2. Soviet
Union — Economic policy — 1966- I. T.
HC336.23.F43 1972     330.9/47/085     *LC* 72-145952

**Katz, Abraham, 1926-.**      **4.2399**
The politics of economic reform in the Soviet Union. — New York: Praeger, [1972] viii, 230 p.; 25 cm. — (Praeger special studies in international economics and development) 1. Russia — Economic policy — 1966- 2. Russia — Economic policy — 1917- I. T.
HC336.23.K33     338.947     *LC* 74-180846

**Berliner, Joseph S.**      **4.2400**
The innovation decision in Soviet industry / Joseph S. Berliner. — Cambridge, Mass.: MIT Press, c1976. xii, 561 p.; 24 cm. Includes index. 1. Industrial organization — Russia. 2. New products 3. Incentives in industry — Russia. 4. Russia — Industries. I. T.
HC336.24.B48     HC336.24 B48.     338/.0947     *LC* 76-2390     *ISBN* 0262021188

**Cole, J. P. (John Peter), 1928-.**      **4.2401**
Geography of the Soviet Union / J.P. Cole. — London; Boston: Butterworths, 1984. xiv, 452 p.: ill., maps; 26 cm. Rev. ed. of: A geography of the U.S.S.R. 2nd ed. 1970. Includes index. 1. Soviet Union — Economic conditions — 1976- 2. Soviet Union — Economic conditions — 1976- — Regional disparities. I. Cole, J. P. (John Peter), 1928- Geography of the U.S.S.R. II. T.
HC336.25.C63 1984     330.947/085 19     *LC* 83-14458     *ISBN* 0408497521

**The Soviet economy: toward the year 2000 / edited by Abram**      **4.2402**
**Bergson and Herbert S. Levine.**
London; Boston: G. Allen & Unwin, 1983. xvi, 452 p.; 25 cm. Includes index. 1. Economic forecasting — Soviet Union — Addresses, essays, lectures. 2. Soviet Union — Economic conditions — 1976- — Addresses, essays, lectures. I. Bergson, Abram, 1914- II. Levine, Herbert Samuel, 1928-
HC336.25.S6834 1983     338.5/443/0947 19     *LC* 82-15611     *ISBN* 0043350453

## HC337 POLAND

**Alton, Thad P. (Thad Paul)**      • **4.2403**
Polish postwar economy. New York Columbia University Press [1955] 330p. (Studies of the Russian Institute, Columbia University) 1. Poland — Economic policy I. T.
HC337 P7 A68     *LC* 55-5751

**Feiwel, George R.**      **4.2404**
Industrialization and planning under Polish socialism [by] George R. Feiwel. — New York: Praeger Publishers, [1971] 2 v.; 25 cm. — (Praeger special studies in international economics and development) 1. Industry and state — Poland. 2. Poland — Economic policy — 1945- I. T.
HC337.P7 F37     330.9438/05     *LC* 79-145951

## HC340 SPECIAL TOPICS, A–Z

**Bergson, Abram, 1914-.**      • **4.2405**
Soviet national income and product, 1940–48 / by Abram Bergson and Hans Heymann, Jr. — New York: Columbia University Press, 1954. xii, 249 p.: ill., map.; 25 cm. 'A research study by the Rand Corporation.' 1. Income — Russia. 2. Gross national product — Russia. I. Heymann, Hans, 1920- II. Rand Corporation. III. T.
HC340.I5 B42     *LC* 54-9364

**McAuley, Alastair, 1938-.**      **4.2406**
Economic welfare in the Soviet Union: poverty, living standards, and inequality / Alastair McAuley. — Madison: University of Wisconsin Press, c1979. xix, 389 p.: ill.; 24 cm. Includes index. 1. Income distribution — Russia. 2. Poor — Russia. I. T.
HC340.I5 M2     HC340I5 M2.     339.2/0947     *LC* 78-53290     *ISBN* 0299076407

**Bergson, Abram, 1914-.**      **4.2407**
Productivity and the social system: the USSR and the West / Abram Bergson. — Cambridge, Mass.: Harvard University Press, 1978. xi, 256 p.; 24 cm. 1. Industrial productivity — Russia. 2. Russia — Economic policy — 1966- I. T.
HC340.I52 B47     338/.0947     *LC* 77-15493     *ISBN* 0674711653

**Industrial innovation in the Soviet Union / edited by Ronald**      **4.2408**
**Amann and Julian Cooper.**
New Haven: Yale University Press, 1982. xxix, 526 p.: ill.; 26 cm. Includes bibliographical references and indexes. 1. Technological innovations — Soviet Union — Case studies. 2. Soviet Union — Industries — Case studies. I. Amann, Ronald, 1943- II. Cooper, Julian, 1945-
HC340.T4 I52 1982     338/.06 19     *LC* 81-70484     *ISBN* 0300027729

**Parrott, Bruce, 1945-.**      **4.2409**
Politics and technology in the Soviet Union / Bruce Parrott. — Cambridge, Mass.: MIT Press, c1983. 428 p.; 24 cm. — (Studies of the Russian Institute.)

Includes index. 1. Technological innovations — Soviet Union. 2. Technology and state — Soviet Union. I. T. II. Series.
HC340.T4 P29 1983     338/.06 19     *LC* 82-22953     *ISBN* 0262160927

## HC341–370 Scandinavia

**Hodne, Fritz.**      **4.2410**
The Norwegian economy, 1920–1980 / Fritz Hodne. — London: Croom Helm; New York: St. Martin's Press, 1983. xviii, 286 p.: ill.; 23 cm. Includes indexes. 1. Norway — Economic conditions — 1918- I. T.
HC365.H553 1983     330.9481/04 19     *LC* 83-13690     *ISBN* 0312579381

**Heckscher, Eli F. (Eli Filip), 1879-1952.**      • **4.2411**
An economic history of Sweden; translated by Goran Ohlin. With a suppl. by Gunnar Heckscher, and a pref. by Alexander Gerschenkron. Cambridge: Harvard University Press, c1954. xlii, 308 p.: ill.; 22 cm. (Harvard economic studies. v. 95) Translation of Svenskt arbete och liv. 1. Sweden — Economic conditions I. T. II. Series.
HC373.H413     *LC* 54-8628

## HC381–390 Spain

**Shafer, Robert Jones, 1915-.**      **4.2412**
The economic societies in the Spanish world, 1763–1821. — [Syracuse, N.Y.] Syracuse University Press, 1958. xiii, 416 p. 1. Spain — Economic policy — Societies, etc. 2. Spain — Colonies — America — Economic policy — Sociètes, etc. I. T.
HC384.S5     *LC* 57-12362

**Harrison, Joseph, 1944-.**      **4.2413**
The Spanish economy in the twentieth century / Joseph Harrison. — New York: St. Martin's Press, 1985. 207 p.; 23 cm. Includes index. 1. Spain — Economic conditions 2. Spain — Economic policy. 3. Spain — Politics and government — 20th century I. T.
HC385.H34 1985     330.946/08 19     *LC* 84-16115     *ISBN* 0312749880

**Lieberman, Sima, 1927-.**      **4.2414**
The contemporary Spanish economy: a historical perspective / Sima Lieberman. — London; Boston: Allen & Unwin, 1982. xii, 378 p.: ill.; 23 cm. Includes index. 1. Spain — Economic conditions — 1975- 2. Spain — Economic conditions I. T.
HC385.L46 1982     330.946 19     *LC* 81-17559     *ISBN* 0043390269

**Burns, Robert Ignatius.**      **4.2415**
Medieval colonialism: postcrusade exploitation of Islamic Valencia / Robert Ignatius Burns. — Princeton, N.J.: Princeton University Press, 1976 (C1975) xxiv, 394 p., [4] leaves of plates: ill.; 24 cm. Includes index. 1. James I, King of Aragon, 1208-1276. 2. Taxation — Valencia — History. 3. Mudéjares 4. Crusades 5. Valencia (Kingdom) — Economic conditions. I. T.
HC387.V3 B87     336.2/00946/76     *LC* 74-25614     *ISBN* 0691052271

**Ringrose, David R.**      **4.2416**
Madrid and the Spanish economy, 1560–1850 / David R. Ringrose. — Berkeley: University of California Press, c1983. xviii, 405 p.: ill.; 24 cm. Includes index. 1. Madrid (Spain) — Economic conditions. 2. Spain — Economic conditions I. T.
HC388.M3 R56 1983     330.946/41 19     *LC* 82-1971     *ISBN* 0520043111

## HC401–407 Balkans. Yugoslavia

**Hoffman, George Walter, 1914-.**      **4.2417**
Regional development strategy in southeast Europe; a comparative analysis of Albania, Bulgaria, Greece, Romania, and Yugoslavia [by] George W. Hoffman. — New York: Praeger, [1972] xx, 322 p.: maps; 25 cm. — (Praeger special studies in international economics and development) 1. Regionalism — Balkan Peninsula. 2. Balkan Peninsula — Economic policy. I. T.
HC405.H6     338/.09496     *LC* 75-181696

**Dobrin, Bogoslav.**      **4.2418**
Bulgarian economic development since World War II. — New York: Praeger Publishers, [1973] xv, 185 p.; 25 cm. — (Praeger special studies in international economics and development) 1. Bulgaria — Economic conditions — 1944- 2. Bulgaria — Economic policy — 1944- I. T.
HC407.B9 D63 1973     330.9/4977/03     *LC* 72-85975

**Moore, John Hampton, 1935-.**      **4.2419**
Growth with self-management: Yugoslav industrialization, 1952–1975 / John H. Moore. — Stanford, Calif.: Hoover Institution Press, Stanford University,

c1980. xvi, 334 p.: graphs; 24 cm. (Hoover Institution publication; 220) Includes index. 1. Industry and state — Yugoslavia. 2. Management — Employee participation — Yugoslavia. 3. Yugoslavia — Industries. I. T.
HC407.M66      338.9497 19      *LC* 79-2464      *ISBN* 0817972013

**Montias, John Michael, 1928-.**           • **4.2420**
Economic development in Communist Rumania. — Cambridge, Mass., M.I.T. Press [1967] xiv, 327 p. illus. 24 cm. — (Studies in international communism, 11) Bibliography: p. 307-310. 1. Rumania — Econ. condit. — 1945- I. T.
HC407.R8M6      338.9498      *LC* 67-16502

**Spigler, Iancu.**                   **4.2421**
Economic reform in Rumanian industry; foreword by Michael Kaser. London, New York, Oxford University Press, 1973. xx, 176 p. maps. 22 cm. (Economic reforms in East European industry) At head of title: Institute of Soviet and East European Studies, University of Glasgow. 1. Planning 2. Industrial management — Romania. 3. Romania — Economic policy — 1945- I. University of Glasgow. Institute of Soviet and East European Studies. II. T. III. Series.
HC407.R8 S627      338.9498      *LC* 74-154732      *ISBN* 0192153390

**Singleton, Frederick Bernard.**            **4.2422**
The economy of Yugoslavia / Fred Singleton and Bernard Carter. — London: Croom Helm; New York: St. Martin's Press, 1982. 279 p.; 23 cm. Includes index. 1. Yugoslavia — Economic conditions 2. Yugoslavia — Economic policy I. Carter, Bernard. II. T.
HC407.S493 1982      330.9497/023 19      *LC* 81-23261      *ISBN* 0312898347

**Tyson, Laura D'Andrea, 1947-.**           **4.2423**
The Yugoslav economic system and its performance in the 1970s / Laura D'Andrea Tyson. — [Berkeley]: Institute of International Studies, University of California, Berkeley, c1980. vii, 112 p.; 24 cm. (Research series - Institute of International Studies, University of California, Berkeley; no. 44) 1. Management — Employee participation — Yugoslavia. 2. Yugoslavia — Economic policy — 1945- 3. Yugoslavia — Politics and government — 1945- I. T.
HC407.T97      338.9497 19      *LC* 80-24650      *ISBN* 0877251444

**Hamilton, F. E. Ian.**               • **4.2424**
Yugoslavia; patterns of economic activity [by] F. E. Ian Hamilton. — New York: Praeger, [1968] xvi, 384 p.: illus., maps.; 23 cm. — (Praeger surveys in economic geography) 1. Yugoslavia — Economic conditions — 1945- I. T.
HC407.Y6 H29      330.9497      *LC* 68-19850

**Milenkovitch, Deborah D.**            **4.2425**
Plan and market in Yugoslav economic thought / by Deborah D. Milenkovitch. — New Haven: Yale University Press, 1971. x, 323 p.: ill.; 23 cm. — (Yale Russian and East European studies, 9) 1. Yugoslavia — Economic policy — 1945- 2. Yugoslavia — Economic conditions — 1945- I. T. II. Series.
HC407.Y6 M47      330.9497/02      *LC* 78-140534      *ISBN* 0300014139

# HC410.7–412 ASIA: GENERAL

**Ashtor, Eliyahu, 1914-.**            **4.2426**
A social and economic history of the Near East in the Middle Ages / E. Ashtor. — Berkeley: University of California Press, c1976. 384 p.: ill.; 24 cm. 1. Islamic Empire — Economic conditions. 2. Islamic Empire — Social conditions. I. T.
HC410.7.A83      309.1/56/01      *LC* 74-29800      *ISBN* 0520029623

**Turner, Bryan Stanley.**            **4.2427**
Capitalism and class in the Middle East: theories of social change and economic development / Bryan S. Turner. — London: Heinemann Educational, 1984. 229 p.; 22 cm. 1. Middle East — Economic conditions. I. T.
HC410.7.T87      330.956/04 19      *ISBN* 0435828932

**Far Eastern economic review.**           • **4.2428**
Yearbook. — Hong Kong: Far Eastern Economic Review. v.: ill. ports. Annual. 1. East Asia — Economic conditions — Yearbooks I. T.
HC 411.F19      *LC* 62-35757

**United Nations. Economic Commission for Asia and the Far**    • **4.2429**
**East.**
Economic survey of Asia and the Far East. 1947–. Bangkok, 1947-. v. maps. annual. Surveys for 1948- issued as United Nations Document E/CN 11 and with the United Nations publications sales numbers. Issued by Dept. of Economic Affairs. Prepared 1948-51 by the commission's Secretariat; 1952 by Research and Statistics Division; 1953- by Research and Planning Division. Surveys for 196 - issued also as part of Economic bulletin for Asia and the Far East. Continued by: United Nations. Economic and Social Commission for Asia and the Pacific. Economic and social survey of Asia and the Pacific. 1. Asia — Economic conditions — 1918- I. United Nations. Dept. of Economic and Social Affairs. II. T. III. Title: Economic bulletin for Asia and the Far East. IV. Title: Economic and social survey of Asia and the Pacific.
HC411.U4 A23      *LC* 49-48996

**The economic history of the Middle East, 1800–1914: a book of**    **4.2430**
**readings / ed. and with an introd. by Charles Issawi.**
Chicago: University of Chicago Press, c1966. xv, 543 p. 1. Middle East — Economic conditions I. Issawi, Charles Philip.
HC412.E265      330.956      *LC* 66-11883

**Fryer, Donald W., 1920-.**            **4.2431**
Emerging Southeast Asia: a study in growth and stagnation / Donald W. Fryer. — 2d ed. — New York: Wiley, 1979. 540 p.: ill.; 24 cm. 'A Halsted Press book.' Includes index. 1. Asia, Southeastern — Economic conditions. I. T.
HC412.F75 1979      330.9/59      *LC* 78-7804      *ISBN* 0470262982

**Hla Myint, U.**               • **4.2432**
Southeast Asia's economy: development policies in the 1970s; a study sponsored by the Asian Development Bank, (by) H. Myint. — Harmondsworth: Penguin, 1972. 189 p.: map.; 19 cm. — (Penguin education) (Penguin modern economics texts: development economics) The overall report of a study undertaken at the request of the Fourth Ministerial Conference for Economic Development of South East Asia by the Asian Development Bank. The entire study, consisting of the overall report and the six sectoral reports has been published under title: Southeast Asia's economy in the 1970's. 1. Asia, Southeastern — Economic conditions — Addresses, essays, lectures. I. Asian Development Bank. II. Southeast Asia's economy in the 1970's. III. T.
HC412.H55 1972      330.9/59      *LC* 73-330833      *ISBN* 0140806563

**International Conference on Economic Development of**    **4.2433**
**Southeast Asia, Kyoto, 1972.**
The economic development of East and Southeast Asia / edited by Shinichi Ichimura. — Honolulu: Distributed [by] University Press of Hawaii, 1975, c1974. 393 p.; 22 cm. (Monographs of the Center for Southeast Asian Studies, Kyoto University. 7) Sponsored by Kyoto University Center for Southeast Asian Studies and Kansai Economic Research Center. 'An East-West Center book.' 1. Asia, Southeastern — Economic conditions — Addresses, essays, lectures. I. Ichimura, Shin'ichi, 1925- ed. II. Kansai Keizai Kenkyū Sentā. III. Kyōto Daigaku. Tōnan Ajia Kenkyū Sentā. IV. T. V. Series.
HC412.I5232 1972      330.9/59      *LC* 74-34060

**Jacobs, Norman, 1924-.**            • **4.2434**
The origin of modern capitalism and eastern Asia. [Hong Kong] Hong Kong University Press, 1958. 243 p. 1. Capitalism 2. Japan — Industries 3. China — Industries I. T.
HC412 J3      *LC* 58-59961

**Myrdal, Gunnar, 1898-.**            • **4.2435**
Asian drama; an inquiry into the poverty of nations. — New York: Twentieth Century Fund, 1968. 3 v. (xxx, 2284 p.): illus., maps (part col.); 25 cm. 1. South Asia — Economic conditions. 2. Asia, Southeastern — Economic conditions. I. Twentieth Century Fund. II. T.
HC412.M9 1968b      330.95      *LC* 67-27845

**Southeast Asia's economy in the 1970s.**           **4.2436**
New York: Praeger Publishers, 1972 (c1971) xxxii, 684 p.: map; 23 cm. Report of a study made by a group of experts for the Asian Development Bank. 1. Asia, Southeastern — Economic conditions — Addresses, essays, lectures. I. Asian Development Bank.
HC412.S596      330.9/59      *LC* 72-174242

**Stamp, Laurence Dudley, 1898-1966.**        • **4.2437**
Asia: a regional and economic geography / by Sir Dudley Stamp. — 12th ed. — London: Methuen, 1967. xvii, 731 p.: maps, diagrs. — (Methuen's advanced geographies) 1. Asia — Economic conditions I. T.
HC412.S7 1967      915      *LC* 67-79077      *ISBN* 0416304001

**Uppal, J. S., 1927-.**               **4.2438**
Economic development in South Asia / Jogindar S. Uppal. New York: St. Martin's Press, c1977. ix, 212 p.; 23 cm. Includes index. 1. South Asia — Economic conditions. 2. South Asia — Social conditions. 3. South Asia — Economic policy. I. T.
HC412.U86      338.959      *LC* 76-28131      *ISBN* 0312230303

**Wong, John, 1939-.**              **4.2439**
ASEAN economies in perspective: a comparative study of Indonesia, Malaysia, the Philippines, Singapore, and Thailand / John Wong. — Philadelphia: Institute for the Study of Human Issues, c1979. xii, 217 p.: ill.; 23 cm. 1. Rural development — Asia, Southeastern. 2. Regional economics 3. Asia, Southeastern — Economic conditions. 4. Asia, Southeastern — Commerce. I. Institute for the Study of Human Issues. II. T.
HC412.W622 1979      330.9/59      *LC* 78-9095      *ISBN* 0915980908

## HC415–415.4 Middle East

**The Islamic Middle East, 700–1900: studies in economic and**    **4.2440**
**social history / edited by A. L. Udovitch.**
Princeton, N.J.: Darwin Press, c1981. 838 p.; 24 cm. — (Princeton studies on
the Near East.) 'Grew out of a research seminar and conference on the
economic history of the Middle East that was conducted at Princeton
University during the spring and summer of 1974.' 1. Middle East —
Economic conditions — Addresses, essays, lectures. 2. Islamic Empire —
Economic conditions — Addresses, essays, lectures. 3. Africa, North —
Economic conditions — Addresses, essays, lectures. I. Udovitch, Abraham L.
II. Series.
HC415.15.I83     330.956/01 19     *LC* 79-52703     *ISBN* 0878500308

**Issawi, Charles Philip.**     **4.2441**
An economic history of the Middle East and North Africa / Charles Issawi. —
New York: Columbia University Press, 1982. xiii, 304 p.; 24 cm. — (Columbia
economic history of the modern world.) Includes index. 1. Middle East —
Economic conditions. 2. Africa, North — Economic conditions I. T.
II. Series.
HC415.15.I84 1982     330.956 19     *LC* 81-19518     *ISBN* 0231034431

**Owen, Edward Roger John.**     **4.2442**
The Middle East in the world economy, 1800–1914 / Roger Owen. — London;
New York: Methuen, 1981. xix, 378 p.; 25 cm. Includes index. 1. Middle East
— Economic conditions. I. T.
HC415.15.O94 1981     330.956 19     *LC* 80-42030     *ISBN* 0416142702

**Flink, Salomon J., 1906- .**     **4.2443**
Israel, chaos and challenge: politics vs. economics / Salomon J. Flink. —
Ramat Gan, Israel; Forest Grove, Or.: Turtledove Pub., 1979. xiii, 265 p.; 25
cm. 1. Israel — Economic policy. I. T.
HC415.25.F5x     338.95694     *LC* 80-110697     *ISBN* 9652000272

**Rubner, Alex.**     • **4.2444**
The economy of Israel: a critical account of the first ten years. — New York:
Praeger [1960, c1959] 307 p.: ill.; 23 cm. 1. Israel — Economic conditions.
I. T.
HC415.25.R8x     *LC* 60-7760

**Gharāybah, Fawzī.**     **4.2445**
The economies of the West Bank and Gaza Strip / Fawzi A. Gharaibeh. —
Boulder, Colo.: Westview Press, 1985. xvi, 182 p.; 23 cm. (Westview special
studies on the Middle East.) Includes index. 1. Israel-Arab War, 1967 —
Occupied territories 2. West Bank — Economic conditions. 3. Ghaza —
Economic conditions. 4. Israel — Economic policy. I. T. II. Series.
HC415.25.Z7 W473 1985     330.95695 19     *LC* 84-19541     *ISBN*
0813370116

**Mazur, Michael P.**     **4.2446**
Economic growth and development in Jordan / Michael P. Mazur. — Boulder,
Colo.: Westview Press, 1979. xvi, 314 p.; 24 cm. — (Westview special studies on
the Middle East) 1. Jordan — Economic conditions. I. T.
HC415.26.M3x     330.9/5695/04     *LC* 78-22518     *ISBN* 0891584552

**Johany, Ali D.**     **4.2447**
The Saudi Arabian economy / Ali D. Johany, Michel Berne, and J. Wilson
Mixon, Jr. — Baltimore: Johns Hopkins University Press, 1986. 189 p.: ill.; 23
cm. Includes index. 1. Petroleum industry and trade — Saudi Arabia. 2. Saudi
Arabia — Economic conditions. I. Berne, Michel. II. Mixon, J. Wilson.
III. T.
HC415.33.J64 1986     330.953/8053 19     *LC* 85-45869     *ISBN*
0801833515

**Moliver, Donald M.**     **4.2448**
The economy of Saudi Arabia / Donald M. Moliver, Paul J. Abbondante. —
New York, N.Y.: Praeger, 1980. xv, 167 p.: graphs; 25 cm. Includes index.
1. Saudi Arabia — Economic conditions. 2. Saudi Arabia — Economic policy.
I. Abbondante, Paul J. joint author. II. T.
HC415.33.M64     330.953/8053 19     *LC* 80-22872     *ISBN*
0030570042

**Economy, society & culture in contemporary Yemen / edited by**    **4.2449**
**B.R. Pridham.**
London; Dover, N.H.: Croom Helm; Exeter, Devon: Centre for Arab Gulf
Studies, University of Exeter, c1985. xii, 257 p.: ill.; 23 cm. 'Papers presented to
a symposium held in July 1983 by Exeter University's Centre for Arab Gulf
Studies.'—P. x. 1. Yemen — Economic conditions — Congresses. 2. Yemen
(People's Democratic Republic) — Economic conditions — Congresses.
3. Yemen — Social conditions — Congresses. 4. Yemen (People's Democratic
Republic) — Social conditions — Congresses. I. Pridham, B. R., 1934-
II. University of Exeter. Centre for Arab Gulf Studies. III. Title: Economy,
society, and culture in contemporary Yemen.
HC415.34.E26 1985     953/.32 19     *LC* 84-23102     *ISBN* 0709920938

**Bahrain and the Gulf: past perspectives and alternative futures /**    **4.2450**
**edited by Jeffrey B. Nugent & Theodore Thomas.**
New York: St. Martin's Press, 1985. 221 p.: ill.; 23 cm. Selected papers from
lectures and a symposium given in the spring semester of 1983 at the University
of Southern California sponsored by the Interdisciplinary Development Study
Group. 1. Bahrain — Economic conditions — Addresses, essays, lectures.
2. Bahrain — Addresses, essays, lectures. I. Nugent, Jeffrey B. II. Thomas,
Theodore H. III. University of Southern California. Interdisciplinary
Development Study Group.
HC415.38.B34 1985     330.953/65053 19     *LC* 84-24808     *ISBN*
0312065663

## HC416–420 Afghanistan

**Michel, Aloys Arthur.**     **4.2451**
The Kabul, Kunduz and Helmand Valleys and the national economy of
Afghanistan: a study of regional resources and the comparative advantages of
development. — Washington: National Academy of Sciences, 1959. xix, 441 p.:
maps.; 28 cm. — (Foreign field research program, report no. 5.) 1. Afghanistan
— Economic conditions I. T.
HC417.M5x     *LC* 60-60660

## HC422–424 Burma. Sri Lanka

**Andrus, James Russell, 1902- .**     • **4.2452**
Burmese economic life / by J. Russell Andrus; foreword by J. S. Furnivall. —
Stanford, Calif.: Stanford University Press, 1948. xxii, 362 p.: fold. maps.
1. Burma — Economic conditions I. T.
HC422.A6x     *LC* 48-5422

**Adas, Michael, 1943- .**     **4.2453**
The Burma delta: economic development and social change on an Asian rice
frontier, 1852–1941. — [Madison]: University of Wisconsin Press, [1974] xv,
256 p.: illus.; 24 cm. 1. Rice trade — Burma, Lower. 2. Burma, Lower —
Economic conditions. 3. Burma, Lower — Social conditions. I. T.
HC422.Z7 B872     330.9/591     *LC* 73-15256     *ISBN* 0299064905

**Johnson, B. L. C. (Basil Leonard Clyde), 1919- .**     **4.2454**
Sri Lanka, land, people, and economy / B.L.C. Johnson and M. LeM.
Scrivenor. — London; Exeter, N.H.: Heinemann Educational Books, 1981. x,
154 p.: ill.; 25 cm. Includes index. 1. Agriculture — Economic aspects — Sri
Lanka. 2. Sri Lanka — Economic conditions. 3. Sri Lanka — Description and
travel. I. Scrivenor, M. LeM. II. T.
HC424.J65     330.9549/303 19     *LC* 81-2504     *ISBN* 0435354892

**Richards, P. J. (Peter J.)**     **4.2455**
Basic needs, poverty, and government policies in Sri Lanka / Peter Richards
and Wilbert Gooneratne. — Geneva: International Labour Office, 1980. 176 p.;
24 cm. (WEP study.) 1. Basic needs — Sri Lanka. 2. Sri Lanka — Economic
conditions. 3. Sri Lanka — Economic policy. I. Gooneratne, Wilbert, 1938-
II. T. III. Series.
HC424.R53     338.9549/3 19     *LC* 83-151000     *ISBN* 9221023168

**Snodgrass, Donald R.**     • **4.2456**
Ceylon; an export economy in transition [by] Donald R. Snodgrass.
Homewood, Ill., R.D. Irwin, 1966. xvii, 416 p. (Publications of the Economic
Growth Center, Yale University) 1. Ceylon — Economic conditions I. T.
HC424.S6x     *LC* 66-14542

## HC426–430 China

**Conference on Modern Chinese Economic History, T'ai-pei,**    **4.2457**
**1977.**
Modern Chinese economic history: proceedings of the Conference on Modern
Chinese Economic History, Academia Sinica, Taipei, Taiwan, Republic of
China, August 26–29, 1977 / edited by Chi–ming Hou, Tzong–shian Yu. —
Taipei: Institute of Economics, Academia Sinica; Seattle: distributed by
University of Washington Press, c1979. xvi, 678 p.: graphs; 26 cm. 1. China —
Economic conditions — Congresses. I. Hou, Chi–ming, 1924- II. Yü, Tzung-
hsien. III. T.
HC426.C65 1977a     330.9/51/05     *LC* 79-114995

**China (People's Republic of China, 1949- )**     • **4.2458**
First five–year plan for development of the national economy of the People's
Republic of China in 1953–1957. — Peking, Foreign Languages Press, 1956.
231 p. 22 cm. 1. China (People's Republic of China, 1949-  ) — Economic
policy. I. T.
HC427.A525     338.951     *LC* 57-47651

**Allen, G. C. (George Cyril), 1900-.**     • **4.2459**
Western enterprise in Far Eastern economic development, China and Japan, by G. C. Allen and Audrey G. Donnithorne. — New York, Macmillan [1954]. 291 p. maps. 23 cm. — (Reprints of economic classics) Reprint of 1954 edition. Bibliography: p. 272-279. Maps at the end. 1. China — Indus. 2. Japan — Indus. 3. Investments, Foreign — China. 4. China — Economic conditions 5. Japan — Economic conditions I. Donnithorne, Audrey. joint author. II. T.
HC427.A58 1968     338     *LC* 54-2001

**Perkins, Dwight Heald.**     **4.2460**
China's modern economy in historical perspective: sponsored by the Social Science Research Council / contributors, Kang Chao ... [et al.]; edited by Dwight H. Perkins. — Stanford, Calif.: Stanford University Press, 1975. xiv, 344 p.; 24 cm. Revised papers from a conference held in Bermuda in June 1973 under the sponsorship of the Subcommittee for Research on the Chinese Economy of the Joint Committee on Contemporary China of the Social Science Research Council and the American Council of Learned Societies. Includes index. 1. Economic development — Addresses, essays, lectures. 2. China — Economic conditions — Addresses, essays, lectures. 3. China — Economic policy — Addresses, essays, lectures. I. Chao, Kang, 1929- II. Social Science Research Council (U.S.) III. T.
HC427.C5598     330.9/52     *LC* 74-82779     *ISBN* 0804708711

**Economic organization in Chinese society. Edited by W. E.**     • **4.2461**
**Willmott.**
Stanford, Calif., Stanford University Press, 1972. xi, 461 p. illus. 24 cm. (Studies in Chinese society) Papers presented at a conference on economic organization in Chinese society held at Sainte-Adèle-en-haut, Aug. 1969. 1. China — Economic conditions — 1945-1976 — Congresses. 2. Taiwan — Economic conditions — 1945-1975 — Congresses. I. Willmott, William E., ed.
HC427.E29     330.9/51/05     *LC* 72-153822     *ISBN* 0804707944

**Gluckstein, Ygael.**     **4.2462**
Mao's China; economic and political survey. Boston: Beacon Press, [1957] 438 p.; 23 cm. 1. China — Economic conditions 2. China — Politics and government I. T.
HC427.G59

**Moulder, Frances V.**     **4.2463**
Japan, China and the modern world economy: toward a reinterpretation of East Asian development ca 1600 to ca 1918 / [by] Frances V. Moulder. Cambridge [etc.]: Cambridge University Press, 1977. x, 255 p.; 22 cm. Index. 1. China — Economic conditions — To 1644 2. China — Economic conditions — 1644-1912 3. Japan — Economic conditions — To 1868 4. Japan — Economic conditions — 1868-1918 I. T.
HC427.M64 1977     330.9/51/03 330.9/52/025     *LC* 76-2230     *ISBN* 0521211743

**Morse, Hosea Ballou, 1855-1934.**     • **4.2464**
The trade and administration of China. New York, Russell & Russell [1967] xv, 505 p. illus., map. 22 cm. Reprint of the 3d rev. ed., 1921. 1. Money — China. 2. China — Commerce 3. China — Politics and government — 1644-1912 4. China — Economic conditions I. T.
HC427.M7 1967     309.151     *LC* 66-24734

**Pan, Ku, 32-92.**     • **4.2465**
Food and money in ancient China; the earliest economic history of China to A.D. 25, Han shu 24, with related texts, Han shu 91 and Shih-chi 129. Translated and annotated by Nancy Lee Swann. Princeton: Princeton University Press, 1950. xiii, 482, [79] p. ill., maps (1 fold.) Ch'ien Han shu, generally attributed to Pan Ku, was begun by his father, Pan Piao, and completed by his sister, Pan Chao. Cf. Introd. 'Reproductions of Chinese texts': [79] p. at end. 1. China — Economic conditions I. Ssu-ma, Ch'ien, ca. 145-ca. 86 B.C. Shi-chi II. Swann, Nancy Lee, 1881-, ed. and tr. III. T.
HC427 P313     *LC* 50-7084

**Chou, Chin-sheng, 1907-.**     **4.2466**
[Chung-kuo ching chi shih. English] An economic history of China, by Chou Chin-sheng. A translation in précis by Edward H. Kaplan. [Bellingham] Program in East Asian Studies, Western Washington State College, 1974. ix, 273 p. illus. 28 cm. (Program in East Asian Studies, Western Washington State College. Occasional paper, no 7) Translation of Chung-kuo ching chi shih. 1. China — Economic conditions — To 1644 2. China — Economic conditions — 1644-1912 I. Kaplan, Edward H., 1936- II. T.
HC427.6.C5513     330.9/51     *LC* 74-620032     *ISBN* 0914584073

**Feuerwerker, Albert.**     • **4.2467**
China's early industrialization; Sheng Hsuan-huai (1844-1916) and Mandarin enterprise. Cambridge, Harvard University Press, 1958. xii, 311, xxxii p. port., diagr. (Harvard East Asian studies, 1) 1. Sheng, Hsüan-huai, 1844-1916. 2. China — Industries I. T. II. Series.
HC427.7 F4     *LC* 58-12967

**Tawney, R. H. (Richard Henry), 1880-1962.**     • **4.2468**
Land and labor in China. With an introd. by Barrington Moore, Jr. Boston, Beacon Press [1966] 207 p. 21 cm. (Beacon paperbacks, BP 235) Originally

written as a memorandum, with the exception of the last chapter, for the conference of the Institute of Pacific Relations held at Shanghai in November 1931. 1. Peasantry — China. 2. China — Economic conditions — 1912-1949 I. T.
HC427.8.T36 1966     330.951     *LC* 67-2097

## HC427.9 1949-

**Authority, participation and cultural change in China; essays by**     **4.2469**
**a European study group. Edited and with an introduction by**
**Stuart R. Schram, with contributions by Marianne Bastid [and**
**others]**
Cambridge [Eng.] University Press, 1973. viii, 350 p. 22 cm. (Contemporary China Institute publications) Revised papers delivered at a conference at Urchfont Manor in September 1972. 1. China — Economic conditions — 1949-1976 — Congresses. 2. China — Social conditions — 1949-1976 — Congresses. I. Schram, Stuart R. ed. II. Bastid, Marianne.
HC427.9.A89     330.9/51/05     *LC* 73-80482     *ISBN* 0521202965
*ISBN* 0521098203

**Barnett, A. Doak.**     • **4.2470**
Communist economic strategy: the rise of mainland China. [Washington] National Planning Association [1959] ix, 106 p. (The Economics of competitive coexistence) 1. China (People's Republic of China, 1949- ) — Economic policy I. T. II. Series.
HC427.9 B3     *LC* 59-14046

**Cheng, Chu-yüan.**     **4.2471**
China's economic development: growth and structural change / Chu-yuan Cheng. — Boulder, Colo.: Westview Press, 1982. xxiii, 535 p.: 1 map; 24 cm. Includes index. 1. China — Economic conditions — 1949-1976 2. China — Economic conditions — 1976- I. T.
HC427.9.C52178     338.951 19     *LC* 81-11671     *ISBN* 0891587888

**Cheng, Chu-yüan.**     • **4.2472**
Communist China's economy, 1949-1962: structural changes and crisis / Cheng Chu-Yuan. — [South Orange, N.J.]: Seton Hall University Press 1963. xii, 217 p.: ill.; 24 cm. 1. China (People's Republic of China, 1949- ) — Economic conditions. I. T.
HC427.9.C532     *LC* 63-11865

**Donnithorne, Audrey.**     • **4.2473**
China's economic system / by Audrey Donnithorne. — New York: Praeger [1967] 592 p.: map (on lining papers); 25 cm. Added t.p. in Chinese. 1. China — Economic conditions — 1949-1976 I. T.
HC427.9.D6 1967b     330.951     *LC* 67-23967

**Eckstein, Alexander, 1915-.**     **4.2474**
China's economic development: the interplay of scarcity and ideology / Alexander Eckstein. — Ann Arbor: University of Michigan Press, c1975. xvi, 399 p.; 24 cm. — (Michigan studies on China). 1. China — Economic conditions — 1949-1976 2. China — Economic policy — 1949-1976 I. T. II. Series.
HC427.9.E27 1975     330.9/51/05     *LC* 74-25951     *ISBN* 0472298720

**Eckstein, Alexander, 1915-.**     **4.2475**
China's economic revolution / Alexander Eckstein. Cambridge; New York: Cambridge University Press, 1977. xii, 340 p.; 24 cm. 1. China — Economic policy 2. China — Economic conditions — 1949- I. T.
HC427.9.E28     330.9/51/05     *LC* 76-9176     *ISBN* 0521212839

**Eckstein, Alexander, 1915-.**     • **4.2476**
Communist China's economic growth and foreign trade: implications for U.S. policy. — [1st ed.]. — New York: Published for the Council on Foreign Relations by McGraw-Hill [1966] xvii, 366 p.: ill.; 22 cm. — (The United States and China in world affairs) Bibliography: p. 335-344. 1. China (People's Republic of China, 1949- ) — Econ. condit. 2. China (People's Republic of China, 1949- ) — Comm. I. Council on Foreign Relations. II. T. III. Series.
HC427.9.E3     330.951     *LC* 65-28588

**Economic reform in the PRC: in which China's economists**     **4.2477**
**make known what went wrong, why, and what should be done**
**about it / edited and translated by George C. Wang.**
Boulder, Colo.: Westview Press, 1982. xii, 155 p.; 24 cm. — (Westview special studies on China and East Asia.) Includes index. 1. China — Economic conditions — 1949-1976 — Addresses, essays, lectures. 2. China — Economic conditions — 1976- — Addresses, essays, lectures. 3. China — Economic policy — 1949-1976 — Addresses, essays, lectures. 4. China — Economic policy — 1976- — Addresses, essays, lectures. I. Wang, George C. II. Series.
HC427.9.E34 1982     338.951 19     *LC* 82-4914     *ISBN* 0865313482

**Economic trends in Communist China.** Edited by Alexander • **4.2478**
Eckstein, Walter Galenson, and Ta–chung Liu.
Chicago: Aldine Pub. Co., [1968] 757 p.; 25 cm. Based on studies for a conference sponsored by the Social Science Research Council Committee on the Economy of China, held at Carmel, Calif., Oct. 1965. 1. China — Economic conditions — 1949- I. Eckstein, Alexander, 1915- ed. II. Galenson, Walter, 1914- ed. III. Liu, Ta-chung. ed. IV. Social Science Research Council. Committee on the Economy of China.
HC427.9.E36    330.951    LC 68-19887

**Howe, Christopher.** **4.2479**
China's economy: a basic guide / Christopher Howe. — New York: Basic Books, 1978. xxxvii, 248 p.: ill.; 25 cm. 1. China — Economic conditions — 1949- I. T.
HC427.9.H66 1978    330.9/51/05    LC 77-20423    ISBN 0465010997

**Hughes, Trevor Jones.** • **4.2480**
The economic development of Communist China, 1949–1960, by T.J. Hughes and D.E.T. Luard. 2d ed. Issued under the auspices of the Royal Institute of International Affairs. London, Oxford University Press, 1961. 229 p.: ill.; 23 cm. 1. China (People's Republic of China, 1949-    ) — Economic policy I. Luard, Evan, 1926- jt. author II. T.
HC427.9 H87 1961    LC 62-1082

**Lardy, Nicholas R.** **4.2481**
Economic growth and distribution in China / Nicholas R. Lardy. — Cambridge [Eng.]; New York: Cambridge University Press, 1978. x, 244 p.; 24 cm. Includes index. 1. China — Economic conditions — 1949- 2. China — Economic policy — 1949- I. T.
HC427.9.L36    330.9/51/05    LC 77-27508    ISBN 0521219043

**Li, Choh-Ming, 1912-.** • **4.2482**
Economic development of Communist China; an appraisal of the first five years of industrialization, by Choh–ming Li. Berkeley, University of California Press, 1959. xvi, 284 p.: tables; 24 cm. (Publications of the Bureau of Business and Economic Research, University of California) 1. China (People's Republic of China, 1949- ) — Economic conditions I. T.
HC427.9 L5    LC 58-13330

**Liu, Ta-chung.** • **4.2483**
The economy of the Chinese mainland: national income and economic development, 1933–1959 [by] Ta–chung Liu [and] Kung–chia Yeh. Princeton, N. J., Princeton University Press, 1965. xvi, 771 p. illus., map. 25 cm. 'This study was undertaken by the Rand Corporation for the United States Air Force.' Bibliography: p. 725-757. 1. China (People's Republic of China, 1949- ) — Economic conditions. I. Yeh, K. C. (K'ung-chia), 1924- joint author. II. Rand Corporation. III. United States. Air Force. IV. T.
HC427.9.L599 1965    330.951    LC 64-12223

**Prybyla, Jan S.** **4.2484**
The Chinese economy: problems and policies / by Jan S. Prybyla. — Columbia: University of South Carolina Press, 1978. xiii, 258 p.: ill.; 24 cm. 1. China — Economic conditions — 1949-1976 2. China — Economic conditions — 1976- 3. China — Economic policy I. T.
HC427.9.P74    338.951    LC 78-1259    ISBN 0872493644

**Riskin, Carl.** **4.2485**
China's political economy: the quest for development since 1949 / Carl Riskin. — Oxford [Oxfordshire]; New York: Oxford University Press, 1986. p. cm. (Economics of the world) Includes index. 1. Agriculture and state — China. 2. China — Economic policy — 1949- I. T. II. Series.
HC427.9.R57 1986    338.951 19    LC 86-16367    ISBN 0198770898

**Swamy, Subramanian.** **4.2486**
Economic growth in China and India, 1952–1970: a comparative appraisal / Subramanian Swamy. — Chicago: University of Chicago Press, 1973. ix, 84 p.; 24 cm. Originally published as v. 21, no. 4, pt. 2 (July 1973) of Economic development and cultural change. 1. China — Economic conditions — 1949- 2. India — Economic conditions — 1947- I. T.
HC427.9.S895    330.9/51/05    LC 72-96344    ISBN 0226783154

**Barnett, A. Doak.** **4.2487**
China's economy in global perspective / A. Doak Barnett. — Washington, D.C.: Brookings Institution, c1981. xxiv, 752 p.; 24 cm. 1. China — Economic conditions — 1976- 2. China — Economic policy — 1976- I. T.
HC427.92.B37    330.951/057 19    LC 81-1193    ISBN 0815708262

**Xue, Muquio, 1904-.** **4.2488**
Current economic problems in China / Xue Muqiao; edited, translated, and with an introduction by K.K. Fung. — Boulder, Colo.: Westview Press, 1982. xxx, 159 p.; 24 cm. — (Westview special studies on China and East Asia.) 1. China — Economic conditions — 1976- — Addresses, essays, lectures. I. Fung, K. K. II. T. III. Series.
HC427.92.H7772 1982    330.951/058 19    LC 82-50237    ISBN 0865314047

**Institutional reform and economic development in the Chinese** **4.2489**
**countryside** / edited by Keith Griffin.
Armonk, N.Y.: M.E. Sharpe, 1984. x, 336 p.: ill.; 23 cm. Papers presented at a seminar at the Institute of Agricultural Economics in Beijing, 1982. 1. Agriculture — Economic aspects — China — Addresses, essays, lectures. 2. Communism — China — Addresses, essays, lectures. 3. China — Economic conditions — 1976- — Addresses, essays, lectures. 4. China — Rural conditions — Addresses, essays, lectures. I. Griffin, Keith B.
HC427.92.I57 1984    338.951/009173/4 19    LC 84-5335    ISBN 0873322851

## HC428–430 LOCAL

**Szczepanik, Edward Franciszek.** • **4.2490**
The economic growth of Hong Kong. [Rev. ed.] London, Oxford University Press [1960] 186 p. illus. Issued under the auspices of the Royal Institute of International Affairs. 1. Hong Kong — Economic conditions. I. T.
HC428.H6 S9 1960    330.95125

**Murphey, Rhoads, 1919-.** • **4.2491**
Shanghai, key to modern China. Cambridge, Harvard University Press, 1953. xii, 232 p. ill., maps. 1. Shanghai (China) — Economic conditions I. T.
HC428 S47 M8    LC 53-5073

**Fei, Hsiao-t'ung.** • **4.2492**
Peasant life in China; a field study of country life in the Yangtze Valley, by Hsiao–Tung Fei, with a preface by Professor Bronislaw Malinowski. New York: Oxford university press, 1946. xx, 300 p.: ill., plates, maps.; 23 cm. (International library of sociology and social reconstruction) 1. Sociology, Rural 2. Villages — China. 3. China — Social life and customs 4. Yangtze, Valley. I. T. II. Series.
HC428.Y3x    309.512

**Chang, Chung-li, 1919-.** • **4.2493**
The income of the Chinese gentry. Introd. by Franz Michael. — Seattle: University of Washington Press, 1962. xvii, 369 p.; 24 cm. — (University of Washington publications on Asia) 'A sequel to The Chinese gentry: studies on their role in nineteenth-century Chinese society.' 1. Income distribution — China 2. Middle classes — China. I. T.
HC430.I5 C47    LC 61-11577

## HC430.5 Taiwan

**Ho, Sam P. S.** **4.2494**
Economic development of Taiwan, 1860–1970 / Samuel P. S. Ho. — New Haven: Yale University Press, 1978. xx, 461 p.; 24 cm. (A Publication of the Economic Growth Center, Yale University) Includes index. 1. Taiwan — Economic conditions — To 1945 2. Taiwan — Economic conditions — 1945-1975 I. T.
HC430.5.H6    330.951/249 19    LC 77-5555    ISBN 0300020872

## HC430.6–440 South Asia. India

**Rosen, George, 1920-.** **4.2495**
Western economists and Eastern societies: agents of change in South Asia, 1950–1970 / George Rosen. — Baltimore: Johns Hopkins University Press, c1985. xxii, 270 p.; 24 cm. (Johns Hopkins studies in development.) Includes index. 1. Technical assistance — South Asia — History. 2. Economic development projects — India — History. 3. Economic development projects — Pakistan — History. 4. Technology transfer — Developing countries — History. I. T. II. Series.
HC430.6.R67 1985    338.91/0954 19    LC 84-4370    ISBN 0801831873

**The Cambridge economic history of India** / edited by Tapan **4.2496**
Raychaudhuri and Irfan Habib.
Cambridge [Eng.]; New York: Cambridge University Press, 1982-. v. <1 >: ill.; 24 cm. Includes index. 1. India — Economic conditions I. Raychaudhuri, Tapan. II. Habib, Irfan, 1931-
HC433.C35 1982    330.954    LC 80-40454    ISBN 0521226929

**Furber, Holden, 1903-.** • **4.2497**
John Company at work; a study of European expansion in India in the late eighteenth century. New York, Octagon Books, 1970 [c1948] xi, 407 p. fold. map. 24 cm. (Harvard historical studies. v. 55) 1. East India Company. 2. Nederlandsche Oost-Indische Compagnie. 3. Nouvelle Compagnie des Indes. 4. Danske asiatiske kompagni. 5. India — Economic conditions 6. India — Politics and government — 1765-1947 I. T. II. Series.
HC434.F8 1970    382/.094/054    LC 70-96181

**Anstey, Vera Powell, 1889-.**     • **4.2498**
The economic development of India. — 4th ed. — London; New York: Longmans, Green, 1952. x, 677 p.: maps (part fold.) diagrs.; 23 cm. Bibliography: p. 639-656. 1. India — Econ. condit. — 1918-1945. 2. India — Indus. 3. India — Soc. condit. I. T.
HC435.A7 1952     330.954     *LC* 52-14815

**Chandra, Bipan.**     **4.2499**
The rise and growth of economic nationalism in India; economic policies of Indian national leadership, 1880–1905. New Delhi People's Pub. House [1966] 783p. 1. India — Economic policy I. T.
HC435 C425

**Mellor, John Williams, 1928-.**     **4.2500**
The new economics of growth: a strategy for India and the developing world / John W. Mellor. — Ithaca, N.Y.: Cornell University Press, 1976. xv, 335 p.: graphs; 22 cm. 'A Twentieth Century Fund study.' 1. India — Economic policy — 1966-1974 2. Developing countries — Economic policy. I. T.
HC435.M39     338.954     *LC* 75-38430     *ISBN* 0801409993

**Rosen, George, 1920-.**     • **4.2501**
Industrial change in India; industrial growth, capital requirements, and technological change, 1937–1955. Glencoe, Ill., Free Press [1958] 243 p. 1. India — Industries I. T.
HC435 R62     *LC* 58-7481

**Singh, V. B. ed.**     • **4.2502**
Economic history of India, 1857–1956. Bombay Allied Publishers [1965] 795p. 1. India — Economic conditions 2. India — History — 20th century I. T.
HC435 S5524

**Chaudhuri, Pramit.**     **4.2503**
The Indian economy: poverty and development / Pramit Chaudhuri. — New York: St. Martin's Press, 1979. ix, 279 p.; 23 cm. Includes indexes. 1. India — Economic policy 2. India — Economic conditions — 1947- I. T.
HC435.2.C4834 1979     330.9/54     *LC* 77-88457     *ISBN* 0312413785

**Chen, Kuan-I, 1926- comp.**     **4.2504**
Comparative development of India and China [by] Kuan–I Chen and J. S. Uppal. — New York: Free Press, [1971] ix, 404 p.; 24 cm. Title on spine: India and China. 1. India — Economic conditions — 1947- — Addresses, essays, lectures. 2. China — Addresses, essays, lectures. I. Uppal, J. S., 1927- joint comp. II. T. III. Title: India and China.
HC435.2.C486     338.951     *LC* 71-142355

**Frankel, Francine R.**     **4.2505**
India's political economy, 1947–1977: the gradual revolution / Francine R. Frankel. — Princeton, N.J.: Princeton University Press, 1979 (c1978). xiv, 600 p.: map; 24 cm. Includes index. 1. Social conflict — India. 2. India — Economic policy — 1947- 3. India — Social conditions — 1947- 4. India — Economic conditions — 1947- 5. India — Politics and government — 1947- I. T.
HC435.2.F7     330.9/54/04     *LC* 78-51164     *ISBN* 0691031207

**Uppal, J. S., 1927-.**     **4.2506**
India's economic problems: an analytical approach / edited by J. S. Uppal. — 2d ed. — New York: St. Martin's Press, 1979, c1978. xiv, 409 p.: ill.; 25 cm. 1. India — Economic conditions — 1947- 2. India — Economic policy — 1966-1974 I. T.
HC435.2.I623 1979     330.954/05 19     *LC* 78-62033     *ISBN* 0312414099

**Jha, Prem Shankar.**     **4.2507**
India, a political economy of stagnation / Prem Shankar Jha. — Delhi: Oxford University Press, 1980. xv, 311 p.: ill.; 23 cm. 1. India — Economic policy — 1947- I. T.
HC435.2.J53     338.954 19     *LC* 80-901823

**Malenbaum, Wilfred.**     • **4.2508**
Modern India's economy; two decades of planned growth. — Columbus, Ohio: C. E. Merrill Pub. Co., [1971] x, 230 p.; 23 cm. — (Merrill's economic systems series) 1. India — Economic conditions — 1947- 2. India — Economic policy — 1947- I. T.
HC435.2.M275     330.954/04     *LC* 72-165986     *ISBN* 0675097606

**Mukherjee, Pranab, 1935-.**     **4.2509**
Beyond survival: emerging dimensions of Indian economy / Pranab Mukherjee. — New Delhi: Vikas, c1984. vii, 257 p.; 23 cm. 1. India — Economic policy — 1947- 2. India — Economic conditions — 1947- I. T.
HC435.2.M825 1984     338.954 19     *LC* 84-901728     *ISBN* 0706926587

**Streeten, Paul.**     • **4.2510**
The crisis of Indian planning: economic planning in the 1960s; edited by Paul Streeten and Michael Lipton; issued under the auspices of the Royal Institute of International Affairs. — London; New York [etc.]: Oxford U.P., 1968. vii,

416 p.; 23 cm. 1. India — Economic policy — 1966-1974 I. Lipton, Michael. II. Royal Institute of International Affairs. III. T.
HC435.2.S8     338.954     *LC* 68-134391

**Uppal, J. S., 1927-.**     **4.2511**
Indian economic planning: three decades of development / J.S. Uppal. — Delhi: Macmillan India Ltd., 1984. 140 p.; 22 cm. 1. India — Economic policy — 1947- I. T.
HC435.2.U64 1984     338.954 19     *LC* 84-901162     *ISBN* 0333904516

**Gillion, Kenneth L.**     • **4.2512**
Ahmedabad; a study in Indian urban history [by] Kenneth L. Gillion. Berkeley, University of California Press, 1968. viii, 195 p. map. 24 cm. 1. Ahmedabad — History. 2. Ahmadābād (India) — Social conditions. 3. Ahmadābād (India) — Economic conditions. I. T.
HC438.A35 G5     309.1/54/75     *LC* 68-25943

**Lambert, Richard D.**     • **4.2513**
Workers, factories, and social change in India. Princeton, N.J., Princeton University Press, 1963. xiii, 247 p. diagrs., tables. 1. Labor and laboring classes — Poona, India (City) 2. Industrialization — Case studies 3. Poona (India) — Industries 4. Poona (India) — Social conditions I. T.
HC438 P6 L24     *LC* 63-7071

**Nafziger, E. Wayne.**     **4.2514**
Class, caste and entrepreneurship: a study of Indian industrialists / E. Wayne Nafziger. — Honolulu: Published for the East-West Center by the University Press of Hawaii, c1978. x, 188 p.; 22 cm. Includes index. 1. Businessmen — India — Visakhapatnam. 2. Businessmen — India 3. Entrepreneurship — Case studies. 4. Social mobility — India — Visakhapatnam. 5. Social mobility — India. I. T.
HC438.V57 N34     301.44/47/0954     *LC* 78-16889     *ISBN* 0824805755

## HC440.5–440.8 Pakistan. Bangladesh

**Ahmed, Viqar.**     **4.2515**
The management of Pakistan's economy, 1947–82 / Viqar Ahmed and Rashid Amjad. — 1st ed. — Karachi; New York: Oxford University Press, 1984. xi, 315 p.: ill.; 24 cm. (UGC monograph series in economics.) 1. Pakistan — Economic policy. I. Amjad, Rashid, 1947- II. T. III. Series.
HC440.5.A723 1984     338.9549/1 19     *LC* 85-159341     *ISBN* 0195773160

**Haq, Mahbub ul, 1934-.**     • **4.2516**
The strategy of economic planning; a case study of Pakistan [by] Mahbub ul Haq. — Karachi: Pakistan Branch, Oxford University Press, [1966, c1963] xvi, 266 p.; 22 cm. 1. Pakistan — Economic policy. I. T.
HC440.5.H37 1966     338.91549     *LC* sa 66-7737

**Lewis, Stephen R.**     • **4.2517**
Economic policy and industrial growth in Pakistan / by Stephen R. Lewis, Jr. — Cambridge, Mass.: M.I.T. Press, [1969] xiii, 191 p.: ill.; 23 cm. Research sponsored by the Pakistan Institute of Development Economics. 1. Pakistan — Industries. 2. Pakistan — Economic policy. I. Pakistan Institute of Development Economics. II. T.
HC440.5.L4 1969b     338.4/09549     *LC* 76-86605

**Pakistan, the roots of dictatorship: the political economy of a**     **4.2518**
**praetorian state / Hassan Gardezi and Jamil Rashid, editors.**
London: Zed Press; Totowa, N.J., U.S.A.: U.S. distributor, Biblio Distribution Center, 1983. xvii, 394 p.: map; 23 cm. Includes index. 1. Debts, External — Pakistan — Addresses, essays, lectures. 2. Islam and politics — Pakistan — Addresses, essays, lectures. 3. Pakistan — Economic policy — Addresses, essays, lectures. 4. Pakistan — Social policy — Addresses, essays, lectures. I. Gardezi, Hassan Nawaz. II. Rashid, Jamil.
HC440.5.P35 1983     338.9549/2 19     *LC* 83-225418     *ISBN* 0862320461

**Papanek, Gustav Fritz.**     • **4.2519**
Pakistan's development, social goals and private incentives [by] Gustav F. Papanek. — Cambridge, Mass.: Harvard University Press, 1967. xxii, 354 p.; 22 cm. 'Written under the auspices of the Center for International Affairs, Harvard University.' 1. Pakistan — Economic policy. 2. Pakistan — Economic conditions. I. Harvard University. Center for International Affairs. II. T.
HC440.5.P38     338.9549     *LC* 67-22871

**Ahmad, Nafis, 1911-.**     **4.2520**
A new economic geography of Bangladesh / Nafis Ahmad. — New Delhi: Vikas Pub. House, c1976. xvi, 249 p., [1] leaf of plates: ill.; 23 cm. Includes index. 1. Bangladesh — Economic conditions. I. T.
HC440.8.A55     330.9/549/205     *LC* 75-908943     *ISBN* 0706904044

**Bangla Desh economy: problems and prospects.** Edited by V. K. • **4.2521**
R. V. Rao.
Delhi, Vikas Publications [1972] vi, 199 p. 23 cm. (Studies in economic growth.
no. 15) 1. Bangladesh — Economic conditions — Addresses, essays, lectures.
I. Rao, V. K. R. V. (Vijendra Kasturi Ranga Varadaraja), 1908- ed. II. Series.
HC440.8.B36     330.9/549/205     *LC* 72-904282     *ISBN* 0706901770

**Dutt, Kalyan, 1924-.**          **4.2522**
Bangladesh economy; an analytical study [by] Kalyan Dutt, Ranajit Dasgupta
[and] Anil Chatterjee. — New Delhi: People's Pub. House, [1973] xi, 267 p.:
maps.; 22 cm. 1. Bangladesh — Economic conditions. I. Dasgupta, Ranajit,
1932- joint author. II. Chatterjee, Anil, 1925- joint author. III. T.
HC440.8.D88     330.9/549/205     *LC* 73-905951

**The Economic development of Bangladesh within a socialist**     **4.2523**
**framework; proceedings of a conference held by the**
**International Economic Association at Dacca.** Edited by E. A.
**G. Robinson and Keith Griffin.**
New York, Wiley [1974] xxii, 330 p. 23 cm. 'A Halsted Press book.'
1. Bangladesh — Economic conditions — Congresses. I. Robinson, E. A. G.
(Edward Austin Gossage), ed. II. Griffin, Keith B. ed. III. International
Economic Association.
HC440.8.E26 1974     338/.09549/2     *LC* 74-8438     *ISBN* 0470728035

**Khan, Azizur Rahman.**          **4.2524**
The economy of Bangladesh. — [London]: Macmillan; [New York]: St.
Martin's Press, [1972] xviii, 196 p.; 22 cm. 1. Bangladesh — Economic
conditions. 2. Bangladesh — Economic policy. I. T.
HC440.8.K53 1972     330.9/549/205     *LC* 72-88005     *ISBN*
0333145461

# HC441–444 Southeast Asia. Indochina

**Crone, Donald K.**          **4.2525**
The ASEAN states: coping with dependence / Donald K. Crone. — New York,
N.Y.: Praeger, 1983. x, 230 p.; 25 cm. Includes index. 1. ASEAN. 2. Asia,
Southeastern — Foreign economic relations. 3. Asia, Southeastern —
Dependency on foreign countries. 4. Asia, Southeastern — Economic policy.
I. T. II. Title: A.S.E.A.N. states.
HC441.C76 1983     337/.0959 19     *LC* 83-2433     *ISBN* 003062911X

**Wawn, Brian.**          **4.2526**
The economies of the ASEAN countries: Indonesia, Malaysia, Philippines,
Singapore, and Thailand / Brian Wawn. — New York: St. Martin's Press, 1982.
ix, 188 p.: ill.; 23 cm. Includes index. 1. Industry and state — Asia,
Southeastern. 2. Asia, Southeastern — Economic policy. 3. Asia, Southeastern
— Economic conditions. I. T.
HC441.W38 1982     330.959/053 19     *LC* 82-5958     *ISBN*
0312236735

**Murray, Martin J.**          **4.2527**
The development of capitalism in colonial Indochina (1870–1940) / Martin J.
Murray. — Berkeley: University of California Press, c1980. xii, 685 p.; 24 cm.
Includes index. 1. Capitalism 2. Indochina — Economic conditions. I. T.
HC442.M87     330.9597/03     *LC* 80-16472     *ISBN* 0520040007

# HC445–460 Thailand. Malaysia. Indonesia. Philippines

**Ingram, James C.**          **4.2528**
Economic change in Thailand, 1850–1970 [by] James C. Ingram. — Stanford,
Calif.: Stanford University Press, 1970. ix, 352 p.: illus., map.; 24 cm. 1955 ed.
published under title: Economic change in Thailand since l850. 1. Thailand —
Economic conditions. I. T.
HC445.I6x     330.9593     *LC* 70-150325     *ISBN* 0804707820

**Young, Kevin, 1945-.**          **4.2529**
Malaysia, growth and equity in a multiracial society / Kevin Young, Willem
C.F. Bussink, Parvez Hasan, coordinating authors. — Baltimore: Published for
the World Bank [by] Johns Hopkins University Press, c1980. xix, 345 p.: map;
24 cm. — (A World Bank country economic report) 1. Malaysia — Economic
conditions. 2. Malaysia — Economic policy. I. Bussink, Willem C. F., 1929-
joint author II. Hasan, Parvez. joint author. III. T.
HC445.5.Y68     330.9595/053 19     *LC* 79-3677     *ISBN* 0801823846

**Singapore development policies and trends** / edited by Peter     **4.2530**
**S.J. Chen.**
Singapore; New York: Oxford University Press, 1983. xiii, 384 p.; 26 cm.
Includes index. 1. Singapore — Economic policy. 2. Singapore — Politics and
government. I. Chen, Peter S. J.
HC445.8.S545 1983     338.9595/7 19     *LC* 83-940892     *ISBN*
0195825144

**Glassburner, Bruce, comp.**          • **4.2531**
The economy of Indonesia; selected readings. Edited, with an introd. by Bruce
Glassburner. — Ithaca: Cornell University Press, [1971] xii, 443 p.; 24 cm.
1. Indonesia — Economic conditions — 1945- — Addresses, essays, lectures.
2. Indonesia — Economic policy — Addresses, essays, lectures. I. T.
HC447.G53     330.9598/03     *LC* 77-127777     *ISBN* 0801406005

**The Indonesian economy** / edited by Gustav F. Papanek.     **4.2532**
New York: Praeger, 1980. xxi, 438 p.: map; 25 cm. 1. Indonesia — Economic
conditions — 1945- — Addresses, essays, lectures. I. Papanek, Gustav Fritz.
HC447.I558     330.9598/037     *LC* 80-18752     *ISBN* 0030574293

**The Indonesian economy during the Soeharto era** / edited by     **4.2533**
**Anne Booth and Peter McCawley.**
Kuala Lumpur; New York: Oxford University Press, 1981. xxv, 329 p.: map; 26
cm. — (East Asian social science monographs.) 1. Indonesia — Economic
conditions — 1945- — Addresses, essays, lectures. 2. Indonesia — Economic
policy — Addresses, essays, lectures. I. Booth, Anne. II. McCawley, Peter.
III. Series.
HC447.I559     330.9598/037 19     *LC* 81-941986     *ISBN* 0195804775

**International Bank for Reconstruction and Development.**     **4.2534**
The Philippines: priorities and prospects for development: report of a mission
sent to the Philippines by the World Bank / Russell J. Cheetham, chief of
mission; Edward K. Hawkins, coordinating author. — Washington: World
Bank, [1976] xx, 573 p. (World Bank country economíc report) Includes index.
1. Philippines — Economic conditions — 1946- I. Cheetham, Russell J.
II. Hawkins, Edward Kenneth. III. T.
HC452.I58 1976     HC452 I58 1976.     330.9/599/04     *LC* 76-17243
    *ISBN* 0801818931

**Baldwin, Robert E.**          **4.2535**
The Philippines / by Robert E. Baldwin. — New York: National Bureau of
Economic Research: distributed by Columbia University Press, 1975. xix,
165 p.; 24 cm. (Foreign trade regimes and economic development; v. 5)
1. Foreign trade regulation — Philippine Islands. 2. Philippines — Economic
conditions — 1946- 3. Philippines — Commercial policy. I. T. II. Series.
HC455.B3x     330.9 s 330.9/599/04     *LC* 74-82373     *ISBN*
0870145053

**Golay, Frank H.**          • **4.2536**
The Philippines: public policy and national economic development. Ithaca,
N.Y., Cornell University Press [1961] 455 p. illus. 24 cm. 1. Philippines —
Economic policy. I. T.
HC455.G6     338.9914     *LC* 61-7869

**Huke, Robert E.**          • **4.2537**
Shadows on the land: an economic geography of the Philippines / Contributing
authors: Jose B. Barcelon [and others.] Manila, Bookmark, 1963. xi, 428 p.
illus., maps. 24 cm. 1. Philippines — Econ. condit. — 1918-. I. T. II. Title: An
economic geography of the Philippines.
HC 455 H92 1963     *LC* 64-4080

**The Philippine economy and the United States: studies in past**     **4.2538**
**and present interactions** / edited by Norman G. Owen.
Ann Arbor: The University of Michigan, Center for South and Southeast Asian
Studies, 1983. xv, 208 p.; 23 cm. (Michigan papers on South and Southeast
Asia. no. 22) 1. Corporations, American — Philippines — Addresses, essays,
lectures. 2. Philippines — Economic conditions — Addresses, essays, lectures.
3. Philippines — Foreign economic relations — United States — Addresses,
essays, lectures. 4. United States — Foreign economic relations — Philippines
— Addresses, essays, lectures. I. Owen, Norman G. II. Series.
HC455.P468 1983     337.599073 19     *LC* 82-74314     *ISBN*
0891480242

**Yoshihara, Kunio, 1939-.**          **4.2539**
Philippine industrialization: foreign and domestic capital / Yoshihara Kunio.
— Quezon City, Metro Manila: Ateneo de Manila University Press; Singapore;
New York: Oxford University Press, 1985. x, 180 p.; 22 cm. Includes index.
1. Investments — Philippines. 2. Investments, Foreign — Philippines.
3. Philippines — Industries. I. T.
HC455.Y67 1985     338.6/041/09599 19     *LC* 86-149596     *ISBN*
9711130432

## HC460.5 East Asia. Far East: General

**Hofheinz, Roy, 1935-.**          4.2540
The Eastasia edge / Roy Hofheinz, Jr., Kent E. Calder. — New York: Basic Books, c1982. ix, 296 p.: ill., maps; 24 cm. Maps on lining papers. 1. East Asia — Economic conditions 2. Asia, Southeastern — Economic conditions. 3. East Asia — Foreign economic relations. 4. Asia, Southeastern — Foreign economic relations. I. Calder, Kent E. II. T.
HC460.5.H63 1982    330.95/0428 19    *LC* 81-68409    *ISBN* 0465017762

## HC461–465 Japan

**Diamond Lead Company.**          4.2541
Diamond's Japan business directory. Tokyo, New York, Diamond Lead Co. v. ill. 27 cm. Annual. 1. Corporations — Japan — Finance. 2. Japan — Industries — Directories. 3. Japan — Commerce — Directories. I. T.
HC461.D5    332.6/7    *LC* 75-647718

**Cohen, Jerome Bernard, 1915-.**      • **4.2542**
Japan's economy in war and reconstruction; with a foreword by Sir George Sansom. Minneapolis, Univ. of Minnesota Press, 1949. xix, 545 p. diagrs. 26 cm. 'Issued under the auspices of the International Secretariat, Institute of Pacific Relations.' Issued also as thesis, Columbia Univ. with title: The Japanese war economy, 1937-1945. Bibliographical footnotes. 1. Japan — Economic conditions — 1918-1945 2. Japan — Economic conditions — 1945- I. T.
HC462.C55    330.952    *LC* 49-9272 rev*

**Lockwood, William Wirt, 1906-.**      • **4.2543**
The economic development of Japan: growth and structural change, 1868–1938. Princeton, N.J., Princeton University Press, 1954. xv, 603 p. ill., map, tables. 1. Japan — Economic conditions 2. Japan — Industries I. T.
HC462 L6    *LC* 54-6077

**Lockwood, William Wirt, 1906-, ed.**      • **4.2544**
The state and economic enterprise in Japan; essays in the political economy of growth. Edited by William W. Lockwood. Contributors: M. Bronfenbrenner [and others] Princeton, N.J., Princeton University Press, 1965. x, 753 p. ill. ([Studies in the modernization of Japan] 2) Contributions to a seminar sponsored by the Conference on Modern Japan and held at Estes Park, Colo., in June 1963. 1. Industry and state — Japan — Addresses, essays, lectures 2. Japan — Economic conditions — Addresses, essays, lectures I. Bronfenbrenner, Martin, 1914- II. Conference on Modern Japan. III. T. IV. Series.
HC462 L78    *LC* 65-15386

**Takekoshi, Yosaburō, 1865-1950.**      • **4.2545**
The economic aspects of the history of the civilization of Japan [by] Yosoburo Takekoshi. — London: Dawsons of Pall Mall, 1967. 3 v.; 25 cm. Label mounted on t.p.: Sole distributors in U.S.A., Paragon Book Gallery, New York. 1. Japan — Economic conditions — To 1868 I. T.
HC462.T2935    330.952    *LC* 68-96138    *ISBN* 0712902066

**Japan's economic security / edited by Nobutoshi Akao.**      4.2546
New York: Published for the Royal Institute of International Affairs by St. Martin's Press, 1983. xii, 279 p.; 22 cm. 1. Natural resources — Japan — Addresses, essays, lectures. 2. Raw materials — Japan — Addresses, essays, lectures. 3. Japan — Commerce — Addresses, essays, lectures. I. Akao, Nobutoshi.
HC462.5.J37 1983    333.7/0952 19    *LC* 82-10257    *ISBN* 0312440642

**Halliday, Jon.**          4.2547
A political history of Japanese capitalism / Jon Halliday. — 1st ed. — New York: Pantheon Books, [1975] xxxiii, 466 p.: map; 25 cm. (The Pantheon Asia library) 1. Japan — Economic conditions — 1868- 2. Japan — Economic policy 3. Japan — Politics and government — 1868- I. T.
HC462.7.H25 1975    330.9/52/03    *LC* 74-4774    *ISBN* 039448391X

**Asia's new giant: how the Japanese economy works / Hugh Patrick and Henry Rosovsky, editors.**      4.2548
Washington: Brookings Institution, c1976. ix, 943 p.: graphs; 24 cm. 1. Japan — Economic policy — 1945- 2. Japan — Economic conditions — 1945- 3. Japan — Social conditions — 1945- I. Patrick, Hugh T. II. Rosovsky, Henry.
HC462.9.A84    330.9/52/04    *LC* 75-42304    *ISBN* 0815769342

**Business and society in Japan: fundamentals for businessmen / edited by Bradley M. Richardson, Taizo Ueda.**      4.2549
New York, N.Y.: Praeger, 1981. xiii, 334 p.; 25 cm. Reports of a study of Japanese business by the East Asian Studies Program of Ohio State University. 1. Japan — Economic conditions — 1945- 2. Japan — Social conditions

3. Japan — Commerce. I. Richardson, Bradley M. II. Ueda, Taizo. III. Ohio State University. East Asian Studies Program.
HC462.9.B86    330.952/048 19    *LC* 81-2710    *ISBN* 0030593212

**Economic policy and development: new perspectives / edited by Toshio Shishido, Ryuzo Sato.**      4.2550
Dover, Mass.: Auburn House; London: Croom Helm, c1985. xv, 320 p.: ill.; 25 cm. 'Contributions ... in honor of Dr. Saburo Okita'—P. ix. 'Saburo Okita: biographical and bibliographical data': p. 317-320. 1. Ōkita, Saburō, 1914- 2. Economic development — Addresses, essays, lectures. 3. Japan — Economic policy — 1945- — Addresses, essays, lectures. 4. Japan — Economic conditions — 1945- — Addresses, essays, lectures. 5. Pacific Area — Economic policy — Addresses, essays, lectures. I. Shishido, Toshio, 1921- II. Satō, Ryūzō, 1931- III. Ōkita, Saburō, 1914-
HC462.9.E236 1985    338.952 19    *LC* 85-6077    *ISBN* 0865691207

**Guillain, Robert, 1908-.**      4.2551
[Japon, troisième grand. English] The Japanese challenge. Translated from the French by Patrick O'Brian. [1st ed. in English] Philadelphia, Lippincott [1970] 352 p. 22 cm. Translation of Japon, troisième grand. 1. Japan — Industries — 1945- I. T.
HC462.9.G7814    330.952    *LC* 73-127086

**Japanese industrial competition to 1990 / by Mary Saso, Stuart Kirby.**      4.2552
Cambridge, Mass.: Abt Books, c1982. xiv, 203 p.: ill.; 26 cm. — (EIU special series. 1) 'Originally published by the Economist Intelligence Unit as Special report nos. 110 and 81'—Verso t.p. 1. Economic forecasting — Japan — Addresses, essays, lectures. 2. Japan — Industries — Addresses, essays, lectures. 3. Japan — Economic conditions — 1945- — Addresses, essays, lectures. 4. Japan — Social conditions — 1945- — Addresses, essays, lectures. I. Saso, Mary. Japanese industry: how to compete and how to cooperate. 1982. II. Kirby, Stuart. Japan's role in the 1980's. 1982. III. Series.
HC462.9.J33 1982    330.952/048 19    *LC* 82-13822    *ISBN* 0890115834

**Ōkawa, Kazushi, 1908-.**      4.2553
Japanese economic growth; trend acceleration in the twentieth century [by] Kazushi Ohkawa & Henry Rosovsky. — Stanford, Calif.: Stanford University Press, 1973. xvi, 327 p.: illus.; 24 cm. — (Studies of economic growth in industrialized countries) 1. Japan — Economic conditions — 1945- I. Rosovsky, Henry. joint author. II. T.
HC462.9.O348    330.9/52/04    *LC* 72-97203    *ISBN* 0804708339

**Pempel, T. J., 1942-.**      4.2554
Policy and politics in Japan: creative conservatism / T.J. Pempel. — Philadelphia: Temple University Press, 1982. xix, 330 p.; 22 cm. — (Policy and politics in industrial states) Includes index. 1. Public administration — Decision making 2. Japan — Economic policy — 1945- 3. Japan — Social policy. 4. Japan — Politics and government — 1945- I. T. II. Series.
HC462.9.P4 1982    338.952 19    *LC* 81-14464    *ISBN* 0877222495

**Pezeu-Massabuau, Jacques.**      4.2555
The Japanese islands: a physical and social geography / Jacques Pezeu-Massabuau; translated and adapted from the French by Paul C. Blum. — Rutland, Vt.: C. E. Tuttle Co., 1978. 283 p., [1] fold. leaf of plates: ill.; 20 cm. Revised translation of Géographie du Japon. Includes index. 1. Japan — Economic conditions — 1945- 2. Japan — Social conditions — 1945- I. Blum, Paul Charles, 1898- II. T.
HC462.9.P4913    309.1/52/04    *LC* 77-82140    *ISBN* 0804811849

**Shinohara, Miyohei, 1919-.**      4.2556
Industrial growth, trade, and dynamic patterns in the Japanese economy / Miyohei Shinohara. — [Tokyo]: University of Tokyo Press, c1982. x, 243 p.: ill.; 24 cm. 1. Industry and state — Japan. 2. Japan — Economic conditions — 1945- 3. Japan — Commerce. I. T.
HC462.9.S5163 1982    330.952/04 19    *LC* 82-227032    *ISBN* 0860082970

**Uchino, Tatsurō, 1925-.**      4.2557
[Sengo Nihon keizaishi. English] Japan's postwar economy: an insider's view of its history and its future / by Tatsurō Uchino; translated by Mark A. Harbison. — 1st English ed. — Tokyo; New York: Kodansha International, 1983. 286 p.: ill.; 23 cm. Revision translation of: Sengo Nihon keizaishi. Ill. on lining papers. Includes index. 1. Japan — Economic conditions — 1945- 2. Japan — Economic policy — 1945- I. T.
HC462.9.U2613 1983    330.952/04 19    *LC* 83-47621    *ISBN* 0870115952

## HC466–470 Korea

**Bartz, Patricia McBride, 1921-.**    • **4.2558**
South Korea, [by] Patricia M. Bartz. — Oxford: Clarendon Press, 1972. xviii, 203 p.: illus., maps.; 27 cm. 1. Korea (South) — Economic conditions 2. Korea (South) — Description and travel. I. T.
HC467.B37    915.19/5    LC 72-196784    ISBN 0198740085

**Cole, David Chamberlin, 1928-.**    • **4.2559**
Korean development; the interplay of politics and economics [by] David C. Cole [and] Princeton N. Lyman. — Cambridge, Mass.: Harvard University Press, 1971. xiii, 320 p.; 24 cm. 'Written under the auspices of the Center for International Affairs, Harvard University.' 1. Korea (South) — Economic conditions — 1960- 2. Korea (South) — Politics and government — 1960- I. Lyman, Princeton N., joint author. II. T.
HC467.C65    330.9519/043    LC 75-131468    ISBN 0674505638

**The Economic and social modernization of the Republic of**    **4.2560**
**Korea / Edward S. Mason ... [et al.].**
Cambridge, Mass.: Council on East Asian Studies, Harvard University: distributed by Harvard University Press, 1981 (c1980). xxxii, 552 p.: ill.; 24 cm. — (Studies in the modernization of the Republic of Korea, 1945-1975.) (Harvard East Asian monographs. 92) Includes index. 1. Korea — Economic conditions — 1945- 2. Korea — Social conditions — 1945- I. Mason, Edward Sagendorph, 1899- II. Harvard University. Council on East Asian Studies. III. Series. IV. Series: Harvard East Asian monographs. 92
HC467.E26 1980    330.9519/5043 19    LC 80-21531    ISBN 0674231759

**Hasan, Parvez.**    **4.2561**
Korea: problems and issues in a rapidly growing economy / Parvez Hasan. — Baltimore: Published for the World Bank [by] the Johns Hopkins University Press, c1976. xv, 277 p.: map; 24 cm. — (A World Bank country economic report) Includes index. 1. Korea (South) — Economic conditions 2. Korea (South) — Commerce. I. World Bank. II. T.
HC467.H37    330.9/519/043    LC 76-17238    ISBN 0801818648. ISBN 0801818656 pbk

**Brun, Ellen.**    **4.2562**
Socialist Korea: a case study in the strategy of economic development / Ellen Brun and Jacques Hersh. — New York: Monthly Review Press, c1976. 422 p., [4] leaves of plates: ill.; 21 cm. 1. Socialism — Korea (North) 2. Korea (North) — Economic conditions. 3. Korea (North) — Economic policy. I. Hersh, Jacques. joint author. II. T.
HC468.A2 B78    330.9/519/3043    LC 76-1651    ISBN 0853453861

**Adelman, Irma.**    **4.2563**
Income distribution policy in developing countries: a case study of Korea / Irma Adelman & Sherman Robinson. — Stanford, Calif.: Published for the World Bank [by] Stanford University Press, 1978. xvii, 346 p.: diagrs.; 24 cm. Includes index. 1. Income distribution — Korea. I. Robinson, Sherman. joint author. II. World Bank. III. T.
HC470.I5 A33    339.2/09519    LC 76-14269    ISBN 0804709254

## HC471–480 Iran. Soviet Central Asia

**Bharier, Julian.**    • **4.2564**
Economic development in Iran, 1900–1970. — London; New York: Oxford University Press, 1971. xviii, 314 p.: 1 ill., map; 23 cm. Map on lining paper. 1. Iran — Economic conditions I. T.
HC475.B5    330.955/05    LC 73-875594    ISBN 0192153420

**Issawi, Charles Philip. comp.**    **4.2565**
The economic history of Iran, 1800–1914. Edited by Charles Issawi. Chicago, University of Chicago Press [1971] xv, 405 p. 25 cm. (Publications of the Center for Middle Eastern studies, no. 8) 1. Iran — Economic conditions 2. Iran — Social conditions. I. T.
HC475.I85    330.9/55/04087    LC 70-153883    ISBN 0226386066

**Conolly, Violet.**    **4.2566**
Siberia today and tomorrow: a study of economic resources, problems, and achievements / Violet Conolly. — New York: Taplinger Pub. Co., 1976, c1975. 248 p., [6] leaves of plates: ill.; 25 cm. Includes index. 1. Siberia — Economic conditions. I. T.
HC487.S5 C62 1976    330.9/57/085    LC 75-26327    ISBN 0800871820

## HC491–495 Turkey

**The Economic history of Turkey, 1800–1914 / [edited by]**    **4.2567**
**Charles Issawi.**
Chicago: University of Chicago Press, 1980. xvi, 390 p.; 25 cm. (Publications of the Center for Middle Eastern Studies; no. 13) 'Companion volume to [editor's] The Economic history of the Middle East ... and The Economic history of Iran.' Includes indexes. 1. Turkey — Economic conditions I. Issawi, Charles Philip.
HC491.E26    330.9561/01    LC 80-444    ISBN 0226386031

**Hale, William M.**    **4.2568**
The political and economic development of modern Turkey / William Hale. — New York: St. Martin's Press, 1981. 279 p.: ill.; 23 cm. Includes index. 1. Turkey — Economic conditions — 1918-1960 2. Turkey — Economic conditions — 1960- 3. Turkey — Economic policy. I. T.
HC492.H34 1981    338.9561 19    LC 81-4970    ISBN 0312620594

**Turkey in the world capitalist system: a study of**    **4.2569**
**industrialisation, power, and class / edited by Huseyin Ramazanoglu.**
Aldershots, Hants, England; Brookfield, Vt., U.S.A.: Gower, c1985. xi, 260 p.; 23 cm. 1. Capitalism — Turkey. 2. Industry and state — Turkey. 3. Turkey — Economic policy. I. Ramazanoglu, Huseyin, 1947-
HC495.C3 T87 1985    338.9561 19    LC 85-17587    ISBN 0566050498

## HC498 Arab Countries: General

**Amin, Samir.**    **4.2570**
[Economie arabe contemporaine. English] The Arab economy today / Samir Amin; introduction by Aidan Foster–Carter; translated by Michael Pallis. — London: Zed Press; Westport, Conn., U.S.A.: U.S. distributor, L. Hill, 1982. 124 p.: ill.; 23 cm. — (Middle East series) 1. Amin, Samir — Addresses, essays, lectures. 2. Arab countries — Economic conditions — Addresses, essays, lectures. I. T.
HC498.A6913 1982    330.917/4927 19    LC 84-108701    ISBN 086232081X

**Ibrahim, Saad Eddin.**    **4.2571**
The new Arab social order: a study of the social impact of oil wealth / Saad Eddin Ibrahim. — Boulder, Colo.: Westview; London, England: Croom Helm, 1982. xiv, 208 p.: ill.; 24 cm. — (Westview's special studies on the Middle East) Includes index. 1. Arab countries — Economic conditions. 2. Arab countries — Social conditions. 3. Arab countries — Politics and government — 1945- I. T.
HC498.I23 1982    306/.3 19    LC 81-16191    ISBN 0865313148

**The Problems of Arab economic development and integration:**    **4.2572**
**proceedings of a symposium held at Yarmouk University, Jordan, November 4 and 5, 1981 / edited by Adda Guecioueur.**
Boulder, Colo.: Westview Press, 1984. xvi, 223 p.: ill.; 24 cm. — (Westview special studies on the Middle East.) 1. Arab countries — Economic integration — Congresses. 2. Arab countries — Economic conditions — Congresses. I. Guecioueur, Adda. II. Series.
HC498.P76 1984    337.1/174927 19    LC 83-1239    ISBN 0865315957

**Rich and poor states in the Middle East: Egypt and the new**    **4.2573**
**Arab order / edited by Malcolm H. Kerr and El Sayed Yassin.**
Boulder, Colo.: Westview Press; Cairo, Egypt: American University in Cairo Press, 1982. x, 482 p.: ill.; 24 cm. (Westview special studies on the Middle East.) 1. Arab countries — Economic policy — Addresses, essays, lectures. I. Kerr, Malcolm H. II. Yāsīn, al-Sayyid. III. Series.
HC498.R5 1982    338.9/00917/4927 19    LC 82-153936    ISBN 0865312753

**Wilson, Rodney.**    **4.2574**
The Arab world: an international statistical directory / Rodney Wilson. — Brighton, Sussex: Wheatsheaf Books; Boulder, Colo.: Westview Press, 1984. 15, [177] p.; 25 cm. 1. Arab countries — Economic conditions — Statistics. I. T.
HC498.W55 1984    330.917/4927/0021 19    LC 85-160625    ISBN 0813300959

## HC501–591 Africa
(see also: HC800-1085)

**Dumont, René, 1904-.**    • **4.2575**
False start in Africa. Translated by Phyllis Nauts Ott. Introd. by Thomas Balogh. With an additional chapter by John Ilatch. — New York, Praeger [1966] 320 p. 23 cm. Translation of L'Afrique noire est mal partie.

Bibliography: p. [318]-320. 1. Africa, Sub-Saharan — Econ. condit. — 1918-
I. T.
HC502.D8413 1966    338.0967    *LC* 66-16593

**Hance, William Adams, 1916-.**    • **4.2576**
African economic development [by] William A. Hance. — Rev. ed. — New
York: Published for the Council on Foreign Relations [by] Praeger, [1967] xiv,
326 p.: maps.; 22 cm. 1. Africa — Economic conditions I. Council on Foreign
Relations. II. T.
HC502.H33 1967    330.96    *LC* 67-20480

**Kamarck, Andrew M.**    • **4.2577**
The economics of African development, by Andrew M. Kamarck. Foreword by
Pierre Moussa. — Rev. ed. — New York: Praeger, [1971] xv, 352 p.: maps.; 21
cm. 1. Africa — Economic conditions I. T.
HC502.K3 1971    330.96    *LC* 70-126778

**Munro, J. Forbes.**    **4.2578**
Africa and the international economy, 1800–1960: an introduction to the
modern economic history of Africa south of the Sahara / J. Forbes Munro.
London: J. M. Dent; Totowa, N.J.: Rowman and Littlefield, 1976. 230 p.: ill.;
23 cm. Includes index. 1. Africa, Sub-Saharan — Economic conditions
2. Africa, Sub-Saharan — Commerce — History. I. T.
HC502.M84    330.9/67    *LC* 76-383031    *ISBN* 0874718937

**Nkrumah, Kwame, 1909-1972.**    **4.2579**
Neo–colonialism: the last stage of imperialism. — [London]: Nelson, [1965] xx,
208 p.: ill., col. map (on lining papers); 24 cm. 1. Investments, Foreign —
Africa. 2. Africa — Foreign economic relations. 3. Africa — Industries. I. T.
HC502.N5 1965    *LC* 66-95948

**Woolf, Leonard, 1880-1969.**    • **4.2580**
Empire & commerce in Africa: a study in economic imperialism by Leonard
Woolf. London, Allen & Unwin, 1968. viii, 374 p. 5 plates, 5 maps. 23 cm.
Originally published 1920. 'Written as a Report for a Committee of the Labour
Research Department.' 1. Economic policy 2. Competition, International
3. Africa — Economic conditions — To 1918 4. Africa — Politics and
government I. Labour Research Department. II. T.
HC502.W6 1968b    382    *LC* 79-355226

**Curtin, Philip D.**    **4.2581**
Economic change in precolonial Africa; Senegambia in the era of the slave trade
[by] Philip D. Curtin. [Madison] University of Wisconsin Press [1975] xxix,
363 p. illus. 24 cm. Accompanied by a supplement entitled Supplementary
evidence (xi, 150 p.) 1. Slave-trade — Africa, West — History. 2. Africa, West
— Economic conditions 3. Africa, West — Commerce — History. I. T.
HC503.W4 C87    330.9/66/301    *LC* 74-5899    *ISBN* 0299066401

**Elliott, Charles, 1939-.**    **4.2582**
Patterns of poverty in the Third World: a study of social and economic
stratification / Charles Elliott, assisted by Francoise de Morsier. — New York:
Praeger, 1975. xii, 416 p.: ill.; 24 cm. (Praeger special studies in international
economics and development) 1. Income — Africa. 2. Income — Asia.
3. Poverty 4. Africa — Economic conditions 5. Asia — Economic conditions
6. Developing countries — Social conditions. I. De Morsier, Francoise, joint
author. II. T.
HC505.P6 E44 1975    330.9/172/4    *LC* 75-1223    *ISBN*
0275099202. *ISBN* 0275893006 pbk

**East Africa; its peoples and resources. Edited by W. T. W.**    **4.2583**
**Morgan.**
2d ed. Nairobi, New York, Oxford University Press, 1973 (c1972). viii, 312 p.
illus. 26 cm. Part of illustrative matter fold. in pocket. 1. Natural resources —
Africa, East. 2. Africa, East — Economic conditions. 3. Africa, East —
Population. I. Morgan, W. T. W. (William Thomas Wilson), 1927- ed.
HC517.E2 E25    333    *LC* 74-166230    *ISBN* 0195720237 *ISBN*
0195720229

**O'Connor, Anthony M. (Anthony Michael)**    • **4.2584**
An economic geography of East Africa [by] A. M. O'Connor. New York,
Praeger [1966] ix, 292 p. 20 maps. 23 cm. (Praeger surveys in economic
geography) 1. Natural resources — Africa, East. 2. Africa, East — Economic
conditions. I. T.
HC517.E2 O28 1966a    330.9676    *LC* 66-22358

**Killick, Tony.**    **4.2585**
Development economics in action: a study of economic policies in Ghana /
Tony Killick. — New York: St. Martin's Press, c1978. xiii, 392 p.: graphs; 23
cm. Includes index. 1. Economic development — Case studies. 2. Ghana —
Economic policy. I. T.
HC517.G6 K54 1978    330.9/667/05    *LC* 77-74764    *ISBN*
0312196822

**Leys, Colin.**    **4.2586**
Underdevelopment in Kenya: the political economy of neo–colonialism,
1964–1971 / Colin Leys. — Berkeley: University of California Press, 1974 [i.e.

1975] xv, 284 p.: maps; 22 cm. 1. Kenya — Economic conditions 2. Kenya —
Politics and government 3. Kenya — Social conditions — 1963- I. T.
HC517.K4 L49    330.9/676/204    *LC* 74-76387    *ISBN* 0520027310.
*ISBN* 0520027701 pbk

**Dike, Kenneth Onwuka.**    • **4.2587**
Trade and politics in the Niger Delta, 1830–1885: an introduction to the
economic and political history of Nigeria. — Oxford: Clarendon Press, 1956. vi,
250 p.: fold. map, tables; 22 cm. — (Oxford studies in African affairs.) 'Grew
out of [the author's] ... thesis for the degree of doctor of philosophy (history) in
the University of London.' 1. Nigeria — Economic conditions 2. Nigeria —
Politics and government I. T. II. Series.
HC517.N48 D5

**Bienen, Henry.**    **4.2588**
The Political economy of income distribution in Nigeria / edited by Henry
Bienen and V. P. Diejomaoh. — New York: Holmes & Meier, 1981. viii, 520 p.;
24 cm. — (Political economy of income distribution in developing countries. 2)
1. Income distribution — Nigeria — Addresses, essays, lectures. 2. Nigeria —
Economic policy — Addresses, essays, lectures. 3. Nigeria — Economic
conditions — Addresses, essays, lectures. I. Diejomaoh, Victor P. II. T.
III. Series.
HC517.N483 I516 1981    339.2/09669    *LC* 80-16860    *ISBN*
0841906181

**Hopkins, A. G. (Anthony G.)**    **4.2589**
An economic history of West Africa [by] A. G. Hopkins. New York, Columbia
University Press, 1973. x, 337 p. illus. 25 cm. (Columbia economic history of
the modern world.) 1. Africa, West — Economic conditions I. T. II. Series.
HC517.W5 H66    330.9/66    *LC* 72-11798    *ISBN* 0231037392

**Mabro, Robert.**    **4.2590**
The Egyptian economy, 1952–1972 / by Robert Mabro. — Oxford: Clarendon
Press, 1974. xii, 254 p.: 21 cm. (Economies of the world) Includes index.
1. Egypt — Economic conditions — 1952- 2. Egypt — Economic policy. I. T.
HC535.M17    330.9/62/05    *LC* 74-188342    *ISBN* 0198770308

**Mabro, Robert.**    **4.2591**
The industrialization of Egypt, 1939–1973: policy and performance / [by]
Robert Mabro and Samir Radwan. Oxford: Clarendon Press, 1976. xii, 279 p.;
23 cm. Index. 1. Egypt — Industries — History I. Radwān, Samīr
Muhammad. II. T.
HC535.M2x    338/.0962    *ISBN* 0198284055

**Amin, Samir.**    **4.2592**
[Afrique de l'Ouest bloquée. English] Neo–colonialism in West Africa.
Translated from the French by Francis McDonagh. New York, Monthly
Review Press [1974, c1973] xviii, 298 p. illus. 21 cm. Translation of L'Afrique
de l'Ouest bloquée. 1. Africa, French-speaking West — Economic policy.
2. Africa, French-speaking West — Economic conditions. I. T.
HC547.W5 A713 1974    330.9/66    *LC* 74-7784    *ISBN* 0853453381

**Pankhurst, Richard Keir Pethick, 1927-.**    **4.2593**
Economic history of Ethiopia, 1800–1935 [by] Richard Pankhurst. — [1st ed.].
— Addis Ababa: Haile Sellassie I University Press, 1968. 772 p.: illus., maps,
ports.; 25 cm. 1. Ethiopia — Economic conditions I. T.
HC591.A3 P24    330.963    *LC* 78-9298

**Zaire, the political economy of underdevelopment / edited by**    **4.2594**
**Guy Gran with the assistance of Galen Hull.**
New York: Praeger, 1979. xviii, 331 p.: maps; 24 cm. Includes index. 1. Zaire
— Economic policy — Addresses, essays, lectures. 2. Zaire — Politics and
government — Addresses, essays, lectures. 3. Zaire — Social conditions —
Addresses, essays, lectures. 4. Zaire — Rural conditions — Addresses, essays,
lectures. 5. Zaire — Foreign relations — 1960- — Addresses, essays, lectures.
I. Gran, Guy. II. Hull, Galen.
HC591.C6 Z37    330.9/675/103    *LC* 79-19512    *ISBN* 0030489164

**Franke, Richard W.**    **4.2595**
Seeds of famine: ecological destruction and the development dilemma in the
west African Sahel / by Richard W. Franke and Barbara H. Chasin. —
Montclair, N.J.: Allanheld, Osmun, 1980. xi, 266 p., [1] leaf of plates: map; 24
cm. (Land Mark studies) Includes index. 1. Famines — Sahel. 2. Rural
development — Sahel. 3. Sahel — Rural conditions. I. Chasin, Barbara H.
joint author. II. T.
HC591.S253 F3433    338.1/9/66    *LC* 79-52471    *ISBN* 0916672263

## HC601–695 Australia. Oceania

**Shaw, A. G. L. (Alan George Lewers), 1916-.**    • **4.2596**
The economic development of Australia / by A. G. L. Shaw. — 3d ed. — London; New York: Longmans, Green, [1955] 212 p.: ill.; 19 cm. 1. Australia — Economic conditions I. T.
HC603.S55

**Ward, Ralph Gerard.**    **4.2597**
Man in the Pacific Islands; essays on geographical change in the Pacific Islands, edited by R. Gerard Ward. — Oxford: Clarendon Press, 1972. x, 339 p.: illus.; 22 cm. 1. Oceania — Economic conditions — Addresses, essays, lectures. 2. Oceania — Social conditions — Addresses, essays, lectures. I. T.
HC683.W37    330.9/9    LC 73-150468    ISBN 0198232101

**Belshaw, Cyril S.**    **4.2598**
Under the ivi tree; society and economic growth in rural Fiji, by Cyril S. Belshaw. Berkeley, University of California Press, 1964. xiii, 336 p. ill., map. 1. Fiji Islands — Economic conditions I. T.
HC687 F5 B4    LC 65-7165

**Kamarck, Andrew M.**    **4.2599**
The tropics and economic development: a provocative inquiry into the poverty of nations / Andrew M. Kamarck. — Baltimore: Published for the World Bank [by] Johns Hopkins University Press, c1976. xiv, 113 p.: maps; 24 cm. Includes index. 1. Tropics — Economic conditions. 2. Developing countries — Economic conditions I. World Bank. II. T.
HC695.K25    338.1/09172/4    LC 76-17242    ISBN 0801818915. ISBN 0801819032 pbk

## HC701–710 Communist Countries: General

**Wilczynski, J. (Jozef), 1922-.**    **4.2600**
Socialist economic development and reforms; from extensive to intensive growth under central planning in the USSR, Eastern Europe, and Yugoslavia [by] J. Wilczynski. New York, Praeger Publishers [1972] xvii, 350 p. 23 cm. 1. Central planning — Communist countries. 2. Communist countries — Economic policy. 3. Communist countries — Economic conditions. I. T.
HC705.W54    330.9/47    LC 73-165528

## HC800–1085 Africa
(see also: HC501-591)

**Accelerated development in Sub–Saharan Africa: an agenda for**    **4.2601**
**action.**
Washington, D.C.: World Bank, [1982] c1981. viii, 198 p.: col. map; 27 cm. 1. Economic assistance — Africa, Sub-Saharan. 2. Africa, Sub-Saharan — Economic conditions — 1960- I. International Bank for Reconstruction and Development.
HC800.A54 1982    338.967 19    LC 81-16828

**Africa in economic crisis / edited by John Ravenhill.**    **4.2602**
New York: Columbia University Press, 1986. xiii, 359 p.; 23 cm. 1. World Bank — Africa, Sub-Saharan — Addresses, essays, lectures. 2. Africa, Sub-Saharan — Economic conditions — Addresses, essays, lectures. I. Ravenhill, John.
HC800.A557 1986    330.967 19    LC 85-26972    ISBN 0231063822

**Ake, Claude.**    **4.2603**
A political economy of Africa / Claude Ake. — Harlow, Essex: Longman, 1981. viii, 196 p.; 23 cm. 1. Africa — Economic conditions 2. Africa — Colonial influence. I. T.
HC800.A65    330.96 19    LC 81-162486    ISBN 0582643708

**ECA and Africa's development, 1983–2008: a preliminary**    **4.2604**
**perspective study.**
Addis Ababa: Economic Commission for Africa, [1983] 103 p.; 25 cm. 'April 1983.' 1. United Nations. Economic Commission for Africa. 2. Africa — Economic conditions — 1960- 3. Africa — Social conditions — 1960- I. United Nations. Economic Commission for Africa. II. Title: E.C.A. and Africa's development, 1983-2008.
HC800.E25 1983    338.96 19    LC 84-980295

**Iliffe, John.**    **4.2605**
The emergence of African capitalism / John Iliffe. — Minneapolis: University of Minnesota Press, c1983. ix, 113 p.; 22 cm. 'The Anstey memorial lectures in the University of Kent at Canterbury, 10-13 May 1982.' Includes index.

1. Capitalists and financiers — Africa, Sub-Saharan — History. 2. Africa, Sub-Saharan — Economic conditions I. T.
HC800.I44 1983    338/.04/0967 19    LC 83-5922    ISBN 0816612366

**Indigenization of African economies / edited by Adebayo**    **4.2606**
**Adedeji.**
New York: Africana Pub. Co., 1981. 413 p.; 23 cm. Includes index. 1. Africanization — Addresses, essays, lectures. 2. Africa — Economic conditions — 1945- — Addresses, essays, lectures. 3. Africa — Colonial influence — Addresses, essays, lectures. I. Adedeji, Adebayo.
HC800.I53 1981    330.96/032 19    LC 81-2712    ISBN 0841907080

**International Bank for Reconstruction and Development.**    **4.2607**
Financing adjustment with growth in sub–Saharan Africa, 1986–90. — Washington, D.C.: World Bank, c1986. x, 120 p.: ill.; 28 cm. 1. Agriculture and state — Africa, Sub-Saharan. 2. Economic assistance — Africa, Sub-Saharan. 3. Africa, Sub-Saharan — Economic policy. I. T.
HC800.I565 1986    338.967 19    LC 86-7754    ISBN 0821307673

**Political economy of contemporary Africa / Peter C.W. Gutkind**    **4.2608**
**and Immanuel Wallerstein, editors.**
2nd ed. — Beverly Hills, Calif.: Sage Publications, c1985. 344 p.; 23 cm. (Sage series on African modernization and development; vol. 1) 1. Africa — Economic conditions — 1960- — Addresses, essays, lectures. 2. Africa — Social conditions — 1960- Addresses, essays, lectures. 3. Africa — Politics and government — 1960- — Addresses, essays, lectures. I. Gutkind, Peter Claus Wolfgang. II. Wallerstein, Immanuel Maurice, 1930-
HC800.P65 1985    338.96 19    LC 84-27647    ISBN 0803920962

**Rodney, Walter.**    **4.2609**
How Europe underdeveloped Africa / by Walter Rodney with a postscript by A.M. Babu. — Rev. ed. — Washington, D.C.: Howard University Press, 1982, c1981. xxiv, 312 p.; 23 cm. 1. Africa — Economic conditions 2. Africa — Colonial influence. 3. Europe — Foreign economic relations — Africa. 4. Africa — Foreign economic relations — Europe. I. T.
HC800.R62 1982    330.96 19    LC 81-6240    ISBN 0882580965

**Sandbrook, Richard.**    **4.2610**
The politics of Africa's economic stagnation / Richard Sandbrook with Judith Barker. — Cambridge [Cambridgeshire]; New York: Cambridge University Press, 1985. xiii, 180 p.: 1 map; 20 cm. (African society today.) Includes index. 1. Africa — Economic conditions — 1960- 2. Africa — Politics and government — 1960- 3. Africa — Social conditions — 1960- I. Barker, Judith. II. T. III. Series.
HC800.S26 1985    960/.328 19    LC 84-28588    ISBN 0521265878

**Sender, John.**    **4.2611**
The development of capitalism in Africa / John Sender and Sheila Smith. — London; New York: Methuen, 1986. p. cm. Includes index. 1. Capitalism — Africa — History. 2. Africa — Economic conditions 3. Africa — Economic policy. I. Smith, Sheila. II. T.
HC800.S448 1986    330.96 19    LC 86-16413    ISBN 0416377300

**Strategies for African development: a study for the Committee**    **4.2612**
**on African Development Strategies / edited by Robert J. Berg,**
**Jennifer Seymour Whitaker; sponsored by the Council on**
**Foreign Relations and the Overseas Development Council.**
Berkeley: University of California Press, c1986. xii, 603 p.; 24 cm. 1. Africa — Economic policy — Addresses, essays, lectures. I. Berg, Robert J. II. Whitaker, Jennifer Seymour, 1938- III. Committee on African Development Strategies (U.S.) IV. Council on Foreign Relations. V. Overseas Development Council.
HC800.S76 1986    338.96 19    LC 85-23304    ISBN 0520057848

**Toward sustained development in sub–Saharan Africa: a joint**    **4.2613**
**program of action.**
Washington, D.C.: World Bank, c1984. ix, 102 p.: ill., map; 27 cm. 1. Economic assistance — Africa, Sub-Saharan. 2. Africa, Sub-Saharan — Economic conditions — 1960- 3. Africa, Sub-Saharan — Economic policy. 4. Africa, Sub-Saharan — Social conditions — 1960- 5. Africa, Sub-Saharan — Social policy. I. International Bank for Reconstruction and Development.
HC800.T69 1984    338.967 19    LC 84-19696    ISBN 0821304232

**Sandbrook, Richard, D. Phil.**    **4.2614**
The politics of basic needs: urban aspects of assaulting poverty in Africa / Richard Sandbrook. — Toronto; Buffalo: University of Toronto Press, 1982. vi, 250 p.: ill.; 23 cm. — (Political economy of world poverty.) 1. Poor — Africa. 2. Urbanization — Africa. 3. Labor and laboring classes — Africa. 4. Social classes — Africa. 5. Basic needs — Africa. 6. Africa — Economic policy. 7. Africa — Social policy. I. T. II. Series.
HC800.Z9 P627 1982    339.4/6/096 19    LC 81-192977    ISBN 0802024289

**Tignor, Robert L.** 4.2615
State, private enterprise, and economic change in Egypt, 1918–1952 / Robert L. Tignor. — Princeton, N.J.: Princeton University Press, c1984. xvi, 317 p.; 23 cm. — (Princeton studies on the Near East.) Includes index. 1. Investments — Egypt — History — 20th century. 2. Middle classes — Egypt — History — 20th century. 3. Egypt — Economic conditions — 1918- 4. Egypt — Industries — Finance — History — 20th century. I. T. II. Series.
HC830.T54 1984    338.962 19    *LC* 83-43097    *ISBN* 0691054169

**Waterbury, John.** 4.2616
The Egypt of Nasser and Sadat: the political economy of two regimes / John Waterbury. — Princeton, N.J.: Princeton University Press, c1983. xxiv, 475 p.: ill.; 24 cm. — (Princeton studies on the Near East.) Includes index. 1. Egypt — Economic policy — 1952- 2. Egypt — Politics and government — 1952- I. T. II. Series.
HC830.W37 1983    338.962 19    *LC* 82-61393    *ISBN* 0691076502

**Ethiopia. Relief and Rehabilitation Commission.** 4.2617
The challenges of drought: Ethiopia's decade of struggle in relief and rehabilitation. — Addis Ababa: Relief and Rehabilitation Commission, 1985. 280 p.: ill. (some col.); 25 cm. Includes index. 1. Droughts — Ethiopia. 2. Ethiopia. Relief and Rehabilitation Commission. 3. Famines — Ethiopia. 4. Disaster relief — Ethiopia. 5. Food relief — Ethiopia. I. T.
HC845.Z9 F335 1985    363.8/83/0963 19    *LC* 86-980251    *ISBN* 0946825017

**Hancock, Graham.** 4.2618
Ethiopia: the challenge of hunger / by Graham Hancock. — London: V. Gollancz, 1985. 127, [1] p.: ill.; 22 cm. 1. Food supply — Ethiopia. 2. Ethiopia — Famines. I. T.
HC845.Z9 F345 1985    363.8/83/0963 19    *LC* 85-170257    *ISBN* 057503680X

**Coulson, Andrew.** 4.2619
Tanzania: a political economy / by Andrew Coulson. — Oxford [Oxfordshire]: Clarendon Press; New York: Oxford University Press, 1982. xiv, 394 p.: maps; 22 cm. Includes index. 1. Tanzania — Economic conditions I. T.
HC885.C68 1982    330.9678 19    *LC* 81-14034    *ISBN* 0198282923

**Nattrass, Jill.** 4.2620
The South African economy: its growth and change / Jill Nattrass. — Cape Town: Oxford University Press, 1981. xx, 328 p.: ill.; 22 cm. Includes index. 1. South Africa — Economic conditions I. T.
HC905.N37    330.968/063 19    *LC* 81-190222    *ISBN* 0195701941

**Asante, S. K. B.** 4.2621
The political economy of regionalism in Africa: a decade of the Economic Community of West African States (ECOWAS) / S.K.B. Asante. — New York: Praeger, 1985. p. cm. Includes index. 1. Economic Community of West African States — History. 2. Africa, West — Economic integration — History. I. T.
HC1000.A86 1985    337.1/66 19    *LC* 85-16740    *ISBN* 003005902X

**Rimmer, Douglas.** 4.2622
The economies of West Africa / Douglas Rimmer. — New York: St. Martin's Press, 1984. xii, 308 p.: ill.; 23 cm. Includes index. 1. Africa, West — Economic conditions — 1960 2. Africa, West — Economic policy. I. T.
HC1000.R56 1984    330.966 19    *LC* 83-40604    *ISBN* 0312236743

**The Political economy of Ivory Coast / edited by I. William** 4.2623
**Zartman and Christopher Delgado.**
New York: Praeger, 1984. vii, 255 p., [1] leaf of plates: map; 25 cm. — (SAIS study on Africa.) Includes index. 1. Ivory Coast — Economic conditions — 1960- — Addresses, essays, lectures. 2. Ivory Coast — Economic policy — Addresses, essays, lectures. I. Zartman, I. William. II. Delgado, Christopher L. III. Series.
HC1025.P64 1984    330.9666/805 19    *LC* 84-1998    *ISBN* 0030640970

**First things first: meeting the basic needs of the people of** 4.2624
**Nigeria: report to the Government of Nigeria / by a JASPA**
**basic needs mission.**
Addis Ababa: International Labour Office, Jobs and Skiils Programme for Africa, 1981. x, 256 p.; 24 cm. 1. Nigeria — Economic conditions — 1970- 2. Nigeria — Social conditions — 1960- 3. Nigeria — Economic policy. 4. Nigeria — Social policy. I. Jobs and Skills Programme for Africa.
HC1055.F57 1981    338.9669 19    *LC* 82-980553    *ISBN* 9221026825

**Kirk-Greene, A. H. M. (Anthony Hamilton Millard)** 4.2625
Nigeria since 1970: a political and economic outline / Anthony Kirk–Greene and Douglas Rimmer. — New York: Africana Publishing Co., 1981. xii, 161 p.: map; 24 cm. 1. Nigeria — Politics and government — 1975- 2. Nigeria — Economic conditions — 1970- 3. Nigeria — Politics and government — 1960-1975 I. Rimmer, Douglas. II. T.
HC1055.K56    330/.9669/05    *LC* 81-3609    *ISBN* 0841907218

**Nafziger, E. Wayne.** 4.2626
The economics of political instability: the Nigerian–Biafran war / E. Wayne Nafziger. — Boulder, Colo.: Westview Press, 1983. xi, 251 p.; 23 cm. — (Westview replica edition) 1. Political stability — Nigeria — History. 2. Nigeria — Politics and government — 1960-1975 3. Nigeria — History — Civil War, 1967-1970 4. Nigeria — Economic conditions — 1960- I. T.
HC1055.N33 1983    330.9669/05 19    *LC* 82-20044    *ISBN* 0865319324

# HD19–91 PRODUCTION

**Cases in operations research / edited by Christoph Haehling von** 4.2627
**Lanzenauer.**
London [Ont.]: Research and Publication Division, School of Business Administration, University of Western Ontario, c1975. xi, 194 p.: ill.; 23 cm. 1. Operations research — Case studies. 2. Industrial management — Case studies. I. Haehling von Lanzenauer, Christoph.
HD20.5.C37    658.4/034    *LC* 76-362790

**Kaufmann, A. (Arnold), 1911-.** • 4.2628
[Invitation à la recherche opérationnelle. English] Introduction to operations research / [by] A. Kaufmann [and] R. Faure; translated by Henry C. Sneyd. — New York: Academic Press, 1968. xi, 300 p.: ill.; 24 cm. (Mathematics in science and engineering. v. 47) Translation of Invitation à la recherche opérationnelle. 1. Operations research 2. Industrial management — Research. I. Faure, Robert. joint author. II. T. III. Series.
HD20.5.K313 1968    658.4    *LC* 67-23162

**Wagner, Harvey M.** 4.2629
Principles of operations research: with applications to managerial decisions / Harvey M. Wagner. — 2d ed. — Englewood Cliffs, N.J.: Prentice-Hall, [1975] xii, 1039 p.: ill.; 25 cm. Includes indexes. 1. Operations research I. T.
HD20.5.W34 1975    001.4/24    *LC* 74-29418    *ISBN* 0137095929

**Classics in scientific management: a book of readings / [edited** 4.2630
**by] Donald Del Mar, Rodger D. Collons.**
University: University of Alabama Press, c1976. xiii, 443 p.; 27 cm. 'The materials for this volume come primarily from ... the Taylor Society bulletins.' 1. Industrial management — Addresses, essays, lectures. 2. Industrial management — United States — Addresses, essays, lectures. I. Del Mar, Donald. II. Collons, Rodger D. III. Taylor Society. Bulletin.
HD21.C64    658.4    *LC* 75-20471    *ISBN* 0817387013

**Drucker, Peter Ferdinand, 1909-.** • 4.2631
The new society: the anatomy of the industrial order. — [1st ed.]. — New York: Harper, [1950] ix, 356 p.; 22 cm. 1. Industry 2. Industrial relations I. T.
HD21.D7    331    *LC* 50-7722

**Kerr, Clark, 1911-.** • 4.2632
Industrialism and industrial man: the problems of labor and management in economic growth, by Clark Kerr [and others. 2d ed.] New York, Oxford University Press, 1964. 263 p. 20 cm. (A Galaxy book) 'GB107.' Bibliographical references included in 'Notes' (p. 251-258) 1. Industrialization 2. Industrial relations I. T.
HD21.K45 1964    338.9    *LC* 64-10063

# HD28–70 Industrial Organization. Industrial Management

**Nystrom, Paul C.** 4.2633
Handbook of organizational design / edited by Paul C. Nystrom and William H. Starbuck. — Oxford; New York: Oxford University Press, 1981. 2 v.: ill.; 25 cm. 1. Organization — Collected works. I. Starbuck, William H., 1934- II. T.
HD30.H24 1981    658.4/02    *LC* 80-40191    *ISBN* 0198272413

**Merrill, Harwood Ferry, 1904- ed.** • 4.2634
Classics in management. Edited by Harwood F. Merrill. — Rev. ed. — [New York]: American Management Association, [1970] xiv, 495 p.; 24 cm. 1. Industrial management — Collections. I. T.
HD30.M45 1970    658/.008    *LC* 74-111466    *ISBN* 0814452310

**Heyel, Carl, 1908-.** 4.2635
The Encyclopedia of management / edited by Carl Heyel. — 3rd ed. — New York: Van Nostrand Reinhold Co., c1982. xxx, 1371 p.: ill.; 26 cm. 1. Industrial management — Dictionaries. I. T.
HD30.15.E49 1982 658/.003/21 19 *LC* 81-16467 *ISBN* 0442251653

**Alter, Steven.** 4.2636
Decision support systems: current practice and continuing challenges / Steven Alter. — Reading, Mass.: Addison-Wesley Pub., c1980. xvi, 316 p.: ill.; 24 cm. — (Addison-Wesley series on decision support.) Includes index. 1. Decision support systems I. T. II. Series.
HD30.23.A44 658.4/03 *LC* 78-67690 *ISBN* 0201001934

**Keen, Peter G. W.** 4.2637
Decision support systems: an organizational perspective / Peter G. W. Keen, Michael S. Scott Morton. — Reading, Mass.: Addison-Wesley Pub. Co., c1978. xv, 264 p.: ill.; 25 cm. — (Addison-Wesley series on decision support.) Includes index. 1. Decision support systems I. Scott Morton, Michael S. joint author. II. T. III. Series.
HD30.23.K35 658.4/03 *LC* 77-90176 *ISBN* 0201036673

**Steiner, George Albert, 1912-.** 4.2638
Strategic planning: what every manager must know / George A. Steiner. — New York: Free Press, c1979. ix, 383 p.: ill.; 24 cm. 1. Strategic planning I. T.
HD30.28.S72 1979 658.4/01 *LC* 78-20647 *ISBN* 0029311101

**The Strategic management handbook / Kenneth J. Albert, editor** 4.2639
**in chief.**
New York: McGraw-Hill, c1983. 546 p. in various pagings: ill.; 24 cm. Includes index. 1. Corporate planning 2. Management I. Albert, Kenneth J., 1943-
HD30.28.S732 1983 658.4/01 19 *LC* 82-17110 *ISBN* 0070009546

**Aggarwal, Raj.** 4.2640
Management science: cases and applications / Raj Aggarwal, Inder Khera. — San Francisco: Holden-Day, c1979. xiii, 229 p.: ill.; 23 cm. 1. Industrial management — Case studies. 2. Operations research I. Khera, Inder. joint author. II. T.
HD31.A34 658 *LC* 79-65492 *ISBN* 0816200963

**Barnard, Chester Irving, 1886-1961.** • 4.2641
The functions of the executive. — Cambridge: Harvard University Press, 1968. xxxvi, 334 p.; 22 cm. 'Thirtieth anniversary edition, with an introduction by Kenneth R. Andrews.' 1. Executives 2. Management 3. Industrial sociology I. T.
HD31.B36 1968 658.42 *LC* 68-28690

**Blau, Peter Michael.** • 4.2642
Formal organizations: a comparative approach / by Peter M. Blau and W. Richard Scott. — San Francisco: Chandler Pub. Co. [1962] 312 p.; 22 cm. (Chandler publications in anthropology) 1. Comparative organization 2. Associations, institutions, etc. I. Scott, W. Richard. joint author. II. T.
HD31.B53 301.4 *LC* 61-17328

**Boulding, Kenneth Ewart, 1910-.** • 4.2643
Linear programming and the theory of the firm [by] Kenneth E. Boulding and W. Allen Spivey, with contributions by Sherrill Cleland [and others] New York, Macmillan [1960] 227 p. ill. 1. Linear programming 2. Industrial management — Mathematical models I. Spivey, W. Allen. II. T.
HD31 B63 *LC* 60-7415

**Caplow, Theodore.** 4.2644
Managing an organization / Theodore Caplow. — 2nd ed. — New York: Holt, Rinehart, and Winston, c1983. vi, 206 p.; 25 cm. Rev. ed. of: How to run any organization. 1st ed. c1976. 1. Management 2. Organization I. T.
HD31.C343 1983 658.4 19 *LC* 83-30 *ISBN* 0030585783

**Classics of organization theory / edited by Jay M. Shafritz,** 4.2645
**Philip H. Whitbeck.**
1st ed. — Oak Park, Ill.: Moore Pub. Co., c1978. xi, 323 p.: ill.; 23 cm. 1. Organization — Addresses, essays, lectures. 2. Management — Addresses, essays, lectures. I. Shafritz, Jay M. II. Whitbeck, Philip H.
HD31.C56 658.4 *LC* 78-27098

**Dalton, Melville.** 4.2646
Men who manage: fusions of feeling and theory in administration / [one of a series of books from the research program of the Institute of Industrial Relations, University of California]. — New York: Wiley [1966, c1959] x, 318 p.: ill.; 24 cm. 1. Industrial management I. T.
HD31.D2 658 *LC* 59-9342

**Drucker, Peter Ferdinand, 1909-.** 4.2647
Management: tasks, responsibilities, practices [by] Peter F. Drucker. — [1st ed.]. — New York: Harper & Row, [1974] xvi, 839 p.; 24 cm. 1. Management I. T.
HD31.D773 1974 658.4 *LC* 72-79655 *ISBN* 0060110929

**Fayol, Henri, 1841-1925.** 4.2648
[Administration industrielle et générale. English] General and industrial management / Henri Fayol; revised by Irwin Gray. — Rev. ed. — New York: Institute of Electrical and Electronics Engineers, c1984. xii, 112 p.; 25 cm. Translation of: Administration industrielle et générale. 'Published under the sponsorship of the IEEE Engineering Management Society.' Includes index. 1. Industrial management 2. Management I. Gray, Irwin. II. T.
HD31.F313 1984 658 19 *LC* 84-10747 *ISBN* 0879421789

**Gouldner, Alvin Ward, 1920-.** • 4.2649
Patterns of industrial bureaucracy. — Glencoe, Ill.: Free Press, [1954] 282 p.; 22 cm. 1. Industrial management 2. Bureaucracy I. T.
HD31.G68 658.01 *LC* 54-8152

**Holt, Charles C.** 4.2650
Planning production, inventories, and work force [by] Charles C. Holt [and others] with contributions by Charles P. Bonini [and] Peter R. Winters. Englewood Cliffs, N.J., Prentice-Hall, 1960. 419 p. ill. (Prentice-Hall International series in management) 1. Production control 2. Inventories 3. Industrial management I. T.
HD31 H62 *LC* 60-16849

**Kast, Fremont Ellsworth, 1926-.** 4.2651
Organization and management: a systems approach [by] Fremont E. Kast [and] James E. Rosenzweig. — 2d ed. — New York: McGraw-Hill, [1974] xiv, 655 p.: illus.; 24 cm. — (McGraw-Hill series in management) 1. Organization 2. Management I. Rosenzweig, James Erwin, 1929- joint author. II. T.
HD31.K33 1974 658.4 *LC* 73-13550 *ISBN* 0070333505

**Kay, Neil M.** 4.2652
The evolving firm: strategy and structure in industrial organization / Neil M. Kay. — New York: St. Martin's Press, 1982. xii, 174 p.: ill.; 23 cm. Includes index. 1. Industrial organization 2. Industrial management 3. Industrial management I. T.
HD31.K35 1982 658.4/02 19 *LC* 81-21436 *ISBN* 0312273169

**Likert, Rensis, 1903-.** 4.2653
New patterns of management. New York: McGraw-Hill, 1961. 270 p.: ill. 1. Industrial management I. T.
HD31 L43 *LC* 61-13167

**Management classics / edited by Michael T. Matteson, John M.** 4.2654
**Ivancevich.**
3rd ed. — Plano, Tex.: Business Publications, 1986. xiii, 430 p.: ill.; 24 cm. 1. Management 2. Industrial management I. Matteson, Michael T. II. Ivancevich, John M.
HD31.M2917 1986 658 19 *LC* 85-71479 *ISBN* 0256034494

**March, James G.** • 4.2655
Organizations, by James G. March and Herbert A. Simon with the collaboration of Harold Guetzkow. — New York: Wiley, [1958] 262 p.: illus.; 24 cm. 1. Organization I. Simon, Herbert Alexander, 1916- joint author. II. T.
HD31.M298 658.01 *LC* 58-13464

**Melman, Seymour.** 4.2656
Dynamic factors in industrial productivity. — New York, Wiley, 1956. 238 p. illus. 23 cm. 1. Industrial management I. T.
HD31.M396 338.01 *LC* 56-4342

**Pugh, Derek Salman.** 4.2657
Organization theory: selected readings / edited by D.S. Pugh. — 2nd ed. — Harmondsworth: Penguin, 1984. 447 p.: ill.; 20 cm. — (Penguin Education.) 1. Organization — Addresses, essays, lectures. 2. Management — Addresses, essays, lecture. 3. Psychology, Industrial — Addresses, essays, lectures. I. T. II. Series.
HD31.O754 1985 302.3/5 19 *ISBN* 014080627X

**Selznick, Philip, 1919-.** 4.2658
Leadership in administration: a sociological interpretation. — Evanston, Ill.: Row, Peterson, [1957] 162 p. 1. Leadership 2. Executives I. T.
HD31 S37 *LC* 57-11350

**Shore, Barry.** 4.2659
Operations management. — New York: McGraw-Hill, [1973] xvi, 550 p.: illus.; 24 cm. — (McGraw-Hill series in management) (Management series) 1. Management 2. Operations research I. T.
HD31.S46 658.4 *LC* 72-10047 *ISBN* 0070570450

**Simon, Herbert Alexander, 1916-.** 4.2660
Administrative behavior: a study of decision–making processes in administrative organization / Herbert A Simon; with a foreword by Chester I. Barnard. — 3d ed. / with new introd. — New York: Free Press, c1976. L, 364 p.; 21 cm. 1. Management 2. Decision-making I. T.
HD31.S55 1976    HD31 S55 1976.    658.4    LC 75-18009    ISBN 0029289718

**Williamson, Oliver E.** 4.2661
Markets and hierarchies, analysis and antitrust implications: a study in the economics of internal organization / Oliver E. Williamson. — New York: Free Press, [1975] xvii, 286 p.: ill.; 25 cm. Includes index. 1. Industrial organization 2. Industrial management 3. Trusts, Industrial I. T.
HD31.W5173    658.4/02    LC 74-27597    ISBN 0029353602

**Woodward, Joan, M.A.** 4.2662
Industrial organization: theory and practice. — London: Oxford University Press, 1965. xii, 281 p.: ill. 1. Industrial management I. T.
HD31 W64    LC 65-6145

**Crozier, Michel.** • 4.2663
The bureaucratic phenomenon / [Translated by the author. — Chicago]: University of Chicago Press [1964] x, 320 p.: ill.; 25 cm. Bibliographical footnotes. 1. Industrial management 2. Bureaucracy I. T.
HD33.C742    658    LC 63-20916

## HD38–69 Special Aspects

**Cyert, Richard Michael, 1921-.** • 4.2664
A behavioral theory of the firm / [by] Richard M. Cyert [and] James G. March; with contributions by G. P. E. Clarkson [and others]. — Englewood Cliffs, N.J.: Prentice-Hall, 1963. 332 p.: ill.; 24 cm. — (Prentice-Hall international series in management) (Prentice-Hall behavioral sciences in business series.) 1. Industrial management — Mathematical models 2. Decision-making — Mathematical models I. March, James G. joint author. II. T.
HD38.C9    658.018    LC 63-13294

**Kepner, Charles Higgins, 1922-.** 4.2665
The rational manager; a systematic approach to problem solving and decision making [by] Charles H. Kepner [and] Benjamin B. Tregoe. Edited with an introd. by Perrin Stryker. New York, McGraw-Hill [1965] vi, 275 p. illus. (part col.) 21 cm. 1. Management 2. Problem solving 3. Decision-making I. Tregoe, Benjamin B. joint author. II. T.
HD38.K44    658.4/03 19    LC 65-21586

**Lawrence, Paul R.** 4.2666
Organization and environment: managing differentiation and integration / [by] Paul R. Lawrence and Jay W. Lorsch; with the research assistance of James S. Garrison. — Boston: Division of Research, Graduate School of Business Administration, Harvard University, 1967. xv, 279 p.: ill.; 22 cm. 1. Organizational effectiveness — Case studies. 2. Organizational behavior — Case studies. 3. Management — Case studies. I. Lorsch, Jay William. joint author. II. T.
HD38.L36 1967    658.4/02 19    LC 67-30338

**Lorsch, Jay William.** 4.2667
Organizations and their members: a contingency approach [by] Jay W. Lorsch [and] John J. Morse. — New York: Harper & Row, [1974] x, 177 p.: illus.; 25 cm. — (Harper & Row's series in organization and management) 1. Industrial organization — Case studies. I. Morse, John J., joint author. II. T.
HD38.L582    301.18/32    LC 74-8622    ISBN 0060440449

**Mintzberg, Henry.** 4.2668
Power in and around organizations / Henry Mintzberg. — Englewood Cliffs, N.J.: Prentice-Hall, c1983. xix, 700 p.: ill.; 24 cm. — (The Theory of management policy series) Includes index. 1. Organization 2. Power (Social sciences) 3. Corporations — United States I. T.
HD38.M4865 1983    302.3/5 19    LC 82-12296    ISBN 0136868576

**Schlaifer, Robert.** • 4.2669
Probability and statistics for business decisions; an introduction to managerial economics under uncertainty. New York, McGraw-Hill, 1959. 732 p. illus. 24 cm. 1. Industrial management — Decision making — Mathematical models. 2. Statistical decision 3. Probabilities I. T.
HD38.S35    658.4/03 19    LC 58-13017

**Thompson, James D.** • 4.2670
Organizations in action: social science bases of administrative theory / James D. Thompson. — New York: McGraw-Hill, 1967. xi, 192 p.; 23 cm. — 1. Industrial organization I. T.
HD38.T448    658.1/1    LC 67-11564    ISBN 0070643806

**Ginzberg, Eli, 1911-.** 4.2671
Beyond human scale: the large corporation at risk / Eli Ginzberg and George Vojta. — New York: Basic Books, c1985. xi, 242 p.; 22 cm. Includes index. 1. Executives — United States. 2. Corporations — United States 3. Employee morale — United States. 4. Personnel management — United States. I. Vojta, George. II. T.
HD38.25.U6 G59 1985    658.4 19    LC 84-45317    ISBN 0465006582

**Jackson, P. M. (Peter McLeod)** 4.2672
The political economy of bureaucracy / P.M. Jackson. — Totowa, N.J.: Barnes & Noble Books, 1983. viii, 295 p.: ill.; 25 cm. Includes index. 1. Bureaucracy I. T.
HD38.4.J32 1983    350/.001 19    LC 82-22674    ISBN 0389203521

**Silver, Edward A. (Edward Allen), 1937-.** 4.2673
Decision systems for inventory management and production planning / Edward A. Silver, Rein Peterson. — 2nd ed. — New York: Wiley, c1985. xxiii, 722 p.: ill.; 24 cm. — (Wiley series in production/operations management.) Peterson's name appears first on the earlier edition. 1. Inventory control — Decision making. 2. Production planning — Decision making. I. Peterson, Rein, 1937- II. T. III. Series.
HD40.P48 1985    658.7/87 19    LC 84-15179    ISBN 0471867829

**Porter, Michael E., 1947-.** 4.2674
Competitive advantage: creating and sustaining superior performance / Michael E. Porter. — New York: Free Press; London: Collier Macmillan, c1985. xviii, 557 p.: ill.; 25 cm. Includes index. 1. Competition 2. Industrial management I. T.
HD41.P668 1985    658 19    LC 83-49518    ISBN 0029250900

**Porter, Michael E., 1947-.** 4.2675
Competitive strategy: techniques for analyzing industries and competitors / Michael E. Porter. — New York: Free Press, c1980. xx, 396 p.: ill.; 25 cm. Includes index. 1. Competition 2. Industrial management I. T.
HD41.P67 1980    658 19    LC 80-65200    ISBN 0029253608

**Telser, Lester G., 1931-.** 4.2676
Competition, collusion, and game theory [by] Lester G. Telser. — Chicago: AldineAtherton, [1972] xix, 380 p.: illus.; 25 cm. — (Aldine treatises in modern economics) 1. Competition — Mathematical models. 2. Prices — Mathematical models. I. T.
HD41.T4    338.6/048    LC 70-141426    ISBN 0202060438

**Little, Ian Malcolm David.** 4.2677
Project appraisal and planning for developing countries, by I. M. D. Little and J. A. Mirrlees. — New York: Basic Books, [1974] xii, 388 p.; 23 cm. 1. Cost effectiveness 2. Capital investments 3. Capital — Accounting I. Mirrlees, James A., joint author. II. T.
HD47.L49    309.2/12/091724    LC 73-91075    ISBN 0465064124

**Braverman, Harry.** 4.2678
Labor and monopoly capital; the degradation of work in the twentieth century. Foreword by Paul M. Sweezy. — New York: Monthly Review Press, c1974. xiii, 465 p.; 21 cm. 1. Division of labor — History. 2. Machinery in industry — History. 3. Industrial management — History. I. T.
HD51.B7 1975    HD51 B7.    331/.09/04    LC 74-7785    ISBN 0853453403

**Durkheim, Emile, 1858-1917.** • 4.2679
[De la division du travail social. English] The division of labor in society. / by Emile Durkheim; translated from the French by George Simpson. — Glencoe, Ill.: Free Press, 1947. xxiv, 439 p.; 22 cm. Translation of De la division du travail social, including a translation of the preface to the 2d ed., 1902, Quelques remarques sur les groupements professionnels. 1. Division of labor I. T. II. Title: De la division du travail social. English
HD51.D962

## HD52–55 Industrial Equipment. Inventory Policy

**Buchan, Joseph.** • 4.2680
Scientific inventory management / Joseph Buchan, Ernest Koenigsberg. — Englewood Cliffs, N.J.: Prentice-Hall, 1963. 523 p.: ill. 1. Inventories — Mathematical models. I. Koenigsberg, Ernest. joint author. II. T.
HD55.B8    LC 63-9168

**Lewis, C. D. (Colin David)** 4.2681
Demand analysis and inventory control / Colin D. Lewis. — Farnborough, Hants: Saxon House; Lexington, Mass.: Lexington Books, 1975. xv, 234 p.: ill.; 24 cm. Includes index. 1. Inventory control — Mathematical models. 2. Supply and demand — Mathematical models. I. T.
HD55.L49    658.7/87    LC 75-312834    ISBN 0347010385

**Naddor, Eliezer.**      **4.2682**
Inventory systems / Eliezer Naddor. — New York: Wiley, 1966. xiv, 341 p.: ill.; 24 cm. Includes index. 1. Inventories I. T.
HD55.N3     658.154     *LC* 65-26850     *ISBN* 0471628301

## HD56–57 Industrial Productivity

**Kendrick, John W.**      **4.2683**
Understanding productivity: an introduction to the dynamics of productivity change / John W. Kendrick. — Baltimore: Johns Hopkins University Press, c1977. vii, 141 p.; 21 cm. — (Policy studies in employment and welfare; no. 31) Includes index. 1. Industrial productivity 2. Industrial productivity — United States. I. T.
HD56.K46     338/.0973     *LC* 77-4786     *ISBN* 0801819962

**Guzzo, Richard A.**      **4.2684**
A guide to worker productivity experiments in the United States, 1976–81 / Richard A. Guzzo, Jeffrey S. Bondy. — New York: Pergamon Press, c1983. xi, 161 p.; 23 cm. Includes indexes. 1. Labor productivity — United States. I. Bondy, Jeffrey S. (Jeffrey Stefan), 1955- II. T.
HD57.G88 1983     331.11/8/0973 19     *LC* 82-13248     *ISBN* 0080295487

**Katzell, Raymond A., 1919-.**      **4.2685**
A guide to worker productivity experiments in the United States, 1971–75: prepared for Work in America Institute, inc., Scarsdale, New York / by Raymond A. Katzell, Penney Bienstock, Paul H. Faerstein. — 1st ed. — New York: New York University Press, 1977. v, 186 p.; 24 cm. 1. Labor productivity — Research — United States. I. Bienstock, Penney, joint author. II. Faerstein, Paul H., joint author. III. Work in America Institute. IV. T. V. Title: Guide to worker productivity experiments in the United States ...
HD57.K337     331.1/18/072073     *LC* 77-368638     *ISBN* 0814745660. *ISBN* 0814745679 pbk

**Salter, W. E. G.**      • **4.2686**
Productivity and technical change, by W. E. G. Salter. — 2nd ed. with an addendum by W. B. Reddaway. — Cambridge: Cambridge U.P., 1966. xiv, 220 p.: tables, diagrs.; 25 cm. — (Cambridge. University. Department of Applied Economics. Monographs, 6) 1. Technological innovations 2. Labor productivity I. T. II. Series.
HD57.S34 1966     338.01     *LC* 66-29362

## HD57.7 Leadership

**Maccoby, Michael, 1933-.**      **4.2687**
The leader: a new face for American management / Michael Maccoby. — New York: Simon and Schuster, c1981. 284 p.; 23 cm. 1. Leadership 2. Organizational effectiveness I. T.
HD57.7.M32     658.4/092 19     *LC* 81-13536     *ISBN* 0671241230

## HD58 Location of Industry

**Estall, Robert C.**      • **4.2688**
Industrial activity and economic geography: a study of the forces behind the geographical location of productive activity in manufacturing industry / R.C. Estall and R. Ogilvie Buchanan. — London: Hutchinson University Library, 1961. 232 p.: maps; 19 cm. — (Geography) 1. Industry — Location I. Buchanan, Robert Ogilvie, 1894- II. T.
HD58.E8     *LC* 61-3844

**Isard, Walter.**      • **4.2689**
Location and space–economy; a general theory relating to industrial location, market areas, land use, trade, and urban structure. [Cambridge] Published jointly by the Technology Press of Massachusetts Institute of Technology and Wiley, New York [1956] 350 p. illus. 24 cm. ([Regional science studies, v. 1]) (Technology Press books in the social sciences.) 1. Industry — Location I. T.
HD58.I7     338     *LC* 56-11026

**Isard, Walter.**      • **4.2690**
Methods of regional analysis; an introduction to regional science, by Walter Isard in association with David F. Bramhall [and others. Cambridge] Published jointly by the Technology Press of the Massachusetts Institute of Technology and Wiley, New York [1960] 784 p. illus. 24 cm. (Regional science studies) 1. Industry — Location I. T.
HD58.I72     338.018     *LC* 60-11723

**Spatial analysis, industry, and the industrial environment:**      **4.2691**
**progress in research and applications** / edited by F.E. Ian Hamilton and G.J.R. Linge.
Chichester, Eng.; New York: Wiley, c1979- < c1983 >. v. < 1-3 > : ill.; 24 cm. 1. Industry — Location — Addresses, essays, lectures. 2. Manufactures — Addresses, essays, lectures. I. Hamilton, F. E. Ian. II. Linge, G. J. R.
HD58.S674     338.6/042     *LC* 78-10298     *ISBN* 0471997382

**Webber, Michael John.**      **4.2692**
Impact of uncertainty on location [by] Michael J. Webber. Canberra, Australian National University Press, 1972. xviii, 310 p. diagrs., graphs, maps, tables. 25 cm. 1. Industry — Location — Mathematical models. I. T.
HD58.W34 1972b     338/.09     *LC* 78-159392     *ISBN* 0708108156

## HD58.7–58.8 Organizational Behavior

**Argyris, Chris, 1923-.**      **4.2693**
Personality and organization: the conflict between system and the individual. — New York: Harper, [1957] 291 p.; 22 cm. 1. Organizational behavior 2. Interorganizational relations 3. Personnel management I. T.
HD58.7.A75 1957     658.3     *LC* 57-11116

**Classics of organizational behavior** / edited by Walter E.      **4.2694**
**Natemeyer.**
1st ed. — Oak Park, Ill.: Moore Pub. Co., c1978. x, 362 p.: ill.; 23 cm. 1. Organizational behavior — Addresses, essays, lectures. 2. Management — Addresses, essays, lectures. I. Natemeyer, Walter E.
HD58.7.C53     658.4     *LC* 78-26983

**Hersey, Paul.**      **4.2695**
Management of organizational behavior: utilizing human resources / Paul Hersey, Kenneth H. Blanchard. — 4th ed. — Englewood Cliffs, N.J.: Prentice-Hall, c1982. xviii, 343 p.: ill.; 23 cm. Includes index. 1. Organizational behavior 2. Management 3. Leadership I. Blanchard, Kenneth H. II. T.
HD58.7.H47 1982     658.3 19     *LC* 81-12097     *ISBN* 0135496187

**Kanter, Rosabeth Moss.**      **4.2696**
Men and women of the corporation / Rosabeth Moss Kanter. — New York: Basic Books, c1977. xv, 348 p.; 24 cm. Includes index. 1. Organizational behavior 2. Industrial organization 3. White collar workers 4. Women white collar workers I. T.
HD58.7.K36     301.18/32     *LC* 76-43464     *ISBN* 0465044522

**Mitroff, Ian I.**      **4.2697**
Stakeholders of the organizational mind / Ian I. Mitroff; foreword by Richard O. Mason. — 1st ed. — San Francisco: Jossey-Bass, 1983. xxv, 178 p.: ill.; 24 cm. — (Jossey-Bass management series.) (Jossey-Bass social and behavioral science series.) Includes index. 1. Organizational behavior 2. Management — Psychological aspects. I. T. II. Series. III. Series: Jossey-Bass social and behavioral science series.
HD58.7.M57 1983     658.4/001/9 19     *LC* 83-48161     *ISBN* 0875895808

**Mohr, Lawrence B.**      **4.2698**
Explaining organizational behavior / Lawrence B. Mohr. — 1st ed. — San Francisco: Jossey-Bass, 1982. xv, 260 p.; 24 cm. — (Jossey-Bass social and behavioral science series.) Includes indexes. 1. Organizational behavior 2. Organization I. T. II. Series.
HD58.7.M63 1982     302.3/5 19     *LC* 81-20747     *ISBN* 087589514X

**Schein, Edgar H.**      **4.2699**
Organizational culture and leadership / Edgar H. Schein. — 1st ed. — San Franciso: Jossey-Bass Publishers, 1985. xx, 358 p.; 24 cm. (A Joint publication in the Jossey-Bass management series and the Jossey-Bass social and behavioral science series) Includes index. 1. Corporate culture 2. Culture 3. Leadership I. T.
HD58.7.S33 1985     302.3/5 19     *LC* 84-43034     *ISBN* 0875896391

**Srivastva, Suresh, 1934-.**      **4.2700**
The executive mind / Suresh Srivastva and associates. — 1st ed. — San Francisco: Jossey-Bass, 1983. xxii, 344 p.: ill.; 24 cm. — (Jossey-Bass management series.) (Jossey-Bass social and behavioral science series.) Based on a symposium held at Case Western Reserve University in 1982. Includes index. 1. Organizational behavior — Congresses. 2. Executives — Congresses. 3. Thought and thinking — Congresses. I. T. II. Series. III. Series: Jossey-Bass social and behavioral science series.
HD58.7.S7 1983     658.4/09 19     *LC* 83-48165     *ISBN* 0875895840

**French, Wendell L., 1923-.**      **4.2701**
Organization development: behavioral science interventions for organization improvement / Wendell L. French, Cecil H. Bell, Jr. — 3rd ed. — Englewood Cliffs, N.J.: Prentice-Hall, c1984. xv, 347 p.: ill.; 23 cm. 1. Organizational change I. Bell, Cecil, 1935- II. T.
HD58.8.F76 1984     658.4/06 19     *LC* 83-24636     *ISBN* 0136416306

## HD59–60.5 Social Aspects. Social Responsibilities

**Bowen, Howard, 1908-.**                                    4.2702
Social responsibilities of the businessman; with a commentary by F. Ernest Johnson. [1st ed.] New York, Harper [1953] xii, 276 p. 22 cm. (Series on ethics and economic life) Bibliography: p. 261-270. 1. Industry — Social aspects I. T.
HD59.B68      658.01      *LC* 53-5434

**Bauer, Raymond Augustine, 1916-.**                          4.2703
The corporate social audit / by Raymond A. Bauer and Dan H. Fenn, Jr. — [New York]: Russell Sage Foundtion, 1972. vi, 102 p.; 24 cm. — (Social science frontiers, 5) 1. Industry — Social aspects 2. Corporations — Auditing I. Fenn, Dan Huntington, 1923- joint author. II. T. III. Series.
H31.S67 no. 5 HD60.B3x      300/.8 s 658.4/08      *LC* 72-83832      *ISBN* 0871541033

**Donaldson, Thomas, 1945-.**                                4.2704
Corporations and morality / Thomas Donaldson. — Englewood Cliffs, N.J.: Prentice-Hall, c1982. ix, 214 p.; 23 cm. 1. Industry — Social aspects I. T.
HD60.D66      658.4/08 19      *LC* 81-12035      *ISBN* 0131770144

**French, Peter A.**                                        4.2705
Collective and corporate responsibility / Peter A. French. — New York: Columbia University Press, 1984. xiv, 215 p.; 24 cm. Includes index. 1. Industry — Social aspects 2. Corporations — Corrupt practices 3. Business ethics 4. Social ethics 5. Criminal liability of juristic persons I. T.
HD60.F74 1984      658.4/08 19      *LC* 84-3226      *ISBN* 0231058365

**Preston, Lee E.**                                         4.2706
Private management and public policy: the principle of public responsibility / Lee E. Preston, James E. Post. — Englewood Cliffs, N.J.: Prentice-Hall, [1975] xv, 157 p.: ill.; 24 cm. (The Prentice-Hall series in economic institutions and social systems) 1. Industry — Social aspects 2. Industry — Social aspects — United States. I. Post, James E., joint author. II. T.
HD60.P73      658.4/08      *LC* 74-26551      *ISBN* 0137109881

**Chamberlain, Neil W.**                                    4.2707
The limits of corporate responsibility / [by] Neil W. Chamberlain. — New York: Basic Books, [1973] v, 236 p.; 24 cm. 1. Industry — Social aspects — United States. I. T.
HD60.5.U5 C473      301.5/5      *LC* 73-81035      *ISBN* 0465041159

**Chamberlain, Neil W.**                                    4.2708
Remaking American values: challenge to a business society / Neil W. Chamberlain. New York: Basic Books, c1977. ix, 193 p.; 22 cm. 1. Industry — Social aspects — United States. 2. Social values 3. Business enterprises — United States I. T.
HD60.5.U5 C475      658.4/08      *LC* 76-28754      *ISBN* 0465069061

**Chamberlain, Neil W.**                                    4.2709
Social strategy and corporate structure / Neil W. Chamberlain. — New York: Macmillan Pub. Co.; London: Collier Macmillian Pub., c1982. xi, 169 p.; 25 cm. — (Studies of the modern corporation.) 1. Industry — Social aspects — United States. 2. Corporations — Social aspects — United States. 3. Industrial organization — United States. 4. Industrial management — United States. I. T. II. Series.
HD60.5.U5 C476 1982      658.4/08 19      *LC* 81-67989      *ISBN* 0029058104

**Committee for Economic Development.**                      4.2710
Social responsibilities of business corporations: a statement on national policy by the Research and Policy Committee of the Committee for Economic Development, June 1971. — [New York, 1971] 74 p.; 28 cm. 1. Industry — Social aspects — U.S. I. T.
HD60.5.U5 C66      658.4/08/0973      *LC* 76-168378

**Heald, Morrell.**                                         • 4.2711
The social responsibilities of business, company, and community, 1900–1960. — Cleveland: Press of Case Western Reserve University, 1970. xix, 339 p.; 24 cm. 1. Industry — Social aspects — United States. I. T.
HD60.5.U5 H4      301.2/4      *LC* 75-84490      *ISBN* 0829501762

**Vogel, David, 1947-.**                                    4.2712
Lobbying the corporation: citizen challenges to business authority / David Vogel. — New York: Basic Books, c1978. xi, 270 p.; 24 cm. Includes index. 1. Industry — Social aspects — United States. 2. Corporations — United States I. T.
HD60.5.U5 V627      301.5/1      *LC* 78-54496      *ISBN* 0465041574

**Whistle blowing: Loyalty and dissent in the corporation** / edited    4.2713
with an introd. and conclusion by Alan F. Westin, with the assistance of Henry I. Kurtz and Albert Robbins.
New York: McGraw-Hill, c1981. x, 181 p.; 24 cm. Spinal title: Whistle-blowing. Sponsored by the Educational Fund for Individual Rights. 1. Whistle

blowing — United States — Congresses. I. Westin, Alan F. II. Kurtz, Henry I. III. Robbins, Albert. IV. Educational Fund for Individual Rights. V. Title: Whistle-blowing.
HD60.5.U5 W47      331/.01      *LC* 80-15800      *ISBN* 0070694834

## HD61 Risk in Industry

**Acceptable risk / Baruch Fischhoff ... [et al.].**        4.2714
Cambridge; New York: Cambridge University Press, 1981. xv, 185 p.: ill.; 24 cm. Includes index. 1. Risk 2. Risk management — Decision making. I. Fischhoff, Baruch, 1946-
HD61.A24      658 19      *LC* 81-9957      *ISBN* 0521241642

## HD62.2–62.8 Management of Special Enterprises

**The Family in business / Paul C. Rosenblatt ... [et al.].**      4.2715
1st ed. — San Francisco: Jossey-Bass Publishers, 1985. xxii, 321 p.; 24 cm. (A Joint publication in the Jossey-Bass management series and the Jossey-Bass social and behavioral science series) Includes indexes. 1. Family corporations — United States — Management. 2. Family corporations — United States — Psychological aspects. I. Rosenblatt, Paul C.
HD62.25.F36 1985      658/.045 19      *LC* 84-43033      *ISBN* 0875896405

**Functioning of the multinational corporation: a global**      4.2716
**comparative study** / edited by Anant R. Negandhi.
New York: Pergamon Press, c1980. ix, 294 p.: ill.; 24 cm. — (Pergamon policy studies on business) 1. International business enterprises — Management — Addresses, essays, lectures. 2. Comparative management — Addresses, essays, lectures. I. Negandhi, Anant R. II. Series.
HD62.4.F86 1980      338.8/8      *LC* 79-27029      *ISBN* 0080250874

**Handbook of international business** / edited by Ingo Walter;      4.2717
**associate editor, Tracy Murray.**
New York: Wiley, 1982. 1 v. (various pagings) 'A Ronald Press publication.' Appendices ( ) A. Sources of information on international business / Betty Jane Punnett — B. A bibliography of international business / Thomas N. Gladwin. Includes index. 1. International business enterprises — Management — Handbooks, manuals, etc. I. Walter, Ingo. II. Murray, Tracy.
HD62.4.H36      658/.049 19      *LC* 81-21960      *ISBN* 0471079499

**Leontiades, James C.**                                    4.2718
Multinational corporate strategy: planning for world markets / James C. Leontiades. — Lexington, Mass.: Lexington Books, c1985. xxi, 228 p.: ill.; 24 cm. Includes index. 1. International business enterprises — Management. 2. Corporate planning I. T.
HD62.4.L46 1985      658.4/012 19      *LC* 83-48686      *ISBN* 0669073814

**Mason, R. Hal (Robert Hal), 1929-.**                      4.2719
The economics of international business [by] R. Hal Mason, Robert R. Miller [and] Dale R. Weigel. New York, Wiley [1975] xiv, 444 p. illus. 24 cm. (The Wiley series in management and administration) 1. International business enterprises — Management. 2. International economic relations I. Miller, Robert R., 1929- joint author. II. Weigel, Dale R., 1938- joint author. III. T.
HD62.4.M37 1975      658/.049 19      *LC* 74-18476      *ISBN* 0471575283

**Vernon, Raymond, 1913-.**                                 4.2720
The economic environment of international business / Raymond Vernon, Louis T. Wells, Jr. — 4th ed. — Englewood Cliffs, N.J.: Prentice-Hall, c1986. viii, 225 p.: ill.; 23 cm. 1. International business enterprises — Management. 2. International economic relations I. Wells, Louis T. II. T.
HD62.4.V47 1986      658/.049 19      *LC* 85-25584      *ISBN* 0132243873

**Killing, J. Peter.**                                      4.2721
Strategies for joint venture success / J. Peter Killing. — [New York]: Praeger, 1983. 133 p.: ill.; 23 cm. Includes index. 1. Joint ventures — Management. 2. International business enterprises — Management. I. T.
HD62.47.K54 1983      658.1/8 19      *LC* 83-13923      *ISBN* 0030639719

**Crimmins, James C.**                                      4.2722
Enterprise in the nonprofit sector / James C. Crimmins and Mary Keil. — Washington, D.C.: Partners for Livable Places; New York: Rockefeller Bros. Fund, c1983. 141 p.; 22 cm. 1. Corporations, Nonprofit — United States — Management. I. T.
HD62.6.C74 1983      658/.048 19      *LC* 83-60521      *ISBN* 0941182037

**Young, Dennis R., 1943-.**                                4.2723
If not for profit, for what?: a behavioral theory of the nonprofit sector based on entrepreneurship / Dennis R. Young. — Lexington, Mass.: LexingtonBooks, c1983. xvii, 170 p.; 24 cm. 1. Corporations, Nonprofit — United States — Management. 2. Entrepreneurship I. T.
HD62.6.Y68 1983      302.3/5 19      *LC* 82-48482      *ISBN* 0669061549

## HD66 Work Groups. Team Work

**Thompson, Philip C.**     **4.2724**
Quality circles: how to make them work in America / Philip C. Thompson. — New York, N.Y.: AMACOM, c1982. viii, 198 p.: ill.; 22 cm. Includes index. 1. Quality circles — United States. I. T.
HD66.T48 1982     658.4/036 19     *LC* 82-4072     *ISBN* 0814457312

## HD69 Other Topics, A–Z

**Consultants and consulting organizations directory.**   **4.2725**
2nd ed. (1973)-   . — Detroit, Mich.: Gale Research Co., c1973-. v.; 29 cm. Triennial. 1. Business consultants — Directories. I. Wasserman, Paul. II. McLean, Janice W. III. Gale Research Company.
HD69.C6 C647     658.4/6/025     *LC* 82-642042

**Fabrycky, W. J. (Wolter J.), 1932-.**     **4.2726**
Economic decision analysis [by] W. J. Fabrycky [and] G. J. Thuesen. Englewood Cliffs, N.J., Prentice-Hall [1974] x, 390 p. illus. 25 cm. 1. Decision-making 2. Decision-making — Mathematical models 3. Capital investments I. Thuesen, G. J., 1938- joint author. II. T.
HD69.D4 F3     658.4/03     *LC* 73-13900     *ISBN* 0132232715

**Schlaifer, Robert.**      • **4.2727**
Analysis of decisions under uncertainty. — New York: McGraw-Hill, [1969] xvi, 729 p.: illus.; 26 cm. 1. Decision-making 2. Statistical decision 3. Probabilities I. T.
HD69.D4 S28     658.4     *LC* 69-19203

**Simon, Herbert Alexander, 1916-.**     **4.2728**
The new science of management decision / Herbert A. Simon. Rev. ed. — Englewood Cliffs, N.J.: Prentice-Hall, c1977. xi, 175 p.; 23 cm. Edition of 1965 published under title: The shape of automation for men and management. 1. Decision-making — Data processing 2. Industrial management — Data processing 3. Automation — Economic aspects I. T.
HD69.D4 S49 1977     658.4/03     *LC* 76-40414     *ISBN* 0136161448

**Fayerweather, John.**      • **4.2729**
The executive overseas: administrative attitudes and relationships in a foreign culture. — [Syracuse, N. Y.]: Syracuse University Press, [c1959] 195 p.: ill.; 24 cm. 1. Executives 2. International business enterprises 3. Mexico — Industries. I. T.
HD 69 F6 F28 1959     *LC* 59-11259

**Barnet, Richard J.**     **4.2730**
Global reach: the power of the multinational corporations / Richard J. Barnet, Ronald E. Müller. — New York: Simon and Schuster, [1974] 508 p.; 25 cm. 1. International business enterprises 2. Corporations, American I. Müller, Ronald E. joint author. II. T.
HD69.I7 B32     338.8/8     *LC* 74-2794     *ISBN* 0671218352

**Behrman, Jack N.**     **4.2731**
National interests and the multinational enterprise; tensions among the North Atlantic countries [by] Jack N. Behrman. — Englewood Cliffs, N.J.: Prentice-Hall, [1970] 194 p.; 23 cm. 1. International business enterprises 2. Corporations, American I. T.
HD69.I7 B42     338.8/8/091821     *LC* 79-112668     *ISBN* 0136097014

**Gladwin, Thomas N.**     **4.2732**
Multinationals under fire: lessons in the management of conflict / Thomas N. Gladwin, Ingo Walter. — New York: Wiley, c1980. xiv, 689 p.; 24 cm. 'A Wiley-Interscience publication.' 1. International business enterprises — Management. 2. International business enterprises — Social aspects 3. Conflict management I. Walter, Ingo. joint author. II. T.
HD69.I7 G54     658.1/8     *LC* 79-21741     *ISBN* 0471019690

**Kolde, Endel Jakob, 1917-.**     **4.2733**
The multinational company; behavioral and managerial analyses [by] E. J. Kolde. — Lexington, Mass.: Lexington Books, [1974] xix, 266 p.: illus.; 23 cm. 1. International business enterprises I. T.
HD69.I7 K65     658.1/8     *LC* 74-2136     *ISBN* 0669933511

**Nationalism and the multinational enterprise; legal, economic**   **4.2734**
**and managerial aspects. Edited by H. R. Hahlo, J. Graham**
**Smith [and] Richard W. Wright.**
Leiden: A. W. Sijthoff; Dobbs Ferry, N.Y.: Oceana Publications, 1973. x, 373 p.; 24 cm. Rev. and expanded versions of papers presented at an international conference held in Montreal in August, 1971. 1. International business enterprises — Addresses, essays, lectures. I. Hahlo, H. R. ed. II. Smith, John Graham, 1936- ed. III. Wright, Richard W. ed.
HD69.I7 N38 1973     658.1/8     *LC* 72-88928     *ISBN* 0379004771

**Stopford, John M.**     **4.2735**
Managing the multinational enterprise; organization of the firm and ownership of the subsidiaries [by] John M. Stopford and Louis T. Wells, Jr. — New York:

Basic Books, [1972] xvi, 223 p.: illus.; 25 cm. — (The Harvard multinational enterprise series) 1. International business enterprises I. Wells, Louis T. joint author. II. T. III. Series.
HD69.I7 S75     658.1/8     *LC* 72-76909     *ISBN* 0465043798

**United Nations. Dept. of Economic and Social Affairs.**   **4.2736**
Multinational corporations in world development. — New York: Praeger, [1974] xiv, 200 p.: illus.; 24 cm. — (Praeger special studies in international economics and development) 1. International business enterprises I. T.
HD69.I7 U45 1974     338.8/8     *LC* 73-18133

**Wilkins, Mira.**     **4.2737**
The maturing of multinational enterprise: American business abroad from 1914 to 1970. — Cambridge, Mass.: Harvard University Press, 1974. xvi, 590 p.; 24 cm. — (Harvard studies in business history. 27) 1. Corporations, American 2. International business enterprises I. T. II. Series.
HD69.I7 W49     338.8/8     *LC* 73-88499     *ISBN* 0674554752

**Gladwin, Thomas N.**     **4.2738**
Environment, planning, and the multinational corporation / by Thomas N. Gladwin; foreword by Maurice F. Strong. — Greenwich, Conn.: Jai Press, c1977. xix, 295 p.: ill.; 25 cm. — (Contemporary studies in economic and financial analysis. v. 8) An adaptation of the author's thesis, University of Michigan, 1975. Includes index. 1. Pollution 2. International business enterprises — Management. 3. Environmental protection 4. Corporate planning I. T. II. Series.
HD69.P6 G55 1977     301.31     *LC* 76-10400     *ISBN* 0892320141

## HD70 Industrial Management, by Country, A–Z

**Caves, Richard E.**     **4.2739**
Competition in the open economy: a model applied to Canada / Richard E. Caves, Michael E. Porter, A. Michael Spence, with John T. Scott. — Cambridge, Mass.: Harvard University Press, 1980. viii, 444 p.; 24 cm. (Harvard economic studies. 150) Includes index. 1. Industrial organization — Canada. 2. Competition, International I. Porter, Michael E., 1947- joint author. II. Spence, A. Michael (Andrew Michael) joint author. III. T. IV. Series.
HD70.C2 C38     338.8/0971 19     *LC* 79-23908     *ISBN* 0674154258

**Granick, David.**     **4.2740**
Enterprise guidance in Eastern Europe: a comparison of four socialist economies / David Granick. — Princeton, N.J.: Princeton University Press, c1975. xvi, 505 p.; 25 cm. 1. Industrial management — Europe, Eastern — Case studies. I. T.
HD70.E7 G68     658.4/00949     *LC* 75-2992     *ISBN* 0691042098

**Negandhi, Anant R.**     **4.2741**
The frightening angels: a study of U.S. multinationals in developing nations / Anant R. Negandhi, S. Benjamin Prasad. — [Kent, Ohio]: Kent State University Press, [1975] xix, 249 p.; ill.; 22 cm. Published in 1971 under title: Comparative management. Includes indexes. 1. Industrial management 2. Corporations, Foreign — Developing countries. 3. Subsidiary corporations — United States. 4. International business enterprises — Developing countries I. Prasad, S. Benjamin. joint author. II. T.
HD70.I4 N43 1975     658.1/8     *LC* 74-30491     *ISBN* 0873381696

**Ouchi, William G.**     **4.2742**
Theory Z: how American business can meet the Japanese challenge / William G. Ouchi. — Reading, Mass.: Addison-Wesley, c1981. xii, 283 p.; 25 cm. Includes index. 1. Industrial management — Japan 2. Industrial management — United States. I. T.
HD70.J3 O88     658.3 19     *LC* 81-8     *ISBN* 0201055244

**Berliner, Joseph S.**      • **4.2743**
Factory and manager in the USSR. — Cambridge: Harvard University Press, 1957. xv, 386 p.; 25 cm. — (Russian Research Center studies, 27) Bibliography: p. [337]-345. Bibliographical references included in 'Notes' (p. [347]-373) 1. Factories — Russia. 2. Factory management — Russia. I. T.
HD70.R9B4     658.5     *LC* 57-9068

**Granick, David.**      • **4.2744**
The Red executive; a study of the organization man in Russian industry. [1st ed.] Garden City, N.Y., Doubleday, 1960. 334 p. ill. 1. Executives — Russia 2. Industrial management — Russia I. T.
HD70 R9 G66     *LC* 60-5929

**Sharpe, Myron E. ed.**     **4.2745**
Planning, profit and incentives in the U. S. S. R. / edited by Myron E. Sharpe. — White Plains, N.Y.: International Arts & Sciences Press 1976. 2 v. 'The material in this collection first appeared in Problems of economics, a journal of translations from Soviet sources.' CONTENTS.-v.1. The Liberman discussion;

a new phase in Soviet economic thought.-v.2. Reform of Soviet economic management. Translated from the Russian. 1. Industrial management — Russia — Addresses, essays, lectures. 2. Profit — Addresses, essays, lectures. 3. Incentives in industry — Addresses, essays, lectures. I. Problems of economics. II. T.
HD70.R9P677      LC 66-20464

**Chandler, Alfred Dupont.**          • **4.2746**
Strategy and structure: chapters in the history of the industrial enterprise. — Cambridge: M.I.T. Press, 1962. xiv, 463 p.: diagrs.; 24 cm. (M.I.T. Press research monographs) 1. Industrial management — United States. 2. Industrial organization — United States. 3. Corporations — United States I. T.
HD70.U5 C5     658     LC 62-11990

**Drucker, Peter Ferdinand, 1909-.**          • **4.2747**
The practice of management. — [1st ed.]. — New York: Harper, [1954] 404 p.; 22 cm. 1. Industrial management — United States. I. T.
HD70.U5 D7     658     LC 54-8946

**Peters, Thomas J.**          **4.2748**
A passion for excellence: the leadership difference / Tom Peters, Nancy Austin. — New York: Random House, c1985. xxv, 437 p.; 25 cm. 1. Industrial management — United States. I. Austin, Nancy. II. T.
HD70.U5 P425 1985     658.4/092/0973 19     LC 84-45767     ISBN 0394544846

# HD72–89 Economic Growth, Development, Planning

(see also: HC59.7-60)

**Pioneers in development / Lord Bauer ... [et al.]; edited by**     **4.2749**
**Gerald M. Meier and Dudley Seers.**
New York: Published for the World Bank, Oxford University Press, 1984. x, 372 p.; 26 cm. 1. Economic development — Addresses, essays, lectures. I. Bauer, P. T. (Péter Tamás) II. Meier, Gerald M. III. Seers, Dudley.
HD74.P56 1984     338.9 19     LC 84-5775     ISBN 0195204522

**Cole, Sam.**          **4.2750**
Worlds apart: technology and North–South relations in the global economy / Sam Cole, Ian Miles. — Brighton, Sussex: Wheatsheaf Books; Totowa, N.J.: Rowman & Allanheld, 1984. xviii, 283 p.: ill.; 23 cm. 1. Economic development 2. Income distribution 3. Economic forecasting 4. International economic relations I. Miles, Ian. II. United Nations Institute for Training and Research. III. T.
HD75.C64 1984     337/.09/048 19     LC 84-125439     ISBN 0710807457

**Meier, Gerald M.**          **4.2751**
Emerging from poverty: the economics that really matters / Gerald M. Meier. — New York: Oxford University Press, 1984. ix, 258 p.; 24 cm. Includes index. 1. Economic development 2. Economic assistance 3. Developing countries I. T.
HD75.M44 1984     338.9/009172/4 19     LC 84-4441     ISBN 0195033744

**Rees, Albert, 1921-.**          **4.2752**
Striking a balance: making national economic policy / Albert Rees. — Chicago: University of Chicago Press, 1984. x, 118 p.: ill.; 23 cm. 1. Economic policy 2. United States — Economic policy I. T.
HD75.R43 1984     338.973 19     LC 83-17881     ISBN 0226707075

**Sylos Labini, Paolo.**          **4.2753**
The forces of economic growth and decline / Paolo Sylos–Labini. — Cambridge, Mass.: MIT Press, c1984. xiv, 253 p.; 24 cm. 1. Economic development — Addresses, essays, lectures. 2. Technological innovations — Addresses, essays, lectures. 3. Industrial organization (Economic theory) — Addresses, essays, lectures. 4. Income distribution — Addresses, essays, lectures. I. T.
HD75.S95 1984     338.9 19     LC 84-9699     ISBN 0262192241

**Education and economic productivity / edited by Edwin Dean.**     **4.2754**
Cambridge, Mass.: Ballinger Pub. Co., c1984. xiv, 223 p.: ill.; 24 cm. 1. Economic development — Effect of education on I. Dean, Edwin.
HD75.7.E38 1984     338.9 19     LC 84-3046     ISBN 0884109437

# HD82 General Works

## HD82 A–C

**Adelman, Irma.**          **4.2755**
Economic growth and social equity in developing countries / [by] Irma Adelman & Cynthia Taft Morris. — Stanford, Calif.: Stanford University Press, 1973. ix, 257 p.; 23 cm. 1. Economic development 2. Political participation — Developing countries 3. Economic development — Social aspects I. Morris, Cynthia Taft, joint author. II. T.
HD82.A533     338.91/172/4     LC 73-80616     ISBN 0804708371

**Backward areas in advanced countries: proceedings of a**     • **4.2756**
**conference held by the International Economic Association [at**
**Varenna, 1957] / edited by E. A. G. Robinson.**
London; Melbourne [etc.]: Macmillan; New York: St. Martin's Press, 1969. xviii, 474 p.: ill., maps; 23 cm. Held jointly with the European Centre for the Co-ordination of Research and Documentation. 1. Economic development — Addresses, essays, lectures. 2. Regional planning — Addresses, essays, lectures. I. Robinson, E. A. G. (Edward Austin Gossage) ed. II. International Economic Association. III. European Coordination Centre for Research and Documentation in Social Sciences.
HD82.B215 1969     338.9     LC 69-13691     ISBN 0333101804

**Baran, Paul A.**          • **4.2757**
The political economy of growth. — New York: Monthly Review Press, 1957. 308 p.; 22 cm. 1. Economic development I. T.
HD82.B29     330.9     LC 57-7953

**Bauer, P. T. (Péter Tamás)**          **4.2758**
Dissent on development: studies and debates in development economics / [by] P. T. Bauer. — Cambridge, Mass.: Harvard University Press, 1972. 550 p.; 23 cm. 1. Economic development 2. Developing countries — Economic conditions I. T.
HD82.B328 1972     330.9/172/4     LC 70-189158     ISBN 0674212819

**Bauer, P. T. (Péter Tamás)**          • **4.2759**
Economic analysis and policy in underdeveloped countries. Durham, N.C.: Published for the Duke University Commonwealth-Studies Center [by] Duke University Press, 1957. 145 p.; 21 cm. (Duke University Commonwealth-Studies Center. Publication no. 4) 1. Underdeveloped areas 2. Economic development I. T.
HD82 B33     LC 57-8814

**Bauer, P. T. (Péter Tamás)**          • **4.2760**
The economics of under–developed countries / by Peter T. Bauer and Basil S. Yamey. — [Chicago]: University of Chicago Press [1957] 271 p.; 20 cm. — (The Cambridge economic handbooks) 1. Underdeveloped areas. 2. Economic development I. Yamey, Basil S. joint author. II. T.
HD82.B332     338.91     LC 57-11204

**Bauer, P. T. (Péter Tamás)**          **4.2761**
Reality and rhetoric: studies in the economics of development / P.T. Bauer. — Cambridge, Mass.: Harvard University Press, 1984. viii, 184 p.; 24 cm. Includes index. 1. Economic development 2. Economic assistance — Developing countries. 3. Developing countries — Economic conditions I. T.
HD82.B333 1984     338.9 19     LC 83-18389     ISBN 0674749464

**Bhagwati, Jagdish N., 1934-.**          **4.2762**
Essays in development economics / Jagdish N. Bhagwati; edited by Gene Grossman. — 1st MIT Press ed. — Cambridge, Mass.: MIT Press, 1985. 2 v.: ill.; 24 cm. 1. Economic development — Addresses, essays, lectures. 2. Developing countries — Economic conditions — Addresses, essays, lectures. I. Grossman, Gene M. II. T.
HD82.B468 1985     338.9 19     LC 85-11343     ISBN 026202229X

**Brown, Lester Russell, 1934-.**          **4.2763**
Building a sustainable society / Lester R. Brown. — 1st ed. — New York: Norton, c1981. xiii, 433 p.: ill.; 21 cm. 'A Worldwatch Institute book.' 1. Economic policy I. Worldwatch Institute. II. T.
HD82.B733 1981     338.9 19     LC 81-11135     ISBN 0393014827

**Cole, J. P. (John P.), 1928-.**          **4.2764**
The development gap: a spatial analysis of world poverty and inequality / by J. P. Cole. — Chichester [Eng.]; New York: J. Wiley, c1981. x, 454 p.: ill.; 25 cm. Includes index. 1. Economic development 2. Developing countries — Economic conditions I. T.
HD82.C5714     338.9     LC 80-40284     ISBN 0471277967

## HD82 D–H

**Daly, Herman E.**      **4.2765**
Steady–state economics: the economics of biophysical equilibrium and moral growth / Herman E. Daly. — San Francisco: W. H. Freeman, c1977. x, 185 p.; 25 cm. 1. Economic development 2. Stagnation (Economics) I. T.
HD82.D31415     338.9     *LC* 77-8264     *ISBN* 0716701863

**Development and the rural–urban divide / edited by John**      **4.2766**
**Harriss and Mick Moore.**
London: Cass, 1984. 166 p.; 23 cm. 1. Economic development 2. Equality 3. Geography, Economic I. Harriss, John. II. Moore, Mick.
HD82.D4x     330.9 19     *ISBN* 0714632414

**Dixit, Avinash K.**      **4.2767**
The theory of equilibrium growth / A. K. Dixit. London: Oxford University Press, 1976. x, 204 p.: diagrs.; 21 cm. Includes index. 1. Economic development 2. Equilibrium (Economics) I. T.
HD82.D5185     339.5     *LC* 76-379719     *ISBN* 0198770804

**Dobb, Maurice Herbert, 1900-.**      • **4.2768**
An essay on economic growth and planning, by Maurice Dobb. — [2d ed.]. — New York: [Monthly Review Press, 1969, c1960] vii, 119 p.; 21 cm. 1. Economic development 2. Economic policy I. T.
HD82.D54 1969     338.9     *LC* 78-87281     *ISBN* 0853451109

**Domar, Evsey D.**      • **4.2769**
Essays in the theory of economic growth. New York, Oxford University Press, 1957. 272 p. ill. 1. Economic development I. T.
HD82 D592     *LC* 57-5768

**Ellman, Michael.**      **4.2770**
Socialist planning / Michael Ellman. — [1st ed. — Cambridge [Eng.]; New York: Cambridge University Press, 1979. xviii, 300 p.: ill.; 22 cm. (Modern Cambridge economics series) Includes index. 1. Economic policy 2. Comparative economics 3. Marxian economics I. T.
HD82.E52     335.43     *LC* 78-57757     *ISBN* 0521222296X

**Fields, Gary S.**      **4.2771**
Poverty, inequality, and development / Gary S. Fields. — Cambridge [Eng.]; New York: Cambridge University Press, 1980. xi, 281 p.: ill.; 22 cm. Includes index. 1. Economic development 2. Income distribution 3. Equality I. T.
HD82.F456     330.9     *LC* 79-21017     *ISBN* 0521225728

**Guha, Ashok S.**      **4.2772**
An evolutionary view of economic growth / Ashok S. Guha. — Oxford [England]: Clarendon Press; New York: Oxford University Press, 1981. 139 p.; 22 cm. 1. Economic development I. T.
HD82.G84     338.9 19     *LC* 82-126655     *ISBN* 0198284314

**Hagen, Everett Einar, 1906-.**      • **4.2773**
On the theory of social change: how economic growth begins. A study from the Center for International Studies, Massachusetts Institute of Technology. — Homewood, Ill.: Dorsey Press, 1962. 557 p.; 24 cm. — (The Dorsey series in anthropology and sociology) 1. Economic development — Social aspects 2. Social change I. Massachusetts Institute of Technology. Center for International Studies. II. T.
HD82.H2     301.24     *LC* 62-16517

**Hayek, Friedrich A. von (Friedrich August), 1899-.**      • **4.2774**
The road to serfdom / by Friedrich A. Hayek; with foreword by John Chamberlain. — Chicago: University of Chicago Press [1944] xi, 250 p.; 21 cm. Bibliographical foot-notes. 'Bibliographical note': p. 242-244. 1. Economic policy 2. Totalitarianism I. T.
HD82.H38 1944a     338.91     *LC* A 44-4381

**Heilbroner, Robert L.**      • **4.2775**
Between capitalism and socialism: essays in political economics, by Robert L. Heilbroner. — [1st ed.]. — New York: Random House, [1970] xviii, 294 p.; 22 cm. 1. Comparative economics I. T.
HD82.H388     330.1     *LC* 79-117700     *ISBN* 0394416651

**Heilbroner, Robert L.**      • **4.2776**
The great ascent; the struggle for economic development in our time. [1st ed.] New York, Harper & Row [c1963] 189 p. 22 cm. 1. Economic development 2. Developing countries — Economic conditions I. T.
HD82.H39     338.9     *LC* 62-17086

**Hirsch, Fred.**      **4.2777**
Social limits to growth / Fred Hirsch. Cambridge, Mass.: Harvard University Press, 1976. x, 208 p.; 24 cm. 'A Twentieth Century Fund study.' Includes index. 1. Economic development — Social aspects 2. Income distribution I. T.
HD82.H484     301.5/1     *LC* 76-18974     *ISBN* 0674813650

**Hirschman, Albert O.**      • **4.2778**
The strategy of economic development. — New Haven: Yale University Press, 1958. xiii, 217 p.: diagrs.; 24 cm. — (Yale studies in economics. 10) 1. Economic development I. T. II. Series.
HD82.H49     338.018     *LC* 58-11254

**Horowitz, Irving Louis.**      **4.2779**
Three worlds of development; the theory and practice of international stratification. — 2d ed. — New York: Oxford University Press, 1972. xxx, 556 p.; 24 cm. 1. Economic development 2. Economic history — 1945- 3. Social history — 1945- 4. World politics — 1945- I. T.
HD82.H618 1972     309     *LC* 79-183868

**Hoselitz, Berthold Frank, 1913-.**      • **4.2780**
Theories of economic growth, by Bert F. Hoselitz [and others]. — Glencoe, Ill.: Free Press, [1961, c1960] 344 p.: diagr.; 24 cm. 'Papers ... of a seminar held at Dartmouth College in July and August of 1956.' 1. Economic development — Addresses, essays, lectures. I. Dartmouth College. II. T.
HD82.H62     330.109     *LC* 60-10898

## HD82 I–M

**International Economic Association.**      • **4.2781**
Economic consequences of the size of nations: proceedings of a conference held by the International Economic Association / edited by E.A.G. Robinson. — London: Macmillan, 1960. xxii, 446 p.: iagrs., tables. 1. States, Small 2. Economic development I. Robinson, E. A. G. (Edward Austin Gossage) II. T.
HD82 I42     *LC* 60-3124

**International Economic Association.**      **4.2782**
Economic growth and resources: proceedings of the fifth world congress of the International Economic Association held in Tokyo, Japan, 1977. — New York: St. Martin's Press, 1979- < 1980 >. v. < 1-4 >: ill.; 22 cm. 1. Economic development — Congresses. 2. Economic policy — Congresses. 3. Natural resources — Congresses. 4. Japan — Economic conditions — 1945- — Congresses. I. Malinvaud, Edmond. II. T.
HD82.I45 1979a     330.9     *LC* 79-4430     *ISBN* 0312233140

**Jumper, Sidney R.**      **4.2783**
Economic growth and disparities: a world view / Sidney R. Jumper, Thomas L. Bell, Bruce A. Ralston. — Englewood Cliffs, N.J.: Prentice-Hall, c1980. vii, 472 p.: ill.; 25 cm. 1. Economic development 2. Economic history — 1971- I. Bell, Thomas L. joint author. II. Ralston, Bruce A. joint author. III. T.
HD82.J85     330.9/047     *LC* 79-23728     *ISBN* 0132256800

**Kahn, Herman, 1922-.**      **4.2784**
World economic development: 1979 and beyond / Herman Kahn, with the Hudson Institute. — Boulder, Colo.: Westview Press, 1979. xxi, 519 p.: ill.; 24 cm. 1. Economic development 2. Economic forecasting I. Hudson Institute. II. T.
HD82.K27 1979     330.9/04     *LC* 79-1737     *ISBN* 0891583920

**Kaldor, Nicholas, 1908-1986.**      **4.2785**
Essays on economic policy / Nicholas Kaldor. — New York: Holmes & Meier Publishers, 1980. 2 v.; 23 cm. (Collected economic essays; v. 3-4) 1. Economic policy — Addresses, essays, lectures. 2. Full employment policies — Addresses, essays, lectures. 3. Inflation (Finance) — Addresses, essays, lectures. 4. Taxation — Addresses, essays, lectures. 5. Economic stabilization — Addresses, essays, lectures. I. T.
HD82.K3 1980     338.9     *LC* 80-18155     *ISBN* 0841904537

**Kitching, G. N.**      **4.2786**
Development and underdevelopment in historical perspective: populism, nationalism, and industrialization / Gavin Kitching. — London; New York: Methuen, 1982. ix, 196 p.: ill.; 22 cm. (Development and underdevelopment.) (Open University set book.) Includes index. 1. Economic development 2. Underdeveloped areas. I. T. II. Series. III. Series: Open University set book.
HD82.K53 1982     338.9 19     *LC* 81-22282     *ISBN* 0416731309

**Kuznets, Simon Smith, 1901-.**      **4.2787**
Modern economic growth: rate, structure, and spread, by Simon Kuznets. — New Haven: Yale University Press, 1966. xvii, 529 p.; 21 cm. — (Studies in comparative economics. 7) 1. Economic development I. T. II. Series.
HD82.K87     338     *LC* 66-21524

**Kuznets, Simon Smith, 1901-.**      **4.2788**
Population, capital, and growth; selected essays [by] Simon Kuznets. New York, Norton [1973] 342 p. 21 cm. 1. Economic development — Addresses, essays, lectures. 2. Population — Addresses, essays, lectures. 3. Capital — Addresses, essays, lectures. I. T.
HD82.K875 1973     330     *LC* 73-12145     *ISBN* 0393054977

**Kuznets, Simon Smith, 1901-.**                                    • 4.2789
Six lectures on economic growth. Glencoe, Ill., Free Press [c1959] 122 p.
1. Economic development I. T.
HD82 K88        LC 59-13596

**Leibenstein, Harvey.**                                    • 4.2790
Economic backwardness and economic growth; studies in the theory of
economic development. One of a series of books from the research program of
the Institute of Industrial Relations, University of California. — New York,
Wiley [1957] 295 p. illus. 24 cm. 1. Economic development 2. Underdeveloped
areas. I. T.
HD82.L34        338.91        LC 57-12296

**Lewis, W. Arthur (William Arthur), 1915-.**                                    • 4.2791
The theory of economic growth / by W. Arthur Lewis. — Homewood, Ill.:
R.D. Irwin, c1955. 453 p. 1. Industry I. T.
HD82.L417 1955a        LC 58-377

**Lindblom, Charles Edward, 1917-.**                                    4.2792
Politics and markets: the world's political economic systems / Charles E.
Lindblom. — New York: Basic Books, c1977. xi, 403 p.; 24 cm.
1. Comparative economics I. T.
HD82.L475        330        LC 77-75250        ISBN 0465059570

**Little, Ian Malcolm David.**                                    4.2793
Economic development: theory, policy, and international relations / Ian M.D.
Little. — New York: Basic Books, c1982. xi, 452 p.; 24 cm. 'A Twentieth
Century Fund book.' Includes indexes. 1. Economic development
2. International economic relations 3. Developing countries — Economic
conditions I. T.
HD82.L49 1982        338.9 19        LC 82-71366        ISBN 0465017878

**McClelland, David Clarence.**                                    • 4.2794
The achieving society. — Princeton, N.J.: Van Nostrand, [1961] 512 p.: illus.;
24 cm. 1. Economic development 2. Achievement motivation 3. Economic
history 4. Entrepreneurship I. T.
HD82.M28        338.9        LC 61-65089

**Meier, Gerald M.**                                    • 4.2795
Leading issues in economic development: studies in international poverty / [by]
Gerald M. Meier. — 2d ed. — [New York]: Oxford University Press, 1970.
xviii, 758 p.; 25 cm. First ed. published in 1964 under title: Leading issues in
development economics. 1. Economic development I. T.
HD82.M44 1970        338.9        LC 74-109932

**Mishan, E. J. (Edward J.), 1917-.**                                    • 4.2796
The costs of economic growth [by] E. J. Mishan. Harmondsworth, Penguin,
1969. 240 p. 18 cm. (Pelican books) 1. Economic development 2. Great Britain
— Economic policy — 1945- I. T.
HD82.M513 1969        330/.09        LC 77-464240        ISBN 0140210903

**Myrdal, Gunnar, 1898-.**                                    • 4.2797
[Development and underdevelopment] Rich lands and poor: the road to world
prosperity. — [1st American ed.] New York: Harper [1958, c1957] xx, 168 p. 20
cm. (World perspectives, v. 16) A revision of the author's Development and
under-development, published in 1956. London ed. (Duckworth) has title:
Economic theory and under-developed regions. 1. Economic development
I. T.
HD82.M9 1958        330.9        LC 57-11787

## HD82 N–Z

**Olson, Mancur.**                                    4.2798
The rise and decline of nations: economic growth, stagflation, and social
rigidities / Mancur Olson. — New Haven: Yale University Press, c1982. xi,
273 p.; 22 cm. 1. Economic development 2. Unemployment — Effect of
inflation on 3. Caste — India 4. Economics I. T.
HD82.O565 1982        338.9/001 19        LC 82-40163        ISBN 0300023073

**Perceptions of development / edited by Sandra Wallman.**                                    4.2799
Cambridge; New York: Cambridge University Press, 1977. 210 p.; 24 cm.
(Perspectives on development) Includes index. 1. Economic development —
Case studies. 2. Social history — Case studies. I. Wallman, Sandra.
HD82.P443        301.24        LC 76-46863        ISBN 052121498X

**The Political economy of development and underdevelopment /**                                    4.2800
**edited by Charles K. Wilber.**
3rd ed. — New York: Random House, c1984. xi, 595 p.: ill.; 24 cm. Includes
indexes. 1. Economic development — Addresses, essays, lectures. I. Wilber,
Charles K.
HD82.P546 1984        330.9172/4 19        LC 83-9558        ISBN 039433597X

**The Political economy of new and old industrial countries /**                                    4.2801
**edited by Christopher Saunders.**
London: Toronto: Butterworths, 1981. ix, 325 p.: ill. — (Butterworths studies
in international political economy.) 1. Economic policy — Addresses, essays,
lectures I. Saunders, Christopher Thomas. II. Series.
HD82 P55        LC 80-41938        ISBN 040810774X

**Reynolds, Lloyd George, 1910-.**                                    4.2802
Image and reality in economic development / Lloyd G. Reynolds. — New
Haven: Yale University Press, 1977. xiii, 497 p.: ill.; 24 cm.— (A publication of
the Economic Growth Center, Yale University) 1. Economic development
I. T.
HD82.R44        HD82 R475.        338.9        LC 77-6458        ISBN
0300020880

**Sundrum, R. M.**                                    4.2803
Development economics: a framework for analysis and policy / R.M. Sundrum.
— Chichester; New York: Wiley, c1983. x, 343 p.: ill.; 24 cm. Includes index.
1. Economic development I. T.
HD82.S8538 1983        338.9 19        LC 82-7066        ISBN 0471103667

**Tinbergen, Jan, 1903-.**                                    • 4.2804
The design of development. Baltimore [Published for] the Economic
Development Institute, International Bank for Reconstruction and
Development [by] the Johns Hopkins Press 1958. 99 p. 1. Economic
development I. T.
HD82 T52        LC 58-9458

**Tinbergen, Jan, 1903-.**                                    • 4.2805
On the theory of economic policy / Jan Tinbergen. — Amsterdam: North-
Holland Pub. Co., 1975. 78 p. — (Contributions to economic analysis. 1)
1. Economic policy I. T. II. Series.
HD82 T53        HD82 T53 1975.        338.01        LC 53-762

**Tinbergen, Jan, 1903-.**                                    • 4.2806
Shaping the world economy: suggestions for an international economic policy.
— New York: Twentieth Century Fund, 1962. xviii, 330 p.: diagrs., tables.
1. Economic development 2. Underdeveloped areas I. T.
HD82 T54        LC 62-20234

**Usher, Dan, 1934-.**                                    4.2807
The measurement of economic growth / Dan Usher. — New York: Columbia
University Press, 1980. x, 306 p.: ill.; 24 cm. 1. Economic development
2. Canada — Economic conditions — 1918- I. T.
HD82.U84        330/.01/8        LC 79-14908        ISBN 0231049048

**Zauberman, Alfred.**                                    4.2808
Mathematical theory in Soviet planning: concepts, methods, techniques /
Alfred Zauberman. — London; New York: Oxford University Press for the
Royal Institute of International Affairs, 1976. xiv, 464 p.; 23 cm. 1. Economic
policy — Mathematical models. 2. Mathematical optimization 3. Control
theory 4. Russia — Economic policy. I. T.
HD82.Z39        338.947        LC 76-356858        ISBN 0192183079

**Peattie, Lisa Redfield.**                                    4.2809
Thinking about development / Lisa Peattie. — New York: Plenum Press,
c1981. x, 198 p.; 22 cm. — (Environment, development, and public policy.
Cities and development.) 1. Economic development — Planning. 2. Technical
assistance — Anthropological aspects I. T. II. Series.
HD87.5.P4        303.4/4 19        LC 81-15858        ISBN 0306407612

# HD101–2210 LAND. AGRICULTURE

# HD101–1395 Land

**Lyle, John Tillman.**                                    4.2810
Design for human ecosystems: landscape, land use, and natural resources /
John Tillman Lyle. — New York: Van Nostrand Reinhold, c1985. vi, 279 p.:
ill.; 29 cm. Includes index. 1. Land use — Planning 2. Land use — Planning —
Case studies. 3. Human ecology 4. Conservation of natural resources
5. Landscape architecture I. T.
HD108.6.L95 1985        333.73/17 19        LC 84-27155        ISBN
0442259433

**Chisholm, Michael, 1931-.**     • **4.2811**
Rural settlement and land use; an essay in location. New York, Science Editions [1967, c1962] 207 p. maps. 22 cm. 1. Farms — Location 2. Villages I. T.
HD111.C47 1967     *LC* 67-5638

**Griswold, Alfred Whitney, 1906-.**     • **4.2812**
Farming and democracy. [1st ed.] New York, Harcourt, Brace [1948] ix, 227 p. 21 cm. 1. Land tenure 2. Democracy 3. Sociology, Rural I. T.
HD111.G7     *LC* 48-6511

**Urban land policy, issues and opportunities / Harold B.**     **4.2813**
**Dunkerley, coordinating editor; with the assistance of Christine M.E. Whitehead.**
New York: Published for the World Bank [by] Oxford University Press, c1983. viii, 214 p.; 24 cm. Includes index. 1. Land use, Urban 2. Urban policy 3. Land tenure I. Dunkerley, Harold B., 1921- II. Whitehead, Christine M. E.
HD111.U7 1983     333.77/17 19     *LC* 82-20247     *ISBN* 0195204034

**King, Russell.**     **4.2814**
Land reform: a world survey / Russell King. Boulder, Colo.: Westview Press, 1977. xvi, 446 p.; 23 cm. (Westview advanced economic geographies) 1. Land reform — Case studies. I. T.
HD156.K54 1977     *LC* 77-24033     *ISBN* 0891588191

## HD166–1130 BY COUNTRY

## HD171–279 United States

**Clawson, Marion, 1905-.**     • **4.2815**
The Bureau of Land Management. — New York: Praeger Publishers, [1971] xiii, 209 p.: illus., maps.; 22 cm. — (Praeger library of U.S. Government departments and agencies, no. 27) 1. United States. Bureau of Land Management. I. T.
HD181.G8 C57     353/.008/232     *LC* 71-101656

**Harris, Marshall Dees, 1903-.**     • **4.2816**
Origin of the land tenure system in the United States, by Marshall Harris. — Westport, Conn.: Greenwood Press, [1970, c1953] xiv, 445 p.: maps.; 23 cm. 1. Land tenure — U.S. — History. I. T.
HD194.H3 1970     333.3/0973     *LC* 70-130038     *ISBN* 0837137314

**Buck, Solon J. (Solon Justus), 1884-1962.**     • **4.2817**
The Granger movement; a study of agricultural organization and its political, economic, and social manifestations, 1870–1880. Lincoln, University of Nebraska Press [1963, c1913] 384 p. illus. 21 cm. (A Bison book) 1. Patrons of Husbandry. 2. Agriculture — United States 3. Agriculture — Economic aspects — United States. 4. Railroads and state — United States 5. Cooperation — United States. I. T.
HD201.B8 1963     338.10973     *LC* 63-9713

**Holley, Donald, 1940-.**     **4.2818**
Uncle Sam's farmers: the New Deal communities in the Lower Mississippi Valley / Donald Holley. — Urbana: University of Illinois Press, [1975] xv, 312 p.; 24 cm. Includes index. 1. Land settlement — Mississippi River Valley. 2. Farmers — Mississippi River Valley — History. 3. New Deal, 1933-1939 4. Mississippi River Valley — Rural conditions. I. T.
HD210.M55 H64     333.1/0976     *LC* 75-20091     *ISBN* 0252005104

**Gates, Paul Wallace, 1901-.**     • **4.2819**
Fifty million acres: conflicts over Kansas land policy, 1854–1890. Ithaca, Cornell University Press [1954] xiii, 311 p. illus., maps. 23 cm. 'Bibliographical note': p. 295-299. 1. Land use — Kansas. 2. Kansas — Public lands. I. T.
HD211.K2G3     333.1     *LC* 54-7385

**Ellis, David Maldwyn.**     • **4.2820**
Landlords and farmers in the Hudson–Mohawk region, 1790–1850. — New York: Octagon Books, 1967 [c1946] xiii, 347 p.: illus.; 21 cm. 1. Land tenure — New York (State) 2. Anti-rent troubles, New York, 1839-1846 3. Agriculture — Economic aspects — New York (State) I. T.
HD211.N7 E5 1967     338.1/09747/3     *LC* 67-18762

### HD216–243 PUBLIC LANDS

**Carstensen, Vernon Rosco, 1907- ed.**     • **4.2821**
The public lands; studies in the history of the public domain. — [General ed.]. — Madison: University of Wisconsin Press, 1963 [c1962] 522 p.: illus.; 25 cm. 1. United States — Public lands I. T.
HD216.C3 1963     333.10973     *LC* 62-21554

**Clawson, Marion, 1905-.**     **4.2822**
The federal lands revisited / Marion Clawson. — Washington, D.C.: Resources for the Future; Baltimore: Distributed by the Johns Hopkins University Press, c1983. xix, 302 p.: ill.; 23 cm. Includes index. 1. United States — Public lands I. T.
HD216.C529 1983     333.1/0973 19     *LC* 83-42904     *ISBN* 0801830982

**Clawson, Marion, 1905-.**     • **4.2823**
The Federal lands since 1956. Washington, Resources for the Future; [1967] xi, 113 p. 26 cm. 1. United States — Public lands I. Clawson, Marion, 1905- The Federal lands; their use and management. II. Resources for the Future. III. T.
HD216.C53     *LC* 67-16034

**Clawson, Marion, 1905-.**     • **4.2824**
Uncle Sam's acres. — Westport, Conn.: Greenwood Press, [1970, c1951] xvi, 414 p.: illus., maps.; 23 cm. 1. U.S. — Public lands. I. T.
HD216.C55 1970     333.1/0973     *LC* 74-106685     *ISBN* 0837133564

**Culhane, Paul J.**     **4.2825**
Public lands politics: interest group influence on the Forest Service and the Bureau of Land Management / Paul J. Culhane. — Baltimore: Published for Resources for the Future by Johns Hopkins University Press, c1981. xv, 398 p.; 24 cm. 1. United States. Forest Service. 2. United States. Bureau of Land Management. 3. Forests and forestry — Government ownership — United States. 4. Forests and forestry — United States — Multiple use. 5. United States — Public lands I. Resources for the Future. II. T.
HD216.C84     333.1/0973 19     *LC* 80-8776     *ISBN* 0801825989

**Valuation of wildland resource benefits / edited by George L.**     **4.2826**
**Peterson and Alan Randall.**
Boulder: Westview Press, 1984. xiii, 258 p.: ill.; 24 cm. (A Westview special study) 'Published in cooperation with the U.S. Department of Agriculture, Forest Service, Rocky Mountain Forest and Range Experiment Station'—P. [iv] 1. Natural areas — Economic aspects — United States — Addresses, essays, lectures. 2. Wilderness areas — Economic aspects — United States — Addresses, essays, lectures. 3. Recreation areas — Economic aspects — United States — Addresses, essays, lectures. 4. Natural resources — United States — Addresses, essays, lectures. 5. United States — Public lands — Addresses, essays, lectures. I. Peterson, George L. II. Randall, Alan, 1944-
HD216.V35 1984     333.78/2 19     *LC* 84-51044     *ISBN* 0813300185

**Foss, Phillip O.**     • **4.2827**
Politics and grass; the administration of grazing on the public domain, Phillip O. Foss. — New York: Greenwood Press, [1969, c1960] ix, 236 p.; 23 cm. 1. Grazing — U.S. 2. U.S. — Public lands. I. T.
HD241.F6 1969     333.7/4     *LC* 75-90508     *ISBN* 0837121361

### HD251–279 REAL ESTATE

**The Real estate handbook / edited by Maury Seldin.**     **4.2828**
Homewood, Ill.: Dow Jones-Irwin, c1980. xxix, 1186 p.: ill.; 24 cm. 1. Real estate business — United States — Handbooks, manuals, etc. I. Seldin, Maury, 1931-
HD255.R38     333.33/02/02     *LC* 79-51783     *ISBN* 0870941844

**Beyond the urban fringe: land use issues of nonmetropolitan**     **4.2829**
**America / Rutherford H. Platt and George Macinko, editors.**
Minneapolis: University of Minnesota Press, c1983. xv, 416 p.: ill.; 24 cm. Includes index. 1. Land use, Rural — United States — Congresses. I. Platt, Rutherford H. II. Macinko, George.
HD256.B49 1983     333.76/13/0973 19     *LC* 83-3518     *ISBN* 0816610991

**Swierenga, Robert P.**     • **4.2830**
Pioneers and profits: land speculation on the Iowa frontier [by] Robert P. Swierenga. — [1st ed.]. — Ames: Iowa State University Press, [1968] xxviii, 260 p.: illus., facsims., maps.; 24 cm. 1. Real estate investment — Iowa — History. I. T.
HD266.I8 S9     333.3/3.09777     *LC* 68-11198

## HD311–320 Canada

**Harris, Richard Colebrook.**     • **4.2831**
The seigneurial system in early Canada; a geographical study. — Madison: University of Wisconsin Press, 1966. xvi, 247 p.: illus., maps.; 26 cm. 1. Land tenure — Canada. 2. Feudalism — Canada. I. T.
HD314.H3     333.30971     *LC* 66-11799

**MacDonald, Norman.**     • **4.2832**
Canada, 1763–1841, immigration and settlement: the administration of the imperial land regulations / by Norman Macdonald. — 1st ed. London, New

York [etc.]: Longmans, Green [1939] xii, 577 p.: fold. map.; 23 cm. 1. Canada — Emigration and immigration. I. T.
HD315.M25    *LC* 40-5487

**Lorimer, James, 1942-.**    **4.2833**
The developers / James Lorimer. — Toronto: J. Lorimer, 1978. xi, 307 p.; 24 cm. 1. Land use, Urban — Canada. 2. Real estate business — Canada. I. T.
HD316.L67    333.3/8/0971    *LC* 79-317913    *ISBN* 0888622198

**Gates, Lillian F.**    • **4.2834**
Land policies of Upper Canada, by Lillian F. Gates. [Toronto] University of Toronto P. [1968] 378 p. 25 cm. (Canadian studies in history and government, 9) 1. Land use — Ontario. 2. Land tenure — Ontario. I. T. II. Series.
HD319.O5 G37    333/.009713    *LC* 68-97201

## HD320.5–580 Latin America

**Singelmann, Peter, 1942-.**    **4.2835**
Structures of domination and peasant movements in Latin America / Peter Singelmann. — Columbia: University of Missouri Press, 1981. 246 p.; 24 cm. Includes index. 1. Peasantry — Latin America. 2. Dominance (Psychology) 3. Latin America — Rural conditions. I. T.
HD320.5.S55    302    *LC* 79-48030    *ISBN* 0826203078

**Stavenhagen, Rodolfo. comp.**    • **4.2836**
Agrarian problems and peasant movements in Latin America. — Garden City., N.Y.: Doubleday, 1970. xi, 583 p.: map.; 19 cm. 1. Land reform — Latin America — Addresses, essays, lectures. 2. Peasantry — Latin America — Addresses, essays, lectures. I. T.
HD320.5.Z63 S8    333.7/6/098    *LC* 73-97704

**McBride, George McCutchen, 1876-.**    • **4.2837**
The land systems of Mexico. With a foreword by Manuel Gamio. — New York: Octagon Books, 1971 [c1923] xii, 204 p.: illus., maps, plans.; 21 cm. — (American Geographical Society. Research series, no. 12) The study, in preliminary form, was presented as the author's thesis, Yale University, 1921. 1. Land tenure — Mexico. I. T.
HD325.M3 1971    333.3/2/0972    *LC* 78-154617    *ISBN* 0374954305

**Simpson, Eyler Newton.**    • **4.2838**
The ejido; Mexico's way out, by Eyler N. Simpson; with a foreword by Lic. Ramón Beteta ... Chapel Hill, The University of North Carolina press, 1937. xxi, 849 p. incl. illus. (maps) tables, diagrs. front., plates. 24 cm. 1. Land tenure — Mexico. 2. Agriculture — Mexico. 3. Mexico — Economic conditions — 1918- 4. Mexico — Social conditions I. T. II. Title: Mexico's way out.
HD325.S5    333.0972    *LC* 37-18116

**Forman, Shepard, 1938-.**    **4.2839**
The Brazilian peasantry / Shepard Forman. — New York: Columbia University Press, 1975. xiii, 319 p.; 24 cm. Includes index. 1. Peasantry — Brazil. 2. Brazil — Rural conditions. 3. Brazil — Politics and government — 1964-1985 I. T.
HD496.F64    301.44/43/0981    *LC* 75-16156    *ISBN* 0231031068

**Loveman, Brian.**    **4.2840**
Struggle in the countryside; politics and rural labor in Chile, 1919–1973. Bloomington, Indiana University Press [1976, c1975] xxxvi, 439 p. maps 24 cm. (International Development Research Center. Studies in development, no. 10) 1. Land tenure — Chile. 2. Land reform — Chile. 3. Chile — Rural conditions. I. T.
HD505.L68 1975    333.1/0983    *LC* 74-6521    *ISBN* 0253355656

**McBride, George McCutchen, 1876-.**    • **4.2841**
Chile: land and society / With a foreword by Carlos Davila. — New York: Octagon Books, 1971 [c1936] xxii, 408 p.: illus., facsims., maps, plans.; 21 cm. — (American Geographical Society. Research series, no. 19) 1. Agriculture — Chile. 2. Land tenure — Chile. 3. Farms — Chile. 4. Chile — Social conditions I. T.
HD505.M3 1971b    333/.00983    *LC* 71-154618    *ISBN* 0374954291

**Ford, Thomas R., 1923-.**    • **4.2842**
Man and land in Peru, by Thomas R. Ford. — New York: Russell & Russell, [1971, c1955] ix, 176 p.: illus., maps.; 23 cm. Originally presented as the author's thesis, Vanderbilt University. 1. Land tenure — Peru. 2. Agriculture — Economic aspects — Peru. I. T.
HD553.F6 1971    333.3/2/0985    *LC* 76-152538

**Blanco, Hugo.**    **4.2843**
Land or death; the peasant struggle in Peru. — [1st ed.]. — New York: Pathfinder Press, 1972. 178 p.: illus.; 22 cm. 1. Land reform — Peru. 2. Peasant uprisings — Peru. 3. Peasantry — Peru. I. T.
HD556.B5513    333.3/2/0985    *LC* 73-186689

**Davies, Keith A.**    **4.2844**
Landowners in colonial Peru / by Keith A. Davies. — 1st ed. — Austin: University of Texas Press, 1984. x, 237 p.: ill.; 24 cm. (Latin American monographs / Institute of Latin American Studies, The University of Texas at Austin; no. 61) 1. Land tenure — Peru — Arequipa (Dept.) — History. 2. Landowners — Peru — Arequipa (Dept.) — History. I. T.
HD559.A73 D38 1984    333.3/0985/32 19    *LC* 83-16749    *ISBN* 0292746393

**Mallon, Florencia E., 1951-.**    **4.2845**
The defense of community in Peru's central highlands: peasant struggle and capitalist transition, 1860–1940 / Florencia E. Mallon. — Princeton, N.J.: Princeton University Press, c1983. xiv, 384 p.: 6 maps; 24 cm. Includes index. 1. Peasantry — Peru — Cordillera Central Region — History. 2. Economic development 3. Capitalism 4. Cordillera Central Region (Peru) — Rural conditions. I. T.
HD559.C67 M34 1983    330.985/206/0880625 19    *LC* 83-42565    *ISBN* 0691076472

## HD581–850 Europe

**Dovring, Folke.**    • **4.2846**
Land and labor in Europe in the twentieth century; a comparative survey of recent agrarian history. 3rd rev. ed. The Hague, M. Nijhoff, 1965. xi, 511 p. illus., fold. map. 26 cm. 1. Land use — Europe. 2. Agriculture — Economic aspects — Europe. I. T.
HD585.D6 1965    *LC* 66-6949

**The Agrarian history of England and Wales / edited by H.P.R.**    • **4.2847**
**Finberg.**
London: Cambridge University Press, 1967-. v.: ill., plates, maps, plans, tables; 23 1/2 cm. Vol. 8, general editor Joan Thirsk. 1. Land use — Great Britain — History. 2. Agriculture — Great Britain — History. I. Finberg, Herbert P.R., 1900- II. Thirsk, Joan.
HD593.A62    333.760942    *LC* 66-19763//r79    *ISBN* 0521084237

**Orwin, Charles Stewart, 1876-.**    • **4.2848**
The open fields / by C.S. and C.S. Orwin. 3rd ed. Oxford: Clarendon P., 1967. xxvi, 196 p.: front., 36 plates (incl. maps, facsims.), maps. 1. Land tenure — Great Britain — History. 2. Agriculture — England — History. 3. Laxton, Nottinghamshire, Eng. 4. Nottinghamshire, England — History — Sources. I. Orwin, Christabel Susan (Lowry). II. T.
HD593.O7 1967    *LC* 67-112039

**Hilton, R. H. (Rodney Howard), 1916-.**    **4.2849**
The English peasantry in the later Middle Ages: the Ford lectures for 1973 and related studies / by R. H. Hilton. — Oxford: Clarendon Press, 1975. 256 p.: map; 23 cm. 1. Peasantry — England — Addresses, essays, lectures. 2. Great Britain — Economic conditions — Addresses, essays, lectures. 3. Great Britain — Social conditions — Addresses, essays, lectures. I. T.
HD594.H54    301.44/43/0942    *LC* 75-316774    *ISBN* 019822432X

**Tawney, Richard Henry.**    • **4.2850**
The agrarian problem in the sixteenth century. London, New York [etc.] Longmans, Green and co., 1912. p. cm. 1. Peasantry — England. 2. Agriculture — England — History. 3. Land tenure — England. I. T.
HD594.T3    *LC* 13-154

**Robinson, Philip S.**    **4.2851**
The plantation of Ulster: British settlement in an Irish landscape, 1600–1670 / Philip S. Robinson. — New York: St. Martin's Press, 1984. xxii, 254 p.: ill., maps. Includes index. 1. Land settlement — Ulster (Northern Ireland and Ireland) — History — 17th century. 2. Plantations — Ulster (Northern Ireland and Ireland) — History — 17th century. 3. Ulster (Northern Ireland and Ireland) — Emigration and immigration — History — 17th century. 4. Ulster (Northern Ireland and Ireland) — History. I. T.
HD620.5.Z8 U477 1984    333.76/09416 19    *LC* 83-13895    *ISBN* 0312614713

**Bloch, Marc Léopold Benjamin, 1886-1944.**    • **4.2852**
[Caractéres originaux de l'histoire rurale française. English] French rural history; an essay on its basic characteristics [by] Marc Bloch. Foreword by Bryce Lyon. Translated from the French by Janet Sondheimer. Berkeley, University of California Press, 1966. xxxiii, 258 p. maps, plans. 23 cm. Translation of Les caractéres originaux de l'histoire rurale française. 1. Land tenure — France — History. 2. Peasantry — France 3. Feudalism — France. I. T.
HD643.B613    630.1144    *LC* 66-15483

**Lefebvre, Georges, 1874-1959.**    • **4.2853**
Les Paysans du Nord pendant la Révolution française. — Bari: Laterza, 1959. 923 p.; 22 cm. — (Collezione storica.) 1. Peasantry — France 2. Land tenure — France. 3. France — Econ. condit. I. T.
HD644.9.L4

**Wright, Gordon, 1912-.**     • **4.2854**
Rural revolution in France; the peasantry in the twentieth century. Stanford, Calif., Stanford University Press, 1964. xi, 271 p. ill., ports., maps. 1. Peasantry — France 2. France — Rural conditions I. T.
HD645 W7     *LC* 64-13356

**Le Roy Ladurie, Emmanuel.**     **4.2855**
[Paysans de Languedoc. English] The peasants of Languedoc. Translated with an introd. by John Day. George Huppert, consulting editor. Urbana, University of Illinois Press [1974] xii, 370 p. 24 cm. 1. Peasantry — France — Languedoc — History. 2. Agriculture — Economic aspects — France — Languedoc — History. I. T.
HD649.L33 L413     301.44/43/09448     *LC* 74-4286     *ISBN* 0252004116

**Field, Daniel, 1938-.**     **4.2856**
The end of serfdom: nobility and bureaucracy in Russia, 1855–1861 / Daniel Field. Cambridge, Mass.: Harvard University Press, 1976. viii, 472 p.; 24 cm. (Russian Research Center studies; 75) Includes index. 1. Land tenure — Russia. I. T.
HD715.F47 1976     333.1/0947     *LC* 75-23191     *ISBN* 0674252403

**Kieniewicz, Stefan.**     **4.2857**
The emancipation of the Polish peasantry. Chicago, University of Chicago Press [1969] xix, 285 p. map. 23 cm. 1. Land tenure — Poland. 2. Land tenure — Galicia (Poland and Ukraine) 3. Land tenure — Silesia. 4. Land tenure — Pomeronia. I. T.
HD728.K47     333.3/2/0943     *LC* 79-92684     *ISBN* 0226435245

**Vassberg, David E. (David Erland), 1936-.**     **4.2858**
Land and society in Golden Age Castile / David E. Vassberg. — Cambridge [Cambridgeshire]; New York: Cambridge University Press, 1984. xvii, 263 p.: maps; 24 cm. (Cambridge Iberian and Latin American studies.) Includes index. 1. Land tenure — Spain — Castile — History. 2. Agriculture — Economic aspects — Spain — Castile — History. 3. Castile (Spain) — Social conditions. I. T. II. Series.
HD779.C29 V37 1984     333.3/0946/3 19     *LC* 83-2029     *ISBN* 0521254701

**Roberts, Henry L.**     **4.2859**
Rumania: political problems of an agrarian state, by Henry L. Roberts. — [Hamden, Conn.]: Archon Books, 1969 [c1951] xiv, 414 p.; 23 cm. 1. Peasantry — Romania. 2. Land tenure — Romania. 3. Romania — Politics and government — 1944- I. T.
HD833.R6 1969     333.3     *LC* 69-13629     *ISBN* 0208006516

## HD850–960 Asia. Middle East

**Stein, Kenneth W., 1946-.**     **4.2860**
The land question in Palestine, 1917–1939 / by Kenneth W. Stein; [maps prepared by Karen L. Wysocki]. — Chapel Hill: University of North Carolina Press, c1984. xviii, 314 p.: ill., maps, ports.; 24 cm. 1. Land tenure — Palestine — History — 20th century. I. T.
HD850.S78 1984     333.3/23/095694 19     *LC* 83-21872     *ISBN* 0807815799

**Gourou, Pierre, 1900-.**     **4.2861**
Man and land in the Far East / Pierre Gourou; translated from the French by S. H. Beaver. — London; New York: Longman; New York: distributed by Longman Inc., 1975. xii, 239 p.: ill.; 23 cm. Translation of La terre et l'homme en Extrême-Orient. Includes index. 1. Peasantry — East Asia. 2. Agriculture — East Asia. 3. East Asia — Social conditions. I. T.
HD855.G613 1975     950     *LC* 73-91779     *ISBN* 0582502403

**Hinton, William.**     • **4.2862**
Fanshen; a documentary of revolution in a Chinese village. New York, Monthly Review Press [1967, c1966] xvii, 637 p. maps. 24 cm. 1. Land tenure — China. 2. Chang-chuang, China (Shansi Province) 3. China — Social conditions — 1949-1976 I. T.
HD866.H5     301.35095117     *LC* 66-23525

**Buck, John Lossing, 1890-.**     • **4.2863**
Land utilization in China: a study of 16,786 farms in 168 localities, and 38,256 farm families in twenty–two provinces in China, 1929–1933. — New York: Paragon Book Reprint Corp., 1964. xxxii, 494 p.: ill., maps; 24 cm. (Paragon reprint oriental series, 26.) 1. Agriculture — China. 2. Agriculture — Economic aspects — China. 3. Food supply — China. I. T. II. Series.
HD868.B8 1964     333.76     *LC* 64-18448

**Stokes, Eric.**     **4.2864**
The peasant and the Raj: studies in agrarian society and peasant rebellion in colonial India / Eric Stokes. — Cambridge; New York: Cambridge University Press, 1978. viii, 308 p.: ill.; 23 cm. — (Cambridge South Asian studies. 23)

1. Land tenure — India — History. 2. Peasantry — India — History. 3. Peasant uprisings — India — History. I. T. II. Series.
HD875.S76     301.44/43/0954     *LC* 77-77731     *ISBN* 0521216842

**Neale, Walter C.**     • **4.2865**
Economic change in rural India: land tenure and reform in Uttar Pradesh, 1800–1955 / by Walter C. Neale. — Port Washington, N.Y.: Kennikat Press, [1973, c1962] xii, 333 p.: ill.; 22 cm. Original ed. issued as no. 12 of the Yale studies in economics. 1. Land tenure — Uttar Pradesh, India — History. I. T.
HD879.U8 N4 1973     333.3/2/0954     *LC* 72-85284     *ISBN* 080461704X

**Cushner, Nicholas P.**     **4.2866**
Landed estates in the colonial Philippines / Nicholas P. Cushner. — New Haven: Yale University South Asia Studies, c1976. vi, 145 p.: maps. — (Monograph series - Yale University Southeast Asia Studies; no. 20) 1. Land tenure — Philippine Islands — History. I. T.
HD904.C87     *LC* 75-27615

**Sturtevant, David Reeves.**     **4.2867**
Popular uprisings in the Philippines, 1840–1940 / David R. Sturtevant. — Ithaca, N.Y.: Cornell University Press, 1976. 317 p.; 23 cm. Includes index. 1. Peasant uprisings — Philippine Islands — History. 2. Radicalism — Philippine Islands — History. I. T.
HD905.S85 1976     *LC* 75-36521     *ISBN* 0801408776

**Huang, Philip C., 1940-.**     **4.2868**
The peasant economy and social change in North China / Philip C.C. Huang. — Stanford, Calif.: Stanford University Press, 1985. xi, 369 p.: maps; 24 cm. Includes index. 1. Peasantry — China — History — Economic aspects. 2. Agriculture — China — History. 3. China — Rural conditions. I. T.
HD923.H83 1985     338.1/095115 19     *LC* 83-40106     *ISBN* 0804712204

**Treadgold, Donald W., 1922-.**     • **4.2869**
The great Siberian migration; government and peasant in resettlement from emancipation to the First World War. Princeton: Princeton University Press, 1957. xiii, 278 p.: ill., ports., maps.; 25 cm. 1. Land settlement — Siberia 2. Peasantry — Siberia I. T.
HD935 T7     *LC* 57-5482

## HD961–1030 Africa

**Prothero, R. Mansell. comp.**     **4.2870**
People and land in Africa south of the Sahara; readings in social geography. Edited by R. Mansell Prothero. New York: Oxford University Press, 1972. iv, 344 p.: illus.; 24 cm. 1. Land use — Africa, Sub-Saharan — Addresses, essays, lectures. 2. Africa, Sub-Saharan — Population — Addresses, essays, lectures. I. T.
HD969.S8 P7     333/.00967     *LC* 72-82995

**Leo, Christopher.**     **4.2871**
Land and class in Kenya / Christopher Leo. — Toronto; Buffalo: University of Toronto Press, c1984. xii, 244 p.: maps; 24 cm. (Political economy of world poverty. 3) Includes index. 1. Land tenure — Kenya — History. 2. Land reform — Kenya — History. 3. Social classes — Kenya — History. I. T. II. Series.
HD983.L46 1984     333.3/096762 19     *LC* 85-123264     *ISBN* 0802025323

**Isaacman, Allen F.**     **4.2872**
Mozambique: the Africanization of a European institution; the Zambesi prazos, 1750–1902 [by] Allen F. Isaacman. — Madison: University of Wisconsin Press, [1972] xviii, 260 p.: illus.; 25 cm. 1. Crown lands — Mozambique — History. 2. Plantations — Mozambique — History. 3. Mozambique — Colonization — History. I. T.
HD1019.M68 I8     333.1/0967/9     *LC* 72-176413     *ISBN* 0299061108

## HD1131 Developing Countries: General

**Blaikie, Piers M.**     **4.2873**
The political economy of soil erosion in developing countries / Piers Blaikie. — London; New York: Longman, 1985. 188 p.: ill.; 22 cm. (Longman development studies) Includes index. 1. Soil conservation — Government policy — Developing countries. 2. Land use — Government policy — Developing countries. 3. Soil erosion — Developing countries. I. T. II. Series.
HD1131.B55 1985     333.76/13 19     *LC* 84-879     *ISBN* 0582300894

## HD1241–1395 Land Tenure

**Apter, David Ernest, 1924-.**     **4.2874**
Against the state: politics and social protest in Japan / David E. Apter and Nagayo Sawa. — Cambridge, Mass.: Harvard University Press, 1984. ix, 271 p., [12] p. of plates: ill.; 25 cm. 1. Shin Tōkyō Kokusai Kūkō. 2. Environmental protection — Japan — Narita-shi — Citizen participation. 3. Eminent domain — Environmental aspects — Japan — Narita-shi. 4. Farmers — Japan — Narita-shi — Political activity. I. Sawa, Nagayo. II. T.
HD1265.J32 N3713 1984    387.7/36/095123 19    *LC* 83-15338
   *ISBN* 0674009207

**Courtenay, P. P. (Percy Philip)**     • **4.2875**
Plantation agriculture / [by] P.P. Courtenay. — New York, Praeger [1966, c1965] viii, 208 p. illus., maps. 23 cm. 1. Plantations 2. Tropical crops I. T.
HD1326.C6    *LC* 65-27030

**Agrarian reform in contemporary developing countries / edited**    **4.2876**
**by Ajit Kumar Ghose.**
London: Croom Helm; New York: St. Martin's Press, 1983. 364 p.: ill.; 23 cm. 'A study prepared for the International Labour Office within the framework of the World Employment Programme.' 1. Land reform — Developing countries — Case studies. I. Ghose, Ajit Kumar, 1947- II. International Labour Office. III. World Employment Programme.
HD1332.A37 1983    333.3/1 19    *LC* 83-13703    *ISBN* 0312014457

**Hinton, William.**     **4.2877**
Shenfan / William Hinton. — 1st ed. — New York: Random House, c1983. xxxix, 785 p., [16] p. of plates: col. ill.; 25 cm. Includes index. 1. Land reform — China — Case studies. 2. Villages — China — Case studies. 3. China — Social conditions — Case studies. I. T.
HD1333.C6 H53 1983    307.7/2/095117 19    *LC* 82-5270    *ISBN* 0394481429

**Moise, Edwin E., 1946-.**     **4.2878**
Land reform in China and North Vietnam: consolidating the revolution at the village level / Edwin E. Moise. — Chapel Hill: University of North Carolina Press, c1983. xiv, 305 p.; 24 cm. Includes index. 1. Land reform — China. 2. Land reform — Vietnam (Democratic Republic) I. T.
HD1333.C6 M64 1983    333.3/1/51 19    *LC* 82-15900    *ISBN* 0807815470

**Yaney, George L.**     **4.2879**
The urge to mobilize: agrarian reform in Russia, 1861–1930 / George Yaney. — Urbana: University of Illinois Press, c1982. viii, 599 p.: ill.; 24 cm. Includes index. 1. Stolypin, Petr Arkad'evich, 1862-1911. 2. Land reform — Soviet Union — History. I. T.
HD1333.S65 Y36 1982    333.3/1/47 19    *LC* 81-11527    *ISBN* 025200910X

**Harding, Susan Friend.**     **4.2880**
Remaking Ibieca: rural life in Aragon under Franco / Susan Friend Harding. — Chapel Hill: University of North Carolina Press, c1984. xvi, 221 p.: ill.; 24 cm. Includes index. 1. Land reform — Spain — Ibieca — History — 20th century. 2. Agriculture — Economic aspects — Spain — Ibieca — History — 20th century. I. T.
HD1333.S712 I243 1984    307.7/2/0946555 19    *LC* 83-21884
   *ISBN* 0807815942

**Hydén, Göran, 1938-.**     **4.2881**
Beyond ujamaa in Tanzania: underdevelopment and an uncaptured peasantry / Göran Hyden. — Berkeley: University of California Press, 1980. x, 270 p.; 23 cm. 1. Peasantry — Tanzania. 2. Peasantry — Africa, Sub-Saharan — Case studies. 3. Collective settlements — Tanzania 4. Socialism — Tanzania 5. Tanzania — Economic conditions I. T.
HD1339.T34 H93 1980b    338.1/09678 19    *LC* 80-135579    *ISBN* 0520039971

**Conflict, politics, and the urban scene / edited by Kevin R. Cox**    **4.2882**
**and R.J. Johnston.**
New York: St. Martin's Press, 1983. 265 p.: ill.; 24 cm. 1. Land use, Urban — Case studies. 2. Cities and towns — Case studies. 3. Municipal government — Case studies. I. Cox, Kevin R., 1939- II. Johnston, R. J. (Ronald John)
HD1391.C66 1982    307/.3 19    *LC* 81-16620    *ISBN* 0312162332

# HD1405–2210 Agriculture

**Distortions of agricultural incentives / edited by Theodore W.**    **4.2883**
**Schultz.**
Bloomington: Indiana University Press, c1978. viii, 343 p.; 24 cm. Papers presented at a 1977 three-day workshop sponsored by the Midwest Center of the American Academy of Arts and Sciences. 1. Agriculture — Economic aspects — Congresses. 2. Agriculture and state — Congresses. I. Schultz, Theodore William, 1902- II. American Academy of Arts and Sciences, Boston. Midwest Center.
HD1405.D57    338.1/8    *LC* 78-3246    *ISBN* 0253318068

**Black, John D. (John Donald), 1883-1960.**     • **4.2884**
Economics for agriculture: selected writings / Edited by James Pierce Cavin with introductory essays. Cambridge, Harvard University Press, 1959. 719 p. illus. (Harvard economic studies. v.111) 1. Agriculture — Economic aspects I. T. II. Series.
HD1411.B49    338.1

**Buse, Rueben C.**     **4.2885**
Applied economics; resource allocation in rural America [by] Rueben C. Buse [and] Daniel W. Bromley. — [1st ed.]. — Ames: Iowa State University Press, 1975. x, 623 p.: illus.; 23 cm. 1. Agriculture — Economic aspects 2. Agriculture — Economic aspects — United States. I. Bromley, Daniel W., 1940- joint author. II. T.
HD1411.B98    338.1/0973    *LC* 74-19097    *ISBN* 081380115X

**Schultz, Theodore William, 1902-.**     **4.2886**
Transforming traditional agriculture. New Haven: Yale University Press, 1964. xiv, 212 p.; 21 cm. (Studies in comparative economics. 3) 1. Agricultural innovations — Developing countries. 2. Agriculture — Economic aspects — Developing countries. I. T. II. Series.
HD1411.S44    338.1    *LC* 64-12661

**Thünen, Johann Heinrich von, 1783-1850.**     • **4.2887**
Isolated state; an English edition of Der isolierte Staat. Translated by Carla M. Wartenberg. Edited with an introd. by Peter Hall. [1st ed.] Oxford, New York, Pergamon Press [1966] lv, 304 p. ill. 22 cm. Abridged and translated from the 2d German ed. 1. Agriculture — Economic aspects 2. Agriculture — Economic aspects — Germany. 3. Rent (Economic theory) I. Hall, Peter Geoffrey. ed. II. T.
IID1411.T4613 1966    *LC* 65-17953

**Food, politics, and agricultural development: case studies in the**    **4.2888**
**public policy of rural modernization / edited by Raymond F.**
**Hopkins, Donald J. Puchala, and Ross B. Talbot.**
Boulder, Colo.: Westview Press, c1979. xv, 311 p.: ill.; 24 cm. — (Westview special studies in social, political, and economic development) 1. Agriculture and state — Addresses, essays, lectures. 2. Food supply — Addresses, essays, lectures. 3. Rural development — Addresses, essays, lectures. I. Hopkins, Raymond F. II. Puchala, Donald James, 1939- III. Talbot, Ross B.
HD1415.F64    338.1/8    *LC* 79-10209    *ISBN* 0891583890

**Hayami, Yūjirō, 1932-.**     **4.2889**
Agricultural development; an international perspective [by] Yujiro Hayami and Vernon W. Ruttan. — Baltimore: Johns Hopkins Press, [1971] xiv, 367 p.; 24 cm. 1. Agriculture — Economic aspects I. Ruttan, Vernon W. joint author. II. T.
HD1415.H318    338.1    *LC* 76-150663    *ISBN* 0801812593

**Johnston, Bruce F., 1919-.**     **4.2890**
Redesigning rural development: a strategic perspective / Bruce F. Johnston and William C. Clark. — Baltimore: Johns Hopkins University Press, c1982. xvi, 311 p.; 24 cm. — (Johns Hopkins studies in development.) Includes indexes. 1. Rural development I. Clark, William C., 1948- II. T. III. Series.
HD1415.J63 1982    338.9/00173/4 19    *LC* 81-17138    *ISBN* 0801827310

**Southworth, Herman McDowell, 1909-.**     • **4.2891**
Agricultural development and economic growth / edited by Herman M. Southworth and Bruce F. Johnston. — Ithaca, N.Y.: Cornell University Press, 1967. xv, 608 p.: ill., col. map.; 24 cm. 1. Agriculture — Economic aspects — Addresses, essays, lectures. 2. Underdeveloped areas — Agriculture. I. Johnston, Bruce F., 1919- II. T.
HD1415.S6    HD1417.A4.    *LC* 67-16792

**Arnon, Itzhak, 1909-.**     **4.2892**
Modernization of agriculture in developing countries: resources, potentials, and problems / I. Arnon. — Chichester [Eng.]; New York: Wiley, c1981. xxiii, 565 p.: ill.; 24 cm. (Environmental monographs and symposia.) 'A Wiley-Interscience publication.' 1. Agriculture — Economic aspects — Developing countries. I. T. II. Series.
HD1417.A76    338.1/09172/4 19    *LC* 80-41588    *ISBN* 0471279285

**Berry, R. Albert.**     **4.2893**
Agrarian structure and productivity in developing countries: a study prepared for the International Labour Office within the framework of the World Employment Programme / R. Albert Berry and William R. Cline. — Baltimore: Johns Hopkins University Press, c1979. x, 248 p.: graphs; 24 cm. 1. Agriculture — Economic aspects — Developing countries. 2. Farms, Size of I. Cline, William R. joint author. II. T.
HD1417.B387    338.1/09172/4    *LC* 78-20524    *ISBN* 0801821908

**Cochrane, Willard Wesley, 1914-.** 4.2894
Agricultural development planning: economic concepts, administrative procedures, and political process / [by] Willard W. Cochrane. — New York: Praeger [1974] xii, 223 p.; 24 cm. (Praeger special studies in international economics and development) 1. Agriculture and state — Developing countries. I. T.
HD1417.C62 338.1/09172/4 *LC* 73-21464 *ISBN* 027508480X

**Cornell University Workshop on Food, Population, and Employment: the Social Impact of Modernizing Agriculture, Ithaca, N.Y., 1971.** 4.2895
Food, population, and employment: the impact of the green revolution / edited by Thomas T. Poleman [and] Donald K. Freebairn. — New York: Praeger Publishers [1973] xiv, 272 p. 25 cm. (Praeger special studies in international economics and development) 'Sponsored by Cornell's Program on Science, Technology, and Society.' 1. Agriculture — Economic aspects — Developing countries — Congresses. 2. Food supply — Congresses. 3. Green Revolution — Congresses. 4. Developing countries — Population — Congresses. I. Poleman, Thomas T. II. Freebairn, Donald K. III. Cornell University. Program on Science, Technology, and Society. IV. T.
HD1417.C67 1971 338.1/09172/4 *LC* 72-92463

**Griffin, Keith B.** 4.2896
The political economy of agrarian change: an essay on the green revolution / Keith Griffin. — Cambridge, Mass.: Harvard University Press, 1974. xv, 264 p.: ill.; 23 cm. 1. Agriculture and state — Developing countries. 2. Green Revolution — Developing countries 3. Agriculture — Economic aspects — Developing countries. I. T.
HD1417.G74 1974b 338.1/09172/4 *LC* 74-80154 *ISBN* 0674685318

**Institutions in agricultural development. Edited by Melvin G. Blase.** 4.2897
[1st ed.] Ames, Iowa State University Press [1971] xii, 247 p. illus. 24 cm. 'The International Rural Institutions Subcommittee of the North Central Land Economics Research Committee (NCR-6) initiated in 1967 the project leading to this book of readings.' 1. Agriculture — Economic aspects — Developing countries — Addresses, essays, lectures. 2. Agriculture and state — Developing countries — Addresses, essays, lectures. I. Blase, Melvin G. ed. II. North Central Land Economics Research Committee. International Rural Institutions Subcommittee.
HD1417.I58 338.1/08 *LC* 72-137088 *ISBN* 0813808553

**Johnston, Bruce F., 1919-.** 4.2898
Agriculture and structural transformation: economic strategies in late-developing countries / Bruce F. Johnston and Peter Kilby. — New York: Oxford University Press, 1975. xxi, 474 p.: ill.; 21 cm. (Economic development series) 1. Agriculture — Economic conditions — Developing countries. I. Kilby, Peter. joint author. II. T.
HD1417.J64 338.1/8/091724 *LC* 74-22880 *ISBN* 0195018702

**Mollett, J. A., 1923-.** 4.2899
Planning for agricultural development / J.A. Mollett. — London: Croom Helm; New York: St. Martin's Press, 1984. 355 p.: ill.; 23 cm. Includes index. 1. Agriculture and state — Developing countries. 2. Agriculture — Economic aspects — Developing countries. I. T.
HD1417.M64 1984 338.1/8/091724 19 *LC* 83-40192 *ISBN* 0709917848

**Morgan, W. B. (William Basil)** 4.2900
Agriculture in the Third World: a spatial analysis / W. B. Morgan. Boulder, Colo.: Westview Press, c1978. xiii, 290 p.: ill., maps; 23cm — (Westview advanced economic geography) Includes index. 1. Underdeveloped areas — Agriculture. 2. Agricultural geography I. T. II. Series.
HD1417.M68 1977 338.1/09172/4 *LC* 77-24064 *ISBN* 0891588191

**Pearse, Andrew Chernocke.** 4.2901
Seeds of plenty, seeds of want: social and economic implications of the green revolution / by Andrew Pearse. — Oxford: Clarendon Press; New York: Oxford University Press, 1980. xi, 262 p.; 23 cm. At head of title: United Nations Research Institute for Social Development. Includes index. 1. Green Revolution — Developing countries I. United Nations Research Institute for Social Development. II. T.
HD1417.P4 338.1/6 19 *LC* 80-40469 *ISBN* 0198771509

**Food and Agriculture Organization of the United Nations.** • 4.2902
World crop statistics: area, production and yield, 1948–64. — Rome, 1966. 458 p.: illus.; 22 x 28 cm. English, French and Spanish. 1. Agriculture — Statistics I. T.
HD1421.F6347 338.1/021/2 *LC* 67-1744

**Food and Agriculture Organization of the United Nations.** 4.2903
FAO production yearbook. Annuaire FAO de la production. Anuario FAO de producción. v. 30- 1976-. Rome, Food and Agriculture Organization of the United Nations. v. ill. 28 cm. (FAO statistics series) Annual. 1. Agriculture — Statistics — Periodicals. I. Food and Agriculture Organization of the United Nations. Annuaire FAO de la production. II. Food and Agriculture Organization of the United Nations. Anuario FAO de producción. III. T.
HD1421.P76 338.1/0212 *LC* 79-649153

**Parker, Robert Alexander Clarke, 1927-.** 4.2904
Coke of Norfolk: a financial and agricultural study, 1707–1842 / by R. A. C. Parker. — [S.l.]: Oxford, 1975. 222 p., [1] leaf of plates: ill.; 23 cm. 1. Leicester, Thomas William Coke, 1st Earl of, 1752-1842. 2. Agriculture — Economic aspects — England — Case studies. 3. Farm management — England — Case studies. I. T.
HD1471.G7 P37 338.1/092/4 B *LC* 76-358558 *ISBN* 0198224036

**Powell, Lawrence N.** 4.2905
New masters: northern planters during the Civil War and Reconstruction / Lawrence N. Powell. — New Haven: Yale University Press, 1980. xiv, 253 p.; 25 cm. — (Yale historical publications. Miscellany. 124) Includes index. 1. Plantations — Southern States — History. 2. Cotton growing — Southern States — History. 3. Afro-American agricultural laborers — Southern States — History. 4. Southern States — History — 1865-1877 I. T. II. Series.
HD1471.U5 P68 338.1/0975 *LC* 79-64226 *ISBN* 0300022174

**Wayne, Michael, 1947-.** 4.2906
The reshaping of plantation society: the Natchez district, 1860–1880 / Michael Wayne. — Baton Rouge: Louisiana State University Press, c1983. xii, 226 p.; 24 cm. Includes index. 1. Plantations — Mississippi — Natchez (District) — History. 2. Natchez (Miss.: District) — Economic conditions. 3. Natchez (Miss.: District) — Social conditions. I. T.
HD1471.U5 W39 1983 307.7/2 19 *LC* 82-7817 *ISBN* 0807110507

**MacFadyen, J. Tevere.** 4.2907
Gaining ground: the renewal of America's small farms / J. Tevere MacFadyen. — 1st ed. — New York: Holt, Rinehart, and Winston, c1984. xi, 242 p.; 22 cm. 'Portions of this book have appeared in different form in Horticulture, Country journal, and Orion nature quarterly'—T.p. verso. Includes index. 1. Farms, Small — United States. I. T.
HD1476.U5 M32 1984 338.1/0973 19 *LC* 83-13003 *ISBN* 0030695635

**Conrad, David Eugene.** • 4.2908
The forgotten farmers; the story of sharecroppers in the New Deal. Urbana, University of Illinois Press, 1965. 223 p. 1. Southern Tenant Farmers' Union. 2. Share-cropping 3. Agriculture — Economic aspects — Southern States I. T.
HD1478 U6 C6 *LC* 65-11734

**Davis, Ronald L. F.** 4.2909
Good and faithful labor: from slavery to sharecropping in the Natchez District, 1860–1890 / Ronald L.F. Davis. — Westport, Conn.: Greenwood Press, 1982. xv, 225 p.: ill.; 22 cm. — (Contributions in American history. 0084-9291; no. 100) Includes index. 1. Share-cropping — History. 2. Afro-Americans — Mississippi — Adams County — Economic conditions. 3. Afro-Americans — Louisiana — Concordia Parish — Economic conditions. 4. Concordia Parish (La.) — Rural conditions. 5. Adams County (Miss.) — Rural conditions. I. T. II. Series.
HD1478.U6 D38 1982 306/.3 19 *LC* 81-13367 *ISBN* 0313231346

**Shaw, Nate.** 4.2910
All God's dangers; the life of Nate Shaw [compiled by] Theodore Rosengarten. [1st ed.] New York, Knopf; [distributed by Random House] 1974. xxv, 561, xii p. map. 25 cm. 1. Shaw, Nate. 2. Share-cropping — History. 3. Afro-Americans — Alabama — Biography. 4. Alabama — Biography. I. Rosengarten, Theodore. II. T.
HD1478.U6 S5 1974 917.61/4/0360924 B *LC* 74-8269 *ISBN* 0394490843

# HD1483–1543 Agricultural Associations. Cooperative Agriculture. Tenancy

**McMath, Robert C., 1944-.** 4.2911
Populist vanguard: a history of the Southern Farmers' Alliance / by Robert C. McMath, Jr. — Chapel Hill: University of North Carolina Press, 1976 (c1975). xiii, 221 p.: ill.; 24 cm. Includes index. 1. National Farmers' Alliance and Industrial Union. 2. Populism — United States — History. I. T.
HD1485.N35 M35 338.1/06/275 *LC* 75-9751 *ISBN* 080781251X

**Morlan, Robert Loren, 1920-.**                                    • **4.2912**
Political prairie fire; the Nonpartisan League, 1915–1922. Minneapolis, University of Minnesota Press [1955] 408 p. illus., ports. 24 cm. 1. National Nonpartisan League. I. T.
HD1485.N4 M6      338.1      *LC* 55-8488

**Berger, Suzanne.**                                                **4.2913**
Peasants against politics; rural organization in Brittany, 1911–1967. Cambridge, Mass., Harvard University Press, 1972. xi, 298 p. illus. 25 cm. 1. Agriculture — France — Côtes-du-Nord (Dept.) — Societies, etc. 2. Agriculture — France — Finistère (Dept.) — Societies, etc. 3. Côtes-du-Nord (France) — Politics and government. 4. Finistère (France) — Politics and government. I. T.
HD1486.F8 B47      322/.2/094411      *LC* 73-174541      *ISBN* 0674659252

**Davies, R. W. (Robert William), 1925-.**                          **4.2914**
The industrialization of Russia / R. W. Davies. — Cambridge, Mass.: Harvard University Press, 1980. 2 v.; 23 cm. Includes indexes. 1. Collectivization of agriculture — Soviet Union — History. 2. Soviet Union — Economic policy — 1928-1932 3. Soviet Union — Industries — History. I. T.
HD1492.R9 D348      338.7/63/0947      *LC* 79-15263      *ISBN* 0674814800

**Stuart, Robert C., 1938-.**                                       **4.2915**
The collective farm in Soviet agriculture [by] Robert C. Stuart. — Lexington, Mass.: Lexington Books, [1972] xx, 254 p.: illus.; 23 cm. 1. Collective farms — Russia. 2. Collective farms — Management I. T.
HD1492.R9 S74      338.1      *LC* 77-175164      *ISBN* 066981265X

**Humphrey, Caroline.**                                             **4.2916**
Karl Marx collective: economy, society, and religion in a Siberian collective farm / Caroline Humphrey. — Cambridge [Cambridgeshire]; New York: Cambridge University Press; Paris: Editions de la Maison des Sciences de l'Homme, 1983. xviii, 522 p.: ill.; 24 cm. — (Cambridge studies in social anthropology. 40) Includes index. 1. State farms — Russian S.F.S.R. — Barguzinskiĭ raĭon — Case studies. I. T. II. Series.
HD1493.S65 H85 1983      338.7/63/09575 19      *LC* 82-19846      *ISBN* 0521244560

**Currie, J. M.**                                                   **4.2917**
The economic theory of agricultural land tenure / J.M. Currie. — Cambridge; New York: Cambridge University Press, 1981. vii, 194 p.: ill.; 24 cm. Includes index. 1. Farm tenancy — Economic aspects 2. Agriculture — Economic aspects I. T.
HD1510.C87      333.3 19      *LC* 80-41114      *ISBN* 0521236347

**Richards, Eric.**                                                 **4.2918**
A history of the Highland clearances: Agrarian transformation and the evictions 1746–1886 / Eric Richards. — London: Croom Helm, c1982. 532 p.; 23 cm. Includes index. 1. Crofters — History. 2. Farm tenancy — Scotland — Highlands — History. 3. Eviction — Scotland — Highlands — History. 4. Highlands (Scotland) — Economic conditions. I. T.
HD1511.G7 R53 1982      333.33/5 19      *LC* 81-208122      *ISBN* 085664496X

**Winters, Donald L.**                                              **4.2919**
Farmers without farms: agricultural tenancy in nineteenth–century Iowa / Donald L. Winters. — Westport, Conn.: Greenwood Press, 1978. xvi, 145 p.: ill.; 22 cm. — (Contributions in American history; no. 79 0084-9219) Includes index. 1. Farm tenancy — Economic aspects — Iowa — History. I. T.
HD1511.U6 I88      333.3/35/09777      *LC* 78-4021      *ISBN* 031320408X

### HD1513–1543 PEASANTS. AGRICULTURAL LABORERS

**Scott, James C.**                                                 **4.2920**
The moral economy of the peasant: rebellion and subsistence in Southeast Asia / James C. Scott. New Haven: Yale University Press, 1976. ix, 246 p.: ill.; 24 cm. 1. Peasantry — Asia, Southeastern. I. T.
HD1513.A755 S36      301.44/43/0959      *LC* 75-43334      *ISBN* 0300018622

**Popkin, Samuel L.**                                               **4.2921**
The rational peasant: the political economy of rural society in Vietnam / Samuel L. Popkin. — Berkeley: University of California Press, c1979. xxi, 306 p.: maps; 22 cm. Includes index. 1. Peasantry — Vietnam — History. 2. Peasantry 3. Vietnam — Rural conditions. I. T.
HD1513.V5 P66      301.44/43/09597      *LC* 77-83105      *ISBN* 0520035615

**Sosnick, Stephen H.**                                             **4.2922**
Hired hands: seasonal farm workers in the United States / by Stephen H. Sosnick. — Santa Barbara: McNally & Loftin, West, c1978. xi, 453 p.; 24 cm.

1. Agricultural laborers — United States 2. Seasonal labor — United States. 3. Migrant agricultural laborers — United States. I. T.
HD1525.S63      331.5/44/0973      *LC* 78-13908      0874613781

**Stein, Walter J.**                                                **4.2923**
California and the Dust Bowl migration / [by] Walter J. Stein. — Westport, Conn.: Greenwood Press, [1973] xiv, 302 p.; 22 cm. — (Contributions in American history, no. 21) Originally presented as the author's thesis, University of California, Berkeley. 1. Agricultural laborers — California. 2. Migration, Internal — United States. 3. California — Emigration and immigration. I. T.
HD1527.C2 S76 1973      331.7/63/09794      *LC* 70-175611      *ISBN* 083716267X

**Horn, Pamela.**                                                   **4.2924**
Labouring life in the Victorian countryside / Pamela Horn. — Toronto: Macmillan of Canada, 1976. 292 p., [8] leaves of plates: ill.; 23 cm. Includes index. 1. Agricultural laborers — Great Britain — History. 2. Great Britain — Rural conditions I. T.
HD1534.H59      301.44/42/0942      *LC* 76-377375      *ISBN* 0717107280

**Newby, Howard.**                                                  **4.2925**
The deferential worker: a study of farm workers in East Anglia / [by] Howard Newby. — London: Allen Lane, 1977. 462 p.; 23 cm. 1. Agricultural laborers — England — East Anglia. I. T.
HD1534.N48      301.44/43/09426      *LC* 78-308049      *ISBN* 0713908920

**Grossman, Lawrence S., 1948-.**                                   **4.2926**
Peasants, subsistence ecology, and development in the highlands of Papua New Guinea / by Lawrence S. Grossman. — Princeton, N.J.: Princeton University Press, c1984. xxi, 302, [9] p. of plates: ill.; 25 cm. Includes index. 1. Peasantry — Papua New Guinea. 2. Rural development — Papua New Guinea. 3. Agriculture — Economic aspects — Papua New Guinea. 4. Human ecology — Papua New Guinea. I. T.
HD1537.P26 G76 1984      305.5/63 19      *LC* 84-42581      *ISBN* 0691094063

### HD1581–1741 Land Reclamation. Water Resources

**Wagret, Paul.**                                                   **4.2927**
Polderlands; translated [from the French] by Margaret Sparks. — London: Methuen, [1972, c1968] xvi, 288 p.: illus., maps.; 23 cm. (University paperbacks) Translation of Les polders. 1. Polders 2. Reclamation of land I. T.
HD1681.W25 1972      333.9/17

**National Symposium on Wetlands, Disneyworld Village, Lake**       **4.2928**
**Buena Vista, Florida, 1978.**
Wetland functions and values: the state of our understanding; proceedings of the National Symposium on Wetlands held in Disneyworld Village, Lake Buena Vista, Florida, November 7–10, 1978 / edited by Phillip E. Greeson, John R. Clark, Judith E. Clark. — Minneapolis, Minn.:American Water Resources Association, 1979. x, 674 p.: ill., cartes. — (Technical publication series - American Water Resources Association; TPS79-2) 'Sponsored by American Water Resources Association, National Wetlands Technical Council'...[et al.]. 1. Wetland ecology — Congresses. 2. Wetlands — United States — Congresses. I. Greeson, Phillip E. II. Clark, John R., 1927- III. Clark, Judith E. IV. United States. National Wetlands Technical Council. V. American Water Resources Association. VI. T.
HD1683.E83 N277 1978      *LC* 79-93316

**Wiener, Aaron.**                                                  **4.2929**
The role of water in development: an analysis of principles of comprehensive planning. — New York; Montreal: McGraw-Hill, c1972. xi, 483 p.; 23 cm. — (McGraw-Hill series in water resources and environmental engineering) 1. Water resources development — Planning. I. T.
HD1691.W49      333.9/1      *LC* 71-154240      *ISBN* 0070701504

**Hirshleifer, Jack.**                                              **4.2930**
Water supply: economics, technology and policy / [by] Jack Hirshleifer, James C. DeHaven [and] Jerome W. Milliman. — Chicago: University of Chicago Press [1969] xiv, 386 p.: ill., maps; 25 cm. "Fourth impression, with new postscript, 1969." 1. Water-rights — U.S. 2. Water resources development — U.S. 3. Water-supply — U.S. I. Milliman, Jerome W. joint author. II. DeHaven, James Charles, 1912- joint author. III. T.
HD1694.A5 H5x

**Water Resources Council (U.S.)**                                  • **4.2931**
The Nation's water resources: the first national assessment. — Washington: [For sale by the Supt. of Docs., U.S. Govt. Print. Off.] 1968. 1 v. (various pagings): ill., maps (both part col.); 26 cm. 1. Water resources development — United States. 2. Water-supply — United States. I. T.
HD1694.A58 1968      333.9/1      *LC* 68-62779

**Anderson, Terry Lee, 1946-.** 4.2932
Water crisis: ending the policy drought / Terry L. Anderson. — Baltimore, Md.: Johns Hopkins University Press, c1983. xii, 121 p.: ill.; 23 cm. 1. Water conservation — Government policy — West (U.S.) 2. Water-supply — West (U.S.) — Rates. 3. Water-rights — West (U.S.) I. T.
HD1695.A17 A59    HD1695A17 A59 1983.    333.91/16/0973 19
LC 83-48046    ISBN 0801830877

**Pisani, Donald J.** 4.2933
From the family farm to agribusiness: the irrigation crusade in California and the West, 1850–1931 / Donald J. Pisani. — Berkeley: University of California Press, c1984. xiii, 521 p., [8] p. of plates: ill.; 24 cm. Includes index. 1. Irrigation — Economic aspects — California — History. 2. Agriculture — Economic aspects — California — History. I. T.
HD1739.C2 P57 1984    338.1/62 19    LC 83-17928    ISBN 0520051270

**Wilkinson, John Craven.** 4.2934
Water and tribal settlement in South–east Arabia: a study of the Aflāj of Oman / J. C. Wilkinson. — New York: Oxford University Press, 1977. xvi, 276 p.: ill.; 27 cm. — (Oxford research studies in geography) Includes index. 1. Water-supply — Oman. 2. Land settlement — Oman. 3. Oman — Social life and customs. I. T.
HD1741.O4 W55    333.9/13/09535    LC 77-7347    ISBN 0198232179

## HD1748–2210 AGRICULTURE, BY COUNTRY

## HD1751–1775 United States

**Farm structure: a historical perspective on changes in the number and size of farms / Committee on Agriculture, Nutrition, and Forestry, United States Senate.** 4.2935
Washington: U.S.G.P.O., 1980. vii, 379 p.: graphs. 1. Farms — United States. I. United States. Congress. Senate. Committee on Agriculture, Nutrition, and Forestry.
HD1753 1980 F3

**Ball, A. Gordon.** 4.2936
Size, structure, and future of farms. Edited by A. Gordon Ball and Earl O. Heady. — [1st ed.]. — Ames: Iowa State University Press, [1972] viii, 404 p.; 23 cm. 1. Farms, Size of — U.S. — Addresses, essays, lectures. 2. Farms — U.S. — Addresses, essays, lectures. I. Heady, Earl Orel, 1916- joint author. II. T.
HD1759.B34    338.1    LC 78-153163    ISBN 0813814405

**Benedict, Murray Reed, 1892-.** • 4.2937
Farm policies of the United States, 1790–1950: a study of their origins and development, by Murray R. Benedict. — New York: Octagon Books, 1966 [c1953] xv, 548 p.; 27 cm. 1. Agriculture and state — United States I. T.
HD1761.B37 1966    338.1/0973    LC 66-28382

**Campbell, Christiana McFadyen, 1915-.** • 4.2938
The Farm Bureau and the New Deal; a study of making of national farm policy, 1933–40. Urbana, University of Illinois Press, 1962. viii, 215 p. tables. 24 cm. Substantially the author's thesis, University of Chicago. Bibliography: p. [196]-201. 1. American Farm Bureau Federation. 2. Agriculture and state — United States I. T.
HD1761.C3 1962    338.10973    LC 62-13210

**Christenson, Reo Millard, 1918-.** • 4.2939
The Brannan plan; farm politics and policy. Ann Arbor, University of Michigan Press [1959] 207 p. 1. Agriculture and state — United States I. T.
HD1761 C5    LC 59-5265

**Cochrane, Willard Wesley, 1914-.** • 4.2940
Farm prices, myth and reality. Minneapolis, University of Minnesota Press [1958] vii, 189 p. diagrs. 24 cm. 1. Agricultural prices — United States. 2. Agriculture — Economic aspects — United States. I. T.
HD1761.C6    LC 58-7556

**Fite, Gilbert Courtland, 1918-.** • 4.2941
George N. Peek and the fight for farm parity. [1st ed.] Norman, University of Oklahoma Press [1954] xiii, 314 p. illus., ports. 23 cm. 1. Peek, George Nelson, 1873-1943. 2. Agriculture — Economic aspects — United States. 3. Agriculture and state — United States I. T.
HD1761.F56    LC 54-5934

**Kirkendall, Richard Stewart, 1928-.** • 4.2942
Social scientists and farm politics in the age of Roosevelt [by] Richard S. Kirkendall. Columbia, University of Missouri Press [1966] ix, 358 p. ports. 1. Agriculture and state — United States I. T.
HD1761 K5    LC 66-14032

**Matusow, Allen J.** • 4.2943
Farm policies and politics in the Truman years, by Allen J. Matusow. — Cambridge, Mass.: Harvard University Press, 1967. 267 p.; 22 cm. — (Harvard historical studies. v. 80) 1. Agriculture and state — United States 2. Agriculture — Economic aspects — United States. 3. United States — Politics and government — 1945-1953 I. T. II. Series.
HD1761.M39    338.1/0973    LC 67-12101

*(handwritten: HD 1761 M44)*

**Peterson, Trudy Huskamp, 1945-.** 4.2944
Agricultural exports, farm income, and the Eisenhower administration / Trudy Huskamp Peterson. — Lincoln: University of Nebraska Press, 1980 (c1979). xii, 222 p.; 23 cm. Includes index. 1. Agriculture — Economic aspects — United States — History. 2. Agriculture and state — United States — History. 3. Farm income — United States — History. 4. United States — Economic policy — 1945-1960 I. T.
HD1761.P42    338.1/873    LC 79-15825    ISBN 080323659X

**Saloutos, Theodore.** 4.2945
The American farmer and the New Deal / Theodore Saloutos. — 1st ed. — Ames: Iowa State University Press, 1982. xviii, 327 p., [10] p. of plates: ill.; 24 cm. — (Henry A. Wallace series on agricultural history and rural studies.) Includes index. 1. Agriculture and state — United States 2. Agriculture — Economic aspects — United States. 3. Farmers — United States 4. New Deal, 1933-1939 5. United States — Economic policy — 1933-1945 I. T. II. Series.
HD1761.S188 1982    338.1/873 19    LC 81-12396    ISBN 0813810760

**Shideler, James H.** • 4.2946
Farm crisis, 1919–1923. Berkeley, University of California Press, 1957. x, 345 p. 25 cm. 'Bibliographical notes': p. 297-301. Bibliographical references included in 'Notes' (p. 303-331) 1. Agriculture — Economic aspects — United States. 2. Agriculture and state — United States I. T.
HD1761.S54    338.15    LC 57-10502

**Shover, John L.** 4.2947
First majority, last minority: the transforming of rural life in America / John L. Shover. — DeKalb: Northern Illinois University Press, c1976. xix, 338 p.: ill.; 22 cm. — (Minorities in American history) Includes index. 1. Agriculture — Economic aspects — United States — History. 2. United States — Rural conditions I. T. II. Series.
HD1761.S556    307.7/2/0973 19    LC 75-26473    ISBN 0875800564

**Taylor, Henry Charles, 1873-.** • 4.2948
The story of agricultural economics in the United States, 1840–1932; men, services, ideas [by] Henry C. and Anne Dewees Taylor. Farm finance section by Norman J. Wall; foreword by Everett E. Edwards; indexed by Adelaide R. Hasse. Ames, Iowa State College Press [1952] xxvi, 1121 p.: ill.; 24 cm. 1. Agriculture — Economic aspects — United States 2. Agriculture and state — United States I. Taylor, Anne (Dewees) II. T. III. Title: Agricultural economics in the United States, 1840-1932.
HD1761.T28    338.1    LC 52-14651

## HD1765 BY DATE

**Shannon, Fred A. (Fred Albert), 1893-1963.** 4.2949
The farmer's last frontier: agriculture, 1860–1897 / by Fred A. Shannon. — White Plains, N.Y.: M. E. Sharpe, [1977] c1945. xii, 434 p., [8] leaves of plates: ill.; 24 cm. Reprint of the ed. published by Farrar & Rinehart, New York, which was issued as v. 5 of the Economic history of the United States. Includes index. 1. Agriculture — Economic aspects — United States — History. I. T.
HD1765 1860.S5 1977    338.1/0973    LC 76-48797    ISBN 0873320999

**Perkins, Van L.** • 4.2950
Crisis in agriculture: the Agricultural Adjustment Administration and the New Deal, 1933 / by Van L. Perkins. — Berkeley, University of California Press, 1969. vii, 245 p.; 24 cm. — (University of California publications in history, v. 81) 1. United States. Agricultural Adjustment Administration. 2. Agriculture and state — United States 3. New Deal, 1933-1939 I. T.
HD1765 1933P4x E173.C15 vol. 81    353.008/23    LC 77-627117

**Baldwin, Sidney, 1922-.** • 4.2951
Poverty and politics; the rise and decline of the Farm Security Administration. [Chapel Hill, University of North Carolina Press, 1968] xvi, 438 p. illus. 24 cm. 1. United States. Farm Security Administration. 2. Agricultural administration — United States. I. T.
HD1765 1935.B3    353.81    LC 68-18052

**Benson, Ezra Taft.** • 4.2952
Cross fire. [1st ed.] Garden City. N.Y., Doubleday, 1962. 627 p. illus. 24 cm.
1. Agriculture and state — United States 2. United States — Politics and
government — 1953-1961 I. T.
HD1765 1953.B46 1962    LC 62-11368

**Schultze, Charles L.** • 4.2953
The distribution of farm subsidies; who gets the benefits? A staff paper [by]
Charles L. Schultze. Washington, Brookings Institution [1971] x, 51 p. 23 cm.
1. Agricultural price supports — United States 2. Subsidies — United States.
I. Brookings Institution. II. T.
HD1765 1971.S39    338.1/873    LC 75-156901    ISBN 0815777531

**Johnson, Glenn L.** 4.2954
The overproduction trap in U.S. agriculture; a study of resource allocation from
World War I to the late 1960's. Edited by Glenn L. Johnson and C. Leroy
Quance. — Baltimore: Published for Resources for the Future by the Johns
Hopkins University Press, [1972] xvii, 211 p.; 23 cm. 1. Agriculture —
Economic aspects — United States — Addresses, essays, lectures.
2. Agriculture and state — United States — Addresses, essays, lectures.
I. Quance, C. Leroy, joint author. II. Resources for the Future. III. T.
HD1765 1972.J63    338.1/873    LC 77-186509    ISBN 0801813875

**Cochrane, Willard Wesley, 1914-.** 4.2955
American farm policy, 1948–1973 / by Willard W. Cochrane and Mary E.
Ryan. — Minneapolis: University of Minnesota Press, c1976. xiv, 431 p.:
graphs; 24 cm. 1. Agriculture and state — United States I. Ryan, Mary Ellen,
1928- joint author. II. T.
HD1765 1976.C6 1976    338.1/873    LC 75-32671    ISBN
0816607834

**1982 census of agriculture.** 4.2956
[Suitland, Md.]: U.S. Dept. of Commerce, Bureau of the Census, < 1984- >.
< v. 1, pt. 48; in 1 >; 28 cm. Includes indexes. 1. Agriculture — United States
— Statistics. I. United States. Bureau of the Census.
HD1769.A14 1984    338.1/0973 19    LC 83-600308

### HD1773–1775 SPECIAL REGIONS

**Russell, Howard S.** 4.2957
A long, deep furrow: three centuries of farming in New England / by Howard S.
Russell. Hanover, N.H.: University Press of New England, 1976. xvi, 672 p.:
ill.; 24 cm. Includes index. 1. Agriculture — Economic aspects — New
England — History. I. T.
HD1773.A2 R87    338.1/0974    LC 73-91314    ISBN 0874510937

**Bogue, Allan G.** • 4.2958
From prairie to corn belt; farming on the Illinois and Iowa prairies in the
nineteenth century. Chicago, University of Chicago Press [1963] 310 p. maps,
diagrs., tables. 1. Agriculture — Economic aspects — Illinois 2. Agriculture
— Economic aspects — Iowa 3. Land settlement — Illinois 4. Land settlement
— Iowa I. T.
HD1773 A3 B6    LC 63-20913

**DeCanio, Stephen J.** 4.2959
Agriculture in the postbellum South: the economics of production and supply
[by] Stephen J. DeCanio. — Cambridge: M.I.T. Press, 1975 (c1974). xii, 335 p.;
23 cm. — (M.I.T. monographs in economics, 12) 1. Agriculture — Economic
aspects — Southern States — History. 2. Agriculture — Economic aspects —
Southern States — Mathematical models. I. T. II. Series.
HD1773.A5 D4    338.1/0975    LC 74-9636    ISBN 0262040476

**Fite, Gilbert Courtland, 1918-.** 4.2960
Cotton fields no more: Southern agriculture, 1865–1980 / Gilbert C. Fite. —
Lexington, Ky.: University Press of Kentucky, c1984. xiii, 273 p., 8 p. of plates:
ill.; 25 cm. (New perspectives on the South.) 1. Agriculture — Economic
aspects — Southern States — History. I. T. II. Series.
HD1773.A5 F58 1984    338.1/0975 19    LC 84-7439    ISBN
0813103061

### HD1781–1900 Canada. Latin America

**Jones, Robert Leslie, 1907-.** • 4.2961
History of agriculture in Ontario, 1613–1880 / by Robert Leslie Jones; with a
foreword by Fred Landon. — Toronto, University of Toronto press, 1946. xvi,
420 p.; 25 cm. — (University of Toronto studies. History and economics; v. 11)
1. Agriculture — Economic aspects — Ontario. 2. Agriculture — Ontario.
I. T.
HD1790.O6 J6    LC 47-27166

**De Janvry, Alain.** 4.2962
The agrarian question and reformism in Latin America / Alain de Janvry. —
Baltimore: The Johns Hopkins University Press, 1982 (c1981). xvi, 311 p.; 24

cm. — (Johns Hopkins studies in development.) Includes index. 1. Agriculture
and state — Latin America. 2. Land reform — Latin America. I. T. II. Series.
HD1790.5.Z8 D4 1981    338.1/88 19    LC 81-4147    ISBN
0801825318

**Lamartine Yates, Paul.** 4.2963
[Campo mexicano. English] Mexico's agricultural dilemma / P. Lamartine
Yates. — Tucson, Ariz.: University of Arizona Press, 1981. xv, 291 p.: ill.; 24
cm. Abridged, rev. and updated version of: El campo mexicano. Includes index.
1. Agriculture — Economic aspects — Mexico. 2. Agriculture — Mexico.
3. Agriculture — Social aspects — Mexico. I. T.
HD1792.L35213    338.1/0972 19    LC 81-10279    ISBN 0816507341

**Collins, Joseph, 1945-.** 4.2964
What difference could a revolution make?: food and farming in the new
Nicaragua / by Joseph Collins, with Frances Moore Lappé and Nick Allen. —
San Francisco, CA: Institute for Food and Development Policy, c1982. x,
185 p.; 22 cm. 1. Agriculture — Economic aspects — Nicaragua. 2. Land
tenure — Nicaragua. 3. Land reform — Nicaragua. 4. Food supply —
Nicaragua. I. Lappé, Frances Moore. II. Allen, Nick, 1950- III. T.
HD1817.C64 1982    338.1/097285 19    LC 82-21032    ISBN
0935028102

**Gudeman, Stephen.** 4.2965
The demise of a rural economy: from subsistence to capitalism in a Latin
American village / Stephen Gudeman. — London; Boston: Routledge & K.
Paul, 1978. 176 p.; 23 cm. — (International library of anthropology.) Includes
index. 1. Agriculture — Economic aspects — Panama — Los Boquerones
region. 2. Sugar growing — Panama — Los Boquerones region. 3. Los
Boquerones region, Panama — Rural conditions. I. T. II. Series.
HD1825.L67 G8    330.9/8/003    LC 79-307023    ISBN 0710088353

**MacEwan, Arthur.** 4.2966
Revolution and economic development in Cuba / Arthur MacEwan. — New
York: St. Martin's Press, 1981. xvi, 265 p.; 23 cm. Includes index.
1. Agriculture — Economic aspects — Cuba. 2. Socialism — Cuba 3. Cuba —
Social conditions — 1959- 4. Cuba — Economic conditions — 1959- I. T.
HD1837.M3 1981    338.1/87291    LC 80-11130    ISBN 0312679807

## HD1916–2055 Europe

**Duby, Georges.** • 4.2967
[Économie rural et la vie des campagnes dans l'occident mediéval. English]
Rural economy and country life in the medieval West. Translated by Cynthia
Postan. Columbia, University of South Carolina Press [1968] xv, 600 p. illus.,
maps. 24 cm. Translation of L'économie rurale et la vie des campagnes dans
l'occident mediéval. 1. Agriculture — Economic aspects — Europe.
2. Agriculture — History I. T.
HD1917.D813    338.1/094    LC 68-20530

**European peasants and their markets: essays in agrarian
economic history / edited by William N. Parker and Eric L.
Jones.** 4.2968
Princeton, N.J.: Princeton University Press, 1976 (c1975). viii, 366 p.: graphs;
24 cm. 1. Agriculture — Economic aspects — Europe — History —
Addresses, essays, lectures. 2. Peasantry — Europe — Addresses, essays,
lectures. 3. Land tenure — Europe — History — Addresses, essays, lectures.
I. Parker, William Nelson. II. Jones, E. L. (Eric Lionel).
HD1917.E86    338.1/094    LC 75-15281

**Slicher van Bath, B. H.** • 4.2969
The agrarian history of Western Europe, A.D. 500–1850 / B. H. Slicher van
Bath; translated by Olive Ordish. — New York: St. Martin's Press, 1963
[i.e.1964] ix, 364 p.: ill. 'Authorized translation from the Dutch De agrarische
geschiedenis van West-Europa (500-1850)' 1. Agriculture — Europe —
History. 2. Peasantry — Europe — History. 3. Europe — Rural conditions.
I. T.
HD1917.S553 1963    LC 64-10299

**Wädekin, Karl Eugen.** 4.2970
Agrarian policies in communist Europe: a critical introduction / by Karl-
Eugen Wädekin; edited by Everett M. Jacobs. — Totowa, N.J.: Allanheld,
Osmun, c1982. x, 324 p.; 24 cm. — (Studies in East European and Soviet
Russian agrarian policy. v. 1) Includes index. 1. Agriculture and state —
Europe, Eastern. 2. Agriculture — Economic aspects — Europe, Eastern.
I. Jacobs, Everett M. II. T. III. Series.
HD1918 1982.W33    338.1/847 19    LC 79-55000    ISBN
0916672409

**Clout, Hugh D.** 4.2971
A rural policy for the EEC? / Hugh Clout. — London; New York: Methuen,
1985 (c1984). xiii, 214 p.: ill.; 23 cm. (Methuen EEC series.) 1. Rural

development — Government policy — European Economic Community countries. I. T. II. Title: Rural policy for the E.E.C.? III. Series.
HD1920.5.Z8 C56    338.94/009173/4 19    *LC* 84-6600    *ISBN* 0416345409

**Hill, Brian E.**                     **4.2972**
The common agricultural policy: past, present, and future / Brian E. Hill. — London; New York: Methuen, 1984. 168 p. (Methuen EEC series.) Includes index. 1. Agriculture and state — European Economic Community countries. 2. Agricultural price supports — European Economic Community countries. 3. Surplus agricultural commodities — European Economic Community countries. 4. Agriculture — Economic aspects — European Economic Community countries. I. T. II. Series.
HD1920.5.Z8 H55 1984    338.1/81/094 19    *LC* 84-4556    *ISBN* 0416321801

**Property, paternalism, and power: class and control in rural**    **4.2973**
**England / Howard Newby ... [et al.].**
Madison: University of Wisconsin Press, c1978. 432 p.; 23 cm. Includes index. 1. Farmers — England — East Anglia. 2. Land tenure — England — East Anglia. 3. Paternalism — England — East Anglia. 4. Sociology, Rural 5. East Anglia (England) — Rural conditions. I. Newby, Howard.
HD1930.E17 P76 1978    307.7/2/09426 19    *LC* 78-20301    *ISBN* 0229078701

**Karcz, Jerzy F, ed.**                    **4.2974**
Soviet and East European agriculture. Edited, with a pref., by Jerzy F. Karcz. Berkeley University of California Press 1967. 445p. (Russian and East European studies.) 1. Agriculture and state — Russia — Addresses, essays, lectures 2. Agriculture and state — Europa, Eastern — Addresses, essays, lectures I. California. University. Center for Slavic and East European Studies II. Conference on Soviet Agricultural and Peasant Affairs, Santa Barbara, Calif., 1965 III. T. IV. Series.
HD1992 C6 1965AA

**Wädekin, Karl Eugen.**                   **4.2975**
Current trends in the Soviet and East European food economy / edited by Karl–Eugen Wädekin = Osteuropas Nahrungswirtschaft Gestern und Morgen / herausgegeben von Karl–Eugen Wädekin. — Berlin: Duncker & Humblot; Manhattan, Kan.: Distribution in the U.S.A. and Canada, Graduate School, Kansas State University, 1982. 368 p.: ill.; 24 cm. (Osteuropastudien der Hochschulen des Landes Hessen. Giessener Abhandlungen zur Agrar- und Wirtschaftsforschung des europäischen Ostens, 0078-6888; Bd. 113) English and German; summary in German. 'This volume is an outgrowth of the Sixth International Conference on Soviet and East European Agricultural Affairs held at Schloss Rauisch-Holzhausen, Germany, June 5-8, 1981'—Pref. 1. Agriculture — Economic aspects — Soviet Union — Congresses. 2. Food supply — Soviet Union — Congresses. 3. Agriculture and state — Soviet Union — Congresses. 4. Agriculture — Economic aspects — Europe, Eastern — Congresses. 5. Food supply — Europe, Eastern — Congresses. 6. Agriculture and state — Europe, Eastern — Congresses. I. International Conference on Soviet and East European Agricultural Affairs. (6th: 1981: Schloss Rauisch-Holzhausen) II. T. III. Title: Osteuropas Nahrungswirtschaft Gestern und Morgen. IV. Series.
HD1992.C87 1982    338.1/9/47 19    *LC* 82-189357    *ISBN* 3428050517

**Jasny, Naum, 1883-1967.**                 • **4.2976**
The socialized agriculture of the USSR; plans and performance. — Stanford, Stanford University Press [1949] xv, 837 p. illus., maps. 24 cm. — (Stanford University. Food Research Institute. Grain economics series, no. 5) 'Sources cited': p. [799]-813. 1. Agriculture — Economic aspects — Russia. I. T. II. Series.
HD1992.J3    338.1    *LC* 49-6913 *

**Johnson, D. Gale (David Gale), 1916-.**           **4.2977**
Prospects for Soviet agriculture in the 1980s / D. Gale Johnson and Karen Brooks. — Bloomington: Indiana University Press, 1983. p. cm. 'Published in association with the Center for Strategic and International Studies, Georgetown University.' 1. Agriculture — Economic aspects — Soviet Union. I. Brooks, Karen (Karen McConnell) II. Georgetown University. Center for Strategic and International Studies. III. T.
HD1992.J56 1983    338.1/0947 19    *LC* 82-15847    *ISBN* 0253346193

**The Soviet rural economy / edited by Robert C. Stuart.**    **4.2978**
Totowa, N.J.: Rowman & Allanheld, 1983. viii, 326 p.; 25 cm. 1. Agriculture — Economic aspects — Soviet Union — Congresses. 2. Agriculture and state — Soviet Union — Congresses. 3. Rural development — Government policy — Soviet Union — Congresses. 4. Soviet Union — Economic policy — 1917- — Congresses. 5. Soviet Union — Rural conditions — Congresses. I. Stuart, Robert C., 1938-
HD1992.S5944 1984    338.1/0947 19    *LC* 83-9668    *ISBN* 0865980926

**Wädekin, Karl Eugen.**                   **4.2979**
The private sector in Soviet agriculture / edited by George Karcz; translated by Keith Bush. — 2d, enl., rev. ed. of Privatproduzenten in der sowjetischen Landwirtschaft. — Berkeley: University of California Press, [1973] xviii, 407 p.; 25 cm. — (Russian and East European studies.) 1. Allotment of land — Russia. 2. Agriculture and state — Russia. I. Karcz, George, ed. II. T. III. Series.
HD1992.W313 1973    338.1/0947    *LC* 76-95322    *ISBN* 0520015584

**Joravsky, David.**                    • **4.2980**
The Lysenko affair. — Cambridge, Mass.: Harvard University Press, 1970. xiii, 459 p.; 24 cm. — (Russian Research Center studies, 61) 1. Lysenko, Trofim Denisovich, 1898-1976. 2. Agriculture and state — Russia. I. T.
HD1993 1970.J6    338.1/847    *LC* 79-113184    *ISBN* 0674539850

**Hedlund, Stefan, 1953-.**                 **4.2981**
Crisis in Soviet agriculture / Stefan Hedlund. — London: Croom Helm; New York: St. Martin's Press, 1984. 228 p.; 23 cm. Includes index. 1. Agriculture and state — Soviet Union. 2. Agriculture — Economic aspects — Soviet Union. 3. Agriculture — Soviet Union. I. T.
HD1993.H43 1984    338.1/847 19    *LC* 83-42998    *ISBN* 0312174012

## HD2056–2195 Asia. Africa. Australia

**Asian Development Bank.**                **4.2982**
Rural Asia: challenge and opportunity / Asian Development Bank. — New York: Praeger, 1978, c1977. 489 p.: ill.; 25 cm. 1. Agriculture — Economic aspects — Asia. 2. Rural development — Asia. 3. Asia — Rural conditions. I. T.
HD2056.A85 1978    338.1/095    *LC* 77-25907

**Agricultural development in the Middle East / edited by Peter**    **4.2983**
**Beaumont and Keith McLachlan.**
Chichester [Sussex]; New York: Wiley, c1985. xii, 349 p.: ill.; 24 cm. 1. Agriculture — Economic aspects — Near East. 2. Agriculture — Near East. I. Beaumont, Peter. II. McLachlan, K. S. (Keith Stanley)
HD2056.5.A64 1985    338.1/0956 19    *LC* 85-6414    *ISBN* 0471907626

**Bardhan, Pranab K.**                  **4.2984**
Land, labor, and rural poverty: essays in development economics / Pranab K. Bardhan. — Delhi: Oxford University Press; New York: Columbia University Press, 1984. ix, 252 p.: ill.; 24 cm. Includes indexes. 1. Agriculture — Economic aspects — India. 2. Agricultural laborers — India. 3. Land tenure — India. 4. Rural poor — India. 5. India — Rural conditions. I. T.
HD2072.B29 1984    338.1/0954 19    *LC* 83-10082    *ISBN* 0231053886

**Franda, Marcus F.**                   **4.2985**
India's rural development: an assessment of alternatives / Marcus Franda. — Bloomington: Indiana University Press, c1979. xi, 306 p.: ill. 1. Rural development — India 2. Agriculture and state — India 3. India — Politics and government — 1947- I. T.
HD2072.F68    HD2072 F68.    338.1/0954    *LC* 79-2177    *ISBN* 025319315X

**Frankel, Francine R.**                  **4.2986**
India's green revolution; economic gains and political costs [by] Francine R. Frankel. — Princeton, N.J.: Princeton University Press, 1971. vii, 232 p.: map.; 23 cm. 1. Agriculture — Economic aspects — India. 2. Green Revolution — India. 3. India — Politics and government — 1947- I. T.
HD2072.F7    338.1/0954    *LC* 74-132237    *ISBN* 0691075360

**Thorner, Daniel.**                    • **4.2987**
Land and labour in India [by] Daniel and Alic Thorner. — Bombay, Asia Pub. House [1962] 227 p. Includes bibliography and bibliographical footnotes. 1. Land use — India. 2. Agriculture — Economic aspects — India. I. Thorner, Alice, 1917- joint author II. T.
HD2072.T48

**Havens, Thomas R. H.**                 **4.2988**
Farm and nation in modern Japan: Agrarian nationalism, 1870–1940, by Thomas R. H. Havens. — Princeton, N.J.: Princeton University Press, [1974] xi, 358 p.; 23 cm. — 1. Agriculture — Economic aspects — Japan. 2. Agriculture and state — Japan. 3. Nationalism — Japan. 4. Japan — Rural conditions I. T.
HD2092.H366    338.1/0952    *LC* 74-3475    *ISBN* 0691031010

**Lardy, Nicholas R.**                  **4.2989**
Agriculture in China's modern economic development / Nicholas R. Lardy. — Cambridge [Cambridgeshire]; New York: Cambridge University Press, 1983. xiii, 285 p.: ill.; 24 cm. Includes index. 1. Agriculture and state — China.

2. Agriculture — Economic aspects — China. 3. Food supply — China. 4. China — Economic policy — 1976- I. T. HD2098.L37 1983    338.1/0951 19    *LC* 82-23555    *ISBN* 0521252466

**Eicher, Carl K.**                                                                 **4.2990**
Research on agricultural development in sub–Saharan Africa: a critical survey / by Carl K. Eicher and Doyle C. Baker. — East Lansing, Mich.: Dept. of Agricultural Economics, Michigan State University, 1982. xi, 335 p.; 28 cm. — (MSU international development papers, 0731-3438; no. 1) 1. Agriculture — Economic aspects — Africa, Sub-Saharan. 2. Agriculture — Africa, Sub-Saharan. 3. Africa, Sub-Saharan — Rural conditions. I. Baker, Doyle C. II. T. III. Series. HD2117.E36 1982    338.1/0967 19    *LC* 82-622612

**Johnston, Bruce F., 1919-.**                                                     • **4.2991**
The staple food economies of western tropical Africa. Stanford, Calif., Stanford University Press, 1958. 305 p. ill. (Stanford University.Food Research Institute. Studies in tropical development) 1. Agriculture — Economic aspects — Africa, West 2. Food supply — Africa, West I. T. HD2117 J6    *LC* 58-11697

**Bates, Robert H.**                                                               **4.2992**
Markets and states in tropical Africa: the political basis of agricultural policies / Robert H. Bates. — Berkeley: University of California Press, c1981. xi, 178 p.; 22 cm. — (California series on social choice and political economy.) Includes index. 1. Agriculture and state — Africa, Sub-Saharan. 2. Agriculture — Economic aspects — Africa, Sub-Saharan. I. T. II. Series. HD2118 1981.B37    338.1/867 19    *LC* 80-39732    *ISBN* 0520042530

**Agrarian policies and rural poverty in Africa / edited by**                      **4.2993**
**Dharam Ghai and Samir Radwan.**
Geneva: International Labour Office, 1983. ix, 311 p.; 25 cm. — (WEP study.) 1. Agriculture and state — Africa. 2. Rural development — Government policy — Africa. 3. Rural poor — Africa. 4. Land reform — Africa. 5. Africa — Rural conditions. I. Ghai, Dharam P. II. Radwan, Samir Muhammad. III. Series. HD2118.A34 1983    338.1/86 19    *LC* 83-140896    *ISBN* 9221031004

**Richards, Alan, 1946-.**                                                         **4.2994**
Egypt's agricultural development, 1800–1980: technical and social change / Alan Richards. — Boulder, Colo.: Westview Press, 1982. xvi, 296 p.: ill.; 24 cm. (A Westview replica edition) Revision of thesis (Ph.D.)—University of Wisconsin—Madison, 1975. Includes index. 1. Agriculture — Economic aspects — Egypt — History. I. T. HD2123.R5 1982    338.1/0962 19    *LC* 81-12919    *ISBN* 0865310998

**Livingstone, Ian.**                                                             **4.2995**
Rural development, employment, and incomes in Kenya: report / prepared for the ILO's Jobs and Skills Programme for Africa (JASPA) by Ian Livingstone. — Addis Ababa: International Labour Office, JASPA, 1981. 2 v. in 1; 21 cm. 1. Rural development — Kenya. 2. Agricultural laborers — Kenya. 3. Kenya — Rural conditions. I. Jobs and Skills Programme for Africa. II. T. HD2126.5.L58 1981    338.9676/2/091734 19    *LC* 82-980600 0922102890

**Meinig, D. W. (Donald William), 1924-.**                                        • **4.2996**
On the margins of the good earth; the South Australian wheat frontier, 1869–1884. — Chicago, Published for the Association of American Geographers by Rand McNally [1962] 231 p. plates, maps. 23 cm. — (The Monograph series of the Association of American Geographers, 2) Bibliographical footnotes. 1. Agriculture — South Australia — History. 2. Land settlement — South Australia. 3. South Australia — Colonization. I. T. HD2177.M4    333.7609942    *LC* 62-7266

# HD2321–4730 INDUSTRY

**Hobson, J. A. (John Atkinson), 1858-1940.**                                     • **4.2997**
The evolution of modern capitalism: a study of machine production. — London: Allen & Unwin; [1949] xvi, 510 p.: maps, diagrs.; 20 cm. 1. Industry — History 2. Capitalism 3. Machinery in industry I. T. HD2321.H6 1949    *LC* 50-4307

**Baumol, William J.**                                                            **4.2998**
Contestable markets and the theory of industry structure / William J. Baumol, John C. Panzar, Robert D. Willig, with contributions by Elizabeth E. Bailey, Dietrich Fischer, Herman C. Quirmbach. — New York: Harcourt Brace Jovanovich, c1982. xxix, 510 p.: ill.; 24 cm. Includes index. 1. Industrial

organization (Economic theory) 2. Microeconomics I. Panzar, John C., 1947- II. Willig, Robert D., 1947- III. T. HD2326.B38 1982    338.6 19    *LC* 81-84084    *ISBN* 015513910X

**Marshall, Alfred, 1842-1924.**                                                  • **4.2999**
Industry & trade; a study of industrial technique and business organization, and of their influences on the conditions of various classes and nations. — 4th ed. — New York: A. M. Kelley, 1970. xxiv, 874 p.; 23 cm. — (Reprints of economic classics) Reprint of the 1923 ed. 1. Industry 2. Commerce 3. Economic history — 1898-1945. 4. Business 5. Trusts, Industrial I. T. HD2326.M3 1970    338/.09    *LC* 72-104007    *ISBN* 0678006024

**Piore, Michael J.**                                                             **4.3000**
The second industrial divide: possibilities for prosperity / Michael J. Piore & Charles F. Sabel. — New York: Basic Books, c1984. ix, 355 p.: ill.; 24 cm. Includes index. 1. Industrialization 2. Mass production 3. Corporations 4. Economic policy I. Sabel, Charles F. II. T. HD2329.P56 1984    338/.06 19    *LC* 83-46080    *ISBN* 0465075622

**Bythell, Duncan.**                                                              **4.3001**
The sweated trades: outwork in nineteenth century Britain / Duncan Bythell. — New York: St. Martin's Press, 1978. 287 p.; 23 cm. 1. Sweating system — Great Britain — History. 2. Home labor — Great Britain — History. I. T. HD2339.G7 B9 1978    338.6/34/0941    *LC* 78-451    *ISBN* 0312779992

**The Small firm: an international survey / edited by David J.**                   **4.3002**
**Storey.**
London: Croom Helm; New York: St. Martin's Press, 1983. 274 p.: ill.; 23 cm. 1. Small business I. Storey, D. J. HD2341.S58 1983    338.6/42 19    *LC* 83-40075    *ISBN* 0312729804

**Aslund, Anders, 1952-.**                                                        **4.3003**
Private enterprise in Eastern Europe: the non–agricultural private sector in Poland and the GDR, 1945–1983 / Anders Åslund; foreword by Włodzimierz Brus. — New York: St. Martin's Press, 1985. xv, 294 p.; 23 cm. Abstract of thesis (doctoral)—St. Anthony's College, Oxford, 1982. Includes index. 1. Small business — Poland. 2. Small business — Germany (East) 3. Informal sector (Economics) — Poland. 4. Informal sector (Economics) — Germany (East) 5. Poland — Economic policy — 1945- 6. Germany (East) — Economic policy. I. T. HD2346.P7 A85 1985    338.6/42/09438 19    *LC* 84-40388    *ISBN* 0312647069

**Drucker, Peter Ferdinand, 1909-.**                                              **4.3004**
Innovation and entrepreneurship: practice and principles / Peter F. Drucker. — 1st ed. — New York: Harper & Row, c1985. ix, 277 p.; 24 cm. Includes index. 1. Small business — United States. 2. New business enterprises — United States. 3. Entrepreneurship I. T. HD2346.U5 D78 1985    658.4/2 19    *LC* 84-48593    *ISBN* 0060154284

**Rock, Howard B., 1944-.**                                                       **4.3005**
Artisans of the New Republic: the tradesmen of New York City in the age of Jefferson / Howard B. Rock. — New York: New York University Press, 1979. xviii, 340 p.: ill.; 24 cm. Includes index. 1. Artisans — New York (City) — History. 2. New York (N.Y.) — Social conditions. I. T. HD2346.U52 N5524    301.44/42    *LC* 78-55570    *ISBN* 0814773796

**Nelson, Daniel, 1941-.**                                                        **4.3006**
Managers and workers: origins of the new factory system in the United States, 1880–1920 / Daniel Nelson. — Madison: University of Wisconsin Press, 1975. x, 234 p.; 24 cm. Includes index. 1. Factory system — United States — History. 2. Personnel management — United States — History. 3. Industrial sociology — United States — History. I. T. HD2356.U5 N44    658.3/00973    *LC* 75-12212    *ISBN* 0299069001

**Winpenny, Thomas R.**                                                           **4.3007**
Industrial progress and human welfare: the rise of the factory system in 19th century Lancaster / Thomas R. Winpenny. — Washington, D.C.: University Press of America, c1982. x, 132 p.; 22 cm. 1. Factory system — Pennsylvania — Lancaster — History — 19th century. 2. Cotton manufacture — Pennsylvania — Lancaster — History — 19th century. 3. Labor and laboring classes — Pennsylvania — Lancaster — History — 19th century. 4. Lancaster (Pa.) — Industries — History — 19th century. I. T. HD2356.U6 L368 1982    338.6/5/0974815 19    *LC* 82-10995    *ISBN* 0819126284

# HD2709–2930 Corporations. Cartels. Trusts

**Parkinson, C. Northcote (Cyril Northcote), 1909-.**     **4.3008**
Big business / C. Northcote Parkinson. — Boston: Little, Brown, c1974. 263 p.: ill.; 26 cm. 1. Big business 2. Trade-unions I. T.
HD2721.P3 1974b     338.7/09     LC 74-3642     ISBN 0297767801

**Baumol, William J.**     **• 4.3009**
Business behavior, value and growth / [by] William J. Baumol. — Rev. ed. — New York: Harcourt, Brace & World [1967] xiii, 159 p.: ill.; 22 cm. Bibliographical footnotes. 1. Oligopolies 2. Economic development I. T.
HD2731.B27 1967     330/.01/8     LC 67-14320

**Berle, Adolf Augustus, 1895-1971.**     **• 4.3010**
The 20th century capitalist revolution. — [1st ed.]. — New York: Harcourt, Brace, [1954] 192 p.; 21 cm. 1. Corporations I. T.
HD2731.B4     338.74     LC 54-11327

**Fellner, William John, 1905-.**     **• 4.3011**
Competition among the few; oligopoly and similar market structures [by] William Fellner. — New York, A. M. Kelley. 1960 [c1949] xv, 328, iii p. illus. 22 cm. — (Reprints of economic classics) Bibliographical footnotes. 1. Competition 2. Oligopolies 3. Trusts, Industrial I. T.
HD2731.F4 1960     338.82     LC 64-17622

**Stocking, George Ward, 1892-.**     **• 4.3012**
Cartels in action: case studies in international business diplomacy / by George W. Stocking and Myron W. Watkins; with the assistance of Alfred E. Kahn and Gertrude Oxenfeldt. — New York: The Twentieth Century Fund, 1946. xii, 533 p.: tables, diagrs.; 24 cm. Sequel: Cartels or competition? 1. Trusts, Industrial I. Watkins, Myron Webster, 1893- joint author. II. Twentieth Century Fund. III. T.
HD2731.S76     LC 46-8321

**Stocking, George Ward, 1892-.**     **• 4.3013**
Monopoly and free enterprise, by George W. Stocking and Myron W. Watkins. With the report and recommendations of the Committee on Cartels and Monopoly. New York, Greenwood Press, 1968 [c1951] xv, 596 p. 24 cm. 1. Cartels I. Watkins, Myron Webster, 1893- joint author. II. Twentieth Century Fund. Committee on Cartels and Monopoly. III. T.
HD2731.S765 1968     338.8/2/0973     LC 68-54439

## HD2741–2756 General Works

**Benston, George J.**     **4.3014**
Conglomerate mergers: causes, consequences, and remedies / George J. Benston. — Washington, D.C.: American Enterprise Institute for Public Policy Research, c1980. 76 p.: ill.; 23 cm. — (Studies in economic policy.) (AEI studies. 270) 1. Consolidation and merger of corporations — United States. 2. Conglomerate corporations — United States. I. T. II. Series. III. Series: AEI studies. 270
HD2741.B39     338.8/3/0973     LC 80-12017     ISBN 0844733733

**Butters, J. Keith (John Keith), 1915-.**     **• 4.3015**
Effects of taxation: corporate mergers / [by] J. Keith Butters, John Lintner [and] William L. Cary. Assisted by Powell Niland. Boston, Division of Research, Graduate School of Business Administration, Harvard University, 1951. Elmsford, N.Y.: Maxwell Reprint Co. [1970] xviii, 364 p.; 21 cm. 1. Consolidation and merger of corporations — United States. 2. Corporations — Taxation — United States I. Lintner, John Virgil, 1916- joint author. II. Cary, William Lucius, 1910- joint author. III. Harvard University. Graduate School of Business Administration. Division of Research. IV. T. V. Title: Corporate mergers.
HD2741.B85 1970     658.1/6     LC 78-104795     ISBN 0827720106

**Vance, Stanley C.**     **4.3016**
Corporate leadership: boards, directors, and strategy / Stanley C. Vance. — New York: McGraw-Hill, c1983. xxii, 292 p.; 24 cm. — (McGraw-Hill series in management.) 1. Directors of corporations — United States. I. T. II. Series.
HD2745.V33 1983     658.4/22 19     LC 82-10040     ISBN 0070668736

**The Determinants and effects of mergers: an international comparison / edited by Dennis C. Mueller.**     **4.3017**
Cambridge, Mass.: Oelgeschlager, Gunn & Hain; Königstein/Ts.: Verlag A. Hain, c1980. xviii, 353 p.: graphs; 24 cm. (Publications of the Science Center Berlin; v. 24) 1. Consolidation and merger of corporations — Case studies. I. Mueller, Dennis C.
HD2746.5.D47     338.8/3 19     LC 80-19381     ISBN 0899460453

**Goode, Richard B.**     **• 4.3018**
The corporation income tax / Richard Goode. — New York: Wiley [1951]. –. xiii, 242 p.: diagrs.; 22 cm. — 1. Corporations — Taxation — United States 2. Income tax — United States I. T.
HD2753.U6 G6     336.243     LC 51-10395

**Casson, Mark, 1945-.**     **4.3019**
Alternatives to the multinational enterprise / by Mark Casson. — New York: Holmes & Meier, 1979. xiii, 116 p.: ill.; 23 cm. 1. International business enterprises 2. Investments, Foreign I. T.
HD2755.5.C39 1979     338.8/8     LC 79-693     ISBN 0841904936

**Caves, Richard E.**     **4.3020**
Multinational enterprise and economic analysis / Richard E. Caves. — Cambridge; New York: Cambridge University Press, 1983 (c1982). xi, 346 p.; 22 cm. — (Cambridge surveys of economic literature) Includes indexes. 1. International business enterprises I. T.
HD2755.5.C395     338.8/8 19     LC 82-4543     ISBN 0521249902

**Dunning, John H.**     **4.3021**
International production and the multinational enterprise / John H. Dunning. — London; Boston: Allen & Unwin, 1981. viii, 439 p.: ill.; 23 cm. 1. International business enterprises I. T.
HD2755.5.D867     338.8/8 19     LC 81-8101     ISBN 0043303196

**Feld, Werner J.**     **4.3022**
Multinational corporations and U.N. politics: the quest for codes of conduct / Werner J. Feld. — New York: Pergamon Press, c1980. ix, 174 p.; 24 cm. (Pergamon policy studies on U.S. and international business.) (Pergamon policy studies) 1. United Nations. 2. International business enterprises — Developing countries 3. Industry and state I. T. II. Title: Codes of conduct. III. Series.
HD2755.5.F44 1980     338.8/8     LC 79-18654     ISBN 0080224881

**Frank, Isaiah, 1917-.**     **4.3023**
Foreign enterprise in developing countries / Isaiah Frank. — Baltimore: Johns Hopkins University Press, c1980. xv, 199 p.; 24 cm. (A Supplementary paper of the Committee for Economic Development) Includes index. 1. International business enterprises — Developing countries I. T.
HD2755.5.F734     338.8/881724 19     LC 79-3722     ISBN 0801823439

**Mirow, Kurt Rudolf.**     **4.3024**
Webs of power: international cartels and the world economy / Kurt Rudolf Mirow and Harry Maurer. — Boston: Houghton Mifflin, 1982. x, 324 p.; 24 cm. 1. International business enterprises 2. Cartels I. Maurer, Harry. II. T.
HD2755.5.M58     338.8/81 19     LC 81-6771     ISBN 0395305365

**Multinational managers and poverty in the Third World / Lee A. Tavis, editor.**     **4.3025**
Notre Dame, Ind.: University of Notre Dame Press, c1982. xii, 269 p.: maps; 24 cm. 1. International business enterprises — Social aspects — Developing countries — Congresses. 2. Poor — Developing countries — Congresses. I. Tavis, Lee A.
HD2755.5.M8345 1982     658.4/08/091724 19     LC 82-50288     ISBN 0268013535

**Political risks in international business: new directions for research, management, and public policy / edited by Thomas L. Brewer.**     **4.3026**
New York: Praeger, 1985. x, 374 p.: ill.; 25 cm. Includes index. 1. International business enterprises — Political aspects — Addresses, essays, lectures. 2. Investments, Foreign — Political aspects — Addresses, essays, lectures. 3. Political stability — Evaluation — Addresses, essays, lectures. I. Brewer, Thomas L., 1941-
HD2755.5.P635 1985     658.1/8 19     LC 84-24801     ISBN 0030637589

**Rugman, Alan M.**     **4.3027**
Inside the multinationals: the economics of internal markets / Alan M. Rugman. — New York: Columbia University Press, 1981. 179 p.: ill.; 23 cm. Includes index. 1. International business enterprises I. T.
HD2755.5.R83     338.8/8 19     LC 81-7691     ISBN 0231053843

**Sigmund, Paul E.**     **4.3028**
Multinationals in Latin America: the politics of nationalization / Paul E. Sigmund. — Madison: University of Wisconsin Press, c1980. xi, 426 p.; 22 cm. 'A Twentieth Century Fund study.' Includes index. 1. International business enterprises — Government ownership — Latin America. 2. Corporations, American — Latin America. 3. Latin America — Foreign economic relations — United States. 4. United States — Foreign economic relations — Latin America. I. T.
HD2755.5.S54     338.8/888     LC 80-5115     0299082101

**Vernon, Raymond, 1913-.**                                    **4.3029**
Storm over the multinationals: the real issues / Raymond Vernon. Cambridge, Mass.: Harvard University Press, 1977. vii, 260 p.: ill.; 24 cm. 1. International business enterprises I. T.
HD2755.5.V473       338.8/8      *LC* 76-30790      *ISBN* 0674838750

**Wagner, Gerrit A.**                                          **4.3030**
[Beschouwingen van een ondernemer. English] Business in the public eye / by G.A. Wagner; translated by Theodore Plantinga. — Grand Rapids, MI.: W.B. Eerdmans Pub. Co., c1982. 125 p.; 21 cm. Translation of: Beschouwingen van een ondernemer. 1. International business enterprises — Addresses, essays, lectures. 2. Industry — Social aspects — Addresses, essays, lectures. 3. Petroleum industry and trade — Addresses, essays, lectures. 4. Energy policy — European Economic Community countries. — Addresses, essays, lectures. I. T.
HD2755.5.W3213 1982       338.8/8 19      *LC* 81-19486      *ISBN* 0802835678

**Wells, Louis T.**                                            **4.3031**
Third World multinationals: the rise of foreign investment from developing countries / Louis T. Wells, Jr. — Cambridge, Mass.: MIT Press, c1983. viii, 206 p.; 24 cm. Includes index. 1. International business enterprises — Developing countries 2. Corporations — Developing countries. I. T.
HD2755.5.W44 1983       338.8/881724 19      *LC* 82-21662      *ISBN* 0262231131

**Wilczynski, J. (Jozef), 1922-.**                             **4.3032**
The multinationals and East–West relations: towards transideological collaboration / J. Wilczynski. — Boulder, Colo.: Westview Press, 1976. x, 235 p.; 22 cm. 1. International business enterprises 2. International economic relations 3. Government business enterprises — Communist countries. I. T.
HD2755.5.W54       338.8/8      *LC* 76-2080      *ISBN* 0891585400

**Biggadike, E. Ralph, 1937-.**                                **4.3033**
Corporate diversification: entry, strategy, and performance / E. Ralph Biggadike. — Boston: Division of Research, Graduate School of Business Administration, Harvard University, c1979. xvi, 220 p.: ill.; 24 cm. Includes index. 1. Diversification in industry — United States. 2. New products 3. Conglomerate corporations — United States. I. Harvard University. Graduate School of Business Administration. Division of Research. II. T.
HD2756.U5 B53       338.8      *LC* 79-84159      *ISBN* 087584118X

**Yoshihara, Kunio, 1939-.**                                   **4.3034**
Sogo shosha: the vanguard of the Japanese economy / Yoshihara Kunio. — Tokyo; New York: Oxford University Press, 1982. xvii, 358 p.; 23 cm. Includes index. 1. Conglomerate corporations — Japan — History. 2. Trusts, Industrial — Japan — History. I. T.
HD2756.2.J3 Y67 1982       338.8/0952 19      *LC* 83-118555      *ISBN* 0195825349

**Yip, George S.**                                             **4.3035**
Barriers to entry: a corporate–strategy perspective / George S. Yip. — Lexington, Mass.: LexingtonBooks, c1982. xv, 222 p.: ill.; 24 cm. Includes index 1. Barriers to entry (Industrial organization) — Mathematical models. 2. Conglomerate corporations — Planning. I. T. II. Title: Corporate-strategy perspective.
HD2756.5.Y36 1982       658.8/02 19      *LC* 81-47993      *ISBN* 0669052256

## HD2757–2930 INDUSTRIAL CONCENTRATION

**Brozen, Yale, 1917-.**                                       **4.3036**
Concentration, mergers, and public policy / Yale Brozen with the assistance of George Bittlingmayer. — New York: Macmillan Pub. Co.; London: Collier Macmillan Publishers, c1982. xxiii, 427 p.: ill.; 25 cm. — (Studies of the modern corporation.) 1. Industrial concentration — Government policy 2. Industrial concentration — Government policy — United States. 3. Trusts, Industrial — Government policy — United States. I. Bittlingmayer, George. II. T. III. Series.
HD2757.B76 1982       338.8/0973 19      *LC* 82-70080      *ISBN* 0029042704

**Sharkey, William W.**                                        **4.3037**
The theory of natural monopoly / William W. Sharkey. — Cambridge [Cambridgeshire]; New York: Cambridge University Press, 1982. viii, 229 p.: ill.; 24 cm. Includes index. 1. Monopolies I. T. II. Title: Natural monopoly.
HD2757.2.S47 1982       338.8/2/01 19      *LC* 82-1136      *ISBN* 0521243947

**Friedman, James W.**                                         **4.3038**
Oligopoly theory / James W. Friedman. — Cambridge [Cambridgeshire]; New York: Cambridge University Press, 1983. xvi, 240 p.: ill; 22 cm. — (Cambridge

surveys of economic literature.) Includes indexes. 1. Oligopolies I. T. II. Series.
HD2757.3.F75 1983       338.8/2 19      *LC* 82-22170      *ISBN* 0521238277

**Crew, Michael A.**                                           **4.3039**
Public utility economics / Michael A. Crew and Paul R. Kleindorfer. — New York: St. Martin's Press, 1979. viii, 246 p.: ill.; 22 cm. Includes index. 1. Public utilities I. Kleindorfer, Paul R. joint author. II. T.
HD2763.C7 1979       338.4/3      *LC* 78-24611      *ISBN* 031265569X

**Kolbe, A. Lawrence.**                                        **4.3040**
The cost of capital, estimating the rate of return for public utilities / A. Lawrence Kolbe and James A. Read, Jr. with George R. Hall. — Cambridge, Mass.: MIT Press, 1985 (c1984). viii, 183 p.: ill.; 24 cm. 'A Charles River Associates study.' Includes index. 1. Public utilities — Rate of return 2. Public utilities — Finance I. Read, James A. II. Hall, George R. III. T.
HD2763.K64 1984       338.4/33636 19      *LC* 84-12241      *ISBN* 0262110946

## HD2766–2930 Corporations, by Country

### HD2766–2798 UNITED STATES

**Analyzing the impact of regulatory change in public utilities /**     **4.3041**
**edited by Michael A. Crew.**
Lexington, Mass.: Lexington Books, c1985. xii, 192 p.: ill.; 24 cm. Based on two seminars held at Rutgers on Oct. 28, 1983 and May 18, 1984. 1. Public utilities — United States — Congresses. 2. Public utilities — Government policy — United States — Congresses. I. Crew, Michael A.
HD2766.A73 1985       363.6/0973 19      *LC* 83-48674      *ISBN* 0669073415

**Gormley, William T., 1950-.**                                **4.3042**
The politics of public utility regulation / William T. Gormley, Jr. — Pittsburgh, Pa.: University of Pittsburgh Press, c1983. xi, 271 p.; 23 cm. 1. Public utilities — United States I. T.
HD2766.G64 1983       363.6/0973 19      *LC* 82-42756      *ISBN* 0822934795

**Lloyd, Henry Demarest, 1847-1903.**                          **● 4.3043**
Wealth against commonwealth / edited and with an introd. by Thomas C. Cochran. — Englewood Cliffs, N.J.: Prentice-Hall [1963] 184 p. (Classics in history series) 1. Standard Oil Company. 2. Trusts, Industrial — United States I. T.
HD2769 O4 L8 1963       *LC* 63-11789

**Tarbell, Ida M. (Ida Minerva), 1857-1944.**                  **● 4.3044**
The history of the Standard oil company; illustrated with portraits, pictures and diagrams. New York: Macmillan, 1937. 2 v.in 1. illus., plates, ports., maps, diagrs. 21 cm. 1. Standard Oil Company. I. T.
HD2769.O4 T2x       *LC* a 40-1979

**Galambos, Louis.**                                           **4.3045**
The public image of big business in America, 1880–1940: a quantitative study in social change / Louis Galambos with the assistance of Barbara Barrow Spence. — Baltimore: Johns Hopkins University Press, [1975] xii, 324 p.: ill.; 24 cm. 1. Big business — United States — History. 2. Industry — Social aspects — United States — History. 3. United States — Social conditions I. Spence, Barbara Barrow, joint author. II. T.
HD2785.G34       338.6/44/0973      *LC* 75-11347      *ISBN* 0801816351

**How to find information about companies: the corporate**     **4.3046**
**intelligence source book / by Washington Researchers**
**Publishing; contributing editors, Lorna M. Daniells, Elizabeth**
**M. Williams, Beth Gibber.**
Ed. 4. — Washington, DC: The Researchers, c1985. 353 p.; 29 cm. (Business research series (Washington, D.C.). v. 3) Includes index. 1. Corporations — Information services — United States. 2. Corporations — United States — Directories. I. Daniells, Lorna M. II. Williams, Elizabeth M. (Elizabeth Marie), 1950- III. Gibber, Beth. IV. Washington Researchers. V. Series.
HD2785.H68 1985       016.3387/4/0973 19      *LC* 86-152265      *ISBN* 0934940304

**Lamoreaux, Naomi R.**                                        **4.3047**
The great merger movement in American business, 1895–1904 / Naomi R. Lamoreaux. — Cambridge [Cambridgeshire]; New York: Cambridge University Press, 1985. xii, 208 p.: ill.; 24 cm. Includes index. 1. Consolidation and merger of corporations — United States — History. I. T.
HD2785.L36 1985       338.8/3/0973 19      *LC* 84-16983      *ISBN* 0521267552

**Mason, Edward Sagendorph, 1899- ed.**     • **4.3048**
The corporation in modern society: edited with an introd. Cambridge: Harvard University Press, 1960. 335 p. 1. Corporations — United States I. T.
HD2785 M359 1960     LC 60-5392

**Mason, Edward Sagendorph, 1899-.**     • **4.3049**
Economic concentration and the monopoly problem. — Cambridge, Harvard University Press, 1957. xvi, 411 p. diagrs., tables. 22 cm. — (Harvard economic studies. v. 100) 1. Big business — U.S. 2. Trusts, Industrial — U.S. I. T. II. Series.
HD2785.M36     338.82     LC 57-6351

**Moody, John, 1868-1958.**     • **4.3050**
The truth about the trusts; a description and analysis of the American trust movement. — New York: Greenwood Press, 1968 [c1904] xxii, 514 p.: illus. (part fold.), fold. map.; 24 cm. 1. Trusts, Industrial — U.S. I. T.
HD2785.M64 1968     338.8/5/0973     LC 68-28643

**Jacoby, Neil H. (Neil Herman), 1909-1979.**     **4.3051**
Corporate power and social responsibility: a blueprint for the future / [by] Neil H. Jacoby; foreword by Arthur F. Burns. — New York: Macmillan [1973] xix, 282 p.; 24 cm. (Studies of the modern corporation.) 1. Corporations — United States 2. Industry — Social aspects — United States. I. T. II. Series.
HD2791.J3     658.4/08     LC 72-14073

**Kristol, Irving.**     **4.3052**
Two cheers for capitalism / Irving Kristol. — New York: Basic Books, c1978. xiv, 274 p.; 22 cm. Includes index. 1. Corporations — United States 2. Capitalism — United States. 3. Social justice 4. United States — Economic conditions I. T.
HD2791.K68     330.12/2/0973     LC 77-20408     ISBN 0465088031

**McGee, John Seneca, 1927-.**     • **4.3053**
In defense of industrial concentration [by] John S. McGee. — New York: Praeger, [1971] xi, 167 p.: illus.; 22 cm. — (New directions in management and economics) 1. Monopolies — U.S. 2. Oligopolies — U.S. 3. Industry and state — U.S. I. T.
HD2791.M3     338.8/2/0973     LC 72-128100

**Scherer, F. M. (Frederic M.)**     **4.3054**
Industrial market structure and economic performance / F.M. Scherer. — 2d ed. — Boston: Houghton Mifflin, 1980. xii, 632 p.: ill.; 25 cm. 1. Industrial organization (Economic theory) 2. Industry and state — United States. I. T.
HD2791.S28     338.7     LC 81-83280     ISBN 0395307260

**Berle, Adolf Augustus, 1895-1971.**     • **4.3055**
The modern corporation and private property [by] Adolf A. Berle and Gardiner C. Means. Rev. ed. New York, Harcourt, Brace & World [1968] xlvi, 380 p. illus. 23 cm. Bibliographical footnotes. 1. Corporations — United States 2. Corporation law — United States I. Means, Gardiner Coit, 1896- joint author. II. T.
HD2795.B53 1968     338.7/4/0973     LC 68-28813

**Clark, John Bates, 1847-1938.**     • **4.3056**
The control of trusts, by John Bates Clark and John Maurice Clark. — Rewritten and enl. ed. With an introductory essay, John Bates and John Maurice Clark on monopoly and competition, by Joseph Dorfman. — New York: A. M. Kelley, 1971. 17, xi, 202 p.; 22 cm. — (Reprints of economic classics) Reprint of the 1914 issue, which was in turn a reprint of the 1912 enlarged edition. The introductory essay is new. 1. Trusts, Industrial I. Clark, John Maurice, 1884- joint author. II. T.
HD2795.C5 1971     338.8/5     LC 70-108000     ISBN 0678006067

**Kaysen, Carl.**     • **4.3057**
Antitrust policy; an economic and legal analysis [by] Carl Kaysen and Donald F. Turner. — Cambridge: Harvard University Press, 1959. xxiii, 345 p.: tables.; 25 cm. — ([Harvard University series on competition in American industry] 7) 1. Trusts, Industrial — United States 2. Trusts, Industrial — United States — Law. I. Turner, Donald F. joint author. II. T. III. Series.
HD2795.K3     338.80973     LC 59-12973

**Vernon, Raymond, 1913-.**     **4.3058**
Sovereignty at bay; the multinational spread of U.S. enterprises. — New York: Basic Books, [1971] x, 326 p.; 22 cm. — (The Harvard multinational enterprise series) 1. International business enterprises 2. Corporations, American I. T. II. Series.
HD2795.V48     338.8/8     LC 73-167766     ISBN 0465080960

**Whitney, Simon Newcomb, 1903-.**     • **4.3059**
Antitrust policies: American experience in twenty industries. — New York: Twentieth Century Fund, 1958. 2 v.: tables; 24 cm. 1. Trusts, Industrial — United States 2. Trusts, Industrial — United States — Law 3. Big business — United States I. T.
HD2795 W5     LC 58-9954

## HD2807-2932 OTHER COUNTRIES

**Profits, progress, and poverty: case studies of international**     **4.3060**
**industries in Latin America / edited by Richard S. Newfarmer.**
Notre Dame, Ind.: University of Notre Dame Press, c1985. xiii, 491 p.; 24 cm. Includes indexes. 1. International business enterprises — Latin America — Case studies. 2. Investments, Foreign — Latin America — Case studies. I. Newfarmer, Richard S.
HD2810.5.P76 1985     338.8/888 19     LC 83-40115     ISBN 0268011524

**International business and Central Europe, 1918–1939 / edited**     **4.3061**
**by Alice Teichova and P.L. Cottrell.**
[Leicester, Leicestershire]: Leicester University Press; New York: St. Martin's Press, 1984 (c1983). xxvii, 459 p.: ill.; 24 cm. Papers presented at the International Symposium in Economic History, held at the University of East Anglia, Sept. 20-22, 1979. 1. Corporations, Foreign — Europe, Eastern — History — Addresses, essays, lectures. 2. International business enterprises — Europe, Eastern — History — Addresses, essays, lectures. 3. Investments, Foreign — Europe, Eastern — History — Addresses, essays, lectures. I. Teichova, Alice. II. Cottrell, P. L. III. International Symposium in Economic History (1979: University of East Anglia)
HD2844.I57 1983     338.8/8843 19     LC 83-13956     ISBN 0312419821

**Tsurumi, Yoshi.**     **4.3062**
The Japanese are coming: a multinational interaction of firms and politics / Yoshi Tsurumi. — Cambridge, Mass.: Ballinger Pub. Co., c1976. xxiii, 333 p.; 24 cm. 1. Corporations, Japanese 2. International business enterprises 3. Investments, Japanese I. T.
HD2907.T73     338.8/8     LC 76-23262     ISBN 0884106519

**Yoshino, M. Y. (Michael Y.)**     **4.3063**
Japan's multinational enterprises / M. Y. Yoshino. — Cambridge: Harvard University Press, 1976. xv, 191 p.; 24 cm. 1. Corporations, Japanese 2. International business enterprises I. T.
HD2907.Y63     338.8/8/0952     LC 76-26602     ISBN 0674472594

**Business in the shadow of apartheid: U.S. firms in South Africa**     **4.3064**
**/ edited by Jonathan Leape, Bo Baskin, Stefan Underhill.**
Lexington, Mass.: Lexington Books, c1985. xxxvii, 242 p.: ill.; 24 cm. 1. Corporations, American — South Africa — Addresses, essays, lectures. 2. Blacks — Employment — South Africa — Addresses, essays, lectures. 3. Industry — Social aspects — Case studies — Addresses, essays, lectures. 4. South Africa — Race relations — Addresses, essays, lectures. I. Leape, Jonathan. II. Baskin, Bo. III. Underhill, Stefan.
HD2922.B87 1985     338.8/8973/068 19     LC 84-47741     ISBN 0669084042

**Akinsanya, Adeoye A.**     **4.3065**
Multinationals in a changing environment: a study of business–government relations in the Third World / Adeoye A. Akinsanya. — New York: Praeger, 1984. xvi, 335 p. Includes index. 1. International business enterprises — Developing countries 2. Industry and state — Developing countries. I. T.
HD2932.A34 1984     338.8/881724 19     LC 83-24592     ISBN 0030598664

# HD2951–3570 Industrial Cooperation. Profit Sharing

**Latta, Geoffrey W., 1947-.**     **4.3066**
Profit sharing, employee stock ownership, savings, and asset formation plans in the Western World / by Geoffrey W. Latta. — Philadelphia: Industrial Research Unit, Wharton School, University of Pennsylvania, 1979. xii, 192 p.; 23 cm. — (Multinational industrial relations series. no. 5 0149-0818) 1. Profit-sharing 2. Employee ownership I. T. II. Title: Asset formation plans in the Western World. III. Series.
HD2971.L33 1981     658.32/25     LC 79-5162     ISBN 0895460157

**Worker cooperatives in America / edited by Robert Jackall,**     **4.3067**
**Henry M. Levin.**
Berkeley: University of California Press, 1985 (c1984). x, 311 p.; 24 cm. Includes index. 1. Producer cooperatives — United States 2. Producer cooperatives — United States — History. 3. Employee ownership — United States. 4. Employee ownership — United States — History. I. Jackall, Robert. II. Levin, Henry M.
HD3134.W67     334/.6/0973 19     LC 84-61     ISBN 0520051173

# HD3611–4730 Industry and State

**Lippincott, Benjamin Evans, 1902-, ed.**    • **4.3068**
On the economic theory of socialism / by Oskar Lange and Fred M. Taylor; Benjamin E. Lippincott, editor. — Minneapolis, Minn.: The University of Minnesota press, 1938. vii, 143 p.: diagr.; 19 cm. (Government control of the economic order, ed. by B.E. Lippincott,. 2) 1. Socialism 2. Industrial organization 3. Industry and state I. Lange, Oskar, 1904-1965. II. Taylor, F. M. (Fred Manville), 1855-1932. III. T. IV. Title: On the economic theory of socialism V. Title: Government control of the economic order
HD3611 L52    *LC* 38-12882

**Kirkpatrick, C. H. (Colin H.), 1944-.**    **4.3069**
Industrial structure and policy in less developed countries / by C.H. Kirkpatrick, N. Lee, and F.I. Nixson. — London, UK; Winchester, Mass., USA: Allen & Unwin, 1984. xv, 263 p.: ill. Includes indexes. 1. Industry and state — Developing countries. 2. Economic development 3. International business enterprises 4. Developing countries — Industries. I. Lee, Norman, 1936- II. Nixson, F. I. III. T.
HD3616.D44 K57 1984    338.9/009172/4 19    *LC* 84-14493    *ISBN* 0043381154

**Industrial policies in Western Europe** / edited by Steven J.    **4.3070**
Warnecke, Ezra N. Suleiman.
New York: Praeger, 1975. x, 249 p.; 25 cm. (Praeger special studies in international politics and government) 1. Industry and state — European Economic Community countries — Addresses, essays, lectures. 2. Trade and professional associations — European Economic Community countries — Addresses, essays, lectures. 3. European Economic Community countries — Economic policy — Addresses, essays, lectures. I. Warnecke, Steven Joshua. II. Suleiman, Ezra N., 1941-
HD3616.E83 I53    338.94    *LC* 75-23998    *ISBN* 0275016706

**Nef, John Ulric, 1899-.**    • **4.3071**
Industry and government in France and England, 1540–1640. — Ithaca, N.Y.: Great Seal Books [1957] x, 162 p. , 19 cm. — 1. Industry and state — France. 2. Industry and state — Great Britain. 3. France — Industry — History 4. Great Britain — Industry — History I. T.
HD3616.F82 N44    *LC* 58-4920

**Turner, Henry Ashby.**    **4.3072**
German big business and the rise of Hitler / Henry Ashby Turner, Jr. — New York: Oxford University Press, 1985. xxi, 504 p.: ill.; 25 cm. Includes index. 1. Nationalsozialistische Deutsche Arbeiter-Partei — History. 2. Industry and state — Germany — History. 3. Big business — Germany — History. 4. National socialism — Germany — History. 5. Germany — Politics and government — 1918-1933 I. T.
HD3616.G35 T87 1985    943.085 19    *LC* 84-5645    *ISBN* 0195034929

**Grant, Wyn.**    **4.3073**
The Confederation of British Industry / Wyn Grant and David Marsh. — London: Hodder and Stoughton, 1977. 226 p.; 25 cm. Imprint covered by label: New York, Holmes & Meier Publishers. 1. Confederation of British Industry. 2. Business and politics — Great Britain. 3. Industry and state — Great Britain. I. Marsh, David C. (David Charles) joint author. II. T.
HD3616.G73 G73    322/.3/0941    *LC* 77-379747    *ISBN* 034017613X. *ISBN* 0340214724 pbk

**Sarti, Roland, 1937-.**    • **4.3074**
Fascism and the industrial leadership in Italy, 1919–1940; a study in the expansion of private power under fascism. — Berkeley: University of California Press, 1971. xii, 154 p.; 25 cm. 1. Industry and state — Italy. 2. Corporate state 3. Fascism — Italy 4. Syndicalism — Italy. 5. Fascism and social status — Italy. I. T.
HD3616.I83 S135    335.6    *LC* 79-138636    *ISBN* 0520018559

**Johnson, Chalmers A.**    **4.3075**
MITI and the Japanese miracle: the growth of industrial policy, 1925–1975 / Chalmers Johnson. — Stanford, Calif.: Stanford University Press, 1982. xvi, 393 p.; 24 cm. Includes index. 1. Japan. Tsūshō Sangyōshō — History. 2. Industry and state — Japan — History. I. T. II. Title: M.I.T.I. and the Japanese miracle.
HD3616.J33 J643 1982    354.520082/06 19    *LC* 81-51330    *ISBN* 0804711283

**Kaplan, Eugene J.**    **4.3076**
Japan: the government–business relationship: a guide for the American businessman / by Eugene J. Kaplan. — Washington: U.S. Bureau of International Commerce; for sale by the Supt. of Docs., U.S. Govt. Print. Off.,

1972. v, 158 p.; 24 cm. 'A United States Department of Commerce publication.' 1. Industry and state — Japan. 2. Japan — Economic policy — 1945- I. T.
HD3616.J33 K34    338/.0952    *LC* 72-601749

**Childs, Marquis William, 1903-.**    • **4.3077**
Sweden; the middle way, by Marquis W. Childs. New rev. and enl. ed. New Haven, Yale university press, 1947. xv, 198 p.: plates, ports., map.; 25 cm. 1. Cooperation — Sweden. 2. Industry and state — Sweden. 3. Sweden — Economic policy. I. T.
HD3616.S53C48 1947    330.9485    *LC* 47-4538 *

**Regulation in perspective: historical essays** / Thomas K.    **4.3078**
McCraw, editor; Morton Keller ... [et al.]; Gerald P. Berk, rapporteur.
Boston: Division of Research, Graduate School of Business Administration, Harvard University; Cambridge, Mass.: Distributed by Harvard University Press, 1982 (c1981). ix, 246 p.; 25 cm. 1. Industry and state — United States — History — Addresses, essays, lectures. 2. Trade regulation — United States — History — Addresses, essays, lectures. I. McCraw, Thomas K.
HD3616.U46 R43    338.973 19    *LC* 81-81141    *ISBN* 087584121X

**Bernstein, Marver H.**    • **4.3079**
Regulating business by independent commission. Princeton, N.J.: Princeton University Press, 1955. xi, 306 p.; 23 cm. 1. Industry and state — United States I. T.
HD3616 U47 B5    *LC* 55-5001

**Breyer, Stephen G., 1938-.**    **4.3080**
Regulation and its reform / Stephen Breyer. — Cambridge, Mass.: Harvard University Press, 1982. xii, 472 p.: ill.; 25 cm. Includes index. 1. Trade regulation — United States. 2. Industry and state — United States. I. T.
HD3616.U47 B68    353.0082 19    *LC* 81-6753    *ISBN* 0674753755

**Instead of regulation: alternatives to federal regulatory agencies**    **4.3081**
/ edited by Robert W. Poole, Jr.
Lexington: Lexington Books, c1982. xi, 404 p.: ill.; 24 cm. 1. Trade regulation — Economic aspects — United States — Addresses, essays, lectures. I. Poole, Robert W., 1944-
HD3616.U47 I48    353.09/1 19    *LC* 81-47333    *ISBN* 0669045853

**Kahn, Alfred E. (Alfred Edward)**    • **4.3082**
The economics of regulation: principles and institutions / [by] Alfred E. Kahn. — New York: Wiley [1970-71] 2 v.; 26 cm. 1. Industry and state — United States. 2. Trade regulation — United States. 3. Monopolies — United States. I. T.
HD3616.U47 K28    338    *LC* 74-116769    *ISBN* 0471454303

**Vogel, Ezra F.**    **4.3083**
Comeback, case by case: building the resurgence of American business / Ezra F. Vogel. — New York: Simon and Schuster, c1985. 320 p.; 25 cm. Includes index. 1. Industry and state — United States. 2. Industry and state — Japan. 3. Competition, International I. T.
HD3616.U47 V64 1985    338.952 19    *LC* 84-22232    *ISBN* 067146079X

*[handwritten: HD 3616 U.47 V64 1985]*

**Wolfson, Nicholas.**    **4.3084**
The modern corporation: free markets versus regulation / Nicholas Wolfson. — New York: Free Press; London: Collier Macmillan, c1984. xi, 191 p.; 25 cm. Includes index. 1. Industry and state — United States. 2. Corporation law — United States 3. Corporations — United States I. T.
HD3616.U47 W57 1984    338.7/4/0973 19    *LC* 84-13645    *ISBN* 0029347009

# HD3840–4730 State Industries. Public Works. Government Ownership

**Walsh, Annmarie Hauck.**    **4.3085**
The public's business: the politics and practices of government corporations / Annmarie Hauck Walsh. — Cambridge, Mass.: MIT Press, c1978. xvi, 436 p.; 24 cm. 'A Twentieth Century Fund study.' Includes index. 1. Corporations, Government — United States. 2. Corporations, Government — United States — Finance. 3. Municipal bonds — United States. I. Twentieth Century Fund. II. T.
HD3887.W34    353.09/2    *LC* 77-15595    *ISBN* 0262230860

**Public corporations and public policy in Canada** / edited by    **4.3086**
Allan Tupper and G. Bruce Doern.
Montreal: Institute for Research on Public Policy; Brookfield, Vt.: Renouf/ USA [distributor], c1981. xviii, 398 p.; 23 cm. Foreword and summary in French. Distributor statement from label on page facing t.p. 1. Corporations,

Government — Canada — Case studies. I. Tupper, Allan, 1950- II. Doern, G. Bruce.
HD4005.P8 1981    354.7109/2 19    *LC* 82-169096    *ISBN* 0920380514

**Trebat, Thomas J.**             **4.3087**
Brazil's state–owned enterprises: a case study of the state as entrepreneur / Thomas J. Trebat. — Cambridge [Cambridgeshire]; New York: Cambridge University Press, 1983. xviii, 294 p.: ill.; 22 cm. — (Cambridge Latin American studies. 45) Includes index. 1. Government business enterprises — Brazil. 2. Corporations, Government — Brazil. I. T. II. Series.
HD4093.T727 1983    354.8109/2 19    *LC* 82-9564    *ISBN* 0521237165

**Saving water in a desert city / William E. Martin ... [et al.].**    **4.3088**
Washington, D.C.: Resources for the Future; [Baltimore]: Distributed by the Johns Hopkins University Press, 1984. xiii, 111 p.: ill.; 26 cm. (Resources for the Future) 1. Water-supply — Arizona — Tucson. 2. Water conservation — Arizona — Tucson. I. Martin, William Edwin.
HD4464.T8 S28 1984    333.91/216/0979177 19    *LC* 83-43263
    *ISBN* 0915707047

**Savas, Emanuel S.**             **4.3089**
The organization and efficiency of solid waste collection / E. S. Savas; with contributions by Daniel Baumol ... [et al.]. — Lexington, Mass.: Lexington Books, c1977. xix, 285 p.: ill.; 24 cm. 1. Refuse collection 2. Refuse and refuse disposal I. Baumol, Daniel. II. T.
HD4482.S38    352/.6    *LC* 76-43606    *ISBN* 0669010952

# HD4801–8943 Labor

**Studies in labor markets / edited by Sherwin Rosen.**    **4.3090**
Chicago: University of Chicago Press, 1981. ix, 395 p.: ill.; 24 cm. — (A Conference report / Universities—National Bureau Committee for Economic Research; no. 31) 1. Labor economics — Congresses. 2. Labor and laboring classes — United States — 1970- — Congresses. I. Rosen, Sherwin.
HD4813.S78    331 19    *LC* 81-7488    *ISBN* 0226726282

**Grossman, Jonathan, 1915-.**          **4.3091**
The Department of Labor [by] Jonathan Grossman. New York, Praeger [1973] x, 309 p. illus. 22 cm. (Praeger library of U.S. Government departments and agencies, no. 37) 1. United States. Dept. of Labor. I. T.
HD4835.U4 G76    353.83    *LC* 73-145947

# HD4841–4854 History

**Kranzberg, Melvin.**             **4.3092**
By the sweat of thy brow: work in the Western world / by Melvin Kranzberg and Joseph Gies. — New York: Putnam, [1975] 248 p.; 21 cm. 1. Labor and laboring classes — History. I. Gies, Joseph. joint author. II. T.
HD4841.K7 1975    331.1/1/09    *LC* 74-79654    *ISBN* 0399113126

**Perlman, Selig, 1888-.**           • **4.3093**
A theory of the labor movement. — New York: A.M. Kelley, 1949, c1928. xii, 321 p.; 17 cm. — (Reprints of economic classics) 1. Labor and laboring classes 2. Trade-unions 3. Labor and laboring classes — Europe. 4. Socialism I. T.
HD4841.P4    *LC* A50-9734

**Burford, Alison.**             **4.3094**
Craftsmen in Greek and Roman society. — Ithaca, N.Y.: Cornell University Press, [1972] 256 p.: ill.; 23 cm. — (Aspects of Greek and Roman life) 1. Artisans — Greece. 2. Artisans — Rome. I. T. II. Series.
HD4844.B85    301.5/5    *LC* 71-37630    *ISBN* 0801407176

**Glotz, Gustave, 1862-1935.**        • **4.3095**
Ancient Greece at work; an economic history of Greece from the Homeric period to the Roman conquest. [Translated by M. R. Dobie] New York, Barnes & Noble [1965] xii, 402 p. illus. 25 cm. ([The History of civilization]) 'First published 1926.' 1. Labor and laboring classes — Greece. 2. Slavery — Greece 3. Greece — Economic conditions I. T.
HD4844.G53 1965    *LC* 65-29891

**Louis, Paul, 1872-1948.**         • **4.3096**
Ancient Rome at work: an economic history of Rome from the origins to the Empire / by Paul–Louis; [translated by E.B.F. Wareing]. — New York: Barnes & Noble, 1965. xiv, 347 p.: ill.; maps. (some fold.), 25 cm. — (The History of

civilization) 1. Labor and laboring classes — Rome. 2. Slavery — Rome 3. Rome — Economic conditions I. Wareing, Eustace Bernard Foley, 1890- II. T. III. Series.
HD4844.L73 1965

**Boissonnade, P. (Prosper), 1862-1935.**      • **4.3097**
Life and work in medieval Europe; the evolution of medieval economy from the fifth to the fifteenth century. Translated by Eileen Power. Pref. to the Torchbook ed. by Lynn White, Jr. New York, Harper & Row [1964] xviii, 394 p. ill. (Harper torchbooks. The Academy library) 'TB1141.' 1. Labor and laboring classes — History 2. Industry — History 3. Europe — Social conditions I. T.
HD4847 B63 1964    *LC* 64-6938

**Galenson, Walter, 1914- ed.**         • **4.3098**
Labor in developing economies. — Berkeley, University of California Press, 1962. x, 299 p. tables. 24 cm. Includes bibliography. 'A publication of the Institute of Industrial Relations, University of California.' Bibliographical footnotes. 1. Labor and laboring classes — Addresses, essays, lectures. I. University of California, Berkeley. Institute of Industrial Relations. II. T.
HD4854.G32 1962    331.1082    *LC* 62-16108

**Gorz, André.**             **4.3099**
Strategy for labor: a radical proposal / translated from the French by Martin A. Nicolaus and Victoria Ortiz. — Boston: Beacon Press [1967] xiv, 199 p. 1. Labor and laboring classes 2. Capitalism 3. Labor and laboring classes — France I. T.
HD4854 G6713    *LC* 67-14111

**Labor in the twentieth century / edited by John T. Dunlop,**    **4.3100**
**Walter Galenson.**
New York: Academic Press, c1978. viii, 329 p.; 24 cm. — (Studies in labor economics.) 1. Labor and laboring classes — History — Case studies. 2. Trade-unions — History — Case studies. 3. Industrial relations — History — Case studies. I. Dunlop, John Thomas, 1914- II. Galenson, Walter, 1914- III. Series.
HD4854.L26    331/.09/04    *LC* 78-3335    *ISBN* 0122243501

# HD4861–4895 Labor Systems

## HD4871–4875 Forced Labor

**Carlton, Richard K., ed.**          • **4.3101**
Forced labor in the 'people's democracies.' New York, Mid-European Studies Center, Free Europe Committee, 1955. 56, 177 p. illus., maps. 28 cm. 1. Forced labor — Europe, Eastern. I. International League for the Rights of Man and the New Democracy, inc. II. T.
HD4871.C33    *LC* 55-9254

**Kloosterboer, Willemina.**          • **4.3102**
Involuntary labour since the abolition of slavery; a survey of compulsory labour throughout the world. Foreword by J. J. Fahrenfort. — Leiden, E. J. Brill, 1960. 215 p. 25 cm. Translation of the author's Proefschrift, Amsterdam. Includes bibliography. 1. Forced labor I. T.
HD4871.K613    *LC* 60-50971

**Lemoine, Maurice.**            **4.3103**
[Sucre amer. English] Bitter sugar: slaves today in the Caribbean / Maurice Lemoine; photographic reportage by the author; translated from the French by Andrea Johnston. — Chicago: Banner Press, c1985. 308 p., [17] leaves of plates: ill.; 22 cm. Translation of: Sucre amer. 1. Contract labor — Dominican Republic. 2. Sugar workers — Dominican Republic. 3. Haitians — Dominican Republic. I. T.
HD4875.D44 L4513 1985    331.5/42/097293 19    *LC* 85-7457
    *ISBN* 0916650189

**Swianiewicz, Stanisław.**          • **4.3104**
Forced labour and economic development; an enquiry into the experience of Soviet industrialization [by] S. Swianiewicz. London, New York, Oxford University Press, 1965. ix, 321 p. 23 cm. 'Issued under the auspices of the Royal Institute of International Affairs.' 1. Forced labor — Soviet Union. 2. Soviet Union — Industries 3. Soviet Union — Economic conditions — 1918-1945 I. T.
HD4875.R9 S9    338.0947    *LC* 65-7645

**Lasker, Bruno, 1880-1965.**                                    • **4.3105**
Human bondage in Southeast Asia. — Westport, Conn.: Greenwood Press, [1972, c1950] 406 p.; 24 cm. 'Published under the auspices of the Institute of Pacific Relations.' 1. Forced labor — Asia, Southeastern. I. T.
HD4875.S57 L3 1972        331.1/173/0959        *LC* 79-138155        *ISBN* 0837156122

**Smith, Abbot Emerson, 1906-.**                                    • **4.3106**
Colonists in bondage; white servitude and convict labor in America, 1607–1776. Chapel Hill, Pub. for the Institute of Early American History and Culture at Williamsburg, Va., by the Univ. of North Carolina Press, 1947. 435 p. 1. Indentured servants 2. Domestics — United States. 3. Penal colonies, British. 4. Crime and criminals — Great Britain. I. Institute of Early American History and Culture (Williamsburg, Va.) II. T.
HD4875.U5 S5        331.54        *LC* 48-5154

## HD4881–4895 APPRENTICESHIP

**Davies, Margaret Gay.**                                    • **4.3107**
The enforcement of English apprenticeship; a study in applied mercantilism, 1563–1642. — Cambridge, Harvard University Press, 1956. x, 319 p. 22 cm. — (Harvard economic studies. v. 97) Bibliography: p. [281]-301. 1. Apprentices — Great Britain. I. T. II. Series.
HD4885.G7 D3x        331.55        *LC* 56-5174

## HD4901–4902 Treatises

**Furniss, Edgar Stephenson, 1890-.**                                    • **4.3108**
The position of the laborer in a system of nationalism; a study in the labor theories of later English mercantilists. New York, Kelley & Millman, 1957. 260 p. 22 cm. 1. Labor economics 2. Mercantile system 3. Labor and laboring classes — Great Britain I. T.
HD4901.F82 1957        *LC* 58-3121

**McNulty, Paul J.**                                    **4.3109**
The origins and development of labor economics: a chapter in the history of social thought / Paul J. McNulty. — Cambridge, Mass.: MIT Press, c1980. viii, 248 p.; 24 cm. 1. Labor economics — History. 2. Economics — History I. T.
HD4901.M22        331/.09        *LC* 80-15320        *ISBN* 0262131625

**Marshall, F. Ray. comp.**                                    **4.3110**
An anthology of labor economics; readings and commentary [by] Ray Marshall [and] Richard Perlman. — New York: Wiley, [c1972] xvii, 965 p.: illus.; 27 cm. 1. Labor economics — Addresses, essays, lectures. I. Perlman, Richard. joint comp. II. T.
HD4901.M28        331/.08        *LC* 78-175794        *ISBN* 0471572985

**Moore, Wilbert Ellis.**                                    • **4.3111**
Industrialization and labor; social aspects of economic development [by] Wilbert E. Moore. — New York, Russell & Russell, 1965 [c1951] xx, 410 p. illus. 23 cm. — (Studies of the Institute of World Affairs) Bibliography: p. [365]-398. 1. Labor and laboring classes 2. Industrialization 3. Labor and laboring classes — Mexico. I. T.
HD4901.M83 1965        331.11091724        *LC* 65-18822

**Moore, Wilbert Ellis. ed.**                                    • **4.3112**
Labor commitment and social change in developing areas. Edited by Wilbert E. Moore and Arnold S. Feldman. — New York, Social Science Research Council, 1960. xv, 378 p. 24 cm. 'Outgrowth of a conference, sponsored by the Committee on Economic Growth of the Social Science Research Council, and held in Chicago on March 28-30, 1958.' Bibliographical footnotes. 1. Labor and laboring classes I. Feldman, Arnold S. joint ed. II. Social Science Research Council (U.S.). Committee on Economic Growth. III. T.
HD4901.M85        331        *LC* 60-53440

**Shister, Joseph.**                                    **4.3113**
Readings in labor economics and industrial relations. 2d ed. Philadelphia: Lippincott, [1956]. 673 p.: 24 cm. — 1. Labor and laboring classes 2. Industrial relations 3. Labor economics I. T.
HD4901.S48 1956        *LC* 56-5020

## HD4903 Discrimination in Employment

**Jain, Harish C.**                                    **4.3114**
Equal employment issues: race and sex discrimination in the United States, Canada, and Britain / Harish C. Jain, Peter J. Sloane. — New York, NY: Praeger, 1981. x, 256 p.; 24 cm. 1. Discrimination in employment 2. Discrimination in employment — Law and legislation I. Sloane, Peter J. II. T.
HD4903.J34 1981        331.13/3 19        *LC* 81-8833        *ISBN* 0030508363

**Becker, Gary Stanley, 1930-.**                                    • **4.3115**
The economics of discrimination [by] Gary S. Becker. 2d ed. Chicago, University of Chicago Press [1971] x, 167 p. 22 cm. (Economics research studies of the Economics Research Center of the University of Chicago) 1. Discrimination in employment — United States 2. Afro-Americans — Employment 3. Afro-Americans — Economic conditions I. T.
HD4903.5.U58 B4 1971        331.1/33/0973        *LC* 73-157422        *ISBN* 0226041158

**Conference on Discrimination in Labor Markets, Princeton**        **4.3116**
**University, 1971.**
Discrimination in labor markets, edited by Orley Ashenfelter and Albert Rees. Princeton, N.J., Princeton University Press 1974 (c1973) xii, 181 p. illus. 22 cm. 'Sponsored by the Industrial Relations Section and the Woodrow Wilson School of Public and International Affairs.' 1. Discrimination in employment — United States — Congresses. I. Ashenfelter, Orley, 1942- ed. II. Rees, Albert, 1921- ed. III. Princeton University. Industrial Relations Section. IV. Woodrow Wilson School of Public and International Affairs. V. T.
HD4903.5.U58 P73 1971        331.1/33/0973        *LC* 72-4037        *ISBN* 0691041709

**Ruchames, Louis, 1917-.**                                    • **4.3117**
Race, jobs & politics; the story of FEPC. New York, Columbia University Press, 1953. x, 255 p. 24 cm. 1. U.S. Committee on Fair Employment Practice (1941-1943) 2. U.S. Committee on Fair Employment Practice (1943-1946) 3. Discrimination in employment — United States 4. Afro-Americans — Employment I. T.
HD4903.5.U58 R8        331.11        *LC* 53-10015

## HD4904–4905 Work: General. Work Ethic

**Friedmann, Georges, 1902-.**                                    • **4.3118**
The anatomy of work; labor, leisure, and the implications of automation. Translated by Wyatt Rawson. [New York] Free Press of Glencoe [1962, c1961] 203 p. 1. Work I. T.
HD4904 F6483        *LC* 61-9165

**Voydanoff, Patricia.**                                    **4.3119**
Work & family: changing roles of men and women / edited by Patricia Voydanoff. — 1st ed. — Palo Alto, Calif.: Mayfield Pub. Co., c1984. viii, 383 p.: ill.; 23 cm. 1. Work and family — Addresses, essays, lectures. I. T. II. Title: Work and family.
HD4904.25.W67 1984        306/.36 19        *LC* 83-61534        *ISBN* 0874845769

**Florence, P. Sargant (Philip Sargant), 1890-.**                                    • **4.3120**
Economics of fatigue and unrest and the efficiency of labour in English and American industry, by P. Sargant Florence. New York, H. Holt and company, 1924. 426 p. illus. 22 cm. Printed in Great Britain. 1. Fatique. 2. Efficiency, Industrial I. T.
HD4904.5.F6        *LC* 25-1390

**Pascarella, Perry.**                                    **4.3121**
The new achievers: creating a modern work ethic / Perry Pascarella. — New York: Free Press; London: Collier Macmillan, c1984. x, 210 p.; 24 cm. 1. Work ethic 2. Job satisfaction 3. Personnel management I. T.
HD4905.P37 1984        658.3/14 19        *LC* 83-49202        *ISBN* 0029248701

**Rose, Michael, 1937-.**                                    **4.3122**
Re–working the work ethic: economic values and socio–cultural politics / Michael Rose. — 1st American ed. — New York: Schocken Books, 1985. ix,

160 p.; 23 cm. (Work and society in the eighties.) Includes index. 1. Work ethic I. T. II. Series.
HD4905.R67 1985     306/.36 19     *LC* 84-23555     *ISBN* 0805239332

# HD4906–5100 Wages

**Brown, Ernest Henry Phelps, 1906-.**     • **4.3123**
A century of pay: the course of pay and production in France, Germany, Sweden, the United Kingdom, and the United States of America, 1860–1960 [by] E. H. Phelps Brown with Margaret H. Browne. — London: Macmillan; New York: St. Martin's P., 1968. 476 p.: illus.; 23 cm. 1. Wages — France — History. 2. Wages — Germany — History. 3. Wages — Sweden — History. 4. Wages — Great Britain — History. 5. Wages — United States — History. I. Browne, Margaret H. II. T.
HD4906.B73     331.2/9/4     *LC* 68-16620

**Reynolds, Lloyd George, 1910-.**     • **4.3124**
The evolution of wage structure, by Lloyd G. Reynolds and Cynthia H. Taft; with a section by Robert M. Macdonald. — New Haven: Yale University Press, 1956 [c1955] xii, 398 p.; 24 cm. — (Yale studies in economics. 6) 1. Wages 2. Wages — United States. I. Morris, Cynthia Taft joint author. II. T. III. Series.
HD4906.R48     331.2     *LC* 56-5945

**Belcher, David W.**     **4.3125**
Compensation administration [by] David W. Belcher. Englewood Cliffs, N.J., Prentice-Hall [1974] xv, 606 p. 24 cm. (Prentice-Hall industrial relations & personnel series) Published in 1955 and 1962 under title: Wage and salary administration. 1. Compensation management 2. Wages I. T.
HD4909.B43 1974     658.3/2 19     *LC* 73-11068     *ISBN* 0131541617

**Cartter, Allan Murray.**     • **4.3126**
Theory of wages and employment. Homewood, Ill., R.D. Irwin, 1959. 193 p. ill. (The Irwin series in economics) 1. Wages I. T.
HD4909 C24     *LC* 59-6113

**Dobb, Maurice Herbert, 1900-.**     • **4.3127**
Wages / by Maurice Dobb; with an introduction by C. W. Guillebaud. — London, J.Nisbet 1956. 201p.;c19cm. (Cambridge economic handbooks.) Includes bibliographies. 1. Wages I. T.
HD4909.D6 1956     331.2     *LC* 57-49867

**Douglas, Paul Howard, 1892-.**     • **4.3128**
The theory of wages, by Paul H. Douglas. With a new foreword and the article, Are there laws of production?. — New York, A. M. Kelley, bookseller, 1964. 41, vii-xx, 3-639 p. illus. 24 cm. — (Reprints of economic classics) Reprint of the 1957 ed. Bibliography: p. 555-610. 1. Wages — U.S. 2. Supply and demand 3. U.S. — Indus. 4. Labor and laboring classes — U.S. — 1914- 5. Capital — U.S. 6. Economics, Mathematical I. T.
HD4909.D63 1964     331.21     *LC* 64-22237

**Dunlop, John Thomas, 1914-.**     **4.3129**
Wage determination under trade unions / John T. Dunlop. — New York: A.M. Kelley, 1950. xi, 230 p.: ill.; 22 cm. 1. Wages 2. Collective bargaining 3. Trade-unions I. T.
HD4909.D8 1950     *LC* 50-58147

**Hicks, John Richard, Sir, 1904-.**     • **4.3130**
The theory of wages. — [2d ed.]. — London, Macmillan; New York, St. Martin's Press [c1963] xix, 388 p. 23 cm. Bibliographical footnotes. 1. Wages 2. Labor economics 3. Unemployed 4. Trade-unions I. T.
HD4909.H5 1963     *LC* 64-35917

**International Economic Association.**     • **4.3131**
The theory of wage determination; proceedings of a conference held by the International Economic Association. Edited by John T. Dunlop. London, Macmillan, 1957. xv, 437 p. diagrs. 1. Wages — Congresses I. Dunlop, John Thomas, 1914- II. T.
HD4909 I55     *LC* 57-3106

**Jaques, Elliott.**     • **4.3132**
Equitable payment; a general theory of work, differential payment, and individual progress. New York, Wiley [1961] 336 p. ill. 1. Wages 2. Work 3. Responsibility I. T.
HD4909 J3     *LC* 61-65959

**Reynolds, Lloyd George, 1910-.**     • **4.3133**
The structure of labor markets; wages and labor mobility in theory and practice, by Lloyd G. Reynolds. — Westport, Conn.: Greenwood Press, [1971, c1951] ix, 328 p.: illus.; 24 cm. 1. Wages 2. Migration, Internal 3. Labor mobility I. T.
HD4909.R38 1971     331.1/2     *LC* 73-109302     *ISBN* 0837138450

**Rothschild, Kurt Wilhelm.**     • **4.3134**
The theory of wages, by K. W. Rothschild. — New York: A. M. Kelley, 1967. viii, 180 p.: illus.; 23 cm. 'Second edition.'—Dust jacket. Reprint of the 1960 ed. 1. Wages I. T.
HD4909.R67 1967     331.2/1     *LC* 67-5911

**Taylor, George William, 1901- ed.**     **4.3135**
New concepts in wage determination, edited by George W. Taylor [and] Frank C. Pierson. Contributors: Leland Hazard [and others]. — New York, McGraw-Hill, 1957. xiii, 336 p. 24 cm. — (McGraw-Hill labor management series) Bibliographical footnotes. 1. Wages I. Pierson, Frank Cook, 1911- joint editor. II. T.
HD4909.T3     331.2     *LC* 56-11057

**Wootton, Barbara, 1897-.**     • **4.3136**
The social foundations of wage policy: a study of contemporary British wage and salary structure [by] Barbara Wooton. 2nd ed., 2nd impression. London, Allen & Unwin, 1964. [5], 200 p. tables. 22 cm. (Unwin university books, 1) 1. Wages 2. Wages — Great Britain. I. T.
HD4909.W6 1964     *LC* 67-97523

**Pen, J. (Jan), 1921-.**     • **4.3137**
The wage rate under collective bargaining. Translated by T.S. Preston. Cambridge, Harvard University Press, 1959. xiv, 216 p. (Wertheim publications in industrial relations.) 1. Wages 2. Collective bargaining I. T. II. Series.
HD4912 P393     *LC* 59-7658

**The Economics of legal minimum wages / edited by Simon**     **4.3138**
**Rottenberg.**
Washington, D.C: American Enterprise Institute for Public Policy Research, c1981. xiv, 534 p.: ill.; 23 cm. — (AEI symposia; 81A) Papers presented at a conference held at the American Enterprise Institute, Washington, D.C., Nov. 1 and 2, 1979. 1. Wages — Minimum wage — United States — Congresses. 2. Labor supply — United States — Congresses. 3. Human capital — United States — Congresses. I. Rottenberg, Simon. II. American Enterprise Institute for Public Policy Research.
HD4918.E26     331.2/3/0973 19     *LC* 80-26563     *ISBN* 0844721972

**Stewart, Charles T., 1922-.**     **4.3139**
Low–wage workers in an affluent society [by] Charles T. Stewart, Jr. — Chicago: Nelson-Hall, [1974] vii, 247 p.; 22 cm. 1. Wages — Minimum wage — United States. 2. Manpower policy — United States I. T.
HD4918.S73     331.2/973     *LC* 73-78912     *ISBN* 0882291017

**Lupton, Tom. comp.**     **4.3140**
Payment systems; selected readings; edited by Tom Lupton. — Harmondsworth: Penguin, 1972. 381 p.: illus.; 18 cm. — (Penguin modern management readings) (Penguin education) 1. Wage payment systems — Addresses, essays, lectures. I. T.
HD4926.L79     331.2/16/08     *LC* 73-153656     *ISBN* 0140801685

**Hart, Robert A.**     **4.3141**
The economics of non–wage labour costs / Robert A. Hart. — London; Winchester, Mass.: Allen & Unwin, 1984. xii, 173 p.: ill.; 23 cm. 1. Employee fringe benefits 2. Labor costs I. T.
HD4928.N6 H37 1984     331.25/5 19     *LC* 83-22328     *ISBN* 0043310966

**The Handbook of employee benefits: design, funding, and**     **4.3142**
**administration / edited by Jerry S. Rosenbloom.**
Homewood, Ill.: Dow Jones-Irwin, c1984. xxiii, 1096 p.: ill.; 24 cm. Includes index. 1. Employee fringe benefits — United States. 2. Employee fringe benefits — Law and legislation — United States. 3. Employee fringe benefits — Taxation — Law and legislation — United States. I. Rosenbloom, Jerry S.
HD4928.N62 U6353 1984     658.3/25/0973 19     *LC* 82-74070     *ISBN* 0870944061

## HD4974–4977 By Country

**Douglas, Paul Howard, 1892-.**     • **4.3143**
Real wages in the United States, 1890–1926. Boston and New York, Houghton Mifflin company, 1930. xxviii, 682 p. tables (1 double) diagrs. 23 cm. 1. Wages — United States. 2. Cost and standard of living — United States. 3. Unemployed — United States. 4. Labor and laboring classes — United States I. T.
HD4975.D6     *LC* 30-12884

**Lewis, Harold Gregg, 1914-.**     • **4.3144**
Unionism and relative wages in the United States; an empirical inquiry. Chicago, University of Chicago Press [1963] xvii, 308 p. diagr., tables. (Studies in economics of the Economics Research Center of the University of Chicago)

'A publication of the Workshop in Labor and Industrial Relations.' 1. Wages — United States — History 2. Trade-unions — United States — History I. T.
HD4975 L47     *LC* 63-20915

**Long, Clarence Dickinson, 1908-.**     • **4.3145**
Wages and earnings in the United States, 1860–1890. A study by the National Bureau of Economic Research, New York. — Princeton: Princeton University Press, 1960. xvii, 169 p.: diagrs., tables; 24 cm. — (National Bureau of Economic Research. General series, no. 67) 1. Wages — United States. I. National Bureau of Economic Research. II. T. III. Series.
HD4975.L57     331.2973     *LC* 60-5756

**Mitchell, Daniel J. B.**     **4.3146**
Unions, wages, and inflation / Daniel J. B. Mitchell. — Washington, D.C.: Brookings Institution, c1980. xiii, 290 p.; 24 cm. 1. Wages — United States. 2. Inflation (Finance) — United States 3. Collective bargaining — United States. 4. Labor economics 5. Trade-unions — United States I. T.
HD4975.M49     331.2/973     *LC* 79-3776     *ISBN* 0815757522

**The Measurement of labor cost / edited by Jack E. Triplett.**     **4.3147**
Chicago: University of Chicago Press, 1983. xi, 539 p.; 24 cm. — (Studies in income and wealth. v. 48) 'Papers and discussion presented at the Conference on the Measurement of Labor Cost held in Williamsburg, Virginia, on 3 and 4 December 1981'—Preface. Includes indexes. 1. Labor costs — United States — Congresses. 2. Employee fringe benefits — United States — Congresses. I. Triplett, Jack E. II. Conference on the Measurement of Labor Cost (1981: Williamsburg, Va.) III. Series.
HD4975.M4x     330 s 338.5/12 19     *LC* 83-5920     *ISBN* 0226812561

**Rees, Albert, 1921-.**     • **4.3148**
Real wages in manufacturing, 1890–1914, by Albert Rees, assisted by Donald P. Jacobs. Princeton, Princeton University Press, 1961. xvi, 163 p. diagrs., tables. (National Bureau of Economic Research. General series, no. 70) 'A study by the National Bureau of Economic Research, New York.' 1. Wages — United States I. T. II. Series.
HD4975 R4     *LC* 61-7401

**United States. Bureau of Labor Statistics.**     • **4.3149**
History of wages in the United States from colonial times to 1928. Washington, U.S. Govt. print. off., 1934. ix, 574 p. incl. tables. 23 cm. 1. Wages — United States. I. Stewart, Estelle M. (Estelle May), 1887-1938. II. Bowen, Jesse Chester, 1865-1948. III. T.
HD4975.U5x     *LC* l 34-109

**Kirsch, Leonard Joel, 1934-.**     **4.3150**
Soviet wages: changes in structure and administration since 1956. Cambridge, Mass., MIT Press [1972] xii, 237 p. 23 cm. 1. Wages — Soviet Union. I. T.
HD5046.K53     331.2/9/47     *LC* 71-173924     *ISBN* 0262110458

# HD5106–5250 Hours

**Cuvillier, Rolande.**     **4.3151**
The reduction of working time: scope and implications in industralised market economies / Rolande Cuvillier. — Geneva: International Labour Office, 1984. vi, 150 p.; 24 cm. 1. Thirty-five hour week I. T.
HD5106.C94 1984     331.25/722 19     *LC* 85-133108     *ISBN* 9221027023

**Dankert, Clyde Edward, 1901- ed.**     • **4.3152**
Hours of work. Edited by Clyde E. Dankert, Floyd C. Mann [and] Herbert R. Northrup. [1st ed.] New York, Harper & Row [1965] viii, 208 p. ill. (Industrial Relations Research Association. Publication no. 32) 1. Hours of labor I. Mann, Floyd Christopher, 1917- II. Northrup, Herbert Roof, 1918- III. T.
HD5106 D33     *LC* 65-21007

**Ronen, Simcha, 1935-.**     **4.3153**
Alternative work schedules: selecting— implementing— and evaluating / Simcha Ronen. — Homewood, Ill.: D. Jones-Irwin, c1984. xiii, 255 p.: ill.; 25 cm. Includes index. 1. Hours of labor, Flexible 2. Part-time employment I. T.
HD5109.R66 1984     658.3/121 19     *LC* 84-70601     *ISBN* 0870945114

**Ronen, Simcha, 1935-.**     **4.3154**
Flexible working hours: an innovation in the quality of work life / by Simcha Ronen. — New York: McGraw-Hill, c1981. xiv, 353 p.: ill.; 24 cm. Includes index. 1. Hours of labor, Flexible — United States. I. T.
HD5109.2.U5 R66     331.25/72/0973     *LC* 80-14614     *ISBN* 0070536074

**Ehrenberg, Ronald G.**     **4.3155**
Longer hours or more jobs?: an investigation of amending hours legislation to create employment / Ronald G. Ehrenberg and Paul L. Schumann. — Ithaca, N.Y.: New York State School of Industrial and Labor Relations, Cornell University, c1982. xii, 177 p.; 24 cm. — (Cornell studies in industrial and labor relations. no. 22) 1. Overtime — United States. 2. Unemployment — United States. 3. Hours of labor — United States. I. Schumann, Paul L., 1955- II. T. III. Series.
HD5111.U5 E52     331.25/72 19     *LC* 81-11284     *ISBN* 0875460909

**Absenteeism / Paul S. Goodman, Robert S. Atkin, and associates.**     **4.3156**
1st ed. — San Francisco: Jossey-Bass, 1984. xxi, 436 p.; 24 cm. — (Jossey-Bass management series.) (Jossey-Bass social and behavioral science series.) 1. Absenteeism (Labor) — Addresses, essays, lectures. I. Goodman, Paul S. II. Atkin, Robert S., 1945- III. Series. IV. Series: Jossey-Bass social and behavioral science series.
HD5115.A175 1984     658.3/14 19     *LC* 84-47985     *ISBN* 0875896170

**Cahill, Marion Cotter, 1901-.**     • **4.3157**
Shorter hours; a study of the movement since the Civil War. New York, AMS Press [1968] 300 p. 22 cm. (Studies in history, economics, and public law, no. 380) Reprint of the 1932 ed. 1. Hours of labor — United States. 2. Labor laws and legislation — United States I. T.
H31.C7 no. 380 1968 HD5124.C3x     331.81/9/73     *LC* 68-54258

**Levitan, Sar A.**     **4.3158**
Shorter hours, shorter weeks: spreading the work to reduce unemployment / Sar A. Levitan and Richard S. Belous. — Baltimore: Johns Hopkins University Press, c1977. ix, 94 p.: ill.; 21 cm. — (Policy studies in employment and welfare; no. 30) 1. Hours of labor — United States. 2. Labor supply — United States. 3. United States — Full employment policies. I. Belous, Richard S. joint author. II. T.
HD5124.L39     331.2/572/0973     *LC* 77-4787     *ISBN* 0801819989

**Bienefeld, M. A.**     **4.3159**
Working hours in British industry: an economic history [by] M. A. Bienefeld. — London: London School of Economics and Political Science; Weidenfeld and Nicolson, [1972] 293 p.; 22 cm. — (L.S.E. research monographs) 1. Hours of labor — Great Britain — History. I. T.
HD5166.B53     331.2/57/0942     *LC* 73-151267     *ISBN* 0297994794

**Langenfelt, Gösta, 1888-.**     **4.3160**
The historic origin of the eight hours day; studies in English traditionalism. Westport, Conn., Greenwood Press [1974] 151 p. 23 cm. Reprint of the 1954 ed. distributed by Almqvist & Wiksell, Stockholm, which was issued as del 87 of Kungl. Vitterhets-, historie- och antikvitetsakademiens handlingar. 1. Alfred, King of England, 849-899. 2. Eight-hour movement — History. I. T.
HD5166.L35     331.2/572     *LC* 73-19224     *ISBN* 0837173140

**Young, Michael Dunlop, 1915-.**     **4.3161**
The symmetrical family, by Michael Young [and] Peter Willmott. With a foreword by Lee Rainwater. — [1st American ed.]. — New York: Pantheon Books, [1974, c1973] xxvii, 398 p.: illus.; 22 cm. 1. Hours of labor — England — London metropolitan area. 2. Leisure — England — London metropolitan area. 3. Time management surveys — England — London metropolitan area. 4. Family — England — London metropolitan area. I. Willmott, Peter. joint author. II. T.
HD5168.Z98 L669 1974     301.5/5/09421     *LC* 73-7009     *ISBN* 0394487273

# HD5306–5450 Strikes. Lockouts

**Kornhauser, Arthur William, 1896- ed.**     • **4.3162**
Industrial conflict, edited by Arthur Kornhauser, Robert Dubin [and] Arthur M. Ross. [Prepared for the Society for the Psychological Study of Social Issues] New York, McGraw-Hill, 1954. 551 p. 1. Strikes and lockouts 2. Trade-unions 3. Industrial relations I. Society for the Psychological Study of Social Issues. II. T.
HD5306 K6     *LC* 53-12870

**Blackman, John L.**     • **4.3163**
Presidential seizure in labor disputes [by] John L. Blackman, Jr. — Cambridge: Harvard University Press, 1967. xvi, 351 p. illus. (Wertheim publications in industrial relations.) 1. Labor disputes — United States. 2. Executive power — United States I. T. II. Series.
HD5324.B53     HD5324 B53.     331.89/8/0973     *LC* 67-20871

**Chamberlain, Neil W.** • **4.3164**
The impact of strikes, their social and ecconomic costs, by Neil W. Chamberlain and Jane Metzger Schilling. [1st ed.] New York, Harper [1954] viii, 257 p. (Yale Labor and Management Center series) 1. Strikes and lockouts — United States 2. Strikes and lockouts — Social aspects I. Schilling, Jane Metzger, jt. author II. T.
HD5324 C42    LC 53-11958

**Yellen, Samuel, 1906-.** • **4.3165**
American labor struggles. — New York: Arno, 1969 [c1936] xviii, 398 p.: illus., maps.; 23 cm. — (American labor (New York, N.Y.) 1. Strikes and lockouts — U.S. — History. I. T. II. Series.
HD5324.Y4 1969    331.89/29/73    LC 70-89773

**Fine, Sidney, 1920-.** • **4.3166**
Sit–down: the General Motors strike of 1936–1937. — Ann Arbor: University of Michigan Press, [1969] ix, 448 p.: illus., ports.; 24 cm. 1. General Motors Corporation Sit-Down Strike, 1936-1937 I. T.
HD5325.A82 1936-1937 .F5    331.881/292    LC 73-83455

**Brody, David, 1930-.** • **4.3167**
Labor in crisis; the steel strike of 1919. [1st ed.] Philadelphia, Lippincott [1965] 208 p. 21 cm. (Critical periods of history) 1. Steel Strike, 1919-1920. 2. Trade-unions — Iron and steel workers — United States — History. I. T.
HD5325.I5 1919.B7    331.89/286/91420973    LC 65-23205

**McGovern, George S. (George Stanley), 1922-.** **4.3168**
The great coalfield war [by] George S. McGovern and Leonard F. Guttridge. Illustrated with photos. and with maps by Samuel H. Bryant. Boston, Houghton Mifflin, 1972. xii, 383 p. illus. 24 cm. 1. Coal Strike, Colorado, 1913-1914. I. Guttridge, Leonard F. joint author. II. T.
HD5325.M63 1913.C853    331.89/282/2330978851    LC 72-177532
ISBN 0395136490

**Eggert, Gerald G.** **4.3169**
Railroad labor disputes; the beginnings of Federal strike policy [by] Gerald G. Eggert. — Ann Arbor: University of Michigan Press, [1967] viii, 313 p.; 24 cm. 1. Strikes and lockouts — Railroads — United States. I. T.
HD5325.R1 E34    331.89/281/385    LC 67-11984

**Lindsey, Almont, 1906-.** • **4.3170**
The Pullman strike, the story of a unique experiment and of a great labor upheaval, by Almont Lindsey ... Chicago, Ill., The University of Chicago press [c1942] 385 p. ill. 1. Chicago Strike, 1894 I. T.
HD5325.R12 1894.C54    331.89    LC 42-50022

**Stevens, Evelyn P.** **4.3171**
Protest and response in Mexico [by] Evelyn P. Stevens. — Cambridge, Mass.: MIT Press, [1974] viii, 372 p.; 21 cm. 1. Strikes and lockouts — Mexico 2. Communication and traffic — Mexico. 3. Violence — Mexico. I. T.
HD5331.A6 S75    301.6/3/0972    LC 74-2232    ISBN 0262191288

**Walsh, Kenneth.** **4.3172**
Strikes in Europe and the United States: measurement and incidence / Kenneth Walsh. — New York: St. Martin's Press, 1983. xiv, 230 p.; 24 cm. Includes index. 1. Strikes and lockouts — European Economic Community countries — Statistical methods. 2. Strikes and lockouts — United States — Statistical methods. I. T.
HD5364.5.A6 W34 1983    331.89/2 19    LC 83-40055    ISBN 0312766416

**Durcan, J. W.** **4.3173**
Strikes in post–war Britain: a study of stoppages of work due to industrial disputes, 1946–73 / J.W. Durcan, W.E.J. McCarthy, and G.P. Redman. — London; Boston: G. Allen & Unwin, 1983. xv, 448 p.: ill.; 24 cm. Includes index. 1. Strikes and lockouts — Great Britain — History — 20th century. I. McCarthy, W. E. J. (William Edward John) II. Redman, G. P. III. T.
HD5365.A6 D87 1983    331.89/2941 19    LC 83-5975    ISBN 0043310931

**The General Strike, 1926 / edited by Jeffrey Skelley.** **4.3174**
London: Lawrence and Wishart, 1976. xiv, 412 p.; 23 cm. 1. General Strike, Great Britain, 1926 I. Skelley, Jeffrey.
HD5366.G46    331.89/25/0941    LC 76-363815    ISBN 085315337X

**Jones, David J. V.** **4.3175**
The last rising: the Newport insurrection of 1839 / David J.V. Jones. — Oxford [Oxfordshire]: Clarendon Press, 1985. 273 p.: ill.; 23 cm. Includes index. 1. Newport Uprising, Wales, 1839 2. Labor disputes — Wales — Newport (Gwent) — History — 19th century. 3. Labor and laboring classes — Wales — Newport (Gwent) — History — 19th century. 4. Social conflict — Wales — Newport (Gwent) — History — 19th century. 5. Chartism — History. I. T.
HD5366.Z9 N495 1985    942.9/91081 19    LC 84-20601    ISBN 0198200765

**Wilks, Ivor.** **4.3176**
South Wales and the rising of 1839: class struggle as armed struggle / Ivor Wilks. — Urbana: University of Illinois Press, c1984. 270 p.; 23 cm. — (Working class in European history.) 1. Frost, John, 1784?-1877. 2. Labor disputes — Wales — Newport (Gwent) — History — 19th century. 3. Labor and laboring classes — Wales — Newport (Gwent) — History — 19th century. 4. Social conflict — Wales — Newport (Gwent) — History — 19th century. 5. Chartism — History. 6. Newport Uprising, Wales, 1839 I. T. II. Series.
HD5366.Z9 N499 1984    303.6/23/0942991 19    LC 84-2530    ISBN 0252011465

**Shorter, Edward.** **4.3177**
Strikes in France, 1830–1968 [by] Edward Shorter [and] Charles Tilly. — [London; New York]: Cambridge University Press, [1974] xxiii, 428 p.: illus.; 24 cm. 1. Strikes and lockouts — France — History. I. Tilly, Charles. joint author. II. T.
HD5374.S55    331.89/2944    LC 73-80475    ISBN 0521202930

# HD5650–5660 Employees' Representation in Management

**Chamberlain, Neil W.** • **4.3178**
The union challenge to management control, by Neil W. Chamberlain. [Hamden, Conn.] Archon Books, 1967 [c1948] xx, 338 p. 23 cm. 1. Industrial management — Employee participation 2. Industrial relations I. T.
HD5650.C54 1967    331.15/2    LC 67-19507

**Jones, Derek C.** **4.3179**
Participatory and self–managed firms: evaluating economic performance / edited by Derek C. Jones, Jan Svejnar. — Lexington, Mass.: Lexington Books, c1982. vii, 358 p.: ill.; 24 cm. Includes index. 1. Management — Employee participation — Case studies. 2. Producer cooperatives — Case studies. I. Svejnar, Jan. II. T.
HD5650.P3335    338.6 19    LC 80-8612    ISBN 0669043281

**The Performance of labor–managed firms / edited by Frank H. Stephen.** **4.3180**
New York: St. Martin's Press, 1982. xv, 280 p.: ill.; 22 cm. Includes index. 1. Works councils — Case studies. 2. Producer cooperatives — Case studies. 3. Management — Employee participation — Case studies. I. Stephen, Frank H., 1946- II. Title: Labor-managed firms.
HD5650.P422 1982    658.3/152 19    LC 81-21216    ISBN 0312600852

**Self–management: economic liberation of man: selected readings / Jaroslav Vanek.** **4.3181**
Harmondsworth, Eng.; Baltimore: Penguin Books, 1975. 478 p.: ill.; 20 cm. (Penguin education) (Penguin modern economic readings) Includes indexes. 1. Management — Employee participation — Addresses, essays, lectures. I. Vanek, Jaroslav.
HD5650.S4    658.31/52    LC 76-355352    ISBN 0140808787

**Sturmthal, Adolf Fox.** • **4.3182**
Workers councils; a study of workplace organization on both sides of the Iron Curtain. Cambridge, Mass., Harvard University Press, 1964. x, 217 p. (Wertheim publications in industrial relations.) 1. Works councils 2. Management — Employee participation I. T. II. Series.
HD5650 S84    LC 64-13429

**Brannen, Peter.** **4.3183**
Authority and participation in industry / Peter Brannen. — New York: St. Martin's, 1983. 168 p. Includes index. 1. Industrial management — Great Britain — Employee participation. 2. Industrial management — Employee participation I. T.
HD5660.G7 B675 1983    658.3/152 19    LC 83-16151    ISBN 0312061234

HD 5660 G7 8675 1983

**Derber, Milton.** • **4.3184**
The American idea of industrial democracy, 1865–1965. Urbana, University of Illinois Press [1970] xv, 553 p. 24 cm. 1. Industrial management — United States — Employee participation — History. 2. Industrial relations — United States — History. I. T.
HD5660.U5 D44    331.15/2    LC 70-100376    ISBN 0252000854

**Kochan, Thomas A.** **4.3185**
Worker participation and American unions: threat or opportunity? / Thomas A. Kochan, Harry C. Katz, Nancy R. Mower. — Kalamazoo, Mich.: W.E. Upjohn Institute for Employment Research, 1984. viii, 202 p.; 23 cm. 1. Industrial management — United States — Employee participation.

2. Trade-unions — United States I. Katz, Harry Charles, 1951- II. Mower, Nancy R. III. T.
HD5660.U5 K62 1984    658.3/152/0973 19    *LC* 84-13071    *ISBN* 0880990228

**Witte, John F.**                                                                 4.3186
Democracy, authority, and alienation in work: workers' participation in an American corporation / John F. Witte. — Chicago: University of Chicago Press, 1980. xii, 216 p.: ill.; 24 cm. Includes index. 1. Management — Employee participation — United States. I. T.
HD5660.U5 W57    658.3/152/0973    *LC* 80-16241    *ISBN* 0226904202

**Worker participation and ownership: cooperative strategies for**      4.3187
**strengthening local economies / William Foote Whyte ... [et al.].**
Ithica [sic], NY: ILR Press, c1983. x, 152 p.; 22 cm. Includes index. 1. Management — Employee participation — United States — Addresses, essays, lectures. 2. Employee ownership — United States — Addresses, essays, lectures. I. Whyte, William Foote, 1914-
HD5660.U5 W67 1983    338.6 19    *LC* 82-23413    *ISBN* 0875460976

**Comisso, Ellen Turkish.**                                                        4.3188
Workers' control under plan and market: implications of Yugoslav self-management / Ellen Turkish Comisso. — New Haven: Yale University Press, 1979. x, 285 p.: ill.; 24 cm. — (Yale studies in political science. 29) 1. Works councils — Yugoslavia. 2. Industrial management — Yugoslavia. 3. Industry and state — Yugoslavia. 4. Socialism — Yugoslavia I. T. II. Series.
HD5660.Y8 C56    338.6    *LC* 79-64227    *ISBN* 0300023340

**Estrin, Saul.**                                                                  4.3189
Self-management: economic theory and Yugoslav practice / Saul Estrin. — Cambridge [Cambridgeshire]; New York: Cambridge University Press, 1984 (c1983). x, 266 p.: ill.; 23 cm. (Soviet and East European studies.) Includes index. 1. Management — Employee participation — Yugoslavia. 2. Income distribution — Yugoslavia. 3. Yugoslavia — Economic conditions — 1945- 4. Yugoslavia — Industries. I. T. II. Series.
HD5660.Y8 E87 1983    658.3/152 19    *LC* 83-5239    *ISBN* 0521244978

**Sacks, Stephen R.**                                                             4.3190
Self-management and efficiency: large corporations in Yugoslavia / Stephen R. Sacks. — London; Boston: Allen and Unwin, 1983. xi, 163 p.: ill.; 23 cm. Includes index. 1. Industrial management — Yugoslavia — Employee participation. 2. Industrial organization — Yugoslavia. 3. Corporations — Yugoslavia. 4. Decentralization in management — Yugoslavia. I. T.
HD5660.Y8 S14 1983    658.3/152/09497 19    *LC* 83-14999    *ISBN* 0043340083

**Wachtel, Howard M.**                                                            4.3191
Workers' management and workers' wages in Yugoslavia; the theory and practice of participatory socialism [by] Howard M. Wachtel. Ithaca [N.Y.] Cornell University Press [1973] xii, 220 p. illus. 22 cm. 1. Management — Yugoslavia — Employee participation. 2. Wages — Yugoslavia. I. T.
HD5660.Y8 W3    658.31/52/09497    *LC* 72-12290    *ISBN* 0801407591

# HD5701–5856 Labor Market. Unemployment

**Beveridge, William Henry Beveridge, Baron, 1879-1963.**            • 4.3192
Unemployment; a problem of industry, 1909 and 1930. — New ed. — New York: AMS Press, [1969] xxvii, 514 p.: illus.; 23 cm. Reprint of the 1930 ed. 'The substance of part I ... was given in lectures delivered in the University of Oxford during Michaelmas term, 1908. The substance of part II was given in lectures delivered in the University of Chicago during December, 1929 ... Part II forms a thesis submitted ... [to] the University of London.' 1. Unemployment 2. Unemployment — Great Britain. I. T.
HD5706.B6 1969    331.1/379/42    *LC* 79-95398

**Garraty, John Arthur, 1920-.**                                                 4.3193
Unemployment in history: economic thought and public policy / by John A. Garraty. 1st ed. — New York: Harper & Row, c1978. 273 p. Includes index. 1. Unemployed — History. I. T.
HD5706.G33 1978    331.1/379    *LC* 76-26227    *ISBN* 0060114576

**Gourvitch, Alexander.**                                                        4.3194
Survey of economic theory on technological change and employment. New York: A.M. Kelley, 1966. 252p. (Reprints of economic classics) First published in 1940. 1. Economics 2. Unemployed — United States 3. United States —

Industries I. T. II. Title: Economic theory on technological change and employment
HD5706 G67

**Killingsworth, Mark R., 1946-.**                                               4.3195
Labor supply / Mark R. Killingsworth. — Cambridge [Cambridgeshire]; New York: Cambridge University Press, 1983. xvi, 493 p.: ill.; 22 cm. — (Cambridge surveys of economic literature.) Includes indexes. 1. Labor supply I. T. II. Series.
HD5706.K57 1983    331.12 19    *LC* 82-14598    *ISBN* 0521233267

**Long, Clarence Dickinson, 1908-.**                                           • 4.3196
The labor force under changing income and employment. Princeton, Princeton University Press, 1958. 440 p. ill. (National Bureau of Economic Research. General series, no. 65) 'A study by the National Bureau of Economic Research, New York.' 1. Labor supply 2. Labor supply — United States I. T. II. Series.
HD5706 L65    *LC* 58-7119

**Pigou, A. C. (Arthur Cecil), 1877-1959.**                                    • 4.3197
The theory of unemployment. New York, A. M. Kelley, 1968. xxv, 319 p. illus. 22 cm. (Reprints of economic classics) Reprint of the 1933 ed. 1. Unemployment I. T.
HD5706.P47 1968    331.1/37/01    *LC* 67-24752

**Universities—National Bureau Committee for Economic**            • 4.3198
**Research.**
The measurement and behavior of unemployment; a conference of the Universities–National Bureau Committee for Economic Research. Princeton, Princeton University Press, 1957. x, 605 p. ill. (National Bureau of Economic Research. Special conference series, 8) 1. Unemployed — Congresses 2. Unemployed — United States — Congresses I. T. II. Series.
HD5706 U66 1957    *LC* 57-5442

**World labour report.**                                                          4.3199
Geneva: International Labour Office, 1984- < 1985 > . v. < 1-2 > : col. ill.; 31 cm. 1. Labor supply 2. Wages 3. Social security 4. Labor supply — Effect of technological innovations on I. International Labour Office.
HD5706.W68 1984    331 19    *LC* 84-166883    *ISBN* 9221036049

**Edwards, Edgar O.**                                                             4.3200
Employment in developing nations: report on a Ford Foundation study / Edgar O. Edwards, editor. — New York: Columbia University Press, 1974. x, 428 p.; 23 cm. 1. Labor supply — Developing countries — Addresses, essays, lectures. 2. Unemployment — Developing countries — Addresses, essays, lectures. 3. Developing countries — Full employment policies — Addresses, essays, lectures. I. Ford Foundation. II. T.
HD5707.E38    331.1/09172/4    *LC* 74-16724    *ISBN* 0231038739

**Harbison, Frederick Harris.**                                                 • 4.3201
Education, manpower, and economic growth; strategies of human resource development [by] Frederick Harbison [and] Charles A. Myers. — New York, McGraw-Hill [1964] xiii, 229 p. diagr., tables. 24 cm. — (McGraw-Hill series in international development) 'A joint project of the Industrial Relations Section, Princeton University, and the Industrial Relations Section, Massachusetts Institute of Technology, as part of the Inter-university Study of Labor Problems in Economic Development. Bibliographical footnotes. 1. Labor supply 2. Education — 1945- 3. Economic development 4. Underdeveloped areas. I. Myers, Charles Andrew, 1913- joint author. II. T.
HD5707.H3    331    *LC* 63-20723

**Unemployment in Western countries: proceedings of a**              4.3202
**conference held by the International Economic Association at**
**Bischenberg, France / edited by Edmond Malinvaud and Jean–**
**Paul Fitoussi.**
New York: St. Martin's Press, 1980. xiv, 551 p.: ill.; 23 cm. — (International Economic Association publications) Includes index. 1. Unemployed — Congresses. 2. Labor supply — Congresses. I. Malinvaud, Edmond. II. Fitoussi, Jean Paul. III. International Economic Association.
HD5707.U45 1980    331.13/79181/2    *LC* 79-29710    *ISBN* 0312832680

**Work in America Institute.**                                                    4.3203
Employment security in a free economy / directed by Jerome M. Rosow and Robert Zager. — New York: Pergamon Press, c1984. xi, 180 p.: ill.; 24 cm. — (Work in America Institute policy study.) 1. Job security — United States. I. Rosow, Jerome M. II. Zager, Robert. III. T. IV. Series.
HD5708.45.U6 W67 1984    658.3/142 19    *LC* 84-19067    *ISBN* 0080309755

**Gordus, Jeanne P.**                                                             4.3204
Plant closings and economic dislocation / Jeanne Prial Gordus, Paul Jarley, Louis A. Ferman. — Kalamazoo, Mich.: W.E. Upjohn Institute for Employment Research, c1981. xiii, 173 p.; 23 cm. 1. Plant shutdowns 2. Unemployed 3. Labor mobility 4. Personnel management 5. Employees,

Relocation of I. Jarley, Paul. II. Ferman, Louis A. III. W.E. Upjohn Institute for Employment Research. IV. T.
HD5708.5.G67 1981     338.6/042 19     *LC* 81-16188     *ISBN* 091155890X

**Bluestone, Barry.**             **4.3205**
The deindustrialization of America: plant closings, community abandonment, and the dismantling of basic industry / Barry Bluestone, Bennett Harrison. — New York: Basic Books, c1982. x, 323 p.: ill.; 24 cm. 1. Plant shutdowns — United States. 2. Capital movements — United States. 3. United States — Industries I. Harrison, Bennett. II. T.
HD5708.55.U6 B58 1982     338.6/042 19     *LC* 82-70844     *ISBN* 0465015905

**Community and capital in conflict: plant closings and job loss /**    **4.3206**
**edited by John C. Raines, Lenora E. Berson, and David McI. Gracie.**
Philadelphia: Temple University Press, 1982. xvii, 318 p.: ill.; 22 cm. 1. Plant shutdowns — United States — Congresses. 2. Unemployment — United States — Congresses. 3. United States — Industries — Location — Congresses. 4. United States — Economic policy — Congresses. I. Raines, John C. II. Berson, Lenora E. III. Gracie, David McI., 1932-
HD5708.55.U6 C65 1982     338.6/042 19     *LC* 82-707     *ISBN* 0877222703

**Martin, Philip L., 1949-.**            **4.3207**
Labor displacement and public policy / Philip L. Martin. — Lexington, Mass.: Lexington Books, c1983. xv, 125 p.: ill.; 24 cm. 1. Layoff systems — United States. 2. Insurance, Unemployment — United States. 3. Supplemental unemployment benefits — United States. 4. Trade adjustment assistance — United States. I. T.
HD5708.55.U6 M37 1983     362.8/5 19     *LC* 82-48099     *ISBN* 0669059692

**McKenzie, Richard B.**            **4.3208**
Fugitive industry: the economics and politics of deindustrialization / by Richard B. McKenzie; foreword by Finis Welch. — San Francisco, Calif.: Pacific Institute for Public Policy Research; Cambridge, Mass.: Ballinger Pub. Co., c1984. xxvi, 281 p.: ill.; 24 cm. — (Pacific studies in public policy.) Includes index. 1. Plant shutdowns — United States. 2. Plant shutdowns — Law and legislation — United States. I. T. II. Series.
HD5708.55.U6 M38 1984     338.6/042 19     *LC* 83-22413     *ISBN* 0884109518

**Meade, James E. (James Edward).**         **4.3209**
Stagflation: vol. 1: wage–fixing / James Meade. — London; Boston: G. Allen & Unwin, 1982. 233 p. 1. Unemployment — Effect of inflation on — Collected works. 2. Wage-price policy — Collected works. I. T.
HD5710.S7     339.5 19     *LC* 81-12717     *ISBN* 0043390234

**Weitzman, Martin L., 1942-.**          **4.3210**
The share economy: conquering stagflation / Martin L. Weitzman. — Cambridge, Mass: Harvard University Press, 1984. vi, 167 p.; 22 cm. Includes index. 1. Unemployment 2. Business cycles 3. Profit-sharing I. T.
HD5710.W45 1984     339.5 19     *LC* 84-665     *ISBN* 0674805828

**Parnes, Herbert S., 1919-.**           **4.3211**
Peoplepower: elements of human resource policy / Herbert S. Parnes. — Beverly Hills [Calif.]: Sage Publications, c1984. 303 p.: ill.; 23 cm. Includes index. 1. Manpower policy 2. Human capital 3. Labor supply I. T.
HD5713.P37 1984     331.11 19     *LC* 84-2085     *ISBN* 0803922760

**Mueller, Charles F. (Charles Francis)**       **4.3212**
The economics of labor migration: a behavioral analysis / Charles F. Mueller. — New York: Academic Press, c1982. xii, 199 p.; 24 cm. — (Studies in urban economics.) Originally presented as the author's thesis (Ph.D.—Boston College) Includes index. 1. Labor mobility 2. Emigration and immigration 3. Migration, Internal I. T. II. Series.
HD5717.M83     331.12/79 19     *LC* 81-19046     *ISBN* 0125095805

**Rosenbaum, James E., 1943-.**          **4.3213**
Career mobility in a corporate hierarchy / James E. Rosenbaum. — Orlando, Fla.: Academic Press, 1984. xviii, 328 p.: graphs; 24 cm. Includes index. 1. Occupational mobility 2. Promotions 3. Occupational mobility — Longitudinal studies. 4. Promotions — Longitudinal studies. I. T.
HD5717.R67 1984     305/.9 19     *LC* 83-22406     *ISBN* 0125970803

# HD5721–5852 By Country

## HD5721–5726 United States

**Work in America; report of a special task force to the Secretary**    **4.3214**
**of Health, Education, and Welfare.**
Cambridge, Mass.: MIT Press, [1973] xix, 262 p.; 22 cm. 1. Manpower policy — United States 2. Labor supply — United States. 3. Job satisfaction I. United States. Dept. of Health, Education, and Welfare.
HD5723.W67     331/.0973     *LC* 73-278     *ISBN* 026208063X

**Blau, Peter Michael.**           • **4.3215**
The American occupational structure [by] Peter M. Blau and Otis Dudley Duncan, with the collaboration of Andrea Tyree. — New York: Wiley, [1967] xvii, 520 p.: illus.; 24 cm. 1. Labor supply — United States. 2. United States — Occupations I. Duncan, Otis Dudley. joint author. II. T.
HD5724.B48     331/.112/0973     *LC* 67-19939

**Bowen, William G.**           • **4.3216**
The economics of labor force participation, by William G. Bowen and T. Aldrich Finegan. — Princeton, N.J.: Princeton University Press, 1969. xxvi, 897 p.: illus.; 25 cm. 1. Labor supply — U.S. 2. Unemployed — U.S. I. Finegan, Thomas Aldrich, 1929- joint author. II. T.
HD5724.B63     331.1/1/0973     *LC* 69-17396

**Creating jobs: public employment programs and wage subsidies:**    **4.3217**
**a study sponsored jointly by the Institute for Research on**
**Poverty and the Brookings Institution / John L. Palmer, editor.**
Washington: The Institution, c1978. 379 p.: ill.; 24 cm. (Studies in social economics. 18) (Monograph series - Institute for Research on Poverty) 1. Public service employment — United States — Addresses, essays, lectures. 2. Employment subsidies — United States — Addresses, essays, lectures. I. Palmer, John Logan. II. Series.
HD5724.C78     331.1/377/0973     *LC* 78-12241     *ISBN* 0815768923.
*ISBN* 0815768915 pbk

**Doeringer, Peter B.**           **4.3218**
Internal labor markets and manpower analysis [by] Peter B. Doeringer [and] Michael J. Piore. Lexington, Mass., Heath [1971] viii, 214 p. illus. 23 cm. 'Prepared for the Manpower Administration, U.S. Department of Labor.' 1. Labor supply — United States. 2. Personnel management — United States. 3. Labor supply — United States — Effect of technological innovations on. I. Piore, Michael J. joint author. II. United States. Dept. of Labor. Manpower Administration. III. T.
HD5724.D588 1971     331.1/0973     *LC* 73-147365

**The Impact of government manpower programs in general, and**    **4.3219**
**on minorities and women / by Charles R. Perry ... [et al.].**
[Philadelphia]: Industrial Research Unit, Wharton School, University of Pennsylvania, c1975. xxxii, 511 p.; 24 cm. (Manpower and human resources studies. no. 4) (Major Industrial Research Unit studies. no. 53) Includes index. 1. Manpower policy — United States 2. Minorities — Employment — United States. I. Perry, Charles R. II. Wharton School. Industrial Research Unit. III. Series. IV. Series: Major Industrial Research Unit studies. no. 53
HD5724.I4     331.1/1/0973     *LC* 74-13177     *ISBN* 0812290879

**Jobs for disadvantaged workers: the economics of employment**    **4.3220**
**subsidies / Robert H. Haveman and John L. Palmer, editors.**
Washington, D.C.: Brookings Institution, c1982. 336 p.: ill.; 24 cm. — (Studies in social economics.) 'Papers and formal discussion ... delivered at a conference held at the Brookings Institution on April 3-4, 1980'—Foreword. 1. Employment subsidies — United States. I. Haveman, Robert H. II. Palmer, John Logan. III. Series.
HD5724.J68     362.8/5 19     *LC* 81-38544     *ISBN* 0815735065

**Myers, Charles Andrew, 1913-.**         • **4.3221**
The dynamics of a labor market; a study of the impact of employment changes on labor mobility, job satisfactions, and company and union policies [by] Charles A. Myers [and] George P. Shultz. New York, Prentice-Hall [1951] x, 219 p. 1. Unemployed — United States I. Shultz, George Pratt, 1920- jt. author II. T.
HD5724 M93     *LC* 51-11694

**Toward a manpower policy. Edited by Robert Aaron Gordon.**    • **4.3222**
New York: Wiley, [1967] x, 372 p.: illus.; 22 cm. — (Wiley books in research program on unemployment) Fourth and final conference of the Research Program on Unemployment, conducted by the Institute of Industrial Relations, University of California, Berkeley, and held in New York, June 1966. 1. Manpower policy — United States I. Gordon, Robert Aaron. ed. II. California. University. Research Program on Unemployment.
HD5724.T65     331/.0973     *LC* 67-19448

**Wilcock, Richard Carrington.**                                  • 4.3223
Unwanted workers; permanent layoffs and long–term unemployment [by] Richard C. Wilcock and Walter H. Franke. — [New York][New York] Free Press of Glencoe [1963] 340 p. illus. 23 cm. Includes bibliography. 1. Unemployed — U.S. I. Franke, Walter Henry, 1928- joint author. II. T.
HD5724.W443      331.137973      *LC* 63-8425

**Rees, Albert, 1921-.**                                          • 4.3224
Workers and wages in an urban labor market [by] Albert Rees and George P. Shultz, with the assistance of Mary T. Hamilton, David P. Taylor [and] Joseph C. Ullman. — Chicago: University of Chicago Press, [1970] xv, 236 p.: illus.; 24 cm. — (Studies in business and society) 1. Labor supply — Illinois — Chicago metropolitan area. 2. Wages — Illinois — Chicago metropolitan area. I. Shultz, George Pratt, 1920- joint author. II. T.
HD5726.C4 R4      331.2/2/0977311      *LC* 75-110114      *ISBN* 0226707059

**Pressman, Jeffrey L.**                                          4.3225
Implementation: how great expectations in Washington are dashed in Oakland: or, why it's amazing that federal programs work at all, this being a saga of the Economic Development Administration as told by two sympathetic observers who seek to build morals on a foundation of ruined hopes / Jeffrey L. Pressman and Aaron Wildavsky. — 3rd ed. — Berkeley: University of California Press, c1984. xxvi, 281 p.: ill.; 22 cm. (Oakland Project series.) Includes indexes. 1. United States. Economic Development Administration. 2. Manpower policy — California — Oakland. 3. Oakland (Calif.) — Public works. I. Wildavsky, Aaron B. II. T. III. Series.
HD5726.O22 P73 1984      353.0084/84/0979466 19      *LC* 83-17987
*ISBN* 0520052323

## HD5728–5852 Other Countries

**Reubens, Beatrice G.**                                          • 4.3226
The hard–to–employ: European programs [by] Beatrice G. Reubens. Foreword by Eli Ginzberg. — New York: Columbia University Press, 1970. xxii, 420 p.; 24 cm. A report prepared for the Manpower Administration, U.S. Dept. of Labor, under research contract no. 26231-26244. 1. Hard-core unemployed — Europe. 2. Manpower policy — Europe I. United States. Dept. of Labor. Manpower Administration. II. T.
HD5764.A6 R48      331.1/12/094      *LC* 78-117018      *ISBN* 0231033885

**Hughes, James J.**                                             4.3227
The economics of unemployment: a comparative analysis of Britain and the United States / James J. Hughes and Richard Perlman. — Cambridge [Cambridgeshire]; New York: Cambridge University Press, 1984. xiii, 258 p.: ill.; 23 cm. 1. Unemployment — Great Britain. 2. Unemployment — United States. I. Perlman, Richard. II. T.
HD5765.A6 H83 1984      331.13/7941 19      *LC* 84-7648      *ISBN* 0521267889

**Moon, Jeremy, 1955-.**                                          4.3228
Unemployment in the UK: politics and policies / Jeremy Moon, J.J. Richardson. — Aldershot, Hants, England; Brookfield, Vt., U.S.A.: Gower, c1985. xi, 201 p.; 23 cm. 1. Unemployment — Great Britain. 2. Unemployment — Government policy — Great Britain. 3. Great Britain — Full employment policies. I. Richardson, J. J. (Jeremy John) II. T.
HD5765.A6 M66 1985      331.13/7941 19      *LC* 85-5515      *ISBN* 0566008920

**Beveridge, William Henry Beveridge, Baron, 1879-1963.**    • 4.3229
Full employment in a free society: a report / by William H. Beveridge. — London: G. Allen & Unwin ltd., 1944. — 429 p.: ill.; 22 cm. 1. Unemployment — Great Britain. 2. Employment — Great Britain. 3. Great Britain — Economic policy I. Great Britain. Inter-departmental Committee on Social Insurance and Allied Services. Social Insurance and Allied Services. II. T.
HD5767.B42 1944      331.1      *LC* 44-47997

**Employment policies in the Soviet Union and Eastern Europe /**    4.3230
**edited by Jan Adam.**
New York: St. Martin's Press, 1982. xvii, 216 p.: ill.; 23 cm. 1. Manpower policy — Soviet Union — Addresses, essays, lectures. 2. Manpower policy — Europe, Eastern — Addresses, essays, lectures. I. Adam, Jan, 1920-
HD5796.E47 1982      331.11/0947 19      *LC* 81-18289      *ISBN* 0312244622

**Moskoff, William.**                                            4.3231
Labour and leisure in the Soviet Union: the conflict between public and private decision–making in a planned economy / William Moskoff. — New York: St. Martin's Press, 1984. xv, 225 p.; 23 cm. Includes index. 1. Labor supply — Soviet Union. 2. Leisure — Soviet Union. 3. Labor policy — Soviet Union. 4. Women — Employment — Soviet Union. 5. Households — Soviet Union — Decision making. I. T.
HD5796.M67 1984      331.13/6/0947 19      *LC* 83-24701      *ISBN* 0312462417

**Sacks, Michael Paul.**                                          4.3232
Work and equality in Soviet society: the division of labor by age, gender, and nationality / Michael Paul Sacks. — New York, N.Y.: Praeger, 1982. xv, 206 p.; 24 cm. 'A direct outgrowth of the author's previous study, Women's work in Soviet Russia: continuity in the midst of change (1976)'—Introd. Includes index. 1. Labor supply — Soviet Union. 2. Women — Employment — Soviet Union. 3. Minorities — Employment — Soviet Union. 4. Age and employment — Soviet Union. I. T.
HD5796.S23 1982      306/.3 19      *LC* 82-278      *ISBN* 0030461413

**Sirageldin, Ismail Abdel-Hamid.**                               4.3233
Saudis in transition: the challenges of a changing labor market / Ismail A. Sirageldin, Naiem A. Sherbiny, M. Ismail Serageldin. — New York: Published for the World Bank [by] Oxford University Press, c1984. viii, 189 p.: ill.; 25 cm. 1. Labor supply — Saudi Arabia. I. Sherbiny, Naiem A. II. Serageldin, Ismail, 1944- III. International Bank for Reconstruction and Development. IV. T.
HD5812.35.A6 S57 1984      331.12/0953/8 19      *LC* 84-1104      *ISBN* 0195204573

**Employment policy in a developing country: a case–study of**    4.3234
**India: proceedings of a joint conference of the International**
**Economic Association and the Indian Economic Association held**
**in Pune, India / edited by Austin Robinson, P.R. Brahmananda**
**and L.K. Deshpande; the record of discussions by John Toye.**
London: Macmillan 1983. 2 v. (xiii, 738 p.): ill. 1. Manpower policy — India — Congresses 2. Unemployed — India — Congresses 3. Labor supply — India — Congresses 4. Underemployment — India — Congresses I. Robinson, Austin, 1897- II. Brahmananda, P. R. III. Deshpande, L. K. IV. International Economic Association. V. Indian Economic Association.
HD5819 E54 1983      *ISBN* 0333346475

**Collier, Paul.**                                               4.3235
Labour and poverty in Kenya, 1900–1980 / Paul Collier and Deepak Lal. — Oxford: Clarendon Press; New York: Oxford University Press, 1986. xi, 296 p.; 24 cm. Includes index. 1. Labor supply — Kenya. 2. Poor — Kenya. 3. Income distribution — Kenya. I. Lal, Deepak. II. T.
HD5840.5.A6 C65 1986      331.12/09676/2 19      *LC* 86-1352      *ISBN* 0198285051

**Squire, Lyn, 1946-.**                                          4.3236
Employment policy in developing countries: a survey of issues and evidence / Lyn Squire. — New York: Published for the World Bank [by] Oxford University Press, c1981. xiii, 229 p.; 25 cm. (World Bank research publication.) Includes index. 1. Labor supply — Developing countries 2. Manpower policy — Developing countries 3. Developing countries — Full employment policies. I. World Bank. II. T. III. Series.
HD5852.S65      331.12/042/091724 19      *LC* 81-2844      *ISBN* 019520266X

**Trade and employment in developing countries / edited by Anne**    4.3237
**O. Krueger ... [et al.].**
Chicago: University of Chicago Press, 1981-<1983 >. v. <1, 3 >; 24 cm. '[Results] from the research project sponsored by the National Bureau of Economic Research on alternate trade strategies and employment.' 1. Foreign trade and employment — Developing countries — Addresses, essays, lectures. 2. Developing countries — Commerce — Addresses, essays, lectures. I. Krueger, Anne O. II. National Bureau of Economic Research.
HD5852.T7      331.12/09172/4      *LC* 80-15826      *ISBN* 0226454924

## HD5860–6000 Employment Agencies

**Library of Congress. Economics Division.**                      4.3238
Readings on public employment services. Washington, U. S. Govt. Print. Off., 1965. vxi, 766 p. illus., maps. 24 cm. 1. Employment agencies — United States — Addresses, essays, lectures. I. United States. Congress. House. Committee on Education and Labor. Select Subcommittee on Labor. II. T.
HD5873.A546      *LC* 65-61260

**Blau, Peter Michael.**                                          • 4.3239
The structure of organizations / [by] Peter M. Blau [and] Richard A. Schoenherr. — New York: Basic Books, [1971] xix, 445 p.: ill.; 24 cm. 1. Employment agencies — U.S. 2. Organization I. Schoenherr, Richard A., joint author. II. T.
HD5875.B55      301.18/32      *LC* 74-126956      *ISBN* 0465082408

## HD6050–6223 Woman Labor

**Equal employment policy for women: strategies for**     **4.3240**
**implementation in the United States, Canada, and Western**
**Europe / edited by Ronnie Steinberg Ratner.**
Philadelphia: Temple University Press, 1980. xxii, 520 p.: ill.; 24 cm. Revised
papers prepared for conference convened May 1978 by Wellesley College
Center for Research on Women. Includes index. 1. Women — Employment —
Congresses. 2. Sex discrimination in employment — Congresses. I. Steinberg,
Ronnie, 1947- II. Wellesley College. Center for Research on Women.
HD6052.E6    331.4    *LC* 79-19509    *ISBN* 0877221561

**The Economics of women and work / edited by Alice H.**     **4.3241**
**Amsden.**
New York, NY: St. Martin's Press, 1980. 409 p.: graphs; 22 cm. 1. Women —
Employment — Addresses, essays, lectures. I. Amsden, Alice Hoffenberg.
HD6053.E26 1980    331.4    *LC* 80-15970    *ISBN* 0312236700

**Myrdal, Alva Reimer, 1902-.**     ● **4.3242**
Women's two roles: home and work, by Alva Myrdal & Viola Klein. — 2nd ed.
(revised and reset). — London: Routledge & K. Paul, 1968. xvii, 213 p.: illus.;
22 cm. — (International library of sociology and social reconstruction)
1. Wives — Employment 2. Women — Social conditions I. Klein, Viola. joint
author. II. T.
HD6053.M9 1968    331.4/3    *LC* 68-77517    *ISBN* 071003489X

**Women returning to work: policies and progress in five countries**     **4.3243**
**/ edited by Alice M. Yohalem; foreword by Eli Ginzberg.**
Montclair, N.J.: Allanheld, Osmun, 1980. xii, 292 p.; 24 cm. — (Conservation
of human resources series. 12) (LandMark studies) 1. Women — Employment
— Case studies. 2. Labor mobility — Case studies. I. Yohalem, Alice M.
II. Series.
HD6053.W64    331.4    *LC* 79-55819    09166720514

**Women working: theories and facts in perspective / edited by**     **4.3244**
**Ann H. Stromberg and Shirley Harkess.**
1st ed. — Palo Alto, Calif.: Mayfield Pub. Co., 1978. xxvii, 458 p.: ill.; 22 cm.
1. Women — Employment — Addresses, essays, lectures. 2. Pay equity —
Addresses, essays, lectures. I. Stromberg, Ann. II. Harkess, Shirley.
HD6053.W66    331.4    *LC* 77-89921    *ISBN* 0874843014

**Yohalem, Alice M.**     **4.3245**
The careers of professional women: commitment and conflict / by Alice M.
Yohalem; foreword by Eli Ginzberg. — Montclair, N.J.: Allanheld, Osmun,
1979. xiv, 224 p.; 24 cm. 'Landmark studies.' 1. Women college graduates —
Employment — United States. 2. Women in the professions — United States.
3. Sex discrimination in employment — United States. 4. Sex discrimination
against women — United States. I. T.
HD6053.6.U5 Y63 1979    331.4/0973    *LC* 77-10187    *ISBN*
0876638213

**Adams, Carolyn Teich.**     **4.3246**
Mothers at work: public policies in the United States, Sweden, and China /
Carolyn Teich Adams, Kathryn Teich Winston. — New York: Longman,
c1980. 312 p.; 24 cm. 1. Mothers — Employment — United States. 2. Mothers
— Employment — Sweden. 3. Mothers — Employment — China. 4. Family
policy — United States. 5. Family policy — Sweden. 6. Family policy —
China. I. Winston, Kathryn Teich, 1946- joint author. II. T.
HD6055.A3    331.4    *LC* 79-18670    *ISBN* 0582280648

**Hurst, Marsha.**     **4.3247**
Determinants and consequences of maternal employment: an annotated
bibliography, 1968–1980 / Marsha Hurst and Ruth E. Zambrana. —
[Washington, D.C.] (2012 Massachusetts Ave., N.W., Washington 20036):
Business and Professional Women's Foundation, [c1981] iii, 85 p.; 22 cm.
1. Mothers — Employment — United States — Abstracts. 2. Children of
working mothers — United States — Abstracts. I. Zambrana, Ruth E. II. T.
III. Title: Maternal employment.
HD6055.2.U6 H87 1981    016.3314/4 19    *LC* 82-173458

**Wandersee, Winifred D.**     **4.3248**
Women's work and family values, 1920–1940 / Winifred D. Wandersee. —
Cambridge, Mass.: Harvard University Press, 1981. 165 p.; 24 cm. Includes
index. 1. Wives — Employment — United States. 2. Work and family —
United States. 3. Cost and standard of living — United States. 4. United States
— Economic conditions — 1918-1945 I. T.
HD6055.2.U6 W36    331.4/3/0973 19    *LC* 80-21100    *ISBN*
0674955358

**Unplanned careers: the working lives of middle–aged women /**     **4.3249**
**edited by Lois Banfill Shaw.**
Lexington, Mass.: LexingtonBooks, c1983. viii, 149 p.: ill.; 24 cm. Based on
interviews made by the National Longitudinal Surveys of Labor Market
Experience during the years from 1967 to 1977. Includes index. 1. Middle aged
women — United States — Longitudinal studies. I. Shaw, Lois Banfill.
II. National Longitudinal Surveys of Labor Market Experience (U.S.)
HD6056.2.U6 U56 1983    331.3/94/088042 19    *LC* 82-47925
   *ISBN* 0669057010

**Jones, Jacqueline, 1948-.**     **4.3250**
Labor of love, labor of sorrow: Black women, work, and the family from slavery
to the present / Jacqueline Jones. — New York: Basic Books, c1985. xiii, 432 p.:
ill.; 25 cm. Includes index. 1. Afro-American women — Employment —
History. 2. Afro-American women — History. 3. Afro-Americans — Families
— History. I. T.
HD6057.5.U5 J66 1985    305.4/8896073 19    *LC* 84-24310    *ISBN*
0465037569

## HD6058–6059 Occupations for Women

**Bose, Christine E.**     **4.3251**
Jobs and gender: a study of occupational prestige / by Christine E. Bose. —
New York: Praeger, 1985. p. cm. Includes index. 1. Women — Employment —
United States. 2. Occupational prestige — United States. I. T.
HD6058.B67 1985    305.4/3/00973 19    *LC* 85-6305    *ISBN*
0030716926

**Doss, Martha Merrill.**     **4.3252**
The directory of special opportunities for women: a national guide of
educational opportunities, career information, networks, and peer counseling
assistance for entry or reentry into the work force / edited by Martha Merrill
Doss. — Garrett Park, Md.: Garrett Park Press, c1981. 293 p.: ill.; 28 cm.
Includes index. 1. Women — Employment — Information services — United
States — Directories. I. T.
HD6058.D8    331.4/128 19    *LC* 80-85274

**Women and work in preindustrial Europe / edited by Barbara**     **4.3253**
**A. Hanawalt.**
Bloomington: Indiana University Press, c1986. xviii, 233 p.; 25 cm. 1. Women
— Employment — Europe — History — Addresses, essays, lectures.
2. Women — Europe — Economic conditions — Addresses, essays, lectures.
3. Europe — Occupations — History — Addresses, essays, lectures.
I. Hanawalt, Barbara.
HD6059.5.E85 W65 1986    331.4/094 19    *LC* 85-42829    *ISBN*
0253366100

## HD6060 Sex Discrimination in Employment

**Meehan, Elizabeth M.**     **4.3254**
Women's rights at work: campaigns and policy in Britain and the United States
/ Elizabeth M. Meehan. — New York: St. Martin's Press, 1985. xvii, 253 p.; 23
cm. Includes index. 1. Sex discrimination in employment — Great Britain.
2. Sex discrimination in employment — United States. 3. Women —
Employment — Great Britain. 4. Women — Employment — United States.
I. T.
HD6060.M44 1985    331.4/133/0941 19    *LC* 84-15997    *ISBN*
0312887930

**Scott, Hilda, 1915-.**     **4.3255**
Working your way to the bottom: the feminization of poverty / Hilda Scott. —
London; Boston: Pandora Press, 1985 (c1984). xii, 192 p.; 20 cm. Includes
index. 1. Sex discrimination in employment 2. Sex discrimination against
women 3. Women heads of households 4. Poverty I. T.
HD6060.S39    331.4 19    *LC* 84-15913    *ISBN* 0863580114

**Sex segregation in the workplace: trends, explanations, remedies**     **4.3256**
**/ Barbara F. Reskin, editor; Committee on Women's**
**Employment and Related Social Issues, Commission on**
**Behavioral and Social Sciences and Education, National**
**Research Council.**
Washington, D.C.: National Academy Press, 1984. viii, 313 p.; 25 cm. Revised
versions of papers originally presented at a workshop held in May, 1982. 1. Sex
discrimination in employment — United States — Congresses. 2. Sex
discrimination against women — United States — Congresses. I. Reskin,
Barbara F. II. National Research Council (U.S.). Committee on Women's
Employment and Related Social Issues.
HD6060.5.U5 S475 1984    331.4/133/0973 19    *LC* 84-8342    *ISBN*
0309034450

## HD6061–6066 Wages. Hours

**Comparable worth: issues and alternatives / edited by E. Robert Livernash.**                                    **4.3257**
2nd ed. — Washington, D.C.: Equal Employment Advisory Council, c1984. xviii, 299 p.: ill.; 23 cm. 1. Equal pay for equal work — United States — Addresses, essays, lectures. 2. Job evaluation — United States — Addresses, essays, lectures. 3. Sex discrimination in employment — United States — Addresses, essays, lectures. 4. Sex discrimination against women — United States — Addresses, essays, lectures. 5. Equal pay for equal work — Addresses, essays, lectures. I. Livernash, E. Robert (Edward Robert) II. Equal Employment Advisory Council.
HD6061.2.U6 C642 1984      331.2/1 19      *LC* 84-81267      *ISBN* 0937856088

**Gold, Michael Evan.**                                    **4.3258**
A dialogue on comparable worth / Michael Evan Gold. — Ithaca, N.Y.: ILR Press: New York State School of Industrial and Labor Relations, Cornell University, c1983. vii, 111 p.; 21 cm. 1. Pay equity — United States. I. T.
HD6061.2.U6 G64 1983      331.2/1 19      *LC* 83-8508      *ISBN* 0875460992

**Hutner, Frances Cornwall.**                                    **4.3259**
Equal pay for comparable worth: the working women's issue of the eighties / Frances C. Hutner. — New York: Praeger, 1986. xiii, 227 p.; 24 cm. Includes index. 1. Equal pay for equal work — United States. 2. Equal pay for equal work — United States — Case studies. 3. Equal pay for equal work I. T.
HD6061.2.U6 H88 1986      331.4/21/0973 19      *LC* 85-19427      *ISBN* 0030628733

**Women, work, and wages: equal pay for jobs of equal value / Donald J. Treiman and Heidi I. Hartmann, editors; Committee on Occupational Classification and Analysis, Assembly of Behavioral and Social Sciences, National Research Council.**                                    **4.3260**
Washington, D.C.: National Academy Press, 1981. xii, 136 p.: ill.; 23 cm. 1. Wages — Women — United States. 2. Pay equity — United States. 3. Sex discrimination in employment — United States. 4. Sex discrimination against women — United States. 5. Job evaluation — United States. I. Treiman, Donald J. II. Hartmann, Heidi I. III. Assembly of Behavioral and Social Sciences (U.S.). Committee on Occupational Classification and Analysis.
HD6061.2.U6 W65      331.2/1 19      *LC* 81-82863      *ISBN* 030903177X

**Kamerman, Sheila B.**                                    **4.3261**
Maternity policies and working women / Sheila B. Kamerman, Alfred J. Kahn, and Paul Kingston. — New York: Columbia University Press, 1983. 183 p.; 24 cm. 1. Maternity leave — United States. 2. Insurance, Maternity — United States. I. Kahn, Alfred J., 1919- II. Kingston, Paul W. III. T.
HD6065.5.U6 K35 1983      331.4/25763 19      *LC* 83-7624      *ISBN* 0231057504

## HD6068 Factory Labor

**Glickman, Rose L.**                                    **4.3262**
Russian factory women: workplace and society, 1880–1914 / Rose L. Glickman. — Berkeley: University of California Press, c1984. xiii, 325 p.; 22 cm. Includes index. 1. Women — Employment — Soviet Union — History. 2. Factory system — Soviet Union — History. I. T.
HD6068.2.S65 G54 1984      331.4/87/0947 19      *LC* 83-6968      *ISBN* 0520048105

## HD6072 Domestic Service

**Katzman, David M. (David Manners), 1941-.**                                    **4.3263**
Seven days a week: women and domestic service in industrializing America / David M. Katzman. — Urbana; London: University of Illinois Press, 1981, c1978. xviii, 374 p.: ill.; 21 cm. 1. Domestics — United States — History. 2. Women — Employment — United States — History. I. T.
HD6072.2.U5      640/.46/0973 18      640/.46/088042 19      *LC* 77-13714      *ISBN* 0252008820

**Dudden, Faye E.**                                    **4.3264**
Serving women: household service in nineteenth–century America / Faye E. Dudden. — 1st ed. — Middletown, Conn.: Wesleyan University Press; Scranton, Pa.: Distributed by Harper & Row, c1983. viii, 344 p.: ill.; 23 cm. 1. Domestics — United States — History — 19th century. I. T.
HD6072.2.U5 D82 1983      305.4/364 19      *LC* 83-1263      *ISBN* 0819550728

## HD6073 Special Industries or Trades, A–Z

**A Needle, a bobbin, a strike: women needleworkers in America / edited by Joan M. Jensen and Sue Davidson.**                                    **4.3265**
Philadelphia: Temple University Press, 1984. xxii, 304 p.: ill.; 22 cm. — (Women in the political economy.) 1. Women clothing workers — United States — History — Addresses, essays, lectures. 2. Strikes and lockouts — Clothing trade — United States — Addresses, essays, lectures. 3. Trade-unions — Clothing workers — United States — Addresses, essays, lectures. I. Jensen, Joan M. II. Davidson, Sue, 1925- III. Series.
HD6073.C62 U56 1984      331.4/887/0773 19      *LC* 83-24338      *ISBN* 0877223408

**Goldberg, Roberta.**                                    **4.3266**
Organizing women office workers: dissatisfaction, consciousness, and action / by Roberta Goldberg. — New York, N.Y.: Praeger, 1983. vi, 152 p.; 25 cm. Originally presented as the author's thesis (doctoral—American University) Includes index. 1. Baltimore Working Women (Organization) 2. Women clerks — Maryland — Baltimore — Case studies. 3. Job satisfaction — Maryland — Baltimore — Case studies. I. T.
HD6073.M392 U525 1983      331.4/816513/097526 19      *LC* 82-18907      *ISBN* 0030632870

**Valli, Linda, 1947-.**                                    **4.3267**
Becoming clerical workers / Linda Valli. — Boston: Routledge & Kegan Paul, 1986. xv, 261 p.; 23 cm. (Critical social thought.) Includes index. 1. Women clerks — United States. 2. Women clerks — Training of — United States. I. T. II. Series.
HD6073.M392 U58 1986      305.4/3651 19      *LC* 85-2499      *ISBN* 0710203365

**Dublin, Thomas, 1946-.**                                    **4.3268**
Women at work: the transformation of work and community in Lowell, Massachusetts, 1826 1860 / Thomas Dublin. — New York: Columbia University Press, 1979. xiii, 312 p., [4] leaves of plates: ill.; 24 cm. Includes index. 1. Women — Employment — Massachusetts — Lowell — History. 2. Textile workers — Massachusetts — Lowell — History. 3. Cotton manufacture — Massachusetts — Lowell — History. 4. Labor and laboring classes — Massachusetts — Lowell — History. 5. Lowell (Mass.) — Social conditions. I. T.
HD6073.T42 U52      331.4/87/70097444      *LC* 79-10701      *ISBN* 0231041667

## HD6079 Women in Trade Unions

**Women and trade unions in eleven industrialized countries / edited by Alice H. Cook, Val R. Lorwin, and Arlene Kaplan Daniels.**                                    **4.3269**
Philadelphia: Temple University Press, 1984. xiii, 327 p.; 24 cm. — (Women in the political economy.) 1. Women in trade-unions — Case studies. I. Cook, Alice Hanson. II. Lorwin, Val R. (Val Rogin), 1907- III. Daniels, Arlene Kaplan, 1930- IV. Series.
HD6079.W56 1984      331.4 19      *LC* 83-17946      *ISBN* 087722319X

**Foner, Philip Sheldon, 1910-.**                                    **4.3270**
Women and the American labor movement: from World War I to the present / Philip S. Foner. — New York: Free Press, 1980. 682 p.: ill. Includes indexes. 1. Women in trade-unions — United States — History. 2. Women — Employment — United States — History. I. T.
HD6079.2.U5 F65      331.4 19      *LC* 79-63035      *ISBN* 0029103703

**Foner, Philip Sheldon, 1910-.**                                    **4.3271**
Women and the American labor movement: from colonial times to the eve of World War I / Philip S. Foner. — New York: Free Press, c1979. xi, 621 p., [4] leaves of plates: ill.; 25 cm. Includes index. 1. Women in trade-unions — United States — History. 2. Women — Employment — United States — History. I. T.
HD6079.2.U5 F65 1979      331.88      *LC* 79-63035      *ISBN* 0029103703

**Women, work, and protest: a century of US women's labor history / edited by Ruth Milkman.**                                    **4.3272**
Boston: Routledge & Kegan Paul, 1985. 333 p. Includes index. 1. Women in trade-unions — United States — History — 20th century — Addresses, essays, lectures. 2. Sex discrimination against women — United States — History — 20th century — Addresses, essays, lectures. I. Milkman, Ruth, 1954-
HD6079.2.U5 W66 1985      331.4/0973 19      *LC* 84-27732      *ISBN* 0710099401

**Dye, Nancy Schrom, 1947-.**                                    **4.3273**
As equals and as sisters: feminism, the labor movement, and the Women's Trade Union League of New York / Nancy Schrom Dye. — Columbia: University of Missouri Press, 1981 (c1980). 200 p.; 24 cm. Includes index.

1. Women's Trade Union League of New York — History. 2. Women in trade-unions — New York (City) — History. 3. Feminism — New York (City) — History. I. T.
HD6079.2.U52 N483      331.88/3      *LC* 80-16751      *ISBN* 0826203183

# HD6091–6220.7 By Region or Country

## HD6093–6096 UNITED STATES

### HD6095 A–L

**Abbott, Edith, 1876-1957.**      • **4.3274**
Women in industry; a study in American economic history. — New York: Arno, 1969. xxii, 408 p.; 23 cm. — (American labor (New York, N.Y.) Reprint of the 1910 ed. 1. Women — Employment — United States — History. 2. United States — Economic conditions I. T. II. Series.
HD6095.A6 1969      331.4/0973      *LC* 70-89714

**America's working women / compiled and edited by Rosalyn**      **4.3275**
**Baxandall, Linda Gordon and Susan Reverby.**
New York: Random House, c1976. xxii, 408, ix p., [10] leaves of plates: ill.; 24 cm. 1. Women — Employment — United States — History — Sources. 2. Women — Employment — United States — History — Addresses, essays, lectures. I. Baxandall, Rosalyn Fraad, 1939- II. Gordon, Linda. III. Reverby, Susan.
HD6095.A662 1976      331.4/0973      *LC* 76-10574      *ISBN* 0394491505

**Davies, Margery W.**      **4.3276**
Woman's place is at the typewriter: office work and office workers, 1870–1930 / Margery W. Davies. — Philadelphia: Temple University Press, 1982. x, 217 p.; 22 cm. — (Class and culture.) Revision of thesis (Ph.D.)—Brandeis University. 1. Women — Employment — United States — History. 2. Clerks — United States — History. 3. Sex role in the work environment — United States — History. I. T. II. Series.
HD6095.D37 1982      305.4/3651 19      *LC* 82-13694      *ISBN* 0877222916

**Dex, Shirley.**      **4.3277**
The sexual division of work: conceptual revolutions in the social sciences / Shirley Dex. — New York: St. Martin's Press, 1985. 234 p.; 23 cm. Includes index. 1. Women — Employment — United States. 2. Women — Employment — Great Britain. 3. Sexual division of labor — United States. 4. Sexual division of labor — Great Britain. I. T.
HD6095.D47 1985      305.4/3/0941 19      *LC* 85-8301      *ISBN* 0312713495

**Eisenstein, Sarah.**      **4.3278**
Give us bread but give us roses: working women's consciousness in the United States, 1890 to the First World War / Sarah Eisenstein. — London; Boston: Routledge & K. Paul, 1983. 207 p.; 22 cm. Includes index. 1. Women — Employment — United States — History — Addresses, essays, lectures. I. T.
HD6095.E35 1983      331.4/0973 19      *LC* 83-4538      *ISBN* 0710094795

**Epstein, Cynthia Fuchs.**      • **4.3279**
Woman's place; options and limits in professional careers. — Berkeley: University of California Press, 1970. x, 221 p.; 23 cm. 1. Women — Employment — United States. 2. Women — United States 3. Sex role I. T.
HD6095.E64      301.41/22/0973      *LC* 75-98139

**Fox, Mary Frank.**      **4.3280**
Women at work / Mary Frank Fox, Sharlene Hesse–Biber. — 1st ed. — [Palo Alto, Calif.]: Mayfield Pub. Co., c1984. xiv, 276 p.: ill.; 23 cm. Includes indexes. 1. Women — Employment — United States. I. Hesse-Biber, Sharlene Janice. II. T.
HD6095.F69 1984      331.4/0973 19      *LC* 83-61533      *ISBN* 0874845254

**Greenwald, Maurine Weiner, 1944-.**      **4.3281**
Women, war, and work: the impact of World War I on women workers in the United States / Maurine Weiner Greenwald. — Westport, Conn.: Greenwood Press, 1980. xxvii, 309 p.: ill.; 22 cm. — (Contributions in women's studies. no. 12 0147-104X) Includes index. 1. Women — Employment — United States — History. 2. World War, 1914-1918 — Economic aspects — United States. I. T. II. Series.
HD6095.G72      331.4/0973 19      *LC* 80-540      *ISBN* 0313213550

**Kessler-Harris, Alice.**      **4.3282**
Out to work: a history of wage–earning women in the United States / Alice Kessler–Harris. — New York: Oxford University Press, 1982. xvi, 400 p.: ill.;

24 cm. 1. Women — Employment — United States — History. 2. Working class women — United States — History. I. T.
HD6095.K449 1982      331.4/0973 19      *LC* 81-11237      *ISBN* 0195030249

**Kessler-Harris, Alice.**      **4.3283**
Women have always worked: a historical overview / Alice Kessler–Harris; [photo research by Flavia Rando]. — Old Westbury, N.Y.: Feminist Press; New York: McGraw-Hill, c1981. xiii, 193 p.: ill.; 24 cm. — (Women's lives, women's work.) 1. Women — Employment — United States — History. I. T. II. Series.
HD6095.K45      331.4/0973      *LC* 80-13400      *ISBN* 091267086X

**Lloyd, Cynthia B., 1943-.**      **4.3284**
The economics of sex differentials / Cynthia B. Lloyd and Beth T. Niemi. — New York: Columbia University Press, 1980 (c1979). xvi, 355 p.: ill.; 24 cm. Includes index. 1. Women — Employment — United States. 2. Sex discrimination in employment — United States. 3. Sex discrimination against women — United States. I. Niemi, Beth T., 1942- joint author. II. T.
HD6095.L558      331.4/0973      *LC* 79-9569      *ISBN* 0231040385

**Lloyd, Cynthia B., 1943- comp.**      **4.3285**
Sex, discrimination, and the division of labor / Cynthia B. Lloyd, editor. — New York: Columbia University Press, 1975. xiv, 431 p.: ill.; 23 cm. 1. Women — Employment — United States — Addresses, essays, lectures. 2. Sex discrimination in employment — United States — Addresses, essays, lectures. 3. Sex discrimination against women — United States — Addresses, essays, lectures. 4. Feminism — United States — Addresses, essays, lectures. I. T.
HD6095.L56      331.4/0973      *LC* 74-32175      *ISBN* 0231037503

### HD6095 M–Z

**My troubles are going to have trouble with me: everyday trials**      **4.3286**
**and triumphs of women workers / Karen Brodkin Sacks and**
**Dorothy Remy, editors.**
New Brunswick, N.J.: Rutgers University Press, c1984. ix, 263 p.; 22 cm. (Douglass series on women's lives and the meaning of gender.) Based on papers from a symposium organized at the 1979 meetings of the American Anthropological Association and from a 1982 conference on 'Research to Make a Better Living for Working Women.' 1. Women — Employment — United States — Addresses, essays, lectures. 2. Sex discrimination in employment — United States — Addresses, essays, lectures. I. Sacks, Karen. II. Remy, Dorothy, 1943- III. Series.
HD6095.M9 1984      331.4 19      *LC* 83-23079      *ISBN* 0813510384

**Not as far as you think: the realities of working women /**      **4.3287**
**[edited by] Lynda L. Moore.**
Lexington, Mass.: Lexington Books, c1986. xii, 201 p.; 24 cm. 1. Women — Employment — United States — Addresses, essays, lectures. 2. Sex discrimination in employment — United States — Addresses, essays, lectures. 3. Women — United States — Psychology — Addresses, essays, lectures. I. Moore, Lynda L.
HD6095.N625 1986      331.4/0973 19      *LC* 85-40109      *ISBN* 0669108367

**Outsiders on the inside: women & organizations / [edited by]**      **4.3288**
**Barbara L. Forisha, Barbara H. Goldman.**
Englewood Cliffs, N.J.: Prentice-Hall, c1981. xxiv, 312 p.; 21 cm. — (A Spectrum book) 1. Women — Employment — United States — Psychological aspects — Addresses, essays, lectures. 2. Sexism — United States — Addresses, essays, lectures. 3. Power (Social sciences) — Addresses, essays, lectures. 4. Organizational change — United States — Addresses, essays, lectures. I. Forisha-Kovach, Barbara. II. Goldman, Barbara H.
HD6095.O9      302.3/5/088042 19      *LC* 80-39705      *ISBN* 0136453821

**Scharf, Lois.**      **4.3289**
To work and to wed: female employment, feminism, and the Great Depression / Lois Scharf. — Westport, Conn.: Greenwood Press, c1980. xiii, 240 p.; 22 cm. — (Contributions in women's studies. no. 15 0147-104X) Includes index. 1. Wives — Employment — United States — History. 2. Feminism — United States — History. 3. Sex discrimination in employment — United States — History. 4. Women — Employment — United States — History. 5. Sex discrimination against women — United States — History. I. T. II. Series.
HD6095.S3      331.4/3/0973 19      *LC* 79-52325      *ISBN* 031321445X

**Sealander, Judith.**      **4.3290**
As minority becomes majority: federal reaction to the phenomenon of women in the work force, 1920–1963 / Judith Sealander. — Westport, Conn.: Greenwood Press, 1983. xiii, 201 p.: ill.; 22 cm. — (Contributions in women's studies. 0147-104X; no. 40) Includes index. 1. Women — Employment — United States — History — 20th century. 2. Women — Government policy — United States — History — 20th century. 3. Labor policy — United States — History — 20th century. I. T. II. Series.
HD6095.S43 1983      331.4/125/0973 19      *LC* 82-15820      *ISBN* 0313237506

**Sokoloff, Natalie J.**     **4.3291**
Between money and love: the dialectics of women's home and market work / Natalie J. Sokoloff; foreword by Elise Boulding. — New York: Praeger, 1980. xix, 299 p.; 24 cm. Includes index. 1. Women — Employment — United States. 2. Marxian economics I. T.
HD6095.S64     *LC* 80-17101     *ISBN* 0030552966

**The Subtle revolution: women at work / Ralph E. Smith, editor.**     **4.3292**
Washington: Urban Institute, c1979. xvi, 279 p.: graphs; 23 cm. Includes index. 1. Women — Employment — United States — Addresses, essays, lectures. I. Smith, Ralph Ely, 1944- II. Urban Institute.
HD6095.S79     331.4/0973     *LC* 79-66788     *ISBN* 0877662606

**Tentler, Leslie Woodcock.**     **4.3293**
Wage–earning women: industrial work and family life in the United States, 1900–1930 / Leslie Woodcock Tentler. — New York: Oxford University Press, 1979. 266 p.; 22 cm. Includes index. 1. Women — Employment — United States — History. 2. Women — United States — History. 3. Sex role I. T.
HD6095.T44     331.4/0973     *LC* 79-12802     *ISBN* 0195026276

**Tsuchigane, Robert.**     **4.3294**
Economic discrimination against women in the United States: measures and changes [by] Robert Tsuchigane [and] Norton Dodge. — Lexington, Mass.: Lexington Books, [1974] xiv, 152 p.; 23 cm. 1. Women — Employment — United States. 2. Sex discrimination in employment — United States. I. Dodge, Norton T. joint author. II. T.
HD6095.T77 1974     331.1/33     *LC* 73-11651     *ISBN* 0669895083

**Walshok, Mary Lindenstein.**     **4.3295**
Blue–collar women: pioneers on the male frontier / Mary Lindenstein Walshok. — 1st ed. — Garden City, N.Y.: Anchor Books, 1981. xxiii, 310 p.; 21 cm. 1. Women — Employment — United States. 2. Labor and laboring classes — United States I. T.
HD6095.W19     331.4/8 19     *LC* 81-43069     *ISBN* 0385153368

**Wertheimer, Barbara M.**     **4.3296**
We were there: the story of working women in America / Barbara Mayer Wertheimer, with the research assistance of Ida Goshkin and Ellen Wertheimer. 1st ed. — New York: Pantheon Books, c1977. xx, 427 p.: ill.; 24 cm. Includes index. 1. Women — Employment — United States — History. 2. Women in trade-unions — United States — History. I. T.
HD6095.W47 1977     331.4/0973     *LC* 76-9597     *ISBN* 039449590X

**Women in the workplace / edited by Phyllis A. Wallace.**     **4.3297**
Boston, Mass.: Auburn House Pub. Co., c1982. xvi, 240 p.; 24 cm. 1. Women — Employment — United States — Addresses, essays, lectures. I. Wallace, Phyllis Ann.
HD6095.W6963 1982     331.4/0973 19     *LC* 81-12775     *ISBN* 0865690693

## HD6096 Special Localities

**The Factory girls: a collection of writings on life and struggles in the New England factories of the 1840's / by the factory girls themselves, and the story, in their own words, of the first trade unions of women workers in the United States; edited by Philip S. Foner.**     **4.3298**
Urbana: University of Illinois Press, c1977. xxvii, 360 p.: ill.; 24 cm. 1. Women — Employment — New England — History — Sources. 2. Factory system — New England — History — Sources. 3. Women in trade-unions — United States — History — Sources. I. Foner, Philip Sheldon, 1910-
HD6096.A11 F3     331.4/0974     *LC* 77-22410     *ISBN* 0252004221

## HD6097–6220.7 Other Regions and Countries

**Tilly, Louise.**     **4.3299**
Women, work, and family / Louise A. Tilly and Joan W. Scott. — New York: Holt, Rinehart and Winston, c1978. xiv, 274 p.: ill.; 24 cm. Includes index. 1. Women — Employment — Great Britain — History. 2. Women — Employment — France — History. 3. Work and family — Great Britain — History. 4. Work and family — France — History. I. Scott, Joan Wallach. joint author. II. T.
HD6135.T54     301.5/1     *LC* 74-19821     *ISBN* 0030333261

**McAuley, Alastair, 1938-.**     **4.3300**
Women's work and wages in the Soviet Union / Alastair McAuley. — London; Boston: Allen & Unwin, 1981. viii, 228 p.; 24 cm. Includes index. 1. Women — Employment — Soviet Union. 2. Wages — Women — Soviet Union. 3. Sex discrimination in employment — Soviet Union. I. T.
HD6166.M38     331.4/0947 19     *LC* 81-144436     *ISBN* 004339020X

**Cook, Alice Hanson.**     **4.3301**
Working women in Japan: discrimination, resistance, and reform / Alice H. Cook and Hiroko Hayashi. — Ithaca, N.Y.: New York State School of Industrial and Labor Relations, c1980. 124 p.; 20 cm. (Cornell international industrial and labor relations reports. no. 10) Includes index. 1. Women — Employment — Japan. 2. Sex discrimination in employment — Japan. 3. Sex discrimination against women — Japan. I. Hayashi, Hiroko, 1943- joint author. II. T. III. Series.
HD6197.C66     331.4/133/0952     *LC* 80-17706     *ISBN* 087546078X

**Boserup, Ester.**     **4.3302**
Woman's role in economic development. New York: St. Martin's Press, [1970] 283 p.: ill.; 23 cm. 1. Women — Employment — Developing countries 2. Women — Developing countries I. T.
HD6223.B68 1970b     331.4/09172/4     *LC* 70-118569

## HD6228–6305 Special Groups of Workers by Age, etc

**Taylor, Ronald B.**     **4.3303**
Sweatshops in the sun; child labor on the farm, by Ronald B. Taylor. Foreword by Carey McWilliams. — Boston: Beacon Press, [1973] xvii, 216 p.: illus.; 21 cm. 1. Children — Employment — United States. 2. Agricultural laborers — United States I. T.
HD6247.A4 U57     331.3/83/0973     *LC* 72-6233     *ISBN* 0807005169

**Reubens, Beatrice G.**     **4.3304**
The youth labor force, 1945–1995: a cross–national analysis / by Beatrice G. Reubens, John A.C. Harrisson, Kalman Rupp; foreword by Eli Ginzberg. — Totowa, N.J.: Allanheld, Osmun, 1982 (c1981). xxii, 387 p.: ill.; 25 cm. — (Conservation of human resources series. 13) (LandMark studies) Includes index. 1. Youth — Employment I. Harrisson, John A. C. II. Rupp, Kalman. III. T. IV. Series.
HD6270.R48     331.3/4125 19     *LC* 80-67390     *ISBN* 0865980276

**Osterman, Paul.**     **4.3305**
Getting started: the youth labor market / Paul Osterman. — Cambridge, Mass.: MIT Press, c1980. 197 p.; 24 cm. 1. Youth — Employment — United States I. T.
HD6273.O87     331.3/412/0973 19     *LC* 80-18932     *ISBN* 0262150212

**Youth and the labor market: analyses of the National Longitudinal Survey / Michael E. Borus, editor.**     **4.3306**
Kalamazoo, Mich.: W.E. Upjohn Institute for Employment Research, 1984. x, 295 p.: ill.; 23 cm. 1. Youth — Employment — United States — Longitudinal studies. 2. High school graduates — Employment — United States — Longitudinal studies. I. Borus, Michael E. II. National Longitudinal Surveys of Labor Market Experience (U.S.)
HD6273.Y648 1984     331.3/412/0973 19     *LC* 84-2367     *ISBN* 0880990163

**The Youth labor market problem: its nature, causes, and consequences / edited by Richard B. Freeman and David A. Wise.**     **4.3307**
Chicago: University of Chicago Press, 1982. ix, 555 p.: ill.; 24 cm. (A National Bureau of Economic Research conference report) 1. Youth — Employment — Congresses. I. Freeman, Richard B. (Richard Barry), 1943- II. Wise, David A.
HD6273.Y656 1982     331.3/412 19     *LC* 81-11438     *ISBN* 0226261611

**Freeman, Richard B. (Richard Barry), 1943-.**     **4.3308**
The overeducated American / Richard B. Freeman. — New York: Academic Press, c1976. xi, 218 p.: ill.; 24 cm. 1. College graduates — Employment — United States. 2. Labor supply — United States. I. T.
HD6278.U5 F73 1976     331.7/1     *LC* 75-36646     *ISBN* 012267250X. *ISBN* 0122672526 pbk

**Rumberger, Russell W.**     **4.3309**
Overeducation in the U.S. labor market / Russell W. Rumberger; foreword by Henry M. Levin. — New York: Praeger, 1981. x, 148 p.: ill.; 24 cm. Includes index. 1. College graduates — Employment — United States. 2. Education, Higher — Economic aspects — United States. 3. Labor supply — United States. 4. Job satisfaction — United States. I. T.
HD6278.U5 R85     331.11/423 19     *LC* 80-24648     *ISBN* 0030579643

**Windle, J. L.**     **4.3310**
Review of research: career planning and development, placement, and recruitment of college–trained personnel / by J. L. Windle, Adrian P. VanMondfrans, and Richard S. Kay. — Bethlehem, Pa.: College Placement Council, [1972] x, 151 p.; 28 cm. 1. College graduates — Employment —

United States — Abstracts. 2. Recruiting of employees — United States — Abstracts. 3. Vocational interests — Abstracts. I. Van Mondfrans, Adrian P., joint author. II. Kay, Richard S. joint author. III. T.
HD6278.U5 W5    331.1/28    *LC* 72-192450

**Bers, Melvin K.**      • **4.3311**
Union policy and the older worker / Melvin K. Bers. Westport, Conn.: Greenwood Press, 1976, c1957. v, 87 p.; 24 cm. Reprint of the 1957 ed. published by the Institute of Industrial Relations, University of California, Berkeley. 1. Age and employment — United States 2. Old age pensions — United States. 3. Trade-unions — United States I. T.
HD6280.B4 1976    331.3/98/0973    *LC* 76-14986    *ISBN* 0837186552

**Doering, Mildred.**      **4.3312**
The aging worker: research and recommendations / Mildred Doering, Susan R. Rhodes, Michael Schuster. — Beverly Hills: Sage Publications, c1983. 391 p.: ill.; 23 cm. Includes index. 1. Age and employment — United States I. Rhodes, Susan R. II. Schuster, Michael R. III. T.
HD6280.D63 1983    658.3/042 19    *LC* 82-23176    *ISBN* 0803919492

**Sheppard, Harold L.**      **4.3313**
The graying of working America: the coming crisis in retirement–age policy / Harold L. Sheppard, Sara E. Rix. — New York: Free Press, c1977. xvii, 174 p.: ill.; 22 cm. 1. Age and employment — United States 2. Retirement age — United States. I. Rix, Sara E. joint author. II. T.
HD6280.S53    331.3/98    *LC* 77-2528    *ISBN* 0029286603

**Piore, Michael J.**      **4.3314**
Birds of passage: migrant labor and industrial societies / Michael J. Piore. — Cambridge; New York: Cambridge University Press, 1979. x, 229 p.; 22 cm. Includes index. 1. Alien labor 2. Alien labor — United States. 3. Emigration and immigration I. T.
HD6300.P56    331.6/2    *LC* 78-12067    *ISBN* 0521224527

**Levin, Nora.**      **4.3315**
While Messiah tarried: Jewish socialist movements, 1871–1917 / Nora Levin. — New York: Schocken Books, 1977. xi, 554 p., [5] leaves of plates: ill.; 24 cm. 1. Allgemeyner Idisher arbeyterbund in Lita, Poylen un Rusland. 2. Jewish trade-unions 3. Jewish socialists 4. Jews — United States — Politics and government. 5. Jews — Soviet Union — Politics and government. 6. Labor Zionism I. T.
HD6305.J3 L46    331.6    *LC* 75-7769    *ISBN* 0805236155

# HD6331 Labor and Machinery. Automation

**Mayo, Elton, 1880-1949.**      • **4.3316**
The human problems of an industrial civilization, by Elton Mayo ... Boston, Division of research, Graduate school of business administration, Harvard university [1946] 5 p. l., 194 p. diagrs. 21 cm. 'Second edition.' Includes a description of the experiments undertaken by the Western electric company at its Hawthorne works in Chicago. 1. Western Electric Company, inc. 2. Fatigue 3. Labor and laboring classes — 1914- 4. Social problems 5. Efficiency, Industrial I. T.
HD6331.M3x    338.4    *LC* A 47-1197

**Microprocessors, manpower, and society: a comparative, cross–**    **4.3317**
**national approach / edited by Malcolm Warner.**
New York: St. Martin's Press, 1984. xi, 367 p.; 23 cm. 1. Machinery in industry — Addresses, essays, lectures. 2. Automation — Addresses, essays, lectures. 3. Microelectronics — Social aspects — Addresses, essays, lectures. 4. Industrial relations — Addresses, essays, lectures. I. Warner, Malcolm.
HD6331.M5 1984    338.4/54 19    *LC* 83-40148    *ISBN* 0312531877

**Shaiken, Harley.**      **4.3318**
Work transformed: automation and labor in the computer age / Harley Shaiken. — 1st ed. — New York: Holt, Rinehart, and Winston, 1985, c1984. xiv, 306 p.; 22 cm. 1. Labor supply — Effect of automation on I. T.
HD6331.S475 1985    331.25 19    *LC* 84-4675    *ISBN* 0030426812

**Somers, Gerald George. ed.**      • **4.3319**
Adjusting to technological change. Editors: Gerald G. Somers, Edward L. Cushman [and] Nat Weinberg. [1st ed.] New York, Harper & Row [1963] viii, 230 p. (Industrial Relations Research Association. Publication no. 29) 1. Machinery in industry I. T.
HD6331 S65    *LC* 63-10630

**Jones, Barry O.**      **4.3320**
Sleepers, wake!: technology and the future of work / Barry Jones. — Melbourne; New York: Oxford University Press, 1983, c1982. 285 p.: ill.; 21 cm. Includes index. 1. Machinery in industry — Australia. 2. Technological innovations — Social aspects — Australia. 3. Unemployment, Technological — Australia. 4. Electronic data processing — Social aspects — Australia. 5. Machinery in industry 6. Technological innovations — Social aspects. I. T.
HD6331.2.A8 J66 1982    303.4/83/0994 19    *LC* 83-125170    *ISBN* 0195543432

**Computerized manufacturing automation: employment,**    **4.3321**
**education, and the workplace.**
Washington, D.C.: Congress of the U.S., Office of Technology Assessment: For sale by the Supt. of Docs., U.S. G.P.O., [1984] ix, 471 p.: ill., maps; 27 cm. 'April 1984'—P. [4] of cover. 'OTA-CIT-235'—P. [4] of cover. S/N 052-003-00949-8 Item 1070-M 1. Labor supply — United States — Effect of automation on. 2. Automation — Economic aspects — United States. 3. Occupational training — United States. I. United States. Congress. Office of Technology Assessment.
HD6331.2.U5 C66 1984    303.4/834 19    *LC* 84-601053

**Hunt, H. Allan.**      **4.3322**
Human resource implications of robotics / by H. Allan Hunt and Timothy L. Hunt. — Kalamazoo, Mich.: W.E. Upjohn Institute for Employment Research, c1983. xiii, 207 p.; 23 cm. 1. Unemployment, Technological — United States. 2. Robotics — Social aspects — United States. 3. Robotics — Economic aspects — United States. I. Hunt, Timothy L. II. T.
HD6331.2.U5 H86 1983    331.12/929892/0973 19    *LC* 83-6201    *ISBN* 0880990090

# HD6350–6940 Trade Unions. Labor Unions

## HD6451–6483 History. General Works

**Busch, G. K.**      **4.3323**
The political role of international trades unions / Gary K. Busch. — New York: St. Martin's Press, 1983. ix, 287 p.; 23 cm. Includes index. 1. International labor activities 2. Trade-unions — Political activity I. T.
HD6475.A1 B87 1983    322/.2 19    *LC* 82-16818    *ISBN* 0312624476

**Haas, Ernst B.**      • **4.3324**
Beyond the nation–state: functionalism and international organization / [by] Ernst B. Haas. — Stanford, Calif.: Stanford University Press, 1964. x, 595 p.; 24 cm. Bibliographical references included in 'Notes' (p. [519]-586) 1. International Labor Organization. I. T.
HD6475.A1H17    341.11    *LC* 64-21999

**Weinberg, Paul.**      **4.3325**
European labor and multinationals / Paul J. Weinberg. — New York: Praeger, 1978. vii, 112 p.; 25 cm. 1. International labor activities 2. Trade-unions — Europe. 3. International business enterprises I. T.
HD6475.A1 W44    331.88/091    *LC* 78-9449    *ISBN* 0030442567

**Lorwin, Lewis Levitzki, 1883-1970.**      • **4.3326**
The international labor movement: history, policies, outlook. [1st ed.] New York, Harper [1953] xviii, 366 p. 1. Trade-unions — History I. T.
HD6476 L67    *LC* 53-8542

**Addison, John T.**      **4.3327**
Trade unions and society: some lessons of the British experience / John T. Addison and John Burton. — Vancouver, B.C., Canada: Fraser Institute, 1984. xxviii, 190 p.; 22 cm. (Labour market series. 3) Includes index. 1. Trade-unions 2. Trade-unions — Great Britain. I. Burton, John, 1945- II. T. III. Series.
HD6483.A26 1984    331.88 19    *LC* 84-184353    *ISBN* 0889750564

**Atherton, Wallace N.**      **4.3328**
Theory of union bargaining goals [by] Wallace N. Atherton. — Princeton, N.J.: Princeton University Press, [1973] x, 168 p.: illus.; 24 cm. 1. Collective bargaining — Mathematical models. I. T.
HD6483.A76    331.89/01/51    *LC* 72-14017    *ISBN* 0691041997

**Galenson, Walter, 1914- ed.**      **4.3329**
Labor and trade unionism: an interdisciplinary reader / edited by Walter Galenson and Seymour Martin Lipset. — New York: Wiley, 1960. 379 p.; 25 cm. 1. Trade-unions — Collections. 2. Industrial relations — Collections. I. Lipset, Seymour Martin. joint ed. II. T.
HD6483.G268    331/.88082    *LC* 60-10314

Institute on the Structure of the Labor Market, American          • 4.3330
University, Washington, D.C., 1950.
The impact of the union; eight economic theorists evaluate the labor union
movement: John Maurice Clark [and others] Edited by David McCord Wright.
New York, Harcourt, Brace [1951] ix, 405 p. diagrs. 1. Trade-unions 2. Wages
3. Economic policy I. Clark, John Maurice, 1884- II. Wright, David McCord,
1909- III. T.
HD6483 I5 1950        LC 51-3959

Mulvey, Charles.                                                    4.3331
The economic analysis of trade unions / Charles Mulvey. — New York: St.
Martin's Press, 1978. viii, 159 p.: ill.; 24 cm. Includes indexes. 1. Trade-unions
2. Labor economics I. T.
HD6483.M78        331.88        LC 78-9094        ISBN 0312226845

Ross, Arthur Max.                                                  • 4.3332
Trade union wage policy. Berkeley, Univ. of California Press, 1948. viii, 133 p.
1. Wages 2. Trade-unions 3. Collective bargaining I. T.
HD6483 R67        LC 48-7683

Ross, Philip.                                                      • 4.3333
The Government as a source of union power; the role of public policy in
collective bargaining. Providence, Brown University Press [1965] xiv, 320 p.
(Brown University bicentennial publications. Studies in the fields of general
scholarship) 1. Collective bargaining — United States I. T.
HD6483 R7        LC 65-10155

Stevens, Carl M.                                                   • 4.3334
Strategy and collective bargaining negotiation. — New York, McGraw-Hill
[1963] 192 p. 25 cm. — (Publications of the Wertheim Committee) Includes
bibliography. 1. Collective bargaining I. T.
HD6483.S68        331.116        LC 62-21805

Sturmthal, Adolf Fox.                                              4.3335
The international labor movement in transition; essays on Africa, Asia, Europe,
and South America. Edited by Adolf Sturmthal and James G. Scoville. —
Urbana: University of Illinois Press, [1973] x, 294 p.: illus.; 24 cm. 1. Trade-
unions — Addresses, essays, lectures. 2. Collective bargaining — Addresses,
essays, lectures. 3. Industrial relations — Addresses, essays, lectures.
I. Scoville, James G., 1940- joint author. II. T.
HD6483.S74        331.88        LC 72-85611        ISBN 0252003047

Trade unions in the developed economies / edited by E. Owen          4.3336
Smith.
New York: St. Martin's, 1982. 218 p.; 22 cm. 1. Trade-unions — Case studies.
I. Owen Smith, E.
HD6483.T673        331.88/09172/2 19        LC 81-51469        ISBN
0312812221

# HD6490 Special Topics

Chaison, Gary N.                                                    4.3337
When unions merge / Gary N. Chaison. — Lexington, Mass.: Lexington
Books, c1986. viii, 186 p.; 24 cm. 1. Trade-unions — United States —
Consolidation. 2. Trade-unions — Canada — Consolidation. 3. Trade-unions
— Great Britain — Consolidation. I. T.
HD6490.C622 U63 1986        331.87 19        LC 85-40455        ISBN
0669110817

Schuster, Michael H.                                               4.3338
Union–management cooperation: structure, process, impact / Michael H.
Schuster. — Kalamazoo, Mich.: W.E. Upjohn Institute for Employment
Research, 1984. xiv, 235 p.: ill.; 23 cm. 1. Labor-management committees —
United States. 2. Industrial relations — United States. I. T.
HD6490.L33 S38 1984        331/.01/12 19        LC 84-17373        ISBN
0880990244

Fulmer, William E.                                                 4.3339
Union organizing: management and labor conflict / William E. Fulmer. — New
York, N.Y.: Praeger, 1982. 228 p.; 24 cm. 1. Trade-unions — United States —
Organizing. I. T.
HD6490.O72 U64 1982        331.89/12 19        LC 82-16172        ISBN
003062603X

Foner, Philip Sheldon, 1910-.                                     4.3340
Organized labor and the Black worker, 1619–1973 [by] Philip S. Foner. New
York, Praeger [1974] xi, 489 p. 25 cm. 1. Trade-unions — United States —
Afro-American membership — History. 2. Afro-Americans — Employment
— History. I. T.
HD6490.R2 F65        331.6/9/96073 19        LC 70-143968

Batstone, Eric.                                                    4.3341
Shop stewards in action: the organization of workplace conflict and
accommodation / Eric Batstone, Ian Boraston, Stephen Frenkel. — Oxford:

Blackwell, 1978 (c1977). xx, 316 p.; 23 cm. — (Warwick studies in industrial
relations.) Includes index. 1. Shop stewards — Great Britain. I. Boraston, Ian,
joint author. II. Frenkel, Stephen. joint author. III. T. IV. Series.
HD6490.S5 B35        331.87/3        LC 77-372030        ISBN 0631172602

# HD6500–6940 By Country

## HD6501–6509 UNITED STATES

### HD6508.A–F

Adamic, Louis, 1899-1951.                                         • 4.3342
Dynamite: the story of class violence in America. — Rev. ed. — Gloucester,
Mass.: P. Smith, 1960 [c1934] 495 p.: illus.; 21 cm. 1. Trade-unions — United
States — History. 2. Labor and laboring classes — United States — History.
3. Strikes and lockouts — United States — History. 4. United States — Social
conditions I. T.
HD6508.A413 1960        331.89/3/0973 19        LC 61-4062

Bakke, E. Wight (Edward Wight), 1903- comp.                        • 4.3343
Unions, management, and the public: readings and text / E. Wight Bakke,
Clark Kerr, Charles W. Anrod. — 3d ed. — New York: Harcourt, Brace &
World, 1967. xvii, 790 p.: ill. 1. Trade-unions — United States 2. Industrial
relations — United States. I. Kerr, Clark, 1911- joint comp. II. Anrod,
Charles W joint comp. III. T.
HD6508.B28 1967        HD6508 B28 1967.        LC 67-14628

Barbash, Jack.                                                     • 4.3344
Labor's grass roots; a study of the local union. [1st ed.] New York, Harper
[1961] 250 p. 1. Trade-unions — United States I. T.
HD6508 B352        LC 61-14839

Barbash, Jack. ed.                                                 • 4.3345
Unions and union leadership: their human meaning. — [1st ed.]. — New York:
Harper, [1959] 348 p.; 22 cm. 1. Trade-unions — United States I. T.
HD6508.B354        331.880973        LC 59-9937

Bok, Derek Curtis.                                                 • 4.3346
Labor and the American community, by Derek C. Bok and John T. Dunlop. —
New York: Simon and Schuster, [1970] 542 p.; 22 cm. 1. Trade-unions — U.S.
2. Collective bargaining — U.S. I. Dunlop, John Thomas, 1914- joint author.
II. T.
HD6508.B59        331/.0973        LC 78-92184        ISBN 0671203665

Bradley, Philip D., ed.                                           4.3347
The public stake in union power. Charlottesville, University of Virginia Press,
1959. x, 382 p. diagrs. 25 cm. 1. Trade-unions — United States — Collections.
I. T.
HD6508.B77        LC 59-11490

Brody, David.                                                      4.3348
Workers in industrial America: essays on the twentieth century struggle /
David Brody. — New York: Oxford University Press, 1980. ix, 257 p.; 21 cm.
1. Trade-unions — United States — History — Addresses, essays, lectures.
2. Labor and laboring classes — United States — History — Addresses, essays,
lectures. I. T.
HD6508.B8113        331.88/0973 19        LC 78-27157        ISBN 0195024907

Collective bargaining, contemporary American experience /          4.3349
Gerald G. Somers, editor; authors, Jack Barbash ... [et al.].
1st ed. — Madison, WI (7226 Social Science, University of Wisconsin, Madison
53706): Industrial Relations Research Association, 1980. vi, 588 p.: ill.; 24 cm.
— (Industrial Relations Research Association series.) 1. Collective bargaining
— United States — Case studies. I. Somers, Gerald George. II. Barbash, Jack.
III. Industrial Relations Research Association. IV. Series.
HD6508.C654        331.89/0973 19        LC 79-90030

Craypo, Charles, 1936-.                                           4.3350
The economics of collective bargaining: case studies in the private sector /
Charles Craypo. — Washington, D.C.: BNA Books, c1986. xiv, 259 p.: ill.; 24
cm. 1. Collective bargaining — United States — Case studies. I. T.
HD6508.C74 1986        331.89/0973 19        LC 85-28373        ISBN
087179490X

Derber, Milton. ed.                                                • 4.3351
Labor and the New Deal, edited by Milton Derber and Edwin Young. New
York, Da Capo Press, 1972 [c1957] xi, 392 p. 23 cm. (Franklin D. Roosevelt
and the era of the New Deal.) 1. Trade-unions — United States 2. Labor and
laboring classes — United States — 1914- 3. New Deal, 1933-1939 I. Young,
Edwin. joint ed. II. T. III. Series.
HD6508.D44 1972        331.88/0973 19        LC 70-169656        ISBN
0306703645

**Foner, Philip Sheldon, 1910-.**      4.3352
History of the labor movement in the United States / by Philip S. Foner. — 2d ed. — New York: International Publishers, [1975-. v. < 2, 5 >; 21 cm. (New World paperbacks) 1. Trade-unions — United States — History. 2. Labor and laboring classes — United States — History. I. T.
HD6508.F57    331.88/0973    LC 75-315606    ISBN 071780092X. ISBN 0717803880 pbk

**Freeman, Richard B. (Richard Barry), 1943-.**      4.3353
What do unions do? / Richard B. Freeman & James L. Medoff. — New York: Basic Books, c1984. viii, 293 p.: ill.; 24 cm. 1. Trade-unions — United States I. Medoff, James L., 1947- II. T.
HD6508.F73 1984    331.88/0973 19    LC 81-68407    ISBN 0465091334

## HD6508.G–R

**Galenson, Walter, 1914-.**      • 4.3354
The CIO challenge to the AFL; a history of the American labor movement, 1935–1941. — Cambridge, Harvard University Press, 1960. xix, 732 p. illus., ports., tables. 25 cm. — (Wertheim publications in industrial relations. Studies in labor-management history) Bibliographical references included in 'Notes' (p. [647]-714) 1. Congress of Industrial Organizations. 2. American Federation of Labor. 3. Trade-unions — U.S. — Hist. I. T.
HD6508.G28    331.880973    LC 60-5390

**Grob, Gerald N., 1931-.**      • 4.3355
Workers and Utopia; a study of ideological conflict in the American labor movement, 1865–1900. [Evanston, Ill.] Northwestern University Press, 1961. 220 p. (Northwestern University studies in history, no. 2) 1. Trade-unions — United States — History I. T. II. Series.
HD6508 G75    LC 61-12384

**Hardman, J. B. S. (Jacob Benjamin Salutsky), 1882-1968. ed.**      4.3356
The house of labor; internal operations of American unions, edited by J. B. S. Hardman [and] Maurice F. Neufeld. New York, Prentice-Hall, 1951. xviii, 555 p. 24 cm. (Prentice-Hall industrial relations and personnel series) 'Prepared under the auspices of the Inter-union Institute, inc.' 1. Trade-unions — United States I. Neufeld, Maurice F. joint ed. II. Inter-union Institute for Labor and Democracy. III. T.
HD6508.H27    331.88/0973    LC 51-2599    ISBN 0837133599

**Hirsch, Barry T., 1949-.**      4.3357
The economic analysis of unions: new approaches and evidence / Barry T. Hirsch, John T. Addison. — Boston: Allen & Unwin, 1986. xi, 337 p.; 25 cm. Includes indexes. 1. Trade-unions — United States 2. Wages — United States. 3. Cost and standard of living — United States. 4. Industrial relations — United States. I. Addison, John T. II. T.
HD6508.H48 1986    331.88/0973 19    LC 85-18690    ISBN 0043310974

**Laslett, John H. M.**      • 4.3358
Labor and the left; a study of socialist and radical influences in the American labor movement, 1881–1924 [by] John H. M. Laslett. New York, Basic Books [1970] vi, 326 p. 25 cm. 1. Trade-unions — United States — History. 2. Socialism — United States I. T.
HD6508.L28    335.43/8/331880973    LC 78-110774    ISBN 0465037429

**Leiserson, William Morris, 1883-1957.**      • 4.3359
American trade union democracy. With a foreword by Sumner H. Slichter. — New York: Columbia University Press, 1959. 354 p.; 24 cm. 1. Trade-unions — United States I. T.
HD6508.L43    331.880973    LC 59-8112

**Mills, C. Wright (Charles Wright), 1916-1962.**      • 4.3360
The new men of power; America's labor leaders, by C. Wright Mills with the assistance of Helen Schneider. New York, A. M. Kelley [1971, c1948] 323 p. 22 cm. (Library of American labor history) (Reprints of economic classics) 1. Trade-unions — United States — History. 2. Labor and laboring classes — United States — History. I. Schneider, Helen. II. T.
HD6508.M583 1971    331.873/0973    LC 68-56261    ISBN 0678007152

**Perlman, Mark.**      4.3361
Labor union theories in America: background and development. Evanston, Ill., Row, Peterson [1958] 313 p. 1. Trade-unions — United States I. T.
HD6508 P39    LC 57-13195

**Perlman, Selig, 1888-.**      • 4.3362
A history of trade unionism in the United States. New York, A. M. Kelley, 1950 [c1922] viii, 313 p. 17 cm. 'Part 1 ... is based on the History of labor in the United States, by Commons and Associates.' 1. Trade-unions — United States — History. I. T.
HD6508.P4 1950    LC 64-4989

**Petro, Sylvester, 1917-.**      • 4.3363
Power unlimited; the corruption of union leadership; a report on the McClellan Committee hearings. New York, Ronald Press Co. [1959] 323 p. 1. United States. Congress. Senate. Select Committee on Improper Activities in the Labor or Management Field 2. Unfair labor practices — United States 3. Trade-unions — United States I. T.
HD6508 P44    LC 59-9560

**Rees, Albert, 1921-.**      • 4.3364
The economics of trade unions. — [Chicago] University of Chicago Press [1962] 208 p. illus. 20 cm. — (Cambridge economic handbooks) 1. Trade-unions — U.S. I. T.
HD6508.R38    331.880973    LC 62-9741

## HD6508.S–Z

**Saposs, David Joseph, 1886-.**      • 4.3365
Communism in American unions. New York, McGraw-Hill, 1959. 279 p. (McGraw-Hill labor management series) 1. Trade-unions — United States 2. Communism — United States — 1917- I. T.
HD6508 S24    LC 59-7318

**Sayles, Leonard R.**      • 4.3366
The local union [by] Leonard R. Sayles [and] George Strauss. Rev. ed. New York, Harcourt, Brace & World [1967] ix, 174 p. illus. 23 cm. (The Harbrace series in business and economics) Bibliographical footnotes. 1. Trade-unions — United States I. Strauss, George, 1923- joint author. II. T.
HD6508.S33 1967    331.88/0973    LC 67-17182

**Seidman, Joel Isaac, 1906-.**      • 4.3367
The worker views his union [by] Joel Seidman [and others. Chicago] University of Chicago Press [1958] 299 p. 'The research project on which this volume reports was sponsored by the Industrial Relations Center of the University of Chicago.' 1. Trade-unions — United States I. T.
HD6508.S373    331.88097    LC 58-5686

**Should the federal government significantly curtail the powers of**      4.3368
**labor unions in the United States?: intercollegiate debate topic, 1981–1982, pursuant to Public Law 88–246 / compiled by the Congressional Research Service, Library of Congress.**
Washington: U.S. G.P.O., 1981. xv, 681 p.: ill.; 24 cm. (Document / House of Representatives, 97th Congress, 1st session; 97-89) Item 996-A, 996-B (microfiche) 1. Trade-unions — United States — Addresses, essays, lectures. 2. Industrial relations — United States — Addresses, essays, lectures. 3. Labor policy — United States — Addresses, essays, lectures. I. United States. Congress. House. II. Library of Congress. Congressional Research Service.
HD6508.S522 1981    331.88/0973 19    LC 82-601136

**Slichter, Sumner H. (Sumner Huber), 1892-1959.**      • 4.3369
Union policies and industrial management. New York, Greenwood Press, 1968 [c1941] xiv, 597 p. 24 cm. (Institute of Economics of the Brookings Institution. Publication no. 85) 1. Trade-unions — United States 2. Industrial management — United States. 3. Industrial relations — United States. I. T.
HD6508.S55 1968    331.88/0973    LC 68-23330

**Taft, Philip, 1902-.**      • 4.3370
Organized labor in American history. — [1st ed.]. — New York: Harper & Row, [1964] xxi, 818 p.; 24 cm. 1. Trade-unions — United States — History. I. T.
HD6508.T25    331.880973    LC 64-12712

**Ulman, Lloyd.**      • 4.3371
The rise of the national trade union; the development and significance of its structure, governing institutions, and economic policies. Cambridge, Harvard University Press, 1955. xix, 639 p. diagrs., tables. 25 cm. (Wertheim publications in industrial relations) 1. Trade-unions — United States — History. I. T.
HD6508.U4    LC 56-5175

**Unions in crisis and beyond: perspectives from six countries /**      4.3372
**edited by Richard Edwards, Paolo Garonna, Franz Tödtling.**
Dover, Mass.: Auburn House Pub. Co., c1986. xii, 340 p.: ill.; 25 cm. Revised papers prepared for conferences held in Sperlonga, Italy, July 1984 and in Vienna, Jan. 1985. Includes index. 1. Trade-unions — United States — Addresses, essays, lectures. 2. Trade-unions — Europe — Addresses, essays, lectures. I. Edwards, Richard, 1944- II. Garonna, P., 1948- III. Tödtling, Franz.
HD6508.U45 1986    331.88 19    LC 85-26646    ISBN 0865691274

**Van Tine, Warren R.**      4.3373
The making of the labor bureaucrat: union leadership in the United States, 1870–1920 [by] Warren R. Van Tine. — Amherst: University of Massachusetts Press, 1973. xi, 230 p.; 22 cm. 1. Trade-unions — United States — Officials and employees — History. I. T.
HD6508.V25    331.88/0973    LC 73-79508

**Wilensky, Harold L.** • **4.3374**
Intellectuals in labor unions; organizational pressures on professional roles. Glencoe, Ill., Free Press [1956] 336 p. 1. Trade-unions — United States — Officials and employees I. T.
HD6508 W5    *LC* 56-6877

**Levy, Jacques E.** **4.3375**
Cesar Chavez: autobiography of La Causa / Jacques E. Levy. — 1st ed. — New York: Norton, [1975] xxv, 546 p., [16] leaves of plates: ill.; 24 cm. Includes index. 1. Chavez, Cesar, 1927- 2. United Farm Workers. 3. Migrant agricultural laborers — United States. I. Chavez, Cesar, 1927- II. T.
HD6509.C48 L48 1975    331.88/13/0924 B    *LC* 75-15747    *ISBN* 0393074943

## HD6515 By Industry, A–Z

**Meister, Dick.** **4.3376**
A long time coming: the struggle to unionize America's farm workers / Dick Meister and Anne Loftis. New York: Macmillan, c1977. xi, 241 p., [8] leaves of plates: ill.; 25 cm. Includes index. 1. Trade-unions — Agricultural laborers — United States — History. I. Loftis, Anne, joint author. II. T.
HD6515.A29 M44    331.88/13/0973    *LC* 76-54510    *ISBN* 0025839209

**Galarza, Ernesto, 1905-.** **4.3377**
Farm workers and agri–business in California, 1947–1960 / Ernesto Galarza. — Notre Dame: University of Notre Dame Press, c1977. xvii, 405 p.; 24 cm. Includes index. 1. Trade-unions — Agricultural laborers — California — History. I. T.
HD6515.A292 C33    331.88/13/09794    *LC* 76-51615    *ISBN* 0268009414

**Taylor, Ronald B.** **4.3378**
Chavez and the farm workers / Ronald B. Taylor. — Boston: Beacon Press, [1975] ix, 342 p.: ill.; 21 cm. Includes index. 1. Chavez, Cesar, 1927- 2. Trade-unions — Agricultural laborers — California. I. T.
HD6515.A292 C38 1975    331.88/13/0924 B    *LC* 74-16671    *ISBN* 0807004987

**Stieber, Jack, 1919-.** • **4.3379**
Governing the UAW. New York, Wiley [1962] 188 p. (Trade unions monograph series) 1. International Union, United Automobile, Aircraft, and Agricultural Implement Workers of America. I. T.
HD6515 A8 S75    *LC* 62-21005

**Galenson, Walter, 1914-.** **4.3380**
The United Brotherhood of Carpenters: the first hundred years / Walter Galenson. — Cambridge, Mass.: Harvard University Press, 1983. vii, 440 p.; 25 cm. — (Wertheim publications in industrial relations.) 1. United Brotherhood of Carpenters and Joiners of America — History. I. T. II. Series.
HD6515.C2 U54 1983    331.88/194/0973 19    *LC* 82-23402    *ISBN* 0674921968

**Arnold, June, 1926- Jesse Thomas.** **4.3381**
Competition and collective bargaining in the needle trades, 1910–1967. — Ithaca: New York State School of Industrial and Labor Relations, Cornell University, 1972. xx, 910 p.: port.; 24 cm. — (Cornell studies in industrial and labor relations. v. 17) 1. Collective bargaining — Clothing industry — United States. 2. Clothing trade — United States. I. T. II. Series.
HD6515.C5 C33    331.89/048/70973    *LC* 79-630987    *ISBN* 0875460356

**Mangum, Garth L.** **4.3382**
The Operating Engineers: the economic history of a trade union. Cambridge, Harvard University Press, 1964. xiv, 344 p. illus., map, diagrs. 25 cm. (Wertheim publications in industrial relations. Studies in labor-management history) Bibliographical footnotes. 1. International Union of Operating Engineers. I. T.
HD6515.E5M3 1964    *LC* 63-19144

**Bensman, David, 1949-.** **4.3383**
The practice of solidarity: American hat finishers in the nineteenth century / David Bensman. — Urbana: University of Illinois, c1985. xxi, 240 p., [8] p. of plates: ill.; 24 cm. (Working class in American history.) Includes index. 1. Trade-unions — Hat trade — United States — History — 19th century. 2. Hatters — United States — History — 19th century. 3. Boycott — United States — History — 19th century. I. T. II. Series.
HD6515.H3 B46 1985    331.88/18741/0973 19    *LC* 83-6592    *ISBN* 0252010930

**Herling, John.** **4.3384**
Right to challenge; people and power in the Steelworkers Union. — [1st ed.]. — New York: Harper & Row, [1972] xi, 415 p.; 24 cm. 1. United Steelworkers of America. I. T.
HD6515.I5 H47    331.88/33    *LC* 67-22526    *ISBN* 0060118342

**Livernash, E. Robert (Edward Robert)** • **4.3385**
Collective bargaining in the basic steel industry; a study of the public interest and the role of Government [by E. Robert Livernash and others. Washington] U.S. Dept. of Labor, 1961. ix, 317 p. diagrs., tables. 24 cm. 1. Strikes and lockouts — [Iron and] steel industry — United States. 2. Iron and steel workers — United States 3. Collective bargaining — United States. I. T.
HD6515.I5L5    331.18691    *LC* L 61-17

**Jensen, Vernon H.** **4.3386**
Strife on the waterfront; the Port of New York since 1945 [by] Vernon H. Jensen. — Ithaca [N.Y.]: Cornell University Press, [1974] 478 p.; 25 cm. 1. Collective bargaining — Stevedores — New York (City) I. T.
HD6515.L82 N474    331/.041/387164097471    *LC* 73-14137    *ISBN* 0801407893

**Perlman, Mark.** • **4.3387**
The machinists: a new study in American trade unionism. Cambridge, Harvard University Press, 1961. 333 p. ill. (Wertheim publications in industrial relations. Studies in labor-management history) 1. International Association of Machinists. I. T.
HD6515 M2 I535    *LC* 61-16695

**Perry, Charles R.** **4.3388**
Collective bargaining and the decline of the United Mine Workers / by Charles R. Perry. — Philadelphia, Pa., U.S.A.: Industrial Research Unit, the Wharton School, University of Pennsylvania, c1984. xi, 273 p.: ill.; 24 cm. — (Major Industrial Research Unit studies. 0149-0818; no. 60) 1. United Mine Workers of America — History. 2. Collective bargaining — Coal mining industry — United States. 3. Trade-unions — Coal-miners — United States. I. T. II. Series.
HD6515.M615 P47 1984    331.88/122/0973 19    *LC* 84-47503    *ISBN* 0895460432

**Aurand, Harold W.** **4.3389**
From the Molly Maguires to the United Mine Workers; the social ecology of an industrial union, 1869–1897 [by] Harold W. Aurand. Philadelphia, Temple University Press, 1972 (c1971) x, 221 p. illus. 24 cm. 1. United Mine Workers of America — History. 2. Trade-unions — Coal miners — Pennsylvania — History. 3. Coal miners — Pennsylvania — History. I. T.
HD6515.M616 P42    331.88/12/209748    *LC* 73-157737    *ISBN* 0877220069

**Baratz, Morton S.** • **4.3390**
The union and the coal industry. New Haven, Yale University Press, 1955. xvii, 170 p. map, diagrs., tables. 24 cm. 1. United Mine Workers of America. 2. Coal miners — United States I. T.
HD6515.M7 U772    *LC* 55-5515

**Harris, William Hamilton, 1944-.** **4.3391**
Keeping the faith: A. Philip Randolph, Milton P. Webster, and the Brotherhood of Sleeping Car Porters, 1925–37 / William H. Harris. — Urbana: University of Illinois Press, c1977. xiv, 252 p., [4] leaves of plates: ill.; 24 cm. — (Blacks in the New World.) Includes index. 1. Randolph, A. Philip (Asa Philip), 1889- 2. Webster, Milton P., 1887-1965. 3. Brotherhood of Sleeping Car Porters. I. T. II. Series.
HD6515.R36 H37    331.88/11/385220973    *LC* 77-8389    *ISBN* 0252004531

**Goldberg, Joseph Philip, 1918-.** • **4.3392**
The maritime story; a study in labor–management relations. Cambridge, Harvard University Press, 1958. 361 p. (Wertheim publications in industrial relations. Studies in labor-management history) 1. Merchant seamen — United States — Societies, etc. 2. Industrial relations — United States I. T.
HD6515 S4 G6    *LC* 58-8077

**Leiter, Robert David, 1922-.** • **4.3393**
The Teamsters Union, a study of its economic impact. New York, Bookman Associates [1957] 304 p. ill. 1. International Brotherhood of Teamsters, Chauffeurs, Warehousemen, and Helpers of America. I. T.
HD6515 T2 L4    *LC* 57-3540

**James, Ralph C., 1929-.** **4.3394**
Hoffa and the teamsters; a study of union power. Princeton, N.J., Van Nostrand [1965] xviii, 430 p. 24 cm. 1. Hoffa, James R. (James Riddle), 1913- I. James, Estelle. joint author. II. T.
HD6515.T3 J3    *LC* 65-26466

**Lembcke, Jerry, 1943-.** **4.3395**
One union in wood / Jerry Lembcke and William M. Tattam. — Madeira Park, B.C.: Harbour Pub. Co.; New York: International Publishers, 1985 (c1984). x, 229 p.; 23 cm. (New World paperbacks) Includes index. 1. International Woodworkers of America — History. 2. Trade-unions — Woodworkers — United States — History. 3. Trade-unions — Woodworkers — Canada — History. I. Tattam, William M., 1941- II. T.
HD6515.W6 L45    331.88/194/0973 19    *LC* 84-15808    *ISBN* 0717806197

## HD6517 Special Localities

**Marshall, F. Ray.**      • **4.3396**
Labor in the South [by] F. Ray Marshall. Cambridge, Mass., Harvard University Press, 1967. xiv, 406 p. 24 cm. (Wertheim publications in industrial relations.) Bibliographical references included in 'Notes' (p. 353-393) 1. Trade-unions — Southern States. I. T. II. Series.
HD6517.A13M3     331.88/0975     *LC* 67-22870

## HD6521–6651 CANADA. LATIN AMERICA

**Jamieson, Stuart Marshall.**      **4.3397**
Industrial relations in Canada [by] Stuart Jamieson. — 2d ed. — New York: St. Martin's Press, [1973] 156 p.; 22 cm. 1. Trade-unions — Canada. I. T.
HD6524.J3 1973     331.88/0971     *LC* 72-14047     *ISBN* 077051023X

**Alexander, Robert Jackson, 1918-.**      • **4.3398**
Organized labor in Latin America [by] Robert J. Alexander. New York, Free Press [1965] x, 274 p. (Studies in contemporary Latin America) 1. Trade-unions — Latin America 2. Labor and laboring classes — Latin America I. T.
HD6530.5 A75     *LC* 65-23024

**Clark, Marjorie Ruth, 1899-.**      **4.3399**
Organized labor in Mexico. — New York: Russell & Russell, [1973] 315 p.; 23 cm. 'First published in 1934.' 1. Trade-unions — Mexico. 2. Labor and laboring classes — Mexico. 3. Labor laws and legislation — Mexico. I. T.
HD6532.C55 1973     331.88/0972     *LC* 72-84983     *ISBN* 0846216825

**Poblete Troncoso, Moisés, 1893-.**      • **4.3400**
The rise of the Latin American labor movement / [by] Moisés Poblete Troncoso [and] Ben G. Burnett. New York: Bookman Associates [1960] 179 p. 1. Trade-unions — Latin America I. Burnett, Ben G., jt. author II. T.
HD6597 P62     *LC* 60-14561

## HD6656–6796 EUROPE

**Galenson, Walter, 1914-.**      • **4.3401**
Trade union democracy in Western Europe. Berkeley, University of California Press, 1961. 96 p. 'A publication of the Institute of Industrial Relations, University of California.' 1. Trade-unions — Europe I. T.
HD6657 G3     *LC* 61-6779

**Sturmthal, Adolf Fox.**      **4.3402**
Left of center: European labor since World War II / Adolf Sturmthal. — Urbana: University of Illinois Press, c1983. xv, 302 p.; 24 cm. Includes index. 1. Trade-unions — Europe — History — 20th century. 2. Industrial relations — Europe — History — 20th century. 3. Socialist parties — Europe — History — 20th century. I. T.
HD6657.S85 1983     331.88/094 19     *LC* 82-11022     *ISBN* 0252010086

**Clinton, Alan.**      **4.3403**
The trade union rank and file: trades councils in Britain, 1900–40 / Alan Clinton. — Manchester: Manchester University Press; Totowa, N.J.: Rowman and Littlefield, 1978 (c1977). x, 262 p.: ill.; 23 cm. Includes index. 1. Trade-unions — Great Britain — History. I. T.
HD6664.C3876     331.87/2     *LC* 79-307831     *ISBN* 0874719828

**Currie, Robert.**      **4.3404**
Industrial politics / Robert Currie. — Oxford: Clarendon Press; New York: Oxford University Press, 1979. viii, 294 p.; 23 cm. 1. Labour Party (Great Britain) — History. 2. Collective bargaining — Great Britain — History. 3. Industrial relations — Great Britain — History. 4. Trade-unions — Great Britain — History. 5. Management — Employee participation — Great Britain — History. I. T.
HD6664.C83     331/.0941     *LC* 78-40480     *ISBN* 019827419X

**May, Timothy C.**      **4.3405**
Trade unions and pressure group politics / [by] Timothy C. May. — Farnborough, Hants.: Saxon House; Lexington, Mass.: Lexington Books, 1975. vii, 149 p.; 24 cm. (Saxon House studies) Includes index. 1. Trade-unions — Great Britain — Political activity. I. T.
HD6664.M35     322/.3     *LC* 76-355517     *ISBN* 034701058X

**Webb, Sidney, 1859-1947.**      • **4.3406**
The History of trade unionism / by Sidney and Beatrice Webb, (1894). — New York: A.M. Kelley, 1965. 784 p. — (Reprints of economic classics) 1. Trade-unions — Great Britain. I. Webb, Beatrice Potter, (Mrs. Sidney Webb), 1858- II. T.
HD6664.P3     *LC* 65-23215

**Webb, Sidney, 1859-1947.**      • **4.3407**
Industrial democracy, by Sidney & Beatrice Webb. New York, A. M. Kelley, 1965. lxi, 929 p. 21 cm. (Reprints of economic classics) 'Original edition 1897.

Reprinted 1965 from the 1920 edition.' Bibliography: p. [879]-900. 1. Trade-unions — Great Britain. I. Webb, Beatrice Potter, 1858-1943. joint author. II. T.
HD6664.P33 1965     331.880942     *LC* 65-18330

**Pelling, Henry.**      **4.3408**
A history of British trade unionism. — 2d ed. — [London]: Macmillan; [New York]: St Martin's Press, 1972. xiii, 310 p.: illus.; 23 cm. 1. Trade-unions — Great Britain — History. I. T.
HD6664.P4 1972     331.88/0942     *LC* 72-82154     *ISBN* 0333143019

**Roberts, B. C. (Benjamin Charles), 1917-.**      • **4.3409**
Trade union government and administration in Great Britain. Cambridge, Harvard University Press, 1956. viii, 570 p. diagrs., tables. 1. Trade-unions — Great Britain I. T.
HD6664.R684x     *LC* a 56-8630

**Taylor, Robert, 1943-.**      **4.3410**
The Fifth estate: Britain's unions in the seventies / Robert Taylor. — London; Boston: Routledge & K. Paul, 1978. xvi, 368 p.: ill.; 23 cm. Includes index. 1. Trade-unions — Great Britain. I. T.
HD6664.T4 1978     331.88/0941     *LC* 77-30402     *ISBN* 0710087519

**Brown, Henry Phelps, Sir, 1906-.**      **4.3411**
The origins of trade union power / by Henry Phelps Brown. — Oxford: Clarendon Press; New York: Oxford University Press, 1983. vi, 320 p.; 24 cm. 1. Trade-unions — Great Britain — Political activity — History. 2. Labor policy — Great Britain — History. 3. Trade-unions — Political activity 4. Labor policy I. T.
HD6667.B76 1983     322/.2/0941 19     *LC* 83-1920     *ISBN* 0198771150

**Hinton, James.**      **4.3412**
Labour and socialism: a history of the British labour movement, 1867–1974 / James Hinton. — Amherst, Mass.: University of Massachusetts Press, 1983. ix, 212 p.; 23 cm. Includes index. 1. Labour Party (Great Britain) — History. 2. Labor and laboring classes — Great Britain — Political activity — History. 3. Trade-unions — Great Britain — Political activity — History. 4. Socialism — Great Britain — History. I. T.
HD6667.H56 1983     322/.2/0941 19     *LC* 82-21798     *ISBN* 0870233939

**Unions and economic crisis: Britain, West Germany, and**      **4.3413**
**Sweden / Peter Gourevitch ... [et al.].**
London; Boston: Allen & Unwin, 1984. viii, 394 p.: ill.; 25 cm. 'Second volume of the Harvard Center for European Studies Project on European Trade Union Responses to Economic Crisis'—P. [v] 1. Trade-unions — Great Britain — Political activity. 2. Trade-unions — Germany (West) — Political activity. 3. Trade-unions — Sweden — Political activity. 4. Great Britain — Economic policy — 1945- 5. Germany (West) — Economic policy 6. Sweden — Economic policy. I. Gourevitch, Peter Alexis. II. Harvard University. Center for European Studies.
HD6667.U54 1984     331.88/094 19     *LC* 83-25784     *ISBN* 004331094X

**The French workers' movement: economic crisis and political**      **4.3414**
**change / edited by Mark Kesselman with the assistance of Guy Groux; translated by Edouardo Diaz, Arthur Goldhammer, and Richard Shyrock.**
London; Boston: G. Allen & Unwin, 1984. viii, 350 p.; 24 cm. Includes index. 1. Trade-unions — France — Addresses, essays, lectures. 2. France — Economic conditions — 1945- — Addresses, essays, lectures. I. Kesselman, Mark. II. Groux, Guy.
HD6684.F74 1984     331.88/0944 19     *LC* 84-9238     *ISBN* 0043310958

**Lefranc, Georges, 1904-.**      • **4.3415**
Le Mouvement syndical sous la Troisième République. Paris Payot 1967. 455p. (Bibliothèque historique) 1. Syndicalism — France 2. Trade-unions — France I. T.
HD6684 L27

**Horowitz, Daniel L.**      • **4.3416**
The Italian labor movement. Cambridge, Harvard University Press, 1963. 356 p. (Werthelm publications in industrial relations) 1. Trade-unions — Italy I. T. II. Series.
HD6709 H67     *LC* 63-10866

**Roberts, David D., 1943-.**      **4.3417**
The syndicalist tradition and Italian fascism / by David D. Roberts. — Chapel Hill: University of North Carolina Press, c1979. x, 410 p.; 24 cm. Based on the author's thesis, University of California at Berkeley, 1971. Includes index. 1. Syndicalism — Italy. 2. Fascism — Italy 3. Corporate state — Italy I. T.
HD6709.R58     335/.82/0945     *LC* 78-23347     *ISBN* 0807813516

**Brown, Emily Clark, 1895-.**                                       • **4.3418**
Soviet trade unions and labor relations. — Cambridge, Harvard University Press, 1966. ix, 394 p. 22 cm. Includes bibliographical references. 1. Trade-unions — Russia. 2. Industrial relations — Russia. I. T.
HD6732.B7      331.1947      LC 66-21332

**Johnston, T. L.**                                                   • **4.3419**
Collective bargaining in Sweden. Cambridge, Mass., Harvard University Press, 1962. 358 p. diagrs., tables. 23 cm. 1. Collective bargaining — Sweden. I. T.
HD6757.J6      LC 62-5728

## HD6800–6940 Asia. Africa

**Beling, Willard A.**                                                • **4.3420**
Pan–Arabism and labor. — Cambridge, Distributed for the Center for Middle Eastern Studies of Harvard University by Harvard University Press, 1960. 127 p. 21 cm. — (Harvard Middle Eastern monographs, 4) Includes bibliography. 1. Trade-unions — Mohammedan countries. 2. Labor and laboring classes — Mohammedan countries. I. T.
HD6800.5.B4      331.88091      LC 60-15082

**Sinha, Ramesh P.**                                                    **4.3421**
Social dimension of trade unionism in India / R.P. Sinha. — New Delhi: Uppal Pub. House, c1984. xiii, 193 p.; 22 cm. Includes index. 1. Trade-unions — India. I. T.
HD6812.S56 1984      331.88/0954 19      LC 84-900975

**Ayusawa, Iwao Frederick, 1894-.**                                   • **4.3422**
A history of labor in modern Japan, by Iwao F. Ayusawa. — Honolulu: East-West Center Press, [c1966] xvi, 406 p.; 24 cm. 1. Trade-unions — Japan — History. I. T.
HD6832.A97      331.88/0952      LC 66-30068

**Cook, Alice Hanson.**                                               • **4.3423**
An introduction to Japanese trade unionism, by Alice H. Cook. Ithaca, New York State School of Industrial and Labor Relations, Cornell University [1966] ix, 216 p. 1. Trade-unions — Japan I. T. II. Title: Japanese trade unionism
HD6832 C6      LC 66-63380

**Roberts, B. C. (Benjamin Charles), 1917-.**                         • **4.3424**
Collective bargaining in African countries, by B.C. Roberts and L. Greyfié de Bellecombe. London, Macmillan, 1967. xviii, 158 p. tables. At head of title: International Institute for Labour Studies. 1. Collective bargaining — Africa, Sub-Saharan I. Greyfié de Bellecombe, Louis. joint author II. International Institute for Labour Studies. III. T.
HD6857 R6      LC 67-14192

# HD6941–6948 Employers' Associations

**Employers associations and industrial relations: a comparative**      **4.3425**
**study** / edited by John P. Windmuller and Alan Gladstone.
Oxford [Oxfordshire]: Clarendon Press; New York: Oxford University Press, c1984. xii, 370 p.; 24 cm. — (Publication of the International Institute for Labour Studies.) 1. Employers' associations — Case studies. I. Windmuller, John P. II. Gladstone, Alan. III. Series.
HD6943.E46 1984      658.3/15/06 19      LC 83-17212      ISBN 019827260X

# HD6951–6976 Industrial Sociology. Social Conditions of Labor. Industrial Relations

**Hirszowicz, Maria.**                                                 **4.3426**
Industrial sociology: an introduction / Maria Hirszowicz; with a guide to the literature by Peter Cook. — New York: St. Martin's Press, 1982. ix, 303 p.; 23 cm. Includes indexes. 1. Industrial sociology I. T.
HD6955.H55 1982      306/.3 19      LC 81-21435      ISBN 0312415591

**Storey, John.**                                                      **4.3427**
Managerial prerogative and the question of control / John Storey. — London; Boston: Routledge & K. Paul, 1983. viii, 243 p.: ill.; 24 cm. Includes index.

1. Industrial sociology 2. Industrial relations 3. Management rights 4. Division of labor I. T.
HD6955.S87 1983      658.3/15 19      LC 82-18572      ISBN 0710092032

**Thompson, Paul.**                                                    **4.3428**
The nature of work: an introduction to debates on the labour process / Paul Thompson. — London: Macmillan Press, 1984 (c1983). xvi, 305 p.; 23 cm. Includes index. 1. Industrial sociology 2. Labor and laboring classes I. T.
HD6955.T53      306/.36 19      ISBN 0333330269

**Edwards, Richard, 1944-.**                                           **4.3429**
Contested terrain: the transformation of the workplace in the twentieth century / Richard Edwards. — New York: Basic Books, c1979. ix, 261 p.; 24 cm. Includes index. 1. Labor and laboring classes — United States 2. Industrial organization — United States. 3. Industrial sociology — Case studies. I. T.
HD6957.U6 E35      301.5/5      LC 78-19942      ISBN 0465014127

**Blauner, Robert.**                                                   • **4.3430**
Alienation and freedom; the factory worker and his industry. — Chicago: University of Chicago Press, [1964] xvi, 222 p.: illus.; 24 cm. 1. Industrial sociology — United States — Case studies. I. T. II. Title: The factory worker and his industry.
HD6961.B57      331.8      LC 64-15820

**Chandler, Margaret K.**                                             • **4.3431**
Management rights and union interests. New York, McGraw-Hill [1964] xiv, 329 p. diagrs. 1. Industrial relations I. T.
HD6961 C48      LC 63-22727

**Inter-university Study of Labor Problems in Economic**               **4.3432**
**Development.**
Industrialism and industrial man reconsidered: some perspectives on a study over two decades of the problems of labor and management in economic growth: final report of the Inter–university Study of Labor Problems in Economic Development (later designated as the Inter–university Study of Human Resources in National Development) / John T. Dunlop ... [et al.]. — Princeton, N.J.: [Inter-university Study of Human Resources in National Development], 1975. 99 p.; 22 cm. 1. Industrial relations 2. Economic development I. Dunlop, John Thomas, 1914- II. Inter-university Study of Human Resources in National Development. III. T.
HD6961.I675 1975      331      LC 75-322485

**Moore, Wilbert Ellis.**                                             • **4.3433**
Industrial relations and the social order. Rev. ed. New York, Macmillan [1951] 660 p. illus. 22 cm. 1. Industrial relations I. T.
HD6961.M64 1951      658.3      LC 51-12535

**Barbash, Jack.**                                                     **4.3434**
The elements of industrial relations / Jack Barbash. — Madison, Wis.: University of Wisconsin Press, 1984. xi, 153 p.; 23 cm. Includes index. 1. Industrial relations I. T.
HD6971.B34 1984      331 19      LC 83-40258      ISBN 0299096106

**Bean, R. (Ron), 1938-.**                                            **4.3435**
Comparative industrial relations: an introduction to cross-national perspectives / by R. Bean. — New York: St. Martin's Press, 1985. 261 p.; 23 cm. Includes indexes. 1. Industrial relations I. T.
HD6971.B368 1985      331 19      LC 84-22889      ISBN 031215335X

**Dunlop, John Thomas, 1914-.**                                       • **4.3436**
Industrial relations systems. — New York: Holt, [1958] 399 p.; 21 cm. 'A Holt-Dryden book.' 1. Industrial relations I. T.
HD6971.D85      331.1      LC 59-5752

**International handbook of industrial relations: contemporary**       **4.3437**
**developments and research** / edited by Albert A. Blum.
Westport, Conn.: Greenwood Press, 1981. xiv, 698 p.; 24 cm. Includes index. 1. Industrial relations — Case studies. I. Blum, Albert A.
HD6971.I62      331      LC 79-8586      ISBN 0313213038

**Multinationals, unions, and labor relations in industrialized**      **4.3438**
**countries** / Robert F. Banks and Jack Stieber, editors.
Ithaca: New York State School of Industrial & Labor Relations, Cornell University, 1977. viii, 200 p.; 24 cm. (Cornell international industrial and labor relations reports. no. 9) 1. Industrial relations — Congresses. 2. International business enterprises — Congresses. 3. Collective bargaining — International business enterprises — Congresses. I. Banks, Robert F., 1936- II. Stieber, Jack, 1919- III. Series.
HD6971.M79      331      LC 77-4463      ISBN 087546064X

**Wilczynski, J. (Jozef), 1922-.**                                     **4.3439**
Industrial relations in planned economies, market economies, and the third world: a comparative study of ideologies, institutions, practices, and problems / J. Wilczynski. — New York: St. Martin's Press, 1983. viii, 256 p.; 23 cm. 1. Industrial relations I. T.
HD6971.W6 1983      331 19      LC 82-20551      ISBN 0312415133

**Worker militancy and its consequences, 1965–75: new directions**    **4.3440**
**in Western industrial relations / edited by Solomon Barkin.**
New York: Praeger Publishers, 1975. xxxvi, 408 p.; 24 cm. — (Praeger special studies in international economics and development) 1. Industrial relations — History — Case studies. 2. Trade-unions — History — Case studies. 3. Labor and laboring classes — History — Addresses, essays, lectures. I. Barkin, Solomon, 1907-
HD6971.W855      331/.09181/2     LC 75-3745     ISBN 0275074102 pbk

**Jones, R. Merfyn.**                            **4.3441**
The North Wales quarrymen, 1874–1922 / by R. Merfyn Jones. — Cardiff: University of Wales Press, published on behalf of the History and Law Committee of the Board of Celtic Studies, 1981. x, 359 p., [1] leaf of plates: ill., maps. —. (Studies in Welsh history. 0141-030X; 4) Maps on lining papers. 1. Stone-cutters — Wales, North — History 2. Slate industry — Wales, North — History 3. Industrial relations — Wales, North — History 4. Trade-unions — Stone-cutters — Wales, North — History I. T. II. Series.
HD6976S72 W34     ISBN 0708307760

# HD6977–7080 Wages and Cost of Living. Standard of Living

**Brown, Henry Phelps, Sir, 1906-.**              **4.3442**
A perspective of wages and prices / Henry Phelps Brown and Sheila V. Hopkins. — London; New York: Methuen, 1981. xvii, 214 p.: ill.; 24 cm. 1. Cost and standard of living — Great Britain — History — Addresses, essays, lectures. 2. Wages — Great Britain — History — Addresses, essays, lectures. 3. Income distribution — Great Britain — History — Addresses, essays, lectures. 4. Wages — Building trades — Great Britain — History — Addresses, essays, lectures. I. Hopkins, Sheila V. II. T.
HD7023.B78 1981     331.2/941 19     LC 81-188230     ISBN 0416319505

**Chapman, Janet G.**                           • **4.3443**
Real wages in Soviet Russia since 1928. Cambridge, Harvard University Press, 1963. xiv, 395 p. 'Both a dissertation under the auspices of the Department of Economics of Columbia University and part of a research program conducted by the Rand Corporation for the United States Air Force.' 1. Cost and standard of living — Russia I. T.
HD7035 C45     LC 63-13809

# HD7090–7256 Social Insurance. Social Security. Pensions. Disability

**The Evolution of social insurance, 1881–1981: studies of**    **4.3444**
**Germany, France, Great Britain, Austria, and Switzerland /**
**edited by Peter A. Köhler and Hans F. Zacher in collaboration**
**with Martin Partington.**
London: F. Pinter; New York: St. Martin's Press on behalf of the Max-Planck-Institut für Ausländisches und Internationales Sozialrecht, 1982. viii, 453 p.; 24 cm. Includes bibliographies and index. 1. Social security — Collected works. I. Köhler, Peter A. II. Zacher, Hans Friedrich, 1928- III. Partington, Martin. IV. Max-Planck-Institut für Ausländisches und Internationales Sozialrecht.
HD7091.E86 1982     368.4 19     LC 81-23258     ISBN 0312272855

**Rimlinger, Gaston V., 1926-.**                  **4.3445**
Welfare policy and industrialization in Europe, America, and Russia / [by] Gaston V. Rimlinger. — New York: Wiley [1971] xi, 362 p.; 24 cm. 1. Social security — History — Case studies. 2. Public welfare — History — Case studies. I. T.
HD7091.R48     368.4     LC 74-132856     ISBN 0471722200

**Social security in international perspective; essays in honor of**   • **4.3446**
**Eveline M. Burns. Edited by Shirley Jenkins. Contributors:**
**Henning Friis [and others]**
New York, Columbia University Press, 1969. xii, 255 p. port. 23 cm. (Social work and social issues.) 1. Social security — Addresses, essays, lectures. I. Burns, Eveline Mabel Richardson, 1900- II. Jenkins, Shirley. ed. III. Friis, Henning Kristian, 1911- IV. Series.
HD7091.S6     LC 71-94628

**Struthers, James, 1950-.**                       **4.3447**
No fault of their own: unemployment and the Canadian welfare state, 1914–1941 / James Struthers. — Toronto; Buffalo: University of Toronto Press, c1983. x, 268 p.; 24 cm. — (State and economic life. 6) Revision of thesis (doctoral)—Trent University. 1. Insurance, Unemployment — Canada — History — 20th century. 2. Unemployment — Canada — History — 20th century. 3. Welfare state — History — 20th century. 4. Unemployment — Government policy — Canada — History — 20th century. I. T. II. Series.
HD7096.C2 S87 1983     368.4/4/00971 19     LC 83-177072     ISBN 0802024807

**Haber, William, 1899-.**                      • **4.3448**
Unemployment insurance in the American economy; an historical review and analysis [by] William Haber and Merrill G. Murray. Homewood, Ill., R.D. Irwin, 1966. xx, 538 p. (The Irwin series in risk and insurace) 1. Insurance, Unemployment — United States I. Murray, Merrill Garver, 1900- jt. author II. T.
HD7096 U5 H26     LC 66-24617

**Hamermesh, Daniel S.**                       **4.3449**
Jobless pay and the economy / Daniel S. Hamermesh. Baltimore: Johns Hopkins University Press, c1977. viii, 114 p.; 21 cm. (Policy studies in employment and welfare; no. 29) 1. Insurance, Unemployment — United States. I. T.
HD7096.U5 H275     368.4/4/00973     LC 76-47369     ISBN 080181927X

# HD7101–7104 Public Health Insurance. Accident Insurance

**Feder, Judith M.**                           **4.3450**
Insuring the nation's health: market competition, catastrophic, and comprehensive approaches / Judith Feder, Jack Hadley, John Holahan. — Washington, D.C.: Urban Institute Press, c1981. xix, 227 p.: ill.; 23 cm. 1. Insurance, Health — United States I. Hadley, Jack. II. Holahan, John. III. T.
HD7102.U4 F37     368.4/2/00973 19     LC 81-51345     ISBN 0877662983

**Feldstein, Martin S.**                         **4.3451**
Hospital costs and health insurance / Martin Feldstein. — Cambridge, Mass.: Harvard University Press, 1981. ix, 327 p.: ill.; 24 cm. Consists of papers previously published, 1971-1977, by the author, with a new introd. Includes index. 1. Insurance, Health — United States — Addresses, essays, lectures. 2. Hospitals — United States — Rates — Addresses, essays, lectures. I. T.
HD7102.U4 F44     368.3/82/00973 19     LC 80-18226     ISBN 0674406753

**National health insurance: conflicting goals and policy choices /**    **4.3452**
**edited by Judith Feder, John Holahan, Theodore Marmor.**
Washington, D.C.: Urban Institute, c1980. xxi, 721 p.; 24 cm. 'UI 261-5057-1.' Includes index. 1. Insurance, Health — United States — Addresses, essays, lectures. 2. Medical economics — United States — Addresses, essays, lectures. I. Feder, Judith M. II. Holahan, John. III. Marmor, Theodore R.
HD7102.U4 N27     368.4/2/00973 19     LC 80-80045     ISBN 0877662711

**Stevens, Robert Bocking.**                     **4.3453**
Welfare medicine in America: a case study of Medicaid / [by] Robert Stevens & Rosemary Stevens. — New York: Free Press, [1974] xxii, 386 p.; 24 cm. 1. Medicaid I. Stevens, Rosemary. joint author. II. T.
HD7102.U4 S83     368.4/2/00973     LC 74-2870     ISBN 0029315204

# HD7105–7250 Pensions. Retirement

**Schulz, James H.**                           **4.3454**
The economics of aging / James H. Schulz. — 3rd ed. — New York: Van Nostrand Reinhold, c1985. xii, 212 p.: ill.; 25 cm. Includes index. 1. Old age pensions — United States. 2. Retirement income — United States. 3. Aged — United States — Economic conditions. I. T. II. Title: Aging.
HD7105.35.U6 S38 1985b     330.973/0927/0880565 19     LC 84-23340     ISBN 0442281323

**Andrews, Emily S.**                           **4.3455**
The changing profile of pensions in America / by Emily S. Andrews. — Washington, DC: Employee Benefit Research Institute, c1985. xxvii, 234 p.; 23 cm. (EBRI-ERF policy study.) Includes index. 1. Pension trusts — United

States. 2. Retirement income — United States. 3. Retirement — Economic aspects — United States. I. T. II. Series.
HD7105.45.U6 A53 1985     332.6/7254 19     *LC* 85-25296     *ISBN* 0866430385

**Munnell, Alicia Haydock.**                                               **4.3456**
The economics of private pensions / Alicia H. Munnell. — Washington, D.C.: Brookings Institution, c1982. xiii, 240 p.: ill.; 24 cm. — (Studies in social economics.) 1. Old age pensions — United States. I. T. II. Series.
HD7106.U5 M83 1982     331.25/2/0973 19     *LC* 82-4223     *ISBN* 0815758944

## HD7121–7250 By Region or Country

**Altmeyer, Arthur Joseph, 1891-.**                                    • **4.3457**
The formative years of social security [by] Arthur J. Altmeyer. Madison, University of Wisconsin Press, 1966. xi, 314 p. facsim., ports. 'Official documents of social security, 1935-65': p. 288-294. 1. United States. Social Security Act I. T.
HD7124 A65     *LC* 66-11801

**Douglas, Paul Howard, 1892-.**                                       • **4.3458**
Social security in the United States [by] Paul H. Douglas. New York, Arno Press, 1971 [c1936] xi, 384 p. 23 cm. (Poverty, U.S.A.: the historical record) 1. United States. Social Security Act 2. Social security — United States. I. United States. Laws, statutes, etc. II. T. III. Series.
HD7124.D6 1971     368.4/00973     *LC* 71-137164     *ISBN* 0405031025

**Aaron, Henry J.**                                                         **4.3459**
Economic effects of social security / Henry J. Aaron. — Washington, D.C.: Brookings Institution, c1982. xii, 84 p.: ill.; 24 cm. — (Studies of government finance.) 1. Social security — United States. I. T. II. Series.
HD7125.A178 1982     368.4/3/00973 19     *LC* 82-73654     *ISBN* 081570030X

**A Challenge to social security: the changing roles of women and         4.3460
men in American society / edited by Richard V. Burkhauser,
Karen C. Holden.**
New York: Academic Press, c1982. xxii, 272 p.; 24 cm. — (Institute for Research on Poverty monograph series.) Includes index. 1. Social security — United States. 2. Survivors' benefits — United States. 3. Family policy — United States. I. Burkhauser, Richard V. II. Holden, Karen C. III. Series.
HD7125.C476 1982     368.4/3/00973 19     *LC* 82-1596     *ISBN* 0121446808

**Controlling the cost of social security / edited by Colin D.           4.3461
Campbell.**
Lexington, Mass.: Lexington Books, c1984. xvii, 269 p.; 24 cm. Papers originally presented at a conference sponsored by the American Enterprise Institute for Public Policy Research in Washington, D.C., June 25-26, 1981. 'An American Enterprise Institute book.' 1. Social security — United States — Addresses, essays, lectures. I. Campbell, Colin Dearborn, 1917- II. American Enterprise Institute for Public Policy Research.
HD7125.C649 1984     353.0082/56 19     *LC* 83-12053     *ISBN* 0669069183

**The Crisis in social security: problems and prospects / Michael       4.3462
J. Boskin, editor; George F. Break ... [et al., contributors].**
San Francisco: Institute for Contemporary Studies, c1977. xiii, 214 p.: graphs; 21 cm. 1. Social security — United States — Addresses, essays, lectures. I. Boskin, Michael J. II. Break, George F.
HD7125.C74     368.4/00973     *LC* 77-72542     *ISBN* 0917616162

**Derthick, Martha.**                                                       **4.3463**
Policymaking for social security / Martha Derthick. — Washington: Brookings Institution, c1979. xiv, 446 p.; 24 cm. 1. Social security — United States. I. T.
HD7125.D48     368.4/00973     *LC* 78-24811     *ISBN* 0815718160

**Ferrara, Peter J., 1956-.**                                              **4.3464**
Social security: the inherent contradiction / Peter J. Ferrara. — San Francisco, Calif.: Cato Institute, c1980. ix, 484 p.: ill.; 24 cm. — (Studies in public policy) 1. Social security — United States. I. T.
HD7125.F47     368.4/3/00973 19     *LC* 80-18949     *ISBN* 0932790240

**Ippolito, Richard A.**                                                    **4.3465**
Pensions, economics, and public policy / Richard A. Ippolito. — Homewood, Ill.: Published for the Pension Research Council, Wharton School, University of Pennsylvania by Dow Jones-Irwin, 1986. xxiii, 267 p.: ill.; 24 cm. Includes index. 1. Pensions — United States I. Wharton School. Pension Research Council. II. T.
HD7125.I58 1986     331.25/2/0973 19     *LC* 85-73289     *ISBN* 0870947605

**Lubove, Roy.**                                                          • **4.3466**
The struggle for social security, 1900–1935. Cambridge, Harvard University Press, 1968. viii, 276 p. 22 cm. (A publication of the Center for the Study of the History of Liberty in America, Harvard University) 1. Social security — United States — History. I. T.
HD7125.L8     368.4/3/00973 19     *LC* 68-14265

**Munnell, Alicia Haydock.**                                               **4.3467**
The future of social security / Alicia H. Munnell. Washington: Brookings Institution, c1977. xiii, 190 p.: ill.; 24 cm. (Studies in social economics.) 1. Social security — United States. I. T. II. Series.
HD7125.M75     368.4/00973     *LC* 76-51883     *ISBN* 0815758960

**Pensions, labor, and individual choice / edited by David A.           4.3468
Wise.**
Chicago: University of Chicago Press, 1985. viii, 453 p.: ill.; 24 cm. (National Bureau of Economic Research project report.) 1. Pensions — United States — Addresses, essays, lectures. 2. Pension trusts — United States — Addresses, essays, lectures. I. Wise, David A. II. Series.
HD7125.P393 1985     331.25/2/0973 19     *LC* 85-1118     *ISBN* 0226902935

**Ricardo-Campbell, Rita.**                                                **4.3469**
Social security: promise and reality / Rita Ricardo Campbell. — Stanford, Calif.: Hoover Institution Press, Stanford University, c1977. xvi, 351 p.: graphs; 24 cm. (Hoover Institution publication; 179) Includes index. 1. Social security — United States. I. T.
HD7125.R5     368.4/00973     *LC* 77-152469     *ISBN* 0817967915

**Social security financing / edited by Felicity Skidmore.              4.3470**
Cambridge, Mass.: MIT Press, c1981. xiii, 295 p.; 24 cm. Papers from a symposium on alternate methods of social security financing held in Washington, D.C., Apr. 21-22, 1980. 1. Social security — United States — Finance — Congresses. I. Skidmore, Felicity.
HD7125.S5983     353.0082/56 19     *LC* 81-5963     *ISBN* 0262191962

**Stein, Bruno, 1930-.**                                                    **4.3471**
Social security and pensions in transition: understanding the American retirement system / Bruno Stein. — New York: Free Press, c1980. xx, 308 p.: ill.; 25 cm. Includes index. 1. Social security — United States. 2. Old age pensions — United States. I. T.
HD7125.S73     368.4/00973     *LC* 79-7632     *ISBN* 002930850X

**Weaver, Carolyn L.**                                                      **4.3472**
The crisis in social security: economic and political origins / Carolyn L. Weaver. — Durham, N.C.: Duke University Press, 1982. x, 249 p.: ill.; 24 cm. — (Duke Press policy studies.) 1. Social security — United States — History. I. T. II. Series.
HD7125.W397 1982     368.4/3/00973 19     *LC* 82-9623     *ISBN* 0822304740

**Mesa-Lago, Carmelo, 1934-.**                                             **4.3473**
Social security in Latin America: pressure groups, stratification, and inequality / Carmelo Mesa-Lago. — Pittsburgh: University of Pittsburgh Press, c1978. xix, 351 p.; 25 cm. (Pitt Latin American series) 1. Social security — Latin America — Case studies. I. T.
HD7130.5.M47     368.4/0098     *LC* 77-15732     *ISBN* 0822933683

## HD7255–7256 REHABILITATION OF THE DISABLED

**Burkhauser, Richard V.**                                                 **4.3474**
Disability and work: the economics of American policy / Richard V. Burkhauser and Robert H. Haveman with the assistance of George Parsons. — Baltimore: Johns Hopkins University Press, c1982. vii, 131 p.; 21 cm. — (Policy studies in employment and welfare. no. 38) Includes index. 1. Handicapped — Employment — United States. 2. Handicapped — Government policy — United States. I. Haveman, Robert H. II. Parsons, George. III. T. IV. Series.
HD7256.U5 B87 1982     331.5/9/0973 19     *LC* 82-113     *ISBN* 0801828341

**Haveman, Robert H.**                                                      **4.3475**
Public policy toward disabled workers: cross–national analyses of economic impacts / Robert H. Haveman, Victor Halberstadt, Richard V. Burkhauser. — Ithaca: Cornell University Press, 1985 (c1984). xi, 583 p.; 25 cm. 1. Vocational rehabilitation — Government policy — United States. 2. Insurance, Disability — Government policy — United States. 3. Vocational rehabilitation — Government policy. 4. Insurance, Disability — Government policy. I. Halberstadt, Victor. II. Burkhauser, Richard V. III. T.
HD7256.U5 H39     362.8/5/0973 19     *LC* 83-73115     *ISBN* 0801416264

**Levitan, Sar A.**       **4.3476**
Jobs for the disabled / Sar A. Levitan and Robert Taggart. Baltimore: Johns Hopkins University Press, c1977. xiii, 129 p.: ill.; 21 cm. (Policy studies in employment and welfare; no. 28) 1. Handicapped — Employment — United States. 2. Vocational rehabilitation — United States. I. Taggart, Robert, 1945- joint author. II. T.
HD7256.U5 L48     331.5/9/0973     *LC* 76-49910     *ISBN* 0801819253

# HD7262–7269 Industrial Safety. Accidents

**Blake, Roland Patton, ed.**       **4.3477**
Industrial safety / edited by Roland P. Blake. 3d ed. Englewood Cliffs, N.J.: Prentice-Hall, 1963. ix, 405 p.: ill.; 24 cm. 1. Industrial safety I. T.
HD7262.B5 1963     331.823     *LC* 63-14723     *ISBN* 0134631331

**Grimaldi, John V., 1916-.**       **4.3478**
Safety management / John V. Grimaldi, Rollin H. Simonds. — 4th ed. — Homewood, Ill.: R.D. Irwin, 1984. xv, 638 p.: ill.; 25 cm. 1. Industrial safety — Management. I. Simonds, Rollin H. II. T.
HD7262.G76 1984     658.3/82 19     *LC* 83-81171     *ISBN* 025602507X

**Lagadec, Patrick.**       **4.3479**
[Risque technologique majeur. English] Major technological risk: an assessment of industrial disasters / Patrick Lagadec; translated from the French by H. Ostwald; technical editor, J.C. Chicken. — 1st ed. — Oxford; New York: Pergamon Press, 1982. xix, 516 p.: ill.; 24 cm. Translation of: Le risque technologique majeur. 1. Industrial accidents 2. Industrial safety 3. Health risk assessment I. T.
HD7262.L2413 1982     363.1/1 19     *LC* 82-3678     *ISBN* 0080289134

**Bacow, Lawrence S.**       **4.3480**
Bargaining for job safety and health / Lawrence S. Bacow. — Cambridge, Mass.: MIT Press, c1980. x, 159 p.; 24 cm. Includes index. 1. Industrial safety — United States. 2. Industrial hygiene — United States. 3. Collective bargaining — United States. I. T.
HD7262.5.U6 B32     331.89     *LC* 80-16602     *ISBN* 0262021528

# HD7285–7390 Housing

**Housing needs and policy approaches: trends in thirteen**       **4.3481**
**countries / edited by Willem van Vliet—, Elizabeth Huttman, and Sylvia Fava.**
Durham: Duke University Press, 1985. xi, 376 p.: ill.; 24 cm. (Duke Press policy studies.) Includes indexes. 1. Housing policy 2. Housing policy — Developing countries 3. Housing — Social aspects. I. Van Vliet, Willem. II. Huttman, Elizabeth D., 1929- III. Fava, Sylvia Fleis, 1927- IV. Series.
HD7287.H68 1985     363.5/8 19     *LC* 85-4549     *ISBN* 0822305879

**Housing and identity: cross–cultural perspectives / edited by**       **4.3482**
**James S. Duncan.**
New York: Holmes & Meier, 1982. 250 p.; 23 cm. Includes index. 1. Housing — Addresses, essays, lectures. 2. Housing — Psychological aspects — Addresses, essays, lectures. 3. Architecture, Domestic — Addresses, essays, lectures. I. Duncan, James S. (James Stuart), 1945-
HD7287.5.H46 1982     363.5 19     *LC* 81-4837     *ISBN* 0841907013

**Boléat, Mark.**       **4.3483**
National housing finance systems: a comparative study / Mark Boleat. — London: Croom Helm in association with The International Union of Building Societies and Savings Associations, c1985. 489 p.; 25 cm. 1. Housing — Finance. I. International Union of Building Societies and Savings Associations. II. T.
HD7287.55.Bx     338.4/33635 19     *ISBN* 0709932499

**Rent control, myths & realities: international evidence of the**       **4.3484**
**effects of rent control in six countries / contributors include, Milton Friedman, Friedrich Hayek, and Basil Kalymon; co-edited by Walter Block and Edgar Olsen.**
Vancouver, B.C., Canada: Fraser Institute, 1981. xxiii, 335 p.: ill.; 22 cm. 1. Rent control — Addresses, essays, lectures. I. Friedman, Milton, 1912- II. Hayek, Friedrich A. von (Friedrich August), 1899- III. Kalymon, Basil, 1944- IV. Block, Walter, 1941- V. Olsen, Edgar O. VI. Title: Rent control, myths and realities.
HD7288.82.R45 1981b     363.5/6 19     *LC* 82-213742     *ISBN* 0889750335

## HD7291–7390 BY REGION OR COUNTRY

**North American housing markets into the twenty–first century /**       **4.3485**
**edited by George W. Gau and Michael A. Goldberg.**
Cambridge, Mass.: Ballinger Pub. Co., c1983. xxv, 383 p.: ill.; 24 cm. Papers presented at a symposium held at the University of British Columbia in July 1981. 1. Housing — North America — Forecasting — Congresses. 2. Population forecasting — North America — Congresses. 3. Twenty-first century — Forecasts — Congresses. I. Gau, George W. II. Golberg, Michael A.
HD7292.A3 N67 1983     381/.456908/097 19     *LC* 82-18495     *ISBN* 0884108805

**Grigsby, William G., 1927-.**       • **4.3486**
Housing markets and public policy. Philadelphia: University of Pennsylvania Press [1963] 346 p.: diagrs., tables; 22 cm. (City planning series) 1. Housing — United States I. T.
HD7293 A3 G7     *LC* 63-15010

**America's housing crisis: what is to be done? / edited by**       **4.3487**
**Chester Hartman (The Institute for Policy Studies).**
Boston: Routledge & Kegan Paul, 1983. xi, 249 p.; 22 cm. — (Alternative policies for America.) 1. Housing policy — United States — Addresses, essays, lectures. I. Hartman, Chester W. II. Institute for Policy Studies. III. Series.
HD7293.A6877 1983     363.5/8/0973 19     *LC* 83-11228     *ISBN* 0710200390

**America's housing: prospects and problems / [edited by] George**       **4.3488**
**Sternlieb, James W. Hughes, and Robert W. Burchell ... [et al.].**
New Brunswick, N.J.: Center for Urban Policy Research, Rutgers University, c1980. xiv, 562 p.: ill.; 24 cm. 1. Housing — United States — Addresses, essays, lectures. I. Sternlieb, George. II. Hughes, James W.
HD7293.A688     363.5/0973     *LC* 80-10700     *ISBN* 0882850636

**The Great housing experiment / edited by Joseph Friedman and**       **4.3489**
**Daniel H. Weinberg.**
Beverly Hills: Sage Publications, c1983. 287 p.: ill.; 23 cm. (Urban affairs annual reviews. v. 24) 1. Housing policy — United States — Addresses, essays, lectures. 2. Housing subsidies — United States — Addresses, essays, lectures. I. Friedman, Joseph, 1944- II. Weinberg, Daniel H. III. Series.
HD7293.Ax     307.7/6 s 363.5/8 19     *LC* 83-3062     *ISBN* 0803919913

**Solomon, Arthur P.**       **4.3490**
Housing the urban poor: a critical evaluation of Federal housing policy / [by] Arthur P. Solomon. — Cambridge, Mass.: MIT Press, [1974] xv, 229 p.; 24 cm. (A Publication of the Joint Center for Urban Studies of the Massachusetts Institute of Technology and Harvard University) 1. Housing policy — United States. 2. Cities and towns — United States. 3. Urban poor — United States. I. T.
HD7293.S63     301.5/4     *LC* 73-22360     *ISBN* 0262191202

**Starr, Roger.**       **4.3491**
Housing and the money market / Roger Starr. — New York: Basic Books, [1975] vi, 250 p.; 25 cm. 1. Housing — United States. 2. Housing — United States — Finance. I. T.
HD7293.S66     333.3/3     *LC* 73-91083     *ISBN* 0465030726

**Lubove, Roy.**       • **4.3492**
The progressives and the slums: tenement house reform in New York City, 1890–1917 / forewords by Samuel P. Hays & Philip S. Broughton. — [Pittsburgh]: University of Pittsburgh Press [1963, c1962] 284 p.: ill.; 24 cm. Includes bibliography. 1. Slums — New York (City) 2. Progressivism (U.S. politics) I. T.
HD7304.N5L8     331.833     *LC* 62-14380

**Kain, John F.**       **4.3493**
Housing markets and racial discrimination: a microeconomic analysis / John F. Kain; John M. Quigley. — New York: National Bureau of Economic Research: distributed by Columbia University Press, 1975. xx, 393 p.: ill.; 24 cm. (Urban and regional studies; no. 3) Includes index. 1. Discrimination in housing — St. Louis metropolitan area. 2. Discrimination in housing — St. Louis metropolitan area — Mathematical models. 3. Housing — St. Louis metropolitan area — Mathematical models. I. Quigley, John M. joint author. II. T.
HD7304.S2 K34     301.5/4     *LC* 75-17521     *ISBN* 0870142704

**Meehan, Eugene J.**       **4.3494**
The quality of federal policymaking: programmed failure in public housing / Eugene J. Meehan. — Columbia: University of Missouri Press, 1979. 230 p., [8] leaves of plates: ill.; 24 cm. Includes index. 1. Public housing — Missouri — St. Louis. I. T.
HD7304.S2 M433     301.5/4     *LC* 78-27663     *ISBN* 0826202721

**Daunton, M. J. (Martin J.)**                              **4.3495**
House and home in the Victorian city: working class housing, 1850–1914 / M.J.
Daunton. — London; Baltimore, Md., USA: E. Arnold, 1983. ix, 320 p., [22] p.
of plates: ill.; 24 cm. — (Studies in urban history. 7) 1. Housing policy — Great
Britain — History — 19th century. 2. Housing — Great Britain — History —
19th century. 3. Labor and laboring classes — Dwellings — Great Britain —
History — 19th century. 4. Housing policy — Great Britain — History — 20th
century. 5. Housing — Great Britain — History — 20th century. 6. Labor and
laboring classes — Dwellings — Great Britain — History — 20th century. I. T.
II. Series.
HD7333.A3 D38 1983      363.5/56/0941 19      *LC* 83-243936      *ISBN*
0713163844

**Gauldie, Enid.**                              **4.3496**
Cruel habitations; a history of working–class housing 1780–1918. — New York:
Barnes and Noble Books, [1974] 363 p.: illus.; 23 cm. 1. Housing — Great
Britain — History. 2. Labor and laboring classes — Great Britain — History
I. T.
HD7333.A3 G38      301.5/4      *ISBN* 0604923347

**Burnett, John, 1925-.**                              **4.3497**
A social history of housing, 1815–1970 / John Burnett; illustrated by
Christopher Powell. — Newton Abbot [Eng.]; North Pomfret, Vt.: David and
Charles, 1978. viii, 344 p., [8] leaves of plates: ill.; 24 cm. 1. Housing —
England — History. I. T.
HD7334.A3 B87      363.5/0941 19      *LC* 77-91461      *ISBN* 0715375245

**Wohl, Anthony S.**                              **4.3498**
The eternal slum: housing and social policy in Victorian London / Anthony S.
Wohl. — Montreal: McGill-Queen's University Press, 1977. xxiv, 386 p., [8]
leaves of plates: ill., graphs, maps, plans, ports.; 24 cm. — (Studies in urban
history. 5) 'A note on sources': p. 341-355. Includes index. 1. Housing —
England — London — History. 2. Housing policy — England — London —
History. 3. Slums — England — London — History. 4. London (England) —
Social policy — History. I. T. II. Series.
HD7334.L6 W63 1977      301.5/4      *LC* 78-310875      *ISBN* 0773503110

**Andrusz, Gregory D.**                              **4.3499**
Housing and urban development in the USSR / Gregory D. Andrusz. —
Albany: State University of New York Press, c1984. xix, 354 p.; 23 cm. Includes
index. 1. Housing — Soviet Union. 2. Housing policy — Soviet Union. 3. City
planning — Soviet Union. I. T.
HD7345.A3 A68 1984      363.5/0947 19      *LC* 83-24258      *ISBN*
0873959116

**Wiebe, Paul D.**                              **4.3500**
Social life in an Indian slum / Paul D. Wiebe. — Durham, N.C.: Carolina
Academic Press, c1975. vii, 179 p.: map; 23 cm. Includes index. 1. Slums —
India. 2. City and town life — India. 3. India — Social conditions — 1947-
I. T.
HD7361.A3 W53      301.36/3      *LC* 75-5480      *ISBN* 089089051X

**Rosenzweig, Roy.**                              **4.3501**
Eight hours for what we will: workers and leisure in an industrial city,
1870–1920 / Roy Rosenzweig. — Cambridge [Cambridgeshire]; New York:
Cambridge University Press, 1983. xi, 304 p.; 23 cm. — (Interdisciplinary
perspectives on modern history.) 1. Labor and laboring classes —
Massachusetts — Worcester — Recreation — History. 2. Worcester, Mass —
Social conditions. I. T. II. Series.
HD7395.R4 R67 1983      306/.48/097443 19      *LC* 82-25256      *ISBN*
0521239168

# HD7651–7801 Industrial Hygiene.
# Welfare Services. International
# Organizations

**Ashford, Nicholas Askounes.**                              **4.3502**
Crisis in the workplace: occupational disease and injury: a report to the Ford
Foundation / Nicholas Askounes Ashford. — Cambridge, Mass.: MIT Press,
c1976. xii, 588 p.; 24 cm. Includes index. 1. United States. Occupational Safety
and Health Administration. 2. Industrial hygiene — United States.
3. Industrial safety — United States. I. Ford Foundation. II. T.
HD7654.A77      614.8/52      *LC* 75-28424      *ISBN* 0262010453

**Masi, Dale A.**                              **4.3503**
Human services in industry / Dale A. Masi. — Lexington, Mass.: Lexington
Books, c1982. xvi, 246 p.; 24 cm. 1. Welfare work in industry — United States.
2. Social service — United States. I. T.
HD7654.M36      658.3/8/0973 19      *LC* 81-47872      *ISBN* 0669051047

**Mendeloff, John M.**                              **4.3504**
Regulating safety: an economic and political analysis of occupational safety and
health policy / John Mendeloff. — Cambridge, Mass.: MIT Press, c1979. xiii,
219 p.: ill.; 24 cm. Includes index. 1. United States. Occupational Safety and
Health Administration. 2. Industrial hygiene — United States. 3. Industrial
safety — United States. I. T.
HD7654.M46      614.8/52      *LC* 78-10637      *ISBN* 026213148X

**Viscusi, W. Kip.**                              **4.3505**
Risk by choice: regulating health and safety in the workplace / W. Kip Viscusi.
— Cambridge, Mass.: Harvard University Press, 1983. vii, 200 p.; 25 cm.
Includes index. 1. Industrial hygiene — United States. 2. Industrial safety —
United States. 3. Industry and state — United States. I. T.
HD7654.V57 1983      363.1/15/0973 19      *LC* 82-15591      *ISBN*
0674773020

**Alcock, Antony Evelyn.**                              **4.3506**
History of the International Labor Organization, by Antony Alcock. [1st
American ed.] New York, Octagon Books, 1971. x, 384 p. 23 cm.
1. International Labour Organisation — History. I. T.
HD7801.A53 1971b      331/.061/1      *LC* 78-144821      *ISBN*
0374901279

**Millis, Harry Alvin, 1873-1948.**                              **• 4.3507**
From the Wagner act to Taft–Hartley; a study of national labor policy and labor
relations, by Harry A. Millis and Emily Clark Brown. [Chicago] University of
Chicago Press [1950] x, 723 p. 1. United States. Labor Management Relations
Act, 1947. 2. Labor laws and legislation — United States I. Brown, Emily
Clark, 1895- II. T.
HD7834 M55      *LC* 50-7091

# HD8001–8013 Government
# Employees

**Kaye, Seymour P.**                              **4.3508**
International manual on collective bargaining for public employees. Edited by
Seymour P. Kaye [and] Arthur Marsh. Foreword by Theodore W. Kheel. —
New York: Praeger, [1973] xxii, 389 p.; 25 cm. — (Praeger special studies in
international politics and government) 1. Collective labor agreements —
Government employees — Addresses, essays, lectures. I. Marsh, Arthur Ivor.
joint author. II. T.
HD8005.5.K3x      344.01/89/04135      *LC* 71-130530

**Levitan, Sar A.**                              **4.3509**
Working for the sovereign: employee relations in the Federal Government / Sar
A. Levitan, Alexandra B. Noden. — Baltimore: Johns Hopkins University
Press, c1983. x, 152 p.: ill.; 21 cm. — (Policy studies in employment and
welfare. no. 39) 1. Collective bargaining — Government employees — United
States. 2. Civil service — United States — Personnel management.
3. Employee-management relations in government — United States. 4. United
States — Officials and employees I. Noden, Alexandra B. II. T. III. Series.
HD8005.6.U5 L479 1983      331/.041353 19      *LC* 82-49064      *ISBN*
0801830281

**Hart, Wilson R.**                              **• 4.3510**
Collective bargaining in the Federal civil service; a study of labor–management
relations in United States Government employment. [1st ed.] New York,
Harper [1961] 302 p. 1. Collective bargaining — United States 2. Civil service
— United States I. T.
HD8008 H3      *LC* 61-7926

**Moskow, Michael H.**                              **• 4.3511**
Collective bargaining in public employment [by] Michael H. Moskow, J. Joseph
Loewenberg [and] Edward Clifford Koziara. — New York: Random House,
[1970] xiv, 336 p.; 22 cm. 1. Collective bargaining — Government employees
— U.S. I. Loewenberg, J    Joseph. joint author. II. Koziara, Edward
Clifford. joint author. III. T.
HD8008.M6      353.001/74      *LC* 78-101742

**Schick, Richard P.**                              **4.3512**
The public interest in government labor relations / Richard P. Schick, Jean J.
Couturier. Cambridge, Mass.: Ballinger Pub. Co., c1977. xvi, 264 p.; 24 cm.
Includes index. 1. Collective bargaining — Government employees — United
States — Case studies. 2. Public interest I. Couturier, Jean J., joint author.
II. T.
HD8008.S36      331.89/041/35      *LC* 76-46642      *ISBN* 0884102459

**Wellington, Harry H.**                              **• 4.3513**
The unions and the cities [by] Harry H. Wellington and Ralph K. Winter, Jr.
Washington, Brookings Institution [1972, c1971] xiii, 226 p. 24 cm. (Studies of
unionism in government) 1. Collective bargaining — Municipal employees —

United States. I. Winter, Ralph K., 1935- joint author. II. Brookings Institution. III. T. IV. Series.
HD8008.W4     331.89/041/352005     LC 79-179327     ISBN 0815792948

**Caiden, Gerald E.**        • 4.3514
Public employment compulsory arbitration in Australia / Gerald E. Caiden. — Ann Arbor: Institute of Labor and Industrial Relations, The University of Michigan-Wayne State University, 1971. 152 p. — (Comparative studies in public employment labor relations) 1. Arbitration, Industrial — Australia. 2. Collective bargains — Government employees — Australia. I. Institute of Labour and Industrial Relations (University of Michigan-Wayne State University) II. T. III. Series.
HD8013.A938 C133 1971     LC 79-634392

**Blanpain, R. (Roger), 1932-.**        • 4.3515
Public employee unionism in Belgium. Ann Arbor, Institute of Labor and Industrial Relations, University of Michigan—Wayne State University, 1971. v, 99 p. 23 cm. (Comparative studies in public employment labor relations) 1. Trade-unions — Government employees — Belgium. 2. Employee-management relations in government — Belgium. I. T. II. Series.
HD8013.B6 B5     331.88/09493     LC 76-634393     ISBN 0877360030 ISBN 0877360049

**Arthurs, H. W. (Harry William), 1935-.**        • 4.3516
Collective bargaining by public employees in Canada: five models [by] H. W. Arthurs. Ann Arbor, Institute of Labor and Industrial Relations, University of Michigan-Wayne State University, 1971. vii, 166 p. 23 cm. (Comparative studies in public employment labor relations.) 1. Collective bargaining — Government employees — Canada. I. T. II. Series.
HD8013.C23 A7     331.89     LC 70-634394     ISBN 0877360057 ISBN 0877360065

**McPherson, William Heston, 1902-.**        • 4.3517
Public employee relations in West Germany [by] William H. McPherson. Ann Arbor, Institute of Labor and Industrial Relations, University of Michigan-Wayne State University, 1971. xii, 251 p. 23 cm. (Comparative studies in public employment labor relations) 1. Employee-management relations in government — Germany (West) 2. Collective bargaining — Government employees — Germany (West) I. T. II. Series.
HD8013.G23 M32     331.89/041/35443     LC 77-634396     ISBN 0877360090 ISBN 0877360103

**Hepple, B. A.**        • 4.3518
Public employee trade unionism in the United Kingdom: the legal framework [by] B. A. Hepple [and] Paul O'Higgins. Ann Arbor, Institute of Labor and Industrial Relations, University of Michigan-Wayne State University, 1971. 221 p. 23 cm. (Comparative studies in public employment labor relations.) 1. Collective labor agreements — Government employees — Great Britain. 2. Employee-management relations in government — Great Britain. I. O'Higgins, Paul. joint author. II. T. III. Series.
LAW     HD8013.G53H4.     344/.42/018     LC 70-634397     ISBN 0877360111 ISBN 087736012X

**Lefkowitz, Jerome.**        • 4.3519
Public employee unionism in Israel. Ann Arbor, Institute of Labor and Industrial Relations, University of Michigan-Wayne State University, 1971. 91 p. 23 cm. (Comparative studies in public employment labor relations) 1. Collective labor agreements — Government employees — Israel. 2. Strikes and lockouts — Civil service — Law and legislation — Israel. 3. Employee-management relations in government — Law and legislation — Israel. I. T. II. Series.
LAW     HD8013.P15 L4x.     344/.5694/018     LC 78-634400
    ISBN 0877360170 ISBN 0877360189

# HD8038 Professions: General

**Shapero, Albert.**        4.3520
Managing professional people: understanding creative performance / Albert Shapero. — New York: Free Press; London: Collier Macmillan, c1985. xviii, 252 p.; 24 cm. Includes index. 1. Professions 2. Personnel management I. T.
HD8038.A1 S53 1985     658.3/044 19     LC 84-18728     ISBN 0029288703

# HD8039 Labor, by Industry or Trade, A–Z

## HD8039.A–L

**Chinoy, Ely.**        • 4.3521
Automobile workers and the American dream. Garden City, N.Y., Doubleday, 1955. 139 p. (Doubleday publications in sociology and anthropology) 1. Automobile industry workers — United States I. T.
HD8039 A82 U63     LC 55-6609

**Dawley, Alan, 1943-.**        4.3522
Class and community: the industrial revolution in Lynn / Alan Dawley. — Cambridge, Mass.: Harvard University Press, 1976. viii, 301 p.: ill.; 24 cm. (Harvard studies in urban history.) Includes index. 1. Shoemakers — Lynn, Mass. 2. Social classes — Lynn, Mass. 3. Shoe industry — Massachusetts — Lynn. I. T. II. Series.
HD8039.B72 U618     331/.045/3097445     LC 75-29049     ISBN 0674133900

**Faler, Paul G. (Paul Gustaf), 1940-.**        4.3523
Mechanics and manufacturers in the early industrial revolution: Lynn, Massachusetts, 1760–1860 / Paul G. Faler. — Albany: State University of New York Press, c1981. xvii, 267 p.; 24 cm. — (SUNY series in American social history.) Includes index. 1. Shoemakers — Massachusetts — Lynn — History. 2. Boots and shoes — Trade and manufacture — Massachusetts — Lynn — History. 3. Labor and laboring classes — Massachusetts — Lynn — History. 4. Lynn (Mass.) — Social conditions. I. T. II. Series.
HD8039.B72 U657     HD8039S72 U657.     331.7/68531/0097445 19
    LC 80-21619     ISBN 0873955048

**Mills, Daniel Quinn.**        4.3524
Industrial relations and manpower in construction. — Cambridge, Mass.: M.I.T. Press, [1972] x, 297 p.; 24 cm. 1. Construction workers — United States. 2. Collective bargaining — Construction industry — United States. 3. Construction industry — United States. I. T.
HD8039.B92U649     338.4/7/6240973     LC 77-161850     ISBN 0262130785

**Fairchilds, Cissie C.**        4.3525
Domestic enemies: servants & their masters in Old Regime France / Cissie Fairchilds. — Baltimore: Johns Hopkins University Press, c1984. xvi, 325 p.: ill.; 24 cm. Includes index. 1. Domestics — France — History — 18th century. 2. Master and servant — France — History — 18th century. I. T.
HD8039.D52 F837 1984     305.4/364 19     LC 83-48059     ISBN 080182978X

**Maza, Sarah C., 1953-.**        4.3526
Servants and masters in eighteenth–century France: the uses of loyalty / Sarah C. Maza. — Princeton, N.J.: Princeton University Press, c1983. xiv, 368 p.: ill.; 23 cm. Includes index. 1. Domestics — France — History — 18th century. 2. Master and servant — France — History — 18th century. I. T.
HD8039.D52 F85 1983     305.4/364 19     LC 83-42566     ISBN 0069053944

**Schatz, Ronald W., 1949-.**        4.3527
The electrical workers: a history of labor at General Electric and Westinghouse, 1923–1960 / Ronald W. Schatz. — Urbana: University of Illinois Press, c1983. xv, 279 p.: ill.; 24 cm. — (Working class in American history.) Includes index. 1. General Electric Company — History. 2. Westinghouse Electric Corporation — History. 3. Trade-unions and communism — United States — History. 4. Electric industry workers — United States — History. 5. Trade-unions — Electric industry workers — United States — History. I. T. II. Series.
HD8039.E32 U67 1983     331.88/12138/0973 19     LC 82-20284
    ISBN 0252010310

**Fite, Gilbert Courtland, 1918-.**        4.3528
American farmers: the new minority / Gilbert C. Fite. — Bloomington: Indiana University Press, c1981. ix, 265 p., [10] p. of plates: ill.; 24 cm. — (Minorities in modern America.) 1. Farmers — United States 2. Farmers — United States — Political activity. 3. Agriculture — Economic aspects — United States. 4. Agriculture and state — United States 5. United States — Rural conditions I. T. II. Series.
HD8039.F32 U64     306/.3 19     LC 80-8843     ISBN 0253301823

**Horowitz, Morris Aaron.**        • 4.3529
The New York hotel industry; a labor relations study. Cambridge, Mass., Harvard University Press, 1960. 265 p. illus. 25 cm. (Wertheim publications in industrial relations.) Includes bibliography. 1. Hotels, taverns, etc —

Employees — New York (City) 2. Industrial relations — New York (City) I. T. II. Series.
HD8039.H82U63     331.184794     *LC* 60-7992

**Brody, David, 1930-.**     • **4.3530**
Steelworkers in America; the nonunion era. — New York: Russell & Russell, [1970, c1960] viii, 303 p.; 22 cm. — (Harvard historical monographs. 45) 'Revision of a dissertation ... Harvard University.' 1. Iron and steel workers — United States I. T. II. Series.
HD8039.I52U52 1970     331.7/66/91420973     *LC* 76-83855

**Kornblum, William.**     **4.3531**
Blue collar community / William Kornblum; with a foreword by Morris Janowitz. — Chicago: University of Chicago Press, 1975 (c1974). xvii, 260 p.; ill.; 23 cm. (Studies of urban society) Includes index. 1. Iron and steel workers — Illinois — Chicago. 2. Trade-unions — Iron and steel workers — Illinois — Chicago. 3. Iron and steel workers — Illinois — Chicago — Political activity. 4. Chicago — Social conditions. I. T.
HD8039.I52 U56     301.44/42/0977311     *LC* 74-5733     *ISBN* 0226450376

**Walkowitz, Daniel J.**     **4.3532**
Worker city, company town: iron and cotton-worker protest in Troy and Cohoes, New York, 1855–84 / Daniel J. Walkowitz. — Urbana: University of Illinois Press, c1978. xv, 292 p.; ill.; 24 cm. (Working class in American history.) Based on the author's thesis, University of Rochester, 1972. Includes index. 1. Iron and steel workers — New York (State) — Troy — History. 2. Textile workers — New York (State) — Cohoes — History. 3. Cotton manufacture — New York (State) — Cohoes — History. 4. Troy (N.Y.) — Social conditions. 5. Cohoes (N.Y.) — Social conditions. I. T. II. Series.
HD8039.I52 U67     301.44/42/0974741     *LC* 78-18305     *ISBN* 0252006674

**Larrowe, Charles P.**     • **4.3533**
Shape-up and hiring hall; a comparison of hiring methods and labor relations on the New York and Seattle waterfronts. Berkeley, University of California Press, 1955. ix, 250 p. illus., ports., map. 25 cm. 1. Stevedores — New York (N.Y.) 2. Stevedores — Seattle. 3. Hiring halls I. T.
HD8039.L82 U654     *LC* 55-10806

## HD8039.M–Z

**Wyman, Mark.**     **4.3534**
Hard rock epic: western miners and the industrial revolution, 1860–1910 / Mark Wyman. — Berkeley: University of California Press, c1979. x, 331 p.: ill.; 25 cm. Includes index. 1. Miners — West (U.S.) — History. 2. Trade-unions — Miners — West (U.S.) — History. 3. Mines and mineral resources — West (U.S.) — History. I. T.
HD8039.M61 U69     331.7/62/23420978     *LC* 78-54805     *ISBN* 0520036786

**Francis, Hywel.**     **4.3535**
The Fed, a history of the South Wales miners in the twentieth century / Hywel Francis and David Smith. — London: Lawrence and Wishart, 1980. xix, 530 p., [32] p. of plates: ill.; 22 cm. 1. Mines and mineral resources — Wales, South — History. 2. Miners — Wales, South — History. I. Smith, David, 1945- II. T.
HD8039.M62F7x     331.88/122334/094294 19     *LC* 82-235042
    *ISBN* 0853155240

**Benson, John.**     **4.3536**
British coal-miners in the nineteenth century: a social history / John Benson. — New York: Holmes & Meier, 1980. 276 p.: maps; 22 cm. Includes index. 1. Coal miners — Great Britain — History. I. T.
HD8039.M62 G723     941.081/088622 19     *LC* 80-11338     *ISBN* 0841905924

**Bodnar, John E., 1944-.**     **4.3537**
Anthracite people: families, unions, and work, 1900–1940 / John Bodnar. — Harrisburg: Commonwealth of Pennsylvania, Pennsylvania Historical and Museum Commission, 1983. 100 p.: ill.; 23 cm. 1. Coal miners — Pennsylvania — Wyoming Valley — History. 2. Labor and laboring classes — Pennsylvania — Wyoming Valley — History. 3. Family — Pennsylvania — Wyoming Valley — History. 4. Trade-unions — Pennsylvania — Wyoming Valley — History. 5. Wyoming Valley (Pa.) — History I. T.
HD8039.M62 U6174 1983     331.7/622335/0974832 19     *LC* 83-622932
    *ISBN* 0892710233

**Corbin, David.**     **4.3538**
Life, work, and rebellion in the coal fields: the southern West Virginia miners, 1880–1922 / David Alan Corbin. — Urbana: University of Illinois Press, c1981. xix, 294 p., [3] leaves of plates: ill.; 23 cm. (The Working class in American history) Includes index. 1. Coal miners — West Virginia — History. 2. Labor

disputes — West Virginia — History. 3. Trade-unions — Coal miners — West Virginia — History. I. T.
HD8039.M62 U61775     331.7/622334/09754 19     *LC* 80-25493
    *ISBN* 0252008502

**Nash, June C., 1927-.**     **4.3539**
We eat the mines and the mines eat us: dependency and exploitation in Bolivian tin mines / June Nash. — New York: Columbia University Press, 1979. xxi, 363 p.: ill.; 24 cm. Includes index. 1. Tin miners — Bolivia. 2. Tin mines and mining — Bolivia. 3. Trade-unions — Tin miners — Bolivia. 4. Bolivia — Social life and customs. I. T.
HD8039.M72 B65     331.7/62/234530984     *LC* 79-11623     *ISBN* 023104710X

**Cottrell, William Frederick, 1903-.**     • **4.3540**
Technological change and labor in the railroad industry; a comparative study. — Lexington, Mass.: Heath Lexington Books, [1970] x, 159 p.; 24 cm. 1. Railroads — Employees — Case studies. 2. Railroads — Automation — Case studies. 3. Technological innovations — Case studies. I. T.
HD8039.R1 C65     385     *LC* 71-114364

**Licht, Walter, 1946-.**     **4.3541**
Working for the railroad: the organization of work in the nineteenth century / Walter Licht. — Princeton, N.J.: Princeton University Press, c1983. xx, 328 p.: ill.; 23 cm. Includes index. 1. Railroads — United States — Employees — History. 2. Railroads — United States — Personnel management — History. I. T.
HD8039.R12 U648 1983     331.7/61385/0973 19     *LC* 82-61372
    *ISBN* 0691047006

**Mintz, Sidney Wilfred, 1922-.**     • **4.3542**
Worker in the cane; a Puerto Rican life history. New Haven, Yale University Press [c1960] 288p. illus. (Caribbean series, 2) 1. Sugar workers — Puerto Rico. 2. Puerto Rico — Rural conditions. I. T.
HD8039.S86 P86     *LC* 60-6606

**Bythell, Duncan.**     • **4.3543**   *HD 8039 T42 G72*
The handloom weavers: a study in the English cotton industry during the Industrial Revolution. — London: Cambridge U.P., 1969. xiv, 302 p.: map.; 22 cm. 1. Weavers — Great Britain. I. T.
HD8039.T42 G72     338.4/7/67721     *LC* 69-10487     *ISBN* 0521075807

**Hareven, Tamara K.**     **4.3544**
Amoskeag: life and work in an American factory-city / by Tamara K. Hareven and Randolph Langenbach. — 1st ed. — New York: Pantheon Books, c1978. xiii, 395 p.: ill.; 24 cm. 1. Amoskeag Manufacturing Company — History. 2. Textile workers — New Hampshire — Manchester — Biography. 3. Manchester (N.H.) — History. I. Langenbach, Randolph, 1945- joint author. II. T.
HD8039.T42 U648 1978     338.7/67/70097428     *LC* 78-52862     *ISBN* 0394488417

# HD8045–8942 Labor, by Country

## HD8051–8085 UNITED STATES

**Directory of national and international labor unions in the**     • **4.3545**
**United States.**
1943-. Washington, D.C.: U.S. Dept. of Labor, Bureau of Labor Statistics: for sale by the Supt. of Docs., U.S. G.P.O., 1943-. v.: ill., ports.; 24-28 cm. (Bulletin / United States Department of Labor, Bureau of Labor Statistics) Biennial. 1. Trade-unions — United States — Directories. I. United States. Bureau of Labor Statistics.
HD8051.A62     331.88/025/73 19     *LC* 44-36

**Clague, Ewan, 1896-1987.**     • **4.3546**
The Bureau of Labor Statistics. — New York: Praeger, [1968] xv, 271 p.: illus., facsim., ports.; 22 cm. — (Praeger library of U.S. Government departments and agencies, no. 13) 1. United States. Bureau of Labor Statistics. I. T.
HD8051.A9 L3 1968     331/.061/73     *LC* 68-30832

## HD8055–8057 Associations

**Goldberg, Arthur J.**     • **4.3547**
AFL–CIO: labor united. — New York: McGraw-Hill, 1956. 319 p.; 21 cm. — (McGraw-Hill labor management series) A history of the AFL and CIO as

labor federations, 1933-52; how they merged, and the consequences that followed therefrom. 1. AFL-CIO. I. T.
HD8055.A5 G66     *LC* 56-11047

**Lorwin, Lewis Levitzki, 1883-1970.**       • **4.3548**
The American Federation of Labor; history, policies, and prospects. Clifton [N.J.] A. M. Kelley, 1972. xix, 573 p. 22 cm. (Reprints of economic classics) (Library of American labor history) Reprint of the 1933 ed. published by the Brookings Institution, Washington, which was issued as publication no. 50 of its Institute of Economics. 1. American Federation of Labor. I. T.
HD8055.A5 L6 1972     331.88/32/0973     *LC* 70-174559     *ISBN* 0678008809

**Morris, James Oliver, 1923-.**       • **4.3549**
Conflict within the AFL; a study of craft versus industrial unionism, 1901–1938. Ithaca, N.Y., Cornell University [c1958] 319 p. (Cornell studies in industrial and labor relations. v. 10) 1. American Federation of Labor. 2. Trade-unions — United States — History I. T. II. Series.
HD8055 A5 M6     *LC* 58-14320

**Taft, Philip, 1902-.**       • **4.3550**
The A.F. of L. from the death of Gompers to the merger. — New York: Octagon Books, 1970 [c1959] xi, 499 p.; 24 cm. The second and concluding volume of the author's 'study' begun with The A.F. of L. in the time of Gompers. 1. American Federation of Labor. I. T.
HD8055.A5T28 1970     331.88/0973     *LC* 75-96193

**Taft, Philip, 1902-.**       • **4.3551**
The A.F. of L. in the time of Gompers. — New York: Octagon Books, 1970 [c1957] xx, 508 p.; 24 cm. 1. American Federation of Labor. I. T.
HD8055.A5 T3 1970     331.88/0973     *LC* 71-96192

**Kampelman, Max M., 1920-.**       • **4.3552**
The Communist Party vs. the C.I.O. [by] Max M. Kampelman. New York, Arno, 1971 [c1957] xv, 299 p. 23 cm. (American labor (New York, N.Y.) 1. Congress of Industrial Organizations (U.S.) 2. Communist Party of the United States of America. 3. Trade-unions — United States I. T. II. Series.
HD8055.C75 K32 1971     331.88/33/0973     *LC* 78-156445     *ISBN* 0405029292

**Lichtenstein, Nelson.**       **4.3553**
Labor's war at home: the CIO in World War II / Nelson Lichtenstein. — Cambridge [Cambridgeshire]; New York: Cambridge University Press, 1983 (c1982). xii, 319 p.; 24 cm. Revision of thesis (Ph.D.)—University of California at Berkeley. Includes index. 1. Congress of Industrial Organizations (U.S.) — History. 2. Labor policy — United States — History — 20th century. I. T.
HD8055.C75 L5     331.88/33/0973 19     *LC* 82-4349     *ISBN* 0521234727

**Brissenden, Paul Frederick, 1885-.**       • **4.3554**
The I. W. W.; a study of American syndicalism. — [2d ed.]. — New York, Russell & Russell [1957] xxii, 438 p. fold. diagr. 22 cm. Bibliography: p. 387-428. 1. Industrial Workers of the World. 2. Syndicalism — U.S. I. T.
HD8055.I5B55 1957     331.886     *LC* 57-6911

**Dubofsky, Melvyn, 1934-.**       • **4.3555**
We shall be all; a history of the Industrial Workers of the World. — Chicago: Quadrangle Books, 1969. xviii, 557 p.: illus.; 25 cm. 1. Industrial Workers of the World. I. T.
HD8055.I5 D8     331.88/0973     *LC* 75-78306

**Fink, Leon, 1948-.**       **4.3556**
Workingmen's democracy: the Knights of Labor and American politics / Leon Fink. — Urbana: University of Illinois Press, c1983. xvii, 249 p.; 24 cm. — (Working class in American history.) Includes index. 1. Knights of Labor — History. 2. Labor and laboring classes — United States — Political activity — History. I. T. II. Series.
HD8055.K7 F56 1983     322/.2/0973 19     *LC* 82-6902     *ISBN* 0252009991

## HD8066 History: General

**Commons, John Rogers, 1862-1945.**       • **4.3557**
History of labour in the United States, by John R. Commons [and others] With an introductory note by Henry W. Farnam. New York, A. M. Kelley, 1966. 4 v. illus. 23 cm. (Reprints of economic classics) First published 1918-35. Vols. 3-4 have title: History of labor in the United States, 1896-1932. 1. Labor and laboring classes — United States 2. Trade-unions — United States I. T.
HD8066.C7 1966     331.0973     *LC* 66-18557

**Gordon, David M.**       **4.3558**
Segmented work, divided workers: the historical transformation of labor in the United States / David M. Gordon, Richard Edwards, Michael Reich. — Cambridge [Cambridgeshire]; New York: Cambridge University Press, 1982.

xii, 288 p.; 24 cm. Includes index. 1. Labor and laboring classes — United States — History. 2. Labor supply — United States — History. 3. Capitalism — United States — History. I. Edwards, Richard, 1944- II. Reich, Michael. III. T.
HD8066.G65     331/.0973 19     *LC* 81-17010     *ISBN* 0521237211

**Rayback, Joseph G.**       • **4.3559**
A history of American labor. New York, Macmillan, 1959. 459 p. 1. Labor and laboring classes — United States — History 2. Trade-unions — United States — History I. T.
HD8066 R3     *LC* 59-5344

## HD8068–8072 By Period

**Morris, Richard Brandon, 1904-.**       • **4.3560**
Government and labor in early America / by Richard B. Morris. — New York: Columbia University Press, c1946. xvi, 557 p. 1. Labor and laboring classes — United States — History. I. T.
HD8068.M65     *LC* a46-961

**Ware, Norman Joseph, 1886-.**       • **4.3561**
The industrial worker, 1840–1860; the reaction of American industrial society to the advance of the industrial revolution. Boston New York, Houghton Mifflin company, 1924. xxi, 249 p. 21 cm. 1. Labor and laboring classes — United States 2. United States — Social conditions I. T.
HD8070.W3     *LC* 24-4600

**Aronowitz, Stanley.**       **4.3562**
False promises; the shaping of American working class consciousness. New York, McGraw-Hill [1973] xii, 465 p. 24 cm. 1. Labor and laboring classes — United States — History. 2. Trade-unions — United States — History. 3. Class consciousness — United States — History. I. T.
HD8072.A687     301.44/42/0973     *LC* 73-5679     *ISBN* 0070023158

**Berg, Ivar E.**       **4.3563**
Managers and work reform: a limited engagement / Ivar Berg, Marcia Freedman, and Michael Freeman. — New York: Free Press, c1978. xiv, 316 p.; 24 cm. 1. Labor and laboring classes — United States 2. Job satisfaction — United States. 3. Labor productivity — United States. 4. Personnel management — United States. 5. Industrial relations — United States. I. Freedman, Marcia K. joint author. II. Freeman, Michael, joint author. III. T.
HD8072.B358     658.31/5     *LC* 77-83165     *ISBN* 0029029007

**Bernstein, Irving, 1916-.**       **4.3564**
A caring society: the New Deal, the worker, and the Great Depression: a history of the American worker, 1933–1941 / Irving Bernstein. — Boston: Houghton Mifflin, 1985. 338 p., [24] p. of plates: ill., ports.; 24 cm. Includes index. 1. Labor and laboring classes — United States — 1914- 2. Labor policy — United States — History. 3. Unemployment — United States — History. I. T. II. Title: History of the American worker, 1933-1941.
HD8072.B365 1985     362.8/5/0973 19     *LC* 84-25129     *ISBN* 0395331161

**Bernstein, Irving, 1916-.**       • **4.3565**
The lean years; a history of the American worker, 1920–1933. Boston, Houghton Mifflin, 1960. 577 p. illus. 23 cm. 1. Labor and laboring classes — United States — 1914- 2. Trade-unions — United States — History — 20th century. I. T. II. Title: History of the American worker, 1920-1933.
HD8072.B37     331.0973     *LC* 60-9143

**Bernstein, Irving, 1916-.**       • **4.3566**
Turbulent years; a history of the American worker, 1933–1941. Boston, Houghton Mifflin, 1970 [c1969] xiv, 873 p. illus., ports. 22 cm. 1. Labor and laboring classes — United States — 1914- I. T. II. Title: History of the American worker, 1933-1941.
HD8072.B38     331/.0973     *LC* 76-80419

**Dubofsky, Melvyn, 1934-.**       **4.3567**
Industrialism and the American worker, 1865–1920 / Melvyn Dubofsky. — 2nd ed. — Arlington Heights, Ill.: H. Davidson, c1985. xiii, 167 p.; 21 cm. (The American history series) Includes index. 1. Labor and laboring classes — United States — History. 2. Trade-unions — United States — History. I. T.
HD8072.D846 1985     331/.0973 19     *LC* 84-27407     *ISBN* 0882958313

**Gutman, Herbert George, 1928-.**       **4.3568**
Work, culture, and society in industrializing America: essays in American working–class and social history / Herbert G. Gutman. — 1st ed. — New York: Knopf: distributed by Random House, c1976. xiv, 343, xvi p.; 22 cm. 1. Labor and laboring classes — United States — History — Addresses, essays, lectures. 2. Industrial relations — United States — History — Addresses, essays, lectures. 3. United States — Social conditions — 1865-1918 —

Addresses, essays, lectures. 4. United States — Social conditions — To 1865 — Addresses, essays, lectures. I. T.
HD8072.G98     301.44/42/0973     LC 75-35733     ISBN 0394496949

**Labor and management. Richard B. Morris, advisory editor.**     4.3569
[S.l.]: Arno, 1973. x, 508 p.: illus.; 29 cm. — (Great contemporary issues.) Selected articles from the New York times. 1. Industrial relations — United States — History — Addresses, essays, lectures. I. Morris, Richard Brandon, 1904- ed. II. New York times III. Series.
HD8072.L215     331/.0973     LC 72-5019     ISBN 0405041632

**Lee, R. Alton.**     • 4.3570
Truman and Taft–Hartley; a question of mandate [by] R. Alton Lee. Lexington, University of Kentucky Press, 1966. viii, 254 p. 23 cm. 'Bibliographical note.': p. [240]-244. 1. Truman, Harry S., 1884-1972. 2. United States. Labor Management Relations Act, 1947. 3. Labor policy — United States — History. 4. United States — Politics and government — 1945-1953 I. T.
HD8072.L33 1966     331/.0973 19     LC 66-26689

**Montgomery, David, 1927-.**     4.3571
Workers' control in America: studies in the history of work, technology, and labor struggles / David Montgomery. — Cambridge [Eng.]; New York: Cambridge University Press, 1979. x, 189 p.; 24 cm. 1. Labor and laboring classes — United States — History. 2. Trade-unions — United States — History. 3. Industrial relations — United States — History. I. T.
HD8072.M74     331.8/0973     LC 78-32001     ISBN 0521225809

**Nadworny, Milton J.**     • 4.3572
Scientific management and the unions, 1900–1932. Cambridge, Harvard University Press, 1955. 187 p. 22 cm. 1. Industrial relations — United States 2. Industrial management — United States. I. T.
HD8072.N23     LC 55-11606

**Ramirez, Bruno.**     4.3573
When workers fight: the politics of industrial relations in the progressive era, 1898–1916 / Bruno Ramirez. — Westport, Conn.: Greenwood Press, 1978. viii, 241 p.; 22 cm. — (Contributions in labor history; no. 2 0146-3608) Includes index. 1. Industrial relations — United States — History. 2. Trade-unions — United States — History. I. T.
HD8072.R34     331/.0973     LC 77-83895     ISBN 0837198267

**Rodgers, Daniel T.**     4.3574
The work ethic in industrial America, 1850–1920 / Daniel T. Rodgers. — Chicago: University of Chicago Press, 1978. xv, 300 p.; 23 cm. 1. Labor and laboring classes — United States — History. 2. Work ethic — United States — History. 3. Middle classes — United States — History. I. T.
HD8072.R76     301.5/5     LC 77-81737     ISBN 0226723518

**Slichter, Sumner H. (Sumner Huber), 1892-1959.**     • 4.3575
The impact of collective bargaining on management, by Sumner H. Slichter, James J. Healy [and] E. Robert Livernash. Washington, Brookings Institution [1960] xv, 982 p. 24 cm. 1. Collective bargaining — United States. 2. Industrial relations — United States. 3. Industrial management — United States. I. T.
HD8072.S6167     331.1973     LC 60-53058

**Stone, Morris, 1912-.**     • 4.3576
Managerial freedom and job security. [1st ed.] New York, Harper & Row [c1964] viii, 262 p. 1. Collective labor agreements — United States I. T.
HD8072 S85     LC 63-20329

**Ware, Norman Joseph, 1886-.**     • 4.3577
The labor movement in the United States, 1860–1895: a study in democracy / by Norman J. Ware. — New York; London: D. Appleton & Co., 1929. xviii, 409 p. 1. Knights of Labor. 2. Labor and laboring classes — United States 3. Trade-unions — United States I. T.
HD8072.W263 1959     LC 29-4787

**The worker and the job: coping with change. [Edited by Jerome M. Rosow].**     4.3578
Englewood Cliffs, N.J.: Prentice-Hall, [1974] x, 208 p.; 21 cm. — (A Spectrum book) At head of title: The American Assembly, Columbia University. Background papers for the 43d American Assembly, Arden House, Harriman, N.Y., Nov. 1973. 1. Labor and laboring classes — United States — Congresses. 2. Job satisfaction — Congresses. I. Rosow, Jerome M. ed. II. American Assembly.
HD8072.W818     331.2     LC 74-765     ISBN 0139653696

**Challenges and choices facing American labor / edited by Thomas A. Kochan.**     4.3579
Cambridge, Mass.: MIT Press, c1985. viii, 356 p.; 24 cm. 1. Industrial relations — United States — Addresses, essays, lectures. 2. Trade-unions — United States — Addresses, essays, lectures. I. Kochan, Thomas A.
HD8072.5.C47 1985     331/.0973 19     LC 84-19372     ISBN 0262110954

**Dunlop, John Thomas, 1914-.**     4.3580
Dispute resolution: negotiation and consensus building / John T. Dunlop. — Dover, Mass.: Auburn House, c1984. xx, 296 p.; 25 cm. 1. Industrial relations — United States. 2. Collective bargaining — United States. 3. Arbitration, Industrial — United States. 4. Mediation and conciliation, Industrial — United States. I. T.
HD8072.5.D86 1984     331.89/14/0973 19     LC 83-27531     ISBN 0865691231

**Gibson, Mary.**     4.3581
Workers' rights / Mary Gibson. — Totowa, N.J.: Rowman & Allanheld, 1983. x, 166 p.; 25 cm. — (Philosophy and society.) Includes index. 1. Employee rights — United States — Case studies. 2. Industrial hygiene — United States — Case studies. 3. Industrial safety — United States — Case studies. 4. Industrial relations — United States — Case studies. I. T. II. Series.
HD8072.5.G52 1983     331/.01/1 19     LC 83-17788     ISBN 0847667561

**Siegel, Irving Herbert.**     4.3582
Labor–management cooperation: the American experience / Irving H. Siegel, Edgar Weinberg. — Kalamazoo, Mich.: W.E. Upjohn Institute for Employment Research, 1982. xi, 316 p.; 23 cm. 1. Industrial relations — United States. I. Weinberg, Edgar. II. W.E. Upjohn Institute for Employment Research. III. T.
HD8072.5.S57 1982     331.89/0973 19     LC 82-8487     ISBN 0911558993

# HD8073 Biography

**Gompers, Samuel, 1850-1924.**     • 4.3583
Seventy years of life and labor; an autobiography. Revised and edited by Philip Taft and John A. Sessions. With a foreword by George Meany. — New York, Dutton, 1957. 334 p. 22 cm. 1. American Federation of Labor. 2. Labor and laboring classes — U.S. I. T.
HD8073.G6A3 1957     923.273     LC 56-8330

**Gompers, Samuel, 1850-1924.**     4.3584
Seventy years of life and labor: an autobiography / Samuel Gompers; edited and with an introduction by Nick Salvatore. — Ithaca, NY: ILR Press, New York State School of Industrial and Labor Relations, Cornell University, c1984. xli, 236 p.: ports.; 23 cm. Includes index. 1. Gompers, Samuel, 1850-1924. 2. American Federation of Labor. 3. Trade-unions — United States — Officials and employees — Biography. 4. Labor and laboring classes — United States I. Salvatore, Nick, 1943- II. T.
HD8073.G6 A3 1984     331.88/32/0924 B 19     LC 84-10765     ISBN 0875461123

**Mandel, Bernard, 1920-.**     • 4.3585
Samuel Gompers, a biography. With an introd.: Samuel Gompers, labor statesman or labor faker? by Louis Filler. [Yellow Springs, Ohio] Antioch Press, 1963. xxii, 566 p. ill., ports. 1. Gompers, Samuels, 1850-1924 I. T.
HD8073 G6 M34     LC 63-14380

**Haywood, Big Bill, 1869-1928.**     • 4.3586
Bill Haywood's book; the autobiography of William D. Haywood. New York, International publishers, [c1929] 368 p. front. 23 cm. 1. Labor and laboring classes — United States 2. Trade-unions — United States I. T.
HD8073.H3 A3     LC 29-1577

**Smith, Gibbs M.**     • 4.3587
[Joe Hill] Labor martyr: Joe Hill [by] Gibbs M. Smith. New York, Grosset & Dunlap [c1969] 286 p. illus. 24 cm. (The Universal library) Originally published under title: Joe Hill. 1. Hill, Joe, 1879-1915. 2. Industrial Workers of the World — Biography. I. T.
HD8073.H55 S63 1969     331.88/6 B     LC 72-190149     ISBN 0448011417

**Wechsler, James Arthur, 1915-.**     • 4.3588
Labor baron: a portrait of John L. Lewis, by James A. Wechsler. — Westport, Conn.: Greenwood Press, [1972, c1944] viii, 278 p.; 22 cm. 1. Lewis, John Llewellyn, 1880-1969. I. T.
HD8073.L4 W4 1972     331.88/33/0924 B     LC 72-143312     ISBN 0837159687

**Goulden, Joseph C.**     4.3589
Meany [by] Joseph C. Goulden. [1st ed.] New York, Atheneum, 1972. 504 p. 25 cm. 1. Meany, George, 1894 2. AFL CIO — History 3. Trade-unions — United States — Officials and employees — Biography. I. T.
HD8073.M4 G6     331.88/33/0924 B     LC 72-82681

**Ashbaugh, Carolyn.**     4.3590
Lucy Parsons: American revolutionary / by Carolyn Ashbaugh. — Chicago: Charles H. Kerr Publishing, 1976. 288 p.: ill.; 20 cm. Published for the Illinois Labor History Society. 1. Parsons, Lucy Eldine Gonzalez. 2. Labor and

laboring classes — United States. — History. I. Illinois Labor History Society. II. T.
HD8073.P36 A85     HD8073P36 A85.     *LC* 75-23909     *ISBN* 0882860053

**Martin, George Whitney.**       **4.3591**
Madam Secretary, Frances Perkins / by George Martin. Boston: Houghton Mifflin, 1976. xv, 589 p., [8] leaves of plates: ill.; 24 cm. Includes index. 1. Perkins, Frances, 1882-1965. 2. Politicians — United States — Biography. 3. Labor policy — United States — History. I. T.
HD8073.P38 M37     973.917/092/4 B     *LC* 75-38637     *ISBN* 0395242932

**Mohr, Lillian Holmen, 1926-.**       **4.3592**
Frances Perkins, that woman in FDR's cabinet! / By Lillian Holmen Mohr. — [Croton-on-Hudson, N.Y.]: North River Press, c1979. viii, 328 p.: ill.; 24 cm. Includes index. 1. Perkins, Frances, 1882-1965. 2. Women in politics — United States — Biography. 3. Labor policy — United States — History. I. T.
HD8073.P38 M63     973.917/092/4 B     *LC* 78-23597     088427010X

**Powderly, Terence Vincent, 1849-1924.**       • **4.3593**
The path I trod; the autobiography of Terence V. Powderly. Edited by Harry J. Carman, Henry David and Paul N. Guthrie. — New York: AMS Press, [1968] xiv, 460 p.: illus.; 23 cm. Reprint of the 1940 ed., which was issued as no. 6 of Columbia studies in American culture. 1. Powderly, Terence Vincent, 1849-1924. 2. Knights of Labor. 3. Labor and laboring classes — United States I. T.
HD8073.P69 A3 1968     331.88/092/4 B     *LC* 77-181971

**Cormier, Frank.**       • **4.3594**
Reuther [by] Frank Cormier and William J. Eaton. Englewood Cliffs, N.J., Prentice-Hall [1970] 475 p. port. 24 cm. 1. Reuther, Walter, 1907-1970. I. Eaton, William J., joint author. II. T.
HD8073.R4 C67     331.881/292/0924 B     *LC* 71-131869     *ISBN* 0137793146

**Grossman, Jonathan, 1915-.**       • **4.3595**
William Sylvis, pioneer of American labor; a study of the labor movement during the era of the civil war. New York Columbia University Press 1945. 302p. (Studies in history, economics and public law, ed. by the Faculty of political science of Columbia university. No. 516) 1. Sylvis, William H., 1828-1869 2. International Molders' and Foundry Workers' Union of North America 3. National Labor Union (U.S.) I. T.
HD8073 S9 G7

# HD8076–8079 Labor in Politics

**Calkins, Fay.**       • **4.3596**
The CIO and the Democratic Party. [Chicago] University of Chicago Press [1952] xiii, 162 p. ill. 1. Congress of Industrial Organizations. Political Action Committee 2. United States — Politics and government — 1933-1953 I. T.
HD8076 C3     *LC* 52-12225

**Greenstone, J. David.**       • **4.3597**
Labor in American politics [by] J. David Greenstone. New York: Knopf, [1969] xviii, 408 L p.; 22 cm. 1. Trade-unions — United States — Political activity. I. T.
HD8076.G67     322/.2/0973     *LC* 68-24675

**Karson, Marc.**       • **4.3598**
American labor unions and politics. Foreword by Selig Perlman. Carbondale, Southern Illinois University Press, 1958-. v. 1. Trade-unions — United States — Political activity I. T.
HD8076 K3     *LC* 58-8253

**Montgomery, David, 1927-.**       **4.3599**
Beyond equality; labor and the radical Republicans, 1862–1872. [1st ed.] New York, Knopf, 1967. xi, 508, xix p. 22 cm. 1. Republican Party (U.S.: 1854- ) — History. 2. Labor and laboring classes — United States — Political activity. 3. Trade-unions — United States 4. United States — Politics and government — 1849-1877 I. T.
HD8076.M65     331/.0973     *LC* 67-18610

**Piven, Frances Fox.**       **4.3600**
Poor people's movements: why they succeed, how they fail / by Frances Fox Piven and Richard A. Cloward. — 1st ed. — New York: Pantheon Books, c1977. xiv, 381 p.; 25 cm. 1. Labor and laboring classes — United States — Political activity — History. 2. Afro-Americans — Civil rights — History. 3. Welfare rights movement — United States — History. I. Cloward, Richard A. joint author. II. T.
HD8076.P55     322.4/4/0973     *LC* 77-5298     *ISBN* 0394488407

**Steffen, Charles G., 1952-.**       **4.3601**
The mechanics of Baltimore: workers and politics in the age of revolution, 1763–1812 / Charles G. Steffen. — Urbana: University of Illinois Press, c1984. xv, 296 p.; 24 cm. — (Working class in American history.) Revision of the author's thesis. 1. Skilled labor — Maryland — Baltimore — Political activity — History. 2. Labor and laboring classes — Maryland — Baltimore — Political activity — History. 3. Baltimore (Md.) — Politics and government I. T. II. Series.
HD8079.B2 S73 1984     322/.2/097526 19     *LC* 83-6891     *ISBN* 0252010884

**Nash, Michael, 1946-.**       **4.3602**
Conflict and accommodation: coal miners, steel workers, and socialism, 1890–1920 / Michael Nash. — Westport, Conn.: Greenwood Press, 1982. xix, 197 p.; 22 cm. (Contributions in labor history. 0146-3608; no. 11) Includes index. 1. Coal miners — Pennsylvania — Political activity — History. 2. Iron and steel workers — Pennsylvania — Political activity — History. 3. Elections — Pennsylvania — History. 4. Socialism — United States — History. I. T. II. Series.
HD8079.P4 N37 1982     322/.2 19     *LC* 81-6691     *ISBN* 0313228388

# HD8081–8085 Immigrant Labor. Minority Labor

**Cummings, Scott, 1944-.**       **4.3603**
Immigrant minorities and the urban working class / Scott Cummings. — Port Washington, N.Y.: Associated Faculty Press, 1983. 151 p.; 24 cm. — (National university publications) 1. Minorities — Employment — United States — History. 2. Labor and laboring classes — United States — Political activity — History. 3. Minorities — United States — Political activity — History. 4. United States — Emigration and immigration — History. I. T.
HD8081.A5 C85 1983     305.5/62/0973 19     *LC* 83-17243     *ISBN* 0804693382

**Erickson, Charlotte.**       • **4.3604**
American industry and the European immigrant, 1860–1885. — New York: Russell & Russell, [1967, c1957] x, 269 p.; 22 cm. — (Studies in economic history) 1. Labor and laboring classes — United States 2. Contract labor — United States. 3. United States — Emigration and immigration I. T.
HD8081.A5 E7 1967     331.6/2/4073     *LC* 66-27065

**Feldstein, Stanley, 1937- comp.**       **4.3605**
The ordeal of assimilation: a documentary history of the white working class. Edited by Stanley Feldstein and Lawrence Costello. [1st ed.] Garden City, N.Y., Anchor Press, 1974. xxiii, 500 p. 21 cm. 1. Alien labor — United States — Addresses, essays, lectures. 2. Working class whites — United States. 3. United States — Foreign population — Addresses, essays, lectures. I. Costello, Lawrence, joint comp. II. T.
HD8081.A5 F43     331.6/2     *LC* 73-16504     *ISBN* 0385048769

**Parmet, Robert D., 1938-.**       **4.3606**
Labor and immigration in industrial America / by Robert D. Parmet. — Boston, Mass.: Twayne, 1981. 268 p.: front.; 21 cm. — (Immigrant heritage of America series.) Includes index. 1. Alien labor — United States — History. 2. Trade-unions — United States — History. 3. Labor and laboring classes — United States — History. 4. United States — Emigration and immigration — History. I. T. II. Series.
HD8081.A5 P37     331.6/2/0973 19     *LC* 81-1438     *ISBN* 0805784187

**Pride against prejudice: work in the lives of older Blacks and young Puerto Ricans: [oral histories / compiled by] Dean W. Morse; foreword by Eli Ginzberg.**       **4.3607**
Montclair, N.J.: Allanheld, Osmun, 1980. xi, 238 p.; 24 cm. — (Conservation of human resources series; 9) (LandMark studies) 'Prepared under contract number 21-36-73-51 from the Employment and Training Administration, U.S. Department of Labor.' 1. Minorities — Employment — New York (City) 2. Afro-Americans — Employment — New York (N.Y.) 3. Puerto Ricans in New York (City) — Employment. 4. Minorities — New York (City) — Interviews. 5. Afro-Americans — New York (City) — Interviews. 6. Puerto Ricans in New York (City) — Interviews. I. Morse, Dean.
HD8081.A5 P74     331.6     *LC* 78-65534     0876638396

**Harris, William Hamilton, 1944-.**       **4.3608**
The harder we run: Black workers since the Civil War / William H. Harris. — New York: Oxford University Press, 1982. ix, 259 p.: ill.; 22 cm. Includes index. 1. Afro-Americans — Employment — History. I. T.
HD8081.A65 H37     331.6/3/96073009 19     *LC* 80-27897     *ISBN* 0195029402

**Trotter, Joe William, 1945-.**       **4.3609**
Black Milwaukee: the making of an industrial proletariat, 1915–45 / Joe William Trotter, Jr. — Urbana: University of Illinois Press, c1985. xvii, 302 p.: ill.; 24 cm. (Blacks in the New World.) Revision of thesis (Ph. D.)—University

of Minnesota. Includes index. 1. Afro-Americans — Employment — Wisconsin — Milwaukee — History. 2. Discrimination in employment — Wisconsin — Milwaukee — History. 3. Race discrimination — Wisconsin — Milwaukee — History. 4. Afro-Americans — Wisconsin — Milwaukee — Social conditions — To 1964. I. T. II. Series.
HD8081.A65 T76 1985    331.6/3/96073077595 19    LC 84-83
    ISBN 0252011244

**Ch'iu, P'ing.**         • 4.3610
Chinese labor in California, 1850–1880, an economic study. Madison, State Historical Society of Wisconsin for the Dept. of History, University of Wisconsin, 1963. 180 p. 23 cm. (Logmark editions) Includes bibliography. 1. Chinese in California. 2. Labor and laboring classes — California — History. I. T.
HD8081.C5C45    331.6251    LC 63-63578

**American labor and immigration history, 1877–1920s: recent**    4.3611
**European research / edited by Dirk Hoerder.**
Urbana: University of Illinois Press, c1983. ix, 286 p.; 24 cm. — (Working class in American history.) Papers prepared for a conference at the University of Bremen, Nov. 1978. Includes index. 1. Labor and laboring classes — United States — History — Congresses. 2. European Americans — History — Congresses. 3. United States — Foreign population — History — Congresses. I. Hoerder, Dirk. II. Series.
HD8081.E93 A45 1983    305.5/6 19    LC 81-23078    ISBN 0252009630

**Hispanics in the U.S. economy / edited by George J. Borjas,**    4.3612
**Marta Tienda.**
Orlando: Academic Press, 1985. xx, 374 p.; 24 cm. Includes index. 1. Hispanic Americans — Employment — Addresses, essays, lectures. 2. Wages — Hispanic Americans — Addresses, essays, lectures. 3. Hispanic Americans — Economic conditions — Addresses, essays, lectures. 4. Hispanic Americans — Social conditions — Addresses, essays, lectures. I. Borjas, George J. II. Tienda, Marta.
HD8081.H7 H58 1985    331.6/3/6873 19    LC 84-14611    ISBN 0121186407

**Davidson, John, 1947-.**         4.3613
The long road north / by John Davidson. — Austin, Tex.: Texas Monthly Press, c1981. 145 p.; 22 cm. 1. Alien labor, Mexican — Texas. 2. Mexicans — Texas. I. T.
HD8081.M6 D38 1981    331.6/2/72073 19    LC 81-8742    ISBN 0932012159

**Fogel, Walter A.**         4.3614
Mexican illegal alien workers in the United States / by Walter Fogel. — Los Angeles: Institute of Industrial Relations, University of California, c1978. 204 p.; 22 cm. (Monograph series - Institute of Industrial Relations, University of California, Los Angeles; 20) 1. Alien labor, Mexican — United States. I. T. II. Title: Illegal alien workers in the United States.
HD8081.M6 F62    331.6/2/72073    LC 78-623108

**Reisler, Mark.**         4.3615
By the sweat of their brow: Mexican immigrant labor in the United States, 1900–1940 / Mark Reisler. — Westport, Conn.: Greenwood, Press, 1976. 298 p. Includes index. 1. Alien labor, Mexican — United States — History. 2. United States — Emigration and immigration — History. I. T.
HD8081.M6 R44 1976    331.6/2/72073    LC 76-5329    ISBN 0837188946

**Siracusa, Carl.**         4.3616
A mechanical people: perceptions of the industrial order in Massachusetts, 1815–1880 / Carl Siracusa. — 1st ed. — Middletown, Conn.: Wesleyan University Press, c1979. 313 p.; 24 cm. Includes index. 1. Labor policy — Massachusetts — History. 2. Labor and laboring classes — Massachusetts — History. 3. Factory system — Massachusetts — History. 4. Massachusetts — Industries — History. I. T.
HD8083.M4 S55    331.1/1/09744    LC 78-26715    ISBN 0819550299

**Greenberg, Brian.**         4.3617
Worker and community: response to industrialization in a nineteenth-century American city, Albany, New York, 1850–1884 / Brian Greenberg. — Albany: State University of New York Press, c1985. ix, 227 p.: maps; 24 cm. (SUNY series in American social history.) Maps on endpapers. Includes index. 1. Labor and laboring classes — New York (State) — Albany — History — 19th century. 2. Industrial relations — New York (State) — Albany — History — 19th century. 3. Convict labor — New York (State) — Albany — History — 19th century. 4. Albany (N.Y.) — Industries — History — 19th century. I. T. II. Series.
HD8085.A43 G74 1985    305.5/62/0974743 19    LC 84-26774
    ISBN 0887060463

**Fried, Marc.**         4.3618
The world of the urban working class, by Marc Fried with Ellen Fitzgerald [and others] Cambridge, Harvard University Press, 1973. ix, 410 p. illus. 24 cm.

1. Labor and laboring classes — Massachusetts — Boston. 2. Slums — Massachusetts — Boston. I. T.
HD8085.B63 F75    301.44/42/0942    LC 73-81673    ISBN 0674961951

**Cumbler, John T.**         4.3619
Working–class community in industrial America: work, leisure, and struggle in two industrial cities, 1880–1930 / John T. Cumbler. — Westport, Conn.: Greenwood Press, 1979. xiv, 283 p.: ill.; 22 cm. (Contributions in labor history. no. 8 0146-3608) Includes index. 1. Labor and laboring classes — Massachusetts — Lynn — History. 2. Labor and laboring classes — Massachusetts — Fall River — History. 3. Lynn (Mass.) — Social conditions. 4. Fall River (Mass.) — Social conditions. I. T. II. Series.
HD8085.L963 C85    301.44/42/0973    LC 78-57768    ISBN 0313206155

**Wilentz, Sean.**         4.3620
Chants democratic: New York City & the rise of the American working class, 1788–1850 / Sean Wilentz. — New York: Oxford University Press, 1984. xii, 446 p., [12] p. of plates: ill.; 25 cm. Includes index. 1. Labor and laboring classes — New York (N.Y.) — History. I. T.
HD8085.N53 W54 1984    305.5/62/097471 19    LC 83-2352    ISBN 0195033426

**Hirsch, Susan E.**         4.3621
Roots of the American working class: the industrialization of crafts in Newark, 1800–1860 / Susan E. Hirsch. — Philadelphia: University of Pennsylvania Press, 1978. xx, 170 p.; 24 cm. 1. Skilled labor — New Jersey — Newark — History. 2. Labor and laboring classes — New Jersey — Newark — History. 3. Newark (N.J.) — Social conditions. I. T.
HD8085.N63 H57    301.44/42/0974932    LC 78-51784    ISBN 0812277473

**Laurie, Bruce.**         4.3622
Working people of Philadelphia, 1800–1850 / Bruce Laurie. — Philadelphia: Temple University Press, 1980. xiii, 273 p.: map; 22 cm. Includes index. 1. Labor and laboring classes — Pennsylvania — Philadelphia — History. I. T.
HD8085.P53 L38    305.5/6    LC 79-28679    ISBN 0877221685

**Griffen, Clyde, 1929-.**         4.3623
Natives and newcomers: the ordering of opportunity in mid–nineteenth-century Poughkeepsie / Clyde and Sally Griffen. — Cambridge, Mass.: Harvard University Press, 1978. xvi, 291 p.; 24 cm. (Harvard studies in urban history.) 1. Occupational mobility — New York (State) — Poughkeepsie — History. 2. Labor and laboring classes — New York (State) — Poughkeepsie — History. 3. Poughkeepsie (N.Y.) — Social conditions. I. Griffen, Sally, 1936- joint author. II. T. III. Series.
HD8085.P713 G74    331.1/27/0974733    LC 77-3553    ISBN 0674603257

## HD8101–8370 CANADA. LATIN AMERICA

**Kwavnick, David.**         4.3624
Organized labour and pressure politics; the Canadian Labour Congress, 1956–1968. — Montreal: McGill-Queen's University Press, 1972. 287 p.; 24 cm. 1. Canadian Labour Congress. 2. Trade-unions — Canada — Political activity. I. T.
HD8102.C275 K85    322/.2/0971    LC 72-82247    ISBN 0773500898

**Woods, H. D.**         4.3625
Labour policy in Canada / H. D. Woods. — 2d ed. / by H. D. Woods, Sylvia Ostry, Mahmood A. Zaidi. — New York: St. Martin's, 1973. 377 p.; 24 cm. — (His Labour policy and labour economics in Canada; v. 1) 1. Labor policy — Canada 2. Industrial relations — Canada. I. T. II. Series.
HD8106.5.W6 vol.1 1973    ISBN 0770510817

**Horowitz, Gad.**         • 4.3626
Canadian labour in politics. — [Toronto]: University of Toronto Press, [1968] 273 p.; 24 cm. — (Studies in the structure of power, decision-making in Canada. 4) 1. Trade-unions — Canada — Political activity. I. T. II. Series.
HD8108.H6    322/.2/0971    LC 68-101781

**Córdova, Efrén.**         4.3627
Industrial relations in Latin America / edited by Efrén Córdova. — New York: Praeger, 1984. xi, 273 p.; 25 cm. 1. Industrial relations — Latin America — Addresses, essays, lectures. I. T.
HD8110.5.C67 1984    331/.098 19    LC 83-24480    ISBN 0030702844

## HD8371–8660 EUROPE

**Geary, Dick.** **4.3628**
European labour protest, 1848–1939 / Dick Geary. — New York, NY: St. Martin's Press, 1981. 195 p.; 23 cm. Includes index. 1. Labor and laboring classes — Europe — History. 2. Labor disputes — Europe — History. I. T.
HD8376.G4 1981 331.89/294 19 *LC* 81-4474 *ISBN* 0312269749

**Blue–collar workers in Eastern Europe / edited by Jan F.** **4.3629**
**Triska, Charles Gati.**
London; Boston: Allen & Unwin, 1981. xvi, 302 p.: ill.; 25 cm. Mostly contributions presented at a conference held at Stanford University, May 1980. 1. Labor and laboring classes — Europe, Eastern — Addresses, essays, lectures. I. Triska, Jan F. II. Gati, Charles.
HD8376.5.B58 305.5/6 19 *LC* 81-10864 *ISBN* 0043210279

**Industrial Democracy in Europe. International Research Group.** **4.3630**
European industrial relations / by Industrial Democracy in Europe (IDE), International Research Group. — Oxford: Clarendon Press; New York: Oxford University Press, 1981. 265 p.: ill. 1. Industrial relations — Europe. 2. Industrial relations — Israel. 3. Management — Employee participation — Europe. 4. Management — Employee participation — Israel. I. T.
HD8376.5.I53 1981 331/.094 19 *LC* 80-41055 *ISBN* 0198272545

**Barbash, Jack.** **4.3631**
Trade unions and national economic policy [by] Jack Barbash, with the assistance of Kate Barbash. — Baltimore: Johns Hopkins Press, [1972] xiv, 206 p.; 24 cm. 1. Trade-unions — Europe — Political activity. 2. Manpower policy — Europe. 3. Europe — Economic policy. I. T.
HD8378.B33 330.9/4/055 *LC* 75-173460 *ISBN* 0801813425

**Castles, Stephen.** **4.3632**
Here for good: Western Europe's new ethnic minorities / Stephen Castles, with Heather Booth and Tina Wallace. — London: Pluto Press, 1984. 259 p.; 20 cm. Includes index. 1. Alien labor — Europe. 2. Children of alien laborers — Europe. 3. Minorities — Europe. I. Booth, Heather, 1950- II. Wallace, Tina. III. T.
HD8378.5.A2 C378 1984 305.8/0094 19 *LC* 84-132547 *ISBN* 0861047524

**Castles, Stephen.** **4.3633**
Immigrant workers and class structure in Western Europe / by Stephen Castles and Godula Kosack. — 2nd ed. — Oxford [Oxfordshire]; New York: Oxford University Press, 1985. xv, 534 p.; 23 cm. Includes index. 1. Alien labor — Europe — Case studies. I. Kosack, Godula. II. T.
HD8378.5.A2 C38 1985 305.8/0094 19 *LC* 84-25553 *ISBN* 0198780184

## HD8381–8300 Britain. Ireland

**Dorfman, Gerald Allen, 1939-.** **4.3634**
British trade unionism against the Trades Union Congress / Gerald A. Dorfman. — Stanford, Calif.: Hoover Institution Press, Stanford University, c1983. vii, 158 p.; 23 cm. (Hoover Press publication; 281) 1. Trades Union Congress. 2. Trade-unions — Great Britain — Political activity. I. T.
HD8383.D67 1983 331.88/0941 19 *LC* 82-83300 *ISBN* 0817978119

**Dorfman, Gerald Allen, 1939-.** **4.3635**
Government versus trade unionism in British politics since 1968 / Gerald A. Dorfman. — Stanford, Calif.: Hoover Institution Press, Stanford University, 1979. vii, 179 p.; 23 cm. (Hoover Institution publication; 224) 1. Trades Union Congress. 2. Trade-unions — Great Britain — Political activity. 3. Wage-price policy — Great Britain. 4. Great Britain — Politics and government — 1964-1979 I. T.
HD8383.T74 D66 322/.2/0941 *LC* 78-70886 *ISBN* 0817972412

**Dorfman, Gerald Allen, 1939-.** **4.3636**
Wage politics in Britain, 1945–1967: government vs. the TUC. — [1st ed.] Ames: Iowa State University Press, 1973. x, 180 p.; 22 cm. 1. Trades Union Congress. 2. Wage-price policy — Great Britain. 3. Great Britain — Economic policy — 1945- I. T.
HD8383.T74 D67 331.2/942 *LC* 72-1833 *ISBN* 0813803004

**Meacham, Standish.** **4.3637**
A life apart: the English working class, 1890–1914 / Standish Meacham. — Cambridge, Mass.: Harvard University Press, 1977. 272 p., [8] leaves of plates: ill.; 25 cm. Includes index. 1. Labor and laboring classes — England — History. I. T.
HD8386.M4 1977b 301.44/42/0942 *LC* 77-72673 *ISBN* 0674530756

**Proletarianization and family history / edited by David Levine.** **4.3638**
Orlando: Academic Press, 1984. xii, 315 p.: ill.; 24 cm. (Studies in social discontinuity.) 1. Labor and laboring classes — Great Britain — History 2. Family — Great Britain — History. 3. Proletariat — History. I. Levine, David, 1946- II. Series.
HD8388.P76 1984 305.5/62/0941 19 *LC* 84-6301 *ISBN* 0124449808

**Robertson, N. (Norman)** **4.3639**
British trade unionism; select documents [by] N. Robertson and K. I. Sams. With a foreword by George Woodcock. Totowa, N.J., Rowman and Littlefield [1972] 2 v. (xxviii, 607 p.) 25 cm. 1. Industrial relations — Great Britain — History — Sources. 2. Trade-unions — Great Britain — History — Sources. I. Sams, K. I. joint author. II. T.
HD8388.R6 1972 331/.0942 *LC* 72-170855 *ISBN* 0874710987

**Rogers, James Edwin Thorold, 1823-1890.** **4.3640**
Six centuries of work and wages. The history of English labour. — London[etc.] T.F. Unwin, 1949. 591 p. 23 cm. 1st edition, 1884. 1. Great Britain — Econ. condit. 2. Wages — Great Britain. 3. Labor and laboring classes — Great Britain I. T.
HD8388.R7 *LC* 08-8219

**Thompson, E. P. (Edward Palmer), 1924-.** • **4.3641**
The making of the English working class. New York, Pantheon Books [1964, c1963] 848 p. 23 cm. 1. Labor and laboring classes — England I. T.
HD8388.T47 331.44 *LC* 64-10769

**Brown, Henry Phelps, Sir, 1906-.** **4.3642**
The growth of British industrial relations; a study from the standpoint of 1906–14. — London, Macmillan; New York, St. Martin's Press, 1960. 414 p. illus. 23 cm. Includes bibliography. 1. Industrial relations — Great Britain. 2. Labor and laboring classes — Great Britain 3. Trade-unions — Great Britain. I. T.
HD8390.B88 1960 331.0942 *LC* 59-16509

**Middlemas, Keith, 1935-.** **4.3643**
Politics in industrial society: the experience of the British system since 1911 / Keith Middlemas. — London: A. Deutsch, 1980 (c1979). 512 p.; 25 cm. 1. Industrial relations — Great Britain — History. 2. Industry and state — Great Britain — History. 3. Great Britain — Politics and government — 20th century I. T.
HD8390.M52 331/.0941 *LC* 80-468589 *ISBN* 0233971297

**Tholfsen, Trygve R.** **4.3644**
Working class radicalism in mid–Victorian England / Trygve R. Tholfsen. New York: Columbia University Press, 1977. 332 p.; 23 cm. 1. Labor and laboring classes — Great Britain — Political activity — History. 2. Radicalism — Great Britain — History. 3. Great Britain — Social conditions — 19th century I. T.
HD8390.T5 1977 322/.2/0941 *LC* 76-43323 *ISBN* 0231042345

**Flanders, Allan D.** • **4.3645**
Management and unions: the theory and reform of industrial relations, by Allan Flanders. — London: Faber, 1970. 3-317 p.; 23 cm. 1. Industrial relations — Great Britain. 2. Collective bargaining — Great Britain. I. T.
HD8391.F553 331.1/9/42 *LC* 72-517399 *ISBN* 0571092802

**Jenkins, Peter George James, 1934-.** **4.3646**
The battle of Downing Street [by] Peter Jenkins. London, Knight, 1970. xiv, 171 p. 22 cm. 1. Labour Party (Great Britain) 2. Trade-unions — Great Britain — Political activity. 3. Great Britain — Politics and government — 1945- I. T.
HD8391.J45 320.9/42/085 *LC* 75-556154 *ISBN* 0853140685

**Wright, A. W.** **4.3647**
G. D. H. Cole and socialist democracy / A. W. Wright. — Oxford: Clarendon Press; New York: Oxford University Press, 1979. 301 p., [1] leaf of plates: port.; 23 cm. 1. Cole, G. D. H. (George Douglas Howard), 1889-1959. 2. Guild socialism I. T.
HD8393.C57 W74 335/.1 *LC* 78-40644 *ISBN* 0198274211

**McLean, Iain.** **4.3648**
Keir Hardie / Iain McLean. — New York: St. Martin's Press, c1975. viii, 183 p.; 23 cm. — (British political biography) 1. Hardie, James Keir, 1856-1915. 2. Labour Party (Great Britain) — History. 3. Socialism — Great Britain I. T.
HD8393.H3 M32 1975b 329.9/41 *LC* 75-18038

**Larkin, Emmet J., 1927-.** • **4.3649**
James Larkin, Irish labour leader, 1876-1947, by Emmet Larkin. Cambridge, M.I.T. Press [1965] xviii, 334 p. ill., ports. 1. Larkin, James, 1876-1947. 2. Trade-unions — Ireland 3. Labor and laboring classes — Ireland I. T.
HD8393 L3 L3 *LC* 64-22134

**Hindess, Barry.**      **4.3650**
The decline of working–class politics. — London: MacGibbon & Kee, 1971. 191 p.; 23 cm. 1. Labor and laboring classes — Great Britain — Political activity. 2. Great Britain — Politics and government — 1945- I. T.
HD8395.H58     323.3     *LC* 74-569620     *ISBN* 0261632108

**McKenzie, Robert Trelford.**      **4.3651**
Angels in marble: working class Conservatives in urban England / [by] Robert McKenzie and Allan Silver. — Chicago: University of Chicago Press, [1968] xi, 295 p.: ill.; 23 cm. — (Studies in contemporary sociology) 1. Conservative Party (Great Britain) 2. Labor and laboring classes — Great Britain I. Silver, Allan, joint author. II. T. III. Title: Working class Conservatives in urban England.
HD8395.M22     323.3     *LC* 67-30555

**Richter, Irving.**      **4.3652**
Political purpose in trade unions. — London: Allen & Unwin, [1973] 258 p.; 22 cm. 1. Amalgamated Engineering Union. 2. Trade-unions — Great Britain — Political activity. I. T.
HD8395.R52     322/.2/0942     *LC* 73-172905     *ISBN* 0043310567

**Williams, Gwyn A.**      **• 4.3653**
Artisans and sans–culottes; popular movements in France and Britain during the French revolution, by Gwyn A. Williams. — New York: Norton, [1969] vi, 128 p.; 21 cm. — (Foundations of modern history) 1. Artisans — Great Britain — Political activity — History. 2. Sansculottes 3. Great Britain — History — 1789-1820 4. France — History — Revolution, 1789-1799 I. T.
HD8395.W48     331.7/94/0942     *LC* 69-14476

**Thompson, Dorothy, 1923-.**      **4.3654**
The Chartists: popular politics in the Industrial Revolution / Dorothy Thompson. — 1st American ed. — New York: Pantheon Books, c1984. 399 p.; 25 cm. 1. Chartism 2. Labor and laboring classes — Great Britain — Political activity — History — 19th century. 3. Labor and laboring classes — Great Britain — History — 19th century I. T.
HD8396.T44 1984     322/.2/0941 19     *LC* 83-21984     *ISBN* 0394511409

**Calhoun, Craig J., 1952-.**      **4.3655**
The question of class struggle: social foundations of popular radicalism during the industrial revolution / Craig Calhoun. — Chicago: University of Chicago Press, 1982. xiv, 321 p.; 24 cm. Includes index. 1. Labor and laboring classes — England — History. 2. Populism — England — History. 3. Radicalism — England — History. I. T.
HD8399.E52 C34     305.5/6 19     *LC* 81-2018     *ISBN* 0226090906

## HD8401–8650.5 Other European Countries

**Hamilton, Richard F.**      **• 4.3656**
Affluence and the French worker in the Fourth Republic [by] Richard F. Hamilton. Princeton, N.J., Princeton University Press, 1967. 323 p. illus., forms, map. 25 cm. 'Published for the Center of International Studies, Princeton University.' 1. Labor and laboring classes — France 2. Political psychology I. Woodrow Wilson School of Public and International Affairs. Center of International Studies. II. T.
HD8435.H3     331/.0944     *LC* 67-11033

**Anderson, Evelyn.**      **• 4.3657**
Hammer or anvil; the story of the German working–class movement, by Evelyn Anderson ... — London, V. Gollancz ltd, 1945. 207 p. 19.5 cm. 1. Labor and laboring classes — Germany — Hist. 2. Germany — Economic policy I. T.
HD8450.A5     331     *LC* 45-10279

**Moore, Barrington, 1913-.**      **4.3658**
Injustice: the social bases of obedience and revolt / Barrington Moore, Jr. — White Plains, N.Y.: M. E. Sharpe; [New York]: distributed by Pantheon Books, c1978. xviii, 540 p.; 24 cm. Includes index. 1. Labor and laboring classes — Germany — History. 2. Radicalism — Germany — History. 3. Social justice 4. Revolutions I. T.
HD8450.M66     301.44/42/0943     *LC* 77-91862     *ISBN* 0873321146

**Spencer, Elaine Glovka, 1939-.**      **4.3659**
Management and labor in imperial Germany: Ruhr industrialists as employers, 1896–1914 / Elaine Glovka Spencer. — New Brunswick, N.J.: Rutgers University Press, c1984. x, 208 p.; 23 cm. Includes index. 1. Industrial relations — Germany (West) — Ruhr (Region) — History. 2. Steel industry and trade — Germany (West) — Ruhr (Region) — History. 3. Iron industry and trade — Germany (West) — Ruhr (Region) — Personnel management — History. 4. Coal mines and mining — Germany (West) —

Ruhr (Region) — Personnel management — History. 5. Employers' associations — Germany (West) — Ruhr (Region) — History. I. T.
HD8459.R8 S68 1984     331/.0943/55 19     *LC* 83-11089     *ISBN* 0813510171

**Neufeld, Maurice F.**      **• 4.3660**
Italy: school for awakening countries; the Italian labor movement in its political, social, and economic setting from 1800 to 1960. Ithaca, New York State School of Industrial and Labor Relations, Cornell University, 1961. viii, 589 p. map (on lining papers) (Cornell international industrial and labor relations reports, no. 5) 1. Labor and laboring classes — Italy 2. Trade-unions — Italy 3. Italy — Social conditions I. T. II. Series.
HD8478 N4     *LC* 60-63276

**The Russian worker: life and labor under the tsarist regime /**      **4.3661**
**edited, with an introduction and annotations by Victoria E. Bonnell.**
Berkeley: University of California Press, c1983. xvii, 216 p.: ill.; 24 cm. 'The five selections in this volume have been chosen and translated from longer works originally published in Russian'—P. xv. 1. Labor and laboring classes — Soviet Union — History — Addresses, essays, lectures. 2. Labor and laboring classes — Soviet Union — Biography — Addresses, essays, lectures. I. Bonnell, Victoria E.
HD8526.R89 1983     305.5/62/0947 19     *LC* 83-47856     *ISBN* 0520048377

**McAuley, Mary.**      **• 4.3662**
Labour disputes in Soviet Russia, 1957–1965. — Oxford: Clarendon P., 1969. ix, 269 p.; 22 cm. 1. Industrial relations — Russia. 2. Trade-unions — Russia. I. T.
HD8526.5.M23     331.89/0947     *LC* 75-386695     *ISBN* 0198282427

**Solidarité. English.**      **4.3663**
Solidarity: the analysis of a social movement: Poland, 1980–1981 / Alain Touraine ... [et al.]; in collaboration with Grażyna Gesicka ... [et al.]; translated by David Denby. — Cambridge [Cambridgeshire]; New York: Cambridge University Press; Paris: Editions de la Maison des sciences de l'homme, 1983. xvi, 203 p.: ill.; 24 cm. Translation of: Solidarité. 1. NSZZ 'Solidarność' (Labor organization) 2. Trade-unions — Poland. 3. Poland — Social conditions — 1980- 4. Poland — Politics and government — 1980- I. Touraine, Alain. II. T.
HD8537.N783 S6413 1983     322/.2/09438 19     *LC* 83-1859     *ISBN* 0521254078

**Galenson, Walter, 1914-.**      **• 4.3664**
The Danish system of labor relations; a study in industrial peace. New York, Russell & Russell [1969, c1952] xii, 321 p. illus. 25 cm. (Wertheim Fellowship publications) 'Mediation act': p. [296]-302. 'Labor Court act': p. [303]-309. 1. Industrial relations — Denmark. I. Denmark. Laws, statutes, etc. Lov om udnaevnelse af en forligsmand i arbejdsstridigheder. English. 1969. II. Denmark. Laws, statutes, etc. Lov om oprettelse af en fast voldgiftsret. English. 1969. III. T.
HD8546.G3 1969     331.1/9/489     *LC* 68-27059

**Peirats, José.**      **• 4.3665**
La C.N.T. [Confederación nacional del trabajo] en la revolución española ... [2a edición.] Paris Ruedo ibérico 1971. (España contemporánea) 1. Confederación Nacional del Trabajo (Spain) 2. Spain — Politics and government I. T.
HD8582 C583 P45 1971

## HD8661–8930 Asia. Africa. Australia. New Zealand

**Myers, Charles Andrew, 1913-.**      **• 4.3666**
Industrial relations in India [by] Charles A. Myers [and] Subbiah Kannappan. — [2d rev. and enl. ed.]. — New York: Asia Pub. House, [1970] xvii, 426 p.; 23 cm. First ed. published in 1958 under title: Labor problems in the industrialization of India. 1. Industrial relations — India. I. Kannappan, Subbiah. joint author. II. T.
HD8686.5.M9 1970     331/.0954     *LC* 70-23145     *ISBN* 0210336803

**Taira, Koji, 1926-.**      **• 4.3667**
Economic development & the labor market in Japan. New York, Columbia University Press, 1970. xiii, 282 p. illus. 25 cm. (Studies of the East Asian Institute) 1. Industrial relations — Japan. 2. Labor policy — Japan. 3. Wages — Japan. I. T.
HD8724.T34     331/.0952     *LC* 78-111459     *ISBN* 0231032722

**Contemporary industrial relations in Japan** / edited by Taishiro    **4.3668**
Shirai.
Madison, Wis.: University of Wisconsin Press, 1983. xxvi, 421 p.: ill.; 24 cm.
Includes index. 1. Industrial relations — Japan — Addresses, essays, lectures.
I. Shirai, Taishirō.
HD8726.5.C65 1983      331/.0952 19    *LC* 83-47770    *ISBN*
0299092801

**Walder, Andrew George.**    **4.3669**
Communist neo–traditionalism: work and authority in Chinese society /
Andrew G. Walder. — Berkeley: University of California Press, c1986. p. cm.
Includes index. 1. Industrial relations — China. 2. Communism — China.
3. Labor and laboring classes — China. I. T.
HD8736.5.W34 1986      306/.36/0951 19    *LC* 85-27093    *ISBN*
0520054393

**The Development of an African working class: studies in class**    **4.3670**
**formation and action** / edited by Richard Sandbrook, Robin
Cohen.
London: Longman, c1975. vii, 330 p.; 25 cm. Consists chiefly of papers
presented at a conference on workers, unions, and development held at the
University of Toronto, April 6-8, 1973. 1. Labor and laboring classes — Africa,
Sub-Saharan — Congresses. 2. Trade-unions — Africa, Sub-Saharan —
Congresses. I. Sandbrook, Richard. II. Cohen, Robin.
HD8776.5.D48      301.44/42/0967    *LC* 76-362061    *ISBN*
0582641799

**Beling, Willard A.**    • **4.3671**
Modernization and African labor; a Tunisian case study [by] Willard A. Beling.
New York, Praeger [1966] xv, 259 p. (Praeger special studies in international
economics and development) 1. Labor and laboring classes — Tunisia I. T.
HD8809 T8 B4      *LC* 65-21101

**Donn, Clifford B.**    **4.3672**
The Australian Council of Trade Unions: history and economic policy /
Clifford B. Donn. — Lanham, [MD]: University Press of America, 1984. xxxiii,
366 p.; 22 cm. 1. Australian Council of Trade Unions. 2. Trade-unions —
Australia. 3. Industrial relations — Australia. I. T.
HD8842.A873 D66      331.88/0994 19    *LC* 82-15951    *ISBN*
0819127280

**Sutch, William Ball, 1904-.**    • **4.3673**
The quest for security in New Zealand, 1840 to 1966. — Wellington; New York
[etc.]: Oxford University Press, 1966. xvi, 512 p.; 20 cm. Illus. lining-papers.
The first third of this book was published by Penguin in 1942.—Dust jacket.
1. Labor and laboring classes — New Zealand. 2. New Zealand — Economic
conditions — 1918- 3. New Zealand — Social conditions. I. T.
HD8866.S8 1966      331/.09931    *LC* 67-88840

## HD8943 Developing Countries

**Peasants and proletarians: the struggles of Third World workers**    **4.3674**
/ edited by Robin Cohen, Peter C. W. Gutkind, and Phyllis
Brazier.
New York: Monthly Review Press, c1979. 505 p.; 22 cm. 1. Labor and laboring
classes — Developing countries — Addresses, essays, lectures. 2. Trade-unions
— Developing countries — Addresses, essays, lectures. 3. Peasantry —
Developing countries — Addresses, essays, lectures. I. Cohen, Robin.
II. Gutkind, Peter Claus Wolfgang. III. Brazier, Phyllis.
HD8943.P42      331/.09172/4    *LC* 79-10020    *ISBN* 0853454213

**Proletarianisation in the Third World: studies in the creation of**    **4.3675**
**a labour force under dependent capitalism** / edited by B.
Munslow and H. Finch.
London; Dover, N.H.: Croom Helm, c1984. 320 p.; 23 cm. Includes index.
1. Labor and laboring classes — Developing countries 2. Labor supply —
Developing countries 3. Poor — Developing countries 4. Proletariat
I. Munslow, Barry. II. Finch, M. H. J. (Martin Henry John)
HD8943.P76 1984      305.5/62/091724 19    *LC* 84-12739    *ISBN*
0709917643

# HD9000–9999 Special Industries and Trades

## HD9000–9490 Agricultural Products. Plant and Animal Products

**Abelson, Philip Hauge.**    **4.3676**
Food: politics, economics, nutrition, and research / edited by Philip H.
Abelson. — Washington: American Association for the Advancement of
Science, c1975. v, 202 p.: ill.; 28 cm. — (AAAS miscellaneous publication; 75-7)
'A special Science compendium.' 1. Food supply — Addresses, essays, lectures.
2. Agriculture — Research — Addresses, essays, lectures. 3. Nutrition —
Addresses, essays, lectures. I. Science. II. T.
HD9000.5.A2x Q181.A1.A68 no.75-7      338.1/9    *LC* 75-18785
   *ISBN* 087168215X. *ISBN* 0871682265 pbk

**Lamartine Yates, Paul.**    • **4.3677**
Food, land, and manpower in Western Europe. — London, Macmillan; New
York, St. Martin's Press, 1960. 294 p. illus. 23 cm. 1. Food supply
2. Agriculture — Economic aspects I. T.
HD9000.5.L3      338.1094    *LC* 60-3985

**The lessons of wage and price controls, the food sector** / edited    **4.3678**
by John T. Dunlop and Kenneth J. Fedor.
Boston: Division of Research, Graduate School of Business Administration,
Harvard University; Cambridge, Mass.: distributed by Harvard University
Press, 1977. xii, 344 p.: graphs; 25 cm. 1. Food prices — United States.
2. Agricultural prices — United States. 3. Wage-price policy — United States.
I. Dunlop, John Thomas, 1914- II. Fedor, Kenneth J.
HD9004.L45      338.1/9/73    *LC* 77-86591    *ISBN* 0875841171

**The Food manufacturing industries: structure, strategies,**    **4.3679**
**performance, and policies** / John M. Connor ... [et al.].
Lexington, Mass.: Lexington Books, c1985. xxii, 474 p.: ill.; 24 cm. Includes
indexes. 1. Food industry and trade — United States. I. Connor, John M.
HD9005.F659 1985      338.4/7664/00973 19    *LC* 83-49504    *ISBN*
0669082031

**Breimyer, Harold F.**    **4.3680**
Economics of the product markets of agriculture / Harold F. Breimyer. — 1st
ed. — Ames: Iowa State University Press, 1976. x, 208 p.: ill.; 24 cm. 1. Farm
produce — United States — Marketing. 2. Agriculture — Economic aspects —
United States. I. T.
HD9006.B67      381/.41/0973    *LC* 75-44220    *ISBN* 0813818400

**Doyle, Jack, 1947-.**    **4.3681**
Altered harvest: agriculture, genetics, and the fate of the world's food supply /
by Jack Doyle. — New York, N.Y., U.S.A.: Viking, 1985. xix, 502 p.; 24 cm.
Includes index. 1. Food industry and trade — Technological innovations —
Government policy — United States. 2. Agricultural innovations —
Government policy — United States. 3. Genetic engineering industry —
Government policy — United States. 4. Biotechnology industries —
Government policy — United States. 5. Pharmaceutical industry —
Government policy — United States. 6. Seed industry and trade —
Technological innovations — Government policy — United States.
7. Agricultural chemicals industry — Government policy — United States.
8. Food adutation and inspection — Government policy — United States. I. T.
HD9006.D65 1985      338.1/9/73 19    *LC* 84-40458    *ISBN*
067011524X

**Grennes, Thomas.**    **4.3682**
The economics of world grain trade / Thomas Grennes, Paul R. Johnson, Marie
Thursby. — New York: Praeger, 1978 (c1977). xii, 129 p.; 24 cm. 1. Grain
trade 2. Grain trade — Mathematical models. I. Johnson, Paul R. (Paul
Reynold), 1929- joint author. II. Thursby, Marie. joint author. III. T.
HD9030.5.G83 1978      382/.41/3    *LC* 77-13715    *ISBN* 0030228360

**Walker, Kenneth R. (Kenneth Richard)**    **4.3683**
Food grain procurement and consumption in China / Kenneth R. Walker. —
Cambridge [Cambridgeshire]; New York: Cambridge University Press, 1984.
xxi, 329 p.: ill.; 23 cm. — (Contemporary China Institute publications.)
1. Grain trade — China. 2. Food consumption — China. 3. Grain trade —
Government policy — China. 4. Food supply — Government policy — China.
I. T. II. Series.
HD9046.C62 W335 1984      381/.4131/0951 19    *LC* 83-7820    *ISBN*
0521256496

**Hadwiger, Don Frank, 1930-.** • **4.3684**
Federal wheat commodity programs [by] Don F. Hadwiger. — [1st ed.]. — Ames: Iowa State University Press, [1970] xi, 407 p.: illus.; 24 cm. 1. Wheat trade — United States. 2. Agricultural price supports — United States 3. Agriculture and state — United States I. T.
HD9049.W5 U4286      353.008/2      LC 72-92693      ISBN 0813806305

**Woodman, Harold D.** • **4.3685**
King cotton & his retainers; financing & marketing the cotton crop of the South, 1800–1925 [by] Harold D. Woodman. — Lexington: University of Kentucky Press, 1968. xiv, 386 p.: illus., col. map (on lining papers); 25 cm. 1. Cotton trade — United States. I. T.
HD9075.W58      338.1/7/3510973      LC 67-29337

**Daniel, Pete.** **4.3686**
Breaking the land: the transformation of cotton, tobacco, and rice cultures since 1880 / Pete Daniel. — Urbana: University of Illinois Press, c1985. xvi, 352 p.: ill.; 24 cm. Includes index. 1. Cotton trade — Southern States — History. 2. Tobacco industry — Southern States — History. 3. Rice trade — Southern States — History. I. T.
HD9077.A13 D36 1985      306/.3 19      LC 84-197      ISBN 0252011473

**Eichner, Alfred S.** • **4.3687**
The emergence of oligopoly; sugar refining as a case study [by] Alfred S. Eichner. — Baltimore: Johns Hopkins Press, [1969] xi, 388 p.: illus., maps.; 24 cm. 1. Sugar — Manufacture and refining — U.S. I. T.
HD9105.E4      338.4/7/6641      LC 74-79300      ISBN 080181068X

**Schwartz, Stuart B.** **4.3688**
Sugar plantations in the formation of Brazilian society: Bahia, 1550–1835 / Stuart B. Schwartz. — Cambridge [Cambridgeshire]; New York: Cambridge University Press, 1985. xxiii, 616 p.: ill.; 24 cm. (Cambridge Latin American studies. 52) Includes index. 1. Sugar trade — Brazil — Bahia (State) — History. 2. Plantations — Brazil — Bahia (State) — History. 3. Slavery — Brazil — Bahia (State) — History. 4. Bahia (Brazil: State) — Race relations. 5. Bahia (Brazil: State) — Social conditions. 6. Bahia (Brazil: State) — Economic conditions. I. T. II. Series.
HD9114.B7 B347 1985      306/.0981/42 19      LC 85-6716      ISBN 0521309344

**Owen, Norman G.** **4.3689**
Prosperity without progress: Manila hemp and material life in the colonial Philippines / Norman G. Owen. — Berkeley: University of California Press, c1984. xxii, 311 p.: ill.; 24 cm. 'This volume is sponsored by the Center for South and Southeast Asia Studies, University of California, Berkeley'—Half-t.p. Includes index. 1. Manila hemp industry — Philippines — History. 2. Philippines — Social conditions. I. University of California, Berkeley. Center for South and Southeast Asia Studies. II. T.
HD9156.M352 P66 1984      338.1/73571/09599 19      LC 82-2024      ISBN 0520044703

## HD9195–9398 Food Products. Groceries

**McMenamin, Michael.** **4.3690**
Milking the public: political scandals of the dairy lobby from L. B. J. to Jimmy Carter / Michael McMenamin and Walter McNamara. — Chicago: Nelson-Hall, c1980. xvi, 300 p.; 23 cm. 1. Milk trade — Political aspects — United States. 2. Milk — Prices — Political aspects — United States. 3. Corruption (in politics) — United States I. McNamara, Walter (Walter J.) joint author. II. T.
HD9282.U4 M25      328.73/078      LC 80-11546      ISBN 0882295527

**Manchester, Alden Coe, 1922-.** **4.3691**
The public role in the dairy economy: why and how governments intervene in the milk business / Alden C. Manchester. — Boulder, Colo.: Westview Press, 1983. xviii, 323 p.: ill.; 24 cm. — (Westview special studies in agriculture science and policy.) Includes index. 1. Milk trade — Government policy — United States. 2. Milk trade — United States — Price policy. 3. Dairy products — United States — Price policy. 4. Agricultural price supports — United States I. T. II. Series.
HD9282.U4 M324 1983      338.1/873 19      LC 83-6957      ISBN 0865315906

**Mueller, Willard Fritz.** • **4.3692**
Changes in market structure of grocery retailing [by] Willard F. Mueller [and] Leon Garoian. Madison, University of Wisconsin, 1961. 215 p. ill. 1. Grocery trade — United States 2. Chain stores — United States I. Garoian, Leon. jt. author II. T.
HD9321.5 M8      LC 60-11444

**Adelman, Morris Albert.** • **4.3693**
A & P.: a study in price–cost behavior and public policy. — Cambridge: Harvard University Press, 1959. xiv, 537 p.: diagrs., tables; 22 cm. (Harvard economic studies. v. 113) Bibliographical footnotes. 1. Great Atlantic & Pacific Tea Company. 2. Pricing — Case studies. I. T. II. Series.
HD9321.9.G7A6      338.52      LC 59-14733

**Cochran, Thomas Childs, 1902-.** • **4.3694**
The Pabst Brewing Company: the history of an American business / Thomas C. Cochran. — New York: New York University Press, 1948. xii, 451 p., [4] leaves of plates: ports. — (New York University. Graduate School of Business Administration. Business history series) 1. Pabst Brewing Company, Milwaukee, Wis. I. T. II. Series.
HD9397.U54 P23      LC 48-7477

## HD9410–9490 Animal Industries. Fisheries

**Shultz, George Pratt.** • **4.3695**
Strategies for the displaced worker: confronting economic change [by] George P.Shultz and Arnold R.Weber. New York: Harper and Row, 1966. 221 p. 1. Armour and Company. 2. Unemployment, Technological I. Weber, Arnold Robert. II. T.
HD9419.A85 S5      658.386      LC 66-13925

**Simpson, James R.** **4.3696**
The world's beef business / James R. Simpson, Donald E. Farris. — 1st ed. — Ames, Iowa: Iowa State University Press, 1982. x, 334 p.: ill.; 23 cm. 1. Beef industry 2. Cattle trade I. Farris, Donald E. II. T.
HD9433.A2 S53 1982      338.1/76213 19      LC 81-20770      ISBN 0813809606

**Smith, Peter H.** **4.3697**
Politics and beef in Argentina; patterns of conflict and change [by] Peter H. Smith. New York, Columbia University Press, 1969. x, 292 p. 25 cm. 1. Cattle trade — Argentina. 2. Meat industry and trade — Argentina. 3. Argentina — Politics and government I. T.
HD9433.A72 S6      338.1/7/62130982      LC 68-8878

**Breen, David.** **4.3698**
The Canadian prairie west and the ranching frontier, 1874–1924 / David H. Breen. — Toronto; Buffalo: University of Toronto Press, c1983. xiii, 302 p., [4] p. of plates: ill., ports.; 24 cm. Includes index. 1. Cattle trade — Prairie Provinces — History. 2. Land use, Rural — Prairie Provinces — History. 3. Ranchers — Prairie Provinces — Political activity — History. I. T.
HD9433.C22 P733 1983      338.1/762/009712 19      LC 83-143575      ISBN 0802055486

**Cunningham, Stephen.** **4.3699**
Fisheries economics: an introduction / Stephen Cunningham, Michael R. Dunn, and David Whitmarsh. — London: Mansell Pub.; New York: St. Martin's Press, 1985. xi, 372 p.: ill.; 24 cm. 1. Fisheries — Economic aspects 2. Fish trade 3. Fishery policy I. Dunn, Michael R. II. Whitmarsh, David. III. T.
HD9450.5.C86 1985      338.3/727 19      LC 84-12577      ISBN 072011702X

**Lawson, Rowena M.** **4.3700**
Economics of fisheries development / Rowena Lawson. — New York: Praeger, 1984. 283 p.: ill. Includes index 1. Fisheries — Economic aspects 2. Fishery management 3. Fisheries — Economic aspects — Developing countries. 4. Fishery management — Developing countries. I. T.
HD9450.5.L38 1984      338.3/72709172/4 19      LC 84-15074      ISBN 0030012430

**Ozanne, Robert W.** **4.3701**
A century of labor–management relations at McCormick and International Harvester. Madison, University of Wisconsin Press, 1967. vii, 300 p. illus. facsims., ports. 24 cm. A companion volume to Wages in practice and theory; McCormick and International Harvester, 1860-1960. 1. International Harvester Company. 2. Industrial relations — United States. I. T.
HD9486.U6 I77      331.1/88/17      LC 67-25939

## HD9502–9505 Energy Industries: General

**Bohi, Douglas R.** **4.3702**
Analyzing demand behavior: a study of energy elasticities / Douglas R. Bohi. — Baltimore: Published for Resources for the Future by the Johns Hopkins University Press, c1981. xiv, 177 p.; 24 cm. Includes index. 1. Energy consumption — Mathematical models. 2. Power resources — Prices — Mathematical models. 3. Elasticity (Economics) — Mathematical models. I. Resources for the Future. II. T.
HD9502.A2 B65      333.79/12/0724 19      LC 81-47616      ISBN 0801827051

**Chapman, P. F. (Peter F.), 1944-.**      4.3703
Metal resources and energy / P.F. Chapman, F. Roberts. — London: Butterworths, 1983. ix, 238 p.: ill.; 24 cm. — (Butterworths monographs in materials.) 1. Power resources I. Roberts, F. II. T. III. Series.
HD9502.A2 C42     HD9502A2 C45 1983.     333.79 19     *ISBN* 0408108010

**Commoner, Barry, 1917-.**      4.3704
The poverty of power: energy and the economic crisis / Barry Commoner. — 1st ed. — New York: Knopf: distributed by Random House, 1976. 314 p.; 22 cm. 1. Power resources 2. Power (Mechanics) 3. Energy policy — United States. 4. Economic history 5. United States — Economic policy — 1971-1981 I. T.
HD9502.A2 C643 1976     333.7     *LC* 75-36798     *ISBN* 0394403711

**Darmstadter, Joel, 1928-.**      4.3705
How industrial societies use energy: a comparative analysis / Joel Darmstadter, Joy Dunkerley, Jack Alterman. — Baltimore: Published for Resources for the Future by the Johns Hopkins University Press, c1977. xvi, 282 p.; 24 cm. 1. Energy consumption 2. Energy consumption — United States. I. Dunkerley, Joy. joint author. II. Alterman, Jack. joint author. III. Resources for the Future. IV. T.
HD9502.A2 D37     333.7     *LC* 77-83780     *ISBN* 0801820413

**Gordon, Richard L., 1934-.**      4.3706
An economic analysis of world energy problems / Richard L. Gordon. — Cambridge, Mass.: MIT Press, c1981. xvii, 282 p.: ill.; 24 cm. Includes index. 1. Energy policy 2. Power resources I. T.
HD9502.A2 G67     333.79 19     *LC* 80-28663     *ISBN* 0262070804

**Handbook of natural resource and energy economics / edited by**      4.3707
**Allen V. Kneese and James L. Sweeney.**
Amsterdam; New York: North-Holland; New York, N.Y., U.S.A.: Sole distributors for the U.S.A. and Canada, Elsevier Science Pub. Co., 1985. 3 v.: ill.; 25 cm. (Handbooks in economics; 6) 1. Energy industries 2. Natural resources 3. Conservation of natural resources 4. Power resources 5. Environmental protection I. Kneese, Allen V. II. Sweeney, James L.
HD9502.A2 H257 1985     333.7 19     *LC* 85-10322     *ISBN* 0444876464

**Webb, Michael Gordon.**      4.3708
The economics of energy / Michael G. Webb and Martin J. Ricketts. — New York: Wiley, c1980. xiii, 315 p.: graphs; 23 cm. 'A Halsted Press book.' 1. Energy policy 2. Economic policy 3. Power resources I. Ricketts, Martin J. joint author. II. T.
HD9502.A2 W4 1980     333.7     *LC* 79-18708     *ISBN* 0470268417

**World energy outlook / International Energy Agency.**      4.3709
Paris: Organisation for Economic Co-operation and Development; Washington D.C.: Distributed by OECD Publications and Information Center, 1982. 473 p.: ill.; 24 cm. 1. Energy industries 2. Energy development 3. Power resources 4. Petroleum industry and trade I. International Energy Agency.
HD9502.A2 W6694 1982     333.79 19     *LC* 82-232560     *ISBN* 9264123601

**Yager, Joseph A., 1916-.**      4.3710
The energy balance in Northeast Asia / Joseph A. Yager with the assistance of Shelley M. Matsuba. — Washington, D.C.: Brookings Institution, c1984. xiv, 249 p.; 24 cm. 1. Power resources — Economic aspects — East Asia. 2. Power resources — Political aspects — East Asia. 3. Energy policy — East Asia. I. Matsuba, Shelley M., 1953- II. Brookings Institution. III. T.
HD9502.A782 Y33 1984     333.79/095 19     *LC* 84-45276     *ISBN* 0815796722

**Cheng, Chu-yüan.**      4.3711
The demand and supply of primary energy in mainland China / Chu–yuan Cheng. — Taipei, Taiwan, Republic of China: Chung-Hua Institution for Economic Research; Seattle: Distributed by University of Washington Press, 1985 (c1984). viii, 178 p.; 26 cm. (Mainland China economic series. no. 3) Pages 178 blank. 1. Energy industries — China. 2. Energy consumption — China. I. T. II. Series.
HD9502.C62 C49 1984     333.79/11/0951 19     *LC* 84-231216

**Hoffman, George Walter, 1914-.**      4.3712
The European energy challenge: East and West / George W. Hoffman with contributions by Leslie Dienes. — Durham, NC: Duke University Press, 1985. xxvii, 207 p.: ill.; 24 cm. (Duke Press policy studies.) Includes index. 1. Energy industries — Europe. I. Dienes, Leslie. II. T. III. Series.
HD9502.E8 H64 1985     333.79/094 19     *LC* 84-24748     *ISBN* 0822305755

**Bohi, Douglas R.**      4.3713
U.S. energy policy: alternatives for security / Douglas R. Bohi, Milton Russell. — Baltimore: Published for Resources for the Future by the Johns Hopkins University Press, [1975] x, 131 p.; 23 cm. Includes summary of the RFF-NSF conference on 'U.S. energy policy: alternatives for security,' held Oct. 3, 1974,
to discuss the first draft of the authors' work. 1. Energy policy — United States. 2. Petroleum industry and trade I. Russell, Milton, 1933- joint author. II. Resources for the Future. III. T.
HD9502.U52 B63     338.4     *LC* 75-4209     *ISBN* 0801817323

**Breyer, Stephen G., 1938-.**      4.3714
Energy regulation by the Federal Power Commission [by] Stephen G. Breyer [and] Paul W. MacAvoy. — Washington: Brookings Institution, [1974] x, 163 p.: illus.; 24 cm. — (Studies in the regulation of economic activity.) 1. United States. Federal Power Commission. 2. Energy policy — United States. I. MacAvoy, Paul W. joint author. II. T. III. Series.
HD9502.U52 B7     353.008/72     *LC* 74-273     *ISBN* 0815710763

**Energy future: report of the energy project at the Harvard**      4.3715
**Business School / Robert Stobaugh, Daniel Yergin, editors; I.C.**
**Bupp ... [et al.].**
New rev. 3rd ed. — New York: Vintage Books, 1983, c1980. xii, 459 p.; 21 cm. 'First Vintage Books edition'—Verso t.p. 1. Energy policy — United States. 2. Power resources — United States. I. Stobaugh, Robert B. II. Yergin, Daniel. III. Harvard University. Graduate School of Business Administration.
HD9502.U52 E4914 1983     333.79/0973 19     *LC* 81-40078     *ISBN* 039474750X

**Energy, the next twenty years: report / by a study group**      4.3716
**sponsored by the Ford Foundation and administered by**
**Resources for the Future; Hans H. Landsberg, chairman;**
**Kenneth J. Arrow ... [et al.].**
Cambridge, Mass.: Ballinger Pub. Co., c1979. xxviii, 628 p.: graphs; 23 cm. 1. Energy policy — United States. 2. Power resources — United States. I. Landsberg, Hans H. II. Arrow, Kenneth Joseph, 1921- III. Ford Foundation. IV. Resources for the Future.
HD9502.U52 E56     333.7     *LC* 79-5226     *ISBN* 0884100928

**Energy use: the human dimension / Paul C. Stern and Elliot**      4.3717
**Aronson, editors; Committee on Behavioral and Social Aspects**
**of Energy Consumption and Production, Commission on**
**Behavioral and Social Sciences and Education, National**
**Research Council.**
New York: W.H. Freeman, 1984. xii, 237 p.: ill.; 24 cm. Includes index. 1. Energy consumption — United States — Psychological aspects. 2. Energy industries — Social aspects — United States. I. Stern, Paul C., 1944- II. Aronson, Elliot. III. National Research Council (U.S.). Committee on Behavioral and Social Aspects of Energy Consumption and Production.
HD9502.U52 E565 1984     306/.3 19     *LC* 84-1633     *ISBN* 0716716216

**Human welfare: the end use for power: prepared for the Electric**      4.3718
**Power Task Force of the Scientists' Institute for Public**
**Information and the Power Study Group of the American**
**Association for the Advancement of Science Committee on**
**Environmental Alterations / edited by Barry Commoner,**
**Howard Boksenbaum, Michael Corr.**
New York: Macmillan Information, [1975] xvi, 185 p.: ill.; 24 cm. (Energy and human welfare; v. 3) 1. Energy consumption — United States — Addresses, essays, lectures. I. Commoner, Barry, 1917- II. Boksenbaum, Howard. III. Corr, Michael. IV. Scientists' Institute for Public Information. Electric Power Task Force. V. American Association for the Advancement of Science. Committee on Environmental Alterations. Power Study Group. VI. Series.
HD9502.U52 H84     333.7     *LC* 75-8992     *ISBN* 0024684406

**Landsberg, Hans H.**      4.3719
High energy costs—uneven, unfair, unavoidable? / Hans H. Landsberg and Joseph M. Dukert. — Baltimore: Published for Resources for the Future by Johns Hopkins University Press, c1981. xiii, 104 p.: ill.; 22 cm. 1. Energy consumption — United States — Costs — Congresses. 2. Poor — United States — Energy assistance — Congresses. I. Dukert, Joseph M. II. Resources for the Future. III. T.
HD9502.U52 L347     339 19     *LC* 81-15648     *ISBN* 0801827825

**Resources for the Future.**      • 4.3720
Energy in the American economy, 1850–1975: an economic study of its history and prospects / by Sam H. Schurr and Bruce C. Netschert, with Vera F. Eliasberg, Joseph Lerner, Hans H. Landsberg. — Baltimore: Published by Resources for the Future, Inc. by the Johns Hopkins Press, 1960. xxii, 774 p.: ill.; 24 cm. 1. Power resources — United States. 2. Energy consumption — United States — History. I. Schurr, Sam H. II. Netschert, Bruce Carlton. III. T.
HD9502.U52 R46     333.7     *LC* 60-14304

# HD9506–9678 Mineral and Metal Industries

**Bosson, Rex, 1943-.**                                                    **4.3721**
The mining industry and the developing countries / Rex Bosson and Bension Varon. New York: Published for the World Bank [by] Oxford University Press, c1977. xii, 292 p.: ill.; 24 cm. (World Bank research publication.) Includes index. 1. Mineral industries 2. Underdeveloped areas — Mineral industries. I. Varon, Bension. joint author. II. T. III. Series.
HD9506.A2 B67    338.2/09172/4    *LC* 77-2983    *ISBN* 0199200963

**Economics of the mineral industries: a series of articles by**          **4.3722**
**specialists.**
4th ed., completely rev. and rewritten / edited by William A. Vogely; Carla Sydney Stone and Richard T. Newcomb, associate editors. — New York: American Institute of Mining, Metallurgical, and Petroleum Engineers, 1985. xii, 660 p.: ill.; 27 cm. (Seeley W. Mudd series.) 1. Mineral industries — Addresses, essays, lectures. 2. Mineral industries — United States — Addresses, essays, lectures. I. Vogely, William A. II. Stone, Carla Sydney. III. Newcomb, Richard T. IV. American Institute of Mining, Metallurgical, and Petroleum Engineers. V. Series.
HD9506.A2 E235 1985    338.2 19    *LC* 85-70525    *ISBN* 089520438X

**Labys, Walter C., 1937-.**                                              **4.3723**
Market structure, bargaining power, and resource price information / Walter C. Labys. — Lexington, Mass.: Lexington Books, c1980. xiv, 238 p.: ill.; 24 cm. Includes index. 1. Mineral industries — Prices. 2. Mineral industries — Consolidation. 3. Commodity control I. T.
HD9506.A2 L23    338.2/3    *LC* 78-19541    *ISBN* 0669025119

**Park, Charles Frederick, 1903-.**                                       **4.3724**
Earthbound: minerals, energy, and man's future / Charles F. Park, Jr., in collaboration with Margaret C. Freeman. — San Francisco: Freeman, Cooper, [1974] c1975. 279 p.: ill.; 25 cm. Includes index. 1. Mines and mineral resources 2. Power resources I. Freeman, Margaret C. II. T.
HD9506.A2 P37 1975    333.8    *LC* 73-87688    *ISBN* 0877353174

**Van Rensburg, W. C. J.**                                                **4.3725**
The economics of the world's mineral industries / W.C.J. Van Rensburg, S. Bambrick. — 1st ed. — Johannesburg; Montréal: McGraw-Hill, c1978. [10], 366p.: ill, cartes. 1. Mineral industries I. Bambrick, S. (Susan) II. T.
HD9506    HD9506A2 V35.    *ISBN* 0070913595

**Van Rensburg, W. C. J.**                                                **4.3726**
Strategic minerals / W.C.J. van Rensburg. — Englewood Cliffs, N.J.: Prentice-Hall, c1986. 2 v.: ill.; 29 cm. (Prentice-Hall international series in world resources, energy, and minerals.) Vol. 2 by W.C.J. van Rensburg, with Paul Anaejionu. Includes indexes. 1. Mineral industries — Government policy — Case studies. 2. Metal trade — Government policy — Case studies. 3. Strategic materials — Government policy — Case studies. I. Anaejionu, Paul. II. T. III. Series.
HD9506.A2 V36 1986    333.8 19    *LC* 85-6569    *ISBN* 0138513872

**World mineral trends and U.S. supply problems / Leonard L.**            **4.3727**
**Fischman, project director.**
Washington, D.C.: Resources for the Future; Baltimore, Md.: Distributed by the Johns Hopkins University Press, 1980. xxxiv, 535 p.: ill.; 26 cm. (Research paper / Resources for the Future; R-20) 1. Metal trade 2. Mines and mineral resources 3. Strategic materials 4. Metal trade — United States. 5. Mines and mineral resources — United States. 6. Strategic materials — Government policy — United States. 7. United States — National security I. Fischman, Leonard L. II. Resources for the Future.
HD9506.A2 W636    333.8/5 19    *LC* 80-8025    *ISBN* 0801824915

**Shusterich, Kurt Michael.**                                             **4.3728**
Resource management and the oceans: the political economy of deep seabed mining / Kurt Michael Shusterich. — Boulder, Colo.: Westview Press, 1982. xx, 344 p.: ill.; 23 cm. — (A Westview replica edition) Includes index. 1. Ocean mining — Government policy — United States. I. T.
HD9506.U62 S53 1982    338.2 19    *LC* 82-4748    *ISBN* 0865319014

**Malone, Michael P.**                                                    **4.3729**
The battle for Butte: mining and politics on the northern frontier, 1864–1906 / by Michael P. Malone. — Seattle: University of Washington Press, c1981. xiv, 281 p., [12] leaves of plates: ill.; 24 cm. — (Emil and Kathleen Sick lecture-book series in western history and biography. 4) Includes index. 1. Mineral industries — Montana — Butte — History. 2. Mines and mineral resources — Montana — Butte — History. 3. Butte (Mont.) — Politics and government. I. T. II. Series.
HD9506.U63 B875    338.2/74/0978668 19    *LC* 81-1283    *ISBN* 0295958375

**Sklar, Richard L.**                                                     **4.3730**
Corporate power in an African state: the political impact of multinational mining companies in Zambia / Richard L. Sklar. — Berkeley: University of California Press, 1975. x, 245 p.: maps; 24 cm. — (Perspectives on Southern Africa. 16) Includes index. 1. Mineral industries — Zambia. 2. International business enterprises — Zambia. 3. Zambia — Politics and government — 1964-4. Zambia — Economic conditions — 1964- I. T. II. Series.
HD9506.Z32 S54    338.2/09689/4    *LC* 74-81440    *ISBN* 0520028147

## HD9510–9529 Iron and Steel

**Hogan, William Thomas, 1919-.**                                         **4.3731**
World steel in the 1980s: a case of survival / William T. Hogan. — Lexington, Mass.: Lexington Books, c1983. xvi, 272 p.; 24 cm. Includes index. 1. Steel industry and trade I. T.
HD9510.5.H57 1983    338.4/7669142 19    *LC* 75-41587    *ISBN* 0669004650

**Manners, Gerald.**                                                      **4.3732**
The changing world market for iron ore, 1950–1980: an economic geography. — Baltimore: Published for Resources for the Future, inc. by the Johns Hopkins Press, [1971] xv, 384 p.; 24 cm. 1. Iron industry and trade I. T.
HD9510.5.M25    338.2/7/3    *LC* 70-146734    *ISBN* 0801813085

**Technological progress and industrial leadership: the growth of**       **4.3733**
**the U.S. steel industry, 1900–1970 / Bela Gold ... [et al.].**
Lexington, Mass.: Lexington Books, c1984. xxix, 798 p.: ill.; 24 cm. 1. Steel industry and trade — United States — Technological innovations. I. Gold, Bela.
HD9515.T35 1984    338.4/76691/0973 19    *LC* 83-48756    *ISBN* 0669075353

**Levine, Michael K.**                                                    **4.3734**
Inside international trade policy formulation: a history of the 1982 US–EC steel arrangements / by Michael K. Levine. — New York: Praeger, 1985. xi, 164 p. Includes index. 1. Steel industry and trade — Government policy — United States. 2. Steel industry and trade — Government policy — European Economic Community countries. 3. United States — Foreign economic relations — European Economic Community countries. 4. European Economic Community countries — Foreign economic relations — United States. I. T.
HD9516.L48 1985    382/.45669142/0973 19    *LC* 85-3724    *ISBN* 0030033683

**McCloskey, Donald N.**                                                  **4.3735**
Economic maturity and entrepreneurial decline; British iron and steel, 1870–1913 [by] Donald N. McCloskey. — Cambridge, Mass.: Harvard University Press, 1973. xiv, 157 p.: illus.; 22 cm. — (Harvard economic studies. v. 142) 1. Iron industry and trade — Great Britain. 2. Steel industry and trade — Great Britain. I. T. II. Series.
HD9521.5.M33    338.4/7/6720942    *LC* 72-92131    *ISBN* 0674228758

**Feldman, Gerald D.**                                                    **4.3736**
Iron and steel in the German inflation, 1916–1923 / Gerald D. Feldman. Princeton, N.J.: Princeton University Press, c1977. xix, 518 p.; 25 cm. 1. Iron industry and trade — Germany — History. 2. Steel industry and trade — Germany — History. 3. Trusts, Industrial — Germany — History. 4. Industry and state — Germany — History. 5. Inflation (Finance) — Germany — History. I. T.
HD9523.5.F44    338.4/7/66910943    *LC* 76-41900    *ISBN* 0691042152

## HD9536–9539 Other Metals

**Bakewell, P. J. (Peter John), 1943-.**                                  **4.3737**
Silver mining and society in colonial Mexico: Zacatecas, 1546–1700, by P. J. Bakewell. Cambridge [Eng.] University Press, 1971. xiii, 294 p. maps. 22 cm. (Cambridge Latin American studies. 15) 1. Silver mines and mining — Mexico — Zacatecas (State) 2. Zacatecas (Mexico: State) — Social conditions. 3. Zacatecas (Mexico: State) — History. I. T. II. Series.
HD9536.M43 Z33    338.2/7/42109724    *LC* 78-158553    *ISBN* 0521082277

**Brecher, Jeremy.**                                                      **4.3738**
Brass Valley: the story of working people's lives and struggles in an American industrial region / the Brass Workers History Project; compiled and edited by Jeremy Brecher, Jerry Lombardi, and Jan Stackhouse. — Philadelphia: Temple University Press, 1982. xvi, 284 p.: ill.; 24 cm. 1. American Brass Company — History. 2. Trade-unions — Brass industry employees — Connecticut — Naugatuck River Valley — History. 3. Brass industry and trade — Connecticut — Naugatuck River Valley — Employees — Interviews. 4. Ethnology — Connecticut — Naugatuck River Valley. 5. Brass industry and trade — Connecticut — Naugatuck River Valley — History. 6. Naugatuck

River Valley (Conn.) — Social conditions. 7. Naugatuck River Valley (Conn.) — Biography. 8. Naugatuck River Valley (Conn.) — Economic conditions. I. Lombardi, Jerry. II. Stackhouse, Jan. III. Brass Workers History Project. IV. T.
HD9539.B8 U538 1982     331.7/6733/097467 19     *LC* 82-5770
   ISBN 0877222711

**Mikesell, Raymond Frech.**          **4.3739**
The world copper industry: structure and economic analysis / Raymond F. Mikesell. — Baltimore: Published for Resources for the Future by Johns Hopkins University Press, c1979. xvi, 393 p.: ill.; 23 cm. 1. Copper industry and trade 2. Copper industry and trade — Finance. I. Resources for the Future. II. T.
HD9539.C6 M54     338.2/7/43     *LC* 79-4581     *ISBN* 0801822572

**Prain, Ronald, Sir, 1907-.**          **4.3740**
Copper: the anatomy of an industry / Sir Ronald Prain. — London: Mining Journal Books, 1975. 298 p.; 22 cm. Includes index. 1. Copper industry and trade 2. Copper industry and trade — Great Britain. I. T.
HD9539.C6 P7     338.2/7/43     *LC* 76-351109     *ISBN* 0900117079

**Baldwin, William Lee.**          **4.3741**
The world tin market: political pricing and economic competition / William L. Baldwin. — Durham, N.C.: Duke University Press, 1983. xii, 273 p.: ill.; 25 cm. — (Duke Press policy studies.) Includes index. 1. Tin industry I. T. II. Series.
HD9539.T5 B34 1983     338.2/7453 19     *LC* 83-8888     *ISBN* 0822305054

**Neff, Thomas L.**          **4.3742**
The international uranium market / Thomas L. Neff. — Cambridge, Mass.: Ballinger Pub. Co., 1984. xxiv, 333 p.: ill.; 24 cm. 1. Uranium industry I. T.
HD9539.U7 N44 1984     382/.424932 19     *LC* 84-9255     *ISBN* 0884108503

**Gupta, Satyadev.**          **4.3743**
The world zinc industry / Satyadev Gupta. — Lexington, Mass.: Lexington Books, c1982. xiii, 203 p.: ill.; 24 cm. Includes index. 1. Zinc industry and trade I. T.
HD9539.Z5 G86     338.2/7452 19     *LC* 81-47075     *ISBN* 066904587X

## HD9540–9559 Coal

**Christenson, Carroll Lawrence, 1902-.**          • **4.3744**
Economic redevelopment in bituminous coal: the special case of technological advance in United States coal mines, 1930–1960. Cambridge, Harvard University Press, 1962. 312 p. illus. 24 cm. (Wertheim publications in industrial relations) 1. Coal mines and mining — United States. I. T.
HD 9545 C55     *LC* 62-8178L

**Landsberg, Hans H.**          • **4.3745**
Energy in the United States: sources, uses, and policy issues / Hans H. Landsberg [and] Sam H. Schurr. — New York: Random House, 1968. x, 242 p.: ill.; 22 cm. 'A Resources for the Future study.' 1. Power resources — United States. 2. Energy policy — United States. I. Schurr, Sam H. II. T.
HD9545.L3     333.7     *LC* 68-13467

**Vietor, Richard H. K., 1945-.**          **4.3746**
Environmental politics and the coal coalition / by Richard H. K. Vietor. — 1st ed. — College Station: Texas A&M University Press, c1980. xiv, 285 p.; 24 cm. — (Environmental history series. no. 2) Includes index. 1. Coal mines and mining — Environmental aspects — United States. 2. Industry and state — United States. I. T. II. Series.
HD9545.V54     363.7/392     *LC* 79-5277     *ISBN* 0890960941

**Zimmerman, Martin B.**          **4.3747**
The U.S. coal industry: the economics of policy choice / Martin B. Zimmerman. — Cambridge, Mass.: MIT Press, c1981. xiv, 205 p.: ill.; 24 cm. — (The Press energy laboratory series; 3) 1. Coal trade — United States. 2. Coal trade — United States — Mathematical models. I. T.
HD9545.Z55     338.2/724/0973 19     *LC* 81-1124     0262240230

**Alm, Alvin L.**          **4.3748**
Coal myths and environmental realities: industrial fuel use decisions in a time of change / Alvin L. Alm with Joan P. Curhan. — Boulder, Colo.: Westview Press, 1984. xviii, 154 p.: ill.; 24 cm. — (Westview special studies in natural resources and energy management.) 1. Coal trade — Government policy — United States. 2. Fossil fuels — Environmental aspects — United States. 3. Fossil fuels — United States — Costs. 4. Air — Pollution — Law and legislation — United States. 5. United States — Industries — Power supply — Decision making. I. Curhan, Joan P. II. T. III. Series.
HD9546.A45 1984     333.8/22/0973 19     *LC* 83-16940     *ISBN* 0865317127

**National Coal Policy Project.**          **4.3749**
Where we agree: report of the National Coal Policy Project / edited by Francis X. Murray. — Boulder, Colo.: Westview Press, 1978. 2 v.: ill.; 24 cm. — (Westview special studies in natural resources and energy management) Includes index. 1. Coal trade — United States. 2. Energy policy — United States. I. Murray, Francis X., 1937- II. T.
HD9546.N34 1978     333.8/22/0973 19     *LC* 78-55420     *ISBN* 0891581758

**Moyer, Reed.**          • **4.3750**
Competition in the midwestern coal industry. Cambridge: Harvard University Press, 1964. xii, 226 p.: ill., maps; 22 cm. (Harvard economic studies. v. 122) 1. Coal mines and mining — Middle West 2. Coal trade — Middle West I. T. II. Series.
HD9547.A13 M67     *LC* 65-11194

**Flinn, Michael W. (Michael Walter), 1917-.**          **4.3751**
The history of the British coal industry, 1700–1830: the Industrial Revolution / by Michael W. Flinn with the assistance of David S. Stoker. — Oxford [Oxfordshire]: Clarendon Press; New York: Oxford University Press, c1984. xviii, 491 p., [8] p. of plates: ill., maps; 24 cm. Includes index. 1. Coal trade — Great Britain — History. 2. Coal mines and mining — Great Britain — History. I. Stoker, David S. II. T.
HD9551.5.F58     338.2/724/0941 19     *LC* 83-4194     *ISBN* 0198282834

**Hodgkins, Jordan Atwood, 1920-.**          • **4.3752**
Soviet power: energy resources, production and potentials. Englewood Cliffs, N.J., Prentice-Hall, 1961. xviii, 190 p. maps, diagrs., tables. 1. Power resources — Russia I. T.
HD9555 R8 H6     *LC* 61-12382

## HD9560–9581 Petroleum. Natural Gas

**OPEC behavior and world oil prices / [edited by] James M. Griffin, David J. Teece; with contributions from Morris Adelman ... [et al.].**          **4.3753**
London; Boston: Allen & Unwin, 1982. viii, 231 p.: ill.; 23 cm. Includes index. 1. Organization of Petroleum Exporting Countries. 2. Petroleum products — Prices I. Griffin, James M. II. Teece, David J. III. Adelman, Morris Albert. IV. Title: O.P.E.C. behavior and world oil prices.
HD9560.4.O6 1982     338.2/3 19     *LC* 82-6840     *ISBN* 0043381022

**Pindyck, Robert S.**          **4.3754**
The structure of world energy demand / Robert S. Pindyck. — Cambridge, Mass.: MIT Press, c1979. x, 299 p.: graphs; 24 cm. 1. Petroleum industry and trade 2. Energy consumption — Mathematical models. I. T.
HD9560.4.P5     333.7     *LC* 79-12565     *ISBN* 0262160749

**Verleger, Philip K.**          **4.3755**
Oil markets in turmoil: an economic analysis / Philip K. Verleger, Jr.; foreword by Bill Bradley; contribution by Marshall Thomas. — Cambridge, Mass.: Ballinger Pub. Co., c1982. xxxi, 289 p.: ill.; 24 cm. Includes index. 1. Petroleum products — Prices 2. Petroleum industry and trade I. T.
HD9560.4.V47 1982     338.2/3 19     *LC* 81-22810     *ISBN* 0884108678

**Adelman, Morris Albert.**          **4.3756**
The world petroleum market, by M. A. Adelman. — Baltimore: Published for Resources for the Future by Johns Hopkins University Press, 1973 (c1972) xviii, 438 p.: illus.; 26 cm. 1. Petroleum industry and trade I. T.
HD9560.5.A34     338.2/7/282     *LC* 72-4029     *ISBN* 0801814227

**Alnasrawi, Abbas.**          **4.3757**
OPEC in a changing world economy / Abbas Alnasrawi. — Baltimore: Johns Hopkins University Press, c1985. xi, 188 p.; 24 cm. Includes index. 1. Organization of Petroleum Exporting Countries. 2. Petroleum industry and trade I. T. II. Title: O.P.E.C. in a changing world economy.
HD9560.5.A5153 1985     341.7/5472282/0601 19     *LC* 84-7196
   *ISBN* 0801832160

**Brossard, E. B.**          **4.3758**
Petroleum—politics and power / E.B. Brossard. — Tulsa, Okla.: Pennwell Books, c1983. xvi, 254 p.: maps; 24 cm. Includes index. 1. Petroleum industry and trade — Government policy — History — 20th century. 2. Petroleum industry and trade — Government policy — United States — History — 20th century. 3. Gas industry — Government policy — History — 20th century. 4. Gas industry — Government policy — United States — History — 20th century. I. T.
HD9560.5.B74 1983     333.8/23 19     *LC* 82-24638     *ISBN* 087814224X

**Hartshorn, J.E.**                                                  • **4.3759**
Politics and world oil economics: an account of the international oil industry in its political environment / [by] J.E. Hartshorn. — Rev. ed. New York: Praeger [1967] 410 p.: maps; 23 cm. 1. Petroleum industry and trade I. T.
HD9560.5 H35 1967a      LC 67-13871

**Jacoby, Neil H. (Neil Herman), 1909-1979.**                        **4.3760**
Multinational oil: a study in industrial dynamics / Neil H. Jacoby. — New York: Macmillan, [1974] xxvi, 323 p.: ill.; 24 cm. (Studies of the modern corporation.) 1. Petroleum industry and trade 2. Energy policy 3. International business enterprises I. T. II. Series.
HD9560.5.J26      338.4/7/6655      LC 74-22381      ISBN 0029159903. ISBN 0029159806 pbk

**Odell, Peter R.**                                                  **4.3761**
The future of oil: world oil resources and use / Peter R. Odell and Kenneth E. Rosing. — 2nd, fully rev. ed. — London: Kogan Page; New York: Nichols Pub. Co., 1983. 224 p.: ill.; 24 cm. 1. Petroleum — Reserves — Mathematical models. 2. Petroleum industry and trade — Forecasting. 3. Energy policy I. Rosing, Kenneth Earl. II. T.
HD9560.5.O32 1983      333.8/232/0724 19      LC 82-19104      ISBN 0893971464

**Odell, Peter R.**                                                  **4.3762**
Oil and world power / Peter R. Odell. — 7th ed. — Harmondsworth, Middlesex, England; New York, N.Y., U.S.A.: Penguin Books, 1983. 188 p. (Pelican books) Includes index. 1. Petroleum industry and trade — Political aspects. 2. World politics — 1975-1985 3. International economic relations I. T.
HD9560.5.O3x 1983      338.2/7282 19      LC 84-673187      ISBN 0140222847

**Pachauri, R. K.**                                                  **4.3763**
The political economy of global energy / R.K. Pachauri. — Baltimore: Johns Hopkins University Press, c1985. xiii, 191 p.: ill.; 24 cm. Includes index. 1. Petroleum industry and trade 2. Energy industries 3. Energy consumption 4. International economic relations I. T.
HD9560.5.P23 1985      333.79 19      LC 84-21825      ISBN 0801824699

**Penrose, Edith Tilton.**                                           • **4.3764**
The large international firm in developing countries: the international petroleum industry / by Edith T. Penrose; with a chapter on the oil industry in Latin America by P. R. Odell. — Cambridge, Mass.: MIT Press, [1969] 311 p.: ill.; 24 cm. 1. Petroleum industry and trade 2. International business enterprises I. T.
HD9560.5.P38 1969      338.8/8      LC 69-13595

**Cowhey, Peter F., 1948-.**                                         **4.3765**
The problems of plenty: energy policy and international politics / Peter F. Cowhey. — Berkeley: University of California Press, c1985. xiii, 447 p.: ill.; 24 cm. (Science, technology, and the changing world order.) 1. Petroleum industry and trade — Political aspects. 2. Energy industries — Political aspects. 3. International economic relations 4. World politics — 1945- 5. Energy policy — Political aspects — United States. 6. United States — Foreign relations — 1945- I. T. II. Series.
HD9560.6.C68 1985      333.79 19      LC 83-9275      ISBN 0520046935

**Vertical integration in the oil industry / edited by Edward J.**   **4.3766**
**Mitchell.**
Washington: American Enterprise Institute for Public Policy Research, 1976. 214 p.; 23 cm. (National energy study; no. 11) On cover: National Energy Project. 1. Petroleum industry and trade — Vertical integration — Addresses, essays, lectures. 2. Petroleum industry and trade — Vertical integration — United States — Addresses, essays, lectures. 3. Trusts, Industrial — Addresses, essays, lectures. I. Mitchell, Edward John, 1937- II. AEI National Energy Project. III. Series.
HD9560.6.V43      338.8/5      LC 76-20267      ISBN 084473215X

## HD9561–9578 By Region or Country

**Kalt, Joseph P.**                                                  **4.3767**
The economics and politics of oil price regulation: federal policy in the post-embargo era / Joseph P. Kalt. — Cambridge, Mass.: MIT Press, c1981. xx, 327 p.: ill.; 24 cm. — (MIT Press series on the regulation of economic activity; 3) Includes index. 1. Petroleum — Prices — United States. 2. Price regulation — United States. 3. Petroleum industry and trade — United States 4. Petroleum law and legislation — United States. I. T. II. Series.
HD9564.K34      338.2/3 19      LC 81-4411      ISBN 0262110792

**De Chazeau, Melvin Gardner.**                                      • **4.3768**
Integration and competition in the petroleum industry / by Melvin G. de Chazeau and Alfred E. Kahn. — Port Washington, N.Y.: Kennikat Press [1973, c1959] xviii, 598 p.; 23 cm. (Monograph series on the petroleum industry) Original ed. issued as v. 3 of Petroleum monograph series.

1. Petroleum industry and trade — United States I. Kahn, Alfred E. (Alfred Edward) joint author. II. T. III. Series.
HD9565.D4 1973      338.4/7/66550973      LC 72-85302      ISBN 0804617112

**Engler, Robert.**                                                  • **4.3769**
The politics of oil: a study of private power and democratic directions. — New York: Macmillan, 1961. 565 p.; 22 cm. 1. Petroleum industry and trade — United States I. T.
HD9565.E5      338.27282      LC 61-17192

**Hamilton, Daniel Corning, 1918-.**                                 • **4.3770**
Competition in oil. Cambridge: Harvard University Press, 1958. 233 p. 1. Petroleum industry and trade — United States 2. Marketing — Case studies. I. T. II. Title: The gulf coast refinery market, 1925-1950.
HD9565.H3 1958      LC 58-7249

**McLean, John Godfrey, 1917-.**                                     • **4.3771**
The growth of integrated oil companies / [by] John G. McLean [and] Robert Wm. Haigh. — Boston: Division of Research, Graduate School of Business Administration, Harvard University, 1954. xxiv, 728 p.: ill. 1. Petroleum industry and trade — United States I. Haigh, Robert William, 1926- II. T.
HD9565.M282

**Bohi, Douglas R.**                                                 **4.3772**
Limiting oil imports: an economic history and analysis / Douglas R. Bohi and Milton Russell. — Baltimore: Published for Resources for the Future by the Johns Hopkins University Press, c1978. xvi, 356 p.: ill.; 24 cm. 1. Petroleum industry and trade — United States 2. Import quotas — United States. 3. Energy policy — United States — History. I. Russell, Milton, 1933- joint author. II. Resources for the Future. III. T.
HD9566.B59      382/.42/2820973      LC 77-18881      ISBN 0801821061

**Bohi, Douglas R.**                                                 **4.3773**
Oil prices, energy security, and import policy / Douglas R. Bohi, W. David Montgomery. — Washington, D.C.: Resources for the Future; Baltimore: Distributed by the Johns Hopkins University Press, c1982. xiv, 203 p.: ill.; 24 cm. Includes index. 1. Petroleum industry and trade — Government policy — United States. 2. Energy policy — United States. I. Montgomery, W. David (William David), 1944- II. T.
HD9566.B6 1982      333.79/0973 19      LC 82-15083      ISBN 080182821X

**Oppenheimer, Bruce Ian.**                                          **4.3774**
Oil and the congressional process; the limits of symbolic politics. Lexington, Mass., Lexington Books [1974] xvi, 198 p. 23 cm. 1. Petroleum industry and trade — United States 2. Petroleum law and legislation — United States. 3. Water — Pollution — Law and legislation — United States. 4. Petroleum — Taxation — United States. 5. Symbolism in politics I. T.
HD9566.O64      338.2/7/2820973      LC 74-312      ISBN 0669927341

**Randall, Stephen J., 1944-.**                                      **4.3775**
United States foreign oil policy, 1919–1948: for profits and security / Stephen J. Randall. — Kingston: McGill-Queen's University Press, c1985. viii, 328 p.: ill.; 24 cm. Includes index. 1. Petroleum industry and trade — Government policy — United States — History — 20th century. 2. Petroleum industry and trade — Political aspects — United States. 3. United States — Foreign relations — 20th century I. T.
HD9566.R36 1985      338.2/7282/0973 19      LC 85-211907      ISBN 0773504494

**Rustow, Dankwart A.**                                              **4.3776**
Oil and turmoil: America faces OPEC and the Middle East / Dankwart A. Rustow. — 1st ed. — New York: Norton, c1982. 320 p.; 22 cm. 1. Organization of Petroleum Exporting Countries. 2. Petroleum industry and trade — Political aspects — Near East. 3. Petroleum industry and trade — Political aspects — United States. 4. Middle East — Foreign relations — United States. 5. United States — Foreign relations — Near East. I. T.
HD9566.R84 1982      338.2/7282/0956 19      LC 82-2208      ISBN 0393015971

**Lieuwen, Edwin, 1923-.**                                           • **4.3777**
Petroleum in Venezuela; a history. — New York: Russell & Russell, [1967] 160 p.: maps.; 22 cm. Reprint of the 1954 ed., which was based on thesis, University of California. 1. Petroleum industry and trade — Venezuela. I. T.
HD9574.V42 L5 1967      338.2/7/2820987      LC 66-27118

**Grayson, Leslie E.**                                               **4.3778**
National oil companies / Leslie E. Grayson. — Chichester [West Sussex]; New York: Wiley, c1981. vii, 269 p.: ill.; 24 cm. 1. Petroleum industry and trade — Europe. 2. Corporations, Government — Europe. I. T.
HD9575.A2 G7      338.7/6223382/094 19      LC 80-41436      ISBN 0471278610

**Woodard, Kim.**      4.3779
The international energy relations of China / Kim Woodard. — Stanford, Calif.: Stanford University Press, 1980. xxi, 717 p.: ill.; 25 cm. Includes index. 1. Petroleum industry and trade — China. 2. Energy industries — China. 3. Energy policy — China. 4. China — Foreign economic relations. I. T.
HD9575.C5x     333.79/0951 19     LC 77-92949     ISBN 0804710082

**Chapman, Keith.**      4.3780
North Sea oil and gas: a geographical perspective / [by] Keith Chapman. Newton Abbot; North Pomfret, Vt.: David and Charles, 1976. 240 p.: ill., maps; 23 cm. (Problems in modern geography) 1. Petroleum in submerged lands — North Sea. 2. Petroleum industry and trade — North Sea. I. T.
HD9575.N57 C5     333.8/2     LC 76-4369     ISBN 0715371835

**Campbell, Robert Wellington.**      • 4.3781
The economics of Soviet oil and gas / by Robert W. Campbell. — Baltimore: Published for Resources for the Future by the Johns Hopkins Press [1968] xv, 279 p.: ill., maps; 24 cm. 1. Petroleum industry and trade — Soviet Union. I. Resources for the Future. II. T.
HD9575.R82 C3     338.2/7/280947     LC 68-22277

**Klinghoffer, Arthur Jay, 1941-.**      4.3782
The Soviet Union & international oil politics / Arthur Jay Klinghoffer. New York: Columbia University Press, 1977. ix, 389 p.: maps; 24 cm. 1. Petroleum industry and trade — Russia. 2. World politics — 1975-1985 3. Russia — Foreign economic relations. I. T.
HD9575.R82 K57     338.2/7/2820947     LC 76-52411     ISBN 0231041047

**Goldman, Marshall I.**      4.3783
The enigma of Soviet petroleum: half-full or half-empty? / Marshall I. Goldman. — London; Boston: Allen & Unwin, 1980. 214 p.; 22 cm. Includes index. 1. Petroleum industry and trade — Soviet Union. I. T.
HD9575.S652 G64     338.2/7282/0947 19     LC 80-40544     ISBN 0043330150

**Longrigg, Stephen Hemsley.**      • 4.3784
Oil in the Middle East: its discovery and development / Stephen Hemsley Longrigg. — 3d ed. — London: Issues under the auspices of the Royal Institute of International Affairs by Oxford University Press, 1968. xii, 519 p.: ill., maps. 1. Petroleum industry and trade — Near East. I. Royal Institute of International Affairs. II. T.
HD9576.A2 L6 1967     LC 67-114585

**Siddayao, Corazon M.**      4.3785
The off-shore petroleum resources of South-east Asia: potential conflict situations and related economic considerations / Corazón Morales Siddayao. — Kuala Lumpur; New York: Oxford University Press, 1978. xx, 205 p.: ill.; 23 cm. — (Natural resources of South-east Asia.) 'Issued under the auspices of the Institute of Southeast Asian Studies in Singapore.' Includes index. 1. Petroleum industry and trade — Asia, Southeastern. 2. Petroleum in submerged lands — Asia, Southeastern. 3. Maritime law — Asia, Southeastern. I. Institute of Southeast Asian Studies. II. T. III. Series.
HD9576.A6892 S56     333.8/232/0959     LC 78-106246     ISBN 0195803957

**Stocking, George Ward, 1892-.**      • 4.3786
Middle East oil; a study in political and economic controversy [by] George W. Stocking. — [Nashville]: Vanderbilt University Press, 1970. xii, 485 p.; 25 cm. 1. Petroleum industry and trade — Near East. I. T.
HD9576.N36 S7     338.2/7/2820956     LC 73-115095     ISBN 0826511562

**Anderson, Irvine H., 1928-.**      4.3787
Aramco, the United States, and Saudi Arabia: a study of the dynamics of foreign oil policy, 1933–1950 / Irvine H. Anderson. — Princeton, N.J.: Princeton University Press, c1981. xiii, 259 p.; 23 cm. Includes index. 1. Arabian American Oil Company. 2. Petroleum industry and trade — Saudi Arabia. 3. Petroleum industry and trade — United States 4. United States — Foreign economic relations — Saudi Arabia. 5. United States — Foreign relations — Saudi Arabia. I. T.
HD9576.S35 A72     338.7/6223382/09538 19     LC 80-8535     ISBN 0691046794

### HD9579 Special Products

**Glasner, David.**      4.3788
Politics, prices, and petroleum: the political economy of energy / by David Glasner; foreword by Paul W. MacAvoy; introduction by Benjamin Zycher. — San Francisco, Calif.: Pacific Institute for Public Policy Research; Cambridge, Mass.: Ballinger Pub. Co., c1985. xlvi, 297 p.: ill.; 24 cm. (Pacific studies in public policy). Includes index. 1. Gasoline industry — Government policy — United States. 2. Petroleum industry and trade — Government policy —

United States. 3. Gas industry — Government policy — United States. 4. Energy policy — United States. I. T. II. Series.
HD9579.G5 U5435 1985     330.2/7282/0973 19     LC 84-19134     ISBN 0884109534

### HD9580–9581 Pipelines

**Johnson, Arthur Menzies, 1921-.**      • 4.3789
The development of American petroleum pipelines: a study in private enterprise and public policy, 1862–1906. — Ithaca, N. Y.: Published for the American Historical Association [by] Cornell University Press, [1956]. xiii, 307 p.: ill., ports., maps (part fold.); 24 cm. 1. Petroleum — Pipe lines 2. Petroleum industry and trade — United States I. T.
HD9580.U5 J6

**MacAvoy, Paul W.**      4.3790
Price controls and the natural gas shortage / Paul W. MacAvoy and Robert S. Pindyck. — Washington: American Enterprise Institute for Public Policy Research, 1975. 81 p.: ill.; 23 cm. (National energy study; 7) Presented by the AEI National Energy Project. 1. Gas, Natural — United States 2. Price regulation — United States — Case studies. 3. Gas, Natural — United States — Mathematical models. I. Pindyck, Robert S. joint author. II. AEI National Energy Project. III. T. IV. Series.
HD9581.U5 M27     338.2/3     LC 75-10769     ISBN 0844731617

**MacAvoy, Paul W.**      • 4.3791
Price formation in natural gas fields: a study of competition, monopsony, and regulation. — New Haven: Yale University Press, 1962. xix, 281 p.: maps, diagrs., tables; 23 cm. (Yale studies in economics. 14) 1. Gas fields — United States. 2. Monopsonies — United States. I. T. II. Series.
HD9581.U5 M28     338.27285     LC 62-16237

### HD9623–9675 Chemical Industries. Drugs

**Chandler, Alfred Dupont.**      • 4.3792
Pierre S. Du Pont and the making of the modern corporation, by Alfred D. Chandler, Jr. and Stephen Salsbury, with the assistance of Adeline Cook Strange. — [1st ed.]. — New York: Harper & Row, [1971] xxii, 722 p.: illus., facsims., geneal. table, ports.; 25 cm. 1. DuPont, Pierre Samuel, 1870-1954. 2. DuPont de Nemours (E. I.) and Company. 3. General Motors Corporation. I. Salsbury, Stephen. joint author. II. T.
HD9651.9.D8 C5     338.8/0924 B     LC 78-123920     ISBN 0060107014

**Dorian, Max.**      • 4.3793
The du Ponts: from gunpowder to nylon / translated by Edward B. Garside; with photos. by Dixie Reynolds. — Boston: Little, Brown, [c1962] 303 p.: ill. 1. Du Pont family (Pièrre Samuel Du Pont de Nemours, 1739-1817) 2. E.I. du Pont de Nemours & Company. I. T.
HD9651.9.D8 D63

**Taylor, Graham D., 1944-.**      4.3794
Du Pont and the international chemical industry / Graham D. Taylor and Patricia E. Sudnik. — Boston, Mass.: Twayne, c1984. xxi, 251 p.: ports.; 23 cm. — (Evolution of American business.) Includes index. 1. E.I. du Pont de Nemours & Company — History. 2. Chemical industry — United States — History. 3. Chemical industry — History. I. Sudnik, Patricia E. II. T. III. Title: DuPont and the international chemical industry. IV. Series.
HD9651.9.D8 T39 1984     338.8/87 19     LC 84-8933     ISBN 0805798056

**Tucker, David.**      4.3795
The world health market: the future of the pharmaceutical industry / David Tucker. — New York, N.Y.: Facts on File, c1984. x, 220 p.: ill.; 26 cm. 1. Pharmaceutical industry 2. Nonprescription drug industry 3. Market surveys I. Facts on File, Inc. II. T.
HD9665.5.T83 1984     380.1/456151 19     LC 84-13609     ISBN 0871969130

**Statman, Meir.**      4.3796
Competition in the pharmaceutical industry: the declining profitability of drug innovation / Meir Statman. — Washington: American Enterprise Institute for Public Policy Research, c1983. 84 p.; 24 cm. (Studies in health policy.) 1. Pharmaceutical industry — United States. 2. Drugs — Research — United States — Costs. 3. Drugs — Generic substitution — Economic aspects — United States. 4. Competition — United States. I. T. II. Series.
HD9666.5.S79 1983     338.4/36151/0973 19     LC 83-3880     ISBN 0844735140

## HD9680–9712 Mechanical Industries

### HD9685–9697 Electrical Utilities and Industries. Electronic Industries

**Turvey, Ralph.**      **4.3797**
Electricity economics: essays and case studies / Ralph Turvey and Dennis Anderson. — Baltimore: Published for the World Bank [by] Johns Hopkins University Press, c1977. xvii, 364 p.: ill.; 23 cm. — (World Bank research publication.) Includes index. 1. Electric utilities — Rates 2. Electric utilities — Costs I. Anderson, Dennis, 1937- joint author. II. World Bank. III. T. IV. Series.
HD9685.A2 T85     338.4/3     LC 76-9031     ISBN 0801818664. ISBN 0801818672 pbk

**Bourassa, Robert, 1933-.**      **4.3798**
Power from the North / Robert Bourassa; with a foreword by James Schlesinger. — Scarborough, Ont.: Prentice-Hall Canada, c1985. x, 181 p., [16] p. of plates: ill.; 24 cm. 1. James Bay Hydroelectric Project 2. Water resources development — James Bay Region (Ont. and Québec) 3. Electric power production — Economic aspects — James Bay Region (Ont. and Québec) I. T.
HD9685.C3 J363 1985     333.79/3215/097141 19     LC 85-158461     ISBN 0136883672

**Wildavsky, Aaron B.**      • **4.3799**
Dixon–Yates: a study in power politics. New Haven: Yale University Press, 1962. xx, 351 p.: ill.; 23 cm. (Yale studies in political science. 3) 1. Dixon-Yates contract, 1954 2. United States — Politics and government — 1953-1961 I. T. II. Series.
HD9685 U42 W64     LC 61-14440

**United States. Federal Power Commission.**      • **4.3800**
National power survey: a report by the Federal Power Commission. — Washington, D.C.: U.S. G.P.O., 1964. 2 v.: ill., maps; 26 cm. 1. Electric Utilities — United States 2. Electric power supply — United States 3. Electric power systems — United States I. T.
HD9685.U5 A545

**Creative financing for energy conservation and cogeneration /**      **4.3801**
**[edited] by F. William Payne.**
Atlanta, Ga.: Fairmont Press, c1984. xi, 277 p.: ill.; 24 cm. 1. Electric power-plants — Energy conservation — Economic aspects — United States. 2. Public utilities — Energy conservation — Economic aspects — United States. 3. Buildings — Energy conservation — Economic aspects — United States. 4. Energy conservation — United States — Equipment and supplies — Finance. 5. Cogeneration of electric power and heat — United States — Equipment and supplies — Finance. 6. Industrial development bonds — United States. I. Payne, F. William, 1924-
HD9685.U5 C75 1984     338.4/362119 19     LC 83-80094     ISBN 091558669X

**Hellman, Richard, 1913-.**      **4.3802**
The competitive economics of nuclear and coal power / Richard Hellman, Caroline J.C. Hellman. — Lexington, Mass.: LexingtonBooks, c1983. xviii, 183 p.; 24 cm. Includes index. 1. Electric Utilities — United States — Costs — Case studies. 2. Nuclear power plants — United States — Costs — Case studies. 3. Coal-fired power plants — United States — Costs — Case studies. I. Hellman, Caroline J. C. II. T.
HD9685.U5 H39 1983     338.2/3 19     LC 82-47500     ISBN 0669055336

**Joskow, Paul L.**      **4.3803**
Markets for power: an analysis of electric utility deregulation / Paul L. Joskow and Richard Schmalensee. — Cambridge, Mass.: MIT Press, c1983. xi, 269 p.; 24 cm. Includes index. 1. Electric Utilities — Government policy — United States. 2. Electric Utilities — United States — Price policy. I. Schmalensee, Richard. II. T.
HD9685.U5 J67 1983     338.4/336362 19     LC 83-13527     ISBN 0262100282

**Principles for electric power policy / Technology Futures, Inc.**      **4.3804**
**and Scientific Foresight, Inc.**
Westport, Conn.; London, England: Quorum Books, 1984. xx, 448 p.; 24 cm. 1. Electric Utilities — Government policy — United States. I. Technology Futures, Inc. II. Scientific Foresight, Inc.
HD9685.U5 P75 1984     333.79/32 19     LC 84-4692     ISBN 0899300952

**Selznick, Philip, 1919-.**      • **4.3805**
TVA and the grass roots: a study in the sociology of formal organization / by Philip Selznick. — New York: Harper & Row, 1966. xvi, 274 p. — (Harper torchbooks.The Academy library.) 1. Tennessee Valley Authority. I. T.
HD9685U61A1395     353.008722

**Brown, D. Clayton (Deward Clayton), 1941-.**      **4.3806**
Electricity for rural America: the fight for the REA / D. Clayton Brown. — Westport, Conn.: Greenwood Press, 1980. xvi, 178 p.; 22 cm. — (Contributions in economics and economic history; no. 29 0084-9235) Includes index. 1. United States. Rural Electrification Administration — History. 2. Rural electrification — United States — History. I. T.
HD9688.U52 B76     353.008/72208/09     LC 79-8287     ISBN 0313214786

**Young, George, 1928-.**      **4.3807**
Venture capital in high–tech companies: the electronics industry in perspective / George Young. — Westport, Conn.: Quorum Books, 1985. vii, 213 p.: ill.; 24 cm. 1. Electronic industries — Finance. 2. Venture capital I. T.
HD9696.A2 Y68 1985     621.381/7/0681 19     LC 85-12057     ISBN 0899301460

**Fisher, Franklin M.**      **4.3808**
IBM and the U.S. data processing industry: an economic history / Franklin M. Fisher, James W. McKie, Richard B. Mancke. — New York, N.Y., U.S.A.: Praeger, 1983. xii, 532 p.; 25 cm. — (Praeger studies in select basic industries.) 1. International Business Machines Corporation — History. 2. Computer industry — United States — History. I. McKie, James W. II. Mancke, Richard B., 1943- III. T. IV. Title: I.B.M. and the US data processing industry. V. Series.
HD9696.C64 I4843 1983     338.7/62138195/0973 19     LC 83-3988     ISBN 0030630592

**Wilson, Robert W.**      **4.3809**
Innovation, competition, and government policy in the semiconductor industry / Robert W. Wilson, Peter K. Ashton, Thomas P. Egan. — Lexington, Mass.: Lexington Books, c1980. xv, 219 p.: ill.; 24 cm. 'A Charles River Associates research study.' Includes index. 1. Semiconductor industry — United States. 2. Technological innovations — United States. 3. Industry and state — United States. I. Ashton, Peter K. joint author. II. Egan, Thomas P. joint author. III. Charles River Associates. IV. T.
HD9696.S43 U59     338.4/762138152/0973     LC 80-8317     ISBN 0669039950

### HD9698 Nuclear Power Industry

**The Nuclear connection: a reassessment of nuclear power and**      **4.3810**
**nuclear proliferation / edited by Alvin Weinberg, Marcelo**
**Alonso, Jack N. Barkenbus.**
New York: Paragon House Publishers, c1985. 295 p.: ill.; 24 cm. 'A Washington Institute book.' 1. Nuclear industry — Addresses, essays, lectures. 2. Nuclear nonproliferation — Addresses, essays, lectures. I. Weinberg, Alvin Martin, 1915- II. Alonso, Marcelo. III. Barkenbus, Jack N. IV. Washington Institute for Values in Public Policy.
HD9698.A2 N77 1985     333.79/24 19     LC 84-26786     ISBN 0887022049

**Willrich, Mason.**      **4.3811**
Nuclear theft: risks and safeguards: a report to the Energy Policy Project of the Ford Foundation / [by] Mason Willrich [and] Theodore B. Taylor. — Cambridge, Mass.: Ballinger Pub. Co. [1974] xvi, 252 p.: ill.; 24 cm. 1. Nuclear industry — Security measures. I. Taylor, Theodore B., 1925- joint author. II. Ford Foundation. Energy Policy Project. III. T.
HD9698.A2 W54     658.4/7     LC 73-19861     ISBN 0884102076 ISBN 0884102084

**Allardice, Corbin.**      **4.3812**
The Atomic Energy Commission [by] Corbin Allardice and Edward R. Trapnell. New York: Praeger [1974] xv, 236 p.: ill.; 22 cm. (Praeger library of U.S. Government departments and agencies, no. 42) 1. U.S. Atomic Energy Commission. I. Trapnell, Edward R., joint author. II. T.
HD9698.U52 A63     353.008/55     LC 76-122088     ISBN 0275554601

**Del Sesto, Steven L.**      **4.3813**
Science, politics, and controversy: civilian nuclear power in the United States, 1946–1974 / Steven L. Del Sesto. — Boulder, Colo.: Westview Press, 1979. xvi, 259 p.; 24 cm. (Westview special studies in science, technology, and public policy.) Based on the author's thesis, Brown University, 1978. Includes index. 1. Nuclear industry — United States — History. I. T. II. Series.
HD9698.U52 D44     333.79/24/0973 19     LC 79-5227     ISBN 0891585664

**Garvey, Gerald, 1935-.**      **4.3814**
Nuclear power and social planning: the city of the second sun / Gerald Garvey. Lexington, Mass.: Lexington Books, c1977. xxi, 159 p.: ill.; 24 cm. Includes index. 1. Nuclear industry — United States. 2. United States — Social policy I. T.
HD9698.U52 G37     309.2/12     LC 76-54556     ISBN 066901303X

## HD9710–9711.5 Automotive and Aerospace Industries

**World motor vehicle data.**     **4.3815**
Annual. Detroit: Motor Vehicle Manufacturers Association of the United States, 1982. 1 v.; 28 cm. 1. Motor vehicles — Statistics. I. Motor Vehicle Manufacturers Association of the United States.
HD9710.A1 W67      338.4/7/62922      *LC* 73-640507

**Bloomfield, G. T. (Gerald Taylor)**     **4.3816**
The world automotive industry / Gerald Bloomfield. — Newton Abbot; North Pomfret, Vt.: David and Charles, 1978. 368 p.: ill.; maps; 25 cm. (Problems in modern geography) 1. Automobile industry and trade I. T.
HD9710.A2 B56      338.4/7/6292      *LC* 77-91774      *ISBN* 0715375393

**The Future of the automobile: the report of MIT's International**     **4.3817**
**Automobile Program / by Alan Altshuler ... [et al.]; with**
**contributions by Hermann Appel ... [et al.].**
Cambridge, Mass.: MIT Press, c1984. xi, 321 p.: ill.; 24 cm. Includes index. 1. Automobile industry and trade I. Altshuler, Alan A., 1936- II. Massachusetts Institute of Technology. III. International Automobile Program.
HD9710.A2 F87 1984      338.4/76292 19      *LC* 84-12269      *ISBN* 026201081X

**Sakiya, Tetsuo, 1926-.**     **4.3818**
[Honda chōhassō keiei. English] Honda Motor: the men, the management, the machines / Tetsuo Sakiya; translated by Kiyoshi Ikemi; adapted by Timothy Porter. — 1st ed. — Tokyo: Kodansha International; New York: Kodansha International/USA: distributed by Harper & Row, 1982. 242 p.: ill.; 22 cm. Rev. translation of: Honda chōhassō keiei. 1. Honda, Sōichirō, 1906- 2. Fujisawa, Takeo, 1910- 3. Honda Giken Kōgyō Kabushiki Kaisha. I. Porter, Timothy. II. T.
HD9710.J34 H65713 1982      338.7/6292/0952 19      *LC* 82-80983      *ISBN* 0870115227

**Chandler, Alfred Dupont. comp. and ed.**     •**4.3819**
Giant enterprise: Ford, General Motors, and the automobile industry; sources and readings. — New York: Harcourt Brace & World, [1964] xiii, 242 p.: illus.; 23 cm. — (The Forces in American economic growth series) 1. Automobile industry and trade — United States. I. T.
HD9710.U52 C38      *LC* 64-12560

**The Competitive status of the U.S. auto industry: a study of the**     **4.3820**
**influences of technology in determining international industrial**
**competitive advantage / prepared by Automobile Panel,**
**Committee on Technology and International Economic and**
**Trade Issues of the Office of the Foreign Secretary, National**
**Academy of Engineering and the Commission on Engineering**
**and Technical Systems, National Research Council.**
Washington, D.C.: National Academy Press, [1982] xii, 202 p.: ill.; 23 cm. 1. Automobile industry and trade — United States. I. National Academy of Engineering. Committee on Technology and International Economic and Trade Issues. Automobile Panel. II. National Research Council (U.S.). Commission on Engineering and Technical Systems.
HD9710.U52 C58 1982      338.4/76292/0973 19      *LC* 82-12506      *ISBN* 030903289X

**Weisberger, Bernard A., 1922-.**     **4.3821**
The dream maker: William C. Durant, founder of General Motors / by Bernard A. Weisberger. — 1st ed. — Boston: Little, Brown, c1979. xix, 396 p.: ill.; 25 cm. Includes index. 1. Durant, William Crapo, 1861-1947. 2. General Motors Corporation — History. 3. Businessmen — United States — Biography. I. T.
HD9710.U52 D858      338.7/6292/0924 B      *LC* 79-90456      *ISBN* 0316928747

**Harbridge House, inc.**     **4.3822**
Corporate strategies of the automotive manufacturers / John B. Schnapp, project director; Jennifer Cassettari, research coordinator; project team, Patricia A. Comer ... [et al.]. — Lexington, Mass.: Lexington Books, c1979. xv, 196 p.; 24 cm. Results of a study prepared for the National Highway Traffic Safety Administration. 1. Automobile industry and trade — United States — Management. 2. Products liability — Automobiles — United States. I. Schnapp, John B. II. United States. National Highway Traffic Safety Administration. III. T.
HD9710.U52 H32 1979      658/.92/920973      *LC* 79-2788      *ISBN* 0669032433

**May, George Smith, 1924-.**     **4.3823**
R. E. Olds, auto industry pioneer / by George S. May. — Grand Rapids: Eerdmans, c1977. viii, 458 p.: ill.; 24 cm. Includes index. 1. Olds, Ransom Eli, 1864-1950. 2. Automobile industry and trade — United States — History. 3. Businessmen — United States — Biography. I. T.
HD9710.U52 O435      338.7/62/920924 B      *LC* 77-7988      *ISBN* 0802870287

**Rae, John Bell, 1911-.**     •**4.3824**
The American automobile; a brief history, by John B. Rae. Chicago, University of Chicago Press [1965] xiv, 265 p. ill., maps, ports. (The Chicago history of American civilization) 1. Automobile industry and trade — United States — History I. T.
HD9710 U52 R29      *LC* 65-24981

**Rae, John Bell, 1911-.**     **4.3825**
The American automobile industry / John B. Rae. — Boston, Mass.: Twayne Publishers, c1984. xii, 212 p.: ill.; 23 cm. — (The Evolution of American business: industries, institutions, and entrepreneurs) Includes index. 1. Automobile industry and trade — United States — History. I. T.
HD9710.U52 R297 1984      338.4/76292/0973 19      *LC* 84-6744      *ISBN* 080579803X

**Rae, John Bell, 1911-.**     •**4.3826**
American automobile manufacturers: the first forty years. — [1st ed.] Philadelphia: Chilton Co., Book Division [1959] 223 p.: ill.; 24 cm. 1. Automobile industry and trade — United States I. T.
HD9710 U52 R3      *LC* 59-5769

**Regulating the automobile / Robert W. Crandall ... [et al.].**     **4.3827**
Washington, D.C.: Brookings Institution, c1986. xiii, 202 p.; 24 cm. (Studies in the regulation of economic activity.) 1. Automobiles — Safety regulations — United States — Cost effectiveness. 2. Automobiles — Motors — Exhaust gas — Law and legislation — Cost effectiveness. 3. Automobiles — Fuel consumption — Law and legislation — United States — Cost effetiveness. I. Crandall, Robert W. II. Series.
HD9710.U52 R39 1986      343.73/078629222 347.30378629222 19      *LC* 85-48171      *ISBN* 0815715943

**White, Lawrence J.**     •**4.3828**
The automobile industry since 1945 [by] Lawrence J. White. — Cambridge, Mass.: Harvard University Press, 1971. xii, 348 p.: illus.; 25 cm. A revision of the author's thesis, Harvard University, 1969. 1. Automobile industry and trade — U.S. I. T.
HD9710.U52 W52      338.4/7/62922220973      *LC* 76-148939      *ISBN* 0674054709

**Homze, Edward L.**     **4.3829**
Arming the Luftwaffe: the Reich Air Ministry and the German aircraft industry, 1919–39 / Edward L. Homze. — Lincoln: University of Nebraska Press, c1977. xv, 296 p., [8] leaves of plates: ill.; 24 cm. Includes index. 1. Aircraft industry — Germany — History. 2. Germany Luftwaffe — History. I. T.
HD9711.G32 H65      338.4/7/629133340943      *LC* 75-38055      *ISBN* 0803208723

**Stekler, Herman O.**     •**4.3830**
The structure and performance of the aerospace industry / by Herman O. Stekler. — Berkeley: University of California Press, 1965. xvi, 223 p.; 25 cm. (Publications of the Institute of Business and Economic Research, University of California) 1. Aerospace industries — United States I. T.
HD9711.5 U6 S7      *LC* 65-17984

**Goldman, Nathan C.**     **4.3831**
Space commerce: free enterprise on the high frontier / Nathan C. Goldman. — Cambridge, Mass.: Ballinger Pub. Co., c1985. xiii, 186 p.: ill.; 24 cm. Includes index. 1. Space industrialization — Government policy — United States. I. T.
HD9711.75.U62 G65 1985      338.4 19      *LC* 84-16761      *ISBN* 0887300030

## HD9720–9739 Manufactures

**Arpan, Jeffrey S.**     **4.3832**
Directory of foreign manufacturers in the United States / Jeffrey S. Arpan, David A. Ricks. — 3rd ed. — Atlanta, Ga.: Business Pub. Division, College of Business Administration, Georgia State University, 1985. xxi, 384 p.; 29 cm. 'Compiled by the Business Publishing Division, a unit of the College of Business Administration, Georgia State University, Atlanta, Georgia. R. Cary Bynum, director, was responsible for the overall compilation'-P. ix. 1. Corporations, Foreign — United States — Directories. 2. Subsidiary corporations — United States — Directories. 3. United States — Manufactures — Directories. I. Ricks, David A. II. Bynum, R. Cary. III. Georgia State University. College of Business Administration. Business Publishing Division. IV. T.
HD9723.A76 1985      338.8/8873/025 19      *LC* 85-237330      *ISBN* 0884061639

**Census of manufactures (1982)**     **4.3833**
1982 census of manufactures. — [Washington, D.C.]: U.S. Dept. of Commerce, Bureau of the Census, 1984-. p. cm. 1. United States — Manufactures — Statistics I. United States. Bureau of the Census. II. T.
HD9724.C4 1984      338.4/767/0973 19      *LC* 83-600153

**Baranson, Jack.**    4.3834
Robots in manufacturing: key to international competitiveness / Jack Baranson. — Mt. Airy, Md.: Lomond Publications, 1983. xii, 152 p.: ill.; 24 cm. 1. Robots, Industrial 2. Manufacturing processes — Automation. 3. Competition, International 4. United States — Manufactures — Automation. 5. Japan — Manufactures — Automation. 6. Europe — Manufactures — Automation. I. T.
HD9725.B37 1983    338.4/54 19    *LC* 83-81240    *ISBN* 0912338393

**Creamer, Daniel Barnett, 1909-.**    • 4.3835
Capital expansion and capacity in postwar manufacturing / by Daniel Creamer. — New York: National Industrial Conference Board, 1961. 88 p.: diagrs., tables.; 23 cm. 1. Capital — United States. 2. United States — Manufactures I. T.
HD9725.C69    338/.0973    *LC* 77-10056    *ISBN* 0837197759

**Prais, S. J.**    4.3836
The evolution of giant firms in Britain: a study of the growth of concentration in manufacturing industry in Britain, 1909–70 / by S. J. Prais. — Cambridge; New York: Cambridge University Press, 1977 (c1976) xvii, 321 p.: ill.; 24 cm. — (The National Institute of Economic and Social Research. Economic and social studies; 30) Includes index. 1. Industrial concentration — Great Britain — History. 2. Industries, Size of 3. Industrial concentration — History. 4. Great Britain — Manufactures. I. T. II. Series.
HD9731.5.P72    338.6/44/0941    *LC* 76-18410    *ISBN* 0521213568

# HD9743 Munitions. Arms Trade

**Stockholm International Peace Research Institute.**    4.3837
The arms trade with the Third World / by Frank Blackaby and others. — Stockholm: Almqvist & Wiksell; New York: Humanities Press [1971] xxxi, 910 p.: ill., maps; 24 cm. 1. Munitions 2. Firearms industry and trade — Developing countries. 3. Munitions — Developing countries. I. T.
HD9743.A2 S76 1971    327/.174    *LC* 72-169792    *ISBN* 0391001973

**Peck, Merton J.**    • 4.3838
The weapons acquisition process: an economic analysis / [by] Merton J. Peck [and] Frederic M. Scherer. — Boston: Division of Research, Graduate School of Business Administration, Harvard University, 1962. xxxii, 736 p.: diagrs.; 22 cm. Bibliography: p. 712-725. 1. Munitions — United States. 2. Defense contracts — United States. 3. United States — Armed Forces — Procurement I. Scherer, F. M. (Frederic M.) joint author. II. T.
HD9743.U6P4    338.476234    *LC* 62-10300

**Arms transfers and American foreign policy / edited by Andrew J. Pierre.**    4.3839
New York: New York University Press, 1979. x, 331 p.; 22 cm. 1. Munitions — United States — Addresses, essays, lectures. 2. United States — Foreign relations — 1974- — Addresses, essays, lectures. I. Pierre, Andrew J.
HD9743.U6 A73    382/.45/62340973    *LC* 79-2057    *ISBN* 0814265750

# HD9750–9769 Forest Products

**Tillman, David A.**    4.3840
Forest products: advanced technologies and economic analyses / David A. Tillman. — Orlando: Academic Press, 1985. xii, 283 p.: ill.; 24 cm. 1. Forest products industry 2. Forest products industry — Technological innovations. I. T.
HD9750.5.T55 1985    338.1/7498 19    *LC* 85-70363    *ISBN* 012691270X

**Carroll, Charles F., 1936-.**    4.3841
The timber economy of Puritan New England [by] Charles F. Carroll. — Providence [R.I.]: Brown University Press, [1974, c1973] xiii, 221 p.: maps.; 24 cm. 1. Lumber trade — New England — History. 2. Forests and forestry — New England — History. 3. New England — Economic conditions. I. T.
HD9757.A1 C35    380.1/41/490974    *LC* 73-7122    *ISBN* 0870571427

**Lower, Arthur Reginald Marsden, 1889-.**    4.3842
Great Britain's woodyard; British America and the timber trade, 1763–1867 [by] Arthur R. M. Lower. — Montreal: McGill-Queen's University Press, 1973. xiv, 271 p.: illus.; 26 cm. 1. Lumber trade — Great Britain — History. 2. Lumber trade — Canada — History. I. T.
HD9761.5.L65    380.1/45/6740942    *LC* 72-82249    *ISBN* 0773500960

**Shineberg, Dorothy Lois.**    4.3843
They came for sandalwood: a study of the sandalwood trade in the south–west Pacific, 1830–1865 / [by] Dorothy Shineberg. — [Melbourne]: Melbourne

University Press; London; New York: Cambridge University Press, [1967] xiv, 299 p.: ill., facsims., maps, ports., tables; 23 cm. 1. Sandalwood trade — New Caledonia. 2. Sandalwood trade — New Caledonia — Loyalty Islands. 3. Sandalwood trade — Vanuatu. I. T.
HD9769.S33 N47    382/.41/497394099    *LC* 67-30710

## HD9850–9949 Textiles. Clothing

**Jeremy, David John, 1939-.**    4.3844
Transatlantic industrial revolution: the diffusion of textile technologies between Britain and America, 1790–1830s / David J. Jeremy. — North Andover, Mass.: Merrimack Valley Textile Museum; Cambridge, Mass.: MIT Press, c1981. xvii, 384 p.: ill.; 21 x 25 cm. Based on the author's thesis (Ph.D.)—University of London, 1978. Includes index. 1. Textile industry — United States — Technological innovations — History. 2. Textile industry — Great Britain — Technological innovations — History. 3. Diffusion of innovations — United States — History. 4. Diffusion of innovations — Great Britain — History. 5. Technology transfer — History. I. Merrimack Valley Textile Museum. II. T.
HD9855.J47    338.4/5677/00941 19    *LC* 81-517    *ISBN* 0262100223

**The New England mill village, 1790–1860 / edited by Gary Kulik, Roger Parks, Theodore Z. Penn.**    4.3845
Cambridge, Mass.: MIT Press, c1982. xxxv, 520 p.: ill.; 24 cm. — (Documents in American industrial history. v. 2) 1. Textile industry — New England — History — Sources. 2. Textile factories — New England — History — Sources. 3. Textile workers — New England — History — Sources. 4. Cities and towns — New England — History — Sources. 5. Villages — New England — History — Sources. 6. New England — Social conditions — Sources. I. Kulik, Gary. II. Parks, Roger N. III. Penn, Theodore Z. IV. Series.
HD9857.A11 N48 1982    307.7/6 19    *LC* 81-23665    *ISBN* 0262110849

**Carlton, David L. (David Lee), 1948-.**    4.3846
Mill and town in South Carolina, 1880–1920 / David L. Carlton. — Baton Rouge: Louisiana State University Press, c1982. xii, 313 p.: map; 24 cm. Map on lining papers. Includes index. 1. Textile industry — Social aspects — South Carolina — History. I. T.
HD9857.S6 C37 1982    307.7/66/09757 19    *LC* 82-7753    *ISBN* 0807110426

**Scranton, Philip.**    4.3847
Proprietary capitalism: the textile manufacture at Philadelphia, 1800–1885 / Philip Scranton. — Cambridge [Cambridgeshire]; New York: Cambridge University Press, 1983. xiii, 431 p.: ill., maps; 24 cm. 1. Textile industry — Pennsylvania — Philadelphia — History — 19th century. I. T.
HD9858.P5 S35 1983    338.4/7677/00974811 19    *LC* 83-10155    *ISBN* 0521252458

**Tucker, Barbara M.**    4.3848
Samuel Slater and the origins of the American textile industry, 1790–1860 / Barbara M. Tucker. — Ithaca: Cornell University Press, 1984. 268 p.: ill.; 24 cm. 1. Slater, Samuel, 1768-1835. 2. Textile industry — United States — Biography. 3. Textile industry — United States — History. I. T.
HD9860.S5 T83 1984    677/.21/0924 B 19    *LC* 84-45145    *ISBN* 0801415942

**Reddy, William M.**    4.3849
The rise of market culture: the textile trade and French society, 1750–1900 / William M. Reddy. — Cambridge [Cambridgeshire]; New York: Cambridge University Press; Paris: Editions de la Maison des sciences de l'homme, 1984. xii, 402 p.: ill.; 24 cm. Includes index. 1. Textile industry — France — History. I. T.
HD9862.5.R43 1984    381/.45677/0944 19    *LC* 83-25232    *ISBN* 0521256534

**Cloth and clothing in medieval Europe: essays in memory of Professor E.M. Carus–Wilson / edited by N.B. Harte and K.G. Ponting.**    4.3850
London: Heinemann Educational Books; [Edington]: Pasold Research Fund, 1983. xiv, 401 p.: ill.; 23 cm. (Pasold studies in textile history. 2) 1. Carus-Wilson, E. M. (Eleanora Mary), 1897-1977 — Addresses, essays, lectures. 2. Carus-Wilson, E. M. (Eleanora Mary), 1897-1977 — Bibliography. 3. Textile industry — Europe — History — Addresses, essays, lectures. 4. Clothing trade — Europe — History — Addresses, essays, lectures. 5. Textile finishing — Europe — History — Addresses, essays, lectures. 6. Clothing and dress — Europe — History — Addresses, essays, lectures. I. Carus-Wilson, E. M. (Eleanora Mary), 1897-1977. II. Harte, N. B. III. Ponting, Kenneth G. IV. Series.
HD9865.A2 C56 1983    338.4/7677/009678 19    *LC* 81-210848    *ISBN* 0435323822

**Ware, Caroline Farrar, 1899-.**    4.3851
The early New England cotton manufacture: a study in industrial beginnings. — Boston: Houghton Mifflin, 1931. 349 p. ill. (Hart Schaffner & Marx prize essays, 48) History of American economy: studies and materials for study; a

series of reprints. 1. Cotton manufacture — New England 2. Industry — History I. T.
HD9877 A1 W3 1931A

**Wallace, Anthony F. C., 1923-.**      **4.3852**
Rockdale: the growth of an American village in the early industrial revolution / Anthony F. C. Wallace; technical drawings by Robert Howard. — 1st ed. — New York: Knopf, c1978. xx, 553 p.: ill.; 25 cm. Includes index. 1. Cotton trade — Pennsylvania — Rockdale — History. 2. Rockdale (Pa.) — Industries — History. 3. Rockdale (Pa.) — Social conditions. 4. Rockdale (Pa.) — Religious life and customs — History. I. T.
HD9878.R6 W34 1978    974.8/14    *LC* 77-20346    *ISBN* 0394421205

**Farnie, Douglas Antony.**      **4.3853**
The English cotton industry and the world market, 1815–1896 / by D. A. Farnie. — Oxford: Clarendon Press; New York: Oxford University Press, 1979. vii, 399 p.: 2 ill.; 23 cm. Includes index. 1. Cotton trade — England — History — 19th century. I. T.
HD9881.5.F37 1979    338.4/7/677210942    *LC* 78-40646    *ISBN* 0198224788

**Sandberg, Lars G.**      **4.3854**
Lancashire in decline: a study in entrepreneurship, technology, and international trade, by Lars G. Sandberg. — Columbus: Ohio State University Press, [1974] xii, 276 p.; 24 cm. 1. Cotton trade — Lancashire, Eng. 2. Cotton manufacture — Lancashire, Eng. 3. Cotton machinery I. T.
HD9881.8.L3 S25    338.4/7/67721094272    *LC* 73-18435    *ISBN* 0814201997

**Stein, Stanley J.**      **4.3855**
The Brazilian cotton manufacture: textile enterprise in an underdeveloped area, 1850–1950 / Stanley J. Stein. — Cambridge, Mass.: Harvard University Press, 1957. xii, 273 p. — (Studies in entrepreneurial history.) 1. Cotton trade — Brazil. 2. Cotton manufacture — Brazil. I. T.
HD9884.B82 S7    *LC* 57-7617

**Jenkins, D. T.**      **4.3856**
The British wool textile industry, 1770–1914 / D.T. Jenkins and K.G. Ponting. — London: Heinemann Educational Books: Pasold Research Fund, 1983 (c1982). xii, 388 p.; 23 cm. Includes index. 1. Wool trade and industry — Great Britain — History. I. Ponting, Kenneth G. II. T.
HD9901.5.J46    338.4/767731/0941 19    *LC* 82-125943    *ISBN* 0435324691

**Coleman, D. C. (Donald Cuthbert), 1920-.**      **4.3857**
Courtaulds: an economic and social history [by] D. C. Coleman. [S.l.]: Oxford, 1969-1980. 3 v. illus., facsims., tables, maps, ports. 24 cm. 1. Courtaulds ltd. I. T.
HD9929.2.G74 C683    338.7/677/00941 19    *LC* 75-413391    *ISBN* 0198282354

**Schmiechen, James A., 1940-.**      **4.3858**
Sweated industries and sweated labor: the London clothing trades, 1860–1914 / James A. Schmiechen. — Urbana: University of Illinois Press, c1984. 209 p.; 24 cm. — (Working class in European history.) Revision of thesis (Ph. D.)— University of Illinois, Champaign-Urbana, 1974. 1. Clothing trade — England — London — History. 2. Clothing workers — England — London — History. 3. Sweating system — England — London — History. 4. Trade-unions — Clothing workers — England — London — History. 5. Labor laws and legislation — Great Britain — History. I. T. II. Series.
HD9940.G82 L67 1984    331.7/687/09421 19    *LC* 82-17357    *ISBN* 0252010248

**Jarnow, Jeannette A.**      **4.3859**
Inside the fashion business: text and readings / Jeannette A. Jarnow, Miriam Guerreiro, Beatrice Judelle. — 4th ed. — New York: Macmillan, c1987. xvii, 525 p.: ill.; 24 cm. 1. Fashion merchandising — United States. 2. Clothing trade — United States. I. Guerreiro, Miriam. II. Judelle, Beatrice, 1908- III. T.
HD9940.U4 J3 1987    338.4/7687/0973 19    *LC* 86-16359    *ISBN* 0023600004

**Francis, Daniel.**      **4.3860**
Partners in furs: a history of the fur trade in Eastern James Bay, 1600–1870 / Daniel Francis and Toby Morantz. — Kingston: McGill-Queen's University Press, c1983. xvi, 203 p.: ill.; 24 cm. Includes index. 1. Fur trade — James Bay Region (Ont. and Québec) — History. 2. Indians of North America — James Bay Region (Ont. and Québec) — Trapping — History. I. Morantz, Toby Elaine, 1943- II. T.
HD9944.C23 J364 1983    380.1/456753/0971314 19    *LC* 83-197138    *ISBN* 0773503854

**Karamanski, Theodore J., 1953-.**      **4.3861**
Fur trade and exploration: opening the Far Northwest, 1821–1852 / by Theodore J. Karamanski. — 1st ed. — Norman: University of Oklahoma Press,

c1983. xxii, 330 p.: ill., maps; 23 cm. Includes index. 1. Fur trade — Northwest, Pacific — History — 19th century. 2. Northwest, Pacific — Discovery and exploration. I. T.
HD9944.U46 A193 1983    380.1/456753/09795 19    *LC* 82-40453    *ISBN* 0806118334

**Kersey, Harry A., 1935-.**      **4.3862**
Pelts, plumes, and hides: white traders among the Seminole Indians, 1870–1930 / Harry A. Kersey, Jr. — Gainesville: University Presses of Florida, 1975. xi, 158 p., [4] leaves of plates: ill.; 24 cm. 'A Florida Atlantic University book.' Includes index. 1. Fur trade — Florida — History. 2. Seminole Indians — History. I. T.
HD9944.U46 F64    381/.439    *LC* 75-16137    *ISBN* 0813005159

## HD9980–9999 Service Industries. Other Industries

**Fuchs, Victor R.**      **• 4.3863**
The service economy [by] Victor R. Fuchs. New York, National Bureau of Economic Research; distributed by Columbia University Press [1968] xxviii, 280 p. illus. 24 cm. (National Bureau of Economic Research. General series, no. 87) 1. Service industries — United States. 2. Service industries — United States — Labor productivity. I. T. II. Series.
HD9980.5.F83    338.4    *LC* 68-8802

**Census of service industries (1982)**      **4.3864**
1982 census of service industries. — Washington: U.S. Dept. of Commerce, Bureau of the Census, 1984-. p. cm. 1. Service industries — United States — Statistics. I. United States. Bureau of the Census. II. T.
HD9981.4.C46 1984    338.4/7/000973 19    *LC* 83-600218

**Services, the new economy / Thomas M. Stanback, Jr. ... [et al.]; foreword by Eli Ginzberg.**      **4.3865**
Totowa, N.J.: Allanheld, Osmun, 1981. xvii, 156 p.; 25 cm. (Conservation of human resources series. 20) (LandMark studies) Includes index. 1. Service industries — United States. 2. United States — Economic conditions — 1971-1981 I. Stanback, Thomas M. II. Series.
HD9981.5.S45    330.973/0927 19    *LC* 81-10905    *ISBN* 0916672638

**Sueno, Akira, 1913-.**      **4.3866**
Entrepreneur and gentleman: a case history of a Japanese company / Akira Sueno; translated by Neal Donner. Rutland, Vt.: C. E. Tuttle Co., 1977. 249 p.: ill.; 22 cm. Translation of Waga shōkon ni kuinashi. 1. Sueno, Akira, 1913-2. Shōwa Bōeki Kabushiki Kaisha. 3. Industrial management — Japan — Case studies. 4. Business enterprises — Japan — Case studies. I. T.
HD9999.C74 S8413    658.4/0092/4 B    *LC* 76-51611    *ISBN* 0804811997

## HE TRANSPORTATION. COMMUNICATION

**Georgano, G. N.**      **4.3867**
Transportation through the ages / edited by G. N. Georgano. — New York: McGraw-Hill, [1972] xii, 311 p.: ill.; 29 cm. 1. Transportation — History I. T.
HE151.G34 1972    380.5/09    *LC* 76-99198    *ISBN* 0070231311

**Glaister, Stephen.**      **4.3868**
Fundamentals of transport economics / Stephen Glaister. — New York: St. Martin's Press, 1981. xi, 194 p.; 23 cm. Includes index. 1. Transportation 2. Choice of transportation — Cost effectiveness. I. T.
HE151.G54 1981    380.5 19    *LC* 81-52181    *ISBN* 0312311524

**Kneafsey, James T.**      **4.3869**
Transportation economic analysis / James T. Kneafsey. — Lexington, Mass.: Lexington Books, [1975] xxvii, 418 p.: ill.; 24 cm. 1. Transportation — United States. 2. Urban transportation — United States. 3. Transportation — Passenger traffic 4. Freight and freightage I. T.
HE151.K57    380.5/0973    *LC* 74-2203    *ISBN* 0699932116

**Kraft, Gerald.**      **4.3870**
The role of transportation in regional economic development: a Charles River Associates research study / [by] Gerald Kraft, John R. Meyer [and] Jean–Paul Valette. — Lexington, Mass.: Lexington Books, [1971] ix, 129 p.: ill.; 23 cm. 1. Transportation 2. Regional planning I. Meyer, John Robert. joint author. II. Valette, Jean Paul. joint author. III. Charles River Associates. IV. T.
HE151.K68    380.5    *LC* 72-158829    *ISBN* 0669624100

**Stone, Tabor R.**    • **4.3871**
Beyond the automobile; reshaping the transportation environment [by] Tabor R. Stone. — Englewood Cliffs, N.J.: Prentice-Hall, [1971] xi, 148 p.: illus.; 21 cm. — (A Spectrum book) 1. Transportation 2. Urban transportation 3. High speed ground transportation I. T.
HE151.S745    388/.0973    LC 72-140266    ISBN 0130760269

**Techniques of transport planning. John R. Meyer, editor.**    **4.3872**
Washington: Brookings Institution, Transport Research Program, [1971] 2 v.: illus., col. maps.; 24 cm. 1. Transportation 2. Transportation — Research I. Meyer, John Robert. ed. II. Straszheim, Mahlon R., 1939- III. Kresge, David T. IV. Roberts, Paul O. V. Brookings Institution, Washington, D.C. Transport Research Program.
HE151.T43    380.5    LC 79-108833    ISBN 0815756909

**Kanafani, Adib K.**    **4.3873**
Transportation demand analysis / Adib Kanafani. — New York: McGraw-Hill, c1983. xi, 320 p.: ill.; 25 cm. (McGraw-Hill series in transportation.) 1. Transportation — Planning 2. Demand (Economic theory) I. T. II. Series.
HE152.5.K36 1983    380.5/068 19    LC 82-13015    ISBN 0070332711

**Leighton, Albert C.**    • **4.3874**
Transport and communication in early medieval Europe, A.D. 500–1100 / [by] Albert C. Leighton . — New York: Barnes & Noble, [1972] 257 p.: ill.; 23 cm. 1. Transportation — History I. T.
HE181.L45 1972b    380.5/09    LC 72-192853    ISBN 0389046132

**Fromm, Gary. ed.**    • **4.3875**
Transport investment and economic development. Washington, Brookings Institution, Transport Research Program [1965] x, 314 p. ill.; maps. Papers prepared for a series of Harvard University seminars, which are part of the Brookings Transport Research Program. 1. Transportation — Addresses, essays, lectures I. Brookings Institution, Washington, D.C. Transport Research Program II. T.
HE193 F75    LC 65-15416

**Williams, Ernest William, 1916-.**    • **4.3876**
Freight transportation in the Soviet Union, including comparisons with the United States [by] Ernest W. Williams, Jr. with the assistance of George Novak and Holland Hunter. A study by the National Bureau of Economic Research. Princeton, N.J., Princeton University Press, 1962. xxi, 221 p. map (on lining papers), diagrs., tables. (National Bureau of Economic Research. General series, no. 76) 1. Freight and freightage — Russia 2. Freight and freightage — United States I. T. II. Series.
HE199 R8 W5 1962    LC 62-11951

**Friedlaender, Ann Fetter.**    • **4.3877**
The dilemma of freight transport regulation / [by] Ann F. Friedlaender. — Washington: Brookings Institution [1969] xiii, 216 p.: ill.; 24 cm. (Studies in the regulation of economic activity.) 'A background paper prepared for a conference of experts at the Brookings Institution, together with a summary of the conference discussion.' 1. Freight and freightage — United States. I. Brookings Institution. II. T. III. Series.
HE199.U5 F7    380.5/2    LC 69-18820    ISBN 0815729367

**Manheim, Marvin L.**    **4.3878**
Fundamentals of transportation systems analysis / Marvin L. Manheim. — Cambridge, Mass.: MIT Press, c1979-. v.: ill.; 24 cm. (MIT Press series in transportation studies. 4-) Includes index. 1. Transportation — Planning 2. Transportation — Mathematical models. 3. System analysis I. T. II. Series.
HE199.9.M34    380.5    LC 78-11535    ISBN 0262131293

# HE201–300 By Country

**Census of transportation (1982)**    **4.3879**
1982 census of transportation. — [Washington]: U.S. Dept. of Commerce, Bureau of the Census, [1984] p. cm. 'Issued May 1983.' 'TC-82-ST' (v. 1) 'TC-82-CS' (v. 2) 'TC82-T-1-< >; TC82-T-51' (v. 3) 1. Transportation — United States — Statistics. I. United States. Bureau of the Census. II. T.
HE203.C44 1984    380.5/0973 19    LC 83-600222

**Farris, Martin T. comp.**    • **4.3880**
Modern transportation; selected readings. Edited by Martin T. Farris [and] Paul T. McElhiney. — 2d ed. — Boston: Houghton Mifflin Co., [1972, c1973] ix, 466 p.; 24 cm. 1. Transportation — United States — Addresses, essays, lectures. I. McElhiney, Paul T. joint comp. II. T.
HE203.F36 1973    380.5/0973    LC 73-1571    ISBN 039514034X

**Harper, Donald Victor, 1927-.**    **4.3881**
Transportation in America: users, carriers, government / Donald V. Harper. — Englewood Cliffs, N.J.: Prentice-Hall, c1978. xxii, 599 p.: ill.; 24 cm. 1. Transportation — United States. 2. Transportation and state — United States. I. T.
HE203.H26    380.5/0973    LC 77-12222    ISBN 013930214X

**Meyer, Balthasar Henry, 1866- ed.**    • **4.3882**
History of transportation in the United States before 1860 / prepared under the direction of Balthasar Henry Meyer, by Caroline E. MacGill and a staff of collaborators. — [New York]: P. Smith, 1948. xi, 678 p.: 5 maps (1 fold.); 25 cm. (Contributions to American economic history [3]) Carnegie Institution of Washington. Publication no. 215C. 1. Transportation — History I. MacGill, Caroline Elizabeth. II. T.
HE203.M4 1948    LC A 48-9999

**Norton, Hugh Stanton, 1921-.**    • **4.3883**
Modern transportation economics [by] Hugh S. Norton. — 2d ed — Columbus, Ohio: Merrill, [1971] viii, 470 p.: illus.; 24 cm. 1. Transportation — U.S. I. T.
HE203.N6 1971    380.5/0973    LC 74-138466    ISBN 0675092620

**Schonberger, Howard B.**    • **4.3884**
Transportation to the seaboard; the communication revolution and American foreign policy, 1860–1900 [by] Howard B. Schonberger. — Westport, Conn.: Greenwood Pub. Corp., [1971] xix, 265 p.; 22 cm. — (Contributions in American history, no. 8) 1. Transportation — U.S. — History. I. T.
HE205.S33    380.5/0973    LC 75-105979    ISBN 0837133068

**Dearing, Charles Lee, 1903-.**    • **4.3885**
National transportation policy / by Charles L. Dearing and Wilfred Owen. — Washington: Brookings Institution, 1949. xiv, 459 p.: diagrs. 'Based in part on a study...which the authors undertook at the request of the Hoover Commission on Government Reorganization.' 1. Transportation — United States. I. Owen, Wilfred. II. Brookings Institution. III. United States. Commission on Organization of the Executive Branch of the Government. IV. T.
HE206.D4

**Locklin, David Philip, 1897-.**    • **4.3886**
Economics of transportation [by] D. Philip Locklin. — 7th ed. — Homewood, Ill.: R. D. Irwin, 1972. xi, 913 p.: illus.; 24 cm. — (The Irwin series in economics) 1. Transportation — United States. 2. Railroads — United States I. T.
HE206.L6 1972    380.5    LC 76-187057

**Meyer, John Robert.**    • **4.3887**
The economics of competition in the transportation industries / [by] John R. Meyer [and others] — Cambridge: Harvard University Press, 1959. 359 p.: ill.; 22 cm. (Harvard economic studies. v. 107) Includes bibliography. 1. Transportation — United States. I. T. II. Series.
HE206.M4    385.0973    LC 59-6160

**Pegrum, Dudley Frank, 1898-.**    • **4.3888**
Transportation: economics and public policy / Dudley F. Pegrum. — Rev. ed. — Homewood, Ill.: R.D. Irwin, 1968. xx, 680 p.: ill.; 24 cm. — (The Irwin series in economics) 1. Transportation — United States 2. Transportation — United States — Law and regulation I. T.
HE206.P4 1968    LC 67-30243

**Smerk, George M. comp.**    • **4.3889**
Readings in urban transportation. Edited by George M. Smerk. — Bloomington: Indiana University Press, [1968] x, 336 p.: illus.; 25 cm. 1. Urban transportation — United States — Addresses, essays, lectures. I. T.
HE206.S6    380.5/0973    LC 68-14613

**Ullman, Edward Louis, 1912-1976.**    • **4.3890**
American commodity flow; a geographical interpretation of rail and water traffic based on principles of spatial interchange. Seattle, University of Washington Press, 1957. xxii, 215 p. maps. 1. Transportation — United States 2. United States — Commerce I. T.
HE206 U4    LC 57-9184

**Fellmeth, Robert C.**    • **4.3891**
The interstate commerce omission, the public interest and the ICC; The Ralph Nader study group report on the Interstate Commerce Commission and transportation, [by] Robert C. Fellmeth, project director [and others] New York, Grossman Publishers, 1970. xv, 423 p. 19 cm. 1. United States. Interstate Commerce Commission. 2. Transportation — United States. I. Nader, Ralph. II. T. III. Title: Ralph Nader study group report on the Interstate Commerce Commission and transportation.
HE206.2.F4    380.5/0973    LC 70-112514

**The Future of American transportation / [Edited by Ernest W. Williams, Jr.].**    • **4.3892**
Englewood Cliffs, N.J.: Prentice-Hall, [1971] v, 211 p.; 22 cm. — (A Spectrum book) At head of title: The American Assembly, Columbia University.

'Designed ... as advance reading for the thirty-ninth American Assembly ... Arden House, Harriman, N.Y., April 15-18, 1971. 1. Transportation — U.S. — Addresses, essays, lectures. I. Williams, Ernest William, 1916- ed. II. American Assembly.
HE206.2.F8      380.5/0973      *LC* 72-160529      *ISBN* 013345827X

**Perspectives on Federal transportation policy / edited by James**      **4.3893**
**C. Miller III.**
Washington: American Enterprise Institute for Public Policy Research, [1975] 218 p.: graphs; 24 cm. Proceedings of a conference held in Washington, D.C., Feb. 1974, sponsored by American Enterprise Institute for Public Policy Research. 1. Transportation and state — United States — Congresses. I. Miller, James Clifford. II. American Enterprise Institute for Public Policy Research.
HE206.2.P47      380.5/0973      *LC* 74-29369      *ISBN* 0844720569

**Sampson, Roy J.**                                                   **4.3894**
Domestic transportation: practice, theory, and policy / Roy J. Sampson, Martin T. Farris, David L. Shrock. — 5th ed. — Boston: Houghton Mifflin Co., c1985. xiv, 640 p.: ill.; 25 cm. 1. Transportation — United States. 2. Freight and freightage — United States. I. Farris, Martin T. II. Shrock, David L. III. T.
HE206.2.S25 1985      380.5/0973 19      *LC* 84-80269      *ISBN* 0395357136

**Kirkland, Edward Chase, 1894-.**                               • **4.3895**
Men, cities, and transportation; a study in New England history, 1820–1900. — New York: Russell & Russell, [1968, c1948] 2 v.: illus., facsims., maps, ports.; 25 cm. — (Studies in economic history) 1. Transportation — New England. 2. Railroads — New England. I. T. II. Series.
HE207.K5 1968      380.5/0974      *LC* 68-15132

**Baughman, James P.**                                           • **4.3896**
Charles Morgan and the development of Southern transportation [by] James P. Baughman. — Nashville: Vanderbilt University Press, 1968. xxxi, 302 p.: illus., maps, ports.; 25 cm. 1. Morgan, Charles, 1795-1878. 2. Transportation — Southern States — History. I. T.
HE208.B38      380.5/0924      *LC* 68-17281

**Stokes, Charles J.**                                           • **4.3897**
Transportation and economic development in Latin America [by] Charles J. Stokes. — New York: F. A. Praeger, [1968] xv, 204 p.: illus., maps.; 25 cm. — (Praeger special studies in international economics and development) 1. Transportation — South America. 2. Roads — South America. I. T.
HE230.A1 S7      380.5/098      *LC* 68-18930

**Nash, C. A. (Christopher Alfred), 1947-.**                         **4.3898**
Economics of public transport / C.A. Nash. — London: Longman, 1982. x, 194 p.: ill.; 24 cm. — (Modern economics.) 1. Transportation — Great Britain. I. T. II. Series.
HE243.A2 N37 1982      380.5/0941 18      380.5/9/0941 19      *LC* 81-215543      *ISBN* 0582446317

**Stubbs, P. C. (Peter C.), 1937-.**                                **4.3899**
Transport economics / P. C. Stubbs, W. J. Tyson, M. Q. Dalvi. — London; Boston: G. Allen & Unwin, 1980. viii, 216 p.: ill.; 22 cm. (Studies in economics; 15) Includes index. 1. Transportation — Great Britain. I. Tyson, W. J. (William James), 1946- joint author. II. Dalvi, M. Q. (M. Quasim) joint author. III. T.
HE243.S8      380.5/0941 19      *LC* 80-502906      *ISBN* 0043380883

**Hunter, Holland.**                                            • **4.3900**
Soviet transportation policy. Cambridge, Harvard University Press, 1957. xxiii, 416 p. fold. map, diagrs., tables. (Russian Research Center studies, 28) 1. Transportation — Russia I. T.
HE255 H8 1957      *LC* 57-11657

# HE300–311 Urban Transportation

## (see also: HE4201-5260)

**Hutchinson, B. G.**                                               **4.3901**
Principles of urban transport systems planning [by] B. G. Hutchinson. — Washington: Scripta Book Co., [1974] xx, 444 p.: illus.; 24 cm. 1. Urban transportation policy 2. Traffic estimation I. T.
HE305.H87      388.4      *LC* 73-20309      *ISBN* 0070315396

**International Conference on Personal Rapid Transit, 2d,**         **4.3902**
**University of Minnesota, 1973.**
Personal rapid transit II: progress, problems, and potential in a promising new form of public transportation reported at the 1973 International Conference on Personal Rapid Transit / J. Edward Anderson, general editor, Sherry H.

Romig, assistant editor, ... [et al.]. — Minneapolis: University of Minnesota, 1974. xii, 648 p.: ill.; 27 cm. 1. Personal rapid transit — Congresses. I. Anderson, John Edward. II. Romig, Sherry H. III. T.
HE305.I56 1973      388.4/1      *LC* 75-332287

**Metropolitan transportation planning / John W. Dickey, senior**     **4.3903**
**author, ... [et al.].**
2nd ed. — Washington, D.C.: Hemisphere Pub. Corp.; [New York]: McGraw-Hill, c1983. xiii, 607 p.: ill.; 25 cm. — (McGraw-Hill series in transportation.) 1. Urban transportation policy 2. Urban transportation — Mathematical models. I. Dickey, John W., 1941- II. Series.
HE305.M47 1983      388.4/068 19      *LC* 82-23319      *ISBN* 0891162712

**Meyer, Michael D.**                                               **4.3904**
Urban transportation planning: a decision–oriented approach / Michael D. Meyer, Eric J. Miller. — New York: McGraw-Hill, c1984. xvii, 524 p.: ill.; 25 cm. — (McGraw-Hill series in transportation.) 1. Urban transportation — Planning. I. Miller, Eric J. II. T. III. Series.
HE305.M49 1984      388.4/068 19      *LC* 83-25573      *ISBN* 0070417520

**National Conference on Personal Rapid Transit, 1st, University**     **4.3905**
**of Minnesota, 1971.**
Personal rapid transit; a selection of papers on a promising new mode of public transportation. Edited by J. Edward Anderson [and others. — Minneapolis]: Institute of Technology, University of Minnesota, 1972. viii, 502 p.: illus.; 23 cm. 1. Personal rapid transit — Congresses. I. Anderson, John Edward. ed. II. T.
HE305.N34 1971      388.4/1      *LC* 72-612184

**Organisation for Economic Co-operation and Development.**         **4.3906**
The automobile and the environment: an international perspective / prepared by the Organisation for Economic Co–operation and Development; edited by Ralph Gakenheimer. — Cambridge, Mass.: MIT Press, c1978. xiii, 494 p.: ill.; 24 cm. (MIT Press series in transportation studies. 1) 1. Transportation — Environmental aspects — Addresses, essays, lectures. 2. Automobiles — Environmental aspects — Addresses, essays, lectures. I. Gakenheimer, Ralph A. II. T. III. Series.
HE305.O73 1978      388.4      *LC* 78-2493      *ISBN* 0262070707

**Owen, Wilfred.**                                              • **4.3907**
The accessible city [by] Wilfred Owen with the assistance of Inai Bradfield. — Washington, D.C.: Brookings Institution, [1972] viii, 150 p.: illus.; 24 cm. 1. Urban transportation I. T.
HE305.O9      388.4      *LC* 76-39698      *ISBN* 0815767706

**Public transportation: planning, operations, and management /**     **4.3908**
**editors, George E. Gray, Lester A. Hoel.**
Englewood Cliffs, N.J.: Prentice-Hall, c1979. xviii, 749 p.: ill.; 25 cm. 1. Urban transportation — Addresses, essays, lectures. 2. Local transit — Management — Addresses, essays, lectures. 3. Transportation — Planning — Addresses, essays, lectures. I. Gray, George E., 1927- II. Hoel, Lester A.
HE305.P8      388.4      *LC* 78-11618      *ISBN* 0137391692

**Pushkarev, Boris.**                                               **4.3909**
Public transportation and land use policy / Boris S. Pushkarev, Jeffrey M. Zupan. — Bloomington: Indiana University Press, c1977. ix, 242 p.: ill.; 29 cm. 'A Regional Plan Association book.' 1. Urban transportation policy. 2. Choice of transportation 3. Land use, Urban I. Zupan, Jeffrey M. joint author. II. Regional Plan Association (New York, N.Y.) III. T.
HE305.P87 1977      388.4      *LC* 76-29299      *ISBN* 0253346827

**Richards, Brian, 1928-.**                                         **4.3910**
Moving in cities / Brian Richards. — Boulder, Colo.: Westview Press, c1976. 104 p.: ill.; 22 cm. 1. Urban transportation 2. Local transit I. T.
HE305.R53 1976      388.4      *LC* 75-22380      *ISBN* 0891585133

**Stopher, Peter Robert.**                                          **4.3911**
Urban transportation modeling and planning / [by] Peter R. Stopher, Arnim H. Meyburg. Lexington, Mass.; London: D.C. Heath, 1975. xix, 347 p.: ill., forms, maps, plans; 24 cm. 'Lexington books'. 1. Urban transportation — United States — Mathematical models. I. Meyburg, Arnim Hans. II. T.
HE305.S84      388.4/0973      *LC* 74-21876      *ISBN* 0669969419

**Strobel, Horst.**                                                 **4.3912**
Computer controlled urban transportation / Horst Strobel; International Institute for Applied Systems Analysis. — Chichester; Toronto: J. Wiley, 1982. xv, 500 p.: ill., maps. — (International series on applied systems analysis. 10) 'A Wiley-interscience publication'. 1. Urban transporation — Data processing 2. Automatic control — Data processing I. International Institute for Applied Systems Analysis. II. T. III. Series.
HE305 S85      *ISBN* 0471100366

**Urban transport economics / edited by David A. Hensher.** 4.3913
Cambridge; New York: Cambridge University Press, 1977. viii, 277 p.: ill.; 24
cm. 1. Urban transportation — Addresses, essays, lectures. I. Hensher, David
A., 1947-
HE305.U69        388.4/042        *LC* 76-11061        *ISBN* 052121128X

**Yago, Glenn.** 4.3914
The decline of transit: urban transportation in German and U.S. cities,
1900–1970 / Glenn Yago. — Cambridge [Cambridgeshire]; New York:
Cambridge University Press, 1984. ix, 293 p.: ill.; 24 cm. Includes index.
1. Urban transportation — United States — History — 20th century. 2. Urban
transportation policy — United States — History — 20th century. 3. Urban
transportation — Germany (West) — History — 20th century. 4. Urban
transportation policy — Germany (West) — History — 20th century. I. T.
HE305.Y33 1984        388.4/0943 19        *LC* 83-7297        *ISBN* 052125633X

**Altshuler, Alan A., 1936-.** 4.3915
The urban transportation system: politics and policy innovation / Alan
Altshuler, with James P. Womack, John R. Pucher. — Cambridge, Mass.: MIT
Press, c1979. xii, 558 p.; 24 cm. — (MIT Press series in transportation studies.
2) (A Publication of the Joint Center for Urban Studies of the Massachusetts
Institute of Technology and Harvard University) 1. Urban transportation
policy — United States. 2. Local transit — United States. I. Womack, James
P. joint author. II. Pucher, John R. joint author. III. T. IV. Series.
HE308.A63        388.4/0973        *LC* 78-25805        *ISBN* 0262010550

**Jones, Ian Shore.** 4.3916
Urban transport appraisal / Ian S. Jones. New York: Wiley, c1977. x, 144 p.:
ill.; 23 cm. (Studies in planning) 'A Halsted Press book.' 1. Urban
transportation — United States. 2. Urban transportation — United
States — Costs. I. T. II. Series.
HE308.J65 1977        388.4/0973        *LC* 76-54811        *ISBN* 0470990325

**Meyer, John Robert.** 4.3917
Autos, transit, and cities / John R. Meyer, José A. Gómez-Ibáñez. —
Cambridge, Mass.: Harvard University Press, 1981. x, 360 p.; 24 cm. 'A
Twentieth Century Fund report.' 1. Urban transportation policy — United
States. I. Gómez-Ibáñez, José A., 1948- II. T.
HE308.M49        388.4/0973 19        *LC* 81-6477        *ISBN* 0674054857

**Owen, Wilfred.** 4.3918
Transportation for cities: the role of Federal policy / Wilfred Owen. —
Washington: Brookings Institution, c1976. x, 70 p.; 23 cm. 1. Urban
transportation policy — United States. 2. Federal aid to transportation —
United States. 3. Transportation and state — United States. I. T.
HE308.O9        388.4/0973        *LC* 75-44508        *ISBN* 0815767730

**Para–transit: neglected options for urban mobility / Ronald F.** 4.3919
**Kirby ... [et al.].**
Washington: Urban Institute, [1974?] xv, 319 p., [4] leaves of plates: ill.; 23 cm.
Includes indexes. 1. Paratransit services — United States. 2. Urban
transportation — United States. I. Kirby, Ronald F. II. Urban Institute.
HE308.P3        388.4        *LC* 75-325780        *ISBN* 0877661219

**Pikarsky, Milton.** 4.3920
Urban transportation policy and management / Milton Pikarsky, Daphne
Christensen. Lexington, Mass.: Lexington Books, c1976. xiv, 255 p.: ill.; 24 cm.
1. Urban transportation policy — United States. 2. Transportation — United
States — Passenger traffic. I. Christensen, Daphne, joint author. II. T.
HE308.P44        388.4/0973        *LC* 76-21933        *ISBN* 0669009555

**Smerk, George M.** 4.3921
Urban mass transportation; a dozen years of Federal policy [by] George M.
Smerk. — Bloomington: Indiana University Press, [1974] xvi, 388 p.; 24 cm.
1. Urban transportation policy — United States. I. T.
HE308.S53 1974        388.4/0973        *LC* 73-21242        *ISBN* 0253361702

**Cheape, Charles W., 1945-.** 4.3922
Moving the masses: urban public transit in New York, Boston, and
Philadelphia, 1880–1912 / Charles W. Cheape. — Cambridge, Mass.: Harvard
University Press, 1980. vii, 285 p.: ill.; 25 cm. (Harvard studies in business
history. 31) Includes index. 1. Transportation — Massachusetts — Boston —
History. 2. Transportation — New York (N.Y.) — History. 3. Transportation
— Pennsylvania — Philadelphia — History. 4. Local transit — United States
— History — Case studies. I. T. II. Series.
HE310.B6 C45        388.4/0974        *LC* 79-15875        *ISBN* 0674588274

# HE331–373 Traffic Engineering. Roads

**Antoniou, Jim.** 4.3923
Environmental management planning for traffic / by Jim Antoniou. — London;
New York: McGraw-Hill, 1972 (c1971) 171 p.: ill.; 31 cm. 1. Traffic
engineering 2. Environmental policy I. T.
HE333.A57        388.4/131        *LC* 72-181422        *ISBN* 0070942226

**Appleyard, Donald.** 4.3924
Livable streets / Donald Appleyard, with M. Sue Gerson and Mark Lintell. —
Berkeley: University of California Press, c1981. xvii, 364: ill.; 26 cm. Includes
index. 1. City traffic 2. Streets 3. Neighborhood — Environmental aspects.
4. Urban policy I. Gerson, M. Sue. joint author. II. Lintell, Mark. joint
author. III. T.
HE333.A65 1981        388.4/1        *LC* 78-54789        *ISBN* 0520036891

**Drew, Donald R.** • 4.3925
Traffic flow theory and control / [by] Donald R. Drew. — New York:
McGraw-Hill, [1968] 467 p.: ill.; 22 cm. — (McGraw-Hill series in
transportation) 1. Traffic flow I. T.
HE333.D7        388.3/1        *LC* 68-13626

**Hobbs, F. D. (Frederick Derek)** 4.3926
Traffic planning and engineering / by F. D. Hobbs. — 2d rev. ed. — Oxford;
New York: Pergamon Press, 1979. xvi, 543 p.: ill.; 22 cm. — (Pergamon
international library of science, technology, engineering, and social studies) Ed.
for 1967 by F. D. Hobbs and B. D. Richardson published under title: Traffic
engineering. 1. Traffic engineering I. T.
HE333.H6 1979        388.3/1        *LC* 78-40001        *ISBN* 0080226965

**Leibbrand, Kurt.** • 4.3927
[Verkehr und Städtebau. English] Transportation and town planning.
Translated by Nigel Seymer. Cambridge, Mass., M.I.T. Press [1970, c1964] x,
381 p. illus., maps. 26 cm. Translation of Verkehr und Städtebau. 1. Traffic
engineering 2. City planning I. T.
HE333.L3813 1970        388.4        *LC* 70-138300        *ISBN* 0262120402

**Thomson, J. Michael (John Michael), 1928-.** 4.3928
Great cities and their traffic / J. Michael Thompson. — London: Gollancz,
1977. 344 p.: ill.; 21 cm. Includes index. 1. City traffic I. T.
HE333.T53        388.4/1        *LC* 77-374314        *ISBN* 0575021462

**Transportation and traffic engineering handbook / Wolfgang S.** 4.3929
**Homburger, editor; Louis E. Keefer and William R. McGrath,**
**associate editors.**
2nd ed. — Englewood Cliffs, N.J.: Prentice-Hall, c1982. xii, 883 p.: ill.; 29 cm.
At head of title: Institute of Transportation Engineers. 1. Traffic engineering
2. Transportation I. Homburger, Wolfgang S. II. Keefer, Louis E.
III. McGrath, William R. (William Restore), 1922- IV. Institute of
Transportation Engineers.
HE333.T68 1982        388.3/1 19        *LC* 82-340        *ISBN* 0139303626

**Wohl, Martin.** • 4.3930
Traffic system analysis [by] Martin Wohl [and] Brian V. Martin. — New York:
McGraw-Hill, [1967] xvi, 558 p.: illus.; 23 cm. — (McGraw-Hill series in
transportation) 1. Traffic engineering I. Martin, Brian V. joint author. II. T.
HE333.W58        711/.73        *LC* 67-26355

**International Conference on Behavioral Travel Demand (1975:** 4.3931
**Asheville, N.C.)**
Behavioral travel–demand models: [proceedings] / edited by Peter R. Stopher,
Arnim H. Meyburg. — Lexington, Mass.: Lexington Books, c1976. xix, 296 p.:
ill.; 24 cm. Conference sponsored by the U.S. Dept. of Transportation and the
Engineering Foundation. 1. Choice of transportation — Mathematical models
— Congresses. 2. Human behavior — Mathematical models — Congresses.
I. Stopher, Peter R. II. Meyburg, Arnim H. III. United States. Dept. of
Transportation. IV. Engineering Foundation (U.S.) V. T.
HE336.C5 I57 1975        380.5/0724 19        *LC* 76-14666        *ISBN*
066900734X

**Mohring, Herbert.** • 4.3932
Highway benefits: an analytical framework / by Herbert Mohring and Mitchell
Harwitz. — [Evanston, Ill.]: Published for the Transportation Center at
Northwestern University by Northwestern University Press, 1962. 209 p.: ill.;
23 cm. 1. Roads — Economic aspects I. Harwitz, Mitchell, jt. author II. T.
HE336 E3 M64        *LC* 61-17086

**Wilson, George Wilton, 1928-.**                            • **4.3933**
The impact of highway investment on development, by George W. Wilson [and others]. — Washington: Brookings Institution. Transport Research Program, [1966] xxii, 226 p.: illus., maps.; 24 cm. 1. Roads — Economic aspects I. T.
HE336.E3 W45        388.1/1 19        LC 66-13625

**Inose, Hiroshi, 1927-.**                                    **4.3934**
[Dōro kōtsū kansei. English] Road traffic control / by Hiroshi Inose and Takashi Hamada; translation edited by Edward C. Posner. — [Tokyo]: University of Tokyo Press, c1975. xvi, 331 p.: ill.; 24 cm. Translation of Dōro kōtsū kansei. 1. Traffic flow — Mathematical models. 2. Traffic engineering — Mathematical models. I. Hamada, Takashi, 1941- II. T.
HE336.T7 I5613        388.3/1        LC 76-368437

**Burch, Philip H.**                                          • **4.3935**
Highway revenue and expenditure policy in the United States. — New Brunswick, N.J.: Rutgers University Press, [1962]. xiv, 315 p.: ill. 1. Roads — United States — Finance. I. T.
HE355.B8

**Leavitt, Helen, 1932-.**                                    • **4.3936**
Superhighway—superhoax. — [1st ed.]. — Garden City, N.Y.: Doubleday, 1970. 324 p.: illus., map (on lining papers); 22 cm. 1. Express highways — U.S. I. T.
HE355.L4        388.1        LC 70-86890

**Meyer, John Robert.**                                       • **4.3937**
The urban transportation problem [by] J. R. Meyer, J. F. Kain [and] M. Wohl. — Cambridge: Harvard University Press, 1965. xix, 427 p.: illus., maps.; 25 cm. — ([A Rand Corporation research study]) 1. Traffic engineering — United States. 2. Local transit — United States. I. Kain, John F. joint author. II. Wohl, Martin. joint author. III. T.
HE355.M46        380.5091732        LC 65-13848

**Owen, Wilfred.**                                            • **4.3938**
The metropolitan transportation problem. — Rev. ed. — Garden City, N.Y.: Anchor Books, [1966] xiii, 266 p.: illus.; 19 cm. 'A Brookings Institution study.' 1. Traffic engineering — United States. I. T.
HE355.O848 1966        380.5091732        LC 66-21151

**Rae, John Bell, 1911-.**                                    • **4.3939**
The road and the car in American life [by] John B. Rae. — Cambridge, Mass.: MIT Press, [1971] xiv, 390 p.; 24 cm. 1. Roads — U.S. 2. Automobiles — U.S. 3. Urban transportation — U.S. I. T.
HE355.R33        388/.0973        LC 70-148972        ISBN 0262180499

**Robinson, John, 1909-.**                                    • **4.3940**
Highways and our environment. — New York: McGraw-Hill, [1971] xii, 340 p.: illus., map., ports.; 27 cm. 1. Roads — U.S. 2. Environmental policy — U.S. 3. Transportation and state — U.S. I. T.
HE355.R6        388.1/0973        LC 74-133810        ISBN 0070533156

**Rose, Mark H., 1942-.**                                     **4.3941**
Interstate: express highway politics, 1941–1956 / Mark H. Rose. — Lawrence: Regents Press of Kansas, c1979. xii, 169 p.; 24 cm. Includes index. 1. Express highways — United States — History. 2. Express highways — Law and legislation — United States — History. 3. Transportation and state — United States — History. I. T.
HE355.R675        388.1/2        LC 78-14940        ISBN 0700601864

**Jordan, Philip Dillon, 1903-.**                             • **4.3942**
The National Road / by Philip D. Jordan. — Gloucester, Mass.: Peter Smith, 1966 [c1948] 442 p.: ill., map (on lining-papers); 23 cm. (The American trails series) 'Bibliographical note': p. 415-431. Bibliographical footnotes. 1. Cumberland Road 2. Northwest, Old — History I. T. II. Series.
HE356.C8J6 1966        388.1        LC 48-6393 *

**Institute of Transportation Engineers.**                    **4.3943**
Manual of traffic engineering studies / authors: Paul C. Box, Joseph C. Oppenlander. — 4th ed. — Arlington, Va: The Institute, 1976. v, 233 p., [25] leaves of plates: ill., forms. First - 2d editions by the Accident Prevention Dept. Association of Casualty and Surety Companies. Companion publication to the Institute's Transportation and traffic engineering handbook. 1. Traffic engineering 2. Traffic accidents I. Box, Paul C. II. Oppenlander, Joseph C. III. Association of Casualty and Surety Companies. Accident Prevention Dept. Manual of traffic engineering studies IV. T.
HE369 I53        HE369 I53 1976.

# HE381–971 Water Transportation

## HE381–560 Waterways. Ports

**Goodrich, Carter, 1897-1971. ed.**                          **4.3944**
Canals and American economic development / by Carter Goodrich [and others]; edited by Carter Goodrich. — Port Washington, N.Y.: I. J. Friedman Division, Kennikat Press, [1972, c1961] vi, 303 p.: ill.; 22 cm. 1. Canals — United States. 2. United States — Economic conditions I. T.
HE395.A3 G6 1972        386.4/0973        LC 72-86271        ISBN 0804617651

**Scheiber, Harry N.**                                        • **4.3945**
Ohio canal era; a case study of government and the economy, 1820–1861, by Harry N. Scheiber. — Athens: Ohio University Press, 1969 [c1968] xviii, 430 p.: maps.; 22 cm. 1. Canals — Ohio — History. 2. Ohio — Economic conditions. I. T.
HE395.O47 S3        353.9771/008/764        LC 68-20936

**Hadfield, Charles, 1909-.**                                 **4.3946**
World canals: inland navigation past and present / Charles Hadfield. — New York, N.Y.: Facts on File, c1986. 432 p.: ill., maps; 25 cm. Includes index. 1. Canals — History. 2. Inland navigation — History. I. T.
HE526.H33 1986        387.4/09 19        LC 85-29272        ISBN 0816013764

**Folkman, David I.**                                         **4.3947**
The Nicaragua route [by] David I. Folkman, Jr. Salt Lake City, University of Utah Press [1972] xii, 173 p. illus. 26 cm. (University of Utah publications in the American West, v. 8) 1. Nicaragua Canal (Nicaragua) I. T.
HE536.F64        386/.445        LC 73-180827        ISBN 0874800323

**Du Val, Miles Percy, 1896-.**                               • **4.3948**
Cadiz to Cathay: the story of the long diplomatic struggle for the Panama Canal / by Miles P. DuVal, Jr. — New York: Greenwood Press, 1968 [c1947] xix, 548 p.: ill., facsims., maps, ports.; 24 cm. 1. Panama Canal (Panama) 2. Nicaragua Canal (Nicaragua) 3. United States — Foreign relations I. T.
HE537.8.D87 1968        386/.444        LC 68-23284

**Atkins, Warren H.**                                         **4.3949**
Modern marine terminal operations and management / Warren H. Atkins, in cooperation with the Maritime Division of the Port of Oakland; edited by Raymond A. Boyle. — Oakland, Calif.: The Port, c1983. vii, 327 p.: ill. (some col.), plans; 23 x 28 cm. Plans on lining papers. Errata sheet inserted. Includes index. 1. Marine terminals — Management. I. Boyle, Raymond A. II. Port of Oakland. Maritime Division. III. T.
HE551.A84 1983        387.1/6 19        LC 83-62161

**Branch, Alan E.**                                           **4.3950**
Elements of port operation and management / Alan E. Branch. — London; New York: Chapman and Hall, 1986. xiv, 265 p.: ill.; 23 cm. Includes index. 1. Harbors — Management. I. T.
HE551.B52 1986        387.1/068 19        LC 85-24301        ISBN 0412252503

**Rudolph, Wolfgang, 1923-.**                                 **4.3951**
[Hafenstadt. English] Harbor and town: a maritime cultural history / Wolfgang Rudolph. — [Leipzig]: Edition Leipzig, c1980. 250 p.: chiefly ill. (some col.); 28 cm. Translation of: Die Hafenstadt. Includes index. 1. Harbors — Social aspects. 2. Seafaring life I. T.
HE551.R813x 1980        LC 84-673362

**Albion, Robert Greenhalgh, 1896-.**                         • **4.3952**
The rise of New York port, 1815–1860. With the collaboration of Jennie Barnes Pope. New York, Scribner [1970, c1939] xvi, 481 p. illus., maps, ports. 25 cm. 1. Harbors — New York (N.Y.) — History. 2. New York (N.Y.) — Commerce — History — 19th century. I. T.
HE554.N7 A6 1970        387.1/097471        LC 71-123329

**Bird, James Harold, 1923-.**                                • **4.3953**
The major seaports of the United Kingdom. — London: Hutchinson, [c1963] 454 p.: ill., maps. 1. Harbors — Great Britain. I. T.
HE557.G7 B5        LC 64-30992

## HE561–971 Shipping

**Alexandersson, Gunnar.**                                    • **4.3954**
World shipping: an economic geography of ports and seaborne trade / Gunnar Alexandersson [and] Göran Norström. — New York: Wiley, [c1963] 507 p.:

ill., maps, port. 1. Shipping 2. Harbors 3. International economic relations I. Norström, Göran. II. T.
HE563.A3 A4

**Maxtone-Graham, John.**      **4.3955**
The only way to cross / with a foreword by Walter Lord. — New York: Macmillan, [1972] xiii, 434 p.: ill.; 24 cm. 1. Ocean liners I. T.
HE566.O25 M38     387.5/42/091631     LC 72-75351

**Branch, Alan E.**      **4.3956**
Dictionary of shipping/international trade terms and abbreviations / by Alan E. Branch. — 2nd ed. — London: Witherby, 1982. xv, 279 p.: ill.; 22 cm. — 1. Shipping — Dictionaries. 2. Shipping — Abbreviations. 3. Commerce — Dictionaries. 4. Commerce — Abbreviations. I. T.
HE567.B65     387.5/44/03     ISBN 0900886706

**Abrahamsson, Bernhard J.**      **4.3957**
International ocean shipping: current concepts and principles / Bernhard J. Abrahamsson. — Boulder, Colo.: Westview Press, 1980. xv, 232 p.; 24 cm. Includes index. 1. Shipping 2. Merchant marine 3. Commerce I. T.
HE571.A2 1980     387.5/44     LC 79-26674     ISBN 0891588752

**Advances in maritime economics / edited by R. O. Goss;**      **4.3958**
**contributors, B. M. Gardner ... [et al.]**
Cambridge; New York: Cambridge University Press, 1977. 294 p.: ill.; 24 cm. Companion volume to the editor's Studies in maritime economics. 1. Shipping — Addresses, essays, lectures. 2. Merchant marine — Addresses, essays, lectures. I. Goss, R. O.
HE571.A36     387.5/1     LC 76-1135     ISBN 0521212324

**Beth, Hans Ludwig.**      **4.3959**
25 years of world shipping / by Hans Ludwig Beth, Arnulf Hader and Robert Kappel. — London: Fairplay Publications Ltd., 1984. 205 p.: ill. 1. Shipping — History I. Hader, Arnulf II. Kappel, Robert. III. T. IV. Title: Twenty-five years of world shipping.
HE571.B47     ISBN 0905045610

**Goss, R. O.**      • **4.3960**
Studies in maritime economics [by] R. O. Goss. — London: Cambridge U.P., 1968. viii, 194 p.: illus.; 23 cm. 1. Shipping I. T.
HE571.G67     387     LC 68-29328     ISBN 0521073294

**Kendall, Lane C., 1912-.**      **4.3961**
The business of shipping / by Lane C. Kendall. — 5th ed. — Centreville, Md.: Cornell Maritime Press, 1986. x, 512 p.: ill.; 24 cm. Includes index. 1. Shipping I. T.
HE571.K4 1986     387.5/068 19     LC 85-48287     ISBN 087033350X

**Harbron, John D.**      • **4.3962**
Communist ships and shipping. New York: Praeger, [1963] x, 262 p. ill., maps. 1. Shipping — Communist countries. 2. Shipbuilding — Communist countries. I. T.
HE581.H3 1963     LC 63-18832

**Marx, Daniel.**      • **4.3963**
International shipping cartels: a study of industrial self–regulation by shipping conferences. By Daniel Marx, Jr. — New York: Greenwood Press, [1969] xii, 323 p.; 23 cm. 1. Shipping conferences I. T.
Law     HE581.M37 1969.     338.8/8     LC 69-13988

**Beth, H. L.**      **4.3964**
Economics of regulation in shipping / H.L. Beth. — Bremen: Institute of Shipping Economics Bremen, 1984. 20 p.; 24 cm. — (Lectures & contributions / Institute of Shipping Economics Bremen, 0724-1232; no. 37) 1. Maritime law 2. Shipping I. Institut für Seeverkehrswirtschaft Bremen. II. T.
HE582.B4x

**Harper, Lawrence Averell, 1901-.**      • **4.3965**
The English navigation laws; a seventeenth–century experiment in social engineering. New York, Octagon Books, 1964 [c1939] xiv, 503 p. Issued also as thesis, Columbia University. 1. Maritime law — Great Britain 2. Shipping — Great Britain — History 3. Great Britain — Commerce — History I. T.
HE587 G7 H3 1964     LC 64-16382

**Euroship 84: a collection of papers on the EEC's Maritime**      **4.3966**
**requirements for the 1990s.**
England: Marine Management (Holdings) Ltd., 1984. (The Institute of Marine Engineers; Conference No. 17)
HE597.E86     ISBN 0907206107

**Whitlark, Frederick Louis.**      • **4.3967**
Introduction to the lakes: an introduction to the Great Lakes and St. Lawrence Seaway. — [1st ed.] New York: Greenwich Book Publishers [1959] 256 p.: ill.; 21 cm. 1. Shipping — Great Lakes 2. Saint Lawrence Seaway I. T.
HE630 G7 W5     LC 59-8801

**Ambler, Charles Henry, 1876-1957.**      • **4.3968**
A history of transportation in the Ohio Valley, with special reference to its waterways, trade and commerce from the earliest period to the present time. Westport, Conn., Greenwood Press [1970, c1931] 465 p. illus., maps. 23 cm. 1. Shipping — Ohio River Valley. 2. Ohio River Valley — Commerce. I. T.
HE630.O5 A6 1970     386/.3/0977     LC 72-98804     ISBN 0837129052

**Michigan Business Executives Research Conference.**      • **4.3969**
The St. Lawrence Seaway, by Carlos E. Toro, project coordinator, and Laurence P. Dowd, director, assisted by James M. Washburne [and others] Ann Arbor, Bureau of Business Research, School of Business Administration, University of Michigan, 1961. xii, 66 p. (Michigan business reports, no. 37. International series) 1. Saint Lawrence Seaway 2. Shipping — Michigan I. Toro, Carlos E. II. Dowd, Laurence Phillips, 1914- III. T.
HE630 S17 M5     LC 61-64277

## HE731–953 MERCHANT MARINE

**Carlisle, Rodney P.**      **4.3970**
Sovereignty for sale: the origins and evolution of the Panamanian and Liberian flags of convenience / Rodney Carlisle. — Annapolis, Md.: Naval Institute Press, c1981. xvii, 278 p.: ill., map; 24 cm. Map on lining papers. Includes index. 1. Flags of convenience — Panama — History. 2. Flags of convenience — Liberia — History. 3. Ships — Registration and transfer — Panama — History. 4. Ships — Registration and transfer — Liberia — History. I. T. II. Title: Flags of convenience.
HE736.C37     387.2/45 19     LC 81-607020     ISBN 0870216686

**An Assessment of maritime trade and technology.**      **4.3971**
Washington, D.C.: Congress of the U.S., Office of Technology Assessment: For sale by the Supt. of Docs., U.S. G.P.O., 1983. vii, 231 p.: ill., maps; 26 cm. 'October 1983'—P. [4] of cover. 'OTA-0-220'—P. [4] of cover. S/N 052-003-00931-5 Item 1070-M 1. Merchant marine — United States 2. Shipping — United States 3. Shipping bounties and subsidies — United States. 4. Shipbuilding — Technological innovations. I. United States. Congress. Office of Technology Assessment. II. Title: Maritime trade and technology.
HE745.A87 1983     387.5/0973 19     LC 83-600606

**The Economic value of the United States merchant marine, by**      • **4.3972**
**Allen R. Ferguson [and others]**
Evanston, Transportation Center at Northwestern University [1961] xxii, 545 p. diagrs., tables. 1. Merchant marine — United States 2. Shipping bounties and subsidies — United States I. Ferguson, Allen Richmond II. Northwestern University (Evanston, Ill.). Transportation Center.
HE745 E25     LC 61-14135

**Frankel, Ernst G.**      **4.3973**
Management and operations of American shipping / Ernst G. Frankel. — Boston, Mass.: Auburn House, c1982. xviii, 260 p.: ill.; 24 cm. Includes index. 1. Shipping — United States 2. Merchant marine — United States I. T.
HE745.F729 1982     387.5/068 19     LC 81-22873     ISBN 0865691002

**Frankel, Ernst G.**      **4.3974**
Regulation and policies of American shipping / Ernst G. Frankel. — Boston, Mass.: Auburn House Pub. Co., c1982. xviii, 347 p.: ill.; 24 cm. Includes index. 1. Shipping — United States 2. Merchant marine — United States 3. Maritime law — United States. I. T.
HE745.F73 1982     387.5/0973 19     LC 81-12721     ISBN 0865690995

**Marine transportation in the United States: constraints and**      **4.3975**
**opportunities: national ocean goals and objectives for the 1980's.**
Washington, D.C.: National Advisory Committee on Oceans and Atmosphere: For sale by the Supt. of Docs., U.S. G.P.O., [1983] xiii, 88 p.: ill.; 28 cm. 'January 1983.' S/N 052-003-00905-6 Item 1070-J 1. Merchant marine — United States 2. Shipping — United States I. United States. National Advisory Committee on Oceans and Atmosphere.
HE745.M38 1983     387.5/0973 19     LC 83-601988

**Whitehurst, Clinton H., 1927-.**      **4.3976**
The U.S. merchant marine: in search of an enduring maritime policy / by Clinton H. Whitehurst, Jr. — Annapolis, Md.: Naval Institute Press, c1983. xviii, 314 p.: ill., maps; 24 cm. Includes index. 1. Merchant marine — United States — Addresses, essays, lectures. 2. Shipping — United States — Addresses, essays, lectures. I. T. II. Title: US merchant marine. III. Title: United States merchant marine.
HE745.W495 1983     387.5/068 19     LC 83-13467     ISBN 0870217372

**Great Britain. Committee of Inquiry into Shipping.**      **4.3977**
Report. London, H.M. Stationery Off., 1970. xvii, 497 p. 25 cm. ([Great Britain. Parliament. Papers by command] cmnd.; 4337) Chairman: Viscount Rochdale.

1. Merchant marine — Great Britain 2. Shipping — Great Britain.
I. Rochdale, John Durival Kemp, Viscount, 1906- II. T.
HE823.A484      387.5/0942      *LC* 74-512627      *ISBN* 0101433700

# HE1001–3560 Railroads

**Westwood, J. N.**                                                                    **4.3978**
Railways at war / John Westwood. — 1st ed. — San Diego, Calif.: Howell-North Books, 1981 (c1980). 224 p.: ill.; 26 cm. Includes index. 1. Railroads — History — 20th century. 2. World politics — 20th century I. T.
HE1021.W47 1981      385/.09/04 19      *LC* 80-25429      *ISBN* 0831071389

**Fontgalland, Bernard de.**                                                           **4.3979**
[Système ferroviaire dans le monde. English] The world railway system / Bernard de Fontgalland. — Cambridge [Cambridgeshire]; New York: Cambridge University Press, 1984. xiv, 209 p.: ill.; 24 cm. Translation of: Le système ferroviaire dans le monde. Includes index. 1. Railroads I. T.
HE1031.F6513 1984      385 19      *LC* 84-1820      *ISBN* 0521245419

**Lardner, Dionysius, 1793-1859.**                                                   • **4.3980**
Railway economy; a treatise on the new art of transport, its management, prospects & relations ... — New York: A. M. Kelley, 1968. xxiii, 442 p.; 22 cm. — (Reprints of economic classics) Reprint of the 1850 ed. 1. Railroads I. T.
HE1031.L32 1968      385      *LC* 67-29509

**Goodrich, Carter, 1897-1971.**                                                     • **4.3981**
Government promotion of American canals and railroads, 1800–1890. New York: Columbia University Press, 1960. x, 382 p.: map; 24 cm. 1. Railroads and state — United States 2. Canals — United States 3. Inland water transportation — United States I. T.
HE1051 G6      *LC* 60-6546

**Martin, Albro.**                                                                   • **4.3982**
Enterprise denied; origins of the decline of American railroads, 1897–1917. — New York: Columbia University Press, 1971. xiv, 402 p.; 23 cm. 1. Railroads and state — U.S. I. T.
HE1051.M37      385/.0973      *LC* 71-159673      *ISBN* 023103508X

**Nelson, James Cecil, 1908-.**                                                      • **4.3983**
Railroad transportation and public policy. Washington, Brookings Institution [1959] xiii, 512 p. diagrs., tables. 1. Railroads and state — United States I. T.
HE1061 N4      *LC* 59-10493

**Summers, Mark W. (Mark Wahlgren), 1951-.**                                           **4.3984**
Railroads, reconstruction, and the gospel of prosperity: aid under the radical Republicans, 1865–1877 / Mark W. Summers. — Princeton, N.J.: Princeton University Press, c1984. xiii, 361 p.; 25 cm. Includes index. 1. Republican Party (U.S.) — History — 19th century. 2. Reconstruction 3. Railroads and state — Southern States — History — 19th century. 4. United States — Politics and government — 1865-1877 I. T.
HE1061.S94 1984      385/.1 19      *LC* 83-43094      *ISBN* 0691046956

**Wyckoff, D. Daryl.**                                                                 **4.3985**
Railroad management / D. Daryl Wyckoff. — Lexington, Mass.: Lexington Books, [1976] xviii, 193 p.: ill.; 24 cm. Includes index. 1. Railroads — Management 2. Railroads — United States I. T.
HE1626.W93      658/.91/385      *LC* 75-5237      *ISBN* 0669997706

**Horowitz, Morris Aaron.**                                                          • **4.3986**
Manpower utilization in the railroad industry; an analysis of working rules and practices. Boston, Bureau of Business and Economic Research, Northeastern University, 1960. viii, 68 p. diagrs., tables. 1. Railroads — United States — Employees 2. Railroads — Management I. T.
HE1741 H67

**MacAvoy, Paul W.**                                                                 • **4.3987**
Regulation of transport innovation: the ICC and unit coal trains to the East Coast / by Paul W. MacAvoy and James Sloss. — New York: Random House, [1967] 143 p.; 19 cm. — (Random House series in industrial economics) 1. Railroads — United States — Rates. 2. Coal — United States — Transportation. I. Sloss, James, joint author. II. T.
HE2116.C7 M28      353/.00875/2403      *LC* 67-10910

**Greenberg, Dolores.**                                                                **4.3988**
Financiers and railroads, 1869–1889: a study of Morton, Bliss & Company / Dolores Greenberg. — Newark: University of Delaware Press; London: Associated University Presses, c1980. 286 p.: ill.; 24 cm. Includes index. 1. Morton, Bliss & Company — History. 2. Railroads — United States — Finance — History. I. T.
HE2236.G73      385/.1      *LC* 78-66830      *ISBN* 0874131480

**Friedlaender, Ann Fetter.**                                                          **4.3989**
Freight transport regulation: equity, efficiency, and competition in the rail and trucking industries / Ann F. Friedlaender, Richard H. Spady. — Cambridge, Mass.: MIT Press, c1981. xv, 366 p.: ill.; 24 cm. — (MIT Press series on the regulation of economic activity. 1) Includes index. 1. Railroads — United States — Freight. 2. Trucking — United States. 3. Transportation and state — United States. 4. Freight and freightage — United States. I. Spady, Richard H., 1952- II. T. III. Series.
HE2355.F74      388/.044/0973 19      *LC* 80-23879

**The American railway: its construction, development,**                               **4.3990**
**management, and appliances / by Thomas Curtis Clarke [and**
**others]; with an introd. by Thomas M. Cooley.**
New York: B. Blom, 1972. xxviii, 456 p.: ill.; 27 cm. Reprint of the 1897 ed. 1. Railroads — United States — Addresses, essays, lectures. I. Clarke, Thomas Curtis, 1827-1901.
HE2741.A5 1972      385/.0973      *LC* 74-189048

**Chandler, Alfred Dupont. ed.**                                                       **4.3991**
The railroads, the Nation's first big business; sources and readings. Compiled and edited by Alfred D. Chandler, Jr. New York, Harcourt, Brace & World [1965] ix, 213 p. map. 23 cm. (The Forces in American economic growth series) 1. Railroads — United States — History — Addresses, essays, lectures. I. T.
HE2751.C45      385.0973      *LC* 65-12850

**Fishlow, Albert.**                                                                 • **4.3992**
American railroads and the transformation of the antebellum economy. Cambridge, Harvard University Press, 1965. XV, 452 p. maps. (Harvard economic studies. 127) 1. Railroads — United States — History 2. United States — Economic conditions I. T. II. Series.
HE2751 F53      *LC* 65-22068

**Fogel, Robert William.**                                                           • **4.3993**
Railroads and American economic growth: essays in econometric history. — Baltimore: Johns Hopkins Press, [1964] xv, 296 p.: illus., maps (1 fold.); 24 cm. 1. Railroads — United States — History. 2. United States — Economic conditions I. T.
HE2751.F65      385.0973      *LC* 64-25069

**Hultgren, Thor, 1902-.**                                                           • **4.3994**
American transportation in prosperity and depression. New York: National Bureau of Economic Research [c1948] 397 p. (Studies in business cycles. no. 00003) 1. Railroads — United States 2. Business cycles I. T. II. Series.
HE2751.H84      *LC* 49-643

**Johnson, Arthur Menzies, 1921-.**                                                  • **4.3995**
Boston capitalists and western railroads: a study in the nineteenth–century railroad investment process / [by] Arthur M. Johnson and Barry E. Supple. — Cambridge: Harvard University Press, 1967. x, 392p.: maps.-. (Harvard studies in business history. 23) 1. Railroads — United States — Finance I. Supple, Barry Emanuel, jt. author II. T. III. Series.
HE2751.J57      658.1/5938      *LC* 67-13254

**Kerr, K. Austin (Kathel Austin)**                                                  • **4.3996**
American railroad politics, 1914–1920; rates, wages, and efficiency [by] K. Austin Kerr. [Pittsburgh] University of Pittsburgh Press [1968] viii, 250 p. 23 cm. Based on thesis, University of Pittsburgh. 1. Railroads — United States 2. Railroads and state — United States I. T.
HE2751.K47      385/.0973      *LC* 68-21628

**Stilgoe, John R., 1949-.**                                                           **4.3997**
Metropolitan corridor: railroads and the American scene / John R. Stilgoe. — New Haven: Yale University Press, c1983. xiii, 397 p.: ill.; 26 cm. Includes index. 1. Railroads — United States — History. 2. Railroads — United States — Right of way — History. 3. Railroads — Social aspects — United States — History. I. T.
HE2751.S68 1983      385/.0973 19      *LC* 83-3585      *ISBN* 0300030428

**Stover, John F.**                                                                  • **4.3998**
American railroads. [Chicago] University of Chicago Press [1961] 302 p. ill. (The Chicago history of American civilization) 1. Railroads — United States — History I. T.
HE2751 S7      *LC* 61-8081

**Stover, John F.**                                                                  • **4.3999**
The life and decline of the American railroad [by] John F. Stover. — New York: Oxford University Press, 1970. xi, 324 p.: ill., maps.; 22 cm. 1. Railroads — U.S. — History. I. T.
HE2751.S74      385/.0973      *LC* 77-83054

**Martin, Albro.**                                                                     **4.4000**
James J. Hill and the opening of the Northwest / Albro Martin. — New York: Oxford University Press, 1976. xii, 676 p.: ill.; 24 cm. 1. Hill, James Jerome, 1838-1916. 2. Great Northern Railway (U.S.) 3. Businessmen — United States — Biography. I. T.
HE2754.H5 M37      385/.092/4 B      *LC* 75-46362      *ISBN* 0195020707

**Conant, Michael.** • 4.4001
Railroad mergers and abandonments. Berkeley: University of California Press, 1964. xiii, 212 p. (Publications of the Institute of Business and Economic Research, University of California.) 1. Railroads — United States — History. 2. Railroads — United States — Consolidation. I. T.
HE2757 1964 C6     LC 64-22705

**Keeler, Theodore E.** 4.4002
Railroads, freight, and public policy / Theodore E. Keeler. — Washington, D.C.: Brookings Institution, c1983. xi, 180 p.: ill.; 24 cm. — (Studies in the regulation of economic activity.) 1. Railroads and state — United States 2. Railroads — United States — Freight. I. T. II. Series.
HE2757.K43 1983     385/.068 19     LC 82-45985     ISBN 0815748566

## HE2771–2791 UNITED STATES

## HE2771 By State, A–Z

**Baker, George Pierce, 1903-.** • 4.4003
The formation of the New England railroad systems; a study of railroad combination in the nineteenth century. — New York: Greenwood Press, 1968 [c1937] xxxi, 283 p.: illus.; 23 cm. 'This study was originally ... written as a doctor's thesis.' 1. Railroads — New England. I. T.
HE2771.A11 B3 1968     385/.0974     LC 68-8936

**Parks, Robert J.** • 4.4004
Democracy's railroads; public enterprise in Jacksonian Michigan [by] Robert J. Parks. — Port Washington, N.Y.: Kennikat Press, 1972. 261 p.: illus.; 24 cm. — (Kennikat Press national university publications. Series in American studies) 1. Railroads and state — Michigan. I. T.
HE2771.M5 P37     385/.09774     LC 79-189557     ISBN 0804690278

**Benson, Lee.** • 4.4005
Merchants, farmers & railroads: railroad regulation and New York politics, 1850–1887. — New York: Russell & Russell, [1969, c1955] x, 310 p.: ill., maps.; 24 cm. — (Studies in economic history) 1. Railroads — New York (State) 2. Railroad law — New York (State) I. T.
HE2771.N7 B4 1969     385     LC 68-27048

**Carson, Robert Barry, 1934-.** • 4.4006
Main line to oblivion; the disintegration of New York railroads in the twentieth century [by] Robert B. Carson. — Port Washington, N.Y.: Kennikat Press, [1971] ix, 273 p.: maps.; 23 cm. — (Kennikat Press national university publications. Series in American studies) 1. Railroads — New York (State) I. T.
HE2771.N7 C37     385/.09747     LC 75-139352     ISBN 0804690030

## HE2781 By City, A–Z

**Condit, Carl W.** 4.4007
The port of New York / Carl W. Condit. — Chicago: University of Chicago Press, c1980-1981. 2 v.: ill.; 25 cm. 1. Railroads — New York (N.Y.) — History. 2. Railroad terminals — New York (N.Y.) — History. 3. New York (N.Y.) — History I. T.
HE2781.N7 C66     385/.09747/1     LC 79-16850     ISBN 0226114600

## HE2791 By Railroad, A–Z

**Overton, Richard Cleghorn, 1907-.** • 4.4008
Burlington route; a history of the Burlington lines [by] Richard C. Overton. [1st ed.]. New York, Knopf, 1965. xxviii, 623, xl p. illus., maps, ports. 25 cm. 1. Chicago, Burlington & Quincy Railroad Company. I. T.
HE2791.C643 O79     385.0973     LC 64-19106

**Overton, Richard Cleghorn, 1907-.** • 4.4009
Gulf to Rockies; the heritage of the Fort Worth and Denver–Colorado and Southern Railways, 1861–1898, by Richard C. Overton. With pen sketches by Reginald Marsh. Westport, Conn., Greenwood Press [1970, c1953] xiii, 410 p. illus., facsim., maps, ports. 23 cm. 1. Fort Worth and Denver City Railway. 2. Colorado and Southern Railway. I. T.
HE2791.F7375 O8 1970     385/.0978     LC 76-100234     ISBN 0837130352

**Gates, Paul Wallace, 1901-.** • 4.4010
The Illinois Central Railroad and its colonization work / by Paul W. Gates. — New York: Johnson Reprint Corp., 1968. vii, xiii, 374 p.: ill., maps.; 23 cm. — (History of American economy) Reprint of the 1934 ed., with a new introd.

1. Illinois Central Railroad. 2. Railroad land grants — Illinois. 3. Illinois — History I. T.
HE2791.I3 G3 1968     385/.09773     LC 68-29513

**Athearn, Robert G.** • 4.4011
Union Pacific country, by Robert G. Athearn. Chicago, Rand McNally [1971] 480 p. illus., maps, ports. 24 cm. 1. Union Pacific Railroad — History. 2. West (U.S.) — History I. T.
HE2791.U55 A37     385/.0978     LC 73-140766

**Ames, Charles Edgar, 1895-.** • 4.4012
Pioneering the Union Pacific; a reappraisal of the builders of the railroad. — New York: Appleton-Century-Crofts, [1969] xvii, 591 p.: illus., facsims., maps, ports.; 24 cm. 1. Union Pacific Railroad Company. I. T.
HE2791.U55 A4     338.4/7/6251     LC 69-13448

**Fogel, Robert William.** • 4.4013
The Union Pacific Railroad: a case in premature enterprise. — Baltimore: Johns Hopkins Press, 1960. 129 p.; 24 cm. (Johns Hopkins University studies in historical and political science. ser. 78, no. 2) 1. Union Pacific Railroad Company (1862-1880) I. T. II. Series.
HE2791.U55 F6x     LC 60-14850

## HE2801–3560 OTHER COUNTRIES

**Irwin, Leonard Bertram, 1904-.** • 4.4014
Pacific railways and nationalism in the Canadian–American Northwest, 1845–1873. New York, Greenwood Press, 1968 [c1939] xii, 246 p. 24 p. First published in 1939 as thesis, University of Pennsylvania. 1. Canadian Pacific Railway 2. Northern Pacific Railroad Company. 3. Pacific railroads — Early projects 4. Railroads and state — Canada. 5. Northwest, Canadian I. T.
HE2807.I78 1968     385/.097     LC 69-10107

**Stevens, G. R. (George Roy), 1895-.** 4.4015
History of the Canadian National Railways [by] G. R. Stevens. New York, Macmillan [1973] xii, 538 p. illus. 24 cm. (Railroads of America) 1. Canadian National Railways — History. 2. Railroads — Canada — History. I. T.
HE2810.C14 S73     385/.0971     LC 72-75352

**Berton, Pierre, 1920-.** 4.4016
The impossible railway; the building of the Canadian Pacific. — [1st American ed.]. — New York: Knopf, 1972. xx, 574, xvii p.: illus.; 25 cm. First published in 2 v. under titles: The national dream (1970) and The last spike (1971) 1. Canadian Pacific Railway 2. Railroads and state — Canada. 3. Canada — History — 1867-1914 I. T.
HE2810.C2 B44 1972     385/.0971     LC 72-2236     ISBN 0394465695

**The CPR West: the iron road and the making of a nation /** 4.4017
**edited by Hugh A. Dempsey.**
Vancouver: Douglas & McIntyre, c1984. 333 p.: ill.; 24 cm. Includes index. 1. Canadian Pacific Railway — History — Addresses, essays, lectures. 2. Canada, Western — History — Addresses, essays, lectures. I. Dempsey, Hugh Aylmer, 1929-
HE2810.C2 C67 1984     385/.0971 19     LC 85-126528     ISBN 0888944241

**Lamb, W. Kaye (William Kaye), 1904-.** 4.4018
History of the Canadian Pacific Railway / W. Kaye Lamb. — New York: Macmillan, 1977. xv, 491 p.: ill.; 24 cm. (Railroads of America) Includes index. 1. Canadian Pacific Railway — History. I. T.
HE2810.C2L3x     385/.0971     LC 76-13593     ISBN 0025676601

**Currie, Archibald William.** • 4.4019
The Grand Trunk Railway of Canada. — Toronto, University of Toronto Press, 1957. 556 p. illus. 24 cm. 1. Grand Trunk Railway Company of Canada. I. T.
HE2810.G7C8     385.065     LC 57-59353

**Pletcher, David M.** • 4.4020
Rails, mines, and progress: seven American promoters in Mexico, 1867–1911, by David M. Pletcher. Port Washington, N.Y., Kennikat Press [1972, c1958] x, 321 p. maps. 23 cm. 1. Railroads — Mexico — History. 2. Mineral industries — Mexico. 3. Investments, American — Mexico — Case studies. I. T.
HE2818.P59 1972     385/.0972     LC 79-153237     ISBN 0804615470

**Sun, E-tu Zen, 1921-.** • 4.4021
Chinese railways and British interests, 1898–1911. — New York: Russell & Russell, [1971, c1954] viii, 230 p.: 2 maps.; 22 cm. 1. Railroads — China — History. 2. Investments, British — China. I. T.
HE3288.S8 1971     385/.0951     LC 74-152540

**Tupper, Harmon.**                                                        **4.4022**
To the great ocean; Siberia and the Trans–Siberian Railway. [1st ed.] Boston, Little, Brown [1965] xv, 536 p. ill., maps, ports. 1. Velikaia Sibirskaia magistral'. I. T.
HE3380 T7 T85      *LC* 65-10900

# HE3601–5260 Local Railways. Local Transit

**McKay, John P.**                                                        **4.4023**
Tramways and trolleys: the rise of urban mass transport in Europe / by John P. McKay. — Princeton, N.J.: Princeton University Press, c1976. xv, 266 p.: ill.; 23 cm. Includes index. 1. Street-railroads — Europe — History. 2. Urban transportation — Europe — History. I. T.
HE3812.M33 1976      388.4/094      *LC* 76-3746      *ISBN* 0691052409

**Berry, Donald Stilwell, 1911-.**                                        • **4.4024**
The technology of urban transportation, by Donald S. Berry [and others]. Evanston, Ill.] Published for the Transportation Center at Northwestern University, by Northwestern University Press [c1963] xiv, 145 p. maps, diagrs., tables. (The Metropolitan transportation series) 1. Local transit 2. Traffic engineering I. T.
HE4211 B4      *LC* 63-11943

**Lang, Albert Scheffer.**                                                • **4.4025**
Urban rail transit: its economics and technology [by] A. Scheffer Lang [and] Richard M. Soberman. Cambridge, Published for the Joint Center for Urban Studies of the Massachusetts Institute of Technology and Harvard University by the M.I.T. Press, Massachusetts Institute of Technology [1964] xii, 139 p. ill., diagrs. 1. Local transit 2. Local transit — United States I. Soberman, Richard M. jt. author II. T.
HE4211 L28      *LC* 63-23379

**Vuchic, Vukan R.**                                                      **4.4026**
Urban public transportation: systems and technology / Vukan R. Vuchic. — Englewood Cliffs, N.J.: Prentice-Hall, c1981. xiv, 673 p.: ill.; 24 cm. 1. Local transit I. T.
HE4211.V83      388.4 19      *LC* 80-21081      *ISBN* 0139394966

**Urban transit: the private challenge to public transportation /**      **4.4027**
**edited by Charles A. Lave; foreword by John Meyer.**
San Francisco, Calif.: Pacific Institute for Public Policy Research; Cambridge, Mass.: Ballinger Pub. Co., 1985. xxii, 372 p.: ill.; 24 cm. (Pacific studies in public policy.) Includes index. 1. Local transit — United States — Addresses, essays, lectures. 2. Paratransit services — United States — Addresses, essays, lectures. I. Lave, Charles A. II. Series.
HE4441.U735 1985      388.4/0973 19      *LC* 84-21529      *ISBN* 0884109690

**Fitch, Lyle C. (Lyle Craig)**                                          **4.4028**
Urban transportation and public policy [by] Lyle C. Fitch and associates. Based on memoranda prepared by Alan Cripe [and others] San Francisco, Chandler Pub. Co. [1964] xv, 279 p. ill. (Chandler publications in political science) 'Based upon a 1961 study prepared by the Institute of Public Administration for the U.S. Department of Commerce and the Housing and Home Finance Agency.' 1. Local transit — United States I. T.
HE4451 F53      *LC* 64-15743

**Hilton, George Woodman.**                                              • **4.4029**
The electric interurban railways in America [by] George W. Hilton and John F. Due. Stanford, Calif., Stanford University Press, 1960. ix, 463 p. ill., maps. 1. Street-railroads — United States — History I. Due, John Fitzgerald. jt. author II. T.
HE4451 H55      *LC* 60-5383

**Urban mass transit planning / Edited by Wolfgang S.**                  • **4.4030**
**Homburger.**
Berkeley, Calif.; 1967. v, 212 p.: ill.; maps; 28 cm. (Institute of Transportation and Traffic Engineering, University of California. Course notes) 'In the fall of 1966 a short course on 'urban mass transit planning' was developed by the Polytechnic Institute of Brooklyn with the assistance of the New York State Science and Technology Foundation and the cooperation of the U.S. Bureau of Public Roads ... Presented herein is an expansion and revision of the original notes.' 1. Local transit — United States — Addresses, essays, lectures. I. Homburger, Wolfgang S. ed. II. Polytechnic Institute of Brooklyn. III. Institute of Transportation and Traffic Engineering.
HE4451.U72      711/.7/0973      *LC* 68-64018

# HE5601–5720 Automotive Transportation

**Bendixson, Terence.**                                                   **4.4031**
[Instead of cars] Without wheels: alternatives to the private car / Terence Bendixson. — Bloomington: Indiana University Press, 1975, c1974. 256 p.: ill.; 22 cm. First published in 1974 under title: Instead of cars. Includes index. 1. Transportation, Automotive 2. Transportation, Automotive — Great Britain. 3. Urban transportation policy 4. Urban transportation policy — Great Britain. I. T.
HE5611.B43 1975      338.4      *LC* 74-21680      *ISBN* 0253365600

**Skomal, Edward N.**                                                     **4.4032**
Automatic vehicle locating systems / Edward N. Skomal. — New York: Van Nostrand Reinhold, c1981. viii, 323 p.: ill.; 24 cm. Includes index. 1. Motor vehicles — Automatic location systems 2. Transportation, Automotive — Data processing I. T.
HE5613.S55      388.3/21 19      *LC* 80-22346      *ISBN* 0442244959

**Arthur D. Little, Inc.**                                                • **4.4033**
The state of the art of traffic safety; a comprehensive review of existing information. Prepared by Arthur D. Little, inc., for the Automobile Manufacturers Association, inc. New York, Praeger [1970] xxi, 624 p. 25 cm. (Praeger special studies in international politics and public affairs) 1. Traffic safety I. Automobile Manufacturers Association. II. T.
HE5614.L58 1970      614.8/62      *LC* 71-105411

**Walters, A. A. (Alan Arthur), 1926-.**                                 • **4.4034**
The economics of road user charges [by] A. A. Walters. — [Washington: International Bank for Reconstruction and Development]; distributed by Johns Hopkins Press, Baltimore, [1968] xiii, 243 p.: illus.; 23 cm. — (World Bank staff occasional papers, no. 5) 1. Transportation, Automotive — Taxation 2. Transportation, Automotive — Cost of operation 3. User charges I. T. II. Series.
HE5618.W3      388      *LC* 68-8702

**Gusfield, Joseph R., 1923-.**                                          **4.4035**
The culture of public problems: drinking–driving and the symbolic order / Joseph R. Gusfield. — Chicago: University of Chicago Press, 1981. xiv, 263 p.; 24 cm. Includes index. 1. Drunk driving — California — San Diego Co. 2. Traffic violations — California — San Diego Co. 3. Sociology — Research — Case studies. 4. Social problems — Case studies. 5. National characteristics, American — Case studies. I. T.
HE5620.D7 G87      353.0087/83      *LC* 80-17007      *ISBN* 0226310930

**Wagenaar, Alexander C.**                                               **4.4036**
Alcohol, young drivers, and traffic accidents: effects of minimum–age laws / Alexander C. Wagenaar. — Lexington, Mass.: LexingtonBooks, c1983. xii, 151 p.: ill.; 24 cm. Includes index. 1. Drinking and traffic accidents — United States. 2. Youth — United States — Alcohol use. I. T.
HE5620.D7 W33 1983      363.1/251 19      *LC* 83-47515      *ISBN* 0669066966

**Berger, Michael L., 1943-.**                                           **4.4037**
The devil wagon in God's country: the automobile and social change in rural America, 1893–1929 / Michael L. Berger. — Hamden, Conn.: Archon Books, 1979. 269 p.: ill.; 23 cm. Includes index. 1. Automobiles — Social aspects — United States — History. 2. United States — Rural conditions I. T.
HE5623.B45      301.24/3      *LC* 79-17185      *ISBN* 0208017046

**Buel, Ronald A.**                                                      • **4.4038**
Dead end: the automobile in mass transportation [by] Ronald A. Buel. — Englewood Cliffs, N.J.: Prentice-Hall, [1972] 231 p.; 24 cm. 1. Transportation, Automotive — U.S. 2. Urban transportation — U.S. I. T.
HE5623.B82      388.3/0973      *LC* 75-175808      *ISBN* 0131969803

**Gilbert, Gorman, 1943-.**                                              **4.4039**
The taxicab: an urban transportation survivor / Gorman Gilbert & Robert E. Samuels. — Chapel Hill: University of North Carolina Press, c1982. xiv, 200 p.; 21 cm. Includes index. 1. Taxicabs — United States — History. I. Samuels, Robert E., 1913- II. T.
HE5623.G53 1982      388.4/1321 19      *LC* 82-2726      *ISBN* 0807815284

**Regulation of entry and pricing in truck transportation / edited**     **4.4040**
**by Paul W. MacAvoy and John W. Snow.**
Washington: American Enterprise Institute for Public Policy Research, c1977. 301 p.: graphs; 23 cm. — (Ford Administration papers on regulatory reform) (Studies in government regulation.) (AEI studies; 162) 1. Trucking — United States. 2. Industry and state — United States. I. MacAvoy, Paul W. II. Snow, John W. III. Series. IV. Series: Studies in government regulation.
HE5623.R43      388.3/24/0973      *LC* 77-89167

**Taff, Charles Albert, 1916-.**                                          **4.4041**
Commercial motor transportation / Charles A. Taff. — 7th ed. — Centreville, Md.: Cornell Maritime Press, 1986. xi, 434 p.: ill.; 24 cm. Includes index. 1. Transportation, Automotive — United States. I. T.
HE5623.T3 1986        388.3/0973 19        *LC* 85-47905        *ISBN* 0870333453

**Vidich, Charles.**                                                     **4.4042**
The New York cab driver and his fare / Charles Vidich. — Cambridge, Mass.: Schenkman Pub. Co., c1976. 186 p.: ill.; 24 cm. 1. Taxicabs — New York (City) 2. Taxicab drivers — New York (City) I. T.
HE5634.N5 V53        388.3/21/097471        *LC* 74-80370        *ISBN* 0870739255

**Button, Kenneth John.**                                                **4.4043**
The economics of urban freight transport / K.J. Button and A.D. Pearman. — New York: Holmes & Meier Publishers, c1981. x, 218 p.: ill.; 23 cm. Publisher from label on t.p. Includes indexes. 1. Transportation, Automotive — Great Britain — Freight. 2. Delivery of goods I. Pearman, A. D. joint author. II. T.
HE5663.A6 B88 1981        388.4/1324        *LC* 79-21942        *ISBN* 0333248082

# HE5736–5739 Bicycles

**Forester, John, 1929-.**                                               **4.4044**
Bicycle transportation / John Forester. — Cambridge, Mass.: MIT Press, c1983. xiii, 394 p.: ill.; 24 cm. Rev. ed. of: Cycling transportation engineering. c1977. Includes index. 1. Bicycle commuting 2. Bicycle commuting — United States. I. T.
HE5736.F67 1983        388.4/132 19        *LC* 83-7932        *ISBN* 026206085X

# HE6000–7500 Postal Service

**Fuller, Wayne Edison, 1919-.**                                    • **4.4045**
The American mail: enlarger of the common life / [by] Wayne E. Fuller. — Chicago: University of Chicago Press, [1972] xi, 378 p.; 21 cm. — (Chicago history of American civilization.) 1. Postal service — United States — History. I. T. II. Series.
HE6371.F84        383/.49/73        *LC* 72-78254        *ISBN* 0226268845

**Hafen, Le Roy Reuben, 1893-.**                                    • **4.4046**
The overland mail, 1849–1869; promoter of settlement, precursor of railroads, by Le Roy R. Hafen. — New York: AMS Press, [1969] 361 p.: illus., map, ports.; 23 cm. Reprint of the 1926 ed. 1. Postal service — U.S. — History. I. T.
HE6375.H3 1969        383/.49/73        *LC* 73-90099

**Fuller, Wayne Edison, 1919-.**                                    • **4.4047**
RFD, the changing face of rural America / [by] Wayne E. Fuller. — Bloomington: Indiana University Press [1964] xii, 361 p.: ill.; 22 cm. 1. Rural free delivery 2. United States — Rural conditions I. T.
HE6455 F8        *LC* 64-19374

# HE7601–9715 Telecommunication. Radio. Television. Telephone

(see also: PN1990-1992, TK6630-6720)

**Telecommunications: an interdisciplinary text / edited by**              **4.4048**
**Leonard Lewin.**
Dedham, MA: Artech House, c1984. xxii, 687 p.: ill.; 24 cm. Rev. and expanded edition of: Telecommunications, an interdisciplinary survey. c1979. 1. Telecommunication — Addresses, essays, lectures. 2. Telecommunication policy — Addresses, essays, lectures. 3. Telecommunication systems — Addresses, essays, lectures. I. Lewin, Leonard, 1919- II. Telecommunications, an interdisciplinary survey.
HE7631.T443 1984        384 19        *LC* 84-70225        *ISBN* 0890061408

**Williams, Frederick, 1933-.**                                          **4.4049**
The communications revolution / Frederick Williams. — Beverly Hills: Sage Publications, c1982. 291 p.: ill.; 23 cm. Includes index. 1. Telecommunication I. T.
HE7631.W54 1982        384 19        *LC* 81-18498        *ISBN* 0803917821

**Brock, Gerald W.**                                                     **4.4050**
The telecommunications industry: the dynamics of market structure / Gerald W. Brock. — Cambridge, Mass.: Harvard University Press, 1981. xi, 336 p.; 24 cm. — (Harvard economic studies. v. 151) 1. Telecommunication — United States. 2. Telecommunication — Law and legislation — United States. 3. Telecommunication policy — United States. 4. Telecommunication — Europe. I. T. II. Series.
HE7775.B68        384/.0973 19        *LC* 80-25299        *ISBN* 0674872851

**The Economics of competition in the telecommunications**              **4.4051**
**industry / by John R. Meyer ... [et al.].**
Cambridge, Mass.: Oelgeschlager, Gunn & Hain, Inc., c1980. xvii, 341 p.; 24 cm. 1. Telecommunication — United States. 2. Telephone — United States I. Meyer, John Robert.
HE7775.E28 1980        384/.065/73        *LC* 80-17414        *ISBN* 0899460569

**Communications policy and the political process / edited by**         **4.4052**
**John J. Havick.**
Westport, Conn.: Greenwood Press, 1983. x, 223 p.; 25 cm. — (Contributions in political science. 0147-1066; no. 101) Includes index. 1. Telecommunication policy — United States — Addresses, essays, lectures. I. Havick, John J. II. Series.
HE7781.C644 1983        384/.068 19        *LC* 83-1673        *ISBN* 0313232342

**Saunders, Robert J.**                                                  **4.4053**
Telecommunications and economic development / Robert J. Saunders, Jeremy J. Warford, Bjorn Wellenius. — Baltimore: Published for the World Bank [by] the Johns Hopkins University Press, c1983. xvi, 395 p.: ill.; 25 cm. Includes index. 1. Telecommunication — Developing countries. 2. Telecommunication — Mathematical models. I. Warford, Jeremy J. II. Wellenius, Bjorn. III. International Bank for Reconstruction and Development. IV. T.
HE8635.S28 1983        384/.09172/4 19        *LC* 82-49065        *ISBN* 0801828287

**Broadcasting cablecasting yearbook.**                                  **4.4054**
1982-        . — [Washington: Broadcasting Publications, c1982-. v.: ill.; 28 cm. Annual. Title from cover. 1. Broadcasting — Directories. 2. Radio advertising — Directories. 3. Television advertising — Directories. 4. Cable television — Directories.
HE8689.B77        384.54/0973        *LC* 82-643037

**Head, Sydney W.**                                                      **4.4055**
World broadcasting systems: a comparative analysis / Sydney W. Head. — Belmont, Calif.: Wadsworth Pub. Co., c1985. xix, 457 p.: ill.; 25 cm. (Wadsworth series in mass communication.) Includes index. 1. Broadcasting I. T. II. Series.
HE8689.4.H43 1985        384.54 19        *LC* 84-21019        *ISBN* 0534047343

**Unesco. Division of Statistics on Culture and Communication.**        **4.4056**
Statistics on radio and television: 1960–1976 / Division of Statistics on Culture and Communication, Office of Statistics, Paris 1978. — Paris: Unesco, 1979. 124 p.: graphs; 30 cm. (Statistical reports and studies; no. 23) Errata slip inserted. 1. Broadcasting — Statistics. I. T.
HE8689.4.U54 1979        384.54/021/2 19        *LC* 79-319352        *ISBN* 9231016814

**Sterling, Christopher H., 1943-.**                                     **4.4057**
Electronic media: a guide to trends in broadcasting and newer technologies, 1920–1983 / Christopher H. Sterling. — New York: Praeger, 1984. xxix, 337 p. 1. Broadcasting — United States — Statistics. I. T.
HE8689.8.S7295 1984        384.54/0973 19        *LC* 83-27019        *ISBN* 0030714680

**Sterling, Christopher H., 1943-.**                                     **4.4058**
Stay tuned: a concise history of American broadcasting / Christopher H. Sterling and John M. Kittross. — Belmont, Calif.: Wadsworth Pub. Co., c1978. xiv, 562 p.: ill.; 24 cm. Includes index. 1. Broadcasting — United States — History. I. Kittross, John M., 1929- joint author. II. T.
HE8689.8.S73        HE8689.8 S73.        384.54/0973        *LC* 77-10628
        *ISBN* 0534005144

**Head, Sydney W.**                                                      **4.4059**
Broadcasting in Africa; a continental survey of radio and television. Edited by Sydney W. Head. — Philadelphia: Temple University Press, [1974] xvi, 453 p.: illus.; 24 cm. — (International and comparative broadcasting) 1. Radio broadcasting — Africa. I. T.
HE8689.9.A35 H4        384.54/096        *LC* 73-79478        *ISBN* 0877220271

**Broadcasting in Asia and the Pacific: a continental survey of**       **4.4060**
**radio and television / edited by John A. Lent.**
Philadelphia: Temple University Press, c1978. xx, 429 p.; 23 cm. — (International and comparative broadcasting) Includes index. 1. Broadcasting — Asia — Addresses, essays, lectures. 2. Broadcasting — Oceanica — Addresses, essays, lectures. I. Lent, John A.
HE8689.9.A7 B76        384/.095        *LC* 75-44708        *ISBN* 0877220689

**Paulu, Burton, 1910-.**        4.4061
Radio and television broadcasting in Eastern Europe / by Burton Paulu. — Minneapolis: University of Minnesota Press, [1974] xi, 592 p.; 24 cm. Includes index. 1. Broadcasting — Europe, Eastern. I. T.
HE8689.9.E22 P38 1974     HE8689.9 E22 P38 1974.     384.54/0947
    *LC* 74-79505     *ISBN* 0816607214

**Katz, Elihu, 1926-.**        4.4062
Broadcasting in the Third World: promise and performance / Elihu Katz and George Wedell, with Michael Pilsworth and Dov Shinar. — Cambridge: Harvard University Press, 1977. xvi, 305 p.; 24 cm. 1. Broadcasting — Developing countries I. Wedell, E. G. (Eberhard George), 1927- joint author. II. T.
HE8689.95.K37     384.55/4/091724     *LC* 77-8282     *ISBN* 0674083415

**Beville, Hugh Malcolm.**        4.4063
Audience ratings: radio, television, and cable / Hugh Malcolm Beville, Jr. — Hillsdale, N.J.: L. Erlbaum Associates, 1985. xvi, 362 p., [1] leaf of plates: ill.; 24 cm. (Communication) Includes index. 1. Radio programs — Rating 2. Television programs — Rating I. T.
HE8697.A8 B46 1985     384.54/3 19     *LC* 85-1529     *ISBN* 0898595355

**Browne, Donald R.**        4.4064
International radio broadcasting: the limits of the limitless medium / Donald R. Browne. — New York, N.Y.: Praeger, 1982. xii, 369 p.; 24 cm. Includes index. 1. International broadcasting 2. Radio broadcasting 3. Radio in propaganda I. T.
HE8697.P6 B76 1982     384.54 19     *LC* 81-22707     *ISBN* 003059619X

**Briggs, Asa, 1921-.**        • 4.4065
The history of broadcasting in the United Kingdom. London; New York: Oxford University Press, 1961-70. 3 v.: ill., ports.; 22 cm. 1. British Broadcasting Corporation. 2. Radio broadcasting — Great Britain — History. I. T. II. Title: Broadcasting in the United Kingsom.
HE8699.G7 B65     *LC* 61-16211

## HE8700 Television

**Bower, Robert T.**        4.4066
The changing television audience in America / Robert T. Bower. — New York: Columbia University Press, 1985. 172 p.: ill.; 24 cm. Includes index. 1. Television audiences — United States — Attitudes — History. I. T.
HE8700.66.U6 B68 1985     384.55/44/0973 19     *LC* 85-6674     *ISBN* 0231061145

**Frank, Ronald Edward, 1933-.**        4.4067
Audiences for public television / Ronald E. Frank and Marshall G. Greenberg. — Beverly Hills, Calif.: Sage Publications, c1982. 230 p.; 23 cm. 1. Television audiences — United States. 2. Public television — United States. I. Greenberg, Marshall G., 1935- II. T.
HE8700.7.A8 F69 1982     384.55/44 19     *LC* 82-16754     *ISBN* 0803907648

**Baldwin, Thomas F.**        4.4068
Cable communication / Thomas F. Baldwin, D. Stevens McVoy. — Englewood Cliffs, N.J.: Prentice-Hall, c1983. xv, 416 p.: ill.; 24 cm. 1. Cable television I. McVoy, D. Stevens. II. T.
HE8700.7.C6 B34 1983     384.55/56 19     *LC* 82-7584     *ISBN* 0131101714

**The Cable/broadband communications book.**        4.4069
1977/78-. Washington, Communications Press. v. 28 cm. Biennial. 1. Cable television — United States — Periodicals. 2. Telecommunication — United States — Periodicals.
HE8700.7.C6 C315     384.55/47     *LC* 78-642239

**Greenfield, Jeff.**        4.4070
Television: the first fifty years / Jeff Greenfield; [editor, Lory Frankel]. — New York: H. N. Abrams, c1977. 280 p.: ill. (some col.), ports. 1. Television — United States — History. 2. Television programs — United States — History. I. T.
HE8700.8.G74     791.45 791/.45/0973     *LC* 77-9159     *ISBN* 0810916517

**Levin, Harvey Joshua, 1924-.**        4.4071
Fact and fancy in television regulation: an economic study of policy alternatives / Harvey J. Levin. — New York: Russell Sage Foundation, c1980. xvii, 505 p.; 24 cm. — (Publications of Russell Sage Foundation) 1. Television broadcasting policy — United States. 2. Television broadcasting — United States. I. T.
HE8700.8.L48     384.55/443 19     *LC* 79-90148     *ISBN* 0871545314

**Mankiewicz, Frank, 1924-.**        4.4072
Remote control: television and the manipulation of American life / Frank Mankiewicz and Joel Swerdlow. — New York: Times Books, c1978. viii, 308 p.; 25 cm. Includes index. 1. Television broadcasting — Social aspects — United States. I. Swerdlow, Joel L. joint author. II. T.
HE8700.8.M36 1978     301.24/3     *LC* 76-9726     *ISBN* 0812906497

**Television and human behavior / by George Comstock ... [et**        4.4073
**al.], with the assistance of Thomas Bowers ... [et al.].**
New York: Columbia University Press, 1978. xviii, 581 p.: ill. Includes index. 1. Television — Psychological aspects 2. Television broadcasting — Social aspects — United States. 3. Television and children I. Comstock, George A.
HE8700.8.T34     HE8700.8 T34.     384.55/01/9     *LC* 78-5915
    *ISBN* 0231044208

## HE8701–9715 Telephone Industry

**The Social impact of the telephone / Ithiel de Sola Pool, editor.**        4.4074
Cambridge, Mass.: MIT Press, c1977. viii, 502 p.: ill., maps.; 24 cm. — (MIT Bicentennial studies; 1) 1. Telephone — Social aspects — Addresses, essays, lectures. I. Pool, Ithiel de Sola, 1917-
HE8735.S65     301.16/1     *LC* 77-4110     *ISBN* 0262160668

**Smith, George David.**        4.4075
The anatomy of a business strategy: Bell, Western Electric, and the origins of the American telephone industry / George David Smith. — Baltimore: Johns Hopkins University Press, c1985. xxii, 237 p.: ill.; 24 cm. (The Johns Hopkins/AT&T series in telephone history) Includes index. 1. American Telephone and Telegraph Company — History. 2. Western Electric Company — History. 3. Telephone — United States — History. I. T. II. Series.
HE8846.A55 S65 1985     384.6/065/73 19     *LC* 84-23419     *ISBN* 0801827108

## HE9761–9900 Air Transportation

**Gidwitz, Betsy.**        4.4076
The politics of international air transport / Betsy Gidwitz. — Lexington, Mass.: Lexington Books, c1980. xii, 259 p.: maps; 24 cm. Includes index. 1. Aeronautics, Commercial — Political aspects. 2. Aeronautics, Commercial — Law and legislation I. T.
HE9777.G53     341.7/567 19     *LC* 79-2706     *ISBN* 0669032344

**Sampson, Anthony.**        4.4077
Empires of the sky: the politics, contests and cartels of world airlines / Anthony Sampson. — 1st American ed. — New York: Random House, c1984. 254 p.; 25 cm. 1. Airlines I. T.
HE9780.S26 1984     387.7/065 19     *LC* 84-23787     *ISBN* 0394533437

**Pillai, K. G. J.**        • 4.4078
The air net; the case against the world aviation cartel [by] K. G. J. Pillai. New York, Grossman Publishers, 1969. xix, 212 p. 21 cm. 1. International Air Transport Association. 2. Airlines — Rates 3. Cartels I. T.
HE9783.5.P5     387.7     *LC* 77-88566

**Eads, George C., 1942-.**        4.4079
The local service airline experiment [by] George C. Eads. — Washington: Brookings Institution, [1972] xiii, 223 p.: illus.; 23 cm. — (Studies in the regulation of economic activity.) 1. Local service airlines — United States. I. T. II. Series.
HE9785.E2     387.7/42/0973     *LC* 72-141     *ISBN* 081572022X

**Straszheim, Mahlon R., 1939-.**        • 4.4080
The international airline industry / [by] Mahlon R. Straszheim. — Washington: Brookings Institution, Transport Research Program, [1969] viii, 297 p.; 24 cm. 1. Aeronautics, Commercial I. Brookings Institution, Washington, D.C. Transport Research Program. II. T.
HE9786.S7     338.4/7/3877     *LC* 67-30604

**Baker, Robert Fulton, 1917-.**        • 4.4081
Technology and decisions in airport access [by] Robert F. Baker and Raymond M. Wilmotte. Prepared for the Urban Transportation Research Council. — New York: American Society of Civil Engineers, 1970. xii, 152 p.; 22 cm. 1. Access to airports — U.S. 2. Urban transportation — U.S. I. Wilmotte, Raymond Maurice, 1901- joint author. II. American Society of Civil Engineers. Urban Transportation Research Council. III. T. IV. Title: Airport access.
HE9797.4.A2 B3     387.7/36     *LC* 76-283480

**Airline deregulation: the early experience / John R. Meyer and**    **4.4082**
**Clinton V. Oster, Jr., editors; [authors] John R. Meyer ... [et.**
**al.].**
Boston, Mass.: Auburn House Pub. Co., c1981. xx, 287 p.: ill.; 24 cm.
1. Aeronautics, Commercial — United States — History. 2. Aeronautics,
Commercial — Law and legislation — United States — History.
3. Aeronautics and state — United States — History. 4. Airlines — United
States — History. I. Meyer, John Robert. II. Oster, Clinton V.
HE9803.A3 A36      387.7/0973 19      *LC* 81-3620      *ISBN* 0865690782

**Kane, Robert M.**    **4.4083**
Air transportation / Robert M. Kane, Allan D. Vose. — 8th ed. — Dubuque,
Iowa: Kendall/Hunt Pub. Co., c1982. ix, 419 p.: ill. (Aviation management
series.) Includes index. 1. Aeronautics, Commercial — United States I. Vose,
Allan D. II. T. III. Series.
HE9803.A3 K3 1982      387.7/0973 19      *LC* 83-126468      *ISBN*
0840326394

**Solberg, Carl, 1915-.**    **4.4084**
Conquest of the skies: a history of commercial aviation in America / by Carl
Solberg. — 1st ed. — Boston: Little, Brown, c1979. vi, 441 p.: ill.; 24 cm.
Includes index. 1. Aeronautics, Commercial — United States — History. I. T.
HE9803.A3 S64      387.7/0973      *LC* 79-15993      *ISBN* 0316803308

**Biederman, Paul.**    **4.4085**
The U.S. airline industry: end of an era / Paul Biederman. — New York, N.Y.:
Praeger, 1982. xxiii, 198 p.; 25 cm. — (Praeger studies in select basic
industries.) Includes index. 1. Aeronautics, Commercial — United States I. T.
II. Title: US airline industry. III. Series.
HE9803.A35 B5 1982      387.7/065/73 19      *LC* 81-17845      *ISBN*
0030603242

**Deregulation and the new airline entrepreneurs / John R.**    **4.4086**
**Meyer and Clinton V. Oster, Jr., with Marni Clippinger ... [et**
**al.].**
Cambridge, Mass.: MIT Press, c1984. xvi, 240 p.: ill.; 24 cm. — (MIT Press
series on the regulation of economic activity. 9) 1. Aeronautics, Commercial —
United States 2. Airlines — United States. 3. Aeronautics and state — United
States. I. Meyer, John Robert. II. Oster, Clinton V. III. Clippinger, Marni.
IV. Series.
HE9803.A35 D47 1984      387.7/12 19      *LC* 84-7935      *ISBN*
0262131986

**Bailey, Elizabeth E.**    **4.4087**
Deregulating the airlines / Elizabeth E. Bailey, David R. Graham, Daniel P.
Kaplan. — Cambridge, Mass.: MIT Press, c1985. xiv, 243 p.: ill.; 25 cm. (MIT
Press series on the regulation of economic activity. 10) Includes index.
1. Aeronautics, Commercial — Government policy — United States.
2. Aeronautics, Commercial — Law and legislation — United States.
I. Graham, David R. II. Kaplan, Daniel P. III. T. IV. Series.
HE9803.A4 B32 1985      387.7/068 19      *LC* 84-21816      *ISBN*
0262022133

**Douglas, George W. (George Warren), 1938-.**    **4.4088**
Economic regulation of domestic air transport; theory and policy [by] George
W. Douglas [and] James C. Miller III. Washington, Brookings Institution
[1974] xii, 211 p. illus. 24 cm. (Studies in the regulation of economic activity.)
1. United States. Civil Aeronautics Board. 2. Aeronautics and state — United
States. 3. Aeronautics, Commercial — United States I. Miller, James Clifford.
joint author. II. T. III. Series.
HE9803.A4 D68      387.7/1/0973 19      *LC* 74-17435      *ISBN* 0815757247

**Jordan, William A.**    **• 4.4089**
Airline regulation in America; effects and imperfections [by] William A.
Jordan. — Baltimore: Johns Hopkins Press, [1970] xvi, 352 p.; 24 cm. 1. U.S.
Civil Aeronautics Board. 2. Aeronautics and state — U.S. 3. Airlines — U.S.
I. T.
HE9803.A4 J6      387.7/0973      *LC* 75-118837      *ISBN* 0801810620

**Nance, John J.**    **4.4090**
Splash of colors: the self–destruction of Braniff International / John J. Nance.
— 1st ed. — New York: Morrow, 1984. 426 p.: ill.; 24 cm. 1. Braniff Airways.
I. T.
HE9803.B73 N36 1984      387.7/065/73 19      *LC* 83-25072      *ISBN*
0688035868

# HF1–4040 COMMERCE

**World trade annual.**    **• 4.4091**
1963-. [New York: Walker] v.; 24 cm. Annual. Issued in 4 vols. each with
distinctive title. 1. Commerce — Yearbooks. 2. Commerce — Directories.
I. United Nations. Statistical Office.
HF53.W6      382      *LC* 64-66238

**Ohlin, Bertil Gotthard, 1899-.**    **• 4.4092**
Interregional and international trade [by] Bertil Ohlin. Rev. ed. Cambridge,
Harvard University Press, 1967. xv, 324 p. 25 cm. (Harvard economic studies.
v. 39) Bibliographical footnotes. 1. Prices 2. Commerce 3. Foreign exchange
I. T. II. Title: International trade. III. Series.
HF81.O5 1967      382      *LC* 67-17317

# HF351–499 History

**Hasebroek, Johannes, 1893-.**    **4.4093**
Trade and politics in ancient Greece / by Johannes Hasebroek; translated by L.
M. Fraser and D. C. Macgregor. — London: G. Bell, 1933. xi, 187 p. 22 cm.
Translation of Staat und Handel im alten Griechenland. 1. Greece —
Commerce — History. 2. Greece — Economic policy. I. T.
HF375.H33      382.0938      *LC* 34-11758

**Trade in the ancient economy / edited by Peter Garnsey, Keith**    **4.4094**
**Hopkins, and C.R. Whittaker.**
Berkeley: University of California Press, 1983. xxv, 230 p.; 23 cm. Includes
indexes. 1. Greece — Commerce — History — Addresses, essays, lectures.
2. Rome — Commerce — History — Addresses, essays, lectures. I. Garnsey,
Peter. II. Hopkins, Keith, 1934- III. Whittaker, C. R.
HF375.T73 1983      382/.093 19      *LC* 82-13652      *ISBN* 0520048032

**Lopez, Robert Sabatino, 1910-.**    **4.4095**
The commercial revolution of the Middle Ages, 950–1350 [by] Robert S. Lopez.
Englewood Cliffs, N.J., Prentice-Hall [1971] xi, 177 p. illus. 21 cm. (The
Economic civilization of Europe) (A Spectrum book) 1. Commerce — History
— Medieval, 500-1500 2. Economic history — Medieval, 500-1500 I. T.
HF395.L64      330.9/02      *LC* 79-160536      *ISBN* 013152934X

**Schafer, Edward H.**    **4.4096**
The golden peaches of Samarkand; a study of T'ang exotics. Berkeley,
University of California Press, 1963. xiii, 399 p. plates, map (on lining papers)
1. China — Commerce — History 2. China — History — T'ang dynasty,
618-907 I. T.
HF408 S3      *LC* 63-8922

**Davies, David William, 1908-.**    **4.4097**
A primer of Dutch seventeenth century overseas trade. — The Hague: Nijhoff,
1961. xii, 160 p. ill. (part fold., part col.) port., maps (part fold.) 1. Colonial
companies 2. Netherlands — Commerce — History. I. T.
HF482.D3      382.09492      *LC* 63-201

**Chaudhuri, K. N.**    **4.4098**
The trading world of Asia and the English East India Company, 1660–1760 /
K. N. Chaudhuri. — Cambridge [Eng.]; New York: Cambridge University
Press, 1978. xviii, 628 p.: ill.; 24 cm. Includes index. 1. East India Company —
History. 2. Europe — Commerce — Asia — History. 3. Asia — Commerce —
Europe — History. I. T.
HF486.E6 C44      382/.06/55      *LC* 77-77745      *ISBN* 0521217164

**Ball, J. N.**    **4.4099**
Merchants and merchandise: the expansion of trade in Europe 1500–1630 / J.
N. Ball. — New York: St. Martin's Press, 1977. 226 p.: map; 23 cm. Includes
index. 1. Merchants — Europe — History. 2. Europe — Commerce —
History. I. T.
HF493.B34 1977b      382/.094      *LC* 77-74803      *ISBN* 0312530080

**Maizels, Alfred.**    **• 4.4100**
Industrial growth and world trade: an empirical study of trends in production,
consumption and trade in manufactures from 1899–1959; with a discussion of
probable future trends. — Cambridge [Eng.]: University Press, 1963. xxiii,
563 p.: diagrs., tables.; 24 cm. (Economic and social studies. 21) 1. Commerce
2. Industrialization I. T. II. Series.
HF499.M33

# HF1002 Dictionaries: Bilingual

**Collin, Françoise, 1928-.**      4.4102
Harrap's French and English business dictionary / edited by Françoise Collin, Jane Pratt, and Peter Collin. — London: Harrap, 1981. ix, 235, 23, 212 p.; 24 cm. 1. Business — Dictionaries. 2. English language — Dictionaries — French. 3. Business — Dictionaries — French. 4. French language — Dictionaries — English. I. Pratt, Jane. II. Collin, P. H. (Peter Hodgson) III. T.
HF1002.C58 1981     650/.03/21 19     LC 81-167430     ISBN 0245534555

# HF1003–1010 General Works

**Allen, William Richard, 1924- ed.**      • 4.4103
International trade theory: Hume to Ohlin / edited, with an introd. by William R. Allen. — New York: Random House, [1965] 210 p.: ill.; 19 cm. (Random House studies in economics, SE 9) 1. Commerce I. T.
HF1007 A39     LC 65-23330

**American Economic Association.**      • 4.4104
Readings in the theory of international trade, selected by a committee of the American Economic Assn. — Philadelphia, Blakiston Co., 1949. xvii, 637 p. diagrs. 22 cm. — (Blakiston series of republished articles on economics, v. 4) 'Selection committee ... Howard S. Ellis, Lloyd A. Metzler.' 'Classified bibliography of articles on international economics': p. 555-625. 1. Commerce I. Ellis, Howard Sylvester, 1898- comp. II. T.
HF1007.A5     382.082     LC 49-1493 *

**Bhagwati, Jagdish N., 1934-.**      • 4.4105
Trade, tariffs and growth: essays in international economics. — London: Weidenfeld & Nicolson, 1969. ix, 371 p.: illus.; 23 cm. 1. Commerce 2. Tariff 3. Economic development I. T.
HF1007.B44 1969     382     LC 71-437853     ISBN 0297178296

**Johnson, Harry G. (Harry Gordon), 1923-1977.**      • 4.4106
International trade and economic growth; studies in pure theory. Cambridge, Harvard University Press [c1958] 204 p. diagrs. 23 cm. Based on the author's thesis, Harvard University. Bibliographical footnotes. 1. Commerce I. T.
HF1007.J62     382     LC A 59-7736

**Lewis, W. Arthur (William Arthur), 1915-.**      4.4107
The evolution of the international economic order / W. Arthur Lewis. — Princeton: Princeton University Press, c1978. 81 p.; 22 cm. (The Eliot Janeway lectures on historical economics in honor of Joseph Schumpeter; 1977) Includes index. 1. International economic relations — Addresses, essays, lectures. I. T. II. Series.
HF1007.L68     382.1     LC 77-15374     ISBN 0691042195. ISBN 0691003602 pbk

**Marshall, Alfred, 1842-1924.**      • 4.4108
The pure theory of foreign trade: the pure theory of domestic values / by Alfred Marshall. — London: The London School of Economics and Political Science, 1930. 2 p. l., facsim.: 28, 37, [1] p.: fold. diagrs.; 22 cm. (Series of reprints of scarce tracts in economic and political science. no. 1) Facsimile reprint of two papers printed for private circulation in 1879. 1. Commerce 2. Value 3. Economics, Mathematical I. T. II. Title: The pure theory of domestic values.
HF1007.M35     382     LC 32-4479

**Taussig, Frank William, 1859-1940.**      • 4.4109
International trade / by F.W. Taussig. — New York: A. M. Kelley, 1966. xxi, 425 p.: ill.; 22 cm. — (Reprints of economic classics) 1. Commerce 2. Foreign exchange I. T.
HF1007.T25 1966     LC 66-19696

**Viner, Jacob, 1892-1970.**      • 4.4110
International trade and economic development: lectures delivered at the National University of Brazil. — Glencoe, Ill.: Free Press, [1952] 154 p.; 21 cm. 1. Commerce 2. Commercial policy I. T.
HF1007.V53 1952     382.04     LC 52-14627

**International marketing management / edited by Erdener**      4.4111
**Kaynak.**
New York: Praeger, 1984. 361 p.: ill. Includes index. 1. Export marketing — Management — Addresses, essays, lectures. I. Kaynak, Erdener.
HF1009.5.I544 1984     658.8/48 19     LC 84-15927     ISBN 0030717140

**Keegan, Warren J.**      4.4112
Multinational marketing management / Warren J. Keegan. — 3rd ed. — Englewood Cliffs, N.J.: Prentice-Hall, c1984. xxii, 698 p.: ill.; 25 cm. — (Prentice-Hall series in marketing.) (Prentice-Hall international series in management.) 1. Export marketing — Management. I. T. II. Series. III. Series: Prentice-Hall international series in management.
HF1009.5.K39 1984     658.8/48 19     LC 83-24751     ISBN 0136050492

**Piercy, Nigel.**      4.4113
Export strategy, markets and competition / Nigel Piercy. — London; Boston: Allen & Unwin, 1982. xv, 265 p.; 22 cm. Includes index. 1. Export marketing 2. Price policy. I. T.
HF1009.5.P44 1982     658.8/48 19     LC 82-8774     ISBN 0043820379

# HF1014–1027 Balance of Trade. Trade Statistics. Commercial Geography

**Meade, J. E. (James Edward), 1907-.**      • 4.4114
A geometry of international trade. London: Allen & Unwin, [1952] 112 p.: ill.; 22 cm. 1. Balance of trade 2. Commerce 3. Geometry I. T.
HF1014 M4     LC 53-613

**Yearbook of international trade statistics.**      • 4.4115
1st-     issue; 1950-. New York, Dept. of Economic and Social Affairs, Statistical Office, United Nations [etc.] v. 28 cm. ([Document] - United Nations ST/STAT/Ser.G) Annual. Issued with the United Nations publications sales numbers. No. 1 issued without symbol of United Nations Document. Issues for 1956-59 issued in 2 volumes. 1. Commercial statistics — Periodicals. I. United Nations. Statistical Office. Dept. of Economic and Social Affairs. II. United Nations. Statistical Office.
HF1014.Y4x     382.058     LC 51-8987

**Barter in the world economy / edited by Bart S. Fisher,**      4.4116
**Kathleen M. Harte.**
New York: Praeger, 1985. vii, 293 p. 1. Barter — Addresses, essays, lectures. I. Fisher, Bart S. II. Harte, Kathleen M.
HF1019.B37 1985     382 19     LC 85-6257     ISBN 0030716098

**Alexander, John W. (John Wesley), 1918-.**      4.4117
Economic geography / John W. Alexander, Lay James Gibson. — 2d ed. — Englewood Cliffs, N.J.: Prentice-Hall, c1979. xiv, 480 p.: ill.; 28 cm. 1. Geography, Economic I. Gibson, Lay James. joint author. II. T.
HF1025.A53 1979     330.9     LC 78-15735     ISBN 0132251515

**Butler, Joseph H.**      4.4118
Economic geography: spatial and environmental aspects of economic activity / Joseph H. Butler. — New York: Wiley, c1980. xiv, 402 p.: ill.; 24 cm. Includes index. 1. Geography, Economic I. T.
HF1025.B86     330.9     LC 80-14542     ISBN 0471126810

**Ginsburg, Norton Sydney.**      • 4.4119
Essays on geography and economic development / by Brian J.L.Berry and others. Chicago: University of Chicago, 1960. xx, 173 p.: ill., maps.; 23 cm. (Research paper (University of Chicago. Dept. of Geography) no.62.) 1. Geography, Economic — Addresses, essays, lectures. I. Berry, Brian Joe Lobley, 1934- II. T. III. Title: Geography and economic development. IV. Series.
HF1025.G5     LC 60-2105

**Lloyd, Peter E.**      4.4120
Location in space: a theoretical approach to economic geography / Peter E. Lloyd & Peter Dicken. — 2d ed. — London; New York: Harper & Row, c1977. xii, 474 p.: ill.; 26 cm. Includes index. 1. Geography, Economic 2. Space in economics 3. Industry — Location I. Dicken, Peter. joint author. II. T.
HF1025.L584 1977     330.9     LC 77-23256     ISBN 0060440481

**McCarty, Harold Hull, 1901-.**      • 4.4121
A preface to economic geography [by] Harold H. McCarty and James B. Lindberg. — Englewood Cliffs, N. J., Prentice-Hall [1966] x, 261 p. illus. 23 cm.

Includes bibliographies. 1. Geography, Economic I. Lindberg, James B. joint author. II. T.
HF1025.M27      330.9      *LC* 66-13726

**Smith, Robert Henry Tufrey. comp.**                                    • **4.4122**
Readings in economic geography; the location of economic activity, edited by Robert H. T. Smith, Edward J. Taaffe [and] Leslie J. King. — Chicago, Rand McNally [1968] 406 p. illus., maps. 25 cm. — (Rand McNally geography series) 1. Geography, Economic 2. Industry — Location 3. Space in economics I. Taaffe, Edward James, joint comp. II. King, Leslie J. joint comp. III. T.
HF1025.S62      330.91/08      *LC* 68-10126

**Stamp, L. Dudley (Laurence Dudley), 1898-1966.**                        **4.4123**
Chisholm's handbook of commercial geography / entirely rewritten by Dudley Stamp. — 20th ed. / rev. by G. Noel Blake and Audrey N. Clark. — London; New York: Longman, 1980. xxxii, 983 p.: ill.; 25 cm. Includes index. 1. Geography, Commercial 2. Commercial products I. Blake, G. Noel, 1914- II. Clark, Audrey N. III. T.
HF1025.S689 1980      338/.09      *LC* 79-42772      *ISBN* 0582300150

**Stamp, L. Dudley (Laurence Dudley), 1898-1966.**                        **4.4124**
A commercial geography [by] Sir Dudley Stamp. — [9th ed. — London]: Longman, [1973] viii, 824 p.: illus., maps.; 22 cm. 1. Geography, Commercial I. T.
HF1025.S69 1973      330.9      *LC* 74-155452      *ISBN* 0582310431

**Stamp, L. Dudley (Laurence Dudley), 1898-1966.**                        **4.4125**
[Regional geography for higher certificate and intermediate courses] A regional geography for advanced and scholarship courses, by Sir Dudley Stamp. London, Longmans, 1968-. v. illus., charts, maps. 23 cm. (The University geographical series) First ed. published in 1930-34 under title: A regional geography for higher certificate and intermediate courses. 1. Geography, Commercial. 2. Commercial products. I. T. II. Series.
HF1025.S7382      330.9      *LC* 77-860929

**Thoman, Richard S., 1919-.**                                            **4.4126**
The geography of economic activity [by] Richard S. Thoman [and] Peter B. Corbin. — 3d ed. — New York: McGraw-Hill, [1974] viii, 420 p.: illus.; 24 cm. — (McGraw-Hill series in geography) 1. Geography, Economic I. Corbin, Peter B., joint author. II. T.
HF1025.T47 1974      330.9      *LC* 74-5756      *ISBN* 0070642079

**Zimmermann, Erich W. (Erich Walter), 1888-.**                          • **4.4127**
[World resources and industries] Zimmermann's World resources and industries. 3d ed. [by] W. N. Peach [and] James A. Constantin. New York, Harper & Row [1972] xiv, 575 p. illus. 27 cm. 1. Natural resources 2. Industry 3. Agriculture — Economic aspects 4. Geography, Economic I. Peach, William Nelson. II. Constantin, James A. III. T. IV. Title: World resources and industries.
HF1025.Z5 1972      330.9/047      *LC* 72-187048      *ISBN* 0060450959

# HF1040–1054 Commodities

**Commodity year book.**                                                  • **4.4128**
-1984. — New York, N.Y.: Commodity Research Bureau. v.: ill.; 29 cm. Annual. Began in 1939. Description based on: 1981; title from cover. Publication suspended, 1943-1947. 1. Commercial products — Periodicals. 2. Commercial products — Prices — Periodicals. 3. Commercial statistics — Periodicals. I. Commodity Research Bureau (New York, N.Y.)
HF1041.C56      380.1/029/4 19      *LC* 39-11418

**United States. Office of Management and Budget.**                       **4.4129**
Standard industrial classification manual. — [Rev. ed.] [Washington;: For sale by National Technical Information Service], 1987. 705 p.; 26 cm. Originally issued by the U.S. Technical Committee on Industrial Classification. PB87-100 012/HCQ. 1. Commercial products — United States — Classification. I. United States. Technical Committee on Industrial Classification. Standard industrial classification manual. II. T.
HF1042.A55 1987

**Resources for the Future.**                                             • **4.4130**
Trends in natural resource commodities: statistics of prices, output, consumption, foreign trade, and employment in the United States, 1870–1957 / [by] Neal Potter and Francis T. Christy, Jr. [research associates; edited by Pauline Manning] — Baltimore: Published for Resources for the Future by Johns Hopkins Press, 1962. ix, 568 p.: diagrs., tables; 33 cm. 1. Raw materials — United States 2. Natural resources — United States I. Potter, Neal II. Christy, Francis T. III. T.
HF1051 R48      *LC* 62-11711

**Page, Talbot.**                                                         **4.4131**
Conservation and economic efficiency: an approach to materials policy / Talbot Page. Baltimore: Published for Resources for the Future by the Johns Hopkins University Press, c1977. xvii, 266 p.: ill.; 24 cm. 1. Raw materials — United States. 2. Conservation of natural resources — United States 3. Recycling (Waste, etc.) I. Resources for the Future. II. T.
HF1052.P33      338/.0973      *LC* 76-22846      *ISBN* 0801819040

# HF1401–1650 Commercial Policy

**Balassa, Bela A.**                                                       • **4.4132**
The theory of economic integration. Homewood, Ill., R. D. Irwin [c1961] 304 p.; 24 cm. (The Irwin series in economics.) 1. International economic integration I. T.
HF1408.B2      *LC* 61-16921

**Balassa, Bela A.**                                                       • **4.4133**
Trade prospects for developing countries / by Bela Balessa. — Homewood, Ill.: R. D. Irwin, 1964. xii, 450 p.: ill.; 23 cm. — (Publications of the Economic Growth Center) 1. International economic relations 2. Underdeveloped areas — Commerce. I. T.
HF1408.B23      *LC* 64-17248

**Trade, balance of payments and growth; papers in international**         • **4.4134**
**economics in honor of Charles P. Kindleberger. Edited by**
**Jagdish N. Bhagwati, Ronald W. Jones, Robert A. Mundell**
**[and] Jaroslav Vanek.**
Amsterdam: North-Holland Pub. Co., 1971. xi, 532 p.: port.; 23 cm. 'Sole distributors for the U.S.A. and Canada: American Elsevier Publishing Company ... New York ... .' 1. International economic relations — Addresses, essays, lectures. 2. Commerce — Addresses, essays, lectures. 3. Balance of payments — Addresses, essays, lectures. I. Kindleberger, Charles Poor, 1910- II. Bhagwati, Jagdish N., 1934- ed.
HF1408.T7      382/.1      *LC* 71-157041      *ISBN* 0444100946

**The New international economic order: the North–South debate**          **4.4135**
/ Jagdish N. Bhagwati, editor.
Cambridge, Mass.: MIT Press, c1977. xiv, 390 p.; 24 cm. (MIT Bicentennial studies) Based largely on a workshop held at MIT in May 1976. 1. International economic relations — Congresses. 2. Developing countries — Foreign economic relations — Congresses. I. Bhagwati, Jagdish N., 1934-
HF1410.N4835      382.1      *LC* 77-7062      *ISBN* 0262021269. *ISBN*
0262520427 pbk

# HF1411–1412 General Works

## HF1411 A–L

**American Economic Association.**                                         • **4.4136**
Readings in international economics. Selected by a committee of the American Economic Association. Selection Committee for this volume Richard E. Caves and Harry G. Johnson. Homewood, Ill., Published for the Association by R. D. Irwin, 1968. xvi, 604 p. illus. 24 cm. (The Series of republished articles on economics, v. 11) 1. International economic relations — Addresses, essays, lectures. 2. Commerce — Addresses, essays, lectures. I. Caves, Richard E. comp. II. Johnson, Harry G. (Harry Gordon), 1923-1977. comp. III. T.
HF1411.A4585      382/.08      *LC* 67-21001

**Bedjaoui, Mohammed.**                                                   **4.4137**
[Pour un nouvel ordre économique international. English] Towards a new international economic order / Mohammed Bedjaoui. — New York: Holmes & Meier, 1979. 287 p.; 24 cm. Translation of Pour un nouvel ordre économique international. 1. International economic relations I. T.
HF1411.B3313      382.1      *LC* 79-22943      *ISBN* 0841905851

**Bhagwati, Jagdish N., 1934-.**                                          **4.4138**
Essays in international economic theory / Jagdish Bhagwati; edited by Robert C. Feenstra. — Cambridge, Mass.: MIT Press, c1983. 2 v.: ill.; 24 cm. 1. International economic relations — Collected works. I. Feenstra, Robert C. II. T.
HF1411.B466 1983      337 19      *LC* 83-857      *ISBN* 026202196X

**Clement, Meredith O.**                                                  • **4.4139**
Theoretical issues in international economics / by M. O. Clement, Richard L. Pfister [and] Kenneth J. Rothwell. — Boston: Houghton Mifflin, [1967] xiii, 449 p.: ill.; 24 cm. 1. International economic relations 2. International finance I. Pfister, Richard L. joint author. II. Rothwell, Kenneth J. joint author. III. T.
HF1411.C434      382      *LC* 67-1952

**Frey, Bruno S.**      **4.4140**
International political economics / Bruno S. Frey. — New York: Basil Blackwell, 1985 (c1984). viii, 183 p.: ill.; 24 cm. 1. International economic relations I. T.
HF1411.F735     337 19     *LC* 84-12477     *ISBN* 0855207485

**Hoyt, Ronald E.**      **4.4141**
Winners and losers in East–West trade: a behavioral analysis of U.S.–Soviet détente (1970–1980) / Ronald E. Hoyt. — New York, N.Y.: Praeger, 1983. xiii, 239 p.; 25 cm. Includes index. 1. East-West trade (1945- ) 2. United States — Commerce — Soviet Union. 3. Soviet Union — Commerce — United States. I. T.
HF1411.H69 1983     382/.0973/047 19     *LC* 82-18613     *ISBN* 003062486X

**Independent Commission on International Development Issues.**      **4.4142**
North–South, a programme for survival: report of the Independent Commission on International Development Issues. — 1st MIT Press paperback ed. — Cambridge, Mass.: MIT Press, 1980. 304 p.; 18 cm. 1. International economic relations 2. Economic development 3. Developing countries — Foreign economic relations. I. T.
HF1411.I368 1980     337/.09/04     *LC* 80-50086     *ISBN* 0262520591

**Independent Commission on International Development Issues.**      **4.4143**
Common crisis North–South: cooperation for world recovery / The Brandt Commission; Willy Brandt ... [et al.]. — 1st MIT Press pbk. ed. — Cambridge, Mass.: MIT Press, 1983. 174 p.: ill.; 18 cm. 1. International economic relations 2. Developing countries — Foreign economic relations. 3. Economic development I. Brandt, Willy, 1913- II. T.
HF1411.I368 1983     337/.09/048 19     *LC* 83-60614     *ISBN* 0262520850

**Jones, Charles A., 1949-.**      **4.4144**
The north–south dialogue: a brief history / Charles A. Jones. — New York: St. Martin's Press, 1983. xi, 153 p.; 24 cm. (Studies in international political economy) Includes index. 1. International economic relations I. T.
HF1411.J57 1983     337/.09/048 19     *LC* 82-10410     *ISBN* 0312578946

**Keohane, Robert O. (Robert Owen), 1941-.**      **4.4145**
After hegemony: cooperation and discord in the world political economy / Robert O. Keohane. — Princeton, N.J.: Princeton University Press, c1984. ix, 290 p.; 24 cm. Includes index. 1. International economic relations 2. World politics — 1945- I. T.
HF1411.K442 1984     337 19     *LC* 84-42576     *ISBN* 0691076766

**Knorr, Klaus Eugen, 1911-.**      **4.4146**
The power of nations: the political economy of international relations / Klaus Knorr. New York: Basic Books, [1975] x, 353 p.; 25 cm. 'Written under the auspices of the Center of International Study, Princeton University.' 1. International economic relations 2. International relations I. T.
HF1411.K584     382.1     *LC* 74-25920     *ISBN* 0465061427

**Lindert, Peter H.**      **4.4147**
International economics / Peter H. Lindert. — 8th ed. — Homewood, Ill.: Irwin, 1986. 1 v. (various pagings): ill.; 25 cm. — (Irwin publications in economics) 1. International economic relations 2. Commercial policy 3. Foreign exchange I. T.
HF1411.L536 1986     337 19     *LC* 85-81465     *ISBN* 0256033420

**Loehr, William.**      **4.4148**
Threat to development: pitfalls of the NIEO / William Loehr and John P. Powelson. — Boulder, Colo.: Westview Press, 1983. xiv, 170 p.: ill.; 24 cm. (Westview special studies in social, political, and economic development.) 1. International economic relations 2. Developing countries — Foreign economic relations. I. Powelson, John P., 1920- II. T. III. Series.
HF1411.L554 1983     337 19     *LC* 82-4777     *ISBN* 0865311285

## HF1411 M–Z

**MacBean, Alasdair I.**      **4.4149**
International institutions in trade and finance / A.I. MacBean and P.N. Snowden. — London; Boston: Allen & Unwin, 1981. xiv, 255 p.; 23 cm. — (Studies in economics; 18) Includes index. 1. International economic relations 2. International agencies 3. Financial institutions, International I. Snowden, P. N. (P. Nicholas) II. T.
HF1411.M22 1981     337/.06/01 19     *LC* 82-208792     *ISBN* 0043820328

**Meade, J. E. (James Edward), 1907-.**      • **4.4150**
Problems of economic unions. — Chicago: University of Chicago Press, [1953] 102 p. (Charles R. Walgreen Foundation lectures) 1. Commercial policy 2. Balance of trade 3. Internatonal cooperation. I. T. II. Series.
HF1411.M38

**Meier, Gerald M.**      • **4.4151**
The international economics of development; theory and policy [by] Gerald M. Meier. — New York: Harper & Row, [1968] xi, 338 p.: illus.; 24 cm. 'A revised and expanded edition of [the author's] International trade and development.' 1. International economic relations 2. Economic development I. T.
HF1411.M44 1968     338.91     *LC* 68-10874

**Myrdal, Gunnar, 1898-.**      • **4.4152**
Beyond the welfare state: economic planning and its international implications. — New Haven: Yale University Press, 1960. 287 p.; 23 cm. — (Yale Law School. Storrs lectures on jurisprudence, 1958) 1. International economic relations 2. Economic policy I. T.
HF1411.M92     338.91     *LC* 60-7828

**Patterson, Gardner.**      • **4.4153**
Discrimination in international trade: the policy issues, 1945–1965. Princeton, N.J., Princeton University Press, 1966. xiv, 414 p.; 21 cm. 1. Commercial policy I. T.
HF1411 P336     *LC* 66-14314

**Pisar, Samuel.**      • **4.4154**
Coexistence and commerce: guidelines for transactions between East and West. — [1st ed.]. — New York: McGraw-Hill, [1970] xv, 558 p.; 23 cm. 1. East-West trade (1945- ) 2. Communist countries — Commercial policy. 3. Commercial law — Communist countries. 4. Foreign trade regulation — Communist countries. I. T.
HF1411.P54     382/.09171/3/01717     *LC* 79-112842

**Policy alternatives for a new international economic order: an**      **4.4155**
**economic analysis / edited by William R. Cline.**
New York: Published for the Overseas Development Council [by] Praeger Publishers, 1979. xiv, 392 p.; 24 cm. 1. International economic relations — Addresses, essays, lectures. 2. Commodity control — Addresses, essays, lectures. 3. Food supply — Addresses, essays, lectures. 4. Developing countries — Commerce — Addresses, essays, lectures. I. Cline, William R. II. Overseas Development Council.
HF1411.P583     382.1     *LC* 79-87553     *ISBN* 0030494664

**Scammell, W. M.**      **4.4156**
The international economy since 1945 / W. M. Scammell. — New York: St. Martin's Press, 1980. x, 226 p.; 25 cm. 1. International economic relations 2. Economic history — 1945- I. T.
HF1411.S292     337/.09/04     *LC* 79-27416     *ISBN* 0312421915

**Social and cultural issues of the new international economic**      **4.4157**
**order / edited by Jorge Lozoya, Haydee Birgin.**
New York: Published for UNITAR and the Center for Economic and Social Studies of the Third World (CEESTEM) [by] Pergamon Press, c1981. xvii, 212 p.; 24 cm. — (Pergamon policy studies on the new international economic order.) 'A volume in the New international economic order (NIEO) library.' 1. International economic relations — Addresses, essays, lectures. 2. International economic relations — Social aspects — Addresses, essays, lectures. I. Lozoya, Jorge Alberto. II. Birgin, Haydee. III. United Nations Institute for Training and Research. IV. Centro de Estudios Económicos y Sociales del Tercer Mundo. V. Series.
HF1411.S55 1981     337/.09/048 19     *LC* 81-2028     *ISBN* 0080251234

**Tinbergen, Jan, 1903-.**      • **4.4158**
International economic integration. 2d rev. ed. Amsterdam, Elsevier, 1965. xix, 142 p. ill., map. 1. International economic integration I. T.
HF1411 T47 1965     *LC* 64-15301

**Viner, Jacob, 1892-1970.**      • **4.4159**
International economics: studies. — Glencoe, Ill.: Free Press, [1951] 381 p.; 25 cm. 1. Commercial policy 2. Investments, Foreign 3. United States — Commercial policy I. T.
HF1411.V5     330.4     *LC* 52-6313/L

**Wilczynski, J. (Jozef), 1922-.**      • **4.4160**
The economics and politics of East–West trade. New York: Praeger, [1969] 416 p.; 23 cm. 1. East-West trade (1945- ) I. T.
HF1411.W55     382/.09171/301717     *LC* 72-93449

**World politics and international economics / C. Fred Bergsten**      **4.4161**
**and Lawrence B. Krause, editors; contributions by C. Fred**
**Bergsten ... [et al.].**
Washington: Brookings Institution, [1975] xi, 359 p.; 24 cm. Originally published as the winter 1975 special issue (v. 29, no. 1) of International organization. Includes index. 1. International economic relations — Addresses, essays, lectures. 2. International finance — Addresses, essays, lectures. 3. World politics — 1965-1975 — Addresses, essays, lectures. I. Bergsten, C. Fred, 1941- II. Krause, Lawrence B.
HF1411.W66     338.91     *LC* 75-15684     *ISBN* 0815709161

## HF1412-1413 Developing Countries

Rich country interests and Third World development / edited by **4.4162**
Robert Cassen ... [et al.].
New York: St. Martins Press, 1982. 369 p.; 22 cm. 1. International economic
relations 2. Developing countries — Economic conditions I. Cassen, Robert.
HF1412.R53 1982          337/.09/048 19          *LC* 82-42561          *ISBN*
0312681011

Balassa, Bela A.                                                    **4.4163**
The newly industrializing countries in the world economy / Bela Balassa. —
New York: Pergamon Press, c1981. xxiii, 461 p.; 24 cm. 1. Developing
countries — Commerce — Addresses, essays, lectures. I. T.
HF1413.B345 1981          330.9172/4 19          *LC* 80-20787          *ISBN*
0080263364

Maizels, Alfred.                                                    • **4.4164**
Exports and economic growth of developing countries: a theoretical and
empirical study of the relationships between exports and economic growth, with
illustrative projections for 1975 for the main overseas sterling countries, by
Alfred Maizels assisted by L. F. Campbell–Boross and P. B. W. Rayment.
London, Cambridge U.P., 1968. xx, 443 p. illus. 24 cm. (Economic and social
studies, 25) 1. Developing countries — Commerce. 2. Sterling area
I. Campbell-Boross, Laszlo Ferenc. II. Rayment, Paul Bernard Walter.
III. T.
HF1413.M3          382/.6/091724          *LC* 68-26987          *ISBN* 0521069599

The New Communist Third World: an essay in political          **4.4165**
economy / edited by Peter Wiles.
New York: St. Martin's Press, 1982. 392 p.; 23 cm. Includes index.
1. Developing countries — Commerce — Addresses, essays, lectures.
2. Communist countries — Commerce — Addresses, essays, lectures. I. Wiles,
Peter John de la Fosse.
HF1413.N495 1982          337/.09172/4 19          *LC* 81-13620          *ISBN*
0312566077

## HF1416-1430 International Economic Relations. Foreign Commercial Policy

Knorr, Klaus Eugen, 1911-.                                         **4.4166**
Power and wealth; the political economy of international power [by] Klaus
Knorr. — New York: Basic Books, [1973] x, 210 p.; 22 cm. — (The Political
economy of international relations series) 1. International economic relations
2. International relations 3. Power (Social sciences) I. T.
HF1416.K56          327/.11          *LC* 72-89187          *ISBN* 0465061400

Behrman, Jack N.                                                    **4.4167**
Industrial policies: international restructuring and transnationals / Jack N.
Behrman. — Lexington, Mass.: Lexington Books, c1984. xiv, 254 p.; 24 cm.
1. International economic integration 2. International business enterprises
3. Industry and state I. T.
HF1418.5.B44 1984          337.1 19          *LC* 83-49533          *ISBN* 0669082759

Newbery, David M. G.                                               **4.4168**
The theory of commodity price stabilization: a study in the economics of risk /
David M.G. Newbery and Joseph E. Stiglitz. — Oxford: Clarendon Press;
Oxford; New York: Oxford University Press, 1981. xv, 462 p.; ill.; 25 cm.
Includes index. 1. Commodity control 2. Risk I. Stiglitz, Joseph E. II. T.
III. Title: Commodity price stabilization.
HF1428.N485          338.5/2 19          *LC* 81-201605          *ISBN* 0198284179

Baldwin, Robert E.                                                 • **4.4169**
Nontariff distortions of international trade [by] Robert E. Baldwin. —
Washington: Brookings Institution, [1970] viii, 210 p.; 24 cm. 1. Nontariff
trade barriers I. T.
HF1430.B34          382/.3          *LC* 78-109436          *ISBN* 081570786X

Griffiths, Brian.                                                  **4.4170**
Invisible barriers to invisible trade / by Brian Griffiths. — New York: Holmes
& Meier, 1976. xvii, 178 p.; 23 cm. Includes index. 1. Nontariff trade barriers
2. Invisible items of trade I. T.
HF1430.G74 1975          382.1

## HF1451-1650 By Country

## HF1451-1478 United States

Bauer, Raymond Augustine, 1916-.                                  • **4.4171**
American business and public policy: the politics of foreign trade / by Raymond
A. Bauer, Ithiel de Sola Pool, & Lewis Anthony Dexter; foreword by Max F.
Millikan. — New York: Atherton Press, 1963. xxvii, 499 p.: ill.; 24 cm. — (The
Atherton Press political science series) Includes bibliography. 1. U.S. —
Commercial policy. 2. Pressure groups — Case studies. 3. Lobbying — Case
studies. 4. Industry and state — U.S. I. T.
HF1455.B33          337.9173          *LC* 63-8171

Gilpin, Robert.                                                    **4.4172**
U.S. power and the multinational corporation: the political economy of foreign
direct investment / Robert Gilpin. — New York: Basic Books, [1975] xii,
291 p.; ill.; 22 cm. — (The Political economy of international relations series)
1. International business enterprises 2. International economic relations
3. United States — Foreign economic relations 4. United States — Foreign
relations I. T.
HF1455.G5          382.1/0973          *LC* 75-7265          *ISBN* 0465089518

Kaufman, Burton Ira.                                               **4.4173**
Trade and aid: Eisenhower's foreign economic policy, 1953–1961 / Burton I.
Kaufman. — Baltimore: Johns Hopkins University Press, c1982. xiv, 279 p.; 24
cm. — (Johns Hopkins University studies in historical and political science.
100th ser., 1) Includes index. 1. Eisenhower, Dwight D. (Dwight David),
1890-1969. 2. United States — Foreign economic relations I. T. II. Series.
HF1455.K282 1982          337.73 19          *LC* 81-15594          *ISBN* 0801826233

Pastor, Robert A.                                                  **4.4174**
Congress and the politics of U.S. foreign economic policy, 1929–1976 / Robert
A. Pastor. — Berkeley: University of California Press, c1980. xiii, 366 p.; 24 cm.
Based on the author's thesis, Harvard. Includes index. 1. United States.
Congress. 2. United States — Foreign economic relations I. T.
HF1455.P28          337.73          *LC* 79-63552          *ISBN* 0520039041

Krause, Lawrence B.                                                **4.4175**
U.S. economic policy toward the Association of Southeast Asian Nations:
meeting the Japanese challenge / Lawrence B. Krause. — Washington, D.C.:
Brookings Institution, c1982. x, 98 p.; 24 cm. 1. ASEAN. 2. Asia,
Southeastern — Foreign economic relations — United States. 3. Japan —
Foreign economic relations — Asia, Southeastern. 4. Asia, Southeastern —
Foreign economic relations — Japan. 5. United States — Foreign economic
relations — Asia, Southeastern. I. T.
HF1456.5.A7 K72 1982          337.73059 19          *LC* 82-9656          *ISBN*
0815750269

Abegglen, James C.                                                 **4.4176**
The strategy of Japanese business / James C. Abegglen. — Cambridge, Mass.:
Ballinger Pub. Co., c1984. xxvii, 227 p.: ill.; 24 cm. 'An Abt Books/Ballinger
publication'–B. [ii]. 1. Industrial management — Japan 2. Research,
Industrial — Japan. 3. United States — Foreign economic relations — Japan.
4. Japan — Foreign economic relations — United States. I. T.
HF1456.5.J3 A54 1984          337.52073 19          *LC* 84-12423          *ISBN*
0884109267

Coping with U.S.–Japanese economic conflicts / edited by I.M.          **4.4177**
Destler, Hideo Sato.
Lexington, Mass.: Lexington Books, c1982. viii, 293 p.; 24 cm. 1. United States
— Foreign economic relations — Japan — Case studies — Addresses, essays,
lectures. 2. Japan — Foreign economic relations — United States — Case
studies — Addresses, essays, lectures. 3. United States — Commerce — Japan
— Case studies — Addresses, essays, lectures. 4. Japan — Commerce —
United States — Case studies — Addresses, essays, lectures. I. Destler, I. M.
II. Sato, Hideo, 1942-
HF1456.5.J3 C66          382/.0973/052 19          *LC* 81-47897          *ISBN*
0669051446

## HF1479-1529 Canada. Latin America

Stovel, John A.                                                    • **4.4178**
Canada in the world economy / by John A. Stovel. — Cambridge: Harvard
University Press, 1959. xiii, 364 p.: diagrs.; 22 cm. — (Harvard economic
studies. v.108) 'Revised extended, and reorganized version of a doctoral
dissertation ... Harvard University.' 1. Canada — Foreign economic relations.
I. T. II. Series.
HF1479.S7

Latin America and world economy: a changing international **4.4179**
order / edited by Joseph Grunwald.
Beverly Hills, Calif.: Sage Publications, c1978. 323 p.; 23 cm. — (Latin
American international affairs series; v. 2) (Sage library of social research)
1. Latin America — Foreign economic relations — Addresses, essays, lectures.
2. Latin America — Economic integration — Addresses, essays, lectures.
I. Grunwald, Joseph, 1920- II. Series.
HF1480.5.L383      338.91/8      *LC* 77-17031      *ISBN* 0803908644

**Albert, Bill.** **4.4180**
South America and the world economy from Independence to 1930 / prepared
for the Economic History Society by Bill Albert. — London: Macmillan, 1983.
96 p.: maps; 22 cm. (Studies in economic and social history.) Includes index.
1. Investments, Foreign — Latin America. 2. Investments, Foreign — South
America. 3. Latin America — Foreign economic relations. 4. South America
— Foreign economic relations. I. Economic History Society. II. T. III. Series.
HF1480.52.A5x 1983      337.8 19      *LC* 83-229962      *ISBN* 0333342232

**Smith, Robert Freeman, 1930-.** **4.4181**
The United States and revolutionary nationalism in Mexico, 1916–1932. —
Chicago: University of Chicago Press, [1972] xv, 288 p.; 23 cm. 1. Nationalism
— Mexico. 2. Mexico — Foreign economic relations — United States.
3. United States — Foreign economic relations — Mexico. 4. Mexico —
Foreign relations — United States. 5. United States — Foreign relations —
Mexico. I. T.
HF1482.5.U5 S6      382/.09/72073      *LC* 73-182872      *ISBN*
0226765067

## HF1531–1583 Europe

**Holzman, Franklyn D.** **4.4182**
International trade under communism: politics and economics / Franklyn D.
Holzman. New York: Basic Books, c1976. xvi, 239 p.; 22 cm. 1. East-West
trade (1945- ) 2. Communist countries — Commercial policy. 3. Communist
countries — Foreign economic relations. I. T.
HF1531.H65      382/.09171/7      *LC* 76-7489      *ISBN* 0465033814

**Meade, J. E. (James Edward), 1907-.** • **4.4183**
Case studies in European economic union; the mechanics of integration [by] J.
E. Meade, H. H. Liesner [and] S. J. Wells. Edited, with an introd. by J. E.
Meade. — London, New York, Oxford University Press, 1962. vii, 424 p. fold.
maps, diagrs., tables. 23 cm. 'Issued under the auspices of the Royal Instutute of
International Affairs.' Bibliography: p. [417]-419. 1. Europe — Economic
integration 2. International economic integration I. T.
HF1531.M4      338.914      *LC* 62-6742

**Hine, R. C.** **4.4184**
The political economy of European trade: an introduction to the trade policies
of the EEC / R.C. Hine. — Brighton, Sussex: Wheatsheaf Books; New York: St.
Martin's Press, 1985. xviii, 294 p.: ill.; 23 cm. Includes indexes. 1. European
Economic Community countries — Commercial policy. 2. European
Economic Community countries — Foreign economic relations. I. T.
HF1532.92.H56 1985      382/.3/094 19      *LC* 84-16035      *ISBN*
0710801246

**Barratt Brown, Michael.** • **4.4185**
After imperialism / Michael Barratt–Brown. — London: Heinemann, 1963.
xvii, 521 p.; 22 cm. 1. Commonwealth of Nations — Economic policy.
2. Underdeveloped areas. 3. Great Britain — Foreign economic relations
4. Great Britain — Colonies — Economic policy I. T.
HF1533.B74      *LC* 64-56337

**Graham, Gerald Sandford, 1903-.** • **4.4186**
British policy and Canada, 1774–1791; a study in 18th century trade policy.
London, New York [etc.]: Longmans, Green, 1930. xi, 161 p.: maps; 23 cm.
(Imperial studies; no. 4) 1. Great Britain — Commercial policy. 2. Great
Britain — Colonies — Commerce 3. Canada — Commerce I. T. II. Series.
HF1533.G7      382.30942      *LC* 31-1459

**Graham, Gerald Sandford, 1903-.** • **4.4187**
Sea power and British North America, 1783–1820; a study in British colonial
policy, by Gerald S. Graham ... — Cambridge, Harvard University press;
London, H. Milford, Oxford University Press, 1941. xii p., 2 l., [3]-302 p. incl.
tables, diagrs., maps (part double) 23 cm. — (Half-title: Harvard historical
studies ... vol. XLVI) Bibliographical foot-notes. 'Bibliographical note': p.
[291]-294. 1. Gt. Brit. — Commercial policy. 2. Gt. Brit. — Comm.
3. Canada — Comm. 4. U.S. — Comm. I. T.
HF1533.G72      325.342097      *LC* A 41-3159

**Platt, D. C. M. (Desmond Christopher Martin), 1934-.** • **4.4188**
Finance, trade, and politics in British foreign policy 1815–1914 [by] D. C. M.
Platt. Oxford, London, Clarendon P., 1968. xl, 454 p. 6 maps. 23 cm. 1. Great
Britain — Foreign economic relations — History. 2. Great Britain — Foreign

relations — 19th century 3. Great Britain — Foreign relations — 1901-1910
I. T.
HF1533.P58      327.42      *LC* 68-93648      *ISBN* 0198213778

**West Germany, a European and global power / edited by** **4.4189**
**Wilfrid L. Kohl, Giorgio Basevi.**
Lexington, Mass.: Lexington Books, c1980. xv, 224 p.: graphs; 24 cm. Based on
papers presented at a conference held at the Bologna Center of Johns Hopkins
University, Oct. 5-7, 1978. 1. European Economic Community — Germany,
West — Congresses. 2. Germany (West) — Foreign economic relations —
Congresses. 3. Germany (West) — Foreign relations — Congresses. I. Kohl,
Wilfrid L. II. Basevi, Giorgio, 1938-
HF1545.W45      337.43      *LC* 79-2391

**Valkenier, Elizabeth Kridl.** **4.4190**
The Soviet Union and the Third World: an economic bind / Elizabeth Kridl
Valkenier. — New York, N.Y.: Praeger, 1983. xiv, 188 p.; 24 cm. (Studies of the
Harriman Institute.) Includes indexes. 1. International economic relations
2. Economic assistance, Russian — Developing countries. 3. Soviet Union —
Foreign economic relations — Developing countries. 4. Developing countries
— Foreign economic relations — Soviet Union. I. T. II. Series.
HF1557.V34 1983      337.470172/4 19      *LC* 83-6304      *ISBN*
0030621496

## HF1585–1650 Asia

**Dutt, Srikant, 1954-1981.** **4.4191**
India and the Third World: altruism or hegemony / Dutt Srikant. — London:
Zed Books, 1984. xiii, 184 p.; 23 cm. (Third World studies.) 1. India — Foreign
economic relations — Developing countries. 2. Developing countries —
Foreign economic relations — India. I. T. II. Series.
HF1590.15.D44 D87 1984      337.540172/4 19      *LC* 84-116744      *ISBN*
0862320909

**Islam, Nurul.** **4.4192**
Foreign trade and economic controls in development: the case of United
Pakistan / Nurul Islam. — New Haven [Conn.]: Yale University Press, c1981.
xv, 271 p.; 25 cm. — (A Publication of the Economic Growth Center, Yale
University) 1. Pakistan — Commercial policy — History. 2. Pakistan —
Economic policy. 3. Pakistan — Economic conditions. I. T.
HF1590.5.I84      382/.095491 19      *LC* 81-1122      *ISBN* 0300025351

**Higashi, Chikara.** **4.4193**
Japanese trade policy formulation / Chikara Higashi; forewords by Yasuhiro
Nakasone and Michio Watanabe. — New York, N.Y.: Praeger, 1983. xii,
179 p.; 25 cm. Includes index. 1. Japan — Commercial policy. I. T.
HF1601.H49 1983      382/.3/0952 19      *LC* 83-13878      *ISBN*
0030635098

**Tsurumi, Yoshi.** **4.4194**
Sogoshosha: engines of export–based growth / Yoshi Tsurumi, with the
contribution of Rebecca R. Tsurumi. — Montreal: Institute for Research on
Public Policy; [Brookfield, Vt.: distributed by Renouf/USA], 1980. xvii, 94 p.;
23 cm. Distributor from label mounted on p. 2 of cover. 1. Foreign trade
promotion — Japan. 2. Conglomerate corporations — Japan 3. Foreign trade
promotion 4. Conglomerate corporations I. Tsurumi, Rebecca R. joint author.
II. T.
HF1601.T78      338.8/8852 19      *LC* 80-670195      *ISBN* 0920380581

## HF1701–2701 Tariff Policy

**Bastable, Charles Francis, 1855-.** • **4.4195**
The commerce of nations / by C. F. Bastable; revised by T. E. Gregory. — 10th
ed. London: Methuen & co. ltd., [1927] viii p., 1 l., 212 p.; 20 cm. 1. Commerce
2. Free trade and protection 3. Tariff — History. 4. Commercial policy
I. Gregory, Theodor Emanuel Gugenheim II. T.
HF1711.B3 1927      *LC* 23-11802

**Johnson, Harry G. (Harry Gordon), 1923-1977.** **4.4196**
Aspects of the theory of tariffs, by Harry G. Johnson. Cambridge, Mass.,
Harvard University Press, 1972 [c1971] xii, 451 p. illus. 23 cm. 1. Tariff I. T.
HF1713.J6 1972      382.7/01      *LC* 73-173414      *ISBN* 0674049918

**Johnson, Harry G. (Harry Gordon), 1923-1977. comp.** • **4.4197**
New trade strategy for the world economy; edited by Harry G. Johnson.
London, Allen & Unwin, 1969. [11], 344 p. 23 cm. 1. Free trade and protection
— Free trade 2. North Atlantic Region — Economic integration. I. T.
HF1713.J62      382/.71/091821      *LC* 78-397277      *ISBN* 0043301436

**Johnson, Harry G. (Harry Gordon), 1923-1977.**　　　　**4.4198**
Trade strategy for rich and poor nations / edited by Harry G. Johnson. —
[Toronto]: University of Toronto, 1971. [7], 232 p.; 23 cm. 1. Free trade and
protection — Free trade 2. Commercial policy 3. Investments, American
4. Developing countries — Commercial policy. I. T.
HF1713.J64　　　382/.71/08　　　*LC* 78-591426　　　*ISBN* 0043500269

**Yeager, Leland B.**　　　　**4.4199**
Foreign trade and U.S. policy: the case for free international trade / Leland B.
Yeager, David G. Tuerck. — New York: Praeger, 1976. x, 295 p.; 24 cm.
(Praeger special studies in international business, finance, and trade) 1. Free
trade and protection — Free trade 2. Free trade and protection 3. United
States — Commercial policy I. Tuerck, David G. joint author. II. T.
HF1713.Y38　　　382.7/1/0973　　　*LC* 75-19832　　　*ISBN* 0275562700

**Murray, Tracy.**　　　　**4.4200**
Trade preferences for developing countries / Tracy Murray. — New York:
Wiley, 1977. xiv, 172 p.; 24 cm. (Problems of economic integration) 'A Halsted
Press book.' Includes index. 1. Tariff — Developing countries 2. Tariff
preferences — Developing countries I. T.
HF1721.M87 1977　　　382.7　　　*LC* 76-58546　　　*ISBN* 0470990805

## HF1750–2580 BY COUNTRY

**Taussig, Frank William, 1859-1940.**　　　　**• 4.4201**
The tariff history of the United States. Including a consideration of the tariff of
1930. New York: A. M. Kelley, 1967. xii, 536 p.; 22 cm. (Reprints of economic
classics.) Reprint of the 8th ed., 1931. 1. Tariff — United States — History.
I. T.
HF1753.T3 1967　　　*LC* 67-27415

**George, Henry, 1839-1897.**　　　　**• 4.4202**
Protection or free trade: an examination of the tariff question, with especial
regard to the interests of labor / by Henry George. — New York: Robert
Schalkenbach Foundation, [1940] xii, 335 p.; 19cm. 1. Free trade and
protection — Free trade 2. Tariff — United States I. T.
HF1755.G355 1940　　　382.7/0973

**Schattschneider, Elmer Eric, 1892-1971.**　　　　**• 4.4203**
Politics, pressures and the tariff; a study of free private enterprise in pressure
politics, as shown in the 1929–1930 revision of the tariff. [Unaltered and
unabridged ed.] Hamden, Conn., Archon Books, 1963. xi, 301 p. diagrs. 23 cm.
Issued also as thesis—Columbia University. 1. Tariff — United States
2. Lobbying 3. United States — Politics and government — 1923-1929 I. T.
HF1756S38 1963　　　*LC* 63-19636

**Taussig, F. W. (Frank William), 1859-1940.**　　　　**• 4.4204**
Some aspects of the tariff question: an examination of the development of
American industries under protection. — 3d enl. ed. continued to 1930 with the
coöperation of H. D. White. New York: AMS Press, [1971] xiii, 499 p.; 23 cm.
Reprint of the 1931 ed. 1. Tariff — United States 2. Free trade and protection
I. T.
HF1756.T34 1971　　　382/.7　　　*LC* 72-137297　　　*ISBN* 0404063489

**Dales, John Harkness, 1920-.**　　　　**• 4.4205**
The protective tariff in Canada's development; eight essays on trade and tariffs
when factors move with special reference to Canadian protectionism 1870–1955
[by] J. H. Dales. — [Toronto] University of Toronto Press [c1966] v, 168 p. 23
cm. — (Canadian university paperbacks, 58) Bibliographical footnotes.
1. Tariff — Canada. 2. Canada — Commercial policy. 3. Free trade and
protection I. T.
HF1763.D3　　　382/.7/0971　　　*LC* 67-83529

**Wonnacott, Ronald J.**　　　　**• 4.4206**
Free trade between the United States and Canada, the potential economic
effects [by] Ronald J. Wonnacott and Paul Wonnacott. — Cambridge, Harvard
University Press, 1967. xx, 430 p. illus., map. 22 cm. — (Harvard economic
studies. v. 129) Bibliographical footnotes. 1. Free trade and protection — Free
trade 2. Canada — Commercial policy. 3. U.S. — Commercial policy.
I. Wonnacott, Paul. joint author. II. T. III. Series.
HF1766.W6　　　382/.09/71073　　　*LC* 67-17323

**Johnson, Harry G. (Harry Gordon), 1923-1977.**　　　　**• 4.4207**
Harmonization of national economic policies under free trade [by] Harry G.
Johnson, Paul Wonnacott [and] Hirofumi Shibata. [Toronto] Published for the
Private Planning Association of Canada by University of Toronto Press [c1968]
84 p. 23 cm. (Canada in the Atlantic economy, 3) 1. Free trade and protection
— Free trade 2. Tariff — Europe. I. Wonnacott, Paul. II. Shibata, Hirofumi,
1929- III. Private Planning Association of Canada. IV. T. V. Series.
HF2036.J6　　　382/.71　　　*LC* 68-101428

**Semmel, Bernard.**　　　　**• 4.4208**
The rise of free trade imperialism; classical political economy, the empire of free
trade and imperialism 1750–1850. — Cambridge [Eng.]: University Press, 1970.
x, 250 p.; 24 cm. 1. Free trade and protection — Free trade 2. Imperialism
3. Gt. Brit. — Commerce. I. T.
HF2046.S45　　　382/.71　　　*LC* 71-112473　　　*ISBN* 0521077257

**Meade, J. E. (James Edward), 1907-.**　　　　**• 4.4209**
The theory of customs unions. — Amsterdam: North-Holland Pub. Co., 1955.
121 p.; 20 cm. (Professor Dr. F. de Vries lectures; [1955]) 1. Convention
douantière belgo-luxembourgeoise-néerlandaise. 2. Customs unions I. T.
HF2135.M4　　　*LC* 56-5042

# HF3001–4050 Commerce, by Region or Country

## HF3001–3163 United States

**American export register.**　　　　**4.4210**
1980-. New York: Thomas International Pub. Co. v.: ill.; 29 cm. Annual. 'A
Thomas international publication.' 1. United States — Commerce —
Directories.
HF3010.A6　　　382/.6/029473　　　*LC* 80-648882

**Business organizations, agencies, and publications directory.**　　　　**4.4211**
3rd ed. (1986)-　　.— Detroit, Mich.: Gale Research Co., c1986-. v.; 29 cm.
Annual. Issued in 2 vol. 1. Trade and professional associations — United States
— Directories. 2. Business — Information services — United States —
Directories. 3. Business literature — Publishing — United States —
Directories. 4. Reference books — Business — Bibliography — Periodicals.
5. United States — Commerce — Directories. 6. United States — Industries
— Directories.
HF3010.B86　　　061/.3 19　　　*LC* 86-645427

**Barger, Harold.**　　　　**• 4.4212**
Distribution's place in the American economy since 1869. Princeton: Princeton
University Press, 1955. xviii, 222 p.: diagrs., tables; 24 cm. (National Bureau of
Economic Research. General series, no. 58) 'A study by the National Bureau of
Economic Research, New York.' 1. United States — Commerce — History
I. T. II. Series.
HF3021 B3　　　*LC* 55-10677

**Cochran, Thomas Childs, 1902-.**　　　　**• 4.4213**
Business in American life: a history, by Thomas C. Cochran. — New York:
McGraw-Hill, [1972] x, 402 p.; 24 cm. 1. United States — Commerce —
History I. T.
HF3021.C55　　　917.3/03　　　*LC* 78-38740　　　*ISBN* 0070115206

**Krooss, Herman Edward, 1912-1975.**　　　　**• 4.4214**
American business history [by] Herman E. Krooss [and] Charles Gilbert. —
Englewood Cliffs, N.J.: Prentice-Hall, [1972] x, 358 p.; 24 cm. 1. United States
— Commerce — History I. Gilbert, Charles, 1913- joint author. II. T.
HF3021.K76　　　380.1/0973　　　*LC* 71-172403　　　*ISBN* 0130240915

**Miller, William, 1912- ed.**　　　　**• 4.4215**
Men in business: essays on the historical role of the entrepreneur; with 2
additional essays on American business leaders, not included in the original
edition. — New York: Harper & Row [1962] 389 p.; 21 cm. — (Harper
torchbooks, TB1081. The Academy library) Includes bibliography.
1. Capitalists and financiers — U.S. 2. Entrepreneurship I. T.
HF3023.A2M5 1962　　　338.7　　　*LC* 62-52879

**Shepherd, James F.**　　　　**4.4216**
Shipping, maritime trade, and the economic development of colonial North
America, by James F. Shepherd and Gary M. Walton. — Cambridge [Eng.]:
University Press, 1972. ix, 255 p.: illus.; 24 cm. 1. Shipping — United States —
History 2. United States — Commerce — History 3. United States — History
— Colonial period, ca. 1600-1775 I. Walton, Gary M. joint author. II. T.
HF3025.S717　　　382/.0973　　　*LC* 76-176256　　　*ISBN* 0521084091

**Cohen, Stephen D.**　　　　**4.4217**
Uneasy partnership: competition and conflict in U.S.–Japanese trade relations /
Stephen D. Cohen. — Cambridge, Mass.: Ballinger Pub. Co., c1985. xvi, 228 p.;
24 cm. Includes index. 1. United States — Commerce — Japan. 2. Japan —
Commerce — United States. I. T.
HF3127.C64 1985　　　382/.0952/073 19　　　*LC* 84-16924　　　*ISBN*
0887300200

### HF3151–3163 LOCAL COMMERCE

**Albion, Robert Greenhalgh, 1896-.**     **4.4218**
New England and the sea, by Robert G. Albion, William A. Baker [and] Benjamin W. Labaree. Marion V. Brewington, picture editor. — [1st ed.]. — Middletown, Conn.: Published for the Marine Historical Association, Mystic Seaport, by Wesleyan University Press, [1972] xiv, 299 p.: illus.; 27 cm. — (American maritime library. v. 5) 1. Shipping — New England — History. 2. New England — Commerce — History. I. Baker, William A. joint author. II. Labaree, Benjamin Woods. joint author. III. T. IV. Series.
HF3151.A65      387/.0974      *LC* 72-3694      *ISBN* 0819540528

**Horlick, Allan Stanley, 1941-.**     **4.4219**
Country boys and merchant princes; the social control of young men in New York. Lewisburg [Pa.] Bucknell University Press [1975] 278 p. illus. 22 cm. 1. Merchants — New York (City) — History. 2. Occupational mobility — New York (City) — History. 3. New York (N.Y.) — Social conditions. I. T.
HF3163.N7 H66      301.44/42/097471      *LC* 73-2887      *ISBN* 0838713610

**Goldstein, Jonathan.**     **4.4220**
Philadelphia and the China trade, 1682–1846: commercial, cultural, and attitudinal effects / Jonathan Goldstein. — University Park: Pennsylvania State University Press, c1978. 121 p., [2] leaves of plates: ill.; 24 cm. Originally presented as the author's thesis, University of Pennsylvania. Includes index. 1. Philadelphia (Pa.) — Commerce — China — History. 2. China — Commerce — Philadelphia — History. I. T.
HF3163.P5 G64 1978      382/.09748/11051      *LC* 77-1638      *ISBN* 0271005122

### HF3211 The Americas: General

**Liss, Peggy K.**     **4.4221**
Atlantic empires: the network of trade and revolution, 1713–1826 / Peggy K. Liss. — Baltimore: Johns Hopkins University Press, c1983. xiii, 348 p.; 24 cm. — (Johns Hopkins studies in Atlantic history and culture.) 1. America — Commerce — History. 2. Europe — Commerce — History. 3. United States — History — Revolution, 1775-1783 — Influence 4. Latin America — Colonial influence. I. T. II. Series.
HF3211.L57 1983      382/.094/08 19      *LC* 82-13099      *ISBN* 0801827426

### HF3221–3490 Canada. Latin America

**McCalla, Douglas, 1942-.**     **4.4222**
The Upper Canada trade, 1834–1872: a study of the Buchanans' business / Douglas McCalla. — Toronto: University of Toronto Press, c1979. viii, 231 p.: ill.; 24 cm. Includes index. 1. Buchanan, Isaac, 1810-1883. 2. Wholesale trade — Ontario — History. 3. Ontario — Commerce — History. I. T.
HF3229.O5 M32      382/.09713      *ISBN* 0802054420

**Socolow, Susan Migden, 1941-.**     **4.4223**
The merchants of Buenos Aires, 1778–1810: family and commerce / Susan Migden Socolow. — Cambridge [Eng.]; New York: Cambridge University Press, 1979 (c1978). xv, 253 p.: ill.; 22 cm. — (Cambridge Latin American studies. 30) Includes index. 1. Merchants — Argentine Republic — Buenos Aires — History. I. T. II. Series.
HF3390.B8 S62      381/.0982/1      *LC* 77-82516      *ISBN* 0521218128

### HF3491–3760 Europe

#### HF3501–3540 Britain

**Schumpeter, Elizabeth Boody.**     • **4.4224**
English overseas trade statistics, 1697–1808 / with an introd. by T.S. Ashton and a memoir of Mrs. Schumpeter by Elizabeth W. Gilboy. — Oxford: Clarendon Press, 1960 [i.e. 1961] vii, 72 p.: tables; 26 x 36 cm. 1. Great Britain — Commerce — History. I. T.
HF3501.S35

**Andrews, Kenneth R.**     **4.4225**
Trade, plunder, and settlement: maritime enterprise and the genesis of the British Empire, 1480–1630 / Kenneth R. Andrews. –– Cambridge [Cambridgeshire]; New York: Cambridge University Press, 1985 (c1984). ix, 394 p.: maps; 24 cm. Includes index. 1. Colonial companies 2. Great Britain — Commerce — History. 3. Great Britain — Colonies — History 4. Great Britain — History — Modern period, 1485- I. T.
HF3505.A68      382/.0942 19      *LC* 84-5044      *ISBN* 0521257603

**Power, Eileen Edna, 1889-1940.**     • **4.4226**
Studies in English trade in the fifteenth century, edited by Eileen Power and M. M. Postan. — New York: Barnes & Noble, [1966] xx, 435 p.: maps.; 25 cm. 1. Great Britain — Commerce — History. I. Postan, M. M. (Michael Moïssey), 1899-1981. joint author. II. T. III. Title: English trade in the fifteenth century.
HF3505.1.P6 1966      380/.0942      *LC* 67-3939

**Supple, Barry Emanuel.**     • **4.4227**
Commercial crisis and change in England, 1600–1642: a study in the instability of a mercantile economy. Cambridge [Eng.] University Press, 1959. xii, 296 p.; 23 cm. (Cambridge studies in economic history) 1. Wool trade and industry — Great Britain. 2. Great Britain — Commerce — History. I. T. II. Series.
HF3505.4 S8      *LC* 60-16026

**Imlah, Albert Henry, 1901-.**     • **4.4228**
Economic elements in the Pax Britannica; studies in British foregin trade in the nineteenth century. — Cambridge, Harvard University Press, 1958. xiii, 224 p. diagrs., tables. 24 cm. Bibliographical footnotes. 1. Great Britain — Comm. I. T.
HF3505.8.I4      382.0942      *LC* A 58-8639 rev

**Saul, S. B.**     • **4.4229**
Studies in British overseas trade, 1870–1914 / by S.B. Saul. — [Liverpool]: Liverpool University Press, 1960. vi, 246 p.: diagrs., tables.; 24 cm. 1. Great Britain — Commerce — History. I. T. II. Title: British overseas trade, 1870-1914.
HF3506.S25 1960      *LC* 61-4326

**Schlote, Werner.**     • **4.4230**
British overseas trade from 1700 to the 1930s / translated by W.O. Henderson and W.H. Chaloner. Oxford: Blackwell, 1952. xvi, 181 p.: diagrs., tables; 23 cm. 1. Great Britain — Commerce — History. I. T.
HF3506.S33      *LC* 53-1272

**Greenberg, Michael.**     • **4.4231**
British trade and the opening of China, 1800–42 / by Michael Greenberg. — Cambridge [Eng.]: University Press, 1951. xii, 238 p.; 22 cm. — (Cambridge studies in economic history) 1. Opium trade — China. 2. Great Britain — Commerce — China. 3. China — Commerce — Great Britain. 4. China — History — War of 1840-1942. I. T.
HF3508.C5 G73 1951a

**Thrupp, Sylvia Lettice, 1903-.**     • **4.4232**
The merchant class of medieval London, 1300–1500 / by Sylvia L. Thrupp. — Chicago: University of Chicago P., c1948. xix, 401 p.; 24 cm. 1. Merchants, British. 2. London (England) — Social life and customs 3. London (England) — Commerce. I. T.
HF3510L8 T4      323.32      *LC* 48-3697

### HF3541–3760 Other European Countries

**Erhard, Ludwig.**     • **4.4233**
Germany's comeback in the world market / by Ludwig Erhard with the assistance of Dr. von Maltzan; edited by Herbert Gross; translated by W. H. Johnston. — London: Allen & Unwin [1954] 276 p.: ill.; 23 cm. 1. Germany (West) — Commerce. I. T.
HF3566.E674      382      *LC* 55-3185

**Kaiser, David E., 1947-.**     **4.4234**
Economic diplomacy and the origins of the Second World War: Germany, Britain, France, and Eastern Europe, 1930–1939 / David E. Kaiser. — Princeton, N.J.: Princeton University Press, c1980. xvi, 346 p.; 25 cm. Includes index. 1. Economic history — 1918-1945 2. Germany — Commerce — Europe, Eastern. 3. Europe, Eastern — Commerce — Germany. 4. Great Britain — Commerce — Europe, Eastern. 5. Europe, Eastern — Commerce — Great Britain. 6. France — Commerce — Europe, Eastern. 7. Europe, Eastern — Commerce — France. I. T.
HF3568.E35 K34      382/.094      *LC* 80-7536      *ISBN* 069105312X

**Holzman, Franklyn D.**     **4.4235**
Foreign trade under central planning [by] Franklyn D. Holzman. Cambridge, Harvard University Press, 1974. xiii, 436 p. illus. 25 cm. (Russian Research Center studies, 73) A collection of essays written over the past decade. 1. Central planning — Soviet Union. 2. Soviet Union — Commerce — Addresses, essays, lectures. 3. Soviet Union — Commercial policy — Addresses, essays, lectures. 4. Communist countries — Commerce — Addresses, essays, lectures. I. T.
HF3626.H6      382/.0947      *LC* 73-83966      *ISBN* 0674308859

**Fisher, John Robert.**     **4.4236**
Commercial relations between Spain and Spanish America in the era of free trade, 1778–1796 / John Fisher. — Liverpool, U.K.: Centre for Latin-American Studies, University of Liverpool, 1985. 158 p.: ill.; 21 cm. (Monograph series / Centre for Latin American Studies, University of

Liverpool; no. 13) 1. Spain — Commerce — Latin America — History — 18th century. 2. Latin America — Commerce — Spain — History — 18th century. 3. Spain — Commercial policy — History — 18th century. I. T.
HF3688.L3 F57 1985    382/.0946/08 19    *LC* 86-156898    *ISBN* 0902806122

# HF3761–4040.7 Asia. Africa

**Islam and the trade of Asia; a colloquium, edited by D. S.**    **4.4237**
**Richards.**
Oxford [Eng.] B. Cassirer [Philadelphia] University of Pennsylvania Press [1970] vi, 266 p. illus. (part col.) 25 cm. (Papers on Islamic history. 2) English or French. Held by the Near Eastern History Group at Oxford, June 26-30, 1967. 1. Middle East — Commerce — Asia. 2. Asia — Commerce — Near East. 3. Islamic Empire — Commerce — Asia. 4. Asia — Commerce — Islamic Empire. I. Richards, Donald Sidney, ed. II. Near Eastern History Group, Oxford. III. Series.
HF3760.8.Z7A8    382/.09176/7105    *LC* 70-120112    *ISBN* 0812276191

**Fairbank, John King, 1907-.**    • **4.4238**
Trade and diplomacy on the China coast; the opening of the treaty ports, 1842–1854. Cambridge, Harvard University Press, 1953. 2 v. port., maps. (Harvard historical studies. v. 62-63) 1. Harbors — China 2. Customs administration — China 3. China — Commerce — History 4. China — Foreign relations I. T. II. Series.
HF3776 F3    *LC* 52-12260

**Bhagwati, Jagdish N., 1934-.**    **4.4239**
India / by Jagdish N. Bhagwati, T. N. Srinivasan. — New York: National Bureau of Economic Research: distributed by Columbia University Press, 1975. xxiv, 261 p.: ill.; 24 cm. (Foreign trade regimes and economic development; v. 6) 1. Foreign exchange problem — India. 2. India — Commerce. 3. India — Commercial policy. 4. India — Economic conditions — 1947- I. Srinivasan, T. N., 1933- joint author. II. T. III. Series.
HF3786.5.B3x    330.9 s 330.9/54/04    *LC* 74-82374    *ISBN* 0870145061

**Wolf, Martin, 1946-.**    **4.4240**
India's exports / Martin Wolf. — New York: Published for the World Bank [by] Oxford University Press, 1983 (c1982). xiv, 203 p.: ill.; 24 cm. Includes index. 1. India — Commerce. 2. India — Commercial policy. I. T.
HF3786.5.W64 1982    382/.6/0954 19    *LC* 82-6309    *ISBN* 0195202112

**Hall, Kenneth R.**    **4.4241**
Maritime trade and state development in early Southeast Asia / Kenneth R. Hall. — Honolulu: University of Hawaii Press, c1985. xv, 368 p.: ill., maps; 24 cm. Includes index. 1. Asia, Southeastern — Commerce — History. 2. Asia, Southeastern — History I. T.
HF3790.8.H35 1985    382/.0959 19    *LC* 84-22777    *ISBN* 0824809599

**Foreign trade of Japan / compiled by Ministry of International**    • **4.4242**
**Trade and Industry.**
194—1971. — Tokyo: Japan External Trade Organization, 194—1971. v.: ill.; 28 cm. Annual. Description based on: report for 1965. 1. Foreign trade promotion — Japan — Statistics. 2. Japan — Commerce — Statistics. 3. Japan — Economic conditions — 1945- — Statistics. I. Japan. Tsūshō Sangyōshō. II. Nihon Bōeki Shinkōkai.
HF 3821.5 F72    382/.0952

**Rowe, William T.**    **4.4243**
Hankow: commerce and society in a Chinese city, 1796–1889 / William T. Rowe. — Stanford, Calif.: Stanford University Press, 1984. viii, 436 p.: ill.; 24 cm. Includes index. 1. Guilds — China — Han-k'ou — History — 19th century. 2. Han-k'ou (China) — Commerce — History — 19th century. 3. Han-k'ou (China) — Social conditions. I. T.
HF3840.H36 R68 1984    380.1/0951/212 19    *LC* 82-61784    *ISBN* 0804712042

**Gray, Richard, 1929-.**    **4.4244**
Pre–Colonial African Trade: essays on trade in Central and Eastern Africa before 1900; edited by Richard Gray and David Birmingham. — London, New York, Oxford U.P., 1970. x, 308 p. maps. 23 cm. 1. Africa — Commerce I. Birmingham, David. joint author. II. T.
HF3876.G68    380.1/0967    *LC* 77-505054    *ISBN* 19215639X 50/-

**Alpers, Edward A.**    **4.4245**
Ivory and slaves: changing pattern of international trade in East Central Africa to the later nineteenth century / Edward A. Alpers. — Berkeley: University of California Press, 1975. xviii, 296 p.: ill.; 23 cm. Half title and title on spine: Ivory & slaves in East Central Africa. Includes index. 1. Ivory 2. Slave-trade

— Africa, Eastern — History. 3. Africa, Eastern — Commerce — History. I. T. II. Title: Ivory & slaves in East Central Africa.
HF3899.E3 A46 1975    382/.0967    *LC* 73-93046    *ISBN* 0520026896

**Harms, Robert W., 1946-.**    **4.4246**
River of wealth, river of sorrow: the central Zaire basin in the era of the slave and ivory trade, 1500–1891 / Robert W. Harms. — New Haven: Yale University Press, c1981. xv, 277 p.: ill., maps; 22 cm. Includes index. 1. Investments — Congo River watershed — History. 2. Congo River watershed — Commerce — History. 3. Congo River watershed — Social conditions. I. T.
HF3914.H37    380.1/09675/1 19    *LC* 81-1702    *ISBN* 0300026161

**International business in the Pacific Basin / edited by R. Hal**    **4.4247**
**Mason.**
Lexington, Mass.: Lexington Books, c1978. xiv, 213 p.; 23 cm. Based on a research symposium held at UCLA. 1. International business enterprises — Congresses. 2. Pacific Area — Commerce — Congresses. I. Mason, R. Hal (Robert Hal), 1929-
HF4030.7.A25    382/.099    *LC* 78-2373    *ISBN* 066902189X

# HF5000–6191 Business

**The ... Dow Jones–Irwin business and investment almanac.**    **4.4248**
1982-     . — Homewood, Ill.: Dow Jones-Irwin, c1982-. v.: ill.; 24 cm. Annual. 1. Business — Periodicals 2. Investments — United States — Periodicals. 3. Corporations — United States — Finance — Periodicals. 4. United States — Economic conditions — 1971- — Periodicals. I. Levine, Sumner N. II. Dow Jones-Irwin.
HF5003.D68a    330.9/005    *LC* 82-643830

**Aitken, Hugh G. J.**    • **4.4249**
Explorations in enterprise / edited by Hugh G.J. Aitken. — Cambridge: Harvard University Press, 1965. x, 420 p. 1. Entrepreneurship — Addresses, essays, lectures 2. Business — Addresses, essays, lectures I. T.
HF5011 A5    *LC* 65-12782

**Bursk, Edward Collins, 1907- ed.**    • **4.4250**
The world of business; a selected library of the literature of business from the accounting code of Hammurabi to the 20th century 'Administrator's prayer.' Edited with commentaries and notes by three members of the faculty of the Harvard Business School: Edward C. Bursk, Donald T. Clark [and] Ralph W. Hidy. — New York: Simon and Schuster, 1962. 4 v. (xii, 2655 p.): illus., ports., facsims.; 23 cm. 1. Business — Addresses, essays, lectures. I. T.
HF5011.B75    650.82    *LC* 62-14278

**Million dollar directory.**    **4.4251**
1979-. Parsippany, N.J. [etc.] Dun's Marketing Services. v. 29 cm. Annual. Annual index has title: Master index. Vols. for 1979- issued in 2 vols.: v. 2 called The Middle market; vols for < 1982-> issued in 3 vols.; vols. for < 1985-> issued in 5 v.: v. [1-4] called Series, v. [5] called Top 50,000 companies. I. Dun and Bradstreet, inc. Marketing Services Division. II. Dun's Marketing Services. III. Middle market.
HF5035.D8    *LC* sc 80-1582

**Beard, Miriam, 1901-.**    • **4.4252**
A history of business / by Miriam Beard. — [Ann Arbor] University of Michigan Press, 1962-1963. 2 v. 21 cm. — (Ann Arbor paperbacks, AA 76) 1. Business 2. Commerce — History 3. Industry — History I. T.
HF5341.B4 1962    650.9    *LC* 62-4735 rev

**Gras, Norman Scott Brien, 1884-1956.**    • **4.4253**
Business and capitalism; an introduction to business history [by] N.S.B. Gras ... New York, F.S. Crofts, 1939. xxii, 408 p. front., ill., plates, ports., diagrs. 1. Business 2. Capitalism I. T.
HF5341 G7    *LC* 39-16191

**Berg, Ivar E.**    • **4.4254**
The business of America / edited by Ivar Berg. — New York: Harcourt, Brace & World, c1968. x, 437 p.; 24 cm. — (The Harbrace series in business and economics) 1. United States — Commerce I. T.
HF5343.B4    650/.0973    *ISBN* 0155056352

**Chamberlain, Neil W.**    **4.4255**
The place of business in America's future; a study in social values [by] Neil W. Chamberlain. — New York: Basic Books, [1973] vii, 338 p.; 24 cm. 1. Business enterprises — United States 2. Social values 3. Industry — Social aspects — United States. I. T.
HF5343.C58    301.5/5/0973    *LC* 72-89186    *ISBN* 0465057780

**Chandler, Alfred Dupont.**      **4.4256**
The visible hand: the managerial revolution in American business / Alfred D. Chandler, Jr. — Cambridge, Mass.: Harvard University Press, 1977. xvi, 608 p.; 24 cm. 1. Business enterprises — United States — Management — History. 2. Industrial organization — United States — History. 3. United States — Industries I. T.
HF5343.C584     658.4/00973     *LC* 77-1529     *ISBN* 0674940512

**McGuire, Joseph William.**      • **4.4257**
Business and society. — New York: McGraw-Hill, [1963] 312 p.; 21 cm. 1. Business I. T.
HF5343.M2     650     *LC* 63-13013

**The Dynamics of Victorian business: problems and perspectives**      **4.4258**
**to the 1870s / edited by Roy Church.**
London; Boston: Allen & Unwin, 1980. xii, 274 p.: graphs; 23 cm. Includes index. 1. Business enterprises — Great Britain — History — Addresses, essays, lectures. I. Church, Roy A.
HF5349.G7 D96     338.4/0941 19     *LC* 79-41410     *ISBN* 0043303005

**Veblen, Thorstein, 1857-1929.**      • **4.4259**
The theory of business enterprise / by Thorstein Veblen. — New York: C. Scribner's sons, 1935. vii, 400 p.; 21 cm. First published 1904. 'Of the chapters included in the volume, the fifth, on Loan credit, is taken, without substantial change, from volume IV of the Decennial publications of the University of Chicago, where it appears as a monograph.'—Pref. 1. Business 2. Capital I. T.
HF5351.V38 1935     658     *LC* 39-1058

**Directory of business and financial services.**      • **4.4260**
[1st]- ; 1924-. New York [etc.]: Special Libraries Association. v.; 20-26 cm. Separately paged supplements accompany some vols. 1. Business — Information services — Directories. 2. Investments — Information services — United States — Directories. 3. Investments — Information services — Canada — Directories. I. Special Libraries Association. Committee on Commercial Information Services. II. Special Libraries Association. Financial Division. III. Special Libraries Association. Business and Finance Division.
HF5353.D56     027.6/9/025     *LC* 25-4599

**Encyclopedia of business information sources: a bibliographic**      **4.4261**
**guide to approximately 22,000 citations covering more than**
**1,100 primary subjects of interest to business personnel ... /**
**James Woy, editor.**
6th ed. — Detroit, Mich.: Gale Research Co., 1986. — 878 p.; 29 cm. 1. Business — Information services — Directories. 2. Management — Information services — Directories. 3. Reference books — Business — Bibliography. 4. Reference books — Management — Bibliography. 5. Business — Bibliography 6. Management — Bibliography I. Woy, James B.
HF5353.E9 1986     *LC* 84-643366     *ISBN* 0810303647

# HF5381–5391 Vocational Guidance. Business Ethics

**Occupational outlook handbook.**      • **4.4262**
1949-     . — [Washington]: Bureau of Labor Statistics: for sale by the Supt. of Docs., U. S. Govt. Print. Off. v.: ill., maps.; 28 cm. — (Bulletin / U.S. Dept. of Labor, Bureau of Labor Statistics; 2075) Annual. 'Employment information on occupations for use in guidance.' Vols. for 1949-     issued in the congressional series as House documents. 1. Vocational guidance 2. United States — Occupations I. United States. Bureau of Labor Statistics. II. United States. Veterans Administration. III. Series.
HF5381.A1 O36     331.702

**Handbook of vocational psychology / edited by W. Bruce Walsh**      **4.4263**
**and Samuel H. Osipow.**
Hillsdale, N.J.: Lawrence Erlbaum Associates, 1983-. 2 v.: ill.; 24 cm. 1. Vocational guidance — Addresses, essays, lectures. 2. Occupations — Psychological aspects — Addresses, essays, lectures. 3. Personality and occupation — Addresses, essays, lectures. 4. Occupations — Handbooks, manuals, etc. 5. Vocational guidance — Handbooks, manuals, etc. 6. Psychology — Handbooks, manuals, etc. I. Walsh, W. Bruce, 1936- II. Osipow, Samuel H.
HF5381.H1335 1983     158.6 19     *LC* 83-8856     *ISBN* 0898592852

**Healy, Charles C.**      **4.4264**
Career development: counseling through the life stages / Charles C. Healy. — Boston, Mass.: Allyn and Bacon, c1982. ix, 662 p.: ill.; 25 cm. Includes indexes. 1. Vocational guidance I. T.
HF5381.H338     331.7/02 19     *LC* 81-8056     *ISBN* 0205075576

**Bolles, Richard Nelson.**      **4.4265**
What color is your parachute? / Richard Nelson Bolles. — 1971-     . Berkeley, Calif.: Ten Speed Press, 1971-. v.: ill.; 23-24 cm. Annual. 'A practical manual for job-hunters & career changers.' 1. Job hunting — Periodicals. 2. Career changes — Periodicals. 3. Vocational guidance — Periodicals. I. T.
HF5382.7.B64     650.1/4/05 19     *LC* 84-649334

**Dickhut, Harold W., 1911-.**      **4.4266**
The professional resume and job search guide / Harold W. Dickhut. — [5th ed.]. — Englewood Cliffs, N.J.: Prentice-Hall, c1981. 218 p.; 29 cm. — (A Spectrum book) First-4th ed. published under title: Professional resume/job search guide. 1. Résumés (Employment) 2. Applications for positions 3. Employment interviewing I. T.
HF5383.D47 1981     650.1/4     *LC* 80-15824     *ISBN* 0137257058

**Adams, Jane.**      **4.4267**
Women on top: success patterns and personal growth / Jane Adams. — New York: Hawthorn Books, c1979. ix, 227 p.; 24 cm. Includes index. 1. Success in business 2. Women in business — United States. I. T.
HF5386.A513 1979     650.1/02/4042     *LC* 79-84666     *ISBN* 0801587883

**Ethical theory and business / edited by Tom L. Beauchamp,**      **4.4268**
**Norman E. Bowie.**
Englewood Cliffs, N.J.: Prentice-Hall, c1979. xii, 642 p.; 24 cm. 1. Business ethics — Addresses, essays, lectures. 2. Business ethics — Case studies — Addresses, essays, lectures. 3. Industry — Social aspects — United States — Addresses, essays, lectures. 4. Industry — Social aspects — United States — Case studies — Addresses, essays, lectures. 5. Corporation law — United States I. Beauchamp, Tom L. II. Bowie, Norman E., 1942-
HF5387.E82     174/.4     *LC* 78-20875

**National Conference on Business Ethics. 1st, Bentley College,**      **4.4269**
**1977.**
Business values and social justice: compatibility or contradiction?: Proceedings of the first National Conference on Business Ethics, March 11 and 12, 1977 / edited by W. Michael Hoffman; sponsored by the Center for Business Ethics, Bentley College. — Waltham, Mass.: The Center, c1977. viii, 134 p.: ill.; 23 cm. 1. Business ethics — Congresses. I. Hoffman, W. Michael. II. Bentley College. Center for Business Ethics. III. T.
HF5387.N37 1977     174/.4     *LC* 78-103071

**National Conference on Business Ethics. 2d, Bentley College,**      **4.4270**
**1978.**
Power and responsibility in the American business system: proceedings of the second National Conference on Business Ethics, April 7 & 8, 1978 / edited by W. Michael Hoffman; sponsored by the Center for Business Ethics, Bentley College. — Washington, D.C.: University Press of America, c1979. x, 547 p. 1. Business ethics — Congresses. I. Hoffman, W. Michael. II. Bentley College. Center for Business Ethics. III. T.
HF5387.N37 1978     174./4     *LC* 79-64514     *ISBN* 081910762X

**National Conference on Business Ethics. 3d, Bentley College,**      **4.4271**
**1979.**
The work ethic in business: proceedings of the Third National Conference on Business Ethics / sponsored by the Center for Business Ethics, Bentley College; edited by W. Michael Hoffman, Thomas J. Wyly. — Cambridge, Mass.: Oelgeschlager, Gunn & Hain; Washington, D.C.: Ethics Resource Center, c1981. xxxiii, 349 p.: ill.; 24 cm. 1. Work ethic — United States — Congresses. 2. Labor and laboring classes — United States — 1970- — Congresses. I. Hoffman, W. Michael. II. Wyly, Thomas J. III. Bentley College. Center for Business Ethics. IV. T.
HF5387.N37 1979x     331/.01/3 19     *LC* 80-22708     *ISBN* 0899460682

**National Conference on Business Ethics (4th: 1981: Bentley**      **4.4272**
**College)**
Ethics and the management of computer technology: proceedings of the Fourth National Conference on Business Ethics / sponsored by the Center for Business Ethics, Bentley College; edited by W. Michael Hoffman, Jennifer Mills Moore. — Cambridge, Mass.: Oelgeschlager, Gunn & Hain, c1982. xix, 175 p.: ill.; 23 cm. 1. Electronic data processing — Moral and ethical aspects — Congresses. 2. Business ethics — Congresses. I. Hoffman, W. Michael. II. Moore, Jennifer Mills. III. Bentley College. Center for Business Ethics. IV. T.
HF5387.N37 1981x     174/.4 19     *LC* 82-3562     *ISBN* 0899461441

**National Conference on Business Ethics. (5th: 1983: Bentley**      **4.4273**
**College)**
Corporate governance and institutionalizing ethics: proceedings of the Fifth National Conference on Business Ethics / sponsored by the Center for Business Ethics, Bentley College; edited by W. Michael Hoffman, Jennifer Mills Moore, David A. Fedo. — Lexington, Mass.: Lexington Books, c1984. xx, 313 p.: ill.; 24 cm. 1. Business ethics — Congresses. 2. Corporations — Social aspects — Congresses. I. Hoffman, W. Michael. II. Moore, Jennifer Mills. III. Fedo, David A. IV. Bentley College. Center for Business Ethics. V. T.
HF5387.N37 1983     174/.4 19     *LC* 84-47818     *ISBN* 0669082597

**National Conference on Business Ethics. (6th: 1985: Waltham,**   4.4273a
**Mass.)**
Ethics and the multinational enterprise: proceedings of the Sixth National
Conference on Business Ethics, October 10 and 11, 1985 / sponsored by Center
for Business Ethics, Bentley College, Waltham, Massachusetts; edited by W.
Michael Hoffman, Ann E. Lange, David A. Fedo. — Lanham, MD: University
Press of America, c1986. xlix, 530 p.: ill.; 23 cm. 1. International business
enterprises — Moral and ethical aspects — Congresses. 2. Business ethics —
Congresses. I. Hoffman, W. Michael. II. Lange, Ann E. III. Fedo, David A.
IV. Bentley College. Center for Business Ethics. V. T.
HF5387.N37 1985x     174/.4 19     LC 86-19038

**Profit and responsibility: issues in business and professional**   4.4274
**ethics / edited by Patricia Werhane and Kendall D'Andrade.**
New York: E. Mellen Press, c1985. ix, 285 p.; 24 cm. (Studies in religion and
society; v. 12) 1. Business ethics — Addresses, essays, lectures. I. Werhane,
Patricia Hogue. II. D'Andrade, Kendall.
HF5387.P75 1985     174/.4 19     LC 84-27279     ISBN 0889468621

# HF5410–5417.5 Marketing. Distribution

**Alderson, Wroe.**   • 4.4275
Planning and problem solving in marketing, by Wroe Alderson and Paul E.
Green. — Homewood, Ill.: R. D. Irwin, 1964. x, 661 p.: illus.; 24 cm.
1. Marketing 2. Decision-making in marketing. I. Green, Paul E. joint author.
II. T.
HF5415.A393     658.8     LC 64-21029

**Bartels, Robert, 1913-.**   4.4276
The history of marketing thought / by Robert Bartels. — 2d ed. — [Columbus,
Ohio]: Grid [inc.], c1976. 327 p.; 24 cm. (Grid series in marketing) First
published in 1962 under title: The development of marketing thought. Includes
indexes. 1. Marketing I. T.
HF5415.B36 1976     658.8/009     LC 75-6015     ISBN 0882440853

**Bonoma, Thomas V.**   4.4277
Segmenting the industrial market / Thomas V. Bonoma, Benson P. Shapiro. —
Lexington, Mass.: Lexington Books, c1983. xi, 126 p.; 24 cm. Includes index.
1. Industrial marketing 2. Market segmentation I. Shapiro, Benson P. II. T.
HF5415.B525 1983     658.8 19     LC 82-49325     ISBN 0669065781

**Dawson, John A.**   4.4278
The marketing environment / John A. Dawson. — New York: St. Martin's
Press, 1979. 379 p.: ill.; 22 cm. 1. Marketing I. T.
HF5415.D38     381     LC 78-31580     ISBN 0312515308

**Douglas, Edna.**   4.4279
Economics of marketing / Edna Douglas. — New York: Harper & Row, [1975]
viii, 728 p.: ill.; 27 cm. 1. Marketing I. T.
HF5415.D73     380.1     LC 75-3527     ISBN 0060416955

**Engel, James F.**   4.4280
Promotional strategy: managing the marketing communications process /
James F. Engel, Martin R. Warshaw, Thomas C. Kinnear. — 5th ed. —
Homewood, Ill.: R.D. Irwin, 1983. xv, 655 p., [4] p. of plates: ill. (some col.); 25
cm. — (Irwin series in marketing.) 1. Marketing 2. Advertising 3. Marketing
— Management I. Warshaw, Martin R. II. Kinnear, Thomas C., 1943- III. T.
IV. Series.
HF5415.E65 1983     658.8/2 19     LC 82-84060     ISBN 025602846X

**Fisher, Lawrence.**   4.4281
Industrial marketing: an analytical approach to planning and execution /
Lawrence Fisher. — 2d ed. — London: Business Books, 1976. xiv, 270 p.; 25
cm. 1. Industrial marketing I. T.
HF5415.F535 1976     658.8     LC 77-365309     ISBN 0220662924

**Halbert, Michael.**   • 4.4282
The meaning and sources of marketing theory. New York, McGraw-Hill [1965]
xxx, 330 p. 25 cm. (McGraw-Hill Marketing Science Institute series)
Bibliography: p. 295-315. 1. Marketing I. T.
HF5415.H178     658.801     LC 64-66043

**Handbook of modern marketing / Victor P. Buell, editor.**   4.4283
2nd ed. — New York: McGraw-Hill, c1986. 1 v. (various pagings): ill.; 24 cm.
1. Marketing — Addresses, essays, lectures. I. Buell, Victor P.
HF5415.H1867 1986     658.8 19     LC 85-14903     ISBN 0070088543

**Levitt, Theodore, 1925-.**   • 4.4284
Innovation in marketing, new perspectives for profit and growth. — New York:
McGraw-Hill, 1962. 253 p.; 21 cm. — (McGraw-Hill series in marketing and
advertising) 1. Marketing I. T.
HF5415.L48     658.8     LC 62-13817

**Mallen, Bruce E. comp.**   • 4.4285
The marketing channel; a conceptual viewpoint. New York, Wiley [1967] xiii,
308 p. illus. 26 cm. 1. Marketing — Addresses, essays, lectures. I. T.
HF5415.M2696     LC 67-17344

**Means, Gardiner Coit, 1896-.**   • 4.4286
Pricing power & the public interest: a study based on steel. — [1st ed.] New
York: Harper [1962] 359 p.: ill.; 22 cm. 1. Pricing 2. Steel — Prices I. T.
HF5415 M43     LC 61-12230

**Palda, Kristian S.**   • 4.4287
Pricing decisions and marketing policy [by] Kristian S. Palda. — Englewood
Cliffs, N.J.: Prentice-Hall, [1971] x, 116 p.; 23 cm. — (Prentice-Hall
Foundations of marketing series) 1. Price policy. 2. Marketing I. T.
HF5415.P233     658.8/16     LC 78-139413     ISBN 0136996604

**Risley, George, 1910-.**   4.4288
Modern industrial marketing. New York, McGraw-Hill [1972] xiv, 363 p. 24
cm. 1. Industrial marketing 2. Marketing — Management I. T.
HF5415.R552     658.8     LC 72-6106     ISBN 0070529418

**Stone, Merlin, 1948-.**   4.4289
Marketing and economics / by Merlin Stone. — New York: St. Martin's Press,
1980. vii, 181 p.; 23 cm. 1. Marketing 2. Economics I. T.
HF5415.S859     658.8     LC 79-22206     ISBN 0312515278

**Webster, Frederick E.**   4.4290
Industrial marketing strategy / Frederick E. Webster, Jr. — 2nd ed. — New
York: Wiley, c1984. xv, 321 p.: ill.; 24 cm. (Ronald series on marketing
management.) 'A Ronald Press publication.' 1. Industrial marketing I. T.
II. Series.
HF5415.W358 1984     658.8 19     LC 84-7390     ISBN 0471879584

**Porter, Glenn.**   • 4.4291
Merchants and manufacturers; studies in the changing structure of nineteenth-
century marketing [by] Glenn Porter and Harold C. Livesay. Baltimore, Johns
Hopkins Press [1971] x, 257 p. 24 cm. 1. Marketing — Management — United
States — History. 2. United States — Commerce — History I. Livesay,
Harold C., joint author. II. T.
HF5415.1.P55     658.8/00973     LC 72-156071     ISBN 0801812518

**Anderson, Dole A., 1917-.**   • 4.4292
Marketing and development: the Thailand experience, by Dole A. Anderson. —
East Lansing: Institute for International Business and Economic Development
Studies, Michigan State University, 1970. xx, 214 p.: map.; 24 cm. — (MSU
international business and economic studies) 1. Marketing — Thailand.
2. Thailand — Economic conditions. I. T. II. Series.
HF5415.12.T45 A62     380.1/09593     LC 78-631957

# HF5415.123–5415.129 Information. Marketing Channels

**Haley, Russell I.**   4.4293
Developing effective communications strategy: a benefit segmentation approach
/ Russell I. Haley. — New York: Wiley, 1985. xii, 510 p.: ill.; 24 cm. (Ronald
series on marketing management. 0275-875X) 'A Ronald Press publication.'
1. Communication in marketing 2. Market segmentation I. T. II. Series.
HF5415.123.H35 1985     658.8/02 19     LC 84-26983     ISBN
0471812625

**Marketing information: a professional reference guide / edited**   4.4294
**by Jac L. Goldstucker; compiled by Dennis W. Goodwin, with**
**the staff of the Business Publishing Division, Georgia State**
**University.**
Atlanta, Ga.: Business Pub. Division, College of Business Administration, the
University, 1982. xxv, 369 p.; 29 cm. Includes indexes. 1. Marketing —
Information services — United States. 2. Marketing research — United States
— Directories. 3. Marketing — Bibliography I. Goldstucker, Jac L.
II. Goodwin, Dennis W. III. Georgia State University. College of Business
Administration. Business Publishing Division.
HF5415.124.M37 1982     658.8/0025/73 19     LC 82-623031

**Mallen, Bruce E.**   4.4295
Principles of marketing channel management: interorganizational distribution
design and relations / Bruce Mallen. — Lexington, Mass.: Lexington Books,

c1977. xx, 353 p.; 24 cm. 1. Marketing channels 2. Marketing — Management
I. T.
HF5415.125.M34    658.8    *LC* 76-27923    *ISBN* 0669009857

**Stern, Louis W., 1935-.**    **4.4296**
Marketing channels / Louis W. Stern, Adel I. El–Ansary. — Englewood Cliffs,
N.J.: Prentice-Hall, c1977. xiii, 590 p.; ill.; 24 cm. (Prentice-Hall international
series in management) 1. Marketing channels I. Ansary, Adel I. joint author.
II. T.
HF5415.125.S76    658.8/4    *LC* 76-23417    *ISBN* 0135571243

**Dannhaeuser, Norbert, 1943-.**    **4.4297**
Contemporary trade strategies in the Philippines: a study in marketing
anthropology / Norbert Dannhaeuser. — New Brunswick, N.J.: Rutgers
University Press, c1983. xiii, 279 p.; 24 cm. Includes index. 1. Marketing
channels — Philippines — Case studies. 2. Economic anthropology —
Philippines — Case studies. I. T.
HF5415.129.D36 1983    381/.09599 19    *LC* 82-5382    *ISBN*
0813509505

# HF5415.13–5415.157 Marketing Management

**Wiechmann, Ulrich E.**    **4.4298**
Marketing management in multinational firms: the consumer packaged goods
industry / Ulrich E. Wiechmann. — New York: Praeger, 1976. xi, 103 p.: ill.;
24 cm. — (Praeger special studies in international economics and development)
1. Marketing — Management 2. International business enterprises I. T.
HF5415.13.W53 1976    658.8    *LC* 75-19831    *ISBN* 0275558509

**Marketing decision models / edited by Randall L. Schultz,**    **4.4299**
**Andris A. Zoltners.**
New York: North Holland, c1981. xii, 298 p.: ill.; 24 cm. 1. Marketing —
Management — Decision making — Mathematical models. 2. Marketing —
Mathematical models I. Schultz, Randall L. II. Zoltners, Andris A.
HF5415.135.M37    658.8 19    *LC* 80-20618    *ISBN* 0444004262

## HF5415.15–5415.153 Product Management

**Urban, Glen L.**    **4.4300**
Design and marketing of new products / Glen L. Urban, John R. Hauser. —
Englewood Cliffs, N.J.: Prentice-Hall, c1980. xx, 618 p.: ill.; 24 cm. —
(Prentice-Hall international series in management.) Includes indexes. 1. New
products 2. Design, Industrial — United States. I. Hauser, John R. joint
author. II. T. III. Series.
HF5415.15.U7    658.5/038    *LC* 80-11707    *ISBN* 0132012693

**New–product forecasting: models and applications / edited by**    **4.4301**
**Yoram Wind, Vijay Mahajan, Richard N. Cardozo.**
Lexington, Mass.: Lexington Books, c1981. x, 564 p.: ill.; 24 cm. 1. New
products — Mathematical models — Addresses, essays, lectures. 2. Product
management — Mathematical models — Addresses, essays, lectures. 3. Sales
forecasting — Mathematical models — Addresses, essays, lectures. I. Wind,
Yoram. II. Mahajan, Vijay. III. Cardozo, Richard N.
HF5415.153.N48    658.5/75/0724    *LC* 80-8388    *ISBN* 0669041025

# HF5415.2–5415.3 Marketing Research. Market Surveys

**Cox, William Edwin, 1930-1978.**    **4.4302**
Industrial marketing research / William E. Cox, Jr. — New York: Wiley,
c1979. xii, 468 p.: ill.; 24 cm. (Ronald series on marketing management) 'A
Ronald Press publication.' 1. Industrial marketing — Research. 2. Marketing
research — United States. I. T.
HF5415.2.C68 1979    658.8/3    *LC* 78-11480    *ISBN* 0471034673

**Ferber, Robert, 1922-.**    **4.4303**
Handbook of marketing research. Robert Ferber, editor–in–chief. — New
York: McGraw-Hill, [1974] 1 v. (various pagings): illus.; 23 cm. 1. Marketing
research — Handbooks, manuals, etc. I. T.
HF5415.2.F419    658.8/3    *LC* 73-12967    *ISBN* 0070204624

**Green, Paul E.**    **4.4304**
Research for marketing decisions / Paul E. Green, Donald S. Tull. — 4th ed. —
Englewood Cliffs, N.J.: Prentice-Hall, c1978. xiii, 673 p.: ill.; 24 cm. —
(Prentice-Hall international series in management) Includes index.
1. Marketing research I. Tull, Donald S. joint author. II. T.
HF5415.2.G68 1978    658.8/3    *LC* 77-24414    *ISBN* 0137741588

**Honomichl, Jack J.**    **4.4305**
Marketing/research people: their behind–the–scenes stories / Jack J.
Honomichl. — Chicago, IL: Crain Books, c1984. x, 190 p.: ill.; 23 cm.
1. Marketing research — United States — Case studies. 2. Marketing —
United States — Case studies. 3. Advertising — United States — Case studies.
I. T.
HF5415.2.H625 1984    658.8/3 19    *LC* 83-72176    *ISBN*
0872510905

**Myers, John G.**    **4.4306**
Marketing research and knowledge development: an assessment for marketing
management / John G. Myers, William F. Massy, Stephen A. Greyser. —
Englewood Cliffs, N.J.: Prentice-Hall, c1980. xiv, 306 p.: ill.; 24 cm.
1. Marketing research — United States. I. Massy, William F. joint author.
II. Greyser, Stephen A. joint author. III. T.
HF5415.2.M945    658.8/3973 19    *LC* 80-13929    *ISBN* 0135576865

**Perceived quality: how consumers view stores and merchandise /**    **4.4307**
**edited by Jacob Jacoby, Jerry C. Olson.**
Lexington, Mass.: LexingtonBooks, c1985. xiv, 311 p.: ill.; 24 cm. (Advances in
retailing series.) 1. Consumers' preferences — Addresses, essays, lectures.
2. Quality of products — Addresses, essays, lectures. 3. Selectivity
(Psychology) — Addresses, essays, lectures. I. Jacoby, Jacob. II. Olson, Jerry
C. (Jerry Corrie), 1944- III. Series.
HF5415.2.P455 1985    658.8/343 19    *LC* 83-49531    *ISBN*
0669082724

**Foxall, G. R.**    **4.4308**
Consumer choice / Gordon R. Foxall. — New York: St. Martin's Press, 1983.
viii, 149 p.; 23 cm. Includes index. 1. Consumers 2. Consumers — Attitudes
3. Motivation research (Marketing) I. T.
HF5415.3.F642 1983    658.8/34 19    *LC* 83-2897    *ISBN*
0312166125

**Marketing to the changing household: management and research**    **4.4309**
**perspectives / edited by Mary Lou Roberts and Lawrence H.**
**Wortzel.**
Cambridge, Mass.: Ballinger Pub. Co., c1984. xxv, 349 p.: ill.; 24 cm. Includes
index. 1. Households — United States — Addresses, essays, lectures.
2. Marketing research — Addresses, essays, lectures. 3. Marketing —
Management — Addresses, essays, lectures. I. Roberts, Mary Lou.
II. Wortzel, Lawrence H.
HF5415.3.M278 1984    658.8 19    *LC* 84-12288    *ISBN* 0884109860

**Personal values and consumer psychology / edited by Robert E.**    **4.4310**
**Pitts, Jr., Arch G. Woodside.**
Lexington, Mass.: Lexington Books, c1984. xii, 318 p.: ill.; 24 cm.
1. Consumers — Addresses, essays, lectures. 2. Values — Addresses, essays,
lectures. I. Pitts, Robert E. II. Woodside, Arch G.
HF5415.3.P45 1984    658.8/342 19    *LC* 83-48123    *ISBN*
066906937X

**Prince, Melvin.**    **4.4311**
Consumer research for management decisions / Melvin Prince, with the
collaboration of Irene A. Silbert. — New York: Wiley, c1982. xiii, 210 p.; 24
cm. — (Ronald series on marketing management. 0275-875X) 'A Ronald Press
publication.' Includes index. 1. Consumers — Research 2. Marketing research
I. Silbert, Irene A. II. T. III. Series.
HF5415.3.P74    658.8/34 19    *LC* 81-16509    *ISBN* 0471097152

**Bowersox, Donald J.**    **4.4312**
Logistical management: a systems integration of physical distribution
management and materials management / Donald J. Bowersox. — 2d ed. —
New York: Macmillan, c1978. xii, 528 p.: ill.; 24 cm. Includes indexes.
1. Physical distribution of goods — Management 2. Materials management
I. T.
HF5415.7.B66 1978    658.7 19    *LC* 77-4670    *ISBN* 0023131101

# HF5416.5–5417 Price Policy

**Kaplan, A. D. H. (Abraham David Hannath), 1893-.**    **4.4313**
Pricing in big business: a case approach / by A. D. H. Kaplan, Joel B. Dirlam,
Robert F. Lanzillotti. — Westport, Conn.: Greenwood Press, 1980, c1958. xiv,
344 p.: ill.; 23 cm. Reprint of the ed. published by Brookings Institution,
Washington. 1. Price policy — Case studies. I. Dirlam, Joel B. joint author.
II. Lanzillotti, Robert Franklin, 1921- joint author. III. T.
HF5416.5.K36 1980    658.8/16    *LC* 79-28354    *ISBN* 0313222916

**Oxenfeldt, Alfred Richard, 1917-.**    **4.4314**
Pricing strategies / Alfred R. Oxenfeldt. — New York: Amacom, [1975] x,
255 p.; 24 cm. 1. Price policy. I. T.
HF5417.O94    338.5/26    *LC* 74-78207    *ISBN* 0814453686

## HF5419–5430 Wholesale Trade. Retail Trade

**Bartels, Robert, 1913- ed.**                                    **4.4315**
Comparative marketing; wholesaling in fifteen countries. Sponsored by the American Marketing Association. — Homewood, Ill., R. D. Irwin [1963] xii, 317 p. diagrs., tables. 24 cm. Studies prepared by the Comparative Marketing Committee, American Marketing Association under the chairmanship of R. Bartels. Bibliography: p. [309]-317. Essays on wholesaling in West Germany, Finland, Italy, the Netherlands, Turkey, Egypt, Israel, India, Japan, Australia, Tropical Africa, Central America, the U.S.S.R., Communist China, Yugoslavia. 1. Wholesale trade I. American Marketing Association. Comparative Marketing Committee. II. T.
HF5421.B3      658.86      LC 63-19881

**Census of wholesale trade (1982). Geographic area series.**      **4.4316**
1982 census of wholesale trade. Geographic area series. — [Washington, D.C.]: U.S. Dept. of Commerce, Bureau of the Census, [1984-. v. ; 28 cm. 'April 1984'—V. 1, t.p. 'WC82-A-51.' 1. Wholesale trade — United States — Statistics. I. United States. Bureau of the Census. II. T.
HF5421.C4 1984      381/.2/0973 19      LC 83-600198

**Census of wholesale trade (1982). Industry series.**            **4.4317**
1982 Census of wholesale trade. Industry series. Miscellaneous subjects. — [Washington, D.C.]: U.S. Dept. of Commerce, Bureau of the Census: for sale by the Supt. of Docs., U.S. G.P.O., 1985. 1 v. (various paging): forms. 'WC82-I-4'—T.p. 'Issued October 1985'—T.p. 1. Wholesale trade — United States — Statistics. I. United States. Bureau of the Census. II. T. III. Title: Miscellaneous subjects. IV. Title: Industry series, miscellaneous subjects.
HF5421.C42 1984

**Duncan, Delbert J.**                                            **4.4318**
Modern retailing management: basic concepts and practices / Delbert J. Duncan, Stanley C. Hollander, Ronald Savitt. — 10th ed. — Homewood, Ill.: R.D. Irwin, 1983. xvii, 683 p.: ill.; 25 cm. 1. Retail trade — Management 2. Retail trade I. Hollander, Stanley C., 1919- II. Savitt, Ronald. III. T.
HF5429.D83 1983      658.8/7 19      LC 82-83829      ISBN 0256025320

**Vaughn, Charles L., 1911-.**                                    **4.4319**
Franchising: its nature, scope, advantages, and development / by Charles L. Vaughn. — Lexington, Mass.: Lexington Books, [1974] xiv, 197 p.; 24 cm. Based in part upon a content analysis of the proceedings of the annual international management conferences on franchising held at Boston College as well as research publications on the subject. 1. Franchises (Retail trade) I. T.
HF5429.V36      658.8/4      LC 73-19738      ISBN 066991777X

**Wingate, John Williams, 1899-.**                              • **4.4320**
Retail merchandise management [by] John W. Wingate, Elmer O. Schaller [and] F. Leonard Miller. Englewood Cliffs, N.J., Prentice-Hall [1972] xiii, 386 p. illus. 25 cm. 1. Retail trade — Management I. Schaller, Elmer O. (Elmer Otto) joint author. II. Miller, F. Leonard, joint author. III. T.
HF5429.W5855      658.8/7      LC 73-168617      ISBN 0137787537

**Luxenberg, Stan.**                                              **4.4321**
Roadside empires: how the chains franchised America / by Stan Luxenberg. — New York, N.Y., U.S.A.: Viking, 1985. viii, 313 p.; 24 cm. Includes index. 1. Franchises (Retail trade) — United States. I. T.
HF5429.235.U5 L88 1985      381/.13/0973 19      LC 83-40231      ISBN 0670326585

**Census of retail trade (1982). Geographic area series.**        **4.4322**
1982 census of retail trade. Geographic area series. — [Washington, D.C.]: U.S. Dept. of Commerce, Bureau of the Census, 1984-. v. : 28 cm. 'April 1984'—V. 1, t.p. 'RC82-A-51.' 1. Retail trade — United States — Statistics — Collected works. I. United States. Bureau of the Census. II. T.
HF5429.3.C4 1984      381/.1/0973 19      LC 83-600162

**Census of retail trade (1982). Industry series.**              **4.4323**
1982 census of retail trade. Industry series. — Washington, D.C.: U.S. Dept. of Commerce, Bureau of the Census: For sale by Supt. of Docs., U.S. G.P.O., 1985-. v.: forms; 28 cm. 'RC82-I-1'- 1. Retail trade — United States — Statistics. I. United States. Bureau of the Census. II. T. III. Title: Industry series.
HF5429.3.C433 1985

## HF5437–5459 Buying. Selling

**Purchasing handbook.**                                          **4.4324**
Aljian's Purchasing handbook / formerly edited by George W. Aljian. — 4th ed. / sponsored by the National Association of Purchasing Management; coordinating editor, Paul V. Farrell. — New York: McGraw-Hill, c1982. 1 v. (various pagings); 24 cm. 1. Purchasing — Handbooks, manuals, etc. I. Aljian, George W. II. Farrell, Paul V. III. National Association of Purchasing Management. IV. T.
HF5437.P795 1982      658.7/2 19      LC 81-8350      ISBN 0070458995

**Blake, Robert Rogers, 1918-.**                                • **4.4325**
The grid for sales excellence; benchmarks for effective salesmanship [by] Robert R. Blake [and] Jane Srygley Mouton. — New York: McGraw-Hill, [1970] ix, 209 p.; 23 cm. 1. Selling I. Mouton, Jane Srygley. joint author. II. T.
HF5438.B663      658.85      LC 71-104737

**Bursk, Edward Collins, 1907- comp.**                          • **4.4326**
Salesmanship and sales force management. Edited by Edward C. Bursk and G. Scott Hutchison. — Cambridge, Mass.: Harvard University Press, 1971. ix, 191 p.: illus.; 29 cm. 'Articles selected from the Harvard business review for the series entitled The business administrator.' 1. Selling — Addresses, essays, lectures. 2. Sales Management — Addresses, essays, lectures. I. Hutchison, George Scott, joint comp. II. T.
HF5438.B8464      658.81/008      LC 78-150007      ISBN 0674785304

**The Direct marketing handbook / Edward L. Nash, editor in**     **4.4327**
**chief.**
New York: McGraw-Hill, c1984. xxiii, 946 p.: ill.; 24 cm. 1. Direct selling 2. Marketing I. Nash, Edward L.
HF5438.25.D555 1984      658.8/4 19      LC 83-9871      ISBN 0070460175

**Personal selling: theory, research, and practice / edited by**  **4.4328**
**Jacob Jacoby, C. Samuel Craig.**
Lexington, Mass.: Lexington Books, c1984. xvi, 316 p.: ill.; 24 cm. — (Advances in retailing series.) Papers presented at a conference, co-sponsored by the Institute for Retail Management and the Association for Consumer Research. 1. Selling — Congresses. I. Jacoby, Jacob. II. Craig, C. Samuel. III. New York University. Institute of Retail Management. IV. Association for Consumer Research (U.S.) V. Series.
HF5438.25.P46 1984      658.8/5 19      LC 83-48825      ISBN 0669076066

**Strang, Roger A.**                                              **4.4329**
The promotional planning process / Roger A. Strang. — New York, N.Y.: Praeger, 1980. xii, 127 p.; 25 cm. Includes index. 1. Sales promotion — Planning. 2. Marketing I. T.
HF5438.5.S77      658.8/2 19      LC 80-18848      ISBN 0030491010

## HF5461–5485 Special Types of Stores. Warehousing

**The Retail revolution: market transformation, investment, and**  **4.4330**
**labor in the modern department store / Barry Bluestone ... [et al.].**
Boston, Mass.: Auburn House Pub. Co., 1981 [c1980] xvi, 160 p.: ill.; 25 cm. Includes index. 1. Department stores I. Bluestone, Barry.
HF5461.R47      658.8/71 19      LC 80-26036      ISBN 0865690529

**Benson, Susan Porter, 1943-.**                                  **4.4331**
Counter cultures: saleswomen, managers, and customers in American department stores, 1890–1940 / Susan Porter Benson. — Urbana: University of Illinois Press, c1986. xvi, 322 p.: ill.; 24 cm. — (Working class in American history.) 1. Department stores — United States — History. 2. Department stores — Employees — United States — History. 3. Women clerks (Retail trade) — United States — History. I. T. II. Series.
HF5465.U5 B45 1986      381/.1/0973 19      LC 85-21012      ISBN 0252012526

**Hower, Ralph Merle, 1903-.**                                  • **4.4332**
History of Macy's of New York, 1858–1919: chapters in the evolution of the department store / by Ralph M. Hower. — Cambridge, Mass.: Harvard University Press, 1943. xxvii, 500 p. incl. tables, diagrs. front., plates, ports., facsims.; 22 cm. (Half-title: Harvard studies in business history. VII) 'Notes and

references': p. [423]-480. 1. Macy (R. H.) & co., New York. I. T. II. Title: Macy's of New York.
HF5465.U6M27    658.871    *LC* A 43-1889

**Emmet, Boris, 1885-.**    • 4.4333
Catalogues and counters; a history of Sears, Roebuck and Company, by Boris Emmet & John E. Jeuck. — [Chicago]: University of Chicago Press, [1950] xix, 788 p.: illus., ports., map (on lining papers); 25 cm. 1. Sears, Roebuck and Company. I. Jeuck, John E., joint author. II. T.
HF5467.S4 E5    658.872065    *LC* 50-7387

**Lebhar, Godfrey Montague, 1882-.**    • 4.4334
Chain stores in America, 1859–1962. 3d ed. New York, Chain Store Pub. Corp. [1963] 430 p. ill. 1. Chain stores — United States I. T.
HF5468 L4 1963    *LC* 63-2856

**Beals, Ralph Leon, 1901-.**    4.4335
The peasant marketing system of Oaxaca, Mexico / Ralph L. Beals. — Berkeley: University of California Press, [1975] ix, 419 p.: ill.; 24 cm. Includes index. 1. Markets — Mexico — Oaxaca (State) 2. Farm produce — Mexico — Oaxaca (State) — Marketing. 3. Cost and standard of living — Mexico — Oaxaca (State) I. T.
HF5473.M62 O392    381    *LC* 73-76098    *ISBN* 0520024354

**Ackerman, Kenneth B.**    4.4336
Practical handbook of warehousing / Kenneth B. Ackerman. — 2nd ed. — Washington: Traffic Service Corp., c1986. xxvii, 612 p.: ill.; 24 cm. 1. Warehouses I. T. II. Title: Warehousing.
HF5485.A24 1986    658.7/85 19    *LC* 86-137932    *ISBN* 0874080363

**Frey, Stephen L. (Stephen Louis), 1939-.**    4.4337
Warehouse operations, a handbook / Stephen L. Frey. — Beaverton, Or.: M/A Press, c1983. viii, 295 p.: ill. (some col.); 24 cm. 1. Warehouses — Management — Handbooks, manuals, etc. I. T.
HF5485.F75 1983    658.7/85 19    *LC* 81-12380    *ISBN* 0930206142

# HF5500–5599 Business Organization and Administration

**Marshall, Judi.**    4.4338
Women managers: travellers in a male world / Judi Marshall. — Chichester [Sussex]; New York: Wiley, c1984. vii, 251 p.: ill.; 23 cm. Includes index. 1. Women executives I. T.
HF5500.2.M248 1984    658.4/09/088042 19    *LC* 83-23579    *ISBN* 0471904198

**Davis, George, 1939-.**    4.4339
Black life in corporate America: swimming in the mainstream / George Davis and Glegg Watson. — 1st ed. — Garden City, N.Y.: Anchor Press/Doubleday, 1982. 204 p.; 22 cm. Includes index. 1. Afro-American executives 2. Afro-Americans in business I. Watson, Glegg. II. T.
HF5500.3.U54 D38 1982    658.4/09/08996073 19    *LC* 81-22760    *ISBN* 0385147015

**Fernandez, John P., 1941-.**    4.4340
Racism and sexism in corporate life: changing values in American business / John P. Fernandez. — Lexington, Mass.: Lexington Books, c1981. xxiii, 359 p.: ill.; 24 cm. Includes index. 1. Minority executives — United States. 2. Women executives — United States. 3. Discrimination in employment — United States 4. Corporations — United States — Personnel management. I. T.
HF5500.3.U54 F474 1981    658.3/041 19    *LC* 80-8945    *ISBN* 0669044776

**Larwood, Laurie.**    4.4341
Women in management / Laurie Larwood, Marion M. Wood. Lexington, Mass.: Lexington Books, c1977. xiv, 199 p.; 24 cm. 1. Women executives — United States. 2. Executive ability I. Wood, Marion M. joint author. II. T.
HF5500.3.U54 L37    331.4/81/658400973    *LC* 76-27033    *ISBN* 0669009733

**Steiner, George Albert, 1912-.**    4.4342
The new CEO / George A. Steiner. — New York: Macmillan; London: Collier Macmillan, c1983. xiv, 133 p.; 25 cm. — (Studies of the modern corporation.) 1. Executives — United States. I. T. II. Title: CEO. III. Series.
HF5500.3.U54 S746 1983    658.4/00973 19    *LC* 82-48599    *ISBN* 0029312507

## HF5546–5547 Office Practice

**Hutchinson, Lois Irene.**    • 4.4343
Standard handbook for secretaries [by] Lois Irene Hutchinson. — 8th ed. — [New York]: McGraw-Hill, 1969. x, 638 p.: map.; 23 cm. 1. Office practice 2. English language — Rhetoric 3. English language — Grammar — 1950- I. T.
HF5547.H77 1969    650    *LC* 69-19201

**Benét, Mary Kathleen.**    4.4344
The secretarial ghetto. — [1st ed. in the U.S.]. — New York: McGraw-Hill, [1973, c1972] v, 181 p.; 22 cm. 1. Secretaries 2. Women — Employment I. T.
HF5547.5.B42 1973    331.4/81/6513741    *LC* 72-10053    *ISBN* 0070045364

**Vinnicombe, Susan.**    4.4345
Secretaries, management, and organizations / Susan Vinnicombe. — London: Heinemann Educational Books, 1980. vi, 122 p.: ill.; 22 cm. — (An H.E.B. paperback) 1. Secretaries 2. Organization 3. Office management I. T.
HF5547.5.V56    651.3/741 19    *LC* 80-670216    0432828967

## HF5548.2 Electronic Data Processing

**Hussain, Donna.**    4.4346
Information resource management / Donna Hussain, K.M. Hussain. — Homewood, Ill.: R.D. Irwin, 1984. xiii, 645 p.: ill.; 25 cm. (Irwin series in information and decision sciences.) 1. Information resources management I. Hussain, Khateeb M., 1924- II. T. III. Series.
HF5548.2.H856 1984    658/.054 19    *LC* 83-81770    *ISBN* 0256029903

**Martin, James, 1933-.**    4.4347
Security, accuracy, and privacy in computer systems. — Englewood Cliffs, N.J.: Prentice-Hall, [1973] xiv, 626 p.: illus.; 24 cm. — (Prentice-Hall series in automatic computation) 1. Electronic data processing departments — Security measures 2. Electronic data processing 3. Privacy, Right of I. T.
HF5548.2.M342    658.4/7    *LC* 73-14961    *ISBN* 0137989911

**Norman, Adrian R. D.**    4.4348
Computer insecurity / Adrian R.D. Norman. — London; New York: Chapman and Hall, 1983. xiv, 351 p.: ill.; 25 cm. 1. Electronic data processing departments — Security measures — Case studies. 2. Computers — Access control — Case studies. 3. Computer crimes — Case studies. I. T.
HF5548.2.N575 1983    658.4/78 19    *LC* 83-5267    *ISBN* 0412223104

**Wooldridge, Susan, 1940-.**    4.4349
Security standards for data processing / [by] Susan Wooldridge, Colin R. Corder [and] Claude R. Johnson. — New York: Wiley, [1973] viii, 186 p.: ill.; 23 cm. 'A Halsted Press book.' 1. Electronic data processing departments — Security measures I. Corder, Colin R. joint author. II. Johnson. Claude R., joint author. III. T.
HF5548.2.W655 1973    658.4/7    *LC* 73-3759    *ISBN* 0470961018

## HF5548.8 Industrial Psychology

**Handbook of industrial and organizational psychology / Marvin**    4.4350
**D. Dunnette, editor.**
Chicago: Rand McNally College Pub. Co., c1976. xxvii, 1740 p.: ill.; 25 cm. 1. Psychology, Industrial — Addresses, essays, lectures. 2. Organizational behavior — Addresses, essays, lectures. I. Dunnette, Marvin D.
HF5548.8.H265    158.7    *LC* 74-18664    *ISBN* 0528629123

**Leavitt, Harold J. ed.**    4.4351
Readings in managerial psychology / edited by Harold J. Leavitt and Louis R. Pondy. — 2d ed. — Chicago: University of Chicago Press, 1974 (c1973) xii, 787 p.: ill.; 24 cm. 1. Psychology, Industrial — Addresses, essays, lectures. 2. Industrial management — Addresses, essays, lectures. I. Pondy, Louis R. joint ed. II. T.
HF5548.8.L36 1973    658    *LC* 72-96499    *ISBN* 0226469840

**Tiffin, Joseph, 1905- joint author.**    4.4352
Industrial psychology / [by] Ernest J. McCormick [and] Joseph Tiffin. — 6th ed. Englewood Cliffs, N.J.: Prentice-Hall [1974] xii, 625 p.: ill.; 24 cm. Authors' names in reverse order in previous editions. 1. Psychology, Industrial I. McCormick, Ernest J. (Ernest James) II. T.
HF5548.8.M18    158.7    *LC* 73-9733    *ISBN* 0134631250

**Vroom, Victor Harold, 1932-.**     • **4.4353**
Work and motivation [by] Victor H. Vroom. — New York: Wiley, [1964] ix, 331 p.; 24 cm. 1. Psychology, Industrial 2. Work — Psychological aspects I. T.
HF5548.8.V7     658.01     *LC* 64-17155

**Zander, Alvin Frederick, 1913-.**     **4.4354**
Groups at work / Alvin Zander. — 1st ed. — San Francisco: Jossey-Bass, 1977. xiv, 144 p.; 24 cm. — (The Jossey-Bass social and behavioral science series) Includes index. 1. Work groups 2. Psychology, Industrial 3. Organizational behavior I. T.
HF5548.8.Z233     158.7     *LC* 77-82918     *ISBN* 0875893473

**Human stress and cognition in organizations: an integrated**     **4.4355**
**perspective / edited by Terry A. Beehr, Rabi S. Bhagat.**
New York: Wiley, c1985. xv, 453 p.: ill.; 25 cm. (Wiley series on organizational assessment and change.) 1. Job stress — Addresses, essays, lectures. 2. Stress (Psychology) — Addresses, essays, lectures. 3. Organizational behavior — Addresses, essays, lectures. I. Beehr, Terry A. II. Bhagat, Rabi S. III. Series.
HF5548.85.H86 1985     158.7 19     *LC* 84-20868     *ISBN* 0471869546

**Pelletier, Kenneth R.**     **4.4356**
Healthy people in unhealthy places: stress and fitness at work / Kenneth R. Pelletier. — New York, N.Y.: Delacorte Press/Seymour Lawrence, c1984. xii, 225 p.; 24 cm. 'A Merloyd Lawrence book.' 1. Job stress 2. Psychology, Industrial 3. Occupational health services I. T.
HF5548.85.P44 1984     158.7 19     *LC* 83-7837     *ISBN* 0385292759

# HF5549 Personnel Management

**Famularo, Joseph J.**     **4.4357**
Handbook of modern personnel administration. Joseph J. Famularo, editor-in-chief. — New York: McGraw-Hill, [1972] 1 v. (various pagings): illus.; 24 cm. 1. Personnel management — Addresses, essays, lectures. I. T.
HF5549.F29     658.3     *LC* 70-161666     *ISBN* 0070199124

**Fleishman, Edwin A. ed.**     **4.4358**
Studies in personnel and industrial psychology / editors: Edwin A. Fleishman [and] Alan R. Bass. — 3d ed. — Homewood, Ill.: Dorsey Press, 1974. xiv, 623 p.: ill.; 23 cm. — (The Dorsey series in psychology) 1. Personnel management — Addresses, essays, lectures. 2. Psychology, Industrial — Addresses, essays, lectures. I. Bass, Alan R., joint ed. II. T.
HF5549.F582 1974     658.3/008     *LC* 73-84299     *ISBN* 0256010854

**Fombrun, Charles J.**     **4.4359**
Strategic human resource management / Charles J. Fombrun, Noel M. Tichy, Mary Anne Devanna. — New York: Wiley, c1984. xv, 499 p.: ill.; 25 cm. Includes indexes. 1. Personnel management I. Tichy, Noel M. II. Devanna, Mary Anne. III. T.
HF5549.F587 1984     658.3 19     *LC* 84-15223     *ISBN* 0471810797

**Gellerman, Saul W.**     **4.4360**
Managers and subordinates / Saul W. Gellerman. Hinsdale, Ill.: Dryden Press, c1976. xiii, 208 p.; 22 cm. Includes index. 1. Personnel management I. T.
HF5549.G373     658.3     *LC* 76-385     *ISBN* 0030899281

**McGregor, Douglas.**     **4.4361**
The human side of enterprise: 25th anniversary printing / Douglas McGregor; foreword by Warren Bennis. — New York: McGraw-Hill, c1985. x, 246 p.: ill.; 21 cm. 1. Personnel management I. T.
HF5549.M27 1985     658.3 19     *LC* 85-61506     *ISBN* 0070450986

**Managing human assets / Michael Beer ... [et al.].**     **4.4362**
New York: Free Press; London: Collier Macmillan, c1984. xi, 209 p.: ill.; 25 cm. Includes index. 1. Personnel management — Addresses, essays, lectures. I. Beer, Michael.
HF5549.M31347 1984     658.3 19     *LC* 84-14996     *ISBN* 0029023904

**Miner, John B.**     **4.4363**
Personnel and industrial relations: a managerial approach / John B. Miner, Mary Green Miner. — 4th ed,. — New York: Macmillan; London: Collier Macmillan, 1985. xvi, 683 p.: ill.; 25 cm. 1. Personnel management 2. Industrial relations I. Miner, Mary Green. II. T.
HF5549.M522 1985     658.3 19     *LC* 84-7175     *ISBN* 0023816201

**Heneman, Herbert Gerhard, 1944-.**     **4.4364**
Personnel/human resource management / Herbert G. Heneman III ... [et al.]. — 3rd ed. — Homewood, Ill.: Irwin, 1986. xv, 745 p.: col. ill.; 25 cm. (Irwin series in management and the behavioral sciences.) 1. Personnel management I. T. II. Series.
HF5549.P4514 1986     658.3 19     *LC* 85-82004     *ISBN* 0256033609

**Pigors, Paul John William, 1900-.**     **4.4365**
Personnel administration: a point of view and a method / Paul Pigors, Charles A. Myers; [new drawings by J&R Services, inc.]. — 9th ed. — New York: McGraw-Hill, c1981. xv, 588 p.: ill.; 24 cm. 1. Personnel management I. Myers, Charles Andrew, 1913- joint author. II. T.
HF5549.P468 1981     658.3     *LC* 80-14506     *ISBN* 0070499713

**Walker, James W., 1941-.**     **4.4366**
Human resource planning / James W. Walker. — New York: McGraw-Hill, c1980. xii, 418 p.: ill.; 25 cm. — (McGraw-Hill series in management.) Includes indexes. 1. Personnel management 2. Manpower planning I. T. II. Series.
HF5549.W3116     658.3     *LC* 79-21956     *ISBN* 0070678405

**Whyte, William Foote, 1914-.**     • **4.4367**
Money and motivation: an analysis of incentives in industry / by William Foote Whyte and Melville Dalton [and others. — 1st ed.]. — New York: Harper, [1955] 268 p.: ill.; 22 cm. 1. Personnel management 2. Industrial relations I. T.
HF5549.W483     658.32     *LC* 55-8549

## HF5549.2–.5 SPECIAL ASPECTS, A–Z

**Foulkes, Fred K.**     **4.4368**
Personnel policies in large nonunion companies / Fred K. Foulkes. — Englewood Cliffs, N.J.: Prentice-Hall, c1980. xiv, 354 p.; 24 cm. Includes index. 1. Personnel management — United States. I. T.
HF5549.2.U5 F68     658.3/03 19     *LC* 80-10695     *ISBN* 0136603084

**Alcoholism and its treatment in industry / Carl J. Schramm,**     **4.4369**
**editor.**
Baltimore: Johns Hopkins University Press, c1977. xii, 191 p.; 24 cm. 1. Alcoholism and employment — Addresses, essays, lectures. 2. Alcoholism — Treatment — Addresses, essays, lectures. I. Schramm, Carl J.
HF5549.5.A4 A4     658.38/2     *LC* 77-4783     *ISBN* 0801819733

**Trice, Harrison Miller, 1920-.**     **4.4370**
Spirits and demons at work: alcohol and other drugs on the job / Harrison M. Trice and Paul M. Roman. — 2d ed. — Ithaca: New York State School of Industrial and Labor Relations, Cornell University, c1978. xxv, 268 p.; 23 cm. — (ILR paperback. no. 11) Includes index. 1. Alcoholism and employment 2. Drugs and employment I. Roman, Paul M. joint author. II. T. III. Series.
HF5549.5.A4 T72 1978     362.2/9     *LC* 78-23804     *ISBN* 0875460720

**Hall, Douglas T., 1940-.**     **4.4371**
Career development in organizations / Douglas T. Hall and associates; foreword by Raymond A. Katzell. — 1st ed. — San Francisco: Jossey-Bass, 1986. xxv, 366 p.: ill.; 24 cm. — (Jossey-Bass management series.) (Jossey-Bass social and behavioral science series.) 1. Career development. I. T. II. Series. III. Series: Jossey-Bass social and behavioral science series.
HF5549.5.C35 H35 1986     650.1/4 19     *LC* 86-2932     *ISBN* 0875896812

**Lawshe, Charles Hubert, 1908-.**     • **4.4372**
Principles of personnel testing [by] C. H. Lawshe [and] Michael J. Balma. — 2d ed. — New York: McGraw-Hill, [1966] viii, 427 p.: illus.; 24 cm. 1. Ability testing 2. Employment tests I. Balma, Michael J., joint author. II. T.
HF5549.5.E5 L3 1966     658.3     *LC* 66-15181

**Lopez, Felix M.**     **4.4373**
Personnel interviewing, theory and practice / Felix M. Lopez. — 2d ed. — New York: McGraw-Hill, [1975] xiii, 356 p.: ill.; 24 cm. Includes indexes. 1. Employment interviewing I. T.
HF5549.5.I6 L6 1975     658.4/52     *LC* 75-1047     *ISBN* 0070387265

**Job satisfaction—a reader / [selected by] Michael M.**     **4.4374**
**Gruneberg.**
New York: Wiley, 1976. xiv, 254 p.: ill.; 23 cm. 'A Halsted Press book.' 1. Job satisfaction — Addresses, essays, lectures. I. Gruneberg, Michael M.
HF5549.5.J63 J6     658.31/42     *LC* 75-43852     *ISBN* 0470329114

**Burack, Elmer H.**     **4.4375**
Career management in organizations: a practical human resource planning approach / Elmer H. Burack, Nicholas J. Mathys. — Lake Forest, IL: Brace-Park Press, c1980. xxix, 427 p.: ill.; 24 cm. Includes index. 1. Manpower planning 2. Career development. 3. Vocational guidance I. Mathys, Nicholas J. joint author. II. T.
HF5549.5.M3 B87     650.1/4     *LC* 79-55540

**Burack, Elmer H.**     **4.4376**
Human resource planning: a pragmatic approach to manpower staffing and development / Elmer H. Burack, Nicholas J. Mathys. — Lake Forest, IL: Brace-Park Press, 1980, c1979. xxvii, 371 p.: ill.; 24 cm. 1. Manpower planning 2. Vocational guidance 3. Personnel management I. Mathys, Nicholas J. joint author. II. T.
HF5549.5.M3 B88     658.3     *LC* 79-55539

*HF 5549.5 I6 L6 1975*

**Tracey, William R.** 4.4377
Human resources management and development handbook / edited by William R. Tracey. — New York: American Management Associations, c1985. xvii, 1550 p.: ill.; 26 cm. Spine title: Human resources management & development handbook. 1. Manpower planning — Addresses, essays, lectures. 2. Personnel management — Addresses, essays, lectures. I. T. II. Title: Human resources management & development handbook.
HF5549.5.M3 H85 1985    658.3 19    LC 84-274    ISBN 0814401015

**Schein, Edgar H.** 4.4378
Career dynamics: matching individual and organizational needs / Edgar H. Schein. — Reading, Mass.: Addison-Wesley Pub. Co., c1978. xii, 276 p.: ill.; 21 cm. — (Addison-Wesley series on organization development) 1. Manpower planning 2. Vocational guidance I. T.
HF5549.5.M3 S33    650/.14    LC 77-93330    ISBN 0201068346

**Landy, Frank J.** 4.4379
The measurement of work performance: methods, theory, and applications / Frank J. Landy, James L. Farr. — New York: Academic Press, 1983. xii, 342 p.: ill.; 24 cm. — (Organizational and occupational psychology.) Includes indexes. 1. Employees, Rating of I. Farr, James L. II. T. III. Title: Work performance. IV. Series.
HF5549.5.R3 L35 1983    658.3/125 19    LC 82-22657    ISBN 0124356605

**Craig, Robert L.** 4.4380
Training and development handbook: a guide to human resource development / edited by Robert L. Craig; sponsored by the American Society for Training and Development. — 2d ed. — New York: McGraw-Hill, c1976. p. cm. 1. Employees, Training of I. American Society for Training and Development. II. T.
HF5549.5.T7 C7 1976    658.31/24    LC 76-15295    ISBN 007001521X

**Taylor, Bernard, 1931-.** 4.4381
Management development and training handbook / editors: Bernard Taylor and Gordon L. Lippitt. — London; New York: McGraw Hill, [1975] xxiii, 650 p.: ill.; 23 cm. 1. Executives — Training of — Addresses, essays, lectures. I. Lippitt, Gordon L. joint author. II. T.
HF5549.5.T7 T295    658.4/07/124    LC 74-13384    ISBN 0070844461

# HF5550–5585 Finance. Credit Management

**Anderson, David R.** 4.4382
Practical controllership / [by] David R. Anderson, Leo A. Schmidt [and] Andrew M. McCosh. — 3d ed. — Homewood, Ill.: Irwin, 1973. xvii, 628 p.: ill.; 24 cm. — (The Willard J. Graham series in accounting) 1. Controllership I. Schmidt, Leo Anton, joint author. II. McCosh, Andrew M. joint author. III. T.
HF5550.A65 1973    658.1/5    LC 72-92414    ISBN 0256000085

**Beckman, Theodore N., 1894-.** • 4.4383
[Credits and collections in theory and practice] Credits and collections: management and theory / [by] Theodore N. Beckman [and] Ronald S. Foster. — 8th ed. New York: McGraw-Hill [1969] xii, 724 p.: ill., forms.; 24 cm. First published in 1924 under title: Credits and collections in theory and practice. 1. Credit — Management 2. Collecting of accounts I. Foster, Ronald S., joint author. II. T.
HF5566.B35 1969    658.88    LC 68-55262

**Forman, Martin.** 4.4384
Factoring and finance / Martin Forman and John Gilbert. — New York: Wiley, 1976. x, 142 p.: ill.; 21 cm. 'A Halsted Press book.' Includes index. 1. Factoring (Finance) 2. Working capital I. Gilbert, John, 1946- joint author. II. T.
HF5569.F67    658.1/5    LC 75-10115    ISBN 0470266260

# HF5601–5689 Accounting

**Littleton, A. C. (Ananias Charles), 1886-.** 4.4385
Accounting evolution to 1900 / by A. C. Littleton. — University of Alabama Press ed. — University, Ala.: University of Alabama Press, 1981. ix, 373 p.; 21 cm. (Accounting history classics series) Revised version of the author's thesis.

Reprint of the 1933 ed. published by American Institute Pub. Co., New York, with a new foreword by V.K. Zimmerman. 1. Accounting — History. I. T.
HF5605.L5 1981    657/.09 19    LC 80-22353    ISBN 0817300651

**Littleton, A. C. (Ananias Charles), 1886-.** • 4.4386
Studies in the history of accounting: edited on behalf of the Association of University Teachers of Accounting and the American Accounting Association / by A.C. Littleton and B.S. Yamey. — Homewood, Ill.: R.D. Irwin, 1956. 392 p.: ill.; 24 cm. 1. Accounting — History. I. Yamey, Basis S. II. T.
HF5605.L52 1956a    HF5605.L52 1956.    LC 58-1428

**Oldham, K. Michael (Kenneth Michael)** 4.4387
Accounting systems and practice in Europe / K. Michael Oldham. — 3rd ed. — Aldershot, Hants, England; Brookfield, Vt., U.S.A.: Gower Pub. Co., c1987. 1 v. Includes index. 1. Accounting — Europe. I. T.
HF5616.E8 O43 1987    657/.094 19    LC 86-19570    ISBN 0566026120

**Briloff, Abraham J.** 4.4388
Unaccountable accounting [by] Abraham J. Briloff. — New York: Harper & Row, [1972] xvii, 365 p.; 22 cm. 1. Accounting — History — United States. 2. Accounting I. T.
HF5616.U5 B74 1972    657/.0973    LC 71-156509    ISBN 0060104716

**Previts, Gary John.** 4.4389
A history of accounting in America: an historical interpretation of the cultural significance of accounting / Gary John Previts, Barbara Dubis Merino. — New York: Wiley, c1979. xii, 378 p.: ill.; 24 cm. 'A Ronald Press publication.' Includes index. 1. Accounting — United States — History. I. Merino, Barbara Dubis. joint author. II. T.
HF5616.U5 P72    657/.0973    LC 79-616    ISBN 0471051721

**Stevens, Mark, 1947-.** 4.4390
The Big Eight / Mark Stevens. — New York: Macmillan, c1981. 240 p.; 24 cm. Includes index. 1. Accounting firms — United States. 2. Big business — United States. I. T.
HF5616.U5 S75    338.7/61657/0973 19    LC 81-8403    ISBN 0026144204

**Kohler, Eric Louis, 1892-1976.** 4.4391
[Dictionary for accountants] Kohler's Dictionary for accountants / edited by W.W. Cooper, Yuji Ijiri. — 6th ed. — Englewood Cliffs, N.J.: Prentice-Hall, c1983. xi, 574 p.; 25 cm. — (Prentice-Hall series in accounting.) Rev. ed. of: A dictionary for accountants. 5th ed. 1975. Includes index. 1. Accounting — Dictionaries. I. Cooper, William W. (William Wager), 1914- II. Ijiri, Yuji. III. T. IV. Title: Dictionary for accountants. V. Series.
HF5621.K6 1983    657/.03/21 19    LC 82-13354    ISBN 0135166586

**Chambers, R. J. (Raymond J.), 1917-.** • 4.4392
Accounting, evaluation, and economic behavior / [by] Raymond J. Chambers. — Englewood Cliffs, N.J.: Prentice-Hall [1966] xii, 388 p.: ill.; 24 cm. (Prentice-Hall international series in management) 1. Accounting I. T.
HF5625.C47    657    LC 66-13944

**Hendriksen, Eldon S. comp.** 4.4393
Contemporary accounting theory [compiled by] Eldon S. Hendriksen [and] Bruce P. Budge. — Encino, Calif.: Dickenson Pub. Co., [1974] viii, 350 p.; 23 cm. — (Dickenson series on contemporary thought in accounting) 1. Accounting I. Budge, Bruce P., joint comp. II. T.
HF5625.H46    657/.01    LC 73-81294    ISBN 0822101165

**Buckley, John W.** 4.4394
The accounting profession [by] John W. Buckley and Marlene H. Buckley. — Los Angeles: Melville Pub. Co., [1974] xvii, 209 p.: illus.; 24 cm. — (Melville series on management, accounting, and information systems) 1. Accounting — Vocational guidance I. Buckley, Marlene H., 1938- joint author. II. T.
HF5629.B78    657/.023    LC 74-8880    ISBN 0471116106

**Moonitz, Maurice. ed.** • 4.4395
Significant accounting essays / edited by Maurice Moonitz [and] A.C. Litt. — Englewood Cliffs, N.J.: Prentice-Hall [1965] x, 529 p. 1. Accounting — Addresses, essays, lectures I. Littleton, A. C. (Ananias Charles), 1886- II. T.
HF5629 M6    LC 65-16940

**Windal, Floyd W.** 4.4396
The accounting professional: ethics, responsibility, and liability / Floyd W. Windal and Robert N. Corley. — Englewood Cliffs, N.J.: Prentice-Hall, c1980. xiv, 456 p.; 24 cm. 1. Accountants — Professional ethics I. Corley, Robert Neil. joint author. II. T.
HF5629.W55    174/.9657 19    LC 79-9537    ISBN 0130030201

**Belkaoui, Ahmed, 1943-.** 4.4397
Accounting theory / Ahmed Belkaoui. — New York: Harcourt Brace Jovanovich, c1981. xii, 318 p.: ill.; 23 cm. 1. Accounting I. T.
HF5635.B4167    657/.01 19    LC 80-82704    ISBN 0155004700

**Handbook of modern accounting / edited by Sidney Davidson**          **4.4398**
**and Roman L. Weil.**
3rd ed. — New York: McGraw-Hill, c1983. 1 v. (various pagings); 24 cm.
1. Accounting — Handbooks, manuals, etc. I. Davidson, Sidney, 1919-
II. Weil, Roman L.
HF5635.H23 1983          657 19          LC 83-952          *ISBN* 0070154929

**Lasser, J. K. (Jacob Kay), 1896-1954.**          **4.4399**
Handbook of accounting methods. Edited by J.K. Lasser Institute: Lee Gray,
Bernard Greisman [and] T.R. Lasser. 3d ed. Princeton, N.J., Van Nostrand
[1964] ix, 970 p. ill. ([Van Nostrand accounting and business books])
1. Accounting I. T.
HF5635 L35 1964          LC 64-22335

**Littleton, A. C. (Ananias Charles), 1886-.**          • **4.4400**
Essays on accountancy: a collection of readings / published for the Dept. of
Accountancy, University of Illinois. — Urbana: University of Illinois Press,
1961. 637 p.; 26 cm. 'The essays ... are for the most part extracts from ... [the
author's] articles.' 1. Accounting — Addresses, essays, lectures 2. Accounting
— Vocational guidance 3. Accounting — Study and teaching I. T.
HF5635 L73          LC 60-8341

**Paton, William Andrew, 1889-.**          • **4.4401**
Essentials of accounting / by William A. Paton and Robert L. Dixon. — New
York: Macmillan [1958] 800 p.: ill.; 22 cm. 1. Accounting I. Dixon, Robert L.
joint author. II. T.
HF5635.P314 1958          657          LC 58-7137

## HF5667 Auditing

**Arens, Alvin A.**          **4.4402**
Auditing, an integrated approach / Alvin A. Arens, James K. Loebbecke. — 2d
ed. — Englewood Cliffs, N.J.: Prentice-Hall, c1980. xvi, 776 p.: ill.; 24 cm. —
(Prentice-Hall series in accounting) Includes index. 1. Auditing I. Loebbecke,
James K. joint author. II. T.
HF5667.A69 1980          657/.45 19          LC 79-28407          *ISBN* 0130516562

**Lasser, J. K. (Jacob Kay), 1896-1954.**          • **4.4403**
Handbook of auditing methods. — New York: Van Nostrand, 1953. 769 p.
1. Auditing I. T. II. Title: Auditing methods.
HF5667.L36

**Robertson, Jack C.**          **4.4404**
Auditing / Jack C. Robertson, Frederick G. Davis. — 4th ed. — Plano, Tex.:
Business Publications, 1985. xxii, 794 p.: ill.; 24 cm. 1. Auditing I. Davis,
Frederick G. II. T.
HF5667.R72 1985          657/.45 19          LC 84-71559          *ISBN* 0256032742

**Thornhill, William T., 1926-.**          **4.4405**
Complete handbook of operational and management auditing / William T.
Thornhill. — Englewood Cliffs, N.J.: Prentice-Hall, c1981. 592 p.; 29 cm.
Includes index. 1. Auditing, Internal — Handbooks, manuals, etc. I. T.
HF5668.25.T49          657/.458/0202 19          LC 81-7340          *ISBN*
0131611410

## HF5679 Electronic Data Processing in Accounting

**Perry, William E.**          **4.4406**
The accountants' guide to computer systems / William E. Perry. — New York:
Wiley, c1982. xi, 286 p.: ill.; 24 cm. — (Modern accounting perspectives and
practices series.) 'A Ronald Press publication.' Includes index. 1. Accounting
— Data processing I. T. II. Series.
HF5679.P42 1982          001.64/024657 19          LC 81-19859          *ISBN*
0471089923

## HF5681–5686 Special Aspects. Cost Accounting

**Briloff, Abraham J.**          **4.4407**
More debits than credits: the burnt investor's guide to financial statements /
Abraham J. Briloff. — 1st ed. — New York: Harper & Row, c1976. xv, 453 p.:
ill.; 22 cm. 1. Financial statements 2. Accounting — United States — History.
I. T.
HF5681.B2 B72 1976          657/.3          LC 74-15812          *ISBN* 0060104767

**Foster, George, 1948-.**          **4.4408**
Financial statement analysis / George Foster. — 2nd ed. — Englewood Cliffs,
N.J.: Prentice-Hall, c1985. xii, 625 p.; 24 cm. (Prentice-Hall series in
accounting.) 1. Financial statements I. T. II. Series.
HF5681.B2 F64 1986          657/.3 19          LC 85-28112          *ISBN* 0133163172

**Lev, Baruch.**          **4.4409**
Financial statement analysis: a new approach. — Englewood Cliffs, N.J.:
Prentice-Hall, [1974] xvii, 262 p.: ill.; 24 cm. — (Prentice-Hall contemporary
topics in accounting series) (Prentice-Hall foundations of finance series)
1. Financial statements I. T.
HF5681.B2 L56          657/.3          LC 74-3287          *ISBN* 0133162656

**Industry norms and key business ratios.**          **4.4410**
Library ed. — 1982-83 ed.-          . — [New York]: Dun & Bradstreet Credit
Services. v.; 28 cm. (Dun's financial profiles.) Annual. 1. Ratio analysis —
Periodicals. 2. Line of business reporting — United States — Statistics —
Periodicals. 3. United States — Industries — Statistics — Periodicals. I. Dun
& Bradstreet Credit Services. II. Series.
HF5681.R25 I53          338.0973 19          LC 84-647330

**Troy, Leo.**          **4.4411**
Almanac of business and industrial financial ratios / by Leo Troy. — 1981-82
ed. — Englewood Cliffs, N.J.: Prentice-Hall, c1982. xxvii, 373 p.; 28 cm. Tables.
Includes index. 1. Ratio analysis 2. United States — Industries — Statistics
I. T.
HF5681.R25 T68 1982          338.5/0973 19          LC 82-238989          *ISBN*
0130227498

**Horngren, Charles T., 1926-.**          **4.4412**
Cost accounting: a managerial emphasis / Charles T. Horngren, George Foster.
— 6th ed. — Englewood Cliffs, N.J.: Prentice-Hall, 1987. 1 v. Includes index.
1. Cost accounting 2. Costs, Industrial I. Foster, George, 1948- II. T.
HF5686.C8 H59 1987          658.1/511 19          LC 86-21274          *ISBN*
0131795082

**Lasser, J. K. (Jacob Kay), 1896-1954. ed.**          • **4.4413**
Handbook of cost accounting methods. New York: D. Van Nostrand Co., 1949.
vii, 1344 p.: diagrs., form.; 24 cm. 1. Cost accounting I. T.
HF5686.C8 L275          657          LC 49-1897

**The Managerial and cost accountant's handbook / edited by**          **4.4414**
**Homer A. Black, James Don Edwards.**
Homewood, Ill.: Dow Jones-Irwin, c1979. xxv, 1297 p.: ill.; 24 cm. 1. Cost
accounting — Addresses, essays, lectures. 2. Managerial accounting —
Addresses, essays, lectures. I. Black, Homer A., 1923- II. Edwards, James
Don.
HF5686.C8 M263          658.1/511          LC 78-61201          *ISBN* 0870941739

**Matz, Adolph, 1905-.**          **4.4415**
Cost accounting: planning and control / Adolph Matz, Milton F. Usry;
consulting editor, Lawrence H. Hammer. — 8th ed. — Cincinnati: South-
Western Pub. Co., c1984. xii, 786 p.: ill. (some col.); 24 cm. 'A87.' 1. Cost
accounting I. Usry, Milton F. II. Hammer, Lawrence H. III. T.
HF5686.C8 M344 1984          657/.42 19          LC 83-61249          *ISBN*
0538018704

**Multinational accounting: a research framework for the eighties**          **4.4416**
**/ edited by Frederick D.S. Choi.**
Ann Arbor, Mich.: UMI Research Press, c1981. xii, 248 p.; 24 cm. —
(Research for business decisions. no. 46) 1. International business enterprises
— Accounting. I. Choi, Frederick D. S., 1942- II. Series.
HF5686.I56 M84          657/.95 19          LC 81-16448          *ISBN* 0835712672

## HF5691–5716 Business Mathematics. Tables

**Kemeny, John G.**          **4.4417**
Finite mathematics with business applications [by] John G. Kemeny [and
others]. — 2d ed. — Englewood Cliffs, N.J.: Prentice-Hall, [1972] xiii, 529 p.:
illus.; 24 cm. 1. Business — Mathematical models 2. Business mathematics
I. T.
HF5695.K4 1972          510          LC 75-171841          *ISBN* 0133173216

**Cox, Edwin Burk, 1930-.**          • **4.4418**
Basic tables in business and economics / edited by Edwin B. Cox. New York:
McGraw-Hill [1967] xiv, 399 p.: ill.; 23 cm. (McGraw-Hill basic tables series)
1. Ready-reckoners 2. Business mathematics — Tables, etc. 3. United States
— Statistics I. T.
HF5699.C892          511/.8          LC 66-19284

# HF5801–6191 Advertising

**Ogilvy, David, 1911-.**                                                • 4.4419
Confessions of an advertising man. — [1st ed.]. — New York: Atheneum, 1963.
172 p.; 24 cm. 1. Ogilvy, David, 1911- 2. Advertising — United States —
Biography. I. T.
HF5810.O34 A3        659.1        LC 63-17855

**Presbrey, Frank, 1855-1936.**                                          4.4420
The history and development of advertising / with more than three hundred
and fifty illustrations. — New York: Greenwood Press, 1968 [c1929] ix, 642 p.:
ill. 1. Advertising — History. I. T.
HF5811.P7 1968

**Backman, Jules, 1910-.**                                              • 4.4421
Advertising and competition. New York, New York University Press, 1967.
xvi, 239 p. ill. 1. Advertising — United States I. T.
HF5813.U6 B28        LC 67-17108

**Berman, Ronald.**                                                      4.4422
Advertising and social change / Ronald Berman. — Beverly Hills: Sage
Publications, c1981. 159 p.; 23 cm. — (Sage commtext series. v. 8) Includes
index. 1. Advertising — Social aspects — United States. I. T. II. Series.
HF5813.U6 B39        659.1/042/0973 19        LC 81-14326        ISBN
0803917376

**Marchand, Roland.**                                                    4.4423
Advertising the American dream: making way for modernity, 1920–1940 /
Roland Marchand. — Berkeley: University of California Press, c1985. xxii,
448 p.: ill. (some col.); 26 cm. Includes index. 1. Advertising — United States
— History. I. T.
HF5813.U6 M26 1985        659.1/0973 19        LC 84-28082        ISBN
0520052536

**Schudson, Michael.**                                                   4.4424
Advertising, the uneasy persuasion: its dubious impact on American society /
Michael Schudson. — New York: Basic Books, c1984. xii, 288 p.; 24 cm.
1. Advertising — United States — History. I. T.
HF5813.U6 S38 1984        659.1/042/0973 19        LC 84-45076        ISBN
0465000789

**Albion, Mark S., 1951-.**                                              4.4425
Advertising's hidden effects: manufacturers' advertising and retail pricing /
Mark S. Albion. — Boston, Mass.: Auburn House Pub. Co., c1983. xxi, 311 p.;
25 cm. Includes index. 1. Advertising — Economic aspects. I. T.
HF5821.A398 1983        381/.1 19        LC 82-6776        ISBN 0865691118

**Borden, Neil Hopper, 1895-.**                                         • 4.4426
The economic effects of advertising, by Neil H. Borden ... Chicago, R. D. Irwin,
inc., 1942. xl, 988 p. tables (1 fold.) diagrs., forms (1 fold.) 23.5 cm.
1. Advertising I. T.
HF5821.B57        659.1        LC 42-1977

**Pope, Daniel, 1946-.**                                                 4.4427
The making of modern advertising / Daniel Pope. — New York: Basic Books,
c1983. x, 340 p.; 22 cm. 1. Advertising I. T.
HF5821.P64 1983        338.4/76591 19        LC 82-72404        ISBN
0465043259

**Schmalensee, Richard.**                                                4.4428
The economics of advertising. — Amsterdam: North-Holland Pub. Co., 1972.
xiii, 312 p.; 23 cm. — (Contributions to economic analysis. 80) 1. Advertising
I. T. II. Series.
HF5821.S413        659.1        LC 70-183284        ISBN 0720431808

**Bauer, Raymond Augustine, 1916-.**                                    • 4.4429
Advertising in America; the consumer view [by] Raymond A. Bauer and
Stephen A. Greyser, in collaboration with Donald L. Kanter and William M.
Weilbacher, with the assistance of Alice E. Courtney and Christopher Gale. —
Boston: Division of Research, Graduate School of Business Administration,
Harvard University, 1968. xxvi, 473 p.; 21 cm. 'A report and interpretation of
the American Association of Advertising Agencies' study on the consumer
judgment of advertising.' 1. Advertising — Psychological aspects
2. Consumers — United States I. Greyser, Stephen A. joint author.
II. Kanter, Donald Lucky, 1925- III. Weilbacher, William M. IV. American
Association of Advertising Agencies. V. Harvard University. Graduate School
of Business Administration. Division of Research. VI. T.
HF5822.B335        659.1/01/9        LC 68-18720

**Packard, Vance Oakley, 1914-.**                                        • 4.4430
The hidden persuaders. — New York: D. McKay Co., [1957] 275 p.; 21 cm.
1. Advertising — Psychological aspects 2. Propaganda I. T.
HF5822.P3        659.1015        LC 57-13787

**Psychological processes and advertising effects: theory, research,**        4.4431
**and applications / edited by Linda F. Alwitt and Andrew A.**
**Mitchell.**
Hillsdale, N.J.: L. Erlbaum Associates, 1985. ix, 305 p.: ill.; 24 cm. Papers from
the Second Annual Conference on Advertising and Consumer Psychology held
in Chicago, Ill., May 1983. 1. Advertising — Psychological aspects —
Addresses, essays, lectures. I. Alwitt, Linda F. II. Mitchell, Andrew A., 1939-
III. Conference on Advertising and Consumer Psychology. (2nd: 1983:
Chicago, Ill.)
HF5822.P78 1985        659.1/01/9 19        LC 84-28773        ISBN
0898595150

**Barton, Roger, 1903-.**                                               • 4.4432
Handbook of advertising management. Roger Barton, editor. New York,
McGraw-Hill [1970] 1 v. (various pagings) illus. 21 cm. 1. Advertising —
Management — Handbooks, manuals, etc. I. T.
HF5823.B314        659.1/02/02        LC 74-96237

**Kleppner, Otto, 1899-.**                                               4.4433
[Advertising procedure] Otto Kleppner's Advertising procedure / Thomas
Russell, Glenn Verrill. — 9th ed. — Englewood Cliffs, NJ: Prentice-Hall,
c1986. xvii, 665 p.: ill. (some col.); 27 cm. (Prentice-Hall series in marketing.)
Includes index. 1. Advertising I. Russell, Thomas. II. Verrill, Glenn. III. T.
IV. Series.
HF5823.K45 1986        659.1 19        LC 85-12374        ISBN 0136432557

**Ogilvy, David, 1911-.**                                                4.4434
Ogilvy on advertising / David Ogilvy. — 1st American ed. — New York:
Crown, c1983. 224 p.: ill. (some col.); 26 cm. 1. Advertising I. T.
HF5823.O36 1983        659.1 19        LC 83-1877        ISBN 051755075X

**Albion, Mark S., 1951-.**                                              4.4435
The advertising controversy: evidence on the economic effects of advertising /
Mark S. Albion, Paul W. Farris. — Boston, Mass.: Auburn House Pub. Co.,
c1981. xxi, 226 p.: ill.; 24 cm. Includes index. 1. Advertising media planning
2. Advertising — Economic aspects. 3. Advertising — Management I. Farris,
Paul. joint author. II. T.
HF5826.5.A43        659.1/11 19        LC 80-24645        ISBN 086569057X

**Boddewyn, J. J. (Jean J.)**                                            4.4436
Comparison advertising: a worldwide study / J. J. Boddewyn, Katherin
Marton; with the special assistance of IAA national chapters; Rita Bari ... [et
al.]. — New York: Hastings House, c1978. x, 245 p.: ill.; 24 cm. —
(Communication arts book) 'A worldwide study sponsored by the International
Advertising Association.' Includes index. 1. Advertising, Comparison
I. Marton, Katherin. joint author. II. International Advertising Association
(1938- ) III. T.
HF5827.B577        659.13        LC 78-5546        ISBN 0803812493

**Young, Robert F. (Robert Freeman), 1940-.**                           4.4437
Managing cooperative advertising: a strategic approach / Robert F. Young,
Stephen A. Greyser. — Lexington, Mass.: LexingtonBooks, c1983. x, 170 p.:
ill.; 24 cm. 1. Cooperative advertising I. Greyser, Stephen A. II. T.
HF5827.4.Y68 1983        659.1 19        LC 82-48572        ISBN 0669063010

**Heighton, Elizabeth J.**                                               4.4438
Advertising in the broadcast and cable media / Elizabeth J. Heighton, Don R.
Cunningham. — 2nd ed. — Belmont, Calif.: Wadsworth Pub. Co., c1984. xv,
368 p.: ill.; 25 cm. — (Wadsworth series in mass communication.) Includes
index. Rev. ed. of: Advertising in the broadcast media. 1976. 1. Broadcast
advertising 2. Cable television advertising I. Cunningham, Don R. II. T.
III. Series.
HF6146.B74 H44 1984        659.14 19        LC 83-5805        ISBN 0534029140

**Poltrack, David.**                                                     4.4439
Television marketing: network, local, and cable / David Poltrack. — New
York: McGraw-Hill, c1983. xii, 395 p.: ill.; 24 cm. 1. Television advertising
2. Cable television advertising I. T.
HF6146.T42 P64 1983        659.14/3 19        LC 83-851        ISBN
0070504067

**Fritschler, A. Lee, 1937-.**                                           4.4440
Smoking and politics; policymaking and the Federal bureaucracy [by] A. Lee
Fritschler. — 2d ed. — Englewood Cliffs, N.J.: Prentice-Hall, [1975] x, 180 p.;
21 cm. 1. United States. Federal Trade Commission. 2. Cigarettes — Labeling
— United States. 3. Advertising — Cigarettes I. T.
HF6161.C35 F7 1975        659.1/967973/0973 19        LC 74-12381        ISBN
0138150192

**Fox, Charles Philip, 1913-.**                                    **4.4441**
Billers, banners, and bombast: the story of circus advertising / Charles Philip Fox and Tom Parkinson. — 1st ed. — Boulder, Colo.: Pruett Pub. Co., c1985. 266 p., 16 p. of plates: ill. (some col.); 22 x 26 cm. Includes index. 1. Advertising — Circus I. Parkinson, Tom. II. T.
HF6161.C424 F69 1985        659.1/97913 19      *LC* 82-16561        *ISBN* 0871086093

# HG FINANCE

**Rao, Dileep.**                                    **4.4442**
Handbook of business finance and capital sources. 1979-. Minneapolis, MN, InterFinance Corp. v. ill. 29 cm. Annual. 1. Finance — United States — Periodicals. 2. Financial institutions — United States — Periodicals. 3. Corporations — United States — Periodicals. 4. Business enterprises — United States — Periodicals. I. T.
HG61.R36        332.1/0973        *LC* 79-643216

**Munn, Glenn G. (Glenn Gaywaine), 1890-.**                                    **4.4443**
Encyclopedia of banking and finance / Glenn G. Munn. — 8th ed., rev. and expanded / F.L. Garcia. — Boston: Bankers Pub. Co., 1983. xiii, 1024 p.: ill.; 29 cm. 1. Banks and banking — Dictionaries. 2. Finance — Dictionaries. 3. Banks and banking — United States — Dictionaries. I. Garcia, F. L. (Ferdinand Lawrence), 1909- II. T.
HG151.M8 1983        332/.03/21 19      *LC* 83-8845        *ISBN* 0872670422

**Directory of business and financial services / editors, Mary**                **4.4444**
**McNierney Grant, Riva Berleant–Schiller.**
8th ed. — New York: Special Libraries Association, c1984. x, 189 p.; 26 cm. Includes indexes. 1. Finance — Information services — Directories. 2. Business — Information services — Directories. 3. Investments — Information services — Directories. I. Grant, Mary McNierney. II. Berleant-Schiller, Riva.
HG151.7.D57 1984        332/.025/73 19      *LC* 83-20300        *ISBN* 0871112876

**Stigum, Marcia L.**                                    **4.4445**
The money market: myth, reality, and practice / Marcia Stigum. — Homewood, Ill.: Dow Jones-Irwin, c1978. xviii, 578 p.: ill.; 24 cm. Includes index. 1. Money market I. T.
HG153.S74        332/.0412 19      *LC* 78-59224        *ISBN* 0870941674

**Feis, Herbert, 1893-1972.**                                    • **4.4446**
Europe: the world's banker, 1870–1914; an account of European foreign investment and the connection of world finance with diplomacy before the war. With an introd. by Charles P. Howland. Published for the Council on Foreign Relations. New Haven, Yale University Press, 1930. 469 p. (Publications of the Council on Foreign Relations) 1. Finance — Europe 2. Europe — Politics — 1871-1918 I. T.
HG171 F4

**Handbook of financial markets and institutions / edited by**                **4.4447**
**Edward I. Altman; associate editor Mary Jane McKinney.**
6th ed. — New York: Wiley, c1987. 1197 p. in various pagings: ill.; 24 cm. — (Wiley professional banking and finance series.) Rev. ed. of: Financial handbook, 5th ed. c1981. 1. Finance — Handbooks, manuals, etc. 2. Finance — United States — Handbooks, manuals, etc. 3. Corporations — Finance — Handbooks, manuals, etc. 4. International finance — Handbooks, manuals, etc. I. Altman, Edward I., 1941- II. McKinney, Mary Jane. III. Title: Financial handbook. IV. Series.
HG173.H33 1987        658.1/5 19      *LC* 86-11125        *ISBN* 0471819549

**Madden, John Thomas, 1882-1948.**                                    • **4.4448**
The international money markets / by John T. Madden and Marcus Nadler. — New York: Greenwood Press, 1968 [c1935] xiii, 548 p.; 24 cm. 1. Money market I. Nadler, Marcus, 1895- joint author. II. T. III. Title: Money markets.
HG173.M25 1968        332.4/5        *LC* 68-23311

**Shaw, Edward Stone.**                                    **4.4449**
Financial deepening in economic development / [by] Edward S. Shaw. — New York: Oxford University Press, 1973. xii, 260 p.; 22 cm. (Economic development series) 1. Finance — Developing countries. I. T.
HG174.S49        332/.09172/4      *LC* 72-92298

**Grant proposals that succeeded / edited by Virginia White.**                **4.4450**
New York: Plenum Press, c1983. viii, 240 p.: ill.; 28 cm. — (Nonprofit management and finance.) 1. Fund raising — Case studies. 2. Research grants — Case studies. 3. Proposal writing in research — Case studies. I. White, Virginia P. II. Series.
HG177.G69 1983        001.4/4 19      *LC* 82-22262        *ISBN* 0306408732

**Amling, Frederick.**                                    **4.4451**
Personal financial management / Frederick Amling, Wiliam G. Droms. — 2nd ed. — Homewood, Ill.: Irwin, 1986. xvii, 590 p.: ill.; 25 cm. 1. Finance, Personal I. Droms, William G., 1944- II. T.
HG179.A555 1986        332.024 19      *LC* 85-81405        *ISBN* 025603351X

**Neufeld, Edward Peter.**                                    **4.4452**
The financial system of Canada; its growth and development [by] E. P. Neufeld. — [Toronto]: Macmillan of Canada, [1972] 645 p.; 25 cm. 1. Finance — Canada. 2. Financial institutions — Canada. I. T.
HG185.C2 N48        332.1/0971      *LC* 70-178200        *ISBN* 0770508588

**Kindleberger, Charles Poor, 1910-.**                                    **4.4453**
A financial history of Western Europe / Charles P. Kindleberger. — London; Boston: Allen & Unwin, 1984. xviii, 525 p.: ill., maps; 24 cm. Includes index. 1. Finance — Europe — History. I. T.
HG186.A2 K56 1984        332/.094 19      *LC* 83-72852        *ISBN* 0043320880

**Schuker, Stephen A., 1939-.**                                    **4.4454**
The end of French predominance in Europe: the financial crisis of 1924 and the adoption of the Dawes plan / by Stephen A. Schuker. — Chapel Hill: University of North Carolina Press, c1976. xv, 444 p.; 24 cm. Includes index. 1. Finance — France — History — 20th century. 2. Money — France — History — 20th century. 3. World War, 1914-1918 — Reparations. I. T.
HG186.F8 S34        332/.0944      *LC* 75-38799        *ISBN* 0807812536

**Cairncross, Alexander Kirkland.**                                    • **4.4455**
Home and foreign investment, 1870–1913; studies in capital accumulation. Cambridge [Eng.] University Press, 1953. xvi, 251 p. ill., tables. 1. Capital — Great Britain 2. Investments — Great Britain 3. Investments, British I. T.
HG186 G7 C3        *LC* 53-11731

**Jenks, Leland Hamilton, 1892-.**                                    • **4.4456**
The migration of British capital to 1875. New York, Nelson [1963, c1927] 442 p. 1. Investments, British 2. Finance — Great Britain 3. Great Britain — Economic conditions 4. Great Britain — Economic policy I. T.
HG186 G7 J4 1963        *LC* 63-23667

**Garvy, George.**                                    **4.4457**
Money, financial flows, and credit in the Soviet Union / George Garvy. — New York: National Bureau of Economic Research, 1977. xii, 223 p.; 24 cm. — (Studies in international economic relations; 7) Includes index. 1. Finance — Russia. 2. Money — Russia. 3. Banks and banking — Russia. 4. Credit — Russia. I. T. II. Series.
HG186.R8 G37        332/.0947      *LC* 76-58491        *ISBN* 0870145185

**Financial institutions and markets in Southeast Asia: a study of**                **4.4458**
**Brunei, Indonesia, Malaysia, Philippines, Singapore, and**
**Thailand / edited by Michael T. Skully.**
New York: St. Martin's Press, 1984. xviii, 411 p.: ill., maps; 23 cm. Includes index. 1. Financial institutions — Asia, Southeastern — Addresses, essays, lectures. 2. Finance — Asia, Southeastern — Addresses, essays, lectures. I. Skully, Michael T.
HG187.A789 F56 1984        332.1/0959 19      *LC* 83-13892        *ISBN* 0312289642

**Uppal, J. S., 1927-.**                                    **4.4459**
Public financial institutions in India / J.S. Uppal. — Delhi: Macmillan India, 1984. 111 p.; 23 cm. 1. Government financial institutions — India. I. T.
HG187.I4 U66 1984        332.2 19      *LC* 84-903343        *ISBN* 0333904605

**Nasution, Anwar.**                                    **4.4460**
Financial institutions and policies in Indonesia / Anwar Nasution. — Singapore: Institute of Southeast Asian Studies, c1983. xvii, 182 p.: ill.; 27 cm. 1. Finance — Indonesia. 2. Financial institutions — Indonesia. 3. Indonesia — Economic policy. I. T.
HG187.I7 N37 1983        332.1/09598 19      *LC* 83-941889        *ISBN* 9971902605

**Eshag, Eprime.**                                    **4.4461**
Fiscal and monetary policies and problems in developing countries / Éprime Eshag. — Cambridge [Cambridgeshire]; New York: Cambridge University Press, 1983. xxii, 287 p.: ill.; 23 cm. (Modern Cambridge economics.) 1. Finance — Developing countries. 2. Fiscal policy — Developing countries 3. Monetary policy — Developing countries. I. T. II. Series.
HG195.E83 1983        336/.09172/4 19      *LC* 82-17831        *ISBN* 0521249007

# HG201–1496 Money

**Dormael, Armand van, 1916-.**     **4.4462**
Bretton Woods: birth of a monetary system / Armand van Dormael. — New York: Holmes & Meier Publishers, c1978. xi, 322 p.; 22 cm. 1. United Nations Monetary and Financial Conference, Bretton Woods, N.H., 1944 — History. 2. International finance — History. I. T.
HG205 1944.D67 1978    332.4/5/09    *LC* 77-10651    *ISBN* 0841903263

**Managing foreign exchange risk: essays commissioned in honor**     **4.4463**
**of the centenary of the Wharton School, University of**
**Pennsylvania / edited by Richard J. Herring.**
Cambridge [Cambridgeshire]; New York, NY: Cambridge University Press, 1983. 235 p. Based on essays and perspectives presented at a conference entitled Managing international risk, held in Philadelphia, Oct. 26-27, 1981, sponsored jointly by the Global Interdependence Center, the Group of Thirty, and the Wharton School, University of Pennsylvania. 1. Wharton School. 2. Foreign exchange administration — Congresses. 3. Foreign exchange problem — Congresses. I. Herring, Richard. II. Global Interdependence Center. III. Group of Thirty. IV. Wharton School. V. Title: Foreign exchange risk.
HG205 1981a    658.1/55 19    *LC* 82-21999    *ISBN* 052125079X

**Exchange rates and international macroeconomics / edited by**     **4.4464**
**Jacob A. Frenkel.**
Chicago: University of Chicago Press, 1983. x, 382 p.: ill.; 23 cm. — (A conference report / National Bureau of Economic Research) Papers and comments presented at a conference held in Cambridge, Mass., Nov. 20-21, 1981; sponsored by the National Bureau of Economic Research. 1. Foreign exchange — Congresses. 2. International finance — Congresses. I. Frenkel, Jacob A. II. National Bureau of Economic Research.
HG205 1981c    332.4/56 19    *LC* 83-14524    *ISBN* 0226262499

**Exchange rate theory and practice / edited by John F. O.**     **4.4465**
**Bilson and Richard C. Marston.**
Chicago: University of Chicago Press, 1985 (c1984). ix, 528 p.: ill.; 24 cm. (A National Bureau of Economic Research conference report) Papers presented at a conference held in Jan. 1982 at the Rockefeller Foundation's Bellagio Conference Center on Lake Como in northern Italy, and sponsored by the National Bureau of Economic Research. 1. Foreign exchange — Congresses. I. Bilson, John F. O. II. Marston, Richard C. III. National Bureau of Economic Research.
HG205 1984    332.4/5 19    *LC* 84-2441    *ISBN* 0226050963

## HG220–230 Theory

**Friedman, Milton, 1912- ed.**     • **4.4466**
Studies in the quantity theory of money. With essays by Milton Friedman [and others. Chicago] University of Chicago Press [1956] v, 265 p. ill. (Studies in economics of the Economics Research Center of the University of Chicago) 1. Quantity theory of money 2. Inflation (Finance) I. T.
HG221 F78    *LC* 56-10999

**Gale, Douglas.**     **4.4467**
Money, in disequilibrium / Douglas Gale. — Welwyn [Hertfordshire]: J. Nisbet; New York: Cambridge University Press, 1983. xi, 368 p.: ill.; 23 cm. (The Cambridge economic handbooks) Bibliography: p. [357]-364. Includes index. 1. Money 2. Equilibrium (Economics) I. T. II. Series.
HG221.G238 1983    332.4 19    *LC* 84-241377    *ISBN* 0521262917

**Gale, Douglas.**     **4.4468**
Money, in equilibrium / Douglas Gale. — Welwyn [Hertfordshire]: J. Nisbet; Cambridge; New York: Cambridge University Press, 1982. ix, 349 p.: ill.; 23 cm. — (Cambridge economic handbooks) Includes index. 1. Money 2. Equilibrium (Economics) I. T. II. Series.
HG221.G24 1982    332.4 19    *LC* 82-215957    *ISBN* 0521246946

**Goodhart, C. A. E. (Charles Albert Eric).**     **4.4469**
Money, information, and uncertainty / C. A. E. Goodhart. — New York: Barnes & Noble, 1975. ix, 331 p.: graphs; 25 cm. Includes index. 1. Money I. T.
HG221.G674 1975b    332.4    *LC* 76-351659    *ISBN* 0064924920

**Hawtrey, R. G. (Ralph George), 1879-.**     • **4.4470**
Currency and credit / Ralph George Hawtrey. — 4th ed. — London: Longmans, Green, 1950. ix, 475 p.; 23 cm. — 1. Money 2. Credit 3. International finance I. T.
HG221.H33 1950    332.4    *LC* 50-8721

**Hayek, Friedrich A. von (Friedrich August), 1899-.**     **4.4471**
Money, capital, and fluctuations: early essays / F.A. Hayek; edited by Roy McCloughry. — Chicago, IL: University of Chicago Press; London: Routledge & Kegan Paul, 1984. xi, 196 p.; 23 cm. 1. Money — Addresses, essays, lectures. 2. Capital — Addresses, essays, lectures. 3. Business cycles — Addresses, essays, lectures. I. McCloughry, Roy. II. T.
HG221.H346 1984    332.4 19    *LC* 84-227    *ISBN* 0226320928

**Jevons, William Stanley, 1835-1882.**     • **4.4472**
Investigations in currency & finance [by] W. Stanley Jevons. New York, A.M. Kelley, bookseller, 1964. xiiv, 428 p. illus. (2 fold. in pocket) (Reprints of economic classics.) 'Edited, with an introduction, by H.S. Foxwell.' Includes index. 1. Money 2. Finance 3. Prices 4. Depressions 5. Bimetallism 6. Precious metals 7. Currency question — Great Britain. I. Foxwell, Herbert Somerton, 1849-1936. II. T. III. Series.
HG221.J46    332.41    *LC* 64-22238

**Johnson, Harry G. (Harry Gordon), 1923-1977.**     • **4.4473**
Essays in monetary economics [by] Harry G. Johnson. London, Allen & Unwin, 1967. 3-332 p. diagrs. 22 1/2 cm. 1. Money 2. Monetary policy 3. Fiscal policy I. T.
HG221.J663    332.4/01    *LC* 67-88230

**Johnson, Harry G. (Harry Gordon), 1923-1977.**     **4.4474**
Further essays in monetary economics [by] Harry G. Johnson. Cambridge, Mass., Harvard University Press, 1973 [c1972] 366 p. illus. 22 cm. 1. Money 2. Monetary policy 3. International finance I. T.
HG221.J6634    332.4    *LC* 72-95183    *ISBN* 0674335252

**Milton Friedman's monetary framework: a debate with his**     **4.4475**
**critics / edited by Robert J. Gordon; Milton Friedman ... [et**
**al.].**
Chicago: University of Chicago Press, 1975 (c1974). xii, 192 p.; 24 cm. Includes index. 1. Friedman, Milton, 1912- A theoretical framework for monetary analysis. 2. Money — Addresses, essays, lectures. 3. Quantity theory of money — Addresses, essays, lectures. I. Gordon, Robert J. (Robert James), 1940- II. Friedman, Milton, 1912-
HG221.M655    332.4/01    *LC* 73-92599    *ISBN* 0226264076. *ISBN* 0226264084 pbk

**Myrdal, Gunnar, 1898-.**     • **4.4476**
Monetary equilibrium / by Gunnar Myrdal. — London [etc.]: Hodge, 1939. xi, 214 p.; 22 cm. 1. Wicksell, Knut, 1851-1926. 2. Money I. T.
HG221 M87 1939

**Niehans, Jürg.**     **4.4477**
The theory of money / Jurg Niehans. — Baltimore: Johns Hopkins University Press, c1978. xi, 312 p.; 24 cm. Includes indexes. 1. Money I. T.
HG221.N66    332.4/01    *LC* 77-17247    *ISBN* 0801820553

**Patinkin, Don.**     • **4.4478**
Money, interest, and prices: an integration of monetary and value theory / Don Patinkin. — 2d ed. New York: Harper & Row, [1965] xxv, 708 p.: ill.; 22 cm. 1. Money 2. Interest and usury 3. Value I. T.
HG221.P335 1965    332.401    *LC* 65-16252

**Patinkin, Don.**     **4.4479**
Studies in monetary economics. — New York: Harper & Row, [1972] 262 p.: illus.; 25 cm. 1. Monetary policy I. T.
HG221.P33524    332.4/6    *LC* 78-170625    *ISBN* 0060450312

**Robertson, Dennis Holme, 1890-.**     • **4.4480**
Essays in monetary theory / by D.H. Robertson. — London: P.S. King & Son, 1940. ix, 234 p.; 22 cm. 1. Keynes, John Maynard, 1888-1946. 2. Money 3. Interest and usury. 4. Business cycles I. T.
HG221.R557    *LC* a 41-490

**Robertson, Dennis Holme, Sir, 1890-1963.**     • **4.4481**
Money. [Chicago] University of Chicago Press [1959] 187 p. 19 cm. (The Cambridge economic handbooks) 1. Money I. T.
HG221.R56 1959    332.4    *LC* 59-9825

**Thorn, Richard S. ed.**     **4.4482**
Monetary theory and policy: major contributions to contemporary thought / edited by Richard S. Thorn. [Rev. ed.]. — New York: Praeger, c1976. xi, 689 p.; 23 cm. 1. Money — Addresses, essays, lectures. 2. Monetary policy — Addresses, essays, lectures. I. T.
HG221.T44 1976    332.4    *LC* 75-41865    *ISBN* 0275228002

**Varieties of monetary experience. Edited and with an introd. by**     • **4.4483**
**David Meiselman. With essays by John V. Deaver [and others].**
Chicago: University of Chicago Press, [1970] 391 p.: illus.; 24 cm. — (Economics research studies of the Economics Research Center of the University of Chicago) 1. Money — Addresses, essays, lectures. 2. Quantity

theory of money — Addresses, essays, lectures. 3. Monetary policy — Addresses, essays, lectures. I. Meiselman, David, ed.
HG221.V35    332.4    *LC* 70-116027    *ISBN* 0226519309

**Desai, Meghnad.**             **4.4484**
Testing monetarism / Meghnad Desai. — New York: St. Martin's Press, 1982, c1981. 246 p.: ill.; 22 cm. Includes index. 1. Money — Mathematical models. 2. Monetary policy — Mathematical models. 3. Chicago school of economics I. T. II. Title: Monetarism.
HG221.3.D48 1982    332.4/6/0724 19    *LC* 81-21360    *ISBN* 0312793561

## HG229 Money and Prices. Inflation

**Flemming, John Stanton, 1941-.**        **4.4485**
Inflation / by J. S. Flemming. — London: Oxford University Press, 1976. 136 p.: ill.; 21 cm. 1. Inflation (Finance) 2. Inflation (Finance) — Great Britain. I. T.
HG229.F624    332.4/1    *LC* 76-377976    *ISBN* 0198770855

**Frisch, Helmut.**               **4.4486**
Theories of inflation / Helmut Frisch. — Cambridge [Cambridgeshire]; New York: Cambridge University Press, 1984 (c1983). ix, 262 p.: ill.; 22 cm. — (Cambridge surveys of economic literature.) Based on: Die neue Inflationstheorie. Göttingen: Vandenhoeck und Ruprecht, 1980. Includes indexes. 1. Inflation (Finance) I. T. II. Series.
HG229.F723    332.4/1/01 19    *LC* 83-1871    *ISBN* 0521224705

**Hayek, Friedrich A. von (Friedrich August), 1899-.**    • **4.4487**
Prices and production. [2d ed., rev. and enl.] New York: A. M. Kelley, [1967] xiv, 162 p.: ill.; 20 cm. (London School of Economics and Political Science. Studies in economics and political science; series of monographs, no. 107) Reprint of the 1935 ed. 1. Money 2. Prices 3. Currency question I. T.
HG229 H3

**Inflation, causes and effects / edited by Robert E. Hall.**    **4.4488**
Chicago: University of Chicago Press, 1983 (c1982). ix, 290 p.: ill.; 24 cm. — (National Bureau of Economic Research project report.) 1. Inflation (Finance) — Addresses, essays, lectures. 2. Inflation (Finance) — United States — Addresses, essays, lectures. I. Hall, Robert Ernest, 1943- II. Series.
HG229.I4512    332.4/1 19    *LC* 82-10932    *ISBN* 0226313239

**Laidler, David E. W.**            **4.4489**
Essays on money and inflation / D. E. W. Laidler. — Chicago: University of Chicago Press, 1976 (c1975). xiii, 246 p.: ill.; 23 cm. (Studies in inflation) Includes indexes. 1. Inflation (Finance) 2. Monetary policy — Mathematical models. I. T. II. Series.
HG229.L2    332.4/1    *LC* 75-22170    *ISBN* 0226467937

**Wicksell, Knut, 1851-1926.**          • **4.4490**
Interest and prices (Geldzins und Güterpreise) A study of the causes regulating the value of money. Translated by R.F. Kahn. With an introd. by Bertil Ohlin, and the article The enigma of business cycles, translated by Carl G. Uhr. New York, A.M. Kelley, 1965. xxxi, 239 p. (Reprints of economic classics) 1. Money 2. Prices 3. Quantity theory of money 4. Interest and usury I. T.
HG229 W523 1965    *LC* 65-16993

**Worldwide inflation: theory and recent experience / Lawrence**    **4.4491**
**B. Krause, Walter S. Salant, editors.**
Washington: Brookings Institution, c1977. xi, 686 p.: graphs; 24 cm. 1. Inflation (Finance) — Addresses, essays, lectures. I. Krause, Lawrence B. II. Salant, Walter S.
HG229.W664    332.4/1    *LC* 76-51580    *ISBN* 0815750293 pbk. *ISBN* 0815750307

**Marshall, Alfred, 1842-1924.**         • **4.4492**
Money, credit & commerce. — New York: A.M. Kelley, 1965. vx, 368 p.: ill. — (Reprints of economics classics) Original editions 1923. 1. Money 2. Commerce 3. Credit 4. Banks and banking — Great Britain. I. T.
HG230.M3 1965    *LC* 65-16984

## HG230.3–313 Monetary Policy.
## Gold Standard

**Laidler, David E. W.**            **4.4493**
Monetarist perspectives / David Laidler. — Cambridge, Mass.: Harvard University Press, 1983 (c1982). xii, 218 p.; 23 cm. Includes indexes. 1. Monetary policy 2. Macroeconomics I. T.
HG230.3.L34    332.4/1 19    *LC* 82-15406    *ISBN* 0674582403

**Bloomfield, Arthur I. (Arthur Irving)**      • **4.4494**
Monetary policy under the international gold standard: 1880–1914. [New York, Federal Reserve Bank of New York] 1959. 62 p. diagrs. 1. Currency question 2. Banks and banking, Central I. Federal Reserve Bank of New York. II. T.
HG253 B59    *LC* 59-64275

**A Retrospective on the classical gold standard, 1821–1931 /**    **4.4495**
**edited by Michael D. Bordo, Anna J. Schwartz.**
Chicago: University of Chicago Press, c1984. xi, 681 p.: ill.; 24 cm. (A Conference report / National Bureau of Economic Research) Papers from a conference sponsored by the National Bureau of Economic Research, held in March, 1982. 1. Gold standard — History — Congresses. I. Bordo, Michael D. II. Schwartz, Anna Jacobson. III. National Bureau of Economic Research.
HG297.R44 1984    332.4/222 19    *LC* 84-2440    *ISBN* 0226065901

**Jastram, Roy W., 1915-.**           **4.4496**
Silver: the restless metal / Roy W. Jastram. — New York: Wiley, c1981. xvii, 224 p., [3] fold. leaves of plates: ill.; 24 cm. 'A Ronald Press publication.' 1. Silver — England — History. 2. Silver — United States — History. I. T.
HG307.E5 J37    332.4/223/09 19    *LC* 80-28361    *ISBN* 0471039128

## HG451–1486 By Country

## HG451–645 United States

**Friedman, Milton, 1912-.**           **4.4497**
Monetary trends in the United States and the United Kingdom, their relation to income, prices, and interest rates, 1867–1975 / Milton Friedman and Anna J. Schwartz. — Chicago: University of Chicago Press, 1982. xxxi, 664 p.: ill.; 24 cm. — (National Bureau of Economic Research monograph.) Includes indexes. 1. Money supply — United States — History. 2. Money supply — Great Britain — History. 3. United States — Economic conditions 4. Great Britain — Economic conditions I. Schwartz, Anna Jacobson. II. T. III. Series.
HG501.F74 1982    332.9/973 19    *LC* 81-16273    *ISBN* 0226264092

**Ernst, Joseph Albert.**           **4.4498**
Money and politics in America, 1755–1775; a study in the Currency act of 1764 and the political economy of revolution. Chapel Hill, Published for the Institute of Early American History and Culture, by the University of North Carolina Press [1973] xix, 403 p. illus. 24 cm. 1. Currency question — United States 2. Monetary policy — History. 3. United States — Politics and government — Colonial period, ca. 1600-1775 4. Great Britain — Colonies — America — Financial questions. I. Institute of Early American History and Culture (Williamsburg, Va.) II. T.
HG508.E75    973.3/1    *LC* 73-6858    *ISBN* 080781217X

**Bowen, William G.**           **4.4499**
The wage–price issue; a theoretical analysis. — Princeton, N. J., Princeton University Press, 1960. 447 p. illus. 23 cm. 'A project of the Industrial Relations Section, Princeton University.' Includes bibliography. 1. Inflation (Finance) — U.S. 2. Prices — U.S. 3. Wages — U.S. I. Princeton University. Industrial Relations Section. II. T.
HG538.B74    332.413    *LC* 60-5742

**Cagan, Phillip.**           **4.4500**
The financial effects of inflation / Phillip Cagan and Robert E. Lipsey. — Cambridge, Mass.: Published for the National Bureau of Economic Research by Ballinger Pub. Co., 1978. xiv, 87 p.: graphs; 24 cm. — (General series - National Bureau of Economic Research; 103) Includes index. 1. Inflation (Finance) — United States 2. Finance — United States. I. Lipsey, Robert E. joint author. II. National Bureau of Economic Research. III. T.
HG538.C16    332.4/1    *LC* 78-13124    *ISBN* 0884104869

**Chandler, Lester Vernon, 1905-.**      • **4.4501**
American monetary policy, 1928–1941 [by] Lester V. Chandler. — New York: Harper & Row, [1971] viii, 371 p.; 25 cm. 1. Monetary policy — U.S. — History. I. T.
HG538.C47    332.4/9/73    *LC* 71-132665

**Friedman, Milton, 1912-.**        • **4.4502**
A monetary history of the United States, 1867–1960 [by] Milton Friedman [and] Anna Jacobson Schwartz. Princeton, Princeton University Press, 1963. xxiv, 860 p. diagrs., tables. 24 cm. (National Bureau of Economic Research. Studies in business cycles, 12) 1. Money — United States — History 2. Currency question — United States — History. 3. Monetary policy — United States — History. I. Schwartz, Anna Jacobson. joint author. II. T.
HG538.F86    332.4973    *LC* 63-7521

**Friedman, Milton, 1912-.**        • **4.4503**
Monetary statistics of the United States: estimates, sources, methods [by] Milton Friedman [and] Anna Jacobson Schwartz. New York, National Bureau of Economic Research, 1970. xx, 629 p. illus. 24 cm. (National Bureau of

Economic Research. Studies in business cycles, 20) 1. Money — United States 2. Money — United States — Statistics. I. Schwartz, Anna Jacobson. joint author. II. T.
HG538.F863    332.4/9/73    *LC* 78-85410    *ISBN* 0870142100

**Friedman, Milton, 1912-.**    • 4.4504
The optimum quantity of money, and other essays. — Chicago: Aldine Pub. Co., [1969] vi, 296 p.: illus.; 25 cm. 1. Money supply — United States — Addresses, essays, lectures. 2. Monetary policy — United States — Addresses, essays, lectures. 3. Money — Addresses, essays, lectures. I. T.
HG538.F866    332.4/9/73    *LC* 68-8148

**Friedman, Milton, 1912-.**    • 4.4505
A program for monetary stability. — New York, Fordham University Press, 1959. 110 p. 24 cm. — (The Millar lectures, no. 3) Includes bibliography. 1. Currency question — U.S. I. T.
HG538.F87    332.4973    *LC* 60-9782

**Wicker, Elmus R.**    • 4.4506
Federal Reserve monetary policy, 1917–1933 [by] Elmus R. Wicker. New York, Random House [c1966] xiv, 221 p. 22 cm. 1. Monetary policy — United States. I. T.
HG538.W62    332.4/973    *LC* 67-10164

**Mayer, Thomas, 1927-.**    4.4507
Money, banking, and the economy / Thomas Mayer, James S. Duesenberry, Robert Z. Aliber. — 1st ed. — New York: Norton, c1981. xii, 755 p.: ill.; 24 cm. 1. Money — United States 2. Banks and banking — United States 3. Monetary policy — United States. I. Duesenberry, James Stemble, 1918- joint author. II. Aliber, Robert Z. joint author. III. T.
HG540.M39 1981    332.1/0973 19    *LC* 80-29109    *ISBN* 0393951219

**Mitchell, Wesley Clair, 1874-1948.**    • 4.4508
A history of the greenbacks: with special reference to the economic consequences of their issue, 1862–65 / Wesley Mitchell. — [Chicago]: University of Chicago Press, [1960, c1903] 577 p.: ill., tables; 23 cm. — (Chicago reprint series.) 1. Greenbacks — History I. T.
HG604 M68

**Unger, Irwin.**    • 4.4509
The greenback era; a social and political history of American finance, 1865–1879. — Princeton, N.J.: Princeton University Press, 1964. 467 p.; 25 cm. 1. Greenbacks — History. 2. Currency question — United States — History. 3. United States — Politics and government — 1865-1877 I. T.
HG604.U5    332.4973    *LC* 63-18651

## HG660.5 Latin America

**Pazos, Felipe.**    4.4510
Chronic inflation in Latin America [by] Felipe Pazos. Translated by Ernesto Cuesta in collaboration with the author. New York, Praeger Publishers [1972] xvi, 186 p. illus. 25 cm. (Praeger special studies in international economics and development) Rev. and updated translation of Medidas para detener la inflación crónica en América Latina published in 1969. 1. Inflation (Finance) — Latin America. 2. Latin America — Economic policy. I. T.
HG660.5.P3513 1972    332.4/1    *LC* 71-180848

## HG921–1201 Europe

**Triffin, Robert.**    • 4.4511
Europe and the money muddle; from bilateralism to near–convertibility, 1947–1956. — New Haven, Yale University Press, 1957. xxvii, 351 p. diagrs., tables. 24 cm. — (Yale studies in economics. 7) 1. Currency question — Europe. 2. Foreign exchange problem — Europe. I. T. II. Series.
HG924.T69    332.494    *LC* 57-6878

**Ungerer, Horst.**    4.4512
The European monetary system: the experience, 1979–82 / by Horst Ungerer, with Owen Evans, and Peter Nyberg. — Washington, D.C.: International Monetary Fund, [1983] v, 41 p.: ill.; 28 cm. (Occasional paper / International Monetary Fund, 0251-6365; no. 19) 1. Money — European Economic Community countries I. Evans, Owen, 1953- II. Nyberg, Peter. III. T.
HG930.5.U49 1983    332.4/5/094 19    *LC* 83-166479

**Capie, Forrest.**    4.4513
A monetary history of the United Kingdom, 1870–1982 / Forrest Capie, Alan Webber. — London; Boston: Allen & Unwin, 1985. 596 p. Includes index. 1. Money — Great Britain — History. 2. Money — Great Britain — Statistics — History. I. Webber, Alan, 1954- II. T.
HG939.C29 1985    332.4/0941 19    *LC* 84-20431    *ISBN* 004332097X

**Moggridge, D. E. (Donald Edward), 1943-.**    4.4514
British monetary policy, 1926–1931, the Norman conquest of $4.86 [by] D. E. Moggridge. Cambridge [Eng.] University Press, 1972. x, 301 p. 24 cm. (University of Cambridge. Dept. of Applied Economics. Monographs, 21) 1. Monetary policy — Great Britain. 2. Gold standard I. T.
HG939.M578    332.4/942    *LC* 76-169576    *ISBN* 0521082250

**Moggridge, D. E. (Donald Edward), 1943-.**    4.4515
The return to gold, 1925: the formulation of economic policy and its critics, by D. E. Moggridge. London, Cambridge U.P., 1969. 119 p. 24 cm. (University of Cambridge. Dept. of Applied Economics. Occasional papers, 19) 1. Monetary policy — Great Britain. 2. Gold standard I. T.
HG939.M58    332.4/22/0942    *LC* 77-85730    *ISBN* 0521076668

**Howson, Susan, 1945-.**    4.4516
Domestic monetary management in Britain, 1919–38 / Susan Howson. — Cambridge; New York: Cambridge University Press, 1975. ix, 213 p.: ill.; 25 cm. (Occasional papers - University of Cambridge, Department of Applied Economics; 48) 1. Monetary policy — Great Britain. I. T.
HG939.5.H65    332.4/941    *LC* 75-21032    *ISBN* 0521210593

**The Money supply and the exchange rate / edited by W.A. Eltis**    4.4517
**and P.J.N. Sinclair.**
Oxford: Clarendon Press; New York: Oxford University Press, 1981. 364 p.: ill.; 24 cm. 1. Money supply — Great Britain — Addresses, essays, lectures. 2. Monetary policy — Great Britain — Addresses, essays, lectures. 3. Foreign exchange problem — Great Britain — Addresses, essays, lectures. I. Eltis, W. A. (Walter Alfred) II. Sinclair, P. J. N.
HG939.5.M625    332.4/941 19    *LC* 81-201760    *ISBN* 0198771681

**Miskimin, Harry A.**    4.4518
Money and power in fifteenth–century France / Harry A. Miskimin. — New Haven: Yale University Press, c1984. x, 303 p.; 25 cm. — (Yale series in economic history.) Includes index. 1. Money — France — History — 15th century. 2. Monetary policy — France — History — 15th century. 3. Fiscal policy — France — History — 15th century. 4. France — Politics and government — 1328-1589 I. T. II. Series.
HG976.M49 1984    332.4/944 19    *LC* 83-21754    *ISBN* 0300031327

**Harris, Seymour Edwin, 1897-.**    • 4.4519
The assignats, by S. E. Harris. — New York: AMS Press, [1969] xix, 293 p.: illus.; 23 cm. Reprint of the 1930 ed. 1. Assignats 2. France — History — Revolution, 1789-1799 — Finance I. T.
HG978.2.H3 1969    332.5/3/0944    *LC* 74-98625

**Bresciani-Turroni, Costantino.**    • 4.4520
The economics of inflation; a study of currency depreciation in post–war Germany. With a foreword by Lionel Robbins. Translated by Millicent E. Savers. — [New York]: A. M. Kelley, [1968] 464 p.: illus.; 23 cm. — (A Sir Halley Stewart publication) Rev. English version of Le vicende del marco tedesco. 'First published in English, 1937 ... third impression, 1968.' 1. Currency question — Germany. 2. Inflation (Finance) — Germany. 3. Germany — Economic conditions — 1918-1945 I. T.
HG999.B73 1968    332.4/9/43    *LC* 68-6120    *ISBN* 0043320058

## HG1211–1311 Asia

**Chou, Shun-hsin, 1915-.**    • 4.4521
The Chinese inflation, 1937–1949. New York, Columbia University Press, 1963. xiii, 319 p. diagrs. (Studies of the East Asian Institute) 1. Inflation (Finance) — China I. T.
HG1224 C52    *LC* 62-18260

**Hsiao, Katharine H. Y. Huang (Katharine Huei-Ying Huang),**    4.4522
**1923-.**
Money and banking in the Chinese Mainland / Katharine H.Y. Huang Hsiao. — Taipei, Taiwan, Republic of China: Chung-Hua Institution for Economic Research; Seattle: Distributed by University of Washington Press, 1985 (c1984). viii, 98 p.: ill.; 26 cm. (Mainland China economic series. no. 1) 'June 1984.' 1. Money — China. 2. Banks and banking — China. I. T. II. Series.
HG1285.H73 1984    332.1/0951 19    *LC* 84-231124

**Trescott, Paul B.**    4.4523
Thailand's monetary experience: the economics of stability / [by] Paul B. Trescott. — New York: Praeger Publishers, [1971] xxiv, 342 p.: ill.; 25 cm. — (Praeger special studies in international economics and development) 1. Monetary policy — Thailand. 2. Thailand — Economic policy. I. T.
HG1300.5.T73    332.4/9/593    *LC* 71-153838

## HG1496 Developing Countries

**Cline, William R.**       **4.4524**
World inflation and the developing countries / William R. Cline and associates; William R. Cline ... [et al.]. — Washington, D.C.: Brookings Institution, c1981. xiv, 266 p.: ill.; 24 cm. 1. Inflation (Finance) — Developing countries — Addresses, essays, lectures. I. T.
HG1496.C56    332.4/1/091724 19    *LC* 80-25426    *ISBN* 0815714688

**Thirlwall, A. P.**       **4.4525**
Inflation, saving and growth in developing economies / A. P. Thirlwall. — New York: St. Martin's Press, 1975 (c1974). xiii, 256 p.; 23 cm. 1. Inflation — Finance — Developing countries — Mathematical models. 2. Savings and investment — Developing countries — Mathematical models. 3. Monetary policy — Developing countries — Mathematical models. I. T.
HG1496.T53 1974b    332.4/1/091724    *LC* 74-15568

# HG1501–3540 Banking

**Bank performance annual.**       **4.4526**
1986-      . — Boston, Mass.: Warren, Gorham & Lamont, c1986-. v.; 26 cm. Annual. 1. Banks and banking — Handbooks, manuals, etc. 2. Finance — Handbooks, manuals, etc. 3. Banks and banking — United States — Handbooks, manuals, etc. 4. Finance — United States — Handbooks, manuals, etc.
HG1611.B19    332 11    *LC* 86-645426

**Irons, Edward D.**       **4.4527**
Black managers: the case of the banking industry / Edward D. Irons and Gilbert W. Moore; foreword by Phyllis Wallace. — New York: Praeger, 1985. xviii, 184 p.: ill.; 25 cm. 'Praeger special studies. Praeger scientific.' 1. Afro-American bankers 2. Banks and banking — United States — Vocational guidance. I. Moore, Gilbert W. II. T.
HG1615.7.M5 I76 1985    332.1/023/73 19    *LC* 84-18304    *ISBN* 0030719380

**Homer, Sidney, 1902-.**       **4.4528**
A history of interest rates / Sidney Homer. — 2d ed., completely rev. — New Brunswick, N.J.: Rutgers University Press, c1977. xvi, 615 p.: ill.; 24 cm. 1. Interest rates — History. 2. Credit — History. I. T.
HG1621.H6 1977    332.8/09    *LC* 77-3872    *ISBN* 0813508401

## HG2401–3540 BY COUNTRY

## HG2401–2626 United States

**Miller, Richard B.**       **4.4529**
Bankers almanac / Richard B. Miller. — 1985. — Boston, MA: Bankers Pub. Co., c1985. 454 p. (Bankers reference series.) 1. Banks and banking — United States — Handbooks, manuals, etc. 2. Banks and banking — United States — Periodicals. I. Miller, Richard Bradford, 1927- II. T. III. Series.
HG2401.B36    332.1/0973 19    *LC* 86-648271

**Timberlake, Richard Henry, 1922-.**       **4.4530**
The origins of central banking in the United States / Richard H. Timberlake, Jr. — Cambridge, Mass.: Harvard University Press, 1978. ix, 272 p.; 24 cm. 1. Monetary policy — United States — History. 2. Banks and banking, Central — United States — History. I. T.
HG2461.T55    332.1/1/0973    *LC* 78-4622    *ISBN* 0674644808

**Hammond, Bray.**       • **4.4531**
Banks and politics in America, from the Revolution to the Civil War. — Princeton: Princeton University Press, 1957. xi, 771 p.; 25 cm. 1. Banks and banking — United States — History. I. T.
HG2472.H3    332.1    *LC* 57-8667

**Cooper, S. Kerry.**       **4.4532**
Banking deregulation and the new competition in financial services / Kerry Cooper, Donald R. Fraser. — Cambridge, Mass.: Ballinger Pub. Co., c1984. xvii, 278 p.: ill.; 24 cm. Includes index. 1. Banks and banking — United States 2. Financial institutions — United States. 3. Banking law — United States. 4. Banks and banking 5. Banking law I. Fraser, Donald R. II. T.
HG2491.C67 1984    332.1/0973 19    *LC* 84-6223    *ISBN* 0884107124

**Board of Governors of the Federal Reserve System (U.S.)**    **4.4533**
Banking and monetary statistics. — Washington: Board of Governors of the Federal Reserve System, 1914/41-. v. 27 cm. 1. Banks and banking — United States — Statistics. 2. Finance — United States — Statistics. 3. Money — United States — Statistics. I. T.
HG2493.U56x    332/.0973

**Board of Governors of the Federal Reserve System (U.S.)**    • **4.4534**
The Federal funds market, a study by a Federal Reserve System committee. Washington [1959] vii, 111 p. diagrs., tables. 23 cm. ([Federal Reserve technical papers]) 1. Federal funds market (U.S.) I. T. II. Series.
HG2562.F8 A53    332.17    *LC* 59-60040

**Willis, Parker B. (Parker Brown), 1907-.**       **4.4535**
The Federal funds market, its origin and development / by Parker B. Willis. 5th ed. — [Boston]: Federal Reserve Bank of Boston, 1970 i.e. 1972. vii, 128 p.: graphs; 23 cm. 1. Federal funds market (United States) I. T.
HG2562.F8 W54 1972    332.1/13    *LC* 77-601197

**Board of Governors of the Federal Reserve System (U.S.)**    • **4.4536**
The Federal Reserve System: purpose and functions. 1st- ed.; 1939-. Washington, Board of Governors of the Federal Reserve System. v. ill. 21 cm. Irregular. Subtitle varies slightly. 1. Federal Reserve banks — Periodicals. 2. Banks and banking — United States — Periodicals. I. T.
HG2563.A32    332.110973    *LC* 39-26719

**Chandler, Lester Vernon, 1905-.**       • **4.4537**
Benjamin Strong, central banker. Washington, Brookings Institution [1958] 495 p. ill. 1. Strong, Benjamin, 1872-1928. 2. Federal Reserve banks 3. Banks and banking, Central I. T.
HG2563 C52    *LC* 58-13996

**Osthaus, Carl R.**       **4.4538**
Freedmen, philanthropy, and fraud: a history of the Freedman's Savings Bank / Carl R. Osthaus. — Urbana: University of Illinois Press, c1976. 257 p.; 24 cm. (Blacks in the New World.) Includes index. 1. Freedman's Savings and Trust Company, Washington, D.C. — History. I. T. II. Series.
HG2613.W34 F85    332.2/1/09753    *LC* 75-23214    *ISBN* 0252003055

## HG2701–3540 Other Countries

**Neufeld, Edward Peter.**       • **4.4539**
Bank of Canada operations and policy. [Toronto] University of Toronto Press, 1958. 253 p. ill. 1. Bank of Canada, Ottawa I. T.
HG2706 N4 1958    *LC* 59-31031

**Meyer. Richard Hemmig.**       • **4.4540**
Bankers' diplomacy; monetary stabilization in the twenties. — New York: Columbia University Press, 1970. xi, 170 p.; 24 cm. — (Columbia studies in economics. 4) 1. Banks and banking, Central — Europe. 2. Monetary policy — Europe. 3. International finance I. T. II. Series.
HG2976.M4 1970    332.1/1/094    *LC* 79-111120    *ISBN* 0231033257

**Clapham, John Harold, Sir, 1873-.**       • **4.4541**
The Bank of England, a history by Sir John Clapham. Cambridge [Eng.] The University press, 1944. 2 v. fronts., ports., facsims., diagrs. 24 cm. 1. Bank of England. I. T.
HG2994.C5    332.1    *LC* 44-9869

**Sayers, R. S. (Richard Sidney), 1908-.**       **4.4542**
The Bank of England, 1891–1944 / R. S. Sayers. Cambridge; New York: Cambridge University Press, 1976. 3 v.; 24 cm. Vol. [3]: Appendixes. 1. Bank of England. I. T.
HG2994.S29 1976    332.1/1/0941    *LC* 76-46116    *ISBN* 0521210674

**März, Eduard.**       **4.4543**
[Österreichische Bankpolitik in der Zeit der grossen Wende 1913-1923. English] Austrian banking and financial policy: Creditanstalt at a turning point, 1913–1923 / Eduard März; translated by Charles Kessler. — New York: St. Martin's Press, 1985 (c1984). xxvi, 627 p., [8] p. of plates: ill.; 24 cm. Translation of: Österreichische Bankpolitik in der Zeit der grossen Wende 1913-1923. 1. Österreichische Credit-Anstalt für Handel und Gewerbe — History. 2. Banks and banking — Austria — History. 3. World War, 1914-1918 — Finance — Austria. 4. Austria — Economic conditions I. T.
HG3020.V54 O47513    332.1/09436 19    *LC* 84-15148    *ISBN* 0312061242

**Iklé, Max.**       **4.4544**
[Schweiz als internationaler Bank- und Finanzplatz. English] Switzerland: an international banking and finance center. Translated from the German by Eric Schiff. Stroudsburg, Pa., Dowden, Hutchinson & Ross [1972] 156 p. 24 cm. Translation of Die Schweiz als internationaler Bank- und Finanzplatz.

1. Banks and banking — Switzerland. 2. Banks and banking, International I. T.
HG3204.I3513     332.1/09494     LC 72-76544     ISBN 0879330023

**Badrud-Din, Abdul-Amir.**     **4.4545**
The Bank of Lebanon: central banking in a financial centre and entrepôt / Abdul-Amir Badrud-Din. — London; Dover, N.H.: F. Pinter, 1984. xii, 230 p.; 23 cm. Originally presented as the author's thesis (doctoral—Oxford) 1. Bank of Lebanon. 2. Banks and banking — Lebanon. 3. Money — Lebanon. I. T.
HG3259.A7 B33 1984     332.1/1/095692 19     LC 83-43270     ISBN 0861874617

**Prindl, Andreas R.**     **4.4546**
Japanese finance: a guide to banking in Japan / Andreas R. Prindl. — Chichester; New York: Wiley, c1981. xii, 137 p.; 24 cm. Includes index. 1. Banks and banking — Japan. 2. Finance — Japan. I. T.
HG3324.P74 1981     332.1/0952 19     LC 81-212198     ISBN 0471099821

**Wilson, Rodney.**     **4.4547**
Banking and finance in the Arab Middle East / Rodney Wilson. — New York: St. Martin's Press, 1983. xii, 208 p.; 23 cm. Cover title: Banking & finance in the Arab Middle East. 1. Banks and banking, Arab countries 2. Finance — Arab countries. I. T. II. Title: Banking & finance in the Arab Middle East.
HG3366.A6 W53 1983     332.1/0917/5927 19     LC 81-21432     ISBN 0312066309

**Landes, David S.**     • **4.4548**
Bankers and pashas; international finance and economic imperialism in Egypt [by] David S. Landes. — New York: Harper & Row, [1969, c1958] xvii, 354 p.: illus., map, ports.; 21 cm. — (Harper torchbooks, TB 1412) 1. Dervieu, Edouard, 1824-1904. 2. Banks and banking, Foreign — Egypt — History. 3. Investments, Foreign — Egypt — History. 4. Egypt — Foreign economic relations. I. T.
HG3386.L35 1969     332.1/5/0962     LC 75-3718

# HG3701–3781 Credit. Government Lending

**Cole, Robert Hartzell.**     **4.4549**
Consumer and commercial credit management / Robert H. Cole. — 7th ed. — Homewood, Ill.: R.D. Irwin, 1984. xvi, 511 p.: ill.; 24 cm. — (Irwin series in marketing.) 1. Credit — Management 2. Consumer credit I. T. II. Series.
HG3751.C64 1984     658.8/8 19     LC 83-80580     ISBN 0256030154

**Baron, David P.**     **4.4550**
The Export–Import Bank: an economic analysis / David P. Baron. — New York: Academic Press, 1983. xi, 342 p.; 24 cm. — (Economic theory, econometrics, and mathematical economics.) 1. Export-Import Bank of the United States. 2. Export credit — United States. I. T. II. Series.
HG3754.U5 B37 1983     332.1/54 19     LC 82-24379     ISBN 0120790807

**Caplovitz, David.**     **4.4551**
Consumers in trouble; a study of debtors in default [by] David Caplovitz. With the assistance of Eric Single. — New York: Free Press, [1974] xiv, 352 p.; 25 cm. 1. Consumer credit — United States. 2. Debtor and creditor — United States. I. T.
HG3756.U54 C38     332.7/43     LC 73-14747     ISBN 0029052602

# HG3810–3877 Foreign Exchange

**The Economics of exchange rates: selected studies / edited by**     **4.4552**
**Jacob A. Frenkel, Harry G. Johnson.**
Reading, Mass.: Addison-Wesley Pub. Co., c1978. xvii, 218 p.; graphs; 24 cm. — (Addison-Wesley series in economics) 1. Foreign exchange — Addresses, essays, lectures. I. Frenkel, Jacob A. II. Johnson, Harry G. (Harry Gordon), 1923-1977.
HG3821.E3     332.4/5     LC 77-88058     ISBN 0201023741. ISBN 0201023768 pbk

**Niehans, Jürg.**     **4.4553**
International monetary economics / Jürg Niehans. — Baltimore: Johns Hopkins University Press, 1984. xii, 340 p.; 24 cm. Includes indexes. 1. Foreign exchange 2. International finance 3. Monetary policy I. T.
HG3821.N595 1984     332/.042 19     LC 83-14960     ISBN 0801830214

**Sohmen, Egon.**     • **4.4554**
Flexible exchange rates. — Rev. ed. — Chicago: University of Chicago Press, [1969] xvi, 263 p.: illus.; 23 cm. 1. Foreign exchange problem I. T.
HG3821.S63 1969     332.4/5     LC 69-18375     ISBN 0226767817

**Einzig, Paul, 1897-1973.**     • **4.4555**
The Euro–dollar system: practice and theory of international interest rates. — 4th ed. — London: Macmillan, 1970. xviii, 208 p.; 23 cm. 1. Foreign exchange 2. Banks and banking, International 3. Euro-dollar market I. T.
HG3826.E35 1970     332.4/5     LC 79-107887     ISBN 0333053354

**Ellis, Howard Sylvester, 1898-.**     • **4.4556**
Exchange control in central Europe, by Howard S. Ellis. — Westport, Conn.: Greenwood Press, [1971, c1941] xiv, 413 p.: illus.; 23 cm. 'Originally published as 'Exchange control in Austria and Hungary' and 'Exchange control in Germany' in the Quarterly journal of economics, volume 54, no. 1, part 2, November, 1939 and volume 54, no. 4, part 2, August, 1940.' 1. Foreign exchange 2. Currency question — Austria. 3. Currency question — Hungary. 4. Currency question — Germany. I. T.
HG3834.E55 1971     332.4/01     LC 69-13892     ISBN 0837144620

**Black, Stanley W.**     **4.4557**
Floating exchange rates and national economic policy / Stanley W. Black. — New Haven: Yale University Press, 1977. xvii, 204 p.: ill.; 22 cm. 1. Foreign exchange 2. Economic policy I. T.
HG3851.B5     332.4/5     LC 77-76296     ISBN 0300021240

**Krueger, Anne O.**     **4.4558**
Exchange–rate determination / Anne O. Krueger. — Cambridge [Cambridgeshire]; New York: Cambridge University Press, 1983. ix, 218 p.; 22 cm. — (Cambridge surveys of economic literature.) Includes index. 1. Foreign exchange I. T. II. Series.
HG3851.K7 1983     332.4/56 19     LC 82-14649     ISBN 0521253047

**Einzig, Paul, 1897-1973.**     • **4.4559**
A dynamic theory of forward exchange. — 2nd ed. — London, Melbourne [etc.]: Macmillan; New York: St. Martin's P., 1967. xxvi, 601 p. 1. Forward exchange I. T.
HG3853.F6 E5 1967

**Bergsten, C. Fred, 1941-.**     **4.4560**
The dilemmas of the dollar: the economics and politics of United States international monetary policy / C. Fred Bergsten. — [New York]: New York University Press, 1975. xv, 584 p.; 22 cm. 'A Council on Foreign Relations book.' 1. Foreign exchange problem — United States. 2. Balance of payments — United States. 3. International economic relations I. T.
HG3863.B43     332.4/5/0973     LC 74-101654     ISBN 0814710018

# HG3879–4000 International Finance. International Monetary System. International Banking

**Aliber, Robert Z.**     **4.4561**
The international money game / Robert Z. Aliber. — 4th ed., rev. and expanded. — New York: Basic Books, c1983. xii, 356 p.: ill.; 21 cm. Includes index. 1. International finance I. T.
HG3881.A44 1983     332.4/5 19     LC 82-72393     ISBN 0465033776

**Allen, Polly Reynolds.**     **4.4562**
Asset markets and exchange rates: modeling an open economy / Polly Reynolds Allen, Peter B. Kenen. — [Abridged ed.] — Cambridge [Eng.]; New York: Cambridge University Press, 1983. xi, 321 p.: ill.; 23 cm. 1. International finance — Mathematical models. 2. Foreign exchange — Mathematical models. 3. International economic integration — Mathematical models. I. Kenen, Peter B., 1932- II. T.
HG3881.A447     332.4/5     LC 79-16874     ISBN 0521274060

**Allen, Polly Reynolds.**     **4.4563**
Asset markets, exchange rates, and economic integration: a synthesis / Polly Reynolds Allen, Peter B. Kenen. — Cambridge [Eng.]; New York: Cambridge University Press, 1980. xiv, 585 p.: ill.; 24 cm. 1. International finance — Mathematical models. 2. Foreign exchange — Mathematical models.

3. International economic integration — Mathematical models. I. Kenen, Peter B., 1932- joint author. II. T.
HG3881.A447    332.4/5    *LC* 79-16874    *ISBN* 0521229820

**Corden, W. M. (Warner Max)**      **4.4564**
Inflation, exchange rates, and the world economy: lectures on international monetary economics / W.M. Corden. — 3rd ed., enlarged and rev. — Chicago: University of Chicago Press, 1986. viii, 195 p.: ill.; 22 cm. Includes index.
1. International finance 2. Balance of payments 3. Inflation (Finance) 4. Petroleum products — Prices 5. Money — European Economic Community countries I. T.
HG3881.C674 1986    332.4/5 19    *LC* 85-51490    *ISBN* 0226115828

**Dam, Kenneth W.**      **4.4565**
The rules of the game: reform and evolution in the international monetary system / Kenneth W. Dam. — Chicago: University of Chicago Press, 1982. xviii, 382 p.; 24 cm. Includes index. 1. International finance I. T.
HG3881.D326    332/.042 19    *LC* 81-10416    *ISBN* 0226134997

**The Future of the international monetary system / edited by**    **4.4566**
**Tamir Agmon, Robert G. Hawkins, Richard M. Levich.**
Lexington, Mass.: Lexington Books, c1984. ix, 301 p.: ill.; 24 cm.
1. International finance — Congresses. I. Agmon, Tamir. II. Hawkins, Robert G. III. Levich, Richard M.
HG3881.F872 1984    332.4/5 19    *LC* 83-47657    *ISBN* 0669067210

**Henning, Charles N.**      **4.4567**
International financial management / Charles N. Henning, William Pigott, Robert Haney Scott. — New York: McGraw-Hill, c1978. xv, 576 p.: ill.; 25 cm. (McGraw-Hill series in finance) 1. International finance 2. International business enterprises — Finance. I. Pigott, William, 1927- joint author. II. Scott, Robert Haney. joint author. III. T.
HG3881.H427    658.1/5    *LC* 77-24757    *ISBN* 0070281750

**International Bank for Reconstruction and Development.**    **4.4568**
IDA in retrospect: the first two decades of the International Development Association. — New York: Published for the World Bank [by] Oxford University Press, 1983 (c1982). xvi, 142 p.: ill. (some col.), map, ports.; 27 cm. 1. International Development Association. I. T. II. Title: I.D.A. in retrospect.
HG3881.I5723 1982    332.1/53 19    *LC* 82-14224    *ISBN* 0195204077

**International finance handbook / edited by Abraham M.**    **4.4569**
**George, Ian H. Giddy.**
New York: Wiley, c1983. 2 v.: ill.; 24 cm. 'A Wiley-Interscience publication.'
1. International finance — Handbooks, manuals, etc. 2. International business enterprises — Finance — Handbooks, manuals, etc. I. George, Abraham M. II. Giddy, Ian H.
HG3881.I57633 1983    332/.042 19    *LC* 82-23824    *ISBN* 0471098612

**The International monetary system under flexible exchange**    **4.4570**
**rates: global, regional, and national: essays in honor of Robert**
**Triffin / edited by Richard N. Cooper ... [et al.].**
Cambridge, Mass.: Ballinger Pub. Co., c1982. xvi, 320 p.: ill.; 24 cm.
1. International finance — Addresses, essays, lectures. 2. Foreign exchange problem — Addresses, essays, lectures. I. Triffin, Robert. II. Cooper, Richard N.
HG3881.I57673    332.4/5 19    *LC* 81-12861    *ISBN* 0884108538

**McKinnon, Ronald I.**      **4.4571**
Money in international exchange: the convertible currency system / Ronald I. McKinnon. — New York: Oxford University Press, 1979. xii, 294 p.; 24 cm.
1. International finance 2. Monetary unions 3. Foreign exchange problem I. T.
HG3881.M2737    332.4/5    *LC* 78-673    *ISBN* 0195024087

**Mason, Edward Sagendorph, 1899-.**      **4.4572**
The World Bank since Bretton Woods; the origins, policies, operations, and impact of the International Bank for Reconstruction and Development and the other members of the World Bank group: the International Finance Corporation, the International Development Association [and] the International Centre for Settlement of Investment Disputes [by] Edward S. Mason [and] Robert E. Asher. Washington, Brookings Institution [1973] xxiii, 915 p. 23 cm. 1. World Bank. I. Asher, Robert E., 1910- joint author. II. T.
HG3881.M355    332.1/53    *LC* 73-1089    *ISBN* 0815754922

**Moffitt, Michael, 1951-.**      **4.4573**
The world's money: international banking, from Bretton Woods to the brink of insolvency / Michael Moffitt. — New York: Simon and Schuster, c1983. 284 p.; 23 cm. 1. International finance I. T.
HG3881.M575 1983    332/.042 19    *LC* 83-402    *ISBN* 0671446827

**Odell, John S., 1945-.**      **4.4574**
U.S. international monetary policy: markets, power, and ideas as sources of change / John S. Odell. — Princeton, N.J.: Princeton University Press, c1982.

xvi, 385 p.: ill.; 23 cm. Revision of thesis (Ph.D.)—University of Wisconsin, 1976. 1. International finance 2. Monetary policy — United States. 3. Devaluation of currency — United States. 4. United States — Foreign economic relations I. T. II. Title: US international monetary policy.
HG3881.O27 1982    332.4/5/0973 19    *LC* 82-47607    *ISBN* 0691076421

**Oliver, Robert W.**      **4.4575**
International economic co–operation and the World Bank / Robert W. Oliver; foreword by Irving Friedman. — New York: Holmes & Meier, 1975. xxii, 421 p.; 23 cm. Includes index. Imprint from label on t.p. 1. International Bank for Reconstruction and Development. 2. International finance 3. International economic relations I. T.
HG3881.O42    332.1/53

**Rodriguez, Rita M., 1944-.**      **4.4576**
International financial management / Rita M. Rodriguez, E. Eugene Carter. — Englewood Cliffs, N.J.: Prentice-Hall, c1976. xix, 619 p.: ill.; 24 cm.
1. International finance I. Carter, E. Eugene. joint author. II. T.
HG3881.R584    658.1/5    *LC* 75-40208    *ISBN* 0134730097

**Sanford, Jonathan E.**      **4.4577**
U.S. foreign policy and multilateral development banks / Jonathan E. Sanford. — Boulder, Colo.: Westview Press, 1982. xiv, 279 p.; 24 cm. — (Westview special studies in international relations.) Includes index. 1. Financial institutions, International 2. Development banks 3. Economic assistance, American 4. United States — Foreign relations — 1945- I. T. II. Title: United States foreign policy and multilateral development banks. III. Title: US foreign policy and multilateral development banks. IV. Series.
HG3881.S1873 1982    332.1/53 19    *LC* 82-50178    *ISBN* 0865311897

**Solomon, Robert.**      **4.4578**
The international monetary system, 1945–1976: an insider's view / Robert Solomon. — 1st ed. — New York: Harper & Row, c1977. xiii, 381 p.; 24 cm.
1. International finance I. T.
HG3881.S5574 1977    332.4/5    *LC* 76-10094    *ISBN* 006013898X

**Tew, Brian.**      **4.4579**
The evolution of the international monetary system, 1945–77 / Brian Tew. — New York: Wiley, 1977. 254 p.; 23 cm. 'A Halsted Press book.' Includes index.
1. International finance — History. I. T.
HG3881.T44 1977    332.4/5/09    *LC* 77-7132    *ISBN* 0470992107

**Williamson, John, 1937-.**      **4.4580**
The failure of world monetary reform, 1971–74 / John Williamson. — New York: New York University Press, 1977. xiii, 221 p.: 1 ill.; 23 cm. Includes index. 1. International finance I. T.
HG3881.W493 1977    332.4/5    *LC* 77-71278    *ISBN* 0814791735

**The IMF and stabilization: developing country experiences /**    **4.4581**
**directed and edited by Tony Killick; contributors, Graham Bird**
**... [et al.].**
New York: St. Martin's Press, 1984. viii, 216 p.: ill.; 23 cm. Companion vol.: The Quest for economic stabilization. 1984. 1. International Monetary Fund. 2. Economic stabilization — Developing countries. 3. Developing countries — Economic policy. 4. Balance of payments — Developing countries I. Killick, Tony. II. Bird, Graham R. III. Title: I.M.F. and stablization.
HG3881.5.I58 I39 1984    332.1/52 19    *LC* 83-40190    *ISBN* 0312402295

**IMF conditionality / edited by John Williamson.**      **4.4582**
Washington, D.C.: Institute for International Economics; Cambridge: Distributed by MIT Press, 1983. xvi, 679 p.; 24 cm. Based on a conference which was held at Airlie House, Virginia, Mar. 24-26, 1982, sponsored by the Institute. 1. International Monetary Fund — Congresses. 2. Loans, Foreign — Congresses. I. Williamson, John, 1937- II. Institute for International Economics (U.S.) III. Title: I.M.F. conditionality. IV. Title: Conditionality.
HG3881.5.I58 I4 1983    332.1/52 19    *LC* 82-21352    *ISBN* 0881320064

**The Quest for economic stabilization: the IMF and the Third**    **4.4583**
**World / directed and edited by Tony Killick; contributors,**
**Graham Bird ... [et al.].**
New York: St. Martin's Press, 1984. ix, 340 p.; 23 cm. Companion vol. to: The IMF and stabilization. 1984. Includes indexes. 1. International Monetary Fund. 2. Economic stabilization — Developing countries. 3. Developing countries — Economic policy. 4. Balance of payments — Developing countries I. Killick, Tony. II. Bird, Graham R.
HG3881.5.I58 Q47 1984    332.1/52 19    *LC* 83-40191    *ISBN* 0312660278

Technology, finance, and development: an analysis of the World   **4.4584**
Bank as a technological institution / edited by Charles Weiss,
Nicolas Jéquier.
Lexington, Mass.: LexingtonBooks, 1984. vi, 342 p., [4] p. of plates: ill. (some
col.); 24 cm. 1. World Bank. 2. Technical assistance 3. Technology transfer —
Developing countries. I. Weiss, Charles. II. Jéquier, Nicolas, 1941-
HG3881.5.W57 T42 1984     338.91 19     *LC* 83-49213     *ISBN*
0669077623

## HG3882–3891 BALANCE OF PAYMENTS. FOREIGN LOANS

**Aubrey, Henry G.**                                • **4.4585**
The dollar in world affairs: an essay in international financial policy. — [1st ed.]
New York: Published for the Council on Foreign Relations by Harper & Row
[1964] xii, 295 p.; 22 cm. 1. Balance of payments — United States I. T.
HG3883 U7 A85     *LC* 63-21750

**Balassa, Bela A. ed.**                             **4.4586**
Changing patterns in foreign trade and payments / edited with an introd. by
Bela Balassa. — 3d ed. — New York: Norton, c1978. xii, 302 p.; 21 cm. —
(Problems of the modern economy) 1. Balance of payments — United States —
Addresses, essays, lectures. 2. International economic relations — Addresses,
essays, lectures. 3. International finance — Addresses, essays, lectures.
4. International business enterprises — Addresses, essays, lectures.
5. Investments, Foreign — Addresses, essays, lectures. I. T.
HG3883.U7 B25 1978     332.4/5     *LC* 77-11985     *ISBN* 0393056627

**Williamson, Jeffrey G., 1935-.**                           • **4.4587**
American growth and the balance of payments, 1820–1913; a study of the long
swing. Chapel Hill, University of North Carolina Press [1964] xviii, 298 p. ill.
1. Balance of payments — United States I. T.
HG3883 U7 W5 1964     *LC* 64-13563

**Makin, John H.**                                   **4.4588**
The global debt crisis: America's growing involvement / John H. Makin. —
New York: Basic Books, c1984. xiv, 281 p.; 24 cm. Includes index. 1. Loans,
Foreign — Developing countries 2. Debts, External — Developing countries
3. Loans, American — Developing countries. I. T.
HG3891.5.M34 1984     336.3/435/091724 19     *LC* 84-45075     *ISBN*
0465026818

## HG3894–4000 MONETARY UNIONS. CURRENCY AREAS

**Dufey, Gunter.**                                 **4.4589**
The international money market / Gunter Dufey, Ian H. Giddy. — Englewood
Cliffs, N.J.: Prentice-Hall, c1978. xvi, 283 p.: ill.; 24 cm. — (Prentice-Hall
foundations of finance series) 1. Euro-dollar market 2. Euro-bond market
3. International finance I. Giddy, Ian H. joint author. II. T.
HG3897.D83 1978     332.4/5     *LC* 78-1298     *ISBN* 0134709225

**Eurocurrencies and the international monetary system / edited**   **4.4590**
**by Carl H. Stem, John H. Makin, and Dennis E. Logue.**
Washington: American Enterprise Institute for Public Policy Research, c1976.
413 p.: graphs; 25 cm. 'Proceedings of an October 1974 conference sponsored
jointly by the American Enterprise Institute and the United States Department
of the Treasury.' 1. Euro-dollar market — Congresses. 2. International finance
— Congresses. I. Stem, Carl H. II. Makin, John H. III. Logue, Dennis E.
IV. American Enterprise Institute for Public Policy Research. V. U.S.
Treasury Dept.
HG3897.E9     332.4/54     *LC* 76-29115     *ISBN* 0844720917

**Hogan, W. P. (Warren Pat), 1929-.**                       **4.4591**
The incredible Eurodollar / W.P. Hogan and I.F. Pearce. — London; Boston:
G. Allen & Unwin, 1982. viii, 144 p.; 22 cm. Rev. ed. published as: The
incredible Eurodollar, or, Why the world's money system is collapsing. Rev. ed.
1983. 1. Euro-dollar market 2. International finance I. Pearce, I. F. (Ivor F.)
II. T.
HG3897.H63 1982     332.4/5 19     *LC* 81-19154     *ISBN* 0043320813

**Gowa, Joanne S.**                                 **4.4592**
Closing the gold window: domestic politics and the end of Bretton Woods /
Joanne Gowa. — Ithaca: Cornell University Press, 1983. 208 p.; 25 cm.
(Cornell studies in political economy.) Includes index. 1. Foreign exchange
problem — United States. 2. Devaluation of currency — United States.
3. International finance 4. United States — Foreign economic relations —

Case studies. 5. United States — Politics and government — 1969-1974 I. T.
II. Series.
HG3903.G68 1983     332.4/560973 19     *LC* 83-7184     *ISBN*
0801416221

**Ellis, Howard Sylvester, 1898-.**                       • **4.4593**
Exchange control in Germany / [by] Howard S. Ellis. — Cambridge, Mass.,:
Harvard University Press, 1940. 220 p.: tables, diagrs.; 24 cm. — (The
Quarterly journal of economics; Vol. LIV, no. 4, pt. 1.) 1. Foreign exchange —
Law — Germany 2. Currency question — Germany I. T.
HG3949.E5x

## HG4001–4495 Corporation Finance

**Manser, W. A. P. (William Arthur Peete)**                **4.4594**
The financial role of multinational enterprises [by] W. A. P. Manser. New York,
J. Wiley [1973] 176 p. 25 cm. 'A Halsted Press book.' 1. International business
enterprises — Finance. I. T.
HG4011.M236     338.8/8     *LC* 72-12259     *ISBN* 047056766X

**Willson, James D.**                                **4.4595**
Controllership, the work of the managerial accountant / James D. Willson and
John B. Campbell. — 3d ed. — New York: Wiley, c1981. ix, 889 p.: ill.; 24 cm.
Second ed. by J. B. Heckert and J. D. Willson published in 1963. 'A Ronald
Press publication.' Includes index. 1. Controllership 2. Managerial accounting
I. Campbell, John B., joint author. II. Heckert, J. Brooks (Josiah Brooks),
1893- Controllership. III. T.
HG4026.H43 1981     658.1/51 19     *LC* 80-39552     *ISBN* 0471057118

**Neave, Edwin H.**                                  **4.4596**
Financial management, theory and strategies / Edwin H. Neave, John C.
Wiginton. — Englewood Cliffs, N.J.: Prentice-Hall, c1981. xvi, 394 p.; ill.; 24
cm. 1. Corporations — Finance 2. Business enterprises — Finance 3. Finance
I. Wiginton, John C. joint author. II. T.
HG4026.N4     658.1/5 19     *LC* 80-19224     *ISBN* 0133161099

**Robbins, Sidney M.**                               **4.4597**
Money in the multinational enterprise; a study of financial policy [by] Sidney M.
Robbins and Robert B. Stobaugh. With a simulation model constructed by
Daniel M. Schydlowsky. — New York: Basic Books, [1973] xix, 231 p.: illus.;
25 cm. — (The Harvard multinational enterprise series) 1. International
business enterprises — Finance. I. Stobaugh, Robert B. joint author. II. T.
III. Series.
HG4026.R6     658.1/5     *LC* 73-76366     *ISBN* 0465047157

**Milling, Bryan E.**                                 **4.4598**
Financial tools for the non–financial executive / Bryan E. Milling. — Radnor,
Pa.: Chilton, c1983. xi, 201 p.: ill.; 24 cm. Includes index. 1. Corporations —
Finance — Handbooks, manuals, etc. 2. Business enterprises — Finance —
Handbooks, manuals, etc. I. T.
HG4027.3.M54 1983     658.1/5 19     *LC* 82-70779     *ISBN* 0801973910

**Handbook of international financial management / edited by**   **4.4599**
**Allen Sweeny and Robert Rachlin.**
New York: McGraw-Hill, c1984. 1 v. (various pagings): ill.; 24 cm.
1. International business enterprises — Finance — Handbooks, manuals, etc.
I. Sweeny, Allen. II. Rachlin, Robert, 1937-
HG4027.5.H36 1984     658.1/599 19     *LC* 83-25581     *ISBN*
0070625786

**Kettell, Brian.**                                  **4.4600**
The finance of international business / Brian Kettell; foreword by Andreas R.
Prindl; with a new introd. by the author. — Westport, Conn.: Quorum Books,
1981. xviii, 275 p.: ill.; 24 cm. Includes index. 1. International business
enterprises — Finance. 2. International finance I. T.
HG4027.5.K47 1981     658.1/599 19     *LC* 80-28878     *ISBN*
0899300111

**Managing international risk: essays commissioned in honor of**   **4.4601**
**the centenary of the Wharton School, University of**
**Pennsylvania / edited by Richard J. Herring.**
Cambridge [Cambridgeshire]; New York, NY: Cambridge University Press,
1983. 273 p. Based on essays and perspectives presented at a conference entitled
'Managing international risk,' held in Philadelphia, Oct. 26-27, 1981, sponsored
jointly by the Global Interdependence Center, the Group of Thirty, and the
Wharton School, University of Pennsylvania. 1. International business
enterprises — Finance — Congresses. 2. International finance — Congresses.
3. Risk management — Congresses. I. Herring, Richard. II. Global
Interdependence Center. III. Group of Thirty. IV. Wharton School.
HG4027.5.M36 1983     658.1/5 19     *LC* 82-19930     *ISBN* 0521250781

**Lurie, Adolph G.**                                    **4.4602**
How to read annual reports intelligently: a stockholder's guide / Adolph Lurie. — Englewood Cliffs, N.J.: Prentice-Hall, c1984. viii, 168 p.: ill.; 24 cm. 'A Spectrum book.' Includes index. 1. Corporation reports I. T.
HG4028.B2 L87 1984     338.7/4 19     LC 84-11719     ISBN 0134305620

**Corporate cash management: techniques and analysis / edited by**     **4.4603**
**Frank J. Fabozzi and Leslie N. Masonson.**
Homewood, Ill.: Dow Jones-Irwin, c1985. xv, 373 p.: ill.; 24 cm. 1. Cash management — United States. 2. Cash management I. Fabozzi, Frank J. II. Masonson, Leslie N.
HG4028.C45 C58 1985     658.1/5244 19     LC 84-71295     ISBN 0870944770

**The Corporate finance sourcebook.**                   **4.4604**
1979-. New York, McGraw-Hill Book Co. v. 30 cm. Annual. 1. Corporations — United States — Finance — Directories. 2. Finance — United States — Directories.
HG4057.A1565     332/.025/73     LC 79-642719

**Directory of corporate affiliations.**               **4.4605**
1973-    . — Skokie, Ill.: National Register Pub. Co., [1973-. v.; 28 cm. Annual. 'Who owns whom, the family tree of every major corporation in America.' Updating supplements issued quarterly during 1973. 1. Corporations — United States — Directories. 2. Holding companies — United States — Directories.
HG4057.A217     338.8/025/73 19     LC 83-641510

**Ward's directory of ... private U.S. companies.**     **4.4606**
[1984]. — Petaluma, CA: B.H. Ward, [c1984-. v. Annual. Indicates coverage by number in title, e.g., 1984 has 49,000. Lacks numeric and chronological designation. Called v. 2 of a set of directories issued by B.H. Ward. 1. Corporations — United States — Rankings — Directories. I. Baldwin H. Ward Publications, Inc.
HG4057.A57     338.7/4/02573 19     LC 85-642676

# HG4501–6270 Investments. Speculation

**Stigum, Marcia L.**                                   **4.4607**
Money market calculations: yields, break–evens, and arbitrage / Marcia Stigum, in collaboration with John Mann. — Homewood, Ill.: Dow Jones-Irwin, c1981. xii, 199 p.: ill.; 29 cm. Includes index. 1. Investments — Mathematics 2. Money market — Mathematics. I. Mann, John. II. T.
HG4515.3.S8     332.63/2 19     LC 80-66022     ISBN 0870941925

**Reuber, Grant L.**                                    **4.4608**
Private foreign investment in development [by] Grant L. Reuber, with H. Crookell, M. Emerson [and] G. Gallais–Hamonno. Oxford, Clarendon Press, 1973. xiv, 371 p. maps. 22 cm. At head of title: Development Centre of the Organization for Economic Co-operation and Development, Paris. 1. Investments, Foreign — Developing countries I. Organisation for Economic Co-operation and Development. Development Centre. II. T.
HG4517.R46     332.6/73/091724     LC 74-153096     ISBN 0198281927     ISBN 019828196X

**Levine, Sumner N.**                                   **4.4609**
Financial analyst's handbook. Edited by Sumner N. Levine. — Homewood, Ill.: Dow Jones-Irwin, 1975. 2 v.: illus.; 24 cm. 1. Investment analysis I. T.
HG4521.L625     332.6     LC 74-81386     ISBN 0870940821

**Geisst, Charles R.**                                  **4.4610**
A guide to the financial markets / Charles R. Geisst. — New York: St. Martin's Press, 1982. xv, 144 p.: ill.; 22 cm. 1. Capital market 2. Hedging (Finance) I. T. II. Title: Financial markets.
HG4523.G44 1982     332.6/78 19     LC 81-18514     ISBN 0312352948

**Darst, David M., 1947-.**                             **4.4611**
The handbook of the bond and money markets / David M. Darst. — New York: McGraw-Hill, c1981. xv, 461 p.: ill.; 24 cm. Includes index. 1. Bonds — Handbooks, manuals, etc. 2. Investments — Handbooks, manuals, etc. 3. Money market — Handbooks, manuals, etc. I. T.
HG4527.D37     332.63/23     LC 80-36816     ISBN 0070154015

**Cairncross, Alec, Sir, 1911-.**                       **4.4612**
Control of long–term international capital movements; a staff paper [by] Sir Alec Cairncross. Washington, Brookings Institution [1973] xiv, 104 p. 23 cm.

1. Investments, Foreign 2. Balance of payments I. Brookings Institution. II. T.
HG4538.C22     332.6/73     LC 73-12634     ISBN 0815712375

**Faith, Nicholas, 1933-.**                             **4.4613**
The infiltrators: the European business invasion of America. — [1st ed.]. — New York: Dutton, 1972 [c1971] xvii, 242 p.: map.; 22 cm. 1. Investments, Foreign — United States. 2. Business enterprises, Foreign — United States. I. T.
HG4538.F24 1972     332.6/73/0973     LC 72-173028     ISBN 0525133054

**Lall, Sanjaya.**                                      **4.4614**
Foreign investment, transnationals, and developing countries / Sanjaya Lall and Paul Streeten. — Boulder, Colo.: Westview Press, 1977. xii, 280 p.; 23 cm. Includes index. 1. Investments, Foreign — Developing countries 2. International business enterprises 3. Investments, Foreign I. Streeten, Paul. joint author. II. T.
HG4538.L275 1977     332.6/73/091724     LC 77-7024     ISBN 0891588000

**Mattione, Richard P.**                                **4.4615**
OPEC's investments and the international financial system / Richard P. Mattione. — Washington, D.C.: Brookings Institution, c1985. xi, 201 p.; 25 cm. 1. Organization of Petroleum Exporting Countries. 2. Investments, Foreign 3. Investments, Arab 4. Petroleum industry and trade — Finance. 5. International finance I. T. II. Title: O.P.E.C's investments and the international financial system.
HG4538.M38 1985     332.6/7314 19     LC 84-23242     ISBN 0815755104

**Rugman, Alan M.**                                     **4.4616**
International diversification and the multinational enterprise / Alan M. Rugman. — Lexington, Mass.: Lexington Books, c1979. xviii, 137 p.; 24 cm. Includes index. 1. Investments, Foreign 2. International business enterprises — Finance. I. T.
HG4538.R82     338.8/8 19     LC 78-20603     ISBN 0669027723

**Sobel, Robert, 1931 Feb. 19-.**                       **• 4.4617**
Panic on Wall Street: a history of America's financial disasters. — New York: Macmillan, [1968] 469 p.; 22 cm. 1. Wall Street 2. Depressions 3. Speculation I. T.
HG4572.S674     338.54/2/0973     LC 68-25715

# HG4905–5990 By Country

## HG4905–5131 United States

**Rosenberg, Jerry Martin.**                            **4.4618**
Inside the Wall Street journal: the history and the power of Dow Jones & Company and America's most influential newspaper / Jerry M. Rosenberg. — New York: Macmillan; London: Collier Macmillan, c1982. xi, 335 p., [16] p. of plates: ill.; 25 cm. Includes index. 1. Dow Jones & Co — History. 2. Wall Street journal — History. I. T.
HG4910.R69 1982     071/.47/1 19     LC 82-13005     ISBN 0026048604

**The Dow Jones averages, 1885–1980 / edited by Phyllis S.**     **4.4619**
**Pierce.**
Homewood, Ill.: Dow Jones-Irwin, c1982. ca. 400 p.: ill.; 29 cm. 1. Stocks — Prices — United States — Statistics. I. Pierce, Phyllis S. II. Dow Jones & Co. III. Dow Jones-Irwin.
HG4915.D64 1982     332.63/222/0973 19     LC 82-72368     ISBN 0870943537

**The Unlisted market guide.**                          **4.4620**
Glen Head, NY (P.O. Box 106, Glen Head 11545): Unlisted Market Service Corp., c1984. 3 v. (loose-leaf); 26 cm. Cover title. Includes index. 1. Stocks — United States — Tables. 2. Corporations — United States — Finance. I. Unlisted Market Service Corporation.
HG4916.U54 1984     338.7/4/0973 19     LC 85-124707

**Deregulating Wall Street: commercial bank penetration of the**     **4.4621**
**corporate securities market / Ingo Walter, editor.**
New York: Wiley, c1985. xii, 315 p.: ill.; 24 cm. (Wiley professional banking and finance series. 0733-8945) 'A Wiley-Interscience publication.' 1. Investment banking — United States. 2. Banks and banking — United States 3. Wall Street I. Walter, Ingo. II. Title: De-regulating Wall Street. III. Series.
HG4930.5.D46 1985     332.1/754/0973 19     LC 85-5321     ISBN 0471817139

**Moody's industrial manual.**    4.4622
New York: Moody's Investors Service. v.; 30 cm. Annual. Began with: 1954. Cf. New serial titles. 'Covering New York, American & regional stock exchanges & international companies.' Description based on: 1979. Vols. for 1972- issued in parts. 1. Corporations — United States — Periodicals. 2. Securities — United States — Periodicals. I. Moody's Investors Service.
HG4961.M67     *LC* 56-14721

**Carosso, Vincent P.**    • 4.4623
Investment banking in America: a history / [by] Vincent P. Carosso; research associates: Marian V. Sears [and] Irving Katz. — Cambridge, Mass.: Harvard University Press, 1970. xiii, 569 p.; 25 cm. — (Harvard studies in business history. 25) 1. Investment banking — U.S. I. T. II. Series.
HG4963.C37     332.6/6/0973     *LC* 70-99515     *ISBN* 0674465741

**Kozmetsky, George.**    4.4624
Financing and managing fast–growth companies: the venture capital process / George Kozmetsky, Michael D. Gill, Jr., Raymond W. Smilor. — Lexington, Mass.: Lexington Books, c1985. xxii, 144 p.: ill.; 24 cm. Includes index. 1. Venture capital — United States. 2. Venture capital I. Gill, Michael D. II. Smilor, Raymond W. III. T.
HG4963.K69 1985     658.1/52 19     *LC* 84-48473     *ISBN* 0669094811

## HG5151–5990 Other Countries

**Aitken, Hugh G. J.**    • 4.4625
American capital and Canadian resources. Cambridge, Harvard University Press, 1961. xii, 217 p. diagrs., tables. 1. Investments, American — Canada I. T.
HG5152 A7     *LC* 61-13733

**Buckley, Kenneth.**    • 4.4626
Capital formation in Canada, 1896–1930. [Toronto] University of Toronto Press, 1955. x, 163 p. diagrs., tables. (Canadian studies in economics, no. 2) 1. Saving and investment — Canada I. T. II. Series.
HG5152 B8

**Baklanoff, Eric N.**    4.4627
Expropriation of U.S. investments in Cuba, Mexico, and Chile / Eric N. Baklanoff. — New York: Praeger, 1975. xviii, 170 p.; 25 cm. (Praeger special studies in international economics and development) 1. Investments, American — Chile. 2. Investments, American — Cuba. 3. Investments, American — Mexico. I. T.
HG5160.5.A3 B34     332.6/7373     *LC* 74-6731     *ISBN* 0275097803

**Barry, Tom, 1950-.**    4.4628
The other side of paradise: foreign control in the Caribbean / by Tom Barry, Beth Wood, and Deb Preusch. — 1st hardcover ed. — New York: Grove Press, 1984. viii, 405 p.; 25 cm. (Grove Press Latin America series.) Includes index. 1. Investments, Foreign — Caribbean Area. 2. International business enterprises — Caribbean Area. 3. Caribbean Area — Dependency on foreign countries. 4. Caribbean Area — Economic conditions — 1945- I. Wood, Beth. II. Preusch, Deb. III. T. IV. Series.
HG5242.B37 1984     332.6/73/091821 19     *LC* 83-49370     *ISBN* 0394538528

**Platt, D. C. M. (Desmond Christopher Martin), 1934-.**    4.4629
Foreign finance in continental Europe and the United States, 1815–1870: quantities, origins, functions, and distribution / D.C.M. Platt. — London; Boston: G. Allen & Unwin, 1984. viii, 216 p.; 23 cm. Includes index. 1. Investments, Foreign — Europe — History — 19th century. 2. Investments, Foreign — United States — History — 19th century. 3. Railroads — Europe — Finance — History — 19th century. 4. Railroads — United States — Finance — History — 19th century. I. T.
HG5422.P56 1984     332.6/73/094 19     *LC* 83-72851     *ISBN* 0043303366

**Teichova, Alice.**    4.4630
An economic background to Munich; international business and Czechoslovakia 1918–1938. [London, New York] Cambridge University Press [1974] xix, 422 p. 23 cm. (Soviet and East European studies.) 1. Investments, Foreign — Czechoslovakia. I. T. II. Series.
HG5462.5.C9 T44     332.6/73/09437     *LC* 72-89811     *ISBN* 0521200652

**Hou, Chi-ming, 1924-.**    • 4.4631
Foreign investment and economic development in China, 1840–1937. Cambridge: Harvard University Press, 1965. xiii, 306 p. (Harvard East Asian series, 21) 1. Investments, Foreign — China 2. China — Economic conditions I. T.
HG5722 H6     *LC* 65-22069

**Ray, Rajat Kanta.**    4.4632
Industrialization in India: growth and conflict in the private corporate sector, 1914–47 / Rajat K. Ray. — New York: Oxford University Press, 1979. xi, 384 p.; 23 cm. Includes index. 1. Investments — India. 2. India — Industries. I. T.
HG5732.R33     332.6/72/0954     *LC* 79-903614

**Carr, David William, 1936-.**    4.4633
Foreign investment and development in the southwest Pacific, with special reference to Australia and Indonesia / David William Carr. — New York: Praeger, 1978. xii, 197 p.; 24 cm. Includes index. 1. Investments, Foreign — Indonesia. 2. Investments, Foreign — Australia. 3. Investments, Foreign — Oceania. I. T.
HG5752.C37 1978     332.6/73/099     *LC* 78-8598     *ISBN* 003042271X

**Ho, Sam P. S.**    4.4634
China's open door policy: the quest for foreign technology and capital: a study of China's special trade / Samuel P.S. Ho and Ralph W. Huenemann. — Vancouver: University of British Columbia Press, 1984. viii, 277 p.; 24 cm. (Asian studies monographs. 5) Includes indexes. 1. Investments, Foreign — China. 2. Technology transfer — China. 3. China — Foreign economic relations. I. Huenemann, Ralph William, 1939- II. T. III. Series.
HG5782.H6 1984     338.951/026 19     *LC* 84-212061     *ISBN* 0774801972

**Makgetla, Neva.**    4.4635
Outposts of monopoly capitalism: Southern Africa in the changing global economy / by Neva Makgetla and Ann Seidman. — Westport, Conn.: L. Hill, c1980. xiii, 370 p.; 21 cm. 'A Lawrence Hill-Zed Press book.' 1. Investments, American — South Africa. 2. Corporations, American — South Africa. 3. South Africa — Economic conditions — 1961- I. Seidman, Ann Willcox, 1926- joint author. II. T.
HG5851.A3 M34 1980     338.8/8973/068 19     *LC* 80-80525     *ISBN* 0882081144

## HG6001–6270 Speculation. Lotteries

**Handbook of futures markets: commodity, financial, stock index,**    4.4636
**and options / Perry J. Kaufman.**
New York: Wiley, c1984. 1 v. (various pagings): ill.; 26 cm. 'A Wiley-Interscience publication.' 1. Commodity exchanges — Handbooks, manuals, etc. I. Kaufman, Perry J.
HG6046.H36 1984     332.63/28 19     *LC* 84-3504     *ISBN* 0471087149

**Ezell, John Samuel.**    • 4.4637
Fortune's merry wheel: the lottery in America. Cambridge: Harvard University Press, 1960. vii, 331 p.: facsims., tables; 25 cm. 1. Lotteries — United States I. T.
HG6126 E9     *LC* 60-8448

## HG8011–9970 Insurance

**The Business insurance handbook / compiled and edited by**    4.4638
**Gray Castle, Robert F. Cushman, Peter R. Kensicki.**
Homewood, Ill.: Dow Jones-Irwin, c1981. xvii, 753 p.: ill., forms, ports.; 24 cm. 1. Insurance, Business — Handbooks, manuals, etc. 2. Risk management — Handbooks, manuals, etc. I. Castle, Gray. II. Cushman, Robert Frank, 1931- III. Kensicki, Peter R.
HG8059.B87     368.8/1/00202 19     *LC* 80-70437     *ISBN* 0870942379

**Levy, Michael H.**    • 4.4639
A handbook of personal insurance terminology / by Michael H. Levy. — Lynbrook, N.Y.: Farnsworth Pub. Co., 1968. xi, 595 p.; 24 cm. 1. Insurance, Life — Dictionaries. 2. Insurance, Health — Dictionaries. I. T.
HG8759.L4     368.3/2/0014     *LC* 68-3253

**Hogg, Robert V.**    4.4640
Loss distributions / Robert V. Hogg, Stuart A. Klugman, with the assistance of Charles C. Hewitt and Gary Patrik. — New York: Wiley, c1984. x, 235 p.; 23 cm. — (Wiley series in probability and mathematical statistics. Applied probability and statistics.) Includes index. 1. Insurance — Statistical methods 2. Insurance — Mathematical models. I. Klugman, Stuart A., 1949- II. T. III. Series.
HG8781.H63 1984     368/.015 19     *LC* 83-19663     *ISBN* 0471879290

**Weare, Walter B.**     **4.4641**
Black business in the New South; a social history of the North Carolina Mutual Life Insurance Company [by] Walter B. Weare. — Urbana: University of Illinois Press, [1973] x, 312 p.: illus.; 24 cm. — (Blacks in the New World.) 1. North Carolina Mutual Life Insurance Company. I. T. II. Series.
HG8963.N9553 W4    368.3/2/0065756563    *LC* 72-92690    *ISBN* 0252002857

**Rokes, Willis Park.**     **4.4642**
No–fault insurance. — Santa Monica, Calif.: Insurors Press, 1971. xxi, 416 p.; 24 cm. — (Insurance management and education series) 1. Insurance, No-fault automobile — U.S. I. T.
HG9970.A5 R58    368.2/32    *LC* 72-173308

# HJ PUBLIC FINANCE

**Musgrave, Richard Abel, 1910- comp.**     • **4.4643**
Classics in the theory of public finance, edited by Richard A. Musgrave and Alan T. Peacock. London; New York: Macmillan, 1958. xix, 244 p.: ill.; 26 cm. (International Economic Association publications.) 1. Finance, Public — Addresses, essays, lectures I. Peacock, Alan T., jt. comp. II. T. III. Series.
HJ117 M8

**Buchanan, James M.**     • **4.4644**
The demand and supply of public goods, by James M. Buchanan. — Chicago: Rand McNally, [1968] ix, 214 p.: illus.; 22 cm. — (Rand McNally economics series) 1. Public goods I. T.
HJ135.B83    336    *LC* 68-16834

**Peacock, Alan T., 1922-.**     **4.4645**
The economic theory of fiscal policy, by Alan Peacock and G. K. Shaw. — New York: St. Martin's Press, 1972 (c1971) 214 p.: illus.; 24 cm. 1. Fiscal policy — Mathematical models. I. Shaw, G. K. (Graham Keith), 1938- joint author. II. T.
HJ135.P4    336.3    *LC* 78-163472

**Musgrave, Richard Abel, 1910-.**     **4.4646**
Public finance in a democratic society: collected papers of Richard A. Musgrave. — New York: New York University Press, 1986. 2 v.: ill.; 25 cm. 1. Finance, Public I. T.
HJ141.M796 1986    336 19    *LC* 85-32053    *ISBN* 0814754287

**Musgrave, Richard Abel, 1910-.**     • **4.4647**
The theory of public finance; a study in public economy. New York, McGraw-Hill, 1959. 628 p. illus. 24 cm. 1. Fiscal policy 2. Welfare economics I. T.
HJ141.M8    350.72    *LC* 58-8852

**Rose, Richard, 1933-.**     **4.4648**
Can government go bankrupt? / Richard Rose & Guy Peters. — New York: Basic Books, c1978. xv, 283 p.; 22 cm. 1. Finance, Public 2. Debts, Public 3. Bankruptcy I. Peters, Guy. joint author. II. T.
HJ141.R64    336.3/4/01    *LC* 78-54493    *ISBN* 0465008348

**Oates, Wallace E.**     • **4.4649**
Fiscal federalism / [by] Wallace E. Oates. — New York: Harcourt Brace Jovanovich, [1972] xvi, 256 p.: ill.; 22 cm. — (The Harbrace series in business and economics) 1. Intergovernmental fiscal relations 2. Grants-in-aid 3. Finance, Public I. T.
HJ192.O18    336.1/85    *LC* 78-185772    *ISBN* 015527452X

**Goffart, Walter A.**     **4.4650**
Caput and colonate: towards a history of late Roman taxation / Walter Goffart. — Toronto: Buffalo: University of Toronto Press, [1974] 165 p.; 24 cm. — (Phoenix supplementary volume; 12) 1. Taxation — Rome. I. T.
HJ225.G64    336.2/00937/6    *LC* 73-85096    *ISBN* 0802052894

# HJ241–1839 History, by Country

## HJ241–789 United States

**Myers, Margaret G. (Margaret Good), 1899-.**     • **4.4651**
A financial history of the United States / by Margaret G. Myers. New York: Columbia University Press, 1970. viii, 451 p.: ill., facsims.; 25 cm. 1. Finance,

Public — United States — History. 2. Finance — United States — History. I. T.
HJ241.M93    332/.0973    *LC* 70-104900    *ISBN* 0231024428

**Phelps, Edmund S. ed.**     • **4.4652**
Private wants and public needs: issues surrounding the size and scope of Government expenditure / edited with an introd. by Edmund S. Phelps. — Rev. ed. — New York: W. W. Norton, [1965] xiii, 178 p.; 21 cm. — (Problems of the modern economy) 1. Fiscal policy — United States. I. T.
HJ257.P45 1965    350    *LC* 65-12517

**Rees, David, 1928-.**     **4.4653**
Harry Dexter White: a study in paradox. — New York: Coward, McCann & Geoghegan, [1973] 506 p.; 24 cm. 1. White, Harry Dexter, 1892-1948. I. T.
HJ257.R43    330.9/2/4 B    *LC* 72-94121    *ISBN* 0698105249

**Stein, Herbert, 1916-.**     • **4.4654**
The fiscal revolution in America. — Chicago: University of Chicago Press, [1969] xiv, 526 p.; 24 cm. — (Graduate School of Business. University of Chicago. Third series: Studies in business and society [14]) 1. Fiscal policy — United States. 2. Monetary policy — United States. I. T.
HJ257.S78    336.73    *LC* 69-14828

**The Economics of public finance; essays by Alan S. Blinder and [others].**     **4.4655**
Washington: Brookings Institution, [1974] xvi, 435 p.: illus.; 24 cm. — (Studies of government finance) 1. Finance, Public — United States — Addresses, essays, lectures. 2. Finance, Public — Addresses, essays, lectures. I. Blinder, Alan S. II. Series.
HJ257.2.E25    336.73    *LC* 74-276    *ISBN* 0815709986

**Fisher, Louis.**     **4.4656**
Presidential spending power / Louis Fisher. — Princeton, N.J.: Princeton University Press, [1975] xiii, 345 p.; 23 cm. 1. Budget — United States 2. Finance, Public — United States 3. United States — Appropriations and expenditures I. T.
HJ257.2.F57    353.007/222    *LC* 75-4408    *ISBN* 0691075751

**O'Connor, James (James R.)**     **4.4657**
The fiscal crisis of the state / [by] James O'Connor. — New York: St. Martin's Press, [1973]. –. 276 p.; 21 cm. — 1. Finance, Public — United States 2. Budget — United States 3. Taxation — United States I. T.
HJ257.2.O26 1973    353.007/2    *LC* 72-95747

**Pechman, Joseph A., 1918-.**     **4.4658**
Federal tax policy / Joseph A. Pechman. — 4th ed. — Washington, D.C.: Brookings Institution, c1983. xix, 410 p.: ill.; 24 cm. — (Studies of government finance.) 1. Fiscal policy — United States. 2. Taxation — United States I. T. II. Series.
HJ257.2.P4 1983    336.2/00973 19    *LC* 83-23126    *ISBN* 0815769644

**Aronson, J. Richard (Jay Richard), 1937-.**     **4.4659**
Financing state and local governments. — 4th ed. / J. Richard Aronson and John L. Hilley. — Washington, D.C.: Brookings Institution, c1986. xvii, 265 p.: ill.; 24 cm. (Studies of government finance.) Third ed. by James A. Maxwell and J. Richard Aronson. Includes index. 1. Finance, Public — United States — States 2. Local finance — United States. 3. Intergovernmental fiscal relations — United States. I. Hilley, John L. II. Maxwell, James Ackley, 1897-1975. Financing state and local governments. III. T. IV. Series.
HJ275.A83 1986    336.73 19    *LC* 85-48207    *ISBN* 081575518X

**Barfield, Claude E.**     **4.4660**
Rethinking federalism: block grants and federal, state, and local responsibilities / Claude E. Barfield. — Washington: American Enterprise Institute for Public Policy Research, c1981. ix, 99 p.; 23 cm. — (AEI studies. 349) 1. Block grants — United States. 2. Intergovernmental fiscal relations — United States. 3. Federal government — United States. I. T. II. Series.
HJ275.B29    336.1/85 19    *LC* 81-17602    *ISBN* 0844734799

**Break, George F.**     **4.4661**
Financing government in a Federal system / George F. Break. — Washington, D.C.: Brookings Institution, c1980. xi, 276 p.; 24 cm. — (Studies of government finance.) 1. Intergovernmental fiscal relations — United States. 2. Finance, Public — United States I. T. II. Series.
HJ275.B66    336.1/85/0973    *LC* 79-3775    *ISBN* 0815710682

**Dommel, Paul R., 1933-.**     **4.4662**
The politics of revenue sharing [by] Paul R. Dommel. Bloomington, Indiana University Press [1974] 211 p. 22 cm. 1. Intergovernmental fiscal relations — United States. 2. Grants-in-aid — United States. 3. United States — Politics and government — 1969-1974 I. T.
HJ275.D65    336.1/85/0973    *LC* 74-376    *ISBN* 0253345510

**Nathan, Richard P.**    4.4663
Revenue sharing: the second round / Richard P. Nathan, Charles F. Adams, Jr., and associates, with the assistance of André Juneau and James W. Fossett. — Washington: Brookings Institution, c1977. xvi, 268 p.; 24 cm. Includes index. 1. Revenue-sharing — United States. I. Adams, Charles F., 1945- joint author. II. Brookings Institution. III. T.
HJ275.N273    336.1/85    LC 76-51884    ISBN 081575986X. ISBN 0815759851 pbk

**Wright, Deil Spencer, 1930-.**    4.4664
Understanding intergovernmental relations: public policy and participants' perspectives in local, state, and national governments / Deil S. Wright. — North Scituate, Mass.: Duxbury Press, c1978. xv, 410 p.; 24 cm. — (The Duxbury Press series on public policy) Includes index. 1. Intergovernmental fiscal relations — United States. I. T.
HJ275.W72    350/.725/0973    LC 77-26967    ISBN 0878721525

## HJ790–1839 Other Countries

**Ward, Norman.**    • 4.4665
The public purse; a study in Canadian democracy. — [Toronto] University of Toronto Press [1962] 334 p. 24 cm. — (Canadian government series, 11) Includes bibliography. 1. Canada. Parliament. House of Commons — Hist. 2. Finance, Public — Canada — Hist. I. T.
HJ793.W3    336.71    LC 62-5636

**TePaske, John Jay.**    4.4666
The royal treasuries of the Spanish Empire in America / John J. TePaske, Herbert S. Klein. — Durham, N.C.: Duke University Press, 1982. 3 v.; 29 cm. Vol. 1: With the collaboration of Kendall W. Brown. 1. Finance, Public — South America — History. 2. South America — History — To 1806 3. South America — History — Wars of Independence, 1806-1830 I. Klein, Herbert S. II. Brown, Kendall W., 1949- III. T.
HJ891.T46 1982    336.8 19    LC 82-2457    ISBN 0822304864

**Andrien, Kenneth J., 1951-.**    4.4667
Crisis and decline: the Viceroyalty of Peru in the seventeenth century / Kenneth J. Andrien. — 1st ed. — Albuquerque: University of New Mexico Press, c1985. x, 287 p.: map; 24 cm. Includes index. 1. Finance, Public — Peru — History — 17th century. 2. Finance, Public — Spain — Colonies — History — 17th century. 3. Spain — Colonies — America — Economic policy. I. T.
HJ971.A53 1985    336.85 19    LC 84-23436    ISBN 0826307914

**Harriss, G. L.**    4.4668
King, Parliament, and public finance in medieval England to 1369 / G. L. Harriss. — Oxford: Clarendon Press, 1975. xii, 554 p.; 22 cm. Includes index. 1. Finance, Public — England — History. 2. Taxation — England — History. I. T.
HJ1005.H37    336.42    LC 75-328267    ISBN 0198224354

**Bullion, John L., 1944-.**    4.4669
A great and necessary measure, George Grenville and the genesis of the Stamp Act, 1763–1765 / John L. Bullion. — Columbia: University of Missouri Press, 1982. xiv, 317 p.; 24 cm. Includes index. 1. Grenville, George, 1712-1770. 2. Finance, Public — United States — To 1789 3. United States — History. 4. Finance, Public — Great Britain — 1688-1815 5. Great Britain — Colonies — America — History. I. T.
HJ1013.B84 1982    336.2/00973 19    LC 82-2775    ISBN 0826203752

**Hicks, Ursula Kathleen (Webb), 1896-.**    • 4.4670
British public finances, their structure and development, 1880–1952. — London, New York, Oxford University Press, 1954. 225 p. illus. 18 cm. 1. Finance, Public — Gt. Brit. I. T.
HJ1023.H456    336.42    LC 54-9922

**Beer, Samuel Hutchison, 1911-.**    • 4.4671
Treasury control: the co-ordination of financial and economic policy in Great Britain. — Oxford: Clarendon Press, 1956. 138 p.: ill. 1. Great Britain. Treasury. 2. Finance, Public — Great Britain 3. Great Britain — Economic policy I. T.
HJ1030.B4    LC 56-4176

**Harris, Robert D.**    4.4672
Necker, reform statesman of the Ancien Régime / Robert D. Harris. — Berkeley: University of California Press, c1979. 259 p.: port.; 25 cm. Includes index. 1. Necker, Jacques, 1732-1804. 2. Finance, Public — France — To 1789 I. T.
HJ1075.H37    354/.44/00720924    LC 77-93464    0520036477

**Bushnell, Amy.**    4.4673
The king's coffer: proprietors of the Spanish Florida treasury, 1565–1702 / Amy Bushnell. — Gainesville: University Presses of Florida, 1981. ix, 198 p.: map; 24 cm. 'A University of Florida book.' Includes index. 1. Finance, Public — Spain — History. 2. Finance, Public — Florida — History. I. T.
HJ1242.B87    354.460072/09 19    LC 81-7403    ISBN 0813006902

**Zelin, Madeleine.**    4.4674
The magistrate's tael: rationalizing fiscal reform in eighteenth–century Ch'ing China / Madeleine Zelin. — Berkeley: University of California Press, c1984. xviii, 385 p.; 24 cm. Includes index. 1. Finance, Public — China — History. 2. Fiscal policy — China — History. 3. China — History — Ch'ing dynasty, 1644-1912 I. T.
HJ1402.Z44 1984    336.51 19    LC 83-13515    ISBN 0520049306

**Young, Arthur N. (Arthur Nichols), 1890-.**    • 4.4675
China and the helping hand, 1937–1945. — Cambridge, Harvard University Press, 1963. xx, 502 p. map (on lining papers) 25 cm. — (Harvard East Asian series. 12) 'Bibliographical note': p. [449]-451. 1. Finance, Public — China. 2. Economic assistance, American — China. 3. China — Hist. — 1937-1945. 4. World War, 1939-1945 — Finance — China. I. T. II. Series.
HJ1414.Y65    336.51    LC 63-20774

**Goode, Richard B.**    4.4676
Government finance in developing countries / Richard Goode. — Washington, D.C.: Brookings Institution, c1984. xii, 334 p.; 24 cm. (Studies of government finance.) 1. Finance, Public — Developing countries. I. T. II. Series.
HJ1620.G66 1984    336/.09172/4 19    LC 83-20989    ISBN 0815731965

## HJ2005–2199 Income and Expenditure. Budget

**Novick, David.**    4.4677
Current practice in program budgeting (PPBS); analysis and case studies covering government and business. David Novick, editor. — New York: Crane, Russak, [1973] vii, 242 p.; 24 cm. 1. Program budgeting — Addresses, essays, lectures. I. T.
HJ2031.N68    658.1/54    LC 72-91627    ISBN 0844801534

**United States. Office of Management and Budget.**    4.4678
[Budget of the United States Government (Department edition)] Budget of the United States Government. — [Dept. ed.]. — Washington, D.C.: Executive Office of the President, Office of Management and Budget: For sale by the Supt. of Docs., U.S. G.P.O. v.: ill.; 24 cm. Annual. Began with 1971/72. Title varies slightly. Description based on: Fiscal year 1982. Report covers fiscal year. Supplements accompany some issues. *Other editions available:* United States. Office of Management and Budget. Budget of the United States Government (Document edition) (DLC)sn 87042035 (OCoLC)6018330 1. Budget — United States — Periodicals. I. T.
HJ2051.A59    353.007/22    LC 70-611049

**United States. Bureau of the Budget.**    • 4.4679
The Federal budget in brief.: July 1950/June 1951– / U.S. Bureau of the Budget. — [Washington: U.S. Govt. Print. Off.] v.: ill.; 23 cm. 1. Budget — United States I. T.
HJ2051.A5974    LC 50-60126

**The Guide to the federal budget / Stanley E. Collender.**    4.4680
[Washington, D.C.]: Urban Institute Press [etc.], 1985. 1 v.: ill.; 23 cm. (1984- : An Urban Institute paperback) Annual. 1. Budget — United States — Periodicals. I. Collender, Stanley E. II. Northeast-Midwest Institute (U.S.) III. Urban Institute. IV. Title: The new guide to the federal budget.
HJ2051.G84    353.0072/252/05    LC 82-643840 sn 82000823

**Schick, Allen.**    4.4681
Congress and money: budgeting, spending, and taxing / Allen Schick. — Washington, D.C.: Urban Institute, c1980. xiii, 604 p.; 24 cm. 1. Budget — United States 2. Finance, Public — United States 3. Government spending policy — United States I. T.
HJ2051.S34    353.0072 19    LC 80-53322    ISBN 0877662789

**Setting national priorities: the budget. 1971–.**    • 4.4682
Annual. Washington: The Brookings Institution. v.; 23 cm. Annual. 1. Budget — United States I. Schultze, Charles L. II. Brookings Institution.
HJ2051.S47    353.007/22    LC 74-161599

**Schick, Allen.**    4.4683
Manual on the Federal budget process / Allen Schick. Washington: [s.n.], [1982] 143 p. I. Keith, Robert. II. Library of Congress. Congressional Research Service. III. T.
HJ2051.S4x

**Wildavsky, Aaron B.**                                    **4.4684**
The politics of the budgetary process / Aaron Wildavsky. — 4th ed. — Boston:
Little, Brown, c1984. xxxvi, 323 p.; 21 cm. Includes index. 1. Budget — United
States I. T.
HJ2051.W485 1984        353.0072/221 19        *LC* 83-13588        *ISBN*
0316940410

**Ippolito, Dennis S.**                                    **4.4685**
Congressional spending / Dennis S. Ippolito. — Ithaca, N.Y.: Cornell
University Press, 1982 (c1981). 286 p.; 22 cm. 'A Twentieth Century Fund
report.' 1. Government spending policy — United States 2. United States —
Appropriations and expenditures I. Twentieth Century Fund. II. T.
HJ2052.I77        336.3/9/0973 19        *LC* 81-67971        *ISBN* 0801492300

**Schultze, Charles L.**                                    • **4.4686**
The politics and economics of public spending [by] Charles L. Schultze. —
Washington: Brookings Institution, [c1968] viii, 143 p.; 24 cm. — (The H.
Rowan Gaither lectures in systems science) 'Lectures delivered May 1968, at
the University of California, Berkeley, under the sponsorship of the Graduate
School of Business Administration and the Center for Research in Management
Science.' 1. Budget — U.S. 2. Program budgeting — U.S. I. T. II. Series.
HJ2052.S36        336.73        *LC* 69-18824

**Schick, Allen.**                                    • **4.4687**
Budget innovation in the States. Washington: Brookings Institution [1971] x,
223 p. 24 cm. 1. Budget — United States — States 2. Program budgeting —
United States — States. I. Brookings Institution. II. T.
HJ2053.A1 S35        353.9/3/722        *LC* 76-161594        *ISBN* 0815777302

**Peacock, Alan T., 1922-.**                                    **4.4688**
The growth of public expenditure in the United Kingdom / by Alan T. Peacock
and Jack Wiseman; assisted by Jindrich Veverka. A study by the National
Bureau of Economic Research. — Princeton: Priceton University Press, 1961.
xxxi, 213 p.: diagrs., tables; 24 cm. (National Bureau of Economic Research.
General series, no. 72) Bibliographical footnotes. 1. Finance, Public — Great
Britain 2. Great Britain — Appropriations and expenditures. I. Wiseman,
Jack. joint author. II. T. III. Series.
HJ2096.P4        336.42        *LC* 61-7409

# HJ2240–7395 Revenue. Taxation

**American Economic Association.**                                    • **4.4689**
Readings in the economics of taxation, selected by a committee of the American
Economic Association. Selection committee for this volume: Richard A.
Musgrave [and] Carl S. Shoup. Homewood, Ill., Published for the association
by R. D. Irwin, 1959. 581 p. illus. 24 cm. (The Series of republished articles on
economics, v. 9) 1. Taxation — Collections. I. Musgrave, Richard Abel, 1910-
ed. II. T. III. Title: The economics of taxation.
HJ2240.A6        336.2082        *LC* 59-7389

**The Economics of taxation / Henry J. Aaron and Michael J.**        **4.4690**
**Boskin, editors.**
Washington, D.C.: Brookings Institution, c1980. xviii, 418 p.; 24 cm. —
(Studies of government finance.) 1. Taxation — Addresses, essays, lectures.
2. Taxation — United States — Addresses, essays, lectures. 3. Fiscal policy —
Addresses, essays, lectures. 4. Fiscal policy — United States — Addresses,
essays, lectures. I. Aaron, Henry J. II. Boskin, Michael J. III. Series.
HJ2305.E27        336.2/00973        *LC* 79-3774        *ISBN* 0815700148

**Lewis, Stephen R.**                                    **4.4691**
Taxation for development: principles and applications / Stephen R. Lewis. —
New York: Oxford University Press, 1984. xix, 306 p.: ill.; 22 cm. 1. Taxation
2. Taxation — Developing countries I. T.
HJ2305.L48 1984        336.2/009172/4 19        *LC* 83-19308        *ISBN*
0195030524

**Pechman, Joseph A., 1918-.**                                    **4.4692**
Who paid the taxes, 1966–85? / Joseph A. Pechman. — Washington, D.C.:
Brookings Institution, c1985. xi, 84 p.: ill.; 24 cm. (Studies of government
finance.) 1. Tax incidence — United States. 2. Taxation — United States I. T.
II. Series.
HJ2322.A3 P42 1985        336.2/94/0973 19        *LC* 83-45845        *ISBN*
0815769970

**Kalven, Harry.**                                    • **4.4693**
The uneasy case for progressive taxation / by Harry Kalven Jr., and Walter J.
Blum. — [Chicago, 1952] 417-520 p.; 25 cm. 1. Taxation, Progressive
2. Income tax — United States I. Blum, Walter J., joint author. II. T.
HJ2327.U5 K3        *LC* 53-33386

**Bird, Richard Miller, 1938- comp.**                                    **4.4694**
Readings on taxation in developing countries / edited by Richard M. Bird and
Oliver Oldman. — 3d ed. — Baltimore: Johns Hopkins University Press, 1975.
ix, 555 p.; 23 cm. 1. Taxation — Developing countries — Addresses, essays,
lectures. I. Oldman, Oliver Sanford. joint comp. II. T.
HJ2351.B5 1975        336.2/009172/4        *LC* 74-24385        *ISBN*
0801816939

**Due, John Fitzgerald.**                                    **4.4695**
Indirect taxation in developing economies; the role and structure of customs
duties, excises, and sales taxes [by] John F. Due. Baltimore, Johns Hopkins
Press [1970] viii, 201 p. 24 cm. 1. Taxation — Developing countries I. T.
HJ2351.D8        336.2/71/091724        *LC* 70-119108        *ISBN* 0801811678

**Taxation and development / edited by N. T. Wang.**                **4.4696**
New York: Praeger, 1976. xvii, 287 p.; 25 cm. — (Praeger special studies in
international economics and development) 1. Taxation — Developing
countries — Addresses, essays, lectures. I. Wang, N. T. (Nian-Tzu), 1917-
HJ2351.T39        336.2/009172/4        *LC* 75-27023        *ISBN* 0275560104

**United States. Congress. Joint Economic Committee.**                • **4.4697**
The Federal revenue system: facts and problems, 1961; materials assembled by
the committee staff. — New York: Greenwood Press, [1968] xi, 290 p.; 27 cm.
Reprint of the 1961 ed. At head of title: 87th Congress, 1st session. Joint
committee print. 1. Taxation — U.S. I. T.
HJ2381.A524 1968        336.2/00973        *LC* 68-55110

**How taxes affect economic behavior / Henry J. Aaron and**        **4.4698**
**Joseph A. Pechman, editors.**
Washington, D.C.: Brookings Institution, c1981. xvi, 456 p.: ill.; 24 cm. —
(Studies of government finance.) 1. Taxation — United States — Addresses,
essays, lectures. 2. Fiscal policy — United States — Addresses, essays, lectures.
3. United States — Economic policy — 1961-1971 — Addresses, essays,
lectures. 4. United States — Economic policy — 1971-1981 — Addresses,
essays, lectures. I. Aaron, Henry J. II. Pechman, Joseph A., 1918-
III. Brookings Institution. IV. Series.
HJ2381.H68        336.2/00973 19        *LC* 81-1040        *ISBN* 0815700121

**Thurow, Lester C.**                                    • **4.4699**
The impact of taxes on the American economy / [by] Lester C. Thurow. —
New York: Praeger [1971] xiv, 171 p.: ill.; 22 cm. (New directions in
management and economics) 1. Taxation — United States 2. Fiscal policy —
United States. 3. United States — Economic conditions — 1971-1981 I. T.
HJ2381.T53        330.973        *LC* 70-141363

**The Economics of the Caribbean Basin / edited by Michael B.**        **4.4700**
**Connolly and John McDermott.**
New York: Praeger, 1985. xxiii, 355 p.: ill.; 25 cm. 1. Taxation — Caribbean
Area. 2. Tariff — Caribbean Area. 3. Debts, External — Latin America.
4. Monetary policy — Caribbean Area. 5. Foreign exchange administration —
Latin America. I. Connolly, Michael B. (Michael Bahaamonde), 1941-
II. McDermott, John, 1951-
HJ2479.E26 1985        330.9182/1 19        *LC* 85-3419        *ISBN* 0030016746

**Mitchell, Sydney Knox.**                                    **4.4701**
Studies in taxation under John and Henry III. New Haven, Yale University
Press, 1914. xiii, 407 p. (Yale historical publications. Studies, 2) 1. England —
Finance and taxation — History I. T.
HJ2605.M5

**Strayer, Joseph Reese, 1904-.**                                    • **4.4702**
Studies in early French taxation, by Joseph R. Strayer and Charles H. Taylor.
— Westport, Conn.: Greenwood Press, [1972, c1939] xiii, 200 p.; 22 cm.
Original ed. issued as vol. 12 of Harvard historical monographs series.
1. Taxation — France — History. I. Taylor, Charles Holt, 1899- II. T.
HJ2646.S75 1972        336.2/00944        *LC* 78-138187        *ISBN* 0837156440

**Holzman, Franklyn D.**                                    • **4.4703**
Soviet taxation; the fiscal and monetary problems of a planned economy.
Cambridge, Harvard University Press, 1955. xix, 376 p. tables. (Russian
Research Center studies, 16) 1. Taxation — Russia I. T.
HJ2802 H6        *LC* 55-5061

# HJ4101–4449 Property Tax

**Aaron, Henry J.**                                    **4.4704**
Who pays the property tax?: A new view / Henry J. Aaron. — Washington:
Brookings Institution, [1975] xii, 110 p.: ill.; 24 cm. — (Studies of government
finance.) 1. Property tax — United States. I. T. II. Series.
HJ4120.A62        336.2/2/0973        *LC* 75-19270        *ISBN* 0815700229

**Property taxes, housing and the cities / [by] George E.**      **4.4705**
**Peterson [and others].**
Lexington, Mass.: Lexington Books, [1973] xv, 203 p.; 23 cm. 1. Property tax
— United States. 2. Cities and towns — United States. I. Peterson, George E.
HJ4120.P673      336.2/2/0973      *LC* 73-11673      *ISBN* 0669910252

**The Taxation of income from capital. Arnold C. Harberger and**    • **4.4706**
**Martin J. Bailey, editors.**
Washington: Brookings Institution, [1969] xviii, 331 p.: illus.; 24 cm. —
(Studies of government finance) 1. Capital levy — United States — Addresses,
essays, lectures. I. Harberger, Arnold C. ed. II. Bailey, Martin J., ed.
III. Series.
HJ4120.T34      336.2/3      *LC* 68-31834

**Bird, Richard Miller, 1938-.**      **4.4707**
Taxing agricultural land in developing countries [by] Richard M. Bird.
Cambridge, Harvard University Press, 1974. xvi, 361 p. 25 cm. On half t.p.:
Harvard Law School International Tax Program. 1. Land value taxation —
Developing countries. 2. Agriculture — Taxation — Developing countries.
I. Harvard Law School. International Tax Program. II. T.
HJ4153.B57      336.2/2/091724      *LC* 73-77991      *ISBN* 0674868552

**Netzer, Dick, 1928-.**      • **4.4708**
Economics of the property tax / [by] Dick Netzer. — Washington: Brookings
Institution [1966] xviii, 326 p.: ill. (Studies of government finance) 1. Real
property tax — United States I. T.
HJ4181 N43      *LC* 65-28602

## HJ4621–4824 Income Tax

**Kaldor, Nicholas, 1908-1986.**      • **4.4709**
An expenditure tax. London, Allen & Unwin [1955] 249 p. 23 cm. 1. Taxation
I. T.
HJ 4639 K14      *LC* 56-1276

**McLure, Charles E.**      **4.4710**
Must corporate income be taxed twice?: A report of a conference sponsored by
the Fund for Public Policy Research and the Brookings Institution / Charles E.
McLure, Jr. — Washington: Brookings Institution, c1979. xvii, 262 p.; 24 cm.
— (Studies of government finance.) 1. Income tax 2. Corporations — Taxation
3. Dividends — Taxation I. Fund for Public Policy Research. II. Brookings
Institution. III. T. IV. Series.
HJ4639.M32      336.2/43/0973      *LC* 78-27905      *ISBN* 0815756208

**Goode, Richard B.**      **4.4711**
The individual income tax / Richard Goode. — Rev. ed. — Washington:
Brookings Institution, c1976. xiv, 346 p.; 24 cm. — (Studies of government
finance; 2d ser.) 1. Income tax — United States I. T. II. Series.
HJ4652.G6 1976      336.2/42/0973      *LC* 75-38735      *ISBN* 0815731981

**Comprehensive income taxation: a report of a conference**      **4.4712**
**sponsored by the Fund for Public Policy Research and the**
**Brookings Institution / Joseph A. Pechman, editor.**
Washington: Brookings Institution, c1977. xvi, 311 p.; 24 cm. — (Studies of
government finance.) Includes index. 1. Income tax — United States —
Addresses, essays, lectures. I. Pechman, Joseph A., 1918- II. Brookings
Institution. III. Series.
HJ4652.P427      336.2/42      *LC* 77-24246      *ISBN* 0815769822. *ISBN*
0815769814 pbk

**Simons, Henry Calvert, 1899-1946.**      • **4.4713**
Personal income taxation: the definition of income as a problem of fiscal policy /
by Henry C. Simons. — Chicago: The University of Chicago Press [c1938] xi,
238 p.; 21 cm. 1. Income tax — United States I. T.
HJ 4652 S62 1938      *LC* 38-27193

**Frey, Donald E., 1941-.**      **4.4714**
Tuition tax credits for private education: an economic analysis / Donald E.
Frey. — 1st ed. — Ames, Iowa: Iowa State University Press, 1983. ix, 119 p.:
ill.; 21 cm. 1. Tuition tax credits — United States I. T.
HJ4653.C73 F73 1983      336.24/216 19      *LC* 83-12676      *ISBN*
0813818265

**Penniman, Clara.**      **4.4715**
State income taxation / Clara Penniman. — Baltimore: Johns Hopkins
University Press, c1980. xiii, 292 p.; 24 cm. Includes index. 1. Income tax —
United States — States. 2. Tax administration and procedure — United States
— States. I. T.
HJ4655.A1 P43      353.9/3/724 19      *LC* 79-20081      *ISBN* 0801822904

## HJ5703–5715 Consumption Taxes. Sales Tax

**Cnossen, Sijbren.**      **4.4716**
Excise systems: a global study of the selective taxation of goods and services /
Sijbren Cnossen. — Baltimore: Johns Hopkins University Press, c1977. ix,
192 p.; 26 cm. Includes index. 1. Taxation of articles of consumption 2. Sales
tax I. T.
HJ5711.C55      336.2/71      *LC* 77-1407      *ISBN* 0801819628

**Sullivan, Clara Katherine, 1916-.**      **4.4717**
The tax on value added [by] Clara K. Sullivan. New York, Columbia University
Press, 1965. ix, 340 p. Based on thesis, Columbia University. 1. Sales tax I. T.
HJ5711 S8      *LC* 65-14322

**The Value–added tax: lessons from Europe / Henry J. Aaron,**      **4.4718**
**editor.**
Washington, D.C.: Brookings Institution, c1981. xi, 107 p.; 24 cm. — (Studies
of government finance.) 1. Value-added tax — Europe — Addresses, essays,
lectures. 2. Value-added tax — United States — Addresses, essays, lectures.
I. Aaron, Henry J. II. Brookings Institution. III. Series.
HJ5715.E9 V29      336.2/714/094 19      *LC* 81-38475      *ISBN*
0815700288

**Due, John Fitzgerald.**      **4.4719**
Sales taxation: state and local structure and administration / John F. Due and
John L. Mikesell. — Baltimore: Johns Hopkins University Press, c1983. xvii,
350 p.: ill.; 24 cm. Includes index. 1. Sales tax — United States — States.
2. Tax administration and procedure — United States — States. I. Mikesell,
John L. II. T.
HJ5715.U6 D77 1983      350.72/47 19      *LC* 82-13968      *ISBN*
0801828422

## HJ7451–7983 Expenditure

**Burkhead, Jesse.**      • **4.4720**
Public expenditure / [by] Jesse Burkhead [and] Jerry Miner. — Chicago:
Aldine, Atherton, [1971] x, 346 p.; 25 cm. — (Aldine treatises in modern
economics) 1. Expenditures, Public I. Miner, Jerry, 1929- joint author. II. T.
HJ7451.B87      336.3/9      *LC* 76-91725      *ISBN* 020206042X

**Sivard, Ruth Leger.**      **4.4721**
World military and social expenditures. [Leesburg, Va., WMSE Publications,
etc.] 28 cm. 1. Expenditures, Public I. T.
HJ7469.S58      336.3/9      *LC* 75-300012

**Heclo, Hugh.**      **4.4722**
The private government of public money: community and policy inside British
politics / [by] Hugh Heclo and Aaron Wildavsky. — Berkeley: University of
California Press [1974] xxiii, 399 p.: ill.; 23 cm. 1. Government spending policy
— Great Britain. 2. Great Britain — Appropriations and expenditures.
3. Great Britain — Politics and government — 1964-1979 I. Wildavsky,
Aaron B. joint author. II. T.
HJ7766.H4      354/.41/0072      *LC* 73-79474      *ISBN* 0520024974

## HJ8003–8897 Public Debts

**Buchanan, James M.**      • **4.4723**
Public principles of public debt: a defense and restatement / by James M.
Buchanan. — Homewood, Ill.: R.D. Irwin, 1958. xi, 223 p. 1. Debts, Public
I. T.
HJ8015.B8      *LC* 58-8652

**Ferguson, James Milton. ed.**      • **4.4724**
Public debt and future generations / edited by James M. Ferguson. — Chapel
Hill: University of North Carolina Press [1964] 234 p.: ill.; 24 cm. 1. Debts,
Public — United States 2. Fiscal policy — United States I. T.
HJ8119 F4      *LC* 64-22528

**Griffith-Jones, Stephany.**      **4.4725**
International finance and Latin America / Stephany Griffith–Jones. — New
York: St. Martins [i.e. Martin's] Press, 1984. 113 p.; 23 cm. Includes index.

1. Debts, External — Latin America. 2. Loans, Foreign — Latin America. 3. International finance I. T.
HJ8514.5.G75 1984     332.1/5/098 19     *LC* 84-15908     *ISBN* 0312421966

**Politics and economics of external debt crisis: the Latin**     **4.4726**
**American experience / edited by Miguel S. Wionczek, in**
**collaboration with Luciano Tomassini.**
Boulder: Westview Press, 1985. xiii, 481 p.; 24 cm. (Westview special studies on Latin America and the Caribbean.) 1. Debts, External — Latin America — Addresses, essays, lectures. 2. Latin America — Economic policy — Addresses, essays, lectures. I. Wionczek, Miguel S. II. Tomassini, Luciano. III. Series.
HJ8514.5.P65 1985     336.3/435/098 19     *LC* 84-15377     *ISBN* 0865317976

**African debt and financing / edited by Carol Lancaster and**     **4.4727**
**John Williamson.**
Washington, DC: Institute for International Economics, 1986. 223 p.; 23 cm. (Special reports; 5) 1. Debts, External — Africa — Congresses. 2. Loans, Foreign — Africa — Congresses. I. Lancaster, Carol. II. Williamson, John, 1937-
HJ8826.A36 1986     336.3/435/096 19     *LC* 86-7421     *ISBN* 0881320447

**Carvounis, Chris C.**     **4.4728**
The debt dilemma of developing nations: issues and cases / Chris C. Carvounis. — Westport, Conn.: Quorum Books, 1984. xvi, 189 p.; 25 cm. Includes index. 1. Debts, External — Developing countries 2. Debts, External — Developing countries — Case studies. I. T.
HJ8899.C37 1984     336.3/435/091724 19     *LC* 84-1981     *ISBN* 0899300626

# HJ9000–9698 Local Finance

**Lamb, Robert.**     **4.4729**
Municipal bonds: the comprehensive review of tax–exempt securities and public finance / by Robert Lamb & Stephen P. Rappaport. — New York: McGraw-Hill, c1980. xiv, 379 p.; 24 cm. 1. Municipal finance — United States. 2. Municipal bonds — United States. 3. Securities, Tax-exempt — United States. I. Rappaport, Stephen P. joint author. II. T.
HJ9145.L35     336.3/1     *LC* 79-27105     *ISBN* 0070360820

# HJ9701–9995 Public Accounting

**Lynn, Edward S.**     **4.4730**
Fund accounting: theory and practice / Edward S. Lynn, Robert J. Freeman. — 2nd ed. — Englewood Cliffs, N.J.: Prentice-Hall, c1983. xiv, 930 p.: ill.; 24 cm. 1. Municipal finance — United States — Accounting. 2. Local finance — United States — Accounting. 3. Finance, Public — United States — Accounting. 4. Fund accounting — United States. I. Freeman, Robert J. II. T.
HJ9777.A3 L95 1983     657/.835/00973 19     *LC* 82-21587     *ISBN* 0133324117

**Mosher, Frederick C.**     **4.4731**
A tale of two agencies: a comparative analysis of the General Accounting Office and the Office of Management and Budget / Frederick C. Mosher. — Baton Rouge: Louisiana State University Press, c1984. xxvi, 219 p.; 24 cm. — (Miller Center series on the American presidency.) Includes index. 1. United States. General Accounting Office. 2. United States. Office of Management and Budget. I. T. II. Series.
HJ9802.M682 1984     353.0071 19     *LC* 83-10634     *ISBN* 0807111155

## HM SOCIOLOGY: THEORY. SOCIAL PSYCHOLOGY

**American Society for Political and Legal Philosophy.**    4.4732
Community / edited by Carl J. Friedrich. New York: Liberal Arts Press, [c1959]. viii, 293 p. (Nomos; 2) 1. Sociology — Collections. 2. Community. 3. Law — Philosophy. I. Friedrich, Carl J. (Carl Joachim), 1901- II. T. III. Series.
HM15.A5    *LC* 59-11790

**Parsons, Talcott, 1902-.**    • 4.4733
Essays in sociological theory. — Rev. [i.e. 2d] ed. — Glencoe, Ill.: Free Press, [1954] 459 p.: illus; 22 cm. 1. Sociology — Addresses, essays, lectures. I. T. II. Title: Sociological theory.
HM15.P3 1954    301    *LC* 54-14940

**Theories of society: foundations of modern sociological theory /**    • 4.4734
**edited by Talcott Parsons ... [et al.].**
New York: Free Press of Glencoe, 1961. 2 v.: ill. 1. Sociology — Collections. I. Parsons, Talcott, 1902-
HM15.T46    301/.082    *LC* 61-9171

**The International encyclopedia of sociology / edited by Michael**    4.4735
**Mann.**
New York: Continuum, 1984. xi, 434 p.; 25 cm. Also published under title: The Macmillan student encyclopedia of sociology. 1. Sociology — Dictionaries. I. Mann, Michael, 1942-
HM17.I53 1984    301/.0321 19    *LC* 83-15340    *ISBN* 0826402380

**Theodorson, George A.**    • 4.4736
A modern dictionary of sociology [by] George A. Theodorson and Achilles G. Theodorson. — New York: Crowell, [1969] viii, 469 p.; 24 cm. 1. Sociology — Dictionaries. I. Theodorson, Achilles G., joint author. II. T.
HM17.T5    301/.03    *LC* 69-18672

## HM19–22 History

**Aron, Raymond, 1905-.**    • 4.4737
[Grandes doctrines de sociologie historique. English] Main currents in sociological thought / translated by Richard Howard & Helen Weaver. — New York: Basic Books [1965-. v. 25 cm. Translation of Les grandes doctrines de sociologie historique. 1. Sociology — History I. T.
HM19.A73    301.09    *LC* 65-13345

**Barnes, Harry Elmer, 1889-1968. ed.**    • 4.4738
An introduction to the history of sociology. Chicago, Univ. of Chicago Press [1948] xvi, 960 p. 34 cm. Includes bibliographies. 1. Sociology — History I. T.
HM19.B265    309    *LC* 47-12522 *

**Coser, Lewis A., 1913-.**    4.4739
Masters of sociological thought: ideas in historical and social context / Lewis A. Coser; under the general editorship of Robert K. Merton. 2d ed. — New York: Harcourt Brace Jovanovich, c1977. xxv, 611 p.: ill.; 25 cm. Includes index. 1. Sociology — History 2. Sociologists I. T.
HM19.C67 1977    301/.092/2    *LC* 77-72745    *ISBN* 0155551302

**Giddens, Anthony.**    4.4740
Capitalism and modern social theory: an analysis of the writings of Marx, Durkheim and Max Weber. — Cambridge [Eng.]: University Press, 1971. xvii, 261 p.; 24 cm. 1. Marx, Karl, 1818-1883. 2. Durkheim, Emile, 1858-1917. 3. Weber, Max, 1864-1920. I. T.
HM19.G53    301/.045    *LC* 70-161291    *ISBN* 0521082935

**Giddens, Anthony.**    4.4741
New rules of sociological method: a positive critique of interpretative sociologies / Anthony Giddens. New York: Basic Books, c1976. 192 p.; 23 cm. Includes index. 1. Sociology — History 2. Sociology — Methodology I. T.
HM19.G532    301/.09    *LC* 76-9672    *ISBN* 0465050832

**Halfpenny, Peter.**    4.4742
Positivism and sociology: explaining social life / Peter Halfpenny. — London; Boston: Allen & Unwin, 1982. 141 p.; 23 cm. — (Controversies in sociology. 13) Includes index. 1. Sociology — History 2. Positivism 3. Sociology — Methodology I. T. II. Series.
HM19.H18 1982    301 19    *LC* 82-11558    *ISBN* 0043000843

**A History of sociological analysis / Tom Bottomore & Robert**    4.4743
**Nisbet, editors.**
New York: Basic Books, c1978. xvi, 717 p.; 24 cm. 1. Sociology — History — Addresses, essays, lectures. I. Bottomore, T. B. II. Nisbet, Robert A.
HM19.H53    301/.09    *LC* 77-20429    *ISBN* 0465030238

**Martindale, Don.**    • 4.4744
The nature and types of sociological theory / Don Martindale. — 2nd ed. — Boston: Houghton Mifflin, c1981. xv, 656 p.: ill., ports.; 25 cm. Includes index. 1. Sociology — History I. T.
HM19.M36 1981    301/.09 19    *LC* 80-68142    *ISBN* 039529732X

**Nisbet, Robert A.**    • 4.4745
The sociological tradition / [by] Robert A. Nisbet. — New York: Basic Books, [c1966] xii, 349 p.; 25 cm. 1. Sociology — History I. T.
HM19.N5    301/.09    *LC* 66-28636

**Nisbet, Robert A.**    4.4746
Sociology as an art form / Robert Nisbet. — New York: Oxford University Press, 1976. 145 p.; 22 cm. Includes index. 1. Sociology — History — 19th century. 2. Intellectual life 3. Art and society 4. Sociology — Philosophy I. T.
HM19.N53    301/.01    *LC* 76-9278    *ISBN* 0195021029

**Strasser, Hermann, 1941-.**    4.4747
The normative structure of sociology: conservative and emancipatory themes in social thought / Hermann Strasser. — London; Boston: Routledge & K. Paul, 1976. ix, 275, 14 p.; 23 cm. (International library of sociology) Includes indexes. 1. Sociology — History I. T.
HM19.S83 1976    301/.09    *LC* 76-372936    *ISBN* 0710081669

## HM22 BY COUNTRY, A–Z

**Seidman, Steven.**    4.4748
Liberalism and the origins of European social theory / Steven Seidman. — Berkeley: University of California Press, c1983. xii, 419 p.; 22 cm. Includes index. 1. Sociology — Europe — History. 2. Socialism — Europe — History. 3. Liberalism — France — History. 4. Liberalism — Germany — History. I. T.
HM22.E9 S44 1983    301/.094 19    *LC* 82-21802    *ISBN* 0520047419

**Thompson, Kenneth, 1923-.**    4.4749
Auguste Comte: the foundation of sociology / Kenneth Thompson. — New York: Wiley, 1976 (c1975) xiv, 220 p. 'A Halsted Press book.' Includes index. 1. Comte, Auguste, 1798-1857. I. T.
HM22.F8 C75    301/.092/4    *LC* 75-12566    *ISBN* 0470859881

**Durkheim, Emile, 1858-1917.**    4.4750
On morality and society; selected writings. Edited and with an introd. by Robert N. Bellah. — Chicago: University of Chicago Press, [1973] 1 v, 244 p.; 22 cm. — (The Heritage of sociology) 1. Durkheim, Emile, 1858-1917. 2. Sociology I. T.
HM22.F8 D779 1973    301/.092/4    *LC* 73-76594    *ISBN* 0226173356

**Fenton, Steve, 1942-.**    4.4751
Durkheim and modern sociology / Steve Fenton, with Robert Reiner and Ian Hamnett. — Cambridge; New York: Cambridge University Press, 1984. vi, 276 p.; 24 cm. Includes index. 1. Durkheim, Emile, 1858-1917. 2. Durkheimian school of sociology 3. Sociology I. T.
HM22.F8 D788 1984    301 19    *LC* 83-26248    *ISBN* 0521259231

**Giddens, Anthony.**    4.4752
Emile Durkheim / Anthony Giddens. — New York: Viking Press, 1979. 132 p.; 19 cm. — (Modern masters.) Includes index. 1. Durkheim, Emile, 1858-1917. 2. Sociologists — France — Biography. I. T.
HM22.F8 D82 1979    301/.092/4 B    *LC* 78-26657    *ISBN* 0670292834

**LaCapra, Dominick, 1939-.**　　　　　4.4753
Emile Durkheim: sociologist and philosopher / by Dominick LaCapra. — Chicago: University of Chicago Press, 1985. xi, 317 p.; 21 cm. Reprint. Originally published: Ithaca, N.Y.: Cornell University Press, 1972. Includes index. 1. Durkheim, Emile, 1858-1917. 2. Durkheimian school of sociology I. T.
HM22.F8 D83 1985　　301/.092/4 19　　*LC* 85-1190　　*ISBN* 0226467260

**Lukes, Steven.**　　　　　4.4754
Emile Durkheim; his life and work, a historical and critical study. — [1st U.S. ed.]. — New York: Harper & Row, [c1972] xi, 676 p.; 25 cm. 1. Durkheim, Emile, 1858-1917. 2. Sociology — History 3. France — Social conditions I. T.
HM22.F8 D845 1972　　301/.092/4 B　　*LC* 75-156534　　*ISBN* 0060127279

**Nisbet, Robert A.**　　　　　• 4.4755
Émile Durkheim [by] Robert A. Nisbet. With selected essays. — Englewood Cliffs, N.J.: Prentice-Hall, [1965] x, 179 p.; 21 cm. — (Makers of modern social science) Spectrum book, S-118. 1. Durkheim, Emile, 1858-1917. I. T. II. Series.
HM22.F8 D86　　301.01　　*LC* 65-14994

**Durkheim, Emile, 1858-1917.**　　　　　4.4756
Selected writings. Edited, translated, and with an introduction by Anthony Giddens. — Cambridge: University Press, 1972. x, 272 p.; 23 cm. 1. Sociology I. T.
HM22.F8 D875 1972　　301　　*LC* 72-75773　　*ISBN* 0521085047

**Wolff, Kurt H., 1912- ed.**　　　　　• 4.4757
Emile Durkheim, 1858–1917; a collection of essays, with translations and a bibliography. Contributors: Charles Blend [and others]. — Columbus: Ohio State University Press, [1960] 463 p.; illus.; 22 cm. Translations from the works of Emile Durkheim: p. [315]-436. I. Durkheim, Emile, 1858-1917. II. T.
HM22.F8 D88　　923　　*LC* 60-10077

**Alpert, Harry, 1912-.**　　　　　• 4.4758
Emile Durkheim and his sociology. New York: Russell & Russell, 1961 [c1939] 233 p.; 23 cm. (Studies in history, economics, and public law, 445) Reprint: originally published New York, Columbia University Press, 1939. 1. Durkheim, Emile, 1858-1917. 2. Sociology I. T.
HM22.F8D8x H31.C7 no.445 1965　　*LC* 61-13089

**Le Play, Frédéric, 1806-1882.**　　　　　4.4759
Frédéric Le Play on family, work, and social change / edited, translated, and with an introduction by Catherine Bodard Silver. — Chicago: University of Chicago Press, 1982. xii, 340 p.; 21 cm. (Heritage of sociology.) 1. Le Play, Frédéric, 1806-1882. 2. Sociology — France — History. 3. Sociology — France — Methodology. 4. Work and family — France — History. 5. Social change I. T. II. Series.
HM22.F8 L435 1982　　301/.0944 19　　*LC* 81-23125　　*ISBN* 0226472663

**Aron, Raymond, 1905-.**　　　　　• 4.4760
German sociology / Translated by Mary and Thomas Bottomore. — Glencoe, Ill.: Free Press [1957] 141 p.; 23 cm. 1. Sociology — History — Germany. I. T.
HM22.G2A713　　*LC* 57-4467

**Marcuse, Herbert, 1898-.**　　　　　• 4.4761
Reason and revolution; Hegel and the rise of social theory. With a new pref. A note on dialectic, by the author. — [2d ed.]. — Boston: Beacon Press, [1960] 431 p.; 21 cm. — (Beacon paperback no. 110) 1. Hegel, Georg Wilhelm Friedrich, 1770-1831. 2. Sociology — History 3. Dialectic 4. Positivism I. T.
HM22.G3 H43 1960　　301　　*LC* 60-52176

**Loader, Colin, 1941-.**　　　　　4.4762
The intellectual development of Karl Mannheim: culture, politics, and planning / Colin Loader. — Cambridge [Cambridgeshire]; New York: Cambridge University Press, 1985. ix, 261 p.; 24 cm. Includes index. 1. Mannheim, Karl, 1893-1947. 2. Sociologists — Germany — Biography. I. T.
HM22.G3 M3254 1985　　301/.092/4 B 19　　*LC* 84-20040　　*ISBN* 0521265673

**Mitzman, Arthur, 1931-.**　　　　　4.4763
Sociology and estrangement: three sociologists of Imperial Germany. — [1st ed.]. — New York: Knopf; [distributed by Random House], 1973. xii, 375, viii p.; 22 cm. Revision of the author's thesis, Brandeis. 1. Michels, Robert, 1876-1936. 2. Sombart, Werner, 1863-1941. 3. Tönnies, Ferdinand, 1855-1936. I. T.
HM22.G3 M55 1973　　301/.092/2　　*LC* 71-111240　　*ISBN* 0394446046

**Wagner, Helmut R.**　　　　　4.4764
Alfred Schutz: an intellectual biography / Helmut R. Wagner. — Chicago: University of Chicago Press, 1983. xiii, 357 p.; 24 cm. — (Heritage of sociology.) Includes indexes. 1. Schutz, Alfred, 1899-1959. 2. Sociology — Philosophy 3. Phenomenology I. T. II. Series.
HM22.G3 S299 1983　　301/.092/4 B 19　　*LC* 82-13630　　*ISBN* 0226869369

**Bendix, Reinhard.**　　　　　• 4.4765
Max Weber; an intellectual portrait. — [1st ed.]. — Garden City, N. Y.: Doubleday, 1960. 480 p.; 22 cm. 1. Weber, Max, 1864-1920. I. T.
HM22.G3 W42　　923.343　　*LC* 60-5953

**Brubaker, Rogers.**　　　　　4.4766
The limits of rationality: an essay on the social and moral thought of Max Weber / Rogers Brubaker. — London; Boston: Allen & Unwin, 1984. viii, 119 p.; 23 cm. — (Controversies in sociology. 16) Includes index. 1. Weber, Max, 1864-1920. 2. Sociology — Germany. 3. Rationalism 4. Rationalism — Moral and ethical aspects. I. T. II. Series.
HM22.G3 W42367 1984　　301/.092/4 19　　*LC* 83-15152　　*ISBN* 0043011721

**Freund, Julien.**　　　　　• 4.4767
[Sociologie de Max Weber. English] The sociology of Max Weber / translated from the French by Mary Ilford. — [1st American ed.] New York: Pantheon Books [1968] ix, 310 p.; 22 cm. 1. Weber, Max, 1864-1920. I. T.
HM22.G3 W4413 1968　　301/.0924　　*LC* 67-19174

**Turner, Bryan S.**　　　　　4.4768
For Weber: essays on the sociology of fate / Bryan S. Turner. — Boston: Routledge & K. Paul, 1981. x, 408 p.; 22 cm. Includes index. 1. Weber, Max, 1864-1920. 2. Sociology — History 3. Political sociology 4. Religion and sociology I. T.
HM22.G3 W4586　　301/.01 19　　*LC* 81-183509　　*ISBN* 0710007809

**Wiltshire, David.**　　　　　4.4769
The social and political thought of Herbert Spencer / by David Wiltshire. — Oxford [Eng.]; New York: Oxford University Press, 1978. 269 p.; 23 cm. — (Oxford historical monographs) A revision of the author's thesis, Oxford, 1973. Includes index. 1. Spencer, Herbert, 1820-1903. 2. Social evolution 3. Social history I. T.
HM22.G8 S78　　301/.092/4　　*LC* 77-30202　　*ISBN* 0198218737

**Davis, Harold Eugene, 1902-.**　　　　　4.4770
Latin American social thought; the history of its development since independence, with selected readings. [Washington] University Press of Washington, D.C. [1961] iv, 557 p.; 21 cm. 1. Sociology — Latin America — History 2. Sociology — Collected works I. T.
HM22.S76 D3　　309.8　　*LC* 61-11238/L

# HM22.U5–.U6 United States

**Bierstedt, Robert, 1913-.**　　　　　4.4771
American sociological theory: a critical history / Robert Bierstedt. — New York: Academic Press, c1981. xiv, 525 p.; 24 cm. 1. Sociology — United States — History. 2. Sociologists — United States — Biography. I. T.
HM22.U5 B45　　301/.0973 19　　*LC* 81-10820　　*ISBN* 0120974800

**Black sociologists: historical and contemporary perspectives /**　　　　　4.4772
**edited by James E. Blackwell and Morris Janowitz.**
Chicago: University of Chicago Press, 1974. xxii, 415 p.; 21 cm. — (The heritage of sociology) Papers based on a National Conference on Black Sociologists, University of Chicago, May 5-6, 1972. 1. Afro-American sociologists — Congresses. I. Blackwell, James Edward, 1925- II. Janowitz, Morris. III. National Conference on Black Sociologists, University of Chicago, 1972.
HM22.U5 B55　　301/.0973　　*LC* 73-84187　　*ISBN* 0226055655

**Hofstadter, Richard, 1916-1970.**　　　　　• 4.4773
Social Darwinism in American thought. — Rev. ed. — New York: G. Braziller, 1959 [c1955] 248 p.; 22 cm. 1. Social evolution 2. Sociology — History — United States. I. T.
HM22.U5 H6 1959　　301　　*LC* 59-9543

**Sumner, William Graham, 1840-1910.**　　　　　• 4.4774
Social Darwinism; selected essays. With an introd. by Stow Persons. Englewood Cliffs, N.J., Prentice-Hall [1963] 180 p. 22 cm. (Classics in history series, S-CH-7) A Spectrum book. 1. Social Darwinism — Addresses, essays, lectures. I. T.
HM22.U5 S8　　301.082　　*LC* 63-11806

**Horowitz, Irving Louis.**　　　　　4.4775
C. Wright Mills: an American utopian / Irving Louis Horowitz. — New York: Free Press, c1983. x, 341 p.: port.; 24 cm. 1. Mills, C. Wright (Charles Wright), 1916-1962 — Biography. I. T.
HM22.U6 M427 1983　　301/.092/4 B 19　　*LC* 83-5619　　*ISBN* 0029149703

**Tilman, Rick.** 4.4776
C. Wright Mills: a native radical and his American intellectual roots / Rick Tilman. — University Park [Pa.]: Pennsylvania State University Press, c1984. 244 p.; 24 cm. Includes index. 1. Mills, C. Wright (Charles Wright), 1916-1962. 2. Sociology I. T.
HM22.U6 M466 1984    301/.092/4 19    *LC* 83-43034    *ISBN* 027100360X

**Matthews, Fred H.** 4.4777
Quest for an American sociology: Robert E. Park and the Chicago school / Fred H. Matthews. — Montreal: McGill-Queen's University Press, 1977. ix, 278 p.; 24 cm. Includes index. 1. Park, Robert Ezra, 1864-1944. 2. Chicago school of sociology — History. 3. Sociology — United States — History. I. T.
HM22.U6 P345    301/.092/4    *LC* 77-373940    *ISBN* 0773502432

**Raushenbush, Winifred.** 4.4778
Robert E. Park: biography of a sociologist / Winifred Raushenbush; with a foreword and an epilogue by Everett C. Hughes. — Durham, N.C.: Duke University Press, 1979. xii, 206 p.; 25 cm. Includes index. 1. Park, Robert Ezra, 1864-1944. 2. Sociologists — United States — Biography. I. T.
HM22.U6 P347    301/.092/4 B    *LC* 77-88063    *ISBN* 0822304023

**Ward, Lester Frank, 1841-1913.** • 4.4779
Lester Frank Ward: [selections from his work / with an introd. by] Israel Gerver. — New York: Crowell, [1963] 91 p.; 22 cm. — (Major contributors to social science series) 1. Sociology I. Gerver, Israel, ed. II. T.
HM22.U6 W13    301.082    *LC* 63-9194

# HM24 Philosophy

## HM24 A–F

**Alexander, Jeffrey C.** 4.4780
Theoretical logic in sociology / Jeffrey C. Alexander. — Berkeley: University of California Press, c1982. 234 p. 1. Sociology — History — Collected works. 2. Sociology — Philosophy — Collected works. 3. Sociology — Methodology — Collected works. I. T.
HM24.A465 1982    301 19    *LC* 75-17305    *ISBN* 0520030621

**Atkinson, Dick.** 4.4781
Orthodox consensus and radical alternative: a study in sociological theory. New York, Basic Books [1972] ix, 307 p. 1 illus. 24 cm. 1. Sociology — Methodology 2. Sociology — History I. T.
HM24.A85    301/.01    *ISBN* 0435820303

**Bell, Daniel.** 4.4782
The winding passage: essays and sociological journeys, 1960–1980 / Daniel Bell. — Cambridge, Mass.: Abt Books, c1980. xxiv, 370 p.; 25 cm. 1. Sociology — Addresses, essays, lectures. 2. Social history — 1960-1970 — Addresses, essays, lectures. 3. Social history — 1970- — Addresses, essays, lectures. 4. Social change — Addresses, essays, lectures. I. T.
HM24.B386    301 19    *LC* 79-57350    *ISBN* 0890115451

**Bottomore, T. B.** 4.4783
Sociology and socialism / Tom Bottomore. — New York: St. Martin's Press, 1984. 212 p.; 23 cm. 1. Sociology 2. Paradigms (Social sciences) 3. Socialism 4. Capitalism I. T.
HM24.B619 1984    301 19    *LC* 83-22930    *ISBN* 0312740042

**Causal models in panel and experimental designs / edited by** 4.4784
**H.M. Blalock, Jr.**
New York: Aldine Pub. Co., c1985. x, 287 p.: ill.; 24 cm. 1. Sociology — Methodology — Addresses, essays, lectures. 2. Panel analysis — Addresses, essays, lectures. 3. Sociology — Mathematical models — Addresses, essays, lectures. I. Blalock, Hubert M.
HM24.C32 1985    301/.01/8 19    *LC* 84-24276    *ISBN* 0202303152

**Collins, Randall, 1941-.** 4.4785
Conflict sociology: toward an explanatory science. With a contribution by Joan Annett. — New York: Academic Press, [1975] xi, 584 p.; 24 cm. 1. Sociology 2. Social conflict I. T.
HM24.C65    301    *LC* 74-5688    *ISBN* 0121813509

**De Coppens, Peter Roche, 1938-.** 4.4786
Ideal man in classical sociology: the views of Comte, Durkheim, Pareto, and Weber / Peter Roche de Coppens. [University Park]: Pennsylvania State University Press, c1976. vii, 174 p.; 24 cm. Includes index. 1. Sociology — Methodology 2. Sociology — History 3. Man I. T.
HM24.D38    301/.01    *LC* 75-27174    *ISBN* 0271012064

**Dollard, John, 1900-.** • 4.4787
Criteria for the life history, with analyses of six notable documents. New York, P. Smith, 1949. iv, 288 p. 1. Social sciences — Methodology 2. Sociology — Methodology 3. Social psychology I. T.
HM24 D6 1949    *LC* 49-9863

**Durkheim, Emile.** • 4.4788
The rules of sociological method / by Emile Durkheim. — 8th ed. / translated by Sarah A. Solovay and John H. Mueller and edited by George E. G. Catlin. — New York: The Free Press, [1964, c1938]. ix, 146 p. (A Free Press paperback) 1. Sociology — Methodology I. T.
HM24    HM24.D8x.    *LC* 64-57427

**Ekeh, Peter P.** 4.4789
Social exchange theory: the two traditions / Peter P. Ekeh. — Cambridge, Mass.: Harvard University Press, 1974. xv, 237 p.; 22 cm. Includes index. 1. Sociology 2. Social psychology I. T.
HM24.E37    301/.01    *LC* 74-79403    *ISBN* 0674812018

**Fararo, T. J.** 4.4790
Mathematical sociology: an introduction to fundamentals [by] Thomas J. Fararo. — New York: Wiley, [1973] xxvi, 802 p.: illus.; 23 cm. 'A Wiley-Interscience publication.' 1. Sociology — Methodology 2. Sociology — Mathematical models. 3. Game theory I. T.
HM24.F35    301/.01/51    *LC* 73-3204    *ISBN* 0471254606

**Friedrichs, Robert Winslow, 1923-.** 4.4791
A sociology of sociology, by Robert W. Friedrichs. — New York: Free Press, [1970]. xxiii, 429 p.; 24 cm. 1. Sociology I. T.
HM24.F74    301    *LC* 77-91882

## HM24 G–M

**Garfinkel, Harold.** • 4.4792
Studies in ethnomethodology. Englewood Cliffs, N.J., Prentice-Hall [1967] xvi, 288 p. illus. 22 cm. 1. Ethnomethodology I. T.
HM24.G3    306/.072 19    *LC* 67-22565

**Giddens, Anthony.** 4.4793
Central problems in social theory: action, structure, and contradiction in social analysis / Anthony Giddens. — Berkeley: University of California Press, 1979. 294 p.; 23 cm. 1. Sociology 2. Structuralism 3. Functionalism (Social sciences) I. T.
HM24.G446    301    *LC* 79-64667    *ISBN* 0520039726

**Giddens, Anthony.** 4.4794
The constitution of society: outline of the theory of structuration / Anthony Giddens. — Berkeley: University of California Press, 1985 (c1984). xxxvii, 402 p.: ill.; 24 cm. Includes index. 1. Sociology 2. Social structure 3. Social institutions 4. Political sociology I. T.
HM24.G4465    301 19    *LC* 84-40290    *ISBN* 0520052927

**Giddens, Anthony.** 4.4795
Profiles and critiques in social theory / Anthony Giddens; chapter 2 contributed by Fred Dallmayr. — Berkeley: University of California Press, c1982. xi, 239 p.; 23 cm. 1. Sociology — Philosophy 2. Hermeneutics 3. Positivism 4. Social structure 5. Political sociology I. Dallmayr, Fred R. (Fred Reinhard), 1928- II. T.
HM24.G4483 1982    301/.01 19    *LC* 82-20231    *ISBN* 0520049330

**Giddens, Anthony.** 4.4796
Studies in social and political theory / Anthony Giddens. — New York: Basic Books, c1977. 416 p.; 23 cm. 1. Sociology — Addresses, essays, lectures. 2. Hermeneutics — Addresses, essays, lectures. I. T.
HM24.G449    301    *LC* 77-74568    *ISBN* 046508270X

**Gouldner, Alvin Ward, 1920-.** • 4.4797
The coming crisis of Western sociology / [by] Alvin W. Gouldner. — New York: Basic Books, [1970] xv, 528 p.; 25 cm. — (His Studies in the series on the social origins of social theory) 1. Sociology 2. Sociology — History I. T.
HM24.G65    301/.09    *LC* 77-110771    *ISBN* 0465012787

**Held, David.** 4.4798
Introduction to critical theory: Horkheimer to Habermas / David Held. — Berkeley: University of California Press, c1980. 511 p.; 23 cm. Includes index. 1. Habermas, Jürgen. 2. Horkheimer, Max, 1895-1973. 3. Frankfurt school of sociology 4. Criticism (Philosophy) 5. Social institutions I. T.
HM24.H457    301/.01    *LC* 80-10535    *ISBN* 0520041216

**Kilminster, Richard.** 4.4799
Praxis and method: a sociological dialogue with Lukács, Gramsci and the early Frankfurt School / Richard Kilminster. — London; Boston: Routledge & Kegan Paul, 1979. xi, 333 p.; 23 cm. (International library of sociology)

Includes index. 1. Marxian school of sociology 2. Practice (Philosophy) 3. Communism and society I. T.
HM24.K53     301/.01     LC 79-40376     ISBN 0710000944

**Lazarsfeld, Paul Felix.**                                                **4.4800**
The varied sociology of Paul F. Lazarsfeld: writings / collected and edited by Patricia L. Kendall. — New York: Columbia University Press, 1982. xiii, 417 p.: port.; 24 cm. Includes indexes. 1. Sociology 2. Sociology — Methodology 3. Sociology — Statistical methods 4. Social sciences — Research I. Kendall, Patricia L. II. T.
HM24.L364 1982     301 19     LC 81-24205     ISBN 0231051220

**Lemert, Charles C., 1937-.**                                             **4.4801**
Sociology and the twilight of man: homocentrism and discourse in sociological theory / by Charles C. Lemert. — Carbondale: Southern Illinois University Press, c1979. xiii, 260 p.; 24 cm. — (Perspectives in sociology.) Includes index. 1. Sociology — Addresses, essays, lectures. I. T. II. Series.
HM24.L435 1979     301     LC 78-17146     ISBN 0809308517

**Mannheim, Karl, 1893-1947.**                                          • **4.4802**
[Ideologie und Utopie. English] Ideology and utopia: an introduction to the sociology of knowledge / by Karl Mannheim; with a preface by Louis Wirth. — London: K. Paul, Trench, Trubner & co., ltd.; New York: Harcourt, Brace and company, 1936. xxxi, 318 p.; 22 cm. — (International library of psychology, philosophy, and scientific method.) 'The present volume combines a number of different writings of the author. Parts II-IV represent Professor Mannheim's Ideologie und utopie ... Part V consists of his article 'Wissenssoziologie,' originally published in Alfred Vierkandt's Handwörterbuch der soziologie ... Part I was especially written to introduce the present volume to the Anglo-Saxon reader.'—Foreword 'Translated from the German by Louis Wirth and Edward Shils.' 1. Sociology — Methodology 2. Knowledge, Sociology of 3. Ideology 4. Utopias I. Wirth, Louis, 1897-1952. tr. II. Shils, Edward Albert, 1911- joint tr. III. T. IV. Series.
HM24.M27     301     LC 37-370

**Mehan, Hugh, 1941-.**                                                    **4.4803**
The reality of ethnomethodology / Hugh Mehan, Houston Wood. — New York: Wiley, [1975] x, 259 p.: ill.; 24 cm. 'A Wiley-Interscience publication.' Includes index. 1. Ethnomethodology I. Wood, Houston, 1944- joint author. II. T.
HM24.M446     306/.01/8 19     LC 75-1190     ISBN 0471590606

**Merton, Robert King, 1910-.**                                            **4.4804**
Sociological ambivalence and other essays / Robert K. Merton. New York: Free Press, c1976. xii, 287 p.; 24 cm. 1. Sociology 2. Social structure 3. Ethnic attitudes I. T.
HM24.M472     301     LC 76-1033     ISBN 0029211204

## HM24 N–Z

**Plummer, Kenneth.**                                                      **4.4805**
Documents of life: an introduction to the problems and literature of a humanistic method / Ken Plummer. — London; Boston: G. Allen & Unwin, 1983. xiv, 175 p.; 23 cm. — (Contemporary social research series.) Includes index. 1. Sociology — Biographical methods 2. Social sciences — Biographical methods I. T. II. Series.
HM24.P58 1983     300/.72 19     LC 83-2800     ISBN 0043210295

**Qualitative and quantitative social research: papers in honor of**       **4.4806**
**Paul F. Lazarsfeld / edited by Robert K. Merton, James S.**
**Coleman, Peter H. Rossi.**
New York: Free Press, c1979. xviii, 413 p.: port.; 24 cm. 1. Lazarsfeld, Paul Felix. 2. Lazarsfeld, Paul Felix — Bibliography. 3. Sociology — Methodology — Addresses, essays, lectures. I. Lazarsfeld, Paul Felix. II. Merton, Robert King, 1910- III. Coleman, James Samuel, 1926- IV. Rossi, Peter Henry, 1921-
HM24.Q34     301/.01/8     LC 78-24752     ISBN 0029209307

**Quinney, Richard.**                                                      **4.4807**
Social existence: metaphysics, Marxism, and the social sciences / Richard Quinney. — Beverly Hills, Calif.: Sage Publications, c1982. 193 p.: ill.; 22 cm. — (Sage library of social research. v. 141) 1. Sociology — Philosophy 2. Knowledge, Sociology of 3. Metaphysics I. T. II. Series.
HM24.Q55 1982     301/.01 19     LC 82-5903     ISBN 080390830X

**Ritzer, George.**                                                        **4.4808**
Sociology: a multiple paradigm science / George Ritzer. — Rev. ed. — Boston: Allyn and Bacon, c1980. 292 p.; 24 cm. 1. Sociology I. T.
HM24.R494 1980     301     LC 80-10175     ISBN 0205070736

**Rogers, Mary F. (Mary Frances), 1944-.**                                 **4.4809**
Sociology, ethnomethodology, and experience: a phenomenological critique / Mary F. Rogers. — Cambridge [Cambridgeshire]; New York: Cambridge University Press, 1983. xi, 219 p.; 24 cm. — (Arnold and Caroline Rose

monograph series of the American Sociological Association.) Includes indexes. 1. Phenomenological sociology 2. Ethnomethodology I. T. II. Series.
HM24.R648 1983     301/.01 19     LC 82-23579     ISBN 0521253896

**Slater, Phil.**                                                          **4.4810**
Origin and significance of the Frankfurt School: a Marxist perspective / Phil Slater. — London; Boston: Routledge & K. Paul, 1977. xvi, 185 p.; 23 cm. — (International library of sociology) Includes index. 1. Frankfurt school of sociology — History. 2. Institut für Sozialforschung (Frankfurt am Main, Germany) I. T.
HM24.S495     301/.01     LC 77-356661     ISBN 0710084382

**Smart, Barry.**                                                          **4.4811**
Sociology, phenomenology and Marxian analysis: a critical discussion of the theory and practice of a science of society / [by] Barry Smart. — London: Routledge and Kegan Paul, 1976. xiii, 206 p.; 23 cm. (International library of sociology) Includes index. 1. Sociology — Methodology 2. Phenomenalism 3. Communism and society I. T.
HM24.S524     301     LC 76-372946     ISBN 0710083726

**Thomas, William Isaac, 1863-1947.**                                   • **4.4812**
W. I. Thomas on social organization and social personality; selected papers. Edited and with an introd. by Morris Janowitz. — Chicago: University of Chicago Press, [1966] lviii, 311 p.; 21 cm. — (The Heritage of sociology) 1. Sociology — Addresses, essays, lectures. I. Janowitz, Morris. ed. II. T. III. Title: On social organization and social personality.
HM24.T55     301     LC 66-23701

**Turner, Jonathan H.**                                                    **4.4813**
The structure of sociological theory / Jonathan H. Turner. — 3rd ed. — Homewood, Ill.: Dorsey Press, 1982. xv, 488 p.: ill.; 24 cm. — (Dorsey series in sociology.) 1. Sociology I. T. II. Series.
HM24.T84 1982     301/.01 19     LC 80-85476     ISBN 0256026807

**Znaniecki, Florian, 1882-1958.**                                      • **4.4814**
The method of sociology. — New York: Octagon Books, 1968. xii, 338 p.; 21 cm. Reprint of the 1934 ed. 1. Sociology — Methodology I. T.
HM24.Z6 1968     301/.01/8     LC 68-9670

# HM26–39 Sociology of Particular Subjects

**Mannheim, Karl, 1893-1947.**                                          • **4.4815**
Essays on the sociology of knowledge / Edited by Paul Kecskemeti. New York, Oxford University Press, 1952. 327 p. 1. Sociology 2. Knowledge, Theory of I. T.
HM26.M3     301     LC 52-14918

**The View from Goffman / edited by Jason Ditton.**                        **4.4816**
New York: St. Martin's Press, 1980. v, 289 p.; 22 cm. 1. Goffman, Erving — Addresses, essays, lectures. 2. Goffman, Erving — Bibliography. 3. Life style — Addresses, essays, lectures. 4. Sociology — Philosophy — Addresses, essays, lectures. I. Ditton, Jason.
HM26.V53 1980     301/.01     LC 79-25202     0312845984

**Mills, C. Wright (Charles Wright), 1916-1962.**                       • **4.4817**
Sociology and pragmatism: the higher learning in America / [by] C. Wright Mills; edited with an introd. by Irving Louis Horowitz. — New York: Paine-Whitman Publishers [1964] 475 p.; 23 cm. A revision of the author's thesis, University of Wisconsin, with title: A sociological account of pragmatism. 1. Sociology 2. Pragmatism I. T.
HM27.M5 1964     191     LC 64-19448

**Stinchcombe, Arthur L.**                                                 **4.4818**
Economic sociology / Arthur L. Stinchcombe. — New York: Academic Press, 1983. ix, 269 p.; 24 cm. — (Studies in social discontinuity.) Includes index. 1. Sociology 2. Marxian economics 3. Human ecology 4. Technology — Social aspects 5. Population 6. Production (Economic theory) I. T. II. Series.
HM35.E246 1983     306/.3 19     LC 82-13717     ISBN 0126713804

**Buchan, Alastair.**                                                    • **4.4819**
War in modern society: an introduction / by Alastair Buchan. — London: Watts, 1966. xvi, 207 p.; 19 cm. (New thinker's library, no.14) 1. War and society I. T. II. Series.
HM36.5.B8     327.1     LC 67-71325

**Elites, ethnographic issues / edited by George E. Marcus.**             **4.4820**
1st ed. — Albuquerque: University of New Mexico Press, c1983. x, 305 p.; 25 cm. (School of American Research advanced seminar series.) 'A School of

American Research book.' Includes index. 1. Elite (Social sciences) 2. Ethnology I. Marcus, George E. II. Series.
HM37.E44 1983     305.5/2 19     *LC* 83-14526     *ISBN* 0826306586

**Lundberg, George Andrew, 1895-1966.**     • **4.4821**
Can science save us? / by George A. Lundberg. — 2d ed. — New York, McKay 1961. vi, 150 p.; 19 cm. 1. Science — Methodology 2. Sociology I. T.
HM38.L8 1961     *LC* 61-12658

# HM45–47 Study. Teaching

**Bulmer, Martin.**     **4.4822**
The Chicago school of sociology: institutionalization, diversity, and the rise of sociological research / Martin Bulmer. — Chicago: University of Chicago Press, c1984. xix, 285 p.: ill.; 24 cm. (Heritage of sociology.) Includes index. 1. Chicago school of sociology I. T. II. Series.
HM47.U62 C43 1984     301/.07/1177311 19     *LC* 84-8494     *ISBN* 0226080048

**The Research craft: an introduction to social research methods /**     **4.4823**
**John B. Williamson ... [et al.]; in collaboration with Stephen T. Barry, Richard S. Dorr.**
2nd ed. — Boston: Little, Brown, c1982. xi, 434 p.: ill.; 24 cm. Rev. ed. of: The research craft / John B. Williamson, David A. Karp, John R. Dalphin. 1st ed. c1977. 1. Sociology — Research 2. Social sciences — Research I. Williamson, John B.
HM48.R47 1982     300/.72 19     *LC* 81-81757     *ISBN* 0316943649

**Tilly, Charles.**     **4.4824**
Big structures, large processes, huge comparisons / Charles Tilly. — New York: Russell Sage Foundation, 1984. 176 p. (Russell Sage Foundation 75th anniversary series) 1. Social science research. 2. Social structure 3. Social change I. T. II. Series.
HM48.T555     *LC* 84-60264     *ISBN* 0871548798

# HM51–68 General Works, by Original Language

## HM51 English

### HM51 A–M

**Applied sociology / Howard E. Freeman ... [et al.], editors.**     **4.4825**
San Francisco, Calif.: Jossey-Bass, c1983. xxvi, 490 p.: ill.; 24 cm. — (Jossey-Bass social and behavioral science series.) 1. Sociology 2. Sociologists — Employment. 3. Sociology — Study and teaching I. Freeman, Howard E. II. Series.
HM51.A66 1983     301 19     *LC* 82-49035     *ISBN* 0875895638

**Bendix, Reinhard.**     • **4.4826**
Embattled reason: essays on social knowledge. — New York: Oxford University Press, 1970. xi, 395 p.; 22 cm. 1. Sociology — Addresses, essays, lectures. 2. Social change — Addresses, essays, lectures. I. T.
HM51.B394 1970     301     *LC* 79-111644

**Berger, Peter L.**     • **4.4827**
Invitation to sociology: a humanistic perspective. — [1st ed.]. — Garden City, N.Y.: Doubleday, 1963. 191 p.; 18 cm. — (Anchor books) 1. Sociology I. T.
HM51.B45     301     *LC* 63-8758

**Burgess, Ernest Watson, 1886-1966.**     **4.4828**
On community, family, and delinquency: selected writings / edited by Leonard S. Cottrell, Jr., Albert Hunter [and] James F. Short, Jr. — Chicago: University of Chicago Press, 1974 (c1973) ix, 337 p.: ill.; 22 cm. (The Heritage of sociology) 1. Community — Addresses, essays, lectures. 2. Family — Addresses, essays, lectures. 3. Juvenile delinquency — Addresses, essays, lectures. I. T.
HM51.B948     301     *LC* 73-83572     *ISBN* 0226080579

**Coser, Lewis A., 1913- ed.**     • **4.4829**
Sociological theory: a book of readings / edited by Lewis A. Coser, Bernard Rosenberg. — 5th ed. — New York: Macmillan, c1982. xviii, 603 p.; 24 cm.

1. Sociology — Addresses, essays, lectures. I. Rosenberg, Bernard, 1923- II. T.
HM51.C645 1982     301 19     *LC* 81-474     *ISBN* 0023252200

**Dahrendorf, Ralf.**     • **4.4830**
Essays in the theory of society. — Stanford, Calif.: Stanford University Press, 1968. x, 300 p.; 24 cm. 1. Sociology — Addresses, essays, lectures. I. T.
HM51.D25     301     *LC* 67-26526

**Hawley, Amos Henry.**     • **4.4831**
Human ecology: a theory of community structure / by Amos H. Hawley. — New York: Ronald Press, 1950. xvi, 456 p.: ill. 1. Human ecology I. T.
HM51.H38     *LC* 50-7591

**Mannheim, Karl, 1893-1947.**     • **4.4832**
Essays on sociology and social psychology. New York, Oxford University Press, 1953. 319 p. 23 cm. 1. Sociology — Addresses, essays, lectures. 2. Social psychology — Addresses, essays, lectures. I. T.
HM51.M24 1953     *LC* 53-13111

**Merton, Robert King, 1910-.**     • **4.4833**
Social theory and social structure [by] Robert K. Merton. — 1968 enl. ed. — New York: Free Press, [1968] xxiii, 702 p.; 24 cm. 1. Sociology 2. Social structure I. T.
HM51.M393 1968     301/.01     *LC* 68-28789

**Mulkay, M. J. (Michael Joseph), 1936-.**     **4.4834**
Functionalism, exchange and theoretical strategy [by] M. J. Mulkay. New York, Schocken Books [1971] ix, 260 p. 23 cm. 1. Sociology I. T.
HM51.M78 1971b     301/.044     *LC* 70-144783

## HM51 N–Z

**Park, Robert Ezra, 1864-1944.**     **4.4835**
The collected papers of Robert Ezra Park. — New York: Arno Press, 1974. xxii, 403, 278, 358 p.: illus.; 23 cm. — (Perspectives in social inquiry) Reprint of the author's Race and culture, first published in 1950, by Free Press, Glencoe, Ill.; of the author's Human communities, first published 1952, by Free Press, Glencoe, Ill.; and of the author's Society, first published 1955, by Free Press, Glencoe, Ill. 1. Sociology — Addresses, essays, lectures. I. Park, Robert Ezra, 1864-1944. Race and culture. 1974. II. Park, Robert Ezra, 1864-1944. Human communities. 1974. III. Park, Robert Ezra, 1864-1944. Society. 1974. IV. Series.
HM51.P25 1974     301     *LC* 73-14174     *ISBN* 040505517X

**Park, Robert Ezra, 1864-1944.**     • **4.4836**
Introduction to the science of sociology, including the original index to basic sociological concepts [by] Robert E. Park and Ernest W. Burgess. With an introd. by Morris Janowitz. — 3d ed. rev. — Chicago: University of Chicago Press, [1969] xxiv, 1040 p.; 22 cm. — (The Heritage of sociology) 1. Sociology I. Burgess, Ernest Watson, 1886-1966. joint author. II. T.
HM51.P3 1969     301     *LC* 69-15366

**Park, Robert Ezra, 1864-1944.**     • **4.4837**
On social control and collective behavior. Selected papers, edited and with an introd. by Ralph H. Turner. — [1st Phoenix ed.]. — Chicago: University of Chicago Press, [1967] xlvi, 274 p.; 21 cm. — (The Heritage of sociology) 1. Sociology I. Turner, Ralph H. ed. II. T.
HM51.P312     301     *LC* 67-25084

**Parsons, Talcott, 1902-.**     • **4.4838**
The social system. — Glencoe, Ill.: Free Press, [1951] 575 p.; 22 cm. 1. Social systems I. T.
HM51.P35     301     *LC* 51-13850

**Parsons, Talcott, 1902-.**     • **4.4839**
Sociological theory and modern society. — New York: Free Press, [1967] xii, 564 p.; 24 cm. Essays. 1. Sociology I. T.
HM51.P37     301     *LC* 67-12517

**Sorokin, Pitirim Aleksandrovich, 1889-1968.**     • **4.4840**
Fads and foibles in modern sociology and related sciences. — Chicago: Regnery 1956. viii, 357 p.; 24 cm. — 1. Sociology I. T.
HM51.S67     *LC* 56-6176

**Spencer, Herbert, 1820-1903.**     **4.4841**
[Selected works] On social evolution; selected writings. Edited and with an introd. by J. D. Y. Peel. Chicago, University of Chicago Press [1972] li, 270 p. 21 cm. (The Heritage of sociology) 1. Sociology 2. Social evolution 3. Social sciences — Methodology I. Peel, J. D. Y. (John David Yeadon), 1941- ed. II. T.
HM51.S6987 1972     301.24     *LC* 76-172616     *ISBN* 0226768910 *ISBN* 0226768929

**Spencer, Herbert, 1820-1903.**    **• 4.4842**
Social statics; or, The conditions essential to human happiness specified, and the first of them developed. — New York: A. M. Kelley, 1969. viii, 476 p.; 22 cm. — (Man in society) (Reprints of economic classics.) Reprint of the 1851 ed. 1. Social sciences 2. Sociology I. T.
HM51.S7 1969    300    *LC* 69-20304

**Spencer, Herbert.**    **• 4.4843**
The study of sociology / Herbert Spencer; introd. by Talcott Parsons. — Ann Arbor: University of Michigan Press, 1961. 411 p. 1. Sociology 2. Sociology — Study and teaching I. T.
HM51.S75 1961    301    *LC* 61-42488

**Spencer, Herbert, 1820-1903.**    **• 4.4844**
Principles of sociology / Edited by Stanislav Andreski. — [Abridged ed. — Hamden, Conn.]: Archon Books, 1969. xxxvi, 821 p.; 23 cm. 1. Sociology I. T.
HM51.S81112    301    *LC* 73-6040

**Spencer, Herbert, 1820-1903.**    **• 4.4845**
[Principles of sociology. Selections] The evolution of society; selections from Herbert Spencer's Principles of sociology. Edited and with an introd. by Robert L. Carneiro. Chicago, University of Chicago Press [1967] lvii, 241 p. 23 cm. (Classics in anthropology) 1. Sociology I. Carneiro, Robert L. (Robert Leonard), 1927- ed. II. T.
HM51.S8112    301    *LC* 67-20581

**Thomas, William Isaac, 1863-1947.**    **• 4.4846**
Social behavior and personality: contributions of W. I. Thomas to theory and social research / edited by Edmund H. Volkart. — New York: Social Science Research Council, 1951. ix, 338 p.: port.; 24 cm. Bibliographical footnotes. 'Bibliography of W. I. Thomas [compiled by A. Paul Hare]': p. 319-322. 1. Sociology I. Volkart, Edmund Howell, 1919- ed. II. T.
HM51.T58    301    *LC* 51-5300

**Van den Berghe, Pierre L.**    **4.4847**
Man in society: a biosocial view / Pierre L. van den Berghe. — New York: Elsevier, [1975] xiv, 300 p.; 22 cm. Includes index. 1. Sociology 2. Social sciences I. T.
HM51.V33    301    *LC* 74-32422    *ISBN* 0444990003

**Ward, Lester Frank, 1841-1913.**    **• 4.4848**
Dynamic sociology; or, Applied social science, as based upon statical sociology and the less complex sciences. — New York: Greenwood Press, 1968 [c1911] 2 v.; 22 cm. 1. Sociology I. T. II. Title: Applied social science.
HM51.W28 1968b    301    *LC* 69-10167

**Wirth, Louis, 1897-1952.**    **• 4.4849**
Louis Wirth on cities and social life; selected papers. Edited and with an introd. by Albert J. Reiss, Jr. — Chicago: University of Chicago Press, [1964] xxx, 350 p.; 21 cm. — (The Heritage of sociology) 1. Sociology — Addresses, essays, lectures. I. T. II. Title: On cities and social life.
HM51.W54    301.081    *LC* 64-24970

**Znaniecki, Florian, 1882-1958.**    **• 4.4850**
Social actions. — New York: Russell & Russell, [1967] xix, 746 p.; 23 cm. 'First published in 1936.' 1. Sociology I. T.
HM51.Z55 1967    301    *LC* 66-24773

## HM55–63 Other Languages

**Comte, Auguste, 1798-1857.**    **• 4.4851**
System of positive polity / by Auguste Compte. — New York: Burt Franklin, [1968?] 4 v.; 23 cm. (Burt Franklin research and source works series; no. 125.) (Burt Franklin philosophy monograph series; no. 4 (v.2-4 only).) Translation of Système de politique positive. 1. Positivism 2. Sociology I. T.
HM55.C76 1968    146.4    *LC* 66-20689    *ISBN* 0833706403

**Durkheim, Emile, 1858-1917.**    **4.4852**
Émile Durkheim, contributions to L'Année sociologique / edited by Yash Nandan; translated by John French ... [et al.]. — New York: Free Press, c1980. xix, 522 p.; 25 cm. 1. Sociology 2. Sociology — Book reviews. 3. Année sociologique. I. Nandan, Yash. II. Année sociologique. III. T. IV. Title: Contributions to L'Année sociologique.
HM55.D848 1980    301    *LC* 79-54670    *ISBN* 0029079802

**Durkheim, Emile, 1858-1917.**    **• 4.4853**
Émile Durkheim; [selections from his work, with an introd. and commentaries by] George Simpson. New York, Crowell [1963] 129 p. 22 cm. (Major contributors to social science series) 1. Sociology — Addresses, essays, lectures. I. T.
HM55.D85    308.1    *LC* 63-9195

**Durkheim, Emile, 1858-1917.**    **• 4.4854**
Sociology and philosophy. Translated by D. F. Pocock. With an introd. by J. G. Peristiany. Glencoe, Ill., Free Press, 1953. xli, 97 p. 22 cm. 1. Sociology 2. Philosophy I. T.
HM55.D98    *LC* a 54-2835

**Marx, Karl, 1818-1883.**    **• 4.4855**
[Selections. English] Selected writings in sociology & social philosophy / newly translated by T. B. Bottomore; edited, with an introd. and notes, by Mr. Bottomore and Maximilien Rubel, and with a foreword by Erich Fromm. — [1st McGraw-Hill ed.] New York: McGraw-Hill [1964] xviii, 268 p.; 21 cm. 1. Sociology 2. Capitalism I. T.
HM57.M33 1964    301    *LC* 64-5474

**Schutz, Alfred, 1899-1959.**    **• 4.4856**
The phenomenology of the social world / Alfred Schutz; translated by George Walsh and Frederick Lehnert; with an introd. by George Walsh. — [Evanston, Ill.]: Northwestern University Press, c1967. xxxvi, 255 p.; 24 cm. — (Northwestern University studies in phenomenology & existential philosophy) Translation of Der sinnhafte Aufbau der sozialen Welt. 1. Weber, Max, 1864-1920. 2. Sociology 3. Social psychology I. T. II. Series.
HM57.S413    301/.01    *LC* 67-16716    *ISBN* 0810103907

**Simmel, Georg, 1858-1918.**    **• 4.4857**
The sociology of Georg Simmel; translated, edited, and with an introd., by Kurt H. Wolff. — Glencoe, Ill.: Free Press, [1950] lxiv, 445 p.; 22 cm. Contains translations of the author's Grundfragen der Soziologie, part of Soziologie, and the lecture, Die Grossstädte und das Geistesleben. 1. Sociology I. Wolff, Kurt H., 1912- ed. and tr. II. T.
HM57.S482    301    *LC* 50-7406

*[handwritten: HM 57 S482]*

**Tönnies, Ferdinand, 1855-1936.**    **• 4.4858**
[Gemeinschaft und Gesellschaft. English] Community & society (Gemeinschaft und Gesellschaft) Translated and edited by Charles P. Loomis. East Lansing: Michigan State University Press [1957] xii, 298 p.: port.; 24 cm. 1. Sociology I. T.
HM57.T62 1957    301    *LC* 57-8428

**Weber, Max, 1864-1920.**    **• 4.4859**
Economy and society; an outline of interpretive sociology. Edited by Guenther Roth and Claus Wittich. Translators: Ephraim Fischoff [and others]. — New York: Bedminster Press, 1968. 3 v. (cviii, 1469, lxiv p.); 25 cm. Translation of the 4th German ed. of Wirtschaft und Gesellschaft, with appendices from Gesammelte Aufsätze zur Wissenschaftslehre and Gesammelte politische Schriften. 1. Sociology 2. Economics I. T.
HM57.W342    300/.1    *LC* 68-27095

**Weber, Max, 1864-1920.**    **• 4.4860**
[Wirtschaft und Gesellschaft. English v. 1] Basic concepts in sociology. Translated and with an introd. by H. P. Secher. New York, Greenwood Press [1969, c1962] 123 p. 23 cm. First chapter of vol. 1 of the author's Wirtschaft und Gesellschaft. 1. Sociology I. T.
HM57.W343 1969    301    *LC* 77-88968    *ISBN* 0837121469

**Ferrarotti, Franco.**    **4.4861**
[Sociologia alternativa. English] An alternative sociology / by Franco Ferrarotti; edited and with a foreword by J. W. Freiberg; translated from Italian by Pasqualino and Barbara Columbaro. — New York: Irvington Publishers: distributed by Halsted Press, c1979. 200 p.; 22 cm. — (Irvington critical sociology series) Translation of Una sociologia alternativa. 1. Sociology — Italy. 2. Marxian school of sociology — Italy. I. Freiberg, J. W. II. T. III. Series.
HM59.F41313    301    *LC* 78-26022    *ISBN* 047026599X

**Pareto, Vilfredo, 1848-1923.**    **• 4.4862**
Sociological writings / selected and introduced by S. E. Finer; translated by Derick Mirfin. — New York: Praeger, [1966] viii, 335 p.: ill.; 23 cm. 1. Sociology I. Finer, S. E. (Samuel Edward), 1915- ed. II. T.
HM59.P1813    301    *LC* 66-12277

**Pareto, Vilfredo, 1848-1923.**    **• 4.4863**
The mind and society: a treatise on general sociology / by Vilfredo Pareto; translated by Andrew Bongiorno and Arthur Livingston with the advice and active cooperation of James Harvey Rogers; edited by Arthur Livingston. — New York: Dover Publication, 1963. 4 v.. in 2: ill., port. Translation of Trattato di sociologia generale. 1. Sociology I. T.
HM59.P25 1963    *LC* 63-4505

**Sorokin, Pitirim Aleksandrovich, 1889-1968.**    **• 4.4864**
Social and cultural mobility. — Glencoe, Ill.: Free Press, [1959] 645 p.; 22 cm. 'Complete reprints of [the author's] Social mobility and chapter V from volume IV of Social and cultural dynamics.' 1. Sociology 2. Social history I. T.
HM61.S6 1959    301.44    *LC* 59-13122

## HM66–73 Special Aspects

**Parsons, Talcott, 1902-.**     • **4.4865**
The structure of social action: a study in social theory with special reference to a group of recent European writers. — [2d ed.] Glencoe, Ill.: Free Press, 1949. A-F, xii, 817 p.; 23 cm. 1. Sociology I. T.
HM 66 P271 1949

**Chorover, Stephan L.**     **4.4866**
From genesis to genocide: the meaning of human nature and the power of behavior control / Stephan L. Chorover. — Cambridge, Mass.: MIT Press, c1979. xiii, 238 p.; 24 cm. 1. Social control 2. Human behavior 3. Power (Social sciences) I. T.
HM73.C49    301.15    *LC* 78-21107    *ISBN* 0262030683

*[handwritten: HM 73 C49]*

**Mitchell, Jack N.**     **4.4867**
Social exchange, dramaturgy, and ethnomethodology: toward a paradigmatic synthesis / Jack N. Mitchell. — New York: Elsevier, c1978. x, 187 p.; 24 cm. Includes index. 1. Social exchange 2. Drama — Technique 3. Sociology — Methodology I. T.
HM73.M57    301/.01    *LC* 78-13198    *ISBN* 0444990577

**Schwartz, Barry, 1938-.**     **4.4868**
Queuing and waiting: studies in the social organization of access and delay / Barry Schwartz. — Chicago: University of Chicago Press, 1975. v, 217 p.; 23 cm. Includes index. 1. Time management 2. Queuing theory 3. Social interaction I. T.
HM73.S358    301.5    *LC* 75-11607    *ISBN* 0226742105

**Using sociology: an introduction from the clinical perspective /**     **4.4869**
**[edited by] Roger A. Straus.**
Bayside, N.Y.: General Hall, c1985. 200 p.; 24 cm. 1. Clinical sociology I. Straus, Roger A. (Roger Austin), 1948-
HM73.U85 1985    301 19    *LC* 84-81428    *ISBN* 093039058X

## HM101–121 Civilization. Culture. Progress

**Bauman, Zygmunt.**     **4.4870**
Culture as praxis. — London; Boston: Routledge & K. Paul, [1973] v, 198 p.; 23 cm. — (Monographs in social theory) 1. Culture 2. Social structure 3. Sociology — Methodology 4. Anthropology I. T.
HM101.B285 1973    301.2/01    *LC* 73-79108    *ISBN* 0710076061

**Wuthnow, Robert.**     **4.4871**
Cultural analysis: the work of Peter L. Berger, Mary Douglas, Michel Foucault, and Jürgen Habermas / Robert Wuthnow ... [et al.]. — Boston; London: Routledge & Kegan Paul, 1984. viii, 273 p.; 23 cm. Includes index. 1. Berger, Peter L. 2. Douglas, Mary. 3. Foucault, Michel. 4. Habermas, Jürgen. 5. Culture 6. Social change I. T.
HM101.C86 1984    306 19    *LC* 83-17781    *ISBN* 0710098944

**The Essential Frankfurt School reader / edited by Andrew**     **4.4872**
**Arato & Eike Gebhardt; introd. by Paul Piccone.**
New York: Urizen Books, c1978. xxiii, 559 p.; 23 cm. Includes index. 1. Mass society — Addresses, essays, lectures. 2. Political science — Addresses, essays, lectures. 3. Economics — Addresses, essays, lectures. 4. Social sciences — Methodology — Addresses, essays, lectures. I. Arato, Andrew. II. Gebhardt, Eike.
HM101.E745    300/.8    *LC* 76-30906    *ISBN* 091635430X

**Etzioni-Halevy, Eva. comp.**     **4.4873**
Social change: sources, patterns, and consequences. Edited by Eva Etzioni-Halevy and Amitai Etzioni. — 2d ed. — New York: Basic Books, [c1973] xii, 559 p.; 24 cm. Compilers' names in reverse order in the 1964 ed. 1. Social change — Addresses, essays, lectures. I. Etzioni, Amitai. joint comp. II. T.
HM101.E8218 1973    301.24    *LC* 73-81392    *ISBN* 0465078559

**Geography & ethnic pluralism / edited by Colin Clarke, David**     **4.4874**
**Ley, and Ceri Peach.**
London; Boston: G. Allen & Unwin, 1984. xvii, 294 p.: ill.; 24 cm. Contributions by former students of Paul Paget, presented to commemorte his interests and teaching. 1. Pluralism (Social sciences) 2. Ethnic relations 3. Race relations 4. Developing countries — Social conditions. 5. Great Britain — Social conditions I. Clarke, Colin G. II. Ley, David. III. Peach, Ceri. IV. Paget, Paul, 1918- V. Title: Geography and ethnic pluralism.
HM101.G296 1984    303.4/82 19    *LC* 84-6319    *ISBN* 0043091075

**Sorokin, Pitirim Aleksandrovich, 1889-1968.**     • **4.4875**
Social and cultural dynamics / by Pitirim A. Sorokin. — New York: The Bedminster Press, 1962 [c1937]. 4 v. : ill., diagrs. Vol. 1 includes bibliographical references. 1. Civilization — Philosophy 2. History — Philosophy 3. Culture I. T.
HM101 H7512 1962    *LC* 62-4504

*[handwritten: HM 101 S71]*

**Johnson, Lesley.**     **4.4876**
The cultural critics: from Matthew Arnold to Raymond Williams / Lesley Johnson. — London; Boston: Routledge & Kegan Paul, 1979. viii, 235 p.; 23 cm. — (International library of sociology) Includes index. 1. Culture 2. Authors, English — Political and social views I. T.
HM101.J585    301.2/0942    *LC* 78-41306    *ISBN* 0710076789

**Kroeber, Alfred Louis, 1876-1960.**     • **4.4877**
Culture; a critical review of concepts and definitions, by A. L. Kroeber and Clyde Kluckhohn, with the assistance of Wayne Untereiner and appendices by Alfred G. Meyer. Cambridge, Mass., The Museum, 1952. viii, 223 p. 27 cm. (Papers of the Peabody Museum of American Archæology and Ethnology, Harvard University, v. 47, no. 1) 1. Culture 2. Civilization I. Kluckhohn, Clyde, 1905-1960. joint author. II. T.
HM101.K7 1952    901

**Malinowski, Bronislaw, 1884-1942.**     • **4.4878**
Freedom and civilization / by Bronislaw Malinowski. — New York: Roy publishers, [1944] xiv, 338 p.: diagrs.; 22 cm. 1. Civilization 2. Liberty. 3. Democracy 4. Totalitarianism I. T.
HM101 M24    *LC* 44-8875

**Mannheim, Karl, 1893-1947.**     **4.4879**
[Strukturen des Denkens. English] Structures of thinking / Karl Mannheim; text and translation edited and introduced by David Kettler, Volker Meja, and Nico Stehr; translated by Jeremy J. Shapiro and Shierry Weber Nicholsen. — London; Boston: Routledge & Kegan Paul, 1982. 292 p.; 23 cm. — (International library of sociology.) Translation of: Structuren des Denkens. 1. Culture 2. Knowledge, Sociology of I. Kettler, David. II. Meja, Volker. III. Stehr, Nico. IV. T. V. Series.
HM101.M26213 1982    306 19    *LC* 81-13824    *ISBN* 0710009364

**Marcuse, Herbert, 1898-.**     • **4.4880**
One dimensional man; studies in the ideology of advanced industrial society. Boston, Beacon Press [c1964] xvii, 260 p. 24 cm. 1. Civilization, Modern — 20th century I. T.
HM101.M268    301.243    *LC* 64-10088

**Mead, Margaret, 1901-1978.**     **4.4881**
Culture and commitment: the new relationships between the generations in the 1970s / Margaret Mead. — Rev. and updated ed. — New York: Columbia University Press, 1978. xx, 178 p.; 22 cm. Includes index. 1. Culture 2. Social change 3. Conflict of generations I. T.
HM101.M38 1978b    301.2    *LC* 78-14589    *ISBN* 0231046324

**Mills, C. Wright (Charles Wright), 1916-1962.**     • **4.4882**
Power, politics, and people: the collected essays of C. Wright Mills / edited and with an introd. by Irving Louis Horowitz. — New York: Oxford University Press, 1963. 657 p.: ill.; 22 cm. 1. Social change — Addresses, essays, lectures. 2. Power (Social sciences) — Addresses, essays, lectures. 3. United States — Social life and customs — 1945-1970 I. T.
HM101.M59 1963a    308.1    *LC* 63-1444

**Nisbet, Robert A.**     **4.4883**
History of the idea of progress / Robert Nisbet. — New York: Basic Books, c1980. xi, 370 p.; 24 cm. Includes index. 1. Progress I. T.
HM101.N574 1980    303.4    *LC* 79-1979    *ISBN* 0465030254

**Ogburn, William Fielding, 1886-1959.**     • **4.4884**
On culture and social change; selected papers. Edited and with an introd. by Otis Dudley Duncan. — Chicago: University of Chicago Press, [1964] xxii, 360 p.: illus.; 21 cm. — (The Heritage of sociology) 'Scientific writings of William Fielding Ogburn': p. [349]-360. 1. Social change 2. Civilization 3. Technology and civilization I. T.
HM101.O38    301.2    *LC* 64-23418

*[handwritten: HM 101 O34]*

**Rogers, Everett M.**     **4.4885**
Diffusion of innovations / Everett M. Rogers. — 3rd ed. — New York: Free Press; London: Collier Macmillan, c1983. xix, 453 p.: ill.; 25 cm. Rev. ed. of: Communication of innovations. 2nd ed. 1971. Includes indexes. 1. Diffusion of innovations 2. Diffusion of innovations — Study and teaching — History. I. T.
HM101.R57 1983    303.4/84 19    *LC* 82-70998    *ISBN* 0029266505

Sorel, Georges, 1847-1922.                                              • 4.4886
[Illusions du progrès. English] The illusions of progress. Translated by John and
Charlotte Stanley with a foreword by Robert A. Nisbet and an introd. by John
Stanley. Berkeley, University of California Press, 1969. li, 222 p. 24 cm.
1. Progress 2. Socialism I. T.
HM101.S713        301.2/45        LC 69-16511

Sorokin, Pitirim Aleksandrovich, 1889-1968.                            • 4.4887
The crisis of our age; the social and cultural outlook, by Pitirim A. Sorokin ....
— New York: Dutton, [c1941] 338 p.: illus.; 19 cm. Based upon four volumes of
the author's Social and cultural dynamics. 1. Civilization — Philosophy
2. History — Philosophy 3. Culture I. Sorokin, Pitirim Aleksandrovich,
1899-1968. Social and cultural dynamics. II. T.
HM101.S76        901        LC 41-51942

Sorokin, Pitirim Aleksandrovich, 1889-1968.                            • 4.4888
Society, culture, and personality: their structure and dynamics; a system of
general sociology. — New York: Cooper Square Publishers, 1962. 742 p.: illus.;
27 cm. 1. Social groups I. T.
HM101.S763 1962        301        LC 62-19527

Laszlo, Ervin, 1932- ed.                                               4.4889
The world system: models, norms, applications. Edited by Ervin Laszlo. —
New York: G. Braziller, [1973] x, 215 p.: illus.; 22 cm. — (The International
library of systems theory and philosophy) 1. System theory — Congresses.
2. Social systems — Congresses. 3. Social values — Congresses. I. Systems
Philosophy Symposium, 1st, State University of New York at Geneseo, 1973.
II. T. III. Series.
HM101.S97 1973        003        LC 73-79050        ISBN 0807606952

Zaltman, Gerald.                                                       4.4890
Processes and phenomena of social change [by] Gerald Zaltman and [others].
— New York: J. Wiley, [1973] xi, 463 p.: illus.; 23 cm. 'A Wiley-Interscience
publication.' 1. Social change — Addresses, essays, lectures. 2. Diffusion of
innovations — Addresses, essays, lectures. I. T.
HM101.Z285        301.24        LC 72-13021        ISBN 0471981303

## HM106–108 Evolution. Biological and Anthropological Sociology

Bannister, Robert C.                                                   4.4891
Social Darwinism: science and myth in Anglo–American social thought /
Robert C. Bannister. — Philadelphia: Temple University Press, 1979. 292 p.; 24
cm. — (American civilization.) 1. Social Darwinism — Great Britain —
History. 2. Social Darwinism — United States — History. I. T. II. Series.
HM106.B255        301/.0424        LC 79-615        ISBN 0877221553

Dobzhansky, Theodosius Grigorievich, 1900-1975.                        • 4.4892
The biological basis of human freedom / Theodosius Dobzhansky. — New
York: Columbia University Press, 1960. vi, 139 p.; 21 cm. — (Page-Barbour
lectures; 1954) 1. Evolution 2. Man I. T.
HM106.D6        575.1        ISBN 0231085109 pbk

Habermas, Jürgen.                                                      4.4893
Communication and the evolution of society / Jürgen Habermas; translated and
with an introd. by Thomas McCarthy. — Boston: Beacon Press, 1979, c1976.
xxiv, 239 p.; 21 cm. 1. Social evolution 2. Pragmatics 3. Historical
materialism 4. State, The 5. Social sciences — Philosophy I. T.
HM106.H313        301.14        LC 77-88324        ISBN 0807015121

Montagu, Ashley, 1905-.                                                • 4.4894
On being human. New York, H. Schuman [1950] 125 p. 1. Sociology
2. Evolution 3. Cooperation I. T.
HM106 M65        LC 50-7952

Linton, Ralph, 1893-1953.                                             • 4.4895
The cultural background of personality / by Ralph Linton. — New York;
London: D. Appleton-Century company, incorporated, [1945] xix, 157 p.; 20
cm. — (The Century psychology series) Five lectures delivered at Swarthmore
college under the auspices of the Cooper foundation, February, 1943. cf. Pref.
1. Personality and culture 2. Ethnopsychology I. T.
HM107.L5        301.15        LC 45-2477

Shibutani, Tamotsu, 1920-.                                            4.4896
Ethnic stratification; a comparative approach [by] Tamotsu Shibutani and Kian
M. Kwan, with contributions by Robert H. Billigmeier. New York, Macmillan
[1965] xiv, 626 p. 1. Sociology 2. Ethnology 3. Social classes 4. Social mobility
I. Kwan, Kian Moon, 1929-, jt. author II. Billigmeier, Robert H. III. T.
HM107 S5        LC 65-11877

## HM131–133 Social Groups

Blau, Peter Michael.                                                   4.4897
On the nature of organizations [by] Peter M. Blau. New York, Wiley [1974] ix,
358 p. illus. 23 cm. 'A Wiley-Interscience publication.' 1. Organization
2. Organization — Research 3. Bureaucracy I. T.
HM131.B592        301.18/32        LC 74-7392        ISBN 0471080373

Coleman, James Samuel, 1926-.                                         4.4898
The asymmetric society / James S. Coleman. — 1st ed. — Syracuse, N.Y.:
Syracuse University Press, 1982. xii, 191 p.; 22 cm. — (Frank W. Abrams
lectures.) Includes index. 1. Social structure 2. Interpersonal relations
3. Organizational behavior 4. Social role 5. Social change I. T. II. Series.
HM131.C7419 1982        305 19        LC 81-23255        ISBN 0815601727

The Dying community / edited by Art Gallaher, Jr. and                  4.4899
Harland Padfield.
1st ed. — Albuquerque: University of New Mexico Press, c1980. xiv, 305 p.; 24
cm. (School of American Research advanced seminar series.) Based on a
seminar held in September 1976 at the School of American Research, Santa Fe.
'A School of American Research book.' Includes index. 1. Community —
Congresses. 2. Community life — Congresses. 3. Cities and towns — United
States — Congresses. I. Gallaher, Art, 1925- II. Padfield, Harland. III. Series.
HM131.D98        307        LC 79-56814        ISBN 0826305350

Etzioni, Amitai.                                                       • 4.4900
A comparative analysis of complex organizations: on power, involvement, and
their correlates. — [New York]: Free Press of Glencoe [1961] 366 p.; 25 cm.
1. Comparative organization I. T.
HM131.E78        301.4        LC 61-14107

Goffman, Erving.                                                       4.4901
Relations in public: microstudies of the public order. — New York: Basic
Books, [1971] xvii, 396 p.; 25 cm. 1. Social interaction 2. Human behavior
I. T.
HM131.G55        301.11        LC 76-167764        ISBN 0465068952

Golembiewski, Robert T.                                               • 4.4902
The small group; an analysis of research concepts and operations. [Chicago]
University of Chicago Press [1962] xii, 303 p. diagrs., tables. Part of thesis, Yale
University. 1. Small groups I. T.
HM131 G57        LC 62-12633

*(handwritten note in right margin: HM 131 G62)*

Hartsock, Nancy C. M.                                                 4.4903
Money, sex, and power: toward a feminist historical materialism / Nancy C.M.
Hartsock. — New York: Longman, c1983. x, 310 p.; 24 cm. — (Longman series
in feminist theory.) 1. Power (Social sciences) 2. Power (Philosophy)
3. Feminism 4. Exchange 5. Historical materialism 6. Masculinity
(Psychology) I. T. II. Series.
HM131.H32 1983        303.3/3 19        LC 82-17157        ISBN 0582282799

Katz, Daniel, 1903-.                                                  4.4904
The social psychology of organizations / Daniel Katz, Robert L. Kahn. — 2d
ed. — New York: Wiley, c1978. vi, 838 p.: ill.; 24 cm. Includes indexes.
1. Organization 2. Social psychology I. Kahn, Robert Louis, 1918- joint
author. II. T.
HM131.K35 1978        301.18/32        LC 77-18764        ISBN 0471023558

Kropotkin, Petr Alekseevich, kniaz', 1842-1921.                      4.4905
Mutual aid; a factor of evolution, [by] Peter Kropotkin; edited and with an
introd. by Paul Avrich. New York, New York University Press, 1972. vi, 278 p.
23 cm. Translation of Vzaimnaia pomoshch', kak faktor évoliutsii.
1. Cooperation 2. Social groups 3. Sociology I. T.
HM131.K92 1972        335/.83        LC 79-188872

March, James G. ed.                                                  • 4.4906
Handbook of organizations. Edited by James G. March. Chicago, Rand
McNally [1965] xvi, 1247 p. 25 cm. (Rand McNally sociology series)
1. Organizational behavior 2. Organization 3. Management I. T.
HM131.M335        301.4        LC 65-14104

Meyer, John W.                                                        4.4907
Organizational environments: ritual and rationality / John W. Meyer, W.
Richard Scott with the assistance of Brian Rowan and Terrance E. Deal. —
Beverly Hills: Sage, c1983. 302 p.: ill.; 23 cm. Includes index. 1. Organization
— Addresses, essays, lectures. I. Scott, W. Richard. II. T.
HM131.M469 1983        302.3/5 19        LC 83-13698        ISBN 0803920814

**Meyer, Marshall W.**     **4.4908**
Environments and organizations / Marshall W. Meyer and associates. — 1st ed. — San Francisco: Jossey-Bass, 1978. xiv, 407 p.: ill.; 24 cm. — (The Jossey-Bass social and behavioral science series) Includes index. 1. Organization I. T.
HM131.M47     301.18/32     *LC* 76-50706     *ISBN* 0875893740

**Meyer, Marshall W. comp.**     **4.4909**
Structures, symbols, and systems: readings on organizational behavior / edited by Marshall W. Meyer. — Boston: Little, Brown, [1971] vi, 458 p.; 24 cm. 1. Organizational behavior — Addresses, essays, lectures. I. T.
HM131.M48 1971     301.18/32     *LC* 74-157476

**Parsons, Talcott, 1902-.**     • **4.4910**
Structure and process in modern societies. — Glencoe, Ill.: Free Press, [1960] 344 p.; 22 cm. 1. Organization I. T.
HM131.P33     301.4     *LC* 59-6821

**Perrow, Charles.**     **4.4911**
Complex organizations: a critical essay / Charles Perrow; academic consultants, Albert J. Reiss, Jr., Harold L. Wilensky. — 3rd ed. — New York: Random House, c1986. x, 307 p.; 24 cm. Includes index. 1. Organization I. T.
HM131.P382 1986     302.3/5 19     *LC* 85-14489     *ISBN* 0394344979

**Perrow, Charles.**     • **4.4912**
Organizational analysis: a sociological view. — Belmont, Calif.: Wadsworth Pub. Co., [1970] xiii, 192 p.; 22 cm. — (Behavioral science in industry series) 1. Organization I. T.
HM131.P383     301.4     *LC* 70-98404

**Redfield, Robert, 1897-.**     **4.4913**
The little community, and Peasant society and culture. — Chicago, University of Chicago Press [1973, c1956] v, 182, 92 p.; 21 cm. 'First published in Sweden as vol. 5 of the Gottesman lectures, Uppsala University.' Includes bibliography. I. Redfield, Robert, 1897- II. T.
HM131.R37     *ISBN* 0226706494

**Scott, W. Richard.**     **4.4914**
Organizations: rational, natural, and open systems / W. Richard Scott. — Englewood Cliffs, N.J.: Prentice-Hall, c1981. xviii, 381 p. Includes indexes. 1. Organization I. T.
HM131.S385     HM131 S385.     302.3 19     *LC* 80-24640     *ISBN* 0136419771

**Sherif, Muzafer, 1905-.**     • **4.4915**
Groups in harmony and tension: an integration of studies on intergroup relations / Muzafer Sherif and Carolyn W. Sherif. — New York: Octagon books, 1966, t.p. 1973, c1953. xiii, 316 p., [4] leaves of plates: ill.; 24 cm. 1. Social groups I. Sherif, Carolyn W. II. T.
HM131.S45 1973     301.15     *ISBN* 0374973342

**Stoneall, Linda.**     **4.4916**
Country life, city life: five theories of community / Linda Stoneall. — New York, N.Y.: Praeger, 1983. xiii, 321 p.: ill.; 25 cm. Includes indexes. 1. Community life — Case studies. 2. Sociology, Urban — Case studies. 3. Sociology, Rural — Case studies. 4. City and town life — United States — Case studies. 5. Country life — United States — Case studies. I. T.
HM131.S8257 1983     307 19     *LC* 83-2427     *ISBN* 003061712X

**Katz, Daniel, 1903-.**     **4.4917**
The study of organizations / Daniel Katz, Robert L. Kahn, J. Stacy Adams, editors. — 1st ed. — San Francisco, Calif.: Jossey-Bass, 1980. xx, 567 p.: ill.; 26 cm. — (The Jossey-Bass social and behavioral science series) 1. Organization 2. Organizational effectiveness I. Kahn, Robert Louis, 1918- joint author. II. Adams, J. Stacy. joint author. III. T.
HM131.S832     302.3/5     *LC* 80-15488     *ISBN* 087589464X

**Voluntary associations. Edited by J. Roland Pennock and John**     **4.4918**
**W. Chapman.**
[1st ed.] New York, Atherton Press, 1969. xvi, 291 p. 22 cm. (Nomos 11) 'Yearbook of the American Society for Political and Legal Philosophy.' 1. Associations, institutions, etc. 2. Pluralism (Social sciences) I. Pennock, J. Roland (James Roland), 1906- II. Chapman, John William, 1923- ed. III. American Society for Political and Legal Philosophy. IV. Series.
HM131.V6     301.18/3     *LC* 68-27525

**Weick, Karl E.**     **4.4919**
The social psychology of organizing / Karl E. Weick. — 2d ed. — Reading, Mass.: Addison-Wesley Pub. Co., c1979. ix, 294 p.: ill.; 24 cm. — (Topics in social psychology) Includes index. 1. Organization — Psychological aspects. I. T.
HM131.W39 1979     301.18/32     *LC* 79-10015     *ISBN* 0201085917

**White, Ralph K.**     • **4.4920**
Autocracy and democracy: an experimental inquiry / [by] Ralph K. White [and] Ronald Lippitt. — Westport, Conn.: Greenwood Press, [1972, c1960] x,

330 p.: charts; 22 cm. 1. Social groups 2. Democracy 3. Leadership I. Lippitt, Ronald. joint author. II. T.
HM131.W45 1972     301.18     *LC* 71-138137     *ISBN* 0837157102

## HM132–134 Interpersonal Relations

**Attribution: perceiving the causes of behavior [by] Edward E.**     **4.4921**
**Jones [and others]**
Morristown, N.J.: General Learning Press, [1972] xiii, 186 p.; 24 cm. 1. Attribution (Social psychology) 2. Interpersonal relations I. Jones, Edward Ellsworth, 1926-
HM132.A87     301.11     *LC* 72-86668

**Bennis, Warren G. ed.**     • **4.4922**
Interpersonal dynamics; essays and readings on human interaction, edited by Warren G. Bennis [and others]. — Rev. ed. — Homewood, Ill.: Dorsey Press, 1968. xvi, 766 p.: illus.; 24 cm. — (The Dorsey series in psychology) 1. Interpersonal relations — Addresses, essays, lectures. I. T.
HM132.B45 1968     301.15/08     *LC* 68-23345

**Berne, Eric.**     • **4.4923**
Games people play; the psychology of human relationships. — New York: Grove Press, [1964] 192 p.: illus.; 21 cm. 1. Interpersonal relations 2. Social interaction I. T.
HM132.B46 1964     301.11     *LC* 64-13783

**Caughey, John L., 1941-.**     **4.4924**
Imaginary social worlds: a cultural approach / John L. Caughey. — Lincoln: University of Nebraska Press, c1984. viii, 280 p.; 23 cm. 1. Interpersonal relations 2. Fantasy 3. Psychology, Pathological 4. Mass media — Psychological aspects. 5. Popular culture I. T.
HM132.C38 1984     302 19     *LC* 83-6702     *ISBN* 0803214219

**Gordon, Suzanne, 1945-.**     **4.4925**
Lonely in America / Suzanne Gordon. — New York: Simon and Schuster, c1976. 318 p.; 22 cm. 1. Loneliness 2. Social isolation 3. United States — Social conditions — 1960- I. T.
HM132.G66     301.11/3     *LC* 75-28318

**Handbook of social cognition / edited by Robert S. Wyer, Jr.,**     **4.4926**
**Thomas K. Srull.**
Hillsdale, N.J.: L. Erlbaum Associates, 1984. 3 v.: ill. 1. Social perception — Addresses, essays, lectures. 2. Cognition I. Wyer, Robert S. II. Srull, Thomas K.
HM132.H343 1984     302/.12 19     *LC* 84-6021     *ISBN* 0898593409

**Hinde, Robert A.**     **4.4927**
Towards understanding relationships / Robert A. Hinde. — London; New York: Published in cooperation with European Association of Experimental Social Psychology by Academic Press, 1979. xii, 367 p.: ill.; 24 cm. — (European monographs in social psychology. 18) Includes index. 1. Interpersonal relations I. T. II. Series.
HM132.H53     302     *LC* 79-40921     *ISBN* 0123492505

**Lofland, John.**     **4.4928**
Doing social life: the qualitative study of human interaction in natural settings / John Lofland. New York: Wiley, c1976. xix, 328 p.; 24 cm. 'A Wiley-Interscience publication.' 1. Interpersonal relations 2. Social interaction 3. Social role 4. Social psychology — Experiments — History. 5. Participant observation I. T.
HM132.L63     301.11     *LC* 76-25077     *ISBN* 0471015636

**Rubin, Theodore Isaac.**     **4.4929**
One to one: understanding personal relationships / Theodore Isaac Rubin. — New York: Viking Press, 1983. xvi, 242 p.; 24 cm. 1. Interpersonal relations — Case studies. I. T.
HM132.R845 1983     302.3/4 19     *LC* 82-70123     *ISBN* 0670435961

**Tamir, Lois M., 1954-.**     **4.4930**
Communication and the aging process: interaction throughout the life cycle / Lois M. Tamir. — New York: Pergamon Press, 1980 (c1979). xix, 195 p.; 24 cm. — (Pergamon general psychology series; v. 86) Includes indexes. 1. Interpersonal communication 2. Maturation (Psychology) 3. Aging I. T. II. Title: Live cycle.
HM132.T36 1979     301.14     *LC* 79-17115     *ISBN* 0080246214

**Anderson, Elijah.**     **4.4931**
A place on the corner / Elijah Anderson. — Chicago: University of Chicago Press, 1978. x, 237 p.; 22 cm. — (Studies of urban society) Includes index. 1. Small groups — Case studies. 2. Social status — Illinois — Chicago — Case studies. 3. Participant observation 4. Chicago — Social conditions. I. T.
HM133.A55     301.44/0977311     *LC* 78-1879     *ISBN* 0226019535

**Back, Kurt W.**      **4.4932**
Beyond words; the story of sensitivity training and the encounter movement [by] Kurt W. Back. New York, Russell Sage Foundation [1972] xii, 266 p. 24 cm. 1. Group relations training 2. Social movements I. T.
HM133.B325     301.11/4     *LC* 73-182935     *ISBN* 0871540770

**Bales, Robert Freed, 1916-.**      • **4.4933**
Personality and interpersonal behavior. — New York: Holt, Rinehart, and Winston, [1969, c1970] xiv, 561 p.: illus.; 24 cm. 1. Small groups 2. Interpersonal relations 3. Social interaction I. T.
HM133.B34     301.1     *LC* 71-84682     *ISBN* 0030804507

**Cartwright, Dorwin, ed.**      • **4.4934**
Group dynamics; research and theory, edited by Dorwin Cartwright [and] Alvin Zander. — 3d ed. — New York: Harper & Row, [1968] ix, 580 p.: illus.; 27 cm. 1. Small groups I. Zander, Alvin Frederick, 1913- joint ed. II. T.
HM133.C35 1968     301.15/08     *LC* 68-12274

**Egan, Gerard.**      **4.4935**
Encounter; group processes for interpersonal growth [by] Gerard Egan. — Belmont, Calif.: Brooks/Cole Pub. Co., [1970] 424 p.; 23 cm. 1. Group relations training I. T.
HM133.E45     301.15     *LC* 71-113403

**Smith, Henry Clay, 1913-.**      **4.4936**
Sensitivity training: the scientific understanding of individuals. — New York: McGraw-Hill, [1973] xii, 271 p.; 23 cm. Published in 1966 under title: Sensitivity to people. 1. Group relations training 2. Social perception 3. Empathy I. T.
HM133.S68 1973     301.11     *LC* 72-10309     *ISBN* 0070584818

**Blumberg, Arthur, 1923-.**      **4.4937**
Learning and change in groups / Arthur Blumberg and Robert T. Golembiewski. Harmondsworth, Eng.; Baltimore: Penguin Books, 1976. 208 p.; 18 cm. (Penguin education) (Penguin modern psychology) (Occupational and organizational psychology) 1. Group relations training I. Golembiewski, Robert T. joint author. II. T.
HM134.B58 1976     301.18/5     *LC* 76-377700     *ISBN* 0140805745

# HM136 Social Conflict

**Boulding, Kenneth Ewart, 1910-.**      • **4.4938**
Conflict and defense: a general theory. — New York: Harper [1962] 349 p.: ill.; 22 cm. 'A publication from the Center for Research in Conflict Resolution at the University of Michigan.' 1. Social conflict 2. International relations I. T.
HM136 B6     *LC* 61-14737

**Coser, Lewis A., 1913-.**      **4.4939**
Continuities in the study of social conflict [by] Lewis A. Coser. — New York: Free Press, [1967] x, 272 p.; 22 cm. Essays. 1. Social conflict I. T.
HM136.C73     301.2     *LC* 67-25330

**Coser, Lewis A., 1913-.**      • **4.4940**
The functions of social conflict. — Glencoe, Ill.: Free Press, [1956] 188 p.; 22 cm. 1. Social conflict I. T.
HM136.C74     301.23     *LC* 56-6874

**Deutsch, Morton, 1920-.**      **4.4941**
The resolution of conflict; constructive and destructive processes. New Haven, Yale University Press, 1973. xi, 420 p. illus. 24 cm. 1. Social conflict 2. Competition (Psychology) 3. Cooperation 4. Conflict management I. T.
HM136.D39 1973     301.6/3     *LC* 73-80080     *ISBN* 0300016832

**Schellenberg, James A., 1932-.**      **4.4942**
The science of conflict / James A. Schellenberg. — New York: Oxford University Press, 1982. x, 291 p.: ill.; 22 cm. Includes index. 1. Social conflict 2. Violence 3. Peace I. T.
HM136.S283     303.6 19     *LC* 81-4796     *ISBN* 0195029739

**Sibley, David.**      **4.4943**
Outsiders in urban societies / David Sibley. — New York: St. Martin's Press, 1981. x, 212 p.; 24 cm. Includes index. 1. Marginality, Social 2. Gypsies — Great Britain — Case studies. 3. Sociology, Urban 4. Social structure I. T.
HM136.S5 1981     305.5/6 19     *LC* 81-9292     *ISBN* 0312591926

**Simmel, Georg, 1858-1918.**      • **4.4944**
[Streit. English] Conflict, translated by Kurt H. Wolff. The web of groupaffiliations, translated by Reinhard Bendix. With a foreword by Everett C. Hughes. Glencoe, Ill., Free Press [1955] 195 p. 22 cm. The essays appeared originally as chapters in the author's Soziologie, under the title: Der Streit and Die Kreuzung sozialer Kreise. 1. Social conflict 2. Social groups I. Simmel, Georg, 1858-1918. The web of group-affiliations. II. T. III. Title: Web of group-affiliations.
HM136.S633     301.1532 301.23*     *LC* 54-10671

# HM141 Leadership

**Burns, James MacGregor.**      **4.4945**
Leadership / James MacGregor Burns. — 1st ed. — New York: Harper & Row, c1978. ix, 530 p.; 24 cm. 1. Leadership I. T.
HM141.B847 1978     301.15/53     *LC* 76-5117     *ISBN* 0060105887

**Doob, Leonard William, 1909-.**      **4.4946**
Personality, power, and authority: a view from the behavioral sciences / Leonard W. Doob. — Westport, Conn.: Greenwood Press, 1983. viii, 218 p.: ill.; 24 cm. — (Contributions in psychology. 0736-2714; no. 1) Includes index. 1. Leadership 2. Interpersonal relations 3. Personality 4. Power (Social sciences) 5. Authority I. T. II. Series.
HM141.D59 1983     303.3 19     *LC* 83-1688     *ISBN* 0313239207

**Ethnic leadership in America / edited by John Higham.**      **4.4947**
Baltimore: Johns Hopkins University Press, c1978. x, 214 p.; 24 cm. (Johns Hopkins symposia in comparative history. 9th) Papers from a symposium held at Johns Hopkins University Feb. 5-6, 1976. 1. Leadership — Congresses. 2. Ethnicity — United States — Congresses. 3. Minorities — United States — Congresses. I. Higham, John. II. Series.
HM141.E86     301.15/53     *LC* 77-17257     *ISBN* 0801820367

**Goode, William Josiah.**      **4.4948**
The celebration of heroes: prestige as a social control system / William J. Goode. — Berkeley: University of California Press, c1978. xv, 407 p.; 25 cm. 1. Prestige 2. Interpersonal relations 3. Social interaction 4. Social control I. T.
HM141.G576     301.15     *LC* 77-20322     *ISBN* 0520036026

**Gouldner, Alvin Ward, 1920-.**      • **4.4949**
Studies in leadership: leadership and democratic action / edited by Alvin W. Gouldner. — New York: Russell & Russell, 1965 (c1950) xvi, 736 p.: ill.; 22 cm. 1. Leadership I. T.
HM141 G65 1965     *LC* 64-66395

**Hunter, Floyd.**      • **4.4950**
Community power structure; a study of decision makers. — Chapel Hill: University of North Carolina Press, [1953] xiv, 297 p.: diagrs.; 21 cm. 1. Community leadership 2. Power (Social sciences) I. T.
HM141.H83     301.155     *LC* 53-10042

**Kahn, Si.**      **4.4951**
Organizing, a guide for grassroots leaders / Si Kahn. — 1st McGraw Hill ed. — New York: McGraw-Hill, 1982. xi, 387 p.; 22 cm. Includes index. 1. Leadership 2. Community development I. T.
HM141.K29     303.3/4 19     *LC* 81-8380     *ISBN* 0070331995

**Keller, Suzanne Infeld, 1927-.**      • **4.4952**
Beyond the ruling class; strategic elites in modern society. — New York: Random House, [c1963] 354 p.; 22 cm. 1. Elite (Social sciences) 2. Power (Social sciences) 3. Social classes 4. Prestige I. T.
HM141.K4     301.441     *LC* 63-8270

**Rustow, Dankwart A. comp.**      • **4.4953**
Philosophers and kings; studies in leadership. Edited by Dankwart A. Rustow. — New York: G. Braziller, [1970] vii, 526 p.; 22 cm. — (The Daedalus library) 1. Leadership I. T. II. Series.
HM141.R83     301.15/5     *LC* 77-107778

**Stogdill, Ralph Melvin, 1904-.**      **4.4954**
Stogdill's handbook of leadership: a survey of theory and research. — Rev. and expanded ed. / Bernard M. Bass. — New York: Free Press, c1981. p. cm. Previously published as: Handbook of leadership. Includes index. 1. Leadership — Abstracts. 2. Leadership — Bibliography. I. Bass, Bernard M. II. T. III. Title: Handbook of leadership.
HM141.S83 1981     016.3023/4 19     *LC* 80-70210     *ISBN* 002901820X

**Verba, Sidney.**      • **4.4955**
Small groups and political behavior; a study of leadership. — Princeton, N.J.: Princeton University Press, 1961. 273 p.; 23 cm. 1. Leadership 2. Small groups 3. Political psychology I. T.
HM141.V4     301.155     *LC* 61-6291

**Yukl, Gary A., 1940-.**    **4.4956**
Leadership in organizations / Gary A. Yukl. — Englewood Cliffs, N.J.: Prentice-Hall, c1981. xii, 340 p.: ill.; 24 cm. Includes indexes. 1. Leadership 2. Decision-making 3. Organization I. T.
HM141.Y84    303.3/4 19    *LC* 80-27044    *ISBN* 0135271762

# HM146 Equality

**Blumberg, Paul.**    **4.4957**
Inequality in an age of decline / Paul Blumberg. — New York: Oxford University Press, 1980. xv, 290 p., [1] leaf of plates: ill.; 22 cm. 1. Equality 2. Social mobility — United States. 3. United States — Economic conditions — 1971-1981 I. T.
HM146.B59    305.5    *LC* 80-16047    *ISBN* 019502804X

**Gardner, John William, 1912-.**    **4.4958**
Excellence: can we be equal and excellent too? / John W. Gardner. — Rev. ed. — New York: Norton, c1984. 175 p. 1. Equality 2. Individuality 3. Leadership 4. Academic achievement I. T.
HM146.G29 1984    305 19    *LC* 83-25070    *ISBN* 0393018482

**Rae, Douglas W.**    **4.4959**
Equalities / Douglas Rae and Douglas Yates ... [et al.]. — Cambridge, Mass.: Harvard University Press, 1981. viii, 210 p.: ill.; 24 cm. Includes index. 1. Equality I. Yates, Douglas, 1944- II. T.
HM146.R33    305.5 19    *LC* 81-4157    *ISBN* 0674259807

**Tawney, R. H. (Richard Henry), 1880-1962.**    • **4.4960**
Equality / [by] R. H. Tawney; with an introd. by Richard M. Titmuss. — [4th ed., rev.]. — New York: Barnes & Noble, [1965, c1964] 255 p. 1. Equality I. T.
HM146.T3 1965

# HM201–221 Social Elements

**Parsons, Talcott, 1902- ed.**    • **4.4961**
Toward a general theory of action / [by] Talcott Parsons [and] Edward A. Shils, editors; Edward C. Tolman [and others]. — Cambridge: Harvard University Press, 1951. xi, 506 p.: diagrs.; 25 cm. 1. Sociology I. Shils, Edward Albert, 1911- joint ed. II. T.
HM201.P28    301    *LC* 51-14629

**Parsons, Talcott, 1902-.**    • **4.4962**
Working papers in the theory of action / by Talcott Parsons, Robert F. Bales, and Edward A. Shils. — New York: Free Press, [1953]. –. 269 p.: diagrs.; 21 cm. — 1. Sociology I. T.
HM201.P283    301    *LC* 53-9671

# HM206 Environmental

**Dubos, René J. (René Jules), 1901-.**    • **4.4963**
So human an animal / [by] René Dubos. — New York: Scribner [1968] xiv, 267 p.; 24 cm. 1. Human ecology 2. Man — Influence of environment 3. Technology and civilization I. T.
HM206.D87    301.3    *LC* 68-27794

# HM211 Economic

**Arendt, Hannah.**    • **4.4964**
The human condition. — [Chicago]: University of Chicago Press, [1958] 332 p.; 24 cm. — (Charles R. Walgreen Foundation lectures) 1. Sociology 2. Economics 3. Technology I. T.
HM211.A7    301    *LC* 58-5535

**Caplow, Theodore.**    • **4.4965**
The sociology of work. — Minneapolis: University of Minnesota Press, [1954] 330 p.; 24 cm. 1. Occupations 2. Sociology 3. Social classes I. T.
HM211.C3    301.4*    *LC* 54-8208

# HM213 Intellectual

**Abercrombie, Nicholas.**    **4.4966**
The dominant ideology thesis / Nicholas Abercrombie, Stephen Hill, Bryan S. Turner. — London; Boston: G. Allen & Unwin, 1980. x, 212 p.; 23 cm. Includes index. 1. Ideology I. Hill, Stephen. joint author. II. Turner, Bryan S. joint author. III. T.
HM213.A23    301/.01 19    *LC* 80-40546    *ISBN* 0043011179

**Hollander, Paul, 1932-.**    **4.4967**
Political pilgrims: travels of Western intellectuals to the Soviet Union, China, and Cuba, 1928–1978 / Paul Hollander. — New York: Oxford University Press, 1981. xvi, 524 p.; 24 cm. Includes index. 1. Intellectuals — Europe. 2. Intellectuals — Europe — Political activity. 3. Communist countries — Politics and government 4. Ideology I. T.
HM213.H57    305.5/5 19    *LC* 80-29417    *ISBN* 0195029372

# HM216 Ethical

**Durkheim, Emile, 1858-1917.**    • **4.4968**
Professional ethics and civic morals / translated by Cornelia Brookfield. — Glencoe, Ill.: Free Press [1958] xliv, 228 p.; 22 cm. (International library of sociology and social reconstruction) 1. Social ethics 2. State, The 3. Property I. T.
HM216 D8713 1958    *LC* A60-2811

**Friedrich, Carl J. (Carl Joachim), 1901- ed.**    **4.4969**
Responsibility. New York, Liberal Arts Press [1960] x, 308 p. (Nomos. 3) 'Built on the foundations laid by the papers and discussions of the third annual meeting of the American Society for Political and Legal Philosophy.' 1. Responsibility I. American Society for Political and Legal Philosophy. II. Series.
HM216.F84    *LC* 60-12943

**Huxley, Aldous, 1894-1963.**    • **4.4970**
Brave new world revisited. [1st ed.] New York, Harper [1958] 147 p. 22 cm. 1. Huxley, Aldous, 1894-1963. Brave new world. 2. Culture 3. Propaganda 4. Brainwashing I. T.
HM216.H8    301.152    *LC* 58-12451

**John Rawls' theory of social justice: an introduction / H. Gene**    **4.4971**
**Blocker, Elizabeth H. Smith, editors.**
Athens: Ohio University Press, c1980. xxiii, 520 p.; 24 cm. Based on a conference sponsored by the Ohio Program in the Humanities and held at Ohio University in 1976. Includes index. 1. Rawls, John, 1921- — Congresses. 2. Social justice — Congresses. I. Blocker, H. Gene. II. Smith, Elizabeth H., 1939-
HM216.J58    320/.01/1    *LC* 80-11272    *ISBN* 0821404458

**The Justice motive in social behavior: adapting to times of**    **4.4972**
**scarcity and change / edited by Melvin J. Lerner and Sally C.**
**Lerner.**
New York: Plenum Press, c1981. xxii, 494 p.; 24 cm. — (Critical issues in social justice.) Based on papers presented at a meeting prior to the annual conference of the American Psychological Association, 1978, Toronto, Canada. 1. Social justice — Psychological aspects — Congresses. 2. Social change — Psychological aspects — Congresses. 3. Adaptability (Psychology) — Congresses. I. Lerner, Melvin J., 1929- II. Lerner, Sally C., 1931- III. Series.
HM216.J88    303.4 19    *LC* 81-10605    *ISBN* 0306406756

**Maguire, Daniel C.**    **4.4973**
A new American justice: ending the white male monopolies / Daniel C. Maguire. — 1st ed. — Garden City, N.Y.: Doubleday, 1980. xiii, 218 p.; 22 cm. 1. Social justice 2. Justice, Administration of — United States. 3. Affirmative action programs — United States. 4. Affirmative action programs — Law and legislation — United States. 5. United States — Race relations I. T. II. Title: White male monopolies.
HM216.M264    361.2    *LC* 78-20084    *ISBN* 0385143257

**Niebuhr, Reinhold, 1892-1971.**    • **4.4974**
Moral man and immoral society; a study in ethics and politics. New York, London, C. Scribner's sons, 1932. 4 p.l., xi-xxv p., 1 l., 284 p. 21 cm. 1. Social ethics 2. Political ethics I. T.
HM216.N5    *LC* 33-1231

**Phillips, Derek L.**    **4.4975**
Toward a just social order / Derek L. Phillips. — Princeton, N.J.: Princeton University Press, c1986. x, 460 p.; 25 cm. Includes index. 1. Social justice 2. Social norms 3. Moral conditions I. T.
HM216.P53 1986    303.3/72 19    *LC* 85-43303    *ISBN* 0691094225

**Shinn, Roger Lincoln.**    **4.4976**
Forced options: social decisions for the 21st century / Roger Lincoln Shinn. — 1st ed. — San Francisco: Harper & Row, c1982. xxv, 267 p.; 21 cm. (Religious

perspectives. v. 27) 1. Social ethics 2. Christian ethics 3. Distributive justice 4. Decision-making — Social aspects. 5. Technology — Social aspects I. T. II. Series.
HM216.S463 1982    306 19    *LC* 82-47755    *ISBN* 006067282X

**Sorokin, Pitirim Aleksandrovich, 1889-1968.**    • **4.4977**
Power and morality: who shall guard the guardians? / by Pitirim A. Sorokin [and] Walter A. Lunden. — Boston: P. Sargent [1959] 204 p.; 23 cm. (An Extending horizons book) Includes bibliography. 1. Power (Social sciences) 2. Social ethics I. Lunden, Walter Albin, 1899- joint author. II. T.
HM216.S59    301.155    *LC* 59-4189

# HM221 Technology and Civilization

**Ellul, Jacques.**    **4.4978**
[Système technicien. English] The technological system / Jacques Ellul; translated from the French by Joachim Neugroschel. — New York: Continuum, 1980. vi, 362 p.; 24 cm. Translation of Le système technicien. 1. Technology and civilization I. T.
HM221.E4313    303.4/83    *LC* 80-15344    0816401101

# HM251–291 Social Psychology

## HM251 General Works

### HM251 A–L

**American Society for Political and Legal Philosophy.**    **4.4979**
Rational decision. Edited by Carl J. Friedrich. New York, Atherton Press, 1964. xii, 228 p. 22 cm. (Nomos. 7) 1. Decision-making 2. Judicial process — United States. I. Friedrich, Carl J. (Carl Joachim), 1901- II. T. III. Series.
HM251.A6    *LC* 64-19823

**Aronson, Elliot.**    **4.4980**
The social animal / Elliot Aronson. — 3d ed. — San Francisco: W. H. Freeman, c1980. xvi, 377 p.: ill.; 24 cm. — (A Series of books in psychology) 1. Social psychology I. T.
HM251.A79 1980    302    *LC* 79-27721    *ISBN* 0716712296

**Brown, Roger William, 1925-.**    **4.4981**
Social psychology, the second edition / Roger Brown. — New York: Free Press; London: Collier Macmillan, c1986. xiv, 704 p.: ill.; 25 cm. 1. Social psychology I. T.
HM251.B73 1986    302 19    *LC* 85-13114

**Cooley, Charles Horton, 1864-1929.**    • **4.4982**
Human nature and the social order / introd. by Philip Rieff; foreword by Herbert Mead. — New York: Schocken Books, [1964] xxxviii, 444 p.; 21 cm. — (Schocken paperbacks) 'SB72.' 1. Social psychology 2. Sociology 3. Individualism I. T.
HM251.C8 1964    301.15    *LC* 64-15221

**Cooley, Charles Horton, 1864-1929.**    • **4.4983**
Social organization: a study of the larger mind / introd. by Philip Rieff. — New York: Schocken Books [1962] 425 p.; 21 cm. (Schocken paperbacks, SB22) 1. Sociology 2. Social psychology I. T.
HM251.C85 1962    301.4    *LC* 62-13136

**Deutsch, Morton, 1920-.**    • **4.4984**
Theories in social psychology / [by] Morton Deutsch and Robert M. Krauss. — New York: Basic Books, [1965] x, 244 p.: ill.; 22 cm. — (Basic topics in psychology: social psychology) 1. Social psychology I. Krauss, Robert M., joint author. II. T.
HM251.D47    301.101    *LC* 65-25230

**Festinger, Leon, 1919-.**    • **4.4985**
Social pressures in informal groups: a study of human factors in housing / by Leon Festinger, Stanley Schachter and Kurt Back. — Stanford, Calif.: Stanford University Press [1963, c1950] 197 p.: ill.; 22 cm. 1. Social pressure 2. Sociometry 3. Housing management I. T.
HM251 F4 1963    *LC* 63-4103

**The Handbook of social psychology / [edited by] Gardner**    **4.4986**
**Lindzey, Elliot Aronson.**
3rd ed. — New York: Knopf, c1985. p. cm. Includes index. 1. Social psychology I. Lindzey, Gardner. II. Aronson, Elliot.
HM251.H224 1985    302 19    *LC* 84-18509    *ISBN* 0394350499

**Homans, George Caspar, 1910-.**    • **4.4987**
The human group. — New York: Harcourt, Brace, [1950] xxvi, 484 p.: ill., maps.; 22 cm. 1. Social psychology I. T.
HM251.H66    301.15    *LC* 50-10140

**Kardiner, Abram, 1891-.**    • **4.4988**
The psychological frontiers of society / by Abram Kardiner, with the collaboraton of Ralph Linton, Cora Du Bois and James West [pseud.]. — New York: Columbia university press, [1945] xxiv, 475 p.: ill. 1. Social psychology 2. Ethnopsychology I. Linton, Ralph, 1893-1953. II. Du Bois, Cora Alice, 1903- III. Withers, Carl. IV. T.
HM251.K34

**Lewin, Kurt, 1890-1947.**    • **4.4989**
Resolving social conflicts: selected papers on group dynamics [1935–1946] / ed. by Gertrud Weiss Lewin; foreword by Gordon W. Allport. — [1st ed.] New York: Harper [1948] xvii, 230 p.: ill.; 22 cm. (Michigan. University. Research Center for Group Dynamics. Publication [1]) 1. Social psychology I. Lewin, Gertrud (Weiss) II. T.
HM251 L474    *LC* 48-3764

## HM251 M–Z

**Mead, George Herbert, 1863-1931.**    • **4.4990**
Mind, self & society from the standpoint of a social behaviorist / [by] George H. Mead; edited, with introduction, by Charles W. Morris. — Chicago, Ill.: The University of Chicago press, [1934] xxxviii, 400, [1] p.; 24 cm. 1. Social psychology 2. Behaviorism (Psychology) 3. Self 4. Experience 5. Language and languages I. Morris, Charles William, 1901- ed. II. T.
HM251.M4    301.15    *LC* 35-292

**Mead, George Herbert, 1863-1931.**    **4.4991**
[Selections. 1982] The individual and the social self: unpublished work of George Herbert Mead / edited with an introduction by David L. Miller. — Chicago: University of Chicago Press, 1982. vii, 229 p.; 23 cm. Includes index. 1. Social psychology 2. Self 3. Consciousness 4. Socialization I. Miller, David L., 1903- II. T.
HM251.M4192 1982    302 19    *LC* 82-4885    *ISBN* 0226516733

**Proshansky, Harold M., 1920- ed.**    • **4.4992**
Basic studies in social psychology / edited and with introductions by Harold Proshansky [and] Bernard Seidenberg. — New York: Published for the Society for the Psychological Study of Social Issues [by] Holt, Rinehart and Winston, [1965] xvii, 743 p.: ill.; 24 cm. Companion volume to current studies in social psychology, edited by Ivan D. Steiner and Martin Fishbein. 1. Social psychology — Addresses, essays, lectures. I. Seidenberg, Bernard, joint ed. II. T.
HM251.P75    301.15    *LC* 65-14870

**Retrospections on social psychology / edited by Leon Festinger.**    **4.4993**
New York: Oxford University Press, 1980. xiv, 297 p.; 24 cm. 1. Social psychology — United States — History — Addresses, essays, lectures. I. Festinger, Leon, 1919-
HM251.R474    302    *LC* 80-10919    *ISBN* 0195027515

**Robinson, John P.**    **4.4994**
Measures of social psychological attitudes / John P. Robinson, Phillip R. Shaver. — Rev. ed. — Ann Arbor, Mich.: Survey Research Center, Institute for Social Research, 1973, 1978 printing. viii, 750 p.; 26 cm. 'IRS code no. 2928.' 1. Social psychology 2. Attitude (Psychology) — Testing I. Shaver, Phillip R. II. T.
HM251.R739 1973    302 19    *LC* 79-627967    *ISBN* 0879440694

**Rose, Jerry D., 1933-.**    **4.4995**
Outbreaks, the sociology of collective behavior / Jerry D. Rose. — New York: Free Press, c1982. viii, 278 p.; 24 cm. Includes indexes. 1. Collective behavior I. T.
HM251.R775 1982    302 19    *LC* 81-67439    *ISBN* 0029267900

**Sherif, Muzafer, 1905-.**    • **4.4996**
Social psychology [by] Muzafer Sherif and Carolyn W. Sherif. — New York: Harper & Row, [1969] xx, 616 p.: illus.; 27 cm. 1948 and 1956 eds. published under title: An outline of social psychology. 1. Social psychology I. Sherif, Carolyn W. joint author. II. T.
HM251.S54 1969    301.1    *LC* 69-14987

**Sherif, Muzafer, 1905-.**    • 4.4997
Social interaction process and products; selected essays. — Chicago: Aldine Pub. Co., [1967] vii, 512 p.: illus.; 24 cm. 1. Social psychology I. T.
HM251.S56    301.1    *LC* 67-27398

**Smelser, Neil J.**    4.4998
Theory of collective behavior. — New York: Free Press of Glencoe, [1963] xi, 436 p.: illus.; 22 cm. 1. Collective behavior I. T. II. Title: Collective behavior.
HM251.S628    301.15    *LC* 62-15350

**Steiner, Ivan Dale, 1917- ed.**    • 4.4999
Current studies in social psychology / edited by Ivan D. Steiner [and] Martin Fishbein. — New York: Published for the Society for the Psychological Study of Social Issues [by] Holt, Rinehart and Winston, [1965] xii, 532 p.: ill.; 25 cm. Companion volume to Basic studies in social psychology, edited by Harold Proshansky and Bernard Seidenberg. 1. Social psychology I. Fishbein, Martin, joint ed. II. Society for the Psychological Study of Social Issues. III. T.
HM251.S765    301.15    *LC* 65-12813

**Wallas, Graham, 1858-1932.**    • 4.5000
The great society; a psychological analysis, by Graham Wallas ... New York, The Macmillan company, 1914. xii, 383 p. 21 cm. 1. Social psychology I. T.
HM 251 W19    *LC* 14-11250

## HM258 Communication. Mass Media

**Barnlund, Dean C. comp.**    • 4.5001
Interpersonal communication; survey and studies [compiled by] Dean C. Barnlund. — Boston: Houghton Mifflin, [1968] xi, 727 p.: illus.; 25 cm. 1. Communication — Addresses, essays, lectures. I. T.
HM258.B37    301.16    *LC* 68-3285

*[handwritten: HM 258 B26]*

**Brantlinger, Patrick, 1941-.**    4.5002
Bread & circuses: theories of mass culture as social decay / by Patrick Brantlinger. — Ithaca: Cornell University Press, 1983. 307 p.; 24 cm. 1. Mass media — Social aspects — History. 2. Mass society — History. 3. Culture 4. Popular culture 5. Classicism I. T. II. Title: Bread and circuses.
HM258.B735 1983    302.2/34 19    *LC* 83-45134    *ISBN* 0801415985

**Comparative mass media systems / [edited by] L. John Martin, Anju Grover Chaudhary.**    4.5003
New York, N.Y.: Longman, c1983. viii, 356 p.: ill.; 24 cm. (Longman series in public communication.) 1. Mass media — Social aspects 2. Mass media — Developing countries 3. Mass media — Communist countries. I. Martin, L. John (Leslie John), 1921- II. Chaudhary, Anju Grover, 1945- III. Series.
HM258.C58916 1983    302.2/34 19    *LC* 82-14908    *ISBN* 0582283280

**DeFleur, Melvin L. (Melvin Lawrence), 1923-.**    4.5004
Theories of mass communication / Melvin L. De Fleur, Sandra Ball–Rokeach. — 4th ed. — New York: Longman, c1982. xiii, 263 p.: ill.; 24 cm. 1. Mass media — Social aspects — History. 2. Mass media — Social aspects — United States — History. I. Ball-Rokeach, Sandra. II. T.
HM258.D35 1982    302.2/34 19    *LC* 81-8215    *ISBN* 0582282780

**Hall, Edward Twitchell, 1914-.**    4.5005
Beyond culture / Edward T. Hall. — 1st ed. — Garden City, N.Y.: Anchor Press, 1976. 256 p.; 22 cm. Includes indexes. 1. Intercultural communication 2. Cultural lag 3. Social evolution 4. Personality and culture I. T.
HM258.H29    301.2/1    *LC* 74-3550    *ISBN* 0385087470

**Handbook of intercultural communication / editors, Molefi Kete Asante, Eileen Newmark, Cecil A. Blake.**    4.5006
Beverly Hills: Sage Publications, c1979. 479 p.: ill.; 23 cm. 1. Intercultural communication — Addresses, essays, lectures. I. Asante, Molefi K., 1942- II. Newmark, Eileen. III. Blake, Cecil A.
HM258.H354    301.14    *LC* 78-2468    *ISBN* 0803909543

**Lowery, Shearon.**    4.5007
Milestones in mass communication research: media effects / Shearon Lowery, Melvin L. DeFleur. — New York: Longman, c1983. xvi, 398 p.: ill.; 24 cm. 1. Mass media 2. Mass society I. DeFleur, Melvin L. (Melvin Lawrence), 1923- II. T.
HM258.L68 1983    302.2/34 19    *LC* 82-14043    *ISBN* 0582283523

**The Mediating person: bridges between cultures / edited by Stephen Bochner.**    4.5008
Boston, Mass.: G.K. Hall; Cambridge, Mass.: Schenkman Pub. Co., c1981. x, 323 p.; 25 cm. Includes bibliographies and indexes. 1. Intercultural communication — Addresses, essays, lectures. 2. Cross-cultural studies — Addresses, essays, lectures. 3. Cultural relations — Addresses, essays, lectures. I. Bochner, Stephen.
HM258.M375 1981    306/.4 19    *LC* 81-6358    *ISBN* 081619016X

**Meyrowitz, Joshua.**    4.5009
No sense of place: the impact of electronic media on social behavior / Joshua Meyrowitz. — New York: Oxford University Press, 1985. xv, 416 p.; 24 cm. Includes index. 1. Mass media — Social aspects 2. Communication — Social aspects 3. Social change 4. Mass media — United States — Social aspects. 5. Communication — United States — Social aspects. 6. United States — Social conditions I. T.
HM258.M49 1985    302.2/34 19    *LC* 84-3950    *ISBN* 0195034740

**Propaganda and communication in world history / edited by Harold D. Lasswell, Daniel Lerner, Hans Speier.**    4.5010
Honolulu: Published for the East-West Center by the University Press of Hawaii, 1979-1980. 3 v.; 24 cm. 1. Communication — Social aspects — History — Collected works. 2. Public opinion — History — Collected works. 3. Symbolism in communication — History — Collected works. 4. Propaganda — History — Collected works. I. Lasswell, Harold Dwight, 1902- II. Lerner, Daniel. III. Speier, Hans.
HM258.P74    301.14    *LC* 78-23965    *ISBN* 0824804961

*[handwritten: HM 258 P74]*

**Real, Michael R., 1940-.**    4.5011
Mass–mediated culture / Michael R. Real. — Englewood Cliffs, N.J.: Prentice-Hall, c1977. xii, 289 p.: ill.; 23 cm. Includes index. 1. Mass media — Social aspects — Case studies. 2. Mass media — Moral and religious aspects — Case studies. 3. Popular culture — History — 20th century — Case studies. I. T.
HM258.R343    301.2/1    *LC* 76-30265    *ISBN* 0135592119

**Schwartz, Tony.**    4.5012
The responsive chord. — 1st ed. — Garden City, N.Y.: Anchor Press, 1973. xv, 173 p.: ill. 1. Communication — Social aspects 2. Advertising — Psychological aspects I. T.
HM258.S32    302.23    *LC* 73-81420    *ISBN* 0385088957 795

**Turow, Joseph.**    4.5013
Media industries: the production of news and entertainment / Joseph Turow. — New York: Longman, c1984. x, 213 p.; 24 cm. — (Annenberg/Longman communication books.) Includes index. 1. Mass media — Social aspects 2. Power (Social sciences) I. T. II. Series.
HM258.T87 1984    302.2/34 19    *LC* 83-17519    *ISBN* 0582283590

## HM261–263 Public Opinion. Public Relations. Propaganda

**Backstrom, Charles Herbert, 1926-.**    4.5014
Survey research / Charles H. Backstrom, Gerald Hursh–César. — 2nd ed. — New York: Wiley, c1981. xxvii, 436 p.: ill.; 24 cm. 1. Public opinion polls 2. Social science research. I. Hursh-César, Gerald. II. T.
HM261.B18 1981    303.3/8 19    *LC* 81-1738    *ISBN* 0471025437

**Buchanan, William, 1918-.**    • 4.5015
How nations see each other; a study in public opinion [by] William Buchanan and Hadley Cantril, with the assistance of Virginia Van S. Zerega, Henry Durant [and] James R. White. Westport, Conn., Greenwood Press [1972] ix, 220 p. 24 cm. Prepared under the auspices of the United Nations Educational, Scientific and Cultural Organization. Reprint of the 1953 ed. 1. Public opinion 2. Public opinion polls 3. International relations I. Cantril, Hadley, 1906-1969. joint author. II. Unesco. III. T.
HM261.B8 1972    301.15/4    *LC* 70-138210    *ISBN* 0837155657

**Graber, Doris A. (Doris Appel), 1923-.**    4.5016
Processing the news: how people tame the information tide / Doris A. Graber. — New York: Longman, c1984. xiii, 241 p.: ill.; 23 cm. — (Longman professional studies in political communication and policy.) Includes index. 1. Public opinion — United States — Case studies. 2. Human information processsing — Case studies. 3. Political socialization — United States — Case studies. 4. Mass media — Political aspects — United States — Case studies. 5. Democracy I. T. II. Series.
HM261.G78 1984    306/.2 19    *LC* 83-19537    *ISBN* 0582283949

**Lippmann, Walter, 1889-.**    • 4.5017
Public opinion / by Walter Lippmann. — New York: Harcourt, Brace, 1922. 427 p.: ill.; 22 cm. 1. Public opinion 2. Social psychology 3. United States — Politics and government I. T.
HM261.L75 1922    *LC* 22-6527

**Sherif, Muzafer, 1905-.**    • 4.5018
Social judgment; assimilation and contrast effects in communication and attitude change, by Muzafer Sherif and Carl I. Hovland. New Haven, Yale University Press, 1961. xii, 218 p. (Yale studies in attitude and communication. v. 4) 1. Attitude change 2. Judgment 3. Communication I. Hovland, Carl Iver, 1912- jt. author II. T. III. Series.
HM261 S46    *LC* 61-14432

**Ellul, Jacques.**    • **4.5019**
[Propagandes. English] Propaganda; the formation of men's attitudes. Translated from the French by Konrad Kellen and Jean Lerner. With an introd. by Konrad Kellen. [1st American ed.] New York, Knopf, 1965. xxii, 320, vii p. 25 cm. 1. Propaganda I. T. II. Title: The formation of men's attitudes.
HM263.E413    301.1523    *LC* 64-17708

# HM271–278 Authority and Freedom. Passive Resistance

**Altemeyer, Bob, 1940-.**    **4.5020**
Right–wing authoritarianism / Bob Altemeyer. — [Winnipeg]: University of Manitoba Press, c1981. 352 p.; 24 cm. Includes index. 1. Authoritarianism 2. Conservatism I. T.
HM271.A46 1981    303.3/8 19    *LC* 81-195833    *ISBN* 0887551246

**Arrow, Kenneth Joseph, 1921-.**    • **4.5021**
Social choice and individual values. — 2d ed. — New York: Wiley, [c1963] xi, 124 p.; 24 cm. — (Cowles Foundation for Research in Economics at Yale University. Monograph 12) 1. Social choice 2. Liberty. 3. Social values I. T. II. Series.
HM271.A7 1963    301.151    *LC* 63-23124

**The Authoritarian personality /** by T. W. Adorno [and others.    • **4.5022**
1st ed.] New York: Harper [1950] xxxiii, 990 p.; 24 cm. (Studies in prejudice) (The American Jewish Committee. Social studies series, publication no. 3.) 1. Dogmatism 2. Prejudices 3. Ethnocentrism 4. Antisemitism I. Adorno, Theodor W., 1903-1969. II. Series.
HM271.A8    303.3/6 19    *LC* 50-6315

**Christie, Richard, 1918-.**    • **4.5023**
Studies in the scope and method of 'The Authoritarian personality.' Edited by Richard Christie and Marie Jahoda. Glencoe, Ill., Free Press [1954] 279 p. diagr. (Continuities in social research, [2]) 1. The Authoritarian personality I. Jahoda, Marie. II. T.
HM271 A8 C45    *LC* 54-8151

**Fromm, Erich, 1900-.**    • **4.5024**
Escape from freedom, by Erich Fromm. — New York [etc.]: Farrar & Rinehart, inc., [1941] ix, p. 2 l., 3-305 p.; 22 cm. London edition (K. Paul, Trench, Trubner & co., ltd.) has title: The fear of freedom. 1. Liberty. 2. Democracy 3. Totalitarianism 4. Social psychology I. T.
HM271.F74    323.44    *LC* 41-14128

**Fromm, Erich, 1900-.**    • **4.5025**
The sane society. — New York: Rinehart, [1955] 370 p.; 22 cm. 1. Civilization 2. Social psychology 3. Liberty. I. T.
HM271.F75    323.44    *LC* 55-8006

**Lane, Robert Edwards.**    • **4.5026**
Political ideology: why the American common man believes what he does. — New York: Free Press of Glencoe, [1962] xi, 509 p.; 24 cm. 1. Ideology 2. Liberty. 3. Democracy I. T.
HM271.L2    320.15    *LC* 62-15344

**Milgram, Stanley.**    **4.5027**
Obedience to authority: an experimental view. — [1st ed.]. — New York: Harper & Row, [1974] xvii, 224 p.: ill.; 25 cm. 1. Authority 2. Obedience I. T.
HM271.M47    301.15/52    *LC* 71-138748    *ISBN* 0060129387

**Pennock, J. Roland (James Roland), 1906-.**    • **4.5028**
Coercion / edited by J. Roland Pennock and John W. Chapman. — Chicago: AldineAtherton, 1972. xiv, 328 p.; 23 cm. (Nomos. 14) 'Yearbook of the American Society for Political and Legal Philosophy.' 1. Persuasion (Psychology) 2. Duress (Law) 3. Authoritarianism 4. Power (Social sciences) I. Chapman, John William, 1923- ed. II. American Society for Political and Legal Philosophy. III. T. IV. Series.
HM271.P44    301.15/2    *LC* 71-169505    *ISBN* 0202241165

**Polanyi, Michael, 1891-.**    • **4.5029**
The logic of liberty; reflections and rejoinders. — [Chicago] University of Chicago Press [1951] ix, 206 p. 23 cm. Bibliographical footnotes. 1. Liberty. 2. Research I. T.
HM271.P6    323.44    *LC* 51-8809

**Sennett, Richard, 1943-.**    **4.5030**
Authority / Richard Sennett. — 1st ed. — New York: Knopf: distributed by Random House, 1980. 206 p.; 22 cm. Includes index. 1. Authority I. T.
HM271.S36 1980    303.3/6    *LC* 79-3492    *ISBN* 039442803X

**Hobhouse, L. T. (Leonard Trelawney), 1864-1929.**    • **4.5031**
Liberalism / L. T. Hobhouse; introduction by Alan P. Grimes. — New York: Oxford University Press, 1964. 130 p. — (A Galaxy book; GB 120) Includes index. 1. Liberalism — Great Britain 2. Great Britain — Politics and government — 1837-1901 I. T.
HM276.H7 1964    *LC* 64-19723

**Laski, Harold Joseph, 1893-1950.**    • **4.5032**
The rise of European liberalism: an essay in interpretation / Harold J. Laski. — London: Allen & Unwin, 1936. 287 p. In some degree an historical background to the author's The state in theory and practice published last year. 'Part of the book was delivered at Trinity college, Dublin as the Donellan lectures in February of this year.' 1. Liberalism 2. Political science — History I. T.
HM276.L3    *LC* 36-16525

**Lowi, Theodore J.**    **4.5033**
The end of liberalism: the second republic of the United States / Theodore J. Lowi. — 2d ed. — New York: Norton, c1979. xviii, 331 p.: ill.; 24 cm. 1. Liberalism — United States. I. T.
HM276.L57 1979    320.5/1/0973    *LC* 78-27093    *ISBN* 0393057100

**Unger, Roberto Mangabeira.**    **4.5034**
Knowledge & politics / Roberto Mangabeira Unger. — New York: Free Press, [1975] ix, 336 p.; 24 cm. 1. Liberalism 2. Knowledge, Theory of 3. Political science — History I. T.
HM276.U53    320.5/1    *LC* 74-15369    *ISBN* 0029328403

**Bondurant, Joan Valérie, 1918-.**    • **4.5035**
Conquest of violence; the Gandhian philosophy of conflict, by Joan V. Bondurant. Rev. ed. Berkeley, University of California Press, 1965. xxiii, 271 p. 21 cm. 1. Gandhi, Mahatma, 1869-1948. 2. Passive resistance — India. I. T.
HM278.B6 1965    301.153    *LC* 65-23153

**Gandhi, Mahatma, 1869-1948.**    • **4.5036**
Non–violent resistance (Satyagraha) New York, Schocken Books [1961, c1951] xiv, 404 p. Compiled and edited by Bharatan Kumarappa. 1. Passive resistance to government 2. India — Politics and government — 1919-1947 I. Kumarappa, Bharatan, 1896-1957 II. T.
HM278 G35 1961    *LC* 61-16650

**Lakey, George.**    **4.5037**
Strategy for a living revolution. — New York: Grossman Publishers, 1973. xx, 234 p.; 24 cm. — (A World order book) 1. Nonviolence 2. Revolutions I. T.
HM278.L32 1973    301.6/32    *LC* 72-9898    *ISBN* 0670677949

**Lynd, Staughton. ed.**    **4.5038**
Nonviolence in America; a documentary history. — Indianapolis: Bobbs-Merrill, [1966] xlix, 535 p.; 21 cm. — (The American heritage series) 1. Passive resistance — United States — Addresses, essays, lectures. I. T.
HM278.L9    323.20973    *LC* 65-23010

**Singer, Peter.**    **4.5039**
Democracy and disobedience. — New York: Oxford University Press, 1973. viii, 150 p.; 20 cm. 1. Passive resistance 2. Government, Resistance to I. T.
HM278.S54 1974    323.6/5    *LC* 74-12810    *ISBN* 0198245041

# HM281–283 Crowds. Revolutions

**Bandura, Albert, 1925-.**    **4.5040**
Aggression: a social learning analysis. — Englewood Cliffs, N.J.: Prentice-Hall, [1973] ix, 390 p.: ill.; 24 cm. — (The Prentice-Hall series in social learning theory) 1. Aggressiveness (Psychology) 2. Violence I. T.
HM281.B25    301.1    *LC* 72-12990    *ISBN* 0130207438

**Barrows, Susanna, 1944-.**    **4.5041**
Distorting mirrors: visions of the crowd in late nineteenth–century France / Susanna Barrows. — New Haven: Yale University Press, c1981. ix, 221 p.; 22 cm. — (Yale historical publications. Miscellany. 127) Includes index. 1. Collective behavior 2. Crowds — France. 3. France — Social conditions I. T. II. Series.
HM281.B276    302.3/3 19    *LC* 81-3014    *ISBN* 0300025882

**Camus, Albert, 1913-1960.**    • **4.5042**
[Homme révolté. English] The rebel; an essay on man in revolt. With a foreword by Sir Herbert Read. A rev. and complete translation of L'homme révolté by Anthony Bower. [1st Vintage ed.] New York, Vintage Books, 1956. 306 p. 19 cm. (Vintage books, K30) 1. Revolutions I. T.
HM281.C3513 1956    301.6/333    *LC* 56-13684

**Collective violence** / edited by James F. Short, Jr. [and] Marvin E. Wolfgang.     **4.5043**
Chicago: Aldine-Atherton, [1972] viii, 387 p.; 25 cm. — (Law in action) Expanded ed. of the essays originally published in 1970 as an issue of the Annals of the American Academy of Political and Social Science. 1. Violence — Addresses, essays, lectures. 2. Violence — United States — Addresses, essays, lectures. I. Short, James F. ed. II. Wolfgang, Marvin E., 1924- ed.
HM281.C55 1972     301.6/33/0973     *LC* 74-149843     *ISBN* 0202230090

**Gurr, Ted Robert, 1936-.**     **4.5044**
Why men rebel. Princeton, N.J.: Published for the Center of International Studies, Princeton University [by] Princeton University Press, 1970. xi, 421 p.; ill.; 25 cm. 1. Revolutions 2. Violence I. Woodrow Wilson School of Public and International Affairs. Center of International Studies. II. T.
HM281.G82     301.2/4     *LC* 74-84865     *ISBN* 069107528X

**Hoffer, Eric.**     • **4.5045**
The true believer; thoughts on the nature of mass movements. — [1st ed.]. — New York: Harper, [1951] xiii, 176 p.; 20 cm. 1. Social groups 2. Social psychology 3. Fanaticism I. T.
HM281.H6     301.1582     *LC* 51-1405

**Johnson, Chalmers A.**     • **4.5046**
Revolutionary change [by] Chalmers Johnson. — Boston: Little, Brown, [1966] xviii, 191 p.; 21 cm. — (Basic studies in politics) 1. Revolutions 2. Social change I. T.
HM281.J6     301.24     *LC* 66-26489

**Le Bon, Gustave, 1841-1931.**     • **4.5047**
The crowd: a study of the popular mind / by Gustave Le Bon; with a new introduction by Robert K. Merton. — New York: Viking Press, 1960. xxxix, 207 p. — (Compass books; C66) 1. Crowds I. T.
HM281.L53 1960     *LC* 74-19736     *ISBN* 0670000663

**Park, Robert Ezra, 1864-1944.**     **4.5048**
[Masse und Publikum. English] The crowd and the public, and other essays. Edited and with an introd. by Henry Elsner, Jr. Chicago, University of Chicago Press [1972] xxxii, 146 p. 21 cm. (The Heritage of sociology) 'The crowd and the public [Masse und Publikum] translated by Charlotte Elsner. Note on The crowd and the public by Donald N. Levine.' 1. Social psychology 2. Crowds I. T.
HM281.P2213 1972     301.18/2     *LC* 78-189361     *ISBN* 0226646092

**Rudé, George F. E.**     **4.5049**
Ideology and popular protest / by George Rudé. — 1st American ed. — New York: Pantheon Books, c1980. 176 p.; 22 cm. Includes index. 1. Revolutions — History. 2. Social movements — History. 3. Ideology I. T.
HM281.R8     303.6/4/09     *LC* 80-8030     *ISBN* 039451372X

**Sorokin, Pitirim Aleksandrovich, 1889-1968.**     • **4.5050**
The sociology of revolution, by Pitirim A. Sorokin. — New York: H. Fertig, 1967. 428 p.; 21 cm. Reprint of the 1925 ed. 1. Revolutions 2. Sociology 3. Social psychology I. T.
HM281.S6 1967     301.2     *LC* 67-24598

**Billington, James H.**     **4.5051**
Fire in the minds of men: origins of the revolutionary faith / James H. Billington. — New York: Basic Books, c1980. viii, 677 p.; 24 cm. 1. Revolutions — History — 19th century. 2. Revolutionists — History — 19th century. I. T.
HM283.B54     303.6/4/09034     *LC* 79-2750     *ISBN* 046502405X

**Skocpol, Theda.**     **4.5052**
States and social revolutions: a comparative analysis of France, Russia, and China / Theda Skocpol. — Cambridge; New York: Cambridge University Press, 1979. xvii, 407 p.: ill.; 24 cm. Includes index. 1. Revolutions — Case studies. 2. Revolutions — France — History. 3. Revolutions — Russia — History. 4. Revolutions — China — History. I. T.
HM283.S56     301.6/333     *LC* 78-14314     *ISBN* 052122439X. *ISBN* 0521294991 pbk

# HM291 Social Interaction. Deviant Behavior

**Akers, Ronald L.**     **4.5053**
Deviant behavior: a social learning approach / Ronald L. Akers. — 3rd ed. — Belmont, Calif.: Wadsworth Pub. Co., c1985. xxv, 421 p.; 24 cm. Includes indexes. 1. Deviant behavior 2. Socialization I. T.
HM291.A42 1985     302.5/42 19     *LC* 84-15187     *ISBN* 0534039154

**Bales, Robert Freed, 1916-.**     • **4.5054**
Interaction process analysis: a method for the study of small groups. — Cambridge, Mass.: Addison-Wesley Press, 1950 [i.e. 1949] xi, 203 p.: ill.; 24 cm. 1. Social interaction I. T.
HM291.B25     *LC* 50-5315

**Barber, Bernard.**     **4.5055**
The logic and limits of trust / Bernard Barber. — New Brunswick, N.J.: Rutgers University Press, c1983. 189 p.; 24 cm. Includes index. 1. Trust (Psychology) — Social aspects. 2. Confidence — Social aspects. 3. Social institutions I. T.
HM291.B279 1983     306 19     *LC* 81-23447     *ISBN* 0813509580

**Birenbaum, Arnold.**     **4.5056**
Norms and human behavior / Arnold Birenbaum, Edward Sagarin. New York: Praeger, 1976. x, 178 p.; 21 cm. (Viewpoints in sociology) (Praeger university series) Includes index. 1. Deviant behavior 2. Social control I. Sagarin, Edward, 1913- joint author. II. T.
HM291.B478     301.6/2     *LC* 74-2688     *ISBN* 0275520900

**Blumer, Herbert, 1900-1987.**     • **4.5057**
Symbolic interactionism; perspective and method. — Englewood Cliffs, N.J.: Prentice-Hall, [1969] x, 208 p.; 22 cm. 1. Symbolic interactionism — Addresses, essays, lectures. 2. Sociology — Methodology — Addresses, essays, lectures. I. T.
HM291.B57     301     *LC* 76-80731     *ISBN* 0138799245

**Boissevain, Jeremy.**     **4.5058**
Friends of friends: networks, manipulators and coalitions / Jeremy Boissevain. — New York: St. Martin's Press, 1975 (c1974). xv, 285 p.: ill.; 23 cm. Includes index. 1. Social interaction 2. Interpersonal relations I. T.
HM291.B634 1974     301.11     *LC* 74-83521

**Brittan, Arthur.**     **4.5059**
Meanings and situations. — London; Boston: Routledge & K. Paul, [1973] v, 215 p.; 22 cm. — (International library of sociology) 1. Social interaction I. T.
HM291.B74     301.11     *LC* 72-90009     *ISBN* 071007509X

**Cantril, Hadley, 1906-1969.**     • **4.5060**
The psychology of social movements / by Hadley Cantril. — New York: J. Wiley & sons, inc.; London: Chapman & Hall, limited, 1941. xv. 274 p.: diagr.; 24 cm. — (Wiley books in psychology) 1. Social movements 2. Crowds I. T.
HM291.C3     301.15     *LC* 41-10411

**Cicourel, Aaron Victor, 1928-.**     **4.5061**
Cognitive sociology: language and meaning in social interaction / Aaron V. Cicourel. — New York: Free Press, 1974. 189 p.; 21 cm. Includes indexes. 1. Social interaction 2. Sociolinguistics I. T.
HM291.C56 1974     301.2/1     *LC* 73-18771

**Clinard, Marshall Barron, 1911-.**     **4.5062**
Sociology of deviant behavior / Marshall B. Clinard, Robert F. Meier. — 6th ed. — New York: Holt, Rinehart, and Winston, c1985. x, 403 p.; 25 cm. Includes indexes. 1. Deviant behavior 2. Criminal psychology I. Meier, Robert F. (Robert Frank), 1944- II. T.
HM291.C58 1985     302.5/42 19     *LC* 84-19321     *ISBN* 0030635861

**Cohen, Albert Kircidel.**     • **4.5063**
Deviance and control [by] Albert K. Cohen. — Englewood Cliffs, N.J.: Prentice-Hall, [1966] viii, 120 p.; 24 cm. — (Foundations of modern sociology series) 1. Deviant behavior 2. Social control I. T.
HM291.C59     301.1     *LC* 66-27669

**Cullen, Francis T.**     **4.5064**
Rethinking crime and deviance theory: the emergence of a structuring tradition / Francis T. Cullen. — Totowa, N.J.: Rowman & Allanheld, 1984, c1983. 190 p.: 1 ill.; 24 cm. Includes index. 1. Deviant behavior 2. Criminal psychology I. T.
HM291.C86 1984     302.5/42 19     *LC* 83-17796     *ISBN* 086598073X

**Dollard, John, 1900-.**     • **4.5065**
Frustrations and aggression, by John Dollard, Neal E. Miller, Leonard W. Doob, O. H. Mowrer [and] Robert R. Sears, in collaboration with Clellan S. Ford, Carl Iver Hovland, Richard T. Sollenberger, Institute of human relations, Yale University. — New Haven: Pub. for the Institute of human relations by Yale university press; London: H. Milford, Oxford university press, 1939. viii p., 1 l., 209 p.; 24 cm. 1. Frustration 2. Aggressiveness (Psychology) I. Doob, Leonard William, 1909- joint author. II. Miller, Neal Elgar, 1909- joint author. III. Mowrer, Orval Hobart, 1907- joint author. IV. Sears, Robert Richardson, 1908- joint author. V. Yale university. Institute of human relations. VI. T.
HM291.D6     301.15     *LC* 39-6842

**Goffman, Erving.**                                                          • **4.5066**
Encounters; two studies in the sociology of interaction. — Indianapolis: Bobbs-Merrill, [1961] 152 p.; 22 cm. 1. Social interaction 2. Social distance I. T.
HM291.G58      301.151      LC 61-16844

**Goffman, Erving.**                                                          • **4.5067**
The presentation of self in everyday life. — Garden City, N.Y.: Doubleday, 1959. 255 p.; 18 cm. — (Doubleday anchor books, A174) 1. Self 2. Social role I. T.
HM291.G6 1959      301.15      LC 59-9138

**Homans, George Caspar, 1910-.**                                            • **4.5068**
Social behavior: its elementary forms. Under the general editorship of Robert K. Merton. — New York: Harcourt, Brace & World, [1961] 404 p.: illus.; 22 cm. 1. Social interaction I. T.
HM291.H64      301.15      LC 60-14855

**Matza, David.**                                                            • **4.5069**
Becoming deviant. — Englewood Cliffs, N.J.: Prentice-Hall, [1969] ix, 203 p.; 24 cm. 1. Deviant behavior I. T.
HM291.M38      301.1      LC 70-82903      ISBN 0130734373

**Ollman, Bertell.**                                                         **4.5070**
Alienation: Marx's conception of man in capitalist society. — Cambridge [Eng.]: University Press, 1971. xvi, 325 p.; 23 cm. — (Cambridge studies in the history and theory of politics) 1. Marx, Karl, 1818-1883. 2. Alienation (Social psychology) 3. Communism and society I. T.
HM291.O58      301.6/2      LC 75-158547      ISBN 052108086X

**Research on deviance / edited by Jack D. Douglas.**                        **4.5071**
[1st ed.]. — New York: Random House, [1972] ix, 270 p.; 24 cm. 1. Deviant behavior — Addresses, essays, lectures. 2. Social psychology — Research. I. Douglas, Jack D. ed.
HM291.R45      301.6/2      LC 74-162703      ISBN 039431154X

**Rosenberg, Stanley D.**                                                    **4.5072**
The cold fire: alienation and the myth of culture / by Stanley D. Rosenberg and Bernard J. Bergen. — Hanover, N.H.: Published for Dartmouth College by the University Press of New England, 1977 (c1976). vii, 214 p.; 23 cm. 1. Alienation (Social psychology) 2. Mass society 3. Personality and culture I. Bergen, Bernard J. joint author. II. Dartmouth College. III. T.
HM291.R594      301.6/2      LC 76-3918      ISBN 0874511283

**Schur, Edwin M.**                                                          **4.5073**
Labeling deviant behavior; its sociological implications [by] Edwin M. Schur. New York: Harper & Row, [1971] x, 177 p.; 21 cm. — (Harper & Row monograph series in sociology) 1. Deviant behavior — Labeling theory 2. Interpersonal relations 3. Social control I. T.
HM291.S37      301.6/2      LC 75-168359      ISBN 0060458127

**Schur, Edwin M.**                                                          **4.5074**
The politics of deviance: stigma contests and the uses of power / Edwin M. Schur. — Englewood Cliffs, N.J.: Prentice-Hall, c1980. xi, 241 p.; 21 cm. — (A Spectrum book) 1. Deviant behavior 2. Deviant behavior — Political aspects. 3. Stigma (Social psychology) 4. Power (Social sciences) 5. Social problems 6. Social movements I. T.
HM291.S373 1980      302.5      LC 80-13643      ISBN 0136847536

**Scott, Robert A., 1935-.**                                                 **4.5075**
Theoretical perspectives on deviance / edited by Robert A. Scott and Jack D. Douglas. — New York: Basic Books, [1972] viii, 373 p.; 24 cm. 1. Deviant behavior — Addresses, essays, lectures. I. Douglas, Jack D. joint author. II. T.
HM291.S39      301.6/2      LC 79-174828      ISBN 0465084206

**The Sociology of deviance / edited by M. Michael Rosenberg,**             **4.5076**
**Robert A. Stebbins, Allan Turowetz.**
New York: St. Martin's Press, c1982. ix, 369 p.; 24 cm. Includes index. 1. Deviant behavior — Addresses, essays, lectures. 2. Sociology — Addresses, essays, lectures. I. Rosenberg, M. Michael. II. Stebbins, Robert A., 1938- III. Turowetz, Allan.
HM291.S592 1982      302.5/42 19      LC 81-51864      ISBN 0312740646

**Stanage, Sherman M. (Sherman Miller)**                                     **4.5077**
Reason and violence; philosophical investigations, edited by Sherman M. Stanage. — Totowa, N.J.: Littlefield, Adams, 1974. xv, 253 p.; 21 cm. — (A Littlefield, Adams quality paperback, no. 255) 1. Violence — Addresses, essays, lectures. I. T.
HM291.S78      301.6/33/01      LC 72-85273      ISBN 0822602555

**Taylor, Laurie, 1935-.**                                                   **4.5078**
Deviance and society. — London: Joseph, 1971. xi, 216 p.; 23 cm. — (Tutor books) 1. Deviant behavior 2. Crime and criminals I. T.
HM291.T37      301.6/2      LC 72-176180      ISBN 0718108809

**Toward a general theory of social control / edited by Donald**            **4.5079**
**Black.**
New York: Academic Press, 1984. 2 v.: ill.; 24 cm. (Studies on law and social control.) 1. Social control — Addresses, essays, lectures. 2. Deviant behavior — Addresses, essays, lectures. 3. Sociological jurisprudence — Addresses, essays, lectures. I. Black, Donald J. II. Series.
HM291.T66 1984      303/.3/3 19      LC 83-11886      ISBN 0121028011

**Vanderbilt Sociology Conference. 3d, Vanderbilt University,**             **4.5080**
**1974.**
The labelling of deviance: evaluating a perspective: [proceedings] / edited by Walter R. Gove. [Beverly Hills]: Sage Publications; New York: distributed by Halsted Press, [1975] 313 p.; 24 cm. 1. Deviant behavior — Labeling theory — Congresses. I. Gove, Walter R. II. T.
HM291.V33 1974      301.6/2      LC 75-14102      ISBN 0470319305

---

# HN SOCIAL HISTORY AND CONDITIONS. PROBLEMS. REFORM

---

**The Poverty of progress: changing ways of life in industrial**           **4.5081**
**societies / edited by Ian Miles, John Irvine with Monica**
**Wemegah, and Dag Poleszynski.**
1st ed. — Oxford; New York: Pergamon Press, 1982. xxiii, 344 p.: ill.; 22 cm. 'Selected proceedings of two international conferences on 'alternative ways of life', organized by the Goals, Processes, and Indicators of Development Project of the United Nations University and by the Society for International Development, held in Cartigny, Switzerland, 1978, and Trappeto, Sicily, 1979.' 1. Social history — 1970- — Congresses. 2. Quality of life — Congresses. 3. Social change — Congresses. I. Miles, Ian. II. Irvine, John, fl. 1979- III. United Nations University. IV. Society for International Development.
HN3.P68 1982      303.4 19      LC 81-17779      ISBN 0080289061

**Sinclair, Upton, 1878-1968. ed.**                                          • **4.5082**
The cry for justice; an anthology of the literature of social protest. New ed., rev. and ed. with the cooperation of Edward Sagarin and Albert Teichner. New York, L. Stuart [1964, c1963] 638 p. illus. 24 cm. 1. Social problems I. T.
HN5.S5 1964      808.8893      LC 63-7041

---

# HN8–19 History

**Carlton, Eric.**                                                           **4.5083**
Ideology and social order / Eric Carlton. — London; Boston: Routledge & K. Paul, 1977. 320 p.; 23 cm. — (International library of sociology) Includes index. 1. Athens (Greece) — Social conditions. 2. Egypt — Social conditions I. T.
HN9.C36      301.4/00932      LC 77-362406      ISBN 0710084749

**Duby, Georges.**                                                           **4.5084**
The chivalrous society / Georges Duby; translated by Cynthia Postan. — Berkeley: University of California Press, 1978 (c1977). viii, 246 p.: ill.; 25 cm. 1. Social classes — Europe — History. I. T.
HN11.D78      309.1/4/01      LC 74-81431      ISBN 0520028139

**Social historians in contemporary France; essays from Annales.**         **4.5085**
**Edited and translated by the staff of Annales, Paris.**
New York, Harper & Row [1972] 327 p. illus. 21 cm. (Harper torchbooks, HR 1571) 1. Social history — Modern — Addresses, essays, lectures. I. Annales; économies, sociétés, civilisations.
HN13.S65      309.1/44      LC 72-159633      ISBN 0061315712

**Tilly, Charles.**                                                          **4.5086**
As sociology meets history / Charles Tilly. — New York: Academic Press, c1981. xiii, 237 p.; 24 cm. — (Studies in social discontinuity.) Includes index. 1. Social history 2. Sociology — Methodology 3. History — Methodology 4. Historiography I. T. II. Series.
HN13.T54      907/.2 19      LC 81-12728      ISBN 0126912807

**Barnes, Harry Elmer, 1889-1968.**                                          • **4.5087**
Social institutions in an era of world upheaval, by Harry Elmer Barnes. New York, Prentice-Hall, inc., 1946, c1942. xviii, 927 p. incl. tables, diagrs. 24 cm. (Prentice-Hall sociology series, ed. by Herbert Blumer) 1. Social problems 2. Sociology 3. United States — Social conditions I. T.
HN15.B22      300      LC 42-21948

**Barnes, Harry Elmer, 1889-1968.** • 4.5088
Society in transition. — 2d ed. — New York: Greenwood Press, 1968 [c1952]
xiii, 878 p.: illus., ports.; 24 cm. 1. Social problems 2. United States — Social
conditions I. T.
HN15.B23 1968    309.1/73    LC 68-23271

**Heberle, Rudolf, 1896-.** • 4.5089
Social movements; an introduction to political sociology. New York, Appleton-
Century-Crofts [1951] 478 p. illus. 23 cm. (Appleton-Century-Crofts sociology
series) 1. Social problems 2. Social history I. T.
HN15.H47    LC 51-8413

**Mannheim, Karl, 1893-1947.** • 4.5090
Men and society in an age of reconstruction; studies in modern social structure.
With a bibliographical guide to the study of modern society. New York,
Harcourt, Brace & World [1967] xxii, 469 p. 21 cm. (A Harvest book, HB119)
'Based on Mensch und Gesellschaft im Zeitalter des umbaus, Leiden (Holland)
1935. Translated from the German by Edward Shils. Revised and considerably
enlarged by the author, London, 1940.' 1. Social history — 20th century
2. Sociology 3. Planning 4. Social psychology I. Shils, Edward Albert, 1911-
tr. II. T.
HN15.M263 1967    LC 67-5016

**Moore, Barrington, 1913-.** • 4.5091
Social origins of dictatorship and democracy: lord and peasant in the making of
the modern world / by Barrington Moore, Jr. — Boston: Beacon Press, [1966]
xix, 559 p.; 24 cm. 1. Social history — Modern. 2. Economic history
3. Revolutions 4. Social classes 5. Asia — Politics and government I. T.
HN15.M775    309    LC 66-23782

**Rose, Arnold Marshall, ed.** • 4.5092
Institutions of advanced societies. Minneapolis: University of Minnesota Press,
1958. 691 p. bibl. 1. Social history I. T.
HN 15.R59    301.1536    LC 57-11006

**Swingewood, Alan.** 4.5093
The myth of mass culture / Alan Swingewood. — Atlantic Highlands, N.J.:
Humanities Press, 1977. xii, 146 p.; 23 cm. Includes index. 1. Mass society
2. Popular culture — History 3. 20th century. 3. Socialism and literature
4. Socialism and culture 5. Communism and culture I. T.
HN15.S955 1977    301    LC 77-4699    ISBN 0391006991. ISBN
0391007246 pbk

**Taylor, Charles Lewis.** 4.5094
World handbook of political and social indicators, by Charles Lewis Taylor and
Michael C. Hudson. With the collaboration of Katherine H. Dolan [and others]
2d ed. New Haven, Yale University Press, 1972. xiv, 443 p. illus. 26 cm. First
ed. by Bruce M. Russett, published in 1964. 1. Social indicators. 2. Political
indicators. I. Hudson, Michael C., joint author. II. Russett, Bruce M. World
handbook of political and social indicators. III. T.
HN15.T37 1972    301/.01/8    LC 70-179479    ISBN 0300015550

**Lasch, Christopher.** 4.5095
The world of nations; reflections on American history, politics, and culture. —
[1st ed.]. — New York: Knopf; [distributed by Random House], 1973. xii, 348,
xiv p.; 22 cm. 1. Social history — Modern. I. T.
HN15.5.L37    309.1/04    LC 73-4309    ISBN 0394483944

**Goldthorpe, J. E.** 4.5096
The sociology of the Third World: disparity and involvement / J. E.
Goldthorpe. — Cambridge [Eng.]; New York: Cambridge University Press,
1975. ix, 325 p.; 23 cm. 1. Social history — 20th century 2. Social policy
3. Developing countries — Social conditions. I. T.
HN16.G65    309.1/172/4    LC 74-12979

**Roszak, Theodore, 1933-.** 4.5097
Person/planet: the creative disintegration of industrial society / Theodore
Roszak. — 1st ed. — Garden City, N.Y.: Anchor Press/Doubleday, 1978. xxx,
347 p.; 22 cm. 1. Social history — 20th century 2. Social psychology
3. Human ecology 4. Individuality I. T.
HN16.R63    301.1    LC 75-6165    ISBN 0385000634

**Friedman, Kathi V., 1943-.** 4.5098
Legitimation of social rights and the western welfare state: a Weberian
perspective / by Kathi V. Friedman. — Chapel Hill: University of North
Carolina Press, c1981. xii, 269 p.; 24 cm. Includes index. 1. Weber, Max,
1864-1920 — Addresses, essays, lectures. 2. Welfare state — Addresses, essays,
lectures. 3. Social policy — Addresses, essays, lectures. 4. United States —
Social policy — Addresses, essays, lectures. I. T.
HN17.F74    361.6/5 19    LC 80-29600    ISBN 0807814806

**Huxley, Aldous, 1894-1963.** • 4.5099
Ends and means; an inquiry into the nature of ideals and into the methods
employed for their realization. New York, Greenwood Press [1969, c1937] v,
386 p. 23 cm. 1. Social problems I. T.
HN17.H84 1969    301    LC 79-90533    ISBN 083712252X

**Social movements and social change / edited by Robert H.** 4.5100
**Lauer.**
Carbondale: Southern Illinois University Press, c1976. xxviii,292 p.; 23 cm.
1. Social movements — Addresses, essays, lectures. 2. Social change —
Addresses, essays, lectures. I. Lauer, Robert H., editor.
HN17.S59    301.24/2    LC 76-18747    ISBN 0809307715

**Bell, Daniel.** 4.5101
The coming of post–industrial society: a venture in social forecasting. — New
York: Basic Books, [1973] xiii, 507 p.; ill.; 25 cm. 1. Social history — 20th
century 2. Social prediction 3. United States — Social conditions — 1945-
I. T.
HN17.5.B38    309.1/04    LC 72-89178    ISBN 0465012817

**Biklen, Douglas.** 4.5102
Community organizing: theory and practice / Douglas Biklen. — Englewood
Cliffs, N.J.: Prentice-Hall, c1983. xii, 321 p.; 24 cm. 1. Community
organization 2. Social action 3. Social problems I. T.
HN17.5.B53 1983    361.8 19    LC 82-16599    ISBN 0131536761

**Estes, Richard J.** 4.5103
The social progress of nations / by Richard J. Estes. — New York, N.Y.:
Praeger, 1984. xvi, 223 p. 1. Social history — 1970- 2. Progress 3. Social
indicators I. T.
HN17.5.E79 1984    303.4/4 19    LC 84-9802    ISBN 0030595827

**Institutions of rural development for the poor: decentralization** 4.5104
**and organizational linkages / David K. Leonard & Dale Rogers**
**Marshall, editors.**
[Berkeley]: Institute of International Studies, University of California,
Berkeley, 1983. xii, 237 p.; 24 cm. — (Research series / Institute of
International Studies, University of California, Berkeley, 0068-6093; no. 49)
1. Rural development I. Leonard, David K. II. Marshall, Dale Rogers.
HN17.5.I53 1982    307.7/2 19    LC 82-15651    ISBN 0877251495

**Kumar, Krishan.** 4.5105
Prophecy and progress: the sociology of industrial and post–industrial society /
[by] Krishan Kumar. — Harmondsworth; New York [etc.]: Penguin, 1978.
416 p.; 19 cm. Includes index. 1. Social history — 20th century 2. Social
prediction 3. Progress I. T. II. Title: Post-industrial society.
HN17.5.K83 1978b    301.2    LC 79-321072    ISBN 0713911468

**Major social issues: a multidisciplinary view / edited by J.** 4.5106
**Milton Yinger and Stephen J. Cutler.**
New York: Free Press, c1978. xvi, 575 p.; ill.; 24 cm. 'A publication of the
American Sociological Association.' Includes indexes. 1. Social problems —
Addresses, essays, lectures. 2. Social history — 1945- — Addresses, essays,
lectures. I. Yinger, J. Milton (John Milton), 1916- II. Cutler, Stephen J.
III. American Sociological Association.
HN17.5.M337 1978    309    LC 78-50846    ISBN 002935840X

**Toffler, Alvin.** • 4.5107
Future shock. — New York: Random House, [1970] xii, 505 p.; 23 cm.
1. Social history — 1945- 2. Social change 3. Civilization, Modern — 1950-
4. Regression (Civilization) I. T.
HN17.5.T64    301.2/4    LC 67-12744

**Weitz, Raanan, 1913-.** 4.5108
From peasant to farmer; a revolutionary strategy for development. With the
assistance of Levia Applebaum. — New York: Columbia University Press,
1971. xvi, 292 p.; 22 cm. 1. Rural development 2. Economic development —
Social aspects 3. Agriculture — Economic aspects I. T.
HN17.5.W42    301.3/5    LC 76-170926    ISBN 0231035926

**Wilensky, Harold L.** 4.5109
The welfare state and equality: structural and ideological roots of public
expenditures / by Harold L. Wilensky. — Berkeley: University of California
Press, [1974] c1975. xvii, 151 p.; ill.; 24 cm. Includes index. 1. Welfare state
2. Equality I. T.
HN17.5.W55 1975    361.6    LC 74-79146    ISBN 0520028007

**Yinger, J. Milton (John Milton), 1916-.** 4.5110
Countercultures: the promise and the peril of a world turned upside down / J.
Milton Yinger. — New York: Free Press; London: Collier Macmillan
Publisher, c1982. xi, 371 p.; 24 cm. Includes indexes. 1. Subculture 2. Social
change 3. Social problems 4. Religion and culture 5. Minorities I. T.
HN17.5.Y55    306/.1 19    LC 81-17276    ISBN 0029358906

**Merton, Robert King, 1910- ed.** 4.5111
Contemporary social problems / edited by Robert K. Merton and Robert
Nisbet. — 4th ed. — New York: Harcourt Brace Jovanovich, c1976. xi, 782 p.:
ill.; 24 cm. 1. Social problems I. Nisbet, Robert A. joint ed. II. T.
HN18.M414 1976    301    LC 76-4690    ISBN 015513793X

Smith, David Marshall, 1936-. 4.5112
Human geography: a welfare approach / David M. Smith. — New York: St. Martin's Press, 1977. xii, 402 p.: ill.; 24 cm. Includes index. 1. Social policy 2. Social problems 3. Anthropo-geography I. T.
HN18.S613 1977    304.2 19    *LC* 77-70203    *ISBN* 0312399464

Esler, Anthony. comp. 4.5113
The youth revolution: the conflict of generations in modern history / edited and with an introd. by Anthony Esler. — Lexington, Mass.: Heath, [1974] xxiii, 173 p.: ill.; 21 cm. — (Problems in European civilization) 1. Conflict of generations 2. Youth movement — Addresses, essays, lectures. I. T. II. Series.
HN19.E8    322.4/4    *LC* 74-5567    *ISBN* 0669909289

Laqueur, Walter, 1921-. • 4.5114
Young Germany; a history of the German youth movement. With an introd. by R. H. S. Crossman. — New York, Basic Books Pub. Co. [1962] 253 p. illus. 22 cm. Includes bibliography. 1. Youth movement — Germany. I. T.
HN19.L3 1962a    301.431943    *LC* 62-14623

## HN28–29 Philosophy. Methodology. Social Surveys

Parten, Mildred Bernice, 1902-. 4.5115
Surveys, polls, and samples; practical procedures. New York, Harper [1950] xii, 624 p. (Harper's social science series) 1. Social surveys 2. Public opinion polls I. T.
HN29 P36    *LC* 50-6574

## HN30–40 The Church and Social Problems

Troeltsch, Ernst, 1865-1923. • 4.5116
The social teaching of the Christian churches. Translated by Olive Wyon. With an introductory note by Charles Gore. London, Allen & Unwin [1956] 2 v. (1019 p.) (Halley Stewart publications, 1) 1. Church and social problems — History 2. Church history I. T.
HN31 T75 1956    *LC* 63-25855

Day, Dorothy, 1897-1980. 4.5117
By little and by little: the selected writings of Dorothy Day / edited and with an introduction by Robert Ellsberg. — 1st ed. — New York: Knopf, 1983. xli, 371 p.: port.; 25 cm. Includes index. 1. Church and social problems — Catholic Church — Addresses, essays, lectures. I. Ellsberg, Robert, 1955- II. T.
HN37.C3 D358 1983    261.8/3 19    *LC* 82-48887    *ISBN* 0394524993

The Gospel of peace and justice: Catholic social teaching since 4.5118
Pope John / presented by Joseph Gremillion.
Maryknoll, N.Y.: Orbis Books, c1976. xiv, 623 p.; 24 cm. 1. John XXIII, Pope, 1881-1963. 2. Paul VI, Pope, 1897-1978. 3. Church and social problems — Catholic Church — Papal documents. 4. Social justice I. Gremillion, Joseph.
HN37.C3 G66    261.8/3    *LC* 75-39892    *ISBN* 0883441659

Gutiérrez, Gustavo, 1928-. 4.5119
[Fuerza histórica de los pobres. English] The power of the poor in history: selected writings / Gustavo Gutierrez; translated from the Spanish by Robert R. Barr. — Maryknoll, NY: Orbis Books, 1983. xvi, 240 p.; 24 cm. Translation of: La fuerza historica de los pobres. 1. Church and social problems — Latin America — Addresses, essays, lectures. 2. Poor — Latin America — Addresses, essays, lectures. I. T.
HN39.L3 G8413 1983    261.8/3/098 19    *LC* 82-22252    *ISBN* 0883443880

Link, Eugene P., 1907-. 4.5120
Labor–religion prophet: the times and life of Harry F. Ward / Eugene P. Link; with a foreword by Corliss Lamont and illustrations by Lynd Ward. — Boulder, Colo.: Westview Press, 1984. xxiii, 351 p.: ill.; 24 cm. — (Academy of Independent Scholars retrospections series.) Includes index. 1. Ward, Harry Fredrick, 1873-1966. 2. Church and labor — United States — History. 3. Church and social problems — United States — History. 4. Sociology, Christian — United States — History. I. T. II. Series.
HN39.U5L5x    261.8/34562/0924 19    *LC* 83-17108    *ISBN* 086531621X

Levy, Reuben. 4.5121
The social structure of Islam / by Reuben Levy. — 2d ed. — Cambridge: University Press, 1957, 1962 printing. vii, 536 p.: maps; 22 cm. 1. Sociology, Islamic I. T.
HN40.M6 L4 1962

## HN50–940 Social History and Conditions, by Country

## HN51–90 UNITED STATES

## HN57 Early to 1945

### HN57 A–L

Allen, Robert L., 1942-. 4.5122
Reluctant reformers; racism and social reform movements in the United States, by Robert L. Allen with the collaboration of Pamela P. Allen. Washington, Howard University Press, 1974. 324 p. 25 cm. 1. Social movements 2. United States — Social conditions 3. United States — Race relations I. Allen, Pamela P., joint author. II. T.
HN57.A57    301.24/2/0973    *LC* 73-85495    *ISBN* 0882580027

Anonymous Americans: explorations in nineteenth–century • 4.5123
social history / edited by Tamara K. Hareven.
Englewood Cliffs, N.J.: Prentice-Hall, [1971] xxii, 314 p.: ill.; 21 cm. 1. U.S. — History — Addresses, essays, lectures. 2. U.S. — Social conditions — Addresses, essays, lectures. I. Hareven, Tamara K. ed.
HN57.A67    309.1/73    *LC* 77-143813    *ISBN* 0130383988

Baltzell, E. Digby (Edward Digby), 1915-. • 4.5124
The Protestant establishment: aristocracy & caste in America / by E. Digby Baltzell. New York: Random House [1964] xviii, 429 p.: ill.; 22 cm. 1. Social classes — United States. 2. Protestants — United States 3. United States — Social conditions I. T.
HN57.B26    301.440973    *LC* 64-14840

Bell, Daniel. • 4.5125
The end of ideology: on the exhaustion of political ideas in the fifties. — Glencoe, Ill.: Free Press [1960] 416 p.; 25 cm. Includes bibliography. 1. U.S. — Soc. condit. 2. U.S. — Civilization. 3. Social sciences — Hist. — U.S. I. T.
HN57.B45    309.173    *LC* 59-12186

Berthoff, Rowland Tappan, 1921-. • 4.5126
An unsettled people: social order and disorder in American history / [by] Rowland Berthoff. — [1st ed.]. — New York: Harper & Row, [1971] xvi, 528 p.: ill., maps.; 24 cm. 1. U.S. — Social conditions. I. T.
HN57.B47    309.1/73    *LC* 79-123915

Colonial America: essays in politics and social development. 4.5127
3rd ed. / edited by Stanley N. Katz and John M. Murrin. — New York: Knopf, c1983. xv, 596 p.: maps; 21 cm. 1. United States — Social conditions — To 1865 — Addresses, essays, lectures. 2. United States — Politics and government — Colonial period, ca. 1600-1775 — Addresses, essays, lectures. I. Katz, Stanley Nider. II. Murrin, John M.
HN57.C584 1983    306/.0973 19    *LC* 82-21149    *ISBN* 0394330447

Fine, Sidney, 1920-. • 4.5128
Laissez faire and the general–welfare state: a study of conflict in American thought, 1865–1901. — Ann Arbor: University of Michigan Press [1956] x, 468 p.; 24 cm. (University of Michigan publications. History and political science, v. 22) 1. Laissez-faire 2. United States — Social policy 3. United States — Economic policy I. T.
HN57.F54    *LC* 56-62500

Gallaher, Art, 1925-. • 4.5129
Plainville fifteen years later. New York: Columbia University Press, 1961. 301 p.; 23 cm. 1. Cities and towns — United States 2. Social surveys — United States 3. United States — Social conditions I. T.
HN57 G2    *LC* 61-15104

**Gordon, Milton Myron, 1918-.**　　　　　　● 4.5130
Assimilation in American life: the role of race, religion, and national origins. — New York: Oxford University Press, 1964. 276 p.: illus.; 21 cm. 1. Assimilation (Sociology) 2. Social groups 3. United States — Social conditions I. T.
HN57.G6　　　301.23　　　*LC* 64-15010

**Graham, Hugh Davis.**　　　　　　● 4.5131
[Violence in America] The history of violence in America: historical and comparative perspectives / edited by Hugh Davis Graham and Ted Robert Gurr. Special introd. by John Herbers. — New York: F. A. Praeger [1969] xxxvi, 822 p.: ill.; 22 cm. 'A New York times book.' Commonly known as the Graham report. 'A report [of the Task Force on Historical and Comparative Perspectives] submitted to the National Commission on the Causes and Prevention of Violence.' First published in June 1969 under title: Violence in America. 1. Violence — United States. I. Gurr, Ted Robert, 1936- joint author. II. United States. National Commission on the Causes and Prevention of Violence. Task Force on Historical and Comparative Perspectives. III. T. IV. Title: Violence in America. V. Title: Graham report on violence in America.
HN57.G65 1969c　　　301.2　　　*LC* 70-93570

**Greer, Thomas H.**　　　　　　● 4.5132
American social reform movements: their pattern since 1865 / by Thomas H. Greer. — New York: Prentice-Hall, 1949. ix, 313 p. — (Prentice-Hall sociology series.) 1. Trade-unions — United States 2. Agriculture — Societies, etc — United States. 3. United States — Social conditions 4. United States — Politics and government I. T. II. Series.
HN57.G7　　　301.1535　　　*LC* 49-1202

**Janowitz, Morris.**　　　　　　4.5133
The last half–century: societal change and politics in America / Morris Janowitz. — Chicago: University of Chicago Press, c1978. p. cm. Includes indexes. 1. Social change 2. Social institutions 3. United States — Social conditions — 20th century. 4. United States — Politics and government — 20th century I. T.
HN57.J2479　　　309.1/73/09　　　*LC* 78-17715　　　*ISBN* 0226393062

**Goldmark, Josephine Clara, 1877-1950.**　　　　　　● 4.5134
Impatient crusader: Florence Kelley's life story / by Josephine Goldmark. Urbana: University of Illinois Press, 1953. xii, 217 p.; 24 cm. 1. Kelley, Florence, 1859-1932. I. T.
HN57.K4 G6　　　301.24/20924 B　　　*LC* 76-23383　　　*ISBN* 0837190118

**Lantz, Herman R.**　　　　　　● 4.5135
People of Coal Town / by Herman R. Lantz with the assistance of J. S. McCrary. New York: Columbia University Press, 1958. 310 p.; 24 cm. 1. Coal miners — United States 2. United States — Social conditions I. T.
HN57.L33　　　*LC* 58-7169

**Lasch, Christopher.**　　　　　　4.5136
The agony of the American left. — [1st ed.]. — New York: Knopf, 1969. ix, 212, viii p.; 22 cm. 1. Radicalism — U.S. 2. U.S. — Social conditions. I. T.
HN57.L37　　　301.15/3　　　*LC* 69-10708

*[handwritten in margin: HN 57 L37]*

**Lynd, Robert Staughton, 1892-.**　　　　　　● 4.5137
Middletown: a study in contemporary American culture / by Robert S. Lynd and Helen Merrell Lynd; foreword by Clark Wissler. — New York: Harcourt, Brace, 1929. 550 p.; 23 cm. The Institute of social and religious research...financed the investigation.Pref. The city will be called Middletown...and is in the east-north central group of states that includes Ohio, Indiana, Illinois,Michigan, and Wisconsin. 1. Cities and towns — United States. 2. Cost and standard of living — United States. 3. United States — Social conditions I. T.
HN57.L8　　　*LC* 29-26177

**Lynd, Robert Staughton, 1892-.**　　　　　　● 4.5138
Middletown in transition; a study in cultural conflicts, by Robert S. Lynd & Helen Merrell Lynd. New York, Harcourt, Brace and company [c1937] xviii, 604 p. diagr. 24 cm. Illustrated lining-papers. 'First edition.' 1. Cities and towns — United States. 2. Community life 3. United States — Economic conditions — 1918-1945 4. United States — Religion — 1901-1945 5. United States — Social conditions I. Lynd, Helen Merrell, 1896- joint author. II. T.
HN57.L84　　　309.173　　　*LC* 37-27243

## HN57 M–Z

**Main, Jackson Turner.**　　　　　　● 4.5139
The social structure of revolutionary America. — Princeton, N.J.: Princeton University Press, 1965. viii, 330 p.; 21 cm. 1. United States — Social conditions — To 1865 2. United States — Social life and customs — Colonial period, ca. 1600-1775 I. T.
HN57.M265　　　309.173　　　*LC* 65-17146

**Polenberg, Richard.**　　　　　　● 4.5140
War and society: the United States, 1941–1945. — Philadelphia: Lippincott, [1972] 298 p.; 21 cm. — (Critical periods of history) 1. World War, 1939-1945 — Economic aspects — United States. 2. United States — Social conditions — 1933-1945 3. United States — Politics and government — 1933-1945 I. T.
HN57.P568　　　309.1/73/0917　　　*LC* 76-155879　　　*ISBN* 0397472250

**Polsky, Ned.**　　　　　　● 4.5141
Hustlers, beats, and others. — Chicago: Aldine Pub. Co., [1967] 218 p.; 22 cm. — (Observations) 1. Deviant behavior 2. Pool (Game) 3. United States — Social conditions I. T.
HN57.P57　　　301.18　　　*LC* 67-11416

**Sieber, Sam D.**　　　　　　4.5142
Fatal remedies: the ironies of social intervention / Sam D. Sieber. — New York: Plenum Press, c1981. xx, 234 p.; 22 cm. — (Environment, development, and public policy. Public policy and social services.) Includes index. 1. Evaluation research (Social action programs) — United States. 2. Social action 3. United States — Social policy I. T. II. Title: Social intervention. III. Series.
HN57.S52　　　361.6/1/0973 19　　　*LC* 81-13832　　　*ISBN* 0306407175

**Thomas, John L.**　　　　　　4.5143
Alternative America: Henry George, Edward Bellamy, Henry Demarest Lloyd, and the adversary tradition / John L. Thomas. — Cambridge, Mass.: Harvard University Press, c1983. viii, 399 p., [10] p. of plates: ill.; 24 cm. Includes index. 1. George, Henry, 1839-1897. Progress and poverty. 2. Bellamy, Edward, 1850-1898. Looking backward. 3. Lloyd, Henry Demarest, 1847-1903. Wealth against commonwealth. 4. Utopias 5. Social reformers — United States. 6. United States — Social conditions — 1865-1918 I. T.
HN57.T48 1983　　　303.4/84 19　　　*LC* 82-15448　　　*ISBN* 0674016769

**A Vision shared: a classic portrait of America and its people,**　　　4.5144
**1935–1943 / Text by Hank O'Neal; foreword by Bernarda**
**Shahn; afterword by Paul S. Taylor; photos. & comments by**
**John Collier ... [et al.].**
New York: St. Martin's Press, c1976. 309 p.: ill.; 33 cm. A collection of photos. taken by the photographers of the U.S. Farm Security Administration. Includes index. 1. Photography, Documentary 2. Photographers — United States — Biography. 3. United States — Rural conditions — Pictorial works I. O'Neal, Hank. II. Collier, John, 1913- III. United States. Farm Security Administration.
HN57.V54　　　779/.9/3091730917　　　*LC* 76-5381

**Warner, W. Lloyd (William Lloyd), 1898-1970.**　　　　　　● 4.5145
Democracy in Jonesville; a study of quality and inequality, by W. Lloyd Warner with the collaboration of Wilfrid C. Bailey [and others. 1st ed.] New York, Harper [1949] xviii, 313 p. diagrs. 22 cm. 1. Community life 2. Democracy 3. United States — Social conditions — 1945- I. T.
HN57.W3　　　309.173　　　*LC* 49-10212

**Warner, W. Lloyd (William Lloyd), 1898-1970.**　　　　　　● 4.5146
Yankee City / by W. Lloyd Warner [and others] New Haven: Yale University Press, 1963. 432 p.: ill.; 21 cm. (A Yale paperbound, Y-72) 'One volume, abridged edition, selected and edited by W. Lloyd Warner.' 1. Social classes — United States. 2. Corporations — United States 3. Minorities — United States 4. United States — Social conditions I. T.
HN57.W34　　　301.36　　　*LC* 63-7588

**Watson, J. Wreford (James Wreford), 1915-.**　　　　　　4.5147
Social geography of the United States / J. Wreford Watson. — London; New York: Longman, 1979. 290 p.: ill.; 24 cm. 1. Anthropo-geography — United States. 2. Minorities — United States — History. 3. Social problems 4. United States — Social conditions I. T.
HN57.W352　　　309.1/73　　　*LC* 77-30747　　　*ISBN* 0582481961

**Weiss, Richard, 1934-.**　　　　　　● 4.5148
The American myth of success: from Horatio Alger to Norman Vincent Peale. — New York: Basic Books [1969] 276 p.; 22 cm. 1. Success — United States. 2. Success in literature 3. United States — Social conditions I. T.
HN57.W45　　　309.1/73　　　*LC* 73-78457

**Withers, Carl.**　　　　　　● 4.5149
Plainville, U. S. A. [by] James West [pseud.] New York, Columbia university press [c1945] 238 p. ill. 1. Cities and towns — United States. 2. Social surveys 3. United States — Social conditions I. T.
HN57.W58　　　301.35　　　*LC* a 45-1863 rev

## HN58 1945–1960

**Domhoff, G. William.**　　　　　　● 4.5150
The higher circles; the governing class in America, by G. William Domhoff. — [1st ed.]. — New York: Random House, [1970] xii, 367 p.; 22 cm. 1. Upper

classes — U.S. 2. U.S. — Social conditions — 1945- 3. U.S. — Foreign relations — 1945- 4. U.S. — Politics and government — 1945- I. T.
HN58.D575      301.44      *LC* 79-102332

**Domhoff, G. William.**                                                                    • **4.5151**
Who rules America? [By] G. William Domhoff. — Englewood Cliffs, N.J.: Prentice-Hall, [1967] 184 p.; 21 cm. — (A Spectrum book) 1. Upper classes — U.S. 2. United States — Social conditions — 1945- 3. United States — Economic conditions — 1945- 4. United States — Politics and government — 1945- I. T.
HN58.D58      301.44/0973      *LC* 67-25926

**Harrington, Michael, 1928-.**                                                             **4.5152**
The next America: the decline and rise of the United States / Michael Harrington; photographs by Bob Adelman; designed by Neil Shakery. — 1st ed. — New York: Holt, Rinehart, and Winston, c1981. vi, 154 p.: ill.; 23 x 29 cm. 1. Radicalism — United States. 2. United States — Social conditions — 1945- 3. United States — Politics and government — 1945- I. Adelman, Bob. II. T.
HN58.H245 1981      973.92 19      *LC* 81-1086      *ISBN* 0030574684

**Henry, Jules, 1904-1969.**                                                               • **4.5153**
Culture against man. — New York: Random House, [1963] xiv, 495 p.; 22 cm. 1. National characteristics, American 2. United States — Social conditions — 1945- 3. United States — Civilization — 1945- I. T.
HN58.H4      309.173      *LC* 63-8268

**Jones, Landon Y., 1943-.**                                                               **4.5154**
Great expectations: America and the baby boom generation / Landon Y. Jones. — New York: Ballantine Books, 1981, c1980. viii, 453 p., [4] p. of plates: ill.; 18 cm. Includes index. 1. Youth — United States 2. Fertility, Human — United States. 3. United States — Social conditions — 1945-1960. 4. United States — Economic conditions — 1945- 5. United States — Population I. T.
HN58.J66      973.92      *ISBN* 0345297504

**Sundquist, James L.**                                                                    • **4.5155**
Politics and policy: the Eisenhower, Kennedy, and Johnson years / [by] James L. Sundquist. — Washington: Brookings Institution [1968] viii, 560 p.: ill.; 24 cm. 1. United States — Social conditions — 1945- 2. United States — Politics and government — 1945- I. Brookings Institution. II. T.
HN58.S8      309.1/73      *LC* 68-31837

# HN59 1960–

**U.S. National Commission on the Causes and Prevention of**                               • **4.5156**
**Violence.**
To establish justice, to insure domestic tranquility; final report. — Washington;: For sale by the Supt. of Docs., U.S. Govt. Print. Off., [1969] xxxii, 338 p.: ill., ports.; 24 cm. 1. Violence — U.S. I. T.
HN59.A514      301      *LC* 75-604476

**Califano, Joseph A., 1931-.**                                                            **4.5157**
Governing America: an insider's report from the White House and the Cabinet / Joseph A. Califano, Jr. — New York: Simon and Schuster, c1981. 474 p., [4] p. of plates: ill.; 24 cm. Includes index. 1. Califano, Joseph A., 1931- 2. United States. Dept. of Health, Education, and Welfare. 3. Social legislation — United States. 4. United States — Social policy I. T.
HN59.C26      361.6/1/0973 19      *LC* 81-652      *ISBN* 0671254286

**Clecak, Peter.**                                                                         **4.5158**
America's quest for the ideal self: dissent and fulfillment in the 60s and 70s / Peter Clecak. — New York: Oxford University Press, 1983. xii, 395 p.; 22 cm. 1. United States — Social conditions — 1945- 2. United States — Civilization — 1945- I. T.
HN59.C57 1983      973.92 19      *LC* 82-14532      *ISBN* 0195032268

**Harris, Marvin, 1927-.**                                                                 **4.5159**
America now: the anthropology of a changing culture / Marvin Harris. — New York: Simon and Schuster, c1981. 208 p.; 23 cm. Includes index. 1. United States — Social conditions — 1980- I. T.
HN59.H27      973.92 19      *LC* 81-9132      *ISBN* 067143148X

**Hodgson, Godfrey.**                                                                      **4.5160**
America in our time / Godfrey Hodgson. 1st ed. — Garden City, N.Y.: Doubleday, 1976. x, 564 p.; 24 cm. Includes index. 1. United States — Social conditions — 1960- 2. United States — Civilization — 1945- 3. United States — Politics and government — 1945- 4. United States — Foreign relations — 1945- I. T.
HN59.H59      309.1/73/092      *LC* 75-36625      *ISBN* 0385115725

**Patterson, James T.**                                                                    **4.5161**
America's struggle against poverty, 1900–1980 / James T. Patterson. — Cambridge, Mass.: Harvard University Press, 1981. ix, 268 p.; 24 cm. Includes

index. 1. Public welfare — United States — History — 20th century. 2. United States — Social policy 3. United States — Economic conditions I. T.
HN59.P39      361/.973 19      *LC* 81-4620      *ISBN* 0674031202

**Reich, Charles A.**                                                                      **4.5162**
The greening of America; how the youth revolution is trying to make America livable [by] Charles A. Reich. — [1st ed.]. — New York: Random House, [1970] 399 p.; 22 cm. 1. Young adults — U.S. 2. Youth — U.S. 3. U.S. — Social conditions — 1960- I. T.
HN59.R38      309.1/73      *LC* 71-117689      *ISBN* 0394427300

**Skolnick, Jerome H.**                                                                    • **4.5163**
The politics of protest; a report, submitted by Jerome H. Skolnick. — New York: Simon and Schuster, [1969] xxvii, 419 p.: illus.; 22 cm. Commonly known as the Skolnick report. Report submitted by the director of the Task Force on Violent Aspects of Protest and Confrontation of the National Commission on the Causes and Prevention of Violence. 1. Violence — U.S. 2. U.S. — Social conditions — 1960- I. U.S. Task Force on Demonstrations, Protests, and Group Violence. II. T. III. Title: Skolnick report on violent aspects of protest and confrontation.
HN59.S5 1969      309.1/73      *LC* 75-91304      *ISBN* 0671203819

**Teodori, Massimo, 1938- comp.**                                                          **4.5164**
The new left: a documentary history. — Indianapolis: Bobbs-Merrill, [1969] xiv, 501 p.; 24 cm. 1. Radicalism — U.S. — Addresses, essays, lectures. 2. U.S. — Social conditions — 1960- — Addresses, essays, lectures. I. T.
HN59.T46      301.15/3/0973      *LC* 70-81291

**Urban America.**                                                                         • **4.5165**
One year later: an assessment of the Nation's response to the crisis described by the National Advisory Commission on Civil Disorders / [by] Urban America, and the Urban Coalition; forewords by John W. Gardner and Terry Sanford. — New York: Praeger [1969] xi, 122 p.; 22 cm. 1. Afro-Americans — Economic conditions 2. Afro-Americans — Social conditions 3. United States — Social conditions — 1960- I. Urban Coalition. II. T.
HN59.U7      309.1/73      *LC* 71-82148

**Yankelovich, Daniel.**                                                                   **4.5166**
New rules, searching for self-fulfillment in a world turned upside down / Daniel Yankelovich. — 1st ed. — New York: Random House, c1981. xxi, 278 p.: ill.; 24 cm. 1. Self-realization 2. United States — Social conditions — 1960- 3. United States — Moral conditions I. T.
HN59.Y33 1981      973 19      *LC* 80-6011      *ISBN* 0394502035

**Ordinary people and everyday life: perspectives on the new**                             **4.5167**
**social history / edited by James B. Gardner and George Rollie**
**Adams.**
Nashville, Tenn.: American Association for State and Local History, c1983. viii, 215 p.: ill.; 24 cm. 1. United States — Social conditions — 1960- — Addresses, essays, lectures. 2. United States — Historiography — Addresses, essays, lectures. I. Gardner, James B., 1950- II. Adams, George Rollie. III. American Association for State and Local History.
HN59.2.O72 1983      973 19      *LC* 83-3707      *ISBN* 091005066X

# HN61–65 Social Reform Literature

**Addams, Jane, 1860-1935.**                                                               • **4.5168**
Democracy and social ethics / edited by Anne Firor Scott. — Cambridge: Belknap Press of Harvard University Press, 1964. lxxvii, 281 p.; 19 cm. 1. Social sciences 2. Social ethics 3. United States — Social conditions I. T.
HN64.A2 1907a      *LC* 64-25050

**Commager, Henry Steele, 1902- ed.**                                                      • **4.5169**
The era of reform, 1830–1860. — Princeton, N.J.: Van Nostrand, [1960] 192 p.; 19 cm. — (Van Nostrand anvil books no. 48) 1. Social reformers — United States. 2. United States — Social conditions — To 1865 I. T.
HN64.C727      335      *LC* 60-13458

**Croly, Herbert David, 1869-1930.**                                                       • **4.5170**
The promise of American life / Edited by Arthur M. Schlesinger, Jr. — Cambridge: Belknap Press of Harvard University Press, 1965. xxvii, 468 p.; 22 cm. (John Harvard library.) Bibliographical footnotes. 1. United States — Politics and government 2. United States — Social conditions I. T. II. Series.
HN64.C89 1965      320.973      *LC* 65-13851

**Gamson, William A.**                                                                     **4.5171**
The strategy of social protest / William A. Gamson. — Homewood, Ill.: Dorsey Press, 1975. xiv, 217 p.: graphs; 23 cm. (The Dorsey series in sociology) Includes index. 1. Pressure groups 2. Social movements 3. Pluralism (Social sciences) 4. Elite (Social sciences) I. T.
HN64.G23      301.24/2      *LC* 74-12926      *ISBN* 0256016844

**Lasch, Christopher.** • **4.5172**
The new radicalism in America, 1889–1963: the intellectual as a social type. [1st ed.] New York: Knopf, 1965. xviii, 349, ix p.; 22 cm. 1. Intellectuals — United States. 2. Progressivism (United States politics) 3. United States — Social conditions 4. United States — Civilization — 20th century I. T.
HN64.L29    301.153    *LC* 65-11126

**Lippmann, Walter, 1889-.** • **4.5173**
Drift and mastery: an attempt to diagnose the current unrest / with an introd. and notes by William E. Leuchtenburg. — Englewood Cliffs, N.J.: Prentice-Hall, [1961] 177 p.; 21 cm. — (A Spectrum book: Classics in history series, S-CH-2) 1. United States — Social conditions 2. United States — Politics and government I. T.
HN64.L53 1961    309.173    *LC* 61-14156

**Lippmann, Walter, 1889-.** • **4.5174**
A preface to politics. [Ann Arbor]: University of Michigan Press [1962] 238 p.; 21 cm. (Ann Arbor paperbacks, AA65) 1. Social problems 2. United States — Politics and government I. T.
HN64.L55 1962    *LC* 62-2937

**Woodhull, Victoria C. (Victoria Claflin), 1838-1927.**    **4.5175**
The Victoria Woodhull reader / edited by Madeleine B. Stern. — Weston, Mass.: M&S Press, 1974. 640 p. in various pagings: ill.; 24 cm. 1. United States — Social conditions — 1865-1918 — Addresses, essays, lectures. I. T.
HN64.M393 1974    309.1/73/08    *LC* 74-193236    *ISBN* 0877300097

**Sumner, William Graham, 1840-1910.** • **4.5176**
What social classes owe to each other. — New York: Arno Press, 1972. 169 p.; 22 cm. — (The Right wing individualist tradition in America) Reprint of the 1883 ed. 1. Social ethics 2. Economics I. T. II. Series.
HN64.S9 1972    301.44    *LC* 70-172234    *ISBN* 0405004435

**Walters, Ronald G.**    **4.5177**
American reformers, 1815–1860 / Ronald G. Walters; consulting editor, Eric Foner. — 1st ed. — New York: Hill and Wang, 1978. xiv, 235 p.; 22 cm. — (American century series) Includes index. 1. Social reformers — United States — History. I. T.
HN64.W2136 1978    301.24/2/0973    *LC* 78-7545    *ISBN* 0809025574

**Weinberg, Arthur, 1915- comp.** • **4.5178**
The muckrakers: the era in journalism that moved America to reform, the most significant magazine articles of 1902–1912 / edited and with notes by Arthur and Lila Weinberg. — New York: Simon and Schuster, 1961. 449 p.; 25 cm. 1. Corruption (in politics) — United States 2. United States — Social conditions — 1865-1918 I. Weinberg, Lila Shaffer. joint comp. II. T.
HN64.W433    309.173    *LC* 61-16557

## HN65 1945-

**Alinsky, Saul David, 1909-1972.**    **4.5179**
Rules for radicals; a practical primer for realistic radicals [by] Saul D. Alinsky. — [1st ed.]. — New York: Random House, [1971] xxvi, 196 p.; 22 cm. 1. Community organization 2. Political participation — United States. 3. Radicalism — United States. I. T.
HN65.A675    301.5    *LC* 70-117651    *ISBN* 0394443411

**American social attitudes data sourcebook, 1947–1978 / Philip**    **4.5180**
**E. Converse ... [et at.].**
Cambridge, Mass.: Harvard University Press, 1980. xi, 441 p.: graphs; 31 cm. Chiefly tables. 1. Public opinion — United States. 2. United States — Social conditions — 1945- 1. Public opinion. I. Converse, Philip E., 1928-
HN65.A6819    303.3/8/0973 19    *LC* 79-25398    *ISBN* 0674028805

**Clark, Kenneth Bancroft, 1914-.**    **4.5181**
Pathos of power [by] Kenneth B. Clark. — [1st ed.]. — New York: Harper & Row, [1974] xviii, 188 p.; 22 cm. 1. Power (Social sciences) 2. Social ethics 3. Social scientists 4. United States — Social conditions I. T.
HN65.C53 1974    155.2/34    *LC* 73-14250    *ISBN* 0060107995

**Discrimination in organizations / Rodolfo Alvarez, Kenneth G.**    **4.5182**
**Lutterman, and associates.**
1st ed. — San Francisco: Jossey-Bass, c1979. xxvi, 425 p. — (Jossey-Bass social and behavioral science series.) Includes index. 1. Racism — United States. 2. Sexism — United States. 3. Social indicators — United States. 4. Organizational behavior 5. Organizational change I. Alvarez, Rodolfo, 1936- II. Lutterman, Kenneth G. III. Series.
HN65.D496    HN65 D496.    301.18/32    *LC* 78-62567    *ISBN* 0875894291

**Etzioni, Amitai.**    **4.5183**
Social problems / Amitai Etzioni. — Englewood Cliffs, N.J.: Prentice-Hall, c1976. x, 182 p.; 23 cm. (Prentice-Hall foundations of modern sociology series) 1. Social problems 2. Sociology — Methodology 3. Social policy 4. United States — Social conditions — 1960- I. T.
HN65.E88    309.1/73/092    *LC* 75-38703    *ISBN* 0138174113

**Heidenheimer, Arnold J.**    **4.5184**
Comparative public policy: the politics of social choice in Europe and America / Arnold J. Heidenheimer, Hugh Heclo, Carolyn Teich Adams. — 2nd ed. — New York: St. Martin's Press, c1983. xvi, 367 p.: ill.; 24 cm. Includes index. 1. United States — Social policy 2. Europe — Social policy. I. Heclo, Hugh. II. Adams, Carolyn Teich. III. T.
HN65.H4 1983    361.6/1/094 19    *LC* 82-60471    *ISBN* 031215366X

**Hollander, Paul, 1932-.**    **4.5185**
Soviet and American society; a comparison. New York, Oxford University Press, 1973. xx, 476 p. 24 cm. 1. United States — Social conditions — 1960- 2. Soviet Union — Social conditions I. T.
HN65.H56    309.1/47    *LC* 72-96610

**Lasch, Christopher.**    **4.5186**
The culture of narcissism: American life in an age of diminishing expectations / Christopher Lasch. — 1st ed. — New York: Norton, 1979 (c1978) xviii, 268 p.; 22 cm. 1. Social values 2. United States — Social conditions — 1960- 3. United States — Moral conditions I. T.
HN65.L33 1978    309.1/73/092    *LC* 78-16233    *ISBN* 0393011771

**Marris, Peter.**    **4.5187**
Dilemmas of social reform: poverty and community action in the United States / [by] Peter Marris and Martin Rein. — 2d ed. — Chicago: Aldine Pub. Co., [1973] x, 309 p.; 22 cm. 1. Community organization — Case studies. 2. Poor — United States. 3. United States — Social policy I. Rein, Martin. joint author. II. T.
HN65.M3 1973    361/.973    *LC* 72-78217    *ISBN* 0202302555

**Ryan, William, 1923-.**    **4.5188**
Blaming the victim / by William Ryan. Rev., updated ed. — New York: Vintage Books, 1976. xv, 351 p.; 18 cm. 1. United States — Social conditions — 1960- I. T.
HN65.R9 1976    309.1/73/092    *LC* 76-378867    *ISBN* 0394717627

**Savitch, H. V.**    **4.5189**
Urban policy and the exterior city: Federal, State, and corporate impacts upon major cities / H. V. Savitch. — New York: Pergamon Press, c1979. xv, 359 p.: ill.; 24 cm. — (Pergamon policy studies on urban affairs; no. 41) 1. Urban policy — United States. 2. Power (Social sciences) I. T. II. Series.
HN65.S32 1979    301.36/3    *LC* 79-11552    *ISBN* 0080233902

**Theobald, Robert.**    **4.5190**
Beyond despair: a policy guide to the communications era / Robert Theobald. — Rev. ed. — Cabin John, Md.: Seven Locks Press, c1981. xxix, 167 p.; 24 cm. Includes index. 1. Communication — Social aspects 2. Communication — Psychological aspects 3. Twenty-first century — Forecasts 4. United States — Social policy 5. United States — Economic policy I. T.
HN65.T443 1981    973.92 19    *LC* 81-5348    *ISBN* 0932020046

**Thernstrom, Stephan.** • **4.5191**
Poverty and progress: social mobility in a nineteenth century city. — Cambridge: Harvard University Press, 1964. xii, 286 p.; 22 cm. (A Publication of the Joint Center for Urban Studies of the Massachusetts Institute of Technology and Harvard University) 1. Social mobility — United States. 2. Newburyport (Mass.) I. T.
HN65.T45    309.17445    *LC* 64-21793

**Turner, Jonathan H.**    **4.5192**
American society: problems of structure [by] Jonathan H. Turner. — New York, Harper & Row [1972] xix, 299 p. 24 cm. 1. United States — Social conditions — 1960- 2. United States — Civilization — 1945- I. T.
HN65.T87    309.1/73/092    *LC* 72-84323    *ISBN* 0060467134

# HN79–80 Local History and Conditions

## HN79 By Region or State, A–Z

**Barron, Hal S.**    **4.5193**
Those who stayed behind: rural society in nineteenth–century New England / Hal S. Barron. — Cambridge [Cambridgeshire]; New York: Cambridge University Press, 1984. xiii, 184 p.: ill.; 24 cm. — (Interdisciplinary perspectives on modern history.) Includes index. 1. Rural-urban migration — New England — History — 19th century — Case studies. 2. Chelsea (Vt.: Town) — History. 3. New England — Population, Rural — Case studies. 4. New England — Rural conditions — Case studies. I. T. II. Series.
HN79.A11 B37 1984    307.7/2/0974 19    *LC* 83-26354    *ISBN* 0521257840

**The Invisible minority: urban Appalachians / ed. by William W.**   **4.5194**
**Philliber & Clyde B. McCoy; with Harry C. Dillingham.**
Lexington, Ky.: University Press of Kentucky, c1981. 192 p.; 24 cm. Papers from a conference sponsored by the Academy for Contemporary Problems and the Urban Appalachian Council, held in Columbus, Ohio, Mar. 27-29, 1974. Includes index. 1. Rural-urban migration — United States — Congresses. 2. Mountain whites (Southern States) — Congresses. 3. Appalachian Region — Social conditions — Congresses. I. Philliber, William W., 1943- II. McCoy, Clyde B., 1941- III. Dillingham, Harry C.
HN79.A13 I58      974      *LC* 79-4008      *ISBN* 0813113954

**McKinney, John C., 1920- ed.**      • **4.5195**
The South in continuity and change / edited by John C. McKinney and Edgar T. Thompson. — Durham, N.C.: Duke University Press, 1965. xii, 511 p.: maps; 24 cm. 1. Southern States — Social conditions 2. Southern States — Economic conditions I. Thompson, Edgar Tristan, 1900- joint ed. II. Southern Sociological Society (U.S.) III. Duke University, Durham, N.C. Center for Southern Studies in the Social Sciences and the Humanities. IV. T.
HN79.A13 M214      *LC* 65-19448

**Olmsted South, old South critic, new South planner / edited by**   **4.5196**
**Dana F. White and Victor A. Kramer; [visual materials**
**compiled and arr. by Howard L. Preston and Dana F. White,**
**with Colleen Keegan].**
Westport, Conn.: Greenwood Press, 1979. xxxvi, 259 p.: ill.; 24 cm. (Contributions in American studies; no. 43 0084-9227) 'About Olmsted, a bibliographical essay': p. [247]-252. 1. Olmsted, Frederick Law, 1822-1903. 2. Regional planning — Southern States. 3. Civic improvement — Southern States. 4. Social scientists — United States — Biography. 5. Landscape architects — United States — Biography. 6. Southern States — Social conditions I. White, Dana F. II. Kramer, Victor A.
HN79.A13 O55      309.2/5/0924      *LC* 78-20019      *ISBN* 0313207240

**Such as us: Southern voices of the thirties / edited by Tom E.**   **4.5197**
**Terrill, Jerrold Hirsch.**
Chapel Hill: University of North Carolina Press, c1978. xxvi, 302 p.: ill.; 24 cm. Includes index. 1. Southern States — Social conditions — Case studies. I. Terrill, Tom E. II. Hirsch, Jerrold, 1948-
HN79.A13 S87      309.1/75      *LC* 77-14248      *ISBN* 0807813184

**Davis, Allison, 1902-.**      • **4.5198**
Deep South: a social anthropological study of caste and class / written by Allison Davis, Burleigh B. Gardner and Mary R. Gardner; directed by W. Lloyd Warner. — Chicago, Ill.: The University of Chicago press [1941] xv, 558 p. incl. tables, diagrs., forms; 20 cm. 1. Afro-Americans — Southern States 2. Southern States — Social conditions 3. Southern States — Economic conditions I. Gardner, Burleigh B. (Burleigh Bradford), 1902- joint author. II. Gardner, Mary R., joint author. III. Warner, W. Lloyd (William Lloyd), 1898-1970. ed. IV. T.
HN79.A2 D3      309.175      *LC* 41-23645

**Herring, Harriet Laura.**      • **4.5199**
Passing of the mill village: revolution in a Southern institution. — Chapel Hill: University of North Carolina Press [1949] vii, 137 p.; 21 cm. 1. Villages — Southern States. 2. Cotton manufacture — Southern States. 3. Southern States — Social conditions I. T.
HN79.A2 H4      *LC* 50-5080

**Ladd, Everett Carll.**      • **4.5200**
Ideology in America: change and response in a city, a suburb, and a small town ... — [1st ed.] Ithaca: Cornell University Press [1969] xlii, 378 p.: ill.; 22 cm. 1. Ideology — Case studies. 2. Connecticut — Social conditions — Case studies. 3. Connecticut — Politics and government — 1951- — Case studies. I. T.
HN79.C8 L3      309.1/746      *LC* 69-18214

**Curti, Merle Eugene, 1897-.**      • **4.5201**
The making of an American community: a case study of democracy in a frontier county / by Merle Curti; with the assistance of Robert Daniel [and others]. — Stanford, Calif.: Stanford University Press, 1959. vii, 483 p.: maps, diagrs.; 25 cm. 1. Democracy 2. Frontier and pioneer life — Case studies. 3. Trempealeau County (Wis.) — Social conditions. I. T.
HN79.W62 T73      309.177549      *LC* 59-5051

## HN80 By City, A–Z

**Holmes, Richard, 1951-.**      **4.5202**
Communities in transition: Bedford and Lincoln Massachusetts, 1729–1850 / by Richard Holmes. — Ann Arbor, Mich.: UMI Research Press, c1980. vi, 213 p.; 24 cm. (Studies in American history and culture; no. 16) Includes index. 1. Social change — Case studies. 2. Bedford (Mass.) — Rural conditions. 3. Lincoln (Mass.) — Rural conditions. I. T. II. Series.
HN80.B45 H64 1980      307.7/2/097444      *LC* 80-18459      *ISBN* 083571098X

**Gans, Herbert J.**      • **4.5203**
The urban villagers: group and class in the life of Italian–Americans / foreword by Erich Lindemann. — [New York]: Free Press of Glencoe, [1962] xvi, 367 p.; 22 cm. 1. Sociology, Urban 2. Italian Americans — Massachusetts. I. T.
HN80.B7 G2      301.45      *LC* 62-15362

**Story, Ronald.**      **4.5204**
The forging of an aristocracy: Harvard & the Boston upper class, 1800–1870 / Ronald Story. — 1st ed. — Middletown, Conn.: Wesleyan University Press; Irvington, N.Y.: distributed by Columbia University Press, c1980. xv, 256 p.; 24 cm. 1. Harvard University — History — 19th century. 2. Elite (Social sciences) — Massachusetts — Boston — History — 19th century. 3. Elite (Social sciences) — New England — History — 19th century. 4. Boston (Mass.) — Social conditions. I. T.
HN80.B7 S76      305.5/2/09 19      *LC* 80-460      *ISBN* 0819550442

**Thernstrom, Stephan.**      **4.5205**
The other Bostonians: poverty and progress in the American metropolis, 1880–1970. — Cambridge, Mass.: Harvard University Press, 1973. xvi, 345 p.; 25 cm. (Harvard studies in urban history.) 1. Social mobility — United States. 2. Social classes — United States. 3. Occupational mobility 4. Boston (Mass.) — Social conditions. I. T. II. Series.
HN80.B7 T45      301.44/0973      *LC* 73-77469      *ISBN* 0674644956

**Warner, Sam Bass, 1928-.**      • **4.5206**
Streetcar suburbs: the process of growth in Boston, 1870–1900. Cambridge, Harvard University Press, 1962. xxi, 208 p. illus., maps, tables. 25 cm. (Publications of the Joint Center for Urban Studies) 1. Boston Suburban Area (Mass.) — History. I. T.
HN80.B7 W3      *LC* 62-17228

**Fish, John Hall, 1932-.**      **4.5207**
Black power/white control; the struggle of the Woodlawn Organization in Chicago, by John Hall Fish. Princeton, N.J., Princeton University Press [1973] xii, 356 p. 23 cm. (Studies in religion and society) 1. Woodlawn Organization. 2. Black power — Illinois — Chicago. I. T.
HN80.C5 F58      322.4/4/0977311      *LC* 72-5379      *ISBN* 069109358X

**Hunter, Albert.**      **4.5208**
Symbolic communities: the persistence and change of Chicago's local communities / Albert Hunter; with a foreword by Morris Janowitz. — Chicago: University of Chicago Press, 1974. xviii, 253 p.: ill.; 23 cm. — (Studies of urban society) Includes index. 1. Community organization — Illinois — Chicago. 2. Social structure — Illinois — Chicago. 3. Chicago — Social conditions. I. T.
HN80.C5 H85      301.36/0977311      *LC* 74-75612      *ISBN* 0226360806

**Slayton, Robert A.**      **4.5209**
Back of the yards: the making of a local democracy / Robert A. Slayton. — Chicago: University of Chicago Press, c1986. xiv, 278 p., [24] p. of plates: ill.; 24 cm. Includes index. 1. Community organization — Illinois — Chicago — Case studies. 2. Packing-house workers — Illinois — Chicago — Case studies. 3. Neighborhood — Illinois — Chicago — Case studies. I. T.
HN80.C5 S56 1986      307/.14/0977311 19      *LC* 85-16518      *ISBN* 0226761983

**Suttles, Gerald D.**      • **4.5210**
The social order of the slum; ethnicity and territory in the inner city [by] Gerald D. Suttles. Chicago, University of Chicago Press [1968] xxii, 243 p. illus. 24 cm. (Studies of urban society) 1. Slums — Illinois — Chicago. 2. Poor — Illinois — Chicago. 3. Minorities — Illinois — Chicago. 4. Chicago (Ill.) — Social conditions. I. T.
HN80.C5 S97      309.1/773/11      *LC* 68-26762

**Wolf, Stephanie Grauman.**      **4.5211**
Urban village: population, community and family structure in Germantown, Pennsylvania, 1683–1800 / [by] Stephanie Grauman Wolf. Princeton; Guildford: Princeton University Press, [1977] xi, 361, [1] p.: ill., map; 23 cm. Index. 1. Germantown, Pa. — Social conditions. I. T.
HN80.G46W6x      309.1/748/11      *LC* 76-3025      *ISBN* 0691046328

**Blumin, Stuart M.**      **4.5212**
The urban threshold: growth and change in a nineteenth–century American community / Stuart M. Blumin. — Chicago: University of Chicago Press, c1976. 298 p.: ill.; 23 cm. Includes index. 1. Cities and towns — United States — Case studies. 2. Urbanization — United States — Case studies. 3. Kingston (N.Y.) — Social conditions. 4. Kingston (N.Y.) — Economic conditions. I. T.
HN80.K5 B55 1976      309.1/747/34      *LC* 75-27891      *ISBN* 0226061698

**Gans, Herbert J.**      • **4.5213**
The Levittowners: ways of life and politics in a new suburban community / by Herbert J. Gans. — New York: Pantheon Books, [1967] xxix, 474 p.; 25 cm. 1. Suburban life — Case studies. 2. Willingboro. I. T.
HN80.L4 G3      301.3/62/0974961      *LC* 66-17359

**Shevky, Eshref.** • **4.5214**
The social areas of Los Angeles: analysis and typology / by Eshref Shevky and Marilyn Williams. — Westport, Conn.: Greenwood Press [1972, c1949] xvi, 172 p.: ill.; 23 cm. 'Published for the John Randolph Haynes and Dora Haynes Foundation.' 1. Los Angeles (Calif.) — Social conditions. I. Williams, Marilyn, 1921- joint author. II. T.
HN80.L7 S5 1972     309.1/794/94     *LC* 72-138180     *ISBN* 0837156378

**Philadelphia: work, space, family, and group experience in the** **4.5215**
**nineteenth/century: essays toward an interdisciplinary history of**
**the city / edited by Theodore Hershberg.**
New York: Oxford University Press, 1981. xviii, 525 p.: ill.; 25 cm. Essays based on data compiled by the Philadelphia Social History Project. Includes index. 1. Philadelphia (Pa.) — Social conditions — Addresses, essays, lectures. 2. Philadelphia (Pa.) — Economic conditions — Addresses, essays, lectures. 3. Philadelphia (Pa.) — Population — History — 19th century — Addresses, essays, lectures. I. Hershberg, Theodore. II. Philadelphia Social History Project.
HN80.P5 P48     974.8/11041     *LC* 80-10843     *ISBN* 0195027523

**Ahlbrandt, Roger S.** **4.5216**
Neighborhoods, people, and community / Roger S. Ahlbrandt, Jr. — New York: Plenum Press, c1984. xvii, 238 p.: ill.; 22 cm. — (Environment, development, and public policy. Cities and development.) Includes index. 1. Neighborhood — Pennsylvania — Pittsburgh. 2. Urban policy — Pennsylvania — Pittsburgh. 3. Community life 4. Community organization 5. Pittsburgh (Pa.) — Social conditions. I. T. II. Series.
HN80.P6 A35 1984     307/.3362/0974886 19     *LC* 84-8339     *ISBN* 0306415429

**Bodnar, John E., 1944-.** **4.5217**
Immigration and industrialization: ethnicity in an American mill town, 1870–1940 / John Bodnar. — Pittsburgh: University of Pittsburgh Press, c1977. xix, 213 p.; 22 cm. Includes index. 1. Social classes — Pennsylvania — Steelton — History. 2. Alien labor — Pennsylvania — Steelton — History. 3. Iron and steel workers — Pennsylvania — Steelton — History. 4. Steelton, Pa — Social conditions. I. T.
HN80.S78 B6     309.1/748/18     *LC* 77-74549     *ISBN* 0822933489

# HN90 Special Topics, A–Z

## HN90.C6 Community

**Downs, Anthony.** **4.5218**
Neighborhoods and urban development / Anthony Downs. — Washington, D.C.: Brookings Institution, c1981. xii, 189 p.: ill.; 24 cm. 1. Community development, Urban — United States. 2. Urbanization — United States. I. T.
HN90.C6 D68     307.7/6/0973 19     *LC* 81-66190     *ISBN* 0815719205

**Kettl, Donald F.** **4.5219**
The regulation of American federalism / Donald F. Kettl. — Baton Rouge: Louisiana State University Press, c1983. xviii, 195 p.; 24 cm. — (Miller Center series on the American presidency.) Includes index. 1. Federal aid to community development — United States. 2. Block grants — United States. 3. United States — Social policy I. T. II. Series.
HN90.C6 K47 1983     353.0081/8/09746 19     *LC* 83-9904     *ISBN* 080711121X

**Wireman, Peggy.** **4.5220**
Urban neighborhoods, networks, and families: new forms for old values / Peggy Wireman. — Lexington, Mass.: Lexington Books, c1984. xxiii, 194 p.: ill.; 24 cm. Includes index. 1. Neighborhood — United States. 2. Community development, Urban — United States. 3. Family — United States 4. Social interaction — United States. 5. Community life I. T.
HN90.C6 W47 1984     307/.3362/0973 19     *LC* 80-9016     *ISBN* 0669045039

## HN90.E4 Elites

**Domhoff, G. William.** **4.5221**
Who rules America now?: a view for the '80s / G. William Domhoff. — Englewood Cliffs, N.J.: Prentice-Hall, c1983. xi, 230 p.; 23 cm. Continues: Who rules America? 'A Spectrum book.' 1. Elite (Social sciences) — United States. 2. Power (Social sciences) I. T.
HN90.E4 D652 1983     305.5/2/0973 19     *LC* 83-3104     *ISBN* 0139584056

**Dye, Thomas R.** **4.5222**
Who's running America?—the Reagan years / Thomas R. Dye. — 3rd ed. — Englewood Cliffs, N.J.: Prentice-Hall, c1983. xiii, 285 p.; 23 cm. Rev. ed. of: Who's running America?: The Carter years. 2nd ed. c1979. 1. Elite (Social

sciences) — United States. 2. United States — Politics and government — 1981- I. T.
HN90.E4 D93 1983     305.5/2 19     *LC* 82-3853     *ISBN* 0139584706

## HN90.M3 Mass Media

**Czitrom, Daniel J., 1951-.** **4.5223**
Media and the American mind: from Morse to McLuhan / by Daniel J. Czitrom. — Chapel Hill: University of North Carolina Press, c1982. xiv, 254 p.: ill.; 24 cm. Includes index. 1. Mass media — Social aspects — United States. 2. United States — Popular culture I. T.
HN90.M3 C96 1982     302.2/3 19     *LC* 81-14810     *ISBN* 0807815004

**Media power in politics / Doris A. Graber, editor.** **4.5224**
Washington, D.C.: CQ Press, c1984. xii, 348 p. 1. Mass media — Political aspects — United States. 2. Mass media — Social aspects — United States. I. Graber, Doris A. (Doris Appel), 1923-
HN90.M3 G72 1984     302.2/34 19     *LC* 83-23921     *ISBN* 0871872854

## HM90.M6 Morality

**Haller, John S.** **4.5225**
The physician and sexuality in Victorian America [by] John S. Haller, Jr. and Robin M. Haller. — Urbana: University of Illinois Press, [1974] xv, 331 p.: illus.; 24 cm. 1. Women — United States — Social conditions. 2. Women — Health and hygiene 3. Physicians — United States 4. United States — Moral conditions I. Haller, Robin M. joint author. II. T.
HN90.M6 H34 1974     301.41/7973     *LC* 73-2456     *ISBN* 0252002075

## HN90.P8 Public Opinion

**Bennett, W. Lance.** **4.5226**
Public opinion in American politics / W. Lance Bennett; under the general editorship of James David Barber. — New York: Harcourt Brace Jovanovich, c1980. xi, 420 p.: ill.; 22 cm. 1. Public opinion — United States. 2. Public opinion 3. Political socialization — United States. 4. Political socialization I. Barber, James David. II. T.
HN90.P8 B46     HN90P8 B46.     303.3/8     *LC* 79-92686     *ISBN* 0155738100

**Gallup, George Horace, 1901-.** **4.5227**
The Gallup Poll; public opinion, 1935–1971 [by] George H. Gallup. — [1st ed.]. — New York: Random House, [1972] 3 v. (xliv, 2388 p.); 25 cm. 1. Public opinion — United States. I. T.
HN90.P8 G3     301.15/43/32900973     *LC* 77-39867     *ISBN* 0394472705

**Gallup, George Horace, 1901-.** **4.5228**
The Gallup poll: public opinion, 1972–1977 / George H. Gallup. — Wilmington, Del.: Scholarly Resources, 1978. 2 v. (xxxvii, 1334 p.); 25 cm. A complete compilation of all the public opinion polls conducted by the American Institute of Public Opinion, 1972-1977. Includes index. 1. Public opinion — United States. I. American Institute of Public Opinion. II. T.
HN90.P8 G32     301.15/4/0973     *LC* 77-25755     *ISBN* 0842021299

**McClosky, Herbert.** **4.5229**
The American ethos: public attitudes toward capitalism and democracy / Herbert McClosky, John Zaller. — Cambridge, Mass.: Harvard University Press, 1984. xviii, 342 p.: ill.; 24 cm. (Twentieth Century Fund report.) Includes index. 1. Public opinion — United States. 2. Capitalism — Public opinion. 3. Democracy — Public opinion. I. Zaller, John, 1949- II. T. III. Series.
HN90.P8 M4 1984     330.12/2 19     *LC* 84-12793     *ISBN* 0674023307

## HN90.R3 Radicalism

**Adamson, Madeleine, 1951-.** **4.5230**
This mighty dream: social protest movements in the United States / Madeleine Adamson and Seth Borgos. — Boston: Routledge & Kegan Paul, 1984. 143 p.: ill.; 28 cm. 1. Radicalism — United States. 2. Social movements — United States. 3. United States — Social conditions I. Borgos, Seth, 1952- II. T.
HN90.R3 A3 1984     322.4/4/0973 19     *LC* 84-16111     *ISBN* 0710200404

**Baritz, Loren, 1928- comp.** **4.5231**
The American Left: radical political thought in the twentieth century. — New York: Basic Books, [1971] xxi, 522 p.; 24 cm. 1. Radicalism — U.S. — Addresses, essays, lectures. I. T.
HN90.R3 B35     320.5     *LC* 71-158440     *ISBN* 0465001440

**Bouchier, David.**                                           **4.5232**
Idealism and revolution: new ideologies of liberation in Britain and the United States / David Bouchier. — New York: St. Martin's Press, 1978. ix, 190 p.; 23 cm. Includes index. 1. Radicalism — United States. 2. Radicalism — Great Britain. 3. Ideology 4. Social movements I. T.
HN90.R3 B595 1978        301.5/92        *LC* 78-17007        *ISBN* 0312404395

**Clecak, Peter.**                                           **4.5233**
Radical paradoxes: dilemmas of the American left: 1945–1970. — [1st ed.]. — New York: Harper & Row, [1973] x, 358 p.; 22 cm. 1. Radicalism — United States — Addresses, essays, lectures. 2. Right and left (Political science) — Addresses, essays, lectures. I. T.
HN90.R3 C55 1973        322.4/4/0973        *LC* 73-4072        *ISBN* 0060108193

**Dellinger, David T., 1915-.**                                           **4.5234**
More power than we know: the people's movement toward democracy / Dave Dellinger. — 1st ed. — Garden City, N.Y.: Anchor Press, 1975. viii, 326 p.; 22 cm. Includes index. 1. Radicalism — United States. 2. United States — Social conditions — 1960- I. T.
HN90.R3 D47        322.4/4/0973        *LC* 73-173272        *ISBN* 0385001622

**King, R. (Richard)**                                           • **4.5235**
The party of Eros: radical social thought and the realm of freedom. — Chapel Hill: University of North Carolina Press, [1972] 227 p.; 23 cm. 1. Radicalism — United States. 2. United States — Intellectual life I. T.
HN90.R3 K54        301/.01        *LC* 73-174785        *ISBN* 0807811874

**Miller, Sally M., 1937-.**                                           **4.5236**
The radical immigrant, by Sally M. Miller. — New York: Twayne Publishers, [1974] 212 p.; 22 cm. — (The Immigrant heritage of America series) 1. Radicalism — United States — History. 2. United States — Emigration and immigration — History. I. T.
HN90.R3 M5        322.4/4        *LC* 73-15847        *ISBN* 0805732667

## HN90.S6 Social Class

**Gilbert, Dennis.**                                           **4.5237**
The American class structure: a new synthesis / Dennis Gilbert, Joseph A. Kahl. — 3rd ed. — Homewood, Ill.: Dorsey Press, 1987. xvi, 386 p.: ill.; 24 cm. (Dorsey series in sociology.) Rev. ed. of: The American class structure / Joseph Alan Kahl. 1957. Includes indexes. 1. Social classes — United States. 2. United States — Social conditions I. Kahl, Joseph Alan, 1923- II. Kahl, Joseph Alan, 1923- American class structure. III. T. IV. Series.
HN90.S6 G54        305.5/0973 19        *LC* 81-70947        *ISBN* 0256026785

**Jackman, Mary R.**                                           **4.5238**
Class awareness in the United States / Mary R. Jackman and Robert W. Jackman. — Berkeley: University of California Press, 1983. x, 231 p. 1. Social classes — United States. I. Jackman, Robert W., 1946- II. T.
HN90.S6 J3        HN90S6 J3.        305.5/0973 19        *LC* 82-2766        *ISBN* 0520046749

**Jernegan, Marcus Wilson, 1872-1949.**                                           • **4.5239**
Laboring and dependent classes in colonial America, 1607–1783. — New York: Ungar, [1960] 256 p.; 25 cm. — (American classics) 1. Social classes — United States — History. 2. Slavery in the United States. 3. Labor and laboring classes — United States — History. 4. Public schools — United States — History. 5. Public welfare — Law and legislation — United States — History. I. T.
HN90.S6 J47 1960        305.5/6 19        *LC* 60-13985

**Marwick, Arthur, 1936-.**                                           **4.5240**
Class: image and reality in Britain, France, and the USA since 1930 / Arthur Marwick. — New York: Oxford University Press, 1980. 416 p.; 22 cm. Includes index. 1. Social classes — United States. 2. Social classes — Great Britain 3. Social classes — France. I. T.
HN90.S6 M35        305.5/0941 19        *LC* 80-135297        *ISBN* 0195202031

**Power structure research / edited by G. William Domhoff.**                                           **4.5241**
Beverly Hills, Calif.: Sage Publications, c1980. 270 p.; 23 cm. — (Sage focus editions. v. 17) 1. Social classes — United States — Addresses, essays, lectures. 2. Power (Social sciences) — Addresses, essays, lectures. 3. United States — Politics and government — 1974-1977 — Addresses, essays, lectures. I. Domhoff, G. William. II. Series.
HN90.S6 P68        301.44/0973        *LC* 79-25255        *ISBN* 0803914318

**Hauser, Robert Mason.**                                           **4.5242**
The process of stratification: trends and analyses / Robert M. Hauser, David L. Featherman. — New York: Academic Press, c1977. xxviii, 372 p.; 24 cm. — (Studies in population.) 1. Social mobility — United States. 2. Occupational mobility — United States. I. Featherman, David L. joint author. II. T. III. Series.
HN90.S65 H38        301.44/044/0973        *LC* 76-19487        *ISBN* 0123330505

## HN90.V5 Violence

**Fogelson, Robert M.**                                           • **4.5243**
Violence as protest: a study of riots and ghettos / [by] Robert M. Fogelson. — Garden City, N.Y.: Doubleday, 1971. xviii, 265 p.; 22 cm. 1. Violence — U.S. 2. Riots — U.S. 3. U.S. — Social conditions — 1960- I. T.
HN90.V5 F64        301.2        *LC* 72-121579

**Jeffreys-Jones, Rhodri.**                                           **4.5244**
Violence and reform in American history / Rhodri Jeffreys–Jones. — New York: New Viewpoints, 1978. x, 242 p.; 21 cm. Includes index. 1. Violence — United States — History. I. T.
HN90.V5 J43        301.6/33/0973        *LC* 78-4279        *ISBN* 0531054047

**Justifying violence: attitudes of American men / [by] Monica D.**                                           • **4.5245**
**Blumenthal [and others].**
Ann Arbor: Institute for Social Research, the University of Michigan [1972] xii, 367 p.: ill.; 23 cm. 1. Violence — United States. 2. Violence — Research — United States. 3. Attitude (Psychology) I. Blumenthal, Monica D.
HN90.V5 J87        301.15/43/301633072073        *LC* 74-169101        *ISBN* 0879441143 *ISBN* 0879441135

## HN101–110 Canada

**Clark, S. D. (Samuel Delbert), 1910-.**                                           • **4.5246**
The social development of Canada. Toronto, Can., The University of Toronto press, 1942. x, 484 p. 24 cm. 1. Canada — Social conditions 2. Canada — Social life and customs I. T.
HN103.C55        *LC* a 42-3395

**Clark, S. D. (Samuel Delbert), 1910- ed.**                                           • **4.5247**
Urbanism and the changing Canadian society. [Toronto] University of Toronto Press [1961] 150 p. 1. Cities and towns — Canada — Addresses, essays, lectures 2. Canada — Social conditions — Addresses, essays, lectures I. T.
HN103 C57        *LC* 61-66023

**Porter, John A.**                                           • **4.5248**
The vertical mosaic; an analysis of social class and power in Canada [by] John Porter. — [Toronto] University of Toronto Press [1965] xxi, 626 p. 24 cm. — (Studies in the structure of power, decision-making in Canada. no. 2) Bibliographical footnotes. 1. Canada — Soc. condit. 2. Social classes — Canada. I. T. II. Series.
HN103.5.P6        301.440971        *LC* 65-3947

**Clement, Wallace.**                                           **4.5249**
The Canadian corporate elite: an analysis of economic power / Wallace Clement; with a foreword by John Porter. Toronto: McClelland and Stewart, [1975] xvii, 479 p.; 19 cm. (Carleton library; no. 89) Includes index. 1. Elite (Social sciences) — Canada. 2. Capitalists and financiers — Canada. 3. Social mobility — Canada. 4. Corporations — Canada. I. T.
HN110.E4 C53        301.44/92/0971        *LC* 75-319029        *ISBN* 0771097891

**McRoberts, Kenneth.**                                           **4.5250**
Quebec: social change and political crisis / Kenneth McRoberts, Dale Posgate. — Toronto: McClelland and Stewart, c1976. vi, 216 p.; 21 cm. (Canada in transition series) 1. Québec (Province) — Social conditions. 2. Québec (Province) — Economic conditions. 3. Québec (Province) — Politics and government I. Posgate, Dale. joint author. II. T.
HN110.Q4 M32        309.1/714        *LC* 76-373940        *ISBN* 0771071752

**Artibise, Alan F. J.**                                           **4.5251**
Winnipeg: a social history of urban growth, 1874–1914 / Alan F. J. Artibise. — Montreal: McGill-Queen's University Press, 1975. xiv, 382 p., [8] leaves of plates: ill.; 24 cm. Includes index. 1. Urbanization — Winnipeg, Man. 2. Winnipeg (Man.) — Social conditions. I. T.
HN110.W5 A74        309.1/7127/4        *LC* 75-325419        *ISBN* 0773502025

## HN110.5–370 Latin America

**Heath, Dwight B. ed.**                                           **4.5252**
Contemporary cultures and societies of Latin America; a reader in the social anthropology of Middle and South America. Edited, with introductions and notes, by Dwight B. Heath. — 2d ed. — New York: Random House, [1973, c1974] xvii, 572 p.: illus.; 24 cm. 1. Latin America — Social conditions — 1945- — Addresses, essays, lectures. 2. Latin America — Economic conditions — 1918-1945 — Addresses, essays, lectures. I. T.
HN110.5.A8 H4 1974        309.1/8/003        *LC* 73-13642        *ISBN* 0394317726

**Masses in Latin America** / edited by Irving Louis Horowitz. —   **4.5253**
New York: Oxford University Press, 1970. 608 p.; 24 cm. 'All of the articles in this volume, with the exception of the essay by Bryan Roberts, first appeared in Studies in comparative international development.' 1. Latin America — Social conditions — 1945- — Addresses, essays, lectures. 2. Latin America — Economic conditions — 1945- — Addresses, essays, lectures. I. Horowitz, Irving Louis.
HN110.5.A8 H58      309.1/8      LC 73-83045

**Structure and process in Latin America: patronage, clientage,**   **4.5254**
**and power systems** / edited by Arnold Strickon and Sidney M.
Greenfield.
[1st ed.] Albuquerque: University of New Mexico Press, 1973 (c1972) xii, 256 p.; 25 cm. 'A School of American Research book.' 'Product of a seminar sponsored by the School of American Research and a symposium ... of the American Anthropological Association.' 1. Social structure — Case studies — Addresses, essays, lectures. 2. Patron and client — Latin America — Case studies — Addresses, essays, lectures. 3. Power (Social sciences) — Case studies — Addresses, essays, lectures. 4. Latin America — Social conditions — 1945- — Case studies — Addresses, essays, lectures. I. Strickon, Arnold. ed. II. Greenfield, Sidney M. ed. III. School of American Research (Santa Fe, N.M.) IV. American Anthropological Association.
HN110.5.A8 S77      301.11/098      LC 72-86819      ISBN 0826302599

**Cities & society in colonial Latin America** / edited by Louisa   **4.5255**
Schell Hoberman and Susan Migden Socolow.
1st ed. — Albuquerque: University of New Mexico Press, c1986. p. cm. 1. Social classes — Latin America — History — Addresses, essays, lectures. 2. Elites — Latin America — History — Addresses, essays, lectures. 3. Cities and towns — Latin America — History — Addresses, essays, lectures. 4. Latin America — Economic conditions — Addresses, essays, lectures. 5. Spain — Colonies — History — Addresses, essays, lectures. I. Hoberman, Louisa Schell, 1942- II. Socolow, Susan Migden, 1941- III. Title: Cities and society in colonial Latin America.
HN110.5.C58 1986      306/.098 19      LC 85-20855      ISBN 0826308449

**Lomnitz, Larissa Adler de.**   **4.5256**
[Cerrada del Cóndor. English] Networks and marginality: life in a Mexican shantytown / Larissa Adler Lomnitz; translated by Cinna Lomnitz; foreword by Eric R. Wolf. — New York: Academic Press, c1977. xvi, 230 p.: ill.; 24 cm. (Studies in anthropology) Translation of Cerrada del Cóndor. Includes index. 1. Squatter settlements — Mexico — Mexico (City) 2. Rural-urban migration — Mexico — Mexico (City) 3. Mexico City (Mexico) — Social conditions. I. T.
HN120.M45 L6513      305.5/6 19      LC 76-55974      ISBN 012456450X

**Foster, George McClelland, 1913-.**   **4.5257**
Tzintzuntzan: Mexican peasants in a changing world / George M. Foster. — Rev. ed. — New York: Elsevier-New York, c1979. 392 p.: ill.; 21 cm. Includes index. 1. Villages — Mexico — Case studies. 2. Tzintzuntzan (Mexico) — Social conditions. I. T.
HN120.T95 F6 1979      309.1/72/3      LC 79-9496      ISBN 0444990690

**Smith, Peter H.**   **4.5258**
Labyrinths of power: political recruitment in twentieth–century Mexico / Peter H. Smith. — Princeton, N.J.: Princeton University Press, c1979. xvi, 384 p.: ill.; 25 cm. Includes index. 1. Elite (Social sciences) — Mexico. 2. Power (Social sciences) 3. Mexico — Politics and government I. T.
HN120.Z9 E47      301.44/92/0972      LC 78-51191      ISBN 0691075921

**Adams, Richard Newbold, 1924-.**   • **4.5259**
Crucifixion by power: essays on Guatemalan national social structure, 1944–1966 / with chapters by Brian Murphy and Bryan Roberts. — Austin: University of Texas Press, [1970] xiv, 553 p.: ill., maps.; 24 cm. 1. Social classes — Guatemala. 2. Guatemala — Social conditions. I. T.
HN143.5.A63      309.1/7281      LC 79-121125      ISBN 0292700350

**Lowenthal, David. comp.**   **4.5260**
Consequences of class and color: West Indian perspectives, edited and introduced by David Lowenthal and Lambros Comitas. — Garden City, N.Y.: Doubleday, 1973. xx, 334 p.; 19 cm. (Anchor books.) 1. Social classes — West Indies — Addresses, essays, lectures. 2. West Indies — Social conditions — Addresses, essays, lectures. 3. West Indies — Race question — Addresses, essays, lectures. I. Comitas, Lambros. joint author. II. T.
HN192.5.L65      301.44/09729      LC 72-84928      ISBN 038504402X

**Nelson, Lowry, 1893-.**   • **4.5261**
Rural Cuba. — New York: Octagon Books, 1970 [c1950] x, 285 p.: illus., map.; 24 cm. 1. Cuba — Rural conditions. I. T.
HN203.N4 1970      309.1/7291      LC 71-111634

**Lewis, Oscar.**   **4.5262**
Living the revolution: an oral history of contemporary Cuba / Oscar Lewis, Ruth M. Lewis, Susan M. Rigdon. — Urbana: University of Illinois Press, c1977. 2 v.: ill.; 24 cm. 1. Family — Cuba — Case studies. 2. Cuba — Social conditions 3. Cuba — Poor. 4. Cuba — Politics and government — 1959-

I. Lewis, Ruth M., 1916- joint author. II. Rigdon, Susan M., 1943- joint author. III. T.
HN203.5.L48 1977      309.1/7291/064      LC 76-54878

**Curtin, Philip D.**   • **4.5263**
Two Jamaicas; the role of ideas in a tropical colony, 1830–1865 [by] Philip D. Curtin. — New York: Greenwood Press, 1968 [c1955] xii, 270 p.: illus., map, ports.; 23 cm. 1. Jamaica — Social conditions. I. T.
HN223.C8 1968      309.1/7292      LC 69-10082

**Steward, Julian Haynes, 1902-1972.**   • **4.5264**
The people of Puerto Rico; a study in social anthropology, by Julian H. Steward [and others. — Urbana]: University of Illinois Press, 1956. ix, 540 p.: illus., maps, diagrs.; 29 cm. 'A Social Science Research Center study, College of Social Sciences, University of Puerto Rico.' 1. Puerto Rico — Social conditions I. University of Puerto Rico (Río Piedras Campus). Social Science Research Center. II. T.
HN233.S7      572.7*      LC 56-5682

**Tumin, Melvin Marvin, 1919-.**   • **4.5265**
Social class and social change in Puerto Rico, by Melvin M. Tumin with Arnold S. Feldman. — 2d ed. — Indianapolis: Bobbs-Merrill, [1971] xxv, 549 p.; 23 cm. — (A Social Science Research Center study) 1. Social classes — Puerto Rico. 2. Puerto Rico — Social conditions — 1952- I. Feldman, Arnold S. joint author. II. T.
HN240.Z9 S67 1971      301.44/097295      LC 70-145756

**Smith, M. G. (Michael Garfield)**   • **4.5266**
The plural society in the British West Indies, by M.G. Smith. Berkeley, University of California Press, 1965. xix, 359 p. ill. map. 1. West Indies, British — Social conditions I. T.
HN245 S6 1965      LC 65-10236

**Scobie, James R., 1929-.**   **4.5267**
Buenos Aires: plaza to suburb, 1870–1910 / James R. Scobie. — New York: Oxford University Press, 1974. xvii, 323 p.: ill.; 24 cm. Includes index. 1. Buenos Aires (Argentina) — Social conditions. 2. Buenos Aires (Argentina) — Economic conditions. 3. Buenos Aires (Argentina) — History. I. T.
HN270.B8 S3      309.1/82/1      LC 74-79629      ISBN 0195018214

**McEwen, William J.**   **4.5268**
Changing rural society: a study of communities in Bolivia / William J. McEwen, with the support of the Bolivia Project Staff. — New York: Oxford University Press, 1975. xiv, 463 p.: ill.; 23 cm. Report of a research project conducted by the Research Institute for the Study of Man. Published in 1969 under title: Changing rural Bolivia. Includes index. 1. Social surveys — Bolivia. 2. Rural development — Bolivia. 3. Bolivia — Rural conditions. I. Research Institute for the Study of Man. II. T.
HN277.M24 1975      301.35/2/0984      LC 74-21822      ISBN 0195018931

**Smith, T. Lynn (Thomas Lynn), 1903-.**   **4.5269**
Brazil; people and institutions [by] T. Lynn Smith. 4th ed. Baton Rouge, Louisiana State University Press, 1972. xx, 778 p. illus. 25 cm. 1. Social institutions — Brazil. 2. Brazil — Social conditions — 1964- 3. Brazil — Population. I. T.
HN283.5.S58 1972      309.1/81      LC 73-168396      ISBN 0807109495

**Pastore, José, 1935-.**   **4.5270**
[Desigualdade e mobilidade social no Brasil. English] Inequality and social mobility in Brazil / José Pastore; translated by Robert M. Oxley. — Madison: University of Wisconsin Press, 1982. xviii, 194 p.; 24 cm. Translation of: Desigualdade e mobilidade social no Brasil. Includes index. 1. Social mobility — Brazil. 2. Equality 3. Brazil — Economic conditions I. T.
HN284.P3713 1982      305.5/13/0981 19      LC 81-69826      ISBN 0299088308

**Perlman, Janice E.**   **4.5271**
The myth of marginality: urban poverty and politics in Rio de Janeiro / Janice E. Perlman. — Berkeley: University of California Press, c1976. xxi, 341 p.: ill.; 24 cm. Includes index. 1. Marginality, Social — Brazil — Rio de Janeiro. 2. Poor — Brazil — Rio de Janeiro. 3. Rio de Janeiro (Brazil) — Politics and government. I. T.
HN290.R47 P47      301.44/94/09815      LC 73-87246      ISBN 0520025962

**Jesus, Carolina Maria de.**   **4.5272**
Child of the dark; the diary of Carolina Maria de Jesus. Translated from the Portuguese by David St. Clair. [1st ed.] New York: Dutton, 1962. 190 p. illus. Translation of Quarto de despejo. 1. São Paulo (Brazil) — Social conditions. 2. São Paulo (Brazil) — Poor. I. T.
HN290.S33 J43      LC 62-14719

**Bauer, Arnold J.**   **4.5273**
Chilean rural society from the Spanish conquest to 1930 / Arnold J. Bauer. — Cambridge [Eng.]; New York: Cambridge University Press, 1975. xviii, 265 p.,

[2] leaves of plates: ill.; 21 cm. (Cambridge Latin American studies. 21) Includes index. 1. Chile — Rural conditions. I. T. II. Series.
HN293.B38        309.1/83        *LC* 75-2724        *ISBN* 0521207274

**Cultural transformations and ethnicity in modern Ecuador /**        4.5274
**edited by Norman E. Whitten, Jr.**
Urbana: University of Illinois Press, c1981. xvii, 811 p.: ill.; 24 cm. 1. Indians of South America — Ecuador — Social conditions. 2. Minorities — Ecuador. 3. Ecuador — Social conditions. I. Whitten, Norman E.
HN317.C8        986.6 19        *LC* 81-4402        *ISBN* 0252008324

**Hurtado, Osvaldo.**        4.5275
[Poder político en el Ecuador. English] Political power in Ecuador / by Osvaldo Hurtado; translated by Nick D. Mills, Jr. — 1st English ed. — Albuquerque: University of New Mexico Press, c1980. xxvi, 398 p., [8] leaves of plates: ill.; 24 cm. Translation of El poder politico en el Ecuador, published in 1977. Includes index. 1. Elite (Social sciences) — Ecuador. 2. Power (Social sciences) 3. Ecuador — Economic conditions 4. Ecuador — Social conditions. 5. Ecuador — Politics and government I. T.
HN320.Z9 E4313        306/.2/09866        *LC* 79-56822        *ISBN* 0826305334

**Peruvian contexts of change / edited by William W. Stein.**        4.5276
New Brunswick [N.J.] U.S.A.: Transaction Books, c1985. x, 400 p.; 24 cm. 1. Urbanization — Peru — Addresses, essays, lectures. 2. Rural development — Peru — Addresses, essays, lectures. 3. Peru — Social conditions — Addresses, essays, lectures. 4. Peru — Economic conditions — Addresses, essays, lectures. I. Stein, William W.
HN343.5.P42 1985        306/.0985 19        *LC* 84-67        *ISBN* 0887380131

**Lobo, Susan.**        4.5277
A house of my own: social organization in the squatter settlements of Lima, Peru / Susan Lobo. — Tucson, Ariz.: University of Arizona Press, c1982. xix, 190 p.: ill.; 24 cm. Includes index. 1. Squatter settlements — Peru — Lima. 2. Community development, Urban — Peru — Lima. 3. Lima (Peru) — Social conditions. I. T.
HN344.L6        307.7/6 19        *LC* 81-16275        *ISBN* 0816507392

**Peattie, Lisa Redfield.**        4.5278
The view from the barrio. Ann Arbor, University of Michigan Press [1968] 147 p. illus. 24 cm. 1. Ciudad Guayana (Venezuela) — Social conditions. I. T.
HN370.C5 P4        309.1/87/6        *LC* 68-16441


# HN371–660 Europe

**Ethnic diversity and conflict in Eastern Europe / Peter F.**        4.5279
**Sugar, editor.**
Santa Barbara, Calif.: ABC—Clio, c1980. xii, 553 p.; 24 cm. (The Joint Committee on Eastern Europe publication series; no. 8) Based on a conference on ethnicity in Eastern Europe held June 11-13, 1976, in Seattle, Wash., sponsored by the Joint Committee on Eastern Europe. 1. Nationalism — Europe, Eastern — Congresses. 2. Ethnicity — Europe, Eastern — Congresses. 3. Anthropological linguistics — Europe, Eastern — Congresses. 4. Europe, Eastern — Ethnic relations — Congresses. I. Sugar, Peter F. II. Joint Committee on Eastern Europe.
HN372.E74        305.8/00947        *LC* 80-12032        *ISBN* 0874362970

**Barber, Bernard.**        • 4.5280
European social class: stability and change [by] Bernard Barber and Elinor G. Barber. — New York, Macmillan [1965] xii, 145 p. 21 cm. — (Main themes in European history) 1. Social classes — Europe. I. Barber, Elinor G. joint author. II. T. III. Series.
HN373.B3        301.440942        *LC* 65-12727

**Blum, Jerome, 1913-.**        4.5281
The end of the old order in rural Europe / Jerome Blum. — Princeton, N.J.: Princeton University Press, c1978. xiii, 505 p.: ill.; 24 cm. Includes index. 1. Peasantry — Europe — History. 2. Feudalism — Europe — History. 3. Social classes — Europe — History. 4. Europe — Rural conditions. I. T.
HN373.B55        309.2/63/094        *LC* 77-85530        *ISBN* 0691052662

**Forster, Robert, 1926- comp.**        • 4.5282
European society in the eighteenth century, edited by Robert and Elborg Forster. New York, Walker [1969] xi, 424 p. 24 cm. (The Documentary history of Western civilization) 1. Europe — Social conditions — 18th century — Sources. I. Forster, Elborg, 1931- joint comp. II. T.
HN373.F64 1969b        914/.03/253        *LC* 74-4160

**Houston, J. M. (James Macintosh), 1922-.**        • 4.5283
A social geography of Europe, by J. M. Houston. — New York: F. A. Praeger, [1968, c1963] 271 p.: illus., maps, plans.; 23 cm. 1. Cities and towns — Europe. 2. Europe — Rural conditions. 3. Europe — Population. I. T.
HN373.H68 1968        301.3/094        *LC* 68-13725

**Huggett, Frank Edward.**        4.5284
The land question and European society since 1650 / Frank E. Huggett. — 1st American ed. — [New York]: Harcourt Brace Jovanovich, 1975. 179 p.: ill.; 21 cm. (History of European civilization library) Includes index. 1. Peasantry — Europe — History. 2. Agriculture — Economic aspects — Europe — History. 3. Europe — Rural conditions. I. T.
HN373.H83 1975        309.1/4        *LC* 75-788        *ISBN* 0155490052

**Kamen, Henry Arthur Francis.**        4.5285
The iron century; social change in Europe, 1550–1660 [by] Henry Kamen. New York, Praeger Publishers 1972 (c1971) xiv, 464 p. illus. 25 cm. (History of civilisation) 1. Social classes — Europe — History. 2. Europe — Social conditions — 16th century 3. Europe — Social conditions — 17th century I. T.
HN373.K34        301.29/4        *LC* 74-100937

**Rudé, George F. E.**        4.5286
Europe in the eighteenth century; aristocracy and the bourgeois challenge [by] George Rudé. — New York: Praeger, [1973, c1972] ix, 290 p.: illus.; 25 cm. — (History of civilization) 1. Europe — Social conditions — 18th century. I. T.
HN373.R83 1973        914/.03/253        *LC* 74-187279

**Schlesinger, Rudolf.**        • 4.5287
Central European democracy and its background; economic and political group organization. London, Routledge & Paul [1953] xiv, 402p. 23cm. (International library of sociology and social reconstruction) 1. Labor and laboring classes — Central Europe 2. Central Europe — Social conditions 3. Central Europe — Politics and government I. T.
HN373.S3        *LC* 53-13380

**Stearns, Peter N.**        • 4.5288
European society in upheaval; social history since 1800 [by] Peter N. Stearns. — New York, Macmillan [1967] xix, 425 p. 22 cm. Bibliography: p. 406-418. 1. Europe — Soc. condit. I. T.
HN373.S68        309.14        *LC* 67-13147

**Tannenbaum, Edward R.**        4.5289
1900, the generation before the Great War / Edward R. Tannenbaum. — 1st ed. — Garden City, N.Y.: Anchor Press, 1976, c1977. xii, 463 p.: ill.; 24 cm. 1. Europe — Social conditions — 20th century I. T.
HN373.T33        309.1/4/0288        *LC* 76-18369        *ISBN* 0385004311

**Watts, S. J. (Sheldon J.)**        4.5290
A social history of Western Europe, 1450–1720: tensions and solidarities among rural people / Sheldon J. Watts. — London; Dover, N.H., USA: Hutchinson University Library, 1984. 275 p., [2] p. of plates: ill., maps; 24 cm. (Hutchinson university library for Africa.) Includes index. 1. Social history — Modern, 1500- 2. Europe — Rural conditions. I. T. II. Series.
HN373.W37 1984        306/.094 19        *LC* 84-159439        *ISBN* 0091560810

**Contemporary Europe: social structures and cultural patterns /**        4.5291
**edited by Salvador Giner and Margaret Scotford Archer.**
London; Boston: Routledge & K. Paul, 1978. viii, 323 p.; 23 cm. — (International library of sociology) 1. Europe — Social conditions — Addresses, essays, lectures. I. Giner, Salvador. II. Archer, Margaret Scotford.
HN373.5.C66        301.4/0094        *LC* 77-30716        *ISBN* 071008790X

**Knox, Paul L.**        4.5292
The geography of western Europe: a socio–economic survey / Paul Knox. — Totowa, N.J.: Barnes & Noble Books, 1984. ix, 229 p.: ill.; 24 cm. Includes index. 1. Anthropo-geography — Europe. 2. Europe — Social conditions — 20th century 3. Europe — Economic conditions — 20th century I. T.
HN375.5.K55 1984        306/.094 19        *LC* 84-12330        *ISBN* 0389205125

**Modern European social history, edited by Robert J. Bezucha.**        4.5293
**Selections by James J. Sheehan [and others].**
Lexington, Mass.: D. C. Heath, [1972] xix, 386 p.: illus.; 23 cm. 1. Europe — Social conditions — Addresses, essays, lectures. I. Bezucha, Robert J., ed. II. Sheehan, James J.
HN376.M6        309.1/4        *LC* 79-172910        *ISBN* 0669611433

**Cépède, Michel.**        • 4.5294
Rural problems in the Alpine region: an international study / by Michel Cépède and E.S. Abensour; with the collaboration of Paul and Germaine Veyret. — Rome: Food and Agriculture Organization of the United Nations, 1961. vii, 201 p.: diagrs., tables. 1. Alps — Rural conditions I. Abensour, Emmanuel S., (jt. author) II. T.
HN380A4 C4        HN380A4 C4.        *LC* 61-65025

**Pitt-Rivers, Julian Alfred. ed.**        • 4.5295
Mediterranean countrymen; essays in the social anthropology of the Mediterranean. Edited by Julian Pitt–Rivers. Contributors: A. M. Abou Zeid [and others]. — Paris, Mouton, 1963. 236 p. 25 cm. — (Recherches méditerranéennes. Études, 1) 1. Mediterranian region — Soc. condit. I. T. II. Series.
HN380.M4P5        309.14        *LC* 64-6680

**Connor, Walter D.** 4.5296
Socialism, politics, and equality: hierarchy and change in Eastern Europe and the USSR / Walter D. Connor. New York: Columbia University Press, 1978. x, 389 p.; 23 cm. 1. Social classes — Europe, Eastern. 2. Social classes — Soviet Union 3. Social mobility — Europe, Eastern. 4. Social mobility — Soviet Union I. T.
HN380.Z9 S638     *LC* 78-14780     *ISBN* 023104318X

**Consciousness and class experience in nineteenth–century** 4.5297
**Europe / edited by John M. Merriman.**
New York: Holmes & Meier Publishers, 1979. vii, 261 p., [6] leaves of plates: ill.; 24 cm. Includes index. 1. Social classes — Europe — Case studies. 2. Labor and laboring classes — Europe — Case studies. I. Merriman, John M.
HN380.Z9 S6385 1979     301.44/094     *LC* 79-16032     *ISBN* 0841904448

## HN381–400 Britain

HN → 383 L3

**Laslett, Peter.** • 4.5298
The world we have lost. New York: Scribner, [1966, c1965] xvi, 280 p.; 24 cm. 'Notes to the text': p. [241]-272. 1. Great Britain — Civilization 2. Great Britain — Social conditions I. T.
HN383.L3 1966     914.203     *LC* 66-18543

**Glass, D. V. (David Victor), 1911-.** • 4.5299
Social mobility in Britain / edited by David Victor Glass; with contributions by J. Berent and others. London: Routledge and Paul, 1954. 412 p. — (International library of sociology and social reconstruction (London).) 1. Social classes 2. Social classes 3. Great Britain — Social conditions I. Berent, Jerzy. II. T.
HN385.G62     323.3     *LC* 54-4266     *ISBN* 0710033273

**Gregg, Pauline.** 4.5300
A social and economic history of Britain, 1760–1980 / by Pauline Gregg. — 8th ed., rev. — London: Harrap, 1982. 636 p.; 22 cm. 1. Great Britain — Social conditions 2. Great Britain — Economic conditions I. T.
HN385.G7 1982     306/.0941 19     *LC* 83-174304     *ISBN* 0245539387

**Heclo, Hugh.** 4.5301
Modern social politics in Britain and Sweden: from relief to income maintenance. — New Haven: Yale University Press, 1974. xii, 349 p.: ill.; 25 cm. — (Yale studies in political science. 25) 1. Income maintenance programs — Great Britain. 2. Income maintenance programs — Sweden. 3. Great Britain — Social policy. 4. Sweden — Social policy. I. T. II. Series.
HN385.H39     362/.942     *LC* 73-86898     *ISBN* 0300014805

**Hobsbawm, E. J. (Eric J.), 1917- ed.** 4.5302
Labour's turning point, 1880–1900: extracts from contemporary sources / edited by Eric J. Hobsbawm. — 2d ed. — Rutherford, N.J.: Fairleigh Dickinson University Press, 1975 (c1974). xxvi, 166 p.; 19 cm. 1. Labor and laboring classes — Great Britain — History 2. Trade-unions — Great Britain — History. I. T.
HN385.H57 H6     331.88/0941     *LC* 74-498     *ISBN* 0838615422

**Lynd, Helen Merrell, 1896-.** • 4.5303
England in the eighteen–eighties; toward a social basis for freedom. New York, A. M. Kelley, 1968. viii, 508 p. 23 cm. (Reprints of economic classics) Reprint of the 1945 ed. 1. England — Social conditions — 19th century I. T.
HN385.L9 1968b     309.1/42     *LC* 68-20035

**Marsh, David C. (David Charles)** • 4.5304
The changing social structure of England and Wales, 1871–1951. London, Routledge & Paul; New York, Humanities Press [1958] xiv, 273, 15 p. illus. 23 cm. (International library of sociology and social reconstruction) 1. Great Britain — Social conditions I. T.
HN385.M29     *LC* 59-90

**Miller, Edward, 1915-.** 4.5305
Medieval England: rural society and economic change, 1086–1348 / Edward Miller and John Hatcher. — London; New York: Longman, 1978. xviii, 302 p.: map; 22 cm. (Social and economic history of England.) 1. England — Social conditions 2. England — Social life and customs — Medieval period, 1066-1485 3. England — Economic conditions — Medieval period, 1066-1485 4. England — Rural conditions. I. Hatcher, John. joint author. II. T. III. Series.
HN385.M488     309.1/42/02     *LC* 77-21445     *ISBN* 0582482186

**Mingay, G. E.** • 4.5306
English landed society in the eighteenth century. London: Routledge and Paul, 1963. 292 p.; 23 cm. (Studies in social history.) 1. Great Britain — Social conditions 2. Great Britain — Gentry 3. Land tenure — Great Britain. I. T.
HN385.M5     333.0942     *LC* 63-25746

**Roberts, David, 1923-.** 4.5307
Paternalism in early Victorian England / David Roberts. — New Brunswick, N.J.: Rutgers University Press, c1979. x, 337 p.; 24 cm. Includes index. 1. Paternalism — England — History. I. T.
HN385.R57     301.44/92/0942     *LC* 79-14669     *ISBN* 0813508681

**Roberts, David, 1923-.** • 4.5308
Victorian origins of the British welfare state. — [Hamden, Conn.]: Archon Books, 1969 [c1960] xiii, 369 p.; 24 cm. — (Yale historical publications. Miscellany. 73) 1. Gt. Brit. — Social policy. I. T. II. Series.
HN385.R59 1969     361/.9/42     *LC* 69-11553     *ISBN* 0208006923

**Roebuck, Janet.** 4.5309
The making of modern English society from 1850. — New York: Scribner, [1973] xii, 205 p.: illus.; 24 cm. — (Development of English society) 1. Great Britain — Social conditions I. T. II. Series.
HN385.R62     309.1/42/08     *LC* 72-11321     *ISBN* 0684132753

**Rowse, A. L. (Alfred Leslie), 1903-.** 4.5310
The Elizabethan Renaissance: the life of the society / [by] A. L. Rowse. — New York: Scribner, 1972 (c1971) 2 v. illus. 24 cm. (His The Elizabethan age [3]) 1. Great Britain — Social conditions 2. England — Civilization — 16th century I. T.
HN385.R66 1972     914.2/03/55     *LC* 70-172948     *ISBN* 0684126826

**Thompson, F. M. L. (Francis Michael Longstreth)** • 4.5311
English landed society in the nineteenth century, by F. M. L. Thompson. London, Routledge & K. Paul [1963] xiii, 374 p. map. 23 cm. (Studies in social history) Bibliography: p. 346-354. 1. Land tenure — Great Britain. 2. Great Britain — Gentry 3. Great Britain — Social conditions I. T.
HN385.T45     309.142     *LC* 64-4509

**Cawson, Alan.** 4.5312
Corporatism and welfare: social policy and state intervention in Britain / Alan Cawson. — London: Heinemann Educational Books, 1982. 145 p.: ill.; 23 cm. — (Studies in social policy and welfare. 17) 1. Public welfare — Great Britain. 2. Corporations — Great Britain. 3. Great Britain — Social policy. I. T. II. Series.
HN385.5.C38 1982     361.6/1/0941 19     *LC* 82-125817     *ISBN* 0435821369

**Clout, Hugh D.** 4.5313
Rural geography; an introductory survey, by Hugh D. Clout. — [1st ed.]. — Oxford; New York: Pergamon Press, [1972] xii, 204 p.: illus.; 26 cm. — (The Commonwealth and international library. Pergamon Oxford geographies) 1. Agriculture — Economic aspects — Great Britain. 2. Agriculture — Economic aspects — Europe. 3. Great Britain — Rural conditions 4. Europe — Rural conditions. I. T.
HN385.5.C58 1972     301.35/094     *LC* 72-87827     *ISBN* 0080170412

**Johns, Edward Alistair.** 4.5314
The social structure of modern Britain / by E. A. Johns. — 3d ed. — Oxford; New York: Pergamon Press, 1979. xiv, 284 p.; 21 cm. — (Pergamon international library of science, technology, engineering, and social studies) 1. Great Britain — Social conditions — 1945- I. T.
HN385.5.J6 1979     HN385.5 J6 1979.     309.1/42/085     *LC* 78-40531     *ISBN* 0080233430

**Marwick, Arthur, 1936-.** 4.5315
British society since 1945 / Arthur Marwick. — London: A. Lane, 1982. 303 p.; 23 cm. — (Pelican social history of Britain.) Includes index. 1. Great Britain — Social conditions — 1945- I. T. II. Series.
HN385.5.M364 1982     306/.0941 19     *LC* 82-196764     *ISBN* 0713910755

**Fields, Rona M.** 4.5316
Society under siege: a psychology of Northern Ireland / Rona M. Fields. — Philadelphia: Temple University Press, 1977, c1976. xvi, 267 p.; 24 cm. 1. Irish question 2. Stress (Physiology) — Case studies. 3. Violence — Northern Ireland. 4. Northern Ireland — Social conditions — 1969- I. T.
HN387.5.A8 F53     309.1/416     *LC* 76-21895     *ISBN* 0877220743

**Carlyle, Thomas, 1795-1881.** • 4.5317
Past and present / by Thomas Carlyle; edited with an introd. and notes by Richard D. Altick. — Boston: Houghton Mifflin, 1965. xviii, 294 p.; 21 cm. — (Riverside editions; B92) 1. Social problems 2. Great Britain — Social conditions I. T.
HN388.C33 1965     309.142     *LC* 65-5711

**Arnold, Matthew, 1822-1888.** • 4.5318
Culture and anarchy / Matthew Arnold; edited with an introd. by J. Dover Wilson. — Cambridge: University Press, 1960. xl, 241 p.; 19 cm. 1. Culture 2. Great Britain — Social conditions I. Wilson, John Dover, 1881-1969. II. T.
HN389 A72 1960     824.8     *LC* 60-51224

**Ginsberg, Morris, 1889-1970.**                                • 4.5319
Law and opinion in England in the 20th century. — Berkeley: University of California Press, 1959. viii, 407 p. 1. Law — Great Britain — History and criticism 2. Great Britain — Social policy. I. T.
HN389.G45 1959

**Thompson, Paul Richard, 1935-.**                               4.5320
The Edwardians: the remaking of British society / Paul Thompson. — Bloomington: Indiana University Press, [1975] xi, 382 p., [8] leaves of plates: ill.; 23 cm. 1. Social classes — Great Britain 2. Great Britain — Social conditions — 20th century I. T.
HN389.T43 1975        309.1/41/082        LC 75-10897        ISBN 0253319412

**Titmuss, Richard Morris, 1907-1973.**                          • 4.5321
Essays on 'the welfare state' [by] Richard M. Titmuss. Boston, Beacon Press [1969] 262 p. 21 cm. (Europe in the twentieth century) Reprint of the 2d ed., 1963, with a new introd. by S. R. Graubard. 1. National Health Service (Great Britain) 2. Welfare state 3. Great Britain — Social policy. I. T.
HN389.T58 1969        309.1/41/08        LC 77-88219

**Trends in British society since 1900; a guide to the changing**        4.5322
**social structure of Britain. Edited by A. H. Halsey.**
[London]: Macmillan; [New York]: St. Martin's Press, [1972] xxvi, 578 p.; 24 cm. 1. Great Britain — Social conditions 2. Great Britain — Economic conditions 3. Great Britain — Politics and government — 20th century I. Halsey, A. H. ed.
HN389.T83        309.1/42/082        LC 71-163473        ISBN 0333105494

**Saunders, Laurance James.**                                    • 4.5323
Scottish democracy, 1815–1840. Oliver and Boyd [1950] 444 p. 1. Scotland — Social conditions. I. T.
HN398.A2 S25        LC 51-2416

**Meller, Helen Elizabeth.**                                     4.5324
Leisure and the changing city, 1870–1914 / H. E. Meller. — London; Boston: Routledge & Paul, 1976. 308 p., [4] leaves of plates: ill.; 23 cm. Includes index. 1. Urbanization — England — Bristol (Avon) — History. 2. City and town life — England — History. 3. Recreation — England — Bristol (Avon) 4. Bristol (Avon) — Recreational activities — History. I. T.
HN398.B73 M44 1976        942.3/93/081        LC 76-383866        ISBN 0710084307

**Martin, Ernest Walter, 1914-.**                                • 4.5325
The shearers and the shorn: a study of life in a Devon community, by E. W. Martin. London, Routledge & K. Paul [1965] vii, 250 p. illus., fold. map. 23 cm. (Dartington Hall studies in rural sociology) Label mounted on t.p.: Humanities Press, New York. 1. Social classes — Devon, Eng. 2. Devon — Social conditions. I. T.
HN398.D44 M3        LC 65-3218

**Harrison, J. F. C. (John Fletcher Clews)**                     4.5326
The English common people: a social history from the Norman Conquest to the present / J.F.C. Harrison. — Totowa, N.J.: Barnes & Noble Books, 1984. 445 p. Includes index. 1. Labor and laboring classes — England — Social conditions. 2. England — Social conditions I. T.
HN398.E5 H37 1984        306/.0942 19        LC 84-437        ISBN 0389204706

**Mingay, G. E.**                                                4.5327
Rural life in Victorian England / G. E. Mingay. — New York: Holmes & Meier, 1978, c1976. 212 p.: ill.; 23 cm. Includes index. 1. Social classes — England. 2. England — Rural conditions. 3. England — Population, Rural. I. T.
HN398.E5 M56 1978        309.1/42/081        LC 78-14590        ISBN 0841961018

**Perkin, Harold James.**                                        4.5328
The structured crowd: essays in English social history / Harold Perkin. — Brighton, Sussex: Harvester Press; Totowa, N.J.: Barnes & Noble, 1981. xi, 238 p.; 23 cm. 1. Social history — Addresses, essays, lectures. 2. England — Social conditions — 20th century — Addresses, essays, lectures. 3. England — Social conditions — 19th century — Addresses, essays, lectures. I. T.
HN398.E5 P47 1981        306/.0942 19        LC 81-215098        ISBN 0855274131

**Walvin, James.**                                               4.5329
English urban life, 1776–1851 / James Walvin. — London; Dover, N.H., USA: Hutchinson, 1984. 216 p.; 25 cm. (Hutchinson social history of England.) Includes index. 1. Cities and towns — England — Growth. 2. England — Social conditions — 18th century 3. England — Social conditions — 19th century I. T. II. Series.
HN398.E5 W35 1984        306/.0942 19        LC 84-12941        ISBN 0091561507

**Youings, Joyce A.**                                            4.5330
Sixteenth–century England / Joyce Youings. — London: A. Lane, 1984. 444 p.; 23 cm. — (Pelican social history of Britain.) Includes index. 1. England — Social conditions — 16th century I. T. II. Series.
HN398.E5 Y68 1984        942.05/5 19        LC 84-133761        ISBN 071391243X

**Williams, William Morgan, 1926-.**                             • 4.5331
Gosforth: the sociology of an English village. Glencoe, Ill., Free Press [1956] 246 p. illus. 22 cm. London ed. (Routledge & Paul) has title: The sociology of an English village. 1. Gosforth (Northumberland) 2. England — Rural conditions — Case studies. I. T.
HN398.G7 W5        LC 56-2722 rev

**George, M. Dorothy (Mary Dorothy)**                            • 4.5332
London life in the eighteenth century. — New York: Harper, 1965, c1964. xviii, 452 p.: ill.; 21 cm. (Harper torchbooks) 1. Labor and laboring classes — London. 2. London (England) — Social conditions. 3. London (England) — Poor. I. T.
HN398.L7 G4        309.1421        LC 65-2607

**Roberts, Robert, 1905-1974.**                                  4.5333
The classic slum: Salford life in the first quarter of the century. Manchester, Manchester University Press, 1971. xiii, 219 p., 13 plates; 13 illus. 23 cm. 1. Poor — England — Salford (Greater Manchester) 2. Salford (Greater Manchester) — Social conditions. I. T.
HN398.S2 R6        942.7/32        LC 74-855642        ISBN 0719004535

**Camic, Charles.**                                              4.5334
Experience and enlightenment: socialization for cultural change in eighteenth–century Scotland / Charles Camic. — Chicago: University of Chicago Press, 1983. x, 301 p.; 23 cm. Includes index. 1. Enlightenment 2. Socialization 3. Scotland — Intellectual life. 4. Scotland — Social conditions. 5. Scotland — History — 18th century I. T.
HN398.S3 C35 1983        306/.09411 19        LC 83-4992        ISBN 0226092380

**Orlans, Harold, 1921-.**                                       • 4.5335
Stevenage; a sociological study of a new town. — Westport, Conn.: Greenwood Press, [1971] xv, 313 p.: illus.; 23 cm. Reprint of the 1952 ed. 1. Stevenage (Hertfordshire) I. T.
HN398.S8 O7 1971        309.1/425/8        LC 71-139142        ISBN 0837157587

**Davies, Elwyn, ed.**                                           4.5336
Welsh rural communities / byDavid Jenkins [and others]; edited by Elwyn Davies and Alwyn D. Rees. — [2d ed.] Cardiff: University of Wales Press, 1962. xi, 254 p.: plates, maps, diagrs., tables. 1. Wales — Rural conditions I. Rees, Alwyn D. II. Jenkins, David Clay, 1926- III. T.
HN398 W26 D3 1962        LC 60-35505

**Jones Pierce, Thomas, 1905-1964.**                             4.5337
Medieval Welsh society: selected essays by T. Jones Pierce; edited by J. Beverley Smith. — Cardiff: University of Wales Press, 1972. 452 p., leaf.: maps, port.; 22 cm. 1. Wales — Social conditions. I. Smith, J. Beverley. ed. II. T.
HN398.W26 J63 1972        309.1/429        LC 73-164114        ISBN 0708304478

## HN400 Special Topics, A–Z

**Eysenck, H. J. (Hans Jurgen), 1916-.**                         4.5338
Sex, violence, and the media / H. J. Eysenck & D. K. B. Nias. — New York: St. Martin's Press, 1978. 306 p.; 23 cm. Includes index. 1. Violence in mass media — Great Britain — Psychological aspects. 2. Sex in mass media — Great Britain — Psychological aspects. 3. Pornography — Great Britain. 4. Censorship — Great Britain. I. Nias, D. K. B. joint author. II. T.
HN400.M3 E93 1978        301.16/1        LC 78-69824        ISBN 0312713401

**Macfarlane, L. J. (Leslie John), 1924-.**                      4.5339
Issues in British politics since 1945 / L.J. Macfarlane. — 3rd ed. — Harlow, Essex, England; White Plains, N.Y.: Longman, 1985. p. cm. (Political realities.) Includes index. 1. Public opinion — Great Britain. 2. Great Britain — Politics and government — 1945- I. T. II. Series.
HN400.P8 M32 1985        941.085 19        LC 85-24233        ISBN 0582355605

**Goldthorpe, John H.**                                          4.5340
Social mobility and class structure in modern Britain / John H. Goldthorpe, in collaboration with Catriona Llewellyn and Clive Payne. — Oxford: Clarendon Press; New York: Oxford University Press, 1980. viii, 310 p.: ill.; 25 cm. Includes index. 1. Social classes — Great Britain 2. Social mobility — Great Britain. I. Llewellyn, Catriona. joint author. II. Payne, Clive, joint author. III. T.
HN400.S6 G64        305.5/0941 19        LC 79-41051        ISBN 0198272391

**Neale, R. S.**     4.5341
Class and ideology in the nineteenth century [by] R. S. Neale. — London; Boston: Routledge and Z. Paul, 1972. viii, 200 p.: 1 illus.; 23 cm. 1. Social classes — Great Britain 2. Great Britain — Social conditions — 19th century 3. Great Britain — Politics and government — 19th century I. T.
HN400.S6 N4     301.44/0942     LC 72-196870     ISBN 0710073315

**Westergaard, John H.**     4.5342
Class in a capitalist society: a study of contemporary Britain / John Westergaard and Henrietta Resler. — New York: Basic Books, 1975. xv, 432 p.: graphs; 25 cm. 1. Social classes — Great Britain 2. Equality — Great Britain. 3. Power (Social sciences) 4. Social mobility — Great Britain. 5. Great Britain — Social conditions I. Resler, Henrietta, joint author. II. T.
HN400.S6 W47 1975b     301.44/0941     LC 75-39185     ISBN 0465011446

**Clutterbuck, Richard L.**     4.5343
Britain in agony: the growth of political violence / [by] Richard Clutterbuck. — Revised ed. — Harmondsworth; New York [etc.]: Penguin, 1980. 368 p.: 2 maps; 18 cm. Includes index. 1. Violence — Great Britain. 2. Great Britain — Politics and government — 1964-1979 3. Great Britain — Politics and government — 1979- I. T.
HN400.V5 C56 1980     322.4/2/0941 19     LC 80-513703     ISBN 014005099X

**Bowen, Kurt Derek.**     4.5344
Protestants in a Catholic state: Ireland's privileged minority / Kurt Bowen. — Kingston: McGill-Queen's University Press; Dublin; New York: Gill and Macmillan, c1983. x, 237 p.; 24 cm. Includes index. 1. Protestants — Ireland — History — 20th century. 2. Ireland — Social conditions. I. T.
HN400.3.A8 B69 1983     305.6/30417 19     LC 84-192877     ISBN 0773504125

# HN420.5 Hungary

**Bell, Peter D.**     4.5345
Peasants in Socialist transition: life in a collectivized Hungarian village / Peter D. Bell. — Berkeley: University of California Press, c1984. ix, 322 p.: ill.; 25 cm. Includes index. 1. Villages — Hungary — Case studies. 2. Collective farms — Hungary — Case studies. 3. Kislapos (Hungary) — Social conditions. 4. Hungary — Rural conditions — Case studies. I. T.
HN420.5.K56 B44 1984     307.7/2/09439 19     LC 80-25126     ISBN 0520041577

# HN421–440 France

**Duby, Georges.**     4.5346
[Trois ordres. English] The three orders: feudal society imagined / Georges Duby; translated by Arthur Goldhammer; with a foreword by Thomas N. Bisson. — Chicago: University of Chicago Press, 1980. x, 382 p.; 24 cm. Translation of Les trois ordres. 1. Feudalism — France. 2. France — Social conditions I. T.
HN425.D78313     HN425 D78313.     321.3/0944     LC 80-13158     ISBN 0226167712

**Dupeux, Georges.**     4.5347
[Société française, 1789-1970. English] French society, 1789–1970 / Georges Dupeux; translated by Peter Wait. — New York: Barnes & Noble, 1976. 294 p.: ill.; 22 cm. Translation of La société française, 1789-1970. Includes index. 1. France — Social conditions 2. France — Economic conditions I. T.
HN425.D813 1976     309.1/44     LC 76-358143     ISBN 0416652506

**Lewis, P. S. (Peter Shervey)**     4.5348
Later medieval France: the polity [by] P. S. Lewis. London, Melbourne, [etc.] Macmillan; New York, St. Martin's P., 1968. xiv, 418 p. tables, 2 maps. 23 cm. 1. Social classes — France — History. 2. France — Social conditions 3. France — History — Medieval period, 987-1515 I. T.
HN425.L48     309.1/44     LC 68-10531

**McCloy, Shelby Thomas, 1898-.**     • 4.5349
The humanitarian movement in eighteenth–century France. — [Lexington] University of Kentucky Press [1957] 274 p. 24 cm. Bibliographical footnotes. 1. France — Soc. condit. I. T.
HN425.M3     309.144     LC 57-5835

**Mousnier, Roland.**     4.5350
[Institutions de la France sous la monarchie absolue, 1598-1789. English] The institutions of France under the absolute monarchy, 1598–1789 / Roland Mousnier; translated by Arthur Goldhammer. — Chicago: University of Chicago Press, 1984. 695 p. Translation of: Les institutions de la France sous la monarchie absolue, 1598-1789. 1. Social classes — France — History.

2. France — Social conditions 3. France — Politics and government — 1589-1789 I. T.
HN425.M6813     306/.0944 19     LC 78-26857     ISBN 0226543277

**Tilly, Charles.**     4.5351
The rebellious century, 1830–1930 / Charles Tilly, Louise Tilly, and Richard Tilly. Cambridge: Harvard University Press, 1975. xi, 354 p., [7] leaves of plates: ill.; 25 cm. Includes index. 1. Violence 2. France — Social conditions — 19th century 3. Italy — Social conditions 4. Germany — Social conditions I. Tilly, Louise. joint author. II. Tilly, Richard H. joint author. III. T.
HN425.T54     309.1/4/028     LC 74-16802     ISBN 0674749553

**Mendras, Henri.**     • 4.5352
[Fin des paysans. English] The vanishing peasant; innovation and change in French agriculture. Translated by Jean Lerner. Cambridge, Mass., MIT Press [1970] viii, 289 p. 21 cm. (M.I.T. studies in comparative politics series) Translation of La fin des paysans. 1. Peasantry — France 2. Agriculture — Economic aspects — France. 3. France — Rural conditions. I. T. II. Series.
HN425.5.M3713     309.1/44     LC 79-118349     ISBN 0262130653

**Weber, Eugen Joseph, 1925-.**     4.5353
Peasants into Frenchmen: the modernization of rural France, 1870–1914 / Eugen Weber. Stanford, Calif.: Stanford University Press, 1976. xv, 615 p.: maps; 25 cm. Includes index. 1. Peasantry — France — History. 2. France — Rural conditions. 3. France — Social conditions — 19th century I. T.
HN426.W4 1976     309.2/63/0944     LC 75-7486     ISBN 0804708983

**Sewell, William Hamilton, 1940-.**     4.5354
Structure and mobility: the men and women of Marseille, 1820–1870 / William H. Sewell, Jr. — Cambridge [Cambridgeshire]; New York: Cambridge University Press; Paris: Editions de la Maison des Sciences de l'Homme, 1985. xvi, 377 p.: ill., maps; 24 cm. Includes index. 1. Social indicators — France — Marseille. 2. Social mobility — France — Marseille — History — 19th century. 3. Social structure — France — Marseille — History — 19th century. 4. Labor and laboring classes — France — Marseille — History — 19th century. 5. Marseille (France) — Social conditions. I. T.
HN438.M35 S48 1985     305/.0944/912 19     LC 84-5860     ISBN 0521262372

**Rudé, George F. E.**     4.5355
Paris and London in the eighteenth century; studies in popular protest [by] George Rudé. New York, Viking Press [1971] 350 p. 22 cm. 1. Riots — France — Paris. 2. Riots — England — London. 3. Paris (France) — Social conditions. 4. London (England) — Social conditions. I. T.
HN438.P3 R8 1971     301.6/332/09421     LC 73-148267     ISBN 0670538329

**Morin, Edgar.**     • 4.5356
[Commune en France, la métamorphose de Plodémet. English] The red and the white: report from a French village. Translated by A. M. Sheridan–Smith. [1st American ed.] New York, Pantheon Books [1970] xxiv, 263 p. maps. 22 cm. Translation of Commune en France, la métamorphose de Plodémet. 1. Plozédet (France) — Social conditions. I. T.
HN438.P5 M613 1970     309.1/44/1     LC 69-20183     ISBN 0394442601

**Tilly, Charles.**     • 4.5357
The Vendee. Cambridge, Mass., Harvard University Press, 1964. xi, 373 p. ill., maps. 1. Vendée — Social conditions 2. Vendean War, 1793-1800 I. T.
HN438 V4 T5     LC 64-21247

**Elites in France: origins, reproduction, and power / edited by Jolyon Howorth, Philip G. Cerny.**     4.5358
New York: St. Martin's Press, 1981. vi, 253 p.; 23 cm. Papers presented at the First Annual Conference of the Association for the Study of Modern and Contemporary France, held at the University of Aston, Sept. 18-20, 1980. 1. Elite (Social sciences) — France — History. 2. France — Politics and government I. Howorth, Jolyon. II. Cerny, Philip G., 1946- III. Association for the Study of Modern and Contemporary France (Great Britain)
HN440.E4 E43 1981     305.5/2 19     LC 81-9147     ISBN 0312242425

**Nye, Robert A.**     4.5359
Crime, madness, & politics in modern France: the medical concept of national decline / Robert A. Nye. — Princeton, N.J.: Princeton University Press, c1984. xv, 367 p.: ill.; 25 cm. Includes index. 1. Public opinion — France — History — 19th century. 2. Deviant behavior — France — Public opinion — History — 19th century. 3. Physicians — France — Attitudes — History — 19th century. 4. Degeneration — Public opinion — History — 19th century. 5. Criminal justice, Administration of — France — History — 19th century. 6. France — Politics and government — 1870-1940 I. T. II. Title: Crime, madness, and politics in modern France.
HN440.P8 N94 1984     302.5/42/0944 19     LC 83-43087     ISBN 0691054142

## HN441–460 Germany

**Dahrendorf, Ralf.**      • **4.5360**
[Gesellschaft und Demokratie in Deuschland. English] Society and democracy in Germany. [1st ed. in U.S.A.] Garden City, N.Y., Doubleday, 1967. xvi, 482 p. 22 cm. Translation of Gesellschaft und Demokratie in Deutschland. 1. National characteristics, German 2. Germany — Social conditions 3. Germany — Politics and government — 1871- I. T.
HN445.D313     309.143     *LC* 67-19118

**Sagarra, Eda.**      **4.5361**
A social history of Germany, 1648–1914 / Eda Sagarra. — New York: Holmes & Meier, 1977. 473 p.; 24 cm. Includes index. 1. Social classes — Germany — History. 2. Germany — Social conditions 3. Germany — Economic conditions I. T.
HN445.S23 1977     309.1/43     *LC* 77-24201     *ISBN* 0841903328

**Kershaw, Ian.**      **4.5362**
Popular opinion and political dissent in the Third Reich, Bavaria 1933–1945 / Ian Kershaw. — Oxford, [Oxfordshire]; Clarendon Press; New York: Oxford University Press, 1983. xii, 425 p.; 23 cm. Includes index. 1. Public opinion — Germany, West. 2. Public opinion — Germany, West — Bavaria. 3. National socialism — Public opinion. 4. Bavaria (Germany) — Politics and government — 1918-1945 5. Germany — Politics and government — 1933-1945 I. T.
HN460.P8 K47 1983     303.3/8/09433 19     *LC* 82-12617     *ISBN* 0198219229

**Kocka, Jürgen.**      **4.5363**
[Klassengesellschaft im Krieg. English] Facing total war: German society, 1914–1918 / Jürgen Kocka; translated from the German by Barbara Weinberger. — Cambridge, Mass.: Harvard University Press, 1984. 278 p.; 23 cm. Translation of: Klassengesellschaft im Krieg. Includes index. 1. Social classes — Germany. 2. World War, 1914-1918 — Economic aspects — Germany. I. T.
HN460.S6 K613 1984     306/.0943 19     *LC* 84-19269     *ISBN* 0674290313

## HN471–520 Italy. Netherlands

**Banfield, Edward C.**      • **4.5364**
The moral basis of a backward society, by Edward C. Banfield with the assistance of Laura Fasano Banfield. Photos. by the author. Glencoe, Ill., Free Press; [Chicago] Research Center in Economic Development and Cultural Change, University of Chicago [1958] 204 p. illus., map. 24 cm. 1. Community life — Case studies. 2. Italy, Southern — Social conditions — 1945- — Case studies. I. T.
HN475.B3     309.145     *LC* 58-9398

**Belmonte, Thomas, 1946-.**      **4.5365**
The broken fountain / Thomas Belmonte. — New York: Columbia University Press, 1979. xv, 151 p.; 24 cm. 1. Poor — Italy — Naples — Case studies. 2. Family — Italy — Naples — Case studies. 3. Naples (Italy) — Social conditions — Case studies. I. T.
HN488.N3 B4     309.1/45/73     *LC* 78-32167     *ISBN* 0231045425

**Weissman, Ronald F. E.**      **4.5366**
Ritual brotherhood in Renaissance Florence / Ronald F.E. Weissman. — New York: Academic Press, c1981. xiii, 254 p.; 24 cm. — (Population and social structure. Advances in historical demography) Includes index. 1. Social structure — Italy — History. 2. Confraternities — Italy — Florence — History. 3. Florence (Italy) — Social conditions. 4. Florence (Italy) — Religious life and customs. I. T. II. Series.
HN490.S6 W44     945 19     *LC* 81-17536     *ISBN* 0127444807

**Violence and civil disorder in Italian cities, 1200–1500. Edited**      • **4.5367**
**by Lauro Martines.**
Berkeley, University of California Press, 1972. viii, 353 p. 24 cm. (UCLA Center for Medieval and Renaissance Studies contributions, 5) 1. Violence — Italy — History — Congresses. 2. Cities and towns — Italy — History — Congresses. I. Martines, Lauro. ed.
HN490.V5 V56     309.1/45     *LC* 71-145791     *ISBN* 0520019067

**Goudsblom, Johan.**      • **4.5368**
Dutch society. — New York: Random House, [1967] xii, 175 p.: fold. map.; 19 cm. — (Studies in modern societies, SS31) (A Random House study in sociology.) 1. Netherlands — Social conditions I. T.
HN513.5.G6     309.1/492     *LC* 67-10914

## HN521–539 Soviet Union

**Hare, Richard.**      • **4.5369**
Portraits of Russian personalities between reform and Revolution / Richard Hare. — London; New York: Oxford University Press, 1959. 360 p.: ill.; 23 cm. 1. Reformers 2. Social sciences — History — Russia. 3. Russia — Social conditions. I. T.
HN523.H27     309.147

**Joint Committee on Slavic Studies.**      • **4.5370**
The transformation of Russian society; aspects of social change since 1861, edited by Cyril E. Black. — Cambridge, Mass., Harvard University Press, 1960. vii, 695 p. 25 cm. 'Papers ... originally presented at a conference held at Arden House, in Harriman, New York, on April 25-27, 1958, under the auspices of the Joint Committee on Slavic Studies of the American Council of Learned Societies and the Social Sciences Research Council.' Bibliographical footnotes. 1. Russia — Soc. condit. I. Black, Cyril Edwin, 1915- ed. II. T.
HN523.J6     947.08     *LC* 60-13286

**Pethybridge, Roger William, 1934-.**      **4.5371**
The social prelude to Stalinism / Roger Pethybridge. — New York: St. Martin's Press, 1974. 343 p.; 23 cm. Includes index. 1. Russia — Social conditions — 1917- I. T.
HN523.P48 1974     309.1/47/084     *LC* 74-75011

**Walicki, Andrzej.**      **4.5372**
[Rosyjska filozofia i myśl społeczna od oświecenia do marksizmu. English] A history of Russian thought from the enlightenment to marxism / Andrzej Walicki; translated from the Polish by Hilda Andrews–Rusiecka. — Stanford, Calif.: Stanford University Press, 1979. xvii, 456 p.; 24 cm. Translation of Rosyjska filozofia i myśl społeczna do oświecenia do marksizmu. 1. Intellectuals — Russia. 2. Socialism — Soviet Union 3. Philosophy, Russian I. T.
HN523.W3413     320.5/0947     *LC* 78-66181     *ISBN* 0804710260

**Kerblay, Basile H.**      **4.5373**
[Société soviétique contemporaine. English] Modern Soviet society / Basile Kerblay; translated by Rupert Swyer. — 1st American ed. — New York: Pantheon Books, c1983. xxvi, 321 p.: ill.; 24 cm. Translation of: La société soviétique contemporaine. Includes index. 1. Soviet Union — Social conditions — 1970- 2. Soviet Union — Economic conditions — 1976- I. T.
HN523.5.K413 1983     306/.0947 19     *LC* 82-24646     *ISBN* 0394513169

**The Soviet rural community; a symposium. Edited and with an**      **4.5374**
**introd. by James R. Millar.**
Urbana, University of Illinois Press [1971] xv, 420 p. 24 cm. Papers presented at a symposium held at the University of Illinois in Apr., 1969, and sponsored by the University's Russian and East European Center, the James Buchanan Duke Memorial Fund, and the Center for International Comparative Studies of the University of Illinois. 1. Agriculture and state — Soviet Union — Congresses. 2. Soviet Union — Rural conditions — Congresses. I. Millar, James R., 1936- ed. II. Illinois. University at Urbana-Champaign. Russian and East European Center. III. Illinois. University at Urbana-Champaign. Center for International Comparative Studies.
HN523.5.S66     309.1/47     *LC* 70-122913     *ISBN* 0252001249

**Radishchev, Aleksandr Nikolaevich, 1749-1802.**      • **4.5375**
A journey from St. Petersburg to Moscow. Translation by Leo Wiener. Edited with an introd. and notes by Roderick Page Thaler. — Cambridge, Harvard University Press, 1958. viii, 286 p. port., map. 22 cm. Bibliography: p. [253]-255. 1. Serfdom — Russia. 2. Russia — Soc. condit. 3. Russia — Descr. & trav. I. T.
HN525.R313     309.147     *LC* 58-6580

**Alekseeva, Liudmila, 1927-.**      **4.5376**
[Istoriia inakomysliia v SSSR. English] Soviet dissent: contemporary movements for national, religious, and human rights / by Ludmilla Alexeyeva; translated by Carol Pearce and John Glad. — Middletown, Conn.: Wesleyan University Press, c1985. xiii, 521 p., [32] p. of plates: ill.; 25 cm. Rev. translation of: Istoriia inakomysliia v SSSR. 1. Social movements — Soviet Union — History. 2. Dissenters — Soviet Union — History. 3. Civil rights — Soviet Union — History. 4. Soviet Union — Social conditions — 1945- I. T.
HN527.A4713 1985     303.4/84 19     *LC* 84-11811     *ISBN* 0819551244

**Fainsod, Merle, 1907-1972.**      • **4.5377**
Smolensk under Soviet rule. Cambridge, Harvard University Press, 1958. x, 484 p. maps, diagrs., facsims. 25 cm. 'Bibliographical note': p. [456] 1. Smolensk, Russia (Government) — Social conditions. 2. Smolenskaia oblast' (R.S.F.S.R.) — Social conditions. 3. Zapadnaia oblast', Russia — Social conditions. I. T.
HN530.S6F3     309.147     *LC* 58-10407

**Matthews, Mervyn.**     **4.5378**
Privilege in the Soviet Union: a study of elite life–styles under communism / Mervyn Matthews. — London; Boston: G. Allen & Unwin, 1978. 197 p.; 23 cm. Includes index. 1. Elite (Social sciences) — Russia — Addresses, essays, lectures. 2. Social mobility — Russia — Addresses, essays, lectures. 3. Equality — Addresses, essays, lectures. I. T.
HN530.Z9 E45    301.44/92/0947    LC 78-315486    ISBN 0043230202

*[handwritten margin note: HN 530 Z9 M35]*

**Hollander, Gayle Durham.**     **4.5379**
Soviet political indoctrination; developments in mass media and propaganda since Stalin. New York, Praeger [1972] xviii, 244 p. 25 cm. (Praeger special studies in international politics and public affairs) 1. Mass media — Political aspects — Soviet Union. 2. Mass media — Social aspects — Soviet Union. 3. Communication in politics — Soviet Union. 4. Communication — Social aspects — Soviet Union. I. T.
HN530.Z9 M35    301.15/43/32    LC 70-163927

**Yanowitch, Murray. comp.**     **4.5380**
Social stratification and mobility in the USSR. Edited and translated with an introd. by Murray Yanowitch and Wesley A. Fisher. With a commentary by S. M. Lipset. White Plains, N.Y.: International Arts and Sciences Press [c1973] xxxi, 402 p.: ill.; 24 cm. 1. Social classes — Soviet Union — Addresses, essays, lectures. 2. Social mobility — Soviet Union — Addresses, essays, lectures. I. Fisher, Wesley A. joint comp. II. T.
HN530.Z9 S6483    301.44/044/0947    LC 72-77202    ISBN 0873320085

**Matejko, Alexander J.**     **4.5381**
Social change and stratification in Eastern Europe; an interpretive analysis of Poland and her neighbors [by] Alexander Matejko. New York, Praeger [1974] xxiii, 272 p. 25 cm. (Praeger special studies in international economics and development) 1. Social classes — Poland. 2. Social classes — Europe, Eastern. 3. Europe, Eastern — Economic conditions 4. Europe, Eastern — Social conditions. I. T.
HN539.5.S6 M38    301.44/0943    LC 74-9424    ISBN 0275095703

## HN540–580 Scandinavia

**Nelson, George R., ed.**     • **4.5382**
Freedom and welfare; social patterns in the northern countries of Europe, edited by George R. Nelson, assisted by Aune Mäkinen–Ollinen [and others]. — Westport, Conn.: Greenwood Press, [1970] xiii, 539 p.: illus.; 24 cm. Reprint of the 1953 ed. 1. Public welfare — Scandinavia. 2. Scandinavia — Social conditions. I. T.
HN540.A8 N4 1970    309.1/48    LC 72-98784    ISBN 0837129036

**Fleisher, Wilfrid, 1897-.**     • **4.5383**
Sweden, the welfare state. — New York: J. Day Co., [1956] 255 p.: ill. 1. Public welfare — Sweden. 2. Sweden — Social conditions I. T.
HN573.F55

**Scott, Hilda, 1915-.**     **4.5384**
Sweden's 'right to be human' sex role equality: the goal and the reality / Hilda Scott. — Armonk, N.Y.: M.E. Sharpe, c1982. xiii, 191 p.; 23 cm. 1. Sex role — Sweden. 2. Women — Employment — Sweden. 3. Day care centers — Sweden. 4. Vocational guidance — Sweden. 5. Sweden — Social policy. I. T.
HN577.S36    362.8/356/09485 19    LC 81-5239    ISBN 0873321820

## HN581–650.5 Spain. Portugal. Switzerland. Greece

**Gilmore, David D., 1943-.**     **4.5385**
The people of the plain: class and community in lower Andalusia / David D. Gilmore. — New York: Columbia University Press, 1980. xi, 247 p.: ill.; 24 cm. Includes index. 1. Social classes — Spain — Fuenmayor. 2. Fuenmayor (Spain) — Social conditions. I. T.
HN590.F8 G54    301.44/0946/354    LC 79-20048    ISBN 0231047541

**Pike, Ruth, 1931-.**     **4.5386**
Aristocrats and traders; Sevillian society in the sixteenth century. Ithaca [N.Y.] Cornell University Press [1972] xiii, 243 p. 22 cm. 1. Social classes — Spain — Seville — History. 2. Seville (Spain) — Social conditions. I. T.
HN590.S4 P54    309.1/46/86    LC 76-37756    ISBN 0801406994

**Weisser, Michael R.**     **4.5387**
The peasants of the Montes: the roots of rural rebellion in Spain / Michael R. Weisser. — Chicago: University of Chicago Press, 1977 (c1976). xi, 143 p.: ill.;

21 cm. 1. Peasantry — Spain — Toledo Mountains Region — History. 2. Toledo Mountains Region, Spain — Rural conditions. I. T.
HN590.T63 W44    301.44/43    LC 75-43231    ISBN 0226891585

**Cutileiro, José.**     **4.5388**
A Portuguese rural society. — [London: Oxford Univ. Press, 1971] xvii, 314 p., 10 plates;: illus, map.; 23 cm. — (Oxford monographs on social anthropology) 1. Villages — Portugal — Case studies. 2. Portugal — Rural conditions — Case studies. I. T.
HN593.5.C86    301.29/469/5    LC 79-881336    ISBN 0198231733

**Schmid, Carol L.**     **4.5389**
Conflict and consensus in Switzerland / Carol L. Schmid. — Berkeley: University of California Press; London: University of California Press, Ltd., c1981. vii, 198 p.: ill.; 24 cm. Includes index. 1. Pluralism (Social sciences) 2. Minorities — Switzerland. 3. Religion and state — Switzerland. 4. Multilingualism — Switzerland. 5. Switzerland — Ethnic relations. 6. Switzerland — Politics and government I. T.
HN603.S35    305.8/009494    LC 80-18458    ISBN 0520040791

**Du Boulay, Juliet.**     **4.5390**
Portrait of a Greek mountain village / Juliet Du Boulay. — Oxford: Clarendon Press, 1974. viii, 296 p., [8] leaves of plates: ill.; 23 cm. — (Oxford monographs on social anthropology) Includes index. 1. National characteristics, Greek 2. Greece — Rural conditions. I. T.
HN650.D8x    301.29/495/1    LC 75-307040

**Friedl, Ernestine, 1920-.**     • **4.5391**
Vasilika; a village in modern Greece. New York, Holt, Rinehart and Winston [1962] 110 p. illus. 24 cm. (Case studies in cultural anthropology) 1. Villages — Greece — Case studies. 2. Vasiliká, Greece (Boeotia) I. T.
HN650.F7x    301.35    LC 62-14950

**Sanders, Irwin Taylor, 1909-.**     • **4.5392**
Rainbow in the rock; the people of rural Greece. Cambridge, Harvard University Press, 1962. 363 p. illus. 24 cm. 1. Greece — Rural conditions. I. T.
HN650.S3x    LC 62-7337

**McNeill, William Hardy, 1917-.**     **4.5393**
The metamorphosis of Greece since World War II / William H. McNeill. — Chicago: University of Chicago Press, 1978. viii, 264 p.: map; 23 cm. Includes index. 1. Greece — Social conditions 2. Greece — Economic conditions — 1918-1974 3. Greece — Politics and government — 20th century 4. Greece — Economic conditions — 1974- I. T.
HN650.5.A8 M33    309.1/495/07    LC 77-26105    ISBN 0226561569

## HN651–770 Asia: General. Middle East

**Baer, Gabriel.**     **4.5394**
Fellah and townsman in the Middle East: studies in social history / Gabriel Baer. — London; Totowa, N.J.: F. Cass, 1982. ix, 338 p.; 23 cm. 1. Middle East — Social conditions — Addresses, essays, lectures. 2. Egypt — Social conditions — Addresses, essays, lectures. I. T.
HN656.A8 B33 1982    956 19    LC 82-183738    ISBN 0714631264

**Gerber, Haim.**     **4.5395**
The social origins of the modern Middle East / Haim Gerber. — Boulder, Colo.: L. Rienner; London, England: Mansell, 1987. vii, 221 p.; 24 cm. Includes index. 1. Agriculture and state — Turkey — History. 2. Agriculture — Social aspects — Near East — History. 3. Land tenure — Near East — History. 4. Middle East — Social conditions. 5. Middle East — History — 1517- 6. Middle East — Politics and government. I. T.
HN656.G47 1987    306/.0956 19    LC 86-21925    ISBN 0931477638

**Elites in the Middle East / edited by I. William Zartman.**     **4.5396**
New York: Praeger, 1980. x, 252 p.: ill.; 24 cm. Includes index. 1. Elite (Social sciences) — Middle East — Addresses, essays, lectures. 2. Elite (Social sciences) — Addresses, essays, lectures. I. Zartman, I. William.
HN656.Z9 E43    301.44/92/0956    LC 79-22932    ISBN 0030559618

**Smooha, Sammy.**     **4.5397**
Israel: pluralism and conflict / Sammy Smooha; foreword by Leo Kuper. — Berkeley: University of California Press, 1978. xviii, 462 p.; 23 cm. Includes index. 1. Pluralism (Social sciences) — Israel. 2. Jews, Oriental — Israel 3. Judaism — Israel. 4. Jewish-Arab relations 5. Israel — Social conditions. I. T.
HN660.A8 S6 1978b    301.45    LC 74-76390    ISBN 0520027221

**The Sociology of the Palestinians** / edited by Khalil Nakhleh            **4.5398**
**and Elia Zureik.**
New York: St. Martin's Press, 1980. 238 p.: ill.; 23 cm. Includes index.
1. Palestinian Arabs — Social conditions — Addresses, essays, lectures.
I. Nakhleh, Khalil. II. Zureik, Elia.
HN660.A8 S63 1980      301.45/19/275694      *LC* 79-12706      *ISBN*
0312740735

**Studies of Israeli society** / editor, Ernest Krausz.                     **4.5399**
New Brunswick: Transaction Books, c1980- < 1985 >. v. < 1-3 >: ill.; 24 cm.
(Publication series of the Israel Sociological Society.) Vol. 2: Editor, Ernest
Krausz; assistant editor, David Glanz. 1. Kibbutzim — Israel — Collected
works. 2. Israel — Social conditions — Collected works. 3. Israel —
Emigration and immigration — Collected works. 4. Israel — Ethnic relations
— Collected works. I. Krausz, Ernest. II. Glanz, David. III. Series.
HN660.A8 S83      306/.095694 19      *LC* 79-93045      *ISBN* 087855369X

**Eisenstadt, S. N. (Shmuel Noah), 1923-.**                             • **4.5400**
Israeli society / [by] S. N. Eisenstadt. — London: Weidenfeld & Nicolson,
1967. xi, 451 p.; 24 cm. (Publication series in the history of Zionism and the
Yishuv, the Institute of Contemporary Jewry, the Hebrew University of
Jerusalem) (The Nature of human society series) 1. Israel — Social conditions.
I. T.
HN660.E5x      309.1/5694      *LC* 68-77314

**Israel: social structure and change.** Edited by Michael Curtis         **4.5401**
[and] Mordecai S. Chertoff.
New Brunswick, N.J.: Transaction Books; distributed by Dutton, [1973] 443 p.:
illus.; 24 cm. 'Based in part on the proceedings of the 1971-72 conferences of the
American Academic Association for Peace in the Middle East.' 1. Israel —
Social conditions — Addresses, essays, lectures. 2. Israel — Economic
conditions — Addresses, essays, lectures. 3. Israel — Politics and government
— Addresses, essays, lectures. I. Curtis, Michael, 1923- ed. II. Chertoff,
Mordecai S., 1922- ed. III. American Academic Association for Peace in the
Middle East.
HN660.I8x      309.1/5694/05      *LC* 73-78696      *ISBN* 0878550801

**Halpern, Manfred.**                                                    • **4.5402**
The politics of social change in the Middle East and North Africa. Princeton,
N.J. Princeton University Press, 1963. xxv, 431 p. fold. col. map. 1. Middle
East — Social conditions 2. Middle East — Politics I. T.
HN660.8 H2      *LC* 63-12670

**Eberhard, Wolfram, 1909-.**                                            • **4.5403**
Collected papers. — [Hong Kong]: Hong Kong University Press; [New York:
Oxford University Press, agents], 1967-. v.         : illus., maps, ports.; 23 cm.
1. Land settlement — China. 2. Cities and towns — China. 3. Asia — Social
conditions — Addresses, essays, lectures. I. T.
HN663.E2      309.15      *LC* 67-6764

**Wertheim, W. F. (Willem Frederik), 1907-.**                            • **4.5404**
East–West parallels: sociological approaches to modern Asia. — [1st American
ed.] Chicago: Quadrangle Books, [1965, c1964]. vii, 284 p.: map; 22 cm.
1. Asia, Southeastern — Social conditions. 2. Asia, Southeastern — Politics.
I. T.
HN663.5.W4      309.159      *LC* 63-11847

**Stevenson, Thomas B., 1945-.**                                          **4.5405**
Social change in a Yemeni highlands town / Thomas B. Stevenson. — Salt Lake
City: University of Utah Press, c1985. xxiii, 190 p.: ill.; 24 cm. Includes index.
1. 'Amrān (Yemen) — Social conditions. I. T.
HN664.A8 S73 1985      306/.0953/32 19      *LC* 85-5322      *ISBN*
0874801125

**Modernization in South–East Asia**, edited by Hans–Dieter              **4.5406**
**Evers.**
Singapore; New York: Oxford University Press, 1973. xix, 249 p.; 26 cm. Papers
from a conference held under the auspices of the Institute of Southeast Asian
Studies, Singapore. 1. Asia, Southeastern — Social conditions — Congresses.
2. Asia, Southeastern — Economic conditions — Congresses. I. Evers, Hans-
Dieter. ed. II. Institute of Southeast Asian Studies.
HN667.M63      301.24/0959      *LC* 73-941797

**Ismael, Jacqueline S.**                                                 **4.5407**
Kuwait, social change in historical perspective / Jacqueline S. Ismael. — 1st ed.
— Syracuse, N.Y.: Syracuse University Press, c1982. xii, 202 p.: ill.; 24 cm. —
(Contemporary issues in the Middle East.) Includes index. 1. Kuwait — Social
conditions. 2. Kuwait — Economic conditions. I. T. II. Series.
HN669.A8 I82      953/.67 19      *LC* 81-21244      *ISBN* 0815622546

**Zonis, Marvin, 1936-.**                                                 **4.5408**
The political elite of Iran. — [Princeton]: Princeton University Press, 1971. xvi,
389 p.; 24 cm. — (Princeton studies on the Near East.) 1. Elite (Social sciences)
— Iran. 2. Iran — Politics and government — 1941-1979 I. T. II. Series.
HN670.Z6x      301.44/92      *LC* 74-90966      *ISBN* 0691030839

**Continuity and change in modern Iran** / Michael E. Bonine and         **4.5409**
**Nikki R. Keddie, editors.**
Albany: State University of New York Press, c1981. x, 359 p.: ill.; 23 cm.
1. Iran — Social conditions — Addresses, essays, lectures. 2. Iran — Politics
and government — Addresses, essays, lectures. I. Bonine, Michael E., 1942-
II. Keddie, Nikki R.
HN670.2.A8 C66      955/.053 19      *LC* 80-19468      *ISBN* 0873954661

# HN671–680 China
(see also: HN731-740)

**Ch'ü, T'ung-tsu.**                                                      • **4.5410**
Han social structure. Edited by Jack L. Dull. — Seattle: University of
Washington Press, [1972] xix, 550 p.; 25 cm. — (Han Dynasty, China, 1)
'Documents on Han social structure': p. 251-506. 1. China — Social conditions
— 221 B.C.-960 A.D. I. T. II. Series.
HN673.C43      309.1/31      *LC* 69-14206      *ISBN* 0295950684

**Chang, Chung-li, 1919-.**                                              • **4.5411**
The Chinese gentry; studies on their role in nineteenth–century Chinese society.
Introd. by Franz Michael. — Seattle, University of Washington Press, 1955.
xxi, 250 p. diagrs. 24 cm. — (University of Washington publications on Asia,
no.3) Bibliography: p. 232-243. 1. Middle classes — China. 2. China — Soc.
condit. I. T.
HN673.C5      323.32      *LC* 55-6738

**Eberhard, Wolfram, 1909-.**                                            • **4.5412**
Conquerors and rulers; social forces in medieval China. 2d, rev. ed. Leiden, E. J.
Brill, 1965. 191 p. 25 cm. On label mounted on t.p.: W. Heinman, New York.
1. Middle classes — China. 2. China — Social conditions — 960-1644 I. T.
HN673.E2 1965      301.44      *LC* 65-9562

**Fei, Hsiao-t'ung.**                                                    • **4.5413**
China's gentry; essays in rural–urban relations. Revised & edited by Margaret
Park Redfield, with six life–histories of Chinese gentry families collected by
Yung–teh How, and an introd. by Robert Redfield. Chicago, University of
Chicago Press [1953] v, 289 p. ill. 1. Sociology, Rural 2. China — Social
conditions I. Redfield, Margaret Park. II. Chou, Jung-tê, 1915- III. T.
HN673 F4      *LC* 53-11440

**Ho, Ping-ti.**                                                         • **4.5414**
The ladder of success in Imperial China; aspects of social mobility, 1368–1911.
— New York, Columbia University Press, 1962. xviii, 385 p. tables. 24 cm. —
(Studies of the East Asian Institute, Columbia University) Bibliography: p.
[357]-376. 1. Social mobility — China. I. T.
HN673.H58      301.440951      *LC* 62-10451

**Hsü, Cho-yün, 1930-.**                                                 • **4.5415**
Ancient China in transition; an analysis of social mobility, 722–222 B. C. —
Stanford, Calif., Stanford University Press, 1965. viii, 238 p. illus., geneal.
tables, maps. 24 cm. — (Stanford studies in the civilizations of eastern Asia)
Bibliography: p. [221]-229. 1. China — Soc. condit. 2. Social mobility —
China. I. T. II. Series.
HN673.H75      301.440951      *LC* 65-13110

**Conflict and control in late Imperial China** / edited by Frederic     **4.5416**
**Wakeman, Jr. and Carolyn Grant.**
Berkeley: University of California Press, c1975. xx, 328 p.: maps; 25 cm.
Selected papers originally presented at a conference sponsored by the Center for
Chinese Studies at the University of California, Berkeley, and the Committee on
Studies of Chinese Civilization of the American Council of Learned Societies
held at East-West Center, Honolulu, June, 1971. 1. Power (Social sciences) —
Congresses. 2. China — Social conditions — 1644-1912 — Congresses.
3. China — History — Ch'ing dynasty — 1644-1912 — Congresses.
I. Wakeman, Frederic E. II. Grant, Carolyn. III. University of California,
Berkeley. Center for Chinese Studies. IV. American Council of Learned
Societies. Committee on Studies of Chinese Civilization.
HN676.C66      301.5/92/0951      *LC* 73-87247      *ISBN* 0520025970

**Fried, Morton H. (Morton Herbert), 1923-1986.**                        • **4.5417**
Fabric of Chinese society; a study of the social life of a Chinese county seat, by
Morton H. Fried. — New York: Octagon Books, 1969 [c1953] xi, 243 p.: illus.,
map.; 22 cm. 1. Chu-hsien, China (Anhwei Province) — Social conditions.
I. T.
HN680.C55 F7 1969      309.1/51/225      *LC* 76-75993

**Yang, C. K., 1910-.**                                                  • **4.5418**
A Chinese village in early Communist transition. Cambridge, Technology
Press, Massachusetts Institute of Technology; distributed by Harvard
University Press, 1959. 284 p. 24 cm. 1. Villages — China — Case studies.
2. Agriculture, Cooperative — China — Case studies. 3. China — Rural
conditions — Case studies. 4. Nan-ching, China (Kwangtung Province) I. T.
HN680.N3 Y32      301.35095127      *LC* 59-11517

**Johnson, David G. (David George), 1938-.**     **4.5419**
The medieval Chinese oligarchy / David G. Johnson. — Boulder, Colo.: Westview Press, c1977. xiii, 281 p.; 24 cm. (Westview special studies on China and East Asia) (Columbia University Studies of the East Asian Institute) Includes index. 1. Elite (Social sciences) — China. 2. Oligarchy I. T.
HN680.Z9 E44 1977     301.44/92/0951     *LC* 76-44875     *ISBN* 0891581405

**Pasternak, Burton.**     **4.5420**
Kinship & community in two Chinese villages. — Stanford, Calif.: Stanford University Press, 1972. ix, 174 p.: ill.; 23 cm. 1. Family — Taiwan. 2. Ta-T'ieh, Formosa — Rural conditions. 3. Chung-she, Formosa — Rural conditions. I. T.
HN680.5.T3 P37     309.1/51/249     *LC* 72-78870     *ISBN* 0804708231

## HN681–690.5 India. Pakistan

**Elites in South Asia; edited by Edmund Leach and S. N. Mukherjee.**     • **4.5421**
Cambridge [Eng.] University Press, 1970. xiv, 266 p. 2 maps (1 fold.) 24 cm. Papers originally prepared for a seminar held at St. John's College, Cambridge, in April, 1968 under the auspices of the University Centre of South Asian Studies. 1. Upper classes — India — Congresses. 2. Elite (Social sciences) — India — Congresses. 3. India — Social conditions — Congresses. I. Leach, Edmund Ronald. ed. II. Mukherjee, S. N. III. St. John's College (University of Cambridge) IV. University of Cambridge. Centre for South Asian Studies.
HN682.E44 1970     301.44     *LC* 78-101446     *ISBN* 0521077109

**Heimsath, Charles Herman, 1928-.**     • **4.5422**
Indian nationalism and Hindu social reform, by Charles H. Heimsath. — Princeton, N. J., Princeton University Press, 1964. xiii, 379 p. 25 cm. Bibliography: p. 357-371. 1. India — Soc. condit. I. T.
HN683.H4     309.154     *LC* 63-20660

**Lewis, Oscar, 1914-1970.**     • **4.5423**
Village life in northern India; studies in a Delhi village. With the assistance of Victor Barnouw. — Urbana: University of Illinois Press, 1958. xiii, 384 p.: illus.; 27 cm. 1. Villages — India — Case studies. 2. India — Rural conditions — Case studies. I. T.
HN683.L4     323.354 301.35*     *LC* 57-6953

**Marriott, McKim, ed.**     • **4.5424**
Village India; studies in the little community, papers by Alan R. Beals [and others. — Chicago]: University of Chicago Press, [1955] xix, 269 p.: illus., map.; 25 cm. — (Comparative studies of cultures and civilizations) 'Published also as Memoir no. 83 of the American Anthropological Association.' 1. Villages — India — Case studies. 2. India — Social conditions — 1947- I. Beals, Alan R. II. T.
HN683.M3     323.3     *LC* 55-9326

**Panikkar, K. M. (Kavalam Madhava), 1896-1963.**     • **4.5425**
Hindu society at cross roads. — [3d ed.]. — New York: Asia Pub. House, [1961] 139 p. 1. India — Social conditions I. T.
HN683.P3 1961

**Weber, Max, 1864-1920.**     **4.5426**
The Hindu social system / translated and edited by Hans Gerth and Don Martindale; with an introd. by Don Martindale and a bibliography on Max Weber by Hans Gerth and Hedwig Ide Gerth. — [Minneapolis]: [s.n.], c1950. 48, 63-128, xxvii p.; 28 cm. — (University of Minnesota Sociology.Bulletin; no. 1. Historical series; v. 1.) 1. Hinduism 2. India — Social conditions I. Gerth, Hans Heinrich, 1908- II. T.
HN683.W42     *LC* 50-13994

**Mandelbaum, David Goodman, 1911-.**     • **4.5427**
Society in India [by] David G. Mandelbaum. — Berkeley: University of California Press, 1970. 2 v. (xi, 665, 37, 14 p.): map (on lining papers); 24 cm. 1. Caste — India 2. Family — India. 3. Social mobility — India. 4. India — Social conditions — 1947- I. T.
HN683.5.M344     309.1/54     *LC* 70-99952     *ISBN* 0520016238

**Mohanti, Prafulla.**     **4.5428**
My village, my life: portrait of an Indian village. — New York: Praeger Publishers, [1974, c1973] 230 p.: illus.; 25 cm. 1. Villages — India — Case studies. I. T.
HN683.5.M58 1974     301.35/2/0954     *LC* 73-16895

**Rosen, George, 1920-.**     • **4.5429**
Democracy and economic change in India. Berkeley; University of California Press, 1966. 337 p.,maps. 1. India — Social conditions 2. India — Economic conditions I. T.
HN683.5 R6     309.154     *LC* 66-13986

**Srinivas, Mysore Narasimhachar.**     **4.5430**
Social change in modern India [by] M. N. Srinivas. — Berkeley: University of California Press, 1966. xv, 194 p.; 21 cm. — (The Rabindranath Tagore memorial lectures, 1963) 1. India — Social conditions — 1947- I. T. II. Series.
HN683.5.S7 1966     309.154     *LC* 66-14413

**Klass, Morton, 1927-.**     **4.5431**
From field to factory: community structure and industrialization in West Bengal / Morton Klass. — Philadelphia, Pa.: Institute for the Study of Human Issues, c1978. 264 p.: ill.; 24 cm. Includes index. 1. West Bengal (India) — Rural conditions. 2. Villages — India — West Bengal. 3. West Bengal (India) — Industries. I. T.
HN690.B4 K53     301.35/2/095414     *LC* 78-1552     *ISBN* 0915980347

**Dube, S. C. (Shyama Charan), 1922-.**     • **4.5432**
Indian village / foreword by Morris Edward Opler. — New York: Harper & Row, 1967. 248 p.: illus. — (Harper colophon books) First published in 1955. 1. Villages — India — Case studies. 2. Shamirpet (India). 3. India — Rural consitions — Case studies. I. T.
HN690.D8     *LC* 67-19600

**Orenstein, Henry.**     • **4.5433**
Gaon: conflict and cohesion in an Indian village. Princeton, N.J., Princeton University Press, 1965. viii, 341 p. ill., maps. 1. Villages — India — Poona (District) — Case studies 2. Poona (India: District) — Rural conditions — Case studies I. T.
HN690 P6 O7     *LC* 65-12991

**Srinivas, Mysore Narasimhachar.**     **4.5434**
The remembered village / M. N. Srinivas. — Berkeley: University of California Press, c1976. xvi, 356 p., [4] leaves of plates: ill.; 23 cm. 'Sponsored by the Center for South and Southeast Asia Studies, University of California, Berkeley.' Includes index. 1. Villages — India — Rāmpura (Karnataka) 2. Rāmpura, India (Karnataka) — Rural conditions. I. University of California, Berkeley. Center for South and Southeast Asia Studies. II. T.
HN690.R35 S74     301.35/2/095487     *LC* 75-7203     *ISBN* 0520029976

**Beck, Brenda E. F.**     **4.5435**
Peasant society in Koṅku: a study of right and left subcastes in South India / [by] Brenda E. F. Beck. — Vancouver: University of British Columbia Press [1972] xix, 334 p.; 24 cm. 1. Caste — India — Tamil Nadu. 2. Social structure — India — Tamil Nadu. 3. Tamil Nadu (India) — Social conditions. I. T.
HN690.T3 B4     301.29/54/82     *LC* 72-81828     *ISBN* 0774800143

**Hussain, Asaf.**     **4.5436**
Elite politics in an ideological state: the case of Pakistan / Asaf Hussain. — Folkestone, Eng.: Dawson, 1979. 212 p.; 23 cm. Includes index. 1. Elite (Social sciences) — Pakistan. 2. Pakistan — Politics and government — 1971- I. T.
HN690.5.Z9 E43 1979     323.3     *LC* 79-308121     *ISBN* 0712908609

## HN691–720 Indochina. Indonesia. Philippines

**Hildebrand, George C.**     **4.5437**
Cambodia: starvation and revolution / George C. Hildebrand, Gareth Porter. — New York: Monthly Review Press, c1976. 124 p.: ill.; 21 cm. 1. Starvation 2. Food supply — Cambodia. 3. Cambodia — Rural conditions. 4. Cambodia — History — Civil War, 1970-1975 I. Porter, Gareth, 1942- joint author. II. T.
HN700.C32 H54     320.9/596/04     *LC* 76-1646     *ISBN* 0853453829

**Ngô Vĩnh Long.**     **4.5438**
Before the revolution: the Vietnamese peasants under the French. — Cambridge, Mass.: MIT Press, [1973] xvi, 292 p.; 23 cm. 1. Villages — Vietnam — Addresses, essays, lectures. 2. Vietnam — Rural conditions — Addresses, essays, lectures. I. T.
HN700.V5 N43     309.1/597/03     *LC* 73-5779     *ISBN* 0262120658

**Singapore: society in transition / edited by Riaz Hassan.**     **4.5439**
Kuala Lumpur; New York: Oxford University Press, 1976. xix, 371 p.: ill.; 26 cm. (East Asian social science monographs) Includes index. 1. Ethnology — Singapore. 2. Singapore — Social conditions. 3. Singapore — Economic conditions. 4. Singapore — Politics and government. I. Riaz Hassan.
HN700.67.A8 S57     309.1/595/2     *LC* 77-151870     *ISBN* 0195803523

**Wertheim, W. F. (Willem Frederik), 1907-.**     • **4.5440**
Indonesian Society in transition: a study of social change / by W. F. Wertheim. — 2d rev. ed. — The Hague: W. van Hoeve, 1959, c1956. xiv, 394 p.; 23 cm. An extension of the author's The effects of Western civilization. 1. Indonesia — Social conditions. I. Institute of Pacific Relations. II. T.
HN703.W45     309.1/598     *LC* 60-823

HN
683
M35

**Kartodirdjo, Sartono, 1921-.**     4.5441
Protest movements in rural Java; a study of agrarian unrest in the nineteenth and early twentieth centuries. — Singapore; New York: Oxford University Press, 1974 (c1973). xv, 229 p.: maps.; 23 cm. 'Issued under the auspices of the Institute of Southeast Asian Studies, Singapore.' 1. Peasant uprisings — Indonesia — Java — History. 2. Java (Indonesia) — Rural conditions. I. Institute of Southeast Asian Studies. II. T.
HN710.J3 S25    322.4/4/095982    *LC* 74-168174

**Geertz, Clifford.**     ● **4.5442**
The social history of an Indonesian town. — Cambridge, Mass., M.I.T. Press [1965] v, 217 p. illus., maps. 22 cm. Bibliographical footnotes. 1. Indonesia — Soc. condit. — Case studies. 2. Modjokerto, Indonesia. I. T.
HN710.M6G4    309.1922    *LC* 65-23599

**Philippine social history: global trade and local transformations**  **4.5443**
**/ edited by Alfred W. McCoy & Ed. C. de Jesus.**
Honolulu: University Press of Hawaii;Published in cooperation with Ateneo de Manila University Press, Quezon City, Metro Manila, 1982. vi, 479 p.: ill.; 23 cm. — (Southeast Asia publications series; no. 7) 1. Philippines — Social conditions — Addresses, essays, lectures. 2. Philippines — Commerce — Addresses, essays, lectures. I. McCoy, Alfred W. II. De Jesus, Ed. C.
HN713.P45 1982    306/.09599 19    *LC* 82-244917    *ISBN* 0824808037

**Lewis, Henry T.**     **4.5444**
Ilocano rice farmers; a comparative study of two Philippine barrios [by] Henry T. Lewis. Honolulu, University of Hawaii Press, 1971. xi, 209 p. maps. 24 cm. 1. Ilokanos 2. Luzon (Philippines) — Rural conditions — Case studies. 3. Luzon (Philippines) — Social conditions — Case studies. I. T.
HN720.L8 L4    301.3/5/095991    *LC* 70-127330    *ISBN* 0870224603

**Larkin, John A.**     ● **4.5445**
The Pampangans: colonial society in a Philippine province / [by] John A. Larkin. — Berkeley: University of California Press, 1972. xvii, 340 p.: ill.; 24 cm. 'This volume is sponsored by the Center for South and Southeast Asia Studies, University of California, Berkeley.' 1. Pampanga (Philippines) — Social conditions. I. T.
HN720.P28 L37    309.1/599/1    *LC* 74-165232    *ISBN* 0520020766

## HN721–730 Japan

**Aspects of social change in modern Japan, edited by R. P. Dore.**  ● **4.5446**
**Contributors: Reinard Bendix [and others].**
Princeton, N.J.: Princeton University Press, 1967. x, 474 p.; 21 cm. — ([Studies in the the modernization of Japan]) Contributions to a seminar sponsored by the Conference on Modern Japan and held at Bermuda in Jan., 1963. 1. Japan — Social conditions — Addresses, essays, lectures. I. Dore, Ronald Philip. ed. II. Bendix, Reinhard. III. Conference on Modern Japan. IV. Series.
HN723.A8    309.152    *LC* 66-11973

**Beardsley, Richard King, 1918-.**     ● **4.5447**
Village Japan [by] Richard K. Beardsley, John W. Hall [and] Robert E. Ward. — [Chicago]: University of Chicago Press, [1959] 498 p.: illus.; 25 cm. 1. Villages — Japan — Case studies. 2. Japan — Rural conditions — Case studies. I. T.
HN723.B4    309.15219    *LC* 58-13802

**Hane, Mikiso.**     **4.5448**
Peasants, rebels, and outcastes: the underside of modern Japan / by Mikiso Hane. — 1st ed. — New York: Pantheon, c1982. xiii, 297 p.: maps; 25 cm. 1. Japan — Social conditions 2. Japan — History — 19th century 3. Japan — History — 20th century I. T.
HN723.H36 1982    952 19    *LC* 81-18912    *ISBN* 0394519639

**Nakane, Chie, 1926-.**     **4.5449**
[Tateshakai no ningen kankei. English] Japanese society. Berkeley, University of California Press, 1970. xi, 157 p. illus. 23 cm. Translation of Tateshakai no ningen kankei. 1. Social groups 2. Social values 3. Japan — Social conditions I. T.
HN723.N31513    309.1/52/04    *LC* 71-100021    *ISBN* 0520016424

**Smith, Robert John, 1927-.**     **4.5450**
Japanese society: tradition, self, and the social order / Robert J. Smith. — Cambridge; New York: Cambridge University Press, 1983. xii, 176 p.; 22 cm. — (Lewis Henry Morgan lectures. 1980) Includes indexes. 1. Social structure — Japan. 2. Japan — Social conditions I. T. II. Series.
HN723.S59 1983    306/.0952 19    *LC* 83-7498    *ISBN* 052125843X

**Smith, Thomas Carlyle.**     ● **4.5451**
The agrarian origins of modern Japan. Stanford, Calif., Stanford University Press, 1959. xi, 250 p. ill., map. (Stanford studies in the civilizations of eastern Asia) 1. Land tenure — Japan 2. Agriculture — Economic aspects — Japan 3. Japan — Rural conditions I. T. II. Series.
HN723 S6    *LC* 59-7429

**Tsurumi, Kazuko, 1918-.**     **4.5452**
Social change and the individual; Japan before and after defeat in World War II. — Princeton, N.J.: Princeton University Press, 1970. xiv, 441 p.; 25 cm. 1. Japan — Social conditions I. T.
HN723.T75    309.1/52    *LC* 69-18073    *ISBN* 0691093474

**De Vos, George A.**     **4.5453**
Socialization for achievement; essays on the cultural psychology of the Japanese, by George A. De Vos. With contributions by Hiroshi Wagatsuma, William Caudill, and Keiichi Mizushima. — Berkeley: University of Calif. Press, [1973] xv, 597 p.: illus.; 25 cm. 1. National characteristics, Japanese 2. Socialization 3. Deviant behavior 4. Japan — Social conditions I. T.
HN723.5.D48    301.15/7/0952    *LC* 78-132420    *ISBN* 0520018273

**Vogel, Ezra F.**     **4.5454**
Japan as number one: lessons for America / Ezra F. Vogel. — Cambridge, Mass.: Harvard University Press, 1979. xi, 272 p.; 24 cm. Includes index. 1. Japan — Social conditions — 1945- 2. Japan — Economic conditions — 1945- 3. Japan — Politics and government — 1945- I. T.
HN723.5.V63    309.1/52/04    *LC* 78-24059    *ISBN* 0674472152

**Smith, Robert John, 1927-.**     **4.5455**
Kurusu: the price of progress in a Japanese village, 1951–1975 / Robert J. Smith. — Stanford, Calif.: Stanford University Press, 1978. xvi, 269 p.: ill.; 24 cm. Includes index. 1. Villages — Japan — Case studies. 2. Family life surveys 3. Social change 4. Shionoe-chō, Japan — Rural conditions. I. T.
HN730.S534 S63    301.35/2/09523    *LC* 77-79999    *ISBN* 0804709629

## HN731–755 China. Hong Kong

**Freedman, Maurice.**     **4.5456**
The study of Chinese society: essays / by Maurice Freedman; selected and introduced by G. William Skinner. — Stanford, Calif.: Stanford University Press, 1979. xxiv, 491 p.; 24 cm. 1. Chinese in Southeastern Asia. 2. China — Social conditions I. Skinner, G. William (George William), 1925- II. T.
HN733.F73    309.1/51    *LC* 78-65395    *ISBN* 0804709645

**Chan, Anita.**     **4.5457**
Chen Village: the recent history of a peasant community in Mao's China / Anita Chan, Richard Madsen, and Jonathan Unger. — Berkeley: University of California Press, c1984. viii, 293 p.: ill.; 22 cm. 'Sponsored by the Center for Chinese Studies, University of California, Berkeley'—First prelim. p. 1. China — Rural conditions — Case studies. 1. Madsen, Richard, 1941- II. Unger, Jonathan. III. University of California, Berkeley. Center for Chinese Studies. IV. T.
HN733.5.C42 1984    307.7/2/0951 19    *LC* 82-16094    *ISBN* 0520047206

**Mosher, Steven W.**     **4.5458**
Broken earth: the rural Chinese / Steven W. Mosher. — New York: Free Press; London: Collier Macmillan, c1983. xii, 317 p., [16] p. of plates: ill.; 25 cm. 1. China — Rural conditions. I. T.
HN733.5.M67 1983    306/.0951 19    *LC* 83-47982    *ISBN* 0029217008

**Frolic, B. Michael, 1937-.**     **4.5459**
Mao's people: sixteen portraits of life in revolutionary China / B. Michael Frolic. — Cambridge: Harvard University Press, 1980. 278 p.: map. 1. Chinese in Hongkong — Interviews. 2. China — Social conditions — 1949-1976 — Case studies. I. T.
HN737.F76    HN737 F76.    309.1/51/05    *LC* 79-23013    *ISBN* 0674548469

**Leeming, Frank.**     **4.5460**
Rural China today / Frank Leeming. — London; New York: Longman, 1985. xii, 201 p., [8] p. of plates: ill.; 25 cm. Includes index. 1. Rural development — China. 2. Regional planning — China. 3. China — Rural conditions. I. T.
HN740.Z9 C64 1985    307.7/2/0951 19    *LC* 83-25617    *ISBN* 0582301440

**Watson, Rubie S. (Rubie Sharon), 1945-.**     **4.5461**
Inequality among brothers: class and kinship in South China / Rubie S. Watson. — Cambridge [Cambridgeshire]; New York: Cambridge University Press, 1985. xiii, 193 p.: ill.; 24 cm. (Cambridge studies in social anthropology; 53) Rev. version of thesis (Ph. D.)—London School of Economics, 1982. Includes index. 1. Social classes — Hong Kong — Case studies. 2. Kinship — Hong Kong — Ha Tsuen — Case studies. 3. Ha Tsuen (Hong Kong) — Rural

conditions — Case studies. 4. Hong Kong — Rural conditions — Case studies.
I. T.
HN755.2.C6 W37 1985      305.5/0951/25 19      *LC* 84-14991      *ISBN*
0521267706

# HN766 Arab Countries: Collective

**Arab society: social science perspectives** / edited by Saad Eddin          **4.5462**
Ibrahim, Nicholas S. Hopkins.
2nd ed. — [Cairo]: American University in Cairo Press, c1985. 507 p.; 23 cm.
First ed. published under title: Arab society in transition. 1. Arab countries —
Social conditions. 2. Arab countries — Politics and government — 1945-
I. Ibrahim, Saad Eddin. II. Hopkins, Nicholas S. III. American University at
Cairo. IV. Title: Arab society in transition.
HN766.A8 A7  1985      309.1/17/4927      *ISBN* 9774241266

# HN771–839 Africa

**The Roots of rural poverty in central and southern Africa** /          **4.5463**
edited by Robin Palmer, Neil Parsons.
Berkeley: University of California Press, 1977. xviii, 430 p.: ill.; 23 cm. —
(Perspectives on Southern Africa. 25) Includes index. 1. Rural poor — Africa,
Central — Addresses, essays, lectures. 2. Rural poor — Africa, Southern —
Addresses, essays, lectures. 3. Agriculture — Economic aspects — Africa,
Central — Addresses, essays, lectures. 4. Agriculture — Economic aspects —
Africa, Southern — Addresses, essays, lectures. 5. Africa, Central — Rural
conditions — Addresses, essays, lectures. 6. Africa, Southern — Rural
conditions — Addresses, essays, lectures. I. Palmer, Robin H. II. Parsons,
Neil. III. Series.
HN773.R66 1977b      330.9/67      *LC* 76-24600      *ISBN* 0520033183

**Social stratification in Africa.** Edited by Arthur Tuden and      • **4.5464**
Leonard Plotnicov.
New York: The Free Press, [1970] viii, 392 p.: illus.; 24 cm. 1. Social classes —
Africa — Addresses, essays, lectures. 2. Africa — Social conditions — 1960- —
Addresses, essays, lectures. I. Tuden, Arthur, ed. II. Plotnicov, Leonard, ed.
HN773.S62      301.44/096      *LC* 78-91223

**Lloyd, Peter Cutt.**                                              • **4.5465**
Africa in social change; West African societies in transition [by] P. C. Lloyd.
New York, Praeger [1968] 363 p. maps. 22 cm. 1. Africa, West — Social
conditions — 1960- 2. Africa, West — Politics and government I. T.
HN773.5.L4 1968      309.1/66      *LC* 68-24100

**Mazrui, Ali Al'Amin.**                                           • **4.5466**
Violence and thought; essays on social tensions in Africa [by] Ali A. Mazrui.
[New York] Humanities Press [1969] vii, 351 p. 20 cm. 1. Violence — Africa.
2. Social conflict — Africa. 3. Africa — Social conditions I. T.
HN773.5.M28      309.1/6      *LC* 70-8406

**Sub–Saharan Africa** / edited by Chris Allen and Gavin          **4.5467**
Williams.
New York: Monthly Review Press, c1982. xxi, 217 p.; 23 cm. — (Sociology of
'developing societies.' 2) Includes index. 1. Africa, Sub-Saharan — Social
conditions — Addresses, essays, lectures. I. Allen, Christopher. II. Williams,
Gavin. III. Series.
HN773.5.S9 1982      967 19      *LC* 81-16902      *ISBN* 085345597X

**Hunter, Guy.**                                                   • **4.5468**
The new societies of tropical Africa; a selective study. London, Oxford
University Press, 1962. xviii, 376 p. ill., fold. maps, tables. 1. Africa, Sub-
Saharan — Social conditions I. T.
HN777 H8      *LC* 62-5071

**Baer, Gabriel.**                                                 • **4.5469**
Studies in the social history of modern Egypt. Chicago, University of Chicago
Press [1969] xx, 259 p. 24 cm. (Publications of the Center for Middle Eastern
Studies, no. 4) 1. Egypt — Social conditions I. T.
HN783.B32      309.1/62      *LC* 69-17537

**Anderson, Lisa, 1950-.**                                          **4.5470**
The state and social transformation in Tunisia and Libya, 1830–1980 / Lisa
Anderson. — Princeton, N.J.: Princeton University Press, c1986. xxiv, 325 p.:
maps; 23 cm. — (Princeton studies on the Near East.) Includes index. 1. Social
structure — Tunisia. 2. Social structure — Libya. 3. Tunisia — Rural
conditions. 4. Libya — Rural conditions. 5. Tunisia — Politics and
government. 6. Libya — Politics and government. I. T. II. Series.
HN784.A8 A53 1986      305/.0961/1 19      *LC* 85-43266      *ISBN*
0691054622

**Binder, Leonard.**                                               **4.5471**
In a moment of enthusiasm: political power and the second stratum in Egypt /
Leonard Binder. — Chicago: University of Chicago Press, 1978. xxii, 437 p.:
ill.; 24 cm. Includes index. 1. Elite (Social sciences) — Egypt. 2. Middle classes
— Egypt. 3. Egypt — Rural conditions. 4. Egypt — Politics and government
— 1970- I. T.
HN786.Z9 E43      301.44/92/0962      *LC* 77-15480      *ISBN* 0226051447

**Fakhouri, Hani.**                                                **4.5472**
Kafr el-Elow: an Egyptian village in transition. — New York: Holt, Rinehart
and Winston, [1972] x, 134 p.: ill.; 24 cm. — (Case studies in cultural
anthropology.) 1. Kafr al 'Ilw, Egypt — Social conditions. I. T. II. Series.
HN790.K33 F34      309.1/62/16      *LC* 72-84770      *ISBN* 0030862167

**Barrett, Stanley R.**                                            **4.5473**
Two villages on stilts; economic and family change in Nigeria [by] Stanley R.
Barrett. — New York: Chandler Pub. Co., [1974] xi, 115 p.: illus.; 23 cm. —
(Case studies in social and economic change) 1. Villages — Nigeria — Case
studies. 2. Collective settlements — Nigeria — Case studies. 3. Family —
Nigeria — Case studies. I. T.
HN800.N5 B35      301.42/3/09669      *LC* 73-19765      *ISBN* 0810204754

**Kaunda, Kenneth D. (Kenneth David), 1924-.**                     **4.5474**
[Kaunda on violence] The riddle of violence / Kenneth Kaunda; edited by
Colin M. Morris. — 1st U.S. ed. — San Francisco: Harper & Row, [1981]
c1980. 184 p.; 22 cm. First published in 1980 under title: Kaunda on violence.
1. Violence — Zambia. 2. Nonviolence I. Morris, Colin M. II. T.
HN803.Z9 V54 1981      303.6/2/096894 19      *LC* 80-8348      *ISBN*
0062504509

**Knight, C. Gregory.**                                            **4.5475**
Ecology and change: rural modernization in an African community [by] C.
Gregory Knight. New York, Academic Press [1974] xx, 300 p. illus. 25 cm.
1. Agriculture — Tanzania. 2. Social change 3. Tanzania — Rural conditions.
4. Tanzania — Social conditions — 1964- I. T.
HN814.T32 K57      309.1/678/04      *LC* 73-7446      *ISBN* 0127854355

**Hlophe, Stephen S.**                                             **4.5476**
Class, ethnicity, and politics in Liberia: a class analysis of power struggles in the
Tubman and Tolbert administrations, from 1944–1975 / Stephen S. Hlophe. —
Washington, D.C.: University Press of America, c1979. 317 p.; 23 cm. 1. Social
classes — Liberia. 2. Social conflict — Liberia. 3. Liberia — Ethnic relations.
4. Liberia — Politics and government — 1944-1971 5. Liberia — Politics and
government — 1971-1980 I. T.
HN835.Z9 S65      306/.2/096662 19      *LC* 79-63261      *ISBN*
0819107212

**Levine, Donald Nathan, 1931-.**                                  **4.5477**
Greater Ethiopia: the evolution of a multiethnic society / Donald N. Levine. —
Chicago: University of Chicago Press, 1974. xv, 229 p.: ill.; 23 cm. Includes
index. 1. Ethnology — Ethiopia 2. Ethiopia — Social conditions I. T.
HN840.E82 L48      309.1/63      *LC* 73-91233      *ISBN* 0226475581

# HN863–940 New Zealand. Oceania

**Fuchs, Lawrence H.**                                             • **4.5478**
Hawaii pono: a social history / Lawrence H. Fuchs. — New York: Harcourt,
Brace & World, c1961. ix, 501 p.: map; 22 cm. 1. Hawaii — Social conditions.
I. T.
HN933.F8      *LC* 61-13347

**Belshaw, Cyril S.**                                              • **4.5479**
Changing Melanesia: social economics of culture contact. — Melbourne:
Oxford University Press, 1954. x, 197 p.: maps. 1. New Caledonia — Social
conditions. 2. Vanuatu — Social conditions. 3. Solomon Islands — Social
conditions. I. T.
HN935.B4

# HN980 Developing Areas

**Lehmann, David.**                                                **4.5480**
Development theory: four critical studies / edited by David Lehmann. —
London: Cass, 1979. vii, 106 p.; 24 cm. 1. Economic development —
Addresses, essays, lectures. 2. Developing countries — Economic conditions
— Addresses, essays, lectures. I. T.
HN980.D5 1979      309.2/3/091724      *LC* 79-314142      *ISBN*
0714630942

**Essays on modernization of underdeveloped societies. Editor: A.**    **4.5481**
**R. Desai.**
New York, Humanities Press, 1972. 2 v. illus. 26 cm. Papers presented at a seminar organized by the Dept. of Sociology, University of Bombay, on the occasion of its 1969 golden jubilee. 1. Social history — Modern, 1500- — Addresses, essays, lectures. 2. Developing countries — Social conditions — Addresses, essays, lectures. I. Desai, Akshayakumar Ramanlal. II. Bombay. University. Dept. of Sociology.
HN980.E883     309.1/172/4     *LC* 72-188891     *ISBN* 0391002147

**Introduction to the sociology of 'developing societies' / edited**    **4.5482**
**by Hamza Alavi and Teodor Shanin.**
New York: Monthly Review Press, c1982. xii, 474 p.; 22 cm. (Sociology of 'developing societies.' 1) 1. Developing countries — Social conditions — Addresses, essays, lectures. I. Alavi, Hamza, 1921- II. Shanin, Teodor. III. Series.
HN980.I59 1982     909/.09724 19     *LC* 81-16892     *ISBN* 0853455953

**Long, Norman.**     **4.5483**
An introduction to the sociology of rural development / Norman Long. — Boulder, Colo.: Westview Press, 1977. 221 p.; 23 cm. Includes indexes. 1. Rural development — Socioliological aspects. I. T.
HN980.L66     309.2/63     *LC* 77-72956     *ISBN* 0891588019

**Women and development: the sexual division of labor in rural**    **4.5484**
**societies: a study / prepared for the International Labour Office**
**within the framework of the World Employment Programme:**
**edited by Lourdes Benería.**
New York, N.Y.: Praeger, 1982. xxiii, 257 p.: ill.; 24 cm. 1. Women in rural development 2. Sexual division of labor 3. Rural development 4. Women — Employment — Developing countries I. Benería, Lourdes. II. International Labour Office. III. World Employment Programme.
HN980.W65 1982     306/.36 19     *LC* 82-606     *ISBN* 0030618029

# HQ FAMILY. MARRIAGE. WOMAN

**Households: comparative and historical studies of the domestic**    **4.5485**
**group / edited by Robert McC. Netting, Richard R. Wilk, Eric**
**J. Arnould.**
Berkeley: University of California Press, c1984. xxxviii, 480 p.: ill.; 24 cm. Papers presented at a conference held Oct. 9-15, 1981 at the Seven Springs Conference Center, Mt. Kisco, N.Y., sponsored by the Wenner-Gren Foundation for Anthropological Research. 1. Households — Congresses. 2. Family — Congresses. 3. Social change — Congresses. 4. Culture — Congresses. I. Netting, Robert McC. II. Wilk, Richard R. III. Arnould, Eric J. IV. Wenner-Gren Foundation for Anthropological Research.
HQ7.H68 1984     306.8/5 19     *LC* 83-17975     *ISBN* 0520049969

# HQ10–471 Sexual Life

**Bullough, Vern L.**     **4.5486**
Sexual variance in society and history / Vern L. Bullough. — New York: Wiley, c1976. xvi, 715 p.; 24 cm. 'A Wiley-Interscience publication.' Includes index. 1. Sex customs — History. 2. Sexual deviation — History. I. T.
HQ12.B84     301.41/79     *LC* 75-38911     *ISBN* 0471120804

**Hyde, Janet Shibley.**     **4.5487**
Understanding human sexuality / Janet Shibley Hyde. — 3rd ed. — New York: McGraw-Hill, c1986. xxiii, 740 p., [2] p. of plates: ill. (some col.); 26 cm. Includes index. 1. Sex 2. Sex customs 3. Hygiene, Sexual 4. Sex (Psychology) I. T.
HQ12.H82 1986     612.6 19     *LC* 85-7875     *ISBN* 0070315817

**Bullough, Vern L.**     **4.5488**
Sexual practices & the medieval church / Vern L. Bullough & James Brundage. — Buffalo, N.Y.: Prometheus Books, 1982. xii, 289 p.; 24 cm. Includes index. 1. Sex customs — History — Addresses, essays, lectures. 2. Sex (Theology) — History of doctrines — Middle Ages — 600-1500 — Addresses, essays, lectures. I. Brundage, James A. II. T. III. Title: Sexual practices and the medieval church.
HQ14.B84 1982     261.8/357 19     *LC* 80-85227     *ISBN* 087975141X

**Easlea, Brian.**     **4.5489**
Science and sexual oppression: patriarchy's confrontation with woman and nature / Brian Easlea. — London: Weidenfeld and Nicolson, c1981. xiv, 314 p.;

24 cm. Includes indexes. 1. Sexism 2. Science 3. Masculinity (Psychology) I. T.
HQ16.E18 1981     305.3 19     *LC* 81-165289     *ISBN* 0297778935

**Human sexual behavior; variations in the ethnographic**    **4.5490**
**spectrum. Edited by Donald S. Marshall and Robert C. Suggs.**
New York, Basic Books [1971] xviii, 302 p. 25 cm. (Studies in sex and society) Based on papers presented at the May 1965 Central States Anthropological Society meeting at Lexington, Ky. 1. Sex customs — Case studies. I. Marshall, Donald Stanley, 1919- ed. II. Suggs, Robert C. (Robert Carl), 1932- ed. III. Central States Anthropological Society (U.S.) IV. Series.
HQ16.H85     392/.6     *LC* 78-135552     *ISBN* 0465031579

**Mosse, George L. (George Lachmann), 1918-.**     **4.5491**
Nationalism and sexuality: respectability and abnormal sexuality in modern Europe / George L. Mosse. — 1st ed. — New York: H. Fertig, 1985. viii, 232 p., [10] p. of plates: ill.; 24 cm. Includes index. 1. Sex customs — Europe — History. 2. Sexual ethics — Europe — History. 3. Middle classes — Europe — Conduct of life. 4. Sex customs — Germany — Case studies. 5. Fascist ethics 6. Sex customs — Great Britain — Case studies. I. T.
HQ18.E8 M67 1985     306.7/094 19     *LC* 84-6082     *ISBN* 0865273502

**Weeks, Jeffrey, 1945-.**     **4.5492**
Sex, politics, and society: the regulation of sexuality since 1800 / Jeffrey Weeks. — London; New York: Longman, 1981. xiii, 306 p.; 23 cm. — (Themes in British social history) 1. Sex customs — Great Britain — History — 19th century. 2. Sex customs — Great Britain — History — 20th century. 3. Great Britain — Moral conditions. I. T.
HQ18.G7 W43     306.7/0941 19     *LC* 80-40862     *ISBN* 0582483336

**Barker-Benfield, G. J.**     **4.5493**
The horrors of the half-known life: male attitudes toward women and sexuality in nineteenth-century America / G. J. Barker-Benfield. — 1st ed. — New York: Harper & Row, c1976. xiv, 352 p.; 24 cm. 1. Sex role 2. Masculinity (Psychology) 3. Sex customs — United States — History. 4. Gynecologists — United States. I. T.
HQ18.U5 B3     301.41/0973     *LC* 75-6327     *ISBN* 0060102241

**Kinsey, Alfred Charles, 1894-1956.**     • **4.5494**
Sexual behavior in the human male [by] Alfred C. Kinsey. Wardell B. Pomeroy [and] Clyde E. Martin. — Philadelphia: W. B. Saunders Co., 1948. xv, 804 p.: diagrs.; 24 cm. 'Based on surveys made by members of the staff of Indiana University, and supported by the National Research Council's Committee for Research on Problems of Sex by means of funds contributed by the Medical Division of the Rockefeller Foundation.' 1. Sexual behavior surveys — United States. I. Pomeroy, Wardell Baxter. joint author. II. Martin, Clyde Eugene, joint author. III. T.
HQ18.U5 K5     392.6     *LC* 48-5195

**Reiss, Ira L.**     • **4.5495**
Premarital sexual standards in America; a sociological investigation of the relative social and cultural integration of American sexual standards. Glencoe, Ill., Free Press [1960] 286 p. illus. 22 cm. 1. Premarital sex — United States. 2. Sex customs — United States. 3. Sexual ethics — United States. I. T.
HQ18.U5 R4     392.6     *LC* 60-7095

**Robinson, Paul A., 1940-.**     **4.5496**
The modernization of sex: Havelock Ellis, Alfred Kinsey, William Masters, and Virginia Johnson / Paul Robinson. — 1st ed. — New York: Harper & Row, c1976. viii, 200 p.; 22 cm. 1. Ellis, Havelock, 1859-1939. 2. Kinsey, Alfred Charles, 1894-1956. 3. Masters, William H. 4. Johnson, Virginia E. 5. Sexologists I. T.
HQ18.3.R6     301.41/792/2     *LC* 75-24500     *ISBN* 0060135832

**Pomeroy, Wardell Baxter.**     **4.5497**
Dr. Kinsey and the Institute for Sex Research / Wardell B. Pomeroy. — 1982 ed. — New Haven: Yale University Press, [1982], c1972. xvi, 479 p.; 24 cm. Originally published: 1st ed. New York: Harper & Row, 1972. With new foreword. Includes index. 1. Kinsey, Alfred Charles, 1894-1956. 2. Alfred C. Kinsey Institute for Sex Research. I. T. II. Title: Doctor Kinsey and the Institute for Sex Research.
HQ18.32.K56 P65 1982     155.3/092/4 B 19     *LC* 82-4924     *ISBN* 0300029160

**Chafetz, Janet Saltzman.**     **4.5498**
Sex and advantage: a comparative, macro-structural theory of sex stratification / Janet Saltzman Chafetz. — Totowa, N.J.: Rowman & Allanheld, 1984. x, 134 p.: ill.; 25 cm. Includes index. 1. Sex discrimination against women 2. Social structure 3. Discrimination in employment 4. Family 5. Multivariate analysis I. T.
HQ21.C449 1984     305.4/2 19     *LC* 83-19077     *ISBN* 0865981590

**Crooks, Robert, 1941-.**     4.5499
Our sexuality / Robert Crooks, Karla Baur. — 3rd ed. — Menlo Park, Calif.: Benjamin/Cummings Pub. Co., c1987. p. cm. Includes index. 1. Sex 2. Sex customs — United States. I. Baur, Karla. II. T.
HQ21.C698 1987    612.6 19    *LC* 86-21598    *ISBN* 0805319093

**Ellis, Havelock, 1859-1939.**     • 4.5500
Studies in the psychology of sex, by Havelock Ellis. — New York: Random house, [1940] 2 v.: port., diagrs.; 22 cm. Published by the same publisher in four volumes in 1936. 1. Sex (Psychology) I. T. II. Title: Psychology of sex.
HQ21.E58 1940    136.1 159.9221    *LC* 41-17137

**Ford, Clellan Stearns, 1909-.**     • 4.5501
Patterns of sexual behavior / by Clellan S. Ford, and Frank A. Beach; with a foreword by Robert Latou Dickinson. — [1st ed. New York]: Harper [1951] viii, 307: map, diagrs.; 25 cm. 1. Sex I. Beach, Frank Ambrose, 1911- jt. author II. T.
HQ21 F693    *LC* 51-9766

**Freud, Sigmund, 1856-1939.**     • 4.5502
Three essays on the theory of sexuality / Translated and newly edited by James Stachey. New York: Basic Books, [1963] c1962. xviii, 130 p.; 22 cm. 1. Sex I. T.
HQ21.F813 1975    155.3    *LC* 62-11202

**Human sexuality in four perspectives / Frank A. Beach, editor;**     4.5503
**Milton Diamond ... [et al.].**
Baltimore: Johns Hopkins University Press, c1977. 330 p.: ill.; 24 cm. 1. Sex — Addresses, essays, lectures. I. Beach, Frank Ambrose, 1911- II. Diamond, Milton.
HQ21.H74    612.6    *LC* 76-17235    *ISBN* 0801818451

**Masters, William H.**     4.5504
Human sexuality / William H. Masters, Virginia E. Johnson, Robert C. Kolodny. — 2nd ed. — Boston: Little, Brown, c1985. xxi, 698 p.: ill.; 24 cm. Includes index. 1. Sex 2. Sex (Psychology) 3. Sex (Biology) 4. Sexual disorders I. Johnson, Virginia E. II. Kolodny, Robert C. III. T.
HQ21.M46157 1985    612/.6 19    *LC* 84-17171    *ISBN* 0316549959

**Mead, Margaret, 1901-1978.**     • 4.5505
Male and female, a study of the sexes in a changing world. New York, W. Morrow, 1949. xii, 477 p. 22 cm. 'The substance of this book was given as the Jacob Gimbel lectures in sex psychology under the auspices of Stanford University and the University of California, San Francisco, California, November, 1946.' 'Sources and experience in American culture': p. [451]-463. 1. Sex 2. Women 3. Man I. T.
HQ21.M464    392    *LC* 49-10784

**Powers of desire: the politics of sexuality / edited by Ann**     4.5506
**Snitow, Christine Stansell, and Sharon Thompson.**
New York: Monthly Review Press, c1983. 489 p.; 22 cm. — (New feminist library.) 1. Sex — History — 19th century. 2. Sex — History — 20th century. 3. Power (Social sciences) I. Snitow, Ann Barr, 1943- II. Stansell, Christine. III. Thompson, Sharon. IV. Series.
HQ21.P68 1983    306.7 19    *LC* 82-48037    *ISBN* 0853456097

**Rougemont, Denis de, 1906-.**     • 4.5507
[Amour et l'Occident. English] Love in the Western World. Translated by Montgomery Belgion. Rev. and augm. ed. [New York] Pantheon [c1956] 336 p. 24 cm. Translation of L'amour et l'occident. 1. Tristan — Romances — History and criticism. 2. Love 3. Courtly love 4. Love in literature 5. Albigenses I. T.
HQ21.R86 1956    306.7/09182/1 19    *LC* 56-12212

**Van de Velde, Th. H.**     • 4.5508
Ideal marriage: its physiology and technique / Th. H. Van de Velde. — 2d ed. / rev. by Margaret Smyth. — London: Heinemann Medical Books, 1965. xxi, 257 p.: ill. 1. Marriage 2. Sex in marriage I. Smyth, Margaret. II. T.
HQ21.V415 1965    613.96    *LC* 66-51907

**Aït Sabbah, Fatna.**     • 4.5509
[Femme dans l'inconscient musulman. English] Woman in the Muslim unconscious / Fatna A. Sabbah; translated by Mary Jo Lakeland. — New York: Pergamon Press, c1984. 132 p.; 24 cm. (Athene series.) Translation of: La femme dans l'inconscient musulman. 1. Women, Muslim — Sexual behavior. 2. Women, Muslim — Conduct of life I. T. II. Series.
HQ29.A3613 1984    297/.19783442 19    *LC* 84-11343    *ISBN* 0080316263

**Institute for Sex Research.**     • 4.5510
Sexual behavior in the human female, by the staff of the Institute for Sex Research, Indiana University: Alfred C. Kinsey [and others]. — Philadelphia: Saunders, 1953. xxx, 842 p.: diagrs.; 24 cm. 1. Women — Sexual behavior I. Kinsey, Alfred Charles, 1894-1956. II. T.
HQ29.I57 1953    301.41/76/33    *LC* 53-11127

**Mosher, Clelia Duel, 1863-1940.**     4.5511
The Mosher survey: sexual attitudes of 45 Victorian women / Clelia Duel Mosher; edited by James MaHood and Kristine Wenburg; introd. by Carl N. Degler. — New York: Arno Press, 1980. xix, 469 p.; 23 cm. 1. Women — United States — Sexual behavior — History. 2. Sex customs — United States — History. I. MaHood, James. II. Wenburg, Kristine. III. T.
HQ29.M67 1980    306.7/088042    *LC* 79-48014    *ISBN* 0405130902

**Pleasure and danger: exploring female sexuality / edited by**     4.5512
**Carole S. Vance.**
[S.l.]: Methuen, 1984. xx, 462 p.: ill. Papers presented at the Scholar and the feminist IX conference, held Apr. 24, 1982 at Barnard College, New York City. Includes index. 1. Women — Sexual behavior — Congresses. 2. Feminism — Congresses. I. Vance, Carole S.
HQ29.P54 1984    306.7/088042 19    *LC* 84-8402    *ISBN* 0710099746

**Human sexuality, new directions in American Catholic thought:**     4.5513
**a study / commissioned by the Catholic Theological Society of**
**America; Anthony Kosnik, chairperson ... [et al.].**
New York: Paulist Press, c1977. xvi, 322 p.; 24 cm. Includes index. 1. Sexual ethics — United States. 2. Sex — Religious aspects — Christianity I. Kosnik, Anthony. II. Catholic Theological Society of America.
HQ32.H822    261.8/343 19    *LC* 77-74586    *ISBN* 0809102234

**Lieberman, E. James, 1934-.**     4.5514
Sex & birth control: a guide for the young / [by] E. James Lieberman & Ellen Peck; introd. by Mary S. Calderone. — New York: Crowell, [1973] xiv, 299 p.: ill.; 21 cm. 1. Sex instruction for youth 2. Birth control — United States. I. Peck, Ellen, 1942- joint author. II. T.
HQ35.L544    613.9/5    *LC* 73-7806    *ISBN* 0690729855

**Herman, Judith Lewis, 1942-.**     4.5515
Father–daughter incest / Judith Lewis Herman with Lisa Hirschman. — Cambridge, Mass.: Harvard University Press, 1981. xi, 282 p.; 25 cm. 1. Incest — United States. 2. Fathers and daughters I. Hirschman, Lisa. II. T.
HQ71.H46    306.7 19    *LC* 81-2534    *ISBN* 0674295056

**Krafft-Ebing, R. von (Richard von), 1840-1902.**     • 4.5516
[Psychopathia sexualis. English] Psychopathia sexualis; a medico–forensic study. With an introd. by Ernest van den Haag. Translated from the Latin by Harry E. Wedeck. 1st unexpurgated ed. in English. New York, Putnam [1965] 512 p. 24 cm. 1. Sexual deviation I. T.
HQ71.K9 1965    132.75    *LC* 65-15139

**Plummer, Kenneth.**     4.5517
Sexual stigma: an interactionist account / Kenneth Plummer. — London: Routledge and Kegan Paul, 1975. viii, 258 p.; 23 cm. — (International library of sociology) Includes index. 1. Sexual deviation 2. Homosexuality 3. Stigma (Social psychology) 4. Social interaction I. T.
HQ71.P54    301.41/5    *LC* 75-313397    *ISBN* 0710080603

**Sexually abused children and their families / edited by Patricia**     4.5518
**Beezley Mrazek and C. Henry Kempe.**
1st ed. — Oxford; New York: Pergamon Press, 1981. xii, 271 p.; 26 cm. 1. Sexually abused children — Family relationships — Addresses, essays, lectures. 2. Incest victims — Family relationships — Addresses, essays, lectures. 3. Child molesting — Addresses, essays, lectures. 4. Sex offenders — Addresses, essays, lectures. I. Mrazek, Patricia Beezley. II. Kempe, C. Henry.
HQ71.S424 1981    306.7 19    *LC* 80-42146    *ISBN* 0080267963

**Schlesinger, Benjamin.**     4.5519
Sexual abuse of children: a resource guide and annotated bibliography / Benjamin Schlesinger. — Toronto; Buffalo: University of Toronto Press, c1982. xiii, 200 p.; 21 cm. Includes index. 1. Child molesting — Canada — Addresses, essays, lectures. 2. Incest — Canada — Addresses, essays, lectures. 3. Child molesting — Abstracts. I. T.
HQ72.C3 S35 1982    016.3627/044 19    *LC* 82-165925    *ISBN* 0802064817

**Ruggiero, Guido, 1944-.**     4.5520
The boundaries of eros: sex crime and sexuality in Renaissance Venice / Guido Ruggiero. — New York: Oxford University Press, 1985. viii, 223 p.; 25 cm. (Studies in the history of sexuality.) Includes index. 1. Sex crimes — Italy — Venice — History. 2. Sex customs — Italy — Venice — History. 3. Marriage — Italy — Venice — History. 4. Family — Italy — Venice — History. 5. Renaissance — Italy — Venice. I. T. II. Series.
HQ72.I8 R83 1985    306.7/0945/31 19    *LC* 84-931    *ISBN* 0195034651

**Rubin, Rick, 1949-.**     4.5521
Incest, the last taboo: an annotated bibliography / Rick Rubin, Greg Byerly. — New York: Garland Pub., 1983. xi, 169 p.; 23 cm. — (Garland reference library of social science. v. 143) Includes indexes. 1. Incest — United States — Abstracts. I. Byerly, Greg, 1949- II. T. III. Series.
HQ72.U53 R8 1983    306.7/77 19    *LC* 82-49181    *ISBN* 082409185X

## HQ75–76 Homosexuality

**Lesbian studies: present and future / edited by Margaret**  4.5522
**Cruikshank.**
1st ed. — Old Westbury, N.Y.: Feminist Press, c1982. xviii, 286 p.; 24 cm.
Includes index. 1. Lesbians — Biography. 2. Lesbianism — Study and
teaching. 3. Women's studies I. Cruikshank, Margaret.
HQ75.3.L48 1982      306.7/663/07 19      *LC* 82-4972      *ISBN*
0935312064

**Faderman, Lillian.**  4.5523
Surpassing the love of men: romantic friendship and love between women from
the Renaissance to the present / Lillian Faderman. — 1st ed. — New York:
Morrow, 1981. 496 p.: ill.; 25 cm. 1. Lesbianism — History I. T.
HQ75.5.F33 1981b      306.7/6/09 19      *LC* 80-24482      *ISBN*
068803733X

*Handwritten left margin: HQ 75.5 F33 1981*

**Black lesbians: an annotated bibliography / compiled by JR**  4.5524
**Roberts; foreword by Barbara Smith.**
1st ed. — Tallahassee, Fla.: Naiad Press, 1981. xv, 93 p.: ill., ports.; 22 cm.
Includes index. 1. Afro-American lesbians — Abstracts. I. Roberts, JR.
HQ75.6.U5 R6      306.7/6 19      *LC* 81-80662      *ISBN* 0930044215

**Women–identified women / edited by Trudy Darty and Sandee**  4.5525
**Potter; with a foreword by Judith Schwarz.**
1st ed. — Palo Alto, Calif.: Mayfield Pub. Co., 1984. xix, 316 p.; 23 cm.
1. Lesbians — United States — Social conditions. I. Darty, Trudy, d. 1983.
II. Potter, Sandee.
HQ75.6.U5 W65 1984      306.7/663/0973 19      *LC* 83-62837      *ISBN*
0874845734

**Bell, Alan P., 1932-.**  4.5526
Sexual preference, its development in men and women / Alan P. Bell, Martin S.
Weinberg, Sue Kiefer Hammersmith. — Bloomington: Indiana University
Press, c1981. xii, 242 p.: ill.; 24 cm. + statistical appendix (321 p.:ill.) 'An
official publication of the Alfred C. Kinsey Institute for Sex Research.'
1. Homosexuality 2. Homosexuality — Social aspects. 3. Homosexuality —
Psychological aspects. 4. Homosexuality — Statistics. I. Weinberg, Martin S.
II. Hammersmith, Sue Kiefer. III. Alfred C. Kinsey Institute for Sex
Research. IV. T.
HQ76.B438 1981      306.7/6 19      *LC* 81-47006      *ISBN* 0253166721

**Historical perspectives on homosexuality / compiled and edited**  4.5527
**by Salvatore J. Licata and Robert P. Petersen.**
New York: Haworth Press: Stein and Day, 1982 (c1981). 224 p., [1] leaf of
plate: col. ill.; 24 cm. — (Research on homosexuality. v. 2) (Journal of
homosexuality, 0091-8369; v. 6, no. 1-2) Includes bibliographical references and
index. 1. Homosexuality, Male — History — Addresses, essays, lectures.
I. Licata, Salvatore J. II. Petersen, Robert P. III. Series. IV. Series: Journal of
homosexuality, v. 6, no. 1-2
HQ76.Hx      306.7/6/09 19      *LC* 80-6262      *ISBN* 0917724275

**Bell, Alan P., 1932-.**  4.5528
Homosexualities: a study of diversity among men and women / Alan P. Bell,
Martin S. Weinberg. — New York: Simon and Schuster, c1978. 505 p.; 25 cm.
Report of a study made by the Institute for Sex Research. Includes index.
1. Homosexuality — United States. I. Weinberg, Martin S. joint author.
II. Institute for Sex Research. III. T.
HQ76.2.U5 B45      301.41/57/0973      *LC* 78-7398      *ISBN* 0671242121

**Harry, Joseph.**  4.5529
The social organization of gay males / Joseph Harry, William B. DeVall. —
New York: Praeger, 1978. xii, 223 p.; 25 cm. 1. Homosexuality, Male —
United States. 2. Social interaction 3. Sex role 4. Gay liberation movement —
United States. I. DeVall, William B. joint author. II. T.
HQ76.2.U5 H37      301.41/57      *LC* 78-8381

**Bullough, Vern L.**  4.5530
Homosexuality, a history / by Vern L. Bullough. — New York: New American
Library, c1979. ix, 196 p.; 21 cm. 'A Meridian book.' 1. Homosexuality —
History. I. T.
HQ76.25.B84      306.7/6/09      *LC* 79-84263      *ISBN* 0452005167

**Homosexual behavior: a modern reappraisal / edited by Judd**  4.5531
**Marmor.**
New York: Basic Books, c1980. xv, 416 p.; 24 cm. 1. Homosexuality —
Addresses, essays, lectures. I. Marmor, Judd.
HQ76.25.H673      306.7/6 19      *LC* 78-24659      *ISBN* 0465030459

**Boswell, John.**  4.5532
Christianity, social tolerance, and homosexuality: gay people in Western
Europe from the beginning of the Christian era to the fourteenth century / John
Boswell. — Chicago: University of Chicago Press, c1980. xviii, 424 p., [6] leaves

of plates: ill.; 25 cm. Includes indexes. 1. Homosexuality — Europe — History.
2. Homosexuality — Religious aspects — Christianity — History. I. T.
HQ76.3.E8 B67      306.7/66/094 19      *LC* 79-11171      *ISBN*
0226067106

**Dover, Kenneth James.**  4.5533
Greek homosexuality / K. J. Dover. — Cambridge, Mass.: Harvard University
Press, 1978. x, 244 p., [29] leaves of plates: ill.; 24 cm. Includes indexes.
1. Homosexuality — Greece. 2. Homosexuality — Law and legislation —
Greece. 3. Homosexuality and art 4. Homosexuality in literature 5. Literature
and morals I. T.
HQ76.3.G8 D68 1978      301.41/57/0938      *LC* 77-22423      *ISBN*
0674362616

**Altman, Dennis.**  4.5534
The homosexualization of America: the Americanization of the homosexual /
Dennis Altman. — 1st ed. — New York: St. Martin's Press, c1982. xiv, 242 p.;
22 cm. Includes index. 1. Homosexuality — United States. I. T.
HQ76.3.U5 A4 1982      306.7/66/0973 19      *LC* 81-23193      *ISBN*
0312388888

**Katz, Jonathan.**  4.5535
Gay American history: lesbians and gay men in the U.S.A.: A documentary /
by Jonathan Katz. — New York: Crowell, c1976. xiv, 690 p.: ill.; 26 cm.
Includes index. 1. Homosexuality — United States — History. 2. Lesbianism
— United States — History. I. T.
HQ76.3.U5 K37 1976      301.41/57/0973      *LC* 76-2039      *ISBN*
0690011652

**Rossman, Parker.**  4.5536
Sexual experience between men and boys: exploring the pederast underground /
Parker Rossman. — New York: Association Press, c1976. 247 p.; 22 cm.
Includes index. 1. Homosexuality — United States. 2. Boys — Sexual behavior
I. T.
HQ76.3.U5 R69      301.41/57      *LC* 76-9029      *ISBN* 0809619113

**D'Emilio, John.**  4.5537
Sexual politics, sexual communities: the making of a homosexual minority in
the United States, 1940–1970 / John D'Emilio. — Chicago: University of
Chicago Press, 1983. x, 257 p.; 24 cm. Based on the author's thesis (Ph. D.)—
Columbia University, 1981. 1. Gay liberation movement — United States —
History. I. T.
HQ76.8.U5 D45 1983      306.7/66/0973 19      *LC* 82-16000      *ISBN*
0226142655

**Katz, Jonathan.**  4.5538
Gay/lesbian almanac: a new documentary in which is contained, in
chronological order, evidence of the true and fantastical history of those persons
now called lesbians and gay men ... / Jonathan Ned Katz. — 1st ed. — New
York: Harper & Row, c1983. xxviii, 764 p.: ill.; 23 cm. Includes indexes.
1. Homosexuality, Male — United States — History. 2. Lesbianism — United
States — History. I. T.
HQ76.8.U5 K37 1983      306.7/66/0973 19      *LC* 81-48237      *ISBN*
0060909668

## HQ101–440 Prostitution

**Rosen, Ruth.**  4.5539
The lost sisterhood: prostitution in America, 1900–1918 / Ruth Rosen. —
Baltimore: Johns Hopkins University Press, c1982. xvii, 245 p.: ill.; 24 cm.
Includes index. 1. Prostitution — United States. I. T.
HQ144.R76 1982      306.7/4/0973 19      *LC* 81-23678      *ISBN*
0801826640

**Butler, Anne M., 1938-.**  4.5540
Daughters of joy, sisters of misery: prostitutes in the American West, 1865–90 /
Anne M. Butler. — Urbana: University of Illinois Press, c1985. xx, 179 p.,
[24] p. of plates: ill., ports.; 24 cm. Includes index. 1. Prostitutes — West (U.S.)
— History — 19th century. 2. Prostitution — West (U.S.) — History — 19th
century. I. T.
HQ145.A17 B88 1985      306.7/42/0978 19      *LC* 84-195      *ISBN*
0252011392

**Cohen, Bernard, 1937-.**  4.5541
Deviant street networks: prostitution in New York City / Bernard Cohen. —
Lexington, Mass.: Lexington Books, c1980. xvii, 200 p.: ill.; 24 cm. Includes
index. 1. Prostitution — New York (City) 2. Social sciences — Field work
I. T.
HQ146.N7 C63      306.7/4/097471 19      *LC* 80-8039      *ISBN*
0669039497

**Walkowitz, Judith R.**  4.5542
Prostitution and Victorian society: women, class, and the state / Judith R.
Walkowitz. — Cambridge; New York: Cambridge University Press, 1980. ix,

347 p.; 24 cm. Includes index. 1. Prostitution — Great Britain — History — 19th century. 2. Sexually transmitted diseases — Great Britain — History — 19th century. 3. Sexually transmitted diseases — Law and legislation — Great Britain — History — 19th century. I. T.
HQ185.A5 W34　　301.41/54/0941　　*LC* 79-21050　　*ISBN* 0521223342

## HQ450–471 Erotica. Pornography

**U.S. Commission on Obscenity and Pornography.**　　**4.5543**
The report. — [Washington: For sale by the Supt. of Docs., U.S. Govt. Print. Off.], 1970. 646 p.; 25 cm. 1. Erotica 2. Obscenity (Law) — U.S. I. T.
HQ460.U53　　364.17/4　　*LC* 70-609906

**Foxon, David Fairweather.**　　**4.5544**
Libertine literature in England: 1660–1745 / David Foxon. — New Hyde Park, N.Y.: University Books, [1966, c1965] xi, 70 p.: ill., facsims. 1. Erotic literature — History and criticism 2. English literature — 18th century — History and criticism. 3. Engish literature — Early modern, (1500-1700) — History and criticism. I. T.
HQ462.F6 1965　　809.933　　*LC* 65-24310

**Dworkin, Andrea.**　　**4.5545**
Pornography: men possessing women / Andrea Dworkin. — New York: Putnam, c1981. 300 p.; 21 cm. Includes index. 1. Pornography — Social aspects I. T.
HQ471.D96 1981b　　363.4/7 19　　*LC* 80-28830　　*ISBN* 0399126198

**Goldstein, Michael J. (Michael Joseph), 1930-.**　　**4.5546**
Pornography and sexual deviance; a report of the Legal and Behavioral Institute, Beverly Hills, California [by] Michael J. Goldstein and Harold Sanford Kant, with John J. Hartman. Berkeley: University of California Press, 1973. 194 p.: illus.; 25 cm. 1. Pornography 2. Sexual deviation I. Kant, Harold Sanford, joint author. II. Legal and Behavioral Institute. III. T.
HQ471.G62　　364.1/74　　*LC* 72-97735　　*ISBN* 0520024060

**Pornography and sexual aggression / edited by Neil M.**　　**4.5547**
**Malamuth, Edward Donnerstein.**
Orlando, Fla.: Academic Press, 1984. xviii, 333 p.: ill.; 24 cm. 1. Pornography — Social aspects — Addresses, essays, lectures. 2. Aggressiveness (Psychology) — Addresses, essays, lectures. 3. Women — Crimes against — Addresses, essays, lectures. 4. Violent crimes — Addresses, essays, lectures. I. Malamuth, Neil M. II. Donnerstein, Edward I.
HQ471.P646 1984　　363.4/7 19　　*LC* 84-3086　　*ISBN* 0124662803

**Take back the night: women on pornography / edited by Laura**　　**4.5548**
**Lederer.**
1st ed. — New York: Morrow, 1980. 359 p.; 24 cm. Includes index. 1. Pornography — Addresses, essays, lectures. 2. Pornography — Social aspects — United States. 3. Pornography — Religious aspects 4. Pornography — Psychological aspects. 5. Sex crimes — United States. 6. Feminism — United States. I. Lederer, Laura.
HQ471.T27 1980b　　363.4/7　　*LC* 80-17084　　*ISBN* 0688037283

**Thompson, Roger, 1933-.**　　**4.5549**
Unfit for modest ears: a study of pornographic, obscene, and bawdy works written or published in England in the second half of the seventeenth century / Roger Thompson. — Totowa, N.J.: Rowman and Littlefield, 1979. xii, 233 p.; 23 cm. 1. Literature, Immoral 2. Pornography 3. English literature — Early modern, 1500-1700 — History and criticism. I. T.
HQ471.T46 1979　　820/.9/3538　　*LC* 79-15070　　*ISBN* 0847661954

**Women against censorship / edited by Varda Burstyn; essays by**　　**4.5550**
**Varda Burstyn ... [et al.].**
Vancouver: Douglas & McIntyre, c1985. 210 p.; 23 cm. 1. Pornography — Social aspects — Addresses, essays, lectures. 2. Censorship — Addresses, essays, lectures. 3. Feminism — Addresses, essays, lectures. I. Burstyn, Varda.
HQ471.W66 1985　　363.4/7 19　　*LC* 85-146745　　*ISBN* 0888944551

**Zurcher, Louis A.**　　**4.5551**
Citizens for decency: antipornography crusades as status defense / by Louis A. Zurcher, Jr., and R. George Kirkpatrick, with the collaboration of Robert G. Cushing ... [et al.]. — Austin: University of Texas Press, c1976. xv, 412 p.; 24 cm. Includes index. 1. Pornography — Social aspects — United States. I. Kirkpatrick, Robert George, 1943- joint author. II. T.
HQ471.Z87　　301.2/1　　*LC* 75-22048　　*ISBN* 0292710321

## HQ503–1058 Family. Marriage. Children

**Briffault, Robert, 1876-1948.**　　● **4.5552**
The mothers: a study of the origins of sentiments and institutions / by Robert Briffault. — New York: The Macmillan company, 1927. 3 v.: ill.; 26 cm. 1. Mothers 2. Women — History and condition of women. 3. Marriage 4. Society, Primitive 5. Anthropology 6. Sociology I. T.
HQ503.B6　　*LC* 27-27779

**Laslett, Peter.**　　**4.5553**
Family life and illicit love in earlier generations: essays in historical sociology / Peter Laslett. — Cambridge; New York: Cambridge University Press, 1977. vii, 270 p.: ill.; 24 cm. Includes index. 1. Genealogy 2. Illegitimate children — Great Britain. 3. Orphans — Great Britain. 4. Slavery — United States I. T.
HQ503.L375　　301.42/09　　*LC* 76-21010　　*ISBN* 0521214084. *ISBN* 0521292212 pbk

**Mitterauer, Michael.**　　**4.5554**
[Vom Patriarchat zur Partnerschaft. English] The European family: patriarchy to partnership from the Middle Ages to the present / Michael Mitterauer and Reinhard Sieder; translated by Karla Oosterveen and Manfred Hörzinger. — Chicago: University of Chicago Press, 1982. xv, 235 p.; 24 cm. Translation of: Vom Patriarchat zur Partnerschaft. 1. Genealogy 2. Family — Europe — History. I. Sieder, Reinhard. II. T.
HQ503.M513 1982　　306.8/094 19　　*LC* 81-21954　　*ISBN* 0226532402

**Queen, Stuart Alfred, 1890-.**　　● **4.5555**
The family in various cultures / by Stuart A. Queen, Robert W. Habenstein. — 3d ed. — Philadelphia: Lippincott, 1967. 346 p. 1. Family I. Habenstein, Robert W., joint author. II. T.
HQ503.Q4 1967　　*LC* 67-15520

**Westermarck, Edward, 1862-1939.**　　● **4.5556**
The history of human marriage, by Edward Westermarck. 5th ed., rewritten. London, Macmillan, 1921. New York, Johnson Reprint Corp., 1971. 3 v. 23 cm. (Landmarks in anthropology) 1. Marriage — History. I. T.
HQ503.W5 1971　　301.42/09　　*LC* 75-184261

**Engels, Friedrich, 1820-1895.**　　● **4.5557**
[Ursprung der Familie. English] The origin of the family, private property, and the state, in the light of the researches of Lewis H. Morgan / With an introd. and notes by Eleanor Burke Leacock. [1st ed.] New York: International Publishers [1972, c1942] 285 p.; 21 cm. Translation of Der Ursprung der Familie. 1. Morgan, Lewis Henry, 1818-1881. Ancient society. 2. Genealogy 3. Property — History. 4. State, The 5. Society, Primitive I. Leacock, Eleanor Burke, 1922- ed. II. T.
HQ504.E6 1972　　301.42/1　　*LC* 79-184309　　*ISBN* 0717803384 *ISBN* 0717803597

**Malinowski, Bronislaw, 1884-1942.**　　● **4.5558**
Sex and repression in savage society, by Bronislaw Malinowski. London, K. Paul, Trench, Trubner & co., ltd; New York, Harcourt, Brace & company, inc., 1927. xiv, 285 p. 23 cm. (International library of psychology, philosophy and scientific method) 1. Family 2. Sex 3. Psychoanalysis 4. Society, Primitive 5. Anthropology I. T.
HQ504.M34　　*LC* 27-17344

**Malinowski, Bronislaw, 1884-1942.**　　● **4.5559**
The sexual life of savages in north–western Melanesia: an ethnographic account of courtship, marriage, and family life among the natives of the Trobriand islands, British New Guinea / by Bronislaw Malinowski; with a preface by Havelock Ellis. — 3d ed., with special foreword. London: Routledge & Kegan Paul, 1932. L, 505, 1 p.: front., ill. (plan) plates, maps.; 26 cm. On verso of t.-p.: Robert Mond expedition to New Guinea, 1914-1918. 1. Family 2. Sex 3. Society, Primitive 4. Ethnology — Trobriand islands. I. T.
HQ504.M36 1932a　　*LC* 33-3066

**Lacey, W. K. (Walter Kirkpatrick)**　　**4.5560**
The family in classical Greece [by] W. K. Lacey. Ithaca, N.Y., Cornell University Press [1968] 342 p. illus. 23 cm. (Aspects of Greek and Roman life (Ithaca, N.Y.) 1. Family — Greece. 2. Marriage — Greece. I. T. II. Series.
HQ510.L3　　301.42/0938　　*LC* 68-14817

**Bernard, Jessie Shirley, 1903-.**　　**4.5561**
The future of marriage [by] Jessie Bernard. New York: World Pub., [1972] xvi, 367 p.; 24 cm. 1. Marriage 2. Sex role I. T.
HQ518.B47 1972　　301.42　　*LC* 77-183085　　*ISBN* 0529045214

**Blitsten, Dorothy Rubovits, 1907-.** • **4.5562**
The world of the family: a comparative study of family organizations in their social and cultural settings. — New York: Random House, [1963] xiv, 303 p.; 22 cm. 1. Family I. T.
HQ518.B63    301.42    *LC* 63-8262

**Family in transition: rethinking marriage, sexuality, child rearing, and family organization / [compilers] Arlene S. Skolnick, Jerome H. Skolnick.** **4.5563**
5th ed. — Boston: Little, Brown, c1986. xiii, 598 p.; 23 cm. 1. Family — Addresses, essays, lectures. I. Skolnick, Arlene S., 1933- II. Skolnick, Jerome H.
HQ518.F336 1986    306.8/5 19    *LC* 85-19773    *ISBN* 0316797413

**Lasch, Christopher.** **4.5564**
Haven in a heartless world: the family besieged / Christopher Lasch. — New York: Basic Books, c1977. xviii, 230 p.; 24 cm. 1. Genealogy 2. Marriage — History. 3. Socialization I. T.
HQ518.L27    301.42    *LC* 77-75246    *ISBN* 0465028837

**Ghazzālī, 1058-1111.** **4.5565**
[Iḥyā' 'ulūm al-dīn. Book 12. English] Marriage and sexuality in Islam: a translation of al-Ghazālī's book on the etiquette of marriage from the Iḥyā' / by Madelain Farah. — Salt Lake City, Utah: University of Utah Press, 1984. xii, 185 p.; 24 cm. Translation of the twelfth book of the author's Iḥyā' 'ulūm al-dīn. Originally presented as the translator's thesis (doctoral—University of Utah) Includes index. 1. Marriage — Religious aspects — Islam — Early works to 1800. I. Farah, Madelain. II. T.
HQ525.I8 G5513 1984    297/.19783581 19    *LC* 83-27365    *ISBN* 0874802318

## HQ531–727 BY COUNTRY

## HQ531–557 United States

**American family history: a historical bibliography.** **4.5566**
Santa Barbara, Calif.: ABC-Clio Information Services, c1984. xii, 282 p.; 24 cm. (ABC-Clio research guides.) Drawn from ABC-Clio Information Services' 1973-1982 history database. Includes indexes. 1. Family — United States — History — Abstracts. 2. Family — Canada — History — Abstracts. 3. United States — Genealogy — Abstracts. 4. Canada — Genealogy — Abstracts. I. ABC-Clio Information Services. II. Series.
HQ535.A587 1984    016.3068/5/0973 19    *LC* 84-2955    *ISBN* 0874363802

**Bossard, James Herbert Siward, 1888-1960.** • **4.5567**
Ritual in family living: a contemporary study / by James H.S. Bossard and Eleanor S. Boll. — Philadelphia: University of Pennsylvania Press, 1950. 228 p.; 23 cm. 1. Family — United States 2. United States — Social conditions I. Boll, Eleanor Stoker. II. T.
HQ535.B68    *LC* 50-10690

**Calhoun, Arthur Wallace, 1885-.** • **4.5568**
A social history of the American family from colonial times to the present, by Arthur W. Calhoun. Cleveland, The Arthur H. Clark company, 1917-19. 3 v. 25 cm. 1. Family 2. Women — United States 3. United States — Social life and customs 4. United States — Social conditions I. T. II. Title: The American family.
HQ535.C2    *LC* 17-23329

**Caplow, Theodore.** **4.5569**
Middletown families: fifty years of change and continuity / Theodore Caplow and Howard M. Bahr ... [et al.]. — Minneapolis: University of Minnesota Press, c1982. ix, 436 p., [16] p. of plates: ill.; 24 cm. 'Based on the research of the Middletown III project, 1976-1981, under a grant from the National Science Foundation — T. p. verso. Includes indexes. 1. Family — United States — Longitudinal studies. 2. Cities and towns — United States — Longitudinal studies. 3. Community life — Longitudinal studies. I. T.
HQ535.C25 1982    306.8 19    *LC* 81-14757    *ISBN* 0816610738

**Censer, Jane Turner, 1951-.** **4.5570**
North Carolina planters and their children, 1800–1860 / Jane Turner Censer. — Baton Rogue: Louisiana State University Press, c1984. xxv, 191 p.: 2 maps; 24 cm. Includes index. 1. Family — North Carolina — History — 19th century. 2. Plantation owners — North Carolina — History — 19th century. 3. Plantation life — North Carolina — History — 19th century. 4. North Carolina — Social life and customs I. T.
HQ535.C38 1984    305.5/232/09756 19    *LC* 83-19966    *ISBN* 080711135X

**Cherlin, Andrew J., 1948-.** **4.5571**
Marriage, divorce, remarriage / Andrew J. Cherlin. — Cambridge, Mass.: Harvard University Press, c1981. xiv, 142 p.: ill.; 25 cm. (Social trends in the United States.) 1. Marriage — United States 2. Divorce — United States. 3. Remarriage — United States. 4. Family — United States 5. Afro-Americans — Families I. T. II. Series.
HQ535.C415    306.8/0973 19    *LC* 81-2901    *ISBN* 0674550803

**Cottle, Thomas J.** **4.5572**
A family album: portraits of intimacy and kinship / Thomas J. Cottle. — New York: Harper & Row, 1975 (c1974). xiv, 224 p.; 21 cm. (Harper colophon books; CN 365) 1. Family — United States 2. Interpersonal relations 3. Parent and child I. T.
HQ535.C68    301.42/7    *LC* 74-3589    *ISBN* 006136150X lib. bdg

**Ditzion, Sidney Herbert, 1908-.** • **4.5573**
Marriage, morals, and sex in America: a history of ideas / [by] Sidney Ditzion. — Expanded ed., with a new chapter by the author. — New York: Octagon Books, 1969 [c1953] 460 p.; 24 cm. 1. Family — U.S. 2. Marriage — U.S. 3. U.S. — Moral conditions. I. T.
HQ535.D5 1969    301.42    *LC* 72-96179

**Gordon, Michael, 1940- comp.** **4.5574**
The American family in social–historical perspective / Michael Gordon, editor. — 2d ed. — New York: St. Martin's Press, c1978. x, 580 p.: ill.; 25 cm. 1. Family — United States — History — Addresses, essays, lectures. I. T.
HQ535.G66 1978    301.42/0973    *LC* 77-86000    *ISBN* 031202312X

**Holmstrom, Lynda Lytle.** • **4.5575**
The two–career family. Cambridge, Mass., Schenkman Pub. Co.; distributed by General Learning Press [Morristown, N.J., 1972] vii, 203 p. 24 cm. 1. Dual-career families — United States — Case studies. 2. Professions 3. Husband and wife I. T.
HQ535.H58    301.42/7    *LC* 70-189095

**Kanter, Rosabeth Moss.** **4.5576**
Work and family in the United States: a critical review and agenda for research and policy / by Rosabeth Moss Kanter. — New York: Russell Sage Foundation, 1977. 116 p.; 24 cm. (Social science frontiers; 9) 1. Work and family — United States. I. T. II. Series.
HQ535.K3x    300/.8 s 301.42/0973    *LC* 76-46870    *ISBN* 0871544334

**Koller, Marvin R.** **4.5577**
Families: a multigenerational approach [by] Marvin R. Koller. New York, McGraw-Hill [1974] xi, 339 p. illus. 23 cm. 1. Family — United States 2. Family life education — United States. I. T.
HQ535.K65    301.42/0973    *LC* 73-13932    *ISBN* 007035331X

**LeMasters, E. E.** **4.5578**
Parents in contemporary America: a sympathetic view / E.E. LeMasters, John DeFrain. — 4th ed. — Homewood, Ill.: Dorsey Press, 1983. xiii, 309 p.; 23 cm. — (Dorsey series in sociology.) Rev. ed. of: Parents in modern America. 3rd ed. 1977. 1. Family — United States 2. Parent and child — United States. I. DeFrain, John D. II. T. III. Series.
HQ535.L38 1983    306.8/74/0973 19    *LC* 82-72877    *ISBN* 0256026793

**Muncy, Raymond Lee.** **4.5579**
Sex and marriage in utopian communities: 19th century America. — Bloomington: Indiana University Press, [1973] 275 p.; 25 cm. 1. Marriage — United States 2. Sex customs — United States. 3. Utopias I. T.
HQ535.M85    301.42/3/0973    *LC* 72-85852    *ISBN* 0253180643

**Ogburn, William Fielding, 1886-1959.** • **4.5580**
Technology and the changing family [by] W. F. Ogburn [and] M. F. Nimkoff. — Boston: Houghton Mifflin, [c1955] v, 329 p.: diagrs., tables.; 22 cm. 1. Family — United States 2. United States — Social conditions I. Nimkoff, Meyer Francis, 1904- joint author. II. T.
HQ535.O35    392.3 301.42*    *LC* 55-14040

**Schneider, David Murray, 1918-.** **4.5581**
American kinship: a cultural account / David M. Schneider. — 2d ed. — Chicago: University of Chicago Press, 1980. x, 137 p.; 24 cm. 1. Kinship — United States. 2. Family — United States I. T.
HQ535.S33 1980    301.42/1/0973    *LC* 79-18185    *ISBN* 0226739295

**Schur, Edwin M. ed.** • **4.5582**
The family and the sexual revolution: selected readings / edited by Edwin M. Schur. — Bloomington: Indiana University Press, 1964. xv, 427 p.; 22 cm. 1. Family — Addresses, essays, lectures. 2. Family — United States — Addresses, essays, lectures. 3. Sex customs — United States — Addresses, essays, lectures. 4. Women — United States — Addresses, essays, lectures. 5. Birth control — United States — Addresses, essays, lectures. I. T.
HQ535.S34    301.42082    *LC* 64-18819

**Seward, Rudy Ray.** 4.5583
The American family: a demographic history / Rudy Ray Seward; foreword by Herman R. Lantz. — Beverly Hills, Calif.: Sage Publications, c1978. 223 p.; 22 cm. — (Sage library of social research; v. 70) 1. Family — United States — History. 2. Family — Research — United States. 3. Urbanization — United States. 4. Industrialization I. T.
HQ535.S44 301.42/0973 *LC* 78-19609 *ISBN* 0803911122. *ISBN* 0803911130 pbk

**Bane, Mary Jo.** 4.5584
Here to stay: American families in the twentieth century / Mary Jo Bane. New York: Basic Books, c1976. xvi, 195 p.; 24 cm. Includes index. 1. Family — United States I. T.
HQ536.B3 301.42/0973 *LC* 76-44877 *ISBN* 0465029272

**Blood, Robert O.** • 4.5585
Husbands & wives: the dynamics of married living, by Robert O. Blood, Jr., and Donald M. Wolfe. — Glencoe, Ill.: Free Press, [1960]. 293 p.; 22 cm. 1. Marriage — United States 2. Family — United States I. Wolfe, Donald M. joint author. II. T.
HQ536.B55 301.42 *LC* 59-6824

**Bohen, Halcyone H., 1937-.** 4.5586
Balancing jobs and family life: do flexible work schedules help? / Halcyone H. Bohen, Anamaria Viveros–Long. — Philadelphia: Temple University Press, 1981. xxiv, 336 p.: ill.; 22 cm. (Family Impact Seminar series) Includes index. 1. Work and family — United States — Case studies. 2. Hours of labor, Flexible — United States. 3. United States — Officials and employees — Family relationships. I. Viveros-Long, Anamaria, 1942- joint author. II. T.
HQ536.B63 306.8/7 19 *LC* 80-25165 *ISBN* 0877221995

**Dual–career couples / edited by Fran Pepitone–Rockwell.** 4.5587
Beverly Hills: Sage Publications, c1980. 294 p.; 23 cm. — (Sage focus editions. 24) 1. Dual-career families — United States. I. Pepitone-Rockwell, Fran. II. Series.
HQ536.D797 306.8/7 *LC* 80-15747 *ISBN* 0803914369

**England, Paula.** 4.5588
Households, employment, and gender: a social, economic, and demographic view / Paula England and George Farkas. — New York: Aldine Pub. Co., c1986. ix, 237 p.: ill.; 24 cm. Includes indexes. 1. Households — United States. 2. Cost and standard of living — United States. 3. Women — Employment — United States. 4. Sex discrimination in employment — United States. I. Farkas, George, 1946- II. T.
HQ536.E54 1986 304.6 19 *LC* 85-18628 *ISBN* 0202303225

**Families, what makes them work / David H. Olson ... [et al.];** 4.5589
**foreword by Reuben Hill.**
Beverly Hills, Calif.: Sage Publications, c1983. 312 p.: ill.; 23 cm. 'Olson, McCubbin, and associates'—Spine. 1. Family — United States — Simulation methods. 2. Stress (Psychology) — Simulation methods. 3. Life cycle, Human I. Olson, David H. L.
HQ536.F335 1983 306.8/5/0973 19 *LC* 83-4516 *ISBN* 0803920113

**Fuchs, Lawrence H.** 4.5590
Family matters, by Lawrence H. Fuchs. — New York: Random House, [1972] xix, 266 p.; 22 cm. 1. Family — United States 2. United States — Social conditions — 1960- I. T.
HQ536.F9 301.42/0973 *LC* 78-37037 *ISBN* 0394475488

**Gelles, Richard J.** 4.5591
The violent home: a study of physical aggression between husbands and wives / Richard J. Gelles. — Beverly Hills, Calif.: Sage Publications, [1974] c1972. 230 p.: ill.; 22 cm. — (Sage library of social research; v. 13) Includes indexes. 1. Conjugal violence 2. Child abuse 3. Wife abuse 4. Aggressiveness (Psychology) — Case studies. I. T.
HQ536.G44 1974 301.42/7 *LC* 73-94288 *ISBN* 0803903812

**Kobrin, Frances E.** 4.5592
The ethnic factor in family structure and mobility / Frances E. Kobrin, Calvin Goldscheider. — Cambridge, Mass.: Ballinger Pub. Co., 1978. xxiii, 257 p.; 24 cm. 1. Marriage — Rhode Island — Case studies. 2. Ethnology — Rhode Island — Case studies. 3. Ethnic groups 4. Social mobility — United States. I. Goldscheider, Calvin. joint author. II. T.
HQ536.K62 301.42/1 *LC* 77-25838 *ISBN* 0884103587

**Masnick, George S., 1942-.** 4.5593
The nation's families, 1960–1990 / George Masnick and Mary Jo Bane, with Neal Baer ... [et al.]. — Boston, Mass.: Auburn House Pub. Co., c1980. xv, 175 p.: ill.; 24 cm. (Joint Center outlook report.) 1. Family — United States — Statistics. 2. Households — United States — Statistics. I. Bane, Mary Jo. II. T. III. Series.
HQ536.M326 1980 306.8/0973 19 *LC* 80-20531 *ISBN* 0865690502

**Pleck, Joseph H.** 4.5594
Working wives, working husbands / Joseph H. Pleck. — Beverly Hills, Calif.: Published in cooperation with the National Council on Family Relations [by] Sage Publications, c1985. 167 p.; 23 cm. (New perspectives on family.) 1. Married people — Employment — Social aspects — United States. 2. Sexual division of labor — United States. 3. Sex role — United States. 4. Time management — United States. 5. Family life surveys — United States. I. National Council on Family Relations. II. T. III. Series.
HQ536.P59 1985 306.8/7 19 *LC* 85-11974 *ISBN* 0803924895

**Rethinking the family: some feminist questions / edited by** 4.5595
**Barrie Thorne with Marilyn Yalom; prepared under the auspices of the Center for Research on Women, Stanford University.**
New York: Longman, c1982. x, 246 p.; 23 cm. 1. Family — United States — Addresses, essays, lectures. 2. Feminism — United States — Addresses, essays, lectures. I. Thorne, Barrie. II. Yalom, Marilyn. III. Stanford University. Center for Research on Women.
HQ536.R454 1982 306.8/0973 19 *LC* 81-2427 *ISBN* 0582282659

**Ross, Heather L.** 4.5596
Time of transition: the growth of families headed by women / Heather L. Ross and Isabel V. Sawhill; with the assistance of Anita R. MacIntosh. — Washington, D.C.: Urban Institute, c1975. xii, 223 p.: ill.; 24 cm. 1. Single-parent family — United States. 2. Paternal deprivation I. Sawhill, Isabel V. joint author. II. MacIntosh, Anita R. joint author. III. Urban Institute. IV. T.
HQ536.R66 306.8 19 *LC* 75-38209 8776614909

**Rubin, Lillian B.** 4.5597
Worlds of pain: life in the working–class family / Lillian Breslow Rubin. New York: Basic Books, c1976. xii, 268 p.; 24 cm. Includes index. 1. Family — United States 2. Labor and laboring classes — United States 3. United States — Social conditions — 1960- I. T.
HQ536.R8 301.42/0973 *LC* 76-21648 *ISBN* 0465092454

**Scanzoni, John H., 1935-.** 4.5598
Shaping tomorrow's family: theory and policy for the 21st century / John Scanzoni; foreword by Jessie Bernard. — Beverly Hills: Sage Publications, c1983. 272 p.; 23 cm. — (Sage library of social research. v. 143) 1. Family — Moral and ethical aspects. 2. Twenty-first century — Forecasts 3. Family policy — United States. 4. Right and left (Political science) 5. Family — United States I. T. II. Series.
HQ536.S337 1983 306.8/5/0973 19 *LC* 82-16876 *ISBN* 0803919204

**Scanzoni, John H., 1935-.** 4.5599
Sex roles, life styles, and childbearing: changing patterns in marriage and the family / John H. Scanzoni. New York: Free Press, [1975] ix, 259 p.; 25 cm. 'This investigation was carried out under contract no. 70-2192 from the Center for Population Research, National Institutes for Child Health and Human Development.' Includes indexes. 1. Family — United States 2. Family size — United States. 3. Sex role 4. Birth control — United States. I. T.
HQ536.S34 301.42/0973 *LC* 74-28939 *ISBN* 0029277205

**Scanzoni, John H., 1935-.** 4.5600
Sexual bargaining: power politics in the American marriage [by] John Scanzoni. — Englewood Cliffs, N.J.: Prentice-Hall, [1972] viii, 180 p.; 21 cm. — (A Spectrum book, S-266) 1. Marriage — United States 2. Husband and wife — United States. 3. Sex role I. T.
HQ536.S35 301.42 *LC* 71-39749 *ISBN* 0138074615

**Steiner, Gilbert Yale, 1924-.** 4.5601
The futility of family policy / Gilbert Y. Steiner. — Washington, D.C.: Brookings Institution, c1981. viii, 221 p.; 24 cm. 1. Family — United States 2. Family policy — United States. I. T.
HQ536.S74 306.8/0973 19 *LC* 80-26448 *ISBN* 0815781245

**Two paychecks: life in dual–earner families / edited by Joan** 4.5602
**Aldous.**
Beverly Hills: Sage Publications, c1982. 247 p.; 23 cm. — (Sage focus editions; 56) 'Portions of this book are reproduced from a special issue of the Journal of family issues, June 1981'—T.p. verso. Includes bibliographies. 1. Dual-career families — United States. 2. Married people — Employment — United States. I. Aldous, Joan.
HQ536.T85 1982 306.8/7 19 *LC* 82-10538 *ISBN* 0803918828

## HQ537–557 Special Regions

**Faragher, John Mack, 1945-.** 4.5603
Women and men on the overland trail / John Mack Faragher. — New Haven: Yale University Press, 1979. xiii, 281 p.: map; 25 cm. (Yale historical publications. Miscellany. 121) Includes index. 1. Family — West (U.S.) — History — 19th century. 2. Women — West (U.S.) — History — 19th century. 3. Frontier and pioneer life — West (U.S.) — History — 19th century. 4. Overland journeys to the Pacific I. T. II. Series.
HQ553.F37 301.42/0978 *LC* 78-10290 *ISBN* 0300022670

**Smith, Daniel Blake.**                                                        **4.5604**
Inside the great house: planter family life in eighteenth–century Chesapeake
Society / Daniel Blake Smith. — Ithaca, N.Y.: Cornell University Press, c1980.
305 p.; 23 cm. 1. Family — Chesapeake Bay region — History — 18th century.
2. Plantation life — Chesapeake Bay region — History — 18th century. I. T.
HQ555.C46 S63 1980        306.8/09755/18        *LC* 80-14557        *ISBN*
0801413133

**Ryan, Mary P.**                                                              **4.5605**
Cradle of the middle class: the family in Oneida County, New York, 1790–1865
/ Mary P. Ryan. — Cambridge, Eng.; New York: Cambridge University Press,
1981. xiv, 321 p.: ill.; 24 cm. — (Interdisciplinary perspectives on modern
history.) Includes index. 1. Family — New York (State) — Oneida Co. —
History. 2. Middle classes — New York (State) — Oneida Co. — History. I. T.
II. Series.
HQ555.N7 R9        306.8/09747/62        *LC* 80-18460        *ISBN* 0521232007

**Sennett, Richard, 1943-.**                                                  • **4.5606**
Families against the city; middle class homes of industrial Chicago, 1872–1890.
Cambridge, Mass., Harvard University Press, 1970. x, 258 p. illus., maps. 22
cm. 1. Family — Illinois — Chicago. 2. Middle classes — Illinois — Chicago.
3. Chicago (Ill.) — Social conditions. I. T.
HQ557.C5 S45        301.44/1        *LC* 73-115190        *ISBN* 0674292251

**Adams, Bert N.**                                                            • **4.5607**
Kinship in an urban setting [by] Bert N. Adams. — Chicago: Markham Pub.
Co., [1968] xvii, 228 p.; 22 cm. 1. Kinship — North Carolina — Greensboro.
2. Family — Greensboro, N.C. I. T.
HQ557.G7 A64        301.42/7/091732        *LC* 68-20258

**Demos, John.**                                                              • **4.5608**
A little commonwealth: family life in Plymouth Colony. — New York: Oxford
University Press, 1970. xvi, 201 p.: ill., facsims., port.; 22 cm. 1. Family —
Plymouth, Mass. 2. Plymouth (Mass.) — Social life and customs. I. T.
HQ557.P5 D4        301.42/09744/8        *LC* 75-83040

## HQ560.5–609 Latin America

**Balmori, Diana.**                                                            **4.5609**
Notable family networks in Latin America / Diana Balmori, Stuart F. Voss,
Miles Wortman. — Chicago: University of Chicago Press, 1984. vii, 290 p.; 24
cm. Includes index. 1. Family — Latin America — History — Case studies.
2. Elite (Social sciences) — Latin America — History — Case studies. I. Voss,
Stuart F. II. Wortman, Miles L., 1944- III. T.
HQ560.5.A15 1984        306.8/5/098 19        *LC* 84-2423        *ISBN*
0226036391

**Kinship ideology and practice in Latin America / edited by**               **4.5610**
**Raymond T. Smith.**
Chapel Hill: University of North Carolina Press, c1984. vi, 341 p.: ill.; 24 cm.
Papers resulting from meetings held in New York in Sept. 1980 and in Ixtapan
de la Sal, Mexico in Sept. 1981, both sponsored by the Joint Committee on Latin
American Studies. 1. Family — Latin America — History — Congresses.
2. Kinship — Latin America — History — Congresses. 3. Latin America —
Social life and customs — Congresses. I. Smith, Raymond Thomas, 1925-
II. Joint Committee on Latin American Studies.
HQ560.5.K56 1984        306.8/5/098 19        *LC* 83-26082        *ISBN*
0807816078

**Lewis, Oscar, 1914-1970.**                                                  • **4.5611**
The children of Sánchez, autobiography of a Mexican family. New York,
Random House [1961] 499 p. 24 cm. 1. Family — Mexico — Case studies.
2. Poor — Mexico — Mexico City. 3. Mexico — Social conditions I. T.
HQ562.L38        309.172        *LC* 61-6270

**Lewis, Oscar, 1914-1970.**                                                  • **4.5612**
Five families; Mexican case studies in the culture of poverty. With a foreword
by Oliver La Farge. — New York: Basic Books, [1959] 351 p.: illus.; 25 cm.
1. Family — Mexico — Case studies. 2. Mexico — Social conditions I. T.
HQ562.L4        309.172        *LC* 59-10644

**Martinez Alier, Verena.**                                                    **4.5613**
Marriage, class and colour in nineteenth–century Cuba; a study of racial
attitudes and sexual values in a slave society. — [London; New York]:
Cambridge University Press, [1974] x, 202 p.; 23 cm. — (Cambridge Latin
American studies. 17) Based on the author's thesis, Oxford. 1. Interracial
marriage — Cuba — History. 2. Social classes — Cuba — History. 3. Cuba —
Social conditions I. T. II. Series.
HQ579.M37 1974        HQ579 M37 1974.        301.42/9097291        *LC*
73-82463        *ISBN* 0521204127

**Blake, Judith.**                                                            • **4.5614**
Family structure in Jamaica: the social context of reproduction / in
collaboration with J. Mayone Stycos and Kingsley Davis. — [New York]: Free

Press of Glencoe [1962] x, 262 p.: tables. 1. Family — Jamaica 2. Sex customs
— Jamaica 3. Birth control — Jamaica 4. Fertility, Human I. T.
HQ584 B55        *LC* 60-10893

## HQ611–663 Europe

**Ozment, Steven E.**                                                          **4.5615**
When fathers ruled: family life in Reformation Europe / Steven Ozment. —
Cambridge, Mass.: Harvard University Press, 1983. viii, 238 p.: ill.; 24 cm. —
(Studies in cultural history.) Includes index. 1. Marriage — Europe — History.
2. Family — Europe — History. 3. Husbands — Europe — History.
4. Fathers — Europe — History. 5. Children — Europe — History.
6. Reformation — Europe — History. I. T. II. Series.
HQ611.O97 1983        306.8/094 19        *LC* 83-6098        *ISBN* 0674951204

**Kamerman, Sheila B.**                                                        **4.5616**
Child care, family benefits, and working parents: a study in comparative policy
/ Sheila B. Kamerman, Alfred J. Kahn. — New York: Columbia University
Press, 1981. xii, 327 p.: ill.; 24 cm. 1. Family policy — Europe. 2. Family
policy — United States. 3. Children of working parents — Government policy
— Europe. 4. Children of working parents — Government policy — United
States. 5. Child welfare — Government policy — Europe. 6. Child welfare —
Government policy — United States. I. Kahn, Alfred J., 1919- joint author.
II. T.
HQ612.K35        362.8/2 19        *LC* 80-39690        *ISBN* 0231051700

**Gillis, John R.**                                                           **4.5617**
For better, for worse: British marriages, 1600 to the present / John R. Gillis. —
New York: Oxford University Press, 1985. x, 417 p.: ill.; 25 cm. Includes index.
1. Marriage — Great Britain — History. 2. Courtship — Great Britain —
History. I. T.
HQ613.G55 1985        306.8/0941 19        *LC* 85-13701        *ISBN*
019503614X

**Rose, Phyllis, 1942-.**                                                     **4.5618**
Parallel lives: five Victorian marriages / Phyllis Rose; drawings by David
Schorr. — 1st ed. — New York: Knopf, 1983. 318 p.: ports.; 22 cm. 'A Borzoi
book'—T.p. verso. Includes index. 1. Marriage — Great Britain — History —
19th century — Case studies. 2. Married people — Great Britain — Biography.
3. Authors, English — 19th century — Biography — Marriage. I. T.
HQ613.R67 1983        306.8/1/0941 19        *LC* 83-47785        *ISBN*
0394524322

**Anderson, Michael.**                                                        **4.5619**
Family structure in nineteenth century Lancashire. Cambridge [Eng.]
University Press, 1971. ix, 230 p. 24 cm. (Cambridge studies in sociology, 5)
1. Family — Lancashire — England. 2. Kinship 3. Lancashire — Social
conditions. I. T.
HQ614.A7        301.42/3/094272        *LC* 79-164448        *ISBN* 0521082374

**Macfarlane, Alan.**                                                         **4.5620**
Marriage and love in England: modes of reproduction, 1300–1840 / Alan
Macfarlane. — Oxford, UK; New York, NY, USA: B. Blackwell, 1986. xi,
380 p.; 24 cm. Includes index. 1. Marriage — England — History. 2. Family
— England — History. 3. Malthusianism 4. Family size — England —
History. I. T.
HQ615.M33 1986        306.8/1/0942 19        *LC* 85-13351        *ISBN*
0631139923

**Stone, Lawrence.**                                                          **4.5621**
The family, sex and marriage in England, 1500–1800 / Lawrence Stone. — New
York: Harper and Row, c1977. xxxi, 800, [12] leaves of plates: ill. 1. Family —
England — History. 2. Marriage — England — History. 3. Sex customs —
England — History. I. T.
HQ615.S76        *LC* 77-50        *ISBN* 0060141425

**Duby, Georges.**                                                            **4.5622**
[Chevalier, la femme, et le prêtre. English] The knight, the lady, and the priest:
the making of modern marriage in medieval France / Georges Duby; translated
by Barbara Bray. — 1st American ed. — New York: Pantheon Books, [1984]
xx, 311 p.; 24 cm. Translation of: Le chevalier, la femme et le prêtre.
1. Marriage — France — History. 2. Marriage — Religious aspects —
Catholic Church 3. Social history — Medieval, 500-1500 I. T.
HQ623.D8313        306.8/1/0944 19        *LC* 83-4000        *ISBN* 0394524454

**Flandrin, Jean Louis.**                                                     **4.5623**
[Familles. English] Families in former times: kinship, household, and sexuality
/ by Jean–Louis Flandrin; translated by Richard Southern. — Cambridge
[Eng.]; New York: Cambridge University Press, 1979. xi, 265 p.: ill.; 24 cm. —
(Themes in the social sciences.) Translation of Familles. 1. Family — France
— History. I. T. II. Series.
HQ623.F5513        301.42/0944        *LC* 78-18095        *ISBN* 0521223237.
*ISBN* 0521294495 pbk

**Kertzer, David I., 1948-.**      4.5624
Family life in central Italy, 1880–1910: sharecropping, wage labor, and coresidence / David I. Kertzer. — New Brunswick, N.J.: Rutgers University Press, c1984. xvii, 250 p.; 24 cm. Includes index. 1. Family — Italy — Bertalia — History. 2. Kinship — Italy — Bertalia. 3. Share-cropping — Italy — Bertalia. 4. Labor and laboring classes — Italy — Bertalia. 5. Italy — History — 1870-1915 6. Italy — Rural conditions. I. T.
HQ629.K47 1984    306.8/5/09456 19    LC 82-22958    ISBN 0813509785

**The Family in Imperial Russia:new lines of historical research /**    4.5625
**edited by David L. Ransel.**
Urbana: University of Illinois Press, c1978. 342 p.; 24 cm. Papers presented at a symposium held at the University of Illinois at Urbana-Champaign in Oct. 1976. Includes index. 1. Family — Russia — History — Congresses. 2. Social classes — Russia — History — Congresses. I. Ransel, David L.
HQ637.F35     HQ637 F35.     301.42/0947    LC 78-17579    ISBN 0252007018

**Geiger, H. Kent.**     • 4.5626
The family in Soviet Russia / by H. Kent Geiger. — Cambridge, Mass.: Harvard University Press, 1968. xii, 381 p.; 24 cm. (Russian Research Center studies, 56) 1. Family — Soviet Union. I. T.
HQ637.G37    301.42/0947    LC 68-15637

## HQ665–689 Asia

**Yang, C. K., 1910-.**     • 4.5627
The Chinese family in the communist revolution / with a foreword by Talcott Parsons. — [Cambridge]: Technology Press, Massachusetts Institute of Technology; distributed by Harvard University Press, 1959. 246 p.; 24 cm. 1. Family 2. China — Social conditions I. T.
HQ667 Y3 1959    LC 59-14897

**Veen, Klaas W. van der.**     4.5628
[Huwelijk en hiërarchie bij de Anavil Brahman van Zuid Gujarat. English] I give thee my daughter. A study of marriage and hierarchy among the Anavil Brahmans of South Gujarat. [By] Klaas W. van der Veen. [Translated from the Dutch Nanette Jockin]. Assen, Van Gorcum, 1972. 307 p., 12 p. of photos. 25 cm. (Studies of developing countries. 13) Translation of the author's thesis, Amsterdam, 1969. Translation of Huwelijk en hiërarchie bij de Anavil Brahman van Zuid Gujarat. 1. Marriage — India — Gujarat. 2. Caste — India — Gujarat. I. T. II. Series.
HQ669.V413    301.42/0954/75    LC 72-196027    ISBN 9023209141

**Vatuk, Sylvia.**     4.5629
Kinship and urbanization; white collar migrants in north India. Berkeley, University of California Press [1972] xv, 219 p. illus. 24 cm. 1. Family — Meerut, India (City) 2. Meerut (India) — Social conditions. I. T.
HQ670.V36    301.42/1    LC 75-161993    ISBN 0520020642

**Baker, Hugh D. R.**     4.5630
Chinese family and kinship / Hugh D. R. Baker. — New York: Columbia University Press, 1979. xii, 243 p.: ill.; 28 cm. Includes index. 1. Family — China — History. 2. Kinship — China — History. I. T.
HQ684.A15 1979    301.42/0951    LC 78-26724    ISBN 0231047681

**Parish, William L.**     4.5631
Village and family in contemporary China / William L. Parish, Martin King Whyte. — Chicago: University of Chicago Press, 1978. xiii, 419 p.: ill.; 24 cm. 1. Rural families — China. 2. Villages — China — Case studies. 3. China — Rural conditions. I. Whyte, Martin King. joint author. II. T.
HQ684.P37    301.42/0951    LC 78-3411    ISBN 0226645908

**Stacey, Judith.**     4.5632
Patriarchy and socialist revolution in China / Judith Stacey. — Berkeley: University of California Press, c1983. xi, 324 p.; 22 cm. Includes index. 1. Family — China. 2. Patriarchy — China. 3. Women and socialism — China. 4. Family policy — China. 5. China — Social conditions — 1949-1976 I. T.
HQ684.S7 1983    306.8/5/0951 19    LC 82-8482    ISBN 0520048253

## HQ728–743 FAMILY. MARRIAGE: GENERAL WORKS

**Angell, Robert Cooley, 1899-.**     • 4.5633
The family encounters the depression [by] Robert Cooley Angell ... New York, Chicago [etc.] C. Scribner's sons [c1936] 4 p. l., 309 p. 20 cm. 'The present study ... has sought to find out something about the effect of the depression on family life, and ... to make a contribution to the theory and method of social research.'

—p. 1. 1. Family 2. Adaptability (Psychology) 3. Social psychology 4. Sociology — Methodology 5. United States — Social conditions I. T.
HQ728.A73    LC 36-7913

**Bernard, Jessie Shirley, 1903-.**     • 4.5634
Remarriage, a study of marriage, by Jessie Bernard. — New York: Russell & Russell, [1971, c1956] 372 p.; 23 cm. 1. Remarriage I. T.
HQ728.B476 1971    301.42/7    LC 79-151539

**Bossard, James Herbert Siward, 1888-1960.**     • 4.5635
The large family system: an original study in the sociology of family behavior / with the aid and partial collaboration of Eleanor Stoker Boll. — Philadelphia: University of Pennsylvania Press [1956] 325 p.; 22 cm. 1. Family 2. Child study. I. T.
HQ728.B715    LC 56-9346

**Bott, Elizabeth.**     • 4.5636
Family and social network; roles, norms, and external relationships in ordinary urban families. Pref. by Max Gluckman. — 2d ed. — New York: Free Press, [c1971] xxx, 363 p.; 21 cm. 1. Family I. T.
HQ728.B717 1971b    301.42/1    LC 71-161235

**Burgess, Ernest Watson, 1886-1966.**     • 4.5637
The family; from traditional to companionship [by] Ernest W. Burgess, Harvey J. Locke [and] Mary Margaret Thomes. — 4th ed. — New York: Van Nostrand Reinhold Co., [1971] xii, 644 p.: illus., maps.; 24 cm. 1. Family I. Locke, Harvey James, 1900- joint author. II. Thomes, Mary Margaret, joint author. III. T.
HQ728.B8 1971    301.42    LC 76-146603

**Contemporary theories about the family / edited by Wesley R.**    4.5638
**Burr ... [et al.].**
New York: Free Press, c1979. 2 v.: ill.; 24 cm. 1. Family — Addresses, essays, lectures. I. Burr, Wesley R., 1936-
HQ728.C618    306.8 19    LC 77-81430    ISBN 0029049407

**Economics of the family: marriage, children, and human**    4.5639
**capital:a conference report of the National Bureau of Economic**
**Research / edited by Theodore W. Schultz.**
Chicago: Published for the National Bureau of Economic Research by the University of Chicago Press, 1974. 584 p.: ill.; 24 cm. Contains papers presented at two conferences held in June 1972 and June 1973, sponsored by NBER and the Population Council. First published as supplements to the Journal of political economy, 1973-1974. Includes index. 1. Family — Congresses. 2. Marriage — Congresses. 3. Family size — Economic aspects — Congresses. 4. Fertility, Human — Economic aspects — Congresses. I. Schultz, Theodore William, 1902- II. National Bureau of Economic Research. III. Population Council.
HQ728.E3    301.42    LC 73-81484    ISBN 0226740854

**Goode, William Josiah.**     • 4.5640
World revolution and family patterns. — [New York]: Free Press of Glencoe, [1963] 432 p.; 24 cm. 1. Family 2. Social change 3. Marriage I. T.
HQ728.G59    301.423    LC 63-13538

**Heiss, Jerold. comp.**     4.5641
Family roles and interaction: an anthology / edited by Jerold Heiss. — 2d ed. — Chicago: Rand McNally College Pub. Co., c1976. xiii, 495 p.; 23 cm. (Rand McNally sociology series) 1. Family — Addresses, essays, lectures. 2. Marriage — Addresses, essays, lectures. I. T.
HQ728.H39 1976    301.42    LC 75-11327    ISBN 0528680706

**Henry, Jules, 1904-1969.**     • 4.5642
Pathways to madness. — [1st ed.]. — New York: Random House, [1971] xxii, 477 p.; 25 cm. 1. Family — United States — Case studies. 2. Interpersonal relations 3. Psychology, Pathological I. T.
HQ728.H395    616.8/9/071    LC 77-159349    ISBN 039447323X

**Hill, Reuben, 1912-.**     • 4.5643
Families under stress: adjustment to the crises of war separation and reunion / with chapters in collaboration with Elise Boulding; assisted by Lowell Dunigan and Rachel Ann Elder. — Westport, Conn.: Greenwood Press, [1971, c1949] x, 443 p.: ill.; 23 cm. 1. Family — U.S. 2. U.S. — Social conditions. I. T.
HQ728.H48 1971    301.42/8    LC 73-90529    ISBN 0837131081

**Komarovsky, Mirra, 1906-.**     • 4.5644
Blue–collar marriage. With the collaboration of Jane H. Philips. New York, Random House [1964] xv, 395 p. 1. Marriage — Case studies I. T.
HQ728 K64    LC 64-20031

**Laing, Ronald David.**     4.5645
The politics of the family, and other essays [by] R. D. Laing. New York, Vintage Books [1972, c1971] 133 p. 19 cm. Original ed. issued in series: World of man. 1. Family — Addresses, essays, lectures. 2. Mentally ill — Family relationships — Addresses, essays, lectures. I. T.
HQ728.L335 1972    301.42/08    LC 72-1118    ISBN 0394718097

**Normal family processes** / edited by Froma Walsh; foreword by   **4.5646**
Roy R. Grinker.
New York: Guilford Press, c1982. xxi, 486 p.; 25 cm. — (Guilford family therapy series.) 1. Family — Research I. Walsh, Froma. II. Series.
HQ728.N83 1982     306.8 19    *LC* 81-7197    *ISBN* 0898620511

**Reiss, David, 1937-.**  **4.5647**
The family's construction of reality / David Reiss. — Cambridge, Mass.: Harvard University Press, 1981. xiii, 426 p.: ill.; 24 cm. Includes index.
1. Family — Attitudes. 2. Reality 3. Model theory 4. Social interaction — Psychological aspects. I. T.
HQ728.R383 1981     306.8 19    *LC* 81-2703    *ISBN* 0674294157

**Waller, Willard Walter, 1899-1945.**  ● **4.5648**
The family, a dynamic interpretation. Revised by Reuben Hill. — New York, Dryden Press [1951] xviii, 637 p. 25 cm. Includes bibliographies. 1. Family 2. Marriage I. Hill, Reuben, 1912- II. T.
HQ728.W3 1951     392.3    *LC* 51-10632

**Winch, Robert Francis, 1911-.**  ● **4.5649**
Mate–selection; a study of complementary needs. — New York: Harper, [1958] 349 p.; 22 cm. — (Harper's social science series) 1. Marriage I. T.
HQ728.W548     392.4 301.425*    *LC* 58-5106

**Berger, Brigitte.**  **4.5650**
The war over the family: capturing the middle ground / by Brigitte Berger and Peter L. Berger. — Garden City, N.Y.: Anchor Press/Doubleday, 1983. ix, 252 p.; 22 cm. 1. Family 2. Middle classes 3. Family policy 4. Social change I. Berger, Peter L. II. T.
HQ734.B56 1983     306.8/5 19    *LC* 82-45237    *ISBN* 0385180012

**Blumstein, Philip.**  **4.5651**
American couples: money, work, sex / Philip Blumstein & Pepper Schwartz. — 1st ed. — New York: Morrow, 1983. 656 p.: ill.; 24 cm. 1. Marriage — United States 2. Family — Economic aspects — United States. 3. Married people — Employment — Social aspects — United States. 4. Sex in marriage — United States. 5. Unmarried couples — United States. I. Schwartz, Pepper. II. T.
HQ734.B659 1983     306.8/0973 19    *LC* 83-62066    *ISBN* 0688037720

**Families that work: children in a changing world** / Sheila B.   **4.5652**
Kamerman and Cheryl D. Hayes, editors; Panel on Work, Family, and Community, Committee on Child Development Research and Public Policy, Assembly of Behavioral and Social Sciences, National Research Council.
Washington, D.C.: National Academy Press, 1982. xi, 341 p.; 23 cm. 1. Work and family — Addresses, essays, lectures. 2. Children of working parents — Addresses, essays, lectures. 3. Child development — Addresses, essays, lectures. I. Kamerman, Sheila B. II. Hayes, Cheryl D. III. National Research Council (U.S.). Panel on Work, Family, and Community.
HQ734.F228 1982     306.8/7 19    *LC* 82-81829    *ISBN* 0309032822

**Gilman, Charlotte Perkins, 1860-1935.**  **4.5653**
The home: its work and influence. — Urbana: University of Illinois Press [1972] xxiii, 347 p.; 21 cm. Reprint of the 1903 ed. published by McClure, Phillips, New York; with an introd. by William L. O'Neill. 1. Home I. T.
HQ734.G5 1972     643    *LC* 72-76863    *ISBN* 0252002784 *ISBN* 0252002776

**Parsons, Talcott, 1902-.**  ● **4.5654**
Family, socialization and interaction process / by Talcott Parsons and Robert F. Bales; in collaboration with James Olds [and others]. — Glencoe, Ill.: Free Press, [1955] xvii, 422 p.: diagrs., tables.; 22 cm. 1. Family 2. Family — United States I. Bales, Robert Freed, 1916- joint author. II. T.
HQ734.P23     392 301.42*    *LC* 55-7343

**Rogers, Carl R. (Carl Ransom), 1902-.**  **4.5655**
Becoming partners: marriage and its alternatives, by Carl R. Rogers. New York, Delacorte Press [1972] 243 p. 24 cm. 1. Marriage I. T.
HQ734.R69     301.42/2    *LC* 72-3868

**Shorter, Edward.**  **4.5656**
The making of the modern family / Edward Shorter. — New York: Basic Books, c1975. xiv, 369 p., [4] leaves of plates: ill.; 24 cm. Includes index.
1. Family I. T.
HQ734.S577     301.42    *LC* 75-7266    *ISBN* 0465043275

**Stress and the family** / edited by Hamilton I. McCubbin &   **4.5657**
Charles R. Figley.
New York: Brunner/Mazel, c1983. 2 v.; 24 cm. Vol. 2 edited by Charles R. Figley & Hamilton I. McCubbin. 1. Family — Addresses, essays, lectures. 2. Stress (Psychology) — Addresses, essays, lectures. 3. Life change events — Addresses, essays, lectures. I. McCubbin, Hamilton I. II. Figley, Charles R., 1944-
HQ734.S9735 1983     306.8/5 19    *LC* 83-6048    *ISBN* 0876303211

# HQ750–799 Eugenics. Parenthood

**Warren, Mary Anne.**  **4.5658**
Gendercide: the implications of sex selection / Mary Anne Warren. — Totowa, N.J.: Rowman & Allanheld, 1985. viii, 209 p.; 22 cm. (New feminist perspectives.) 1. Eugenics 2. Sex preselection 3. Sex of children, Parental preferences for 4. Feminism I. T. II. Series.
HQ751.W37 1985     305.3 19    *LC* 85-14452    *ISBN* 0847673308

**Daniels, Pamela, 1937-.**  **4.5659**
Sooner or later: the timing of parenthood in adult lives / Pamela Daniels, Kathy Weingarten. — 1st ed. — New York: Norton, c1982. xi, 366 p.; 24 cm.
1. Parenthood — Psychological aspects. 2. Life cycle, Human I. Weingarten, Kathy. II. T.
HQ755.83.D36 1982     306.8 19    *LC* 81-11006    *ISBN* 0393014843

**Fatherhood and family policy** / edited by Michael E. Lamb,   **4.5660**
Abraham Sagi.
Hillsdale, N.J.: L. Erlbaum, 1983. xi, 276 p. 1. Fathers — Addresses, essays, lectures. 2. Father and child — Addresses, essays, lectures. 3. Family policy — Addresses, essays, lectures. 4. Child rearing — Addresses, essays, lectures. 5. Custody of children — Addresses, essays, lectures. I. Lamb, Michael E., 1953- II. Sagi, Abraham.
HQ756.F38 1983     HQ756 F38.    *LC* 82-18282    *ISBN* 0898591902

**Mackey, Wade C.**  **4.5661**
Fathering behaviors: the dynamics of the man–child bond / Wade C. Mackey. — New York: Plenum Press, c1985. xviii, 203 p.: ill.; 24 cm. (Perspectives in developmental psychology.) Includes indexes. 1. Father and child — Cross-cultural studies. 2. Developmental psychology — Cross-cultural studies 3. Family — United States 4. Father and child — United States. I. T. II. Series.
HQ756.M25 1985     306.8/742 19    *LC* 85-6599    *ISBN* 0306418681

**Russell, Graeme, 1947-.**  **4.5662**
The changing role of fathers? / Graeme Russell. — St. Lucia [Queensland]; New York: University of Queensland Press, c1983. x, 250 p.; 23 cm. Includes index. 1. Fathers — Australia. 2. Child rearing — Australia. 3. Father and child I. T.
HQ756.R86 1983     306.8/742 19    *LC* 82-20041    *ISBN* 0702219428

**André, Rae.**  **4.5663**
Homemakers, the forgotten workers / Rae André. — Chicago: University of Chicago Press, c1981. xi, 299 p.; 24 cm. Includes index. 1. Housewives — United States. 2. Displaced homemakers — United States. I. T.
HQ759.A5     305.4/3 19    *LC* 80-21258    *ISBN* 0226019934

**Between ourselves: letters between mothers and daughters,**   **4.5664**
**1750–1982** / edited by Karen Payne.
Boston: Houghton Mifflin, 1983. xvi, 416 p.; 25 cm. Includes index. 1. Mothers — Correspondence. 2. Daughters — Correspondence. 3. Mothers and daughters — History. 4. Feminism — History. I. Payne, Karen.
HQ759.B53 1983     306.8/743 19    *LC* 83-10803    *ISBN* 0395339693

**Boulton, Mary Georgina.**  **4.5665**
On being a mother: a study of women with pre–school children / Mary Georgina Boulton. — London; New York: Tavistock Publications, 1983. 241 p.; 23 cm. Includes indexes. 1. Mothers 2. Mother and child 3. Family I. T.
HQ759.B75 1983     306.8/743 19    *LC* 83-9150    *ISBN* 0422785407

**Chodorow, Nancy.**  **4.5666**
The reproduction of mothering: psychoanalysis and the sociology of gender / Nancy Chodorow. — Berkeley: University of California Press, c1978. viii, 263 p.; 25 cm. Includes index. 1. Mothers 2. Women — Psychology 3. Mother and child 4. Women and psychoanalysis I. T.
HQ759.C56     301.42/7    *LC* 75-27922    *ISBN* 0520031334

**Dally, Ann G.**  **4.5667**
Inventing motherhood: the consequences of an ideal / by Ann Dally. — New York: Schocken Books, 1983, c1982. 360 p.; 24 cm. Includes index. 1. Motherhood I. T.
HQ759.D248 1983     649/.1 19    *LC* 82-10517    *ISBN* 0805238301

**Finch, Janet.**  **4.5668**
Married to the job: wives' incorporation in men's work / Janet Finch. — London; Boston: G. Allen & Unwin, 1983. x, 182 p.; 23 cm. Includes index. 1. Wives — Effect of husband's employment on I. T.
HQ759.F47 1983     306.8/72 19    *LC* 82-16435    *ISBN* 0043011497

**Fowlkes, Martha R., 1940-.**  **4.5669**
Behind every successful man: wives of medicine and academe / Martha R. Fowlkes. — New York: Columbia University Press, 1980. xv, 223 p.; 24 cm. Includes index. 1. Wives — United States. 2. Professions — United States.

3. Physicians' wives — United States. 4. Teachers' wives — United States. I. T.
HQ759.F68     301.42/7 19     *LC* 79-24901     *ISBN* 0231047762

**Mothering: essays in feminist theory / edited by Joyce**    **4.5670**
**Trebilcot.**
Totowa, N.J.: Rowman & Allanheld, 1984, c1983. viii, 336 p.; 22 cm. — (New feminist perspectives.) 1. Motherhood — Addresses, essays, lectures. 2. Mothers — Addresses, essays, lectures. 3. Feminism — Addresses, essays, lectures. 4. Patriarchy — Addresses, essays, lectures. I. Trebilcot, Joyce. II. Series.
HQ759.M88 1984     306.8/58 19     *LC* 83-4517     *ISBN* 0847671151

**Rich, Adrienne Cecile.**    **4.5671**
Of woman born: motherhood as experience and institution / Adrienne Rich. — 1st ed. — New York: Norton, c1976. 318 p.; 22 cm. 1. Motherhood 2. Mother and child 3. Feminism I. T.
HQ759.R53 1976     301.42/7     *LC* 76-18744     *ISBN* 0393087506

**Anastasiow, Nicholas J.**    **4.5672**
The adolescent parent / by Nicholas J. Anastasiow with Mary Anastasiow ... [et al.]. — Baltimore: P.H. Brookes Pub. Co., c1982. x, 142 p.; 24 cm. 1. Teenage parents — Addresses, essays, lectures. 2. Child development — Addresses, essays, lectures. I. Anastasiow, Mary, 1952- II. T.
HQ759.64.A5 1982     362.7/96 19     *LC* 81-18190     *ISBN* 0933716257

# HQ763–766 Birth Control

**Rogers, Everett M.**    **4.5673**
Communication strategies for family planning / [by] Everett M. Rogers. — New York: Free Press, [1973] xx, 451 p.; 25 cm. 1. Birth control 2. Communication in birth control I. T.
HQ763.R63     301     *LC* 73-1049

**Bean, Lee L.**    **4.5674**
Population and family planning, manpower and training [by] Lee L. Bean, Richmond K. Anderson [and] Howard J. Tatum. — [Bridgeport, Conn.: Distributed for the Population Council by Key Book Service, 1971] xvi, 118 p.; 23 cm. — (An Occasional paper of the Population Council) 1. Birth control — Study and teaching — U.S. 2. Demography — Study and teaching — U.S. I. Anderson, Richmond K., 1907- joint author. II. Tatum, Howard J., 1915- joint author. III. T.
HQ763.6.U5 B4     331.1/26     *LC* 71-155737     *ISBN* 0878340033

**Sanger, Margaret, 1879-1966.**    ● **4.5675**
Margaret Sanger; an autobiography. First edition. New York, W. W. Norton & company, [1938] 504 p. front. (port.) 25 cm. 1. Birth control I. T.
HQ764.S3 A3     *LC* 38-28918

**Hau'ofa, Epeli.**    **4.5676**
Our crowded islands / by Epeli Hau'ofa. — Suva, Fiji: Institute of Pacific Studies, University of the South Pacific, 1977. 1 v. 1. Birth control — Tonga. 2. Tonga — Population. I. University of the South Pacific. Institute of Pacific Studies. II. T.
HQ765.5.T6 H38

**Chandrasekhar, S. (Sripati), 1918-.**    **4.5677**
'A dirty filthy book': the writings of Charles Knowlton and Annie Besant on reproductive physiology and birth control and an account of the Bradlaugh–Besant trial: with the definitive texts of Fruits of philosophy, by Charles Knowlton, The law of population, by Annie Besant, Theosophy and the law of population, by Annie Besant / by S. Chandrasekhar. — Berkeley: University of California Press, c1981. xi, 217 p., [2] leaves of plates: ill.; 22 cm. Includes indexes. 1. Bradlaugh, Charles, 1833-1891. 2. Birth control 3. Malthusianism 4. Population policy 5. Birth control — Religious aspect — Theosophy. I. Knowlton, Charles, 1800-1850. Fruits of philosophy. 1981. II. Besant, Annie Wood, 1847-1933. Law of population. 1981. III. Besant, Annie Wood, 1847-1933. Theosophy and the law of population. 1981. IV. T.
HQ766.C483     304.6/6     *LC* 80-15570     *ISBN* 0520041682

**Cuca, Roberto, 1940-.**    **4.5678**
Experiments in family planning: lessons from the developing world / Roberto Cuca and Catherine S. Pierce; foreword by Bernard Berelson. — Baltimore: Published for the World Bank by Johns Hopkins University Press, c1977. xvi, 261 p.; 24 cm. 1. Underdeveloped areas — Birth control. I. Pierce, Catherine S., 1942- II. T.
HQ766.C9     362.8/2     *LC* 77-4602     *ISBN* 0801820138

**Demerath, Nicholas J., 1913-.**    **4.5679**
Birth control and foreign policy: the alternatives to family planning / Nicholas J. Demerath. — New York: Harper & Row, c1976. x, 228 p.; 21 cm. Includes index. 1. Birth control 2. Population policy 3. Fertility, Human 4. Birth

control — Developing countries 5. Technical assistance, American — Developing countries. I. T.
HQ766.D39     301.32/1     *LC* 76-2040     *ISBN* 0060416165

**Field, Marilyn Jane.**    **4.5680**
The comparative politics of birth control: determinants of policy variation and change in the developed nations / by Marilyn Jane Field. — New York, NY, USA: Praeger, 1983. 305 p.: ill.; 25 cm. — (Landmark dissertations in women's studies series.) Originally presented as the author's thesis (Ph. D.—University of Michigan). 1. Birth control — Government policy. 2. Birth control — Political aspects. I. T. II. Series.
HQ766.F49 1983     363.9/6 19     *LC* 83-16006     *ISBN* 0030695279

**Srikantan, K. S., 1930-.**    **4.5681**
The family planning program in the socioeconomic context / K. S. Srikantan. — New York: Population Council, c1977. xii, 240 p.; 23 cm. 1. Birth control 2. Population policy 3. Fertility, Human 4. Social indicators I. T.
HQ766.S7     301.32/.1     *LC* 77-21847     *ISBN* 0878340270

**Symonds, Richard, 1918-.**    **4.5682**
The United Nations and the population question, 1945–1970, by Richard Symonds and Michael Carder. New York, McGraw-Hill [1973] xviii, 236 p. 24 cm. 'A Population Council book.' 1. United Nations — Technical assistance 2. Birth control — Developing countries 3. Developing countries — Population. I. Carder, Michael, joint author. II. T.
HQ766.S888     301.32     *LC* 72-2008     *ISBN* 0070626510

**Viel Vicuña, Benjamin.**    **4.5683**
The demographic explosion: the Latin American experience / Benjamin Viel; translated from the Spanish and updated by James Walls. — New York: Irvington Publishers: distributed by Halsted Press, c1976. xiii, 249 p.: ill.; 25 cm. (The Irvington population and demography series) Edition for 1966 published under title: La explosión demográfica; ?cuántos son demasiados? At head of title: A Population Reference Bureau book. 1. Birth control 2. Population 3. Latin America — Population. I. T.
HQ766.V5 1976     301.32/1     *LC* 75-15837     *ISBN* 0470905050

**Noonan, John Thomas, 1926-.**    ● **4.5684**
Contraception: a history of its treatment by the Catholic theologians and canonists / [by] John T. Noonan, Jr. — Cambridge: Belknap Press of Harvard University Press, 1965. x, 561 p.: ill.; 25 cm. 1. Birth control — Religious aspects — Catholic Church — History of doctrines. 2. Contraception — Religious aspects — Catholic Church — History of doctrines. I. T.
HQ766.3.N6     261.83     *LC* 65-16687

**China's one–child family policy / edited by Elisabeth Croll,**    **4.5685**
**Delia Davin, and Penny Kane.**
New York: St. Martin's Press, 1985. xvi, 237 p.; 23 cm. 1. Birth control — China — Addresses, essays, lectures. 2. Population policy — China — Addresses, essays, lectures. 3. Family policy — China — Addresses, essays, lectures. 4. China — Social conditions — 1976- — Addresses, essays, lectures. I. Croll, Elisabeth J. II. Davin, Delia. III. Kane, Penny.
HQ766.5.C6 C452 1985     363.9/6/0951 19     *LC* 84-26756     *ISBN* 0312133561

**Hernandez, Donald J.**    **4.5686**
Success or failure?: family planning programs in the Third World / Donald J. Hernandez; foreword by Robert F. Boruch. — Westport, Conn.: Greenwood Press, 1984. xviii, 161 p.: ill.; 25 cm. (Studies in population and urban demography. 0147-1104; no. 4) Includes index. 1. Birth control — Developing countries I. T. II. Series.
HQ766.5.D44 H47 1984     363.9/6/091716 19     *LC* 84-6653     *ISBN* 0313244014

**Soloway, R. A.**    **4.5687**
Birth control and the population question in England, 1877–1930 / Richard Allen Soloway. — Chapel Hill: University of North Carolina Press, c1982. xix, 418 p.; 24 cm. Includes index. 1. Birth control — England — History — Public opinion — Addresses, essays, lectures. 2. Public opinion — England — History — Addresses, essays, lectures. 3. Family size — England — History — Addresses, essays, lectures. 4. England — Population — History — Addresses, essays, lectures. I. T.
HQ766.5.G7 S64 1982     304.6/6 19     *LC* 81-14791     *ISBN* 0807815047

**Stycos, J. Mayone.**    **4.5688**
Clinics, contraception, and communication: evaluation studies of family planning programs in four Latin American countries / [by] J. Mayone Stycos; with Alan B. Keller [and others]. — New York: Appleton-Century-Crofts, [1973] 207 p.: ill.; 22 cm. — (ACC population and demography series) 1. Birth control — Latin America — Case studies. 2. Birth control clinics — Latin America — Case studies. 3. Public relations — Birth control clinics — Case studies. I. T.
HQ766.5.L3 S78     362.8/2     *LC* 79-184865

**Gordon, Linda.**                                                                   **4.5689**
Woman's body, woman's right: a social history of birth control in America / Linda Gordon. — New York: Grossman, 1976. xviii, 479 p.: ill.; 24 cm. 1. Birth control — United States — History. I. T.
HQ766.5.U5 G67        301.32/1        *LC* 76-22691        *ISBN* 0670778176

**Luker, Kristin.**                                                                  **4.5690**
Taking chances: abortion and the decision not to contracept / Kristin Luker. Berkeley: University of California Press, 1976 (c1975). xii, 207 p.; 23 cm. Includes index. 1. Birth control — California. 2. Contraception — Psychological aspects. 3. Abortion — California. 4. Risk-taking (Psychology) I. T.
HQ766.5.U5 L84        301        *LC* 74-22965        *ISBN* 0520028724

**Piotrow, Phyllis Tilson.**                                                         **4.5691**
World population crisis; the United States response. Foreword by George H. Bush, Jr. New York, Praeger [1973] xxiii, 276 p. 25 cm. (Law and population book series, no. 4) (Praeger special studies in international economics and development) 1. Birth control — United States. 2. Birth control — Developing countries 3. United States — Population 4. Developing countries — Population. I. T. II. Series.
HQ766.5.U5 P54        301.32/1        *LC* 72-79545

**Rainwater, Lee.**                                                                  • **4.5692**
And the poor get children; sex, contraception, and family planning in the working class. Assisted by Karol Kane Weinstein. With a pref. by J. Mayone Stycos. — Chicago: Quadrangle Books, 1960. 202 p.; 22 cm. — (Social research studies in contemporary life) 1. Birth control — United States. 2. Labor and laboring class — United States. I. T.
HQ766.5.U5 R3        301.426        *LC* 60-10881

**Reed, James, 1944-.**                                                              **4.5693**
From private vice to public virtue: the birth control movement and American society since 1830 / James Reed. — New York: Basic Books, c1978. xvi, 456 p., [4] leaves of plates: ill., ports. 1. Birth control — United States — History. 2. Contraception — United States — History. I. T.
HQ766.5.U5 R44        HQ766.5U5 R44.        301.32/1        *LC* 77-74571
     *ISBN* 046502582X

**Westoff, Leslie Aldridge.**                                                        • **4.5694**
From now to zero; fertility, contraception and abortion in America, by Leslie Aldridge Westoff and Charles F. Westoff. — Boston: Little, Brown, [1971] xxi, 358 p.; 22 cm. 1. Birth control — U.S. 2. Abortion — U.S. 3. U.S. — Population. I. Westoff, Charles F. joint author. II. T.
HQ766.5.U5 W44        301.3/2/0973        *LC* 73-149473

**World population control: rights and restrictions / edited by the**                **4.5695**
**staff of Columbia human rights law review.**
New York: Family Service Association of America, [1976?], c1975. 575 p. Papers from two symposia on law and population. 1. Population — Law and legislation 2. Population policy — Addresses, essays, lectures 3. Birth control — Addresses, essays, lectures I. Columbia human rights law review.
HQ766.7 W66        *LC* 75-27963        *ISBN* 0873041437

# HQ767 Abortion

**Callahan, Daniel, 1930-.**                                                         • **4.5696**
Abortion: law, choice, and morality / [by] Daniel Callahan. — [New York]: Macmillan [1970] xv, 524 p.; 24 cm. 1. Abortion I. T.
HQ767.C25        179/.7        *LC* 78-99788

**Francome, Colin.**                                                                 **4.5697**
Abortion freedom: a worldwide movement / Colin Francome. — London; Boston: Allen & Unwin, 1984. 241 p.: ill.; 23 cm. Includes index. 1. Abortion — History. 2. Abortion — Law and legislation — History. 3. Birth control — History. 4. Abortion — Great Britain. 5. Abortion — United States. 6. Abortion — Europe. I. T.
HQ767.F72 1984        363.4/6 19        *LC* 83-15558        *ISBN* 0041790014

**Harrison, Beverly Wildung, 1932-.**                                                **4.5698**
Our right to choose: toward a new ethic of abortion / Beverly Wildung Harrison. — Boston: Beacon Press, c1983. xi, 334 p.; 24 cm. 1. Abortion — Moral and ethical aspects 2. Abortion — Religious aspects — Christianity. 3. Abortion — Political aspects — United States. 4. Pro-choice movement — United States. 5. Feminism I. T.
HQ767.3.H37 1983        179/.76 19        *LC* 81-70488        *ISBN* 0807015083

**Tooley, Michael, 1941-.**                                                          **4.5699**
Abortion and infanticide / Michael Tooley. — Oxford: Clarendon Press; New York: Oxford University Press, c1983. ix, 441 p.; 22 cm. Includes index. 1. Abortion — Moral and ethical aspects 2. Infanticide — Moral and ethical aspects. I. T.
HQ767.3.T66 1983        363.4/6 19        *LC* 83-6261        *ISBN* 0198246749

**Abortion: understanding differences / edited by Sidney Callahan**                   **4.5700**
**and Daniel Callahan.**
New York: Plenum Press, c1984. xxii, 338 p.; 24 cm. — (Hastings Center series in ethics.) 1. Abortion — United States — Addresses, essays, lectures. 2. Pro-life movement — United States — Addresses, essays, lectures. 3. Pro-choice movement — United States — Addresses, essays, lectures. 4. Social values — Addresses, essays, lectures. I. Callahan, Sidney Cornelia. II. Callahan, Daniel, 1930- III. Series.
HQ767.5.U5 A28 1984        363.4/6 19        *LC* 84-9965        *ISBN* 0306416409

**Jaffe, Frederick S.**                                                              **4.5701**
Abortion politics: private morality and public policy / by Frederick S. Jaffe, Barbara L. Lindheim, Philip R. Lee. — New York: McGraw-Hill, c1981. viii, 216 p.; 24 cm. 1. Abortion — United States. I. Lindheim, Barbara L. joint author. II. Lee, Philip R. joint author. III. T.
HQ767.5.U5 J33        363.4/6/0973        *LC* 80-17035        *ISBN* 0070321892

**Luker, Kristin.**                                                                  **4.5702**
Abortion and the politics of motherhood / Kristin Luker. — Berkeley: University of California Press, 1984. xvi, 324 p. — (California series on social choice and political economy.) Includes index. 1. Abortion — United States. 2. Abortion — Political aspects — United States. 3. Pro-life movement — United States. 4. Motherhood — United States — Moral and ethical aspects. I. T. II. Series.
HQ767.5.U5 L84 1984        363.4/6/0973 19        *LC* 83-47849        *ISBN* 0520043146

**Perspectives on abortion / edited by Paul Sachdev.**                               **4.5703**
Metuchen, N.J.: Scarecrow Press, 1985. xi, 281 p.; 23 cm. 1. Abortion — United States — Addresses, essays, lectures. 2. Abortion — Canada — Addresses, essays, lectures. 3. Abortion — United States — Public opinion — Addresses, essays, lectures. 4. Public opinion — United States — Addresses, essays, lectures. 5. Abortion — Addresses, essays, lectures. I. Sachdev, Paul.
HQ767.5.U5 P47 1985        363.4/6/0973 19        *LC* 84-10573        *ISBN* 081081708X

# HQ767.8–792 Children. Child Development

**Pollock, Linda A.**                                                                **4.5704**
Forgotten children: parent–child relations from 1500 to 1900 / Linda A. Pollock. — Cambridge [Cambridgeshire]; New York: Cambridge University Press, 1983. xi, 334 p.; 24 cm. Revision of thesis (doctoral)—University of St. Andrews, 1981. 1. Children — History. 2. Children — Public opinion — History. 3. Parent and child — History. 4. Child development — History. 5. Public opinion — History. I. T.
HQ767.87.P64 1983        305.2/3/09 19        *LC* 83-5315        *ISBN* 0521250099

**Lomax, Elizabeth M. R.**                                                           **4.5705**
Science and patterns of child care / Elizabeth M. R. Lomax, in collaboration with Jerome Kagan, Barbara G. Rosenkrantz. — San Francisco: W. H. Freeman, c1978. xiv, 247 p.; 22 cm. — (A Series of books in psychology) 1. Child development 2. Child psychology 3. Child rearing — History. I. Kagan, Jerome. joint author. II. Rosenkrantz, Barbara Gutmann, joint author. III. T.
HQ767.9.L65        649/.1        *LC* 78-4972        *ISBN* 0716702967

**Mead, Margaret, 1901-1978. ed.**                                                   • **4.5706**
Childhood in contemporary cultures / edited by Margaret Mead and Martha Wolfenstein. — [Chicago]: University of Chicago Press [1955] xi, 473 p.: ill.; 24 cm. 1. Children — Collections. I. Wolfenstein, Martha, 1911-1976. joint ed. II. T.
HQ768.M4        392.3        *LC* 55-10248

**Six cultures; studies of child rearing, edited by Beatrice B.**                     • **4.5707**
**Whiting. Contributors: John L. Fischer [and others] Senior**
**investigators: Irvin L. Child, William W. Lambert [and] John**
**W. M. Whiting.**
New York: Wiley, [1963] vi, 1017 p.: illus., maps.; 24 cm. 1. Socialization — Case studies. 2. Children I. Whiting, Beatrice Blyth. ed. II. Child, Irvin Long, 1915-
HQ768.S49        392.3        *LC* 63-8908

**Bettelheim, Bruno.**                                                               • **4.5708**
Love is not enough; the treatment of emotionally disturbed children. Glencoe, Ill., Free Press [1950] ix, 386 p. illus. 22 cm. A report on the 'day-to-day' life at the University of Chicago's Sonia Shankman Orthogenic School. 'Publications on the School': p. 376. 1. Sonia Shankman Orthogenic School. 2. Child rearing 3. Emotional problems of children I. T.
HQ769.B525        136.708        *LC* 50-8083

**Chess, Stella.**     • **4.5709**
Your child is a person; a psychological approach to parenthood without guilt [by] Stella Chess, Alexander Thomas [and] Herbert G. Birch. — New York: Viking Press, [1965] ix, 213 p.; 22 cm. 1. Child rearing I. Thomas, Alexander, 1914- joint author. II. Birch, Herbert George, 1918-1973. joint author. III. T.
HQ769.C437     649.122     *LC* 65-24005

**Raising children in modern America: problems and prospective**    **4.5710**
**solutions / Nathan B. Talbot, editor.**
1st ed. — Boston: Little, Brown, c1976. xiii, 590 p.: ill.; 24 cm. Includes index. 1. Child rearing — Congresses. 2. Children — United States — Congresses. I. Talbot, Nathan Bill, 1909-
HQ769.R17     649/.1/0973     *LC* 75-19236     *ISBN* 0316831352

**Rubin, Zick.**     **4.5711**
Children's friendships / Zick Rubin. — Cambridge, Mass.: Harvard University Press, 1980. 165 p.: ports; 21 cm. (The Developing child series) Includes index. 1. Childhood friendship 2. Child development I. T.
HQ769.R7647     305.2/3     *LC* 79-25644     *ISBN* 0674116186

**Sears, Robert Richardson, 1908-.**     • **4.5712**
Patterns of child rearing / by Robert R. Sears, Eleanor E. Maccoby [and] Harry Levin; in collaboration with Edgar L. Lowell, Pauline S. Sears, and John W. M. Whiting; illus. by Jean Berwick. — Evanston, Ill.: Row, Peterson, [1957] 549 p.: ill.; 24 cm. 'A report ... from the Laboratory of Human Development, Graduate School of Education, Harvard University.' 1. Child rearing I. T.
HQ769.S38     649.1     *LC* 57-2291

**Spock, Benjamin, 1903-.**     • **4.5713**
Problems of parents. Boston, Houghton Mifflin, 1962. 308 p. 23 cm. 1. Child rearing I. T.
HQ769.S68     649.1     *LC* 62-20073

**Whiting, John Wesley Mayhew, 1908-.**     • **4.5714**
Child training and personality; a cross–cultural study, by John W. M. Whiting and Irvin L. Child. New York, Yale University Press, 1953. vi, 353 p. diagrs, 25 cm. 1. Child rearing — Cross-cultural studies 2. Personality and culture — Cross-cultural studies I. Child, Irvin Long, 1915- joint author. II. T.
HQ769.W58     392.3 301.427*     *LC* 52-12079

**Bowlby, John.**     • **4.5715**
Child care and the growth of love / John Bowlby; Abridged and ed. by Margery Fry. — [Harmondsworth, Eng.] Penguin Books [1953] 190 p. — (Pelican books: A271) Based, by permission of the World Health Organization, on the author's report: Maternal care and child health. 1. Child rearing 2. Parent and child 3. Child development I. Fry, Margery, 1874-1958 ed. II. T.
HQ772.B64

**Buhler, Charlotte Malachowski, 1893-1974.**     • **4.5716**
[Kind und familie. English] The child and his family, by Charlotte Buhler. With the collaboration of Edeltrud Baar [and others] Translated by Henry Beaumont. Westport, Conn., Greenwood Press [1972, c1939] viii, 187 p. charts. 22 cm. Translation of Kind und familie. 1. Child psychology 2. Parent and child 3. Family I. T.
HQ772.B93 1972     301.42/7     *LC* 72-156177     *ISBN* 0837161207

**Burlingham, Dorothy.**     • **4.5717**
Infants without families: the case for and against residential nurseries, by Anna Freud and Dorothy Burlingham. New York, N.Y., Medical war books, International university press [1944] 128 p. 1. Child study 2. Children — Institutional care 3. Foster home care I. Freud, Anna, 1895- jt. author II. Hampstead Nurseries, London III. T.
HQ772 B95 1944     *LC* 44-6589

**Elkin, Frederick.**     • **4.5718**
The child and society; the process of socialization. — New York: Random House, [c1960] 121 p.; 19 cm. — (Studies in sociology, SS19) 1. Child study. 2. Socialization I. T.
HQ772.E4     136.732     *LC* 60-16607

**Gesell, Arnold, 1880-1961.**     **4.5719**
The child from five to ten, by Arnold Gesell [and] Frances L. Ilg in collaboration with Louise Bates Ames [and] Glenna E. Bullis. — New York and; London: Harper & Brothers, c1946. xii p., 1 l., 475 p.: illus., diagrs.; 25 cm. 'First edition.' 1. Child study. I. Ilg, Frances Lillian, 1902- joint author. II. Ames, Louise Bates. III. Bullis, Glenna E. IV. T.
HQ772.G38     136.7     *LC* 46-6211

**Gesell, Arnold, 1880-1961.**     • **4.5720**
Studies in child development. — Westport, Conn.: Greenwood Press, [1971, c1948] x, 224 p.: ill.; 23 cm. 1. Child development I. T.
HQ772.G43 1971     155.4/08     *LC* 76-138114     *ISBN* 0837156904

**Redl, Fritz.**     • **4.5721**
The aggressive child, by Fritz Redl and David Wineman. — Glencoe, Ill.: Free Press, [1957] 575 p.; 22 cm. 'A one volume edition, containing in their entirety,

Children who hate...and Controls from within.' 1. Detroit Pioneer House. 2. Problem children 3. Juvenile delinquency I. Wineman, David, joint author. II. T. III. Title: Children who hate. IV. Title: Controls from within.
HQ773.R4     136.763     *LC* 57-9317

**Cataldo, Christine Z.**     **4.5722**
Infant and toddler programs: a guide to very early childhood education / Christine Z. Cataldo. — Reading, Mass.: Addison-Wesley Pub. Co., c1983. xii, 244 p.: ill., ports.; 24 cm. Includes index. 1. Infants — Care and hygiene. 2. Education of children I. T.
HQ774.C376 1983     372/.21 19     *LC* 82-11418     *ISBN* 0201110202

**Schachter, Frances Fuchs, 1930-.**     **4.5723**
Everyday mother talk to toddlers: early intervention / Frances Fuchs Schachter, with Ruth E. Marquis ... [et al.]; foreword by Herbert Zimiles. — New York: Academic Press, 1979. xviii, 211 p.: ill.; 24 cm. Includes index. 1. Domestic education — United States. 2. Children — Language 3. Oral communication 4. Speech acts (Linguistics) 5. Mother and child I. T.
HQ774.5.S3     372.6     *LC* 78-20049     *ISBN* 0126213607

**Weiss, Robert Stuart, 1925-.**     **4.5724**
Going it alone: the family life and social situation of the single parent / Robert S. Weiss. — New York: Basic Books, c1979. xvi, 303 p.; 24 cm. 1. Single-parent family — United States. I. T.
HQ777.4.W44     301.42/7     *LC* 78-19936     *ISBN* 0465026885

**Kamerman, Sheila B.**     **4.5725**
Parenting in an unresponsive society: managing work and family life / Sheila B. Kamerman. — New York: Free Press; London: Collier Macmillan Publishers, c1980. x, 196 p.; 25 cm. Includes index. 1. Children of working mothers — United States. 2. Parenting — United States. 3. Work and family — United States. I. T.
HQ777.6.K35 1980     306.8/7     *LC* 80-641     *ISBN* 0029167302

**Visher, Emily B., 1918-.**     **4.5726**
Stepfamilies: a guide to working with stepparents and stepchildren / Emily B. Visher and John S. Visher. — New York: Brunner/Mazel, c1979. xx, 280 p.; 24 cm. Includes index. 1. Stepparents — United States. 2. Stepchildren — United States. I. Visher, John S., 1921- joint author. II. T.
HQ777.7.V57     HQ777.7 V57.     301.42/7     *LC* 78-25857     *ISBN* 0876301901

## HQ781–792 CHILD LIFE: DESCRIPTIVE WORKS

**Erikson, Erik H. (Erik Homburger), 1902-.**     **4.5727**
Childhood and society / Erik H. Erikson. — 35th anniversary ed. — New York: W.W. Norton, [1985], c1963. 445 p.: ill.; 22 cm. 'Afterthoughts 1985'—p. [4]-11. 'Published writings ... since the first edition of Childhood and society'— p. 427-430. Includes index. 1. Child development 2. Socialization 3. Child psychology 4. Identity (Psychology) — Case studies. I. T.
HQ781.E75 1985     305.2/3 19     *LC* 86-192911     *ISBN* 0393022951

**Mergen, Bernard.**     **4.5728**
Play and playthings: a reference guide / Bernard Mergen. — Westport, Conn.: Greenwood Press, 1982. xi, 281 p.: ill.; 25 cm. — (American popular culture. 0193-6859) Includes index. 1. Play — United States — History. 2. Children — United States 3. Play — United States — Bibliography. I. T. II. Series.
HQ782.M47 1982     790.1/922 19     *LC* 82-6139     *ISBN* 0313221367

**Mussen, Paul Henry.**     **4.5729**
Roots of caring, sharing, and helping: the development of prosocial behavior in children / Paul Mussen, Nancy Eisenberg–Berg. — San Francisco: W. H. Freeman, c1977. ix, 212 p.; 23 cm. — (A series of books in psychology) 1. Socialization 2. Child development I. Eisenberg, Nancy. II. T.
HQ783.M83     301.15/72     *LC* 77-22750     *ISBN* 071670045X. *ISBN* 0716700441 pbk

**Tallman, Irving.**     **4.5730**
Adolescent socialization in cross–cultural perspective: planning for social change / Irving Tallman, Ramona Marotz–Baden, Pablo Pindas. — New York: Academic Press, 1983. xvii, 325 p.: ill.; 24 cm. — (Quantitative studies in social relations.) Includes index. 1. Socialization — Cross-cultural studies 2. Youth — Mexico — Cross-cultural studies. 3. Youth — United States — Cross-cultural studies. 4. Problem solving in children — Cross-cultural studies 5. Social change — Cross-cultural studies I. Marotz-Baden, Ramona. II. Pindas, Pablo. III. T. IV. Series.
HQ783.T34 1983     303.3/2 19     *LC* 83-2511     *ISBN* 0126831807

**Whiting, Beatrice Blyth.**     **4.5731**
Children of six cultures: a psycho–cultural analysis / Beatrice B. Whiting and John W. M. Whiting, in collaboration with Richard Longabaugh; based on data collected by John and Ann Fischer ... [et al.]. — Cambridge, Mass.: Harvard University Press, 1975. xiv, 237 p.: ill.; 21 cm. Includes index. 1. Socialization 2. Child rearing — Cross-cultural studies 3. Personality and culture

4. Children — Research I. Whiting, John Wesley Mayhew, 1908- joint author. II. Longabaugh, Richard. joint author. III. T.
HQ783.W53     301.15/72     *LC* 74-80941     *ISBN* 0674116453

**Greenstein, Fred I.**          **4.5732**
Children and politics / by Fred I. Greenstein. — New Haven: Yale University Press, 1965. viii, 199 p.; 23 cm. — (Yale studies in political science. 13)
1. Children and politics I. T. II. Series.
HQ784.P5 G7     301.154072     *LC* 65-11181

**Hess, Robert D.**          • **4.5733**
The development of political attitudes in children / [by] Robert D. Hess and Judith V. Torney. — Chicago: Aldine Pub. Co., [1967]. xviii, 288 p.: ill.
1. Children and politics I. Torney-Purta, Judith, 1937- II. T.
HQ784.P5 H4     320.01

**Goldman, Ronald.**          **4.5734**
Children's sexual thinking: a comparative study of children aged 5 to 15 years in Australia, North America, Britain, and Sweden / Ronald and Juliette Goldman. — London; Boston: Routledge & K. Paul, 1982. xviii, 485 p.: ill.; 23 cm. Includes indexes. 1. Children and sex — Cross-cultural studies 2. Children — Attitudes — Cross-cultural studies I. Goldman, Juliette. II. T.
HQ784.S45 G64 1982     305.2/3 19     *LC* 81-15353     *ISBN* 071000883X

**The Effects of television advertising on children: review and**      **4.5735**
**recommendations / Richard P. Adler ... [et al.].**
Lexington, Mass.: D.C. Heath, c1980. xi, 367 p.: ill.; 24 cm. Includes index.
1. Television advertising and children I. Adler, Richard.
HQ784.T4 E35     791.45/01/3     *LC* 78-24714     *ISBN* 0669028142

**Liebert, Robert M., 1942-.**          **4.5736**
The early window: effects of television on children and youth. — 2nd ed. / Robert M. Liebert, Joyce N. Sprafkin, Emily S. Davidson. — New York: Pergamon Press, c1982. x, 257 p.: ill.; 24 cm. — (Pergamon general psychology series. 34) Includes indexes. 1. Television and children I. Sprafkin, Joyce N., 1949- II. Davidson, Emily S., 1948- III. T. IV. Series.
HQ784.T4 L48 1982     305.2/3 19     *LC* 82-5327     *ISBN* 0080275486

**Singer, Jerome L.**          **4.5737**
Television, imagination, and aggression: a study of preschoolers / Jerome L. Singer, Dorothy G. Singer. — Hillsdale, N.J.: L. Erlbaum Associates, 1981. x, 213 p.; 24 cm. Includes indexes. 1. Television and children — Longitudinal studies. 2. Imagination in children 3. Aggressiveness in children I. Singer, Dorothy G. joint author. II. T.
HQ784.T4 S56     791.45/01/3     *LC* 80-36810     *ISBN* 0898590604

**Television and behavior: ten years of scientific progress and**      **4.5738**
**implications for the eighties.**
Rockville, Md.: U.S. Dept. of Health and Human Services, Public Health Service, Alcohol, Drug Abuse, and Mental Health Administration, National Institute of Mental Health: [Supt. of Docs., U.S. G.P.O. distributor], 1982. 2 v.; 27 cm. — (DHHS publication. no. (ADM) 82-1195- (ADM) 82-1196) 'An update and elaboration of information presented in the 1972 report of the Surgeon General's Advisory Committee on Television and Behavior' v. 1, p. iii. S/N 017-024-01129-1 (v. 1) S/N 017-024-01141-0 (v. 2) Item 507-B-5 1. Television and children — United States. 2. Television programs — United States — Psychological aspects. I. Pearl, David, 1921- II. Bouthilet, Lorraine. III. Lazar, Joyce B. IV. United States. Surgeon General's Scientific Advisory Committee on Television and Social Behavior. V. National Institute of Mental Health (U.S.) VI. Series.
HQ784.T4 T439 1982     305.2/3 19     *LC* 82-600539

**Freud, Anna, 1895-.**          • **4.5739**
War and children. [New York] Medical war books, 1943. 4 p.l., 11-191 p. 20 cm. 1. Hampstead nurseries. 2. Child study. 3. World War, 1939-1945 — Children I. Burlingham, Dorothy. joint author. II. T.
HQ784.W3 F7     *LC* 43-51246

**Goldstein, Bernard, 1925-.**          **4.5740**
Children and work: a study of socialization / Bernard Goldstein, Jack Oldham. — New Brunswick, N.J.: Transaction Books, c1979. xii, 195 p.; 24 cm. Includes index. 1. Work 2. Child development 3. Socialization 4. Vocational interests I. Oldham, Jack, 1947- joint author. II. T.
HQ784.W6 G64     301.15/72     *LC* 78-62894     *ISBN* 0878552855

**Cohen, Howard, 1944-.**          **4.5741**
Equal rights for children / by Howard Cohen. — Totowa, N.J.: Littlefield, Adams, 1980. x, 172 p.; 21 cm. — (Littlefield, Adams quality paperback series; 350) Includes index. 1. Children's rights — United States. I. T.
HQ789.C63 1980b     305.2/3/0973     *LC* 80-16005     *ISBN* 0822603500

**Mead, Margaret, 1901-1978.**          • **4.5742**
Growth and culture: a photographic study of Balinese childhood / by Margaret Mead and Frances Cooke Macgregor; based upon photos. by Gregory Bateson,

analyzed in Gesell categories. — New York: Putnam [1951] xvi, 223 p.: (p. [65]-[179] ill.) 1. Children in Bali 2. Balinese I. Macgregor, Frances M. Cooke, 1906- II. T.
HQ792 B3 M4     *LC* 51-14875

**Ariès, Philippe.**          **4.5743**
[Enfant et la vie familiale sous l'Ancien Régime. English] Centuries of childhood; a social history of family life. Translated from the French by Robert Baldick. New York, Knopf, 1962. 447 p. illus. 22 cm. Translation of L'enfant et la vie familiale sous l'Ancien Régime. 1. Children — France 2. Family — France. I. T.
HQ792.F7 A73     301.42     *LC* 62-8680

**Rabin, Albert I.**          **4.5744**
Twenty years later: Kibbutz children grown up / A.I. Rabin, Benjamin Beit–Hallahmi. — New York: Springer, c1982. xi, 244 p.; 24 cm. Includes index. 1. Children — Israel — Longitudinal studies. 2. Kibbutzim — Israel — Longitudinal studies. 3. Family — Israel — Longitudinal studies. I. Beit-Hallahmi, Benjamin. II. T.
HQ792.I75 R3 1982     305.2/3/095694 19     *LC* 82-821     *ISBN* 082613310X

**Bettelheim, Bruno.**          • **4.5745**
The children of the dream. [New York] Macmillan [1969] xiii, 363 p. 22 cm. 1. Children — Israel 2. Kibbutzim I. T.
HQ792.P3 B47     301.43/1/095694     *LC* 69-10505

**Clarke-Stewart, Alison, 1943-.**          **4.5746**
Child care in the family: a review of research and some propositions for policy / Alison Clarke–Stewart. — New York: Academic Press, 1977. xvii, 151 p.; 24 cm. (A Carnegie Council on Children monograph) Includes index. 1. Child development 2. Child rearing 3. Children — United States 4. Children — Care and hygiene. I. T.
HQ792.U5 C56     649/.1     *LC* 77-12797     *ISBN* 012175250X

**Ginzberg, Eli, 1911-.**          • **4.5747**
Values and ideals of American youth / edited by Eli Ginzberg; with a foreword by John W. Gardner. — New York: Columbia University Press, 1961. xii, 338 p. 24 cm. 1. Children in the United States. 2. Youth — United States I. T.
HQ792.U5 G5     HQ792.U5 V3.     301.431973     *LC* 61-13560

**Zelizer, Viviana A. Rotman.**          **4.5748**
Pricing the priceless child: the changing social value of children / Viviana A. Zelizer. — New York: Basic Books, c1985. x, 277 p.; 22 cm. Includes index. 1. Children — Economic aspects — United States — History. 2. Child rearing — United States — Costs. 3. Children — Employment — United States. 4. Children — United States — Public opinion — History. 5. Public opinion — United States — History. 6. Social values I. T.
HQ792.U5 Z45 1985     305.2/0973 19     *LC* 84-45302     *ISBN* 046506325X

# HQ793–799 Youth. Adolescence

**Weiner, Rex.**          **4.5749**
Woodstock census: the nationwide survey of the sixties generation / Rex Weiner and Deanne Stillman; research consultant, Linda Z. Waldman. — New York: Viking Press, 1979. xi, 273 p.: ill.; 24 cm. Includes index. 1. Youth — United States — Attitudes. 2. Conflict of generations 3. Radicalism — United States. 4. United States — Social Conditions — 1960- I. Stillman, Deanne. joint author. II. T.
HQ793.W26     301.43/15/0973     *LC* 79-13665     *ISBN* 0670782068

**Blos, Peter.**          • **4.5750**
On adolescence, a psychoanalytic interpretation. — [New York]: Free Press of Glencoe, [1962] 269 p.; 22 cm. 1. Adolescent psychology I. T.
HQ796.B48     136.7354     *LC* 61-14110

**Cavan, Sherri.**          **4.5751**
Hippies of the Haight. — [1st ed.]. — St. Louis: New Critics Press, 1972. 213 p.; 22 cm. 1. Hippies — San Francisco. I. T.
HQ796.C395     301.44/94     *LC* 72-146984     *ISBN* 0878530037

**Coleman, James Samuel, 1926-.**          • **4.5752**
The adolescent society; the social life of the teenager and its impact on education, by James S. Coleman with the assistance of John W. C. Johnstone and Kurt Jonassohn. — [New York]: Free Press of Glencoe, [1961] xvi, 368 p.: diagrs.; 24 cm. 1. Adolescence 2. Education, Secondary — 1945- I. T.
HQ796.C64     301.431     *LC* 61-14725

**Friedenberg, Edgar Zodiag, 1921-.**          **4.5753**
The vanishing adolescent / by Edgar Z. Friedenberg; with an introduction by David Riesman. — Westport, Conn.: Greenwood Press, 1985, c1964. xxv,

144 p.; 23 cm. Reprint. Originally published: Boston: Beacon Press, c1964.
1. Adolescence 2. Adolescent psychology 3. Youth — United States I. T.
HQ796.F77 1985　　305.2/35 19　　*LC* 85-950　　*ISBN* 0313249202

**Gesell, Arnold, 1880-1961.**　　　　　　　　　　　　　• **4.5754**
Youth: the years from ten to sixteen, by Arnold Gesell, Frances L. Ilg [and]
Louise Bates Ames. — [1st ed.]. — New York: Harper, [1956] 542 p.; 25 cm.
1. Adolescence 2. Child study. I. T.
HQ796.G44　　136.7354 136.73*　　*LC* 56-6023

**Gillis, John R.**　　　　　　　　　　　　　　　　　**4.5755**
Youth and history: tradition and change in European age relations,
1770–present / John R. Gillis. — Expanded student ed. — New York:
Academic Press, [1981] xiv, 250 p.: ill.; 23 cm. — (Studies in social
discontinuity.) Includes index. 1. Youth — Europe — History. 2. Adolescence
I. T. II. Series.
HQ796.G514 1981　　305.2/3/09 19　　*LC* 81-7919　　*ISBN*
0127852646

**Handlin, Oscar, 1915-.**　　　　　　　　　　　　　• **4.5756**
Facing life: youth and the family in American history / by Oscar Handlin and
Mary F. Handlin. — [1st ed.]. — Boston: Little, Brown, [1971] ix, 326 p.; 22
cm. 'An Atlantic Monthly Press book.' 1. Youth — U.S. — History. 2. Young
adults — U.S. — History. 3. U.S. — Social conditions. I. Handlin, Mary Flug,
1913- joint author. II. T.
HQ796.H256　　301.43/15/0973　　*LC* 74-161852

*HQ →*
*796*
*K16*

**Kagan, Jerome.**　　　　　　　　　　　　　　　　**4.5757**
Twelve to sixteen: early adolescence / edited by Jerome Kagan and Robert
Coles; essays by J. M. Tanner [and others]. — New York: Norton, 1973 (c1972)
xii, 356 p.; 24 cm. 1. Adolescence I. Coles, Robert. joint author. II. Tanner, J.
M. (James Mourilyan) III. T.
HQ796.K16　　301.43/15　　*LC* 72-4446　　*ISBN* 0393010929

**Lipsitz, Joan.**　　　　　　　　　　　　　　　　　**4.5758**
Growing up forgotten: a review of research and programs concerning early
adolescence: a report to the Ford Foundation / Joan Lipsitz. — Lexington,
Mass.: Lexington Books, c1977. xvi, 267 p.; 24 cm. Includes index.
1. Adolescence 2. Adolescent psychology 3. Social work with youth —
United States. 4. Youth — Research — United States. I. Ford Foundation.
II. T.
HQ796.L54　　301.43/15　　*LC* 76-28621　　*ISBN* 066900975X

**National Commission on Resources for Youth.**　　　　**4.5759**
New roles for youth in the school and the community / National Commission
on Resources for Youth. — New York: Citation Press, 1974. ix, 245 p.: ill.; 21
cm. 1. Youth volunteers in social service — United States. 2. Youth volunteers
in community development — United States. 3. Youth — United States —
Political activity. 4. Volunteer workers in education I. T.
HQ796.N313 1974　　361　　*LC* 74-81188　　*ISBN* 0590095854

**Youniss, James.**　　　　　　　　　　　　　　　　**4.5760**
Adolescent relations with mothers, fathers, and friends / James Youniss and
Jacqueline Smollar. — Chicago: University of Chicago Press, 1985. viii, 201 p.;
24 cm. Companion vol. to: Parents and peers in social development. Includes
index. 1. Youth 2. Interpersonal relations in children 3. Parent and child
4. Friendship 5. Children and adults I. Smollar, Jacqueline. II. T.
HQ796.Y583 1985　　305.2/35 19　　*LC* 84-28067　　*ISBN* 0226964876

**Sherif, Muzafer, 1905-.**　　　　　　　　　　　　　• **4.5761**
Reference groups; exploration into conformity and deviation of adolescents [by]
Muzafer Sherif and Carolyn W. Sherif. — New York: Harper and Row, [1964]
xiv, 370 p.: diagrs.; 22 cm. 1. Teenage boys 2. Reference groups I. Sherif,
Carolyn W. joint author. II. T.
HQ797.S45　　301.431　　*LC* 64-10594

**Jenkins, Richard, 1952-.**　　　　　　　　　　　　　**4.5762**
Lads, citizens, and ordinary kids: working–class youth life–styles in Belfast /
Richard Jenkins. — London; Boston: Routledge & Kegan Paul, 1983. xi,
159 p.; 24 cm. — (Routledge direct editions) Includes index. 1. Youth —
Northern Ireland — Belfast. 2. Labor and laboring classes — Northern Ireland
— Belfast. 3. Life style I. T.
HQ799.G72 B444 1983　　305.2/35/094167 19　　*LC* 83-3339　　*ISBN*
0710095740

**Sigel, Roberta S.**　　　　　　　　　　　　　　　　**4.5763**
The political involvement of adolescents / Roberta S. Sigel and Marilyn B.
Hoskin. — New Brunswick, N.J.: Rutgers University Press, c1981. xiii, 353 p.:
ill.; 24 cm. Includes indexes. 1. Youth — United States — Political activity.
2. Political socialization — United States. I. Hoskin, Marilyn B., 1945- joint
author. II. T.
HQ799.2.P6 S52　　305/.2/088055 19　　*LC* 80-22270　　*ISBN*
0813508975

**Roberts, Albert R.**　　　　　　　　　　　　　　　　**4.5764**
Runaways and non–runaways in an American suburb: an exploratory study of
adolescent and parental coping / by Albert R. Roberts with an introduction by
Albert S. Allissi. — New York, N. Y.: John Jay Press, 1981. xv, 117 p.; 22 cm.
(A Criminal Justice Center Monograph, # 13.) 1. Stress (Psychology)
2. Problem children 3. Youth — United States 4. Adolescent psychology
5. Runaway teenagers I. T.
HQ 799.2 R8

**Cook, Bruce, 1932-.**　　　　　　　　　　　　　　　• **4.5765**
The beat generation. -- New York: Scribner, [1971] 248 p.; 24 cm.
1. Bohemianism — U.S. I. T.
HQ799.7.C66 1971　　301.44/94　　*LC* 73-143950　　*ISBN* 0684123711

**Keniston, Kenneth.**　　　　　　　　　　　　　　　• **4.5766**　*HQ*
Young radicals; notes on committed youth. — [1st ed.]. — New York:　　*799.7*
Harcourt, Brace & World, [1968] xi, 368 p.; 22 cm. 1. Young adults — United　*K33*
States — Political activity. 2. Youth — United States — Political activity.
3. Radicalism — United States. I. T.
HQ799.7.K45　　301.43/15/0973　　*LC* 68-23578

**Keniston, Kenneth.**　　　　　　　　　　　　　　　• **4.5767**
Youth and dissent: the rise of a new opposition. — [1st ed.]. — New York:
Harcourt Brace Jovanovich, [1971] xii, 403 p.; 25 cm. 1. Young adults — U.S.
— Political activity. 2. Alienation (Social psychology) 3. Radicalism — U.S.
I. T.
HQ799.7.K46　　301.6/3　　*LC* 71-160404　　*ISBN* 0151998906

# HQ800 Celibacy

**Stein, Peter J., 1937-.**　　　　　　　　　　　　　　**4.5768**
Single / Peter J. Stein. — Englewood Cliffs, N.J.: Prentice-Hall, c1976. x,
134 p.; 21 cm. — (A Spectrum book; S-406) Includes index. 1. Single people —
United States. I. T.
HQ800.S77　　HQ800 S77.　　301.44　　*LC* 76-12642　　*ISBN*
0138105723

**McNamara, Jo Ann, 1931-.**　　　　　　　　　　　　**4.5769**
A new song: celibate women in the first three Christian Centuries / Jo Ann
McNamara. — New York: Institute for Research in History: Haworth Press,
c1983. 154 p.: ill.; 22 cm. 'Has also been published as Women & history,
numbers 6/7, summer/fall 1983'—T.p. verso. Includes index. 1. Celibacy —
History. 2. Single women — Religious life — History. 3. Asceticism —
History — Early church, ca. 30-600 I. T.
HQ800.15.M38 1983　　306.7/32/09 19　　*LC* 83-10852　　*ISBN*
0866562494

**Chambers-Schiller, Lee Virginia, 1948-.**　　　　　　**4.5770**
Liberty, a better husband: single women in America: the generations of
1780–1840 / Lee Virginia Chambers–Schiller. — New Haven: Yale University
Press, c1984. x, 285 p.; 24 cm. Includes index. 1. Single women — United
States — History. 2. United States — Social life and customs — 1783-1865
I. T.
HQ800.2.C43 1984　　305.4/890652 19　　*LC* 84-3524　　*ISBN*
0300031645

**Vicinus, Martha.**　　　　　　　　　　　　　　　　**4.5771**
Independent women: work and community for single women, 1850–1920 /
Martha Vicinus. — Chicago: University of Chicago Press, c1985. xv, 396 p.,
[24] p. of plates: ill.; 24 cm. (Women in culture and society.) Includes index.
1. Single women — England — Social conditions. 2. Middle classes —
England — History — 19th century. 3. Single women — Employment —
England — History — 19th century. 4. Community life I. T. II. Series.
HQ800.2.V53 1985　　305.4/890652 19　　*LC* 84-16158　　*ISBN*
0226855678

**Peterson, Nancy L.**　　　　　　　　　　　　　　　**4.5772**
Our lives for ourselves: women who have never married / Nancy L. Peterson.
— New York: Putnam, c1981. 264 p.; 24 cm. 1. Single women — United
States. I. T.
HQ800.4.U6 P47 1981　　305.4/8 19　　*LC* 80-23101　　*ISBN*
0399124764

**Staples, Robert.**　　　　　　　　　　　　　　　　**4.5773**
The world of Black singles: changing patterns of male/female relations / Robert
Staples. — Westport, Conn.: Greenwood Press, 1981. xxi, 259 p.; 22 cm. —
(Contributions in Afro-American and African studies. no. 57 0069-9624)
Includes index. 1. Afro-American single people — California — San Francisco
Bay Area — Case studies. 2. Afro-American single people I. T. II. Series.
HQ800.4.U62 S267　　305　　*LC* 80-1025　　*ISBN* 0313224781

## HQ801 Courtship

**Rothman, Ellen K., 1950-.**                                          **4.5774**
Hands and hearts: a history of courtship in America / Ellen K. Rothman. — New York: Basic Books, Inc., c1984. xi, 370 p.: facsim.; 25 cm. 1. Courtship — United States — History. 2. United States — Social life and customs I. T.
HQ801.R85 1984      306.7/34/0973 19      *LC* 83-45261      *ISBN* 0465028802

**Brucker, Gene A.**                                                  **4.5775**
Giovanni and Lusanna: love and marriage in Renaissance Florence / Gene Brucker. — Berkeley: University of California Press, c1986. x, 138 p.: ill.; 22 cm. 1. Adultery — Italy — Florence — Case studies. 2. Marriage — Italy — Florence — Case studies. 3. Social classes — Italy — Florence — Case studies. 4. Social history — Medieval, 500-1500 — Case studies. 5. Florence (Italy) — Social conditions — Case studies. 6. Florence (Italy) — History — Sources. I. T.
HQ806.B78 1986      306.8/1/094551 19      *LC* 85-16556      *ISBN* 0520056558

## HQ809 Family Violence

**The Dark side of families: current family violence research /**      **4.5776**
**edited by David Finkelhor ... [et al.].**
Beverly Hills: Sage Publications, c1983. 384 p.: ill.; 23 cm. Based on papers presented at the National Conference for Family Violence Researchers, Durham, N.H., 1981. 1. Family violence — United States — Addresses, essays, lectures. 2. Wife abuse — United States — Addresses, essays, lectures. 3. Child abuse — United States — Addresses, essays, lectures. 4. Child molesting — United States — Addresses, essays, lectures. 5. Rape in marriage — United States — Addresses, essays, lectures. I. Finkelhor, David. II. National Conference for Family Violence Researchers (1981: Durham, N.H.)
HQ809.3.U5 D37 1983      306.8/7 19      *LC* 82-21496      *ISBN* 0803919344

**Gelles, Richard J.**                                                **4.5777**
Family violence / Richard J. Gelles. — Beverly Hills, Calif.: Sage Publications, c1979. 219 p.; 22 cm. — (Sage library of social research; v. 84) 1. Family violence — United States. I. T.
HQ809.3.U5 G44      301.42/7      *LC* 79-14813      *ISBN* 080391234X

**Stacey, William A.**                                                **4.5778**
The family secret: domestic violence in America / William Stacey, Anson Shupe. — Boston: Beacon Press, c1983. xxi, 237 p.; 21 cm. Includes index. 1. Family violence — United States. 2. Family violence — Texas. I. Shupe, Anson D. II. T.
HQ809.3.U5 S77 1983      306.8/7/0973 19      *LC* 82-73965      *ISBN* 0807041440

**Star, Barbara.**                                                    **4.5779**
Helping the abuser: intervening effectively in family violence / Barbara Star. — New York: Family Service Association of America, c1983. xvii, 262 p.; 23 cm. 1. Family violence — United States. 2. Family social work — United States. I. T.
HQ809.3.U5 S777 1983      362.8/2 19      *LC* 83-48129      *ISBN* 0873042026

**Straus, Murray Arnold, 1926-.**                                     **4.5780**
Behind closed doors: violence in the American family / Murray A. Straus, Richard J. Gelles, Suzanne K. Steinmetz. — 1st ed. — Garden City, N.Y.: Anchor Press/Doubleday, 1980. viii, 301 p.: ill.; 22 cm. Includes index. 1. Family violence — United States. I. Gelles, Richard J. joint author. II. Steinmetz, Suzanne K. joint author. III. T.
HQ809.3.U5 S87      301.42      *LC* 78-22741      *ISBN* 0385142595

**Unhappy families: clinical and research perspectives on family**     **4.5781**
**violence / [edited by] Eli H. Newberger, Richard Bourne.**
Littleton, Mass.: PSG, c1985. x, 190 p. 1. Family violence — United States. 2. Child abuse — United States. 3. Child molesting — United States. I. Newberger, Eli H. II. Bourne, Richard.
HQ809.3.U5 U5 1985      362.8/2 19      *LC* 85-3573      *ISBN* 0884165043

## HQ811–960 Divorce

**Epstein, Joseph, 1937-.**                                           **4.5782**
Divorced in America: marriage in an age of possibility. — [1st ed.]. — New York: Dutton, 1974. 318 p.; 25 cm. 1. Divorce 2. Divorce — United States. I. T.
HQ834.E67 1974      HQ834 E67 1974.      301.42/84/0973      *LC* 73-20270      *ISBN* 0525093753

**Halem, Lynne Carol.**                                               **4.5783**
Separated and divorced women / Lynne Carol Halem. — Westport, Conn.: Greenwood Press, 1982. xiv, 335 p.; 25 cm. — (Contributions in women's studies. 0147-104X; no. 32) Includes index. 1. Divorced women — United States. I. T. II. Series.
HQ834.H33      306.8/9 19      *LC* 81-13178      *ISBN* 0313231605

**Women in Transition Inc.**                                          **4.5784**
Women in transition: a feminist handbook on separation and divorce / Women in Transition, inc. — New York: Scribner, [1975] xiv, 538 p.: ill.; 28 cm. — (Emblem edition) (The Scribner library) Developed from The women's survival manual, published in 1972. Includes index. 1. Divorce — United States. 2. Divorced women — Life skills guides 3. Women — Employment I. T.
HQ834.W68 1975      301.42/8      *LC* 75-15728      *ISBN* 0684142589

## HQ961–975 Free Love. Communal Living

**Constantine, Larry L.**                                             **4.5785**
Group marriage; a study of contemporary multilateral marriage [by] Larry L. and Joan M. Constantine. — New York: Macmillan, [1973] xii, 299 p.: illus.; 22 cm. 1. Free love 2. Marriage — United States I. Constantine, Joan M., joint author. II. T.
HQ964.C65      301.42/2      *LC* 72-87157

**Sex roles in contemporary American communes / edited by Jon**       **4.5786**
**Wagner.**
Bloomington: Indiana University Press, c1982. ix, 242 p.; 25 cm. 1. Communal living — United States — Addresses, essays, lectures. 2. Sex role — United States — Addresses, essays, lectures. I. Wagner, Jon.
HQ971.S48 1982      307.7 19      *LC* 81-47571      *ISBN* 0253351871

**Zablocki, Benjamin David, 1941-.**                                  **4.5787**
Alienation and charisma: a study of contemporary American communes / Benjamin Zablocki. — New York: Free Press, c1980. xxiv, 455 p.: ill.; 24 cm. Includes indexes. 1. Communal living — United States — History. 2. Collective settlements — United States — History. 3. Communal living — History. 4. Decision-making, Group — United States. 5. Alienation (Social psychology) 6. Leadership I. T.
HQ971.Z3      307.7      *LC* 79-55938      *ISBN* 0029357802

**Berger, Bennett M.**                                                **4.5788**
The Survival of a counterculture: ideological work and everyday life among rural communards / by Bennett M. Berger. — Berkeley: University of California Press, c1981. xiv, 264 p.; 22 cm. Includes index. 1. Communal living — California — Case studies. 2. Social sciences — Field work 3. Ideology 4. Knowledge, Sociology of I. T.
HQ971.5.C2 B47      307.7 19      *LC* 72-93531      *ISBN* 0520023889

## HQ998–999 Illegitimacy

**Bastardy and its comparative history: studies in the history of**    **4.5789**
**illegitimacy and marital nonconformism in Britain, France,**
**Germany, Sweden, North America, Jamaica, and Japan / edited**
**by Peter Laslett, Karla Oosterveen, and Richard M. Smith.**
Cambridge, Mass.: Harvard University Press, 1980. xv, 431 p.: ill.; 24 cm. — (Studies in social and demographic history.) Based in part on research by the Cambridge Group for the History of Population and Social Structure. Includes index. 1. Illegitimate children — History. I. Laslett, Peter. II. Oosterveen, Karla, 1905- III. Smith, Richard Michael, 1946- IV. Cambridge Group for the History of Population and Social Structure. V. Series.
HQ998.B3      306.7      *LC* 79-27692      *ISBN* 0674063384

## HQ1031 Mixed Marriages

**Berman, Louis Arthur.**                                             **• 4.5790**
Jews and intermarriage: a study in personality and culture / by Louis A. Berman. — New York: T. Yoseloff [1968] 707 p.; 22 cm. 1. Intermarriage 2. Jews — Psychology 3. Marriage — Religious aspects — Judaism I. T.
HQ1031.B42      301.42/2      *LC* 68-14411

## HQ1058 Widows. Widowers

**Lopata, Helena Znaniecka, 1925-.**                                  **4.5791**
Women as widows: support systems / Helena Znaniecka Lopata. — New York: Elsevier, c1979. 485 p.; 24 cm. Includes index. 1. Widows 2. Widows — Illinois — Chicago — Case studies. I. T.
HQ1058.L66      301.42/86      *LC* 78-21255      *ISBN* 0444990534

**Hyman, Herbert Hiram, 1918-.**      4.5792
Of time and widowhood: nationwide studies of enduring effects / Herbert H. Hyman. — Durham, N.C.: Duke University Press, 1983. 118 p.; 24 cm. — (Duke Press policy studies.) Includes index. 1. Widows — United States — Longitudinal studies. 2. Widowers — United States — Longitudinal studies. 3. Family life surveys — United States. 4. Family — United States I. T. II. Series.
HQ1058.5.U5 H95 1983     306.8/8 19     *LC* 82-25138     *ISBN* 0822305046

**Lopata, Helena Znaniecka, 1925-.**      4.5793
Widowhood in an American city. — Cambridge, Mass.: Schenkman Pub. Co.; distributed by General Learning Press [Morristown, N.J., 1973] xii, 369 p.; 24 cm. 1. Widows — United States. I. T.
HQ1058.5.U5 L6     306.8/8 19     *LC* 77-137491

# HQ1059–1064 Middle Age. Old Age

**Farrell, Michael P., 1942-.**      4.5794
Men at midlife / Michael P. Farrell, Stanley D. Rosenberg. — Boston: Auburn House, c1981. xiv, 242 p.; 24 cm. Includes index. 1. Middle aged men — United States. 2. Middle aged men — United States — Case studies. 3. Middle age — United States. 4. Life cycle, Human I. Rosenberg, Stanley D. II. T.
HQ1059.5.U5 F37 1981     305.2/4 19     *LC* 81-3624     *ISBN* 0865690731

**Aging, social change / edited by Sara B. Kiesler, James N. Morgan, Valerie Kincade Oppenheimer, editors; James G. March, editor–in–chief.**      4.5795
New York: Academic Press, c1981. xxiv, 631 p.: ill.; 24 cm. Papers from a workshop entitled 'The elderly of the future,' held May 3-5, 1979, in Annapolis, Md., which was organized by the Committee on Aging, National Research Council and sponsored by the National Institute on Aging. 1. Aging — Social aspects — Congresses. 2. Aged — United States — Socioeconomic status — Congresses. I. Kiesler, Sara B., 1940- II. Morgan, James N. III. Oppenheimer, Valerie Kincade. IV. Assembly of Behavioral and Social Sciences (U.S.). Committee on Aging. V. National Institute on Aging.
HQ1061.A484 1981     305.2/6 19     *LC* 81-14959     *ISBN* 0120400022

**Clark, Robert Louis, 1949-.**      • 4.5796
The economics of individual and population aging / Robert L. Clark, Joseph J. Spengler. — Cambridge; New York: Cambridge University Press, 1980. viii, 211 p.; 22 cm. (Cambridge surveys of economic literature) Includes index. 1. Old age — Economic aspects. 2. Aging — Economic aspects. 3. Retirement — Economic aspects. 4. Aged — Economic conditions 5. Old age assistance I. Spengler, Joseph John, 1902- joint author. II. T.
HQ1061.C52     301.43/5     *LC* 79-19495     *ISBN* 0521228832

**Fontana, Andrea.**      4.5797
The last frontier: the social meaning of growing old / Andrea Fontana; preface by Fred Davis. Beverly Hills, Calif.: Sage Publications, c1977. 215 p.; 22 cm. (Sage Library of social research; v. 42) Includes index. 1. Aged I. T.
HQ1061.F59     301.43/5     *LC* 77-23186     *ISBN* 0803908326

**Handbook of aging and the social sciences / editors, Robert H. Binstock, Ethel Shanas; with the assistance of associate editors, George L. Maddox, George C. Myers, James H. Schulz.**      4.5798
2nd ed. — New York: Van Nostrand Reinhold Co., c1985. xiv, 809 p.: ill.; 27 cm. 1. Gerontology — Addresses, essays, lectures. 2. Aging — Social aspects — Addresses, essays, lectures. I. Binstock, Robert H. II. Shanas, Ethel.
HQ1061.H336 1985     305.2/6 19     *LC* 84-25729     *ISBN* 0442264801

**Independent aging: family and social systems perspectives / editors, William H. Quinn, George A. Hughston.**      4.5799
Rockville, Md.: Aspen Systems Corp., 1984. xviii, 300 p.: ill.; 24 cm. 'An Aspen publication.' 1. Aged — Family relationships — Addresses, essays, lectures. 2. Aged — Social conditions — Addresses, essays, lectures. 3. Aged — Care and hygiene — Addresses, essays, lectures. 4. Dependency (Psychology) — Addresses, essays, lectures. I. Quinn, William H. II. Hughston, George A.
HQ1061.I49 1984     646.7/8 19     *LC* 84-14445     *ISBN* 0894435507

**International handbook on aging: contemporary developments and research / edited by Erdman Palmore.**      4.5800
Westport, Conn.: Greenwood Press, 1980 (c1979). xviii, 529 p.: 24 cm. 1. Gerontology — Addresses, essays, lectures. I. Palmore, Erdman Ballagh, 1930-
HQ1061.I535     301.43/5     *LC* 78-73802     *ISBN* 0313208905

**Life's career—aging: cultural variations on growing old / edited by Barbara G. Myerhoff, Andrei Simić.**      4.5801
Beverly Hills: Sage Publications, c1978. 252 p.: ill.; 24 cm. (Cross-cultural research and methodology series) 1. Old age — Addresses, essays, lectures. 2. Aging — Social aspects — Cross-cultural studies — Addresses, essays, lectures. I. Myerhoff, Barbara G. II. Simić, Andrei.
HQ1061.L478     301.43/5     *LC* 77-14268     *ISBN* 0803908679

**Stub, Holger Richard.**      4.5802
The social consequences of long life / by Holger R. Stub. — Springfield, Ill.: C.C. Thomas, c1982. x, 277 p.; 23 cm. 1. Longevity — Social aspects. 2. Life expectancy — Social aspects. 3. Old age — Social aspects. I. T.
HQ1061.S843 1982     305.2/6 19     *LC* 82-5775     *ISBN* 0398047235

**Themes of work and love in adulthood / edited by Neil J. Smelser and Erik H. Erikson.**      4.5803
Cambridge, Mass.: Harvard University Press, 1980. x, 297 p.; 24 cm. Revised papers from a conference under the auspices of the Western Center of the American Academy of Arts and Sciences which was held May 8-9, 1977 at the Center for Advanced Study of the Behavioral Sciences in Palo Alto, Calif. 1. Adulthood — Congresses. 2. Work — Congresses. 3. Love — Congresses. I. Smelser, Neil J. II. Erikson, Erik H. (Erik Homburger), 1902-
HQ1061.T47     301.43/4     *LC* 79-26130     *ISBN* 0674877500

**Unruh, David R.**      4.5804
Invisible lives: social worlds of the aged / David R. Unruh; foreword by Anselm Strauss. — Beverly Hills: Sage Publications, c1983. 199 p.: ill.; 23 cm. — (Sociological observations. 14) Includes index. 1. Aged 2. Social integration 3. Social structure 4. Social interaction I. T. II. Series.
HQ1061.U57 1983     305.2/6 19     *LC* 82-23116     *ISBN* 0803919549

**The world of the older woman: conflicts and resolutions / edited by Gari Lesnoff–Caravaglia.**      4.5805
New York, N.Y.: Human Sciences Press, 1985 (c1984). 189 p.: ill.; 22 cm. (Frontiers in aging series. 0271-955X; v. 3) 1. Aged women — Social conditions — Addresses, essays, lectures. I. Lesnoff-Caravaglia, Gari. II. Series.
HQ1061.W67 1984     305.2/6 19     *LC* 83-12658     *ISBN* 0898850894

**Retirement and economic behavior / Henry J. Aaron and Gary Burtless, editors.**      4.5806
Washington, D.C.: Brookings Institution, c1984. xv, 352 p.: ill.; 24 cm. — (Studies in social economics.) Papers presented at a conference held at the Brookings Institution, Oct. 21-22, 1982. 1. Retirement — Economic aspects — United States — Addresses, essays, lectures. 2. Aged — United States — Economic conditions — Addresses, essays, lectures. 3. Retirement income — United States — Addresses, essays, lectures. I. Aaron, Henry J. II. Burtless, Gary T., 1950- III. Series.
HQ1062.R43 1984     306/.38 19     *LC* 83-45961     *ISBN* 0815700369

**Smithers, Janice A., 1931-.**      4.5807
Determined survivors: community life among the urban elderly / Janice A. Smithers. — New Brunswick, N.J.: Rutgers University Press, c1985. xiv, 225 p.: ill.; 23 cm. Includes index. 1. Retirement communities — California — Los Angeles — Case studies. 2. Aged — California — Los Angeles — Case studies. 3. Single people — California — Los Angeles — Case studies. I. T.
HQ1063.S595 1985     305.2/6/0979494 19     *LC* 84-17794     *ISBN* 0813510791

**Teski, Marea.**      4.5808
Living together: an ethnography of a retirement hotel / Marea Teski. — Washington: University Press of America, c1979. 187 p.: ill., charts, plan. 1. Retirement, Places of — United States — Case studies I. T. II. Title: An ethnography of a retirement hotel
HQ1063 T4     *LC* 79-88268     *ISBN* 0819107697

**Wachs, Martin.**      4.5809
Transportation for the elderly: changing lifestyles, changing needs / Martin Wachs. — Berkeley: University of California Press, c1979. xix, 262 p.: ill.; 24 cm. 1. Aged — Transportation 2. Aged — California — Los Angeles Co. — Transportation. I. T.
HQ1063.5.W32     362.6/3     *LC* 78-63091     *ISBN* 0520036913

## HQ1064 Old Age

**Achenbaum, W. Andrew.**      4.5810
Old age in the new land: the American experience since 1790 / W. Andrew Achenbaum. — Baltimore: Johns Hopkins University Press, 1979 (c1978). xii, 237 p.: ill.; 24 cm. Includes index. 1. Aged — United States — History. 2. Aged — United States — Public opinion. 3. Public opinion — United States. I. T.
HQ1064.U5 A26     301.43/5/0973     *LC* 77-28666     *ISBN* 080182107X

**Aging and retirement: prospects, planning, and policy / edited**    **4.5811**
**by Neil G. McCluskey, Edgar F. Borgatta.**
Beverly Hills: Sage Publications, c1981. 233 p.: ill.; 23 cm. — (Sage focus editions) 1. Retirement — United States — Addresses, essays, lectures. I. McCluskey, Neil Gerard. II. Borgatta, Edgar F., 1924-
HQ1064.U5 A6335        305.2/6 19        *LC* 81-14415        *ISBN* 0803917562

**Becerra, Rosina M.**                                                **4.5812**
The Hispanic elderly: a research reference guide / Rosina M. Becerra, David Shaw. — Lanham: University Press of America, c1984. viii, 144 p.; 23 cm. 1. Gerontology literature — United States. 2. Hispanic American aged 3. Hispanic American aged — Research. 4. Hispanic American aged — Bibliography. I. Shaw, David, M.A. II. T.
HQ1064.U5 B325 1984        305.2/6/072 19        *LC* 83-21659        *ISBN* 0819136263

**Berghorn, Forrest J., 1932-.**                                      **4.5813**
The dynamics of aging: original essays on the processes and experiences of growing old / Forrest J. Berghorn, Donna E. Schafer, and associates. — Boulder, Colo.: Westview Press, 1981. xix, 510 p.: ill.; 24 cm. Includes index. 1. Gerontology — United States — Addresses, essays, lectures. 2. Aging — Addresses, essays, lectures. 3. Geriatrics — Addresses, essays, lectures. 4. Aged — Services for — United States. I. Schafer, Donna E. joint author. II. T.
HQ1064.U5 B374        305.2/6        *LC* 80-36687        *ISBN* 0891587810

**Blau, Zena Smith, 1922-.**                                          **4.5814**
Old age in a changing society. New York, New Viewpoints, 1973. xiv, 285 p. 21 cm. Second ed. published in 1981 under title: Aging in a changing society. 1. Aged — United States 2. United States — Social conditions — 1960- I. T.
HQ1064.U5 B43        301.43/5/0973        *LC* 74-190126        *ISBN* 0531063542 *ISBN* 0531064808

**Gelfand, Donald E.**                                                **4.5815**
Aging, the ethnic factor / Donald E. Gelfand. — Boston: Little, Brown, c1982. x, 113 p.; 24 cm. — (Little, Brown series on gerontology.) 1. Minority aged — United States 2. Ethnicity — United States. 3. Aging — United States. 4. Aged — United States I. T. II. Series.
HQ1064.U5 G38        HQ1064U5 G38.        305.2/6 19        *LC* 81-14786        *ISBN* 0316307130

**Johnson, Elizabeth S.**                                             **4.5816**
Growing old: the social problems of aging / Elizabeth S. Johnson, John B. Williamson. — New York: Holt, Rinehart, and Winston, c1980. viii, 196 p.; 24 cm. 1. Aged — United States — Social conditions. 2. Aging 3. Age discrimination — United States. 4. Aged — Psychology I. Williamson, John B. joint author. II. T.
HQ1064.U5 J64        301.43/5/0973        *LC* 78-67459        *ISBN* 0030403162

**Lammers, William W.**                                               **4.5817**
Public policy and the aging / William W. Lammers. — Washington, D.C.: CQ Press, c1983. xv, 265 p.; 23 cm. — (Issues in public policy.) Includes index. 1. Aged — Government policy — United States. I. T. II. Series.
HQ1064.U5 L29 1983        362.6/0973 19        *LC* 82-22138        *ISBN* 0871872463

**Maas, Henry S.**                                                    **4.5818**
From thirty to seventy / Henry S. Maas, Joseph A. Kuypers. — 1st ed. — San Francisco: Jossey-Bass Publishers, 1974. xii, 240 p.; 24 cm. — (Jossey-Bass behavioral science series) Half-title: From thirty to seventy: a forty-year longitudinal study of adult life styles and personality. Includes index. 1. Aging — Psychological aspects 2. Aged — United States 3. Family life surveys — United States. I. Kuypers, Joseph A., joint author. II. T.
HQ1064.U5 M13        301.43/5        *LC* 74-6742        *ISBN* 0875892345

**Minority aging: sociological and social psychological issues /**    **4.5819**
**edited by Ron C. Manuel.**
Westport, Conn.: Greenwood Press, 1982. xvii, 285 p.; 25 cm. — (Contributions in ethnic studies. 0196-7088; no. 8) Includes index. 1. Minority aged — United States — Addresses, essays, lectures. 2. Minority aged — Services for — United States — Addresses, essays, lectures. 3. Afro-American aged — United States — Addresses, essays, lectures. 4. Ethnic relations — Addresses, essays, lectures. I. Manuel, Ron C. II. Series.
HQ1064.U5 M55 1982        305.2/6 19        *LC* 82-930        *ISBN* 0313225419

**Olson, Laura Katz, 1945-.**                                         **4.5820**
The political economy of aging: the state, private power, and social welfare / Laura Katz Olson. — New York: Columbia University Press, 1982. xii, 272 p.; 24 cm. 1. Aged — Government policy — United States. 2. Aging — Economic aspects — United States. 3. United States — Social policy — 1980- — Citizen participation. I. T.
HQ1064.U5 O44 1982        362.6/0973 19        *LC* 82-1315        *ISBN* 0231054505

**Palmore, Erdman Ballagh, 1930-.**                                   **4.5821**
Social patterns in normal aging: findings from the Duke longitudinal study / Erdman Palmore. — Durham, N.C.: Duke University Press, 1981. xii, 135 p.: ill.; 25 cm. Includes index. 1. Aging — Social aspects — United States — Longitudinal studies. I. T.
HQ1064.U5 P26        305.2/6 19        *LC* 81-9800        *ISBN* 0822304589

**Rich, Bennett Milton, 1909-.**                                      **4.5822**
The aging, a guide to public policy / Bennett M. Rich and Martha Baum. — Pittsburgh, Pa.: University of Pittsburgh Press, c1984. xiii, 275 p.; 23 cm. (Contemporary community health series.) (Pitt series in policy and institutional studies.) Includes index. 1. Aged — Government policy — United States. 2. Aged — Legal status, laws, etc. — United States. 3. Old age assistance — United States. I. Baum, Martha. II. T. III. Series. IV. Series: Pitt series in policy and institutional studies.
HQ1064.U5 R512 1984        362.6/0973 19        *LC* 84-40228        *ISBN* 0822953641

**Sourcebook on aging.**                                              **4.5823**
2d ed. — Chicago, Ill.: Marquis Academic Media, c1979. vii, 539 p.: graphs; 29 cm. 1. Aged — United States — Handbooks, manuals, etc. 2. Gerontology — United States — Handbooks, manuals, etc. I. Marquis Academic Media.
HQ1064.U5 S63 1979        305.2/6/0973        *LC* 79-89697        *ISBN* 0837944023

**Williamson, John B.**                                               **4.5824**
Aging and public policy: social control or social justice? / by John B. Williamson, Judith A. Shindul, Linda Evans. — Springfield, Ill., U.S.A.: C.C. Thomas, c1985. xvii, 332 p.; 24 cm. Includes indexes. 1. Aged — Government policy — United States. 2. Pensions — Government policy — United States. 3. Medical policy — United States. I. Shindul, Judith A. II. Evans, Linda. III. T.
HQ1064.U5 W5923 1985        362.6/0973 19        *LC* 84-26735        *ISBN* 0398051046

**Golant, Stephen M.**                                                **4.5825**
A place to grow old: the meaning of environment in old age / Stephen M. Golant. — New York: Columbia University Press, 1984. xi, 421 p.: ill.; 24 cm. — (Columbia studies of social gerontology and aging.) Includes index. 1. Aged — Illinois — Evanston — Social conditions. 2. Human ecology — Illinois — Evanston. 3. Aged — Illinois — Evanston — Dwellings. 4. Aged — Illinois — Evanston — Attitudes. 5. Individuality I. T. II. Series.
HQ1064.U6 I28 1984        305.2/6 19        *LC* 84-5042        *ISBN* 0231048408

**A City revitalized: the elderly lose at monopoly / Marea Teski**    **4.5826**
**... [et al.].**
Lanham, MD: University Press of America, c1983. xxii, 191 p.: ill.; 23 cm. 1. Aged — New Jersey — Atlantic City — Economic conditions. 2. Aged — New Jersey — Atlantic City — Social conditions. 3. Gambling — New Jersey — Atlantic City. 4. Atlantic City (N.J.) — Economic conditions. I. Teski, Marea.
HQ1064.U6 N255 1983        305.2/6/0974985 19        *LC* 83-5786        *ISBN* 0819131652

# HQ1073 Death. Dying

**McManners, John.**                                                  **4.5827**
Death and the enlightenment: changing attitudes to death among Christians and unbelievers in eigthteenth–century France / John McManners. — Oxford [Oxfordshire]: Clarendon Press; New York: Oxford University Press, 1982 (c1981). vii, 619 p.; 23 cm. Includes indexes. 1. Death — History — 18th century. 2. France — Social life and customs — 18th century. 3. France — Intellectual life — History — 18th century. I. T.
HQ1073.5.F8 M25        155.9/37/0944 19        *LC* 82-136773        *ISBN* 0198264402

**Sourcebook on death and dying / consulting editor, James A.**       **4.5828**
**Fruehling.**
1st ed. — Chicago, Ill.: Marquis Professional Publications, c1982. 788 p.: ill.; 29 cm. Includes index. 1. Death — Handbooks, manuals, etc. 2. Death — Societies, etc. — Directories. 3. Undertakers and undertaking — United States — Directories. 4. Undertakers and undertaking — Canada — Directories. I. Fruehling, James A. II. Title: Death and dying.
HQ1073.5.U6 S68 1982        306/.9 19        *LC* 82-82013        *ISBN* 0837958016

## HQ1075 Sex Role

**Changing boundaries: gender roles and sexual behavior / edited**   **4.5829**
**by Elizabeth Rice Allgeier and Naomi B. McCormick;**
**[contributors, Elizabeth Rice Allgeier ... et al.].**
1st ed. — Palo Alto, Calif.: Mayfield Pub. Co., 1983. xvi, 347 p.: ill.; 23 cm.
Includes index. 1. Sex role — Addresses, essays, lectures. 2. Sex — Addresses,
essays, lectures. I. Allgeier, Elizabeth R. II. McCormick, Naomi B.
HQ1075.C5 1983          305.3 19          LC 82-60885          ISBN 087484536X

**A Dictionary of sexist quotations / [compiled by] Simon James.**   **4.5830**
Brighton, Sussex: Harvester Press; Totowa, N.J.: Barnes & Noble, 1984. xii,
206 p.; 23 cm. Includes indexes. 1. Sex role — Dictionaries. 2. Sex role —
Anecdotes, facetiae, satire, etc. 3. Sexism — Dictionaries. 4. Sexism —
Anecdotes, facetiae, satire, etc. I. James, Simon R.
HQ1075.D52 1984          305.3/03/21 19          LC 84-11108          ISBN
038920501X

**Sanday, Peggy Reeves.**   **4.5831**
Female power and male dominance: on the origins of sexual inequality / Peggy
Reeves Sanday. — Cambridge; New York: Cambridge University Press, 1981.
xvii, 295 p.; 24 cm. Includes index. 1. Sex role 2. Sexism 3. Power (Social
sciences) 4. Symbolism (Psychology) 5. Sex (Psychology) 6. Cross-cultural
studies I. T.
HQ1075.S26          305.3          LC 80-18461          ISBN 0521236185

**Women, gender, and social psychology / edited by Virginia E.**   **4.5832**
**O'Leary, Rhoda Kesler Unger, Barbara Strudler Wallston.**
Hillsdale, NJ: L. Erlbaum, 1985. xii, 381 p.; 24 cm. 1. Sex role 2. Women —
Psychology 3. Social psychology I. O'Leary, Virginia E., 1943- II. Unger,
Rhoda Kesler. III. Wallston, Barbara Strudler.
HQ1075.W67 1985          305.3 19          LC 84-23114          ISBN 0898594472

**Gender roles in development projects: a case book / editors,**   **4.5833**
**Catherine Overholt ... [et al.].**
West Hartford, Conn.: Kumarian Press, c1985. xiii, 326 p.: ill.; 23 cm.
(Kumarian Press case studies series.) 1. Sex role — Developing countries —
Case studies. 2. Women — Developing countries — Economic conditions —
Case studies. 3. Women in business — Developing countries — Case studies.
4. Women — Employment — Developing countries — Case studies.
I. Overholt, Catherine, 1942- II. Series.
HQ1075.5.D44 G46 1985          305.3 19          LC 84-23325          ISBN
0931816157

## HQ1090 Men

**Fasteau, Marc Feigen.**   **4.5834**
The male machine. — New York: McGraw-Hill, [1974] xv, 225 p.; 24 cm.
1. Men — Psychology 2. Sex role 3. Interpersonal relations I. T.
HQ1090.F3x          301.41/1          LC 74-9858          ISBN 007019985X

**Herzfeld, Michael, 1947-.**   **4.5835**
The poetics of manhood: contest and identity in a Cretan mountain village /
Michael Herzfeld. — Princeton, N.J.: Princeton University Press, c1985. xviii,
313 p.: ill.; 25 cm. Includes index. 1. Men — Greece — Crete. 2. Social
interaction — Greece — Crete. 3. Identity (Psychology) — Greece — Crete.
4. Ethnology — Greece — Crete. 5. Folklore — Greece 6. Crete — Rural
conditions. 7. Crete — Social life and customs. I. T.
HQ1090.7.G8 H46 1985          305.3/1/094998 19          LC 84-26530          ISBN
0691094101

## HQ1101–2030 Women. Feminism

**International Congress of Anthropological and Ethnological**   **4.5836**
**Sciences. 9th, Chicago, 1973.**
Women cross–culturally: change and challenge / editor, Ruby Rohrlich–
Leavitt. — The Hague: Mouton; Chicago: distributed in the USA and Canada
by Aldine, [1975] xiv, 669 p., [2] leaves of plates: ill.; 24 cm. (World
anthropology.) 1. Women and socialism — Congresses. 2. Anthropologists,
Women — Congresses. 3. Women — Social conditions — Congresses.
I. Rohrlich, Ruby. II. T. III. Series.
HQ1106 1973.I57          301.41/2          LC 76-355232          ISBN 020201147X

**Beyond domination: new perspectives on women and philosophy**   **4.5837**
**/ edited by Carol C. Gould.**
Totowa, N.J.: Rowman & Allanheld, 1984, c1983. xii, 321 p.; 22 cm. (New
feminist perspectives series.) Includes papers given at the Annette Walters
Memorial Conference on the Philosophy of Women's Liberation, May 15-17,
1981, Milwaukee, Wis., organized by the Institute of Women Today.
1. Feminism — Philosophy — Congresses. I. Gould, Carol C. II. Institute of
Women Today. III. Annette Walters Memorial Conference on the Philosophy
of Women's Liberation (1981: Milwaukee, Wis.) IV. Series.
HQ1106.B49 1984          305.4/2 19          LC 83-10894          ISBN 0847672026

**The Psychology of women: future directions in research / edited**   **4.5838**
**by Julia A. Sherman & Florence L. Denmark.**
New York, N.Y.: Psychological Dimensions, inc., 1979 (c1978). xxii, 758 p.; 24
cm. Sponsored by the Committee on Women of the American Psychological
Association, the National Institute of Mental Health, and the Ford Foundation.
1. Women — Social conditions — Congresses. 2. Women — Sexual behavior
— Congresses. 3. Women — Psychology — Congresses. 4. Women —
Employment — Congresses. I. Sherman, Julia Ann, 1934- II. Denmark,
Florence. III. American Psychological Association. Committee on Women.
IV. National Institute of Mental Health (U.S.) V. Ford Foundation.
HQ1106.P78 1978          301.41/2 19          LC 78-31824          ISBN 0884370097

**Cardinale, Susan.**   **4.5839**
Anthologies by and about women: an analytical index / compiled by Susan
Cardinale with Jay Casey. — Westport, Conn.: Greenwood Press, 1982. xxvii,
822 p.; 25 cm. 1. Women — Indexes. I. Casey, Jay. II. T.
HQ1111.C35 1982          016.3054 19          LC 81-13423          ISBN 0313221804

**Woman's almanac: 12 how–to handbooks in one / compiled and**   **4.5840**
**edited by Kathryn Paulsen and Ryan A. Kuhn; designed by**
**Holly Alderman McLellan.**
1st ed. — New York: Lippincott, c1976. 624 p.: ill.; 28 cm. On cover: Illustrated
Woman's almanac. Includes index. 1. Women's encyclopedias and dictionaries
2. Women — Societies and clubs — Directories. I. Paulsen, Kathryn.
II. Kuhn, Ryan A. III. Title: Illustrated woman's almanac.
HQ1115.I37          301.41/2          LC 76-2055          ISBN 039701113X. ISBN
0397011385 pbk

## HQ1121–1154 History

**Beard, Mary Ritter, 1876-1958.**   ● **4.5841**
Woman as force in history; a study in traditions and realities, by Mary R. Beard.
New York, The Macmillan company, 1946. viii p., 2 l., 369 p. 22 cm. 'First
printing.' 'An illustrative bibliography': p. 333-358. 1. Women — History and
condition of women I. T.
HQ1121.B36          396          LC 46-1638

**Chafetz, Janet Saltzman.**   **4.5842**
Female revolt: women's movements in world and historical perspective / Janet
Saltzman Chafetz, Anthony Gary Dworkin with the assistance of Stephanie
Swanson. — Totowa, N.J.: Rowman & Allanheld, 1986. x, 260 p.: ill.; 24 cm.
Includes index. 1. Feminism — History. 2. Feminism — Cross cultural
studies. 3. Women's rights — History. I. Dworkin, Anthony Gary.
II. Swanson, Stephanie. III. T.
HQ1121.C45 1986          305.4/2/09 19          LC 85-22141          ISBN
0847673596

**Woman in Western thought / edited by Martha Lee Osborne.**   **4.5843**
1st ed. — New York: Random House, c1979. xx, 341 p.; 24 cm. 1. Women —
Addresses, essays, lectures. 2. Women — Social conditions — Addresses,
essays, lectures. 3. Women — History — Addresses, essays, lectures.
I. Osborne, Martha Lee, 1928-
HQ1121.W88          301.41/2          LC 78-16116          ISBN 039432112X

**Allen, Prudence.**   **4.5844**
The concept of woman: the Aristotelian revolution, 750 BC–AD 1250 /
Prudence Allen. — Montréal: Eden Press, c1985. vii, 577 p.: ill.; 24 cm.
Includes index. 1. Femininity (Philosophy) 2. Women I. T.
HQ1122.A44 1985          305.4 19          ISBN 092079243X

**Beard, Mary Ritter, 1876-1958.**   ● **4.5845**
On understanding women. [1st ed.] New York: Greenwood Press, 1968 [c1931]
viii, 541 p.; 22 cm. 1. Women 2. Women — History 3. Civilization I. T.
HQ1122.B4 1968          301.41/2          LC 68-54773

**Sayers, Janet.**   **4.5846**
Biological politics: feminist and anti–feminist perspectives / Janet Sayers. —
London; New York: Tavistock, 1982. 235 p.; 23 cm. Includes indexes.
1. Feminism 2. Human biology — Social aspects I. T.
HQ1122.S24 1982          305.4/2 19          LC 81-16841          ISBN 0422778702

**Women's life in Greece and Rome / [compiled by] Mary R.**        **4.5847**
**Lefkowitz and Maureen B. Fant.**
Baltimore, Md.: Johns Hopkins University Press, 1982. xiii, 294 p.; 24 cm. Rev.
and enl. ed. of: Women in Greece and Rome. 1977. 1. Women — Rome.
2. Women — Greece. I. Lefkowitz, Mary R., 1935- II. Fant, Maureen B.
HQ1127.W653 1982        305.4/0938 19        *LC* 82-7756        *ISBN*
0801828651

**Pomeroy, Sarah B.**        **4.5848**
Goddesses, whores, wives, and slaves: women in classical antiquity / Sarah B.
Pomeroy. — New York: Schocken Books, 1975. xiii, 265 p. [3] leaves of plates:
ill.; 21 cm. Includes index. 1. Women — History — To 500 2. Greece — Social
conditions — To 146 B.C. 3. Rome — Social conditions. I. T.
HQ1134.P64        301.41/2/0938        *LC* 74-8782        *ISBN* 0805235620

**Reflections of women in antiquity / [compiled by] Helene P.**        **4.5849**
**Foley.**
New York: Gordon and Breach Science Publishers, c1981. xvii, 420 p., [11] p.
of plates: ill.; 24 cm. 1. Sappho. 2. Women in literature 3. Women — History
— To 500 I. Foley, Helene P., 1942-
HQ1134.R4 1981        305.4/09/01 19        *LC* 81-13352        *ISBN*
0677163703

**Schaps, David M.**        **4.5850**
Economic rights of women in ancient Greece / David M. Schaps. —
Edinburgh: University Press, [c1979] 165 p. 1. Women — Grece. 2. Women's
rights — Greece. 3. Right of property — Greece. 4. Property (Greek law)
I. T.
HQ1134.S4        *ISBN* 0852243431

**Women in the ancient world: the Arethusa papers / John**        **4.5851**
**Peradotto and J.P. Sullivan, editors.**
Albany: State University of New York Press, 1983. 377 p.: ill.; 24 cm. (SUNY
series in classical studies.) 1. Women — Greece — Addresses, essays, lectures.
2. Women — Rome — Addresses, essays, lectures. 3. Civilization, Classical —
Addresses, essays, lectures. I. Peradotto, John, 1933- II. Sullivan, J. P. (John
Patrick) III. Series.
HQ1134.W63 1983        305.4/0938 19        *LC* 83-4975        *ISBN*
0873957725

**Gardner, Jane F.**        **4.5852**
Women in Roman law & society / Jane F. Gardner. — Bloomington: Indiana
University Press, 1986. 281 p.; 23 cm. Includes index. 1. Women — Rome —
Social conditions. 2. Women's rights — Rome. 3. Women — Legal status,
laws, etc. — Rome. I. T. II. Title: Women in Roman law and society.
HQ1136        HQ1136 G37.        305.4/2/0937 19        *ISBN* 0709911785

**Hallett, Judith P., 1944-.**        **4.5853**
Fathers and daughters in Roman society: women and the elite family / Judith P.
Hallett. — Princeton, N.J.: Princeton University Press, c1984. xix, 422 p.
1. Women — Rome — Social conditions. 2. Fathers and daughters — Rome
— History. 3. Family — Rome — History. 4. Upper classes — Rome —
History. 5. Rome — History I. T.
HQ1136.H35 1984        305.4/2/0945632 19        *LC* 83-43074        *ISBN*
0691035709

**Pomeroy, Sarah B.**        **4.5854**
Women in Hellenistic Egypt: from Alexander to Cleopatra / Sarah B. Pomeroy.
— New York: Schocken Books, 1984. xxii, 241 p.: ill.; 22 cm. Includes index.
1. Women — Egypt — History. 2. Greeks — Egypt — History. 3. Egypt —
History — 332-30 B.C. I. T.
HQ1137.E3 P65 1984        305.4/0932 19        *LC* 84-3122        *ISBN*
0805239111

**Kleinbaum, Abby Wettan.**        **4.5855**
The war against the Amazons / Abby Wettan Kleinbaum. New York: McGraw
Hill, c1983. viii, 240 p.: ill.; 24 cm. Includes index. 1. Amazons 2. Amazons in
literature. 3. Sex role I. T.
HQ1139.K57        305.3 19        *LC* 82-7781        *ISBN* 0070350337

**Gies, Frances.**        **4.5856**
Women in the Middle Ages / Frances and Joseph Gies. — 1st ed. — New York:
Crowell, c1978. 264 p.: ill.; 21 cm. Includes index. 1. Women — History —
Middle Ages, 500-1500 2. Women — Europe — Biography. 3. Women —
Europe — Social conditions. I. Gies, Joseph. joint author. II. T.
HQ1143.G53 1978        301.41/2/0902        *LC* 77-25832        *ISBN*
0690017243

**Medieval women / edited by Derek Baker; dedicated and**        **4.5857**
**presented to Professor Rosalind M. T. Hill on the occasion of**
**her seventieth birthday.**
Oxford: Published for the Ecclesiastical History Society by B. Blackwell, 1978.
xii, 399 p., [9] leaves of plates: ill.; 22 cm. (Studies in church history. Subsidia. 1)
1. Hill, Rosalind, M. T. — Addresses, essays, lectures. 2. Hill, Rosalind M. T.

— Bibliography. 3. Women — History — Middle ages, 500-1500 — Addresses,
essays, lectures. I. Baker, Derek. II. Hill, Rosalind M. T. III. Series.
HQ1143.M43        305.4/2/094 19        *LC* 80-499721        *ISBN* 0631192603

**Power, Eileen Edna, 1889-1940.**        **4.5858**
Medieval women / Eileen Power; edited by M. M. Postan. — Cambridge
[Eng.]; New York: Cambridge University Press, 1976 (c1975). 112 p.: ill.; 21
cm. Texts of lectures given by the author at various places and times. Includes
index. 1. Women — History — Middle Ages, 500-1500 2. Women — Europe
— Social conditions. I. Postan, M. M. (Michael Moïssey), 1899-1981. II. T.
HQ1143.P68        301.41/2/0902        *LC* 75-7212        *ISBN* 0521099463 pbk

**Women in medieval society / Brenda M. Bolton ... [et al.];**        **4.5859**
**edited, with an introd., by Susan Mosher Stuard.**
[Philadelphia]: University of Pennsylvania Press, 1976. 219 p.: graphs; 24 cm.
(The Middle ages) Includes index. 1. Women — History — Middle ages,
500-1500 — Addresses, essays, lectures. 2. Social history — Medieval,
500-1500 — Addresses, essays, lectures. I. Bolton, Brenda. II. Stuard, Susan
Mosher.
HQ1143.W64        301.41/2/0902        *LC* 75-41617        *ISBN* 0812277082

**Dillard, Heath, 1933-.**        **4.5860**
Daughters of the reconquest: women in Castilian town society, 1100–1300 /
Heath Dillard. — Cambridge; New York: Cambridge University Press, 1984.
xii, 272 p., [8] p. of plates: ill.; 24 cm. (Cambridge Iberian and Latin American
studies.) Includes index. 1. Urban women — Spain — Castile. 2. Castile
(Spain) — Social conditions. I. T. II. Series.
HQ1147.C37 D54 1984        305.4/2/09463 19        *LC* 83-23220        *ISBN*
0521259223

**Stafford, Pauline.**        **4.5861**
Queens, concubines, and dowagers: the king's wife in the early Middle Ages /
Pauline Stafford. — Athens, Ga.: University of Georgia Press, c1983. xiii,
248 p.: ill.; 25 cm. Includes index. 1. Queens — Social conditions. 2. Princesses
— Social conditions. 3. Middle Ages — History 4. Europe — History —
392-814 I. T.
HQ1147.E85 S73 1983        305.4/890655 19        *LC* 82-13368        *ISBN*
0820306398

**Women of the medieval world: essays in honor of John H.**        **4.5862**
**Mundy / edited by Julius Kirshner and Suzanne F. Wemple.**
Oxford, OX, UK; New York, NY, USA: B. Blackwell, 1985. ix, 380 p., [1] leaf
of plates: port.; 24 cm. Includes index. 1. Mundy, John Hine, 1917- 2. Women
— Europe — History — Middle Ages, 500-1500 — Addresses, essays, lectures.
I. Mundy, John Hine, 1917- II. Kirshner, Julius. III. Wemple, Suzanne
Fonay.
HQ1147.E85 W66 1985        305.4/09/02 19        *LC* 84-20342        *ISBN*
0631138722

**Gold, Penny Schine.**        **4.5863**
The lady & the Virgin: image, attitude, and experience in twelfth–century
France / Penny Schine Gold. — Chicago: University of Chicago Press, 1985.
xxiv, 182 p., [8] p. of plates: ill.; 23 cm. (Women in culture and society.)
Substantial and thorough revision of author's dissertation. Includes index.
1. Mary, Blessed Virgin, Saint — Symbolism 2. Women — France — History
— Middle ages, 500-1500. 3. Social history — Medieval, 500-1500 I. T.
II. Title: Lady and the Virgin. III. Series.
HQ1147.F7 G65 1985        305.4/0944 19        *LC* 84-23701        *ISBN*
0226300870

**Lucas, Angela M.**        **4.5864**
Women in the Middle Ages: religion, marriage, and letters / Angela M. Lucas.
— New York: St. Martin's Press, c1983. xvi, 214 p.; 23 cm. Includes index.
1. Women — England — History — Middle Ages, 500-1500. 2. Women —
Europe — History — Middle Ages, 500-1500. I. T.
HQ1147.G7 L82 1983        305.4/2/0942 19        *LC* 82-42578        *ISBN*
0312887434

**French women and the Age of Enlightenment / edited by Samia**        **4.5865**
**I. Spencer.**
Bloomington: Indiana University Press, 1985 (c1984). xv, 429 p.; 25 cm.
1. Women — France — History — 18th century — Addresses, essays, lectures.
2. Women — France — Social conditions — Addresses, essays, lectures.
I. Spencer, Samia I., 1943-
HQ1149.F8 F73        305.4/0944 19        *LC* 83-48403        *ISBN* 0253324815

**Wiesner, Merry E., 1952-.**        **4.5866**
Working women in Renaissance Germany / Merry E. Wiesner. — New
Brunswick, N.J.: Rutgers University Press, c1986. xiii, 263 p.: ill.; 24 cm. —
(Douglass series on women's lives and the meaning of gender.) Includes index.
1. Women — Germany — History — Renaissance, 1450-1600. 2. Women —
Germany — Economic conditions. 3. Women — Employment — Germany —
History. I. T. II. Series.
HQ1149.G3 W54 1986        305.4/3/00943 19        *LC* 85-14451        *ISBN*
0813511380

**Boxer, C. R. (Charles Ralph), 1904-.**     **4.5867**
Women in Iberian expansion overseas, 1415–1815: some facts, fancies and personalities / C. R. Boxer. — New York: Oxford University Press, 1975. 142 p., [1] leaf of plates: col. ill.; 23 cm. 1. Women — Spain — Colonies — History. 2. Women — Portugal — Colonies — History. 3. Women — Spain — Colonies — Biography. 4. Women — Portugal — Colonies — Biography. I. T.
HQ1149.S7 B68    301.41/2/0946    *LC* 74-32645    *ISBN* 0195198174

**Connecting spheres: women in the Western world, 1500 to the**    **4.5868**
**present** / edited by Marilyn J. Boxer and Jean H. Quataert; foreword by Joan W. Scott.
New York: Oxford University Press, 1987. p. cm. Includes index. 1. Women — History — Cross-cultural studies. 2. Women — History — United States. 3. Women — History — Europe. 4. Feminism — History — Cross-cultural studies. I. Boxer, Marilyn J. II. Quataert, Jean H.
HQ1150.C66 1987    305.4 19    *LC* 86-17949    *ISBN* 0195041232

**Spender, Dale.**     **4.5869**
Feminist theorists: three centuries of key women thinkers / edited by Dale Spender; introduction by Ellen Carol DuBois. — 1st American ed. — New York: Pantheon Books, c1983. xiii, 402 p.; 21 cm. Reprint. Originally published: Women's Press, 1983. With new introd. 1. Feminists — Biography — Addresses, essays, lectures. I. T.
HQ1150.F46 1983    305.4/2/0922 19    *LC* 83-47747    *ISBN* 0394721977

**Thompson, Roger, 1933-.**     **4.5870**
Women in Stuart England and America; a comparative study. — London; Boston: Routledge and K. Paul, 1974. ix, 276 p.; 23 cm. 1. Women — England — History. 2. Women — Massachusetts — History. 3. Women — Virginia — History. I. T.
HQ1150.T48 1974    301.41/2/0942    *LC* 73-93638    *ISBN* 0710078226

# HQ1154 19th–20th Centuries

**Banks, Olive.**     **4.5871**
Faces of feminism: a study of feminism as a social movement / Olive Banks. — New York: St. Martin's Press, 1981. 285 p.; 24 cm. Includes indexes. 1. Feminism — History. I. T.
HQ1154.B268 1981    305.4/2/09 19    *LC* 81-13582    *ISBN* 0312279523

**Brittan, Arthur.**     **4.5872**
Sexism, racism, and oppression / Arthur Brittan and Mary Maynard. — Oxford, UK; New York, NY: Blackwell, 1985 (c1984). 236 p.; 22 cm. Includes index. 1. Sex discrimination against women 2. Race discrimination 3. Oppression (Psychology) I. Maynard, Mary. II. T.
HQ1154.B833    305 19    *LC* 84-12483    *ISBN* 0855206748

**Daly, Mary.**     **4.5873**
Beyond God the Father: toward a philosophy of women's liberation / by Mary Daly. — Boston: Beacon Press, 1985, c1973. xxxiv, 225 p.: ill.; 21 cm. Includes index. 1. Feminism 2. Women in Christianity I. T.
HQ1154.D3 1985    305.4/2 19    *LC* 84-45067    *ISBN* 0807015024

**Daly, Mary.**     **4.5874**
Gyn/ecology, the metaethics of radical feminism / Mary Daly. — Boston: Beacon Press, c1978. xviii, 485 p.; 24 cm. 1. Feminism 2. Social ethics I. T.
HQ1154.D312    301.41/2    *LC* 78-53790    *ISBN* 0807015105

**Daly, Mary.**     **4.5875**
Pure lust: elemental feminist philosophy / Mary Daly. — Boston: Beacon Press, c1984. xiv, 471 p.; 24 cm. Includes indexes. 1. Feminism 2. Social ethics I. T.
HQ1154.D314 1984    305.4/2/01 19    *LC* 83-71944    *ISBN* 0807015040

**Deckard, Barbara Sinclair.**     **4.5876**
The women's movement, political, socioeconomic, and psychological issues / Barbara Sinclair Deckard. — 3rd ed. — New York: Harper & Row, c1983. xii, 500 p.; 21 cm. Includes index. 1. Women — History 2. Women — United States — History. 3. Feminism I. T.
HQ1154.D35 1983    305.4/2/09 19    *LC* 82-15768    *ISBN* 0060416157

**Discovering reality: feminist perspectives on epistemology,**    **4.5877**
**metaphysics, methodology, and philosophy of science / edited by**
**Sandra Harding and Merrill B. Hintikka.**
Dordrecht, Holland; Boston: D. Reidel; Hingham, MA: Sold and distributed in the USA and Canada by Kluwer Boston, c1983. xix, 332 p.; 23 cm. — (Synthese library; v. 161) 1. Feminism — Addresses, essays, lectures. 2. Philosophy — History — Addresses, essays, lectures. 3. Science — Philosophy — Addresses,

essays, lectures. 4. Social sciences — Philosophy — Addresses, essays, lectures. I. Harding, Sandra G. II. Hintikka, Merrill B., 1939-
HQ1154.D538 1983    305.4/2 19    *LC* 82-16507    *ISBN* 9027714967

**Eisenstein, Zillah R.**     **4.5878**
The radical future of liberal feminism / Zillah R. Eisenstein. — New York: Longman, c1981. xi, 260 p.; 24 cm. — (Longman series in feminist theory.) 1. Feminism 2. Liberalism 3. Radicalism I. T. II. Series.
HQ1154.E44    305.4/2    *LC* 80-19464    *ISBN* 0582282055

**Evans, Richard J.**     **4.5879**
The feminists: women's emancipation movements in Europe, America, and Australasia, 1840–1920 / Richard J. Evans. London: Croom Helm; New York: Barnes & Noble, 1977. p. cm. Includes index. 1. Feminism — History. I. T.
HQ1154.E8 1977    322.4/4    *LC* 77-77490    *ISBN* 0064920372

**Feminism and materialism: women and modes of production /**    **4.5880**
**edited by Annette Kuhn and AnnMarie Wolpe.**
London; Boston: Routledge and Paul, 1978. xi, 328 p.; 28 cm. 1. Women — Social conditions 2. Sexual division of labor I. Kuhn, Annette. II. Wolpe, AnnMarie.
HQ1154.F443 1978    305.4/2 19    *LC* 78-40670    *ISBN* 0710000723

**Feminist quotations: voices of rebels, reformers, and visionaries**    **4.5881**
/ compiled by Carol McPhee, Ann FitzGerald.
1st ed. — New York: Crowell, c1979. xiv, 271 p.; 24 cm. Includes indexes. 1. Feminism — Quotations, maxims, etc. I. McPhee, Carol. II. FitzGerald, Ann.
HQ1154.F446 1979    301.41/2/08    *LC* 78-3308    *ISBN* 0690017707

**Frye, Marilyn.**     **4.5882**
The politics of reality: essays in feminist theory / by Marilyn Frye. — Trumansburg, N.Y.: Crossing Press, c1983. xvi, 176 p.; 22 cm. — (Crossing Press feminist series.) 1. Feminism — Addresses, essays, lectures. I. T. II. Series.
HQ1154.F78 1983    305.4/2 19    *LC* 83-2082    *ISBN* 0895941007

**Gornick, Vivian. comp.**     • **4.5883**
Woman in sexist society: studies in power and powerlessness / edited by Vivian Gornick and Barbara K. Moran. — New York: Basic Books, [1971] xxv, 515 p.; 25 cm. 1. Women — History — Modern period, 1600- — Addresses, essays, lectures. I. Moran, Barbara K., joint comp. II. T.
HQ1154.G63    301.41/2/08    *LC* 70-157125    *ISBN* 0465091997

**Kelly, Joan, 1928-1982.**     **4.5884**
Women, history & theory: the essays of Joan Kelly / Joan Kelly. — Chicago: University of Chicago Press. 1984. xxvi, 163 p.; 23 cm. (Women in culture and society.) 1. Feminism — Addresses, essays, lectures. 2. Women — History — Addresses, essays, lectures. I. T. II. Series.
HQ1154.K38 1984    305.4/09 19    *LC* 84-2558    *ISBN* 0226430278

**Millett, Kate.**     **4.5885**
Sexual politics. — [1st ed.]. — Garden City, N.Y.: Doubleday, 1970. xii, 393 p.; 25 cm. 1. Women — History — Modern period, 1600- 2. Sex role 3. Women in literature 4. Sex in literature I. T.
HQ1154.M5    301.41/2    *LC* 70-103769

**Mitchell, Juliet, 1940-.**     • **4.5886**
Woman's estate. [1st American ed. New York] Pantheon Books [1972, c1971] 182 p. 22 cm. Includes bibliographical references. 1. Feminism 2. Women — History and condition of women. I. T.
HQ1154.M53 1972    323.4    *LC* 77-164419    *ISBN* 0394473426

**The New women's movement: feminism and political power in**    **4.5887**
**Europe & the USA / edited by Drude Dahlerup.**
London: Sage, 1986. [288] p.: ill.; 22 cm. (Sage modern politics series; v.12) 1. Feminism — History — 20th century. I. Dahlerup, Drude.
HQ1154.N47 1986    305.4/2/091812 19    *ISBN* 0803980108

**Oakley, Ann.**     **4.5888**
Subject women / Ann Oakley. — 1st American ed. — New York: Pantheon Books, c1981. x, 406 p.: ill.; 22 cm. Includes index. 1. Women's rights — History — 20th century. 2. Feminism — History — 20th century. I. T.
HQ1154.O18 1981    305.4/2 19    *LC* 81-47208    *ISBN* 0394749049

**O'Barr, Jean Fox, 1942-.**     **4.5889**
Third world women: factors in their changing status. — Durham, N. C.: Duke University, Center for International Studies, 1976. vii, 94 p. — (Duke University. Center for International Studies. Occasional paper; no. 2) 1. Women — History and condition of women 2. Women — Social conditions I. T.
HQ1154 O2    *LC* 76-23703

**Fuller, Margaret, 1810-1850.**     • **4.5890**
Woman in the nineteenth century: and kindred papers relating to the sphere, condition, and duties of woman / edited by Arthur B. Fuller. — New and

complete ed., with an introd. by Horace Greeley. — New York: Greenwood Press, 1968. 420 p.; 20 cm. Reprint of the 1874 ed. 1. Women — History — Modern period, 1600- I. Fuller, Arthur Buckminster, 1822-1862, ed. II. T.
HQ1154.O8 1968    301.41/2/09034    *LC* 68-54430

**Perceiving women / edited by Shirley Ardener.**    **4.5891**
New York: Wiley, [1975] xxiii, 167 p.: ill.; 26 cm. 'A Halsted Press book.' 1. Women — Addresses, essays, lectures. 2. Feminism — Addresses, essays, lectures. I. Ardener, Shirley.
HQ1154.P427 1975    301.41/2    *LC* 75-12662    *ISBN* 0470033096

**The Politics of women's spirituality: essays on the rise of**    **4.5892**
**spiritual power within the feminist movement / edited by**
**Charlene Spretnak.**
1st ed. — Garden City, N.Y.: Anchor Books, 1982. xxx, 590 p.; 22 cm. 1. Feminism — Religious aspects — Addresses, essays, lectures. 2. Spirituality — Addresses, essays, lectures. 3. Women (in religion, folklore, etc.) — Addresses, essays, lectures. I. Spretnak, Charlene, 1946-
HQ1154.P6    305.4/2 19    *LC* 80-2876    *ISBN* 0385172419

**Rossi, Alice S., 1922- comp.**    • **4.5893**
Essays on sex equality [by] John Stuart Mill & Harriet Taylor Mill. Edited and with an introductory essay by Alice S. Rossi. Chicago, University of Chicago Press [1970] ix, 242 p. ports. 22 cm. 1. Women — History — Modern period, 1600- Addresses, essays, lectures. I. Mill, John Stuart, 1806-1873. II. Mill, Harriet Hardy Taylor, 1807-1858. III. T.
HQ1154.R745    301.41/2/08    *LC* 78-133381    *ISBN* 0226525457

**Rossi, Alice S., 1922- comp.**    **4.5894**
The feminist papers: from Adams to de Beauvoir. Edited and with introductory essays by Alice S. Rossi. — New York: Columbia University Press, 1973. xix, 716 p.; 21 cm. 1. Women — History — Modern period, 1600- 2. Women's rights — Addresses, essays, lectures. 3. Feminism — Addresses, essays, lectures. I. T.
HQ1154.R746    301.41/2/08    *LC* 73-8828    *ISBN* 0231037953

**Ruether, Rosemary Radford.**    **4.5895**
New woman, new earth: sexist ideologies and human liberation / Rosemary Radford Ruether. — New York: Seabury Press, [1975] xiv, 221 p.; 22 cm. 'A Crossroad book.' Includes index. 1. Sexism — Addresses, essays, lectures. 2. Women in Christianity — Addresses, essays, lectures. 3. Race discrimination — Addresses, essays, lectures. 4. Sex role — Religious aspects — Christianity — Addresses, essays, lectures. I. T.
HQ1154.R83    261.8/34/1    *LC* 75-17649    *ISBN* 0816412057

**Sisterhood is global: the international women's movement**    **4.5896**
**anthology / compiled, edited, and with an introduction by Robin**
**Morgan.**
1st ed. — Garden City, N.Y.: Anchor Press/Doubleday, 1984. xxiii, 815 p.; 24 cm. Includes index. 1. Feminism — Addresses, essays, lectures. 2. Women's rights — Addresses, essays, lectures. I. Morgan, Robin.
HQ1154.S54 1984    305.4/2 19    *LC* 82-45332    *ISBN* 0385177968

**Spender, Lynne.**    **4.5897**
Intruders on the rights of men: women's unpublished heritage / Lynne Spender. — London; Boston: Pandora Press, 1983. xii, 136 p.: ill.; 20 cm. Includes index. 1. Feminism 2. Publishers and publishing 3. Power (Social sciences) I. T.
HQ1154.S63 1983    305.4/2 19    *LC* 82-22251    *ISBN* 0863580009

**The Technological woman: interfacing with tomorrow / edited**    **4.5898**
**by Jan Zimmerman.**
New York: Praeger, c1983. viii, 296 p.; 24 cm. Based on papers from the Conference on Future, Technology, and Woman, held at San Diego State University, March 1981. 1. Women — Addresses, essays, lectures. 2. Technology — Addresses, essays, lectures. 3. Home economics — Addresses, essays, lectures. 4. Women — Employment — Addresses, essays, lectures. 5. Human reproduction — Addresses, essays, lectures. I. Zimmerman, Jan. II. Conference on Future, Technology, and Woman (1981: San Diego State University)
HQ1154.T38 1983    305.4 19    *LC* 82-14033    *ISBN* 0030628296

**What is feminism? / edited by Juliet Mitchell and Ann Oakley.**    **4.5899**
Oxford: Basil Blackwell, 1986. ix, 252 p.; 22 cm. 1. Feminism I. Mitchell, Juliet, 1940- II. Oakley, Ann.
HQ1154.W53    305.4/2 19    *ISBN* 0631148426

**Woman, new dimensions / edited by Walter J. Burghardt.**    **4.5900**
New York: Paulist Press, c1977. viii, 189 p.; 23 cm. 1. Women — Social conditions — Addresses, essays, lectures. 2. Women's rights — Addresses, essays, lectures. 3. Women in Christianity — Addresses, essays, lectures. I. Burghardt, Walter J.
HQ1154.W85    301.41/2    *LC* 76-50969    *ISBN* 0809120119

**Women and philosophy: toward a theory of liberation / edited**    **4.5901**
**by Carol C. Gould and Marx W. Wartofsky.**
New York: Putnam, c1976. viii, 364 p.; 22 cm. 'Based on a recent special issue of the quarterly journal, The philosophical forum, (volume v, nos. 1-2).' 1. Feminism — History — Addresses, essays, lectures. I. Gould, Carol C. II. Wartofsky, Marx W. III. Philosophical forum.
HQ1154.W878 1976    301.41/2/09    *LC* 75-33604    *ISBN* 0399116524

**Women in the world: a comparative study / Lynne B. Iglitzin,**    **4.5902**
**Ruth Ross, editors.**
Santa Barbara, Calif.: Clio Books, c1976. xviii, 427 p.; 23 cm. (Studies in comparative politics; no. 6) 'This volume is the result of a series of seminar meetings sponsored jointly by the Department of Political Science of the University of California, Santa Barbara, and the Center for the Study of Democratic Institutions.' 1. Women — Social conditions — Addresses, essays, lectures. 2. Women — Legal status, laws, etc. — Addresses, essays, lectures. I. Iglitzin, Lynne B., 1931- II. Ross, Ruth A., 1933- III. California. University, Santa Barbara. Dept. of Political Science. IV. Center for the Study of Democratic Institutions.
HQ1154.W8838    301.41/2    *LC* 74-14197    *ISBN* 0874362008

**Women: roles and status in eight countries / edited by Janet**    **4.5903**
**Zollinger Giele, Audrey Chapman Smock.**
New York: Wiley, c1977. xiii, 443 p.; 24 cm. 'A Wiley-Interscience publication.' 1. Women — Social conditions — Addresses, essays, lectures. 2. Women's rights — Addresses, essays, lectures. 3. Women in politics — Addresses, essays, lectures. I. Giele, Janet Zollinger. II. Smock, Audrey C.
HQ1154.W884    301.41/2    *LC* 76-39950    *ISBN* 0471015040

**Women in development: a resource guide for organization and**    **4.5904**
**action / ISIS Women's International Information and**
**Communication Service; forword by Boston Women's Health**
**Book Collective.**
Philadelphia: New society publishers, 1984. 225 p.: ill.; 30 cm. 1. Women — Economic conditions. 2. Women — Social conditions 3. Women — Employment 4. Women in rural development 5. Women — Bibliography. I. ISIS (Organization)
HQ1154.W8842 1983    305.4 19

**Women united, women divided: comparative studies of ten**    **4.5905**
**contemporary cultures / edited by Patricia Caplan and Janet M.**
**Bujra.**
Bloomington: Indiana University Press, c1979. 288 p.; 19 cm. 1. Women — Addresses, essays, lectures. 2. Solidarity — Addresses, essays, lectures. I. Caplan, Patricia. II. Bujra, Janet M.
HQ1154.W889 1979    301.41/2    *LC* 78-14085    *ISBN* 0253122155

# HQ1166–1172 SPECIAL ETHNIC GROUPS

**Pescatello, Ann M.**    **4.5906**
Power and pawn: the female in Iberian families, societies, and cultures / Ann M. Pescatello. — Westport, Conn.: Greenwood Press, 1976. xix, 281 p.; 21 cm. — (Contributions in intercultural and comparative studies; no. 1) Includes index. 1. Women — History 2. Women — Social conditions 3. National characteristics, Spanish 4. National characteristics, Portuguese. I. T.
HQ1166.P47 1976    301.41/2/0946    *LC* 75-35352    *ISBN* 0837185831

**Mernissi, Fatima.**    **4.5907**
Beyond the veil: male–female dynamics in modern Muslim society / by Fatima Mernissi. — Rev. ed., 1st Midland Book ed. — Bloomington: Indiana University Press, 1987. p. cm. Includes index. 1. Women, Muslim 2. Women — Morocco. I. T.
HQ1170.M46 1987    305.4/862971 19    *LC* 86-46034    *ISBN* 0253311624

**Middle Eastern Muslim women speak / edited by Elizabeth**    **4.5908**
**Warnock Fernea and Basima Qattan Bezirgan.**
Austin: University of Texas Press, c1977. xxxvi, 402 p., [28] leaves of plates: ill.; 24 cm. — (The Dan Danciger publication series) 1. Women — Near East — Addresses, essays, lectures. 2. Women, Muslim — Addresses, essays, lectures. I. Fernea, Elizabeth Warnock. II. Bezirgan, Basima Qattan, 1933-
HQ1170.M53    301.41/2/0956    *LC* 76-16845    *ISBN* 0292750331

**Strobel, Margaret, 1946-.**    **4.5909**
Muslim women in Mombasa, 1890–1975 / Margaret Strobel. — New Haven: Yale University Press, 1979. xiii, 258 p.: maps; 22 cm. Includes index. 1. Women, Muslim 2. Women — Kenya — Mombasa. I. T.
HQ1170.S87    301.41/2/0967623    *LC* 79-10721    *ISBN* 0300023022

**Women in the Muslim world / edited by Lois Beck and Nikki Keddie.**      4.5910
Cambridge, Mass.: Harvard University Press, 1978. xi, 698 p.: ill.; 24 cm. 1. Women, Muslim — Addresses, essays, lectures. I. Beck, Lois, 1944- II. Keddie, Nikki R.
HQ1170.W59     301.41/2/0917671     LC 78-3633     ISBN 0674954807

**The Jewish woman: new perspectives / edited by Elizabeth Koltun.**      4.5911
New York: Schocken Books, 1976. xx, 294 p.; 21 cm. 1. Women, Jewish — Addresses, essays, lectures. 2. Women in Judaism — Addresses, essays, lectures. I. Koltun, Elizabeth.
HQ1172.J48     301.41/2     LC 75-35445     ISBN 0805236147

**Marcus, Jacob Rader, 1896-.**      4.5912
The American Jewish woman, 1654–1980 / by Jacob R. Marcus. — New York: Ktav Pub. House; Cincinnati: American Jewish Archives, 1981. xiv, 231 p., [8] leaves of plates: ill.; 24 cm. Includes index. 1. Women, Jewish — United States — History. 2. Jews — United States — History. 3. Women — United States — History. 4. United States — Ethnic relations I. T.
HQ1172.M37     305.4/8 19     LC 81-1720     ISBN 0870687514

**The American Jewish woman: a documentary history / by Jacob R. Marcus.**      4.5913
New York: Ktav Pub. House; Cincinnati: American Jewish Archives, 1981. xvii, 1047 p., [39] leaves of plates: ports; 24 cm. 'Intended as a supplement to Jacob R. Marcus, The American Jewish woman, 1654-1980.'—Pref. 1. Women, Jewish — United States — History — Sources. 2. Jews — United States — History — Sources. 3. Women — United States — History — Sources. 4. United States — Ethnic relations — Sources. I. Marcus, Jacob Rader, 1896-
HQ1172.M37 Suppl     205.4/8 19     LC 81-1966     ISBN 0870687522

## HQ1180–1399 WOMEN'S STUDIES. WOMEN: SPECIAL ASPECTS

**Beere, Carole A., 1944-.**      4.5914
Women and women's issues: a handbook of tests and measures / Carole A. Beere. — 1st ed. — San Francisco: Jossey-Bass, 1979. xvi, 550 p.; 26 cm. (The Jossey-Bass social and behavioral science series) 1. Women's studies — Methodology — Handbooks, manuals, etc. 2. Sex role — Testing — Handbooks, manuals, etc. 3. Social role — Testing — Handbooks, manuals, etc. I. T.
HQ1180.B43     301.41/2/018     LC 79-88106     ISBN 0875894186

**Theories of women's studies / edited by Gloria Bowles and Renate Duelli Klein.**      4.5915
London; Boston: Routledge & Kegan Paul, 1983. xiv, 277 p.; 21 cm. Includes index. 1. Women's studies — Addresses, essays, lectures. I. Bowles, Gloria. II. Duelli-Klein, Renate.
HQ1180.T48 1983     305.4/2/072 19     LC 82-19512     ISBN 0710094884

## HQ1201–1205 GENERAL WORKS

**Astell, Mary, 1668-1731.**      4.5916
An essay in defence of the female sex. Written by a Lady. [New York] Source Book Press, 1971 (c1970) 133p. 1. Women I. A Lady II. T.
HQ1201 A85 1970

**History of ideas on woman: a source book / [edited by] Rosemary Agonito.**      4.5917
New York: Putnam, c1977. 414 p.; 23 cm. Includes index. 1. Women — Addresses, essays, lectures. I. Agonito, Rosemary.
HQ1201.H67 1977     301.41/2     LC 77-5061     ISBN 0399119647

**Bardwick, Judith M.**      4.5918
Psychology of women: a study of bio–cultural conflicts / [by] Judith M. Bardwick. — New York: Harper & Row, 1972 (c1971) vii, 242 p.; 24 cm. 1. Women — Psychology I. T.
HQ1206.B23     155.6/33     LC 70-137799     ISBN 0060404973(pbk)

**Barnett, Rosalind C.**      4.5919
The competent woman: perspectives on development / by Rosalind C. Barnett and Grace K. Baruch; with an afterword by Carolyn G. Heilbrun. — New York: Irvington Publishers: distributed by Halsted Press, c1978. 184 p.; 22 cm. — (Irvington social relations series) Includes index. 1. Women — Psychology 2. Socialization 3. Success 4. Ability I. Baruch, Grace K. joint author. II. T.
HQ1206.B26 1978     155.6/33     LC 78-8380     ISBN 0470264241

**Becoming female: perspectives on development / edited by Claire B. Kopp, in collaboration with Martha Kirkpatrick.**      4.5920
New York: Plenum Press, c1979. xviii, 469 p.; 24 cm. — (Women in context.) 1. Women — Psychology — Addresses, essays, lectures. 2. Developmental psychology — Addresses, essays, lectures. 3. Child development — Addresses, essays, lectures. 4. Women — United States — Socialization — Addresses, essays, lectures. I. Kopp, Claire B. II. Kirkpatrick, Martha. III. Series.
HQ1206.B34     301.41/2     LC 79-9970     ISBN 0306402297

**Bernard, Jessie Shirley, 1903-.**      4.5921
The female world / Jessie Bernard. — New York: Free Press, c1981. x, 614 p.: ill.; 24 cm. Includes indexes. 1. Women — Psychology 2. Women — Social conditions I. T.
HQ1206.B374     305.4/2 19     LC 80-69880     ISBN 0029030005

**Butler, Pamela.**      4.5922
Self–assertion for women: a guide to becoming androgynous / Pamela Butler. — San Francisco: Canfield Press, c1976. 307 p.: ill.; 24 cm. 1. Women — Psychology 2. Assertiveness (Psychology) 3. Androgyny (Psychology) I. T.
HQ1206.B85     155.6/33 19     LC 76-44230     ISBN 0063812185

**Deutsch, Helene, 1884-.**      • 4.5923
The psychology of women / a psychoanalytic interpretation by Helene Deutsch ... Foreword by Stanley Cobb ... — New York: Grune & Stratton, 1944-. v.; 23 cm. 1. Women I. T.
HQ1206.D4     396     LC 44-5287

**Female psychology: the emerging self / [edited by] Sue Cox.**      4.5924
2nd ed. — New York: St. Martin's Press, c1981. x, 494 p.: ill.; 24 cm. 1. Women — Psychology — Addresses, essays, lectures. 2. Feminism — Addresses, essays, lectures. I. Cox, Sue.
HQ1206.F424 1981     155.6/33 19     LC 80-52382     ISBN 0312287437

**Feminine personality and conflict [by] Judith M. Bardwick [and others].**      • 4.5925
Belmont, Calif., Brooks/Cole Pub. Co. [1970] vii, 102 p. illus. 23 cm. (Contemporary psychology series) 1. Women — Psychology I. Bardwick, Judith M., 1933-
HQ1206.F43     155.6/33     LC 73-131872

**'Femininity,' 'masculinity,' and 'androgyny': a modern philosophical discussion / edited by Mary Vetterling–Braggin.**      4.5926
Totowa, N.J.: Rowman and Littlefield, c1982. x, 326 p.; 21 cm. 1. Women — Psychology 2. Men — Psychology 3. Sex differences (Psychology) 4. Androgyny (Psychology) 5. Woman (Philosophy) I. Vetterling-Braggin, Mary.
HQ1206.F44 1982b     305.3 19     LC 82-529     ISBN 0847670708

**Gilligan, Carol, 1936-.**      4.5927
In a different voice: psychological theory and women's development / Carol Gilligan. — Cambridge, Mass.: Harvard University Press, 1982. vi, 184 p.; 24 cm. Includes index. 1. Women — Psychology — Longitudinal studies. 2. Developmental psychology — Longitudinal studies. 3. Moral development — Longitudinal studies. I. T.
HQ1206.G58 1982     305.4/2 19     LC 81-13478     ISBN 0674445430

**Heilbrun, Carolyn G., 1926-.**      4.5928
Reinventing womanhood / Carolyn G. Heilbrun. — 1st ed. — New York: Norton, c1979. 244 p.; 22 cm. Includes index. 1. Women — Psychology 2. Sex role 3. Women in literature 4. Fiction — Women authors — History and criticism. I. T.
HQ1206.H43 1979     301.41/2     LC 78-25607     ISBN 0393012107

**Horney, Karen, 1885-1952.**      • 4.5929
Feminine psychology; [papers] Edited and with an introd. by Harold Kelman. — [1st ed.]. — New York: W. W. Norton, [1967] 269 p.; 22 cm. 'Sponsored by the Association for the Advancement of Psychoanalysis.' 1. Women — Psychology 2. Sex (Psychology) I. Association for the Advancement of Psychoanalysis. II. T.
HQ1206.H6     155.3/33     LC 67-12439

**Jaggar, Alison M.**      4.5930
Feminist politics and human nature / Alison M. Jaggar. — Totowa, N.J.: Rowman & Allanheld, 1983. vi, 408 p.; 24 cm. — (Philosophy and society.) 1. Feminism — Philosophy. 2. Feminism — Political aspects. 3. Women and socialism I. T. II. Series.
HQ1206.J33 1983     305.4/2 19     LC 83-3402     ISBN 084767181X

**Luke, Helen M., 1904-.**      4.5931
Woman: Earth and spirit, the feminine in symbol and myth / Helen M. Luke. — New York: Crossroad, 1981. 102 p.; 22 cm. 1. Women — Psychology 2. Women (in religion, folklore, etc.) 3. Women and religion 4. Femininity (Psychology) I. T.
HQ1206.L843     305.4/2 19     LC 81-209     ISBN 0824500180

McMillan, Carol, 1954-. **4.5932**
Women, reason, and nature: some philosophical problems with feminism / Carol McMillan. — Princeton, N.J.: Princeton University Press, c1982. x, 165 p.; 23 cm. Includes index. 1. Feminism — Philosophy. 2. Woman (Philosophy) 3. Women's studies — Philosophy. I. T.
HQ1206.M37 1982      305.4/2 19      LC 82-12207      ISBN 0691072744

Miller, Jean Baker. comp. **4.5933**
Psychoanalysis and women; contributions to new theory and therapy. — New York: Brunner/Mazel, [1973] xiii, 418 p.; 22 cm. 1. Women — Psychology 2. Women — Mental health I. T.
HQ1206.M5 1973      155.6/33      LC 72-97730      ISBN 0876300697

Montagu, Ashley, 1905-. **4.5934**
The natural superiority of women. — Rev. ed. — New York: Macmillan, [1968] xvi, 235 p.; 22 cm. 1. Women I. T.
HQ1206.M65 1968      301.41/2      LC 68-18873

O'Brien, Mary. **4.5935**
The politics of reproduction / Mary O'Brien. — Boston: Routledge & Kegan Paul, 1981. x, 240 p.; 22 cm. Includes index. 1. Feminism 2. Reproduction I. T.
HQ1206.O24      320/.01/1 19      LC 81-203741      ISBN 0710008104

Okin, Susan Moller. **4.5936**
Women in Western political thought / Susan Moller Okin. — Princeton, N.J.: Princeton University Press, c1979. 371 p.; 23 cm. Based on the author's thesis. Includes index. 1. Plato — Political science. 2. Rousseau, Jean-Jacques, 1712-1778 — Political science. 3. Mill, John Stuart, 1806-1873 — Political science. 4. Women 5. Sex role 6. Feminism I. T.
HQ1206.O38      301.41/2      LC 79-84004      ISBN 0691076138

O'Leary, Virginia E., 1943-. **4.5937**
Toward understanding women / Virginia E. O'Leary. — Monterey, Calif.: Brooks/Cole Pub. Co., c1977. x, 253 p.: ill.; 24 cm. Includes indexes. 1. Women — Psychology 2. Sex role I. T.
HQ1206.O74      155.6/33      LC 77-5103      ISBN 0818502282

Philosophy of woman: an anthology of classic and current **4.5938**
concepts / edited by Mary Briody Mahowald.
2nd ed. — Indianapolis, Ind.: Hackett, 1983. xv, 454 p.; 22 cm. 1. Woman (Philosophy) I. Mahowald, Mary Briody.
HQ1206.P46 1983      305.4/2 19      LC 83-8433      ISBN 0915144492

Rosaldo, Michelle Zimbalist. **4.5939**
Woman, culture, and society / edited by Michelle Zimbalist Rosaldo and Louise Lamphere. Contributors: Joan Bamberger [and others]. — Stanford, Calif.: Stanford University Press, 1974. xi, 352 p.; 24 cm. 1. Women — History — Modern period, 1600- — Addresses, essays, lectures. I. Lamphere, Louise. joint author. II. Bamberger, Joan. III. T.
HQ1206.R65      301.41/2      LC 73-89861      ISBN 0804708509

Schur, Edwin M. **4.5940**
Labeling women deviant: gender, stigma, and social control / Edwin M. Schur. — Philadelphia: Temple University Press, 1983. x, 286 p.; 22 cm. Includes index. 1. Women — Social conditions 2. Deviant behavior — Labeling theory 3. Sex discrimination against women 4. Stigma (Social psychology) 5. Social norms I. T.
HQ1206.S443 1983      305.4/2 19      LC 83-10942      ISBN 0877223327

Sherman, Julia Ann, 1934-. **4.5941**
On the psychology of women; a survey of empirical studies, by Julia A. Sherman. — Springfield, Ill.: Thomas, [1971] ix, 304 p.; 24 cm. 1. Women — Psychology I. T.
HQ1206.S48      155.6/33      LC 77-149194

Spender, Dale. **4.5942**
Women of ideas and what men have done to them: from Aphra Behn to Adrienne Rich / Dale Spender. — London; Boston: Routledge & Kegan Paul, 1982. xii, 586 p.; 25 cm. Includes indexes. 1. Women intellectuals 2. Women intellectuals — Case studies. 3. Sex discrimination against women I. T.
HQ1206.S68 1982      305.4 19      LC 82-12208      ISBN 0710093535

Strouse, Jean. comp. **4.5943**
Women & analysis: dialogues on psychoanalytic views of femininity. — New York: Grossman Publishers, 1974. viii, 375 p.; 24 cm. 1. Women — Psychology — Addresses, essays, lectures. 2. Femininity (Psychology) — Addresses, essays, lectures. I. T.
HQ1206.S86 1974      155.6/33      LC 73-7313      ISBN 0670778419

Taylor, Barbara, 1950-. **4.5944**
Eve and the New Jerusalem: socialism and feminism in the nineteenth century / Barbara Taylor. — 1st American ed. — New York: Pantheon Books, c1983.

xviii, 394 p.: ports.; 22 cm. Includes index. 1. Feminism — History — 19th century. 2. Women and socialism — History — 19th century. I. T.
HQ1206.T33 1983      305.4/2/09034 19      LC 82-19007      ISBN 0394527666

Ulanov, Ann Belford. • **4.5945**
The feminine in Jungian psychology and in Christian theology. Evanston [Ill.] Northwestern University Press, 1971. xi, 347 p. 23 cm. 1. Jung, C. G. (Carl Gustav), 1875-1961. 2. Femininity (Psychology) 3. Psychology, Religious I. T.
HQ1206.U47      LC 74-149922      ISBN 0810103516

Williams, Juanita H., 1922-. **4.5946**
Psychology of women: behavior in a biosocial context / Juanita H. Williams. — 3rd ed. — New York: Norton, c1987. 444 p.: ill. Includes index. 1. Women — Psychology 2. Women — Physiology 3. Women — Social behavior. I. T.
HQ1206.W72 1987      155.6/33 19      LC 86-231655      ISBN 0393955672

*[handwritten: HQ 1206 W72 1977]*

Woman, dependent or independent variable? / Edited and **4.5947**
authored by Rhoda Kesler Unger & Florence L. Denmark.
New York: Psychological Dimensions, [1975] 828 p.: ill.; 24 cm. 1. Women — Psychology — Addresses, essays, lectures. 2. Sex role — Addresses, essays, lectures. 3. Women — Health and hygiene — Addresses, essays, lectures. I. Unger, Rhoda Kesler. II. Denmark, Florence.
HQ1206.W854      155.6/33      LC 75-7628      ISBN 0884370003

The Woman question: selections from the writings of Karl • **4.5948**
Marx, Frederick Engels, V.I. Lenin, Joseph Stalin.
New York: International Publishers, 1951. 96 p. — (Little New World paperbacks; LNW-19) 1. Women — Social conditions 2. Women and socialism I. Marx, Karl, 1818-1883.
HQ1206.W86      LC 51-5114

Woman's nature: rationalizations of inequality / [edited by] **4.5949**
Marian Lowe, Ruth Hubbard.
New York: Pergamon Press, c1983. xii, 155 p.: ill.; 24 cm. — (Athene series.) 1. Women — Social conditions — Addresses, essays, lectures. 2. Equality — Addresses, essays, lectures. 3. Feminism — Addresses, essays, lectures. 4. Rationalization (Psychology) — Addresses, essays, lectures. I. Lowe, Marian. II. Hubbard, Ruth, 1924- III. Series.
HQ1206.W865 1983      HQ1206 W865 1983.      305.4 19      LC 83-4066      ISBN 0080301436

Beauvoir, Simone de, 1908-. • **4.5950**
[Deuxième sexe. English] The second sex; translated and edited by H. M. Parshley. [1st American ed.] New York, Knopf, 1953 [c1952] xxx, 732, xiv p. 25 cm. 1. Women I. T.
HQ1208.B352      396      LC 52-6407

Women in culture and politics: a century of change / edited by **4.5951**
Judith Friedlander ... [et al.].
Bloomington: Indiana University Press, c1986. xvii, 394 p.; 25 cm. Translation of: Stratégies des femmes. Based on papers presented at three meetings of the New Family and New Woman Research Planning Group held in France in 1979 and 1980 and in the United States in 1982. 1. Women — Europe — Congresses. 2. Women — United States — Congresses. 3. Feminism — Europe — Congresses. 4. Feminism — United States — Congresses. I. Friedlander, Judith. II. New Family and New Woman Research Planning Group.
HQ1208.S7713 1986      305.4/094 19      LC 85-45098      ISBN 0253313287

## HQ1221 ETHICS

Harrison, Beverly Wildung, 1932-. **4.5952**
Making the connections: essays in feminist social ethics / Beverly Wildung Harrison; edited by Carol S. Robb. — Boston: Beacon Press, c1985. xxii, 312 p.; 24 cm. Includes index. 1. Feminism — Moral and ethical aspects — Addresses, essays, lectures. 2. Social ethics — Addresses, essays, lectures. 3. Christian ethics — Addresses, essays, lectures. I. Robb, Carol S. II. T.
HQ1221.H27 1985      305.4/2 19      LC 84-45718      ISBN 0807015245

Women's consciousness, women's conscience: a reader in **4.5953**
feminist ethics / edited by Barbara Hilkert Andolsen, Christine
E. Gudorf, Mary D. Pellauer.
Minneapolis: Winston Press, c1985. xxvi, 310 p.; 24 cm. 'A Seabury book.' 1. Feminism — Moral and ethical aspects. 2. Feminism — Religious aspects 3. Social ethics 4. Feminism — United States. I. Andolsen, Barbara Hilkert. II. Gudorf, Christine E. III. Pellauer, Mary D.
HQ1221.W893 1985      305.4/2 19      LC 85-50124      ISBN 0866839585

## HQ1236–1391 WOMEN IN POLITICS

**Baxter, Sandra, 1945-.**     **4.5954**
Women and politics: the visible majority / Sandra Baxter, Marjorie Lansing. — Rev. ed. — Ann Arbor: University of Michigan Press, 1983. ix, 259 p.: ill.; 24 cm. — (Women and culture series.) Includes index. 1. Women in politics — United States. 2. Feminism — United States. 3. Voting — United States. 4. Politics, Practical I. Lansing, Marjorie, 1916- II. T. III. Series.
HQ1236.B28 1983     305.4/2 19     LC 83-6555     ISBN 0472100432

**Elshtain, Jean Bethke, 1941-.**     **4.5955**
Public man, private woman: women in social and political thought / Jean Bethke Elshtain. — Princeton, N.J.: Princeton University Press, c1981. xviii, 378 p.; 23 cm. Includes index. 1. Women in politics 2. Political science — History 3. Knowledge, Theory of I. T. II. Title: Women in social and political thought.
HQ1236.E47     305.4/2 19     LC 81-47122     ISBN 0691076324

**The Extended family: women and political participation in India and Pakistan / edited by Gail Minault.**     **4.5956**
1st ed. — Delhi: Chanakya Publications, 1981. xiii, 312 p.; 23 cm. 1. Women in politics — India — Addresses, essays, lectures. 2. Women in politics — Pakistan — Addresses, essays, lectures. 3. Women's rights — India — Addresses, essays, lectures. 4. Women's rights — Pakistan — Addresses, essays, lectures. I. Minault, Gail, 1939-
HQ1236.E97 1981     305.4/0954 19     LC 81-904986

**Kelly, Rita Mae.**     **4.5957**
The making of political women: a study of socialization and role conflict / Rita Mae Kelly & Mary Boutilier. — Chicago: Nelson-Hall, c1978. x, 368 p.; 23 cm. 1. Women in politics — United States. 2. Sex role 3. Statesmen's wives — Biography. I. Boutilier, Mary A. joint author. II. T.
HQ1236.K45     301.41/2/0973     LC 77-17081     ISBN 0882292900

**Pharr, Susan J.**     **4.5958**
Political women in Japan: the search for a place in political life / Susan J. Pharr. — Berkeley, Calif.: University of California Press, 1981. xiv, 239 p.: ill.; 22 cm. Includes index. 1. Women in politics — Japan. 2. Political socialization I. T.
HQ1236.P46     305.4/2/0952     LC 80-12984     ISBN 0520040716

**The Politics of the second electorate: women and public participation: Britain, USA, Canada, Australia, France, Spain, West Germany, Italy, Sweden, Finland, Eastern Europe, USSR, Japan / edited by Joni Lovenduski and Jill Hills.**     **4.5959**
London; Boston: Routledge & Kegan Paul, 1981. xviii, 332 p.; 22 cm. 1. Women in politics — Addresses, essays, lectures. I. Lovenduski, Joni. II. Hills, Jill.
HQ1236.P64     324/.088/042 19     LC 81-199239     ISBN 0710008066

**Randall, Vicky.**     **4.5960**
Women and politics / Vicky Randall. — New York: St. Martin's Press, 1982. x, 227 p.; 23 cm. Includes index. 1. Women in politics — United States. 2. Feminism — United States. I. T.
HQ1236.R26 1982     305.4/2/0973 19     LC 82-10657     ISBN 0312887299

**Sapiro, Virginia.**     **4.5961**
The political integration of women: roles, socialization, and politics / Virginia Sapiro. — Urbana: University of Illinois Press, c1983. 205 p.; 24 cm. Includes index. 1. Women in politics — United States. 2. Political socialization — United States. 3. Sex role — United States. I. T.
HQ1236.S27 1983     306/.2 19     LC 82-2672     ISBN 0252009207

**Women in Washington: advocates for public policy / edited by Irene Tinker.**     **4.5962**
Beverly Hills: Sage Publications, c1983. 327 p.; 23 cm. — (Sage yearbooks in women's policy studies. v. 7) Includes index. 1. Women in politics — Washington (D.C.) — Addresses, essays, lectures. 2. Women — Government policy — United States — Addresses, essays, lectures. 3. Women in politics — Washington (D.C.) — Case studies — Addresses, essays, lectures. 4. Lobbying — Washington (D.C.) — Case studies — Addresses, essays, lectures. I. Tinker, Irene. II. Series.
HQ1236.W638 1983     305.4/2 19     LC 83-7761     ISBN 0803920695

**Women, war, and revolution / edited by Carol R. Berkin and Clara M. Lovett.**     **4.5963**
New York: Holmes & Meier, 1980. xiii, 310 p., [4] leaves of plates: ill.; 24 cm. Includes index. 1. Women in politics — History — Congresses. 2. War — Congresses. 3. Revolutions — Congresses. 4. Women and peace — Congresses. I. Berkin, Carol. II. Lovett, Clara Maria, 1939-
HQ1236.W65 1979     301.41/2     LC 79-26450     ISBN 0841905029

**Women, state, and party in Eastern Europe / edited by Sharon L. Wolchik and Alfred G. Meyer.**     **4.5964**
Durham: Duke University Press, 1985. xiv, 453 p.; 24 cm. (Duke Press policy studies.) Revised and updated papers first presented at the Conference on Changes in the Status of Women in Eastern Europe held at George Washington University, December 4-6, 1981. Series statement from jacket. Includes index. 1. Women — Europe, Eastern — Congresses. 2. Women in politics — Europe, Eastern — Congresses. 3. Women and socialism — Europe, Eastern — Congresses. 4. Feminism — Europe, Eastern — Congresses. I. Wolchik, Sharon L. II. Meyer, Alfred G. III. Conference on Changes in the Status of Women in Eastern Europe (1981: George Washington University) IV. Series.
HQ1236.5.E85 W65 1985     305.4/0947 19     LC 85-16262     ISBN 0822306603

**Women and politics in Western Europe / edited by Sylvia Bashevkin.**     **4.5965**
London: Cass, 1985. 101 p.: ill.; 23 cm. 1. Women in politics — Europe. I. Bashevkin, Sylvia B.
HQ1236.5.E87 W44     323.3/4/094 19     LC gb 85-38379     ISBN 0714632759

**Mansbridge, Jane J.**     **4.5966**
Why we lost the ERA / Jane J. Mansbridge. — Chicago: University of Chicago Press, 1986. xii, 327 p.; 24 cm. Includes index. 1. Women's rights — United States 2. Equal rights amendments — United States. 3. Feminism — United States. I. T.
HQ1236.5.U6 M37 1986     305.4/2/0973 19     LC 86-6954     ISBN 0226503577

**Vallance, Elizabeth (Elizabeth M.)**     **4.5967**
Women in the House: a study of women members of Parliament / by Elizabeth Vallance. — London: Athlone Press; [Atlantic Highlands] N.J.: distributed in U.S. and Canada by Humanities Press, 1979. 212 p.; 23 cm. Includes index. 1. Great Britain. Parliament. House of Commons. 2. Women in politics — Great Britain. 3. Legislators — Great Britain. I. T.
HQ1391.G7 V34     306/.2     LC 79-321679     ISBN 0485111861

**Carroll, Susan J., 1950-.**     **4.5968**
Women as candidates in American politics / Susan J. Carroll. — Bloomington: Indiana University Press, c1985. xv, 236 p.; 24 cm. Includes index. 1. Women in politics — United States. 2. Elections — United States I. T.
HQ1391.U5 C37 1985     305.4/3329 19     LC 84-42836     ISBN 0253366151

**Diamond, Irene, 1947-.**     **4.5969**
Sex roles in the state house / Irene Diamond. — New Haven: Yale University Press, 1977. xii, 214 p.: graphs; 22 cm. 1. Women in politics — New England. 2. Legislators — New England. 3. Sex role I. T.
HQ1391.U5 D52     301.41/2/0974     LC 76-49708     ISBN 0300021151

**Kirkpatrick, Jeane J.**     **4.5970**
Political woman / Jeane J. Kirkpatrick. — New York: Basic Books, [1974] xiii, 274 p.; 25 cm. 1. Women in politics — United States. 2. Political participation — United States. 3. Power (Social sciences) I. T.
HQ1391.U5 K57     329     LC 73-90130     ISBN 0465059708

**Mandel, Ruth B.**     **4.5971**
In the running: the new woman candidate / Ruth B. Mandel. — New Haven: Ticknor & Fields, 1981. xxi, 280 p.; 24 cm. 1. Women in politics — United States. 2. Women — United States 3. Feminism — United States. 4. Electioneering — United States. I. T.
HQ1391.U5 M36     305.4/2 19     LC 80-24190     ISBN 0899190278

**A Portrait of marginality: the political behavior of the American woman / edited by Marianne Githens and Jewel L. Prestage.**     **4.5972**
New York: D. McKay Co., c1977. xvii, 428 p.; 23 cm. 1. Women in politics — United States — Addresses, essays, lectures. 2. Marginality, Social — United States — Addresses, essays, lectures. I. Githens, Marianne. II. Prestage, Jewel Limar, 1931-
HQ1391.U5 P67     301.5/92     LC 76-58484     ISBN 0679303332 pbk

**Rossi, Alice S., 1922-.**     **4.5973**
Feminists in politics: a panel analysis of the First National Women's Conference / Alice S. Rossi. — New York: Academic Press, c1982. xxvii, 411 p.: ill.; 24 cm. 1. National Women's Conference (1st: 1977: Houston, Tex.) — Evaluation. 2. Women in politics — United States — Congresses — Evaluation. 3. Feminism — United States — Congresses — Evaluation. I. T.
HQ1391.U5 R67 1982     320/.088/042 19     LC 82-8807     ISBN 0125982801

## HQ1393–1395 WOMEN AND RELIGION

**The Feminist mystic, and other essays on women and spirituality / edited by Mary E. Giles.**     **4.5974**
New York: Crossroad, 1982. vii, 159 p.; 21 cm. 1. Women and religion I. Giles, Mary E.
HQ1393.F44 1982     305.4 19     LC 81-22130     ISBN 0824504321

**Daly, Mary.**　　　　　　　　　　　　　　　**4.5975**
The church and the second sex / Mary Daly, with the feminist postChristian introduction and new archaic afterwords by the author. — Boston: Beacon Press, c1985. xxx, 231 p.; 21 cm. Includes bibliographical references and index. 1. Catholic Church — Controversial literature 2. Feminism — Religious aspects — Christianity 3. Feminism — Religious aspects — Catholic Church 4. Sexism in religion 5. Women in Christianity I. T.
HQ1394.D28 1985　　261.8/344 19　　*LC* 85-47519　　*ISBN* 0807011010

**Stanton, Elizabeth Cady, 1815-1902.**　　　　　　**4.5976**
The woman's Bible. — New York: Arno Press, 1972 [c1895-98] 2 v. in 1.; 24 cm. — (American women: images and realities) 1. Bible — Commentaries 2. Women in the Bible I. Bible. English. Selections. 1972. II. T. III. Series.
HQ1395.S72　　220.8/30141/2　　*LC* 72-2626　　*ISBN* 040504481X

## HQ1399 OTHER SPECIAL TOPICS

**Men's studies modified: the impact of feminism on the academic** **4.5977**
**disciplines / editor, Dale Spender.**
1st ed. — Oxford; New York: Pergamon Press, 1981. xiii, 248 p.; 25 cm. (Athene series. 1) 1. Feminism — Addresses, essays, lectures. 2. Knowledge, Theory of — Addresses, essays, lectures. 3. Men — Addresses, essays, lectures. 4. Dominance (Psychology) — Addresses, essays, lectures. 5. Power (Social sciences) — Addresses, essays, lectures. I. Spender, Dale. II. Series.
HQ1399.M4 1981　　305.4/2 19　　*LC* 80-41818　　*ISBN* 008026770X

## HQ1402–1870.9 WOMEN, BY REGION OR COUNTRY

## HQ1402–1439 United States

**The Women's annual, ... the year in review.**　　**4.5978**
1980-1981. — Boston: G.K. Hall & Co., c1981-c1982. 2 v.; 25 cm. (Reference publication in women's studies.) Annual. 1. Feminism — United States — Yearbooks. I. Haber, Barbara. II. G.K. Hall & Company. III. Series.
HQ1402.W65　　305.4/2/0973　　*LC* 82-641994

**Women's rights almanac.**　　　　　　　　　　**4.5979**
1974-. Bethesda, Md.: Elizabeth Cady Stanton Pub. Co. v.: ill.; 21 cm. Annual. 1. Women — United States — Yearbooks. 2. Women's rights — United States — Yearbooks. 3. Almanacs, American
HQ1406.W65　　301.41/2/0973　　*LC* 74-77527

## HQ1410 History, General

**Clinton, Catherine, 1952-.**　　　　　　　　　**4.5980**
The other civil war: American women in the nineteenth century / Catherine Clinton; consulting editor, Eric Foner. — New York: Hill and Wang, c1984. xiii, 242 p.; 22 cm. — (American century series.) Includes index. 1. Women — United States — History — 19th century. 2. Feminism — United States — History — 19th century. I. T. II. Series.
HQ1410.C44 1984　　305.4/0973 19　　*LC* 84-525　　*ISBN* 0809074605

**Conway, Jill K., 1934-.**　　　　　　　　　　**4.5981**
The female experience in eighteenth– and nineteenth–century America: a guide to the history of American women / Jill K. Conway, with the assistance of Linda Kealey and Janet E. Schulte. — Princeton, N.J.: Princeton University Press, 1985, c1982. xxiv, 290 p.; 22 cm. Cover title: The female experience in 18th and 19th century America. Reprint. Originally published: New York: Garland Pub., 1982. 1. Women — United States — History — Sources. 2. Women — United States — History — 18th century — Bibliography. 3. Women — United States — History — 19th century — Bibliography. I. Kealey, Linda, 1947- II. Schulte, Janet E., 1958- III. T. IV. Title: Female experience in 18th and 19th century America.
HQ1410.C66 1985　　016.3054/0973 19　　*LC* 85-42665　　*ISBN* 0691005990

**Cott, Nancy F. comp.**　　　　　　　　　　　**4.5982**
Root of bitterness; documents of the social history of American women. Edited, and with an introd., by Nancy F. Cott. — [1st ed.]. — New York: Dutton, 1972. vii, 373 p.; 21 cm. 1. Women — United States — Social conditions. I. T.
HQ1410.C68　　301.41/2/0973　　*LC* 72-194870　　*ISBN* 0525473289

**Flexner, Eleanor, 1908-.**　　　　　　　　　　**4.5983**
Century of struggle: the woman's rights movement in the United States / Eleanor Flexner. Rev. ed. — Cambridge, Mass.: Belknap Press of Harvard University Press, 1975. xiii, 405 p., [6] leaves of plates: ill.; 25 cm. 1. Women —

United States 2. Women — Suffrage — United States. 3. Women's rights — United States I. T.
HQ1410.F6 1975　　301.41/2/0973　　*LC* 74-34542　　*ISBN* 0674106512

**Hooks, Bell.**　　　　　　　　　　　　　　**4.5984**
Ain't I a woman: black women and feminism / by Bell Hooks. — Boston, Mass.: South End Press, c1981. 205 p. Includes index. 1. Afro-American women 2. Feminism — United States — History. 3. United States — Race relations I. T.
HQ1410.H68　　HQ1410 H68.　　305.48/0973　　*LC* 81-51392　　*ISBN* 0896081281

**Kennedy, Susan Estabrook.**　　　　　　　　　**4.5985**
If all we did was to weep at home: a history of white working–class women in America / Susan Estabrook Kennedy. — Bloomington: Indiana University Press, c1979. xx, 331 p.; 22 cm. — (Minorities in modern America.) Includes index. 1. Women — United States — Social conditions. 2. Labor and laboring classes — United States 3. Social mobility — United States. 4. Working class women — United States. 5. Working class whites — United States. I. T. II. Series.
HQ1410.K45　　301.41/2/0973　　*LC* 78-20431　　*ISBN* 0253191548

**Kraditor, Aileen S. comp.**　　　　　　　　●**4.5986**
Up from the pedestal; selected writings in the history of American feminism, edited with an introd. by Aileen S. Kraditor. — Chicago: Quadrangle Books, [1968] 372 p.; 25 cm. 1. Feminism — United States — History — Addresses, essays, lectures. I. T.
HQ1410.K7　　301.41/2/0973　　*LC* 68-26443

**Matthaei, Julie A.**　　　　　　　　　　　　**4.5987**
An economic history of women in America: women's work, the sexual division of labor, and the development of capitalism / Julie A. Matthaei. — New York: Schocken Books; Brighton, Sussex: Harvester Press, 1982. xiv, 381 p.: ill.; 21 cm. 1. Women — United States — Economic conditions. 2. Sexual division of labor — History. 3. United States — Economic conditions — 1971- I. T.
HQ1410.M37 1982　　305.4/3 19　　*LC* 81-84111　　*ISBN* 0805238042

**Myres, Sandra L.**　　　　　　　　　　　　**4.5988**
Westering women and the frontier experience, 1800–1915 / Sandra L. Myres. — 1st ed. — Albuquerque: University of New Mexico Press, c1982. xxii, 365 p.: ill.; 24 cm. — (Histories of the American frontier.) 1. Women — West (U.S.) — History — 19th century. 2. Frontier and pioneer life — West (U.S.) I. T. II. Series.
HQ1410.M96 1982　　305.4/2/0978 19　　*LC* 82-6956　　*ISBN* 082630625X

**O'Neill, William L.**　　　　　　　　　　　●**4.5989**
Everyone was brave: the rise and fall of feminism in America / [by] William L. O'Neill. — Chicago: Quadrangle Books, 1969. xi, 369 p.; 22 cm. 1. Feminism — United States. 2. Women — United States I. T.
HQ1410.O64　　301.41/2/0973　　*LC* 71-78313

**Rosenberg, Rosalind, 1946-.**　　　　　　　　**4.5990**
Beyond separate spheres: intellectual roots of modern feminism / Rosalind Rosenberg. — New Haven: Yale University Press, c1982. xxii, 288 p.: ports.; 25 cm. Includes index. 1. Feminism — United States — Philosophy. 2. Women social scientists — United States — Attitudes — History. 3. Women college graduates — United States — Attitudes — History. I. T.
HQ1410.R67 1982　　305.4/2/0973 19　　*LC* 81-15967　　*ISBN* 0300026951

**Baird, Jo.**　　　　　　　　　　　　　　**4.5991**
Index to the first ten years, 1972–1982 / compiled by Jo Baird, Shirley Frank, and Beth Stafford; introduction by Florence Howe. — Old Westbury, NY: The Feminist Press, 1984. 48 p.; 28 cm. — Index of: Women's Studies Newsletter, Women's Studies Quarterly, Women's Studies International. 1. Women — Bibliography. I. Frank, Shirley II. Stafford, Beth III. Women's Studies Newsletter. IV. Women's Studies Quarterly. V. Women's Studies International. VI. T.
Z7961.B163 HQ1410.W612x

**Women of America: a history / Carol Ruth Berkin, Mary Beth** **4.5992**
**Norton.**
Boston: Houghton Mifflin Co., c1979. xv, 442 p.: ill.; 24 cm. Includes index. 1. Women — United States — History — Addresses, essays, lectures. I. Berkin, Carol. II. Norton, Mary Beth.
HQ1410.W65　　301.41/2/0973　　*LC* 78-69589　　*ISBN* 0395270677

## HQ1412 Biography, Collective

**Cantarow, Ellen.**　　　　　　　　　　　　**4.5993**
Moving the mountain: women working for social change / Ellen Cantarow, with Susan Gushee O'Malley and Sharon Hartman Strom. — Old Westbury, N.Y.: Feminist Press; New York: McGraw-Hill, c1980. xli, 166 p.: ill.; 23 cm. — (Women's lives, women's work.) Report of interviews with Florence

Luscomb, Ella Baker, and Jessie Lopez De La Cruz. Includes index. 1. Feminists — United States — Biography. 2. Women social reformers — United States — Biography. 3. Women in politics — United States — History. 4. United States — Social conditions I. O'Malley, Susan Gushee, 1942- II. Strom, Sharon Hartman. III. Luscomb, Florence, 1887- IV. Baker, Ella, 1903-1986. V. De La Cruz, Jessie Lopez, 1919- VI. T. VII. Series.
HQ1412.C36     301.24/2/0922     *LC* 79-11840     *ISBN* 0070204438

**Coles, Robert.**            **4.5994**
Women of crisis: lives of struggle and hope / Robert Coles and Jane Hallowell Coles. — New York: Delacorte Press/S. Lawrence, c1978. vi, 291 p.; 24 cm. (Radcliffe biography series.) 'A Merloyd Lawrence book.' 1. Women — United States — Biography. 2. Labor and laboring classes — United States — Addresses, essays, lectures. 3. Working class women — United States — Biography. 4. United States — Social conditions — Addresses, essays, lectures. I. Coles, Jane Hallowell. joint author. II. T. III. Series.
HQ1412.C64 1978     301.41/2/0973     *LC* 78-5068     *ISBN* 0440095360

**Coles, Robert.**            **4.5995**
Women of crisis II: lives of work and dreams / Robert Coles and Jane Hallowell Coles. — New York: Delacorte Press/S. Lawrence, c1980. xii, 237 p.; 24 cm. (Radcliffe biography series.) 'A Merloyd Lawrence book.' 1. Women — United States — Biography — Addresses, essays, lectures. 2. Labor and laboring classes — United States — Addresses, essays, lectures. 3. Working class women — United States — Biography — Addresses, essays, lectures. 4. United States — Social conditions — Addresses, essays, lectures. I. Coles, Jane Hallowell. joint author. II. T. III. Series.
HQ1412.C642     301.41/2/0973     *LC* 79-25210     *ISBN* 0440096359

**Flexner, James Thomas, 1908-.**            **4.5996**
An American saga: the story of Helen Thomas and Simon Flexner / by James Thomas Flexner. — 1st ed. — Boston: Little, Brown, c1984. xviii, 494 p.: ill.; 24 cm. Includes index. 1. Flexner, Helen Thomas, 1871-1956. 2. Flexner, Simon, 1863-1946. 3. Johns Hopkins University — History. 4. Pathologists — United States — Biography. 5. Feminists — United States — Biography. I. T.
HQ1412.F57 1984     616/.07/0924 B 19     *LC* 83-19918     *ISBN* 0316286117

**Herman, Kali.**            **4.5997**
Women in particular: an index to American women / by Kali Herman. — Phoenix, AZ: Oryx Press, 1984. xviii, 740 p.: ill.; 29 cm. Includes index. 1. Women — United States — Biography — Indexes. 2. Women — United States — Registers. I. T.
HQ1412.H47 1984     016.3054/0973 19     *LC* 84-1019     *ISBN* 0897740882

**Scott, Anne Firor, 1921-.**            **4.5998**
Making the invisible woman visible / Anne Firor Scott. — Urbana: University of Illinois Press, c1984. xxvii, 387 p.; 24 cm. 1. Women — United States — Biography. 2. Women — United States — History. 3. Women — Southern States — History. 4. Women — United States — Societies and clubs — History. 5. Women — United States — Addresses, essays, lectures. I. T.
HQ1412.S36 1984     305.4/0973 19     *LC* 83-17962     *ISBN* 0252011104

**Stanton, Elizabeth Cady, 1815-1902.**            **4.5999**
Elizabeth Cady Stanton, Susan B. Anthony, correspondence, writings, speeches / edited and with a critical commentary by Ellen Carol DuBois; foreword by Gerda Lerner. — New York: Schocken Books, 1981. xv, 272 p.: port.; 20 cm. — (Studies in the life of women) 1. Stanton, Elizabeth Cady, 1815-1902. 2. Anthony, Susan B. (Susan Brownell), 1820-1906. 3. Feminists — United States — Correspondence. 4. Feminism — United States — History — 19th century — Addresses, essays, lectures. I. Anthony, Susan B. (Susan Brownell), 1820-1906. II. DuBois, Ellen Carol, 1947- III. T.
HQ1412.S72 1981     305.4/092/2 19     *LC* 80-27603     *ISBN* 0805237593

## HQ1413 Biography, Individual, A–Z
(Too general to class elsewhere)

**Sklar, Kathryn Kish.**            **4.6000**
Catharine Beecher: a study in American domesticity. — New Haven: Yale University Press, 1973. xv, 356 p.: ill.; 25 cm. 1. Beecher, Catharine Esther, 1800-1878. I. T.
HQ1413.B4 S54     301.41/2/0924 B     *LC* 73-77166     *ISBN* 0300015801

**Eckhardt, Celia Morris, 1935-.**            **4.6001**
Fanny Wright: rebel in America / Celia Morris Eckhardt. — Cambridge, Mass.: Harvard University Press, 1984. xii, 337 p.: ill.; 25 cm. Includes index. 1. Wright, Frances, 1795-1852. 2. Feminists — United States — Biography. I. T.
HQ1413.D2 E25 1984     303.4/84 B 19     *LC* 83-8571     *ISBN* 0674294351

**Moynihan, Ruth Barnes.**            **4.6002**
Rebel for rights, Abigail Scott Duniway / Ruth Barnes Moynihan. — New Haven: Yale University Press, c1983. xv, 273 p., [8] p. of plates: ill.; 24 cm. — (Yale historical publications. Miscellany. 130) Based on the author's thesis (Ph. D.)—Yale University. Includes index. 1. Duniway, Abigail Scott, 1834-1915. 2. Suffragettes — United States — Biography. 3. Women's rights — United States — History — 19th century. 4. Women — Suffrage — United States — History — 19th century. 5. Women — Suffrage — Oregon — History — 19th century. I. T. II. Series.
HQ1413.D86 M69 1983     324.6/23/0924 B 19     *LC* 83-1142     *ISBN* 0300029527

**Hill, Mary Armfield.**            **4.6003**
Charlotte Perkins Gilman: the making of a radical feminist, 1860–1896 / Mary A. Hill. — Philadelphia: Temple University Press, 1980. xi, 362 p.: ill.; 24 cm. Includes index. 1. Gilman, Charlotte Perkins, 1860-1935. 2. Feminists — United States — Biography. I. T.
HQ1413.G54 H54     301.41/2/0924 B     *LC* 79-22395     *ISBN* 087722160X

**Bacon, Margaret Hope.**            **4.6004**
Valiant friend: the life of Lucretia Mott / by Margaret Hope Bacon. — New York, N.Y.: Walker, 1980. x, 265 p., [4] leaves of plates: ill.; 24 cm. Includes index. 1. Mott, Lucretia, 1793-1880. 2. Feminists — United States — Biography. 3. Abolitionists — United States — Biography. I. T.
HQ1413.M68 B33     361.2/092/4 B 19     *LC* 79-91253     *ISBN* 0802706452

**Griffith, Elisabeth.**            **4.6005**
In her own right: the life of Elizabeth Cady Stanton / Elisabeth Griffith. — New York: Oxford University Press, 1984. xx, 268 p., [16] p. of plates: ill.; 25 cm. 1. Stanton, Elizabeth Cady, 1815-1902. 2. Feminists — United States — Biography. 3. Suffragettes — United States — Biography. 4. Women's rights — United States — History. I. T.
HQ1413.S67 G74 1984     324.6/23/0924 B 19     *LC* 83-25120     *ISBN* 0195034406

## HQ1416–1419 History, to 1920

**Berg, Barbara J.**            **4.6006**
The remembered gate: origins of American feminism: the woman and the city, 1800–1860 / Barbara J. Berg. — New York: Oxford University Press, 1978. xvi, 334 p.; 22 cm. — (The Urban life in America series) Includes index. 1. Women — United States — History. 2. Women — United States — Social conditions. 3. Feminism — United States — History. 4. Urbanization — United States — History. I. T.
HQ1418.B5     301.41/2/0973     *LC* 76-51709     *ISBN* 0195022807

**Cott, Nancy F.**            **4.6007**
The bonds of womanhood: 'woman's sphere' in New England, 1780–1835 / Nancy F. Cott. New Haven: Yale University Press, 1977. xii, 225 p.; 22 cm. Includes index. 1. Women — New England — Social conditions. 2. Women — New England — History. I. T.
HQ1418.C67     301.41/2/09     *LC* 76-49728     *ISBN* 0300020236

**Degler, Carl N.**            **4.6008**
At odds: women and the family in America from the Revolution to the present / Carl N. Degler. — New York: Oxford University Press, 1980. xiv, 527 p.; 24 cm. 1. Women — United States — History. 2. Family — United States — History. I. T.
HQ1418.D44     301.41/2/0973     *LC* 79-17438     *ISBN* 0195026578

**James, Janet Wilson, 1918-.**            **4.6009**
Changing ideas about women in the United States, 1776–1825 / Janet Wilson James. — New York: Garland Pub., 1981. xxix, 337 p.; 24 cm. — (Modern American history.) Includes index. 1. Women — United States — Public opinion — History. 2. Public opinion — United States — History. I. T. II. Series.
HQ1418.J35 1981     305.4/2/0973 19     *LC* 80-8474     *ISBN* 082404858X

**Kerber, Linda K.**            **4.6010**
Women of the Republic: intellect and ideology in Revolutionary America / Linda K. Kerber. — Chapel Hill: Published for the Institute of Early American History and Culture by the University of North Carolina Press, c1980. xiv, 304 p.: ill.; 24 cm. Includes index. 1. Women — United States — History. 2. United States — History — Revolution, 1775-1783 I. T.
HQ1418.K47     305.4/2/0973     *LC* 79-28683     *ISBN* 0807814407

**Norton, Mary Beth.**            **4.6011**
Liberty's daughters: the Revolutionary experience of American women, 1750–1800 / Mary Beth Norton. — 1st ed. — Boston: Little, Brown, c1980. xvi, 384 p.: ill.; 24 cm. Includes index. 1. Women — United States — History — Colonial period, ca. 1600-1775 — Sources. 2. Women — United States — History — Revolution, 1775-1783 — Sources. 3. Women — United States —

History — 1783-1815 — Sources. 4. Women in politics — United States — History — Sources. I. T.
HQ1418.N67     301.41/2/0973     *LC* 79-25245     *ISBN* 0316612510

**Scott, Anne Firor, 1921-.**        • **4.6012**
The Southern lady: from pedestal to politics, 1830–1930. — Chicago: University of Chicago Press, [1970] xv, 247 p.; 23 cm. 1. Women — Southern States — History. I. T.
HQ1418.S38     301.41/2/0975     *LC* 73-123750     *ISBN* 0226743462

**Jensen, Joan M.**        **4.6013**
With these hands: women working on the land / Joan M. Jensen. — Old Westbury, N.Y.: Feminist Press; New York: McGraw-Hill, c1981. xxiii, 295 p.: ill.; 24 cm. (Women's lives, women's work.) Includes bibliographical references and index. 1. Rural women — United States — History. 2. Women farmers — United States — History. 3. Women in agriculture — United States — History. 4. Rural women in literature — History. 5. Minority women — United States — History. I. T. II. Series.
HQ1419.J39     305.4/3 19     *LC* 80-13944     *ISBN* 0912670908

**Leach, William, 1944-.**        **4.6014**
True love and perfect union: the feminist reform of sex and society / William Leach. — New York: Basic Books, c1980. xii, 449 p.; 24 cm. 1. Feminism — United States — History — 19th century. 2. Women — United States — History — 19th century. 3. Women — United States — Social conditions. I. T.
HQ1419.L4     305.4/2/0973 19     *LC* 80-50557     *ISBN* 0465087523

**Smith-Rosenberg, Carroll.**        **4.6015**
Disorderly conduct: visions of gender in Victorian America / Carroll Smith-Rosenberg. — 1st ed. — New York: Oxford University Press, 1986, c1985. viii, 357 p., [8] p. of plates: ill.; 25 cm. 1. Women — United States — History — 19th century. 2. Women — United States — Social conditions 3. Middle classes — United States — History. 4. Sex role — United States — History. I. T.
HQ1419.S58 1986     305.4/0973 19     *ISBN* 0195040392

## HQ1420 1920–

**Anderson, Karen, 1947-.**        **4.6016**
Wartime women: sex roles, family relations, and the status of women during World War II / Karen Anderson. — Westport, Conn.: Greenwood Press, 1981. 198 p.; 22 cm. — (Contributions in women's studies. ISSN 0147-104X; no. 20) Includes index. 1. Women — United States — History — 20th century. 2. World War, 1939-1945 — Social aspects — United States. I. T. II. Series.
HQ1420.A65     HQ1420 A65.     305.4/2/0973 19     *LC* 80-1703     *ISBN* 0313208840

**Bernard, Jessie Shirley, 1903-.**        **4.6017**
Women, wives, mothers: values and options / Jessie Bernard. — Chicago: Aldine Pub. Co., 1975. viii, 286 p.; 24 cm. 1. Women — United States — Social conditions. 2. Women — Psychology 3. Sex role I. T.
HQ1420.B47     301.41/2     *LC* 74-18210     *ISBN* 0202302806

**Friedan, Betty.**        • **4.6018**
The feminine mystique. New York, Norton [1963] 410 p. 22 cm. 1. Feminism — United States. 2. Women — United States — Social and moral conditions. 3. Women — Psychology 4. United States — Social conditions — 1945- I. T.
HQ1420.F7     396     *LC* 62-10097

**Gerson, Kathleen.**        **4.6019**
Hard choices: how women decide about work, career, and motherhood / Kathleen Gerson. — Berkeley: University of California Press, c1985. xix, 312 p.; 24 cm. (California series on social choice and political economy.) Includes index. 1. Women — United States — Social conditions. 2. Mothers — United States — Social conditions. 3. Women — Employment — United States — History. 4. Mothers — Employment — United States — History. 5. Family size — United States — History. 6. Women — United States — Psychology. I. T. II. Series.
HQ1420.G4 1985     305.4/0973 19     *LC* 84-8602     *ISBN* 0520051742

**Hartmann, Susan M.**        **4.6020**
The home front and beyond: American women in the 1940s / Susan M. Hartmann. — Boston: Twayne Publishers, c1982. xi, 235 p.: ill.; 23 cm. — (American women in the twentieth century.) Includes index. 1. Women — United States — History — 20th century. 2. World War, 1939-1945 — Women 3. Women — Employment — United States — History. 4. Women — United States — Social conditions. I. T. II. Series.
HQ1420.H34 1982     HQ1420 H34 1982.     305.4/0973 19     *LC* 82-6209     *ISBN* 080579901X

**Kaledin, Eugenia.**        **4.6021**
Mothers and more: American women in the 1950s / Eugenia Kaledin. — Boston: Twayne Publishers, c1984. 260 p., [2] p. of plates: ill., ports.; 23 cm. (American women in the twentieth century.) Includes index. 1. Women — United States — History — 20th century — Addresses, essays, lectures.

2. Mothers — United States — History — 20th century — Addresses, essays, lectures. 3. Feminism — United States — History — 20th century — Addresses, essays, lectures. I. T. II. Series.
HQ1420.K35 1984     305.4/0973 19     *LC* 84-15656     *ISBN* 0805799044

**Our American sisters: women in American life and thought /**     **4.6022**
[compiled by] Jean E. Friedman, William G. Shade.
3rd ed. — Lexington, Mass.: D.C. Heath, c1982. ix, 593 p.: ill.; 24 cm. 1. Women — United States — History — Addresses, essays, lectures. 2. Women — United States — Social conditions — Addresses, essays, lectures. I. Friedman, Jean E. II. Shade, William G.
HQ1420.O93 1982     305.4/0973 19     *LC* 81-84827     *ISBN* 0669047554

**Sapiro, Virginia.**        **4.6023**
Women in American society: an introduction to women's studies / Virginia Sapiro. — Palo Alto, Calif.: Mayfield Pub. Co., c1986. xvi, 502 p.: ill.; 24 cm. Includes index. 1. Women — United States 2. Women's studies — United States. I. T.
HQ1420.S27 1986     305.4/0973 19     *LC* 85-62622     *ISBN* 0874847087

**Simms, Margaret C.**        **4.6024**
Slipping through the cracks: the status of black women / edited by Margaret C. Simms and Julianne Malveaux. — New Brunswick, N.J.: Transaction Books, c1986. 302 p. — (Black studies sociology, 0034-6446) Papers from a conference. 1. Afro-American women — United States — Congresses I. Malveaux, Julianne. II. T. III. Series.
HQ1420 S55 1986     *ISBN* 0887386628

**Zelman, Patricia G.**        **4.6025**
Women, work, and national policy: the Kennedy–Johnson years / by Patricia G. Zelman. — Ann Arbor, Mich.: UMI Research Press, c1982. x, 160 p.; 24 cm. — (Studies in American history and culture. no. 33) Revision of thesis (Ph.D.)—Ohio State University, 1980. Includes index. 1. Women — Government policy — United States — History. I. T. II. Series.
HQ1420.Z44 1982     305.4/0973 19     *LC* 81-16351     *ISBN* 0835712826

## HQ1423–1426 REFORM LITERATURE

**DuBois, Ellen Carol, 1947-.**        **4.6026**
Feminism and suffrage: the emergence of an independent women's movement in America, 1848–1869 / Ellen Carol DuBois. — Ithaca: Cornell University Press, 1978. 220 p.; 22 cm. Includes index. 1. Feminism — United States — History. 2. Women's rights — United States — History. I. T.
HQ1423.D8     322.4/4/0973     *LC* 77-90902     *ISBN* 0801410436

**Epstein, Barbara Leslie, 1944-.**        **4.6027**
The politics of domesticity: women, evangelism, and temperance in nineteenth-century America / by Barbara Leslie Epstein. — 1st ed. — Middletown, Conn.: Wesleyan University Press; Irvington, N.Y.: distributed by Columbia University Press, c1981. 188 p.; 24 cm. Includes index. 1. Feminism — United States — History — 19th century. 2. Temperance — History — 19th century. 3. Women in Christianity — United States — History — 19th century. 4. Revivals — United States — History — 19th century. 5. United States — Church history I. T.
HQ1423.E67     305.4/2     *LC* 80-16671     *ISBN* 0819550507

**Grimké, Sarah Moore, 1792-1873.**        • **4.6028**
Letters on the equality of the sexes and the condition of woman, addressed to Mary S. Parker. — New York: B. Franklin, [1970] 128 p.; 19 cm. — (Selected essays in history, economics, and social science, 188) (Burt Franklin research and source works series, 575.) Reprint of the 1838 ed. 1. Women's rights — United States 2. Women — United States I. Parker, David. Mary S. II. T.
HQ1423.G8 1970     301.41/2     *LC* 79-133542     *ISBN* 0833714597

**Hersh, Blanche Glassman, 1928-.**        **4.6029**
The slavery of sex: feminist-abolitionists in America / Blanche Glassman Hersh. — Urbana: University of Illinois Press, c1978. xi, 280 p.; 24 cm. Includes index. 1. Feminism — United States — History. 2. Women's rights — United States — History. 3. Feminists — United States — History. 4. Abolitionists — History. I. T.
HQ1423.H47     301.41/2/0973     *LC* 78-14591     *ISBN* 025200695X

**Lebsock, Suzanne.**        **4.6030**
The free women of Petersburg: status and culture in a southern town, 1784–1860 / Suzanne Lebsock. — 1st ed. — New York: Norton, c1984. xx, 326 p.: map; 22 cm. Includes index. 1. Women — Virginia — Petersburg — History — 19th century. 2. Women — Virginia — Petersburg — Social conditions. 3. Women — Virginia — Petersburg — Economic conditions.

4. Afro-American women — Virginia — Petersburg — History — 19th century. 5. Petersburg (Va.) — History — 19th century. I. T.
HQ1423.L39 1984    305.4/2/09755581 19    *LC* 83-8065    *ISBN* 0393017389

## HQ1426 1860/70–

### HQ1426 A–D

**Bergmann, Barbara R.**    4.6031
The economic emergence of women / Barbara R. Bergmann. — New York: Basic Books, c1986. x, 372 p. Includes index. 1. Women — United States — Economic conditions. 2. Women — Employment — United States. 3. Sex discrimination against women — United States. 4. Housewives — United States. I. T.
HQ1426.B429 1986    305.4/2/0973 19    *LC* 85-73876    *ISBN* 0465017967

**Blau, Francine D.**    4.6032
The economics of women, men, and work / Francine D. Blau, Marianne A. Ferber. — Englewood Cliffs, N.J.: Prentice-Hall, c1986. xiv, 365 p.; 24 cm. 1. Women — United States — Economic conditions. 2. Women — United States — Social conditions. 3. Women — Employment — United States. 4. Housewives — United States. 5. Sexual division of labor — United States. I. Ferber, Marianne A., 1923- II. T.
HQ1426.B62 1986    305.3/0973 19    *LC* 85-30746    *ISBN* 0132337193

**Boles, Janet K., 1944-.**    4.6033
The politics of the equal rights amendment: conflict and the decision process / Janet K. Boles. — New York: Longman, c1979. x, 214 p.; 21 cm. Includes index. 1. Equal Rights Amendment Project. 2. Equal rights amendments — United States. I. T.
HQ1426.B68    342/.73/087    *LC* 78-11052    *ISBN* 0582280915.
*ISBN* 0582280907 pbk

**Borenstein, Audrey, 1930-.**    4.6034
Chimes of change and hours: views of older women in twentieth–century America / Audrey Borenstein. — Rutherford [N.J.]: Fairleigh Dickinson University Press; London: Associated University Presses, c1983. 518 p.; 24 cm. Includes indexes. 1. Middle aged women — United States — Social conditions. 2. Aged women — United States — Social conditions. I. T.
HQ1426.B685 1983    305.2/44/0973 19    *LC* 82-48159    *ISBN* 0838631703

**Buhle, Mari Jo, 1943-.**    4.6035
Women and American socialism, 1780–1920 / Mari Jo Buhle. — Urbana: University of Illinois Press, c1981. p. cm. — (The Working class in American history) Includes index. 1. Feminism — United States — History. 2. Women and socialism — United States — History. 3. United States — History — 1865-1921 I. T.
HQ1426.B82    305.4/2/0973 19    *LC* 80-719    *ISBN* 0252008731

**Building feminist theory: essays from Quest.**    4.6036
New York, N.Y.: Longman, c1981. xxiii, 280 p.; 23 cm. Includes index. 1. Feminism — United States — Addresses, essays, lectures. I. Quest (Washington, D.C.)
HQ1426.B83    305.4/2/0973 19    *LC* 80-28842    *ISBN* 0582282101

**Capitalist patriarchy and the case for socialist feminism / edited**    4.6037
**by Zillah R. Eisenstein.**
New York: Monthly Review Press, c1979 [i.e. c1978] vii, 394 p.; 21 cm. 1. Feminism — United States — Addresses, essays, lectures. 2. Women and socialism — Addresses, essays, lectures. I. Eisenstein, Zillah R.
HQ1426.C244    301.41/2    *LC* 77-76162    *ISBN* 0853454191

**Chafe, William Henry.**    • 4.6038
The American woman; her changing social, economic, and political roles, 1920–1970. — New York: Oxford University Press, 1972. xiii, 351 p.; 22 cm. Based on author's dissertation, Columbia. 1. Women — United States — History. 2. Women's rights — United States I. T.
HQ1426.C45    301.41/2/0973    *LC* 72-77496    *ISBN* 0195015789

**Chafe, William Henry.**    4.6039
Women and equality: changing patterns in American culture / William H. Chafe. — New York: Oxford University Press, 1977. xiii, 207 p.; 22 cm. 1. Women — Social conditions 2. Feminism — United States. 3. Sex role 4. Equality — United States. I. T.
HQ1426.C453    301.41/2/0973    *LC* 76-42639    *ISBN* 0195021584

**Dignity: lower income women tell of their lives and struggles:**    4.6040
**oral histories / compiled by Fran Leeper Buss; introduction by**
**Susan Contratto.**
Ann Arbor: University of Michigan Press, c1985. 290 p.: ill.; 23 cm. (Women and culture series.) 1. Working class women — United States — Case studies. 2. Urban women — United States — Case studies. 3. Women, Poor — United States — Case studies. 4. Women — Employment — United States — Case studies. I. Buss, Fran Leeper, 1942- II. Series.
HQ1426.D54 1985    305.4/3 19    *LC* 85-990    *ISBN* 047206357X

**Douglass, Frederick, 1817?-1895.**    4.6041
Frederick Douglass on women's rights / Philip S. Foner, editor. Westport, Conn.: Greenwood Press, 1976. x, 190 p.: ill.; 22 cm. (Contributions in Afro-American and African studies. no. 25) 1. Douglass, Frederick, 1817?-1895. 2. Women's rights — United States — Addresses, essays, lectures. I. Foner, Philip Sheldon, 1910- II. T. III. Series.
HQ1426.D82 1976    323.4    *LC* 76-5326    *ISBN* 0837188954

### HQ1426 E–G

**Ehrenreich, Barbara.**    4.6042
For her own good: 150 years of the experts' advice to women / Barbara Ehrenreich, Deirdre English. — 1st ed. — Garden City, N.Y.: Anchor Press/Doubleday, 1978. x, 325 p.; 22 cm. 1. Mother and child — History. 2. Women's health services — Social aspects — United States — History. 3. Women's rights — United States — History. 4. Women — United States — Social conditions. I. English, Deirdre. II. T.
HQ1426.E38    305.4    *LC* 77-76234    *ISBN* 0385126506

**Eisenstein, Hester.**    4.6043
Contemporary feminist thought / Hester Eisenstein. — Boston: G.K. Hall, c1983. xx, 196 p.; 23 cm. — (Publication in women's studies.) Includes index. 1. Feminism — United States — History. 2. Feminism — United States. I. T. II. Series.
HQ1426.E39 1983    305.4/2/0973 19    *LC* 83-11867    *ISBN* 0816190429

**Eisenstein, Zillah R.**    4.6044
Feminism and sexual equality: crisis in liberal America / Zillah Eisenstein. — New York: Monthly Review Press, c1984. 266 p.; 21 cm. 1. Feminism — Political aspects — United States. 2. Liberalism — United States. 3. Conservatism — United States. 4. Sex discrimination against women — United States. 5. United States — Politics and government — 1981- I. T.
HQ1426.E395 1984    305.4/2/0973 19    *LC* 84-4606    *ISBN* 0853456453

**Evans, Sara M. (Sara Margaret), 1943-.**    4.6045
Personal politics: the roots of women's liberation in the civil rights movement and the new left / by Sara Evans. — 1st ed. — New York: Knopf: distributed by Random House, 1979. xii, 274 p. Includes index. 1. Women — United States — Social conditions. 2. Radicalism — United States. 3. Feminism — United States. 4. Civil rights — United States I. T.
HQ1426.E9 1979    HQ1426 E9 1979.    301.41/2/0973    *LC* 78-54929    *ISBN* 0394419111

*[handwritten: HQ 1426 E9 1979]*

**Feminism and philosophy / edited by Mary Vetterling–Braggin,**    4.6046
**Frederick A. Elliston, Jane English.**
Totowa, N.J.: Littlefield, Adams, 1977. xii, 452 p.; 21 cm. — (A Littlefield, Adams quality paperback; no. 335) 1. Feminism — United States — Addresses, essays, lectures. 2. Sex role — Addresses, essays, lectures. 3. Sex discrimination against women — United States — Addresses, essays, lectures. 4. Women's rights — United States — Addresses, essays, lectures. I. Vetterling-Braggin, Mary. II. Elliston, Frederick. III. English, Jane, 1947-
HQ1426.F45    301.41/2/0973    *LC* 77-24207

**Feminist theory: a critique of ideology / edited by Nannerl O.**    4.6047
**Keohane, Michelle Z. Rosaldo, and Barbara C. Gelpi.**
Chicago: University of Chicago Press, 1982. xii, 306 p.; 23 cm. Articles originally published in vol. 6, no. 4, and vol. 7, no. 1 & 2 of Signs. 1. Feminism — United States — Addresses, essays, lectures. I. Keohane, Nannerl O., 1940- II. Rosaldo, Michelle Zimbalist. III. Gelpi, Barbara Charlesworth.
HQ1426.F474 1982    305.4/2 19    *LC* 82-6953    *ISBN* 0226431630

**Ferree, Myra Marx.**    4.6048
Controversy and coalition: the new feminist movement / Myra Marx Ferree, Beth B. Hess. — Boston: Twayne Publishers, c1985. xi, 215 p.: ill.; 23 cm. (Social movements past & present) Includes index. 1. Feminism — United States. I. Hess, Beth B., 1928- II. T.
HQ1426.F475 1985    305.4/2/0973 19    *LC* 84-22421    *ISBN* 0805797076

**Fishburn, Katherine, 1944-.**    4.6049
Women in popular culture: a reference guide / Katherine Fishburn. — Westport, Conn.: Greenwood Press, 1982. 267 p.; 25 cm. — (American popular

culture. 0193-6859) 1. Women in popular culture — United States — History. I. T. II. Series.
HQ1426.F685 1982     305.4/0973 19     *LC* 81-13421     *ISBN* 0313221529

**Freeman, Jo.**           **4.6050**
The politics of women's liberation: a case study of an emerging social movement and its relation to the policy process / Jo Freeman. — New York: McKay, [1975] xvi, 268 p.; 22 cm. Includes index. 1. Feminism — United States. 2. Women's rights — United States I. T.
HQ1426.F84     301.41/2/0973     *LC* 74-25208     *ISBN* 0679302840

**Fulenwider, Claire Knoche.**           **4.6051**
Feminism in American politics: a study of ideological influence / Claire Knoche Fulenwider. — New York, N.Y.: Praeger, c1980. xi, 165 p.; 24 cm. (American political parties and elections.) 'Copublished with the Eagleton Institute of Politics, Rutgers University.' Includes index. 1. Feminism — United States. 2. Women in politics — United States. I. Eagleton Institute of Politics. II. T. III. Series.
HQ1426.F88     301.41/2/0973     *LC* 79-25131     *ISBN* 0030534615

**Gelb, Joyce, 1940-.**           **4.6052**
Women and public policies / Joyce Gelb and Marian Lief Palley. — Princeton, N.J.: Princeton University Press, c1982. xiv, 198 p.; 22 cm. 1. Women in politics — United States. 2. Feminism — United States. 3. United States — Social policy I. Palley, Marian Lief, 1939- II. T.
HQ1426.G35 1982     305.4/2/0973 19     *LC* 82-400     *ISBN* 0691076391

**Gilman, Charlotte Perkins, 1860-1935.**     • **4.6053**
Women and economics. [New York] Source Book Press [1970, c1898] vii, 340 p. 22 cm. 1. Women — Economic conditions. I. T.
HQ1426.G45 1970     301.41/2     *LC* 78-134188     *ISBN* 0876810814

## *HQ1426 H–M*

**Hayden, Dolores.**           **4.6054**
The grand domestic revolution: a history of feminist designs for American homes, neighborhoods, and cities / Dolores Hayden. — Cambridge, Mass.: MIT Press, c1981. 367 p.: ill.; 24 cm. 1. Feminism — United States — Addresses, essays, lectures. 2. Division of labor — Addresses, essays, lectures. 3. Housewives — United States — Addresses, essays, lectures. 4. Home economics — United States — Addresses, essays, lectures. 5. Women and socialism — United States — Addresses, essays, lectures. 6. Architecture, Domestic — United States — Addresses, essays, lectures. I. T.
HQ1426.H33     305.4/2 19     *LC* 80-18917     *ISBN* 0262081083

**Hole, Judith.**     • **4.6055**
Rebirth of feminism / [by] Judith Hole and Ellen Levine. — [New York]: Quadrangle Books [1971] xiii, 488 p.: ill.; 24 cm. 1. Feminism — United States. 2. Women — United States 3. Women's rights — United States I. Levine, Ellen, joint author. II. T.
HQ1426.H67     301.41/2/0973     *LC* 70-162808

**Hooks, Bell.**           **4.6056**
Feminist theory from margin to center / Bell Hooks. — Boston, MA: South End Press, c1984. 174 p.; 22 cm. 1. Feminism — United States — Evaluation. 2. Afro-American women — Attitudes. 3. Marginality, Social — United States. I. T.
HQ1426.H675 1984     305.4/2/0973 19     *LC* 84-50937     *ISBN* 0896082229

**Feminist frameworks: alternative theoretical accounts of the**     **4.6057**
**relations between women and men / Alison M. Jaggar, Paula S. Rothenberg.**
2nd ed. — New York: McGraw-Hill, c1984. xviii, 446 p.; 24 cm. 1. Feminism — United States — Addresses, essays, lectures. 2. Sexism — Addresses, essays, lectures. 3. Social institutions — Addresses, essays, lectures. 4. Women's rights — Addresses, essays, lectures. 5. Social change — Addresses, essays, lectures. I. Rothenberg, Paula S., 1943- II. Jaggar, Alison M.
HQ1426.J325 1984     305.4/2 19     *LC* 83-17518     *ISBN* 0070322511

**Joseph, Gloria I.**           **4.6058**
Common differences: conflicts in black and white feminist perspectives / by Gloria I. Joseph and Jill Lewis. — 1st ed. — New York: Anchor Press/Doubleday, 1981. xii, 300 p.; 21 cm. Includes index. 1. Feminism — United States — Addresses, essays, lectures. 2. Afro-American women — Addresses, essays, lectures. 3. United States — Race relations — Addresses, essays, lectures. I. Lewis, Jill. joint author. II. T.
HQ1426.J67     305.4/2/0973 19     *LC* 79-6885     *ISBN* 0385142714

**Klein, Ethel, 1952-.**           **4.6059**
Gender politics: from consciousness to mass politics / Ethel Klein. — Cambridge, Mass.: Harvard University Press, 1984. x, 209 p.: ill.; 25 cm. Includes index. 1. Women in politics — United States — History — 20th

century. 2. Feminism — United States — History — 20th century. 3. Women's rights — United States — History — 20th century. 4. Sex role — United States — History — 20th century. I. T.
HQ1426.K58 1984     305.4/2/0973 19     *LC* 84-8992     *ISBN* 0674341961

**Lemons, J. Stanley.**     • **4.6060**
The woman citizen; social feminism in the 1920's [by] J. Stanley Lemons. — Urbana: University of Illinois Press, [1973] xiii, 266 p.; 24 cm. 1. Feminism — United States. 2. Women — United States — Social conditions. 3. Women in politics — United States. I. T.
HQ1426.L45     301.41/2/0973     *LC* 72-75488     *ISBN* 0252002679

**Melder, Keith.**           **4.6061**
Beginnings of sisterhood: the American woman's rights movement, 1800–1850 / Keith E. Melder. — New York: Schocken Books, 1977. 199 p.; 21 cm. — (Studies in the life of women) Includes index. 1. Women's rights — United States — History. 2. Feminism — United States — History. I. T.
HQ1426.M44 1977     301.41/2/0973     *LC* 76-53611     *ISBN* 080523649X

**Men's ideas/women's realities: Popular science, 1870–1915 /**     **4.6062**
**edited by Louise Michele Newman.**
New York: Pergamon Press, c1985. xxviii, 337 p.; 24 cm. — (Athene series.) 1. Feminism — United States — History — Addresses, essays, lectures. 2. Women's rights — United States — History — Addresses, essays, lectures. 3. Women — United States — Social conditions — Addresses, essays, lectures. I. Newman, Louise Michele. II. Popular science (New York, N.Y.) III. Series.
HQ1426.M46 1985     305.4/2/0973 19     *LC* 84-1072     *ISBN* 0080319300

**Morgan, Robin.**           **4.6063**
Going too far: the personal chronicle of a feminist / by Robin Morgan. — 1st ed. — New York: Random House, c1977. xiii, 333 p.; 25 cm. Includes index. 1. Morgan, Robin. 2. Feminism — United States — History — Addresses, essays, lectures. 3. Feminists — United States — Correspondence. I. T.
HQ1426.M84     301.41/2/0924     *LC* 76-53507     *ISBN* 0394482271

**Morgan, Robin. comp.**     • **4.6064**
Sisterhood is powerful; an anthology of writings from the women's liberation movement. — [1st ed.]. — New York: Random House, [1970] xli, 602 p.; illus.; 22 cm. 1. Women's rights — United States — Addresses, essays, lectures. 2. Feminism — United States — Addresses, essays, lectures. I. T.
HQ1426.M85     301.41/2/08     *LC* 70-117694

## *HQ1426 N–Z*

**NASW Conference on Social Work Practice with Women (1st:**     **4.6065**
**1980: Washington, D.C.)**
Women, power, and change: selected papers from Social Work Practice in Sexist Society: First NASW Conference on Social Work Practice with Women, September 14–16, 1980, Washington, D.C. / Ann Weick and Susan T. Vandiver, editors. — Washington, D.C.: National Association of Social Workers, c1982. xviii, 214 p.; 23 cm. 'NASW catalog no.: CPB-092-C'—T.p. verso. 1. Women — United States — Social conditions — Addresses, essays, lectures. 2. Sex discrimination against women — United States — Addresses, essays, lectures. 3. Women — Services for — United States — Addresses, essays, lectures. 4. Power (Social sciences) — Addresses, essays, lectures. 5. Social change — Addresses, essays, lectures. I. Weick, Ann. II. Vandiver, Susan T. III. National Association of Social Workers. IV. T. V. Title: Social work practice in sexist society.
HQ1426.N37 1980     305.4/2/0973 19     *LC* 81-83429     *ISBN* 0871010925

**The New woman's survival catalog. [Editors: Kirsten Grimstad**     **4.6066**
**and Susan Rennie]**
New York, Coward, McCann & Geoghegan [1973] 223 p. illus. 37 cm. 1. Feminism — Information services — United States. 2. Feminism — United States — Bibliography. I. Grimstad, Kirsten. ed. II. Rennie, Susan, ed.
HQ1426.N48 1973     016.30141/2/0973     *LC* 73-85371     *ISBN* 0698105672

**Porterfield, Amanda, 1947-.**           **4.6067**
Feminine spirituality in America: from Sarah Edwards to Martha Graham / Amanda Porterfield. — Philadelphia: Temple University Press, 1980. 238 p.; 22 cm. 1. Women — United States — Attitudes. 2. Feminism — United States. 3. Sex role in literature 4. Spirituality — Christianity. I. T.
HQ1426.P67     305.4/2/0973     *LC* 80-12116     *ISBN* 0877221758

**Robinson, Lillian S.**           **4.6068**
Sex, class, and culture / Lillian S. Robinson. — Bloomington: Indiana University Press, c1978. xxxiii, 349 p.; 21 cm. 1. Feminism — United States — Addresses, essays, lectures. 2. Culture — Addresses, essays, lectures.

3. Criticism (Philosophy) — Addresses, essays, lectures. 4. Women and literature — United States — Addresses, essays, lectures. I. T.
HQ1426.R72     305.4/0973 19     *LC* 85-29838     *ISBN* 0416012418

**Weibel, Kathryn.**                                                            **4.6069**
Mirror, mirror: images of women reflected in popular culture / Kathryn Weibel. Garden City, N.Y.: Anchor Books, 1977. xxii, 256 p., [4] leaves of plates: ill.; 18 cm. 1. Women in popular culture 2. Women — United States — Social conditions. 3. Sex role 4. United States — Popular culture I. T.
HQ1426.W423     301.41/2/0973     *LC* 76-47835     *ISBN* 0385111312

**Welter, Barbara.**                                                           **4.6070**
Dimity convictions: the American woman in the nineteenth century / Barbara Welter. — Athens: Ohio University Press, 1976. 230 p. 1. Feminism — United States — History. 2. American literature — Women authors — History and criticism. 3. United States — Social life and customs — 19th century I. T.
HQ1426.W425     HQ1426 W425.     *LC* 76-8305     *ISBN* 0821403524

**Freeman, Jo.**                                                               **4.6071**
Women: a feminist perspective / edited by Jo Freeman. — 3rd ed. — Palo Alto, Calif.: Mayfield Pub. Co., c1984. xxiv, 615 p.; 23 cm. 1. Women — United States — Social conditions — Addresses, essays, lectures. 2. Feminism — United States — Addresses, essays, lectures. I. T.
HQ1426.W62 1984     305.4/2/0973 19     *LC* 83-62829     *ISBN* 0874845688

**Women, power, and policy / edited by Ellen Boneparth.**                      **4.6072**
New York: Pergamon Press, c1982. xii, 319 p.; 24 cm. 1. Feminism — United States — Political aspects — Addresses, essays, lectures. I. Boneparth, Ellen, 1945-
HQ1426.W645 1982     305.4/2/0973 19     *LC* 81-13825     *ISBN* 008028048X

## HQ1438–1439 BY STATE OR CITY

**Clinton, Catherine, 1952-.**                                                 **4.6073**
The plantation mistress: woman's world in the old South / Catherine Clinton. — 1st ed. — New York: Pantheon Books, 1983 (c1982). xix, 331 p.; 25 cm. Includes index. 1. Plantation owners' wives — Southern States. 2. Women plantation owners — Southern States. 3. Slaveholders — Southern States. 4. Patriarchy — Southern states. 5. Southern States — Social life and customs — 1775-1865 I. T.
HQ1438.A13 C58 1982     305.4/2/0975 19     *LC* 82-3549     *ISBN* 0394516869

**Fairbanks, Carol, 1935-.**                                                   **4.6074**
Farm women on the prairie frontier: a sourcebook for Canada and the United States / by Carol Fairbanks and Sara Brooks Sundberg; illustrations by Ted F. Myers. — Metuchen, N.J.: Scarecrow Press, 1983. xiii, 237 p.: ill.; 23 cm. Includes index. 1. Rural women — West (U.S.) — History — Addresses, essays, lectures. 2. Rural women — Northwest, Canadian — History — Addresses, essays, lectures. 3. Frontier and pioneer life — West (U.S.) — History — Addresses, essays, lectures. 4. Frontier and pioneer life — Northwest, Canadian — History — Addresses, essays, lectures. 5. American literature — Women authors — Bibliography. 6. Canadian literature — Women authors — Bibliography. I. Sundberg, Sara Brooks, 1951- II. T.
HQ1438.A17 F34 1983     305.4/0971 19     *LC* 83-4498     *ISBN* 0810816253

**Stratton, Joanna L.**                                                        **4.6075**
Pioneer women: voices from the Kansas frontier / Joanna L. Stratton; introd. by Arthur M. Schlesinger, Jr. — New York: Simon and Schuster, c1981. 319 p., [16] leaves of plates: ill.; 24 cm. Includes index. 1. Women pioneers — Kansas — History. 2. Frontier and pioneer life — Kansas. I. T.
HQ1438.K2 S77     305.4/2/09781     *LC* 80-15960     *ISBN* 0671226118

**Jeffrey, Julie Roy.**                                                        **4.6076**
Frontier women: the trans–Mississippi West, 1840–1880 / Julie Roy Jeffrey. — 1st ed. — New York: Hill and Wang, 1979. xvi, 240 p.; 22 cm. (American century series) Includes index. 1. Women — West (U.S.) — History. 2. Frontier and pioneer life — West (U.S.) I. T.
HQ1438.W45 J43 1979     301.41/2/0978     *LC* 79-12279     *ISBN* 0809048035

**Hewitt, Nancy A., 1951-.**                                                   **4.6077**
Women's activism and social change: Rochester, New York, 1822–1872 / Nancy A. Hewitt. — Ithaca, N.Y.: Cornell University Press, 1984. 281 p.; 24 cm. 1. Feminism — New York (State) — Rochester — History — 19th century. 2. Rochester (N.Y.) — Social conditions. I. T.
HQ1439.R62 H48 1984     305.4/2/0974789 19     *LC* 83-45940     *ISBN* 0801416167

**Blackwelder, Julia Kirk, 1943-.**                                            **4.6078**
Women of the Depression: caste and culture in San Antonio, 1929–1939 / by Julia Kirk Blackwelder. — 1st ed. — College Station: Texas A & M University

Press, c1984. xviii, 279 p.: ill.; 24 cm. — (Texas A & M southwestern studies. no. 2) Includes index. 1. Women — Texas — San Antonio — Economic conditions. 2. Working class women — Texas — San Antonio — Economic conditions. 3. Afro-American women — Texas — San Antonio — Economic conditions. 4. Mexican American women — Texas — San Antonio — Economic conditions. 5. Depressions — 1929 — United States 6. San Antonio (Tex.) — Race relations. I. T. II. Series.
HQ1439.S2 B42 1984     305.4/09764/351 19     *LC* 83-40496     *ISBN* 0890961778

## HQ1451–1590 Canada. Latin America

**A Flannel shirt and liberty: British emigrant gentlewomen in the**           **4.6079**
**Canadian West, 1880–1914 / edited by Susan Jackel.**
Vancouver: University of British Columbia Press, c1982. xxvii, 229 p., [12] p. of plates: ill.; 24 cm. 1. Women — Canada, Western — History — Addresses, essays, lectures. 2. British — Canada — History — Addresses, essays, lectures. 3. Canada, Western — Emigration and immigration — History — Addresses, essays, lectures. I. Jackel, Susan.
HQ1453.F55 1982     305.4/8821/0712 19     *LC* 82-183238     *ISBN* 0774801492

**Luxton, Meg.**                                                               **4.6080**
More than a labour of love: three generations of women's work in the home / Meg Luxton. — Toronto, Ont.: Women's Press, c1980. 260 p.: ill.; 22 cm. — (Women's Press domestic labour series. v. 2) 1. Housewives — Canada — Longitudinal studies. 2. Wives — Canada — Longitudinal studies. 3. Mothers — Canada — Longitudinal studies. 4. Home economics — Canada — Longitudinal studies. I. T. II. Series.
HQ1455.L89 1980     305.4/3 19     *LC* 81-173398     *ISBN* 0889610622

**Silverman, Eliane Leslau.**                                                  **4.6081**
The last best West: women on the Alberta frontier, 1880–1930 / by Eliane Leslau Silverman. — 1st ed. — Montréal: Eden Press, c1984. xiii, 183 p.: ill.; 23 cm. 1. Women — Alberta — History. 2. Women — Alberta — Social conditions. 3. Frontier and pioneer life — Alberta. I. T.
HQ1459.A4 S55 1984     305.4/097123 19     *LC* 84-178150     *ISBN* 0920792294

**Latin American women: historical perspectives / edited by**                  **4.6082**
**Asunción Lavrin.**
Westport, Conn.: Greenwood Press, 1978. xiv, 343 p., [5] leaves of plates: ill.; 24 cm. — (Contributions in women's studies. no. 3) 1. Women — Latin America — History — Addresses, essays, lectures. 2. Women — Latin America — Social conditions — Addresses, essays, lectures. I. Lavrin, Asunción. II. Series.
HQ1460.5.L37     301.41/2/098     *LC* 77-94758     *ISBN* 0313203091

**Sex and class in Latin America: women's perspectives on**                    **4.6083**
**politics, economics, and the family in the Third World / edited**
**by June Nash, Helen Icken Safa.**
Brooklyn, N.Y.: J. F. Bergin Publishers, 1980. xiii, 330 p.: ill.; 23 cm. 1. Women — Latin America. 2. Sex discrimination against women — Latin America. 3. Social classes — Latin America. I. Nash, June C., 1927- II. Safa, Helen Icken.
HQ1460.5.S49 1980     305.4/098     *LC* 80-13644     *ISBN* 0897890043

**Women and change in Latin America / June Nash, Helen Safa,**                 **4.6084**
**and contributors.**
South Hadley, Mass.: Bergin & Garvey Publishers, 1986, c1985. 372 p.: ill.; 24 cm. 1. Women — Latin America — Economic conditions — Addresses, essays, lectures. 2. Women — Latin America — Social conditions — Addresses, essays, lectures. 3. Women — Employment — Latin America — Addresses, essays, lectures. 4. Sexual division of labor — Latin America — Addresses, essays, lectures. 5. Feminism — Latin America — Addresses, essays, lectures. I. Nash, June C., 1927- II. Safa, Helen Icken.
HQ1460.5.W6 1986     305.4/098 19     *LC* 85-18563     *ISBN* 0897890698

**Elmendorf, Mary L. (Mary Lindsay)**                                          **4.6085**
Nine Mayan women: a village faces change. Cambridge, Mass., Schenkman Pub. Co. [c1976] xxiv, 159 p. illus. 23 cm. A revision of the author's thesis, Union Graduate School, 1972, published under title: The Mayan woman and change. 1. Women — Mexico — Chan Kom — Case studies. 2. Mayas — Social life and customs. 3. Mayas — Religion and mythology I. T.
HQ1465.C5 E45 1976     301.41/2/09726     *LC* 74-12464     *ISBN* 0470238623 *ISBN* 047023864X

**Randall, Margaret, 1936-.**                                                  **4.6086**
Women in Cuba, twenty years later / by Margaret Randall; with photographs by Judy Janda. — New York, N.Y.: Smyrna Press, 1980. 167 p., [32] p. of

plates: ill.; 22 cm. 1. Women — Cuba — History — 20th century. 2. Women and socialism — Cuba — History — 20th century. I. Janda, Judy. II. T.
HQ1507.R37 1981      305.4/2/097291 19      *LC* 80-54055      *ISBN* 0918266149

**Barrios de Chungara, Domitila.**      **4.6087**
[Si me permiten hablar. English] Let me speak!: Testimony of Domitila, a woman of the Bolivian mines / by Domitila Barrios de Chungara with Moema Viezzer; translated by Victoria Ortiz. — New York: Monthly Review Press, c1978. 235 p.: ill.; 21 cm. Translation of Si me permiten hablar. 1. Barrios de Chungara, Domitila. 2. Women in community development — Bolivia — Biography. 3. Women in trade-unions — Bolivia — Biography. 4. Tin mines and mining — Bolivia. 5. Tin miners — Bolivia. 6. Feminists — Bolivia — Biography. I. Viezzer, Moema. joint author. II. T.
HQ1537.B37713      984      *LC* 77-91757      *ISBN* 0853454450

**Martín, Luis.**      **4.6088**
Daughters of the conquistadores: women of the Viceroyalty of Peru / Luis Martín. — 1st ed. — Albuquerque: University of New Mexico Press, c1983. xiii, 354 p.: ill.; 24 cm. Includes index. 1. Women — Peru — History. 2. Spaniards — Peru — History. 3. Peru — History — 1548-1820 I. T.
HQ1572.M37 1983      305.4/0985 19      *LC* 83-6625      *ISBN* 0826307078

# HQ1586–1725.5 Europe

**Scott, Hilda, 1915-.**      **4.6089**
Does socialism liberate women? Experiences from Eastern Europe. — Boston: Beacon Press, [1974] xii, 240 p.; 22 cm. 1. Women — Europe, Eastern. 2. Women and socialism — Europe, Eastern. 3. Discrimination in employment I. T.
HQ1587.S36 1974      301.41/2/0947      *LC* 74-212      *ISBN* 0807041629

**Robertson, Priscilla Smith.**      **4.6090**
An experience of women: pattern and change in nineteenth–century Europe / Priscilla Robertson; with an appendix by Steve Hochstadt. — Philadelphia: Temple University Press, 1982. xii, 673 p.; 24 cm. Includes index. 1. Women — Europe — History — 19th century. 2. Feminism — Europe — History — 19th century. I. T.
HQ1588.R6 1982      305.4/2/094 19      *LC* 81-9315      *ISBN* 0877222347

**Women, the family, and freedom: the debate in documents /**      **4.6091**
**edited by Susan Groag Bell & Karen M. Offen.**
Stanford, Calif.: Stanford University Press, 1983. 2 v.; 24 cm. 1. Feminism — Europe — History — Sources. 2. Feminism — United States — History — Sources. 3. Women's rights — Europe — History — Sources. 4. Women's rights — United States — History — Sources. 5. Family — Europe — History — Sources. 6. Family — United States — History — Sources. I. Bell, Susan G. II. Offen, Karen M.
HQ1588.W645 1983      305.4/09 19      *LC* 82-61081      *ISBN* 0804711704

# HQ1591–1600 Britian. Ireland

**Currell, Melville.**      **4.6092**
Political woman / Melville E. Currell. — London: Croom Helm; Totowa, N.J.: Rowman & Littlefield, 1974. 201 p.; 23 cm. Includes index. 1. Women in politics — Great Britain. 2. Women — Great Britain — Social conditions. I. T.
HQ1593.C83      329      *LC* 74-195267      *ISBN* 0874715644

**Fraser, Antonia, 1932-.**      **4.6093**
The weaker vessel / Antonia Fraser. — 1st American ed. — New York: Knopf: Distributed by Random House, c1984. xvi, 544 p., [24] p. of plates: ill., ports.; 24 cm. Includes index. 1. Women — England — History — 17th century. I. T.
HQ1593.F7 1984      305.4/0942 19      *LC* 84-47751      *ISBN* 0394513517

**Wilson, Elizabeth, 1936-.**      **4.6094**
Only halfway to paradise: women in postwar Britain, 1945–1968 / Elizabeth Wilson. — London; New York: Tavistock Publications, 1980. 233 p.; 19 cm. Includes indexes. 1. Women — Great Britain — Social conditions. 2. Women — Great Britain — History — 20th century. 3. Great Britain — Social conditions — 1945- I. T.
HQ1593.W54 1980      305.4/2/0941 19      *LC* 80-142364      *ISBN* 0422768707

**Hogrefe, Pearl.**      **4.6095**
Women of action in Tudor England: nine biographical sketches / Pearl Hogrefe. 1st ed. — Ames: Iowa State University Press, 1977. xxiv, 263 p.: ill.; 24 cm. Includes index. 1. Women — England — Biography. I. T.
HQ1595.A3 H63      920.72/0942      *LC* 76-28496      *ISBN* 081380910X

**Flexner, Eleanor, 1908-.**      **4.6096**
Mary Wollstonecraft: a biography. — New York: Coward, McCann & Geoghegan, [1972] 307 p.: ill.; 24 cm. 1. Wollstonecraft, Mary, 1759-1797 — Biography. I. T.
HQ1595.W64 F5      301.41/2/0924 B      *LC* 72-76664      *ISBN* 0698104471

**Hogrefe, Pearl.**      **4.6097**
Tudor women: commoners and queens / Pearl Hogrefe. — 1st ed. — Ames: Iowa State University Press, 1976 (c1975). xiv, 170 p., [4] leaves of plates: ill.; 23 cm. Includes index. 1. Women — England — Social conditions. 2. Women — England — History. I. T.
HQ1596.H63      301.41/2/0942      *LC* 75-20248      *ISBN* 0813816955

**Vicinus, Martha.**      • **4.6098**
Suffer and be still: women in the Victorian age / edited by Martha Vicinus. — Bloomington: Indiana University Press, [1972] xv, 239 p.: ill.; 25 cm. 1. Women — Great Britain 2. Women — Great Britain — Social conditions. I. T.
HQ1596.V5 1972      301.41/2/0942      *LC* 71-184524      *ISBN* 0253355729

**Warnicke, Retha M.**      **4.6099**
Women of the English Renaissance and Reformation / Retha M. Warnicke. — Westport, Conn.: Greenwood Press, 1983. viii, 228 p.; 24 cm. — (Contributions in women's studies. 0147-104X; no. 38) Includes index. 1. Women — England — History — 16th century. 2. Humanists — England — History — 16th century. 3. Women — Education — England — History — 16th century. 4. Women — England — Religious life — History — 16th century. 5. Great Britain — Social life and customs — 16th century 6. Great Britain — History — Tudors, 1485-1603 I. T. II. Series.
HQ1596.W37 1983      305.4/0942 19      *LC* 82-12180      *ISBN* 0313236119

**A Widening sphere: changing roles of Victorian women / edited**      **4.6100**
**by Martha Vicinus.**
Bloomington: Indiana University Press, c1977. xix, 326 p.: ill.; 24 cm. Includes index. 1. Women — Great Britain — History — Addresses, essays, lectures. 2. Women — Great Britain — Social conditions — Addresses, essays, lectures. 3. Feminism — Great Britain — Addresses, essays, lectures. 4. Great Britain — Social conditions — 19th century — Addresses, essays, lectures. I. Vicinus, Martha.
HQ1596.W44 1977      301.41/2/0941      *LC* 76-26433      *ISBN* 0253365406

**Wollstonecraft, Mary, 1759-1797.**      **4.6101**
A vindication of the rights of woman: an authoritative text, backgrounds, criticism / Mary Wollstonecraft; edited by Carol H. Poston. 1st ed. — New York: Norton, c1975. ix, 240 p.; 22 cm. (A Norton critical edition) 'The text ... is the second 1792 London edition.' 1. Women — Social and moral questions 2. Women's rights I. Poston, Carol H. II. T.
HQ1596.W6 1975b      301.41/2      *LC* 75-37775      *ISBN* 0393044270

**Bouchier, David.**      **4.6102**
The feminist challenge: the movement for women's liberation in Britain and the USA / David Bouchier. — 1st American ed. — New York: Schocken Books, 1984. xi, 252 p.; 23 cm. Includes index. 1. Feminism — Great Britain — History. 2. Feminism — United States — History. 3. Feminism — Philosophy. I. T.
HQ1597.B69 1984      305.4/2/0941 19      *LC* 83-14296      *ISBN* 0805238816

**Oakley, Ann.**      **4.6103**
The sociology of housework / Ann Oakley. — 1st American ed. — New York: Pantheon Books, [1975] c1974. x, 242 p.; 22 cm. 1. Women — Great Britain — Social conditions. 2. Feminism 3. Home economics I. T.
HQ1597.O15 1975      301.41/2      *LC* 75-4668      *ISBN* 0394497740

**Richards, Janet Radcliffe.**      **4.6104**
The sceptical feminist: a philosophical enquiry / Janet Radcliffe Richards. — London; Boston: Routledge & Kegan Paul, 1980. x, 306 p.; 23 cm. Includes index. 1. Feminism — Great Britain. I. T.
HQ1597.R5      305.4/2 19      *LC* 80-40879      *ISBN* 071000673X

**Women in the labour movement: the British experience / edited**      **4.6105**
**by Lucy Middleton; foreword by James Callaghan.**
London: Croom Helm; Totowa, N.J.: Rowman and Littlefield, 1977. 221 p.; 23 cm. Includes index. 1. Labour Party (Great Britain) — History — Addresses, essays, lectures. 2. Women in politics — Great Britain — History — Addresses, essays, lectures. 3. Women in trade-unions — Great Britain — History — Addresses, essays, lectures. I. Middleton, Lucy.
HQ1597.W57 1977      301.41/2      *LC* 76-54160      *ISBN* 0874719429

**Jeffreys, Sheila.**      **4.6106**
The spinster and her enemies: feminism and sexuality, 1880–1930 / Sheila Jeffreys. — London; Boston: Pandora Press, 1985. vii, 232 p.; 20 cm. Includes

index. 1. Feminism — England — History. 2. Sexual ethics — England — History. 3. Single women — England — Sexual behavior — History. I. T. HQ1599.E5 J44 1985    305.4/2/0942 19    *LC* 85-9279    *ISBN* 0863580505

**Lewis, Jane (Jane E.)**              **4.6107**
Women in England, 1870–1950: sexual divisions and social change / Jane Lewis. — Brighton, Sussex: Wheatsheaf Books; Bloomington: Indiana University Press, 1984. xv, 240 p.; 25 cm. 1. Working class women — England — History. 2. Middle class women — England — History. 3. Mothers — England — History. 4. Family — England — History. 5. Sexual division of labor — England — History. I. T.
HQ1599.E5 L49 1984    305.4/0942 19    *LC* 84-48437    *ISBN* 0253366089

**Rogers, Katharine M.**                **4.6108**
Feminism in eighteenth–century England / Katharine M. Rogers. — Urbana: University of Illinois Press, c1982. 291 p.; 24 cm. 1. Feminism — England — History — 18th century. I. T.
HQ1599.E5 R63 1982    305.4/2/0942 19    *LC* 81-16236    *ISBN* 0252009002

*HQ*
*1599*
*E5*
*R63*
*1982*

**Smith, Hilda L., 1941-.**                **4.6109**
Reason's disciples: seventeenth–century English feminists / Hilda L. Smith. — Urbana: University of Illinois Press, c1982. xx, 237 p.; 24 cm. Includes index. 1. Feminism — England — History — 17th century. 2. Women authors I. T.
HQ1599.E5 S62 1982    305.4/2/0942 19    *LC* 81-14834    *ISBN* 0252009126

**Women in English society, 1500–1800 / edited by Mary Prior.**    **4.6110**
London; New York: Methuen, 1985. xvi, 294 p.: ill.; 23 cm. 1. Women — England — History — 16th century — Addresses, essays, lectures. 2. Women — England — History — 17th century — Addresses, essays, lectures. 3. Women — England — History — 18th century — Addresses, essays, lectures. I. Prior, Mary.
HQ1599.E5 W64 1985    305.4/0942 19    *LC* 84-20547    *ISBN* 0416357008

**The Women of England: from Anglo–Saxon times to the**    **4.6111**
**present: interpretive bibliographical essays / edited with an**
**introd. by Barbara Kanner.**
Hamden, Conn.: Archon Books, 1979. 429 p.; 24 cm. Includes index. 1. Women — England — History — Sources. 2. Women — England — History — Bibliography. I. Kanner, Barbara, 1925-
HQ1599.E5 W65    301.41/2/0942    *LC* 78-32166    *ISBN* 0208016392

**Marshall, Rosalind Kay.**              **4.6112**
Virgins and viragos: a history of women in Scotland from 1080 to 1980 / Rosalind K. Marshall. — Chicago, Ill.: Academy Chicago, 1983. 365 p., [8] p. of plates: ill.; 24 cm. Spine title: Virgins & viragos. 1. Women — Scotland — History. I. T. II. Title: Virgins & viragos.
HQ1599.S35 M37 1983    305.4/09411 19    *LC* 82-24439    *ISBN* 0897330749

**Women in Irish society: the historical dimension / edited by**    **4.6113**
**Margaret MacCurtain and Donncha Ó Corráin.**
Westport, Conn.: Greenwood Press, 1979. 125 p.; 24 cm. — (Contributions in women's studies. no. 11 0147-104X) 1. Women — Ireland — History — Addresses, essays, lectures. 2. Women — Ireland — Social conditions — Addresses, essays, lectures. 3. Women — Ireland — Economic conditions — Addresses, essays, lectures. I. MacCurtain, Margaret. II. Ó Corráin, Donnchadh. III. Series.
HQ1600.3.W65    301.41/2/09415    *LC* 79-964    *ISBN* 0313212546

## HQ1611–1630 France. Germany

**Bidelman, Patrick Kay.**              **4.6114**
Pariahs stand up!: the founding of the liberal feminist movement in France, 1858–1889 / Patrick Kay Bidelman. — Westport, Conn.: Greenwood Press, 1982. xxviii, 285 p.; 22 cm. — (Contributions in women's studies. 0147-104X; no. 31) Includes index. 1. Women — France — History — 19th century. 2. Men — France — History — 19th century. 3. Feminism — France — History — 19th century. 4. Women — France — Societies and clubs — History — 19th century. 5. Women's rights — France — History — 19th century. 6. Liberalism — France — History — 19th century. 7. Women — Suffrage — France — History — 19th century. I. T. II. Series.
HQ1613.B5 1982    305.4/2/0944 19    *LC* 81-4222    *ISBN* 0313230064

**Duchen, Claire.**                 **4.6115**
Feminism in France: from May '68 to Mitterand / Claire Duchen. — London; Boston: Routledge & Kegan Paul, 1986. x, 165 p.: ill.; 22 cm. Includes index.

1. Feminism — France — History — 20th century. 2. Women in politics — France — History — 20th century. I. T.
HQ1613.D8 1986    305.4/2/0944 19    *LC* 85-10705    *ISBN* 0710204558

**Smith, Bonnie G., 1940-.**             **4.6116**
Ladies of the leisure class: the bourgeoises of northern France in the nineteenth century / Bonnie G. Smith. — Princeton, N.J.: Princeton University Press, c1981. x, 303 p., [4] leaves of plates: ill.; 23 cm. Includes index. 1. Middle class women — France — History — 19th century. 2. Middle classes — France — History — 19th century. I. T.
HQ1613.S54    305.4/0944 19    *LC* 81-47157    *ISBN* 0691053308

**Moses, Claire Goldberg, 1941-.**           **4.6117**
French feminism in the nineteenth century / Claire Goldberg Moses. — Albany: State University of New York Press, c1984. xiii, 311 p.: ill.; 23 cm. (SUNY series in European social history) Cover title: French feminism in the 19th century. Includes index. 1. Feminism — France — History — 19th century. I. T. II. Title: French feminism in the 19th century.
HQ1615.M67 1984    305.4/2/0944 19    *LC* 83-18040    *ISBN* 0873958594

**Lougee, Carolyn C., 1942-.**            **4.6118**
Le paradis des femmes: women, salons, and social stratification in seventeenth–century France / by Carolyn C. Lougee. — Princeton, N.J.: Princeton University Press, 1976. ix, 252 p.; 24 cm. Includes index. 1. Women — France — History. 2. Feminism — France. 3. Salons — France. I. T.
HQ1616.L68    301.41/2/0944    *LC* 76-3266    *ISBN* 0691052395

**McMillan, James F., 1948-.**            **4.6119**
Housewife or harlot: the place of women in French society, 1870–1940 / James F. McMillan. — New York: St. Martin's Press, 1981. 229 p.; 23 cm. Includes index. 1. Women — France — Social conditions. 2. Women — France — History. 3. Housewives — France — History. 4. Women — Employment — France — History. 5. Feminism — France — History. 6. France — History — Third Republic, 1870-1940 I. T.
HQ1617.M26 1981    305.4/2/0944 19    *LC* 80-18675    *ISBN* 0312393474

**New French feminisms: an anthology / edited and with**    **4.6120**
**introductions by Elaine Marks and Isabelle de Courtivron.**
Amherst: University of Massachusetts Press, 1980. xiii, 279 p.; 24 cm. Includes index. 1. Feminism — France — Addresses, essays, lectures. I. Marks, Elaine. II. De Courtivron, Isabelle.
HQ1617.N43    305.4/2/0944 19    *LC* 79-4698    *ISBN* 0870232800

**Stephenson, Jill.**                  **4.6121**
The Nazi organisation of women / Jill Stephenson. — London: Croom Helm; Totowa, N.J.: Barnes & Noble, 1981. 246 p.: map; 23 cm. Includes index. 1. Reichsfrauenführung (Germany) 2. Women — Germany — Societies, clubs, etc. 3. Women — Germany — History — 20th century. 4. Germany — History — 1933-1945 I. T.
HQ1623.S72 1981    324.243/038 19    *LC* 81-147241    *ISBN* 0389201138

**Stephenson, Jill.**                  **4.6122**
Women in Nazi society / Jill Stephenson. — New York: Barnes & Noble Books, 1975. 223 p.; 23 cm. Originally presented as the author's thesis, Edinburgh University. Includes index. 1. Nationalsozialistische Deutsche Arbeiter-Partei. 2. Women — Germany — Social conditions. 3. Germany — Politics and government — 1933-1945 I. T.
HQ1623.S73 1975    301.41/2/0943    *LC* 76-355728    *ISBN* 0064965287

**When biology became destiny: women in Weimar and Nazi**    **4.6123**
**Germany / edited by Renate Bridenthal, Atina Grossmann, and**
**Marion Kaplan.**
New York: Monthly Review Press, 1985 (c1984). xiv, 364 p.: ill.; 21 cm. (New feminist library.) 1. Women — Germany — History — 20th century — Addresses, essays, lectures. 2. Right and left (Political science) — Addresses, essays, lectures. 3. Germany — Politics and government — 1918-1933 — Addresses, essays, lectures. 4. Germany — Politics and government — 1933-1945 — Addresses, essays, lectures. I. Bridenthal, Renate. II. Grossmann, Atina. III. Kaplan, Marion A. IV. Series.
HQ1623.W475 1984    305.4/0943 19    *LC* 84-18969    *ISBN* 0853456429

**German feminism: readings in politics and literature / edited by**    **4.6124**
**Edith Hoshino Altbach ... [et al.].**
Albany, N.Y.: State University of New York Press, c1984. xii, 389 p.; 24 cm. 1. Feminism — Germany (West) — Addresses, essays, lectures. 2. German prose literature — Germany (West) — Women authors. 3. German prose literature — 20th century. I. Altbach, Edith Hoshino.
HQ1625.G465 1984    305.4/2/0943 19    *LC* 83-17849    *ISBN* 0873958403

**German women in the nineteenth century: a social history /**    **4.6125**
**edited by John C. Fout.**
New York: Holmes & Meier, 1984. xi, 439 p.; 23 cm. 1. Women — Germany — History — 19th century — Addresses, essays, lectures. I. Fout, John C., 1937-
HQ1625.G467 1984     305.4/0943 19     *LC* 83-18596     *ISBN* 0841908435

**Pore, Renate, 1943-.**    **4.6126**
A conflict of interest: women in German social democracy, 1919–1933 / Renate Pore. — Westport, Conn.: Greenwood Press, 1981. xviii, 129 p.; 22 cm. — (Contributions in women's studies. no. 26 0147-104X) Includes index. 1. Sozialdemokratische Partei Deutschlands. 2. Women's rights — Germany — History. 3. Feminism — Germany — History. 4. Women in politics — Germany — History. 5. Women and socialism — Germany — History. 6. Germany — History — 1918-1933 I. T. II. Series.
HQ1627.P73     305.4/2/0943 19     *LC* 80-27183     *ISBN* 0313228566

**Quataert, Jean H.**    **4.6127**
Reluctant feminists in German Social Democracy, 1885–1917 / Jean H. Quataert. — Princeton, N.J.: Princeton University Press, c1979. xiii, 310 p.; 23 cm. Includes index. 1. Women — Germany — Social conditions. 2. Feminism — Germany — History. 3. Women and socialism — Germany — History. 4. Women in politics — Germany — History. 5. Women — Germany — Biography. I. T.
HQ1627.Q37     301.41/2/0943     *LC* 79-84011     *ISBN* 069105276X

### HQ1661–1665 Soviet Union

**Clements, Barbara Evans, 1945-.**    **4.6128**
Bolshevik feminist: the life of Aleksandra Kollontai / Barbara Evans Clements. — Bloomington: Indiana University Press, c1979. xiii, 352 p., [5] leaves of plates: ill.; 24 cm. Includes index. 1. Kollontaĭ, A. (Aleksandra), 1872-1952. 2. Socialists — Russia — Biography. I. T.
HQ1662.K6 C55     335.43/092/4 B     *LC* 78-3240     *ISBN* 0253312094

**Kollontaĭ, A. (Aleksandra), 1872-1952.**    **4.6129**
[Selected works. English] Selected writings of Alexandra Kollontai / translated with an introd. and commentaries by Alix Holt. — Westport, Conn.: L. Hill, 1978 (c1977). 335 p.; 23 cm. Translated from the Russian. Includes index. 1. Kommunisticheskaia partiia Sovetskogo Soiuza — Party work — Addresses, essays, lectures. 2. Communists — Russia — Biography — Addresses, essays, lectures. 3. Women — Russia — Addresses, essays, lectures. 4. Communist ethics — Addresses, essays, lectures. 5. Russia — Politics and government — 1917- — Addresses, essays, lectures. I. Holt, Alix. II. T.
HQ1662.K61313 1977     335.43/092/4     *LC* 77-88786     *ISBN* 088208092X

**Stites, Richard.**    **4.6130**
The women's liberation movement in Russia: feminism, nihilism, and bolshevism, 1860–1930 / Richard Stites. — Princeton, N.J.: Princeton University Press, c1978. xx, 464 p.; 25 cm. Includes index. 1. Feminism — Russia — History. 2. Nihilism 3. Women — Russia — History. I. T.
HQ1662.S735     301.41/2/0947     *LC* 77-72137     *ISBN* 0691052549

**Women, work, and family in the Soviet Union /** edited with an    **4.6131**
**introduction by Gail Warshofsky Lapidus; [translated by**
**Vladimir Talmy].**
Armonk, N.Y.: M.E. Sharpe, c1982. xlvi, 311 p.; 24 cm. Translated from the Russian. 'Published simultaneously as vol. XXIV, no. 5-7 of Problems of Economics'—T.p. verso. 1. Women — Soviet Union — Addresses, essays, lectures. 2. Women — Employment — Soviet Union — Addresses, essays, lectures. 3. Work and family — Soviet Union — Addresses, essays, lectures. I. Lapidus, Gail Warshofsky.
HQ1662.W63     305.4/0947 19     *LC* 81-9281     *ISBN* 0873321812

**Edmondson, Linda Harriet.**    **4.6132**
Feminism in Russia, 1900–17 / Linda Harriet Edmondson. — Stanford, Calif.: Stanford University Press, 1984. xi, 197 p.; 23 cm. Includes index. 1. Feminism — Soviet Union — History — 20th century. I. T.
HQ1663.E35 1984     305.4/2/0947 19     *LC* 83-45338     *ISBN* 0804712123

**Engel, Barbara Alpern.**    **4.6133**
Mothers and daughters: women of the intelligentsia in nineteenth century Russia / Barbara Alpern Engel. — Cambridge; New York: Cambridge University Press, 1983. x, 230 p.; 24 cm. Includes index. 1. Women in politics — Soviet Union — History — 19th century. 2. Mothers — Soviet Union — History — 19th century. 3. Daughters — Soviet Union — History — 19th century. 4. Intellectuals — Soviet Union — History — 19th century. 5. Radicalism — Soviet Union — History — 19th century. 6. Soviet Union — Social conditions — 1801-1917 I. T.
HQ1663.E53 1983     305.4/2/0947 19     *LC* 82-14611     *ISBN* 0521251257

**Lapidus, Gail Warshofsky.**    **4.6134**
Women in Soviet society: equality, development, and social change / Gail Warshofsky Lapidus. — Berkeley: University of California Press, c1978. x, 381 p.; 25 cm. Includes index. 1. Women — Soviet Union — Social conditions. 2. Women's rights — Soviet Union. 3. Sex role I. T.
HQ1663.L33     305.4/0947     *LC* 74-16710     *ISBN* 0520028686

**Women and Russia: feminist writings from the Soviet Union /**    **4.6135**
**Tatyana Mamonova, editor; with the assistance of Sarah**
**Matilsky; foreword by Robin Morgan; translated by Rebecca**
**Park and Catherine A. Fitzpatrick.**
Boston: Beacon Press, c1984. xxiii, 273 p.: ports.; 22 cm. 1. Feminism — Soviet Union — Addresses, essays, lectures. I. Mamonova, Tatyana, 1943- II. Matilsky, Sarah. III. Park, Rebecca. IV. Fitzpatrick, Catherine A.
HQ1663.W63 1984     305.4/2/0947 19     *LC* 82-73963     *ISBN* 0807067083

### HQ1726–1785 Asia. Middle East

**Dorsky, Susan, 1946-.**    **4.6136**
Women of 'Amran: a Middle Eastern ethnographic study / Susan Dorsky. — Salt Lake City: University of Utah Press, c1986. 230 p.: ill.;; 24 cm. Includes index. 1. Women — Yemen — 'Amrān — Social conditions. 2. Women, Muslim — Yemen — 'Amrān. 3. 'Amrān (Yemen) — Social life and customs. I. T.
HQ1730.7.Z8 A473 1986     305.4/0953/32 19     *LC* 85-26534     *ISBN* 0874802504

**Wikan, Unni, 1944-.**    **4.6137**
Behind the veil in Arabia: women in Oman / Unni Wikan. — Baltimore: Johns Hopkins University Press, c1982. xiii, 314 p.: ill., map; 24 cm. Includes index. 1. Women — Oman — Suhār. 2. Sex customs — Oman — Suhār. 3. Marriage — Oman — Suhār. 4. Suhār (Oman) — Social life and customs. I. T.
HQ1731.Z8 S838 1982     305.4/2/09538 19     *LC* 81-18622     *ISBN* 0801827299

**Smedley, Agnes, 1890-1950.**    **4.6138**
Portraits of Chinese women in revolution / by Agnes Smedley; edited with an introd. by Jan MacKinnon and Steve MacKinnon; with an afterword by Florence Howe. — Old Westbury, N.Y.: Feminist Press, 1977. xxxv, 203 p.: ill.; 22 cm. 1. Smedley, Agnes, 1890-1950. 2. Women — China — History. I. T.
HQ1737.S56     301.41/2/0951     *LC* 76-18896     *ISBN* 0912670444

**Women in Chinese society /** edited by Margery Wolf and    **4.6139**
Roxane Witke; contributors, Emily M. Ahern ... [et al.].
Stanford, Calif.: Stanford University Press, 1975. x, 315 p.; 24 cm. (Studies in Chinese society). 1. Women — China — Social conditions — Addresses, essays, lectures. I. Wolf, Margery. II. Witke, Roxane. III. Ahern, Emily M.
HQ1737.W65     301.41/2/0951     *LC* 74-82782     *ISBN* 0804708746

**Wolf, Margery.**    **4.6140**
Women and the family in rural Taiwan. — Stanford, Calif.: Stanford University Press, 1972. x, 235 p.: illus.; 23 cm. 1. Women — Taiwan. 2. Family — Taiwan. I. T.
HQ1740.5.W65     301.42/1     *LC* 70-183895     *ISBN* 0804708088

**Jain, Devaki, 1933-.**    **4.6141**
Women's quest for power: five Indian case studies / Devaki Jain, assisted by Nalini Singh, Malini Chand. — Sahibabad, Distt. Ghaziabad: Vikas, c1980. vi, 272 p., [1] leaf of plates: ill.; 23 cm. 'By the same author': p. [ii] 1. Women — India — Social conditions — Case studies. I. Singh, Nalini. II. Chand, Malini. III. T.
HQ1743.J33     305.4/2/0954 19     *LC* 80-901719     *ISBN* 0706910214

**Socio–economic status of Indian women /** edited by K. Murali    **4.6142**
**Manohar.**
1st ed. — Delhi: Seema Publications, 1983. xii, 137 p.; 22 cm. Includes index. 1. Women — India — Social conditions. 2. Women — India — Economic conditions. I. Murali Manohar, K.
HQ1743.S6 1983     305.4/2/0954 19     *LC* 83-901653

**Roy, Manisha, 1936-.**    **4.6143**
Bengali women / Manisha Roy. — Chicago: University of Chicago Press, 1976 (c1975). xvii, 205 p.: ports.; 23 cm. Includes index. 1. Women — India — West Bengal. 2. Women, Hindu — India — West Bengal. 3. Upper classes — India — West Bengal. I. T.
HQ1744.B4 R68     301.41/2/095414     *LC* 74-33521     *ISBN* 0226730417

**Usha Rao, N. J. (Nandalike Jagannath)**    **4.6144**
Women in a developing society / N.J. Usha Rao. — New Delhi: Ashish, 1983. vi, 180 p.: 1 folded map; 23 cm. Includes index. 1. Women — India — Karnataka — Social conditions — Addresses, essays, lectures. 2. Women —

India — Karnataka — Economic conditions — Addresses, essays, lectures. I. T.
HQ1744.K36 U83 1983     305.4/2/095487 19     *LC* 83-904297

**Robins-Mowry, Dorothy, 1921-.**       **4.6145**
The hidden sun: women of modern Japan / Dorothy Robins–Mowry; with a foreword by Edwin O. Reischauer. — Boulder, Colo.: Westview Press, 1983. xxii, 394 p.; ill.; 23 cm. Includes index. 1. Women — Japan — Social conditions. I. T.
HQ1762.R6 1983     305.4/0952 19     *LC* 82-20230     *ISBN* 0865314217

**Women in changing Japan / edited by Joyce Lebra, Joy**    **4.6146**
**Paulson, Elizabeth Powers.**
Boulder, Colo.: Westview Press, 1976. xi, 322 p.; 24 cm. (Westview special studies on China and East Asia.) 1. Women — Japan — Addresses, essays, lectures. 2. Women's rights — Japan — Addresses, essays, lectures. I. Lebra-Chapman, Joyce, 1925- II. Paulson, Joy. III. Powers, Elizabeth, 1944-IV. Series.
HQ1762.W65     301.41/2/0952     *LC* 75-33663     *ISBN* 0891580190

**Lebra, Takie Sugiyama, 1930-.**       **4.6147**
Japanese women: constraint and fulfillment / Takie Sugiyama Lebra. — Honolulu: University of Hawaii Press, c1984. xi, 345 p.; 24 cm. Includes index. 1. Women — Japan — Social conditions — Case studies. 2. Life cycle, Human — Case studies. 3. Sex role — Japan — Case studies. 4. Participant observation I. T.
HQ1763.L4 1984     305.4/0952 19     *LC* 83-18029     *ISBN* 0824808681

**Sievers, Sharon L.**       **4.6148**
Flowers in salt: the beginnings of feminist consciousness in modern Japan / Sharon L. Sievers. — Stanford, Calif.: Stanford University Press, 1983. xiv, 240 p.; ill.; 23 cm. 1. Feminism — Japan — History — 19th century. 2. Japan — Social conditions — 1868- I. T.
HQ1763.S57 1983     305.4/2/0952 19     *LC* 82-60104     *ISBN* 0804711658

**Yamazaki, Tomoko, 1932-.**       **4.6149**
[Ameyuki-san no uta. English] The story of Yamada Waka: from prostitute to feminist pioneer / Tomoko Yamazaki; trans. by Wakako Hironaka, Ann Kostant. — Tokyo; New York: Kodansha International; New York, N.Y.: Distributed by Harper & Row, 1985. p. cm. Ameyuki-san no uta: Yamada Waka no sukinaru shōgai. 1. Yamada, Waka, 1879-1957. 2. Feminists — Japan — Biography. I. T.
HQ1763.Y3913 1985     305.4/2/0924 B 19     *LC* 85-40042     *ISBN* 4770012330

**Spence, Jonathan D.**       **4.6150**
The death of woman Wang / Jonathan D. Spence. — New York: Viking Press, 1978. xvii, 169 p.: maps; 22 cm. 1. Women — China — History. 2. Runaway wives — China. I. T.
HQ1767.S63 1978     951     *LC* 77-29134     *ISBN* 0670262323

**Women and the family in the Middle East: new voices of change**    **4.6151**
**/ edited by Elizabeth Warnock Fernea.**
1st ed. — Austin: University of Texas Press, c1985. xii, 356 p.; 24 cm. 1. Women — Arab countries — Addresses, essays, lectures. 2. Family — Arab countries — Addresses, essays, lectures. 3. Women — Iran — Addresses, essays, lectures. 4. Arab countries — Social life and customs — Addresses, essays, lectures. I. Fernea, Elizabeth Warnock.
HQ1784.W65 1985     305.4/2/09174927 19     *LC* 84-11944     *ISBN* 0292755287

## HQ1786–1870 Africa. Australia

**The Black woman cross–culturally / edited by Filomina Chioma**    **4.6152**
**Steady.**
Cambridge, Mass.: Schenkman Pub. Co., c1981. ix, 645 p.: ill.; 22 cm. 1. Women, Black — Africa — Addresses, essays, lectures. 2. Women, Black — Caribbean Area — Addresses, essays, lectures. 3. Women, Black — Latin America — Addresses, essays, lectures. 4. Afro-American women — Addresses, essays, lectures. I. Steady, Filomina Chioma.
HQ1787.B56 1981     305.4/08896     *LC* 80-17214     *ISBN* 0870733451

**Oliver, Caroline.**       **4.6153**
Western women in colonial Africa / Caroline Oliver. — Westport, Conn.: Greenwood Press, 1982. xv, 201 p.; 22 cm. — (Contributions in comparative colonial studies. 0163-3813; no. 12) Includes index. 1. Women — Africa — Biography. 2. Explorers, Women — Biography. 3. Women missionaries — Africa — Biography. 4. Travelers — Africa — Biography. I. T. II. Series.
HQ1787.O4 1982     960/.088042 B 19     *LC* 81-24194     *ISBN* 0313233888

**African women south of the Sahara / edited by Margaret Jean**    **4.6154**
**Hay and Sharon Stichter.**
London; New York: Longman, 1984. xiv, 225 p.: ill.; 23 cm. Includes index. 1. Women — Africa, Sub-Saharan — Economic conditions. 2. Women — Africa, Sub-Saharan — Social conditions. 3. Women — Africa, Sub-Saharan — Political activity. I. Hay, Margaret Jean. II. Stichter, Sharon.
HQ1788.A57 1984     305.4/0967 19     *LC* 83-7905     *ISBN* 0582643732

**Rural development and women in Africa.**       **4.6155**
Geneva, Switzerland: International Labour Office, 1984. x, 157 p. — (WEP study.) 'This publication is the outcome of a WEP project.' 1. Women in rural development — Africa. 2. Rural development — Africa. I. World Employment Programme. II. International Labour Office.
HQ1788 D489 1984     *ISBN* 9221036332

**Obbo, Christine.**       **4.6156**
African women: their struggle for economic independence / Christine Obbo. — London: Zed Press, 1980. x, 166 p.; 23 cm. 1. Women — Africa, East — Economic conditions. I. T.
HQ1788.O2     305.4/2/096 19     *LC* 80-670250     *ISBN* 0905762339

**Perspectives on power: women in Africa, Asia, and Latin**    **4.6157**
**America / Jean F. O'Barr, editor.**
Durham, N.C.: Duke University, Center for International Studies, 1982. x, 120 p.; 23 cm. — (Occasional paper series / Duke University, Center for International Studies; no. 13) Proceedings of a conference held Mar. 27-28, 1981, at Duke University. 1. Women — Africa — Addresses, essays, lectures. 2. Women — Asia — Addresses, essays, lectures. 3. Women — Latin America — Addresses, essays, lectures. 4. Power (Social sciences) I. O'Barr, Jean F. II. Duke University. Center for International Studies.
HQ1788.P47 1982     305.4/095 19     *LC* 82-50929     0916994247

**Women in Africa: studies in social and economic change /**    **4.6158**
**edited by Nancy J. Hafkin and Edna G. Bay.**
Stanford, Calif.: Stanford University Press, 1976. x, 306 p.: maps; 23 cm. Includes index. 1. Women — Africa, Sub-Saharan — Social conditions — Addresses, essays, lectures. 2. Women — Africa, Sub-Saharan — Economic conditions — Addresses, essays, lectures. I. Hafkin, Nancy J. II. Bay, Edna G.
HQ1788.W58     301.41/2/0966     *LC* 75-44901     *ISBN* 0804709068

**Davis, Susan Schaefer.**       **4.6159**
Patience and power: women's lives in a Moroccan village / by Susan Schaefer Davis. — Cambridge, Mass.: Schenkman, c1983. 198 p.: ill.; 22 cm. Includes index. 1. Rural women — Morocco. 2. Village communities — Morocco. 3. Women, Muslim I. T.
HQ1791.D38 1983     305.4/0964 19     *LC* 82-866     *ISBN* 0870735039

**Maher, Vanessa.**       **4.6160**
Women and property in Morocco: their changing relation to the process of social stratification in the Middle Atlas / Vanessa Maher. — London; New York: Cambridge University Press, 1974. xii, 238 p.; 24 cm. (Cambridge studies in social anthropology; 10) Includes index. 1. Women — Morocco — Social conditions. 2. Marriage — Morocco. 3. Morocco — Social conditions. I. T.
HQ1816.M62 M3     301.41/2/0964     *LC* 74-80351     *ISBN* 0521205484

**Robertson, Claire C., 1944-.**       **4.6161**
Sharing the same bowl?: a socioeconomic history of women and class in Accra, Ghana / Claire C. Robertson. — Bloomington: Indiana University Press, c1984. x, 299 p.: ill.; 25 cm. Includes index. 1. Women — Ghana — Accra — Economic conditions. 2. Women — Ghana — Accra — Social conditions. 3. Women — Ghana — Accra — Case studies. 4. Social classes — Ghana — Accra. 5. Gā (African people) I. T.
HQ1816.Z8 A277 1984     305.4/2/09667 19     *LC* 83-48112     *ISBN* 0253352053

**Urdang, Stephanie.**       **4.6162**    HQ
Fighting two colonialisms: women in Guinea–Bissau / by Stephanie Urdang. —   1818
New York: Monthly Review Press, c1979. 320 p.: ill.; 21 cm. 1. Women —   U69
Guinea-Bissau. 2. Women's rights — Guinea-Bissau. 3. Guinea-Bissau —
Colonial influence. I. T.
HQ1818.U69     301.41/2/096657     *LC* 79-2329     *ISBN* 0853455112

**Dixson, Miriam.**       **4.6163**
The real Matilda: woman and identity in Australia, 1788–1975 / [by] Miriam Dixson. Ringwood, Australia: Penguin Books Australia, 1976. 280 p.; 19 cm. (Pelican books) Includes index. 1. Women — Australia — History. 2. Women's rights I. T.
HQ1822.D58     301.41/2/0994     *LC* 76-369485     *ISBN* 0140219382

**Matthews, Jill Julius.**       **4.6164**
Good and mad women: the historical construction of femininity in twentieth–century Australia / Jill Julius Matthews. — North Sydney, NSW, Australia; Winchester, Mass, USA: Allen & Unwin Australia, 1984. ix, 223 p.; 22 cm.

Includes index. 1. Women — Australia — Social conditions. 2. Femininity (Psychology) 3. Feminism — Australia — History — 20th century. I. T.
HQ1822.M35 1984     305.4/2/0994 19     *LC* 84-71002     *ISBN* 0868616575

**Women, class, and history: feminist perspectives on Australia**     **4.6165**
**1788–1978 / edited by Elizabeth Windschuttle.**
[Auckland, N.Z.?]: Fontana, 1982 (c1980). ix, 604 p.; 20 cm. 1. Women — Australia — History — Addresses, essays, lectures. 2. Women — Australia — Social conditions — Addresses, essays, lectures. I. Windschuttle, Elizabeth.
HQ1823.W654     305.4/2/0994 19     *LC* 81-128749     *ISBN* 0006357229

## HQ1870.9 Developing Countries: General

**Charlton, Sue Ellen M.**     **4.6166**
Women in Third World development / Sue Ellen M. Charlton. — Boulder, Colo.: Westview Press, 1984. xiv, 240 p.: ill.; 24 cm. 1. Women — Developing countries — Social conditions. 2. Women — Developing countries — Economic conditions. 3. Women in rural development 4. Women in community development I. T.
HQ1870.9.C47 1984     305.4/2 19     *LC* 84-2403     *ISBN* 0865317348

**Comparative perspectives of Third World women: the impact of**     **4.6167**
**race, sex, and class / edited by Beverly Lindsay.**
New York: Praeger, 1980. xi, 318 p.; 24 cm. 1. Women — Developing countries — Addresses, essays, lectures. 2. Minority women — United States — Addresses, essays, lectures. I. Lindsay, Beverly.
HQ1870.9.C65     301.41/2     *LC* 78-19793     *ISBN* 0030466512

**Huston, Perdita, 1936-.**     **4.6168**
Third World women speak out: interviews in six countries on change, development, and basic needs / Perdita Huston. — New York: Published in cooperation with the Overseas Development Council [by] Praeger, 1979. xix, 153 p.; 24 cm. 1. Women — Developing countries — Attitudes. 2. Basic needs — Developing countries. 3. Developing countries — Social conditions. I. Overseas Development Council. II. T.
HQ1870.9.H87     301.41/2/091724     *LC* 78-32180

**Rogers, Barbara, 1945-.**     **4.6169**
The domestication of women: discrimination in developing societies / Barbara Rogers. — New York, N.Y.: St. Martin's Press, 1980, c1979. 200 p.; 23 cm. 1. Women — Developing countries 2. Women in rural development — Developing countries. 3. Sex discrimination against women — Developing countries. 4. Division of labor I. T.
HQ1870.9.R64 1980     305.4 19     *LC* 79-26691     *ISBN* 0312216270

**Technology and rural women: conceptual and empirical issues /**     **4.6170**
**edited by Iftikhar Ahmed.**
London, UK; Winchester, Mass., USA: Allen & Unwin, 1985. xvi, 383 p.; 23 cm. 'A study prepared for the International Labour Office within the framework of the World Employment Programme.' Includes index. 1. Rural women — Developing countries — Addresses, essays, lectures. 2. Women in rural development — Developing countries — Addresses, essays, lectures. 3. Technology — Social aspects — Developing countries — Addresses, essays, lectures. 4. Technological innovations — Developing countries — Addresses, essays, lectures. I. Ahmad, Iftikhar. II. International Labor Office. World Employment Programme.
HQ1870.9.T43 1985     305.4/3/0091734 19     *LC* 84-29778     *ISBN* 0043820433

## HQ1871–2030 Women's Clubs

**Women's organizations: a national directory / edited by Martha**     **4.6171**
**Merrill Doss.**
Garrett Park, MD: Garrett Park Press, c1986. 302 p.: ill.; 28 cm. Includes indexes. 1. Women — United States — Societies and clubs — Directories. I. Doss, Martha Merrill.
HQ1903.W66 1986     305.4/06/073 19     *LC* 86-81710     *ISBN* 0912048425

**Blair, Karen J.**     • **4.6172**
The clubwoman as feminist: true womanhood redefined, 1868–1914 / Karen J. Blair; pref. by Annette K. Baxter. — New York: Holmes & Meier Publishers, 1980. xv, 199 p.; 24 cm. Includes index. 1. Women — United States — Societies and clubs — History. 2. Women in public life — United States — History. 3. Feminism — United States — History. I. T.
HQ1904.B56     301.41/2/0973     *LC* 79-26390     *ISBN* 084190538X

## HS Associations. Societies

**Schmidt, Alvin J.**     **4.6173**
Fraternal organizations / Alvin J. Schmidt; advisory editor, Nicholas Babchuk. — Westport, Conn.: Greenwood Press, 1980. xxxiii, 410 p.; 24 cm. — (Greenwood encyclopedia of American institutions. 3) Includes index. 1. Friendly societies — United States — History. 2. Friendly societies — Canada — History. 3. Friendly societies — United States — Directories. 4. Friendly societies — Canada — Directories. 5. Voluntarism — United States. 6. Voluntarism — Canada. I. Babchuk, Nicholas. II. T. III. Series.
HS17.S3     366/.00973     *LC* 79-6187     *ISBN* 0313214360

**Wirsing, Robert.**     **4.6174**
Socialist society and free enterprise politics: a study of voluntary assocations in urban India / Robert G. Wirsing. — Durham, N.C.: Carolina Academic Press, c1977. xiv, 214 p.; 23 cm. Includes index. 1. Associations, institutions, etc — India — Nagpur (City) I. T.
HS81.I5 W57     329     *LC* 76-6775     *ISBN* 0890890668

**Dumenil, Lynn, 1950-.**     **4.6175**
Freemasonry and American culture, 1880–1930 / Lynn Dumenil. — Princeton, N.J.: Princeton University Press, c1984. xviii, 305 p., [4] p. of plates; ill.; 23 cm. Includes index. 1. Freemasonry — United States — History — 19th century. 2. Freemasonry — United States — History — 20th century. 3. WASPs (Persons) 4. United States — Social conditions — 1918-1932 5. United States — Social conditions — 1865-1918 I. T.
HS529.D86 1984     366/.1/0973 19     *LC* 84-42594     *ISBN* 0691047162

**Muraskin, William A.**     **4.6176**
Middle–class Blacks in a white society: Prince Hall Freemasonry in America / by William A. Muraskin. — Berkeley: University of California Press, c1975. xi, 318 p.; 25 cm. Includes index. 1. Afro-American freemasons 2. Afro-Americans 3. Middle classes — United States. I. T.
HS883.M87     366/.1     *LC* 73-94435     *ISBN* 0520027051

**Gosden, P. H. J. H.**     **4.6177**
Self–help: voluntary associations in 19th century Britain [by] P. H. J. H. Gosden. — New York: Barnes & Noble, [1974] viii, 295 p.; 23 cm. — 1. Friendly societies — Great Britain — History. 2. Self-help groups — Great Britain — History. 3. Cooperative societies — Great Britain — History. I. T.
HS1508.G7 G67     366

**Domhoff, G. William.**     **4.6178**
The Bohemian Grove and other retreats; a study in ruling–class cohesiveness, by G. William Domhoff. [1st ed.] New York, Harper & Row [1974] xvi, 250 p. map (on lining papers) 22 cm. 1. Bohemian Club (San Francisco, Calif.) 2. Upper classes — United States. 3. Elite (Social sciences) I. T.
HS2725.S4 B774     367/.973     *LC* 73-14253     *ISBN* 0060110481

**Macleod, David I.**     **4.6179**
Building character in the American boy: the Boy Scouts, YMCA, and their forerunners, 1870–1920 / David I. Macleod. — Madison: University of Wisconsin Press, 1983. xx, 404 p.; 24 cm. 1. Boy Scouts of America. 2. YMCA of the USA. I. T.
HS3313.M25 1983     369.43/0973 19     *LC* 83-47763     *ISBN* 0299094006

## HT51–485 Communities

**Bell, Colin.**     **4.6180**
Community studies: an introduction to the sociology of the local community / [by] Colin Bell and Howard Newby. — New York: Praeger Publishers, [1972, c1971] 262 p.; 22 cm. 1. Community 2. Social classes 3. Power (Social sciences) I. Newby, Howard. joint author. II. T.
HT65.B44     301.34     *LC* 71-185773

# HT101–351 The City. Urban Sociology

**The Many facets of human settlements: science and society:**    **4.6181**
**papers prepared for AAAS activities in connection with**
**HABITAT, the U.N. Conference on Human Settlements /**
**editors, Irene Tinker and Mayra Buvinić.**
1st ed. — Oxford; New York: Pergamon Press, 1977. vi, 405 p.: ill.; 26 cm.
Symposium sponsored by the Office of International Science of the American
Association for the Advancement of Science during the AAAS annual meeting
held in Boston, Feb. 18-24, 1976. Also issued by Pergamon Press as v. 2, no. 1-4,
of Habitat. 1. Cities and towns — Congresses. 2. Human ecology —
Congresses. 3. Environmental policy — Congresses. I. Tinker, Irene.
II. Buvinić, Mayra. III. American Association for the Advancement of
Science. Office of International Science.
HT107.M36 1977     301.36     LC 77-6307     ISBN 0080219942

**Burgess, Ernest Watson, 1886-1966.**    ● **4.6182**
Contributions to urban sociology, edited by Ernest W. Burgess and Donald J.
Bogue. — Chicago: University of Chicago Press, [1964] xi, 673 p.: maps,
diagrs., tables.; 24 cm. Abridged ed. published in 1967 under title: Urban
sociology. 1. Sociology, Urban — Collections. I. Bogue, Donald Joseph, 1918-
joint ed. II. T.
HT108.B8     301.36082     LC 63-21309

## HT111–150 History

**Fischer, Claude S., 1948-.**    **4.6183**
To dwell among friends: personal networks in town and city / Claude S.
Fischer. — Chicago: University of Chicago Press, 1982. xii, 451 p.: ill.; 23 cm.
Includes index. 1. Sociology, Urban 2. Social structure 3. Quality of life I. T.
II. Title: Personal networks in town and city.
HT111.F56     307 19     LC 81-11505     ISBN 0226251373

**Gutkind, Erwin Anton, 1886-.**    ● **4.6184**
International history of city development / [By] E.A. Gutkind. [New York]:
Free Press of Glencoe [1964-c1972] 8 v.: ill., maps; 29 cm. 1. Cities and towns
— History 2. Cities and towns — Planning — History I. T.
HT111 G8     LC 64-13231

**Light, Ivan Hubert.**    **4.6185**
Cities in world perspective / Ivan Light. — New York: Macmillan; London:
Collier Macmillan, c1983. xiv, 466 p.: ill., maps; 25 cm. Lectures accompanied
by slides to further explain and elaborate points in the book are available from
the author. 1. Sociology, Urban 2. Cities and towns 3. Urbanization I. T.
HT111.L53 1983     307.7/64 19     LC 82-15288     ISBN 0023706805

**Mingione, Enzo.**    **4.6186**
Social conflict and the city / Enzo Mingione. — New York: St. Martin's Press,
c1981. 207 p.: ill.; 24 cm. 1. Urbanization 2. Urbanization — Italy — Case
studies. 3. Marxian school of sociology 4. Regional economics 5. Capitalism
I. T.
HT111.M55 1981     307.7/6 19     LC 81-1393     ISBN 0312731639

**Mumford, Lewis, 1895-.**    ● **4.6187**
The city in history: its origins, its transformations, and its prospects. — [1st
ed.]. — New York: Harcourt, Brace & World, [1961] xi, 657 p.: plates, maps.;
25 cm. 1. Cities and towns — History. I. T.
HT111.M8     301.36     LC 61-7689

**Vance, James E.**    **4.6188**
This scene of man: the role and structure of the city in the geography of Western
civilization / James E. Vance, Jr. New York: Harper's College Press, c1977. xx,
437 p.: ill.; 24 cm. (Harper & Row series in geography) 1. Cities and towns —
History. 2. Cities and towns — Growth — History. 3. Urban economics
4. Urbanization — History. I. T. II. Title: Geography of western civilization.
HT111.V29     301.36/3/09     LC 77-852     ISBN 0061674079

**Sjoberg, Gideon.**    ● **4.6189**
The preindustrial city, past and present. — Glencoe, Ill.: Free Press, [1960]
353 p.; 22 cm. 1. Cities and towns — History. I. T.
HT113.S5     301.36     LC 60-10903

**White, Morton Gabriel, 1917-.**    ● **4.6190**
The intellectual versus the city, from Thomas Jefferson to Frank Lloyd Wright
[by] Morton and Lucia White. — Cambridge: Harvard University Press, 1962.
270 p.; 25 cm. — (Publications of the Joint Center for Urban Studies)
1. Sociology, Urban — Addresses, essays, lectures. 2. Cities and towns —
United States. I. White, Lucia. joint author. II. T.
HT113.W53     301.36     LC 62-17229

**Hammond, Mason, 1903-.**    **4.6191**
The city in the ancient world, by Mason Hammond, assisted by Lester J.
Bartson. — Cambridge, Mass.: Harvard University Press, 1972. xiv, 617 p.:
maps.; 25 cm. — (Harvard studies in urban history.) 1. Cities and towns,
Ancient 2. Cities and towns, Ancient — Bibliography. I. T. II. Series.
HT114.H35     301.36/093     LC 73-180153

**Castells, Manuel.**    **4.6192**
The city and the grassroots: a cross–cultural theory of urban social movements
/ Manuel Castells. — Berkeley: University of California Press, c1983. xxi,
450 p.: ill.; 26 cm. — (California series in urban development; [2]) Includes
index. 1. Sociology, Urban — Cross-cultural studies. 2. Cities and towns —
History — Cross-cultural studies. 3. Social movements — History — Cross-
cultural studies. 4. Urbanization — History — Cross-cultural studies.
5. Social change — History — Cross-cultural studies. I. T.
HT119.C29 1983     307.7/6 19     LC 82-40099     ISBN 0520047567

**The City in cultural context / edited by John A. Agnew, John**    **4.6193**
**Mercer, and David E. Sopher.**
Boston: Allen & Unwin, 1984. xiv, 299 p., [8] p. of plates: ill.; 25 cm. 1. Cities
and towns — Cross-cultural studies. 2. Urbanization — Cross-cultural studies.
3. Social change — Cross-cultural studies I. Agnew, John A. II. Mercer,
John, 1934- III. Sopher, David Edward.
HT119.C59 1984     307.7/6 19     LC 84-2851     ISBN 0043011764

**Hauser, Philip Morris, 1909- ed.**    ● **4.6194**
The study of urbanization, edited by Philip M. Hauser [and] Leo F. Schnore. —
New York: Wiley, [1965] viii, 554 p.; 24 cm. 1. Urbanization 2. Cities and
towns — Growth I. Schnore, Leo Francis, 1927- joint ed. II. T.
HT119.H3     301.364     LC 65-24223

**Patterns of urbanization: comparative country studies / edited**    **4.6195**
**by Sidney Goldstein and David F. Sly; with contributions by**
**Ashish Bose ... [et al.].**
Dolhain: Ordina Editions, [1977] 2 v.: ill.; 25 cm. (Working paper -
International Union for the Scientific Study of Population; 3) 1. Urbanization
— Case studies. I. Goldstein, Sidney, 1927- II. Sly, David. III. Bose, Ashish.
IV. International Union for the Scientific Study of Population.
HT119.P38     301.36/1     LC 78-302076

**Smith, Michael P.**    **4.6196**
The city and social theory / Michael P. Smith. — New York: St. Martin's Press,
c1979. xiii, 315 p.; 24 cm. 1. Sociology, Urban I. T.
HT119.S6     307.7/6     LC 75-38024     ISBN 0312140002

**Urbanization and settlement systems: international perspectives**    **4.6197**
**/ edited by L.S. Bourne, R. Sinclair, K. Dziewoński, for**
**International Geographical Union, Commission on National**
**Settlement Systems.**
Oxford [Oxfordshire]; New York: Oxford University Press, 1984. vi, 475 p.: ill.,
maps; 24 cm. 1. Urbanization — Addresses, essays, lectures. 2. Human
settlements — Addresses, essays, lectures. I. Bourne, Larry S. II. Sinclair,
Robert, 1930- III. Dziewoński, Kazimierz. IV. International Geographical
Union. Commission on National Settlement Systems.
HT119.U72 1984     307.7/6 19     LC 83-15409     ISBN 0198232438

**Yeates, Maurice.**    **4.6198**
The North American city / Maurice Yeates, Barry Garner; [cover design, Al
Burkhardt]. — 3d ed. — San Francisco: Harper & Row, c1980. xv, 557 p.: ill.;
25 cm. Includes index. 1. Cities and towns — North America. I. Garner,
Barry J., 1937- joint author. II. T.
HT122.Y4 1980     307.7/6/097     LC 80-10703     ISBN 0060473347

### HT123–149 BY COUNTRY

### HT123 United States

#### *HT123 A–L*

**Abrams, Charles, 1902-1970.**    ● **4.6199**
The city is the frontier. — [1st ed.]. — New York: Harper & Row, [1965] xii,
394 p.; 22 cm. 1. City planning — United States. I. T.
HT123.A6     711/.59/0973     LC 64-25145

**American urban history: an interpretive reader with**    **4.6200**
**commentaries / edited by Alexander B. Callow, Jr.**
3rd ed. — New York: Oxford University Press, 1982. x, 566 p.: ill.; 23 cm.
1. Cities and towns — United States — History. I. Callow, Alexander B.
HT123.A666 1982     307.7/6/0973     LC 81-4465     ISBN 019502981X

**Barth, Gunther Paul.**                                          **4.6201**
City people: the rise of modern city culture in nineteenth–century America / Gunther Barth. — New York: Oxford University Press, 1980. viii, 289 p., [6] leaves of plates: ill.; 22 cm. Includes index. 1. Cities and towns — United States — Growth — History — 19th century. 2. Urbanization — United States — History — 19th century. I. T.
HT123.B297     307.7/6/0973     *LC* 80-10875     *ISBN* 0195027558

**Bender, Thomas.**                                               **4.6202**
Toward an urban vision: ideas and institutions in nineteenth–century America / Thomas Bender. — Lexington: University Press of Kentucky, [1975] xv, 277 p.; 25 cm. Includes index. 1. Cities and towns — United States — History. 2. Urbanization — United States — History. 3. Sociology, Urban — United States. 4. Lowell (Mass.) — History. I. T.
HT123.B36     301.36/0973     *LC* 74-18930     *ISBN* 0813113261

**Bogue, Donald Joseph, 1918-.**                               • **4.6203**
The structure of the metropolitan community; a study of dominance and subdominance, by Donald J. Bogue. — New York: Russell & Russell, [1971] x, 210 p.: illus.; 29 cm. — (University of Michigan. Contributions of the Institute for Human Adjustment. Social Science Research Project) 'First published in 1950.' 1. Cities and towns — United States. 2. United States — Statistics, Vital I. T.
HT123.B6 1971     301.3/63/0973     *LC* 75-139904

**Boyer, Paul S.**                                                **4.6204**
Urban masses and moral order in America, 1820–1920 / Paul Boyer. — Cambridge, Mass.: Harvard University Press, 1978. xvi, 387 p., [13] leaves of plates: ill.; 24 cm. 1. Urbanization — United States — History. 2. United States — Moral conditions I. T.
HT123.B67     301.36/3/0973     *LC* 78-15973     *ISBN* 0674931092

**Bradbury, Katharine L.**                                        **4.6205**
Urban decline and the future of American cities / Katharine L. Bradbury, Anthony Downs, Kenneth A. Small. — Washington, D.C.: Brookings Institution, c1982. xiii, 309 p.; 24 cm. 1. Cities and towns — United States — Growth. 2. Urban policy — United States. I. Downs, Anthony. II. Small, Kenneth A. III. T.
HT123.B695 1982     307.7/64/0973 19     *LC* 82-70888     *ISBN* 0815710542

**Cities of the mind: images and themes of the city in the social**     **4.6206**
**sciences / edited by Lloyd Rodwin and Robert M. Hollister.**
New York: Plenum Press, c1984. xiii, 356 p.; 24 cm. — (Environment, development, and public policy. Cities and development.) 1. Cities and towns — United States — Addresses, essays, lectures. 2. Social sciences — United States — Addresses, essays, lectures. 3. Cities and towns — Addresses, essays, lectures. 4. Social sciences — Addresses, essays, lectures. I. Rodwin, Lloyd. II. Hollister, Robert M. III. Series.
HT123.C4967 1984     307.7/6/0973 19     *LC* 84-1991     *ISBN* 0306414260

**Contemporary metropolitan America / Association of American**     **4.6207**
**Geographers, Comparative Metropolitan Analysis Project; John**
**S. Adams, editor.**
Cambridge, Mass.: Ballinger Pub. Co., c1976. 4 v.: ill.; 26 cm. 1. Cities and towns — United States. I. Adams, John S., 1938- II. Association of American Geographers. Comparative Metropolitan Analysis Project.
HT123.C635     301.36/3/0973     *LC* 76-56167     *ISBN* 0884104257

**Duncan, Otis Dudley.**                                        • **4.6208**
Metropolis and region [by] Otis Dudley Duncan [and others] Baltimore, Published for Resources for the Future by Johns Hopkins Press [1960] xviii, 587 p. maps, diagrs., tables. 24 cm. 1. Cities and towns — United States. 2. Metropolitan areas — United States I. Resources for the Future. II. T.
HT123.D78     307.7/6 19     *LC* 60-10656

**The Economics of neighborhood / edited by David Segal.**         **4.6209**
New York: Academic Press, 1979. xiii, 296 p.: graphs; 24 cm. — (Studies in urban economics.) 1. Urban economics — Addresses, essays, lectures. 2. Neighborhood — Mathematical models — Addresses, essays, lectures. 3. Neighborhood — Economic aspects — United States — Addresses, essays, lectures. 4. Land use, Urban — United States — Addresses, essays, lectures. 5. Residential mobility — United States — Addresses, essays, lectures. I. Segal, David. II. Series.
HT123.E3     330.9/173/2     *LC* 78-22534     *ISBN* 0126362505

**Glaab, Charles Nelson, 1927-.**                               • **4.6210**
A history of urban America [by] Charles N. Glaab [and] A. Theodore Brown. New York, Macmillan [1967] 328 p. 1. Cities and towns — United States I. Brown, A. Theodore (Andrew Theodore), 1923- joint author II. T.
HT123 G56     *LC* 67-15198

**Goist, Park Dixon.**                                            **4.6211**
From Main Street to State Street: town, city, and community in America / Park Dixon Goist. — Port Washington, N.Y.: Kennikat Press, 1977. 180 p.; 23 cm.

— (Interdisciplinary urban series) (National University publications) Includes index. 1. Cities and towns — United States. 2. Urbanization — United States. 3. Community 4. Cities and towns in literature 5. United States — Social conditions I. T.
HT123.G573     301.36/0973     *LC* 77-2923     *ISBN* 0804691851

**Hansen, Niles M.**                                              **4.6212**
The challenge of urban growth: the basic economics of city size and structure / Niles M. Hansen. Lexington, Mass.: Lexington Books, [1975] xiv, 173 p.: ill.; 24 cm. 1. Cities and towns — United States — Growth. 2. Urban economics I. T.
HT123.H34     301.36/3/0973     *LC* 74-25089     *ISBN* 0669977098

**Harrison, Bennett.**                                            **4.6213**
Urban economic development; suburbanization, minority opportunity, and the condition of the central city. — Washington: Urban Institute, [1974] xiv, 200 p.: illus.; 24 cm. 1. Cities and towns — United States. 2. Urban economics — Case studies. I. T.
HT123.H37     330.9/173/2     *LC* 73-86699     *ISBN* 0877660980

**Hollingsworth, J. Rogers (Joseph Rogers), 1932-.**             **4.6214**
Dimensions in urban history: historical and social science perspectives on middle–size American cities / J. Rogers Hollingsworth and Ellen Jane Hollingsworth. — Madison: University of Wisconsin Press, 1979. viii, 184 p.; 24 cm. Includes index. 1. Cities and towns — United States — History. 2. Cities and towns — Wisconsin — Case studies. 3. Urbanization — United States — History. 4. Sociology, Urban — United States. 5. United States — Social conditions — 1865-1918 I. Hollingsworth, Ellen Jane. joint author. II. T.
HT123.H65     301.36/0973     *LC* 78-65011     *ISBN* 0299078205

**Levy, John M.**                                                 **4.6215**
Economic development programs for cities, counties, and towns / John M. Levy. — New York, N.Y.: Praeger, 1981. ix, 175 p.; 24 cm. Includes index. 1. Urban policy — United States. 2. Community development, Urban — United States. 3. Federal aid to community development — United States. I. T.
HT123.L39     338.973 19     *LC* 81-2716     *ISBN* 0030578914

## *HT123 M–Z*

**McKelvey, Blake, 1903-.**                                      • **4.6216**
The emergence of metropolitan America, 1915–1966. — New Brunswick, N.J.: Rutgers University Press, [1968] x, 311 p.: illus., maps, ports.; 24 cm. Continues the author's The urbanization of America, 1860-1915. 1. Urbanization — United States. I. T.
HT123.M22     301.3/64/0973     *LC* 68-18695

**McKelvey, Blake, 1903-.**                                      • **4.6217**
The urbanization of America, 1860–1915. — New Brunswick, N.J.: Rutgers University Press, [1963] 370 p.: illus.; 25 cm. 1. Urbanization — United States. 2. United States — Economic conditions — 1865-1918 I. T.
HT123.M23     301.36     *LC* 62-21248

**Macdonald, Michael C. D.**                                      **4.6218**
America's cities: a report on the myth of urban renaissance / by Michael C.D. Macdonald. — New York: Simon and Schuster, c1984. 428 p.; 23 cm. Includes index. 1. Cities and towns — United States. 2. Urban renewal — United States. 3. Urban economics I. T.
HT123.M284 1984     307.7/6/0973 19     *LC* 84-5426     *ISBN* 0671439138

**The Martial metropolis: U.S. cities in war and peace / edited by**     **4.6219**
**Roger W. Lotchin.**
New York: Praeger, 1984. xiii, 242 p.; 25 cm. 1. Cities and towns — United States — History — 20th century. 2. Sociology, Military — United States. I. Lotchin, Roger W.
HT123.M299 1984     306/.27 19     *LC* 83-21250     *ISBN* 0030603919

**Miller, Roberta Balstad.**                                      **4.6220**
City and hinterland: a case study of urban growth and regional development / Roberta Balstad Miller. — Westport, Conn.: Greenwood Press, 1979. xiv, 179 p.: maps; 22 cm. — (Contributions in American history; no. 77 0084-9219) Includes index. 1. Cities and towns — Growth — United States. 2. Regional economics — History. 3. Regional planning — United States — History. I. T.
HT123.M538     301.36/1/0974765     *LC* 78-55340     *ISBN* 0313205248

**Mohl, Raymond A.**                                              **4.6221**
The urban experience; themes in American history. Edited by Raymond A. Mohl [and] James F. Richardson. — Belmont, Calif.: Wadsworth Pub. Co., [1973] xi, 265 p.; 23 cm. 1. Cities and towns — United States — Addresses, essays, lectures. I. Richardson, James F., 1931- joint author. II. T.
HT123.M62     301.36/1/0973     *LC* 72-97322     *ISBN* 0534002870

**Rethinking urban policy: urban development in an advanced**    **4.6222**
**economy / Royce Hanson, editor.**
Washington, D.C.: National Academy Press, 1983. xiv, 215 p.: ill.; 23 cm.
'Committee on National Urban Policy, Commission on Behavioral and Social
Sciences and Education, National Research Council.' Includes index. 1. Urban
policy — United States. 2. Urban economics I. Hanson, Royce. II. National
Research Council (U.S.). Commission on Behavioral and Social Sciences and
Education. Committee on National Urban Policy.
HT123.R456 1983    338.973/09173/2 19    *LC* 83-19422    *ISBN*
0309034264

**Rossi, Peter Henry, 1921-.**    **4.6223**
The roots of urban discontent: public policy, municipal institutions, and the
ghetto [by] Peter H. Rossi, Richard A. Berk [and] Bettye K. Eidson. — New
York: Wiley, [1974] xxv, 499 p.; 23 cm. — (The Wiley series in urban research)
'A publication of the Center for Metropolitan Planning and Research of the
Johns Hopkins University.' 'A Wiley-Interscience publication.' 1. Cities and
towns — United States — Case studies. 2. Sociology, Urban 3. United States
— Social conditions — 1960- I. Berk, Richard A. joint author. II. Eidson,
Bettye K., joint author. III. Johns Hopkins University. Center for
Metropolitan Planning and Research. IV. T.
HT123.R67    301.36/0973    *LC* 73-22219    *ISBN* 0471737704

**Schlesinger, Arthur Meier, 1888-1965.**    • **4.6224**
The rise of the city, 1878–1898. — Chicago: Quadrangle Books, [1971, c1933]
xiv, 494 p.; 21 cm. — (History of American life. v. 10) (Quadrangle paperbacks,
QP410) 1. Cities and towns — U.S. 2. U.S. — Social conditions — 1865-1918.
3. U.S. — Social life and customs. 4. U.S. — Civilization — 1865-1918. I. T.
II. Series.
HT123.S3 1971    917.3/03/8    *LC* 78-29656

**Stein, Maurice Robert, 1926-.**    • **4.6225**
The eclipse of community; an interpretation of American studies. — Princeton,
N.J.: Princeton University Press, 1960. 354 p.; 23 cm. 1. Cities and towns —
United States. 2. Community life — Research. I. T.
HT123.S78    301.360973    *LC* 60-5757

*[handwritten left margin: HT 123 S81, arrow pointing to Stein entry]*

**Strauss, Anselm L.**    **4.6226**
Images of the American city / by Anselm L. Strauss. — New Brunswick, N.J.:
Transaction Books, c1976. xiv, 306 p.: ill. 1. Cities and towns — United States.
I. T.
HT123.S786 1976    *LC* 75-43358

**Street, David.**    **4.6227**
Handbook of contemporary urban life / David Street and associates. — 1st ed.
— San Francisco: Jossey-Bass, 1978. xxii, 741 p.; 24 cm. — (The Jossey-Bass
social and behavioral science series) Includes indexes. 1. City and town life —
United States — Addresses, essays, lectures. 2. Urbanization — United States
— Addresses, essays, lectures. I. T.
HT123.S787    301.36/0973    *LC* 78-1155    *ISBN* 0875893724

**Suttles, Gerald D.**    • **4.6228**
The social construction of communities [by] Gerald D. Suttles. — Chicago:
University of Chicago Press, [1972] x, 278 p.; 23 cm. — (Studies of urban
society) 1. Sociology, Urban 2. Community 3. Social groups I. T.
HT123.S83    301.36    *LC* 74-177310    *ISBN* 0226781895

**Thompson, Wilbur Richard, 1923-.**    • **4.6229**
A preface to urban economics / [by] Wilbur R. Thompson. Baltimore:
Published for Resources for the Future by Johns Hopkins Press [1968] xv,
413 p.; 21 cm. 1. Cities and towns — United States. 2. City planning — United
States. 3. United States — Economic conditions — 1945- I. Resources for the
Future. II. T.
HT123.T48 1968    301.3/64/0973    *LC* 68-4313

**Tunnard, Christopher.**    • **4.6230**
American skyline: the growth and form of our cities and towns / [by]
Christopher Tunnard and Henry Hope Reed; drawings by John Cohen. —
Boston: Houghton Mifflin, 1955. 302 p.: ill.; 22 cm. 1. Cities and towns —
United States I. Reed, Henry Hope. jt. author II. T.
HT123 T85    *LC* 55-6553

**Urban policymaking and metropolitan dynamics: a comparative**    **4.6231**
**geographical analysis / John S. Adams, editor.**
Cambridge, Mass.: Ballinger Pub. Co., c1976. xxii, 576 p.: ill.; 26 cm. A study
commissioned by the Comparative Metropolitan Analysis Project, Association
of American Geographers. 1. Urban policy — United States — Addresses,
essays, lectures. 2. Metropolitan areas — United States — Addresses, essays,
lectures. I. Adams, John S., 1938- II. Association of American Geographers.
Comparative Metropolitan Analysis Project.
HT123.U748    301.36/3/0973    *LC* 76-25165    *ISBN* 0884104265

**Warner, Sam Bass, 1928-.**    **4.6232**
The urban wilderness: a history of the American city / by Sam Warner. — [1st
ed.]. — New York: Harper & Row, [1972] xvii, 303 p.: ill.; 25 cm. 1. Cities and
towns — United States. I. T.
HT123.W235    301.36/3/0973    *LC* 72-79700    *ISBN* 0060145315

**Warren, Roland Leslie, 1915-.**    • **4.6233**
The community in America [by] Roland L. Warren. — 2d ed. — Chicago:
Rand McNally, [1971, c1972] xii, 418 p.; 24 cm. — (Rand McNally sociology
series) 1. Community life 2. Cities and towns — U.S. 3. U.S. — Social
conditions. I. T.
HT123.W25 1972    301.3/4/0973    *LC* 75-178231

**Weimer, David R. (David Rhoads) ed.**    • **4.6234**
City and country in America. — New York, Appleton-Century-Crofts [1962]
399 p. illus. 21 cm. 1. Cities and towns — United States — Addresses, essays,
lectures. I. T.
HT123.W4    301.340973    *LC* 62-12332

*[handwritten right margin: HT 123 W42]*

**Wood, Robert Coldwell, 1923-.**    **4.6235**
The necessary majority: middle America and the urban crisis / [by] Robert C.
Wood. — New York: Columbia University Press, 1972. x, 95 p.; 21 cm.
1. Cities and towns — U.S. I. T.
HT123.W56    301.36/3/0973    *LC* 70-183228    *ISBN* 0231036175

## HT123.5 Regions of the United States

**Garner, John S., 1945-.**    **4.6236**
The model company town: urban design through private enterprise in
nineteenth-century New England / John S. Garner. — Amherst: University of
Massachusetts Press, 1984, c1982. xiv, 288 p.: ill.; 19 x 24 cm. Includes index.
1. Company towns — New England — History — 19th century. 2. Company
towns — New England — History — 19th century — Case studies. 3. City
planning — New England — History — 19th century. 4. City planning — New
England — History — 19th century — Case studies. 5. City planning —
Massachusetts — Hopedale — History — 19th century. I. T.
HT123.5.A11 G37 1984    307.7/67/0974 19    *LC* 84-8636    *ISBN*
0870234420

**Gottmann, Jean.**    • **4.6237**
Megalopolis; the urbanized northeastern seaboard of the United States. New
York, Twentieth Century Fund, 1961. xi, 810 p. ill., maps, tables. 1. Cities and
towns — Atlantic States 2. Cities and towns — Growth 3. Metropolitan areas
— Atlantic States I. T.
HT123.5 A12 G6    *LC* 61-17298

**Goldfield, David R., 1944-.**    **4.6238**
Cotton fields and skyscrapers: southern city and region, 1607–1980 / David R.
Goldfield. — Baton Rouge: Louisiana State University Press, c1982. xiv, 232 p.:
ill.; 24 cm. Includes index. 1. Cities and towns — Southern States — History.
2. Sectionalism (United States) — History. 3. Agriculture — Economic
aspects — Southern States. 4. Conservatism — Southern States — History.
5. Southern States — Race relations. I. T.
HT123.5.A13 G64 1982    307.7/6/0975 19    *LC* 82-6582    *ISBN*
0807110299

**The Metropolitan Midwest: policy problems and prospects for**    **4.6239**
**change / edited by Barry Checkoway and Carl V. Patton.**
Urbana: University of Illinois Press, c1985. 309 p.: ill.; 24 cm. 1. Cities and
towns — Middle West — Economic conditions. 2. Cities and towns — Middle
West — Social conditions. 3. Urban policy — Middle West. 4. City planning
— Middle West. 5. Urban renewal — Middle West. 6. Metropolitan areas —
Middle West. I. Checkoway, Barry. II. Patton, Carl V.
HT123.5.A14 M47 1985    307.7/64/0977 19    *LC* 83-18213    *ISBN*
0252011147

**The Rise of the Sunbelt cities / edited by David C. Perry and**    **4.6240**
**Alfred J. Watkins.**
Beverly Hills, Calif.: Sage Publications, c1977. 309 p.; 23 cm. — (Urban affairs
annual reviews. v. 14) 1. Cities and towns — Sunbelt States — Addresses,
essays, lectures. I. Perry, David C. II. Watkins, Alfred J. III. Series.
HT123.5.A163R5x    301.36/08 s 301.36/3/0976    *LC* 77-93698
   *ISBN* 0803910290. *ISBN* 0803910304 pbk

**Sunbelt cities: politics and growth since World War II / edited**    **4.6241**
**by Richard M. Bernard and Bradley R. Rice.**
1st ed. — Austin: University of Texas Press, 1984. x, 346 p.: maps; 24 cm.
1. Cities and towns — Sunbelt States. I. Bernard, Richard M., 1948- II. Rice,
Bradley Robert, 1948-
HT123.5.A163 S93 1984    307.7/64/0973 19    *LC* 83-10222    *ISBN*
0292775768

**Reps, John William.**    **4.6242**
Cities of the American West: a history of frontier urban planning / John W.
Reps. — Princeton, N.J.: Princeton University Press, c1979. xii, 827 p., 32 [i.e.

16] leaves of plates: ill.; 23 x 27 cm. Includes index. 1. Cities and towns — West (U.S.) — History. 2. Urbanization — West (U.S.) I. T.
HT123.5.A17 R46    301.36/3/0978    *LC* 78-51187    *ISBN* 0691046484

**Hudson, John C.** 4.6243
Plains country towns / John C. Hudson. — Minneapolis: University of Minnesota Press, c1985. xi, 189 p.: ill.; 24 cm. Includes index. 1. Cities and towns — North Dakota — History. 2. Railroads — North Dakota — History. I. T.
HT123.5.N9 H82 1985    307.7/62/09784 19    *LC* 84-13049    *ISBN* 0816613478

**Withey, Lynne.** 4.6244
Urban growth in colonial Rhode Island: Newport and Providence in the eighteenth century / Lynne Withey. — Albany: State University of New York Press, c1984. xiv, 183 p.; 24 cm. Includes index. 1. Urbanization — Rhode Island — History. 2. Rhode Island — History — Colonial period, ca. 1600-1775 3. Newport (R.I.) — Economic conditions. 4. Providence (R.I.) — Economic conditions. 5. Newport (R.I.) — Social conditions. 6. Providence (R.I.) — Social conditions. I. T.
HT123.5.R4 W55 1984    307.7/64/097452 19    *LC* 83-438    *ISBN* 0873957512

**The City in southern history: the growth of urban civilization in** 4.6245
**the South / edited by Blaine A. Brownell and David R.**
**Goldfield; contributors, Blaine A. Brownell ... [et al.].**
Port Washington, N.Y.: Kennikat Press, 1977. 228 p.: ill.; 24 cm. (National university publications) 1. Cities and towns — Southern States — Addresses, essays, lectures. 2. Urbanization — Southern States — Addresses, essays, lectures. I. Brownell, Blaine A. II. Goldfield, David R., 1944-
HT123.5.S6 C57    301.36/3/0975    *LC* 76-41235    *ISBN* 0804690782

## HT127–129 Canada. Latin America

**The Canadian city: essays in urban and social history / edited** 4.6246
**by Gilbert A. Stelter and Alan F.J. Artibise.**
Rev. and enl. — Ottawa, Canada: Carleton University Press; Don Mills, Ont., Canada: Distributed by Oxford University Press Canada, 1984. 503 p.: ill.; 20 cm. (Carleton library series. 132) 1. Cities and towns — Canada — History. 2. City and town life — Canada — History. I. Stelter, Gilbert Arthur, 1933- II. Artibise, Alan F. J. III. Series.
HT127.C36 1984    307.7/64/0971 19    *LC* 85-161039    *ISBN* 088629018X

**Roberts, Bryan R., 1939-.** 4.6247
Cities of peasants: the political economy of urbanization in the Third World / Bryan Roberts. — Beverly Hills, Calif.: Sage Publications, 1979, c1978. vi, 207 p.; 22 cm. (Explorations in urban analysis; v. 1) Includes indexes. 1. Urbanization — Latin America. I. T. II. Series.
HT127.5.R62 1979    301.36/1/098    *LC* 79-87589    *ISBN* 0803912900

**Urbanization in contemporary Latin America: critical** 4.6248
**approaches to the analysis of urban issues / edited by Alan**
**Gilbert, in association with Jorge E. Hardoy and Ronaldo**
**Ramírez.**
Chichester; New York: J. Wiley, c1982. xv, 286 p.: ill.; 24 cm. 1. Urban policy — Latin America — Addresses, essays, lectures. 2. Social classes — Latin America — Addresses, essays, lectures. 3. Social conflict — Addresses, essays, lectures. 4. Housing policy — Latin America — Addresses, essays, lectures. I. Gilbert, Alan, 1944- II. Hardoy, Jorge Enrique. III. Ramírez, Ronaldo.
HT127.5.U718 1982    307.7/6/098 19    *LC* 81-21876    *ISBN* 0471101834

**The Urban explosion in Latin America: a continent in process of** • 4.6249
**modernization / Glenn H. Beyer, editor.**
Ithaca, N.Y.: Cornell University Press, [1967] xx, 360 p.: map.; 24 cm. 'The role of the city in the modernization of Latin America, the conference that served as the basis for this volume, was a feature of the Cornell Latin America Year, 1965-1966.' 1. Urbanization — Latin America. 2. Cities and towns — Latin America. I. Beyer, Glenn H. ed. II. Cornell University. III. T.
HT129.L3 U7    301.3/64/098    *LC* 67-23759

## HT131–145 Europe

**Dickinson, Robert Eric, 1905-.** • 4.6250
The west European city; a geographical interpretation. — London: Routledge & Paul, [1951] xviii, 580 p.: illus., maps (part fold.); 23 cm. — (International library of sociology and social reconstruction) 1. Cities and towns — Europe. I. T.
HT131.D5    323.352    *LC* 51-8811

**Hohenberg, Paul M.** 4.6251
The making of urban Europe, 1000–1950 / Paul M. Hohenberg, Lynn Hollen Lees. — Cambridge, Mass.: Harvard University Press, 1985. xiv, 398 p.: ill.; 25 cm. (Harvard studies in urban history.) Includes index. 1. Urbanization — Europe — History. 2. Cities and towns — Europe — Growth — History. 3. Urban economics — History. I. Lees, Lynn Hollen. II. T. III. Series.
HT131.H58 1985    307.7/6/094 19    *LC* 84-25333    *ISBN* 0674543602

**Urban life in Mediterranean Europe: anthropological** 4.6252
**perspectives / edited by Michael Kenny and David I. Kertzer.**
Urbana: University of Illinois Press, c1983. x, 338 p.: ill., maps; 24 cm. 1. Cities and towns — Europe, Southern. 2. Urban anthropology I. Kenny, Michael, 1923- II. Kertzer, David I., 1948-
HT131.U69 1983    307.7/64/094 19    *LC* 82-1890    *ISBN* 0252009584

**Clark, Peter.** 4.6253
English Towns in transition 1500–1700 / Peter Clark and Paul Slack. — London; New York: Oxford University Press, 1976. 176 p.; 21 cm. Includes index. 1. Cities and towns — England — History. 2. Cities and towns — England — Growth. I. Slack, Paul. joint author. II. T.
HT133.C542    301.36/3/0941    *LC* 77-360863    *ISBN* 0192158163

**Dyos, H. J. (Harold James), 1921-1978.** 4.6254
The Victorian city: images and realities, edited by H. J. Dyos and Michael Wolff. London, Boston, Routledge & Kegan Paul [1973] 2 v. (xxxii, 957 p.) illus. 25 cm. 1. Cities and towns — Great Britain — History. 2. Great Britain — Social conditions — 19th century I. Wolff, Michael, 1927- joint author. II. T.
HT133.D89    301.36/3/0942    *LC* 73-76088    *ISBN* 0710073844

**The Early modern town: a reader / edited with an introd. by** 4.6255
**Peter Clark.**
New York: Longman, 1976. viii, 332 p.; 22 cm. 1. Cities and towns, Medieval — Great Britain — Addresses, essays, lectures. I. Clark, Peter, 1944-
HT133.E2    301.36/3/0942    *LC* 76-7041    *ISBN* 0582484049

**Elliott, Brian A.** 4.6256
The city: patterns of domination and conflict / Brian Elliott and David McCrone. — New York: St. Martin's Press, 1982. vi, 173 p.; 23 cm. 1. Sociology, Urban — Great Britain. 2. Social conflict 3. Urban economics 4. Power (Social sciences) 5. Marxian school of sociology I. McCrone, David. II. T.
HT133.E4 1982    307.7/64 19    *LC* 81-51614    *ISBN* 0312139845

**Lloyd, David Wharton.** 4.6257
The making of English towns: a vista of 2000 years / David W. Lloyd. — [London]: V. Gollancz in association with P. Crawley, 1984. 290 p.: ill.; 26 cm. 1. Cities and towns — England — History. I. T.
HT133.L56 1984    307.7/6/0941 19    *LC* 83-239565    *ISBN* 0575033371

**Platt, Colin.** 4.6258
The English medieval town / Colin Platt. — New York: McKay, c1976. 219 p.: ill.; 26 cm. Includes index. 1. Cities and towns, Medieval — Great Britain. I. T.
HT133.P58 1976    301.36/3/0942    *LC* 76-363578    *ISBN* 0679505849

**Smailes, Arthur E.** • 4.6259
The geography of towns [by] Arthur E. Smailes. — [1st U.S. ed.]. — Chicago: Aldine Pub. Co., [1968, c1966] 160 p.: illus., maps.; 21 cm. — (University library of geography) 1. Cities and towns — History. 2. Cities and towns — Great Britain. I. T.
HT133.S6 1968    301.3/6    *LC* 68-19873

**French cities in the nineteenth century / edited by John M.** 4.6260
**Merriman.**
New York: Holmes & Meier, 1981. 304 p.: ill.; 23 cm. Includes index. 1. Urbanization — France — History — 19th century. 2. Municipal government — France — History — 19th century. 3. France — Industries — History — 19th century. I. Merriman, John M.
HT135.F76 1981    307.7/6/0944 19    *LC* 81-2520    *ISBN* 0841904642

**Walker, Mack.** 4.6261
German home towns: community, state, and general estate, 1648–1871. — Ithaca: Cornell University Press, [1971] xi, 473 p.: map.; 24 cm. 1. Cities and towns — Germany — History. 2. Sociology, Urban — Germany. I. T.
HT137.W33 1971    301.3/6    *LC* 76-162540    *ISBN* 0801406706

**The City in Russian history / Michael F. Hamm, editor.** 4.6262
Lexington: University Press of Kentucky, c1976. 349 p.: ill.; 24 cm. Includes index. 1. Cities and towns — Russia — Addresses, essays, lectures.

2. Urbanization — Russia — Addresses, essays, lectures. 3. City planning — Russia — Addresses, essays, lectures. I. Hamm, Michael F.
HT145.R9 C58      301.36/3/0947      *LC* 75-3544      *ISBN* 0813113288

**Harris, Chauncy Dennison, 1914-.**                                    • **4.6263**
Cities of the Soviet Union: studies in their functions, size, denisty, and growth / [by] Chauncy D. Harris. — Chicago: Published for Association of American Geographers by Rand McNally [1970] xxviii, 484 p.: ill., maps; 23 cm. (The Monograph series of the Association of American Geographers, 5) 1. Cities and towns — Soviet Union. I. T.
HT145.R9 H37      301.3/64/0947      *LC* 72-98437

**The Socialist city: spatial structure and urban policy / edited by**      **4.6264**
**R. A. French & F. E. Ian Hamilton.**
Chichester; New York: Wiley, c1979. xviii, 541 p.: ill.; 24 cm. 1. Cities and towns — Russia — Addresses, essays, lectures. 2. Cities and towns — Europe, Eastern — Addresses, essays, lectures. I. French, Richard Anthony. II. Hamilton, F. E. Ian.
HT145.R9 S63      309.2/62/0947      *LC* 78-16828      *ISBN* 0471996890

# HT147–149 Asia. Africa

**Asia urbanizing: population growth & concentration & the**      **4.6265**
**problems thereof: a comparative symposium by Asian and**
**Western experts in search of wise approaches / edited by Social**
**Science Research Institute, International Christian University.**
Tokyo: Simul Press, 1976. ii, 178 p.; 21 cm. 1. Urbanization — Asia — Congresses. 2. Cities and towns — Growth — Congresses. I. Kokusai Kirisutokyō Daigaku, Tokyo. Shakai Kagaku Kenkyūjo.
HT147.A2 A84      HT147A2 A84.      301.36/095      *LC* 77-366223

**The Chinese city between two worlds / edited by Mark Elvin**      **4.6266**
**and G. William Skinner.**
Stanford, Calif.: Stanford University Press, 1974. xiii, 458 p.: ill.; 24 cm. (Studies in Chinese society) 'Eight of the papers ... were presented ... at a conference held in St. Croix, Virgin Islands, in December-January 1968-69.' 1. Cities and towns — China — Addresses, essays, lectures. I. Elvin, Mark. ed. II. Skinner, G. William (George William), 1925- ed.
HT147.C48 C43      301.36/3/0951      *LC* 73-89858      *ISBN* 0804708533

**The City in Communist China. Edited by John Wilson Lewis.**      **4.6267**
**Contributors: Jerome Alan Cohen [and others].**
Stanford, Calif.: Stanford University Press, 1971. xii, 449 p.: maps.; 24 cm. — (Studies in Chinese society) 'Eight of the papers ... were originally presented at a research conference held in St. Croix, Virgin Islands, at the end of 1968.' 1. Cities and towns — China — Addresses, essays, lectures. I. Lewis, John Wilson, 1930- ed. II. Cohen, Jerome Alan.
HT147.C48 C55      309.1/51      *LC* 78-130828      *ISBN* 0804707480

**The City in late imperial China / edited by G. William Skinner;**      **4.6268**
**contributors, Hugh D. R. Baker ... [et al.].**
Stanford, Calif.: Stanford University Press, 1977. xvii, 820 p.: ill.; 24 cm. (Studies in Chinese society) 1. Cities and towns — China — History — Addresses, essays, lectures. I. Skinner, G. William (George William), 1925- II. Baker, Hugh D. R.
HT147.C48 C56      301.36/3/0951      *LC* 75-184      *ISBN* 0804708924

**Kirkby, R. J. R. (Richard J. R.)**      **4.6269**
Urbanization in China: town and country in a developing economy, 1949-2000 A.D. / R.J.R. Kirkby. — New York: Columbia University Press, 1985. 289 p.: ill. Includes index. 1. Urbanization — China. 2. Cities and towns — China. 3. China — Economic condititions — 1976- 4. China — Population. I. T.
HT147.C48 K57 1985      307.7/6/0951 19      *LC* 84-23063      *ISBN* 0231061501

**Rozman, Gilbert.**      **4.6270**
Urban networks in Ch'ing China and Tokugawa Japan. — Princeton, N.J.: Princeton University Press, [1974, c1973] xiv, 355 p.: illus.; 25 cm. 1. Cities and towns — China. 2. Cities and towns — Japan. 3. Sociology, Urban — Case studies. I. T.
HT147.C48 R69      301.36/3/0951      *LC* 72-1986      *ISBN* 0691030820

**Whyte, Martin King.**      **4.6271**
Urban life in contemporary China / Martin King Whyte, William L. Parish. — Chicago: University of Chicago Press, 1984. viii, 408 p., [8] p. of plates: ill.; 24 cm. 1. Cities and towns — China. 2. Urban economics 3. Family — China. 4. Quality of life — China. I. Parish, William L. II. T.
HT147.C48 W59 1984      307.7/6/0951 19      *LC* 83-7779      *ISBN* 0226895467

**Efrat, Elisha.**      **4.6272**
Urbanization in Israel / Elisha Efrat. — London: C. Helm; New York: St. Martin's Press, 1984. 225 p.: ill.; 22 cm. Includes index. 1. Cities and towns — Israel. 2. Urbanization — Israel. 3. Israel — Social conditions. I. T.
HT147.I7 E38 1984      307.7/6/095694 19      *LC* 83-24718      *ISBN* 0709909314

**Dore, Ronald Philip.**      • **4.6273**
City life in Japan; a study of a Tokyo ward. — Berkeley, University of California Press, 1958. x, 472 p. illus. 22 cm. Bibliographical references included in 'Notes' (p. 437-461) 1. Cities and towns — Japan. I. T.
HT147.J3D6      301.360952135      *LC* 59-16060

**The Middle East city: ancient traditions confront a modern**      **4.6274**
**world / edited by Abdulaziz Y. Saqqaf.**
New York: Paragon House, c1986. xx, 393 p.: ill. (some col.); 26 cm. Proceedings of a conference sponsored by the Middle East Chapter of the Professors World Peace Academy. 'A PWPA book.' 1. Cities and towns, Islamic — Near East — History — Congresses. 2. Urbanization — Near East — History — Congresses. 3. Rural-urban migration — Near East — History — Congresses. I. Saqqaf, Abdulaziz Y., 1951- II. Professors World Peace Academy. Middle East Chapter.
HT147.N4 M52 1987      307.7/6/0956 19      *LC* 86-12385      *ISBN* 0943852137

**Roberts, M. Hugh P.**      **4.6275**
An urban profile of the Middle East / M. Hugh P. Roberts. — New York: St. Martin's Press, 1979. 239 p.: ill.; 24 cm. 1. Cities and towns — Middle East. 2. Cities and towns — Africa, North. 3. Urbanization — Middle East. 4. Urbanization — Africa, North. 5. City planning — Middle East. 6. City planning — Africa, North. I. T.
HT147.N4 R6 1979      309.2/62/0956      *LC* 78-27185      *ISBN* 0312834675

**Lapidus, Ira M. (Ira Marvin)**      **4.6276**
Muslim cities in the later Middle Ages / Ira M. Lapidus. — Student ed. — Cambridge [Cambridgeshire]; New York: Cambridge University Press, 1984. xvi, 208 p.; 25 cm. Includes index. 1. Cities and towns, Islamic — Near East. 2. Islamic Empire — Social conditions. I. T.
HT147.5.L36 1984      307.7/64/0917671 19      *LC* 83-20858      *ISBN* 0521263611

**Raymond, André.**      **4.6277**
The great Arab cities in the 16th–18th centuries: an introduction / André Raymond. — New York: New York University Press, 1984. xvi, 155 p.: ill., maps; 28 cm. (Hagop Kevorkian series on Near Eastern art and civilization.) Translated from the French. 'Printed version of four lectures given in April and May 1983 at the Hagop Kevorkian Center at New York University'—Pref. Includes index. 1. Cities and towns — Arab countries. 2. Arab countries — Social conditions. I. T. II. Series.
HT147.5.R39 1984      307.7/64/09174927 19      *LC* 84-9895      *ISBN* 0814773915

**El-Shakhs, Salah. comp.**      **4.6278**
Urbanization, national development, and regional planning in Africa. Edited by Salah El-Shakhs [and] Robert Obudho. New York, Praeger Publishers [1974] xiii, 232 p. illus. 23 cm. (Praeger special studies in international economics and development) 1. Urbanization — Africa. 2. City planning — Africa. 3. Regional planning — Africa. I. Obudho, Robert A. joint comp. II. T.
HT148.A2 E47      301.36/3/096      *LC* 73-9387

**Hanna, William John, 1931-.**      **4.6279**
Urban dynamics in Black Africa: an interdisciplinary approach / [by] William John Hanna [and] Judith Lynne Hanna. — Chicago: Aldine, Atherton, [1971] x, 390 p.: ill.; 24 cm. 1. Cities and towns — Africa. 2. Cities and towns — Africa — Bibliography. 3. Urbanization — Africa. 4. Urbanization — Africa — Bibliography. I. Hanna, Judith Lynne. joint author. II. T.
HT148.A2 H3 1971      307.7/64/0967 19      *LC* 73-149840      *ISBN* 020224038X

**O'Connor, Anthony M. (Anthony Michael)**      **4.6280**
The African city / Anthony O'Connor. — New York: Africana Pub. Co., 1983. 359 p.: maps; 23 cm. Includes index. 1. Cities and towns — Africa, Sub-Saharan. 2. Rural-urban migration — Africa, Sub-Saharan. 3. Housing — Africa, Sub-Saharan. 4. Ethnic groups 5. Urban economics I. T.
HT148.A357 O25 1983      307.7/64/096 19      *LC* 83-10648      *ISBN* 0841908818

**Mabogunje, Akin L.**      **4.6281**
Urbanization in Nigeria. — London: University of London P., 1968. 3-353 p.: 16 plates, illus., maps.; 23 cm. 1. Urbanization — Nigeria. I. T.
HT148.N5 M3      301.3/64/09669      *LC* 79-365499      *ISBN* 0340093900

**Living under apartheid: aspects of urbanization and social** **4.6282**
**change in South Africa / edited by David M. Smith.**
London; Boston: Allen & Unwin, 1982. xiii, 256 p.: ill.; 25 cm. — (London
research series in geography. 2) Includes index. 1. Urban policy — South
Africa — Addresses, essays, lectures. 2. Urbanization — South Africa — Case
studies. 3. Blacks — South Africa — Segregation — Case studies. I. Smith,
David Marshall, 1936- II. Series.
HT148.S6 L58 1982      305.8/00968 19      *LC* 82-11605      *ISBN*
0043091105

**Hanna, William John, 1931-.** **4.6283**
Urban dynamics in black Africa: an interdisciplinary approach / William John
Hanna, Judith Lynne Hanna. — 2nd rev. ed. — New York: Aldine Pub. Co.,
1981. vii, 260 p.: ill.; 24 cm. Includes index. 1. Cities and towns — Africa, Sub-
Saharan. 2. Cities and towns — Africa, Sub-Saharan — Bibliography.
3. Urbanization — Africa, Sub-Saharan. 4. Urbanization — Africa, Sub-
Saharan — Bibliography. I. Hanna, Judith Lynne. II. T.
HT148.S8 H36 1981      307.7/64/0967 19      *LC* 80-69655      *ISBN*
0202241580

**Hull, Richard W., 1940-.** **4.6284**
African cities and towns before the European conquest / by Richard W. Hull.
— 1st ed. — New York: Norton, c1976. xxi, 138 p.: ill.; 22 cm. Includes index.
1. Cities and towns — Africa, Sub-Saharan — History. 2. Africa, Sub-Saharan
— Civilization — History. I. T.
HT148.S8 H85 1976      301.36/3/096      *LC* 76-16038      *ISBN*
0393055817

**Gugler, Josef.** **4.6285**
Urbanization and social change in West Africa / Josef Gugler, William G.
Flanagan. — Cambridge; New York: Cambridge University Press, 1978. xiv,
235 p.: maps; 24 cm. — (Urbanization in developing countries) Includes
indexes. 1. Urbanization — Africa, West. 2. Africa, West — Social conditions
I. Flanagan, William G. joint author. II. T.
HT148.W4 G83 1978      307.7/6/0966 19      *LC* 76-9175      *ISBN*
0521213487

**Peil, Margaret.** **4.6286**
Cities and suburbs: urban life in west Africa / Margaret Peil. — New York:
Africana Pub. Co., 1981. 322 p., [7] leaves of plates: ill.; 24 cm. Includes index.
1. Cities and towns — Africa, West. 2. Urbanization — Africa, West. I. T.
HT148.W4 P44 1981      307.7/6/0966 19      *LC* 80-26440      *ISBN*
0841906858

# HT151–155 General Works

**Anderson, Nels, 1889-.** • **4.6287**
The industrial urban community; historical and comparative perspectives. —
New York: Appleton-Century-Crofts, [1971] xii, 438 p.; 24 cm. 1. Cities and
towns 2. Urbanization 3. Sociology, Urban I. T.
HT151.A597      301.3/6      *LC* 71-131432      *ISBN* 0390031011

**Berry, Brian Joe Lobley, 1934-.** **4.6288**
Comparative urbanization: divergent paths in the twentieth century / Brian
J.L. Berry. — Rev. and enl. 2nd ed. — New York: St. Martin's Press, c1981. xv,
235 p.: ill.; 22 cm. — (Making of the 20th century.) Rev. ed. of: The human
consequences of urbanisation. 1973. Includes index. 1. Sociology, Urban
2. Urbanization I. Berry, Brian Joe Lobley, 1934- Human consequences of
urbanisation. II. T. III. Series.
HT151.B4337 1981      307.7/6 19      *LC* 82-61562      *ISBN* 0312154755

**Beshers, James M.** • **4.6289**
Urban social structure. — [New York]: Free Press of Glencoe, [1962] 207 p.; 22
cm. 1. Cities and towns 2. Cities and towns — United States. 3. Sociology —
Mathematical models. I. T.
HT151.B44      301.360973      *LC* 62-11844

**Castells, Manuel.** **4.6290**
[Question urbaine. English] The urban question: a Marxist approach / Manuel
Castells; translated by Alan Sheridan. — Cambridge, Mass.: MIT Press, 1977.
x, 502 p., [1] fold. leaf of plates; 24 cm. — (Social structure and social change; 1)
Translation of La question urbaine. Includes index. 1. Cities and towns
2. Urbanization I. T. II. Series.
HT151.C37613 1977b      301.36      *LC* 77-75345      *ISBN* 0262030632

**Current issues in urban economics / edited by Peter** **4.6291**
**Mieszkowski and Mahlon Straszheim.**
Baltimore: Johns Hopkins University Press, c1979. xiv, 589 p.; 24 cm. 1. Cities
and towns — United States — Addresses, essays, lectures. 2. Urban economics
— Addresses, essays, lectures. I. Mieszkowski, Peter M. II. Straszheim,
Mahlon R., 1939-
HT151.C87      330.9/173/2      *LC* 78-14947      *ISBN* 0801821096

**Fischer, Claude S., 1948-.** **4.6292**
The urban experience / Claude S. Fischer; under the general editorship of
Robert K. Merton. — 2nd ed. — San Diego: Harcourt Brace Jovanovich,
c1984. xi, 371 p.: ill.; 21 cm. Includes index. 1. Sociology, Urban — United
States. 2. Cities and towns — United States. I. T.
HT151.F495 1984      307.7/6/0973 19      *LC* 83-82508      *ISBN*
0155934988

**Greer, Scott A.** • **4.6293**
The emerging city; myth and reality. — [New York]: Free Press of Glencoe,
[1962] 232 p.; 22 cm. 1. Sociology, Urban I. T.
HT151.G68      301.36      *LC* 62-11851

**Harvey, David, 1935-.** **4.6294**
Social justice and the city. [Baltimore]: Johns Hopkins University Press, [1973]
336 p.; 24 cm. (Johns Hopkins studies in urban affairs.) 1. Sociology, Urban
2. Urbanization 3. Social justice 4. Land use, Urban I. T. II. Series.
HT151.H34 1973      309.2/62      *LC* 73-7183      *ISBN* 080181524X

**Hawley, Amos Henry.** **4.6295**
Urban society; an ecological approach [by] Amos H. Hawley. — New York:
Ronald Press Co., [1971] ix, 348 p.: illus.; 24 cm. 1. Urbanization 2. Sociology,
Urban I. T.
HT151.H358      307.7/6 19      *LC* 79-155207

**Mumford, Lewis, 1895-.** • **4.6296**
The culture of cities [by] Lewis Mumford. New York, Harcourt, Brace and
company [c1938] xii, 586 p. plates. 24 cm. 1. Cities and towns 2. City planning
3. Regional planning I. T.
HT151.M78      323.352      *LC* 38-27277

**Palen, J. John.** **4.6297**
The urban world [by] J. John Palen. New York, McGraw-Hill [1975] xv, 480 p.
illus. 24 cm. 1. Cities and towns 2. Cities and towns — United States.
3. Urbanization — Developing countries I. T.
HT151.P283      301.36/0973      *LC* 74-10730      *ISBN* 0070480885

**Park, Robert Ezra, 1864-1944.** • **4.6298**
The city / [by] Robert E. Park, Ernest W. Burgess [and] Roderick D.
McKenzie; with an introd. by Morris Janowitz. — Chicago: University of
Chicago Press, [1967] x, 239 p.; 21 cm. — (The Heritage of sociology)
1. Sociology, Urban I. Burgess, Ernest Watson, 1886-1966. joint author.
II. McKenzie, Roderick Duncan, 1885-1940. joint author. III. T.
HT151.P3 1967      301.3/64      *LC* 66-23694

**Robson, William Alexander, 1895- ed.** **4.6299**
Great cities of the world: their government, politics, and planning / edited by
William A. Robson and D. E. Regan. — Beverly Hills, Calif.: Sage
Publications, [1972] 2 v. (1114 p.): maps; 24 cm. 1. Cities and towns
2. Municipal government I. Regan, David E. joint author. II. T.
HT151.R585 1972b      352/.008      *LC* 75-167875      *ISBN* 0803901550

**Weber, Max, 1864-1920.** • **4.6300**
The city. Translated and edited by Don Martindale and Gertrud Neuwirth. —
Glencoe, Ill.: Free Press, [1958] 242 p.; 22 cm. 1. Cities and towns I. T.
HT151.W413      323.352 301.36*      *LC* 58-6492

**Barker, Roger Garlock, 1903-.** • **4.6301**
Qualities of community life [by] Roger G. Barker [and] Phil Schoggen. — [1st
ed.]. — San Francisco: Jossey-Bass, 1973. xii, 562 p.: illus.; 27 cm. — (The
Jossey-Bass behavioral science series) 1. Sociology, Urban — Case studies.
2. Cities and towns — United States — Case studies. 3. Cities and towns —
Great Britain — Case studies. I. Schoggen, Phil, joint author. II. T.
HT153.B34      301.36      *LC* 72-13601      *ISBN* 0875891721

**City classification handbook: methods and applications / edited** **4.6302**
**by Brian J. L. Berry; with the assistance of Katherine B. Smith.**
New York: Wiley-Interscience, 1972. x, 394 p.: ill.; 23 cm. (Wiley series in
urban research) 1. Cities and towns — Addresses, essays, lectures. 2. Cities
and towns — Research — Addresses, essays, lectures. I. Berry, Brian Joe
Lobley, 1934- ed.
HT153.C57      301.3/63/0973      *LC* 71-171911      *ISBN* 0471071153

**La Gory, Mark, 1947-.** **4.6303**
Urban social space / Mark La Gory, John Pipkin. — Belmont, Calif.:
Wadsworth Pub. Co., c1981. xii, 356 p.; 24 cm. Includes index. 1. Sociology,
Urban 2. City planning — History. 3. Human ecology 4. Space (Architecture)
5. Social change 6. Residential mobility I. Pipkin, John. joint author. II. T.
HT153.L26      307.7/6 19      *LC* 80-29675      *ISBN* 053400864X

**Handlin, Oscar, 1915- ed.** • **4.6304**
The historian and the city. Edited by Oscar Handlin and John Burchard. —
[Cambridge, Mass.]: M.I.T. Press, 1963. xii, 299 p.; 25 cm. — (Publications of
the Joint Center for Urban Studies of the Massachusetts Institute of Technology
and Harvard University.) Includes papers delivered at a conference convened
by the Joint Center for Urban Studies, in August, 1961. 1. Cities and towns —

Addresses, essays, lectures. 2. Sociology, Urban — Addresses, essays, lectures. I. Burchard, John Ely, 1898- joint ed. II. Joint Center for Urban Studies. III. T.
HT155.H2     301.36082     *LC* 63-18004

## HT161–169 City Planning

**Fishman, Robert, 1946-.**                               **4.6305**
Urban utopias in the twentieth century: Ebenezer Howard, Frank Lloyd Wright, and Le Corbusier / Robert Fishman. — New York: Basic Books, c1977. xiv, 332 p., [16] leaves of plates: ill.; 25 cm. Includes index. 1. Howard, Ebenezer, Sir, 1850-1928. 2. Wright, Frank Lloyd, 1867-1959. 3. Le Corbusier, 1887-1965. 4. City planning 5. Cities and towns I. T.
HT161.F57     309.2/62     *LC* 76-43457     *ISBN* 046508933X

**Howard, Ebenezer, Sir, 1850-1928.**                    • **4.6306**
Garden cities of to–morrow / by Ebenezer Howard; edited, with a pref., by F.J. Osborn. With an introductory essay by Lewis Mumford. — Cambridge, Mass.: M.I.T. Press, 1965. 168 p.: illus., plans.; 19 cm. — (MIT paperback series) Includes the 2 prefaces and text of the 1946 ed., first published in 1898 under title: Tomorrow, a peaceful path to real reform. 1. Garden cities I. Osborn, Frederic J. II. Howard, Ebenezer, Sir, 1850-1928. Garden cities of to-morrow. III. T.
HT161.H6     *LC* 65-10521     *ISBN* 0571061893

**Barnett, Jonathan.**                                    **4.6307**
Urban design as public policy; practical methods for improving cities. Foreword by John V. Lindsay. — [New York]: Architectural Record Books, [1974] 200 p.: illus.; 24 cm. 1. City planning — United States. I. T.
HT166.B375     309.2/62/0973     *LC* 73-88222

**Blumenfeld, Hans.**                                     • **4.6308**
The modern metropolis: its origins, growth, characteristics, and planning / selected essays; edited by Paul D. Spreiregen. — Cambridge, Mass.: MIT Press [1971] xvi, 379 p.: ill.; 21 cm. 'MIT 191.' 1. City planning I. T.
HT166.B54 1971     309.2/62     *LC* 76-31874     *ISBN* 026202022X
*ISBN* 0262520281

**Encyclopedia of urban planning. Arnold Whittick, editor–in–    4.6309
chief.**
New York: McGraw-Hill, [1974] xxi, 1218 p.: illus.; 25 cm. 1. City planning — Dictionaries. I. Whittick, Arnold, 1898- ed.
HT166.E5     309.2/62/03     *LC* 73-19757     *ISBN* 0070700753

**Galantay, Ervin Y.**                                    **4.6310**
New towns: antiquity to the present / Ervin Y. Galantay. — New York: G. Braziller, [1975] ix, 180 p.: ill.; 26 cm. (Planning and cities) Includes index. 1. New towns I. T.
HT166.G25 1975     301.36/3     *LC* 74-81216     *ISBN* 0807607665

**International Conference on the History of Urban and Regional    4.6311
Planning. 1st, London, 1977.**
The rise of modern urban planning, 1800–1914 / edited by Anthony Sutcliffe. — New York: St. Martin's Press, 1980. xi, 235 p.: ill.; 24 cm. 1. City planning — History — 19th century — Congresses. 2. Regional planning — History — 19th century — Congresses. I. Sutcliffe, Anthony, 1942- II. T.
HT166.I6113 1977     307.7/6     *LC* 80-17273     *ISBN* 0312684304

**Lynch, Kevin, 1918-.**                                  **4.6312**
A theory of good city form / Kevin Lynch. — Cambridge, Mass.: MIT Press, c1981. 514 p.: ill.; 24 cm. Includes index. 1. City planning — Philosophy. 2. Sociology, Urban 3. Cities and towns — History. I. T.
HT166.L96     307.7/6/01 19     *LC* 80-26348     *ISBN* 0262120852

**Morris, A. E. J. (Anthony Edwin James)**               **4.6313**
History of urban form: before the industrial revolutions / A. E. J. Morris. — 2d ed. — New York: Wiley, 1979. x, 317 p.: ill.; 26 cm. 'A Halsted Press book.' Includes indexes. 1. City planning — History. 2. Cities and towns, Ancient 3. Cities and towns, Medieval I. T.
HT166.M59 1979     307.7/6/09     *LC* 79-41117     *ISBN* 0470266147

**Rykwert, Joseph, 1926-.**                               **4.6314**
The idea of a town: the anthropology of urban form in Rome, Italy and the ancient world / Joseph Rykwert. — Princeton, N.J.: Princeton University Press, c1976. 242 p.: ill.; 26 cm. 1. City planning — History. 2. Cities and towns, Ancient I. T.
HT166.R94     309.2/62/093     *LC* 75-31901     *ISBN* 0691039011

**Urban Europe / by Leo van den Berg ... [et al.] for the         4.6315
European Coordination Centre for Research and Documentation
in Social Sciences.**
1st ed. — Oxford; New York: Pergamon Press, 1982. 162 p.: maps. (Cross national comparative series) 1. City planning 2. Urban policy 3. Urban policy

— Europe — Evaluation. I. Berg, Leo van den. II. European Coordination Centre for Research and Documentation in Social Sciences.
HT166.U735 1982     307.7/64/094 19     *LC* 81-81233     *ISBN* 008023156X

### HT167–169 By Country

### HT167–168 United States

**The American planner: biographies and recollections / edited by   4.6316
Donald A. Krueckeberg.**
New York: Methuen, 1983. xiii, 433 p.: ill.; 24 cm. 1. City planners — United States — Addresses, essays, lectures. 2. City planners — United States — Biography — Addresses, essays, lectures. 3. Regional planning — United States — Addresses, essays, lectures. I. Krueckeberg, Donald A.
HT167.A5767 1983     307/.12/0922 B 19     *LC* 82-6461     *ISBN* 0416333605

**Conference on New Communities, Washington, D.C., 1971.         4.6317**
New towns in America; the design and development process. Edited by James Bailey. Foreword by Carrell S. McNulty, Jr. — New York: Wiley, [1974] xii, 165 p.: illus.; 29 cm. At head of title: The American Institute of Architects. 1. New towns — United States. I. Bailey, James, 1932- ed. II. American Institute of Architects. III. T.
HT167.C64 1974     309.2/62/0973     *LC* 73-77292     *ISBN* 047100975X

**Frieden, Bernard J.**                                    **4.6318**
The politics of neglect: urban aid from model cities to revenue sharing / Bernard J. Frieden and Marshall Kaplan. — Cambridge, Mass.: MIT Press, [1975] x, 281 p.; 23 cm. — (A Publication of the Joint Center for Urban Studies) 1. City planning — United States. 2. Urban renewal — United States. 3. Federal-city relations — United States. I. Kaplan, Marshall. joint author. II. T.
HT167.F74     309.2/62/0973     *LC* 75-6792     *ISBN* 0262060612

**Gans, Herbert J.**                                       • **4.6319**
People and plans; essays on urban problems and solutions [by] Herbert J. Gans. New York, Basic Books [1968] xvii, 395 p. 25 cm. 1. City planning — United States. 2. United States — Social policy I. T.
HT167.G35     309.2/6/0973     *LC* 68-54134

**Introduction to planning history in the United States / edited    4.6320
by Donald A. Krueckeberg.**
New Brunswick, N.J.: Center for Urban Policy Research, c1983. xiii, 302 p.: ill.; 23 cm. Includes index. 1. City planning — United States — History — Addresses, essays, lectures. I. Krueckeberg, Donald A.
HT167.I57 1983     307/.12/0973 19     *LC* 82-14572     *ISBN* 0882850830

**Lubove, Roy.**                                           • **4.6321**
The urban community: housing and planning in the progressive era. Englewood Cliffs, N.J., Prentice-Hall [1967] ix, 148 p. 21 cm. (American historical sources series: research and interpretation) 1. City planning — United States — Addresses, essays, lectures. I. T.
HT167.L8     307.7/6/0973 19     *LC* 67-10119

**Olmsted, Frederick Law, 1822-1903.**                     **4.6322**
Civilizing American cities; a selection of Frederick Law Olmsted's writings on city landscapes. Edited by S. B. Sutton. — Cambridge, Mass.: MIT Press, [1971] 310 p.: illus.; 24 cm. 1. Cities and towns — Planning — United States. 2. Parks — United States. I. T.
HT167.O44     711/.558/0973     *LC* 72-113729     *ISBN* 0262190702

**The Practice of local government planning / editors, Frank S.     4.6323
So ... [et al.].**
Washington: Published in cooperation with the American Planning Association by the International City Management Association, c1979. 676 p.: ill.; 28 cm. — (Municipal management series) Previous ed. published under title: Principles and practice of urban planning. Includes index. 1. City planning — United States. I. So, Frank S. II. Principles and practice of urban planning. III. Series.
HT167.P7     352/.96/0973     *LC* 79-21380     *ISBN* 0873260201

**Scott, Mel, 1906-.**                                     • **4.6324**
American city planning since 1890; a history commemorating the fiftieth anniversary of the American Institute of Planners [by] Mel Scott. Berkeley, University of California Press, 1969. xxii, 745 p. illus., plans. 27 cm. 1. American Institute of Planners. 2. City planning — United States — History. I. T.
HT167.S3     711/.4/0973     *LC* 70-84533     *ISBN* 0520013824

**McFarland, M. Carter.**    **4.6325**
Federal Government and urban problems: HUD: successes, failures, and the fate of our cities / M. Carter McFarland; with an introd. by Paul Ylvisaker. — Boulder, Colo.: Westview Press, 1978. xviii, 277 p.; 24 cm. 1. United States. Dept. of Housing and Urban Development. 2. Housing policy — United States. 3. Cities and towns — United States. I. T.
HT167.2.M33 1978    301.36/3/0973    *LC* 77-26301    *ISBN* 0891580859

**Reps, John William.**    **4.6326**
Tidewater towns: city planning in colonial Virginia and Maryland / by John W. Reps. — Williamsburg, Va.: Colonial Williamsburg Foundation; distributed by the University Press of Virginia, Charlottesville, [1972] xii, 345 p.: ill.; 24 x 32 cm. (Williamsburg architectural studies.) 1. City planning — Virginia — History. 2. City planning — Maryland — History. I. T. II. Series.
HT167.5.V8 R46    711/.4/097521    *LC* 77-154342    *ISBN* 0910412871

**Lubove, Roy.**    • **4.6327**
Twentieth–century Pittsburgh: government, business, and environmental change. — New York: Wiley [1969] x, 189 p.: ill., maps; 22 cm. (New dimensions in history. Historical cities.) 1. City planning — Pennsylvania — Pittsburgh. 2. Urban renewal — Pennsylvania — Pittsburgh. 3. Pittsburgh (Pa.) — Politics and government. 4. Pittsburgh (Pa.) — Social conditions. I. T. II. Series.
HT168.P48 L6    711/.4/0974886    *LC* 69-19234    *ISBN* 047155250X

**Silver, Christopher, 1951-.**    **4.6328**
Twentieth–century Richmond: planning, politics, and race / Christopher Silver. — Knoxville: University of Tennessee Press, c1984. x, 342 p.: ill.; 23 cm. (Twentieth-century America series.) Includes index. 1. City planning — Virginia — Richmond — History — 20th century. 2. Urban renewal — Virginia — Richmond. 3. Afro-Americans — Housing — Virginia — Richmond. 4. Richmond (Va.) — Politics and government. I. T. II. Title: 20th-century Richmond. III. Series.
HT168.R5 S54 1984    307/.12/09755451 19    *LC* 83-16848    *ISBN* 087049421X

**United States. National Capital Planning Commission.**    **4.6329**
Worthy of the nation: the history of planning for the national capital / National Capital Planning Commission; Frederick Gutheim, consultant. — Washington: Smithsonian Institution Press, c1977. xvii, 415 p.: ill.; 27 cm. (National Capital Planning Commission historical studies) Includes index. 1. City planning — Washington (D.C.) — History. I. Gutheim, Frederick Albert, 1908- II. T.
HT168.W3 U52 1977    309.2/62/09753    *LC* 77-120    *ISBN* 0874744962. *ISBN* 0874744970 pbk

## HT169 Other Countries

**Evenson, Norma.**    **4.6330**
Paris: a century of change, 1878–1978 / Norma Evenson. — New Haven: Yale University Press, c1979. xvii, 382 p.: ill.; 29 cm. Includes index. 1. Urban renewal — France — Paris. 2. City planning — France — Paris. I. T.
HT169.F72 P356    309.2/62/0944361    *LC* 78-10257    *ISBN* 0300022107

**Cherry, Gordon Emanuel.**    **4.6331**
Urban change and planning; a history of urban development in Britain since 1750 [by] Gordon E. Cherry. — Henley-on-Thames [Eng.]: G. T. Foulis, [1972] 254 p.: illus.; 25 cm. 1. City planning — Great Britain. 2. Urban renewal — Great Britain. 3. Cities and towns — Great Britain. I. T.
HT169.G7 C46    309.2/62/0942    *LC* 72-191984    *ISBN* 0854291199

**Osborn, Frederic James, Sir, 1885-.**    • **4.6332**
The new towns: the answer to megalopolis / [by] Frederic J. Osborn and Arnold Whittick; introd. by Lewis Mumford. — [Completely rev. and reset]. — Cambridge, Mass.: M.I.T. Press, [1969, c1963] 456 p.: ill., maps, plans.; 26 cm. 1. New towns — Great Britain. I. Whittick, Arnold, 1898- II. T.
HT169.G7 O8 1969    309.2/62/0941    *LC* 71-96902    *ISBN* 0262150107

**British town planning: the formative years / edited by Anthony Sutcliffe.**    **4.6333**
New York: St. Martin's Press, 1981. xi, 211 p.: ill., plans, ports. 1. City planning — Great Britain — History — Addresses, essays, lectures. I. Sutcliffe, Anthony, 1942-
HT169.G7 S97 1981    307.7/6/0941 19    *LC* 81-51916    *ISBN* 0312105452

**Olsen, Donald J.**    **4.6334**
The growth of Victorian London / Donald J. Olsen. — New York: Holmes & Meier, 1976. 384 p.: ill.; 26 cm. Includes index. 1. City planning — England —

London — History — 19th century. 2. Architecture — England — London — History. 3. London (England) — History — 1800-1950 I. T.
HT169.G72 L6474 1976    301.36/3/09421    *LC* 76-25164    *ISBN* 0841902844

**Geddes, Patrick, Sir, 1854-1932.**    **4.6335**
City development: a report to the Carnegie Dunfermline Trust / with an introd. by Peter Green. — New Brunswick, N.J.: Rutgers University Press [1973] 33, 231 p.: ill.; 30 cm. 'A complete and unabridged photolithographic facsimile of the first edition' published in 1904 by Geddes and Co., Edinburgh. 1. City planning — Scotland — Dunfermline (Fife) 2. Parks — Scotland — Dunfermline (Fife) I. Carnegie Dunfermline Trust. II. T.
HT169.G72 S454 1904a    711/.4/094133    *LC* 73-161930    *ISBN* 0813507480

**Gutkind, Peter Claus Wolfgang.**    **4.6336**
Urban anthropology: perspectives on third world urbanisation and urbanism / by Peter C. W. Gutkind. — New York: Barnes & Noble, 1974. 262 p.: map; 25 cm. Includes indexes. 1. Urbanization — Developing countries 2. Sociology, Urban I. T.
HT169.5.G87 1974    301.36/3/091724    *LC* 75-305307    *ISBN* 0064926109

**King, Anthony D.**    **4.6337**
Colonial urban development: culture, social power, and environment / Anthony D. King. — London; Boston: Routledge & Paul, 1976. xvi, 328 p.: ill.; 25 cm. Includes indexes. 1. Urbanization — Developing countries 2. Cities and towns — Developing countries 3. Sociology, Urban I. T.
HT169.5.K55    301.36/3/091724    *LC* 76-383717    *ISBN* 0710084048

**Third world urbanization / edited by Janet Abu–Lughod, Richard Hay, Jr.**    **4.6338**
Chicago: Maaroufa Press, c1977. 395 p.; 23 cm. Includes index. 1. Urbanization — Developing countries — Addresses, essays, lectures. I. Abu-Lughod, Janet. II. Hay, Richard.
HT169.5.T52    301.36/1/091724    *LC* 76-53367    *ISBN* 0884250059

**Rodwin, Lloyd.**    **4.6339**
Cities and city planning / Lloyd Rodwin, with Hugh Evans ... [et al.]. — New York: Plenum Press, c1981. viii, 309 p., [8] p. of plates: ill.; 21 cm. (Environment, development, and public policy. Cities and development.) 1. New towns — Addresses, essays, lectures. 2. Metropolitan areas — Addresses, essays, lectures. 3. Regional planning — Developing countries — Addresses, essays, lectures. 4. City planning — Addresses, essays, lectures. 5. Cities and towns — Addresses, essays, lectures. I. T. II. Series.
HT169.55.R62    307.7/6 19    *LC* 81-13956    *ISBN* 0306406667

**Costonis, John J.**    **4.6340**
Space adrift: landmark preservation and the marketplace / John J. Costonis. — Urbana: Published for the National Trust for Historic Preservation by the University of Illinois Press, [1974] xx, 207 p.: ill.; 26 cm. Includes index. 1. Development rights transfer — United States. 2. Historic buildings — United States — Conservation and restoration. 3. Development rights transfer — Illinois — Chicago. 4. Chicago (Ill.) — Buildings, structures, etc. I. T.
HT169.9.D4 C6    309.2/62    *LC* 73-5405    *ISBN* 0252004027

## HT170–178 Urban Renewal

**Marris, Peter.**    **4.6341**
Community planning and conceptions of change / Peter Marris. — London; Boston: Routledge & Kegan Paul, 1982. vii, 140 p.; 23 cm. Includes index. 1. Urban renewal 2. Community development, Urban 3. Land use, Urban 4. Social action 5. Urban economics I. T.
HT170.M33 1982    307/.12 19    *LC* 82-13175    *ISBN* 0710093497

**Gentrification, displacement, and neighborhood revitalization / edited by J. John Palen and Bruce London.**    **4.6342**
Albany: State University of New York Press, c1984. viii, 271 p.; 24 cm. — (SUNY series in urban public policy) 1. Urban renewal — United States — Addresses, essays, lectures. 2. Neighborhood — United States — Addresses, essays, lectures. 3. Residential mobility — United States — Addresses, essays, lectures. 4. Middle classes — United States — Addresses, essays, lectures. 5. Gentrification — United States — Addresses, essays, lectures. I. Palen, J. John. II. London, Bruce.
HT175.G47 1984    307/.342/0973 19    *LC* 83-5038    *ISBN* 0873957849

**Wilson, James Q. ed.**    • **4.6343**
Urban renewal: the record and the controversy / edited by James Q. Wilson. — Cambridge, Mass.: M.I.T. Press, [1966] xix, 683 p.: ill., plans.; 25 cm. — (Publications of the Joint Center for Urban Studies of the Massachusetts

Institute of Technology and Harvard University) 1. Urban renewal — United States. I. T.
HT175.U6 W5     711.59     *LC* 66-14344

**Stone, Clarence N. (Clarence Nathan), 1935-.**     **4.6344**
Economic growth and neighborhood discontent: system bias in the urban renewal program of Atlanta / by Clarence N. Stone. — Chapel Hill: University of North Carolina Press, c1976. xv, 256 p.; 24 cm. Includes index. 1. Urban renewal — Georgia — Atlanta. I. T.
HT177.A77 S76     309.2/62/09758231     *LC* 75-22274     *ISBN* 0807812625

**Rossi, Peter Henry, 1921-.**     **• 4.6345**
The politics of urban renewal: the Chicago findings / Peter H. Rossi and Robert A. Dentler; with the assistance of Nelson W. Polsby [and others]. — New York: Free Press of Glencoe, 1961. 308 p.: ill., map. 1. Urban renewal — Illinois — Chicago. I. Dentler, Robert A., 1928- II. T.
HT177.C5R6     711.590977311     *LC* 59-13865

## HT321 Urban Economics

**Jacobs, Jane, 1916-.**     **• 4.6346**
The economy of cities. — New York: Random House, [1969] 268 p.: illus.; 22 cm. 1. Urban economics 2. Industry — Social aspects 3. Economic development I. T.
HT321.J32     338/.09173/2     *LC* 69-16413

**Marxism and the metropolis: new perspectives in urban political**     **4.6347**
**economy / edited by William K. Tabb and Larry Sawers.**
2nd ed. — New York: Oxford University Press, 1984. x, 390 p.; 25 cm. Papers from a second conference on new perspectives in the urban economy held at American University, Washington, D.C., in May 1981. Only four of the papers in the first edition are repeated. 1. Urban economics — Addresses, essays, lectures. 2. Marxian economics — Addresses, essays, lectures. 3. Cities and towns — United States — Addresses, essays, lectures. I. Tabb, William K. II. Sawers, Larry, 1942-
HT321.M24 1984     338.973/009173/2 19     *LC* 82-25965     *ISBN* 0195033078

**Neenan, William B., 1929-.**     **• 4.6348**
Political economy of urban areas / [by] William B. Neenan. — Chicago: Markham Pub. Co., [1972] xix, 344 p.: ill.; 22 cm. — (Markham series in public policy analysis) 1. Urban economics 2. Municipal finance I. T.
HT321.N43     330.9/73     *LC* 75-184324     *ISBN* 0841009252

**Urbanization in the world–economy / edited by Michael**     **4.6349**
**Timberlake.**
Orlando: Academic Press, 1985. xv, 387 p.: ill.; 24 cm. (Studies in social discontinuity.) Includes index. 1. Urbanization — Addresses, essays, lectures. 2. Urban economics — Addresses, essays, lectures. 3. International economic relations — Addresses, essays, lectures. I. Timberlake, Michael. II. Series.
HT321.U34 1985     307.7/6 19     *LC* 84-12511     *ISBN* 0126912904

## HT330–334 Metropolitan Areas

**Metropolis, 1890–1940 / edited by Anthony Sutcliffe.**     **4.6350**
Chicago: University of Chicago Press, 1984. viii, 458 p.: ill.; 25 cm. 1. Metropolitan areas — History — 20th century — Congresses. 2. Cities and towns — Growth — History — 20th century — Congresses. 3. Urbanization — History — 20th century — Congresses. 4. City planning — History — 20th century — Congresses. I. Sutcliffe, Anthony, 1942-
HT330.M45 1984     307.7/64 19     *LC* 83-40340     *ISBN* 0226780252

**Cox, Kevin R., 1939-.**     **4.6351**
Conflict, power, and politics in the city: a geographic view [by] Kevin R. Cox. — New York: McGraw-Hill, [1973] xiii, 133 p.: illus.; 23 cm. — (McGraw-Hill problems series in geography) 1. Metropolitan areas — United States 2. Metropolitan government — United States. I. T.
HT334.U5 C68     301.5/92     *LC* 72-6644     *ISBN* 0070132739

**Popenoe, David, 1932-.**     **4.6352**
Private pleasure, public plight: American metropolitan community life in comparative perspective / David Popenoe. — New Brunswick, U.S.A.: Transaction Books, c1985. viii, 162 p.; 24 cm. 1. Metropolitan areas — United States 2. Sociology, Urban — United States. 3. Community life 4. Social problems I. T.
HT334.U5 P66 1985     307.7/64/0973 19     *LC* 84-16411     *ISBN* 0887380301

**Post–industrial America: metropolitan decline & inter–regional**     **4.6353**
**job shifts / edited by George Sternlieb and James W. Hughes.**
New Brunswick, N.J.: Center for Urban Policy Research, Rutgers - the State University of New Jersey, c1975. 267 p.: ill.; 24 cm. 1. Metropolitan areas — United States — Addresses, essays, lectures. 2. Migration, Internal — United States — Addresses, essays, lectures. 3. United States — Industries — Addresses, essays, lectures. 4. United States — Social conditions — 1960- Addresses, essays, lectures. I. Sternlieb, George. II. Hughes, James W. III. Rutgers University. Center for Urban Policy Research.
HT334.U5 P67     301.36/4/0973     *LC* 75-34000     *ISBN* 088285027X

## HT351–384 Suburbs. City Growth

**Berger, Bennett M.**     **• 4.6354**
Working–class suburb: a study of auto workers in suburbia. Berkeley: University of California Press, 1960. xiii, 143 p.: tables; 25 cm. 1. Suburban life — Case studies. 2. Milpitas (Calif.) I. T.
HT351.B4     *LC* 60-11846

**Muller, Peter O.**     **4.6355**
Contemporary suburban America / Peter O. Muller. — Englewood Cliffs, N.J.: Prentice-Hall, c1981. xii, 218 p.: ill.; 23 cm. Based on the author's The outer city. Includes indexes. 1. Suburbs — United States — History. 2. Metropolitan areas — United States — History. 3. Suburban life — United States — History. 4. Suburbs — Economic aspects — United States. I. T.
HT351.M84     307.7/4/0973 19     *LC* 80-25653     *ISBN* 0131706470

**Seeley, John R.**     **• 4.6356**
Crestwood Heights; a study of the culture of suburban life [by] John R. Seeley, R. Alexander Sim [and] Elizabeth W. Loosley. Introd. by David Riesman. — [1st ed.]. — New York: Basic Books, [1956] xv, 505 p.: illus.; 24 cm. 1. Suburban life I. T.
HT351.S3     323.353 301.36*     *LC* 56-9099

**Fligstein, Neil.**     **4.6357**
Going north, migration of Blacks and whites from the South, 1900–1950 / Neil Fligstein. — New York: Academic Press, c1981. xvi, 230 p.: ill., map.; 24 cm. — (Quantitative studies in social relations.) Originally presented as the author's thesis. Includes index. 1. Rural-urban migration — United States — History — 20th century. I. T. II. Series.
HT361.F55 1981     304.8/0975 19     *LC* 81-14901     *ISBN* 0122607201

**Jackson, Kenneth T.**     **4.6358**
Crabgrass frontier: the suburbanization of the United States / Kenneth T. Jackson. — New York: Oxford University Press, 1985. x, 396 p.: ill.; 24 cm. 1. Suburbs — United States — History. 2. Suburban life 3. Housing — United States — History. 4. United States — Social conditions I. T.
HT384.U5 J33 1985     307.7/4/0973 19     *LC* 85-4844     *ISBN* 0195036107

## HT390–395 Regional Planning

**Coastal area management and development / United Nations,**     **4.6359**
**Department of International Economic and Social Affairs,**
**Ocean Economics and Technology Branch.**
1st ed. — Oxford; New York: Pergamon Press, 1982. xii, 188 p.; 24 cm. 1. Coastal zone managment. 2. Economic development 3. Coastal zone management I — Law and legislation 4. Developing countries — Economic conditions I. United Nations. Ocean Economics and Technology Branch.
HT391.C497 1982     333.91/715 19     *LC* 82-14991     *ISBN* 0080233937

**Development from above or below?: The dialectics of regional**     **4.6360**
**planning in developing countries / edited by Walter B. Stöhr**
**and D.R. Fraser Taylor.**
Chichester [Eng.]; New York: Wiley, 1981. xii, 488 p.: maps.; 24 cm. 1. Regional planning — Developing countries — Case studies. I. Stöhr, Walter B. II. Taylor, D. R. F. (David Ruxton Fraser), 1937-
HT391.D39     361.6/09172/4 19     *LC* 80-40850     *ISBN* 0471278238

**Hewing, Geoffrey J. D.**     **4.6361**
Regional industrial analysis and development / Geoffrey J. D. Hewings. — New York: St. Martin's Press, 1977. 180 p.: ill. — (The Field of geography) 1. Regional planning 2. Regional economics 3. Industry — Location I. T.
HT391.H43     309.2/5     *LC* 77-76803     *ISBN* 0312669100

**Regional analysis / edited by Carol A. Smith.**     **4.6362**
New York: Academic Press, 1976. 2 v.: ill.; 24 cm. (Studies in anthropology) 1. Regional economics — Addresses, essays, lectures. 2. Central places —

Addresses, essays, lectures. 3. Social systems — Economic aspects — Addresses, essays, lectures. 4. Developing countries — Commerce — Addresses, essays, lectures. I. Smith, Carol A.
HT391.R29    380.1/09172/4    *LC* 75-30474    *ISBN* 0126521018

**Jorgensen-Dahl, Arnfinn, 1939-.**         **4.6363**
Regional organization and order in South–East Asia / Arnfinn Jorgensen-Dahl. — London: St. Martin's, 1982. xvii, 278 p.; 23 cm. 1. Asia, Southeastern — Foreign relations. I. T.
DS526.7    HT395.A75 J6.    321/.04 18    321/.04 19    *ISBN* 0333306635

**Regional development in Western Europe / edited by Hugh D.**    **4.6364**
**Clout.**
2d ed. — Chichester [Eng.]; New York: J. Wiley, c1981. xiv, 417 p.: ill.; 26 cm. 1. Regional planning — Europe — Addresses, essays, lectures. 2. Europe — Economic conditions — 1945- — Addresses, essays, lectures. I. Clout, Hugh D.
HT395.E8 R4 1981    361.6/094 19    *LC* 80-40852    *ISBN* 0471278459

# HT401–485 Rural Sociology

**Nelson, Lowry, 1893-.**         • **4.6365**
Rural sociology: its origin and growth in the United States. — Minneapolis: University of Minnesota Press, [1969] viii, 221 p.; 24 cm. 1. Sociology, Rural — History — U.S. I. T.
HT415.N4    301.3/5/0973    *LC* 78-77654

**Our forgotten past: seven centuries of life on the land / texts by**    **4.6366**
**Jerome Blum ... [et al.]; edited by Jerome Blum.**
London: Thames and Hudson, c1982. 240 p.: ill. (some col.); 28 cm. Includes index. 1. Farm life — History — Addresses, essays, lectures. 2. Rural conditions — Addresses, essays, lectures. 3. Peasantry — History — Addresses, essays, lectures. I. Blum, Jerome, 1913-
HT415.O93 1982    307.7/2 19    *LC* 82-161501    *ISBN* 0500250804

**The Keeping of animals: adaptation and social relations in**    **4.6367**
**livestock producing communities / edited by Riva Berleant–**
**Schiller and Eugenia Shanklin.**
Totowa, N.J.: Allanheld, Osmun, 1983. xxi, 186 p.: ill.; 25 cm. 1. Sociology, Rural — Addresses, essays, lectures. 2. Shepherds — Addresses, essays, lectures. 3. Peasantry — Addresses, essays, lectures. 4. Herders — Addresses, essays, lectures. 5. Ranchers — Addresses, essays, lectures. 6. Livestock — Social aspects. I. Berleant-Schiller, Riva. II. Shanklin, Eugenia, 1939-
HT421.K43 1983    307.7/62 19    *LC* 81-65015    *ISBN* 0865980330

**Loomis, Charles Price, 1905-.**         **4.6368**
A strategy for rural change / by Charles P. Loomis and J. Allan Beegle. — Cambridge, Mass.: Schenkman Pub. Co.; New York: distributed by Halsted Press, [1975] xv, 525 p.: ill.; 24 cm. 1. Sociology, Rural — United States. 2. United States — Rural conditions I. Beegle, J. Allan (Joseph Allan), 1918- joint author. II. T.
HT421.L564    309.1/173/4    *LC* 74-22100    *ISBN* 0470544805

**The Rural sociology of the advanced societies: critical**    **4.6369**
**perspectives / edited by Frederick H. Buttel and Howard**
**Newby.**
Montclair, N.J.: Allanheld, Osmun, 1980. ix, 529 p.; 24 cm. 1. Sociology, Rural — Addresses, essays, lectures. 2. Agriculture — Economic aspects — Addresses, essays, lectures. 3. Agriculture and state — Addresses, essays, lectures. I. Buttel, Frederick H. II. Newby, Howard.
HT421.R85    301.35    *LC* 79-5177    *ISBN* 0916672301

**Sanders, Irwin Taylor, 1909-.**         **4.6370**
Rural society / Irwin T. Sanders. — Englewood Cliffs, N.J.: Prentice-Hall, c1977. xiv, 170 p.: ill.; 24 cm. — (Prentice-Hall foundations of modern sociology series) Includes index. 1. Sociology, Rural I. T.
HT421.S25 1977    307.7/2 19    *LC* 76-30737    *ISBN* 0137844476

**Sorokin, Pitirim Aleksandrovich, 1889-1968. ed.**      • **4.6371**
A systematic source book in rural sociology, edited by Pitirim A. Sorokin, Carle C. Zimmerman and Charles J. Galpin. New York, Russell & Russell, 1965, [c1930-1932] 3 v. 23 cm. Bibliographical footnotes. 1. Sociology, Rural 2. Social psychology 3. Population I. Zimmerman, Carle Clark, 1897- joint ed. II. Galpin, Charles Josiah, 1864- joint editor. III. T.
HT421.S64    301.35    *LC* 66-11362

**Bunce, M. F.**         **4.6372**
Rural settlement in an urban world / Michael Bunce. — New York: St. Martin's Press, 1982. 219 p.: ill.; 23 cm. 1. Villages 2. Social change 3. Rural conditions I. T.
HT431.B86 1982    307.7/2 19    *LC* 81-52986    *ISBN* 0312696051

**Vidich, Arthur J.**         • **4.6373**
Small town in mass society: class, power and religion in a rural community / by Arthur J. Vidich and Joseph Bensman. — [Rev. ed.] Princeton, N.J.: Princeton University Press, 1968. xxviii, 493 p.; 21 cm. (Princeton paperbacks, no. 131) 1. Villages — United States. 2. United States — Rural conditions I. Bensman, Joseph. joint author. II. T.
HT431.V5 1968    301.3/5/0973    *LC* 68-27411

# HT601–1595 CLASSES. RACES

# HT601–1445 Classes

**Bendix, Reinhard. ed.**         • **4.6374**
Class, status, and power; social stratification in comparative perspective, edited by Reinhard Bendix and Seymour Martin Lipset. — 2d ed. — New York: Free Press, [1966] xviii, 677 p.: illus.; 28 cm. 1. Social classes — Collections. I. Lipset, Seymour Martin. joint ed. II. T.
HT605.B4 1966    323.3    *LC* 65-23025

**Barber, Bernard.**         • **4.6375**
Social stratification; a comparative analysis of structure and process. Under the general editorship of Robert K. Merton. — New York: Harcourt, Brace, [1957] 540 p.: illus.; 22 cm. 1. Social classes I. T.
HT609.B25    323.3    *LC* 57-241

**Centers, Richard.**         • **4.6376**
The psychology of social classes; a study of class consciousness. New York: Russell & Russell, 1961 [c1949] xii, 244 p.: diagrs., tables; 22 cm. (Studies in public opinion) 1. Social classes 2. Class consciousness I. T. II. Series.
HT609.C4 1961    301.44    *LC* 61-13778

**Cole, G. D. H. (George Douglas Howard), 1889-1959.**      • **4.6377**
Studies in class structure. [London] Routledge and Paul [1955] vii, 195 p. tables. 23 cm. (International library of sociology and social reconstruction) 1. Social clases — Great Britain. I. T. II. Title: Class structure.
HT609.C66    *LC* 56-329

**Cox, Oliver Cromwell, 1901-.**         • **4.6378**
Caste, class, & race; a study in social dynamics. Introd. by Joseph S. Roucek. New York: Monthly Review Press, 1959. xxxviii, 624 p.: diagrs.; 24 cm. 1. Caste 2. Social classes 3. Race relations I. T.
HT609 C7 1959    *LC* 59-8866       *HT 609 C7*

**Dahrendorf, Ralf.**         • **4.6379**
[Soziale Klassen und Klassenkonflikt in der industriellen Gesellschaft. English] Class and class conflict in industrial society. [Translated, rev., and expanded by the author] Stanford, Calif., Stanford University Press, 1959. 336 p. 25 cm. 1. Social conflict 2. Industrial relations I. T.
HT609.D313    301.44    *LC* 59-7425

**Giddens, Anthony.**         **4.6380**
The class structure of the advanced societies. — New York: Barnes & Noble, [1973] 336 p.; 22 cm. — 1. Social classes I. T.
HT609.G47    301.44

**Lenski, Gerhard Emmanuel, 1924-.**         • **4.6381**
Power and privilege; a theory of social stratification [by] Gerhard E. Lenski. New York, McGraw-Hill [1966] xiv, 495 p. ill. (McGraw-Hill series in sociology) 1. Social classes I. T.
HT609 L44    *LC* 65-28594

**Lipset, Seymour Martin.**         • **4.6382**
Social mobility in industrial society [by] Seymour Martin Lipset and Reinhard Bendix. Berkeley, University of California Press, 1959. xxi, 309 p. illus. 25 cm. At head of title: A publication of the Institute of Industrial Relations, University of California. 1. Social mobility I. Bendix, Reinhard. joint author. II. University of California, Berkeley. Institute of Industrial Relations. III. T.
HT609.L52    301.44    *LC* 58-12829

**Packard, Vance Oakley, 1914-.**                                    **4.6383**
The status seekers; an exploration of class behavior in America and the hidden barriers that affect you, your community, your future. — New York: D. McKay Co., [1959] 376 p.; 21 cm. 1. Social classes — United States. I. T.
HT609.P3        301.44        *LC* 59-9387

**Smelser, Neil J. ed.**                                          • **4.6384**
Social structure and mobility in economic development, edited by Neil J. Smelser and Seymour Martin Lipset. Chicago: Aldine Pub. Co. [1966] ix, 399 p.; 24 cm. Papers presented at a conference on social structure, social mobility, and economic development held in San Francisco, January 30-February 1, 1964 and sponsored by the Committee on Economic Growth of the Social Science Research Council. 1. Social mobility — Addresses, essays, lectures. 2. Social structure — Addresses, essays, lectures. 3. Economic development — Addresses, essays, lectures. I. Lipset, Seymour Martin. joint ed. II. Social Science Research Council (U.S.). Committee on Economic Growth. III. T.
HT609.S6        301.44        *LC* 65-12458

**Tumin, Melvin Marvin, 1919-.**                                    **4.6385**
Social stratification: the forms and functions of inequality / Melvin M. Tumin. — 2nd ed. — Englewood Cliffs, N.J.: Prentice-Hall, c1985. x, 166 p.; 23 cm. (Prentice-Hall foundations of modern sociology series.) 1. Social classes 2. Equality I. T. II. Series.
HT609.T8 1985        305 19        *LC* 84-17772        *ISBN* 0138186596

**Warner, W. Lloyd (William Lloyd), 1898-1970.**                    • **4.6386**
Social class in America; a manual of procedure for the measurement of social status [by] W. Lloyd Warner with Marchia Meeker and Kenneth Eells. With a new essay, Theory and method for the comparative study of social stratification, by W. Lloyd Warner. New York, Harper [1960] 298 p. illus. 21 cm. (Harper torchbooks, TB1013. The Academy library) 1. Social classes — United States. I. T.
HT609.W28 1960        301.44        *LC* 60-2697

**Warner, W. Lloyd (William Lloyd), 1898-1970.**                    • **4.6387**
The social life of a modern community, by W. Lloyd Warner and Paul S. Lunt. New Haven, Yale university press; London, H. Milford, Oxford university press, 1941. xx, 460 p. incl. illus. (map), tables, diagrs. 24 cm. (Yankee City series, v. 1) 1. Cities and towns 2. Social classes 3. Culture I. Lunt, Paul Sanborn, joint author. II. T. III. Series.
HT609.W3        301.1523        *LC* 42-2549

**Warner, W. Lloyd (William Lloyd), 1898-1970.**                    • **4.6388**
The status system of a modern community, by W. Lloyd Warner and Paul S. Lunt. New Haven: Yale University Press, 1942. xx, 246 p.: incl. ill. (diagrs.) tables; 24 cm. (Yankee City series, vol. II) 'Published on the Richard Teller Crane, Jr., memorial fund.' 1. Sociology, Urban 2. Social classes I. Lunt, Paul Sanborn, jt. author II. T.
HT609 W32        *LC* A42-3288

**Wright, Erik Olin.**                                            **4.6389**
Class, crisis, and the state / Erik Olin Wright. — London: NLB, c1978. 266 p.: ill.; 22 cm. On jacket: Distributed in U.S. by Schocken Books, New York. Includes indexes. 1. Social classes 2. Depressions 3. Bureaucracy 4. Capitalism I. T.
HT609.W7        305.5 19        *LC* 78-319053        *ISBN* 0902308939

## HT641–657 Hereditary Classes

**Elias, Norbert.**                                              **4.6390**
[Höfische Gesellschaft. English] The court society / by Norbert Elias; translated by Edmund Jephcott. — 1st American ed. — New York: Pantheon Books, c1983. 301 p.; 24 cm. Translation of: Die höfische Gesellschaft. 1. Aristocracy I. T.
HT647.E5313 1983        305.5/2 19        *LC* 83-4236        *ISBN* 0394532821

**Emmons, Terence.**                                            • **4.6391**
The Russian landed gentry and the peasant emancipation of 1861. London, Cambridge U.P., 1968. xi, 484 p. 2 plates, ports, 23 cm. 1. Land tenure — Soviet Union. 2. Soviet Union — Gentry. I. T.
HT647.E6        323.3/0947        *LC* 68-29654        *ISBN* 0521073405

**Forster, Robert, 1926-.**                                      • **4.6392**
The nobility of Toulouse in the eighteenth century; a social and economic study. New York: Octagon Books, 1971 [c1960] 212 p.: ill.; 24 cm. (The Johns Hopkins University studies in historical and political science, ser. 78, no. 1) 1. Catholic Church. Diocese of Toulouse (France) — Rural conditions. 2. France — Nobility I. T.
HT653.F7 F6 1971        333.3/0944/86 19        *LC* 79-159186        *ISBN* 0374928177

**Girouard, Mark, 1931-.**                                        **4.6393**
Life in the English country house: a social and architectural history / Mark Girouard. — New Haven: Yale University Press, 1978. v, 344 p.: ill. (some col.); 27 cm. Based on the author's Slade lectures given at Oxford University in 1975-76. 1. Upper classes — Great Britain — History. 2. Country homes — Great Britain — History. 3. Architecture and society — Great Britain — History. I. T.
HT653.G7 G57        301.44/1        *LC* 78-9088        *ISBN* 0300022735

**McFarlane, K. B. (Kenneth Bruce)**                              **4.6394**
The nobility of later medieval England: the Ford lectures for 1953 and related studies, by K. B. McFarlane. [S.l.]: Oxford, 1973. xlii, 315 p., leaf. ports. 23 cm. 1. Great Britain — Nobility I. T.
HT653.G7 M3        301.44/2        *LC* 73-157237        *ISBN* 0198223625

**Mingay, G. E.**                                                **4.6395**
The gentry: the rise and fall of a ruling class / G. E. Mingay. — London; New York: Longman, 1976. 216 p.: map. (Themes in British social history) Includes index. 1. Great Britain — Gentry I. T.
HT657.M54        929.7/2        *LC* 76-13576        *ISBN* 0582484022

**Stone, Lawrence.**                                              **4.6396**
An open elite?: England, 1540–1880 / by Lawrence Stone and Jeanne C. Fawtier Stone. — Oxford [Oxfordshire]: Clarendon Press; New York: Oxford University Press, 1984. xxv, 566 p., [16] p. of plates: ill.; 25 cm. Includes index. 1. Elite (Social sciences) — England — Case studies. 2. Architecture, Domestic — England 3. Country homes — England — History. 4. England — Gentry — History. I. Stone, Jeanne C. Fawtier. II. T.
HT657.S86 1984        305.5/232/0942 19        *LC* 83-8221        *ISBN* 0198226454

## HT675–690 Occupational Classes. Middle Class

**Bendix, Reinhard.**                                            • **4.6397**
Work and authority in industry; ideologies of management in the course of industrialization. New York, Wiley [1956] 466 p. illus. 24 cm. 1. Industrial management 2. Industrial relations I. T.
HT685.B4        323.3        *LC* 56-6479

**Elliott, Philip Ross Courtney.**                                **4.6398**
The sociology of the professions [by] Philip Elliott. — [New York]: Herder and Herder, [1972] x, 180 p.; 23 cm. — (New perspectives in sociology) 1. Professions 2. Professions — Great Britain — Sociological aspects. 3. Professions — United States — Sociological aspects. I. T.
HT687.E44 1972b        301.5/5        *LC* 75-188934

**Moore, Wilbert Ellis.**                                        • **4.6399**
The professions: roles and rules [by] Wilbert E. Moore. — New York: Russell Sage Foundation, [1970] xi, 303 p.; 24 cm. 1. Professions 2. Professions — U.S. I. T.
HT687.M63        331.7/1        *LC* 78-104184        *ISBN* 0871546043

**Barber, Elinor G.**                                            • **4.6400**
The bourgeoisie in 18th century France. — Princeton: Princeton University Press, 1955. x, 165 p.; 23 cm. Based on thesis, Radcliffe College. 1. Middle classes — France. I. T.
HT690.F8 B3        323.32        *LC* 55-10680

**Singer, Barnett.**                                              **4.6401**
Village notables in nineteenth–century France: priests, mayors, schoolmasters / Barnett Singer. — Albany: State University of New York Press, c1983. viii, 199 p.; 24 cm. — (SUNY series in European social history) Includes index. 1. Middle classes — France — History — 19th century. 2. France — Rural conditions. I. T.
HT690.F8 S55 1983        305.5/53 19        *LC* 82-3195        *ISBN* 087395629X

**Vogel, Ezra F.**                                                **4.6402**
Japan's new middle class; the salary man and his family in a Tokyo suburb, by Ezra F. Vogel. — [2d ed.]. — Berkeley: University of California Press, 1971 [c1963] xiii, 313 p.; 21 cm. 1. Middle classes — Japan. 2. Japan — Social conditions I. T.
HT690.J3 V6 1971        301.44/1/0952        *LC* 76-181439        *ISBN* 0520020928

**Halttunen, Karen, 1951-.**                                      **4.6403**
Confidence men and painted women: a study of middle–class culture in America, 1830–1870 / Karen Halttunen. — New Haven: Yale University Press, 1983 (c1982). xviii, 262 p.: ill.; 22 cm. — (Yale historical publications. Miscellany. 129) Includes index. 1. Middle classes — United States — History

— 19th century. 2. Social values 3. Hypocrisy 4. Sincerity 5. United States — Moral conditions I. T. II. Series.
HT690.U6 H34 1982      305.5/5/0973 19      *LC* 82-8336      *ISBN* 0300028350

**Mills, C. Wright (Charles Wright), 1916-1962.**                          • 4.6404
White collar; the American middle classes. New York, Oxford University Press, 1951. xx, 378 p. 22 cm. 1. Middle classes — United States. 2. White collar workers — United States. I. T.
HT690.U6 M5      323.32      *LC* 51-5298

## HT713–725 Caste System

**Dumont, Louis, 1911-.**                                          4.6405
[Homo hierarchicus. English] Homo hierarchicus: the caste system and its implications / Louis Dumont; translated [from the French] by Mark Sainsbury, Louis Dumont, and Basia Gulati. — Complete rev. English ed. — Chicago: University of Chicago Press, 1980. li, 488 p.: ill.; 23 cm. Includes index. 1. Caste — India I. T.
HT720.D813 1980      305.5/0954      *LC* 80-16480      *ISBN* 0226169626

**Karve, Irawati Karmarkar, 1905-1970.**                          4.6406
Hindu society: an interpretation / [by] Irawati Karve. — [2d ed. — Poona: Deshmukh Prakashan, 1968] x, 180 p.: ill., maps; 22 cm. 1. Caste — India I. T.
HT720.K3 1968      *LC* 74-928489

**Rudolph, Lloyd I.**                                          • 4.6407
The modernity of tradition: political development in India [by] Lloyd I. Rudolph [and] Susanne Hoeber Rudolph. Chicago, University of Chicago Press [1967] x, 306 p. 23 cm. 1. Gandhi, Mahatma, 1869-1948. 2. Caste — India 3. Law — India. I. Rudolph, Susanne Hoeber. joint author. II. T.
HT720.R83      301.44/0954      *LC* 67-25527

**Structure and change in Indian society. Edited by Milton Singer**      • 4.6408
**and Bernard S. Cohn.**
Chicago, Aldine Pub. Co. [1968] xvi, 507 p. illus., maps (part col.) 26 cm. (Viking Fund publications in anthropology. no. 47) 'Papers ... were presented ... to a conference on social structure and social change in India held at the University of Chicago, June 3-5, 1965.' Co-sponsored by the Wenner-Gren Foundation for Anthropological Research and the Committee on Southern Asian Studies of the University of Chicago. 1. Caste — India — Addresses, essays, lectures. 2. India — Social conditions — Addresses, essays, lectures. I. Singer, Milton B. ed. II. Cohn, Bernard S., ed. III. Wenner-Gren Foundation for Anthropological Research. IV. University of Chicago. Committee on Southern Asian Studies. V. Series.
HT720.S8      309.1/54      *LC* 67-17609

## HT751–815 Serfdom

**Hyams, Paul R.**                                          4.6409
King, lords, and peasants in medieval England: the common law of villeinage in the twelfth and thirteenth centuries / by Paul R. Hyams. — Oxford [Eng.]: Clarendon Press, 1980. xxii, 295 p.; 22 cm. (Oxford historical monographs) Includes index. 1. Serfdom — England — History. I. T.
HT781.H9 1980      306/.3      *LC* 79-42923      *ISBN* 019821880X

**Blum, Jerome, 1913-.**                                          4.6410
Lord and peasant in Russia, from the ninth to the nineteenth century. Princeton, N.J., Princeton University Press, 1961. x, 656 p. maps. 1. Serfdom — Russia 2. Peasantry — Russia 3. Russia — Social conditions I. T.
HT807 B55      *LC* 61-7413

## HT851–1445 Slavery
(Slavery in the United States: see: E451-453)

**Africans abroad: a documentary history of the Black Diaspora**      4.6411
**in Asia, Latin America, and the Caribbean during the age of**
**slavery / Graham W. Irwin.**
New York: Columbia University Press, 1977. xvi, 408 p.; 24 cm. Includes index. 1. Slavery — History. 2. Blacks — History I. Irwin, Graham W.
HT861.A4      301.45/19/6      *LC* 77-457      *ISBN* 0231039360

**Davis, David Brion.**                                          4.6412
Slavery and human progress / David Brion Davis. — New York: Oxford University Press, 1984. xix, 374 p.; 24 cm. Includes index. 1. Slavery — History. 2. Progress 3. Slavery — Emancipation — History. 4. Slavery and the church I. T.
HT861.D38 1984      306/.362/09 19      *LC* 83-25115      *ISBN* 0195034392

**Finley, M. I. (Moses I.), 1912-.**                                          4.6413
Ancient slavery and modern ideology / M. I. Finley. — New York: Viking Press, 1980. 202 p.; 23 cm. Four lectures presented at the Collège de France in November and December 1978. Includes index. 1. Slavery — Greece 2. Slavery — Rome I. T.
HT863.F48      306/.362/0938 19      *LC* 80-15012      *ISBN* 0670122777

**Greek and Roman slavery: a sourcebook / Thomas Wiedemann.**      4.6414
Baltimore: Johns Hopkins University Press, 1981. 284 p.: maps; 22 cm. 1. Slavery — Greece — History — Sources. 2. Slavery — Rome — History — Sources. I. Wiedemann, Thomas E. J.
HT863.G73 1981      306/.3 19      *LC* 80-25432      *ISBN* 0801825156

**Hopkins, Keith.**                                          4.6415
Conquerors and slaves / by Keith Hopkins. — Cambridge; New York: Cambridge University Press, 1978 (c1977). 268 p. (Sociological studies in Roman history. v. 1) Includes index. 1. Slavery in Rome. 2. Social structure 3. Rome — Social conditions. 4. Rome — History I. T. II. Series.
HT863.H66      301.44/93/09376      *LC* 77-90209      *ISBN* 0521219450

**Vogt, Joseph, 1895-.**                                          4.6416
[Sklaverei und Humanität. English] Ancient slavery and the ideal of man / Joseph Vogt; translated by Thomas Wiedemann. — Cambridge, Mass.: Harvard University Press, 1975. x, 227 p.; 22 cm. Translation of Sklaverei und Humanität, 2d ed. Includes index. 1. Slavery in Greece. 2. Slavery in Rome. I. T.
HT863.V613      301.44/93/0938      *LC* 74-17885      *ISBN* 0674034406

**Westermann, William Linn, 1873-1954.**                          4.6417
The slave systems of Greek and Roman antiquity. Philadelphia: American Philosophical Society, 1955. xii, 180 p. (Memoirs of the American Philosophical Society, v. 40) 1. Slavery in Greece 2. Slavery in Rome I. T.
HT863 W4      *LC* 54-9107

**Bloch, Marc Léopold Benjamin, 1886-1944.**                          4.6418
[Mélanges historiques. English. Selections] Slavery and serfdom in the Middle Ages: selected essays / by Marc Bloch; translated by William R. Beer. — Berkeley: University of California Press, 1975. ix, 276 p.; 24 cm. — (Publications of the Center for Medieval and Renaissance Studies, UCLA; 8) 'Translated and extracted from [the author's] Mélanges historiques.' 1. Slavery — History. 2. Slavery — Europe — History. 3. Serfdom — Europe — History. I. T.
HT865.B5713 1975      301.44/93/094      *LC* 79-123627      *ISBN* 0520027676

**Davis, David Brion.**                                          4.6419
The problem of slavery in Western culture. — Ithaca, N.Y.: Cornell University Press, [1966] xiv, 505 p.; 24 cm. 1. Slavery 2. Slavery and the church I. T.
HT871.D3      326      *LC* 66-14348

**Patterson, Orlando, 1940-.**                                          4.6420
Slavery and social death: a comparative study / Orlando Patterson. — Cambridge, Mass.: Harvard University Press, 1982. xiii, 511 p.: maps; 25 cm. 1. Slavery 2. Slaves — Psychology. 3. Slaveholders — Psychology. I. T.
HT871.P37 1982      306/.362 19      *LC* 82-1072      *ISBN* 0674810821

**Klein, Herbert S.**                                          4.6421
The middle passage: comparative studies in the Atlantic slave trade / Herbert S. Klein. — Princeton, N.J.: Princeton University Press, c1978. xxiii, 282 p.; 25 cm. Includes index. 1. Slave-trade — History. I. T.
HT975.K55      380.1/44      *LC* 77-85545      *ISBN* 0691031193

**Rawley, James A.**                                          4.6422
The transatlantic slave trade: a history / James A. Rawley. — 1st ed. — New York: Norton, c1981. xiv, 452 p.: ill.; 24 cm. 1. Slave-trade — History. I. T.
HT985.R38 1981      382/.44/09 19      *LC* 81-2863      *ISBN* 0393014711

**Furneaux, Robin.**                                          4.6423
William Wilberforce. — London: Hamilton, 1974. iii-xvi, 506 p., [16] p. of plates.: illus., ports.; 24 cm. Includes index. 1. Wilberforce, William, 1759-1833. I. T.
HT1029.W5 F87 1974      326/.092/4 B      *LC* 74-176482      *ISBN* 0241022029

**Foner, Eric.**                                          4.6424
Nothing but freedom: emancipation and its legacy / Eric Foner. — Baton Rouge: Louisiana State University Press, c1983. xii, 142 p.; 23 cm. (Walter Lynwood Fleming lectures in southern history.) 1. Slavery — Emancipation 2. Slavery — United States — Emancipation 3. Reconstruction 4. Liberty. 5. Labor and laboring classes — United States — History — 19th century. I. T. II. Series.
HT1031.F66 1983      326/.0973 19      *LC* 83-7906      *ISBN* 080711118X

## HT1048–1445 SLAVERY, BY REGION

**Neither slave nor free; the freedman of African descent in the** 4.6425
**slave societies of the New World. Edited with an introd. by**
**David W. Cohen and Jack P. Greene.**
Baltimore, Johns Hopkins University Press [1972] xi, 344 p. 24 cm. (Johns
Hopkins symposia in comparative history. 3rd) 'This volume grew out of a
symposium ... held at the Johns Hopkins University on April 8 and 9, 1970.
Sponsored by the Department of History and the Institute of Southern History.'
1. Freedmen — America — Congresses. 2. Slavery — America — Congresses.
I. Cohen, David William. ed. II. Greene, Jack P. ed. III. Series.
HT1048.N43    301.45/19/607    LC 79-184238    ISBN 0801813743

**Price, Richard, 1941- comp.** 4.6426
Maroon societies: rebel slave communities in the Americas / edited by Richard
Price. — 2d ed. — Baltimore: Johns Hopkins University Press, 1979. ix, 445 p.:
ill.; 20 cm. — (A Johns Hopkins paperback) Includes index. 1. Fugitive slaves
— America — Addresses, essays, lectures. 2. Maroons — Addresses, essays,
lectures. I. T.
HT1048.P74 1979    301.44/93    LC 79-16806    ISBN 0801822475

**Mellafe R., Rolando.** 4.6427
Negro slavery in Latin America / Roland Mellafe; translated by J. W. S. Judge.
— Berkeley: University of California Press, c1975. 172 p., [5] leaves of plates:
ill.; 24 cm. Includes index. 1. Slavery — Latin America — History. 2. Slave-
trade — Latin America — History. I. T.
HT1052.5.M4413    301.44/93/098    LC 78-170720    ISBN
0520021061

**Palmer, Colin A., 1942-.** 4.6428
Slaves of the white God: Blacks in Mexico, 1570–1650 / Colin A. Palmer.
Cambridge: Harvard University Press, 1976. 234 p.: map; 24 cm. Includes
index. 1. Slavery — Mexico — History. I. T. II. Title: Blacks in Mexico,
1570-1650.
HT1053.P35    301.44/93/0972    LC 75-34054    ISBN 0674810856

**Comitas, Lambros. comp.** 4.6429
Slaves, free men, citizens; West Indian perspectives. Edited and introduced by
Lambros Comitas and David Lowenthal. — Garden City, N.Y.: Anchor Books,
1973. xvii, 340 p.: illus.; 18 cm. 1. Slavery — West Indies — Addresses, essays,
lectures. 2. Freedmen in the West Indies — Addresses, essays, lectures.
3. West Indies — Social conditions — Addresses, essays, lectures.
I. Lowenthal, David. joint comp. II. T.
HT1071.C67    309.1/729    LC 72-84929    ISBN 0385042892

**Mintz, Sidney Wilfred, 1922-.** 4.6430
Caribbean transformations / Sidney W. Mintz. — Chicago: Aldine Pub. Co.,
1974. xii, 355 p.; 23 cm. Includes index. 1. Slavery — Caribbean Area
2. Peasantry — Caribbean Area. 3. Plantations — Caribbean Area.
4. Caribbean Area — Politics and government I. T.
HT1071.M56    305.5/67/09729 19    LC 74-82602    ISBN
0202011259

**Murray, David R.** 4.6431
Odious commerce: Britain, Spain, and the abolition of the Cuban slave trade /
David R. Murray. — Cambridge [Eng.]; New York: Cambridge University
Press, 1980. xi, 423 p.; 23 cm. — (Cambridge Latin American studies. 37)
Includes index. 1. Slave-trade — Cuba. 2. Great Britain — Foreign relations
— Spain. 3. Spain — Foreign relations — Great Britain. I. T. II. Series.
HT1077.M87    382/.44/097291    LC 79-41365    ISBN 0521228670

**Hall, Gwendolyn Midlo.** 4.6432
Social control in slave plantation societies; a comparison of St. Domingue and
Cuba. Baltimore, Johns Hopkins Press [c1971] xiii, 166 p. 24 cm. (The Johns
Hopkins University studies in historical and political science. ser. 89, 1) Based
on the author's thesis, University of Michigan. 1. Slavery — Dominican
Republic 2. Slavery — Cuba 3. Social control I. T.
HT1081.H35 1971    301.44/93/097291    LC 79-163195    ISBN
0801812526

**Buckley, Roger Norman, 1937-.** 4.6433
Slaves in red coats: the British West India regiments, 1795–1815 / Roger
Norman Buckley. — New Haven: Yale University Press, 1979. xi, 210 p.: ill.; 24
cm. Includes index. 1. Great Britain. Army — Colonial forces — West Indies,
British — History. 2. Slavery — West Indies, British 3. Soldiers, Black —
West Indies, British — History. I. T.
HT1091.B77    355.3/52    LC 78-16830    ISBN 0300022166

**Drescher, Seymour.** 4.6434
Econocide: British slavery in the era of abolition / Seymour Drescher. —
Pittsburgh: University of Pittsburgh Press, c1977. xiv, 279 p.: graphs; 24 cm.
Includes index. 1. Slavery in Great Britain — Anti-slavery movements.
2. Slavery — West Indies, British 3. Slave-trade — Great Britain. 4. Slave-
trade — West Indies, British. I. T.
HT1093.D7 1977    301.44/93/0941    LC 76-50887    ISBN
0822933446

**Higman, B. W., 1943-.** 4.6435
Slave population and economy in Jamaica, 1807–1834 / B. W. Higman.
Cambridge; New York: Cambridge University Press, 1976. vii, 327 p.: ill.; 24
cm. Includes index. 1. Slavery — Jamaica — History. I. T.
HT1096.H53    301.44/93    LC 75-28627    ISBN 0521210534

**Turner, Mary, 1931-.** 4.6436
Slaves and missionaries: the disintegration of Jamaican slave society, 1787–1834
/ Mary Turner. — Urbana: University of Illinois Press, c1982. 223 p.: maps; 24
cm. (Blacks in the New World.) Includes index. 1. Slavery — Jamaica
2. Missionaries — Jamaica — History. 3. Slavery and the church 4. Race
relations — Religious aspects 5. Jamaica — Race relations. I. T. II. Series.
HT1096.T87 1982    305.5/67/097292 19    LC 82-6983    ISBN
0252009614

**Handler, Jerome S.** 4.6437
Plantation slavery in Barbados: an archaeological and historical investigation /
Jerome S. Handler and Frederick W. Lange, with the assistance of Robert V.
Riordan. — Cambridge: Harvard University Press, 1978. xiii, 368 p.: ill.; 24 cm.
Includes index. 1. Slavery — Barbados — History. 2. Plantation life —
Barbados — History. 3. Barbados — Antiquities. I. Lange, Frederick W.,
1944- joint author. II. Riordan, Robert V., joint author. III. T.
HT1105.B3 H34    301.44/93/0972981    LC 77-22312    ISBN
0674672755

**Goveia, Elsa V.** 4.6438
Slave society in the British Leeward Islands at the end of the eighteenth century
/ Elsa V. Goveia. — Westport, Conn.: Greenwood Press, 1980, c1965. ix,
370 p.: map; 24 cm. Reprint of the ed. published by Yale University Press, New
Haven, which was issued as no. 8 of Caribbean series. 1. Slavery — Leeward
Islands (West Indies) — Case studies. 2. Sugar trade — Leeward Islands.
3. Leeward Islands — Politics and government. 4. Leeward Islands — Social
conditions. I. T.
HT1105.L4 G66 1980    305.5/6    LC 80-13    ISBN 0313221561

**Toplin, Robert Brent, 1940-.** 4.6439
The abolition of slavery in Brazil. — [1st ed.]. — New York: Atheneum, 1972
[c1971] xvii, 299 p.; 23 cm. — (Studies in American Negro life) Based on the
author's thesis, Rutgers. 1. Slavery — Brazil I. T.
HT1128.T66    301.44/93/0981    LC 79-139329

**Bowser, Frederick P.** 4.6440
The African slave in colonial Peru, 1524–1650 [by] Frederick P. Bowser.
Stanford, Calif., Stanford University Press, 1974. xiv, 439 p. illus. 24 cm.
1. Slavery — Peru 2. Slave-trade — Peru. 3. Blacks — Peru — History. I. T.
HT1147.B67    301.44/93/0985    LC 73-80619    ISBN 0804708401

**Craton, Michael.** 4.6441
Sinews of empire; a short history of British slavery. — [1st ed.]. — Garden City,
N.Y.: Anchor Press, 1974. xxii, 413 p.: illus.; 18 cm. 1. Slavery in Great Britain
— History. 2. Slave-trade — Great Britain — History. I. T.
HT1161.C64 1974    301.44/93/09171241    LC 73-16502    ISBN
0385063393

**Miers, Suzanne.** 4.6442
Britain and the ending of the slave trade. — New York: Africana Pub. Corp.,
[1975] xv, 405 p.: illus.; 25 cm. 1. Slave-trade — Great Britain. 2. Slavery in
Great Britain — Anti-slavery movements. I. T.
HT1162.M53 1975    382/.44/0942    LC 74-18052    ISBN
0841901872

**Fladeland, Betty, 1919-.** 4.6443
Abolitionists and working–class problems in the age of industrialization / Betty
Fladeland. — Baton Rouge: Louisiana State University Press, 1984. xiv, 232 p.;
23 cm. Includes index. 1. Abolitionists — Great Britain — Attitudes —
History — 19th century. 2. Slavery — United States — Anti-slavery
movements — Public opinion — History — 19th century. 3. Social reformers
— Great Britain — Attitudes — History — 19th century. 4. Labor and
laboring classes — Great Britain — History — 19th century 5. Public opinion
— Great Britain — History — 19th century. I. T.
HT1163.F57 1984    326/.0941 19    LC 83-82561    ISBN 0807111678

**Hellie, Richard.** 4.6444
Slavery in Russia, 1450–1725 / Richard Hellie. — Chicago: University of
Chicago Press, 1982. xix, 776 p.: ill.; 24 cm. Includes index. 1. Slavery — Soviet
Union — History. I. T.
HT1206.H44 1982    306/.3 19    LC 81-12954    ISBN 0226326470

**Nwulia, Moses D. E., 1932-.** 4.6445
The history of slavery in Mauritius and the Seychelles, 1810–1875 / Moses D.E.
Nwulia. — Rutherford, N.J.: Fairleigh Dickenson University Press; London:
Associated University Presses, c1981. 246 p.: maps; 22 cm. Includes index.
1. Slavery — Mauritius 2. Slavery — Seychelles I. T.
HT1315.I4 N88    301.44/93/096982    LC 79-15363    ISBN
0838623980

## HT1321–1427 Africa

**Lovejoy, Paul E.**                                                4.6446
Transformations in slavery: a history of slavery in Africa / Paul E. Lovejoy. — Cambridge [Cambridgeshire]; New York: Cambridge University Press, 1983. xvi, 349 p.: maps; 24 cm. (African studies series. 36) Includes index. 1. Slavery — Africa — History. 2. Slave-trade — Africa — History. I. T. II. Series.
HT1321.L68 1983    306/.362/096 19    *LC* 82-12849    *ISBN* 0521243696

**Slaves and slavery in Muslim Africa / edited with an**    4.6447
**introduction by John Ralph Willis.**
London, England; Totowa, N.J.: F. Cass, 1985. 2 v.; 23 cm. 1. Slavery — Africa 2. Slavery and Islam — Africa. I. Willis, John Ralph.
HT1321.S56 1985    306.3/62/096 19    *LC* 83-24313    *ISBN* 0714632015

**Women and slavery in Africa / edited by Claire C. Robertson**    4.6448
**and Martin A. Klein.**
Madison, Wis.: University of Wisconsin Press, 1984. x, 380 p.: ill.; 24 cm. 1. Slavery — Africa — Addresses, essays, lectures. 2. Women — Africa — Addresses, essays, lectures. 3. Slave-trade — Africa — Addresses, essays, lectures. I. Robertson, Claire C., 1944- II. Klein, Martin A.
HT1321.W66 1983    305.5/67/096 19    *LC* 83-47769    *ISBN* 029909460X

**Anstey, Roger.**                                               4.6449
The Atlantic slave trade and British abolition, 1760–1810 / Roger Anstey. — Atlantic Highlands, N.J.: Humanities Press, 1975. xxiv, 456 p., [4] leaves of plates: ill.; 22 cm. Includes index. 1. Slave-trade — Africa, West. 2. Slavery in Great Britain — Anti-slavery movements. I. T.
HT1322.A67    382/.44    *LC* 74-28042    *ISBN* 0391003712

**Cooper, Frederick, 1947-.**                                    4.6450
Plantation slavery on the east coast of Africa / Frederick Cooper. New Haven [Conn.]: Yale University Press, 1977. xviii, 314 p.; 24 cm. (Yale historical publications. Miscellany. 113) Includes index. 1. Slavery — Africa, East — History. 2. Slavery and Islam — Africa, East. 3. Plantation life — Africa, East — History. I. T. II. Series.
HT1326.C66    301.44/93/0967    *LC* 76-41308    *ISBN* 0300020414

**Slavery in Africa: historical and anthropological perspectives /**    4.6451
**edited by Suzanne Miers and Igor Kopytoff.**
Madison: University of Wisconsin Press, 1977. xvii, 474 p.: maps; 24 cm. 1. Slavery — Africa, Sub-Saharan — Addresses, essays, lectures. I. Miers, Suzanne. II. Kopytoff, Igor.
HT1427.S8 S58    301.44/93/0967    *LC* 76-53653    *ISBN* 0299073300

## HT1501–1595 Races

**Chase, Allan, 1913-.**                                         4.6452
The legacy of Malthus: the social costs of the new scientific racism / Allan Chase. — 1st ed. — New York: Knopf: distributed by Random House, 1976. xxvii, 686, xviii p. — Includes index. 1. Race discrimination — History. 2. Eugenics — History. 3. Genetics — History. I. T.
HT1521.C43 1976    HT1521 C43 1977.    301.45/1/042    *LC* 76-13726    *ISBN* 0394480457

**Kuper, Leo.**                                                  4.6453
The pity of it all: polarisation of racial and ethnic relations / Leo Kuper. — Minneapolis: University of Minnesota Press, 1977. 302 p.; 23 cm. Includes index. 1. Race relations 2. Violence — Africa — Case studies. 3. Terrorism — Africa — Case studies. 4. Pluralism (Social sciences) — Africa — Case studies. 5. Africa — Race relations — Case studies. I. T.
HT1521.K77 1977b    301.45/1/042096    *LC* 77-78351    *ISBN* 0816608172

**Tinker, Hugh.**                                                4.6454
Race, conflict, and the international order: from Empire to United Nations / Hugh Tinker. — New York: St. Martin's Press, 1977. 157 p.: maps; 23 cm. — (The Making of the 20th century) Includes index. 1. Race relations 2. Racism 3. Social history — 20th century 4. International relations I. T.
HT1521.T56 1977    301.2    *LC* 77-79017    *ISBN* 0312661304

**Van den Berghe, Pierre L.**                                    4.6455
The ethnic phenomenon / Pierre L. van den Berghe. — New York: Elsevier, c1981. xiv, 301 p.; 24 cm. Includes indexes. 1. Racism 2. Ethnicity 3. Sociobiology 4. Social ethics I. T.
HT1521.V25    305.8 19    *LC* 80-21092    *ISBN* 0444015507

**Wilson, William J., 1935-.**                                   4.6456
Power, racism, and privilege; race relations in theoretical and sociohistorical perspectives [by] William J. Wilson. New York, Macmillan [1973] xi, 224 p. 21 cm. 1. Race relations 2. Power (Social sciences) 3. United States — Race relations 4. South Africa — Race relations I. T.
HT1521.W57    301.45/1/042    *LC* 72-87160

**World minorities.**                                            4.6457
Sunbury: Quartermaine House Ltd. [for the] Minority Rights Group, 1977-1978. 2 v.: map; 22 cm. Vol. 1-<3 > edited by Georgina Ashworth. Label mounted on t.p.: Transatlantic Arts, Levittown, N.Y., sole distributor for the U.S.A. 1. Minorities — Addresses, essays, lectures. 2. Race discrimination — Addresses, essays, lectures. I. Ashworth, Georgina.
HT1521.W67    301.45    *LC* 78-310796    *ISBN* 0905898001

**Gist, Noel Pitts, 1899-.**                                     4.6458
The blending of races: marginality and identity in world perspective [edited by] Noel P. Gist and Anthony Gary Dworkin. — New York: Wiley-Interscience, [1972] xii, 289 p.; 23 cm. 1. Race relations — Addresses, essays, lectures. 2. Miscegenation — Addresses, essays, lectures. 3. Minorities — Addresses, essays, lectures. I. T.
HT1523.G57    301.45    *LC* 72-5122    *ISBN* 0471302538

**Rex, John.**                                                   4.6459
Race, colonialism and the city. — London; Boston: Routledge and Kegan Paul, 1973. xx, 310 p.; 23 cm. 1. Race relations 2. Colonies 3. Sociology, Urban I. T.
HT1523.R43    301.45/1/091732    *LC* 72-95125    *ISBN* 0710074123

**Congress of African Peoples, Atlanta, 1970.**                  4.6460
African congress; a documentary of the first modern pan–African congress. Edited with an introd. by Imamu Amiri Baraka (LeRoi Jones). New York, Morrow, 1972. xiv, 493 p. 22 cm. 1. Black race — Congresses. 2. Blacks — Congresses. I. Baraka, Imamu Amiri, 1934- II. T.
HT1581.C58 1970    910/.039/6    *LC* 78-159735

## HV1–5840 SOCIAL PATHOLOGY. SOCIAL WELFARE

**The International foundation directory / consultant editor, H.V.**    4.6461
**Hodson.**
3rd ed., rev. and enl. — Detroit, MI: Gale Research Co., 1983. xxviii, 401 p.; 25 cm. Includes indexes. 1. Endowments — Directories. I. Hodson, H. V. (Henry Vincent), 1906-
HV7.I57 1983b    361.7/632/025 19    *LC* 84-181779    *ISBN* 0810320320

**O'Neil, Maria Joan, 1937-.**                                   4.6462
The general method of social work practice / Maria Joan O'Neil; with a foreword by Carel B. Germain. — Englewood Cliffs, N.J.: Prentice-Hall, c1984. xiv, 351 p.: ill.; 24 cm. 1. Social work education 2. Social work education — Curricula. 3. Social service 4. Holism I. T.
HV11.O58 1984    361.3 19    *LC* 83-21239    *ISBN* 0133505545

**Polansky, Norman Alburt, 1918- ed.**                           4.6463
Social work research: methods for the helping professions / edited by Norman A. Polansky. — Rev. ed. — Chicago: University of Chicago Press, 1975. ix, 314 p.; 24 cm. 1. Social service — Research I. T.
HV11.P64 1975    361/.007/2    *LC* 74-26798    *ISBN* 0226672190

**Shulman, Lawrence.**                                           4.6464
The skills of helping: individuals and groups / Lawrence Shulman. — 2nd ed. — Itasca, Ill.: F.E. Peacock Publishers, c1984. xvii, 432 p.: ill.; 25 cm. Includes indexes. 1. Social work education I. T.
HV11.S493 1984    361.3 19    *LC* 83-63542    *ISBN* 087581302X

**Tripodi, Tony.**                                               4.6465
Uses & abuses of social research in social work. New York, Columbia University Press, 1974. xii, 222 p. 23 cm. 1. Social service — Research 2. Social service 3. Sociology — Research I. T.
HV11.T75    361/.007/2    *LC* 73-17280    *ISBN* 0231036620 *ISBN* 0231036639

**Timms, Noel.**                                                 4.6466
Dictionary of social welfare / Noel and Rita Timms. — London; Boston: Routledge & K. Paul, 1982. vi, 217 p.; 23 cm. 1. Social service — Dictionaries. 2. Social policy — Dictionaries. I. Timms, Rita. II. T.
HV12.T54 1982    361/.003/21 19    *LC* 82-5385    *ISBN* 0710090846

**Social problems.** • **4.6467**
The other side: perspectives on deviance / edited by Howard S. Becker. — [New York]: Free Press of Glencoe, [1964] 297 p.; 22 cm. Papers chiefly from the Fall, 1962, issue of Social problems, with the addition of others which appeared in the same periodical before or after that date. 1. Deviant behavior — Addresses, essays, lectures. 2. Handicapped — Addresses, essays, lectures. I. Becker, Howard Saul, 1928- ed. II. T. III. Title: Perspectives on deviance.
HV13.S6      364.2      *LC* 64-16953

**The Development of welfare states in Europe and America /**    **4.6468**
**edited by Peter Flora and Arnold J. Heidenheimer.**
New Brunswick, U.S.A.: Transaction Books, c1981. 417 p.; ill.; 24 cm. 1. Welfare state — Addresses, essays, lectures. I. Flora, Peter, 1944- II. Heidenheimer, Arnold J.
HN17.5.D48      361.6/5      *LC* 79-65227      *ISBN* 0878553576

**Davis, Allen Freeman, 1931-.**    **4.6469**
American heroine: the life and legend of Jane Addams [by] Allen F. Davis. — New York: Oxford University Press, 1973. xx, 339 p.: illus.; 24 cm. 1. Addams, Jane, 1860-1935. I. T.
HV28.A35 D38      361/.92/4 B      *LC* 73-82664      *ISBN* 0195016947

**Parker, Franklin, 1921-.**    **4.6470**
George Peabody: a biography / foreword by Merle Curti. — Nashville: Vanderbilt University Press, 1971. x, 233 p.: port.; 25 cm. 1. Peabody, George, 1795-1869. I. T.
HV28.P4 P29 1971      361.7/4/0924 B      *LC* 79-157741      *ISBN* 0826511708

# HV30–516 Social Welfare. Social Work

**Northen, Helen.**    **4.6471**
Clinical social work / by Helen Northen. — New York: Columbia University Press, 1982. xii, 369 p.; 24 cm. Includes index. 1. Social service 2. Social case work 3. Medical social work I. T.
HV31.N67      361.3/2 19      *LC* 81-10235      *ISBN* 0231038003

**Promoting competence in clients: a new/old approach to social**    **4.6472**
**work practice / Anthony N. Maluccio, editor.**
New York: Free Press; London: Collier Macmillan Publishers, c1981. xiv, 370 p.; 25 cm. Includes index. 1. Social service — Addresses, essays, lectures. I. Maluccio, Anthony N.
HV31.P76      361 19      *LC* 80-1056      *ISBN* 0029198305

**Encyclopedia of social work.**    **4.6473**
1st- issue; 1929-. New York: National Association of Social Workers. v.; 25 cm. 1. Social service — Yearbooks. I. Hall, Fred S. (Fred Smith), 1870-1946. ed. II. Kurtz, Russell Harold, 1890- ed. III. Hodges, Margaret B., ed. IV. Lurie, Harry Lawrence, 1892-1973, ed. V. National Association of Social Workers. VI. Russell Sage Foundation. VII. American Association of Social Workers.
HV35.S6      361/.003      *LC* 30-30948

**Compton, Beulah Roberts.**    **4.6474**
Social work processes / Beulah Roberts Compton and Burt Galaway. — 3rd ed. — Homewood, Ill.: Dorsey Press, 1984. xxii, 609 p.: ill.; 25 cm. — (Dorsey series in social welfare.) 1. Social service — Addresses, essays, lectures. 2. Social case work — Addresses, essays, lectures. I. Galaway, Burt. II. T. III. Series.
HV37.C62 1984      361.3 19      *LC* 83-72197      *ISBN* 0256028664

**Social work treatment: interlocking theoretical approaches /**    **4.6475**
**edited by Francis J. Turner; with a foreword by Katherine A. Kendall.**
3rd ed. — New York: Free Press; London: Collier Macmillan, c1986. xxxvii, 682 p.; 25 cm. 1. Social service — Addresses, essays, lectures. I. Turner, Francis Joseph, 1929-
HV37.S579 1986      361 19      *LC* 85-24717      *ISBN* 0029331005

**Theory and practice of community social work / edited by**    **4.6476**
**Samuel H. Taylor and Robert W. Roberts.**
New York: Columbia University Press, 1985. xiii, 442 p.; 24 cm. 1. Social service — Addresses, essays, lectures. 2. Community organization — Addresses, essays, lectures. I. Taylor, Samuel H. II. Roberts, Robert W.
HV37.T465 1985      361.8 19      *LC* 84-15628      *ISBN* 0231053681

**The Field of social work / [edited by] Arthur E. Fink, Jane H.**    **4.6477**
**Pfouts, Andrew W. Dobelstein.**
8th ed. — Beverly Hills, Calif.: Sage Publications, c1985. 400 p.; 24 cm. 1. Social service — Addresses, essays, lectures. 2. Social service — United States — Addresses, essays, lectures. I. Fink, Arthur E. (Arthur Emil), 1903- II. Pfouts, Jane H. (Jane Hoyer), 1921-1982. III. Dobelstein, Andrew W.
HV40.F45 1985      361.3 19      *LC* 84-18082      *ISBN* 080392268X

**Goldstein, Howard, 1922-.**    **4.6478**
Social work practice: a unitary approach. — [1st ed.]. — Columbia: University of South Carolina Press, [1973] xv, 288 p.; 24 cm. 1. Social service 2. Social service — History. I. T.
HV40.G64      361      *LC* 73-4687      *ISBN* 0872492850

**Meyer, Carol H., 1924-.**    **4.6479**
Social work practice / Carol H. Meyer. 2d ed. — New York: Free Press, c1976. xv, 268 p.; 21 cm. Includes index. 1. Social service I. T.
HV40.M516 1976      361.3      *LC* 75-20949      *ISBN* 0029211409

**Richmond, Mary Ellen, 1861-1928.**    **4.6480**
Social diagnosis. New York Free Press [1965] 511p. 1. Charity organization 2. Charities 3. Social service I. T.
HV40 R5 1965

**Siporin, Max.**    **4.6481**
Introduction to social work practice / Max Siporin. — New York: Macmillan, [1975] xii, 468 p.; 24 cm. 1. Social service I. T.
HV40.S587      361      *LC* 74-7713      *ISBN* 0024108502

**Social support networks: informal helping in the human services**    **4.6482**
**/ [edited by] James K. Whittaker, James Garbarino, and associates.**
Hawthorne, N.Y.: Aldine Pub. Co., 1983. xx, 479 p.; 24 cm. Includes indexes. 1. Social service 2. Helping behavior 3. Friendship 4. Interpersonal relations I. Whittaker, James K. II. Garbarino, James.
HV40.S617 1983      362 19      *LC* 83-11761      *ISBN* 0202360318

**Towle, Charlotte.**    • **4.6483**
Common human needs / by Charlotte Towle. — Rev. ed. — New York, N.Y.: National Association of Social Workers, 1957. 132 p.; 22 cm. First ed. published: Washington: Federal Security Agency, 1945. 1. Public welfare 2. Social service I. T.
HV 40 T74 1957      *LC* 58-1629

**Weissman, Harold H.**    **4.6484**
Agency–based social work: neglected aspects of clinical practice / Harold Weissman, Irwin Epstein, and Andrea Savage. — Philadelphia: Temple University Press, 1983. xviii, 344 p.; 24 cm. 1. Social work administration — Addresses, essays, lectures. I. Epstein, Irwin. II. Savage, Andrea. III. T.
HV40.W435 1983      361/.0068 19      *LC* 83-9314      *ISBN* 087722322X

**Whittaker, James K.**    **4.6485**
Social treatment; an approach to interpersonal helping [by] James K. Whittaker. — Chicago: Aldine Pub. Co., [1974] viii, 270 p.; 22 cm. — (Modern applications of social work) 1. Social service I. T.
HV40.W485      361      *LC* 71-172856      *ISBN* 0202360113

**Bloom, Martin, 1934-.**    **4.6486**
The paradox of helping: introduction to the philosophy of scientific practice. — New York: Wiley, [1975] xiv, 283 p.: illus.; 24 cm. 1. Social service 2. Counseling 3. Social case work I. T.
HV41.B45      361      *LC* 74-13524      *ISBN* 047108235X

**Fischer, Joel.**    **4.6487**
Planned behavior change: behavior modification in social work / Joel Fischer, Harvey L. Gochros. — New York: Free Press, [1975] xviii, 525 p.: ill.; 24 cm. Includes indexes. 1. Social service 2. Behavior modification 3. Professional ethics I. Gochros, Harvey L. joint author. II. T.
HV41.F47      361/.06      *LC* 74-34554      *ISBN* 0029102502

**Furniss, Norman, 1944-.**    **4.6488**
The case for the welfare state: from social security to social equality / Norman Furniss and Timothy Tilton. Bloomington: Indiana University Press, c1977. xii, 249 p.; 22 cm. Includes index. 1. Welfare state 2. Public welfare I. Tilton, Timothy Alan, joint author. II. T.
HV41.F95 1977      361.6      *LC* 76-26414      *ISBN* 0253313228

**Kadushin, Alfred.**    **4.6489**
Consultation in social work / Alfred Kadushin. — New York: Columbia University Press, 1977. xi, 236 p.; 24 cm. Includes index. 1. Social service 2. Social service — Team work 3. Medical consultation 4. Psychiatric consultation I. T.
HV41.K22      361/.06      *LC* 77-24345      *ISBN* 0231041241

**Lipsky, Michael.**    **4.6490**
Street–level bureaucracy: dilemmas of the individual in public services / Michael Lipsky. — New York: Russell Sage Foundation, c1980. xviii, 244 p.; 24 cm. — (Publications of Russell Sage Foundation.) Includes bibliographical references and index. 1. Social workers 2. Social policy I. T. II. Series.
HV41.L53      361.3/01      *LC* 79-7350      *ISBN* 0871545241

**Reamer, Frederic G., 1953-.**                                    **4.6491**
Ethical dilemmas in social service / Frederic G. Reamer. — New York:
Columbia University Press, 1982. xiii, 280 p.; 24 cm. 1. Social service — Moral
and ethical aspects. 2. Social service — United States. I. T.
HV41.R4 1982          174/.9362 19          *LC* 81-18071          *ISBN* 0231051883

**Weiner, Myron E.**                                    **4.6492**
Human services management: analysis and applications / Myron E. Weiner. —
Homewood, Ill.: Dorsey Press, 1982. xvi, 640 p.: ill.; 24 cm. — (Dorsey series in
social welfare.) Includes indexes. 1. Social work administration I. T.
II. Series.
HV41.W368 1982          361/.0068 19          *LC* 81-70943          *ISBN* 0256027455

## HV43 SOCIAL CASE WORK

**Clinical social work in the eco–systems perspective / Carol H.**          **4.6493**
**Meyer, editor.**
New York: Columbia University Press, 1983. xii, 262 p.: ill.; 24 cm. — (Social
work and social issues.) 1. Social case work — Addresses, essays, lectures.
I. Meyer, Carol H., 1924- II. Series.
HV43.C534 1983          361.3/2 19          *LC* 83-2124          *ISBN* 0231051948

**Differential diagnosis and treatment in social work / edited by**          **4.6494**
**Francis J. Turner; with a foreword by Florence Hollis.**
3rd ed. — New York: Free Press; London: Collier Macmillan, c1983. xlvi,
897 p.; 24 cm. 1. Social case work — Addresses, essays, lectures. 2. Psychiatric
social work — Addresses, essays, lectures. 3. Medical social work —
Addresses, essays, lectures. I. Turner, Francis Joseph, 1929-
HV43.D56 1983          361.3 19          *LC* 82-48390          *ISBN* 0029329906

**Germain, Carel B.**                                    **4.6495**
The life model of social work practice / Carel B. Germain, Alex Gitterman. —
New York: Columbia University Press, 1980. xiii, 376 p.; 24 cm. 1. Social case
work 2. Man — Influence of environment I. Gitterman, Alex, 1938- joint
author. II. T.
HV43.G47          361          *LC* 79-17816          *ISBN* 0231041527

**Hamilton. Gordon.**                                    • **4.6496**
Theory and practice of social case work. — 2d ed., rev. — New York: Published
for the New York School of Social Work, Columbia University, by Columbia
University Press, 1951. 328 p.; 23 cm. 1. Social case work I. T.
HV43.H3 1951          361.8          *LC* 51-12493

**Handbook of clinical social work / Aaron Rosenblatt, Diana**          **4.6497**
**Waldfogel, general editors.**
1st ed. — San Francisco, Calif.: Jossey-Bass, 1983. xxviii, 1181 p.; 27 cm.
1. Social service — Addresses, essays, lectures. 2. Social case work —
Addresses, essays, lectures. I. Rosenblatt, Aaron. II. Waldfogel, Diana.
III. Title: Clinical social work.
HV43.H315 1983          361.3/2 19          *LC* 82-49042          *ISBN* 087589562X

**Hollis, Florence.**                                    **4.6498**
Casework, a psychosocial therapy / Florence Hollis and Mary E. Woods. — 3d
ed. — New York: Random House, c1981. xvi, 534 p.; 24 cm. Includes index.
1. Social casework. 2. Psychotherapy — Social aspects I. Woods, Mary E.,
1930- II. T.
HV43.H58 1981          361.3/2 19          *LC* 80-29399          *ISBN* 0394323688

**Kadushin, Alfred.**                                    **4.6499**
The social work interview / Alfred Kadushin. — 2nd ed. — New York:
Columbia University Press, 1983. 423 p.; 25 cm. Includes index.
1. Interviewing 2. Social service I. T.
HV43.K26 1983          361.3/22 19          *LC* 82-23670          *ISBN* 0231047622

**Perlman, Helen Harris.**                                    • **4.6500**
Social casework, a problem–solving process. — [Chicago]: University of
Chicago Press, [1957] 268 p.; 24 cm. 1. Social case work I. T.
HV43.P46          361.8 361.3*          *LC* 57-6270

**Reid, William James, 1928-.**                                    **4.6501**
The task–centered system / William J. Reid. — New York: Columbia
University Press, 1978. xi, 354 p.; 24 cm. Includes indexes. 1. Social case work
2. Social group work I. T.
HV43.R382          361.3          *LC* 78-2488          *ISBN* 023103797X

**Schwartz, Arthur.**                                    **4.6502**
Social casework: a behavioral approach / Arthur Schwartz and Israel
Goldiamond, with Michael W. Howe. — New York: Columbia University
Press, 1975. xiii, 315 p.; 23 cm. Includes indexes. 1. Social case work
I. Goldiamond, Israel, 1919- joint author. II. Howe, Michael W., joint author.
III. T.
HV43.S34          361.3          *LC* 75-2298          *ISBN* 0231037783

**Wilson, Suanna J., 1943-.**                                    **4.6503**
Confidentiality in social work: issues and principles / Suanna J. Wilson. — New
York: Free Press, c1978. xiii, 274 p.; 24 cm. Includes index. 1. Confidential
communications — Social case work 2. Privacy, Right of I. T.
HV43.W518 1978          361.3/2          *LC* 77-18475          *ISBN* 0029347505

## HV45 SOCIAL GROUP WORK

**Perspectives on social group work practice: a book of readings /**          **4.6504**
**edited by Albert S. Alissi.**
New York: Free Press, c1980. x, 405 p.; 24 cm. 1. Social group work —
Addresses, essays, lectures. I. Alissi, Albert S.
HV45.P46 1980          361.4          *LC* 79-7633          *ISBN* 0029004802

**Theories of social work with groups / Robert W. Roberts and**          **4.6505**
**Helen Northen, editors.**
New York: Columbia University Press, 1976. xviii, 401 p.; 24 cm. 1. Social
group work — Collected works. I. Roberts, Robert W. II. Northen, Helen.
HV45.T48          361.4          *LC* 76-4967          *ISBN* 0231038852

## HV85–516 By Country

### HV85–99 United States

**Foundations / editors–in–chief, Harold M. Keele and Joseph C.**          **4.6506**
**Kiger.**
Westport, Conn.: Greenwood Press, 1984. xxix, 516 p.; 25 cm. — (The
Greenwood encyclopedia of American institutions, 0271-9509; no. 8)
1. Charities — United States — Societies, etc. 2. Social service —
United States — Societies, etc. — History. 3. Corporations — United States —
Charitable contributions — History. 4. Endowments — United States —
History. I. Keele, Harold M. II. Kiger, Joseph Charles.
HV88.F68 1984          361.7/632/09 19          *LC* 83-10750          *ISBN*
0313225567

**Social service organizations / editor–in–chief Peter**          **4.6507**
**Romanofsky, advisory editor Clarke A. Chambers.**
Westport, Conn.: Greenwood Press, 1978. 2 v.; 24 cm. — (Greenwood
encyclopedia of American institutions. [2]) Series numbering from
bibliography. Includes index. 1. Charities — United States — Societies, etc. —
History. 2. Charities, Medical — United States — History. 3. Social service —
Societies, etc. — History. 4. Charities — United States — Societies, etc. —
Directories. 5. Charities, Medical — United States — Directories. 6. Social
service — Societies, etc. — Directories I. Romanofsky, Peter. II. Chambers,
Clarke A. III. Series.
HV88.S59          361.7/0973          *LC* 77-84754          *ISBN* 0837198291

**Kruzas, Anthony Thomas.**                                    **4.6508**
Social service organizations and agencies directory: a reference guide to
national and regional social service organizations, including advocacy groups,
voluntary associations, professional societies, federal and state agencies,
clearinghouses, and information centers / compiled and edited by Anthony T.
Kruzas; assistant editors, Robert Fitch Allen ... [et al.]. — 1st ed. — Detroit,
Mich.: Gale Research Co., c1982. xii, 525 p.; 29 cm. Includes index. 1. Social
service — United States — Directories. 2. Associations, institutions, etc —
United States — Directories. I. T.
HV89.K78 1982          361.8/025/73 19          *LC* 82-206132          *ISBN*
0810303299

**National Association of Social Workers.**                                    **4.6509**
Directory of agencies: U.S. voluntary, international voluntary,
intergovernmental. — Washington, D.C.: National Association of Social
Workers, c1980. 104 p.; 25 cm. Includes index. 1. Social service — United
States — Directories. 2. Social service — Directories. I. T.
HV89.N223 1980          362/.025/73 19          *LC* 80-81981          0871010854

**Ehrenreich, John, 1943-.**                                    **4.6510**
The altruistic imagination: a history of social work and social policy in the
United States / John H. Ehrenreich. — Ithaca: Cornell University Press, 1985.
271 p.; 24 cm. Includes index. 1. Social service — United States — History.
2. United States — Social policy — History. I. T.
HV91.E38 1985          361.3/0973 19          *LC* 84-45807          *ISBN* 0801417643

**Feagin, Joe R.**                                    **4.6511**
Subordinating the poor: welfare and American beliefs / Joe R. Feagin. —
Englewood Cliffs, N.J.: Prentice-Hall, [1975] x, 180 p.; 21 cm. (A Spectrum
book) 1. Public welfare — United States 2. Poor — United States. 3. Public
welfare — United States — Public opinion. 4. Poor — United States — Public
opinion. 5. Public opinion — United States. I. T.
HV91.F38          362.5/0973          *LC* 75-4941          *ISBN* 0138591407

**Ginsberg, Leon H.**     **4.6512**
The practice of social work in public welfare / Leon H. Ginsberg. — New York: Free Press; London: Collier Macmillan, c1983. xiii, 226 p.; 24 cm. — (Fields of practice series.) Includes index. 1. Public welfare — United States 2. Social service — United States. 3. Social case work — United States. I. T. II. Series.
HV91.G47 1983    361.3/0973 19    LC 82-71888    ISBN 0029117607

**Harrington, Michael, 1928-.**     • **4.6513**
The other America; poverty in the United States. New York, Macmillan, 1962. 191 p. 22 cm. 1. Poor — United States. I. T.
HV91.H3    301.44    LC 62-8555

**Kahn, Alfred J., 1919-.**     **4.6514**
Shaping the new social work. Alfred J. Kahn, editor. — New York: Columbia University Press, 1973. ix, 221 p.; 23 cm. — (Social work and social issues) 1. Social service — United States — Addresses, essays, lectures. 2. Social service — Vocational guidance — Addresses, essays, lectures. I. T.
HV91.K29    361/.973    LC 73-4189

**Katz, Michael B.**     **4.6515**
In the shadow of the poorhouse: a social history of welfare in America / Michael B. Katz. — New York: Basic Books, c1986. xiv, 338 p.; 24 cm. Includes index. 1. Public welfare — United States — History. 2. Social service — United States — History. 3. United States — Social policy I. T.
HV91.K349 1986    362.5/8/0973 19    LC 85-73875    ISBN 0465032257

**Katz, Michael B.**     **4.6516**
Poverty and policy in American history / Michael B. Katz. — New York: Academic Press, c1983. xii, 289 p.: ill.; 24 cm. (Studies in social discontinuity.) 1. Public welfare — United States — History. 2. Poor — United States — History. 3. Poor — Government policy — United States — History. 4. Almshouses — United States — History. 5. Tramps — United States — History. 6. Dependency (Psychology) — History. I. T. II. Series.
HV91.K35 1983    361.6/0973 19    LC 83-3700    ISBN 0124017606

**Leiby, James.**     **4.6517**
A history of social welfare and social work in the United States / James Leiby. — New York: Columbia University Press, 1978. viii, 426 p.; 24 cm. Includes index. 1. Public welfare — United States — History. 2. Social service — United States — History. I. T.
HV91.L37    361/.973    LC 78-3774    ISBN 0231033524

**Lubove, Roy.**     • **4.6518**
The professional altruist; the emergence of social work as a career, 1880–1930. — Cambridge: Harvard University Press, 1965. viii, 291 p.; 22 cm. — (A Publication of the Center for the Study of the History of Liberty in America, Harvard University) 1. Social workers — United States. 2. Charities — United States I. T.
HV91.L8    361.973    LC 65-12786

**Rothman, David J.**     **4.6519**
Conscience and convenience: the asylum and its alternatives in progressive America / David J. Rothman. — 1st ed. — Boston: Little, Brown, c1980. xii, 464 p.; 22 cm. Continues The discovery of the asylum. 1. Public institutions — United States — History. 2. Asylums — United States — History. 3. Prisons — United States — History. I. T.
HV91.R727    361/.973    LC 79-23331    ISBN 0316757748

**Segalman, Ralph.**     **4.6520**
Poverty in America: the welfare dilemma / Ralph Segalman, Asoke Basu. — Westport, Conn.: Greenwood Press, c1981. xvi, 418 p.; 24 cm. — (Contributions in sociology; no. 39 0084-9278) Includes index. 1. Public welfare — United States 2. Poverty — United States. I. Basu, Asoke, 1938- joint author. II. T.
HV91.S33    362.5/0973    LC 79-6568    ISBN 0313207518

**Trattner, Walter I.**     **4.6521**
From poor law to welfare state: a history of social welfare in America / Walter I. Trattner. — 3rd ed. — New York: Free Press; London: Collier Macmillan, c1984. xx, 362 p.; 22 cm. 1. Public welfare — United States — History. 2. Social service — United States — History. I. T.
HV91.T7 1984    361/.973 19    LC 83-48725    ISBN 0029330106

**Wilensky, Harold L.**     • **4.6522**
Industrial society and social welfare: the impact of industrialization on the supply and organization of social welfare services in the United States / by Harold L. Wilensky [and] Charles N. Lebeaux. — New York: Free Press, 1965. lii, 397 p. 1. Public welfare — United States 2. Industrialization 3. United States — Social conditions I. Lebeaux, Charles Nathan, 1913- joint author. II. T.
HV91.W5    360.973    LC 65-8899

**Kamerman, Sheila B.**     **4.6523**
Social services in the United States: policies and programs / Sheila B. Kamerman and Alfred J. Kahn. — Philadelphia: Temple University Press,

1976. xii, 561 p.; 22 cm. 1. Social service — United States. I. Kahn, Alfred J., 1919- joint author. II. T.
HV95.K32    362/.973    LC 75-35492    ISBN 0877220654

**Lerman, Paul, 1926-.**     **4.6524**
Deinstitutionalization and the welfare state / Paul Lerman. — New Brunswick, N.J.: Rutgers University Press, c1982. xvi, 246 p.; 24 cm. Includes index. 1. Institutional care — United States. 2. United States — Social policy I. T.
HV95.L46 1982    361.6/8 19    LC 81-5909    ISBN 0813509343

**Piven, Frances Fox.**     • **4.6525**
Regulating the poor; the functions of public welfare [by] Frances Fox Piven and Richard A. Cloward. [1st ed.] New York, Pantheon Books [1971] xvii, 389 p. 22 cm. 1. Public welfare — United States I. Cloward, Richard A. joint author. II. T.
HV95.P57    361.6/0973 19    LC 70-135368    ISBN 0394460383

**Rein, Mildred.**     **4.6526**
Dilemmas of welfare policy: why work strategies haven't worked / Mildred Rein. — New York: Praeger Publishers, 1982. xii, 179 p.: ill.; 24 cm. Includes index. 1. Public welfare — United States 2. Welfare recipients — Employment — United States I. T.
HV95.R434 1982    362.5/82/0973 19    LC 82-3726    ISBN 003056137X

**Corporate 500. The Directory of corporate philanthropy.**     **4.6527**
[1980]- . — San Francisco: Public Management Institute, [1980?-. v.; 28 cm. 1. Endowments — United States — Directories. I. Public Management Institute.
HV97.A3 C63    361.7/65/02573    LC 82-643221

**West, Guida.**     **4.6528**
The national welfare rights movement: the social protest of poor women / Guida West. — New York, N.Y.: Praeger, 1981. xxi, 451 p.; 24 cm. Includes index. 1. National Welfare Rights Organization. 2. Welfare rights movement — United States. 3. Women, Poor — United States. I. T.
HV97.N34 W47    362.5/82/06073 19    LC 80-39554    ISBN 0030521661

**Human services and resource networks / Seymour B. Sarason ... [et al.].**     **4.6529**
1st ed. — San Francisco: Jossey-Bass, 1977. xvi, 201 p.; 24 cm. (The Jossey-Bass behavioral science series) Includes index. 1. Social service — Connecticut — Essex. 2. Social structure 3. Social change 4. Leadership I. Sarason, Seymour Bernard, 1919-
HV99.E87 H85    361    LC 76-57307    ISBN 0875893090

## HV101–516 Other Countries

**Mencher, Samuel, 1918-1967.**     • **4.6530**
Poor law to poverty program: economic security policy in Britain and the United States / Samuel Mencher. — Pittsburgh: University of Pittsburgh Press, 1967. xix, 476 p.; 24 cm. 1. Public welfare — Great Britain — History. 2. Public welfare — United States — History. 3. Economic security — Great Britain — History. 4. Economic security — United States — History. I. T.
HV245.M39    360    LC 67-13926

**Pritchard, Colin.**     **4.6531**
Social work: reform or revolution? / Colin Pritchard and Richard Taylor. — London; Boston: Routledge & K. Paul, 1978. 162 p.; 23 cm. (Library of social work 0305-4381) Includes index. 1. Social service — Great Britain — Political aspects. I. Taylor, R. K. S. (Richard K. S.) joint author. II. T.
HV245.P87 1978    361/.941    LC 78-326338    ISBN 0710088825

**Algie, Jimmy.**     **4.6532**
Social values: objectives and action / Jimmy Algie. — New York: Wiley, [1975] 491 p.; 23 cm. 'A Halsted Pressbook.' Includes indexes. 1. Social service — Great Britain. I. T.
HV248.A45 1975    362/.941    LC 75-12902    ISBN 0470022507

**Forrest, Alan I.**     **4.6533**
The French Revolution and the poor / Alan Forrest. — New York: St. Martin's Press, 1981. x, 198 p.; 25 cm. Includes indexes. 1. Charities — France — History — 18th century. 2. Poor — France — History — 18th century. 3. France — History — Revolution, 1789 I. T.
HV265.F64 1981    362.5/8/0944 19    LC 80-29105    ISBN 0312305249

**Martz, Linda.**     **4.6534**
Poverty and welfare in Habsburg Spain: the example of Toledo / Linda Martz. — Cambridge [Cambridgeshire]; New York: Cambridge University Press, 1983. xvii, 266 p.: ill.; 24 cm. (Cambridge Iberian and Latin American studies.)

Includes index. 1. Charities — Spain — Toledo — History. 2. Poor — Spain — Toledo — History. 3. Toledo (Spain) — Social policy. I. T. II. Series.
HV343.M37 1983        362.5/8/094643 19        *LC* 82-19725        *ISBN* 0521239524

**Lieberman, Morton A., 1931-.**                                    **4.6535**
Self–help groups for coping with crisis: origins, members, processes, and impact / Morton A. Lieberman, Leonard D. Borman, and associates; with special contributions by Gary R. Bond, Paul Antze and Leon H. Levy. — 1st ed. — San Francisco: Jossey-Bass, c1979. xvi, 462 p.; 24 cm. — (Jossey-Bass social and behavioral science series.) Includes index. 1. Self-help groups — United States — Addresses, essays, lectures. I. Borman, Leonard D. joint author. II. T. III. Series.
HV547.L53        361.7        *LC* 79-88772        *ISBN* 0875894356

# HV553–640.5 Disaster Relief. Refugees

**Erikson, Kai T.**                                    **4.6536**
Everything in its path: destruction of community in the Buffalo Creek flood / Kai T. Erikson. — New York: Simon and Schuster, c1976. 284 p.: ill.; 22 cm. 1. Floods — West Virginia — Buffalo Creek. 2. Disasters — Psychological aspects I. T.
HV610 1972.E74        363        *LC* 76-26462        *ISBN* 0671223674

**Refugees and world politics; edited by Elizabeth G. Ferris.**                                    **4.6537**
New York: Praeger, 1985. 224 p. Includes index. 1. Refugees — Addresses, essays, lectures. 2. World politics — Addresses, essays, lectures. I. Ferris, Elizabeth G.
HV640.R432 1985        362.8/7 19        *LC* 85-495        *ISBN* 0030720435

**Conference on Ethical Issues and Moral Principles in United**                                    **4.6538**
**States Refugee Policy (1983: Washington, D.C.)**
American refugee policy: ethical and religious reflections / edited by Joseph M. Kitagawa. — [New York?]: Presiding Bishops Fund for World Relief, Episcopal Church, in collaboration with Winston Press, Minneapolis, Minn., 1985 (c1984). x, 170 p.; 23 cm. Sponsored by the United States Coordinator for Refugee Affairs and the Religious Advisory Committee on Refugee and Migration Affairs, held in Washington, D.C., 1983. 1. Refugees — Government policy — United States — Congresses. 2. Refugees — Government policy — Religious aspects — Congresses. 3. Refugees — Government policy — Moral and ethical aspects — Congresses. 4. Church and state — United States — Congresses. I. Kitagawa, Joseph Mitsuo, 1915- II. Religious Advisory Committee on Refugee and Migration Affairs (U.S.) III. Presiding Bishop's Fund for World Relief (Episcopal Church) IV. T.
HV640.4.U54 C66 1983        362.8/7/0973 19        *LC* 84-40507        *ISBN* 0866839755

# HV687–689 Medical and Psychiatric Social Work

**Wallace, Stephen R.**                                    **4.6539**
Clinical social work in health care: new biopsychosocial approaches / Stephen R. Wallace, Richard J. Goldberg, Andrew E. Slaby. — New York, NY: Praeger, 1984. ix, 242 p.; 25 cm. 1. Medical social work 2. Psychiatric social work I. Goldberg, Richard J. II. Slaby, Andrew Edmund. III. T.
HV687.W34 1984        362.1/0425 19        *LC* 83-13744        *ISBN* 0030641837

**Germain, Carel B.**                                    **4.6540**
Social work practice in health care: an ecological perspective / Carel Bailey Germain. — New York: Free Press, c1984. xix, 296 p.: ill.; 25 cm. — (Fields of practice series.) Includes indexes. 1. Medical social work — United States. I. T. II. Series.
HV687.5.U5 G47 1984        362.1/0425/0973 19        *LC* 83-48757        *ISBN* 0029116600

**Social work issues in health care / edited by Rosalind S. Miller,**                                    **4.6541**
**and Helen Rehr.**
Englewood Cliffs, N.J.: Prentice-Hall, c1983. xi, 291 p.; 24 cm. 1. Medical social work — United States. I. Miller, Rosalind S., 1923- II. Rehr, Helen.
HV687.5.U5 S645 1983        362.1/0425 19        *LC* 82-12294        *ISBN* 0138195323

**Wodarski, John S.**                                    **4.6542**
Behavioral social work / John S. Wodarski, Dennis A. Bagarozzi. — New York: Human Sciences Press, c1978. 335 p.; 21 cm. 1. Psychiatric social work 2. Behavior modification I. Bagarozzi, Dennis A. joint author. II. T.
HV689.W62        362.2/04/25        *LC* 78-26356        *ISBN* 0877053758

# HV697–4959 Protection. Assistance

**Hartman, Ann.**                                    **4.6543**
Family–centered social work practice / Ann Hartman, Joan Laird. — New York: Free Press; London: Collier Macmillan, c1983. xii, 419 p.; 24 cm. Includes index. 1. Family social work — United States. I. Laird, Joan. II. T.
HV699.H35 1983        362.8/2 19        *LC* 83-47656        *ISBN* 0029141001

**Maluccio, Anthony N.**                                    **4.6544**
Learning from clients: interpersonal helping as viewed by clients and social workers / Anthony N. Maluccio. — New York: Free Press, c1979. xii, 322 p.; 24 cm. Includes index. 1. Family social work — United States. 2. Social service — Research — United States. 3. Social service — United States — Evaluation. 4. Helping behavior I. T.
HV699.M33        361/.06        *LC* 78-67753        *ISBN* 0029198208

# HV701–1416 Children

**Child abuse: commission and omission / edited by Joanne**                                    **4.6545**
**Valiant Cook and Roy Tyler Bowles.**
Toronto: Butterworths, 1981. xv, 509 p.; 24 cm. 1. Child abuse — Addresses, essays, lectures. I. Cook, Joanne Valiant. II. Bowles, Roy Tyler.
HV713.C3824        362.7/044 19        *LC* 80-514757        *ISBN* 0409824100

**Child, family, neighborhood: a master plan for social service**                                    **4.6546**
**delivery / June Brown ... [et al.].**
New York, N.Y.: Child Welfare League of America, c1982. x, 63 p.; 23 cm. 'CW-34.'–P. [4] of cover. 1. Child welfare — Mathematical models. 2. Children — Services for — Mathematical models. I. Brown, June. II. Child Welfare League of America.
HV713.C3825 1982        362.7/042 19        *LC* 81-21678        *ISBN* 0878682090

**Costin, Lela B.**                                    **4.6547**
Child welfare: policies and practice / [by] Lela B. Costin. — New York: McGraw-Hill, [1972] xii, 423 p.: ill.; 24 cm. 1. Child welfare 2. Child welfare — United States. I. T.
HV713.C67        362.7/0973        *LC* 70-37091        *ISBN* 007013202X

**Goldstein, Joseph.**                                    **4.6548**
Beyond the best interests of the child [by] Joseph Goldstein, Anna Freud [and] Albert J. Solnit. — New York: Free Press, [1973] xiv, 170 p.; 21 cm. 1. Custody of children 2. Children — Legal status, laws, etc. 3. Custody of children — United States. 4. Child welfare I. Freud, Anna, 1895- joint author. II. Solnit, Albert J. joint author. III. T.
HV713.G54        362.7        *LC* 73-9136        *ISBN* 0029123003

**Group care for children: concept and issues / edited by Frank**                                    **4.6549**
**Ainsworth and Leon C. Fulcher.**
London; New York: Tavistock, 1981. xvi, 308 p.; 22 cm. 1. Group homes for children — Addresses, essays, lectures. 2. Day care centers — Addresses, essays, lectures. 3. Children — Institutional care — Addresses, essays, lectures. I. Ainsworth, Frank. II. Fulcher, Leon C.
HV713.G76 1981        362.7/32 19        *LC* 81-207187        *ISBN* 0422772909

**Garbarino, James.**                                    **4.6550**
Protecting children from abuse and neglect: developing and maintaining effective support systems for families / James Garbarino, S. Holly Stocking, with Alice H. Collins ... [et al.]. — 1st ed. — San Francisco: Jossey-Bass, 1980. xv, 222 p.; 24 cm. — (Jossey-Bass social and behavioral science series.) Includes index. 1. Child abuse — Services — Addresses, essays, lectures. 2. Child abuse — Services — United States — Addresses, essays, lectures. I. Stocking, S. Holly. joint author. II. T. III. Series.
HV713.P76        362.7/1        *LC* 79-24239        *ISBN* 0875894429

**Zietz, Dorothy.**                                    **● 4.6551**
Child welfare: services and perspectives. — 2d ed. — New York: Wiley, [1969] xi, 346 p.: illus.; 23 cm. First ed. published in 1959 under title: Child welfare; principles and methods. 1. Child welfare 2. Child welfare — U.S. I. T.
HV713.Z5 1969        362.7/0973        *LC* 79-81335        *ISBN* 047198275X

**Billingsley, Andrew.**     **4.6552**
Children of the storm: black children and American child welfare [by] Andrew Billingsley [and] Jeanne M. Giovannoni. New York, Harcourt, Brace, Jovanovich [1972] xvii, 263 p. illus. 22 cm. 1. Child welfare — United States. 2. Afro-American children I. Giovannoni, Jeanne M. joint author. II. T.
HV741.B5     362.7     LC 72-75593     *ISBN* 0151173400 *ISBN* 0155072714

**Bremner, Robert Hamlett, 1917- comp.**     **4.6553**
Children and youth in America: a documentary history / editor, Robert H. Bremner; associate editors, John Barnard, Tamara K. Hareven [and] Robert M. Mennel. — Cambridge, Mass.: Harvard University Press, 1974. 2 v.: ill., facsims., music; 27 cm. 1. Child welfare — United States — History. 2. Children — United States — History. 3. Youth — United States — History. I. T.
HV741.B77     362.7/0973     LC 74-115473     *ISBN* 0674116100

**Damaged parents, an anatomy of child neglect / Norman A.**     **4.6554**
**Polansky ... [et al.].**
Chicago: University of Chicago Press, 1981. xii, 271 p.; 24 cm. Includes indexes. 1. Child abuse — United States — Addresses, essays, lectures. 2. Socially handicapped children — United States — Addresses, essays, lectures. 3. Social work with the socially handicapped — United States — Addresses, essays, lectures. I. Polansky, Norman Alburt, 1918-
HV741.D35     362.7/044 19     LC 80-22793     *ISBN* 0226672212

**Fredericksen, Hazel, 1897-.**     **4.6555**
The child and his welfare [by] Hazel Fredericksen [and] R. A. Mulligan. — 3d ed. — San Francisco: W. H. Freeman, [1972] x, 434 p.: illus.; 24 cm. 1. Children — Services for — United States. I. Mulligan, Raymond A., 1915- joint author. II. T.
HV741.F75 1972     362.7/0973     LC 70-172242     *ISBN* 0716709058

**Garbarino, James.**     **4.6556**
Understanding abusive families / James Garbarino, Gwen Gilliam. — Lexington, Mass.: Lexington Books, c1980. xvi, 263 p.: graphs; 24 cm. 1. Child abuse — United States. 2. Child molesting — United States. 3. Youth — United States — Family relationships. 4. Youth — United States — Crimes against. 5. Human ecology I. Gilliam, Gwen. joint author. II. T.
HV741.G37     362.8/2     LC 79-47983     *ISBN* 0669036218

**A Handbook of child welfare: context, knowledge, and practice**     **4.6557**
**/ Joan Laird and Ann Hartman, editors.**
New York: Free Press; London: Collier Macmillan, c1985. xxvi, 864 p.: ill.; 25 cm. Includes indexes. 1. Child welfare — United States. 2. Social work with children — United States. I. Laird, Joan. II. Hartman, Ann.
HV741.H32 1985     362.7/95/0973 19     LC 84-18769     *ISBN* 0029180902

HV
741
H47
→ **Helfer, Ray E.**     • **4.6558**
The battered child, edited by Ray E. Helfer and C. Henry Kempe. With a foreword by Katherine B. Oettinger. Chicago, University of Chicago Press [1968] xv, 268 p. illus. 25 cm. 1. Child abuse — United States — Addresses, essays, lectures. I. Kempe, C. Henry. joint author. II. T.
HV741.H4     364.15     LC 68-16695

**Kadushin, Alfred.**     **4.6559**
Child welfare services / Alfred Kadushin. — 3d ed. — New York: Macmillan, c1980. xi, 718 p.; 27 cm. 1. Child welfare — United States. I. T.
HV741.K26 1980     362.7/0973     LC 79-13416     *ISBN* 0033618108

**Kempe, Ruth S.**     **4.6560**
Child abuse / Ruth S. Kempe and C. Henry Kempe. — Cambridge, Mass.: Harvard University Press, 1978. 136 p.; 21 cm. — (Developing child.) Includes index. 1. Child abuse — United States. I. Kempe, C. Henry. joint author. II. T. III. Series.
HV741.K44     362.7/1     LC 78-5104     *ISBN* 0674114256. *ISBN* 0674114264 pbk

**Maluccio, Anthony N.**     **4.6561**
Permanency planning for children: concepts and methods / Anthony N. Maluccio, Edith Fein, and Kathleen A. Olmstead. — New York: Tavistock Publications, 1986. xiii, 328 p.; 24 cm. Includes indexes. 1. Social work with children — United States. 2. Child welfare — United States. 3. Custody of children — United States. I. Fein, Edith. II. Olmstead, Kathleen A. III. T.
HV741.M344 1986     362.7/95 19     LC 85-17333     *ISBN* 0422788406

**Martin, Judith A., 1945-.**     **4.6562**
Gender–related behaviors of children in abusive situations / by Judith Martin. — Saratoga, Calif.: R & E Publishers, c1983. vii, 135 p.; 21 cm. 1. Child abuse — Research — United States. 2. Child abuse — United States. 3. Social surveys — United States. I. T.
HV741.M346 1983     362.7/044 19     LC 81-86006     *ISBN* 0882476858

**Mayhall, Pamela D. (Pamela Douglass), 1939-.**     **4.6563**
Child abuse and neglect: sharing responsibility / Pamela D. Mayhall, Katherine Eastlack Norgard. — New York: Wiley, c1983. xiv, 400 p.; 24 cm. 1. Child abuse — United States. 2. Abandoned children — United States. I. Norgard, Katherine Eastlack, 1941- II. T.
HV741.M35 1983     362.7/044 19     LC 82-24799     *ISBN* 0471099295

**National directory of children & youth services.**     **4.6564**
1979-. Denver, Colo., American Association for Protecting Children (American Humane Association); Longmont, Colo. [etc.] Bookmakers Guild [etc.] v. 28 cm. Annual. 1. Youth — Services for — United States — Directories. 2. Child welfare — United States — Directories. I. American Association for Protecting Children. II. Child protection report.
HV741.N3157     362.7/025/73     LC 80-644422

**Nelson, Barbara J., 1949-.**     **4.6565**
Making an issue of child abuse: political agenda setting for social problems / Barbara J. Nelson. — Chicago: University of Chicago Press, 1984. xiv, 169 p.; 24 cm. 1. Child abuse — Government policy — United States. I. T.
HV741.N39 1984     362.7/044 19     LC 83-18044     *ISBN* 0226572005

**Schorr, Alvin Louis, 1921-.**     **4.6566**
Children and decent people / edited by Alvin L. Schorr. — New York: Basic Books, [1974] xvii, 222 p.; 22 cm. 1. Children — Services for — United States — Addresses, essays, lectures. 2. Children — Institutional care — United States — Addresses, essays, lectures. 3. Day care centers — United States — Addresses, essays, lectures. 4. Children — Care and hygiene — Addresses, essays, lectures. I. T.
HV741.S35     362.7/0973     LC 73-82894     *ISBN* 0465010415

**Stein, Theodore J.**     **4.6567**
Decision making at child welfare intake: a handbook for practitioners / Theodore J. Stein and Tina L. Rzepnicki. — New York, N.Y.: Child Welfare League of America, c1983. xiv, 130 p.; 23 cm. 1. Child welfare — United States. 2. Foster home care — United States. I. Rzepnicki, Tina L. II. T.
HV741.S744 1983     362.7/1 19     LC 83-2030     *ISBN* 0878682139

**Steiner, Gilbert Yale, 1924-.**     **4.6568**
The children's cause / Gilbert Y. Steiner, with the assistance of Pauline H. Milius. — Washington: Brookings Institution, c1976. viii, 265 p.; 24 cm. 1. Child welfare — United States. 2. Children — Legal status, laws, etc. — United States. I. Milius, Pauline H., joint author. II. Brookings Institution. III. T.
HV741.S75     362.7/0973     LC 75-43465     *ISBN* 0815781202

**Walters, David R., 1934-.**     **4.6569**
Physical and sexual abuse of children: causes and treatment / David R. Walters. — Bloomington: Indiana University Press, [1975] xii, 192 p.: form ; 22 cm. Includes index. 1. Child abuse — United States. I. T.
HV741.W25 1975     364.1/5     LC 75-1940     *ISBN* 0253344905

**Giovannoni, Jeanne M.**     **4.6570**
Defining child abuse / Jeanne M. Giovannoni and Rosina M. Becerra. — New York: Free Press, c1979. xviii, 302 p.; 24 cm. Includes index. 1. Child abuse — California. 2. Child abuse — United States — Case studies. 3. Child welfare — United States — Case studies. I. Becerra, Rosina M. joint author. II. T.
HV742.C2 G46 1979     362.7/1     LC 79-7180     *ISBN* 002911750X

**Jaffe, Eliezer David, 1933-.**     **4.6571**
Child welfare in Israel / Eliezer David Jaffe. — New York, N.Y.: Praeger, 1982. xiii, 319 p.: ill.; 25 cm. (Praeger special studies in social welfare.) Includes index. 1. Child welfare — Israel. I. T. II. Series.
HV800.I8 J33 1982     362.7/95/095694 19     LC 81-15422     *ISBN* 0030577527

## HV851–868 NURSERIES. DAY CARE

**Clarke-Stewart, Alison, 1943-.**     **4.6572**
Daycare / Alison Clarke-Stewart. — Cambridge, Mass.: Harvard University Press, 1982. 173 p.: ill.; 21 cm. — (The Developing child series) Includes index. 1. Day care centers 2. Child development I. T.
HV851.C55 1982     362.7/12 19     LC 82-956     *ISBN* 0674194039

**Day care: scientific and social policy issues / edited by Edward**     **4.6573**
**F. Zigler, Edmund W. Gordon; under the auspices of the**
**American Orthopsychiatric Association.**
Boston, Mass.: Auburn House Pub. Co., c1982. xix, 515 p.; 24 cm. Includes bibliographies and index. 1. Day care centers — United States — Addresses, essays, lectures. 2. Day care centers — Government policy — United States — Addresses, essays, lectures. I. Zigler, Edward, 1930- II. Gordon, Edmund W. III. American Orthopsychiatric Association.
HV854.D39 1982     362.7/12/0973 19     LC 81-12838     *ISBN* 0865690987

**Sidel, Ruth.**      4.6574
Women and child care in China: a firsthand report / Ruth Sidel; photographs by Victor W. Sidel. — Rev. ed. — New York, N.Y.: Penguin, 1982. xlii, 211 p.: ill.; 20 cm. Includes index. 1. Day care centers — China. 2. Child rearing — China. 3. Child rearing 4. Women — China — Social conditions. I. T.
HV861.C5 S53 1982    362.7/95/0951 19    *LC* 82-432    *ISBN* 0140037187

## HV873–881 FOSTER CARE. ADOPTION

**Wolins, Martin. comp.**      4.6575
Successful group care: explorations in the powerful environment. — Chicago: Aldine Pub. Co., [1974] ix, 463 p.; 25 cm. 1. Children — Institutional care — Addresses, essays, lectures. I. T.
HV873.W57    362.7/32/08    *LC* 73-75709    *ISBN* 0202360172

**Kline, Draza.**      4.6576
Foster care of children; nurture and treatment [by] Draza Kline [and] Helen–Mary Forbush Overstreet. — New York: Columbia University Press, 1972. xii, 316 p.; 23 cm. — (Studies of the Child Welfare League of America) 1. Foster home care I. Overstreet, Helen Mary, joint author. II. T.
HV875.K592 1972    362.7/33    *LC* 78-186386    *ISBN* 0231036019

**Feigelman, William.**      4.6577
Chosen children: new patterns of adoptive relationships / William Feigelman and Arnold R. Silverman. — New York, NY, U.S.A.: Praeger, 1983. xxiv, 261 p.; 24 cm. Includes index. 1. Adoption — United States. 2. Foster parents — United States — Family relationships. 3. Children, Adopted — United States — Family relationships. 4. Social case work with children 5. Family social work — United States. I. Silverman, Arnold R., 1940- II. T.
HV875.64.F44 1983    362.7/34/0973 19    *LC* 83-13972    *ISBN* 003062343X

**Coles, Robert.**      4.6578
Uprooted children; the early life of migrant farm workers. — [Pittsburgh]: University of Pittsburgh Press, [1970] xxiii, 142 p.; 20 cm. — (Horace Mann lecture, 1969) 1. Children of migrant laborers — United States. 2. Migrant agricultural laborers — United States. I. T. II. Series.
HV881.C62    917.3/03/924    *LC* 70-98270    *ISBN* 0822931923

**Fanshel, David.**      4.6579
Children in foster care: a longitudinal investigation / David Fanshel and Eugene B. Shinn. — New York: Columbia University Press, 1978. xiv, 520, [2] p.; 24 cm. Includes index. 1. Foster home care — United States — Longitudinal studies. I. Shinn, Eugene B., joint author. II. T.
HV881.F36    362.7/33/0973    *LC* 77-2872    *ISBN* 0231035764

## HV888–907 HANDICAPPED CHILDREN

**Dinnage, Rosemary.**      4.6580
The handicapped child: research review. — London: Longman, in association with the National Bureau for Co-operation in Child Care, 1970- v. ; 22 cm. — (Studies in child development) 1. Handicapped children — Research. I. National Bureau for Co-operation in Child Care. II. T.
HV888.D5    362.7/8/3    *LC* 72-501429    *ISBN* 0582324491

**Parents speak out: then and now / [edited by] H. Rutherford**    4.6581
**Turnbull III, Ann P. Turnbull.**
2nd ed. — Columbus: C.E. Merrill Pub. Co., c1985. xii, 287 p.: ill.; 23 cm. 1. Handicapped children — Family relationships — Addresses, essays, lectures. I. Turnbull, H. Rutherford. II. Turnbull, Ann P., 1947-
HV888.P38 1985    362.4/088054 19    *LC* 84-61748    *ISBN* 0675204046

**Edgerton, Robert B., 1931-.**      4.6582
Mental retardation / Robert B. Edgerton. — Cambridge, Mass.: Harvard University Press, 1979. 125 p.: ill.; 21 cm. — (Developing child.) Includes index. 1. Mentally handicapped children 2. Mentally handicapped I. T. II. Series.
HV891.E34 1979    362.3    *LC* 78-27199    *ISBN* 0674568850. *ISBN* 0674568869 pbk

**Koch, Richard, 1921-.**      4.6583
The mentally retarded child and his family: a multidisciplinary handbook / edited by Richard Koch and James C. Dobson. — Rev. ed. — New York: Brunner/Mazel, c1976. xiii, 546 p.: ill.; 24 cm. 1. Mentally handicapped children 2. Mentally handicapped children — Family relationships. I. Dobson, James C., 1936- joint author. II. T.
HV891.K58 1976    362.7/8/3    *LC* 75-42133    *ISBN* 0876301219

**Buck, Pearl S. (Pearl Sydenstricker), 1892-1973.**      4.6584
The child who never grew. New York, J. Day Co. [1960] 62 p. 20 cm. 'Appeared as an article in the Ladies' home journal, May, 1950.' 1. Vineland, N.J. Training School. 2. Mentally handicapped children — Biography. I. T.
HV897.N5 V56    362.2    *LC* 50-9500

**Powell, Thomas H.**      4.6585
Brothers & sisters—a special part of exceptional families / by Thomas H. Powell and Peggy Ahrenhold Ogle. — Baltimore: Brookes Pub. Co., c1985. xv, 226 p.; 23 cm. Includes index. 1. Handicapped children — Family relationships. 2. Brothers and sisters I. Ogle, Peggy Ahrenhold, 1952- II. T. III. Title: Brothers and sisters—a special part of exceptional families.
HV903.P69 1985    362.8/2 19    *LC* 84-19923    *ISBN* 0933716451

## HV1445 Women

**Rousseau, Ann Marie, 1946-.**      4.6586
Shopping bag ladies: homeless women speak about their lives / by Ann Marie Rousseau; preface by Alix Kates Shulman. — New York: Pilgrim Press, c1981. [160] p.: ill.; 19 x 26 cm. 1. Homeless women — United States. 2. Homeless women — Services for — United States. I. T.
HV1445.R68    305.4/8 19    *LC* 81-407    *ISBN* 0829804137

**Women helping women: a state–by–state directory of services.**    4.6587
1st ed. — New York, N.Y.: Women's Action Alliance: Distributed by Neal-Schuman Publishers, c1981. xxiii, 179 p.; 24 cm. 1. Women — Services for — United States — States — Directories. 2. Social work with women — United States — States — Directories. I. Women's Action Alliance.
HV1445.W65 1981    362.8/3/02573 19    *LC* 82-140956    *ISBN* 0960582800

## HV1451–1493 Aged

**Beauvoir, Simone de, 1908-.**      • 4.6588
[Vieillesse. English] The coming of age / translated by Patrick O'Brian. — [1st American ed.] New York: Putnam [1972] 585 p.; 24 cm. Translation of La vieillesse. 1. Aged I. T.
HV1451.B413 1972b    301.43/5    *LC* 75-189781

**Reaching the aged: social services in forty–four countries /**    4.6589
**editors, Morton I. Teicher, Daniel Thursz, Joseph L. Vigilante.**
Beverly Hills: Sage Publications, c1979. 256 p.; 23 cm. — (Social service delivery systems; v. 4) 1. Aged — Services for — Addresses, essays, lectures. 2. Social work with the aged — Addresses, essays, lectures. 3. Aged — Family relationships — Addresses, essays, lectures. 4. Aged — Care and hygiene — Addresses, essays, lectures. I. Teicher, Morton I. II. Thursz, Daniel. III. Vigilante, Joseph L.
HV1451.R4    362.6    *LC* 79-18525    *ISBN* 0803913656

**Abuse of the elderly: a guide to resources and services / [edited**    4.6590
**by] Joseph J. Costa.**
Lexington, Mass.: Lexington Books, c1984. xiii, 289 p.; 24 cm. Includes index. 1. Aged — United States — Abuse of. 2. Abused aged — Services for — United States. I. Costa, Joseph J.
HV1461.A28 1984    362.8/8/0880565 19    *LC* 82-48472    *ISBN* 0669061425

**Huttman, Elizabeth D., 1929-.**      4.6591
Social services for the elderly / Elizabeth D. Huttman. — New York: Free Press, c1985. vii, 296 p.; 25 cm. Includes index. 1. Aged — Services for — United States. 2. Old age assistance — United States. 3. Social work with the aged — United States I. T.
HV1461.H88 1985    362.6/0973 19    *LC* 85-1593    *ISBN* 0029156009

**Steinberg, Raymond M.**      4.6592
Case management and the elderly: a handbook for planning and administering programs / Raymond M. Steinberg, Genevieve W. Carter. — Lexington, Mass.: LexingtonBooks, c1983. xii, 211 p.; 24 cm. Includes index. 1. Social work with the aged — United States — Handbooks, manuals, etc. 2. Social work administration — United States — Handbooks, manuals, etc. I. Carter, Genevieve W. II. T.
HV1461.S83 1983    362.6/042 19    *LC* 82-17127    *ISBN* 0669060895

**Francis, Doris, 1940-.**      4.6593
Will you still need me, will you still feed me, when I'm 84? / Doris Francis. — Bloomington: Indiana University Press, c1984. xii, 252 p.: ill.; 24 cm. Includes index. 1. Jewish aged — Ohio — Cleveland. 2. Jews — Ohio — Cleveland — Social conditions. 3. Jewish aged — England — Leeds (West Yorkshire) 4. Jews — England — Leeds (West Yorkshire) — Social conditions.

5. Cleveland (Ohio) — Social conditions. 6. Leeds (West Yorkshire) — Social conditions. I. T.
HV1471.C58 F7 1984    305.2/6/089924077132 19    *LC* 82-49351    *ISBN* 0253365457

## HV1551–3024 Handicapped

**Katz, Alfred H. (Alfred Hyman), 1916-.**                      **4.6594**
A handbook of services for the handicapped / Alfred H. Katz and Knute Martin. — Westport, Conn.: Greenwood Press, 1982. xiii, 291 p.; 25 cm. 1. Handicapped — Services for — United States — Handbooks, manuals, etc. I. Martin, Knute. II. T.
HV1553.K37 1982    362.4/0458/0973 19    *LC* 81-20314    *ISBN* 0313213852

**United States. Congress. Office of Technology Assessment.**   **4.6595**
Technology and handicapped people / Office of Technology Assessment Congress of the United States. — New York: Springer, 1983. ix, 212 p.: ill. 1. Handicapped — Services for — United States. 2. Self-help devices for the disabled — United States. 3. Technology — Social aspects — United States. I. T.
HV1553.T42 1983    362.4/0483 19    *LC* 82-600546    *ISBN* 0826144307

**Discovery ('83-    ) (1984: Chicago, Ill.)**                  **4.6596**
Discovery '84: technology for disabled persons: conference papers / edited by Christopher Smith. — Menomonie, WI: Materials Development Centre, Stout Vocational Rehabilitation Institute, University of Wisconsin-Stout, c1985. — ix, 251 p.: ill.; 29 cm. Discovery '84 held in Chicago, Ill. on October 1-3, 1984. 1. Self-help devices for the disabled — Congresses 2. Handicapped — Rehabilitation — Congresses 3. Computers — Congresses I. Smith, Christopher. II. T.
HV1568.D4    *ISBN* 0916671615

**With the power of each breath: a disabled women's anthology /**   **4.6597**
**[edited by] Susan E. Browne, Debra Connors, Nanci Stern.**
1st ed. — Pittsburgh: Cleis Press, c1985. 354 p.; 22 cm. 1. Handicapped women — United States — Case studies. I. Browne, Susan E. II. Connors, Debra. III. Stern, Nanci.
HV1569.3.W65 W58 1985    362.4/088/042 19    *LC* 85-71206    *ISBN* 0939416069

**Tuttle, Dean W.**                                             **4.6598**
Self-esteem and adjusting with blindness: the process of responding to life's demands / by Dean W. Tuttle; with a foreword by Gil L. Johnson.. — Springfield, Ill., U.S.A.: C.C. Thomas, c1984. xix, 316 p.: ill.; 24 cm. Includes index. 1. Blindness — Psychological aspects. 2. Self-respect 3. Blind — Rehabilitation I. T.
HV1593.T87 1984    362.4/12/019 19    *LC* 83-5037    *ISBN* 0398048878

**Barraga, Natalie.**                                           **4.6599**
Visual handicaps and learning / Natalie Barraga. — Rev. ed. — Astin, Tex.: Exceptional Resources, c1983. xi, 166 p.; 21 cm. Cover title: Visual handicaps & learning. 1. Visually handicapped — Education. I. T. II. Title: Visual handicaps & learning.
HV1626.B37 1983    362.4/1 19    *LC* 83-206352    *ISBN* 093559406X

**Lowenfeld, Berthold.**                                        **4.6600**
The visually handicapped child in school. Edited by Berthold Lowenfeld. — New York: John Day Co., [1973] xvi, 384 p.; 25 cm. — (John Day books in special education) 1. Visually handicapped children — Education — Addresses, essays, lectures. I. T.
HV1626.L75    371.9/11    *LC* 72-12303    *ISBN* 0381970973

**Deaf children: developmental perspectives / edited by Lynn S.**   **4.6601**
**Liben.**
New York: Academic Press, 1979. xv, 246 p.: ill.; 24 cm. — (Developmental psychology series.) 1. Children, Deaf — Addresses, essays, lectures. I. Liben, Lynn S. II. Series.
HV2390.D42    155.4/5/12    *LC* 77-77237    *ISBN* 0124479502

**Higgins, Paul C.**                                            **4.6602**
Outsiders in a hearing world: a sociology of deafness / Paul C. Higgins; foreword by Robert A. Scott. — Beverly Hills, Calif.: Sage Publications, c1980. 205 p.; 22 cm. — (Sociological observations. v. 10) 1. Deaf 2. Deafness — Social aspects. I. T. II. Series.
HV2395.H53    305    *LC* 80-12150    *ISBN* 0803914210

**Levine, Edna Simon, 1910-.**                                  **4.6603**
The ecology of early deafness: guides to fashioning environments and psychological assessments / Edna Simon Levine. — New York: Columbia University Press, 1981. xv, 422 p.: ill.; 24 cm. 1. Deafness — Psychological aspects. 2. Man — Influence of environment 3. Human ecology I. T.
HV2395.L39    362.4/2/019 19    *LC* 80-27138    *ISBN* 0231038860

**Moores, Donald F.**                                           **4.6604**
Educating the deaf: psychology, principles, and practices / Donald F. Moores. — 2nd ed. — Boston: Houghton Mifflin Co., c1982. xvii, 375 p.: ill.; 25 cm. Includes indexes. 1. Deaf — Education 2. Deafness 3. Deaf — Education — United States. I. T.
HV2430.M66 1982    371.91/2 19    *LC* 81-82565    *ISBN* 039531707X

**Quigley, Stephen Patrick, 1927-.**                            **4.6605**
Language and deafness / Stephen P. Quigley, Peter V. Paul. — San Diego, Calif.: College-Hill Press, c1984. xvi, 277 p.: ill.; 24 cm. Spine title: Language & deafness. Includes indexes. 1. Deaf — Education 2. Children, Deaf — Language 3. Deaf — Means of communication — Study and teaching. 4. Deaf — Education — United States. I. Paul, Peter V. II. T. III. Title: Language & deafness.
HV2471.Q52 1984    371.91/2 19    *LC* 83-26144    *ISBN* 0933014147

**Costello, Elaine.**                                           **4.6606**
Signing: how to speak with your hands / Elaine Costello; illustrated by Lois A. Lehman. — Toronto; New York: Bantam Books, 1983. xvii, 248 p.: ill.; 28 cm. Includes index. 1. Sign language I. Lehman, Lois A. II. T.
HV2474.C67 1983    419 19    *LC* 82-45947    *ISBN* 0553014587

**Lane, Harlan L.**                                             **4.6607**
When the mind hears: a history of the deaf / Harlan Lane. — 1st ed. — New York: Random House, c1984. xvii, 537 p.: ill., ports.; 24 cm. Includes index. 1. Deaf — United States — History. 2. Deaf — United States — Biography. I. T.
HV2530.L36 1984    305/.908162/0973 19    *LC* 83-43201    *ISBN* 0394508785

**Conley, Ronald W.**                                           **4.6608**
The economics of mental retardation [by] Ronald W. Conley. — Baltimore: Johns Hopkins University Press, [1973] xiii, 377 p.; 23 cm. 1. Mentally handicapped I. T.
HV3004.C65 1973    362.3    *LC* 72-12345    *ISBN* 0801814103

**Kugel, Robert B.**                                            **4.6609**
Changing patterns in residential services for the mentally retarded. Edited by Robert B. Kugel and Wolf Wolfensberger. Washington: President's Committee on Mental Retardation, 1969. 435 p.; 27 cm. 1. Mentally handicapped — Institutional care — United States. 2. Mentally handicapped — Services for — United States. I. Wolfensberger, Wolf. joint author. II. United States. President's Committee on Mental Retardation. III. T.
HV3004.K8    362.3    *LC* 79-600494

**MacMillan, Donald L.**                                        **4.6610**
Mental retardation in school and society / Donald L. MacMillan. — 2nd ed. — Boston: Little, Brown, c1982. xii, 655 p.: ill.; 24 cm. Includes index. 1. Mentally handicapped 2. Mentally handicapped — Education I. T.
HV3004.M26 1982    362.3 19    *LC* 81-84230    *ISBN* 0316542725

**Achievements in residential services for persons with disabilities:**   **4.6611**
**toward excellence / edited by Tony Apolloni, Joanna**
**Cappuccilli, and Thomas P. Cooke.**
Baltimore: University Park Press, c1980. xiv, 205 p.: ill.; 23 cm. Proceedings of a conference held in Pomona, Calif., Dec. 14-15, 1977. 1. Developmentally disabled — Services for — United States — Congresses. 2. Community mental health services — United States — Congresses. I. Apolloni, Tony. II. Cappuccilli, Joanna. III. Cooke, Thomas P. IV. Title: Toward excellence.
HV3006.A3 A25    362.3/0973    *LC* 79-22077    *ISBN* 0839115415

**The Mentally retarded and society: a social science perspective**   **4.6612**
**/ edited by Michael J. Begab and Stephen A. Richardson.**
Baltimore: University Park Press, [1975] xix, 492 p.; 26 cm. Proceedings of a conference held in Niles, Mich., Apr. 18-20, 1974, sponsored by the National Institute of Child Health and Human Development and the Rose Kennedy Center at Albert Einstein College of Medicine. 1. Mentally handicapped — United States — Congresses. I. Begab, Michael J. II. Richardson, Stephen A. III. National Institute of Child Health and Human Development (U.S.) IV. Rose F. Kennedy Center for Research in Mental Retardation and Human Development.
HV3006.A3 M45    362.3/0973    *LC* 75-33173    *ISBN* 083910751X

**Deinstitutionalization and community adjustment of mentally**   **4.6613**
**retarded people / edited by Robert H. Bruininks ... [et al.].**
Washington, D.C. (5101 Wisconsin Ave., N.W., Washington 20016): American Association on Mental Deficiency, c1981. xvi, 412 p.: ill.; 24 cm. (Monograph of the American Association on Mental Deficiency; no. 4) 1. Mental retardation facilities — United States — Addresses, essays, lectures. I. Bruininks, Robert H.
HV3006.A4 D473    362.3/85 19    *LC* 80-70191

**Shaping the future: community–based residential services and facilities for mentally retarded people** / edited by Philip Roos, Brian M. McCann, and Max R. Addison; National Association for Retarded Citizens.    **4.6614**
Baltimore: University Park Press, c1980. xi, 169 p.: ill.; 23 cm. 'Based on a national conference held December 4-5, 1978 in Phoenix, Arizona ... planned and sponsored by the National Association for Retarded Citizens (NARC) Research and Demonstration Institute and the NARC's Residential Services and Facilities Committee.' 1. Mentally handicapped — Services for — United States — Congresses. I. Roos, Philip. II. McCann, Brian M. III. Addison, Max. R. IV. National Association for Retarded Citizens. Research and Demonstration Institute. V. National Association for Retarded Citizens. Residential Services and Facilities Committee.
HV3006.A4 S63    362.3    *LC* 79-23618    0839115563

## HV3176–3198 Special Ethnic Groups

**Devore, Wynetta.**    **4.6615**
Ethnic–sensitive social work practice / Wynetta Devore, Elfriede G. Schlesinger. — St. Louis: C. V. Mosby Co., 1981. xi, 285 p.: ill.; 23 cm. 1. Social work with minorities I. Schlesinger, Elfriede G. joint author. II. T.
HV3176.D46    361.3 19    *LC* 80-27538    *ISBN* 0801612683

**Jenkins, Shirley.**    **4.6616**
The ethnic dilemma in social services / Shirley Jenkins. — New York: Free Press; London: Collier Macmillan Publishers, c1981. xii, 237 p.; 25 cm. Includes index. 1. Social work with minorities — United States. 2. Ethnic attitudes — United States — Case studies. I. T.
HV3176.J45    361.3/089 19    *LC* 80-2155    *ISBN* 0029164001

**Black heritage in social welfare, 1860–1930** / compiled and edited by Edyth L. Ross.    **4.6617**
Metuchen, N.J.: Scarecrow Press, 1978. xviii, 488 p. Includes index. 1. Afro-Americans — Social work with — History — Addresses, essays, lectures. 2. Afro-Americans — Charities — History — Addresses, essays, lectures. 3. Social service — United States — History — Addresses, essays, lectures. I. Ross, Edyth L., 1916-
HV3181.B55    HV3181 B55.    362.8/4    *LC* 78-8403    *ISBN* 0810811456

**Solomon, Barbara Bryant, 1934-.**    **4.6618**
Black empowerment: social work in oppressed communities / Barbara Bryant Solomon. New York: Columbia University Press, 1976. viii, 438 p.; 24 cm. 1. Afro-Americans — Social work with I. T.
HV3181.S64    362.8/4    *LC* 76-26972    *ISBN* 0231040865

## HV4023–5630 Urban Poor. Homeless

**Auletta, Ken.**    **4.6619**
The underclass / Ken Auletta. — 1st ed. — New York: Random House, c1982. xviii, 348 p.; 25 cm. Includes index. 1. Socially handicapped — United States. 2. Poor — United States. I. T.
HV4045.A9 1982    362.8 19    *LC* 81-48274    *ISBN* 0394523431

**Mohl, Raymond A.**    • **4.6620**
Poverty in New York, 1783–1825 / [by] Raymond A. Mohl. — New York: Oxford University Press, 1971. xv, 318 p.: maps; 22 cm. (The Urban life in America series) 1. Poor — New York (N.Y.) — History. 2. Social service — New York (N.Y.) — History. I. T.
HV4046.N6 M65    362.5/097471    *LC* 72-140913    *ISBN* 0195013670

**Riis, Jacob A. (Jacob August), 1849-1914.**    • **4.6621**
How the other half lives; studies among the tenements of New York. Edited by Sam Bass Warner, Jr. Cambridge, Belknap Press of Harvard University Press, 1970. xix, 246 p. illus., plans. 24 cm. (John Harvard library) Reprint of the 1890 ed. 1. Tenement-houses — New York (N.Y.) 2. Poor — New York (N.Y.) I. T. II. Series.
HV4046.N6 R55 1970    301.44/1    *LC* 70-120321    *ISBN* 0674410068

**Lawless, Paul.**    **4.6622**
Urban deprivation and government initiative / Paul Lawless. — London; Boston: Faber, 1979. 251 p.; 22 cm. Includes index. 1. Poor — Great Britain. 2. Community development, Urban — Great Britain. 3. Great Britain — Social policy. I. T.
HV4085.A5 L38    362.5/0941    *LC* 79-670243    *ISBN* 0571113370

**Himmelfarb, Gertrude.**    **4.6623**
The idea of poverty: England in the early Industrial Age / Gertrude Himmelfarb. — 1st ed. — New York: Knopf, 1984. x, 596 p., [16] p. of plates: ill.; 25 cm. 1. Poor — England — History — 19th century. 2. Poor — England

— History — 18th century. 3. Great Britain — Economic conditions — 1760-1860 I. T.
HV4086.A3 H55 1984    362.5/0942 19    *LC* 83-47964    *ISBN* 0394530624

**Booth, Charles, 1840-1916.**    • **4.6624**
[Life and labour of the people in London. Selections] Charles Booth's London: a portrait of the poor at the turn of the century, drawn from his Life and labour of the people in London / selected and edited by Albert Fried and Richard M. Elman. — New York: Pantheon Books [1967, c1968] xxxix, 342 p.: map (on lining papers); 25 cm. 1. Labor and laboring classes — England — London. 2. Poor — England — London. 3. London (England) — Social conditions. I. Elman, Richard M. ed. II. Fried, Albert. ed. III. T. IV. Title: London; a portrait of the poor at the turn of the century.
HV4088.L8 B76 1968    301.44/1    *LC* 67-19173

**Mayhew, Henry, 1812-1887.**    • **4.6625**
London labour and the London poor. With a new introd. by John D. Rosenberg. New York, Dover Publications [1968] 4 v. illus., facsims., maps, ports. 26 cm. 'An unabridged republication of the work as published ... in 1861-1862, to which has been added a new introduction.' 1. Poor — England — London. 2. Labor and laboring classes — England — London. 3. Crime and criminals — England — London. 4. Charities — England — London — Societies, etc. 5. Prostitution — England — London. 6. London (England) — Social conditions. I. T.
HV4088.L8 M52 1968    301.45/23/09421    *LC* 68-19549

**Hufton, Olwen H.**    **4.6626**
The poor of eighteenth–century France 1750–1789 / Olwen H. Hufton. — Oxford [Eng.]: Clarendon Press, 1974. x, 414 p., [4] leaves of plates: ill.; 22 cm. Includes index. 1. Poor — France — History. 2. France — Social conditions I. T.
HV4094.H84    362.5/0944    *LC* 75-308049    *ISBN* 0198225199

**Addams, Jane.**    • **4.6627**
Twenty years at Hull–house / with autobiographical notes, by Jane Addams; with illus. by Norah Hamilton. — New York: Macmillan, 1911. 462 p.: ill. "More than a third of the material in the book has appeared in the American magazine, one chapter of it in McClure's magazine." 1. Hull House (Chicago, Ill.) 2. Chicago — Social conditions. I. T.
HV4196.C4 H7 1938    *LC* 13-7309

**Harper, Douglas A.**    **4.6628**
Good company / Douglas A. Harper. — Chicago: University of Chicago Press, c1982. ix, 172 p., [52] p. of plates: ill., ports.; 25 cm. 1. Tramps — United States. I. T.
HV4505.H37 1982    305.5/6 19    *LC* 81-11367    *ISBN* 0226316866

**Hombs, Mary Ellen.**    **4.6629**
Homelessness in America: a forced march to nowhere / by Mary Ellen Hombs and Mitch Snyder; with a foreword by Daniel Berrigan. — Washington, D.C. (1345 Euclid St., N.W., Washington 20009): Community for Creative Non-violence, c1982. xviii, 146 p.: ill.; 28 cm. 1. Homelessness — United States. 2. United States — Social policy I. Snyder, Mitch. II. Community for Creative Non-violence (Washington, D.C.) III. T.
HV4505.H65 1982    362.5/0973 19    *LC* 83-163724

## HV4701–4759 Protection of Animals

**Regan, Tom.**    **4.6630**
The case for animal rights / Tom Regan. — Berkeley: University of California Press, c1983. xv, 425 p.; 24 cm. 1. Animals, Treatment of — Philosophy. I. T.
HV4708.R43 1983    179/.3 19    *LC* 83-1087    *ISBN* 0520049047

**Regan, Tom.**    **4.6631**
All that dwell therein: animal rights and environmental ethics / Tom Regan. — Berkeley: University of California Press, c1982. x, 249 p.; 23 cm. 'Papers and lectures written and delivered over the past six years or so on the general topic of human obligations to nonhumans'–Pref. Includes index. 1. Animals, Treatment of — Addresses, essays, lectures. 2. Animals, Treatment of — Law and legislation — Addresses, essays, lectures. I. T.
HV4711.R36 1982    179/.3 19    *LC* 81-16469    *ISBN* 0520045718

# HV5001–5720 Alcoholism

**Cohen, Sidney, 1910-.**　　　　　　　　　　　　　**4.6632**
The alcoholism problems: selected issues / Sidney Cohen. — New York: Haworth Press, c1983. ix, 193 p.; 24 cm. 1. Alcoholism — Addresses, essays, lectures. I. T.
HV5035.C63 1983　　　616.86/1 19　　　*LC* 83-179　　　*ISBN* 0866562095

**Royce, James E.**　　　　　　　　　　　　　　　**4.6633**
Alcohol problems and alcoholism: a comprehensive survey / James E. Royce. — New York: Free Press, c1981. xiii, 383 p.; 25 cm. Includes index. 1. Alcoholism I. T.
HV5035.R9　　　362.2/92 19　　　*LC* 81-67421　　　*ISBN* 0029275407

**Prevention of alcohol abuse / edited by Peter M. Miller and**　　**4.6634**
**Ted D. Nirenberg.**
New York: Plenum Press, c1984. xvi, 520 p.; 24 cm. 1. Alcoholism — Prevention — Addresses, essays, lectures. I. Miller, Peter M. (Peter Michael), 1942- II. Nirenberg, Ted D., 1952-
HV5047.P73 1984　　　362.2/927 19　　　*LC* 83-19203　　　*ISBN* 0306413280

**Drinking and crime: perspectives on the relationships between**　　**4.6635**
**alcohol consumption and criminal behavior / edited by James J.**
**Collins, Jr.; foreword by Marvin E. Wolfgang.**
New York: Guilford Press, c1981. xix, 356 p.; 24 cm. — (The Guilford alcohol studies series) Includes indexes. 1. Alcoholism and crime — Addresses, essays, lectures. I. Collins, James J., 1936-
HV5053.D74　　　364.2/4 19　　　*LC* 80-28046　　　*ISBN* 0898621631

**Alcohol and the family / edited by Jim Orford and Judith**　　**4.6636**
**Harwin.**
New York: St. Martin's Press, 1982. 295 p.; 23 cm. Includes indexes. 1. Alcoholics — Family relationships — Addresses, essays, lectures. I. Orford, Jim. II. Harwin, Judith.
HV5132.A43 1982　　　362.8/2 19　　　*LC* 82-50090　　　*ISBN* 0312017065

**Deutsch, Charles, 1947-.**　　　　　　　　　　**4.6637**
Broken bottles, broken dreams: understanding and helping the children of alcoholics / Charles Deutsch. — New York: Teachers College, Columbia University, c1982. xiv, 213 p.; 24 cm. Includes index. 1. Children of alcoholics I. T.
HV5132.D43　　　362.8/28 19　　　*LC* 81-5729　　　*ISBN* 0807726648

**Seixas, Judith S.**　　　　　　　　　　　　　　**4.6638**
Children of alcoholism: a survivor's manual / by Judith S. Seixas and Geraldine Youcha. — 1st ed. — New York: Crown Publishers, c1985. xiv, 208 p.; 23 cm. Includes index. 1. Children of alcoholics — United States — Case studies. 2. Alcoholics — United States — Family relationships — Case studies. I. Youcha, Geraldine. II. T.
HV5132.S44 1985　　　362.2/92 19　　　*LC* 84-17450　　　*ISBN* 0517555999

**Youth, Alcohol, and Social Policy Conference (1978: Arlington,**　　**4.6639**
**Va.)**
Youth, alcohol, and social policy / edited by Howard T. Blane and Morris E. Chafetz. — New York: Plenum Press, c1979. xxvi, 424 p.: ill.; 24 cm. Papers presented at the conference organized by the Health Education Foundation and held Oct. 18-20, 1978 in Arlington, Va. 1. Youth — United States — Alcohol use — Congresses. 2. Alcoholism — United States — Prevention — Congresses. 3. Liquor problem — United States — Congresses. I. Blane, Howard T., 1926- II. Chafetz, Morris E. III. Health Education Foundation (Washington, D.C.) IV. T.
HV5135.Y68 1978　　　362.2/92/0973 19　　　*LC* 79-9094　　　*ISBN* 030640253X

**Sandmaier, Marian.**　　　　　　　　　　　　**4.6640**
The invisible alcoholics: women and alcohol abuse in America / Marian Sandmaier. — New York: McGraw-Hill, c1980. xviii, 298 p.; 24 cm. Includes index. 1. Women — United States — Alcohol use. I. T.
HV5137.S25　　　362.2/92　　　*LC* 79-17819　　　*ISBN* 0070546606

**Duis, Perry, 1943-.**　　　　　　　　　　　　**4.6641**
The saloon: public drinking in Chicago and Boston, 1880–1920 / Perry R. Duis. — Urbana: University of Illinois Press, c1983. 380 p., [24] p. of plates: ill.; 24 cm. 1. Hotels, taverns, etc — Social aspects — Illinois — Chicago — Case studies. 2. Hotels, taverns, etc — Social aspects — Massachusetts — Boston — Case studies. 3. Prohibition — Social aspects — United States — History. 4. United States — Social conditions — 1865-1918 I. T.
HV5201.S6 D84 1983　　　647/.9573 19　　　*LC* 83-6971　　　*ISBN* 0252010108

**Bordin, Ruth Birgitta Anderson, 1917-.**　　　　**4.6642**
Woman and temperance: the quest for power and liberty, 1873–1900 / Ruth Bordin. — Philadelphia: Temple University Press, 1981. xviii, 221 p.: ill.; 24 cm. — (American civilization.) 1. Woman's Christian Temperance Union — History. 2. Temperance — History. 3. Women in public life — United States — History. I. T. II. Series.
HV5229.B67　　　363.4/1/0973 19　　　*LC* 80-21140　　　*ISBN* 087722157X

**Alcoholics Anonymous comes of age, by a co–founder [Bill W.**　　● **4.6643**
**1st ed.].** — New York: Harper, [1957] 335 p.: illus.; 22 cm. 1. Alcoholics Anonymous. I. A co-founder. II. W., Bill.
HV5278.A78 A4　　　178.6 616.86*　　　*LC* 57-10949

**Heather, Nick.**　　　　　　　　　　　　　　**4.6644**
Controlled drinking / Nick Heather and Ian Robertson. — London; New York: Methuen, 1981. x, 294 p.; 24 cm. Includes indexes. 1. Alcoholism — Treatment I. Robertson, Ian, 1951- II. T.
HV5278.H4 1981　　　616.86/106 19　　　*LC* 82-106111　　　*ISBN* 0416719708

**Kurtz, Ernest.**　　　　　　　　　　　　　　**4.6645**
Not–God: a history of Alcoholics Anonymous / Ernest Kurtz. — Center City, Minn.: Hazelden Educational Services, c1979. xiii, 363 p.; 22 cm. Includes indexes. 1. Alcoholics Anonymous — History. I. T.
HV5278.K85　　　362.2/9286　　　*LC* 79-88264　　　*ISBN* 0894860658

**Kerr, K. Austin (Kathel Austin)**　　　　　　　**4.6646**
Organized for prohibition: a new history of the Anti–saloon League / K. Austin Kerr. — New Haven: Yale University Press, c1985. xvii, 293 p., [8] p. of plates: ill.; 24 cm. 1. Anti-saloon League of America — History. 2. Prohibition — United States — History. I. T.
HV5287.A64 K47 1985　　　363.4/1/06073 19　　　*LC* 85-3131　　　*ISBN* 0300032935

**Alcohol and alcohol problems: new thinking and new directions**　　**4.6647**
**/ edited by William J. Filstead, Jean J. Rossi, Mark Keller.**
Cambridge, Mass.: Ballinger Pub. Co., c1976. viii, 304 p.; 24 cm. Outgrowth of a symposium held at the Alcoholism Rehabilitation Center of the Lutheran General Hospital, Park Ridge, Ill., in the spring of 1973. 1. Alcoholism — Congresses. 2. Alcoholism — Treatment — Congresses. 3. Alcoholism — Prevention — Congresses. I. Filstead, William J. II. Rossi, Jean J. III. Keller, Mark, 1907-
HV5288.A38　　　362.2/92　　　*LC* 76-7401　　　*ISBN* 0884101150

**Rorabaugh, W. J.**　　　　　　　　　　　　　**4.6648**
The alcoholic republic, an American tradition / W. J. Rorabaugh. — New York: Oxford University Press, 1979. xvi, 302 p.: ill.; 22 cm. Includes index. 1. Alcoholism — United States — History. 2. United States — Social conditions — To 1865 I. T.
HV5291.R67　　　362.2/92　　　*LC* 79-650　　　*ISBN* 0195025849

**Alcohol, reform, and society: the liquor issue in social context /**　　**4.6649**
**edited by Jack S. Blocker, Jr.**
Westport, Conn.: Greenwood Press, 1979. x, 289 p.: ill.; 22 cm. — (Contributions in American history; no. 83 0084-9219) Includes index. 1. Temperance societies — United States — History — Addresses, essays, lectures. 2. Prohibition — United States — Addresses, essays, lectures. 3. Liquor problem — United States — History — Addresses, essays, lectures. I. Blocker, Jack S.
HV5292.A384　　　322.4/4/0973　　　*LC* 78-73800　　　*ISBN* 0313208891

**Drinking: alcohol in American society, issues and current**　　**4.6650**
**research / editors, John A. Ewing, Beatrice A. Rouse.**
Chicago: Nelson-Hall, c1978. xi, 443 p.; 23 cm. 1. Liquor problem — United States — Addresses, essays, lectures. 2. Alcoholism and employment — Addresses, essays, lectures. I. Ewing, John A. II. Rouse, Beatrice A.
HV5292.D75　　　362.2/92/0973　　　*LC* 76-47522　　　*ISBN* 0882291297

**Gusfield, Joseph R., 1923-.**　　　　　　　　　**4.6651**
Symbolic crusade: status politics and the American temperance movement / Joseph R. Gusfield. — 2nd ed. — Urbana: University of Illinois Press, c1986. viii, 226 p.; 21 cm. 1. Temperance 2. Prohibition — United States — History. I. T.
HV5292.G8 1986　　　363.4/1/0973 19　　　*LC* 85-28858　　　*ISBN* 0252013212

**Lender, Mark E., 1947-.**　　　　　　　　　　**4.6652**
Drinking in America: a history / by Mark Edward Lender, James Kirby Martin. — New York: Free Press; London: Macmillan, c1982. xv, 222 p.: ill.; 25 cm. Includes index. 1. Alcoholism — United States — History. I. Martin, James Kirby, 1943- II. T.
HV5292.L4 1982　　　394.1/3/0973 19　　　*LC* 82-70076　　　*ISBN* 0029185300

**Mendelson, Jack H. (Jack Harold), 1929-.** 4.6653
Alcohol, use and abuse in America / Jack H. Mendelson, Nancy K. Mello. —
1st ed. — Boston: Little, Brown, c1985. xii, 395 p.: ill.; 24 cm. Includes index.
1. Alcoholism — United States — History. 2. Alcohol — Physiological effect
I. Mello, Nancy K. II. T.
HV5292.M4 1985    362.2/92/0973 19    *LC* 85-6959    *ISBN*
0316566632

# HV5800–5840 Drug Abuse

**Gerstel, David U., 1945-.** 4.6654
Paradise, Incorporated—Synanon: a personal account / by David U. Gerstel.
— Novato, CA: Presidio Press, c1982. x, 288 p.; 22 cm. 1. Synanon
(Foundation) — History. I. T.
HV5800.S93 G47 1982    362.2/93/06079493 19    *LC* 82-312    *ISBN*
0891411127

**Blum, Richard H.** 4.6655
Drug dealers—taking action / [by] Richard H. Blum and associates. — [1st ed.]
San Francisco: Jossey-Bass, 1973. xxii, 312 p.: ill.; 24 cm. (The Jossey-Bass
behavioral science series) 1. Narcotics dealers — Addresses, essays, lectures.
2. Narcotics, Control of — Addresses, essays, lectures. 3. Narcotic laws —
Addresses, essays, lectures. 4. Drug abuse — Treatment — Addresses, essays,
lectures. I. T.
HV5801.B569    362.2/93    *LC* 76-187065    *ISBN* 0875891667

**Blum, Richard H.** • 4.6656
Society and drugs; social and cultural observations, [by] Richard H. Blum &
associates. — [1st ed.]. — San Francisco: Jossey-Bass, 1969. xvi, 400 p.; 24 cm.
— (His Drugs, 1) (The Jossey-Bass behavioral science series.) 'A publication of
the Institute for the Study of Human Problems, Stanford University.' 1. Drug
abuse — Social aspects I. Stanford University. Institute for the Study of
Human Problems. II. T.
HV5801.B57    301.47/686/3    *LC* 73-75936    *ISBN* 0875890334

**Laurie, Peter.** • 4.6657
Drugs: medical, psychological and social facts. — 2nd ed. — Harmondsworth:
Penguin, 1971. 191 p.: 1 illus., facsim.; 18 cm. — (Pelican books) 1. Narcotic
habit 2. Narcotics I. T.
HV5801.L35 1971    362.2/93    *LC* 72-188035    *ISBN* 0140211047

**Abel, Ernest L., 1943-.** 4.6658
A dictionary of drug abuse terms and terminology / Ernest L. Abel. —
Westport, Conn.: Greenwood Press, 1984. xi, 187 p.; 25 cm. 1. Drug abuse —
Dictionaries. I. T.
HV5804.A23 1984    362.2/93/0321 19    *LC* 83-22867    *ISBN*
0313240957

**O'Brien, Robert, 1932-.** 4.6659
The encyclopedia of drug abuse / Robert O'Brien and Sidney Cohen. — New
York: Facts on File, c1984. xxvii, 454 p.; 26 cm. Includes index. 1. Drug abuse
— Dictionaries. 2. Drugs — Dictionaries. I. Cohen, Sidney, 1910- II. T.
III. Title: Drug abuse.
HV5804.O24 1984    362.2/9 19    *LC* 82-5034    *ISBN* 0871966905

**Grinspoon, Lester, 1928-.** 4.6660
Cocaine: a drug and its social evolution / Lester Grinspoon & James B. Bakalar.
— New York: Basic Books, c1976. x, 308 p.; 24 cm. Includes index. 1. Cocaine
— History. 2. Cocaine habit — United States. I. Bakalar, James B., 1943- joint
author. II. T.
HV5810.G73    362.2/93    *LC* 76-7675    *ISBN* 0465011896

**Courtwright, David T., 1952-.** 4.6661
Dark paradise: opiate addiction in America before 1940 / David T.
Courtwright. — Cambridge, Mass.: Harvard University Press, 1982. 270 p.; 24
cm. Includes index. 1. Opium habit — History. 2. Opium — Therapeutic use
— History. 3. Morphine habit 4. Heroin habit 5. Narcotic addicts — History.
6. Opium trade — Law and legislation — United States — History. I. T.
HV5816.C648    362.2/93/0973 19    *LC* 81-6958    *ISBN* 0674192613

**Furst, Peter T.** 4.6662
Hallucinogens and culture / Peter T. Furst. — San Francisco: Chandler &
Sharp, c1976. xii, 194 p.: ill.; 23 in. (Chandler & Sharp series in cross-cultural
themes) Includes index. 1. Hallucinogenic drugs 2. Hallucinogenic drugs and
religious experience I. T.
HV5822.H25 F87    301.2/2    *LC* 75-25442    *ISBN* 0883165171

**Kaplan, John.** 4.6663
The hardest drug: heroin and public policy / John Kaplan. — Chicago:
University of Chicago Press, c1983. x, 247 p.; 24 cm. — (Studies in crime and

justice.) 1. Heroin 2. Narcotics, Control of — Government policy — United
States. I. T. II. Series.
HV5822.H4 K36 1983    362.2/93 19    *LC* 82-17514    *ISBN*
0226424278

**Life with heroin: voices from the inner city / edited by Bill** 4.6664
**Hanson ... [et al.].**
Lexington, Mass.: Lexington Books, c1985. vi, 210 p.; 24 cm. 1. Heroin habit
— United States — Addresses, essays, lectures. 2. Afro-Americans — Drug
use — Addresses, essays, lectures. 3. Narcotic addicts — United States —
Addresses, essays, lectures. I. Hanson, Bill.
HV5822.H4 L53 1985    306/.1 19    *LC* 84-40722    *ISBN*
0669099333

**Himmelstein, Jerome L.** 4.6665
The strange career of marihuana: politics and ideology of drug control in
America / Jerome L. Himmelstein. — Westport, Conn.: Greenwood Press,
1983. xii, 179 p.; 22 cm. — (Contributions in political science. 0147-1066; no.
94) Includes index. 1. Marihuana 2. Narcotics, Control of — United States —
History. 3. Marihuana — Law and legislation — United States. I. T.
II. Series.
HV5822.M3 H55 1983    363.4/5 19    *LC* 82-12181    *ISBN*
0313235171

**Hochman, Joel Simon.** 4.6666
Marijuana and social evolution. — Englewood Cliffs, N.J.: Prentice-Hall,
[1972] viii, 184 p.; 22 cm. — (A Spectrum book) 1. Marihuana — Social
aspects. 2. Drug abuse — Social aspects — United States. I. T.
HV5822.M3 H62    362.2/93    *LC* 72-8952    *ISBN* 0135562171

**Youth drug abuse: problems, issues, and treatment / edited by** 4.6667
**George M. Beschner, Alfred S. Friedman.**
Lexington, Mass.: Lexington Books, c1979. xxxi, 681 p.: ill.; 24 cm. 1. Drugs
and youth — United States — Addresses, essays, lectures. 2. Drug abuse —
United States — Addresses, essays, lectures. 3. Drug abuse — United States —
Prevention — Addresses, essays, lectures. I. Beschner, George M.
II. Friedman, Alfred S.
HV5824.Y68 Y68    362.7/8/2930973    *LC* 78-21197    *ISBN*
0669028045

**Becker, Howard Saul, 1928-.** • 4.6668
Outsiders; studies in the sociology of deviance. — London: Free Press of
Glencoe, [c1963] 179 p.; 22 cm. 1. Narcotic addicts — United States.
2. Musicians — United States. I. T.
HV5825.B4    301.246    *LC* 63-8413

**Criminal justice and drugs: the unresolved connection / edited** 4.6669
**by James C. Weissman and Robert L. DuPont.**
Pt. Washington, N.Y.: Kennikat Press, 1982. xii, 204 p. — (Multi-disciplinary
studies in the law.) (National university publications) 1. Drug abuse — United
States — Addresses, essays, lectures. 2. Drug abuse — Treatment — United
States — Addresses, essays, lectures. 3. Drug abuse and crime — United States
— Addresses, essays, lectures. 4. Narcotic addicts — Rehabilitation — United
States — Addresses, essays, lectures. 5. Criminal justice, Administration of —
United States — Addresses, essays, lectures. 6. Drugs — Law and legislation
— United States — Evolution — Addresses, essays, lectures. I. Weissman,
James C., 1947- II. DuPont, Robert L., 1936- III. Series.
HV5825.C74    HV5825 C74.    363.4/5 19    *LC* 81-3701    *ISBN*
0804692912

**Drug Abuse Council (Washington, D.C.)** 4.6670
The facts about 'drug abuse' / The Drug Abuse Council. — New York: Free
Press, c1980. xi, 291 p.: ill.; 24 cm. 1. Drug abuse — United States —
Addresses, essays, lectures. 2. Narcotics, Control of — United States —
Addresses, essays, lectures. I. T.
HV5825.D772 1980    362.2/93/0973    *LC* 79-54668    *ISBN*
0029077206

**Helmer, John.** 4.6671
Drugs and minority oppression / John Helmer. — New York: Seabury Press,
[1975] xi, 192 p.; 24 cm. (A Continuum book) 1. Drug abuse — United States.
2. Minorities — United States 3. United States — Social conditions I. T.
HV5825.H43    362.8/4    *LC* 75-2114    *ISBN* 0816492166

**Lidz, Charles W.** 4.6672
Heroin, deviance, and morality / Charles W. Lidz and Andrew L. Walker, with
the assistance of Leroy C. Gould. — Beverly Hills, Calif.: Sage Publications,
c1980. 269 p.; 23 cm. — (Sage library of social research; v. 112) Includes index.
1. Drug abuse — United States. 2. Deviant behavior 3. United States —
Moral conditions I. Walker, Andrew L. joint author. II. Gould, Leroy C.
III. T.
HV5825.L46    362.2/93/0973 19    *LC* 80-23327    *ISBN* 0803915497

**Rachal, Patricia, 1952-.** 4.6673
Federal narcotics enforcement: reorganization and reform / Patricia Rachal. —
Boston, Mass.: Auburn House Pub. Co., c1982. xiii, 170 p.; 24 cm.

1. Narcotics, Control of — United States — Management. 2. United States — Executive departments — Management I. T.
HV5825.R32 1982    353.0076/5 19    LC 82-1722    ISBN 0865690898

**Street ethnography: selected studies of crime and drug use in natural settings / Robert S. Weppner, editor.**    4.6674
Beverly Hills, Calif.: Sage Publications, c1977. 288 p.; 24 cm. (Sage annual reviews of drug and alcohol abuse. v. 1) 1. Drug abuse and crime — United States — Addresses, essays, lectures. 2. Deviant behavior — Addresses, essays, lectures. I. Weppner, Robert S. II. Series.
HV5825.S77    362.2/93/0973    LC 76-50446    ISBN 0803908083

# HV6001–9920 CRIMINOLOGY

**Encyclopedia of crime and justice / Sanford H. Kadish, editor in chief.**    4.6675
New York: Free Press, c1983. 4 v. (xxxvi, 1790 p.); 29 cm. 1. Crime and criminals — Dictionaries. 2. Criminal justice, Administration of — Dictionaries. I. Kadish, Sanford H. II. Title: Crime and justice.
HV6017.E52 1983    364/.03/21 19    LC 83-7156    ISBN 0029181100

**Gibbons, Don C.**    4.6676
The criminological enterprise: theories and perspectives / Don C. Gibbons. — Englewood Cliffs, N.J.: Prentice-Hall, c1979. xiii, 226 p.; 23 cm. 1. Crime and criminals — United States — History. 2. Crime and criminals — History. I. T.
HV6021.G5    364/.09    LC 78-15736    ISBN 0131936158

**Cortés, Juan B.**    4.6677
Delinquency and crime: a biopsychosocial approach: empirical, theoretical, and practical aspects of criminal behavior / [by] Juan B. Cortés; with Florence M. Gatti. — New York: Seminar Press, 1972. x, 468 p.; 24 cm. 1. Crime and criminals 2. Criminal anthropology 3. Criminal psychology I. Gatti, Florence M. II. T.
HV6025.C65    364.2    LC 76-154390    ISBN 0128169508

**Criminology: a cross–cultural perspective / edited by Dae H. Chang.**    4.6678
Durham: Carolina Academic Press, c1976. 2 v. (xiv, 1039, xiv): ill.; 23 cm. 1. Crime and criminals — Cross-cultural studies I. Chang, Dae H.
HV6025.C74 1976    364    LC 75-5478    ISBN 0890890536

**Mannheim, Hermann, 1889- ed.**    • 4.6679
Pioneers in criminology / Edited and introduced by Hermann Mannheim. — 2d ed., enl. — Montclair, N.J.: Patterson Smith, 1972. xv, 505 p.; 23 cm. — (Patterson Smith reprint series in criminology, law enforcement, and social problems. Publication no. 121) 1. Criminologists I. T.
HV6025.M322 1972    364/.092/2 B    LC 78-108238    ISBN 0875851215

**Michael, Jerome, 1890-1953.**    • 4.6680
[Institute of criminology and of criminal justice] Crime, law, and social science, by Jerome Michael & Mortimer J. Adler. Reprinted with a new introd. by Gilbert Geis. Montclair, N.J., Patterson Smith, 1971 [c1933] xliii, 440 p. illus. 23 cm. (Patterson Smith reprint series in criminology, law enforcement, and social problems. Publication no. 118) First published in 1932 under title: An institute of criminology and of criminal justice. 1. Crime and criminals 2. Criminal justice, Administration of I. Adler, Mortimer Jerome, 1902- joint author. II. T.
HV6025.M5 1971    364/.973    LC 77-108235    ISBN 0875851185

**Radzinowicz, Leon.**    • 4.6681
Ideology and crime / Leon Radzinowicz. — New York: Columbia University Press, 1966. xii, 152 p. — (James S. Carpentier lectures. 1965) 1. Crime and criminals I. T. II. Series.
HV6025.R37 1966    364    LC 66-15724

**Shelley, Louise I.**    4.6682
Crime and modernization: the impact of industrialization and urbanization on crime / Louise I. Shelley. — Carbondale: Southern Illinois University Press, c1981. xxii, 186 p.; 24 cm. (Science and international affairs series.) Includes index. 1. Crime and criminals 2. Crime and criminals — Developing countries. 3. Technology — Social aspects I. T. II. Series.
HV6025.S458    364.2/5 19    LC 80-24044    ISBN 0809309831

**Taylor, Ian R.**    4.6683
The new criminology: for a social theory of deviance, [by] Ian Taylor, Paul Walton [and] Jock Young; [with a foreword by Alvin W. Gouldner]. — London: Routledge and Kegan Paul, 1973. xv, 325 p.; 23 cm. — (International library of sociology) 1. Crime and criminals 2. Deviant behavior I. Walton, Paul. joint author. II. Young, Jock. joint author. III. T.
HV6025.T38    364.2/5    LC 72-95127    ISBN 0710074727

**Sutherland, Edwin Hardin, 1883-1950.**    • 4.6684
The Sutherland papers / edited by Albert Cohen, Alfred Lindesmith [and] Karl Schuessler. — Bloomington: Indiana University Press, 1956. vi, 330 p.: port., diagrs., tables; 23 cm. (Indiana University publications. Social science series, no. 15) 'Selected bibliography of the writings of Edwin Sutherland': p. 327-330. Bibliographical footnotes. 1. Crime and criminals — Addresses, essays, lectures I. Cohen, Albert Kircidel. ed. II. T.
HV6028.S8    364.081    LC 56-63616 rev

**Archer, Dane, 1946-.**    4.6685
Violence and crime in cross–national perspective / Dane Archer and Rosemary Gartner. — New Haven: Yale University Press, c1984. ix, 341 p.: ill.; 24 cm. Includes index. 1. Crime and criminals — History — 20th century — Cross-cultural studies. 2. Violent crimes — History — 20th century — Cross-cultural studies. I. Gartner, Rosemary, 1952- II. T.
HV6030.A73 1984    364/.042 19    LC 83-21700    ISBN 0300031491

**Block, Alan A.**    4.6686
Organizing crime / Alan A. Block, William J. Chambliss. — New York, N.Y.: Elsevier, c1981. 238 p.; 24 cm. 1. Organized crime 2. Crime and criminals 3. Organized crime — United States 4. Crime and criminals — United States I. Chambliss, William J. joint author. II. T.
HV6030.B55    364.1/06 19    LC 80-25099    ISBN 0444990798

# HV6035–6250 Criminal Anthropology. Criminals. Victims

**Vold, George B. (George Bryan), 1896-1967.**    4.6687
Theoretical criminology / by George B. Vold and Thomas J. Bernard. — 3rd ed. — New York: Oxford University Press, 1986. xiv, 374 p.; 24 cm. 1. Criminal anthropology 2. Crime and criminals 3. Deviant behavior 4. Social conflict I. Bernard, Thomas J. II. T.
HV6035.V6 1986    364.2 19    LC 85-11558    ISBN 0195036166

**Lombroso-Ferrero, Gina, 1872-1944.**    • 4.6688
Criminal man: according to the classification of Cesare Lombroso / with an introd. by Cesare Lombroso; reprinted with a new introd. by Leonard D. Savitz. — Montclair, N.J.: Patterson Smith, 1972. xxxvii, 322 p.: ill.; 22 cm. — (Patterson Smith reprint series in criminology, law enforcement, and social problems, publication no. 134) Reprint of the 1911 ed., which was issued as no. 27 of The Science series. 1. Crime and criminals 2. Criminal anthropology I. Lombroso, Cesare, 1835-1909. II. T.
HV6045.L83 1972    364.1    LC 70-129338    ISBN 0875851347

**The Female offender / edited by Laura Crites.**    4.6689
Lexington, Mass.: Lexington Books, c1976. xii, 230 p.; 24 cm. 1. Female offenders — United States — Addresses, essays, lectures. 2. Women prisoners — United States — Addresses, essays, lectures. 3. Criminal justice, Administration of — United States — Addresses, essays, lectures. I. Crites, Laura L.
HV6046.F373    364.3/74/0973    LC 76-2933    ISBN 0669006351

**Jones, Ann, 1937-.**    4.6690
Women who kill / Ann Jones. — 1st ed. — New York: Holt, Rinehart, and Winston, c1980. xviii, 408 p.; 24 cm. 1. Female offenders 2. Murder I. T.
HV6046.J66    364.1/523/088042    LC 80-12329    ISBN 0030407117

**Mann, Coramae Richey, 1931-.**    4.6691
Female crime and delinquency / Coramae Richey Mann. — University, Ala.: University of Alabama Press, c1984. xv, 331 p.: ill.; 25 cm. Includes index. 1. Female offenders 2. Female offenders — United States. 3. Delinquent girls 4. Delinquent girls — United States. 5. Sex discrimination against women — United States. I. T.
HV6046.M36 1984    364.3/74/0973 19    LC 82-16052    ISBN 0817301445

**Pollak, Otto, 1908-.**    • 4.6692
The criminality of women. Philadelphia, University of Pennsylvania Press, 1950. xxi, 180 p. 23 cm. 1. Female offenders I. T.
HV6046.P6    364.373    LC 50-8040

**Smart, Carol.**    4.6693
Women, crime, and criminology: a feminist critique / Carol Smart. London; Boston: Routledge & K. Paul, 1977 [i.e. 1976] xv, 208 p.; 23 cm. Began as the

author's thesis (M.A.). Includes indexes. 1. Female offenders 2. Female offenders — Great Britain. 3. Female offenders — United States. I. T.
HV6046.S62      364.3/74      *LC* 77-350404      *ISBN* 0710084498

**Thomas, William Isaac, 1863-1947.**      • **4.6694**
The unadjusted girl; with cases and standpoint for behavior analysis. Foreword by Mrs. W. F. Dummer. — Montclair, N.J.: Patterson Smith, 1969 [c1923] xvii, 261 p.; 22 cm. — (Patterson Smith reprint series in criminology, law enforcement, and social problems. Publication no. 26) 1. Delinquent girls — Case studies. I. T.
HV6046.T4 1969      364.36/4      *LC* 69-14951      *ISBN* 087585026X

**The Pains of imprisonment** / edited by Robert Johnson, Hans    **4.6695**
Toch; foreword by Christopher S. Dunn.
Beverly Hills: Sage Publications, c1982. 335 p.: ill.; 23 cm. 1. Prison psychology 2. Stress (Psychology) 3. Prisoners — Mental health — United States. 4. Criminal psychology I. Johnson, Robert, 1948- II. Toch, Hans.
HV6089.P34 1982      365/.01/9 19      *LC* 82-16761      *ISBN* 0803919026

**McCord, William Maxwell, 1930-.**      • **4.6696**
Origins of crime: a new evaluation of the Cambridge–Somerville Youth Study / [by] William McCord and Joan McCord, with Irving Kenneth Zola. — Montclair, N.J.: Patterson Smith, 1969 [c1959] xvi, 219 p.; 23 cm. — (Patterson Smith reprint series in criminology, law enforcement, and social problems, no. 49) 1. Cambridge-Somerville Youth Study. 2. Criminal anthropology I. McCord, Joan, joint author. II. Zola, Irving Kenneth, 1935- III. T.
HV6115.M3 1969      364.2      *LC* 69-14939      *ISBN* 0875850499

**Quinney, Richard.**      **4.6697**
Class, state, & crime / Richard Quinney. — 2d ed. — New York: Longman, c1980. x, 213 p.; 21 cm. 1. Crime and criminals — Economic aspects. 2. Capitalism 3. Criminal justice, Administration of I. T.
HV6171.Q54 1980      364      *LC* 79-24840      *ISBN* 0582281563

**Newman, Oscar.**      **4.6698**
Defensible space; crime prevention through urban design. — New York: Macmillan, [1972] xvii, 264 p.: illus.; 24 cm. 1. Crime prevention — New York (City) 2. Crime and criminals — New York (City) 3. Architecture, Domestic — New York (City) I. T.
HV6177.N49      364.4/4      *LC* 73-187075

**David, Pedro R.**      **4.6699**
The world of the burglar: five criminal lives / edited by Pedro R. David. — 1st ed. — Albuquerque: University of New Mexico Press, [1974] xi, 298 p.; 25 cm. 1. Crime and criminals — Interviews. 2. Burglary I. T.
HV6245.D33      364.1/62/0922 B      *LC* 73-82774      *ISBN* 0826303048

**Wideman, John Edgar.**      **4.6700**
Brothers and keepers / John Edgar Wideman. — 1st ed. — New York: Holt, Rinehart and Winston, c1984. 243 p.; 22 cm. 1. Wideman, Robert Douglas, 1950- 2. Wideman, John Edgar. 3. Afro-American criminals — Biography. 4. Brothers — United States — Biography. I. T.
HV6245.W733 1984      364.3/092/4 B 19      *LC* 84-6582      *ISBN* 0030617545

**[Conwell, Chic] d. 1933.**      • **4.6701**
The professional thief, by a professional thief; annotated and interpreted by Edwin H. Sutherland. — Chicago, Ill.: The University of Chicago press, [1937] xiii, 256, [1] p.; 20 cm. — (The University of Chicago sociological series) 'The professional thief ... was known as Chic Conwell.'—Introd., signed: Edwin H. Sutherland. 1. Thieves — United States. 2. Crime and criminals — United States I. Sutherland, Edwin Hardin, 1883-1950. II. T.
HV6248.C66 A3      364      *LC* 37-36112

**King, Harry.**      **4.6702**
Box man; a professional thief's journey, by Harry King. As told to and edited by Bill Chambliss. With commentary by Bill Chambliss. — New York: Harper & Row, [1972] xi, 179 p.; 21 cm. — (Harper torchbooks, TB 1667) 1. King, Harry. I. Chambliss, William J. II. T.
HV6248.K52 A3      364.1/62/0924 B      *LC* 72-76245      *ISBN* 0061316679

**I, Pierre Rivière, having slaughtered my mother, my sister, and**    **4.6703**
**my brother ...: a case of parricide in the 19th century** / edited
**by Michel Foucault; translated by Frank Jellinek.**
1st American ed. — New York: Pantheon Books, [1975] 288 p. Translation of Moi, Pierre Rivière, ayant égorgé ma mère, ma soeur et mon frère ... un cas de parricide au XIXe siècle. 'This work is the outcome of a joint research project by a team engaged in a seminar at the Collège de France. The authors are Blandine Barret-Kriegal ... [et al.]' 1. Rivière, Pierre, 1815-1840. 2. Parricide — France — Case studies. 3. Medical jurisprudence — France — Case studies. I. Foucault, Michel. ed. II. Barret-Kriegel, Blandine.
HV6248.R57 M6413 1975      364.1/523      *LC* 74-26205      *ISBN* 0394493109

**Sacco, Nicola, 1891-1927.**      • **4.6704**
The letters of Sacco and Vanzetti. Edited by Marion Denman Frankfurter and Gardner Jackson. New York, Octagon Books, 1971 [c1928] xi, 414 p. facsims., ports. 21 cm. 1. Sacco-Vanzetti case I. Vanzetti, Bartolomeo, 1888-1927. II. T.
HV6248.S3 A4 1971      364.15/23/0922 B      *LC* 76-159224      *ISBN* 0374970033

**Klockars, Carl B.**      **4.6705**
The professional fence [by] Carl B. Klockars. — New York: Free Press, [1974] xii, 242 p.; 22 cm. Originally presented as the author's thesis, University of Pennsylvania. 1. Swaggi, Vincent Norfior, 1914- 2. Receiving stolen goods — United States. 3. Crime and criminals — United States — Biography. I. T.
HV6248.S75 K56 1974      364.1/62 B      *LC* 74-483      *ISBN* 0029175607

**Elias, Robert, 1950-.**      **4.6706**
Victims of the system: crime victims and compensation in American politics and criminal justice / Robert Elias. — New Brunswick, N.J.: Transaction Books, c1983. xix, 340 p.: ill.; 24 cm. 1. Victims of crimes — United States. 2. Reparation — United States. 3. Criminal justice, Administration of — United States I. T.
HV6250.3.U5 E45 1983      362.8/8 19      *LC* 83-383      *ISBN* 087855470X

**Hindelang, Michael J.**      **4.6707**
Victims of personal crime: an empirical foundation for a theory of personal victimization / Michael J. Hindelang, Michael R. Gottfredson, James Garofalo. — Cambridge, Mass.: Ballinger Pub. Co., c1978. xxiv, 324 p.: ill.; 24 cm. Includes indexes. 1. Victims of crimes — United States. 2. Victims of crimes surveys — United States. I. Gottfredson, Michael R. joint author. II. Garofalo, James. joint author. III. T.
HV6250.3.U5 H57      364      *LC* 77-15981      *ISBN* 0884107930

**Schechter, Susan.**      **4.6708**
Women and male violence: the visions and struggles of the battered women's movement / Susan Schechter. — Boston: South End Press, c1982. ii, 367 p.: ill.; 22 cm. Includes index. 1. Abused women — United States. 2. Abused wives — United States. 3. Abused wives — Services for — United States. 4. Wife abuse — United States — Prevention. 5. Feminism — United States. I. T.
HV6250.4.W65 S33 1982      *LC* 82-61150      *ISBN* 0896081591

**Stanko, Elizabeth Anne, 1950-.**      **4.6709**
Intimate intrusions: women's experience of male violence / Elizabeth A. Stanko. — London; Boston: Routledge & Kegan Paul, 1985. xi, 211 p.: ill.; 22 cm. Includes index. 1. Women — Crimes against 2. Victims of crimes — Great Britain. 3. Victims of crimes — United States. 4. Violent crimes — Great Britain. 5. Violent crimes — United States. 6. Sex discrimination in criminal justice administration — Great Britain. 7. Sex discrimination in criminal justice administration — United States. I. T.
HV6250.4.W65 S73 1985      362.8/8 19      *LC* 84-9765      *ISBN* 0710200692

**Wilson, Carolyn F.**      **4.6710**
Violence against women: an annotated bibliography / Carolyn F. Wilson. — Boston, Mass.: G.K. Hall, c1981. xiii, 111 p.; 25 cm. — (Reference publication in women's studies.) Includes indexes. 1. Women — United States — Crimes against — Abstracts. 2. Violence (Law) — United States — Abstracts. 3. Rape — United States — Abstracts. 4. Wife abuse — United States — Abstracts. 5. Incest — United States — Abstracts. 6. Pornography — United States — Abstracts. I. T. II. Series.
HV6250.4.W65 W54      016.3628/3 19      *LC* 81-6232      *ISBN* 0816184976

# HV6251–7220 Crimes and Offenses

**Gurr, Ted Robert, 1936-.**      **4.6711**
Rogues, rebels, and reformers: a political history of urban crime and conflict / Ted Robert Gurr, in collaboration with Peter N. Grabosky ... [et al.]. Beverly Hills, Calif.: Sage Publications, c1976. xii, 192 p.: ill.; 24 cm. 1. Crime and criminals — Case studies. 2. Offenses against public safety — Case studies. 3. Criminal justice, Administration of — Case studies. 4. Crime prevention — Case studies. I. T.
HV6251.G87      364/.9173/2      *LC* 76-17370      *ISBN* 0803906811

# HV6254–6492 Offenses Against Public Order

**Kupperman, Robert H., 1935-.** 4.6712
Terrorism: threat, reality, response / Robert H. Kupperman, Darrell M. Trent; foreword by Walter Laqueur. — Stanford, Calif.: Hoover Institution Press, Stanford University, c1979. xxiii, 450 p.: ill.; 24 cm. (Hoover Institution publication; 204) Includes index. 1. Terrorism — Addresses, essays, lectures. I. Trent, Darrell Melvin, 1938- joint author. II. T.
HV6431.K87    364.1/31    *LC* 78-70394    *ISBN* 081797041X

**Laqueur, Walter, 1921-.** 4.6713
Terrorism / Walter Laqueur. — 1st ed. — Boston: Little, Brown, c1977. 277 p.; 25 cm. Includes index. 1. Terrorism I. T.
HV6431.L36    301.6/33    *LC* 77-4872    *ISBN* 0316514705

**Schmid, Alex Peter.** 4.6714
Political terrorism: a research guide to concepts, theories, data bases, and literature / Alex P. Schmid; with a bibliography by the author and a world directory of 'Terrorist' organizations by A.J. Jongman. — Amsterdam: North-Holland; New Brunswick, U.S.A.: Distributors, Transaction Books, [1984], c1983. xiv, 585 p.; 24 cm. (C.O.M.T.-Publication; no. 12) At head of title: SWIDOC, Royal Netherlands Academy of Arts and Sciences, Social Science Information- and Documentation Centre. Centre for the Study of Social Conflicts (C.O.M.T.), State University of Leiden. Includes index. 1. Terrorism 2. Terrorism — Directories. 3. Terrorism — Bibliography. I. Jongman, A. J. II. Sociaal-Wetenschappelijk Informatie- en Documentatiecentrum (Koninklijke Nederlandse Akademie van Wetenschappen) III. Rijksuniversiteit te Leiden. Centrum voor Onderzoek van Maatschappelijke Tegenstellingen. IV. T.
HV6431.S35x 1984    *LC* 86-672072    *ISBN* 0444856021

**Whyte, William Foote, 1914-.** 4.6715
Street corner society; the social structure of an Italian slum. — Enl. [2d] ed. — [Chicago]: University of Chicago Press, [1955] xxii, 366 p.: diagrs.; 22 cm. 1. Gangs — United States. 2. Italians in the United States. 3. Cities and towns — United States. I. T.
HV6439.U5 W5 1955    323.352 301.45*    *LC* 55-5152

**Thrasher, Frederic M.** • 4.6716
The gang: a study of 1,313 gangs in Chicago / by Frederic M. Thrasher. — 2d rev. ed. Chicago, Ill.: The University of Chicago Press, [c1936] xxi, 605 p.: ill. (incl. facsims.) diagrs.; 20 cm. (The University of Chicago sociological series) 'Chicago's gangland': folded map in envelope laid in. 'Selected bibliography': p. 554-580. 1. Gangs 2. Chicago — Social conditions. I. T. II. Title: Gangs in Chicago.
HV6439.U7C4 1936    136.77    *LC* 36-35233

**Kwitny, Jonathan.** 4.6717
Vicious circles: the Mafia in the marketplace / Jonathan Kwitny. — 1st ed. — New York: Norton, c1979. ix, 422 p.; 24 cm. Includes index. 1. Mafia — United States. 2. Organized crime — United States 3. Crime and criminals — Economic aspects — United States. 4. United States — Commerce I. T.
HV6446.K95 1979    364.1/06/073    *LC* 78-13183    *ISBN* 0393011887

**Reuter, Peter.** 4.6718
Disorganized crime: the economics of the visible hand / Peter Reuter. — Cambridge, Mass.: MIT Press, c1983. xiv, 233 p.; 24 cm. Includes index. 1. Organized crime — United States 2. Mafia — United States. 3. Racketeering — United States. I. T.
HV6446.R48 1983    338.4/73641/06073 19    *LC* 82-22940    *ISBN* 026218107X

**Blok, Anton.** 4.6719
The Mafia of a Sicilian village, 1860–1960: a study of violent peasant entrepreneurs / Anton Blok; with a foreword by Charles Tilly. — New York: Harper & Row; Toronto: Fitzhenry and Whiteside, 1975, c1974. xxxiii, 293 p., [4] leaves of plates: ill.; 21 cm. (State and revolution) (Harper torchbooks) Includes index. 1. Mafia 2. Peasantry — Italy — Sicily — Case studies. 3. Sicily — Rural conditions — Case studies. I. T.
HV6453.I82 S6123 1975    364.1/06    *LC* 73-7450    *ISBN* 0061361305

**Wells-Barnett, Ida B., 1862-1931.** 4.6720
On lynchings: Southern horrors, A red record, Mob rule in New Orleans / [by] Ida B. Wells-Barnett. — New York: Arno Press, 1969. 24, 101, 48 p.: ill., ports.; 23 cm. (American Negro, his history and literature.) With reproductions of the original t.p. of each work published in 1892, 1895, and 1900 respectively. 1. Lynching I. T. II. Series.
HV6457.B37    364.1/34    *LC* 72-75854

**Hall, Jacquelyn Dowd.** 4.6721
Revolt against chivalry: Jessie Daniel Ames and the women's campaign against lynching / Jacquelyn Dowd Hall. — New York: Columbia University Press,

1979. xiv, 373 p.: ill.; 24 cm. Based on the author's thesis, Columbia University. Includes index. 1. Ames, Jessie Daniel, 1883-1972. 2. Lynching 3. Social reformers — Biography. I. T.
HV6457.H34    364.6/6/0924    *LC* 78-11815    *ISBN* 0231040407

**Zangrando, Robert L.** 4.6722
The NAACP crusade against lynching, 1909–1950 / Robert L. Zangrando. — Philadelphia: Temple University Press, c1980. ix, 309 p.; 24 cm. Includes index. 1. National Association for the Advancement of Colored People. 2. Lynching I. T.
HV6457.Z36    364.6/6    *LC* 80-13926    *ISBN* 087722174X

**Grant, Donald Lee, 1919-.** 4.6723
The anti-lynching movement, 1883–1932 / by Donald L. Grant. — San Francisco: R and E Research Associates, 1975. xi, 205 p.; 28 cm. Includes index. 1. Lynching I. T.
HV6459.G7    364.6/6    *LC* 75-18122    *ISBN* 0882473484

**Button, James W., 1942-.** 4.6724
Black violence: political impact of the 1960s riots / James W. Button. — Princeton, N.J.: Princeton University Press, c1978. xii, 248 p.: ill.; 22 cm. Includes index. 1. Riots — United States. 2. Afro-Americans — Social conditions — 1964-1975 3. Economic assistance, Domestic — United States 4. United States — Politics and government — 1963-1969 5. United States — Politics and government — 1969-1974 I. T.
HV6477.B87    301.5/92/0973    *LC* 78-51158    *ISBN* 069107531X

**Feldberg, Michael, 1943-.** 4.6725
The turbulent era: riot & disorder in Jacksonian America / Michael Feldberg. — New York: Oxford University Press, 1980. vi, 136 p.; 22 cm. Includes index. 1. Riots — United States — History — 19th century. 2. Riots — Pennsylvania — Philadelphia. 3. Violence — United States — History — 19th century. 4. Philadelphia (Pa.) — Ethnic relations. I. T.
HV6477.F44    301.6/332/0973    *LC* 79-17705    *ISBN* 0195026772

**Platt, Anthony M. comp.** • 4.6726
The politics of riot commissions, 1917–1970; a collection of official reports and critical essays. Edited and introduced by Anthony Platt. Contributors: Elliott Currie [and others]. — New York: Macmillan, [1971] x, 534 p.; 22 cm. 'From the research program of the Center for the Study of Law and Society, University of California, Berkeley.' 1. Riots — U.S. — History. 2. Governmental investigations — U.S. — History. I. California. University. Center for the Study of Law and Society. II. T.
HV6477.P5    364.14/3    *LC* 79-150069

**Richter, Donald C., 1934-.** 4.6727
Riotous Victorians / by Donald C. Richter. — Athens: Ohio University Press, c1981. xi, 185 p.: ill.; 24 cm. Includes index. 1. Riots — England — History — 19th century. 2. Demonstrations — England — History — 19th century. 3. Great Britain — History — Victoria, 1837-1901 I. T.
HV6485.G72 E57    303.6/2 19    *LC* 80-25055    *ISBN* 0821405713

# HV6493–6631 Crimes Against the Person. Suicide

**Schur, Edwin M.** 4.6728
Crimes without victims; deviant behavior and public policy: abortion, homosexuality, drug addiction [by] Edwin M. Schur. — Englewood Cliffs, N.J.: Prentice-Hall, [1965] ix, 180 p.; 21 cm. — (A Spectrum book, S-111) 1. Crimes without victims — United States. 2. Abortion I. T.
HV6493.S3    364    *LC* 65-12304

**Wolfgang, Marvin E., 1924-.** • 4.6729
Patterns in criminal homicide. — Philadelphia: University of Pennsylvania, [1958] xiv, 413 p.: maps, forms, tables.; 22 cm. An analysis of all criminal homicides listed by police in Philadelphia between Jan. 1, 1948 and Dec. 31, 1952. 1. Homicide — Case studies. 2. Homicide — Philadelphia. I. T.
HV6534.P5 W6    364.38 364.15*    *LC* 56-11803

**Douglas, Jack D.** • 4.6730
The social meanings of suicide, by Jack D. Douglas. Princeton. N.J., Princeton University Press, 1967. xiv, 398 p. 23 cm. 1. Durkheim, Emile, 1858-1917. Le suicide. 2. Suicide — Sociological aspects. I. T.
HV6545.D6    301.1    *LC* 67-14408

**Durkheim, Emile, 1858-1917.** • 4.6731
[Suicide, étude de sociologie. English. 1951] Suicide, a study in sociology / translated by John A. Spaulding and George Simpson; edited, with an introd., by George Simpson. — Glencoe, Ill.: Free Press [1951] 405 p.: maps; 22 cm. 1. Suicide — Sociological aspects. I. T.
HV6545.D812    394.8    *LC* 51-9585

## HV6558–6626 Violence Against Women

**Brownmiller, Susan.** 　　　　　　　　　　**4.6732**
Against our will: men, women, and rape / Susan Brownmiller. — New York:
Simon and Schuster, [1975] 472 p.; 25 cm. 1. Rape I. T.
HV6558.B76　　364.1/53　　*LC* 75-12705　　*ISBN* 0671220624

**Groth, A. Nicholas.** 　　　　　　　　　　**4.6733**
Men who rape: the psychology of the offender / A. Nicholas Groth, with H.
Jean Birnbaum. — New York: Plenum Press, c1979. xviii, 227 p.; 24 cm.
1. Rape 2. Criminal psychology I. Birnbaum, H. Jean. joint author. II. T.
HV6558.G76　　364.1/53　　*LC* 79-18624　　*ISBN* 0306402688

**Katz, Sedelle, 1923-.** 　　　　　　　　　　**4.6734**
Understanding the rape victim: a synthesis of research findings / Sedelle Katz,
Mary Ann Mazur. — New York: Wiley, c1979. xvi, 340 p.; 24 cm. — (Wiley
series on personality processes) 'A Wiley-Interscience publication.' Includes
index. 1. Rape 2. Victims of crimes 3. Sex crimes I. Mazur, Mary Ann, 1946-
joint author. II. T.
HV6558.K37　　362.8/8　　*LC* 78-25704　　*ISBN* 0471035734

**The Rape crisis intervention handbook: a guide for victim care /** 　　**4.6735**
**edited by Sharon L. McCombie.**
New York: Plenum Press, c1980. xv, 235 p.; 24 cm. 1. Rape victims — Services
for — Addresses, essays, lectures. I. McCombie, Sharon L.
HV6558.R35　　362.8/8　　*LC* 80-14191　　*ISBN* 030640401X

**Bart, Pauline.** 　　　　　　　　　　**4.6736**
Stopping rape: successful survival strategies / Pauline B. Bart, Patricia H.
O'Brien. — New York: Pergamon Press, c1985. xii, 201 p.; 24 cm. (Athene
series.) Includes index. 1. Rape — United States. 2. Rape — United States —
Prevention. I. O'Brien, Patricia H. (Patricia Helen), 1949- II. T. III. Series.
HV6561.B367 1985　　362.8/83 19　　*LC* 85-6589　　*ISBN* 0080328148

**Rape and sexual assault: a research handbook / Ann Wolbert** 　　**4.6737**
**Burgess, editor.**
New York: Garland Pub., 1985. xvi, 433 p.; 23 cm. (Garland reference library
of social science; vol. 203) 1. Rape — United States — Prevention —
Addresses, essays, lectures. 2. Rape victims — United States — Addresses,
essays, lectures. 3. Rapists — United States — Addresses, essays, lectures.
4. Violence in mass media — United States — Addresses, essays, lectures.
I. Burgess, Ann Wolbert.
HV6561.R37 1985　　362.8/83/0973 19　　*LC* 83-48217　　*ISBN*
0824090497

**Russell, Diana E. H.** 　　　　　　　　　　**4.6738**
Rape in marriage / Diana E.H. Russell. — New York: Macmillan, c1982. xvi,
412 p.; 24 cm. Includes index. 1. Rape in marriage — United States. I. T.
HV6561.R89 1982　　362.8/3 19　　*LC* 82-7874　　*ISBN* 0026061902

**Schwendinger, Julia R.** 　　　　　　　　　　**4.6739**
Rape and inequality / Julia R. and Herman Schwendinger. — Beverly Hills,
Calif.: SAGE Publications, Inc., c1983. 240 p.; 23 cm. — (Sage library of social
research. v. 148) Includes index. 1. Rape — United States. 2. Sexism — United
States. 3. Violence — United States. 4. Victims of crimes — United States.
5. Rape — United States — Prevention. I. Schwendinger, Herman. II. T.
III. Series.
HV6561.S37 1983　　364.1/532/09 19　　*LC* 82-24092　　*ISBN*
0803919670

**Sussman, Les, 1944-.** 　　　　　　　　　　**4.6740**
The rapist file / Les Sussman and Sally Bordwell; with an introduction by Ellen
Frankfort. — New York: Chelsea House, 1981. 215 p.; 24 cm. 1. Rapists —
United States — Interviews. I. Bordwell, Sally, 1947- II. T.
HV6561.S93　　364.1/532/0973 19　　*LC* 81-10269　　*ISBN* 0877540942

**Williams, Joyce E.** 　　　　　　　　　　**4.6741**
The second assault: rape and public attitudes / Joyce E. Williams & Karen A.
Holmes. — Westport, Conn.: Greenwood Press, 1982. xvi, 232 p.; 24 cm. —
(Contributions in women's studies. 0147-104X; no. 27) Includes index. 1. Rape
— United States. 2. Rape — United States — Public opinion. 3. Rape victims
— United States — Attitudes. 4. Public opinion — United States. I. Holmes,
Karen A. joint author. II. T. III. Series.
HV6561.W54　　364.1/532/0973 19　　*LC* 81-339　　*ISBN* 0313225427

**Russell, Diana E. H.** 　　　　　　　　　　**4.6742**
Sexual exploitation: rape, child sexual abuse, and workplace harassment /
Diana E.H. Russell. — Beverly Hills, Calif.: Sage Publications, c1984. 319 p.;
23 cm. (Sage library of social research. v. 155) Includes indexes. 1. Rape —
California. 2. Child molesting — California. 3. Sexual harassment —
California. I. T. II. Series.
HV6565.C2 R87 1984　　364.1/532/09794 19　　*LC* 84-6950　　*ISBN*
0803923546

**Gilder, George F., 1939-.** 　　　　　　　　　　**4.6743**
Visible man: a true story of post–racist America / by George Gilder. — New
York: Basic Books, c1978. xiii, 249 p.; 22 cm. 1. Rape — New York (State) —
Albany — Case studies. 2. Racism — New York (State) — Albany. I. T.
HV6568.A4 G54　　364.1/53　　*LC* 77-20411　　*ISBN* 0465090419

**McCahill, Thomas W.** 　　　　　　　　　　**4.6744**
The aftermath of rape / Thomas W. McCahill, Linda C. Meyer, Arthur M.
Fischman. — Lexington, Mass.: Lexington Books, 1979. xx, 258 p.; 24 cm.
1. Rape — Pennsylvania — Philadelphia — Case studies. 2. Victims of crimes
— Pennsylvania — Philadelphia — Case studies. 3. Criminal justice,
Administration of — Pennsylvania — Philadelphia — Case studies. I. Meyer,
Linda C. joint author. II. Fischman, Arthur M. joint author. III. T.
HV6568.P5 M23　　364.1/53　　*LC* 79-1952　　*ISBN* 066903018X

**Bowker, Lee H.** 　　　　　　　　　　**4.6745**
Beating wife–beating / Lee H. Bowker. — Lexington, Mass.: Lexington Books,
c1983. xi, 154 p.; 24 cm. 1. Abused wives — Wisconsin — Milwaukee —
Attitudes — Case studies. 2. Wife abuse — Wisconsin — Milwaukee — Case
studies. 3. Family violence — Wisconsin — Milwaukee — Case studies.
4. Abused wives — Services for — Wisconsin — Milwaukee — Case studies.
5. Social work with women — Wisconsin — Milwaukee — Case studies. I. T.
HV6626.B68 1983　　362.8/3 19　　*LC* 82-48603　　*ISBN* 0669063452

**Dobash, R. Emerson.** 　　　　　　　　　　**4.6746**
Violence against wives: a case against the patriarchy / R. Emerson Dobash,
Russell Dobash. — New York: Free Press, c1979. xii, 339 p.; 24 cm. Includes
index. 1. Wife abuse 2. Patriarchy 3. Social history I. Dobash, Russell. joint
author. II. T.
HV6626.D6 1979　　362.8/2　　*LC* 79-7181　　*ISBN* 0029073200

**Giles-Sims, Jean.** 　　　　　　　　　　**4.6747**
Wife battering, a systems theory approach / Jean Giles–Sims; foreword by
Murray A. Straus. — New York: Guilford Press, c1983. xiv, 193 p.; 24 cm. —
(Perspectives on marriage and the family.) Includes index. 1. Wife abuse —
United States. 2. System analysis I. T. II. Series.
HV6626.G54 1983　　362.8/3 19　　*LC* 82-15555　　*ISBN* 0898620759

*HV*
*6626*
*G54*
*1983*

**Walker, Lenore E.** 　　　　　　　　　　**4.6748**
The battered woman syndrome / Lenore E. Walker. — New York: Springer
Pub. Co., c1984. xiv, 256 p.: ill.; 24 cm. — (Springer series, focus on women. v.
6) Includes index. 1. Wife abuse — United States. 2. Abused wives — United
States — Psychology. I. T. II. Series.
HV6626.W345 1984　　362.8/3 19　　*LC* 84-1324　　*ISBN* 0826143202

## HV6635–6773 Crimes Against Property. White Collar Crime

**Geis, Gilbert. comp.** 　　　　　　　　　　**4.6749**
White–collar crime: offenses in business, politics, and the professions / edited,
with introd. and notes by Gilbert Geis and Robert F. Meier. — Rev. ed. — New
York: Free Press, c1977. xii, 356 p.; 24 cm. First ed. published in 1968 under
title: White-collar criminal. Includes index. 1. White collar crimes — United
States — Addresses, essays, lectures. I. Meier, Robert F. (Robert Frank), 1944-
II. T.
HV6635.G35 1977　　364/.1　　*LC* 76-27223　　*ISBN* 0029115906.
*ISBN* 0029116007 pbk

**White–collar and economic crime: multidisciplinary and cross–** 　　**4.6750**
**national perspectives / edited by Peter Wickman, Timothy**
**Dailey.**
Lexington, Mass.: Lexington Books, c1982. xviii, 285 p.; 24 cm. Papers
presented at a symposium held Feb. 7-9, 1980 at the State University of New
York College at Potsdam and sponsored by the Research Committee on
Deviance and Social Control of the International Sociological Association.
1. White collar crimes — United States — Congresses. 2. Corporations —
United States — Corrupt practices — Congresses. I. Wickman, Peter M.
II. Dailey, Timothy. III. International Sociological Association. Research
Committee on Deviance and Social Control.
HV6635.W44　　364.1/68 19　　*LC* 81-47561　　*ISBN* 0669046655

**White–collar crime: theory and research / Gilbert Geis and** 　　**4.6751**
**Ezra Stotland, editors.**
Beverly Hills: Sage Publications, c1980. 320 p.: graphs; 23 cm. — (Sage
criminal justice system annuals. v. 13) 1. White collar crimes — Addresses,
essays, lectures. 2. White collar crimes — United States — Addresses, essays,
lectures. I. Geis, Gilbert. II. Stotland, Ezra, 1924- III. Series.
HV6635.W45　　364.1/68　　*LC* 79-26672　　*ISBN* 0803914040

**Wooden, Wayne S.** 　　　　　　　　　　**4.6752**
Children and arson: America's middle class nightmare / Wayne S. Wooden and
Martha Lou Berkey. — New York: Plenum Press, c1984. ix, 267 p.; 22 cm.
Includes index. 1. Arson — United States — Psychological aspects — Case

studies. 2. Juvenile delinquents — United States — Attitudes — Case studies. 3. Adolescent psychology — United States — Case studies. 4. Criminal psychology — Case studies. I. Berkey, Martha Lou. II. T.
HV6638.5.U6 W66 1984     364.1/64 19     LC 84-11731     ISBN 0306417731

**Cameron, Mary Owen.**                     • **4.6753**
The booster and the snitch: department store shoplifting. London, Free Press of Glencoe [1964] 202 p. maps, diagrs. 1. Shoplifting 2. Department stores I. T.
HV6652 C3     LC 64-16954

**Abadinsky, Howard, 1941-.**                   **4.6754**
The criminal elite: professional and organized crime / Howard Abadinsky. — Westport, Conn.: Greenwood Press, 1983. xv, 190 p.: ill.; 22 cm. — (Contributions in criminology and penology. 0732-4464; no. 1) Includes indexes. 1. Jewel thieves — New York Metropolitan Area. 2. Organized crime — United States 3. Italian American criminals — United States. I. T. II. Series.
HV6661.N7 A49 1983     364.1/62 19     LC 83-1445     ISBN 0313238332

**Hunt, Morton M., 1920-.**                     **4.6755**
The mugging [by] Morton Hunt. — [1st ed.]. — New York: Atheneum, 1972. xiii, 488 p.; 25 cm. 1. Robbery — Bronx (Borough) — Case studies. 2. Mugging — New York (State) — Bronx (Borough) — Case studies. 3. Criminal justice, Administration of — Bronx (Borough) — Case studies. I. T.
HV6661.N72 H8 1964     364.1/55     LC 75-184726

**Cressey, Donald Ray, 1919-.**                 • **4.6756**
Other people's money; a study in the social psychology of embezzlement [by] Donald R. Cressey. — Belmont, Calif.: Wadsworth Pub. Co., [1971, c1953] 191 p.; 22 cm. — (The Wadsworth series in analytical ethnography) 1. Embezzlement I. T.
HV6675.C72 1971     364.16/2     LC 78-174667     ISBN 0534001424

**McClintick, David, 1940-.**                   **4.6757**
Indecent exposure: a true story of Hollywood and Wall Street / David McClintick. — 1st ed. — New York: Morrow, 1982. 544 p.: ill.; 24 cm. Includes index. 1. Begelman, David. 2. Robertson, Cliff. 3. Columbia Pictures Industries. 4. Embezzlement — New York (N.Y.) 5. Motion picture actors and actresses — California — Los Angeles. 6. Extortion — New York (N.Y.) 7. Hollywood (Los Angeles, Calif.) — Industries. 8. Los Angeles (Calif.) — Industries. I. T.
HV6684.N5 M35 1982     364.1/62 19     LC 82-3574     ISBN 068801349X

## HV6705–6727 Obscenity. Censorship
### (see also: KF9444)

**Broun, Heywood, 1888-1939.**                • **4.6758**
Anthony Comstock: roundsman of the Lord / by Heywood Broun & Margaret Leech. — New York: A. & C. Boni, 1927. 6 p.: l., 11-285 p., plates, ports., facsims.; 23 cm. 'Trade edition.' Bibliography: p. 277-280. 1. Comstock, Anthony, 1844-1915. I. Leech, Margaret. II. T.
HV6705.B7     LC 27-5428

**Ernst, Morris Leopold, 1888-.**                 **4.6759**
To the pure ... A study of obscenity and the censor, by Morris L. Ernst and William Seagle. New York, The Viking press, 1928. xiv p., 1 l., 336 p. 21 cm. Bibliography: p. 311-321. 1. Censorship — United States. 2. Obscenity (Law) — United States. I. Seagle, William, 1898- joint author. II. T.
HV6727.E73     LC 28-30424

## HV6768–6773 Corporate Crime. Computer Crime

**Jacoby, Neil H. (Neil Herman), 1909-1979.**        **4.6760**
Bribery and extortion in world business: a study of corporate political payments abroad / Neil H. Jacoby, Peter Nehemkis, Richard Eells. — New York: Macmillan, c1977. xx, 294 p.; 25 cm. 1. Corporations — Corrupt practices 2. Bribery 3. International business enterprises I. Nehemkis, Peter Raymond. joint author. II. Eells, Richard Sedric Fox, 1917- joint author. III. T.
HV6768.J3     364.1/32     LC 77-6942     ISBN 0029160006

**Vaughan, Diane.**                       **4.6761**
Controlling unlawful organizational behavior: social structure and corporate misconduct / Diane Vaughan. — Chicago: University of Chicago Press, 1983. xiv, 174 p.; 23 cm. (Studies in crime and justice.) Includes index. 1. Revco Drug Stores, Inc — Case studies. 2. White collar crimes — United States. 3. Corporations — United States — Corrupt practices. 4. Interorganizational

relations — United States. 5. Computer crimes — United States. 6. Organizational behavior — Case studies. I. T. II. Series.
HV6768.V38 1983     364.1/06/073 19     LC 83-3489     ISBN 0226851710

**Clinard, Marshall Barron, 1911-.**             **4.6762**
Corporate crime / Marshall B. Clinard and Peter C. Yeager, with the collaboration of Ruth Blackburn Clinard. — New York: Free Press; London: Collier Macmillan, c1980. xiii, 386 p.; 24 cm. Includes index. 1. Corporations — United States — Corrupt practices. 2. Commercial crimes — United States. I. Yeager, Peter C. joint author. II. Clinard, Ruth Blackburn. joint author. III. T.
HV6769.C56 1980     364.1/68/0973 19     LC 80-2156     ISBN 0029057108

**Sutherland, Edwin Hardin, 1883-1950.**        **4.6763**
White collar crime: the uncut version / Edwin H. Sutherland; with an introduction by Gilbert Geis and Colin Goff. — New Haven: Yale University Press, c1983. xxxiii, 291 p.; 24 cm. 1. White collar crimes — United States. 2. Corporations — United States — Corrupt practices. I. T.
HV6769.S93 1983     364.1/68/0973 19     LC 82-48911     ISBN 0300029217

**Parker, Donn B.**                        **4.6764**
Fighting computer crime / Donn B. Parker. — New York: Scribner, c1983. xiii, 352 p.: ill.; 24 cm. Includes index. 1. Computer crimes — Prevention. I. T.
HV6773.C65 P37 1983     364.1/68 19     LC 83-3217     ISBN 068417796X

## HV6774–7220 Criminology, by Region or Country

## HV6774–6795 United States

**Uniform crime reports for the United States.**       **4.6765** [REF] HV 6787 U58
Vol. 1 (Jan.-July 1930)-     . — Washington, D.C.: U.S. Dept. of Justice, Federal Bureau of Investigation: For sale by the Supt. of Docs., U.S. G.P.O., 1986. 1 v.: ill.; 26-28 cm. (Uniform crime reports) Annual. Each edition is kept up to date by quarterly cumulated releases. Issues for 1930-57 called v. 1-28. 1. Criminal statistics — United States — Periodicals. I. United States. Federal Bureau of Investigation.
HV6787.A3     LC 30-27005

**Sourcebook of criminal justice statistics, 1984 / by Michael J.**    **4.6766**
**Hindelang [and others.**
Washington]: U.S. National Criminal Justice Information and Statistics Service; [for sale by the Supt. of Docs., U.S. Govt. Print. Off.], 1985. 1 v. 1. Criminal statistics — United States. 2. Criminal justice, Administration of — United States — Statistics. 3. Corrections — United States — Statistics. I. Hindelang, Michael J. comp. II. United States. National Criminal Justice Information and Statistics Service.
HV6787.S68     364     LC 74-601963

**U.S. President's Commission on Law Enforcement and**    • **4.6767**
**Administration of Justice.**
The challenge of crime in a free society; a report. Introd. and afterword by Isidore Silver. — New York: Dutton, 1968 [i.e. 1969] 814 p.: illus.; 24 cm. Commonly known as the Crime commission report. 1. Crime and criminals — U.S. I. T. II. Title: Crime commission report.
HV6789.A33 1969     364/.9/73     LC 69-16914

**United States. Task Force on Organized Crime.**      • **4.6768**
Task Force report; organized crime, annotations and consultants' papers. — [Washington: For sale by the Supt. of Docs., U.S. Govt. Print. Off., 1967] vii, 126 p.: illus.; 28 cm. 1. Organized crime — United States I. T. II. Title: Organized crime.
HV6789.A343     364.1/0973     LC 67-61470

**Crime in city politics / edited by Anne Heinz, Herbert Jacob,**    **4.6769**
**and Robert L. Lineberry.**
New York, N.Y.: Longman, c1983. xii, 288 p.: ill.; 23 cm. — (Longman professional studies in law and public policy.) 1. Crime and criminals — United States — Addresses, essays, lectures. 2. Political crimes and offenses — United States — Addresses, essays, lectures. I. Heinz, Anne M. II. Jacob, Herbert, 1933- III. Lineberry, Robert L. IV. Series.
HV6789.C693 1983     364.1/32/0973 19     LC 82-9921     ISBN 058228368X

**Crime in society** / [edited by] Leonard D. Savitz, Norman    **4.6770**
Johnston.
New York: Wiley, c1978. xii, 963 p.: ill.; 24 cm. 1. Crime and criminals —
United States — Addresses, essays, lectures. 2. Criminal behavior, Prediction
of — Addresses, essays, lectures. 3. Criminal psychology — Addresses, essays,
lectures. I. Savitz, Leonard D. II. Johnston, Norman Bruce, 1921-
HV6789.C695    364/.973    *LC* 78-806    *ISBN* 0471033855

**Sifakis, Carl.**    **4.6771**
The encyclopedia of American crime / by Carl Sifakis. — New York, NY:
Facts on File, c1982. xii, 802 p.: ill., ports.; 28 cm. Includes index. 1. Crime and
criminals — United States — Dictionaries. I. T. II. Title: American crime.
HV6789.S54    364/.973/0321 19    *LC* 81-600    *ISBN* 0871966204

**Silberman, Charles E., 1925-.**    **4.6772**
Criminal violence, criminal justice / Charles E. Silberman. — 1st ed. — New
York: Random House, c1978. xviii, 540 p.; 25 cm. Includes index. 1. Crime
and criminals — United States 2. Criminal justice, Administration of —
United States 3. Violence — United States. I. T.
HV6789.S55    364/.973    *LC* 77-5981    *ISBN* 0394483065

**Wilson, James Q.**    **4.6773**
Thinking about crime / James Q. Wilson. — Rev. ed., 2nd. — New York: Basic
Books, c1983. x, 293 p.; 25 cm. 1. Crime and criminals — United States —
Addresses, essays, lectures. 2. Criminal justice, Administration of — United
States — Addresses, essays, lectures. I. T.
HV6789.W53 1983    364/.973 19    *LC* 83-70752    *ISBN* 0465085504

**American violence and public policy: an update of the National**    **4.6774**
**Commission on the Causes and Prevention of Violence** / edited
by Lynn A. Curtis.
New Haven: Yale University Press, c1985. xi, 263 p.; 24 cm. 1. Violent crimes
— Government policy — United States — Addresses, essays, lectures.
I. Curtis, Lynn A. II. United States. National Commission on the Causes and
Prevention of Violence.
HV6791.A72 1985    364.1 19    *LC* 84-40194    *ISBN* 0300032315

**Anderson, Annelise Graebner.**    **4.6775**
The business of organized crime: a Cosa Nostra family / Annelise Graebner
Anderson. — Stanford, Calif.: Hoover Institution Press, c1979. 179 p.; 24 cm.
(Hoover Institution publication; 201) Includes index. 1. Organized crime —
United States 2. Mafia — United States. I. T.
HV6791.A76    364.1/06/0973    *LC* 78-59464    *ISBN* 0817970118

**Curtis, Lynn A.**    **4.6776**
Criminal violence: national patterns and behavior / Lynn A. Curtis. Lexington,
Mass.: Lexington Books, [1974] xxi, 231 p.: ill.; 24 cm. Includes indexes. 1.
1. Crime and criminals — United States 2. Violence — United States.
3. Victims of crimes — United States. I. T.
HV6791.C87    364/.973    *LC* 74-15535    *ISBN* 0669960241

**Elderly criminals** / Evelyn S. Newman, Donald J. Newman,    **4.6777**
**Mindy L. Gewirtz and associates.**
Cambridge, Mass.: Oelgeschlager, Gunn & Hain, c1984. xxvi, 252 p.: ill.; 24 cm.
Includes index. 1. Aged offenders — United States — Addresses, essays,
lectures. I. Newman, Evelyn S. II. Newman, Donald J. III. Gewirtz, Mindy
L.
HV6791.E38 1984    364.3/7 19    *LC* 83-8227    *ISBN* 0899462030

**Graber, Doris A. (Doris Appel), 1923-.**    **4.6778**
Crime news and the public / Doris A. Graber. — New York: Praeger, 1980.
xviii, 239 p.: ill.; 24 cm. Includes index. 1. Crime and criminals — United
States — Public opinion. 2. Mass media — Social aspects — United States.
3. Crime and the press — United States. 4. Public opinion — United States.
I. T.
HV6791.G69    364/.973    *LC* 80-16032    *ISBN* 0030557569

**Ianni, Francis A. J.**    **4.6779**
Black Mafia; ethnic succession in organized crime [by] Francis A. J. Ianni. New
York, Simon and Schuster [1974] 381 p. 24 cm. 1. Organized crime — United
States 2. Mafia — United States. 3. Afro-American criminals I. T.
HV6791.I2    364.1/06/073    *LC* 74-113    *ISBN* 067121764X

**Judge, lawyer, victim, thief: women, gender roles, and criminal**    **4.6780**
**justice** / [edited by] Nicole Hahn Rafter, Elizabeth Anne
Stanko.
[Boston]: Northeastern University Press, c1982. xii, 383 p.; 24 cm. 1. Sex
discrimination in criminal justice administration — United States — Addresses,
essays, lectures. 2. Women — United States — Crimes against — Addresses,
essays, lectures. 3. Female offenders — United States — Addresses, essays,
lectures. 4. Women prisoners — United States — Addresses, essays, lectures.
I. Rafter, Nicole Hahn, 1939- II. Stanko, Elizabeth Anne, 1950-
HV6791.J83 1982    364/.088042 19    *LC* 82-2285    *ISBN*
0930350294

**Parker, J. A., 1936-.**    **4.6781**
What the Negro can do about crime [by] J. A. Parker and Allan C. Brownfeld.
New Rochelle, N.Y., Arlington House [1974] 206 p. 24 cm. 1. Crime and
criminals — United States 2. Victims of crimes — United States. 3. Afro-
Americans 4. Crime prevention — United States. I. Brownfeld, Allan C.,
1939- joint author. II. T.
HV6791.P37    364    *LC* 74-6195    *ISBN* 0870002317

**Pearce, Frank.**    **4.6782**
Crimes of the powerful: Marxism, crime, and deviance / Frank Pearce;
foreword by Jock Young. London: Pluto Press, 1976. 172 p.; 20 cm. 1. Crime
and criminals — United States 2. Commercial crimes — United States.
3. White collar crimes — United States. 4. Organized crime — United States
I. T.
HV6791.P4 1976    364/.973    *LC* 76-379315    *ISBN* 0904383059

**Simon, Rita James.**    **4.6783**
Women and crime / Rita James Simon. — Lexington, Mass.: Lexington Books,
[1975] xvi, 126 p.; 24 cm. Includes index. 1. Female offenders — United States.
2. Criminal justice, Administration of — United States I. T.
HV6791.S54    364.3/74/0973    *LC* 74-25067    *ISBN* 0669974285

**Peterson, Mark A., 1944-.**    **4.6784**
[Doing crime] Who commits crimes: a survey of prison inmates / Mark A.
Peterson, Harriet B. Braiker; with Suzanne M. Polich. — Cambridge, Mass.:
Oelgeschlager, Gunn & Hain, c1981. xxix, 267 p.: ill.; 26 cm. Reprint.
Originally published: Doing crime: a survey of California prison inmates. Santa
Monica, CA: Rand, 1980. 'R-2200-DOJ.' 1. Crime and criminals — California.
2. Prisoners — California. I. Braiker, Harriet B., 1948- II. Polich, Suzanne
M., 1943- III. Rand Corporation. IV. T.
HV6793.C2 P48 1981    364.3/09794 19    *LC* 81-9478    *ISBN*
0899461034

# HV6801-7220 Other Countries

**Crime and the law: the social history of crime in Western**    **4.6785**
**Europe since 1500** / edited by V.A.C. Gatrell, Bruce Lenman,
and Geoffrey Parker.
London: Europa Publications, 1980. xii, 381 p.; 25 cm. — (Europa social
history of human experience.) 1. Crime and criminals — Europe — History —
Addresses, essays, lectures. 2. Criminal law — Europe — History —
Addresses, essays, lectures. I. Gatrell, V. A. C., 1941- II. Lenman, Bruce.
III. Parker, Geoffrey, 1943- IV. Title: Crime & the law. V. Series.
HV6937.A2 1980    364/.94 19    *LC* 81-177088    *ISBN* 0905118545

**Albion's fatal tree: crime and society in eighteenth-century**    **4.6786**
**England** / Douglas Hay ... [et al.].
1st American ed. — New York: Pantheon Books, c1975. 352 p., [6] leaves of
plates: ill.; 22 cm. 1. Crime and criminals — England — History — Addresses,
essays, lectures. I. Hay, Douglas.
HV6943.A54 1975    364/.942    *LC* 75-23256    *ISBN* 0394471202

**Crime in England, 1550-1800** / edited by J. S. Cockburn.    **4.6787**
Princeton, N.J.: Princeton University Press, c1977. xiv, 364 p.: graphs; 25 cm.
Includes index. 1. Crime and criminals — England — History — Addresses,
essays, lectures. 2. Criminal justice, Administration of — England — History
— Addresses, essays, lectures. I. Cockburn, J. S.
HV6943.C74    364/.942    *LC* 77-2867    *ISBN* 0691052581

**Tobias, J. J. (John Jacob)**    **4.6788**
Nineteenth-century crime in England: prevention and punishment [by] J. J.
Tobias. New York, Barnes & Noble [1972] 183 p. 23 cm. (Sources for social &
economic history) 1. Crime and criminals — England. 2. Police — England
3. Punishment — England. I. T.
HV6944.T63 1972    364/.942    *LC* 73-152567    *ISBN* 0064969304

**Salgādo, Gāmini, 1929-.**    **4.6789**
The Elizabethan underworld / Gāmini Salgādo. — London: J. M. Dent;
Totowa, N.J.: Rowman and Littlefield, 1977. 221 p.: ill.; 24 cm. 1. Rogues and
vagabonds — England — London — History. 2. Crime and criminals —
England — London — History. I. T.
HV6946.Z8 L657 1977    364/.9421    *LC* 77-377365    *ISBN*
0874719674

**Wright, Gordon, 1912-.**    **4.6790**
Between the guillotine and liberty: two centuries of the crime problem in France
/ Gordon Wright. — New York: Oxford University Press, 1983. ix, 290 p.: ill.;
22 cm. Includes index. 1. Crime and criminals — France — History — 19th
century. 2. Crime and criminals — France — History — 20th century. I. T.
HV6963.W74 1983    364/.944 19    *LC* 82-12520    *ISBN* 0195032438

**Greene, Graham, 1904-.**    **4.6791**
J'accuse, the dark side of Nice / Graham Greene. — London: Bodley Head,
1982. 69 p.: ill.; 22 cm. English and French. Title on p. 37: J'accuse, ou, Nice

côté-ombre. 1. Criminal justice, Administration of — France — Nice. I. T. II. Title: J'accuse, ou, Nice côté-ombre.
HV6967.G73 1982      364/.944941 19      *LC* 82-148261      *ISBN* 0370309308

**Chevalier, Louis, 1911-.**                    **4.6792**
[Classes laborieuses et classes dangereuses ... English] Laboring classes and dangerous classes in Paris during the first half of the nineteenth century. Translated from the French by Frank Jellinek. [1st American ed.] New York, H. Fertig, 1973. viii, 505 p. 24 cm. 1. Crime and criminals — Paris — History. 2. Paris (France) — Social conditions. I. T.
HV6970.P3 C513      364/.944/36      *LC* 72-6702

**Zehr, Howard.**                               **4.6793**
Crime and the development of modern society: patterns of criminality in nineteenth century Germany and France / Howard Zehr. London: Croom Helm; Totowa, N.J.: Rowman and Littlefield, 1976. 188 p.: graphs; 23 cm. Includes index. 1. Crime and criminals — Germany — History. 2. Crime and criminals — France — History. 3. Social history — 19th century I. T.
HV6974.Z43 1976      364/.943      *LC* 76-19109      *ISBN* 0874718619

**Connor, Walter D.**                          **4.6794**
Deviance in Soviet society: crime, delinquency, and alcoholism / [by] Walter D. Connor. — New York: Columbia University Press, 1972. viii, 327 p.; 23 cm. 1. Crime and criminals — Soviet Union. 2. Juvenile delinquency — Soviet Union. 3. Liquor problem — Soviet Union. I. T.
HV7012.C65      364/.947      *LC* 71-180044      *ISBN* 0231034393

**Clinard, Marshall Barron, 1911-.**              **4.6795**
Cities with little crime: the case of Switzerland / Marshall B. Clinard. — Cambridge [Eng.]; New York: Cambridge University Press, 1978. xv, 208 p.; 24 cm. — (The Arnold and Caroline Rose monograph series) 1. Crime and criminals — Switzerland. 2. Criminal justice, Administration of — Switzerland. I. T.
HV7053.C58      364/.9494      *LC* 77-88672      *ISBN* 0521219604

---

# HV7231–9920 Penology: General

## HV7551–8280 Police

**Messick, Hank.**                            **4.6796**
John Edgar Hoover; an inquiry into the life and times of John Edgar Hoover, and his relationship to the continuing partnership of crime, business, and politics. New York, McKay [1972] 276 p. 22 cm. 1. Hoover, J. Edgar (John Edgar), 1895-1972. I. T.
HV7911.H6 M46      364/.092/4 B      *LC* 70-188259

**Carte, Gene E.**                             **4.6797**
Police reform in the United States: the era of August Vollmer, 1905–1932 / by Gene E. Carte and Elaine H. Carte. — Berkeley: University of California Press, c1975. x, 137 p., [3] leaves of plates: ill.; 24 cm. Includes index. 1. Vollmer, August, 1876-1955. 2. Police — California — Berkeley — History. 3. Police — United States — History. I. Carte, Elaine H., joint author. II. T.
HV7911.V6 C37      363.2/092/4 B      *LC* 73-87248      *ISBN* 0520025997

**Power and authority in law enforcement** / edited by Terry R.     **4.6798**
**Armstrong, Kenneth M. Cinnamon; with a foreword by Donald Kreps.**
Springfield, Ill.: Thomas, c1976. xv, 190 p.; 24 cm. 1. Police — Addresses, essays, lectures. 2. Power (Social sciences) — Addresses, essays, lectures. 3. Authority — Addresses, essays, lectures. 4. Law enforcement — Addresses, essays, lectures. I. Armstrong, Terry R., 1946- II. Cinnamon, Kenneth M.
HV7921.P67 1976      363.2      *LC* 76-7384      *ISBN* 0398035717

**Thibault, Edward A., 1939-.**                  **4.6799**
Proactive police management / Edward A. Thibault, Lawrence M. Lynch, R. Bruce McBride. — Englewood Cliffs, N.J.: Prentice-Hall, c1985. x, 342 p.; 24 cm. 1. Police administration I. Lynch, Lawrence M., 1927- II. McBride, R. Bruce. III. T.
HV7935.T47 1985      351.74 19      *LC* 84-13364      *ISBN* 0137114419

**Vanagunas, Stanley.**                        **4.6800**
Administration of police organizations / Stanley Vanagunas and James F. Elliott. — Boston: Allyn and Bacon, c1980. ix, 386 p.: ill.; 24 cm. Includes index. 1. Police administration 2. Police administration — United States. I. Elliott, J. F. (James Franklin), 1924- joint author. II. T.
HV7935.V33      363.2      *LC* 79-11877      *ISBN* 0205066666

**Brown, Michael K.**                          **4.6801**
Working the street: police discretion and the dilemmas of reform / Michael K. Brown. — New York: Russell Sage Foundation, c1981. xvi, 349 p.; 24 cm. — (Publications of Russell Sage Foundation.) Includes index. 1. Police discretion — California. 2. Police patrol — California. 3. Police discretion — Political aspects — California. 4. Police — California. 5. Public relations — Police 6. Police discretion — United States. I. T. II. Series.
HV7936.D54 B76 1981      363.2/32 19      *LC* 80-69175      *ISBN* 0871541904

**Radelet, Louis A.**                          **4.6802**
The police and the community / [by] Louis A. Radelet, with research and complementary materials prepared by Hoyt Coe Reed. — Beverly Hills: Glencoe Press, [1973] xiii, 751 p.; 25 cm. — (Glencoe Press criminal justice series) 1. Public relations — Police 2. Police — United States I. Reed, Hoyt Coe. II. T.
HV7936.P8 R3      659.2/9/36320973      *LC* 72-93310

**Marchand, Donald A.**                      **4.6803**
The politics of privacy, computers, and criminal justice records: controlling the social costs of technological change / Donald A. Marchand. — Arlington, Va.: Information Resources Press, 1980. xvi, 433 p.: ill.; 24 cm. Includes index. 1. Information storage and retrieval systems — Criminal justice, Administration of 2. Computers — Access control 3. Privacy, Right of I. T.
HV7936.A8 M28      651.5/042 19      *LC* 80-80675      *ISBN* 0878150307

**Horne, Peter.**                              **4.6804**
Women in law enforcement / by Peter Horne; with a foreword by Lewis J. Sherman. — 2d ed. — Springfield, Ill.: Thomas, 1980. xvii, 269 p.: ill.; 24 cm. Includes index. 1. Policewomen — United States. 2. Policewomen I. T.
HV8023.H67 1980      363.2/088042 19      *LC* 79-24230      *ISBN* 0398040303

**Martin, Susan Ehrlich.**                      **4.6805**
Breaking and entering: policewomen on patrol / Susan Ehrlich Martin. — Berkeley: University of California Press, c1980. xvi, 265 p., [4] leaves of plates: ill.; 22 cm. Originally presented as the author's thesis, American University. Includes index. 1. Policewomen — United States. I. T.
HV8023.M37 1980      363.2/088042 19      *LC* 79-63555      *ISBN* 0520039084

**Kennett, Lee B.**                            **4.6806**
The gun in America: the origins of a national dilemma / Lee Kennett and James La Verne Anderson. — Westport, Conn.: Greenwood Press, 1975. x, 339 p.; 21 cm. (Contributions in American history; no. 37) Includes index. 1. Gun control — United States — History. 2. Firearms — Law and legislation — United States — History. 3. Firearms industry and trade — United States — History. I. Anderson, James L. II. T.
HV8059.K45      363.3      *LC* 74-5990      *ISBN* 0837175305

**Sherrill, Robert.**                           **4.6807**
The Saturday night special: and other guns with which Americans won the West, protected bootleg franchises, slew wildlife, robbed countless banks, shot husbands purposely and by mistake, and killed presidents—together with the debate over continuing same / Illustrated by Julio Fernandez. New York: Charterhouse [1973] xiii, 338 p.: ill.; 22 cm. 1. National Rifle Association of America. 2. Gun control — United States. 3. Firearms — Law and legislation — United States. I. T.
HV8059.S47      363.3/3      *LC* 73-84076      *ISBN* 0883270161

**Allison, Harrison C.**                        **4.6808**
Personal identification / [by] Harrison C. Allison.; Vern L. Folley, consulting editor. — Boston: Holbrook Press, [1973] xiv, 402 p.: ill.; 25 cm. 1. Identification 2. Crime and criminals — Identification I. T.
HV8073.A59      364.12/5      *LC* 72-86561

**Forensic science: scientific investigation in criminal justice** /     **4.6809**
**edited by Joseph L. Peterson.**
New York: AMS Press, [1975] 439 p.: ill.; 24 cm. Includes index. 1. Criminal investigation — Addresses, essays, lectures. 2. Crime laboratories — Addresses, essays, lectures. 3. Criminal justice, Administration of — Addresses, essays, lectures. I. Peterson, Joseph L., 1945-
HV8073.F59      364.12/1      *LC* 75-11812      *ISBN* 0404131395

**O'Hara, Charles E.**                          **4.6810**
An introduction to criminalistics: the application of the physical sciences to the detection of crime / [by] Charles E. O'Hara & James W. Osterburg. — Bloomington: Indiana University Press, [1972] xxii, 705 p.: ill.; 25 cm. 1. Criminal investigation I. Osterburg, James W. joint author. II. T. III. Title: Criminalistics.
HV8073.O4 1972      364.12      *LC* 72-182990      *ISBN* 025333103X

**Lykken, David Thoreson.**	**4.6811**
A tremor in the blood: uses and abuses of the lie detector / David Thoreson Lykken. — New York: McGraw-Hill, [1980] 317 p. 1. Lie detectors and detection I. T.
HV8078.L94	363.2/54	*LC* 80-10697	*ISBN* 0070392102

**Manning, Peter K.**	**4.6812**
The narc's game: organizational and informational limits on drug law enforcement / Peter K. Manning. — Cambridge, Mass.: MIT Press, c1980. xiv, 316 p.: ill.; 24 cm. Includes index. 1. Narcotics, Control of 2. Narcotics, Control of — United States. I. T.
HV8079.N3 M36	363.4/5	*LC* 79-24620	*ISBN* 0262131544

**Police and the elderly / edited by Arnold P. Goldstein, William	4.6813
J. Hoyer, Phillip J. Monti.**
New York: Pergamon Press, c1979. x, 116 p.; 24 cm. — (Pergamon general psychology series; v. 78) 1. Police services for the aged — Addresses, essays, lectures. 2. Aged — Crimes against — Addresses, essays, lectures. I. Goldstein, Arnold P. II. Hoyer, William J. III. Monti, Phillip J.
HV8079.225.P64 1979	364	*LC* 78-27400	*ISBN* 0080238947

**Morn, Frank, 1937-.**	**4.6814**
'The eye that never sleeps': a history of the Pinkerton National Detective Agency / Frank Morn. — Bloomington: Indiana University Press, c1982. xi, 244 p.; 24 cm. Includes index. 1. Pinkerton's National Detective Agency. 2. Police, Private — United States — History. 3. Watchmen — United States — History. I. T.
HV8087.M67 1982	338.7/61363289/0973 19	*LC* 81-47776	*ISBN* 0253320860

## HV8130–8280 By Country

### HV8130–8148 UNITED STATES

**Black, Donald J.**	**4.6815**
The manners and customs of the police / Donald Black. — New York: Academic Press, 1981 (c1980). xiii, 274 p.; 24 cm. Includes indexes. 1. Police — United States — Addresses, essays, lectures. I. T.
HV8138.B5	363.2/0973 19	*LC* 80-1675	*ISBN* 0121028801

**Blacks and criminal justice / edited by Charles E. Owens,	4.6816
Jimmy Bell.**
Lexington, Mass.: Lexington Books, c1977. ix, 151 p.; 24 cm. 1. Criminal justice, Administration of — United States — Addresses, essays, lectures. 2. Afro-Americans — Addresses, essays, lectures. 3. Afro-American criminals — Addresses, essays, lectures. 4. Prisoners — Education — United States — Addresses, essays, lectures. I. Owens, Charles E. II. Bell, Jimmy.
HV8138.B53	364/.973	*LC* 76-43639	*ISBN* 0669011010

**Cooper, John L., 1936-.**	**4.6817**
The police and the ghetto / John L. Cooper. — Port Washington, N.Y.: Kennikat Press, 1980. 158 p.; 23 cm. — (Multi-disciplinary studies in the law.) (National university publications) 1. Police — United States 2. Public relations — Police 3. Afro-American police 4. United States — Race relations I. T. II. Series.
HV8138.C65	363.2	*LC* 79-19261	*ISBN* 0804692505

**Elliff, John T.**	**4.6818**
The reform of FBI intelligence operations / John T. Elliff; written under the auspices of the Police Foundation. — Princeton, N.J.: Princeton University Press, c1979. xi, 248 p.; 22 cm. Includes index. 1. United States. Federal Bureau of Investigation. 2. Intelligence service — United States 3. United States — National security I. Police Foundation (U.S.) II. T.
HV8138.E57	353.007/4	*LC* 78-70290	*ISBN* 0691076073

**Fogelson, Robert M.**	**4.6819**
Big-city police / Robert M. Fogelson. Cambridge, Mass.: Harvard University Press, 1977. xi, 374 p.; 25 cm. (An Urban Institute study) 1. Police — United States — History. I. T.
HV8138.F55	363.2/0973	*LC* 77-5096	*ISBN* 0674072812

**Investigating the FBI. Edited by Pat Watters and Stephen	4.6820
Gillers.**
[1st ed.] Garden City, N.Y., Doubleday, 1973. xxxiii, 518 p. 22 cm. 'A book of the Committee for Public Justice.' Based on a conference on the FBI held at Princeton University, Oct. 29-30, 1971. 1. United States. Federal Bureau of Investigation — Addresses, essays, lectures. I. Watters, Pat. ed. II. Gillers, Stephen, 1943- ed. III. Committee for Public Justice (U.S.)
HV8138.I58	364.12/06/173	*LC* 72-76219	*ISBN* 0385066848

**Justice and corrections / [edited by] Norman Johnston, Leonard	4.6821
D. Savitz.**
New York: Wiley, c1978. xii, 989 p.: ill.; 24 cm. 1. Criminal justice, Administration of — United States — Addresses, essays, lectures. I. Johnston, Norman Bruce, 1921- II. Savitz, Leonard D.
HV8138.J88	364/.973	*LC* 78-748	*ISBN* 0471033847

**Monkkonen, Eric H., 1942-.**	**4.6822**
Police in urban America, 1860–1920 / Eric H. Monkkonen. — Cambridge [Eng.]; New York: Cambridge University Press, 1981. xv, 220 p.: graphs; 23 cm. — (Interdisciplinary perspectives on modern history.) 1. Police — United States — History. I. T. II. Series.
HV8138.M65	363.2/0973 19	*LC* 80-16762	*ISBN* 0521234549

**Powers, Richard Gid, 1944-.**	**4.6823**
G-men, Hoover's FBI in American popular culture / Richard Gid Powers. — Carbondale: Southern Illinois University Press, c1983. xix, 356 p.: ill., ports.; 24 cm. 1. Hoover, J. Edgar (John Edgar), 1895-1972. 2. United States. Federal Bureau of Investigation. 3. Criminal investigation in mass media — United States. 4. Detectives in mass media — United States. 5. United States — Popular culture I. T. II. Title: G-men, Hoover's F.B.I. in American popular culture.
HV8138.P68 1983	353.0074 19	*LC* 83-632	*ISBN* 0809310961

**Reiman, Jeffrey H.**	**4.6824**
The rich get richer and the poor get prison: ideology, class and criminal justice / Jeffrey H. Reiman. — New York: Wiley, c1979. xii, 214 p.; 23 cm. 1. Criminal justice, Administration of — United States I. T.
HV8138.R42	364/.973	*LC* 78-23986	*ISBN* 0471047260

**Sullivan, William C.**	**4.6825**
The Bureau: my thirty years in Hoover's FBI / William C. Sullivan, with Bill Brown. — 1st ed. — New York: Norton, c1979. 286 p.: ill.; 24 cm. Includes index. 1. Hoover, J. Edgar (John Edgar), 1895-1972. 2. United States. Federal Bureau of Investigation. I. Brown, Bill, 1930- II. T.
HV8138.S93 1979	353.007/4	*LC* 79-15416	*ISBN* 0393012360

**Sykes, Richard E., 1932-.**	**4.6826**
Policing, a social behaviorist perspective / Richard E. Sykes, Edward E. Brent. — New Brunswick, N.J.: Rutgers University Press, c1983. xviii, 310 p.: ill.; 24 cm. — (Crime, law, and deviance series.) Includes index. 1. Police — United States 2. Public relations — United States — Police. 3. Social interaction — United States — Mathematical models. 4. Human behavior — Mathematical models I. Brent, Edward E., 1949- II. T. III. Series.
HV8138.S97 1983	363.2/3 19	*LC* 82-10229	*ISBN* 0813509718

**Trojanowicz, Robert C., 1941-.**	**4.6827**
Criminal justice and the community [by] Robert C. Trojanowicz [and] Samuel Dixon. — Englewood Cliffs, N.J.: Prentice-Hall, [1974] xiii, 424 p.; 24 cm. 1. Criminal justice, Administration of — United States 2. Law enforcement — United States. 3. Public relations — Police I. Dixon, Samuel L., 1934- joint author. II. T.
HV8138.T76	364	*LC* 74-875	*ISBN* 0131935577

**Wilson, James Q.**	**4.6828**
The investigators: managing FBI and narcotics agents / James Q. Wilson. — New York: Basic Books, c1978. xi, 228 p.; 22 cm. 1. United States. Federal Bureau of Investigation — Management. 2. United States. Drug Enforcement Administration — Management. 3. Criminal investigation — United States. 4. Narcotics, Control of — United States. I. T.
HV8138.W633	364.12	*LC* 77-20428	*ISBN* 0465035892

**Blackstock, Nelson.**	**4.6829**
Cointelpro: the FBI's secret war on political freedom / by Nelson Blackstock; with an introd. by Noam Chomsky. — New York: Vintage Books, 1976, c1975. xiii, 216 p.; 21 cm. 1. United States. Federal Bureau of Investigation. 2. Political rights — United States. 3. Civil rights — United States I. T.
HV8141.B6 1976	364.1/32/0973	*LC* 76-10583	*ISBN* 0394721861

**Farmer, David John, 1935-.**	**4.6830**
Crime control: the use and misuse of police resources / David John Farmer. — New York: Plenum Press, c1984. xix, 233 p.; 22 cm. — (Criminal justice and public safety.) Includes index. 1. Police administration — United States. I. T. II. Series.
HV8141.F37 1984	350.74/0973 19	*LC* 84-11470	*ISBN* 0306416883

**Scharf, Peter, 1945-.**	**4.6831**
The badge and the bullet: police use of deadly force / Peter Scharf, Arnold Binder. — New York, NY, USA: Praeger, 1983. ix, 254 p.; 25 cm. 1. Police shootings — United States. I. Binder, Arnold. II. T.
HV8141.S29 1983	363.2/32 19	*LC* 83-4106	*ISBN* 0030629632

**Stark, Rodney.** 4.6832
Police riots; collective violence and law enforcement. — Belmont, Calif.: Wadsworth Pub. Co., [1972] vi, 250 p.; 21 cm. — (Focus books) 1. Police — U.S. 2. Violence — U.S. I. T.
HV8141.S8    363.2/3    *LC* 78-178816    *ISBN* 0534001459

**Commission of Inquiry into the Black Panthers and the Police.** 4.6833
Search and destroy; a report. Roy Wilkins and Ramsey Clark, chairmen. [1st ed.] New York, Metropolitan Applied Research Center [1973] xii, 284 p. illus. 22 cm. 1. Black Panther Party. 2. Police — Illinois — Chicago. 3. Public relations — Police I. Wilkins, Roy, 1901- II. Clark, Ramsey, 1927- III. T.
HV8148.C42 C65 1973    363.2/34    *LC* 73-7068    *ISBN* 0060108282

**Reuss-Ianni, Elizabeth, 1944-.** 4.6834
Two cultures of policing: street cops and management cops / Elizabeth Reuss-Ianni. — New Brunswick, [N.J.]: Transaction Books, c1983. 145 p.; 24 cm. (New observations) Includes index. 1. Police administration — New York (N.Y.) 2. Police patrol — New York (N.Y.) 3. New York (N.Y.) — Police. I. T.
HV8148.N5 R48 1983    352.2/09747/1 19    *LC* 82-7079    *ISBN* 0878554696

**New York (City). Knapp Commission.** 4.6835
The Knapp Commission report on police corruption. — New York: G. Braziller, [1973?] 2, 3, xiii, ii, 283 p.: map.; 24 cm. 1. Police corruption — New York (City) I. T.
HV8148.N52 A46    364.1/32    *LC* 73-76969    *ISBN* 080760688X

## HV8149–8280 OTHER COUNTRIES

**Reiner, Robert, 1946-.** 4.6836
The blue–coated worker: a sociological study of police unionism / Robert Reiner. — Cambridge [Eng.]; New York: Cambridge University Press, 1978. 295 p.; 24 cm. — (Cambridge studies in sociology; 10) Includes index. 1. Trade-unions — Police — Great Britain. 2. Police — Great Britain — Attitudes. 3. Police — Great Britain. I. T.
HV8195.A2 R44    331.88/11/36320941    *LC* 77-85695    *ISBN* 0521218896

**Whitaker, Ben, 1934-.** 4.6837
The police in society / Ben Whitaker. — London: Methuen, 1979. 351 p.: ill.; 23 cm. Includes index. 1. Police — Great Britain. I. T.
HV8195.A2 W48    363.2/0941    *LC* 79-310622    *ISBN* 041334200X

**Rumbelow, Donald.** 4.6838
I spy blue: the police and crime in the City of London from Elizabeth I to Victoria. London, Macmillan; New York, St. Martin's Press, 1971. 250 p., 8 plates. illus., map, ports. 24 cm. Illus. on lining papers. 1. Police — England — London — History. 2. Crime and criminals — London — History. I. T.
HV8198.L7 R9    363.2/09421    *LC* 70-171584    *ISBN* 0333106520

**Barron, John, 1930-.** 4.6839
KGB: the secret work of Soviet secret agents / John Barron. — [1st ed.]. — New York: Reader's Digest Press; distributed by E. P. Dutton, 1974. xiv, 462 p.: illus.; 25 cm. 'Portions of this material have appeared in Reader's digest in slightly different form.' 1. Soviet Union. Komitet gosudarstvennoĭ bezopasnosti. I. T.
HV8225.B37    HV8225 B37.    327/.12/0947    *LC* 73-79532    *ISBN* 0883490099

**Barron, John, 1930-.** 4.6840
KGB today: the hidden hand / John Barron. — New York: Reader's Digest Press, 1983. 489 p., [8] p. of plates: ill.; 24 cm. 1. Soviet Union. Komitet gosudarstvennoĭ bezopasnosti. I. T. II. Title: K.G.B. today.
HV8225.B373 1983    363.2/83/0947 19    *LC* 83-4645    *ISBN* 0883491648

## HV8301–9025 Prisons. Punishment. Prison Violence

**Barnes, Harry Elmer, 1889-1968.** 4.6841
The story of punishment; a record of man's inhumanity to man. — 2d ed. rev. — Montclair, N.J.: Patterson Smith, 1972. xv, 292 p.: illus.; 22 cm. — (Patterson Smith reprint series in criminology, law enforcement, and social problems. Publication no. 112) Reprint of the 1930 ed., except for those pages the author revised prior to his death, and which have been reset. 1. Punishment 2. Prisons 3. Crime and criminals I. T.
HV8497.B3 1972    364.6    *LC* 74-108229    *ISBN* 0875851126

**Maestro, Marcello T., 1907-.** 4.6842
Cesare Beccaria and the origins of penal reform [by] Marcello Maestro. Foreword by Norval Morris. Philadelphia, Temple University Press [1973] xii, 179 p. 22 cm. 1. Beccaria, Cesare, marchese di, 1738-1794. 2. Punishment I. T.
HV8661.B5 M3    364.6/092/4 B    *LC* 72-91133    *ISBN* 0877220247

**Bowker, Lee H.** 4.6843
Prisoner subcultures / Lee H. Bowker. — Lexington, Mass.: Lexington Books, c1977. xii, 173 p.; 24 cm. 1. Prisoners 2. Subculture I. T.
HV8665.B68    365/.6    *LC* 77-6182    *ISBN* 066901429X

**Toch, Hans.** 4.6844
Living in prison: the ecology of survival / Hans Toch, with contributions by John Gibbs, John Seymour, Daniel Lockwood. — New York: Free Press, c1977. xii, 318 p.: graphs; 25 cm. Includes index. 1. Prisons 2. Prison psychology 3. Prisoners I. T.
HV8665.T6    365/.3    *LC* 77-4570    *ISBN* 002932680X

**Zimring, Franklin E.** 4.6845
Deterrence; the legal threat in crime control [by] Franklin E. Zimring [and] Gordon J. Hawkins. With a foreword by James Vorenberg. Chicago: University of Chicago Press, [1973] xiv, 376 p.: illus.; 23 cm. — (Studies in crime and justice.) 1. Punishment in crime deterrence 2. Crime prevention 3. Punishment — Research. I. Hawkins, Gordon, 1919- joint author. II. T. III. Series.
HV8665.Z55    364.6    *LC* 72-89584    *ISBN* 0226983501

**Foucault, Michel.** 4.6846
[Surveiller et punir. English] Discipline and punish: the birth of the prison / Michel Foucault; translated from the French by Alan Sheridan. — 1st American ed. — New York: Pantheon Books, 1978 (c1977). 333 p., [3] leaves of plates: ill.; 25 cm. Translation of Surveiller et punir. 1. Prisons 2. Prison discipline 3. Punishment I. T.
HV8666.F6813 1977    365    *LC* 77-5301    *ISBN* 0394499425

**Meiners, Roger E.** 4.6847
Victim compensation: economic, legal, and political aspects / Roger E. Meiners. — Lexington, Mass.: Lexington Books, c1978. xv, 123 p.: ill.; 24 cm. A revision of the author's thesis, Virginia Polytechnic Institute. Includes index. 1. Reparation 2. Victims of crimes I. T.
HV8688.M44 1978    362.8/8    *LC* 77-80772    *ISBN* 0669016675

**Berns, Walter, 1919-.** 4.6848
For capital punishment: crime and the morality of the death penalty / Walter Berns. — New York: Basic Books, c1979. x, 214 p.; 22 cm. 1. Capital punishment 2. Capital punishment — United States. I. T.
HV8694.B5    364.6/6    *LC* 78-73763    *ISBN* 0465024734

**Black, Charles Lund, 1915-.** 4.6849
Capital punishment: the inevitability of caprice and mistake / Charles L. Black, Jr. — 2nd ed. augm. — New York: Norton, c1981. 174 p.; 22 cm. 'First Edition'—Verso t.p. 1. Capital punishment I. T.
HV8698.B47 1981    364.6/6 19    *LC* 81-2824    *ISBN* 0393013332

**Bowers, William J.** 4.6850
Executions in America, [by] William J. Bowers. With the assistance of Andrea Carr and Glenn L. Pierce. Lexington, Mass. Heath [1977] 489p. (Lexington books) 1. Capital punishment — United States 2. Executions and executioners — United States 3. Race discrimination — United States I. T.
HV8699 U5 B68

**McCafferty, James A., comp.** 4.6851
Capital punishment. Edited by James A. McCafferty. — Chicago: Aldine-Atherton, [1972] xii, 273 p.; 22 cm. — (An Atherton controversy) 1. Capital punishment — United States — Addresses, essays, lectures. I. T. II. Series.
HV8699.U5 M3    364.6/6/08    *LC* 74-169503    *ISBN* 0202302385

**Magee, Doug, 1947-.** 4.6852
Slow coming dark: interviews on death row / Doug Magee. — New York: Pilgrim Press, c1980. 181 p.: ill.; 24 cm. 1. Death row — United States — Case studies. 2. Prisoners — United States — Interviews. I. T.
HV8699.U5 M33    364.6/6/0922 B 19    *LC* 80-19747    *ISBN* 0829804005

**Van den Haag, Ernest.** 4.6853
The death penalty: a debate / pro, Ernest van den Haag, con, John P. Conrad. — New York: Plenum Press, c1983. xiv, 305 p.; 23 cm. 1. Capital punishment — United States — Addresses, essays, lectures. I. Conrad, John Phillips, 1913- II. T.
HV8699.U5 V36 1983    364.6/6/0973 19    *LC* 83-11079    *ISBN* 0306414163

**On prison education / edited by Lucien Morin.**    **4.6854**
Quebec: Canadian Government Publishing Centre, Supply & Services Canada, 1982. 332 p.;23 cm. 1. Prisoners — Education I. Morin, Lucien.
HV8875.O6    HV8875 O5.

**Swan, L. Alex (Llewelyn Alex), 1938-.**    **4.6855**
Families of Black prisoners: survival and progress / L. Alex Swan. — Boston, Mass.: G.K. Hall, c1981. x, 163 p.; 24 cm. 1. Prisoners' families — United States. 2. Afro-American prisoners — Family relationships. I. T.
HV8886.U5 S96 1981    362.8/2 19    *LC* 80-25223    *ISBN* 0816184127

**Rudé, George F. E.**    **4.6856**
Protest and punishment: the story of the social and political protesters transported to Australia, 1788–1868 / by George Rudé. — Oxford [Eng.]: Clarendon Press; New York: Oxford University Press, 1978. x, 270 p.; 23 cm. Includes indexes. 1. Penal colonies — Great Britain — History. 2. Dissenters — Great Britain — History. 3. Dissenters — Canada — History. 4. Penal colonies — Australia. 5. Australia — Exiles — History. I. T.
HV8950.A8 R83    365/.3    *LC* 77-30539    *ISBN* 0198224303

**Kopelev, Lev, 1912-.**    **4.6857**
[Khranit' vechno. English] To be preserved forever / Lev Kopelev; translated and edited by Anthony Austin; published and translated under the auspices of Ardis. — Philadelphia: Lippincott, c1977. 268 p., [4] leaves of plates: ill.; 25 cm. Continued by the author's The education of a true believer, published in 1980. Abridged translation of Khranit' vechno. 1. Kopelev, Lev, 1912- 2. Political prisoners — Russia — Biography. I. Austin, Anthony. II. T.
HV8959.R9 K6613 1977    365/.45/0924 B    *LC* 77-1926    *ISBN* 0397011407

**Eriksson, Torsten, 1906-1977.**    **4.6858**
The reformers: an historical survey of pioneer experiments in the treatment of criminals / Torsten Eriksson; translated from the original Swedish text by Catherine Djurklou. — New York: Elsevier Scientific Pub. Co., c1976. 310 p., [7] leaves of plates: ill.; 24 cm. 1. Corrections — History. 2. Prisons — History. I. T.
HV8975.E74    364.6/09    *LC* 76-25049    *ISBN* 0444990305

**Bowker, Lee H.**    **4.6859**
Prison victimization / Lee H. Bowker. — New York: Elsevier, c1980. x, 231 p.; 24 cm. Includes index. 1. Prison violence — United States. I. T.
HV9025.B68    365/.641    *LC* 80-15727    *ISBN* 0444990771

# HV9051–9230 Juvenile Delinquency

## HV9069 GENERAL WORKS

### HV9069 A–H

**Empey, LaMar Taylor, 1923-.**    **4.6860**
Explaining delinquency: construction, test, and reformulation of a sociological theory [by] LaMar T. Empey [and] Steven G. Lubeck, with Ronald L. LaPorte. — Lexington, Mass.: Heath Lexington Books, [1971] xv, 223 p.: ill.; 23 cm. 1. Juvenile delinquency I. Lubeck, Steven G., joint author. II. T.
HV9069.E573 1971    364.36    *LC* 70-158950    *ISBN* 066974641X

**Griffin, Brenda S.**    **4.6861**
Juvenile delinquency in perspective / Brenda S. Griffin, Charles T. Griffin. — New York: Harper & Row, c1978. xxi, 452 p.: ill.; 24 cm. Includes index. 1. Juvenile delinquency 2. Juvenile justice, Administration of 3. Juvenile delinquency — Prevention I. Griffin, Charles T., joint author. II. T.
HV9069.G84    364.36    *LC* 77-13315    *ISBN* 0060425121

**Johnson, Richard E., 1949-.**    **4.6862**
Juvenile delinquency and its origins: an integrated theoretical approach / Richard E. Johnson. — Cambridge [Eng.]; New York: Cambridge University Press, 1979. x, 182 p.; 24 cm. — (The Arnold and Caroline Rose monograph series of the American Sociological Association) Includes index. 1. Juvenile delinquency 2. Criminal behavior, Prediction of I. T.
HV9069.J57    364.3/6 19    *LC* 78-67263    *ISBN* 0521224772

**Juvenile delinquency: a book of readings / [edited by] Rose**    **4.6863**
**Giallombardo.**
4th ed. — New York: Wiley, 1982. viii, 591 p.; 24 cm. 1. Juvenile delinquency — Addresses, essays, lectures. 2. Juvenile justice, Administration of —

Addresses, essays, lectures. 3. Juvenile delinquency — Prevention — Addresses, essays, lectures. 4. Rehabilitation of juvenile delinquents — Addresses, essays, lectures. I. Giallombardo, Rose.
HV9069.J79 1982    364.3/6 19    *LC* 81-6927    *ISBN* 0471083445

### HV9069 K–Z

**Reckless, Walter Cade.**    **4.6864**
The prevention of juvenile delinquency: an experiment / [by] Walter C. Reckless [and] Simon Dinitz. — Columbus: Ohio State University Press, 1972. xvii, 253 p.; 21 cm. Chiefly based on a report of the Ohio State University Research Foundation to the National Institute of Mental Health, May 31, 1970. 1. Juvenile delinquency I. Dinitz, Simon. joint author. II. Ohio State University. Research Foundation. III. T.
HV9069.R413    364.36    *LC* 72-6750    *ISBN* 0814201822

*[handwritten margin note: HV 9069 R413]*

**Sanders, William B., 1944-.**    **4.6865**
Juvenile delinquency / William B. Sanders. — New York: Praeger, 1976. xv, 238 p.; 21 cm. — (Viewpoints in sociology) (Praeger University series) Includes index. 1. Juvenile delinquency 2. Juvenile justice, Administration of I. T.
HV9069.S25    364.36    *LC* 74-15685    *ISBN* 0275223604

**Stott, D. H. (Denis Herbert), 1909-.**    **4.6866**
Delinquency: the problem and its prevention / by Denis Stott. — New York: SP Medical & Scientific Books, c1982. 345 p.; 24 cm. Includes index. 1. Juvenile delinquency 2. Juvenile delinquency — Prevention 3. Juvenile delinquency — United States. 4. Juvenile delinquency — United States — Prevention. I. T.
HV9069.S764 1982    364.3/6 19    *LC* 80-25928    *ISBN* 0893351458

## HV9073–9096 SPECIAL ASPECTS. JUVENILE COURTS

**Hart, Hastings Hornell, 1851-1932.**    **4.6867**
Juvenile court laws in the United States / edited by Hastings H. Hart. — New York: Charities Publication Committee, 1910. [Dubuque, Iowa: Brown Reprints, 1972?]. vii, 150 p. — (The Russell Sage Foundation reprint series) 'A summary by states, by Thomas J. Homer; a topical abstract, by Grace Abbott; and the new juvenile court law of Monroe County, N.Y.' I. Homer, Thomas Johnston, 1858- II. Abbott, Grace, 1878-1939. III. New York (State). Laws, statutes, etc. IV. T.
HV9078.H3x

## HV9101–9230 JUVENILE DELINQUENCY, BY COUNTRY

## HV9103–9106 United States

**Back on the street: the diversion of juvenile offenders /**    **4.6868**
**[compiled by] Robert M. Carter, Malcolm W. Klein.**
Englewood Cliffs, N.J.: Prentice-Hall, 1976. xv, 368 p.: ill.; 23 cm. 1. Juvenile justice, Administration of — United States — Addresses, essays, lectures. 2. Social work with delinquents and criminals — United States — Addresses, essays, lectures. 3. Police services for juveniles — United States — Addresses, essays, lectures. I. Carter, Robert Melvin, 1929- II. Klein, Malcolm W.
HV9104.B33    362.7/4    *LC* 75-22449    *ISBN* 0130553190

**Bartollas, Clemens.**    **4.6869**
Juvenile victimization: the institutional paradox / Clemens Bartollas, Stuart J. Miller, Simon Dinitz. — [Beverly Hills]: Sage Publications; New York: distributed by Halsted Press, c1976. xv, 324 p.: ill.; 24 cm. Includes indexes. 1. Juvenile corrections — United States. 2. Rehabilitation of juvenile delinquents — United States. 3. Prison psychology I. Miller, Stuart J., 1938- joint author. II. Dinitz, Simon. joint author. III. T.
HV9104.B35    365.973    *LC* 76-3476    *ISBN* 0470054905

**Cottle, Thomas J.**    **4.6870**
Children in jail: seven lessons in American justice / Thomas J. Cottle. — Boston: Beacon Press, c1977. xiii, 178 p.; 21 cm. 1. Juvenile delinquency — United States — Case studies. 2. Juvenile corrections — United States — Case studies. I. T.
HV9104.C59 1977    365/.42/0973    *LC* 75-77440    *ISBN* 0807004928

**Elliott, Delbert S.**    **4.6871**
Delinquency and dropout / [by] Delbert S. Elliott [and] Harwin L. Voss. — Lexington, Mass.: Lexington Books, [1974] xvii, 264 p.: ill.; 23 cm. 1. Juvenile

delinquency — United States. 2. Dropouts I. Voss, Harwin L. joint author. II. T.
HV9104.E44    364.36/0973    *LC* 73-19727    *ISBN* 0669919349

**Empey, LaMar Taylor, 1923-.**    **4.6872**
American delinquency, its meaning and construction / LaMar T. Empey. — Homewood, Ill.: Dorsey Press, 1978. xv, 617 p.; 24 cm. — (Dorsey series in sociology.) Includes bibliographies and indexes. 1. Juvenile delinquency — United States. 2. Juvenile justice, Administration of — United States. I. T. II. Series.
HV9104.E56    364.3/6/0973 19    *LC* 77-85787    *ISBN* 0256019851

**Finestone, Harold.**    **4.6873**
Victims of change: juvenile delinquents in American society / Harold Finestone. — Westport, Conn.: Greenwood Press, 1976. 235 p. — (Contributions in sociology; no. 20) Includes index. 1. Juvenile delinquency — United States. I. T.
HV9104.F525    364.36/0973    *LC* 76-5327    *ISBN* 0837188970

**The Juvenile justice system / Malcolm W. Klein, editor.**    **4.6874**
Beverly Hills, Calif.: Sage Publications, c1976. 287 p.; 24 cm. — (Sage criminal justice system annuals. v. 5) 1. Juvenile justice, Administration of — United States — Addresses, essays, lectures. I. Klein, Malcolm W. II. Series.
HV9104.J87    364.3/6/0973 19    *LC* 75-14632    *ISBN* 0803904509.
*ISBN* 0803904517 pbk

**Katkin, Daniel.**    **4.6875**
Juvenile delinquency and the juvenile justice system / Daniel Katkin, Drew Hyman, John Kramer. — North Scituate, Mass.: Duxbury Press, c1976. xv, 462 p.: ill.; 24 cm. Cover title: Delinquency and the juvenile justice system. 1. Juvenile justice, Administration of — United States. 2. Juvenile delinquency — United States. I. Hyman, Drew. joint author. II. Kramer, John, 1943- joint author. III. T. IV. Title: Delinquency and the juvenile justice system.
HV9104.K37    364.3/6/0973 19    *LC* 75-41972    *ISBN* 0878721045

**Kobrin, Solomon.**    **4.6876**
Community treatment of juvenile offenders: the DSO experiments / Solomon Kobrin, Malcolm W. Klein, written with Elaine M. Corry ... [et al.]. — Beverly Hills: Sage Publications, c1983. 341 p.: ill.; 23 cm. Includes indexes. 1. Status offenders — United States. 2. Community-based corrections — United States. 3. Juvenile justice, Administration of — United States — Evaluation. 4. Juvenile delinquency — United States — Prevention. I. Klein, Malcolm W. II. T.
HV9104.K64 1983    364.6/8 19    *LC* 83-13758    *ISBN* 080392108X

**Mennel, Robert M.**    **4.6877**
Thorns & thistles: juvenile delinquents in the United States, 1825–1940 / [by] Robert M. Mennel. — Hanover: Published for the University of New Hampshire by the University Press of New England, 1973. xxvii, 231 p.; 24 cm. 1. Juvenile delinquency — United States — History. 2. Rehabilitation of juvenile delinquents — United States — History. 3. Juvenile courts — United States — History. I. T.
HV9104.M45    364.36/0973    *LC* 72-95187    *ISBN* 0874510708

**Muehlbauer, Gene.**    **4.6878**
The losers: gang delinquency in an American suburb / Gene Muehlbauer and Laura Dodder. — New York, N.Y.: Praeger, 1983. xii, 138 p.; 25 cm. Includes index. 1. Juvenile delinquency — United States — Case studies. 2. Gangs — United States — Case studies. 3. Deviant behavior — Case studies. I. Dodder, Laura. II. T.
HV9104.M82 1983    364.3/6/0973 19    *LC* 82-25497    *ISBN* 0030603137

**Richards, Pamela.**    **4.6879**
Crime as play: delinquency in a middle class suburb / Pamela Richards, Richard A. Berk, Brenda Forster. — Cambridge, Mass.: Ballinger Pub. Co., c1979. xii, 259 p.; 24 cm. Includes index. 1. Juvenile delinquents — United States. 2. Middle classes — United States. 3. Suburban crimes — United States. I. Berk, Richard A. joint author. II. Forster, Brenda, joint author. III. T.
HV9104.R52 1979    364.36    *LC* 79-12772    *ISBN* 0884107981

**Wadsworth, Michael Edwin John.**    **4.6880**
Roots of delinquency: infancy, adolescence, and crime / Michael Wadsworth. — New York: Barnes & Noble Books, 1979. ix, 150 p.; 23 cm. Includes indexes. 1. Juvenile delinquency — United States. 2. Criminal behavior, Prediction of 3. Juvenile delinquents — United States. I. T.
HV9104.W33    364.36/0973    *LC* 79-10065    *ISBN* 0064973050

**Lerman, Paul, 1926-.**    **4.6881**
Community treatment and social control: a critical analysis of juvenile correctional policy / Paul Lerman. — Chicago: University of Chicago Press, [1975] xv, 254 p.; 23 cm. (Studies in crime and justice.) Includes index. 1. Rehabilitation of juvenile delinquents — California. 2. Community-based corrections — California. 3. Social control I. T. II. Series.
HV9105.C2 L47    364.36/09794    *LC* 74-11629    *ISBN* 0226473074

**Shaw, Clifford Robe, 1896- ed.**    • **4.6882**
The jack–roller, a delinquent boy's own story. Chicago, University of Chicago Press [1930] 205 p. ill. (Behavior research fund monographs) The story of 'Stanley' with comments by C.R. Shaw and E.W. Burgess. 1. Juvenile delinquency — Chicago 2. Reformatories — Illinois 3. Child welfare — Chicago I. Burgess, Ernest Watson, 1886-1966. II. T.
HV9105 I3 S5    *LC* 30-16374

**Bakal, Yitzhak.**    **4.6883**
Reforming corrections for juvenile offenders: alternatives and strategies / Yitzhak Bakal, Howard W. Polsky. — Lexington, Mass.: Lexington Books, c1979. xxii, 213 p.: graphs; 24 cm. Includes index. 1. Juvenile corrections — Massachusetts. 2. Community-based corrections — Massachusetts. I. Polsky, Howard W., joint author. II. T.
HV9105.M4 B34    364.6    *LC* 73-11680    *ISBN* 0669902098

**McEwen, Craig A.**    **4.6884**
Designing correctional organizations for youths: dilemmas of subcultural development / Craig A. McEwen; Center for Criminal Justice, Harvard Law School. — Cambridge, Mass.: Ballinger Pub. Co., c1978. xxx, 246 p.; 24 cm. — (Series on Massachusetts youth correction reforms) Includes index. 1. Juvenile corrections — Massachusetts. 2. Community-based corrections — Massachusetts. 3. Subculture I. Harvard University. Center for Criminal Justice. II. T. III. Series.
HV9105.M4 M2    364.6    *LC* 77-27488    *ISBN* 0884107892

**Jack-Roller.**    **4.6885**
The Jack–Roller at seventy: a fifty–year follow–up / the Jack–Roller and Jon Snodgrass, Gilbert Geis, James F. Short, Jr., Solomon Kobrin. — Lexington, Mass.: Lexington Books, c1982. ix, 173 p.; 24 cm. 1. Juvenile delinquency — Illinois — Chicago — Longitudinal studies. I. Snodgrass, Jon. II. T.
HV9106.C4 J24 1982    364.3/6/0977311 19    *LC* 81-47825    *ISBN* 0669049123

**Wolfgang, Marvin E., 1924-.**    **4.6886**
Delinquency in a birth cohort [by] Marvin E. Wolfgang, Robert M. Figlio [and] Thorsten Sellin. Chicago: University of Chicago Press, [1972] x, 327 p.; 23 cm. — (Studies in crime and justice.) 1. Juvenile delinquency — Pennsylvania — Philadelphia — Case studies. I. Figlio, Robert M., joint author. II. Sellin, Johan Thorsten, 1896- III. T. IV. Series.
HV9106.P5 W64    364.36/09748/11    *LC* 75-187929    *ISBN* 0226905535

## HV9107–9230 Other Countries

**West, D. J. (Donald James), 1924-.**    **4.6887**
Delinquency, its roots, careers, and prospects / D.J. West. — Cambridge, Mass.: Harvard University Press, 1982. 186 p.; 23 cm. Includes indexes. 1. Juvenile delinquency — England — London. I. T.
HV9146.L65 W47 1982    HV9146L65 W47.    364.3/6/09421 19

**Melossi, Dario, 1948-.**    **4.6888**
[Carcere e fabbrica. English] The prison and the factory: origins of the penitentiary system / Dario Melossi and Massimo Pavarini; translated by Glynis Cousin. — Totowa, N.J.: Barnes and Noble Books, 1981. xii, 243 p.; 22 cm. Translation of: Carcere e fabbrica. 1. Prisons — Italy — History. 2. Convict labor — Italy — History. I. Pavarini, Massimo, 1947- II. T.
HV9163.M4413 1981    365/.945 19    *LC* 81-10838    *ISBN* 0389201901

**Wagatsuma, Hiroshi, 1927-.**    **4.6889**
Heritage of endurance: family patterns and delinquency formation in urban Japan / Hiroshi Wagatsuma and George A. De Vos. — Berkeley: University of California Press, c1984. xii, 500 p.: ill.; 24 cm. Includes index. 1. Juvenile delinquency — Japan — Tokyo — Psychological aspects. 2. Family — Japan — Tokyo — Psychological aspects. 3. Personality and culture — Japan — Tokyo. I. De Vos, George A. II. T.
HV9207.A5 W33 1984    364.3/6/0952135 19    *LC* 76-7770    *ISBN* 0520032225

## HV9261–9430 Reformation. Rehabilitation

**Fox, Vernon Brittain, 1916-.**    **4.6890**
Community–based corrections / Vernon Fox. Englewood Cliffs, N.J.: Prentice-Hall, c1977. xv, 320 p.: ill.; 24 cm. Includes index. 1. Community-based corrections 2. Community-based corrections — United States. I. T.
HV9275.F67    364.6    *LC* 76-6879    *ISBN* 0131532545

**Palmer, Ted.**      **4.6891**
Correctional intervention and research: current issues and future prospects / Ted Palmer. — Lexington, Mass.: Lexington Books, c1978. xxiii, 273 p.; 24 cm. Includes index. 1. Corrections 2. Corrections — Research. 3. Corrections — United States. I. T.
HV9275.P34    364.6    *LC* 77-25777    *ISBN* 0669021660

**United States. Task Force on Corrections.**     • **4.6892**
Task Force report: corrections. — [Washington: For sale by the Supt. of Docs., U.S. Govt. Print. Off., 1967] xiii, 222 p.: illus.; 28 cm. 1. Corrections — United States. I. T. II. Title: Corrections.
HV9304.A5 1967    364/.9/73    *LC* 67-61469

**Bartollas, Clemens.**      **4.6893**
Correctional treatment: theory and practice / Clemens Bartollas. — Englewood Cliffs, N.J.: Prentice-Hall, c1985. xvi, 304 p.: ill.; 24 cm. Includes index. 1. Corrections — United States. 2. Rehabilitation — United States. 3. Prisoners — Psychiatric care — United States. 4. Correctional psychology I. T.
HV9304.B36 1985    364.6/0973 19    *LC* 84-4702    *ISBN* 0131783289

**Clear, Todd R.**      **4.6894**
Controlling the offender in the community: reforming the community supervision function / Todd R. Clear, Vincent O'Leary. — Lexington, Mass.: Lexington Books, c1983. xvii, 189 p.; 24 cm. 1. Community-based corrections — United States. I. O'Leary, Vincent. II. T.
HV9304.C58 1983    364.6/8 19    *LC* 81-47444    *ISBN* 0669046337

**Corrections and punishment** / David F. Greenberg, editor.      **4.6895**
Beverly Hills, Calif.: Sage Publications, c1977. 288 p.; 23 cm. — (Sage criminal justice system annuals. v. 8) 1. Corrections — Social aspects — United States — Addresses, essays, lectures. 2. Punishment — Social aspects — United States — Addresses, essays, lectures. I. Greenberg, David F. II. Series.
HV9304.C675    364.6/0973    *LC* 77-79870    *ISBN* 0803906005

**Hickey, Joseph E.**      **4.6896**
Toward a just correctional system / Joseph E. Hickey, Peter L. Scharf. — 1st ed. — San Francisco: Jossey-Bass, 1980. xx, 202 p.; 24 cm. — (The Jossey-Bass social and behavioral science series) Includes index. 1. Corrections — United States. 2. Prisons — United States. 3. Prisoners — Legal status, laws, etc. — United States. I. Scharf, Peter, 1945- joint author. II. T.
HV9304.H53    365/.973 19    *LC* 79-88112    *ISBN* 0875893961

**Schmidt, Janet.**      **4.6897**
Demystifying parole / Janet Schmidt. Lexington, Mass.: Lexington Books, c1977. xviii, 177 p.; 24 cm. Includes bibliographical references and index. 1. United States. Board of Parole. 2. Parole — United States. I. T.
IIV9304.S34    364.6/2/0973    *LC* 76-48375    *ISBN* 0669011452

**Stanley, David T.**      **4.6898**
Prisoners among us: the problem of parole / David T. Stanley. — Washington: Brookings Institution, c1976. xvii, 205 p.; 24 cm. Includes index. 1. Parole — United States. 2. Parole officers — United States. 3. Community-based corrections — United States. I. T.
HV9304.S7    364.6/2/0973    *LC* 75-44506    *ISBN* 0815781067

**Hosford, Ray E., 1933-.**      **4.6899**
The crumbling walls: treatment and counseling of prisoners / edited by Ray E. Hosford and C. Scott Moss. — Urbana: University of Illinois Press, [1975] xiv, 257 p.: ill.; 24 cm. 1. Rehabilitation of criminals — California — Addresses, essays, lectures. 2. Correctional psychology — Addresses, essays, lectures. 3. Corrections — California — Addresses, essays, lectures. I. Moss, Claude Scott, 1924- joint author. II. T.
HV9305.C2 H68 1975    364.6    *LC* 74-23266    *ISBN* 0252004248

**Augustus, John, 1785-1859.**      **4.6900**
[Report of the labors of John Augustus] John Augustus: first probation officer. John Augustus' original Report of his labors (1852) with an introd. by Sheldon Glueck. Reprinted with a new pref. and an index. Montclair, N.J., Patterson Smith, 1972. xxix, 110 p. illus. 22 cm. (Patterson Smith reprint series in criminology, law enforcement, and social problems. Publication no. 130) First published in 1852 under title: A report of the labors of John Augustus, for the last ten years, in aid of the unfortunate ... Reprint of the 1939 ed. 1. Probation — Massachusetts — Boston. 2. Charities — Massachusetts — Boston. I. T.
HV9306.B7 A8 1972    364.6/3/0924 B    *LC* 79-129308    *ISBN* 0875851304

**Hartjen, Clayton A 1943-.**      **4.6901**
Delinquency in India: a comparative analysis / Clayton A. Hartjen, S. Priyadarsini. — New Brunswick, N.J.: Rutgers University Press, c1984. xiv, 252 p.: ill.; 24 cm. — (Crime, law, and deviance series.) Includes index. 1. Juvenile delinquency — India — Tamil Nadu. 2. Juvenile justice, Administration of — India — Tamil Nadu. 3. Juvenile delinquency — India —

Tamil Nadu — Public opinion. 4. Public opinion — India — Tamil Nadu. I. Priyadarsini, S., 1943- II. T. III. Series.
HV9399.T35 H37 1984    364.3/6/095482 19    *LC* 82-16693    *ISBN* 0813509971

# HV9441-9920 PENOLOGY, BY COUNTRY

## HV9456-9499 United States

**Freedman, Estelle B., 1947-.**      **4.6902**
Their sisters' keepers: women's prison reform in America, 1830–1930 / Estelle B. Freedman. — Ann Arbor: University of Michigan Press, c1981. viii, 248 p.; 24 cm. — (Women and culture series.) Based on the author's thesis, Columbia University. Includes index. 1. Reformatories for women — United States — History. 2. Prison reformers — United States — History. I. T. II. Series.
HV9466.F73    365/.43/0973 19    *LC* 80-24918    *ISBN* 0472100084

**McKelvey, Blake, 1903-.**      **4.6903**
American prisons: a history of good intentions / Blake McKelvey. Montclair, N.J.: P. Smith, c1977. xv, 408 p., [10] leaves of plates: ill.; 24 cm. 1. Prisons — United States — History. I. T.
HV9466.M3 1977    365/.973    *LC* 75-14556    *ISBN* 0875857043

**Stastny, Charles.**      **4.6904**
Who rules the joint?: the changing political culture of maximum–security prisons in America / Charles Stastny, Gabrielle Tyrnauer. — Lexington, Mass.: Lexington Books, c1982. xix, 234 p.: ill.; 24 cm. Includes index. 1. Prisons — United States — History. 2. Prison administration — United States — History. 3. Prison reformers — United States — History. 4. Power (Social sciences) I. Tyrnauer, Gabrielle. II. T.
HV9466.S7 1982    365/.973 19    *LC* 78-14157    *ISBN* 0669026611

**Abbott, Jack Henry, 1944-.**      **4.6905**
In the belly of the beast: letters from prison / Jack Henry Abbott; with an introduction by Norman Mailer. — 1st ed. — New York: Random House, c1981. xvi, 166 p.; 22 cm. 1. Abbott, Jack Henry, 1944- 2. Prisoners — United States — Biography. 3. Prisons — United States. I. T.
HV9468.A22 A37    365/.44/0924 B 19    *LC* 80-6038    *ISBN* 0394518586

**Coed prison** / [edited by] John Ortiz Smykla.      **4.6906**
New York: Human Sciences Press, c1980. 306 p.; 22 cm. Includes index. 1. Prisons, Coeducational — United States — Addresses, essays, lectures. 2. Prisons, Coeducational — United States — Bibliography. 3. Women prisoners — United States — Addresses, essays, lectures. I. Smykla, John Ortiz.
HV9469.C63    365/.3 19    *LC* 79-17202    *ISBN* 087705410X

**Cordilia, Ann.**      **4.6907**
The making of an inmate: prison as a way of life / by Ann Cordilia. — Cambridge, Mass.: Schenkman Pub. Co. c1983. xvi, 133 p.; 22 cm. 1. Prisoners — United States — Attitudes. 2. Ex-convicts — United States — Attitudes. 3. Socialization 4. Prison psychology I. T.
HV9471.C667 1983    365/.6/019 19    *LC* 82-20447    *ISBN* 0870737228

**Corrections in the community: success models in correctional reform** / [edited by] E. Eugene Miller, M. Robert Montilla.      **4.6908**
Reston, Va.: Reston Pub. Co., c1977. xxiii, 291 p.; 24 cm. 1. Community-based corrections — United States — Addresses, essays, lectures. I. Miller, E. Eugene. II. Montilla, M. Robert.
HV9471.C67    364.6    *LC* 76-56136    *ISBN* 0879091746

**Davis, Angela Yvonne, 1944-.**      **4.6909**
If they come in the morning; voices of resistance [by] Angela Y. Davis [and others] Foreword by Julian Bond. — New York: Third Press, [1971] vi, 281 p.; 21 cm. 'A Joseph Okpaku book.' 1. Political prisoners — United States. 2. Prisons — United States. 3. Prisoners' writings — United States. I. T.
HV9471.D38    365/.45    *LC* 71-169154    *ISBN* 0893880221

**Goldfarb, Ronald L.**      **4.6910**
Jails, the ultimate ghetto / Ronald Goldfarb. — 1st ed. — Garden City, N.Y.: Anchor Press, 1975. 470 p. 22 cm. 1. Jails — United States. 2. Juvenile detention homes — United States. I. T.
HV9471.G64    365/.973    *LC* 74-9450    *ISBN* 0385097840

**Keve, Paul W.**      **4.6911**
Prison life and human worth / by Paul W. Keve. — Minneapolis: University of Minnesota Press, [1974] vi, 199 p.; 23 cm. Includes index. 1. Prisons — United

*[handwritten margin notes: BL ST] E 185.61 D38 1971]*

States. 2. Correctional institutions — United States. 3. Parole — United States. I. T.
HV9471.K4    365/.973    *LC* 74-84252    *ISBN* 0816607346

**Mitford, Jessica, 1917-.**    **4.6912**
Kind and usual punishment; the prison business. [1st ed.] New York, Knopf; [distributed by Random House] 1973. xi, 340, xi p. 22 cm. 1. Prisons — United States. 2. Corrections — United States. I. T.
HV9471.M58 1973    365/.973    *LC* 73-7263    *ISBN* 0394476026

**Pontell, Henry N., 1950-.**    **4.6913**
A capacity to punish: the ecology of crime and punishment / Henry N. Pontell. — Bloomington: Indiana University Press, c1984. xii, 140 p.: ill.; 24 cm. Includes index. 1. Criminal justice, Administration of — United States 2. Crime and criminals — United States 3. Punishment — United States. 4. Crime prevention — United States. I. T.
HV9471.P66 1984    364/.973 19    *LC* 83-48107    *ISBN* 0253313090

**Alabama bound: forty–five years inside a prison system / [edited    4.6914
by] Ray A. March.**
University: University of Alabama Press, c1978. ix, 204 p., [3] leaves of plates: ill.; 22 cm. Includes index. 1. Prisons — Alabama. 2. Punishment — Alabama. 3. Corrections — Alabama. 4. Prisons — Alabama — Officials and employees — Interviews. I. March, Ray A., 1934-
HV9475.A2 A5    365/.9761    *LC* 77-3352    *ISBN* 0817344063

**Yee, Min S.**    **4.6915**
The melancholy history of Soledad Prison: in which a utopian scheme turns bedlam / [by] Min S. Yee. — [1st ed.]. — New York: Harper's Magazine Press, [1973] xv, 268 p.; 22 cm. 1. Jackson, George, 1941-1971. 2. Soledad Correctional Training Facility. 3. Prison riots — California — Case studies. I. T.
HV9475.C3 S68 1973    365/.9794/76    *LC* 72-12097    *ISBN* 006129800X

**New York (State). Special Commission on Attica.**    **4.6916**
Attica; the official report of the New York State Special Commission on Attica. New York, Praeger, c1972. 533 p. ill. 21 cm. 1. Attica Prison. 2. Prison riots — Attica, New York. I. T.
HV 9475 N716 N53 1972    *LC* 72-92084

**Cardozo-Freeman, Inez.**    **4.6917**
The joint: language and culture in a maximum security prison / by Inez Cardozo–Freeman, in collaboration with Eugene P. Delorme; with the technical assistance of David W. Maurer and Robert A. Freeman; with a foreword by Simon Dinitz. — Springfield, Ill., U.S.A.: Thomas, c1984. xxi, 579 p.; 24 cm. Includes index. 1. Washington State Penitentiary. 2. Prisoners — Washington (State) — Language. 3. Prisoners — Washington (State) — Attitudes. 4. Prison psychology I. Delorme, Eugene P. II. T.
HV9475.W22 W373 1984    365/.6/0979748 19    *LC* 83-9266    *ISBN* 0398049114

## HV9501–9920 Other Countries

**Ignatieff, Michael.**    **4.6918**
A just measure of pain: the penitentiary in the industrial revolution, 1750–1850 / Michael Ignatieff. — 1st ed. — New York: Pantheon Books, c1978. xiii, 257 p., [8] leaves of plates: ill.; 24 cm. Originally presented as the author's thesis, Harvard. 1. Prisons — Great Britain — History. I. T.
HV9644.I36 1978    365/.942    *LC* 78-51808    *ISBN* 0394410416

**Fitzgerald, Mike, 1951-.**    **4.6919**
British prisons / Mike Fitzgerald and Joe Sim. — 2nd ed. — Oxford: Blackwell, 1982. 182 p.; 22 cm. Includes index. 1. Prisons — Great Britain. 2. Prisoners — Great Britain. 3. Imprisonment — Great Britain. I. Sim, Joe. II. T.
HV9647.F5 1982    365/.941 19    *LC* 81-174513    *ISBN* 0631126066

**Jones, Howard, 1918-.**    **4.6920**
Open prisons / Howard Jones and Paul Cornes; assisted by Richard Stockford. — London; Boston: Routledge & K. Paul, 1977. ix, 275 p.; 22 cm. — (International library of social policy) 1. Open prisons — Great Britain. I. Cornes, Paul. joint author. II. Stockford, Richard. III. T.
HV9647.J66    365/.3    *LC* 77-30063    *ISBN* 0710086024

**Spierenburg, Petrus Cornelis.**    **4.6921**
The spectacle of suffering: executions and the evolution of repression: from a preindustrial metropolis to the European experience / Pieter Spierenburg. — Cambridge [Cambridgeshire]; New York: Cambridge University Press, 1984. xii, 274 p.; 24 cm. Revision of the author's thesis (University of Amsterdam, 1978) under the title: Judicial violence in the Dutch Republic. Includes index. 1. Punishment — Amsterdam — History. 2. Punishment — Netherlands — History. 3. Punishment — Europe — History. I. T.
HV9710.A47 S64 1984    364.6/094 19    *LC* 84-3195    *ISBN* 0521261864

**Solzhenitsyn, Aleksandr Isaevich, 1918-.**    **4.6922**
[Arkhipelag GULag, 1918-1956. English] The Gulag Archipelago, 1918–1956; an experiment in literary investigation [by] Aleksandr I. Solzhenitsyn. Translated from the Russian by Thomas P. Whitney. [1st ed.] New York, Harper & Row [1974-78] 3 v. illus. 24 cm. Translation of Arkhipelag GULag, 1918-1956. Vol. 3 translated by H. Willetts. 1. Prisons — Soviet Union. 2. Political prisoners — Soviet Union. 3. Concentration camps — Soviet Union. I. T.
HV9713.S6413 1974    365/.45/0947    *LC* 73-22756    *ISBN* 0060139145

**Soyinka, Wole.**    **4.6923**
The man died: prison notes of Wole Soyinka. — [1st U.S. ed.]. — New York: Harper & Row, [c1972] 317 p.; 22 cm. 1. Political prisoners — Nigeria — Personal narratives. I. T.
HV9849.N5 S68 1972    365/.6/0924 B    *LC* 72-10685    *ISBN* 0060139722

# HX1–15 SOCIETIES. COLLECTIONS

**The American radical press, 1880–1960. Edited with an introd.** **4.6924**
**by Joseph R. Conlin.**
Westport, Conn.: Greenwood Press, [1974] 2 v. (xiv, 720 p.); 21 cm. Essays on various periodicals, many having been written as introductions for Greenwood Press' Radical reprint series. 1. Socialism — Periodicals — History. 2. Communism — Periodicals — History. 3. Radicalism — Periodicals — History. 4. Labor and laboring classes — United States — Periodicals — History. I. Conlin, Joseph Robert. ed.
HX1.A49    335/.00973    LC 72-9825    ISBN 083716625X

**MacKenzie, Norman Ian.** **4.6925**
The Fabians / Norman and Jeanne MacKenzie. — New York: Simon and Schuster, c1977. 446 p., [8] leaves of plates: ill.; 24 cm. 1. Fabian Society (Great Britain) I. MacKenzie, Jeanne. joint author. II. T.
HX11.F5 M33    335/.14    LC 76-41350    ISBN 067122347X

**Communist International.** **4.6926**
The Communist International, 1919–1943; documents, selected and edited by Jane Degras. — [London]: F. Cass, 1971. 3 v.; 25 cm. 'Originally issued under the auspices of the Royal Institute of International Affairs.' Reprint of the 1956-65 ed. 1. Communism — History — Sources. I. Degras, Jane Tabrisky, 1905- ed. II. Royal Institute of International Affairs. III. T.
HX11.I5 A5314 1971    329/.072    LC 72-182920    ISBN 0714615544

**Joll, James.** **4.6927**
The Second International, 1889–1914 / James Joll. — Rev. and extended ed. — London; Boston: Routledge & K. Paul, 1975 (c1974). viii, 224 p.; 23 cm. Includes index. 1. International Socialist Congress. I. T.
HX11.I5 J6 1974    324/.1 19    LC 75-306923    ISBN 0710079664

# HX21–63 HISTORY. BIOGRAPHY

**Laidler, Harry Wellington, 1884-1970.** • **4.6928**
History of socialism; a comparative survey of socialism, communism, trade unionism, cooperation, utopianism, and other systems of reform and reconstruction [by] Harry W. Laidler. — [Updated and expanded ed.]. — New York: Crowell, [1968] xx, 970 p.: illus., ports.; 24 cm. 1944 and 1949 ed. published under title: Social-economic movements. 1. Socialism — History. 2. Communism — History 3. Utopias I. T.
HX21.L37 1968    335/.009    LC 67-29698

# HX36–39 19th Century

**Berki, R. N.** **4.6929**
Socialism / R. N. Berki. — New York: St. Martin's Press, 1976 (c1975). 184 p.; 22 cm. Includes index. 1. Socialism I. T.
HX36.B43 1975b    335/.009    LC 75-7713

**Buber, Martin, 1878-1965.** • **4.6930**
Paths in Utopia. Translated by R.F.C. Hull; introd. by Ephraim Fischoff. Boston: Beacon Hill, 1958. 152 p.; 21 cm. 1. Socialism — History. 2. Communism — History 3. Cooperation — History. I. T.
HX36.B8 1958    335.09    LC 59-375

**Cole, G. D. H. (George Douglas Howard), 1889-1959.** • **4.6931**
A history of socialist thought. New York: St. Martin's Press, 1953-60. 5 v.; 23 cm. Bibliography: v. 1, p. 317-332. 1. Socialism — History I. T.
HX36.C58    335.09    LC 53-1067

**Harrington, Michael, 1928-.** **4.6932**
Socialism. — New York: Saturday Review Press, [1972] 436 p.; 25 cm. 1. Socialism I. T.
HX36.H36    335    LC 76-154260    ISBN 0841501416

**Hobsbawm, E. J. (Eric J.), 1917-.** **4.6933**
Revolutionaries: contemporary essays / [by] E. J. Hobsbawm. — [1st American ed.] New York: Pantheon Books [1973] viii, 278 p.; 23 cm. 1. Communism — Addresses, essays, lectures. 2. Anarchism and anarchists — Addresses, essays, lectures. 3. Violence — Addresses, essays, lectures. I. T.
HX36.H57    322.4/2    LC 73-4973    ISBN 0394487753

**Hunt, Robert Nigel Carew.** • **4.6934**
The theory and practice of communism, an introduction. — [5th rev. ed.]. — New York: Macmillan, 1957. 286 p.; 22 cm. 1. Communism — History I. T.
HX36.H8 1957a    335.409    LC 57-9367

**Jacoby, Russell.** **4.6935**
Dialectic of defeat: contours of Western Marxism / Russell Jacoby. — Cambridge; New York: Cambridge University Press, 1981. x, 202 p.; 24 cm. 1. Marx, Karl, 1818-1883. 2. Communism — History 3. Communism and philosophy I. T.
HX36.J22    335.4/09 19    LC 81-3904    ISBN 052123915X

**Kiernan, V. G. (Victor Gordon), 1913-.** **4.6936**
Marxism and imperialism: studies / by V. G. Kiernan. — New York: St. Martin's Press, 1975, c1974. xi, 260 p.; 23 cm. 1. Socialism — History. 2. Communism — History 3. Imperialism — History. I. T.
HX36.K5 1975    321/.03    LC 74-17723

**Kołakowski, Leszek.** **4.6937**
[Główne nurty marksizmu. English] Main currents of Marxism: its rise, growth, and dissolution / by Leszek Kołakowski; translated from the Polish by P. S. Falla. — Oxford: Clarendon Press, 1978. 3 v.; 22 cm. Translation of Główne nurty marksizmu. 1. Socialism — History. 2. Communism — History I. T.
HX36.K61813    335.4/09    LC 78-40247    ISBN 0198245475

**Lichtheim, George, 1912-.** • **4.6938**
Marxism: an historical and critical study / by George Lichtheim. — New York: Praeger, 1961. xx, 412 p. — (Books that matter) 1. Socialism — History. 2. Communism — History I. T.
HX36.L48    LC 61-8694

**McLellan, David.** **4.6939**
Marxism after Marx: an introduction / David McLellan. — 1st U.S. ed. — New York: Harper & Row, [1980] c1979. ix, 355 p.; 24 cm. 1. Communism — History I. T.
HX36.M23 1980    335.43/09    LC 79-1675    ISBN 0060130261

**Ulam, Adam Bruno, 1922-.** **4.6940**
The unfinished revolution: Marxism and communism in the modern world / Adam B. Ulam. — Rev. ed. — Boulder, Colo.: Westview Press, 1979. xiii, 287 p.; 24 cm. 1. Socialism — History. 2. Communism — History I. T.
HX36.U42 1979    335/.009 19    LC 79-700    ISBN 0891584854

**Wilson, Edmund, 1895-1972.** • **4.6941**
To the Finland station: a study in the writing and acting of history / with a new introd. — New York: Farrar, Straus and Giroux, [1972] xviii, 590 p.; 20 cm. 1. Socialism — History. 2. Communism — History 3. History — Philosophy I. T.
HX36.W5 1972    335/.009    LC 77-187695    ISBN 0374278334

**Lichtheim, George, 1912-.** • **4.6942**
The origins of socialism. — New York: Praeger, [1969] xii, 302 p.; 21 cm. 1. Socialism — History. I. T.
HX39.L48    335/.009    LC 69-10520

**Taylor, Keith.** **4.6943**
The political ideas of the utopian socialists / Keith Taylor. — London; Totowa, N.J.: Cass, 1982. ix, 238 p.; 22 cm. Includes index. 1. Socialism — History — 19th century. 2. Socialism — Philosophy — History — 19th century. 3. Utopias — History — 19th century. 4. Socialists — Biography. I. T.
HX39.T38 1982    321/.07 19    LC 82-184995    ISBN 0714630896

## HX39.5 Karl Marx

**Marx, Karl, 1818-1883.**     **4.6944**
[Works. English. 1975] Karl Marx, Frederick Engels: collected works / [translators: Richard Dixon and others] New York: International Publishers, 1975. 2 v.: ill.; 23 cm. Includes index. 1. Socialism — Collected works. 2. Economics — Collected works. I. Engels, Friedrich, 1820-1895. Works. English. 1975 II. T.
HX39.5.A213 1975    335.4 19    *LC* 73-84671    *ISBN* 0717804070

**Marx, Karl, 1818-1883.**     **4.6945**
[Selections. English] Karl Marx: economy, class and social revolution / edited and with an introductory essay by Z. A. Jordan. — New York: Scribner, [1975] c1971. xi, 332 p.; 23 cm. Includes index. 1. Socialism — Collected works. 2. Sociology — Collected works. I. Jordan, Zbigniew A. ed. II. T. III. Title: Economy, class and social revolution.
HX39.5.A224 1975    335.4/12    *LC* 74-3770    *ISBN* 0684139464

**Marx, Karl, 1818-1883.**     **4.6946**
[Selections] Selected writings / Karl Marx; edited by David McLellan. — Oxford [Eng.]: Oxford University Press, 1977. ix, 625 p.; 25 cm. Includes indexes. 1. Socialism — Collected works. I. McLellan, David. II. T.
HX39.5.A224 1977b    335.4/1    *LC* 77-5704    *ISBN* 019876037X. *ISBN* 0198760388 pbk

**Marx, Karl, 1818-1883.**     • **4.6947**
The Marx–Engels reader / edited by Robert C. Tucker. — 2d ed. — New York: Norton, c1978. xlii, 788 p.; 22 cm. 1. Communism — Collected works. 2. Socialism — Collected works. I. Engels, Friedrich, 1820-1895. II. Tucker, Robert C. III. T.
HX 39.5 A224 M39 1978    *LC* 77-16635    *ISBN* 0393056848

**Avineri, Shlomo.**     • **4.6948**
[Mishnato ha-hevratit veha-medinit shel Karl Marks. English] The social and political thought of Karl Marx. London, Cambridge U.P., 1968. viii, 269 p. 23 cm. (Cambridge studies in the history and theory of politics) Translation of Mishnato ha-hevratit veha-medinit shel Karl Marks. 1. Marx, Karl, 1818-1883. I. T.
HX39.5.A853    335.4    *LC* 68-12055    *ISBN* 052104071X

**Berlin, Isaiah, Sir.**     • **4.6949**
Karl Marx; his life and environment. — 3d ed. — London; New York: Oxford University Press, 1963. 295 p.; 17 cm. — (The Home university library of modern knowledge, 189) 1. Marx, Karl, 1818-1883. I. T.
HX39.5.B4 1963    .923.343    *LC* 64-1146

**Buchanan, Allen E., 1948-.**     **4.6950**
Marx and justice: the radical critique of liberalism / Allen E. Buchanan. — London: Methuen, 1982. xiv, 206 p.; 24 cm. Includes index. 1. Marx, Karl, 1818-1883. 2. Liberalism 3. Justice 4. Civil rights I. T.
HX39.5.B79 1982b    335.4/01 19    *ISBN* 0416334504

**Elster, Jon, 1940-.**     **4.6951**
Making sense of Marx / Jon Elster. — Cambridge [Cambridgeshire]; New York: Cambridge University Press; Paris: Editions de la Maison des sciences de l'homme, 1985. xv, 556 p.; 24 cm. (Studies in Marxism and social theory.) Includes indexes. 1. Marx, Karl, 1818-1883. 2. Marxian school of sociology I. T. II. Series.
HX39.5.E44 1985    335.4 19    *LC* 84-17640    *ISBN* 0521228964

**Evans, Michael, 1936-.**     **4.6952**
Karl Marx. — Bloomington: Indiana University Press, [1975] 215 p.; 23 cm. 1. Marx, Karl, 1818-1883. I. T.
HX39.5.E9 1975    320.5/32/0924 B    *LC* 74-15712    *ISBN* 0253331722

**Fromm, Erich, 1900- ed.**     • **4.6953**
Marx's concept of man / with a translation from Marx's Economic and philosophical manuscripts by T. B. Bottomore. — New York: F. Ungar Pub. Co. [1961] xii, 260 p. (Milestones of thought in the history of ideas) 1. Marx, Karl, 1818-1883. I. Marx, Karl, 1818-1883. II. T.
HX39.5 F7    *LC* 61-11935

**Harrington, Michael, 1928-.**     **4.6954**
The twilight of capitalism / by Michael Harrington. — New York: Simon and Schuster, c1976. 446 p.; 22 cm. Includes index. 1. Marx, Karl, 1818-1883. 2. United States — Economic policy — 1971-1981 3. United States — Social policy I. T.
HX39.5.H28    335.4    *LC* 75-41465    *ISBN* 0671221965

**McLellan, David.**     **4.6955**
Karl Marx: his life and thought. — [1st U.S. ed.]. — New York: Harper & Row, 1973. xii, 498 p.; ill.; 24 cm. 1. Marx, Karl, 1818-1883. I. T.
HX39.5.M26    335.4/092/4 B    *LC* 73-4104    *ISBN* 0060128291

**McLellan, David.**     • **4.6956**
Marx before Marxism. — [1st U.S. ed.]. — New York: Harper & Row, [1970] viii, 233 p.: map.; 22 cm. 1. Marx, Karl, 1818-1883. I. Marx, Karl, 1818-1883. II. T.
HX39.5.M27 1970b    335.4/0924 B    *LC* 70-105231

**Maguire, John M.**     **4.6957**
Marx's Paris writings: an analysis / John Maguire; with an introd. by David McLellan. — New York: Harper & Row, 1973. xxiv, 170 p. 1. Marx, Karl, 1818-1883. 2. Socialism I. T.
HX39.5.M32 1973    *ISBN* 0064945057

**Marxism / edited by J. Roland Pennock and John W. Chapman.**     **4.6958**
New York: New York University Press, 1983. xv, 342 p.; 22 cm. — (Nomos; 26) Includes index. 1. Marx, Karl, 1818-1883 — Congresses. I. Pennock, J. Roland (James Roland), 1906- II. Chapman, John William, 1923- III. Series.
HX39.5.M377 1983    335.4 19    *LC* 83-8360    *ISBN* 0814765866

**Mehring, Franz, 1846-1919.**     • **4.6959**
Karl Marx: the story of his life / by Franz Mehring; translated by Edward Fitzgerald; new introd. by Max Shactman. — [Ann Arbor, Mic.]: University of Michigan Press, 1962. 575 p.: ill. (Ann Arbor paperbacks for the study of communism and Marxism; AA73) 1. Marx, Karl, 1818-1883. 2. Communists — Biography. I. T.
HX39.5.M4163 1962    335.40924    *LC* 62-53142    *ISBN* 0472060732 pbk

**Seigel, Jerrold E.**     **4.6960**
Marx's fate: the shape of a life / by Jerrold Seigel. — Princeton, N.J.: Princeton University Press, c1978. ix, 451 p.; 24 cm. 1. Marx, Karl, 1818-1883. 2. Communists — Biography. 3. Socialism I. T.
HX39.5.S36    335.4/092/4 B    *LC* 77-85563    *ISBN* 069105259X

**Suchting, W. A. (Wallis Arthur)**     **4.6961**
Marx, an introduction / W.A. Suchting. — New York: New York University Press, 1983. xxii, 242 p.: ill.; 23 cm. Includes index. 1. Marx, Karl, 1818-1883. I. T.
HX39.5.S92 1983    335.4/092/4 19    *LC* 83-8034    *ISBN* 0814778313

**Swingewood, Alan.**     **4.6962**
Marx and modern social theory / Alan Swingewood. — New York: Wiley, [1975] 247 p.; 22 cm. 'A Halsted Press book.' Includes index. 1. Marx, Karl, 1818-1883. 2. Communism and society 3. Sociology — History I. T.
HX39.5.S97 1975    335.4/1    *LC* 75-4554    *ISBN* 0470839988

**Tönnies, Ferdinand, 1855-1936.**     **4.6963**
[Karl Marx, Leben und Lehre. English] Karl Marx, his life and teachings (Leben und Lehre) / by Ferdinand Tönnies; translated from the German by Charles P. Loomis and Ingeborg Paulus. — [East Lansing]: Michigan State University Press, 1974. xvi, 169 p.; 24 cm. Translation of Karl Marx, Leben und Lehre. 1. Marx, Karl, 1818-1883. I. T.
HX39.5.T5613 1974    335.4/092/4 B    *LC* 73-91768    *ISBN* 0870131818

**Tucker, Robert C.**     • **4.6964**
The Marxian revolutionary idea / [by] Robert C. Tucker. — [1st ed.] New York: Norton [1969] xi, 240 p.; 22 cm. 'A publication of the Center of International Studies, Princeton University.' 1. Marx, Karl, 1818-1883. 2. Socialism 3. Revolutions 4. Communism and society I. Woodrow Wilson School of Public and International Affairs. Center of International Studies. II. T.
HX39.5.T8    335.41/0924    *LC* 69-20038

# HX40–44 20th Century

**Claudín, Fernando.**     **4.6965**
[Crisis del movimiento comunista. English] The Communist movement: from Comintern to Cominform / Fernando Claudin. — New York: Monthly Review Press, 1976 (c1975). 2 v.; 21 cm. Translation of La crisis del movimiento comunista. Pt. 1 translated by B. Pearce; pt. 2 translated by F. MacDonagh. 1. Communism — History I. T.
HX40.C59813    335.43    *LC* 74-25015    *ISBN* 0853453667

**Comparative communism: the Soviet, Chinese, and Yugoslav models / [compiled by] Gary K. Bertsch and Thomas W. Ganschow.**     **4.6966**
San Francisco: W. H. Freeman, c1976. ix, 463 p.; 24 cm. 1. Communism — 20th century — Addresses, essays, lectures. 2. Communism — Russia — Addresses, essays, lectures. 3. Communism — China — Addresses, essays,

lectures. 4. Communism — Yugoslavia — Addresses, essays, lectures. I. Bertsch, Gary Kenneth, 1944- II. Ganschow, Thomas W. HX40.C735    HX40 C675.    335.43/4    LC 75-20464    *ISBN* 0716707330

**Hook, Sidney, 1902-.**                                                      • **4.6967**
Marx and the Marxists; the ambiguous legacy. — Princeton, N.J.: Van Nostrand, [1955] 254 p.; 18 cm. — (An Anvil original, no. 7) 1. Socialism — History. 2. Communism — History I. T. HX40.H6    335.4/09 19    *LC* 55-11286

**Lane, David Stuart.**                                                       **4.6968**
Leninism: a sociological interpretation / David Lane. — Cambridge [Eng.]; New York: Cambridge University Press, 1981. x, 150 p.; 24 cm. — (Themes in the social sciences.) Includes index. 1. Communism — History I. T. II. Series. HX40.L245    335.43 19    *LC* 80-41533    *ISBN* 0521238552

**Lens, Sidney.**                                                            **4.6969**
The promise and pitfalls of revolution. — Philadelphia: United Church Press, [1974] 287 p.; 22 cm. 'A Pilgrim Press book.' 1. Communism — History 2. Capitalism — History. 3. Revolutions — History. 4. Economic history — 20th century 5. Radicalism — United States. I. T. HX40.L3872    330.9/04    *LC* 73-19810    *ISBN* 0829802541

**Merleau-Ponty, Maurice, 1908-1961.**                                        • **4.6970**
[Humanisme et terreur. English] Humanism and terror: an essay on the Communist problem / translated and with notes, by John O'Neill. — Boston: Beacon Press [1969] xlvii, 189 p.; 22 cm. 1. Communism 2. Terrorism 3. Communism — Soviet Union I. T. HX40.M4213    335.43/0947 19    *LC* 71-84796

**Meyer, Alfred G.**                                                         • **4.6971**
Communism / Alfred G. Meyer. — 4th ed. — New York: Random House, c1984. ix, 195 p.; 21 cm. Includes index. 1. Communism 2. Communism — Soviet Union I. T. HX40.M43 1984    335.43 19    *LC* 83-11188    *ISBN* 039433163X

**Narkiewicz, Olga A.**                                                      **4.6972**
Marxism and the reality of power, 1919–1980 / Olga A. Narkiewicz. — New York: St. Martin's Press, 1981. 337 p.; 23 cm. Includes index. 1. Communism — History 2. Communist parties — History. I. T. HX40.N32 1981    324/.1 19    *LC* 81-9423    *ISBN* 0312518498

**Seton-Watson, Hugh.**                                                      • **4.6973**
From Lenin to Khrushchev, the history of world communism. [2d ed.] New York: Praeger [1960] 432 p.; 22 cm. (Books that matter) 1. Communism — History I. T. HX40 S39 1960    *LC* 60-6999

**Trotsky, Leon, 1879-1940.**                                                **4.6974**
The age of permanent revolution; a Trotsky antology. Edited, with an introd., by Isaac Deutscher (with the assistance of George Novack) [New York, Dell Pub. Co., 1964] 384 p. (Dell Laurel edition) 1. Revolutions — Addresses, essays, lectures 2. Communism — Addresses, essays, lectures 3. Socialism — Addresses, essays, lectures 4. Russia — Politics and government — 20th century — Addresses, essays, lectures I. Deutscher, Isaac, 1907-1967. II. T. HX40 T713 1964    *LC* 64-55028

**Western Marxism: a critical reader / Gareth Stedman Jones ...**              **4.6975**
[et al.]; edited by New left review.
London: NLB; Atlantic Highlands: Humanities Press, c1977. 354 p.; 22 cm. Essays originally appearing in New left review. 1. Communism — Addresses, essays, lectures. I. Jones, Gareth Stedman. HX40.W46 1977    335.4/094    *LC* 77-4105    *ISBN* 0391007203

## HX44 1945–

**Black, Cyril Edwin, 1915- ed.**                                            • **4.6976**
Communism and revolution: the strategic uses of political violence / edited by Cyril E. Black and Thomas P. Thornton. — Princeton, N.J.: Princeton University Press, 1964. ix, 467 p.; 25 cm. Essays resulting from research activity of the Center of International Studies. 1. Communism — History 2. Revolutions I. Thornton, Thomas Perry. joint ed. II. Woodrow Wilson School of Public and International Affairs. Center of International Studies. III. T. HX44.B55    335.4309    *LC* 63-18640

**Garaudy, Roger.**                                                          **4.6977**
[Grand tournant du socialisme. English] The crisis in communism: the turning-point of socialism / translated from the French by Peter and Betty Ross. — New York: Grove Press; [Distributed by Random House, c1970] 255 p.; 21 cm. Translation of Le grand tournant du socialisme. 1. Socialism I. T. HX44.G3513 1970b    335    *LC* 74-155124    *ISBN* 0394475879 *ISBN* 0394177630

**Leonhard, Wolfgang.**                                                      **4.6978**
Three faces of Marxism: the political concepts of Soviet ideology, Maoism, and humanist Marxism / translated by Ewald Osers. — New York: Holt, Rinehart and Winston, [1974] xiv, 497 p.; 24 cm. Translation of Die Dreispaltung des Marxismus. 1. Communism — 1945- 2. Communism — Russia. 3. Communism — China. 4. Communist strategy I. T. HX44.L39813    335.43    *LC* 71-182771    *ISBN* 0030886201

**Self–governing socialism: a reader / edited by Branko Horvat,**             **4.6979**
Mihailo Marković, Rudi Supek.
White Plains, N.Y.: International Arts and Sciences Press, c1975. 2 v.; 23 cm. 1. Socialism — History. 2. Social systems 3. Democracy 4. Management — Employee participation 5. Political sociology I. Horvat, Branko. II. Marković, Mihailo, 1923- III. Supek, Rudi, 1913- HX44.S39    335    *LC* 73-92805

# HX51–63 Special Systems and Movements

**Bahro, Rudolf, 1935-.**                                                    **4.6980**
The alternative / by Rudolf Bahro. — [New York]: Times Books, [1978] 463 p. Translation of Die Alternative. Includes index. 1. Socialism 2. Communism I. T. HX56.B2613    335    *LC* 78-53300    *ISBN* 0812907663

**Marcuse, Herbert, 1898-.**                                                 • **4.6981**
Soviet Marxism, a critical analysis. — New York: Columbia University Press, 1958. 271 p.; 21 cm. — (Studies of the Russian Institute, Columbia University) 1. Communism 2. Communist ethics I. T. HX56.M318    335.4    *LC* 57-10943

**Crossman, R. H. S. (Richard Howard Stafford), 1907-1974. ed.**             • **4.6982**
The God that failed, by Arthur Koestler [and others. 1st ed.] New York, Harper [1950, c1949] v, 273 p. 22 cm. 1. Communism — Addresses, essays, lectures. I. Koestler, Arthur, 1905- II. T. HX59.C75    335.4    *LC* 50-5050

**Schumpeter, Joseph Alois, 1883-1950.**                                     • **4.6983**
Capitalism, socialism, and democracy. 3d ed. New York, Harper [1950] xiv, 431 p. 22 cm. 1. Socialism 2. Capitalism 3. Democracy I. T. HX72.S38 1950    335    *LC* 50-8700

**Gorman, Robert A.**                                                        **4.6984**
Neo–Marxism, the meanings of modern radicalism / Robert A. Gorman. — Westport, Conn.: Greenwood Press, 1982. x, 309 p.; 24 cm. — (Contributions in political science. 0147-1066; no. 77) Includes index. 1. Communism 2. Radicalism I. T. II. Series. HX73.G67 1982    335.4/01 19    *LC* 81-13404    *ISBN* 0313232644

**Nove, Alec.**                                                              **4.6985**
The economics of feasible socialism / Alec Nove. — London; Boston: G. Allen & Unwin, 1983. xi, 244 p.; 25 cm. 1. Socialism 2. Socialism — History. 3. Marxian economics 4. Economic history I. T. HX73.N67 1983    338.9/009171/7 19    *LC* 82-18169    *ISBN* 0043350488

# HX80–516 Socialism, Communism, by Country

## HX81–92 United States

### HX83 History

**Bell, Daniel.**                                                            **4.6986**
Marxian socialism in the United States. — Princeton, N.J., Princeton University Press, 1967. xiii, 212 p. 21 cm. First published in 1952 as chapter 6 of Socialism and American life (Princeton studies in American civilization, no. 4) edited by Donald Drew Egbert and Stow Persons. 1. Socialism — United States — History. I. T. HX83.B4    335.4/0973    *LC* 67-30481

**Diggins, John P.**              4.6987
Up from communism: conservative odysseys in American intellectual history / John P. Diggins. — 1st ed. — New York: Harper & Row, [1975] xvii, 522 p., [8] leaves of plates: ill.; 22 cm. 1. Communism — United States — History. 2. United States — Intellectual life I. T.
HX83.D48 1975     335.43/0973     *LC* 74-24505     *ISBN* 0060110422

**Draper, Theodore, 1912-.**         ● 4.6988
American communism and Soviet Russia: the formative period. — New York: Viking Press, 1960. 558 p.; 22 cm. — (Communism in American life) 1. Communism — U.S. I. T.
HX83.D68     335.430973     *LC* 60-7672

**Draper, Theodore, 1912-.**          4.6989
The roots of American communism. New York, Viking Press, 1957. x, 498 p. ill., ports., facsims. (Communism in American life) 1. Communism — United States I. T.
HX83 D7     *LC* 57-6433

**Gornick, Vivian.**             4.6990
The romance of American Communism / Vivian Gornick. — New York: Basic Books, c1977. xiii, 265 p.; 24 cm. 1. Communism — United States — 1917- I. T.
HX83.G6     335.43/0973     *LC* 77-75248     *ISBN* 0465071104

**Kivisto, Peter, 1948-.**          4.6991
Immigrant socialists in the United States: the case of Finns and the Left / Peter Kivisto. — Rutherford [N.J.]: Fairleigh Dickinson University Press; London; Cranbury, N.J.: Associated University Presses, c1984. 243 p.: ill.; 24 cm. Includes index. 1. Communists — United States — History. 2. Finnish Americans — History. I. T.
HX83.K47 1984     335.4/08994541073 19     *LC* 83-48835     *ISBN* 0838632033

**Klehr, Harvey.**            4.6992
The heyday of American communism: the depression decade / Harvey Klehr. — New York: Basic Books, c1984. xiv, 511 p.; 25 cm. 1. Communist Party of the United States of America — History — 20th century. 2. Communism — United States — History — 20th century. 3. United States — Economic conditions — 1918-1945 4. United States — Politics and government — 1919-1933 5. United States — Politics and government — 1933-1945 I. T.
HX83.K55 1984     335.43/0973 19     *LC* 83-70762     *ISBN* 0465029450

**Quint, Howard H.**          ● 4.6993
The forging of American socialism; origins of the modern movement [by] Howard H. Quint. Indianapolis, Bobbs-Merrill [1964, c1953] ix, 409 p. (The American heritage series, 24) 1. Socialism — United States I. T.
HX83 Q5 1964     *LC* 64-16709

**Weinstein, James, 1926-.**        ● 4.6994
The decline of socialism in America, 1912–1925. — New York: Monthly Review Press, [1967] xi, 367 p.; 22 cm. 1. Socialist Party (U.S.) 2. Socialism — United States I. T.
HX83.W4     335/.00973     *LC* 67-19258

## HX84 Biography

**Debs, Eugene V. (Eugene Victor), 1855-1926.**     ● 4.6995
Writings and speeches of Eugene V. Debs. / Introd. by Arthur M. Schlesinger, Jr. — New York: Hermitage Press, 1948. xvii, 486 p.: ports.; 22 cm. 1. Socialism — United States 2. Labor and laboring classes — United States 3. United States — Social conditions I. T.
HX84.D3 A313     335     *LC* 48-3028

**Currie, Harold W.**           4.6996
Eugene V. Debs / by Harold W. Currie. — Boston: Twayne Publishers, c1976. 157 p.: port.; 21 cm. — (Twayne's United States authors series; TUAS 267) Includes index. 1. Debs, Eugene V. (Eugene Victor), 1855-1926. I. T.
HX84.D3 C87     335/.3/0924 B     *LC* 76-3780     *ISBN* 0805771670

**Ginger, Ray.**             ● 4.6997
The bending cross; a biography of Eugene Victor Debs. New York, Russell & Russell [1969, c1949] x, 516 p. port. 23 cm. 1. Debs, Eugene V. (Eugene Victor), 1855-1926. I. T.
HX84.D3 G5 1969     335/.3/0924 B     *LC* 70-83848

**Salvatore, Nick, 1943-.**          4.6998
Eugene V. Debs: citizen and socialist / Nick Salvatore. — Urbana: University of Illinois Press, c1982. xiv, 437 p., [12] p. of plates: ill.; 24 cm. — (Working class in American history) Includes index. 1. Debs, Eugene V. (Eugene Victor), 1855-1926. 2. Socialists — United States — Biography. I. T. II. Series.
HX84.D3 S23 1982     335/.3/0924 B 19     *LC* 82-1860     *ISBN* 0252009673

**Haywood, Harry, 1898-.**          4.6999
Black Bolshevik: autobiography of an Afro–American Communist / Harry Haywood. — Chicago: Liberator Press, c1978. x, 700 p., [7] leaves of plates: ill.; 23 cm. 1. Haywood, Harry, 1898- 2. Communists — United States — Biography. 3. Afro-Americans — Biography. 4. Communism — United States — History. I. T.
HX84.H38 A32     335.43/092/4 B     *LC* 77-77464     *ISBN* 0930720520

**Painter, Nell Irvin.**          4.7000
The narrative of Hosea Hudson, his life as a Negro Communist in the South / Nell Irvin Painter. — Cambridge, Mass.: Harvard University Press, 1979. xiii, 400 p.: ill.; 25 cm. Includes index. 1. Hudson, Hosea. 2. Afro-American communists — Southern States — Biography. 3. Afro-Americans — Southern States — Biography. 4. Trade-unions — Southern States — Officials and employees — Biography. 5. Iron and steel workers — Southern States — Biography. I. T.
HX84.H8 P34     335.43/092/4 B     *LC* 79-4589     *ISBN* 0674601106

**Lens, Sidney.**           4.7001
Unrepentant radical: an American activist's account of five turbulent decades / Sideny Lens. — Boston: Beacon Press, c1980. 438 p.; 21 cm. Includes index. 1. Lens, Sidney. 2. Socialists — United States — Biography. 3. Socialism — United States 4. Radicalism — United States. I. T.
HX84.L37 A35     335/.00973     *LC* 79-53757     *ISBN* 0807032069

**Johnpoll, Bernard K.**         ● 4.7002
Pacifist's progress: Norman Thomas and the decline of American socialism / by Bernard K. Johnpoll. — Chicago: Quadrangle Books, 1970. xiii, 336 p.; 22 cm. 1. Thomas, Norman, 1884-1968. 2. Socialist Party (U.S.) 3. Socialism — United States I. T.
HX84.T47 J65     329/.81 B     *LC* 70-116078     *ISBN* 0812901525

## HX85–89 General Works

**Fried, Albert. comp.**          ● 4.7003
Socialism in America: from the Shakers to the Third International; a documentary history. — [1st ed.]. — Garden City, N.Y., Doubleday, 1970. xi, 580 p. 22 cm. 1. Socialism — United States — History — Addresses, essays, lectures. I. T.
HX86.F817     335/.00973     *LC* 76-97702

**Mayo, Henry Bertram, 1911-.**       ● 4.7004
Introduction to Marxist theory. New York, Oxford University Press, 1960. 334 p. 1. Communism 2. Democracy I. T.
HX86 M36 1960     *LC* 60-5276

**Meyer, Alfred G.**          ● 4.7005
Marxism: the unity of theory and practice: a critical essay / by Alfred G. Meyer. — Cambridge: Harvard University Press, 1970. xxx, 182 p.; 22 cm. (Russian Research Center studies, 14) Reprint of the 1954 ed., with a new introd. 1. Socialism I. T.
HX86.M468 1970     335.4     *LC* 73-123568     *ISBN* 0674551028

**Sombart, Werner, 1863-1941.**       4.7006
[Warum gibt es in den Vereinigten Staaten keinen Sozialismus? English] Why is there no socialism in the United States? / Werner Sombart; translated by Patricia M. Hocking and C. T. Husbands; edited and with an introductory essay by C. T. Husbands, and with a foreword by Michael Harrington. — White Plains, N.Y.: International Arts and Sciences Press, 1976. xliii, 187 p.; 23 cm. Translation of Warum gibt es in den Vereinigten Staaten keinen Sozialismus? Includes index. 1. Socialism — United States 2. Labor and laboring classes — United States I. T.
HX86.S6613 1976     335/.00973     *LC* 76-8031     *ISBN* 0873320832

## HX101–235 Canada. Latin America

**Horn, Michiel, 1939-.**          4.7007
The League for Social Reconstruction: intellectual origins of the democratic left in Canada, 1930–1942 / Michiel Horn. — Toronto: University of Toronto Press, 1980. xii, 270 p.: ill.; 24 cm. Includes index. 1. League for Social Reconstruction — History. 2. Socialism — Canada — History. 3. Intellectuals — Canada — History. 4. Radicalism — Canada — History. 5. Right and left (Political science) I. T.
HX101.L43 H67 1980     324.271/0972 19     *LC* 81-141608     *ISBN* 0802054870

**Penner, Norman.**          4.7008
The Canadian left: a critical analysis / Norman Penner. — Scarborough, Ont.; Englewood Cliffs, N.J.: Prentice-Hall, c1977. 287 p.; 23 cm. Includes index. 1. Socialism — Canada — History. 2. Communism — Canada — History. I. T.
HX103.P46 1977     335/.00971 19     *LC* 82-210280     *ISBN* 0131131265

**McCormack, Andrew Ross, 1943-.**      **4.7009**
Reformers, rebels, and revolutionaries: the Western Canadian radical movement, 1899–1919 / A. Ross McCormack. — Toronto: University of Toronto Press, c1977. xi, 228 p., [4] leaves of plates: ill.; 24 cm. Includes index. 1. Socialism — Canada — History. 2. Radicalism — Canada — History. 3. Trade-unions — Canada — Political activity — History. I. T.
HX109.M3    320.5/315/0971    *LC* 77-4338    *ISBN* 0802053858

**Liss, Sheldon B.**      **4.7010**
Marxist thought in Latin America / Sheldon B. Liss. — Berkeley: University of California Press, c1984. x, 374 p.; 22 cm. Includes index. 1. Communism — Latin America. I. T.
HX110.5.A6 L57 1984    335.43/098 19    *LC* 83-4838    *ISBN* 0520050215

**Ratliff, William E.**      **4.7011**
Castroism and communism in Latin America, 1959–1976: the varieties of Marxist–Leninist experience / William E. Ratliff. Washington: American Enterprise Institute for Public Policy Reearch, 1976. xx, 240 p.; 23 cm. (AEI-Hoover policy studies; 19) (Hoover Institution studies; 56) 1. Communism — Latin America. 2. Communism — Cuba. I. T. II. Series. III. Series: Hoover Institution studies; 56
HX110.5.A6 R38    329/.07/098    *LC* 76-28554    *ISBN* 0844732206

**Communism in Central America and the Caribbean / edited by**      **4.7012**
**Robert Wesson.**
Stanford, Calif.: Hoover Institution Press, c1982. xiv, 177 p.; 23 cm. (Hoover international studies.) (Hoover Press publication; 261) 1. Communism — Central America — Addresses, essays, lectures. 2. Communism — Caribbean Area — Addresses, essays, lectures. I. Wesson, Robert G. II. Series.
HX118.5.C65 1982    335.43/09728 19    *LC* 81-82707    *ISBN* 0817976124

**Guevara, Ernesto, 1928-1967.**      • **4.7013**
Venceremos!: The speeches and writings of Ernesto Che Guevara / edited, annotated, and with an introd. by John Gerassi. — New York: Macmillan, [1968] xix, 442 p.; 24 cm. 1. Communism — Cuba — Addresses, essays, lectures. I. T.
HX157.G816    335.43/0924    *LC* 68-22126

**Dumont, René, 1904-.**      **4.7014**
[Cuba, est-il socialiste? English] Is Cuba socialist? / René Dumont; translated by Stanley Hochman. — New York: Viking Press [1974] 159 p.; 22 cm. Translation of Cuba, est-il socialiste? 1. Communism — Cuba. 2. Cuba — Economic conditions — 1959- 3. Cuba — Economic policy. I. T.
HX158.5.D8213 1974    335.43/4/097291    *LC* 70-164991    *ISBN* 0670401927

# HX236–380 Europe

**Anderson, Perry.**      **4.7015**
Considerations on Western Marxism / [by] Perry Anderson. London: NLB, 1976. ix, 125 p.; 22 cm. 1. Socialism — Europe — History. I. T.
HX237.A52 1976    335.4    *LC* 77-353200    *ISBN* 090230867X

**Burks, Richard Voyles, 1913-.**      • **4.7016**
The dynamics of communism in Eastern Europe. — Princeton, N. J., Princeton University Press, 1961. xii, 244 p. maps, tables. 23 cm. Bibliographical footnotes. 1. Communism — Europe, Eastern. I. T.
HX237.B8    335.43094    *LC* 61-7400

**Lindemann, Albert S.**      **4.7017**
A history of European socialism / Albert S. Lindemann. — New Haven: Yale University Press, c1983. xxi, 385 p.; 24 cm. Includes index. 1. Marx, Karl, 1818-1883. 2. Communism — Europe — History. 3. Socialism — Europe — History. I. T.
HX237.L536 1983    335/.0094 19    *LC* 82-40167    *ISBN* 0300027974

*HX 237 L536 1983* (handwritten)

**Skilling, H. Gordon (Harold Gordon), 1912-.**      • **4.7018**
Communism, national and international; Eastern Europe after Stalin [by] H. Gordon Skilling. — [Toronto] University of Toronto Press [1964] ix, 168 p. 23 cm. Bibliographical footnotes. 1. Communism — Europe, Eastern. 2. Europe, Eastern — Politics. I. T.
HX237.S4    335.4    *LC* 64-56966

**Howard, Dick, 1943-.**      **4.7019**
The Unknown dimension: European Marxism since Lenin / edited by Dick Howard and Karl E. Klare. — New York: Basic Books, 1972. x, 418 p.; 24 cm. 1. Socialism — Europe — History 2. Communism — Europe — History 3. Dialectical materialism I. Klare, Karl E. II. T.
HX237.U53    HX44.H6.    *LC* 71-188889 (in bk.)    *ISBN* 0465088775

**Boggs, Carl.**      **4.7020**
The impasse of European communism / Carl Boggs. — Boulder, Colo.: Westview Press, 1982. xiii, 181 p.; 24 cm. 1. Communism — Europe. I. T.
HX238.5.B63 1982    335.43/094 19    *LC* 81-22005    *ISBN* 0891587845

**Communism in Eastern Europe / edited by Teresa Rakowska–**      **4.7021**
**Harmstone and Andrew Gyorgy.**
Bloomington: Indiana University Press, c1979. viii, 338 p.: map; 24 cm. 1. Communism — Europe, Eastern — Addresses, essays, lectures. I. Rakowska-Harmstone, Teresa. II. Gyorgy, Andrew, 1917-
HX238.5.C65    335.43/0947    *LC* 78-20402    *ISBN* 0253337917. *ISBN* 0253202256 pbk

**The European Left: Italy, France, and Spain / edited by**      **4.7022**
**William E. Griffith.**
Lexington, Mass.: Lexington Books, c1979. vii, 260 p.; 24 cm. 1. Communism — Italy — Addresses, essays, lectures. 2. Socialism — Italy — Addresses, essays, lectures. 3. Communism — France — Addresses, essays, lectures. 4. Socialism — France — Addresses, essays, lectures. 5. Communism — Spain — Addresses, essays, lectures. 6. Socialism — Spain — Addresses, essays, lectures. I. Griffith, William E.
HX238.5.E88    335.43/094    *LC* 79-7711    *ISBN* 0669031992

**Marzani, Carl.**      **4.7023**
The promise of Eurocommunism / by Carl Marzani; introd. by John Cammett. — Westport, Conn.: L. Hill, c1980. xxii, 346 p.; 21 cm. Includes index. 1. Communism — Europe. I. T.
HX238.5.M395    335.43/094    *LC* 80-80526    *ISBN* 0882081101

**Pelinka, Anton, 1941-.**      **4.7024**
[Sozialdemokratie in Europa. English] Social democratic parties in Europe / Anton Pelinka. — New York, N.Y., U.S.A.: Praeger, 1983. xvi, 190 p.; 25 cm. Translation of: Sozialdemokratie in Europa. Includes index. 1. Socialism — Europe 2. Socialist parties — Europe. I. T.
HX238.5.P4413 1983    324.24072 19    *LC* 82-18940    *ISBN* 0030623626

**The Politics of Eurocommunism: socialism in transition / edited**      **4.7025**
**by Carl Boggs and David Plotke.**
1st ed. — Boston: South End Press, c1980. 479 p.; 21 cm. 1. Communism — Europe — Addresses, essays, lectures. I. Boggs, Carl. II. Plotke, David.
HX238.5.P64    335.43/094 19    *LC* 79-66993    *ISBN* 0896080528

**Leonhard, Wolfgang.**      **4.7026**
[Eurokommunismus. English] Eurocommunism: challenge for East and West / Wolfgang Leonhard; translated by Mark Vecchio. — New York: Holt, Rinehart, and Winston, 1980, c1978. x, 398 p.; 24 cm. Translation of Eurokommunismus: Herausforderung für Ost und West. 1. Communism — Europe. 2. Communist parties I. T.
HX239.L4613 1979    335.43/094    *LC* 79-11290    *ISBN* 0030449510

*TITLE IS IN LIBRARY BUT CALL # IS NOT LISTED IN ONLINE CAT* (handwritten)

**Communism and political systems in Western Europe / David**      **4.7027**
**E. Albright, editor.**
Boulder, Colo.: Westview Press, 1979. xx, 379 p.; 24 cm. — (Westview special studies in west European politics and society) 1. Communism — Europe — Addresses, essays, lectures. 2. Communist parties — Addresses, essays, lectures. 3. Europe — Politics and government — 1945- — Addresses, essays, lectures. I. Albright, David E.
HX239.Z7 C63    335.43/094    *LC* 78-19054    *ISBN* 0891583084

**Tannahill, Neal R., 1949-.**      **4.7028**
The Communist parties of Western Europe: a comparative study / R. Neal Tannahill. — Westport, Conn.: Greenwood Press, 1978. xvi, 299 p.; 22 cm. (Contributions in political science. no. 10 0147-1066) Includes index. 1. Communism — Europe. 2. Communist parties 3. Europe — Politics and government — 1945- I. T. II. Series.
HX239.Z7 T36    335.43/094    *LC* 77-94750    *ISBN* 0313203180

## HX241–250 Britain

**Cole, Margaret, 1893-1980.**      • **4.7029**
The story of Fabian socialism. Stanford, Calif., Stanford University Press [1961] 366 p. illus. 22 cm. 1. Fabian Society (Great Britain) 2. Socialism — Great Britain — History. I. T.
HX243.C53    335.14    *LC* 61-16949

**Thomas, Hugh, 1931-.**      **4.7030**
John Strachey. — [1st U.S. ed.]. — New York: Harper & Row, [1973] 319 p.; 22 cm. 1. Strachey, John, 1901-1963. I. T.
HX243.S86 T56    320/.92/4 B    *LC* 73-4129    *ISBN* 0060142715

**Terrill, Ross.**      **4.7031**
R. H. Tawney and his times; socialism as fellowship. Cambridge, Mass., Harvard University Press, 1973. x, 373 p. illus. 25 cm. 1. Tawney, R. H.

(Richard Henry), 1880-1962. 2. Tawney, R. H. (Richard Henry), 1880-1962 — Bibliography. I. T.
HX243.T38 T47      335/.0092/4 B     *LC* 72-83392      *ISBN* 0674743768

**Winter, J. M.**                                                                       **4.7032**
Socialism and the challenge of war; ideas and politics in Britain, 1912–18 [by] J. M. Winter. — London; Boston: Routledge & K. Paul, [1974] ix, 310 p.: illus.; 23 cm. 1. Socialism — Great Britain 2. Great Britain — Politics and government — 1910-1936 I. T.
HX243.W54      335/.00941     *LC* 74-75861      *ISBN* 0710078390

**The Future that doesn't work: social democracy's failures in**               **4.7033**
**Britain / edited by R. Emmett Tyrrell, Jr.; [contributors]**
**Samuel Brittan ... et al.].**
1st ed. — Garden City, N.Y.: Doubleday, 1977. vi, 208 p.; 22 cm. 1. Socialism — Great Britain — Addresses, essays, lectures. I. Tyrrell, R. Emmett. II. Brittan, Samuel.
HX244.F87      309.1/41/085     *LC* 76-9482      *ISBN* 0385121865

**Webb, Beatrice Potter, 1858-1943.**                                          **4.7034**
The diary of Beatrice Webb / edited by Norman and Jeanne MacKenzie. — Cambridge, Mass.: Belknap Press of Harvard University Press, 1982-1985. 4 v.: ill.; 24 cm. 1. Webb, Beatrice Potter, 1858-1943 — Collected works. 2. Socialists — Great Britain — Biography — Collected works. 3. Great Britain — Social conditions — Collected works. I. MacKenzie, Norman Ian. II. MacKenzie, Jeanne. III. T.
HX244.7.W42 A33 1982      335/.14/0924 19     *LC* 82-9159     *ISBN* 0674202872

**Cole, G. D. H. (George Douglas Howard), 1889-1959.**                        • **4.7035**
What Marx really meant. Westport, Conn.: Greenwood Press [1970] 309, vi p.; 23 cm. Reprint of the 1934 ed. 1. Socialism 2. Marxian economics I. T.
HX246.C65 1970      335.4     *LC* 79-90489      *ISBN* 0837130824

**Crossman, R. H. S. (Richard Howard Stafford), 1907-1974.**                  • **4.7036**
New Fabian essays [by] R. H. S. Crossman [& others]; preface by C. R. Attlee. 1st ed. reprinted; edited & with a new introduction by R. H. S. Crossman. London, Dent, 1970. [1], xvi, 215 p. 23 cm. 1. Socialism — Addresses, essays, lectures. 2. Economic policy — Addresses, essays, lectures. 3. Socialism — Great Britain — Addresses, essays, lectures. I. T.
HX246.C88 1970      335/.14     *LC* 73-519554      *ISBN* 0460039490

**Crosland, Anthony, 1918-.**                                                  • **4.7037**
The future of socialism / by C. A. R. Crosland. Rev. ed. — New York: Schocken Books, 1964, c1963. 368 p.; 21 cm. (Schocken paperbacks) 1. Socialism — Great Britain I. T.
HX246.C94      335/.00941     *LC* 63-18395

**Fabian essays in socialism, by G. Bernard Shaw [and others]**               • **4.7038**
**Edited by G. Bernard Shaw.**
Gloucester, Mass., P. Smith, 1967. 280 p. 21 cm. Reprint of the 1889 ed. 1. Socialism — Addresses, essays, lectures. 2. Socialism — Great Britain I. Shaw, Bernard, 1856-1950. ed.
HX246.F2 1967      335/.14/08     *LC* 67-1807

**Holland, Stuart.**                                                           **4.7039**
The socialist challenge / Stuart Holland. — London: Quartet Books, 1975. 414 p.: ill.; 22 cm. Errata slip inserted. 1. Socialism 2. Socialism — Great Britain I. T.
HX246.H585      335/.009/047     *LC* 75-327638      *ISBN* 0704320509

**Jay, Douglas, 1907-.**                                                       • **4.7040**
Socialism in the new society. — New York: St Martin's Press, 1963 [c1962] vi, 414 p.; 23 cm. 1. Socialism 2. Socialism — Great Britain I. T.
HX246.J348      335.10942     *LC* 63-8228

**Shaw, Bernard, 1856-1950.**                                                  • **4.7041**
The intelligent woman's guide to socialism, capitalism, sovietism, and fascism. New York, Random House [1971, c1928] xlvi, 529 p. 22 cm. 1928 ed. published under title: The intelligent woman's guide to socialism and capitalism. 1. Socialism 2. Capitalism 3. Communism 4. Fascism I. T.
HX246.S53 1971      330.12     *LC* 74-159375      *ISBN* 0394473159

**Stretton, Hugh.**                                                            **4.7042**
Capitalism, socialism, and the environment / Hugh Stretton. — Cambridge, Eng.; New York: Cambridge University Press, 1976. vi, 332 p.; 22 cm. 1. Socialism 2. Capitalism 3. Environmental policy I. T.
HX246.S822      335     *LC* 76-15285      *ISBN* 0521210577

## HX251–260.5 Austria. Hungary

**Austro–Marxism / texts translated and edited by Tom**                       **4.7043**
**Bottomore and Patrick Goode; with an introd. by Tom**
**Bottomore.**
Oxford [Eng.]: Clarendon Press, 1978. viii, 308 p.; 23 cm. Includes index. 1. Communism — Austria — Addresses, essays, lectures. 2. Communism and social sciences — Addresses, essays, lectures. I. Bottomore, T. B. II. Goode, Patrick.
HX256.A9      335.43/09436     *LC* 77-30292      *ISBN* 0198272294

**Lukács, György, 1885-1971.**                                                • **4.7044**
[Geschichte und Klassenbewusstsein. English] History and class consciousness: studies in Marxist dialectics / [by] Georg Lukács; translated by Rodney Livingstone. — Cambridge, Mass.: MIT Press [1971] xlvii, 356 p.; 23 cm. Translation of Geschichte und Klassenbewusstsein. 1. Socialism 2. Proletariat 3. Capitalism 4. Communism 5. Class consciousness I. T.
HX260.H8 L783      335.41/08     *LC* 70-146824      *ISBN* 0262120356

**Kovrig, Bennett.**                                                          **4.7045**
Communism in Hungary: from Kun to Kádár / Bennett Kovrig. — Stanford, Calif.: Hoover Institution Press, c1979. xviii, 525 p.: map; 23 cm. (Histories of ruling Communist parties.) (Hoover Institution publication; 211) Includes index. 1. Communism — Hungary — History. 2. Hungary — Politics and government — 20th century I. T. II. Series.
HX260.5.A6 K68      335.43/09439     *LC* 78-59863      *ISBN* 0817971122

## HX261–270 France

**Before Marx: socialism and communism in France, 1830–48 /**                 **4.7046**
**edited by Paul E. Corcoran.**
New York: St. Martin's Press, 1983. xii, 237 p.; 23 cm. Includes index. 1. Socialism — France — History — 19th century. 2. Communism — France — History — 19th century. I. Corcoran, Paul E., 1944-.
HX263.B36 1983      335/.00944 19     *LC* 82-21557      *ISBN* 0312071582

**Loubère, Leo A.**                                                           • **4.7047**
Louis Blanc: his life and his contribution to the rise of French Jacobin-socialism. [Evanston, Ill.] Northwestern University Press, 1961. xii, 256 p. (Northwestern University studies in history, no. 1) 1. Blanc, Louis, 1811-1882. 2. Socialism — France I. T. II. Series.
HX263 B54 L6      *LC* 61-6042

**Spitzer, Alan B. (Alan Barrie), 1925-.**                                    • **4.7048**
The revolutionary theories of Louis Auguste Blanqui [by] Alan B. Spitzer. — New York: AMS Press, [1970] 208 p.; 23 cm. — (Columbia studies in the social sciences, no. 594) Reprint of the 1957 ed. 1. Blanqui, Louis Auguste, 1805-1881. I. T. II. Series.
HX263.B56 S6 1970      320.5/31/0924     *LC* 70-120198      *ISBN* 0404515940

**Kelly, Michael P.**                                                         **4.7049**
Modern French Marxism / Michael Kelly. — Baltimore, Md.: Johns Hopkins University Press, 1982. 240 p.; 24 cm. Includes index. 1. Marx, Karl, 1818-1883. 2. Communism — France. I. T.
HX263.K44 1982      335.43/0944 19     *LC* 82-47973      *ISBN* 0801829062

**Lichtheim, George, 1912-.**                                                 • **4.7050**
Marxism in modern France. — New York, Columbia University Press, 1966. ix, 212 p. 24 cm. 'Sponsored by the Research Institute on Communist Affairs of Columbia University.' Bibliography: p. [199]-207. 1. Socialism — France — Hist. 2. Communism — France — Hist. I. Columbia University. Research Institute on Communist Affairs. II. T.
HX263.L43      335.40944     *LC* 66-14788

**Hyams, Edward, 1912-1975.**                                                 **4.7051**
Pierre–Joseph Proudhon, his revolutionary life, mind, and works / Edward Hyams. — New York: Taplinger Pub. Co., 1979. 304 p.; 22 cm. 1. Proudhon, P.-J. (Pierre-Joseph), 1809-1865. 2. Socialists — France — Biography. 3. Anarchism and anarchists — France — Biography. I. T.
HX263.P75 H92 1979      335/.2 B     *LC* 78-72023      *ISBN* 0800865529

**The French Socialist experiment / edited by John S. Ambler.**               **4.7052**
Philadelphia: Institute for the Study of Human Issues, c1985. x, 224 p.; 25 cm. 1. Socialism — France — Addresses, essays, lectures. 2. France — Economic policy — 1945- — Addresses, essays, lectures. 3. France — Social policy — Addresses, essays, lectures. 4. France — Politics and government — 1981- — Addresses, essays, lectures. I. Ambler, John S. (John Steward)
HX264.F73 1985      335/.00944 19     *LC* 84-707      *ISBN* 0897270576

**Saint-Simon, Henri, comte de, 1760-1825.**                                  **4.7053**
[Selections. English. 1975] Henri Saint–Simon (1760–1825): selected writings on science, industry, and social organization / translated and edited by Keith

Taylor. — New York: Holmes and Meier Publishers, 1975. 312 p.; 23 cm. 1. Socialism, Christian 2. Socialism and society I. T.
HX265.S224 1975     335/.2     LC 75-15653     ISBN 0841902127

**Caute, David.**       • **4.7054**
Communism and the French intellectuals, 1914–1960 / David Caute. — New York: Macmillan, 1964. 412 p. 1. Parti communiste français. 2. Communism — France. 3. France — Intellectual life I. T.
HX266.C38     LC 64-12166

## HX271–280 Germany

**Korsch, Karl, 1886-1961.**       **4.7055**
Karl Korsch: revolutionary theory / edited by Douglas Kellner. — Austin: University of Texas Press, c1977. vi, 299 p. 1. Korsch, Karl, 1886-1961. 2. Communism — Collected works. 3. Revolutions — Collected works. I. Kellner, Douglas, 1943- II. T.
HX271.K67 1977     HX271 K67 1977.     335.43     LC 76-56182
ISBN 0292743017

**Bebel, August, 1840-1913.**       • **4.7056**
My life, by August Bebel. London [etc.]: T.F. Unwin, 1912. 343 p.: port.; 23 cm. Translated from the German. I. T.
HX273 B42     LC 13-12024

**Bernstein, Eduard, 1850-1932.**       • **4.7057**
Evolutionary socialism: a criticism and affirmation. [Translated by Edith C. Harvey]. — New York, Schocken Books [1961] 224 p. 21 cm. — (Schocken paperbacks, SB11) Translation of Die Voraussetzungen des Sozialismus und die Aufgaben der Sozialdemokratie. 1. Socialism I. T.
HX273.B553 1961     335     LC 61-16649

**Salvadori, Massimo L.**       **4.7058**
[Kautsky e la rivoluzione socialista, 1880-1938. English] Karl Kautsky and the socialist revolution, 1880–1938 / Massimo Salvadori; translated by Jon Rothschild. — London: NLB, 1979. 357 p.; 22 cm. Translation of Kautsky e la rivoluzione socialista, 1880-1938. Includes index. 1. Kautsky, Karl, 1854-1938. 2. Socialists — Germany — Biography. 3. Socialism — History. I. T.
HX273.K34 S2413     335.4/092/4 B     LC 79-320776     ISBN 0860910156

**Luxemburg, Rosa, 1871-1919.**       **4.7059**
Selected political writings of Rosa Luxemburg. Edited and introd. by Dick Howard. New York [Monthly Review Press, 1971] 441 p. 22 cm. 1. Luxemburg, Rosa, 1871-1919. 2. Socialism I. T.
HX273.L8215 1971     335.4/08     LC 75-142991     ISBN 0853451427

**Geras, Norman, 1943-.**       **4.7060**
The legacy of Rosa Luxemburg / [by] Norman Geras. — London: NLB, 1976. 210 p.; 22 cm. Includes index. 1. Luxemburg, Rosa, 1871-1919. I. T.
HX273.L83 G47 1976     335.4/092/4     LC 77-353222     ISBN 0902308289

**Nettl, J. P.**       • **4.7061**
Rosa Luxemburg [by] J. P. Nettl. — London, New York [etc.] Oxford U. P., 1966. 2 v. (xviii, 984 p.) 2 fronts, 24 plates (incl. facsims., ports.) 22 1/2 cm. Bibliography: v. 2, p. [863]-934. 1. Luxemburg, Rosa, 1871-1919. I. T.
HX273.L83N4     335.40924 (B)     LC 66-2563

**Plamenatz, John Petrov.**       • **4.7062**
German Marxism and Russian communism. — London, New York: Longmans, Green [1954] 356 p.; 23 cm. 1. Communism — Germany 2. Communism — Russia. I. T.
HX273.P45     335.4     LC 54-3188

**Roth, Guenther.**       • **4.7063**
The Social Democrats in Imperial Germany; a study in working–class isolation and national integration. Pref. by Reinhard Bendix. — Totowa, N. J., Bedminster Press, 1963. xiv, 352 p. 22 cm. Bibliography: p. [327]-343. 1. Socialism — Germany — Hist. 2. Germany — Pol. & govt. — 1871-1918. I. T.
HX273.R58     335.5     LC 63-13891

**Engels, Friedrich, 1820-1895.**       • **4.7064**
Socialism, Utopian and scientific, by Frederick Engels; translated by Edward Aveling. New York: International publishers [c1935] 93 p. 22 cm. (Marxist library ... vol. II) 1. Socialism I. Aveling, Edward Bibbins, 1851-1898. tr. II. T.
HX276.E55 1935     335     LC 36-13815

**Engels, Friedrich, 1820-1895.**       • **4.7065**
[Herrn Eugen Dühring's Umwälzung der Wissenschaft. English] Anti–Dühring: Herr Eugen Dühring's revolution in science. Moscow, Progress Publishers, 1969. 502 p. port. 21 cm. Translation of Herrn Eugen Dühring's Umwälzung der Wissenschaft. 1. Dühring, Eugen Karl, 1833-1921. 2. Socialism 3. Philosophy 4. Economics 5. Dialectical materialism I. T.
HX276.E565 1969     335     LC 76-441866

**Mayer, Gustav, 1871-1948.**       • **4.7066**
[Friedrich Engels. English] Friedrich Engels; a biography. Translated from the German for the first time by Gilbert and Helen Highet. The translation edited by R. H. S. Crossman. New York, H. Fertig, 1969 [c1936] viii, 332, xii p. illus., ports. 23 cm. 1. Engels, Friedrich, 1820-1895. I. T.
HX276.E6 M32 1969     335.40924 B     LC 68-9596

**Gay, Peter, 1923-.**       • **4.7067**
The dilemma of democratic socialism; Eduard Bernstein's challenge to Marx. — New York, Collier Books [1962] 348 p. 19 cm. — (Collier books, AS19Y) Includes bibliography. 1. Bernstein, Eduard, 1850-1932. 2. Socialism 3. Democracy 4. Sozialdemokratische Partei Deutschlands. I. T.
HX276.G3 1962     335.5     LC 62-12075

**Kautsky, Karl, 1854-1938.**       **4.7068**
The road to power / by Karl Kautsky ... authorized translation by A.M. Simons. — Chicago, Ill.: S. A. Bloch, 1909. 127 p. 20 cm. 1. Socialism I. Simons, A. M., tr. II. T.
HX276.K384     LC 09-28001

**Marx, Karl, 1818-1883.**       • **4.7069**
[Selections. English] Basic writings on politics and philosophy [by] Karl Marx and Friedrich Engels. Edited by Lewis S. Feuer. [1st ed.] Garden City, N.Y., Doubleday, 1959. 497 p. 19 cm. (Anchor books, A185) 1. Socialism — Collections. I. Engels, Friedrich, 1820-1895. joint author. II. T.
HX276.M2773 1959     335     LC 59-12053

**Marx, Karl, 1818-1883.**       • **4.7070**
[Selected works. English. 1968] Selected works [of] Karl Marx and Frederick Engels. Moscow, Progress, 1968. 800 p., 2 l. of illus. 22 cm. 1. Socialism — Collections. 2. Economics — Collections. I. Engels, Friedrich, 1820-1895. II. T.
HX276.M2773 1968b     335.4/08     LC 73-393771

**Marx, Karl, 1818-1883.**       • **4.7071**
[Deutsche Ideologie. English. Selections] The German ideology, by Karl Marx and Friedrich Engels. Part one, with selections from parts two and three, together with Marx's 'Introduction to a critique of political economy; edited and with introduction by C. J. Arthur, translated from the German. London, Lawrence & Wishart, 1970. iii-viii, 158 p. 22 cm. 1. Feuerbach, Ludwig, 1804-1872. 2. Socialism 3. Communism 4. Idealism 5. Materialism I. Engels, Friedrich, 1820-1895. joint author. II. Arthur, C. J. (Christopher John), 1940- ed. III. Marx, Karl, 1818-1883. Einleitung zu einer Kritik der politischen Ökonomie. English. 1970. IV. Marx, Karl, 1818-1883. Thesen über Feuerbach. English. 1970. V. T.
HX276.M2782 1970     LC 71-574036     ISBN 0853152179

**Marx, Karl, 1818-1883.**       • **4.7072**
Critique of the Gotha programme, by Karl Marx; with appendices by Marx, Engels and Lenin; a revised translation. — New York, International publishers [c1938] vii, 116 p. 22 cm. — (Little Marx library) 'Edited by C. P. Dutt.' 'The present edition is a revised translation of an earlier edition issued by International publishers in 1933, and is based upon the Russian edition of the Marx-Engels-Lenin institute.'—Publishers' note. 1. Sozialdemokratische Partei Deutschlands. 2. Socialism — Germany 3. Communism I. Engels, Friedrich, 1820-1895. II. Lenin, Vladimir Il'ich, 1870-1924. III. Dutt, C. P., ed. IV. Moscow. Institut Marksa-Engel'sa-Lenina. V. T. VI. Title: The Gotha programme. VII. Series.
HX276.M283 1938     335.0943     LC 38-23740

**Marx, Karl, 1818-1883.**       • **4.7073**
[Manifest der Kommunistischen Partei. English] The Communist manifesto [by] Karl Marx and Friedrich Engels. Principles of communism [by] Friedrich Engels; a new translation by Paul M. Sweezy. The Communist manifesto after 100 years [by] Paul M. Sweezy and Leo Huberman. New York, Monthly Review Press [1964] v, 113 p. 23 cm. The Communist manifesto is a reproduction of the limited edition of 1933. The Principles of communism was translated from the text of the Marx-Engels Gesamtausgabe, 1st division, v. 6, pt. 1, p. 503-522. 'The Communist manifesto after 100 years' was first published in the Monthly review, Aug., 1949. 1. Communism I. Engels, Friedrich, 1820-1895. joint author. II. Engels, Friedrich, 1820-1895. Grundsätze des Kommunismus. English. 1964. III. Sweezy, Paul Marlor, 1910- The Communist manifesto after 100 years. 1964. IV. T. V. Title: Principles of communism. VI. Title: Communist manifesto after 100 years.
HX276.M3 1964a     335.42     LC 64-21175

**Marx, Karl, 1818-1883.**       • **4.7074**
[Manifest der Kommunistischen Partei. English] Birth of the Communist manifesto, with full text of the Manifesto, all prefaces by Marx and Engels, early drafts by Engels and other supplementary material. Edited and annotated, with an introd. by Dirk J. Struik. [1st ed.] New York, International Publishers [1971] 224 p. illus., ports. 21 cm. 1. Marx, Karl, 1818-1883. Manifest der

Kommunistischen Partei. I. Engels, Friedrich, 1820-1895. joint author.
II. Struik, Dirk Jan, 1894- ed. III. T.
HX276.M3 1971   335.42/2   *LC* 77-148513   *ISBN* 0717802884

## HX286–295 Italy

**Gramsci, Antonio, 1891-1937.**   **4.7075**
Selections from political writings (1921–1926) / Antonio Gramsci; with
additional texts by other Italian Communist leaders; translated and edited by
Quintin Hoare. — London: Lawrence and Wishart, c1978. xxviii, 516 p.; 22 cm.
1. Communism — Italy — Addresses, essays, lectures. 2. Italy — Politics and
government — 1922-1945 — Addresses, essays, lectures. I. Hoare, Quintin.
II. T.
HX288.G69213 1978b   335.43/0945   *LC* 78-6715   *ISBN*
0717805557 pbk

**Gramsci, Antonio, 1891-1937.**   **4.7076**
Selections from the prison notebooks of Antonio Gramsci / edited and
translated by Quintin Hoare and Geoffrey Nowell Smith. — New York:
International Publishers, 1972 (c1971). xcvi, 483 p.; 23 cm. — (New World
paperbacks for the study of Marxist sources; 0397) On spine: Prison notebooks.
1. Communism — Italy — Addresses, essays, lectures. 2. Socialism — Italy —
Addresses, essays, lectures. I. Hoare, Quintin. ed. II. Nowell-Smith, Geoffrey.
ed. III. T. IV. Title: Prison notebooks.
HX288.G7 A23   335.430945   *LC* 73-77646   *ISBN* 071780397X

**Gramsci, Antonio, 1891-1937.**   **4.7077**
[Selections. English] Antonio Gramsci: selections from political writings,
1910–1920: with additional texts by Bordiga and Tasca / selected and edited by
Quintin Hoare; translated by John Mathews. — New York: International
Publishers, c1977. xxi, 393 p.; 22 cm. 1. Communism — Italy — Addresses,
essays, lectures. 2. Italy — Politics and government — 1915-1922 —
Addresses, essays, lectures. I. Hoare, Quintin. II. T.
HX288.G7 A23 1977   335.43/0945   *LC* 76-54252   *ISBN*
0717804852

**Cammett, John McKay, 1927-.**   • **4.7078**
Antonio Gramsci and the origins of Italian Communism [by] John M.
Cammett. — Stanford, Calif.: Stanford University Press, 1967. xiv, 306 p.; 24
cm. 1. Gramsci, Antonio, 1891-1937. I. T.
HX288.G7 C27   HX288G7 C27.   335.40945   *LC* 66-22983

**Clark, Martin.**   **4.7079**
Antonio Gramsci and the revolution that failed / Martin Clark. New Haven:
Yale University Press, 1977. x, 225 p.; 23 cm. Includes index. 1. Gramsci,
Antonio, 1891-1937. 2. Trade-unions — Italy — Political activity — History.
3. Communism — Italy — History. 4. Italy — History — 1914-1945 I. T.
HX288.G7 C52 1977   335.4/092/4 B   *LC* 76-49754   *ISBN*
0300020775

**Spriano, Paolo.**   **4.7080**
Antonio Gramsci and the Party: the prison years / by Paolo Spriano; translated
by John Fraser. — London: Lawrence and Wishart, 1979. 192 p.; 22 cm.
Translation of Gramsci in carcere e il Partito. 1. Gramsci, Antonio, 1891-1937.
2. Partito comunista italiano — History 3. Communists — Italy — Biography
I. T.
HX288.G7 S6713

**Hostetter, Richard.**   • **4.7081**
The Italian Socialist movement. Princeton, N. J., Van Nostrand [1950-. v. 24
cm. Bibliographical footnotes. 1. Socialism — Italy — History. I. T.
HX288.H6   335   *LC* 58-13833

**Boggs, Carl.**   **4.7082**
The two revolutions: Antonio Gramsci and the dilemmas of western Marxism /
by Carl Boggs. — 1st ed. — Boston, MA: South End Press, c1984. xii, 311 p.; 23
cm. 1. Gramsci, Antonio, 1891-1937. 2. Communists — Italy — Biography.
3. Communism — History I. T.
HX289.7.G73 B63 1984   335.4/092/4 B 19   *LC* 84-13871   *ISBN*
0896082261

**Gramsci, Antonio, 1891-1937.**   • **4.7083**
The modern prince, and other writings. New York, International Publishers
[1967, c1957] 192 p. 21 cm. (New world paperbacks) 'Translated into English
by Dr. Louis Marks, who has also contributed the biographical introductions.'
1. Communism 2. Communism — Italy. 3. Social sciences — Addresses,
essays, lectures. I. T.
HX291.G7 1967   335.43   *LC* 67-25646

## HX311–315.7 Russia

**Balabanoff, Angelica, 1878-1965.**   • **4.7084**
My life as a rebel. — [3d ed.]. — New York: Greenwood Press, 1968 [c1938] ix,
324 p.; 22 cm. 1. Balabanoff, Angelica, 1878-1965. 2. Communism — History
3. Socialism — History. I. T.
HX312.B3 1968   335.43/0924 B   *LC* 68-23270

**Daniels, Robert Vincent.**   • **4.7085**
The conscience of the revolution: Communist opposition in Soviet Russia. —
Cambridge, Harvard University Press, 1960. xi, 526 p. diagrs. 25 cm. —
(Russian Research Center studies, 40) '[Begun] as a doctoral dissertation 'The
Left opposition in the Russian Communist Party, to 1924,' Harvard University,
1950.' Bibliography: p. [439]-448. 1. Communism — Russia. 2. Russia — Pol.
& govt. — 1917-1936. I. T.
HX312.D34   947.0841   *LC* 60-10035

**Mendel, Arthur P.**   • **4.7086**
Dilemmas of progress in tsarist Russia: legal Marxism and legal Populism.
Cambridge, Harvard University Press, 1961. viii, 310 p. (Russian Research
Center studies, 43) 1. Socialism — Soviet Union — History 2. Populism in
Russia (Narodnichestvo) I. T.
HX312 M44   *LC* 61-13738

**Baron, Samuel Haskell, 1921-.**   • **4.7087**
Plekhanov; the father of Russian Marxism. — Stanford, Calif., Stanford
University Press, 1963. 400 p.: ill.; 24 cm. Includes bibliography. 1. Plekhanov,
Georgiĭ Valentinovich, 1856-1918. I. T.
HX312.P63B3   923.247   *LC* 63-10732

**Lerner, Warren.**   • **4.7088**
Karl Radek, the last internationalist. — Stanford, Calif.: Stanford University
Press, 1970. x, 240 p.: illus., ports.; 23 cm. Based on the author's thesis,
Columbia University. 1. Radek, Karl, 1885-1939. I. T.
HX312.R3 L4 1970   335.43/0924 B   *LC* 70-97915   *ISBN*
0804707227

**Weeks, Albert Loren, 1929-.**   • **4.7089**
The first Bolshevik; a political biography of Peter Tkachev, by Albert L. Weeks.
New York: New York University Press, 1968. xiv, 221 p. facsims., ports. 24 cm.
1. Tkachev, Petr Nikitich, 1844-1886. 2. Communists — Soviet Union —
Biography. I. T.
HX312.T55 W4   335.4/0924   *LC* 68-15336

**Howe, Irving.**   **4.7090**
Leon Trotsky / Irving Howe. — New York: Viking Press, 1978. viii, 214 p.; 22
cm. Includes index. 1. Trotsky, Leon, 1879-1940. I. T.
HX312.T75 H68 1978   335.43/092/4 B   *LC* 77-26978   *ISBN*
0670423726

**Venturi, Franco.**   **4.7091**
[Populismo russo. English] Roots of revolution: a history of the populist and
socialist movements in nineteenth century Russia / Franco Venturi; translated
from the Italian by Francis Haskell; with an introduction by Isaiah Berlin. —
Chicago: University of Chicago Press, 1983, c1960. xxxvi, 850 p.; 23 cm.
Translation of: Il populismo russo. Reprint. Originally published: New York:
Knopf, 1960. 1. Communism — Soviet Union — History — 19th century.
2. Populism — Soviet Union — History — 19th century. I. T.
HX312.V44513 1983   947.08 19   *LC* 82-21811   *ISBN* 0226852709

**Gombin, Richard, 1939-.**   **4.7092**
The radical tradition: a study in modern revolutionary thought / Richard
Gombin; translated by Rupert Swyer. — New York: St. Martin's Press, 1979.
153 p.; 23 cm. Includes index. 1. Communism — Russia — History.
2. Socialism — Soviet Union — History. I. T.
HX313.G65 1979   322.4/2/094   *LC* 78-31150   *ISBN* 031266186X

**Haimson, Leopold Henri.**   • **4.7093**
The Russian Marxists & the origins of bolshevism. — Cambridge, Harvard
University Press, 1955. viii, 246 p. ports. 25 cm. — (Russian Research Center
studies, 19) Bibliography: p. [235]-240. 1. Socialism — Soviet Union — Hist.
2. Revolutionists, Russian. I. T.
HX313.H3   335.4   *LC* 55-10972

**Stalinism: essays in historical interpretation / edited by Robert**   **4.7094**
**C. Tucker; with contributions by Wlodzimierz Brus ... [et al.].**
1st ed. — New York: Norton, c1977. xx, 332 p.; 25 cm. Based on papers
presented at a conference on 'Stalinism and Communist political culture' held
at Bellagio, Italy, July 25-31, 1975 and sponsored by the Planning Group on
Comparative Communist Studies of the American Council of Learned
Societies. 1. Communism — Russia — History — Congresses. I. Tucker,
Robert C. II. Brus, Włodzimierz. III. American Council of Learned Societies
Devoted to Humanistic Studies. Planning Group on Comparative Communist
Studies.
HX313.S683 1977   335.43/0947   *LC* 76-56110   *ISBN* 0393056082

**Tuominen, Arvo, 1894-.** 4.7095
The bells of the Kremlin: an experience in communism / by Arvo Tuominen; Piltti Heiskanen, editor; Lily Leino, translator; with an introduction by Harrison E. Salisbury. — Hanover: University Press of New England, 1983. xvi, 333 p., [16] p. of plates: ill.; 24 cm. Excerpts from 5 books and taped interviews. Includes index. 1. Communism — Soviet Union — History — 20th century. 2. Communism — Finland — History — 20th century. I. Heiskanen, Piltti. II. T.
HX313.T86 1983      335.43/0947 19      LC 82-17647      ISBN 0874512492

**Bukharin, Nikolaĭ Ivanovich, 1888-1938.** • 4.7096
[Azbuka kommunizma. English] The ABC of communism [by] N. Bukharin and E. Preobrazhensky. Introd. by E. H. Carr. [Translated from the Russian by Eden and Cedar Paul] Baltimore: Penguin Books [1969] 480 p.; 18 cm. (The Pelican classics, AC 5) Translation of Azbuka kommunizma. 1. Kommunisticheskaia partiia Sovetskogo Soiuza. 2. Communism — Soviet Union I. Preobrazhenskiĭ, E. A. (Evgeniĭ Alekseevich), 1886-1937. joint author. II. T.
HX314.B822 1969      335.43/0947      LC 72-5714

**Bukharin, Nikolaĭ Ivanovich, 1888-1938.** • 4.7097
Historical materialism: a system of sociology / authorized translation from the 3d Russian ed. — New York: Russell & Russell, 1965. 318 p.; 23 cm. 1. Socialism 2. Dialectical materialism I. T.
HX314.B85 1965

**Lenin, Vladimir Ilʹich, 1870-1924.** • 4.7098
[Chto delatʹ? English] What is to be done?: burning questions of our movement / [translated by J. Fineberg and G. Hanna; edited by V. J. Jerome]. — New York: International Publishers [1969] vi, 198, [1] p.; 21 cm. (New World paperbacks, NW-107) Translation of Chto delatʹ? 1. Rossiĭskaia sotsial-demokraticheskaia rabochaia partiia. 2. Socialism — Soviet Union I. T.
HX314.L342 1969      335.43/0947      LC 69-18884

**Lenin, Vladimir Ilʹich, 1870-1924.** • 4.7099
State and revolution; Marxist teaching about the theory of the state and the tasks of the proletariat in the revolution. Rev. translation. [Special ed.] New York: International Publishers [1935] 104 p. (Little Lenin library; v.14) 1. Marx, Karl, 1818-1883. 2. Socialism 3. State, The 4. Revolutions I. T.
HX314 L352 1935

**Polan, A. J.** 4.7100
Lenin and the end of politics / A.J. Polan. — Berkeley: University of California Press, 1984. viii, 229 p.; 22 cm. Based on the author's thesis (Ph. D.)— University of Durham. 1. Lenin, Vladimir Ilʹich, 1870-1924. Gosudarstvo i revoliutsiia. 2. Marx, Karl, 1818-1883. 3. Socialism 4. State, The 5. Revolutions 6. Soviet Union — Politics and government — 1917- I. T.
HX314.L3529 P65 1984      320.1 19      LC 84-2489      ISBN 0520053141

**Lenin, Vladimir Ilʹich, 1870-1924.** • 4.7101
Marx, Engels, Marxism / V. I. Lenin. — 4th English ed. — Moscow: Foreign Languages Pub. House, 1951. 580 p., [3] leaves of plates: ports. I. Marx, Karl, 1818-1883. II. Engels, Friedrich, 1820-1895. III. T.
HX314 L3547 1951

**Meyer, Alfred G.** • 4.7102
Leninism. — New York, Praeger [1962, c1957] 324 p. 21 cm. — (Praeger Paperback PPS-81) Includes bibliography. 1. Communism — Russia. I. T.
HX314.M49 1962      335.430947      LC 62-10312

## HX336–340 Sweden

**Tingsten, Herbert Lars Gustaf, 1896-.** 4.7103
[Svenska socialdemokratins idéutveckling. English] The Swedish social democrats; their ideological development [by] Herbert Tingsten. Translated by Greta Frankel and Patricia Howard–Rosen. Introd. by Richard Tomasson. [Totowa, N.J.] Bedminster Press, 1973. xxxii, 719 p. 24 cm. Translation of Den svenska socialdemokratins idéutveckling. 1. Socialism — Sweden I. T.
HX337.T513      335/.009485      LC 72-94562      ISBN 0870870327

## HX365.5–375.5 Yugoslavia. Greece

**Zukin, Sharon.** 4.7104
Beyond Marx and Tito: theory and practice in Yugoslav socialism / Sharon Zukin. — London; New York: Cambridge University Press, 1975. x, 302 p.; 22 cm. Includes index. 1. Communism — Yugoslavia. 2. Management — Yugoslavia - Employee participation. 3. Yugoslavia — Politics and government — 1945- I. T.
HX365.5.A6 Z8      335.43/4/09497      LC 74-12978      ISBN 0521206308

**Djilas, Milovan, 1911-.** • 4.7105
The new class; an analysis of the communist system, by Milovan Djilas. New York, Praeger [1958] 214 p. 21 cm. 1. Communism — Yugoslavia. 2. Communism 3. Communism — Soviet Union I. T.
HX365.5.D49      335.4      LC 57-9496

**Macridis, Roy C.** 4.7106
Greek politics at a crossroads: what kind of socialism? / Roy C. Macridis. — Stanford, Calif.: Hoover Institution Press, 1984. x, 72 p.; 23 cm. — (Hoover international studies.) (Hoover Press publication; 299) 1. Socialism — Greece 2. Communism — Greece. 3. Greece — Politics and government — 1974- I. T. II. Series.
HX375.5.A6 M32 1984      949.5/076 19      LC 84-3772      ISBN 0817979921

## HX381–466 Asia. Africa

**Peasant rebellion and Communist revolution in Asia / contributors: John Badgley [and others]; edited by John Wilson Lewis.** 4.7107
Stanford, Calif.: Stanford University Press, 1974. xiv, 364 p.; 23 cm. 'Papers ... were first presented at a research conference held in St. Croix, Virgin Islands, in January 1973.' 1. Communism — Asia — Congresses. 2. Peasant uprisings — Asia — Congresses. 3. Revolutions — Asia — Congresses. I. Badgley, John H., 1930- II. Lewis, John Wilson, 1930- ed.
HX382.P4      322.4/2/095      LC 73-89860      ISBN 0804708568

**Rose, Saul.** • 4.7108
Socialism in southern Asia. London: Oxford University Press, 1959. 278 p.: ill.; 23 cm. 1. Socialism — Asia I. T.
HX382 R6      LC 59-3232

**Brandt, Conrad.** • 4.7109
A documentary history of Chinese communism, by Conrad Brandt, Benjamin Schwartz, and John K. Fairbank. New York, Atheneum, 1966. 552 p.; 21 cm. (Atheneum paperbacks, 87) Reprint of the work first published in 1952. 1. Communism — China — History. 2. Chung-kuo kung chʹan tang — History. I. Schwartz, Benjamin Isadore, 1916- joint author. II. Fairbank, John King, 1907- joint author. III. T.
HX387.B7 1966      LC 66-6102

**Hsiao, Tso-liang, 1910-.** • 4.7110
Power relations within the Chinese communist movement, 1930–1934. Seattle: University of Washington Press, 1961. x, 404 p.; 24 cm. (University of Washington publications on Asia) 1. Communism — China. I. T.
HX387.H75      LC 61-11573

**Meisner, Maurice J., 1931-.** • 4.7111
Li Ta–chao and the origins of Chinese Marxism, by Maurice Meisner. — Cambridge: Harvard University Press, 1967. xvii, 326 p.; 24 cm. — (Harvard East Asian series. 27) Revision of the author's thesis, University of Chicago. 1. Li, Ta-chao, 1888-1927. 2. Communism — China. I. T. II. Series.
HX387.L48 M4      335.4/0951      LC 67-10904

**Schwartz, Benjamin Isadore, 1916-.** • 4.7112
Communism and China: ideology in flux / by Benjamin I. Schwartz. — Cambridge, Mass.: Harvard University Press, 1968. vi, 254 p.; 22 cm. 1. Communism — China. 2. Soviet Union — Relations — China 3. China — Relations — Soviet Union I. T.
HX387.S33      335.43/0951      LC 68-28696

**Selden, Mark.** 4.7113
The Yenan Way in revolutionary China. — Cambridge: Harvard University Press, 1972, (c1971). xi, 311 p.: maps.; 25 cm. — (Harvard East Asian series. 62) 1. Communism — China. I. T. II. Series.
HX387.S42      335.43/4/0951      LC 79-152272      ISBN 0674965604

**Ghose, Sankar, 1925-.** 4.7114
Socialism and communism in India. — Bombay: Allied Publishers, 1972 (c1971) xiii, 468 p.; 22 cm. 1. Socialism — India 2. Communism — India I. T.
HX392.G46      LC 70-919988

**Mohan Ram, 1933-.** • 4.7115
Indian communism: split within a split. — [Delhi]: Vikas Publications, [1969] ix, 293 p.; 22 cm. 1. Communism — India 2. Communism — 1945- 3. Communist revisionism — Case studies. I. T.
HX393.5.M62      335.43/0954      LC 72-909962

**Mohan Ram, 1933-.** 4.7116
Maoism in India / Mohan Ram. — New York: Barnes & Noble, 1971. vii, 196 p.; 23 cm. 1. Communism — India I. T.
HX393.5.M63      335.43/4/0951      ISBN 038904198x

**Sen, Chanakya, 1921-.**      **4.7117**
Communism in Indian politics / [by] Bhabani Sen Gupta. — New York: Columbia University Press, 1972. xx, 455 p.; 23 cm. 1. Communist Party of India. 2. Communist Party of India (Marxist) 3. Communism — India I. T. HX394.Z7 S45     335.43/0954     *LC* 73-190190     *ISBN* 0231035683 *ISBN* 0231083033

**Nossiter, T. J. (Thomas Johnson)**      **4.7118**
Communism in Kerala: a study in political adaptation / by T.J. Nossiter. — Berkeley: University of California Press for the Royal Institute of International Affairs, London, 1982. xv, 426 p.; ill.; 22 cm. Includes index. 1. Communism — India — Kerala — History. I. Royal Institute of International Affairs. II. T. HX395.K4 N67 1982     335.43/0954/83 19     *LC* 81-71762     *ISBN* 0520046676

**Franda, Marcus F.**      • **4.7119**
Radical politics in West Bengal [by] Marcus F. Franda. — Cambridge, Mass.: M.I.T. Press, [1971] xiv, 287 p.; 24 cm. — (Studies in communism, revisionism, and revolution 16) 1. Communism — India — West Bengal. 2. Political parties — India — West Bengal. I. T. II. Series. HX395.W4 F7     329.9/54/14     *LC* 76-138839     *ISBN* 026206040X

**Communism in Indochina: new perspectives / edited byJoseph J.**      **4.7120**
**Zasloff, MacAlister Brown.**
Lexington, Mass.: Lexington Books, [1975] xi, 295 p.; 24 cm. Papers originally presented at an ad hoc seminar held Sept. 30-Oct. 2, 1974 in New York and sponsored by the Southeast Asia Development Advisory Group of the Asia Society. 1. Communism — Indochina — Congresses. I. Zasloff, Joseph Jermiah. II. Brown, MacAlister. III. Southeast Asia Development Advisory Group. HX398.5.C65     335.43/09597     *LC* 75-18761     *ISBN* 0669001619

**Lê, Duân, 1907-.**      • **4.7121**
The Vietnamese revolution; fundamental problems and essential tasks. [1st ed.] New York, International Publishers [1971] vii, 151 p. (incl. cover) 21 cm. 'Based upon the English version published in 1970 by the Foreign Languages Publishing House, Hanoi, which has been completely reedited for this edition.' 1. Communism — Vietnam (Democratic Republic, 1946- ) 2. Communist strategy 3. Vietnam (Democratic Republic) — Economic policy. I. T. HX400.V5 L4213 1971     335.43/4     *LC* 71-171528     *ISBN* 0717803457 *ISBN* 0717803317

**Huỳnh, Kim Khánh.**      **4.7122**
Vietnamese communism, 1925–1945 / Huỳnh Kim Khánh. — Ithaca: Published under the auspices of the Institute of Southeast Asian Studies, Singapore, by Cornell University Press, 1982. 379 p.; ill.; 22 cm. Includes index. 1. Communism — Vietnam — History. I. T. HX400.5.A6 H89 1982     335.43/09597 19     *LC* 81-70696     *ISBN* 0801413699

**Kublin, Hyman.**      **4.7123**
Asian revolutionary; the life of Sen Katayama. Princeton, N.J., Princeton University Press, 1964. xiii, 370 p. ports. 23 cm. Bibliography: p. 341-362. 1. Katayama, Sen, 1859-1933. 2. Socialism — Japan I. T. HX412.K33K8     923.252     *LC* 63-7156

**Bernstein, Gail Lee.**      **4.7124**
Japanese Marxist: a portrait of Kawakami Hajime, 1879–1946 / Gail Lee Bernstein. — Cambridge, Mass.: Harvard University Press, 1976. xiv, 222 p.; 24 cm. (Harvard East Asian series. 86) Includes index. 1. Kawakami, Hajime, 1879-1946. I. T. II. Series. HX412.K345 B47     335.43/092/4 B     *LC* 76-20516     *ISBN* 0674471938

**Scalapino, Robert A.**      **4.7125**
Communism in Korea [by] Robert A. Scalapino & Chong-sik Lee. — Berkeley: University of California Press, 1973 (c1972). 2 v. (xxi, 1533 p.): illus.; 25 cm. 'Published under the auspices of the Center for Japanese and Korean Studies, University of California, Berkeley.' 'Index for Part I and Part II' ([41] p.) in pocket at end of pt. 1. 1. Communism — Korea — History. 2. Communism — Korea (Democratic People's Republic) I. Lee, Chong-Sik, 1931- joint author. II. T. HX415.5.A6 S35     321.9/2/095193     *LC* 79-165236     *ISBN* 0520020804

**Suh, Dae-sook, 1931-.**      • **4.7126**
The Korean Communist movement, 1918–1948. Princeton, N.J., Princeton University Press, 1967. xix, 406 p. maps. 24 cm. (Studies of the East Asian Institute, Columbia University) Revision of the author's thesis, Columbia University, 1964. 1. Communism — Korea — History. I. T. HX415.5.A6 S9 1967     329.9/519     *LC* 66-17711

**Thaxton, Ralph, 1944-.**      **4.7127**
China turned rightside up: revolutionary legitimacy in the peasant world / Ralph Thaxton. — New Haven: Yale University Press, c1983. xxi, 286 p.: ill.;

25 cm. 1. Communism — China — History — 20th century. 2. Peasant uprisings — China — History — 20th century. 3. China — Politics and government — 20th century I. T. HX417.T48 1983     303.6/4/0951 19     *LC* 82-40165     *ISBN* 0300027079

**Nkrumah, Kwame, 1909-1972.**      • **4.7128**
Consciencism; philosophy and ideology for de–colonization. [Rev. ed.] New York, Monthly Review Press [1970] 122 p. 22 cm. 1. Socialism — Africa 2. Philosophy, African I. T. HX437.N55 1970     335.41/1     *LC* 72-15010     *ISBN* 0853451389

**Ottaway, David.**      **4.7129**
Afrocommunism / David and Marina Ottaway. — 2nd ed. — New York: Africana Pub. Co., 1985. p. cm. Includes index. 1. Communism — Africa. 2. Socialism — Africa I. Ottaway, Marina. II. T. HX438.5.O87 1985     335.43/096 19     *LC* 85-7535     *ISBN* 0841910340

**Socialism in sub–Saharan Africa: a new assessment / edited by**      **4.7130**
**Carl G. Rosberg & Thomas M. Callaghy.**
Berkeley: Institute of International Studies, University of California, c1979. x, 426 p.; 23 cm. (Research series - Institute of International Studies, University of California, Berkeley; no. 38) 1. Socialism — Africa, Sub-Saharan — Addresses, essays, lectures. 2. Africa, Sub-Saharan — Politics and government — Addresses, essays, lectures. I. Rosberg, Carl Gustav. II. Callaghy, Thomas M. HX438.5.S63     335/.00967     *LC* 79-84635     *ISBN* 087725138X

**Friedland, William H. ed.**      • **4.7131**
African socialism. Edited by William Friedland [and] Carl G. Rosberg, Jr. Stanford, Calif., Published for the Hoover Institution on War, Revolution, and Peace by Stanford University Press, 1964. xi, 313 p. 23 cm. (Hoover Institution publications) 1. Socialism — Africa I. Rosberg, Carl Gustav. joint ed. II. T. HX439.F7     335.096     *LC* 64-14553

**Pratt, Cranford.**      **4.7132**
The critical phase in Tanzania, 1945–1968: Nyerere and the emergence of a socialist strategy / Cranford Pratt. — Cambridge, Eng.; New York: Cambridge University Press, 1976. x, 309 p., [4] leaves of plates: ill.; 24 cm. Includes index. 1. Nyerere, Julius K. (Julius Kambarage), 1922- 2. Socialism — Tanzania 3. Tanzania — Politics and government 4. Tanganyika — Politics and government. I. T. HX448.5.A6 P7     320.9/678     *LC* 75-22979     *ISBN* 0521208246

**Nyerere, Julius K. (Julius Kambarage), 1922-.**      **4.7133**
Ujamaa—essays on socialism [by] Julius K. Nyerere. Dar es Salaam, Oxford University Press, 1968. viii, 186 p. 18 cm. 1. Socialism 2. Socialism — Tanzania 3. Collective settlements — Tanzania I. T. HX457.T3 N92     335     *LC* 76-9146

# HX518–550 SPECIAL TOPICS

**Lowenthal, Richard, 1908-.**      **4.7134**
Model or ally?: The Communist powers and the developing countries / Richard Lowenthal. — New York: Oxford University Press, 1977. x, 400 p.; 22 cm. 1. Communist strategy 2. Communist state 3. Developing countries — Politics and government. I. T. HX518.S8 L63     917.3/04/925     *LC* 76-9273     *ISBN* 0195021053

**Lang, Berel. comp.**      **4.7135**
Marxism and art; writings in aesthetics and criticism. Edited by Berel Lang and Forrest Williams. — New York: McKay, [1972] viii, 470 p.; 23 cm. 1. Communism and art I. Williams. Forrest, joint comp. II. T. HX521.L34     701     *LC* 77-185134

**Williams, Raymond.**      **4.7136**
Marxism and literature / Raymond Williams. — Oxford [Eng.]: Oxford University Press, 1977. 217 p.; 21 cm. — (Marxist introductions) Includes index. 1. Communism and literature I. T. HX531.W47     335.43/8/80195     *LC* 77-5728     *ISBN* 0198760566

**Miranda, José Porfirio.**      **4.7137**
[Cristianismo de Marx. English] Marx against the Marxists: the Christian humanism of Karl Marx / José Porfirio Miranda; translated from the Spanish by John Drury. — Maryknoll, N.Y.: Orbis Books, c1980. xiii, 316 p.; 24 cm. Translation of El cristianismo de Marx. 1. Marx, Karl, 1818-1883. 2. Communism and Christianity I. T. HX536.M5413     335.4/01     *LC* 80-14415     *ISBN* 0883443228

**Mojzes, Paul.**      4.7138
Christian–Marxist dialogue in Eastern Europe / Paul Mojzes. — Minneapolis: Augsburg Pub. House, c1981. 336 p.; 22 cm. 1. Communism and Christianity — Europe, Eastern. I. T.
HX536.M59 1981     261.2/1 19     *LC* 81-65659     *ISBN* 0806618957

**Religion and atheism in the U.S.S.R. and Eastern Europe /**      4.7139
**edited by Bohdan R. Bociurkiw and John W. Strong, assisted by**
**Jean K. Laux.**
Toronto; Buffalo: University of Toronto Press, 1975. xviii, 412 p.; 23 cm. (The Carleton series in Soviet and East European studies) 'The idea of this volume was conceived at an international symposium ... organised at Carleton University in April 1971 by the Institute of Soviet and East European Studies.' 1. Communism and religion — Addresses, essays, lectures. 2. Church and state in Russia — Addresses, essays, lectures. 3. Church and state — Europe, Eastern — Addresses, essays, lectures. I. Bociurkiw, Bohdan R. II. Strong, John W., 1930- III. Laux, Jean K. IV. Series.
HX536.R437 1975     261.7/0947     *LC* 73-89059     *ISBN* 0802021158

**Woodbey, George Washington, b. 1854.**      4.7140
Black socialist preacher: the teachings of Reverend George Washington Woodbey and his disciple, Reverend G.W. Slater, Jr. / edited and with an introduction by Philip S. Foner; foreword by Ronald V. Dellums. — San Francisco, Calif.: Synthesis Publications, c1983. iii, 363 p.; port.; 21 cm. 1. Socialism and religion — United States — Addresses, essays, lectures. 2. Afro-Americans — Social conditions — To 1964 — Addresses, essays, lectures. 3. Socialism — United States — Addresses, essays, lectures. I. Slater, George W. II. Foner, Philip Sheldon, 1910- III. T.
HX536.W72 1983     261.2/1 19     *LC* 83-17927     *ISBN* 0899350267

**Fleron, Frederic J., 1937- comp.**      4.7141
Communist studies and the social sciences: essays on methodology and empirical theory / Edited by Frederic J. Fleron, Jr. — Chicago: Rand McNally, [1969] xiii, 481 p.; 23 cm. 1. Communism and social sciences I. T.
HX541.5.F54     335.43/8/3     *LC* 69-17208

**Colletti, Lucio.**      4.7142
[Ideologia e società. English] From Rousseau to Lenin: studies in ideology and society / [translated from the Italian by John Merrington and Judith White]. — London, NLB, 1972. [6], 240 p. 22 cm. Translation of Ideologia e società. 1. Communism and society I. T.
HX542.C6213 1972     335.4     *LC* 72-171217     *ISBN* 0902308718

**Gouldner, Alvin Ward, 1920-.**      4.7143
The dialectic of ideology and technology: the origins, grammar, and future of ideology / Alvin W. Gouldner. — New York: Seabury Press, c1976. xvi, 304 p.; 24 cm. — ([His The dark side of the dialectic; v. 1]) (A Continuum book) 1. Communism and society I. T.
HX542.G68     335.4/112     *LC* 75-29393     *ISBN* 0816492751

**Stojanović, Svetozar.**      4.7144
[Izmedu ideala i stvarnosti. English] Between ideals and reality; a critique of socialism and its future. Translated by Gerson S. Sher. New York, Oxford University Press, 1973. xvii, 222 p. 22 cm. Translation of Izmedu ideala i stvarnosti. 1. Communism and society 2. Dialectical materialism 3. Alienation (Philosophy) I. T.
HX542.S78713     335.4/1     *LC* 72-91017

**European women on the left: socialism, feminism, and the**      4.7145
**problems faced by political women, 1880 to the present / edited**
**by Jane Slaughter and Robert Kern.**
Westport, Conn.: Greenwood Press, 1981. vi, 245 p.; 22 cm. — (Contributions in women's studies. no. 24 0147-104X) Includes index. 1. Women and socialism — Europe — History — Addresses, essays, lectures. 2. Feminism — Europe — History — Addresses, essays, lectures. I. Slaughter, Jane, 1941- II. Kern, Robert, 1934- III. Series.
HX546.E9     335/.0094 19     *LC* 80-23553     *ISBN* 0313225435

**Lenin, Vladimir Il'ich, 1870-1924.**      • 4.7146
[Selections. English. 1969] The emancipation of women; from the writings of V. I. Lenin. Pref. by Nadezhda K. Krupskaya. With an appendix, 'Lenin on the woman question,' by Clara Zetkin. New York, International Publishers [1969] 135 p. 21 cm. (New World paperbacks, NW-130) 1. Women and socialism I. T.
HX546.L4313     335.43/8/3014121     *LC* 74-15197     *ISBN* 0717802906

**Mullaney, Marie Marmo.**      4.7147
Revolutionary women: gender and the socialist revolutionary role / Marie Marmo Mullaney. — New York, N.Y.: Praeger, 1983. x, 401 p.; ports.; 25 cm. Includes index. 1. Women and socialism 2. Women revolutionists — Biography. 3. Communists — Biography. I. T.
HX546.M83 1983     335/.0088042 19     *LC* 82-22437     *ISBN* 0030619270

**Sowerwine, Charles, 1943-.**      4.7148
[Femmes et le socialisme. English] Sisters or citizens?: women and socialism in France since 1876 / Charles Sowerwine. — Cambridge; New York: Cambridge University Press, 1982. xx, 248 p.; 24 cm. Revision and translation of: Les Femmes et le socialisme. Includes index. 1. Women and socialism — France — History. I. T.
HX546.S6813     335/.0088/042 19     *LC* 81-7692     *ISBN* 0521234840

**Vogel, Lise.**      4.7149
Marxism and the oppression of women: toward a unitary theory / Lise Vogel. — New Brunswick, N.J.: Rutgers University Press, 1984 (c1983). xiii, 218 p.; 24 cm. Includes index. 1. Marx, Karl, 1818-1883. 2. Women and socialism I. T.
HX546.V63 1983     335.4/088042 19     *LC* 82-24047     *ISBN* 0813509955

**Women and revolution: a discussion of the unhappy marriage of**      4.7150
**Marxism and feminism / edited by Lydia Sargent.**
Boston, MA: South End Press, c1981. xxxii, 373 p.; 22 cm. (South End Press political controversies series. #2) Series for hardbound ed. appears only on jacket. 1. Women and socialism — Addresses, essays, lectures. 2. Feminism — Addresses, essays, lectures. I. Sargent, Lydia. II. Series.
HX546.W615 1981     *LC* 80-54829     *ISBN* 0896080617

**Dyson, Lowell K., 1929-.**      4.7151
Red harvest: the Communist Party and American farmers / Lowell K. Dyson. — Lincoln: University of Nebraska Press, c1982. xii, 259 p.; 23 cm. 1. Communist Party of the United States of America. 2. Communism and agriculture — United States. I. T.
HX550.A37 D97 1982     324.273/75 19     *LC* 81-8200     *ISBN* 0803216599

**Soviet nationalities in strategic perspective / edited by S.**      4.7152
**Enders Wimbush.**
New York: St. Martin's Press, 1985. xxviii, 253 p.; 23 cm. 1. Nationalism and socialism — Soviet Union — Addresses, essays, lectures. I. Wimbush, S. Enders.
HX550.N3 S657 1985     323.1/47 19     *LC* 84-40374     *ISBN* 0312748477

# HX626–795 UTOPIAN SOCIALISM. COLLECTIVE SETTLEMENTS

**Popenoe, Oliver.**      4.7153
Seeds of tomorrow: new age communities that work / Oliver and Cris Popenoe. — 1st ed. — San Francisco: Harper & Row, c1984. xii, 289 p.: ill.; 24 cm. 1. Collective settlements — Case studies. I. Popenoe, Cris. II. T.
HX632.P67 1984     335/.9/09048 19     *LC* 83-48425     *ISBN* 0062506803

**Fogarty, Robert S.**      4.7154
Dictionary of American communal and utopian history / Robert S. Fogarty. — Westport, Conn.: Greenwood Press, 1980. xxvi, 271 p.; 25 cm. Includes index. 1. Collective settlements — United States. 2. Utopias 3. Socialists — United States — Biography. I. T.
HX653.F65     335/.9/73     *LC* 79-7476     *ISBN* 031321347X

**Hayden, Dolores.**      4.7155
Seven American utopias: the architecture of communitarian socialism, 1790–1975 / Dolores Hayden. — Cambridge, Mass.: MIT Press, c1976. ix, 401 p.: ill.; 26 cm. Includes index. 1. Utopias I. T.
HX653.H39     335/.973     *LC* 75-23148     *ISBN* 0262080826

**Kanter, Rosabeth Moss.**      4.7156
Commitment and community: communes and utopias in sociological perspective. — Cambridge, Mass.: Harvard University Press, 1972. x, 303 p.; 24 cm. 1. Collective settlements — United States — History. 2. Utopias I. T.
HX653.K35     335/.973     *LC* 72-76565     *ISBN* 0674145755

**Melville, Keith.**      4.7157
Communes in the counter culture: origins, theories, styles of life. — New York: Morrow, 1972. 256 p.; 22 cm. 1. Communal living — United States — History. 2. Radicalism — United States. 3. Social values 4. United States — Social conditions — 1960- I. T.
HX653.M44     335/.9/73     *LC* 77-151927

**Veysey, Laurence R.**      4.7158
The communal experience: anarchist and mystical counter–cultures in America / [by] Laurence Veysey. — [1st ed.]. — New York: Harper & Row, [1973] xi,

495 p.; 24 cm. 1. Collective settlements — United States. 2. Radicalism — United States. I. T.
HX654.V48     335/.9/73     *LC* 73-4135     *ISBN* 0060145013

**Thomas, Robert David, 1939-.**          4.7159
The man who would be perfect: John Humphrey Noyes and the Utopian impulse / Robert David Thomas. [Philadelphia]: University of Pennsylvania Press, 1977. xii, 199 p.: port.; 24 cm. Includes index. 1. Noyes, John Humphrey, 1811-1886. 2. Oneida Community. 3. Social reformers — United States — Biography. I. T.
HX656.O5 N697     335/.9/74764 B     *LC* 76-53198     *ISBN* 0812277244

**Robertson, Constance Noyes. comp.**          4.7160
Oneida Community: an autobiography, 1851–1876 / edited, with an introd. and prefaces, by Constance Noyes Robertson. — [1st ed. Syracuse]: Syracuse University Press [1970] xvi, 364 p.: ill., ports.; 24 cm. 1. Noyes, John Humphrey, 1811-1886. 2. Oneida Community. I. T.
HX656.O5 R62     335/.9747/64     *LC* 75-115417     *ISBN* 0815600690

**Owen, Robert, 1771-1858.**          • 4.7161
A new view of society and other writings / [by] Robert Owen. — London: J.M. Dent & sons, ltd. [193-?] xx, 298 p., 1 l.; 18 cm. (Everyman's library, ed. by Ernest Rhys. Science, [no. 799]) Introduction by G.D.H. Cole. 1. Communism — Great Britain 2. Socialism I. T.
HX696 O9 1930     *LC* 36-37604

**Cole, G. D. H. (George Douglas Howard), 1889-1959.**          • 4.7162
The life of Robert Owen. New introd. by Margaret Cole. [3d ed. Hamden, Conn.] Archon Books, 1966. xxii, 349 p.: ill., port. 1. Owen, Robert, 1771-1858. 2. Socialism — Great Britain 3. Cooperation — Great Britain I. T.
HX696 O9 C6 1966     *LC* 66-864

**Harrison, J. F. C. (John Fletcher Clews)**          4.7163
Quest for the new moral world; Robert Owen and the Owenities in Britain and America [by] J. F. C. Harrison. New York, Scribner [1969] xi, 392 p. illus., ports. 25 cm. London ed. (Routledge and K. Paul) has title: Robert Owen and the Owenites in Britain and America. 1. Owen, Robert, 1771-1858. I. T.
HX696.O9 H34 1969b     335/.12     *LC* 68-17343

**Johnson. Christopher H.**          4.7164
Utopian communism in France: Cabet and the Icarians, 1839–1851 / Christopher H. Johnson. — Ithaca, N.Y.: Cornell University Press, 1974. 324 p.; 23 cm. Includes index. 1. Cabet, Étienne, 1788-1856. 2. Socialism — France — History. 3. France — Politics and government — 1830-1848 I. T.
HX703.J62 1974     335/.2/0924     *LC* 74-10409     *ISBN* 0801408954

**Fourier, Charles, 1772-1837.**          • 4.7165
[Selected works. English] The Utopian vision of Charles Fourier; selected texts on work, love, and passionate attraction. Translated, edited and with an introd. by Jonathan Beecher and Richard Bienvenu. Boston, Beacon Press [1971] xiv, 427 p. 22 cm. 1. Collective settlements — Collected works. 2. Socialism — Collected works. 3. Utopias — Collected works. I. Beecher, Jonathan. ed. II. Bienvenu, Richard. ed. III. T.
HX704.F7212     321/.07     *LC* 72-136222     *ISBN* 0807015385

**Gerson, Menachem, 1908-.**          4.7166
Family, women, and socialization in the kibbutz / Menachem Gerson. — Lexington, Mass.: Lexington Books, c1978. xiii, 142 p.; 23 cm. 1. Kibbutzim 2. Family — Israel. 3. Women — Israel. I. T.
HX742.2.A3 G47     334/.683/095694     *LC* 78-57188     *ISBN* 066902371X

**Lieblich, Amia, 1939-.**          4.7167
Kibbutz Makom: report from an Israeli kibbutz / by Amia Lieblich. — 1st ed. — New York: Pantheon Books, 1982. xxvi, 318 p. (Pantheon village series) 1. Collective settlements — Israel — Case studies I. T.
HX742.2.A3 L53     307.7 19     *LC* 81-47204     *ISBN* 039450724X

**Shepher, Israel.**          4.7168
The kibbutz: an anthropological study / by Israel Shepher; foreword by Uri Leviatan; Joseph Blasi, editor–in–chief. — Norwood, PA: Norwood Editions, 1983. x, 298 p.; 26 cm. — (Kibbutz, communal society, and alternative social policy series.) (Kibbutz studies book series. v. 8) 1. Collective settlements — Israel — Case studies. 2. Quality of work life — Israel — Case studies. I. Blasi, Joseph R. II. T. III. Series. IV. Series: Kibbutz studies book series. v. 8
HX742.2.A3 S52 1983     307.7/76/095694 19     *LC* 83-13161     *ISBN* 0848264649

**Spiro, Melford E.**          • 4.7169
Kibbutz: venture in utopia / [by] Melford E. Spiro. — New, augmented ed. — New York: Schocken Books, [1971] xxii, 306 p.; 21 cm. — (Studies in the

libertarian and utopian tradition) (Schocken paperbacks) 1. Kibbutzim — Case studies. I. T.
HX765.P3 S7 1971     334/.683/095694     *LC* 70-132260     *ISBN* 0805200630

# HX806–811 UTOPIAS

**Ferguson, John, 1921-.**          4.7170
Utopias of the classical world / John Ferguson. — Ithaca, N.Y.: Cornell University Press, 1975. 228 p.; 23 cm. (Aspects of Greek and Roman life) 1. Utopias — History. I. T. II. Series.
HX806.F43     321/.07     *LC* 74-7700     *ISBN* 0801409322

**Kateb, George.**          • 4.7171
Utopia and its enemies. London, Free Press of Glencoe [1963] 244 p. 1. Utopias I. T.
HX806 K38     *LC* 63-8418

**Manuel, Frank Edward. ed.**          • 4.7172
Utopias and Utopian thought, edited by Frank E. Manuel. — Boston: Houghton Mifflin, 1966. xxiv, 321 p.; 24 cm. — (The Daedalus library) 1. Utopias — Addresses, essays, lectures. I. T.
HX806.M35     321.07     *LC* 66-11232

**Mumford, Lewis, 1895-.**          • 4.7173
The story of Utopias / by Lewis Mumford; with an introduction by Hendrik Willem Van Loon. — New York: P. Smith, 1941. xii p., 1 l., 11-315 p.: ill.; 22 cm. 1. Utopias I. T.
HX806.Mx     *LC* a 42-1728

**Walsh, Chad, 1914-.**          4.7174
From Utopia to nightmare. Westport, Conn., Greenwood Press [1972, c1962] 190 p. 22 cm. 1. Utopias — History. 2. Dystopias — History. I. T.
HX806.W2 1972     321/.07     *LC* 71-38130     *ISBN* 0837163250

**More, Thomas, Sir, Saint, 1478-1535.**          • 4.7175
Utopia / edited with introd. and notes by Edward Surtz. — New Haven: Yale University Press, 1964. xxxiv, 158 p.: front.; 21 cm. (The Yale edition of the works of St. Thomas More: selected works) 1. Utopias I. Surtz, Edward L. II. T.
HX811 1516 E964     *LC* 64-56154

**Logan, George M., 1941-.**          4.7176
The meaning of More's Utopia / by George M. Logan. — Princeton, N.J.: Princeton University Press, c1983. xv, 296 p.; 23 cm. Includes index. 1. More, Thomas, Sir, Saint, 1478-1535. Utopia I. T.
HX811 1516.Z5 L63 1983     321/.07 19     *LC* 82-16147     *ISBN* 0691065578

**Campanella, Tommaso, 1568-1639.**          4.7177
[Civitas Solis. English & Italian] La città del sole: dialogo poetico = The City of the Sun: a poetical dialogue / Tommaso Campanella; translated with introd. and notes by Daniel J. Donno. — Berkeley: University of California Press, c1981. 144 p.; 21 cm. (Biblioteca italiana) Translation of Civitas Solis. Translation based on the Italian text edited by Luigi Firpo. Text in English and Italian; introd. and notes in English. 1. Utopias I. Donno, Daniel John, 1920- II. T. III. Title: City of the Sun.
HX811 1623.E980     335/.02 19     *LC* 80-20133     *ISBN* 0520040368

**Lytton, Edward Bulwer Lytton, Baron, 1803-1873.**          4.7178
The coming race. — London: Oxford University Press; 1928. vi, 186, 27 p. 23 cm. 1. Utopias I. T.
HX811 1886.L9     321/.07

**Bellamy, Edward, 1850-1898.**          • 4.7179
Looking backward, 2000–1887. Edited by John L. Thomas. — Cambridge: Belknap Press of Harvard University Press, 1967. 314 p.; 22 cm. — (John Harvard library) First published in 1888. Reprinted from the corrected MS. Sequel: Equality. 1. Utopias I. Thomas, John L. ed. II. T. III. Series.
HX811 1887.B3342     813/.4 19     *LC* 67-14337

# HX821–999 ANARCHISM

**Guérin, Daniel, 1904-.**                                                    **4.7180**
[Anarchisme, de la doctrine à l'action. English] Anarchism; from theory to practice. Introd. by Noam Chomsky. Translated by Mary Klopper. New York, Monthly Review Press [1970] xx, 166 p. 21 cm. Translation of L'anarchisme, de la doctrine à l'action. 1. Anarchism and anarchists — History. I. T.
HX828.G813       335/.83/09       LC 71-105316

**Joll, James.**                                                    **• 4.7181**
The anarchists. — [1st American ed.]. — Boston: Little, Brown, [1965, c1964] 303 p.: illus., ports.; 22 cm. 'An Atlantic Monthly Press book.' 1. Anarchism and anarchists. I. T.
HX828.J6 1965       321.9       LC 65-10901

**Kropotkin, Petr Alekseevich, kniaz', 1842-1921.**               **4.7182**
[Selected works. 1975] The essential Kropotkin / edited by Emile Capouya and Keitha Tompkins. — 1st ed. — New York: Liveright, [1975] xxiii, 294 p.; 22 cm. 1. Anarchism and anarchists. 2. Socialism 3. Social history — 20th century I. Capouya, Emile, ed. II. Tompkins, Keitha, ed. III. T.
HX828.K73 1975       320.5/7       LC 74-28041       ISBN 0871405911

**Shatz, Marshall. comp.**                                           **4.7183**
The essential works of anarchism / edited by Marshall S. Shatz. — New York: Quadrangle Books, [c1972] xxix, 604 p.; 22 cm. 1. Anarchism and anarchists — Collected works. I. T.
HX828.S5       335/.83/08       LC 71-183192

**Thomas, Paul.**                                                    **4.7184**
Karl Marx and the anarchists / Paul Thomas. — London; Boston: Routledge & Kegan Paul, 1980. ix, 406 p.; 23 cm. Includes index. 1. Marx, Karl, 1818-1883. 2. Anarchism and anarchists. I. T.
HX828.T47       335/.83 19       LC 79-41564       ISBN 0710004273

**Woodcock, George, 1912-.**                                         **• 4.7185**
Anarchism: a history of libertarian ideas and movements / George Woodcock. — Cleveland: Meridian Books, 1962. 504 p. — (An original Meridian book; M133) Includes index. 1. Anarchism and anarchists. I. T.
HX828.W6       LC 62-12355

**Anarchism / edited by J. Roland Pennock and John W.**              **4.7186**
**Chapman.**
New York: New York University Press, 1978. xlv, 375 p.; 22 cm. — (Nomos. 19) Includes index. 1. Anarchism and anarchists — Addresses, essays, lectures. I. Pennock, James Roland, 1906- II. Chapman, John William, 1923- III. Series.
HX833.A568       335/.83       LC 77-84158       ISBN 0814765726

**The Anarchist reader / edited by George Woodcock.**               **4.7187**
Hassocks, Eng.: Harvester Press; Atlantic Highlands, N.J.: Humanities Press, 1978 (c1977). 383 p.; 23 cm. 1. Anarchism and anarchists — Addresses, essays, lectures. I. Woodcock, George, 1912-
HX833.A57 1977       335/.83       LC 77-2990       ISBN 0391007092

**Bookchin, Murray, 1921-.**                                         **• 4.7188**
Post-scarcity anarchism / by Murray Bookchin, Lewis Herber. — Berkeley [Calif.]: Ramparts Press, [1971] 288 p.; 22 cm. Errata slip inserted. 1. Anarchim. 2. Radicalism I. Bookchin, Murray. II. T.
HX833.H38       335/.83       LC 75-158914       ISBN 087867005X

**Read, Herbert Edward, Sir, 1893-1968.**                            **• 4.7189**
Poetry and anarchism. — Freeport, N.Y.: Books for Libraries Press, [1972] 126 p.; 23 cm. — (Essay index reprint series) Reprint of the 1938 ed. 1. Anarchism and anarchists. 2. Socialism and the arts I. T.
HX833.R253 1972       824/.9/12       LC 72-290       ISBN 0836928199

**Ritter, Alan, 1937-.**                                             **4.7190**
Anarchism, a theoretical analysis / Alan Ritter. — Cambridge [Eng.]; New York: Cambridge University Press, 1981 (c1980). vii, 187 p.; 23 cm. 1. Anarchism and anarchists. I. T.
HX833.R55       335/.83/01 19       LC 80-40589       ISBN 0521233240

**Taylor, Michael, Ph. D.**                                          **4.7191**
Community, anarchy, and liberty / Michael Taylor. — Cambridge [Cambridgeshire]; New York: Cambridge University Press, 1982. 184 p.; 23 cm. Includes index. 1. Anarchism and anarchists. 2. Community 3. Liberty. I. T.
HX833.T39 1982       335/.83 19       LC 82-1173       ISBN 0521246210

**Goldman, Emma, 1869-1940.**                                        **• 4.7192**
Red Emma speaks: selected writings and speeches / compiled and edited by Alix Kates Shulman. — [1st ed.] New York: Random House [1972] 413 p.: port.; 22 cm. 1. Goldman, Emma, 1869-1940. 2. Women and socialism — Addresses, essays, lectures. 3. Communism — Addresses, essays, lectures. 4. Anarchism and anarchists — Addresses, essays, lectures. 5. Revolutions — Addresses, essays, lectures. I. T.
HX844.G62 1972       335/.83/0924       LC 77-37077       ISBN 0394470958

**Hart, John M. (John Mason), 1935-.**                               **4.7193**
Anarchism & the Mexican working class, 1860–1931 / John M. Hart. — Austin: University of Texas Press, c1978. x, 249 p.: ill.; 24 cm. Includes index. 1. Anarchism and anarchists — Mexico — History. 2. Labor and laboring classes — Mexico — History. I. T.
HX851.H37       335/.83/0972       LC 77-16210       ISBN 0292703317

**Kropotkin, P. A.**                                                 **• 4.7194**
Selected writings on anarchism and revolution / P. A. Kropotkin; edited, with an introd., by Martin A. Miller. — Cambridge, Mass.: M.I.T. Press, 1970. viii, 374 p.; 21 cm. 1. Anarchism and anarchists — Addresses, essays, lectures. 2. Revolutions — Addresses, essays, lectures. I. T.
HX914.K67       335/.83       LC 73-107994       ISBN 0262110377

**Woodcock, George.**                                                **• 4.7195**
The anarchist prince: a biographical study of Peter Kropotkin / by George Woodcock and Ivan Avakumović. — New York: Schocken Books, [1971] 465 p.: ports.; 21 cm. — (Studies in the libertarian and utopian tradition) Includes index. 1. Kropotkin, Petr Alekseevich, kniaz', 1842-1921. I. Avakumovic, Ivan. joint author. II. T.
HX914.K7 W6 1971       947.08/0924 B       LC 70-152571       ISBN 0805203052 Pbk

**Bakunin, Mikhail Aleksandrovich, 1814-1876.**                     **• 4.7196**
Bakunin on anarchy; selected works by the activist–founder of world anarchism. Edited, translated and with an introd. by Sam Dolgoff. Pref. by Paul Avrich. — [1st ed.]. — New York: A. A. Knopf, 1972. xxvii, 405, vii p.: port.; 26 cm. 1. Anarchism and anarchists — Collected works. I. T.
HX915.B164       320.5/7/08       LC 79-136351       ISBN 0394416015

**Bakunin, Mikhail Aleksandrovich, 1814-1876.**                     **• 4.7197**
The political philosophy of Bakunin: scientific anarchism, compiled and edited by G.P. Maximoff. Pref. by Bert F. Hoselitz; introd. by Rudolf Rocker; biographical sketch of Bakunin, by Max Nettlau. Glencoe, Ill., Free Press, 1953. 434 p. 1. Anarchism and anarchists I. Maksimov, Grigoriĭ Petrovich, 1893-1950. II. T.
HX915 B1642       LC 53-9076

**Carr, Edward Hallett, 1892-.**                                     **• 4.7198**
Michael Bakunin. [1st ed.] New York: Vintage Books [1961, c1937] 511 p.; 19 cm. (Vintage Russian library, V-725) 1. Bakunin, Mikhail Aleksandrovich, 1814-1876. 2. Anarchism and anarchists I. T.
HX915 B3 C3 1961       LC 61-2306

**Mintz, Jerome R.**                                                 **4.7199**
The anarchists of Casas Viejas / Jerome R. Mintz. — Chicago: University of Chicago Press, 1982. xvi, 336 p., [40] p. of plates: ill.; 24 cm. Includes index. 1. Anarchism and anarchists — Spain — Casas Viejas — History. 2. Syndicalism — Spain — Casas Viejas — History. 3. Peasant uprisings — Spain — Casas Viejas — History. 4. Casas Viejas (Cadiz, Spain) — History. I. T.
HX928.C34 M54 1982       335/.83/094688 19       LC 81-19696       ISBN 0226531066

**Stanley, Thomas A., 1946-.**                                       **4.7200**
Ōsugi Sakae, anarchist in Taishō Japan: the creativity of the ego / Thomas A. Stanley. — Cambridge, Mass.: Council on East Asian Studies, Harvard University: Distributed by Harvard University Press, 1982. xviii, 232 p.: port.; 24 cm. — (Harvard East Asian monographs. 102) Includes index. 1. Ōsugi, Sakae, 1885-1923. 2. Anarchism and anarchists — Japan — Biography. I. T. II. Series.
HX947.O84 S72 1982       335/.83/0924 B 19       LC 81-6916       ISBN 067464493X

## J1–981 OFFICIAL DOCUMENTS

**United States. Continental Congress.** **4.7201**
A decent respect to the opinions of mankind: Congressional State papers, 1774–1776 / compiled and edited by James H. Hutson, coordinator, American Revolution Bicentennial Office. — Washington: Library of Congress: for sale by the Supt. of Docs., U.S. Govt. Print. Off.; 1975. v, 154 p.; 24 cm. 1. United States — Politics and government — Revolution, 1775-1783 2. United States — History — Revolution, 1775-1783 — Causes I. Hutson, James H. II. Library of Congress. American Revolution Bicentennial Office. III. T.
J10.D74 1975     973.3/1     LC 75-619135     ISBN 084440165X

**United States. Congress. Senate. (1st: 1789-1791).**     • **4.7202**
Senate legislative journal. Linda Grant De Pauw, editor; Charlene Bangs Bickford [and] LaVonne Marlene Siegel, assistant editor[s] Baltimore, Johns Hopkins University Press [1972] xxiv, 774 p. 24 cm. (Documentary history of the First Federal Congress of the United States of America, March 4, 1789-March 3, 1791. v. 1) The 'Journal of the first session of the Senate of the United States of America (New York: Thomas Greenleaf, 1789). E-22207; Journal of the second session of the Senate of the United States of America (New York: John Fenno, 1790). E-22982; Journal of the third session of the Senate of the United States of America (Philadelphia: John Fenno, 1791). E-23901' have been taken as the basic text for this edition. 1. Legislative journals — United States. 2. United States — Politics and government — 1789-1797 — Sources. I. De Pauw, Linda Grant. II. T. III. Series.
J31 1972x vol. 1     328.73/09 s 328.73/01 19     LC 72-189461     ISBN 0801812801

**United States. Congress. Senate. (1st: 1789-1791).**     **4.7203**
Senate executive journal and related documents. Linda Grant De Pauw, editor; Charlene Bangs Bickford [and] La Vonne Marlene Siegel, assistant editor[s] Baltimore, Johns Hopkins University Press [1974] xvii, 574 p. illus. 23 cm. (Documentary history of the First Federal Congress of the United States of America, March 4, 1789-March 3, 1791. v. 2) 1. Legislative journals — United States. 2. United States — Politics and government — 1789-1797 — Sources. I. De Pauw, Linda Grant. II. T. III. Series.
J31 1972x vol. 2     328.73/09 s 328.73/01 19     LC 73-13443     ISBN 080181572X

**United States. Congress. Senate.** **4.7204**
The Journal of the Senate, including the Journal of the Executive proceedings of the Senate. 1st-14th Congress; Mar./Sept. 1789-Dec. 1816/Mar. 1817. Wilmington, Del.: M. Glazier, inc., 1977. 14 v.; 23-29 cm. (The Congressional journals of the United States) (National State papers of the United States series, 1789-1817) Other editions available: Journal of the Senate of the United States of America nyu Other editions available: Journal of the Executive proceedings of the Senate nyu 1. Legislation — United States — Periodicals. 2. United States — Politics and government — Periodicals. I. United States. Congress. Senate. Journal of the Executive proceedings of the Senate. II. T. III. Series. IV. Series: National State papers of the United States series, 1789-1817
J31 1977x     328.73/009/033     LC 78-646663

**United States. Congress. House.** **4.7205**
Journal of the House of Representatives. 1st-14th Congress; Mar./Sept. 1789-Dec. 1816/Mar. 1817. Wilmington, Del.: M. Glazier, inc., 1977. 14 v.; 23-29 cm. (The Congressional journals of the United States) (National State papers of the United States series, 1789-1817) Other editions available: Journal of the House of Representatives of the United States 1. Legislation — United States — Periodicals. 2. United States — Politics and government — Periodicals. I. T. II. Series. III. Series: National State papers of the United States series, 1789-1817
J32 1977x     328.73/009/033     LC 78-646662

**United States. President.**     • **4.7206**
Public papers of the presidents of the United States. — Washington: Federal Register Division, National Archives and Records Service, General Services Administration; For sale by the Supt. of Docs., U.S. G.P.O. v.: col. ill., ports.; 26 cm. Annual. 'Containing the public messages, speeches, and statements of the President', < 1956- > Description based on: 1956. Vols. for -1956 published retrospectively. Vols. for some years issued in parts. 1. Presidents — United States — Messages — Periodicals. 2. United States — Politics and government — Periodicals. I. United States. Office of the Federal Register. II. United States. Federal Register Division. III. T.
J80.A283     353.03/5 19     LC 58-61050

**The Cumulated indexes to the public papers of the Presidents of the United States.** **4.7207**
Millwood, N.Y.: KTO Press. 5 v. 1. Presidents — United States 2. United States — Politics and government — Addresses, essays, lectures — Indexes. I. KTO Press. II. United States. President. Public papers of the Presidents of the United States. III. Title: Public papers of the Presidents of the United States.
J80.A28x     354.73

## JA COLLECTIONS. GENERAL WORKS

**Storing, Herbert J., 1928- ed.**     • **4.7208**
Essays on the scientific study of politics [by] Walter Berns [and others] Edited by Herbert J. Storing. New York, Holt, Rinehart and Winston [1962] vii, 333 p. 1. Political science — Addresses, essays, lectures I. T.
JA37 S67     LC 62-7453

**Strauss, Leo.**     • **4.7209**
What is political philosophy? and other studies. — Glencoe, Ill., Free Press [1959] 315 p. 22 cm. 1. Political science — Addresses, essays, lectures. I. T.
JA37.S7     320.4     LC 58-12852

**Lasswell, Harold Dwight, 1902-.**     • **4.7210**
The analysis of political behaviour; an empirical approach, by Harold D. Lasswell. — [Hamden, Conn.]: Archon Books, 1966. ix, 314 p.; 23 cm. 1. Political science — Addresses, essays, lectures. I. T.
JA38.L4 1966     320.01     LC 66-9781

**Niebuhr, Reinhold, 1892-1971.**     **4.7211**
Reinhold Niebuhr on politics: his political philosophy and its application to our age as expressed in his writings / edited by Harry R. Davis and Robert C. Good. — New York: Scribner's, 1960. xviii, 364 p.; 24 cm. 1. Political science — Collected works. I. T.
JA38.N5     LC 60-6326

**Barker, Ernest, Sir, 1874-1960.**     • **4.7212**
Church, state, and education. With a new pref. by the author. 1st American ed. [Ann Arbor] University of Michigan Press [1957] 217 p. (Ann Arbor paperbacks, AA10) 1. Church and state 2. Political science — Addresses, essays, lectures I. T.
JA41 B3 1957     LC 57-4682

**Laslett, Peter.**     • **4.7213**
Philosophy, politics and society: a collection / edited by Peter Laslett. — Oxford: Blackwell, 1956. 184 p.; 14 cm. 1. Political science — Addresses, essays, lectures. I. T.
JA41.L36     LC 56-58956     ISBN 0631168109

**The Statesman's year–book.**     • **4.7214**
[1st]- ed; 1864-. New York [etc.] St. Martin's Press [etc.] v. maps (part fold., part col.) 19 cm. Annual. 'Statistical and historical annual of the states of the world. Rev. after official returns.' In 1899 in addition to the regular ed. there was pub. an 'American edition.' 1. Political science — Yearbooks. I. Martin, Frederick, 1830-1883, ed. II. Keltie, Sir John Scott, 1840-1927, ed. III. Renwick, Isaac Parker Anderson, ed. IV. Epstein, Mortimer, 1880-1946. ed. V. Steinberg, S. H. (Sigfrid Henry), 1899-1969. ed. VI. Paxton, John, 1923-ed.
JA51.S7     LC 04-3776

**Chandler, Ralph C., 1934-.**     **4.7215**
The public administration dictionary / Ralph C. Chandler, Jack C. Plano. — New York: Wiley, c1982. ix, 406 p.; 24 cm. Includes index. 1. Public administration — Dictionaries. I. Plano, Jack C. II. T.
JA61.C47     350/.0003 19     LC 81-12945     ISBN 0471091219

**Scruton, Roger.**     **4.7216**
A dictionary of political thought / Roger Scruton. — 1st U.S. ed. — New York: Harper & Row, c1982. 499 p.; 22 cm. 1. Political science — Dictionaries. I. T.
JA61.S37 1982     320/.03 19     LC 82-47532     ISBN 0060150440

**Bentley, Arthur Fisher, 1870-1957.**      • 4.7217
The process of government [by] Arthur F. Bentley. Edited by Peter H. Odegard. — Cambridge: Belknap Press of Harvard University Press, 1967. xliii, xiii, 501 p.; 22 cm. — (John Harvard library.) First published in 1908. 1. Political science 2. Political psychology I. T. II. Series.
JA66.B4 1967     320     *LC* 66-14458

**Friedrich, Carl J. (Carl Joachim), 1901-.**      4.7218
An introduction to political theory; twelve lectures at Harvard [by] Carl J. Friedrich. New York, Harper & Row [1967] viii, 182 p. 22 cm. 1. Political science I. T.
JA66.F7     320/.01     *LC* 67-11648

**Huntington, Samuel P.**      4.7219
Political order in changing societies, by Samuel P. Huntington. — New Haven: Yale University Press, 1968. xi, 488 p.; 24 cm. 'Written under the auspices of the Center for International Affairs, Harvard University.' 'Delivered in part as the Henry L. Stimson lectures, Yale University.' 1. Political science I. Harvard University. Center for International Affairs. II. T.
JA66.H795     320     *LC* 68-27756

**Duverger, Maurice, 1917-.**      • 4.7220
[Introduction à la politique] The idea of politics. Translated by Robert North and Ruth Murphy. Indianapolis, Bobbs-Merrill Co. [1966] xiv, 238 p. 22 cm. Translation of Introduction à la politique. 1. Political science I. T.
JA67.D843     320.01     *LC* 66-18595

## JA71–73 Theory. Method

**Brecht, Arnold, 1884-.**      • 4.7221
Political theory; the foundations of twentieth–century political thought. — Princeton, N.J.: Princeton University Press, 1959. 603 p.; 25 cm. 1. Political science — Methodology. 2. Political science — History I. T.
JA71.B73     320.1     *LC* 59-5591

**Crick, Bernard R.**      • 4.7222
In defence of politics. London, Weidenfeld and Nicolson [c1962] 156 p. (The Nature of human society) 1. Political science I. T.
JA71 C7     *LC* 62-17138

**Crick, Bernard R.**      4.7223
Political theory and practice [by] Bernard Crick. — New York: Basic Books, [1974, c1973] xii, 243 p.; 23 cm. 1. Political science — Addresses, essays, lectures. I. T.
JA71.C72 1974     320/.08     *LC* 72-89853     *ISBN* 0465059430

**Easton, David, 1917-.**      • 4.7224
The political system; an inquiry into the state of political science. — 2d ed. — New York: Knopf, [1971] xx, 377, x p.; 21 cm. 1. Political science 2. Political science — United States — History. I. T.
JA71.E3 1971     320 19     *LC* 78-137991     *ISBN* 0394315367

**Eisenstadt, S. N. (Shmuel Noah), 1923-.**      • 4.7225
The political systems of empires. London: Free Press of Glencoe [1963] 524 p. 1. Comparative government 2. Monarchy 3. Bureaucracy 4. Power (Social science) I. T.
JA71 E38     *LC* 63-7656

**Germino, Dante L.**      • 4.7226
Beyond ideology; the revival of political theory [by] Dante Germino. — New York: Harper & Row, [1967] ix, 254 p.; 22 cm. 1. Political science I. T.
JA71.G4     320.5     *LC* 67-25976

**Laslett, Peter.**      4.7227
Philosophy, politics and society, fourth series; a collection, edited by Peter Laslett, W. G. Runciman and Quentin Skinner. New York, Barnes & Noble Books [1972] 219 p. 23 cm. 1. Political science — Addresses, essays, lectures. I. Runciman, W. G. (Walter Garrison), 1934- joint author. II. Skinner, Quentin, joint author. III. T.
JA71.L28 1972b     320/.01/1 19     *LC* 73-168245     *ISBN* 0064940650

**Lasswell, Harold Dwight, 1902-.**      • 4.7228
The future of political science. New York, Atherton Press, 1963. 256 p. (The American Political Science Association series) 1. Political science I. T.
JA71 L3 1963     *LC* 63-16401

**Oakeshott, Michael Joseph, 1901-.**      • 4.7229
Rationalism in politics, and other essays. — New York: Basic Books Pub. Co., [1962] 333 p.; 22 cm. 1. Political science — Addresses, essays, lectures. 2. Rationalism — Addresses, essays, lectures. I. T.
JA71.O24 1962     320/.08     *LC* 62-15834

**Philosophy, politics, and society, fifth series: a collection /**      4.7230
**edited by Peter Laslett and James Fishkin.**
New Haven: Yale University Press, 1979. 312 p.: ill.; 23 cm. 1. Political science — Addresses, essays, lectures. 2. Democracy — Addresses, essays, lectures. 3. Justice — Addresses, essays, lectures. I. Laslett, Peter. II. Fishkin, James S.
JA71.P48 1979     320/.01/1     *LC* 78-64932     *ISBN* 0300023375

**Friedrich, Carl J. (Carl Joachim), 1901-.**      • 4.7231
Man and his government: an empirical theory of politics. — New York: McGraw-Hill [1963] xiii, 737 p.; 25 cm. 1. Political science — Methodology. I. T.
JA73.F68     320.18     *LC* 63-15892

**Lasswell, Harold Dwight, 1902-.**      • 4.7232
Political writings. — Glencoe, Ill., Free Press, 1951. 525 p. 22 cm. Includes bibliographies. 1. Political science 2. Psychoanalysis I. T.
JA73.L28     320.81     *LC* 51-11212

**Lasswell, Harold Dwight, 1902-.**      • 4.7233
Politics: who gets what, when, how. New York, P. Smith, 1950,[c1936]. ix, 264 p. 1. Political science I. T.
JA73 L3     *LC* A51-8949

**Van Dyke, Vernon, 1912-.**      • 4.7234
Political science: a philosophical analysis / Vernon Van Dyke. — Stanford, Calif.: Stanford University Press, 1960. xv, 235 p. Includes index. 1. Political science — Methodology. I. T.
JA73.V3     *LC* 60-11836

## JA74 Political Psychology

**Almond, Gabriel Abraham, 1911-.**      • 4.7235
The civic culture; political attitudes and democracy in five nations, by Gabriel A. Almond and Sidney Verba. — Princeton, N.J.: Princeton University Press, 1963. xi, 562 p.: diagrs., tables.; 25 cm. 1. Political pscyhology. 2. Social participation 3. Social history — 1945- I. Verba, Sidney. joint author. II. T.
JA74.A4     306/.2 19     *LC* 63-12666

**Easton, David, 1917-.**      • 4.7236
A systems analysis of political life. New York, Wiley [1965] xvi, 507 p. illus. 24 cm. 1. Political psychology 2. Political science — Research I. T.
JA74.E23     320/.01/8     *LC* 65-12714

**Eulau, Heinz, 1915-.**      • 4.7237
The behavioral persuasion in politics. — New York: Random House, [1963] 141 p.; 19 cm. — (Random House studies in political science) 'PS42.' 1. Political psychology I. T.
JA74.E88     329     *LC* 62-21335

**Handbook of political communication/ edited by Dan D. Nimmo**      4.7238
**and Keith R. Sanders.**
Beverly Hills: Sage Publications, c1981. 732 p. 1. Communication in politics — Addresses, essays, lectures. I. Nimmo, Dan D. II. Sanders, Keith R.
JA74.H34     JA74 H46.     306/.2 19     *LC* 81-9362     *ISBN* 0803917147

**Janowitz, Morris. ed.**      • 4.7239
Community political systems. Contributors: Victor Ayoub [and others] Edited by Morris Janowitz. Glencoe, Ill., Free Press [1961] 259 p. diagrs., tables. (International yearbook of political behavior research, v. 1) 1. Political psychology 2. Community 3. Power (Social sciences) I. T. II. Series.
JA74 J2     *LC* 59-13864

**Key, V. O. (Valdimer Orlando), 1908-1963.**      • 4.7240
A primer of statistics for political scientists. New York, Crowell, 1954. 209 p. illus. 22 cm. 1. Political statistics I. T.
JA74.K48     311.2     *LC* 54-5502

**Lane, Robert Edwards.**      • 4.7241
Political life: why people get involved in politics. — Glencoe, Ill.: Free Press, [1959] 374 p.: illus.; 25 cm. 1. Political psychology 2. United States — Politics and government I. T.
JA74.L25     329     *LC* 58-6485

**Lasswell, Harold Dwight, 1902-.**      • 4.7242
Language of politics; studies in quantitative semantics, by Harold D. Lasswell, Nathan Leites, and associates. Cambridge, Massachusetts Institute of Technology Press [1965, c1949] vii, 398 p. ill. 'Most of the work ... was done at the University of Chicago or in connection with the War Communications Research Project at the Library of Congress.' 1. Political science —

Terminology 2. Semantics (Philosophy) I. Leites, Nathan Constantin, 1912- II. T.
JA74 L3 1965    *LC* 65-8781

**Minogue, Kenneth R.**    **4.7243**
Alien powers: the pure theory of ideology / Kenneth Minogue. — New York: St. Martin's Press, 1985. vi, 255 p.; 25 cm. Includes index. 1. Ideology 2. Political science I. T.
JA74.M535 1985    320.5 19    *LC* 84-22340    *ISBN* 0312018606

**Weldon, Thomas Dewar, 1897-1958.**    • **4.7244**
The vocabulary of politics / T.D. Weldon. — Harmondsworth: Penguin Books, 1953. 199 p. 18 cm. — (A Pelican book) 1. Political science I. T.
JA74.W4    *LC* A 55-3000

**Du Preez, Wilhelmus Petrus.**    **4.7245**
The politics of identity: ideology and the human image / Peter du Preez. — New York: St. Martin's Press, 1980. 178 p.; 23 cm. Includes index. 1. Political psychology 2. Identity (Psychology) 3. South Africa — Politics and government 4. South Africa — Ethnic relations. I. T.
JA74.5.D8 1980    320/.01/9 19    *LC* 80-19996    *ISBN* 0312626975

**Handbook of political psychology.** Jeanne N. Knutson, general    **4.7246**
editor.
[1st ed.]. — San Francisco: Jossey-Bass Publishers, 1973. xvi, 542 p.; 27 cm. — (The Jossey-Bass behavioral science series) 1. Political psychology I. Knutson, Jeanne Nickell, ed.
JA74.5.H35    320/.01/9    *LC* 72-5893    *ISBN* 0875891748

**Human nature in politics** / edited by J. Roland Pennock and    **4.7247**
John W. Chapman.
New York: New York University Press, 1977. x, 348 p.: ill.; 23 cm. (Nomos; 17 0078-0979) Includes index. 1. Political psychology — Addresses, essays, lectures. I. Pennock, J. Roland (James Roland), 1906- II. Chapman, John William, 1923- III. Series.
JA74.5.H85    320/.01/9    *LC* 76-23506    *ISBN* 0814765688

**Renshon, Stanley Allen.**    **4.7248**
Psychological needs and political behavior: a theory of personality and political efficacy. — New York: Free Press, [1974] xiv, 300 p.; 21 cm. 1. Political psychology 2. Personality 3. Political participation — United States. I. T.
JA74.5.R45    320/.01/9    *LC* 73-11735    *ISBN* 0029263204

## JA75–80 Political Sociology

**Authority revisited** / edited by J. Roland Pennock and John W.    **4.7249**
Chapman.
New York: New York University Press, 1987. xii, 344 p.; 22 cm. — (Nomos; 29) 1. Authority. 2. Political science. 3. Law — Philosophy. I. Pennock, J. Roland (James Roland), 1906- II. Chapman, John William, 1923- III. Series.
JA75.A97 1987    320.2 19    *LC* 86-21071    *ISBN* 0814766013

**Kirchheimer, Otto.**    • **4.7250**
Political justice; the use of legal procedure for political ends. Princeton, N.J., Princeton University Press, 1961. 452 p. 1. Law and politics I. T.
JA75 K5    *LC* 61-7418

**Aron, Raymond, 1905-.**    • **4.7251**
[Sociologie des sociétés industrielles. English] Democracy and totalitarianism. Translated by Valence Ionescu. New York, Praeger [1969, c1968] xiv, 262 p. 23 cm. Translation of Démocratie et totalitarisme which was first published under title: Sociologie des sociétés industrielles. 1. Political sociology I. T.
JA76.A7513 1969    320/.01    *LC* 69-12900

**Bendix, Reinhard. comp.**    • **4.7252**
State and society; a reader in comparative political sociology, edited by Reinhard Bendix, in collaboration with Coenraad Brand [and others] Boston, Little, Brown [1968] viii, 648 p. 24 cm. 1. Political sociology — Addresses, essays, lectures. I. Brand, C. M. (Coenraad M.) II. T.
JA76.B4    320/.01    *LC* 68-23013

**Kraus, Sidney.**    **4.7253**
The effects of mass communication on political behavior / Sidney Kraus and Dennis Davis. — University Park: Pennsylvania State University Press, c1976. xiii, 308 p.; 23 cm. 1. Communication in politics 2. Mass media — Political aspects 3. Political socialization I. Davis, Dennis. joint author. II. T.
JA76.K72    JA76 K72.    301.5/92    *LC* 76-3480    *ISBN* 0271012269

**Laslett, Peter.**    • **4.7254**
Philosophy, politics and society (second series), a collection edited by Peter Laslett and W.G. Runciman. Oxford, B. Blackwell, 1962. 229 p. 22 cm. 1. Political science — Addresses, essays, and lectures. I. Runciman, W. G. (Walter Garrison), 1934- II. T.
JA 76 L34 1962    *LC* 63-5934

**Compromise in ethics, law, and politics** / edited by J. Roland    **4.7255**
Pennock and John W. Chapman.
New York: New York University Press, 1979. xiv, 212 p.; 22 cm. (Nomos; 21) 1. Political ethics — Addresses, essays, lectures. 2. Compromise (Ethics) — Addresses, essays, lectures. 3. Compromise (Law) — Addresses, essays, lectures. I. Pennock, J. Roland (James Roland), 1906- II. Chapman, John William, 1923- III. Series.
JA79.C65    320/.01    *LC* 79-63469    *ISBN* 0814765742

**Justification** / edited by J. Roland Pennock and John W.    **4.7256**
Chapman.
New York: New York University Press, 1986. xv, 368 p.; 22 cm. — (NOMOS; 28) 1. Political ethics — Addresses, essays, lectures. 2. Justification (Theory of knowledge) — Addresses, essays, lectures. 3. Law — Philosophy — Addresses, essays, lectures. I. Pennock, J. Roland (James Roland), 1906- II. Chapman, John William, 1923-
JA79.J87 1986    172 19    *LC* 85-13811    *ISBN* 0814765955

**Morgenthau, Hans Joachim, 1904-.**    • **4.7257**
Scientific man vs. power politics, by Hans J. Morgenthau. Chicago, Ill., The University of Chicago press [1946] ix, 244 [1] p. 20 cm. 1. Political science 2. Science 3. International relations I. T.
JA80.M6    *LC* a 46-23

## JA81–84 History of Political Thought

**Bluhm, William Theodore, 1923-.**    **4.7258**
Theories of the political system: classics of political thought & modern political analysis / [by] William T. Bluhm. — Englewood Cliffs, N.J.: Prentice-Hall [1965] ix, 502 p. (Prentice-Hall series in political science) 1. Political science — History I. T.
JA81 B625    *LC* 65-10147

**Kirk, Russell.**    **4.7259**
The roots of American order. — [1st ed.]. — LaSalle, Ill.: Open Court, [1974] xvi, 534 p.; 24 cm. 1. Political science — History 2. Law — History and criticism I. T.
JA81.K55    320/.09    *LC* 74-13521    *ISBN* 0875482929

**McIlwain, Charles Howard, 1871-1968.**    • **4.7260**
The growth of political thought in the West, from the Greeks to the end of the Middle Ages. — New York: Cooper Square Publishers, 1968 [c1932] vii, 417 p.; 23 cm. 1. Political science — History I. T.
JA81.M26 1968    320/.09    *LC* 68-55171

**Nisbet, Robert A.**    **4.7261**
The social philosophers: community and conflict in Western thought [by] Robert Nisbet. — New York: Crowell, [1973] xii, 466 p.: illus.; 25 cm. 1. Political science — History 2. Sociology — History I. T.
JA81.N57    301/.01    *LC* 72-83132    *ISBN* 0690744064

**Sabine, George Holland, 1880-1961.**    • **4.7262**
A history of political theory. — 3d ed. — New York: Holt, Rinehart and Winston, [1961] 948 p.; 22 cm. 1. Political science — History I. T.
JA81.S3 1961    320.9    *LC* 61-12771

**Skinner, Quentin.**    **4.7263**
The foundations of modern political thought / Quentin Skinner. — Cambridge; New York: Cambridge University Press, 1978. 2 v.; 24 cm. Vol. 1: 1979 printing. 1. Political science — History — Collected works. I. T.
JA81.S54    320.5/09/03    *LC* 78-51676    *ISBN* 0521220238

**Strauss, Leo. ed.**    • **4.7264**
History of political philosophy, edited by Leo Strauss [and] Joseph Cropsey. — Chicago: Rand McNally, [1963] 790 p.; 24 cm. — (Rand McNally political science series) 1. Political science — History I. Cropsey, Joseph. joint ed. II. T. III. Title: Political philosophy.
JA81.S75    320.9    *LC* 63-7143

**Vaughan, Charles Edwyn, 1854-1922.**    • 4.7265
Studies in the history of political philosophy before and after Rousseau. Edited by A.G. Little. New York, Russell & Russell, 1960. 2 v. 1. Political science — History 2. Philosophy, Modern — History I. T. II. Title: Political philosophy
JA81 V3 1960    LC 60-6034

**Wolin, Sheldon S.**    • 4.7266
Politics and vision; continuity and innovation in Western political thought. — Boston: Little, Brown, [1960] 529 p.; 25 cm. 1. Political science — History I. T.
JA81.W6    320.9    LC 60-10499

## JA82 MEDIEVAL

**Carlyle, Robert Warrand, Sir, 1859-1934.**    • 4.7267
A history of mediæval political theory in the West, by Sir R. W. Carlyle and A. J. Carlyle. Edinburgh, London, W. Blackwood & sons ltd., 1928-36. 6 v. 23 cm. 1. Political science — History I. Carlyle, A. J. (Alexander James), 1861-1943. II. T.
JA82.C3 1928    320.9    LC 38-4080

**Gierke, Otto Friedrich von, 1841-1921.**    • 4.7268
Political theories of the Middle Age / by Otto Gierke; translated with an introd. by Frederic William Maitland. — Boston: Beacon Press, 1958, 1959 printing. lxxx, 197 p. (Beacon paperback; no. 67) Translation of Die publicistischen Lehren des Mittelalters, a section of v.3 of Das deutsche Genossenschaftsrecht. 1. Political science — History 2. Civilization, Medieval I. T.
JA82.G4    LC 58-4118

**Lerner, Ralph. ed.**    4.7269
Medieval political philosophy: a sourcebook. Edited by Ralph Lerner and Muhsin Mahdi, with the collaboration of Ernest L. Fortin. — Ithaca, N.Y.: Cornell University Press, [1972, c1963] xii, 532 p.; 23 cm. — (Cornell paperbacks) (Agora paperback editions) 1. Political science — Early works to 1700 — Addresses, essays, lectures. 2. Philosophy, Medieval — Addresses, essays, lectures. I. Mahdi, Muhsin. joint ed. II. T.
JA82.L4 1972    320.9/02    LC 72-4326    ISBN 0801491398

**Morrall, John B.**    • 4.7270
Political thought in medieval times [by] John B. Morrall. — 3rd ed. — London: Hutchinson University Library, 1971. 154 p.; 23 cm. — (Hutchinson University Library) 1. Political science — History I. T.
JA82.M6 1971    320/.09/02    LC 72-187548    ISBN 0091076803

**Passerin d'Entrèves, Alessandro, 1902-.**    • 4.7271
The medieval contribution to political thought, Thomas Aquinas, Marsilius of Padua, Richard Hooker, by Alexander Passerin D'Entrèves ... — [London] Oxford university press, 1939. viii, 148 p. 23 cm. Lectures ... delivered in the University of Oxford during the summer term, 1938 ... The argument of the first four lectures mainly corresponds to that of my Italian book, Lafilosofia politica medioevale, published in 1934.'—Pref. 'A note about the literature': p. [143]-146. 1. Thomas, Aquinas, Saint, 1225?-1274. 2. Marsilius, of Padua, d. 1342? 3. Political science — Hist. 4. Hooker, Richard, 1553or 4 — 1600. I. T.
JA82.P32    320.902    LC 39-15662

**Rosenthal, Erwin Isak Jakob, 1904-.**    4.7272
Political thought in medieval Islam: an introductory outline / by Erwin I.J. Rosenthal. — Westport, Conn.: Greenwood Press, 1985. xi, 323 p.; 22 cm. Reprint. Originally published: Cambridge: University Press, 1958. Includes index. 1. Political science — Islamic Empire — History. 2. Islam and state I. T.
JA82.R6 1985    297/.1977 19    LC 85-21909    ISBN 0313250944

## JA83 MODERN

**Allen, J. W. (John William), 1865-1944.**    • 4.7273
A history of political thought in the sixteenth century. London, Methuen [1957] 527 p. 23 cm. 1. Political science — History — 16th century. 2. Reformation 3. Church and state — Europe — History — 16th century. 4. State, The I. T.
JA83.A6 1957    320/.01/09 19    LC 57-1901

**Collini, Stefan, 1947-.**    4.7274
That noble science of politics: a study in nineteenth-century intellectual history / Stefan Collini, Donald Winch, John Burrow. -- Cambridge [Cambridgeshire]; New York: Cambridge University Press, 1983. x, 385 p.; 24 cm. 1. Political science — History — 19th century. I. Winch, Donald. II. Burrow, J. W. (John Wyon), 1935- III. T.
JA83.C633 1983    320.5/09/034 19    LC 83-7696    ISBN 052125762X

**Gierke, Otto Friedrich von, 1841-1921.**    • 4.7275
Natural law and the theory of society, 1500 to 1800, by Otto Gierke, with a lecture on The ideas of natural law and humanity, by Ernest Troeltsch; translated with an introduction by Ernest Barker ... — Cambridge [Eng.] The University press, 1934. 2 v. 24 cm. A translation of five subsections in the fourth volume of Gierke's 'Das deutsche genossenschaftsrecht'. cf. Introd. 'List of authors cited': v. 2, p. [401]-417. 1. Natural law 2. State, The 3. Political science — Hist. I. Troeltsch, Ernest, 1865-1923. II. Barker, Ernest, Sir, 1874-1960. tr. III. T.
JA83.G5    LC 34-29519

**Laslett, Peter.**    • 4.7276
Philosophy, politics, and society, third series: a collection / edited by Peter Laslett and W. G. Runciman. — New York: Barnes & Noble, 1967. 232 p.; 23 cm. 1. Political science — History I. Runciman, W. G. (Walter Garrison), 1934- joint author. II. T.
JA83.L3    LC 67-9504

**Plamenatz, John Petrov.**    • 4.7277
Man and society, political and social theory. New York, McGraw-Hill [1963] 2 v. 23 cm. 1. Political science — History 2. Social sciences — History I. T.
JA83.P53    320.9    LC 63-11940

**Voegelin, Eric, 1901-.**    4.7278
From Enlightenment to Revolution / Eric Voegelin; edited by John H. Hallowell. — Durham, N.C.: Duke University Press, 1975. ix, 307 p.; 25 cm. 1. Political science — History I. T.
JA83.V57    320/.09    LC 74-81864    ISBN 0822303264

## JA84 BY COUNTRY, A–Z

**Monière, Denis, 1947-.**    4.7279
[Développement des idéologies au Québec. English] Ideologies in Quebec: the historical development / Denis Monière; translated by Richard Howard. — Toronto; Buffalo: University of Toronto Press, 1981. x, 328 p.; 23 cm. Translation with revisions of: Le développement des idéologies au Québec. 1. Political science — Québec (Province) — History. 2. Economics — Québec (Province) — History. 3. Québec (Province) — Politics and government 4. Québec (Province) — Economic conditions. I. T.
JA84.C3 M6613 1981    971.4 19    LC 81-189566    ISBN 0802054528

**Taylor, Charles, 1935-.**    4.7280
Radical Tories: the conservative tradition in Canada / Charles Taylor. — Toronto: Anansi, c1982. 231 p.; 23 cm. Includes index. 1. Conservatism — Canada — History — 20th century. 2. Canada — Politics and government — 20th century I. T.
JA84.C3 T39 1982    320.5/2/0971 19    LC 82-242421    ISBN 0887840965

**De Grazia, Sebastian. comp.**    • 4.7281
Masters of Chinese political thought; from the beginnings to the Han Dynasty. Pref. by Frederick W. Mote. New York: Viking Press, [1973] xiv, 430 p.; 21 cm. 1. Political science — China — History. I. T.
JA84.C6 D4    320.5/0951    LC 72-78989    ISBN 0670462012

**Hsiao, Kung-ch'üan, 1897-.**    4.7282
[Chung-kuo cheng chih ssu hsiang shih. English] A history of Chinese political thought: v. 1: from the beginnings to the sixth century A.D. / tr. F.W. Mote. — Princeton, N.J.: Princeton University Press, 1979. 778 p. (Princeton library of Asian translations.) Translation of Chung-kuo cheng chih ssu hsiang shih. Includes index. 1. Poltical science — China — History. 2. Philosophy, Chinese I. T. II. Series.
JA84.C6 H6813    320.5/0951    LC 77-85553    ISBN 0691031169

**Hourani, Albert Habib.**    4.7283
Arabic thought in the liberal age, 1798–1939. Issued under the auspices of the Royal Institute of International Affairs. London, New York, Oxford University Press, 1962. 403 p. 23 cm. Includes bibliography. 1. Political science — History — Arabic countries. I. T.
JA84.E3H6 1962    320.953    LC 63-185

**Dyson, Kenneth H. F.**    4.7284
The state tradition in Western Europe: a study of an idea and institution / Kenneth H.F. Dyson. — New York: Oxford University Press, 1980. viii, 310 p.; 24 cm. Includes indexes. 1. Political science — Europe — History. I. T.
JA84.E9 D94    320.1/094 19    LC 80-17234    ISBN 0195202090

**Keohane, Nannerl O., 1940-.**    4.7285
Philosophy and the state in France: the Renaissance to the Enlightenment / Nannerl O. Keohane. — Princeton, N.J.: Princeton University Press, c1980. xii, 501 p.; 25 cm. Includes index. 1. Political science — France — History. 2. Philosophy, French — 17th century I. T.
JA84.F8 K46    320.1/01/0944    LC 79-3219    ISBN 0691076111

**Lloyd, Howell A.** 4.7286
The State, France, and the sixteenth century / Howell A. Lloyd. — London; Boston: G. Allen & Unwin, 1983. xx, 233 p.; 23 cm. — (Early modern Europe today.) Includes index. 1. Political science — France — History. 2. France — Politics and government — 16th century I. T. II. Series.
JA84.F8 L56 1983   320.1/01/0944 19   *LC* 82-16471   *ISBN* 0049400665

**Lough, John.** 4.7287
The Philosophes and post–revolutionary France / by John Lough. — Oxford: Clarendon Press; New York: Oxford University Press, 1982. 284 p.; 22 cm. Includes index. 1. Political science — France — History. 2. Social sciences — France — History. I. T.
JA84.F8 L65 1982   320/.01/0944 19   *LC* 81-18673   *ISBN* 0198219210

**Barker, Ernest, Sir, 1874-1960.** • 4.7288
Political thought in England 1848 to 1914. — 2d ed. — London, New York, Oxford University Press [1959] 232 p. 18 cm. — (The Home university library of modern knowledge, 104) First published in 1915 under title: Political thought in England from Herbert Spencer to the present day. Bibliography: p. [225]-228. 1. Political science — Hist. — Gt. Brit. I. T.
JA84.G7B3 1950   *LC* A 51-434

**Brinton, Crane, 1898-1968.** • 4.7289
English political thought in the nineteenth century / by Crane Brinton. — Cambridge: Harvard University Press, 1949. vii, 311 p. Includes bibliography. 1. Political science — History — Great Britain. 2. Philosophers, English. I. T.
JA84.G7B67 1949   320.942   *LC* 50-5654

**Cobban, Alfred.** • 4.7290
Edmund Burke and the revolt against the eighteenth century; a study of the political and social thinking of Burke, Wordsworth, Coleridge, and Southey. [2d ed.] New York, Barnes & Noble [1961, c1960] 280 p. 21 cm. Includes bibliography. 1. Burke, Edmund, 1729-1797. 2. Wordsworth, William, 1770-1850 — Political and social views. 3. Coleridge, Samuel Taylor, 1772-1834 — Political and social views. 4. Southey, Robert, 1774-1843. 5. Eighteenth century 6. Political science — History — Great Britain. I. T.
JA84.G7C6 1961   320.942   *LC* 61-1721

**Dickinson, H. T.** 4.7291
Liberty and property: political ideology in eighteenth–century Britain / H. T. Dickinson. — New York: Holmes and Meier Publishers, 1978 (c1977). 369 p.; 22 cm. 1. Political science — Great Britain — History. 2. Great Britain — Politics and government — 18th century I. T.
JA84.G7 D48   320.5/0941   *LC* 77-13477   *ISBN* 0841903514

**Greenleaf, W. H.** • 4.7292
Order, empiricism, and politics; two traditions of English political thought, 1500–1700 [by] W. H. Greenleaf. — London; New York: Published for the University of Hull by The Oxford University Press, 1964. vi, 299 p.; 23 cm. — (University of Hull publications) 1. Political science — Great Britain — History. I. T.
JA84.G7 G85 1964   320.5/0942   *LC* 65-320

**Hanson, Donald W.** 4.7293
From kingdom to commonwealth; the development of civic consciousness in English political thought, by Donald W. Hanson. Cambridge, Mass.: Harvard University Press, 1970. xiv, 469 p.; 25 cm. — (Harvard political studies) 1. Political science — Great Britain — History. I. T. II. Series.
JA84.G7 H28   320/.09   *LC* 77-105371   *ISBN* 0674324757

**Laski, Harold Joseph, 1893-1950.** • 4.7294
Political thought in England from Locke to Bentham / by Harold J. Laski. — New York: H. Holt, c1920. 323 p.; 17 cm. (Home university library of modern knowledge; 103) 1. Political science — Great Britain — History. I. T. II. Series.
JA84.G7 L3 1973   JA84.G7 L3 1920.   320.9/41   *LC* 20-14002

**Hardy, Peter.** • 4.7295
Partners in freedom and true Muslims. The political thought of some Muslim scholars in British India 1912–1947. Lund, Studentlitteratur, 1971. 63 p. 23 cm. (Scandinavian Institute of Asian Studies. Monograph series no. 5) 1. Political science — India — History. 2. Islam and state — India — History. I. T.
JA84.I4 H33   320/.0954   *LC* 74-594707

**Maruyama, Masao, 1914-.** 4.7296
[Nihon seiji shisō shi kenkyū. English] Studies in the intellectual history of Tokugawa Japan / Masao Maruyama; translated by Mikiso Hane. — Tokyo: University of Tokyo Press, 1974. xxxvii, 383 p.; 24 cm. Translation of Nihon seiji shisō shi kenkyū. Includes index. 1. Political science — Japan — History. I. T.
JA84.J3 M313   952/.025   *LC* 70-90954   *ISBN* 0691075662

**Jorrín, Miguel.** • 4.7297
Latin–American political thought and ideology, by Miguel Jorrín and John D. Martz. — Chapel Hill: University of North Carolina Press, [1970] xiii, 453 p.; 24 cm. 1. Political science — History — Latin America. I. Martz, John D. II. T.
JA84.L3 J65   320/.098   *LC* 71-109461   *ISBN* 0807811440

**Karpat, Kemal H. comp.** • 4.7298
Political and social thought in the contemporary Middle East,, edited by Kemal H. Karpat. London, Pall Mall P., 1968. xiii, 397 p. 24 cm. ([Pall Mall library of Middle Eastern affairs]) 1. Nationalism — Middle East — Addresses, essays, lectures. 2. Socialism in the Middle East — Addresses, essays, lectures. 3. Turkey — Politics and government — 1909- — Addresses, essays, lectures. 4. Arab countries — Politics and government — 1945- — Addresses, essays, lectures. I. T.
JA84.N18 K3 1968   320.9/56   *LC* 77-376933

**Political and social thought in the contemporary Middle East / edited by Kemal H. Karpat.** 4.7299
Rev. and enl. ed. — New York, N.Y.: Praeger, 1982. xliv, 557 p.; 24 cm. 1. Political science — Middle East — History. 2. Middle East — Politics and government I. Karpat, Kemal H.
JA84.N18 P64 1982   320.5 19   *LC* 81-11877   *ISBN* 0030576091

**Anderson, Thornton, 1915-.** • 4.7300
Russian political thought, an introduction. Ithaca, N.Y., Cornell University Press [1967] xiii, 444 p. 24 cm. 1. Political science — History — Soviet Union. I. T.
JA84.R9 A7   320.9/47   *LC* 67-12902

**Hill, Ronald J., 1943-.** 4.7301
Soviet politics, political science, and reform / Ronald J. Hill. — Oxford: M. Robertson; White Plains, N.Y.: M. E. Sharpe, 1980. x, 221 p.; 23 cm. Includes indexes. 1. Political science — Russia. 2. Russia — Politics and government — 1953- I. T.
JA84.R9 H54 1980   320/.0947 19   *LC* 79-55751   *ISBN* 0873321561

**Fernández-Santamaría, J. A., 1936-.** 4.7302
The state, war and peace: Spanish political thought in the Renaissance, 1516–1559 / J. A. Fernández–Santamaria. — Cambridge [Eng.]; New York: Cambridge University Press, 1977. xiv, 316 p.; 24 cm. — (Cambridge studies in early modern history) Includes index. 1. Political science — Spain — History. 2. Spain — Politics and government — 1516-1556 I. T.
JA84.S7 F47   320.5/0946   *LC* 76-27903   *ISBN* 0521214386

# JA84.U5 United States

**Appleby, Joyce Oldham.** 4.7303
Capitalism and a new social order: the Republican vision of the 1790s / Joyce Appleby. — New York: New York University Press, 1984. x, 110 p.; 24 cm. — (Anson G. Phelps lectureship on early American history.) 1. Republican Party (U.S.: 1792-1828) — History — 18th century. 2. Political science — United States — History — 18th century. 3. United States — Politics and government — 1789-1815 I. T. II. Series.
JA84.U5 A75 1984   320.5/0973 19   *LC* 83-13359   *ISBN* 0814705812

**Boorstin, Daniel J. (Daniel Joseph), 1914-.** • 4.7304
The genius of American politics. [Chicago] University of Chicago Press [1953] 201 p. 22 cm. (Charles R. Walgreen Foundation lectures) 1. Political science — United States — History. 2. United States — Politics and government I. T.
JA84.U5 B6   320.973   *LC* 53-9434

**Crick, Bernard R.** • 4.7305
The American science of politics: its origins and conditions. Berkeley: University of California Press, 1959. 252 p. 1. Political science — History — United States I. T.
JA84 U5 C7 1959A   *LC* 59-3487

**Dahl, Robert Alan, 1915-.** • 4.7306
Pluralist democracy in the United States: conflict and consent [by] Robert A. Dahl. Chicago, Rand McNally [1967] xix, 471 p. illus. 24 cm. (Rand McNally political science series) Second ed. published in 1972 under title: Democracy in the United States. 1. Pluralism (Social sciences) — United States. 2. Democracy 3. Political science — United States — History. I. T.
JA84.U5 D3   320.9/73   *LC* 66-30520

**Diggins, John P.** 4.7307
The lost soul of American politics: virtue, self–interest, and the foundations of liberalism / John Patrick Diggins. — New York: Basic Books, c1984. xiii, 409 p.; 25 cm. Includes index. 1. Liberalism — United States — History.

2. Materialism — United States — History. 3. Political science — United States — History. 4. United States — Politics and government I. T.
JA84.U5 D53 1984     320.5/1/0973 19     *LC* 83-46079     *ISBN* 0465042430

**Harbour, William R.**                                        4.7308
The foundations of conservative thought: an Anglo–American tradition in perspective / William R. Harbour. — Notre Dame, Ind.: University of Notre Dame Press, c1982. 220 p.; 23 cm. Includes index. 1. Conservatism — United States. 2. Conservatism — Great Britain. 3. Conservatism I. T.
JA84.U5 H37 1982     320.5/2 19     *LC* 82-11011     *ISBN* 0268009597

**Kolkey, Jonathan Martin.**                                   4.7309
The New Right, 1960–1968: with epilogue, 1969–1980 / Jonathan Martin Kolkey. — Washington, D.C.: University Press of America, c1983. xi, 403 p.; 23 cm. Includes index. 1. Conservatism — United States. 2. United States — Politics and government — 1945- I. T.
JA84.U5 K54 1983     320.5/2/0973 19     *LC* 82-23821     *ISBN* 0819129933

**Lora, Ronald.**                                            • 4.7310
Conservative minds in America. — Chicago: Rand McNally, [c1971] xiii, 274 p.; 22 cm. — (The Rand McNally series on the history of American thought and culture) 1. Conservatism — United States. 2. Conservatism I. T.
JA84.U5 L67 1971     320.5/2/0973     *LC* 78-170893

**McCloskey, Robert Green.**                                 • 4.7311
American conservatism in the age of enterprise; a study of William Graham Sumner, Stephen J. Field, and Andrew Carnegie. Cambridge, Harvard University Press, 1951. xi, 193 p. (Harvard political studies) 1. Sumner, William Graham, 1840-1910. 2. Field, Stephen Johnson, 1816-1899. 3. Carnegie, Andrew, 1835-1919. 4. Conservatism 5. Political science — History — United States I. T.
JA84 U5 M35     *LC* 51-13468

**McCoy, Charles Allan, 1920- comp.**                        • 4.7312
Apolitical politics; a critique of behavioralism. Edited by Charles A. McCoy [and] John Playford. New York, Crowell [1968, c1967] viii, 246 p. 23 cm. 1. Political science — United States — History — Addresses, essays, lectures. I. Playford, John. joint comp. II. T.
JA84.U5 M37     320/.08     *LC* 67-26837

**Merriam, Charles Edward, 1874-1953.**                      • 4.7313
American political ideas; studies in the development of American political thought, 1865–1917, by Charles E. Merriam. — New York: Johnson Reprint Corp., 1969. vii, 481 p.; 20 cm. — (Reprints in government and political science) Reprint of the 1920 ed., with a new introd. by Robert E. Merriam. 1. U.S. — Politics and government. I. T.
JA84.U5 M5 1969b     320.9/73     *LC* 71-76213

**Miles, Michael W., 1945-.**                                4.7314
The odyssey of the American right / Michael W. Miles. — New York: Oxford University Press, 1980. x, 371 p.; 22 cm. 1. Conservatism — United States. 2. United States — Politics and government — 1945- I. T.
JA84.U5 M62     320.5/2/0973     *LC* 80-14532     *ISBN* 0195027744

**Ostrom, Vincent, 1919-.**                                  4.7315
The intellectual crisis in American public administration. University, Ala.: University of Alabama Press, [1973] xiii, 165 p.; 21 cm. 1. Political science — United States — History. 2. Public administration 3. Democracy I. T.
JA84.U5 O88     353     *LC* 73-38     *ISBN* 0817348174

**Peele, Gillian, 1949-.**                                   4.7316
Revival and reaction: the right in contemporary America / by Gillian Peele. — Oxford: Clarendon Press; New York: Oxford University Press, 1984. xiii, 266 p.; 23 cm. Includes index. 1. Conservatism — United States. 2. United States — Politics and government — 1981- I. T.
JA84.U5 P39 1984     320.5/2/0973 19     *LC* 84-246256     *ISBN* 0198211309

**Steinfels, Peter.**                                        4.7317
The neoconservatives: the men who are changing America's politics / Peter Steinfels. — New York: Simon and Schuster, c1979. 335 p.; 25 cm. 1. Conservatism — United States. I. T.
JA84.U5 S74     320.5/2/0973     *LC* 79-574     *ISBN* 0671226657

**Thom, Gary, 1941-.**                                       4.7318
Bringing the Left back home: a critique of American social criticism / Gary Thom. — New Haven: Yale University Press, 1979. x, 303 p.: 22 cm. 1. Political science — United States 2. Sociology — United States 3. Democracy I. T.
JA84.U5 T47     301.5/92/0973     *LC* 79-14712     *ISBN* 0300023324

**Wood, Gordon S.**                                          4.7319
The creation of the American Republic, 1776–1787, by Gordon S. Wood. Chapel Hill, Published for the Institute of Early American History and Culture

at Williamsburg, Va., by the University of North Carolina Press [1969] xiv, 653 p. 24 cm. Includes bibliographical references. 1. Political science — United States — History. I. Institute of Early American History and Culture (Williamsburg, Va.) II. T.
JA84.U5 W6     320/.0973     *LC* 71-78861

**Wright, Benjamin Fletcher, 1900-.**                        • 4.7320
American interpretations of natural law, a study in the history of political thought. New York, Russell & Russell, 1962 [c1931] 360 p. 1. Natural law — History — United States I. T.
JA84 U5 W67 1962     *LC* 62-10697

# JC POLITICAL THEORY. THE STATE

# JC20–45 Primitive State

**Maine, Henry Sumner, Sir, 1822-1888.**                     • 4.7321
Ancient law / by Sir Henry James Sumner Maine. — London & Toronto: J. M. Dent & sons, ltd.; New York: E. P. Dutton & co., 1931. xviii, 237 p.; 17 cm. — (Half-title: Everyman's library, ed. by Ernest Rhys. History. [no. 734]) Introduction by J. H. Morgan. Bibliography: p. xvi. 1. Law — History and criticism I. Morgan, John Hartman, 1876- ed. II. T.
JC21.M2     *LC* A 18-315

**Morgan, Lewis Henry, 1818-1881.**                          • 4.7322
Ancient society / by Lewis H. Morgan; edited by Leslie A. White. — Cambridge: Belknap Press of Harvard University Press, 1964. xlv, 471 p.: facsim.; 25 cm. 1. Society, Primitive 2. Civilization 3. Sociology I. T.
JC21.M84 1964     *LC* 64-21789

# JC47–50 Oriental State

**Lambton, Ann Katharine Swynford.**                         4.7323
State and government in medieval Islam: an introduction to the study of Islamic political theory: the jurists / by Ann K. S. Lambton. — Oxford; New York : Oxford University Press, 1981. xviii, 364 p.; 22 cm. — (London oriental series. v. 36) Includes index. 1. Islam and state 2. Political science — Islamic Empire — History. I. T. II. Series.
JC49.L35     322/.1/0917671 19     *LC* 80-41454     *ISBN* 0197136001

**Nizām al-Mulk, 1018-1092.**                                4.7324
[Siyāsatnāmah. English] The book of government: or, Rules for kings: the Siyar al–muluk or Siyasat–nama of Nizam al–Mulk / translated from the Persian by Hubert Darke. — 2d ed. — London; Boston: Routledge & K. Paul, 1978. xxiv, 264 p.; 23 cm. (Persian heritage series; v. 32) Includes index. 1. Political science — Early works to 1800 2. Islamic Empire — History I. Darke, Hubert, ed. and tr. II. T. III. Title: Rules for Kings.
JC49.N43 1978     320/.01     *LC* 78-369906     *ISBN* 0710086199

**Piscatori, James P.**                                      4.7325
Islam in a world of nation–states / James P. Piscatori. — Cambridge [Cambridgeshire]; New York: Cambridge University Press, 1986. viii, 193 p.: ill.; 24 cm. 'Published in association with the Royal Institute of International Affairs.' Includes index. 1. Islam and state 2. Islam — 20th century I. Royal Institute of International Affairs. II. T.
JC49.P57 1986     322/.1/0917671 19     *LC* 86-8275     *ISBN* 052132985X

**Watt, W. Montgomery (William Montgomery)**                 4.7326
Islamic political thought: the basic concepts [by] W. Montgomery Watt. Edinburgh, Edinburgh U.P., 1968. xi, 186 p. 21 cm. (Islamic surveys, 6) 1. Political science — Islamic Empire — History. 2. Islamic Empire — Politics and government. I. T.
JC49.W3x     320/.09176/7     *LC* 68-22846     *ISBN* 0852240325

**Ghoshal, Upendra Nath, 1886-1969.**                        • 4.7327
A history of Indian political ideas; the ancient period and the period of transition to the Middle Ages. [Bombay] Oxford University Press, 1959. xxii, 589 p. 1. Hindus 2. Political science — History — India 3. India — Politics and goverment — Ancient period I. T.
JC50 G6 1959     *LC* 59-65390

Kautalya.                                                                • 4.7328
The Kautilīya Arthaśāstra [by] R.P. Kangle. [Bombay] University of Bombay,
1960-65. 3 v. (University of Bombay studies: Sanskrit, Prakrit and Pali, no. 1-3)
1. Administrative law — India 2. India — Social life and customs I. Kangle,
R.P. II. T.
JC50 K28 1960        *LC* SA64-8212

Kautalya.                                                                • 4.7329
Kautilya's Arthaśāstra, translated by Dr. R. Shamasastry ... with an
introductory note by the late Dr. J.F. Fleet. [7th ed.] Mysore, Mysore Printing
and Pub. House [1961] xxxix, 484 p. 1. Administrative law — India 2. India —
Social life and customs I. T.
JC50 K283 1961

Shang, Yang, d. 338 B.C.                                                 • 4.7330
The book of Lord Shang; a classic of the Chinese school of law. Translated from
the Chinese with introd. and notes by J. J. L. Duyvendak. [Chicago] University
of Chicago Press [1963, c1928] 346p. (UNESCO collection of representative
works. Chinese series.) Title also in Chinese. 1. Political science — China —
History. 2. Philosophy, Chinese I. Duyvendak, J. J. L. (Jan Julius Lodewijk),
1889- tr. II. T. III. Series.
JC50.K8 1963        *LC* 63-22585

Creel, Herrlee Glessner, 1905-.                                          4.7331
Shen Pu-hai: a Chinese political philosopher of the fourth century B. C. /
Herrlee G. Creel. Chicago: University of Chicago Press, 1975 (c1974). ix,
446 p.: map; 24 cm. Includes selections from Shen's Shen tzu. Includes index.
1. Shen, Pu-hai, 400-337 B.C. 2. Political science — China — History.
I. Shen, Pu-hai, 400-337 B.C. Shen tzu. English and Chinese. Selections. 1974.
II. T.
JC50.S495 C73        320.1/092/4 B        *LC* 73-77130        *ISBN* 0226120279

## JC51–95 Ancient State

Finley, M. I. (Moses I.), 1912-.                                         4.7332
Politics in the ancient world / M.I. Finley. — Cambridge [Cambridgeshire];
New York: Cambridge University Press, 1983. viii, 152 p.; 23 cm. — (Wiles
lectures. 1980) Includes index. 1. Greece — Politics and government —
Addresses, essays, lectures. 2. Rome — Politics and government — Addresses,
essays, lectures. I. T. II. Series.
JC51.F55 1983        320.938 19        *LC* 83-1771        *ISBN* 0521254892

Fustel de Coulanges, 1830-1889.                                         • 4.7333
[Cité antique. English] The ancient city: a study on the religion, laws and
institutions of Greece and Rome. — Garden City, N.Y.: Doubleday, 1956.
396 p.; 18 cm. (A Doubleday anchor book, A76) 1. Cities and towns, Ancient
2. Rome — Politics and government 3. Greece — Politics and government
I. T.
JC51.F95 1956        938        *LC* 55-12307

Fustel de Coulanges, 1830-1889.                                         4.7334
[Cité antique. English] The ancient city: a study on the religion, laws, and
institutions of Greece and Rome / Numa Denis Fustel de Coulanges; with a
new foreword by A. Momigliano and S. C. Humphreys. — Baltimore: Johns
Hopkins University Press, c1980. xxiii, 388 p.; 21 cm. Translation of La cité
antique. 1. Cities and towns, Ancient 2. Rome — Politics and government
3. Greece — Politics and government I. T.
JC51.F95 1980        938        *LC* 79-3703        *ISBN* 0801823048

Halliday, William Reginald, 1886-.                                      • 4.7335
The growth of the city state: lectures on Greek and Roman history. Liverpool,
The University of Liverpool ltd; London, Hodder and Stoughton ltd., 1923.
264 p. 22 cm. 1. Cities and towns, Ancient 2. Greece — Politics and
government 3. Rome — Politics and government I. T. II. Title: The city state,
The growth of.
JC51.H3        *LC* 24-3548

Hammond, Mason, 1903-.                                                   • 4.7336
City-state and world state in Greek and Roman political theory until Augustus.
Cambridge Harvard University Press 1951. 217p. 1. State, The 2. Political
science — History 3. Internationalism I. T.
JC51 H33        *LC* 51-11285

Romilly, Jacqueline de.                                                  4.7337
The rise and fall of states according to Greek authors / Jacqueline de Romilly.
Ann Arbor: University of Michigan Press, c1977. 100 p.; 22 cm. (Jerome
lectures. 11th ser.) 1. Political science — History 2. Greece — Politics and
government 3. Rome — Politics and government I. T. II. Series.
JC51.R56 1977        320.1/01        *LC* 75-31054        *ISBN* 0472087622

## JC71–79 Greece

Aristotle and Xenophon on democracy and oligarchy /          4.7338
translations with introductions and commentary by J. M.
Moore.
Berkeley: University of California Press, [1975] 320 p.: maps; 23 cm. 1. Athens
(Greece) — Constitutional history — Collected works. 2. Athens (Greece) —
Politics and government — Collected works. 3. Sparta (Ancient city) —
Politics and government — Collected works. I. Moore, J. M. (John Michael)
JC71.A1 A74 1975b        320.9/38        *LC* 74-16713        *ISBN* 0520028635.
*ISBN* 0520029097 pbk

Aristotle.                                                               • 4.7339
Politics of Aristotle / Translated with an introd., notes and appendixes, by
Ernest Barker. Oxford: Clarendon, 1946. 411 p. — 1. Political science
I. Barker, Ernest, Sir. II. T.
JC71.A41 B3        *LC* 47-692

Aristotle.                                                               4.7340
[Politics. English] The politics / Aristotle; translated, and with an introduction,
notes, and glossary by Carnes Lord. — Chicago: University of Chicago Press,
c1984. 284 p.; 24 cm. Translation of: Politica. Includes index. 1. Political
science — Early works to 1800 I. Lord, Carnes. II. T.
JC71.A41 L67 1984        320.1 19        *LC* 84-215        *ISBN* 0226026671

Rhodes, P. J. (Peter John)                                              4.7341
A commentary on the Aristotelian Athenaion politeia / by P.J. Rhodes. —
Oxford: Clarendon Press; New York: Oxford University Press, 1981. xiii,
795 p.: ill.; 23 cm. Includes indexes. 1. Aristotle. Athēnaiōn politeia I. T.
JC71.A41 R48 1981        342.38/502 343.85022 19        *LC* 82-140073
        *ISBN* 0198140045

Stalley, R. F.                                                           4.7342
An introduction to Plato's Laws / R. F. Stalley. — Indianapolis: Hackett Pub.
Co., c1983. x, 208 p.; 23 cm. Includes index. 1. Plato. Laws. 2. Law —
Philosophy. 3. State, The 4. Statutes 5. Constitutional law I. Plato. Laws.
English. II. T.
JC71.P2S7x        340/.109 19        *LC* 83-81848        *ISBN* 0915145847

Plato.                                                                   4.7343
[Laws. English.] The laws of Plato / translated with notes and an interpretive
essay by Thomas L. Pangle. — New York: Basic Books, c1980. xiv, 562 p.; 24
cm. 1. Political science — Early works to 1800 2. State, The I. Pangle,
Thomas L. II. T.
JC71.P2633 1980        321/.07        *LC* 79-7344        *ISBN* 0465038565

Plato.                                                                   • 4.7344
[Statesman English. 1957] Statesman. Translated by J.B. Skemp; edited, with an
introd., by Martin Ostwald. New York, Liberal Arts Press [1957] 100 p. (The
Library of liberal arts, no. 57) 1. Political science I. Skemp, Joseph Bright
II. T.
JC71 P313 1957        *LC* 57-14633

Plato.                                                                   4.7345
The Republic. Translated by G. M. A. Grube. Indianapolis, Hackett Pub. Co.
[1974] vii, 263 p. 21 cm. 1. Political science — Early works to 1800 2. Utopias
I. Grube, G. M. A. (George Maximilian Anthony) II. T.
JC71.P343        321/.07        *LC* 73-91951

Plato.                                                                   4.7346
[Republic. English] The Republic. Translated, with notes and an interpretive
essay, by Allan Bloom. New York, Basic Books [1968] xx, 487 p. 25 cm.
1. Political science — Early works to 1800 2. Utopias I. Bloom, Allan David,
1930- tr. II. T.
JC71.P35 1968        321/.07        *LC* 68-54141

Annas, Julia.                                                           4.7347
An introduction to Plato's Republic / by Julia Annas. — Oxford: Clarendon
Press; New York: Oxford University Press, 1981. viii, 362 p.; 22 cm. Includes
index. 1. Plato. Republic. I. T.
JC71.P6 A544 1981        321/.07 19        *LC* 80-41901        *ISBN* 0198274289

Averroës, 1126-1198.                                                    4.7348
[Be'ur le-sefer hanhagat ha-medinah le-Aplaton. English] Averroes on Plato's
Republic. Translated, with an introd. and notes, by Ralph Lerner. Ithaca [N.Y.]
Cornell University Press [1974] xxix, 176 p. 21 cm. Translation of Be'ur le-sefer
hanhagat ha-medinah le-Aplaton. 1. Plato. Republic. I. Lerner, Ralph. ed.
II. T.
JC71.P6 A83 1974        321/.07        *LC* 73-18521        *ISBN* 0801408210

Foster, Michael Beresford.                                             4.7349
The political philosophies of Plato and Hegel, by M. B. Foster. New York,
Russell & Russell, 1965. xii, 207 p. 23 cm. 'First published in 1935.' 1. Plato.

Republic. 2. Hegel, Georg Wilhelm Friedrich, 1770-1831. Grundlinien der Philosophie des Rechts 3. State, The I. T.
JC71.P6 F6 1965    LC 65-17893

**Hall, Robert William.**    **4.7350**
Plato / Robert W. Hall. — London; Boston: G. Allen & Unwin, 1981. 168 p.; 22 cm. — (Political thinkers. 9) Includes index. 1. Plato — Political science. I. T. II. Series.
JC71.P6 H34    321/.07 19    LC 81-10943    ISBN 0043201458

**White, Nicholas P., 1942-.**    **4.7351**
A companion to Plato's Republic / Nicholas P. White. — Indianapolis: Hackett Pub. Co., c1979. viii, 275 p.; 24 cm. Includes index. 1. Plato. Republic. I. Plato. Republic. II. T.
JC71.P6 W47    321/.07    LC 78-70043    ISBN 0915144565

**Kraut, Richard, 1944-.**    **4.7352**
Socrates and the state / Richard Kraut. — Princeton; Guildford: Princeton University Press, c1984. ix, 338 p.; 23 cm. 1. Political science I. T.
JC71.S62    320.5/092/4 19    LC 83-17113    ISBN 0691076669

**Arnheim, M. T. W. (Michael T. W.)**    **4.7353**
Aristocracy in Greek society / M. T. W. Arnheim. — London: Thames and Hudson, [c1977] 221 p.; 22 cm. — (Aspects of Greek and Roman life) Includes index. 1. Greece — Politics and government — To 146 B.C. 2. Greece — Nobility. I. T. II. Series.
JC73.A74    301.44/2/0938    LC 76-43353    ISBN 0500400318

**Barker, Ernest, Sir, 1874-1960.**    • **4.7354**
Greek political theory; Plato and his predecessors. — London, Methuen; New York, Barnes & Noble [1960] 468 p. 21 cm. — (University paperbacks, UP-3) 1. Plato. 2. Political science — Hist. — Greece. I. T.
JC73.B23 1960    320.938    LC 60-51504

**Barker, Ernest, Sir, 1874-1960.**    • **4.7355**
The Political thought of Plato and Aristotle / by E. Barker. — New York: Russell & Russell, 1959. 559 p.; 24 cm. 1. Plato. Republic. 2. Aristotle. Politics. 3. Political science — Greece — History I. T.
JC73.B25 1959    320.938    LC 59-7621

**Ehrenberg, Victor, 1891-.**    • **4.7356**
[Griechische und der hellenistische Staat. English] The Greek state. 2nd ed. London: Methuen, 1969. xii, 308 p.; 23 cm. 'Distributed in the U.S.A. by Barnes & Noble.' Translation of Der griechische und der hellenistische Staat. 1. Greece — Politics and government I. T.
JC73.E353 1969    320.9/38    LC 70-443245    ISBN 0416128203

**Greenidge, A. H. J. (Abel Hendy Jones), 1865-1906.**    • **4.7357**
A handbook of Greek constitutional history, by A. H. J. Greenidge. London, Macmillan and co., limited, 1920. xvii, 276 p. front. (fold. map) 20 cm. (Handbooks of archaeology and antiquities) 'First edition 1896; reprinted ... 1920.' 1. Greece — Constitutional history. I. T.
JC73.G82 1920    LC 32-33357

**Kagan, Donald.**    • **4.7358**
The great dialogue; history of Greek political thought from Homer to Polybius. New York, Free Press [1965] xi, 274 p. (History of Western political thought) 1. Political science — History — Greece I. T.
JC73 K28    LC 65-11888

**Larsen, Jakob Aall Ottesen.**    • **4.7359**
Representative government in Greek and Roman history / [by] J.A.O. Larsen. — Berkeley: University of California Press, 1955. vi, 249 p.; 22 cm. (Sather classical lectures. v. 28) 1. Greece — Politics and government 2. Rome — Politics and government I. T. II. Series.
JC73.L3 1966    321.4/0938    LC 55-6998

**Sinclair, T. A. (Thomas Alan), 1899-1961.**    **4.7360**
A history of Greek political thought, by T. A. Sinclair. [2d ed. with an additional chapter on the Early Roman Empire] Cleveland, World Pub. Co. [1968, c1967] vi, 345 p. 21 cm. 1. Political science — Greece — History. I. T.
JC73.S5 1968    320/.0938    LC 67-26539

**Starr, Chester G., 1914-.**    **4.7361**
Individual and community: the rise of the polis, 800–500 B.C. / Chester G. Starr. — New York: Oxford University Press, 1986. x, 213 p.; 22 cm. Includes index. 1. Greece — Politics and government — To 146 B.C. I. T.
JC73.S68 1986    320.938 19    LC 85-15360    ISBN 0195039718

**Staveley, E. S.**    **4.7362**
Greek and Roman voting and elections / [by] E. S. Staveley. — Ithaca, N.Y.: Cornell University Press, [1972] 271 p.: ill.; 23 cm. — (Aspects of Greek and Roman life) 1. Voting — Greece. 2. Voting — Rome. 3. Elections — Greece. 4. Elections — Rome. I. T. II. Series.
JC73.S73    324/.2/0938    LC 75-37004    ISBN 0801406935

**Strauss, Leo.**    **4.7363**
The city and man. — Chicago, Rand McNally [1964] 245 p. 24 cm. — (Rand McNally political science series) 'An enlarged version of the Page-Barbour lectures ... delivered at the University of Virginia in the spring of 1962.' Bibliographical footnotes. 1. Aristotle. Politics. 2. Plato. Republic. 3. Thucydides. History of the Peloponnesian War 4. Political science I. T.
JC73.S8    LC 64-14116

**Finley, M. I. (Moses I.), 1912-.**    **4.7364**
Democracy ancient and modern, by M. I. Finley. New Brunswick, N.J., Rutgers University Press [1973] x, 118 p. 21 cm. (Mason Welch Gross lectureship series.) 1. Democracy — History — Addresses, essays, lectures. 2. Athens (Greece) — Politics and government — Addresses, essays, lectures. I. T. II. Series.
JC79.A8 F5    320.9/38/5    LC 73-1814    ISBN 0813507510

**Jones, A. H. M. (Arnold Hugh Martin), 1904-1970.**    **4.7365**
Athenian democracy. New York, Praeger [1958] 198 p.: ill. 1. Athens (Greece) — Politics and government. 2. Athens (Greece) — Social conditions. I. T.
JC79.A8 J6 1958    LC 58-11136

## JC81–95 Rome. Byzantine Empire

**Fritz, Kurt von, 1900-.**    • **4.7366**
The theory of the mixed constitution in antiquity; a critical analysis of Polybius' political ideas. — New York, Columbia University Press, 1954. xiv, 490 p. 24 cm. Bibliographical references included in 'Notes' (p. [405]-474) Bibliography: p. [475]-477. 1. Polybius. 2. State, The I. T.
JC81.P767F7    320.15    LC 54-10329

**Homo, Léon Pol, 1872-1957.**    • **4.7367**
Roman political institutions: from city to state / by Léon Homo; [translated by M.R. Dobie]. — New York: Barnes & Noble, 1962. xvii, 426 p.; 24 cm. Translation of Les institutions politiques romaines: de la cité à l'Etat. 1. Rome — Politics and government I. T.
JC83 H74    LC 62-5834

**Hopkins, Keith, 1934-.**    **4.7368**
Death and renewal / Keith Hopkins. — Cambridge [Cambridgeshire]; New York: Cambridge University Press, 1983. xx, 276 p.: maps; 24 cm. — (Sociological studies in Roman history. v. 2) Includes indexes. 1. Heads of state — Rome — Succession. 2. Elite (Social sciences) — Rome. 3. Gladiators 4. Funeral rites and ceremonies — Rome. 5. Mourning customs — Rome. 6. Rome — Politics and government — 30 B.C.-284 A.D. 7. Rome — Politics and government — 265-30 B.C. I. T. II. Series.
JC83.H76 1983    305.5/2/0937 19    LC 82-17887    ISBN 0521249910

**Sherwin-White, A. N. (Adrian Nicholas)**    **4.7369**
The Roman citizenship / by A. N. Sherwin-White. — 2nd ed. — Oxford: Clarendon Press, 1980. 1. Citizenship — Rome I. T.
JC85.C5    323.6/0937    LC 79-41370    ISBN 019814847X pa

**Talbert, Richard J. A., 1947-.**    **4.7370**
The Senate of Imperial Rome / Richard J.A. Talbert. — Princeton, N.J.: Princeton University Press, c1984. xvii, 583 p.: ill.; 24 cm. Includes indexes. 1. Rome. Senate. 2. Rome — Politics and government — 30 B.C.-284 A.D. I. T.
JC85.S4 T17 1984    328/.3/0937 19    LC 83-42580    ISBN 0691054002

**Griffin, Miriam T. (Miriam Tamara)**    **4.7371**
Seneca: a philosopher in politics / by Miriam T. Griffin. — Oxford: Clarendon Press, 1976. xii, 504 p.; 23 cm. Includes index. 1. Seneca, Lucius Annaeus, ca. 4 B.C.-65 A.D. 2. Seneca, Lucius Annaeus, ca. 4 B.C.-65 A.D — Political science. 3. Political science — Early works to 1800 4. Rome — Politics and government — 30 B.C.-68 A.D. I. T.
JC89.G67    320.5/092/4    LC 76-371997    ISBN 0198143656

**Barker, Ernest, Sir, 1874-1960. ed. and tr.**    • **4.7372**
Social and political thought in Byzantium, from Justinian I to the last Palaeologus; passaged from Byzantine writers and documents. Translated with an introd. and notes by Ernest Barker. Oxford: Clarendon Press, 1957. 239 p., 22 cm. 1. Byzantine Empire — Constitutional history — Sources. 2. Social sciences — History — Byzantine Empire— — Sources I. T.
JC 93 .B3    LC 57-59133

## JC101–126 Medieval State

**Ullmann, Walter, 1910-.**      • **4.7373**
Principles of government and politics in the Middle Ages. New York: Barnes & Noble, [1961]. 320 p. ill. 1. State, The I. T. II. Title: Government and politics in the Middle Ages
JC101 U44     LC 61-66673

**Coulborn, Rushton, comp.**      **4.7374**
Feudalism in history. [Unaltered and unabridged ed.] Hamden, Conn.: Archon Books, 1965, c1956. 438 p. 1. Feudalism I. T.
JC111.C6 1965     321.3     LC 65-24506

**John, of Salisbury, Bishop of Chartres, d. 1180.**      **4.7375**
[Policraticus. English] Policraticus: the statesman's book / John of Salisbury; abridged and edited, with an introd., by Murray F. Markland. — New York: F. Ungar Pub. Co., c1979. xxviii, 161 p.; 21 cm. — (Milestones of thought in the history of ideas) 1. Political science — Early works to 1800 I. Markland, Murray F. II. T. III. Series.
JC121.J582 1979     320/.01     LC 78-4305     ISBN 0804424136

**John, of Salisbury, Bishop of Chartres, d. 1180.**      • **4.7376**
The statesman's book of John of Salisbury: being the fourth, fifth, and sixth books, and selections from the seventh and eighth books, of the Policraticus / translated into English with an introduction by John Dickinson. — New York, Russell & Russell, 1963 [c1955] xc, 410 p. 23 cm. — (Political science classics) 1. Political science I. Dickinson, John, 1894-1952. II. T.
JC121.J6 1963     320.1     LC 62-16195

JC
121
M323
1956
v1+v2

**Marsilius, of Padua, d. 1342?**      • **4.7377**
Marsilius of Padua, the defender of peace. — New York, Columbia University Press, 1951-56. 2 v. 24 cm. — (Records of civilization, sources and studies. no. 46) Bibliography: v. 1, p. [319]-326. Bibliographical footnotes. 1. Church and state 2. State, The 3. Political science — Hist. I. Gewirth, Alan. Marsilius of Padua and medieval political philosophy. II. T. III. Series.
JC121.M323 1951     320.15     LC 51-11283 rev 3

**McGrade, Arthur S.**      **4.7378**
The political thought of William of Ockham; personal and institutional principles [by] Arthur Stephen McGrade. [London, New York] Cambridge University Press [1974] xiii, 269 p. 24 cm. (Cambridge studies in medieval life and thought. 3d ser., v. 7.) 1. William, of Ockham, ca. 1285-ca. 1349 — Political science. I. T. II. Series.
JC121.O34 M33     320.5/092/4     LC 73-86044     ISBN 0521202841

**Thomas, Aquinas, Saint, 1225?-1274.**      • **4.7379**
Selected political writings / Aquinas; edited with an introd. by A.P. D'Entrèves; translated by J.G. Dawson. — Oxford: Blackwell, 1948. xxxvi, 199 p. — (Blackwell's political texts) Latin and English. 1. Political science I. T.
JC121.T43 1948     LC 49-6611

**Gilby, Thomas, 1902-.**      • **4.7380**
The political thought of Thomas Aquinas. [Chicago] University of Chicago Press [1958] 357 p. 1. Thomas Aquinas, Saint — Political science 2. Political science — History I. Gilby, Thomas, 1902- Principality and polity II. T.
JC121 T5 G5 1958A     LC 58-5539

## JC131–273 Modern State

**Deutsch, Karl Wolfgang, 1912- ed.**      • **4.7381**
Nation–building, edited by Karl W. Deutsch and William J. Foltz. — [1st ed.]. — New York, Atherton Press, 1966. xix, 171 p. 22 cm. — (An Atheling book, SP-505) 'Grew out of a panel discussion of the September 1962, meeting of the American Political Science Association.' 'A selection of recent works on nation building, bibliography [by] Donald J. Puchala': p. 132-150. Includes bibliographical references. 1. States, New 2. Nationalism I. Foltz, William J. joint ed. II. American Political Science Association. III. T.
JC131.D4 1966     320.15     LC 66-6982

**Meinecke, Friedrich, 1862-1954.**      • **4.7382**
Machiavellism; the doctrine of raison d'état and its place in modern history. Translated from the German by Douglas Scott, with a general introd. to Friedrich Meinecke's work by W. Stark. New Haven, Yale University Press, 1957. xlvi, 438 p. (Rare masterpieces of philosophy and science) 1. Reason of state I. T.
JC131 M42     LC 57-4318

## JC134–145 16th Century

**Bodin, Jean, 1530-1596.**      • **4.7383**
The six bookes of a commonweale. A facsimile reprint of the English translation of 1606, corrected and supplemented in the light of a new comparison with the French and Latin texts. Edited with an introd. by Kenneth Douglas McRae. Cambridge, Harvard University Press, 1962. Axii, A103 p., facsim. (x. 794 p.), A105-A214 p. (Harvard political classics) 'Out of the French and Latine copies, done into English, by Richard Knolles.' - original t. p. 1. Political science 2. State, The I. Knelles, Richard, 1550?-1610 II. McRae, Kenneth D. (Kenneth Douglas) III. T. IV. Series.
JC139 B743 1606A     LC 60-10039

**Franklin, Julian H.**      **4.7384**
Jean Bodin and the rise of absolutist theory [by] Julian H. Franklin. Cambridge [Eng.] University Press, 1973. viii, 124 p. 24 cm. (Cambridge studies in the history and theory of politics) 1. Bodin, Jean, 1530-1596. 2. Despotism 3. Political science — France — History. 4. Political science — Europe — History. I. T.
JC139.B8 F7     321.6/092/4     LC 72-83666     ISBN 0521200008

**Calvin, Jean, 1509-1564.**      • **4.7385**
John Calvin on God and political duty / edited with an introd. by John T. McNeill. — [2d ed.]. — New York: Liberal Arts Press, [1956]. xxvi, 102 p. (Library of liberal arts. 23) Selections from the author's Institutes of the Christian religion, Commentaries on Romans, and Commentaries on Daniel 1. Political science I. McNeill, John Thomas, 1885- II. T. III. Title: God and political duty. IV. Series.
JC139.C3 A3 1956

**Languet, Hubert, 1518-1581.**      • **4.7386**
A defence of liberty against tyrants; a translation of the Vindiciae contra tyrannos, by Hunius Brutus [pseud.] With an historical introd. by Harold J. Laski. Gloucester, Mass., P. Smith, 1963. 229 p. 21 cm. Also attributed to Duplessis-Mornay, and formerly to Beza, Hotman and others. Cf. Nouv. biog. Générale. Reprint of the translation of 1689 with reproduction of t. p. 1. Political science 2. Kings and rulers — Duties 3. Despotism I. Mornay, Philippe de, seigneur du Plessis-Marly, 1549-1623. II. T.
JC139.L22

**Cargill Thompson, W. D. J. (William David James) 1930-1978.**      **4.7387**
The political thought of Martin Luther / W.D.J. Cargill Thompson; edited by Philip Broadhead and with a preface by A.G. Dickens. — Brighton, Sussex: Harvester Press; Totowa, N.J.: Barnes & Noble Books, 1984. xi, 187 p.; 23 cm. 1. Luther, Martin, 1483-1546 — Political science. I. Broadhead, Philip. II. T.
JC141.L8 C37 1984     320.5/5/0924 19     LC 83-27521     ISBN 0389204684

**Machiavelli, Niccolò, 1469-1527.**      • **4.7388**
Chief works, and others. Translated by Allan Gilbert. — Durham, N.C.: Duke University Press, 1965. 3 v. (xii, 1514 p.): illus., facsims., port.; 25 cm. 1. Political science — Early works to 1800 2. Political ethics I. Gilbert, Allan H., 1888- ed. and tr. II. T.
JC143.M1529 1965     320.1     LC 64-16192

JC
143
M14
1965
v.1,2,3

**Machiavelli, Niccolò, 1469-1527.**      **4.7389**
The portable Machiavelli / newly translated and edited and with a critical introd. by Peter Bondanella and Mark Musa. — New York: Viking Press, [1979] 574 p. 1. Machiavelli, Niccolò, 1469-1527. 2. Political science — Early works to 1800 I. Bondanella, Peter E., 1943- II. Musa, Mark. III. T.
JC143.M1463 1979     JC143 M1529 1979.     320.1/092/4     LC 78-13961     ISBN 0670445223

**Machiavelli, Niccolò, 1469-1527.**      **4.7390**
[Discorsi sopra la prima deca de Tito Livio. English] The discourses of Niccolò Machiavelli / [translated from the Italian, with an introd. and notes by Leslie J. Walker; with a new introd. and appendices by Cecil H. Clough]. — London; Boston: Routledge and Paul, 1975. 2 v.: port; 23 cm. Includes indexes. 1. Livy. 2. Political science — Early works to 1800 I. Walker, Leslie Joseph, 1877- II. Clough, Cecil H. III. T.
JC143.M163 1975     320.1     LC 76-372039     ISBN 071008076X

**Mansfield, Harvey Claflin, 1932-.**      **4.7391**
Machiavelli's new modes and orders: a study of the Discourses on Livy / Harvey C. Mansfield, Jr. — Ithaca: Cornell University Press, 1979. 460 p.; 24 cm. 1. Machiavelli, Niccolò, 1469-1527. Discorsi sopra la prima deca di Tito Livio. 2. Livy. 3. Political science — Early works to 1800 I. Machiavelli, Niccolò, 1469-1527. Discorsi sopra la prima deca di Tito Livio. English. 1979. II. T.
JC143.M163 1979     320.1/01 19     LC 79-12380     ISBN 0801411823

**Machiavelli, Niccolò, 1469-1527.**      **4.7392**
[Discorsi sopra la prima deca di Tito Livio. English] The discourses. Edited with an introd. by Bernard Crick, using the translation of Leslie J. Walker with revisions by Brian Richardson. [Harmondsworth, Eng.] Penguin Books [1984] 543 p. 18 cm. (Pelican classics, AC14) Translation of Discorsi sopra la prima

deca di Tito Livio. 1. Livy. 2. Political science — Early works to 1800 I. Crick, Bernard R. ed. II. T.
JC143.M163 1970     320.9/37     *ISBN* 0140444289

**Machiavelli, Niccolò, 1469-1527.**                                    • 4.7393
[Principe. English] The prince and The discourses, by Niccolò Machiavelli, with an introduction by Max Lerner. New York, The Modern library [c1940] xlvi, 540 p. 18 cm. (The Modern library of the world's best books) 1. Livy. 2. Political science 3. Political ethics I. Ricci, Luigi, 1842-1915, tr. II. Vincent, Eric Reginald Pearce, 1894- ed. III. Detmold, Christian Edward, 1810-1887. tr. IV. Lerner, Max, 1902- V. Machiavelli, Niccolò, 1469-1527. Discorsi sopra la prima deca di Tito Livio. English. 1940. VI. T.
JC143.M38 1940     320.1     *LC* 40-27343

**Machiavelli, Niccolò, 1469-1527.**                                    4.7394
[Principe. English] The prince: a new translation, backgrounds, interpretations, peripherica / Niccolo Machiavelli; translated and edited by Robert M. Adams. — 1st ed. — New York: Norton, c1977. xix, 283 p.; 22 cm. (A Norton critical edition) Includes index. 1. Political science — Early works to 1800 2. Political ethics I. Adams, Robert Martin, 1915- II. T.
JC143.M38 1977     320.1     *LC* 77-3581     *ISBN* 0393044483. *ISBN* 039309149X pbk

**Machiavelli, Niccolò, 1469-1527.**                                    4.7395
[Principe. English] The prince / Niccolo Machiavelli; edited with an introduction by Peter Bondanella; translated by Peter Bondanella and Mark Musa. — Oxford [Oxfordshire]; New York: Oxford University Press, 1984. xxiv, 101 p.; 19 cm. — (The World's classics) Translation of: Il principe. 1. Political science — Early works to 1800 2. Political ethics I. Bondanella, Peter E., 1943- II. T.
JC143.M38 1984     320.1 19     *LC* 83-13059     *ISBN* 0192816020

**Machiavelli, Niccolò, 1469-1527.**                                    4.7396
[Principe. English] The prince / Niccolò Machiavelli; a new translation, with an introduction, by Harvey C. Mansfield, Jr. — Chicago: University of Chicago Press, 1985. xxvii, 124 p.; 21 cm. Translation of: Il principe. Includes index. 1. Political science — Early works to 1800 2. Political ethics I. Mansfield, Harvey Claflin, 1932- II. T.
JC143.M38 1985     320.1 19     *LC* 85-2536     *ISBN* 0226500373

**Chabod, Federico.**                                    • 4.7397
Machiavelli & the Renaissance. [Essays] Translated from the Italian by David Moore, with an introd. by A.P. d'Entrèves. Cambridge, Harvard University Press, 1958. xviii, 258 p. 1. Machiavelli, Niccolò, 1469-1527. 2. Machiavelli, Niccolò, 1469-1527. Il principe 3. Renaissance — Italy I. T.
JC143 M4 C413     *LC* A61-4033

**Pitkin, Hanna Fenichel.**                                    4.7398
Fortune is a woman: gender and politics in the thought of Niccolò Machiavelli / Hanna Fenichel Pitkin. — Berkeley: University of California Press, c1984. ix, 354 p.: port.; 24 cm. Includes index. 1. Machiavelli, Niccolò, 1469-1527 — Political science. 2. Machiavelli, Niccolò, 1469-1527 — Political and social views. 3. Autonomy (Psychology) 4. Sex role I. T.
JC143.M4 P57 1984     320/.01/10924 19     *LC* 83-6541     *ISBN* 0520049322

**Pocock, J. G. A. (John Greville Agard), 1924-.**                                    4.7399
The Machiavellian moment: Florentine political thought and the Atlantic republican tradition [by] J. G. A. Pocock. [Princeton, N.J.] Princeton University Press [1975] x, 602 p. 25 cm. 1. Machiavelli, Niccolò, 1469-1527 — Political and social views. 2. Political science — Italy — History. 3. Political science — Great Britain — History. 4. Political science — United States — History. I. T.
JC143.M4 P6     320.1/092/4     *LC* 73-2490     *ISBN* 0691075603

**Erasmus, Desiderius, d. 1536.**                                    • 4.7400
The education of a Christian prince. Translated with an introduction on Erasmus and on ancient and medieval political thought by Lester K. Born. — New York: Octagon Books, 1965 [c1936] ix, 277 p.; 24 cm. — (Records of civilization, sources and studies. no. 27) Translation of Institutio principis Christiani. 1. Education of princes 2. Kings and rulers — Duties 3. Peace I. Born, Lester Kruger, 1903- ed. and tr. II. T. III. Series.
JC145.E65 1965     320.01     *LC* 65-20969

## JC151–163 17th Century

**Gough, J. W. (John Wiedhofft)**                                    • 4.7401
John Locke's political philosophy: eight studies / by J. W. Gough. — Oxford: Clarendon Press, c1950. vii, 204 p. 1. Locke, John, 1632-1704. I. T.
JC153.G68     *LC* 50-13071

**Harrington, James, 1611-1677.**                                    • 4.7402
Political writings: representative selections. Edited with an introd. by Charles Blitzer. — New York, Liberal Arts Press [1955] 165 p. 21 cm. — (The Library

of liberal arts, no. 38. Political science) 1. Political science 2. Gt. Brit. — Pol. & govt. I. T.
JC153.H325     320.81     *LC* 55-2880

**Downs, Michael.**                                    4.7403
James Harrington / by Michael Downs. — Boston: Twayne Publishers, c1977. 151 p.; 21 cm. — (Twayne's English authors series; TEAS 188) Includes index. 1. Harrington, James, 1611-1677. I. T.
JC153.H4 D68     320.5/092/4     *LC* 77-21418     *ISBN* 0805766936

**Hobbes, Thomas, 1588-1679.**                                    • 4.7404
De cive; or, The citizen. Ed. with an introd. by Sterling P. Lamprecht. New York, Appleton-Century-Crofts [1949] xxxi, 211 p. (Appleton-Century philosophy source-books) 1. Political science 2. Natural law 3. Authority I. T.
JC153 H633     *LC* 49-9268

**Hobbes, Thomas, 1588-1679.**                                    • 4.7405
Leviathan: or, The matter, forme and power of a commonwealth, ecclesiasticall and civil / edited by Michael Oakeshott; with an introduction by Richard S. Peters. — New York: Collier Books, [1962] 511 p.; 18 cm. — (Collier classics in the history of thought) 1. Political science 2. State, The I. Oakeshott, Michael Joseph, 1901- II. T.
JC153.H65 1962     320.15     *LC* a 62-8701

**Bowle, John.**                                    • 4.7406
Hobbes and his critics; a study in seventeenth century constitutionalism. — New York: Barnes & Noble, [1969] 215 p.; 23 cm. 1. Hobbes, Thomas, 1588-1679 — Political science. I. T.
JC153.H66 B68 1969     320.5/092/4     *LC* 78-9350     *ISBN* 0389010561

**Oakeshott, Michael Joseph, 1901-.**                                    4.7407
Hobbes on civil association / Michael Oakeshott. — Berkeley: University of California Press, 1975. 154 p.; 23 cm. 1. Hobbes, Thomas, 1588-1679 — Political science. I. T.
JC153.H66 02 1975b     320/.01     *LC* 74-27295     *ISBN* 0520029321

**Raphael, D. D. (David Daiches), 1916-.**                                    4.7408
Hobbes: morals and politics / D. D. Raphael. — London: Allen & Unwin, 1977. 104 p.; 22 cm. (Political thinkers; no. 6) 1. Hobbes, Thomas, 1588-1679 — Political science. 2. Political ethics I. T.
JC153.H66 R36     172     *LC* 77-368975     *ISBN* 0043201180

**Strauss, Leo.**                                    • 4.7409
The political philosophy of Hobbes, its basis and its genesis; translated from German manuscript by Elsa M. Sinclair. — [Chicago]: University of Chicago Press, [1952] xx, 172 p.; 22 cm. 1. Hobbes, Thomas, 1588-1679 — Political science. 2. Political science I. T.
JC153.H66 S7 1952     320.1     *LC* 52-9720

**Warrender, Howard.**                                    • 4.7410
The political philosophy of Hobbes, his theory of obligation. Oxford, Clarendon Press, 1957. ix, 346 p. 1. Hobbes, Thomas, 1588-1679. 2. Natural obligations 3. Political science I. T.
JC153 H66 W3     *LC* A57-7367

**Locke, John, 1632-1704.**                                    • 4.7411
Two treatises of government; a critical edition with an introd. and apparatus criticus by Peter Laslett. Cambridge [Eng.] University Press, 1960. xii, 520 p. Original title page reads: Two treatises of government: in the former, the false principles and foundation of Sir Robert Filmer, and his followers, are detected and overthrown. The latter is an essay concerning the true original, extent, and end of civil-government London, Printed for Awnsham and J. Churchill at the Black Swan 1968. 1. Filmer, Robert, Sir, d. 1653. Patriarcha 2. Political science 3. Liberty. I. Laslett, Peter. II. T.
JC153 L8 1960     *LC* 60-4458

**Locke, John, 1632-1704.**                                    • 4.7412
Treatise of civil government and A letter concerning toleration, by John Locke; edited by Charles L. Sherman. New York, D. Appleton-Century company, incorporated [c1937] xv, 224 p. (Appleton-Century philosophy sourcebooks; S.P. Lamprecht, editor) 'A letter concerning toleration' was first published in 1689 and 'An essay concerninw the true original, extent and end of civil government' in 1690. cf. Introd. 1. Political science 2. Liberty. 3. Toleration I. Sherman, Charles Lawton, 1894- II. T. III. Title: A letter concerning toleration
JC153 L85 1937     *LC* 37-997

**Locke, John, 1632-1704.**                                    • 4.7413
The second treatise of government: (An essay concerning the true original extent and end of civil government) and A letter concerning toleration / edited, with a rev. introduction by J.W. Gough. — New York: Barnes & Noble, 1966. xlvii, 167 p. 1. Political science 2. Liberty. 3. Toleration I. Gough, J. W. (John Wiedhofft) II. T.
JC153.L85 1966a

**Dunn, Mary Maples.**                                                    • 4.7414
William Penn, politics and conscience. — Princeton, N.J.: Princeton University Press, 1967. x, 206 p.; 23 cm. 1. Penn, William, 1644-1718. I. T.
JC153.P4 D8        320.1        *LC* 66-21831

**Gierke, Otto Friedrich von, 1841-1921.**                                • 4.7415
[Johannes Althusius und die Entwicklung der naturrechtlichen Staatstheorien. English] The development of political theory. Translated by Bernard Freyd. New York, H. Fertig, 1966. 364 p. 24 cm. Translation of Johannes Althusius und die Entwicklung der naturrechtlichen Staatstheorien. 1. Althusius, Johannes, 1557-1638. 2. Political science — History I. T.
JC156.A5 G52 1966        320.1        *LC* 66-24346

**Spinoza, Benedictus de, 1632-1677.**                                    • 4.7416
The political works: The Tractatus theologico–politicus in part, and the Tractatus politicus in full / edited and translated with an introduction and notes by A. G. Wernham. Oxford,: Clarendon Press, 1958. — x, 463 p., 22 cm. Latin and English. 1. Political science I. Wernham, A. G. II. T.
JC163.S74        *LC* 58-1191

## JC171–189 18th Century

**Burke, Edmund, 1729-1797.**                                            • 4.7417
Philosophy of Edmund Burke; a selection from his speeches and writings / Edited with an introd.by Louis I.Bredvold and Ralph G.Ross. — Ann Arbor: University of Michigan Press, c1960. 276p. 1. Political science I. Bredvold, Louis I. II. Ross,Ralph Gilbert III. T.
JC176.B8253        320.1        *LC* 60-13177

**Burke, Edmund, 1729-1797.**                                            4.7418
[Selections. 1976] Edmund Burke on government, politics, and society / selected and edited by B. W. Hill. — New York: International Publications Service, 1975. 382 p.; 22 cm. Includes index. 1. Political science — Collected works. 2. State, The — Collected works. I. Hill, Brian W. II. T.
JC176.B826        320/.092/4 19        *LC* 75-23385        *ISBN* 0800201612

**Fasel, George W.**                                                     4.7419
Edmund Burke / by George Fasel. — Boston: Twayne Publishers, c1983. 151 p.: port.; 23 cm. (Twayne's English authors series. TEAS 286) Includes index. 1. Burke, Edmund, 1729-1797 — Political science. I. T. II. Series.
JC176.B83 F35 1983        320/.01/0924 19        *LC* 83-8581        *ISBN* 0805768610

**Godwin, William, 1756-1836.**                                          4.7420
Enquiry concerning political justice and its influence on morals and happiness. Photographic facsimile of the 3d ed., corr. and ed., with variant readings of the 1st and 2d editions and with a critical introd. and notes by F. E. L. Priestley. [Toronto] Univ. of Toronto Press, 1946. 3 v. 24 cm. (Toronto. University. Dept. of English. Studies and texts, no.2) 1. Political ethics I. Priestley, F. E. L. (Francis Ethelbert Louis), 1905- ed. II. T.
JC176.G83 1946        320        *LC* 48-18278

**Winch, Donald.**                                                       4.7421
Adam Smith's politics: an essay in historiographic revision / Donald Winch. — Cambridge; New York: Cambridge University Press, 1978. xi, 206 p.; 22 cm. — (Cambridge studies in the history and theory of politics) Includes index. 1. Smith, Adam, 1723-1790 — Political science. I. T.
JC176.S63 W56        320.5/092/4        *LC* 77-82525        *ISBN* 0521218276

**Swift, Jonathan, 1667-1745.**                                          4.7422
A discourse of the contests and dissentions between the nobles and the commons in Athens and Rome: with the consequences they had upon both those states; edited with an introduction and notes textual, critical, and historical by Frank H. Ellis. Oxford, Clarendon P., 1967. xiv, 270 p. 2 plates (ports.), facsim., diagr. 22 1/2 cm. 1. Political science 2. Rome — Politics and government 3. Athens (Greece) — Politics and government. I. Ellis, Frank H. (Frank Hale), 1916- ed. II. T.
JC176.S9 1967        320.9/42        *LC* 67-84550

**Paine, Thomas, 1737-1809.**                                            4.7423
The complete writings of Thomas Paine, collected and edited by Philip S. Foner, with a biographical essay, and notes and introductions presenting the historical background of Paine's writings. New York, Citadel Press, 1945. 2 v. port. 22 cm. 1. Paine, Thomas, 1737-1809. I. Foner, Philip Sheldon, 1910- II. T.
JC177.A3 1945        *LC* 45-2289 REV

**Conway, Moncure Daniel, 1832-1907.**                                   • 4.7424
The life of Thomas Paine. — New York: B. Blom, 1969 [i.e. 1970] xvi, 352 p.: port.; 27 cm. Reprint of the 1909 ed., with a new introd. Appendices (p. 328-348):—A. The Cobbett papers.—B. The Hall manuscripts.—C. Portraits of Paine.—D. Brief list of Paine's works (p. 348) 1. Paine, Thomas, 1737-1809. I. T.
JC178.V2 C7 1970        320.5/1/0924 B        *LC* 68-56506

**Hawke, David Freeman.**                                                4.7425
Paine. — [1st ed.]. — New York: Harper & Row, [1974] x, 500 p.: ill.; 24 cm. — 1. Paine, Thomas, 1737-1809. I. T.
JC178.V2 H34 1974        320.5/1/0924 B        *LC* 73-14264        *ISBN* 0060117842

**Barnave, Joseph, 1761-1793.**                                          4.7426
Power, property, and history; Barnave's Introduction to the French Revolution and other writings. Translated, with an introductory essay by Emanuel Chill. New York, Harper & Row [1971] vii, 156 p. 21 cm. (Harper torchbooks, TB1556) 1. State, The 2. France — History — Revolution, 1789-1799 — Causes I. Chill, Emanuel, 1924- ed. II. T.
JC179.B3        944.04/01        *LC* 77-147078        *ISBN* 0061315567

**Montesquieu, Charles de Secondat, baron de, 1689-1755.**               4.7427
The political theory of Montesquieu / [selected and translated by] Melvin Richter. — Cambridge; New York: Cambridge University Press, 1977. xi, 355 p.; 24 cm. 1. Political science — Collected works. 2. State, The — Collected works. I. Richter, Melvin, 1921- II. T.
JC179.M68 1977        320        *LC* 76-4753        *ISBN* 0521211565. *ISBN* 0521290619 pbk

**Montesquieu, Charles de Secondat, baron de, 1689-1755.**               • 4.7428
The spirit of the laws; translated by Thomas Nugent, with an introd. by Franz Neumann. — New York, Hafner Pub. Co., 1949. 2 v. in 1. 21 cm. — (The Hafner library of classics, 9) Bibliographical footnotes. 1. Political science 2. State, The 3. Law — Philosophy. 4. Jurisprudence I. T.
JC179.M        JC179.M74 1949.        *LC* A 50-3300

**Durkheim, Emile, 1858-1917.**                                          • 4.7429
Montesquieu and Rousseau: forerunners of sociology. Foreword by Henri Peyre. Durkheim, Montesquieu, and Rousseau, by Georges Davy. Note, by A. Cuvillier. [Translated by Ralph Manheim] Ann Arbor, University of Michigan Press [1960] xvi, 155 p. 1. Montesquieu, Charles de Secondat, baron de, 1689-1755. De l'esprit des lois. 2. Rousseau, Jean Jacques. Contrat social 3. Sociology — History I. T.
JC179 M8 D83        *LC* 60-5669

**Pangle, Thomas L.**                                                    4.7430
Montesquieu's philosophy of liberalism; a commentary on the Spirit of the laws [by] Thomas L. Pangle. Chicago, University of Chicago Press [1973] x, 336 p. 22 cm. 1. Montesquieu, Charles de Secondat, baron de, 1689-1755. De l'esprit des lois. 2. Liberalism I. T.
JC179.M8 P35        320.1        *LC* 73-77139        *ISBN* 0226645436

**Shackleton, Robert.**                                                  • 4.7431
Montesquieu; a critical biography. [London] Oxford University Press, 1961. xiv, 432 p. ill., port. 1. Montesquieu, Charles de Secondat, baron de, 1689-1755. I. T.
JC179 M8 S35        *LC* 61-4884

**Rousseau, Jean-Jacques, 1712-1778.**                                   • 4.7432
[Selections. 1971] The political writings of Jean Jacques Rousseau. Edited from the original manuscripts and authentic editions, with introductions and notes by C. E. Vaughan. New York, B. Franklin [1971] 2 v. facsim. 24 cm. (Burt Franklin research and source works series, 771. Philosophy monograph series, 65) Reprint of the 1915 ed. 1. Political science — Collected works. 2. Social contract — Collected works. I. Vaughan, Charles Edwyn, 1854-1922. ed. II. T.
JC179.R7 1971        320/.01 19        *LC* 71-165348        *ISBN* 0833743554

**Rousseau, Jean-Jacques, 1712-1778.**                                   • 4.7433
The social contract and Discourses / translated with an introd. by G. D. H. Cole. — New York: Dutton, 1950. liv, 330 p.; 19 cm. — (Everyman's library: Philosophy and theology; 660A) 1. Political science 2. Social contract I. T.
JC179.R86 1950        *LC* 50-7348

**Rousseau, Jean-Jacques, 1712-1778.**                                   4.7434
[Du contrat social English] On the social contract, with Geneva manuscript and Political economy / Jean–Jacques Rousseau; edited by Roger D. Masters; translated by Judith R. Masters. — New York: St. Martin's Press, c1978. viii, 245 p.; 22 cm. Translation of Contrat social and discours sur l'oeconomie politique. The Geneva manuscript is the first draft of the Social contract. 1. Political science 2. Social contract I. Masters, Roger D. II. Masters, Judith R. III. Rousseau, Jean-Jacques, 1712-1778. Discours sur l'oeconomie politique. English. 1978. IV. T. V. Title: On the social contract.
JC179.R86 1978        320/.01 19        *LC* 78-106287        *ISBN* 0312694458

**Gildin, Hilail.**                                                      4.7435
Rousseau's Social contract: the design of the argument / Hilail Gildin. — Chicago: University of Chicago Press, c1983. vii, 206 p.; 23 cm. 1. Rousseau, Jean-Jacques, 1712-1778. Du contrat social I. T.
JC179.R88 G54 1983        320./01 19        *LC* 82-20148        *ISBN* 0226293688

**Shklar, Judith N.**                                                    • **4.7436**
Men and citizens: a study of Rousseau's social theory, by Judith N. Shklar. — London: Cambridge U.P., 1969. viii, 245 p.; 22 cm. — (Cambridge studies in the history and theory of politics) 1. Rousseau, Jean Jacques, 1712-1778 — Political science. I. T.
JC179.R9 S55        320.1/1/0924        LC 75-75828        ISBN 0521075742

**Kant, Immanuel, 1724-1804.**                                          **4.7437**
Kant's political writings. Edited with an introd. and notes by Hans Reiss. Translated by H. B. Nisbet. — Cambridge [Eng.]: University Press, 1970. xi, 210 p.; 23 cm. — (Cambridge studies in the history and theory of politics) 1. Kant, Immanuel, 1724-1804 — Political science. I. Reiss, Hans Siegbert. ed. II. T.
JC181.K295        320/.01        LC 72-93710        ISBN 0521077176

## JC201-248 19th Century

**Bagehot, Walter, 1826-1877.**                                         • **4.7438**
Physics and politics; or, Thoughts on the application of the principles of 'natural selection' and 'inheritance' to political society. Introd. by Hans Kohn. Boston, Beacon Press [1956] 164 p. (Beacon paperbacks, 25) 1. Political science 2. Nationalism 3. Evolution I. T.
JC223 B14 1956        LC 56-2727

**Bentham, Jeremy, 1748-1832.**                                         • **4.7439**
A fragment on government / by Jeremy Bentham; edited with an introduction by F.C. Montague. — London: Oxford University Press, 1931. xii, 241 p.; 23 cm. 1. Blackstone, William, Sir, 1723-1780. Commentaries on the laws of England 2. Political science 3. Constitutional law I. Montague, Francis Charles, 1858-1935. II. T.
JC223 B48        LC 32-2642

**Bosanquet, Bernard, 1848-1923.**                                      • **4.7440**
The Philosophical theory of the state / by Bernard Bosanquet. — 4th ed. reprinted. — London: Macmillan; New York: St. Martin's P., 1965 [i.e. 1966] lxii, 320 p.; 22 cm. 1. Political science 2. State, The I. T.
JC223.B74 1966        320.1        LC 66-75109

**Greengarten, I. M., 1949-.**                                          **4.7441**
Thomas Hill Green and the development of liberal-democratic thought / I.M. Greengarten. — Toronto; Buffalo: University of Toronto Press, c1981. x, 151 p.; 24 cm. Cover title: Thomas Hill Green & the development of liberal-democratic thought. 1. Green, Thomas Hill, 1836-1882 — Political science. I. T. II. Title: Thomas Hill Green & the development of liberal-democratic thought.
JC223.G8 G73 1981        192 19        LC 81-156441        ISBN 0802055036

**Ten, C. L.**                                                          **4.7442**
Mill on liberty / C. L. Ten. — Oxford: Clarendon Press; New York: Oxford University Press, c1980. x, 195 p.; 22 cm. Includes index. 1. Mill, John Stuart, 1806-1873 — Political science. 2. Liberty. I. T.
JC223.M66 T45        323.44 19        LC 80-40977        ISBN 0198246439

**Dodge, Guy Howard.**                                                  **4.7443**
Benjamin Constant's philosophy of liberalism: a study in politics and religion / by Guy Howard Dodge. — Chapel Hill: University of North Carolina Press, c1980. xii, 194 p.; 23 cm. Includes index. 1. Constant, Benjamin, 1767-1830 — Political science. 2. Liberalism I. T.
JC229.C8 D62        320.5/12/0924 19        LC 79-26784        ISBN 0807814334

**Holmes, Stephen, 1948-.**                                             **4.7444**
Benjamin Constant and the making of modern liberalism / Stephen Holmes. — New Haven: Yale University Press, c1984. vii, 337 p.; 24 cm. Includes index. 1. Constant, Benjamin, 1767-1830 — Political science. 2. Liberalism I. T.
JC229.C8 H64 1984        320.5/12/0924 19        LC 84-5118        ISBN 0300030835

**Ritter, Alan, 1937-.**                                                • **4.7445**
The political thought of Pierre-Joseph Proudhon. Princeton, N.J., Princeton University Press, 1969. xii, 222 p. port. 23 cm. 1. Proudhon, P.-J. (Pierre-Joseph), 1809-1865. I. T.
JC229.P8 R54        320/.01        LC 68-56319        ISBN 0691075263

**Tocqueville, Alexis de, 1805-1859.**                                  **4.7446**
[Selections. English.] Alexis de Tocqueville on democracy, revolution, and society: selected writings / edited and with an introd. by John Stone and Stephen Mennell. — Chicago: University of Chicago Press, 1980. x, 391 p.; 22 cm. (The Heritage of sociology) Includes index. 1. Political science — Collected works. 2. Sociology — Collected works. I. Stone, John, D. Phil. II. Mennell, Stephen. III. T.
JC229.T7713 1980        301.5/92/08        LC 79-21204        ISBN 0226805263

**Drescher, Seymour.**                                                  **4.7447**
Tocqueville and England. — Cambridge, Harvard University Press, 1964. viii, 263 p. 21 cm. — (Harvard historical monographs. 55) Bibliography: p. [231]-254. 1. Tocqueville, Alexis de, 1805-1859. 2. Gt. Brit. — Pol. & govt. — 1800-1837. I. T. II. Series.
JC229.T8D7 1964        LC 63-20764

**Zetterbaum, Marvin.**                                                 **4.7448**
Tocqueville and the problem of democracy. — Stanford, Calif., Stanford University Press, 1967. ix, 185 p. 23 cm. Bibliography: p. [173]-177. 1. Tocqueville, Alexis de, 1805-1859. 2. Democracy I. T.
JC229.T8Z4        321.8/0924        LC 67-13664

**Kaufmann, Walter Arnold. comp.**                                      • **4.7449**
Hegel's political philosophy. Edited by Walter Kaufmann. — [1st ed.]. — New York: Atherton Press, 1970. 179 p.; 23 cm. 1. Hegel, Georg Wilhelm Friedrich, 1770-1831 Georg Wilhelm Friedrich, — Political science — Addresses, essays, lectures. 2. State, The — Addresses, essays, lectures. I. T.
JC233.H46 K36        320.1/0924        LC 79-105606

**Pelczynski, Z. A.**                                                   • **4.7450**
Hegel's political philosophy—problems and perspectives; a collection of new essays, edited by Z. A. Pelczynski. — Cambridge [Eng.]: University Press, 1971. viii, 246 p.; 24 cm. 1. Hegel, Georg Wilhelm Friedrich, 1770-1831 Georg Wilhelm Friedrich, — Political science — Addresses, essays, lectures. I. T.
JC233.H46 P4        320.5        LC 71-160096        ISBN 0521081238

**The State and civil society: studies in Hegel's political**          **4.7451**
**philosophy / edited by Z.A. Pelczynski.**
Cambridge [Cambridgeshire]; New York: Cambridge University Press, 1984. ix, 327 p.; 24 cm. Includes index. 1. Hegel, Georg Wilhelm Friedrich, 1770-1831 — Political science — Addresses, essays, lectures. I. Pelczynski, Z. A.
JC233.H46 S7 1984        320/.01 19        LC 84-3144        ISBN 0521247934

**Hunt, Richard N.**                                                    **4.7452**
Classical Marxism, 1850–1895 / Richard N. Hunt. — Pittsburgh, Pa.: University of Pittsburgh Press, c1984. xiii, 421 p.; 24 cm. (The Political ideas of Marx and Engels; 2) Includes index. 1. Marx, Karl, 1818-1883 — Political science. 2. Engels, Friedrich, 1820-1895 — Political science. 3. Communist state I. T.
JC233.M299 H85 vol. 2        320.5/315 s 320.5/315 19        LC 84-5218
  ISBN 0822934965

**Treitschke, Heinrich Gotthard von, 1834-1896.**                       • **4.7453**
Politics. Abridged, edited, and with an introd. by Hans Kohn. [Translated from the German by Blanche Dugdale and Torben de Bille]. — New York, Harcourt, Brace & World [1963] xxv, 338 p. 21 cm. 'HO33.' Bibliographical references included in 'Notes' (p. 309-322) 1. State, The 2. Political science I. T.
JC233.T832        320.1        LC 63-20972

**Hegel's social and political thought: the philosophy of objective**   **4.7454**
**spirit / edited by Donald Phillip Verene.**
[Atlantic Highlands], N.J.: Humanities Press; [Brighton], Sussex: Harvester Press, 1980. vi, 250 p.; 24 cm. 'Papers ... from the ... biennial conference of the Hegel Society of America, held at Villanova University, Villanova, Pennsylvania, November 11-13, 1976.' 1. Hegel, Georg Wilhelm Friedrich, 1770-1831 — Political science — Congresses. I. Verene, Donald Phillip, 1937- II. Hegel Society of America.
JC234.H36 H43 1980        320.5/092/4        LC 77-26183        ISBN 039100543X

## JC249-273 20th Century

**Poulantzas, Nicos Ar.**                                               **4.7455**
[État, le pouvoir, le socialisme. English] State, power, socialism / [by] Nicos Poulantzas; translated [from the French] by Patrick Camiller. — London: NLB, 1979 (c1978). 269 p.; 22 cm. Translation of L'état, le pouvoir, le socialisme. 1. State, The 2. Communist state 3. Social classes I. T.
JC249.P6713        320.1/01        LC 79-306225        ISBN 086091013X

**Poulantzas, Nicos Ar.**                                               **4.7456**
[Pouvoir politique et classes sociales. English] Political power and social classes / [by] Nicos Poulantzas; translation ... [from the French edited by] Timothy O'Hagan. — London: NLB; Sheed and Ward, 1974 (c1973) 367 p.; 22 cm. Translation of Pouvoir politique et classes sociales. Includes index. 1. State, The 2. Communist state 3. Social classes I. T.
JC249.P6813        301.5/92        LC 73-168461        ISBN 0722073046

## JC251–252 UNITED STATES

**Young-Bruehl, Elisabeth.**     4.7457
Hannah Arendt, for love of the world / Elisabeth Young–Bruehl. — New Haven: Yale University Press, c1982. xxv, 563 p., [12] p. of plates: ill.; 24 cm. Includes index. 1. Arendt, Hannah. 2. Political scientists — Biography. I. T. JC251.A74 Y68 1982    320.5/3/0424 B 19     *LC* 81-16114    *ISBN* 0300026609

**Cassirer, Ernst, 1874-1945.**     • 4.7458
The myth of the state / by Ernst Cassirer; [edited by Charles W. Hendel]. — New Haven, Yale University Press, 1946. xii, 303 p. 1. State, The 2. Political science 3. Mythology I. Handel, Charles William 1890- II. T. JC251.C3    *LC* a 46-5936    *ISBN* 0300003528

**Lippmann, Walter, 1889-.**     • 4.7459
Essays in the public philosophy. — [1st ed.]. — Boston: Little, Brown, [c1955] 189 p.; 22 cm. 1. Democracy 2. Political science I. T. II. Title: The public philosophy. JC251.L47    321.82*    *LC* 55-6533

**Lippmann, Walter, 1889-.**     • 4.7460
The essential Lippmann; a political philosophy for liberal democracy. Edited by Clinton Rossiter & James Lare. — New York: Random House, [1963] 552 p.; 22 cm. 1. Political science I. T. JC251.L48    320.81    *LC* 63-11623

**MacIver, Robert M. (Robert Morrison), 1882-1970.**     • 4.7461
The web of government [by] R. M. MacIver. — Rev. ed. — New York: Free Press, [1965] viii, 373 p.; 22 cm. — (Free Press paperbacks) 1. Political science I. T. JC251.M2 1965    320    *LC* 65-19015

**Merriam, Charles Edward, 1874-1953.**     • 4.7462
Political power / Charles E. Merriam; with a new introd. by Harold D. Lasswell. — New York: Collier Books, 1964. 317 p.; 18 cm. 'BS196.' 1. Power (Social sciences) 2. Political science I. T. JC251.M4 1964    *LC* 63-10946

**Merriam, Charles Edward, 1874-1953.**     • 4.7463
The role of politics in social change, by Charles Edward Merriam. New York, New York university press; London, H. Milford, Oxford university press, 1936. 5 p. l., 13-149 p. 24 cm. (James Stokes lectureship on politics. New York university. Stokes foundation.) 1. Political science 2. Fascism 3. Communism 4. Public opinion I. T. JC251.M43    320.1    *LC* 36-28567

**Santayana, George, 1863-1952.**     • 4.7464
Dominations and powers; reflections on liberty, society, and government. — Clifton [N.J.]: A. M. Kelley, 1972 [c1951] xv, 481 p.; 22 cm. — (Scribner reprint editions) 1. Political science I. T. JC251.S33 1972    320.5    *LC* 75-158153    *ISBN* 0678027757

**Voegelin, Eric, 1901-.**     • 4.7465
The new science of politics, an introduction. Chicago, University of Chicago Press [1952] xiii, 193 p. (Charles R. Walgreen Foundation lectures) 1. Political science 2. Representative government and representation I. T. JC251 V64    *LC* 52-13531

**Burnham, James, 1905-1987.**     • 4.7466
The managerial revolution. — Bloomington: Indiana University Press, [1960] 285 p.; 20 cm. — (A Midland book, MB23) 1. World politics — 20th century 2. Social problems 3. Capitalism 4. Socialism I. T. JC252.B8 1960    330.15    *LC* 60-8308

**Merriam, Charles Edward, 1874-1953.**     • 4.7467
Public & private goverment, by Charles E. Merriam. New Haven, Yale university press; London, H. Milford, Oxford university press, 1944. 5 p. l., 78 p. 21 cm. (Powell lectures on philosophy at Indiana university: W. H. Jellema, editor. 8th ser.) 'Published for Indiana university.' 1. Political science 2. Democracy 3. Sovereignty 4. Association and associations. I. T. JC252.M45    *LC* a 44-1310

## JC253–273 OTHER COUNTRIES

**Barker, Ernest, Sir, 1874-1960.**     4.7468
Principles of social & political theory. Oxford, Clarendon Press, 1954. 284 p. 1. Political science I. T. JC257 B33

**Catlin, George Edward Gordon, 1896-.**     • 4.7469
The science and method of politics / by G. E. G. Catlin. Hamden, Conn.: Archon Books, 1964. xii, 360 p.; 22 cm. 1. Political science 2. History 3. Ethics I. T. JC257.C3 1964    *LC* 64-25412

**Catlin, George E. G.**     • 4.7470
A study of the principles of politics: being an essay towards political rationalization / by George E. G. Catlin. — New York: Russell & Russell, 1967. 469 p. 1. Political science 2. Authority I. T. II. Title: The principles of politics. JC257.C35 1967    *LC* 66-27049

**Collingwood, R. G. (Robin George), 1889-1943.**     • 4.7471
The new Leviathan; or, Man, society, civilization and barbarism, by R. G. Collingwood ... — Oxford, The Clarendon press, 1942. viii, 387, [1] p. 23 cm. 1. Hobbes, Thomas, 1588-1679. Leviathan 2. Political science 3. Civilization 4. State, The I. T. JC257.C6    320.1    *LC* A 42-5477

**Laski, Harold Joseph, 1893-1950.**     4.7472
A grammar of politics. [5th ed.] London Allen & Unwin [1967] 672p. 1. Political science I. T. JC257 L3 1967

**Miliband, Ralph.**     4.7473
The state in capitalist society. — New York: Basic Books, [1969] x, 292 p.; 22 cm. 1. State, The 2. Capitalism I. T. JC257.M54 1969b    320.1/5    *LC* 78-93689

**Russell, Bertrand, 1872-1970.**     • 4.7474
Power, a new social analysis / by Bertrand Russell. — London: G. Allen & Unwin, 1938. 328 p. 1. Political science 2. Executive power 3. Power (Social sciences) I. T. JC257.R8 1938a    320.1    *LC* 39-7089

**Barker, Ernest, Sir, 1874-1960.**     • 4.7475
Essays on government. 2d ed. Oxford: Clarendon P., 1951. 304p.; 23 cm. 1. Constitutional law — Addresses,essays,lectures. I. T. JC258.B3 1951    342.04    *LC* 51-6482

**Maritain, Jacques, 1882-1973.**     • 4.7476
Man and the state. — Chicago: University of Chicago Press, [1951] x, 219 p.; 22 cm. — (Charles R. Walgreen Foundation Lectures) 1. State, The 2. Democracy 3. Church and social problems — Catholic Church I. T. JC261.M32    320.15    *LC* 51-555

**Maritain, Jacques, 1882-1973.**     • 4.7477
Scholasticism and politics / translation edited by Mortimer J. Adler. 3d ed. London: G. Bles, 1954. 197 p. 1. Scholasticism 2. Political science I. T. JC261.M33 1954    *LC* 55-32607

**Sassoon, Anne Showstack.**     4.7478
Gramsci's politics / Anne Showstack Sassoon. — New York: St. Martin's Press, 1980. 261 p.; 23 cm. Includes index. 1. Gramsci, Antonio, 1891-1937 — Political science. I. T. JC265.G68 S27 1980    335.43/092/4 19    *LC* 79-57375    *ISBN* 0312342381

**Mosca, Gaetano, 1858-1941.**     • 4.7479
The ruling class (Elementi di scienze politica) by Gaetano Mosca. Translated by Hannah D. Kahn. Edited and revised, with an introduction, by Arthur Livingston. 1st ed. New York, McGraw-Hill book company, inc. [1939] xii, 514 p. 1. Political science I. Livingston, Arthur, 1883- II. T. JC265 M623    *LC* 39-2657

**Meisel, James Hans, 1900-.**     • 4.7480
The myth of the ruling class; Gaetano Mosca and the 'elite.' Ann Arbor, University of Michigan Press [1958] vi, 432 p. diagrs. 24 cm. 1. Mosca, Gaetano, 1858-1941. I. T. JC265.M65 M4    *LC* 57-7101

**Onwuanibe, Richard C.**     4.7481
A critique of revolutionary humanism: Frantz Fanon / by Richard C. Onwuanibe. — St. Louis, Mo., U.S.A.: W.H. Green, c1983. xviii, 145 p.: port.; 24 cm. Spine title: Frantz Fanon. Includes indexes. 1. Fanon, Frantz, 1925-1961 — Political science. 2. Humanism 3. Revolutions 4. Africa — Colonial influence. I. T. II. Title: Frantz Fanon. JC273.F36 O58 1983    322.4/2/01 19    *LC* 83-192205    *ISBN* 0875272967

**Iyer, Raghavan Narasimhan.**     4.7482
The moral and political thought of Mahatma Gandhi [by] Raghavan N. Iyer. New York, Oxford University Press, 1973. xiii, 449 p. 22 cm. 1. Gandhi, Mahatma, 1869-1948 — Political science. 2. Political ethics 3. Nonviolence I. T. JC273.G28 I9    181/.4    *LC* 72-96613    *ISBN* 0195016920

## JC311–323 Nationalism

**Apter, David Ernest, 1924-.**     • **4.7483**
Ideology and discontent, edited by David E. Apter. London, Free Press of Glencoe [1964] 342 p. ill. (Interntional yearbook of political behavior research, v. 5) 1. Nationalism 2. Political psychology I. T. II. Series.
JC311 A74 1964     LC 64-20305

**Carr, Edward Hallett, 1892-.**     • **4.7484**
Nationalism and after, by Edward Hallett Carr ... London, Macmillan, 1945. vi, 73, [1] p. 1. Nationalism 2. Inaterntional cooperation I. T.
JC311 C35     LC 45-3864

**Deutsch, Karl Wolfgang, 1912-.**     • **4.7485**
Nationalism and social communication; an inquiry into the foundations of nationality. — [Cambridge]: Published jointly by the Technology Press of the Massachusetts Institute of Technology, and Wiley, New York, [1953] x, 292 p.: maps, diagrs.; 24 cm. 1. Nationalism I. T.
JC311.D43     320.15 321.8*     LC 53-7949

**Emerson, Rupert, 1899-.**     **4.7486**
From empire to nation; the rise to self–assertion of Asian and African peoples. Cambridge, Harvard University Press, 1960. 466 p. 24 cm. 1. Nationalism — Asia. 2. Colonies 3. States, New — Politics and government 4. Nationalism — Africa. I. T.
JC311.E49     320.158     LC 60-5883

**The Future of cultural minorities / edited by Antony E. Alcock,**     **4.7487**
**Brian K. Taylor, John M. Welton.**
New York: St. Martin's Press, 1979. viii, 221 p.; 23 cm. Based on a seminar held at the Richardson Institute for Peace and Conflict Research in May 1977. Includes indexes. 1. Minorities — Congresses. I. Alcock, Antony Evelyn. II. Taylor, Brian K. III. Welton, John M.
JC311.F93 1979     301.45     LC 78-13725     ISBN 0312314701

**Kohn, Hans, 1891-1971.**     • **4.7488**
Nationalism, its meaning and history. Rev. ed. Princeton, N.J., Van Nostrand [1965] 192 p. 19 cm. 1. Nationalism I. T.
JC311.K56 1965     LC 65-5303

**Kohn, Hans, 1891-1971.**     • **4.7489**
The idea of nationalism, a study in its origins and background, y Hans Kohn ... New York, The Macmillan company, 1944. xiii, 735 p. 1. Nationalism I. T.
JC311 K567     LC 44-3540

**Kohn, Hans, 1891-1971.**     • **4.7490**
Prophets and peoples; studies in nineteenth century nationalism, by Hans Kohn. — New York: The Macmillan company, 1946. 4 p. l., 213 p.; 21 cm. 'First printing.' 'This book grew out of five lectures delivered in July, 1945, as the Norman Wait Harris foundation lectures at Northwestern university in Evanston, Illinois.'—Pref. 1. Nationalism and nationality. I. T.
JC311.K568     320.15     LC 46-3346

**Smith, Anthony D.**     **4.7491**
The ethnic revival / Anthony D. Smith. — Cambridge; New York: Cambridge University Press, 1981. xxiv, 240 p.; 24 cm. — (Themes in the social sciences.) Includes index. 1. Nationalism 2. Ethnic groups — Political activity. 3. Ethnicity I. T. II. Series.
JC311.S537 1981     320.5/4 19     LC 80-42149     ISBN 0521232678

**Tagore, Rabindranath, 1861-1941.**     • **4.7492**
Nationalism, by Sir Rabindranath Tagore. New York, The Macmillan company, 1917. 159 p. 19 cm. 1. Nationalism and nationality. I. T.
JC311.T26     LC 17-22891

**Talmon, J. L. (Jacob Leib), 1916-.**     • **4.7493**
Political Messianism: the romantic phase. — New York: Praeger, [1961, c1960] 607 p. (Books that matter) 1. Messianism, Political I. T.
JC315.T2 1961

## JC319 Geopolitics

**Brunn, Stanley D.**     **4.7494**
Geography and politics in America [by] Stanley D. Brunn. — New York: Harper & Row, [1974] xviii, 443 p.: illus.; 24 cm. — (Harper & Row series in geography) 1. Geography, Political 2. Political sociology 3. Regionalism — United States. 4. United States — Politics and government I. T.
JC319.B78     320.1/2     LC 73-17670     ISBN 0060410183

**Cohen, Saul Bernard.**     **4.7495**
Geography and politics in a world divided. — 2d ed. — New York: Oxford University Press, 1973. xxi, 334 p.: illus.; 21 cm. 1. Geopolitics I. T.
JC319.C58 1973     320.1/2     LC 73-77923     ISBN 0195016955

**Gottmann, Jean.**     • **4.7496**
La politique des états et leur géographie / Jean Gottmann. — Paris: A. Colin, 1952. xi, 228 p.; 23 cm. — (Sciences politiques) 1. Geopolitics I. T.
JC319 G65     LC 52-2344

**Jackson, W. A. Douglas (William Arthur Douglas), 1923- ed.**     • **4.7497**
Politics and geographic relationships; readings on the nature of political geography. Englewood Cliffs, N.J., Prentice-Hall [1964] xii, 411 p. ill., maps. 1. Geopolitics — Collections 2. Political science — Collections I. T.
JC319 J24     LC 63-13284

**Paddison, Ronan.**     **4.7498**
The fragmented state: the political geography of power / Ronan Paddison. — New York: St. Martin's Press, 1983. x, 315 p.: ill.; 24 cm. Includes index. 1. Geography, Political 2. Power (Social sciences) I. T.
JC319.P23 1983     320.1/2 19     LC 83-4490     ISBN 0312302444

**Pluralism and political geography: people, territory, and state /**     **4.7499**
**edited by Nurit Kliot and Stanley Waterman.**
London: Croom Helm; New York: St. Martin's Press, 1983. 323 p.: ill.; 23 cm. 1. Geography, Political — Addresses, essays, lectures. 2. Pluralism (Social sciences) — Addresses, essays, lectures. I. Kliot, Nurit. II. Waterman, Stanley.
JC319.P58 1983     320.1/2 19     LC 83-6212     ISBN 0312617666

**Political studies from spatial perspectives: Anglo–American**     **4.7500**
**essays on political geography / edited by Alan D. Burnett and**
**Peter J. Taylor.**
Chichester [Eng.]; New York: J. Wiley, c1981. xv, 519 p.: ill.; 26 cm. Based on a seminar held under the auspices of the Political Geography Working Party at the annual conference of the Institute of British Geographers, Lancaster University, Jan. 1980. Errata slip inserted. 1. Geography, Political — Congresses. I. Burnett, Alan D. II. Taylor, Peter J. (Peter James), 1944- III. Political Geography Working Party.
JC319.P62     320.1/2 19     LC 80-41384     ISBN 0471279099

**Taylor, Peter J. (Peter James), 1944-.**     **4.7501**
Political geography: world–economy, nation–state and locality / Peter J. Taylor. — London; New York: Longman, 1985. x, 238 p.: ill.; 24 cm. Includes index. 1. Geography, Political 2. Geopolitics I. T.
JC319.T34 1985     320.1/2 19     LC 84-5790     ISBN 0582300886

## JC323 Frontiers

**Curzon of Kedleston, George Nathaniel Curzon, 1st Marquis,**     • **4.7502**
**1859-1925.**
Frontiers. 2d ed. — Oxford, Clarendon Press, 1908. 58 p. (The Romanes Lecture, 1907) I. T.
JC323.C88 1908     LC 21-19687

## JC325–347 Nature, Entity, Concept of the State. Symbols

**De Grazia, Sebastian.**     • **4.7503**
The political community, a study of anomie. — Chicago, Univ. of Chicago Press [1948] xx, 258 p. 24 cm. — (Phoenix books, P116.) Bibliographical references included in 'Notes' (p. [193]-242) 1. Anomy 2. Belief and doubt 3. State, The I. T.
JC325.D37     320.15     LC 48-9544 *

**Hobhouse, L. T. (Leonard Trelawney), 1864-1929.**     • **4.7504**
The metaphysical theory of the state: a criticism / by L. T. Hobhouse. — London: G. Allen & Unwin; New York: Macmillan, 1918. 156 p.; 22 cm. — (Studies in economics and political science. 51) Includes index. 1. Hegel, Georg Wilhelm Friedrich, 1770-1831. 2. State, The I. T. II. Series.
JC325.H6     LC 18-22760

**Jouvenel, Bertrand de, 1903-.**     • **4.7505**
On power, its nature and the history of its growth; pref. by D. W. Brogan. Translation by J. F. Huntington. — New York, Viking Press, 1949 [c1948] xix, 421 p. 22 cm. Bibliographical references included in 'Notes' (p. 383-421) 1. Authority 2. State, The I. T.
JC325.J62 1949     320.1     LC 49-8896 *

**Niebuhr, Reinhold, 1892-1971.**     • **4.7506**
The structure of nations and empires; a study of the recurring patterns and problems of the political order in relation to the unique problems of the nuclear age. New York, Scribner [1959] xi, 306 p. 1. State, The 2. Imperialism 3. Internationalism I. T.
JC325 N5     *LC* 59-11324

**Statemaking and social movements: essays in history and theory**     **4.7507**
/ edited by Charles Bright and Susan Harding.
Ann Arbor: University of Michigan Press, c1984. 404 p.; 24 cm. 1. State, The — Addresses, essays, lectures. 2. Social movements — Addresses, essays, lectures. I. Bright, Charles, 1943- II. Harding, Susan Friend.
JC325.S7354 1984     306/.2 19     *LC* 84-7430     *ISBN* 0472100505

**Jouvenel, Bertrand de, 1903-.**     • **4.7508**
Sovereignty; an inquiry into the political good. Translated by J. F. Huntington. — [Chicago] University of Chicago Press [1957] 319 p. 22 cm. Translation of De la souveraineté. 1. Sovereignty 2. Liberty. I. T.
JC327.J613     320.157     *LC* 57-9548

**Laski, Harold Joseph, 1893-1950.**     • **4.7509**
Studies in the problem of sovereignty. — New York, H. Fertig, 1968. x, 297 p. 21 cm. Reprint of the 1917 ed. Bibliographical footnotes. 1. Sovereignty 2. Church and state I. T.
JC327.L3 1968     320.1/57     *LC* 67-24584

**Laski, Harold Joseph, 1893-1950.**     • **4.7510**
Authority in the modern state. — [Hamden, Conn.]: Archon Books, 1968 [c1919] x, [15]-398 p.; 22 cm. 'An unaltered and unabridged [reprint] edition.' 1. State, The 2. Sovereignty 3. Church and state I. T. II. Title: Modern state.
JC327.L35 1968     320.1     *LC* 68-21685

## JC328 Allegiance. Resistance to Government

**Bedau, Hugo Adam. comp.**     • **4.7511**
Civil disobedience; theory and practice. — New York: Pegasus, [1969] 282 p.; 21 cm. 1. Government, Resistance to I. T.
JC328.B38     322/.4     *LC* 68-27984

**Bickel, Alexander M.**     **4.7512**
The morality of consent / Alexander M. Bickel. — New Haven: Yale University Press, 1975. vii, 156 p.; 22 cm. Based on the William C. DeVane lectures at Yale University in 1973. Includes index. 1. Allegiance 2. Government, Resistance to I. T.
JC328.B53     323.6/5     *LC* 75-10988     *ISBN* 0300019114

**Grodzins, Morton Melvin.**     • **4.7513**
The loyal and the disloyal; social boundaries of patriotism and treason. Chicago, University of Chicago Press, [1956] 319 p. 23 cm. 1. Loyalty 2. Patriotism I. T.
JC328.G7     *LC* 56-7201

**Hamburger, Joseph, 1922-.**     • **4.7514**
James Mill and the art of revolution. New Haven, Yale University Press, 1963. xiii, 289 p. (Yale studies in political science. 8) 1. Mill, James, 1773-1836. 2. Government, Resistance to 3. Great Britain — Politics and government — 1830-1837 I. T. II. Series.
JC328 H25     *LC* 63-13963

**Pateman, Carole.**     **4.7515**
The problem of political obligation: a critical analysis of liberal theory / Carole Pateman. — Chichester; New York: Wiley, c1979. xi, 205 p.; 24 cm. Includes indexes. 1. Allegiance 2. Liberalism 3. Democracy 4. Political obligation I. T.
JC328.P27     323.6/5/01     *LC* 78-18460     *ISBN* 0471996998

**Political and legal obligation. Edited by J. Roland Pennock and**     • **4.7516**
**John W. Chapman.**
[1st ed.] New York, Atherton Press, 1970. xxiii, 455 p. 22 cm. (Nomos. 12) 'Yearbook of the American Society for Political and Legal Philosophy.' 1. Allegiance — Addresses, essays, lectures. 2. Government, Resistance to — Addresses, essays, lectures. I. Pennock, J. Roland (James Roland), 1906- ed. II. Chapman, John William, 1923- ed. III. American Society for Political and Legal Philosophy. IV. Series.
JC328.P58     320.1/5     *LC* 70-105609

**Ginsberg, Benjamin.**     **4.7517**
The consequences of consent: elections, citizen control, and popular acquiescence / Benjamin Ginsberg. — Reading, Mass.: Addison-Wesley, 1982. xiii, 271 p.: ill.; 21 cm. Includes index. 1. General will 2. Representative

government and representation 3. Consensus (Social sciences) 4. Elections 5. Pressure groups 6. Consent (Law) I. T.
JC328.2.G56     320/.01/1 19     *LC* 81-3581     *ISBN* 0201040794

**Goodman, Paul, 1911-1972.**     **4.7518**
Drawing the line: the political essays of Paul Goodman / edited by Taylor Stoehr. — 1st ed. — New York: Free Life Editions, 1977. xxxii, 272 p.; 22 cm. 1. Government, Resistance to — Addresses, essays, lectures. 2. Social sciences — Addresses, essays, lectures. I. Stoehr, Taylor, 1931- II. T.
JC328.3.G67 1977     309.1/73/092     *LC* 77-71943     *ISBN* 0914156179

**Walzer, Michael.**     • **4.7519**
Obligations; essays on disobedience, war, and citizenship. — Cambridge: Harvard University Press, 1970. xvi, 244 p.; 22 cm. 1. Government, Resistance to 2. War 3. Citizenship I. T.
JC328.3.W34     323.6/5     *LC* 70-111489     *ISBN* 0674630009

**Grundy, Kenneth W.**     **4.7520**
The ideologies of violence / [by] Kenneth W. Grundy [and] Michael A. Weinstein. — Columbus, Ohio: Merrill, [1974] vii, 117 p.; 23 cm. 1. Violence 2. Ideology I. Weinstein, Michael A. joint author. II. T.
JC328.6.G78     301.6/33     *LC* 73-91055     *ISBN* 0675088356

**Wilkinson, Paul.**     **4.7521**
Terrorism and the liberal state / Paul Wilkinson. — 2nd ed., rev., extended, and updated. — New York: New York University Press, 1986. xiv, 322 p.; 22 cm. Includes index. 1. Violence 2. Terrorism 3. Liberalism I. T.
JC328.6.W54 1986     322.4/2 19     *LC* 85-15303     *ISBN* 0814792065

## JC330 Power

**Dahl, Robert Alan, 1915-.**     • **4.7522**
Modern political analysis [by] Robert A. Dahl. — 2d ed. — Englewood Cliffs, N.J.: Prentice-Hall, [1970] viii, 118 p.: illus.; 24 cm. — (Foundations of modern political science series) 1. Power (Social sciences) 2. Political science I. T.
JC330.D34 1970     320     *LC* 70-93290     *ISBN* 0135970474

**Putnam, Robert D.**     **4.7523**
The beliefs of politicians: ideology, conflict, and democracy in Britain and Italy [by] Robert D. Putnam. — New Haven: Yale University Press, 1973. xii, 309 p.: illus.; 25 cm. — (Yale studies in political science. 24) 1. Elite (Social sciences) 2. Ideology 3. Social conflict 4. Democracy 5. Legislators — Great Britain. 6. Legislators — Italy. I. T. II. Series.
JC330.P87     320.5     *LC* 72-75207     *ISBN* 0300014988

**Aunger, Edmund A.**     **4.7524**
In search of political stability: a comparative study of New Brunswick and Northern Ireland / Edmund A. Aunger. — Montreal: McGill-Queen's University Press, c1981. xiv, 224 p.: ill.; 23 cm. Includes index. 1. Political stability — New Brunswick — History. 2. Political stability — Northern Ireland — History. 3. New Brunswick — Politics and government. 4. Northern Ireland — Politics and government I. T.
JC330.2.A93 1981     306/.2 19     *LC* 81-174075     *ISBN* 0773503668

## JC331–341 Special Theories of the State. Social Contract

**Barker, Ernest, Sir, 1874-1960.**     • **4.7525**
Social contract; essays by Locke, Hume and Rousseau. London, New York, Oxford University Press [1952] lxiii, 440 p. 16 cm. (The world's classics, 511) 1. Social contract 2. State, The I. T.
JC336.B27 1952     320.1     *LC* 51-13405

**Coker, Francis William, 1878-.**     • **4.7526**
Organismic theories of the state; nineteenth century interpretations of the state as organism or as person, by F. W. Coker. — New York: AMS Press, 1967. 209 p.; 23 cm. — (Studies in history, economics, and public law, v. 38, no. 2, whole no. 101) Reprint of the 1910 ed. 1. State, The I. T.
JC336.C8 1967     320.1/1     *LC* 74-120061

**Gough, J. W. (John Wiedhofft)**     • **4.7527**
The social contract, a critical study of its development. 2d ed. Oxford, Clarendon Press, 1957. viii, 259 p. 1. Social contract I. T.
JC336 G6 1957     *LC* A57-3247

**Oppenheimer, Franz, 1864-1943.**     • **4.7528**
The state; its history and development viewed sociologically. [Authorized translation by John M. Gitterman]. — New York: Arno Press, 1972. xv, 302 p.;

22 cm. — (The Right wing individualist tradition in America) Reprint of the 1926 ed. 1. State, The I. T.
JC336.O6213 1972      320.1      *LC* 73-172224      *ISBN* 0405004338

**Smith, Whitney.**                                                     **4.7529**
Flags and arms across the world / Whitney Smith. — New York: McGraw-Hill, c1980. 256 p.: ill.; 19 cm. Revision of a section of Flags through the ages and across the world. Includes index. 1. Flags I. Smith, Whitney. Flags through the ages and across the world. II. T.
JC345.S56      929.9      *LC* 79-13271      *ISBN* 007059094X

**Smith, Whitney.**                                                     **4.7530**
Flags through the ages and across the world / Whitney Smith; designed by Emil Bührer. — New York: McGraw-Hill, [1975] 357 p.: ill. (some col.); 29 cm. Includes index. 1. Flags — History. I. T.
JC345.S57      929.9      *LC* 75-12602      *ISBN* 0070590931

# JC348–497 Forms of the State

## JC359 Imperialism

**Betts, Raymond F.**                                                   • **4.7531**
Europe overseas: phases of imperialism [by] Raymond F. Betts. — New York: Basic Books, [1968] ix, 206 p.; 22 cm. 1. Imperialism 2. World politics I. T.
JC359.B45      321/.03/094      *LC* 68-19772

**De Schweinitz, Karl, 1920-.**                                         **4.7532**
The rise and fall of British India: imperialism as inequality / Karl de Schweinitz, Jr. — London; New York: Methuen, 1983. 275 p.; 22 cm. Includes index. 1. Imperialism — Case studies. 2. India — History — British occupation, 1765-1947 I. T.
JC359.D36 1983      325/.341/0954 19      *LC* 82-20868      *ISBN* 0416335306

**Folz, Robert.**                                                       • **4.7533**
[Idée d'empire en Occident du V au XIV siècle. English] The concept of empire in Western Europe from the fifth to the fourteenth century; translated [from the French] by Sheila Ann Ogilvie. London, Edward Arnold, 1969. xv, 250 p. 23 cm. Translation of L'idée d'empire en Occident du V. au XIV siècle. 1. Imperialism 2. Europe — History — 476-1492 I. T.
JC359.F613      321/.03/094      *LC* 71-443272      *ISBN* 0713154519

**Headrick, Daniel R.**                                                 **4.7534**
The tools of empire: technology and European imperialism in the nineteenth century / Daniel R. Headrick. — New York: Oxford University Press, 1981. x, 221 p.; 22 cm. 1. Technology — History. 2. Imperialism — History. I. T.
JC359.H4      303.4/83/09034      *LC* 80-18099      *ISBN* 0195028317

**Koebner, Richard, 1885-1958.**                                        • **4.7535**
Imperialism; the story and significance of a political word, 1840–1960, by Richard Koebner and Helmut Dan Schmidt. — Cambridge [Eng.]: University Press, 1964. xxv, 432 p.; 24 cm. 1. Imperialism I. Schmidt, Helmut Dan, joint author. II. T.
JC359.K6      321.03      *LC* 64-4156

**Lichtheim, George, 1912-.**                                           • **4.7536**
Imperialism. — New York: Praeger, [1971] vii, 183 p.; 21 cm. — (Praeger paperbacks, P-300) 1. Imperialism I. T.
JC359.L53      321/.03      *LC* 70-117474

**Mommsen, Wolfgang J., 1930-.**                                        **4.7537**
[Imperialismustheorien. English] Theories of imperialism / Wolfgang J. Mommsen; translated from the German by P. S. Falla. — 1st American ed. — New York: Random House, 1981 (c1980). x, 180 p.; 22 cm. Translation of Imperialismustheorien. Includes index. 1. Imperialism I. T.
JC359.M5813      325/.32/09 19      *LC* 80-5279      *ISBN* 0394509323

**Reynolds, Charles.**                                                  **4.7538**
Modes of imperialism / Charles Reynolds. — New York: St. Martin's Press, 1981. viii, 263 p.; 24 cm. Includes index. 1. Imperialism I. T.
JC359.R47 1981      325/.32 19      *LC* 81-82752      *ISBN* 0312543131

**Schumpeter, Joseph Alois, 1883-1950.**                                • **4.7539**
Imperialism and social classes. Translated by Heinz Norden; edited and with an introd. by Paul M. Sweezy. New York, A. M. Kelley, 1951. xxv, 221 p. 20 cm. Translations of Zur Soziologie der Imperialismen and Die sozialen Klassen im ethnisch homogenen Milieu, which originally appeared in Archiv für Sozialwissenschaft und Sozialpolitik. 1. Imperialism 2. Social conflict I. T.
JC359.S36      *LC* A 51-4379

**Strachey, John, 1901-1963.**                                          • **4.7540**
The end of empire. — [1st U.S. ed.]. — New York, Random House [1960, c1959] 351 p. 23 cm. 'The second volume in a projected series of studies on the Principles of democratic socialism, of which the first volume was entitled Contemporary capitalism.' 1. Imperialism 2. Commonwealth of Nations 3. India — Pol. & govt. I. T.
JC359.S77 1960      321.03      *LC* 60-5459

**Thornton, A. P. (Archibald Paton)**                                   • **4.7541**
Doctrines of imperialism [by] A.P. Thornton. New York, Wiley [1965] ix, 246 p. (New dimensions in history; essays in comparative history) 1. Imperialism I. T. II. Series.
JC359 T45      *LC* 65-27652

**Thornton, A. P. (Archibald Paton)**                                   **4.7542**
Imperialism in the twentieth century / by A. P. Thornton. — Minneapolis: University of Minnesota Press, 1978 (c1977). xii, 363 p.; 23 cm. Includes index. 1. Imperialism I. T.
JC359.T46      327/.11      *LC* 77-81211      *ISBN* 0816608202

**Wesson, Robert G.**                                                   • **4.7543**
The imperial order [by] Robert G. Wesson. — Berkeley: University of California Press, 1967. 547 p.; 25 cm. 1. Imperialism I. T.
JC359.W47      321/.03      *LC* 67-11938

**Woolf, Leonard, 1880-1969.**                                          • **4.7544**
Imperialism and civilization. With a new introd. for the Garland ed. by Sylvia Strauss. New York, Garland Pub., 1971 [i.e. 1972] 11, 134 p. 23 cm. (The Garland library of war and peace) Reprint of the 1928 ed. 1. Imperialism 2. Civilization 3. World politics 4. Nationalism 5. Eastern question (Far East) 6. Africa — Colonization I. T. II. Series.
JC359.W6 1972      325/.3      *LC* 79-148377      *ISBN* 0824004590

## JC361–363 World State. Internationalism

**Goodman, Elliot Raymond, 1923-.**                                     • **4.7545**
The Soviet design for a world state. With a foreword by Philip E. Mosly. New York, Columbia University Press, 1960. xviii, 512 p. (Studies of the Russian Institute, Columbia University) 1. Internationalism 2. International organization 3. Communism 4. Russia — Foreign relations I. T.
JC361 G66 1960      *LC* 60-7625

**Deutsch, Karl Wolfgang, 1912-.**                                      • **4.7546**
Political community at the international level; problems of definition and measurement, by Karl W. Deutsch. — [Garden City, N.Y.]: Archon Books, 1970 [c1954] x, 70 p.; 23 cm. 1. International organization I. T.
JC362.D45 1970      321/.04      *LC* 71-104710      *ISBN* 0208009035

**Mitrany, David, 1888-.**                                              **4.7547**
A working peace system: an argument for the functional development of international organization / by David Mitrany. — London: Royal Institute of International Affairs; New York: Oxford University Press, 1943. 56 p.; 22 cm. 'On cover: Post war problems.' 1. International organization I. T.
JC362.M53      *LC* 43-14506

## JC365 Small States. New States

**Chicago. University. Committee for the Comparative Study of New Nations.**   • **4.7548**
Old societies and new States; the quest for modernity in Asia and Africa. Edited by Clifford Geertz. — [New York] Free Press of Glencoe [1963] viii, 310 p. illus. 22 cm. Bibliographical footnotes. 1. States, New 2. Asia 3. Africa I. Geertz, Clifford. ed. II. T.
JC365.C47      915      *LC* 63-8416

**Vital, David.**                                                       • **4.7549**
The inequality of states: a study of the small power in international relations. — Oxford: Clarendon P., 1967. [9] 198 p.: tables. 1. States, Small I. T.
JC365.V5

## JC375–393 Monarchy

**Bendix, Reinhard.**                                                   **4.7550**
Kings or people: power and the mandate to rule / Reinhard Bendix. — Berkeley: University of California Press, c1978. xii, 692 p.: ill.; 24 cm. 1. Kings and rulers — History. 2. Prerogative, Royal — History. 3. National state — History. I. T.
JC375.B45      301.5/92      *LC* 72-85525      *ISBN* 0520023021

**Eccleshall, Robert.**     **4.7551**
Order and reason in politics: theories of absolute and limited monarchy in early modern England / Robert Eccleshall. — Oxford; New York: Published for the University of Hull by Oxford University Press, 1978. 197 p.; 23 cm. 'The adolescent phase of this project was a Ph.D. thesis submitted in the University of Hull.' Includes index. 1. Monarchy 2. Political science — Great Britain — History. I. T.
JC375.E33    321.6    *LC* 77-30452    *ISBN* 0197134319

**Franklin, Julian H., comp.**     • **4.7552**
Constitutionalism and resistance in the sixteenth century; three treatises by Hotman, Beza, & Mornay. Translated and edited by Julian H. Franklin. New York, Pegasus [1969] ix, 208 p. 21 cm. 1. Kings and rulers I. Hotman, François, sieur de Villiers Saint Paul, 1524-1590. Francogallia. English. 1969. II. Bèze, Théodore de, 1519-1605. Du droit des magistrats sur leur subiets. English. 1969. III. Languet, Hubert, 1518-1581. Vindiciae contra tyrannos. English. 1969. IV. T.
JC385.F73    321    *LC* 71-77131

**Kantorowicz, Ernst Hartwig, 1895-1963.**     • **4.7553**
The King's two bodies: a study in medieval political theology / by Ernst H. Kantorowicz. — Princeton, N.J.: Princeton University Press, 1957. xvi, 568 p.: ill.; 25 cm. 1. Kings and rulers 2. Great Britain — Kings and rulers I. T.
JC385.K25    321.6    *LC* 57-5448

**Figgis, John Neville, 1866-1919.**     • **4.7554**
The divine right of kings. — 2d ed. Cambridge, University press, 1914. xi, [1], 406 p. 20 cm. First edition appeared in 1896 under title 'The theory of the divine right of kings', being an enlargement of the author's Prince consort dissertation, 1892. 1. Divine right of kings 2. Great Britain — Kings and rulers — Succession I. T.
JC389.F5 1914    *LC* a 14-2574

**Kern, Fritz, 1884-1950.**     • **4.7555**
Kingship and law in the middle ages: I. The divine right of kings and the right of resistance in the early middle ages. II. Law and constitution in the middle ages. Studies by Fritz Kern ... translated with an introduction by S. B. Chrimes ... Oxford, B. Blackwell, 1939. xxxi, [1], 214 p. 23 cm. ([Studies in mediaeval history, edited by Geoffrey Barraclough. 4]) 'The whole text of the Gottesgnadentum [und widerstandsrecht im früheren mittelalter] incorporating a number of revisions ... supplied by the author himself, together with only about one eighth of the foot-notes, is here edited and translated ... [Also] a translation, with some of the footnotes, of very nearly the whole of another of the author's works, his article entitled Recht und verfassung im mittelalter, which appeared in the Historische Zeitschrift in 1919.'—Pref. 1. Monarchy 2. Divine right of kings 3. Law — Hist. & crit. 4. Constitutional history 5. Middle Ages I. Chrimes, S. B. (Stanley Bertram), 1907- tr. II. T. III. Title: The divine right of kings and the right of resistance. IV. Title: Law and constitution.
JC389.K43    *LC* 40-6717

**Elyot, Thomas, Sir 1490?-1546.**     • **4.7556**
The book named The governor / Edited with an introd. by S. E. Lehmberg. — New ed. — London, Dent; New York Dutton 1963. xiv, 241 p. 19 cm. — (Everyman's library, no. 227) 1. Kings and rulers — Duties 2. Education of princes I. T. II. Title: The governor.
JC393.B3 E5 1963

## JC414 Despotism

**Wittfogel, Karl August, 1896-.**     • **4.7557**
Oriental despotism; a comparative study of total power. — New Haven, Yale University Press, 1957. xix, 556 p. 24 cm. Bibliography: p. 491-529. 1. Despotism 2. Civilization, Oriental 3. Irrigation I. T.
JC414.W5    321.6    *LC* 56-10873

## JC421–458 Democracy

**Bryce, James Bryce, Viscount, 1838-1922.**     • **4.7558**
Modern democracies, by James Bryce (Viscount Bryce) ... — New York, The Macmillan company, 1921. 2 v. 23 cm. 1. Democracy 2. Political science I. T.
JC421.B8    *LC* 21-5466

**Crozier, Michel.**     **4.7559**
The crisis of democracy: report on the governability of democracies to the Trilateral Commission / Michel Crozier, Samuel P. Huntington, Joji Watanuki. — [New York]: New York University Press, 1975. 220 p.; 21 cm. — (Triangle papers. [8]) 1. Democracy 2. Europe — Politics and government 3. United States — Politics and government 4. Japan — Politics and government I. Huntington, Samuel P. joint author. II. Watanuki, Jōji, 1931- joint author. III. Trilateral Commission. IV. T. V. Series.
JC421.C86    321.8    *LC* 75-27167    *ISBN* 0814713645

**Everdell, William R.**     **4.7560**
The end of kings: a history of republics and republicans / William R. Everdell. — New York: Free Press; London: Collier-Macmillan, c1983. xii, 370 p.; 24 cm. Includes index. 1. Republics — History. I. T.
JC421.E94 1983    321.8/6 19    *LC* 83-48070    *ISBN* 0029099307

**Padover, Saul Kussiel, 1905-.**     **4.7561**
Sources of democracy: voices of freedom, hope and justice / selected with commentary by Saul K. Padover. — New York: McGraw-Hill Book Co., [1973] xxxiv, 402 p.; 25 cm. 1. Democracy — Addresses, essays, lectures. 2. Political science — History — Addresses, essays, lectures. 3. Political science — United States — History — Addresses, essays, lectures. I. T.
JC421.P33    320.5/1    *LC* 72-10247    *ISBN* 0070480737

**Smith, Bruce James, 1946-.**     **4.7562**
Politics & remembrance: republican themes in Machiavelli, Burke, and Tocqueville / Bruce James Smith. — Princeton, N.J.: Princeton University Press, c1985. xii, 287 p.; 23 cm. (Studies in moral, political, and legal philosophy.) Includes index. 1. Machiavelli, Niccolò, 1469-1527 — Political science. 2. Burke, Edmund, 1729-1797 — Political science. 3. Tocqueville, Alexis de, 1805-1859 — Political science. 4. Republicanism 5. Political participation 6. Memory I. T. II. Title: Politics and remembrance. III. Series.
JC421.S55 1985    323/.042 19    *LC* 84-15946    *ISBN* 0691076812

**Bachrach, Peter.**     • **4.7563**
The theory of democratic elitism; a critique. — Boston: Little, Brown, [1967] xiv, 109 p.; 21 cm. — (Basic studies in politics) 1. Democracy 2. Elite (Social sciences) I. T.
JC423.B19    320.5    *LC* 67-12114

**Barber, Benjamin R., 1939-.**     **4.7564**
Strong democracy: participatory politics for a new age / Benjamin R. Barber. — Berkeley: University of California Press, c1984. xvi, 320 p.; 24 cm. 1. Democracy 2. Liberalism 3. Citizenship 4. Community 5. Political participation I. T.
JC423.B243 1984    321.8 19    *LC* 83-4842    *ISBN* 0520051157

**Buchanan, James M.**     • **4.7565**
The calculus of consent, logical foundations of constitutional democracy [by] James M. Buchanan and Gordon Tullock. — Ann Arbor: University of Michigan Press, [1962] x, 361 p.: diagrs.; 24 cm. 1. Democracy 2. Decision-making 3. Voting I. Tullock, Gordon. joint author. II. T.
JC423.B86    321.8    *LC* 62-7705

**Cahn, Edmond Nathaniel, 1906-1964.**     • **4.7566**
The predicament of democratic man. — New York: Macmillan, 1961. 194 p.; 22 cm. 1. Democracy I. T.
JC423.C23    321.8    *LC* 61-10343

**Dahl, Robert Alan, 1915-.**     • **4.7567**
A preface to democratic theory. — [Chicago]: University of Chicago Press, [1956] 155 p.: illus.; 21 cm. — (Charles R. Walgreen Foundation lectures) 1. Democracy I. T.
JC423.D25    321.82*    *LC* 56-6642

**Friedrich, Carl J. (Carl Joachim), 1901-.**     • **4.7568**
The new image of the common man. [Enl. ed.] Boston, Beacon Press, 1950. xxvi, 382 p. 1. Democracy 2. Political science 3. Public opinion I. T.
JC423 F76 1950    *LC* 50-14808

**Green, Philip, 1932-.**     **4.7569**
Retrieving democracy: in search of civic equality / Philip Green. — Totowa, N.J.: Rowman & Allanheld, 1985. ix, 278 p.; 22 cm. 1. Democracy 2. Equality I. T.
JC423.G74 1985    321.8 19    *LC* 84-23798    *ISBN* 0847674053

**Hallowell, John H. (John Hamilton), 1913-.**     • **4.7570**
The moral foundation of democracy. [Chicago] University of Chicago Press [1954] 134 p. (Charles R. Walgreen Foundation lectures, 1952) 1. Democracy I. T.
JC423 H36    *LC* 54-11938

**Hook, Sidney, 1902-.**     • **4.7571**
Political power and personal freedom; critical studies in democracy, communism, and civil rights. New York, Criterion Books [1959] 462 p. 22 cm. 1. Democracy 2. Communism and liberty 3. Socialism I. T.
JC423.H75    323.44    *LC* 59-6126

**Liberal democracy / edited by J. Roland Pennock and John W. Chapman.**     **4.7572**
New York: New York University Press, 1983. xv, 453 p.: ill.; 22 cm. — (Nomos; 25) 'A quarter-century of NOMOS (Index)': p. 431-446. 1. Democracy — Addresses, essays, lectures. 2. Liberalism — Addresses, essays, lectures. 3. Judicial review — Addresses, essays, lectures. I. Pennock, J. Roland (James Roland), 1906- II. Chapman, John William, 1923- III. Series.
JC423.L517 1983    321.8 19    *LC* 82-14430    *ISBN* 081476584X

**Lippincott, Benjamin Evans, 1902-.**     • **4.7573**
Victorian critics of democracy: Carlyle, Ruskin, Arnold, Stephen, Maine, Lecky. New York, Octagon Books, 1964 [c1938] viii, 276 p. 24 cm. 1. Carlyle, Thomas, 1795-1881. 2. Ruskin, John, 1819-1900. 3. Arnold, Matthew, 1822-1888. 4. Stephen, James Fitzjames, Sir, 1829-1894. 5. Maine, Henry Sumner, Sir, 1822-1888. 6. Lecky, William Edward Hartpole, 1838-1903. 7. Democracy I. T.
JC423.L57 1964     *LC* 64-24850

**Lipset, Seymour Martin.**     • **4.7574**
Political man; the social bases of politics. — [1st ed.]. — Garden City, N.Y.: Doubleday, 1960. 432 p.: illus.; 22 cm. 1. Democracy 2. Elections 3. Voting 4. Political parties — United States 5. Trade-unions — United States 6. United States — Politics and government I. T.
JC423.L58     306/.2 19     *LC* 60-5943

**Macpherson, C. B. (Crawford Brough), 1911-.**     **4.7575**
Democratic theory: essays in retrieval / [by] C. B. Macpherson. — Oxford: Clarendon Press, 1973. xii, 255 p.; 22 cm. 1. Democracy — Addresses, essays, lectures. I. T.
JC423.M159     320.5/1     *LC* 73-157532     *ISBN* 0198271875

**Macpherson, C. B. (Crawford Brough), 1911-.**     **4.7576**
The life and times of liberal democracy / C. B. Macpherson. — Oxford [Eng.]; New York: Oxford University Press, 1977. 120 p.; 21 cm. Includes index. 1. Democracy I. T.
JC423.M1593 1977     321.8     *LC* 77-30093     *ISBN* 0192191209. *ISBN* 0192891065 pbk

**Maine, Henry Sumner, Sir, 1822-1888.**     **4.7577**
Popular government / by Sir Henry Sumner Maine; with an introd. by George W. Carey. — Indianapolis: Liberty Classics, c1976. 254 p.; 24 cm. Includes index. 1. Representative government and representation 2. Democracy 3. United States — Constitutional history I. T.
JC423.M19 1976     321.8     *LC* 76-26329     *ISBN* 0913966142

**Mayo, Henry Bertram, 1911-.**     • **4.7578**
An introduction to democratic theory. — New York: Oxford University Press, 1960. vi, 316 p.; 21 cm. 1. Democracy I. T. II. Title: Democratic theory.
JC423.M38     321.8     *LC* 60-7063

**Mill, John Stuart, 1806-1873.**     • **4.7579**
Considerations on representative government / introd. by F. A. Hayek. — Chicago: Regnery, [1962] 365 p. (A Gateway edition, 6072) 1. Representative government and representation I. T.
JC423.M6 1962

**Niebuhr, Reinhold, 1892-1971.**     • **4.7580**
The children of light and the children of darkness; a vindication of democracy and a critique of its traditional defence. — New York, Scribner [1960] xv, 190 p. 21 cm. — (The Scribner library, SL18) Bibliographical footnotes. 1. Democracy I. T.
JC423.N5 1960     321.8     *LC* 60-4748

**Pennock, J. Roland (James Roland), 1906-.**     • **4.7581**
Liberal democracy: its merits and prospects. New York, Rinehart [1950] xii, 403 p. 1. Democracy 2. Liberalism I. T.
JC423 P46     *LC* 50-10692

**Pool, Ithiel de Sola, 1917-.**     • **4.7582**
Symbols of democracy, by Ithiel de Sola Pool with the collaboration of Harold D. Lasswell and Daniel Lerner [and others] Introd. by Peter H. Odegard. [Stanford] Stanford University Press, 1952. xi, 80 p. illus. 23 cm. (Hoover Institute studies. Symbols. no. 4) Bibliographical references included in 'Notes' (p. 77-80) 1. Democracy I. T. II. Series.
JC423.P58     *321.82     *LC* 52-5968

**Sartori, Giovanni.**     • **4.7583**
Democratic theory. Based on the author's translation of Democrazia e definizione (2nd edition). — Detroit, Wayne State University Press, 1962. 479 p. 21 cm. — (Waynebook no. 6) Includes bibliography. 1. Democracy I. T.
JC423.S273 1962     321.4     *LC* 62-7184

**Spitz, Elaine, 1932-.**     **4.7584**
Majority rule / Elaine Spitz. — Chatham, N.J.: Chatham House, c1984. xvi, 238 p. — (Chatham House series on change in American politics.) Includes index. 1. Democracy 2. Majorities I. T. II. Series.
JC423.S74 1984     321.8 19     *LC* 83-23151     *ISBN* 0934540217

**Walzer, Michael.**     **4.7585**
Radical principles: reflections of an unreconstructed democrat / Michael Walzer. — New York: Basic Books, c1980. viii, 310 p.; 22 cm. 1. Democracy — Addresses, essays, lectures. 2. Liberalism — Addresses, essays, lectures. 3. Socialism — Addresses, essays, lectures. I. T.
JC423.W292     320.5     *LC* 79-56371     *ISBN* 0465068243

## JC474 Communist State

**Balbus, Isaac D.**     **4.7586**
Marxism and domination: a neo–Hegelian, feminist, psychoanalytic theory of sexual, political, and technological liberation / Isaac D. Balbus. — Princeton, N.J.: Princeton University Press, c1982. xiii, 417 p. Includes index. 1. Communist state 2. Communism and psychology 3. Communism and society 4. Dominance (Psychology) I. T.
JC474.B336     JC474 B336.     335.4/1 19     *LC* 82-47582     *ISBN* 0691076219

**Mesa-Lago, Carmelo, 1934-.**     **4.7587**
Comparative socialist systems: essays on politics and economics / Carmelo Mesa–Lago and Carl Beck, editors. — Pittsburgh: University of Pittsburgh Center for International Studies, 1975. xv, 441 p.: graphs; 23 cm. 1. Communist state — Addresses, essays, lectures. 2. Communist countries — Economic conditions — Addresses, essays, lectures. I. Beck, Carl, 1930- II. T.
JC474.C67     335     *LC* 75-331585     *ISBN* 0916002012

**Lane, David Stuart.**     **4.7588**
The socialist industrial state: towards a political sociology of state socialism / David Lane. Boulder, Colo.: Westview Press, 1976. 230 p.; 23 cm. Includes index. 1. Communist state I. T.
JC474.L25     321.9/2     *LC* 75-33036     *ISBN* 0891585230

**Miliband, Ralph.**     **4.7589**
Marxism and politics / Ralph Miliband. — Oxford: Oxford University Press, 1977. 199 p.; 21 cm. — (Marxist introductions.) Includes index. 1. Communist state I. T. II. Series.
JC474.M52     320.5/315     *LC* 77-372361     *ISBN* 0198760590

**Political culture and political change in Communist States /**     **4.7590**
**edited by Archie Brown and Jack Gray.**
2d ed. — New York: Holmes & Meier Publishers, 1979. xiv, 286 p.; 23 cm. 1. Communist state 2. Communist countries — Politics and government. I. Brown, Archie, 1938- II. Gray, Jack, 1926-
JC474.P59 1979     301.5/92/091717     *LC* 79-14698     *ISBN* 0841905088. *ISBN* 0841905096 pbk

*[handwritten: [Peace St.] JC 474 P59 1977]*

**White, Stephen, 1945-.**     **4.7591**
Communist political systems: an introduction / Stephen White, John Gardner, George Schöpflin. — 2nd ed. — New York: St. Martin's Press, 1987. p. cm. Includes index. 1. Communist state 2. Communist countries — Politics and government. I. Gardner, John, 1939 Nov. 1- II. Schöpflin, George. III. T.
JC474.W48 1987     321.9/2 19     *LC* 87-4262     *ISBN* 0312007221

## JC478 Corporate State

**Pike, Fredrick B.**     **4.7592**
The new corporatism; social–political structures in the Iberian world. Fredrick B. Pike and Thomas Stritch, editors. — Notre Dame: University of Notre Dame Press, [1974] xxii, 218 p.; 24 cm. — (International studies of the Committee on International Relations, University of Notre Dame) 1. Corporate state — Addresses, essays, lectures. 2. Latin America — Politics and government — 1948- — Addresses, essays, lectures. 3. Spain — Politics and government — 1939-1975 — Addresses, essays, lectures. I. Stritch, Thomas, joint author. II. T.
JC478.P45     320.5/31     *LC* 73-22583     *ISBN* 0268005389

## JC481 Totalitarianism. Fascism

**Arendt, Hannah.**     • **4.7593**
The origins of totalitarianism. — New ed. — New York: Harcourt, Brace & World, [1966] xxxi, 526 p.; 24 cm. 1. Totalitarianism 2. Imperialism 3. Antisemitism I. T.
JC481.A6 1966     321.9     *LC* 66-22273

**Authoritarian politics in modern society; the dynamics of**     • **4.7594**
**established one–party systems, edited by Samuel P. Huntington**
**and Clement H. Moore.**
New York, Basic Books [1970] x, 533 p. 25 cm. 1. Totalitarianism — Addresses, essays, lectures. 2. One party systems — Addresses, essays, lectures. I. Huntington, Samuel P. ed. II. Moore, Clement Henry. ed.
JC481.A915     321.9/08     *LC* 78-94304     *ISBN* 0465005691

**Bowen, Ralph Henry, 1919-.**     • **4.7595**
German theories of the corporative state, with special reference to the period 1870–1919, by Ralph H. Bowen. — New York: Russell & Russell, [1971, c1947] viii, 243 p.; 23 cm. 1. Corporate state 2. Trade and professional associations I. T.
JC481.B67 1971     335.6/0943     *LC* 73-151540

JC
481
C87

**Curtis, Michael, 1923-.** **4.7596**
Totalitarianism / Michael Curtis. — New Brunswick, N.J.: Transaction Books, c1979. 128 p.; 21 cm. 1. Totalitarianism I. T.
JC481.C87     321.9     *LC* 78-66238     *ISBN* 087855288X

**Dahl, Robert Alan, 1915-.** **• 4.7597**
Controlling nuclear weapons: democracy versus guardianship / Robert Dahl. — 1st ed. — Syracuse, N.Y.: Syracuse University Press, 1985. ix, 113 p.; 23 cm. (Frank W. Abrams lectures.) Includes index. 1. Authoritarianism 2. Democracy 3. Nuclear arms control I. T. II. Series.
JC481.D33 1985     321.9 19     *LC* 85-4783     *ISBN* 0815623348

**Fascism: a reader's guide: analyses, interpretations, bibliography** **4.7598**
/ edited by Walter Laqueur.
Berkeley: University of California Press, c1976. x, 478 p.; 24 cm. 1. Fascism — Addresses, essays, lectures. I. Laqueur, Walter, 1921-
JC481.F334     320.5/33     *LC* 75-13158     *ISBN* 0520030338

**Friedrich, Carl J. (Carl Joachim), 1901-.** **• 4.7599**
Totalitarian dictatorship and autocracy [by] Carl J. Friedrich and Zbigniew K. Brzezinski. 2d ed., rev. by Carl J. Friedrich. Cambridge, Harvard University Press, 1965. xvi, 439 p. 22 cm. 1. Totalitarianism I. Brzezinski, Zbigniew K., 1928- joint author. II. T.
JC481.F74 1965     321.64     *LC* 65-13843

**Gregor, A. James (Anthony James), 1929-.** **4.7600**
The Fascist persuasion in radical politics, by A. James Gregor. Princeton, N.J., Princeton University Press [1974] xiii, 472 p. 23 cm. 1. Fascism 2. Radicalism 3. Socialism I. T.
JC481.G686     320.5/33     *LC* 73-2463     *ISBN* 0691075565

**Kornhauser, William.** **• 4.7601**
The politics of mass society. Glencoe, Ill.: Free Press, [1959] 256 p.; 22 cm. 1. Totalitarianism 2. Democracy 3. Mass society I. T.
JC481.K6     321.64     *LC* 59-6820

JC
481
N49
1965

**Neumann, Sigmund, 1904-.** **• 4.7602**
Permanent revolution; totalitarianism in the age of international civil war. — 2d ed. — New York, Praeger [1965] xxii, 402 p. 21 cm. Bibliography: p. [311]-389. 1. Totalitarianism 2. Dictators I. T.
JC481.N37 1965     321.9     *LC* 65-21107

**Payne, Stanley G.** **4.7603**
Fascism, Comparison and definition / Stanley G. Payne. — Madison: University of Wisconsin Press, c1980. viii, 3-234 p.; 23 cm. Includes index. 1. Fascism 2. Fascism — History. I. T.
JC481.P374     320.5/33     *LC* 79-5415     *ISBN* 0299080609

**Revel, Jean François.** **4.7604**
[Tentation totalitaire. English] The totalitarian temptation / by Jean-François Revel; translated by David Hapgood. — 1st ed. — Garden City, N.Y.: Doubleday, 1977. 311 p.; 22 cm. 1. Totalitarianism 2. Communism 3. Socialism 4. Liberalism I. T.
JC481.R4813     320.5/32     *LC* 76-48604     *ISBN* 0385122748

**Schapiro, Leonard Bertram, 1908-.** **4.7605**
Totalitarianism [by] Leonard Schapiro. — New York: Praeger, [1972] 144 p.; 23 cm. — (Key concepts in political science) 1. Totalitarianism I. T. II. Series.
JC481.S35     321.9     *LC* 76-100924

**Schlesinger, Arthur Meier, 1917-.** **• 4.7606**
The vital center; the politics of freedom. Boston, Houghton Mifflin Co., 1949. x, 274 p. 22 cm. 1. Totalitarianism 2. Communism 3. Liberalism 4. United States — Politics and government — 1901-1953 I. T.
JC481.S38     320.5/1 19     *LC* 49-5453

**Talmon, J. L. (Jacob Leib), 1916-.** **• 4.7607**
The origins of totalitarian democracy / by J. L. Talmon. — New York: Praeger, 1960, 1961 printing. xi, 366 p. — (Books that matter) 1. Totalitarianism I. T.
JC481.T32 1960     *LC* 60-14072

**Weber, Eugen Joseph, 1925-.** **• 4.7608**
Varieties of fascism: doctrines of revolution in the twentieth century / Eugen Joseph Weber. — Princeton, N.J.: Van Nostrand, 1964. 191 p. — (Anvil original; 73) 1. Fascism 2. Fascism — Collections I. T. II. Title: Doctrines of revolution in the twentieth century.
JC481.W38     821.644     *LC* 64-4892     *ISBN* 0442000731 pa

**Who were the Fascists: social roots of European Fascism /** **4.7609**
**edited by Stein Ugelvik Larsen, Bernt Hagtvet, Jan Petter**
**Myklebust, with the assistance of Gerhard Botz ... [et al.].**
Bergen: Universitetsforlaget; Irvington-on-Hudson, N.Y.: Columbia University Press [distributor], c1980. 816 p.: ill.; 23 cm. 1. Fascism — Europe — History. 2. Europe — Politics and government — 1918-1945 I. Larsen, Stein Ugelvik. II. Hagtvet, Bernt. III. Myklebust, Jan Petter.
JC481.W48     320.5/33/094 19     *LC* 80-151530     *ISBN* 8200053318

## JC491–497 Revolutions

**American Society for Political and Legal Philosophy.** **• 4.7610**
Revolution; yearbook. Edited by Carl J. Friedrich. [1st ed.] New York, Atherton Press, 1966. x, 246 p. (Nomos. 8) 1. Revolutions I. Friedrich, Carl J. (Carl Joachim), 1901- II. T. III. Series.
JC491 A5     *LC* 65-28141

**Arendt, Hannah.** **• 4.7611**
On revolution. — New York: Viking Press, [1963] 343 p.; 22 cm. 1. Revolutions I. T.
JC491.A68     321.09     *LC* 63-8855

**Brinton, Crane, 1898-1968.** **• 4.7612**
The anatomy of revolution. — [Rev. ed.]. — New York, Prentice-Hall [1952] xi, 324 p. 24 cm. Bibliography: p. [295]-315. 1. Revolutions I. T.
JC491.B7 1952     321.092     *LC* 52-8598

**Leiden, Carl.** **• 4.7613**
The politics of violence: revolution in the modern world / Carl Leiden and Karl M. Schmitt. — Englewood Cliffs, N.J.: Prentice-Hall, 1968. x, 244 p. (Spectrum book) Includes bibliographical references and index. 1. Revolutions 2. Revolutions — Case studies. I. Schmitt, Karl Michael, 1922- joint author. II. T.
JC491.L36 1980     322.4/2 19     *LC* 68-14469

**Oppenheimer, Martin.** **• 4.7614**
The urban guerrilla. Chicago, Quadrangle Books [1969] 188 p. 22 cm. 1. Revolutions 2. Afro-Americans I. T.
JC491.O6     323.2     *LC* 69-20159

**Wilkinson, Paul.** **4.7615**
Political terrorism. — New York: Wiley, [1975, c1974] 159, [1] p.; 22 cm. 'A Halsted Press book.' 1. Revolutions 2. Terrorism I. T.
JC491.W55 1975     322.4/2     *LC* 74-18470     *ISBN* 0470946210

**Jászi, Oszkár, 1875-1957.** **• 4.7616**
Against the tyrant; the tradition and theory of tyrannicide, by Oscar Jászi and John D. Lewis. — Glencoe, Ill., Free Press [1957] 288 p. 22 cm. Bibliographical references included in 'Notes' (p. 257-279) 1. Dictators 2. Government, Resistance to I. Lewis, John Donald, 1905- joint author. II. T.
JC495.J3     321.6     *LC* 57-1024

## JC501–628 Purpose, Functions and Relations of the State

**Viereck, Peter Robert Edwin, 1916-.** **• 4.7617**
Conservatism: from John Adams to Churchill. — Princeton, N.J.: Van Nostrand, [1956] 192 p.; 18 cm. — (An Anvil original, no. 11) 1. Conservatism I. T.
JC501.V48     320.1     *LC* 56-6883

**Viereck, Peter Robert Edwin.** **• 4.7618**
Conservatism revisited. Rev. and enl. ed. / With the addition of: The new conservatism - What went wrong? New York: Colliers Books, 1962. 192p. 1. Metternich-Winneburg, Clemens Lothar Wenzel, Fürst von. 2. Conservatism I. T. II. Title: New conservatism - What went wrong?
JC501.V5 1965     320.1     *LC* 62-19968

**American Society for Political and Legal Philosophy.** **4.7619**
Authority / edited by Carl J. Friedrich. — Cambridge: Harvard University Press, 1958. 234 p. — (Nomos. 1) I. Friedrich, Carl J. (Carl Joachim), 1901- II. T. III. Series.
JC507.A49

**American Society for Political and Legal Philosophy.** **• 4.7620**
The public interest. Edited by Carl J. Friedrich. New York, Atherton Press, 1962. xiii, 256 p. (Nomos. 5) 1. Public interest I. Friedrich, Carl J. (Carl Joachim), 1901- II. T. III. Series.
JC507 A5     *LC* 62-19400

**Schubert, Glendon A.** **• 4.7621**
The public interest; a critique of the theory of a political concept. Glencoe, Ill., Free Press [1964, c1960] x, 244 p. 22 cm. 1. Public interest I. T.
JC507.S35     *LC* 60-10902

## JC571–628 The State and the Individual

**Ackerman, Bruce A.**      4.7622
Social justice in the liberal state / Bruce A. Ackerman. — New Haven: Yale University Press, c1980. xii, 392 p.; 24 cm. 1. Liberalism 2. Justice I. T.
JC571.A135    320.5/1    *LC* 80-12618    *ISBN* 0300024398

**Acton, John Emerich Edward Dalberg Acton, Baron, 1834-1902.**    • 4.7623
Essays on Freedom and power / Selected, and with a new introd, by Gertrude Himmelfarb. New York: Published by Noonday Press, 1955, [c1948] 350 p.; 18 cm. (Meridian books, M12.) 1. Liberty. 2. Church history 3. History — Addresses, essays, lectures. I. T.
JC571.A14 1955    323.44    *LC* 55-7581

**Ajami, Fouad.**      4.7624
Human rights and world order politics / Fouad Ajami. — New York, N.Y.: World Order Models Project: Available from Institute for World Order, 1978. 33 p.; 23 cm. — (Working paper / World Order Models Project; no. 4) 1. Civil rights — Addresses, essays, lectures. 2. Social justice — Addresses, essays, lectures. I. Institute for World Order. II. T.
JC571.A25 1978    341.4/81 19    *LC* 83-216080

**Bay, Christian, 1921-.**      4.7625
Strategies of political emancipation / Christian Bay. — Notre Dame: University of Notre Dame Press, c1981. xii, 247 p. — (Loyola lecture series in political analysis) 1. Liberty. 2. Liberalism 3. Need (Psychology) 4. Oppression (Psychology) I. T. II. Series.
JC571.B377   JC571 B377.    323.44 19    *LC* 80-53117    *ISBN* 0268017026

**Bay, Christian, 1921-.**      • 4.7626
The structure of freedom. — Stanford, Calif.: Stanford University Press, [1970] xxvii, 419 p.; 24 cm. 1. Liberty. I. T.
JC571.B378 1970    323.44    *LC* 74-19685    *ISBN* 0804705399

**Cumming, Robert Denoon, 1916-.**      • 4.7627
Human nature and history; a study of the development of liberal political thought. — Chicago: University of Chicago Press, [1969] 2 v.; 24 cm. 1. Liberalism I. T.
JC571.C77    320.5/1    *LC* 68-54081

**Donnelly, Jack.**      4.7628
The concept of human rights / Jack Donnelly. — New York: St. Martin's Press, 1985. 120 p.; 23 cm. Revision of thesis (Ph. D.)—University of California, Berkeley, 1981. Includes index. 1. Civil rights I. T.
JC571.D74 1985    323.4 19    *LC* 84-22863    *ISBN* 0312159412

**Eden, Robert.**      4.7629
Political leadership & nihilism: a study of Weber & Nietzsche / Robert Eden. — Tampa: University Presses of Florida, 1984. xx, 348 p.; 24 cm. 'A University of South Florida book.' Includes index. 1. Weber, Max, 1864-1920 — Political science. 2. Nietzsche, Friedrich Wilhelm, 1844-1900 — Political science. 3. Political leadership 4. Authority 5. Nihilism I. T. II. Title: Political leadership and nihilism.
JC571.E36 1983    320.2 19    *LC* 83-17075    *ISBN* 0813007585

**Falk, Richard A.**      4.7630
Human rights and state sovereignty / Richard Falk. — New York: Holmes & Meier Publishers, 1981. x, 251 p.; 24 cm. 'Written under the auspices of the Center of International Studies, Princeton University.' 1. Civil rights 2. Comparative government I. T.
JC571.F24 1981    323.4 19    *LC* 80-22620    *ISBN* 084190619X

**Forsythe, David P., 1941-.**      4.7631
Human rights and world politics / by David P. Forsythe. — Lincoln: University of Nebraska Press, c1983. xiv, 309 p.: ill.; 22 cm. Includes index. 1. Civil rights 2. World politics 3. United States — Foreign relations I. T.
JC571.F634 1983    323.4 19    *LC* 82-13360    *ISBN* 0803268564

**Green, Thomas Hill, 1836-1882.**      • 4.7632
Lectures on the principles of political obligation. Introd. by Lord Lindsay of Birker. [Ann Arbor] University of Michigan Press [1967] xxxvi, 252 p. 21 cm. (Ann Arbor paperbacks, AA126) 1. Political obligation 2. Liberty. 3. Natural law I. T. II. Title: Principles of political obligation.
JC571.G78 1967    320.1    *LC* 67-2413

**Henkin, Louis.**      4.7633
The rights of man today / Louis Henkin. — Boulder, Colo.: Westview Press, 1978. xiv, 173 p.; 24 cm. — (The Gottesman lectures) 'Derives from lectures delivered at Yeshiva University as Benjamin Gottesman lectures.' 1. Civil rights I. T. II. Series.
JC571.H387    323.4    *LC* 78-6722    *ISBN* 089158174X

**Hook, Sidney, 1902-.**      • 4.7634
The paradoxes of freedom. Berkeley, University of California Press, 1962. 152 p. 23 cm. (Jefferson memorial lectures) 1. Jefferson, Thomas, 1743-1826. 2. Democracy 3. Civil rights 4. Liberty. I. T.
JC571.H64    323.44    *LC* 62-16335

**Human rights / edited by J. Roland Pennock and John W. Chapman.**      4.7635
New York: New York University Press, 1981. xvi, 303 p.; 22 cm. (Nomos. 23) Includes selected papers from meetings of the American Society for Political and Legal Philosophy and the American Political Science Association, held jointly Sept. 1978. 1. Civil rights — Addresses, essays, lectures. I. Pennock, J. Roland (James Roland), 1906- II. Chapman, John William, 1923- III. American Society for Political and Legal Philosophy. IV. American Political Science Association. V. Series.
JC571.H7683    323.4 19    *LC* 80-21253    *ISBN* 0814765785

**Human rights and American foreign policy / edited by Donald P. Kommers and Gilburt D. Loescher.**      4.7636
Notre Dame, Ind.: University of Notre Dame Press, c1979. xii, 333 p.; 24 cm. 1. Civil rights — Addresses, essays, lectures. 2. United States — Foreign relations — 1974- — Addresses, essays, lectures. I. Kommers, Donald P. II. Loescher, Gil.
JC571.H7687    323.4    *LC* 78-62966    *ISBN* 0268010714

**North American human rights directory / edited by Laurie S. Wiseberg and Hazel Sirett, HRI.**      4.7637
Washington, D.C.: Human Rights Internet, c1984. 264 p. Includes index. 1. Civil rights — Societies, etc. — Directories. 2. Social justice — Societies, etc. — Directories. I. Wiseberg, Laurie S. II. Sirett, Hazel. III. Human Rights Internet.
JC571 H769441984    *ISBN* 0939338025

**Joyce, James Avery.**      4.7638
The new politics of human rights / James Avery Joyce. — New York: St. Martin's Press, 1979, c1978. xi, 305 p.; 22 cm. Includes index. 1. Civil rights I. T.
JC571.J66 1979    323.4    *LC* 78-13333    *ISBN* 0312568800

**Leyden, W. von (Wolfgang von), 1911-.**      4.7639
Hobbes and Locke, the politics of freedom and obligation / W. von Leyden. — New York: St. Martin's Press, 1982. x, 253 p.; 22 cm. 1. Hobbes, Thomas, 1588-1679 — Political science. 2. Locke, John, 1632-1704 — Political science. 3. Liberty. 4. Authority 5. Duty I. T.
JC571.L524 1982    323.44/01 19    *LC* 80-26163    *ISBN* 0312388241

**Macfarlane, L. J. (Leslie John), 1924-.**      4.7640
The theory and practice of human rights / L.J. Macfarlane. — New York: St. Martin's Press, 1985. 193 p.; 23 cm. Includes index. 1. Civil rights I. T.
JC571.M2132 1985    323.4 19    *LC* 84-27743    *ISBN* 0312797168

**Machan, Tibor R. comp.**      4.7641
The libertarian alternative: essays in social and political philosophy / Tibor R. Machan, editor. — Chicago: Nelson-Hall Co., [1974] xv, 553 p.; 24 cm. 1. Individualism — Addresses, essays, lectures. 2. Collectivism — Addresses, essays, lectures. 3. Libertarianism — Addresses, essays, lectures. I. T.
JC571.M23    320.5/1    *LC* 73-80501    *ISBN* 0911012729

**Maritain, Jacques, 1882-1973.**      • 4.7642
[Droits de l'homme et la loi naturelle. English] The rights of man and natural law. Translated by Doris C. Anson. New York, Gordian Press, 1971 [c1943] 119 p. 22 cm. Translation of Les droits de l'homme et la loi naturelle. 1. Natural law 2. Liberty. I. Anson, Doris C., tr. II. T.
JC571.M343 1971    323.4/01    *LC* 74-150416    *ISBN* 0877521468

**Newman, Stephen L.**      4.7643
Liberalism at wits' end: the libertarian revolt against the modern state / Stephen L. Newman. — Ithaca: Cornell University, 1984. 184 p.; 24 cm. Includes index. 1. Libertarianism 2. Libertarianism — United States. I. T.
JC571.N48 1984    320.5/12 19    *LC* 84-7108    *ISBN* 0801417473

**Nozick, Robert.**      4.7644
Anarchy, state, and utopia / Robert Nozick. — New York: Basic Books, [1974] xvi, 367 p.; 25 cm. Includes index. 1. State, The 2. Civil rights 3. Anarchism and anarchists. 4. Utopias I. T.
JC571.N68    320.1/01    *LC* 73-91081    *ISBN* 0465002706

**Reading Nozick: essays on Anarchy, state, and Utopia / edited, with an introduction, by Jeffrey Paul.**      4.7645
Totowa, N.J.: Rowman & Littlefield, 1981. xi, 418 p.; 22 cm. — (Philosophy and society) 1. Nozick, Robert Anarchy, state, and Utopia — Addresses, essays, lectures. 2. State, The — Addresses, essays, lectures. 3. Civil rights — Addresses, essays, lectures. 4. Anarchism and anarchists — Addresses, essays,

lectures. 5. Utopias — Addresses, essays, lectures. I. Paul, Jeffrey. II. Nozick, Robert. Anarchy, state, and Utopia. III. Series.
JC571.N683 R4 1981    320.1/01 19    LC 81-12092    ISBN 0847662799

**Power, Jonathan, 1941-.** 4.7646
Amnesty International, the human rights story / Jonathan Power. — New York: McGraw-Hill, c1981. 128 p.: ill.; 26 cm. Includes index. 1. Amnesty International. 2. Civil rights 3. Violence 4. Political prisoners I. T.
JC571.P68    323.4/9/0601 19    LC 81-8158    ISBN 0070505977

**Spencer, Herbert, 1820-1903.** 4.7647
[Selected works] The man versus the state, with four essays on politics and society. Edited with an introd. by Donald MacRae. Baltimore, Penguin Books [1969] 350 p. facsim. 18 cm. (Pelican classics) 1. State, The 2. Individualism 3. Political science I. T.
JC571.S745    320.1    LC 79-14536

**Spitz, David, 1916-.** 4.7648
The real world of liberalism / David Spitz. — Chicago: University of Chicago Press, c1982. xi, 232 p.; 24 cm. 1. Liberalism 2. Conservatism I. T.
JC571.S7723 1982    320.5/1 19    LC 81-16262    ISBN 0226769739

**Strauss, Leo.** • 4.7649
Natural right and history. Chicago, University of Chicago Press [1953] 327 p. (Charles R. Walgreen Foundation lectures) 1. Natural law I. T.
JC571 S83 1953    LC 53-12840

**Van Dyke, Vernon, 1912-.** 4.7650
Human rights, ethnicity, and discrimination / Vernon Van Dyke. — Westport, Conn.: Greenwood Press, 1985. xii, 259 p.; 22 cm. (Contributions in ethnic studies. 0196-7088; no. 10) Includes index. 1. Civil rights 2. Minorities — Civil rights. 3. Discrimination I. T. II. Series.
JC571.V26 1985    323.1 19    LC 84-10328    ISBN 0313246556

**Watkins, Frederick Mundell.** • 4.7651
The political tradition of the West; a study in the development of modern liberalism. Cambridge, Harvard Univ. Press, 1948. xiv, 368 p. 1. Liberalism 2. Political science — History I. T.
JC571.W24    LC 48-8502

## JC575–578 Equality. Justice

**Nielsen, Kai.** 4.7652
Equality and liberty: a defense of radical egalitarianism / Kai Nielsen. — Totowa, N.J.: Rowman and Allanheld, 1985. ix, 320 p.; 25 cm. 1. Equality 2. Liberty. I. T.
JC575.N45 1985    320.5/3 19    LC 84-8223    ISBN 0847667588

**Pennock, J. Roland (James Roland), 1906- ed.** • 4.7653
Equality. Edited by J. Roland Pennock and John W. Chapman. [1st ed.] New York, Atherton Press, 1967. xviii, 313 p. 22 cm. (Nomos. 9) Includes papers of a meeting of the American Society for Political and Legal Philosophy and the American Society of International Law, held in Washington in April, 1965. 1. Equality I. Chapman, John William, 1923- joint ed. II. American Society for Political and Legal Philosophy. III. American Society of International Law. IV. T. V. Series.
JC575.P4    323.42    LC 66-27936

**Verba, Sidney.** 4.7654
Equality in America: the view from the top / Sidney Verba, Gary R. Orren. — Cambridge, Mass.; London, England: Harvard University Press, 1985. x, 334 p.; 24 cm. Includes index. 1. Equality — United States. I. Orren, Gary R. II. T.
JC575.V47 1985    323.4/2/0973 19    LC 84-19756    ISBN 0674259610

**Walzer, Michael.** 4.7655
Spheres of justice: a defense of pluralism and equality / Michael Walzer. — New York: Basic Books, c1983. xviii, 345 p.; 25 cm. 1. Distributive justice 2. Equality 3. Pluralism (Social sciences) I. T.
JC575.W34 1983    320/.01/1 19    LC 82-72409    ISBN 0465081908

**American Society for Political and Legal Philosophy.** 4.7656
Justice. Carl J. Friedrich and John W. Chapman, editors. New York, Atherton Press [1963] x, 325 p. 22 cm. (Nomos. 6) Erratum slip inserted. Bibliographical footnotes. 1. Justice 2. Law — Philosophy. I. Friedrich, Carl J. (Carl Joachim), 1901- II. Chapman, John William, 1923- III. T. IV. Series.
JC578.A7 1963    LC 63-19057

**Barry, Brian M.** 4.7657
The liberal theory of justice: a critical examination of the principal doctrines in A Theory of Justice by John Rawls / by Brian Barry. — Oxford: Clarendon Press, 1973. x, 168 p.; 22 cm. 1. Rawls, John, 1921- A theory of justice. I. T.
JC578.B36    340.1/1    LC 74-150433    ISBN 0198245092

**Posner, Richard A.** 4.7658
The economics of justice / Richard A. Posner. — Cambridge, Mass.: Harvard University Press, 1981. xiii, 415 p.; 24 cm. Includes index. 1. Justice — Addresses, essays, lectures. 2. Social justice — Addresses, essays, lectures. 3. Economics — Addresses, essays, lectures. I. T.
JC578.P67    320/.01/1 19    LC 80-25075    ISBN 0674235258

**Rawls, John, 1921-.** 4.7659
A theory of justice. Cambridge, Mass.: Belknap Press of Harvard University Press, 1971. xv, 607 p.; 24 cm. 1. Justice I. T.
JC578.R38    320/.01/1 19    LC 73-168432    ISBN 0674880102

**Wolff, Robert Paul.** 4.7660
Understanding Rawls: a reconstruction and critique of A theory of justice / Robert Paul Wolff. Princeton, N.J.: Princeton University Press, c1977. x, 224 p.; 22 cm. Includes index. 1. Rawls, John, 1921- A theory of justice. 2. Justice I. T.
JC578.R383 W64    340.1/1    LC 76-49527    ISBN 0691019924

**Reading Rawls: critical studies on Rawls' A theory of justice /** 4.7661
**edited with an introd. by Norman Daniels.**
New York: Basic Books, [1975] xxxiv, 352 p.; graphs; 22 cm. Includes index. 1. Rawls, John, 1921- A theory of justice — Addresses, essays, lectures. 2. Justice — Addresses, essays, lectures. I. Daniels, Norman, 1942-
JC578.R39    340.1/1    LC 74-25908    ISBN 0465068545. ISBN 0465068553 pbk

## JC585–599 Liberty

**American Society for Political and Legal Philosophy.** • 4.7662
Liberty. Edited by Carl J. Friedrich. New York, Atherton Press, 1962. xii, 333 p. (Nomos. 4) 1. Liberty. I. Friedrich, Carl J. (Carl Joachim), 1901- II. T. III. Series.
JC585 A46    LC 62-19416

**Berlin, Isaiah, Sir.** • 4.7663
Four essays on liberty. — London; New York [etc.]: Oxford University P., 1969. lxiii, 213 p.; 20 1/2 cm. — (Galaxy book, 191) (Oxford University Press paperback.) 1. Liberty. I. T.
JC585.B418    323.4    LC 71-403692

**Carlyle, A. J. (Alexander James), 1861-1943.** • 4.7664
Political liberty, a history of the conception in the middle ages and modern times / by A.J. Carlyle. Oxford, The Clarendon press, 1941. viii, 220 p. 23 cm. 1. Liberty. 2. Political science — History I. T.
JC585.C33    LC 41-16208

**Hayek, Friedrich A. von (Friedrich August), 1899-.** • 4.7665
The constitution of liberty. [Chicago] University of Chicago Press [1960] x, 569 p. 1. Liberty. 2. Rule of law 3. Social policy I. T.
JC585 H29    LC 59-11618

**Hayek, Friedrich A. von (Friedrich August von), 1899-.** 4.7666
Law, legislation, and liberty: a new statement of the liberal principles of justice and political economy / F.A. Hayek. — New pbk. ed. — London: Routledge and Kegan Paul, 1982. 3 v. in 1; 22 cm. 1. Liberty. 2. Democracy 3. Economic policy 4. Rule of law 5. Legislation 6. Social justice I. T.
JC585.H293 1982    320/.01/1 19    LC 82-176256    ISBN 0710092113

**Laski, Harold Joseph, 1893-1950.** • 4.7667
Liberty in the modern state. — Clifton [N.J.]: A. M. Kelley, 1972 [c1948] xi, 175 p.; 22 cm. 1. Liberty. 2. Political science I. T.
JC585.L3 1972    323.44    LC 77-122064

**Machan, Tibor R.** 4.7668
The Libertarian reader / edited by Tibor R. Machan. — Totowa, N.J.: Rowman and Littlefield, 1982. viii, 287 p.; 24 cm. — (Philosophy and society.) 1. Libertarianism — Addresses, essays, lectures. 2. Liberty — Addresses, essays, lectures. 3. Laissez-faire — Addresses, essays, lectures. 4. Sociological jurisprudence — Addresses, essays, lectures. I. T. II. Series.
JC585.L39 1982    320.5/12 19    LC 81-22677    ISBN 0847670619

**Mill, John Stuart, 1806-1873.** • 4.7669
On liberty; Representative government; The subjection of women: three essays / by John Stuart Mill; with an introduction by Millicent Garrett Fawcett. — London: Oxford University Press, H. Milford, [1933] xx, 548 p.; 15.5 cm. — (Half-title: The world's classics. CLXX) 'In 'The world's classics' ... first published in one volume in 1912.' 1. Liberty. 2. Representative government and representation 3. Women — Social and moral questions. 4. Women — Rights of women. I. T. II. Title: Representative government. III. Title: The subjection of women.
JC585.M6 1933    323.44    LC 33-27317

**Mill, John Stuart, 1806-1873.**                              **4.7670**
On liberty / John Stuart Mill; annotated text, sources and background, criticism edited by David Spitz. — 1st ed. — New York: Norton, [1975] xi, 260 p.; 22 cm. (A Norton critical edition) Includes index. 1. Liberty. I. Spitz, David, 1916- ed. II. T.
JC585.M6 1975       323.44       *LC* 74-32203       *ISBN* 0393044009

**Van Dyke, Vernon, 1912-.**                                  **4.7671**
Human rights, the United States, and world community. — New York: Oxford University Press, 1970. ix, 292 p.; 24 cm. 1. Civil rights I. T.
JC585.V276       323.4       *LC* 75-94558

**Von Mises, Ludwig, 1881-1973.**                           • **4.7672**
The free and prosperous commonwealth; an exposition of the ideas of classical liberalism. Translated by Ralph Raico. Edited by Arthur Goddard. Princeton, N.J., Van Nostrand [1962] 207 p. (The William Volker Fund series in the humane studies) 1. Liberalism 2. Economics I. T. II. Series.
JC585 V613       *LC* 62-51576

**Berns, Walter, 1919-.**                                    • **4.7673**
Freedom, virtue & the first amendment [by] Walter Berns. New York, Greenwood Press [1969, c1957] xiii, 264 p. 23 cm. 1. Freedom of speech — United States. 2. Civil rights — United States I. T.
JC591.B44 1969       323.44/0973       *LC* 79-90470       *ISBN* 0837121434

**Bosmajian, Haig A.**                                        **4.7674**
The language of oppression / Haig A. Bosmajian. — Washington: Public Affairs Press, [1975] 156 p.; 23 cm. 1. Freedom of speech — United States. 2. Civil rights — United States 3. Freedom of speech I. T.
JC591.B686       323.44/3/0973       *LC* 74-24984

**Chaffee, Zechariah, 1885-.**                               • **4.7675**
Free speech in the United States. — Cambridge, Harvard Univ. Press, 1964. xviii, 634 p. 24 cm. 'Bibliographical note': p. [569]-571. Bibliographical footnotes. 1. Freedom of speech — United States. 2. Sedition I. T.
JC591.C52 1946       323.443       *LC* 48-3488 *

**Levy, Leonard Williams, 1923-.**                          • **4.7676**
Legacy of suppression; freedom of speech and press in early American history. Cambridge, Mass., Belknap Press of Harvard University Press, 1960. xiv, 353 p. 22 cm. 1. Freedom of speech — United States — History. 2. Freedom of the press — United States — History. I. T.
JC591.L2       323.443       *LC* 60-8449

**Meiklejohn, Alexander, 1872-1964.**                        • **4.7677**
Free speech and its relation to self–government. Port Washington, N.Y., Kennikat Press [1972, c1948] xiv, 107 p. 22 cm. 1. Freedom of speech — United States. I. T.
JC591.M4 1972       323.44/3       *LC* 79-153229       *ISBN* 080461539X

**Meiklejohn, Alexander, 1872-1964.**                        • **4.7678**
Political freedom; the constitutional powers of the people. With a foreword by Malcolm Pitman Sharp. [1st ed.] New York, Harper [1960] 166 p. 22 cm. '[Includes] with a minor change, the text of the [author's] book Free speech and its relation to self-government.' 1. Freedom of speech — United States. I. T.
JC591.M42       323.44/3/0973       *LC* 60-5703

**Schauer, Frederick F.**                                    **4.7679**
Free speech: a philosophical enquiry / Frederick Schauer. — Cambridge [Cambridgeshire]; New York: Cambridge University Press, 1982. xiv, 237 p.; 24 cm. Includes index. 1. Freedom of speech I. T.
JC591.S35 1982       323.44/3/01 19       *LC* 82-4170       *ISBN* 0521243408

**Beer, Lawrence Ward, 1932-.**                              **4.7680**
Freedom of expression in Japan: a study in comparative law, politics, and society / Lawrence Ward Beer. — 1st ed. — Tokyo; New York: Kodansha International, 1985 (c1984). 415 p.; 27 cm. 1. Freedom of speech — Japan. 2. Freedom of the press — Japan. I. T.
JC591.2.B44       342.52/0853 345.202853 19       *LC* 83-48288       *ISBN* 0870116320

**Surveillance, dataveillance, and personal freedoms: use and abuse of information technology / a symposium edited by the staff of Columbia human rights law review; foreword by Nat Hentoff; [Rev. and augm. text].**                    **4.7681**
Fair Lawn, N.J.: R. E. Burdick, [1973] 247 p.; 24 cm. 'Original text published as pages 1-235 of the Columbia human rights law review, volume 4, number 1.' 1. Privacy, Right of — Addresses, essays, lectures. 2. Electronic data processing — Addresses, essays, lectures. 3. Intelligence service — Addresses, essays, lectures. I. Columbia human rights law review.
JC597.S95 1973       323.44       *LC* 73-80006       *ISBN* 091363803X

**International Commission of Jurists (1952- )**             **4.7682**
The decline of democracy in the Philippines: a report of missions / by William J. Butler, John P. Humphrey, G. E. Bisson. — Geneva: International Commission of Jurists, 1977. viii, 97 p.; 23 cm. 1. Martial law — Philippine Islands. 2. Civil

rights — Philippine Islands. 3. Political rights — Philippine Islands. 4. Justice, Administration of — Philippine Islands. I. Butler, William Jack, 1919- II. Humphrey, John P. III. Bisson, G. E. IV. T.
JC 599 P5 I62 1977       *LC* 78-323878       *ISBN* 0891921931

## JC599.U4–.U5 United States

**Becker, Carl Lotus, 1873-1945.**                           • **4.7683**
Freedom and responsibility in the American way of life; five lectures delivered ... at the University of Michigan, December 1944; with an introductory essay by George H. Sabine. [1st ed.] New York, A. A. Knopf, 1945. xlii, 122, iv p. 22 cm. (Michigan. University. William W. Cook Foundation. Lectures; v. 1) 1. Civil rights — United States — Addresses, essays, lectures. I. T.
JC599.U5 B35 1945       323.4/0973 19       *LC* 45-9854

**Civil liberties: policy and policy making / edited by Stephen L. Wasby.**                                                    **4.7684**
Carbondale: Southern Illinois University Press, 1977, c1976. xiv, 235 p.; 21 cm. 1. Civil rights — United States — Addresses, essays, lectures. 2. Policy sciences — Addresses, essays, lectures. I. Wasby, Stephen L., 1937-
JC599.U5 C55 1977       323.4/0973       *LC* 76-43318       *ISBN* 0809308177

**Commager, Henry Steele, 1902-.**                           • **4.7685**
Freedom, loyalty, dissent. — New York: Oxford University press, 1954. 155 p.; 20 cm. 1. Liberty. 2. Civil rights — United States I. T.
JC599.U5 C59       323.4       *LC* 54-7131

**Corwin, Edward Samuel, 1878-1963.**                        • **4.7686**
Liberty against government; the rise, flowering and decline of a famous juridical concept. Baton Rouge, Louisiana State Univ. Press, 1948. xiii, 210 p. 21 cm. Bibliographical footnotes. 1. Liberty. 2. Civil rights — United States 3. United States — Constitutional history I. T.
JC599.U5C66       323.44       *LC* 48-8664 *

**Donohue, William A., 1947-.**                              **4.7687**
The politics of the American Civil Liberties Union / William A. Donohue; with a foreword by Aaron Wildavsky. — New Brunswick, U.S.A.: Transaction Books, c1985. xxiv, 366 p.; 24 cm. 1. American Civil Liberties Union. I. T.
JC599.U5 D66 1985       323.4/06/073 19       *LC* 84-16235       *ISBN* 0887380212

**Gibson, James L.**                                         **4.7688**
Civil liberties and Nazis: the Skokie free–speech controversy / James L. Gibson, Richard D. Bingham. — Urbana, Ill.: Praeger, 1985. xi, 227 p.: ill. Includes index. 1. American Civil Liberties Union. 2. National Socialist Party of America. 3. Freedom of speech — United States. 4. Assembly, Right of — United States. 5. Skokie (Ill.) — Demonstration, 1977. I. Bingham, Richard D. II. T.
JC599.U5 G525 1985       323.44/3/0973 19       *LC* 84-26320       *ISBN* 0030016347

**Grimes, Alan Pendleton, 1919-.**                           **4.7689**
Equality in America; religion, race, and the urban majority. New York, Oxford University Press, 1964. x, 136 p. 21 cm. 1. Civil rights — United States 2. Equality — United States I. T.
JC599.U5 G74       323.4       *LC* 64-15012

**Jaffa, Harry V.**                                          **4.7690**
Equality and liberty: theory and practice in American politics [by] Harry V. Jaffa. — New York, Oxford University Press, 1965. xv, 229 p. 21 cm. Bibliographical footnotes. 1. Liberty. 2. Equality I. T.
JC599.U5J24       323.4       *LC* 65-15614

**Lamson, Peggy.**                                           **4.7691**
Roger Baldwin, founder of the American Civil Liberties Union: a portrait / by Peggy Lamson; illustrated with photos. — Boston: Houghton Mifflin, 1976. 304p. cm. Includes index. 1. Baldwin, Roger Nash, 1884- 2. American Civil Liberties Union — History. 3. Civil rights — United States — History. I. T.
JC599.U5 L28       323.4/092/4 B       *LC* 76-25100       *ISBN* 0395247616

**Lasswell, Harold Dwight, 1902-.**                          • **4.7692**
National security and individual freedom, by Harold D. Lasswell. — New York: Da Capo Press, 1971 [c1950] xiii, 259 p.; 24 cm. — (Civil liberties in American history) 1. Civil rights — U.S. 2. War and emergency powers — U.S. 3. U.S. — Defenses. I. T. II. Series.
JC599.U5 L35 1971       323.4       *LC* 71-139193       *ISBN* 0306700859

**Levy, Leonard Williams, 1923-.**                          • **4.7693**
Jefferson & civil liberties; the darker side. — Cambridge, Belknap Press of Harvard University Press, 1963. xv, 225 p. 22 cm. — (A publication of the Center for the Study of the History of Liberty in America, Harvard University) Bibliography: p. 179-186. 1. Jefferson, Thomas, 1743-1826. 2. Civil rights — U.S. I. T.
JC599.U5L45       323.4       *LC* 63-19140

**McClosky, Herbert.**                                                                 **4.7694**
Dimensions of tolerance: what Americans believe about civil liberties / Herbert
McClosky and Alida Brill. — New York: Russell Sage Foundation, c1983. x,
512 p.: ill.; 24 cm. Includes index. 1. Civil rights — United States — Public
opinion. 2. Public opinion — United States. I. Brill, Alida. II. T.
JC599.U5 M38 1983      323.4/0973 19      LC 82-72959      *ISBN*
0871545918

**Murphy, Paul L., 1923-.**                                                           **4.7695**
World War I and the origin of civil liberties in the United States / Paul L.
Murphy. — 1st ed. — New York: Norton, 1980 (c1979). 285 p.; 21 cm. — (The
Norton essays in American history) 1. Civil rights — United States — History.
2. World War, 1914-1918 — Law and legislation — United States. 3. World
War, 1914-1918 — United States. I. T.
JC599.U5 M833      323.4/0973      LC 79-9519      *ISBN* 0393012263

**Project on Computer Databanks (National Academy of**                                **4.7696**
**Sciences)**
Databanks in a free society: computers, record–keeping, and privacy; report /
[by] Alan F. Westin, project director [and] Michael A. Baker, assistant project
director. — [New York]: Quadrangle Books [1972] xxi, 522 p.; 25 cm.
1. Electronic data processing — United States. 2. Privacy, Right of — United
States. 3. Public records — United States. I. Westin, Alan F. ed. II. Baker,
Michael A., ed. III. T.
JC599.U5 N28 1972      029/.9/32344      LC 75-183193      *ISBN*
0812902920

**Neier, Aryeh, 1937-.**                                                              **4.7697**
Dossier: the secret files they keep on you / Aryeh Neier. — New York: Stein
and Day, 1975, c1974. 216 p.; 25 cm. 1. Privacy, Right of — United States.
2. Records I. T.
JC599.U5 N44 1975      323.44/0973      LC 74-78522      *ISBN*
0812817206

**Pound, Roscoe, 1870-1964.**                                                        **• 4.7698**
The development of constitutional guarantees of liberty. — New Haven,
Published for Wabash College by Yale University Press, 1957. 207 p. 21 cm.
1. Civil rights — U.S. 2. Civil rights — Gt. Brit. I. T.
JC599.U5P6      323.4      LC 57-6343

**Privacy. Edited by J. Roland Pennock and John W. Chapman.**                        **• 4.7699**
[1st ed.] New York, Atherton Press, 1971. xx, 255 p. 22 cm. (Nomos. 13)
1. Privacy, Right of — United States — Addresses, essays, lectures.
I. Pennock, J. Roland (James Roland), 1906- ed. II. Chapman, John William,
1923- ed. III. Series.
JC599.U5 P75      323.44      LC 79-140624

**Reverse discrimination / edited by Barry R. Gross.**                               **4.7700**
Buffalo: Prometheus Books, 1977. viii, 401 p.; 24 cm. 1. Affirmative action
programs — United States — Addresses, essays, lectures. 2. Reverse
discrimination — United States — Addresses, essays, lectures. I. Gross, Barry
R., 1936-
JC599.U5 R44      323.42/3/0973      LC 76-53643      *ISBN* 0879750839

**Rothbard, Murray Newton, 1926-.**                                                  **4.7701**
For a new liberty: the libertarian manifesto / Murray N. Rothbard. — Rev. ed.
1st Collier Books ed. — New York: Collier Books, 1978. x, 338 p.; 24 cm.
1. Liberty. 2. Laissez-faire 3. United States — Economic policy 4. United
States — Social policy I. T.
JC599.U5 R66 1978      320.5/1/0973      LC 78-12225      *ISBN*
0020746903

**Thomas, Norman, 1884-1968.**                                                       **• 4.7702**
The test of freedom. [1st ed.] New York, Norton [1954] 211 p. 22 cm.
1. Liberty. 2. Civil rights — United States 3. Subversive activities — United
States. 4. Communism — United States — 1917- I. T.
JC599.U5 T45      LC 54-8184

**United States. Dept. of Health, Education, and Welfare.**                          **4.7703**
**Secretary's Advisory Committee on Automated Personal Data**
**Systems.**
Records, computers, and the rights of citizens / report of the Secretary's
Advisory Committee on Automated Personal Data Systems. — [Cambridge?
Mass.: MIT Press, 1973] xxxv, 344 p.; 22 cm. 1. Privacy, Right of — United
States. 2. Business records — United States. 3. Public records — United
States. 4. Computers and civilization I. T.
JC599.U5 U54 1973a      323.44/0973      LC 73-13449      *ISBN*
026258025X

**Benjamin, Gerald.**                                                                **4.7704**
Race relations and the New York City Commission on Human Rights. Ithaca
[N.Y.]: Cornell University Press, [1974] 274 p.; 22 cm. 1. New York (N.Y.).
City Commission on Human Rights. 2. Civil rights — New York (City)
3. New York (N.Y.) — Race question. I. T.
JC599.U52 N523      352/.98/097471      LC 73-20790      *ISBN*
0801408261

## JC605 PROPERTY

**Property / edited by J. Roland Pennock and John W. Chapman.**                      **4.7705**
New York: New York University Press, 1980. xiv, 418 p.; 22 cm. — (Nomos.
22) Includes papers presented at the American Society for Political and Legal
Philosophy meetings held in New York, Dec. 1977. Includes index. 1. Right of
property — Addresses, essays, lectures. 2. Property — Addresses, essays,
lectures. I. Chapman, John William, 1923- II. Pennock, James Roland.
III. American Society for Political and Legal Philosophy. IV. Series.
JC605.P76      323.4/6      LC 79-55007      *ISBN* 0814765769

# JF Constitutional History and Administration: General. Comparative

# JF31–36 History

**McIlwain, Charles Howard, 1871-1968.**                                             **4.7706**
Constitutionalism, ancient and modern. Rev. ed. Ithaca, N.Y.: Great Seal
Books, [1958, c1947] 180 p.; 19 cm. 1. Constitutional history I. T.
JF31.M28 1958      LC 59-3775

**McIlwain, Charles Howard, 1871-1968.**                                            **• 4.7707**
Constitutionalism & the changing world: collected papers / by C. H. McIlwain.
— New York: The Macmillan company; Cambridge, Eng.: The University
Press, 1939. viii, 312 p.; 23 cm. Printed in Great Britain. 1. Constitutional
history I. T.
JF31.M3 1939a      LC 43-26066

# JF37 Handbooks

**Lambert's Worldwide government directory, with inter–**                           **4.7708**
**governmental organizations / editor, Diane E. Hrabak.**
Washington, D.C.: Lambert Publications, 1981. x, 779 p.; 29 cm. 1. Heads of
state — Directories. 2. Cabinet officers — Directories. 3. International
agencies — Directories. I. Hrabak, Diane E. II. Lambert Publications, Inc.
III. Title: Worldwide government directory, with inter-governmental
organizations.
JF37.L34      351/.2 19      LC 81-80273      *ISBN* 0939304007

**Political handbook of the world.**                                               **• 4.7709**
1927-. New York: Harper and Row for Council on Foreign Relations. v.: col.
maps. Annual. 'Parliaments, parties and press.' Annual supps. published.'The
world this year ,' 1971- N.Y. Simon & Schuster. 1. Political science —
Handbooks, manuals, etc. 2. Newspapers — Directories 3. Political parties
I. Council on Foreign Relations.
JF37.P6      LC 28-12165      *ISBN* 0070036411

# JF45–128 Treatises

**Finer, Herman, 1898-1969.**                                                       **• 4.7710**
Theory and practice of modern government. — Rev. ed., with a new introd. to
the reprint ed. — Westport, Conn.: Greenwood Press, [1970, c1949] xxx,
978 p.; 26 cm. 1. Political science I. T.
JF51.F52 1970      320      LC 69-13895      *ISBN* 0837119898

**Friedrich, Carl J. (Carl Joachim), 1901-.**                                       **• 4.7711**
[Constitutional government and politics] Constitutional government and
democracy: theory and practice in Europe and America / [by] Carl J. Friedrich.
— 4th ed. Waltham, Mass.: Blaisdell Pub. Co. [1968] xxiii, 728 p.; 23 cm. (A
Blaisdell book in political science) First ed. published in 1937 under title:
Constitutional government and politics. 1. Political science 2. Constitutional
history I. T.
JF51.F7 1968      342      LC 68-10378

**Friedrich, Carl J. (Carl Joachim), 1901-.**    • **4.7712**
The impact of American constitutionalism abroad [by] Carl J. Friedrich. Boston, Boston University Press, 1967. vii, 112 p. 22 cm. (The Gaspar G. Bacon lecture[s] on the Constitution of the United States, 1966) 1. Comparative government 2. United States — Constitutional history I. T. II. Series.
JF51.F72      342/.73/09      *LC* 67-25934

**Friedrich, Carl J. (Carl Joachim), 1901-.**    **4.7713**
Limited government: a comparison [by] Carl J. Friedrich. Englewood Cliffs, N.J., Prentice-Hall [1974] xii, 139 p. 23 cm. (Prentice-Hall contemporary comparative politics series) 1. Constitutional history 2. Comparative government I. T.
JF51.F723      320.3      *LC* 74-802      *ISBN* 0135371678 *ISBN* 0135371597

**Kantor, Harry.**    **4.7714**
Patterns of politics and political systems in Latin America. — Chicago: Rand McNally, [1969] xiii, 742 p.: maps.; 25 cm. — (Rand McNally political science series) 1. Comparative government 2. Latin America — Politics and government I. T.
JF51.K3      320.3/098      *LC* 68-16840

**Presidents and prime ministers / edited by Richard Rose and**    **4.7715**
**Ezra N. Suleiman; foreword by Richard E. Neustadt.**
Washington, D.C.: American Enterprise Institute, 1980. 347 p.; 23 cm. — (American Enterprise Institute studies in political and social processes) (AEI studies; 281) 1. Comparative government I. Rose, Richard, 1933- II. Suleiman, Ezra N., 1941-
JF51.P68      351.003/13      *LC* 80-17898      *ISBN* 0844733865

**Uphoff, Norman Thomas. comp.**    **4.7716**
The political economy of development: theoretical and empirical contributions / edited by Norman T. Uphoff and Warren F. Ilchman. — Berkeley: University of California Press [1972] xi, 506 p.; 26 cm. 1. Developing countries — Politics and government — Addresses, essays, lectures. 2. Developing countries — Economic policy — Addresses, essays, lectures. I. Ilchman, Warren Frederick. joint comp. II. T.
JF60.U64      320.9/172/4      *LC* 77-161999      *ISBN* 0520020626 *ISBN* 0520023145

**Wolpin, Miles D.**    **4.7717**
Militarism and social revolution in the Third World / Miles D. Wolpin. — Totowa, N.J.: Allanheld, Osmun, 1981. x, 260 p.; 24 cm. (LandMark studies) Includes index. 1. Civil-military relations — Developing countries. 2. Developing countries — Politics and government. 3. Developing countries — Armed Forces — Political activity. I. T.
JF60.W63      322/.5/091724 19      *LC* 81-65014      *ISBN* 0865980217

**Young, Crawford, 1931-.**    **4.7718**
The politics of cultural pluralism / Crawford Young. — Madison: University of Wisconsin Press, 1976. xii, 560 p.: maps; 24 cm. 1. Pluralism (Social sciences) — Case studies. 2. Developing countries — Politics and government 3. Developing countries — Social conditions. I. T.
JF60.Y67      320.9/172/4      *LC* 74-27318      *ISBN* 0299067408

# JF195–723 Organs and Functions of Government

**Finer, S. E. (Samuel Edward), 1915-.**    • **4.7719**
The man on horseback: the role of the military in politics / S.E. Finer. — New York: Praeger, 1962. 268 p.: ill. — (Books that matter) 1. Civil supremacy over the military I. T.
JF195.M48 F5

**Vile, M. J. C.**    **4.7720**
Constitutionalism and the separation of powers, by M. J. C. Vile. — Oxford: Clarendon P., 1967. vii, 359 p.; 22 1/2 cm. 1. Separation of powers I. T.
JF229.V5      350/.002      *LC* 67-81265

**Rossiter, Clinton Lawrence, 1917-1970.**    • **4.7721**
Constitutional dictatorship: crisis government in the modern democracies. — Princeton: Princeton Univ. Press, 1948. ix, 322 p.; 25 cm. 1. War and emergency powers 2. Dictators I. T. II. Title: Crisis government in the modern democracies.
JF256.R6      *LC* 48-7284

**Bidwell, Robin.**    **4.7722**
Guide to government ministers. — London: Frank Cass, 1973. 1. Cabinet officers — Directories. I. T. II. Title: Bidwell's guide to government ministers. III. Title: Government ministers.
JF331 B58      *LC* 72-92968      *ISBN* 0714629774

**Government coalitions in western democracies / Edited by Eric**    **4.7723**
**C. Browne, John Dreijmanis.**
New York: Longman, c1982. x, 384 p.; 24 cm. Includes indexes. 1. Coalition governments I. Browne, Eric C. II. Dreijmanis, John.
JF331.G63      324/.094 19      *LC* 81-8241      *ISBN* 0582282187

**Dicey, Albert Venn, 1835-1922.**    • **4.7724**
Lectures on the relation between law & public opinion in England, during the nineteenth century / by A. V. Dicey. — London: Macmillan and Co., Ltd., 1914. xciv, 506 p.; 23 cm. '1st ed., 1905; 2d ed., 1914.' 1. Law — Great Britain — History and criticism 2. Public opinion — Great Britain. 3. Great Britain — Politics and government — 19th century I. T.
JF432.G8 D5 1914      *LC* 14-11597

**Referendums: a comparative study of practice and theory /**    **4.7725**
**edited by David Butler and Austin Ranney.**
Washington: American Enterprise Institute for Public Policy Research, c1978. 250 p.: ill.; 23 cm. — (AEI studies; 216) 1. Referendum 2. Comparative government I. Butler, David, 1924- II. Ranney, Austin.
JF491.R38      328/.2      *LC* 78-22045      *ISBN* 0844733180

**Bogdanor, Vernon, 1943-.**    **4.7726**
The people and the party system: the referendum and electoral reform in British politics / Vernon Bogdanor. — Cambridge [Cambridgeshire]; New York: Cambridge University Press, 1981. ix, 285 p.: ill.; 23 cm. Includes index. 1. Referendum — Great Britain. 2. Representative government and representation — Great Britain. 3. Elections — Great Britain. 4. Political parties — Great Britain 5. Great Britain — Politics and government I. T.
JF493.G74 B64      324.6/3/0941 19      *LC* 81-3895      *ISBN* 052124207X

**Herman, Valentine.**    **4.7727**
Parliaments of the world: a reference compendium / prepared by Valentine Herman, with the collaboration of Françoise Mendel. Berlin; New York: DeGruyter, 1976. xii, 985 p.; 24 cm. At head of title: Inter-parliamentary Union. Includes index. 1. Legislative bodies — Handbooks, manuals, etc. I. Mendel, Françoise, joint author. II. Inter-parliamentary Union. III. T.
JF501.H45 1976      328/.3      *LC* 76-17574      *ISBN* 311006975X

**Bentham, Jeremy, 1748-1832.**    **4.7728**
[Book of fallacies] Bentham's handbook of political fallacies. Baltimore, Johns Hopkins Press, 1952. xxxii, 269 p. port. 22 cm. 1. Legislative bodies 2. Political science I. Larrabee, Harold Atkins, 1894- ed. II. T. III. Title: Handbook of political fallacies.
JF511.B5 1952      *LC* 52-12783

**The Role of the legislature in Western democracies / edited by**    **4.7729**
**Norman J. Ornstein.**
Washington: American Enterprise Institute for Public Policy Research, c1981. xvii, 192 p.; 23 cm. — (AEI symposia. 81F) Proceedings of a conference held at Selsdon Park Hotel, Surrey, England, June 8-10, 1979, and sponsored by the American Enterprise Institute for Public Policy Research. 1. Legislative bodies — Congresses. 2. Democracy — Congresses. I. Ornstein, Norman J. II. American Enterprise Institute for Public Policy Research. III. Series.
JF511.R63      328/.3 19      *LC* 81-7923      *ISBN* 0844722146

**Robert, Henry M. (Henry Martyn), 1837-1923.**    **4.7730**
The Scott, Foresman Robert's Rules of order newly revised / Henry M. Robert. — A new and enl. ed. / by Sarah Corbin Robert, with the assistance of Henry M. Robert III, William J. Evans, James W. Cleary. — Glenview, Ill.: Scott, Foresman, [1984] c1981. xlii, 594 p.; 17 cm. Edition of 1970 published under title: Robert's Rules of order newly revised. Includes index. 1. Parliamentary practice I. Robert, Sarah Corbin. II. Robert's Rules of order newly revised. III. T. IV. Title: Rules of order newly revised.
JF515.R692 1984      060.4/2 19      *LC* 84-10551      *ISBN* 0673154718

**Dahl, Robert Alan, 1915-.**    • **4.7731**
Polyarchy; participation and opposition, by Robert A. Dahl. — New Haven: Yale University Press, 1971. 257 p.; 21 cm. 1. Opposition (Political science) 2. Political participation I. T.
JF518.D32      321/.8      *LC* 70-140524      *ISBN* 0300013914

**Dahl, Robert Alan, 1915-.**    **4.7732**
Regimes and oppositions, edited by Robert A. Dahl. — New Haven: Yale University Press, 1973. 411 p.; 25 cm. 1. Opposition (Political science) 2. Comparative government I. T.
JF518.D322      322.4      *LC* 79-151571      *ISBN* 0300013906

**Hayes, Michael T., 1949-.**    **4.7733**
Lobbyists and legislators: a theory of political markets / Michael T. Hayes. — New Brunswick, N.J.: Rutgers University Press, c1981. viii, 200 p.; 24 cm.

Includes index. 1. Lobbyists 2. Pressure groups 3. Legislators 4. Supply and demand I. T.
JF529.H39     328/.38 19     *LC* 80-23430     *ISBN* 0813509106

# JF800–1191 Political Rights. Suffrage. Representation

**Gosnell, Harold Foote, 1896-.**      • **4.7734**
Democracy, the threshold of freedom. New York: Ronald Press Co., [1948] vii, 316 p.; 24 cm. 1. Suffrage 2. Representative government and representation I. T.
JF831 G6     *LC* 48-5188

**Democracy at the polls: a comparative study of competitive**     **4.7735**
**national elections / edited by David Butler, Howard R.**
**Penniman, and Austin Ranney.**
Washington, D.C.: American Enterprise Institute for Public Policy Research, c1981. 367 p.; 23 cm. — (AEI studies; 297) 1. Elections 2. Comparative government I. Butler, David, 1924- II. Penniman, Howard Rae, 1916- III. Ranney, Austin.
JF1001.D45     324.6 19     *LC* 80-22652     *ISBN* 0844734055

**Mueller, Dennis C.**      **4.7736**
Public choice / Dennis C. Mueller. — Cambridge [Eng.]; New York: Cambridge University Press, 1979. xiii, 297 p.: ill.; 22 cm. — (Cambridge surveys of economic literature) Includes index. 1. Elections 2. Democracy 3. Social choice 4. Welfare economics I. T.
JF1001.M78     324/.2     *LC* 78-11197     *ISBN* 0521225507

**Trent, Judith S.**      **4.7737**
Political campaign communication: principles and practices / by Judith S. Trent and Robert V. Friedenberg. — New York, NY: Praeger, 1983. xiii, 319 p. 1. Electioneering 2. Communication in politics I. Friedenberg, Robert V. II. T.
JF1001.T73 1983     JF1001 T73 1983.     324.7 19     *LC* 83-2132
    *ISBN* 0030625270

**Birch, Anthony Harold.**      • **4.7738**
Representation [by] A. H. Birch. — New York: Praeger, [1972] 149 p.; 23 cm. — (Key concepts in political science) 1. Representative government and representation I. T. II. Series.
JF1051.B55     321.8     *LC* 78-100911

**Choosing an electoral system: issues and alternatives / [edited]**     **4.7739**
**by Arend Lijphart, Bernard Grofman.**
New York: Praeger, 1984. xii, 273 p.: ill.; 24 cm. (American political parties and elections.) 'Copublished with the Eagleton Institute of Politics, Rutgers University.' Includes index. 1. Representative government and representation — Addresses, essays, lectures. 2. Proportional representation — Addresses, essays, lectures. 3. Elections — Addresses, essays, lectures. I. Lijphart, Arend. II. Grofman, Bernard. III. Series.
JF1051.C545 1984     324.6/3 19     *LC* 84-18283     *ISBN* 0030695465

**Pennock, J. Roland (James Roland), 1906-.**      • **4.7740**
Representation. Edited by J. Roland Pennock and John W. Chapman. [1st ed.] New York, Atherton Press, 1968. xvii, 317 p. 22 cm. (Nomos. 10) 'Yearbook of the American Society for Political and Legal Philosophy.' 1. Representative government and representation 2. Representative government and representation — United States. I. Chapman, John William, 1923- joint author. II. American Society for Political and Legal Philosophy. III. T. IV. Series.
JF1051.P395     321.8/08     *LC* 68-16404

**Pitkin, Hanna Fenichel.**      • **4.7741**
The concept of representation. — Berkeley: University of California Press, 1967. vi, 323 p.; 23 cm. 1. Representative government and representation I. T.
JF1051.P5     328.2     *LC* 67-25052

**Pole, J. R. (Jack Richon)**      **4.7742**
The gift of government: political responsibility from the English restoration to American independence / J.R. Pole. — Athens: University of Georgia Press, c1983. xiv, 185 p.; 23 cm. (Richard B. Russell lectures. no. 1) 1. Representative government and representation — Great Britain — History. 2. Representative government and representation — United States — History. I. T. II. Series.
JF1051.P58 1983     328/.3/09 19     *LC* 82-13533     *ISBN* 0820306525

**Irvine, William P.**      **4.7743**
Does Canada need a new electoral system? / William P. Irvine. — Kingston, Ont.: Institute of Intergovernmental Relations, Queen's University; Port Credit, Ont.: distributed by P. D. Meany, c1979. xii, 99 p.; 23 cm. — (Queen's

studies on the future of the Canadian communities. 1 0708-3289) 1. Representative government and representation — Canada. 2. Elections — Canada. 3. Political parties — Canada. I. T. II. Series.
JF1059.C2 I78     324/.24/0971     *LC* 79-321294     *ISBN* 0889110115

**Hermens, Ferdinand Aloys, 1906-.**      • **4.7744**
Democracy or anarchy?: A study of proportional representation / [by] F. A. Hermens; with a new supplement by the author. — New York: Johnson Reprint Corp., 1972. xxx, 491 p.; 23 cm. — (Reprints in government and political science) Reprint of the 1941 ed. which was issued as v. 1 of Modern politics, a series of studies in politics and political philosophy. 1. Proportional representation 2. Majorities I. T.
JF1071.H43 1972     328/.3347     *LC* 72-38858

**Bain, Henry M., 1926-.**      • **4.7745**
Ballot position and voter's choice: the arrangement of names on the ballot and its effect on the voter / [by] Henry M. Bain, Jr. and Donald S. Hecock; foreword by V. O. Key, Jr. — Detroit: Wayne State University Press, 1957. xv, 108 p.: ill.; 22 cm. 1. Ballot 2. Voting I. Hecock, Donald Sumner, 1906- joint author. II. T.
JF1091.B3 1973     324/.25     *LC* 72-9371     *ISBN* 0837165784

# JF1321–2112 Government. Administration

**Merton, Robert King, 1910- ed.**      **4.7746**
Reader in bureaucracy, edited by Robert K. Merton [and others]. — Glencoe, Ill.: Free Press, [1952] 464 p.; 25 cm. 1. Bureaucracy — Collections. I. T.
JF1321.M4     351     *LC* 51-13786

**Gladden, Edgar Norman.**      **4.7747**
A history of public administration [by] E. N. Gladden. — London: Cass, 1972. 2 v. (xii, 269 p., 419 p.); 23 cm. 1. Public administration — History. I. T.
JF1341.G57     350/.0009     *LC* 73-155727     *ISBN* 071461310X

**Jacoby, Henry.**      **4.7748**
[Bürokratisierung der Welt. English] The bureaucratization of the world / translated from the German by Eveline L. Kanes. — Berkeley: University of California Press [1973] vii, 241 p.; 24 cm. Translation of Die Bürokratisierung der Welt. 1. Bureaucracy — History. I. T.
JF1341.J313     350/.001     *LC* 74-165224     *ISBN* 0520020839

**Blau, Peter Michael.**      **4.7749**
Bureaucracy in modern society / Peter M. Blau [and] Marshall W. Meyer. — 2rd ed. — New York: Random House, 1971. xi, 180 p. 21 cm. (Random House studies in sociology, SS12) Includes index. 1. Bureaucracy I. Meyer, Marshall W. joint author. II. T.
JF1351.B55 1971     302.3/5 19     *LC* 73-156338     *ISBN* 0394314522

**Blau, Peter Michael.**      • **4.7750**
The dynamics of bureaucracy: a study of interpersonal relations in two Government agencies. — Rev. [2d] ed. — [Chicago]: University of Chicago Press, [1963, c1955] 322 p.: ill.; 22 cm. 1. Public administration — Case studies. 2. Bureaucracy I. T.
JF1351.B56 1963     350     *LC* 63-22822

**Chapman, Brian.**      • **4.7751**
The profession of government: the public service in Europe. London, Allen & Unwin [1959] 352 p. 1. Public administration 2. Europe — Politics I. T.
JF1351 C4     *LC* 59-2798

**Conference on Bureaucracy and Political Development (1962:**      • **4.7752**
**Center for Advanced Study in the Behavioral Sciences)**
Bureaucracy and political development; [Papers] Edited by Joseph LaPombara. Contributors: Carl Beck [and others] Princeton, N.J., Princeton University Press, 1963. xiv, 487 p. 24 cm. (Studies in political development, 2) 'Sponsored by the Committee on Comparative Politics of the Social Science Research Council.' 1. Bureaucracy 2. Public administration I. La Palombara, Joseph G. ed. II. Beck, Carl, 1930- III. Social Science Research Council. Committee on Comparative Politics. IV. T.
JF1351.C6 1962b     351.1     *LC* 63-11059

**Downs, Anthony.**      • **4.7753**
An economic theory of democracy. — New York: Harper, [1957] 310 p.: illus.; 22 cm. 1. Public administration 2. Voting 3. Political parties I. T.
JF1351.D65     351     *LC* 57-10571

**Downs, Anthony.**　　　　　　　　　　　　　**4.7754**
Inside bureaucracy. — Boston: Little, Brown, [1967] xv, 292 p.: illus.; 24 cm. 'A Rand Corporation research study.' 1. Bureaucracy I. Rand Corporation. II. T.
JF1351.D67　301.18　*LC* 67-18259

**Dunsire, Andrew.**　　　　　　　　　　　　**4.7755**
Administration: the word and the science / [by] A. Dunsire. — New York: Wiley [1973] x, 262 p.; 23 cm. 'A Halsted Press book.' 1. Public administration I. T.
JF1351.D78 1973　350　*LC* 73-7176　　*ISBN* 0470227524

**Gulick, Luther Halsey, 1892- ed.**　　　　• **4.7756**
Papers on the science of Administration / by Luther Gulick [and others]; edited by Luther Gulick and L. Urwick. — New York: A. M. Kelley, 1969. 195 p.: ill.; 28 cm. (Reprints of economic classics) First published in 1937. 1. Organization 2. Public administration — Addresses, essays, lectures. I. Urwick, L. F. (Lyndall Fownes), 1891- joint ed. II. T.
JF1351.G8 1969　658　*LC* 68-55727

**Heady, Ferrel.**　　　　　　　　　　　　　**4.7757**
Public administration: a comparative perspective / Ferrel Heady. — 3rd ed., rev. — New York: M. Dekker, c1984. xii, 453 p.; 24 cm. — (Public administration and public policy. 24) 1. Public administration I. T. II. Series.
JF1351.H4 1984　350 19　*LC* 83-26231　　*ISBN* 0824772059

**Morstein Marx, Fritz, 1900-.**　　　　　　　**4.7758**
The administrative state; an introduction to bureaucracy. [Chicago] University of Chicago Press [1957] 202 p. 24 cm. (The Chicago library of comparative politics) 1. Public administration 2. Civil service I. T.
JF1351.M59　*LC* 57-6987

**Riggs, Fred Warren.**　　　　　　　　　　**4.7759**
Administration in developing countries; the theory of prismatic society [by] Fred W. Riggs. — Boston, Houghton Mifflin [1964] xvi, 477 p. illus. 22 cm. Bibliographical footnotes. 1. Public administration 2. Underdeveloped areas. I. T. II. Title: The theory of prismatic society.
JF1351.R48　350　*LC* 64-56355

**Self, Peter.**　　　　　　　　　　　　　　**4.7760**
Administrative theories and politics: an inquiry into the structure and processes of modern government. — [Toronto]: University of Toronto Press, [1973] 308 p.; 22 cm. 1. Public administration I. T.
JF1351.S44 1973　350　*LC* 72-98025　　*ISBN* 0802019889

**Simon, Herbert Alexander, 1916-.**　　　　• **4.7761**
Public administration / [by] Herbert A. Simon, Donald W. Smithburg [and] Victor A. Thompson. — [1st ed.] New York: Knopf, 1950. xv, 582, xviii p.; 22 cm. 1. Public administration I. T.
JF1351 S5 1950　*LC* 50-8992

**Tullock, Gordon.**　　　　　　　　　　　**4.7762**
The politics of bureaucracy / by Gordon Tullock; foreword by James M. Buchanan. — Washington: Public Affairs Press, 1965. 228 p. 1. Bureaucracy 2. Public administration I. T.
JF1351.T8 1965　*LC* 65-14383

**Waldo, Dwight.**　　　　　　　　　　　　• **4.7763**
The administrative state: a study of the political theory of American public administration. — New York: Ronald Press Co. [1948] viii, 227 p.; 24 cm. — (Series in political science) Includes bibliographies. 1. Public administration 2. U.S. — Pol. & govt. I. T. II. Series.
JF1351.W3　350　*LC* 48-6082 *

**Wamsley, Gary L.**　　　　　　　　　　　**4.7764**
The political economy of public organizations: a critique and approach to the study of public administration / [by] Gary L. Wamsley [and] Mayer N. Zald. — Lexington, Mass.: Lexington Books, [1973] x, 110 p.; 24 cm. 1. Public administration 2. Organization I. Zald, Mayer N. joint author. II. T.
JF1351.W35　350　*LC* 72-6283　　*ISBN* 066984814X

**Etzioni-Halevy, Eva.**　　　　　　　　　　**4.7765**
Bureaucracy and democracy: a political dilemma / Eva Etzioni–Halevy. — London; Boston: Routledge & K. Paul, 1983. xi, 266 p.; 23 cm. Includes index. 1. Bureaucracy 2. Democracy I. T.
JF1411.E89 1983　306.2 19　*LC* 83-9498　　*ISBN* 0710095732

**Katz, Elihu, 1926- comp.**　　　　　　　　**4.7766**
Bureaucracy and the public; a reader in official–client relations, edited by Elihu Katz & Brenda Danet. — New York: Basic Books, [1973] ix, 534 p.; 25 cm. 1. Bureaucracy — Addresses, essays, lectures. 2. Organizational change — Addresses, essays, lectures. 3. Political participation — Addresses, essays, lectures. I. Danet, Brenda, joint comp. II. T.
JF1411.K38　301.18/32　*LC* 72-89283　　*ISBN* 0465007732

**Lewis, Eugene.**　　　　　　　　　　　　**4.7767**
Public entrepreneurship: toward a theory of bureaucratic political power: the organizational lives of Hyman Rickover, J. Edgar Hoover, and Robert Moses / Eugene Lewis. — Bloomington: Indiana University Press, c1980. x, 274 p.: diagrs.; 25 cm. 1. Hoover, J. Edgar (John Edgar), 1895-1972. 2. Moses, Robert, 1888-1981. 3. Rickover, Hyman George. 4. Public administration 5. Government executives 6. Power (Social sciences) I. T.
JF1411.L48　301.44/47/0922 19　*LC* 79-2451　　*ISBN* 0253173841

**Page, Edward.**　　　　　　　　　　　　**4.7768**
Political authority and bureaucratic power: a comparative analysis / Edward C. Page. — 1st ed. — Knoxville: University of Tennessee Press, c1985. 193 p.; 23 cm. Includes index. 1. Weber, Max, 1864-1920. 2. Bureaucracy 3. Authority 4. Leadership 5. Comparative government I. T.
JF1501.P34 1985　350/.001 19　*LC* 84-21895　　*ISBN* 0870494546

## JF1525.I6 Intelligence Service

**Hilsman, Roger.**　　　　　　　　　　　• **4.7769**
Strategic intelligence and national decisions. Glencoe, Ill.: Free Press [1956] 187 p.; 22 cm. 1. Intelligence service I. T.
JF1525 I6 H53　*LC* 56-6873

**Kent, Sherman.**　　　　　　　　　　　• **4.7770**
Strategic intelligence for American world policy. Hamden, Conn., Archon Books, 1965 [c1949] xxvii, 226 p. 22 cm. 1. Intelligence service I. T.
JF1525.I6 K4 1965　353.0089　*LC* 65-25395

**Laqueur, Walter, 1921-.**　　　　　　　　**4.7771**
A world of secrets: the uses and limits of intelligence / Walter Laqueur. — New York: Basic Books, c1985. xii, 404 p.; 25 cm. 'A Twentieth Century Fund book.' Includes index. 1. Intelligence service I. T.
JF1525.I6 L37 1985　327.1/2 19　*LC* 85-47567　　*ISBN* 0465092373

## JF1800–1820 Military Government

**Nordlinger, Eric A.**　　　　　　　　　　**4.7772**
Soldiers in politics: military coups and governments / Eric A. Nordlinger. — Englewood Cliffs, N.J.: Prentice-Hall, c1977. xiii, 224 p.; 23 cm. (Prentice-Hall contemporary comparative politics series.) Includes index. 1. Military government — Developing countries. 2. Civil-military relations — Developing countries. 3. Developing countries — Politics and government. I. T.
JF1820.N67　322/.5　*LC* 76-40016　　*ISBN* 0138221634

# JF2011–2112 Political Parties. Practical Politics

**Electoral change in advanced industrial democracies:**　　**4.7773**
**realignment or dealignment? / editors, Russell J. Dalton, Scott Flanagan, Paul Allen Beck; contributors, James Alt ... [et al.].**
Princeton, N.J.: Princeton University Press, 1985 (c1984). xvi, 513 p.; 25 cm. Includes index. 1. Political parties — Addresses, essays, lectures. 2. Elections — Addresses, essays, lectures. 3. Comparative government — Addresses, essays, lectures. I. Dalton, Russell J. II. Flanagan, Scott C. III. Beck, Paul Allen. IV. Alt, James E.
JF2011.E43 1984　324 19　*LC* 84-42592　　*ISBN* 0691076758

**Participation in politics / edited by J. Roland Pennock and**　**4.7774**
**John W. Chapman.**
New York: Lieber-Atherton, 1975. xix, 300 p.; 23 cm. (Nomos. 16 0078-0979) 'Yearbook of the American Society for Political and Legal Philosophy.' 1. Political participation — Addresses, essays, lectures. 2. Political participation — United States — Addresses, essays, lectures. I. Pennock, J. Roland (James Roland), 1906- II. Chapman, John William, 1923- III. American Society for Political and Legal Philosophy. IV. Series.
JF2011.P29　329　*LC* 73-83019　　*ISBN* 0883110210

**Political parties of Europe / edited by Vincent E. McHale;**　　**4.7775**
**Sharon Skowronski, assistant editor.**
Westport, Conn.: Greenwood Press, 1983. 2 v. (xviii, 1297 p.); 24 cm. — (Greenwood historical encyclopedia of the world's political parties.) 1. Political parties — Europe — History — Handbooks, manuals, etc. I. McHale, Vincent E., 1939- II. Skowronski, Sharon. III. Series.
JF2011.P595 1983　JF2011 P595 1983.　324.24/002/02 19　*LC* 82-15408　　*ISBN* 0313214050

**Pye, Lucian W., 1921- ed.** • 4.7776
Political culture and political development, edited by Lucian W. Pye & Sidney Verba. Contributors: Lucian W. Pye [and others]. — Princeton, N.J.: Princeton University Press, 1965. x, 574 p.; 25 cm. — (Studies in political development, 5) 'Sponsored by the Committee on Comparative Politics of the Social Science Research Council.' 1. Comparative government — Collections. 2. World politics — 1955-1965 — Collections. I. Verba, Sidney. joint ed. II. Social Science Research Council. Committee on Comparative Politics. III. T. IV. Series.
JF2011.P9    320.3    LC 65-10840

**World encyclopedia of political systems & parties / edited by** 4.7777
**George E. Delury.**
New York, N.Y.: Facts on File, c1983. 2 v. (xviii, 1296 p.); 29 cm. 1. Political parties — Handbooks, manuals, etc. 2. Comparative government — Handbooks, manuals, etc. I. Delury, George E.
JF2011.W67 1983    324.2/02/02 19    LC 83-1541    ISBN 0871965747

**Michels, Robert, 1876-1936.** • 4.7778
[Zur Sociologie des Parteiwesens. English] Political parties: a sociological study of the oligarchical tendencies of modern democracy / translated by Eden and Cedar Paul; introd. by Seymour Martin Lipset. — New York: Collier Books, [1962] 379 p.; 18 cm. Translation of Zur Soziologie des Parteiwesens in der moderne Demokratie, with an additional chapter written for the English ed. entitled: Party life in war-time. 1. Political parties 2. Democracy I. T.
JF2049.M62 1962    329    LC 61-18564

**Wallas, Graham, 1858-1932.** • 4.7779
Human nature in politics. With an introd. by A.L. Rowse. [3d ed.] Lincoln, University of Nebraska Press, 1962. 313 p. (A Bison book, BB133) 1. Politics, Practical 2. Political ethics I. T.
JF2049 W2 1962A    LC A64-228

**Beyme, Klaus von.** 4.7780
[Parteien in westlichen Demokratien. English] Political parties in Western democracies / Klaus von Beyme; English translation by Eileen Martin. — New York: St. Martin's Press, 1985. xiii, 444 p.: ill.; 23 cm. Translation of: Parteien in westlichen Demokratien. Includes index. 1. Political parties I. T.
JF2051.B4613 1985    324.2/09182/2 19    LC 84-18171    ISBN 0312623755

**Day, Alan J. (Alan John)** 4.7781
Political parties of the world / compiled and edited by Alan J. Day and Henry W. Degenhardt. — Detroit: Gale Research Co., 1980. x, 432 p.; 26 cm. — (Keesing's reference publication.) Includes indexes. 1. Political parties — Directories. I. Degenhardt, Henry W. II. T. III. Series.
JF2051.D39    324.2/025 19    LC 80-83467    ISBN 0810320258

**Duverger, Maurice, 1917-.** • 4.7782
[Partis politiques. English] Political parties, their organization and activity in the modern state. [3d ed.] Translated by Barbara and Robert North. With a foreword by D. W. Brogan. [London] Methuen [1969] xxxvii, 439 p. 21 cm. (University paperbacks, 82) Distributed in the U.S.A. by Barnes and Noble. Translation of Les partis politiques. 1. Political parties I. T.
JF2051.D883 1969    329/.02    LC 70-27893    ISBN 0416683207

**Epstein, Leon D.** • 4.7783
Political parties in Western democracies [by] Leon D. Epstein. — New York: Praeger, [1967] ix, 374 p.; 21 cm. 1. Political parties I. T.
JF2051.E65    329/.02/091812    LC 67-24674

**Key, V. O. (Valdimer Orlando), 1908-1963.** • 4.7784
Politics, parties, & pressure groups. — 5th ed. — New York: Crowell [1964] xiii, 738 p.: ill., maps, diagrs.; 24 cm. Bibliographical footnotes. 1. Politics, Practical 2. Political parties — U.S. 3. Lobbying I. T.
JF2051.K4 1964    329    LC 64-11799

**Ostrogorski, M. (Moisei), 1854-1919.** • 4.7785
[Démocratie et l'organisation des partis politiques. English] Democracy and the organization of political parties. Translated from the French by Frederick Clarke. With a pref. by James Bryce. New York, Haskell House Publishers, 1970. 2 v. 23 cm. Reprint of the 1902 ed. 1. Political parties — Great Britain 2. Political parties — United States I. T.
JF2051.O85 1970    329/.02    LC 72-122620    ISBN 0838310036

**La Palombara, Joseph G. ed.** • 4.7786
Political parties and political development, edited by Joseph LaPalombara and Myron Weiner. Contributors: Leonard Binder [and others]. — Princeton, N.J.: Princeton University Press, 1966. vii, 487 p.: illus.; 25 cm. — (Studies in political development, 6) 1. Political parties — Addresses, essays, lectures. 2. Politics, Practical — Addresses, essays, lectures. I. Weiner, Myron. joint ed. II. T. III. Series.
JF2051.P25    329.02    LC 66-10558

**Sartori, Giovanni.** 4.7787
Parties and party systems: a framework for analysis, Vol.1 / [by] Giovanni Sartori. Cambridge [etc.]: Cambridge University Press, 1976. xiii, 370 p.: ill.; 24 cm. In 2 vols. 1. Political parties I. T.
JF2051.S26    329/.02    LC 76-4756    ISBN 0521212383

**Tugwell, Rexford G. (Rexford Guy), 1891-.** • 4.7788
The art of politics: as practiced by three great Americans, Franklin Delano Roosevelt, Luis Muñoz Marín, and Fiorello H. La Guardia / Rexford G. Tugwell. — Garden City, N.Y.: Doubleday, 1958. xiii, 295 p.; 22 cm. 1. Roosevelt, Franklin D. (Franklin Delano), 1882-1945. 2. Muñoz Marín, Luis, 1898- 3. La Guardia, Fiorello H. (Fiorello Henry), 1882-1947. 4. Politics, Practical — Case studies. 5. United States — Politics and government — 1933-1945 I. T.
JF2051.T8    LC 58-12056

**Diamond, Edwin.** 4.7789
The spot: the rise of political advertising on television / Edwin Diamond and Stephen Bates. — Cambridge, Mass.: MIT Press, c1984. xiv, 416 p.: ill.; 21 cm. Includes index. 1. Advertising, Political — United States. 2. Television advertising — United States. I. Bates, Stephen, 1958- II. T.
JF2112.A4 D53 1984    324.73 19    LC 84-7904    ISBN 0262040751

**Mauser, Gary A.** 4.7790
Political marketing: an approach to campaign strategy / Gary A. Mauser. — New York, N.Y., U.S.A.: Praeger, 1983. xiv, 304 p.: ill.; 24 cm. — (Praeger series in public and nonprofit sector marketing.) Includes index. 1. Campaign management 2. Electioneering 3. Marketing I. T. II. Series.
JF2112.C3 M38 1983    324.7 19    LC 82-25973    ISBN 0030525918

# JK–JQ CONSTITUTIONAL HISTORY, BY COUNTRY

# JK United States

**Congressional quarterly almanac; a service for editors and** • 4.7791
**commentators.**
v. 1- Jan./Mar. 1945-. Washington, Congressional Quarterly News Features [etc.] 1. United States — Politics & government — Periodicals 2. United States. Congress — Periodicals I. Title: Congressional quarterly
JK1.C66    LC 47-41081

**Elliot, Jeffrey M.** 4.7792
The Presidential–Congressional political dictionary / Jeffrey M. Elliot, Sheikh R. Ali. — Santa Barbara, Calif.: ABC-Clio, c1984. xiv, 365 p.; 24 cm. — (Clio dictionaries in political science; #9) Includes index. 1. United States. Congress — Dictionaries. 2. Presidents — United States — Dictionaries. 3. United States — Politics and government — Dictionaries. I. Ali, Sheikh Rustum. II. T.
JK9.E4 1984    320.473/03/21 19    LC 84-6316    ISBN 0874363578

**Plano, Jack C.** 4.7793
The American political dictionary / Jack C. Plano, Milton Greenberg. — 7th ed. — New York: Holt, Rinehart, and Winston, c1985. ix, 606 p.; 24 cm. Includes index. 1. United States — Politics and government — Dictionaries. I. Greenberg, Milton, 1927- II. T.
JK9.P55 1985    320.973/03 19    LC 84-12822    ISBN 0030028442

**Safire, William, 1929-.** 4.7794
[Political dictionary] Safire's political dictionary / by William Safire. — An enl. up-to-date ed. of The new language of politics. [3d ed.]. — New York: Random House, c1978. xxx, 845 p.; 24 cm. Includes index. 1. United States — Politics and government — Dictionaries. I. T. II. Title: Political dictionary.
JK9.S2 1978    320/.03    LC 78-57124    ISBN 0394502612

**Smith, Edward Conrad, 1891- ed.** • 4.7795
Dictionary of American politics [by] Edward C. Smith and Arnold J. Zurcher. — 2d ed. — New York: Barnes & Noble, [1968] vii, 434 p.: illus., maps.; 22 cm. — (Everyday handbooks) 1. United States — Politics and government — Dictionaries. I. Zurcher, Arnold John, 1902- joint ed. II. T.
JK9.S5 1968    320/.0973    LC 67-28530

**Sperber, Hans, 1885-.** • 4.7796
American political terms; an historical dictionary [by] Hans Sperber and Travis Trittschuh. Detroit, Wayne State University Press, 1962. x, 516 p. 1. United

States — Politics and government — Dictionaries I. Trittschuh, Travis, jt. author II. T.
JK9 S65      *LC* 62-11233

# JK11–371 CONSTITUTIONAL HISTORY

**How democratic is the Constitution? / Robert A. Goldwin and**      **4.7797**
**William A. Schambra, editors.**
Washington, D.C.: American Enterprise Institute for Public Policy Research, c1980. 150 p.; 23 cm. — (AEI studies; 294) 1. Representative government and representation — United States. 2. Democracy — Addresses, essays, lectures. 3. United States — Constitutional history — Addresses, essays, lectures. I. Goldwin, Robert A. 1922- II. Schambra, William A.
JK21.H78      321.8/042/0973 19      *LC* 80-24291      *ISBN* 0844734004

**Corwin, Edward Samuel, 1878-1963.**      **4.7798**
The foundations of American constitutional and political thought, the powers of Congress, and the President's power of removal / edited, with an introd. and an epilogue, by Richard Loss. — Ithaca: Cornell University Press, 1981. 392 p.; 25 cm. (His Corwin on the Constitution; v. 1) 1. United States. Congress — Powers and duties 2. Political science — United States — History. 3. United States — Constitutional history I. Loss, Richard. II. T.
JK31.C6x vol. 1      342.73 s 342.73/029 19      *LC* 81-450      *ISBN* 0801413818

**Corwin, Edward Samuel, 1878-1963.**      **4.7799**
The Judiciary / [Edward S. Corwin]; edited with an introd. by Richard Loss. — Ithaca: Cornell University Press, 1987. 399 p. (His Corwin on the Constitution; v.2) 1. United States. Supreme Court. 2. Judicial power — United States. 3. United States — Constitutional history. 4. United States — Politics and government. I. Loss, Richard. II. T.
JK31.C6x vol. 2      342.73 19      *LC* 80-69823      *ISBN* 0801413818

**Dahl, Robert Alan, 1915-.**      **4.7800**
Democracy in the United States: promise and performance / Robert A. Dahl. — 4th ed. — Boston: Houghton Mifflin Co., c1981. xiv, 475 p.: ill.; 24 cm. 1. Representative government and representation — United States. 2. Pluralism (Social sciences) — United States. 3. United States — Politics and government 4. United States — Constitutional history I. T.
JK31.D33 1981      320.973 19      *LC* 80-50967      *ISBN* 0395307937

**Holcombe, Arthur Norman, 1884-.**      ● **4.7801**
Our more perfect union: from eighteenth–century principles to twentieth–century practice. — Cambridge: Harvard University Press, 1950. xiii, 460 p.; 25 cm. Bibliographical references included in 'Notes' (p. 431-446) 1. U.S. — Constitutional history. I. T.
JK31.H7      342.73      *LC* 50-9371

**Ostrander, Gilman Marston, 1923-.**      ● **4.7802**
The rights of man in America, 1606–1861. — Columbia: University of Missouri Press, [1960] 356 p.; 24 cm. 1. Democracy 2. United States — Politics and government 3. United States — Social conditions — To 1865 I. T.
JK31.O8      342.739      *LC* 60-11577

**Rossiter, Clinton Lawrence, 1917-1970.**      ● **4.7803**
Conservatism in America: the thankless persuasion. — 2d ed., rev. — New York: Knopf, 1962. 306 p.; 21 cm. 1. Conservatism — United States. 2. United States — Politics and government I. T.
JK31.R58 1962a      320.5/2/0973 19      *LC* 62-17857

**Rossiter, Clinton Lawrence, 1917-1970.**      ● **4.7804**
Seedtime of the Republic; the origin of the American tradition of political liberty. [1st ed.] New York, Harcourt, Brace [1953] xiv, 558 p. 1. Liberty. 2. Political science — History — United States 3. United States — Constitutional history I. T.
JK31 R6      *LC* 53-5647

**Warren, Charles, 1868-1954.**      ● **4.7805**
The making of the Constitution. — New York: Barnes & Noble, [1967] xii, 832 p.; 22 cm. 1. United States. Constitution 2. United States — Constitutional history I. T.
JK31.W35 1967      342.73/09      *LC* 67-16628

**Tugwell, Rexford G. (Rexford Guy), 1891-.**      **4.7806**
The emerging Constitution / by Rexford G. Tugwell. — [1st ed.] New York: Harper's Magazine Press [1974] xxxvii, 642 p.; 24 cm. 1. United States — Constitutional history I. T.
JK39.T84 1974      342/.73/029      *LC* 73-6316      *ISBN* 0061282251

# JK49–277 By Period

**Kavenagh, W. Keith.**      **4.7807**
Foundations of colonial America: a documentary history. Edited by W. Keith Kavenagh. Foreword by Richard B. Morris. New York, Chelsea House, 1973. 3 v. 26 cm. 1. United States — Politics and government — Colonial period, ca. 1600-1775 — Sources. I. T.
JK49.K38      325/.342/0973      *LC* 72-80866      *ISBN* 0835206246

## JK54–103 COLONIAL PERIOD

**Breen, T. H.**      ● **4.7808**
The character of the good ruler: a study of Puritan political ideas in New England, 1630–1730, by T. H. Breen. — New Haven: Yale University Press, 1970. xx, 301 p.: facsim.; 22 cm. — (Yale historical publications. Miscellany. 92) 1. Leadership 2. Puritans 3. New England — Politics and government — Colonial period, ca. 1600-1775 I. T. II. Series.
JK54.B74      320.9/74      *LC* 76-118726      *ISBN* 0300011865

**McLaughlin, Andrew Cunningham, 1861-1947.**      ● **4.7809**
The foundations of American constitutionalism. With an introd. by Henry Steel Commager. — Gloucester, Mass.: P. Smith, 1972 [c1932] 160 p.; 22 cm. — (Premier Americana) Reprint of the ed. published by the New York University Press, New York, in series: Anson G. Phelps lectureship on early American history. 1. United States — Politics and government — Colonial period, ca. 1600-1775 — Addresses, essays, lectures. 2. New England — Politics and government — Colonial period, ca. 1600-1775 — Addresses, essays, lectures. 3. United States — Constitutional history — Addresses, essays, lectures. I. T.
JK54.M3 1972      973.4      *LC* 73-158191      *ISBN* 0844640158

**Ward, Harry M.**      **4.7810**
Statism in Plymouth Colony [by] Harry M. Ward. — Port Washington, N.Y.: Kennikat Press, [1973] 193 p.; 24 cm. — (Kennikat Press national university publications. Series in American studies) 1. Civil rights — Plymouth, Mass. — History. 2. Massachusetts — Politics and government — Colonial period, ca. 1600-1775 I. T.
JK99.M39 W37      323.4/09744/82      *LC* 72-91177      *ISBN* 0804690367

**Ritchie, Robert C., 1938-.**      **4.7811**
The Duke's province: a study of New York politics and society, 1664–1691 / by Robert C. Ritchie. — Chapel Hill: University of North Carolina Press, c1977. xii, 306 p.; 24 cm. Includes index. 1. New York (State) — Politics and government — Colonial period, ca. 1600-1775 2. New York (State) — Economic conditions. 3. New York (State) — Social conditions. I. T.
JK99.N69 R57      309.1/747/02      *LC* 77-681      *ISBN* 0807812927

**Patterson, Stephen F., 1937-.**      **4.7812**
Political parties in revolutionary Massachusetts [by] Stephen F. Patterson. — [Madison]: University of Wisconsin Press, [1973] ix, 299 p.; 25 cm. 1. Political parties — Massachusetts — History. 2. Massachusetts — Politics and government — Colonial period, ca. 1600-1775 3. Massachusetts — Politics and government — Revolution, 1775-1783 I. T.
JK103.M4 P37      329/.02      *LC* 72-7991      *ISBN* 0299062600

## JK111–181 1776-1820

**American political writing during the founding era, 1760–1805 /**      **4.7813**
**[edited by] Charles S. Hyneman, Donald S. Lutz.**
Indianapolis: Liberty Press, c1983. 2 v. (xviii, 1417 p.); 24 cm. Includes index. 1. United States — Politics and government — Colonial period, ca. 1600-1775 — Sources. 2. United States — Politics and government — Revolution, 1775-1783 — Sources. 3. United States — Politics and government — 1783-1809 — Sources. I. Hyneman, Charles Shang, 1900- II. Lutz, Donald S.
JK113.A716 1983      973.3 19      *LC* 82-24884      *ISBN* 0865970386

**Kenyon, Cecelia M. ed.**      ● **4.7814**
The antifederalists / edited by Cecelia M. Kenyon. — Indianapolis: Bobbs-Merrill [1966] cxxiii, 455 p.; 21 cm. (The American heritage series, 38) 1. United States — Politics and government — 1783-1789 — Sources. 2. United States — Constitutional history — Sources. I. T.
JK116.K4      342.73/024 347.30224 19      *LC* 65-23008

**Main, Jackson Turner.**      ● **4.7815**
The antifederalists: critics of the Constitution, 1781–1788. — Chapel Hill: Published for the Institute of Early American History and Culture at Williamsburg, Va., by the University of North Carolina Press, [1961] xv, 308 p.; 24 cm. Based on the author's thesis. 'Historiographical and bibliographical essay': p. 293-297. Bibliographical footnotes. 1. United States — Constitutional history 2. United States — History — Confederation, 1783-1789 I. T.
JK116.M2      973.4      *LC* 61-17904

**Herring, Edward Pendleton, 1903-.** • **4.7816**
Group representation before Congress, by Pendleton Herring. Baltimore, Md., The Johns Hopkins press, 1929. xxiv, 309 p. 23 cm. (Brookings Institution. Institute for Government Research. Studies in administration, no. 22) 'First published in 1929. Reissued, 1967. ' 1. Lobbying I. T. II. Series.
JK118H4 1929    LC 29-6686

## JK128 Declaration of Independence

**United States.** **4.7817**
[Declaration of Independence] The Declaration of Independence and the Constitution of the United States of America / with an introduction by Richard G. Stevens. — Washington, D.C.: Georgetown University Press, 1984. 64 p.; 15 cm. 1. United States. Declaration of Independence. 2. United States — Constitution. I. Stevens, Richard G., 1925- II. United States. Constitution. 1984. III. T.
JK128.A1x    342.73/023 347.30223 19    LC 84-8116    ISBN 0878404120

**Becker, Carl Lotus, 1873-1945.** • **4.7818**
The Declaration of independence; a study in the history of political ideas, by Carl Becker. Reprinted with an introduction by the author. New York, A. A. Knopf, 1942. 3 p. l., v-xvii p., 3 l., 3-286 p., 1 l. 21 cm. 1. Jefferson, Thomas, 1743-1826. 2. United States. Declaration of Independence. 3. National law. 4. United States — Politics and government — Revolution, 1775-1783 I. T.
JK128.B4 1942    342.73 973.313    LC 42-5563

**Eidelberg, Paul.** **4.7819**
On the silence of the Declaration of independence / Paul Eidelberg. — Amherst: University of Massachusetts Press, 1976. xv, 127 p.; 24 cm. 1. United States. Declaration of Independence. I. T.
JK128.E35    320.5/0973    LC 76-8759    ISBN 0870232169

## JK130–136 Articles of Confederation

**Jensen, Merrill.** **4.7820**
The Articles of confederation: an interpretation of the social–constitutional history of the American Revolution 1774–1781. — Madison: University of Wisconsin Press [1970] xxix, 284 p.; 21 cm. Reprint of the 1940 ed. with a new foreword by the author. 1. United States. Articles of Confederation 2. United States — Constitutional history 3. United States — History — Revolution, 1775-1783 I. T.
JK131.J4x    342/.73    LC 75-26061    ISBN 0299002047

## JK141–170 Constitution, 1787–1788
## (see also: KF4501-5130)

**United States. Constitutional Convention (1787).** • **4.7821**
The debates in the Federal Convention of 1787, which framed the Constitution of the United States of America, reported by James Madison, a delegate from the state of Virginia. International ed. Gaillard Hunt and James Brown Scott, editors. New York, Oxford University Press, 1920. xcvii, 731 p. facsims. (2 fold.) 25 cm. (Publications of the Carnegie endowment for international peace. Division of international law, Washington) 1. United States. Constitution I. Madison, James, 1751-1836. II. Hunt, Gaillard, 1862-1924. ed. III. Scott, James Brown, 1866-1943. joint ed. IV. T.
JK141 1920    LC 20-16222

**Elliot, Jonathan, 1784-1846, ed.** • **4.7822**
The debates in the several State conventions on the adoption of the Federal Constitution as recommended by the general convention at Philadelphia in 1787 ... Collected and rev. from contemporary publications by Johathan Elliot. New York, B. Franklin [1968?] 5 v. 24 cm. (American classics in history and social science 13) (Burt Franklin research and source works series, 109.) 'From the edition of 1888.' Vol. 1-4, 2d ed., with considerable additions. Vol. 5 has title: Debates on the adoption of the Federal Constitution in the convention held at Philadelphia in 1787, with a diary of the debates of the Congress of the Confederation as reported by James Madison. Rev. and newly arranged by Jonathan Elliot. Supplementary to Elliot's Debates. 1. United States. Constitution I. Madison, James, 1751-1836. II. United States. Constitutional Convention (1787). III. T.
JK141 1968    342/.73/024    LC 75-6334

**Beard, Charles Austin, 1874-1948.** **4.7823**
An economic interpretation of the Constitution of the United States, by Charles A. Beard with new introduction. — New York: Macmillan, [c1935] xx, 330 p.; 22 cm. 1. United States — Constitutional history 2. United States. Constitution 3. United States — Economic conditions I. T.
JK146.B5 1935    342/.733    LC 35-15006

**Brown, Robert Eldon, 1907-.** • **4.7824**
Charles Beard and the Constitution: a critical analysis of 'An economic interpretation of the Constitution.'. — Princeton: Princeton University Press,
1956. 219 p.; 23 cm. 1. Beard, Charles Austin, 1874-1948. An economic interpretation of the Constitution of the United States. 2. United States. Constitution I. T.
JK146.B53 B7    342.733    LC 56-8373

**Van Doren, Carl, 1885-1950.** • **4.7825**
The great rehearsal; the story of the making and ratifying of the Constitution of the United States. New York, Viking Press, 1948. xii, 336 p. illus., ports. 22 cm. 1. United States. Constitutional Convention (1787). 2. United States — Constitutional history I. T.
JK146.V3 1948a    342.73/029 347.30229 19    LC 48-657

**Federalist.** • **4.7826**
The enduring Federalist. New York, F. Ungar Pub. Co. [1959]. xvi, 396 p. illus., ports. 22 cm. 1. United States — Constitutional law I. Beard, Charles Austin, 1874-1948. ed. II. T.
JK154 1959    LC 59-9146

**The Federalist.** • **4.7827**
The Federalist. Edited with introd. and notes, by Jacob E. Cooke. — [1st ed.]. — Middletown, Conn., Wesleyan University Press [1961] xxx, 672 p. 24 cm. 1. United States — Constitutional law I. Cooke, Jacob Ernest, 1924- ed. II. T.
JK154 1961b    342.73/024 347.30224 19    LC 61-6971

**Adair, Douglass.** **4.7828**
Fame and the founding fathers: essays / edited by Trevor Colbourn; with a personal memoir by Caroline Robbins and a bibliographical essay by Robert E. Shalhope. — [1st ed.] New York: Published for the Institute of Early American History and Culture at Williamsburg, Va., by Norton [1974] xxxv, 315 p.: music; 24 cm. 1. The Federalist — Addresses, essays, lectures. 2. United States — Constitutional history — Addresses, essays, lectures. I. Institute of Early American History and Culture (Williamsburg, Va.) II. T.
JK155.A32    329/.1/008    LC 73-17356    ISBN 0393054993

**The Complete anti–Federalist / edited, with commentary and** **4.7829**
**notes, by Herbert J. Storing with the assistance of Murray Dry.**
Chicago: University of Chicago Press, 1981. 7 v.; 25 cm. 1. Political science — United States — History — Sources. 2. United States — Constitutional history — Sources. 3. United States — Constitutional law I. Storing, Herbert J., 1928- II. Dry, Murray.
JK155.C65 1981    342.73/029 347.30229 19    LC 81-10287    ISBN 0226775739

**Epstein, David F.** **4.7830**
The political theory of the Federalist / David F. Epstein. — Chicago: University of Chicago Press, 1984. ix, 234 p.; 24 cm. 1. Federalist. 2. Political science — United States — History. I. T.
JK155.E64 1984    342.73/029 347.30229 19    LC 83-17858    ISBN 0226212998

**Rutland, Robert Allen, 1922-.** • **4.7831**
The birth of the Bill of Rights, 1776–1791. Chapel Hill: Published for the Institute of Early American History and Culture by the University of North Carolina Press [1955] vi, 243 p.; 24 cm. Bibliographical footnotes. Appendices (p. [231]-235: A. The Virginia Declaration of rights.—B. The Federal Bill of Rights. 1. United States. Constitution. 1st-10th amendments 2. Civil rights — United States I. Virginia. Declaration of rights. II. T.
JK168.R8    323.4    LC 55-13817

**James, Joseph B. (Joseph Bliss), 1912-.** • **4.7832**
The framing of the Fourteenth amendment. Urbana, University of Illinois Press, 1956. ix, 220 p. 26 cm. (Illinois studies in the social sciences, v. 37) 'Originally ... a doctoral dissertation at the University of Illinois.' 1. United States — Constitutional law — Amendments — 14th I. T.
H31.I4 vol. 37 JK169 14th 1956    323.41    LC 56-5680

## JK171–181 1778–1820

**Beard, Charles Austin, 1874-1948.** • **4.7833**
Economic origins of Jeffersonian democracy / by Charles A. Beard. — New York: Free Press [1965, c1943] ix, 474 p.: ill. (maps) diagr.; 23 cm. (A Free Press paperback) 1. Federal Party (U.S.) 2. United States — Politics and government — Constitutional period, 1789-1809 3. United States — History — Constitutional period, 1789-1809. 4. United States — Economic conditions I. T.
JK171.A1 B2    973.4    LC 65-5633

**The Documentary history of the first Federal elections,** **4.7834**
**1788–1790 / edited by Merrill Jensen, Robert A. Becker.**
Madison: University of Wisconsin Press, 1976- <1986 >. v. <1-3 >: maps; 25 cm. On spine: The first Federal elections, 1788-1790. Vols. 2-<3 >: Gordon DenBoer, editor, Lucy Trumbull Brown, associate editor, Charles D. Hagermann, editorial assistant. 1. Elections — United States — History — Sources. 2. United States — Politics and government — 1789-1797 — Sources.

I. Jensen, Merrill. II. Becker, Robert A., 1943- III. DenBoer, Gordon, 1933-
IV. Title: First Federal elections, 1788-1790.
JK171.A1 D6    329/.023/7303    *LC* 74-5903    *ISBN* 0299066908

**White, Leonard Dupee, 1891-1958.**        • 4.7835
The Federalists: a study in administrative history. — New York: Macmillan
Co., 1948. xii, 538 p.; 22 cm. Bibliographical footnotes. 1. United States —
Politics and government — Constitutional period, 1789-1809 I. T.
JK171.A1W4    973.41    *LC* 48-7016 *

**Cunningham, Noble E., 1926-.**        4.7836
The process of government under Jefferson / by Noble E. Cunningham, Jr. —
Princeton, N.J.: Princeton University Press, c1978. xii, 357 p.; 24 cm. Includes
index. 1. Jefferson, Thomas, 1743-1826. 2. United States — Politics and
government — 1801-1809 I. T.
JK180.C86    320.9/73/046    *LC* 77-85535    *ISBN* 0691046514

**White, Leonard Dupee, 1891-1958.**        • 4.7837
The Jeffersonians; a study in administrative history, 1801-1829. New York,
Macmillan, 1951. xiv, 572 p. 22 cm. 1. United States — Politics and
government — 1783-1865 I. T.
JK180.W5    *LC* 51-12490

## JK201–254 1821–1898/1908

**Randall, J. G. (James Garfield), 1881-1953.**        • 4.7838
Constitutional problems under Lincoln. Rev. ed. Urbana, University of Illinois
Press, 1951. xxxiii, 596 p. map. 24 cm. 1. Lincoln, Abraham, 1809-1865.
2. United States — Politics and government — Civil War, 1861-1865
3. United States — Constitutional history 4. United States — Constitutional
law I. T.
JK201.R3 1951    *LC* 51-1577

**White, Leonard Dupee, 1891-1958.**        • 4.7839
The Jacksonians: a study in administrative history, 1829–1861. — New York:
Macmillan, 1954. xii, 593 p.; 22 cm. 1. United States — Politics and
government — 1815-1861 I. T.
JK201.W45    *LC* 54-12436

**Calhoun, John C. (John Caldwell), 1782-1850.**        • 4.7840
A disquisition on government: and selections from the Discourse / edited with
an introd., by C. Gordon Post. — New York: Liberal Arts Press [1953] xxxv,
104 p.; 21 cm. 1. Political science 2. United States — Politics and government
I. T.
JK216.C17    *LC* 53-4386

**Nelson, William Edward, 1940-.**        4.7841
The roots of American bureaucracy, 1830–1900 / William E. Nelson. —
Cambridge, Mass.: Harvard University Press, 1982. 208 p.; 25 cm. 1.
1. Bureaucracy — United States — History — 19th century. 2. United States
— Politics and government — 19th century 3. United States — Constitutional
history I. T.
JK216.N44 1982    320.973 19    *LC* 82-6214    *ISBN* 0674779452

**Tocqueville, Alexis de, 1805-1859.**        • 4.7842
[De la démocratie en Amérique. English] Democracy in America / edited by J.
P. Mayer and Max Lerner; a new translation by George Lawrence. — [1st ed.]
New York: Harper & Row [1966] 2 v. in 1 (xciii, 802 p.); 24 cm. 'Text is based
on the second revised and corrected text of [Mayer's] 1961 French edition.'
1. Democracy 2. United States — Politics and government 3. United States —
Social conditions — To 1865 I. Mayer, J. P. (Jacob Peter), 1903- ed.
II. Lerner, Max, 1902- ed. III. T.
JK216.T7 1966a    309.173    *LC* 62-14540

**Hyman, Harold Melvin, 1924-.**        4.7843
A more perfect Union: the impact of the Civil War and Reconstruction on the
Constitution / by Harold M. Hyman. — [1st ed.]. — New York: Knopf, 1973.
xix, 562, xviii p.; 25 cm. — (Impact of the Civil War.) 1. United States —
Constitutional history 2. United States — Politics and government — Civil
War, 1861-1865 3. United States — Politics and government — 1865-1877
I. T. II. Series.
JK231.H9    320.9/73/07    *LC* 72-2256    *ISBN* 0394467078

**Skowronek, Stephen.**        4.7844
Building a new American state: the expansion of national administrative
capacities, 1877–1920 / Stephen Skowronek. — Cambridge [Cambridgeshire];
New York: Cambridge University Press, 1982. x, 389 p.; 24 cm. Includes index.
1. United States — Politics and government — 1865-1933 I. T.
JK231.S55 1982    353/.0009 19    *LC* 81-15225    *ISBN* 0521230225

**White, Leonard Dupee, 1891-1958.**        • 4.7845
The Republican era, 1869–1901: a study in administrative history / with the
assistance of Jean Schneider. — New York: Macmillan, 1958. 406 p.; 22 cm.
1. U.S. — Pol. & govt. — 1865-1900. I. T.
JK231.W5    353    *LC* 58-6209

**McPherson, Edward, 1830-1895.**        4.7846
Hand–book of politics / new introd. by Harold M. Hyman and Hans L.
Trefousse. — New York: Da Capo Press, 1972. 4 v.; 24 cm. — (Studies in
American history and government) 'An unabridged republication in four
volumes of the twelve original volumes published biennially in Washington,
D.C., from 1872 through 1894, inclusive.' 1. United States — Politics and
government — 1865-1898 — Handbooks, manuals, etc. I. T.
JK241.M235 1972    320.9/73/08    *LC* 72-146558

**Brownson, Orestes Augustus, 1803-1876.**        4.7847
The American Republic: its Constitution, tendencies, and destiny / edited for
the modern reader by Americo D. Lapati. — New Haven: College & University
Press, 1974 (c1972) 255 p.; 21 cm. — (The Masterworks of literature series,
M-35) Reprint of the 1865 ed. 1. Political science 2. United States — Politics
and government I. T.
JK246.B88 1972b    320.4/73    *LC* 71-143281

**Bryce, James Bryce, Viscount, 1838-1922.**        • 4.7848
The American Commonwealth. Newly edited, abridged, and introduced by
Louis M. Hacker. — New York: Putnam, [1959] 2 v. in 1 (xi, 612 p.): map.; 19
cm. — (Capricorn books, 19a-b) 1. United States — Politics and government
2. United States — Social conditions — 1865-1918 I. T.
JK246.B9 1959    342.73    *LC* 59-11821

**Wilson, Woodrow, 1856-1924.**        • 4.7849
Constitutional government in the United States. New York, Columbia
University Press [1961, c1908] 236 p. 21 cm. (A Columbia paper back, 15)
1. United States — Politics & government. 2. United States — Constitutional
law I. T.
JK246.W82 1961    353    *LC* 61-2275

## JK261–277 1908–

**Brogan, D. W. (Denis William), 1900-1974.**        • 4.7850
Politics in America / by D. W. Brogan. Rev. ed., with a new introd. by the
author. New York: Harper & Row [1969] xxiii, 476 p.; 21 cm. (Harper
torchbooks, TB 1469) London ed. has title: An introduction to American
politics. 1. United States — Politics and government — 20th century I. T.
JK268.B72 1969    329/.00973    *LC* 70-12100

**Barone, Michael.**        4.7851
The almanac of American politics: the Senators, the Representatives—their
records, States, and districts, 1974 [by] Michael Barone, Grant Ujifusa [and]
Douglas Matthews. — [2d ed.]. — Boston: Gambit, [c1973] xxiii, 1240 p.: illus.;
22 cm. 1. United States. Congress — Registers 2. United States. Congress.
House — Election districts — Handbooks, manuals, etc. 3. United States —
Politics and government — 1945- I. Ujifusa, Grant, joint author.
II. Matthews, Douglas. joint author. III. T.
JK271.B343 1974    328.73    *LC* 72-96875    *ISBN* 087645077X

**Buckley, William F. (William Frank), 1925-.**        • 4.7852
Up from liberalism [by] William F. Buckley, Jr. Introd. by Barry Goldwater.
Foreword by John Dos Passos. New Rochelle, Arlington House [1968] xxx,
234 p. 21 cm. 1. Liberalism — United States. 2. United States — Politics and
government — 20th century I. T.
JK271.B723 1968    320.5/1/0973    *LC* 68-18819

**Bundy, McGeorge.**        4.7853
The strength of government. — Cambridge: Harvard University Press, 1968.
xii, 113 p.; 21 cm. — (The Godkin lectures at Harvard University, 1968) Based
on the Godkin lectures delivered at Harvard University in March 1968.
1. United States — Politics and government — 1945- I. T.
JK271.B726    320/.0973    *LC* 68-54016

**Denton, Robert E., Jr.**        4.7854
Political communication in America / Robert E. Denton, Gary C. Woodward.
— New York: Praeger, 1985. xvi, 364 p. 1. Communication — Political aspects
— United States. 2. United States — Politics and government I. Woodward,
Gary C. II. T.
JK271.D46 1985    306/.2/0973 19    *LC* 85-3599    *ISBN* 0030713269

**De Witt, Benjamin Parke.**        • 4.7855
The progressive movement: a non–partisan, comprehensive discussion of
current tendencies in American politics / introd. by Arthur Mann. — Seattle:
University of Washington Press [1968] xx, 376 p.; 23 cm. — (Americana
library) Reprint of the 1915 ed., with a new introd. 1. Progressive Party
(Founded 1912) 2. Municipal government — United States. 3. United States
— Politics and government — 1909-1913 I. T.
JK271.D5    320.9/73    *LC* 68-6751

**Goldwater, Barry M. (Barry Morris), 1909-.**        • 4.7856
The conscience of a Conservative. Shepherdsville, Ky., Victor Pub. Co., 1960.
123 p. 22 cm. 1. United States — Politics and government — 20th century
I. T.
JK271.G668    342.73    *LC* 60-12269

**Lindblom, Charles Edward, 1917-.** 4.7857
The policy–making process / Charles E. Lindblom. — 2d ed. — Englewood Cliffs, N.J.: Prentice-Hall, c1980. xi, 131 p.; 23 cm. — (Prentice-Hall foundations of modern political science series) Includes index. 1. Policy sciences 2. Power (Social sciences) 3. United States — Politics and government I. T.
JK271.L52 1980     320.9/73     LC 79-15539     ISBN 0136865437

**Mendelsohn, Harold A.** • 4.7858
Polls, television, and the new politics [by] Harold Mendelsohn and Irving Crespi. — Scranton: Chandler Pub. Co., [1970] xii, 329 p.: illus.; 21 cm. — (Chandler publications in political science) 1. Public opinion — U.S. 2. Television in politics — U.S. 3. U.S. — Politics and government — 1945- I. Crespi, Irving. joint author. II. T.
JK271.M38     329/.05     LC 76-99782     ISBN 810200104

**Pomper, Gerald M.** • 4.7859
The performance of American Government: checks and minuses [by] Gerald M. Pomper [and others] New York, Free Press [1972] xii, 372 p. 24 cm. 1. Political participation — United States — Addresses, essays, lectures. 2. Afro-Americans — Politics and government — Addresses, essays, lectures. 3. United States — Politics and government — 1945- — Addresses, essays, lectures. I. T.
JK271.P58     320.9/73/09     LC 71-163607

**Schoenberger, Robert A., comp.** • 4.7860
The American right wing; readings in political behavior. Edited by Robert A. Schoenberger. — New York: Holt, Rinehart and Winston, [1969] viii, 308 p.; 23 cm. 1. Right and left (Political science) 2. Political psychology 3. U.S. — Politics and government — 1945- I. T.
JK271.S238     320.9/73     LC 71-82452     ISBN 0030793351

**Schwarz, John E.** 4.7861
America's hidden success: a reassessment of twenty years of public policy / John E. Schwarz. — 1st ed. — New York: Norton, c1983. 208 p.; 22 cm. 1. United States — Politics and government — 1945- I. T.
JK271.S355 1983     320.973 19     LC 83-42646     ISBN 0393018032

**Westin, Alan F.** • 4.7862
The uses of power; 7 cases in American politics [by] Hugh Douglas Price [and others] New York, Harcourt, Brace & World [1962] 376 p. 1. Power (Social sciences) — Case studies 2. United States — Politics and government — 1945- I. Price, Hugh Douglas II. T.
JK271 W39     LC 61-17826

**Blevins, Leon W., 1937-.** 4.7863
The young voter's manual: a topical dictionary of American government and politics / by Leon W. Blevins. — Totowa, N.J.: Littlefield, Adams, 1973. xi, 366 p.; 26 cm. — (A Littlefield, Adams quality paperback no. 260) 1. United States — Politics and government — Handbooks, manuals, etc. I. T.
JK274.B623     320.4/73     LC 73-10377     ISBN 0822602601

## JK305 Separation of Powers

**Fisher, Louis.** 4.7864
The politics of shared power: Congress and the executive / Louis Fisher. — Washington, D.C.: Congressional Quarterly Press, c1981. xiv, 217 p.; 23 cm. — (Politics and public policy series.) Includes indexes. 1. United States. Congress — Powers and duties 2. Separation of powers — United States. 3. Executive power — United States I. T. II. Series.
JK305.F54     320.4 19     LC 81-5442     ISBN 0871871637

**Separation of powers—does it still work? / Robert A. Goldwin** 4.7865
**and Art Kaufman, editors.**
Washington, D.C.: American Enterprise Institute for Public Policy Research, c1986. xi, 193 p.; 23 cm. — (AEI studies. 446) 1. Separation of powers — United States. I. Goldwin, Robert A. 1922- II. Kaufman, Art. III. Series.
JK305.S47 1986     320.473 19     LC 86-14083     ISBN 0844736074

## JK310–339 Federal–State Relations

**Nagel, Paul C.** • 4.7866
One nation indivisible: the union of American thought, 1776–1861. — New York: Oxford University Press, 1964. vii, 328 p.; 22 cm. 1. Federal government — United States 2. State rights 3. United States — Politics and government — 1783-1865 I. T.
JK311 N28     LC 64-11235

**Walker, David Bradstreet, 1927-.** 4.7867
Toward a functioning federalism / David B. Walker. — Cambridge, Mass.: Winthrop, c1981. xiv, 267 p.; 24 cm. — (Winthrop foundations of public management series.) 1. Federal government — United States — History.

2. Intergovernmental fiscal relations — United States — History. I. T. II. Series.
JK311.W18     321.02/0973 19     LC 81-2123     ISBN 0876268947

**Danielson, Michael N.** 4.7868
One nation, so many governments / Michael N. Danielson, Alan M. Hershey, John M. Bayne. Lexington, Mass.: Lexington Books, c1977. xii, 141 p.: ill.; 24 cm. 'A report to the Ford Foundation.' 1. Federal government — United States. 2. Local government — United States. 3. State governments I. Hershey, Alan M. joint author. II. Bayne, John M., joint author. III. Ford Foundation. IV. T.
JK325.D27     320.9/73     LC 76-53868     ISBN 0669012939

**Derthick, Martha.** 4.7869
Between State and Nation; regional organizations of the United States [by] Martha Derthick, with the assistance of Gary Bombardier. — Washington: Brookings Institution, [1974] ix, 242 p.; 23 cm. 1. Federal government — United States — Case studies. 2. Regionalism — United States — Case studies. 3. Regional planning — United States — Case studies. I. Bombardier, Gary, joint author. II. T.
JK325.D46     353.9/292     LC 74-727     ISBN 0815718128

**Glendening, Parris N.** 4.7870
Pragmatic Federalism: an intergovernmental view of American government / Parris N. Glendening, Mavis Mann Reeves. — Pacific Palisades, Calif.: Palisades Publishers, c1977. ix, 334 p.: ill.; 24 cm. 1. Federal government — United States. 2. Intergovernmental fiscal relations — United States. I. Reeves, Mavis Mann. joint author. II. T.
JK325.G57     321.02/3/0973 19     LC 76-29891     ISBN 0913530107. ISBN 0913530093 pbk

**Grodzins, Morton.** • 4.7871
The American system; a new view of government in the United States. Edited by Daniel J. Elazar. — Chicago: Rand McNally, [1966] xviii, 404 p.; 24 cm. — (Rand McNally political science series) 1. Federal government — United States. I. T.
JK325.G78     320.973     LC 66-13444

**Haider, Donald H.** 4.7872
When governments come to Washington: Governors, mayors, and intergovernmental lobbying, by Donald H. Haider. — New York: Free Press, [1974] xvi, 336 p.; 24 cm. 1. Federal government — United States. 2. Intergovernmental fiscal relations — United States 3. Mayors — United States 4. County officials and employees — United States. 5. Lobbying I. T.
JK325.H24     353.9/29     LC 73-17643     ISBN 002913370X

**Henig, Jeffrey R., 1951-.** 4.7873
Public policy and federalism: issues in state and local politics / Jeffrey R. Henig. — New York: St. Martin's Press, c1985. xiii, 401 p.: ill.; 24 cm. Spine title: Public policy & federalism. Includes index. 1. Federal government — United States. 2. Local government — United States. 3. State governments I. T. II. Title: Public policy & federalism.
JK325.H42 1985     321.02/3/0973 19     LC 84-51680     ISBN 0312655576

**Martin, Roscoe Coleman, 1903-1972.** • 4.7874
The cities and the Federal system [by] Roscoe C. Martin. — [1st ed.]. — New York: Atherton Press, [1965] viii, 200 p.; 22 cm. 1. Federal government — United States. 2. Intergovernmental fiscal relations — United States. 3. Grants-in-aid — United States. 4. Metropolitan areas — United States I. T.
JK325.M37     350.0930973     LC 65-24497

**Matheson, Scott.** 4.7875
Out of balance / Scott M. Matheson, with James Edwin Kee. — Salt Lake City: G.M. Smith: P. Smith Books, c1986. xiv, 302 p.: ill.; 23 cm. Includes index. 1. Federal government — United States. 2. Intergovernmental fiscal relations — United States. 3. Governors — United States — Politics and government — 1981- 5. Utah — Politics and government. I. Kee, James Edwin. II. T.
JK325.M38 1986     353.9792 19     LC 86-6760     ISBN 0879052562

**Nice, David C., 1952-.** 4.7876
Federalism: the politics of intergovernmental relations / David C. Nice. — New York: St. Martin's Press, 1987. xi, 226 p.: ill.; 23 cm. 1. Federal government — United States. 2. Federal-city relations — United States. 3. State-local relations — United States. 4. Intergovernmental fiscal relations — United States. I. T.
JK325.N53 1987     321.02/0973 19     LC 86-60643     ISBN 0312285493

**Patterson, James T.** • 4.7877
The New Deal and the States; federalism in transition [by] James T. Patterson. Princeton, N.J., Princeton University Press, 1969. viii, 226 p. 23 cm. 1. Federal government — United States. 2. New Deal, 1933-1939 3. United States —

Economic policy — 1933-1945 4. United States — Politics and government — 1933-1945 I. T.
JK325.P36    321.02/3/0973 19    *LC* 69-17313

**Sundquist, James L.**                • **4.7878**
Making federalism work; a study of program coordination at the community level [by] James L. Sundquist, with the collaboration of David W. Davis. — Washington: Brookings Institution, [1969] viii, 293 p.; 24 cm. 1. Federal government — U.S. 2. Economic assistance, Domestic — U.S. I. Davis, David W., joint author. II. T.
JK325.S86    353    *LC* 78-104334    *ISBN* 0815782187

**Macmahon, Arthur Whittier, 1890-.**    **4.7879**
Administering federalism in a democracy / [by] Arthur W. Macmahon. — New York: Oxford University Press, 1972. x, 196 p.; 21 cm.— (Public administration and democracy) 1. Federal government — United States. I. T.
JK331.M23    320.4/73    *LC* 72-177993

**Reveley, W. Taylor.**    **4.7880**
War powers of the President and Congress: who holds the arrows and olive branch? / W. Taylor Reveley III. — Charlottesville: University Press of Virginia, 1981. 394 p.; 24 cm. — (Virginia legal studies.) Includes index. 1. War and emergency powers — United States — History. I. T. II. Series.
JK339.R48    342.73/041 9    *LC* 80-29046    *ISBN* 0813908086

## JK361 Church–State Relations

**Howe, Mark De Wolfe, 1906-1967.**    **4.7881**
The garden and the wilderness; religion and government in American constitutional history. Chicago, University of Chicago Press [1965] x, 180 p. 21 cm. Lectures sponsored by the Frank L. Weil Institute for Studies in Religion and the Humanities. 1. Church and state — United States I. Frank L. Weil Institute for Studies in Religion and the Humanities. II. T.
JK361.H6    323.4420973    *LC* 65-24977

## JK401–1686 Government.
## Administration

**Basic documents of American public administration, 1776–1950**    **4.7882**
**/ selected and edited by Frederick C. Mosher.**
New York: Holmes & Meier, 1976. xii, 225 p.; 24 cm. Continued by: Basic documents of American public administration since 1950 / selected and edited by Richard J. Stillman II. 1. Civil service — United States — History — Sources. 2. United States — Politics and government — Sources 3. United States — Executive departments — Management — History — Sources. I. Mosher, Frederick C.
JK411.B3    353    *LC* 76-13866    *ISBN* 0841902755. *ISBN* 0841902763 pbk

**Basic documents of American public administration since 1950 /**    **4.7883**
**selected and edited by Richard J. Stillman II.**
New York: Holmes & Meier, 1982. xiii, 311 p.; 23 cm. Continues: Basic documents of American public administration, 1776-1950 / selected and edited by Frederick C. Mosher. 1. Administrative agencies — United States — Management — History — Sources. 2. Civil service — United States — History — Sources. 3. United States — Politics and government — 1945- Sources. 4. United States — Executive departments — Management — History — Sources. I. Stillman, Richard Joseph, 1943-
JK411.B32 1982    353 19    *LC* 82-11726    *ISBN* 0841908184

**Gellhorn, Walter, 1906-.**    • **4.7884**
Individual freedom and governmental restraints. — New York: Greenwood Press, 1968 [c1956] 215 p.; 23 cm. Based on the Edward Douglass White lectures delivered in 1956 at Louisiana State University. 1. Civil rights — United States 2. United States — Politics and government — 20th century I. T.
JK411.G4 1968    323.4    *LC* 68-54421

**Redford, Emmette Shelburn, 1904-.**    **4.7885**
Organizing the executive branch: the Johnson presidency / Emmette S. Redford and Marlan Blissett. — Chicago: University of Chicago Press, 1981. x, 277 p.; 24 cm. — (An Administrative history of the Johnson presidency) 1. United States — Executive departments — Reorganization. 2. United States — Politics and government — 1963-1969 I. Blissett, Marlan. II. T.
JK411.R43    353.07/3 19    *LC* 81-1142    *ISBN* 0226706753

## JK421–464 Treatises

**United States government manual (Washington, D.C.: 1973)**    **4.7886**
The United States government manual. — 1973/74-    . — Washington, D.C.: Office of the Federal Register, National Archives and Records Service, General Services Administration: For sale by the Supt. of Docs., U.S. G.P.O., [1973-. v.: ill.; 24 cm. Annual. Published as a special edition of the Federal register. Published 1935-1972/73 as United States Government organization manual. 1. United States — Executive departments — Handbooks, manuals, etc. 2. United States — Politics and government — Handbooks, manuals, etc. I. United States. Office of the Federal Register. II. Federal register. III. T.
JK421.A3    353    *LC* 73-646537

**United States. President's Committee on Administrative**    • **4.7887**
**Management.**
Report of the Committee: with studies of administrative management in the federal government / submitted to the President and to the Congress in accordance with Public law no. 739, 74th Congress, 2d session. — Washington: U.S. Govt. Print. Off., 1937. xiii, 382 p.: ill.; 29 cm. Louis Brownlow, chairman. Includes index. 1. United States — Politics and government — 1933-1945 2. United States — Executive departments I. Brownlow, Louis, 1879- II. T.
JK421 A45 1937    *LC* 37-26978

**Berman, Larry.**    **4.7888**
The Office of Management and Budget and the Presidency, 1921–1979 / Larry Berman. — Princeton, N.J.: Princeton University Press, c1979. xiii, 180 p.: diagrs.; 23 cm. Includes index. 1. United States. Office of Management and Budget. 2. Presidents — United States I. T.
JK421.B37    353.007/1    *LC* 79-83977    *ISBN* 0691076197

**Gaus, John Merriman, 1894-.**    • **4.7889**
The frontiers of public administration / [by] John M. Gaus, Leonard D. White [and] Marshall E. Dimock. — New York: Russell & Russell, [1967, c1936] ix, 146 p.; 23 cm. (Studies in public administration, v. 6) 1. Public administration 2. United States — Politics and government I. White, Leonard Dupee, 1891-1958. joint author. II. Dimock, Marshall Edward, 1903- joint author. III. T.
JK421.G33 1967    350    *LC* 66-27077

**Goodsell, Charles T.**    **4.7890**
The case for bureaucracy: a public administration polemic / Charles T. Goodsell. — Chatham, N.J.: Chatham House Publishers, c1983. xi, 179 p.; 23 cm. — (Chatham House series on change in American politics.) Includes index. 1. Bureaucracy — United States. I. T. II. Series.
JK421.G64 1983    353/.01 19    *LC* 82-14795    *ISBN* 0934540179

**Government agencies / editor–in–chief Donald R. Whitnah.**    **4.7891**
Westport, Conn.: Greenwood Press, 1983. xxviii, 683 p.; 24 cm. — (Greenwood encyclopedia of American institutions. 0271-9509; 7) Includes index. 1. Administrative agencies — United States. I. Whitnah, Donald Robert, 1925- II. Series.
JK421.G65 1983    353.04 19    *LC* 82-15815    *ISBN* 0313220174

**Herring, Edward Pendleton, 1903-.**    • **4.7892**
Public administration and the public interest. 1st ed. New York, McGraw-Hill, 1936. xii, 416 p. 1. United States — Executive departments 2. United States — Politics & government I. T.
JK421 H4    *LC* 36-6336

**Pemberton, William E., 1940-.**    **4.7893**
Bureaucratic politics: executive reorganization during the Truman administration / William E. Pemberton. — Columbia: University of Missouri Press, 1979. 262 p.; 24 cm. Includes index. 1. United States — Executive departments 2. United States — Politics and government — 1945-1953 I. T.
JK421.P36    353.04    *LC* 78-2990    *ISBN* 0826202446

**Seidman, Harold.**    **4.7894**
Politics, position, and power: from the positive to the regulatory state / Harold Seidman, Robert Gilmour. — 4th ed. — New York: Oxford University Press, 1986. viii, 370 p.; 21 cm. Includes index. 1. United States — Politics and government I. Gilmour, Robert S. (Robert Scott), 1940- II. T.
JK421.S44 1986    353 19    *LC* 85-20514    *ISBN* 0195039912

## JK467–468 Special Topics

**Handler, Edward.**    **4.7895**
Business in politics: campaign strategies of corporate political action committees / Edward Handler, John R. Mulkern. — Lexington, Mass.: Lexington Books, c1982. xii, 128 p.; 24 cm. Includes index. 1. Business and politics — United States. 2. Corporations — United States — Political activity. 3. Political action committees — United States. 4. United States — Politics and government — 1977-1981 I. Mulkern, John R. II. T.
JK467.H27 1982    322/.3 19    *LC* 81-48560    *ISBN* 0669054283

**The PAC handbook: political action for business.**    **4.7896**
Cambridge, Mass.: Ballinger Pub. Co., 1982, c1980. 361 p.: ill. 1. Business and politics — United States. 2. Corporations — United States — Political activity. 3. Political action committees — United States. I. Fraser/Associates. II. Title: P.A.C. handbook.
JK467.P33 1981    322/.3/0973 19    *ISBN* 0884108791

**Silverman, Corinne.**    **4.7897**
The President's economic advisors / by Corinne Silverman. — Syracuse, N.Y.: Inter-University Case Program, 1959. 18 p. (Case study; no. 48) 1. Presidents — United States. I. T.
JK467.S4x

**Encyclopedia of governmental advisory organizations, 1988–89 /**    **4.7898**
**Denise M. Allard and Donna Batten, editors.**
6th ed. — Detroit: Gale Research, c1987. 1207 p.; 29 cm. 'A reference guide to more than 5,400 permanent, continuing, and ad hoc U.S. presidential advisory committees, congressional advisory committees, public advisory committees, interagency committees, and other government-related boards, panels, task forces, commissions, conferences, and other similar bodies serving in a consultative, coordinating, advisory, research, or investigative capacity'. Supplemented by: New governmental advisory organizations. Includes indexes. 1. Executive advisory bodies — United States — Directories. I. Adzigian, Denise Allard. II. Batten, Donna. III. Gale Research Company.
JK468.C7 E52 1987    353.09/2/025    *ISBN* 081030256X

**Wolanin, Thomas R., 1942-.**    **4.7899**
Presidential advisory commissions: Truman to Nixon / Thomas R. Wolanin. — Madison: University of Wisconsin Press, 1975. xii, 298 p.; 24 cm. 1. Executive advisory bodies — United States. 2. United States — Politics and government — 1945- I. T.
JK468.C7 W64    353.09/3    *LC* 74-27317    *ISBN* 0299068609

**Rohr, John A. (John Anthony), 1934-.**    **4.7900**
Ethics for bureaucrats: an essay on law and values / John A. Rohr; foreword by Herbert J. Storing. — New York: M. Dekker, c1978. xii, 292 p.; 24 cm. (Political science; v. 8) 1. Civil service ethics — United States. 2. Civil service — United States 3. Government executives — United States. I. T.
JK468.E7 R56    172/.2    *LC* 78-15327    *ISBN* 082476756X

## JK486.I6 Intelligence Service

**Agee, Philip.**    **4.7901**
Inside the Company: CIA diary / Philip Agee. — American ed. — New York: Stonehill, c1975. 639 p.: diagrs.; 22 cm. Includes index. 1. United States. Central Intelligence Agency. I. T.
JK468.I6 A75 1975b    327/.12/0924    *LC* 75-323312    *ISBN* 0883730286

**Breckinridge, Scott D.**    **4.7902**
The CIA and the U.S. intelligence system / Scott D. Breckinridge. — Boulder: Westview Press, 1986. xviii, 364 p.; 24 cm. (Westview library of federal departments, agencies, and systems.) 1. United States. Central Intelligence Agency. 2. Intelligence service — United States I. T. II. Title: CIA and the United States intelligence system. III. Series.
JK468.I6 B74 1986    327.1/2/0973 19    *LC* 85-20377    *ISBN* 081330282X

**Colby, William Egan, 1920-.**    **4.7903**
Honorable men: my life in the CIA / William Colby and Peter Forbath. — New York: Simon and Schuster, c1978. 493 p., [8] leaves of plates: ill.; 24 cm. Includes index. 1. Colby, William Egan, 1920- 2. United States. Central Intelligence Agency. 3. Intelligence officers — United States — Biography. I. Forbath, Peter, joint author. II. T.
JK468.I6 C59    327/.12/0924 B    *LC* 78-1525    *ISBN* 0671228757

**Corson, William R.**    **4.7904**
The armies of ignorance: the rise of the American intelligence empire / William R. Corson. — New York: Dial Press/J. Wade, c1977. vi, 640 p.; 24 cm. Includes index. 1. Intelligence service — United States I. T.
JK468.I6 C66    327/.12/0973    *LC* 77-88822    *ISBN* 0803702825

**Donner, Frank J.**    **4.7905**
The age of surveillance: the aims and methods of America's political intelligence system / by Frank J. Donner. — 1st ed. — New York: Knopf: distributed by Random House, 1980. xvi, 554 p.; 25 cm. Includes index. 1. Intelligence service — United States I. T.
JK468.I6 D65 1980    353.0074    *LC* 79-3479    *ISBN* 0394402987

**The Intelligence community: history, organization, and issues /**    **4.7906**
**compiled and edited by Tyrus G. Fain, in collaboration with**
**Katharine C. Plant and Ross Milloy; with an introd. by Frank**
**Church.**
New York: R. R. Bowker Co., 1977. xxiii, 1036 p.; 24 cm. — (Public documents series) Includes indexes. 1. United States. Central Intelligence Agency. I. Fain, Tyrus G. II. Plant, Katharine C. III. Milloy, Ross. IV. Series.
JK468.I6 I57    353.008/92    *LC* 77-5854    *ISBN* 0835209598

**Johnson, Loch K., 1942-.**    **4.7907**
A season of inquiry: the Senate intelligence investigation / Loch K. Johnson. — Lexington, Ky.: University Press of Kentucky, c1985. 317 p.: ill.; 24 cm. Includes index. 1. Intelligence service — United States 2. Governmental investigations — United States I. T.
JK468.I6 J64 1985    327.1/2/0973 19    *LC* 84-22106    *ISBN* 0813115353

**Oseth, John M., 1944-.**    **4.7908**
Regulating U.S. intelligence operations: a study in definition of the national interest / John M. Oseth; with a foreword by Roger Hilsman. — Lexington, Ky.: University Press of Kentucky, c1985. xvii, 236 p.; 25 cm. Includes index. 1. Intelligence service — United States I. T. II. Title: Regulating US intelligence operations.
JK468.I6 O84 1985    327.1/2/0973 19    *LC* 84-22105    *ISBN* 0813115345

**Powers, Thomas, 1940 Dec. 12-.**    **4.7909**
The man who kept the secrets: Richard Helms & the CIA / by Thomas Powers. — 1st ed. — New York: Knopf, 1979. xv, 393 p.; 25 cm. Includes index. 1. Helms, Richard. 2. United States. Central Intelligence Agency. I. T.
JK468.I6 P68 1979    327/.12/0924 B    *LC* 79-2210    *ISBN* 0394507770

**Prados, John.**    **4.7910**
Presidents' secret wars: CIA and Pentagon covert operations since World War II / John Prados. — 1st ed. — New York: W. Morrow, c1986. 480 p.; 25 cm. Includes index. 1. United States. Central Intelligence Agency. 2. Intelligence service — United States 3. Military intelligence — United States. 4. United States — Foreign relations — 1945- I. T.
JK468.I6 P7 1986    327.1/2/06073 19    *LC* 86-12854    *ISBN* 068805384X

**Prados, John.**    **4.7911**
The Soviet estimate: U.S. intelligence analysis & Russian military strength / John Prados. — New York: Dial Press, c1982. xv, 367 p.; 24 cm. Includes index. 1. United States. Central Intelligence Agency. 2. Intelligence service — United States 3. Strategic forces — Soviet Union. I. T.
JK468.I6 P72    327.1/2/0973 19    *LC* 81-15232    *ISBN* 0385272111

**Ranelagh, John.**    **4.7912**
The agency: the rise and decline of the CIA / John Ranelagh. — New York: Simon and Schuster, c1986. 847 p., [16] p. of plates: ill.; 24 cm. Includes index. 1. United States. Central Intelligence Agency — History. I. T.
JK468.I6 R29 1986    327.1/2/06073 19    *LC* 85-30329    *ISBN* 0671443186

**Richelson, Jeffrey.**    **4.7913**
The U.S. intelligence community / Jeffrey Richelson. — Cambridge, Mass.: Ballinger Pub. Co., c1985. xxv, 358 p.; 24 cm. 1. Intelligence service — United States I. T.
JK468.I6 R53 1985    327.1/2/0973 19    *LC* 84-24385    *ISBN* 0887300243

**Troy, Thomas F.**    **4.7914**
Donovan and the CIA: a history of the establishment of the Central Intelligence Agency / Thomas F. Troy. — Frederick, Md.: University Publicaitons of America, 1981. xvii, 589 p.: ill.; 26 cm. — (Aletheia books.) Includes index. 1. Donovan, William J. (William Joseph), 1883-1959. 2. United States. Central Intelligence Agency — History. I. T. II. Series.
JK468.I6 T74 1981    327.1/2/06073 19    *LC* 81-12904

**Wise, David.**    **4.7915**
The American police state: the government against the people / David Wise. 1st ed. — New York: Random House, c1976. 437 p.; 25 cm. Includes index. 1. Intelligence service — United States 2. Civil rights — United States 3. United States — Politics and government — 1933-1945 4. United States — Politics and government — 1945- I. T.
JK468.I6 W49    323.4/0973    *LC* 76-14173    *ISBN* 0394496779

**Hendricks, Evan.**    **4.7916**
Former secrets: government records made public through the Freedom of Information Act: 500 case studies on the use of the Freedom of Information Act by business, consumers, scholars, lawyers, reporters, state officials, civil libertarians, unions, and political activists / by Evan Hendricks for the Campaign for Political Rights. — Washington, DC (201 Massachusetts Ave., NE, Washington 20002): The Campaign, c1982. iv, 204 p.; 28 cm. 1. Freedom

of information — United States. 2. Government information — United States. 3. Public records — United States. I. Campaign for Political Rights (U.S.) II. T.
JK468.S6 H46 1982　　353.0071/45 19　　*LC* 82-168555

# JK511–1599 Branches of Government

## JK511–901 EXECUTIVE

### JK511–609 The President

**Barber, James David.**　　　　　　　　　　　　　　**4.7917**
The Presidential character: predicting performance in the White House / by James David Barber. — 2d ed. — Englewood Cliffs, N.J.: Prentice-Hall, c1977. xi, 576 p.; 24 cm. 1. Presidents — United States — Case studies. 2. Presidents — United States — Psychology. 3. Prediction (Psychology) I. T.
JK511.B37 1977　　353.03/1 19　　*LC* 77-4094　　*ISBN* 013697466X.
*ISBN* 0136978479

**Cunliffe, Marcus.**　　　　　　　　　　　　　　**4.7918**
American Presidents and the Presidency. — New York: American Heritage Press, [1972] 446 p.: ill.; 23 cm. 1968 ed. published under title: The American heritage history of the Presidency. 1. Presidents — United States I. T.
JK511.C83 1972　　353.03/13　　*LC* 72-925　　*ISBN* 0070149356

**Goldsmith, William M.**　　　　　　　　　　　　　**4.7919**
The growth of Presidential power; a documented history, by William M. Goldsmith. With an introductory essay by Arthur M. Schlesinger, Jr. — New York: Chelsea House Publishers, 1974. 3 v. (xxvi, 2342 p.); 25 cm. 1. Executive power — United States — History. 2. Presidents — United States — History. I. T.
JK511.G64　　353.03/2　　*LC* 74-9623　　*ISBN* 0835207781

**Polsby, Nelson W. comp.**　　　　　　　　　　　**4.7920**
The modern Presidency. Edited by Nelson W. Polsby. — [1st ed.]. — New York: Random House, [1973] xii, 236 p.; 24 cm. 1. Presidents — United States — Addresses, essays, lectures. 2. United States — Politics and government — 1933-1945 — Addresses, essays, lectures. 3. United States — Politics and government — 1945- — Addresses, essays, lectures. I. T.
JK511.P67　　321.8/042　　*LC* 72-11695　　*ISBN* 0394317467

**Schlesinger, Arthur Meier, 1917-.**　　　　　　　**4.7921**
The imperial Presidency / [by] Arthur M. Schlesinger, Jr. — Boston: Houghton Mifflin, 1973. x, 505 p.; 24 cm. 1. Presidents — United States — History. 2. Executive power — United States — History. I. T.
JK511.S35　　973　　*LC* 73-15805　　*ISBN* 0395177138

**Binkley, Wilfred Ellsworth, 1883-.**　　　　　　• **4.7922**
[Powers of the president] President and Congress. 3d rev. ed. New York, Vintage Books [1962] 403 p. 19 cm. First ed. published in 1937 under title: The powers of the President. 1. United States. Congress — History. 2. Executive power — United States — History. 3. Legislative power — United States — History. I. T.
JK516.B5 1962　　353.03　　*LC* 62-2230

**Cronin, Thomas E.**　　　　　　　　　　　　　　**4.7923**
The state of the Presidency / Thomas E. Cronin. — 2d ed. — Boston: Little, Brown, c1980. vii, 417 p.: graphs; 23 cm. Includes index. 1. Presidents — United States I. T.
JK516.C75 1980　　353.03/1 19　　*LC* 79-90616　　*ISBN* 0316161799

**Edwards, George C.**　　　　　　　　　　　　　**4.7924**
Presidential leadership: politics and policy making / George C. Edwards III, Stephen J. Wayne. — New York: St. Martin's Press, 1985. xiii, 480 p.: ill.; 24 cm. Includes index. 1. Presidents — United States I. Wayne, Stephen J. II. T.
JK516.E32 1985　　353.03/1 19　　*LC* 84-18387　　*ISBN* 0312640374

**Hargrove, Erwin C.**　　　　　　　　　　　　　**4.7925**
The power of the modern Presidency [by] Erwin C. Hargrove. Foreword by Harold D. Lasswell. — [1st ed.]. — Philadelphia: Temple University Press, [1974] xi, 353 p.; 24 cm. 1. Presidents — United States 2. Executive power — United States 3. United States — Politics and government — 1933-1945 4. United States — Politics and government — 1945- I. T.
JK516.H26　　353.03/2　　*LC* 74-9939　　*ISBN* 0394317246

**The Illusion of presidential government / edited by Hugh Heclo**　**4.7926**
**and Lester M. Salamon.**
Boulder, Colo.: Westview Press, 1981. xiv, 359 p.; 24 cm. 'Most of the chapters in this volume were originally prepared during the spring and summer 1980 for use by a panel on presidential management convened by the National Academy of Public Administration'—Pref. 1. Presidents — United States — Addresses,

essays, lectures. I. Heclo, Hugh. II. Salamon, Lester M. III. National Academy of Public Administration.
JK516.I43　　353.03/1 19　　*LC* 81-10343　　*ISBN* 0865312486

**Laski, Harold Joseph, 1893-1950.**　　　　　　• **4.7927**
The American presidency: an interpretation. — Westport, Conn.: Greenwood Press, [1972, c1940] viii, 278 p.; 22 cm. 1. Presidents — United States 2. United States — Politics and government I. T.
JK516.L3 1972　　353/.0313　　*LC* 79-138120　　*ISBN* 0837156963

**Neustadt, Richard E.**　　　　　　　　　　　　　**4.7928**
Presidential power: the politics of leadership from FDR to Carter / Richard E. Neustadt. — New ed. — New York: Wiley, c1980. xv, 286 p.; 23 cm. 1. Presidents — United States 2. Executive power — United States 3. United States — Politics and government — 1945- I. T.
JK516.N4 1980　　353.03/2　　*LC* 79-19474　　*ISBN* 0471059889

**Pious, Richard M., 1944-.**　　　　　　　　　　　**4.7929**
The American Presidency / Richard M. Pious. — New York: Basic Books, c1979. xx, 491 p.; 24 cm. Includes index. 1. Presidents — United States I. T.
JK516.P55　　353.03/13　　*LC* 78-19808　　*ISBN* 0465001831

**The Presidency in the constitutional order / edited by Joseph**　　**4.7930**
**M. Bessette and Jeffrey Tulis.**
Baton Rouge: Louisiana State University Press, c1981. xii, 349 p.; 24 cm. Chiefly papers from workshops held at the White Burkett Miller Center, University of Virginia, 1977-1978. 1. Presidents — United States — Addresses, essays, lectures. I. Bessette, Joseph M. II. Tulis, Jeffrey. III. White Burkett Miller Center.
JK516.P65　　353.03/1　　*LC* 80-14250　　*ISBN* 0807107743

**Reedy, George E., 1917-.**　　　　　　　　　　　**4.7931**
The twilight of the Presidency [by] George E. Reedy. — New York: World Pub. Co., [1970] xvii, 205 p.; 21 cm. 'An NAL book.' 1. Presidents — U.S. I. T.
JK516.R35　　353.03　　*LC* 72-100111

**Rossiter, Clinton Lawrence, 1917-1970.**　　　　• **4.7932**
The American Presidency. — [2d ed.]. — New York: Harcourt, Brace, [1960] 281 p.; 21 cm. — (A Harvest book, HB35) 1. Presidents — United States I. T.
JK516.R6 1960　　353.03　　*LC* 60-5436

**Wildavsky, Aaron B. comp.**　　　　　　　　　　**4.7933**
The Presidency, edited by Aaron Wildavsky. — Boston: Little, Brown, [1969] xv, 795 p.; 24 cm. 1. Presidents — U.S. — Addresses, essays, lectures. I. T.
JK516.W5　　353/.03　　*LC* 71-75397

**Edwards, George C.**　　　　　　　　　　　　　**4.7934**
The public presidency: the pursuit of popular support / George C. Edwards III. — New York: St. Martin's Press, c1983. x, 276 p.; 24 cm. 'Intended for use as a supplementary text for courses both in the Presidency and in Public opinion'—Pref. 1. Presidents — United States — Public opinion. 2. Public opinion — United States. I. T.
JK518.E28 1983　　353.03/5 19　　*LC* 82-60470　　*ISBN* 0312655630

**Grossman, Michael Baruch.**　　　　　　　　　　**4.7935**
Portraying the President: the White House and the news media / Michael Baruch Grossman and Martha Joynt Kumar. — Baltimore: Johns Hopkins University Press, c1981. x, 358 p.: graphs; 24 cm. 1. Presidents — United States — Press conferences 2. Government and the press — United States. 3. Press and politics — United States. I. Kumar, Martha Joynt. joint author. II. T.
JK518.G76　　353.03/5 19　　*LC* 80-24634　　*ISBN* 0801823757

**Hobbs, Edward Henry.**　　　　　　　　　　　　**4.7936**
Behind the President; a study of Executive Office agencies. Washington, Public Affairs Press [1954] vi, 248 p. 24 cm. 1. United States. Executive Office of the President. I. T.
JK518.H6　　*LC* 53-5789

**Light, Paul Charles.**　　　　　　　　　　　　　**4.7937**
The president's agenda: domestic policy choice from Kennedy to Carter (with notes on Ronald Reagan) / Paul Charles Light. — Baltimore: Johns Hopkins University Press, c1982. ix, 246 p.; 24 cm. Revision of thesis (Ph. D.)—University of Michigan. Includes index. 1. Presidents — United States 2. Policy sciences 3. United States — Politics and government — 1945- 4. United States — Social policy I. T.
JK518.L47 1982　　353.03/23 19　　*LC* 81-47607　　*ISBN* 0801826578

**Seymour-Ure, Colin, 1938-.**　　　　　　　　　　**4.7938**
The American president: power and communication / Colin Seymour-Ure. — New York: St. Martin's Press, 1982. xiii, 190 p.; 23 cm. Includes index. 1. Presidents — United States 2. Executive power — United States 3. Communication in politics — United States. 4. United States — Politics and government — 1945- I. T.
JK518.S45 1982　　353.03/2 19　　*LC* 82-5772　　*ISBN* 0312027869

**Studying the Presidency** / edited by George C. Edwards III and   **4.7939**
Stephen J. Wayne.
1st ed. — Knoxville: University of Tennessee Press, c1983. viii, 312 p.; 23 cm.
1. Presidents — United States — Research — Addresses, essays, lectures.
2. Presidents — United States — History — Sources — Addresses, essays,
lectures. I. Edwards, George C. II. Wayne, Stephen J.
JK518.S78 1983     353.03/13/072 19     *LC* 82-17472     *ISBN*
0870493787

## JK521–540 Nomination. Election

**Abramowitz, Alan.**           **4.7940**
Nomination politics: party activists and presidential choice / Alan I.
Abramowitz and Walter J. Stone. — New York: Praeger, 1984. xiii, 158 p.; 24
cm. Includes index. 1. Presidents — United States — Nomination I. Stone,
Walter J. II. T.
JK521.A27 1984     324.5 19     *LC* 84-17891     *ISBN* 0030005191

**Ceaser, James W.**           **4.7941**
Reforming the reforms: a critical analysis of the presidential selection process /
James W. Ceaser. — Cambridge, Mass.: Ballinger Pub. Co., c1982. xi, 201 p.;
24 cm. 1. Presidents — United States — Nomination I. T.
JK521.C4 1982     324.5/0973 19     *LC* 81-21638     *ISBN* 0884108848

**Crotty, William J.**           **4.7942**
Presidential primaries and nominations / William Crotty, John S. Jackson III.
— Washington, D.C.: CQ Press, c1985. xii, 251 p.; ill.; 23 cm. 1. Presidents —
United States — Nomination I. Jackson, John S., 1940- II. T.
JK521.C76 1985     324.5/4 19     *LC* 84-17662     *ISBN* 0871872609

**Keech, William R.**           **4.7943**
The party's choice / William R. Keech and Donald R. Matthews. —
Washington: Brookings Institution, c1976. xii, 258 p.; ill.; 24 cm. (Studies in
presidential selection) 1. Presidents — United States — Nomination
I. Matthews, Donald R. joint author. II. T. III. Series.
JK521.K43     329/.022/0973     *LC* 75-31757     *ISBN* 0815748523

**Polsby, Nelson W.**           **4.7944**
Consequences of party reform / Nelson W. Polsby. — Oxford; New York:
Oxford University Press, 1983. xvi, 267 p.; 22 cm. 1. Presidents — United
States — Nomination I. T.
JK521.P58 1983     324.5/0973 19     *LC* 82-14509     *ISBN* 0195032349

**Davis, James W., 1920-.**           • **4.7945**
Presidential primaries: road to the White House / by James W. Davis. — New
York: Crowell [1967] xii, 324 p.; 21 cm. (Crowell studies in political science.)
1. Primaries 2. Presidents — United States — Election I. T. II. Series.
JK522.D3     329.022'0973     *LC* 67-14300

**Lengle, James I., 1949-.**           **4.7946**
Representation and Presidential primaries: the Democratic Party in the post
reform era / James I. Lengle. — Westport, Conn.: Greenwood Press, 1981. xi,
131 p.; ill.; 24 cm. — (Contributions in political science. no. 57 0147-1066)
Includes index. 1. Democratic Party (U.S.) 2. Primaries — United States.
3. Representative government and representation — United States.
4. Presidents — United States — Nomination I. T. II. Series.
JK522.L46     324.2736 19     *LC* 80-1791     *ISBN* 031322482X

**Ceaser, James W.**           **4.7947**
Presidential selection: theory and development / James W. Ceaser. —
Princeton, N.J.: Princeton University Press, c1979. xiv, 371 p.; 23 cm. Based on
the author's thesis, Harvard, 1977. Includes index. 1. Presidents — United
States — Election — History. 2. Presidents — United States — Nomination —
History. 3. Political science — United States — History. I. T.
JK524.C4     329/.00973     *LC* 78-70282     *ISBN* 0691076022

**Elections Research Center (Governmental Affairs Institute)**    • **4.7948**
America at the polls: a handbook of American presidential election statistics,
1920–1964 / compiled and edited by Richard M. Scammon. — Pittsburgh:
University of Pittsburgh Press, 1965. 521 p. 29 cm. 1. Presidents — United
States — Election — Statistics. I. Scammon, Richard M. ed. II. T.
JK524.G6     324.202173 19     *LC* 65-27801

**Heale, M. J.**           **4.7949**
The presidential quest: candidates and images in American political culture,
1787–1852 / M.J. Heale. — London; New York: Longman, 1982. xi, 268 p.; 22
cm. 1. Presidents — United States — Election — History. I. T.
JK524.H39 1982     324.973/05 19     *LC* 81-8415     *ISBN* 0582295424

**Jamieson, Kathleen Hall.**           **4.7950**
Packaging the presidency: a history and criticism of presidential campaign
advertising / Kathleen Hall Jamieson. — New York: Oxford University Press,
1984. xiii, 505 p.; ill.; 25 cm. Includes index. 1. Presidents — United States —
Election 2. Advertising, Political — United States. 3. United States — Politics
and government — 1945- I. T.
JK524.J36 1984     324.973/092 19     *LC* 84-7134     *ISBN* 0195035046

**Kelley, Stanley.**           **4.7951**
Interpreting elections / by Stanley Kelley, Jr. — Princeton, N.J.: Princeton
University Press, c1983. xv, 267 p.: ill.; 23 cm. 1. Presidents — United States —
Election 2. Elections — United States 3. Voting research — United States.
4. United States — Politics and government — 1945- I. T.
JK524.K34 1983     324.973/092 19     *LC* 82-25184     *ISBN*
0691076545

**Key, V. O. (Valdimer Orlando), 1908-1963.**           • **4.7952**
The responsible electorate; rationality in presidential voting, 1936–1960 [by] V.
O. Key, Jr., with the assistance of Milton C. Cummings, Jr. Foreword by
Arthur Maass. Cambridge, Belknap Press of Harvard University Press, 1966.
xxi, 158 p. port. 22 cm. 1. Presidents — United States — Election 2. United
States — Politics and government — 1933-1953 3. United States — Politics
and government — 1953-1961 I. Cummings, Milton C. II. T.
JK524.K4     324.20973     *LC* 66-13181

**Lazarsfeld, Paul Felix.**           • **4.7953**
The people's choice: how the voter makes up his mind in a presidential
campaign, by Paul F. Lazarsfeld, Bernard Berelson and Hazel Gaudet. — [2d
ed.]. — New York, Columbia University Press, 1948. xxxiii, 178 p. diagrs. 28
cm. Bibliographical references included in 'Footnotes' (p. 159-173) 1. Voting
2. Presidents — U.S. — Election. 3. Political parties — U.S. I. Berelson,
Bernard, 1912- joint author. II. Gaudet, Hazel. joint author. III. T.
JK524.L38 1948     324.73     *LC* 48-8605 *

**Monroe, Kristen R., 1946-.**           **4.7954**
Presidential popularity and the economy / Kristen Renwick Monroe. — New
York: Praeger, 1984. xxiii, 289 p.; 25 cm. Includes index. 1. Presidents —
United States — Election 2. Elections — United States 3. Public opinion —
United States. 4. United States — Economic conditions — 1945- — Public
opinion. I. T.
JK524.M66 1984     324.973/092 19     *LC* 83-13943     *ISBN*
0030635667

**Page, Benjamin I.**           **4.7955**
Choices and echoes in Presidential elections: rational man and electoral
democracy / Benjamin I. Page. — Chicago: University of Chicago Press, c1978.
xvi, 336 p.: ill.; 24 cm. 1. Presidents — United States — Election 2. Voting —
United States. I. T.
JK524.P33     329/.00973     *LC* 78-4997     *ISBN* 0226644707

**The Past and future of Presidential debates / edited by Austin**   **4.7956**
**Ranney.**
Washington: American Enterprise Institute for Public Policy Research, c1979.
226 p.; 23 cm. — (AEI studies; 228) 1. Presidents — United States — Election
— 1960. 2. Presidents — United States — Election — 1976. 3. Television in
politics — United States 4. Campaign debates — United States. I. Ranney,
Austin.
JK524.P36     329/.023/73092     *LC* 78-26778     *ISBN* 084473330X

**Peel, Roy Victor, 1896-.**           • **4.7957**
The 1932 campaign: an analysis / by Roy V. Peel and Thomas C. Donnelly. —
New York: Farrar & Rinehart, 1935. viii, 242 p.; 20 cm. Maps on lining-papers.
1. Presidents — United States — Election — 1932. 2. Politics, Practical
3. New Deal, 1933-1939 4. United States — Politics and government —
1929-1933 I. Donnelly, Thomas C. (Thomas Claude), 1905- joint author.
II. T.
JK526 1932.P432     329/.023/730916     *LC* 35-7208

**Berelson, Bernard, 1912-.**           • **4.7958**
Voting: a study of opinion formation in a presidential campaign / [by] Bernard
R. Berelson, Paul F. Lazarsfeld [and] William N. McPhee. — [Chicago]:
University of Chicago Press [1954] xix, 395 p.: ill.; 24 cm. 1. Voting — United
States. 2. Presidents — United States — Election — 1948. 3. Elections —
United States — Case studies. I. T.
JK526 1948.B4     324.73     *LC* 54-11205

**Mosteller, Frederick, 1916-.**           **4.7959**
The pre-election polls of 1948; report to the Committee on Analysis of Pre-
election Polls and Forecasts, by Frederick Mosteller [and others] with the
collaboration of Leonard W. Doob [and others] New York, Social Science
Research Council, 1949. xx, 396 p. illus. (Bulletin (Social Science Research
Council (U.S.)) 60) 'Appendix A: Report of the Committee on Analysis of Pre-
election Polls and Forecasts': p. 290-315. 1. Public opinion polls 2. United
States — Presidents — Election I. Social Science Research Council.
Committee on Analysis of Pre-election Polls and Forecasts II. T. III. Series.
JK526 1948.M6     *LC* 49-11319

**The Election of 1976: reports and interpretations / Gerald M.**    **4.7960**
**Pomper ... [et al.]; Marlene M. Pomper, editor.**
New York: D. McKay Co., c1977. viii, 184 p.: ill.; 24 cm. 1. Presidents —
United States — Election — 1976 — Addresses, essays, lectures. 2. Elections
— United States — Addresses, essays, lectures. I. Pomper, Gerald M.
JK526 1976.E37     329/.023/730925     *LC* 77-1488    *ISBN*
0679303375

**Patterson, Thomas E.**    **4.7961**
The mass media election: how Americans choose their president / Thomas E.
Patterson; sponsored by the Committee on Mass Communications and Political
Behavior of the Social Science Research Council. — New York: Praeger, 1980.
xvi, 203 p.; 25 cm. (American political parties and elections.) 'Copublished with
the Eagleton Institute of Politics, Rutgers University.' Includes index.
1. Presidents — United States — Election — 1976. 2. Mass media — Political
aspects — United States. I. Social Science Research Council (U.S.). Committee
on Mass Communications and Political Behavior. II. T. III. Series.
JK526 1976.P37     324.7/3/0973     *LC* 80-15986    *ISBN* 0030577292

**The Election of 1980: reports and interpretations / Gerald M.**    **4.7962**
**Pomper ... [et al.]; Marlene Michels Pomper, editor.**
Chatham, N.J.: Chatham House Publishers, c1981. viii, 199 p.; 24 cm.
1. Presidents — United States — Election — 1980 — Addresses, essays,
lectures. I. Pomper, Gerald M.
JK526 1980.E43     324.973/0926 19     *LC* 81-598    *ISBN* 0934540101

**The Election of 1984: reports and interpretations / Gerald M.**    **4.7963**
**Pomper ... [et al.].**
Chatham, N.J.: Chatham House Publishers, c1985. 197 p. 1. United States.
Congress — Elections, 1984 — Addresses, essays, lectures. 2. Presidents —
United States — Election — 1984 — Addresses, essays, lectures. 3. Elections
— United States — Addresses, essays, lectures. I. Pomper, Gerald M.
JK526 1984d     324.973/0927 19     *LC* 85-4223    *ISBN* 093454042X

**Best, Judith.**    **4.7964**
The case against direct election of the President: a defense of the Electoral
College / by Judith Best. — Ithaca: Cornell University Press, 1975. 235 p.; 21
cm. Includes index. 1. Presidents — United States — Election I. T.
JK528.B44 1975     324/.21     *LC* 74-25366    *ISBN* 0801409160

**Brams, Steven J.**    **4.7965**
The Presidential election game / Steven J. Brams. — New Haven: Yale
University Press, 1978. xix, 242 p.: graphs; 22 cm. 1. Presidents — United
States — Election 2. Political games I. T.
JK528.B73     329/.00973     *LC* 78-5815    *ISBN* 0300022549

**Matthews, Donald R.**    **4.7966**
Perspectives on presidential selection. Donald R. Matthews, editor. —
Washington: Brookings Institution, [1973] xii, 246 p.: illus.; 24 cm. — (Studies
in presidential selection) 1. Presidents — United States — Election
2. Presidents — Election I. T. II. Series.
JK528.M33     329/.022     *LC* 73-1078    *ISBN* 0815755082

**Polsby, Nelson W.**    **4.7967**
Presidential elections: strategies of American electoral politics / Nelson W.
Polsby, Aaron Wildavsky. — 6th ed. — New York: Scribner, c1984. xv, 361 p.:
ill.; 23 cm. 1. Presidents — United States — Election I. Wildavsky, Aaron B.
II. T.
JK528.P63 1984     324.973 19     *LC* 83-16410    *ISBN* 0684179911

## *JK558–595 Powers*

**Franck, Thomas M.**    **4.7968**
Foreign policy by Congress / Thomas M. Franck, Edward Weisband. — New
York: Oxford University Press, 1979. ix, 357 p.; 24 cm. 1. United States.
Congress — Powers and duties 2. Executive power — United States 3. United
States — Foreign relations I. Weisband, Edward, 1939- joint author. II. T.
JK573 1979.F7     328.73/07/46     *LC* 79-14857    *ISBN* 0195026357

**Arnold, R. Douglas, 1950-.**    **4.7969**
Congress and the bureaucracy: a theory of influence / R. Douglas Arnold. —
New Haven: Yale University Press, 1979. xiii, 235 p.: graphs; 22 cm. — (Yale
studies in political science. 28) 1. United States. Congress. 2. Government
spending policy — United States 3. Administrative agencies — United States
— Management. 4. Public administration — Decision making I. T. II. Series.
JK585.A78     353.007/21     *LC* 78-65493    *ISBN* 0300023456

**Both ends of the avenue: the presidency, the executive branch,**    **4.7970**
**and Congress in the 1980s / edited by Anthony King.**
Washington: American Enterprise Institute for Public Policy Research, c1983.
273 p.; 23 cm. — (Studies in political and social processes.) (AEI studies. 361)
1. United States. Congress. 2. Presidents — United States I. King, Anthony
Stephen. II. American Enterprise Institute for Public Policy Research.
III. Series. IV. Series: AEI studies. 361
JK585.B55 1983     353.03/72 19     *LC* 82-20706    *ISBN* 0844734977

## JK609.5 Vice President

**Goldstein, Joel K. (Joel Kramer), 1953-.**    **4.7971**
The modern American vice presidency: the transformation of a political
institution / Joel K. Goldstein. — Princeton, N.J.: Princeton University Press,
c1982. xii, 409 p.; 23 cm. Includes index. 1. Vice-Presidents — United States
I. T.
JK609.5.G64 1982     353.03/18 19     *LC* 81-47918    *ISBN* 0691076367

**Light, Paul Charles.**    **4.7972**
Vice–presidential power: advice and influence in the White House / Paul C.
Light. — Baltimore: Johns Hopkins University Press, c1984. vii, 278 p.: ill.; 24
cm. Includes index. 1. Vice-Presidents — United States I. T.
JK609.5.L53 1984     353.03/18 19     *LC* 83-48050    *ISBN* 0801830583

## JK611–616 The Cabinet

**Fenno, Richard F., 1926-.**    • **4.7973**
President's Cabinet: an analysis in the period from Wilson to Eisenhower. —
Cambridge, Mass.: Harvard U.P., 1959. 327 p. — (Harvard political studies)
1. Cabinet officers — United States. I. T. II. Series.
JK611.F4     353.05     *LC* 59-9272

## JK631–900 Executive Departments. Civil Service

**United States. Commission on Organization of the Executive**    • **4.7974**
**Branch of the Government (1947-1949)**
The Hoover Commission report on organization of the Executive Branch of the
Government. Westport, Conn., Greenwood Press [1970] xvi, 524 p. illus. 23
cm. Reprint of the 1949 ed. 1. United States — Executive departments —
Reorganization. I. Hoover, Herbert, 1874-1964. II. T.
JK643.C47 A553 1970     353/.03     *LC* 75-109978    *ISBN* 0837144841

**Van Riper, Paul P.**    • **4.7975**
History of the United States civil service. Evanston, Ill.: Row, Peterson [1958]
588 p.: ill.; 24 cm. 1. Civil service — United States — History I. T.
JK681 V3     *LC* 58-5927

**Crenson, Matthew A., 1943-.**    **4.7976**
The Federal machine: beginnings of bureaucracy in Jacksonian America /
Matthew A. Crenson. — Baltimore: Johns Hopkins University Press, [1975] xii,
186 p.; 23 cm. Includes index. 1. United States — Executive departments —
History. 2. United States — Politics and government — 1829-1837 3. United
States — Social conditions — To 1865 I. T.
JK686.C74     353/.0009/034     *LC* 74-6818    *ISBN* 080181586X

**American Assembly.**    • **4.7977**
The Federal Government service. [Edited by Wallace S. Sayre. 2d ed.]
Englewood Cliffs, N.J., Prentice-Hall [1965] viii, 245 p. (A Spectrum book, S-
AA-14) Originally served as source material for participants in the Sixth
American Assembly at Arden House, Harriman, N.Y. 1. Civil service —
United States I. Sayre, Wallace Stanley, 1905-1972. II. T.
JK691 A52 1965     *LC* 65-20600

**Karl, Barry Dean.**    • **4.7978**
Executive reorganization and reform in the New Deal, the genesis of
administrative management, 1900–1939. Cambridge, Mass.: Harvard
University Press, 1963. 292 p.; 22 cm. 1. Roosevelt, Franklin D. (Franklin
Delano), 1882-1945. 2. United States — Executive departments I. T.
JK691 K35     *LC* 63-13813

**Mosher, Frederick C.**    • **4.7979**
Democracy and the public service [by] Frederick C. Mosher. — New York:
Oxford University Press, 1968. xii, 219 p.; 22 cm. — (Public administration and
democracy) 1. Civil service — United States I. T.
JK691.M65     353/.006     *LC* 68-19768

**Bernstein, Marver H.**    • **4.7980**
The job of the Federal executive. Washington, Brookings Institution [1958]
241 p. 1. Executives — United States 2. United States — Officials and
employees I. T.
JK723 E9 B4     *LC* 58-14472

**Heclo, Hugh.**    **4.7981**
A government of strangers: executive politics in Washington / Hugh Heclo. —
Washington: Brookings Institution, c1977. xvi, 272 p.; 24 cm. 1. Government
executives — United States. 2. Patronage, Political — United States.
I. Brookings Institution. II. T.
JK723.E9 H36     301.5/92/0973     *LC* 76-51882    *ISBN* 0815735367.
*ISBN* 0815735359 pbk

**Kaufman, Herbert, 1922-.**      **4.7982**
The administrative behavior of federal bureau chiefs / Herbert Kaufman. — Washington, D.C.: Brookings Institution, c1981. xii, 220 p.; 24 cm. Includes index. 1. Government executives — United States. I. T.
JK723.E9 K38     353.04 19     *LC* 81-10128     *ISBN* 0815748442

**Schott, Richard L.**      **4.7983**
People, positions, and power: the political appointments of Lyndon Johnson / Richard L. Schott and Dagmar S. Hamilton. — Chicago: University of Chicago Press, c1983. x, 245 p.; 24 cm. — (Administrative history of the Johnson presidency.) 1. Cabinet officers — United States — Appointment, qualifications,tenure, etc. 2. Government executives — United States — Appointment, qualifications, tenure, etc. 3. United States — Officials and employees — Selection and appointment 4. United States — Politics and government — 1963-1969 I. Hamilton, Dagmar S. II. T. III. Series.
JK731.S36 1983     353/.03/2 19     *LC* 83-4814     *ISBN* 0226740161

**Macy, John W., 1917-.**      **4.7984**
America's unelected government: appointing the president's team / John W. Macy, Bruce Adams, J. Jackson Walter; senior consultant, G. Calvin Mackenzie. — Cambridge, Mass.: Ballinger Pub. Co., c1983. xvi, 128 p.; 24 cm. At head of title: National Institute of Public Affairs. 'A National Academy of Public Administration book.' Includes index. 1. Government executives — United States — Appointment, qualifications, tenure, etc. 2. Presidents — United States — Staff 3. United States — Officials and employees — Selection and appointment I. Adams, Bruce, 1947- II. Walter, J. Jackson, 1940- III. National Institute of Public Affairs (U.S.) IV. T.
JK736.M335 1983     353.03/2 19     *LC* 83-15540     *ISBN* 088410964X

**Lee, Robert D.**      **4.7985**
Public personnel systems / by Robert D. Lee, Jr. — Baltimore: University Park Press, c1979. xv, 434 p.; 24 cm. Includes index. 1. Civil service — United States 2. Civil service — United States — States 3. Local officials and employees — United States. 4. Personnel management — United States. I. T.
JK765.L43     353.006     *LC* 79-12468     *ISBN* 0839114524

**Hartman, Robert W.**      **4.7986**
Pay and pensions for federal workers / Robert W. Hartman. — Washington, D.C.: Brookings Institution, c1983. ix, 118 p.: ill.; 24 cm. 1. United States — Officials and employees — Pensions 2. United States — Officials and employees — Salaries, etc. I. T.
JK776.H36 1983     353.001/23 19     *LC* 82-45980     *ISBN* 0815734964

**Informing the people: a public affairs handbook / edited by**      **4.7987**
**Lewis M. Helm ... [et al.].**
New York: Longman, c1981. viii, 359 p.; 26 cm. — (Longman series in public communication.) Includes index. 1. Government publicity — United States. 2. Government information — United States. I. Helm, Lewis M., 1931- II. Series.
JK849.A3 I53     353.0081/9     *LC* 80-18390     *ISBN* 0582282004

**United States. Dept. of State.**      • **4.7988**
The Biographic register. Oct. 1, 1870-. Washington: U.S. Govt. Print. Off. v.: fold. maps; 24-26 cm. Annual. Registers for 1930-74 issued as Its Publications; 1950-74 also as Its Department and Foreign Service series. 1. United States. Dept. of State — Officials and Employees — Biography. I. T.
JK851.A3

**United States. Congress. Senate. Committee on Government**      **4.7989**
**Operations.**
Organizing for national security. — Washington: U.S. Govt. Print. Off., 1961. 3 v. (The American military experience) Hearings held Feb.23-Aug. 24, 1961. 1. National Security Council (U.S.) 2. United States — National security 3. United States — Executive departments 4. United States — Politics and government — 1945- I. T.
JK870.N3U6x     353.04     *LC* 78-22404     *ISBN* 0405118791

### JK901 Independent Regulatory Commissions

**Welborn, David M., 1934-.**      **4.7990**
Governance of Federal regulatory agencies / by David M. Welborn. — 1st ed. — Knoxville: University of Tennessee Press, c1977. viii, 179 p.; 24 cm. Includes index. 1. Independent regulatory commissions — United States. I. T.
JK901.W4     353.09/1     *LC* 77-8012     *ISBN* 0870492160

### JK1000–1447 CONGRESS

**United States. Congress.**      • **4.7991**
Biographical directory of the American Congress, 1774–1971, the Continental Congress, September 5, 1774, to October 21, 1788, and the Congress of the United States, from the First through the Ninety-first Congress, March 4, 1789, to January 3, 1971, inclusive. — [Washington]: U.S. Govt. Print. Off., 1971. 1972 p.; 30 cm. — (92d Congress, 1st session. Senate document; no. 92-8) 'Lawrence F. Kennedy, chief compiler.' 1. United States. Continental Congress

— Biography. 2. United States. Congress — Biography 3. United States — Biography — Dictionaries. I. Kennedy, Lawrence F., comp. II. T.
JK1010.A5 1971     328.73/0922 [B]     *LC* 79-616224

**Politics in America: members of Congress in Washington and at**      **4.7992** [*Ref.*]
**home / Alan Ehrenhalt, editor; Renee Amrine, associate editor.**      *JK 1010 P64 1985*
Washington, D.C.: CQ Press, c1985. xx, 1,758 p.: ill.; 24 cm. Includes index. 1. United States. Congress — Biography 2. United States. Congress — Committees 3. Election districts — United States — Handbooks, manuals, etc. I. Ehrenhalt, Alan, 1947- II. Amrine, Renee. III. Congressional Quarterly, inc.
JK1010.P64 1985     328.73/073/025 19     *LC* 85-12777     *ISBN* 0871873753

**United States. Congress.**      • **4.7993**
Official congressional directory. Washington: U.S. Govt. Print. Off. [etc.] v.: ill.; 15-24 cm. Title varies:     -49th Cong., Congressional directory. Directories for some sessions issued in revised editions. Includes Directory of Congress, and Department and congressional directory. 1. United States. Congress — Registers 2. United States. Congress — Biography 3. Political science — Directories I. T. II. Title: Congressional directory.
JK1011.A318     *LC* 06-35330 REV

**United States. Congress.**      **4.7994**
[Official Congressional Directory] The United States Congressional Directories, 1789–1840. Edited by Perry M. Goldman & James S. Young. New York, Columbia University Press, 1973. 417 p. 23 cm. 1. United States. Congress — Registers I. Goldman, Perry M., ed. II. Young, James Sterling. ed. III. T.
JK1011.U53     328.73/0025     *LC* 73-15907     *ISBN* 0231033656

**The Almanac of American politics.**      **4.7995**
1972-. Washington, D.C. [etc.] Barone & Co. [etc.] v. ill. 22 cm. (A Sunrise book) Biennial. 1. United States. Congress — Biography 2. United States. Congress — Committees 3. Election districts — United States — Handbooks, manuals, etc. I. Barone, Michael. II. Ujifusa, Grant. III. Matthews, Douglas.
JK1012.A44     328.73/005     *LC* 70-160417

**Congressional staff directory.**      • **4.7996**
1959-. Mount Vernon, Va. [etc.] Congressional Staff Directory [etc.] v. 24 cm. Annual. 1. United States. Congress — Directories 2. United States. Congress — Biography — Periodicals. I. Brownson, Charles Bruce, 1914- ed.
JK1012.C65     328.738     *LC* 59-13987

### JK1021–1059 History

**Congressional Quarterly's Guide to Congress.**      **4.7997**
3rd ed. — Washington, DC: Congressional Quarterly Inc., c1982. xx, 1185 p.: ill.; 29 cm. 1. United States. Congress. I. Congressional Quarterly, inc. II. Title: Guide to Congress.
JK1021.C565 1982     328.73 19     *LC* 82-14148     *ISBN* 0871872390

**Fenno, Richard F., 1926-.**      **4.7998**
Congressmen in committees / Richard F. Fenno, Jr. — Boston, Mass.: Little, Brown, 1973. xvii, 302 p.: tables; 22 cm. — (Study of congress series) 1. United States. Congress — Committees 2. Legislators — United States I. T. II. Series.
JK1029.F4     *LC* 72-13634

**Unekis, Joseph K.**      **4.7999**
Congressional committee politics: continuity and change / Joseph K. Unekis and Leroy N. Rieselbach. — New York: Praeger, 1984. 305 p.: ill. Includes index. 1. United States. Congress — Committees I. Rieselbach, Leroy N. II. T.
JK1029.U53 1984     328.73/0765 19     *LC* 84-2141     *ISBN* 0030713331

**The New Congress / edited by Thomas E. Mann and Norman J.**      **4.8000**
**Ornstein.**
Washington: American Enterprise Institute for Public Policy Research, c1981. 400 p.; 23 cm. — (AEI studies; 305) 1. United States. Congress — Addresses, essays, lectures. I. Mann, Thomas E. II. Ornstein, Norman J.
JK1041.N48     328.73 19     *LC* 80-25724     *ISBN* 0844734152

**Vital statistics on Congress / Norman J. Ornstein ... [et al.];**      **4.8001**
**foreword by Richard F. Fenno, Jr.**
1984-1985 ed. — Washington: American Enterprise Institute for Public Policy Research, c1984. xxiii, 261 p.: ill.; 23 cm. — (AEI studies. 410) (American Enterprise Institute studies in political and social processes) Second updated ed. of: Vital statistics on Congress, 1980 / John F. Bibby, Thomas E. Mann, Norman J. Ornstein, c1980. 1. United States. Congress — Statistics. I. Ornstein, Norman J. II. Bibby, John F. Vital statistics on Congress, 1980. III. American Enterprise Institute for Public Policy Research. IV. Series.
JK1041.V58 1984     328.73/00212 19     *LC* 84-20401     *ISBN* 0844735647

**Bibby, John F.**      **4.8002**
On Capitol Hill; studies in the legislative process [by] John F. Bibby [and] Roger H. Davidson. — 2d ed. — Hinsdale, Ill.: Dryden Press, [1972] xii, 300 p.; 23 cm. 1. Legislators — United States — Case studies. I. Davidson, Roger H. joint author. II. T.
JK1051.B5 1972     328.73     *LC* 72-81201     *ISBN* 0030852846

**Mayhew, David R.**      **4.8003**
Party loyalty among congressmen: the difference between Democrats and Republicans, 1947–1962 / [by] David R. Mayhew. — Cambridge: Harvard University Press, 1966. xiv, 189 p.; ill.; 22 cm. — (Harvard political studies) 1. Legislators — United States 2. Party discipline — United States. 3. United States — Politics and government — 1945- I. T. II. Series.
JK1051.M3     329     *LC* 66-21341

**Orfield, Gary.**      **4.8004**
Congressional power: Congress and social change / Gary Orfield; under the general editorship of James David Barber. — New York: Harcourt Brace Jovanovich, [1975] xii, 339 p.; 22 cm. 1. United States. Congress. 2. Legislative power — United States 3. United States — Politics and government — 1945- 4. United States — Social policy I. T.
JK1051.O73     328.73     *LC* 74-23945     *ISBN* 0155130811

**Schneider, Jerrold E.**      **4.8005**
Ideological coalitions in Congress / Jerrold E. Schneider. — Westport, Conn.: Greenwood Press, 1979. xvi, 270 p.; 24 cm. — (Contributions in political science. no. 16 0147-1066) Includes indexes. 1. United States. Congress — Voting. 2. Coalition (Social sciences) 3. Ideology I. T. II. Series.
JK1051.S46     328.73/07/75     *LC* 78-4019     *ISBN* 0313204101

**Shelley, Mack C., 1950-.**      **4.8006**
The permanent majority: the conservative coalition in the United States Congress / Mack C. Shelley II. — University, Ala.: University of Alabama Press, c1983. xiv, 201 p.; 25 cm. Includes index. 1. United States. Congress — Voting — History. 2. Conservatism — United States — History. 3. United States — Politics and government — 1945- 4. United States — Politics and government — 1933-1945 I. T.
JK1051.S56 1983     328.73/0775 19     *LC* 82-16055     *ISBN* 0817301372

## JK1061–1083 Constitution. Powers

**Bailey, Stephen Kemp.**      • **4.8007**
Congress at work / Stephen K. Bailey [and] Howard D. Samuel. — Hamden, Conn.: Archon Books, 1965,[c1952]. x, 502 p.: ill.; 22 cm. — 1. United States. Congress. I. Samuel, Howard D. II. T.
JK1061.B3 1965     328.73     *LC* 65-15011

**Congress reconsidered / edited by Lawrence C. Dodd and Bruce**      **4.8008**
**I. Oppenheimer.**
2d ed. — Washington, D.C.: Congressional Quarterly Press, c1981. x, 442 p.; 23 cm. — (Politics and public policy series.) Includes index. 1. United States. Congress — Addresses, essays, lectures. I. Dodd, Lawrence C., 1946- II. Oppenheimer, Bruce Ian. III. Series.
JK1061.C587 1981     328.73 19     *LC* 80-39915     *ISBN* 0871871629

**Davidson, Roger H.**      **4.8009**
Congress and its members / Roger H. Davidson, Walter J. Oleszek. — Washington, D.C.: Congressional Quarterly Press, c1981. xvi, 470 p.: ill.; 23 cm. — (Politics and public policy series.) Includes index. 1. United States. Congress. 2. Legislators — United States I. Oleszek, Walter J. II. T. III. Series.
JK1061.D29     328.73 19     *LC* 81-5446     *ISBN* 0871872021

**Galloway, George Barnes, 1898-.**      **4.8010**
Congress at the crossroads / by George B. Galloway. — New York, Thomas Y. Crowell company [1946] ix, 374 p. incl. tables, diagrs. 22 cm. 1. United States. Congress. I. T.
JK1061.G3     328.73     *LC* 46-7851

**Galloway, George Barnes, 1898-.**      • **4.8011**
The legislative process in Congress. — New York, Crowell [1962] xii, 689 p. 2 diagrs. (on lining paper) 22 cm. 'In a sense ... a successor to, rather than a revision of,' the author's Congress at the crossroads. Includes bibliographies. 1. United States. Congress. 2. Legislation — U.S. 3. Legislative power — U.S. I. T.
JK1061.G32     328.73     *LC* 53-11621

**Huitt, Ralph K.**      • **4.8012**
Congress; two decades of analysis [by] Ralph K. Huitt [and] Robert L. Peabody. — New York: Harper & Row, [1969] xi, 241 p.; 24 cm. — (Harper's American political behavior series) 1. U.S. Congress. I. Peabody, Robert L. joint author. II. T.
JK1061.H83     328.73/07     *LC* 69-11945

**Jones, Charles O.**      **4.8013**
The United States Congress: people, place, and policy / Charles O. Jones. — Homewood, Ill.: Dorsey Press; Georgetown, Ont.: Irwin-Dorsey, 1982. xxi, 477 p.: ill.; 25 cm. — (Dorsey series in political science.) Includes index. 1. United States. Congress. I. T. II. Series.
JK1061.J64     328.73 19     *LC* 81-68064     *ISBN* 0256026637

**Polsby, Nelson W. comp.**      **4.8014**
Congressional behavior. Edited by Nelson W. Polsby. — [1st ed.]. — New York: Random House, [1971] xii, 269 p.; illus.; 25 cm. 1. U.S. Congress — Addresses, essays, lectures. I. T.
JK1061.P62     328.73     *LC* 70-122483     *ISBN* 0394310233

**Powers of Congress.**      **4.8015**
2nd ed. — [Washington, D.C.]: Congressional Quarterly, Inc., c1982. vi, 380 p.: ill.; 23 cm. Includes index. 1. United States. Congress — Powers and duties I. Congressional Quarterly, inc.
JK1061.P68 1982     328.73/074 19     *LC* 82-14331     *ISBN* 0871872420

**Studies of Congress / edited by Glenn R. Parker.**      **4.8016**
Washington, D.C.: CQ Press, c1985. xv, 570 p.: ill.; 23 cm. Includes index. 1. United States. Congress — Addresses, essays, lectures. I. Parker, Glenn R. II. Congressional Quarterly, inc.
JK1061.S78 1985     328.73 19     *LC* 84-16993     *ISBN* 0871873338

**Sundquist, James L.**      **4.8017**
The decline and resurgence of Congress / James L. Sundquist. — Washington, D.C.: Brookings Institution, c1981. xi, 500 p.; 24 cm. 1. United States. Congress. 2. United States — Politics and government — 20th century I. T.
JK1061.S93     328.73     *LC* 81-66191     *ISBN* 0815782241

**Truman, David Bicknell, 1913-.**      • **4.8018**
The Congressional party: a case study. — New York: Wiley [1959] xii, 336 p.: diagrs., tables; 24 cm. 1. United States. Congress — Case studies 2. United States. 81st Cong., 1949-1951 3. Political parties — United States I. T.
JK1061 T7     *LC* 59-13030

**Vogler, David J.**      **4.8019**
The politics of Congress / David J. Vogler. — 4th ed. — Boston: Allyn and Bacon, c1983. x, 325 p.; 22 cm. 1. United States. Congress. I. T.
JK1061.V63 1983     328.73 19     *LC* 82-24499     *ISBN* 0205079792

**Wilson, Woodrow, 1856-1924.**      • **4.8020**
Congressional government; a study in American politics. Introd. by Walter Lippmann. New York, Meridian Books, 1956. 222 p. (Meridian books, M27) 1. United States. Congress. 2. United States — Politics & government I. T.
JK1061 W54     *LC* 56-6567

**Young, Roland Arnold, 1910-.**      • **4.8021**
The American Congress. New York, Harper & Row [1958] 333 p. 1. United States. Congress. I. T.
JK1061 Y67     *LC* 58-5081

**Jacobson, Gary C.**      **4.8022**
Strategy and choice in congressional elections / Gary C. Jacobson and Samuel Kernell. — New Haven: Yale University Press, c1981. xiii, 111 p.: graphs; 22 cm. 1. United States. Congress — Elections 2. Voting — United States. 3. Politics, Practical 4. Political psychology I. Kernell, Samuel, 1945- II. T.
JK1067.J32     324.7/2/0973 19     *LC* 81-40439     *ISBN* 0300026900

**Mayhew, David R.**      **4.8023**
Congress: the electoral connection / David R. Mayhew. — New Haven: Yale University Press, 1974. vii, 194 p.: diagr.; 21 cm. (Yale studies in political science. 26) 1. United States. Congress — Elections 2. United States. Congress. I. T. II. Series.
JK1067.M3     329     *LC* 74-78471     *ISBN* 0300017774

**Reid, T. R.**      **4.8024**
Congressional odyssey: the saga of a Senate bill / T. R. Reid. — San Francisco: W. H. Freeman, c1980. xi, 140 p., [4] leaves of plates: ill.; 24 cm. Includes index. 1. United States. Congress. 2. Legislation — United States I. T.
JK1067.R44     328.73/077     *LC* 80-10108     *ISBN* 0716711710

**Fiorina, Morris P.**      **4.8025**
Congress, keystone of the Washington establishment / Morris P. Fiorina. New Haven: Yale University Press, 1977. xi, 105 p.: ill.; 21 cm. (A Yale fastback; 18) 1. United States. Congress. 2. Administrative agencies — United States. 3. Representative government and representation — United States. I. T.
JK1071.F55     328.73     *LC* 76-54606     *ISBN* 0300021321

**Johannes, John R., 1943-.**      **4.8026**
To serve the people: Congress and constituency service / John R. Johannes. — Lincoln: University of Nebraska Press, c1984. xv, 294 p.; 23 cm. Includes index.

1. United States. Congress. 2. Representative government and representation — United States. I. T. II. Title: Constituency service.
JK1071.J63 1984    328/.331/0973 19    LC 83-17050    ISBN 080322561X

**Fenno, Richard F., 1926-.**    • 4.8027
The power of the purse: appropriations politics in Congress / [by] Richard F. Fenno, Jr. — Boston: Little, Brown, [1966] xxix, 704 p.; 24 cm. 1. United States. Congress. House. Committee on Appropriations. 2. United States. Congress. Senate. Committee on Appropriations. I. T.
JK1074.F4    328.365    LC 66-22957

**Dahl, Robert Alan, 1915-.**    • 4.8028
Congress and foreign policy. [1st ed.] New York, Harcourt, Brace [1950] x, 305 p. Half title: Institute of International Studies, Yale University. 1. United States. Congress. 2. United States — Foreign relations I. Yale University. Institute of International Studies. II. T.
JK1081 D35    LC 50-8588

**Fox, Harrison W.**    4.8029
Congressional staffs: the invisible force in American lawmaking / Harrison W. Fox, Jr. and Susan Webb Hammond. — New York: The Free Press, c1977. xiv, 227 p.; 25 cm. Includes index. 1. United States. Congress — Officials and employees I. Hammond, Susan Webb, joint author. II. T.
JK1083.F68    328.73/07/6    LC 77-72041    ISBN 0029104203

**Malbin, Michael J.**    4.8030
Unelected representatives: Congressional staff and the future of representative government / Michael J. Malbin. — New York: Basic Books, c1980. viii, 279 p.; 25 cm. 1. United States. Congress — Officials and employees 2. Representative government and representation — United States. I. T.
JK1083.M34    328.73/0761    LC 79-3127    ISBN 046508866X

## JK1091–1128 Procedures. Lobbying

**Froman, Lewis Acrelius, 1935-.**    4.8031
The congressional process: strategies, rules, and procedures / by Lewis A. Froman, Jr. — Boston: Little, Brown, [1967] xvii, 221 p.; 22 cm. — (The Study of Congress series) 1. United States. Congress — Rules and practice I. T. II. Series.
JK1096.F7    328.73/05    LC 67-18261

**Gross, Bertram Myron, 1912-.**    • 4.8032
The legislative struggle: a study in social combat. — New York: McGraw-Hill, 1953. xviii, 472 p.; 24 cm. — (McGraw-Hill series in political science) Bibliographical footnotes. 1. United States. Congress. 2. Legislation — U.S. I. T.
JK1096.G7    328.73    LC 52-11509

**Oleszek, Walter J.**    4.8033
Congressional procedures and the policy process / Walter J. Oleszek. — Washington: Congressional Quarterly Press, c1978. xv, 256 p.; 21 cm. — (Politics and public policy series) Includes index. 1. United States. Congress. I. T.
JK1096.O43    328.73    LC 78-17372    ISBN 0871871531

**Ornstein, Norman J.**    4.8034
Congress in change: evolution and reform / edited by Norman J. Ornstein. — New York: Praeger, 1975. xii, 298 p.: ill.; 22 cm. 1. United States. Congress — Addresses, essays, lectures. I. T.
JK1096.O74    328.73    LC 73-10268    ISBN 0275100502

**Berry, Jeffrey M., 1948-.**    4.8035
Lobbying for the people: the political behavior of public interest groups / Jeffrey M. Berry. — Princeton, N.J.: Princeton University Press, c1977. x, 331 p.; 22 cm. Includes index. 1. Lobbying — United States. 2. Pressure groups — United States. 3. Public interest — United States. I. T.
JK1118.B4    322.4/3/0973    LC 77-71973    ISBN 0691075883

**McFarland, Andrew S., 1940-.**    4.8036
Common Cause: lobbying in the public interest / Andrew S. McFarland. — Chatham, N.J.: Chatham House Publishers, c1984. x, 212 p. — (Chatham House series on change in American politics.) 1. Common Cause (U.S.) I. T. II. Series.
JK1118.M39 1984    322.4/3/0973 19    LC 84-7732    ISBN 0934540292

**Truman, David Bicknell, 1913-.**    • 4.8037
The governmental process; political interests and public opinion. — [1st ed.] — New York: Knopf, 1951. xvi, 544, xv p.; 22 cm. — (Borzoi books in political science) 1. Lobbying — United States. 2. Public opinion — United States. I. T.
JK1118.T7    328.368    LC 51-4187

**Wilson, James Q.**    4.8038
Political organizations, by James Q. Wilson. — New York: Basic Books, [1974, c1973] 359 p.; 25 cm. 1. Lobbying — United States. 2. Pressure groups — United States. I. T.
JK1118.W54    329/.03/0973    LC 73-85991    ISBN 0465059368

**Barth, Alan.**    • 4.8039
Government by investigation / Alan Barth. — New York: Viking Press, 1955. 231 p.; 23 cm. 1. Civil rights 2. Governmental investigations I. T.
JK1123.A2 B3    328/.34    LC 55-6901

## JK1151–1274 Senate

**Rothman, David J.**    • 4.8040
Politics and power; the United States Senate, 1869–1901 [by] David J. Rothman. — Cambridge, Mass., Harvard University Press, 1966. x, 348 p. illus., group ports. 22 cm. — (A Publication of the Center for the Study of the History of Liberty in America, Harvard University) 'Bibliographical note': p. [276]-286. 1. United States. Congress. Senate. 2. U.S. — Pol. & govt. — 1865-1900. I. T.
JK1158.R65    328.73071    LC 66-13185

**Asbell, Bernard.**    4.8041
The Senate nobody knows / Bernard Asbell. — 1st ed. — Garden City, N.Y.: Doubleday, 1978. ix, 466 p.; 22 cm. Includes index. 1. Muskie, Edmund S., 1914- 2. United States. Congress. Senate. I. T.
JK1161.A9    328.73/07/1    LC 77-77646    ISBN 0385042159

**Matthews, Donald R.**    • 4.8042
U.S. Senators and their world. — Chapel Hill: University of North Carolina Press, [1960] xvi, 303 p.: diagrs., tables.; 24 cm. 1. United States. Congress. Senate. I. T.
JK1161.M35    328.73    LC 60-16299

**Ripley, Randall B.**    • 4.8043
Power in the Senate / [by] Randall B. Ripley. — New York: St. Martin's Press, [1969] vii, 246 p.: ill.; 23 cm. 'Literature on the post-1869 Senate': p. 237-239. 1. U.S. Congress. Senate. I. T.
JK1161.R55    328.73/07/1    LC 74-83407

**White, William Smith.**    • 4.8044
Citadel; the story of the U.S. Senate [by] William S. White. — Boston: Houghton Mifflin, 1968 [c1957] xi, 274 p.; 22 cm. 1. United States. Congress. Senate. I. T.
JK1161.W5 1968    328.73/07/1    LC 68-3378

**Clark, Joseph S.**    • 4.8045
The Senate establishment / by Joseph S. Clark, and other Senators; foreword by James MacGregor Burns. — [1st ed.] New York: Hill and Wang [1963] 138 p.; 21 cm. (American century series) 'AC67.' 1. United States. Congress. Senate — Committees — Seniority system — Addresses, essays, lectures. 2. United States — Politics and government — 1961-1963 — Addresses, essays, lectures. I. T.
JK1239.C55    328.73/07652 19    LC 63-19809

**Harris, Joseph Pratt, 1896-.**    • 4.8046
The advice and consent of the Senate; a study of the confirmation of appointments by the United States Senate. Berkeley, University of California Press, 1953. xii, 457 p. 25 cm. 1. United States. Congress. Senate — Rules and practice. 2. United States — Officials and employees — Selection and appointment I. T.
JK1274.H3    LC 53-11239

## JK1304–1447 House of Representatives

**Alexander, Thomas Benjamin, 1918-.**    • 4.8047
Sectional stress and party strength; a study of roll–call voting patterns in the United States House of Representatives, 1836–1860 [by] Thomas B. Alexander. Nashville, Vanderbilt University, 1967. xvii, 284 p. illus. (part col.) 29 cm. 1. United States. Congress. House. 2. Political science — Data processing 3. United States — Politics and government — 1783-1865 I. T.
JK1316.A64    328.73/07/2    LC 67-21652

**Bensel, Richard Franklin, 1949-.**    4.8048
Sectionalism and American political development, 1880–1980 / Richard Franklin Bensel. — Madison, Wis.: University of Wisconsin Press, 1984. xx, 494 p.: ill.; 24 cm. 1. United States. Congress. House — Voting — History. 2. Political parties — United States — History. 3. Sectionalism (United States) — History. 4. United States — Politics and government — 1865-1900 5. United States — Politics and government — 20th century I. T.
JK1316.B43 1984    320.973 19    LC 84-40145    ISBN 0299098303

**Galloway, George Barnes, 1898-.**                     ● **4.8049**
History of the House of Representatives / by George Galloway. — New York: Crowell [1962, c1961] xii, 334 p.: ports., diagr., tables; 24 cm. 1. United States. Congress. House. I. T.
JK1316.G2      *LC* 61-17413

**Hasbrouck, Paul De Witt, 1896-.**                     ● **4.8050**
Party government in the House of Representatives. New York, Macmillan, 1927. ix,265p. 21cm. Without thesis note. 1. United States. Congress. House. 2. Political parties — United States 3. United States — Politics and government I. T.
JK1316.H3      *LC* 27-19400

**Carroll, Holbert N.**                                 ● **4.8051**
The House of Representatives and foreign affairs. Pittsburgh, University of Pittsburgh [1958] 365 p. 24 cm. 1. United States. Congress. House. 2. United States — Foreign relations I. T.
JK1319.C3      *LC* 58-10705

**Deckard, Barbara Sinclair.**                          **4.8052**
Congressional realignment, 1925–1978 / by Barbara Sinclair. — 1st ed. — Austin: University of Texas Press, 1982. 201 p.; 24 cm. Includes index. 1. United States. Congress. House — Voting — History. 2. United States — Politics and government — 20th century I. T.
JK1319.D42 1982      328.73/0775/09 19      *LC* 82-4812      *ISBN* 0292703600

**Gertzog, Irwin N., 1933-.**                           **4.8053**
Congressional women: their recruitment, treatment, and behavior / Irwin N. Gertzog. — New York: Praeger, 1984. xiv, 290 p.; 25 cm. (Women and politics.) Includes index. 1. United States. Congress. House — History — 20th century. 2. Women legislators — United States — History — 20th century. I. T. II. Series.
JK1319.G47 1984      328.73/073/088042 19      *LC* 84-4714      *ISBN* 0030630584

**Miller, Clem, 1916-1962.**                            **4.8054**
Member of the House; letters of a Congressman. Edited, with additional text by John W. Baker. — New York: Scribner, [1962] 195 p.; 21 cm. 'The letters were written in the period of 1959 through 1961.' 1. United States. Congress. House. 2. United States — Politics and government — 1953-1961 I. T.
JK1319.M5      328.73      *LC* 62-19447

**MacRae, Duncan.**                                     **4.8055**
Dimensions of congressional voting; a statistical study of the House of Representatives in the Eighty–first Congress, by Duncan MacRae, Jr., with the collaboration of Fred H. Goldner. Berkeley, University of California Press, 1958. v, 203-390 p. diagrs., tables. (University of California publications in sociology and social institutions, v. 1, no. 3) 1. United States 81st Cong., 1949-1951. House 2. United States — Politics & government — 1945- I. T.
JK1323 1949 M25      *LC* A58-9678

**Shannon, W. Wayne.**                                  ● **4.8056**
Party, constituency, and congressional voting: a study of legislative behavior in the United States House of Representatives / [by] W. Wayne Shannon. — Baton Rouge: Louisiana State University Press [c1968] xii, 202 p.; 24 cm. (Louisiana State University studies. Social science series, no. 14) 1. United States. Congress. House — Voting. 2. United States — Politics and government — 1945- I. T. II. Series.
JK1323 1968.S5      328.73/07/2      *LC* 68-31138

**Fenno, Richard F., 1926-.**                           **4.8057**
Home style: House Members in their districts / Richard F. Fenno, Jr. — Boston: Little, Brown, c1978. xvi, 304 p.; 21 cm. 1. United States. Congress. House. 2. Legislators — United States 3. Electioneering — United States. I. T.
JK1323 1978.F46      328.73/07/3      *LC* 77-94156

**Dexter, Lewis Anthony.**                              ● **4.8058**
The sociology and politics of Congress. With a chapter by Kenneth Kerle. — Chicago: Rand McNally, [c1969] xii, 300 p.; 21 cm. — (Rand McNally political science series) 1. United States. Congress. House. 2. Elections — United States 3. Lobbying — United States. I. T.
JK1331.D47      328.73/07      *LC* 77-112043

**Jones, Charles O.**                                   ● **4.8059**
Every second year: Congressional behavior and the two–year term / [by] Charles O. Jones. — Washington: Brookings Institution [1967] xiii, 118 p.; 24 cm. 1. United States. Congress. House — Term of office. I. Brookings Institution. II. T.
JK1331.J6      328.73/072      *LC* 67-30596

**MacNeil, Neil, 1923-.**                               ● **4.8060**
Forge of democracy: the House of Representatives. — New York, D. McKay [1963] 496 p. 22 cm. Includes bibliography. 1. United States. Congress. House. I. T.
JK1331.M2      328.73      *LC* 63-11721

**Peabody, Robert L. ed.**                              **4.8061**
New perspectives on the House of Representatives / [edited by] Robert L. Peabody and Nelson W. Polsby. 3d. ed. — Chicago: Rand McNally College Pub. Co., c1977. ix, 420 p.: ill.; 23 cm. 1. United States. Congress. House. I. Polsby, Nelson W. joint ed. II. T.
JK1331.P4 1977      328.73/07/2      *LC* 76-17158      *ISBN* 0528651013

**Deckard, Barbara Sinclair.**                          **4.8062**
Majority leadership in the U.S. House / Barbara Sinclair. — Baltimore: Johns Hopkins University Press, 1984 (c1983). xiv, 263 p.; 24 cm. Includes index. 1. United States. Congress. House — Leadership. 2. Democratic Party (U.S.) I. T.
JK1411.D43 1983      328.73/0762 19      *LC* 83-278      *ISBN* 0801829348

**Davidson, Roger H.**                                  **4.8063**
Congress against itself / Roger H. Davidson and Walter J. Oleszek. Bloomington: Indiana University Press, c1977. xiii, 306 p.: ill.; 24 cm. Includes index. 1. United States. Congress. House — Committees. I. Oleszek, Walter J. joint author. II. T.
JK1429.D38 1977      328.73/07/65      *LC* 76-12378      *ISBN* 0253314054

**Manley, John F.**                                     ● **4.8064**
The politics of finance: the House Committee on Ways and Means / [by] John F. Manley. — Boston: Little, Brown, [1970] xvi, 395 p.; 22 cm. — (The Study of Congress series) 1. Mills, Wilbur Daigh, 1909- 2. U.S. Congress. House. Committee on Ways and Means. I. T. II. Series.
JK1430.W32 M33      328.73/07/65      *LC* 70-128558

JK
1430
W32
M33

## JK1511–1599 THE JUDICIARY
### (see also: KF5130, KF8700-9075)

**Frankfurter, Felix, 1882-1965.**                      ● **4.8065**
Law and politics: occasional papers, 1913–1938 / edited by Archibald MacLeish and E. F. Prichard; with a foreword by MacLeish. — New York: Harcourt, Brace, [1939] 352 p.; 22 cm. 1. Law — United States — Addresses, essays, lectures. 2. United States — Politics and government — 20th century I. MacLeish, Archibald, 1892- II. Prichard, Edward Fretwell. III. T.
JK 1521 F82 1939      *LC* 39-27861

**Grossman, Joel B.**                                   ● **4.8066**
Lawyers and judges: the ABA and the politics of judicial selection / [by] Joel B. Grossman. — New York: J. Wiley [1965] xii, 228 p.; 24 cm. 1. American Bar Association. 2. Judges — United States I. T. II. Title: The ABA and the politics of judicial selection
JK1548 J8 G7      *LC* 65-16409

**Congressional Quarterly, Inc.**                       **4.8067**
[Guide to the U.S. Supreme Court] Congressional Quarterly's Guide to the U.S. Supreme Court. — Washington: Congressional Quarterly, inc., c1979. xxii, 1022 p.: ill.; 29 cm. Includes indexes. 1. United States. Supreme Court. I. T. II. Title: Guide to the U.S. Supreme Court.
JK1571.C65 1979      347/.73/26      *LC* 79-20210      *ISBN* 087187184X

## JK1711–2246 POLITICS. CIVIL RIGHTS

**Konvitz, Milton Ridvas, 1908-.**                      **4.8068**
A century of civil rights, by Milton R. Konvitz. With a study of State law against discrimination, by Theodore Leskes. — New York: Columbia University Press, 1961. viii, 293 p.; 24 cm. 'Table of statutes': p. [278]-280. 1. Civil rights — United States — History. 2. Afro-Americans — Civil rights I. Leskes, Theodore. State law against discrimination. II. T.
JK1711.K6      323.40973      *LC* 61-8988

**The New American political system / Samuel H. Beer ... [et al.]; edited by Anthony King.**      **4.8069**
Washington: American Enterprise Institute for Public Policy Research, c1978. 407 p.: ill.; 23 cm. — (AEI studies; 213) 1. United States — Politics and government — 1969-1974 — Addresses, essays, lectures. 2. United States — Politics and government — 1974-1977 — Addresses, essays, lectures. 3. United States — Politics and government — 1977- — Addresses, essays, lectures. I. Beer, Samuel Hutchison, 1911- II. King, Anthony Stephen.
JK1717.N48      320.9/73/092      *LC* 78-11849      *ISBN* 0844733156

**Rice, Stuart Arthur, 1889-.**                         ● **4.8070**
Quantitative methods in politics / by Stuart A. Rice. — New York: Russell & Russell, [1969] xxii, 331 p.; 22 cm. Reprint of the 1928 ed. 1. Politics, Practical

2. Social psychology 3. Public opinion 4. Statistics 5. U.S. — Politics and government. I. T.
JK1726.R5 1969      320.9/73      LC 68-27082

**Schaar, John H.**        • 4.8071
Loyalty in America. Berkeley, University of California Press, 1957. vii, 217 p. 'Composed originally as a doctoral dissertation in political science at the University of California, Los Angeles.' 1. Allegiance — United States 2. Loyalty I. T.
JK1726 S33      LC 56-10748

**Simpson, Dick W.**        4.8072
Strategies for change: how to make the American political dream work / Dick Simpson, George Beam. 1st ed. — Chicago: Swallow Press, c1976. 258 p.: ill.; 23 cm. Includes index. 1. Political participation — United States. 2. Politics, Practical I. Beam, George D., joint author. II. T.
JK1764.S54      329/.00973      LC 75-43482      ISBN 0804006962

**Kettner, James H.**        4.8073
The development of American citizenship, 1608–1870 / by James H. Kettner. — Chapel Hill: Published for the Institute of Early American History and Culture, Williamsburg, Va., by the University of North Carolina Press, c1978. xi, 391 p.; 24 cm. 1. Naturalization — United States — History. 2. Citizenship — United States — History. I. Institute of Early American History and Culture (Williamsburg, Va.) II. T.
JK1814.K47      323.6/0973      LC 78-954      ISBN 0807813265

## JK1846–1936 Suffrage

**Porter, Kirk Harold, 1891-.**        • 4.8074
A history of suffrage in the United States, by Kirk H. Porter. New York, Greenwood Press [1969, c1918] xi, 260 p. 23 cm. 1. Suffrage — United States 2. Afro-Americans — Suffrage 3. Women — Suffrage — United States. I. T.
JK1846.P82 1969      324/.73      LC 69-14039

**United States. President's Commission on Registration and**    • 4.8075
**Voting Participation.**
Report of the President's Commission on Registration and Voting Participation. — [Washington: President's Commission on Registration and Voting Participation], 1963. iii, 69 p. Cover title: Report on registration and voting participation. 1. Voting — United States. I. T. II. Title: Report on registration and voting participation.
JK1853 A44      JK1853 A44 1963.      LC 64-60374

**Campbell, Angus.**        • 4.8076
Group differences in attitudes and votes, a study of the 1954 congressional election, by Angus Campbell and Homer C. Cooper. [Ann Arbor] Survey Research Center, Institute for Social Research, University of Michigan [1956] v, 149 p. (Survey Research Center series, publication no. 15) 1. United States. Congress — Elections 2. Voting — United States 3. Social groups I. Cooper, Homer Choppell, 1923-, jt. author II. T.
JK1853 C36      LC 56-63164

**Fenton, John H.**        • 4.8077
The Catholic vote. New Orleans: Hauser Press [1960] 146 p.; 23 cm. (Galleon books) 1. Catholics in the U.S. 2. Christianity and politics 3. Voting — United States. I. T.
JK1853.F4      LC 60-12512

## JK1880–1911 WOMEN

**Woman's Rights Convention. (1st: 1848: Seneca Falls, N.Y.)**    • 4.8078
Woman's Rights Conventions, Seneca Falls & Rochester, 1848. New York: Arno, 1969. 9, 16 p.; 23 cm. Reprint of the 1870 ed. which was published under title: Proceedings of the Woman's Rights Conventions held at Seneca Falls & Rochester N.Y., July & August, 1848. This work includes Proceedings of the Woman's Rights Convention, held at the Unitarian Church, Rochester, N.Y., August 2, 1848, published in 1870, and Report of the Woman's Rights Convention, held at Seneca Falls, N.Y., July 19 & 20, 1848, published in 1848. 1. Women's rights — United States — Congresses. 2. Women — Suffrage — United States — Congresses. I. Woman's Rights Convention. Rochester, N.Y., 1848. Proceedings. 1969. II. Woman's Rights Convention. (1st: 1848: Seneca Falls, N.Y.). Report. 1969. III. T.
JK1885 1848b      301.41/2      LC 76-79180

**Catt, Carrie Chapman, 1859-1947.**        • 4.8079
Woman suffrage and politics: the inner story of the suffrage movement / by Carrie Chapman Catt and Nettie Rogers Shuler; introd. by T. A. Larson. — Seattle: University of Washington Press [1969, c1926] xxiii, 504 p.; 23 cm. (Americana library, 12) 1. Women — Suffrage — United States. I. Shuler, Nettie Rogers, 1865-1939, joint author. II. T.
JK1896.C3 1969      324/.3/0973      LC 70-8954

**The Concise history of woman suffrage: selections from the**    4.8080
**classic work of Stanton, Anthony, Gage, and Harper / edited by**
**Mari Jo and Paul Buhle.**
Urbana: University of Illinois Press, c1978. xxii, 468 p.; 23 cm. 1. Women — Suffrage — United States — History — Sources. I. Buhle, Paul, 1944- II. Buhle, Mari Jo, 1943- III. Stanton, Elizabeth Cady, 1815-1902. ed. History of woman suffrage.
JK1896.C58      322.4/4      LC 78-1733      ISBN 0252006690 ISBN 0252006917 pbk

**Duniway, Abigail Scott, 1834-1915.**        • 4.8081
Path breaking; an autobiographical history of the equal suffrage movement in Pacific Coast states. With a new introd. by Eleanor Flexner. — 2d ed. — New York: Schocken Books, [1971] xviii, 297 p.: illus.; 21 cm. — (Studies in the life of women) (A Schocken paperback series) 1. Duniway, Abigail Scott, 1834-1915. 2. Women — Suffrage — Oregon. 3. Women — Suffrage — United States. 4. Prohibition 5. Suffragettes — United States — Biography. I. T.
JK1896.D8 1971      324/.3/0924 B      LC 79-162285      ISBN 0805203222

**Grimes, Alan Pendleton, 1919-.**        • 4.8082
The Puritan ethic and woman suffrage / [by] Alan P. Grimes. — New York: Oxford University Press, 1967. xiii, 159 p.; 21 cm. 1. Women — Suffrage — The West I. T.
JK1896 G7      LC 67-15460

*[handwritten: JK 1896 G86]*

**Kraditor, Aileen S.**        • 4.8083
The ideas of the woman suffrage movement, 1890–1920 [by] Aileen S. Kraditor. New York, Columbia University Press, 1965. xii, 313 p. 1. Women — Suffrage — United States I. T.
JK1896 K7      LC 65-14410

**Morgan, David, 1937-.**        • 4.8084
Suffragists and Democrats; the politics of woman suffrage in America. — [East Lansing]: Michigan State University Press, 1972. 225 p.; 22 cm. 1. Women — Suffrage — United States — History. I. T.
JK1896.M66      324/.3/0973      LC 76-150079      ISBN 0870131634

**Dorr, Rheta Louise Childe, 1872-1948.**        • 4.8085
Susan B. Anthony, the woman who changed the mind of a nation. New York, AMS Press [1970] xiii, 367 p. illus., ports. 23 cm. Reprint of the 1928 ed. 1. Anthony, Susan B. (Susan Brownell), 1820-1906. 2. Women — Suffrage — United States. 3. Suffragettes — United States — Biography. I. T.
JK1899.A6 D6 1970      324/.3/0924 B      LC 74-100519      ISBN 0404006264

**Harper, Ida Husted, 1851-1931.**        • 4.8086
Life and work of Susan B. Anthony. New York: Arno, 1969. 3 v. (xxiv, 1633 p.): ill., ports.; 24 cm. Reprint of the 1898-1908 ed. 1. Anthony, Susan B. (Susan Brownell), 1820-1906. I. T.
JK1899.A6 H32      324/.3/0924 B      LC 70-79184

**Lutz, Alma.**        • 4.8087
Susan B. Anthony: rebel, crusader, humanitarian. — Boston: Beacon Press [1959] 340 p.: ill.; 24 cm. 1. Anthony, Susan B. (Susan Brownell), 1820-1906. I. T.
JK1899 A6 L8 1959      LC 59-6164

**Stanton, Elizabeth Cady, 1815-1902.**        • 4.8088
Eighty years and more; reminiscences, 1815–1897. With a new introd. by Gail Parker. — New York: Schocken Books, [1971] xx, 474 p.: ports.; 21 cm. — (Studies in the life of women) Reprint of the 1898 ed. 1. Stanton, Elizabeth Cady, 1815-1902. I. T.
JK1899.S7 A3 1971      324/.3/0924 B      LC 75-162284      ISBN 0805203249

**Stevens, Doris, 1892-.**        • 4.8089
Jailed for freedom. — Freeport, N.Y.: Books for Libraries Press, [1971, c1920] xii, 388 p.: ill., ports.; 23 cm. 1. Women — Suffrage — United States. I. T.
JK1901.S85 1971      324/.3/0973      LC 76-153003      ISBN 0836957571

**Taylor, Antoinette Elizabeth, 1917-.**        • 4.8090
The woman suffrage movement in Tennessee. New York, Bookman Associates [1957] 150 p. 1. Women — Suffrage — Tennessee I. T.
JK1911 T2 T36      LC 57-2117

## JK1923–1929 AFRO-AMERICANS

**Conyers, James E., 1932-.**        4.8091
Black elected officials: a study of Black Americans holding governmental office / James E. Conyers, Walter L. Wallace. — New York: Russell Sage Foundation, c1976. xii, 190 p.; 24 cm. Includes index. 1. Afro-Americans — Politics and government 2. Local officials and employees — United States.

3. United States — Politics and government — 1945- I. Wallace, Walter L. joint author. II. T.
JK1924.C65    320.9/73/092    *LC* 74-30881    *ISBN* 0871542064

**Garrow, David J., 1953-.**      4.8092
Protest at Selma: Martin Luther King, Jr., and the Voting rights act of 1965 / David J. Garrow. — New Haven, Conn.: Yale University Press, 1978. xiii, 346 p.: ill.; 24 cm. Revision of the author's senior honors thesis, Wesleyan University, 1975. 1. Afro-Americans — Southern States — Suffrage. 2. Voter registration — Southern States. 3. Selma-Montgomery Rights March, 1965 I. T.
JK1929.A2 G37    324/.15    *LC* 78-5593    *ISBN* 0300022476

**Keech, William R.**      • 4.8093
The impact of Negro voting; the role of the vote in the quest for equality [by] William R. Keech. Chicago, Rand McNally [1968] ix, 113 p. 24 cm. (American politics research series) 1. Afro-Americans — Suffrage 2. Elections — North Carolina — Durham. 3. Elections — Alabama — Tuskegee. I. T.
JK1929.A2 K4    324/.09174/96    *LC* 68-16841

**Lawson, Steven F., 1945-.**      4.8094
Black ballots: voting rights in the South, 1944–1969 / Steven F. Lawson. — New York: Columbia University Press, 1976. xii, 474 p.; 24 cm. — (Contemporary American history series) Includes index. 1. Afro-Americans — Southern States — Suffrage. I. T.
JK1929.A2 L3    324/.15    *LC* 76-18886    *ISBN* 0231039786. *ISBN* 0231083521 pbk

**Watters, Pat.**      • 4.8095
Climbing Jacob's ladder; the arrival of Negroes in Southern politics [by] Pat Watters [and] Reese Cleghorn. [1st ed.] New York, Harcourt, Brace & World [1967] xvi, 389 p. 24 cm. 1. Afro-Americans — Politics and government 2. Afro-Americans — Southern States I. Cleghorn, Reese, joint author. II. T.
JK1929.A2 W3    320.9/75    *LC* 67-20324

**Frye, Hardy T.**      4.8096
Black parties and political power: a case study / Hardy T. Frye; foreword by William Kornhouser. — Boston, Mass.: G. K. Hall, c1980. xviii, 220 p.: ill.; 24 cm. — (Perspectives on the Black world.) Includes index. 1. National Democratic Party of Alabama. 2. Afro-Americans — Alabama — Politics and government. I. T. II. Series.
JK1929.A4 F79    324.2761/07    *LC* 79-27907    *ISBN* 0816182795

### JK1936 LOCAL PRACTICES

**Bartley, Numan V.**      4.8097
Southern politics and the second reconstruction / by Numan V. Bartley and Hugh D. Graham. — Baltimore: Johns Hopkins University Press, [1975] xvi, 233 p.: ill.; 24 cm. Includes index. 1. Elections — Southern States. 2. Political parties — Southern States. 3. Southern States — Politics and government I. Graham, Hugh Davis. joint author. II. T.
JK1936.A2 B37    324/.2/0975    *LC* 74-24377    *ISBN* 080181667X

**Kousser, J. Morgan.**      4.8098
The shaping of Southern politics: suffrage restriction and the establishment of the one–party South, 1880–1910 / J. Morgan Kousser. — New Haven: Yale University Press, 1974. xvii, 319 p.; 25 cm. (Yale historical publications. Miscellany. 102) Includes index. 1. Suffrage — Southern States — History. 2. Southern States — Politics and government — 1865-1950 I. T. II. Series.
JK1936.A2 K68    324/.1/0975    *LC* 73-86905    *ISBN* 0300016964

## JK1951–2246 Electoral System

**Burnham, Walter Dean.**      • 4.8099
Critical elections and the mainsprings of American politics. — [1st ed.]. — New York: Norton, [1970] xii, 210 p.: ill., maps.; 22 cm. 1. Elections — U.S. — History. I. T.
JK1965.B85    324/.73    *LC* 70-117450    *ISBN* 0393099628

**Cox, Edward Franklin, 1925-.**      • 4.8100
State and national voting in Federal elections, 1910–1970. — [Hamden, Conn.]: Archon Books, 1972. xv, 280 p.; 26 cm. 1. Elections — U.S. — Statistics. 2. Voting — U.S. — Statistics. I. T.
JK1965.C59    329/.023/73    *LC* 70-183138    *ISBN* 0208012613

**Dinkin, Robert J.**      4.8101
Voting in revolutionary America: a study of elections in the original thirteen states, 1776–1789 / Robert J. Dinkin. — Westport, Conn.: Greenwood Press, 1982. x, 184 p.; 22 cm. — (Contributions in American history. no. 99) Continues: Voting in provincial America. Includes index. 1. Elections — United States — History. 2. United States — Politics and government —

Revolution, 1775-1783 3. United States — Politics and government — 1783-1789 I. T. II. Series.
JK1965.D54 1982    324.973/02 19    *LC* 81-13266    *ISBN* 0313230919

**The Evolution of American electoral systems / Paul Kleppner ...**      4.8102
**[et al.].**
Westport, Conn.: Greenwood Press, 1981. xiii, 279 p.: ill.; 24 cm. — (Contributions in American history; no. 95 0084-9219) 1. Elections — United States — History — Addresses, essays, lectures. 2. Political parties — United States — History — Addresses, essays, lectures. I. Kleppner, Paul.
JK1965.E96    324/.0973 19    *LC* 80-24632    *ISBN* 0313213798

**The History of American electoral behavior / edited by Joel H.**      4.8103
**Silbey, Allan G. Bogue, and William H. Flanigan; contributors,**
**Lee Benson ... [et al.].**
Princeton, N.J.: Princeton University Press, c1978. xv, 384 p.: ill.; 25 cm. — (Quantitative studies in history) Papers presented at a conference held at Cornell University in June 1973. 1. Elections — United States — History — Addresses, essays, lectures. I. Silbey, Joel H. II. Bogue, Allan G. III. Flanigan, William H. IV. Benson, Lee. V. Series.
JK1965.H57    324.2    *LC* 77-85565    *ISBN* 0691075905

**Kleppner, Paul.**      4.8104
The third electoral system 1853–1892: parties, voters, and political cultures / by Paul Kleppner. — Chapel Hill: University of North Carolina Press, c1979. xxii, 424 p.: maps; 25 cm. Includes index. 1. Elections — United States — History. 2. Voting — United States — History. 3. United States — Politics and government — 19th century I. T.
JK1965.K53    324/.2    *LC* 78-7949    *ISBN* 0807813281

**Kleppner, Paul.**      4.8105
Who voted?: The dynamics of electoral turnout, 1870–1980 / Paul Kleppner. — New York: Praeger Publishers, 1982. xi, 238 p.; 24 cm. — (American political parties and elections). Includes index. 1. Elections — United States — History. 2. Political participation — United States — History. I. T. II. Series.
JK1965.K54 1982    324.973 19    *LC* 82-3740    *ISBN* 0030589339

**America votes: a handbook of contemporary American election**      • 4.8106
**statistics.**
New York: Macmillan, 1956-. v.: maps.; 29 cm. Editor: v.1- R. M. Scammon. Issued by Governmental Affairs Institute. v. 1- '1945-54' 1. Elections — United States — Statistics. I. Scammon, Richard M. ed. II. Governmental Affairs Institute (U.S.)
JK1967.A8    *LC* 56-10132

**Congressional Quarterly, Inc.**      4.8107
[Guide to U.S. elections] Congressional Quarterly's Guide to U.S. elections. — Washington: CQ, c1975. xvi, 1103 p.: ill.; 29 cm. Includes indexes. 1. Elections — United States — History — Statistics. 2. Political conventions — United States — History. 3. Political parties — United States — History. I. T. II. Title: Guide to U.S. Elections.
JK1967.C66 1975    324.973 19    *LC* 75-659    *ISBN* 087187072X

**Heard, Alexander.**      • 4.8108
Southern primaries and elections, 1920–1949 [by] Alexander Heard and Donald S. Strong. — Freeport, N.Y.: Books for Libraries Press, [1970, c1950] 206 p.; 29 cm. 1. Elections — Southern States. I. Strong, Donald Stuart, 1912- joint author. II. T.
JK1967.H4 1970    324.75    *LC* 70-130551    *ISBN* 0836955242

**Petersen, Svend, 1911-.**      4.8109
A statistical history of the American presidential elections: with supplementary tables covering 1968–1980 / Svend Petersen; introduction 'Our national elections' by Louis Filler. — Westport, Conn.: Greenwood Press, 1981. xxiii, 250, [25] p.; 26 cm. Reprint. Originally published: New York: Ungar, c1968. 1. Presidents — United States — Election — History. I. T.
JK1967.P4 1981    324.973 19    *LC* 81-6348    *ISBN* 031322952X

**Strong, Donald Stuart, 1912-.**      4.8110
Issue voting and party realignment / Donald S. Strong. — University: University of Alabama Press, c1977. viii, 110 p. 1. Voting — United States — Addresses, essays, lectures. 2. Voting research — United States — Addresses, essays, lectures. 3. Party affiliation — United States — Addresses, essays, lectures. I. T.
JK1967.S78    JK1967 S78.    324/.2    *LC* 77-1087    *ISBN* 0817348360

**Wolfinger, Raymond E.**      4.8111
Who votes? / Raymond E. Wolfinger and Steven J. Rosenstone. — New Haven: Yale University Press, 1980. x, 158 p.; 22 cm. — (A Yale fastback) Includes index. 1. Elections — United States 2. Voting — United States. I. Rosenstone, Steven J. joint author. II. T.
JK1967.W64    324.973/092    *LC* 79-48068    *ISBN* 0300025416

A Tide of discontent: the 1980 elections and their meaning /    **4.8112**
edited by Ellis Sandoz and Cecil V. Crabb, Jr.
Washington, D.C.: Congressional Quarterly Press, c1981. xiv, 254 p.: ill.; 23 cm. — (Politics and public policy series.) Includes index. 1. United States. Congress — Elections, 1980 — Addresses, essays, lectures. 2. Presidents — United States — Election — 1980 — Addresses, essays, lectures. I. Sandoz, Ellis, 1931- II. Crabb, Cecil Van Meter, 1924- III. Series.
JK1968 1980.T53      324.973/0926 19      *LC* 81-4586      *ISBN* 0871872056

The American elections of 1982 / edited by Thomas E. Mann    **4.8113**
and Norman J. Ornstein.
Washington: American Enterprise Institute for Public Policy Research, c1983. xii, 203 p.: ill.; 23 cm. — (AEI studies. 389) (American Enterprise Institute studies in political and social processes) 1. United States. Congress — Elections, 1982 — Addresses, essays, lectures. 2. Elections — United States — Addresses, essays, lectures. 3. United States — Politics and government — 1981- — Addresses, essays, lectures. I. Mann, Thomas E. II. Ornstein, Norman J. III. American Enterprise Institute for Public Policy Research. IV. Series.
JK1968 1982      324.973/0927 19      *LC* 83-11843      *ISBN* 0844735310

Barber, James David.    • **4.8114**
The lawmakers: recruitment and adaptation to legislative life. — New Haven: Yale University Press, 1965. xii, 314 p.; 25 cm. — (Yale studies in political science. 11) Bibliography: p. 262-263. Bibliographical references included in 'Notes' (p. 285-310) 1. Politics, Practical 2. U.S. — Pol. & govt. I. T. II. Series.
JK1976.B3      328.73      *LC* 65-11172

Elections and the political order [by] Angus Campbell [and    • **4.8115**
others], Survey Research Center, Institute for Social Research, the University of Michigan.
New York, Wiley [1966] ix, 385 p. illus. 24 cm. 1. Elections — United States 2. Politics, Practical 3. United States — Politics and government — 1945- I. Campbell, Angus. II. University of Michigan. Survey Research Center.
JK1976.E45      324.20973      *LC* 65-27662

Goldenberg, Edie N.    **4.8116**
Campaigning for Congress / Edie N. Goldenberg, Michael W. Traugott. — Washington, D.C.: CQ Press, c1984. xv, 207 p.: ill.; 23 cm. Includes index. 1. United States. Congress — Elections 2. Electioneering — United States. I. Traugott, Michael W. II. T.
JK1976.G64 1984      324.7/0973 19      *LC* 84-1840      *ISBN* 0871872838

University of Michigan. Survey Research Center.    • **4.8117**
The American voter / [by] Angus Campbell [and others] New York: Wiley [1960] viii, 573 p.: diagrs., tables; 24 cm. 1. Elections — United States I. Campbell, Angus. II. T.
JK1976 M5      *LC* 60-11615

Moos, Malcolm Charles, 1916-.    • **4.8118**
Politics, presidents, and coattails / by Malcolm Moos. — New York: Greenwood Press, [1969, c1952] xxi, 237 p.: ill., maps.; 27 cm. 1. U.S. Congress. House — Elections. 2. Voting — U.S. 3. Presidents — U.S. — Election. I. T.
JK1976.M6 1969      324/.2/0973      *LC* 69-14002

## JK1980–2246 Special Topics

Baker, Gordon E.    • **4.8119**
Rural versus urban political power; the nature and consequences of unbalanced representation. Garden City, N.Y., Doubleday, 1955. 70 p. 24 cm. (Doubleday short studies in political science, 20.) 1. Election districts — United States. 2. United States — Politics and government — 20th century I. T.
JK1982.B3      *LC* 55-6671

Merriam, Charles Edward, 1874-1953.    • **4.8120**
Non-voting, causes and methods of control. Chicago, Ill., The University of Chicago press [c1924] xvi, 287 p. incl. forms. front. 21 cm. 1. Elections — Chicago. 2. Ballot I. Gosnell, Harold Foote, joint author. II. T.
JK1986.M4      *LC* 24-21889

## JK1991 Campaign Funds

United States. President's Commission on Campaign Costs.    • **4.8121**
Financing presidential campaigns: report. — [Washington: U.S. Govt. Print. Off.], 1962 [i.e. 1964] 36 p.: ill.; 24 cm. 1. Elections — United States — Campaign funds 2. Presidents — United States — Elections I. T.
JK1991 A4 1964      *LC* 62-61089

Adamany, David W.    **4.8122**
Campaign finance in America / by David W. Adamany. — North Scituate, Mass.: Duxbury Press, [1972] xiv, 274 p.; 24 cm. 1. Campaign funds — United States. I. T.
JK1991.A627      329/.025      *LC* 72-77743      *ISBN* 0878720324

Adamany, David W.    **4.8123**
Political money: a strategy for campaign financing in America / David W. Adamany, George E. Agree. — Baltimore: Johns Hopkins University Press, [1975] x, 242 p.; 23 cm. 1. Elections — United States — Campaign funds. I. Agree, George E., joint author. II. T.
JK1991.A64    JK1991 A64.      329/.025/0973      *LC* 75-11351      *ISBN* 0801817188

Alexander, Herbert E.    **4.8124**
Financing politics: money, elections, and political reform / Herbert E. Alexander. — Washington: Congressional Quarterly Press, c1976. 299 p.: ill.; 21 cm. — (Politics and public policy series) Includes index. 1. Campaign funds — United States. I. T.
JK1991.A6797      324.7/8/0973 19      *LC* 76-22558      *ISBN* 0871870983

Alexander, Herbert E.    **4.8125**
Financing the 1980 election / Herbert E. Alexander with the assistance of Brian A. Haggerty. — Lexington, Mass.: Lexington Books, c1983. xiii, 524 p.; 24 cm. 1. United States. Congress — Elections, 1980. 2. Presidents — United States — Election — 1980. 3. Campaign funds — United States. I. Haggerty, Brian A. II. T.
JK1991.A685 1983      324.7/8/0973 19      *LC* 82-48863      *ISBN* 0669063754

Alexander, Herbert E.    • **4.8126**
Money in politics, by Herbert E. Alexander. Foreword by Tom Wicker. — Washington: Public Affairs Press, [1972] ix, 353 p.; 24 cm. 1. Campaign funds — United States. I. T.
JK1991.A694      329/.025/0973      *LC* 78-188305

Campaign money: reform and reality in the States / edited by    **4.8127**
Herbert E. Alexander.
New York: Free Press, c1976. xiv, 337 p.; 24 cm. 1. Campaign funds — United States. I. Alexander, Herbert E.
JK1991.C35      329/.025/0973      *LC* 76-21180      *ISBN* 0029004101

Heard, Alexander.    • **4.8128**
The costs of democracy. — Chapel Hill: University of North Carolina Press, [1960] xxv, 493 p.: tables.; 24 cm. 1. Campaign funds — United States. I. T.
JK1991.H39      324.273      *LC* 60-10532

Jacobson, Gary C.    **4.8129**
Money in congressional elections / Gary C. Jacobson. — New Haven: Yale University Press, 1980. xix, 251 p.: ill.; 22 cm. 1. United States. Congress — Elections 2. Campaign funds — United States. I. T.
JK1991.J32      329/.025/0973      *LC* 79-20669      *ISBN* 0300024428

Money and politics in the United States: financing elections in    **4.8130**
the 1980s / edited by Michael J. Malbin.
Washington, D.C.: American Enterprise Institute for Public Policy Research; Chatham, N.J.: Chatham House, c1984. 324 p.; 23 cm. 1. Campaign funds — United States — Addresses, essays, lectures. I. Malbin, Michael J.
JK1991.M73 1984      324.7/8/0973 19      *LC* 84-2900      *ISBN* 0934540233

Nichols, David, 1940-.    **4.8131**
Financing elections; the politics of an American ruling class. — New York: New Viewpoints, 1973. ix, 191 p.; 21 cm. 1. Campaign funds — United States. 2. Business and politics — United States. I. T.
JK1991.N5      329/.025      *LC* 73-3420      *ISBN* 0531053520

Overacker, Louise, 1891-.    • **4.8132**
Presidential campaign funds / by Louise Overacker; with an introduction by Theodore Francis Green. — Boston: Boston University Press, 1916. vii, 76 p.; 22 cm. (The Gaspar G. Bacon lectureship on the Constitution of the United States, Boston university lectures 1945) 1. Elections — United States — Campaign funds 2. Presidents — United States — Election I. T.
JK1991.½72      *LC* 46-6165

Roeder, Edward.    **4.8133**
PACs Americana: a directory of political action committees (PACs) and their interests / by Edward Roeder. — Washington, D.C.: Sunshine Services Corp., c1982. xxiv, 859, [69] p.; 28 cm. 1. Campaign funds — United States — Directories. 2. Political action committees — United States — Directories. I. T. II. Title: P.A.C.'s Americana.
JK1991.R63 1982      322.4/3/02573 19      *LC* 81-85581      *ISBN* 0942236009

**Sabato, Larry.** 4.8134
PACs: inside the world of political action committees / Larry J. Sabato. — 1st ed. — New York: Norton, c1984. p. cm. Includes index. 1. Campaign funds — United States. 2. Political action committees — United States. I. T. II. Title: P.A.C.s.
JK1991.S23 1984　　　324.7/8/0973 19　　　*LC* 84-6068

**To enact a law: Congress and campaign financing [by] Robert L. Peabody [and others].** 4.8135
New York: Praeger, [1972] xii, 225 p.: illus.; 25 cm. 1. Campaign funds — United States. 2. Radio in politics — United States 3. Television in politics — United States I. Peabody, Robert L. II. Title: Congress and campaign financing.
JK1991.T6　　　328.73/07/7　　　*LC* 73-160477

**Weinberger, Marvin.** 4.8136
The PAC directory: a complete guide to political action committees / compiled by Marvin Weinberger and David U. Greevy. — Cambridge, Mass.: Ballinger, c1982. 1552 p. in various pagings; 29 cm. 1. Campaign funds — United States. 2. Political action committees — United States — Directories. I. Greevy, David U. II. T. III. Title: P.A.C. directory.
JK1991.W44 1982　　　324.7/8/0973 19　　　*LC* 82-11480　　　*ISBN* 0884108562

## JK2007–2246 Other Topics

**Bean, Louis Hyman, 1896-.** • 4.8137
How to predict elections [by] Louis H. Bean. — Westport, Conn.: Greenwood Press, [1972, c1948] x, 196 p.: illus.; 22 cm. 1. Election forecasting — United States. 2. Elections — United States — Statistics. I. T.
JK2007.B4 1972　　　324/.242/0973　　　*LC* 78-141278　　　*ISBN* 0837158729

**Rosenstone, Steven J.** 4.8138
Forecasting presidential elections / Steven J. Rosenstone. — New Haven: Yale University Press, c1983. xii, 211 p.: ill.; 22 cm. Includes index. 1. Election forecasting — United States. 2. Presidents — United States — Election 3. United States — Politics and government — 1945- I. T.
JK2007.R67 1983　　　324.973 19　　　*LC* 83-42877　　　*ISBN* 0300026919

**United States. Congress. Senate. Library.** • 4.8139
Nomination and election of the President and Vice President of the United States, including the manner of selecting delegates to national political conventions. Compiled under the direction of Francis R. Valeo, secretary of the Senate, by Richard D. Hupman, Senate Library, and Robert L. Tienken, Legislative Reference Service, Library of Congress. Washington, U.S. Govt. Print. Off., 1968. v, 261 p. 24 cm. 1. Primaries — United States. 2. Political conventions — United States. I. Hupman, Richard D. comp. II. Tienken, Robert L., comp. III. Library of Congress. Legislative Reference Service. IV. T.
JK2063.A513 1968　　　329/.02/0973　　　*LC* 68-60675

**Ewing, Cortez Arthur Milton, 1896-1962.** • 4.8140
Primary elections in the South: a study in uniparty politics. — 'First edition'. Norman: University of Oklahoma Press [c1953] xii, 112 p.; 21 cm. 1. Primaries — Southern States I. T.
JK2071 E9　　　*LC* 53-5472

## JK2251–2391 Political Parties

**Bain, Richard C.** 4.8141
Convention decisions and voting records / [by] Richard C. Bain and Judith H. Parris. 2d ed. Washington: Brookings Institution [1973] x, 350, [120] p.; 25 cm. (Studies in presidential selection) 1. Political conventions — United States. I. Parris, Judith H. joint author. II. T. III. Series.
JK2255.B3 1973　　　329/.0221　　　*LC* 73-1082　　　*ISBN* 0815707681

**Chase, James S.** 4.8142
Emergence of the presidential nominating convention, 1789–1832. Urbana: University of Illinois Press, 1974 (c1973) xvii, 332 p.; 24 cm. 1. Political conventions — United States — History. 2. Political parties — United States — History. 3. Presidents — United States — Nomination — History. I. T.
JK2255.C45　　　329/.0221/0973　　　*LC* 72-97157　　　*ISBN* 0252003128

**Davis, James W., 1920-.** 4.8143
National conventions in an age of party reform / James W. Davis; foreword by David S. Broder. — Westport, Conn.: Greenwood Press, 1983. xxi, 304 p.; 24 cm. (Contributions in political science. 0147-1066; no. 91) Includes index. 1. Political conventions — United States. 2. Political parties — United States I. T. II. Series.
JK2255.D428 1983　　　324.5/6/0973 19　　　*LC* 82-9382　　　*ISBN* 031323048X

**Johnson, Donald Bruce, 1921- comp.** 4.8144
National party platforms / compiled by Donald Bruce Johnson. — Rev. ed. — Urbana: University of Illinois Press, c1978. 2 v. (xiii, 1035 p.); 27 cm. Edition for 1973 by D. B. Johnson and K. H. Porter published under title: National party platforms, 1840-1972. Includes indexes. 1. Political parties — United States — Platforms — History. I. T.
JK2255.J64 1978　　　324.2/3/0973 19　　　*LC* 78-17373　　　*ISBN* 0252006925

**McKee, Thomas Hudson.** • 4.8145
[National platforms of all political parties] The national conventions and platforms of all political parties, 1789 to 1905; convention, popular and electoral vote. Also the political complexion of both Houses of Congress at each biennial period. New York, B. Franklin [1971] 414, 33 p. 19 cm. (Burt Franklin research & source works series, 873. American classics in history and social science, 217) Reprint of the 1906 ed. Originally published under title: The national platforms of all political parties. 1. Political parties — United States — Platforms — History. 2. Presidents — United States — Election 3. Political conventions — United States — History. I. T.
JK2255.M2 1971　　　329/.02　　　*LC* 75-132682　　　*ISBN* 0833723316

## JK2260–2263 History

**Buel, Richard, 1933-.** 4.8146
Securing the revolution: ideology in American politics, 1789–1815. — Ithaca [N.Y.]: Cornell University Press, [1972] xii, 391 p.; 24 cm. 1. Political parties — United States — History. 2. United States — Politics and government — 1789-1815 I. T.
JK2260.B8　　　329/.02　　　*LC* 74-38120　　　*ISBN* 0801407052

**Hofstadter, Richard, 1916-1970.** • 4.8147
The idea of a party system: the rise of legitimate opposition in the United States, 1780–1840. — Berkeley: University of California Press, 1969. xiii, 280 p.; 23 cm. — (Jefferson memorial lectures) 1. Political parties — U.S. I. T. II. Series.
JK2260.H73　　　329/.02/0973　　　*LC* 76-82377

**Kelley, Robert Lloyd, 1925-.** 4.8148
The cultural pattern in American politics: the first century / Robert Kelley. — 1st ed. — New York: Knopf, c1979. xiv, 368 p.; 22 cm. Includes index. 1. Political parties — United States — History. 2. United States — Social conditions I. T.
JK2260.K44 1979　　　329/.02　　　*LC* 78-23823　　　*ISBN* 0394502795

**Nichols, Roy F. (Roy Franklin), 1896-1973.** • 4.8149
The invention of the American political parties, by Roy F. Nichols. New York, Macmillan [1967] xii, 416 p. 24 cm. 1. Political parties — United States — History. I. T.
JK2260.N5　　　329.02　　　*LC* 67-12797

**Schapsmeier, Edward L.** 4.8150
Political parties and civic action groups / Edward L. Schapsmeier and Frederick H. Schapsmeier. — Westport, Conn.: Greenwood Press, 1981. xxxiii, 554 p.; 25 cm. — (Greenwood encyclopedia of American institutions. [4]) Series numbering from bibliography. 1. Political parties — United States — Handbooks, manuals, etc. 2. Political clubs — United States — Handbooks, manuals, etc. I. Schapsmeier, Frederick H. joint author. II. T. III. Series.
JK2260.S36　　　324.273/00202 19　　　*LC* 80-1714　　　*ISBN* 0313214425

**Silbey, Joel H.** • 4.8151
The shrine of party: congressional voting behavior, 1841–1852 / [by] Joel H. Silbey. — [Pittsburgh]: University of Pittsburgh Press, [1967] x, 292 p.; 24 cm. 1. Political parties — United States — History. 2. Party discipline — United States. 3. United States — Politics and government — 1815-1861 I. T.
JK2260.S5　　　324.273/09 19　　　*LC* 66-25415

**Zvesper, John, 1948-.** 4.8152
Political philosophy and rhetoric: a study of the origins of American party politics / John Zvesper. Cambridge; New York: Cambridge University Press, 1977. vii, 237 p.; 22 cm. (Cambridge studies in the history and theory of politics) 1. Political parties — United States — History. I. T.
JK2260.Z93　　　329/.02　　　*LC* 76-11097　　　*ISBN* 0521213231

**Bernhard, Winfred E. A., comp.** 4.8153
Political parties in American history / edited by Winfred E. A. Bernhard; general editor: Morton Borden. — New York: Putnam, [1974, c1973-74] 3 v. (xliv, 1324 p.): ill.; 22 cm. Vol. 2 edited by F. A. Bonadio; v. 3 edited by P. L. Murphy. 1. Political parties — United States — History — Addresses, essays, lectures. I. Bonadio, Felice A. II. Murphy, Paul L., 1923- III. T.
JK2261.B47　　　329/.02　　　*LC* 73-76139　　　*ISBN* 0399109919

**Fairlie, Henry, 1924-.** 4.8154
The parties: Republicans and Democrats in this century / Henry Fairlie. — New York: St. Martin's Press, c1978. 236 p.; 22 cm. 1. Republican Party (U.S.:

1854- ) 2. Democratic Party (U.S.) 3. United States — Politics and government — 20th century I. T.
JK2261.F24　　329.3　　*LC* 77-9176　　*ISBN* 031259738X

**Harmel, Robert, 1950-.**　　　　　　　　　　**4.8155**
Parties and their environments: limits to reform? / Robert Harmel, Kenneth Janda. — New York: Longman, c1982. x, 176 p.: ill.; 24 cm. Includes index. 1. Democratic Party (U.S.) 2. Republican Party (U.S.: 1854- ) 3. Political parties — United States I. Janda, Kenneth. II. T.
JK2261.H27　　324.273 19　　*LC* 81-8357　　*ISBN* 0582282993

**Haynes, Frederick Emory, 1868-.**　　　　　• **4.8156**
Social politics in the United States, by Fred E. Haynes. — New York: AMS Press, [1970] xii, 414 p.; 23 cm. Reprint of the 1924 ed. 1. Political parties — U.S. — History. 2. Socialism — United States — History. 3. Trade-unions — U.S. — History. 4. U.S. — Politics and government. 5. U.S. — Social conditions. I. T.
JK2261.H34 1970　　320.9/73　　*LC* 70-126648　　*ISBN* 0404031684

**Ippolito, Dennis S.**　　　　　　　　　　**4.8157**
Political parties, interest groups, and public policy: group influence in American politics / Dennis S. Ippolito, Thomas G. Walker. — Englewood Cliffs, N.J.: Prentice-Hall, c1980. x, 431 p.: ill.; 24 cm. 1. Political parties — United States 2. Pressure groups — United States. I. Walker, Thomas G., joint author. II. T.
JK2261.I66　　329/.02　　*LC* 79-16057　　*ISBN* 0136843573

**Ladd, Everett Carll.**　　　　　　　　　　**4.8158**
Transformations of the American party system: political coalitions from the New Deal to the 1970s / Everett Carll Ladd, Jr., with Charles D. Hadley. — 1st ed. — New York: Norton, [1975] xxv, 371 p.: graphs; 22 cm. 1. Political parties — United States 2. New Deal, 1933-1939 3. United States — Politics and government — 1945- 4. United States — Politics and government — 1933-1945 I. Hadley, Charles D. joint author. II. T.
JK2261.L34 1975　　329/.02　　*LC* 75-22123　　*ISBN* 0393055590.
*ISBN* 0393092038 pbk

**McCormick, Richard Patrick, 1916-.**　　　• **4.8159**
The second American party system: party formation in the Jacksonian era / by Richard P. McCormick. — Chapel Hill: University of North Carolina Press [1966] x, 389 p. 'Publication ... sponsored by the American Association for State and Local History, Nashville, Tennessee.' 1. Political parties — United States — History 2. United States — Politics & government — 1825-1829 3. United States — Politics & government — 1829-1837 I. T.
JK2261 M165　　*LC* 66-10962

**Mazmanian, Daniel A., 1945-.**　　　　　　**4.8160**
Third parties in presidential elections [by] Daniel A. Mazmanian. — Washington: Brookings Institution, [1974] viii, 163 p.: ill.; 24 cm. — (Studies in presidential selection) 1. Third parties (United States politics) 2. Presidents — United States — Election I. T. II. Series.
JK2261.M38　　329/.02　　*LC* 74-281　　*ISBN* 0815755228

**Orth, Samuel Peter, 1873-1922.**　　　　　• **4.8161**
The boss and the machine. New Haven, Yale university press; [etc., etc.] 1919. ix, 203 p. front., plates, ports. 21 cm. 1. Political parties — United States 2. United States — Politics and government I. T.
JK2261.O7 E173.C55 vol. 43　　*LC* 19-3705

**Party organizations and American politics / Cornelius P. Cotter**　　**4.8162**
**... [et al.].**
New York: Praeger, 1984. 203 p.: ill. (American political parties and elections.) 1. Political parties — United States I. Cotter, Cornelius P. II. Series.
JK2261.P314 1984　　324.2/1/0973 19　　*LC* 84-8286　　*ISBN* 0030718317

**Political parties in the eighties / edited by Robert A. Goldwin.**　　**4.8163**
Washington, D.C.: American Enterprise Institute for Public Policy Research, c1980. 152 p.; 23 cm. — (AEI studies; 274) 1. Political parties — United States — Addresses, essays, lectures. I. Goldwin, Robert A. 1922- II. American Enterprise Institute for Public Policy Research. III. Public Affairs Conference Center.
JK2261.P64　　324.273　　*LC* 80-14977　　*ISBN* 0844733822

**Price, David Eugene.**　　　　　　　　　　**4.8164**
Bringing back the parties / David E. Price. — Washington, D.C.: CQ Press, c1984. xiv, 314 p.: ill.; 23 cm. 1. Political parties — United States 2. United States — Politics and government — 1945- I. T.
JK2261.P74 1984　　324.273 19　　*LC* 83-26151　　*ISBN* 0871873044

**Rosenstone, Steven J.**　　　　　　　　　　**4.8165**
Third parties in America: citizen response to major party failure / Steven J. Rosenstone, Roy L. Behr, Edward H. Lazarus. — Princeton, N.J.: Princeton University Press, c1984. viii, 266 p.: ill.; 23 cm. Includes index. 1. Third parties

(United States politics) — History. 2. Elections — United States — History. I. Behr, Roy L., 1958- II. Lazarus, Edward H., 1959- III. T.
JK2261.R67 1984　　324.273/09 19　　*LC* 83-43091　　*ISBN* 0691076731

**Schlesinger, Arthur Meier, 1917-.**　　　　　**4.8166**
History of U.S. political parties. Arthur M. Schlesinger, Jr., general editor. — New York: Chelsea House Publishers, 1973. 4 v. (liv, 3544 p.); 25 cm. 1. Political parties — United States — History. I. T.
JK2261.S35　　329/.02　　*LC* 72-8682　　*ISBN* 0835205940

**Stedman, Murray Salisbury, 1917-.**　　　　• **4.8167**
Discontent at the polls: a study of farmer and labor parties, 1827–1948 / by Murray S. Stedman, Jr., and Susan W. Stedman. — New York: Russell & Russell, [1967, c1950] x, 190 p.: ill.; 22 cm. 1. Political parties — United States 2. United States — Economic conditions I. Stedman, Susan (Winter) joint author. II. T.
JK2261.S84 1967　　329/.00973　　*LC* 66-27154

**Sundquist, James L.**　　　　　　　　　　**4.8168**
Dynamics of the party system: alignment and realignment of political parties in the United States / James L. Sundquist. — Rev. ed. — Washington, D.C.: Brookings Institution, c1983. xiv, 466 p.; 24 cm. 1. Political parties — United States — History. I. T.
JK2261.S9 1983　　324.273/09 19　　*LC* 83-6354　　*ISBN* 0815782268

**Walton, Hanes, 1941-.**　　　　　　　　　**4.8169**
Black political parties; an historical and political analysis. New York, Free Press [1972] xi, 276 p. 23 cm. 1. Political parties — United States — History. 2. Afro-Americans — Politics and government I. T.
JK2261.W33　　329/.894　　*LC* 76-143514

**Schlesinger, Stephen C.**　　　　　　　　**4.8170**
The new reformers: forces for change in American politics / Stephen C. Schlesinger. — Boston: Houghton Mifflin, 1975. xvi, 238 p.; 22 cm. 1. Political parties — United States 2. Social reformers — United States. 3. United States — Politics and government — 1945- I. T.
JK2263 1975.S33　　322.4/0973　　*LC* 75-9943　　*ISBN* 0395207096

# JK2265–2275 Treatises

**The American party systems; stages of political development,**　　• **4.8171**
**edited by William Nisbet Chambers and Walter Dean Burnham.**
**Contributors: Frank J. Sorauf [and others]**
New York, Oxford University Press, 1967. ix, 321 p. illus. 24 cm. Outgrowth of a conference on American political party development, held at Washington University, St. Louis, in April, 1966. 1. Political parties — United States — Addresses, essays, lectures. I. Chambers, William Nisbet, 1916- ed. II. Burnham, Walter Dean. ed. III. Sorauf, Frank J. (Frank Joseph), 1928-
JK2265.A68　　329/.02/0973　　*LC* 67-28029

**American Political Science Association. Committee on Political**　　• **4.8172**
**Parties.**
Toward a more responsible two–party system: a report ... New York: Rinehart, [c1950] 99 p. 'Appeared as a supplement to the American politial science review, vol. XLIV, no. 3, part 2, September, 1950.' 1. Political parties I. T.
JK2265.A7　　*LC* 50-11344

**Burnham, Walter Dean.**　　　　　　　　**4.8173**
The current crisis in American politics / Walter Dean Burnham. — New York: Oxford University Press, 1983 (c1982). ix, 330 p.; 24 cm. 'The writings of Walter Dean Burnham': p. 321-322. 1. Political parties — United States — Addresses, essays, lectures. 2. Elections — United States — Addresses, essays, lectures. 3. Voting — United States — Addresses, essays, lectures. 4. Political participation — United States — Addresses, essays, lectures. I. T.
JK2265.B87 1982　　324/.0973 19　　*LC* 82-6511　　*ISBN* 0195032195

**Herring, Edward Pendleton, 1903-.**　　　　• **4.8174**
The politics of democracy; American parties in action [by] Pendleton Herring. New York, W. W. Norton & Company [c1940] xiv, [21]-468 p. plates. 21 cm. 'First edition.' 1. Political parties — United States 2. Politics, Practical 3. United States — Politics and government I. T.
JK2265.H47　　329　　*LC* 40-27328

**Merriam, Charles Edward, 1874-1953.**　　　• **4.8175**
The American party system / by Charles E. Merriam and Harold Foote Gosnell; with a new introd. by Robert E. Merriam. — 4th ed. New York: Johnson Reprint Corp., 1969. vii, 530 p.: ill., maps.; 21 cm. — (Reprints in government and political science) Reprint of the 1949 ed. 1. Political parties — United States 2. United States — Politics and government I. Gosnell, Harold Foote, 1896- joint author. II. T.
JK2265.M4 1969　　329/.02/0973　　*LC* 75-76214

**Schattschneider, Elmer Eric, 1892-1971.**          • 4.8176
Party government [by] E.E. Schattschneider ... New York, Farrar and
Rinehart, inc. [c1942] xv, 219 p., 1 l. diagrs. (American government in action
series; Phillips Bradley, editor) 1. Political parties — United States 2. United
States — Politics and government I. T.
JK2265 S35          LC 42-2229

**Turner, Julius.**          • 4.8177
Party and constituency: pressures on Congress / [by] Julius Turner. — Rev. ed.
by Edward V. Schneier, Jr. — Baltimore: Johns Hopkins Press, [1970] xvii,
312 p.; 21 cm. 1. U.S. Congress. 2. Political parties — U.S. 3. Legislators —
U.S. I. Schneier, Edward V. joint author. II. T.
JK2265.T87 1970          329/.00973          LC 75-110374          ISBN 0801811236

**Goodnow, Frank Johnson, 1859-1939.**          • 4.8178
Politics and administration; a study in government. — New York: Russell &
Russell, [1967] xiii, 270 p.; 20 cm. 1. Political parties — United States
2. United States — Politics and government I. T.
JK2267.G65 1967          353          LC 66-24696

**Verba, Sidney.**          • 4.8179
Participation in America: political democracy and social equality / [by] Sidney
Verba [and] Norman H. Nie. — New York: Harper & Row, [1972] xxiii, 428 p.;
ill.; 25 cm. 1. Political participation — United States. I. Nie, Norman H. joint
author. II. T.
JK2274.A3 V4          329/.01          LC 72-80128          ISBN 0060468238

**Moon, Henry Lee, 1901-.**          • 4.8180
Balance of power: the Negro vote. [1st ed.] Garden City, N.Y., Doubleday,
1948. 256 p. 22 cm. 1. Negroes — Politics and suffrage. 2. Elections — United
States I. T.
JK2275.N4 M6          LC 48-6926

**Tatum, Elbert Lee.**          • 4.8181
The changed political thought of the Negro, 1915–1940 / with a foreword by
Lawrence A. Davis. — New York: Exposition Press [1951] 205 p.; 23 cm.
1. Negroes — Politics and suffrage. I. T.
JK2275.N4 T3          LC 51-11870

## JK2276–2295 Organization

**Felknor, Bruce L.**          • 4.8182
Dirty politics / [by] Bruce L. Felknor. — [1st ed.]. — New York: Norton,
[1966] 295 p.: ill., ports.; 22 cm. 1. Politics, Practical 2. Elections — United
States — History. I. T.
JK2281.F4          329.023          LC 65-20238

**Sabato, Larry.**          4.8183
The rise of political consultants: new ways of winning elections / Larry J.
Sabato. — New York: Basic Books, c1981. 376 p.: ill.; 24 cm. Includes indexes.
1. Political consultants — United States. 2. Campaign management — United
States. 3. Electioneering — United States. I. T.
JK2281.S2          324.7/0973 19          LC 81-66104          ISBN 046507040X

**Simpson, Dick W.**          4.8184
Winning elections: a handbook in participatory politics [by] Dick Simpson. —
Chicago: Swallow Press, [1972] 194 p.: illus.; 23 cm. 1. Electioneering —
United States — Handbooks, manuals, etc. 2. Campaign management (United
States) — Handbooks, manuals, etc. I. T.
JK2283.S54          324.7/0973 19          LC 78-171874          ISBN 0804005419

## JK2295 Politics, by Locality

**Lockard, Duane, 1921-.**          • 4.8185
New England State politics. — Princeton, N.J.: Princeton University Press,
1959. 347 p.: illus.; 25 cm. 1. Political parties — New England. 2. New
England — Politics and government I. T.
JK2295.A112 L6          329          LC 59-5600

**De Santis, Vincent P.**          • 4.8186
Republicans face the Southern question: the new departure years, 1877–1897.
Baltimore, Johns Hopkins Press, 1959. 275 p. maps. 23 cm. 1. Republican
Party (U.S.: 1854- ) 2. Political parties — Southern States. 3. Soutern States —
Politics and government — 1865- I. T.
H31.J6 ser. 77, no. 1 JK2295.A13 D4x          LC 59-10767

**Tindall, George Brown.**          4.8187
The disruption of the solid South. Athens: University of Georgia Press, [1972]
xiv, 98 p.; 23 cm. (Mercer University Lamar memorial lectures, no. 14)
1. Republican Party (U.S.: 1854- ) 2. Political parties — Southern States.
3. Southern States — Politics and government — 1865- I. T.
JK2295.A13 T55          320.9/75/04          LC 76-169951          ISBN 0820302805

**Cresap, Dean Russell, 1912-.**          • 4.8188
Party politics in the Golden State. Los Angeles, Haynes Foundation, 1954. xi,
126 p. diagrs. 24 cm. (John Randolph Haynes and Dora Haynes Foundation.
Publications. Monograph series, 37) 1. Political parties — California. I. T.
II. Series.
JK2295.C3 C7          329          LC 54-3336

**Risjord, Norman K.**          4.8189
Chesapeake politics, 1781–1800 / Norman K. Risjord. — New York: Columbia
University Press, 1978. 715 p. 1. Political parties — Maryland — History.
2. Political parties — Virginia — History. 3. Political parties — North
Carolina — History. I. T.
JK2295.M32 R57          309.1/75/03          LC 78-7996          ISBN 0231043287

**Baum, Dale, 1943-.**          4.8190
The Civil War party system: the case of Massachusetts, 1848–1876 / by Dale
Baum. — Chapel Hill: University of North Carolina Press, c1984. xviii, 289 p.;
24 cm. Includes index. 1. Political parties — Massachusetts — History — 19th
century. 2. Elections — Massachusetts — History — 19th century.
3. Massachusetts — Politics and government — Civil War, 1861-1865 I. T.
JK2295.M42 B28 1984          324.2744/009 19          LC 83-19687          ISBN
0807815888

**Formisano, Ronald P., 1939-.**          4.8191
The transformation of political culture: Massachusetts parties, 1790s–1840s /
Ronald P. Formisano. — New York: Oxford University Press, 1983. xiii,
496 p.: ill.; 24 cm. 1. Political parties — Massachusetts — History — 19th
century. 2. Political parties — Massachusetts — History — 18th century.
3. Massachusetts — Politics and government — 1775-1865 I. T.
JK2295.M42 F67 1983          324.2744/009 19          LC 82-14517          ISBN
0195031245

**Formisano, Ronald P., 1939-.**          • 4.8192
The birth of mass political parties, Michigan, 1827–1861 [by] Ronald P.
Formisano. Princeton, N.J., Princeton University Press, 1971. xii, 356 p. map.
25 cm. 1. Political parties — Michigan — History. I. T.
JK2295.M52 F6          329/.02          LC 73-154995          ISBN 0691046050

**Scarrow, Howard A.**          4.8193
Parties, elections, and representation in the state of New York / Howard A.
Scarrow. — New York: New York University Press, 1983. ix, 142 p.; 24 cm.
1. Political parties — New York (State) 2. Elections — New York (State)
3. Apportionment (Election law) — New York (State) I. T.
JK2295.N73 S27 1983          324.6/09747 19          LC 83-2147          ISBN
0814778283

**Peel, Roy Victor, 1896-.**          • 4.8194
The political clubs of New York City / by Roy V. Peel. — Port Washington,
N.Y.: I. J. Friedman, [1968] xii, 360 p.: ill., maps; 23 cm. (Empire State
historical publications series, no. 48) Reprint of the 1935 ed. 1. Political clubs
— New York (City) 2. New York (N.Y.) — Clubs. 3. New York (N.Y.) —
Politics and government I. T.
JK2295.N74 P4 1968          329/.006          LC 68-18356

**Adler, Norman, 1942-.**          4.8195
Political clubs in New York / Norman M. Adler, Blanche Davis Blank;
foreword by Roy V. Peel. — New York: Praeger, 1975. xxiv, 275 p.; 25 cm.
(Praeger special studies in U.S. economic, social, and political issues) Continues
R. V. Peel's The political clubs of New York City published in 1935. 1. Political
clubs — New York (City) 2. New York (N.Y.) — Clubs. 3. New York (N.Y.)
— Politics and government I. Blank, Blanche Davis, 1923- joint author.
II. Peel, Roy Victor, 1896- The political clubs of New York City. III. T.
JK2295.N74 P4 1975          329/.0211/097471          LC 72-89642          ISBN
0275288528

**Soukup, James Rudolph, 1928-.**          • 4.8196
Party and factional division in Texas, by James R. Soukup, Clifton McCleskey
[and] Harry Holloway. Austin, University of Texas Press [1964] xviii, 221 p.
maps. 24 cm. 1. Political parties — Texas. I. T.
JK2295.T5 S6          LC 63-16060

## JK2301–2391 Particular Parties

### JK2307–2319 DEMOCRATIC

**Garson, Robert A.**          4.8197
The Democratic Party and the politics of sectionalism, 1941–1948 / Robert A.
Garson. — Baton Rouge: Louisiana State University Press, [1974] xiii, 353 p.;
24 cm. Includes index. 1. Democratic Party (U.S.) — History. 2. States'
Rights Democratic Party. 3. United States — Politics and government —
1933-1953 I. T.
JK2307 1941.G37          329.3/009/044          LC 73-93121          ISBN
0807100706

**Acheson, Dean, 1893-1971.**      • **4.8198**
A Democrat looks at his party. [1st ed.] New York: Harper [1955] 199 p.; 22 cm. 1. Democratic Party (U.S.) 2. United States — Politics and government — 20th century I. T.
JK2316.A25      329.3      *LC* 55-11841

**Baker, Jean H.**      **4.8199**
Affairs of party: the political culture of Northern Democrats in the mid–nineteenth century / Jean H. Baker. — Ithaca: Cornell University Press, c1983. 368 p.: ill.; 24 cm. Includes index. 1. Democratic Party (U.S.) — History. 2. Political socialization — United States — History. 3. United States — Politics and government — 1849-1877 I. T.
JK2316.B34 1983      324.2736/09 19      *LC* 82-14283      *ISBN* 0801415136

**Burner, David, 1937-.**      • **4.8200**
The politics of provincialism; the Democratic Party in transition, 1918–1932. [1st ed.] New York, Knopf, 1968 [c1967] xiii, 293, viii p. 22 cm. 1. Democratic Party (U.S.) — History. I. T.
JK2316.B8      324.2736/09 19      *LC* 67-18618

**Martin, John Frederick.**      **4.8201**
Civil rights and the crisis of liberalism: the Democratic Party, 1945–1976 / John Frederick Martin. — Boulder, Colo.: Westview Press, 1979. xv, 301 p.; 24 cm. 1. Democratic Party (U.S.) 2. Liberalism — United States. 3. Civil rights — United States 4. United States — Politics and government — 1945- I. T.
JK2316.M27      329.3      *LC* 79-10886      *ISBN* 0891584544

**Silbey, Joel H.**      **4.8202**
A respectable minority: the Democratic Party in the Civil War era, 1860–1868 / Joel H. Silbey. — 1st ed. — New York: Norton, c1977. xviii, 267 p.; 21 cm. — (The Norton essays in American history) Includes index. 1. Democratic Party (U.S.) — History. 2. United States — Politics and government — Civil War, 1861-1865 3. United States — Politics and government — 1865-1869 I. T.
JK2317 1860.S57 1977      329.3/009/034      *LC* 77-24048      *ISBN* 0393056481

**Grossman, Lawrence, 1945-.**      **4.8203**
The Democratic Party and the Negro: northern and national politics, 1868–92 / Lawrence Grossman. — Urbana: University of Illinois Press, c1976. xi, 212 p.; 24 cm. — (Blacks in the New World.) A revision of the author's thesis, City University of New York, 1973. Includes index. 1. Democratic Party (U.S.) — History. 2. Afro-Americans — Politics and government 3. United States — Politics and government — 1865-1898. I. T. II. Series.
JK2317 1868.G752      329.3/009/034      *LC* 75-30546      *ISBN* 0252005759

**Andersen, Kristi.**      **4.8204**
The creation of a Democratic majority, 1928–1936 / Kristi Andersen. — Chicago: University of Chicago Press, 1979. xv, 160 p.: ill.; 22 cm. A revision of the author's thesis, University of Chicago. Includes index. 1. Democratic Party (U.S.) — History. 2. United States — Politics and government — 1929-1933 3. United States — Politics and government — 1933-1945 I. T.
JK2317 1928.A53 1979      329/.3/09042      *LC* 78-11660      *ISBN* 0226018849

**Wilson, James Q.**      • **4.8205**
The amateur Democrat; club politics in three cities. [Chicago] University of Chicago Press [1962] 378 p. ill. 1. Democratic party 2. Political clubs I. T.
JK2317 1962 W5      *LC* 62-13564

**Domhoff, G. William.**      **4.8206**
Fat cats and Democrats; the role of the big rich in the party of the common man [by] G. William Domhoff. Englewood Cliffs, N.J., Prentice-Hall [1972] 203 p. 22 cm. 1. Democratic Party (U.S.) 2. Campaign funds — United States. 3. Capitalists and financiers — United States. 4. Upper classes — United States. I. T.
JK2317 1972.D64      329.3/025      *LC* 78-38791      *ISBN* 0133081710

**Parmet, Herbert S.**      **4.8207**
The Democrats: the years after FDR / Herbert S. Parmet. — New York: Macmillan, 1976. xi, 371 p., [8] leaves of plates: ill.; 25 cm. Includes index. 1. Democratic Party (U.S.) 2. United States — Politics and government — 1945- I. T.
JK2317 1976.P37      329.3      *LC* 75-25990      *ISBN* 0025947702

**Shafer, Byron E.**      **4.8208**
Quiet revolution: the struggle for the Democratic Party and the shaping of post–reform politics / Byron E. Shafer. — New York: Russell Sage Foundation, c1983. ix, 618 p.: ill.; 24 cm. Includes index. 1. Democratic Party (U.S.) 2. Presidents — United States — Nomination 3. Political participation — United States. 4. United States — Politics and government — 1945- I. T.
JK2317 1983      324.2736 19      *LC* 83-61130      *ISBN* 0871547651

**Barnard, William D.**      **4.8209**
Dixiecrats and Democrats: Alabama politics, 1942–1950 / [by] William D. Barnard. — University: University of Alabama Press, [1974] viii, 200 p.: ill.; 25 cm. 1. Democratic Party. Alabama. 2. States' Rights Democratic Party. 3. Alabama — Politics and government — 1865-1950 I. T.
JK2318.A3 1942      329.3/009761      *LC* 73-22711      *ISBN* 0817348204

**Semel, Vicki Granet.**      **4.8210**
At the grass roots in the Garden State: reform and regular Democrats in New Jersey / Vicki Granet Semel. Rutherford [N.J.]: Fairleigh Dickinson University Press, c1977. 287 p. Includes index. 1. Democratic Party (N.J.) 2. New Jersey — Politics and government — 1951- I. T.
JK2318.N5 1977      *LC* 75-5246      *ISBN* 0838617379

**Young, Alfred Fabian, 1925-.**      • **4.8211**
The Democratic Republicans of New York; the origins, 1763–1797 [by] Alfred F. Young. Chapel Hill, Published for the Institute of Early American History and Culture, Williamsburg, Va., by the University of North Carolina Press [1967] xv, 636 p. illus., maps. 24 cm. 1. Democratic Party (N.Y.) I. Institute of Early American History and Culture (Williamsburg, Va.) II. T.
JK2318.N7 1967      329.3/009747      *LC* 67-23493

**Guterbock, Thomas M.**      **4.8212**
Machine politics in transition: party and community in Chicago / Thomas M. Guterbock. — Chicago: University of Chicago Press, c1980. xxii, 324 p.: ill.; 23 cm. (Studies of urban society) Includes index. 1. Democratic Party (Ill.) 2. Party affiliation — Illinois — Chicago. 3. Chicago (Ill.) — Politics and government — 1951- I. T.
JK2319.C4 G87      329/.0211 19      *LC* 79-16131      *ISBN* 0226311147

**Moscow, Warren.**      • **4.8213**
The last of the big–time bosses: the life and times of Carmine De Sapio and the rise and fall of Tammany Hall. — New York: Stein and Day [1971] 227 p.; 25 cm. 1. De Sapio, Carmine, 1908- 2. Tammany Hall 3. New York (N.Y.) — Politics and government I. T.
JK2319.N56 M66      329.3/0092/4 B      *LC* 79-160351      *ISBN* 0812814002

**Mushkat, Jerome.**      • **4.8214**
Tammany; the evolution of a political machine, 1789–1865. [1st ed. Syracuse, N.Y.] Syracuse University Press [1971] xii, 476 p. illus., ports. 24 cm. (A New York State study) 1. Tammany Society, or Columbian Order. 2. Tammany Hall 3. New York (N.Y.) — Politics and government — To 1898 I. T.
JK2319.N56 M86      329/.0211/097471      *LC* 78-150346      *ISBN* 0815600798

**Riordon, William L., 1861-1909.**      • **4.8215**
Plunkitt of Tammany Hall: a series of very plain talks on very practical politics / delivered by ex–Senator George Washington Plunkitt, the Tammany philosopher, from his rostrum—the New York County court house bootblack stand; introd. by Arthur Mann. — New York: Dutton, 1963. 98 p.: ill.; 19 cm. 1. Plunkitt, George Washington, 1842-1924. 2. Tammany Hall I. T.
JK2319.N57 R5 1963      329.3      *LC* 63-2648

## JK2320–2358 Republican

**Marcus, Robert D., 1936-.**      • **4.8216**
Grand Old Party; political structure in the gilded age, 1880–1896 [by] Robert D. Marcus. New York, Oxford University Press, 1971. x, 323 p. 22 cm. 1. Republican Party (U.S.: 1854- ) — History. I. T.
JK2320.A7 1880      329.6      *LC* 70-127175

**Cole, Arthur Charles, 1886-.**      • **4.8217**
The Whig Party in the South. Gloucester, Mass., P. Smith, 1962 [c1914] 392 p. illus. 21 cm. (American Historical Association. Prize essays, 1912) 1. Whig Party (U.S.) — Southern States. 2. United States — Politics and government — 1815-1861 I. T. II. Series.
JK2331.C6x      *LC* 62-3244

**Howe, Daniel Walker.**      **4.8218**
The political culture of the American Whigs / Daniel Walker Howe. — Chicago: University of Chicago Press, 1980 (c1979). vii, 404 p.; 24 cm. 1. Whig Party (U.S.) 2. United States — Politics and government — 1783-1865 I. T.
JK2331.H68      329/.4      *LC* 79-12576      *ISBN* 0226354784

**Smith, Theodore Clarke, 1870-1960.**      • **4.8219**
The Liberty and Free Soil Parties in the Northwest. — New York: Arno Press, 1969. xi, 351 p.: maps.; 23 cm. — (The Anti-slavery crusade in America) Reprint of the 1897 ed. 'Liberty and Free Soil press in the Northwest, 1836-1854': p. [318]-324. 1. Liberty Party. 2. Free-Soil Party 3. Slavery in the United States. 4. U.S. — Politics and government — 1815-1861. I. T. II. Series.
JK2336.A6S6 1969      329/.8      *LC* 76-88555

**Blue, Frederick J.**      **4.8220**
The Free Soilers; third party politics, 1848–54 [by] Frederick J. Blue. — Urbana: University of Illinois Press, [1973] xii, 350 p.; 24 cm. 1. Free-Soil Party 2. United States — Politics and government — 1849-1861 I. T.
JK2336.A7 1848.B5     329/.87     *LC* 72-86408     *ISBN* 025200308X

**Mailer, Norman.**      **4.8221**
Miami and the siege of Chicago; an informal history of the Republican and Democratic Conventions of 1968. — New York: World Pub. Co., [1968] 223 p.; 22 cm. 1. Republican Party. National Convention, 29th, Miami, Fla., 1968. 2. Democratic Party. National Convention, Chicago, 1968. I. T.
JK2353 1968.M34     329/.0221/0973     *LC* 68-58886

**Mayer, George H.**      • **4.8222**
The Republican Party, 1854–1966. [by] George H. Mayer. 2d ed. New York, Oxford University Press, 1967. xi, 604 p. 24 cm. 1. Republican Party (U.S.: 1854- ) — History. I. T.
JK2356.M3 1967     329.6/009     *LC* 67-25300

**Reinhard, David W., 1952-.**      **4.8223**
The Republican Right since 1945 / David W. Reinhard. — Lexington, Ky.: University Press of Kentucky, c1983. ix, 294 p.; 25 cm. Includes index. 1. Republican Party (U.S.) 2. Conservatism — United States — History — 20th century. 3. United States — Politics and government — 1945- I. T.
JK2356.R28 1983     324.2734 19     *LC* 82-40460     *ISBN* 0813114845

**Reichard, Gary W., 1943-.**      **4.8224**
The reaffirmation of Republicanism: Eisenhower and the Eighty-third Congress / by Gary W. Reichard. — Knoxville: University of Tennessee Press, [1975] xv, 303 p.; 24 cm. (Twentieth-century America series) Based on the author's thesis, Cornell University. Includes index. 1. Eisenhower, Dwight D. (Dwight David), 1890-1969. 2. Republican Party (U.S.: 1854- ) 3. United States. 83d Cong., 1953-1954. 4. United States — Politics and government — 1953-1961 I. T.
JK2357 1953.R43     329.6     *LC* 75-1017     *ISBN* 0870491679

**Phillips, Kevin P.**      • **4.8225**
The emerging Republican majority / [by] Kevin P. Phillips. — New Rochelle, N.Y.: Arlington House [1969] 482 p.: ill., maps; 24 cm. 1. Republican Party (U.S.: 1854- ) 2. Voting — United States. 3. United States — Politics and government — 1945- I. T.
JK2357 1969.P53     324/.24/0973     *LC* 76-79602     *ISBN* 0870000586

**Nathans, Elizabeth Studley.**      • **4.8226**
Losing the peace; Georgia Republicans and Reconstruction, 1865–1871. — Baton Rouge: Louisiana State University Press, [1969, c1968] xi, 268 p.: map.; 23 cm. 1. Republican Party. Georgia. I. T.
JK2358.G4 1969     329.6/009758     *LC* 68-8942

## JK2361–2391 OTHERS

**Durden, Robert Franklin.**      • **4.8227**
The climax of populism: the election of 1896 [by] Robert F. Durden. — [Lexington]: University of Kentucky Press, [1965] xii, 190 p.; 23 cm. 1. Populist Party (U.S.) I. T.
JK2372.D8     324.2732/7 19     *LC* 65-11824

**Hicks, John Donald, 1890-.**      • **4.8228**
The Populist revolt: a history of the Farmers' alliance and the People's Party. — [Lincoln]: University of Nebraska Press, 1961 [c1959] 473 p.: ill.; 21 cm. (A Bison book, BB111) 1. Populist Party (U.S.) 2. National Farmers' Alliance and Industrial Union. 3. Agriculture — Economic aspects — United States. 4. United States — Politics and government — 1865-1900 I. T.
JK2372.H5 1961     324.2732/7 19     *LC* 61-7237

**Palmer, Bruce, 1942-.**      **4.8229**
'Man over money': the Southern Populist critique of American capitalism / Bruce Palmer. — Chapel Hill: University of North Carolina Press, c1980. xviii, 311 p.; 24 cm. — (The Fred W. Morrison series in Southern studies) Includes index. 1. Populist Party (U.S.) 2. Populism — United States — History. 3. Southern States — Politics and government — 1865-1950 4. United States — Politics and government — 1893-1897 I. T.
JK2372.P34     329/.88/00975     *LC* 79-24698     *ISBN* 080781427X

**Pollack, Norman.**      • **4.8230**
The Populist response to industrial America; midwestern Populist thought. Cambridge, Harvard University Press, 1962. 166 p. 1. Populist Party (U.S.) I. T.
JK2372 P6     *LC* 62-20249

**Shaw, Barton C., 1947-.**      **4.8231**
The wool-hat boys: Georgia's Populist Party / Barton C. Shaw. — Baton Rouge: Louisiana State University Press, c1984. 237 p.: map; 24 cm. Based on the author's thesis, Emory University, 1979. Includes index. 1. Populist Party (Ga.) — History — 19th century. 2. Populism — Georgia — History — 19th century. 3. Georgia — Politics and government — 1865-1950 I. T.
JK2374.G4 S52 1984     324.2759/027 19     *LC* 83-19982     *ISBN* 0807111481

**Nugent, Walter T. K.**      • **4.8232**
The tolerant Populists; Kansas, populism and nativism. Chicago, University of Chicago Press [1963] 256 p. 1. People's Party of the United States. Kansas 2. Kansas — Politics & government — 1865-1950 I. T.
JK2374 K2 1963     *LC* 63-13069

**Duncan-Clark, Samuel John, 1875-1938.**      • **4.8233**
The Progressive movement: its principles and its programme / with an introd. by Theodore Roosevelt. Boston, Small, Maynard. — [New York: AMS Press, 1972] xx, 318 p.; 19 cm. Reprint of the 1913 ed. 1. Progressive Party (Founded 1912) I. T.
JK2387.D8 1972     329/.892     *LC* 72-164808     *ISBN* 0404022170

**Foster, William Z., 1881-1961.**      • **4.8234**
History of the Communist Party of the United States. — New York: Greenwood Press, 1968 [c1952] 600 p.; 24 cm. 1. Communist Party of the United States of America. 2. Socialism — United States 3. Communism — United States — 1917- I. T.
JK2391.C5 F58 1968     329/.82     *LC* 68-30821

**Howe, Irving.**      • **4.8235**
The American Communist Party: a critical history, 1919–1957 / by Irving Howe and Lewis Coser with the assistance of Julius Jacobson. — Boston: Beacon Press [c1957] x, 593 p.; 21 cm. Bibliographical references included in 'Notes' (p. 555-575) 1. Communist Party of the United States of America. 2. Communism — United States — 1917- I. Coser, Lewis A., 1913- joint author. II. T.
JK2391.C5H68     329.8     *LC* 58-6243

**Isserman, Maurice.**      **4.8236**
Which side were you on?: the American Communist Party during the Second World War / Maurice Isserman. — 1st ed. — Middletown, Conn.: Wesleyan University Press, c1982. xx, 305 p., [16] p. of plates: ill.; 24 cm. 1. Communist Party of the United States of America. 2. World War, 1939-1945 — United States. I. T.
JK2391.C5 I83     324.273/75 19     *LC* 81-16350     *ISBN* 0819550590

**Starobin, Joseph Robert, 1913-.**      **4.8237**
American communism in crisis, 1943–1957 / [by] Joseph R. Starobin. — Cambridge: Harvard University Press, 1972. xvii, 331 p.: port.; 25 cm. 1. Communist Party of the United States of America. 2. Communism — U.S. — 1917- I. T.
JK2391.C5 S67     329/.82/009     *LC* 79-172326     *ISBN* 0674022750

**Naison, Mark, 1946-.**      **4.8238**
Communists in Harlem during the depression / Mark Naison. — Urbana: University of Illinois Press, c1983. xxi, 355 p.; 24 cm. — (Blacks in the New World.) 1. Communist Party of the United States of America — History. 2. Communism — New York (N.Y.) — History. 3. Depressions — 1929 — United States 4. Harlem (New York, N.Y.) — History. I. T. II. Series.
JK2391.C53 N56 1983     324.273/75/09 19     *LC* 82-10848     *ISBN* 0252006445

**Gieske, Millard L.**      **4.8239**
Minnesota farmer–laborism: the third–party alternative / by Millard L. Gieske. — Minneapolis: University of Minnesota Press, c1979. ix, 389 p.: ill. 1. Democratic-Farmer-Labor Party. 2. Minnesota — Politics and government I. T.
JK2391.D4 G53     JK2391.D4 G53.     329/.893     *LC* 79-1115     *ISBN* 0816608903

**Green, James R., 1944-.**      **4.8240**
Grass–roots socialism: radical movements in the Southwest, 1895–1943 / James R. Green. — Baton Rouge: Louisiana State University Press, c1978. xxiv, 450 p.: ill.; 24 cm. 1. Socialist Party (U.S.) 2. Socialist Party (U.S.). Oklahoma. 3. Socialism — Southwest, Old I. T.
JK2391.S6 G73     329/.81/00979     *LC* 77-28205     *ISBN* 0807103675

**Shannon, David A.**      • **4.8241**
The Socialist Party of America: a history. — New York: Macmillan, 1955. 320 p.; 22 cm. 1. Socialist Party (U.S.) I. T.
JK2391.S6 S5 1955     *LC* 55-13545

## JK2403–9600 STATE GOVERNMENT

**The Book of the States.**      • **4.8242**
v. 1- 1935-. Lexington, Ky. [etc.] Council of State Governments. v. ill., ports. 26 cm. Biennial. Vol. 1 issued in 2d and 3d eds., with additional material. Vol. 2

issued in 2 pts. Separately paged supplements accompany most issues. 1. State governments — Yearbooks. I. Council of State Governments. II. American Legislators' Association.
JK2403.B6    353.9/3/2    LC 35-11433

**Adrian, Charles R.** 4.8243
Governing our fifty States and their communities / Charles R. Adrian. — 4th ed. — New York: McGraw-Hill, c1978. vi, 138 p.; 21 cm. — (Foundations of American government and political science) 1. State governments 2. Local government — United States. I. T. II. Series.
JK2408.A28 1978    320.9/73    LC 77-11933    ISBN 0070004536

**Dye, Thomas R.** 4.8244
Politics in states and communities / Thomas R. Dye. — 5th ed. — Englewood Cliffs, N.J.: Prentice-Hall, c1985. xvi, 510 p.: ill.; 25 cm. 1. State governments 2. Local government — United States. I. T.
JK2408.D82 1985    320.8/0973 19    LC 84-13407    ISBN 0136851991

**Havard, William C.** 4.8245
The changing politics of the South / edited by William C. Havard. — Baton Rouge: Louisiana State University Press, [1972] xxv, 755 p.: ill.; 24 cm. 1. Southern States — Politics and government — 1951- I. T.
JK2408.H37    320.9/75/04    LC 75-181357    ISBN 0807100463

**Key, V. O. (Valdimer Orlando), 1908-1963.** • 4.8246
American State politics: an introduction. — [1st ed.] New York: Knopf, 1956. 289 p.: ill.; 22 cm. 1. State governments I. T.
JK2408.K4    342.73 320.973*    LC 56-6508

**Politics in the American states: a comparative analysis / edited** 4.8247
**by Virginia Gray, Herbert Jacob, Kenneth N. Vines.**
4th ed. — Boston: Little, Brown, c1983. xx, 474 p.: ill.; 24 cm. 1. State governments I. Gray, Virginia. II. Jacob, Herbert, 1933- III. Vines, Kenneth Nelson, 1924-
JK2408.P64 1983    320.973 19    LC 82-82209    ISBN 0316325775

**Sharkansky, Ira.** 4.8248
The maligned states: policy accomplishments, problems, and opportunities / Ira Sharkansky. — 2d ed. — New York: McGraw-Hill, c1978. xiii, 162 p.: maps; 21 cm. — (Policy impact and political change in America) 1. State governments I. T. II. Series.
JK2408.S46 1978    320.9/73/0924    LC 77-5703    ISBN 0070564345

**Sharkansky, Ira.** • 4.8249
Regionalism in American politics. — Indianapolis: Bobbs-Merrill, [1969, c1970] xiv, 194 p.: maps.; 22 cm. 1. State governments 2. Regionalism — U.S. 3. U.S. — Politics and government — 1945- I. T.
JK2408.S47    353.9    LC 69-13635

**National Municipal League. State Constitutional Studies** • 4.8250
**Project.**
Model State constitution. 6th ed. New York, 1963. x, 118 p. 23 cm. (Its Publications, ser. 1, no. 1) Earlier editions by its Committee on State Government. 1. Constitutions, State — United States. 2. State governments I. National Municipal League. Committee on State Government. Model State constitution. II. T.
JK2417.N3x    LC 65-5259

## JK2443–2525 Administration

**Brock, William Ranulf.** 4.8251
Investigation and responsibility: public responsibility in the United States, 1865–1900 / William R. Brock. — Cambridge [Cambridgeshire]; New York: Cambridge University Press, 1984. viii, 280 p.; 24 cm. Includes index. 1. State government — History — 19th century. 2. United States — Economic policy — To 1933 3. United States — Social policy I. T.
JK2443.B86 1984    353.9 19    LC 83-26205    ISBN 0521258979

**Ransone, Coleman Bernard, 1920-.** • 4.8252
The office of Governor in the United States. — University, Ala.: University of Alabama Press, 1956. xii, 417 p.: diagrs., tables; 24 cm. 1. Governors — United States I. T.
JK2447.R32    353.9    LC 56-7220

**Schlesinger, Joseph A.** • 4.8253
How they became governor; a study of comparative state politics, 1870–1950. Foreword by Robert A. Dahl. East Lansing, Govermental Research Bureau, Michigan State University [1957] 103 p. diagrs., tables. 23 cm. (Governmental Research Bureau, Michigan State University, East Lansing. Political research studies, no. 3) 1. Governors — United States I. T.
JK2447.S35    LC 58-62621

**Campbell, Ballard C., 1940-.** 4.8254
Representative democracy: public policy and Midwestern legislatures in the late nineteenth century / Ballard C. Campbell. — Cambridge, Mass.: Harvard University Press, 1980. xi, 260 p.; 25 cm. 1. Legislative bodies — Middle West — Voting — History. 2. Middle West — Politics and government. I. T.
JK2484.C35    328.77077/09    LC 80-12775    ISBN 0674762754

**Main, Jackson Turner.** 4.8255
Political parties before the Constitution. — Chapel Hill: Published for the Institute of Early American History and Culture at Williamsburg, Va., by the University of North Carolina Press, [1973] xx, 481 p.: illus.; 25 cm. 1. Legislative bodies — United States — States — History. 2. Political parties — United States — History. I. T.
JK2484.M33    329/.02    LC 71-184228    ISBN 0807811947

**Citizens Conference on State Legislatures.** • 4.8256
State legislatures: an evaluation of their effectiveness: the complete report. — New York: Praeger, [1971] xv, 480 p.: ill.; 24 cm. — (Praeger special studies in U.S. economic and social development) 1. Legislative bodies — United States — States. I. T.
JK2488.C5    328.73    LC 72-170026

**Francis, Wayne L.** 4.8257
Legislative issues in the fifty States; a comparative analysis [by] Wayne L. Francis. — Chicago: Rand McNally, [c1967] vii, 129 p.: illus.; 24 cm. — (American politics research series) 1. Legislative bodies — United States I. T.
JK2488.F7    328.73    LC 67-21415

**Jewell, Malcolm Edwin, 1928-.** 4.8258
The State legislature; politics and practice [by] Malcolm E. Jewell. — 2d ed. — New York: Random House, [1969] viii, 152 p.; 19 cm. — (Random House studies in political science, PS37) 1. Legislative bodies — U.S. — States. 2. State governments I. T.
JK2488.J4 1969    328.73    LC 69-14289

**The politics of reapportionment / edited by Malcolm E. Jewell.** • 4.8259
New York: Atherton Press, 1962. 334 p.: ill., maps, 24 cm. (The Atherton Press political science series.) 1. Apportionment (Election law) — United States — States.
JK2493.J4    324.334    LC 62-21052

**Zeigler, L. Harmon (Luther Harmon), 1936-.** • 4.8260
Lobbying; interaction and influence in American state legislatures [by] Harmon Zeigler [and] Michael A. Baer. Belmont, Calif., Wadsworth Pub. Co. [1969] xxi, 210 p. 22 cm. (New frontiers in American politics series) 1. Lobbying — United States. I. Baer, Michael A., joint author. II. T.
JK2498.Z4    328.73/07/68    LC 69-11347

## JK2700–9600 Individual States

**Bryan, Frank M.** 4.8261
Yankee politics in rural Vermont / by Frank M. Bryan. — Hanover, N.H.: University Press of New England, 1974. xviii, 314 p.: ill.; 24 cm. 1. Apportionment (Election law) — Vermont. 2. Political parties — Vermont. 3. Vermont — Politics and government — 1865- I. T.
JK3095.B8    320.9/743/04    LC 73-78913    ISBN 0874510821

**Dennison, George M.** 4.8262
The Dorr War: republicanism on trial, 1831–1861 / George M. Dennison. — Lexington: University Press of Kentucky, c1976. xiv, 250 p.; 23 cm. A revision of the author's thesis, University of Washington, Seattle. Includes index. 1. Dorr, Thomas Wilson, 1805-1854. 2. Rhode Island — Politics and government 3. Rhode Island — Constitutional history. 4. United States — Constitutional history I. T.
JK3225 1842.D45 1976    320.9/745/03    LC 75-3543    ISBN 081311330X

**Underwood, James E.** 4.8263
Governor Rockefeller in New York: the apex of pragmatic liberalism in the United States / James E. Underwood and William J. Daniels. — Westport, Conn.: Greenwood Press, 1982. xvi, 335 p.: ill.; 25 cm. — (Contributions in political science. 0147-1066; no. 75) Includes index. 1. Rockefeller, Nelson A. (Nelson Aldrich), 1908-1979. 2. New York (State) — Politics and government — 1951- I. Daniels, William J. II. T. III. Series.
JK3425 1982.U52    353.974703/1/0924 19    LC 81-13259    ISBN 0313213356

**Connery, Robert Howe, 1907-.** 4.8264
Rockefeller of New York: executive power in the statehouse / by Robert H. Connery and Gerald Benjamin. — Ithaca, N.Y.: Cornell University Press, 1979. 480 p.: ill.; 24 cm. 1. Rockefeller, Nelson A. (Nelson Aldrich), 1908-1979. 2. Executive power — New York (State) 3. New York (State) —

Governors — Powers and duties. 4. New York (State) — Politics and government — 1951- I. Benjamin, Gerald. joint author. II. T.
JK3451.C66    353.9/747/032    *LC* 78-23947    *ISBN* 0801411882

**A Virginia profile, 1960–2000: assessing current trends and** • 4.8265
**problems / edited by John V. Moeser.**
Palisades Park, N.J.: Commonwealth Books, 1983. xi, 290 p.: ill.; 22 cm. — (Commonwealth Books public policy series.) 1. Virginia — Politics and government — 1951- 2. Virginia — Economic policy. 3. Virginia — Social policy. I. Moeser, John V., 1942- II. Series.
JK3925 1981.V55    975.5/043 19    *ISBN* 0940390019

**Thornton, J. Mills, 1943-.** 4.8266
Politics and power in a slave society: Alabama, 1800–1860 / J. Mills Thornton III. — Baton Rouge: Louisiana State University Press, c1978. xxiv, 492 p.: ill.; 24 cm. Includes index. 1. Alabama — Politics and government — To 1865 I. T.
JK4525 1977.T48    320.9/761/05    *LC* 77-4296    *ISBN* 0807102598

**Hyink, Bernard L.** • 4.8267
Politics & government in California / [by] Bernard L. Hyink, Seyom Brown [and] Ernest W. Thacker. — 8th ed. New York: Crowell [1973] viii, 292 p.: ill.; 23 cm. 1. California — Politics and government — 1951- I. Brown, Seyom. joint author. II. Thacker, Ernest W. joint author. III. T.
JK8725 1973.H9    320.9794 19    *LC* 73-4985    *ISBN* 0690001495

## JK9661–9993 CONFEDERATE STATES

**Warner, Ezra J.** 4.8268
Biographical register of the Confederate Congress / Ezra J. Warner and W. Buck Yearns. — Baton Rouge: Louisiana State University Press, c1975. xviii, 319 p., [5] leaves of plates: ill.; 25 cm. 1. Confedcrate States of America. Congress — Biography. 2. Confederate States of America. Congress — Registers. I. Yearns, W. Buck (Wilfred Buck), 1918- joint author. II. T.
JK9663.W3    328.75/092/2 B    *LC* 74-77329    *ISBN* 0807100927

## JL1–500 Canada

**Dawson, Robert MacGregor, 1895-1958.** • 4.8269
The government of Canada [by] R. MacGregor Dawson. 5th ed. rev. by Norman Ward. [Toronto] University of Toronto Press [1970] xiv, 569 p. 24 cm. (Canadian government series, 2) 1. Canada — Politics and government 2. Canada — Constitutional history. I. Ward, Norman, 1918- II. T. III. Series.
JL15.D3 1970    342/.71    *LC* 73-18110

**Martin, Chester Bailey, 1882-1958.** • 4.8270
Empire & commonwealth; studies in governance and self-government in Canada, by Chester Martin ... — Oxford, The Clarendon press, 1929. xxi, 385, [1] p. 23 cm. 1. Canada — Constitutional history. 2. Canada — Pol. & govt. 3. Imperial federation I. T. II. Title: Governance and self-government in Canada.
JL15.M3    *LC* 29-15655

**Armstrong, Christopher, 1942-.** 4.8271
The politics of federalism: Ontario's relations with the Federal Government, 1867–1942 / Christopher Armstrong. — Toronto; Buffalo: University of Toronto Press, c1981. xiv, 279 p.: map; 24 cm. — (Ontario historical studies series. 0380-9188) 'A project of the Board of Trustees of the Ontario Historical Studies Series for the Government of Ontario.' 1. Federal government — Canada — History. 2. Canada — Politics and government — 1867-1914 3. Canada — Politics and government — 1914-1945 4. Ontario — Politics and government. I. T. II. Series.
JL27.A75    321.02/3/0971 19    *LC* 81-157524    *ISBN* 0802024343

**Bakvis, Herman.** 4.8272
Federalism and the organization of political life: Canada in comparative perspective / Herman Bakvis. — Kingston, Ont., Canada: Institute of Intergovernmental Relations, Queen's University; Port Credit, Ont.: Distributed by P.D. Meany Co., c1981. ix, 98 p.; 23 cm. — (Queen's studies on the future of the Canadian communities. 0708-3289; 2) Errata slip inserted. 1. Federal government — Canada. 2. Minorities — Canada. 3. Comparative government I. T. II. Series.
JL27.B34 1981    321.02/0971 19    *LC* 82-210724    *ISBN* 0889110328

**Black, Edwin R.** 4.8273
Divided loyalties: Canadian concepts of federalism / Edwin R. Black. — Montreal: McGill-Queen's University Press, [1975] vii, 272 p.; 24 cm. 1. Federal government — Canada. I. T.
JL27.B53    321/.02    *LC* 75-319658    *ISBN* 0773502300

**Canada and the new constitution: the unfinished agenda / edited** 4.8274
**by Stanley M. Beck and Ivan Bernier.**
Montreal: Institute for Research on Public Policy = l'Institut de recherches politiques, c1983. 2 v.; 23 cm. Includes some text in French. 1. Canada — Constitutional law — Amendments — Addresses, essays, lectures. I. Beck, Stanley M. II. Bernier, Ivan. III. Institute for Research on Public Policy.
JL27.C342    342.71/03 19    *ISBN* 0920380735

**The Future of North America: Canada, the United States, and** 4.8275
**Quebec nationalism / edited by Elliot J. Feldman, Neil Nevitte.**
Cambridge, Mass.: Center for International Affairs, Harvard University; Montreal, Quebec: Institute for Research on Public Policy, c1979. 378; 23 cm. (Harvard studies in international affairs. no. 42) 'Essays ... written originally as papers for presentation at Harvard University's 1977-78 Seminar on Canadian-United States Relations.' 1. Federal government — Canada — Addresses, essays, lectures. 2. Nationalism — Québec (Province) — Addresses, essays, lectures. 3. Canada — Relations — United States — Addresses, essays, lectures. 4. United States — Relations — Canada — Addresses, essays, lectures. I. Feldman, Elliot J. II. Nevitte, Neil. III. Harvard University. Center for International Affairs. IV. Institute for Research on Public Policy. V. Seminar on Canadian-United States Relations. VI. Series.
JL27.F87    321.02/0971 19    *LC* 78-71645    *ISBN* 087674045X

**Gérin-Lajoie, Paul, 1920-.** • 4.8276
Constitutional amendment in Canada. Toronto, University of Toronto Press, 1950. xliii, 340 p. (Canadian government series, 3) Includes the Statute of Westminster, 1931, and the British North America (no. 2) act, 1949. 1. Canada Constitution — Amendments I. Canada. Constitution II. Great Britain. Laws, statutes, etc. Statute of Westminster, 1931 III. T. IV. Series.
JL27 G4    *LC* 51-6660

**Political support in Canada: the crisis years: essays in honor of** 4.8277
**Richard A. Preston / by E. Donald Briggs ... [et al.]; edited by**
**Allan Kornberg and Harold D. Clarke.**
Durham, N.C.: Duke University Press, 1983. xvi, 463 p.; 25 cm. — (Duke University Center for International Studies publication.) 1. Federal government — Canada — Addresses, essays, lectures. 2. Allegiance — Canada — Addresses, essays, lectures. 3. Legitimacy of governments — Canada — Addresses, essays, lectures. 4. Political participation — Canada — Addresses, essays, lectures. I. Preston, Richard Arthur. II. Briggs, E. Donald. III. Kornberg, Allan. IV. Clarke, Harold D. V. Series.
JL27.P64 1983    320.971 19    *LC* 83-11567    *ISBN* 0822305461

**Schwartz, Mildred A.** 4.8278
Politics and territory; the sociology of regional persistence in Canada [by] Mildred A. Schwartz. — Montreal: McGill-Queen's University Press, 1974. xii, 344 p.: illus.; 24 cm. 1. Regionalism — Canada. 2. Political parties — Canada. I. T.
JL27.S36    301.5/92    *LC* 73-79502    *ISBN* 0773501665

**Simeon, Richard.** 4.8279
Federal–provincial diplomacy; the making of recent policy in Canada. — [Toronto; Buffalo, N.Y.]: University of Toronto Press, [1972] xvii, 324 p.; 24 cm. — (Studies in the structure of power, decision-making in Canada. 5) Originally presented as the author's thesis, Yale. 1. Federal government — Canada. I. T. II. Series.
JL27.S5 1972    320.4/71    *LC* 74-163822    *ISBN* 0802017835

**Stevenson, Garth.** 4.8280
Unfulfilled union: Canadian federalism and national unity / Garth Stevenson. — Toronto: Macmillan of Canada, 1979. x, 257 p.; 22 cm. — (Canadian controversies series) 1. Federal government — Canada. I. T.
JL27.S73    321/.02/0971    *LC* 79-319945    *ISBN* 0770517870

**Trudeau, Pierre Elliott.** • 4.8281
[Fédéralisme et la société canadienne-française. English] Federalism and the French Canadians. With an introd. by John T. Saywell. New York, St. Martin's Press, 1968. xxvi, 212 p. 23 cm. Translation of Le Fédéralisme et la société canadienne-française. 1. Federal government — Canada. 2. Canada — English-French relations I. T.
JL27.T713 1968    320/.0971    *LC* 68-29110

**Canada. Parliament, 1865.** • 4.8282
The Confederation debates in the Province of Canada, 1865: a selection / edited and introduced by P. B. Waite. — Toronto: McClelland and Stewart, c1963. 157, [2] p.; 19 cm. — (The Carleton library; no. 2) 1. Canada — Politics and government — 1841-1867 — Sources. 2. Canada — Constitutional history — Sources. I. Waite, Peter B. II. T.
JL55.C26 1963    342.71/024    *LC* 80-455119

**The Politics of Canadian public policy / edited by Michael M.** 4.8283
**Atkinson and Marsha A. Chandler.**
Toronto; Buffalo: University of Toronto Press, c1983. 286 p.; 24 cm. 1. Canada — Politics and government — Addresses, essays, lectures. 2. Canada — Economic policy — Addresses, essays, lectures. 3. Canada — Social policy —

Addresses, essays, lectures. I. Atkinson, Michael M. II. Chandler, Marsha A., 1945-
JL61.P68 1983    361.6/1/0971 19    *LC* 83-171573    *ISBN* 0802024858

**Smiley, Donald V.**    • **4.8284**
The Canadian political nationality, by Donald V. Smiley. — Toronto; London: Methuen, 1967. xv, 142 p.; 23 cm. 1. Canada — Politics and government — 1914- I. T.
JL65.1967.S4    320.9/71    *LC* 67-25014

**Hockin, Thomas A., 1938-.**    **4.8285**
Government in Canada / Thomas A. Hockin. — New York: Norton, 1976 (c1975). 252 p.: maps; 22 cm. — (Comparative modern governments) Includes index. 1. Canada — Politics and government — 1945-1980 I. T.
JL65 1975.H63    320.4/71    *LC* 76-5846    *ISBN* 0393055329. *ISBN* 0393092941 pbk

**McWhinney, Edward.**    **4.8286**
Quebec and the Constitution, 1960–1978 / Edward McWhinney. — Toronto; Buffalo: University of Toronto Press, 1979. xvi, 170 p.; 23 cm. 1. Canada — Constitutional history. 2. Québec (Province) — History — Autonomy and independence movements 3. Québec (Province) — Politics and government — 1960- I. T.
JL65 1979.M32    342.71/05 347.1025 19    *LC* 79-316335    *ISBN* 0802054560

## JL88–185 BRANCHES OF GOVERNMENT

**Apex of power: the Prime Minister and political leadership in Canada / edited by Thomas A. Hockin.**    **4.8287**
2d ed. — Scarborough, Ont.: Prentice-Hall of Canada, c1977. xv, 359 p.: ill.; 23 cm. 1. Prime ministers — Canada — Addresses, essays, lectures. 2. Canada — Politics and government — 1945-1980 — Addresses, essays, lectures.
JL99.H62 1977    320.9/71/06    *LC* 77-373755    *ISBN* 0130386537

**The Biography of an institution; the Civil Service Commission of Canada, 1908–1967 [by] J. E. Hodgetts [and others]**    **4.8288**
Montreal, McGill-Queen's University Press, 1972. xi, 532 p. 24 cm. (Canadian public administration series.) 1. Civil Service Commission of Canada — History. I. Hodgetts, J. E., 1917- II. Series.
JL108.B56    354/.71/006    *LC* 72-87185    *ISBN* 0773501401 *ISBN* 0773501592

**Hodgetts, J. E., 1917-.**    **4.8289**
The Canadian public service; a physiology of government, 1867–1970 [by] J. E. Hodgetts. — [Toronto; Buffalo]: University of Toronto Press, [1973] xiii, 363 p.: ill.; 24 cm. — (Studies in the structure of power, decision-making in Canada.) 1. Civil service — Canada. 2. Canada — Politics and government — 1867- 3. Canada — Executive departments. I. T. II. Series.
JL108.H62    354/.71/04    *LC* 72-90738    *ISBN* 0802018637

**Jackson, Robert J., 1936-.**    **4.8290**
The Canadian legislative system: politicians and policymaking / Robert J. Jackson and Michael M. Atkinson. — 2d rev. ed. — Toronto: Macmillan of Canada, 1980. xiv, 222 p.; 22 cm. — (Canadian controversies series) 1. Canada. Parliament. 2. Canada — Politics and government — 1945-1980 I. Atkinson, Michael M. joint author. II. T.
JL136.J3 1980    328.71 19    *LC* 80-489660    *ISBN* 0770518486

**The Legislative process in Canada: the need for reform: proceedings of a conference held at the University of Victoria and sponsored by the Institute for Research on Public Policy and the Faculty of Law, University of Victoria, March 31–April 1, 1978 / edited by William A. W. Neilson and James C. MacPherson.**    **4.8291**
[Montreal]: Institute for Research on Public Policy; Toronto: distributed by Butterworth and Co. (Canada), 1979 (c1978). xii, 328 p.; 23 cm. Includes summary in French. 1. Legislative bodies — Canada — Congresses. 2. Legislation — Canada — Congresses. I. Neilson, William A. W. II. MacPherson, J. C. (James C.), 1950- III. Institute for Research on Public Policy. IV. University of Victoria (B. C.). Faculty of Law.
JL136.L43    328.71    *LC* 80-452166    *ISBN* 0920380115

**Presthus, Robert Vance.**    **4.8292**
Elite accommodation in Canadian politics [by] Robert Presthus. — Cambridge [Eng.]: University Press, 1973. xii, 372 p.; 24 cm. 1. Pressure groups — Canada. 2. Political participation — Canada. 3. Elite (Social sciences) I. T.
JL167.P7    322.4/3/0971    *LC* 72-83598    *ISBN* 0521086957

## JL191–194 SUFFRAGE. ELECTIONS

**Cleverdon, Catherine Lyle.**    **4.8293**
The woman suffrage movement in Canada [by] Catherine L. Cleverdon. With an introd. by Ramsay Cook. [2d ed. — Toronto; Buffalo]: University of Toronto Press, [1974] xxvi, xiii, 324 p.: illus.; 23 cm. — (Social history of Canada. 18) Originally published as the author's thesis, Columbia University, 1950. 1. Women — Suffrage — Canada. I. T. II. Series.
JL192.C6 1974    324/.3/0971    *LC* 73-82587    *ISBN* 0802021085

**Absent mandate: the politics of discontent in Canada / Harold D. Clarke ... [et al.].**    **4.8294**
Toronto, Ont., Canada: Gage, c1984. xi, 193 p.: ill.; 21 cm. — (Canadian controversies series.) Series statement from CIP data on verso t.p. 1. Elections — Canada. 2. Voting — Canada. 3. Canada — Politics and government — 1945-1980 I. Clarke, Harold D. II. Series.
JL193.A65 1984    324.971/0644 19    *LC* 84-180241    *ISBN* 0771555776

**Canada at the polls, 1979 and 1980: a study of the general elections / edited by Howard R. Penniman.**    **4.8295**
Washington, D.C.: American Enterprise Institute for Public Policy Research, c1981. xiv, 426 p.: ill., map; 23 cm. — (At the polls.) (Studies in political and social processes.) (AEI studies. 345) 1. Elections — Canada — Addresses, essays, lectures. 2. Political parties — Canada — Addresses, essays, lectures. 3. Canada — Politics and government — 1945-1980 — Addresses, essays, lectures. I. Penniman, Howard Rae, 1916- II. American Enterprise Institute for Public Policy Research. III. Series. IV. Series: Studies in political and social processes. V. Series: AEI studies. 345
JL193.C34    324.971/0645 19    *LC* 81-19144    *ISBN* 0844734748

**Canada at the polls: the general election of 1974 / edited by Howard R. Penniman.**    **4.8296**
Washington: American Enterprise Institute for Public Policy Research, 1975. 310 p.: graphs; 23 cm. — (Foreign affairs study; 24) 1. Elections — Canada — Addresses, essays, lectures. 2. Political parties — Canada — Addresses, essays, lectures. 3. Canada — Politics and government — 1945-1980 — Addresses, essays, lectures. I. Penniman, Howard Rae, 1916- II. Series.
JL193.C35    329/.023/710644    *LC* 75-24771    *ISBN* 0844731781

**Meisel, John.**    **4.8297**
Working papers on Canadian politics. — Montreal: McGill-Queen's University Press, 1972. xiii, 220 p.: illus.; 22 cm. 1. Elections — Canada. 2. Political parties — Canada. I. T.
JL193.M45    329/.00971    *LC* 72-78029    *ISBN* 0773501436

**Scarrow, Howard A.**    • **4.8298**
Canada votes; a handbook of Federal and Provincial election data. New Orleans, Hauser Press [1962] x, 238 p. diagrs., tables. (A Galleon book) 1. Canada. Parliament — Elections 2. Local elections — Canada I. T.
JL193 S35    *LC* 62-14822

## JL195–198 POLITICAL PARTIES

**Engelmann, Frederick C.**    • **4.8299**
Political parties and the Canadian social structure / by Frederick C. Engelmann and Mildred A. Schwartz. — Scarborough, Ont.: Prentice-Hall of Canada, 1967. 277p. 1. Political parties — Canada. I. Schwartz, Mildred A. II. T.
JL195.E5    329.971    *LC* 67-18808

**Party politics in Canada / edited by Hugh G. Thorburn.**    **4.8300**
5th ed. — Scarborough, Ont.: Prentice-Hall, c1985. x, 349 p.: ill.; 23 cm. 1. Political parties — Canada. 2. Canada — Politics and government I. Thorburn, Hugh G., 1924-
JL195.P37 1985    324.271 19    *LC* 85-161047    *ISBN* 0136525954

**Political parties of the Americas: Canada, Latin America, and the West Indies / edited by Robert J. Alexander.**    **4.8301**
Westport, Conn.: Greenwood Press, 1982. 2 v. (xix, 864 p.); 25 cm. — (Greenwood historical encyclopedia of the world's political parties.) 1. Political parties — Canada. 2. Political parties — Latin America. 3. Political parties — West Indies. I. Alexander, Robert Jackson, 1918- II. Series.
JL195.P64 1982    324.2/098 19    *LC* 81-6952    *ISBN* 0313214743

**Robin, Martin.**    **4.8302**
Canadian provincial politics, the party systems of the ten provinces, edited by Martin Robin. Scarborough, Ont.: Prentice-Hall of Canada, [1972] 318 p.; 23 cm. 1. Political parties — Canada — Addresses, essays, lectures. 2. State governments — Canada — Addresses, essays, lectures. I. T.
JL195.R6    320.9/71    *LC* 70-109490

**Courtney, John C.** 　　　　　　　　　　　　　　4.8303
The selection of national party leaders in Canada [by] John C. Courtney. [Hamden, Conn.] Archon Books, 1973. xiv, 278 p. 24 cm. 1. Liberal Party of Canada. 2. Progressive Conservative Party (Canada) 3. Leadership I. T.
JL196.C68 1973　　　329.9/71　　　*LC* 72-14046　　　*ISBN* 0208013938

**Avakumovic, Ivan.** 　　　　　　　　　　　　　4.8304
The Communist Party in Canada: a history / Ivan Avakumovic. — Toronto: McClelland and Stewart, c1975. x, 309 p.; 21 cm. Includes index. 1. Communist Party of Canada — History. I. T.
JL197.C5 A9　　　329.9/71　　　*LC* 78-301511　　　*ISBN* 0771009801

**Lipset, Seymour Martin.** 　　　　　　　　　• 4.8305
Agrarian socialism: the Cooperative Commonwealth Federation in Saskatchewan, study in political sociology / S. M. Lipset. — Berkeley: University of California Press, 1950. xvii, 315 p. 1. Co-operative Commonwealth Federation (Saskatchewan) 2. Socialism — Saskatchewan 3. Saskatchewan — Politics and government. I. T.
JL197.C6 L5　　　329.9/7124　　　*LC* 50-10524

**McHenry, Dean Eugene, 1910-.** 　　　　　• 4.8306
The third force in Canada; the Cooperative Commonwealth Federation, 1932–1948. Berkeley, University of California Press, 1950. viii, 351 p. 'Second in a series on labour parties functioning within the British Commonwealth of Nations.' 1. Co-operative Commonwealth Federation I. T.
JL197 C6 M3　　　*LC* 50-5973

**Young, Walter D.** 　　　　　　　　　　　　• 4.8307
The anatomy of a party: the national CCF, 1932–1961 [by] Walter D. Young. — [Toronto]: University of Toronto Press, [c1969] 328 p.; 24 cm. 1. Co-operative Commonwealth Federation. I. T.
JL197.C6 Y6　　　329.9/71　　　*LC* 73-460705　　　*ISBN* 0802052215

**Whitaker, Reginald.** 　　　　　　　　　　　4.8308
The government party: organizing and financing the Liberal Party of Canada, 1930–58 / Reginald Whitaker. — Toronto; Buffalo: University of Toronto Press, c1977. xxiv, 507 p.; 24 cm. (Canadian government series; 20 0068-8835) Originally presented as the author's thesis, University of Toronto. 1. Liberal Party of Canada — History. 2. Canada — Politics and government — 1914-1945 3. Canada — Politics and government — 1945-1980 I. T. II. Series.
JL197.L5 W48 1977　　329.9/71　　*LC* 78-301195　　*ISBN* 0802054013. *ISBN* 0802063209 pbk

**English, John, 1945-.** 　　　　　　　　　　4.8309
The decline of politics: the Conservatives and the party system, 1901–20 / John English. — Toronto; Buffalo: University of Toronto Press, c1977. x, 237 p.; 24 cm. — (Canadian government series; 19 0068-8835) 1. Borden, Robert Laird, Sir, 1854-1937. 2. Progressive Conservative Party (Canada) — History. 3. Canada — Politics and government — 20th century I. T. II. Series.
JL197.P67 E53　　329.9/71　　*LC* 78-321958　　*ISBN* 0802053866

**Granatstein, J. L.** 　　　　　　　　　　　• 4.8310
The politics of survival; the Conservative Party of Canada, 1939–1945 [by] J. L. Granatstein. — [Toronto]: University of Toronto Press, [1967] ix, 231 p.; 24 cm. 1. Progressive Conservative Party (Canada) 2. Canada — Politics and government — 1914- I. T.
JL197.P67 G7　　320.9/71　　*LC* 68-72926

**Perlin, George C.** 　　　　　　　　　　　　4.8311
The Tory syndrome: leadership politics in the Progressive Conservative Party / George C. Perlin. — Montreal: McGill-Queen's University Press, c1980. xii, 250 p.; 24 cm. 1. Progressive Conservative Party (Canada) 2. Leadership 3. Canada — Politics and government — 20th century I. T.
JL197.P67 P47　　324.27104　　*LC* 80-474879　　*ISBN* 0773503501

**Dyck, Perry Rand, 1943-.** 　　　　　　　　4.8312
Provincial politics in Canada / Rand Dyck. — Scarborough, Ont.: Prentice-Hall Canada, 1986. — 626 p.: ill. Includes index. 1. Federal government — Canada I. T.
JL198.D93 1986　　320.971 19　　*LC* 86-223281　　*ISBN* 0137316623

**Kornberg, Allan.** 　　　　　　　　　　　　4.8313
Representative democracy in the Canadian provinces / Allan Kornberg, William Mishler, Harold D. Clarke. — Scarborough, Ont.: Prentice-Hall Canada, c1982. xii, 292 p.: ill.; 23 cm. 1. State governments — Canada. 2. Representative government and representation — Canada — Provinces. I. Mishler, William, 1947- II. Clarke, Harold D. III. T.
JL198.K67 1982　　320.971 19　　*LC* 82-188852　　*ISBN* 0137737548

**Dion, Léon, 1923-.** 　　　　　　　　　　　4.8314
Quebec: the unfinished revolution / Léon Dion; foreword by Hugh Thorburn [; translation by Thérèse Romer]. Montreal [Que.]: McGill-Queen's University Press, 1976. xiii, 218 p.; 24 cm. Translation with revisions of La prochaine

révolution. 1. Québec (Province) — Politics and government 2. Québec (Province) — Economic conditions. I. T.
JL243 1976.D5613　　320.9/714/04　　*LC* 77-352511　　*ISBN* 0773502424

**Saywell, John T., 1929-.** 　　　　　　　　　4.8315
The rise of the Parti québécois 1967–76 / John Saywell. — Toronto; Buffalo: University of Toronto Press, c1977. 174 p.: ill.; 24 cm. Originally published in the Canadian annual review, 1967-1970, and the Canadian annual review of politics and public affairs, 1971-1976. 1. Parti québécois. 2. Québec (Province) — Politics and government — 1960- I. T.
JL259.A56 S28　　329.9/714　　*LC* 77-372992　　*ISBN* 0802022758

**Quinn, Herbert Furlong, 1910-.** 　　　　　4.8316
The Union nationale: Quebec nationalism from Duplessis to Lévesque / Herbert F. Quinn. — 2d enl. ed. — Toronto; Buffalo: University of Toronto Press, 1979. xiii, 342 p.; 24 cm. Includes index. 1. Union nationale (Canada) — History. 2. Nationalism — Québec (Province) — History. 3. Québec (Province) — Politics and government I. T.
JL259.A58 Q56 1979　　324.2714/093　　*LC* 80-472454　　*ISBN* 0802023185

## JL243–500 PROVINCIAL POLITICS

**Beck, J. Murray (James Murray), 1914-.** 　　• 4.8317
The Government of Nova Scotia. — Toronto, University of Toronto Press, 1957. xii, 372 p. diagr., geneal. table, tables. 24 cm. — (Canadian Government series, 8) Bibliographical footnotes. 1. Nova Scotia — Pol. & govt. I. T. II. Series.
JL304.B4　　342.716　　*LC* 58-542

**Smith, David E., 1936-.** 　　　　　　　　　4.8318
Prairie liberalism: the Liberal Party in Saskatchewan, 1905–71 / David E. Smith. — Toronto; Buffalo: University of Toronto Press, [1975] x, 352 p.; 24 cm. (Canadian government series; 18 0068-8835) Includes index. 1. Liberal Party of Canada. 2. Saskatchewan — Politics and government. I. T. II. Series.
JL319.A54 S6 1975　　329.9/7124　　*LC* 74-78676　　*ISBN* 0802053130

**Thorburn, Hugh G., 1924-.** 　　　　　　　• 4.8319
Politics in New Brunswick. — Toronto, University of Toronto Press, 1961. vi, 217 p. maps, diagrs., tables. 24 cm. — (Canadian government series, 10) Bibliographical footnotes. 1. New Brunswick — Pol. & govt. I. T. II. Series.
JL350.T47　　354.715　　*LC* 63-25108

**MacKinnon, Frank.** 　　　　　　　　　　　• 4.8320
The government of Prince Edward Island. — Toronto, University of Toronto Press, 1951. xii, 385 p. 24 cm. — (Canadian Government series, 5) Bibliography: p. 369-371. 1. Prince Edward Island — Pol. & govt. 2. Prince Edward Island — Constitutional history. I. T. II. Series.
JL382.M3　　342.717　　*LC* 53-2186

**Lingard, Charles Cecil, 1901-.** 　　　　　　• 4.8321
Territorial government in Canada; the autonomy question in the old Northwest territories, by C. Cecil Lingard ... — Toronto, The University of Toronto press, 1946. xi, 269 p. illus. (maps) 23 cm. Bibliography: p. [261]-264. 1. Northwest territories, Canada — Constitutional history. I. T.
JL462.L5　　342.71　　*LC* A 47-2812

**Thomas, Lewis Herbert, 1917-.** 　　　　　• 4.8322
The struggle for responsible government in the Northwest Territories, 1870–97 / Lewis Herbert Thomas. — Toronto: University of Toronto Press, 1956. viii, 276 p.: ill., maps. 1. Northwest Territories, Canada — Politics and government I. T.
JL462 T5　　JL462 T5.　　*LC* 56-3490

**Donnelly, Murray S.** 　　　　　　　　　　• 4.8323
The Government of Manitoba. — [Toronto?] University of Toronto Press [c1963] 185 p. 24 cm. — (Canadian government series, 14) 'Ph. D. dissertation ... updated to June 1960.' Bibliography: p. [176]180. 1. Manitoba — Pol. & govt. I. T. II. Series.
JL500.M3D6　　354.71　　*LC* 63-23544

## JL950–3899 Latin America

**Lynch, John, 1927-.** 　　　　　　　　　　• 4.8324
Spanish colonial administration, 1782–1810; the intendant system in the Viceroyalty of the Río de la Plata. New York, Greenwood Press [1969, c1958] xi, 335 p. maps. 23 cm. 1. Río de la Plata (Viceroyaity) 2. Spain — Colonies — America — Administration. I. T.
JL950.L9 1969　　325.3/1/0946　　*LC* 69-13979

**Johnson, John J., 1912-.**     4.8325
Political change in Latin America: the emergence of the middle sectors. — Stanford, Calif.: Stanford University Press, 1958. xiii, 272 p.; 22 cm. — (Stanford studies in history, economics, and political science, 15) 1. Middle classes — Latin America. 2. Latin America — Politics and government 3. Latin America — Social conditions I. T.
JL952.J6     323.32     *LC* 58-11696

**Véliz, Claudio.**     4.8326
The centralist tradition of Latin America / Claudio Véliz. — Princeton, N.J.: Princeton University Press, c1980. xii, 355 p.; 23 cm. Includes index. 1. Decentralization in government — Latin America. 2. Authoritarianism 3. Latin America — Social conditions I. T.
JL956.S8 V44     320.9/8     *LC* 79-84019     *ISBN* 0691052808

**Authoritarianism and corporatism in Latin America / James M.**     4.8327
**Malloy, editor.**
Pittsburgh: University of Pittsburgh Press, x1977. x, 549 p.; 24 cm. — (Pitt Latin American series) 'Outgrowth of a conference ... held at the University of Pittsburgh in April 1974.' Includes index. 1. Corporate state — Latin America — Congresses. 2. Authoritarianism — Latin America — Congresses. 3. Latin America — Politics and government — 1948- — Congresses. I. Malloy, James M.
JL958.A9     320.9/8/003     *LC* 76-6669     *ISBN* 0822933284. *ISBN* 0822952750 pbk

**Denton L., Carlos F.**     4.8328
Latin American politics: a functional approach [by] Charles F. Denton [and] Preston Lee Lawrence. San Francisco, Chandler Pub. Co. [1972] xii, 242 p. illus. 23 cm. (Chandler publications in political science) 1. Latin America — Politics and government — 1948- I. Lawrence, Preston Lee, joint author. II. T.
JL960.D47     320.9/8/003     *LC* 74-179035     *ISBN* 081020455X

**The New authoritarianism in Latin America / David Collier,**     • 4.8329
**editor; contributors, Fernando Henrique Cardoso ... [et al.];**
**sponsored by the Joint Committee on Latin American Studies of**
**the Social Science Research Council and the American Council**
**of Learned Societies.**
Princeton, N.J.: Princeton University Press, c1979. 456 p.: ill.; 24 cm. Includes index. 1. Authoritarianism — Latin America — Addresses, essays, lectures. 2. Bureaucracy — Addresses, essays, lectures. 3. Latin America — Politics and government — 1948- — Addresses, essays, lectures. 4. Latin America — Armed Forces — Political activity — Addresses, essays, lectures. I. Collier, David, 1942- II. Cardoso, Fernando Henrique. III. Joint Committee on Latin American Studies.
JL960.N48     320.9/8/003     *LC* 79-83982     *ISBN* 0691076162

**Parry, J. H. (John Horace), 1914-.**     • 4.8330
The Audiencia of New Galicia in the sixteenth century: a study in Spanish colonial government / by J. H. Parry. — Cambridge, Eng.: University Press, 1948. 204 p.: fold. map. 1. Nueva Galicia, Mexico — Politics and government. I. T.
JL1200.Z9 N83     *LC* 49-21037

**Niemeyer, E. Victor (Eberhardt Victor), 1919-.**     4.8331
Revolution at Querétaro: The Mexican constitutional convention of 1916-1917, by E. V. Niemeyer, Jr. Austin, Published for the Institute of Latin American Studies by the University of Texas Press [1974] xiii, 297 p. illus. 23 cm. (Latin American monographs, no. 33) 1. Mexico. Congreso Constituyente (1916-1917) 2. Mexico — Constitutional history. I. University of Texas at Austin. Institute of Latin American Studies. II. T.
JL1215 1917.N53     342/.72/029     *LC* 73-20203     *ISBN* 0292770057

**Scott, Robert Edwin.**     • 4.8332
Mexican government in transition / by Robert E. Scott. — Rev. ed. — Urbana: University of Illinois Press, 1964. 345 p.; 21 cm. (Illini books, IB-20) Bibliography: p. 319-328. 1. Mexico — Pol. & govt. — 1910-1946. 2. Mexico — Pol. & govt. — 1946- I. T.
JL1231.S35 1964     320.972     *LC* 64-18222

**Needler, Martin C.**     4.8333
Mexican politics: the containment of conflict / Martin C. Needler. — New York, N.Y.: Praeger; Stanford, Calif.: Hoover Institution Press, 1982. xi, 157 p.: ill.; 24 cm. — (Politics in Latin America.) 'SE 155'—Spine. Includes index. 1. Mexico — Politics and government — 1970- I. T. II. Series.
JL1281.N43 1982     972.08/3 19     *LC* 82-5376     *ISBN* 0030620414

**Mabry, Donald J., 1941-.**     4.8334
Mexico's Accion Nacional; a Catholic alternative to revolution [by] Donald J. Mabry. — [1st ed. — Syracuse, N.Y.]: Syracuse University Press, 1973. xiv, 269 p.; 23 cm. 1. Acción Nacional (Mexico) I. T.
JL1298.A3 M24     329.9/72     *LC* 73-9975     *ISBN* 0815600968

**Von Sauer, Franz A.**     4.8335
The alienated 'loyal' opposition: Mexico's Partido Acción Nacional / Franz A. von Sauer. — 1st ed. — Albuquerque: University of New Mexico Press, [1974] xx, 197 p., [4] leaves of plates: ill.; 25 cm. Includes index. 1. Acción Nacional (Mexico) I. T.
JL1298.A3 V65     329.9/72     *LC* 74-80743     *ISBN* 0826303412

**Ropp, Steve C.**     4.8336
Panamanian politics: from guarded nation to national guard / Steve C. Ropp. — New York, N.Y.: Praeger; Stanford, Calif.: Hoover Institution Press, 1982. xvii, 151 p.: ill.; 24 cm. — (Politics in Latin America.) Includes index. 1. Panama Canal Treaties, 1977 2. Panama — Politics and government 3. Panama — Foreign relations. I. T. II. Series.
JL1648.R66 1982     972.87/05 19     *LC* 81-17831     *ISBN* 0030606225

**Romero, José Luis, 1909-.**     • 4.8337
A history of Argentine political thought. Introd. and translation [of the 3d ed.] by Thomas F. McGann. Stanford, Calif., Stanford University Press, 1963. 270 p. ill. 1. Argentina — Constitutional history 2. Argentina — Social conditions I. T.
JL2011 R613     *LC* 63-12042

**Walter, Richard J.**     4.8338
The Socialist Party of Argentina, 1890–1930 / by Richard J. Walter. — Austin: Institute of Latin American Studies, University of Texas at Austin: distributed by the University of Texas Press, c1977. xx, 284 p.: map; 24 cm. (Latin American monographs; no. 42) Includes index. 1. Partido Socialista (Argentina) — History. I. T.
JL2098.S6 W34     329.9/82     *LC* 77-620003     *ISBN* 0292775393. *ISBN* 0292775407 pbk

**Erickson, Kenneth Paul.**     4.8339
The Brazilian corporative state and working-class politics / Kenneth Paul Erickson. — Berkeley: University of California Press, 1978 (c1977). xvii, 225 p.: ill.; 25 cm. Includes index. 1. Corporate state — Brazil. 2. Trade-unions — Brazil — Political activity. 3. Labor and laboring classes — Brazil — Political activity. 4. Brazil — Politics and government — 1964-1985 I. T.
JL2415 1977.E74     322/.2/0981     *LC* 75-40661     *ISBN* 0520031628

**Gil, Federico Guillermo.**     • 4.8340
The political system of Chile / [by] Federico G. Gill. — Boston: Houghton Mifflin [1966] ix, 323 p.: ill., map; 21 cm. Bibliography: p. 315-318. 1. Chile — Pol. & govt. — 1920- 2. Chile — Soc. condit. I. T.
JL2615 1966.G5     320.983     *LC* 66-2177

**Furci, Carmelo.**     4.8341
The Chilean Communist Party and the road to socialism / Carmelo Furci. — London: Zed Books; Totowa, N.J.: U.S. distributor, Biblio Distribution Center, 1985 (c1984). xiv, 204 p.: ill.; 23 cm. Includes index. 1. Partido Comunista de Chile — History. I. T.
JL2698.C5 F87 1984     324.283/075 19     *LC* 84-200157     *ISBN* 0862322367

**Fleet, Michael.**     4.8342
The rise and fall of Chilean Christian democracy / Michael Fleet. — Princeton, N.J.: Princeton University Press, c1985. xv, 274 p.; 25 cm. Includes index. 1. Partido Demócrata-Cristiano (Chile) 2. Christian democracy — Chile. 3. Chile — Politics and government — 1920-1970 4. Chile — Politics and government — 1970-1973 I. T.
JL2698.D4 F54 1985     324.283/072 19     *LC* 84-42885     *ISBN* 0691076847

**Politics of compromise: coalition government in Colombia /**     4.8343
**edited by R. Albert Berry, Ronald G. Hellman, Mauricio**
**Solaún.**
New Brunswick, N.J.: Transaction Books, c1980. xii, 488 p.: ill.; 24 cm. 'A Center for Inter-American Relations book.' 1. Partido Conservador (Colombia) — Addresses, essays, lectures. 2. Partido Liberal (Colombia) — Addresses, essays, lectures. 3. Coalition governments — Colombia — Addresses, essays, lectures. 4. Colombia — Politics and government — 1974- — Addresses, essays, lectures. I. Berry, R. Albert. II. Hellman, Ronald G. III. Solaún, Mauricio.
JL2831.P64     320.9/861/063     *LC* 78-64478     *ISBN* 0878553010

**Blanksten, George I.**     • 4.8344
Ecuador: constitutions and caudillos. New York: Russell & Russell, 1964. xii, 196 p.: map, tables; 23 cm. (University of California publications in political science.) Reprint of the 1951 ed. 1. Ecuador — Constitutional history. 2. Ecuador — Politics and government — 1830- I. T.
JL3011.B55 1964     *LC* 64-16465

**Martz, John D.**     4.8345
Ecuador: conflicting political culture and the quest for progress [by] John D. Martz. — Boston: Allyn and Bacon, [1972] viii, 216 p.: illus.; 22 cm. — (The Allyn and Bacon series in Latin American politics) 1. Ecuador — Politics and

government — 1944- 2. Ecuador — Economic conditions — 1972- 3. Ecuador
— Social conditions. I. T.
JL3031.M35     309.1/866/07     *LC* 70-189205

**Gibson, Charles, 1920-.**     • **4.8346**
The Inca concept of sovereignty and the Spanish administration in Peru. —
New York: Greenwood Press, [1969] 146 p.: map.; 24 cm. — (University of
Texas. Institute of Latin-American studies. Latin-American studies, 4) Reprint
of the 1948 ed. 1. Sovereignty 2. Incas 3. Peru — History — Conquest,
1522-1548 4. Peru — Politics and government — 1548-1820 I. T.
JL3400.G5 1969     320.1/57/0985     *LC* 69-19004

**Fisher, John Robert.**     **4.8347**
Government and society in colonial Peru; the intendant system 1784–1814, by
J. R. Fisher. London, University of London, Athlone P., 1970. xii, 289 p. map.
23 cm. (University of London historical studies, 29) 1. Intendants 2. Peru —
Politics and government — 1548-1820 3. Spain — Colonies — America —
Administration. I. T.
JL3426 1784.F56     325.3/46/0985     *LC* 70-21018     *ISBN*
0485131293

**Stepan, Alfred C.**     **4.8348**
The state and society: Peru in comparative perspective / by Alfred Stepan. —
Princeton, N.J.: Princeton University Press, c1978. xix, 348 p.: ill.; 24 cm.
Includes index. 1. State, The 2. Corporate state 3. Peru — Politics and
government — 1968- 4. Peru — Social policy. 5. Peru — Economic policy.
I. T.
JL3431.S73     321.9     *LC* 77-85567     *ISBN* 0691075913

**Kantor, Harry.**     • **4.8349**
The ideology and program of the Peruvian Aprista movement. — Washington:
Savile Books, 1966. v, 175 p.: port.; 24 cm. Reprint of 1953 ed., published as v.
4, no. 1 of the University of California publications in political science.
Bibliography: p. 151-166. 1. Partido del Pueblo (Peru) 2. Peru — Pol. & govt.
— 1919- I. T.
JL3498.A6K35 1966     329.985     *LC* 66-20722

**Klarén, Peter F., 1938-.**     **4.8350**
Modernization, dislocation, and Aprismo; origins of the Peruvian Aprista
Party, 1870–1932, by Peter F. Klarén. Austin, Published for the Institute of
Latin American Studies by the University of Texas Press [1973] xxiii, 189 p.
illus. 23 cm. (Latin American monographs, no. 32) 1. Partido Aprista Peruano.
I. University of Texas at Austin. Institute of Latin American Studies. II. T.
JL3498.A6 K53     329.9/85     *LC* 73-4915     *ISBN* 0292760019

**Taylor, Philip Bates.**     • **4.8351**
Government and politics of Uruguay / by Philip B. Taylor, Jr. — New Orleans:
Tulane University, 1960, [c1962] 285 p., [2] folded leaves of plates: charts; 24
cm. (Tulane studies in political science. v. 7) Includes index. 1. Uruguay —
Politics and government — 1810- 2. Uruguay — Constitutional history. I. T.
II. Series.
JL3611.T39 1962     320.9895 19     *LC* 62-2464

**Blank, David Eugene.**     **4.8352**
Venezuela, politics in a petroleum republic / David Eugene Blank. — New
York: Praeger, 1984. xi, 225 p.: ill.; 25 cm. — (Politics in Latin America.)
Includes index. 1. Petroleum industry and trade — Venezuela. 2. Petroleum
industry and trade — Government policy — Venezuela. 3. Venezuela —
Politics and government — 1958- I. T. II. Series.
JL3881.B57 1984     987/.0633 19     *LC* 83-24469     *ISBN* 0030697921

**Levine, Daniel H.**     **4.8353**
Conflict and political change in Venezuela / by Daniel H. Levine. —
[Princeton, N.J.]: Princeton University Press, [1973] xiii, 285 p.: ill.; 23 cm.
Earlier version presented as the author's thesis, Yale. 1. Political parties —
Venezuela. 2. Education — Venezuela. 3. Students — Venezuela — Political
activity. 4. Venezuela — Social conditions — 1958- 5. Venezuela — Politics
and government — 1958- I. T.
JL3898.A1 L48 1973     320.9/87/063     *LC* 75-39790     *ISBN*
0691075476

**Herman, Donald L.**     **4.8354**
Christian Democracy in Venezuela / Donald L. Herman. — Chapel Hill:
University of North Carolina Press, c1980. xiv, 289 p.; 24 cm. Includes index.
1. COPEI. 2. Venezuela — Politics and government I. T.
JL3898.S6 H47     329.9/87     *LC* 79-24582     *ISBN* 0807814253

# JN Europe

## JN1–97 General

**The Europa year book.**     • **4.8355**
1st ed. (1959)-     . — London: Europa Publications, 1959-. v.; 26 cm. Annual.
1. European federation — Periodicals. 2. Europe — Politics and government
— Periodicals. I. Europa Publications Limited.
JN1.E85     940.55/05 19     *LC* 59-2942

**Babuscio, Jack.**     **4.8356**
European political facts, 1648–1789 / by Jack Babuscio and Richard Minta
Dunn. — New York, NY: Facts on File, 1984. ix, 387 p.; 25 cm. Includes index.
1. Europe — Politics and government — 1648-1789 2. Europe — Economic
conditions I. Dunn, Richard Minta. II. T.
JN9.B3 1984     940.2/5 19     *LC* 83-25390     *ISBN* 0871969920

**Anderson, Eugene Newton.**     • **4.8357**
Political institutions and social change in continental Europe in the nineteenth
century, by Eugene N. Anderson & Pauline R. Anderson. — Berkeley:
University of California Press, 1967. x, 451 p.; 24 cm. 1. Europe — Politics and
government — 1789-1900 I. Anderson, Pauline Safford (Relyea) joint author.
II. T.
JN10.A5     320.9/4     *LC* 67-21432

**Cook, Chris, 1945-.**     **4.8358**
European political facts, 1848–1918 / Chris Cook and John Paxton. — New
York: Facts on File, 1978. viii, 342 p.; 24 cm. Includes index. 1. Europe —
Politics and government — 1848-1871 2. Europe — Politics and government
— 1871-1918 I. Paxton, John. joint author. II. T.
JN10.C66 1978     940.2/8 19     *LC* 77-21138     *ISBN* 0871963760

**Cook, Chris, 1945-.**     **4.8359**
European political facts, 1918–84 / Chris Cook and John Paxton. — New ed. —
New York, N.Y.: Facts on File, 1986. 280 p.; 25 cm. Includes index.
1. International agencies — Handbooks, manuals, etc. 2. Europe — Politics
and government — 1918-1945 — Handbooks, manuals, etc. 3. Europe —
Politics and government — 1945- — Handbooks, manuals, etc. I. Paxton,
John. II. T.
JN12.C643 1986     320.94/02/02 19     *LC* 85-10162     *ISBN*
0816013012

**Flanz, Gisbert H.**     **4.8360**
Comparative women's rights and political participation in Europe / Gisbert H.
Flanz. — Dobbs Ferry, N.Y.: Transnational Publishers, c1983. xix, 520 p.; 25
cm. Includes index. 1. Women — Legal status, laws, etc. — Europe.
2. Women's rights — Europe. 3. Women in politics — Europe. I. T.
JN12.F5x     346.401/34 344.06134 19     *LC* 82-19317     *ISBN*
0941320022

**Parker, Geoffrey, 1933-.**     **4.8361**
A political geography of Community Europe / Geoffrey Parker. — London;
Boston: Butterworths, 1983. xi, 141 p.: ill.; 24 cm. 1. European communities
2. Geopolitics — Europe. I. T.
JN15.P34 1983     341.24/2 19     *LC* 83-6054     *ISBN* 0408108398

**Butler, David, 1924-.**     **4.8362**
European elections and British politics / David Butler and David Marquand.
— London; New York: Longman, 1981. vi, 193 p.: ill.; 23 cm. 1. European
Parliament. 2. European Parliament — Elections. 3. European Economic
Community — Great Britain 4. Elections — Great Britain. I. Marquand,
David. II. T.
JN36.B876     341.24/2 19     *LC* 80-41086     *ISBN* 0582295289

**Herman, Valentine.**     **4.8363**
The European Parliament and the European community / Valentine Herman,
Juliet Lodge. — New York: St. Martin's Press, 1978. ix, 199 p.; 23 cm. Includes
index. 1. European Parliament. I. Lodge, Juliet. joint author. II. T.
JN36.H4 1978     341.24/2     *LC* 77-26889     *ISBN* 0312270747

**Coalition government in Western Europe / edited by Vernon**     **4.8364**
**Bogdanor.**
London; Exeter, NH: Heinemann Educational Books, 1984 (c1983). 282 p.; 23
cm. At head of title: Policy Studies Institute, European Centre for Political
Studies. 1. Coalition governments — Europe — Addresses, essays, lectures.
2. Europe — Politics and government — 1945- — Addresses, essays, lectures.
I. Bogdanor, Vernon, 1943- II. European Centre for Political Studies.
JN94.A2 C63 1983     324/.094 19     *LC* 84-151615     *ISBN*
0435831046

**The Formation of national States in Western Europe / edited by**   **4.8365**
**Charles Tilly; contributors, Gabriel Ardant ... [et al.].**
Princeton, N.J.: Princeton University Press, 1975. xiv, 711 p.: ill.; 25 cm.
(Studies in political development; 8) Sponsored by the Committee on
Comparative Politics, Social Science Research Council. Includes index.
1. Europe — Politics and government I. Tilly, Charles. ed. II. Ardant,
Gabriel. III. Social Science Research Council. Committee on Comparative
Politics. IV. Series.
JN94.A2 F67      320.9/4      *LC* 74-20941      *ISBN* 0691052190

**Government and administration in Western Europe / edited by**   **4.8366**
**F. F. Ridley.**
New York: St. Martin's Press, 1979. 244 p.; 23 cm. 1. Comparative government
— Addresses, essays, lectures. 2. Europe — Politics and government —
Addresses, essays, lectures. I. Ridley, F. F. (Frederick F.)
JN94.A5 G68 1979      JN94A5 G68 1979.      354/.4      *LC* 79-13518
     *ISBN* 031234113X

**Aberbach, Joel D.**            **4.8367**
Bureaucrats and politicians in western democracies / Joel D. Aberbach, Robert
D. Putnam, Bert A. Rockman; with the collaboration of Thomas J. Anton,
Samuel J. Eldersveld, Ronald Inglehart. — Cambridge, Mass.: Harvard
University Press, 1981. xii, 308 p.: ill.; 25 cm. 1. Government executives —
Europe. 2. Government executives — United States. 3. Politicians — Europe.
4. Politicians — United States I. Putnam, Robert D. II. Rockman, Bert A.
III. T.
JN94.A69 E92      351/.001/094 19      *LC* 81-2899      *ISBN* 0674086252

**Policy styles in Western Europe / edited by Jeremy**   **4.8368**
**Richardson.**
London; Boston: Allen & Unwin, 1982. x, 213 p.; 23 cm. 1. Comparative
government — Addresses, essays, lectures. 2. Policy sciences — Addresses,
essays, lectures. 3. Europe — Politics and government — 1945- — Addresses,
essays, lectures. I. Richardson, J. J. (Jeremy John)
JN94.A91 P64 1982      320.3/094 19      *LC* 82-11415      *ISBN*
0043500625

**Carstairs, Andrew McLaren.**          **4.8369**
A short history of electoral systems in Western Europe / Andrew McLaren
Carstairs. — London; Boston: Allen & Unwin, 1980. 236 p.; 23 cm. Includes
index. 1. Elections — Europe — History. I. T.
JN94.A95 C37      324.6/094 19      *LC* 80-40547      *ISBN* 0043240062

**Democracy and elections: electoral systems and their political**   **4.8370**
**consequences / edited by Vernon Bogdanor and David Butler.**
Cambridge [Cambridgeshire]; New York: Cambridge University Press, 1983.
ix, 267 p.: ill.; 24 cm. 1. Elections — European Economic Community
countries — Addresses, essays, lectures. 2. Elections — Japan — Addresses,
essays, lectures. I. Bogdanor, Vernon, 1943- II. Butler, David, 1924-
JN94.A95 D45 1983      324.21/094 19      *LC* 82-25300      *ISBN*
0521252954

**Sallnow, John.**          **4.8371**
An electoral atlas of Europe, 1968–1981: a political geographic compendium
including 76 maps / John Sallnow and Anna John; cartography by Sarah K.
Webber. — London; Boston: Butterworth Scientific, 1982. 149 p.: ill., maps; 26
cm. (Butterworths European studies.) 1. Elections — Europe. 2. Elections —
Europe — Maps. 3. Europe — Politics and government — 1945- I. John,
Anna. II. Webber, Sarah K. III. T. IV. Series.
JN94.A956 S24 1982      324.94/0557 19      *LC* 82-171318      *ISBN*
0408108002

**The Communist parties of Italy, France, and Spain: postwar**   **4.8372**
**change and continuity: a casebook / edited by Peter Lange,**
**Maurizio Vannicelli; with a foreword by Stanley Hoffmann.**
London: Allen & Unwin, 1981. xii, 385 p.; 25 cm. — (Casebook series on
European politics and society. v. 1) Includes index. 1. Communist parties —
Europe — History. I. Lange, Peter Michael. II. Vannicelli, Maurizio.
III. Series.
JN94.A979 C645      324.24075/09 19      *LC* 80-41833      *ISBN*
0043290337

**Conservative politics in Western Europe / edited by Zig**   **4.8373**
**Layton–Henry.**
New York: St. Martin's Press, 1982. xi, 352 p.: ill.; 23 cm. 1. Political parties —
Europe — Addresses, essays, lectures. 2. Conservatism — Europe —
Addresses, essays, lectures. 3. Europe — Politics and government — 1945- —
Addresses, essays, lectures. I. Layton-Henry, Zig.
JN94.A979 C65 1982      324.2404 19      *LC* 81-710      *ISBN* 0312164181

**Political parties in the European Community / edited by**   **4.8374**
**Stanley Henig.**
London: Allen & Unwin, 1979. 314 p.: ill.; 23 cm. First ed. published in 1969
under title: European political parties. At head of title: European Centre for
Political Studies, European Cultural Foundation. 1. Political parties —

European Economic Community countries. I. Henig, Stanley. II. European
Centre for Political Studies. III. Title: European political parties.
JN94.A979 E85 1979      329/.02/094      *LC* 78-40902      *ISBN*
0043290248

**Middlemas, Keith, 1935-.**          **4.8375**
Power and the party: changing faces of communism in Western Europe / Keith
Middlemas. — London: Deutsch, 1980. 400 p.; 24 cm. 1. Communist parties
— Europe. I. T.
JN94.A979 M53      324.24075 19      *LC* 80-500510      *ISBN* 0233971513

**Moderates and conservatives in Western Europe: political**   **4.8376**
**parties, the European Community, and the Atlantic Alliance /**
**edited by Roger Morgan and Stefano Silvestri.**
1st American ed. — [Rutherford, NJ]: Fairleigh Dickinson University Press,
1983. viii, 280 p.; 23 cm. At head of title: Policy Studies Institute. Includes
index. 1. Center parties — Europe 2. Europe — Politics and government —
1945- I. Morgan, Roger, 1932- II. Silvestri, Stefano. III. Policy Studies
Institute.
JN94.A979 M632 1983      324.24/05 19      *LC* 83-5662      *ISBN*
0838632017

**Stammen, Theo.**          **4.8377**
Political parties in Europe / Theo Stammen; translated from the original by
Gunda Cannon–Kern. — London: J. Martin Pub., 1980. 321 p.; 22 cm.
1. Political parties — Europe. 2. Europe — Politics and government — 1945-
I. T.
JN94.A979 S63      324.24009      *ISBN* 0906237084

**Social democratic parties in Western Europe / edited by**   **4.8378**
**William E. Paterson and Alastair H. Thomas.**
New York: St. Martin's Press, 1977. 444 p.; 23 cm. 1. Political parties —
Europe — Addresses, essays, lectures. 2. Socialist parties — Addresses, essays,
lectures. I. Paterson, William E. II. Thomas, Alastair H.
JN94.A979 S64 1977b      329/.02/094      *LC* 77-77314      *ISBN*
0312731752

**Western European party systems: trends and prospects / Peter**   **4.8379**
**H. Merkl, editor.**
New York: Free Press, c1980. xi, 676 p.; 25 cm. Based on papers given at a
symposium held in Washington, D.C. in the fall of 1977. 1. Political parties —
Europe — Congresses. I. Merkl, Peter H.
JN94.A979 W47 1980      329/.02/094      *LC* 78-22783      *ISBN*
0029200601

# JN101–1371 Britain

## JN111–237 Constitutional History

**Stephenson, Carl, 1886-1954, ed. and tr.**      • **4.8380**
Sources of English constitutional history; a selection of documents from A.D.
600 to the present, edited and translated by Carl Stephenson and Frederick
George Marcham. — New York; London: Harper & brothers, 1937. xxxiv p., 1
l., 906 p.; 22 cm. — (Harper's historical series) 'First edition.' 1. Great Britain
— Constitutional history — Sources. I. Marcham, Frederick George, 1898-
joint ed. and tr. II. T.
JN111.S67      342.4209      *LC* 37-23477

**Bagehot, Walter, 1826-1877.**      • **4.8381**
Walter Bagehot: a study of his life and thought together with a selection from
his political writings, by Norman St. John–Stevas. — Bloomington, Indiana
University Press, 1959. xvi, 485 p. port. 23 cm. Includes bibliographies. 1. Gt.
Brit. — Pol. & govt. — Addresses, essays, lectures. I. St. John-Stevas, Norman.
II. T.
JN113.B3      320.942      *LC* 59-1446

**Maitland, Frederic William, 1850-1906.**      • **4.8382**
The constitutional history of England: a course of lectures delivered / by F.W.
Maitland. — 1st ed. — Cambridge: University Press, c1908. xxviii, 547 p.; 23
cm. Editor: H.A.L. Fisher. Lectures delivered at Cambridge in 1887 and 1888.
1. Great Britain — Constitutional history I. Fisher, Herbert Albert Laurens,
1865-1940 II. T.
JN118.M23      *LC* 80-31630

**Stubbs, William, 1825-1901.**      • **4.8383**
The constitutional history of England in its origin and development. New York,
Barnes & Noble [1967] 3 v. 22 cm. Vol. 1: 6th ed.; v. 2: 4th ed.; v. 3: 5th ed.
Reprint of the 1897 ed. 1. Great Britain — Constitutional history I. T.
JN118.S82 1967      342/.41/029      *LC* 67-6910

**Petit-Dutaillis, Charles Edmond, 1868-1947.**      • **4.8384**
Studies and notes supplementary to Stubbs' Constitutional history, by Ch.
Petit–Dutaillis and Georges Lefebvre. [Manchester] Manchester University

Press; New York, Barnes & Noble [1969, c1930] xv, 518 p. 21 cm. Translation of Notes et études historiques which appeared in Histoire constitutionnelle de l'Angleterre, the French edition of Stubbs' Constitutional history. 1. Great Britain — Constitutional history I. Lefebvre, Georges, 1874-1959. joint author. II. Stubbs, William, 1825-1901. Constitutional history of England. III. T.
JN118.S9 P4 1969    342.41/029 344.10229 19    *LC* 78-4090    *ISBN* 0719003415

**Bagehot, Walter, 1826-1877.**                                    • **4.8385**
The English Constitution. With an introd. by R. H. S. Crossman. — Ithaca, N.Y.: Cornell University Press, [1966] 310 p.; 19 cm. — (Cornell paperbacks, CP-23) 'First published in 1867.' 1. Great Britain — Constitutional law. 2. Great Britain — Politics and government I. T.
JN125.B2 1966    342.4203    *LC* 66-15425

## JN128–171 To 1485

**Loyn, H. R. (Henry Royston)**                                    **4.8386**
The governance of Anglo–Saxon England, 500–1087 / H.R. Loyn. — Stanford, Calif.: Stanford University Press, 1984. xvii, 222 p.: ill.; 24 cm. — (Governance of England. 1) Includes index. 1. Great Britain — Politics and government — 449-1066 I. T. II. Series.
JN131.L69 1984    942.01 19    *LC* 83-50797    *ISBN* 0804712174

**Chrimes, S. B. (Stanley Bertram), 1907-.**                       • **4.8387**
An introduction to the administrative history of mediaeval England, by S. B. Chrimes. [3d ed.] New York, Barnes & Noble, 1966 [c1959] xv, 285 p. 23 cm. (Studies in mediaeval history, v. 7) 1. Great Britain — Politics and government 2. Great Britain — Constitutional history I. T.
JN137.C48 1966    354.420009    *LC* 66-31840

**Lyon, Bryce Dale, 1920-.**                                       • **4.8388**
A constitutional and legal history of medieval England. — New York, Harper [1960] 671 p.: ill.; 25 cm. Includes bibliography. 1. Gt. Brit. — Pol. & govt. — To 1485. 2. Law — Gt. Brit. — Hist. & crit. I. T.
JN137.L9    342.42    *LC* 60-5725

**Poole, Austin Lane, 1889-1963.**                                 • **4.8389**
Obligations of society in the XII and XIII centuries; the Ford lectures delivered in the University of Oxford in Michaelmas term 1944. Oxford, The Clarendon Press, 1946. 4 p.l., 115, [1] p. 23 cm. 1. Feudalism — Great Britain. 2. Great Britain — Social conditions I. T.
JN137.P6    *LC* a 46-4300

**Thompson, Faith, 1893-1961.**                                    **4.8390**
Magna carta; its role in the making of the English Constitution, 1300–1629. New York, Octagon Books, 1972 [c1948] x, 410 p. illus. 24 cm. 1. Magna Carta. 2. Great Britain — Constitutional history I. T.
JN137.T45 1972    342/.42/029    *LC* 70-159233    *ISBN* 0374978700

**Maitland, Frederic William, 1850-1906.**                         • **4.8391**
Domesday book and beyond. Three essays in the early history of England. By Frederic William Maitland ... Cambridge, University press, 1897. xiii, [1] 527, [1] p. maps. 24 1/2 cm. 1. Land tenure — Great Britain — History. 2. Feudalism — Great Britain. 3. Village communities — Great Britain. I. T.
JN141.M2    *LC* 01-18854

**Richardson, H. G. (Henry Gerald), 1884-.**                       • **4.8392**
The governance of mediaeval England from the conquest to Magna carta [by] H. G. Richardson and G. O. Sayles. — Edinburgh, University Press [1963] ix, 514 p. 26 cm. — (Edinburgh University publications; history, philosophy, and economics, no. 16) Bibliography: p. 471-495. 1. Stubbs, William, 1825-1901. Constitutional history of England. 2. Gt. Brit. — Constitutional history. I. Sayles, G. O. (George Osborne), 1901- joint author. II. T.
JN143.R5    342.4209    *LC* 63-3823

**Holt, James Clarke. comp.**                                      **4.8393**
Magna Carta and the idea of liberty. Edited by James C. Holt. New York, Wiley [1972] viii, 192 p. 22 cm. (Major issues in history) 1. Magna Carta — Addresses, essays, lectures. 2. Liberty — Addresses, essays, lectures. I. T.
JN147.H643    323.44    *LC* 70-38963    *ISBN* 047140845X *ISBN* 0471408433

**Chrimes, S. B. (Stanley Bertram), 1907-.**                       • **4.8394**
English constitutional ideas in the fifteenth century, by S. B. Chrimes ... Cambridge [Eng.] The University press, 1936. xx, 415, [1] p. 23 cm. 'Appendix. Extracts from year book cases cited in the text': p. [350]-394. 1. Great Britain — Constitutional history. 2. Great Britain — Constitutional law. 3. Great Britain — Politics and government — 1399-1485 I. T.
JN165.C45    *LC* 37-892

## JN175–215 16th, 17th, 18th Centuries

**Elton, G. R. (Geoffrey Rudolph) ed.**                            • **4.8395**
The Tudor constitution: documents and commentary. Cambridge [Eng.] University Press, 1960. xvi, 496 p.; 24 cm. I. T.
JN181.T32 E4    *LC* 60-16351

**Williams, Penry.**                                               **4.8396**
The Tudor regime / by Penry Williams. — Oxford: Clarendon Press; New York: Oxford University Press, 1979. xii, 486 p.; 23 cm. 1. Great Britain — Politics and government — 1485-1603 2. Great Britain — Social conditions I. T.
JN181.W54    320.9/42/05    *LC* 79-40424    *ISBN* 0198224915

**Elton, G. R. (Geoffrey Rudolph)**                                • **4.8397**
The Tudor revolution in government; administrative changes in the reign of Henry VIII. — Cambridge [Eng.] University Press, 1953. xii, 465 p. 23 cm. Bibliographical footnotes. 1. Great Britain — Pol. & govt. — 1509-1547. I. T.
JN183 1509.E55    354.42    *LC* 53-13334

**Gooch, G. P. (George Peabody), 1873-1968.**                      • **4.8398**
English democratic ideas in the seventeenth century, by G. P. Gooch. 2d ed., with supplementary notes and appendices by H. J. Laski. Cambridge [Eng.] University Press [1927] x, 315 p.; 19 cm. 1. Democracy 2. Great Britain — Politics and government — 1603-1714 I. T.
JN191.G7 1927    *LC* 27-18694

**Tanner, Joseph Robson, 1860-1931.**                              • **4.8399**
English constitutional conflicts of the seventeenth century, 1603–1689 / by J.R. Tanner. — [Students' edition]. — Cambridge: The University Press, 1928. x, 315 p.; 22 cm. 1. Great Britain — Constitutional history 2. Great Britain — History — Stuarts, 1603-1714 I. T.
JN191 T3    *LC* 28-25327

**Judson, Margaret Atwood, 1899-.**                                • **4.8400**
The crisis of the constitution; an essay in constitutional and political thought in England, 1603-1645. New York, Octagon Books, 1964, [c1949] xi, 444 p. 21 cm. (Rutgers studies in history, no.5) 1. Great Britain — Constitutional history 2. Great Britain — Politics and government — 1603-1649 I. T.
JN193.J8 1964    *LC* 64-24846

**Western, John R.**                                               • **4.8401**
Monarchy and revolution; the English state in the 1680's [by] J. R. Western. — Totowa, N.J.: Rowman and Littlefield, [1972] viii, 421 p.: illus.; 21 cm. 1. Great Britain — Politics and government — 1660-1714 I. T.
JN201.W47 1972    914.2/03/6    *LC* 72-189584    *ISBN* 0874710669

**Namier, Lewis Bernstein, Sir, 1888-1960.**                       • **4.8402**
The structure of politics at the accession of George III / by Sir Lewis Namier. — 2d ed. — London, Macmillan; New York, St. Martin's Press, 1957. xvii, 514 p.: facsim., geneal. tables, tables. 23 cm. 1. Great Britain — Politics and government — 1760-1789 I. T.
JN210.N3 1957    342.42    *LC* 57-14066

**Plumb, J. H. (John Harold), 1911-.**                             • **4.8403**
The origins of political stability, England, 1675–1725 [by] J. H. Plumb. Boston, Houghton Mifflin, 1967. xviii, 206 p. 22 cm. (The Ford lectures, 1965) London ed. (Macmillan) has title: The growth of political stability. 1. Political stability — Great Britain — History. 2. Great Britain — Politics and government — 1660-1714 3. Great Britain — Politics and government — 1714-1727 I. T.
JN210.P55 1967a    320.9/42    *LC* 67-11830

**Robbins, Caroline.**                                             **4.8404**
The eighteenth–century commonwealthman; studies in the transmission, development, and circumstance of English liberal thought from the Restoration of Charles II until the War with the Thirteen Colonies. Cambridge, Mass., Harvard University Press, 1959. viii, 462 p. 1. Liberalism 2. Political science — History — Great Britain 3. Great Britain — Constitutional history I. T.
JN210 R6    *LC* 59-7660

**Holmes, Geoffrey S., 1928-.**                                    • **4.8405**
British politics in the age of Anne [by] Geoffrey Holmes. London, Melbourne [etc.] Macmillan; New York, St. Martin's P., 1967. xiv, 546 p. tables. 22 1/2 cm. Bibliographical references included in 'Notes' (p. [459]-518) 1. Great Britain — Politics and government — 1702-1714 I. T.
JN212 1707.H64    320.9/42    *LC* 67-16865

## JN216–237 19th–20th Centuries

**MacDonagh, Oliver.**                                             **4.8406**
Early Victorian government, 1830–1870 / Oliver MacDonagh. New York: Holmes & Meier Publishers, 1977. 242 p.; 22 cm. Includes index. 1. Great Britain — Politics and government — 19th century 2. Great Britain —

Economic conditions — 19th century 3. Great Britain — Social conditions — 19th century I. T.
JN216.M15 1977    309.1/41/081    *LC* 76-57957    *ISBN* 0841903042

**Butler, James Ramsay Montagu, 1889-.**    • **4.8407**
The passing of the great reform bill / by J.R.M. Butler. — London: Longmans, Green and Co., 1914. xiii, 454 p., [8] leaves of plates: ill., ports.; 24 cm. 1. Great Britain. Parliament — Reform 2. Great Britain — Politics and government — 1800-1837 I. T.
JN218 B8    *LC* 14-13951

**Gash, Norman.**    • **4.8408**
Politics in the age of Peel: a study in the technique of parliamentary representation, 1830–1850 / Norman Gash. — London, New York: Longmans, Green, 1953. xxi, 496 p.; 23 cm. — 1. Elections — Great Britain 2. Great Britain — Politics and government — 1830-1837 3. Great Britain — Politics and government — 1937-1901 I. T.
JN223.G3    *LC* 53-9637

**Bentley, Michael, 1948-.**    **4.8409**
The liberal mind, 1914–1929 / Michael Bentley. — Cambridge; New York: Cambridge University Press, 1977. viii, 279 p.; 22 cm. — (Cambridge studies in the history and theory of politics) Includes index. 1. Liberal Party (Great Britain) — History. 2. Liberalism — Great Britain — History. 3. Great Britain — Politics and government — 1910-1936 I. T.
JN231.B45    320.5/1/0941    *LC* 76-11072    *ISBN* 052121243X

**Birch, Anthony Harold.**    **4.8410**
Representative and responsible government: an essay on the British constitution. — London: Allen and Unwin [1964] 252 p. 1. Great Britain — Politics and government — 1945- I. T.
JN231 B57 1964    *LC* 64-5250

**British politics in perspective / edited by R.L. Borthwick and    4.8411
J.E. Spence.**
New York: St. Martin's Press, 1984. 251 p.; 23 cm. Includes index. 1. Great Britain — Politics and government — 1979- — Addresses, essays, lectures. I. Borthwick, R. L. II. Spence, J. E. (John Edward)
JN231.B725 1984    320.941 19    *LC* 83-40608    *ISBN* 0312105088

**Butler, David, 1924-.**    • **4.8412**
British political facts, 1900–1967 by David Butler and Jennie Freeman. London, Macmillan; New York, St. Martin's P., 1968. xix, 314 p. 25 cm. (Papermac, 194) 1. Great Britain — Politics and government — 20th century — Handbooks, manuals, etc. I. Freeman, Jennie joint author. II. T.
JN231.B82    320/.0942    *LC* 67-27323

**Dilemmas of change in British politics / edited by Donley T.    4.8413
Studlar and Jerold L. Waltman.**
Jackson: University Press of Mississippi in association with the Institute of Anglo-American Studies, 1984. xiv, 251 p.; 23 cm. 1. Great Britain — Politics and government — 1979- — Addresses, essays, lecturs. I. Studlar, Donley T. II. Waltman, Jerold L., 1945- III. University of Southern Mississippi. Institute of Anglo-American Studies.
JN231.D55 1984    320.941 19    *LC* 83-14782    *ISBN* 0878051953

**Leys, Colin.**    **4.8414**
Politics in Britain: an introduction / Colin Leys. — Toronto; Buffalo: University of Toronto Press, 1983. x, 350 p.: ill.; 22 cm. 1. Social classes — Great Britain 2. Great Britain — Politics and government — 1945- I. T.
JN231.L49 1983    941.085 19    *LC* 83-213340    *ISBN* 0802065295

**Norton, Philip.**    **4.8415**
The constitution in flux / Philip Norton. — Oxford: M. Robertson, 1982. vii, 312 p.; 23 cm. Includes index. 1. Great Britain — Constitutional history 2. Great Britain — Politics and government — 1964-1979 I. T.
JN231.N67 1982    342.41/029 344.10229 19    *LC* 82-184685    *ISBN* 0855205210

**Rose, Richard, 1933-.**    **4.8416**
United Kingdom facts / Richard Rose and Ian McAllister. — London: Macmillan, 1982. x, 168 p.; 26 cm. 1. Great Britain — Politics and government — 1945- 2. Great Britain — Social conditions — 1945- — Statistics. 3. Great Brtiain — Economic conditions — 1945- — Statistics. I. McAllister, Ian. II. T.
JN231.R67x 1982    *LC* 85-672794    *ISBN* 0333253418

**Rose, Richard, 1933-.**    • **4.8417**
Politics in England, an interpretation. — Boston: Little, Brown, [1964] xi, 266 p.; 21 cm. — (The Little, Brown series in comparative politics) At head of title: A country study. 1. Great Britain — Politics and government I. T.
JN234 1964.R6    320.941 19    *LC* 64-17419

**Jessop, Bob.**    **4.8418**
Traditionalism, conservatism and British political culture / by Bob Jessop. — London: Allen & Unwin [1974] 287 p.; 23 cm. 1. Conservatism — Great

Britain. 2. Voting — Great Britain. 3. Great Britain — Politics and government — 1964-1979 I. T.
JN234 1974.J48    320.9/41/0856    *LC* 75-300266    *ISBN* 0043290175

**Bruce-Gardyne, Jock.**    **4.8419**
The power game: an examination of decision–making in government / Jock Bruce–Gardyne and Nigel Lawson. — Hamden, Conn.: Archon Books, 1976. 204 p.; 23 cm. Includes index. 1. Public administration — Decision making — Case studies. 2. Power (Social sciences) — Case studies. 3. Great Britain — Politics and government — 1945-1964 4. Great Britain — Politics and government — 1964-1979 I. Lawson, Nigel. II. T.
JN234 1976.B78 1976    320.9/41/0856    *LC* 76-6971    *ISBN* 0208015981

**Rose, Richard, 1933- comp.**    **4.8420**
Studies in British politics: a reader in political sociology / contributors, James Alt ... [et al.]; edited by Richard Rose. 3d ed. — New York: St. Martin's Press, 1977 (c1976). xi, 547 p.: ill.; 23 cm. 1. Great Britain — Politics and government — 1945- — Addresses, essays, lectures. 2. Great Britain — Social conditions — 1945- — Addresses, essays, lectures. I. Alt, James E. II. T.
JN234 1976.R6 1976    301.5/92/0941    *LC* 76-11279

**Birch, Anthony Harold.**    **4.8421**
Political integration and disintegration in the British Isles / [by] A. H. Birch. — London; Boston: Allen & Unwin, 1977. 183 p.; 23 cm. Includes index. 1. Regionalism — British Isles. 2. Decentralization in government — British Isles. I. T.
JN234 1977.B54    320.9/41/082    *LC* 78-312362    *ISBN* 0043201237

**Britain, progress and decline / edited by William B. Gwyn and    4.8422
Richard Rose for the British Politics Group.**
New Orleans: Tulane University, 1980. xiii, 164 p.; 22 cm. — (Tulane studies in political science. v. 17) 1. Great Britain — Politics and government — 1945- — Addresses, essays, lectures. 2. Great Britain — Economic conditions — 1945- — Addresses, essays, lectures. 3. Great Britain — Social conditions — 1945- — Addresses, essays, lectures. I. Gwyn, William B. II. Rose, Richard, 1933- III. British Politics Group. IV. Series.
JN234 1980.B7x    320 s 941.085 19    *LC* 81-165801    *ISBN* 0930598180

**Smith, Geoffrey, 1930-.**    **4.8423**
British government and its discontents / Geoffrey Smith & Nelson W. Polsby. — New York: Basic Books, c1981. xvi, 202 p.; 22 cm. 1. Great Britain — Politics and government — 1945- 2. Great Britain — Economic policy — 1945- 3. Great Britain — Foreign relations — 1945- 4. Great Britain — Social policy. I. Polsby, Nelson W. joint author. II. T.
JN234 1981.S64    320.941 19    *LC* 79-56372    *ISBN* 0465007651

**Beer, Samuel Hutchison, 1911-.**    **4.8424**
Britain against itself: the political contradictions of collectivism / by Samuel H. Beer. — 1st ed. — New York: Norton, c1982. xvi, 231 p.; 22 cm. 1. Great Britain — Politics and government — 1979- I. T.
JN234 1982.B43    320.941 19    *LC* 81-18869    *ISBN* 0393015645

**Miliband, Ralph.**    **4.8425**
Capitalist democracy in Britain / Ralph Miliband. — Oxford; New York: Oxford University Press, 1982. 165 p.; 23 cm. Includes index. 1. Political participation — Great Britain. 2. Social classes — Great Britain 3. Great Britain — Politics and government I. T.
JN234 1982.M54    320.941 19    *LC* 82-14103    *ISBN* 0198274459

**Benn, Tony, 1925-.**    **4.8426**
Arguments for democracy / Tony Benn; edited by Chris Mullin. — London: J. Cape, 1981. xiv, 257 p.; 23 cm. 1. Democracy 2. Great Britain — Politics and government — 1979- 3. Great Britain — Politics and government — 1964-1979 I. Mullin, Chris. II. T.
JN237 1981.B46    320.941 19    *LC* 81-170794    *ISBN* 0224018787

## JN248–276 COMMONWEALTH OF NATIONS

**Underhill, Frank Hawkins, 1889-.**    • **4.8427**
The British Commonwealth: an experiment in co–operation among nations / Frank H. Underhill. — Durham, N. C.: Published for the Duke University Commonwealth-Studies Center by Duke University Press, 1956. xxiii, 127 p. 21 cm. — (Publications of the Duke University Commonwealth-Studies Center) 1. Commonwealth of Nations I. T.
JN248.U5    354.4201    *LC* 56-9166

**Hobson, J. A. (John Atkinson), 1858-1940.**    • **4.8428**
Imperialism, a study. New introd. by Philip Siegelman. [Ann Arbor] University of Michigan Press [1965] xx, 386 p. maps. 21 cm. (Ann Arbor paperbacks, AA103) 1. Imperialism 2. Imperial federation 3. Great Britain — Colonies I. T.
JN276.H7 1965    321.03    *LC* 65-6003

**Mansergh, Nicholas.**      • **4.8429**
The Commonwealth and the nations: studies in British Commonwealth relations. — [1st ed.] reprinted. — London: Dawsons, 1968. viii, 229 p.; 19 cm. 'First published 1948.' 1. Imperial federation 2. Commonwealth of Nations I. T.
JN276.M34 1968     320.9/171/242     *LC* 78-392680     *ISBN* 0712903275

**Nairn, Tom.**      **4.8430**
The break–up of Britain: crisis and neo–nationalism / Tom Nairn. — London: NLB, 1977. 368 p.; 22 cm. 'Most of the contents of this book appeared previously in New Left Review.' Includes index. 1. Regionalism — Great Britain. I. T.
JN297.R44 N34     320.5/4/0941     *LC* 78-302049     *ISBN* 0902308572

**Rose, Richard, 1933-.**      **4.8431**
The territorial dimension in government: understanding the United Kingdom / Richard Rose. — Chatham, N.J.: Chatham House, c1982. 228 p.; 23 cm. 1. Regionalism — Great Britain. 2. Great Britain — Politics and government — 1964-1979 3. Great Britain — Politics and government — 1979-. I. T.
JN297.R44 R67 1982     320.1/2/0941 19     *LC* 82-9680     *ISBN* 0934540160

## JN301–869 GOVERNMENT. ADMINISTRATION

### JN309–329 History. Treatises

**Studies in the growth of nineteenth–century government. Edited**      **4.8432**
**by Gillian Sutherland.**
Totowa, N.J.: Rowman and Littlefield, [1972] viii, 295 p.; 23 cm. Based on a colloquium held in 1969 under the auspices of the Past and Present Society. 1. Political science — Great Britain — History — Congresses. 2. Great Britain — Politics and government — 19th century — Congresses. 3. Great Britain — Executive departments — History — Congresses. I. Sutherland, Gillian. ed.
JN309.S78 1972b     354/.42/0009034     *LC* 72-184825     *ISBN* 0874710804

**Gray, Andrew, 1947-.**      **4.8433**
Administrative politics in British government / Andrew Gray, William I. Jenkins. — Sussex: Wheatsheaf Books; New York: St. Martin's Press, 1985. x, 259 p.; 23 cm. Includes indexes. 1. Administrative agencies — Great Britain. 2. Great Britain — Executive departments. 3. Great Britain — Politics and government I. Jenkins, W. I. (William Ieuan) II. T.
JN318.G72 1985     354.4107 19     *LC* 85-2264     *ISBN* 0312004613

**Morrison, Herbert Stanley, 1888-.**      • **4.8434**
Government and Parliament: a survey from the inside / by Lord Morrison of Lambeth. — 3d ed. London; New York: Oxford University Press, 1964. 384 p.; 20 cm. (Oxford paperbacks, 80) 1. Great Britain — Politics and government — 20th century I. T.
JN318.M73 1964     328.42     *LC* 64-4027

**Bogdanor, Vernon, 1943-.**      **4.8435**
Devolution / Vernon Bogdanor. — Oxford; New York: Oxford University Press, 1979. 246 p.; 21 cm. — (Oxford paperbacks university series) Includes index. 1. Decentralization in government — Great Britain — History. I. T.
JN329.D43 B64     354/.41/082     *LC* 78-41055     *ISBN* 0192191284

**Drucker, H. M. (Henry Matthew)**      **4.8436**
The politics of nationalism and devolution / H. M. Drucker and Gordon Brown. — London; New York: Longman, 1980. 138 p.; 20 cm. — (Politics today) Includes index. 1. Decentralization in government — Great Britain. 2. Scotland — Politics and government — 20th century 3. Wales — Politics and government — 20th century I. Brown, J. Gordon. joint author. II. T. III. Series.
JN329.D43 D78     354/.41/082     *LC* 79-41025     *ISBN* 0582295203

**Kimber, Richard, comp.**      **4.8437**
Pressure groups in Britain: a reader. Edited by Richard Kimber and J. J. Richardson. London, Dent; Totowa, N.J., Rowman and Littlefield [1974] vi, 304 p. 24 cm. 1. Pressure groups — Great Britain — Addresses, essays, lectures. I. Richardson, J. J. (Jeremy John) joint comp. II. T.
JN329.P7 K54     322.4/3/0942     *LC* 74-1192     *ISBN* 0874715245

**Richardson, J. J. (Jeremy John)**      **4.8438**
Governing under pressure: the policy process in a post–parliamentary democracy / J. J. Richardson, A. G. Jordan. — Oxford: Robertson, 1979. viii, 212 p.; 23 cm. (Government and administration series) Includes index. 1. Pressure groups — Great Britain. 2. Great Britain — Politics and government — 1945- I. Jordan, A. G. joint author. II. T.
JN329.P7 R5     322.4/3/0941 19     *LC* 79-320759     *ISBN* 0855202378

## JN331–453 The Executive

### JN331–389 The Crown

**Kemp, Betty.**      • **4.8439**
King and Commons, 1660–1832. — London, Macmillan; New York, St. Martin's Press, 1957. 167 p.: ill.; 23 cm. 1. Prerogative, Royal — Gt. Brit. 2. Legislative power — Gt. Brit. I. T.
JN331.K44     354.4203     *LC* 57-14139

**Jolliffe, John Edward Austin, 1891-.**      • **4.8440**
Angevin kingship / by J.E.A. Jolliffe. — 2d ed. — London: A. & C. Black, 1963. xi, 358 p.; 28 cm. 1. Prerogative, Royal — Great Britain. 2. Great Britain — Politics and government — 1154-1399 I. T.
JN337.J6 1963     *LC* 63-5905     *ISBN* 0713604964

**Weston, Corinne Comstock.**      **4.8441**
Subjects and sovereigns: the grand controversy over legal sovereignty in Stuart England / Corinne Comstock Weston, Janelle Renfrow Greenberg. — Cambridge; New York: Cambridge University Press, 1981. viii, 430 p.; 22 cm. Includes index. 1. Monarchy — Great Britain 2. Political science — England — History. I. Greenberg, Janelle Renfrow. II. T.
JN339.W47     320.2/0942 19     *LC* 80-40588     *ISBN* 0521232724

**Martin, Kingsley, 1897-1969.**      • **4.8442**
The crown and the establishment. — London, Hutchinson [1962] 192 p. illus. 22 cm. Includes bibliography. 1. Gt. Brit. — Kings and rulers. 2. Gt. Brit. — Pol. & govt. — 19th cent. 3. Gt. Brit. — Pol. & govt. — 20th cent. I. T.
JN341.M3 1962a     *LC* 62-6814

### JN401–453 The Cabinet. Civil Service

**Daalder, Hans.**      • **4.8443**
Cabinet reform in Britain, 1914–1963. Stanford Calif.: Stanford University Press, 1963. x, 381 p.; 24 cm. 1. Cabinet system — Great Britain 2. Great Britain — Politics and government — 20th century I. T.
JN401 D223     *LC* 63-14127

**Ehrman, John.**      • **4.8444**
Cabinet government and war, 1890–1940. [Hamden, Conn.] Archon Books, 1969. x, 137 p. 21 cm. (The Lees Knowles lectures, 1957) Reprint of the 1958 ed. 1. Cabinet system — Great Britain. 2. World War, 1914-1918 — Great Britain I. T. II. Series.
JN401.E5 1969     354.42/05     *LC* 69-15790     *ISBN* 0208007377

**Punnett, R. M. (Robert Malcolm)**      **4.8445**
Front–bench opposition; the role of the leader of the opposition, the shadow cabinet, and shadow government in British politics [by] R. M. Punnett. New York, St. Martin's Press [1973] xvii, 500 p. illus. 23 cm. 1. Cabinet system — Great Britain. 2. Opposition (Political science) — Great Britain. 3. Great Britain — Politics and government — 1945- I. T.
JN401.P84     320.9/42/085     *LC* 73-85300

**The British Prime Minister / edited, with a preface to the**      **4.8446**
**American edition, by Anthony King.**
2nd ed. — Durham, N.C.: Duke University Press, 1985. xiv, 275 p.; 23 cm. Includes index. 1. Prime ministers — Great Britain — Addresses, essays, lectures. I. King, Anthony Stephen.
JN405.B75 1985     354.4103/13 19     *LC* 84-24711     *ISBN* 0822306344

**Crossman, R. H. S. (Richard Howard Stafford), 1907-1974.**      **4.8447**
The myths of cabinet government / [by] Richard H. S. Crossman. — Cambridge, Mass.: Harvard University Press, 1972. xxix, 126 p.; 21 cm. (The Godkin lectures at Harvard University, 1970) 1. Cabinet system — Great Britain — Addresses, essays, lectures. I. T.
JN405.C76     320.9/42/085     *LC* 71-169860     *ISBN* 0674598350

**Gordon Walker, Patrick Chrestien.**      **4.8448**
The Cabinet [by] Patrick Gordon Walker. — Revised ed. — London: Fontana, 1972. 191 p.; 18 cm. 1. Cabinet system — Great Britain. 2. Great Britain — Politics and government I. T.
JN405.G63 1972     354/.42/05     *LC* 72-185834     *ISBN* 0005329365

**Headey, Bruce W.**      **4.8449**
British Cabinet Ministers: the roles of politicians in executive office / by Bruce Headey. — London: Allen & Unwin, 1974. 3-316 p.; 23 cm. Includes index. 1. Cabinet officers — Great Britain. 2. Cabinet system — Great Britain. I. T.
JN405.H37     354/.41/04     *LC* 75-301084     *ISBN* 0043200982

**Wilson, Harold, Sir, 1916-.** **4.8450**
The governance of Britain / Harold Wilson. — New York: Harper & Row, 1977 (c1976). xiii, 219 p.: port.; 24 cm. 1. Cabinet system — Great Britain. 2. Great Britain — Politics and government I. T.
JN405.W54 1976    354/.41/032    *LC* 76-47262    *ISBN* 0060146761

**Quangos in Britain: government and the networks of public** **4.8451**
**policy–making / edited by Anthony Barker.**
London: Macmillan, 1982. 250 p. Includes indexes. 1. Corporations — Great Britain — Political activity — Addresses, essays, lectures. 2. Associations, institutions, etc — Great Britain — Political activity — Addresses, essays, lectures. 3. Great Britain — Politics and government — 1964-1979 — Addresses, essays, lectures. I. Hayes, M. Vincent. II. Title: Government and the networks of public policy-making.
JN407.Q83    322.0941    *ISBN* 0333294688

**Ashford, Douglas Elliott.** **4.8452**
Policy and politics in Britain: the limits of consensus / Douglas E. Ashford. — Philadelphia: Temple University Press, 1981. xv, 330 p.; 21 cm. — (Policy and politics in industrial states) Includes index. 1. Great Britain — Politics and government — 1945- 2. Great Britain — Economic policy — 1945- 3. Great Britain — Social policy. I. T. II. Series.
JN425.A83    320.941 19    *LC* 80-19771    *ISBN* 0877221944

**Chapman, Richard A.** **4.8453**
The higher Civil Service in Britain, [by] Richard A. Chapman. — London: Constable, 1970. x, 194 p.; 23 cm. — (Sociology and social welfare series) 1. Civil service — Gt. Brit. I. T.
JN425.C47    301.5/5    *LC* 75-559428    *ISBN* 0094556202

**Fry, Geoffrey Kingdon.** **4.8454**
The Administrative 'revolution' in Whitehall: a study of the politics of administrative change in British central government since the 1950s / G.K. Fry. — London: Croom Helm, c1981. 217 p.; 22 cm. Includes index. 1. Administrative agencies — Great Britain — Reorganization. 2. Great Britain — Executive departments — Reorganization. 3. Great Britain — Politics and government — 1945- I. T.
JN425.F78    354.4107/3 19    *LC* 81-192395    *ISBN* 070991010X

**Fry, Geoffrey Kingdon.** **4.8455**
Statesmen in disguise: the changing role of the administrative class of the British home Civil Service, 1853–1966. — London; Melbourne [etc.]: Macmillan, 1969. 479 p.; 23 cm. Revision of thesis, London University. 1. Civil service — Gt. Brit. I. T.
JN425.F79 1969    354.42/006    *LC* 73-411769    *ISBN* 0333002903

## JN500–695 Parliament

**Pollard, A. F. (Albert Frederick), 1869-1948.** • **4.8456**
The evolution of Parliament. 2d ed., rev. with appendices, notes, and illus. New York, Russell & Russell, 1964. xv, 459 p. illus. 23 cm. 'Second edition, 1926; reissued 1964.' 1. Great Britain. Parliament — History. 2. Great Britain. Parliament. I. T.
JN508.P6 1964    *LC* 63-23452

**The English parliament in the Middle Ages / R.G. Davies, J.H.** **4.8457**
**Denton, editors.**
Philadelphia: University of Pennsylvania Press, 1981. x, 214 p.; 24 cm. — (Middle Ages.) Includes index. 1. Great Britain. Parliament — History. 2. Representative government and representation — England — History. 3. England — Constitutional history. I. Davies, R. G. (Richard Garfield), 1947- II. Denton, Jeffrey Howard. III. Series.
JN515.E54    328.42/09 19    *LC* 81-3423    *ISBN* 081227802X

**Sayles, G. O. (George Osborne), 1901-.** **4.8458**
The King's Parliament of England, by G. O. Sayles. [1st ed.] New York, Norton [1974] x, 164 p. 22 cm. (Historical controversies) 1. Great Britain. Parliament — History. 2. Legislative bodies — Great Britain — History. I. T. II. Series.
JN515.S35    328.42/09    *LC* 74-95544    *ISBN* 0393055086 *ISBN* 0393093220

**Cannon, John Ashton.** **4.8459**
Parliamentary reform 1640–1832 [by] John Cannon. — Cambridge [Eng.]: University Press, 1973 (c1972). xiv, 333 p.; 23 cm. 1. Great Britain. Parliament — Reform — History. I. T.
JN521.C3    328.42/09    *LC* 72-83588    *ISBN* 0521086973

**Lehmberg, Stanford E.** **4.8460**
The later Parliaments of Henry VIII, 1536–1547 / Stanford E. Lehmberg. — Cambridge [Eng.]; New York: Cambridge University Press, 1977. ix, 379 p.; 23 cm. Includes index. 1. Great Britain. Parliament — History. 2. Great Britain — Politics and government — 1509-1547 I. T.
JN525.L39    328.42/09    *LC* 76-7804    *ISBN* 0521212561

**Brock, Michael.** **4.8461**
The Great Reform Act. — London: [Hutchinson, 1973] 411 p.; 22 cm. — (Hutchinson university library: history) 1. Great Britain. Parliament — Reform. 2. Great Britain — Politics and government — 1800-1837 I. T.
JN543.B74    324/.42    *LC* 74-150442    *ISBN* 0091159105

**Smith, F. B. (Francis Barrymore), 1932-.** • **4.8462**
The making of the Second Reform Bill / F. B. Smith. — [Melbourne]: Melbourne University Press; London, New York: Cambridge University Press [1966] (7) 297 p.: ill.; 22 cm. 1. Great Britain. Parliament — Reform. 2. Great Britain — Politics and government — 1837-1901 I. T.
JN543.S6 1966    *LC* 66-16531

**Crick, Bernard R.** **4.8463**
The reform of Parliament. — Revised 2nd ed. — London: Weidenfeld and Nicolson, 1970. xxii, 325 p.; 23 cm. 1. Great Britain. Parliament. I. T.
JN550 1964.C73    328.42/09/04    *LC* 72-191090    *ISBN* 029776246X

**McIlwain, Charles Howard, 1871-1968.** • **4.8464**
The High Court of Parliament and its supremacy; an historical essay on the boundaries between legislation and adjudication in England. Hamden, Conn.: Archon Books, 1962 [c1910] xxi, 408 p.; 22 cm. Bibliographical footnotes. I. T.
JN557.M2x

**Ranney, Austin.** **4.8465**
Pathways to Parliament: candidate selection in Britain / Austin Ranney. — London: Macmillan, 1965. xiv, 298 p.: ill. 1. Great Britain. Parliament — Elections 2. Nominations for office — Great Britain. I. T.
JN558.R3 1965b

**McKisack, May.** • **4.8466**
The parliamentary representation of the English boroughs during the Middle Ages. [London] F. Cass [1962] 180 p. 23 cm. Includes bibliography. 1. Great Britain. Parliament — History. 2. Elections — Great Britain. I. T.
JN561.M3 1962    328.42    *LC* 63-564

**Waller, Robert.** **4.8467**
The almanac of British politics / Robert Waller. — London: Croom Helm; New York: St. Martin's Press, 1983. 608 p.: maps; 22 cm. Includes index. 1. Great Britain. Parliament. House of Commons — Election districts 2. Election districts — Great Britain. 3. Great Britain — Economic conditions — 1945- 4. Great Britain — Social conditions — 1945- I. T.
JN561.W28 1983    328.41/07345 19    *LC* 83-3100    *ISBN* 0312021364

## JN617–653 House of Lords

**Weston, Corinne Comstock.** • **4.8468**
English constitutional theory and the House of Lords, 1556–1832. — [1st AMS ed.]. — New York: AMS Press, [1970, c1965] vii, 304 p.: facsims.; 23 cm. — (Columbia studies in the social sciences, no. 607) 1. Gt. Brit. Parliament. House of Lords — History. 2. Gt. Brit. — Constitutional history. I. T. II. Series.
JN621.W44 1970    328.42/09    *LC* 79-127441    *ISBN* 0404516076

**Bromhead, P. A.** **4.8469**
The House of Lords and contemporary politics, 1911–1957. — London, Routledge & Paul [1958] xiii, 283 p. 23 cm. Bibliography: p. 278. Bibliographical footnotes. 1. Great Britain. Parliament. House of Lords. I. T.
JN627.B7    328.42    *LC* 58-1920

## JN671–695 House of Commons

**Who's who of British members of Parliament: a biographical** **4.8470**
**dictionary of the House of Commons based on annual volumes**
**of Dod's Parliamentary companion and other sources / [edited**
**by] Michael Stenton.**
Hassocks, Sussex, Eng.: Harvester Press; Atlantic Highlands, N.J.: Humanities Press, 1976-1981. 4 v.; 24 cm. Vol. 2-4 edited by Michael Stenton and Stephen Lees. Includes indexes. 1. Great Britain. Parliament. House of Commons — Biography. I. Stenton, Michael. II. Lees, Stephen. III. Dod's Parliamentary companion.
JN672.W47 1976    328.41/092/2 B    *LC* 76-12565    *ISBN* 0391006134

**The Commons today.** **4.8471**
Rev. ed. of the Commons in the seventies / edited by S.A. Walkland and Michael Ryle for the Study of Parliament Group. — [London]: Fontana Paperbacks, 1981. 333 p.: ill.; 18 cm. — (Fontana original) Previous ed. published as: The Commons in the seventies. 1977. 1. Great Britain. Parliament. House of Commons — Addresses, essays, lectures. 2. Great

Britain — Politics and government — 1964- — Addresses, essays, lectures. I. Walkland, S. A. II. Ryle, Michael. III. Study of Parliament Group. JN673.C65 1981　328.41/072 19　LC 81-176740　ISBN 0006361870

**Laski, Harold Joseph, 1893-1950.**　　　　　**4.8472**
Reflections on the Constitution: the House of Commons, the Cabinet, the Civil Service / by Harold J. Laski. — Manchester: Manchester University Press, 1951. 220 p. 1. Great Britain. Parliament. House of Commons. 2. Cabinet system 3. Civil service — Great Britain. I. T.
JN673.L3　LC 51-6821/L

**Richards, Peter G.**　　　　　● **4.8473**
Honourable members; a study of the British backbencher [by] Peter G. Richards. — [2d ed.]. — London, Faber and Faber [1964] 294 p. 23 cm. Bibliography: p. 281-283. 1. Great Britain. Parliament. House of Commons. 2. Legislators — Gt. Brit. I. T.
JN673.R5 1964　LC 65-52

**Notestein, Wallace, 1878-1969.**　　　　　● **4.8474**
The House of Commons, 1604–1610. — New Haven: Yale University Press, 1971. xiii, 598 p.; 24 cm. 1. Gt. Brit. Parliament. House of Commons — History. 2. Gt. Brit. — Politics and government — 1603-1625. I. T.
JN675 1604.N6　328.42/09　LC 72-118733　ISBN 0300013566

**Brooke, John, 1920-.**　　　　　● **4.8475**
The House of Commons, 1754–1790: introductory survey. London, Oxford U.P., 1968. viii, 312 p. 21 cm. (Oxford paperback, no. 147) At head of title: The History of Parliament. Originally published as vol. 1 of The history of Parliament: the House of Commons, 1754-1790, by Sir Lewis Namier & John Brooke. 1. Great Britain. Parliament. House of Commons. I. Namier, Lewis Bernstein, Sir, 1888-1960. The House of Commons, 1754-1790. II. T. III. Title: History of Parliament.
JN675 1754.B7　328.42/07/2　LC 71-395379　ISBN 0198811470

**Norton, Philip.**　　　　　**4.8476**
Dissension in the House of Commons: intra–party dissent in the House of Commons' division lobbies, 1945–1974 / compiled and edited by Philip Norton. — London: Macmillan, 1975. xiv, 643 p.; 25 cm. 'The primary source of information ... is Parliamentary debates, House of Commons, fifth series, otherwise known as Hansard.' Includes indexes. 1. Great Britain. Parliament. House of Commons — Voting. 2. Party discipline — Great Britain. 3. Great Britain — Politics and government — 1945- I. Great Britain. Parliament. House of Commons. Parliamentary debates (Hansard). II. T.
JN675 1975.N67　328.41/09 19　LC 75-331855　ISBN 0333181042

**Norton, Philip.**　　　　　**4.8477**
Dissension in the House of Commons, 1974–79 Philip Norton. — Oxford: Clarendon Press; New York: Oxford University Press, 1980. xxxiv, 524 p.; 24 cm. Includes indexes. 1. Great Britain. Parliament. House of Commons — Voting. 2. Great Britain — Politics and government — 1964-1979 I. T.
JN675 1980.N67　328.41/0775　LC 79-41754　ISBN 0198274300

**Norton, Philip.**　　　　　**4.8478**
The Commons in perspective / Philip Norton. — New York, N.Y.: Longman, 1981. vi, 265 p.: ill.; 24 cm. 1. Great Britain. Parliament. House of Commons. I. T.
JN675 1981.N67 1981　328.41/072 19　LC 81-830　ISBN 0582282942

**Taylor, Eric, 1918-.**　　　　　● **4.8479**
The House of Commons at work. — 7th ed. — Harmondsworth: Penguin, 1967. 256 p.; 18 cm. — (Pelican books, A257) 1. Great Britain. Parliament. House of Commons — Rules and practice. I. T.
JN688.T38 1967　328.41/05　LC 68-115650

## JN901–1097 Elections. Suffrage

**Jupp, Peter.**　　　　　**4.8480**
British and Irish elections, 1784–1831. — Newton Abbot: David & Charles; New York: Barnes & Noble, [1973] 212 p.; 22 cm. — (David & Charles sources for social & economic history) 1. Elections — Great Britain — History. 2. Elections — Ireland — History. I. T.
JN951.J86 1973　329/.023/4207　LC 74-160434　ISBN 0604934381

**Butler, David E.**　　　　　● **4.8481**
The British general election of 1951. London: Macmillan, 1952. viii, 289 p.: diagr., facsims.; 22 cm. 1. Great Britain. Parliament — Elections, 1951 2. Great Britain — Politics and government — 1945- I. T.
JN955 B8　LC 52-13620

**Butler, David E.**　　　　　● **4.8482**
The British general election of 1964 / by D.E. Butler and Anthony King. — London: Macmillan; New York: St. Martin's Press, 1965. ix, 401 p.: ill., maps,

ports. 1. Great Britain. Parliament — Elections, 1964. 2. Great Britain — Politics and government — 1945- I. King, Anthony Stephen. II. T.
JN955.B816　LC 65-18642

**Butler, David, 1924-.**　　　　　**4.8483**
The British General Election of 1966, by D. E. Butler and Anthony King. London, Melbourne [etc.] Macmillan; New York, St. Martin's P., 1966. xi, 338 p. illus., 4 plates (incl. ports.) maps, facsims., tables, diagrs. 22 1/2 cm. 1. Great Britain. Parliament — Elections, 1964. 2. Great Britain — Politics and government — 1964-1979 I. King, Anthony Stephen. joint author. II. T.
JN955.B817　324.20942　LC 66-78718

**Butler, David E. 1924-.**　　　　　● **4.8484**
The electoral system in Britain, since 1918. — 2d ed. — Oxford, Clarendon Press, 1963. xiv, 232 p. illus. 23 cm. 'First published in 1953 under the title: The electoral system in Britain, 1918-1951.' 'Bibliographical note': p. [221]-223. 1. Great Britain. Parliament — Elections 2. Elections — Gt. Brit. 3. Election law — Gt. Brit. I. T.
JN955.B82 1963　342.42　LC 63-24311

**Cook, Chris, 1945-.**　　　　　**4.8485**
The age of alignment: electoral politics in Britain, 1922–1929 / Chris Cook. — London: Macmillan; Toronto: University of Toronto Press, 1975. x, 367 p.; 23 cm. — 1. Great Britain. Parliament — Elections 2. Elections — Great Britain 3. Great Britain — Politics and government — 1910-1936 I. T.
JN955.C66　JN955 C64 1975.　ISBN 0802022049

**Hanham, H. J.**　　　　　● **4.8486**
Elections and party management; politics in the time of Disraeli and Gladstone. — [London] Longmans [1959] 468 p. 23 cm. Includes bibliography. 1. Elections — Gt. Brit. I. T.
JN955.H3　329.942　LC 59-4944

**Moore, David Cresap, 1925-.**　　　　　**4.8487**
The politics of deference: a study of the mid–nineteenth century English political system / David Cresap Moore. Hassocks [Eng.]: Harvester Press; New York: Barnes & Noble, 1976. 529 p., [6] leaves of plates: maps; 24 cm. index. 1. Great Britain. Parliament. House of Commons — Election districts 2. Suffrage — Great Britain — History. 3. Voting — Great Britain — History. 4. Great Britain — Politics and government — 19th century I. T.
JN955.M56　301.5/92/0941　LC 74-26187　ISBN 006494932X

**Nicholas, H. G. (Herbert George), 1911-.**　　　　　● **4.8488**
The British General Election of 1950 / by H. G. Nicholas; with an appendix by D. E. Butler. — 1st ed., new impression. London: Cass, 1968. x, 353 p.: 10 plates (2 fold), ill., facsims., maps (1 col.); 22 cm. 1. Great Britain. Parliament — Elections, 1950. 2. Great Britain — Politics and government — 1945-1964 I. T.
JN955.N5 1968　324/.2/0942　LC 68-134006

**Nordlinger, Eric A.**　　　　　**4.8489**
The working–class Tories; authority, deference and stable democracy [by] Eric A. Nordlinger. Berkeley, University of California Press, 1967. 276 p. 22 cm. 1. Conservative Party (Great Britain) 2. Elections — Great Britain. 3. Great Britain — Politics and government — 1945- I. T.
JN955.N6 1967a　323　LC 67-19219

**Pelling, Henry.**　　　　　● **4.8490**
Social geography of British elections, 1885–1910. — London, [etc.] Macmillan; New York, St. Martin's P., 1967. xxxi, 455 p. 24 maps, tables. 22 1/2 cm. Bibliographical footnotes. 1. Great Britain. Parliament — Elections I. T.
JN955.P4　324/.2/0942　LC 67-108494

**Pulzer, Peter G. J.**　　　　　**4.8491**
Political representation and elections in Britain / Peter G.J.Pulzer. — 3rd ed. — London Allen & Unwin 1975. 176 p. — (Studies in political science) Includes index. 1. Representative government and representation — Gt. Brit. 2. Elections — Gt. Brit. 3. Political parties — Gt. Brit. I. T.
JN955 P8 1975　ISBN 004329023x

**Britain at the polls, 1979: a study of the general election /**　　　　　**4.8492**
**edited by Howard R. Penniman.**
Washington: American Enterprise Institute for Public Policy Research, 1981, c1980. 345 p.: ill.; 23 cm. — (AEI's At the polls studies.) (AEI studies; 296) 1. Great Britain. Parliament — Elections, 1979 — Addresses, essays, lectures. 2. Elections — Great Britain — Addresses, essays, lectures. 3. Political parties — Great Britain — Addresses, essays, lectures. I. Penniman, Howard Rae, 1916- II. Series.
JN956.B74　324.9410857 19　LC 80-27536　ISBN 0844734063

**Britain at the polls, 1983: a study of the general election /**　　　　　**4.8493**
**edited by Austin Ranney.**
[Durham, N.C.]: Duke University Press, 1985. xiv, 226 p.: ill.; 24 cm. 'An American Enterprise Institute book.' Includes index. 1. Great Britain. Parliament — Elections, 1983 — Addresses, essays, lectures. 2. Great Britain

— Politics and government — 1979- — Addresses, essays, lectures. I. Ranney, Austin.
JN956.B743 1985    324.941/0858 19    *LC* 84-24646    *ISBN* 0822306190

**Butler, David, 1924-.**      **4.8494**
The British general election of 1983 / by David Butler and Dennis Kavanagh. — New York: St. Martin's Press, 1984. xii, 388 p.: ill.; 22 cm. Includes index. 1. Great Britain. Parliament — Elections, 1983. 2. Elections — Great Britain. I. Kavanagh, Dennis. II. T.
JN956.B82 1984    324.941/0858 19    *LC* 83-26990    *ISBN* 0312102569

**Butler, David, 1924-.**      • **4.8495**
The British general election of 1955, by D. E. Butler. [1st ed.]; new impression. London, Cass, 1969. viii, 236 p., 8 plates. illus., facsims., maps, ports. 23 cm. 1. Great Britain. Parliament — Elections, 1955. I. T.
JN956.B85 1969    324/.2/0942    *LC* 79-506006    *ISBN* 0714615498

**Butler, David, 1924-.**      **4.8496**
The British general election of February, 1974 / by David Butler and Dennis Kavanagh. — New York: St. Martin's Press, 1974. ix, 354 p.: ill.; 23 cm. Includes index. 1. Great Britain. Parliament — Elections, 1974. I. Kavanagh, David, joint author. II. T.
JN956.B85 1974a    329/.023/410857    *LC* 74-16824

**Butler, David, 1924-.**      **4.8497**
The British general election of October 1974 / by David Butler and Dennis Kavanagh. — New York: St. Martin's Press, [1975] 368 p.: ill.; 23 cm. 1. Great Britain. Parliament — Elections, 1974. I. Kavanagh, Dennis. II. T.
JN956.B85 1975b    329/.023/410857    *LC* 75-21706

**Butler, David, 1924-.**      • **4.8498**
The British general election of 1959, by D. E. Butler and Richard Rose. [London] F. Cass, 1970. viii, 293 p. illus., maps, ports. 22 cm. Label mounted on t.p.: Distributed in the U.S.A. by Humanities Press, New York. First published in 1960. 1. Great Britain. Parliament — Elections, 1959. 2. Great Britain — Politics and government — 1945-1964 I. Rose, Richard, 1933- joint author. II. T.
JN956.B86 1970    329/.023/42085    *LC* 73-22706    *ISBN* 0714615501

**Butler, David, 1924-.**      • **4.8499**
The British general election of 1970 / by David Butler and Michael Pinto–Duschinsky. — London: Macmillan; New York: St. Martin's Press, 1971. xviii, 493 p., 8 plates: ill., facsims., ports.; 23 cm. 1. Great Britain. Parliament — Elections, 1970. I. Pinto-Duschinsky, Michael, 1943- joint author. II. T.
JN956.B865    329/.023/42085    *LC* 70-145587    *ISBN* 0333121422

**Butler, David, 1924-.**      **4.8500**
The British general election of 1979 / by David Butler and Dennis Kavanagh. — London: Macmillan, 1980. 443 p.: ill.; 23 cm. 1. Great Britain. Parliament — Elections, 1979. 2. Elections — Great Britain. I. Kavanagh, Dennis. II. T.
JN956.B867 1980    324.9410857 19    *LC* 80-497266    *ISBN* 0333269349

**Butler, David, 1924-.**      **4.8501**
Political change in Britain: the evolution of electoral choice / David Butler, Donald Stokes. — 2d ed. — New York: St. Martin's Press, 1974 [i.e. 1975] xi, 500 p.: ill.; 22 cm. 1. Elections — Great Britain. 2. Voting — Great Britain. 3. Political parties — Great Britain 4. Great Britain — Politics and government — 1945- I. Stokes, Donald E. joint author. II. T.
JN956.B87 1975    301.5/92/0941    *LC* 73-90320

**Dunleavy, Patrick.**      **4.8502**
British democracy at the crossroads: voting and party competition in the 1980s / Patrick Dunleavy and Christopher T. Husbands. — London; Boston: Allen & Unwin, 1985. xx, 251 p.: ill.; 25 cm. Includes index. 1. Elections — Great Britain. 2. Voting — Great Britain. 3. Political parties — Great Britain 4. Great Britain — Politics and government — 1979- I. Husbands, Christopher T. II. T.
JN956.D86 1985    324.941 19    *LC* 84-24264    *ISBN* 0043240100

**Heath, A. F. (Anthony Francis)**      **4.8503**
How Britain votes / Anthony Heath, Roger Jowell, and John Curtice, with the assistance of Julia Field and Clarissa Levine. — 1st ed. — Oxford [Oxfordshire]; New York: Pergamon Press, 1985. xiv, 251 p.: ill.; 24 cm. Includes index. 1. Elections — Great Britain. 2. Voting — Great Britain. 3. Great Britain — Politics and government — 1945- I. Jowell, Roger. II. Curtice, John. III. T.
JN956.H39 1985    324.241/0858 19    *LC* 85-12098    *ISBN* 0080318592

**Himmelweit, Hilde T.**      **4.8504**
How voters decide: a model of vote choice based on a special longitudinal study extending over fifteen years and the British election surveys of 1970–1983 / Hilde T. Himmelweit, Patrick Humphreys, Marianne Jaeger. — Rev. and

updated ed. — Milton Keynes [England]; Philadelphia: Open University Press, [1985]. xi, 283 p.: ill.; 22 cm. Rev. ed. of: How voters decide / Hilde T. Himmelweit ... [et al.]. 1981. Includes indexes. 1. Voting — Great Britain — Longitudinal studies. 2. Great Britain — Politics and government — 1945- I. Humphreys, Patrick. II. Jaeger, Marianne. III. T.
JN956.H68 1985    324.941 19    *LC* 84-19030    *ISBN* 0335105912

**Särlvik, Bo.**      **4.8505**
Decade of dealignment: the Conservative victory of 1979 and electoral trends in the 1970's / Bo Särlvik and Ivor Crewe; with the assistance of Neil Day and Robert MacDermid. — Cambridge [Cambridgeshire]: New York: Cambridge University Press, 1983. xv, 393 p.: ill.; 24 cm. 1. Elections — Great Britain. 2. Political parties — Great Britain 3. Great Britain — Politics and government — 1964-1979 I. Crewe, Ivor. II. T.
JN956.S27 1983    324.941/085 19    *LC* 83-1827    *ISBN* 0521226740

**Alderman, Geoffrey.**      **4.8506**
British elections: myth and reality / [by] Geoffrey Alderman. — London: Batsford, 1978. 236 p.; 23 cm. Includes index. 1. Great Britain. Parliament — Elections 2. Elections — Great Britain. I. T.
JN961.A4    324/.21/0941    *LC* 78-323161    *ISBN* 0713401958

**Rose, Richard, 1933-.**      • **4.8507**
Influencing voters; a study of campaign rationality. — New York: St. Martin's Press, [1967] 288 p.: illus., facsims.; 22 cm. 1. Electioneering — Great Britain. 2. Public relations and politics 3. Elections — Great Britain. I. T.
JN961.R6 1967    329/.023/0942    *LC* 67-12244

## JN976–985 Woman Suffrage

**Garner, Les.**      **4.8508**
Stepping stones to women's liberty: feminist ideas in the women's suffrage movement, 1900–1918 / Les Garner. — 1st American ed. — Rutherford [N.J.]: Fairleigh Dickinson University Press, 1984. viii, 142 p.: ill.; 23 cm. Includes index. 1. Women — Suffrage — Great Britain — History — 20th century. 2. Feminism — Great Britain — History — 20th century. I. T.
JN979.G37 1984    324.6/23/0941 19    *LC* 83-25360    *ISBN* 0838632238

**Harrison, Brian Howard.**      **4.8509**
Separate spheres: the opposition to women's suffrage in Britain / Brian Harrison. — New York: Holmes & Meier, 1978. 274 p.; 23 cm. Includes index. 1. Women — Suffrage — Great Britain — History. I. T.
JN979.H37 1978    324/.3/0941    *LC* 78-4473    *ISBN* 0841903859

**Morgan, David, 1937-.**      **4.8510**
Suffragists and Liberals; the politics of woman suffrage in England. — Totowa, N.J.: Rowman and Littlefield, [1975] vii, 184 p.; 23 cm. 1. Women — Suffrage — Great Britain — History. I. T.
JN979.M67 1975    324/.3/0942    *LC* 74-17334    *ISBN* 0874715830

**Pankhurst, Emmeline, 1858-1928.**      • **4.8511**
My own story / by Emmeline Pankhurst. — New York: Hearst's International Library Co., [1914] 364 p.: ill.; 22 cm. — 1. Women — Suffrage — Great Britain. 2. Women — Great Britain — Biography. 3. Women in politics — Great Britain. I. T.
JN979.P265    324.623

**Pankhurst, E. Sylvia (Estelle Sylvia), 1882-1960.**      • **4.8512**
The suffragette: the history of the women's militant suffrage movement, 1905–1910. — [New York]: Source Book Press, [1970] 517 p.: ill., ports.; 22 cm. Reprint of the 1911 ed. 1. Women — Suffrage — Great Britain. I. T.
JN979.P3 1970    324/.3/0942    *LC* 70-133998    *ISBN* 0876810873

**Rosen, Andrew.**      **4.8513**
Rise up, women!: the militant campaign of the Women's Social and Political Union, 1903–1914 / Andrew Rosen. — London; Boston: Routledge and Kegan Paul, 1974. xix, 312 p., [8] p. of plates: ill., ports.; 23 cm. Includes index. 1. Women's Party (Gt. Brit.) 2. Women — Suffrage — Great Britain — History. I. T.
JN979.R57    324/.3/0941    *LC* 74-81317    *ISBN* 0710079346

**Rover, Constance.**      • **4.8514**
Women's suffrage and party politics in Britain, 1866–1914. — London, Routledge & K. Paul; Toronto, Toronto U.P., 1967. xv, 240 p. tables, diagrs. 22 1/2 cm. — (Studies in political history) Bibliography: p. 225-231. 1. Women — Suffrage — Gt. Brit. I. T.
JN979.R6    324/.3/0942    *LC* 67-104592

## JN1039 Campaign Funds

**Pinto-Duschinsky, Michael, 1943-.**      **4.8515**
British political finance, 1830–1980 / Michael Pinto–Duschinsky. — Washington: American Enterprise Institute for Public Policy Research, c1981.

xviii, 339 p.: ill.; 23 cm. — (AEI studies. 330) Includes index. 1. Campaign funds — Great Britain — History. 2. Political parties — Great Britain — History. I. T. II. Series.
JN1039.P56      324.7/8/0941 19      *LC* 81-7963      *ISBN* 0844734519

## JN1111–1129 POLITICAL PARTIES

**Jennings, Ivor, Sir, 1903-1965.**                                    • **4.8516**
Party politics / by Sir Ivor Jennings. — Cambridge: University Press, 1960-1962. 3 v.: tables; 24 cm. 1. Political parties — Great Britain 2. Great Britain — Politics and government I. T.
JN1117.J38      *LC* 61-1035

**O'Gorman, Frank.**                                    **4.8517**
The emergence of the British two–party system, 1760–1832 / Frank O'Gorman. — London: E. Arnold, 1982. xi, 132 p.; 22 cm. — (Foundations of modern history.) Includes index. 1. Political parties — Great Britain — History — 18th century. 2. Political parties — Great Britain — History — 19th century. I. T. II. Series.
JN1117.O36 1982      324.241/02 19      *LC* 82-134282      *ISBN* 0713162937

**Kenyon, J.P. (John Philipps), 1927-.**                                    **4.8518**
Revolution principles: the politics of party, 1689–1720 / J. P. Kenyon. — Cambridge; New York: Cambridge University Press, 1977. viii, 248 p.; 22 cm. (The Ford lectures; 1975-6) (Cambridge studies in the history and theory of politics) 1. Political parties — Great Britain — History. 2. Great Britain — Politics and government — 1689-1702 3. Great Britain — Politics and government — 1702-1714 4. Great Britain — Politics and government — 1714-1727 I. T.
JN1118.K45      329.9/41      *LC* 76-53518      *ISBN* 0521215420

**Hill, Brian W.**                                    **4.8519**
British parliamentary parties, 1742–1832: from the fall of Walpole to the first Reform Act / B.W. Hill. — London; Boston: Allen & Unwin, 1985. x, 272 p.; 22 cm. Includes index. 1. Political parties — Great Britain — History. 2. Great Britain — Politics and government — 18th century 3. Great Britain — Politics and government — 19th century I. T.
JN1119.H535 1985      324.241/02 19      *LC* 84-24271      *ISBN* 0049421875

**Hill, Brian W.**                                    **4.8520**
The growth of parliamentary parties, 1689–1742 / B. W. Hill. Hamden, Conn.: Archon Books, 1976. 265 p.; 23 cm. Includes index. 1. Political parties — Great Britain — History. 2. Great Britain — Politics and government — 1689-1702 3. Great Britain — Politics and government — 18th century I. T.
JN1119.H54 1976      329.9/41      *LC* 76-21898      *ISBN* 0208015930

**Adversary politics and electoral reform / edited by S. E. Finer.**      **4.8521**
[London]: Anthony Wigram, 1975. x, 374 p.: ill.; 23 cm. Essays. 1. Political parties — Great Britain 2. Elections — Great Britain. I. Finer, S. E. (Samuel Edward), 1915-
JN1121.A64      324/.21/094      *LC* 76-364108      *ISBN* 0950446904

**Finer, S. E. (Samuel Edward), 1915-.**                                    **4.8522**
The changing British party system, 1945–1979 / S. E. Finer. — Washington: American Enterprise Institute for Public Policy Research, c1980. xviii, 244 p.: diag.; 23 cm. — (AEI studies; 265) (American Enterprise Institute studies in political and social processes) 1. Political parties — Great Britain I. T.
JN1121.F56      329/.02/0941      *LC* 79-25084      *ISBN* 0844733687

**Jackson, Robert J., 1936-.**                                    **4.8523**
Rebels and whips: an analysis of dissension, discipline and cohesion in British political parties [by] Robert J. Jackson. — London; Melbourne [etc.]: Macmillan; New York: St. Martin's P., 1968. xii, 346 p.; 23 cm. 1. Party discipline — Great Britain. I. T.
JN1121.J3      324.241 19      *LC* 68-19078

**Multi–party Britain / edited by H. M. Drucker.**                                    **4.8524**
New York: Praeger Publishers, 1979. xiii, 242 p.: ill.; 23 cm. Includes index. 1. Political parties — Great Britain I. Drucker, H. M. (Henry Matthew)
JN1121.M84      324.241      *LC* 79-52940      *ISBN* 0030534461

**Rose, Richard, 1933-.**                                    **4.8525**
Do parties make a difference? / Richard Rose. — Chatham, N.J.: Chatham House Publishers, c1980. xii, 176 p.; 23 cm. — (Chatham House series on change in American politics.) 1. Political parties — Great Britain 2. Elections — Great Britain. 3. Great Britain — Politics and government — 1945- I. T. II. Series.
JN1121.R667      324.241      *LC* 80-15818      *ISBN* 093454008X

**Rose, Richard, 1933-.**                                    **4.8526**
The problem of party government / Richard Rose. — New York: Free Press, [1975] c1974. ix, 502 p.; 24 cm. Includes index. 1. Political parties — Great

Britain 2. Pressure groups — Great Britain. 3. Elections — Great Britain. 4. Great Britain — Politics and government — 1945- I. T.
JN1121.R67 1975      329.9/41      *LC* 74-30329      *ISBN* 0029267803

## JN1129 Political Parties, A–Z

**McKenzie, Robert Trelford.**                                    • **4.8527**
British political parties: the distribution of power within the Conservative and Labour Parties / R.T. McKenzie. — 2d ed. New York: St Martin's Press [1963] xv, 694 p.; 23 cm. 1. Conservative Party (Great Britain) 2. Labour Party (Great Britain) I. T.
JN1129.C62 M3      329.942      *LC* 64-10619

**Pelling, Henry.**                                    • **4.8528**
The British Communist Party; a historical profile. — London: A. and C. Black, [1958] 204 p.: illus.; 23 cm. 1. Communist Party of Great Britain. I. T.
JN1129.C62 P4      329.942      *LC* 59-602

**Stewart, Robert MacKenzie.**                                    **4.8529**
The foundation of the Conservative Party, 1830–1867 / Robert Stewart. — London; New York: Longman, 1978. xvii, 427 p.: ill.; 24 cm. — (A History of the Conservative Party; v. 1) Includes index. 1. Conservative Party (Great Britain) — History. I. T. II. Series.
JN1129.C69 H57 vol. 1      329.9/41      *LC* 77-3280      *ISBN* 058250712X

**Ramsden, John, 1947-.**                                    **4.8530**
The age of Balfour and Baldwin, 1902–1940 / John Ramsden. — London; New York: Longman, 1978. xii, 413 p.: ill.; 24 cm. — (A History of the Conservative Party; v. 3) Originally presented as the author's thesis, Oxford, 1974. Includes index. 1. Conservative Party (Great Britain) — History. 2. Great Britain — Politics and government — 1901-1936 3. Great Britain — Politics and government — 1936-1945 I. T. II. Series.
JN1129.C69 H57 vol. 3 JN1129.C72 1902      329.9/41 s 329.9/41      *LC* 77-30745      *ISBN* 0582507146

**Blake, Robert, 1916-.**                                    **4.8531**
The Conservative Party from Peel to Thatcher / Robert Blake. — Rev. ed. — London: Fontana, 1985. xii, 401 p., 20 p. of plates: ill.; 23 cm. Rev. edition of: The Conservative Party from Peel to Churchill. Includes index. 1. Conservative Party (Great Britain) — History I. T. II. Title: Conservative Party from Peel to Churchill.
JN1129.C7 B54 1985      324.24104/09      *ISBN* 0006860036

**Smith, Paul.**                                    • **4.8532**
Disraelian Conservatism and social reform. London, Routledge & K. Paul; Toronto, Toronto U. P., 1967. x, 358 p. 8 plates (incl. ports., facsims.) 23 cm. (Studies in political history) Bibliography: p. 326-343. 1. Disraeli, Benjamin, Earl of Beaconsfield, 1804-1881. 2. Conservative Party (Great Britain) — History. 3. Great Britain — Social conditions I. T.
JN1129.C7S6      329.9/42      *LC* 67-110084

**Conservative Party politics / edited by Zig Layton–Henry;**      **4.8533**
**foreword by Sir Ian Gilmour.**
London: Macmillan, 1980. xvii, 286 p.; 23 cm. Includes index. 1. Conservative Party (Great Britain) — Addresses, essays, lectures. I. Layton-Henry, Zig.
JN1129.C72 1980b      324.24104      *LC* 80-477031      *ISBN* 0333266013

**Howell, David, 1945-.**                                    **4.8534**
British workers and the Independent Labour Party, 1888–1906 / David Howell. — Manchester (Greater Manchester): Manchester University Press; New York, NY: St. Martin's Press, 1983. ix, 522 p.; 24 cm. Includes index. 1. Independent Labour Party (Great Britain) — History. 2. Labor and laboring classes — Great Britain — History 3. Trade-unions — Great Britain — History. I. T.
JN1129.I52 H68 1983      324.24107/09 19      *LC* 82-24086      *ISBN* 0312105681

**Brand, Carl Fremont.**                                    • **4.8535**
The British Labour Party, a short history [by] Carl F. Brand. — Stanford, Calif.: Stanford University Press, 1964. 340 p.; 24 cm. 1. Labour Party (Great Britain) — History. I. T.
JN1129.L32 B68      329.942      *LC* 64-24293

**Cole, G. D. H. (George Douglas Howard), 1889-1959.**                                    • **4.8536**
A history of the Labour Party from 1914. New York, A. M. Kelley [1969] x, 517 p. illus. 23 cm. Companion to British working-class politics, 1832-1914. 1. Labour Party (Great Britain) 2. Great Britain — Politics and government — 20th century I. T.
JN1129.L32 C6 1969b      329.9/42      *LC* 73-90407      *ISBN* 0678065055

**Hodgson, Geoff.** **4.8537**
Labour at the crossroads: the political and economic challenge to the Labour Party in the 1980s / Geoff Hodgson. — Oxford: M. Robertson, 1981. x, 257 p.: ill.; 23 cm. 1. Labour Party (Great Britain) I. T.
JN1129.L32 H625 1981    324.24106 19    *LC* 81-165141    *ISBN* 0855204621

**Kogan, David.** **4.8538**
The battle for the Labour Party / David Kogan and Maurice Kogan. — London: Kogan Page, 1982. 160 p., [4] p. of plates: ports.; 23 cm. 1. Labour Party (Great Britain) I. Kogan, Maurice. II. T.
JN1129.L32 K63 1982    324.24107 19    *LC* 82-104788    *ISBN* 0850385407

**Minkin, Lewis.** **4.8539**
The Labour Party Conference: a study in the politics of intra–party democracy / Lewis Minkin. — 2nd ed. — Manchester: Manchester University Press, 1980. xv, 448 p.; 24 cm. 1. Labour Party (Great Britain) 2. Labour Party (Great Britain) — Congresses. I. T.
JN1129.L32 M53 1980    324.24107 19    *ISBN* 071900800X

**Pelling, Henry.** • **4.8540**
The origins of the Labour Party, 1880–1900 / Henry Pelling. — 2d ed. — Oxford: Clarendon Press, 1965. ix, 256 p.: ill., ports.; 23 cm. 1. Labour Party (Great Britain) — History. I. T.
JN1129.L32 P36 1965    *LC* 65-3049

**Pelling, Henry.** • **4.8541**
Short history of the Labour Party. London: Macmillan; New York: St. Martin's Press, 1961. 134 p.: illus.; 23 cm. 1. Labour Party (Gt. Brit.) I. T.
JN1129.L32 P42    *LC* 61-17277

**Warde, Alan.** **4.8542**
Consensus and beyond: the development of Labour Party strategy since the Second World War / Alan Warde. — Manchester: Manchester University Press, c1982. 243 p.; 24 cm. 1. Labour Party (Great Britain) — History. 2. Great Britain — Politics and government — 1945- I. T.
JN1129.L32 W34 1982    324.24107/09 19    *LC* 81-208115    *ISBN* 0719008492

**Benn, Tony, 1925-.** **4.8543**
Arguments for socialism / Tony Benn; edited by Chris Mullin. — London: J. Cape, 1982, c1979. 205 p.; 23 cm. Includes index. 1. Labour Party (Great Britain) 2. Socialism — Great Britain I. Mullin, Chris. II. T.
JN1129.L32 W43    320.9/41/085

**Whiteley, Paul.** **4.8544**
The Labour Party in crisis / Paul Whiteley. — London; New York: Methuen, 1983. x, 253 p.: ill.; 25 cm. Includes index. 1. Labour Party (Great Britain) 2. Great Britain — Politics and government — 1945- I. T.
JN1129.L32 W48 1983    324.24107 19    *LC* 83-13176    *ISBN* 0416338607

**McKibbin, Ross.** **4.8545**
The evolution of the Labour Party, 1910–1924 / by Ross McKibbin. — London; New York: Oxford University Press, 1975 (c1974). xviii, 261 p.; 23 cm. (Oxford historical monographs) Includes index. 1. Labour Party (Great Britain) — History. I. T.
JN1129.L33 1910    324.24107/09 19    *LC* 75-308430    *ISBN* 0198218508

**Coates, David.** **4.8546**
Labour in power?: a study of the Labour government 1974–1979 / David Coates. — London; New York: Longman, 1980. xii, 304 p.; 22 cm. Includes index. 1. Labour Party (Great Britain) 2. Great Britain — Politics and government — 1964-1979 I. T.
JN1129.L33 1974d    354.41/0009    *LC* 79-42850    *ISBN* 058229536X

**Coates, David.** **4.8547**
The Labour Party and the struggle for Socialism / David Coates. — London: Cambridge University Press, 1975. xiv, 257 p.; 23 cm. Includes index. 1. Labour Party (Great Britain) 2. Great Britain — Politics and government — 1945- I. T.
JN1129.L33 1975    329.9/41    *LC* 74-19526    *ISBN* 0521207401. *ISBN* 0521099390 pbk

**Drucker, H. M. (Henry Matthew)** **4.8548**
Doctrine and ethos in the Labour Party / H. M. Drucker. — London; Boston: G. Allen & Unwin, 1979. 134 p.; 23 cm. 1. Labour Party (Great Britain) I. T.
JN1129.L33 1979    329.9/41    *LC* 78-40899    *ISBN* 0043290264

**The Politics of the Labour Party / edited by Dennis Kavanagh.** **4.8549**
London; Boston: G. Allen & Unwin, 1982. 228 p.; 23 cm. 'Selection from papers which were originally presented at a conference ... at Nuffield College, Oxford,

in September 1980'—Pref. 1. Labour Party (Great Britain) — Congresses. 2. Great Britain — Politics and government — 1945- — Congresses. I. Kavanagh, Dennis.
JN1129.L33 1982    324.24107 19    *LC* 81-22803    *ISBN* 004329037X

**The First Labour Party, 1906–1914 / edited by K.D. Brown.** **4.8550**
London; Dover, N.H.: Croom Helm, c1985. 297 p.; 23 cm. 1. Labour Party (Great Britain) — History. 2. Great Britain — Politics and government — 1901-1936 I. Brown, Kenneth Douglas.
JN1129.L35 F57 1985    324.24107/09 19    *LC* 85-4190    *ISBN* 070993209X

**Cyr, Arthur I., 1945-.** **4.8551**
Liberal party politics in Britain / by Arthur Cyr; with a foreword by Michael Steed. — New Brunswick, N.J.: Transaction Books, 1977, c1976. 318 p.; 23 cm. Includes index. 1. Liberal Party (Great Britain) — History. I. T.
JN1129.L45 C9 1977    329.9/41    *LC* 76-702    *ISBN* 087855145X

**Hamer, David Allan.** **4.8552**
Liberal politics in the age of Gladstone and Rosebery: a study in leadership and policy [by] D. A. Hamer. Oxford, Clarendon Press, 1972. xv, 368 p. 23 cm. 1. Liberal Party (Great Britain) — History. 2. Great Britain — Politics and government — 1837-1901 I. T.
JN1129.L45 H3    329.9/42    *LC* 72-180137    *ISBN* 0198223501

**Vincent, John Russell.** • **4.8553**
The formation of the British Liberal Party / J.R. Vincent. — New York: Scribner, [1967], 1966. xxxv, 281 p.; 22 cm. First published in 1966 under title: The formation of the Liberal Party, 1857-1868. 1. Liberal Party (Great Britain) I. T.
JN1129.L45 V5 1967    329.9/42    *LC* 67-13310

**Taylor, Stan, 1948-.** **4.8554**
The National Front in English politics / Stan Taylor. — London: MacMillan; New York, N.Y.: Holmes & Meier, 1982. xvii, 212 p.; 23 cm. U.S. imprint from label on verso of t.p. Includes index. 1. National Front. 2. Great Britain — Politics and government — 1979- I. T.
JN1129.N373 T39 1982    324.241/0938 19    *LC* 82-196455    *ISBN* 0333277414

**Bradley, Ian C.** **4.8555**
Breaking the mould?: the birth and prospects of the Social Democratic Party / Ian Bradley. — Oxford: Martin Robertson, 1981. xiv, 172 p.: ill.; 23 cm. Includes index. 1. Social Democratic Party (Great Britain) — History. 2. Great Britain — Politics and government — 1964-1979 3. Great Britain — Politics and government — 1979- I. T.
JN1129.S58 B7    324.241/0972 19    *LC* 81-195678    *ISBN* 0855204680

**Stephenson, Hugh, 1938-.** **4.8556**
Claret and chips: the rise of the SDP / Hugh Stephenson. — London: M. Joseph, 1982. 201 p.; 23 cm. Includes index. 1. Social Democratic Party (Great Britain) 2. Great Britain — Politics and government — 1979- I. T.
JN1129.S58 S74 1982    324.241/072 19    *LC* 85-118399    *ISBN* 0718121899

**Colley, Linda.** **4.8557**
In defiance of oligarchy: the Tory Party, 1714–60 / Linda Colley. — Cambridge; New York: Cambridge University Press, 1982. viii, 375 p.; 24 cm. Based on thesis (Ph.D.)—Cambridge University, 1976. 1. Tories, English 2. Great Britain — Politics and government — 1714-1760 I. T.
JN1129.T72 C64    324.241/02 19    *LC* 81-10004    *ISBN* 0521239826

**Browning, Reed.** **4.8558**
Political and constitutional ideas of the court Whigs / Reed Browning. — Baton Rouge: Louisiana State University Press, c1982. xi, 281 p.; 23 cm. Includes index. 1. Whig Party (Great Britain) 2. Political science — Great Britain — History. 3. Great Britain — Politics and government — 1714-1760 I. T.
JN1129.W62 B76 1982    324.241/02 19    *LC* 81-19372    *ISBN* 0807109800

**Mitchell, Austin Vernon, 1934-.** • **4.8559**
The Whigs in opposition, 1815–1830, by Austin Mitchell. — Oxford, Clarendon P., 1967. xi, 266 p. tables. 22 1/2 cm. Based on thesis, Oxford University. Bibliography: p. [256]-259. 1. Whig Party (Gt. Brit.) 2. Gt. Brit. — Pol. & govt. — 1800-1837. I. T.
JN1129.W65G7    328.42/09    *LC* 67-103758

## JN1150–1159 WALES

**Davies, D. Hywel.** **4.8560**
The Welsh Nationalist Party, 1925–1945: a call to nationhood / D. Hywel Davies. — New York: St. Martin's Press, 1983. ix, 286 p.: ill.; 22 cm. Based on the author's thesis (M. Sc.)—University of Wales, 1979. Includes index.

1. Plaid Cymru — History. 2. Wales — Politics and government — 20th century I. T.
JN1159.A8 P555 1983    324.2429/03 19    *LC* 83-11221    *ISBN* 0312861907

## JN1187–1371 Scotland

**Pryde, George Smith, 1899-1961.**    • **4.8561**
Central and local government in Scotland since 1707. [London, Published for the Historical Association by Routledge and K. Paul] 1960. 26 p.; 22 cm. (General series (Historical Association (Great Britain)) 45) 1. Scotland — Politics and government I. T. II. Series.
JN 1211 P97 1960    *LC* 63-267

**Kellas, James G.**    **4.8562**
The Scottish political system / James G. Kellas. — 3rd ed. — Cambridge [Cambridgeshire]; New York: Cambridge University Press, 1984. xi, 284 p.: map; 23 cm. Includes index. 1. Scotland — Politics and government — 20th century I. T.
JN1213 1984    320.9411 19    *LC* 83-24085    *ISBN* 0521262496

## JN1401–1572 Ireland. Northern Ireland

**Lyons, Francis Stewart Leland, 1923-.**    • **4.8563**
The Irish parliamentary party, 1890–1910. London Faber and Faber [1951] 284p. (Studies in Irish history, v. 4) 1. Political parties — Ireland 2. Ireland — Politics and government — 1837-1901 3. Ireland — Politics and government — 1901-1910 I. T. II. Series.
JN1411 L86    *LC* 51-32169

**Carty, R. Kenneth.**    **4.8564**
Party and parish pump: electoral politics in Ireland / R.K. Carty. — Waterloo, Ont., Canada: W. Laurier University Press; Atlantic Highlands, N.J.: Distributed by Humanities Press, c1981. xiv, 159 p.: ill.; 24 cm. Distributor from label mounted on t.p. 1. Elections — Ireland — History. 2. Ireland — Politics and government — 1922- I. T.
JN1415.C37    324/.09417 19    *LC* 82-109988    *ISBN* 0889201056

**Chubb, Basil.**    **4.8565**
The government and politics of Ireland / Basil Chubb. — 2nd ed. — Stanford, Calif.: Stanford University Press, 1982. xviii, 396 p.: ill.; 24 cm. Includes index. 1. Ireland — Politics and government — 1922-1949 2. Ireland — Politics and government — 1949- I. T.
JN1415.C48 1982    320.9417 19    *LC* 81-50785    *ISBN* 0804711151

**The Irish parliamentary tradition. Edited by Brian Farrell. With three essays on the treaty debate, by F. S. L. Lyons.**    **4.8566**
Dublin: Gill and Macmillan; New York: Barnes & Noble Books, [1973] 286 p.; 23 cm. — (Thomas Davis lectures. 47th-48th ser.) First 16 essays originally broadcast on RTÉ, Jan.-Apr., 1972; the last 3 essays, by F. S. L. Lyons, were broadcast on RTÉ, Dec., 1971. 1. Representative government and representation — Ireland — History — Addresses, essays, lectures. I. Farrell, Brian. ed. II. Series.
JN1463.I74 1973    328.415    *LC* 73-180415    *ISBN* 0064920682

**Gallagher, Michael, Ph. D.**    **4.8567**
Political parties in the Republic of Ireland / Michael Gallagher. — Manchester; Dover, N.H., USA: Manchester University Press, c1985. 174 p.; 22 cm. 1. Political parties — Ireland. I. T.
JN1571.G35 1985    324.2417 19    *LC* 84-17161    *ISBN* 0719017424

## JN1572 Northern Ireland

**Arthur, Paul, 1945-.**    **4.8568**
Government and politics of Northern Ireland / Paul Arthur. — 2nd ed. — London; New York: Longman, 1984. viii, 168 p.: maps; 20 cm. (Political realities.) Includes index. 1. Northern Ireland — Politics and government I. T. II. Series.
JN1572.A2 A77 1984    320.9416 19    *LC* 83-26803    *ISBN* 0582354803

**Wallace, Martin.**    **4.8569**
Northern Ireland: 50 years of self–government. — Newton Abbot: David & Charles, 1971. 192 p.: map.; 23 cm. 1. Northern Ireland — Politics and government I. T.
JN1572.A2W35    320.9/416/09    *LC* 77-574844    *ISBN* 0715352520

**Birrell, Derek.**    **4.8570**
Policy and government in Northern Ireland: lessons of devolution / Derek Birrell and Alan Murie. — Dublin: Gill and Macmillan; [New York]: Barnes & Noble Books, 1980. 353 p.; 22 cm. Includes index. 1. Northern Ireland —

Politics and government 2. Northern Ireland — Economic policy. 3. Northern Ireland — Social policy. I. Murie, Alan. II. T.
JN1572.A58 B57    320.9416 19    *LC* 80-153876    *ISBN* 0389200190

**Rose, Richard, 1933-.**    • **4.8571**
Governing without consensus: an Irish perspective. — Boston: Beacon Press [1971] 567 p.: ill., maps, ports.; 21 cm. 1. Allegiance — Northern Ireland. 2. Northern Ireland — Politics and government — 1969- I. T.
JN1572.A922 R66    320.9/416    *LC* 70-156451    *ISBN* 0807043907

## JN1601–2229 Austria. Czechoslovakia

**Bluhm, William Theodore, 1923-.**    **4.8572**
Building an Austrian nation: the political integration of a western state / by William T. Bluhm. — New Haven: Yale University Press, 1973. xii, 265 p.; 23 cm. 1. Austria — Politics and government — 1945- I. T.
JN2012.3.B58    320.9/436/05    *LC* 72-91288    *ISBN* 0300015852

**Steiner, Kurt, 1912-.**    **4.8573**
Politics in Austria. — Boston: Little, Brown, [1972] xvii, 443 p.: map.; 22 cm. — (Little, Brown series in comparative politics. A country study) 1. Austria — Politics and government — 1945- I. T.
JN2012.3.S75    320.9/436/05    *LC* 79-186058

**Sully, Melanie A.**    **4.8574**
Political parties and elections in Austria / by Melanie A. Sully. — New York: St. Martin's Press, 1981. xiii, 194 p.: ill.; 23 cm. Includes index. 1. Political parties — Austria. 2. Elections — Austria. 3. Austria — Politics and government — 1945- I. T.
JN2030.S85 1981    324.2436 19    *LC* 80-26389    *ISBN* 0312623259

**Suda, Zdeněk.**    **4.8575**
Zealots and rebels: a history of the Communist Party of Czechoslovakia / Zdenek L. Suda. — Stanford, Calif.: Hoover Institution Press, c1980. xi, 412 p.; 23 cm. — (Hoover Institution publication. 234) (Histories of ruling Communist parties.) Includes index. 1. Komunistická strana Československa — History. I. T. II. Series. III. Series: Histories of ruling Communist parties.
JN2229.A5 S778    324.2437075 19    *LC* 80-8332    *ISBN* 0817973427

## JN2301–3007 France

### JN2321–2433 Ancien Regime

**Hotman, François, sieur de Villiers Saint Paul, 1524-1590.**    **4.8576**
Francogallia. Latin text by Ralph E. Giesey; translated by J. H. M. Salmon. — Cambridge [Eng.]: University Press, 1972. xii, 581 p.; 23 cm. — (Cambridge studies in the history and theory of politics) Parallel Latin text and English translation; introd. in English. 1. France — Politics and government 2. France — Constitutional history. I. Giesey, Ralph E. II. Salmon, J. H. M. (John Hearsey McMillan), 1925- tr. III. T.
JN2325.H67 1972    320.9/44    *LC* 73-172835    *ISBN* 0521083796

**Bonney, Richard.**    **4.8577**
Political change in France under Richelieu and Mazarin, 1624–1661 / by Richard Bonney. — Oxford [Eng.]; New York: Oxford University Press, 1978. vi, 508 p.: ill.; 23 cm. Includes index. 1. France — Politics and government — 17th century I. T.
JN2341.B66    320.9/44/032    *LC* 77-30298    *ISBN* 0198225377

**Rowen, Herbert Harvey.**    **4.8578**
The king's State: proprietary dynasticism in early modern France / Herbert H. Rowen. — New Brunswick, N.J.: Rutgers University Press, c1980. viii, 232 p.; 24 cm. Includes index. 1. Monarchy — France — History. 2. France — Kings and rulers — History. 3. France — Politics and government — 16th century 4. France — Politics and government — 1589-1789 I. T.
JN2341.R68    944/.03/0922 19    *LC* 80-13572    *ISBN* 0813508932

**Seyssel, Claude de, 1450?-1520.**    **4.8579**
[Monarchie de France et deux autres fragments politiques. English] The monarchy of France / Claude de Seyssel; translated by J. H. Hexter; edited, annotated, and introduced by Donald R. Kelley; additional translation by Michael Sherman. — New Haven, Conn.: Yale University Press, c1981. viii, 191 p.; 22 cm. Translation of La monarchie de France et deux autres fragments politiques. 1. Monarchy 2. France — Politics and government — 1328-1589 I. Kelley, Donald R. II. T.
JN2341.S413    321.6/0944 19    *LC* 80-23554    *ISBN* 0300025165

**Louis XIV and absolutism / edited by Ragnhild Hatton.**    **4.8580**
Columbus: Ohio State University Press, 1976. xiii, 306 p.: maps; 23 cm. Most of the essays are translated from French. 1. Louis XIV, King of France, 1638-1715 — Addresses, essays, lectures. 2. France — Politics and government

— 1643-1715 — Addresses, essays, lectures. 3. France — Economic conditions — 17th century — Addresses, essays, lectures. I. Hatton, Ragnhild Marie. JN2369.L68  320.9/44/033  *LC* 75-45158  *ISBN* 0814202551

**Major, J. Russell (James Russell), 1921-.**  **4.8581**
Representative government in early modern France / J. Russell Major. — New Haven: Yale University Press, c1980. xiv, 731 p.: map; 24 cm. (Studies presented to the International Commission for the history of representative and parliamentary institutions; 63) Includes index. 1. France. Etats généraux. 2. Representative government and representation — France — History. I. T. JN2413.M317  320.9/44/02  *LC* 79-14711  *ISBN* 0300023006

## JN2441–3007 CONSTITUTIONAL GOVERNMENT

**Godechot, Jacques Léon, 1907-.**  • **4.8582**
Les institutions de la France sous la Révolution et l'émpire. [1. éd.] Paris Presses Universitaires de France 1951. 687p. (Histoire des institutions) 1. France — Politics and government — 1789-1815 I. T. JN2465 G6

**Siegfried, André, 1875-1959.**  • **4.8583**
Tableau politique de la France de l'Ouest sous la Troisième République. Paris: Colin, 1913. xxviii, 535 p.: ill., fold. map; 26 cm. 1. France — Politics and government I. T. JN2593 1913.S4  *LC* 14-2920

**Leites, Nathan Constantin, 1912-.**  • **4.8584**
On the game of politics in France / with a foreword by D.W. Brogan. — Stanford, Calif.: Stanford University Press, 1959. 190 p. 1. Political parties — France 2. France — Politics and government — 1945- I. T. JN2594 L4 1959  *LC* 59-7426

**MacRae, Duncan.**  • **4.8585**
Parliament, parties, and society in France, 1946–1958. — New York: St. Martin's Press, [1967] xiii, 375 p.; 25 cm. 1. France — Politics and government — 1945- I. T. JN2594.M23  320.9/44  *LC* 67-12241

**Williams, Philip Maynard.**  • **4.8586**
Crisis and compromise; politics in the Fourth Republic, by Philip M. Williams. [3d ed.] London] Longmans [1964] x, 546 p. ill., maps. 1. France — Politics and government — 1945- I. T. JN2594 W5 1964  *LC* 64-9269

**Ehrmann, Henry Walter, 1908-.**  **4.8587**
Politics in France / Henry W. Ehrmann. — 4th ed. — Boston: Little, Brown, c1983. xxii, 376 p.: map; 21 cm. — (The Little, Brown series in comparative politics. A Country study) 1. Representative government and representation — France. 2. France — Politics and government — 1958- I. T. JN2594.2.E5 1983  320.944 19  *LC* 82-7235  *ISBN* 0316222895

**Suleiman, Ezra N., 1941-.**  **4.8588**
Politics, power, and bureaucracy in France; the administrative elite [by] Ezra N. Suleiman. — Princeton, N.J.: Princeton University Press, [1974] xviii, 440 p.: illus.; 25 cm. 1. Cabinet officers — France. 2. Government executives — France. 3. France — Politics and government — 20th century 4. France — Executive departments. I. T. JN2728.S94  354/.44/01  *LC* 72-6524  *ISBN* 0691075522

**Williams, Philip Maynard.**  • **4.8589**
The French Parliament: politics in the Fifth Republic [by] Philip M. Williams. New York, F. A. Praeger [1968] 136 p. 23 cm. (Studies in political science, 2) 1. France. Parlement (1946- ). Assemblée nationale. 2. France — Politics and government — 1958- I. T. JN2787.W5  328.44/09  *LC* 67-30060

**Hause, Steven C., 1942-.**  **4.8590**
Women's suffrage and social politics in the French Third Republic / Steven C. Hause with Anne R. Kenney. — Princeton, N.J.: Princeton University Press, c1984. xx, 382 p., [16] p. of plates: ill.; 25 cm. Includes index. 1. Women — Suffrage — France — History. 2. Feminism — France — History. 3. France — Politics and government — 1870-1940 I. Kenney, Anne R., 1950- II. T. JN2954.H38 1984  324.6/23/0944 19  *LC* 84-42579  *ISBN* 0691054274

**Goguel, François, 1909-.**  • **4.8591**
La politique des partis sous la IIIe republique / [par] Francois Goguel. — 3. ed. — Paris: Editions du Seuil, [1958] 566 p. (Collections Esprit. La Cité prochaine) 1. Political parties — France. 2. France — Politics and government — 1870-1940 I. T. JN2997.G6 1958

**Frears, J. R., 1936-.**  **4.8592**
Political parties and elections in the French Fifth Republic / by J. R. Frears. — New York: St. Martin's Press, 1978 (c1977). xi, 292 p.; 23 cm. Includes index.

1. Political parties — France. 2. Elections — France. 3. France — Politics and government — 1958- I. T. JN2999 1977.F7 1977b  320.9/44/083  *LC* 77-82033  *ISBN* 0312597509

## JN3007 Political Parties

**Kriegel, Annie.**  • **4.8593**
[Communistes français. English] The French Communists: profile of a people / translated by Elaine P. Halperin; foreword by Aristide R. Zolberg. — Chicago: University of Chicago Press [1972] xxiv, 408 p.; 22 cm. 1. Parti communiste français. 2. Communism — France. I. T. JN3007.C6 K6813  329.9/44  *LC* 72-171346  *ISBN* 0226452905

**Bell, David Scott.**  **4.8594**
The French Socialist Party: resurgence and victory / D.S. Bell and Byron Criddle. — Oxford [Oxfordshire]: Clarendon Press; New York: Oxford University Press, 1984. x, 311 p.: map; 22 cm. Includes index. 1. Parti socialiste (France) 2. France — Politics and government — 1969-1974 3. France — Politics and government — 1974-1981 4. France — Politics and government — 1981- I. Criddle, Byron. II. T. JN3007.S6 B44 1984  324.244/074 19  *LC* 83-23707  *ISBN* 0198225970

**Greene, Nathanael, 1935-.**  • **4.8595**
Crisis and decline; the French Socialist Party in the Popular Front era. Ithaca, N.Y., Cornell University Press [1969] xv, 361 p. illus., ports. 24 cm. 1. Parti socialiste (France) I. T. JN3007.S6 G7  329.9/44  *LC* 68-31072

**Noland, Aaron.**  • **4.8596**
The founding of the French Socialist Party, 1893–1905. Cambridge, Harvard University Press, 1956. viii, 233 p. (Harvard historical monographs. 29) 1. Parti socialiste (France) 2. Socialism — France I. T. II. Series. JN3007 S6 N6  *LC* 56-8552

## JN3201–4979 Germany

**Kohn, Walter S. G.**  **4.8597**
Governments and politics of the German–speaking countries / Walter S. G. Kohn. — Chicago: Nelson-Hall, [1980] 291 p.: maps; 23 cm. 1. Europe, German-speaking — Politics and government. I. T. JN3221.K58  320.3/094  *LC* 79-16859  *ISBN* 0882292625

**Carsten, F. L. (Francis Ludwig)**  • **4.8598**
Princes and parliaments in Germany, from the fifteenth to the eighteenth century. Oxford, Clarendon Press, 1959. x, 473 p.: fold. map.; 23 cm. Bibliography: p. [445]-455. 1. Estates (Social orders) — Germany. 2. Representative government and representation — Germany. 3. Germany — Constitutional history I. T. JN3250.E7C3  328.4309  *LC* 59-16742

**Meinecke, Friedrich, 1862-1954.**  • **4.8599**
[Weltbürgertum und Nationalstaat. English] Cosmopolitanism and the national state. Translated by Robert B. Kimber. Introd. by Felix Gilbert. Princeton, N.J., Princeton University Press, 1970. xv, 403 p. 24 cm. Translation of Weltbürgertum und Nationalstaat. 1. Nationalism — Germany. 2. Germany — Politics and government I. T. JN3295.M513  320.9/43  *LC* 65-17150  *ISBN* 0691051771

**Childers, Thomas, 1946-.**  **4.8600**
The Nazi voter: the social foundations of fascism in Germany, 1919–1933 / Thomas Childers. — Chapel Hill: University of North Carolina Press, c1983. xvi, 367 p.; 24 cm. Includes index. 1. Elections — Germany — History. 2. Social classes — Germany — Political activity — History. 3. National socialism — History. 4. Germany — Politics and government — 1918-1933 I. T. JN3838.C44 1983  324.943/085 19  *LC* 83-5924  *ISBN* 0807815705

**Hamilton, Richard F.**  **4.8601**
Who voted for Hitler? / Richard F. Hamilton. — Princeton, N.J.: Princeton University Press, c1982. xv, 664 p.: maps; 24 cm. 1. Hitler, Adolf, 1889-1945. 2. Elections — Germany — History. 3. Social classes — Germany — Political activity — History. 4. National socialism — History. 5. Germany — Politics and government — 1918-1933 I. T. JN3838.H35 1982  324.943/085 19  *LC* 81-17811  *ISBN* 0691093954

**Bergsträsser, Ludwig, 1883-1960.**  • **4.8602**
Geschichte der politischen Parteien in Deutschland / Ludwig Bergsträsser; Aufl., völlig überab. und hrsg. von Wilhelm Mommsen; mit einer Bibliographie von Hans–Gerd Schumann. — München: Günter Olzog Verlag, 1965. 395 p.;

23 cm. — (Deutsches Handbuch der Politik; Bd. 2) 1. Political parties — Germany I. Mommsen, Wilhelm 1892- II. T.
JN3925 B4 1965     *LC* 67-90494

**Levy, Richard S.**        **4.8603**
The downfall of the anti–Semitic political parties in imperial Germany / Richard S. Levy. New Haven: Yale University Press, 1975. vii, 335 p.; 24 cm. — (Yale historical publications. Miscellany. 106) Includes index. 1. Political parties — Germany — History. 2. Antisemitism — Germany — History. I. T. II. Series.
JN3933.L48 1975     329/.9/43     *LC* 74-20083     *ISBN* 0300018037

**Kater, Michael H., 1937-.**        **4.8604**
The Nazi Party: a social profile of members and leaders, 1919–1945 / Michael H. Kater. — Cambridge, Mass.: Harvard University Press, 1983. xiv, 415 p.: ill.; 24 cm. Includes indexes. 1. Nationalsozialistische Deutsche Arbeiter-Partei. 2. National socialism 3. Germany — Social conditions — 1918-1933 4. Germany — Social conditions — 1933-1945 I. T.
JN3946.N36 K37 1983     324.243/038 19     *LC* 82-15814     *ISBN* 0674606558

**Lidtke, Vernon L.**        • **4.8605**
The outlawed party; social democracy in Germany, 1878–1890 [by] Vernon L. Lidtke. — Princeton [N.J.]: Princeton University Press, 1966. xii, 374 p.; 25 cm. 1. Sozialdemokratische Partei Deutschlands. I. T.
JN3946.S83 L5     329.943     *LC* 66-14311

**Schorske, Carl E.**        • **4.8606**
German social democracy, 1905–1917; the development of the great schism, by Carl E. Schorske. New York, Russell & Russell [1970, c1955] xiii, 358 p. 23 cm. — (Harvard historical studies. v. 65) 1. Sozialdemokratische Partei Deutschlands — History — 20th century. 2. Socialism — Germany — History — 20th century. 3. Germany — Politics and government — 1888-1918 I. T. II. Series.
JN3946.S83 S33 1970     324.243072 19     *LC* 71-81471

**Golay, John Ford.**        • **4.8607**
The founding of the Federal Republic of Germany. — [Chicago] University of Chicago Press [1958] xii, 299 p. 24 cm. Bibliography: p. 276-286. 'Basic law for the Federal Republic of Germany': p. 217-262. 1. Germany (Federal Republic, 1949-   ) — Constitutional history. I. Germany (West) Grundgesetz II. T.
JN3971.A2G6     342.43     *LC* 57-11205

**Childs, David, 1933-.**        **4.8608**
West Germany, politics and society / David Childs and Jeffrey Johnson. — New York: St. Martin's Press, 1981. 231 p.; 23 cm. 1. Germany (West) — Politics and government 2. Germany (West) — Social conditions. I. Johnson, Jeffrey. joint author. II. T.
JN3971.A5 C46 1981     320.943     *LC* 80-16747     *ISBN* 0312863004

**Merkl, Peter H.**        • **4.8609**
The origin of the West German Republic. New York, Oxford University Press, 1963. 269 p. illus. 21 cm. 1. Germany (West) — Constitutional history. I. T.
JN3971.A71 M4 1963     342.43     *LC* 63-9627

**Germany at the polls: the Bundestag election of 1976 / edited**        **4.8610**
**by Karl H. Cerny.**
Washington: American Enterprise Institute for Public Policy Research, c1978. 251 p.: map; 23 cm. — (AEI's At the polls series.) (AEI studies; 208) 1. Germany (West). Bundestag — Elections — Addresses, essays, lectures. 2. Elections — Germany (West) — Addresses, essays, lectures. I. Cerny, Karl H. II. Series.
JN3971.A95 G48     329/.023/43087     *LC* 78-15362     *ISBN* 0844733105

**Party government and political culture in Western Germany /**        **4.8611**
**edited by Herbert Döring and Gordon Smith.**
New York: St. Martin's Press, 1982. ix, 227 p.; 23 cm. 1. Political parties — Germany (West) — Addresses, essays, lectures. 2. Political parties — Great Britain — Addresses, essays, lectures. 3. Political socialization — Europe — Addresses, essays, lectures. 4. Europe — Politics and government — Addresses, essays, lectures. I. Döring, Herbert. II. Smith, Gordon R. JN3971.A979 P38 1982     320.94 19     *LC* 81-2098     *ISBN* 0312597606

**Capra, Fritjof.**        **4.8612**
Green politics / Fritjof Capra and Charlene Spretnak in collaboration with Rüdiger Lutz. — 1st ed. — New York: Dutton, c1984. xxi, 244 p.; 22 cm. 1. Grünen (Political party) I. Spretnak, Charlene, 1946- II. Lutz, Wulf-Rüdiger. III. T.
JN3971.A98 G7232 1984     324.243/06 19     *LC* 83-27474     *ISBN* 0525242317

**Braunthal, Gerard, 1923-.**        **4.8613**
The West German Social Democrats, 1969–1982: profile of a party in Power / Gerard Braunthal. — Boulder, Colo.: Westview, 1983. xvi, 334 p.: ill.; 23 cm. —

(Westview replica edition.) Includes index. 1. Sozialdemokratische Partei Deutschlands. I. T. II. Series.
JN3971.A98 S57443 1983     JN3971A98 S57443 1983.     324.243/072 19     *LC* 83-3464     *ISBN* 0865319588

**Ludz, Peter Christian, 1931-.**        **4.8614**
The changing party elite in East Germany [by] Peter C. Ludz. — Cambridge, Mass.: MIT Press, [1972] xxi, 509 p.; 24 cm. Abbreviated and rev. translation of Parteielite im Wandel, which was originally presented as the author's Habilitationsschrift, Freie Universität, Berlin, 1966. 1. Sozialistische Einheitspartei Deutschlands. I. T.
JN3971.5.A98 S65 1972d     329.9/43/1     *LC* 76-162918     *ISBN* 0262120534

## JN4421–4483 Prussia

**Rosenberg, Hans, 1904-.**        • **4.8615**
Bureaucracy, aristocracy, and autocracy; the Prussian experience, 1660–1815. — Cambridge, Harvard University Press, 1958. ix, 247 p. 21 cm. — (Harvard historical monographs. 34) Bibliographical footnotes. 1. Prussia — Pol. & govt. 2. Civil service — Prussia. 3. Prussia — Nobility. I. T. II. Series.
JN4431.R76 1958     342.43     *LC* 58-3879

**Dorwart, Reinhold August, 1911-.**        • **4.8616**
The administrative reforms of Frederick William I of Prussia. — Westport, Conn.: Greenwood Press, [1971, c1953] xi, 250 p.: illus., map.; 23 cm. 1. Frederick William I, King of Prussia, 1688-1740. 2. Prussia (Germany) — Politics and government — 1640-1740. I. T.
JN4443.D6 1971     354.43     *LC* 70-138221     *ISBN* 0837155789

**Simon, Walter Michael, 1922-.**        • **4.8617**
The failure of the Prussian reform movement, 1807–1819 [by] Walter M. Simon. New York, H. Fertig, 1971 [c1955] xii, 272 p. 24 cm. 1. Prussia (Kingdom). Armee — History. 2. Prussia (Germany) — Constitutional history. I. T. II. Title: The Prussian reform movement.
JN4445.S5 1971     943/.06     *LC* 73-80591

**Anderson, Eugene Newton.**        • **4.8618**
The social and political conflict in Prussia, 1858–1864, by Eugene N. Anderson. — New York: Octagon Books, 1968 [c1954] x, 445 p.; 24 cm. 1. Prussia (Germany) — Politics and government — 1848-1866. I. T.
JN4451.A54 1968     943/.07     *LC* 68-16772

## JN5001–5185 Greece

**Kaltchas, Nicholas Stavrou, 1895-1937.**        • **4.8619**
Introduction to the constitutional history of modern Greece. New York, AMS Press [1970, c1965] xvi, 187 p. 23 cm. 1. Greece — Constitutional history. I. T.
JN5016.K3 1970     342/.495/09     *LC* 78-110573     *ISBN* 0404036279

**Legg, Keith R., 1935-.**        • **4.8620**
Politics in modern Greece [by] Keith R. Legg. Stanford, Calif., Stanford University Press, 1969. viii, 367 p. illus., map. 24 cm. A revision of the author's thesis, University of California, Berkeley. Bibliography: p. 349-354. 1. Greece, Modern — Politics and government. I. T.
JN5016.L4     320.9/495     *LC* 69-18495     *ISBN* 804707057

**Greece at the polls: the national elections of 1974 and 1977 /**        **4.8621**
**edited by Howard R. Penniman.**
Washington: American Enterprise Institute for Public Policy Research, c1981. xiv, 220 p.: ill.; 23 cm. (AEI's At the polls studies.) (Studies in political and social processes.) (AEI studies. 317) 1. Greece. Voulē — Elections. 2. Legislative bodies — Greece. 3. Greece — Politics and government — 1974- I. Penniman, Howard Rae, 1916- II. Series. III. Series: Studies in political and social processes. IV. Series: AEI studies. 317
JN5123.G67     324.9495/076 19     *LC* 81-8026     *ISBN* 0844734357

## JN5201–5660 Italy

**Kogan, Norman.**        • **4.8622**
The government of Italy. — New York, Crowell [1962] 225 p. illus. 21 cm. — (Crowell comparative government series) Includes bibliography. 1. Italy — Pol. & govt. — 1945- I. T.
JN5451.K6     342.45     *LC* 62-17567

**Adams, John Clarke, 1910-.**        • **4.8623**
The government of republican Italy [by] John Clarke Adams [and] Paolo Barile. 2d ed. Boston, Houghton Mifflin [1966] 251 p. map. 21 cm. 1. Italy —

Politics and government — 1945-1976 2. Italy — Politics and government — Handbooks, manuals, etc. I. Barile, Paolo. joint author. II. T.
JN5468.A65 1966      320.945      LC 66-2839

**La Palombara, Joseph G.**          • 4.8624
Interest groups in Italian politics, by Joseph La Palomabara. Princeton, N.Y., Princeton University Press, 1964. xv, 452 p. 1. Pressure groups 2. Representative government and representation 3. Italy — Politics and government — 1945- I. T.
JN5477 P7 L35      LC 63-23408

**Italy at the polls, 1979: a study of the parliamentary elections /**    4.8625
**[edited by Howard R. Penniman].**
Washington, D.C.: American Enterprise Institute for Public Policy Research, c1981. xiv, 335 p.: ill.; 23 cm. — (At the polls.) (Studies in political and social processes.) (AEI studies. 321) 1. Italy. Parlamento — Elections — Addresses, essays, lectures. 2. Elections — Italy — Addresses, essays, lectures. 3. Italy — Politics and government — 1945- — Addresses, essays, lectures. I. Penniman, Howard Rae, 1916- II. Series. III. Series: Studies in political and social processes. IV. Series: AEI studies. 321
JN5609.I89      324.945/0927 19      LC 81-8106      ISBN 0844734411

**Italy at the polls: the parliamentary elections of 1976 / edited**    4.8626
**by Howard R. Penniman.**
Washington: American Enterprise Institute for Public Policy Research, c1977. 386 p.; 23 cm. — (American Enterprise Institute studies in political and social processes; 169) 1. Italy. Parlamento — Elections — Addresses, essays, lectures. 2. Elections — Italy — Addresses, essays, lectures. 3. Italy — Politics and government — 1945- — Addresses, essays, lectures. I. Penniman, Howard Rae, 1916-
JN5609.I9      329/.023/45092      LC 77-90425      ISBN 0844732680

**Webster, Richard A., 1928-.**          • 4.8627
The cross and the fasces; Christian democracy and fascism in Italy. Stanford, Calif., Stanford University Press, 1960. xiii, 229 p. 1. Centre parties — Italy 2. Fascism — Italy 3. Christian democracy I. T.
JN5651 W4      LC 60-13868

**Galli, Giorgio, 1928-.**          • 4.8628
Patterns of political participation in Italy, by Giorgio Galli and Alfonso Prandi. New Haven, Yale University Press, 1970. xviii, 364 p. illus., maps. 25 cm. Summarized findings of a study carried out by a research team of the Carlo Cattaneo Institute at Bologna, Italy, 1962-1966; translated from Italian MS. by Patricia Poggi. 1. Political parties — Italy. 2. Elections — Italy. I. Prandi, Alfonso, 1920- joint author. II. Istituto Carlo Cattaneo. III. T.
JN5655 1970.G34      329.9/45      LC 78-99824      ISBN 0300012764

**Amyot, Grant.**          4.8629
The Italian Communist Party: the crisis of the popular front strategy / Grant Amyot. — New York: St. Martin's Press, 1981. 252 p.; 22 cm. Includes index. 1. Partito comunista italiano. 2. Italy — Politics and government — 1945- I. T.
JN5657.C63 A788 1981      324.245075 19      LC 80-26959
     0312357141

**Communism in Italy and France / edited by Donald L. M.**    4.8630
**Blackmer and Sidney Tarrow.**
Princeton, N.J.: Princeton University Press, [1975] xii, 651 p. 1. Partito comunista italiano — Addresses, essays, lectures. 2. Parti communiste français — Addresses, essays, lectures. I. Blackmer, Donald L. M. II. Tarrow, Sidney G.
JN5657.C63 C65      JN5657C63 C65.      329.9/45      LC 74-25612
     ISBN 0691087245

**Hobsbawm, E. J. (Eric J.), 1917-.**          4.8631
[Giorgio Napolitano. English] The Italian road to socialism: an interview / by Eric Hobsbawm with Giorgio Napolitano of the Italian Communist Party; translated by John Cammett & Victoria DeGrazia. — 1st U.S. ed. — Westport, Conn.: L. Hill; [New York: distributed by Whirlwind Book Co.], 1977. 118 p.; 22 cm. Translation of Giorgio Napolitano, intervista sul PCI. 1. Partito comunista italiano — Miscellanea. 2. Communism — Italy — Miscellanea. I. Napolitano, Giorgio. II. T.
JN5657.C63 H613 1977      329.9/45      LC 77-83770      ISBN
0882080822

**The Italian Communist Party: yesterday, today, and tomorrow /**    4.8632
**edited by Simon Serfaty and Lawrence Gray.**
Westport, Conn.: Greenwood Press, 1980. xii, 256 p.; 25 cm. — (Contributions in political science. no. 46 0147-1066) Includes index. 1. Partito comunista italiano — History. I. Serfaty, Simon. II. Gray, Lawrence. III. Series.
JN5657.C63 I68      324.245075      LC 79-6833      ISBN 0313209952

**Sassoon, Don.**          4.8633
The strategy of the Italian Communist Party: from the resistance to the historic compromise / by Donald Sassoon; foreword by E. J. Hobsbawm. — New York:

St. Martin's Press, 1981. xi, 259 p. 1. Partito comunista italiano. 2. Communism — Italy. 3. Communist strategy I. T.
JN5657.C63 S27 1981      JN5657C63 S27 1981.      324.245075 19      LC
81-5753      ISBN 0312764782

**Germino, Dante L.**          • 4.8634
The Italian Fascist Party in power; a study in totalitarian rule [by] Dante L. Germino. New York, H. Fertig, 1971 [c1959] x, 181 p. 24 cm. 1. Partito nazionale fascista (Italy) I. T.
JN5657.F33 G4 1971      329.9/45      LC 74-80551

## JN6101–6371 Belgium

**Fitzmaurice, John.**          4.8635
Politics of Belgium: crisis and compromise in a plural society / by John Fitzmaurice; with a foreword by Leo Tindemans. — New York: St. Martin's Press, 1983. xiv, 256 p.; 23 cm. 1. Belgium — Politics and government — 1951-
I. T.
JN6165.F57 1983      949.3/043 19      LC 82-24056      ISBN 0312626398

## JN6500–6625 Soviet Union

**Fischer, George, 1923-.**          • 4.8636
Russian liberalism, from gentry to intelligentsia. — Cambridge, Harvard University Press, 1958. ix, 240 p. ports. 22 cm. — (Russian Research Center studies, 30) Bibliography: p. [209]-226. 1. Liberalism 2. Russia — Pol. & govt. — 19th cent. I. T.
JN6511.F5      342.47      LC 57-13462

**Medvedev, Roy Aleksandrovich, 1925-.**          4.8637
[Kniga o sotsialisticheskoĭ demokratii. English] On socialist democracy / Roy A. Medvedev; translated from the Russian and edited by Ellen DeKadt. — 1st American ed. — New York: Knopf: distributed by Random House, 1975. xxii, 405, xv p.; 22 cm. Translation of Kniga o sotsialisticheskoĭ demokratii. 1. Communist state 2. Soviet Union — Politics and government — 1953- I. T.
JN6511.M4313 1975      320.9/47/085      LC 74-21309      ISBN
0394489608

**Schapiro, Leonard Bertram, 1908-.**          • 4.8638
The government and politics of the Soviet Union [by] Leonard Schapiro. 2nd (revised) ed. London, Hutchinson, 1967. 176 p. tables, diagrs. 22 cm. (Hutchinson university library: Politics) 1. Soviet Union — Politics and government — 1917- 2. Soviet Union — Politics and government — 1953-
I. T.
JN6515 1965.S32      354.47      LC 67-77191

**Ploss, Sidney I. comp.**          • 4.8639
The Soviet political process; aims, techniques, and examples of analysis. Edited, with introductions, by Sidney I. Ploss. — Waltham, Mass.: Ginn, [1970, c1971] viii, 304 p.; 23 cm. 1. Kommunisticheskaia partiia Sovetskogo Soiuza. 2. Russia — Politics and government — 1917- I. T.
JN6515 1971.P58      320.9/47      LC 79-108415

**Reshetar, John Stephen.**          • 4.8640
The Soviet polity; government and politics in the U.S.S.R. [by] John S. Reshetar Jr. — New York: Dodd, Mead, 1971. ix, 412 p.; 21 cm. 1. Russia — Politics and government — 1917- I. T.
JN6515 1971.R47      320.9/47/084      LC 76-143293      ISBN
0396063152

**Osborn, Robert J.**          4.8641
The evolution of Soviet politics [by] Robert J. Osborn. Homewood, Ill., Dorsey Press, 1974. xiii, 574 p. illus. 24 cm. (The Dorsey series in political science) 1. Soviet Union — Politics and government — 1917- I. T.
JN6515 1974.O83      320.9/47/084      LC 73-89118      ISBN 0256015333

**Unger, Aryeh L.**          4.8642
Constitutional development in the USSR: a guide to the Soviet constitutions / Aryeh L. Unger. — New York: Pica Press: Distributed by Universe Books, 1982, c1981. viii, 310 p.; 23 cm. Includes indexes. 1. Russia — Constitutional history. I. T.
LAW      JN6515.1981 U5.      342.47/029 344.70229 19      LC 81-12022
     ISBN 0876637322

**Vyshinskiĭ, Andreĭ IAnuar'evich, 1883-1954.**          • 4.8643
The law of the Soviet State; tr. from the Russian by Hugh W. Babb [under the Russian Translation Project of the American Council of Learned Societies] Introd. by John N. Hazard. New York, Macmillan Co., 1948. xvii, 749 p.; 24 cm. 1. Soviet Union — Constitutional law. I. Babb, Hugh Webster, 1887- II. American Council of Learned Societies Devoted to Humanistic Studies. Russian Translation Project. III. T.
JN6518.V912      342.47      LC 48-9744

Colton, Timothy J., 1947-.                              **4.8644**
Commissars, commanders, and civilian authority: the structure of Soviet military politics / Timothy J. Colton. — Cambridge, Mass.: Harvard University Press, 1979. viii, 365 p.; 25 cm. — (Russian Research Center studies; 79) 1. Kommunisticheskaia partiia Sovetskogo Soiuza. 2. Civil supremacy over the military — Russia. 3. Russia — Armed Forces — Political activity. I. T.
JN6520.C58 C64      322/.5/0947      *LC* 78-23342      *ISBN* 0674145356

Conquest, Robert.                                       ● **4.8645**
Soviet nationalities policy in practice, edited by Robert Conquest. London, Sydney [etc.] Bodley Head, 1967. 160 p. tables.; 23 cm. (His Soviet studies series) 1. Minorities — Russia 2. Nationalism and socialism I. T.
JN6520.M5 C63      *LC* 67-104163      *ISBN*

Barghoorn, Frederick Charles, 1911-.                    ● **4.8646**
Politics in the USSR; a country study [by] Frederick C. Barghoorn. 2d ed. Boston, Little, Brown [1972] xvi, 360 p. illus. 21 cm. (The Little, Brown series in comparative politics) 1. Soviet Union — Politics and government — 1917- I. T.
JN6531.B3 1972      320.9/47/085      *LC* 72-4360

Fainsod, Merle, 1907-1972.                              ● **4.8647**
How Russia is ruled. Rev. ed. Cambridge, Mass., Harvard University Press, 1963. 684 p. illus. 25 cm. (Russian Research Center studies, 11) 1. Soviet Union — Politics and government — 1917- I. T.
JN6531.F3 1963      320.9/47/08      *LC* 63-11418

Hough, Jerry F., 1935-.                                 **4.8648**
How the Soviet Union is governed / Jerry F. Hough and Merle Fainsod. — Cambridge: Harvard University Press, 1979. xiv, 679 p.; 24 cm. 'An extensively revised and enlarged edition by Jerry F. Hough of Merle Fainsod's How Russia is ruled.' 1. Russia — Politics and government — 1917- I. Fainsod, Merle, 1907-1972. joint author. II. Fainsod, Merle, 1907-1972. How Russia is ruled. III. T.
JN6531.F3 1979      320.9/47/08      *LC* 78-22047      *ISBN* 0674410300

Meyer, Alfred G.                                        ● **4.8649**
The Soviet political system; an interpretation [by] Alfred G. Meyer. — New York, Random House [1965] viii, 494 p. 22 cm. 'Bibliographical note': p. [481]-483. 1. Russia — Pol. & govt. — 1917- I. T.
JN6531.M47      320.947      *LC* 65-23338

Schuman, Frederick Lewis, 1904-.                        ● **4.8650**
Government in the Soviet Union [by] Frederick L. Schuman. 2d ed. New York, Crowell [1967] xii, 226 p. 21 cm. (Crowell comparative government series) 1. Soviet Union — Politics and government — 1917- I. T.
JN6531.S38 1967      354.47      *LC* 67-27412

Hazard, John N. (John Newbold), 1909-.                  ● **4.8651**
Settling disputes in Soviet society: the formative years of legal institutions. — New York: Columbia University Press, 1960. xiv, 534 p.: ill.; 24 cm. (Studies of the Russian Institute, Columbia University) 1. Courts — Russia 2. Lawyers — Russia 3. Criminal procedure — Russia 4. Civil procedure — Russia 5. Justice, Administration of — Russia I. T.
JN6571 H39      *LC* 60-11248

Bialer, Seweryn.                                        **4.8652**
Stalin's successors: leadership, stability, and change in the Soviet Union / Seweryn Bialer. — Cambridge [Eng.]; New York: Cambridge University Press, 1980. v, 312 p.; 24 cm. 1. Elite (Social sciences) — Russia. 2. Russia — Politics and government — 1953- I. T.
JN6581.B5      320.947      *LC* 80-12037      *ISBN* 0521235189

Breslauer, George W.                                    **4.8653**
Khrushchev and Brezhnev as leaders: building authority in Soviet politics / George W. Breslauer. — London; Boston: Allen & Unwin, 1982. xiii, 318 p.; 23 cm. Includes index. 1. Khrushchev, Nikita Sergeevich, 1894-1971. 2. Brezhnev, Leonid Il'ich, 1906- 3. Elite (Social sciences) — Soviet Union. 4. Soviet Union — Politics and government — 1953- I. T.
JN6581.B73 1982      947.085 19      *LC* 82-8835      *ISBN* 004329040X

Friedgut, Theodore H.                                   **4.8654**
Political participation in the USSR / Theodore H. Friedgut. — Princeton, N.J.: Princeton University Press, c1979. xv, 353 p.; 22 cm. (Studies of the Russian Institute, Columbia University) Includes index. 1. Political participation — Soviet Union. 2. Soviet Union — Politics and government — 1917- I. T.
JN6581.F74      320.9/47/084      *LC* 78-70293      *ISBN* 0691076081

Nationalism in the USSR & Eastern Europe in the era of                    **4.8655**
Brezhnev & Kosygin: papers and proceedings of the symposium held at University of Detroit on October 3–4, 1975 / George W. Simmonds, editor.
Detroit, Mich.: University of Detroit Press, c1977. 534 p.; 24 cm. 1. Nationalism — Soviet Union — Addresses, essays, lectures. 2. Nationalism — Europe, Eastern — Addresses, essays, lectures. 3. Nationalities, Principle of

— Addresses, essays, lectures. 4. Europe, Eastern — Politics and government — 1945- — Addresses, essays, lectures. 5. Soviet Union — Politics and government — 1953- — Addresses, essays, lectures. I. Simmonds, George W. II. Title: Nationalism in the U.S.S.R. & Eastern Europe in the era of Brezhnev & Kosygin. III. Title: Nationalism in the U.S.S.R. and Eastern Europe in the era of Brezhnev and Kozygin. IV. Title: Nationalism in the USSR and Eastern Europe in the era of Brezhnev and Kosygin.
JN6581.N37      323.1/47 19      *LC* 81-109462

## JN6598 COMMUNIST PARTY

The Twenty–fifth Congress of the CPSU: assessment and            **4.8656**
context / Alexander Dallin, editor.
Stanford, Calif.: Hoover Institution Press, 1977. xii, 127 p.: port.; 23 cm. (Hoover Institution publication; 184) Papers presented at a one day conference sponsored by Center for Russian and East European Studies at Stanford University, Apr. 2, 1976. 1. Kommunisticheskaia partiia Sovetskogo Soiuza. Sezd. (25th: 1976: Moscow, R.S.F.S.R.) I. Dallin, Alexander. II. Stanford University. Center for Russian and East European Studies.
JN6598.K5 1976n      329.9/47      *LC* 77-2445      *ISBN* 0817968423

Russia at the crossroads: the 26th Congress of the CPSU /        **4.8657**
edited by Seweryn Bialer and Thane Gustafson.
London; Boston: Allen & Unwin, 1982. 223 p.; 25 cm. 1. Kommunisticheskaia partiia Sovetskogo Soiuza. Sezd (26th: 1981: Moscow, R.S.F.S.R.) 2. Soviet Union — Economic policy — 1981- — Congresses. 3. Soviet Union — Politics and government — 1953- — Congresses. I. Bialer, Seweryn. II. Gustafson, Thane. III. Kommunisticheskaia partiia Sovetskogo Soiuza. Sezd. (26th: 1981: Moscow, R.S.F.S.R.)
JN6598.K5 1981b      947.085/3 19      *LC* 82-1599      *ISBN* 0043290396

TSK KPSS.                                               ● **4.8658**
History of the Communist party of the Soviet union (bolsheviks) Short course. Edited by a commission of the Central committee of the C. P. S. U. (B.) Authorized by the Central committee of the C. P. S. U. (B.). — New York, International publishers [c1939] xii p., 1 l., 364 p. 22 cm. 1. Kommunisticheskaia partiia Sovetskogo Soiuza. 2. Communism — Russia. I. T.
JN6598.K55E5 1939      335.40947      *LC* 39-15282

Armstrong, John Alexander, 1922-.                       ● **4.8659**
The politics of totalitarianism; the Communist Party of the Soviet Union from 1934 to the present. — New York, Random House [1961] xvi, 458 p. 25 cm. Bibliography: p. 349-427. 1. Kommunisticheskaia partiia Sovetskogo Soiuza. 2. Russia — Pol. & govt. — 1936-1953. 3. Russia — Pol. & govt. — 1953- I. T.
JN6598.K7A67      947.0842      *LC* 61-6242

Nicolaevsky, Boris I., 1887-1966.                       ● **4.8660**
Power and the Soviet elite; 'The letter of an old Bolshevik,' and other essays, by Boris I. Nicolaevsky. Edited by Janet D. Zagoria. New York: Published for the Hoover Institution on War, Revolution, and Peace, by Praeger [1965] xxi, 275 p.; 22 cm. (Praeger publications in Russian history and world communism, no. 159) Hoover Institution publication. 1. Kommunisticheskaia partiia Sovetskogo Soiuza — History — Addresses, essays, lectures. 2. Russia — Politics and government — 1917- — Addresses, essays, lectures. I. Zagoria, Janet D., ed. II. T.
JN6598.K7N55      320.947      *LC* 65-14057

Resolutions and decisions of the Communist Party of the Soviet   **4.8661**
Union / [general ed., Robert H. McNeal].
Toronto; Buffalo: University of Toronto Press, [1974] 4 v.; 24 cm. 1. Kommunisticheskaia partiia Sovetskogo Soiuza — History — Sources. I. McNeal, Robert Hatch, 1930- ed.
JN6598.K7 R455      329.9/47      *LC* 74-81931      *ISBN* 0802021573

Rigby, T. H. (Thomas Henry), 1925-.                     ● **4.8662**
Communist Party membership in the U.S.S.R., 1917–1967 [by] T. H. Rigby. Princeton, N.J., Princeton University Press, 1968. xvii, 573 p. 23 cm. (Studies of the Russian Institute, Columbia University) 1. Kommunisticheskaia partiia Sovetskogo Soiuza — Membership I. T.
JN6598.K7 R5      329.9/47      *LC* 68-20878

Schapiro, Leonard Bertram, 1908-.                       ● **4.8663**
The Communist Party of the Soviet Union, by Leonard Schapiro. — 2d ed., rev. and enl. — New York: Random House, [1970, c1971] xviii, 686 p.: illus., ports.; 25 cm. 1. Kommunisticheskaia partiia Sovetskogo Soiuza — History I. T.
JN6598.K7 S35 1971      329.9/47      *LC* 76-117690      *ISBN* 0394470141

Keep, John L. H.                                        ● **4.8664**
The rise of social democracy in Russia. Oxford, Clarendon Press, 1963. viii, 334 p. 1. Rossiĭskaia sotsial-demokraticheskaia rabochaia partiia — History I. T.
JN6598 S6 K4      *LC* 64-495

The Mensheviks: from the revolution of 1917 to the Second    **4.8665**
World War / edited by Leopold H. Haimson; with contributions
by David Dallin ... [et al.]; translated by Gertrude Vakar.
Chicago: University of Chicago Press, 1974. xxiii, 476 p.; 24 cm. (Hoover
Institution publications; 117) 'This volume is one of a series arising from the
work of the Inter-university Project on the History of the Menshevik
movement.' 1. Rossiĭskaia sotsial-demokraticheskaia rabochaia partiia.
I. Haimson, Leopold H. II. Dallin, David J., 1889-1962. III. Inter-university
Project on the History of the Menshevik movement.
JN6598.S6 M355      329.9/47      LC 73-87302      ISBN 0226312224

## JN6700–6719 Finland

**Nousiainen, Jaakko.**                                            • **4.8666**
[Suomen poliittinen järjestelmä. English] The Finnish political system.
Translated by John H. Hodgson. Cambridge, Mass., Harvard University Press,
1971. x, 454 p. map. 24 cm. Translation based on 3d ed. of the Finnish text of
Suomen poliittinen järjestelmä. 1. Finland — Politics and government — 20th
century I. T.
JN6703 1959.N613      320.9/471/03      LC 76-120320      ISBN
0674302117

**Upton, Anthony F.**                                             **4.8667**
Communism in Scandinavia and Finland: politics of opportunity / [by] A. F.
Upton; with contributions by Peter P. Rohde and A. Sparring. — [1st ed.]. —
Garden City, N.Y.: Anchor Press, 1973. x, 422 p.; 19 cm. — (The History of
communism) 1. Suomen Kommunistinen Puolue. 2. Sveriges kommunistiska
parti (1921-1967). 3. Norges kommunistiske parti. 4. Danmarks
kommunistiske parti. 5. Communist parties — Case studies. I. Rohde, Peter
Preisler, 1902- II. Sparring, Åke. III. T. IV. Series.
JN6719.A5 U68      329.9/48      LC 73-79871      ISBN 0385033656

## JN6750–6769 Poland

**Jedruch, Jacek.**                                               **4.8668**
Constitutions, elections, and legislatures of Poland, 1493–1977: a guide to their
history / Jacek Jedruch. — Washington, D.C.: University Press of America,
c1982. xxi, 590 p.: ill.; 23 cm. Includes index. 1. Legislative bodies — Poland —
History. 2. Representative government and representation — Poland —
History. 3. Poland — Constitutional history. I. T.
JN6752.J43 1982      320.9438 19      LC 81-40301      ISBN 0819125083

**De Weydenthal, Jan B.**                                         **4.8669**
The Communists of Poland: an historical outline / Jan B. de Weydenthal. —
Stanford, Calif.: Hoover Institution Press, Stanford University, 1979 (c1978).
xviii, 217 p.; 23 cm. (Histories of ruling Communist parties.) (Hoover
Institution publication; 202) Includes index. 1. Polska Zjednoczona Partia
Robotnicza — History. 2. Poland — Politics and government — 1945-1980
I. T. II. Series.
JN6769.A52 D49      324.2438/075/09 19      LC 78-59465

## JN7001–7995 Scandinavia

**Elder, Neil.**                                                  **4.8670**
The consensual democracies?: the government and politics of the Scandinavian
states / Neil Elder, Alastair H. Thomas, David Arter. — Oxford: Robertson,
1982. xii, 244 p.: map; 23 cm. Includes index. 1. Scandinavia — Politics and
government I. Thomas, Alastair H. II. Arter, David. III. T.
JN7011.E42 1982      320.948 19      LC 82-149467      ISBN 0855204230

**Nordic democracy: ideas, issues, and institutions in politics,**    **4.8671**
**economy, education, social and cultural affairs of Denmark,**
**Finland, Iceland, Norway, and Sweden / editorial board, Erik**
**Allardt ... [et al.].**
Copenhagen: Det Danske Selskab: Distributed by Munksgaard, 1983 (c1981).
780 p.; 24 cm. Includes index. 1. Education — Scandinavia — Addresses,
essays, lectures. 2. Scandinavia — Economic conditions — Addresses, essays,
lectures. 3. Scandinavia — Politics and government — 1945- 4. Scandinavia
— Social conditions — Addresses, essays, lectures. 5. Scandinavia — Relations
— Foreign countries — Addresses, essays, lectures. I. Allardt, Erik.
II. Danske selskab (Copenhagen, Denmark)
JN7042.N596 1981      948/.08 19      LC 82-146587

**Scandinavia at the polls: recent political trends in Denmark,**     **4.8672**
**Norway, and Sweden / edited by Karl H. Cerny.**
Washington: American Enterprise Institute for Public Policy Research, 1977.
304 p.; 23 cm. — (Studies in political and social processes.) (AEI studies. 143)
'This study is based on a conference which was held on February 10 and 11,
1975, in Washington, D.C.; sponsored by AEI in association with the Graduate
School of Georgetown University.' 1. Scandinavia — Politics and government
— Addresses, essays, lectures. 2. Scandinavia — Social conditions.

3. Scandinavia — Economic conditions — Addresses, essays, lectures.
I. Cerny, Karl H. II. American Enterprise Institute for Public Policy
Research. III. Series. IV. Series: AEI studies. 143
JN7042.S26      329/.023/4808      LC 77-1343      ISBN 0844732400

**Arter, David.**                                                 **4.8673**
The Nordic parliaments: a comparative analysis / by David Arter. — New
York: St. Martin's Press, 1984. x, 421 p.; 23 cm. 1. Legislative bodies —
Scandinavia. 2. Legislative power — Scandinavia. 3. Comparative government
I. T.
JN7056.A77 1984      328/.3/0948 19      LC 84-9803      ISBN
0312577672

**Fitzmaurice, John.**                                            **4.8674**
Politics in Denmark / by John Fitzmaurice. — New York: St. Martin's Press,
1981. xiv, 173 p.; 22 cm. Includes index. 1. Denmark — Politics and
government I. T.
JN7161.F58 1981      320.9489 19      LC 81-1682      ISBN 0312626630

**Logue, John, 1947-.**                                           **4.8675**
Socialism and abundance: radical socialism in the Danish welfare state / John
Logue. — Minneapolis, Minn.: University of Minnesota Press, c1982. xxii,
353 p.; 25 cm. (Nordic series. v. 8) Includes index. 1. Socialistisk folkeparti
(Denmark) 2. Socialism — Denmark I. T. II. Series.
JN7365.S7 L63 1982      324.248907 19      LC 81-14819

**Olsen, Johan P.**                                               **4.8676**
Organized democracy: political institutions in a welfare state, the case of
Norway / by Johan P. Olsen. — Bergen; Oslo: Universitetsforlaget; New York:
Distributed by Columbia University Press, c1983. 246 p.: ill.; 22 cm. Includes
index. 1. Representative government and representation — Norway.
2. Norway — Politics and government — 1945- I. T.
JN7461.O47 1983      320.9481 19      LC 83-140810      ISBN 8200064425

**Lafferty, William M., 1939-.**                                  **4.8677**
Participation and democracy in Norway: the 'distant democracy' revisted [sic] /
William M. Lafferty. — Olso: Universitetsforlaget; Irvington-on-Hudson,
N.Y.: [distributed by] Columbia University Press, c1981. 193 p.; 22 cm.
1. Martinussen, Willy, 1938- The distant democracy. 2. Political participation
— Norway. I. T.
JN7621.L33      323/.042/09481 19      LC 82-102615      ISBN
8200056066

**Håstad, Elis Wilhelm, 1900-1959.**                              • **4.8678**
The Parliament of Sweden. [Translated by Neil C. M. Elder]. — London:
Hansard Society for Parliamentary Government, [1957] 165 p.: illus.; 20 cm.
1. Sweden. Riksdagen. I. T.
JN7915.H2      328.485      LC 58-2204

**Rustow, Dankwart A.**                                           • **4.8679**
The politics of compromise; a study of parties and cabinet government in
Sweden [by] Dankwart A. Rustow. — New York: Greenwood Press, [1969] xi,
257 p.; 23 cm. Reprint of the 1955 ed. 1. Political parties — Sweden. 2. Sweden
— Politics and government I. T.
JN7995.A1 R8 1969      320.9/485      LC 69-14067      ISBN 0837119596

## JN8101–8651 Spain. Portugal

**Coverdale, John F., 1940-.**                                    **4.8680**
The political transformation of Spain after Franco / John F. Coverdale. — New
York: Praeger, 1979. xi, 150 p.: ill.; 24 cm. Includes index. 1. Spain — Politics
and government — 1975- 2. Spain — Economic conditions — 1975- I. T.
JN8209 1979.C68      320.9/46/083      LC 78-19777      ISBN 0030443261

**Kohler-Koch, Beate, 1941-.**                                    **4.8681**
Political forces in Spain, Greece, and Portugal / Beate Kohler; translated by
Frank Carter and Ginnie Hole. — London; Boston: Published in association
with the European Centre for Political Studies by Butterworth Scientific, 1982.
281 p.; 24 cm. — (Butterworths European studies.) 1. Spain — Politics and
government — 1975- 2. Greece — Politics and government — 1974-
3. Portugal — Politics and government — 1974- I. European Centre for
Political Studies. II. T. III. Series.
JN8209.K63 1982      320.946 19      LC 82-238249      ISBN 0408107960

**Alba, Víctor.**                                                 **4.8682**
The Communist Party in Spain / Victor Alba; translated by Vincent G. Smith.
— New Brunswick, N.J.: Transaction Books, c1983. x, 475 p.; 24 cm. Includes
index. 1. Partido Comunista de España — History. I. T.
JN8395.C6 A73 1983      324.246075/09 19      LC 82-19339      ISBN
0878554645

**Hermet, Guy.**                                                  **4.8683**
[Communistes en Espagne. English] The communists in Spain: study of an
underground political movement / Guy Hermet; translated from the French by

S. Seago and H. Fox. — Farnborough, Hants.: Saxon House, 1974. vi, 238 p.; 24 cm. — (Saxon house studies) Translation of Les communistes en Espagne. Includes index. 1. Partido Communista de España. I. T.
JN8395.C6 H4613    329.9/46    *LC* 74-3912    *ISBN* 0347010326

**Morrison, Rodney J., 1934-.**    **4.8684**
Portugal, revolutionary change in an open economy / Rodney J. Morrison. — Boston, Mass.: Auburn House Pub. Co., c1981. xvi, 184 p.; 24 cm. Includes index. 1. Portugal — Politics and government — 1974- 2. Portugal — Economic conditions — 1974- 3. Portugal — Foreign economic relations — Europe. 4. Europe — Foreign economic relations — Portugal. I. T.
JN8502 1981    946.9/044 19    *LC* 81-2099    *ISBN* 0865690774

## JN9600–9679 Bulgaria. Romania. Yugoslavia

**Oren, Nissan.**    • **4.8685**
Bulgarian communism: the road to power, 1934–1944. — New York: Columbia University Press, 1971. xii, 293 p.; 24 cm. (East Central European studies of Columbia University and Research Institute on Communist Affairs, Columbia University) 1. Bŭlgarska komunisticheska partiia — History. 2. Communism — Bulgaria — History. 3. Bulgaria — Politics and government — 1878-1944 I. T.
JN9609.A8 K67818    324.2497/7/07509 19    *LC* 75-147127

**Rothschild, Joseph.**    • **4.8686**
The Communist Party of Bulgaria: origins and development, 1883–1936. — New York: Columbia University Press, 1959. viii, 354 p.; 24 cm. 'First version of this study was written as a doctoral dissertation in the University of Oxford.' 1. Bŭlgarska komunisticheska partiia. I. T.
JN9609.A8 K6847    *LC* 59-10084

**Jowitt, Kenneth.**    **4.8687**
Revolutionary breakthroughs and national development: the case of Romania, 1944–1965. — Berkeley: University of California Press, 1971. 317 p.; 24 cm. 1. Communist state — Case studies. 2. Romania — Politics and government — 1945- I. T.
JN9623 1944.J6    320.9/498/02    *LC* 71-123625    *ISBN* 0520017625

**King, Robert R.**    **4.8688**
A history of the Romanian Communist Party / Robert R. King. — Stanford, Calif.: Hoover Institution Press, Stanford University, c1980. xvi, 190 p.: ill.; 23 cm. — (Histories of ruling Communist parties.) (Hoover Press publication; 233) 1. Partidul Comunist Român — History. I. T. II. Series.
JN9639.A57 K65    324.2498075 19    *LC* 80-8327    *ISBN* 081797332X

**Burg, Steven L., 1950-.**    **4.8689**
Conflict and cohesion in socialist Yugoslavia: political decision making since 1966 / Steven L. Burg. — Princeton, N.J.: Princeton University Press, c1983. xii, 365 p.; 24 cm. Includes index. 1. Yugoslavia — Politics and government — 1945- I. T.
JN9663 1983    949.7/023 19    *LC* 82-61358    *ISBN* 0691076510

**Shoup, Paul.**    • **4.8690**
Communism and the Yugoslav national question. — New York: Columbia University Press, 1968. 308 p.; 24 cm. — (East Central European studies of Columbia University) 1. Savez komunista Jugoslavije. 2. Federal government — Yugoslavia. 3. Regionalism — Yugoslavia. 4. Minorities — Yugoslavia. I. T.
JN9666.S8 S5    320.9/497    *LC* 68-19759

## JQ1–1825 Asia

**Darling, Frank C.**    **4.8691**
The westernization of Asia: a comparative political analysis / Frank C. Darling. — Cambridge, MA: Schenkman Publishing Co., 1980. xxii, 503 p.; 24 cm. 1. Comparative government 2. Asia — Politics and government 3. Asia — Social conditions. 4. Asia — History I. T.
JQ5.D36    950    *LC* 78-20873    *ISBN* 0816190054

**Kahin, George McTurnan. ed.**    • **4.8692**
Major governments of Asia / by Harold C. Hinton [and others]. — 2d ed. — Ithaca, N.Y.: Cornell University Press, [1963] xiii, 719 p.: maps (2 fold.) diagrs.; 25 cm. 1. China — Politics and government — 1949- 2. Japan — Politics and government 3. India — Politics and government 4. Pakistan — Politics and government 5. Indonesia — Politics and government I. Hinton, Harold C. II. T.
JQ5.K3 1963    342    *LC* 63-15940

**Patterns of kingship and authority in traditional Asia / edited**    **4.8693**
**by Ian Mabbett.**
London; Dover, N.H.: Croom Helm, c1985. 202 p.; 23 cm. Mostly papers from a symposium held at the first biennial conference of the Asian Studies Association of Australia, in Melbourne, Aug. 1975. Includes index. 1. Asia — Kings and rulers — Addresses, essays, lectures. I. Mabbett, Ian W.
JQ20.P38 1985    321.6/095 19    *LC* 84-45701    *ISBN* 0709935099

**Political parties of Asia and the Pacific / Haruhiro Fukui,**    **4.8694**
**editor–in–chief; Colin A. Hughes ... [et al.], associate editors.**
Westport, Conn.: Greenwood Press, 1985. 2 v. (xviii, 1346 p.); 25 cm. (Greenwood historical encyclopedia of the world's political parties.) 1. Political parties — Asia. 2. Political parties — Pacific Area. I. Fukui, Haruhiro, 1935- II. Series.
JQ39.A45 P64 1985    324.25 19    *LC* 84-19252    *ISBN* 031321350X

**Explorations in early Southeast Asian history: the origins of**    **4.8695**
**Southeast Asian statecraft / edited by Kenneth R. Hall and**
**John K. Whitmore.**
Ann Arbor: Center for South and Southeast Asian Studies, University of Michigan, 1976. xiv, 358 p.: ill.; 23 cm. (Michigan papers on South and Southeast Asia. 11) On spine: The origins of Southeast Asian statecraft. 1. Asia, Southeastern — Politics and government — Addresses, essays, lectures. 2. Asia, Southeastern — History — Addresses, essays, lectures. I. Hall, Kenneth R. II. Whitmore, John K. III. Title: Origins of Southeast Asian statecraft. IV. Series.
JQ96.A2 E96    320.9/59    *LC* 76-6836    *ISBN* 0891480528

**Kahin, George McTurnan. ed.**    • **4.8696**
Governments and politics of Southeast Asia. Contributors: David A. Wilson [and others]. — 2d ed. — Ithaca, N.Y.: Cornell University Press, [1964] xvii, 796 p.: maps (2 fold.); 24 cm. 1. Asia, Southeastern — Politics and government 2. Asia, Southeastern — Social conditions. I. T.
JQ96.K3 1964    354.59    *LC* 64-17413

## JQ200–459 India

**Menon, V. P. (Vapal Pangunni), 1894-1966.**    • **4.8697**
The transfer of power in India. — Princeton, N. J., Princeton University Press, 1957. 543 p. ports. 25 cm. 'Appendix XII [facsimile] Congress comments on the draft Independence bill, with Nehru's corrections and signature': 9 p. inserted between p. 532 and [533] 1. India — Pol. & govt. — 1919-1947. I. T.
JQ211.M4    342.5409    *LC* 57-2773

**Stokes, Eric.**    • **4.8698**
The English utilitarians and India. — Oxford, Clarendon Press, 1959. xvi, 350 p. 22 cm. Bibliography: p. [334]-338. 1. India — Pol. & govt. — 1765-1947. 2. Utilitarianism I. T.
JQ211.S7    954.03    *LC* 59-648

**Kothari, Rajni.**    **4.8699**
Politics in India. — [New Delhi]: Orient Longman, [1970] xv, 461 p.: map.; 22 cm. 1. India — Politics and government — 1947- I. T.
JQ215 1970.K62    *LC* 72-915897

**Palmer, Norman Dunbar.**    • **4.8700**
The Indian political system [by] Norman D. Palmer. — 2d ed. — Boston: Houghton Mifflin, [1971] ix, 325 p.: map.; 21 cm. — (Contemporary government series) 1. India — Politics and government — 1947- I. T.
JQ215 1971.P3    320.9/54/04    *LC* 77-151750    *ISBN* 039511926X

**Hiro, Dilip.**    **4.8701**
Inside India today / Dilip Hiro. — New York: Monthly Review Press, 1977. xiv, 338 p.; 22 cm. Includes index. 1. India — Politics and government — 1947- I. T.
JQ215 1976.H57    320.9/54/05    *LC* 77-76161    *ISBN* 0853454248

**Pylee, M. V. (Moolamattom Varkey), 1922-.**    **4.8702**
Constitutional government in India / M. V. Pylee. — 4th ed. — New Delhi: S. Claud, 1984. xix, 955 p., [2] leaves of plates: ill.; 22 cm. xx, 699 p., [1] leaves of plates: ill.; 22 cm. Includes index. 1. India — Politics and government — 1947- 2. India — Constitutional history. I. T.
JQ215 1977.P93    342/.54/029 19

**The Indian nationalist movement, 1885–1947: select documents /**    **4.8703**
**edited by B. N. Pandey.**
New York: St. Martin's Press, 1979 (c1978). xxii, 272 p.; 23 cm. Includes index. 1. Political parties — India — History — Sources. 2. India — Politics and government — 1765-1947 I. Pandey, B. N. (Bishwa Nath), 1929-
JQ215 1979.I52    320.9/54/035    *LC* 78-8691    *ISBN* 0312413858

**Hardgrave, Robert L.**    **4.8704**
India: government and politics in a developing nation / Robert L. Hardgrave, Jr., Stanley A. Kochanek. — 4th ed. — New York: Harcourt Brace Jovanovich,

c1986. xii, 395 p.: ill., maps. 1. India — Politics and government — 1947- I. Kochanek, Stanley A. II. T.
JQ215 1986.H37    320.454 19    *LC* 85-80872    *ISBN* 0155413538

**Brass, Paul R.**      **4.8705**
Language, religion and politics in North India / Paul R. Brass. — London: Cambridge University Press, 1974. 467 p.: ill.; 23 cm. Includes index. 1. Languages — Political aspects 2. Religion and state — India. 3. India — Languages I. T.
JQ220.L3 B67 1974    409/.54    *LC* 73-82453    *ISBN* 0521203244

**Kurian, K. Mathew.**      **4.8706**
Centre–State relations / edited by K. Mathew Kurian, P.N. Varughese. — New Delhi: Macmillan India, 1981. viii, 258 p.; 23 cm. 1. Federal government — India. 2. Decentralization in government — India. 3. Intergovernmental fiscal relations — India. I. Varughese, P. N. II. T.
JQ220.S8 C429 1981    321.02/3/0954 19    *LC* 82-901607

**Fox, Richard Gabriel, 1939-.**      **4.8707**
Kin, clan, raja, and rule; statehinterland relations in preindustrial India [by] Richard G. Fox. — Berkeley: University of California Press, 1971. ix, 187 p.: illus., maps.; 23 cm. 1. Political participation — India. 2. Political sociology — Case studies. 3. India — Politics and government I. T.
JQ222.F65    301.44/2/0954    *LC* 76-129614    *ISBN* 0520018079

**Kochanek, Stanley A.**      **4.8708**
Business and politics in India [by] Stanley A. Kochanek. — Berkeley: University of California Press, [1974] xviii, 382 p.; 24 cm. 1. Business and politics — India. I. T.
JQ229.B8 K6    322/.3/0954    *LC* 72-93521    *ISBN* 0520023773

**Pal, R. N., Dr.**      **4.8709**
The Office of the Prime Minister in India / R.N. Pal. — New Delhi: Ghanshyam Publishers & Distributors, [1983] xiv, 279 p.; 22 cm. Revision of the author's thesis (Ph. D.—Himachal Pradesh University) 1. Executive power — India. 2. Prime ministers — India. I. T.
JQ241.P28 1983    354.5403/13 19    *LC* 83-903260

**O'Malley, L. S. S. (Lewis Sydney Steward), 1874-1941.**    • **4.8710**
The Indian civil service, 1601–1930 / L.S.S. O'Malley. — 2d ed. — London: F. Cass, 1965. xiv, 310 p. 1. Civil service — India 2. India — Politics & government I. T.
JQ247 O6 1965    JQ247 O6 1965.    *LC* 65-6997

**Chand, Phul.**      **4.8711**
Indian Parliament / editor, Phul Chand; assistant editor, A. Chunkath. — New Delhi: Institute of Constitutional and Parliamentary Studies: Sole distributors, National Pub. House, 1984. xix, 216, xcvii p.; 25 cm. 1. India. Parliament — Addresses, essays, lectures. I. Chunkath, A. II. T.
JQ256.I56 1984    328.54 19    *LC* 84-900407

**Singh, Baljit, 1929-.**      **4.8712**
Government and politics in India / Baljit Singh and Dhirendra K. Vajpeyi. — New York: Apt Books, c1981. 166 p.; 21 cm. 1. India — Politics and government — 1947- I. Vajpeyi, Dhirendra K. II. T.
JQ281.S56    320.954 19    *LC* 81-65044    *ISBN* 086590006X

**Palmer, Norman Dunbar.**      **4.8713**
Elections and political development: the South Asian experience / by Norman D. Palmer. — Durham, N.C.: Duke University Press, c1975. x, 340 p.: ill.; 23 cm. 1. Elections — India. 2. Elections — South Asia. I. T.
JQ292.P34    324/.54    *LC* 75-4032    *ISBN* 0822303418

**Weiner, Myron.**      **4.8714**
India at the polls, 1980: a study of the parliamentary elections / Myron Weiner. — Washington: American Enterprise Institute for Public Policy Research, c1983. 198 p., [1] leaf of plates: ill.; 23 cm. — (AEI's At the poll studies) (Studies in political and social processes). (AEI studies; 340 [i.e. 341]) 1. Elections — India. 2. India — Politics and government — 1947- I. T. II. Series. III. Series: Studies in political and social processes.
JQ292.W43 1983    320.954/052 19    *LC* 81-19064    *ISBN* 0844734675

**Brass, Paul R.**      **4.8715**
Radical politics in South Asia. Edited by Paul R. Brass and Marcus F. Franda. Contributors: Paul R. Brass [and others]. — Cambridge, Mass.: MIT Press, [1973] xix, 449 p.: illus.; 23 cm. — (Studies in communism, revisionism, and revolution, 19) 1. Political parties — India — Addresses, essays, lectures. 2. Political parties — Bangladesh — Addresses, essays, lectures. 3. Radicalism — India — Addresses, essays, lectures. 4. Communism — India — Addresses, essays, lectures. I. Franda, Marcus F. joint author. II. T. III. Series.
JQ298.A1 B73    320.9/54/05    *LC* 73-402    *ISBN* 0262020998

**Eldersveld, Samuel James.**      **4.8716**
Citizens and politics: mass political behavior in India / Samuel J. Eldersveld and Bashiruddin Ahmed. — Chicago: University of Chicago Press, 1978. xii,

351 p.: ill.; 24 cm. 1. Political participation — India. 2. India — Politics and government — 1947- I. Ahmed, Bashiruddin. joint author. II. T.
JQ298.A1 E48    320.9/54/04    *LC* 77-21395    *ISBN* 0226202801

**Chopra, Pran Nath.**      **4.8717**
A century of Indian National Congress, 1885–1985 / P.N. Chopra, Ram Gopal, M.L. Bhargava. — Delhi: Agam Prakashan, 1986. x, 411 p., [20] p. of plates: ill, ports.; 23 cm. Includes index. 1. Indian National Congress — History. 2. India — Politics and government — 1857-1919 3. India — Politics and government — 20th century I. Ram Gopal, 1912- II. Bhargava, Moti Lal. III. T.
JQ298.I5 C48 1986    324.254/03 19    *LC* 86-157607

**Menon, V. P. (Vapal Pangunni), 1894-1966.**    • **4.8718**
The story of the integration of the Indian States [by] V. P. Menon. New York, Arno Press, 1972 [c1956] 511 p. illus. 24 cm. (World affairs: national and international viewpoints) 1. State governments — India. 2. India — Constitutional history. I. T. II. Title: Integration of the Indian States. III. Series.
JQ298.8.M45 1972    342/.54    *LC* 72-4282    *ISBN* 0405045751

**State politics in contemporary India: crisis or continuity? /**      **4.8719**
**edited by John R. Wood.**
Boulder, Colo.: Westview Press, 1984. xv, 257 p.: map; 22 cm. (A Westview replica edition) Revised and edited papers from a panel at the Thirty-sixth Annual Meeting of the Association for Asian Studies, Washington, D.C., on Mar. 24, 1984. 1. State governments — India — Addresses, essays, lectures. 2. Political parties — India — States — Addresses, essays, lectures. I. Association for Asian Studies. Meeting. (36th: 1984: Washington, D.C.)
JQ298.8.S72 1984    320.2/0954 19    *LC* 84-15243    *ISBN* 0813370027

# JQ442–659 Burma. Pakistan. Rajasthan. Sri Lanka

**Maung Maung Gyi.**      **4.8720**
Burmese political values: the socio–political roots of authoritarianism / Maung Maung Gyi. — New York, N.Y.: Praeger, 1983. xiii, 274 p.; 25 cm. Includes index. 1. Authoritarianism — Burma. 2. Burma — Politics and government 3. Burma — Constitutional history. I. T.
JQ442.M38 1983    320.9591 19    *LC* 83-2169    *ISBN* 0030633389

**Ziring, Lawrence, 1928-.**      **4.8721**
Pakistan: the enigma of political development / Lawrence Ziring. — Folkestone, Kent, Eng.: Dawson; Boulder, Colo.: Westview, 1981 (c1980). 294 p.: maps. 1. Pakistan — Politics and government I. T.
JQ556.Z56 1980    *LC* 80-50285    *ISBN* 0712909540

**Sisson, Richard.**      • **4.8722**
The Congress Party in Rajasthan; political integration and institution–building in an Indian state. Berkeley, University of California Press [1971, c1972] xvii, 347 p. illus. 25 cm. 'Sponsored by the Center for South and Southeast Asia Studies, University of California, Berkeley. 1. Indian National Congress. 2. Political parties — India — Rajasthan — Case studies. I. University of California, Berkeley. Center for South and Southeast Asia Studies. II. T.
JQ620.R2873 57    329.9/54/4    *LC* 70-129607    *ISBN* 0520018087

**Kearney, Robert N.**      **4.8723**
The politics of Ceylon (Sri Lanka) [by] Robert N. Kearney. Ithaca [N.Y.] Cornell University Press [1973] xvii, 249 p. illus. 22 cm. (South Asian political systems) 1. Sri Lanka — Politics and government I. T. II. Series.
JQ653 1973.K4    320.4/549/3    *LC* 73-8702    *ISBN* 0801407982

**Jupp, James.**      **4.8724**
Sri Lanka: Third World democracy / James Jupp. — London; Totowa, N.J.: Cass, 1978. xxi, 423 p.: ill.; 22 cm. — (Studies in Commonwealth politics and history; no. 6) Includes index. 1. Sri Lanka — Politics and government I. T.
JQ655.A1 J86 1978    320.9/549/303    *LC* 78-322381    *ISBN* 0714630934

# JQ670–959 Hong Kong. Malaysia. Singapore. Indonesia

**Endacott, G. B.**      • **4.8725**
Government and people in Hong Kong, 1841–1962, a constitutional history / by G. B. Endacott. — Hong Kong: Hong Kong University Press, 1964. xiv, 263 p.: illus., map, ports; 23 cm. 1. Hong Kong — Politics and government. 2. Hong Kong — Constitutional history. I. T.
JQ673 1964 E5    951.25    *LC* 65-2252

**Milne, R. S. (Robert Stephen), 1919-.**          **4.8726**
Malaysia—new states in a new nation: political development of Sarawak and Sabah in Malaysia [by] R. S. Milne and K. J. Ratnam. London, Frank Cass [1974] x, 501 p. map. 22 cm. (Studies in commonwealth politics and history, no. 2) 1. Federal government — Malaysia. 2. Sarawak — Politics and government. 3. Sabah — Politics and government. I. Ratnam, K. J. joint author. II. T.
JQ713.5.S8 M54 1974     320.9/595/05     *LC* 72-92971     *ISBN* 071462988X

**Yeo, Kim Wah.**          **4.8727**
The politics of decentralization: colonial controversy in Malaya, 1920–1929 / Yeo Kim Wah. — Kuala Lumpur; New York: Oxford University Press, 1982. xiv, 395 p., [16] p. of plates: ill., map, ports.; 23 cm. Revision of the author's thesis (Ph. D.)—Australian National University. Includes index. 1. Federal government — Malaysia — Malaya — History. 2. Decentralization in government — Malaysia — Malaya — History. I. T.
JQ713.5.S8 Y46 1982     320.9595 19     *LC* 82-941394     *ISBN* 0195825241

**Milne, R. S. (Robert Stephen), 1919-.**          **4.8728**
Politics and government in Malaysia / R. S. Milne and Diane K. Mauzy. — Vancouver: University of British Columbia Press, 1978. ix, 406 p.; 23 cm. Includes index. 1. Malaysia — Politics and government. I. Mauzy, Diane K., 1942- joint author. II. T.
JQ715.A1 M53 1978     320.9/595     *LC* 78-321989     *ISBN* 0774800712

**Government and politics of Singapore / edited by Jon S.T.**          **4.8729**
**Quah, Chan Heng Chee, Seah Chee Meow.**
Singapore; New York: Oxford University Press, 1985. xviii, 324 p.: plan; 26 cm. 'Issued under the auspices of the Southeast Asian Studies Program, Insitute of Southeast Asian Studies, Singapore.' Includes index. 1. Singapore — Politics and government. I. Quah, Jon S. T. II. Chan, Heng Chee. III. Seah, Chee Meow. IV. Southeast Asian Studies Program (Institute of Southeast Asian Studies)
JQ745.S5 G68 1985     320.9595/7 19     *LC* 85-941366     *ISBN* 0195826132

**Hindley, Donald.**          • **4.8730**
Communist Party of Indonesia,1951–1963 / D. Hindley. — Berkeley: University of California Press, 1964. xvii, 380 p.: maps.; 25 cm. 1. Communist Party of Indonesia. I. T.
JQ779.A55 H55     329.991     *LC* 64-24889

**Mortimer, Rex Alfred.**          **4.8731**
Indonesian communism under Sukarno; ideology and politics, 1959–1965 [by] Rex Mortimer. — Ithaca [N.Y.]: Cornell University Press, [1974] 464 p.; 24 cm. 1. Partai Komunis Indonesia. 2. Indonesia — Politics and government — 1950-1966 I. T.
JQ779.A55 M67     329.9/598     *LC* 73-19372     *ISBN* 0801408253

## JQ1500–1519 China

**Ch'ien, Tuan-shêng.**          • **4.8732**
The government and politics of China, 1912–1949. — Stanford, Calif.: Stanford University Press, [1970, c1950] xviii, 526 p.: map.; 22 cm. 'SP 113.' 1. China — Constitutional history. I. T.
JQ1502.C46 1970     320.9/51     *LC* 77-108026     *ISBN* 0804707014

**Liu, James Tzŭ-chien, 1919-.**          **4.8733**
Reform in Sung China; Wang An–shih (1021–1086) and his new policies [by] James T. C. Liu. — Cambridge, Harvard University Press, 1959. xiv, 140, xix p. 22 cm. — (Harvard East Asian studies, 3) Bibliography: p. i–xiv (3d group) 1. Wang, An-shih, 1021-1086. 2. China — Pol. & govt. — Early to 1643. I. T. II. Series.
JQ1502.L5     951.02     *LC* 59-9281

**Policy conflicts in post–Mao China: a documentary survey with**          **4.8734**
**analysis / John P. Burns, Stanley Rosen, editors.**
Armonk, N.Y.: M.E. Sharpe, c1986. xii, 372 p.: ill.; 24 cm. Contains material translated from the Chinese press. 'East gate books.' Includes bibliographies. 1. Chinese newspapers 2. China — Politics and government — 1976- — Sources. 3. China — History — 1976- — Sources. I. Burns, John P. II. Rosen, Stanley, 1942-
JQ1502.P65 1986     951.05/7 19     *LC* 86-907     *ISBN* 0873323378

**Cohen, Paul A.**          **4.8735**
Between tradition and modernity: Wang T'ao and reform in late Ch'ing China / Paul A. Cohen. — Cambridge: Harvard University Press, 1974. x, 357 p.: port.; 25 cm. — (Harvard East Asian series. 77) Includes index. 1. Wang, T'ao, 1828-1897. 2. China — Politics and government — 19th century I. T. II. Series.
JQ1508.Cx     301.2/4/0951 B     *LC* 74-75109     *ISBN* 0674068750

**Hsiao, Kung-ch'üan, 1897-.**          • **4.8736**
Rural China; imperial control in the nineteenth century. — Seattle, University of Washington Press, 1960. xiv, 783 p. illus. 24 cm. — (University of Washington publications on Asia) Bibliography: p. 743-776. 1. China — Pol. & govt. — 1862-1899. 2. China — Rural conditions. I. T.
JQ1508.H78     342.51     *LC* 60-15803

**Townsend, James R. (James Roger)**          **4.8737**
Politics in China / James R. Townsend. — 2d ed. — Boston: Little, Brown, c1980. xviii, 380 p., [1] leaf of plates: map; 21 cm. — (The Little, Brown series in comparative politics: A country study) 1. China — Politics and government — 1949-1976 2. China — Politics and government — 1976- I. T.
JQ1508.T68 1980     320.951     *LC* 79-2243     *ISBN* 0316851310

**Harding, Harry, 1946-.**          **4.8738**
Organizing China: the problem of bureaucracy, 1949–1976 / Harry Harding. — Stanford, Calif.: Stanford University Press, 1981. xi, 418 p.: ill.; 24 cm. Includes index. 1. Bureaucracy — China. 2. China — Politics and government — 1949-1976 I. T.
JQ1509 1981     354.5101 19     *LC* 79-67772     *ISBN* 0804710805

**Franke, Wolfgang, 1912-.**          • **4.8739**
The reform and abolition of the traditional Chinese examination system. Cambridge: Center for East Asian Studies, Harvard University; distributed by Harvard University Press, 1960. viii, 100 p.; 28 cm. (Harvard East Asian monographs. 10) Cover title also in Chinese. 1. Civil service — China — Examinations. 2. Examinations — China. I. T. II. Series.
JQ1512.F7     351.30951

**Hucker, Charles O.**          **4.8740**
A dictionary of official titles in Imperial China / Charles O. Hucker. — Stanford, Calif.: Stanford University Press, 1985. viii, 676 p.: ill.; 27 cm. Includes indexes. 1. Titles of honor and nobility — China — Dictionaries — Chinese. 2. Chinese language — Dictionaries — English. 3. China — Officials and employees — Titles — Dictionaries — Chinese. I. T.
JQ1512.Z13 T574 1985     354.51001/03 19     *LC* 82-62449     *ISBN* 0804711933

**Goodman, David S. G.**          **4.8741**
Beijing street voices: the poetry and politics of China's Democracy Movement / David S.G. Goodman. — London: M. Boyars, 1981. xv, 202 p.: ill. — (Open forum) Includes index. 1. Political posters, Chinese. 2. China — Politics and government — 1976- I. T.
JQ1516.G663     JQ1516 G663.     301.16/1     *LC* 79-56846     *ISBN* 0714527033

**Townsend, James R. (James Roger)**          • **4.8742**
Political participation in Communist China [by] James R. Townsend. — Berkeley: University of California Press, 1967. viii, 233 p.; 25 cm. — (Center for Chinese Studies. Publications) 1. Chung-kuo kung ch'an tang. 2. Political participation — China. 3. China — Politics and government I. T.
JQ1519.A45 T6     320.9/51     *LC* 67-11422

**Bartke, Wolfgang.**          **4.8743**
China's new party leadership: biographies and analysis of the Twelfth Central Committee of the Chinese Communist Party / by Wolfgang Bartke and Peter Schier. — Armonk, N.Y.: M.E. Sharpe, c1985. 289 p.: ports.; 29 cm. 'A publication of the Institute of Asian Affairs in Hamburg.' 1. Chung-kuo kung ch'an tang. Chung yang wei yüan hui — Biography. 2. China — Politics and government — 1976- I. Schier, Peter, 1950- II. Institut für Asienkunde (Hamburg, Germany) III. T.
JQ1519.A5 B32 1985     324.251/075/0922 B 19     *LC* 84-14130     *ISBN* 0873322819

**Chang, Kuo-t'ao, 1897-.**          • **4.8744**
The rise of the Chinese Communist Party; the autobiography of Chang Kuo–t'ao. — Lawrence: University Press of Kansas, [1971-72] 2 v.: illus.; 24 cm. 1. Chung-kuo kung ch'an tang — History. I. T.
JQ1519.A5 C374     329.9/51     *LC* 76-141997     *ISBN* 0700600728

**Harrison, James P.**          **4.8745**
The long march to power; a history of the Chinese Communist Party, 1921–72 [by] James Pinckney Harrison. — New York: Praeger Publishers, [1972] xvii, 647 p.: illus.; 25 cm. — (Praeger library of Chinese affairs) 1. Chung-kuo kung ch'an tang — History. I. T.
JQ1519.A5 H266     329.9/51     *LC* 77-168338

**Lewis, John Wilson, 1930-.**          • **4.8746**
Leadership in Communist China. — Ithaca, N.Y.: Cornell University Press, [1963] 305 p.: illus.; 24 cm. 1. Chung-kuo kung ch'an tang. 2. Communism — China. I. T.
JQ1519.A5 L4     354.51     *LC* 63-12090

Mao's China; party reform documents, 1942–44. Translation and    • 4.8747
introd. by Boyd Compton.
Seattle, University of Washington Press, 1952. lii, 278 p. map. 21 cm.
(University of Washington publications on Asia) 1. Chung-kuo kung ch'an
tang. 2. Communism — China. I. Compton, Boyd, ed. and tr.
JQ1519.A5 M3573        329.951 19        LC 51-12273

Yu, George T., 1931-.                                               • 4.8748
Party politics in republican China; the Kuomintang, 1912–1924, by George T.
Yu. Berkeley, University of California Press, 1966. xiv, 203 p. map. 1. Chung-
kuo kuo min tang — History I. T.
JQ1519 A52 Y8        LC 66-13089

# JQ1600–1699 Japan

Stockwin, James Arthur Ainscow.                                     4.8749
Japan: divided politics in a growth economy / J. A. A. Stockwin. — New York:
Norton, [1975] 296 p.: ill.; 21 cm. (The Norton library) (Comparative modern
governments) Includes index. 1. Japan — Politics and government — 1945-
2. Japan — Economic policy — 1945- I. T.
JQ1615 1945.S76        320.9/52/04        LC 74-32234        ISBN 0393055442

Akita, George.                                                      4.8750
Foundations of constitutional government in modern Japan, 1868–1900. —
Cambridge: Harvard University Press, 1967. viii, 292 p.; 24 cm. — (Harvard
East Asian series. 23) 1. Japan — Politics and government — 1868-1912
2. Japan — Constitutional history. I. T. II. Series.
JQ1615 1967.A64        342.52/09        LC 65-13835

Pittau, Joseph.                                                     • 4.8751
Political thought in early Meiji Japan, 1868–1889. Cambridge, Harvard
University Press, 1967. vi, 250 p. 22 cm. (Harvard East Asian series. 24)
1. Political science — Japan — History. 2. Japan — Constitutional history.
I. T. II. Series.
JQ1615.1967.P5        320.9/52        LC 65-22065

Ward, Robert Edward.                                                • 4.8752
Japan's political system [by] Robert E. Ward. — Englewood Cliffs, N.J.:
Prentice-Hall, [1967] ix, 126 p.: illus., map.; 23 cm. — (Comparative Asian
governments series) 1. Japan — Politics and government 2. Japan — Politics
and government — 1945- I. T.
JQ1615 1967.W3        320.9/52        LC 67-20230

Ike, Nobutaka.                                                      4.8753
Japanese politics: patron–client democracy. — 2d ed. — New York: Knopf,
[1972] x, 149 p.; 21 cm. 1. Japan — Politics and government — 1945- 2. Japan
— Social conditions — 1945- 3. Japan — Economic conditions — 1945- I. T.
JQ1618.I39 1972        320.9/52/04        LC 75-38612        ISBN 0394316959

Shillony, Ben-Ami.                                                  4.8754
Politics and culture in wartime Japan / Ben–Ami Shillony. — Oxford:
Clarendon Press; New York: Oxford University Press, 1981. xii, 238 p.; 23 cm.
Includes index. 1. Japan — Politics and government — 1912-1945 2. Japan —
Cultural policy — History. I. T.
JQ1626 1981e        952.03/3 19        LC 82-136768        ISBN 0198215738

Titus, David Anson, 1934-.                                          4.8755
Palace and politics in prewar Japan. New York, Columbia University Press,
1974. x, 360 p. 23 cm. (Studies of the East Asian Institute, Columbia
University) 1. Japan. Kunaishō — History. 2. Japan — Emperors 3. Japan —
Constitutional history. 4. Japan — Politics and government — 1868- I. T.
JQ1641.T55        354/.52/0312        LC 74-6109        ISBN 0231036221

Baerwald, Hans H.                                                   4.8756
Japan's parliament; an introduction [by] Hans H. Baerwald. — [London; New
York]: Cambridge University Press, [1974] 155 p.; 22 cm. 1. Japan. Kokkai.
2. Japan — Politics and government — 1945- I. T.
JQ1654.B33        328.52/09        LC 73-90810        ISBN 0521203872

Richardson, Bradley M.                                              4.8757
The political culture of Japan [by] Bradley M. Richardson. — Berkeley:
University of California Press, [1974] xi, 271 p.; 24 cm. 'Published under the
auspices of the Center for Japanese and Korean Studies, University of
California, Berkeley.' 1. Political participation — Japan. 2. Japan — Politics
and government — 1945- I. T.
JQ1681.R53        301.5/92/0952        LC 76-153551        ISBN 0520020197

Tsurutani, Taketsugu.                                               4.8758
Political change in Japan: response to postindustrial challenge / Taketsugu
Tsurutani. — New York: Longman, c1977. xii, 275 p.: ill.; 23 cm. —
(Comparative studies of political life) Includes index. 1. Political parties —
Japan. 2. Political participation — Japan. 3. Japan — Politics and government
— 1945- I. T.
JQ1681.T75 1977        320.952        LC 80-10282        ISBN 0582281830

Watanuki, Jōji, 1931-.                                              4.8759
Politics in postwar Japanese society / Joji Watanuki. — [Tokyo]: University of
Tokyo Press, c1977. x, 171 p.: ill.; 24 cm. Includes index. 1. Political
participation — Japan. 2. Japan — Politics and government — 1945- I. T.
JQ1681.W34        320.9/52/04        LC 78-318773        ISBN 0860081907

Berger, Gordon Mark, 1942-.                                         4.8760
Parties out of power in Japan, 1931–1941 / Gordon Mark Berger. — Princeton,
N.J.: Princeton University Press, c1977. xv, 413 p.: ill.; 23 cm. Emanates from
the author's thesis, Yale, 1972. Includes index. 1. Political parties — Japan —
History. 2. Japan — Politics and government — 1926-1945 I. T.
JQ1698.A1 B46 1977        329.9/52        LC 76-3243        ISBN 0691031061

Scalapino, Robert A.                                                • 4.8761
Democracy and the party movement in prewar Japan: the failure of the first
attempt. — Berkeley: University of California Press, 1953. xi, 471 p.
1. Political parties — Japan 2. Japan — Politics and government — 1867-1912
3. Japan — Politics and government — 1912-1945 I. T.
JQ1698 A1 S35        LC 53-10608

Scalapino, Robert A.                                                • 4.8762
Parties and politics in contemporary Japan [by] Robert A. Scalapino and
Junnosuke Masumi. — Berkeley: University of California Press, 1962. ix,
190 p.: illus.; 24 cm. 1. Political parties — Japan. 2. Japan — Politics and
government — 1945- I. Masumi, Junnosuke, 1926- joint author. II. T.
JQ1698.A1 S37        329.952        LC 61-14279

Beckmann, George M.                                                 • 4.8763
The Japanese Communist Party 1922–1945, by George M. Beckman & Okubo
Genji. — Stanford, Calif.: Stanford University Press, 1969. 453 p.; 25 cm.
Appendices (p. [279]-361):—A. Draft platform of 1922.—B. Shanghai theses of
1925.—C. Moscow theses of 1926.—D. 1927 theses.—E. 1931 theses.—F. 1932
theses.—G. Nosaka-Yamamoto letter of 1936. 1. Nihon Kyōsantō. I. Okubo,
Genji, joint author. II. T.
JQ1698.K9 B4        329.9/52        LC 68-26776

Langer, Paul Fritz, 1915-.                                          4.8764
Communism in Japan: a case of political naturalization / [by] Paul F. Langer.
— Stanford, Calif.: Hoover Institution Press, [1972] xv, 112 p.; 23 cm. —
(Comparative Communist Party politics) (Hoover Institution studies, 30)
1. Nihon Kyōsantō. 2. Japan — Politics and government — 1945- I. T.
II. Series. III. Series: Hoover Institution studies, 30
JQ1698.K9 L35        329.9/52        LC 73-152426        ISBN 0817933018

Scalapino, Robert A.                                                • 4.8765
The Japanese Communist movement, 1920–1966 [by] Robert A. Scalapino.
Berkeley, University of California Press, 1967. viii, 412 p. 25 cm. 'Sources': p.
[355]-366. Bibliographical footnotes. 1. Nihon Kyosanto. 2. Communism —
Japan. I. T.
JQ1698.K9 S27        329.9/52        LC 67-14443

# JQ1740–1749 Thailand

Wales, Horace Geoffrey Quaritch, 1900-.                             • 4.8766
Ancient Siamese government and administration. New York, Paragon Book
Reprint Corp., 1965. vii, 263 p.; 23 cm. 1. Thailand — Politics and government
I. T.
JQ1742.W3 1965        354.593

Siffin, William J.                                                  • 4.8767
The Thai bureaucracy: institutional change and development / by William J.
Siffin. — Honolulu: East-West Center Press [1966] x, 291 p.; 24 cm.
1. Thailand — Politics and government I. T.
JQ1745 A1 S5        LC 66-13024

Morell, David.                                                      4.8768
Political conflict in Thailand: reform, reaction, revolution / David Morell,
Chai–anan Samudavanija. — Cambridge, Mass.: Oelgeschlager, Gunn & Hain,
c1981. xviii, 362 p.: ill.; 24 cm. Includes index. 1. Thailand — Politics and
government I. Chai'anan Samutwanit. II. T.
JQ1745.M67        320.9593 19        LC 81-3926        ISBN 0899460445

Wilson, David A.                                                    • 4.8769
Politics in Thailand. Ithaca, N. Y., Cornell University Press [1962] 307 p. 22
cm. Includes bibliography. 1. Thailand — Politics and government I. T.
JQ1745.W5        959.3        LC 62-20734

# JQ1780–1825.I Iran. Turkey. Iraq

Behman, M. Reza, 1945-.                                             4.8770
Cultural foundations of Iranian politics / M. Reza Behnam. — Salt Lake City:
University of Utah Press, c1986. 188 p.: map; 24 cm. Includes index. 1. Politics

and culture — Iran. 2. Social structures — Iran. 3. Islam and state — Iran. 4. Iran — Politics and government 5. Iran — History — Revolution, 1979 I. T.
JQ1785.B44 1986     306/.2/0955 19     *LC* 86-15871     *ISBN* 0874802652

**Heper, Metin.**            **4.8771**
The state tradition in Turkey / Metin Heper. — Beverley, North Humberside: Eothen Press; Atlantic Highlands, N.J.: Distributed in the U.S.A. by Humanities Press, c1985. x, 218 p.; 22 cm. Distributor statement from label on t.p. Includes index. 1. State, The 2. Turkey — Politics and government I. T.
JQ1802.H47 1985     320.1/09561 19     *LC* 86-108148     *ISBN* 0906719089

**Tachau, Frank, 1929-.**            **4.8772**
Turkey, the politics of authority, democracy, and development / Frank Tachau. — New York: Praeger, 1984. p. cm. Includes index. 1. Turkey — Politics and government — 1960- 2. Turkey — Economic conditions — 1960- 3. Turkey — Social conditions — 1960- I. T.
JQ1802.T33 1984     320.9561 19     *LC* 84-3451

**Findley, Carter V., 1941-.**            **4.8773**
Bureaucratic reform in the Ottoman Empire: the Sublime Porte, 1789–1922 / Carter V. Findley. — Princeton, N.J.: Princeton University Press, c1980. xxxiii, 455 p., [2] leaves of plates: ill.; 24 cm. — (Princeton studies on the Near East.) Includes index. 1. Bureaucracy — Turkey. 2. Turkey — Politics and government — 19th century I. T. II. Series.
JQ1806.Z1 F55     354/.561/01     *LC* 79-22162     *ISBN* 0691052883

**Batatu, Hanna, 1926-.**            **4.8774**
The old social classes and the revolutionary movements of Iraq: a study of Iraq's old landed and commercial classes and of its Communists, Ba'thists, and Free Officers / Hanna Batatu. — Princeton, N.J.: Princeton University Press, c1978. xxiv, 1283 p., [8] leaves of plates: ill.; 25 cm. — (Princeton studies on the Near East.) Includes indexes. 1. Hizb al-Shuyū'ī al-'Irāqī. 2. Social classes — Iraq. 3. Iraq — Politics and government. I. T. II. Series.
JQ1825.I773 S493     329.9/567     *LC* 78-51157     *ISBN* 0691052417

## JQ1825.J–.N Jordan. Lebanon. Nepal

**Cohen, Amnon, 1936-.**            **4.8775**
Political parties in the West Bank under the Jordanian regime, 1949–1967 / Amnon Cohen. — Ithaca: Cornell University Press, 1982. 278 p.; 24 cm. Translated and emended version of Miflagot ba-Gadah ha-ma'aravit bi-tekufat ha-shilton ha-Yardeni. 1. Political parties — Jordan. 2. Jordan — Politics and government. I. Cohen, Amnon, 1936- Miflagot ba-Gadah ha-ma'aravit bi-tekufat ha-shilton ha-Yardeni. II. T.
JQ1825.J67 C6313 1982     324.25695 19     *LC* 80-25666     *ISBN* 0801413214

**Baaklini, Abdo I.**            **4.8776**
Legislative and political development: Lebanon, 1842–1972 / Abdo I. Baaklini. — Durham, N.C.: Duke University Press, 1976. xv, 316 p.; 25 cm. (Publications of the Consortium for Comparative Legislative Studies; 2) Includes index. 1. Lebanon. Majlis al-Nūwwāb. 2. Legislative bodies — Lebanon. 3. Lebanon — Politics and government I. T.
JQ1825.L45 B3     JQ1825L45 B25.     328.5692/09     *LC* 76-377114

**Chauhan, R. S., 1934-.**            **4.8777**
The political development in Nepal, 1950–70; conflict between tradition and modernity [by] R. S. Chauhan. — New York, Barnes & Noble, 1972 (c1971). x, 336 p.; 22 cm. 1. Nepal — Politics and government. I. T.
JQ1825.N4 C5     320.9/549/6     *LC* 75-923434

**Rose, Leo E.**            • **4.8778**
The politics of Nepal; persistence and change in an Asian monarchy [by] Leo E. Rose and Margaret W. Fisher. — Ithaca, N.Y.: Cornell University Press, [1970] xiii, 197 p.: maps.; 21 cm. — (South Asian political systems) 1. Nepal — Politics and government. I. Fisher, Margaret Welpley, 1903- joint author. II. T. III. Series.
JQ1825.N4 R6     320.9/549/6     *LC* 72-120291     *ISBN* 0801405742

**Shaha, Rishikesh.**            **4.8779**
Nepali politics: retrospect and prospect / Rishikesh Shaha. — Delhi; New York: Oxford University Press, 1975. xii, 208 p.; 22 cm. Includes index. 1. Panchayat — Nepal. 2. Nepal — Politics and government. 3. Nepal — Foreign relations. I. T.
JQ1825.N42 S46 1975     320.9/549/6     *LC* 75-904963

## JQ1825.P3 Palestine. Israel

**Ma'oz, Moshe.**            **4.8780**
Palestinian leadership on the West Bank: the changing role of the Arab mayors under Jordan and Israel / Moshe Ma'oz, with a contribution by Mordechai Nisan. — London; Totowa, N.J.: F. Cass, 1984. xiv, 217 p., [8] p. of plates: ill.; 23 cm. 1. Mayors — West Bank. 2. West Bank — Politics and government. I. T.
JQ1825.P3 A44 1984     320.95695 19     *LC* 83-228501     *ISBN* 0714632341

**Galnoor, Itzhak.**            **4.8781**
Steering the polity: communication and politics in Israel / Itzhak Galnoor. — Beverly Hills: Sage Publications, c1982. xii, 411 p.: ill.; 23 cm. Includes index. 1. Communication in politics — Israel. 2. Israel — Politics and government I. T.
JQ1825.P3 G34 1982     306/.2/095694 19     *LC* 81-21485     *ISBN* 0803913400

**Salpeter, Eliahu.**            **4.8782**
[Mimsad. English] Who rules Israel? / [by] Yuval Elizur and Eliahu Salpeter. — [1st ed.] New York: Harper & Row [1973] x, 342 p.; 22 cm. Translation of ha-Mimsad. 1. Elite (Social sciences) — Israel. 2. Israel — Politics and government I. Elitzur, Yuval. joint author. II. T.
JQ1825.P3 S2713     320.9/5694/05     *LC* 73-5460     *ISBN* 006011164X

**Yaacobi, Gad, 1935-.**            **4.8783**
The government of Israel / Gad Yaacobi. — New York, N.Y. U.S.A.: Praeger, 1982. xii, 329 p.; 25 cm. 1. Israel — Politics and government — 1948- I. T.
JQ1825.P3 Y3 1982     320.95694 19     *LC* 81-21122     *ISBN* 0030599725

**Sager, Samuel.**            **4.8784**
The parliamentary system of Israel / Samuel Sager; with a foreword by Abba Eban. — 1st ed. — Syracuse, N.Y.: Syracuse University Press, 1985. xiii, 259 p.; 24 cm. Includes index. 1. Israel. Keneset. 2. Israel — Politics and government I. T.
JQ1825.P35 S24 1985     328.5694 19     *LC* 85-12631     *ISBN* 0815623356

**Isaac, Rael Jean.**            **4.8785**
Party and politics in Israel: three visions of a Jewish state / Rael Jean Isaac. — New York: Longman, c1981. xi, 228 p.; 24 cm. Includes index. 1. Political parties — Israel. 2. Israel — Politics and government I. T.
JQ1825.P37 I8     324.25694     *LC* 80-17893     *ISBN* 0582281962

**Schiff, Gary S., 1947-.**            **4.8786**
Tradition and politics: the religious parties of Israel / Gary S. Schiff. — Detroit: Wayne State University Press, 1977. 267 p.; 24 cm. — (The Modern Middle East series; v. 9) Includes index. 1. Political parties — Israel — History. 2. Religion and state — Israel — History. 3. Religious Zionism — History. 4. Israel — Politics and government I. T.
JQ1825.P37 S34     324.25694/08/09 19     *LC* 77-5723     *ISBN* 0814315801

**Schnall, David J.**            **4.8787**
Radical dissent in contemporary Israeli politics: cracks in the wall / David J. Schnall. — New York: Praeger, 1979. ix, 229 p.; 24 cm. Includes index. 1. Political parties — Israel. 2. Radicalism — Israel. 3. Israel — Politics and government I. T.
JQ1825.P37 S36     320.9/5694/05     *LC* 78-31209     *ISBN* 003047096X

## JQ1825.Y–1850 Yemen. Arab Countries: General

**Ismael, Tareq Y.**            **4.8788**
The People's Democratic Republic of Yemen: politics, economics, and society: the politics of socialist transformation / Tareq Y. Ismael and Jacqueline S. Ismael. — London: F. Pinter; Boulder, Colo.: L. Rienner, 1986. xxii, 183 p.: ill.; 22 cm. — (Marxist regimes series.) Includes index. 1. Yemen (People's Democratic Republic) — Politics and government. 2. Yemen (People's Democratic Republic) — Economic conditions. 3. Yemen (People's Democratic Republic) — Social conditions. I. Ismael, Jacqueline S. II. T. III. Series.
JQ1825.Y5 I85 1986     953/.32 19     *LC* 86-15442     *ISBN* 0931477964

**Bidwell, Robin Leonard.**            **4.8789**
The Arab world, 1900–1972. Compiled and edited by Robin Bidwell. — [London]: Cass, [1973] xi, 124 p.; 29 cm. — (His Guide to government ministers, v. 2) 1. Arab countries — Registers. I. T.
JQ1850.A4 B53 1973     350/.2/09174927     *LC* 74-162844     *ISBN* 0714630012

# JQ1870–3981 Africa

**Hodder-Williams, Richard.**     **4.8790**
An introduction to the politics of tropical Africa / Richard Hodder–Williams. — London; Boston: G. Allen & Unwin, 1984. xxv, 262 p.; 23 cm. Includes index. 1. Africa, Sub-Saharan — Politics and government 2. Africa, Sub-Saharan — Constitutional history. I. T.
JQ1872.H63 1984    967 19    *LC* 84-9273    *ISBN* 0043201628

**Tordoff, William.**     **4.8791**
Government and politics in Africa / William Tordoff. — Bloomington: Indiana University Press, c1984. xix, 352 p.: maps; 23 cm. Includes index. 1. Africa — Politics and government — 1960- I. T.
JQ1872.T67 1984    320.96 19    *LC* 84-47769    *ISBN* 0253326117

**Bretton, Henry L., 1916-.**     **4.8792**
Power and politics in Africa [by] Henry L. Bretton. — Chicago: Aldine Pub. Co., [1973] xiv, 402 p.: ill.; 25 cm. 1. Power (Social sciences) 2. Africa — Politics and government — 1960- I. T.
JQ1873 1973.B73    320.9/6/03    *LC* 72-78212    *ISBN* 0202241319

**Hailey, William Malcolm Hailey, Baron, 1872-1969.**     ● **4.8793**
Native administration in the British African territories. — London: H.M. Stationery Off., 1950-1953. 5 v. At head of title: pt. 1-4, Colonial Office; v. 5 pt. 5, Commonwealth Relations Office. 1. Great Britain — Colonies — Africa — Administration. 2. Africa — Native races. I. Great Britain. Colonial Office. II. Great Britain. Office of Commonwealth Relations. III. T.
JQ1890.H28    *LC* 51-4697

**Benson, Mary.**     **4.8794**
South Africa: the struggle for a birthright / Mary Benson. — London: International Defence and Aid Fund for Southern Africa, 1985. 314 p.; 22 cm. Reprint. Originally published: Penguin Africa Library, 1966. Rev. ed. of: The African patriots. 1963. Includes index. 1. African National Congress — History. 2. Blacks — South Africa — Political activity — History — 20th century. 3. South Africa — Politics and government — 20th century I. Benson, Mary. African patriots. II. T. III. Title: Struggle for a birthright.
JQ1998.A4 B4 1985    322.4/2/0968 19    *LC* 86-168136    *ISBN* 0904759679

**Butler, Jeffrey.**     **4.8795**
The black homelands of South Africa: the political and economic development of Bophuthatswana and KwaZulu / by Jeffrey Butler, Robert I. Rotberg, and John Adams. — Berkeley: University of California Press, c1977. x, 250 p.: ill.; 25 cm. — (Perspectives on Southern Africa. 21) Includes index. 1. Bophuthatswana (South Africa) — Politics and government. 2. Bophuthatswana (South Africa) — Economic conditions. 3. Kwazulu (South Africa) — Politics and government. 4. Kwazulu (South Africa) — Economic conditions. 5. Homelands (South Africa) I. Rotberg, Robert I. joint author. II. Adams, John, 1938- joint author. III. T. IV. Series.
JQ1999.B63 B87    320.9/68    *LC* 76-7755    *ISBN* 0520032314

**Potholm, Christian P., 1940-.**     **4.8796**
Swaziland; the dynamics of political modernization [by] Christian P. Potholm. — Berkeley: University of California Press, [1972] 183 p.: map.; 23 cm. — (Perspectives on Southern Africa. 8]) 1. Swaziland — Politics and government — 1968- I. T. II. Series.
JQ2721.A2 P68    320.9/68/304    *LC* 74-186117    *ISBN* 0520022009

**Politics in Zambia** / by William Tordoff, editor ... [et al.].     **4.8797**
Berkeley: University of California Press, [1974] xi, 439 p.: maps; 23 cm. — (Perspectives on Southern Africa. 15) Includes index. 1. Political parties — Zambia. 2. Zambia — Politics and government — 1964- I. Tordoff, William. II. Series.
JQ2815 1974.P64    320.96894 19    *LC* 73-86660    *ISBN* 0520025938

**Politics and public policy in Kenya and Tanzania** / edited by Joel D. Barkan.     **4.8798**
Rev. ed. — New York: Praeger, 1984. xviii, 375 p.; 25 cm. Includes index. 1. Rural development — Kenya — Addresses, essays, lectures. 2. Rural development — Tanzania — Addresses, essays, lectures. 3. Kenya — Politics and government — Addresses, essays, lectures. 4. Tanzania — Politics and government — 1964- — Addresses, essays, lectures. 5. Kenya — Social policy — Addresses, essays, lectures. 6. Tanzania — Social policy — Addresses, essays, lectures. I. Barkan, Joel D.
JQ2947.A2 P64 1984    320.9676/2 19    *LC* 84-9829    *ISBN* 0030613582

**Bienen, Henry.**     **4.8799**
Kenya: the politics of participation and control. Princeton, N.J., Princeton University Press [1974] viii, 215 p. 23 cm. 'Written under the auspices of the Center of International Studies, Princeton University, and the Center of International Affairs, Harvard University.' 1. Political participation — Kenya. 2. Political parties — Kenya. 3. Kenya — Economic policy. 4. Kenya — Social conditions — 1963- I. Woodrow Wilson School of Public and International Affairs. Center of International Studies. II. Harvard University. Center for International Affairs. III. T.
JQ2947.A91 B53    320.9/676/2    *LC* 73-2461    *ISBN* 0691030960

**Kuklick, Henrika.**     **4.8800**
The imperial bureaucrat: the colonial administrative service in the Gold Coast, 1920–1939 / Henrika Kuklick. — Stanford, Calif.: Hoover Institution Press, c1979. xvi, 225 p.; 24 cm. (Hoover colonial studies.) (Hoover Institution publication; 217) Includes index. 1. Colonial administrators — Ghana. 2. Ghana — Politics and government — To 1957 3. Great Britain — Colonies — Africa — Administration. I. T. II. Series.
JQ3028.K84    325/.31/4109667    *LC* 79-2463    *ISBN* 0817971718

**Dudley, Billy J.**     **4.8801**
An introduction to Nigerian government and politics / Billy Dudley. — Bloomington: Indiana University Press, c1982. ix, 367 p.; 22 cm. 1. Nigeria — Politics and government — 1960-1975 2. Nigeria — Politics and government — 1975-1979 3. Nigeria — Politics and government — 1979-1983 I. T.
JQ3082.D8 1982    320.9669 19    *LC* 82-47926    *ISBN* 0253331048

**Post, Ken, 1935-.**     **4.8802**
Structure and conflict in Nigeria, 1960–1966 [by] Kenneth Post and Michael Vickers. [Madison] University of Wisconsin Press [1973] vii, 248 p. map (on lining papers) 23 cm. 1. Nigeria — Politics and government — 1960-1975 I. Vickers, Michael, joint author. II. T.
JQ3083 1960.P652    320.9/669/05    *LC* 73-14408    *ISBN* 0299064700

**Eleazu, Uma O.**     **4.8803**
Federalism and nation–building: the Nigerian experience, 1954–1964 / [by] Uma O. Eleazu. — Ilfracombe: Stockwell, 1977. 280 p.: ill., maps; 23 cm. 1. Federal government — Nigeria. 2. Nigeria — Politics and government I. T.
JQ3086.S8 E43 1977    321/.02/09669    *LC* 78-302764    *ISBN* 0722309872

**Cohen, William B., 1941-.**     ● **4.8804**
Rulers of empire: the French colonial service in Africa [by] William B. Cohen. [Stanford, Calif.] Hoover Institution Press, 1971. xv, 279 p. illus. 24 cm. (Hoover Institution publications; 95) 1. Africa, French-speaking West — Politics and government — 1884-1960 2. France — Colonies — Africa — Administration. I. T.
JQ3358.C63    325.3/44/066    *LC* 76-137405    *ISBN* 0817919511

**Cohen, Michael A., 1944-.**     **4.8805**
Urban policy and political conflict in Africa: a study of the Ivory Coast / Michael A. Cohen. — Chicago: University of Chicago Press, 1974. x, 262 p.; 24 cm. Includes index. 1. Political participation — Ivory Coast. 2. City planning — Ivory Coast. 3. Ivory Coast — Politics and government I. T.
JQ3386.A91 C63    301.5/096668    *LC* 73-90942    *ISBN* 0226112233

**Gellar, Sheldon.**     **4.8806**
Structural changes and colonial dependency: Senegal, 1885–1945 / Sheldon Gellar. Beverly Hills, Calif.: Sage Publications, c1976. 80 p.; 22 cm. (Sage research papers in the social sciences; ser. no. 90-036: Studies in comparative modernization series) 1. Senegal — Politics and government 2. Senegal — Economic conditions. 3. France — Colonies — Africa. I. T.
JQ3396.A91 G44    309.1/66/303    *LC* 76-43070    *ISBN* 0803906366

**Weinstein, Brian.**     ● **4.8807**
Gabon: nation–building on the Ogooué. — Cambridge, Mass., M. I. T. Press [c1966] xiv, 287 p. illus., map (on lining paper), port. 25 cm. Bibliography: p. 257-279. 1. Gabon — Pol. & govt. 2. Nationalism — Gabon. I. T.
JQ3407.A2W4    320.9/67/21    *LC* 67-13393

**Saint Véran, Robert.**     **4.8808**
[A Djibouti avec les Afars et les Issas. English] Djibouti, pawn of the Horn of Africa / Robert Tholomier; an abridged translation and postscript by Virginia Thompson and Richard Adloff. — Metuchen, N.J.: Scarecrow Press, 1981. x, 163 p.: map; 23 cm. Abridged translation of: A Djibouti avec les Afars et les Issas. Includes index. 1. Djibouti — Politics and government. 2. Djibouti — Economic conditions. 3. Djibouti — Social conditions. I. Thompson, Virginia McLean, 1903- II. Adloff, Richard. III. T.
JQ3421.A3 1981.S34213    967/.71 19    *LC* 81-143    *ISBN* 0810814153

**Bienen, Henry.**     ● **4.8809**
Tanzania; party transformation and economic development. Princeton, Princeton University Press, 1967. xv, 446 p. illus., map. 23 cm. 'Published for the Center of International Studies, Princeton University.' 1. TANU (Organization) I. Woodrow Wilson School of Public and International Affairs. Center of International Studies. II. T.
JQ3519.A8 T3    329.9678    *LC* 67-21016

The Political economy of Cameroon / edited by Michael G. **4.8810**
Schatzberg and I. William Zartman.
New York: Praeger, 1986. p. cm. (SAIS study on Africa.) Includes index.
1. Cameroon — Politics and government — 1960- — Addresses, essays,
lectures. 2. Cameroon — Economic policy — Addresses, essays, lectures.
3. Cameroon — Economic conditions — 1960- — Addresses, essays, lectures.
I. Schatzberg, Michael G. II. Zartman, I. William. III. Series.
JQ3521.P64 1986      306/.2/096711 19      *LC* 85-20492      *ISBN*
0030030935

Le Vine, Victor T.      **4.8811**
The Cameroon Federal Republic [by] Victor T. Le Vine. Ithaca [N.Y.] Cornell
University Press [1971] xxiii, 205 p. maps. 21 cm. (Africa in the modern world)
1. Cameroon — Politics and government — 1960-1982 I. T.
JQ3522.L4      916.7/11/034      *LC* 70-148025      *ISBN* 0801406374

Joseph, Richard A.      **4.8812**
Radical nationalism in Cameroun: social origins of the U.P.C. rebellion / by
Richard A. Joseph. — Oxford; New York: Clarendon Press, 1977. x, 383 p.:
maps; 22 cm. — (Oxford studies in African affairs.) Includes index. 1. Union
des populations du Cameroun. 2. Cameroon — Politics and government I. T.
II. Series.
JQ3529.A8 U53      322.4/2/096711      *LC* 78-302397      *ISBN*
019822706X

Adgar, Jean Claude.      **4.8813**
Patrimonialism and political change in the Congo. — Stanford, Calif.: Stanford
University Press, 1972. xii, 223 p.: illus.; 24 cm. 1. Zaire — Politics and
government — 1960- I. T.
JQ3603 1972.W5      320.9/675/103      *LC* 79-153821      *ISBN*
0804707936

Abdel-Rahim, Muddathir, 1932-.      • **4.8814**
Imperialism and nationalism in the Sudan: a study in constitutional and
political development, 1899–1956 / by Muddathir 'Abd al-Rahim. — Oxford:
Clarendon P., 1969. xviii, 275 p.: map.; 23 cm. — (Oxford studies in African
affairs.) 'The original version of this study was a thesis submitted ... at the
University of Manchester in April 1964.' 1. Sudan — Politics and government.
I. T. II. Series.
JQ3981.S8 A42      320.9/624      *LC* 75-455729      *ISBN* 0198216483

# JQ4001–6651 Australia. New Zealand. Oceania

Deakin, Alfred, 1856-1919.      • **4.8815**
The federal story: the inner history of the federal cause, 1880–1900. — [2d ed.]
Edited and with an introd. by J.A. La Nauze. [Parkville, Victoria]: Melbourne
University Press, [1963] xii, 182 p.; 23 cm. 1. Australia — Constitutional
history I. T.
JQ4011 D4 1963      *LC* 64-3607

La Nauze, John Andrew, 1911-.      • **4.8816**
The making of the Australian constitution [by] J. A. La Nauze. — [Melbourne]:
Melbourne University Press, [1972] xi, 369 p.: illus.; 24 cm. — (Studies in
Australian federation.) 1. Australia — Constitutional history. I. T. II. Series.
LAW      JQ4011.L3.      342/.94/029      *LC* 72-182931      *ISBN*
0522840167

McMinn, W. G., 1930-.      **4.8817**
A constitutional history of Australia / W. G. McMinn. — Melbourne; New
York: Oxford University Press, 1979. xiii, 213 p.; 22 cm. Includes index.
1. Australia — Constitutional history. 2. Australia — Politics and government
I. T.
JQ4011.M33      342.94/029      *LC* 80-453222      *ISBN* 019550562X

McMillan, John, of Australia.      **4.8818**
Australia's constitution: time for change / John McMillan, Gareth Evans,
Haddon Storey. — Sydney: Law Foundation of New South Wales and George
Allen & Unwin Australia, 1983. xv, 422 p. 1. Australia — Constitutional law
2. Australia — Constitutional history 3. Australia — Politics and government
— 1945- I. Evans Gareth, of Australia II. Storey, Haddon. III. T.
JQ4015 1983 M3      *ISBN* 0868610399

Encel, Sol.      **4.8819**
Cabinet government in Australia / [by] S. Encel. — 2nd ed. — [Carlton South,
Vic.]: Melbourne University Press; Portland, Ore.: [distributed by] ISBS, 1974.
255 p.; 24 cm. Includes index. 1. Cabinet system — Australia. 2. Australia —
Politics and government I. T.
JQ4042.E5 1974      320.9/94      *LC* 75-319561      *ISBN* 0522840639

The Australian Labor Party and federal politics: a documentary      **4.8820**
survey / edited and introduced by Bron Stevens and Pat Weller.
Carlton, [Australia]: Melbourne University Press; Forest Grove, Or.: available
from International Scholarly Book Services, 1977 (c1976). ix, 160 p.; 22 cm.
Includes index. 1. Australian Labor Party. 2. Australia — Politics and
government — 1901-1945 3. Australia — Politics and government — 1945-
I. Stevens, Bronwyn Elizabeth. II. Weller, Patrick Moray.
JQ4098.L3 A88      329/.9/94      *LC* 78-306482      *ISBN* 0522840949

Parker, Robert Stewart.      **4.8821**
The government of New South Wales / [by] R. S. Parker. — St. Lucia, Q.:
University of Queensland Press; Hemel Hempstead, Eng.: distributed by
Prentice-Hall International, 1978. xiv, 462 p.: maps; 23 cm. 1. New South
Wales — Politics and government. I. T.
JQ4515 1978.P37      320.9/944/06      *LC* 79-307928      *ISBN*
0702211397

Hughes, Colin A.      **4.8822**
The government of Queensland / Colin A. Hughes. — St. Lucia, Qld.:
University of Queensland Press; Hemel Hempstead, Herts., England:
distributed by Prentice-Hall International, c1980. viii, 322 p.; 22 cm.
1. Queensland — Politics and government. I. T.
JQ4711.H83 1980      320.4943 19      *LC* 81-144550      *ISBN* 0702215155

Levine, Stephen I.      **4.8823**
The New Zealand political system: politics in a small society / Stephen Levine.
— Sydney; Boston: Allen & Unwin, 1979. 207 p.: ill.; 23 cm. Includes index.
1. New Zealand — Politics and government I. T.
JQ5811.L44      320.9/931/03      *LC* 78-74191      *ISBN* 0868610739

Politics in New Zealand: a reader / edited by Stephen Levine.      **4.8824**
Sydney; Boston: Allen & Unwin; Auckland: distributed by Books Reps ( New
Zealand), 1978. 437 p.: ill.; 23 cm. 1. New Zealand — Politics and government
— Addresses, essays, lectures. I. Levine, Stephen I.
JQ5811.P64 1978      320.9/931/03      *LC* 77-87875      *ISBN* 0868610569

Scott, Kenneth John, 1912-1961.      **4.8825**
The New Zealand Constitution. — Oxford: Clarendon Press, 1962. 188 p.; 23
cm. 1. New Zealand — Constitutional law I. T.
LAW      JQ5815 1962.S63.      *LC* 63-1700

Hill, Larry B.      **4.8826**
The model ombudsman: institutionalizing New Zealand's democratic
experiment / Larry B. Hill. — Princeton, N.J.: Princeton University Press,
c1976. xviii, 411 p.; 23 cm. Based on the author's thesis, Tulane University,
1970. Includes index. 1. Ombudsman — New Zealand. I. T.
JQ5829.O4 H53      354/.931/0091      *LC* 76-3258      *ISBN* 0691075794

Hudson, W. J.      **4.8827**
Australia and Papua New Guinea, edited by W. J. Hudson. — [Sydney]: Sydney
University Press, [1971] viii, 198 p.; 22 cm. 1. Papua-New Guinea (Ter.) —
Politics and government — Addresses, essays, lectures. 2. Papua-New Guinea
(Ter.) — History — Addresses, essays, lectures. I. T.
JQ6311.A2 H84      320.9/95      *LC* 70-135113      *ISBN* 0424062704

Mair, Lucy Philip, 1901-.      **4.8828**
Australia in New Guinea [by] L. P. Mair. [2d ed.] [Melbourne] Melbourne
University Press, c1948] 254 p. 23 cm. 1. Australians — New Guinea
2. Papua New Guinea — Economic conditions. 3. Papua New Guinea —
Politics and government — To 1975 I. T.
JQ6311.A2 M35 1970      919.5      *LC* 72-584975      *ISBN* 0522839576

Heine, Carl.      **4.8829**
Micronesia at the crossroads: a reappraisal of the Micronesian political
dilemma / Carl Heine. — Canberra: Australian National University Press,
1974. xvi, 210 p.; 22 cm. Includes index. 1. Pacific Islands (Trust Territory) —
Politics and government. 2. Micronesia (Federated States) — History. I. T.
JQ6451.A3 1974b      320.9/96/5      *LC* 75-300284      *ISBN* 0708102999

United States. Office of the Chief of Naval Operations.      **4.8830**
United States naval administration of the Trust Territory of the Pacific Islands
/ by Dorothy E. Richard; with a foreword by Arthur W. Radford and an introd.
by Leon S. Fiske. — [Washington]: Office of the Chief of Naval Operations,
1957-[1963] 3 v.: ill. 1. Pacific Islands (Trust Territory) — Politics and
government. I. Richard, Dorothy Elizabeth, 1909- II. T.
JQ6451.A5 A5      *LC* 57-62103

# JS Local Government

**United States. Bureau of the Census.**  •  **4.8831**
[Census of governments: 1967] 1967 census of governments. [Washington, For sale by the Supt. of Docs., U.S. Govt. Print. Off., 1968-. v. in illus., maps. 29 cm. 1. United States — Administrative and political divisions. I. T.
JS3.A257     353/.000021/2     *LC* a 68-7201

**Lumb, R. D.**     **4.8832**
The constitutions of the Australian states / [by] R. D. Lumb. — 4th ed. — St. Lucia, Q.: University of Queensland Press, 1977. 136 p.; 22 cm. Distributed in the United Kingdom by Prentice-Hall International, Hemel Hempstead, Eng. 1. Constitutions, State — Australia. I. T.
JS 10.3 A8 L95 1977     *LC* 77-362698     *ISBN* 0702214523

**Maass, Arthur. ed.**  •  **4.8833**
Area and power: a theory of local government / by Arthur Maass, editor, Paul Ylvisaker and others. — Glencoe, Ill.: Free Press, 1959. 224 p.; 22 cm. 1. Local government 2. Federal government I. T.
JS50.M2     *LC* 58-12850

**Abbott, Frank Frost, 1860-1924.**     **4.8834**
Municipal administration in the Roman Empire / by Frank Frost Abbott and Allan Chester Johnson. — Princeton: Princeton University Press, 1926. vii, 598 p.; 22 cm. Includes index. 'Municipal documents in Greek and Latinfrom Italy and the provinces'. 'Documents from Eygept': p. [247]. 1. Municipal government — Rome I. Johnson, Allan Chester, 1881-1955. II. T.
JS58.A2 1968     352/.008/0937     *LC* 27-20582

**Pirenne, Henri, 1862-1935.**     **4.8835**
Medieval cities, their origins and the revival of trade. Tr. from the French by Frank D. Halsey. — Princeton, Princeton Univ. Press [1969, c1952] 253 p. 21 cm. 'First Princeton paperback printing, 1969.' 1. Cities and towns, Medieval 2. Commerce — Hist. I. T.
JS61.P5 1969     *LC* 25-15374

**Steinberger, Peter J., 1948-.**     **4.8836**
Ideology and the urban crisis / Peter J. Steinberger. — Albany: State University of New York Press, c1985. ix, 175 p.; 24 cm. (SUNY series in urban public policy) Includes index. 1. Urban policy 2. Ideology I. T.
JS91.S73 1985     320.8 19     *LC* 84-8637     *ISBN* 0873959566

# JS300–1565 United States

## JS300–403 Local, Municipal Government

**The County year book.**     **4.8837**
v. 1-4; 1975-78. Washington: National Association of Counties. v. 32 cm. Annual. 'The authoritative source book on county governments.' 1. County government — Yearbooks. I. National Association of Counties. II. International City Management Association.
JS301.C67     352/.0073/0973     *LC* 75-646784

**Allswang, John M.**     **4.8838**
Bosses, machines, and urban voters: an American symbiosis / John M. Allswang. — Port Washington, N.Y.: Kennikat Press, 1977. ix, 157 p.; 23 cm. — (Interdisciplinary urban series) (National university publications) Includes index. 1. Municipal government — United States — History. 2. Politicians — United States — History. I. T.
JS309.A37     352.073     *LC* 77-6299     *ISBN* 0804691940

**Teaford, Jon C.**     **4.8839**
The municipal revolution in America: origins of modern urban government, 1650–1825 / Jon C. Teaford. — Chicago: University of Chicago Press, 1975. viii, 152 p.; 22 cm. Includes index. 1. Municipal government — United States — History. I. T.
JS309.T4     352/.008/0973     *LC* 74-33512     *ISBN* 0226791653

**Town and county: essays on the structure of local government in**     **4.8840**
**the American colonies** / edited by Bruce C. Daniels.
1st ed. — Middletown, Conn.: Wesleyan University Press, c1978. xiv, 279 p.; 23 cm. 1. Local government — United States — History — Addresses, essays, lectures. I. Daniels, Bruce Colin.
JS311.T68     352.073     *LC* 77-14834     *ISBN* 0819550205

**Dorsett, Lyle W.**     **4.8841**
Franklin D. Roosevelt and the city bosses / Lyle W. Dorsett. — Port Washington, N.Y.: Kennikat Press, 1977. x, 134 p.; 23 cm. (Interdisciplinary urban series) (National university publications) Includes index. 1. Roosevelt, Franklin D. (Franklin Delano), 1882-1945. 2. Municipal government — United States — History. 3. United States — Politics and government — 1933-1945 I. T.
JS323.D64     329/.0211     *LC* 77-2657     *ISBN* 080469186X. *ISBN* 0804692033 pbk

**State and local government: the political economy of reform** /     **4.8842**
**edited by Alan K. Campbell and Roy W. Bahl.**
New York: Free Press, c1976. x, 211 p.; 24 cm. 1. Local government — United States — Addresses, essays, lectures. 2. Municipal services — United States — Addresses, essays, lectures. 3. State governments — Addresses, essays, lectures. I. Campbell, Alan K. II. Bahl, Roy W.
JS323.S78     352.073     *LC* 75-43361     *ISBN* 0029051800

**Banfield, Edward C.**  •  **4.8843**
City politics [by] Edward C. Banfield [and] James Q. Wilson. — Cambridge: Harvard University Press, 1963. 362 p.: illus.; 25 cm. — (Publications of the Joint Center for Urban Studies of the Massachusetts Institute of Technology and Harvard University) 1. Municipal government — United States. I. Wilson, James Q. joint author. II. T.
JS331.B28     352.073     *LC* 63-19134

**Liebert, Roland J.**     **4.8844**
Disintegration and political action: the changing functions of city governments in America / by Roland J. Liebert. — New York: Academic Press, c1976. xii, 223 p.; 24 cm. (Quantitative studies in social relations series) Includes indexes. 1. Municipal government — United States. I. T.
JS331.L53 1976     352/.008/0973     *LC* 75-36651     *ISBN* 0124496504

**Martin, David L.**     **4.8845**
Running city hall: municipal administration in America / David L. Martin. — University, Ala.: University of Alabama Press, c1982. viii, 201 p.: ill.; 24 cm. 1. Municipal government — United States. I. T.
JS331.M287 1982     352/.00724/0973 19     *LC* 81-14646     *ISBN* 0817301542

**Rapp, Brian W.**     **4.8846**
Managing local government for improved performance: a practical approach / Brian W. Rapp, Frank M. Patitucci. — Boulder, CO: Westview Press, 1977. xxii, 422 p.; 26 cm. 1. Municipal government — United States. 2. Flint (Mich.) — Politics and government. I. Patitucci, Frank M., joint author. II. T.
JS331.R27     352/.008/0973     *LC* 76-25240     *ISBN* 0891581219

**Colman, William G.**     **4.8847**
Cities, suburbs, and states: governing and financing urban America / William G. Colman. — New York: Free Press, [1975] xi, 350 p.: ill.; 24 cm. 1. Municipal government — United States. 2. Municipal finance — United States. 3. Metropolitan areas — United States I. T.
JS341.C65     352/.008/0973     *LC* 75-2810     *ISBN* 0029064902

**Peterson, Paul E.**     **4.8848**
City limits / Paul E. Peterson. — Chicago: University of Chicago Press, 1981. xvi, 268 p.; 24 cm. Includes index. 1. Municipal government — United States. 2. Federal-city relations — United States. I. T.
JS341.P47     320.8/0973 19     *LC* 80-29043     *ISBN* 0226662926

**Yates, Douglas, 1944-.**     **4.8849**
The ungovernable city: the politics of urban problems and policy making / Douglas Yates. — Cambridge, Mass.: MIT Press, c1977. xvi, 219 p.; 24 cm. — (MIT studies in American politics and public policy. 3) 1. Municipal government — United States. 2. Policy sciences I. T. II. Series.
JS341.Y38     352/.008/0973     *LC* 77-11201     *ISBN* 0262240203

**The Municipal year book.**  •  **4.8850**
1st- ed; 1934-. Washington [etc.] International City Management Association. v. 25-32 cm. Annual. Vols. for 1971- < 84 > do not carry edition designations. 1. Municipal government — United States — Yearbooks. 2. Municipal government by city manager — Yearbooks. I. Ridley, Clarence Eugene, 1891- ed. II. Nolting, Orin Frederyc, 1903- ed. III. International City Management Association. IV. International City Managers' Association.
JS344.C5 A24     *LC* 34-27121

**Stillman, Richard Joseph, 1943-.**     **4.8851**
The rise of the city manager: a public professional in local government / Richard J. Stillman, II. — 1st ed. — Albuquerque: University of New Mexico

Press, [c1974] 170 p.: ill.; 25 cm. Includes index. 1. Municipal government by city manager — United States. I. T.
JS344.C5 S743        352/.0084/0973        LC 74-80742        ISBN 0826303390

**National Municipal League. Advisory committee on the Revision** • **4.8852**
**of the Model City Charter.**
Model city charter. — 6th ed. — New York: National Municipal League, 1964. 76 p. 1. Municipal government — United States. 2. Municipal charters — United States. I. T.
JS354.N3 1964        LC 64-4186

**Ferman, Barbara.**                                                                          **4.8853**
Governing the ungovernable city: political skill, leadership, and the modern mayor / Barbara Ferman. — Philadelphia: Temple University Press, 1985. xii, 281 p.: ill.; 24 cm. Includes index. 1. Mayors — United States 2. Municipal government — United States. I. T.
JS356.F47 1985        352/.0083/0973 19        LC 84-16375        ISBN 0877223769

**Heilig, Peggy, 1942-.**                                                                     **4.8854**
Your voice at city hall: the politics, procedures, and policies of district representation / Peggy Heilig and Robert J. Mundt. — Albany: State University of New York Press, c1984. vii, 171 p.; 24 cm. (SUNY series in urban public policy) Includes indexes. 1. Local elections — United States. 2. Election districts — United States. 3. City council members — United States. 4. Municipal government — United States. I. Mundt, Robert J. II. T.
JS395.H44 1984        324.6/3 19        LC 83-24287        ISBN 0873958217

**Nelson, William E., 1941-.**                                                               **4.8855**
Electing Black mayors; political action in the Black community / William E. Nelson, Jr. and Philip J. Meranto. — Columbus: Ohio State University Press, c1977. 403 p.; 24 cm. 1. Afro-American mayors — Case studies. 2. Afro-Americans — Politics and government — Case studies. 3. Elections — Ohio — Cleveland. 4. Elections — Illinois — East St. Louis. 5. Elections — Indiana — Gary. I. Meranto, Philip J., joint author. II. T.
JS395.N45        329/.023/730923        LC 76-51347        ISBN 0814202705

## JS411–423 Counties. Metropolitan Areas

**Duncombe, Herbert Sydney.**                                                                **4.8856**
Modern county government / Herbert Sydney Duncombe. — Washington: National Association of Counties, c1977. xv, 280 p.: ill.; 24 cm. Includes index. 1. County government — United States. I. T.
JS411.D83        352/.0073/0973        LC 77-80607        ISBN 0911754016

**Torrence, Susan Walker.**                                                                  **4.8857**
Grass roots government; the county in American politics. — Washington: R. B. Luce, [1974] ix, 243 p.: illus.; 23 cm. 1. County government — United States. I. T.
JS411.T67        352/.0073/0973        LC 72-97709        ISBN 0883310279

**Harrigan, John J.**                                                                        **4.8858**
Political change in the metropolis / John J. Harrigan. — Boston: Little, Brown, c1976. xiv, 450 p.; 23 cm. 1. Metropolitan government — United States. 2. Municipal government — United States. 3. Metropolitan areas — United States I. T.
JS422.H33        320.8/0973 19        LC 75-26032

**Mogulof, Melvin B.**                                                                       **4.8859**
Governing metropolitan areas; a critical review of council of governments and the Federal role [by] Melvin B. Mogulof. — Washington: Urban Institute, [c1971] 127 p.; 22 cm. 1. Metropolitan government — United States. I. T.
JS422.M64        352/.0094/0973        LC 76-186305        ISBN 0877660212

**Wikstrom, Nelson.**                                                                        **4.8860**
Councils of governments: a study of political incrementalism / Nelson Wikstrom. Chicago: Nelson-Hall, c1977. xiv, 173 p.: ill.; 23 cm. Includes index. 1. Metropolitan government — United States. I. T.
JS422.W5        352/.0094/0973        LC 76-28784        ISBN 0882293222

**Murphy, Thomas P., 1931-.**                                                                **4.8861**
Urban politics in the suburban era / Thomas P. Murphy, John Rehfuss. — Homewood, Ill.: Dorsey Press, 1976. xvii, 285 p.: ill.; 23 cm. (The Dorsey series in political science) 1. Metropolitan government — United States. 2. Suburbs — United States I. Rehfuss, John, joint author. II. T.
JS423.M87        320.9/73/092        LC 76-363904        ISBN 0256018480

## JS431–451 Regions. States
(State Government: see: JK2403-9600)

**Wellstone, Paul David.**                                                                   **4.8862**
How the rural poor got power: narrative of a grass–roots organizer / Paul David Wellstone. — Amherst: University of Massachusetts Press, 1978. xi, 227 p.; 24 cm. 1. Organization for a Better Rice County. 2. Political participation — Minnesota — Rice Co. 3. Rural poor — Minnesota — Rice Co. 4. Rice County (Minn.) — Politics and government. I. T.
JS451.M69 R58 1978        320.9/776/555        LC 77-22109        ISBN 0870232495

## JS504–1583 Cities, A–Z

**Elazar, Daniel Judah.**                                                                    **4.8863**
The politics of Belleville; a profile of the civil community [by] Daniel J. Elazar. — Philadelphia: Temple University Press, [1972] ix, 165 p.: maps (on lining papers); 22 cm. 1. Belleville (Ill.) — Politics and government. I. T.
JS593.B736 E4        320.9/773/89        LC 70-182890        ISBN 0877220131

**Harris, Carl Vernon, 1937-.**                                                              **4.8864**
Political power in Birmingham, 1871–1921 / by Carl V. Harris. — 1st ed. — Knoxville: University of Tennessee Press, c1977. xvi, 318 p., [8] leaves of plates: ill.; 24 cm. — (Twentieth-century America series) Includes index. 1. Political participation — Alabama — Birmingham — History. 2. Pressure groups — Alabama — Birmingham — History. 3. Birmingham (Ala.) — Politics and government. I. T.
JS598.2.H37        320.9/761/78106        LC 77-1110        ISBN 087049211X

**Kahn, Melvin, 1930-.**                                                                     **4.8865**
The winning ticket: Daley, the Chicago machine, and Illinois politics / by Melvin A. Kahn and Frances J. Majors. — New York: Praeger, 1984. xx, 280 p. — (American political parties and elections.) 'Copublished with the Eagleton Institute of Politics, Rutgers University.' 1. Daley, Richard J., 1902-1976. 2. Nominations for office — Illinois — Chicago. 3. Chicago (Ill.) — Politics and government — 1951- I. Majors, Frances J. II. T. III. Series.
JS708.K27 1984        320.8/09773/11 19        LC 83-24727        ISBN 0030692989

**The Making of the mayor, Chicago, 1983 / editors, Melvin G.**              **4.8866**
**Holli and Paul M. Green.**
Grand Rapids, Mich.: Eerdmans Pub. Co., c1984. xvii, 172 p., [24] p. of plates: ill.; 22 cm. 1. Washington, Harold, 1922-1987 — Addresses, essays, lectures. 2. Mayors — Illinois — Chicago — Election — Addresses, essays, lectures. 3. Elections — Illinois — Chicago — Addresses, essays, lectures. 4. Chicago (Ill.) — Politics and government — 1951- — Addresses, essays, lectures. I. Holli, Melvin G. II. Green, Paul Michael.
JS718.3.M34 1984        324.9773/11043 19        LC 84-5998        ISBN 0802870473

**Tucker, David M., 1937-.**                                                                 **4.8867**
Memphis since Crump: bossism, Blacks, and civic reformers, 1948–1968 / by David M. Tucker. — 1st ed. — Knoxville: University of Tennessee Press, c1980. xvii, 183 p.: ill.; 22 cm. Includes index. 1. Afro-Americans — Memphis — Politics and government. 2. Urban renewal — Tennessee — Memphis. 3. Memphis (Tenn.) — Politics and government. I. T.
JS1092.T8        320.9/768/19        LC 79-12211        ISBN 0870492829

**Dahl, Robert Alan, 1915-.**                                                       • **4.8868**
Who governs?: democracy and power in an American city. — New Haven: Yale University Press, 1961. xii, 355 p.: diagrs., tables; 25 cm. (Yale studies in political science. 4) 1. Municipal government — United States — Case studies. 2. Community power — Case studies. 3. New Haven (Conn.) — Politics and government. I. T. II. Series.
JS1195.2.D2        320.9/746/804        LC 61-16913

**Polsby, Nelson W.**                                                                        **4.8869**
Community power and political theory: a further look at problems of evidence and inference / Nelson W. Polsby. — 2d enl. ed. — New Haven: Yale University Press, 1980. xxvi, 245 p.; 24 cm. 'First edition published as volume 7 in the Yale Studies in Political Science.' 1. Municipal government — United States — Case studies. 2. Community power — Case studies. 3. Social classes — United States. 4. New Haven (Conn.) — Politics and government. I. T.
JS1195.2.P6 1980        301.44/92/0973        LC 79-22966        ISBN 0300024452

**Katznelson, Ira.**                                                                         **4.8870**
City trenches: urban politics and the patterning of class in the United States / Ira Katznelson. — 1st ed. — New York: Pantheon Books, c1981. xiv, 267 p.: maps; 24 cm. 1. Neighborhood government — United States — Case studies. 2. Washington Heights (New York, N.Y.) — Politics and government. 3. Washington Heights (New York, N.Y.) — Social conditions. I. T.
JS1240.W37 K37        320.8/09747/1 19        LC 81-47197        ISBN 039450075X

**Zisk, Betty H., 1930-.** **4.8871**
Local interest politics; a one–way street [by] Betty H. Zisk. Indianapolis, Bobbs-Merrill [1973] xv, 184 p. illus. 21 cm. (Urban governors series.) 1. City council members — California — San Francisco Bay Area. 2. Pressure groups — California — San Francisco Bay Area. I. T. II. Series.
JS1445.A3 Z57    322.4/3/097946    *LC* 77-186245    *ISBN* 0672514923

## JS1701–1819 Canada

**Higgins, Donald J. H., 1943-.** **4.8872**
Urban Canada: its government and politics / Donald J. H. Higgins. — Toronto: Macmillan of Canada, c1977. 322 p.; 23 cm. Includes index. 1. Municipal government — Canada. I. T.
JS1708.H53    352/.008/0971    *LC* 78-315645    *ISBN* 0770516157

## JS3001–6959 Europe

**Jewell, Helen M.** **4.8873**
English local administration in the Middle Ages, [by] Helen M. Jewell. — Newton Abbot: David and Charles; New York: Barnes & Noble Books, 1973 (c1972). 238 p.; 23 cm. 1. Local government — England — History. I. T.
JS3041.J48    352.042    *LC* 73-153472

**Richards, Peter G.** **4.8874**
The reformed local government system / by Peter G. Richards. — 3d ed., rev. — London; Boston: G. Allen & Unwin, 1978. 192 p.; 22 cm. — (New local government series; 5) Includes index. 1. Local government — Great Britain. I. T.
JS3095 1978.R5 1978    352.042    *LC* 78-319616    *ISBN* 0043520685

**Alexander, Alan, 1943-.** **4.8875**
Local government in Britain since reorganisation / Alan Alexander. — London; Boston: G. Allen & Unwin, 1982. ix, 191 p.; 23 cm. — (The New local government series; no. 23) Includes index. 1. Local government — Great Britain. I. T.
JS3095 1982.A39    352.041 19    *LC* 82-1793    *ISBN* 0043521002

**Keith-Lucas, Bryan.** **4.8876**
A history of local government in the twentieth century / by Bryan Keith–Lucas and Peter G. Richards. — London; Boston: G. Allen & Unwin, 1978. 266 p.; 23 cm. — (The New local government series; no. 17) Includes indexes. 1. Local government — Great Britain. I. Richards, Peter G. joint author. II. T.
JS3111.K44    352.041    *LC* 77-30536    *ISBN* 0043520707

**Kesselman, Mark.** • **4.8877**
The ambiguous consensus: a study of local government in France. — New York: Knopf, [1967] xii, 201, v p.; 22 cm. 1. Local government — France 2. France — Politics and government — 1945- I. T.
JS4881.K4    352/.000942    *LC* 67-20625

**Chapman, Brian.** • **4.8878**
Introduction to French local government. London: Allen & Unwin [1953] 238 p.: ill.; 22 cm. 1. Local government — France I. T. II. Title: French local government
JS4883 C45    *LC* 53-3043

**Fried, Robert C.** • **4.8879**
The Italian prefects: a study in administrative politics. — New Haven: Yale University Press, 1963. xix, 343 p.: maps, tables; 23 cm. (Yale studies in political science. 6) 1. Local government — Italy I. T. II. Series.
JS5738 F7    *LC* 63-13960

**Taubman, William.** **4.8880**
Governing Soviet cities; bureaucratic politics and urban development in the USSR. New York, Praeger [1973] xvii, 166 p. 25 cm. (Praeger special studies in international economics and development) 'Sponsored by the Russian Institute of Columbia University.' 1. Municipal government — Soviet Union. I. Columbia University. Russian Institute. II. T.
JS6058.T36    320.4    *LC* 72-92474

**Anton, Thomas Julius.** **4.8881**
Governing greater Stockholm: a study of policy development and system change / by Thomas J. Anton. — Berkeley: Published for the Institute of Governmental Studies [by] University of California Press, [1975] xxii, 237 p.: maps; 25 cm. (Lane studies in regional government.) 1. City planning —

Sweden — Stockholm. 2. Urbanization — Sweden — Stockholm. 3. Stockholm (Sweden) — Politics and government. I. T. II. Series.
JS6272.A84    352/.008/09487    *LC* 73-94447    *ISBN* 0520027183

## JS7001–7819 Asia. Africa

**Heginbotham, Stanley J.** **4.8882**
Cultures in conflict: the four faces of Indian bureaucracy / Stanley J. Heginbotham. — New York: Columbia University Press, 1975. xii, 236 p.; 23 cm. Includes index. 1. Bureaucracy 2. Local officials and employees — Tamil Nadu. 3. Community development — Tamil Nadu. 4. Tamil Nadu (India) — Social conditions. I. T.
JS7025.T33 A43    354/.54/8201    *LC* 74-31206    *ISBN* 0231038887

**Jones, Rodney W.** **4.8883**
Urban politics in India: area, power, and policy in a penetrated system / Rodney W. Jones. — Berkeley: University of California Press, [1974] xviii, 420 p.; 25 cm. 'Sponsored by the Center for South and Southeast Asia Studies, University of California, Berkeley.' Includes index. 1. Indore (India) — Politics and government. I. T.
JS7065.I52 J65    320.4/54    *LC* 73-83052    *ISBN* 0520025458

**Robinson, Marguerite S.** **4.8884**
Political structure in a changing Sinhalese village / Marguerite S. Robinson. — Cambridge [Eng]; New York: Cambridge University Press, 1975. xvi, 376 p.: ill.; 22 cm. — (Cambridge South Asian studies. 15) Includes index. 1. Local government — Sri Lanka — Case studies. 2. Political participation — Sri Lanka — Case studies. 3. Villages — Sri Lanka — Case studies. I. T. II. Series.
JS7122.R63    320.4/549/3    *LC* 74-31806    *ISBN* 0521203740

**Caplan, Lionel.** **4.8885**
Administration and politics in a Nepalese town: the study of a district capital and its environs / Lionel Caplan. London; New York: Oxford University Press, 1975. xiv, 266 p.: maps; 22 cm. Includes indexes. 1. Local government — Nepal — Case studies. I. T.
JS7180.2.C36    352.0549/6    *LC* 76-383279    *ISBN* 0197135854

**Ch'ü, T'ung-tsu.** • **4.8886**
Local government in China under the Ch'ing. Cambridge, Mass.: Harvard University Press, 1962. xiv, 360, L p.: tables; 24 cm. (Harvard East Asian studies, 9) 1. Local government — China I. T. II. Series.
JS7352 A3 C5    *LC* 62-11396

**McKnight, Brian E.** **4.8887**
Village and bureaucracy in Southern Sung China [by] Brian E. McKnight. — Chicago: University of Chicago Press, [1972, c1971] xi, 219 p.; 23 cm. 1. Villages — China. 2. Local government — China. 3. China — History — Sung dynasty, 960-1279 I. T.
JS7352.A3 M3    352.051    *LC* 72-159834    *ISBN* 0226560597

**Shih, Ch'êng-chih.** • **4.8888**
Urban commune experiments in Communist China. [1st ed.] Hong Kong Union Research Institute [1962] 167p. (Communist China problem research series, EC28) 1. Communes (China) I. T. II. Series.
JS7352 S48

**Watt, John Robertson, 1934-.** **4.8889**
The district magistrate in late imperial China [by] John R. Watt. New York, Columbia University Press, 1972. x, 340 p. 23 cm. (Studies of the East Asian Institute) A revision of the author's thesis, Columbia. 1. County government — China. 2. China — Politics and government — 1644-1912 I. T.
JS7353.A8 W35 1972    354/.51    *LC* 79-187299    *ISBN* 0231035357

**Teiwes, Frederick C.** • **4.8890**
Provincial party personnel in mainland China, 1956–1966 [by] Frederick C. Teiwes. — New York: East Asian Institute, Columbia University, [1967] vi, 114 p.; 23 cm. — (Occasional papers of the East Asian Institute, Columbia University) 1. Chung-kuo kung ch'an tang. 2. Local officials and employees — China. I. T.
JS7354.A4 T4    352/.000951    *LC* 66-30779

**Political opposition and local politics in Japan / edited by Kurt** **4.8891**
**Steiner, Ellis S. Krauss, and Scott C. Flanagan.**
Princeton, N.J.: Princeton University Press, 1981 (c1980). ix, 486 p.: ill.; 24 cm. Based on a conference sponsored by the Joint Committee on Japanese Studies of the American Council of Learned Societies and the Social Science Research Council. 1. Local government — Japan — Congresses. 2. Opposition (Political science) — Japan — Congresses. I. Steiner, Kurt, 1912- II. Krauss, Ellis S. III. Flanagan, Scott C. IV. Joint Committee on Japanese Studies.
JS7372.P64    320.8/0952    *LC* 80-7555    *ISBN* 0691076251

**Ruellan, André.**     ● **4.8892**
Local government in Japan. Stanford, Calif., Stanford University Press, 1965.
ix, 564 p. 1. Local government — Japan I. T.
JS7372 S7     *LC* 64-17005

**Hall, John Whitney, 1916-.**     ● **4.8893**
Government and local power in Japan, 500 to 1700: a study based on Bizen
Province. — Princeton, N.J.: Princeton University Press, 1966. x, 446 p.: ill.,
maps; 25 cm. 1. Bizen, Japan (Flef) — Politics and government 2. Local
government — Japan — Case studies I. T.
JS7384 B5 H3     *LC* 65-14307

---

## JV1–5299 COLONIES. IMPERIALISM

---

## JV61–485 History. Administration

**Parry, J. H. (John Horace), 1914-.**     ● **4.8894**
The establishment of the European hegemony, 1415–1715: trade and
exploration in the age of the Renaissance / by J.H. Parry. New York: Harper &
Row, 1963? 202 p. Harper torchbook 1. Colonization — History.
2. Commerce — History I. T.
JV61.P37 1963?     *LC* 65-7512

**Graham, Alexander John.**     **4.8895**
Colony and mother city in ancient Greece, by A. J. Graham. New York: Barnes
& Noble, [1964] xviii, 259 p. 23 cm. 1. Greece — Colonies 2. Greece —
Politics and government I. T.
JV93 G68     *LC* 64-57919

**Betts, Raymond F.**     **4.8896**
The false dawn: European imperialism in the nineteenth century / by Raymond
F. Betts. — Minneapolis: University of Minnesota Press, c1975. xxi, 270 p.: ill.;
24 cm. — (Europe and the world in the Age of Expansion. v. 6) Includes index.
1. Colonies — History. 2. Imperialism — History. I. T. II. Series.
JV105.B47 1975     325/.34     *LC* 75-14683     *ISBN* 0816607621

**Fieldhouse, D. K. (David Kenneth), 1925-.**     ● **4.8897**
The colonial empires; a comparative survey from the eighteenth century, by D.
K. Fieldhouse. [1st American ed.] New York, Delacorte Press [1967, c1966]
xiii, 450 p. illus., maps. 24 cm. (Delacorte world history, v. 29) 1. Colonies —
History. I. T.
JV105.F5 1967     325.309     *LC* 66-23091

**Fieldhouse, D. K. (David Kenneth), 1925-.**     **4.8898**
Colonialism, 1870–1945: an introduction / D. K. Fieldhouse. — New York: St.
Martin's Press, 1981. 151 p.; 23 cm. Includes index. 1. Colonies — History.
I. T.
JV105.F519 1981     325/.3/09 19     *LC* 80-26206     *ISBN* 0312150741

**Fieldhouse, D. K. (David Kenneth), 1925-.**     **4.8899**
Economics and empire, 1830–1914 / D.K. Fieldhouse. — London: Macmillan,
1984. 531 p.: ill., maps; 22 cm. Includes index. 1. Imperialism 2. Economic
history — 1750-1918 I. T.
JV105.F52x 1984     *LC* 84-673314     *ISBN* 0333368274

**Davies, Kenneth Gordon.**     **4.8900**
The North Atlantic world in the seventeenth century / by K. G. Davies. —
Minneapolis: University of Minnesota Press, [1974] xiv, 366 p.: maps; 24 cm. —
(Europe and the world in the Age of Expansion. v. 4) Includes index.
1. Colonies — History. 2. Colonization — History. I. T. II. Series.
JV131.D38 1974     325/.34     *LC* 74-78994     *ISBN* 0816607133

**Ganiage, Jean.**     ● **4.8901**
L'expansion coloniale et les rivalités internationales de 1871 à 1914. Paris,
Centre de documentation universitaire [1964] 3 v. in 1. maps (1 fold.) (Les
Cours de Sorbonne) 1. Colonies — History I. T.
JV145 G3

**Holland, R. F. (Roy Fraser), 1932-.**     **4.8902**
European decolonization, 1918–1981: an introductory survey / R.F. Holland.
— New York: St. Martin's Press, 1985. xiv, 321 p.: maps; 23 cm. Includes
index. 1. Decolonization — History. 2. Europe — Colonies — History — 20th
century. I. T.
JV151.H65 1985     325/.34/09 19     *LC* 84-17980     *ISBN* 0312270607

**Parry, J. H. (John Horace), 1914-.**     **4.8903**
Trade and dominion: the European overseas empires in the eighteenth century
[by] J. H. Parry. New York, Praeger [1971] xvii, 408 p. illus. 25 cm. (Praeger
history of civilization) 1. Colonies — History. 2. Colonies — Commerce.
3. Colonies — Administration I. T.
JV165.P35     325.3/09/033     *LC* 76-100940

**Imperialism: the Robinson and Gallagher controversy / edited**     **4.8904**
**with an introd. by Wm. Roger Louis.**
New York: New Viewpoints, 1976. 252 p.; 22 cm. (Modern scholarship on
European history) Includes index. 1. Gallagher, John, 1919- 2. Robinson,
Ronald Edward, 1920- 3. Colonies in Africa. 4. Imperialism I. Louis, William
Roger, 1936- II. Robinson, Ronald Edward, 1920- III. Gallagher, John, 1919-
JV246.I43     325/.341/096     *LC* 75-26730     *ISBN* 053105375X

**Kiernan, V. G. (Victor Gordon), 1913-.**     ● **4.8905**
The lords of human kind; black man, yellow man, and white man in an age of
empire [by] V. G. Kiernan. [1st American ed.] Boston, Little, Brown [1969]
336 p. illus. 22 cm. 1. Native races 2. Colonies I. T.
JV305.K53 1969b     325.3     *LC* 76-79357

**Maunier, René, 1887-.**     ● **4.8906**
The sociology of colonies; an introduction to the study of race contact. Edited
and translated by E.O. Lorimer. London, Routledge & K. Paul [1949] 2 v. (xii,
767 p.) (International library of sociology and social reconstruction (London)
(International library of sociology and social reconstruction) 1. Colonization
2. Race relations 3. Native races 4. Imperialism I. T. II. Series.
JV305 M314

**Albertini, Rudolf von.**     ● **4.8907**
[Dekolonisation; die Diskussion über Verwaltung und Zukunft der Kolonien,
1919-1960. English] Decolonization; the administration and future of the
colonies, 1919–1960. Translated from the German by Francisca Garvie.
Garden City, N.Y., Doubleday, 1971. xii, 680 p. 25 cm. Translation of
Dekolonisation; die Diskussion über Verwaltung und Zukunft der Kolonien,
1919-1960. 1. Colonies — Administration — History. 2. Decolonization —
History. I. T.
JV308.A6513     325/.31/09 19     *LC* 79-144264

**Birnberg, Thomas B.**     **4.8908**
Colonial development: an econometric study / Thomas B. Birnberg and
Stephen A. Resnick. — New Haven: Yale University Press, 1975. xiii, 347 p.; 25
cm. (A Publication of the Economic Growth Center, Yale University) Includes
index. 1. Colonies — Administration 2. Colonies — Economic conditions.
I. Resnick, Stephen A. joint author. II. T.
JV420.B57 1975     338/.09     *LC* 74-20077     *ISBN* 0300018215

---

## JV1000–5299 Colonizing Nations

(United States: see: E179.5)

---

### JV1000–1099 Great Britain

**Beer, George Louis, 1872-1920.**     ● **4.8909**
The origins of the British colonial system, 1578–1660. New York, P. Smith,
1933. 438 p. 1. Tobacco manufacture and trade 2. Great Britain — Colonies
— Administration 3. Great Britain — Colonies — History I. T.
JV1011 B3 1933

**Beer, George Louis, 1872-1920.**     ● **4.8910**
British colonial policy, 1754–1765. New York, P. Smith, 1933. 327 p. 1. Great
Britain — Colonies 2. Great Britain — Colonies — Administration I. T.
JV1011 B5 1933

**Johnston, W. Ross.**     **4.8911**
Great Britain great empire: an evaluation of the British imperial experience /
W. Ross Johnston. — St. Lucia [Brisbane]; New York: University of
Queensland Press, 1981. xvii, 207 p.; 22 cm. — (The University of Queensland
Press scholars' library) 1. Great Britain — Colonies — History I. T.
JV1011.J64     325/.341/09 19     *LC* 81-4576     *ISBN* 0702215767

**Baumgart, Winfried.**     **4.8912**
[Imperialismus. English] Imperialism: the idea and reality of British and
French colonial expansion, 1880–1914 / by Winfried Baumgart; translated by
the author with the assistance of Ben V. Mast; with a preface by Henri
Brunschwig. — Rev. ed. — New York: Oxford University Press, 1982. xi,
239 p.: map; 22 cm. Translation of: Der Imperialismus. Includes index.
1. Imperialism 2. Great Britain — Colonies 3. France — Colonies I. T.
JV1017.B3813 1982     325/.32/09 19     *LC* 81-22434     *ISBN*
0198730411

**Hyam, Ronald.**    **4.8913**
Britain's imperial century, 1815–1914: a study of empire and expansion / Ronald Hyam. New York: Barnes & Noble Books, 1976. 462 p.: maps; 25 cm. 1. Great Britain — Colonies — History I. T.
JV1017.H92 1976b    325/.341    *LC* 75-41555    *ISBN* 0064930998

**Porter, Bernard.**    • **4.8914**
Critics of empire: British Radical attitudes to colonialism in Africa 1895–1914. — London; Melbourne [etc.]: Macmillan; New York: St. Martin's P., 1968. xvi, 369 p.: 4 plates, illus., facsim., ports.; 23 cm. 1. Colonies in Africa. 2. Great Britain — Colonies I. T.
JV1018.P67    325.3/42/096    *LC* 68-20349

**Thornton, A. P. (Archibald Paton)**    • **4.8915**
The imperial idea and its enemies; a study in British power. London, Macmillan, 1959. 370 p. ill. 1. Imperialism 2. Great Britain — Colonies 3. Public opinion — Great Britain I. T.
JV1018 T5    *LC* 59-16163

**Ward, John M.**    **4.8916**
Colonial self–government: the British experience 1759–1856 / John Manning Ward. Toronto; Buffalo: University of Toronto Press, 1976. viii, 399 p.; 23 cm. Includes index. 1. Great Britain — Colonies — Administration I. T.
JV1025.W37 1976b    320.9/171/241    *LC* 76-375082    *ISBN* 0802022030

**Huttenback, Robert A.**    **4.8917**
Racism and Empire: white settlers and colored immigrants in the British self–governing colonies, 1830–1910 / Robert A. Huttenback. — Ithaca: Cornell University Press, 1976. 359 p.; 22 cm. Includes index. 1. Contract labor — Great Britain — Colonies — History. 2. Great Britain — Colonies — Emigration and immigration — History. I. T.
JV1041.H88 1976    325/.341    *LC* 75-30257    *ISBN* 0801409748

**Halstead, John P.**    **4.8918**
The second British Empire: trade, philanthropy, and good government, 1820–1890 / John P. Halstead. — Westport, Conn.: Greenwood Press, 1983. xiii, 261 p.: maps; 22 cm. — (Contributions in comparative colonial studies. 0163-3813; no. 14) Includes index. 1. Great Britain — Colonies — Administration — History — 19th century. 2. Great Britain — Colonies — Commerce — History — 19th century. 3. Great Britain — Foreign relations — 19th century I. T. II. Series.
JV1060.H34 1983    325/.341/09 19    *LC* 82-20965    *ISBN* 0313235198

**Low, D. A. (Donald Anthony), 1927-.**    **4.8919**
Lion rampant: essays in the study of British imperialism / [by] D. A. Low. — London: Cass, 1973. x, 230 p.; 23 cm. — (Studies in Commonwealth politics and history, no. 1) 1. Great Britain — Colonies — Administration I. T.
JV1060.L68 1973    325/.342    *LC* 72-92970    *ISBN* 0714629863

**Robinson, Kenneth, 1914- ed.**    • **4.8920**
Essays in imperial government. Presented to Margery Perham by Kenneth Robinson and Frederick Madden. Oxford, B. Blackwell, 1963. viii, 293 p. port. 1. Great Britain — Colonies — Administration I. Madden, A. F. II. Perham, Margery Freda, 1896- III. T.
JV1060 R6    *LC* 64-2878

**Webb, Stephen Saunders, 1937-.**    **4.8921**
The Governors–General: the English Army and the definition of the Empire, 1569–1681 / by Stephen Saunders Webb. — Chapel Hill: Published for the Institute of Early American History and Culture, Williamsburg, Va., by the University of North Carolina Press, c1979. xxi, 549 p.: ill.; 25 cm. 1. Military government of dependencies 2. Great Britain — Colonies — Administration I. T.
JV1061.W4    325/.31/0941    *LC* 78-8746    *ISBN* 0807813311

## JV1800–1899 France

**Weinstein, Brian.**    **4.8922**
Eboué. New York, Oxford University Press, 1972. xiii, 350 p. illus. 21 cm. 1. Eboué, Félix, 1884-1944. I. T.
JV1809.E3 W44    967/.4103/0924 B    *LC* 70-173329

**Brunschwig, Henri, 1904-.**    • **4.8923**
French colonialism, 1871–1914: myths and realities / Henri Brunschwig; introd. by Ronald E. Robinson. — New York: Praeger, 1966. x, 228 p.: ill. 1. France — Colonies — History. I. T.
JV1817.B743 1966a    *LC* 65-20084

**Murphy, Agnes, 1912-.**    • **4.8924**
The ideology of French imperialism, 1871–1881. — New York: H. Fertig, 1968 [c1948] viii, 241 p.; 24 cm. 1. Imperialism 2. France — Colonies — History. I. T.
JV1817.M8 1968    325.3/44    *LC* 67-24590

**Power, Thomas Francis, 1916-.**    • **4.8925**
Jules Ferry and the renaissance of French imperialism / by Thomas F. Power. — New York: Octagon Books, 1966. x, 222 p. 1. Ferry, Jules, 1832-1893. 2. Imperialism 3. France — Colonies — History. I. T.
JV1817.P6 1966    *LC* 66-18042

**Delavignette, Robert Louis, 1897-.**    **4.8926**
Robert Delavignette on the French Empire: selected writings / edited by William B. Cohen, with the assistance of Adelle Rosenzweig; selections translated by Camille Garnier. — Chicago: University of Chicago Press, 1977. x, 148 p.: ill.; 25 cm. — (Studies in imperialism) Includes index. 1. France — Colonies — History. 2. France — Colonies — Administration I. Cohen, William B., 1941- II. Rosenzweig, Adelle. III. T.
JV1818.D4    325/.344    *LC* 77-1339    *ISBN* 0226141918

**Sorum, Paul Clay, 1943-.**    **4.8927**
Intellectuals and decolonization in France / by Paul Clay Sorum. — Chapel Hill: University of North Carolina Press, c1977. xiv, 305 p.; 24 cm. Includes index. 1. Intellectuals — France. 2. Decolonization 3. France — Colonies I. T.
JV1818.S67    325/.344    *LC* 76-56186    *ISBN* 0807812951

**Betts, Raymond F.**    • **4.8928**
Assimilation and association in French colonial theory, 1890–1914 [by] Raymond F. Betts. — [New York: AMS Press, 1970, c1960] ix, 224 p.; 23 cm. — (Columbia University studies in the social sciences, 604) 1. France — Colonies — Administration 2. France — Colonies — Native races. I. T.
JV1837.B4 1970b    325.3/44    *LC* 70-130622    *ISBN* 0404516041

## JV2000–2099 Germany

**Smith, Woodruff D.**    **4.8929**
The German colonial empire / by Woodruff D. Smith. — Chapel Hill: University of North Carolina Press, c1978. xiii, 274 p. Includes index. 1. Germany — Colonies — History. 2. Germany — Politics and government — 1871-1918 I. T.
JV2011.S63    JV2011 S63.    325/.343    *LC* 77-18155    *ISBN* 0807813222

**Taylor, A. J. P. (Alan John Percivale), 1906-.**    • **4.8930**
Germany's first bid for colonies, 1884–1885; a move in Bismarck's European policy, by A. J. P. Taylor. New York, Norton [1970] v, 103 p. 20 cm. (Norton library) Reprint of the 1938 ed. 1. Bismarck, Otto, Fürst von, 1815-1898. 2. Germany — Colonies. 3. Germany — Foreign relations — 1871- 4. Europe — Politics and government — 1871-1918 I. T.
JV2017.T3 1970    325.43    *LC* 76-20028    *ISBN* 0393005305

**Henderson, W. O. (William Otto), 1904-.**    • **4.8931**
Studies in German colonial history. — Chicago, Quadrangle Books [1962] 150 p. illus. 23 cm. 1. Germany — Colonies. I. T.
JV2027.H54    325.343    *LC* 62-15843

**Oxford University British commonwealth group.**    • **4.8932**
Germany's colonial demands; edited from the reports of the Oxford University British commonwealth group by A. L. C. Bullock; with a concluding chapter by Vincent Harlow ... — London, Oxford University press, H. Milford, 1939. viii, [4], 274 p., 1 l. illus. (maps) fold. tables. 19 cm. Map on lining-paper. 1. Germany — Colonies. 2. World War, 1914-1918 — Territorial questions. 3. Mandates 4. Africa — Politics. 5. Versailles, Treaty of, June 28, 1949 (Germany) I. Bullock, Alan Louis Charles, ed. II. Harlow, Vincent Todd, 1898- III. T.
JV2027.O9    325.343    *LC* 40-1248

**Schmokel, Wolfe W.**    • **4.8933**
Dream of empire: German colonialism, 1919–1945. New Haven, Yale University Press, 1964. xiv, 204 p. ill. (Yale historical publications. Miscellany 78) 1. Germany — Colonies I. T.
JV2027 S36    *LC* 64-12660

## JV2500–4299 Netherlands. Spain. Portugal. Japan

**Boxer, C. R. (Charles Ralph), 1904-.**    • **4.8934**
The Dutch seaborne empire, 1600–1800, by C.R. Boxer. [1st American ed.] New York, Knopf, 1965. xxvi, 326 p. maps (1 fold.) plates, ports. (The History

of human society) 'Borzoi book' 1. Netherlands — Colonies — Social conditions 2. Netherlands — History — 1648-1714 I. T.
JV2511 B67　　　LC 64-19095

**Parry, J. H. (John Horace), 1914-.**　　　　　　　• 4.8935
The Spanish theory of empire in the sixteenth century. — Cambridge: University Press, 1940. 75 p. 1. Imperialism 2. Spain — Colonies — Administration 3. Spain — Colonies — America I. T.
JV4062.P3　　　LC 41-16610

**Clarence-Smith, W. G., 1948-.**　　　　　　　　4.8936
The third Portuguese empire, 1825–1975: a study in economic imperialism / Gervase Clarence–Smith. — Manchester, U.K.; Dover, N.H.: Manchester University Press, 1985. ix, 246 p.: ill.; 24 cm. Includes index. 1. Portugal — Colonies — Commerce — History. 2. Portugal — Colonies — History. I. T.
JV4211.C53 1985　　　325/.3469/09 19　　　LC 84-9701　　　ISBN 071901719X

**Boxer, C. R. (Charles Ralph), 1904-.**　　　　　• 4.8937
Race relations in the Portuguese colonial empire, 1415–1825. Oxford, Clarendon Press, 1963. vii, 136 p. facsim. 1. Portugal — Colonies — Native races I. T.
JV4235 B6　　　LC 64-201

**Schwartz, Stuart B.**　　　　　　　　　　　4.8938
Sovereignty and society in colonial Brazil; the High Court of Bahia and its judges, 1609–1751 [by] Stuart B. Schwartz. — Berkeley: University of California Press, [1973] xxvii, 438 p.: illus.; 24 cm. 1. Portugal. Relação da Bahia — History. 2. Portugal — Colonies — Administration. 3. Portugal — Colonies — America. 4. Brazil — Social conditions I. T.
JV4266.R4 S38　　　325/.31/09469　　　LC 76-186112　　　ISBN 0520021959

**The Japanese colonial empire, 1895–1945 / edited by Ramon H.**　4.8939
**Myers and Mark R. Peattie; contributors, Ching–chih Chen ... [et al.].**
Princeton, N.J.: Princeton University Press, c1984. x, 540 p., [6] p. of plates: ill.; 24 cm. 'Based on a conference sponsored by the Joint Committee on Japanese Studies of the American Council of Learned Societies and the Social Science Research Council.' 1. Japan — Colonies — East Asia — Administration — History — Addresses, essays, lectures. 2. Japan — Colonies — East Asia — Economic policy — Addresses, essays, lectures. 3. East Asia — Politics and government — Addresses, essays, lectures. I. Myers, Ramon Hawley, 1929- II. Peattie, Mark R., 1930- III. Chen, Ching-chih, 1937 May 24- IV. Joint Committee on Japanese Studies.
JV5260.J36 1984　　　325/.31/52095 19　　　LC 83-42571　　　ISBN 0691053987

# JV6000–9500 Emigration.
## Immigration
(U.S.: see also: E184)

**International Economic Association.**　　　　　　4.8940
Economics of international migration; proceedings of a conference held by the International Economic Association. Edited by Brinley Thomas. — London: Macmillan; New York: St. Martin's Press, 1958. xiii, 501 p.: diagrs., tables.; 23 cm. 1. Emigration and immigration — Economic aspects — Congresses. 2. Labor supply — Congresses. I. Brinley, Thomas, 1906- ed. II. T.
JV6011 1958　　　325.13　　　LC 58-14862

**Thomas, Brinley, 1906-.**　　　　　　　　　4.8941
Migration and economic growth; a study of Great Britain and the Atlantic economy. 2d ed. Cambridge [Eng.] University Press, 1973. xxxi, 498 p. illus. 24 cm. 1. Great Britain — Emigration and immigration — Economic aspects. 2. United States — Emigration and immigration — Economic aspects. 3. Great Britain — Economic conditions 4. United States — Economic conditions I. T.
JV6098.T5 1973　　　325　　　LC 79-171684　　　ISBN 0521085667

**Johnson, Kenneth F.**　　　　　　　　　　4.8942
Illegal aliens in the Western Hemisphere: political and economic factors / Kenneth F. Johnson, Miles W. Williams; epilogue by Stephen P. Mumme. — New York, N.Y.: Praeger, 1981. 207 p.: maps; 24 cm. Includes index. 1. Aliens, Illegal I. Williams, Miles. II. T.
JV6271.J64　　　323.6/31/091812 19　　　LC 81-2729　　　ISBN 003052461X

**Golab, Caroline.**　　　　　　　　　　　4.8943
Immigrant destinations / Caroline Golab. — Philadelphia: Temple University Press, 1977. x, 246 p.; 24 cm. 1. Labor supply — United States — History.

2. Neighborhood 3. United States — Emigration and immigration — History. I. T.
JV6450.G64　　　301.32/4/0974811　　　LC 77-81334　　　ISBN 087722109X

**Kraut, Alan M.**　　　　　　　　　　　　4.8944
The huddled masses: the immigrant in American society, 1880–1921 / Alan M. Kraut. — Arlington Heights, Ill.: Harlan Davidson, c1982. xi, 212 p., [32] p. of plates: ill.; 21 cm. — (The American history series) Includes index. 1. Americanization — History. 2. United States — Emigration and immigration — History. I. T.
JV6450.K7 1982　　　304.8/73 19　　　LC 81-17488　　　ISBN 0882958119

**Taylor, Philip A. M.**　　　　　　　　　　• 4.8945
The distant magnet; European emigration to the U.S.A. [by] Philip Taylor. — New York: Harper & Row, [1971] xvi, 326 p.: illus.; 25 cm. — (A Torchbook library ed.) 1. U.S. — Emigration and immigration — History. 2. Europe — Emigration and immigration — History. I. T.
JV6450.T37 1971　　　325.2/4/0973　　　LC 70-162288　　　ISBN 0061360589

**Hansen, Marcus Lee, 1892-1938.**　　　　　　• 4.8946
The Atlantic migration, 1607–1860: a history of the continuing settlement of the United States / by Marcus Lee Hansen; edited with a foreword by Arthur M. Schlesinger. — Cambridge, Mass.: Harvard University Press, 1940. xvii, 391 p., [9] p. of plates: ill., map. 1. Emigration and immigration 2. United States — Emigration and immigration 3. Europe — Social conditions I. Schlesinger, Arthur Meier, 1888-1965. II. T.
JV6451 H3　　　LC 40-6920

**Hansen, Marcus Lee, 1892-1938.**　　　　　　• 4.8947
The immigrant in American history / by Marcus Lee Hansen; edited with a foreword by Arthur M. Schlesinger. — Cambridge, Mass.: Harvard University Press, 1940. xi, 230 p.; 21 cm. 1. Emigration and immigration 2. United States — Emigration and immigration 3. Immigrants — United States I. Schlesinger, Arthur Meier, 1888-1965. ed. II. T.
JV6451.H33　　　325.73　　　LC 40-35768

**Divine, Robert A.**　　　　　　　　　　　• 4.8948
American immigration policy, 1924–1952, by Robert A. Divine. — New York: Da Capo Press, 1972 [c1957] viii, 220 p.; 24 cm. — (Civil liberties in American history) 1. Refugees, Political 2. United States — Emigration and immigration I. T. II. Series.
JV6455.D5 1972　　　325.73　　　LC 70-166323　　　ISBN 0306702444

**U.S. immigration and refugee policy: global and domestic issues**　4.8949
**/ edited by Mary M. Kritz.**
Lexington, Mass.: Lexington Books, c1983. xxi, 415 p.; 24 cm. 1. Emigration and immigration — Addresses, essays, lectures. 2. Refugees — Addresses, essays, lectures. 3. United States — Emigration and immigration — Addresses, essays, lectures. I. Kritz, Mary M.
JV6455.U17 1983　　　325.73 19　　　LC 82-47513　　　ISBN 0669055433

**Wittke, Carl Frederick, 1892-1971.**　　　　　• 4.8950
We who built America: the saga of the immigrant / by Carl Wittke. — [Rev. ed. Cleveland]: Press of Western Reserve University [1964] xviii, 550 p.; 23 cm. 1. United States — Emigration and immigration 2. Immigrants — United States 3. United States — Nationality. I. T.
JV6455.W55 1964　　　LC 64-20939

**The Unavoidable issue: U.S. immigration policy in the 1980s /**　4.8951
**edited by Demetrios G. Papademetriou and Mark J. Miller.**
Philadelphia: Institute for the Study of Human Issues, c1983. x, 305 p.; 24 cm. 1. United States — Emigration and immigration — Addresses, essays, lectures. I. Papademetriou, Demetrios G. II. Miller, Mark J.
JV6483.U52 1983　　　325.73 19　　　LC 82-15650　　　ISBN 0897270479

**Clamor at the gates: the new American immigration / edited by**　4.8952
**Nathan Glazer.**
San Francisco, Calif.: ICS Press, c1985. ix, 337 p.: ill.; 24 cm. 1. United States — Emigration and immigration — Government policy — Addresses, essays, lectures. 2. United States — Emigration and immigration — Economic aspects — Addresses, essays, lectures. 3. United States — Emigration and immigration — Addresses, essays, lectures. I. Glazer, Nathan.
JV6493.C57 1985　　　325.73 19　　　LC 85-175　　　ISBN 0917616707

**The Gateway: U.S. immigration issues and policies / edited by**　4.8953
**Barry R. Chiswick.**
Washington, D.C.: American Enterprise Institute for Public Policy Research, c1982. 476 p.: ill.; 23 cm. — (AEI symposia. 81I) Proceedings of a conference cosponsored by the American Enterprise Institute for Public Policy Research and the College of Business Administration, University of Illinois at Chicago Circle, and held Apr. 10-11, 1980 at the UICC campus. 1. Emigration and immigration law — United States — Congresses. 2. United States — Emigration and immigration — Congresses. I. Chiswick, Barry R.

II. American Enterprise Institute for Public Policy Research. III. University of Illinois at Chicago Circle. College of Business Administration. IV. Series.
JV6493.G37 1982    325.73 19    *LC* 81-8009    *ISBN* 0844722200

**Morris, Milton D.**    **4.8954**
Immigration—the beleaguered bureaucracy / Milton D. Morris. — Washington, D.C.: Brookings Institution, c1985. x, 150 p.: ill.; 24 cm. 1. United States — Emigration and immigration — Government policy. I. T.
JV6493.M673 1985    325.73 19    *LC* 84-22962    *ISBN* 0815758383

**Loescher, Gil.**    **4.8955**
Calculated kindness: refugees and America's half–open door, 1945 to the present / Gil Loescher, John A. Scanlan. — New York: Free Press; London: Collier Macmillan, c1986. xviii, 346 p.; 25 cm. Includes index. 1. Refugees — Government policy — United States — History — 20th century. 2. Refugees — United States. 3. United States — Emigration and immigration I. Scanlan, John A. II. T.
JV6601.R4 L63 1986    325/.21/0973 19    *LC* 86-12079    *ISBN* 0029273404

**Fenton, Edwin.**    **4.8956**
Immigrants and unions, a case study, Italians and American labor, 1870–1920 / Edwin Fenton. — New York: Arno Press, 1975. 630 p. (The Italian American experience) Reprint of the author's thesis, Harvard, 1957. 1. Italians in the United States. 2. Trade-unions — United States 3. United States — Emigration and immigration 4. Italy — Emigration and immigration. I. T. II. Series.
JV6774.F45 1975    331.88/0973    *LC* 74-28474

**Dinnerstein, Leonard.**    **4.8957**
America and the survivors of the Holocaust / Leonard Dinnerstein. — New York: Columbia University Press, 1982. xiv, 409 p.: ill.; 24 cm. — (Contemporary American history series). Includes index. 1. Jews — United States — History — 20th century. 2. Holocaust survivors — Government policy — United States — History — 20th century. 3. United States — Emigration and immigration — History — 20th century. I. T. II. Series.
JV6895.J5 D55    325.73 19    *LC* 81-15443    *ISBN* 0231041764

**Richardson, Bonham C., 1939-.**    **4.8958**
Caribbean migrants: environment and human survival on St. Kitts and Nevis / Bonham C. Richardson. — 1st ed. — Knoxville: University of Tennessee Press, c1983. xiii, 207 p.: ill.; 24 cm. Includes index. 1. Saint Kitts-Nevis — Emigration and immigration — History. 2. Saint Kitts-Nevis — Social conditions. I. T.
JV7339.S75 R52 1983    304.8/097297/3 19    *LC* 82-7078    *ISBN* 0870493604

**Solberg, Carl E.**    **4.8959**
Immigration and nationalism, Argentina and Chile, 1890–1914, by Carl Solberg. Austin, Published for the Institute of Latin American Studies by the University of Texas Press [1970] xi, 222 p. 24 cm. (University of Texas at Austin. Institute of Latin American Studies. Latin American monographs, no. 18) 1. Nationalism — Argentine Republic. 2. Nationalism — Chile. 3. Argentina — Emigration and immigration. 4. Chile — Emigration and immigration. I. T.
JV7442.S63    325.82    *LC* 76-99916    *ISBN* 0292700202

**Immigrants and minorities in British society / edited by Colin**    **4.8960**
**Holmes.**
London; Boston: Allen & Unwin, 1978. 208 p.; 23 cm. Includes indexes. 1. Minorities — Great Britain — History — Addresses, essays, lectures. 2. Great Britain — Emigration and immigration — History — Addresses, essays, lectures. I. Holmes, Colin, 1938-
JV7620.I55    301.45/0941    *LC* 78-321418    *ISBN* 0049421603

**Sherman, A. J. (Ari Joshua)**    **4.8961**
Island refuge; Britain and refugees from the Third Reich, 1933–1939 [by] A. J. Sherman. Berkeley, University of California Press [c1973] 291 p. 23 cm. 1. Jews — Germany — Persecutions 2. Great Britain — Emigration and immigration — History. I. T.
JV7685.J46 S55    325/.21    *LC* 73-86850

**Brain, Peter J.**    **4.8962**
Population, immigration, and the Australian economy / Peter J. Brain, Rhonda L. Smith, Gerard P. Schuyers, with contributions from B. S. Gray, A. N. E. Jolley and A. W. Smith. — London: Croom Helm, c1979. 404 p.: ill.; 23 cm. Includes index. 1. Australia — Emigration and immigration — Economic aspects. 2. Australia — Economic conditions — 1945- I. Smith, Rhonda L. joint author. II. Schuyers, Gerard P. joint author. III. T.
JV9125.B7    330.994/05    *LC* 80-457453    *ISBN* 0856649864

# JX INTERNATIONAL LAW. INTERNATIONAL RELATIONS. INTERNATIONAL ORGANIZATION

**Studies on a just world order / edited by Richard A. Falk, et al.**    **4.8963**
Vol. 1-    . — Boulder, Colo.: Westview Press, 1982-. v.: ill.; 24 cm. Each volume has also a distinctive title.
JX1.S8x    *LC* sn 84-10550

**Israel, Fred L. comp.**    **• 4.8964**
Major peace treaties of modern history, 1648–1967 / editor: Fred L. Israel; commentaries by Emanuel Chill; with an introductory essay by Arnold Toynbee. — New York: Chelsea House Publishers, 1967-80. 4 v.: illus., maps (part col.); 25 cm. 1. Treaties I. T.
JX121.I8    341.7/3/0265 19    *LC* 67-27855

**Hurst, Michael. comp.**    **4.8965**
Key treaties for the great powers, 1814–1914. Selected and edited by Michael Hurst. — New York: St. Martin's Press, [1972] 2 v. (xviii, 948 p.); 25 cm. 1. Treaties — Collections I. T.
JX151.H87 1972b    341/.026    *LC* 72-188873

**Bowman, M. J.**    **4.8966**
Multilateral treaties: index and current status / compiled and annotated within the University of Nottingham Treaty Centre by M.J. Bowman and D.J. Harris. — London: Butterworths; St. Paul, Minn.: Mason Pub. Co., 1984. xii, 516 p.; 26 cm. Kept up to date by cumulative supplements. 1. Treaties — Indexes. I. Harris, D. J. (David John) II. University of Nottingham. Treaty Centre. III. T.
JX171.B68 1984    341/.0265 19    *LC* 85-214741    *ISBN* 0406252777

**Current international treaties / edited by T.B. Millar with**    **4.8967**
**Robin Ward.**
New York, NY: New York University Press, c1984. 558 p.; 23 cm. 1. Treaties — Collections I. Millar, T. B. (Thomas Bruce) II. Ward, Robin.
JX171.C87 1984    341/.026 19    *LC* 84-8256    *ISBN* 0814753922

**Grenville, J. A. S. (John Ashley Soames), 1928-.**    **4.8968**
The major international treaties, 1914–1973; a history and guide with texts [by] J. A. S. Grenville. New York, Stein and Day [1974] xxix, 575 p. maps. 25 cm. 1. Treaties — Collections 2. World politics — 20th century I. T.
JX171.G74    341/.026    *LC* 75-163352    *ISBN* 0812816544

**International organization and integration: annotated basic**    **4.8969**
**documents and descriptive directory of international**
**organizations and arrangements / board of editors, P.J.G.**
**Kapteyn ... [et al.]; with a foreword by Louis B. Sohn.**
2nd, completely rev. ed. — The Hague; Boston: Martinus Nijhoff Publishers; Hingham, MA: Distributors for the U.S. and Canada, Kluwer Boston, c1981-c1984. < v. 1, pt. A, v. 2, pts. A-K; in 4 >; 25 cm. Vol. 2, pt. < K >: first imprint place: Dordrecht. Tables inserted in each volume. Includes indexes. 1. United Nations. 2. Treaties — Collections 3. International law — Sources I. Kapteyn, P. J. G. (Paul Joan George)
JX171.I54 1981    341.2 19    *LC* 81-18881    *ISBN* 9024725798

**Rohn, Peter H.**    **4.8970**
World treaty index / Peter H. Rohn. — 2nd ed. — Santa Barbara, Calif.: ABC-Clio Information Services, c1983-c1984. 5 v.; 29 cm. 1. Treaties — Indexes. I. T.
JX171.R63 1983    341/.026 19    *LC* 83-3872    *ISBN* 0874361419

**American foreign relations.**    **4.8971**
1938/39-. New York: New York University Press. v.; 21-25 cm. Annual. 'A documentary record.' 'A Council on Foreign Relations book.' Vols. for 1938/39-1951 called v. 2-13. I. World Peace Foundation. II. Council on Foreign Relations.
JX231.D63    *LC* sc 78-20

**United States. Dept. of State.**    **4.8972**
Foreign relations of the United States / Department of State, United States of America. — [Departmental ed.]. — 1932-    . — Washington: For sale by the Supt. of Docs., U.S. G.P.O., 1948-. v.: maps; 24 cm. (Department of State publication.) Annual. Vols. for 1932- issued in parts. 1. United States — Foreign relations — Periodicals. I. T. II. Series.
JX233.A3    327.73 19    *LC* 10-3793

**The Cumulated index to the U.S. Department of State papers**    **4.8973**
**relating to the foreign relations of the United States, 1939–1945**
**/ introduction by Fredrick Aandahl.**
Millwood, N.Y.: Kraus International Publications, c1980. 2 v. (cxcix, 1031 p.);
24 cm. 1. United States. Dept. of State Foreign relations of the United States —
Indexes. 2. United States — Foreign relations — Indexes. I. Aandahl,
Fredrick. II. United States. Dept. of State. Foreign relations of the United
States.
JX233.A3 Suppl     327.73 19     *LC* 81-160874     *ISBN* 0527207446

**United States. Treaties, etc.**      • **4.8974**
Treaties, conventions, international acts, protocols and agreements between the
United States of America and other powers ... Washington, Govt. Print. Off.,
1910–38. Grosse Pointe, Mich., Scholarly Press [1970?] 4 v. (xxvi, 5755 p.) 24
cm. (61st Congress, 2d session. Senate. Document no. 357) Prepared under the
direction of the Committee on Foreign Relations, United States Senate, in
cooperation with the Dept. of State. 1. United States — Foreign relations
I. United States. Congress. Senate. Committee on Foreign Relations.
II. United States. Dept. of State. III. T.
JX236 1910c     341.2/73     *LC* 78-121307

**Detente: a documentary record / [compiled by] Charles E.**    **4.8975**
**Timberlake.**
New York: Praeger Publishers, 1978. xviii, 231 p.; 25 cm. 1. Detente 2. United
States — Foreign relations — Treaties 3. Russia — Foreign relations —
Treaties. I. Timberlake, Charles E.
JX236 1972.D47     341/.0266/73047     *LC* 78-19465     *ISBN*
0030466660

**A Guide to the United States treaties in force.**      **4.8976**
1982 ed.-     . — Buffalo, N.Y.: W.S. Hein Co., 1982-. v.; 28 cm. Annual.
Issues for 1982-    in two parts. 1. United States — Foreign relations —
Treaties — Indexes. I. Kavass, Igor I. II. Sprudzs, Adolf. III. United States.
Treaties in force.
JX236.5.G84     341/.0264/73 19     *LC* 85-641134

**Watt, Donald Cameron.**      • **4.8977**
Documents on the Suez crisis, 26 July to 6 November, 1956 / selected and
introduced by D.C. Watt. — London: Royal Institute of International Affairs
[1957] 88 p.: ill.; 22 cm. 1. Suez Canal I. T.
JX403 W3     *LC* 57-28067

**Germany. Auswärtiges Amt.**      • **4.8978**
[Akten zur deutschen auswärtigen Politik. English] Documents on German
foreign policy, 1918–1945, from the archives of the German Foreign Ministry.
Washington: U.S. Govt. Print. Off., 1949-. v.: fold. maps; 24 cm. ([U.S.] Dept.
of State. Publication 3277, 3558, 3838, 3883, 4964, 5436, 6312, 6462, 6491,
6545, 6750, 6848, 7083, 7384, 7439, 8083, 9338) Edited under the sponsorship
of the U.S. Dept. of State, the British Foreign Off. and the French Govt. Vol. 14
of Series D has imprint: Arlington, Va., Open-Door Press. 1. Germany —
Foreign relations — 1918-1933 2. Germany — Foreign relations — 1933-1945
I. T.
JX691.A45     327.43 19     *LC* 49-46672

**Slusser, Robert M.**      • **4.8979**
A calendar of Soviet treaties, 1917–1957 [by] Robert M. Slusser [and] Jan F.
Triska, with the assistance of George Ginsburgs [and] Wilfred O. Reiners.
Stanford, Calif., Stanford University Press, 1959. xii, 530 p. (Hoover Institution
on War, Revolution, and Peace. Documentary series, no. 4) 1. Russia —
Foreign relations — Treaties I. Triska, Jan F. jt. author II. T.
JX756 1917     *LC* 59-10638

**Ginsburgs, George.**      **4.8980**
A calendar of Soviet treaties, 1958–1973 / George Ginsburgs, Robert M.
Slusser. — Alphen aan den Rijn, Netherlands; Rockville, Md.: Sijthoff &
Noordhoff, 1981. xx, 908 p.; 25 cm. 'A publication issued by the
Documentation Office for East European Law, University of Leyden.' 1. Soviet
Union — Foreign relations — Treaties — Chronology. I. Slusser, Robert M.
II. T.
JX757.5.G56 1981     341/.026447 19     *LC* 80-50453     *ISBN*
9028606092

**Plano, Jack C.**      **4.8981**
The international relations dictionary / Jack C. Plano, Roy Olton. — 3rd ed. —
Santa Barbara, Calif.: ABC-Clio, c1982. xxvi, 488 p.; 24 cm. — (Clio
dictionaries in political science.) Includes index. 1. International relations —
Dictionaries. I. Olton, Roy, 1922- II. T. III. Series.
JX1226.P55 1982     327/.03 19     *LC* 82-3996     *ISBN* 0874363322

**Tunkin, G. I. (Grigoriĭ Ivanovich)**      **4.8982**
[Teoriia mezhdunarodnogo prava. English] Theory of international law / G. I.
Tunkin; translated with an introd. by William E. Butler. — Cambridge, Mass.:
Harvard University Press, 1974. xxv, 497 p.; 24 cm. Translation of Teoriia
mezhdunarodnogo prava. 1. International law — Philosophy I. T.
JX1245.T8113 1974     341/.01     *LC* 73-92258     *ISBN* 0674880013

**Ferencz, Benjamin B. 1920-.**      **4.8983**
Enforcing international law: a way to world peace: a documentary history and
analysis / by Benjamin B. Ferencz; introduction by Louis B. Sohn. — London;
New York: Oceana Publications, c1983. 2 v. (xix, 890 p.): ill.; 27 cm. 1. United
Nations — Armed Forces — History — Sources. 2. International law —
Sources 3. Sanctions (International law) — History — Sources. I. T.
JX1246.F46 1983     341.5/8 19     *LC* 83-42858     *ISBN* 0379121476

**Lauterpacht, Hersch, Sir, 1897-1960.**      • **4.8984**
Private law sources and analogies of international law, with special reference to
international arbitration. [Hamden, Conn.] Archon Books, 1970. xxiv, 326 p.
22 cm. Reprint of the 1927 ed. 1. International law 2. Jurisprudence
3. Arbitration, International I. T.
JX1248.L3 1970     341     *LC* 71-95030     *ISBN* 0208008144

## JX1250–1255 Special Aspects

**Beitz, Charles R.**      **4.8985**
Political theory and international relations / Charles R. Beitz. — Princeton,
N.J.: Princeton University Press, c1979. ix, 212 p.; 23 cm. Includes index.
1. International relations 2. Political science I. T.
JX1250.B4     327     *LC* 79-83976     *ISBN* 0691076146

**McDougal, Myres Smith, 1906-.**      **4.8986**
Studies in world public order / by Myres S. McDougal and associates. — New
Haven: New Haven Press; Dordrecht: M. Nijhoff, 1986. 1 v. Includes index.
1. Public policy (International law) 2. Sociological jurisprudence I. T.
JX1251.M36 1986     341 19     *LC* 85-25849     *ISBN* 0898389003

**Sprout, Harold Hance, 1901-.**      • **4.8987**
Ecological perspective on human affairs: with special reference to international
politics / by Harold and Margaret Sprout. Princeton, N.J.: Published for the
Princeton Center of International Studies, by Princeton U.P., 1965. 236 p. —
(Princeton paperbacks) 1. Human ecology 2. International relations
I. Sprout, Margaret Tuttle, 1903- II. Sprout, Harold Hance, 1901- Man-milieu
relationship hypotheses in the contex of international politics. III. Woodrow
Wilson School of Public and International Affairs. Center of International
Studies. IV. T.
JX1251.S49     301.3     *LC* 65-17161

**Verwey, W. D.**      **4.8988**
Economic development, peace, and international law. [By] Wil D. Verwey.
Assen, Van Gorcum, 1972. xx, 362 p. 23 cm. (Polemogical studies, no. 16)
1. Economic development 2. International law 3. Peace I. T.
JX1252.V47     338.91     *LC* 73-152025     *ISBN* 9023209923

**Frank, Jerome David, 1909-.**      **4.8989**
Sanity and survival in the nuclear age: psychological aspects of war and peace /
Jerome D. Frank. — New York: Random House, 1984. x, 330 p.; 21 cm.
'Formerly entitled: Sanity and survival: psychological aspects of war and peace.'
1. International relations — Psychological aspects I. T.
JX1255.F7 1982     327/.01/9 19     *LC* 82-9872     *ISBN* 0394332296

**Granger, John Van Nuys, 1918-.**      **4.8990**
Technology and international relations / John V. Granger. — San Francisco:
W. H. Freeman, c1979. xi, 202 p.: ill.; 25 cm. 1. International relations
2. Technology — International cooperation 3. Technology and state I. T.
JX1255.G74     327     *LC* 78-15363     *ISBN* 0716710048

**Hoffmann, Stanley.**      **4.8991**
Duties beyond borders: on the limits and possibilities of ethical international
politics / Stanley Hoffmann. — 1st ed. — Syracuse, N.Y.: Syracuse University
Press, 1981. xiv, 252 cm. — (Frank W. Abrams lectures.)
1. International relations 2. International relations — Moral and religious
aspects. I. T. II. Series.
JX1255.H56     327.1/01 19     *LC* 81-2401     *ISBN* 0815601670

**Kelman, Herbert C. ed.**      • **4.8992**
International behavior; a social–psychological analysis, edited by Herbert C.
Kelman. — New York: Holt, Rinehart and Winston, [1965] xiv, 626 p.: illus.;
24 cm. 'Published for the Society for the Psychological Study of Social Issues.'
1. International relations — Psychological aspects — Addresses, essays,
lectures. 2. Social psychology — Addresses, essays, lectures. I. Society for the
Psychological Study of Social Issues. II. T.
JX1255.K47     327.019     *LC* 65-12803

**Nardin, Terry, 1942-.**      **4.8993**
Law, morality, and the relations of states / Terry Nardin. — Princeton, N.J.:
Princeton University Press, c1983. xii, 350 p.; 23 cm. Includes index.
1. International law 2. International relations — Moral and ethical aspects.
I. T.
JX1255.N28 1983     341/.01 19     *LC* 83-42570     *ISBN* 0691076634

**Stagner, Ross, 1909-.**      **4.8994**
Psychological aspects of international conflict. — Belmont, Calif.: Brooks/Cole Pub. Co., [1967] xi, 234 p.: ill.; 23 cm. — (Contemporary psychology series) 1. International relations — Psychological aspects I. T.
JX1255.S8     327/.01/9     *LC* 67-25148

## JX1291–1299 Study. Teaching

**Frost, Mervyn.**      **4.8995**
Towards a normative theory of international relations: a critical analysis of the philosophical and methodological assumptions in the discipline with proposals towards a substantive normative theory / Mervyn Frost. — Cambridge [Cambridgeshire]; New York: Cambridge University Press, 1986. x, 241 p.; 23 cm. Based on the author's thesis (Ph. D.)—University of Stellenbosch, 1983. Includes index. 1. International relations — Methodology. 2. International relations — Research. I. T.
JX1291.F76 1986     327/.072 19     *LC* 85-15165     *ISBN* 0521305128

**Hermann, Charles F., 1938-.**      **4.8996**
International crises: insights from behavioral research / edited by Charles F. Hermann. — New York: Free Press, [1972] x, 334 p.: ill.; 24 cm. 1. International relations — Research — Addresses, essays, lectures. I. T.
JX1291.H47     327/.07/2     *LC* 74-165102

**Jervis, Robert, 1940-.**      **4.8997**
Perception and misperception in international politics / Robert Jervis. — Princeton, N.J.: Princeton University Press, c1976. xi, 445 p. Includes index. 1. International relations — Research. I. T.
JX1291.J47     JX1291 J47.     327/.01/9     *LC* 76-3259     *ISBN* 0691056560

**Mathisen, Trygve.**      • **4.8998**
Methodology in the study of international relations. Oslo, Oslo University Press, 1959. x, 265 p. 24 cm. (Norges almenvitenskapelige forskningsrad. Sect. A. 198-2) 1. International relations — Study and teaching. I. T.
JX1291.Mx     *LC* a 59-6132

**Sprout, Harold Hance, 1901-.**      **4.8999**
Toward a politics of the planet earth / [by] Harold Sprout and Margaret Sprout. — New York: Van Nostrand Reinhold Co., [1971] x, 499 p.: ill.; 24 cm. 1. International relations — Research. 2. Environmental policy I. Sprout, Margaret Tuttle, 1903- joint author. II. T.
JX1291.S665     327/.072     *LC* 74-148558

**Tanter, Raymond.**      **4.9000**
Theory and policy in international relations, edited by Raymond Tanter and Richard H. Ullman. — Princeton, N.J.: Princeton University Press, [1972] 250 p.; 25 cm. 'This book is being issued separately as a supplement to World politics, vol. XXIV, 1972.' 1. International relations — Research. I. Ullman, Richard H. (Richard Henry) joint author. II. T.
JX1291.T35     327/.101     *LC* 70-155087     *ISBN* 0691056447

**Wright, Quincy, 1890-1970.**      • **4.9001**
The study of international relations. New York: Appleton-Century-Crofts [1955] 642 p.: ill.; 24 cm. (The Century political science series) 1. International relations — Study and teaching 2. International relations I. T.
JX1293 U6 W7     *LC* 55-5046

## JX1305–1598 International Relations. Diplomatic History

**Bozeman, Adda Bruemmer, 1908-.**      • **4.9002**
Politics and culture in international history. — Princeton, N.J.: Princeton University Press, 1960. 560 p.; 25 cm. 1. International relations — History. I. T.
JX1305.B65     327.09     *LC* 60-5743

**Corbett, Percy Ellwood, 1892-.**      • **4.9003**
Law in diplomacy. Princeton, N.J., Princeton University Press, 1959. 290 p. 1. International relations 2. Diplomacy 3. International law I. T.
JX1305 C6     *LC* 59-5593

**Akehurst, Michael Barton.**      **4.9004**
A modern introduction to international law / Michael Akehurst. — 6th ed. — London; Boston: Allen and Unwin, c1987. 304 p. 1. International law I. T.
JX1308.A43 1987     341 19     *LC* 86-28828     *ISBN* 0043410367

**Kaplan, Morton A.**      • **4.9005**
System and process in international politics. — [New York: Wiley, 1957] 283 p.; 24 cm. 1. International relations I. T.
JX1308.K3     341     *LC* 57-13362

**Schwarzenberger, Georg, 1908-.**      • **4.9006**
Power politics; a study of world society. — 3d ed. — New York: Praeger, 1964. xxi, 614 p. illus., may (on lining papers) 26 cm. — 'Published under the auspices of the London Institute of World Affairs.' 'Selected bibliography on world affairs, by F. Parkinson in association with J. Burton and O. P. St. John': p. 555-590. 1. International relations I. T.
JX1308.S35 1964a     327     *LC* 64-22793

**Waltz, Kenneth Neal, 1924-.**      • **4.9007**
Man, the state and war: a theoretical analysis / by Kenneth N. Waltz. — New York: Columbia University Press, c1959. viii, 263 p. — (Topical studies in international relations) 1. War 2. International relations I. T. II. Series.
JX1308.W3     *LC* 59-11482     *ISBN* 0231022921

**Dehio, Ludwig, 1888-.**      • **4.9008**
The precarious balance: four centuries of the European power struggle / translated from the German by Charles Fullman. — [1st American ed.] New York: Knopf, 1962. 295 p.; 22 cm. (Borzoi book) 1. Balance of power 2. Imperialism 3. World politics I. T.
JX1318 D423     *LC* 61-9235

**Quester, George H.**      **4.9009**
Offense and defense in the international system / George H. Quester. New York: Wiley, c1977. xii, 219 p.; 22 cm. (International relations series) 'Written under the auspices of the Cornell University Peace Studies Program.' Includes bibliographical references and index. 1. Balance of power — History. 2. World history I. Cornell University. Peace Studies Program. II. T.
JX1318.Q47     327/.112/09     *LC* 76-28329     *ISBN* 0471702552

## JX1391–1395 20th Century

**Beloff, Max, 1913-.**      • **4.9010**
Foreign policy and the democratic process. Baltimore, Johns Hopkins Press, 1955. 134 p. (The Albert Shaw lectures on diplomatic history, 1954) 1. International relations 2. Democracy 3. United States — Foreign relations — 1945- I. T.
JX1391 B4     *LC* 55-9743

**Carr, Edward Hallett, 1892-.**      • **4.9011**
The twenty years' crisis, 1919–1939; an introduction to the study of international relations. [2d ed.] London, Macmillan; New York, St. Martin's Press, 1956. xii, 243 p. 22 cm. 1. International relations 2. World politics I. T.
JX1391.C32 1956     *LC* 58-4654

**Eayrs, James George, 1926-.**      **4.9012**
Diplomacy and its discontents [by] James Eayrs. — [Toronto; Buffalo]: University of Toronto Press, [c1971] xi, 198 p.; 24 cm. 1. International relations 2. Diplomatic and consular service I. T.
JX1391.E18     327/.2     *LC* 73-163811     *ISBN* 0802018076

**Hoffmann, Stanley. ed.**      **4.9013**
Contemporary theory in international relations. — Englewood Cliffs, N.J.: Prentice-Hall, 1960. 293 p.: illus.; 22 cm. 1. International relations — Collections. I. T.
JX1391.H6     327.01     *LC* 59-15939

**Morgenthau, Hans Joachim, 1904-.**      **4.9014**
Politics among nations: the struggle for power and peace / Hans J. Morgenthau, Kenneth W. Thompson. — 6th ed. — New York: Knopf: Distributed by Random House, c1985. xiv, 688 p.: ill., maps; 25 cm. Maps on lining papers. Includes index. 1. International relations I. Thompson, Kenneth W., 1921- II. T.
JX1391.M6 1985     327 19     *LC* 84-17176     *ISBN* 0394541014

**Northedge, F. S.**      **4.9015**
A hundred years of international relations / [by] F. S. Northedge [and] M. J. Grieve. — New York: Praeger, 1972 (c1971) x, 397 p.: maps; 23 cm. 1. International relations — History. I. Grieve, M. J., joint author. II. T.
JX1391.N57 1971b     327/.09/04     *LC* 76-172080

**Soviet strategy in Europe / edited by Richard Pipes.**      **4.9016**
New York: Crane, Russak, c1976. xiv, 316 p.; 24 cm. 'Outgrowth of a study undertaken by the Strategic Studies Center of the Stanford Research Institute.' 'The research on which this work is based was supported by the Advanced Research Projects Agency of the Department of Defense under contract no. DAHC15-73-0380.' 1. Detente — Addresses, essays, lectures. 2. Europe — Foreign relations — Russia — Addresses, essays, lectures. 3. Russia — Foreign

relations — Europe — Addresses, essays, lectures. I. Pipes, Richard. II. Stanford Research Institute. Strategic Studies Center.
JX1393.D46 S68     327.47/04     *LC* 76-1555     *ISBN* 0844808547

**Atkins, G. Pope, 1934-.**         **4.9017**
Latin America in the international political system / G. Pope Atkins. New York: Free Press, c1977. xv, 448 p.; 25 cm. Includes index. 1. Latin America — Foreign relations I. T.
JX1393.L3 A88     327.8     *LC* 76-20882     *ISBN* 0029010608

**Ireland, Timothy P., 1948-.**         **4.9018**
Creating the entangling alliance: the origins of the North Atlantic Treaty Organization / Timothy P. Ireland. — Westport, Conn.: Greenwood Press, 1981. x, 245 p.; 22 cm. — (Contributions in political science. no. 50 0147-1066) Includes index. 1. North Atlantic Treaty Organization. I. T. II. Series.
JX1393.N67 I73     355/.031/091821     *LC* 80-655     *ISBN* 0313220948

**Kaplan, Lawrence S.**         **4.9019**
The United States and NATO: the formative years / Lawrence S. Kaplan. — Lexington, Ky.: University Press of Kentucky, c1984. xi, 276 p.; 25 cm. 1. North Atlantic Treaty Organization — History. 2. United States — Foreign relations — 1945- I. T. II. Title: United States and N.A.T.O.
JX1393.N67 K37 1984     355/.031/091821 19     *LC* 84-5087     *ISBN* 0813115116

**Aron, Raymond, 1905-.**         • **4.9020**
[Paix et guerre entre les nations. English] Peace and war; a theory of international relations. Translated from the French by Richard Howard and Annette Baker Fox. [1st ed.] Garden City, N.Y., Doubleday, 1966. xviii, 820 p. 24 cm. Translation of Paix et guerre entre les nations. 1. International relations 2. Military policy I. T.
JX1395.A7313     327     *LC* 65-13986

**Buchan, Alastair.**         **4.9021**
Power and equilibrium in the 1970s. — New York: Published for the Council on Foreign Relations by Praeger Publishers, [1973] 120 p.; 22 cm. — (Russell C. Leffingwell lectures. 1972) 1. International relations I. Council on Foreign Relations. II. T. III. Series.
JX1395.B79     327     *LC* 72-83002

**Burton, John W. (John Wear), 1915-.**         • **4.9022**
Systems, states, diplomacy and rules [by] J. W. Burton. London, Cambridge U.P., 1968. xii, 251 p. illus. 22 cm. 1. International relations I. T.
JX1395.B863     327     *LC* 68-29653     *ISBN* 0521073162

**Butterfield, Herbert, 1900- ed.**         • **4.9023**
Diplomatic investigations: essays in the theory of international politics / edited by Herbert Butterfield and Martin Wight. — London: Allen & Unwin, 1966. 5-227 p.; 22 cm. Contributors: Hedley Bull, Herbert Butterfield, Michael Howard, G. F. Hudson, Donald Mackinnon, Martin Wight. Bibliographical footnotes. 1. International relations — Addresses, essays, lectures. I. Wight, Martin. joint ed. II. Bull, Hedley. III. T.
JX1395.B868     327.01     *LC* 66-71958

**Butterfield, Herbert, 1900-.**         • **4.9024**
International conflict in the twentieth century; a Christian view. [1st ed.] New York, Harper [1960] 123 p. (Religious perspectives. v. 2) 1. International relations 2. Christianity and international affairs I. T. II. Series.
JX1395 B87     *LC* 60-7954

**Change in the international system / edited by Ole R. Holsti,**         **4.9025**
**Randolph M. Siverson, Alexander L. George.**
Boulder, Colo.: Westview Press, 1980. xxxii, 316 p.; 24 cm. 1. International relations — Addresses, essays, lectures. I. Holsti, Ole R. II. Siverson, Randolph M. III. George, Alexander L.
JX1395.C465     327.1/01     *LC* 80-11913     *ISBN* 0891588469

**Claude, Inis L.**         • **4.9026**
Power and international relations. — New York: Random House, [1962] 310 p.; 22 cm. 1. International relations 2. Balance of power 3. Security, International 4. International organization I. T.
JX1395.C55     327     *LC* 62-16200

**Dougherty, James E.**         **4.9027**
Contending theories of international relations: a comprehensive survey / James E. Dougherty, Robert L. Pfaltzgraff, Jr. — 2d ed. — New York: Harper & Row, c1981. xv, 592 p.; 24 cm. 1. International relations I. Pfaltzgraff, Robert L. joint author, II. T.
JX1395.D67 1981     327.1/01 19     *LC* 80-21038     *ISBN* 0060452153

**Falk, Richard A.**         **4.9028**
A global approach to national policy / Richard A. Falk. — Cambridge, Mass.: Harvard University Press, 1975. x, 320 p.; ill.; 25 cm. 1. International relations 2. International organization 3. United States — Foreign relations — 1945- I. T.
JX1395.F29     327     *LC* 75-326242     *ISBN* 0674354451

**Falk, Richard A. ed.**         **4.9029**
The strategy of world order / edited by Richard A. Falk [and] Saul H. Mendlovitz. — [1st ed.]. — New York: World Law Fund, 1966. 4 v.: ill.; 24 cm. 1. United Nations — Addresses, essays, lectures. 2. International relations — Addresses, essays, lectures. 3. International law — Addresses, essays, lectures. 4. Disarmament — Economic aspects. — Addresses, essays, lectures. I. Mendlovitz, Saul H. joint ed. II. T.
JX1395.F3     327     *LC* 66-14524

**Henkin, Louis.**         **4.9030**
How nations behave: law and foreign policy / Louis Henkin. — 2d ed. — New York: Published for the Council on Foreign Relations by Columbia University Press, 1979. xv, 400 p.; 22 cm. Includes bibliographical references and index. 1. International law 2. International relations I. T.
JX1395.H45 1979     341     *LC* 79-1015     *ISBN* 0231047568

**Hoffmann, Stanley.**         • **4.9031**
The state of war: essays on the theory and practice of international politics. — New York: Praeger, [1965] x, 276 p.; 21 cm. 1. International relations — Addresses, essays, lectures. 2. War (International law) — Addresses, essays, lectures. 3. United States — Foreign relations — 1963-1969 I. T.
JX1395.H62     327.1     *LC* 65-24942

**Keohane, Robert O. (Robert Owen), 1941-.**         **4.9032**
Power and interdependence: world politics in transition / Robert O. Keohane, Joseph S. Nye; [written under the auspices of the Center for International Affairs, Harvard University]. — New York: The Free Press, 1975. xiv, 273 p.; 24 cm. 1. International relations 2. International economic relations I. Nye, Joseph S. joint author. II. T.
JX1395.K428     327

**Linkage politics; essays on the convergence of national and**         • **4.9033**
**international systems. Edited by James N. Rosenau.**
New York, Free Press [1969] xii, 352 p. illus. 24 cm. 'Published for the Princeton Center of International Studies.' Based on essays originally conceived at a two-day conference in January, 1966, sponsored by the Center of International Studies of Princeton University, and later presented at the Annual Meeting of the American Political Science Association, New York City, September, 1966. 1. International relations — Addresses, essays, lectures. I. Rosenau, James N. ed. II. Woodrow Wilson School of Public and International Affairs. Center of International Studies.
JX1395.L522     327     *LC* 69-10482

**Liska, George.**         **4.9034**
Alliances and the third world. — Baltimore: Johns Hopkins Press, [1968] ix, 61 p.; 21 cm. — (Studies in international affairs, no. 5) 1. International relations 2. Alliances I. T.
JX1395.L524     327     *LC* 68-17254

**Liska, George.**         • **4.9035**
International equilibrium: a theoretical essay on the politics and organization of security / George Liska. — Cambridge: Harvard University Press, 1957. 223 p. Includes index. 1. International relations 2. Security, International I. T.
JX1395 L53     JX1395 L53.     *LC* 57-9077

**Reshaping the international order: a report to the Club of Rome**         **4.9036**
**/ Jan Tinbergen, coordinator; Antony J. Dolman, editor; Jan**
**van Ettinger, director.**
1st ed. — New York: Dutton, c1976. 325 p.: ill.; 24 cm. On spine:RIO: reshaping the international order. 1. International relations — Addresses, essays, lectures. 2. Underdeveloped areas. 3. Technical assistance 4. Wealth 5. International economic relations — Addresses, essays, lectures. 6. International organization — Addresses, essays, lectures. I. Tinbergen, Jan, 1903- II. Dolman, Antony J. III. Ettinger, Jan van, 1902- IV. Club of Rome. V. Title: RIO: reshaping the international order.
JX/1395.R42 1976     330.904     *ISBN* 0525192506

**Rosenau, James N.**         **4.9037**
The scientific study of foreign policy / James N. Rosenau. — Rev. and enl. ed. — New York: Nichols Pub. Co., [1980] xvii, 577 p.; 23 cm. Includes index. 1. International relations — Addresses, essays, lectures. I. T.
JX1395.R573 1980     327.1     *LC* 79-25453     *ISBN* 0893970743

**Sprout, Harold Hance, 1901-.**         • **4.9038**
Foundations of international politics / by Harold and Margaret Sprout. — Princeton, N.J.: Van Nostrand, 1962. vi, 734 p. ill. — (Van Nostrand political science series) 1. International relations 2. World politics — 1945- I. Sprout, Margaret Tuttle, 1903- II. T.
JX1395.S65     *LC* 62-20143

## JX1398–1403 INTEROCEANIC CANALS

**Miner, Dwight Carroll, 1904-.**        • **4.9039**
The fight for the Panama route; the story of the Spooner act and the Hay–Herrán Treaty. New York, Octagon Books, 1966 [c1940] xv, 469 p. maps. 24 cm. Issued also as thesis, Columbia University. 1. Hay-Herrán Treaty, 1903. 2. United States — Foreign relations — Colombia. 3. Colombia — Foreign relations — United States. 4. Panama Canal (Panama) I. T.
JX1398.M5 1966     327.730861     LC 66-18054

**Williams, Mary Wilhelmine, 1878-1944.**        • **4.9040**
Anglo–American Isthmian diplomacy, 1815–1915. Gloucester, Mass., P. Smith, 1965 [c1916] xii, 356 p.: ill. 1. Clayton-Bulwer treaty, 1850 2. Panama Canal (Panama) 3. United States — Foreign relations — Great Britain. 4. Great Britain — Foreign relations — United States. I. T.
JX1398.W5 1965a     LC 65-2973

**Bray, Wayne D.**        **4.9041**
The common law zone in Panama: a case study in reception, with some observations on the relevancy thereof to the Panama Canal Treaty controversy / by Wayne D. Bray; introduction by Gustavo A. Mellander; prólogo por Alfonso L. García Martínez, with an English translation. San Juan, P.R.: Inter American University Press, c1977. xxiii, 150 p., [3] leaves of plates: ill.; 26 cm. Includes index. 1. Panama Canal Treaties, 1977 2. Common law — Canal zone. 3. Civil law — Canal zone. I. T.
LAW     JX1398.73.B7.     340/.0972875     LC 76-23354     ISBN 0913480355

## JX1404–1598 INTERNATIONAL RELATIONS, BY COUNTRY

## JX1405–1431 United States

**Bailey, Thomas Andrew, 1902-.**        • **4.9042**
The art of diplomacy; the American experience [by] Thomas A. Bailey. — New York: Appleton-Century-Crofts, [1968] xii, 303 p.; 21 cm. 1. United States — Foreign relations 2. United States — Diplomatic and consular service I. T.
JX1407.B23     327.73     LC 68-11680

**Beard, Charles Austin, 1874-1948.**        • **4.9043**
The idea of national interest: an analytical study in American foreign policy / by Charles A. Beard; with the collaboration of G. H. E. Smith. — New York: Macmillan, 1934. ix, 583 p.: ill. 1. Investments, American 2. United States — Foreign relations 3. United States — Commercial policy I. Smith, George H. E. (George Howard Edward), 1898-1962. joint author II. T.
JX1407.B28     LC 34-3511

**Dennis, Alfred Lewis Pinneo, 1874-.**        **4.9044**
Adventures in American diplomacy, 1896–1906. — New York: E. P. Dutton & company, [1928] 537 p. 1. United States — Foreign relations — 1901-1909 2. United States — Foreign relations — 1897-1901 I. T.
JX1415.D4     LC 28-7286

**United States. Congress. Senate. Committee on Foreign Relations.**        **4.9045**
A decade of American foreign policy: basic documents, 1941–49 / prepared at the request of the Senate Committee on Foreign Relations by the staff of the committee and the Dept. of State. — Washington: U.S. Govt. Print. Off., 1950. xiv, 1381 p.: ill., map; 24 cm. (Document / [U.S.] 81st Cong., 1st sess. [1950] Senate; no.123) 1. United States. Dept. of State. 2. United States — Foreign relations — 1933-1945 3. United States — Foreign relations — 1945- I. United States. Dept. of State. II. T.
JX1416.A47     327.73     LC 50-60544

**Beard, Charles Austin, 1874-1948.**        • **4.9046**
The devil theory of war; an inquiry into the nature of history and the possibility of keeping out of war. New York, Greenwood Press [1969, c1936] 124 p. 23 cm. 'An expansion of three articles published in the New republic.' An analysis of testimony given to the Special Committee to Investigate the Munitions Industry, U.S. Senate, and a proposal for future American action. 1. World War, 1914-1918 — Economic aspects — United States. 2. World War, 1914-1918 — Finance 3. Investments, American 4. United States — Commercial policy 5. United States — Neutrality I. United States. Congress. Senate. Special Committee to Investigate the Munitions Industry. II. T.
JX1416.B37 1969     327.73     LC 68-54771

**Borchard, Edwin Montefiore, 1884-1951.**        • **4.9047**
Neutrality for the United States / by Edwin Borchard and William Potter Lage. — 2d ed., with new material covering 1937-1940. New Haven, Yale University Press, 1940. [New York: AMS Press, 1973] xi, 461 p.; 23 cm. 1. World War, 1914-1918 — United States. 2. United States — Foreign relations — 20th century 3. United States — Neutrality I. Lage, William Potter. joint author. II. T.
JX1416.B65 1973     327.73     LC 78-153305     ISBN 0404046444

**American foreign policy current documents (Washington, D.C.: 1956)**        • **4.9048**
American foreign policy current documents. — 1956-1967. — Washington, D.C.: Historical Division, Bureau of Public Affairs: for sale by the Supt. of Docs., U.S. G.P.O., 1959-1969. v.; 24 cm. (Department of State publication.) Annual. 1. United States — Foreign relations — 1953-1961 — Sources — Periodicals. I. United States. Dept. of State. Historical Division. II. United States. Dept. of State. Historical Office. III. T. IV. Series.
JX1417.A33     327.73     LC 59-64042

**United States. Dept. of State. Historical Office.**        • **4.9049**
[American foreign policy, 1950-1955] American foreign policy; basic documents, 1950-1955. New York, Arno Press, 1971. 2 v. (lix, 3244, xxv p.) illus., maps (part fold.) 24 cm. (Dept. of State. Publication 6446. General foreign policy series, 117) (American foreign policy, 1941-1963) Reprint of the 1957 ed., published under title: American foreign policy, 1950-1955; basic documents. 1. United States — Foreign relations — 1945- — Sources. I. T.
JX1417.A55 1971     327.73     LC 75-138312     ISBN 040501757X

**Hoyt, Edwin C. (Edwin Chase), 1916-.**        **4.9050**
Law & force in American foreign policy / Edwin C. Hoyt. — Lanham: University Press of America, c1985. 270 p.; 23 cm. 1. Intervention (International law) 2. International law — United States. 3. United States — Foreign relations — 1945- I. T. II. Title: Law and force in American foreign policy.
JX1417.H69 1985     327.73 19     LC 84-21969     ISBN 0819144304

**Thompson, Kenneth W., 1921-.**        **4.9051**
Morality and foreign policy / Kenneth W. Thompson. — Baton Rouge: Louisiana State University Press, c1980. xiii, 197 p.; 24 cm. 1. International relations — Moral and religious aspects. 2. United States — Foreign relations — Moral and religious aspects. I. T.
JX1417.T49     172/.4 19     LC 79-23211     ISBN 0807106569

**Waltz, Kenneth Neal, 1924-.**        • **4.9052**
Foreign policy and democratic politics: the American and British experience / [by] Kenneth N. Waltz. — Boston: Little, Brown, [1967] xii, 331 p.: ill.; 23 cm. 'Jointly sponsored by the Institute of War and Peace Studies, School of International Affairs, Columbia University ... and the Center for International Affairs, Harvard University.' 1. United States — Foreign relations — 1945- 2. Great Britain — Foreign relations — 1945- I. Columbia University. Institute of War and Peace Studies. II. Harvard University. Center for International Affairs. III. T.
JX1417.W3     327     LC 66-28737

**Perkins, Dexter, 1889-.**        • **4.9053**
[Hands off] A history of the Monroe doctrine. [Rev. ed.] Boston, Little, Brown [1955] xiv, 462 p. 22 cm. 'A new edition of the book originally published under the title Hands off: a history of the Monroe doctrine.' 1. Monroe doctrine I. T.
JX1425.P384 1955     327.73     LC 55-10752

**Perkins, Dexter, 1889-.**        **4.9054**
The Monroe doctrine, 1823–1826 / Dexter Perkins. — London: H. Milford, Oxford University Press, 1927. xi, 280 p.; 21 cm. — (Harvard historical studies; v. 29) 'Bibliographical note': p. 263-269. 1. Monroe doctrine. I. T.
JX1425.P385 1927     327.73     LC 27-12082

**Perkins, Dexter, 1889-.**        • **4.9055**
The Monroe doctrine, 1826–1867. Baltimore, Johns Hopkins Press, 1933. xi, 580 p. (The Albert Shaw Lectures on Diplomatic History, 1932) 1. Monroe doctrine I. T. II. Series.
JX1425.P386

**Perkins, Dexter, 1889-.**        • **4.9056**
The Monroe doctrine, 1867–1907 / by Dexter Perkins. — Baltimore: The Johns Hopkins press, 1937. ix, 480 p.; 20 cm. (The Albert Shaw lectures on diplomatic history, 1937) 1. Monroe doctrine I. T. II. Series.
JX1425.P387     LC 38-2735

**United States. Interdepartmental Group for Africa.**        **4.9057**
[Southern Africa] The Kissinger study of Southern Africa: National security study memorandum 39 (secret); edited and introduced by Mohamed A. El-Khawas and Barry Cohen; pref. by Edgar Lockwood. — 1st ed. — Westport, Conn.: L. Hill; [New York: distributed by Whirlwind Book Co.], 1976. 189 p.; 21 cm. Reprint, with new introd. and appendices, of the 1969 ed. of a classified national security study entitled: Southern Africa. 1. United States — Foreign relations — Africa, Southern. 2. Africa, Southern — Foreign relations — United States. I. El-Khawas, Mohamed A. II. Cophen, Barry. III. T.
JX1428.A38 U55 1976     327.73/068     LC 76-18043     ISBN 0882080717

**Canada and the United States: transnational and** **4.9058**
**transgovernmental relations / edited by Annette Baker Fox,**
**Alfred O. Hero, Jr., and Joseph S. Nye, Jr.**
New York: Columbia University Press, 1976, c1974. xiii, 443 p.: ill.; 24 cm. Includes index. 1. United States — Foreign relations — Canada — Addresses, essays, lectures. 2. Canada — Foreign relations — United States — Addresses, essays, lectures. I. Fox, Annette Baker, 1912- II. Hero, Alfred O. III. Nye, Joseph S.
JX1428.C2 C3 1976　　327.73/071　　*LC* 75-45495

**Bachrack, Stanley D., 1927-.** **4.9059**
The Committee of One Million: the 'China Lobby' and U.S. policy, 1953–1971 / Stanley D. Bachrack. — New York: Columbia University Press, 1976. xi, 371 p. Includes index. 1. Committee of One Million (against the Admission of Communist China to the United Nations) New York. 2. United Nations — China. 3. United States — Foreign relations — China. 4. China — Foreign relations — United States. I. T.
JX1428.C6 B3　　JX1428C6 B3.　　327.73/051　　*LC* 76-18117
　*ISBN* 0231039336

**Kahn, E. J. (Ely Jacques), 1916-.** **4.9060**
The China hands: America's Foreign Service officers and what befell them / E. J. Kahn, Jr. — New York: Viking, 1975. xii, 337 p.: map; 25 cm. Includes index. 1. United States — Foreign relations — China. 2. China — Foreign relations — United States. 3. United States — Diplomatic and consular service — China. I. T.
JX1428.C6 K34　　327.73/051　　*LC* 75-15767　　*ISBN* 067021857X

**White, Nathan N.** **4.9061**
U.S. policy toward Korea: analysis, alternatives, and recommendations / Nathan N. White. — Boulder, Colo.: Westview Press, c1979. ix, 231 p.; 23 cm. — (A Westview replica edition) 1. United States — Foreign relations — Korea. 2. Korea — Foreign relations — United States. I. T.
JX1428.K8 W54　　327.73/0519　　*LC* 78-20735　　*ISBN* 0891584900

**Barnet, Richard J.** **4.9062**
The giants: Russia and America / Richard J. Barnet. — New York: Simon and Schuster, c1977. 190 p.; 25 cm. Includes index. 1. Detente 2. United States — Foreign relations — Russia. 3. Russia — Foreign relations — United States. I. T.
JX1428.R8 B36　　327.73/047　　*LC* 77-9004　　*ISBN* 0671227416

**The Making of America's Soviet policy / edited by Joseph S.** **4.9063**
**Nye, Jr.**
New Haven: Yale University Press, c1984. x, 369 p.: ill.; 25 cm. 'Council on Foreign Relations books.' 1. United States — Foreign relations — Soviet Union 2. Soviet Union — Foreign relations — United States I. Nye, Joseph S.
JX1428.S65 M34 1984　　327.73047 19　　*LC* 83-51295　　*ISBN* 0300031408

### JX1429–1431 Confederate States of America

**Callahan, James Morton, 1864-1956.** **• 4.9064**
The diplomatic history of the Southern Confederacy. — New York: Greenwood Press, [1968, c1901] 304 p.; 23 cm. — (The Albert Shaw lectures on diplomatic history, 1900) 1. Confederate States of America — Foreign relations I. T. II. Series.
JX1429.C2 1968　　973.72/1　　*LC* 69-13849

## JX1515–1598 Other Countries

**A Foremost nation: Canadian foreign policy and a changing** **4.9065**
**world / edited by Norman Hillmer and Garth Stevenson.**
Toronto: McClelland and Stewart, c1977. 296 p.; 21 cm. — (Carleton contemporaries) 1. Canada — Foreign relations — 1945- Addresses, essays, lectures. 2. Canada — Foreign economic relations — Addresses, essays, lectures. I. Hillmer, Norman. II. Stevenson, Garth.
JX1515.F67　　327.71　　*LC* 77-370888　　*ISBN* 0771099118

**Sorel, Albert, 1842-1906.** **• 4.9066**
Europe under the old regime / by Albert Sorel; translated by Francis H. Herrick. — New York: Harper & Row, 1964. vi, 80 p. — (Harper torchbooks. The Academy library) Translation of the first chapter of v.1 of the author's L'Europe et la révolution française. 1. International relations — History. 2. International law — History — Europe. 3. State, The 4. Europe — Politics. I. Herrick, Francis Herkomer, 1900- II. T.
JX1542 S613 1964　　320.94　　*LC* 65-7775

**Northedge, F. S.** **4.9067**
Descent from power: British foreign policy, 1945–1973 / F. S. Northedge. — London: Allen & Unwin, 1974. 3-382 p.: maps; 23 cm. (Minerva series of students' handbooks; no. 27) Includes index. 1. Great Britain — Foreign relations — 1945- I. T.
JX1543.N67　　327.41　　*LC* 75-317624　　*ISBN* 0043270506

**Wallace, William, 1941-.** **4.9068**
The foreign policy process in Britain / William Wallace. — London: Royal Institute of International Affairs, 1976 (c1975). x, 320 p.; 25 cm. Includes index. 1. Great Britain — Foreign relations — 1945- I. T.
JX1543.W3　　354/.41　　*LC* 76-361550　　*ISBN* 0905031016

**Beloff, Max, 1913-.** **• 4.9069**
New dimensions in foreign policy; a study in British administrative experience, 1947–59. — New York: Macmillan, 1961. 208 p. 23 cm. Bibliographical Footnotes 1. Gt. Brit. — For. rel. — Europe. 2. International agencies I. T.
JX1543.Z7E73　　327.4204　　*LC* 61-19774

**Katzenstein, Peter J.** **4.9070**
Disjoined partners: Austria and Germany since 1815 / Peter J. Katzenstein. Berkeley: University of California Press, c1976. xv, 263 p.: ill.; 23 cm. 1. Austria — Foreign relations — Germany 2. Germany — Foreign relations — Austria I. T.
JX1547.Z7 G475　　327.436/043　　*LC* 74-30526　　*ISBN* 0520029453

**Degras, Jane Tabrisky, 1905-.** **4.9071**
Soviet documents on foreign policy / selected and edited by Jane Degras. — London: Oxford University Press, 1951-1953. 3 v.; 24 cm. Issued under the auspices of the Royal Institute of International Affairs. 1. Soviet Union — Foreign relations — 1917-1945 I. T.
JX1555.A2 D4　　JX1555.A2 S4.　　327.47　　*LC* 51-3107

**Triska, Jan F.** **• 4.9072**
The theory, law, and policy of Soviet treaties / [by] Jan F. Triska [and] Robert M. Slusser. — Stanford, Calif.: Stanford University Press, 1962. xi, 593 p.; 25 cm. (Hoover institution publications) 1. International and municipal law — Soviet Union. 2. Treaty-making power — Soviet Union. 3. Soviet Union — Foreign relations — 1917-1945 — Treaties. 4. Soviet Union — Foreign relations — 1945- — Treaties. I. Slusser, Robert M. joint author. II. T.
JX1555.Z6 T75　　341.2　　*LC* 62-11989

**Sena, Cānakya, 1921-.** **4.9073**
Soviet–Asian relations in the 1970s and beyond: an interperceptional study / Bhabani Sen Gupta [i.e. C. Sen]. — New York: Praeger, 1976. xii, 368 p.; 25 cm. (Praeger special studies in international politics and government) 1. Russia — Foreign relations — Asia. 2. Asia — Foreign relations — Russia. I. T.
JX1555.Z7 A77　　327.47/05　　*LC* 76-24368　　*ISBN* 0275237400

**Soviet foreign policy toward Western Europe / edited by** **4.9074**
**George Ginsburgs, Alvin Z. Rubinstein.**
New York: Praeger, 1978. vii, 295 p.; 25 cm. Includes index. 1. Russia — Foreign relations — Europe. 2. Europe — Foreign relations — Russia. I. Ginsburgs, George. II. Rubinstein, Alvin Z.
JX1555.Z7 E787　　327.47/04　　*LC* 78-17925　　*ISBN* 0030443318

**Kennan, George Frost, 1904-.** **4.9075**
The nuclear delusion: Soviet–American relations in the atomic age / George F. Kennan. — 1st ed. — New York: Pantheon Books, c1982. xxx, 208 p.; 22 cm. 1. Nuclear disarmament 2. United States — Foreign relations — Soviet Union 3. Soviet Union — Foreign relations — United States I. T.
JX1555.Z7 U437 1982　　327.47073 19　　*LC* 82-14111　　*ISBN* 0394529464

**Maude, George.** **4.9076**
The Finnish dilemma: neutrality in the shadow of power / George Maude. London; New York: Published for the Royal Institute of International Affairs by Oxford University Press, 1976. vi, 153 p.; 22 cm. Includes index. 1. Finland — Foreign relations 2. Finland — Neutrality. 3. Finland — History — 1939- I. T.
JX1555.3.M38　　327.471　　*LC* 77-363111　　*ISBN* 0192183192

**Barnett, A. Doak.** **4.9077**
The making of foreign policy in China: structure and process / A. Doak Barnett. — Westview Press / Foreign Policy Institute ed. — Boulder: Westview Press; [Washington, D.C.]: Foreign Policy Institute, School of Advanced International Studies, Johns Hopkins University, 1985. xiii, 160 p.; 24 cm. (SAIS papers in international affairs. no. 9) Includes index. 1. China — Foreign relations — 1976- I. T. II. Series.
JX1570.B37 1985　　327.51 19　　*LC* 85-3319　　*ISBN* 0813302323

**Hsü, Immanuel Chung-yueh, 1923-.** **• 4.9078**
China's entrance into the family of nations: the diplomatic phase, 1858–1880 / [by] Immanuel C.Y. Hsü; foreword by William L. Langer. — Cambridge: Harvard University Press, 1960. xvi, 255, xxxvi p.: tables; 25 cm. (Harvard East Asian studies, 5) 1. International law — History — China 2. China — Foreign relations — To 1912 3. China — Diplomatic and consular service I. T. II. Series.
JX1570 H7　　*LC* 60-5738

O'Leary, Greg. **4.9079**
The shaping of Chinese foreign policy / Greg O'Leary. — New York: St. Martin's Press, 1980. 302 p.; 23 cm. Includes index. 1. China — Foreign relations — 1949-1976 I. T.
JX1570.O43    327.51    *LC* 80-10231    *ISBN* 0312716230

Falk, Richard A. comp. • **4.9080**
The Vietnam war and international law / edited by Richard A. Falk. — Princeton, N.J.: Princeton University Press, 1968-72. 3 v.; 24 cm. Sponsored by the American Society of International Law. 1. Vietnamese Conflict, 1961-1975 — Addresses, essays, lectures. I. American Society of International Law. II. T.
JX1573.F3    341.6    *LC* 67-31295    *ISBN* 0691092141

The Foreign policy of modern Japan / edited by Robert A. **4.9081**
Scalapino; foreword by Edwin O. Reischauer.
Berkeley: University of California Press, c1977. xix, 426 p.: graphs; 25 cm. Papers presented at a conference held on Kauai, Hawaii, Jan. 14-18, 1974, and sponsored by the Joint Committee on Japanese Studies of the American Council of Learned Societies and the Social Science Research Council. 1. Japan — Foreign relations — 1945- — Decision making — Congresses. 2. Japan — Foreign economic relations — Congresses. I. Scalapino, Robert A. II. Joint Committee on Japanese Studies.
JX1577.F76 1977    327.52    *LC* 77-370835    *ISBN* 0520031962

Slonim, Solomon. **4.9082**
South West Africa and the United Nations: an international mandate in dispute. Baltimore: Johns Hopkins University Press [c1973] xix, 409 p.: map; 24 cm. 1. United Nations — Namibia. 2. Mandates — Namibia. I. T.
JX1586.S64 S55    341.2/7    *LC* 72-4020    *ISBN* 0801814308

# JX1621–1894 Diplomacy. The Diplomatic Service

Nicolson, Harold George, Sir, 1886-1968. • **4.9083**
The evolution of diplomatic method, being the Chichele lectures delivered at the University of Oxford in November 1953. London, Constable [1954] 93 p. 1. Diplomacy — History I. T.
JX1635 N5 1954    *LC* 54-14971

Satow, Ernest Mason, Sir, 1843-1929. **4.9084**
[Guide to diplomatic practice] Satow's Guide to diplomatic practice. — 5th ed. / edited by Lord Gore-Booth, assistant editor, Desmond Pakenham. — London; New York: Longman, 1979. xix, 544 p.: port.; 24 cm. 1. Diplomatic and consular service 2. Diplomacy 3. International relations I. T. II. Title: Guide to diplomatic practice.
JX1635.S3 1979    327    *LC* 77-12580    *ISBN* 0582501091

Mattingly, Garrett, 1900-1962. • **4.9085**
Renaissance diplomacy. — London: Cape, [1955] 323 p.: illus.; 23 cm. 1. Diplomacy — History. I. T.
JX1641.M27 1955a    327.09    *LC* 55-2849

Lauren, Paul Gordon. **4.9086**
Diplomats and bureaucrats: the first institutional responses to twentieth-century diplomacy in France and Germany / Paul Gordon Lauren. — Stanford, Calif.: Hoover Institution Press, 1976. xviii, 294 p.: ill.; 24 cm. (Hoover Institution publications; 153) Includes index. 1. France — Diplomatic and consular service — History. 2. Germany — Diplomatic and consular service — History. 3. France — Politics and government — 20th century 4. Germany — Politics and government — 20th century I. T.
JX1661.L38    350/.892    *LC* 75-29785    *ISBN* 0817965319

Kertesz, Stephen Denis, 1904- ed. • **4.9087**
Diplomacy in a changing world / edited by Stephen D. Kertész and M.A. Fitzsimons. — [Notre Dame, Ind.]: University of Notre Dame Press, 1959. viii, 407 p.; 24 cm. (International studies of the Committee on International Relations, University of Notre Dame) 1. Diplomacy 2. International relations 3. World politics — 1955- I. Fitzsimons, M. A. (Matthew Anthony), 1912- II. T.
JX1662 K4    *LC* 59-10416

Nicolson, Harold George, Sir, 1886-1968. • **4.9088**
Diplomacy. 3d ed. London: Oxford U.P., 1963. 268 p.; 17 cm. (Home university library of modern knowledge. 192.) 1. Diplomacy I. T. II. Series.
JX1662.N5 1964    *LC* 63-24986

Pearson, Lester B. • **4.9089**
Diplomacy in the nuclear age [by] Lester B. Pearson. — Westport, Conn.: Greenwood Press, [1969, c1959] vi, 114 p.; 23 cm. 1. Diplomacy — Addresses, essays, lectures. 2. World politics — 1945- — Addresses, essays, lectures. I. T.
JX1662.P35 1969    327/.2    *LC* 77-94616    *ISBN* 0837125324

Thayer, Charles Wheeler, 1910-. • **4.9090**
Diplomat / Foreword by Sir Harold Nicolson. — [1st ed.]. — New York: Harper [1959] 299 p.; 22 cm. Includes bibliography. 1. Diplomatic and consular service 2. U.S. — Diplomatic and consular service. 3. Russia — Diplomatic and consular service. 4. Diplomacy I. T.
JX1662.T5    327.0973    *LC* 59-6320

Webster, Charles Kingsley, Sir, 1886-1961. • **4.9091**
The art and practice of diplomacy. New York, Barnes & Noble, 1962 [c1961] 245 p. 23 cm. 1. Diplomacy I. T.
JX1664.W39    341.7081    *LC* 62-999

The Times survey of foreign ministries of the world / selected **4.9092**
and edited by Zara Steiner.
London: Times Books; Westport, Conn.: Meckler Pub., c1982. 624 p.; 24 cm. 1. Diplomatic and consular service — History. I. Steiner, Zara S. II. Times Books (Firm)
JX1687.T55 1982    351.01 19    *LC* 82-104557    *ISBN* 0723002452

United States. Dept. of State. **4.9093**
Post report. — [Washington], 19. v.: ill.; 27 cm. Cover title. Includes earlier editions of some volumes. 'Notes for travellers' includes 'Recommended reading.' 1. Voyages and travel — Guide-books. 2. United States — Diplomatic and consular service I. T.
JX1705.A286    341/.33    *LC* 70-612480

Wriston, Henry Merritt, 1889-. • **4.9094**
Diplomacy in a democracy, by Henry M. Wriston. — 1st. ed. — New York: Harper, c1956. 115 p.; 22 cm. 1. Diplomatic and consular service 2. United States — Foreign relations 3. United States — Diplomatic and consular service I. T.
JX1705.W7 1974    JX1705 W7 1956.    327.73    *LC* 56-11919

*JX 1705 W95*

Halperin, Morton H. **4.9095**
Bureaucratic politics and foreign policy [by] Morton H. Halperin, with the assistance of Priscilla Clapp and Arnold Kanter. — Washington: The Brookings Institution, [1974] xvii, 340 p.; 24 cm. 1. United States — Foreign relations administration I. Clapp, Priscilla, joint author. II. Kanter, Arnold. joint author. III. T.
JX1706.A4 1974    353.008/92    *LC* 73-22384    *ISBN* 0815734085

Weil, Martin. **4.9096**
A pretty good club: the founding fathers of the U.S. Foreign Service / Martin Weil. — 1st ed. — New York: Norton, c1978. 313 p.: ill.; 24 cm. Includes index. 1. United States. Foreign Service. I. T.
JX1706.Z5 W4 1978    353.008/92    *LC* 77-25104    *ISBN* 0393056589

Nossal, Kim Richard. **4.9097**
The politics of Canadian foreign policy / Kim Richard Nossal. — Scarborough, Ont.: Prentice-Hall Canada, c1985. xvi, 232 p.; 23 cm. 1. Canada — Foreign relations administration. 2. Canada — Politics and government I. T.
JX1729.Nx    327.71 19    *ISBN* 0136843255

Cuttino, George Peddy. **4.9098**
English diplomatic administration, 1259–1339, by G. P. Cuttino. — 2nd ed., revised and enlarged. — Oxford: Clarendon Press, 1972 (c1971). 280 p., plate.: facsim.; 22 cm. — (Oxford historical monographs) 1. Diplomacy — History. 2. Great Britain — Foreign relations — 1154-1399 I. T.
JX1783.A3    327/.2/0942    *LC* 72-190761    *ISBN* 019822348X

Strang, William Strang, Baron, 1893-. • **4.9099**
The Foreign Office / [by] Lord Strang and other members of the Foreign Service. — London: Allen & Unwin; New York: Oxford University Press, [1955] 226 p.; 23 cm. — (The New Whitehall series) 1. Great Britain. Foreign Office. 2. Gt. Brit. — Diplomatic and consular service. I. T.
JX1783.S8    *LC* 55-2817

Boardman, Robert, 1945-. **4.9100**
The management of Britain's external relations, edited by Robert Boardman and A. J. R. Groom. — New York: Barnes & Noble, 1973. x, 362 p.; 22 cm. 1. Great Britain — Foreign relations administration. I. Groom, A. J. R. joint author. II. T.
JX1784.A4 1973    327.2/0942    *LC* 73-330869    *ISBN* 0333122593

Seabury, Paul. • **4.9101**
The Wilhelmstrasse: a study of German diplomats under the Nazi regime / Paul Seabury. — Berkeley: University of California Press. 1954. xiv, 217 p., [2] leaves of plates: ill.; 23 cm. Originally presented as the author's thesis, Columbia University. Includes index. 1. Germany. Auswärtiges Amt. 2. Germany —

Diplomatic and consular service. 3. Germany — Foreign relations — 1933-1945 I. T.
JX1796.S45 1976    327/.2/0943    *LC* 54-11495

**Mêng, S.M.**                • 4.9102
The Tsungli yamen: its organization and functions. Cambridge, East Asian Research Center, Harvard University; distributed by Harvard University Press, 1962. v, 146 p. (Chinese Economic and Political Studies. Monograph series) 1. China. Wai wu pu. 2. China — Foreign relations — To 1912 I. T.
JX1838 A4 M4    *LC* 62-53393

# JX1901–1995 International Arbitration. World Peace. International Organization

**Yearbook of international organizations = Annuaire des**    • 4.9103
**organisations internationales.**
1st ed. (1948)- . — Brussels: Union of International Associations, 1948- . — Biennial. Some vols. issued for 2 year periods. 1. International agencies — Yearbooks. I. Union of International Associations. II. Title: Annuaire des organisations internationales. III. Title: Yearbook of international organisations.
JX1904.A42    JA51.Y39.    *LC* 49-22132

**Boulding, Kenneth Ewart, 1910-.**    4.9104
Stable peace / Kenneth E. Boulding. — Austin: University of Texas Press, c1978. xii, 143 p.: ill.; 21 cm. 1. Peace — Research 2. International relations — Research. I. T.
JX1904.5.B69    327/.172/072    *LC* 78-617    *ISBN* 0292764472

**Reardon, Betty.**    4.9105
Sexism and the war system / Betty A. Reardon; foreword by Patricia Schroeder. — New York: Teachers College Press, c1985. xiv, 111 p.; 23 cm. Includes index. 1. Peace — Research 2. Women and peace 3. Sexism 4. Feminism I. T.
JX1904.5.R43 1985    327.1/72/088042 19    *LC* 85-12619    *ISBN* 0807727695

**Davis, Calvin DeArmond.**    4.9106
The United States and the Second Hague Peace Conference: American diplomacy and international organization, 1899–1914 / Calvin DeArmond Davis. — Durham, N.C.: Duke University Press, 1975, c1976. ix, 398 p.; 25 cm. Includes index. 1. International Peace Conference. 2d, 1907. 2. International organization 3. United States — Foreign relations — 20th century I. T.
JX1916.D32 1976    341.5    *LC* 75-17353    *ISBN* 0822303469

**Brinton, Crane, 1898-1968.**    • 4.9107
From many, one; the process of political integration, the problem of world government. Westport, Conn., Greenwood Press [1971, c1948] vi, 126 p. 23 cm. 'Based on lectures delivered at Pomona College, Claremont, California, in March 1947 under the Joseph Horsfall Johnson Foundation.' 1. International organization I. T.
JX1938.B75 1971    321/.04    *LC* 70-143309    *ISBN* 0837159644

**Brock, Peter, 1920-.**    4.9108
Pacifism in Europe to 1914. — Princeton, N.J.: Princeton University Press, 1972. x, 556 p.; 25 cm. — (His A History of pacifism, v. 1) 1. Pacifism — History. I. T.
JX1938.B76    261.8/73    *LC* 75-166362    *ISBN* 0691046085

**Hemleben, Sylvester John.**    4.9109
Plans for world peace through six centuries. — Chicago, Ill.: The University of Chicago Press, [1943] 227p. 1. Peace 2. International law — History 3. International relations — History 4. Security, International I. T.
JX1938 H43

**Mangone, Gerard J.**    • 4.9110
A short history of international organization. — New York: McGraw-Hill, 1954. 326 p.; 24 cm. — (McGraw-Hill series in political science) 1. International organization — History. I. T.
JX1938.M25    341.1109    *LC* 53-10619

**Schuman, Frederick Lewis, 1904-.**    • 4.9111
The commonwealth of man; an inquiry into power politics and world government. [1st ed.] New York, Knopf, 1952. xvi, 494, xvi p. 22 cm. 1. International organization 2. International relations I. T.
JX1938.S35    *LC* 52-6424

**Brock, Peter, 1920-.**    • 4.9112
Pacifism in the United States / from the colonial era to the First World War. — Princeton, N.J.: Princeton University Press, 1968. xii, 1005 p.; 25 cm. 1. Pacifism — History. I. T.
JX1944.B75    341.1    *LC* 68-11439

**Hinsley, F. H. (Francis Harry), 1918-.**    • 4.9113
Power and the pursuit of peace: theory and practice in the history of relations between states, by F. H. Hinsley. London, Cambridge U.P., 1967. [7], 416 p. 21 cm. 1. International relations — History. 2. Peace I. T.
JX1944.H5 1967    341.1    *LC* 68-92375    *ISBN* 0521094488

**Howard, Michael Eliot, 1922-.**    4.9114
War and the liberal conscience / Michael Howard. — New Brunswick, N.J.: Rutgers University Press, 1978. 143 p.; 23 cm. — (The Trevelyan lectures; 1977) 1. Peace — History. 2. World politics — To 1900 3. World politics — 20th century 4. War — History. 5. Liberalism 6. Europe — Politics and government I. T. II. Series.
JX1944.H68 1978b    327/.172    *LC* 78-50655    *ISBN* 0813508665

**Kant, Immanuel, 1724-1804.**    4.9115
Perpetual peace / edited, with an introd., by Lewis White Beck. — New York: Liberal Arts Press [1957] xviii, 59 p.; 21 cm. — (The Library of liberal arts, no. 54) Translation of Zum ewigen Frieden. Bibliography: p. xvii. 1. Peace I. T.
JX1946.K3 1957    341.6    *LC* 57-3588

**Ralston, Jackson Harvey, 1857-1945.**    4.9116
International arbitration, from Athens to Locarno, by Jackson H. Ralston. — Stanford University, Calif.: Stanford university press; London: H. Milford, Oxford university press, 1929. xvi, 417 p.; 24 cm. — ([Stanford books in world politics]) Companion volume to the author's 'The law and procedure of international tribunals.' cf. Foreword. 1. Arbitration, International — History. 2. International law — History. I. T.
JX1948.R3    *LC* 29-9590

**Kuehl, Warren F., 1924-.**    4.9117
Seeking world order: the United States and international organization to 1920 / [by] Warren F. Kuehl. — Nashville: Vanderbilt University Press, [1969] xi, 385 p.; 25 cm. 1. International organization 2. United States — Foreign relations — To 1865 I. T.
JX1950.K8    341.1/1/0973    *LC* 69-19952    *ISBN* 0826511376

## JX1952–1953 20TH CENTURY

**Brock, Peter, 1920-.**    4.9118
Twentieth-century pacifism. — New York: Van Nostrand Reinhold, [1970] vii, 274 p.; 21 cm. — (New perspectives in political science, 26) 1. Pacifism I. T.
JX1952.B745    341.1    *LC* 71-15767

**Dickinson, Goldsworthy Lowes.**    • 4.9119
Causes of international war. London: Swarthmore Press, 1920. 110 p.; 19 cm. (International Relations Series) 1. International relations 2. War I. T. II. Series.
JX1952.D53

**Doves and diplomats: foreign offices and peace movements in**    4.9120
**Europe and America in the twentieth century / edited by**
**Solomon Wank.**
Westport, Conn.: Greenwood Press, 1978. xi, 303 p.; 22 cm. — (Contributions in political science. no. 4) 1. Peace — Societies, etc. — History — 20th century — Addresses, essays, lectures. I. Wank, Solomon. II. Series.
JX1952.D69    327/.172/0904    *LC* 77-87969    *ISBN* 0313200270

**Reves, Emery.**    • 4.9121
The anatomy of peace, by Emery Reves. New York and London, Harper & brothers [1946] 5 p. l., 293 p. 19.5 cm. 'Eighth edition.' 1. War 2. Peace 3. Sovereignty 4. World War, 1939-1945 — Peace I. T.
JX1952.R44 1946    341    *LC* 46-2213

**Shotwell, James Thomson, 1874-1965.**    • 4.9122
War as an instrument of national policy and its renunciation in the Pact of Paris / by James T. Shotwell. — New York: Harcourt, Brace and company, 1929. x, 310 p. Vol.XIII of a collection entitled: Documents of the third conference, Institute of Pacific relations, Kyoto, Japan. 1929. 1. Renunciation of war treaty, Paris, Aug. 17, 1928. 2. War 3. United States — Foreign relations — 1923-1929 I. T.
JX1952.S65    *LC* 29-3416

**Veblen, Thorstein, 1857-1929.**    • 4.9123
An inquiry into the nature of peace and the terms of its perpetuation / by Thorstein Veblen. — New York: A.M. Kelley, Bookseller, 1964. xiii, 367 p. —

(Reprints of Economic classics) 1. Peace 2. World War, 1914-1918 — Peace. I. T.
JX1952.V38 1964    *LC* 63-23512

**Wright, Quincy, 1890-1970.**    ● **4.9124**
Problems of stability and progress in international relations. — Berkeley, University of California Press, 1954. xiv, 378 p. 24 cm. Bibliographical references included in 'Notes' (p. [333]-360) 1. International relations — Addresses, essays, lectures. I. T.
JX1952.W72    341.04    *LC* 53-11251

**Young, Oran R.**    ● **4.9125**
The politics of force; bargaining during international crises, by Oran R. Young. Princeton, N.J., [Published for the Center of International Studies, Princeton University, by] Princeton University Press, 1968. xii, 438 p. 23 cm. 1. Arbitration, International I. Woodrow Wilson School of Public and International Affairs. Center of International Studies. II. T.
JX1952.Y65    341.6/3    *LC* 68-27408

**Zacher, Mark W.**    **4.9126**
International conflicts and collective security, 1946–1977: the United Nations, Organization of American States, Organization of African Unity, and Arab League / Mark W. Zacher. — New York: Praeger, 1979. x, 297 p.; 24 cm. 1. Security, International 2. Regionalism (International organization) I. T.
JX1952.Z24    327.1/16 19    *LC* 78-19775    *ISBN* 0030442613

**Waskow, Arthur I.**    ● **4.9127**
The worried man's guide to world peace: a Peace Research Institute handbook / [by] Arthur I. Waskow. — [1st ed.] Garden City, N. Y.: Anchor Books, 1963. xiv, 219 p.; 19 cm. 'A377' 1. Peace I. Washington, D. C. Peace Research Institute. II. T.
JX1953.W38    *LC* 63-16627

# JX1954 International Organization

**Bull, Hedley.**    **4.9128**
The anarchical society: a study of order in world politics / Hedley Bull. — New York: Columbia University Press, 1977. xv, 335 p.: ill.; 25 cm. 1. International organization 2. International relations I. T.
JX1954.B79 1977    341.2 19    *LC* 76-21786    *ISBN* 0231041322

**Claude, Inis L.**    **4.9129**
Swords into plowshares: the problems and progress of international organization / [by] Inis L. Claude, Jr. — 4th ed. — New York: Random House, [1971] xii, 514 p.; 24 cm. 1. International organization — History. I. T.
JX1954.C54 1971    341/.2    *LC* 70-122480    *ISBN* 0394310039

**Conflict in world society: a new perspective on international**    **4.9130**
**relations / edited by Michael Banks; foreword by Herbert Kelman.**
New York: St. Martin's Press, 1984. xx, 234 p.; 23 cm. Essays written in honor of John Burton. Includes indexes. 1. Burton, John W. (John Wear), 1915- — Addresses, essays, lectures. 2. International relations — Addresses, essays, lectures. 3. International organization — Addresses, essays, lectures. I. Banks, Michael. II. Burton, John W. (John Wear), 1915-
JX1954.C578455 1984    327.1/1 19    *LC* 84-4834    *ISBN* 0312162294

**Deutsch, Karl Wolfgang, 1912-.**    ● **4.9131**
Political community and the North Atlantic area: international organization in the light of historical experience / by Karl W. Deutsch [and others]. — New York: Greenwood Press, [1969, c1957] xiii, 228 p.; 23 cm. 1. International organization 2. North Atlantic Region I. T.
JX1954.D46 1969    341.18/18/21    *LC* 69-13882    *ISBN* 0837110548

**Dolman, Antony J.**    **4.9132**
Resources, regimes, and world order / Antony J. Dolman with a foreword by Jan Tinbergen. — New York: Published in cooperation with Foundation Reshaping the International Order (RIO) [by] Pergamon Press, c1981. xiv, 413 p.; 24 cm. — (Pergamon policy studies on international development.) Report resulting from a project of the RIO Foundation. Includes indexes. 1. International organization 2. International cooperation I. T. II. Series.
JX1954.D59 1981    327.1/7 19    *LC* 81-11874    *ISBN* 0080280803

**Falk, Richard A.**    **4.9133**
A study of future worlds / Richard A. Falk. — New York: Free Press, [1975] xxxiii, 506 p.: ill.; 24 cm. (Preferred worlds for the 1990's) 1. International organization 2. International relations I. T.
JX1954.F25    341.2    *LC* 74-10139    *ISBN* 0029100607

**Goodrich, Leland Matthew, 1899- comp.**    **4.9134**
International organization: politics & process. Edited by Leland M. Goodrich & David A. Kay. [Madison, Wis.] University of Wisconsin Press [1973] xxii,

465 p. 22 cm. 'The essays in this volume are collected from International organization, volumes 1-26.' 1. International organization — Addresses, essays, lectures. I. Kay, David A., 1940- joint comp. II. International organization. III. T.
JX1954.G618    341.2    *LC* 72-7986    *ISBN* 0299062503 *ISBN* 0299062546

**Kim, Samuel S., 1935-.**    **4.9135**
The quest for a just world order / Samuel S. Kim. — Boulder, Colo.: Westview Press, 1984. xix, 440 p.; 24 cm. — (Westview special studies in international relations.) Includes index. 1. International organization I. T. II. Series.
JX1954.K47 1984    341.2 19    *LC* 83-10327    *ISBN* 0865313652

**Lagos Matus, Gustavo.**    **4.9136**
Revolution of being: a Latin American view of the future / Gustavo Lagos and Horacio H. Godoy. — New York: Free Press, c1977. xxvii, 226 p.; 25 cm. — (Preferred worlds for the 1990's) 1. International organization 2. Twenty-first century 3. Latin America — Economic conditions — 1945- 4. Latin America — Social conditions — 1945- I. Godoy, Horacio H. joint author. II. T.
JX1954.L33    341.2    *LC* 77-3848    *ISBN* 0029178401

**Mangone, Gerard J.**    ● **4.9137**
The idea and practice of world government. — New York: Columbia University Press, 1951. xi, 278 p. 1. International organization I. T.
JX1954.M343    *LC* 51-11232

**Mitrany, David, 1888-.**    **4.9138**
The functional theory of politics / David Mitrany. — [London]: London School of Economics & Political Science; New York: St. Martin's Press, 1976, c1975. xxv, 294 p.; 23 cm. Autobiographical. Includes index. 1. Mitrany, David, 1888- 2. International organization I. T.
JX1954.M498 1976    327    *LC* 75-37253

**Streit, Clarence Kirshman, 1896-.**    ● **4.9139**
Union now: a proposal for an Atlantic federal union of the free. — Postwar ed., with 5 new chapters. — New York: Harper, [1949] 324 p. 'First made public in essence in three Cooper Foundation lectures at Swarthmore College.' Includes the text of the shorter version, first pub. in 1940. 1. International organization 2. Democracy 3. World politics 4. Security, International 5. United States — Foreign relations I. T.
JX1954.S8 1949    *LC* 49-759

# JX1961–1963 Pacifism

**Robbins, Keith.**    **4.9140**
The abolition of war: the 'Peace Movement' in Britain, 1914–1919 / [by] Keith Robbins. — Cardiff: University of Wales Press, 1976. 255 p.; 23 cm. Includes index. 1. World War, 1914-1918 — Protest movements — Great Britain. I. T.
JX1961.G7 R6    940.3/162/0941    *LC* 77-360251    *ISBN* 0708306225

**Chatfield, Charles, 1934-.**    ● **4.9141**
For peace and justice; pacifism in America, 1914–1941. — [1st ed.]. — Knoxville: University of Tennessee Press, [1971] viii, 447 p.: illus., ports.; 24 cm. 1. Pacifism — History. I. T.
JX1961.U6 C5    327/.172    *LC* 70-142143    *ISBN* 0870491261

**Curti, Merle Eugene, 1897-.**    **4.9142**
Peace or war; the American struggle, 1636–1936. New York, W. W. Norton & company [c1936] 374 p. 23 cm. 1. Peace 2. Peace societies. 3. Public opinion — United States. 4. Arbitration, International — History. 5. United States — Foreign relations I. T.
JX1961.U6 C83    *LC* 36-9208

**DeBenedetti, Charles.**    **4.9143**
The peace reform in American history / Charles DeBenedetti. — Bloomington: Indiana University Press, c1980. xvii, 245 p.; 24 cm. Includes index. 1. Peace — History. I. T.
JX1961.U6 D42    327/.172/09    *LC* 79-2173    *ISBN* 0253130956

**Marchand, C. Roland, 1933-.**    ● **4.9144**
The American peace movement and social reform, 1898–1918, by C. Roland Marchand. [Princeton] N.J.: Princeton University Press, [1973, c1972] xix, 441 p.; 25 cm. 1. Peace 2. Peace — Societies, etc. 3. Social movements — United States. I. T.
JX1961.U6 M37    327/.172    *LC* 70-166382    *ISBN* 0691046093

**Patterson, David S., 1937-.**    **4.9145**
Toward a warless world: the travail of the American peace movement, 1887–1914 / by David S. Patterson. Bloomington: Indiana University Press, c1976. xi, 339 p.; 24 cm. 1. Peace — History. I. T.
JX1961.U6 P33 1976    327/.172/0973    *LC* 75-28916    *ISBN* 0253360196

Wittner, Lawrence S.                                    **4.9146**
Rebels against war: the American peace movement, 1933–1983 / Lawrence S. Wittner. — Rev. ed. — Philadelphia: Temple University Press, 1984. viii, 364 p.; 22 cm. Includes index. 1. Peace — History. 2. United States — Foreign relations — 20th century I. T.
JX1961.U6 W53 1984       327.1/72/0973 19       *LC* 83-27523       *ISBN* 0877223467

**My country is the whole world: an anthology of women's work**       **4.9147**
**on peace and war / [compiled by] Cambridge Women's Peace Collective.**
London; Boston: Pandora Press, 1984. xiv, 306 p.: ill., ports.; 21 cm. 1. Women and peace — Addresses, essays, lectures. 2. Peace — Addresses, essays, lectures. 3. War — Addresses, essays, lectures. I. Cambridge Women's Peace Collective.
JX1965.M9 1984       327.1/72/088042 19       *LC* 83-17201       *ISBN* 0863580041

# JX1971 COURTS OF INTERNATIONAL ARBITRATION

**Hudson, Manley Ottmer, 1886-.**                      **4.9148**
The Permanent Court of International Justice, 1920–1942: a treatise / by Manley O. Hudson. — New York: Arno Press, 1972 [c1943] xxiv, 807 p.; 24 cm. — (World affairs: national and international viewpoints) 1. Permanent Court of International Justice. I. T. II. Series.
JX1971.5.H719 1972b       341.5/5       *LC* 72-4277       *ISBN* 0405045719

**Jenks, C. Wilfred (Clarence Wilfred), 1909-1973.**       **• 4.9149**
The prospects of international adjudication, by C. Wilfred Jenks. London, Stevens, 1964. xl, 805 p. (The Law of international institutions) 1. Permanent Court of International Justice. 2. International Court of Justice. I. T.
JX1971.5 J35 1964       *LC* 63-15142

**Lauterpacht, Hersch, Sir, 1897-1960.**                **• 4.9150**
The development of international law by the International Court, being a revised edition of The development of international law by the Permanent Court of International Justice (1934). — New York: Praeger, [1958] 408 p.; 25 cm. 1. Permanent Court of International Justice. 2. International Court of Justice. 3. International law — History. I. T.
JX1971.5.L3 1958b       341.1       *LC* 58-8540

**Lissitzyn, Oliver James, 1912-.**                     **• 4.9151**
The International Court of Justice: its role in the maintenance of international peace and security / by Oliver J. Lissitzyn. — New York: Octagon Books, 1972. 118 p.; 24 cm. Reprint of the 1951 ed., which was issued as no. 6 of United Nations studies. 1. International Court of Justice. I. T.
JX1971.6.L5 1972       341.5/5       *LC* 72-159207       *ISBN* 0374950431

**Rosenne, Shabtai. ed.**                               **4.9152**
Documents on the International Court of Justice / compiled and edited by Shabtai Rosenne. — Leiden: A.W. Sijthoff; Dobbs Ferry, N.Y.: Oceana, 1974. xi, 391 p.; 25 cm. 1. International Court of Justice. I. T.
JX/1971.6.R82       JX1971.6 R58.       *LC* 73-91985       *ISBN* 0379001888

**Rosenne, Shabtai.**                                   **4.9153**
The law and practice of the International Court / by Shabtai Rosenne. — 2nd rev. ed. — Dordrecht: M. Nijhoff, 1985. xxv, 811 p.; 25 cm. Includes index. 1. International Court of Justice. I. T.
JX1971.6.R62 1985       341.5/52 19       *LC* 85-2997       *ISBN* 9024729866

# JX1974 DISARMAMENT

**Becker, Abraham Samuel, 1927-.**                      **4.9154**
Military expenditure limitation for arms control: problems and prospects: with a documentary history of recent proposals / Abraham S. Becker. — Cambridge, Mass.: Ballinger Pub. Co., c1977. xiv, 352 p.; 24 cm. Includes index. 1. Disarmament 2. Armed Forces — Appropriations and expenditures I. T.
JX1974.B366       327/.174       *LC* 77-8224       *ISBN* 0884104702

**Noel-Baker, Philip John, Baron, 1889-.**              **4.9155**
The first world disarmament conference, 1932–1933 and why it failed / by Philip Noel-Baker. — Oxford; New York: Pergamon Press, 1979. xiv, 147 p.; 22 cm. 1. Conference for the Reduction and Limitation of Armaments, Geneva, 1932-1934. 2. Disarmament I. T.
JX1974.C67 N63 1979       327/.174       *LC* 78-40922       *ISBN* 0080233651

**Dallin, Alexander.**                                  **• 4.9156**
The Soviet Union and disarmament: an appraisal of Soviet attitudes and intentions / by Alexander Dallin and others. — New York: Published for the

School of International Affairs, Columbia University, by F. A. Praeger [1964] xi, 282 p. 25 cm. — (Praeger special studies in international politics and administration) Includes bibliographical references. 1. Disarmament 2. Russia — For. rel. — 1945- 3. Russia — Military policy. I. T.
JX1974.D33       341.67       *LC* 64-25591

**Decisionmaking for arms limitation: assessments and prospects /**       **4.9157**
**edited by Hans Guenter Brauch, Duncan L. Clarke.**
Cambridge, Mass.: Ballinger Pub. Co., c1983. xxxi, 332 p.; 24 cm. 1. Arms control — Decision making. I. Brauch, Hans Günter, 1947- II. Clarke, Duncan L.
JX1974.D4 1983       327.1/74 19       *LC* 82-22773       *ISBN* 0884108643

**Dingman, Roger.**                                     **4.9158**
Power in the Pacific: the origins of naval arms limitation, 1914–1922 / Roger Dingman. — Chicago: University of Chicago Press, 1976. xiii, 318 p.: ill.; 24 cm. Includes index. 1. United States. Navy — History 2. Great Britain. Royal Navy — History. 3. Japan. Kaigun — History. 4. Disarmament — History. I. T.
JX1974.D465       327/.172       *LC* 75-36402       *ISBN* 0226153312

**Etzioni, Amitai.**                                    **• 4.9159**
The hard way to peace: a new strategy. [1st ed.] New York: Collier Books [1962] 285 p.; 18 cm. (A Collier Books original, AS212) 1. Nuclear disarmament 2. Disarmament I. T.
JX1974.E75       341.67       *LC* 62-12073

**Millis, Walter, 1899-1968.**                          **• 4.9160**
The abolition of war / [by] Walter Millis & James Real. — New York: Macmillan [1963] 217 p.; 21 cm. 1. Disarmament 2. International organization I. Real, James, joint author. II. T.
JX1974.M52       341.67       *LC* 63-11805

**Saaty, Thomas L.**                                    **• 4.9161**
Mathematical models of arms control and disarmament: application of mathematical structures in politics [by] Thomas L. Saaty. — New York: Wiley, [1968] ix, 190 p.: ill.; 23 cm. — (Operations Research Society of America. Publications in operations research, no. 14) 1. Disarmament — Mathematical models. I. T. II. Series.
JX1974.S115       341.6/7/0182       *LC* 68-9248       *ISBN* 0471748102

**Spanier, John W.**                                    **• 4.9162**
The politics of disarmament: a study in Soviet–American gamesmanship / by John W. Spanier and Joseph L. Nogee. — New York: F. A. Praeger [1962] 226 p.; 21 cm. (Books that matter) 1. Disarmament 2. Nuclear disarmament I. Nogee, Joseph L. joint author. II. T.
JX1974.S64       341.67       *LC* 62-20191

**Stanford Arms Control Group.**                        **4.9163**
International arms control: issues and agreements / by the Stanford Arms Control Group; edited by John H. Barton and Lawrence D. Weiler. — Stanford, Calif.: Stanford University Press, 1976. ix, 444 p.: ill.; 24 cm. Includes index. 1. Disarmament 2. Nuclear arms control I. Barton, John H. II. Weiler, Lawrence D. III. T.
JX1974.S6575 1976       327/.174       *LC* 76-14270       *ISBN* 0804709211

**Stockholm International Peace Research Institute.**       **4.9164**
Arms control: a survey and appraisal of multilateral agreements / Stockholm International Peace Research Institute; [written by Jozef Goldblat]. London: Taylor & Francis; New York: Crane, Russak, 1978. 238 p.; 24 cm. 1. Arms control 2. Nuclear disarmament 3. Treaties I. Goldblat, Jozef. II. T.
JX1974.S78 1978       *LC* 78-54614       *ISBN* 0844813583

**Wainhouse, David Walter, 1900-.**                     **• 4.9165**
Arms control agreements: designs for verification and organization / [by] David W. Wainhouse in association with Bernhard G. Bechhoefer [and others]. — Baltimore: Johns Hopkins Press, [1968] ix, 179 p.; 24 cm. 'A revision and condensation of a study initially prepared by the Washington Center of Foreign Policy Research under a contract for the United States Arms Control and Disarmament Agency.' 1. Arms control I. Washington Center of Foreign Policy Research. II. United States. Arms Control and Disarmament Agency. III. T.
JX1974.W23 1968       341.6/7       *LC* 68-9694

**Wheeler-Bennett, John Wheeler, Sir, 1902-1975.**       **• 4.9166**
The pipe dream of peace: the story of the collapse of disarmament / by John W. Wheeler-Bennett. — New York: H. Fertig, 1971 [c1935] xi, 302 p.; 23 cm. 1. Conference for the Reduction and Limitation of Armaments, Geneva, 1932-1934. 2. Disarmament 3. World politics — 1919-1932 I. T.
JX1974.W53 1971       341/.73       *LC* 76-80601

**Arms, defense policy, and arms control: essays / by Franklin A.**       **4.9167**
**Long ... [et al.]; edited by Franklin A. Long and George W. Rathjens.**
New York: Norton, 1975. 222 p.: ill.; 24 cm. 1. Nuclear arms control — Addresses, essays, lectures. 2. Disarmament — Addresses, essays, lectures.

3. United States — Defenses — Addresses, essays, lectures. 4. Soviet Union — Defenses — Addresses, essays, lectures. I. Long, Franklin A., 1910- II. Rathjens, George W.
JX1974.7.A68 1975    327/.174    *LC* 76-357900    *ISBN* 0393055736

**Barnaby, Frank.**                                                    **4.9168**
Arms uncontrolled / SIPRI, Stockholm International Peace Research Institute; prepared by Frank Barnaby, and Ronald Huisken. — Cambridge, Mass.: Harvard University Press, 1975. xiii, 232 p., [4] leaves of plates: ill.; 25 cm. Includes index. 1. Nuclear nonproliferation 2. Militarism I. Huisken, Ronald. joint author. II. Stockholm International Peace Research Institute. III. T.
JX1974.7.B365    338.4/7/355    *LC* 75-2815    *ISBN* 0674046552

**Beker, Avi.**                                                        **4.9169**
Disarmament without order: the politics of disarmament at the United Nations / Avi Beker. — Westport, Conn.: Greenwood Press, 1985. xii, 212 p.: ill.; 25 cm. (Contributions in political science. 0147-1066; no. 118) Includes index. 1. United Nations. 2. Nuclear disarmament 3. Disarmament I. T. II. Series.
JX1974.7.B44 1985    341.7/33 19    *LC* 84-6722    *ISBN* 031324362X

**Beres, Louis René.**                                                **4.9170**
Apocalypse: nuclear catastrophe in world politics / Louis René Beres; with a foreword by Paul C. Warnke. — Chicago: University of Chicago Press, 1980. xvi, 315 p.; 24 cm. 1. Nuclear disarmament 2. Nuclear warfare 3. International organization I. T.
JX1974.7.B457    327.1/74    *LC* 80-13541    *ISBN* 0226043606

**Disarmament: negotiations and treaties, 1946–1971.**                **4.9171**
New York, Scribner [1972] ix, 385 p. 22 cm. (Keesing's research report) 1. Nuclear disarmament — History.
JX1974.7.D57    341.73    *LC* 72-500    *ISBN* 0684129191 *ISBN* 0684129183

**The dynamics of the arms race / edited by David Carlton and**        **4.9172**
**Carlo Schaerf.**
New York: Wiley, [1975] 244 p.; 23 cm. Articles originally presented at a symposium sponsored by the University of Padua. 'A Halsted Press book.' 1. Nuclear disarmament — Addresses, essays, lectures. I. Carlton, David, 1938- II. Schaerf, Carlo. III. Università di Padova.
JX1974.7.D88    327/.174    *LC* 74-20106    *ISBN* 0470134801

**Galtung, Johan.**                                                    **4.9173**
There are alternatives!: four roads to peace and security / Johan Galtung. — Nottingham, England: Spokesman; Chester Springs, PA: U.S. distributor Dufour Editions, 1984. 221 p.: ill.; 22 cm. Distributor statement from label on t.p. 1. Nuclear disarmament I. T.
JX1974.7.G27 1984    327.1/74 19    *LC* 84-70304    *ISBN* 0851243932

**Nuclear arms control: background and issues / Committee on**         **4.9174**
**International Security and Arms Control, National Academy of**
**Sciences.**
Washington, D.C.: National Academy Press, 1985. x, 378 p.; 23 cm. Includes index. 1. Nuclear arms control — United States. 2. Nuclear arms control — Soviet Union. I. National Academy of Sciences (U.S.). Committee on International Security and Arms Control.
JX1974.7.N812 1985    327.1/74/0973 19    *LC* 84-62287    *ISBN* 0309034914

**Quester, George H.**                                                 **4.9175**
The politics of nuclear proliferation [by] George Quester. — Baltimore: Johns Hopkins University Press, [1973] x, 249 p.; 23 cm. 1. Nuclear nonproliferation 2. Nuclear weapons I. T.
JX1974.7.Q47    327/.174    *LC* 73-8119    *ISBN* 0801814774

**Russell, Bertrand, 1872-1970.**                                      • **4.9176**
Has man a future? / Bertrand Russell. — New York: Simon and Schuster, 1962, c1961. 128 p. 1. Nuclear disarmament I. T.
JX1974.7.R8 1962    327    *LC* 62-9600

**Thompson, E. P. (Edward Palmer), 1924-.**                            **4.9177**
Beyond the cold war: a new approach to the arms race and nuclear annihilation / E.P. Thompson. — 1st American ed. — New York: Pantheon Books, c1982. xxii, 198 p.; 22 cm. 1. Nuclear disarmament 2. Arms race — History — 20th century. I. T.
JX1974.7.T525 1982    327.1/74 19    *LC* 82-47896    *ISBN* 0394527968

**York, Herbert Frank, comp.**                                         **4.9178**
Arms control: readings from Scientific American / with introductions by Herbert F. York. — San Francisco: W. H. Freeman [1973] vi, 427 p.: ill. (part col.); 30 cm. 1. Nuclear arms control I. Scientific American. II. T.
JX1974.7.Y57    327/.174    *LC* 73-4963    *ISBN* 0716708809 *ISBN* 0716708795

**Atlantic Council of the United States. Nuclear Fuels Policy**        **4.9179**
**Working Group.**
Nuclear power and nuclear weapons proliferation: report of the Atlantic Council's Nuclear Fuels Policy Working Group. — [Washington]: Atlantic Council of the United States; Boulder, Colo.: distributed by Westview Press, [1977] 2 v.; 25 cm. (Energy series) (Policy papers) 1. Nuclear nonproliferation 2. Nuclear energy — International control. I. T.
JX1974.73.A88 1977    327/.174    *LC* 78-59089    *ISBN* 0917258134

**Talbott, Strobe.**                                                   **4.9180**
Deadly gambits: the Reagan administration and the stalemate in nuclear arms control / Strobe Talbott. — 1st ed. — New York: Knopf: Distributed by Random House, 1984. xiv, 380 p.; 25 cm. 1. Strategic Arms Reduction Talks. 2. Nuclear arms control 3. United States — Foreign relations — 1981- I. T.
JX1974.76.T34 1984    327.1/74 19    *LC* 84-47781    *ISBN* 0394536371

## JX1975 LEAGUE OF NATIONS

**Bendiner, Elmer.**                                                   **4.9181**
A time for angels: the tragicomic history of the League of Nations / by Elmer Bendiner. 1st ed. — New York: Knopf: distributed by Random House, 1975. xiv, 441, xviii p., [8] leaves of plates: ill.; 25 cm. Includes index. 1. League of Nations — History. I. T.
JX1975.B3644    341.22    *LC* 74-21279    *ISBN* 0394481836

**Burton, Margaret Ernestine, 1885-.**                                 • **4.9182**
The Assembly of the League of Nations / by Margaret E. Burton. — Chicago, Illinois: University of Chicago Press, 1941. xi, 441 p.; 23 cm. 1. League of Nations. Assembly. I. T.
JX1975.B83 1941    341.22/2    *LC* 41-19714

**Fleming, Denna Frank, 1893-.**                                       • **4.9183**
The United States and the League of Nations, 1918–1920 / by D. F. Fleming. — New York: Russell & Russell [1968] 593 p.: ill., ports.; 25 cm. 1. Wilson, Woodrow, 1856-1924. 2. League of Nations — United States. 3. United States. 66th Cong., 1919-1921. Senate. 4. Treaty of Versailles (1919). 5. United States — Foreign relations — 1913-1921 I. T.
JX1975.F585 1968    341.1    *LC* 66-24689

**Greaves, Harold Richard Goring, 1907-.**                             • **4.9184**
The League committees and world order; a study of the permanent expert committees of the League of nations as an instrument of international government, by H.R.G. Greaves ... London, Oxford university press, 1931. xi, 266 p., 1 l. 1. League of Nations. 2. International co-operation 3. Intellectual co-operation I. T.
JX1975.G675

**Henig, Ruth B. (Ruth Beatrice)**                                     **4.9185**
The League of Nations, edited by Ruth B. Henig. Edinburgh, Oliver and Boyd, 1973. x, 203 p. 22 cm. (Evidence and commentary) 1. League of Nations. I. T.
JX1975.H43    341.22    *LC* 74-158008    *ISBN* 0050025929 *ISBN* 0050025899

**Joyce, James Avery.**                                                **4.9186**
Broken star: the story of the League of Nations (1919–1939) / [by] James Avery Joyce. — Swansea: C. Davies, 1978. 231 p.: ill., facsims., maps, ports.; 22 cm. Includes index. 1. League of Nations — History. I. T.
JX1975.J74 1978    341.22    *LC* 79-300195    *ISBN* 0715404199

**Miller, David Hunter, 1875-.**                                       • **4.9187**
The drafting of the Covenant, by David Hunter Miller, with an introduction by Nicholas Murray Butler ... New York, G.P. Putnam's sons, 1928. 2 v. 1. League of Nations. Covenant 2. Paris Peace Conference (1919-1920). I. T.
JX1975 M45    *LC* 28-14675

**Ranshofen-Wertheimer, Egon Ferdinand, 1894-.**                       • **4.9188**
The international secretariat: a great experiment in international administration / by Egon F. Ranshofen–Wertheimer. — Washington, D.C.: Carnegie Endowment for International Peace, 1945. xxvii, 478 p.: ill. — (Studies in the administration of international law and organization; no. 3) 1. League of Nations. Secretariat. 2. International organization I. Carnegie Endowment for International Peace. Division of International Law. II. T. III. Series.
JX 1975 R21 1945

**Schwarzenberger, Georg, 1908-.**                                     • **4.9189**
The League of nations and world order; a treatise on the principle of universality in the theory and practice of the League of nations, by Georg Schwarzenberger ... preface by H.A. Smith ... London, Constable, 1936. xvii, 191 p. (New commonwealth institute monographs. [Ser. A no. 3]) 1. League of Nations. 2. Peace I. T.
JX1975.S29 1936

**Scott, George, 1925-.**    **4.9190**
The rise and fall of the League of Nations. — [1st American ed.]. — New York: Macmillan, [1974, c1973] 432 p.; 24 cm. 1. League of Nations. I. T.
JX1975.S36 1974    341.22    *LC* 73-20179

**Walters, F. P. (Francis Paul), 1888-.**    **4.9191**
A history of the League of Nations / F.P. Walters. — London: Oxford University Press, 1952. 2 v. (xv, 833 p.); 23 cm. 1. League of Nations — History. I. T.
JX1975.W28    341.1209    *LC* 52-7354

**Zimmern, Alfred Eckhard, Sir, 1879-1957.**    • **4.9192**
The League of Nations and the rule of law, 1918–1935. — New York: Russell & Russell, [1969] xiii, 542 p.; 23 cm. Reprint of the 1939 ed. 1. League of Nations. 2. League of Nations. Covenant. 3. International law — History. I. T.
JX1975.Z45 1969    341.12    *LC* 69-17852

**Veatch, Richard, 1926-.**    **4.9193**
Canada and the League of Nations / Richard Veatch. — Toronto; Buffalo: University of Toronto Press, [1975] xi, 224 p.; 24 cm. Includes index. 1. League of Nations — Canada. I. T.
JX1975.5.C2 V43    341.22/71    *LC* 75-19086    *ISBN* 0802053319

**Fleming, Denna Frank, 1893-.**    • **4.9194**
The United States and world organization, 1920–1933. — New York: AMS Press, 1966 [c1938] xiv, 569 p.: ill.; 24 cm. 1. League of Nations — United States. 2. World politics — 1919-1932 3. United States — Foreign relations I. T.
JX1975.5.U5 F6 1966    *LC* 70-168040

**Stone, Ralph A.**    • **4.9195**
The irreconcilables; the fight against the League of Nations [by] Ralph Stone. — [Lexington]: University Press of Kentucky, [1970] 208 p.; 24 cm. 1. League of Nations — U.S. I. T.
JX1975.5.U5 S75    341.12    *LC* 70-94073    *ISBN* 0813111994

# JX1976–1977 United Nations

**Russell, Ruth B.**    • **4.9196**
A history of the United Nations Charter; the role of the United States, 1940–1945, by Ruth B. Russell, assisted by Jeannette E. Muther. Washington, Brookings Institution [1958] xviii, 1140 p. (The Brookings series on the United Nations) 1. United Nations. Charter. 2. United Nations — History 3. United Nations — United States I. T.
JX1976 R8    *LC* 58-14016

**United States. Delegation to the United Nations Conference on**    • **4.9197**
**International Organization, San Francisco, 1945.**
Charter of the United Nations. Report to the President on the results of the San Francisco conference by the chairman of the United States delegation, the Secretary of State. New York, Greenwood Press [1969] 266 p. 23 cm. Commonly known as the Stettinius report. Reprint of the 1945 ed. Edward R. Stettinius, Jr., chairman. 1. United Nations Conference on International Organization (1945: San Francisco, Calif.) I. Stettinius, Edward R. (Edward Reilly), 1900-1949. II. T. III. Title: Stettinius report on the Charter of the United Nations.
JX1976.4.U55 1945mb    341.13/2    *LC* 73-94623    *ISBN* 0837124670

**Annual review of United Nations affairs, 1970–1971 / edited by**    **4.9198**
**Florence Remz.**
1949-. Dobbs Ferry, N.Y. [etc.]: Oceana Publications [etc.], 1972. 197 p.; 24 cm. 1. United Nations — Yearbooks. I. Eagleton, Clyde, 1891-1958, ed. II. New York University. Graduate Program of Studies in United Nations and World Affairs. III. Institute for Annual Review of United Nations Affairs.
JX1977.A1 A5    341.13058    *LC* 50-548

**United Nations. General Assembly.**    • **4.9199**
Rules of procedure. — Dec. 1947-. New York: [s.n.], 1947-. v.; 23 cm. ([Document] (United Nations) A/520) Issued with the United Nations publications sales numbers. 1. United Nations. General Assembly — Rules and practice. I. T. II. Series.
JX1977.A3362 JX1977.A2    341.133

**Dag Hammarskjöld revisited: the UN Secretary–General as a**    **4.9200**
**force in world politics / edited by Robert S. Jordan.**
Durham, N.C.: Carolina Academic Press, c1983. xvi, 197 p.: ill.; 24 cm. (International relations series; no. 8) Includes index. 1. Hammarskjöld, Dag, 1905-1961 — Addresses, essays, lectures. 2. United Nations. Secretary-General — Addresses, essays, lectures. I. Jordan, Robert S., 1929-
JX1977.A362 D33 1983    341.23/24 19    *LC* 81-70434    *ISBN* 0890892334

**Everyone's United Nations.**    **4.9201**
9th-   ed.; 1979-. New York, United Nations. v. 23 cm. 1st-8th editions, 1948-1968, had title: Everyman's United Nations. 1. United Nations. I. United Nations. Dept. of Public Information.
JX1977.A37 E9    341.23    *LC* 80-644223

**United Nations.**    • **4.9202**
Yearbook. 1946/47-. New York: Columbia University Press in co-operation with the United Nations. v.,illus. Annual. United Nations publications.Sales no.:1947.I18,etc. 1. International agencies — Yearbooks. I. United Nations. Dept. of Public Information. II. T. III. Title: United Nations yearbook.
JX1977.A37 Y4    *LC* 47-7191

**Finley, Blanche, 1906-.**    **4.9203**
The structure of the United Nations General Assembly, its committees, commissions, and other organisms, 1946–1973 / by Blanche Finley. — Dobbs Ferry, N.Y.: Oceana Publications, 1977. 3 v. (1463 p.); 26 cm. 1. United Nations. General Assembly. I. T. II. Title: Structure of the United Nations General Assembly ...
JX1977.A495 F56    341.23/2    *LC* 77-72373    *ISBN* 0379102404

**Bailey, Sydney Dawson.**    **4.9204**
The procedure of the UN Security Council / Sydney D. Bailey. — Oxford [Eng.]: Clarendon Press, 1975. xii, 424 p.; 22 cm. 1. United Nations. Security Council. I. T.
JX1977.A593 B34    341.23/2    *LC* 76-355298    *ISBN* 0198271999

**Asher, Robert E., 1910-.**    • **4.9205**
The United Nations and promotion of the general welfare / by Robert E. Asher ... [et al.]. — Washington, D. C.: Brookings Institution, 1957. xvi, 1216 p.; 24 cm. 'Charter of the United Nations':p.1083-1101. 'Universal declaration of human rights':p. 1108-1122. 'Draft covenant on civil and political rights':p. 1112-1122. 'Draft covenant on economic, social and cultural rights':p. 1123-1129. 1. United Nations. 2. Public welfare 3. Civil rights 4. Colonies I. Brookings Institution. II. United Nations. Charter. III. United Nations. General Assembly. Universal Declaration of Human Rights IV. T.
JX1977.A816    341.13    *LC* 57-13368

**Baehr, P. R. (Peter R.)**    **4.9206**
The United Nations: reality and ideal / Peter R. Baehr and Leon Gordenker. — New York: Praeger, 1984. p. cm. Includes index. 1. United Nations. I. Gordenker, Leon, 1923- II. T.
JX1977.B214 1984    341.23 19    *LC* 84-3155    *ISBN* 0030627575

**Bailey, Sydney Dawson.**    • **4.9207**
The General Assembly of the United Nations; a study of procedure and practice [by] Sydney D. Bailey. Rev. ed. New York, Praeger [1964] xv, 374 p. ill. 'Published under the auspices of the Carnegie Endowment for International Peace.' Errata slip inserted. 1. United Nations. General Assembly. I. Carnegie Endowment for International Peace. II. T.
JX1977 B22 1964    *LC* 64-22485

**Bailey, Sydney Dawson.**    **4.9208**
Voting in the Security Council [by] Sydney D. Bailey. — Bloomington: Indiana University Press, [c1969] vii, 275 p.; 24 cm. — (Indiana University international studies) Documents included in appendices (p. [105]-236) 1. United Nations. Security Council. 2. United Nations — Voting I. T.
JX1977.B227    341.13/5    *LC* 69-15990    *ISBN* 025336275X

**Castañeda, Jorge.**    **4.9209**
[Valor jurídico de las resoluciones de las Naciones Unidas. English] Legal effects of United Nations resolutions / translated by Alba Amoia. — New York: Columbia University Press, 1969. viii, 243 p.; 23 cm. (Columbia University studies in international organization, no. 6) Translation of Valor jurídico de las resoluciones de las Naciones Unidas. 1. United Nations — Resolutions I. T. II. Series.
JX1977.C29813    341.13    *LC* 75-94629    *ISBN* 0231033784

**Chamberlin, Waldo, 1905-.**    **4.9210**
A chronology and fact book of the United Nations, 1941–1976 / Waldo Chamberlin, Thomas Hovet, Jr., Erica Hovet; with a pref. by Andrew W. Cordier. Dobbs Ferry, N.Y.: Oceana Publications, 1976. 302 p.; 22 cm. Includes index. 1. United Nations — History. I. Hovet, Thomas. joint author. II. Hovet, Erica. joint author. III. T.
JX1977.C48222 1976    341.23    *LC* 76-18777    *ISBN* 0379001896

**Clark, Grenville.**    **4.9211**
Introduction to world peace through world law / by Grenville Clark and Louis Sohn. — Rev. 1984 ed. — Chicago: World Without War Publications, [1984] 102 p. 1. Sohn, Louis B. 2. United Nations Constitution — Amendments. 3. International law 4. International cooperation I. T. II. Title: World peace through world law.
JX1977.C553 1984

**A Comprehensive handbook of the United Nations: a**    **4.9212**
**documentary presentation in two volumes / compiled and edited**
**by Min–chuan Ku.**
New York: Monarch Press, c1978-. v.; 26 cm. Includes index. 1. United
Nations. I. Ku, Min-chuan.
JX1977.C6123　　　341.23　　　*LC* 77-71588　　　*ISBN* 0671187740

**Diplomacy at the UN / edited and introduced by G.R. Berridge**    **4.9213**
**and A. Jennings.**
New York: St. Martin's Press, 1985. xvii, 227 p.; 23 cm. 1. United Nations —
Addresses, essays, lectures. 2. Diplomacy — Addresses, essays, lectures.
3. International relations — Addresses, essays, lectures. I. Berridge, Geoff.
II. Jennings, Anthony, MA. III. Title: Diplomacy at the U.N.
JX1977.D526 1985　　　341.23 19　　　*LC* 84-11733　　　*ISBN* 0312211171

**Eichelberger, Clark Mell, 1896-.**    **4.9214**
Organizing for peace: a personal history of the founding of the United Nations /
Clark M. Eichelberger. — 1st ed. — New York: Harper & Row, c1977. xiii,
317 p.; 22 cm. — (A Cass Canfield book) Includes index. 1. United Nations.
I. T.
JX1977.E38 1977　　　341.23　　　*LC* 76-5127　　　*ISBN* 0060111143

**Franck, Thomas M.**    **4.9215**
Nation against nation: what happened to the U.N. dream and what the U.S. can
do about it / Thomas M. Franck. — New York: Oxford University Press, 1985.
viii, 334 p.; 24 cm. Includes index. 1. United Nations. 2. United Nations —
United States. I. T.
JX1977.F694 1985　　　341.23 19　　　*LC* 84-25393　　　*ISBN* 0195035879

**The Future of international organization / edited by Rüdiger**    **4.9216**
**Jütte and Annemarie Grosse–Jütte.**
New York: St. Martin's Press, 1981. x, 228 p.; 23 cm. 'A publication of the
Institute of Peace Research and Security Policy at the University of Hamburg'.
1. United Nations — Addresses, essays, lectures. 2. International agencies —
Addresses, essays, lectures. 3. International organization — Addresses, essays,
lectures. I. Jütte, Rüdiger, 1944- II. Grosse-Jütte, Annemarie, 1948-
III. Universität Hamburg. Institut für Friedensforschung und
Sicherheitspolitik.
JX1977.F85 1981　　　341.2 19　　　*LC* 80-21735　　　*ISBN* 0312314760

**Goodrich, Leland Matthew.**    **4.9217**
The United Nations in a changing world / [by] Leland M. Goodrich. New
York: Columbia University Press, [1974] xiii, 280 p.; 23 cm. I. T.
JX1977.G67　　　341.23/09/04　　　*LC* 74-893　　　*ISBN* 0231038240

**Hammarskjöld, Dag, 1905-1961.**    ● **4.9218**
Servant of peace: a selection of the speeches and statements of Dag
Hammarskjold, Secretary–General of the United Nations, 1953–1961 / edited
and introduced by Wilder Foote. — New York: Harper & Row, [1962] 388 p.;
23 cm. 1. United Nations — Addresses, essays, lectures. 2. World politics —
1955- — Addresses, essays, lectures. I. T.
JX1977.H2648　　　*LC* 62-20111

**Kelsen, Hans, 1881-1973.**    ● **4.9219**
The law of the United Nations: a critical analysis of its fundamental problems /
by Hans Kelsen; with supplement. — New York: F.A. Praeger, 1950. xvii,
903 p.; 26 cm. — (Library of world affairs; no. 11) 'Published under the auspices
of the London Institute of World Affairs.' 1. United Nations. I. T. II. Series.
JX1977.K43 1950

**Lie, Trygve, 1896-.**    ● **4.9220**
In the cause of peace; seven years with the United Nations. New York,
Macmillan, 1954. 473 p. ill. 1. United Nations. 2. World politics — 1945- I. T.
JX1977 L47　　　*LC* 54-12462

**Luard, Evan, 1926-.**    **4.9221**
A history of the United Nations / Evan Luard. — New York: St. Martin's
Press, 1982. 404 p.; 23 cm. 1. United Nations — History. I. T.
JX1977.L79 1982　　　341.23/09 19　　　*LC* 81-16701　　　*ISBN* 0312386540

**Murphy, John Francis, 1937-.**    **4.9222**
The United Nations and the control of international violence: a legal and
political analysis / John F. Murphy. — Totowa, N.J.: Allanheld, Osmun
Publishers, 1982. xii, 212 p.; 24 cm. 1. United Nations. 2. Pacific settlement of
international disputes I. T.
JX1977.M827 1982　　　341.23 19　　　*LC* 81-69989　　　*ISBN* 0865980799

**Nicholas, H. G. (Herbert George), 1911-.**    **4.9223**
The United Nations as a political institution / H. G. Nicholas. — 5th ed. —
London: Oxford University Press, 1975. 263 p.; 20 cm. — (A Galaxy book; 105)
'Charter of the United Nations': p. [221]-253. 1. United Nations. I. United
Nations. Charter. II. T.
JX1977.N45 1975　　　JX1977 N45 1975.　　　341/.232　　　*ISBN*
0195198263

**Osmańczyk, Edmund Jan, 1913-.**    **4.9224**
The encyclopedia of the United Nations and international agreements /
Edmund Jan Osmańczyk. — Philadelphia: Taylor and Francis, 1985. xv,
1059 p.; 27 cm. Includes indexes. 1. United Nations — Dictionaries.
2. International relations — Dictionaries. I. T.
JX1977.O8213 1985　　　341.23/03 19　　　*LC* 85-3368　　　*ISBN*
0850663121

**Schwebel, Stephen Myron, 1929-.**    ● **4.9225**
The Secretary–General of the United Nations; his political powers and practice
[by] Stephen M. Schwebel. — New York: Greenwood Press, [1969, c1952] xiv,
299 p.; 23 cm. 1. United Nations. Secretary-General. I. T.
JX1977.S37 1969　　　341.13/7　　　*LC* 75-91773　　　*ISBN* 0837123763

**Sohn, Louis B. ed.**    **4.9226**
Cases on United Nations law, edited by Louis B. Sohn. — 2d ed., rev. —
Brooklyn: Foundation Press, 1967. xxii, 1086 p.; 26 cm. — (University
casebook series). 1. United Nations. 2. International law — Cases. I. T.
II. Title: United Nations law. III. Series.
JX1977.S64 1967　　　341.13　　　*LC* 67-8867

**Stoessinger, John George.**    ● **4.9227**
The United Nations and the superpowers; United States–Soviet interaction at
the United Nations [by] John G. Stoessinger with the assistance of Robert G.
McKelvey. New York, Random House [1965] xvii, 206 p. 19 cm. (Studies in
political science, PS53) 1. United Nations — United States. 2. United Nations
— Soviet Union. I. T.
JX1977.S795　　　341.1309　　　*LC* 65-23342

**United States. Congress. Senate. Committee on Foreign**    ● **4.9228**
**Relations.**
Review of the United Nations Charter: compilation of staff studies prepared for
the use of the Subcommittee on the United Nations Charter of the Committee
on Foreign Relations, pursuant to S. Res. 126, Eighty–third Congress. —
Westport, Conn.: Greenwood Press [1970] vii, 365 p.: ill., fold. maps; 24 cm.
(83d Congress, 2d session. Senate. Document no. 164) Reprint of the 1955 ed.
1. United Nations. Charter. 2. United Nations — United States. I. T.
JX1977.U473 1970　　　341/.232　　　*LC* 68-55114　　　*ISBN* 0837131707

**The US, the UN, and the management of global change / edited**    **4.9229**
**by Toby Trister Gati.**
New York: New York University Press, 1983. xiii, 380 p.; 22 cm. — (UNA-
USA policy studies book series.) 'A UNA-USA book.' 1. United Nations.
2. United Nations — United States. 3. International relations 4. United States
— Foreign relations — 1945- I. Gati, Toby Trister. II. Title: U.S., the U.N.,
and the management of global change. III. Series.
JX1977.U7 1983　　　341.23 19　　　*LC* 83-2304　　　*ISBN* 081472986X

**Who's who in the United Nations and related agencies.**    **4.9230**
1st ed. — New York: Arno Press, 1975. xxxiii, 785 p.; 24 cm. Includes index.
1. United Nations — Biography. 2. International agencies — Biography.
JX1977.W467　　　341.23/092/2 B　　　*LC* 75-4105　　　*ISBN* 040500490X

## JX1977.2–.3 Relations with Individual Countries

**Hovet, Thomas.**    ● **4.9231**
Africa in the United Nations. [Evanston, Ill.,] Northwestern University Press,
1963. xiii, 336 p. map, diagrs. (Northwestern University (Evanston, Ill.)
African studies, no. 10) 1. United Nations — Africa 2. Africa — Politics I. T.
II. Series.
JX1977.2 A4 H68　　　*LC* 62-17804

**Dugard, John, 1936-.**    **4.9232**
The South West Africa/Namibia dispute; documents and scholarly writings on
the controversy between South Africa and the United Nations. Edited by John
Dugard. Berkeley, University of California Press [1973] xix, 585 p. 24 cm.
(Perspectives on Southern Africa. 9) 1. United Nations — Namibia. 2. United
Nations — South Africa. I. T. II. Series.
JX1977.2.A45 D83　　　341.23/68　　　*LC* 76-142052　　　*ISBN* 0520018869

**Oliver, Thomas W.**    **4.9233**
The United Nations in Bangladesh / by Thomas W. Oliver. — Princeton, N.J.:
Princeton University Press, c1978. xix, 231 p.; 23 cm. 1. United Nations —
Bangladesh. 2. International relief — Bangladesh. I. T.
JX1977.2.B27 O57　　　341.23/549/2　　　*LC* 77-85554　　　*ISBN*
069107593X

**Lefever, Ernest W.**    ● **4.9234**
Uncertain mandate; politics of the U.N. Congo operation [by] Ernest W.
Lefever. — Baltimore: Johns Hopkins Press, [1967] xvi, 254 p.: illus., map,
ports.; 24 cm. 1. United Nations — Zaire. I. T.
JX1977.2.C57 L44　　　341.13/9/675　　　*LC* 67-22890

**Xydis, Stephen George.**                                                    • 4.9235
Cyprus: conflict and conciliation, 1954–1958 / [by] Stephen G. Xydis. — Columbus, Ohio: State University Press [1967] xviii, 704 p.; 23 cm. 'A publication of the Mershon Center for Education in National Security.' 1. United Nations — Cyprus I. Mershon Center for Education in National Security. II. T.
JX1977.2C78 X9    *LC* 67-14732

**Berkes, Ross N.**                                                          • 4.9236
The diplomacy of India; Indian foreign policy in the United Nations, by Ross N. Berkes and Mohinder S. Bedi. — Stanford, Calif., Stanford University Press, 1958. 221 p. 23 cm. Photocopy. Ann Arbor, Mich., University Microfilms, A Xerox Co., 1970. 1. United Nations — India. 2. India — For. rel. I. Bedi, Mohinder S., joint author. II. T. III. Title: Indian foreign policy in the United Nations.
JX1977.2.I47B4 1970    341.139    *LC* 58-11695

**Beichman, Arnold.**                                                        • 4.9237
The other State Department: the United States Mission to the United Nations; its role in the making of foreign policy. Foreword by Leland M. Goodrich. — New York: Basic Books, [1968] xxii, 221 p.; 22 cm. 1. United States. Mission to the United Nations. I. T.
JX1977.2.U5 B43 1968    341.13/9/73    *LC* 68-29923

**Finger, Seymour Maxwell, 1915-.**                                          4.9238
Your man at the UN: people, politics, and bureaucracy in making foreign policy / Seymour Maxwell Finger. — New York: New York University Press, c1980. xx, 320 p.; 24 cm. 1. United Nations — United States — History. 2. United States — Foreign relations — 1945- I. T.
JX1977.2.U5 F56    341.23/73    *LC* 79-3657    *ISBN* 081472566X

**Haas, Ernst B.**                                                          4.9239
The web of interdependence; the United States and international organizations [by] Ernst B. Haas. — Englewood Cliffs, N.J.: Prentice-Hall, [1970] 115 p.; 24 cm. — (America's role in world affairs series) 1. United Nations — United States. 2. United States — Foreign relations — 1969-1974 I. T.
JX1977.2.U5 H2    341.13    *LC* 69-14549    *ISBN* 0139478388

**Riggs, Robert Edwon, 1927-.**                                             • 4.9240
Politics in the United Nations: a study of United States influence in the General Assembly. — Urbana: University of Illinois Press, 1958. vi, 208 p.: diagrs., tables.; 26 cm. (Illinois studies in the social sciences, v. 41) 1. United Nations — United States. 2. United States — Foreign relations — 1945- I. T.
JX1977.2.U5 R5    *LC* 58-5601

**Stevenson, Adlai E. (Adlai Ewing), 1900-1965.**                           • 4.9241
Looking outward; years of crisis at the United Nations; [speeches and papers] Edited, with commentary, by Robert L. and Selma Schiffer. Pref. by John F. Kennedy. [1st ed.] New York, Harper & Row [1963] xx, 295 p. 1. United Nations — United States 2. United States — Foreign relations — 1961- I. T.
JX1977.2 U5 S77    *LC* 63-16520

**Stoessinger, John George.**                                               4.9242
The United Nations & the superpowers: China, Russia & America / John G. Stoessinger. 4th ed. — New York: Random House, c1977. xxv, 245 p.; 20 cm. 1. United Nations — United States. 2. United Nations — Russia. 3. United Nations — China. I. T.
JX1977.2.U5 S8 1977    341.23    *LC* 76-48733    *ISBN* 0394312694

## JX1977.8 Special Topics, A–Z

**Alker, Hayward R.**                                                        • 4.9243
World politics in the General Assembly [by] Hayward R. Alker, Jr., and Bruce M. Russett. — New Haven, Yale University Press, 1965. xxvi, 326 p. 24 cm. — (Yale studies in political science. 15) Bibliographical footnotes. 1. United Nations. General Assembly. I. Russett, Bruce M. joint author. II. T. III. Series.
JX1977.8.G4A7    341.133    *LC* 65-22313

**Bailey, Sydney Dawson.**                                                  • 4.9244
The Secretariat of the United Nations [by] Sydney D. Bailey. — Rev. ed. — New York, Praeger [1964] x, 128 p. illus. 21 cm. Includes bibliographical references. 1. United Nations. Secretariat. I. T.
JX1977.8.S4B3 1964    341.137    *LC* 64 22486

**Gordenker, Leon, 1923-.**                                                 • 4.9245
The UN Secretary–General and the maintenance of peace. New York: Columbia University Press, 1967. xx, 380 p.; 24 cm. (Columbia University studies in international organization, no. 4) 1. United Nations. Secretary-General. 2. United Nations — Armed Forces 3. Arbitration, International I. T. II. Series.
JX1977.8S4 G6    *LC* 67-15254

**Nations on record: United Nations General Assembly roll–call**            4.9246
**votes (1946–1973) / Lynn Schopen ... [et al.].**
Oakville-Dundas, Ont.: Canadian Peace Research Institute, c1975. x, 515, 19 p.; 29 cm. 'List of roll-call (recorded) votes taken in the U.N. General Assembly Plenary Meetings, 1946-1973.' Includes index. 1. United Nations — Voting I. Schopen, Lynn. II. United Nations. General Assembly.
JX1977.8.V6 N38    341.23/2    *LC* 76-355296

**Nations on record: United Nations General Assembly Roll–call**            4.9247
**votes (1974–1977). Supplement / Hanna Newcombe ... [et al.].**
Dundas, Ont.: Peace Research Institute-Dundas, c1981. vi, 131, 6 p.; 29 cm. Includes index. 1. United Nations — Voting I. Newcombe, Hanna, 1922-. II. Peace Research Institute-Dundas. III. Title: Nations on record: United Nations General Assembly roll-call votes (1946-1973)
JX1977.8.V6N3x    341.23/22 19    *ISBN* 0919117112

## JX1979 REGIONAL ORGANIZATION

**Etzioni, Amitai.**                                                        • 4.9248
Political unification, a comparative study of leaders and forces. New York: Holt, Rinehart and Winston [1965] xx, 346 p.; 21 cm. 'Sponsored by the Institute of War and Peace Studies of Columbia University.' 1. Regionalism (International organization) I. Columbia University. Institute of War and Peace Studies. II. T.
JX1979 E8    *LC* 65-14882

**Nye, Joseph S. comp.**                                                    4.9249
International regionalism; readings [by] Joseph S. Nye, Jr. — Boston: Little, Brown, [1968] xvi, 432 p.: illus.; 21 cm. 'Written under the auspices of the Center for International Affairs, Harvard University.' 1. Regionalism (International organization) — Addresses, essays, lectures. I. Harvard University. Center for International Affairs. II. T.
JX1979.N9    341.18    *LC* 68-18417

**Regionalism and the United Nations / edited by Berhanykun**               4.9250
**Andemicael.**
Dobbs Ferry, N.Y.: Published for the United Nations Institute for Training and Research [by] Oceana Publications, 1979. xx, 603 p.; 25 cm. 1. United Nations — Addresses, essays, lectures. 2. Regionalism (International organization) — Addresses, essays, lectures. I. Andemicael, Berhanykun. II. United Nations Institute for Training and Research.
JX1979.R43    341.24    *LC* 79-14018    *ISBN* 0379005913

**Russett, Bruce M.**                                                       • 4.9251
International regions and the international system: a study in political ecology / Bruce M. Russett. — Chicago: Rand McNally, 1967. xvi, 252 p.: ill.; 23 cm. Includes index. 1. Regionalism (International organization) I. T.
JX1979.R8    341.24    *LC* 67-14695

## JX1981 U.N. PEACEKEEPING FORCES

**Bailey, Sydney Dawson.**                                                  4.9252
How wars end: the United Nations and the termination of armed conflict 1946–1964 / Sydney D. Bailey. — Oxford: Clarendon Press; New York: Oxford University Press, 1983 (c1982). 2 v.; 23 cm. 1. United Nations — Armed Forces 2. Pacific settlement of international disputes 3. War 4. World politics — 1945- I. T.
JX1981.P7 B26 1982    341.5/8 19    *LC* 82-2080    *ISBN* 0198274246

**Harbottle, Michael.**                                                     4.9253
The Blue Berets. — [Harrisburg, Pa.]: Stackpole Books, [1972, c1971] 157 p.: illus.; 23 cm. 1. United Nations — Armed Forces 2. Arbitration, International I. T.
JX1981.P7 H27 1972    341.5/8    *LC* 70-179598

**Higgins, Rosalyn.**                                                       • 4.9254
United Nations peacekeeping, 1946–1967: documents and commentary. London, [etc.] Issued under the auspices of the Royal Institute of International Affairs by Oxford University Press 1969-1981. 4v.: maps. 1. United Nations — Armed Forces I. Royal Institute of International Affairs. II. T
JX1981 P7 H5

**Moskos, Charles C.**                                                      4.9255
Peace soldiers: the sociology of a United Nations military force / Charles C. Moskos, Jr. — Chicago: University of Chicago Press, 1976. xi, 171 p.; 21 cm. 1. United Nations — Armed Forces I. T.
JX1981.P7 M68    301.5/93    *LC* 75-5070    *ISBN* 0226542254

**Peacekeeping, appraisals & proposals** / edited by Henry **4.9256**
Wiseman.
New York: Pergamon Press, c1983. xiii, 461 p.; 24 cm. 'Published for the
International Peace Academy.' 1. United Nations — Armed Forces
I. Wiseman, Henry. II. Title: Peacekeeping, appraisals and proposals.
JX1981.P7 P39 1983    341.5/8 19    *LC* 82-22575    *ISBN* 0080275540

**Rikhye, Indar Jit, 1920-.**    **4.9257**
The theory & practice of peacekeeping / Indar Jit Rikhye. — New York:
Published for the International Peace Academy by St. Martin's Press, 1984. xiii,
255 p.; maps: 24 cm. 1. United Nations — Armed Forces 2. Security,
International I. International Peace Academy. II. T. III. Title: Theory and
practice of peacekeeping.
JX1981.P7 R528 1984    341.5/8 19    *LC* 83-40193    *ISBN*
0312797184

**Rosner, Gabriella.**    • **4.9258**
The United Nations Emergency Force. New York: Columbia University Press,
1963. 294 p.; 24 cm. (Columbia University studies in international organization,
no. 2) 1. United Nations Emergency Force. I. T. II. Series.
JX1981 P7 R6    *LC* 63-15454

**Wainhouse, David Walter, 1900-.**    **4.9259**
International peace observation: a history and forecast / [by] David W.
Wainhouse in association with Bernhard G. Bechhoefer [and others] Baltimore:
Johns Hopkins Press, 1966. xvii, 663 p. 1. United Nations — Armed Forces
2. Arbitration, International I. T.
JX1981 P7 W25    *LC* 66-14376

**Wainhouse, David Walter, 1900-.**    **4.9260**
International peacekeeping at the crossroads: national support—experience and
prospects / [by] David W. Wainhouse; with the assistance of Frederick P.
Bohannon, James E. Knott, [and] Anne P. Simons. — Baltimore: Johns
Hopkins University Press, [1973] xi, 634 p.: ill.; 26 cm. 'A revision and a
condensation of a study carried out for the United States Arms Control and
Disarmament Agency under the auspices of the Washington Center of Foreign
Policy Research of the Johns Hopkins University School of Advanced
International Studies.' 1. United Nations — Armed Forces 2. International
police I. United States. Arms Control and Disarmament Agency.
II. Washington Center of Foreign Policy Research. III. T.
JX1981.P7 W26 1973    341.5/2    *LC* 73-7887    *ISBN* 0801814782

## JX1985–1989 Arbitration. Treaties

**Ferrell, Robert H.**    • **4.9261**
Peace in their time; the origins of the Kellogg–Briand pact, by Robert H.
Ferrell. — [Hamden, Conn.]: Archon Books, 1968 [c1952] x, 293 p.; 23 cm. —
(Yale historical publications. Miscellany. 55) 'Originally written as a
dissertation for the degree of doctor of philosophy at Yale.' 1. Renunciation of
war treaty, Paris, Aug. 27, 1928. I. T. II. Title: Kellogg-Briand pact.
III. Series.
JX1987.A42 F4 1968    341.2    *LC* 68-8018    *ISBN* 0208006532

## JX1995 International Agencies

**Ameri, Houshang, 1935-.**    **4.9262**
Politics and process in the specialized agencies of the United Nations /
Houshang Ameri. — Aldershot, Hants.: Gower, c1982. xiii, 284 p.; 23 cm.
Includes index. 1. International agencies I. T.
JX1995.A48 1982    341.23/2 19    *LC* 82-202825    *ISBN* 0566005387

**Archer, Clive.**    **4.9263**
International organizations / Clive Archer. — London; Boston: Allen &
Unwin, 1983. xii, 193 p.; 23 cm. — (Key concepts in international relations. 1)
Includes index. 1. International agencies I. T. II. Series.
JX1995.A72 1983    341.2 19    *LC* 83-6329    *ISBN* 0043201563

**Armstrong, J. D. (James David), 1945-.**    **4.9264**
The rise of the international organisation: a short history / David Armstrong.
— New York: St. Martin's Press, 1982. x, 166 p.; 23 cm. — (Making of the 20th
century.) Includes index. 1. Regionalism (International organization)
2. International agencies I. T. II. Series.
JX1995.A75 1982    341.2 19    *LC* 82-16767    *ISBN* 0312684274

**Cox, Robert W., 1926-.**    **4.9265**
The anatomy of influence; decision making in international organization, by
Robert W. Cox and Harold K. Jacobson, and [others]. — New Haven: Yale
University Press, 1974. xiii, 497 p.; 24 cm. 1. International agencies
2. Decision-making I. Jacobson, Harold Karan. II. T.
JX1995.C76    341.24    *LC* 72-75188    *ISBN* 0300015534

**Farley, Lawrence T., 1947-.**    **4.9266**
Change processes in international organizations / by Lawrence T. Farley. —
Cambridge, Mass.: Schenkman Pub. Co., c1982. viii, 167 p.: ill.; 22 cm.
1. International agencies I. T.
JX1995.F28 1982    341.2 19    *LC* 80-25613    *ISBN* 0870730355

**Feld, Werner J.**    **4.9267**
International organizations: a comparative approach / by Werner Feld and
Robert S. Jordan, with Leon Hurwitz. — New York, NY: Praeger, 1983. xxii,
332 p.: ill.; 25 cm. 1. International agencies I. Jordan, Robert S., 1929-
II. Hurwitz, Leon. III. T.
JX1995.F36 1983    341.2 19    *LC* 82-22313    *ISBN* 0030596211

**Jacobson, Harold Karan.**    **4.9268**
Networks of interdependence: international organizations and the global
political system / Harold K. Jacobson. — 2nd ed. — New York: Knopf, c1984.
xxiv, 483 p.: ill.; 25 cm. 1. International agencies 2. International relations
I. T.
JX1995.J28 1984    341.2 19    *LC* 83-24825    *ISBN* 0394331648

**Luard, Evan, 1926-.**    **4.9269**
International agencies: the emerging framework of interdependence / Evan
Luard. — Dobbs Ferry, N.Y.: Published for the Royal Institute of International
Affairs [by] Oceana Publications, c1977. xii, 338 p.; 23 cm. 1. International
agencies I. Royal Institute of International Affairs. II. T.
JX1995.L83 1977b    341.2    *LC* 76-15414    *ISBN* 0379006863

**Peaslee, Amos Jenkins, 1887-.**    **4.9270**
International governmental organizations: constitutional documents / by Amos
J. Peaslee. — Revised 3d ed. - in 5 parts / prepared by Dorothy Peaslee Xydis.
— The Hague: Nijhoff, 1974- <1979>. v. <1, 3-5 in 4>; 25 cm.
1. International agencies I. Xydis, Dorothy Peaslee. II. T.
JX1995.P42    341.2 19    *LC* 75-303002    *ISBN* 9024716012

**Plano, Jack C.**    **4.9271**
Forging world order: the politics of international organization / [by] Jack C.
Plano [and] Robert E. Riggs. — New York: Macmillan, [1967] viii, 600 p.; 24
cm. 1. International agencies I. Riggs, Robert Edwon, 1927- joint author.
II. T.
JX1995.P535    060    *LC* 67-18893

**Rubinstein, Alvin Z.**    • **4.9272**
The Soviets in international organizations: changing policy toward developing
countries, 1953–1963 / with a foreword by Philip E. Jacob. — Princeton:
Princeton University Press, 1964. xix, 380 p.; 23 cm. 1. International agencies
2. Technical assistance, Russian I. T.
JX1995.R8    341.11    *LC* 64-12184

**Taylor, Phillip.**    **4.9273**
Nonstate actors in international politics: from transregional to substate
organizations / Phillip Taylor. — Boulder: Westview Press, 1984. xvii, 247 p.:
ill.; 24 cm. — (Westview special studies in international relations.) Includes
index. 1. International agencies 2. International relations I. T. II. Series.
JX1995.T38 1984    341.2 19    *LC* 83-25997    *ISBN* 086531344X

# JX2001–4494 International Law

## JX3091–3695 20th Century

**Carr, Edward Hallett.**    • **4.9274**
The twenty years' crisis, 1919–1939: an introduction to the study of
international relations / by Edward Hallett Carr. — 2nd ed. — London:
Macmillan, 1946. xii, 243 p. 1. International relations 2. World politics I. T.
JX3091.C3 1946    *LC* 46-7549    *ISBN* 0333069137

**The Future of the international legal order. Edited by Cyril E.**    • **4.9275**
**Black and Richard A. Falk. Written under the auspices of the**
**Center of International Studies, Princeton University.**
[Princeton, N.J., Princeton University Press, 1969- v. 25 cm. 1. International
law 2. International relations I. Black, Cyril Edwin, 1915- ed. II. Falk,
Richard A. ed. III. Woodrow Wilson School of Public and International
Affairs. Center of International Studies.
JX3091.F8    341.2 19    *LC* 68-20866    *ISBN* 069100215X

**Bozeman, Adda Bruemmer, 1908-.**　　　**4.9276**
The future of law in a multicultural world, by Adda B. Bozeman. — Princeton, N.J.: Princeton University Press, 1971. xvii, 229 p.; 23 cm. 1. International law 2. Cultural relations I. T.
JX3110.B6 F85　　340/.2　　*LC* 78-131127　　*ISBN* 0691056439

**Brittin, Burdick H.**　　　**4.9277**
International law for seagoing officers / Burdick H. Brittin. — 5th ed. — Annapolis, Md.: Naval Institute Press, c1986. xv, 503 p.: ill. Includes index. 1. International law I. T.
JX3110.B68 I5 1981　　341 19　　*LC* 81-607005　　*ISBN* 0870213059

**Corbett, Percy Ellwood, 1892-.**　　　• **4.9278**
Law and society in the relations of states. — [1st ed.] New York: Harcourt, Brace, [1951] x, 337 p.; 28 cm. — 1. International law I. T.
JX3110.C6 F73　　341　　*LC* 51-4385

**Friedmann, Wolfgang, 1907-.**　　　**4.9279**
The changing structure of international law, by Wolfgang Friedmann. New York, Columbia University Press, 1964. xvi, 410 p. 1. International law I. T.
JX3110 F7 C45 1964　　*LC* 64-23101

**Jessup, Philip C. (Philip Caryl), 1897-.**　　　• **4.9280**
A modern law of nations; an introduction, by Philip C. Jessup. With a new pref. by the author. — [Hamden, Conn.]: Archon Books, 1968 [c1948] xiv, 236 p.; 22 cm. 1. International law I. T.
JX3140.J4 1968　　341　　*LC* 68-20377

**Kaplan, Morton A.**　　　• **4.9281**
The political foundations of international law [by] Morton A. Kaplan and Nicholas deB. Katzenbach. — New York: Wiley, [1961] 372 p.; 24 cm. 1. International law 2. World politics I. Katzenbach, Nicholas de Belleville, 1922- joint author. II. T.
JX3140.K3 P6　　341　　*LC* 61-11520

**Stone, Julius, 1907-.**　　　**4.9282**
Visions of world order: between state power and human justice / Julius Stone. — Baltimore: Johns Hopkins University Press, c1984. xxix, 246 p.; 24 cm. 1. International law 2. Sociological jurisprudence 3. Justice 4. International organization I. T.
JX3180.S73 V57 1984　　341/.01 19　　*LC* 84-5749　　*ISBN* 0801831741

**Wright, Quincy, 1890-1970.**　　　• **4.9283**
The Role of international law in the elimination of war. — Manchester, Eng.: Manchester University Press; New York: Oceana Publications, 1961. vii, 119 p.; 22 cm. 1. International law I. T.
JX3195.W7 R6　　*LC* 61-18186

**Brierly, James Leslie, 1881-1955.**　　　• **4.9284**
The basis of obligation in international law, and other papers / selected and edited by Hersch Lauterpacht and C. H. M. Waldock. — Oxford: Clarendon Press, 1958. 387 p.: ill.; 22 cm. 1. International law I. T.
JX3225.B67　　341　　*LC* 58-1108

**Brierly, James Leslie, 1888-1955.**　　　• **4.9285**
The law of nations: an introduction to the international law of peace / Edited by Humphrey Waldock. — 6th ed. — New York: Oxford University Press, 1963. 442 p.; 19 cm. 1. International law I. T.
JX3225.B7 1963　　*LC* 63-3113

**Brownlie, Ian.**　　　**4.9286**
Principles of public international law / by Ian Brownlie. — 3d ed. — Oxford [Eng.]: Clarendon Press; New York: Oxford University Press, 1979. xxxviii, 743 p.; 24 cm. 1. International law I. T.
JX3225.B78 1979　　341 19　　*LC* 79-41139　　*ISBN* 0198760663

**Jenks, C. Wilfred (Clarence Wilfred), 1909-1973.**　　　• **4.9287**
The common law of mankind. New York, Praeger [1958] 456 p. 26 cm. (The Library of world affairs, no.41) 1. Internatinal law. I. T.
JX3225.J4　　341　　*LC* 58-8539

**Lauterpacht, Hersch, Sir, 1897-1960.**　　　• **4.9288**
The function of law in the international community. Hamden, Conn.: Archon Books, 1966. xxiv, 469 p.; 22 cm. First published in 1933. 1. International law 2. Arbitration, International I. T.
JX3225.L3 1966　　341　　*LC* 66-16776

**Mitrany, David.**　　　**4.9289**
The progress of international government. — New Haven: Yale University Press 1933. 176p. 1. International law 2. International relations I. T.
JX3225 M5 1933A

**Oppenheim, L. (Lassa), 1858-1919.**　　　**4.9290**
International law, a treatise. Ed. 6, ed. by H. Lauterpacht. London, Longmans [1940-] vol. 2. Contents of vol. 2. Ed. 6: Disputes, war and neutrality. 1. International law I. Lauterpacht, Hersch, Sir, 1897-1960. ed. II. T.
JX3264.I6x

**Schwarzenberger, Georg, 1908-.**　　　• **4.9291**
The frontiers of international law / published under the auspices of the London Institute of World Affairs. — London: Stevens, 1962. 320 p.; 26 cm. (The Library of world affairs, no. 59) 1. International law I. T. II. Series.
JX3275 S28　　*LC* 62-5074

**Schwarzenberger, Georg, 1908-.**　　　**4.9292**
A manual of international law. 6th ed. / by Georg Schwarzenberger and E. D. Brown. — Milton [Eng.]: Professional Books, 1976. lix, 612 p., [1] fold. leaf of plates; 23 cm. Label mounted on t.p.: Distributed in U.S.A. by F. B. Rothman, South Hackensack, N.J. 1. International law I. Brown, E. D. (Edward Duncan) joint author. II. T.
JX3275.S32 1976　　341　　*LC* 77-357791　　*ISBN* 0903486261

**Schwarzenberger, Georg, 1908-.**　　　• **4.9293**
International law. 3d ed. London, Stevens, 1957-. v.; 25 cm. 1. International law I. T.
JX 3275 S41 I6 1957　　*LC* 57-59355

**Visscher, Charles de, 1884-.**　　　• **4.9294**
Theory and reality in public international law / translated from the French by P. E. Corbett. — Rev. ed. Princeton, N. J.: Princeton University Press, 1968. xii, 527 p.; 22 cm. Bibliographical references included in 'Footnotes' (p. 409-498) 1. International law I. T.
JX3375.V5T53 1968　　341　　*LC* 67-21020

**Kelsen, Hans, 1881-1973.**　　　• **4.9295**
Law and peace in international relations / by Hans Kelsen. — Cambridge, Mass.: Harvard University Press, 1942. xi, 181 p.; 21 cm. — (The Oliver Wendell Holmes lectures; 1940-41.) 1. International law 2. Peace 3. International cooperation I. T.
JX3425.K4 L3

**Kelsen, Hans, 1881-1973.**　　　**4.9296**
Principles of international law. — 2d ed., rev. and edited by Robert W. Tucker. — New York: Holt, Rinehart and Winston, [1966] xviii, 602 p. 24 cm. 1. International law I. Tucker, Robert W. ed. II. T.
JX3425.K4P7 1966　　341　　*LC* 66-13303

**McWhinney, Edward.**　　　**4.9297**
Conflict and compromise: international law and world order in a revolutionary age / Edward McWhinney. — New York: Holmes & Meier, 1981. 160 p.; 24 cm. Includes index. 1. International law 2. International relations 3. Revolutions I. T.
JX3695.C2 M29 1981　　341 19　　*LC* 80-29045　　*ISBN* 0841906947

## JX4001–5810 SPECIAL TOPICS

**Liska, George.**　　　• **4.9298**
Nations in alliance; the limits of interdependence. Baltimore, Johns Hopkins Press [1962] 301 p. 1. Alliances I. T.
JX4005 L5　　*LC* 62-14359

**Treaties and alliances of the world / compiled and written by Henry W. Degenhardt; general editor, Alan J. Day.**　　　**4.9299**
4th ed. — Harlow, Essex, U.K.: Longman; Detroit, Mich., USA: Distributed exclusively in the U.S. and Canada by Gale Research Co., 1986. p. cm. — (Keesing's reference publication). Includes index. 1. Alliances 2. Treaties I. Degenhardt, Henry W. II. Day, Alan J. (Alan John) III. Series.
JX4005.T72 1986　　341.2 19　　*LC* 86-21009　　*ISBN* 0582902770

**Crawford, James, 1948-.**　　　**4.9300**
The creation of states in international law / James Crawford. — Oxford: Clarendon Press; New York: Oxford University Press, 1979. xxvii, 498 p.; 23 cm. Originally presented as the author's thesis, Oxford, 1976. Includes index. 1. Sovereignty 2. State succession 3. States, New I. T.
JX4041.C7　　341.26　　*LC* 78-40308　　*ISBN* 0198253478

**Lauterpacht, Hersch, Sir, 1897-1960.**　　　• **4.9301**
Recognition in international law. — Cambridge [Eng.]: Univ. Press, 1947. xix, 442 p.; 23 cm. — (Cambridge studies in international and comparative law, 3) 1. Recognition (International law) I. T. II. Series.
JX4044.L3　　341 19　　*LC* 47-5343

**Cobban, Alfred.**　　　　　　　　　　　　　　　　　　　• 4.9302
The nation state and national self–determination. — [Rev. ed.]. — New York: Crowell, [1970, c1969] 318 p.; 21 cm. 1945 and 1948 editions published under title: National self-determination. 1. Self-determination, National I. T.
JX4054.C6 1970　　320.1/3　　*LC* 73-112487

**Emerson, Rupert, 1899-.**　　　　　　　　　　　　　　　• 4.9303
Self–determination revisited in the era of decolonization / by Rupert Emerson. — [Cambridge, Mass.]: Center for International Affairs, Harvard University, 1964. 64 p. — (Harvard University. Center for International Affairs. Occasional papers in international affairs; no. 9) 1. Self-determination, National I. T. II. Series.
JX4054 E4　　JX4054 E4.　　320.158　　*LC* 64-66005

**Lenin, Vladimir Il'ich, 1870-1924.**　　　　　　　　　　• 4.9304
The right of nations to self–determination; selected writings. New York, International Publishers [1951] 128 p. 21 cm. 1. Self-determination, National I. T.
JX4054.L42 1951　　*LC* 51-14325

**Catudal, Honoré Marc, 1944-.**　　　　　　　　　　　　4.9305
The diplomacy of the Quadripartite Agreement on Berlin: a new era in East–West politics / Honoré M. Catudal jr.; foreword by Kenneth Rush. — Berlin: Berlin-Verlag, 1978-. 335 p.: ill.; 21 cm. (Political studies; Nr. 12) Includes index. 1. Quadripartite Agreement on Berlin (1971) 2. Berlin (Germany) — International status I. T.
JX4084.B38 C38　　341.2/9　　*LC* 78-345065　　*ISBN* 3870611383

**McHenry, Donald F.**　　　　　　　　　　　　　　　　4.9306
Micronesia, trust betrayed: altruism vs self interest in American foreign policy / Donald F. McHenry. — New York: Carnegie Endowment for International Peace, c1975. xiii, 260 p.: map; 23 cm. Includes index. 1. International trusteeships — Pacific Islands (Trust Territory) 2. Pacific Islands (Trust Territory) — Politics and government. 3. Pacific Islands (Trust Territory) — International status. I. Carnegie Endowment for International Peace. II. T.
JX4084.P27 M23　　341.2/9　　*LC* 75-42570　　*ISBN* 0870030000

**Samuels, Marwyn S.**　　　　　　　　　　　　　　　4.9307
Contest for the South China Sea / Marwyn S. Samuels. — New York: Methuen, 1982. xiii, 203 p.: ill.; 24 cm. Includes index. 1. Paracel Islands — International status. 2. Spratly Islands — International status. I. T.
JX4084.P28 S25 1982　　341.2/9/0916472 19　　*LC* 81-18868　　*ISBN* 0416331408

**Jones, Stephen Barr, 1903-.**　　　　　　　　　　　　• 4.9308
Boundary–making: a handbook for statesmen, treaty editors, and boundary commissioners / by Stephen B. Jones; with a foreword by S. Whittemore Boggs. — Washington: Carnegie Endowment for International Peace, 1945. xv, 268 p.: ill., maps; 24 cm. — (Monograph series / Carnegie Endowment for International Peace, Division of International Law; no. 8) 1. Boundaries I. Carnegie Endowment for International Peace. Division of International Law. II. T.
JX4111.J6　　320.128　　*LC* 45-4928

**The law of the sea: offshore boundaries and zones / edited by**　• 4.9309
**Lewis M. Alexander.**
Columbus: Ohio State University Press, 1967. xv, 321 p.: ill., maps. 'A publication of the Law of the Sea Institute and the Mershon Center for Education in National Security.' Papers of a conference held at the Ohio State University, June 27-July 1, 1966, sponsored by the Law of the Sea Institute. 1. Territorial waters — Addresses, essays, lectures. 2. Continental shelf — Addresses, essays, lectures. 3. Maritime law — Addresses, essays, lectures. I. Alexander, Lewis M. II. Law of the Sea Institute.
JX4131.L34　　*LC* 67-16949

**Prescott, J. R. V. (John Robert Victor)**　　　　　　　4.9310
The political geography of the oceans / J. R. V. Prescott. — New York: Wiley, [1975] 247 p.: ill.; 23 cm. (Problems in modern geography) 'A Halsted Press book.' Includes index. 1. Territorial waters 2. Continental shelf 3. Geography, Political I. T.
JX4131.P73 1975　　341.44/8　　*LC* 74-31813　　*ISBN* 0470696729

**Alexander, Lewis M.**　　　　　　　　　　　　　　　4.9311
Offshore geography of northwestern Europe: the political and economic problems of delimitation and control. — London: Murray, 1966. 162 p. ill. (The Monograph series of the Association of American Geographers, 3) 1. Territorial waters — Europe, Northern I. T.
JX4135 A4

**McNair, Arnold D. (Arnold Duncan), baron, 1885-.**　　• 4.9312
The law of treaties / by Lord McNair. — Rev. ed. Oxford: Clarendon Press, 1961. xxi, 789 p.; 24 cm. 1. Treaties 2. International law I. T.
JX4165.M18　　*LC* 64-37745

**Borgese, Elisabeth Mann.**　　　　　　　　　　　　　4.9313
Pacem in maribus. Edited by Elisabeth Mann Borgese. — New York: Dodd, Mead, [1973, c1972] xxxiv, 382 p.; 23 cm. A selection and condensation of material resulting from the Pacem in Maribus Convocation in Malta, 1970, and other projects of the Center for the Study of Democratic Institutions at Santa Barbara, Calif., and of the Pacem in Maribus Institute at the Royal University of Malta. 1. Maritime law — Addresses, essays, lectures. 2. Marine resources conservation — Law and legislation — Addresses, essays, lectures. I. T.
JX4408.B66　　341.44　　*LC* 72-3140　　*ISBN* 0396064175

**The Maritime dimension / edited by R.P. Barston and Patricia**　　4.9314
**Birnie.**
London; Boston: Allen & Unwin, 1980. 194 p.: ill., maps; 23 cm. 1. Maritime law 2. Marine resources conservation — Law and legislation I. Barston, R. P. (Ronald Peter) II. Birnie, Patricia W.
JX4411.M27　　341.4/5 19　　*LC* 80-40751　　*ISBN* 0043410154

**McDougal, Myres Smith, 1906-.**　　　　　　　　　　• 4.9315
The public order of the oceans: a contemporary international law of the sea / by Myres S. McDougal and William T. Burke. — New Haven: Yale University Press, 1962. xxv, 1226 p. 'List of abbreviations' (bibliographical): p. xxi-xxv. Appendices (p. 1143-1191): A. Convention on the territorial sea and the contiguous zone.—B. Convention on the high seas.—C. Convention on fishing and conservation of the living resources of the high seas.—D. Convention on the continental shelf.—E. Ratifications and accessions to the conventions.—F. Declarations and reservations to the conventions. 1. Maritime law I. Burke, William T. joint author II. T.
JX4411 M3　　JX4411 M3.　　341.57　　*LC* 62-16238

**United Nations Conference on the Law of the Sea. (3rd:**　　4.9316
**1973-1982: New York, N.Y., etc.)**
The Law of the sea: official text of the United Nations Convention on the Law of the Sea, with annexes and index: final act of the Third United Nations Conference on the Law of the Sea; introductory material on the convention and the conferences. — London: C. Helm; New York: St. Martin's Press, c1983. xxxvii, 224 p.; 24 cm. 'Contains the official text of the United Nations Convention on the Law of the Sea, signed at Montego Bay, Jamaica, on 10 December 1982'—Prefatory note. 1. Maritime law I. United Nations Convention on the Law of the Sea (1982). 1983. II. T.
JX4421.L38 1983　　*LC* 83-40157　　*ISBN* 0312475551

**Defining international aggression, the search for world peace: a**　　4.9317
**documentary history and analysis / by Benjamin B. Ferencz;**
**with an introd. by Louis B. Sohn.**
Dobbs Ferry, N.Y.: Oceana Publications, 1975. 2 v.; 27 cm. Includes index. 1. Aggression (International law) I. Ferencz, Benjamin B. 1920-
JX4471.D43　　341.5/8　　*LC* 75-16473　　*ISBN* 037900271X

**Falk, Richard A.**　　　　　　　　　　　　　　　　• 4.9318
Law, morality, and war in the contemporary world. — New York: Published for the Center of International Studies, Princeton University [by] Praeger [1963] 120 p.; 21 cm. (Princeton studies in world politics. 5) 1. International law 2. War — Moral and ethical aspects 3. International relations I. T. II. Series.
JX4471 F2　　*LC* 63-13680

**Osgood, Robert Endicott.**　　　　　　　　　　　　• 4.9319
Force, order, and justice / by Robert E. Osgood and Robert W. Tucker. — Baltimore: Johns Hopkins Press [1967] viii, 374 p.; 24 cm. 1. Aggression (International law) 2. War (International law) 3. International relations I. Tucker, Robert W. II. T.
JX4471.O8　　341　　*LC* 67-16915

**Stone, Julius, 1907-.**　　　　　　　　　　　　　　• 4.9320
Aggression and world order. Berkeley, University of California Press, 1958. 226 p. 1. United Nations. 2. Aggression (International law) I. T.
JX4471.S8 1958　　*LC* 58-3285

**Iklé, Fred Charles.**　　　　　　　　　　　　　　　• 4.9321
How nations negotiate. — New York: Praeger, [1967, c1964] xv, 272 p.; 21 cm. — (Praeger university series, U-630) 'Written under the auspices of the Center for International Affairs.' 1. Diplomatic negotiations in international disputes I. Harvard University. Center for International Affairs. II. T.
JX4473.I4 1967　　341.6　　*LC* 67-22334

**Zartman, I. William.**　　　　　　　　　　　　　　4.9322
The practical negotiator / I. William Zartman and Maureen R. Berman. — New Haven: Yale University Press, c1982. xiii, 250 p.; 22 cm. Includes index. 1. Diplomatic negotiations in international disputes 2. Diplomacy 3. Negotiation I. Berman, Maureen R., 1948- II. T.
JX4473.Z37　　327.2 19　　*LC* 81-40435　　*ISBN* 0300025238

## JX4505-5395 Law of War. Neutrality

**Documents on the laws of war** / edited by Adam Roberts and    **4.9323**
Richard Guelff.
Oxford: Clarendon Press; New York: Oxford University Press, 1982. xi, 498 p.;
25 cm. Includes index. 1. War (International law) I. Roberts, Adam.
II. Guelff, Richard, 1950-
JX4505.D62 1982   341.6 19   *LC* 81-14212   *ISBN* 0198761171

**The Law of war** / edited by Richard I. Miller; [general authors:    **4.9324**
Michael Bergner et al.].
Lexington, Mass.: Lexington Books, [1975] xi, 329 p.; 24 cm. 1. War
(International law) I. Miller, Richard I. II. Bergner, Michael.
JX4511.L38   341.6   *LC* 74-16936   *ISBN* 0669958778

**McDougal, Myres Smith, 1906-.**     • **4.9325**
Law and minimum world public order: the legal regulation of international
coercion / by Myres S. McDougal and Florentino P. Feliciano. — New Haven:
Yale University Press, c1961. xxvi, 872 p. 1. War (International law)
2. Sanctions (International law) I. Feliciano, Florentino P. II. T.
JX4511.M2   *LC* 61-14435

**Restraints on war: studies in the limitation of armed conflict** /    **4.9326**
edited by Michael Howard.
Oxford; New York: Oxford University Press, 1979. viii, 173 p.; 23 cm. Includes
index. 1. War (International law) — Addresses, essays, lectures. I. Howard,
Michael Eliot, 1922-
JX4511.R47   341.6 19   *LC* 79-309945   *ISBN* 0198225458

**Stone, Julius, 1907-.**     • **4.9327**
Legal controls of international conflict; a treatise on the dynamics of disputes–
and war–law. 2d impression, rev., with supplement 1953-1958. New York,
Rinehart, 1959. iv, 903 p. (Fletcher School studies in international affairs)
1. War (International law) 2. Pacific settlement of international disputes I. T.
II. Series.
JX4511 S8 1959   *LC* 60-1932

**Fraenkel, Ernst, 1898-.**     • **4.9328**
Military occupation and the rule of law: occupation government in the
Rhineland, 1918–1923 / Ernst Fraenkel. — London; Toronto: Oxford
University Press, 1944. xi, 267 p. — (Studies of the Institute of World Affairs)
'This study is presented in collaboration with the Carnegie Endowment for
International Peace.' 1. Rhineland (German territory under Allied occupation,
1918-1930). Military Occupation. I. Carnegie Endowment for International
Peace. II. T.
JX5003.F7   *LC* 44-47946

**Garrett, Richard.**     **4.9329**
P.O.W. / Richard Garrett. — Newton Abbot [Devon]: David & Charles, 1981.
240 p.: ill.; 24 cm. Includes index. 1. Prisoners of war — History. I. T.
II. Title: POW.
JX5141.G37   355.1/296/09 19   *LC* 81-200969   *ISBN* 0715379860

**Pillar, Paul R., 1947-.**     **4.9330**
Negotiating peace: war termination as a bargaining process / Paul R. Pillar. —
Princeton, N.J.: Princeton University Press, c1983. ix, 282 p.: ill.; 25 cm.
Includes index. 1. Peace 2. Armistices 3. War 4. Negotiation 5. International
relations I. T.
JX5166.P54 1983   327.1/72 19   *LC* 83-42572   *ISBN* 0691076561

**Deák, Francis, 1898-1972.**     • **4.9331**
A Collection of neutrality laws, regulations and treaties of various countries /
edited and annotated by Francis Deák and Philip Jessup. Washington, D.C.:
Carnegie Endowment for International Peace, 1939. 2 v.; 25 cm. (Publications
of the Carnegie Endowment for International Peace. Division of International
Law, Washington.) This material which includes laws, regulations and treaties
covering the period from 1800 until October 1, 1938, has been assembled in the
course of the preparation of a draft Convention on Rights and Duties of Neutral
States in Naval and Aerial War for Research in International Law, under the
auspices of the Faculty of the Harvard Law School. 1. Neutrality 2. Treaties
3. War, Maritime (International law) 4. Aeronautics, Military I. Jessup,
Philip C. (Philip Caryl), 1897- II. Research in international law. III. T.
IV. Title: Neutrality laws, regulations and treaties.
JX5355.D4   341.3   *LC* 39-34164

**Kuper, Leo.**     **4.9332**
Genocide: its political use in the twentieth century / Leo Kuper. — New
Haven: Yale University Press, 1981. 255 p.; 22 cm. Includes index. 1. Genocide
I. T.
JX5418.K86 1981   341.7/7 19   *LC* 81-16151   *ISBN* 0300027958

**Willis, James F.**     **4.9333**
Prologue to Nuremberg: the politics and diplomacy of punishing war criminals
of the First World War / James F. Willis. — Westport, Conn.: Greenwood
Press, 1982. xiii, 292 p.: ill.; 25 cm. — (Contributions in legal studies.

0147-1074; no. 20) Includes index. 1. War crime trials 2. Leipzig Trials,
Leipzig, Germany, 1921 3. War crimes I. T. II. Series.
JX5433.W54 1982   341.6/9/02684321   *LC* 81-1055   *ISBN*
0313214549

**Conot, Robert E.**     **4.9334**
Justice at Nuremberg / Robert E. Conot. — 1st ed. — New York: Harper &
Row, c1983. xiii, 593 p., [16] p. of plates: ill.; 24 cm. Includes index.
1. Nuremberg Trial of Major German War Criminals, Nuremberg, Germany,
1945-1946 I. T.
JX5437.8.C66 1983   341.6/9/02684321 19   *LC* 82-48395   *ISBN*
006015117X

## JX5483-5486 International Claims

**Lillich, Richard B.**     • **4.9335**
International claims: their adjudication by national commissions / Richard B.
Lillich. — Syracuse, N.Y.: Syracuse University Press, 1962. xiv, 140 p.; 24 cm.
1. Claims I. T.
JX5483.L5   *LC* 62-7735

## JX5760-5810 Aeronautics. Space Law

**McDougal, Myres Smith, 1906-.**     • **4.9336**
Law and public order in space, by Myres S. McDougal, Harold D. Lasswell,
and Ivan A. Vlasic. New Haven, Yale University Press, 1963. xxvi, 1147 p.
1. Space law 2. Airspace (International law) I. T.
JX5771 M3   *LC* 63-13968

**McWhinney, Edward.**     **4.9337**
Aerial piracy and international terrorism: the illegal diversion of aircraft and
international law / Edward McWhinney. — 2nd rev. ed. — Dordrecht, the
Netherlands; Boston: M. Nijhoff, 1987. 213 p. (International studies on
terrorism.) Rev. ed. of: Aerial piracy and international law / by Edward
McWhinney and others. 1971. Includes index. 1. Hijacking of aircraft I. Aerial
piracy and international law. II. T. III. Series.
JX5775.C7 M36 1987   341.7/72 19   *LC* 86-18045   *ISBN*
0898389194

**Fawcett, J. E. S. (James Edmund Sandford), 1913-.**     **4.9338**
Outer space: new challenges to law and policy / J.E.S. Fawcett. — New York:
Oxford, 1985 [c1984] vi, 169 p.: ill.; 22 cm. Includes index. 1. Space law I. T.
JX5810.F38 1984   341.4/7 19

---

# JX6731.W3 War Crimes

(see also: D804)

**Falk, Richard A. comp.**     • **4.9339**
Crimes of war: a legal, political–documentary, and psychological inquiry into
the responsibility of leaders, citizens, and soldiers for criminal acts in wars /
edited by Richard A. Falk, Gabriel Kolko, and Robert Jay Lifton. — [1st ed.].
— New York: Random House, [1971] 590 p.; 22 cm. 1. War crimes I. Kolko,
Gabriel. joint comp. II. Lifton, Robert Jay, 1926- joint comp. III. T.
JX6731.W3 F3   341/.69   *LC* 73-127540   *ISBN* 0394414152

**Glueck, Sheldon, 1896-.**     • **4.9340**
War criminals, their prosecution & punishment, by Sheldon Glueck ... New
York, A. A. Knopf, 1944. viii, 250, xii p., 1 l. 22 cm. 'First edition.'
Bibliographical references included in 'Notes' (p. 187-250) Bibliography: p.
216-222. 1. War crimes I. T.
JX6731.W3G5   341.3   *LC* 44-47372

**International War Crimes Tribunal (1st: 1967: Stockholm,**     • **4.9341**
**Sweden and Roskilde, Denmark)**
Against the crime of silence: proceedings of the Russell International War
Crimes Tribunal, Stockholm, Copenhagen / edited by John Duffett; introd. by
Bertrand Russell; foreword by Ralph Schoenman. — [1st ed.] New York:
Bertrand Russell Peace Foundation, 1968. ix, 662 p.: ill., ports.; 21 cm.
1. Vietnamese Conflict, 1961-1975 — Atrocities 2. War crimes I. Duffett,
John. ed. II. Bertrand Russell Peace Foundation. III. T.
JX6731.W3 I46 1967   341.6/9   *LC* 68-55747

**Maugham, Frederic Herbert Maugham, 1st Viscount, 1866-1958.**   • **4.9342**
U.N.O. and war crimes / by Viscount Maugham; with a postscript by Lord
Hankey. — London: John Murray, 1951. 143 p.; 22 cm. 1. United Nations.

2. War crimes 3. Nuremberg Trial of Major German War Criminals, Nuremberg, Germany, 1945-1946 4. War crime trials — Germany. I. T.
JX6731.W3 M38    341.6/9    *LC* 52-1871

**Minear, Richard H.**                **4.9343**
Victors' justice; the Tokyo war crimes trial [by] Richard H. Minear. —
Princeton, N.J.: Princeton University Press, 1971. xv, 229 p.: illus.; 23 cm.
1. Tokyo Trial, Tokyo, Japan, 1946-1948 I. T.
JX6731.W3 M5    341/.69    *LC* 74-163211

# K    Law

## K Law: General. Comparative

**Weber, Max, 1864-1920.**    • 4.9344
Max Weber on law in economy and society / edited with introd. and annotations by Max Rheinstein. — Translation from Max Weber, Wirtschaft und Gesellschaft, 2d ed. (1925) by Edward Shils and Max Rheinstein. Cambridge: Harvard University Press, 1954. 363 p.; 22 cm. (20th century legal philosophy series, v. 6.) 1. Comparative law I. T. II. Title: Law in economy and society.
K.W414 1954    330.1    LC 54-5023

**Pound, Roscoe, 1870-1964.**    • 4.9345
Interpretations of legal history. — Gloucester, Mass.: P. Smith, 1967. xvii, 171 p.; 21 cm. — (Cambridge studies in English legal history.) Reprint of the 1923 ed. 1. Jurisprudence 2. Law — History and criticism I. T. II. Series.
K10.P6x    340/.09    LC 67-5240

**Wigmore, John Henry, 1863-1943.**    • 4.9346
A panorama of the world's legal systems, by John Henry Wigmore ... with five hundred illustrations ... Saint Paul, West publishingg company [c1928] 3 v. illus. Paged continuously. 'The sixteen principal legal systems, past and present, form the subject—Egyptian, Mesopotamian, Hebrew, Chinese, Hindu, Greek, Roman, Japanese, Mohammedan, Keltic, Slavic, Germanic, maritime, ecclesiastical, Romanesque, Anglican.'—Author's note. 1. Law — History and criticism 2. Comparative law I. T. II. Title: The world's legal systems.
K10.W5x    340.9    LC 28-31092

**Walker, David M.**    4.9347
The Oxford companion to law / by David M. Walker. — Oxford; New York: Oxford University Press, 1980. ix, 1366 p.; 25 cm. 1. Law — Dictionaries 2. Law — Great Britain — Dictionaries. I. T.
K48.W34    340/.091812    LC 79-40846    ISBN 019866110X

**Lawyers in early modern Europe and America / edited by**    4.9348
**Wilfrid Prest.**
New York: Holmes & Meier Publishers, 1981. 216 p.: ill.; 23 cm. 1. Lawyers — Europe — History — Addresses, essays, lectures. 2. Lawyers — North America — History — Addresses, essays, lectures. I. Prest, Wilfrid R.
K115.Z9 L28    340/.023/4 19    LC 80-22574    ISBN 0841906793

**Berman, Harold Joseph, 1918-.**    4.9349
Law and revolution: the formation of the Western legal tradition / Harold J. Berman. — Cambridge, Mass.: Harvard University Press, 1983. viii, 657 p.: maps; 24 cm. 1. Law — History and criticism I. T.
K150.B47 1983    340/.09 19    LC 82-15747    ISBN 0674517741

**Fuller, Lon L., 1902-.**    4.9350
Anatomy of the law / Lon L. Fuller. Westport, Conn.: Greenwood Press, 1976, c1968. v, 122 p.; 24 cm. Reprint of the ed. published by Praeger, New York. 1. Law — History and criticism I. T.
K150.F84 1976    340/.09    LC 75-36095    ISBN 0837186226

## K190 Primitive Law. Ethnological Jurisprudence

**Bohannan, Paul. ed.**    • 4.9351
Law and warfare: studies in the anthropology of conflict. — [1st ed.] Garden City, N.Y.: Published for the American Museum of Natural History [New York, by] the Natural History Press, 1967. — xiv, 441 p.: ill., map; 22 cm. (American Museum sourcebooks in anthropology) 1. Law, Primitive — Addresses, essays, lectures. 2. Ethnological jurisprudence — Addresses, essays, lectures. 3. War — Addresses, essays, lectures. I. American Museum of Natural History. II. T. III. Series.
K190.B6x    341.3    LC 67-10386

**Gluckman, Max, 1911-1975.**    • 4.9352
Politics, law and ritual in tribal society. — Chicago: Aldine Pub. Co., [1965] xxxii, 339 p.: ill., maps.; 22 cm. 1. Law, Primitive 2. Society, Primitive I. T.
K190.G5x    321.12    LC 64-21381

**Hoebel, E. Adamson (Edward Adamson), 1906-.**    • 4.9353
The law of primitive man: a study in comparative legal dynamics. — Cambridge: Harvard University Press, 1954. viii, 357 p.; 22 cm. 1. Law, Primitive I. T.
K190.H6x    340.1    LC 54-9331

**Maine, Henry Sumner, Sir, 1822-1888.**    4.9354
Ancient law: its connection with the early history of society, and its relation to modern ideas / Henry Sumner Maine; foreword by Lawrence Rosen. — Tucson: University of Arizona Press, c1986. lxxxi, 400 p.; 22 cm. — (Classics of anthropology) Reprint. Originally published: New York: Holt, 1864. Includes index. 1. Law, Ancient 2. Law, Primitive 3. Comparative law I. T.
K190.M35 1986    340.5/3 19    LC 86-6929    ISBN 0816510067

**Law in culture and society / edited by Laura Nader.**    • 4.9355
Chicago: Aldine Pub. Co. [1969] ix, 454 p.: maps; 25 cm. Papers presented at a 2d Wenner-Gren conference held at Burg Wartenstein, Gloggnitz, Austria, Aug. 3-13, 1966. 1. Ethnological jurisprudence — Addresses, essays, lectures. 2. Law, Primitive — Addresses, essays, lectures. I. Nader, Laura. ed. II. Wenner-Gren Foundation for Anthropological Research.
K190.N3x    340    LC 68-8157

**Newman, Katherine.**    4.9356
Law and economic organization: a comparative study of preindustrial societies / Katherine S. Newman. — Cambridge [Cambridgeshire]; New York: Cambridge University Press, 1983. xii, 264 p.; 23 cm. Revision of thesis (Ph. D.)—University of California, Berkeley, 1979. Includes index. 1. Ethnological jurisprudence I. T.
K190.N48 1983    340/.115 19    LC 83-7169    ISBN 0521247918

**Roberts, Simon.**    4.9357
Order and dispute: an introduction to legal anthropology / Simon Roberts. — New York: St. Martin's Press, 1979. 216 p.; 19 cm. Includes index. 1. Law, Primitive 2. Ethnological jurisprudence 3. Justice, Administration of I. T.
K190.R6    340.1/15    LC 78-24778    ISBN 0312587139

## K201–487 Jurisprudence. Philosophy and Theory of Law

**Hohfeld, Wesley Newcomb, 1879-1918.**    4.9358
Fundamental legal conceptions as applied in judicial reasoning / by Wesley Newcomb Hohfeld; edited by Walter Wheeler Cook; with a new foreword by Arthur L. Corbin. — Westport, Conn.: Greenwood Press, 1978, c1919. xv, 114 p.: 23 cm. Reprint of the 1964 ed. published by Yale Univ. Press, New Haven, which was issued as A Yale paperbound, Y-115. Includes bibliographical references. 1. Law — Methodology 2. Law — Addresses, essays, lectures. I. Cook, Walter Wheeler, 1873-1943. II. T.
K212.H63 1978    340.1    LC 75-31367    ISBN 0837185254

**Cardozo, Benjamin N. (Benjamin Nathan), 1870-1938.**    4.9359
The growth of the law. — Westport, Conn.: Greenwood Press, [1973, c1924] xvi, 145 p.; 20 cm. Reprint of the 1966 ed. published by Yale University Press, New Haven. 1. Law — Philosophy. I. T.
K230.C3x    340.1    LC 73-8154    ISBN 0837169534

**Cohen, Felix S., 1907-1953.**    4.9360
Ethical systems and legal ideals: an essay on the foundations of legal criticism / by Felix S. Cohen. — Westport, Conn.: Greenwood Press, 1976, c1933. xi, 303 p.; 23 cm. Reprint of the ed. published by Falcon Press, New York. 1. Law — Philosophy. 2. Ethics 3. Legal ethics I. T.
K230.C6x    174/.3    LC 75-40440    ISBN 0837186439

**Fuller, Lon L., 1902-.**    4.9361
The morality of law / by Lon L. Fuller. — Rev. ed. — New Haven: Yale University Press, 1977, c1969. xi, 262 p.; 21 cm. — (Storrs lectures on jurisprudence. 1963) 1. Law and ethics I. T. II. Series.
K230.F84 M67 1977    340.1/12    LC 72-93579    ISBN 0300004729

**Hegel, Georg Wilhelm Friedrich, 1770-1831.**    • **4.9362**
[Grundlinien der Philosophie des Rechts English] Philosophy of right. Translated with notes by T. M. Knox. [1st ed.] Oxford, Clarendon Press [1965] xvi, 382 p. 23 cm. Translation of Grundlinien der Philosophie des Rechts. 1. Law — Philosophy. 2. Political science 3. Natural law 4. Ethics I. Knox, T. M. (Thomas Malcolm), 1900- II. T.
K230.H43 P4513 1965     340/.1 19     LC 68-48361

**Pennock, J. Roland (James Roland), 1906-.**    **4.9363**
The limits of law. Edited by J. Roland Pennock and John W. Chapman. New York, Lieber-Atherton, 1974. xii, 276 p. 23 cm. (Nomos, 15) Includes papers presented at a meeting of the American Society for Political and Legal Philosophy held in association with the American Association of Law Schools in Chicago, Dec. 1970. 1. Law — Philosophy — Addresses, essays, lectures. I. Chapman, John William, 1923- joint author. II. American Society for Political and Legal Philosophy. III. Association of American Law Schools. IV. T. V. Series.
K230.L5x     340.1     LC 73-83018     ISBN 0883110083

**Pollock, Frederick, Sir, 1845-1937.**    **4.9364**
Jurisprudence and legal essays / by Sir Frederick Pollock; selected and introduced by A. L. Goodhart. — Westport, Conn.: Greenwood Press, 1978, c1961. xlviii, 243 p.; 23 cm. Reprint of the ed. published by Macmillan, London. Includes index. 1. Jurisprudence I. T.
K230.P6 J8 1978     340.1     LC 77-28352     ISBN 0313202494

**Pound, Roscoe, 1870-1964.**    • **4.9365**
An introduction to the philosophy of law. — Rev. ed. — New Haven: Yale University Press, 1954. 201 p.; 21 cm. 1. Law — Philosophy. I. T.
K230.P6x     340.1     LC 52-12076

**Hart, H. L. A. (Herbert Lionel Adolphus), 1907-.**    **4.9366**
The concept of law / by H. L. A. Hart. — New York: Oxford University Press, 1961 [i.e. 1976] 263 p.; 21 cm. Preface: Mar. 1972. Includes index. 1. Jurisprudence 2. Law — Philosophy. I. T.
K237.H3 1976     340.1     LC 76-379015     ISBN 0198760728 pbk

**Fuller, Lon L., 1902-.**    **4.9367**
Legal fictions / [by] Lon L. Fuller. — Stanford, Calif.: Stanford University Press, 1967. xiii, 142 p.; 23 cm. Bibliographical footnotes. 1. Fictions (Law) I. T.
K274.F8x     340     LC 67-17303

**Hart, H. L. A. (Herbert Lionel Adolphus), 1907-.**    **4.9368**
Essays on Bentham: studies in jurisprudence and political theory / by H.L.A. Hart. — Oxford [Oxfordshire]: Clarendon Press; New York: Oxford University Press, c1982. 272 p.: ill.; 22 cm. 1. Bentham, Jeremy, 1748-1832 — Addresses, essays, lectures. 2. Jurisprudence — Addresses, essays, lectures. 3. Political science — Addresses, essays, lectures. I. T.
K334.H37 1982     340/.1 19     LC 82-3601     ISBN 0198253486

**Durkheim, Emile, 1858-1917.**    **4.9369**
Durkheim and the law / edited by Steven Lukes and Andrew Scull. — New York: St. Martin's Press, 1983. 241 p.; 23 cm. 1. Durkheim, Emile, 1858-1917. 2. Sociological jurisprudence I. Lukes, Steven. II. Scull, Andrew T. III. T.
K369.D87 1983     340/.115 19     LC 83-11031     ISBN 0312222653

**Ethics, economics, and the law / edited by J. Roland Pennock**    **4.9370**
**and John W. Chapman.**
New York: New York University Press, 1982. xix, 323 p.; 22 cm. — (Nomos; 24) 1. Law — Philosophy — Addresses, essays, lectures. 2. Law and ethics — Addresses, essays, lectures. 3. Property — Addresses, essays, lectures. 4. Economics — Addresses, essays, lectures. I. Pennock, J. Roland (James Roland), 1906- II. Chapman, John William, 1923- III. Series.
K486.E83 1982     340/.11 19     LC 81-16882     ISBN 0814765831

**Frank, Jerome, 1889-1957.**    **4.9371**
Law and the modern mind. Gloucester, Mass. Peter Smith 1970. 404p. 1. Law — Psychology 2. Law — Philosophy 3. Psychology, Forensic I. T.
K487.P75F7x

# K520–5570 Comparative Law

**Women and property, women as property / edited by Renee**    **4.9372**
**Hirschon.**
London: Croom Helm; New York: St. Martin's Press, 1984. [v], 222 p. — (Oxford women's series.) 1. Women — Legal status, laws, etc. 2. Married women 3. Property I. Hirschon, Renee. II. Series.
K644.W65 1983     K644 W65 1984.     346.04 342.64 19     LC 83-11029     ISBN 0312887302

**Glendon, Mary Ann, 1938-.**    **4.9373**
The new family and the new property / Mary Ann Glendon. — Toronto, Ont.: Butterworths, 1981. xvii, 269 p. 1. Domestic relations 2. Property 3. Labor laws and legislation I. T.
K670 G43     346.01 19     ISBN 0409834106

**Becker, Lawrence C.**    **4.9374**
Property rights: philosophic foundations / Lawrence C. Becker. — London; Boston: Routledge and K. Paul, 1977. 135 p.; 23 cm. 1. Right of property I. T.
K721.5.B4     323.4/6/01     LC 78-300178     ISBN 0710086792

**Abraham, Henry Julian, 1921-.**    **4.9375**
The judicial process: an introductory analysis of the courts of the United States, England, and France / Henry J. Abraham. — 5th ed. — New York: Oxford University Press, 1986. xvi, 624 p.; 23 cm. Includes indexes. 1. Courts — United States 2. Courts — Great Britain. 3. Courts — France. 4. Judicial process I. T.
K2100.A725 1986     347/.01 342.71 19     LC 85-15261     ISBN 0195037138

**The Disputing process: law in ten societies / Laura Nader and**    **4.9376**
**Harry F. Todd, Jr., editors.**
New York: Columbia University Press, 1978. xx, 372 p.; 24 cm. Includes index. 1. Arbitration and award 2. Negotiation 3. Courts 4. Customary law I. Nader, Laura. II. Todd, Harry F.
K2400.D5     347/.09     LC 78-8729     ISBN 0231045360

**Constitutions of the countries of the world: a series of updated**    **4.9377**
**texts, constitutional chronologies and annotated bibliographies /**
**edited by A.P. Blaustein and G.H. Flanz.**
Permanent ed. Dobbs Ferry, N.Y.: Oceana Publications [1971- 17 v. (loose-leaf) 28 cm. The English translations of some of the constitutions are accompanied by the original texts. Includes unnumbered supplement volume and Historic constitutions volumes. 1. Constitutions I. Blaustein, Albert P., 1921- II. Flanz, Gisbert H.
K3157.A2 B58 1971     342.02/3     LC 76-141327

**Independence documents of the world / [compiled] by Albert P.**    **4.9378**
**Blaustein, Jay Sigler, Benjamin R. Beede, with Wayne E. Olson**
**... [et al.].**
Dobbs Ferry, N.Y.: Oceana Publications, 1977. 2 v. (xiv, 800 p.); 26 cm. 1. Constitutional law — Sources. I. Blaustein, Albert P., 1921- II. Sigler, Jay A. III. Beede, Benjamin R.
K3157.A2 B6     342.02     LC 77-7333     ISBN 0379007940

**Peaslee, Amos Jenkins, 1887-.**    **4.9379**
Constitutions of nations, by Amos J. Peaslee. Rev. 4th ed., prepared by Dorothy Peaslee Xydis. [The Hague, M. Nijhoff, 1984-] v. illus., maps. 25 cm. 1. Constitutions I. Xydis, Dorothy Peaslee. ed. II. T.
K3157.A2P4 1984     342.02/3 342.223 19     LC 83-19506

**Constitutions of dependencies and special sovereignties / edited**    **4.9380**
**by Albert P. Blaustein & Phyllis M. Blaustein.**
Dobbs Ferry, N.Y.: Oceana Publications, 1975-. 6 v; 28 cm. Editors: Albert P. Blaustein & Eric B. Blaustein (1975- < 1985 > ) Loose-leaf for updating. 1. Constitutions 2. Constitutions — Great Britain — Colonies. I. Blaustein, Albert P., 1921- II. Blaustein, Phyllis M. III. Blaustein, Eric B.
K3157.E5 C65 1975     342.02/3 342.223 19     LC 75-21651     ISBN 0379002787

**Constitutionalism / edited by J. Roland Pennock and John W.**    **4.9381**
**Chapman.**
New York: New York University Press, 1979. xv, 398 p.; 22 cm. (Nomos; 20) 1. Constitutional law — Addresses, essays, lectures. 2. Constitutional law — Interpretation and construction — Addresses, essays, lectures. I. Pennock, J. Roland (James Roland), 1906- II. Chapman, John William, 1923- III. Series.
K3165.C6     342.02/9     LC 78-58843     ISBN 0814765734

**Brownlie, Ian. comp.**    **4.9382**
Basic documents on human rights / edited by Ian Brownlie. — 2d ed. — Oxford: Clarendon Press; New York: Oxford University Press, 1981. x, 505 p.; 24 cm. Includes index. 1. Civil rights 2. Human rights I. T.
K3238.A1 B76 1981     323.4 19     LC 80-49923     ISBN 0198761244

**McDougal, Myres Smith, 1906-.**    **4.9383**
Human rights and world public order: the basic policies of an international law of human dignity / by Myres S. McDougal, Harold D. Lasswell, and Lung-chu Chen. — New Haven, Conn.: Yale University Press, 1980. xxiv, 1016 p.; 24 cm. 1. Human rights I. Lasswell, Harold Dwight, 1902- joint author. II. Chen, Lung-chu, 1935- joint author. III. T.
K3240.4.M27     341.48/1     LC 79-18149     ISBN 0300023448

**Mower, A. Glenn (Alfred Glenn)**    **4.9384**
The United States, the United Nations, and human rights: the Eleanor Roosevelt and Jimmy Carter eras / A. Glenn Mower, Jr. — Westport, Conn.: Greenwood Press, 1979. xii, 215 p.; 22 cm. (Studies in human rights. no. 4

0146-3586) Includes index. 1. Human rights 2. Civil rights 3. United States —
Foreign relations — 1945- I. T. II. Series.
K3240.4.M68     341.48/1     LC 78-22134     ISBN 031321090X

**Robertson, A. H. (Arthur Henry), 1913-.**                     **4.9385**
Human rights in the world: an introduction to the study of the international
protection of human rights / by A.H. Robertson. — 2nd ed. — New York: St.
Martin's Press, 1982. viii, 243 p.; 22 cm. 1. Human rights I. T.
K3240.4.R6 1982     341.4/81 19     LC 82-10238     ISBN 0312399618

**Sieghart, Paul.**                                             **4.9386**
The international law of human rights / Paul Sieghart. — Oxford; New York:
Clarendon Press, 1983. xxiv, 569 p.; 24 cm. Includes index. 1. Human rights
I. T.
K3240.4.S49 1983     341.4/81 19     LC 82-14248     ISBN 0198760965

**Dimensions internationales des droits de l'homme. English.**   **4.9387**
The International dimensions of human rights / Karel Vasak, general editor;
revised and edited for the English edition by Philip Alston. — Westport, Conn.:
Greenwood Press; Paris, France: Unesco, 1982. 2 v. (755 p.): 1 ill.; 25 cm.
Translation of: Les dimensions internationales des droits de l'homme.
Illustrative matter on folded leaf in pocket at end of v. 2. Includes indexes.
1. Human rights — Addresses, essays, lectures. 2. Civil rights — Addresses,
essays, lectures. I. Vasak, Karel. II. Alston, Philip. III. Unesco. IV. T.
K3240.6.D5513 1982     341.48/1 19     LC 81-22566     ISBN
0313233942

**The International Bill of Rights: the Covenant on Civil and**   **4.9388**
**Political Rights / Louis Henkin, editor.**
New York: Columbia University Press, 1981. x, 523 p.; 24 cm. 1. Human rights
— Addresses, essays, lectures. I. Henkin, Louis. II. Title: Covenant on Civil
and Political Rights.
K3240.6.I53     341.4/81 19     LC 81-6112     ISBN 0231051808

**Press law in modern democracies: a comparative study / Pnina**   **4.9389**
**Lahav, editor.**
New York: Longman, c1985 [i.e.1984?]. xvi, 366 p.; 24 cm. — (Annenberg/
Longman communication books.) 1. Freedom of the press 2. Press law
I. Lahav, Pnina, 1945- II. Series.
K3255.P73 1985     343/.0998 342.3998 19     LC 83-19595     ISBN
0582284783

**Lillich, Richard B.**                                          **4.9390**
The human rights of aliens in contemporary international law / Richard B.
Lillich. — Manchester [Greater Manchester]; Dover, N.H., U.S.A.:
Manchester University Press, 1985 (c1984). xii, 177 p.; 24 cm. (Melland Schill
monographs in international law.) Parts of this volume were originally
delivered as the Melland Schill lectures at the University of Manchester, Nov.
19-20, 1981. 1. Aliens 2. Human rights I. T. II. Series.
K3274.L55 1984     341.4/84 19     LC 84-15500     ISBN 0719009146

**M'Gonigle, R. Michael.**                                       **4.9391**
Pollution, politics, and international law: tankers at sea / R. Michael
M'Gonigle and Mark W. Zacher. — Berkeley: University of California Press,
c1979. xviii, 394 p.: ill.; 24 cm. — (Science, technology, and the changing world
order.) 1. Oil pollution of the sea — Law and legislation 2. Tankers — Law
and legislation 3. Liability for oil pollution damages I. Zacher, Mark W. joint
author. II. T. III. Series.
K3590.4.M3     341.7/623     LC 78-54799     ISBN 0520036905

**Kline, John M.**                                               **4.9392**
International codes and multinational business: setting guidelines for
international business operations / John M. Kline. — Westport, Conn.:
Quorum Books, 1985. vi, 184 p.; 25 cm. Includes index. 1. Foreign trade
regulation 2. International business enterprises — Law and legislation I. T.
K3943.K58 1985     341.7/53 19     LC 84-18061     ISBN 0899300855

**Glick, Leslie Alan.**                                          **4.9393**
Multilateral trade negotiations: world trade after the Tokyo Round / Leslie
Alan Glick. — Totowa, N.J.: Rowman & Allanheld, 1984. xvi, 423 p.; 25 cm.
1. Tokyo Round (1973-1979) 2. Tariff — Law and legislation 3. Foreign trade
regulation 4. Tariff — Law and legislation — United States. 5. Foreign trade
regulation — United States I. T.
K4603 1973.G55 1984     341.7/54/0265 19     LC 80-70919     ISBN
0865980365

**Hall, Jerome, 1901-.**                                       • **4.9394**
General principles of criminal law / by Jerome Hall. — Indianapolis: Bobbs-
Merrill Co., 1960. xii, 642 p. 1. Criminal law I. T.
K5018.H35 1960     LC 60-3677

**Polyviou, Polyvios G., 1949-.**                                **4.9395**
Search & seizure: constitutional and common law / Polyvios G. Polyviou. —
London: Duckworth, 1982. viii, 391 p.; 26 cm. 'Table of cases': p. [380]-387.

Includes index. 1. Searches and seizures — United States. 2. Searches and
seizures — Great Britain. I. T. II. Title: Search and seizure.
K5438.P64 1982     345.73/0522 347.305522 19     LC 82-144031
ISBN 0715615920

**Parsloe, Phyllida.**                                           **4.9396**
Juvenile justice in Britain and the United States: the balance of needs and rights
/ Phyllida Parsloe. — London: Boston; Routledge & K. Paul, 1978. x, 325 p.;
23 cm. — (Library of social work) 1. Juvenile courts — Great Britain.
2. Juvenile justice, Administration of — Great Britain. 3. Juvenile courts —
United States. 4. Juvenile justice, Administration of — United States. I. T.
K5575.P35     345/.41/08     LC 77-30714     ISBN 0710087721

# KB Ancient Law. Theocratic Systems

**MacDowell, Douglas M. (Douglas Maurice)**                      **4.9397**
The law in classical Athens / Douglas M. MacDowell. — Ithaca, N.Y.: Cornell
University Press, 1978. 280 p.; 23 cm. — (Aspects of Greek and Roman life)
1. Law, Greek 2. Law — Greece — Athens. I. T. II. Series.
KB.M2x     340.5/3/85     LC 78-54141     ISBN 080141198X

**Kunkel, Wolfgang, 1902-.**                                     **4.9398**
An introduction to Roman legal and constitutional history. Translated by J.M.
Kelly. 2d ed., based on the sixth German edition of Römische
Rechtsgeschichte. 2D ed. Oxford Clarendon Press 1973. 236p. 1. Roman law
— History I. T. II. Title: Roman legal and constitutional history
KBD.K8x     LC 73-173382

**Wilkin, Robert Nugen, 1886-.**                                 **4.9399**
Eternal lawyer: a legal biography of Cicero / by Robert N. Wilkin. — New
York: Macmillan Co., 1947. 264 p.: ill. 1. Cicero, Marcus. I. T.
KBD.W5x     928.7     LC 47-3078

**Vinogradoff, Paul, Sir, 1854-1925.**                         • **4.9400**
Roman law in medieval Europe, / by Paul Vinogradoff. — Oxford: The
Clarendon press, 1929. 155 p.; 20 cm. 1. Roman law 2. Law — History and
criticism I. Zulueta Francis de, 1878- ed. II. T.
LAW <Roman Law A>     KBD.V5x.     LC 30-8239

# KD United Kingdom. Anglo-American Law. Common Law

**Anson, William Reynell, Sir, 1843-1914.**                    • **4.9401**
The law and custom of the constitution. Oxford, Clarendon Press, 1886–92.
New York, Johnson Reprint Corp. [1970] 2 v. 23 cm. (Reprints in government
and political science) 1. Great Britain — Constitutional law. 2. Great Britain
— Politics and government I. T.
KD.A6x     342/.42/09     LC 78-18540

**Dicey, Albert Venn, 1835-1922.**                             • **4.9402**
Introduction to the study of the law of the Constitution. — 10th ed., with
introd. by E. C. S. Wade. — London: Macmillan; New York: St. Martin's Press,
1959. cxcviii, 535 p.; 23 cm. 'Short bibliography of modern authorities': p.
500-502. 1. Gt. Brit. — Constitutional law. I. Wade, E. C. S. (Emlyn Capel
Stewart), 1895- ed. II. T.
KD.D5x     342.42     LC 60-50164

**Jennings, Ivor, Sir, 1903-1965.**                            • **4.9403**
The British constitution, by Sir Ivor Jennings. — 5th ed. — Cambridge:
Cambridge U.P., 1966. xi, 218 p.: 8 plates, tables.; 21 cm. 1. Great Britain —
Constitutional law. 2. Great Britain — Politics and government I. T.
KD.J4x     320.942     LC 66-15941

**Pound, Roscoe, 1870-1964.**                                  • **4.9404**
The spirit of the common law, by Roscoe Pound ... Boston, Marshall Jones
Company [1931] xv p., 1 β., 224 p. 21 cm. (Dartmouth alumni lectureships on
the Guernsey Center Moore foundation ... 1921) 'Reprinted November 1931.'
1. Common law 2. Law — History and criticism 3. Law — United States —
History and criticism I. T.
KD.P6x     LC 35-34119

**A Concise dictionary of law.**      **4.9405**
Oxford [Oxfordshire]; New York: Oxford University Press, 1983. 394 p.; 21 cm. Editor, Elizabeth A. Martin. 1. Law — Great Britain — Dictionaries. 2. Law — Great Britain — Terms and phrases. I. Martin, E. A. (Elizabeth A.) II. Oxford University Press.
KD313.C66 1983     349.41/03 344.1003 19     *LC 83-17323*     *ISBN* 0198253990

**Winfield, Percy Henry, Sir, 1878-1953.**      • **4.9406**
The chief sources of English legal history. New York, B. Franklin [c1925] xviii, 374 p. 24 cm. (Burt Franklin bibliography and reference series, no. 35) 1. Law — Great Britain — History and criticism 2. Law — Great Britain — Bibliography 3. Law — Great Britain — Sources. I. T.
KD530.W5x     *LC 63-6681*

**Holdsworth, William Searle, Sir, 1871-1944.**      • **4.9407**
A history of English law. London, Methuen & co., 1903-66. 16 v. illus. Vols. 7-8 are without date of publication; v. 7 has preface dated 1925. Vols. 13-16 edited by A. L. Goodhart and H. G. Hanbury. 1. Law — Great Britain — History and criticism I. Goodhart, Arthur Lehman, Sir, 1891- ed. II. Hanbury, Harold Greville, 1898- ed. III. T.
KD532.H6x     340/.0942     *LC 12-34240*

**Pollock, Frederick, Sir, 1845-1937.**      **4.9408**
The history of English law before the time of Edward I, by Sir Frederick Pollock and Frederic William Maitland. 2nd ed. reissued; with a new introduction and select bibliography by S. F. C. Milsom. London, Cambridge U.P., 1968. 2 v. 24 cm. 1. Law — Great Britain — History and criticism I. Maitland, Frederic William, 1850-1906. joint author. II. T.
KD532.P64 1968     340/.0942     *LC 68-21197*     *ISBN* 0521095158

**Robertson, A. J. (Agnes Jane) ed. and tr.**      • **4.9409**
Anglo–Saxon charters, edited with translation and notes. [2d ed.] Cambridge [Eng.] University Press, 1956. XXV, 555 p. 22 cm. (Cambridge studies in English legal history.) 1. Charters 2. English language — Old English, ca. 450-1100 — Texts. 3. Great Britain — Charters, grants, privileges. 4. Great Britain — History — Anglo-Saxon period, 449-1066 — Sources. I. T. II. Series.
KD555.R6x     *LC 58-846*

**Blackstone, William, Sir, 1723-1780.**      • **4.9410**
Commentaries on the laws of England / adapted by Robert Malcolm Kerr; pref. by Charles M. Haar. — Boston: Beacon Press, 1962. 4 v.; 21 cm. — (Beacon series in classics of the law) (Beacon paperback; 140) 1. Law — Great Britain I. Kerr, Robert Malcolm, 1821-1902. ed. II. T. III. Series.
KD660.B53     340.0942     *LC 63-5513*

**Fifoot, C. H. S. (Cecil Herbert Stuart), 1899-.**      • **4.9411**
History and sources of the common law: tort and contract, by C. H. S. Fifoot. New York, Greenwood Press [1970] xvii, 446 p. 24 cm. Reprint of the 1949 ed. 1. Torts — Great Britain — History. 2. Contracts — Great Britain — History. I. T.
KD671.F5x     347.5/0942     *LC 75-98758*     *ISBN* 0837128145

**Holmes, Oliver Wendell, 1841-1935.**      **4.9412**
The common law. By O. W. Holmes, Jr. Boston, Little, Brown, and company, 1881. xvi, 422 p. 22 cm. 'Year book and early cases': p. xv-xvi. 1. Common law I. T.
KD671.H6x     *LC 03-19966*     *ISBN* 0313671319

**Milsom, S. F. C. (Stroud Francis Charles), 1923-.**      **4.9413**
Historical foundations of the common law / S.F.C. Milsom. — 2nd ed. — London; Boston: Butterworths, 1981. xiii, 475 p.; 22 cm. 1. Common law — Great Britain. I. T.
KD671.M54 1981     349.42/09 344.2009 19     *LC 82-111120*     *ISBN* 0406625026

**Plucknett, Theodore Frank Thomas, 1897-1965.**      • **4.9414**
A concise history of the common law / by Theodore F. T. Plucknett. — 5th ed. — London: Butterworth, 1956. xxvi, 746, 56 p. 1. Common law — Great Britain — History 2. Law — Great Britain — History and criticism I. T.
KD671.P58 1956     *LC 57-1816*

**Palmer, Robert C., 1947-.**      **4.9415**
The Whilton dispute, 1264–1380: a social–legal study of dispute settlement in medieval England / Robert C. Palmer. — Princeton, N.J.: Princeton University Press, c1984. xxii, 295 p.; 23 cm. 1. De Whelton, William, d. 1267 — Estate. 2. Whilton family 3. Real property — England — History. 4. Great Britain — History — Medieval period, 1066-1485 I. T.
KD1514.D4 P35 1984     346.4205/4 344.20554 19     *LC 83-13858*     *ISBN* 0691054045

**Dawson, John Philip.**      • **4.9416**
A history of lay judges. Cambridge, Harvard University Press, 1960. viii, 310 p. 1. Lay judges I. T.
K D2726 H5     *LC 61-5576*

**The New Poor Law in the nineteenth century / edited by Derek Fraser.**      **4.9417**
New York: St. Martin's Press, 1976. 218 p.; 23 cm. (Problems in focus series) Includes index. 1. Poor laws — Great Britain — History. I. Fraser, Derek.
KD3310.N4 1976b     362.5/0942     *LC 75-43484*

**Street, Harry.**      **4.9418**
Constitutional and administrative law. — 5th ed. / edited by Harry Street, Rodney Brazier. — Harmondsworth: Penguin, 1985. 748 p.; 20 cm. Includes index. At head of title: de Smith. On cover: New edition. 'A Pelican book.' 1. Administrative law — Great Britain. 2. Civil rights — Great Britain 3. Justice, Administration of — Great Britain 4. Great Britain — Constitutional law. I. Brazier, Rodney. II. De Smith, Stanley Alexander. III. T.
KD3930.S7x     *ISBN* 0140226109

**Marshall, Geoffrey.**      **4.9419**
Constitutional theory / by Geoffrey Marshall. — Oxford: Clarendon Press; New York: Oxford University Press, 1971. ix, 238 p.; 22 cm. — (Clarendon law series) Includes index. 1. Great Britain — Constitutional law. 2. United States — Constitutional law I. T.
KD3989.M38 1971     342.41/02     *LC 79-29301*

**Street, Harry, 1919-.**      **4.9420**
Freedom, the individual, and the law / [by] H. Street. — 4th ed. — Harmondsworth; New York: Penguin, 1977. 327 p.; 19 cm. 1. Civil rights — Great Britain. I. T.
KD4080.S77 1977     342/.42/085     *LC 77-379989*     *ISBN* 0140206469

**Lester, Anthony.**      **4.9421**
Race and law in Great Britain [by] Anthony Lester and Geoffrey Bindman. — Cambridge: Harvard University Press, 1972. 491 p.; 25 cm. Includes the texts of the Race relations acts of 1965 and 1968. 1. Race discrimination — Law and legislation — Great Britain. I. Bindman, Geoffrey. joint author. II. Great Britain. Laws, statutes, etc. Race relations act 1965. 1972. III. Great Britain. Laws, statutes, etc. Race relations act 1968. 1972. IV. T.
KD4095.L47     342/.42/087     *LC 73-189159*     *ISBN* 0674745701

**Thomas, Donald Serrell.**      **4.9422**
A long time burning; the history of literary censorship in England. — New York: Praeger, [1969] xii, 546 p.: illus.; 23 cm. 1. Censorship — Great Britain — History. 2. English literature — History and criticism I. T.
KD4114.T48 1969b     363.3/1     *LC 73-83392*

**Griffith, J. A. G. (John Aneurin Grey)**      **4.9423**
The politics of the judiciary / J. A. G. Griffith. — 3rd ed. — [London]: Fontana Press, 1985. 255 p.; 20 cm. — (Political issues of modern Britain) On cover: A. Fontana original. 1. Political questions and judicial power — Great Britain. I. T. II. Series.
KD4645.G74     347/.41/014     *ISBN* 0006860206

**Select documents on the constitutional history of the British Empire and Commonwealth: the foundations of a colonial system of government / edited by Frederick Madden with David Fieldhouse.**      **4.9424**
Westport, Conn.: Greenwood Press, 1985-. v. ; 25 cm. (Documents in imperial history, 0749-4831; no. 1-) 1. Commonwealth of Nations — Constitutional history — Sources. 2. Great Britain — Colonies — Constitutional history — Sources. 3. Great Britain — Constitutional history — Sources. I. Madden, A. F. II. Fieldhouse, D. K. (David Kenneth), 1925-
KD5025.S45 1985     342/.029/09171241 342.22909171241 19     *LC* 84-21213     *ISBN* 0313238979

**Jackson, R. M. (Richard Meredith), 1903-.**      **4.9425**
The machinery of justice in England / R. M. Jackson. — 7th ed. — Cambridge; New York: Cambridge University Press, 1977. xii, 627 p.: maps; 24 cm. 1. Courts — Great Britain. 2. Justice, Administration of — Great Britain. I. T.
KD7100.J3 1977     347/.42     *LC 77-4401*     *ISBN* 0521216885

**Turner, Ralph V.**      **4.9426**
The English judiciary in the age of Glanvill and Bracton, c. 1176–1239 / Ralph V. Turner. — Cambridge [Cambridgeshire]; New York: Cambridge University Press, 1985. xiv, 321 p.; 23 cm. (Cambridge studies in English legal history.) 1. Judges — Great Britain — History. 2. Courts — Great Britain — History. I. T. II. Series.
KD7285.T87 1985     347.42/014/09 344.2071409 19     *LC 84-20058*     *ISBN* 052126510X

**Radzinowicz, Leon, Sir.**      • **4.9427**
A history of English criminal law and its administration from 1750 / by Leon Radzinowicz. — London: Stevens, 1948-. v. Published under the auspices of the Pilgrim Trust. 1. Criminal law — Great Britain — History I. Pilgrim Trust (Great Britain) II. T.
KD7850.R3     *LC 49-15181 rev*

**Moran, Richard.**    **4.9428**
Knowing right from wrong: the insanity defense of Daniel McNaughton / Richard Moran. — New York: Free Press; London: Collier Macmillan, c1981. xiii, 234 p.: ill.; 24 cm. Includes indexes. 1. McNaughton, Daniel. 2. Insanity — Jurisprudence — Great Britain. 3. Criminal liability — Great Britain. 4. Criminal psychology I. T.
KD7897.M67 1981    345.41/04 344.1054 19    *LC* 81-65034    *ISBN* 002921890X

**Brandon, Ruth.**    **4.9429**
Wrongful imprisonment; mistaken convictions and their consequences [by] Ruth Brandon and Christie Davies. — [Hamden, Conn.]: Archon Books, 1973. 296 p.; 23 cm. 1. Judicial error — Great Britain. 2. False imprisonment — Great Britain. I. Davies, Christie. joint author. II. T. III. Title: Mistaken convictions and their consequences.
KD8464.B7    345/.42/05    *LC* 72-12829    *ISBN* 0208013377

# KE Canada

**Prang, M. E.**    **4.9430**
N. W. Rowell, Ontario nationalist / Margaret Prang. — Toronto; Buffalo: University of Toronto Press, [1975] x, 553 p., [4] leaves of plates; 24 cm. 1. Rowell, Newton Wesley, 1867-1941. I. T.
KE.P7x    340/.092/4 B    *LC* 73-89843    *ISBN* 0802053009

**Riel, Louis, 1844-1885. defendant.**    **4.9431**
The Queen v Louis Riel. With an introduction by Desmond Morton. [Toronto, Buffalo] University of Toronto Press [1974] xxxv, 383 p. illus. 23 cm. (Social history of Canada. 19) 1. Riel, Louis, 1844-1885. 2. Riel Rebellion, 1885 I. Morton, Desmond. II. T. III. Series.
KE.R5x    345/.71/0231    *LC* 73-91562    *ISBN* 0802021247 *ISBN* 0802062326

**Brode, Patrick, 1950-.**    **4.9432**
Sir John Beverley Robinson: bone and sinew of the compact / Patrick Brode. — Toronto: Published for the Osgoode Society by University of Toronto Press, c1984. x, 326 p., [6] p. of plates: ill.; 24 cm. 1. Robinson, John Beverley, Sir, 1791-1863. 2. Judges — Ontario — Biography. I. Osgoode Society. II. T.
KF406.R63 B76 1984    971.3/02/0924 19    *LC* 85-133805    *ISBN* 0802034063

**Reshaping confederation: the 1982 reform of the Canadian Constitution / edited by Paul Davenport and Richard H. Leach.**    **4.9433**
Durham, N.C.: Duke University Press, 1984. 329 p.; 27 cm. (Duke University Center for International Studies publication.) 'The text of this book was originally published without appendix or index as volume 45, no. 4, of the journal Law & contemporary problems'—Verso t.p. 1. Canada — Constitutional law — Congresses. I. Davenport, Paul. II. Leach, Richard H. III. Series.
KE4218 1982    342.71/03 347.1023 19    *LC* 83-20665    *ISBN* 082230578X

**Cheffins, Ronald I.**    **4.9434**
The revised Canadian Constitution: politics as law / Ronald I. Cheffins, Patricia A. Johnson. — Toronto: McGraw-Hill Ryerson, 1986. — 244 p. — (McGraw-Hill Ryerson series in Canadian politics) Includes index. 1. Canada. Constitution Act, 1982 2. Canada — Constitutional law. 3. Canada — Constitutional law — Amendments. I. Johnson, Patricia A. II. T.
KE4219.Cx    342.71/03 19    *ISBN* 0075488426

**La Forest, G. V. (Gerard V.)**    • **4.9435**
Natural resources and public property under the Canadian Constitution [by] Gerard V. La Forest. [Toronto] University of Toronto Press [1969] xiv, 230 p. 24 cm. 1. Natural resources — Law and legislation — Canada. 2. Canada — Public lands. I. T.
KE5110.L3 1969    340    *LC* 70-429807    *ISBN* 802015166 11.50

# KF United States

## KF1–159 Bibliography. Reference Works

**Mersky, Roy M.**    • **4.9436**
Law books for non-law libraries and laymen; a bibliography. Compiled and edited with annotations by Roy M. Mersky. — Dobbs Ferry, N.Y.: Oceana Publications, 1969. 110 p.; 20 cm. — (Legal almanac series, no. 44) 1. Law — U.S. — Bibliography. I. T.
KF1.M4    016.34/00973    *LC* 69-15494

**Taylor, Betty W.**    **4.9437**
American law publishing, 1860–1900 / by Betty W. Taylor and Robert J. Munro. — Dobbs Ferry, NY: Glanville Publications, c1984. 4 v.: ill.; 26 cm. 1. Law — United States — Bibliography. 2. Legal literature — United States — Publishing — History. 3. Practice of law — United States — History. I. Munro, Robert J. II. T.
KF1.T36 1984    349.73 347.3 19    *LC* 83-9049    *ISBN* 0878020586

**Congressional Quarterly, inc.**    • **4.9438**
Congress and the Nation: a review of government and politics in the postwar years. — [1st ed.] Washington / [1965-69] 2 v.: ill.; 29 cm. Vols. 1-3: 'published by Congressional Quarterly Service.' Vols. 2-6 have subtitle: a review of government and politics. 1. Legislation — United States 2. United States — Politics and government — 1945- I. T.
KF49.C653    973.92 19    *LC* 65-22351    *ISBN* 0871871122

**Nabors, Eugene.**    **4.9439**
Legislative reference checklist: the key to legislative histories from 1789–1903 / Eugene Nabors. — Littleton, Colo.: Rothman, 1982. xv, 440 p.; 24 cm. 1. Bills, Legislative — United States — Tables. 2. Statutes — United States — Tables. 3. Legislative histories — United States — Handbooks, manuals, etc. I. T.
KF49.L43 1982    348.73/28 347.30828 19    *LC* 82-18074    *ISBN* 0837709083

**United States. Supreme Court.**    • **4.9440**
United States Supreme Court reports. — Lawyers' ed. — 2nd ser., v. 1 (Oct. term 1956)- . — Rochester, N.Y.: Lawyers Co-operative Pub. Co., 1957-. v.; 26 cm. Kept up-to-date by advance reports, Later Case Service vols., and pocket supplements. 'Complete with headnotes, summaries of decisions, statements of cases, points and authorities of counsel, annotations, tables, and parallel references.' Numbered also with: United States reports, vols. 352-1. Law reports, digests, etc — United States. I. Lawyers Co-operative Publishing Company. II. T.
KF101.A313    *LC* 17-25985

**Guenther, Nancy Anderman, 1949-.**    **4.9441**
United States Supreme Court decisions: an index to their locations / by Nancy Anderman. — Metuchen, N.J.: Scarecrow Press, 1976. vii, 316 p.; 23 cm. 1. United States. Supreme Court. 2. Law reports, digests, etc — United States — Indexes. I. T.
KF101.6.A5    348/.73/413    *LC* 76-8479    *ISBN* 081080932X

**Blandford, Linda A.**    **4.9442**
Supreme Court of the United States, 1789–1980: an index to opinions arranged by justice / sponsored by the Supreme Court Historical Society; edited by Linda A. Blandford, Patricia Russell Evans. — Millwood, N.Y.: Kraus International Publications, c1983. 2 v. (xxv, 1126 p.); 24 cm. 1. United States. Supreme Court United States reports — Indexes. 2. Law reports, digests, etc — United States — Indexes. 3. Judicial opinions — United States — Indexes. I. Evans, Patricia Russell. II. Supreme Court Historical Society. III. T.
KF101.6.B57 1983    348.73/413 347.30841 19    *LC* 82-48981    *ISBN* 0527279528

**Black, Henry Campbell, 1860-1927.**    **4.9443**
[Dictionary of law] Black's Law dictionary: definitions of the terms and phrases of American and English jurisprudence, ancient and modern / by Henry Campbell Black. — 5th ed. / by the publisher's editorial staff, contributing authors, Joseph R. Nolan and M.J. Connolly. — St. Paul: West Pub. Co., 1979. xiv, 1511 p.; 26 cm. First ed., 1891, has title: A dictionary of law. 1. Law — United States — Dictionaries. 2. Law — Dictionaries I. Nolan, Joseph R. II. Connolly, Michael J. III. T. V. Title: Law dictionary.
KF156.B53 1979    340/.03    *LC* 79-12547    *ISBN* 0829920412

**The guide to American law: everyone's legal encyclopedia.**    **4.9444**
St. Paul [Minn.]: West Pub. Co., 1983-1984. 12 v.: ill. (some col.), ports.; 27 cm.
1. Law — United States — Dictionaries. I. West Publishing Company.
KF156.G77 1983    348.73/6 347.3086 19    *LC* 83-1134    *ISBN*
0314732241

**Law and legal information directory / Paul Wasserman,**    **4.9445**
**managing editor, Marek Kaszubski, associate editor.**
1st ed. — Detroit, Mich.: Gale Research Co., 1980. xiv, 527 p.; 29 cm. Includes
index. 1. Law — Information services — United States — Directories. 2. Law
— United States — Societies, etc. — Directories. 3. Law — Information
services — Canada — Directories. I. Wasserman, Paul. II. Kaszubski, Marek.
III. Gale Research Company.
KF190.L35    KF190 L35.    340/.025/73 19    *LC* 80-20178    *ISBN*
0810301695

---

# KF202–213 Collections

**Black, Hugo LaFayette, 1886-1971.**    • **4.9446**
One man's stand for freedom: Mr. Justice Black and the Bill of rights: a
collection of his Supreme Court opinions / selected and edited, with an introd.
and notes, by Irving Dilliard. — [1st ed.] New York: Knopf, 1963. 504 p.: ill.;
25 cm. 1. Judicial opinions — United States. I. Dilliard, Irving, 1904- ed.
II. United States. Supreme Court. III. T.
KF213.B56 D5    323.40973    *LC* 62-8691

**Brandeis, Louis Dembitz, 1856-1941.**    • **4.9447**
The unpublished opinions of Mr. Justice Brandeis; the Supreme Court at work,
by Alexander M. Bickel. With an introd. by Paul A. Freund. Cambridge,
Belknap Press of Harvard University Press, 1957. xxi, 278 p. ports., facsims. 25
cm. Bibliographical references included in 'Notes' (p. [249]-262) 1. United
States. Supreme Court. 2. Judicial opinions — United States I. Bickel,
Alexander M. II. T.
KF213.B7    347.99/73 (B)    *LC* 57-9069

**Douglas, William O. (William Orville), 1898-.**    **4.9448**
The Douglas opinions / edited by Vern Countryman. — 1st ed. — New York:
Random House, c1977. xiv, 465 p.; 24 cm. Includes index. 1. Douglas, William
O. (William Orville), 1898- 2. Judicial opinions — United States.
I. Countryman, Vern. II. T.
KF213.D6 C63    342/.73/085    *LC* 76-53485    *ISBN* 0394497953

**Frank, Jerome, 1889-1957.**    • **4.9449**
A man's reach, the philosophy of Judge Jerome Frank / edited by Barbara
Frank Kristein. — New York: Macmillan, [c1965] xxviii, 450 p.; 24cm.
1. Judial opinions — United States. 2. Law — United States — Addresses,
essays, lectures. I. Kristein, Barbara (Frank) ed. II. T.
KF213.F67 K7    340.081    *LC* 63-16104

**Frankfurter, Felix, 1882-1965.**    • **4.9450**
Of law and life & other things that matter; papers and addresses of Felix
Frankfurter, 1956–1963. Edited by Philip B. Kurland. Cambridge, Mass.,
Belknap Press of Harvard University Press, 1965. viii, 257 p. port. 22 cm.
1. Law — United States — Addresses, essays, lectures. I. T.
KF213.F73 1965    340.082    *LC* 65-13221

**Friendly, Henry J.**    • **4.9451**
Benchmarks. Chicago, University of Chicago Press [1967] 324 p. 25 cm.
1. Law — United States — Addresses, essays, lectures. I. T.
KF 213 F92 1967    *LC* 67-12149

**Hand, Learned, 1872-1961.**    • **4.9452**
The spirit of liberty; papers and addresses. Collected, and with an introd. and
notes, by Irving Dilliard. — 3d ed., enl. — New York: Knopf, 1960. xxx, 310 p.:
port.; 22cm. 1. Law — United States — Addresses, essays, lectures. 2. United
States — Civilization — Addresses, essays, lectures. I. T.
KF213.H3 1960    304    *LC* 60-10956

---

# KF220–224 Criminal Trials

**Frank, Jerome, 1889-1957.**    • **4.9453**
Not guilty / by Jerome Frank and Barbara Frank in association with Harold M.
Hoffman; foreword by Justice William O. Douglas. — New York: Da Capo
Press, 1971 [c1957] 261 p.; 24 cm. — (Civil liberties in American history)

1. Judicial error — U.S. — Cases. 2. Trials — U.S. I. Kristein, Barbara
Frank, joint author. II. Hoffman, Harold M., 1903- III. T. IV. Series.
KF220.F7 1971    345/.73/05    *LC* 72-138495    *ISBN* 0306700727

**Busch, Francis X. (Francis Xavier), b. 1879.**    • **4.9454**
Prisoners at the bar; an account of the trials of the William Haywood case, the
Sacco–Vanzetti case, the Loeb–Leopold case, the Bruno Hauptmann case, by
Francis X. Busch. Freeport, N.Y., Books for Libraries Press [1970, c1952] ix,
288 p. illus. 23 cm. (Biography index reprint series) 1. Trials (Murder) —
United States. I. T.
KF221.M8 B8 1970    343/.5/230973    *LC* 77-126319    *ISBN*
0836980255

**Matzner, Dorothe.**    **4.9455**
Victims of justice [by] Dorothe Matzner and Margaret English. — [1st ed.]. —
New York: Atheneum, 1973. viii, 371 p.: illus.; 25 cm. 1. Trials (Murder) —
United States. I. English, Margaret. joint author. II. T.
KF221.M8 M38    345/.73/02523    *LC* 72-82691

**Zenger, John Peter, 1697-1746. defendant.**    • **4.9456**
The trial of Peter Zenger / edited and with an introd. and notes by Vincent
Buranelli. — [New York]: New York University Press, 1957. viii, 152 p.; 21 cm.
1. Zenger, John Peter, 1697-1746. 2. New-York weekly journal. I. Buranelli,
Vincent. II. New York (Colony). Supreme Court of Judicature. III. T.
KF223.Z4 B87    342/.73/085    *LC* 57-6370

**Kennebeck, Edwin.**    **4.9457**
Juror number four: the trial of thirteen Black Panthers as seen from the jury
box. — [1st ed.]. — New York: Norton, [1973] 238 p.; 21 cm. 1. Black Panthers
Trial, New York, N.Y., 1970-1971 I. T.
KF224.B55 K4    345/.73/0231    *LC* 72-10228    *ISBN* 0393085465

**Aptheker, Bettina.**    **4.9458**
The morning breaks: the trial of Angela Davis / Bettina Aptheker. — 1st ed. —
New York: International Publishers, 1975. xii, 284 p.; 21 cm. 1. Davis, Angela
Yvonne, 1944- I. T.
KF224.D3 A68    345/.73/02523    *LC* 75-1268    *ISBN* 0717804585

**Martin, Charles H., 1945-.**    **4.9459**
The Angelo Herndon case and southern justice / Charles H. Martin. — Baton
Rouge: Louisiana State University Press, c1976. xv, 234 p., [3] leaves of plates:
ill.; 24 cm. Based on the author's thesis, Tulane University, 1972. Includes
index. 1. Herndon, Angelo, 1913- I. T.
KF224.H47 M3    342/.73/0.850269    *LC* 73-91777    *ISBN*
0807101745

**The United States of America v. one book entitled Ulysses by**    **4.9460**
**James Joyce: documents and commentary: a 50–year**
**retrospective / introduction by Richard Ellmann; edited by**
**Michael Moscato, Leslie LeBlanc.**
Frederick, MD: University Publications of America, c1984. xxvii, 482 p.; 24
cm. 1. Joyce, James, 1882-1941. Ulysses. 2. Random House (Firm) — Trials,
litigation, etc. 3. Trials (Obscenity) — New York (N.Y.) I. Moscato, Michael.
II. LeBlanc, Leslie.
KF224.R33 U53 1984    345.73/0274 347.305274 19    *LC* 83-25929
   *ISBN* 0890935904

**Radosh, Ronald.**    **4.9461**
The Rosenberg file: a search for the truth / Ronald Radosh and Joyce Milton.
— 1st ed. — New York: Holt, Rinehart, and Winston, c1983. xv, 608 p.; 24 cm.
Includes index. 1. Rosenberg, Julius, 1918-1953 — Trials, litigation, etc.
2. Rosenberg, Ethel, 1916-1953 — Trials, litigation, etc. 3. Trials (Espionage)
— New York (N.Y.) 4. Trials (Conspiracy) — New York (N.Y.) I. Milton,
Joyce. II. T.
KF224.R6 R32 1983    345.73/0231 347.305231 19    *LC* 82-15569
   *ISBN* 0030490367

**Russell, Francis, 1910-.**    • **4.9462**
Tragedy in Dedham; the story of the Sacco–Vanzetti case. — 50th anniversary
ed. — New York: McGraw-Hill, [1971] xxiii, 480 p.: ill., maps, ports.; 22 cm.
1. Sacco-Vanzetti case I. T.
KF224.S2 R85    345/.73/02523    *LC* 76-154839    *ISBN* 0070543429

**Carter, Dan T.**    • **4.9463**
Scottsboro; a tragedy of the American South [by] Dan T. Carter. — London;
New York: Oxford University Press, [1971, c1969] xiii, 431 p.: illus.; 21 cm. —
(A Galaxy book 363) 1. Scottsboro case. I. T.
KF224.S34 C3 1971    345/.761/0253    *LC* 73-30836    *ISBN*
0195014901

**Freed, Donald.**    **4.9464**
Agony in New Haven; the trial of Bobby Seale, Ericka Huggins, and the Black
Panther Party. — New York: Simon and Schuster, [1973] 347 p.; 22 cm.
1. Huggins, Ericka. 2. Seale, Bobby, 1936- 3. Black Panther Party. I. T.
KF224.S38 F7    345/.73/02523    *LC* 72-83929    *ISBN* 0671212842

**Mitford, Jessica, 1917-.**     • 4.9465
The trial of Dr. .Spock: the Rev. William Sloane Coffin, Jr., Michael Ferber, Mitchell Goodman, and Marcus Raskin. — [1st ed.] New York: Knopf, 1969. x, 272 p.; 22 cm. Appendices #(p. [249]-272):—1. The indictment.—2. Overt act #1, 'A call to resist illegitimate authority.'—3. Overt act #3, Michael Ferber's speech, 'A time to say no.'—4. Overt act #4, Speech in Boston by the Rev. William Sloane Coffin, Jr.—5. Overt act #6, Statement before the Department of Justice by the Rev. William Sloane Coffin, Jr.—6. The role of the American Civil Liberties Union in the case of the Boston Five. 1. Spock, Benjamin, 1903- I. T.
KF224.S5 M5     343/.3/10926     *LC* 69-10682

**Sirica, John J.**     4.9466
To set the record straight: the break–in, the tapes, the conspirators, the pardon / John J. Sirica. — 1st ed. — New York: Norton, c1979. 394 p.: ill.; 24 cm. 1. Nixon, Richard M. (Richard Milhous), 1913- 2. Sirica, John J. 3. Watergate Trial, Washington, D.C., 1973 4. Watergate Affair, 1972-1974 I. T.
KF224.W33 S57     345/.73/0232     *LC* 79-10039     *ISBN* 0393012344

## KF228 Civil Suits

**Friendly, Fred W.**     4.9467
Minnesota rag: the dramatic story of the landmark Supreme Court case that gave new meaning to freedom of the press / Fred W. Friendly. — 1st ed. — New York: Random House, c1981. 243 p., [4] leaves of plates: ill.; 22 cm. Includes index. 1. Near, Jay M. 2. Saturday press (Minneapolis, Minn.) 3. Freedom of the press — Minnesota. 4. Freedom of the press — United States. I. T.
KF228.N35 F73     342.73/0853/0264 347.3028530264 19     *LC* 80-6018     *ISBN* 0394507525

**Fisher, Franklin M.**     4.9468
Folded, spindled, and mutilated: economic analysis and U.S. v. IBM / Franklin M. Fisher, John J. McGowan, and Joen E. Greenwood. — Cambridge, Mass.: MIT Press, c1983. xvi, 443 p.; 24 cm. — (MIT Press series on the regulation of economic activity. 7) 1. International Business Machines Corporation — Trials, litigation, etc. 2. Antitrust law — United States. 3. Computer industry — Law and legislation — United States. 4. Antitrust law — Economic aspects — United States. 5. Computer industry — Law and legislation — Economic aspects — United States. 6. United States — Trials, litigation, etc. I. McGowan, John J. II. Greenwood, Joen E. III. T. IV. Series.
KF228.U5 F57 1983     343.73/072 347.30372 19     *LC* 83-935     *ISBN* 0262060868

**Jaworski, Leon.**     4.9469
The right and the power: the prosecution of Watergate / Leon Jaworski. — New York: Reader's Digest Press: distributed by Crowell, 1976. 305 p.; 24 cm. Includes index. 1. Nixon, Richard M. (Richard Milhous), 1913- 2. United States. petitioner. 3. Watergate Affair, 1972-1974 I. T.
KF228.U5 J3     345/.73/0232     *LC* 76-22594     *ISBN* 0883491028

## KF240–292 Legal Research. Legal Education

**Cohen, Morris L., 1927-.**     4.9470
Legal research in a nutshell / by Morris L. Cohen. — 4th ed. — St. Paul, Minn.: West Pub. Co., 1985. xxv, 452 p.: ill.; 19 cm. (Nutshell series.) 1. Legal research — United States. I. T. II. Series.
KF240.C54 1985     340/.072073 19     *LC* 84-21929     *ISBN* 0314832432

**Price, Miles Oscar, 1890-1968.**     4.9471
Effective legal research / Miles O. Price, Harry Bitner, Shirley Raissi Bysiewicz. — 4th ed. — Boston: Little, Brown, c1979. xix, 643 p.; 24 cm. 1. Legal research — United States. I. Bitner, Harry, 1916- joint author. II. Bysiewicz, Shirley R. joint author. III. T.
KF240.P7 1979     340/.07/2073     *LC* 79-119241

**Uniform system of citation; form of citation and abbreviations.**     4.9472
Cambridge: Harvard Law Review Association, 19— v.; 15 cm. 1. Annotations and citations (Law) I. Harvard Law Review Association.
KF 245 H33 1949     KF245.U6x.     *LC* 41-12137

**Llewellyn, Karl N. (Karl Nickerson), 1893-1962.**     • 4.9473
The bramble bush: on our law and its study. — New York: Oceana Publications, 1951. 160 p.; 24 cm. Errata slip inserted. 1. Law — Study and teaching — United States. 2. Law — United States — Addresses, essays, lectures. I. T. II. Title: On our law and its study.
KF 272 L79 1951     *LC* 51-1727

**Vanderbilt, Arthur T., 1888-1957. ed.**     • 4.9474
Studying law; selections from the writings of Albert J. Beveridge [and others. 2d. ed. New York] New York University Press, 1955. 753 p. 20 cm. 1. Law — United States — History and criticism 2. Law — Great Britain — History and criticism I. T.
KF 272 V22 1955     *LC* 55-7147

**The Official guide to U.S. law schools.**     4.9475
1986-87-     . — [Newtown, PA]: Published by Law School Admission Council/Law School Admission Services in cooperation with the American Bar Association and the Association of American Law Schools, c1986-. v.; 28 cm. Annual. 'Prelaw handbook.' 1. Law — Study and teaching — United States — Periodicals. 2. Law — Study and teaching — United States — Directories. I. Law School Admission Council. II. Law School Admission Services (U.S.) III. American Bar Association. IV. Association of American Law Schools.
KF273 A87     340 11     *LC* sn 85-3241

## KF294–338 Legal Profession

**Casper, Jonathan D.**     4.9476
Lawyers before the Warren Court: civil liberties and civil rights, 1957–66 / [by] Jonathan D. Casper. — [Urbana: University of Illinois Press, 1972] xi, 221 p.; 24 cm. 1. United States. Supreme Court. 2. Lawyers — United States. 3. Civil rights — United States I. T.
KF298.C27     342/.73/0850269     *LC* 74-186342     *ISBN* 025200244X

**Drinker, Henry Sandwith, 1880-1965.**     4.9477
Legal ethics / by Henry S. Drinker. — Westport, Conn.: Greenwood Press, 1980, c1953. xxii, 448 p.; 24 cm. Reprint of the ed. published by Columbia University Press, New York, which was issued in series: Legal studies of the William Nelson Cromwell Foundation. Includes indexes. 1. Legal ethics — United States. I. T.
KF306.D7 1980     174/.3/0973     *LC* 80-11445     *ISBN* 0313223211

**Warren, Charles, 1868-1954.**     • 4.9478
A history of the American bar. New York: H. Fertig, 1966 [i.e. 1967, c1939] xii, 586 p.; 24 cm. Includes bibliographical references. 1. Lawyers — United States 2. Courts — United States 3. Law — United States — History and criticism I. T.
KF323.W3 1967     340/.0973     *LC* 66-24357

## KF350–374 History of American Law

**Documentary history of the First Federal Congress of the**     4.9479
**United States of America, March 4, 1789–March 3, 1791 /**
**Linda Grant De Pauw, editor.**
Baltimore: Johns Hopkins University Press, 1972. 774 p. Sponsored by the National Historical Publications [and Records] Commission and the George Washington University. 1. United States. Congress (1st: 1789-1791) — Collected works. 2. Law — United States — Sources — Collected works. 3. United States — Politics and government — 1789-1797 — Sources — Collected works. I. De Pauw, Linda Grant. II. Veit, Helen E. III. United States. National Historical Publications and Records Commission. IV. George Washington University. V. Title: Documentary history of the First Federal Congress, 1789-1791.
KF350.D63 1972     328.73/09 19     *LC* 73-155164

**Law in American history. Edited by Donald Fleming & Bernard**     • 4.9480
**Bailyn. Introd. by Byron R. White.**
Boston, Little, Brown [c1971] xi, 677 p. 24 cm. (Perspectives in American history, v. 5) 1. Law — United States — History and criticism — Addresses, essays, lectures. I. Fleming, Donald, 1923- ed. II. Bailyn, Bernard. ed. III. Series.
E171.P47 vol. 5 KF352.A2     973/.08 s 340/.0973     *LC* 70-183855

**Gilmore, Grant.**     4.9481
The ages of American law / Grant Gilmore. New Haven: Yale University Press, 1977. x, 154 p.; 22 cm. (Storrs lectures on jurisprudence. 1974) Includes index.

1. Law — United States — History and criticism — Addresses, essays, lectures. I. T. II. Series.
KF352.A2 G5　　340/.0973　　*LC* 76-49988　　*ISBN* 0300019513

**Pound, Roscoe, 1870-1964.**　　　　　　　　　　• **4.9482**
The formative era of American law. New York: P. Smith, 1950 [c1938] x, 188 p.; 21 cm. 'Four lectures ... delivered at the Law School of Tulane University on the occasion of the centennial of the death of Edward Livingston, October 27-30, 1936.' Bibliographical footnotes. 1. Livingston, Edward, 1764-1836. 2. Law — United States — History and criticism 3. Law — Addresses, essays, lectures I. T.
KF352.A75P68　　*LC* 50-50803

**Friedman, Lawrence Meir, 1930-.**　　　　　　　• **4.9483**
A history of American law [by] Lawrence M. Friedman. New York, Simon and Schuster [1973] 655 p. 23 cm. 1. Law — United States — History and criticism I. T.
KF352.F7　　349.73/09 347.3009 19　　*LC* 72-83930　　*ISBN* 0671212265

**Hurst, James Willard, 1910-.**　　　　　　　　• **4.9484**
The growth of American law: the law makers. Boston, Little, Brown, 1950. 502 p. 1. Law — United States — History & criticism I. T.
KF352.H87　　*LC* 50-6788

**Schwartz, Bernard, 1923-.**　　　　　　　　　**4.9485**
The law in America: a history. — New York: McGraw-Hill c1974. xiii, 382 p.; 24 cm. Includes index. 1. Law — United States — History and criticism I. T.
KF352.S35　　340/.0973　　*LC* 74-5287　　*ISBN* 0070556784

**Flaherty, David H. comp.**　　　　　　　　　• **4.9486**
Essays in the history of early American law. Edited with an introd. by David H. Flaherty. Chapel Hill, Published for the Institute of Early American History and Culture of Williamsburg, Va., by the University of North Carolina Press [1969] x, 534 p. 24 cm. 1. Law — United States — History and criticism — Addresses, essays, lectures. 2. United States — History — Colonial period, ca. 1600-1775 — Addresses, essays, lectures. I. Institute of Early American History and Culture (Williamsburg, Va.) II. T.
KF361.A2F5　　340/.0973　　*LC* 78-80020

**Bloomfield, Maxwell H.**　　　　　　　　　**4.9487**
American lawyers in a changing society, 1776–1876 / Maxwell Bloomfield. — Cambridge, Mass.: Harvard University Press, 1976. ix, 397 p.; 24 cm. (Studies in legal history) 1. Law — United States — History and criticism 2. Lawyers — United States — Biography. I. T.
KF366.B5　　340/.0973　　*LC* 75-14172　　*ISBN* 0674029100

**Levy, Leonard Williams, 1923-.**　　　　　　• **4.9488**
The law of the Commonwealth and Chief Justice Shaw. Cambridge, Harvard University Press, 1957. 383 p. port. 25 cm. 1. Shaw, Lemuel, 1781-1861. 2. Law — Massachusetts — History and criticism. I. T.
KF 368 S5 L66 1957　　*LC* 57-6350

## KF373 20th Century Biography

**Arnold, Thurman Wesley, 1891-1969.**　　　　• **4.9489**
Fair fights and foul: a dissenting lawyer's life / [by] Thurman Arnold. — [1st ed.]. — New York: Harcourt, Brace & World, [1965] 292 p.: ill.; 22 cm. 1. Lawyers — United States — Correspondence, reminiscences, etc. I. T.
KF373.A7 A3　　923.473　　*LC* 65-14716

**Biddle, Francis, 1886-1968.**　　　　　　　• **4.9490**
In brief authority. — [1st ed.]. — Garden City,N.Y.: Doubleday, 1962. 494 p.: illus.; 22cm. A continuation of the author's A casual past. Autobiographical. 1. Lawyers — United States — Correspondence, reminiscences, etc. I. T.
KF373.B5 A32　　923.473　　*LC* 62-16744

**Ware, Gilbert.**　　　　　　　　　　　　**4.9491**
William Hastie: grace under pressure / Gilbert Ware. — New York: Oxford University Press, 1984. x, 305 p.; 25 cm. Includes index. 1. Hastie, William. 2. Afro-American judges — Biography. 3. Civil rights workers — United States — Biography. I. T.
KF373.H38 W37 1984　　347.73/2434 B 347.3073334 B 19　　*LC* 84-5657　　*ISBN* 0195032985

**Yarbrough, Tinsley E., 1941-.**　　　　　　**4.9492**
Judge Frank Johnson and human rights in Alabama / Tinsley E. Yarbrough. — University, Ala.: University of Alabama Press, c1981. ix, 270 p.: ill.; 24 cm. Includes index. 1. Johnson, Frank Minis, 1918- 2. Judges — Alabama — Biography. 3. Civil rights — Alabama. I. T.
KF373.J55 Y37　　347.73/2234 B　　*LC* 80-17433　　*ISBN* 0817300562

**Turow, Scott.**　　　　　　　　　　　　**4.9493**
One L / Scott Turow. — New York: Putnam, c1977. 300 p.; 23 cm. 1. Turow, Scott. 2. Harvard Law School. 3. Law students — Massachusetts — Biography. I. T.
KF373.T88 A33　　340/.07/3　　*LC* 76-57246　　*ISBN* 0399119329

**Williams, Edward Bennett.**　　　　　　　• **4.9494**
One man's freedom / introd. by Eugene V. Rostow. — [1st ed.] New York: Atheneum, 1962. 344 p.; 22 cm. 1. Lawyers — United States — Correspondence, reminiscences, etc. I. T.
KF371.W5　　KF373.W5.　　340.9　　*LC* 62-11689

## KF379–391 Philosophy. General Works

**Dworkin, R. M.**　　　　　　　　　　　**4.9495**
A matter of principle / Ronald Dworkin. — Cambridge, Mass.: Harvard University Press, 1985. 425 p. Includes index. 1. Political questions and judicial power — United States. 2. Law — Philosophy. 3. Jurisprudence 4. Law and politics I. T.
KF380.D85 1985　　340/.1 19　　*LC* 84-25122　　*ISBN* 0674554604

**Levi, Edward Hirsch, 1911-.**　　　　　　　**4.9496**
An introduction to legal reasoning. Chicago: University of Chicago Press [1968, c1948] 104 p.; 21 cm. First published in the University of Chicago law review. 1. Law — U.S. — Interpretation and construction. I. T.
KF380.L4x

**Lieberman, Jethro Koller.**　　　　　　　　**4.9497**
The litigious society / Jethro K. Lieberman. — New York: Basic Books, c1981. x, 212 p. 1. Justice, Administration of — United States. 2. Damages — United States. 3. Actions and defenses — United States I. T.
KF380.L53　　KF380 L53.　　346.7303 347.3063 19　　*LC* 80-68181
　*ISBN* 0465041345

**Rosen, Paul L.**　　　　　　　　　　　**4.9498**
The Supreme Court and social science / [by] Paul L. Rosen. — Urbana: University of Illinois Press, [1972] xii, 260 p.; 24 cm. 1. United States. Supreme Court. 2. Sociological jurisprudence I. T.
KF380.R67　　340.1/15　　*LC* 78-189329　　*ISBN* 0252002350

**Scheingold, Stuart A.**　　　　　　　　　**4.9499**
The politics of rights: lawyers, public policy, and political change / Stuart A. Scheingold. — New Haven: Yale University Press, 1974. xiv, 224 p.; 21 cm. 1. Law — United States 2. Law and politics 3. Civil rights — United States 4. Lawyers — United States. I. T.
KF380.S3　　340.1/15　　*LC* 74-79972　　*ISBN* 0300017839

**Forer, Lois G., 1914-.**　　　　　　　　　**4.9500**
The death of the law / Lois G. Forer. — New York: McKay, [1975] xxx, 352 p.; 22 cm. 1. Justice, Administration of — United States. 2. Law — United States I. T.
KF384.F675　　340/.0973　　*LC* 74-25722　　*ISBN* 0679505237

**Handler, Joel F.**　　　　　　　　　　　**4.9501**
Social movements and the legal system: a theory of law reform and social change / Joel F. Handler. — New York: Academic Press, 1979 (c1978). xiv, 252 p.; 24 cm. (Institute for Research on Poverty monograph series.) Includes index. 1. Law — United States 2. Sociological jurisprudence 3. Social movements — United States. I. T. II. Series.
KF384.H27　　340.1/15　　*LC* 78-11151　　*ISBN* 0123228409

**Gray, John Chipman, 1839-1915.**　　　　　**4.9502**
The nature and sources of the law. — 2d ed., from author's notes, by Roland Gray. — Gloucester, Mass.: P. Smith, 1972. 348 p. Reprint of the 1921 ed. 1. Law. Jurisprudence. I. Gray, Roland, 1878- II. T.
K F385.G7 1972x　　*ISBN* 0844621560

**Kent, James, 1763-1847.**　　　　　　　　• **4.9503**
Commentaries on American law. — New York: Da Capo Press, 1971. 4 v.; 24 cm. — (American constitutional and legal history) Reprint of the 1826-30 ed. 1. Law — U.S. I. T.
KF385.K433　　340/.0973　　*LC* 78-75290　　*ISBN* 0306712938

**Posner, Richard A.**　　　　　　　　　　**4.9504**
Economic analysis of law [by] Richard A. Posner. — Boston: Little, Brown, 1972 [c1973] xi, 415 p.: illus.; 25 cm. 1. Law — United States 2. Trade regulation — United States. I. T.
KF385.P65　　340/.0973　　*LC* 73-6408

# KF398–8228 Special Branches of American Civil Law

## KF465–553 Law of Persons. Family Law

**Chafee, Zechariah, 1885-1957.**                          • **4.9505**
Three human rights in the Constitution of 1787. Lawrence: University of Kansas Press, 1956. 245 p.: ill., ports.; 22 cm. 1. Great Britain. Parliament — Freedom of debate. 2. Attainder 3. Freedom of movement — Great Britain. 4. Freedom of movement — United States. 5. United States. Congress — Freedom of debate I. T.
KF472.C4         LC 56-9451

**Alexander, Shana.**                                          **4.9506**
[State-by-State guide to women's legal rights] Shana Alexander's State-by-State guide to women's legal rights / Barbara Brudno, legal consultant. — 1st ed. — Los Angeles: Wollstonecraft: distributed by Price/Stern/Sloan Publishers, [1975] 224 p.: ill.; 29 cm. 1. Women — Legal status, laws, etc. — United States — States. I. T.
KF478.Z95 A4      346/.73/013      LC 74-10169      ISBN 0883810085

**Who speaks for the child: the problems of proxy consent /**      **4.9507**
**edited by Willard Gaylin and Ruth Macklin.**
New York: Plenum Press, c1982. xii, 315 p.; 22 cm. — (Hastings Center series in ethics.) 1. Children — Legal status, laws, etc. — United States — Addresses, essays, lectures. 2. Informed consent (Medical law) — United States — Addresses, essays, lectures. 3. Parent and child (Law) — United States — Addresses, essays, lectures. I. Gaylin, Willard. II. Macklin, Ruth, 1938- III. Series.
KF479.A75 W46 1982      346.7301/35 347.306135 19      LC 82-5392
     ISBN 0306408600

**The Mentally retarded citizen and the law / sponsored by the**      **4.9508**
**President's Committee on Mental Retardation; edited by**
**Michael Kindred ... [et al.]; with a pref. by Lawrence A. Kane,**
**Jr.**
New York: Free Press, c1976. xxix, 738 p.; 26 cm. 'The President's Committee on Mental Retardation convened a conference in 1973 ... Each of the 22 principal papers appear in a chapter of this volume.' 1. Insanity — Jurisprudence — United States — Congresses. 2. Mental health laws — United States — Congresses. I. Kindred, Michael. II. United States. President's Committee on Mental Retardation.
KF480.A75 M46      346/.73/013      LC 74-21489      ISBN 0029168600

**Bursten, Ben.**                                             **4.9509**
Beyond psychiatric expertise / by Ben Bursten. — Springfield, Ill., U.S.A.: C.C. Thomas, c1984. xvii, 256 p.; 24 cm. — (American lecture series. Monograph in American lectures in behavioral science and law; 1063) Includes index. 1. Insanity — Jurisprudence — United States. 2. Insane — Commitment and detention — United States. 3. Forensic psychiatry — United States. I. T. II. Series.
KF480.B78 1984      344.73/044 347.30444 19      LC 84-2435      ISBN 0398049912

**Weitzman, Lenore J.**                                       **4.9510**
The divorce revolution: the unexpected social and economic consequences for women and children in America / Lenore J. Weitzman. — New York: Free Press; London: Collier Macmillan, c1985. xxiv, 504 p.; 25 cm. Includes index. 1. Divorce — Law and legislation — United States. 2. Marital property — United States. 3. Divorced women — United States — Social conditions. 4. Divorced women — United States — Economic conditions. I. T.
KF535.W43 1985      346.7301/66 347.306166 19      LC 85-6868      ISBN 0029347106

**Goldstein, Joseph.**                                        **4.9511**
Before the best interests of the child / Joseph Goldstein, Anna Freud, Albert J. Solnit. — New York: Free Press, c1979. xii, 288 p.; 18 cm. 1. Custody of children — United States. 2. Children — Legal status, laws, etc. — United States. 3. Parent and child (Law) — United States. 4. Child welfare — United States. I. Freud, Anna, 1895- joint author. II. Solnit, Albert J. joint author. III. T.
KF547.G64      362.7      LC 79-64249      ISBN 0029122201

## KF566–698 Real Property. Land Law

**Vose, Clement E.**                                          • **4.9512**
Caucasians only: the Supreme Court, the NAACP, and the restrictive covenant cases. — Berkeley: University of California Press, 1959. xi, 296 p.: ill., ports., maps; 24 cm. 1. National Association for the Advancement of Colored People. 2. Discrimination in housing — Law and legislation — United States. 3. Afro-Americans — Housing 4. Real covenants — United States. I. T.
LAW      KF662.V6x.      331.833      LC 59-8758

## KF801–1241 Law of Contracts

**Corbin, Arthur L. (Arthur Linton), 1874-1967.**            • **4.9513**
Corbin on contracts / by Arthur Linton Corbin. — One vol. edition. — St. Paul: West Pub. Co., c1952. xi, 1224 p. 1. Contracts — United States. I. T.
KF801.C65      KF801Z9 C65 1952.      347.40973      LC 52-3852

## KF1246–1327 Torts

**Calabresi, Guido, 1932-.**                                 **4.9514**
Ideals, beliefs, attitudes, and the law: private law perspectives on a public law problem / Guido Calabresi. — 1st ed. — Syracuse, N.Y.: Syracuse University Press, 1985. xv, 208 p.; 24 cm. (Frank W. Abrams lectures.) Includes index. 1. Torts — United States. 2. Law and ethics I. T. II. Series.
KF1250.C35 1985      346.7303 347.3063 19      LC 85-2590      ISBN 0815623097

**Harper, Fowler V. (Fowler Vincent), 1897-1965.**          • **4.9515**
The law of torts / Fowler V. Harper, Fleming James, Jr., Oscar S. Gray. — 2nd ed. — Boston: Little, Brown, 1986. 6 v.; 24 cm. Includes index. 1. Torts — United States. I. James, Fleming, 1904- II. Gray, Oscar S., 1926- III. T.
KF1250.H37 1986      346.7303 347.3063 19      LC 84-81757      ISBN 0316325872

**Prosser, William Lloyd, 1898-.**                           • **4.9516**
Handbook of the law of torts, by William L. Prosser. — 4th ed. — St. Paul: West Pub. Co., 1971. xix, 1208 p.; 27 cm. — (Hornbook series.) Cover title: Law of torts. On spine: Torts. 1. Torts — U.S. I. T. II. Title: Law of torts. III. Series.
KF1250.P7 1971      346/.73/03      LC 77-156347

### KF1262 Violation of Privacy

**Chief Justice Earl Warren Conference on Advocacy in the**      **4.9517**
**United States. Cambridge, Mass., 1974.**
Privacy in a free society: final report: annual Chief Justice Earl Warren Conference on Advocacy in the United States, June 7–8, 1974 / sponsored by the Roscoe Pound–American Trial Lawyers Foundation. — [Cambridge, Mass.: Roscoe Pound-American Trial Lawyers Foundation, 1974] 104 p.: port.; 25 cm. 1. Privacy, Right of — United States — Addresses, essays, lectures. I. Roscoe Pound-American Trial Lawyers Foundation. II. T.
KF1262.A75 C45 1974      342/.73/085      LC 74-19797

**O'Brien, David M.**                                         **4.9518**
Privacy, law, and public policy / David M. O'Brien; foreword by C. Herman Pritchett. — New York, N.Y.: Praeger, 1979. xiv, 262 p.; 24 cm. Includes indexes. 1. Privacy, Right of — United States. 2. Public policy (Law) — United States. 3. Freedom of information — United States. I. T.
KF1262.O25      342/.73/085      LC 79-14131      ISBN 0030504066

### KF1266 Libel. Slander

**Lawhorne, Clifton O.**                                      **4.9519**
The Supreme Court and libel / Clifton O. Lawhorne; foreword by Howard Rusk Long. — Carbondale: Southern Illinois University Press, c1981. xviii, 140 p.; 23 cm. — (New horizons in journalism) 1. United States. Supreme Court. 2. Libel and slander — United States — Cases. I. T.
KF1266.A7 L38      346.7303/4 19      LC 80-21161      ISBN 080930998X

### KF1322 Government Torts

**Jacobs, Clyde Edward, 1925-.**                             **4.9520**
The Eleventh amendment and sovereign immunity [by] Clyde E. Jacobs. — Westport, Conn.: Greenwood Press, [1972] viii, 216 p.; 21 cm. — (Contributions in American history, no. 19) 1. Government liability — United States I. T.
KF1322.J3      342/.73/088      LC 71-149959      ISBN 0837160588

## KF1396-1416 Corporations. Securities

**Stone, Christopher D.**                                                      **4.9521**
Where the law ends: the social control of corporate behavior / Christopher D. Stone. — 1st ed. — New York: Harper & Row, [1975] xiii, 273 p.; 22 cm. 1. Corporation law — United States 2. Industry — Social aspects — United States. I. T.
KF1416.S7        346/.73/066        LC 74-20415        ISBN 0060141336

## KF1600-2940 Regulation of Trade, Commerce, Industry

**Litan, Robert E., 1950-.**                                                  **4.9522**
Reforming Federal regulation / Robert E. Litan and William D. Nordhaus. — New Haven: Yale University Press, c1983. x, 204 p.: ill.; 22 cm. 1. Trade regulation — United States. 2. Administrative procedure — United States. I. Nordhaus, William D. II. T.
KF1600.L57 1983        342.73/066 347.30266 19        LC 83-3622        ISBN 0300030452

**Rights and regulation: ethical, political, and economic issues /**     **4.9523**
**edited by Tibor R. Machan and M. Bruce Johnson; foreword by Aaron Wildavsky.**
Cambridge, Mass.: Ballinger Pub. Co., c1983. xxv, 309 p.; 24 cm. — (Pacific studies in public policy.) 1. Industrial laws and legislation — United States. 2. Trade regulation — United States. 3. Public policy (Law) — United States. I. Machan, Tibor R. II. Johnson, M. Bruce. III. Series.
KF1600.R5 1983        343.73/07 347.3037 19        LC 83-11309        ISBN 0884109283

**United States. Attorney General's National Committee to Study**   • **4.9524**
**the Antitrust Laws.**
Report. — Washington: U. S. Govt. Printing Office, 1955. xiii, 393 p.; 24 cm. Cover title. 1. Antitrust law — United States. I. T.
KF 1649 A325 1955        LC 55-60722

**Bork, Robert H.**                                                           **4.9525**
The antitrust paradox: a policy at war with itself / Robert H. Bork. — New York: Basic Books, c1978. xi, 462 p.: ill.; 24 cm. 1. Antitrust law — United States. I. T.
KF1649.B67        343/.73/072        LC 77-74573        ISBN 0465003699

**Letwin, William.**                                                         • **4.9526**
Law and economic policy in America: the evolution of the Sherman antitrust act. — New York: Random House, [1965] xi, 304 p.; 22 cm. 1. Trusts, Industrial — United States — Law. I. T.
KF1649.L4 1965        338.80973        LC 64-21993

**Neale, A. D. (Alan Derrett)**                                              **4.9527**
The antitrust laws of the United States of America: a study of competition enforced by law / by A. D. Neale and D. G. Goyder; with a foreword by Abe Fortas. — 3d ed. — Cambridge [Eng.]; New York: Cambridge University Press, 1980. xvi, 526 p.; 24 cm. (Economic and social studies; 19) Includes indexes. 1. Antitrust law — United States. I. Goyder, D. G. joint author. II. T.
KF1649.N4 1980b        343.73/072 19        LC 80-40661        ISBN 0521235693

## KF1801-1873 Mining

**Tank, Ronald Warren.**                                                      **4.9528**
Legal aspects of geology / Ronald W. Tank. — New York: Plenum Press, c1983. xii, 583 p.; 24 cm. 1. Mining law — United States. 2. Water — Law and legislation — United States. 3. Geologists — Legal status, laws, etc. — United States. I. T.
KF1819.T36 1983        344.73/095 347.30495 19        LC 83-2246        ISBN 0306411598

## KF2161-2849 Transportation. Communication

**Miller, George Hall, 1919-.**                                              • **4.9529**
Railroads and the Granger laws [by] George H. Miller. — Madison: University of Wisconsin Press, [1971] xi, 296 p.: maps.; 23 cm. 1. Railroads — U.S. — Rates. 2. Railroads and state — U.S. I. T.
KF2355.A4 M5        385/.0973        LC 75-138059        ISBN 0299058700

**Paul, James C. N.**                                                         **4.9530**
Federal censorship: obscenity in the mail / by James C. N. Paul and Murray L. Schwartz. — Westport, Conn.: Greenwood Press, 1977, c1961. xv, 368 p.; 23 cm. Reprint of the ed. published by Free Press of Glencoe, New York. Includes index. 1. Postal service — United States — Laws and regulations.

2. Censorship — United States. 3. Obscenity (Law) — United States. I. Schwartz, Murray L. joint author. II. T.
KF2737.P38 1977        344/.73/0531        LC 77-10978        ISBN 0837198186

**Mass media and the Supreme Court: the legacy of the Warren**           **4.9531**
**years / edited, with commentaries and special notes by Kenneth S. Devol.**
3rd ed., rev. and enl. — New York: Hastings House, c1982. xiv, 463 p.; 24 cm. — (Studies in public communication) (Communication arts books) Excerpts from opinions of the Supreme Court, with concurrences and dissents, and articles from various journals of law and mass communication. 1. Press law — United States — Cases. 2. Telecommunication — Law and legislation — United States — Cases. 3. Freedom of the press — United States — Cases. I. Devol, Kenneth S. II. United States. Supreme Court.
KF2750.A7 M37 1982        343.73/099 347.30399 19        LC 82-6242        ISBN 0803847416

**Hemmer, Joseph J.**                                                         **4.9532**
Free speech / Joseph J. Hemmer, Jr. — Metuchen, N.J.: Scarecrow Press, 1979. ix, 297 p.; 23 cm. — (His Communication under law; v. 1) Includes indexes. 1. Freedom of speech — United States. 2. Freedom of the press — United States. I. T.
KF2750.A73 H46 vol. 1 KF4772        343.73/099 s 342.73/0853 19        LC 79-19166        ISBN 0810812487

**Hemmer, Joseph J.**                                                         **4.9533**
Journalistic freedom / Joseph J. Hemmer, Jr. — Metuchen, N.J.: Scarecrow Press, 1980. ix, 411 p.; 23 cm. — (His Communication under law; v. 2) Includes indexes. 1. Press law — United States — Cases. I. T.
KF2750.A73 H46 vol. 2 KF2750        343.73/099 s 343.73/0998        LC 80-7960        ISBN 0810813157

**Denniston, Lyle W.**                                                        **4.9534**
The reporter and the law: techniques of covering the courts / by Lyle W. Denniston; sponsored by the American Bar Association and the American Newspaper Publishers Association Foundation. — New York: Hastings House, c1980. xxii, 289 p.; 24 cm. — (Communication arts books) Includes index. 1. Press law — United States. 2. Newspaper court reporting — United States. 3. Free press and fair trial — United States. 4. Journalism, Legal — United States. I. T.
KF2750.D46        070.4/49/34705        LC 79-24051        ISBN 0803863411

**Pember, Don R., 1939-.**                                                    **4.9535**
Mass media law / Don R. Pember. — 3rd ed. — Dubuque, Iowa: W.C. Brown, c1984. xiii, 610 p.; 24 cm. 1. Mass media — Law and legislation — United States. 2. Press law — United States. I. T.
KF2750.P4 1984        343.73/099 347.30399 19        LC 83-72275        ISBN 0697043657

**Bensman, Marvin R., 1937-.**                                               **4.9536**
Broadcast regulation: selected cases and decisions / Marvin R. Bensman. — Lanham, MD: University Press of America, c1983. i, 100, 36 p.; 22 cm. Includes index. 1. Broadcasting — Law and legislation — United States — Digests. 2. Mass media — Law and legislation — United States — Digests. I. T.
KF2763.36.B46 1983        343.73/09945 347.3039945 19        LC 83-14530        ISBN 0819134414

**Irwin, Manley Rutherford.**                                                **4.9537**
Telecommunications America: markets without boundaries / Manley Rutherford Irwin. — Westport, Conn.: Quorum Books, c1984. xiv, 147 p.: ill.; 25 cm. Includes index. 1. American Telephone and Telegraph Company. 2. Telecommunication — Law and legislation — United States. 3. Telecommunication policy — United States. 4. Telecommunication — United States. I. T.
KF2765.I78 1984        343.73/0994 347.303994 19        LC 83-9448        ISBN 0899300294

**Documents of American broadcasting / Frank J. Kahn, editor.**          **4.9538**
4th ed. — Englewood Cliffs, N.J.: Prentice-Hall, c1984. xvii, 501 p.; 24 cm. 1. Television — Law and legislation — United States. 2. Radio — Law and legislation — United States. I. Kahn, Frank J.
KF2804.D6 1984        343.73/09945 347.3039945 19        LC 83-11025        ISBN 0132171333

**Emery, Walter Byron, 1907-.**                                              **4.9539**
Broadcasting and government: responsibilities and regulations, by Walter B. Emery. — [Rev. — East Lansing]: Michigan State University Press, [1971] viii, 569 p.; 24 cm. 1. Broadcasting — Law and legislation — United States. I. T.
KF2805.E4 1971        343/.73/0994        LC 70-154335        ISBN 0870131591

**Rowan, Ford.**                                                              **4.9540**
Broadcast fairness: doctrine, practice, prospects: a reappraisal of the fairness doctrine and equal time rule / Ford Rowan. — New York: Longman, c1984. xvi, 214 p.; 24 cm. — (Longman series in public communication.) 1. Fairness

doctrine (Broadcasting) — United States. 2. Equal time rule (Broadcasting) — United States. I. T. II. Series.
KF2812.R68 1984     343.73/09945 347.3039945 19     *LC* 83-19998
    *ISBN* 0582284341

**Krasnow, Erwin G.**        **4.9541**
The politics of broadcast regulation / Erwin G. Krasnow, Lawrence D. Longley, Herbert A. Terry; foreword by Newton Minow. — 3rd ed. — New York: St. Martin's Press, c1982. xiv, 304 p.: ill.; 24 cm. Includes index. 1. United States. Federal Communications Commission. 2. Broadcasting — Law and legislation — United States. I. Longley, Lawrence D. II. Terry, Herbert A. III. T.
KF2840.K7 1982     343.73/09945 347.3039945 19     *LC* 81-51850
    *ISBN* 0312626533

**Misregulating television: network dominance and the FCC /**     **4.9542**
**Stanley M. Besen ... [et al.].**
Chicago: University of Chicago Press, 1984. viii, 202 p.; 24 cm. 1. United States. Federal Communications Commission. 2. Television — Law and legislation — United States. 3. Television — Government policy — United States. 4. Television broadcasting — United States.
KF2840.M58 1984     343.73/09946 347.3039946 19     *LC* 84-8738
    *ISBN* 0226044157

**Rivkin, Steven R.**        **4.9543**
A new guide to Federal cable television regulations / Steven R. Rivkin. — Cambridge, Mass.: MIT Press, c1978. xiv, 314 p.: forms; 29 cm. 'A compendium of relevant documents': p. 126-302. 1. Cable television — Law and legislation — United States. I. T.
KF2844.R585     *LC* 77-28389     *ISBN* 0262180898

## KF2901–2940 Professions. Medical Jurisprudence

**Annas, George J.**        **4.9544**
The rights of doctors, nurses, and allied health professionals: a health law primer / George J. Annas, Leonard H. Glantz, and Barbara F. Katz. — Cambridge, Mass.: Ballinger, c1981. xviii, 382 p.; 24 cm. — (American Civil Liberties Union handbook.) 'A Discus book.' 1. Medical laws and legislation — United States. 2. Nursing — Law and legislation — United States. 3. Allied health personnel — Legal status, laws, etc. — United States. I. Glantz, Leonard H. II. Katz, Barbara F. III. T. IV. Series.
KF2905.Z9 A56     344.73/041 347.30441 19     *LC* 80-69898     *ISBN* 0884107272

**DeVries, Raymond G.**        **4.9545**
Regulating birth: midwives, medicine, & the law / Raymond G. DeVries. — Philadelphia: Temple University Press, 1985. xix, 203 p.; 22 cm. (Health, society, and policy.) Includes index. 1. Midwives — Legal status, laws, etc. — United States. I. T. II. Series.
KF2915.M5 D48 1985     344.73/0415 347.304415 19     *LC* 84-16196
    *ISBN* 0877223793

## KF2986–3180 Copyright. Trademarks

**Strong, William S.**        **4.9546**
The copyright book: a practical guide / William S. Strong. — 2nd ed. — Cambridge, Mass.: MIT Press, c1984. xii, 223 p.: 1 form; 21 cm. 1. Copyright — United States. I. T.
KF2994.S75 1984     346.7304/82 347.306482 19     *LC* 84-7925     *ISBN* 0262192349

**Neitzke, Frederic William.**        **4.9547**
A software law primer / Frederic William Neitzke. — New York: Van Nostrand Reinhold, c1984. xi, 157 p.: ill.; 25 cm. Includes index. 1. Copyright — Computer programs — United States. 2. Computer programs — Patents. I. T.
KF3024.C6 N44 1984     346.7304/82 347.306482 19     *LC* 83-23508
    *ISBN* 0442268661

**Oathout, John D.**        **4.9548**
Trademarks: a guide to the selection, administration, and protection of trademarks in modern business practice / John D. Oathout. — New York: Scribner, c1981. viii, 210 p.: ill.; 22 cm. Includes index. 1. Trademarks — United States. I. T.
KF3180.O16     346.7304/88 347.306488 19     *LC* 81-4492     *ISBN* 0684168448

## KF3301–3580 Labor Law

**Koretz, Robert F., 1912- comp.**        • **4.9549**
Labor organization. Editor: Robert F. Koretz. — New York: Chelsea House Publishers, [1970] v, 846 p.; 24 cm. — (Statutory history of the United States) 1. Labor laws and legislation — United States I. T. II. Series.
KF3305.8 1970     340     *LC* 77-10294

**Bailey, Stephen Kemp.**        • **4.9550**
Congress makes a law; the story behind the Employment act of 1946. — New York: Columbia University Press, 1950. xii, 282 p.; 24 cm. 1. United States. Laws, statutes, etc. Employment act of 1946. I. T.
KF3306.5.A16B3x     *LC* 49-49271

**Individual rights in the corporation: a reader on employee rights**     **4.9551**
**/ edited by Alan F. Westin and Stephan Salisbury.**
1st ed. — New York: Pantheon Books, c1980. xx, 473 p.; 25 cm. Includes index. 1. Labor laws and legislation — United States 2. Employee rights — United States. I. Westin, Alan F. II. Salisbury, Stephan.
KF3318.I5     323.4     *LC* 79-1902     *ISBN* 0394507150

**Gregory, Charles Oscar, 1902-.**        **4.9552**
Labor and the law / by Charles O. Gregory and Harold A. Katz. — 3d ed. — New York: Norton, c1979. 719 p.; 21 cm. Includes index. 1. Labor laws and legislation — United States I. Katz, Harold Ambrose, 1921- joint author. II. T.
KF3369.G7 1979     344/.73/01     *LC* 79-4291     *ISBN* 0393012085

**Gross, James A., 1933-.**        **4.9553**
The making of the National Labor Relations Board; a study in economics, politics, and the law [by] James A. Gross. Albany, State University of New York Press, 1974. 265 p.: ill. 1. United States. National Labor Relations Board. I. T. II. Title: Reshaping of the National Labor Relations Board.
KF3372.G76     353.008/3     *LC* 74-5284     *ISBN* 0873952707

**Frank W. Pierce Memorial Conference, Cornell University,**     **4.9554**
**1973.**
Union power and public policy / David B. Lipsky, editor. — Ithaca, N.Y.: New York State School of Industrial and Labor Relations, Cornell University, 1975. xv, 131 p.; 28 cm. — (Frank W. Pierce memorial lectureship and conference series) 1. Trade-unions — Law and legislation — United States — Addresses, essays, lectures. 2. Labor laws and legislation — United States — Addresses, essays, lectures. I. Lipsky, David B., 1939- ed. II. New York State School of Industrial and Labor Relations. III. T. IV. Series.
KF3389.A2 F7 1973     331.8/0973     *LC* 74-620171     *ISBN* 0875460577

**Prasow, Paul.**        • **4.9555**
Arbitration and collective bargaining: conflict resolution in labor relations [by] Paul Prasow [and] Edward Peters. — New York: McGraw-Hill, [1970] xix, 426 p.; 23 cm. — (McGraw-Hill series in management) 1. Arbitration, Industrial — U.S. 2. Collective bargaining — U.S. I. Peters, Edward, 1909- joint author. II. T.
KF3408.P7     331.1/16/0973     *LC* 78-89791

**Stone, Morris, 1912-.**        • **4.9556**
Labor–management contracts at work; analysis of awards reported by the American Arbitration Association. — [1st ed.]. — New York: Harper, [1961] viii, 307 p.; 22 cm. 1. Collective labor agreements — United States. I. T.
KF3408.S63     331.116     *LC* 61-12231

**Wellington, Harry H.**        • **4.9557**
Labor and the legal process, by Harry H. Wellington. New York, Yale University Press, 1968. xi, 409 p. 21 cm. 1. Collective bargaining — United States. 2. Trade-unions — Law and legislation — United States. I. T.
KF3408.W4     340     *LC* 68-27769

**Elkouri, Frank.**        **4.9558**
How arbitration works / by Frank Elkouri and Edna Asper Elkouri. — 4th ed. — Washington, D.C.: Bureau of National Affairs, c1985. xxvi, 873 p.; 27 cm. (Series on arbitration.) Includes index. 1. Arbitration, Industrial — United States. I. Elkouri, Edna Asper. II. T. III. Series.
KF3424.E53 1985     344.73/018914 347.30418914 19     *LC* 85-9641
    *ISBN* 0871794705

**Fleming, Robben Wright, 1916-.**        • **4.9559**
The labor arbitration process [by] R. W. Fleming. — Urbana: University of Illinois Press, 1965. 233 p.; 24 cm. 1. Arbitration, Industrial — United States. I. T.
KF3424.F55     331.1550973     *LC* 65-19569

**Thieblot, Armand J.**        **4.9560**
Union violence: the record and the response by courts, legislatures, and the NLRB / by Armand J. Thieblot, Jr. and Thomas R. Haggard. — Philadelphia, Pa., U.S.A.: Industrial Research Unit, Wharton School, University of

Pennsylvania, c1983. xv, 540 p.; 23 cm. (Labor relations and public policy series. 0075-7470; no. 25) 1. Strikes and lockouts — Law and legislation — United States. 2. Violence (Law) — United States. 3. Trade-unions — Law and legislation — United States. I. Haggard, Thomas R. II. Wharton School. Industrial Research Unit. III. T. IV. Series.
KF3431.T46 1983     344.73/01892 347.3041892 19     *LC* 83-81085
    *ISBN* 0895460408

**Ledvinka, James.**                                                      **4.9561**
Federal regulation of personnel and human resource management / James Ledvinka. — Boston, Mass.: Kent Pub. Co., c1982. xiii, 274 p.: ill.; 22 cm. — (Kent human resource management series.) 1. Labor laws and legislation — United States I. T. II. Series.
KF3455.L42 1982     344.73/01 347.3041 19     *LC* 81-20826     *ISBN* 0534011608

**Fullinwider, Robert K., 1942-.**                                        **4.9562**
The reverse discrimination controversy: a moral and legal analysis / Robert K. Fullinwider. — Totowa, N.J.: Rowman and Littlefield, 1980. xi, 300 p.; 22 cm. — (Philosophy and society series.) Includes index. 1. Affirmative action programs — Law and legislation — United States. 2. Reverse discrimination in employment — Law and legislation — United States. 3. Discrimination — United States. 4. Affirmative action programs — United States. 5. Discrimination in employment — United States I. T. II. Series.
KF3464.F84     344.73/01133     *LC* 79-27344     *ISBN* 084766273X

**Gould, William B.**                                                     **4.9563**
Black workers in white unions: job discrimination in the United States / William B. Gould. Ithaca: Cornell University Press, c1977. 506 p.; 24 cm. 1. Discrimination in employment — Law and legislation — United States. 2. Trade-unions — Afro-American membership I. T.
KF3464.G6     344/.73/01133     *LC* 76-50263     *ISBN* 0801410622

**Williams, Walter E. (Walter Edward), 1936-.**                           **4.9564**
The state against Blacks / Walter E. Williams. — New York: McGraw-Hill, 1982. xvii, 183 p.: ill. 1. Afro-Americans — Employment — Law and legislation 2. Afro-Americans — Legal status, laws, etc. I. T.
KF3464.W54     KF3464 W54.     344.73/016396073 347.30416396073 19     *LC* 82-7232     *ISBN* 0070703787

**Abramson, Joan.**                                                       **4.9565**
Old boys—new women: the politics of sex discrimination / Joan Abramson. — New York: Praeger, 1979. xi, 255 p.; 24 cm. Includes index. 1. Sex discrimination in employment — Law and legislation — United States. 2. Sex discrimination against women — Law and legislation — United States. 3. Women — Employment — Law and legislation — United States. I. T.
KF3467.A92     344/.73/014     *LC* 79-65933     *ISBN* 0030497566

**Fogel, Walter A.**                                                      **4.9566**
The Equal Pay Act: implications for comparable worth / Walter Fogel. — New York: Praeger, 1984. 128 p. Includes indexes. 1. Equal pay for equal work — Law and legislation — United States. 2. Sex discrimination against women — Law and legislation — United States. I. T.
KF3467.F63 1984     344.73/0121 347.304121 19     *LC* 84-11594
    *ISBN* 0030717892

**MacKinnon, Catharine A.**                                               **4.9567**
Sexual harassment of working women: a case of sex discrimination / Catharine A. MacKinnon; foreword by Thomas I. Emerson. — New Haven: Yale University Press, 1979. xiv, 312 p.; 22 cm. 1. Sex discrimination in employment — Law and legislation — United States. 2. Sex discrimination against women — Law and legislation — United States. 3. Sexual harassment of women — United States. I. T.
KF3467.M3     344/.73/014     *LC* 78-9645     *ISBN* 0300022980

**Wood, Stephen B.**                                                    **• 4.9568**
Constitutional politics in the progressive era; child labor and the law [by] Stephen B. Wood. Chicago, University of Chicago Press [1968] xiv, 320 p. 23 cm. 1. Children — Employment — Law and legislation — United States. I. T.
KF3552.W6     331.3/1/0973     *LC* 67-25525

## KF3600–3686 Social Insurance

**Stevens, Robert Bocking.**                                            **• 4.9569**
Income security: statutory history of the United States / editor: Robert B. Stevens. — New York: Chelsea House Publishers, [1970] x, 919 p.; 24 cm. — (Statutory history of the United States.) 1. Social security — Law and legislation — United States. I. T. II. Series.
KF3643.8 1970     344/.73/02     *LC* 71-14384

## KF3775–3829 Public Health. Medical Legislation

**Wenner, Lettie McSpadden.**                                             **4.9570**
The environmental decade in court / Lettie M. Wenner. — Bloomington: Indiana University Press, c1982. xii, 211 p.: ill.; 22 cm. 1. Environmental law — United States — Cases. I. T.
KF3775.A7 W46 1982     344.73/046/02642 347.3044602642 19     *LC* 81-47778     *ISBN* 0253319579

**Air and water pollution control law, 1982: a comprehensive**            **4.9571**
**examination of the law pertaining to the control of air and water pollution with emphasis on recent developments / editors, Phillip D. Reed, Gregory S. Wetstone.**
Washington, DC (1346 Connecticut Ave., N.W., Washington 20036): Environmental Law Institute, c1982. viii, 783 p.; 28 cm. 'A preliminary version of this volume, Air and water pollution control law, 1981, was distributed at the Conference on Water and Air Pollution Law ... November 1981, Washington, D.C.'—T.p. verso. 1. Air — Pollution — Law and legislation — United States. 2. Water — Pollution — Law and legislation — United States. I. Reed, Phillip D. II. Wetstone, Gregory. III. Environmental Law Institute.
KF3812.A95 1982     344.73/04634 347.3044634 19     *LC* 83-145664

**Melnick, R. Shep, 1951-.**                                              **4.9572**
Regulation and the courts: the case of the Clean Air Act / R. Shep Melnick. — Washington, D.C.: Brookings Institution, c1983. x, 404 p.; 24 cm. 1. Air — Pollution — Law and legislation — United States. 2. Judicial review of administrative acts — United States. 3. Administrative procedure — United States. 4. Administrative law — United States. I. T.
KF3812.M44 1983     344.73/046342 347.30446342 19     *LC* 83-7694
    *ISBN* 0815756623

**Christoffel, Tom.**                                                     **4.9573**
Health and the law: a handbook for health professionals / Tom Christoffel. — New York: Free Press; London: Collier Macmillan, c1982. xiii, 450 p.; 24 cm. Includes index. 1. Medical laws and legislation — United States. 2. Public health laws — United States. I. T.
KF3821.C57 1982     344.73/04 347.3044 19     *LC* 82-70808     *ISBN* 0029053706

## KF3885–3894 Drug Laws

**Temin, Peter.**                                                         **4.9574**
Taking your medicine: drug regulation in the United States / Peter Temin. — Cambridge, Mass.: Harvard University Press, 1980. vii, 274 p.; 25 cm. Includes index. 1. Drugs — Law and legislation — United States. 2. Drugs — Law and legislation — Economic aspects — United States. 3. Pharmaceutical industry — United States. I. T.
KF3885.T45 1980     344.73/04233 19     *LC* 80-16680     *ISBN* 0674867254

**Lindesmith, Alfred Ray, 1905-.**                                      **• 4.9575**
The addict and the law / by Alfred R. Lindesmith. — Bloomington: Indiana University Press, [1965] xiii, 337 p.: ill.; 22 cm. 1. Narcotic laws — United States. 2. Narcotic addicts — Legal status, laws, etc. — United States. 3. Narcotic laws I. T.
KF3890.L5     343.57     *LC* 64-18821

**Bonnie, Richard J.**                                                    **4.9576**
Marijuana use and criminal sanctions: essays on the theory and practice of decriminalization / by Richard J. Bonnie. — Charlottesville, Va.: Michie Co., c1980. ix, 264 p.; 24 cm. 1. Marihuana — Law and legislation — United States. 2. Decriminalization — United States. 3. Marihuana — Law and legislation 4. Decriminalization I. T.
KF3891.M2 B66     344.73/0545 347.304545 19     *LC* 79-49271
    *ISBN* 0872152448

**Moller, Richard Jay.**                                                  **4.9577**
Marijuana: your legal rights / Richard Jay Moller; edited by Ralph Warner. — Reading, Mass.: Addison-Wesley, c1981. 271 p.: ill.; 24 cm. 'A Nolo Press book.' Includes index. 1. Marihuana — Law and legislation — United States. 2. Criminal procedure — United States. I. Warner, Ralph E. II. T.
KF3891.M2 M64     345.73/0277 19     *LC* 81-621     *ISBN* 0201047691

## KF3989 Sports Laws

**Berry, Robert C.**                                                      **4.9578**
Law and business of the sports industries / Robert C. Berry, Glenn M. Wong. — Boston, Mass.: Auburn House Pub. Co., c1986. 2 v.: ill.; 25 cm.

1. Professional sports — Law and legislation — United States. I. Wong, Glenn M. II. T.
KF3989.B47 1986　　　344.73/099 347.30499 19　　　*LC* 82-22833　　　*ISBN* 0865690812

# KF4101–4258 Education

**The Yearbook of school law.**　　　　　　　　　　　**4.9579**
1950-. Topeka, Kans. [etc.] National Organization on Legal Problems of Education [etc.] v. 22 cm. Annual. 1. Educational law and legislation — United States I. Garber, Lee Orville, 1900- II. National Organization on Legal Problems of Education.
KF4102.5.Y4　　　379.1473　　　*LC* 52-2403

**Alexander, Kern.**　　　　　　　　　　　**4.9580**
American public school law / Kern Alexander, M. David Alexander. — 2nd ed. — St. Paul: West Pub. Co., c1985. xxxix, 817 p.; 26 cm. 1. Educational law and legislation — United States — Cases. I. Alexander, M. David. II. T.
KF4118.A39 1985　　　344.73/071 347.30471 19　　　*LC* 84-21993　　　*ISBN* 0314852131

**Fellman, David, 1907- ed.**　　　　　　　　　　　**4.9581**
The Supreme Court and education / edited, with an introd. and notes, by David Fellman. — 3d ed. — New York: Teachers College Press, c1976. xxii, 323 p.; 19 cm. — (Classics in education; no. 4) 1. Educational law and legislation — United States — Cases. I. United States. Supreme Court. II. T.
KF4118.F44 1976　　　344/.73/071　　　*LC* 77-14865　　　*ISBN* 0807725110

**School days, rule days: the legalization and regulation of**　　　**4.9582**
**education / edited by David L. Kirp and Donald N. Jensen.**
London; Philadelphia: Falmer Press, 1986. vi, 389 p.; 24 cm. 1. Educational law and legislation — United States 2. Education and state — United States. I. Kirp, David L. II. Jensen, Donald N.
KF4119.A2 S29 1985　　　344.73/071 347.30471 19　　　*LC* 85-1537
　　*ISBN* 1850000174

**Edwards, Newton, 1889-.**　　　　　　　　　　　● **4.9583**
The courts and the public schools: the legal basis of school organization and administration / by Newton Edwards. 3d ed. / with a pref. and an additional chapter by Lee O. Garber. — Chicago: University of Chicago Press, 1971. xviii, 710 p.; 25 cm. 1. Educational law and legislation — United States 2. Teachers — Legal status, laws, etc. — United States. I. Garber, Lee Orville, 1900- II. T.
KF4119.E3 1971　　　344/.73/071　　　*LC* 76-151482　　　*ISBN* 0226186067

**Lapati, Americo D.**　　　　　　　　　　　**4.9584**
Education and the Federal Government: a historical record / Americo D. Lapati. — New York: Mason/Charter, 1975. v, 388 p.; 24 cm. Includes index. 1. Educational law and legislation — United States 2. Educational law and legislation — United States — History. I. T.
KF4119.L35　　　344/.73/07　　　*LC* 75-4696　　　*ISBN* 0884051056

**McCarthy, Martha M.**　　　　　　　　　　　**4.9585**
Public school law: teachers' and students' rights / Martha M. McCarthy, Nelda H. Cambron. — Boston, MA: Allyn & Bacon, c1981. xii, 336 p.; 25 cm. 1. Teachers — Legal status, laws, etc. — United States. 2. Students — Legal status, laws, etc. — United States. I. Cambron-McCabe, Nelda H. II. T.
KF4119.M38　　　344.73/078 347.30478 19　　　*LC* 81-1304　　　*ISBN* 020507278X

**Reutter, E. Edmund, 1924-.**　　　　　　　　　　　**4.9586**
The Supreme Court's impact on public education / E. Edmund Reutter, Jr. — [Bloomington, Ind.]: Phi Delta Kappa; [Topeka, Kan.]: National Organization on Legal Problems of Education, c1982. vii, 205 p.; 23 cm. Includes index. 1. Educational law and legislation — United States I. T.
KF4119.R48 1982　　　344.73/071 347.30471 19　　　*LC* 81-60805　　　*ISBN* 0873677846

**Bailey, Stephen Kemp.**　　　　　　　　　　　**4.9587**
ESEA; the Office of Education administers a law [by] Stephen K. Bailey and Edith K. Mosher. [1st ed. Syracuse, N.Y.] Syracuse University Press [1968] xii, 393 p. illus. 24 cm. 'Public law 89-10, 89th Congress, H.R. 2362, April 11, 1965: an act to strengthen and improve educational quality and educational opportunities in the Nation's elementary and secondary schools': p. 235-266. 1. United States. Office of Education. 2. Federal aid to education — United States I. Mosher, Edith K., joint author. II. United States. Elementary and Secondary Education Act of 1965. 1968. III. T.
KF4137.B3　　　340　　　*LC* 68-27692

**Graglia, Lino A.**　　　　　　　　　　　**4.9588**
Disaster by decree: the Supreme Court decisions on race and the schools / Lino A. Graglia. — Ithaca, N.Y.: Cornell University Press, 1976. 351 p.; 22 cm. 1. Discrimination in education — Law and legislation — United States —

Cases. 2. Busing for school integration — Law and legislation — United States — Cases. I. T.
KF4154.G7　　　344/.73/0798　　　*LC* 75-36997　　　*ISBN* 0801409802

**Dimond, Paul R.**　　　　　　　　　　　**4.9589**
Beyond busing: inside the challenge to urban segregation / Paul R. Dimond. — Ann Arbor: University of Michigan Press, c1985. xii, 411 p.; 24 cm. Includes index. 1. Discrimination in education — Law and legislation — United States. 2. Discrimination in housing — Law and legislation — United States. 3. Busing for school integration — Law and legislation — United States. I. T.
KF4155.D56 1985　　　344.73/0798 347.304798 19　　　*LC* 84-29782
　　*ISBN* 0472100629

**Hogan, John C. (John Charles)**　　　　　　　　　　　**4.9590**
The schools, the courts, and the public interest [by] John C. Hogan. Lexington, Mass., Lexington Books [1974] xvi, 262 p. illus. 22 cm. (Lexington Books politics of education series) 1. Right to education — United States. 2. Educational equalization — United States. 3. Educational law and legislation — United States I. T.
KF4155.H6　　　344/.73/079　　　*LC* 73-1005　　　*ISBN* 0669868922

**Kluger, Richard.**　　　　　　　　　　　**4.9591**
Simple justice: the history of Brown v. Board of Education and Black America's struggle for equality / by Richard Kluger. — 1st ed. — New York: Knopf, 1976, c1975. x, 823, xxiii p., [4] leaves of plates: ill.; 24 cm. Includes indexes. 1. Segregation in education — Law and legislation — United States. I. T.
KF4155.K55 1976　　　344/.73/0798　　　*LC* 75-8221　　　*ISBN* 0394472896

**O'Neill, Timothy J.**　　　　　　　　　　　**4.9592**
Bakke & the politics of equality: friends and foes in the classroom of litigation / Timothy J. O'Neill. — 1st ed. — Middletown, Conn.: Wesleyan University Press; Scranton, Pa.: Distributed by Harper & Row, c1985. xviii, 325 p.; 24 cm. Includes index. 1. Bakke, Allan Paul. 2. Discrimination in education — Law and legislation — United States. 3. Affirmative action programs — Law and legislation — United States. 4. Judicial process — United States. 5. Law and politics 6. Sociological jurisprudence I. T. II. Title: Bakke and the politics of equality.
KF4155.O53 1985　　　344.73/0798 347.304798 19　　　*LC* 83-26122
　　*ISBN* 0819551163

**Wolters, Raymond, 1938-.**　　　　　　　　　　　**4.9593**
The burden of Brown: thirty years of school desegregation / Raymond Wolters. — Knoxville: University of Tennessee Press, c1984. 346 p.; 24 cm. Includes index. 1. Discrimination in education — Law and legislation — United States. 2. School integration — United States — Case studies. I. T.
KF4155.W64 1984　　　344.73/0798 347.304798 19　　　*LC* 83-21620
　　*ISBN* 0870494236

**Dolbeare, Kenneth M.**　　　　　　　　　　　**4.9594**
The school prayer decisions from court policy to local practice [by] Kenneth M. Dolbeare and Phillip E. Hammond. Chicago, University of Chicago Press [1971] xi, 164 p. 23 cm. 1. Religion in the public schools — Law and legislation — United States. I. Hammond, Phillip E., joint author. II. T.
KF4162.D64　　　344/.73/0796　　　*LC* 70-140461　　　*ISBN* 0226155153

**Manwaring, David Roger, 1933-.**　　　　　　　　　　　● **4.9595**
Render unto Caesar; the flag–salute controversy. [Chicago] University of Chicago Press [1962] 320 p. 23 cm. 'This book began as a doctoral dissertation at the University of Wisconsin.' 1. Jehovah's Witnesses 2. Flags — Law and legislation — United States. I. T.
KF4162.M35　　　323.44　　　*LC* 62-13563

**Muir, William Ker.**　　　　　　　　　　　● **4.9596**
Prayer in the public schools; law and attitude change [by] William K. Muir, Jr. Chicago, University of Chicago Press [1967] ix, 170 p. 21 cm. 1. Prayer in the public schools — Law and legislation — United States. 2. Prayer in the public schools — United States. I. T.
KF4162.M8　　　344/.73/0796　　　*LC* 67-28851

**Ingelhart, Louis E. (Louis Edward)**　　　　　　　　　　　**4.9597**
Freedom for the college student press: court cases and related decisions defining the campus fourth estate boundaries / Louis E. Ingelhart. — Westport, Conn.: Greenwood Press, 1985. viii, 229 p.; 25 cm. (Contributions to the study of mass media and communications. 0732-4456; no. 3) Includes index. 1. Journalism, College — Law and legislation — United States. I. T. II. Series.
KF4165.I54 1985　　　344.73/0793 347.304793 19　　　*LC* 84-19183
　　*ISBN* 0313246076

**Fischer, Louis, 1924-.**　　　　　　　　　　　**4.9598**
The civil rights of teachers / [by] Louis Fischer [and] David Schimmel. — New York: Harper & Row, [1973] xv, 220 p.; ill.; 21 cm. — (Critical issues in education) 1. Teachers — Legal status, laws, etc. — United States. 2. Civil rights — United States I. Schimmel, David. joint author. II. T.
KF4175.F58　　　344/.73/078　　　*LC* 72-11495　　　*ISBN* 0060420723

**Levine, Erwin L.**                                                    **4.9599**
PL94-142: an act of Congress / Erwin L. Levine, Elizabeth M. Wexler. — New York: Macmillan Pub. Co.; London: Collier Macmillan Publishers, c1981. xi, 214 p.; 21 cm. 1. United States. Education for All Handicapped Children Act 2. Handicapped children — Education — Law and legislation — United States. I. Wexler, Elizabeth M. joint author. II. T.
KF4210.A314 A164      344.73/0791    *LC* 80-18071      *ISBN*
0023702702

**Special education in America: its legal and governmental**          **4.9600**
**foundations / edited by Joseph Ballard, Bruce A. Ramirez and**
**Frederick J. Weintraub.**
Reston, VA: Council for Exceptional Children, c1982. v, 104 p.; 26 cm. 1. Handicapped children — Education — Law and legislation — United States — Addresses, essays, lectures. 2. Exceptional children — Education — Law and legislation — United States — Addresses, essays, lectures. I. Ballard, Joseph. II. Ramirez, Bruce A. III. Weintraub, Frederick J.
KF4210.A75 S64 1982      344.73/0791 347.304791 19      *LC* 82-71299
*ISBN* 0865861331

**Cremins, James J.**                                                  **4.9601**
Legal and political issues in special education / by James J. Cremins. — Springfield, Ill.: C.C. Thomas, c1983. xi, 119 p.; 24 cm. 1. Handicapped children — Education — Law and legislation — United States. 2. Handicapped children — Education — Government policy — United States. I. T.
KF4210.C73 1983      344.73/0791 347.304791 19      *LC* 83-4841
*ISBN* 0398048789

**Goldberg, Steven S. (Steven Selig), 1950-.**                         **4.9602**
Special education law: a guide for parents, advocates, and educators / Steven S. Goldberg. — New York: Plenum Press, c1982. xi, 229 p.; 24 cm. 1. Handicapped children — Education — Law and legislation — United States. I. T.
KF4210.G64 1982      344.73/0791 347.304791 19      *LC* 82-13190
*ISBN* 0306408481

**Kaplin, William A.**                                                 **4.9603**
The law of higher education: a comprehensive guide to legal implications of administrative decision making / William A. Kaplin. — 2nd ed. — San Francisco: Jossey-Bass Publishers, 1985. xxv, 621 p.; 26 cm. (Jossey-Bass higher education series.) 1. Universities and colleges — Law and legislation — United States. I. T. II. Series.
KF4225.K36 1985      344.73/074 347.30474 19      *LC* 84-47987      *ISBN*
0875896197

**Solutions to ethical and legal problems in social research /**      **4.9604**
**edited by Robert F. Boruch, Joe S. Cecil.**
New York: Academic Press, 1983. xiv, 335 p.: ill.; 24 cm. (Quantitative studies in social relations.) Most chapters were presented at the conference held Feb. 23-25, 1978 in Washington, D.C. and sponsored by the National Science Foundation. 1. Social sciences — Research — Law and legislation — United States — Congresses. 2. Social sciences — Research — United States — Congresses. 3. Social sciences and ethics — Congresses. I. Boruch, Robert F. II. Cecil, Joe S. III. National Science Foundation (U.S.) IV. Series.
KF4280.S6 S65 1983      300/.72 19      *LC* 83-2697      *ISBN* 0121186806

## KF4298-4302 Motion Pictures

**Randall, Richard S.**                                                • **4.9605**
Censorship of the movies; the social and political control of a mass medium [by] Richard S. Randall. — Madison: University of Wisconsin Press, 1968. xvi, 280 p.; 24 cm. 1. Motion pictures — Censorship — United States. I. T.
KF4300.R3      791.43      *LC* 68-14035

## KF4501-5130 Constitutional Law

### KF4501-4530 SOURCES

**The Documentary history of the ratification of the Constitution**   **4.9606**
**/ edited by Merrill Jensen.**
Madison: State Historical Society of Wisconsin, 1976-. v.; 24 cm. Includes indexes. 1. United States — Constitutional history — Sources. I. Jensen, Merrill.
KF4502.D63      342/.73/029      *LC* 75-14149      *ISBN* 0870201530

**United States. Constitution.**                                      **4.9607**
The Constitution of the United States of America: analysis and interpretation: Annotations of cases decided by the Supreme Court of the United States to June 29, 1972 / Prepared by the Congressional Research Service, Library of Congress. Lester S. Jayson, supervising editor. Johnny H. Killian, editor. Sylvia Beckey, associate editor. Thomas Durbin, associate editor. [Rev. ed.]

Washington: U.S. Govt. Print. Off., 1974. xliv, 1961 p. 29 cm. (92d Congress, 2d session. Senate. Document no. 92-82) Kept up to date by cumulative pocket supplements. 1. United States. Constitution 2. United States — Constitutional law I. Jayson, Lester S. ed. II. Killian, Johnny H. ed. III. United States. Supreme Court. IV. Library of Congress. Congressional Research Service. V. T.
KF4527.J39      342/.73/023      *LC* 74-601236

**Constitutions of the United States, national and state.**          **4.9608**
2d ed. — Dobbs Ferry, N.Y.: Oceana Publications, 1974-. v.; 28 cm. 'Published for Legislative Drafting Research Fund of Columbia University'—V. 1, 1985 t.p. Loose-leaf for updating. Includes unnumbered index volume. 1. Constitutions, State — United States. I. Columbia University. Legislative Drafting Research Fund.
KF4530.C6 1974      342/.73/02      *LC* 74-7681

**Swindler, William Finley. comp.**                                   **4.9609**
Sources and documents of United States constitutions, edited and annotated by William F. Swindler. — Dobbs Ferry, N.Y.: Oceana Publications, 1973-1979. 10 v.; 27 cm. 1. Constitutions, State — United States. I. T.
KF4530.S94      342.73/024 347.30224 19      *LC* 73-170979      *ISBN*
0379161753

**Thorpe, Francis Newton, 1857-1926. comp.**                          • **4.9610**
The Federal and State constitutions, colonial charters, and other organic laws of the States, territories, and Colonies, now or heretofore forming the United States of America. Washington, Govt. Print. Off., 1909. Grosse Pointe, Mich., Scholarly Press [1968] 7 v. 23 cm. (59th Congress, 2d session. House of Representatives. Document, no. 357) 1. United States. Constitution 2. Constitutions, State — United States. 3. Charters 4. United States — Constitutional law I. United States. Constitution II. T.
KF4530.T46 1968      342/.73      *LC* 70-8462

## KF4541-4561 CONSTITUTIONAL HISTORY OF THE UNITED STATES

### KF4541 General

**Crosskey, William Winslow.**                                        • **4.9611**
Politics and the Constitution in the history of the United States. — [Chicago]: University of Chicago Press, [1953]-1980. 3 v.; 25 cm. Vol. 3 by W.W. Crosskey and W. Jeffrey, Jr., has special title: The political background of the Federal Convention. 1. United States. Supreme Court. 2. United States — Constitutional law 3. United States — Constitutional history I. Jeffrey, William, 1921- II. T.
KF4541.C7      342.73/029 347.30229 19      *LC* 53-7433      *ISBN*
0226121380

**Farrand, Max, 1869-1945.**                                          **4.9612**
The framing of the Constitution of the United States, by Max Farrand. New Haven, Yale University press; [etc., etc.] 1913. ix p., 3 l., 281 p. 22 cm. This book is founded upon the records of the Federal convention (New Haven, Yale university press, 1911. 3 vols.) edited by the author. cf. Pref. 1. United States. Constitutional Convention (1787). 2. United States. Constitution I. T.
KF4541.F3      *LC* 13-8095

**Hall, Kermit.**                                                     **4.9613**
A comprehensive bibliography of American constitutional and legal history, 1896–1979 / by Kermit L. Hall. — Millwood, N.Y.: Kraus International Publications, c1984. 5 v. (xlix, 3443 p.); 27 cm. Includes indexes. 1. Law — United States — History and criticism — Bibliography. 2. United States — Constitutional history — Bibliography. I. T.
KF4541.H34 1984      016.34973 016.3473 19      *LC* 82-48983      *ISBN*
0527374083

**Levy, Leonard Williams, 1923-.**                                    **4.9614**
Judgments: essays on American constitutional history / by Leonard W. Levy. — Chicago: Quadrangle Books, 1972. viii, 341 p.; 25 cm. 1. Civil rights — United States 2. United States — Constitutional history I. T.
KF4541.L38      342/.73/029      *LC* 70-182508      *ISBN* 0812902432

**Murphy, Paul L., 1923-.**                                           **4.9615**
The Constitution in crisis times, 1918–1969, by Paul L. Murphy. — [1st ed.]. — New York: Harper & Row, [1972, c1971] xviii, 570 p.: ill.; 22 cm. — (The New American Nation series) 1. U.S. — Constitutional history. I. T.
KF4541.M85 1972      342/.73/029      *LC* 70-156570      *ISBN*
0060131187

**Paludan, Phillip S., 1938-.**                                       **4.9616**
A covenant with death: the Constitution, law, and equality in the Civil War era / Phillip S. Paludan. — Urbana: University of Illinois Press, [1975] xiv, 309 p.; 24 cm. Includes index. 1. Reconstruction 2. United States — Constitutional history I. T.
KF4541.P34      342/.73/029      *LC* 74-34324      *ISBN* 025200261X

**Schwartz, Bernard, 1923-.**    **4.9617**
From confederation to nation: the American Constitution, 1835–1877. — Baltimore: Johns Hopkins University Press, [1973] xi, 243 p.; 23 cm. 1. United States — Constitutional history I. T.
KF4541.S35    342/.73/029    *LC* 72-12353    *ISBN* 0801814642

**Corwin, Edward Samuel, 1878-1963.**    • **4.9618**
The 'higher law' background of American constitutional law / by Edward S. Corwin. — Ithaca, N.Y.: Great Seal Books, 1955, c1929. xii, 89 p.; 19 cm. 1. United States — Constitutional law — History. 2. Great Britain — Constitutional law — History. I. T.
LAW    KF4541.Z9 C6.    *LC* 55-3444

## KF4545 Special Topics, A–Z

**Ehrlich, Walter, 1921-.**    **4.9619**
They have no rights: Dred Scott's struggle for freedom / Walter Ehrlich. — Westport, Conn.: Greenwood Press, 1979. xvi, 266 p.: ports.; 22 cm. — (Contributions in legal studies. no. 9 0147-1074) Includes index. 1. Scott, Dred. 2. Slavery in the United States — Law. I. T. II. Series.
KF4545.S5 E35    346/.73/013    *LC* 78-22135    *ISBN* 0313208190

**Fehrenbacher, Don Edward, 1920-.**    **4.9620**
The Dred Scott case, its significance in American law and politics / Don E. Fehrenbacher. — New York: Oxford University Press, 1978. xii, 741 p.; 24 cm. 1. Scott, Dred. 2. Slavery in the United States — Law. 3. Slavery in the United States — Legal status of slaves in free states. 4. United States — History — 1849-1877 I. T.
KF4545.S5 F43    346/.73/013    *LC* 78-4665    *ISBN* 0195024036

**Fehrenbacher, Don Edward, 1920-.**    **4.9621**
[Dred Scott case, its significance in American law and politics] Slavery, law, and politics: the Dred Scott case in historical perspective / Don E. Fehrenbacher. — New York: Oxford University Press, 1981. viii, 326 p.; 22 cm. Abridged ed. of the author's The Dred Scott case, its significance in American law and politics. Includes index. 1. Scott, Dred. 2. Slavery in the United States — Law and legislation. 3. Slavery in the United States — Legal status of slaves in free states. I. T.
KF4545.S5 F432    346.7301/3 19    *LC* 80-25574    *ISBN* 0195028821

**Finkelman, Paul, 1949-.**    **4.9622**
An imperfect union: slavery, Federalism, and comity / Paul Finkelman. — Chapel Hill: University of North Carolina Press, c1981. xii, 378 p.; 24 cm. — (Studies in legal history.) Includes indexes. 1. Slavery — United States — Legal status of slaves in free states I. T. II. Series.
KF4545.S5 F56    346/.73/013    *LC* 79-27526    *ISBN* 0807814385

**Morris, Thomas D., 1938-.**    **4.9623**
Free men all: the personal liberty laws of the North, 1780–1861 [by] Thomas D. Morris. — Baltimore: Johns Hopkins University Press, [1974] xii, 253 p.; 24 cm. 1. Personal liberty laws I. T.
KF4545.S5 M67    342/.73/085    *LC* 73-8126    *ISBN* 0801815053

**Wiecek, William M., 1938-.**    **4.9624**
The sources of antislavery constitutionalism in America, 1760–1848 / William M. Wiecek. — Ithaca: Cornell University Press, 1977. 306 p.; 23 cm. 1. Slavery in the United States — Law and legislation — History. 2. United States — Constitutional history I. T.
KF4545.S5 W53    346/.73/013    *LC* 77-6169    *ISBN* 0801410894

## KF4546–4552 Constitutional Law: General

**Millett, Stephen M., 1947-.**    **4.9625**
A selected bibliography of American constitutional history / Stephen M. Millett; introd. by C. Herman Pritchett. — Santa Barbara: Clio Books, [1975] ix, 116 p.; 23 cm. Includes index. 1. United States — Constitutional law — Bibliography. 2. United States — Constitutional history — Bibliography. I. T.
KF4546.M54    016.342/73/029    *LC* 75-8677    *ISBN* 0874362040

**Chandler, Ralph C., 1934-.**    **4.9626**
The constitutional law dictionary / Ralph C. Chandler, Richard A. Enslen, Peter G. Renstrom. — Santa Barbara, Calif.: ABC-Clio Informations Services, c1985. 507 p.; 24 cm. (Clio dictionaries in political science. 8) Includes index. 1. United States — Constitutional law — Terms and phrases. 2. United States — Constitutional union — Cases I. Enslen, Richard A., 1931- II. Renstrom, Peter G., 1943- III. T. IV. Series.
KF4548.5.C47 1985    342.73 347.302 19    *LC* 84-12320    *ISBN* 0874360315

**Clark, Floyd Barzilia, 1886-.**    • **4.9627**
The Constitutional doctrines of Justice Harlan / by Floyd B. Clark. — New York: Da Capo Press, 1969. vii, 208 p.; 24 cm. Reprint of the 1915 ed.

Originally issued as author's thesis, Johns Hopkins University, 1914. 1. Harlan, John Marshall, 1833-1911. 2. U.S. — Constitutional law. I. T.
KF4550.C53 1969    342/.24    *LC* 74-87560

**Corwin, Edward Samuel, 1878-1963.**    **4.9628**
[Constitution and what it means today] Edward S. Corwin's The Constitution and what it means today / rev. by Harold W. Chase and Craig R. Ducat. — 14th ed. — Princeton, N.J.: Princeton University Press, 1978. xv, 673 p.; 25 cm. Annual supplements entitled Supreme Court decisions update the main work between editions. 1. United States — Constitutional law I. Chase, Harold William, 1922- II. Ducat, Craig R. III. T. IV. Title: The Constitution and what it means today.
KF4550.C64 1978    342/.73/023    *LC* 78-53809    *ISBN* 0691092400

**Pritchett, C. Herman (Charles Herman), 1907-.**    **4.9629**
Constitutional law of the federal system / C. Herman Pritchett. — Englewood Cliffs, N.J.: Prentice-Hall, c1984. xiii, 382 p.; 23 cm. Includes the text of the U.S. Constitution. 1. United States. Supreme Court. 2. Judicial review — United States. 3. Federal government — United States. 4. Separation of powers — United States. 5. United States — Constitutional law — Interpretation and construction. I. United States. Constitution. 1984. II. T.
KF4550.P744 1984    342.73 347.302 19    *LC* 83-16108    *ISBN* 0131679325

**Tribe, Laurence H.**    **4.9630**
Constitutional choices / Laurence H. Tribe. — Cambridge, Mass.: Harvard University Press, 1985. xiv, 458 p.; 25 cm. Includes indexes. 1. United States — Constitutional law — Interpretation and construction. I. T.
KF4550.T786 1985    342.73 347.302 19    *LC* 84-19235    *ISBN* 0674165381

**Hirschfield, Robert S.**    **4.9631**
The Constitution and the Court: the development of the basic law through judicial interpretation. — New York: Random House, [1962] 257 p.; 19 cm. — (Studies in political science, PS40) 1. United States. Supreme Court. 2. Judicial review — United States. 3. United States — Constitutional law I. T.
KF4550.Z9 H55    342.733    *LC* 62-10672

**Pritchett, C. Herman (Charles Herman), 1907-.**    **4.9632**
The American constitutional system / C. Herman Pritchett. — 5th ed. — New York: McGraw-Hill, 1981. viii, 144 p.; 20 cm. (Foundations of American government and political science) Includes index. 1. United States — Constitutional law I. T. II. Series.
KF4550.Z9 P7 1981    342.73    *LC* 80-13462    *ISBN* 0070508933

**Wright, Benjamin Fletcher, 1900-.**    • **4.9633**
The growth of American constitutional law [by] Benjamin F. Wright. With an introd. by Robert G. McCloskey. — Chicago: University of Chicago Press, [1967] xvi, 276 p.; 21 cm. — (The Court and the Constitution) (Phoenix books) 1. United States. Supreme Court. 2. United States — Constitutional law I. T.
KF4552.W7 1967    342.73/09    *LC* 67-12151

## KF4555 Constitution Amendment

**Freedman, Samuel S., 1927-.**    **4.9634**
ERA, may a state change its vote? / Samuel S. Freedman & Pamela J. Naughton. — Detroit: Wayne State University Press, 1978. 170 p.; 22 cm. — (Waynebook; 46) Includes index. 1. Sex discrimination against women — Law and legislation — United States. 2. United States — Constitutional law — Amendments — Ratification. I. Naughton, Pamela J., 1954- joint author. II. T.
KF4555.F73    342/.73/087    *LC* 78-10821    *ISBN* 0814316239

**Grimes, Alan Pendleton, 1919-.**    **4.9635**
Democracy and the amendments to the Constitution / Alan P. Grimes. — Lexington, Mass.: Lexington Books, c1978. xi, 190 p.; 24 cm. 1. United States — Constitutional law — Amendments I. T.
KF4557.G74    342.73/03 347.3023 19    *LC* 78-4342    *ISBN* 0669023442

## KF4565–4578 SEPARATION OF POWERS

**Fisher, Louis.**    **4.9636**
Constitutional conflicts between Congress and the President / Louis Fisher. — Princeton, N.J.: Princeton University Press, c1985. xviii, 372 p.; 23 cm. Rev. ed. of: The Constitution between friends. 1978. Includes indexes. 1. Separation of powers — United States. 2. United States — Constitutional law I. Fisher, Louis. Constitution between friends. II. T.
KF4565.F57 1985    320.473 19    *LC* 83-60462    *ISBN* 0691076804

**Kurland, Philip B.**    **4.9637**
Watergate and the Constitution / Philip B. Kurland. — Chicago: University of Chicago Press, 1978. x, 261 p.; 24 cm. — (The William R. Kenan, Jr., inaugural

JK
268
W94

lectures) 1. Separation of powers — United States. 2. Watergate Affair, 1972-1974 3. United States — Constitutional law I. T. II. Series.
KF4565.K87     342/.73/062     *LC* 77-18338     *ISBN* 0226463931

**Friedman, Leon. comp.**            **4.9638**
United States v. Nixon: the President before the Supreme Court / introductory essay by Alan Westin; edited by Leon Friedman. — New York: Chelsea House Publishers, 1974. xxi, 619 p.; 25 cm. 1. Nixon, Richard M. (Richard Milhous), 1913- 2. Executive privilege (Government information) — United States — Cases. 3. Watergate Affair, 1972-1974 I. T.
KF4570.A7 F74     342/.73/062     *LC* 74-16403     *ISBN* 0835208028

**Berger, Raoul, 1901-.**            **4.9639**
Executive privilege: a constitutional myth. — Cambridge, Mass.: Harvard University Press, 1974. xvi, 430 p.; 25 cm. — (Studies in legal history.) 1. Executive privilege (Government information) — United States. I. T. II. Series.
KF4570.B47     353.03/2     *LC* 73-93837     *ISBN* 0674274253

## KF4575 Judicial Review

**Black, Charles Lund, 1915-.**        • **4.9640**
The people and the court; judicial review in a democracy. — New York: Macmillan, 1960. 238 p.; 22 cm. 1. United States. Supreme Court. 2. Judicial review — United States. I. T.
KF4575.B55     347.9973     *LC* 60-5483

**Bobbitt, Philip.**            **4.9641**
Constitutional fate: theory of the constitution / Philip Bobbitt. — New York: Oxford University Press, 1982. xii, 285 p.: ill.; 22 cm. 1. Judicial review — United States. I. T.
KF4575.B63 1982     347.73/12 347.30712 19     *LC* 82-3480     *ISBN* 0195031202

**Carr, Robert Kenneth, 1908-.**        • **4.9642**
The Supreme Court and judicial review [by] Robert K. Carr. — Westport, Conn.: Greenwood Press, [1970, c1942] xiv, 304 p.; 23 cm. — (American government in action series.) 1. U.S. Supreme Court. 2. Judicial review — U.S. I. T. II. Series.
KF4575.C3 1970     347.99/73     *LC* 74-98215     *ISBN* 0837132614

**Ely, John Hart, 1938-.**            **4.9643**
Democracy and distrust: A theory of judicial review / John Hart Ely. — Cambridge: Harvard University Press, 1980. viii, 268 p.; 24 cm. 1. Judicial review — United States. I. T.
KF4575.E4     347/.73/12     *LC* 79-19859     *ISBN* 0674196368

**Haines, Charles Grove, 1879-1948.**        • **4.9644**
The American doctrine of judicial supremacy. New York, Russell & Russell, 1959. 705 p. 24 cm. (Publications of the University of California at Los Angeles in social sciences) 1. Judicial review — United States. I. T.
KF4575.H35     351.94     *LC* 59-7256

**Beard, Charles Austin, 1874-1948.**        • **4.9645**
The Supreme Court and the Constitution / with an introd. and bibliographies by Alan F. Westin. — Englewood Cliffs, N.J.: Prentice-Hall, [1962] 149 p.; 21 cm. — (A Spectrum book: classics in history series, S-CH-6) 1. United States. Supreme Court. 2. Judicial reviews — United States. 3. United States — Constitutional history I. T.
KF4575.Z9 B4 1962     342.73     *LC* 61-16980

## KF4600–4629 FEDERAL–STATE RELATIONS. CONTRACT CLAUSE

**Cooley, Thomas McIntyre, 1824-1898.**        • **4.9646**
A treatise on the constitutional limitations which rest upon the legislative power of the States of the American Union. — New York: Da Capo Press, 1972. xlvii, 720 p.; 23 cm. — (Da Capo Press reprints in American constitutional and legal history) Reprint of the 1st ed. published in 1868. 1. Legislative power — U.S. — States. 2. State rights 3. U.S. — Constitutional law. I. T.
KF4600.C6 1972     342/.73/05     *LC* 78-87510     *ISBN* 0306714035

**Powell, Thomas Reed, 1880-1955.**        • **4.9647**
Vagaries and varieties in constitutional interpretation. — New York: AMS Press, 1967 [c1956] xv, 229 p.; 23 cm. Original ed. issued in series: James S. Carpentier lectures, 1955. 1. Federal government — United States. 2. Judicial review — United States. 3. United States — Constitutional law — Interpretation and construction. I. T.
KF4600.P68 1967     *LC* 72-187901

**Schmidhauser, John R. (John Richard), 1922-.**        • **4.9648**
The Supreme Court as final arbiter in Federal–State relations, 1789–1957. — Chapel Hill: University of North Carolina Press [1958] viii, 241 p.; 24 cm.

1. United States. Supreme Court. 2. Federal government — United States I. T.
KF4600.S3x     *LC* 58-3675

**United States. Domestic Policy Council. Working Group of**    **4.9649**
**Federalism.**
The status of federalism in America: a report. — Washington, D.C.: [The author], 1986. 86 p.; 28 cm. 1. Federal government — United States. 2. Local government — United States. 3. United States — Constitutional law I. T.
KF4600.U5x

**Wiecek, William M., 1938-.**            **4.9650**
The guarantee clause of the U.S. Constitution, by William M. Wiecek. — Ithaca: Cornell University Press, [1972] 324 p.; 22 cm. — (Cornell studies in civil liberty) 1. Federal government — U.S. 2. State governments 3. Civil rights — U.S. I. T.
KF4600.W55     342/.73/042     *LC* 73-162542     *ISBN* 0801406714

**Hunting, Warren Belknap, 1888-1918.**        • **4.9651**
The obligation of contracts clause of the United States Constitution, by Warren B. Hunting ... Baltimore, The Johns Hopkins press, 1919. x, 11-122 p. (Johns Hopkins University studies in historical and political science. Ser. 37, no. 4) 1. Contracts 2. United States — Constitutional law I. T. II. Series.
KF4608.Hx     *LC* 20-2056

**Wright, Benjamin Fletcher, 1900-.**        • **4.9652**
The contract clause of the Constitution / by Benjamin Fletcher Wright. — Cambridge: Harvard university press, 1938. xv, 287 p.; 23 cm. 1. Contracts — United States. 2. Corporations — Taxation — United States 3. United States — Constitutional law — Cases 4. United States. Supreme Court. I. T.
KF4608.W75     *LC* 39-4050

## KF4741–4788 CIVIL AND POLITICAL RIGHTS AND LIBERTIES

## KF4741–4750 General Works. The Bill of Rights

**Schwartz, Bernard, 1923- comp.**        • **4.9653**
Civil rights / Editor: Bernard Schwartz. — New York: Chelsea House Publishers, [1970] 2 v. (1888 p.); 24 cm. — (Statutory history of the United States) Consists of Federal legislation, extracts from congressional debates, major Supreme Court decisions, etc., with commentary by the compiler. 1. Civil rights — United States I. T. II. Series.
KF4743.8 1970     323.4/0973     *LC* 79-78410

**Schwartz, Bernard, 1923- comp.**        • **4.9654**
The Bill of Rights: a documentary history. New York, Chelsea House Publishers, 1971. 2 v. (xvii, 1234 p.) 24 cm. 1. United States — Constitutional law — Amendments — 1st-10th — Sources. I. T.
KF4744 1971     342/.73/029     *LC* 71-150209     *ISBN* 0070796130

**Emerson, Thomas Irwin, 1907-.**        • **4.9655**
Political and civil rights in the United States; a collection of legal and related materials [by] Thomas I. Emerson, David Haber [and] Norman Dorsen. — 3d ed. — Boston: Little, Brown, 1967. 2 v. (xxviii, 2274 p.); 25 cm. 1. Civil rights — U.S. 2. Civil rights — U.S. — Cases. 3. Political rights — U.S. 4. Political rights — U.S. — Cases. I. Haber, David. joint author. II. Dorsen, Norman. joint author. III. T.
KF4748.E5 1967     342.73/03     *LC* 67-12930

**Konvitz, Milton Ridvas, 1908- ed.**        **4.9656**
Bill of Rights reader; leading constitutional cases [edited by] Milton R. Konvitz. — 5th ed., rev. — Ithaca [N.Y.]: Cornell University Press, [1973] xviii, 747 p.; 25 cm. — (Cornell studies in civil liberty) 1. Civil rights — United States — Cases. I. T.
KF4748.K6 1973     342/.73/085     *LC* 73-8671     *ISBN* 0801407834

**The Supreme Court and individual rights / [editor, Elder Witt].**    **4.9657**
Washington, D.C.: Congressional Quarterly, c1980. 303 p., [1] leaf of plates: ill.; 28 cm. 'December 1979.' 1. United States. Supreme Court. 2. Civil rights — United States — Cases. I. Congressional Quarterly, inc.
KF4748.S9     342/.73/085     *LC* 79-26967     *ISBN* 0871871955

**Hugo Black Symposium in American History. 1st, University of**    **4.9658**
**Alabama, 1976.**
Hugo Black and the Bill of Rights: proceedings of the First Hugo Black Symposium in American History on 'The Bill of Rights and American Democracy' / edited by Virginia Van der Veer Hamilton. — University: Published for the University of Alabama in Birmingham by the University of Alabama Press, c1978. xvii, 104 p.; 22 cm. 1. Black, Hugo LaFayette,

1886-1971 — Congresses. 2. Civil rights — United States — Congresses. I. Hamilton, Virginia Van der Veer. II. T.
KF4749.A2 H8 1976    342/.73/085    LC 77-24689    ISBN 0817393099

**Our endangered rights: the ACLU report on civil liberties today**    **4.9659**
/ edited by Norman Dorsen.
1st ed. — New York: Pantheon Books, c1984. xvi, 333 p.; 24 cm. 1. Civil rights — United States — Addresses, essays, lectures. I. Dorsen, Norman. II. American Civil Liberties Union.
KF4749.A2 O93 1984    342.73/085 347.30285 19    LC 83-43146
   ISBN 0394722299

**The Rights of Americans: what they are—what they should be.**    **• 4.9660**
Edited by Norman Dorsen.
[1st ed.]. — New York: Pantheon Books, [1971, c1970] xxi, 679 p.; 25 cm. 'Essays commemorating the 50th anniversary of the American Civil Liberties Union.' 1. Civil rights — U.S. — Addresses, essays, lectures. I. Dorsen, Norman. ed. II. American Civil Liberties Union.
KF4749.A2R5 1971    323.4/0973    LC 72-128005    ISBN 0394467906

**Six justices on civil rights / edited and with an introduction by**    **4.9661**
Ronald D. Rotunda.
London; New York: Oceana Publications, c1983. 211 p., [1] leaf of plates: port.; 23 cm. — (David C. Baum memorial lectures; 2) 1. Civil rights — United States — Addresses, essays, lectures. I. Rotunda, Ronald D.
KF4749.A2.S69    LC 82-62327    ISBN 0379200449

**Abraham, Henry Julian, 1921-.**    **4.9662**
Freedom and the Court: civil rights and liberties in the United States / [by] Henry J. Abraham. — 2d ed. — New York: Oxford University Press, 1972. xii, 397 p.; 22 cm. 1. United States. Supreme Court. 2. Civil rights — United States I. T.
KF4749.A73 1972    342/.73/085    LC 75-177991    ISBN 0195015266

**Brigham, John, 1945-.**    **4.9663**
Civil liberties and American democracy / John Brigham. — Washington, D.C.: CQ Press, c1984. xiii, 300 p.; 23 cm. Includes indexes. 1. Civil rights — United States 2. United States — Constitutional law I. T.
KF4749.B73 1984    342.73/085 347.30285 19    LC 84-1869    ISBN 0871873036

**Casper, Jonathan D.**    **4.9664**
The politics of civil liberties / Jonathan D. Casper. — New York: Harper and Row, c1972. xi, 322 p. — (Harper's American political behavior series) 1. Civil rights — United States I. T.
KF4749.C33    LC 72-82899    ISBN 0060412135

**Cortner, Richard C.**    **4.9665**
The Supreme Court and the second Bill of Rights: the fourteenth amendment and the nationalization of civil liberties / Richard C. Cortner. — Madison: University of Wisconsin Press, 1981. xi, 360 p.; 24 cm. 1. United States. Constitution. 14th Amendment 2. United States. Supreme Court. 3. Due process of law — United States. 4. Civil rights — United States 5. United States — Constitutional law — Amendments — 1st-10th I. T.
KF4749.C66    342.73/085 19    LC 80-5112    ISBN 029908390X

**Douglas, William O. (William Orville), 1898-.**    **• 4.9666**
The right of the people / by William O. Douglas. — Garden City, N.Y.: Doubleday, 1958. 238 p.; 22 cm. 'This book is in substantial part the North lectures delivered at Franklin and Marshall College in the spring of 1957.' 1. Civil rights — United States 2. Civil supremacy over the military — United States. I. T.
KF4749.D64 1958

**Dumbauld, Edward, 1905-.**    **• 4.9667**
The Bill of rights and what it means today / by Edward Dumbauld. — Norman: University of Oklahoma Press, 1957. 242 p., [4] leaves of plates: ill. 1. United States. Constitution. 1st-10th amendments I. T.
KF4749.D85    LC 57-5954

**The Future of our liberties: perspectives on the Bill of Rights /**    **4.9668**
edited by Stephen C. Halpern.
Westport, Conn.: Greenwood Press, c1982. xvi, 251 p.; 22 cm. — (Contributions in legal studies. 0147-1074; no. 25) Includes index. 1. Civil rights — United States I. Halpern, Stephen C. II. Series.
KF4749.F87 1982    342.73/085 347.30285 19    LC 81-13430    ISBN 0313223661

**Hand, Learned, 1872-1961.**    **• 4.9669**
The Bill of rights. Cambridge: Harvard University Press, 1958. v, 82 p.; 22 cm. (The Oliver Wendell Holmes lectures, 1958) 1. Civil rights — United States I. T. II. Series.
KF4749.H36    342.73    LC 58-8248

**How does the Constitution secure rights? / Robert A. Goldwin**    **4.9670**
and William A. Schambra, editors.
Washington: American Enterprise Institute for Public Policy Research, c1985. xiv, 125 p.; 23 cm. (AEI studies. 380) 'Third in a series in AEI's project 'A Decade of study of the Constitution''—T.p. verso. Continues: How capitalistic is the Constitution? c1982. 1. Civil rights — United States 2. United States — Constitutional law — Amendments — 1st-10th I. Goldwin, Robert A. 1922- II. Schambra, William A. III. Series.
KF4749.H68 1985    342.73/085 347.30285 19    LC 85-4020    ISBN 0844735213

**Konvitz, Milton Ridvas, 1908-.**    **• 4.9671**
Expanding liberties: freedom's gains in postwar America / Milton R. Konvitz. — New York: Viking Press, 1966. xvii, 429 p.; 22 cm. 1. Civil rights — United States 2. Liberty — United States. I. T.
KF4749.K6    323.4/0973    LC 66-11354

**Mykkeltvedt, Roald Y., 1929-.**    **4.9672**
The nationalization of the Bill of Rights: Fourteenth Amendment due process and procedural rights / Roald Y. Mykkeltvedt. — Port Washington, N.Y.: Associated Faculty Press, 1983. xi, 167 p.; 24 cm. (National university publications) Includes index. 1. United States. Supreme Court. 2. Civil rights — United States 3. Due process of law — United States. 4. United States — Constitutional law — Amendments — 1st-10th I. T.
KF4749.M94 1983    342.73/085 347.30285 19    LC 83-829    ISBN 0804693064

**Neither conservative nor liberal: the Burger Court on civil**    **4.9673**
rights and liberties / edited by Francis Graham Lee.
Malabar, Fla.: R.E. Krieger Pub. Co., 1983. 136 p.; 23 cm. 1. Burger, Warren E., 1907- 2. United States. Supreme Court. 3. Civil rights — United States I. Lee, Francis Graham.
KF4749.N44 1983    342.73/085/02643 347.3028502643 19    LC 82-120    ISBN 0898744253

**Perry, Michael J.**    **4.9674**
The Constitution, the courts, and human rights: an inquiry into the legitimacy of constitutional policymaking by the judiciary / Michael J. Perry. — New Haven: Yale University Press, c1982. ix, 241 p.; 24 cm. 1. United States. Supreme Court. 2. Judicial review — United States. 3. Civil rights — United States 4. United States — Constitutional law — Interpretation and construction. I. T.
KF4749.P43 1982    342.73/085 347.30285 19    LC 82-40164    ISBN 0300027451

**Pritchett, C. Herman (Charles Herman), 1907-.**    **4.9675**
Constitutional civil liberties / C. Herman Pritchett. — Englewood Cliffs, N.J.: Prentice-Hall, c1984. x, 406 p.; 23 cm. 1. Civil rights — United States I. T.
KF4749.P74 1984    342.73/085 347.30285 19    LC 83-15940    ISBN 0131678582

**Pritchett, C. Herman (Charles Herman), 1907-.**    **• 4.9676**
Civil liberties and the Vinson Court. [Chicago] University of Chicago Press [1954] xi, 296 p. 24 cm. 1. United States. Supreme Court. 2. Civil rights — United States I. T.
LAW    KF4749.P7x.    323.4    LC 54-8459

**Thomas, William R.**    **4.9677**
The Burger Court and civil liberties / William R. Thomas. — Brunswick, Ohio: King's Court Communications, c1976. 159 p. 1. United States. Supreme Court. 2. Civil rights — United States I. T.
KF4749.T48    LC 76-3209    ISBN 089139012X

**Fraenkel, Osmond Kessler, 1888-.**    **4.9678**
The rights we have. 2d ed., rev. to include the most important decisions of the U. S. Supreme Court through 1973. New York, Crowell, c1974. 246 p. 21 cm. 1. Civil rights — United States — Popular works. I. T.
KF 4750 F82 1974    LC 74-5428    ISBN 0690005857

## KF4753–4757 Civil Rights of Particular Groups

**The Rights of gay people: the basic ACLU guide to a gay**    **4.9679**
person's rights / E. Carrington Boggan ... [et al.].
New York: Discus Books, 1975. xii, 268 p.; 18 cm. (An American Civil Liberties Union handbook) 1. Homosexuality — Law and legislation — United States. 2. Civil rights — United States I. Boggan, E. Carrington.
KF4754.5.Z9 R54 1975    342.73/087 347.30287 19    LC 75-13991    ISBN 0380003910

**Sickels, Robert J.**    **4.9680**
Race, marriage and the law [by] Robert J. Sickels. — Albuquerque: University of New Mexico Press, [1972] viii, 167 p.; 22 cm. 1. Miscegenation — United States. 2. Race discrimination — Law and legislation — United States. 3. Impediments to marriage — United States. I. T.
KF4755.S54    346/.73/016    LC 72-86815    ISBN 0826302564

### KF4756–4757 Afro–Americans

**Whalen, Charles W.**     4.9681
The longest debate: a legislative history of the 1964 Civil Rights Act / Charles and Barbara Whalen. — Cabin John, Md.; Washington, D.C.: Seven Locks Press, c1985. xx, 289 p.: ill.; 24 cm. Ill. on lining papers. Includes index. 1. United States. Civil Rights Act of 1964 2. Afro-Americans — Legal status, laws, etc. 3. Discrimination — United States. I. Whalen, Barbara, 1928- II. T.
KF4756.A315 A168 1985     342.73/0873 347.302873 19     LC 84-20218
    ISBN 0932020348

**Friedman, Leon. ed.**     • 4.9682
Southern justice. With a foreword by Mark DeW. Howe. New York, Pantheon Books [1965] xiii, 306 p. 22 cm. 1. Justice, Administration of — Southern States. 2. Afro-Americans — Legal status, laws, etc. 3. Civil rights — Southern States. I. T.
KF4757.A5 F7     323.4     LC 65-14581

**Barnes, Catherine A.**     4.9683
Journey from Jim Crow: the desegregation of southern transit / Catherine A. Barnes. — New York: Columbia University Press, 1983. xi, 313 p. — (Contemporary American history series.) Based on the author's thesis (Ph.D.)—Columbia University. Includes index. 1. Segregation in transportation — Law and legislation — Southern States — History. 2. Segregation in transportation — Southern States — History. I. T. II. Series.
KF4757.B33 1983     KF4757 B33 1983.     343.73/093 347.30393 19
    LC 83-7566     ISBN 0231053800

**Belz, Herman.**     4.9684
A new birth of freedom: the Republican Party and freedmen's rights, 1861 to 1866 / Herman Belz. — Westport, Conn.: Greenwood Press, 1976. xv, 199 p.; 22 cm. (Contributions in American history; no. 52) Includes index. 1. Republican Party (U.S.: 1854- ) — History. 2. Afro-Americans — Civil rights — History. I. T.
KF4757.B37     342/.73/085     LC 76-5257     ISBN 0837189020

**Berger, Morroe.**     • 4.9685
Equality by statute; the revolution in civil rights. — Rev. ed. — Garden City, N.Y.: Doubleday, 1967. viii, 253 p.; 22 cm. 1. Civil rights — United States 2. Discrimination — United States. I. T.
KF4757.B4 1967     342.73/03     LC 67-16897

**Higginbotham, A. Leon, 1928-.**     4.9686
In the matter of color: the colonial period / A. Leon Higginbotham, Jr. — New York: Oxford University Press, 1978. xxiii, 512 p., [4] leaves of plates: ill.; 24 cm. — (His Race and the American legal process) Includes index. 1. Afro-Americans — Legal status, laws, etc. — History. I. T. II. Series.
KF4757.H53     342/.73/087     LC 76-51713     ISBN 0195023870

**James, Joseph B. (Joseph Bliss), 1912-.**     4.9687
The ratification of the Fourteenth Amendment / Joseph B. James. — [Macon, Ga.]: Mercer University Press, c1984. viii, 331 p.; 24 cm. Includes index. 1. Civil rights — United States 2. Due process of law — United States. 3. United States — Constitutional law — Amendments — 14th 4. United States — Constitutional history I. T.
KF4757.J34 1984     342.73/085 347.30285 19     LC 83-26481     ISBN 0865540985

**Jones, Augustus J.**     4.9688
Law, bureaucracy, and politics: the implementation of Title VI of the Civil Rights Act of 1964 / Augustus J. Jones Jr. — Washington, D.C.: University Press of America, c1982. xv, 300 p.; 22 cm. Includes index. 1. Afro-Americans — Legal status, laws, etc. 2. Afro-Americans — Civil rights I. T.
KF4757.J65 1982     353.0081/1 19     LC 82-1852     ISBN 0819121541

**Miller, Loren.**     • 4.9689
The petitioners: the story of the Supreme Court of the United States and the Negro. — New York: Pantheon Books [1966] xv, 461 p.; 22 cm. 1. United States. Supreme Court. 2. Afro-Americans — Legal status, laws, etc. I. T.
KF4757.M5     342.73     LC 65-14582

**Nieman, Donald G.**     4.9690
To set the law in motion: the Freedmen's Bureau and the legal rights of Blacks, 1865–1868 / Donald G. Nieman. — Millwood, N.Y.: KTO Press, c1979. xvii, 250 p.; 24 cm. — (KTO studies in American history) Includes index. 1. United States. Bureau of Refugees, Freedmen, and Abandoned Lands. 2. Afro-Americans — Civil rights 3. Freedmen I. T. II. Series.
KF4757.N53     342/.73/087     LC 79-12536     ISBN 0527672351

**Wasby, Stephen L., 1937-.**     4.9691
Desegregation from Brown to Alexander: an exploration of Supreme Court strategies / by Stephen L. Wasby, Anthony A. D'Amato, and Rosemary Metrailer; with a foreword by Victor G. Rosenblum. — Carbondale: Southern Illinois University Press, c1977. xx, 489 p.; 24 cm. 1. United States. Supreme Court. 2. Afro-Americans — Civil rights I. D'Amato, Anthony A. joint author. II. Metrailer, Rosemary, 1944- joint author. III. T.
KF4757.W38     342/.73/08502643     LC 76-30792     ISBN 0809308053

**Kalven, Harry.**     • 4.9692
The Negro and the First amendment, by Harry Kalven, Jr. Columbus, Ohio State University Press, 1965. ix, 190 p. 21 cm. (Law forum series) 'Lectures ... originally given for the Ohio State Law Forum on April 7, 8, and 9, 1964.' 1. Afro-Americans — Civil rights 2. Freedom of speech — United States 3. Freedom of association — United States. I. T.
KF4757.Z9K3     323.40973     LC 65-63005

### KF4758–4764 Sex Discrimination. Race Discrimination

**Equal Rights Amendment Project.**     4.9693
The equal rights amendment: a bibliographic study / compiled by the Equal Rights Amendment Project; Anita Miller, project director; Hazel Greenberg, editor and compiler. — Westport, Conn.: Greenwood Press, 1976. xxvii, 367 p.; 24 cm. Includes indexes. 1. Equal rights amendments — United States — Bibliography. I. Miller, Anita, 1928- II. Greenberg, Hazel. III. T.
KF4758.A1 E6     016.342/73/0878 016.347302878 19     LC 76-24999
    ISBN 0837190584

**Hughes, Marija Matich.**     4.9694
The sexual barrier: legal, medical, economic, and social aspects of sex discrimination / Marija Matich Hughes. — [Enl. and rev. ed.]. — Washington: Hughes Press, c1977. xxi, 843 p.; 24 cm. Includes index. 1. Sex discrimination against women — Law and legislation — United States — Bibliography. 2. Women — Legal status, laws, etc. — Bibliography. 3. Women — Bibliography. I. T.
KF4758.A1 H83 1977     016.30141/2/0973     LC 77-83214     ISBN 0912560045

**Lee, Rex E., 1935-.**     4.9695
A lawyer looks at the Equal rights amendment / Rex E. Lee. — Provo, UT: Brigham Young University Press, c1980. xv, 141 p.; 23 cm. 1. Equal rights amendments — United States. I. T.
KF4758.L43     342.73/0878 19     LC 80-22202     ISBN 0842518835

**From the black bar: voices for equal justice / [edited by] Gilbert Ware.**     4.9696
New York: Putnam, c1976. xxxviii, 341 p.: ill.; 22 cm. (New perspectives on Black America) 1. Equality before the law — United States — Addresses, essays, lectures. 2. Afro-Americans — Legal status, laws, etc. — Addresses, essays, lectures. I. Ware, Gilbert. II. Series.
KF4764.A75 F76     340/.0973     LC 75-24957     ISBN 0399114637

**Baer, Judith A.**     4.9697
Equality under the constitution: reclaiming the Fourteenth Amendment / Judith A. Baer. — Ithaca: Cornell University Press, 1983. 308 p.; 24 cm. Includes indexes. 1. Equality before the law — United States 2. Civil rights — United States I. T.
KF4764.B33 1983     342.73/085 347.30285 19     LC 83-6220     ISBN 0801415551

**Pole, J. R. (Jack Richon)**     4.9698
The pursuit of equality in American history / J. R. Pole. — Berkeley: University of California Press, c1978. xv, 380 p.; 24 cm. (Jefferson memorial lectures) 1. Equality before the law — United States — History. 2. Civil rights — United States — History. 3. United States — Constitutional history I. T. II. Series.
KF4764.P64     323.4/0973     LC 76-20020     ISBN 0520032861

**Due process / edited by J. Roland Pennock and John W. Chapman.**     4.9699
New York: New York University Press, 1977. xxxiii, 362 p.; 22 cm. (Nomos; 18) 1. Due process of law — United States — Addresses, essays, lectures. 2. Due process of law — Addresses, essays, lectures. I. Pennock, J. Roland (James Roland), 1906- II. Chapman, John William, 1923- III. Series.
KF4765.A75 D8     347/.73     LC 76-40511     ISBN 0814765696

### KF4770–4783 Freedom of Expression

**Anastaplo, George, 1925-.**     4.9700
The constitutionalist; notes on the first amendment. Dallas, Southern Methodist University Press [1971] xiii, 826 p. 24 cm. 1. Freedom of speech — United States. 2. Freedom of the press — United States. 3. United States — Constitutional history I. T.
KF4770.A953     342/.73/085     LC 72-165793

## KF4772 Freedom of Speech (cont.)

**Berns, Walter, 1919-.**                                    **4.9701**
The First amendment and the future of American democracy / Walter Berns. — New York: Basic Books, c1976. xi, 266 p.; 22 cm. 1. Civil rights — United States 2. United States — Constitutional law — Amendments — 1st. I. T.
KF4770.B396    342/.73/085    *LC* 76-22593    *ISBN* 0465024106

**Canavan, Francis, 1917-.**                                 **4.9702**
Freedom of expression: purpose as limit / Francis Canavan. — Durham, N.C.: Carolina Academic Press and Claremont Institute for the Study of Statesmanship and Political Philosophy, c1984. xv, 181 p. — (Studies in statesmanship) 1. Freedom of speech — United States 2. Freedom of the press — United States I. T.
KF4770 C35 1984    *LC* 83-71826    *ISBN* 0898892695

**Ladenson, Robert F.**                                      **4.9703**
A philosophy of free expression and its constitutional applications / Robert F. Ladenson. — Totowa, N.J.: Rowman and Littlefield, c1983. x, 213 p.; 22 cm. — (Philosophy and society.) Includes index. 1. Freedom of speech — United States. I. T. II. Series.
KF4770.L3 1983    342.73/0853 347.302853 19    *LC* 82-18106
*ISBN* 0847667618

**Oboler, Eli M.**                                           **4.9704**
The fear of the word: censorship and sex, by Eli M. Oboler. — Metuchen, N.J.: Scarecrow Press, 1974. viii, 362 p.; 22 cm. 1. Censorship — United States. 2. Censorship 3. Obscenity (Law) — United States. 4. Obscenity (Law) I. T.
KF4770.O2    363.3/1/0973    *LC* 74-6492    *ISBN* 0810807246

**Van Alstyne, William W.**                                  **4.9705**
Interpretations of the First Amendment / William W. Van Alstyne. — Durham, N.C.: Duke University Press, 1984. x, 136 p.: ill.; 25 cm. — (Duke Press policy studies.) 1. Freedom of speech — United States. 2. Freedom of the press — United States. 3. Mass media — Law and legislation — United States. I. T. II. Series.
KF4770.V36 1984    342.73/085 347.30285 19    *LC* 84-4030    *ISBN* 0822305909

### KF4772 Freedom of Speech

**Downs, Donald Alexander.**                                 **4.9706**
Nazis in Skokie: freedom, community, and the First Amendment / Donald Alexander Downs. — Notre Dame, Ind.: University of Notre Dame Press, c1985. xii, 227 p.; 24 cm. (Notre Dame studies in law and contemporary issues. v. 1) Includes index. 1. National Socialist Party of America. 2. Freedom of speech — United States — Illinois — Skokie. 4. Jews — Illinois — Skokie. 5. Demonstrations — Illinois — Skokie. I. T. II. Series.
KF4772.D69 1985    322.4/4/097731 19    *LC* 84-40294    *ISBN* 0268009686

**Haiman, Franklyn Saul.**                                   **4.9707**
Speech and law in a free society / Franklyn S. Haiman. — Chicago: University of Chicago Press, 1981. x, 499 p.; 24 cm. 1. Freedom of speech — United States. I. T.
KF4772.H345    342.73/0853 347.302853 19    *LC* 81-7546    *ISBN* 0226312135

**Hamlin, David, 1945-.**                                    **4.9708**
The Nazi/Skokie conflict: a civil liberties battle / David Hamlin. — Boston: Beacon Press, 1981 (c1980). 184 p.; 21 cm. 1. National Socialist Party of America. 2. American Civil Liberties Union. 3. Freedom of speech — United States. 4. Assembly, Right of — United States. 5. Demonstrations — Illinois — Skokie. I. T.
KF4772.H36    342.73/085 19    *LC* 80-68165    *ISBN* 0807032301

**Neier, Aryeh, 1937-.**                                     **4.9709**
Defending my enemy: American Nazis, the Skokie case, and the risks of freedom / Aryeh Neier. — 1st ed. — New York: Dutton, c1979. 182 p.; 22 cm. Includes index. 1. National Socialist Party of America. 2. American Civil Liberties Union. 3. Freedom of speech — United States. 4. Assembly, Right of — United States. 5. Demonstrations — Illinois — Skokie. 6. Jews — United States — Politics and government. I. T.
KF4772.N43    323.4/0973    *LC* 78-10180    *ISBN* 0525089721

**Tedford, Thomas L.**                                       **4.9710**
Freedom of speech in the United States / Thomas L. Tedford. — 1st ed. — Carbondale: Southern Illinois University Press, 1985. xvii, 473 p.: ill.; 24 cm. 1. Freedom of speech — United States — History. I. T.
KF4772.T43 1985    323.44/3/0973 19    *LC* 84-27681    *ISBN* 0394332563

### KF4774–4775 Freedom of the Press. Freedom of Information

**Justice Hugo Black and the first amendment: "no law' means no law'** / edited by Everette E. Dennis, Donald M. Gillmor, David L. Grey.                                              **4.9711**
1st ed. — Ames: Iowa State University Press, 1978. vii, 204 p.; 24 cm. Includes indexes. 1. Black, Hugo LaFayette, 1886-1971 — Addresses, essays, lectures. 2. Freedom of speech — United States — Addresses, essays, lectures. 3. Freedom of the press — United States — Addresses, essays, lectures. I. Dennis, Everette E. II. Gillmor, Donald M. III. Grey, David L.
KF4774.A75 J8    342/.73/085    *LC* 78-685    *ISBN* 0813819059

**Levy, Leonard Williams, 1923- ed.**                        **• 4.9712**
Freedom of the press from Zenger to Jefferson: early American libertarian theories / edited by Leonard W. Levy. — Indianapolis: Bobbs-Merrill Co. [1966] lxxxiii, 409 p.; 21 cm. (The American Heritage series, 41) 1. Freedom of the press — United States — Collected works. I. T.
KF4774.A75L4    323.4450973    *LC* 66-14830

**Nelson, Harold L. ed.**                                    **• 4.9713**
Freedom of the press from Hamilton to the Warren Court, edited by Harold L. Nelson. Indianapolis, Bobbs-Merrill [1967] lxviii, 420 p. 21cm. (American heritage series, 74) 1. Freedom of the press — United States — Collected works. I. T.
KF4774.A75 N44    323.4450973    *LC* 66-22578

**Barron, Jerome A.**                                        **4.9714**
Freedom of the press for whom? the right of access to mass media [by] Jerome A. Barron. — Bloomington: Indiana University Press, [1973] xv, 368 p.; 22 cm. 1. Freedom of information — United States. I. T.
KF4774.B36    342/.73/085    *LC* 72-75387    *ISBN* 0253128404

**Barron, Jerome A.**                                        **4.9715**
Handbook of free speech and free press / Jerome A. Barron, C. Thomas Dienes. — Boston: Little, Brown, c1979. xvii, 756 p.; 24 cm. 1. Freedom of the press — United States. 2. Freedom of speech — United States. 3. Press law — United States. I. Dienes, C. Thomas. joint author. II. T.
KF4774.B37    342/.73/085    *LC* 79-83843

**Hachten, William A.**                                      **• 4.9716**
The Supreme Court on freedom of the press: decisions and dissents [by] William A. Hachten. [1st ed.] Ames, Iowa State University Press [1968] xxi, 316 p. 24 cm. Bibliography: p. 309-311. 1. Freedom of the press — United States. I. United States. Supreme Court. II. T.
KF4774.H3    323.44/5/0973    *LC* 68-17492

**Levy, Leonard Williams, 1923-.**                           **4.9717**
Emergence of a free press / Leonard W. Levy. — New York; Oxford: Oxford University Press, 1985. xxii, 383 p.; 25 cm. Rev. ed. of: Legacy of suppression. 1960. Includes index. 1. Freedom of the press — United States — History. 2. Freedom of speech — United States — History. I. Levy, Leonard Williams, 1923- Legacy of suppression. II. T.
KF4774.L48 1985    323.44/5 19    *LC* 84-20653    *ISBN* 0195035062

**Lofton, John.**                                            **4.9718**
The press as guardian of the first amendment / by John Lofton. — 1st ed. — Columbia, SC: University of South Carolina Press, c1980. xiv, 358 p.; 23 cm. Includes index. 1. Freedom of the press — United States — History. 2. Press law — United States — History. I. T.
KF4774.L64    342.73/0853    *LC* 80-10617    *ISBN* 087249389X

**Boyer, Paul S.**                                           **• 4.9719**
Purity in print; the vice–society movement and book censorship in America [by] Paul S. Boyer. — New York: Scribner, [1968] xxi, 362 p.: illus., facsims., ports.; 24 cm. 1. Censorship — United States — History. 2. Obscenity (Law) — United States. I. T.
KF4775.B6    323.44/5/0973    *LC* 68-17340

### KF4783 Freedom of Religion

**Pfeffer, Leo, 1910-.**                                     **4.9720**
Religion, state, and the Burger Court / by Leo Pfeffer. — Buffalo, N.Y.: Prometheus Books, c1984. xiv, 310 p.; 24 cm. Includes index. 1. United States. Supreme Court. 2. Freedom of religion — United States. I. T.
KF4783.P46 1984    342.73/0852 347.302852 19    *LC* 84-43056    *ISBN* 0879752750

### KF4850–4852 INTERNAL SECURITY

**Gellhorn, Walter, 1906-.**                                 **• 4.9721**
The States and subversion / edited by Walter Gellhorn. — Ithaca, Cornell University Press, 1952. vii, 454 p.; 23 cm. (Cornell studies in civil liberty)

Reprint of the ed. published by Cornell University Press, Ithaca, N.Y., in series: Cornell studies in civil liberty. 1. Subversive activities — United States — States. I. T.
KF4850.Z95 G4 1976　　342/.73/088　　LC 52-10508　　*ISBN* 0837181577

## KF4865–4869 Church and State

**Miller, Robert Thomas, 1920-.**　　　　　　　　　　　4.9722
Toward benevolent neutrality: Church, State, and the Supreme Court / by Robert T. Miller and Ronald B. Flowers. — Waco, Tex.: Markham Press Fund, Baylor University Press, c1977. xi, 601 p.; 24 cm. 1. Freedom of religion — United States — Cases. I. Flowers, Ronald B. (Ronald Bruce), 1935- II. T.
KF4865.A7 M54　　342.73/0852　　LC 77-85269　　*ISBN* 0918954207

**Sorauf, Frank J. (Frank Joseph), 1928-.**　　　　　　4.9723
The wall of separation: the constitutional politics of church and state / Frank J. Sorauf. — Princeton, N.J.: Princeton University Press, c1976. xiii, 394 p.; 25 cm. 1. Ecclesiastical law — United States. 2. Church and state — United States I. T.
KF4865.S6　　342/.73/085　　LC 75-3476　　*ISBN* 0691075743

## KF4881 Referendum

**Magleby, David B.**　　　　　　　　　　　　　　　4.9724
Direct legislation: voting on ballot propositions in the United States / David B. Magleby. — Baltimore: Johns Hopkins University Press, c1984. xi, 270 p.: ill.; 24 cm. Includes index. 1. Referendum — United States. I. T.
KF4881.M33 1984　　328/.2 19　　LC 83-22265　　*ISBN* 0801828449

## KF4885–4921 Election Law

**Neuborne, Burt, 1941-.**　　　　　　　　　　　　4.9725
The rights of candidates and voters: the basic ACLU guide for voters and candidates / Burt Neuborne, Arthur Eisenberg. — New York: Avon Books, c1976. 158 p.; 18 cm. — (An American Civil Liberties Union handbook) 'A Discus book.' 1. Election law — United States. 2. Suffrage — United States I. Eisenberg, Arthur. joint author. II. American Civil Liberties Union. III. T.
KF4886.N48　　342/.73/07　　LC 76-15915　　*ISBN* 038000626X

**Elliott, Ward E. Y.**　　　　　　　　　　　　　4.9726
The rise of guardian democracy; the Supreme Court's role in voting rights disputes, 1845–1969, [by] Ward E. Y. Elliott. — Cambridge: Harvard University Press, 1974. xiv, 391 p.; 25 cm. — (Harvard political studies) 1. United States. Supreme Court. 2. Suffrage — United States — History. I. T. II. Series.
KF4891.E43　　342/.73/07　　LC 73-90611　　*ISBN* 0674771567

**Ball, Howard, 1937-.**　　　　　　　　　　　　4.9727
Compromised compliance: implementation of the 1965 Voting Rights Act / Howard Ball, Dale Krane, and Thomas P. Lauth. — Westport, Conn.: Greenwood Press, 1982. xv, 300 p.; 22 cm. — (Contributions in political science. 0147-1066; no. 66) Includes index. 1. Afro-Americans — Suffrage 2. Voter registration — United States. I. Krane, Dale. II. Lauth, Thomas P. III. T. IV. Title: Voting Rights Act. V. Series.
KF4893.B35 1982　　342.73/072/0269 347.302720269 19　　LC 81-6342　　*ISBN* 0313220379

**Hamilton, Charles V.**　　　　　　　　　　　　4.9728
The bench and the ballot; southern Federal judges and Black voters [by] Charles V. Hamilton. New York, Oxford University Press, 1973. xii, 258 p. 22 cm. 1. Voter registration — Southern States. 2. Afro-Americans — Suffrage 3. Judges — Southern States. I. T.
KF4893.H34　　342/.75/07　　LC 73-82668　　*ISBN* 0195017188

**Gillette, William.**　　　　　　　　　　　　• 4.9729
The right to vote: politics and the passage of the Fifteenth amendment. — Baltimore: Johns Hopkins Press [1969] 206 p.: group port.; 21 cm. 1. United States — Constitutional law — Amendments — 15th I. T.
KF4893.Z9G5 1969　　342/.73/01　　LC 74-94492　　*ISBN* 0801802180

**Representation and redistricting issues / edited by Bernard**　4.9730
**Grofman ... [et al.].**
Lexington, Mass.: LexingtonBooks, D.C. Heath, c1982. xiv, 282 p.; 24 cm. — (Policy Studies Organization series.) 'The essays in this volume were initially presented at the 'Conference on Representation and Reapportionment Issues of the 1980s,' San Diego, California, June 11-15, 1980'—Pref. Includes indexes. 1. Apportionment (Election law) — United States — Congresses. 2. Election districts — United States — Congresses. I. Grofman, Bernard. II. Conference on Representation and Reapportionment Issues of the 1980s (1980: San Diego, Calif.) III. Series.
KF4905.A75 R43 1982　　342.73/053 347.30253 19　　LC 81-47689　　*ISBN* 066904718X

**Dixon, Robert Galloway, 1920-.**　　　　　　　• 4.9731
Democratic representation; reapportionment in law and politics [by] Robert G. Dixon, Jr. — New York: Oxford University Press, 1968. xviii, 654 p.; 24 cm. 1. Apportionment (Election law) — United States. I. T.
KF4905.D5　　328.73/07/3452　　LC 68-18563

**Durbin, Thomas M.**　　　　　　　　　　　　4.9732
Nomination and election of the President and Vice President of the United States, 1984: including the manner of selecting delegates to national political conventions / by Thomas M. Durbin for the Committee on Rules and Administration, United States Senate. — Washington: U.S. Govt. Print. Off., 1984. viii, 382 p.; 24 cm. — (S. prt.; 98-150) At head of title: 98th Congress, 1st session, Committee print. Distributed to some depository libraries in microfiche. 'February 1984.' Item 1046-B, 1046-C (microfiche) 1. Election law — United States. 2. Presidents — United States — Election 3. Vice-Presidents — United States — Election I. United States. Congress. Senate. Committee on Rules and Administration. II. T.
KF4910.D87 1984　　342.73/07 347.3027 19　　LC 84-602265

## KF4930–5005 Congress. Powers

**Willett, Edward F.**　　　　　　　　　　　　4.9733
How our laws are made / revised and updated by Edward F. Willett, Jr.; presented by Mr. Rodino. — Washington: U.S. G.P.O.: For sale by the Supt. of Docs., U.S. G.P.O., 1981. vi, 73 p.; 23 cm. (Document / 97th Congress, 1st session, House of Representatives; no. 97-120) 1. Legislation — United States I. Rodino, Peter W. II. T.
KF4945.Z9 W54 1981　　328.73/077 19　　LC 82-601774

## KF4958–4961 Impeachment

**Berger, Raoul.**　　　　　　　　　　　　　4.9734
Impeachment: the Constitutional problems / Raoul Berger. — Cambridge, Mass.: Harvard University Press, 1973. xii, 345 p. — (Studies in legal history) 1. Impeachments — United States. 2. Impeachments — Great Britain. I. T.
KF4958B46　　342.7305　　LC 73-75055　　*ISBN* 0674444752

**Hoffer, Peter C.**　　　　　　　　　　　　4.9735
Impeachment in America, 1635–1805 / Peter Charles Hoffer and N.E.H. Hull. — New Haven: Yale University Press, c1984. xiv, 325 p.; 25 cm. Includes index. 1. Impeachments — United States — History. I. Hull, N. E. H., 1949- II. T.
KF4958.H63 1984　　328.73/07453 19　　LC 83-19772　　*ISBN* 0300030533

**Redman, Eric.**　　　　　　　　　　　　　4.9736
The dance of legislation. — New York: Simon and Schuster, [1973] 319 p.; 22 cm. 1. United States. Congress. Senate. 2. Legislation — United States I. T.
KF4980.R4　　328.73/07/7　　LC 72-93515　　*ISBN* 0671214942

**Price, David Eugene.**　　　　　　　　　　4.9737
Who makes the laws?: creativity and power in Senate committees / [by] David E. Price. — Cambridge, Mass.: Schenkman Pub. Co.; distributed by General Learning Press [Morristown, N.J., c1972] x, 380 p.; 24 cm. 1. United States. Congress. Senate — Committees. 2. Legislation — United States I. T.
KF4986.P7　　328.73/07/7　　LC 72-81509

## KF5050–5125 Executive Branch. Presidency

**Corwin, Edward Samuel, 1878-1963.**　　　　4.9738
The President: office and powers, 1787–1984: history and analysis of practice and opinion / Edward S. Corwin. — 5th rev. ed. / by Randall W. Bland, Theodore T. Hindson, Jack W. Peltason. — New York: New York University Press, 1984. xxii, 565 p.; 24 cm. 1. Executive power — United States — History. 2. Presidents — United States — History. 3. United States — Politics and government I. Bland, Randall Walton. II. Hindson, Theodore T., 1942- III. Peltason, J. W. (Jack Walter), 1923- IV. T.
KF5051.C6 1984　　353.031 19　　LC 84-993　　*ISBN* 0814713904

**Friedman, Leon.**　　　　　　　　　　　　4.9739
Unquestioning obedience to the President; the ACLU case against the illegal war in Vietnam, by Leon Friedman and Burt Neuborne. Introd. by Senator George S. McGovern. — [1st ed.] — New York: Norton, [1972] 284 p.; 21 cm. 1. Berk, Malcolm A. 2. Orlando, Salvatore, 1948- 3. War and emergency powers — United States 4. Vietnamese Conflict, 1961-1975 — United States I. Neuborne, Burt, 1941- joint author. II. T.
KF5060.F7　　342/.73/062　　LC 76-169044　　*ISBN* 0393054624

**Marcus, Maeva, 1941-.**　　　　　　　　　4.9740
Truman and the steel seizure case: the limits of Presidential power / Maeva Marcus. — New York: Columbia University Press, 1977. xiv, 390 p.; 24 cm. (Contemporary American history series) Includes index. 1. Truman, Harry S., 1884-1972. 2. Sawyer, Charles, 1887- 3. Youngstown Sheet and Tube

Company. 4. War and emergency powers — United States 5. Steel industry and trade — Law and legislation — United States. I. T.
KF5060.M37     343.73/078669142 19    *LC* 77-4095     *ISBN* 0231041268

**Sofaer, Abraham D.**                             **4.9741**
War, foreign affairs, and constitutional power / by Abraham D. Sofaer. — Cambridge, Mass.: Ballinger Pub. Co., c1984. 413 p.: ill.; 24 cm. Vol. 2- by Henry Bartholomew Cox. 'A report of the American Bar Association Steering Committee on War, Foreign Affairs, and Constitutional Power'—V. 2, t.p. 1. War and emergency powers — United States — History. 2. Separation of powers — United States — History. 3. United States — Foreign relations — Law and legislation — History. I. Cox, Henry Bartholomew. II. American Bar Association. Steering Committee on War, Foreign Affairs, and Constitutional Power. III. T.
KF5060.S6     342.73/0412 347.302412 19     *LC* 76-15392     *ISBN* 088410222X

**Labovitz, John R., 1943-.**                           **4.9742**
Presidential impeachment / John R. Labovitz. — New Haven: Yale University Press, 1978. xiii, 268 p.; 22 cm. 1. Nixon, Richard M. (Richard Milhous), 1913- — Impeachment 2. Impeachments — United States. I. T.
KF5075.L33     353.03/6     *LC* 77-76300     *ISBN* 0300022131

**Navasky, Victor S.**                            • **4.9743**
Kennedy justice [by] Victor S. Navasky. — [1st ed.]. — New York: Atheneum, 1971. xx, 482 p.; 25 cm. 1. Kennedy, Robert F., 1925-1968. 2. U.S. Dept. of Justice. I. T.
KF5107.N34     353.5     *LC* 77-145633

## KF5130 The Judiciary

**Agresto, John.**                              **4.9744**
The Supreme Court and constitutional democracy / John Agresto. — Ithaca [N.Y.]: Cornell University Press, 1984. 182 p.; 23 cm. 1. United States. Supreme Court. 2. Judicial power — United States. 3. Judicial review — United States. 4. Separation of powers — United States. I. T.
KF5130.A93 1984     347.73/262 347.307352 19     *LC* 83-45928
    *ISBN* 080141623X

**Berger, Raoul, 1901-.**                           **4.9745**
Government by judiciary: the transformation of the fourteenth amendment / Raoul Berger. — Cambridge, Mass.: Harvard University Press, 1977. x, 483 p.; 25 cm. Includes indexes. 1. Judicial power — United States. 2. United States — Constitutional law — Amendments — 14th I. T.
KF5130.B4     347/.73/12     *LC* 77-6777     *ISBN* 0674357957

**Cahill, Fred V.**                              • **4.9746**
Judicial legislation: a study in American legal theory. — New York: Ronald Press Co. [1952] ix, 164 p.; 24 cm. 1. Judge-made law — United States 2. Judicial power — United States 3. Jurisprudence I. T.
KF5130.C3x     *LC* 52-7873

**Ellis, Richard E.**                             • **4.9747**
The Jeffersonian crisis; courts and politics in the young Republic [by] Richard E. Ellis. New York, Oxford University Press, 1971. xii, 377 p. 22 cm. 1. Political questions and judicial power — United States. I. T.
KF5130.E44     320.9/73/046     *LC* 70-141844

**Jaffe, Louis Leventhal.**                        • **4.9748**
English and American judges as lawmakers, by Louis L. Jaffe. — Oxford: Clarendon P., 1969. x, 116 p.; 21 cm. 1. U.S. Supreme Court. 2. Judge-made law — U.S. 3. Judge-made law — Gt. Brit. I. T.
KF5130.J3     347.9     *LC* 72-486082     *ISBN* 0198251939

**Neely, Richard, 1941-.**                          **4.9749**
How courts govern America / Richard Neely. — New Haven, Conn.: Yale University Press, c1981. xvii, 233 p.; 24 cm. Includes index. 1. Judicial power — United States. 2. Political questions and judicial power — United States. 3. Judge-made law — United States. I. T.
KF5130.N43 1981     347.73/1 347.3071 19     *LC* 81-1048     *ISBN* 0300025890

## KF5300 Local Government

**Zimmerman, Joseph Francis, 1928-.**             **4.9750**
State–local relations: a partnership approach / Joseph F. Zimmerman. — New York, NY: Praeger, 1983. viii, 240 p.; 24 cm. Includes index. 1. State-local relations — United States. 2. Intergovernmental fiscal relations — United States. I. T.
KF5300.Z53 1983     342.73/042 347.30242 19     *LC* 82-19004     *ISBN* 003063184X

## KF5399 Civil Service. Police

**Williams, Gregory Howard.**                   **4.9751**
The law and politics of police discretion / Gregory Howard Williams. — Westport, Conn.: Greenwood Press, 1984. xi, 218 p.; 22 cm. (Contributions in criminology and penology. 0732-4464; no. 4) Includes index. 1. Police discretion — United States. 2. Law enforcement — United States. I. T. II. Series.
KF5399.W56 1984     345.73/052 347.30552 19     *LC* 83-22741     *ISBN* 0313240701

# KF5401–5425 Administrative Organization and Procedure

**Davis, Kenneth Culp.**                         • **4.9752**
Administrative law treatise. St. Paul, West Pub. Co., 1958. 4 v. forms. 26 cm. —— Supplement. St. Paul, West Pub. Co., 1970. xxix, 1154 p. 26 cm. 1. Administrative law — United States. I. T.
KF 5402 D264 1958     *LC* 59-557

**Davis, Kenneth Culp.**                         • **4.9753**
Administrative law and government. St. Paul: West Pub. Co., 1960. xxiv, 547 p.; 24 cm. 1. Administrative law — United States. I. T.
KF5402.D3x     351.9     *LC* 60-4435

**Federal regulatory directory.**                    **4.9754**
1979/80-. [Washington]: Congressional Quarterly Inc. v. 24 cm. Annual. 'Comprehensive guide to all federal regulatory activities.' 1. Independent regulatory commissions — United States — Directories. 2. Administrative procedure — United States. 3. United States — Executive departments — Directories. I. Congressional Quarterly, inc.
KF5406.A15 F4     353/.00025     *LC* 79-644368

**Davis, Kenneth Culp.**                         • **4.9755**
Discretionary justice; a preliminary inquiry. — Baton Rouge: Louisiana State University Press, [1969] xii, 233 p.; 24 cm. 1. Administrative discretion — United States. 2. Judicial discretion — United States. I. T.
KF5407.D3     342.73/066 19     *LC* 69-12591

**Tolchin, Susan J.**                            **4.9756**
Dismantling America: the rush to deregulate / Susan J. Tolchin and Martin Tolchin. — Boston: Houghton Mifflin, 1983. x, 323 p.; 22 cm. Includes index. 1. Administrative procedure — United States. 2. Administrative agencies — United States. 3. Consumer protection — Law and legislation — United States. 4. Trade regulation — United States. 5. Law and politics I. Tolchin, Martin. II. T.
KF5407.T64 1983     342.73/066 347.30266 19     *LC* 83-10840     *ISBN* 0395344271

**Landis, James McCauley, 1899-1964.**            **4.9757**
The administrative process. — Westport, Conn.: Greenwood Press, [1974, c1938] xxi, 160 p.; 22 cm. Reprint of the ed. published by Yale University Press, New Haven, which was issued as Storrs lectures on jurisprudence, 1938. 1. Administrative procedure — United States. I. T.
KF5407.Z9 L35 1974     342/.73/066     *LC* 73-17952     *ISBN* 0837172845

# KF5500–5677 Public Property. Water Resources. Public Land

**Kutler, Stanley I.**                            • **4.9758**
Privilege and creative destruction: the Charles River Bridge case / Stanley I. Kutler. Philadelphia: Lippincott, c1971. 191 p.: map.; 21 cm. 1. Charles River Bridge (Boston, Mass.) 2. Warren Bridge (Boston, Mass.) I. T. II. Title: The Charles River Bridge case.
KF5541.C48 K8     346/.744/61044     *LC* 71-148245

**Water rights: scarce resource allocation, bureaucracy, and the**     **4.9759**
**environment** / editor, Terry L. Anderson; foreword by Jack Hirshleifer.
San Francisco, Calif.: Pacific Institute for Public Policy Research; Cambridge, Mass.: Ballinger Pub. Co., c1983. xxiii, 348 p.: ill.; 24 cm. — (Pacific studies in public policy.) 1. Water-rights — United States — Addresses, essays, lectures. I. Anderson, Terry Lee, 1946- II. Pacific Institute for Public Policy Research. III. Series.
KF5569.A2 W37 1983     346.7304/691 347.3064691 19     *LC* 83-3855     *ISBN* 0884103897

**Ducsik, Dennis W., 1946-.** 4.9760
Shoreline for the public: a handbook of social, economic, and legal considerations regarding public recreational use of the Nation's coastal shoreline / [by] Dennis W. Ducsik. — Cambridge, Mass.: MIT Press, [1974] xiii, 257 p.; 23 cm. — (Massachusetts Institute of Technology. Report no. MITSG 74-16) Photocopy of typescript. Index no. 74-616-Cdp. 1. Shore protection — Law and legislation — United States. 2. Outdoor recreation — United States. I. T.
KF5627.D8    346/.73/046917    *LC* 74-4528    *ISBN* 026204045X

# KF5691–5710 Planning. Zoning. Building

**Johnston, R. J. (Ronald John)** 4.9761
Residential segregation, the state, and constitutional conflict in American urban areas / R.J. Johnston. — London; Orlando: Academic Press, 1984. vii, 203 p.: ill.; 26 cm. (Institute of British Geographers special publication, 0073-9006; no. 17) 1. Zoning, Exclusionary — Law and legislation — United States. 2. Discrimination in housing — Law and legislation — United States. 3. Suburbs — United States I. T.
KF5698.J64 1984    305.5/0973 19    *LC* 83-72657    *ISBN* 0123876605

**International Conference of Building Officials.** 4.9762
Uniform building code. — Whittier, Calif.: International Conference of Building Officials, c1984. xxiii, 817 p.; 21 cm. Includes index. Title on spine: UBC 85 1. Building laws — United States. I. T. II. Title: UBC 85.
KF5701.I524 1984    343/.73/078    *LC* 84-62480

**Harman, Thomas L., 1942-.** 4.9763
Guide to the National electrical code / Thomas L. Harman, Charles E. Allen. — Englewood Cliffs, N.J.: Prentice-Hall, c1979. xii, 388 p.: ill.; 29 cm. Includes index. 1. Electric engineering — Law and legislation — United States. I. Allen, Charles E. joint author. II. National Fire Protection Association. National electrical code, 1978. III. T.
KF5704.H37    343/.73/078    *LC* 78-14476    *ISBN* 0133705102

# KF5750–5755 Government Property. Public Records

**O'Brien, David M.** 4.9764
The public's right to know: the Supreme Court and the First Amendment / David M. O'Brien. — New York, N.Y.: Praeger, c1981. x, 205 p.; 24 cm. Includes index. 1. Government information — United States. 2. Public records — Law and legislation — United States. I. T.
KF5753.O24    342.73/0853 19    *LC* 81-988    *ISBN* 0030580293

# KF6200–6795 Public Finance. Taxation

**Break, George F.** 4.9765
Federal tax reform, the impossible dream? / George F. Break and Joseph A. Pechman. — Washington: Brookings Institution, [1975] xiv, 142 p.: ill.; 24 cm. — (Studies of government finance.) Includes index. 1. Taxation — Law and legislation — United States. I. Pechman, Joseph A., 1918- joint author. II. T. III. Series.
KF6289.B74    336.2/00973    *LC* 75-22391    *ISBN* 0815710721

**United States. Internal Revenue Service.** • 4.9766
Your Federal income tax for individuals. 1943- ed. Washington. forms. 24-28 cm. (Publication - Internal Revenue Service) Annual. Issued 1954- as IRS publication. Title varies slightly. No issue for 1945? 1. Income tax — United States — Law and legislation I. T.
KF6369.Ax    336.242    *LC* 44-40552

**Surrey, Stanley S.** 4.9767
Pathways to tax reform: the concept of tax expenditures / [by] Stanley S. Surrey. — Cambridge: Harvard University Press, 1974 (c1973). xi, 418 p.; 25 cm. 1. Income tax — Law and legislation — United States. 2. Income tax — United States — Deductions. I. T.
KF6369.S9    336.2/4/0973    *LC* 73-87686    *ISBN* 0674657896

# KF7201–7755 National Defense. Military Law

**Rossiter, Clinton Lawrence, 1917-1970.** 4.9768
The Supreme Court and the Commander in Chief / by Clinton Rossiter. Expanded ed. / with an introductory note and additional text by Richard P. Longaker. — Ithaca, N.Y.: Cornell University Press, 1976. xxiii, 231 p.; 22 cm. 1. War and emergency powers — United States I. Longaker, Richard P. II. T.
KF7220.Z9 R6 1976    342/.73/062    *LC* 76-12815    *ISBN* 0801410525

**Irons, Peter H., 1940-.** 4.9769
Justice at war / Peter Irons. — New York: Oxford University Press, 1983. xiii, 407 p.; 24 cm. 1. Japanese Americans — Legal status, laws, etc. 2. Japanese Americans — Evacuation and relocation, 1942-1945 I. T.
KF7224.5.I76 1983    342.73/083 347.30283 19    *LC* 83-8190    *ISBN* 019503273X

**Schug, Willis E.** 4.9770
United States law and the Armed Forces; cases and materials on constitutional law, courts-martial, and the rights of servicemen. Edited by Willis E. Schug. — New York: Praeger, [1972] xi, 546 p.; 25 cm. — (Praeger special studies in U.S. economic and social development) 1. Military law — United States — Cases. 2. Courts-martial and courts of inquiry — United States — Cases. I. T.
KF7250.A7S3    343/.73/0143    *LC* 75-167623

# KF8201–8228 Indians

**U.S. Laws, statutes, etc.** 4.9771
Indian affairs. Laws and treaties. Compiled and edited by Charles J. Kappler. Washington, Govt. Print. Off., 1904–41. — [New York: AMS Press, 1971, i.e. 1972] 5 v.; 27 cm. Commonly known as the Kappler report. 1. Indians of North America — Legal status, laws, etc. 2. Indians of North America — Treaties I. Kappler, Charles Joseph, 1868-1946. II. U.S. Treaties, etc. III. T. IV. Title: Kappler report on Indian affairs.
KF8203 1972    342/.73/087    *LC* 78-128994    *ISBN* 0404067107

**Cohen, Felix S., 1907-1953.** 4.9772
[Handbook of federal Indian law] Felix S. Cohen's Handbook of federal Indian law. — 1982 ed. / board of authors and editors, Rennard Strickland, editor-in-chief ... [et al.]; contributing writers, Denis Binder ... [et al.]. — Charlottesville, Va.: Michie: Bobbs-Merrill, c1982. xxviii, 912 p.; 27 cm. Originally published as: Handbook of federal Indian law. 1942. 1. Indians of North America — Legal status, laws, etc. 2. Indians of North America — Treaties I. Strickland, Rennard. II. T. III. Title: Handbook of federal Indian law.
KF8205.C6 1982    342.73/0872 347.302872 19    *LC* 81-86229    *ISBN* 0872154130

**Prucha, Francis Paul. comp.** 4.9773
Documents of United States Indian policy / edited by Francis Paul Prucha. Lincoln: University of Nebraska Press, [1975] ix, 278 p.: 24 cm. Includes index. 1. Indians of North America — Legal status, laws, etc. 2. Indians of North America — Government relations — Sources. I. T.
KF8205.P78    016.3231/19/7073    *LC* 74-14081    *ISBN* 0803208529

**Washburn, Wilcomb E.** • 4.9774
Red man's land/white man's law: a study of the past and present status of the American Indian [by] Wilcomb E. Washburn. — New York: Scribner, [1971] viii, 280 p.: facsim.; 24 cm. 1. Indians of North America — Legal status, laws, etc. I. T.
KF8205.W38    342/.73/087    *LC* 70-143960    *ISBN* 0684124890

**Brodeur, Paul.** 4.9775
Restitution, the land claims of the Mashpee, Passamaquoddy, and Penobscot Indians of New England / by Paul Brodeur; afterword by Thomas N. Tureen. — Boston: Northeastern University Press, c1985. ix, 148 p.: ill.; 24 cm. 1. Mashpee Indians — Claims. 2. Mashpee Indians — Land tenure. 3. Passamaquoddy Indians — Claims. 4. Passamaquoddy Indians — Land tenure. 5. Penobscot Indians — Claims. 6. Penobscot Indians — Land tenure. 7. Indians of North America — New England — Claims. I. T.
KF8208.B76 1985    346.7304/3/08997 347.3064308997 19    *LC* 84-29635    *ISBN* 0930350693

**The Great Sioux nation: sitting in judgement on America: based** 4.9776
**on and containing testimony heard at the 'Sioux treaty hearing'**
**held December, 1974, in Federal District Court, Lincoln,**
**Nebraska / Roxanne Dunbar Ortiz; introd. by Vine Deloria,**
**Jr.; [photos., Michelle Vignes, Melinda Rorick].**
1st ed. — New York: American Indian Treaty Council Information Center: distributed by Random House, c1977. 224 p.: ill.; 28 cm. 'Fort Laramie treaty of 1868': p. 94-99. 1. Dakota Indians — Treaties, 1868. 2. Dakota Indians 3. Dakota Indians — History. 4. Dakota Indians — Government relations 5. Indians of North America — Government relations I. Ortiz, Roxanne

Dunbar. II. United States. District Court. Nebraska. Transcript of the trial on the motion to dismiss for want of jurisdiction. III. United States. Treaties, etc., 1865-1869 (Johnson) Treaty between the United States of America and different tribes of Sioux Indians. 1977.
KF8228.D1 G7     342/.782/087     *LC* 77-78717     *ISBN* 0394422996

# KF8700–9075 Courts. Procedure

**Klein, Fannie J.**        **4.9777**
The administration of justice in the courts: a selected annotated bibliography / compiled and annotated by Fannie J. Klein. Dobbs Ferry, N.Y.: Published for the Institute of Judicial Administration and National Center for State Courts by Oceana Publications, 1976. 2 v. (lx, 1152 p.); 24 cm. Updates and expands the author's Judicial administration and the legal profession. Includes indexes. 1. Justice, Administration of — United States — Bibliography. 2. Courts — United States — Bibliography. I. T.
KF8700.A1 K39     016.347/73/1     *LC* 76-2627     *ISBN* 0379101378

**Courts, judges, and politics: an introduction to the judicial**     **4.9778**
**process** / [edited by] Walter F. Murphy, C. Herman Pritchett.
4th ed. — New York: Random House, c1986. xiv, 657 p.; 24 cm. 1. Judicial process — United States. 2. Law and politics I. Murphy, Walter F., 1929- II. Pritchett, C. Herman (Charles Herman), 1907-
KF8700.A7 C67 1986     347.73/1 347.3071 19     *LC* 85-14404     *ISBN* 0394347404

**Karlen, Delmar.**        • **4.9779**
The citizen in court: litigant, witness, juror, judge. — New York: Holt, Rinehart and Winston [1964] viii, 211 p.; 21 cm. Bibliography: p. 203-205. 1. Courts — United States — Popular works. 2. Procedure (Law) — United States — Popular works. I. T.
KF8700.Z9 K3x     347.90973     *LC* 64-18754

**Guice, John D. W.**        **4.9780**
The Rocky Mountain bench; the territorial supreme courts of Colorado, Montana, and Wyoming, 1861–1890, by John D. W. Guice. — New Haven: Yale University Press, 1972. xi, 222 p.; 23 cm. — (Yale Western Americana series. 23) 1. Colorado (Ter.) Supreme Court. 2. Montana (Ter.) Supreme Court. 3. Wyoming (Ter.) Supreme Court. I. T. II. Series.
KF8736.G8     347/.78/035     *LC* 72-75195     *ISBN* 0300014791

## KF8741–8748 SUPREME COURT

## KF8741–8742 History

**Stephenson, D. Grier.**        **4.9781**
The Supreme Court and the American Republic: an annotated bibliography / D. Grier Stephenson, Jr. — New York: Garland Pub., 1981. xiv, 281 p.; 23 cm. — (Garland reference library of social science; vol. 85) Includes indexes. 1. United States. Supreme Court — Bibliography. I. T.
KF8741.A1 S75 1981     016.34773/26 016.34730735 19     *LC* 80-8978
    *ISBN* 0824093569

**Blaustein, Albert P., 1921-.**        **4.9782**
The first one hundred justices: statistical studies on the Supreme Court of the United States / by Albert P. Blaustein and Roy M. Mersky. — Hamden, Conn.: Archon Books, 1978. 210 p.; 24 cm. Includes index. 1. United States. Supreme Court — Statistics. 2. Judges — United States — Biography. I. Mersky, Roy M. joint author. II. T.
KF8741.A152 B6     347/.73/2634     *LC* 77-23543     *ISBN* 0208012907

**History of the Supreme Court of the United States.**     **4.9783**
[New York, Macmillan, 1971- < 84 > v. < 1, 2, 5, 6, pt. 1; 9 > illus. 24 cm. At head of title: The Oliver Wendell Holmes Devise. 1. United States. Supreme Court — History. I. United States. Permanent Committee for the Oliver Wendell Holmes Devise.
KF8742.A45H55     347.73/26/09 347.3073509 19     *LC* 78-30454
    *ISBN* 0025413600

**Swisher, Carl Brent, 1897-1968.**        **4.9784**
The Taney period, 1836–64. New York, Macmillan [1974] xvii, 1041 p. illus. 24 cm. (History of the Supreme Court of the United States. v. 5) 1. United States. Supreme Court — History — 19th century. I. T. II. Series.
KF8742.A45 H55 vol. 5     347/.73/26     *LC* 72-93318     *ISBN* 0025413805

**Garraty, John Arthur, 1920- ed.**        • **4.9785**
Quarrels that have shaped the Constitution, edited by John A. Garraty. [1st ed.] New York, Harper & Row [1964] x, 276 p. 22 cm. 1. United States. Supreme Court — History. 2. United States — Constitutional history I. T.
KF8742.A5G3     342.73 347.302 19     *LC* 64-18054

**Supreme Court activism and restraint / edited by Stephen C.**     **4.9786**
**Halpern, Charles M. Lamb.**
Lexington, Mass.: Lexington Books, c1982. xi, 436 p.: ill.; 24 cm. 1. United States. Supreme Court — Addresses, essays, lectures. 2. Judicial process — United States — Addresses, essays, lectures. I. Halpern, Stephen C. II. Lamb, Charles M.
KF8742.A5 S86 1982     347.73/26 347.30735 19     *LC* 81-47764
    *ISBN* 0669048550

**Abraham, Henry Julian, 1921-.**        **4.9787**
Justices and Presidents: a political history of appointments to the Supreme Court / [by] Henry J. Abraham. — New York: Oxford University Press, 1974. ix, 310 p.; 22 cm. 1. United States. Supreme Court — History. I. T.
KF8742.A72     347/.73/2634     *LC* 73-90341

**Baum, Lawrence.**        **4.9788**
The Supreme Court / Lawrence Baum; [cover design, Richard Pottern, cover ill. George Rebh. — Washington, D.C.: Congressional Quarterly Press, c1981. xii, 248 p.: ill.; 23 cm. — (Politics and public policy series) Includes indexes. 1. United States. Supreme Court. I. T.
KF8742.B35     347.73/26 347.30735 19     *LC* 80-607841     *ISBN* 0871871602

**Berry, Mary Frances.**        **4.9789**
Stability, security, and continuity: Mr. Justice Burton and decision–making in the Supreme Court, 1945–1958 / Mary Frances Berry. — Westport, Conn.: Greenwood Press, 1978. viii, 286 p.: ill.; 22 cm. — (Contributions in legal studies; no. 1 0147-1074) Includes index. 1. Burton, Harold Hitz, 1888-1964. 2. United States. Supreme Court — History — 20th century. 3. Judicial process — United States. I. T. II. Series.
KF8742.B47     347/.73/2634 B     *LC* 77-84772     *ISBN* 0837197988

**Kutler, Stanley I.**        • **4.9790**
Judicial power and Reconstruction politics [by] Stanley I. Kutler. — Chicago: University of Chicago Press, [1968] ix, 178 p.: port.; 23 cm. 1. United States. Supreme Court — History — 19th century. 2. United States — Politics and government — 1865-1883 I. T.
KF8742.K8     347.99/73     *LC* 68-16702

**Rohde, David W.**        **4.9791**
Supreme Court decision making / David W. Rohde and Harold J. Spaeth. — San Francisco: W. H. Freeman, c1976. xvii, 229 p.: ill.; 25 cm. 1. United States. Supreme Court. 2. Judicial process — United States — Research. I. Spaeth, Harold J. joint author. II. T.
KF8742.R63     347/.73/265     *LC* 75-25645     *ISBN* 0716707179

**Schwartz, Bernard, 1923-.**        **4.9792**
Inside the Warren court / Bernard Schwartz with Stephan Lesher. — 1st ed. — Garden City, N.Y.: Doubleday, 1983. 299 p.; 22 cm. Includes index. 1. United States. Supreme Court — History. I. Lesher, Stephan. II. T.
KF8742.S33 1983     347.73/26/09 347.3073509 19     *LC* 83-1980
    *ISBN* 0385183267

**Semonche, John E., 1933-.**        **4.9793**
Charting the future: the Supreme Court responds to a changing society, 1890–1920 / John E. Semonche. — Westport, Conn.: Greenwood Press, 1978. xiii, 470 p.; 25 cm. — (Contributions in legal studies. no. 5 0147-1074) Includes index. 1. United States. Supreme Court — History. I. T. II. Series.
KF8742.S44     347/.73/2609     *LC* 77-94745     *ISBN* 0313203148

**Steamer, Robert J.**        **4.9794**
The Supreme Court in crisis; a history of conflict [by] Robert J. Steamer. — [Amherst]: University of Massachusetts Press, 1971. viii, 333 p.; 24 cm. 1. U.S. Supreme Court — History. I. T.
KF8742.S74     347/.73/262     *LC* 74-123544

**Wasby, Stephen L., 1937-.**        **4.9795**
The Supreme Court in the Federal judicial system / Stephen L. Wasby. — New York: Holt, Rinehart and Winston, c1978. x, 262 p.; 24 cm. Includes index. 1. United States. Supreme Court. 2. Courts — United States I. T.
KF8742.W38     347/.73/26     *LC* 74-30706     *ISBN* 0030304261

## KF8744–8745 Biography

### KF8744 COLLECTIVE BIOGRAPHY OF JUSTICES

**Dawson, Nelson L.**    **4.9796**
Louis D. Brandeis, Felix Frankfurter, and the New Deal / by Nelson Lloyd Dawson. — Hamden, Conn.: Archon Books, 1980. viii, 272 p.; 23 cm. Includes index. 1. Brandeis, Louis Dembitz, 1856-1941. 2. Frankfurter, Felix, 1882-1965. 3. Law — United States — History and criticism 4. Judges — United States — Biography. 5. New Deal, 1933-1939 6. United States — Politics and government — 1933-1945 I. T.
KF8744.D38    973.917/092/2    *LC* 80-18409    *ISBN* 0208018174

**Friedman, Leon. comp.**    • **4.9797**
The justices of the United States Supreme Court, 1789–1969: their lives and major opinions / Leon Friedman & Fred L. Israel, editors; with an introd. by Louis H. Pollak. — New York: Chelsea House in association with Bowker, 1969. 4 v. (xxiv, 3373 p.); 25 cm. 1. United States. Supreme Court — Biography. I. Israel, Fred L. joint comp. II. T.
KF8744.F75    347.99/22    *LC* 69-13699    *ISBN* 0835202178

**Murphy, Bruce Allen.**    **4.9798**
The Brandeis/Frankfurter connection: the secret political activities of two Supreme Court justices / Bruce Allen Murphy. — New York: Oxford University Press, 1982. x, 473 p.; 24 cm. Includes index. 1. Brandeis, Louis Dembitz, 1856-1941. 2. Frankfurter, Felix, 1882-1965. 3. Judges — United States. 4. Law — United States — History and criticism I. T.
KF8744.M87    347.73/2634 347.3073534 19    *LC* 82-2104    *ISBN* 0195031229

**Silverstein, Mark, 1947-.**    **4.9799**
Constitutional faiths: Felix Frankfurter, Hugo Black, and the process of judicial decision making / Mark Silverstein. — Ithaca: Cornell University Press, 1984. 234 p.; 24 cm. Includes indexes. 1. Frankfurter, Felix, 1882-1965. 2. Black, Hugo LaFayette, 1886-1971. 3. Judges — United States — Biography. 4. Political questions and judicial power — United States. 5. Judicial process — United States. I. T.
KF8744.S56 1984    347.73/2634 B 347.3073534 B 19    *LC* 83-45946    *ISBN* 0801416507

**White, G. Edward.**    **4.9800**
The American judicial tradition: profiles of leading American judges / G. Edward White. New York: Oxford University Press, 1976. x, 441 p.; 24 cm. Includes index. 1. United States. Supreme Court — History. 2. Judges — United States — Biography. I. T.
KF8744.W5    347/.73/2634 B    *LC* 75-32356    *ISBN* 0195020170

### KF8745 INDIVIDUAL JUSTICES, A–Z

### KF8745 A–G

**Dunne, Gerald T.**    **4.9801**
Hugo Black and the judicial revolution / by Gerald T. Dunne. New York: Simon and Schuster, c1977. 492 p., [8] leaves of plates: ill.; 22 cm. Includes index. 1. Black, Hugo LaFayette, 1886-1971. 2. Judges — United States — Biography. I. T.
KF8745.B55 D86    347/.73/2634 B    *LC* 76-44363    *ISBN* 0671223410

**Hamilton, Virginia Van der Veer.**    **4.9802**
Hugo Black; the Alabama years. — Baton Rouge: Louisiana State University Press, [1972] ix, 330 p.: illus.; 24 cm. 1. Black, Hugo LaFayette, 1886-1971. I. T.
KF8745.B55 H34    347/.73/2634 B    *LC* 75-181566    *ISBN* 0807100447

**Magee, James J.**    **4.9803**
Mr. Justice Black, absolutist on the Court / James J. Magee. — Charlottesville: University Press of Virginia, 1980. xv, 214 p.; 24 cm. — (Virginia legal studies.) Includes indexes. 1. Black, Hugo LaFayette, 1886-1971. 2. Judges — United States — Biography. I. T. II. Series.
KF8745.B55 M33    347/.73/2634 B    *LC* 79-11555    *ISBN* 0813907845

**Paper, Lewis J.**    **4.9804**
Brandeis / Lewis J. Paper. — Englewood Cliffs, N.J.: Prentice-Hall, c1983. 442 p., [12] p. of plates: ill.; 24 cm. 1. Brandeis, Louis Dembitz, 1856-1941. 2. Judges — United States — Biography. I. T.
KF8745.B67 P36 1983    347.73/2634 B 347.3073534 B 19    *LC* 83-3020    *ISBN* 0130812994

**Strum, Philippa.**    **4.9805**
Louis D. Brandeis: justice for the people / Philippa Strum. — Cambridge, Mass.: Harvard University Press, 1984. xv, 508 p., [8] p. of plates: ports.; 24 cm. Includes index. 1. Brandeis, Louis Dembitz, 1856-1941. 2. Judges — United States — Biography. I. T.
KF8745.B67 S78 1984    347.73/2634 B 347.3073534 B 19    *LC* 83-18653    *ISBN* 0674539214

**Urofsky, Melvin I.**    **4.9806**
Louis D. Brandeis and the progressive tradition / Melvin I. Urofsky; edited by Oscar Handlin. — Boston: Little, Brown, c1981. 183 p.; 21 cm. — (Library of American biography.) Includes index. 1. Brandeis, Louis Dembitz, 1856-1941. 2. Judges — United States — Biography. I. Handlin, Oscar, 1915- II. T. III. Series.
KF8745.B67 U75    347.73/2634 B 347.3073534 B 19    *LC* 80-81814    *ISBN* 0316887870

**Danelski, David Joseph, 1930-.**    • **4.9807**
A Supreme Court Justice is appointed / [by] David J. Danelski. — New York: Random House [1964] x, 242 p.: ill.; 21 cm. (Random House studies in political science, PS46) Bibliography: p. [229]-236. 1. Butler, Pierce, 1866-1939. 2. United States. Supreme Court. I. T.
KF8745.B8D3    347.9973    *LC* 64-22706

**Douglas, William O. (William Orville), 1898-.**    **4.9808**
Go East, young man: the early years; the autobiography of William O. Douglas. [1st ed.] New York, Random House [1974] xv, 493 p. illus. 24 cm. 1. Douglas, William O. (William Orville), 1898- I. T.
KF8745.D6 A3    347/.73/2634 B    *LC* 73-5025    *ISBN* 0394488342

**Countryman, Vern.**    **4.9809**
The judicial record of Justice William O. Douglas / Vern Countryman. — Cambridge: Harvard University Press, 1974. viii, 418 p.; 25 cm. 1. Douglas, William O. (William Orville), 1898- 2. United States. Supreme Court — History. I. T.
KF8745.D6 C68    347/.73/2634    *LC* 74-76655    *ISBN* 0674488768

**Duram, James C., 1939-.**    **4.9810**
Justice William O. Douglas / by James C. Duram. — Boston: Twayne Publishers, 1981. 159 p.: port.; 21 cm. — (Twayne's United States authors series. TUSAS 405) Includes index. 1. Douglas, William O. (William Orville), 1898- 2. Judges — United States — Biography. I. T. II. Series.
KF8745.D6 D87    347.73/2634 B 347.3073534 B 19    *LC* 81-2926    *ISBN* 0805773347

**Swisher, Carl Brent, 1897-1968.**    • **4.9811**
Stephen J. Field, craftsman of the law. Hamden, Conn., Archon Books, 1963 [c1930] 473 p. illus. 22 cm. 1. Field, Stephen Johnson, 1816-1899. I. T.
KF8745.F5 S9x    923.473    *LC* 63-16037

**Shogan, Robert.**    **4.9812**
A question of judgment; the Fortas case and the struggle for the Supreme Court. — Indianapolis: Bobbs-Merrill, [1972] x, 314 p.; 24 cm. 1. Fortas, Abe. 2. United States. Supreme Court. I. T.
KF8745.F65 S5    347/.73/2634    *LC* 74-173224

**Frankfurter, Felix, 1882-1965.**    **4.9813**
From the diaries of Felix Frankfurter: with a biographical essay and notes / by Joseph P. Lash; assisted by Jonathan Lash. — 1st ed. — New York: Norton, [1975] xiii, 366 p.; 24 cm. 1. Frankfurter, Felix, 1882-1965. 2. Judges — United States — Correspondence, reminiscences, etc. I. Lash, Joseph P., 1909- II. T.
KF8745.F7 A33    347/.73/2634 B    *LC* 75-8675    *ISBN* 0393074889

**Frankfurter, Felix, 1882-1965.**    • **4.9814**
Felix Frankfurter reminisces, recorded in talks with Harlan B. Phillips. New York, Reynal [1960] 310 p. 1. Lawyers — United States — Correspondence, reminiscences, etc. 2. Judges — United States — Correspondence, reminiscences, etc. I. Phillips, Harlan Buddington, 1920- II. T.
KF8745.F7A3x    *LC* 60-9777

**Hirsch, H. N.**    **4.9815**
The enigma of Felix Frankfurter / H. N. Hirsch. — New York: Basic Books, c1981. x, 253 p.; 24 cm. 1. Frankfurter, Felix, 1882-1965. 2. Judges — United States — Biography. I. T.
KF8745.F7 H57    347.73/2634 B 19    *LC* 80-61884    *ISBN* 046501979X

**Parrish, Michael E.**    **4.9816**
Felix Frankfurter and his times: the reform years / Michael E. Parrish. — New York: Free Press; London: Collier Macmillan, c1982. vi, 330 p., [8] p. of plates. 1. Frankfurter, Felix. 2. Judges — United States — Biography. I. T.
KF8745.F7 P37 1982    347.73/2634 B 347.3073534 B 19    *LC* 81-69263    *ISBN* 0029237408

## KF8745 H–R

**Bowen, Catherine Drinker, 1897-1973.**                • **4.9817**
Yankee from Olympus; Justice Holmes and his family [by] Catherine Drinker
Bowen ... — Boston: Little, Brown and company, 1944. xvii p., 2 l., [3]-475 p.:
incl. illus. (facsim.), geneal. tables., front., ports.; 22 cm. 'An Atlantic monthly
press book.' 'Published April 1944, reprinted April 1944 (three times)'
1. Holmes, Oliver Wendell, 1841-1935. I. T.
KF8745.H6 B65 1944        923.473        *LC* 44-3384

**Howe, Mark De Wolfe, 1906-.**                • **4.9818**
Justice Oliver Wendell Holmes / by Mark De Wolfe Howe. — Cambridge,
Massachusetts: Belknap Press of Harvard University Press, 1957-. v.: ill., ports.;
24 cm. 1. Holmes, Oliver Wendell, 1841-1935 — Biography. 2. Judges —
United States — Biography. I. T.
KF8745.H6 H68        PS1981.H6.        923.473        *LC* 57-6348

**Holmes, Oliver Wendell, 1841-1935.**                **4.9819**
Holmes–Pollock letters: the correspondence of Mr. Justice Holmes and Sir
Frederick Pollock, 1874–1932. Edited by Mark De Wolfe Howe with an introd.
by John Gorham Palfrey. Cambridge, Mass., Harvard University Press, 1946
[c1941] 2 v. in 1. ports. 24 cm. 1. Pollock, Frederick, Sir, 1845-1937. 2. Law
3. Judges — United States — Correspondence. I. Howe, Mark De Wolfe,
1906-1967. II. T.
KF 8745 H75 P77 1946        KF8745.H6x.        *LC* 47-2890

**Holmes, Oliver Wendell, 1841-1935.**                • **4.9820**
Holmes–Laski letters: the correspondence of Mr. Justice Holmes and Harold J.
Laski, 1916–1935 / edited by Mark De Wolfe Howe; with a foreword by Felix
Frankfurter. — Cambridge: Harvard University Press, 1953. 2 v. (xvi, 1650 p.):
ports., facsims.; 22 cm. 1. Laski, Harold Joseph, 1893-1950. 2. Holmes, Oliver
Wendell, 1841-1935. 3. Judges — United States — Correspondence. I. Laski,
Harold Joseph, 1893-1950. II. Howe, Mark De Wolfe, 1906-1967. III. T.
KF 8745 H75 H85 1953        *LC* 52-8216

**Baker, Leonard.**                **4.9821**
John Marshall: a life in law. — New York: Macmillan, [1974] x, 845 p.: illus.;
24 cm. 1. Marshall, John, 1755-1835. I. T.
KF8745.M3 B3        347/.73/2634 B        *LC* 73-2751        *ISBN* 002506360X

**Faulkner, Robert Kenneth.**                • **4.9822**
The jurisprudence of John Marshall. — Princeton, N.J.: Princeton University
Press, 1968. xxi, 307 p.; 23 cm. 1. Marshall, John, 1755-1835. I. T.
KF8745.M3 F3        347.99/24        *LC* 67-21022

**Bland, Randall Walton.**                **4.9823**
Private pressure on public law; the legal career of Justice Thurgood Marshall
[by] Randall W. Bland. — Port Washington, N.Y.: Kennikat Press, 1973. xi,
206 p.: ports.; 24 cm. — (Kennikat Press national university publications. Series
in American studies) A revision of the author's thesis, University of Notre
Dame. 1. Marshall, Thurgood, 1908- I. T.
KF8745 M34 B55        347/.73/2634 B        *LC* 72-91170        *ISBN*
0804690359

**Fairman, Charles, 1897-.**                • **4.9824**
Mr. Justice Miller and the Supreme Court, 1862–1890. New York, Russell &
Russell [1966, c1939] vii, 456 p. illus., ports. 22 cm. 'Table of cases cited or
referred to in text and notes': p. 433-441. Bibliographical footnotes. 1. Miller,
Samuel Freeman, 1816-1890. 2. United States. Supreme Court. 3. United
States — Constitutional law — Cases I. T.
KF8745.M54F3        347.9720973 (B)        *LC* 66-24688

**Fine, Sidney, 1920-.**                **4.9825**
Frank Murphy / by Sidney Fine. — Ann Arbor: University of Michigan Press,
c1975-c1984. 3 v.: ill.; 24 cm. Vol. 2 published by the University of Chicago
Press, Chicago. 1. Murphy, Frank, 1890-1949. 2. Judges — United States —
Biography. I. T.
KF8745.M8 F49        347/.73/2634 B 347.3073534 B 19        *LC* 74-25945
        *ISBN* 0472329499

**Howard, J. Woodford.**                • **4.9826**
Mr. Justice Murphy: a political biography / by J. Woodford Howard, Jr. —
Princeton, N.J.: Princeton University Press, 1968. x, 578 p.: ill., ports.; 25 cm.
1. Murphy, Frank, 1890-1949. I. T.
KF8745.M8 H6        347.99/73 B        *LC* 68-11444

## KF8745 S–Z

**Mason, Alpheus Thomas, 1899-.**                • **4.9827**
Harlan Fiske Stone; pillar of the law. — [Hamden, Conn.]: Archon Books, 1968
[c1956] xiii, 914 p.: illus., ports.; 23 cm. 1. Stone, Harlan Fiske, 1872-1946.
I. T.
KF8745.S8 M3 1968        347.99/73        *LC* 68-21687

**Dunne, Gerald T.**                • **4.9828**
Justice Joseph Story and the rise of the Supreme Court [by] Gerald T. Dunne.
— New York: Simon and Schuster, [1971, c1970] 458 p.: port.; 22 cm. 1. Story,
Joseph, 1779-1845. I. T.
KF8745.S83 D84        347/.7326/34 B        *LC* 70-139620        *ISBN*
0671206656

**Newmyer, R. Kent.**                **4.9829**
Supreme Court Justice Joseph Story: statesman of the Old Republic / R. Kent
Newmyer. — Chapel Hill: University of North Carolina Press, c1985. xvii,
490 p.: ill.; 24 cm. (Studies in legal history.) Includes indexes. 1. Story, Joseph,
1779-1845. 2. Judges — United States — Biography. I. T. II. Series.
KF8745.S83 N48 1985        347.73/2634 B 347.3073534 B 19        *LC*
84-11886        *ISBN* 0807816264

**Mason, Alpheus Thomas, 1899-.**                • **4.9830**
William Howard Taft, Chief Justice. New York, Simon and Schuster [1965]
354 p. port. 23 cm. 1. Taft, William H. (William Howard), 1857-1930. I. T.
KF8745.T27 M3        347.9973        *LC* 65-11166

**Magrath, C. Peter.**                • **4.9831**
Morrison R. Waite: the triumph of character. — New York: Macmillan, [1963]
334 p.: ill.; 24 cm. 1. Waite, Morrison Remick, 1816-1888. I. T.
KF8745.W27 M3        923.473        *LC* 63-14340

**Warren, Earl, 1891-1974.**                **4.9832**
The memoirs of Earl Warren / by Earl Warren. 1st ed. — Garden City, N.Y.:
Doubleday, 1977. xii, 394 p., [12] leaves of plates: ill.; 24 cm. Includes index.
1. Warren, Earl, 1891-1974. 2. Judges — United States — Biography. I. T.
KF8745.W3 A35        347/.73/2634 B        *LC* 76-42842        *ISBN*
0385128351

**Pollack, Jack Harrison.**                **4.9833**
Earl Warren, the judge who changed America / Jack Harrison Pollack. —
Englewood Cliffs, N.J.: Prentice Hall, c1979. viii, 386 p., [4] leaves of plates: ill.;
24 cm. Includes index. 1. Warren, Earl, 1891-1974. 2. Judges — United States
— Biography. I. T.
KF8745.W3 P64        347/.73/2634 B        *LC* 78-24234        *ISBN*
0132223155

**Schwartz, Bernard, 1923-.**                **4.9834**
Super chief, Earl Warren and his Supreme Court: judicial biography / by
Bernard Schwartz. — Unabridged ed. — New York: New York University
Press, 1983. xiii, 853 p., [17] p. of plates: ports.; 24 cm. Includes index.
1. Warren, Earl, 1891-1974. 2. Judges — United States — Biography. I. T.
KF8745.W3 S37 1983        347.73/2634 B 347.3073534 B 19        *LC*
82-18868        *ISBN* 0814778259

**White, G. Edward.**                **4.9835**
Earl Warren, a public life / G. Edward White. — New York: Oxford University
Press, 1982. x, 429 p., [4] p. of plates: ports.; 24 cm. 1. Warren, Earl,
1891-1974. 2. Judges — United States — Biography. I. T.
KF8745.W3 W45 1982        347.73/2634 B 347.3073534 B 19        *LC*
82-2105        *ISBN* 0195031210

**Highsaw, Robert Baker, 1917-.**                **4.9836**
Edward Douglass White, defender of the conservative faith / Robert B.
Highsaw. — Baton Rouge: Louisiana State University Press, c1981. xiv, 212 p.,
[3] leaves of plates: ill.; 24 cm. — (Southern biography series.) Includes index.
1. White, Edward Douglass, 1845-1921. 2. Judges — United States —
Biography. I. T. II. Series.
KF8745.W5 H53        347.73/2634 B        *LC* 80-17874        *ISBN*
0807107530

## KF8748 Criticism

**Ball, Howard, 1937-.**                **4.9837**
Judicial craftsmanship or fiat?: Direct overturn by the United States Supreme
Court / Howard Ball. — Westport, Conn.: Greenwood Press, 1978. xiv, 160 p.;
22 cm. — (Contributions in political science. no. 7 0147-1066) Includes index.
1. United States. Supreme Court. 2. Judicial review — United States.
3. Political questions and judicial power — United States. I. T. II. Series.
KF8748.B24        347.73/26        *LC* 77-91102        *ISBN* 0313200351

**The Burger Court: the counter–revolution that wasn't / edited**                **4.9838**
**by Vincent Blasi; foreword by Anthony Lewis.**
New Haven: Yale University Press, c1983. xiv, 326 p.: ill.; 24 cm. Includes
index. 1. Burger, Warren E., 1907- 2. United States. Supreme Court. 3. Civil
rights — United States I. Blasi, Vincent, 1943-
KF8748.B86 1983        347.73/26 347.30735 19        *LC* 83-5828        *ISBN*
0300029411

**Frankfurter, Felix, 1882-1965.**                                  • **4.9839**
The business of the Supreme court; a study in the federal judicial system, by Felix Frankfurter and James M. Landis. New York, The Macmillan company, 1927. viii p., 1 l., 349 p. 24 cm. 1. United States. Supreme Court. 2. Courts — United States 3. United States — Constitutional law I. Landis, James McCauley, 1899-1964. joint author. II. T.
KF8748.F7x        LC 27-24024

**Funston, Richard.**                                               **4.9840**
Constitutional counterrevolution?: The Warren Court and the Burger Court: judicial policy making in modern America / Richard Y. Funston. Cambridge, Mass.: Schenkman Pub. Co.; New York: distributed by Halsted Press, c1977. xiii, 399 p.; 23 cm. Includes indexes. 1. United States. Supreme Court. I. T.
KF8748.F85        347/.73/26        LC 76-49923        ISBN 0470990228

**Jackson, Percival E., 1891-.**                                    • **4.9841**
Dissent in the Supreme Court: a chronology / by Percival E. Jackson. — [1st ed.]. — Norman: University of Oklahoma Press, [1969] xii, 583 p.; 24 cm. 1. U.S. Supreme Court. 2. Dissenting opinions — U.S. I. T.
KF8748.J27        347.99/73        LC 69-10621        ISBN 0806108398

**Kurland, Philip B.**                                              • **4.9842**
Politics, the Constitution, and the Warren Court [by] Philip B. Kurland. — Chicago: University of Chicago Press, [1970] xxv, 222 p.; 22 cm. — (The 1969 Cooley lectures, University of Michigan Law School) 1. U.S. Supreme Court. 2. U.S. — Constitutional law. I. T.
KF8748.K8        347/.7326        LC 74-124734        ISBN 0226464083

**Mason, Alpheus Thomas, 1899-.**                                   • **4.9843**
The Supreme Court from Taft to Burger = originally published as The Supreme Court from Taft to Warren / Alpheus Thomas Mason. — 3d ed., rev. and enl. — Baton Rouge: Louisiana State University Press, c1979. xii, 337 p.; 23 cm. 1. United States. Supreme Court. I. T.
KF8748.M3 1979        347/.73/26        LC 78-19084        ISBN 080710468X

**Mendelson, Wallace.**                                             • **4.9844**
Justices Black and Frankfurter: conflict in the court / Wallace Mendelson. — 2d ed. — Chicago: University of Chicago Press, 1966. xi, 153 p. 1. Black, Hugo LaFayette, 1886-1971. 2. Frankfurter, Felix, 1882-1965. 3. United States. Supreme Court. 4. United States — Constitutional law I. T.
KF8748.Mx        LC 66-4748        ISBN 0226519805

**Rostow, Eugene V. (Eugene Victor), 1913-.**                       • **4.9845**
The sovereign prerogative; the Supreme Court and the quest for law. New Haven, Yale University Press, 1962. 318 p. 22 cm. 1. United States. Supreme Court. 2. Judicial review — United States. I. T. II. Title: The Supreme Court and the quest for law.
KF8748.R65        347.9973        LC 62-16240

**Schmidhauser, John R. (John Richard), 1922-.**                    **4.9846**
The Supreme Court and Congress; conflict and interaction, 1945–1968, by John R. Schmidhauser and Larry L. Berg. New York, Free Press [1972] viii, 197 p. illus. 21 cm. (The Supreme Court in American life) 1. United States. Supreme Court. 2. United States. Congress. 3. Law and politics I. Berg, Larry L. joint author. II. T. III. Series.
KF8748.S27        347.73/26 347.30735 19        LC 77-160068

**Swindler, William Finley.**                                       • **4.9847**
Court and Constitution in the twentieth century / by William F. Swindler. — Indianapolis: Bobbs-Merrill, [1969-. v.; 24 cm. 1. United States. Supreme Court. I. T.
KF8748.S9        347/.73/26        LC 68-11152        ISBN 0672518732

## KF8750–8752 COURTS OF APPEAL

**Schick, Marvin.**                                                 • **4.9848**
Learned Hand's Court. Baltimore, Johns Hopkins Press [1970] xvi, 371 p. port. 24 cm. 1. Hand, Learned, 1872-1961. 2. United States. Court of Appeals (2nd Circuit) I. T.
KF8752 2nd.S3        347/.73/24        LC 73-97491        ISBN 0801812143

**Bass, Jack.**                                                     **4.9849**
Unlikely heroes: the dramatic story of the Southern judges of the Fifth Circuit who translated the Supreme Court's Brown decision into a revolution for equality / Jack Bass. — New York: Simon and Schuster, c1981. 352 p., [8] p. of plates: ill.; 22 cm. Includes index. 1. United States. Court of Appeals (5th Circuit) — History. I. T.
KF8752 5th.B3        347.73/24/09 347.3072409 19        LC 81-1023        ISBN 0671250647

## KF8810–9075 CIVIL PROCEDURE

**Coleman, Lee, 1938-.**                                            **4.9850**
The reign of error: psychiatry, authority, and law / Lee Coleman. — Boston: Beacon Press, c1984. xvi, 300 p.; 22 cm. Includes index. 1. Forensic psychiatry — United States. 2. Insanity — Jurisprudence — United States. 3. Criminal liability — United States. I. T.
KF8922.C64 1984        614/.1 19        LC 83-71943        ISBN 0807004812

**Szasz, Thomas Stephen, 1920-.**                                   • **4.9851**
Psychiatric justice. New York, Macmillan [1965] 283 p. 22 cm. 1. Forensic psychiatry 2. Insanity — Jurisprudence — United States. I. T.
KF8965.S9        LC 65-20171

**Llewellyn, Karl N. (Karl Nickerson), 1893-1962.**                 • **4.9852**
The common law tradition: deciding appeals. Boston, Little, Brown, 1960. 565 p. 1. Appellate procedure — United States 2. Stare decisis — United States 3. Judicial process — United States I. T.
KF9050.L5x        LC 60-14465

**Seide, Katharine, comp.**                                         • **4.9853**
A dictionary of arbitration and its terms; labor, commercial, international; a concise encyclopedia of peaceful dispute settlement. — Dobbs Ferry, N.Y.: Published for the Eastman Library of the American Arbitration Association, by Oceana Publications, 1970. xviii, 334 p.; 25 cm. 1. Arbitration and award — U.S. — Dictionaries. 2. Arbitration and award — Dictionaries. I. Lucius Root Eastman Arbitration Library, New York. II. T.
KF9085.A68S4        331.15/5/03        LC 70-94692        ISBN 0379003864

# KF9201–9760 Criminal Law. Criminal Procedure

**Lermack, Paul.**                                                  **4.9854**
Rights on trial: the Supreme Court and the criminal law / Paul Lermack. — Port Washington, N.Y.: Associated Faculty Press, 1983. 117 p.; 24 cm. — (National university publications) Includes index. 1. United States. Supreme Court. 2. Criminal procedure — United States — Cases. 3. Criminal law — United States — Cases. I. T.
KF9218.L47 1983        345.73 347.305 19        LC 83-2794        ISBN 0804693021

**Joughin, Louis.**                                                 • **4.9855**
The legacy of Sacco and Vanzetti / by G. Louis Joughin and Edmund M. Morgan; With an introd. by Arthur M. Schlesinger.— 1st ed. — New York: Harcourt, Brace, 1948. xviii, 598 p.; 25 cm. 1. Sacco-Vanzetti case I. Morgan, Edmund Morris, 1878-1966. II. T.
KF9219.J6        LC 48-8820

## KF9223 Administration of Criminal Justice

**Chapin, Bradley.**                                                **4.9856**
Criminal justice in colonial America, 1606–1660 / Bradley Chapin. — Athens, Ga.: University of Georgia Press, c1983. 203 p.: ill.; 24 cm. Includes index. 1. Criminal justice, Administration of — United States — History. I. T.
KF9223.C53 1983        345.73/05 347.3055 19        LC 82-2753        ISBN 082030624X

**Powers, Edwin.**                                                  • **4.9857**
Crime and punishment in early Massachusetts, 1620–1692; a documentary history. Boston, Beacon Press [1966.] 647 p. illus. 24 cm. 1. Criminal justice, Administration of — Massachusetts — History. 2. Crime and criminals — Massachusetts — History. I. T.
KF 9223 P88 1966        LC 66-14490

**Casper, Jonathan D.**                                             **4.9858**
American criminal justice: the defendant's perspective [by] Jonathan D. Casper. — Englewood Cliffs, N.J.: Prentice Hall, [1972] xiv, 178 p.; 26 cm. — (A Spectrum book) 1. Criminal justice, Administration of — United States I. T.
KF9223.Z9C35        345/.73/05        LC 72-4484        ISBN 0130240346

## KF9225-9227 Punishment. Penalties

**Rubin, Sol.**      • **4.9859**
The law of criminal correction / With Henry Weihofen, George Edwards [and] Simon Rosenzweig. — St. Paul: West Pub. Co., 1963. xxv, 728 p.; 27 cm. 1. Punishment — United States 2. Sentences (Criminal procedure) — United States I. T.
KF9225 R8     *LC* 63-25370

**Berger, Raoul, 1901-.**      **4.9860**
Death penalties: the Supreme Court's obstacle course / Raoul Berger. — Cambridge, Mass.: Harvard University Press, 1982. vii, 242 p.; 25 cm. Includes indexes. 1. United States. Supreme Court. 2. Capital punishment — United States. I. T.
KF9227.C2 B47 1982     345.73/0773 347.305773 19     *LC* 82-3054     *ISBN* 0674194268

**The Death penalty in America** / edited by Hugo Adam Bedau.      **4.9861**
3rd ed. — New York: Oxford University Press, 1982. xiii, 424 p.: ill.; 24 cm. Includes index. 1. Capital punishment — United States. I. Bedau, Hugo Adam.
KF9227.C2 D42 1982     364.6/6/0973 19     *LC* 81-9565     *ISBN* 0195029860

**Meltsner, Michael, 1937-.**      **4.9862**
Cruel and unusual; the Supreme Court and capital punishment. — [1st ed.]. — New York: Random House, [1973] xii, 338 p.; 22 cm. 1. United States. Supreme Court. 2. Capital punishment — United States. I. T.
KF9227.C2 M4     345/.73/077     *LC* 73-3990     *ISBN* 0394472314

**White, Welsh S., 1940-.**      **4.9863**
Life in the balance: procedural safeguards in capital cases / Welsh S. White; foreword by Hugo Adam Bedau. — Ann Arbor: University of Michigan Press, c1984. viii, 289 p.; 24 cm. 1. Capital punishment — United States — Addresses, essays, lectures. 2. Criminal procedure — United States — Addresses, essays, lectures. I. T.
KF9227.C2 W45 1984     345.73/077 347.30577 19     *LC* 84-7346     *ISBN* 0472100521

## KF9300-9461 PARTICULAR OFFENSES

## KF9305-9329 Offenses Against the Person. Sexual Offenses

**Mohr, James C.**      **4.9864**
Abortion in America: the origins and evolution of national policy, 1800-1900 / James C. Mohr. — New York: Oxford University Press, 1978. xii, 331 p.; 22 cm. 1. Abortion — Law and legislation — United States — History. I. T.
KF9315.M6     344/.73/041     *LC* 77-9430     *ISBN* 0195022491

**Tong, Rosemarie.**      **4.9865**
Women, sex, and the law / Rosemarie Tong. — Towowa, N.J.: Rowman & Allanheld, 1984. vi, 216 p.; 22 cm. — (New feminist perspectives series.) 1. Sex crimes — United States. 2. Sex discrimination against women — Law and legislation — United States. 3. Women — Legal status, laws, etc. — United States. 4. Sex and law — United States. 5. Sexism — United States. 6. Sex role I. T. II. Series.
KF9325.T66 1984     345.73/0253 347.305253 19     *LC* 83-16001     *ISBN* 0847672301

**Marsh, Jeanne C., 1948-.**      **4.9866**
Rape and the limits of law reform / Jeanne C. Marsh, Alison Geist, Nathan Caplan. — Boston, Mass.: Auburn House Pub. Co., c1982. xix, 171 p.: ill.; 24 cm. 1. Rape — United States. I. Geist, Alison. II. Caplan, Nathan S. III. T.
KF9329.M37 1982     364.1/532 19     *LC* 81-20621     *ISBN* 0865690839

## KF9350-9379 Offenses Against Property

**Hall, Jerome, 1901-.**      • **4.9867**
Theft, law, and society. 2d ed. Indianapolis, Bobbs-Merrill [1952.] xxiv, 398 p. 24 cm. 1. Larceny — United States. 2. Larceny — Great Britain. 3. Receiving stolen goods — United States. 4. Embezzlement — United Sttes. 5. Justice, Administration of — United States. 6. Justice, Administration of — Great Britain. I. T.
KF 9352 H17 1952     *LC* 52-11268

## KF9405-9420 Contempt of Congress. Contempt of Court

**Beck, Carl, 1930-.**      • **4.9868**
Contempt of Congress; a study of the prosecutions initiated by the Committee on Un-American Activities, 1945-1957. — New York: Da Capo Press, 1974 [c1959] xii, 263 p.; 22 cm. — (Da Capo Press reprints in American constitutional and legal history) Reprint of the ed. published by Hauser Press, New Orleans. Originally presented as the author's thesis, Duke. 1. United States. Congress. House. Committee on Un-American Activities. 2. Contempt of legislative bodies — United States I. T.
KF9405.B4 1974     345/.73/0231     *LC* 75-166090     *ISBN* 0306702290

**Goldfarb, Ronald L.**      • **4.9869**
The contempt power. New York: Columbia University Press, 1963. 366 p.; 23 cm. Issued also as thesis, Yale University. Bibliography: p. [351]-356. 1. Contempt of court — United States. 2. Contempt of legislative bodies — United States I. T.
KF9415.G6     343.34     *LC* 63-20342

## KF9444 Obscenity

**Obscenity and freedom of expression** / compiled and edited by      **4.9870**
Haig A. Bosmajian.
New York: B. Franklin, 1976. xvii, 348 p.; 31 cm. Includes index. 1. Obscenity (Law) — United States — Cases. I. Bosmajian, Haig A.
KF9444.A7 O3     345/.73/0274     *LC* 75-23138     *ISBN* 0891020349

**Clor, Harry M., 1929-.**      **4.9871**
Obscenity and public morality; censorship in a liberal society [by] Harry M. Clor. — Chicago, University of Chicago Press [1969] xii, 315 p. 23 cm. 1. Obscenity (Law) — United States. 2. Censorship — United States. I. T.
KF9444.C53     343/.7/40973     *LC* 69-16772

**Ernst, Morris Leopold, 1888-.**      **4.9872**
The censor marches on; recent milestones in the administration of the obscenity law in the United States, by Morris L. Ernst and Alexander Lindey. — New York: Da Capo Press, 1971 [c1940] xi, 346 p.; 22 cm. — (Civil liberties in American history) 1. Censorship 2. Censorship — U.S. 3. Obscenity (Law) 4. Sex in literature I. Lindey, Alexander, 1896- joint author. II. T. III. Series.
KF9444.E75 1971     344/.73/0531     *LC* 73-164512     *ISBN* 0306702959

**Haney, Robert W.**      **4.9873**
Comstockery in America: patterns of censorship and control / by Robert W. Haney. — Boston: Beacon Press, c1960. xii, 199 p.; 22 cm. 1. Obscenity (Law) — United States. 2. Censorship — United States. I. T.
KF9444.H35 1974     363.3/1/0973     *LC* 60-10489

**Rembar, Charles.**      **4.9874**
The end of obscenity; the trials of Lady Chatterley, Tropic of Cancer, and Fanny Hill. New York, Random House [c1968] xii, 528 p. 22 cm. 1. Lawrence, D. H. (David Herbert), 1885-1930. Lady Chatterley's lover. 2. Miller, Henry, 1891- Tropic of Cancer. 3. Cleland, John, 1709-1789. Memoirs of a woman of pleasure. 4. Obscenity (Law) — United States. I. T.
KF9444.R4     345.73/0274 347.305274 19     *LC* 67-12743

**Ernst, Morris Leopold, 1888-.**      • **4.9875**
Censorship: the search for the obscene, by Morris L. Ernst and Alan U. Schwartz. With an introd. by Philip Scharper. New York, Macmillan [1964] xvi, 288 p. 21 cm. (Milestones of law series) 1. Obscenity (Law) — United States. 2. Censorship — United States. 3. Obscenity (Law) 4. Censorship I. Schwartz, Alan U., joint author. II. T.
KF9444.Z9 E7     343.7     *LC* 64-17597

**Moretti, Daniel S.**      **4.9876**
Obscenity and pornography: the law under the First Amendment / by Daniel S. Moretti. — London; New York: Oceana Publications, 1984. xii, 147 p.; 19 cm. (Legal almanac series. no. 82) Includes index. 1. Obscenity (Law) — United States — Popular works. 2. Pornography — United States — Popular works. 3. Freedom of the press — United States — Popular works. I. T. II. Series.
KF9444.Z9 M67 1984     344.73/0547 347.304547 19     *LC* 84-18940     *ISBN* 0379111489

## KF9601-9760 Criminal Procedure

**Levy, Leonard Williams, 1923-.**      **4.9877**
Against the law: the Nixon Court and criminal justice / [by] Leonard W. Levy. — [1st ed.]. — New York: Harper & Row, [1974] xvi, 506 p.; 22 cm. 1. United States. Supreme Court. 2. Criminal procedure — United States. I. T.
KF9619.L48     347/.73/265     *LC* 74-1831     *ISBN* 0060125942

**Weinreb, Lloyd L., 1936-.**     **4.9878**
Denial of justice: criminal process in the United States / Lloyd L. Weinreb. New York: Free Press, c1977. xi, 177 p.; 27 cm. 1. Criminal procedure — United States. 2. Law enforcement — United States. I. T.
KF9619.W34     345/.73/05     LC 76-27222     *ISBN* 0029349001

**LaFave, Wayne R.**     **• 4.9879**
Arrest: the decision to take a suspect into custody / by Wayne R. LaFave; Frank J. Remington, editor. — [Boston]: Little, Brown, 1965. xxxiv, 540 p.; 24 cm. (Administration of criminal justice series.) 'Report of the American Bar Foundation's survey of the administration of criminal justice in the United States.' Bibliographical footnotes. 1. Arrest — United States. I. T. II. Series.
KF9625.L3     *LC* 65-16283

**Thomas, Wayne H.**     **4.9880**
Bail reform in America / Wayne H. Thomas, Jr.; foreword by Floyd Feeney. Berkeley: University of California Press, 1977 (c1976). xvi, 272 p.; 23 cm. 1. Bail — United States. I. T.
KF9632.T48     345/.73/072     *LC* 75-27936     *ISBN* 0520031318

**Lewis, Anthony, 1927-.**     **• 4.9881**
Gideon's trumpet. — New York: Random House, [1964] 262 p.; 22 cm. 1. Gideon, Clarence Earl. I. T.
KF9646.L4x     323.42     *LC* 64-11986

**Rosett, Arthur I., 1934-.**     **4.9882**
Justice by consent: plea bargains in the American courthouse / Arthur Rosett, Donald R. Cressey. — Philadelphia: Lippincott, c1976. xvi, 227 p.; 23 cm. 1. Plea bargaining — United States. I. Cressey, Donald Ray, 1919- joint author. II. T.
KF9654.R66     345/.73/072     *LC* 75-41447     *ISBN* 0397473419

**Kamisar, Yale.**     **4.9883**
Police interrogation and confessions: essays in law and policy / by Yale Kamisar. — Ann Arbor: University of Michigan Press, c1980. xx, 323 p.; 24 cm. 1. Confession (Law) — United States — Addresses, essays, lectures. 2. Police questioning — United States — Addresses, essays, lectures. I. T.
KF9664.A75 K35     345.73/052     *LC* 80-10640     *ISBN* 0472093185

**Stephens, Otis H., 1936-.**     **4.9884**
The Supreme Court and confessions of guilt / [by] Otis H. Stephens, Jr. — [1st ed.]. — Knoxville: University of Tennessee Press, [1973] x, 236 p.; 23 cm. 1. United States. Supreme Court. 2. Confession (Law) — United States. I. T.
KF9664.S7     345/.73/06     *LC* 73-8777     *ISBN* 0870491474

**Griswold, Erwin N. (Erwin Nathaniel), 1904-.**     **• 4.9885**
The 5th amendment today; three speeches. Cambridge, Harvard University Press, 1955. 82 p. 21 cm. 1. United States. Constitution. 5th amendment. 2. Due process of law — United States. 3. Self-incrimination — United States. I. T.
KF9668.G75     347.94     *LC* 55-6809

**Lapidus, Edith J.**     **4.9886**
Eavesdropping on trial / [by] Edith J. Lapidus. — Rochelle Park, N.J.: Hayden Book Co., [1974, c1973] 287 p.; 24 cm. 1. Eavesdropping — United States. 2. Wire-tapping — United States. I. T.
KF9670.L37     345/.73/052     *LC* 73-17207

**Loftus, Elizabeth F., 1944-.**     **4.9887**
Eyewitness testimony / Elizabeth F. Loftus. — Cambridge, Mass.: Harvard University Press, 1980 (c1979). xv, 253 p.: ill.; 24 cm. Includes index. 1. Witnesses — United States. 2. Psychology, Forensic 3. Crime and criminals — Identification I. T.
KF9672.L63     345/.73/066     *LC* 79-13195     *ISBN* 0674287754

**Kalven, Harry.**     **• 4.9888**
The American jury [by] Harry Kalven, Jr. [and] Hans Zeisel, with the collaboration of Thomas Callahan and Philip Ennis. Boston, Little, Brown [1966] x, 559 p. illus., forms. 25 cm. 'A result of the study of the American jury system undertaken at the University of Chicago Law School.' 1. Jury — United States. I. Zeisel, Hans. joint author. II. University of Chicago. Law School. III. T.
LAW     KF9680.K3x     347.9973     *LC* 66-19153

**Frankel, Marvin E., 1920-.**     **4.9889**
Criminal sentences; law without order, by Marvin E. Frankel. — New York: Hill and Wang, [1973] x, 124 p.; 22 cm. 1. Sentences (Criminal procedure) — United States. I. T.
KF9685.F7     345/.73/077     *LC* 72-95111     *ISBN* 0809037092

**Kress, Jack M.**     **4.9890**
Prescription for justice: the theory and practice of sentencing guidelines / Jack M. Kress. — Cambridge, Mass.: Ballinger Pub. Co., c1980. xxi, 357 p.; 24 cm. Includes index. 1. Sentences (Criminal procedure) — United States. I. T.
KF9685.K73     345/.73/077     *LC* 79-21141     *ISBN* 0884107922

**Newman, Donald J.**     **• 4.9891**
Conviction; the determination of guilt or innocence without trial, by Donald J. Newman. Frank J. Remington: editor. Boston, Little, Brown, 1966. xxvii, 259 p. 24 cm. (Administration of criminal justice series.) 'Report of the American Bar Foundation's survey of the administration of criminal justice in the United States.' 1. Judgments, Criminal — United States. I. T. II. Series.
KF9685.N4     343.097303     *LC* 66-17210

## KF9701–9756 JUVENILE COURTS. PROBATION. PAROLE. JUDICIAL ERROR

**Sprowls, James T.**     **4.9892**
Discretion and lawlessness: compliance in the juvenile court / James T. Sprowls. — Lexington, Mass.: Lexington Books, c1980. xiii, 121 p.; 24 cm. Includes index. 1. Juvenile courts — United States. I. T.
KF9704.S6x     345.73/08     *LC* 79-6735     *ISBN* 0669035408

**Pursuing justice for the child / edited by Margaret K. Rosenheim; with a foreword by Robert Maynard Hutchins.**     **4.9893**
Chicago: University of Chicago Press, 1976. xix, 361 p.; 23 cm. (Studies in crime and justice.) 1. Juvenile courts — United States — Addresses, essays, lectures. 2. Juvenile justice, Administration of — United States — Addresses, essays, lectures. 3. Juvenile corrections — United States — Addresses, essays, lectures. 1. Rosenheim, Margaret Keeney. II. Series.
KF9709.A2 P87     345/.73/08     *LC* 75-43238     *ISBN* 0226727890

**Schlossman, Steven L.**     **4.9894**
Love & the American delinquent: the theory and practice of 'progressive' juvenile justice, 1825–1920 / Steven L. Schlossman. — Chicago: University of Chicago Press, 1977. xii, 303 p.; 23 cm. Includes index. 1. Juvenile courts — United States — History. 2. Juvenile justice, Administration of — United States — History. 3. Juvenile courts — Wisconsin — Milwaukee — History. 4. Juvenile justice, Administration of — Wisconsin — Milwaukee — History. I. T.
KF9709.S3     345/.73/08     *LC* 76-17699     *ISBN* 0226738574

**Von Hirsch, Andrew.**     **4.9895**
The question of parole: retention, reform, or abolition? / Andrew von Hirsch, Kathleen J. Hanrahan; introd. by Sheldon L. Messinger. — Cambridge, Mass.: Ballinger Pub. Co., c1979. xxx, 178 p.; 24 cm. An enlarged version of the authors' Abolish parole? which was published in 1978. 1. Parole — United States. I. Hanrahan, Kathleen J. joint author. II. T.
KF9750.V66 1979     364.6/2/0973     *LC* 78-21131     *ISBN* 0884107965

**Borchard, Edwin Montefiore, 1884-1951.**     **• 4.9896**
Convicting the innocent: errors of criminal justice / by Edwin M. Borchard; with the collaboration of E. Russell Lutz. — New York: Da Capo Press, 1970 [c1932] xxix, 421 p.; 24 cm. — (Civil liberties in American history) (A Da Capo Press reprint series.) 1. Judicial error — U.S. — Cases. 2. Trials — U.S. 3. Compensation for judicial error — U.S. 4. Perjury — U.S. 5. Crime and criminals — Identification I. Lutz, E. Russell, 1902-1970, joint author. II. T.
KF9756.B6 1970     347.99/73     *LC* 74-107406     *ISBN* 0306718863

# KFA–KFW States, A–W

**Freyer, Tony Allan.**     **4.9897**
The Little Rock crisis: a constitutional interpretation / Tony Freyer. — Westport, Conn.: Greenwood Press, c1984. xii, 186 p.; 22 cm. (Contributions in legal studies. 0147-1074; no. 30) Includes index. 1. Discrimination in education — Law and legislation — Arkansas — Little Rock. 2. School integration — Arkansas — Little Rock. 3. Discrimination in education — Law and legislation — United States. 4. School integration — United States I. T. II. Series.
KFA3992.2.F73 1984     344.767/0798 347.6704798 19     *LC* 83-26663     *ISBN* 0313244162

**Gawalt, Gerard W.**     **4.9898**
The promise of power: the emergence of the legal profession in Massachusetts, 1760–1840 / Gerard W. Gawalt. — Westport, Conn.: Greenwood Press, 1979. x, 254 p.; 22 cm. — (Contributions in legal studies. no. 6 0147-1074) Includes index. 1. Lawyers — Massachusetts — History. 2. Practice of law — Massachusetts — History. I. T. II. Series.
KFM2478.G38     340/.09744     *LC* 78-57765     *ISBN* 0313206120

**Haskins, George Lee, 1915-.**     **• 4.9899**
Law and authority in early Massachusetts: a study in tradition and design. — [Hamden, Conn.]: Archon Books, 1968 [c1960] xvi, 298 p.; 22 cm. 1. Law —

Massachusetts — History and criticism. 2. Massachusetts — History — New
Plymouth, 1620-1691 I. T.
KFM2478.H3 1968     349.744/09 347.44009 19     *LC* 68-26932
    *ISBN* 0208006850

**Nelson, William Edward, 1940-.**        **4.9900**
Americanization of the common law: the impact of legal change on
Massachusetts society, 1760–1830 / William E. Nelson. — Cambridge, Mass.:
Harvard University Press, 1975. ix, 269 p.; 25 cm. (Studies in legal history.)
Includes index. 1. Law — Massachusetts — History and criticism.
2. Sociological jurisprudence — History — Massachusetts. 3. Common law —
United States. I. T. II. Series.
KFM2478.N44     340/.09744     *LC* 74-21231

**Reid, John Phillip.**        **4.9901**
In a defiant stance: the conditions of law in Massachusetts Bay, the Irish
comparison; and the coming of the American Revolution / John Phillip Reid.
— University Park: Pennsylvania State University Press, c1977. 225 p.; 24 cm.
1. Law — Massachusetts — History and criticism. 2. Law — Ireland —
History and criticism. 3. United States — History — Colonial period, ca.
1600-1775 4. Ireland — History — 18th century I. T.
KFM2478.R4     340/.09744     *LC* 76-42453     *ISBN* 0271012404

**Konig, David Thomas, 1947-.**        **4.9902**
Law and society in Puritan Massachusetts: Essex County, 1629–1692 / by
David Thomas Konig. — Chapel Hill: University of North Carolina Press,
c1979. xxi, 215 p.; 25 cm. — (Studies in legal history.) Includes index. 1. Law
— Massachusetts — Essex Co. — History and criticism. 2. Essex County
(Mass.) — History I. T. II. Series.
KFM2999.E8 K66     340/.09744     *LC* 78-26685     *ISBN* 0807813362

**Basch, Norma.**        **4.9903**
In the eyes of the law: women, marriage, and property in nineteenth–century
New York / Norma Basch. — Ithaca: Cornell University Press, 1982. 255 p.; 23
cm. Includes index. 1. Married women — New York (State) — History.
2. Marital property — New York (State) — History. I. T.
KFN5124.B37 1982     346.74701/6 347.470616 19     *LC* 82-2454
    *ISBN* 0801414660

**Zeisel, Hans.**        • **4.9904**
Delay in the court [by] Hans Zeisel, Harry Kalven, Jr. [and] Bernard Bucholz.
Boston, Little, Brown, 1959. xxvii, 313 p. illus. 25 cm. A University of Chicago
Law School study in judicial administration 1. New York (State). Supreme
Court (First District) 2. Court congestion and delay — New York (State)
I. University of Chicago. Law School. II. T.
KFN5956.Z43     347.9973     *LC* 59-9179

**Goebel, Julius, 1892-1973.**        • **4.9905**
Law enforcement in colonial New York; a study in criminal procedure
(1664–1776) [by] Julius Goebel, Jr. [and] T. Raymond Naughton. — Montclair,
N.J.: Patterson Smith, 1970 [c1944] xxxix, 867 p.; 23 cm. — (Patterson Smith
reprint series in criminology, law enforcement, and social problems, publication
no. 122) Conducted under the auspices of the Legal Research Committee of the
Commonwealth Fund. 1. Criminal procedure — New York (Colony)
I. Naughton, Thomas Raymond, 1908- joint author. II. Commonwealth
Fund. Legal Research Committee. III. T.
KFN6155.G6 1970     343/.09747/03     *LC* 71-108239     *ISBN*
0875851223

# KFZ Confederate States

**Lee, Charles Robert.**        • **4.9906**
The Confederate Constitutions. — Chapel Hill: University of North Carolina
Press, 1963. viii, 225 p.; 23 cm. 1. Confederate States of America —
Constitutional history. I. Confederate States of America. Constitution
II. United States. Constitution III. T.
KFZ9000.L4     342/.75/02     *LC* 63-4415

**Robinson, William Morrison, 1891-.**        • **4.9907**
Justice in grey; a history of the judicial system of the Confederate States of
America, by William M. Robinson. — New York: Russell & Russell, [1968,
c1941] xxi, 713 p.; 24 cm. 1. Courts — Confederate States of America.
2. Justice, Administration of — Confederate States of America. I. T.
KFZ9108.R6 1968     347.99/75     *LC* 68-15155

# KG–KH Latin America

**Burkholder, Mark A., 1943-.**        **4.9908**
From impotence to authority: the Spanish Crown and the American audiencias,
1687–1808 / Mark A. Burkholder, D. S. Chandler. — Columbia: University of
Missouri Press, c1977. xii, 253 p.: ill.; 26 cm. Includes indexes. 1. Judges —
Spain — Colonies. I. Chandler, D. S. (Dewitt Samuel), 1938- joint author.
II. T.
KG.B8x     347/.46/014     *LC* 76-45742     *ISBN* 0826202195

**Flory, Thomas, 1947-.**        **4.9909**
Judge and jury in imperial Brazil, 1808–1871: social control and political
stability in the new State / by Thomas Flory. — Austin: University of Texas
Press, c1981. xiii, 268 p.; 24 cm. (Latin American monographs ; no. 53)
Includes index. 1. Judges — Brazil — History. 2. Courts — Brazil — History.
3. Liberalism — Brazil — History. 4. Political stability — Brazil — History.
5. Brazil — Social conditions — 19th century I. T.
KHD.F5x     347.81/01 19     *LC* 80-23447     *ISBN* 0292740158

**Burkholder, Mark A., 1943-.**        **4.9910**
Politics of a colonial career: José Baquíjano and the Audiencia of Lima / Mark
A. Burkholder. — 1st ed. — Albuquerque: University of New Mexico Press,
1981 (c1980). xi, 184 p., [4] leaves of plates; 24 cm. Includes index.
1. Baquíjano y Carrillo, José, d. 1818. 2. Peru. Real Audiencia. 3. Judges —
Peru — Biography. 4. Peru — History — 1548-1820 I. T.
KHQ.B8x     347.85/03534 B 19     *LC* 80-52279     *ISBN* 0826305458

# KJ–KM Europe

**Chapman, Guy.**        **4.9911**
The Dreyfus trials. — New York: Stein and Day, [1972] 282 p.: illus.; 23 cm.
1. Dreyfus, Alfred, 1859-1935. I. T.
KJV.C5x     345/.44/0231     *LC* 71-188172     *ISBN* 0812814878

**Martin, Benjamin F., 1947-.**        **4.9912**
The hypocrisy of justice in the Belle Epoque / Benjamin F. Martin. — Baton
Rouge: Louisiana State University Press, c1984. xii, 251 p.: ill.; 24 cm. Includes
index. 1. Trials — France. 2. Criminal justice, Administration of — France.
3. Female offenders — France. 4. France — History — Third Republic,
1870-1940 I. T.
KJV.M3x     345.44/02 344.4052 19     *LC* 83-16263     *ISBN*
0807111163

**Dawson, Philip.**        **4.9913**
Provincial magistrates and revolutionary politics in France, 1789–1795. —
Cambridge, Mass.: Harvard University Press, 1972. x, 424 p.; 21 cm. —
(Harvard historical monographs. 66) 1. Judges — France. 2. France —
History — Revolution, 1789-1795 I. T. II. Series.
KJW.D3x     944.04     *LC* 74-182816     *ISBN* 0674719603

**Politics and government in the Federal Republic of Germany:**        **4.9914**
**basic documents / edited by Carl–Christoph Schweitzer ... [et**
**al.].**
Leamington Spa [Warwickshire]: Berg, c1984. xix, 444 p.: ill.; 22 cm. Includes
index. 1. Germany (West) — Constitutional history — Sources. 2. Germany
(West) — Politics and government — Sources. I. Schweitzer, Carl Christoph.
KK4443.6.P65 1984b     342.43/029 344.30229 19     *LC* 85-233563
    *ISBN* 0907582133

**Russia. Laws, statutes, etc., 1689-1725 (Peter I)**        **4.9915**
[Dukhovnyĭ reglament. English] The spiritual regulation of Peter the Great.
Translated and edited by Alexander V. Muller. Seattle, University of
Washington Press [1972] xxxviii, 150 p. 25 cm. (Publications on Russia and
Eastern Europe of the Institute for Comparative and Foreign Area Studies, no.
3) Translation of Dukhovnyĭ reglament. 1. Ecclesiastical law — Soviet Union.
I. Muller, Alexander V., ed. II. T.
KM     344/.47/09     *LC* 72-4590     *ISBN* 0295952377

**Berman, Harold Joseph, 1918-.**        • **4.9916**
Justice in the U.S.S.R.: an interpretation of Soviet law. — Rev. ed., enl.
Cambridge: Harvard University Press, 1963. x, 450 p.; 20 cm. (Russian
Research Center studies, 3) First published in 1950 under title: Justice in
Russia. Bibliographical references included in 'Notes' (p. [385]-431) 1. Justice,
Administration of — Russia. 2. Law — Russia. I. T.
KM.B475 1963     340.0947     *LC* 64-4942

**Juviler, Peter H.**                                                        **4.9917**
Revolutionary law and order: politics and social change in the USSR / Peter H. Juviler. New York: Free Press, c1976. xii, 274 p.; 24 cm. Includes index. 1. Criminal law — Russia — History. 2. Criminal justice, Administration of — Russia — History. 3. Crime and criminals — Russia — History. I. T.
KM.J89 1976      364      *LC* 76-12832      *ISBN* 0029168007

**Terts, Abram, 1925- defendant.**                                          **• 4.9918**
On trial: the Soviet State versus 'Abram Tertz' and 'Nikolai Arzhak' / translated, edited and with an introd. by Max Hayward. — [1st ed.] New York: Harper and Row [1966] vi, 183 p.; 22 cm. Trial before the Supreme Court of the R.S.F.S.R., held in Moscow Oblast Court in February 1966. Appendix (p. [161]-178): The heirs of Smerdyakov, by Z. Kedrina [from the] Literary gazette, January 22, 1966.—Bibliography of the works of Abram Tertz (Andrei Sinyavsky) and Nikolai Arzhak (Yuli Daniel) in English and Russian. I. Daniėl', IUliĭ, 1925- defendant II. Hayward, Max. III. Russian S.F.S.R. Verkhovnyĭ Sud. IV. T.
KM.T4x      *LC* 66-24376

## KP–KQ Asia

**Coomaraswamy, Radhika.**                                                  **4.9919**
Sri Lanka: the crisis of the Anglo–American constitutional traditions in a developing society / Radhika Coomaraswamy. — New Delhi: Vikas, c1984. 192 p.; 23 cm. 'The Constitution of the Democratic Socialist Republic of Sri Lanka.': p. [19]-184. Includes index. 1. Sri Lanka — Constitutional history. 2. Sri Lanka — Constitutional law. I. Sri Lanka. Āndukrama Vyavasthāva (1978) II. T.
KQ.C6x      342.549/3 345.49302 19      *LC* 84-900015

**Galanter, Marc, 1931-.**                                                  **4.9920**
Competing equalities: law and the backward classes in India / Marc Galanter. — Berkeley: University of California Press, c1984. xxii, 625 p.: ill.; 24 cm. Includes indexes. 1. Minorities — Legal status, laws, etc. — India. 2. Untouchables — Legal status, laws, etc. — India. 3. Civil rights — India. 4. India — Scheduled tribes — Legal status, laws, etc. I. T.
KQ.G3x      342.54/0873 345.402873 19      *LC* 82-2017      *ISBN* 0520042891

**Ch'ü, T'ung-tsu.**                                                        **• 4.9921**
[Chung-kuo fa lü yü Chung-kuo she hui. English] Law and society in traditional China / T'ung-tsu Ch'ü. Paris; La Haye: Mouton, 1961. 304 p.; 24 cm. (Monde d'outre-mer, passé et présent. Etudes. 4) Original edition published in 1947 under title (romanized): Chung-kuo fa lü yü Chung-kuo she hui. 1. Law — China — History and criticism. I. T. II. Series.
KQK.C5x      340.0951      *LC* 62-19813

**Cohen, Jerome Alan.**                                                     **• 4.9922**
The criminal process in the People's Republic of China, 1949–1963: an introduction. — Cambridge: Harvard University Press, 1968. xvi, 706 p.; 26 cm. (Harvard studies in East Asian law, 2) 1. Criminal procedure — China. 2. Criminal law — China. I. T. II. Series.
KQK.C6x      343/.0951      *LC* 68-14252

**A Great trial in Chinese history: the trial of the Lin Biao and**         **4.9923**
**Jiang Qing counter–revolutionary cliques, Nov. 1980–Jan. 1981.**
1st ed. — Beijing, China: New World Press; Elmsford, N.Y.: Distribution by Pergamon Press, 1981. 521 p.: ill. 1. Lin, Piao, 1908-1971. 2. Chiang, Ch'ing, 1910- 3. Trials (Political crimes and offenses) — China — Peking. 4. Counterrevolutions — China. 5. Chung-kuo kung ch'an tang — Purges 6. Gang of Four Trial, Peking, China, 1980-1981 I. Lin, Piao, 1908-1971. II. Chiang, Ch'ing, 1910-
KQK.G7x      345.51/0231 345.105231 19      *LC* 81-179817      *ISBN* 0080279198

**Noda, Yoshiyuki, 1912-.**                                                 **4.9924**
Introduction to Japanese law. Translated and edited by Anthony H. Angelo. [Tokyo] University of Tokyo Press, c1976. 253 p. 24 cm. Translation of Introduction au droit japonais. 1. Law — Japan — History and criticism. I. Angelo, Anthony H. II. T. III. Title: Japanese law. IV. Title: Droit japonais.
KQP.N6x      *ISBN* 0860081605

## KR Africa

**African women & the law: historical perspectives / edited by**           **4.9925**
**Margaret Jean Hay and Marcia Wright.**
[Boston]: Boston University, African Studies Center, c1982. xiv, 173 p.; 23 cm. — (Papers on Africa. 7) Papers presented at a conference held at Columbia University in April 1979. 1. Women — Legal status, laws, etc. — Africa — History. I. Hay, Margaret Jean. II. Wright, Marcia. III. Columbia University. IV. Title: African women and the law. V. Series.
KR.A4x      960 s 346.601/34 960 s 346.06134 19      *LC* 82-231480

**Elias, T. O. (Taslim Olawale)**                                          **• 4.9926**
The nature of African customary law. [Manchester] Manchester University Press [1956] 318 p. 1. Law, Primitive — Africa I. T.
KR.E4x      *LC* 57-1037

**Kuper, Hilda.**                                                          **• 4.9927**
African law: adaptation and development / edited by Hilda Kuper and Leo Kuper. — Berkeley: University of California Press, 1965. viii, 275 p.; 24 cm. Contributions, in English or French, to the second interdisciplinary seminar arranged by the African Studies Center of the University of California, Los Angeles, and held in the spring of 1963. 1. Law — Africa — Addresses, essays, lectures I. Kuper, Leo. II. University of California, Los Angeles. African Studies Center. III. T.
KR.K8x      *LC* 65-24589

**Nwabueze, B. O. (Benjamin Obi)**                                          **4.9928**
The presidential Constitution of Nigeria / B.O. Nwabueze. — New York: St. Martin's Press, 1982. xvii, 558 p.; 23 cm. 1. Nigeria — Constitutional law. I. T.
KRG.N9x      342.669 346.6902 19      *LC* 82-47637      *ISBN* 0312640323

**Fallers, Lloyd A.**                                                       **4.9929**
Law without precedent: legal ideas in action in the courts of colonial Busoga / [by] Lloyd A. Fallers. — Chicago: University of Chicago Press [1969] xi, 365 p.: ill., maps; 24 cm. 1. Justice, Administration of — Busoga. I. T.
LAW      KRK.F3 1969.      347.99/676/1      *LC* 77-86135      *ISBN* 226236811

## L EDUCATION: GENERAL

**Lagemann, Ellen Condliffe, 1945-.**     **4.9930**
Private power for the public good: a history of the Carnegie Foundation for the Advancement of Teaching / Ellen Condliffe Lagemann. — 1st ed. — Middletown, Conn.: Wesleyan University Press; Scranton, Pa.: Distributed by Harper & Row, c1983. xix, 246 p., [8] p. of plates: ill.; 23 cm. 1. Carnegie Foundation for the Advancement of Teaching — History. I. T.
L13.C433 L34 1983     361.7/632 19     *LC* 83-168179     *ISBN* 081955085X

**The Condition of education.**     **4.9931**
Washington, D.C.: U.S. Dept. of Education, Office of Educational Research and Improvement, National Center for Education Statistics: For sale by the Supt. of Docs., U.S. G.P.O. v.: ill. (some col.); 28 cm. (1975-1979: DHEW publication; no. (NCES) Annual. Began with 1975. Description based on: 1982 ed., [pt. 1] Vols. for 1977- <1982> issued in parts. ERIC version for 1981-1982 distributed to depository libraries in microfiche. 1. Education — United States — 1965- — Statistics — Periodicals. I. United States. Office of Educational Research and Improvement. Center for Education Statistics. II. National Center for Education Statistics.
L112.N377a     370/.973     *LC* 75-643861

**United States. Dept. of Health, Education, and Welfare. Office**     **4.9932**
**of the Secretary.**
The Second Newman report: national policy and higher education / report of a special task force to the Secretary of Health, Education, and Welfare; [Frank Newman, chairman]. — Cambridge, Mass.: MIT Press, 1974. xxiii, 227 p.; 21 cm. The 1st Newman report was published in 1971 under title: Report on higher education, March 1971. 1. Education, Higher — United States. I. Newman, Frank, 1927- II. Report on higher education, March 1971. III. T. IV. Title: National policy and higher education.
L112.S42 1973     378.73     *LC* 73-21475     *ISBN* 0262080710

## L900–901 Directories

**The Gourman report. A rating of graduate and professional**     **4.9933**
**programs in American and international universities.**
[1st ed.] (1980)-     . — Los Angeles, Calif.: National Education Standards, 1980-. v.; 28 cm. Irregular. 1. Universities and colleges — Graduate work — Evaluation. 2. Universities and colleges — Evaluation 3. Universities and colleges — Curricula — Evaluation.
PAR     L900.G68.     *LC* 87-641747

**International handbook of universities.**     **4.9934**
1st ed. (1959). — Paris: International Association of Universities, 1959. 1 v.; 25 cm. Triennial. 1. Universities and colleges — Directories I. International Association of Universities.
L900.I58     378.058     *LC* 59-4778

**International handbook of universities and other institutions of**     **4.9935**
**higher education.**
2nd ed. (1962)-     . — Paris: International Association of Universities, c1962-. v.; 25-29 cm. Triennial. First edition published as International Handbook of Universities. 1. Universities and colleges — Directories I. International Association of Universities.
L900.I58     378 19     *LC* 86-640857

**Accredited institutions of postsecondary education, programs,**     **4.9936**
**candidates / published for the Council on Postsecondary**
**Accreditation.**
Washington, D.C.: American Council on Education. v.; 24 cm. Annual. Began with issue for 1976-77. A directory of accredited institutions, professionally accredited programs, and candidates for accreditation. Description based on: 1980-81. 1. Education, Higher — United States — Directories. I. Council on Postsecondary Accreditation. II. American Council on Education.
L901.A48     378.73     *LC* 81-641495

**American community, technical, and junior colleges.**     **4.9937**
9th ed.-     . — New York: American Council on Education: Macmillan, c1984-. v.; 28 cm. (American Council on Education/Macmillan series in higher education) 1. Community colleges — United States — Directories. 2. Junior colleges — United States — Directories. 3. Technical education — United States — Directories. I. American Council on Education. II. American Association of Community and Junior Colleges. III. Series.
L901.A5x     387 11     *LC* sn 84-6687

**Barron's profiles of American colleges. Descriptions of the**     **4.9938**
**colleges / compiled and edited by the College Division of**
**Barron's Educational Series.**
15th ed. — Woodbury, N.Y.: Barron's Educational Series, c1986. liii, 1225 p.: ill.; 28 cm. Includes index. I. Barron's Educational Series, inc. College Division.
L901.B32 1986     378.73 19     *LC* 86-14711     *ISBN* 0812036565

**Cass, James.**     **4.9939**
Comparative guide to American colleges: for students, parents, and counselors / by James Cass and Max Birnbaum. — 12th ed. — New York: Harper & Row, c1985. xl, 704 p.; 28 cm. 'Perennial Library.' Includes indexes. 1. Universities and colleges — United States — Directories. I. Birnbaum, Max. II. T.
L901.C33 1985     378.73 19     *LC* 85-42557     *ISBN* 0060154632

**Doughty, Harold.**     **4.9940**
Guide to American graduate schools. — 5th ed., completely rev. / by Harold R. Doughty. — New York, N.Y.: Penguin Books, 1986. 581 p.; 28 cm. Includes indexes. 1. Universities and colleges — United States — Directories. 2. Professional education — United States — Directories. I. T.
L901.D65 1986     378/.1553/02573 19     *LC* 86-42541     *ISBN* 0140467254

**Education directory: colleges and universities.**     **4.9941**
[Washington]: National Center for Educational Statistics. v.; 27 cm. On cover: Postsecondary education. 1. Education, Higher — United States — Directories. I. National Center for Education Statistics.
L901.E34     370/.25/73

**The Handbook of private schools.**     • **4.9942**
1st- 1915-. Boston, P. Sargent. illus., maps. 19 cm. (Sargent's handbook series.) Annual. 1. Private schools — United States. 2. Private schools — Canada. I. Sargent, Porter Edward, 1872-1951. II. Series.
L901.H3     *LC* 15-12869

**Internships.**     **4.9943**
1981-     . — Cincinnati, Ohio: Writer's Digest Books, c1981-. v.; 21 cm. Annual. 1. Interns (Education) — United States — Directories. 2. Employees — Training of — United States — Directories.
L901.I66     331.25/922 19     *LC* 81-649753

**The National faculty directory.**     • **4.9944**
1970-. Detroit: Gale Research Co. v.; 29 cm. Annual. 1971-1982 issued in 2 vols.; 1983- issued in 3 vols. Kept up to date with supplements. 1. College teachers — United States — Directories. I. Gale Research Company.
L901.N34     378.1/2/02573 378     *LC* 76-114404

**Patterson's American education.**     • **4.9945**
v. [1]- 1904-. Mount Prospect, Ill. [etc.]: Educational Directories [etc.] v.; 22-28 cm. Annual. Beginning with 1958/59 vol. issued in 2 pts.: pt. 1, School systems; pt. 2, Schools classified. 1. Education — United States — Directories 2. Education — Canada — Directories. I. Patterson, Homer L., ed.
L901.P3     370/.25/73     *LC* 04-12953

## LA HISTORY OF EDUCATION

**Ulich, Robert, 1890- ed.**     • **4.9946**
Three thousand years of educational wisdom: selections from great documents. — 2d ed., enl., with new chapters on John Dewey and the Judaic tradition. — Cambridge: Harvard University Press, 1954. 668 p.; 25 cm. 1. Education — History — Sources. I. T.
LA5.U4 1954     370.973     *LC* 54-12764

**Brickman, William W.**     **4.9947**
Educational historiography: tradition, theory, and technique / by William W. Brickman. — Cherry Hill, N.J.: Emeritus, 1982. 332 p.; 22 cm. Enl. ed. of: Research in educational history. 1973. 1. Education — Historiography. 2. Education — History — Research. I. T.
LA9.B68 1982    370/.722 19    *LC* 82-71738    *ISBN* 0943694000

**Bowen, James, 1928-.**     **4.9948**
A history of Western education / James Bowen. — New York: St. Martin's Press, 1972-1981. 3 v.: ill.; 25 cm. 1. Education — History I. T.
LA11.B622    370/.9    *LC* 79-185251    *ISBN* 0416161103

**Brubacher, John Seiler, 1898-.**     • **4.9949**
A history of the problems of education [by] John S. Brubacher. — 2d ed. — New York: McGraw-Hill, [c1966] xix, 659 p.; 22 cm. — (Foundations in education) 1. Education — History I. T.
LA11.B7 1966    370.9    *LC* 65-21580

**Mayer, Frederick, 1921-.**     • **4.9950**
A history of educational thought. — 2d ed. — Columbus, Ohio: C. E. Merrill Books, [1966] x, 561 p.: ill., ports.; 24 cm. 1. Education — History I. T.
LA11.M35 1966    370.1    *LC* 66-14407

**Ulich, Robert, 1890-.**     • **4.9951**
History of educational thought. — Rev. ed. — [New York]: American Book Co., [1968] xii, 452 p.; 21 cm. 1. Education — Philosophy 2. Education — History I. T. II. Title: Educational thought.
LA11.U4 1968    370.1/09    *LC* 68-5908

**Cubberley, Ellwood Patterson, 1868-1941.**     • **4.9952**
Readings in the history of education: a collection of sources and readings to illustrate the development of educational practice, theory, and organization / by Ellwood P. Cubberley. — Boston: Houghton Mifflin, 1920. xxv, 684 p.: ill. — (Riverside textbooks in education) 1. Education — History I. T.
LA13.C83    *LC* 20-22845

**Rusk, Robert R. (Robert Robertson), 1879-1972.**     • **4.9953**
The doctrines of the great educators / by Robert R. Rusk. — Rev. and enl. ed. Melbourne: Macmillan; New York: St. Martin's Press, 1965. vii, 336 p.; 21 cm. Bibliographical footnotes. 1. Education — History 2. Educators I. T.
LA13.R85 1965    370.1    *LC* 65-28849 rev

# LA21 Special Topics

**Feinberg, Walter, 1937-.**     **4.9954**
Reason and rhetoric: the intellectual foundations of 20th century liberal educational policy. — New York: Wiley, [1975] xiv, 287 p.; 23 cm. 1. Education — Philosophy — History. I. T.
LA21.F44    370.1    *LC* 74-16009    *ISBN* 0471256978

**Smith, Michael P.**     **4.9955**
The libertarians and education / Michael P. Smith. — London; Boston: Allen & Unwin, 1983. 161 p.; 23 cm. — (Unwin education books.) Includes index. 1. Education — Philosophy — History. 2. Libertarianism I. T. II. Series.
LA21.S6 1983    370/.1 19    *LC* 83-8766    *ISBN* 0043701396

**Spring, Joel H.**     **4.9956**
A primer of libertarian education / Joel Spring. — 1st ed. — New York: Free Life Editions, 1976. 157 p.: ill.; 23 cm. 1. Education — Philosophy — History. 2. Education — 1965- I. T.
LA21.S67    370.1    *LC* 75-10122    *ISBN* 0914156128

**Ulich, Robert, 1890-.**     • **4.9957**
The education of nations: a comparison in historical perspective. — Rev. ed. — Cambridge: Harvard University Press, 1967. xv, 365 p.; 25 cm. 1. Education — History I. T.
LA21.U4 1967    370/.9    *LC* 67-27094

**[Benjamin, Harold Raymond Wayne] 1893-1969.**     **4.9958**
Saber-tooth curriculum, including other lectures in the history of paleolithic education, by J. Abner Peddiwell, PH.D. [pseud.] and several tequila daisies, as told to Raymond Wayne [pseud.] with a foreword by Harold Benjamin. New York, London, McGraw-Hill book company, inc., 1939. xiii, 139 p. illus. 20 cm. Illustrated t.-p. on two leaves. I. T.
LA23.B43 1939    *LC* 39-4058

# LA31–133 By Period

## LA31–81 Ancient

**Laurie, Simon Somerville, 1829-1909.**     • **4.9959**
Historical survey of pre–Christian education. — [2d ed.] London, Longmans, Green, 1907. — St. Clair Shores, Mich.: Scholarly Press, 1970 [c1900] xi, 411 p.; 22 cm. 1. Education, Ancient I. T.
LA31.L38 1970    370/.93    *LC* 76-108504    *ISBN* 0403002141

## LA126–133 Modern. 19th–20th Centuries

**Hendley, Brian Patrick, 1939-.**     **4.9960**
Dewey, Russell, Whitehead: philosophers as educators / by Brian Patrick Hendley; foreword by George Kimball Plochmann; introduction by Robert S. Brumbaugh. — Carbondale: Southern Illinois University Press, c1986. xxi, 177 p.; 24 cm. — (Philosophical explorations.) Includes index. 1. Dewey, John, 1859-1952. 2. Russell, Bertrand, 1872-1970. 3. Whitehead, Alfred North, 1861-1947. 4. Education — Philosophy — History. I. T. II. Series.
LA126.H42 1986    370/.1 19    *LC* 85-2148    *ISBN* 0809312298

**Ringer, Fritz K., 1934-.**     **4.9961**
Education and society in modern Europe / Fritz K. Ringer. — Bloomington: Indiana University Press, c1979. 370 p.; 24 cm. Includes index. 1. Comparative education 2. Educational sociology — Germany. 3. Educational sociology — France. 4. Education, Higher — Germany — History. 5. Education, Higher — France — History. I. T.
LA126.R56 1979    370.19/5    *LC* 77-9865    *ISBN* 0253319293

**Kazamias, Andreas M.**     • **4.9962**
Tradition and change in education: a comparative study / Andreas M. Kazamias, Byron G. Massialas. — Englewood Cliffs, N. J.: Prentice-Hall, 1965. 182 p. — (Foundations of education series) 1. Education — History I. Massialas, Byron G. II. T.
LA131.K38    *LC* 65-17805

### LA132–133 1945–

**Brameld, Theodore Burghard Hurt, 1904-.**     • **4.9963**
Ends and means in education; a midcentury appraisal [by] Theodore Brameld. — Westport, Conn.: Greenwood Press, [1969, c1950] xii, 244 p.; 23 cm. 1. Education — 1945-1964 2. Education — Aims and objectives I. T.
LA132.B7 1969    370.1    *LC* 77-98213    *ISBN* 0837128803

**Comparative education / Philip G. Altbach, Robert F. Arnove, Gail P. Kelly, editors.**     **4.9964**
New York: Macmillan, c1982. ix, 533 p.; 25 cm. 1. Comparative education — Addresses, essays, lectures. I. Altbach, Philip G. II. Arnove, Robert F. III. Kelly, Gail Paradise.
LA132.C5967 1982    370.19/5 19    *LC* 81-8437    *ISBN* 0023019204

**Coombs, Philip Hall, 1915-.**     **4.9965**
The world crisis in education: the view from the eighties / Philip H. Coombs. — New York: Oxford University Press, 1985. xiv, 353 p.: ill.; 24 cm. 1. Education I. T.
LA132.C64 1985    370 19    *LC* 84-5713    *ISBN* 019503502X

**Husén, Torsten, 1916-.**     **4.9966**
The learning society / with a foreword by W. Kenneth Richmond. — [London]: Methuen; distributed by Harper & Row, Barnes & Noble Import Division, [1974] xviii, 268 p.; 21 cm. 1. Education — 1965- 2. International education 3. Education — Research I. T.
LA132.H82    370    *LC* 74-174121    *ISBN* 0416794904

**Noah, Harold J.**     **4.9967**
Toward a science of comparative education [by] Harold J. Noah [and] Max A. Eckstein. — [New York]: Macmillan, [1968, c1969] xv, 222 p.; 21 cm. 1. Comparative education I. Eckstein, Max A. joint author. II. T.
LA132.N56 1969    370.19/5    *LC* 69-11406

**Perkinson, Henry J.**     **4.9968**
Learning from our mistakes: a reinterpretation of twentieth–century educational theory / Henry J. Perkinson. — Westport, Conn.: Greenwood Press, 1984. xvi, 209 p.; 22 cm. (Contributions to the study of education.

0196-707X; no. 14) Includes index. 1. Education — Philosophy — History — 20th century. I. T. II. Series.
LA132.P39 1984    370/.1 19    *LC* 83-26670    *ISBN* 0313242399

**Philosophy for education / edited by Seymour Fox.**    **4.9969**
Jerusalem: Van Leer Jerusalem Foundation; [Atlantic Highlands, N.J.: Exclusive distributors in North America, Humanities Press, c1983] 120 p.: port.; 24 cm. (Van Leer Jerusalem Foundation series.) 'Festschrift dedicated to Robert Maynard Hutchins ... based on the proceedings of a conference held at the Center for the Study of Democratic Institutions, in Santa Barbara, California, on April 14-15, 1977'—Verso t.p. 1. Hutchins, Robert Maynard, 1899— Congresses. 2. Education — Philosophy — Congresses. 3. Liberalism — Congresses. I. Fox, Seymour. II. Hutchins, Robert Maynard, 1899- III. Series.
LA132.P494 1983    370/.1 19    *LC* 83-184397    *ISBN* 9652710008

**Scheffler, Israel.**    **4.9970**
Of human potential: an essay in the philosophy of education / Israel Scheffler. — Boston: Routledge & Kegan Paul, 1985. xiii, 141 p.; 23 cm. Includes index. 1. Education — Philosophy 2. Education and state 3. Educational anthropology 4. Intellect 5. Self-actualization (Psychology) I. T.
LA132.S328 1985    370/.1 19    *LC* 85-2140    *ISBN* 0710205716

**Scheffler, Israel.**    **4.9971**
Reason and teaching. — Indianapolis: Bobbs-Merrill, [1973] xi, 203 p.; 21 cm. 1. Education — Philosophy I. T.
LA132.S33 1973b    370.1    *LC* 72-86641    *ISBN* 0672518546

**Bereday, George Z. F.**    **4.9972**
Comparative method in education. — New York: Holt, Rinehart and Winston, [1964] xvi, 302 p.: illus., map.; 22 cm. 1. Comparative education I. T.
LA133.B4    *LC* 64-12922

**Holmes, Brian.**    **4.9973**
Comparative education: some considerations of method / Brian Holmes. — London; Boston: Allen & Unwin, 1981. 195 p.; 23 cm. — (Unwin education books.) Includes indexes. 1. Comparative education — Methodology. I. T. II. Series.
LA133.H64    370.19/5/018 19    *LC* 80-41625    *ISBN* 0043701019

## LA173–186 History of Higher Education

**Compayré, Gabriel, 1843-1913.**    • **4.9974**
Abelard and the origin and early history of universities / New York, Scribner [c1893]. — St. Clair Shores, Mich.: Scholarly Press, [1969] xiii, 315 p.; 22 cm. (The Great educators) 1. Abelard, Peter, 1079-1142. 2. Universities and colleges I. T.
LA177.C7 1969c    378.1/009    *LC* 75-8103

**Rashdall, Hastings, 1858-1924.**    • **4.9975**
The universities of Europe in the Middle Ages. — A new ed., edited by F. M. Powicke and A. B. Emden. — [London]: Oxford University Press, [1958] 3 v.: fronts., fold. map; 23 cm. Cover title: Medieval universities. 'Reprinted lithographically ... from sheets of the new edition [published in 1936]' 1. Universities and colleges — Europe I. Powicke, F. M. (Frederick Maurice), 1879-1963. ed. II. Emden, Alfred Brotherston, 1888- ed. III. T. IV. Title: Medieval universities.
LA177.R25 1958    378.4    *LC* 63-24389

**The University in society. Contributors: Lawrence Stone [and others] Edited by Lawrence Stone.**    **4.9976**
[Princeton, N.J.]: Princeton University Press, [1974] 2 v. (ix, 642 p.): illus.; 25 cm. Product of a research seminar held at the Shelby Cullom Davis Center for Historical Studies, Princeton University, 1969-1971. 1. Education, Higher — History — Addresses, essays, lectures. I. Stone, Lawrence. ed. II. Shelby Cullom Davis Center for Historical Studies.
LA183.U54    378    *LC* 72-14033    *ISBN* 0691052131

## LA186 Student Movements

**Feuer, Lewis Samuel, 1912-.**    • **4.9977**
The conflict of generations; the character and significance of student movements [by] Lewis S. Feuer. — New York, Basic Books [1969] ix, 543 p. 24 cm. 1. Student movements — History. 2. Conflict of generations I. T.
LA186.F4    378.1/98/1    *LC* 68-54130

**Gold, Alice Ross.**    **4.9978**
Fists and flowers: a social psychological interpretation of student dissent / Alice Ross Gold, Richard Christie, Lucy Norman Friedman. — New York: Academic Press, 1976. xi, 204 p.: ill. — (Social psychology) 1. Student movements — United States. 2. Student movements 3. Students — Political activity I. Christie, Richard, 1918- II. Friedman, Lucy Norman. III. T.
LA 186.G59    378.1981    *LC* 75-19640    *ISBN* 0122876504

**Sampson, Edward E.**    **4.9979**
Student activism and protest [by] Edward E. Sampson, Harold A. Korn, and associates. — [1st ed.]. — San Francisco: Jossey-Bass, 1970. xviii, 265 p.; 24 cm. — (The Jossey-Bass series in higher education) 1. Student movements 2. College students — Political activity I. Korn, Harold A., joint author. II. T.
LA186.S26    378.1/98/1    *LC* 77-92898    *ISBN* 0875890520

**Spender, Stephen, 1909-.**    • **4.9980**
The year of the young rebels. — [1st American ed.]. — New York: Random House, [1969] 186 p.; 22 cm. 1. Student movements I. T.
LA186.S6 1969b    378.1/98/1    *LC* 78-78801

## LA201–2270 Education, by Country

## LA201–396 United States

### LA205–209 History

**Butts, R. Freeman (Robert Freeman), 1910-.**    • **4.9981**
A history of education in American culture [by] R. Freeman Butts [and] Lawrence A. Cremin. New York, Holt [1953] 628 p. 25 cm. 1. Education — United States — History. I. Cremin, Lawrence Arthur, 1925- joint author. II. T. III. Title: Education in American culture.
LA205.B88    370.973    *LC* 52-13892

**Cremin, Lawrence Arthur, 1925-.**    **4.9982**
Traditions of American education / Lawrence A. Cremin. New York: Basic Books, c1977. ix, 172 p.; 21 cm. (Merle Curti lectures; 1976) 1. Education — United States — History. 2. Education — Philosophy I. T. II. Series.
LA205.C67    370/.973    *LC* 76-43456    *ISBN* 0465086853

**Cubberley, Ellwood Patterson, 1868-1941.**    **4.9983**
Public education in the United States; a study and interpretation of American educational history; an introductory textbook dealing with the larger problems of present-day education in the light of their historical development, by Ellwood P. Cubberley... Boston, New York [etc.] Houghton Mifflin company [c1919] xxv, [1], 517 p. illus. (incl. maps) plates, ports., diagrs. (1double) 19 cm. Riverside textbooks in education, ed. by E. P. Cubberley... Division of secondary education under the editorial direction of A. Inglis 'Selected references' at end of each chapter except the firs. 1. Public schools — United States. 2. Education — United States — History. I. T.
LA205.C8    *LC* 19-12331

**Hofstadter, Richard, 1916-1970.**    • **4.9984**
The development of academic freedom in the United States, by Richard Hofstadter and Walter P. Metzger. New York, Columbia University Press, 1955. xvi, 527 p. 24 cm. 'Prepared for the American Academic Freedom Project at Columbia University.' 1. Academic freedom — History. 2. Education — United States — History. I. Metzger, Walter P. II. T.
LA205.H55    378.121    *LC* 55-9435

**Karier, Clarence J.**    **4.9985**
The individual, society, and education: a history of American educational ideas / Clarence J. Karier. — 2nd ed. — Urbana: University of Illinois Press, c1986. xxiv, 459 p.; 24 cm. Rev. ed. of: Man, society, and education. 1967. 1. Education — United States — History. 2. Education — Philosophy — History. I. Karier, Clarence J. Man, society, and education. II. T.
LA205.K3 1986    370/.973 19    *LC* 85-24547    *ISBN* 0252012909

**Perkinson, Henry J.**    **4.9986**
Two hundred years of American educational thought / Henry J. Perkinson. — New York: McKay, c1976. xi, 367 p.; 21 cm. (Educational policy, planning, and theory) 1. Education — United States — History. 2. Education — Philosophy I. T.
LA205.P45    370.1/0973    *LC* 75-43907    *ISBN* 0679303057

**Sloan, Douglas. comp.**      **4.9987**
The great awakening and American education: a documentary history / edited, with an introd., by Douglas Sloan. — New York: Teachers College Press, Columbia University, [1973] x, 270 p.; 20 cm. — (Classics in education, no. 46) 1. Education — United States — History — Addresses, essays, lectures. I. T.
LA205.S57     370/.973     *LC* 72-91270

**Spring, Joel H.**      **4.9988**
Education and the rise of the corporate state, by Joel H. Spring. — Boston: Beacon Press, [1972] xiv, 206 p.; 22 cm. 1. Education — United States — History. 2. Education — Aims and objectives 3. Corporations — United States I. T.
LA205.S65 1972     370/.973     *LC* 72-75546     *ISBN* 0807031747

## LA206–209 Early to 1945

**Bailyn, Bernard.**      • **4.9989**
Education in the forming of American society: needs and opportunities for study / by Bernard Bailyn. — Chapel Hill: Published for the Institute of Early American History and Culture at Williamsburg, Va., by the University of North Carolina Press, 1960. xii, 147 p. –. (Needs and opportunities for study series.) 1. Education — United States — History I. T. II. Series.
LA206.B3     *LC* 60-51488

**Hansen, Allen Oscar, 1881-1944.**      • **4.9990**
Liberalism and American education in the eighteenth century / by Allen Oscar Hansen; with an introduction by Edward H. Reisner. — New York: Octagon Books, 1965. xxv, 317 p.; 21 cm. 1. Education — United States — History. I. T.
LA206.H3 1965     *LC* 65-25567

**Knight, Edgar Wallace, 1885-1953. ed.**      • **4.9991**
A documentary history of education in the South before 1860. Chapel Hill, University of North Carolina Press [1949-53] 5 v. 1. Education — Southern States — History — Sources I. T.
LA206 K65     *LC* 49-8813

**Cremin, Lawrence Arthur, 1925-.**      • **4.9992**
The transformation of the school: progressivism in American education, 1876–1957. — [1st ed.]. — New York: Knopf, 1961. 387 p.; 22 cm. 1. Education — United States — History. I. T. II. Title: Progressivism in American education.
LA209.C7     370.973     *LC* 61-11000

**Knight, Edgar Wallace, 1885-1953.**      • **4.9993**
Education in the South. Chapel Hill, N.C.: The University of North Carolina press [c1924] 32 p. 1. Education — Southern states. I. T.
LA209.K4     *LC* e 25-97

**Perkinson, Henry J.**      **4.9994**
The imperfect panacea: American faith in education, 1865–1976 / Henry J. Perkinson. 2d ed. — New York: Random House, c1977. 257 p.; 21 cm. Includes index. 1. Education — United States — History. 2. Education — Philosophy I. T.
LA209.P422 1977     370/.973     *LC* 76-45395     *ISBN* 0394312163

## LA209.2 1945–

**Conant, James Bryant, 1893-1978.**      • **4.9995**
Education in a divided world: the function of the public schools in our unique society / by James Bryant Conant. — New York: Greenwood Press, [1969, c1948] x, 249 p.; 23 cm. 1. Education — United States — 1945-1964. 2. Education — United States — 1965- I. T.
LA209.2.C6 1969     370/.973     *LC* 78-94580     *ISBN* 0837125480

**Hutchins, Robert Maynard, 1899-.**      • **4.9996**
The university of Utopia / by Robert M. Hutchins. — Chicago: University of Chicago Press, 1953. ix, 103 p. — (Charles R. Walgreen Foundation lectures; 1953) 1. Education — United States — 1945- I. T.
LA209.2 H87     LA209.2H87.     *LC* 53-13355

**Keppel, Francis, 1916-.**      • **4.9997**
The necessary revolution in American education. — [1st ed.]. — New York: Harper & Row, [1966] xiv, 201 p.: ill.; 22 cm. 1. Education — United States — 1945- I. T.
LA209.2.K42     370.973     *LC* 65-21005

**The Limits of educational reform / [edited by] Martin Carnoy,**      **4.9998**
**Henry M. Levin.**
New York: D. McKay Co., c1976. xii, 290 p.; 21 cm. (Educational policy, planning, and theory) 1. Education — United States — Addresses, essays, lectures. 2. Educational sociology — United States — Addresses, essays, lectures. I. Carnoy, Martin. II. Levin, Henry M.
LA209.2.L49     370/.973     *LC* 76-5509     *ISBN* 0679303022

**Ravitch, Diane.**      **4.9999**
The troubled crusade: American education, 1945–1980 / Diane Ravitch. — New York: Basic Books, c1983. xiii, 384 p.; 25 cm. 1. Education — United States — History — 20th century. I. T.
LA209.2.R33 1983     370/.973 19     *LC* 83-70750     *ISBN* 0465087566

**Ravitch, Diane.**      **4.10000**
The schools we deserve: reflections on the educational crises of our times / Diane Ravitch. — New York: Basic Books, c1985. ix, 337 p.; 22 cm. Includes index. 1. Education — United States — Aims and objectives. 2. Education — Standards — United States. 3. Education, Humanistic — United States. 4. Education and state — United States. 5. Minorities — Education — United States. 6. School integration — United States I. T.
LA209.2.R38 1985     370/.973 19     *LC* 84-45303     *ISBN* 0465072364

**Rickover, Hyman George.**      • **4.10001**
Education and freedom. Foreword by Edward R. Murrow. Pref. by Charles Van Doren. — [1st ed.]. — New York: Dutton, 1959. 256 p.; 21 cm. 1. Education — United States — 1945- I. T.
LA209.2.R53     370.973     *LC* 59-5810

## LA210 DESCRIPTION. ORGANIZATION. POLICY

**Adler, Mortimer Jerome, 1902-.**      **4.10002**
The Paideia proposal: an educational manifesto / Mortimer J. Adler. — 1st Macmillan paperbacks ed. — New York: Macmillan, 1982. xii, 84 p.; 22 cm. First vol. of the author's trilogy; the 2nd of which is Paideia problems and possibilities, and the 3rd of which is The Paideia program. 1. Education — United States — Aims and objectives. 2. Educational equalization — United States. 3. Education — Philosophy I. T.
LA210.A534 1982     370/.973 19     *LC* 82-7169

**Counts, George S. (George Sylvester), 1889-1974.**      • **4.10003**
Education and American civilization. — New York: Bureau of Publications, Teachers College, Columbia University, 1952. 491 p. 'A publication of the Horace Mann-Lincoln Institute of School Experimentation.' 1. Education — United States 2. United States — Civilization I. Horace Mann-Lincoln Institute of School Experimentation. II. T.
LA210.C63     *LC* 52-9979

**Goodlad, John I.**      **4.10004**
Behind the classroom door / [by] John I. Goodlad, M. Frances Klein, and associates. — Worthington, Ohio: C. A. Jones Pub. Co., [1970] vi, 120 p.: ill.; 22 cm. Published in 1974 under title: Looking behind the classroom door. 1. Education — United States I. Klein, M. Frances. joint author. II. T.
LA210.G63     370/.973     *LC* 70-132450

**Harvard university. Committee on the objectives of a general**      **4.10005**
**education in a free society.**
General education in a free society; report of the Harvard committee. Cambridge [Mass.] The University, 1945. xiii, 267 p. 23 cm. On cover: Advance copy. 1. Education 2. Education — United States I. T.
LA210.H4 1945     *LC* 45-7687

**Illich, Ivan, 1926-.**      **4.10006**
Deschooling society. [1st ed.] New York: Harper & Row [1971] xx, 116 p.; 22 cm. (World perspectives, v. 44) 1. Education — United States 2. Educational sociology — United States. I. T.
LA210.I4 1971     370.19     *LC* 74-138738     *ISBN* 0060121394

**Leonard, George Burr, 1923-.**      • **4.10007**
Education and ecstasy, by George B. Leonard. — New York: Delacorte Press, [1968] 239 p.; 21 cm. 1. Education — United States — 1945- I. T.
LA210.L46     370/.973     *LC* 68-25150

**Racism and American education; a dialogue and agenda for**      **4.10008**
**action. Participants: Harold Howe [and others] Introd. by**
**McGeorge Bundy. Foreword by Averell Harriman. [Edited by**
**Elinor L. Gordon.**
1st ed.]. — New York: Harper & Row, [1970] xv, 164 p.; 22 cm. 'An Urban affairs book.' Report of a conference sponsored by the President's Commission for the Observance of Human Rights Year, 1968, held on Martha's Vineyard, Mass., July, 1968. 1. Education — United States — 1945- 2. Educational equalization — U.S. I. Howe, Harold, 1918- II. Gordon, Eleanor L., ed. III. U.S. President's Commission for the Observance of Human Rights Year, 1968.
LA210.R23 1970     370.19/34/0973     *LC* 77-88629

**Rickover, Hyman George.**      • **4.10009**
American education, a national failure: the problem of our schools and what we can learn from England. — [1st ed.]. — New York: Dutton, 1963. viii, 502 p.: ill., maps., facsims.; 19 cm. 1. Education — United States — 1945- 2. Education — Great Britain — 1945- I. T.
LA210.R48     370     *LC* 63-15788

**Sarason, Seymour Bernard, 1919-.**    **4.10010**
The culture of the school and the problem of change / Seymour B. Sarason. — 2nd ed. — Boston: Allyn and Bacon, c1982. ix, 311 p.; 25 cm. Includes index. 1. Educational innovations — United States. I. T.
LA210.S34 1982    370.19 19    LC 81-12806    *ISBN* 0205077005

**Sexton, Patricia Cayo.**    • **4.10011**
Education and income: inequalities of opportunity in our public schools / P. C. Sexton; foreword by Kenneth B. Clark. — New York: Viking Press, c1961. 298 p.: ill.; 22 cm. — 1. Equality 2. Discrimination in education I. T.
LA210.S4 1961    LA210.S4.    371.96    *LC* 61-10446

## LA212–217 PUBLIC SCHOOL EDUCATION

**Carnoy, Martin.**    **4.10012**
Education as cultural imperialism. — New York: D. McKay Co., [1974] 378 p.; 22 cm. 1. Education — United States — History. 2. Educational sociology — United States. I. T.
LA212.C34    370.19/3    *LC* 73-93964    *ISBN* 0679302468

**Cremin, Lawrence Arthur, 1925-.**    **4.10013**
Public education / Lawrence A. Cremin; foreword by Maxine Greene. — New York: Basic Books, c1976. xi, 100 p.; 21 cm. (The John Dewey Society lecture; no. 15) 1. Public schools — United States. I. T.
LA212.C73    379.73    *LC* 75-36376    *ISBN* 0465067751

**Garbarino, James.**    **4.10014**
Successful schools and competent students / James Garbarino with the assistance of C. Elliott Asp. — Lexington, Mass.: Lexington Books, c1981. iv, 170 p.; 24 cm. 1. Public schools — United States. 2. Academic achievement 3. Prediction of scholastic success I. Asp, C. Elliott. II. T.
LA212.G29    370/.973 19    *LC* 81-47004    *ISBN* 0669045268

**Giroux, Henry A.**    **4.10015**
Ideology, culture & the process of schooling / Henry A. Giroux. — Philadelphia: Temple University Press; London: Falmer Press, 1981. 168 p.; 24 cm. 1. Education — United States — Philosophy — History. 2. Education — Research — United States. 3. Curriculum planning — United States. 4. Positivism I. T. II. Title: Ideology, culture, and the process of schooling.
LA212.G48    370/.973 19    *LC* 81-1732    *ISBN* 0877222282

**Greene, Maxine.**    **4.10016**
The public school and the private vision: a search for America in education and literature / [by] Maxine Greene. — New York: Random House, 1965. viii, 183 p.; 19 cm. — (Random House studies in education) 1. Education — United States — History 2. Philosophy, American I. T. II. Series.
LA212.G7    *LC* 65-23335    *ISBN* 0394306414

**Ravitch, Diane.**    **4.10017**
The revisionists revised: a critique of the radical attack on the schools / Diane Ravitch. — New York: Basic Books, c1978. xii, 194 p.; 22 cm. 1. Education — United States — History — Sources. I. T.
LA212.R36 1978    370/.973    *LC* 77-20417    *ISBN* 0465069436

**Social history of American education** / edited with commentary  • **4.10018**
by Rena L. Vassar.
Chicago: Rand McNally, 1965. 2 v. — (Rand McNally education series) 1. Education — United States — History. I. Vassar, Rena L.
LA212.V3    LA212.S62.    *LC* 65-18594

**Work, technology, and education: dissenting essays in the**    **4.10019**
**intellectual foundations of American education / edited by**
**Walter Feinberg and Henry Rosemont, Jr.**
Urbana: University of Illinois Press, [1975] 222 p.; 24 cm. 1. Education — United States — Addresses, essays, lectures. 2. Education — Philosophy I. Feinberg, Walter, 1937- II. Rosemont, Henry, 1934-
LA212.W67    370/.973    *LC* 75-4854    *ISBN* 0252002520

**Cremin, Lawrence Arthur, 1925-.**    • **4.10020**
The American common school: an historic conception. — New York: Bureau of Publications, Teachers College, Columbia University, 1951. xi, 248 p.; 24 cm. (Teachers College studies in education.) Thesis - Columbia University. 1. Public schools — United States — History. I. T. II. Series.
LA215.C7    379.73    *LC* 51-10599 REV.

**Cremin, Lawrence Arthur, 1925-.**    • **4.10021**
American education; the colonial experience, 1607–1783 [by] Lawrence A. Cremin. — [1st ed.]. — New York: Harper & Row, [1970] xiv, 688 p.; 25 cm. 1. Education — U.S. — History. I. T.
LA215.C73 1970    370/.973    *LC* 79-123923

**Cremin, Lawrence Arthur, 1925-.**    **4.10022**
American education, the national experience, 1783–1876 / Lawrence A. Cremin. — 1st ed. — New York: Harper and Row, c1980. xii, 607 p.; 24 cm. Includes index. 1. Education — United States — History. I. T.
LA215.C74 1980    370/.973    *LC* 79-3387    *ISBN* 0060109122

**Kaestle, Carl F.**    **4.10023**
Pillars of the republic: common schools and American society, 1780–1860 / Carl F. Kaestle; consulting editor, Eric Foner. — 1st ed. — New York: Hill and Wang, 1983. xiv, 266 p.; 21 cm. — (American century series) 1. Public schools — United States — History — 18th century. 2. Public schools — United States — History — 19th century. I. Foner, Eric. II. T.
LA215.K33 1983    371/.01/0973 19    *LC* 82-21163    *ISBN* 0809001543

**Avrich, Paul.**    **4.10024**
The modern school movement: anarchism and education in the United States / Paul Avrich. — Princeton, N.J.: Princeton University Press, c1980. xiii, 447 p., [8] leaves of plates: ill.; 24 cm. Includes index. 1. Ferrer Guardia, Francisco, 1859-1909. 2. Education — United States — Philosophy — History — 20th century. 3. Education — United States — Experimental methods — History — 20th century. 4. Educators — United States — Political activity — History — 20th century. 5. Anarchism and anarchists — United States — History — 20th century. I. T.
LA216.A78    370/.973    *LC* 79-3188    *ISBN* 0691046697

**Cuban, Larry.**    **4.10025**
How teachers taught: constancy and change in American classrooms, 1890–1980 / Larry Cuban. — New York: Longman, c1984. xii, 292 p.: ill.; 24 cm. (Research on teaching monograph series.) Includes index. 1. Education — United States — History — 19th century. 2. Education — United States — History — 20th century. 3. Teaching I. T. II. Series.
LA216.C82 1984    370/.973 19    *LC* 83-17559    *ISBN* 0582284813

**Lieberman, Myron, 1919-.**    • **4.10026**
The future of public education. — [Chicago]: University of Chicago Press, [1960] 294 p.; 23 cm. 1. Public schools — United States. I. T.
LA216.L5    371/.01/0973 19    *LC* 59-15108

**Spring, Joel H.**    **4.10027**
The sorting machine: national educational policy since 1945 / Joel Spring. — New York: McKay, c1976. vi, 309 p.; 21 cm. — (Educational policy, planning, and theory) 1. Education — United States — History — 20th century. 2. Education and state — United States. I. T.
LA216.S67    379.73    *LC* 75-43801    *ISBN* 0679303049

**Academic work and educational excellence: raising student**    **4.10028**
**productivity / edited by Tommy M. Tomlinson and Herbert J.**
**Walberg.**
Berkeley, Calif.: McCutchan Pub. Corp., c1986. x, 307 p.; 24 cm. — (Contemporary educational issues) 1. Education — United States — Aims and objectives. 2. Public schools — United States — Evaluation. 3. Academic achievement
LA217.A57 1986    370/.973 19    *LC* 85-62682    *ISBN* 0821119087

**Barr, Donald.**    **4.10029**
Who pushed Humpty Dumpty?: Dilemmas in American education today. — [1st ed.]. — New York: Atheneum, 1971. ix, 341 p.; 25 cm. 1. Education — U.S. — 1965- I. T.
LA217.B36    370/.973    *LC* 71-139299

**Broudy, Harry S.**    **4.10030**
The real world of the public schools [by] Harry S. Broudy. — [1st ed.]. — New York: Harcourt Brace Jovanovich, [c1973] x, 271 p.; 22 cm. 1. Public schools — United States. 2. Education — United States — 1965- I. T.
LA217.B75 1972    371/.01/0973    *LC* 72-78456    *ISBN* 0151759650

**Fantini, Mario D.**    **4.10031**
Public schools of choice / [by] Mario D. Fantini. — New York: Simon and Schuster, 1974 (c1973) 256 p.; 22 cm. 1. Public schools — United States. 2. Education — Experimental methods I. T.
LA217.F33    371/.01/0973    *LC* 73-10358    *ISBN* 0671215701

**Goodlad, John I.**    **4.10032**
A place called school: prospects for the future / John I. Goodlad. — New York: McGraw-Hill Book Co., c1984. xix, 396 p.: ill.; 24 cm. — (Study of schooling in the United States.) 1. Public schools — United States. I. T. II. Series.
LA217.G654 1984    371/.01/0973 19    *LC* 83-9859    *ISBN* 0070236267

**The Great school debate: which way for American education? /**    **4.10033**
**edited by Beatrice and Ronald Gross.**
New York: Simon & Schuster, c1985. 544 p.; 24 cm. 1. Education — United States — Aims and objectives — Addresses, essays, lectures. 2. Educational equalization — United States — Addresses, essays, lectures. 3. Education — United States — Curricula — Addresses, essays, lectures. 4. Education and

state — United States — Addresses, essays, lectures. 5. Education — United States — Finance — Addresses, essays, lectures. I. Gross, Beatrice. II. Gross, Ronald.
LA217.G74 1985     370/.973 19     *LC* 84-27555     *ISBN* 0671530100

**Heath, Douglas H.**         **4.10034**
Humanizing schools: new directions, new decisions [by] Douglas H. Heath. — New York: Hayden Book Co., [1971] xii, 228 p.; 22 cm. 1. Education — U.S. — 1965- 2. Teaching I. T.
LA217.H4     370.11/2     *LC* 71-169103

**Hechinger, Fred M.**         **4.10035**
Growing up in America / Fred M. & Grace Hechinger. — New York: McGraw-Hill, [1975] 451 p.; 24 cm. Includes index. 1. Education — United States I. Hechinger, Grace. joint author. II. T.
LA217.H43     370/.973     *LC* 75-2083     *ISBN* 007027715X

**Holt, John Caldwell, 1923-.**         • **4.10036**
The underachieving school [by] John Holt. — New York: Pitman Pub. Corp., [1969] ix, 209 p.; 22 cm. 1. Education — U.S. — 1965- 2. Education — Philosophy — 1965- I. T.
LA217.H6     370/.973     *LC* 78-79048

**Kirst, Michael W.**         **4.10037**
Who controls our schools?: American values in conflict / Michael W. Kirst. — New York: Freeman, c1984. xiv, 183 p.: ill.; 24 cm. Includes index. 1. Education — United States — Aims and objectives. 2. Curriculum planning — United States. I. T.
LA217.K57 1984     370/.973 19     *LC* 84-25881     *ISBN* 0716717190

**Kozol, Jonathan.**         **4.10038**
On being a teacher / Jonathan Kozol. — New York: Continuum, 1981. xii, 177 p.; 22 cm. 1. Public schools — United States. 2. Education — United States — Philosophy. 3. Nationalism and education — United States. I. T.
LA217.K688     371/.01/0973 19     *LC* 80-25950     *ISBN* 0826400353

**LaHaye, Tim F.**         **4.10039**
The battle for the public schools / Tim LaHaye. — Old Tappan, N.J.: F.H. Revell Co., c1983. 283 p.: ill.; 21 cm. 1. Public schools — United States. 2. Sex instruction for children 3. Moral education — United States. 4. Christian education of children — United States. I. T.
LA217.L33 1983     371/.01/0973 19     *LC* 82-13257     *ISBN* 0800713206

**Nasaw, David.**         **4.10040**
Schooled to order: a social history of public schooling in the United States / David Nasaw. — New York: Oxford University Press, 1979. xii, 303 p.; 22 cm. Includes index. 1. Public schools — United States — History. 2. Educational sociology — United States — History. I. T.
LA217.N35     371/.01/0973     *LC* 78-10216     *ISBN* 0195025296

**Postman, Neil.**         • **4.10041**
Teaching as a subversive activity [by] Neil Postman [and] Charles Weingartner. — New York: Delacorte Press, [1969] xv, 219 p.; 22 cm. 1. Education — United States — 1965- I. Weingartner, Charles. joint author. II. T.
LA217.P6     370/.973     *LC* 69-11842

**Reimer, Everett W.**         **4.10042**
School is dead: alternatives in education [by] Everett Reimer. — [1st ed.]. — Garden City, N. Y.: Doubleday, 1971. 215 p.; 22 cm. 1. Education — U.S. — 1965- I. T.
LA217.R4     370.11/0973     *LC* 78-157619

**Silberman, Charles E., 1925-.**         • **4.10043**
Crisis in the classroom; the remaking of American education [by] Charles E. Silberman. — [1st ed.]. — New York: Random House, [1970] xiv, 552 p.; 25 cm. 1. Education — U.S. — 1965- I. T.
LA217.S54     370/.973     *LC* 76-102326

**Sizer, Theodore R.**         **4.10044**
Places for learning, places for joy; speculations on American school reform [by] Theodore R. Sizer. — Cambridge, Mass.: Harvard University Press, 1973. xi, 167 p.; 22 cm. 1. Education — United States — 1965- 2. School management and organization — United States. I. T.
LA217.S58     370/.973     *LC* 72-86381     *ISBN* 0674669851

**Sterling, Philip.**         • **4.10045**
The Real teachers / compiled and edited by Philip Sterling. — [1st ed.]. — New York: Random House, [1972] xxii, 440 p.; 22 cm. 1. Education — United States — 1965- 2. Education, Urban — United States. 3. Teachers — United States. I. T.
LA217.S7     371.1/00973     *LC* 72-1813     *ISBN* 0394462254

**United States. National Commission on Excellence in Education.**         **4.10046**
A nation at risk: the imperative for educational reform: a report to the Nation and the Secretary of Education, United States Department of Education / by the National Commission on Excellence in Education. — Washington, D.C.: The Commission: [Supt. of Docs., U.S. G.P.O. distributor], 1983. v, 65 p.; 23 cm. 'An open letter to the American people.' 'April 1983.' S/N 065-000-00177-2 Item 455-B-2 1. Education — United States — 1965- 2. Education — United States — Evaluation. I. T.
LA217.U49 1983     370/.973 19     *LC* 83-602005

## LA219–222 ELEMENTARY AND SECONDARY EDUCATION

**Boyer, Ernest L.**         **4.10047**
High school: a report on secondary education in America / the Carnegie Foundation for the Advancement of Teaching; Ernest L. Boyer. — 1st ed. — New York: Harper & Row, c1983. xviii, 363 p.; 24 cm. 1. High schools — United States — Case studies. I. Carnegie Foundation for the Advancement of Teaching. II. T.
LA222.B68 1983     373.2/38 19     *LC* 83-47528     *ISBN* 0060151935

**Coleman, James Samuel, 1926-.**         **4.10048**
High school achievement: public, Catholic, and private schools compared / James S. Coleman, Thomas Hoffer, Sally Kilgore. — New York: Basic Books, c1982. xxx, 289 p.: ill.; 25 cm. Includes index. 1. High school students — United States — Statistics. 2. Academic achievement I. Hoffer, Thomas. II. Kilgore, Sally. III. T.
LA222.C54 1982     373.18/0973 19     *LC* 81-68411     *ISBN* 0465029566

**Coleman, James Samuel, 1926-.**         **4.10049**
Public and private high schools: the impact of communities / James S. Coleman, Thomas Hoffer. — New York: Basic Books, c1987. xxviii, 254 p.: ill.; 25 cm. Includes index. 1. Education, Secondary — United States. 2. Public schools — United States. 3. Private schools — United States. 4. Academic achievement I. Hoffer, Thomas. II. T.
LA222.C544 1987     373.73 19     *LC* 85-43105     *ISBN* 0465067670

**Conant, James Bryant, 1893-1978.**         • **4.10050**
The child, the parent, and the state. — Cambridge: Harvard University Press, 1959. vi, 211 p.; 22 cm. 1. Education, Secondary — 1945- 2. High schools — United States. I. T.
LA222.C556     373.73     *LC* 59-14735

**Conant, James Bryant, 1893-1978.**         • **4.10051**
The comprehensive high school; a second report to interested citizens, by James B. Conant. [1st ed.] New York, McGraw-Hill [1967] vi, 95 p. 21 cm. 1. Education, Secondary — 1945- 2. Education — United States — 1945- I. T.
LA222.C557 1967     373.1     *LC* 67-16300

**Educational Policies Commission.**         • **4.10052**
Education for all American youth: a further look. — [Rev. ed.] Washington, 1952. 402 p.: ill.; 23 cm. 1. Education — United States I. T.
LA222.E3 1952     *LC* 52-11322

**Hampel, Robert L.**         **4.10053**
The last little citadel: American high schools since 1940 / Robert L. Hampel. — Boston: Houghton Mifflin, 1986. xii, 209 p.; 23 cm. (Study of high schools.) 'The third report from a study of high schools, co-sponsored by the National Association of Secondary School Principals and the Commission on Educational Issues of the National Association of Independent Schools.' Includes index. 1. High schools — United States — History — 20th century. 2. Education, Secondary — United States — History — 20th century. I. National Association of Secondary School Principals (U.S.) II. National Association of Independent Schools. Commission on Educational Issues. III. T. IV. Series.
LA222.H25 1986     373.73 19     *LC* 85-27028     *ISBN* 0395364515

**Krug, Edward August, 1911-.**         • **4.10054**
The shaping of the American high school [by] Edward A. Krug. — New York: Harper & Row, [1964-72] 2 v.; 22 cm. — (Exploration series in education) Vol. 2 has subtitle: 1920-1941, and imprint: Madison, University of Wisconsin Press. Vol. 2 without series note. 1. High schools — United States. 2. Education, Secondary — United States — History. I. T.
LA222.K7     373.73     *LC* 64-12801     *ISBN* 0299059804

**Sizer, Theodore R.**         **4.10055**
Horace's compromise: the dilemma of the American high school: the first report from a study of American high schools, co–sponsored by the National Association of Secondary School Principals and the Commission on Educational Issues of the National Association of Independent Schools /

Theodore R. Sizer. — Boston: Houghton Mifflin, 1984. viii, 241 p.; 24 cm.
1. High schools — United States. I. T.
LA222.S54 1984     373.73 19     *LC* 83-18500     *ISBN* 0395344239

## LA225–228 HIGHER EDUCATION

## LA226 General Works

**American universities and colleges.**        • **4.10056**
[1st]- ; 1928-. Washington [etc.]: American Council on Education [etc.] v.;
23-25 cm. On cover, 1936-40: A handbook of higher education. Publication
suspended 1973-82. 1. Universities and colleges — United States 2. Education
— United States — Directories I. Robertson, David Allan, 1880- ed.
II. MacCracken, John Henry, 1875-1948, ed. III. Marsh, Clarence Stephen,
1882- ed. IV. Brumbaugh, Aaron John, 1890- ed. V. American Council on
Education.
LA226.A65     378.73 370.025 378     *LC* 28-5598

**Barzun, Jacques, 1907-.**        • **4.10057**
The American university: how it runs, where it is going. — New York: Harper
& Row, [1968] xii, 319 p. 1. Universities and colleges — United States
2. Education, Higher — 1945- I. T.
LA226.B37     *LC* 68-15959

**Brubacher, John Seiler, 1898-.**        **4.10058**
Higher education in transition: a history of American colleges and universities,
1636–1976 / John S. Brubacher, Willis Rudy. — 3d ed., rev. and enl. — New
York: Harper & Row, c1976. vii, 536 p.; 24 cm. Includes index. 1. Education,
Higher — United States — History. 2. Universities and colleges — United
States — History. I. Rudy, Willis, 1920- joint author. II. T.
LA226.B75 1976     378.73     *LC* 75-6331     *ISBN* 0060105488

**The College blue book.**        **4.10059**
20th ed. — New York, N.Y.: Macmillan, c1985. 5 v.; 29 cm. Biennial.
1. Universities and colleges — United States — Directories. 2. Universities
and colleges — Canada — Directories. 3. Scholarships — United States —
Directories. 4. Student loan funds — United States — Directories.
5. Vocational education — United States — Directories.
LA226.C685     *ISBN* 0026958309

**Feldman, Kenneth A., 1937-.**        • **4.10060**
The impact of college on students [by] Kenneth A. Feldman [and] Theodore M.
Newcomb. — [1st ed.]. — San Francisco: Jossey-Bass, 1969. 2 v.: illus.; 26 cm.
— (Jossey-Bass series in higher education) 1. Education, Higher — U.S.
2. College students — U.S. I. Newcomb, Theodore Mead, 1903- joint author.
II. T.
LA226.F44     378.1/98/0973     *LC* 79-75940     *ISBN* 0875890369

**Hofstadter, Richard, 1916-1970. ed.**        • **4.10061**
American higher education: a documentary history / edited by Richard
Hofstadter and Wilson Smith. — [Chicago]: University of Chicago Press,
[1961] 2 v.; 25 cm. 1. Universities and colleges — United States — History.
2. Education, Higher — Addresses, essays, lectures. I. Smith, Wilson, joint ed.
II. T.
LA226.H53 1961     378.73     *LC* 61-15935

**Hofstadter, Richard, 1916-1970.**        • **4.10062**
The development and scope of higher education in the United States / by
Richard Hofstadter and C. De Witt Hardy. — New York: Columbia University
Press, for the Commission on Financing Higher Education, 1952. x, 254 p.; 23
cm. Bibliographical footnotes. 1. Education — United States — History
2. Education, Higher I. Hardy, C. De Witt. II. Commission on Financing
Higher Education. III. T.
LA226.H55     378.73     *LC* 52-14741

**Jencks, Christopher.**        • **4.10063**
The academic revolution [by] Christopher Jencks & David Riesman. [1st ed.]
Garden City, N.Y., Doubleday, 1968. xvii, 580 p. 24 cm. 1. Education, Higher
— History. 2. Universities and colleges — United States — History.
I. Riesman, David, 1909- joint author. II. T.
LA226.J4     378.73     *LC* 68-15597

**Jerome, Judson.**        • **4.10064**
Culture out of anarchy; the reconstruction of American higher learning. —
[New York]: Herder and Herder, [1970] xxii, 330 p.; 22 cm. 1. Education,
Higher — U.S. I. T.
LA226.J47     378.73     *LC* 70-129764

**Nisbet, Robert A.**        • **4.10065**
The degradation of the academic dogma: the university in America, 1945–1970,
by Robert Nisbet. Foreword by Ward Madden. — New York: Basic Books,
[1971] xviii, 252 p.; 21 cm. — (The John Dewey Society lecture, no. 12)
1. Universities and colleges — United States — History. I. T.
LA226.N56     378.155/0973     *LC* 75-147013     *ISBN* 0465015883

**Ross, Earle Dudley, 1885-.**        • **4.10066**
Democracy's college; the land–grant movement in the formative state [by] Earle
D. Ross. New York, Arno Press, 1969 [c1942] 267 p. 23 cm. (American
education: its men, ideas, and institutions) 1. School lands — Taxation —
United States. 2. State universities and colleges — United States. 3. Education
— United States — History. I. T.
LA226.R65 1969     379/.123     *LC* 74-89226

**Rudolph, Frederick.**        • **4.10067**
The American college and university, a history / by Frederick Rudolph. — 1st
ed. — New York: Knopf, 1962. xii, 516, xxxvii p.; 22 cm. — (Knopf
publications in education) 'A Borzoi book.' 1. Universities and colleges —
United States — History. I. T. II. Series.
LA226.R72     378.73     *LC* 62-12991

**Veysey, Laurence R.**        **4.10068**
The emergence of the American university [by] Laurence R. Veysey. —
Chicago: University of Chicago Press, [1965] xiv, 505 p.; 25 cm. Revision of
thesis, University of California, Berkeley. 1. Universities and colleges —
United States — History. I. T.
LA226.V47     378.73     *LC* 65-24427

## LA227.1–.2 1800–1965

**Bledstein, Burton J.**        **4.10069**
The culture of professionalism: the middle class and the development of higher
education in America / Burton J. Bledstein. 1st ed. — New York: Norton,
c1976. xii, 354 p.; 22 cm. 1. Education, Higher — United States — History.
2. Middle classes — United States — History. 3. Professional education —
United States — History. 4. Educational sociology — United States —
History. I. T.
LA227.1.B53 1976     301.44/1     *LC* 76-17031     *ISBN* 0393055744

**Levine, David O., 1955-.**        **4.10070**
The American college and the culture of aspiration, 1915–1940 / David O.
Levine. — Ithaca: Cornell University Press, 1986. 281 p.; 24 cm. Includes
index. 1. Universities and colleges — United States — History — 20th century.
2. Student aspirations — United States. 3. Achievement motivation I. T.
LA227.1.L48 1986     378.73 19     *LC* 86-4169     *ISBN* 0801418844

**Grant, Gerald.**        **4.10071**
The perpetual dream: reform and experiment in the American college / Gerald
Grant and David Riesman. — Chicago: University of Chicago Press, 1978,
c1977. vi, 474 p.; 24 cm. Includes indexes. 1. Education, Higher — United
States. I. Riesman, David, 1909- joint author. II. T.
LA227.2.G73     378.73     *LC* 77-11039     *ISBN* 0226306054

## LA227.3 1965–

**Aiken, Henry David, 1912-.**        **4.10072**
Predicament of the university. — Bloomington: Indiana University Press,
[1971] x, 404 p.; 25 cm. 1. Universities and colleges — U.S. 2. Education,
Higher — U.S. — 1965- I. T.
LA227.3.A36 1971     378.73     *LC* 79-143618     *ISBN* 0253129702

**Astin, Alexander W.**        **4.10073**
Four critical years: [effects of college on beliefs, attitudes, and knowledge] /
Alexander W. Astin. — 1st ed. — San Francisco: Jossey-Bass Publishers, 1977.
xvi, 293p.; 24 cm. — — (Jossey-Bass series in higher education) 1. College
students — United States 2. College students — United States — Psychology
3. College students — United States — Attitudes I. T.
LA227.3.A75     *LC* 76-57308     *ISBN* 0875893465

**Bowen, Howard Rothmann, 1908-.**        **4.10074**
Investment in learning: the individual and social value of American higher
education / Howard R. Bowen, with the collaboration of Peter Clecak,
Jacqueline Powers Doud, Gordon K. Douglass. — 1st ed. — San Francisco:
Jossey-Bass Publishers, 1977. xviii, 507 p.; 24 cm. — (The Carnegie Council
series) 'A report ... issued by the Carnegie Council on Policy Studies in Higher
Education.' Includes indexes. 1. Education, Higher — United States.
2. Educational sociology — United States. I. Carnegie Council on Policy
Studies in Higher Education. II. T.
LA227.3.B66     378.73     *LC* 77-82069     *ISBN* 0875893414

**Boyer, Ernest L.**        **4.10075**
College: the undergraduate experience in America / Ernest L. Boyer. — 1st ed.
— New York: Harper & Row, 1987. xix, 328 p.; 26 cm. 'The Carnegie
Foundation for the Advancement of Teaching.' Includes index. 1. Universities
and colleges — United States — Case studies. 2. College students — United
States — Case studies. I. Carnegie Foundation for the Advancement of
Teaching. II. T.
LA227.3.B678 1987     378.73 19     *LC* 85-45182     *ISBN* 0060155078

**Carnegie Commission on Higher Education.**    **4.10076**
Priorities for action: final report. With technical notes and appendixes. — New York: McGraw-Hill, 1973. x, 243 p.; 23 cm. Companion volumes: A digest of reports of the Carnegie Commission on Higher Education and Sponsored research of the Carnegie Commission on Higher Education. The three volumes comprise the Commission's Summary report, 1967-1973. 1. Education, Higher — United States — History. I. T.
LA227.3.C38 1973     378.73     LC 73-15714     ISBN 0070101043

**Carnegie Foundation for the Advancement of Teaching.**    **4.10077**
More than survival: prospects for higher education in a period of uncertainty: a commentary with recommendations / by the Carnegie Foundation for the Advancement of Teaching. — 1st ed. — San Francisco: Jossey-Bass Publishers, 1975. xiv, 166 p.: ill.; 24 cm. (The Carnegie Council series) Includes index. 1. Education, Higher — United States — 1965- I. T.
LA227.3.C39 1975     378.73     LC 75-4481     ISBN 0875892582

**Cross, K. Patricia (Kathryn Patricia), 1926-.**    **4.10078**
Beyond the open door [by] K. Patricia Cross. [1st ed.] San Francisco, Jossey-Bass, 1971. xviii, 200 p. 24 cm. (The Jossey-Bass series in higher education) 'A study sponsored by Educational Testing Service, Center for Research and Development in Higher Education, University of California, Berkeley [and] College Entrance Examination Board.' 1. Universities and colleges — United States — Admission. 2. Education, Higher — United States — 1965- I. Educational Testing Service. II. University of California, Berkeley. Center for Research and Development in Higher Education. III. College Entrance Examination Board. IV. T.
LA227.3.C76     378.1/05/60973     LC 77-170212     ISBN 087589111X

**Hall, Laurence.**    **4.10079**
New colleges for new students / [by] Laurence Hall and associates; foreword by Frank Newman and Russell Edgerton. — [1st ed.]. — San Francisco: Jossey-Bass, 1974. xxi, 210 p.; 24 cm. — (The Jossey-Bass series in higher education) 1. Education, Higher — United States. 2. Educational innovations — United States. I. T.
LA227.3.H23     378.73     LC 73-10933     ISBN 0875891942

**Hefferlin, J. B. Lon.**    **4.10080**
Dynamics of academic reform / [by] J. B. Lon Hefferlin; foreword by Earl F. McGrath. — [1st ed.]. — San Francisco: Jossey-Bass, 1969. xxvi, 240 p.; 24 cm. — (The Jossey-Bass series in higher education) 1. Education, Higher — U.S. — 1965- 2. Universities and colleges — U.S. — Curricula. I. T.
LA227.3.H4     378.73     LC 76-92895     ISBN 0875890482

**Ladd, Everett Carll.**    **4.10081**
The divided academy: professors and politics, by Everett Carll Ladd, Jr., and Seymour Martin Lipset. — New York: McGraw-Hill, [1975] xv, 407 p.; 24 cm. Sponsored by the Carnegie Commission on Higher Education. 1. College teachers — United States — Political activity. 2. United States — Politics and government I. Lipset, Seymour Martin. joint author. II. Carnegie Commission on Higher Education. III. T.
LA227.3.L33     378.1/2     LC 74-17247     ISBN 0070101124

**The Modern American college / Arthur W. Chickering and**    **4.10082**
**associates; foreword by Nevitt Sanford.**
1st ed. — San Francisco: Jossey-Bass, 1981. li, 810 p.: ill.; 26 cm. — (Jossey-Bass series in higher education.) 1. Universities and colleges — United States 2. College students — United States. 3. Continuing education — United States. I. Chickering, Arthur W., 1927- II. Series.
LA227.3.M63     378.73 19     LC 80-8010     ISBN 0875894666

**National Institute of Education (U.S.). Study Group on the**    **4.10083**
**Conditions of Excellence in American Higher Education.**
Involvement in learning: realizing the potential of American higher education: final report of the Study Group on the Conditions of Excellence in American Higher Education. — Washington, D.C.: National Institute of Education, U.S. Dept. of Education: [Supt. of Docs., U.S. G.P.O., distributor, 1984] xi, 99 p.; 26 cm. 'October, 1984.' S/N 065-000-00213-2 Item 461-D-5 1. Education, Higher — United States. 2. Education, Higher — United States — Aims and objectives. I. T.
LA227.3.N34 1984     378.73 19     LC 84-603895

**Newman, Frank, 1927-.**    **4.10084**
Higher education and the American resurgence / Frank Newman; with an introduction by Ernest L. Boyer. — Princeton, N.J.: Carnegie Foundation for the Advancement of Teaching; Lawrenceville, N.J.: Available from the Princeton University Press, c1985. xxii, 268 p.: ill.; 24 cm. (Carnegie Foundation special report.) Includes index. 1. Education, Higher — United States. 2. Competition, International 3. Research — United States I. T. II. Series.
LA227.3.N46 1985     378.73 19     LC 85-21357     ISBN 0931050286

**Parsons, Talcott, 1902-.**    **4.10085**
The American university [by] Talcott Parsons and Gerald M. Platt, with the collaboration of Neil J. Smelser. Editorial associate: Jackson Toby. —

Cambridge: Harvard University Press, 1973. xi, 463 p.; 25 cm. 1. Universities and colleges — United States I. Platt, Gerald M. joint author. II. T.
LA227.3.P37     378.73     LC 73-77470     ISBN 0674029208

**Riesman, David, 1909-.**    **4.10086**
On higher education: the academic enterprise in an era of rising student consumerism / David Riesman. — 1st ed. — San Francisco: Jossey-Bass, 1980. xxxiv, 421 p.; 24 cm. — (The Carnegie Council series) Includes indexes. 1. Universities and colleges — United States 2. College, Choice of — United States. I. T. II. Series.
LA227.3.R53     378.73 19     LC 80-8007     ISBN 0875894844

**Roose, Kenneth D.**    **4.10087**
A rating of graduate programs [by] Kenneth D. Roose [and] Charles J. Andersen. — [Washington]: American Council on Education, [c1970] xi, 115 p.; 28 cm. Study conducted by the American Council on Education. 1. Universities and colleges — U.S. — Graduate work. I. Andersen, Charles J. joint author. II. American Council on Education. III. T.
LA227.3.R65     378.1/553/0973     LC 76-138559     ISBN 0826813712

**Axelrod, Joseph, 1918-.**    **4.10088**
Search for relevance: the campus in crisis / [by] Joseph Axelrod [and others. — 1st ed.]. — San Francisco: Jossey-Bass, 1969. xi, 244 p.; 24 cm. — (The Jossey-Bass series in higher education) 1. Education, Higher — U.S. — 1965- I. T.
LA227.3.S4     378/.001     LC 72-75941     ISBN 0875890385

## LA228 Higher Education. Addresses, Essays, Lectures

**Wilson, Logan, 1907- ed.**    **4.10089**
Universal higher education: costs, benefits, options. Edited by Logan Wilson and Olive Mills. — Washington, [1972] xv, 342 p.; 24 cm. Contains background papers and commentaries presented at the 54th annual meeting of the American Council on Education, held in Washington, D.C., Oct. 6-8, 1971; the background papers were published separately in 1971. 1. Education, Higher — United States — Aims and objectives. I. Mills, Olive, ed. II. American Council on Education. III. T.
LA228.A65     378.73     LC 72-79161     ISBN 0826814050

**Sanford, Nevitt. ed.**    **4.10090**
The American college; a psychological and social interpretation of the higher learning, by Joseph Adelson [and others] Prepared for the Society for the Psychological Study of Social Issues. Editorial committee: Christian Bay [and others]. — New York: Wiley, [1962] xvi, 1084 p.: diagrs., tables.; 24 cm. 1. Universities and colleges — United States 2. Education, Higher — Addresses, essays, lectures. I. Adelson, Joseph. II. Society for the Psychological Study of Social Issues. III. T.
LA228.S3     378.73     LC 61-17362

## LA229 STUDENT LIFE. STUDENT MOVEMENTS

**United States. President's Commission on Campus Unrest.**    **4.10091**
The report of the President's Commission on Campus Unrest; including special reports: the killings at Jackson State, the Kent State tragedy. [Reprint ed.] New York, Arno Press [1970] x, 537 p. illus., maps. 23 cm. 1. Jackson State College. 2. Kent State University. 3. Student movements — United States. I. T.
LA229.A54 1970b     378.1/98/1     LC 71-139710     ISBN 040501712X

**Katz, Joseph, 1920-.**    **4.10092**
No time for youth; growth and constraint in college students [by] Joseph Katz & associates: Harold A. Korn [and others. — 1st ed.]. — San Francisco: Jossey-Bass, 1968. xx, 463 p.; 24 cm. — (The Jossey-Bass series in higher education) 'A publication of the Institute for the Study of Human Problems, Stanford University.' 1. College students — United States. 2. Education, Higher — Aims and objectives I. Korn, Harold Allen. II. Stanford University. Institute for the Study of Human Problems. III. T.
LA229.K32     378.1/98/10973     LC 68-21317

**Levine, Arthur.**    **4.10093**
When dreams and heroes died: a portrait of today's college student: [prepared for the Carnegie Council on Policy Studies in Higher Education] / Arthur Levine. — 1st ed. — San Francisco, Calif.: Jossey-Bass; [New York, N.Y.]: Carnegie Foundation for the Advancement of Teaching, 1980. xix, 157 p.; 24 cm. — (The Carnegie Council series) Includes index. 1. College students — United States — Attitudes. 2. Narcissism I. Carnegie Council on Policy Studies in Higher Education. II. T.
LA229.L42     378/.1981/0973 19     LC 80-8005     ISBN 087589481X

**Novak, Steven J., 1947-.**    **4.10094**
The rights of youth: American colleges and student revolt, 1798–1815 / Steven J. Novak. Cambridge, Mass.: Harvard University Press, 1977. vii, 218 p.: ill.; 23 cm. Includes index. 1. Student movements — United States. 2. College students — Legal status, laws, etc. — United States — History. I. T.
LA229.N68     371.8/1     LC 76-43109     ISBN 0674770161

**Unger, Irwin.**　　　　　　　　　　　**4.10095**
The movement: a history of the American New Left, 1959–1972 / by Irwin Unger; with the assistance of Debi Unger. — New York: Dodd, Mead, 1974. viii, 217 p.; 21 cm. 1. Students for a Democratic Society (U.S.). 2. College students — United States — Political activity. 3. Radicalism — United States. I. Unger, Debi. joint author. II. T.
LA229.U47　　　322.4/4/0973　　　*LC* 73-21168　　　*ISBN* 0396069401

## LA231–396 U.S. Education, by State, A–Z

**Katz, Michael B.**　　　　　　　　　• **4.10096**
The irony of early school reform: educational innovation in mid–nineteenth century Massachusetts / [by] Michael B. Katz. — Cambridge, Mass.: Harvard University Press, 1968. xii, 325 p.; 22 cm. 1. Educational innovations — Massachusetts. 2. Education — Massachusetts — History. I. T.
LA304.K3　　　370/.9744　　　*LC* 68-17626

**Lazerson, Marvin.**　　　　　　　　• **4.10097**
Origins of the urban school; public education in Massachusetts, 1870–1915. — Cambridge, Mass.: Harvard University Press, 1971. xix, 278 p.; 24 cm. — (A Publication of the Joint Center for Urban Studies of the Massachusetts Institute of Technology and Harvard University) 1. Public schools — Massachusetts — History. 2. Education, Urban — Massachusetts — History. I. T.
LA304.L38　　　370.19/348/09744　　　*LC* 77-168433　　　*ISBN* 0674644824

**Schultz, Stanley K.**　　　　　　　　**4.10098**
The culture factory; Boston public schools, 1789–1860 [by] Stanley K. Schultz. New York, Oxford University Press, 1973. xvi, 394 p. illus. 24 cm. (The Urban life in America series) 1. Public schools — Massachusetts — Boston — History. I. T.
LA306.B7 S34　　　370/.9744/61　　　*LC* 72-92297

**Ravitch, Diane.**　　　　　　　　　**4.10099**
The great school wars, New York City, 1805–1973: a history of the public schools as battlefield of social change. — New York: Basic Books, [1974] xviii, 449 p.: ill.; 25 cm. 1. Education — New York (City) — History. I. T.
LA339.N5 R38　　　370.19/3/097471　　　*LC* 73-81136　　　*ISBN* 0465027024

**Rogers, David, 1930-.**　　　　　　　**4.10100**
110 Livingston Street revisited: decentralization in action / David Rogers and Norman H. Chung. — New York: New York University Press, 1984. xvii, 241 p.; 24 cm. Includes index. 1. Politics and education — New York (N.Y.) 2. Schools — Decentralization — New York (N.Y.) I. Chung, Norman H., 1949- II. T. III. Title: One hundred ten Livingston Street revisited.
LA339.N5 R6 1983　　　379.1/535 19　　　*LC* 83-3937　　　*ISBN* 0814773877

## LA417–418 Canada

**Harris, Robin Sutton, 1919-.**　　　　**4.10101**
A history of higher education in Canada, 1663–1960 / Robin S. Harris. — Toronto; Buffalo: University of Toronto Press, c1976. xxiv, 715 p. — (Etudes sur l'histoire d'enseignement supérieur au Canada. 7) Includes index. 1. Education, Higher — Canada — History. I. T. II. Series.
LA417.5.H37　　　LA417.5 H36.　　　378.71　　　*LC* 76-17112　　　*ISBN* 0802033369

## LA420–609 Latin America

**King, Richard G., 1922-.**　　　　　　**4.10102**
The provincial universities of Mexico; an analysis of growth and development [by] Richard G. King, with Alfonso Rangel Guerra, David Kline [and] Noel F. McGinn. — New York: Praeger Publishers, [1971] xxi, 234 p.; 25 cm. — (Praeger special studies in international economics and development) 'A cooperative project of the International Council for Educational Development, New York; Asociación Nacional de Universidades e Institutos de Ensenanza Superior, Mexico City; and Center for Studies in Education and Development, Harvard University.' 1. Universities and colleges — Mexico. 2. Educational planning — Mexico. I. Rangel Guerra, Alfonso. II. International Council for Educational Development. III. T.
LA428.K5　　　378.72　　　*LC* 74-163928

**Kozol, Jonathan.**　　　　　　　　　**4.10103**
Children of the revolution: a Yankee teacher in the Cuban schools / Jonathan Kozol. — New York: Delacorte Press, c1978. xxi, 245 p., [8] leaves of plates: ill.; 22 cm. 1. Education — Cuba — History. I. T.
LA486.K69　　　370/.97291　　　*LC* 78-18522　　　*ISBN* 0440009820

**Education in Latin America / edited by Colin Brock and Hugh**　　**4.10104**
**Lawlor.**
London; Dover, N.H.: Croom Helm, c1985. 196 p.: ill.; 22 cm. 1. Education — Latin America — Addresses, essays, lectures. I. Brock, Colin. II. Lawlor, Hugh.
LA541.E277 1985　　　370/.98 19　　　*LC* 85-3750　　　*ISBN* 0709932731

**Haussman, Fay, 1922-.**　　　　　　**4.10105**
Education in Brazil / Fay Haussman and Jerry Haar. — Hamden, Conn.: Archon Books, 1978. 169 p.: ill.; 23 cm. — (World education series) Includes index. 1. Education — Brazil. I. Haar, Jerry, 1947- joint author. II. T.
LA556.H34　　　370/.981　　　*LC* 77-17797　　　*ISBN* 0208017054

**Silvert, Kalman H.**　　　　　　　　**4.10106**
Education, class, and nation: the experiences of Chile and Venezuela / Kalman H. Silvert, Leonard Reissman. New York: Elsevier, c1976. xvi, 242 p.: ill.; 24 cm. 1. Education — Chile. 2. Education — Venezuela. 3. Educational sociology — Chile. 4. Educational sociology — Venezuela. I. Reissman, Leonard. joint author. II. T.
LA561.S54　　　370/.983　　　*LC* 75-40653　　　*ISBN* 0444990186

## LA620–1040 Europe

**Brickman, William W.**　　　　　　**4.10107**
Educational roots and routes in western Europe / William W. Brickman. — Cherry Hill, N.J.: Emeritus, 1985. viii, 404 p.; 23 cm. 1. Education — Europe — History — Addresses, essays, lectures. 2. Educational literature — Europe — Addresses, essays, lectures. 3. Education — Europe — History — Bibliography. I. T.
LA621.B74 1985　　　370/.94 19　　　*LC* 85-70176　　　*ISBN* 0943694019

**Thorndike, Lynn, 1882-1965.**　　　　• **4.10108**
University records and life in the Middle Ages. — New York: Octagon Books, 1971 [c1944] xvii, 476 p.: fold. map.; 24 cm. — (Records of civilization, sources and studies. no. 38) 1. Universities and colleges — Europe 2. Education, Medieval I. T. II. Series.
LA627.T45 1971　　　378.4　　　*LC* 77-145546

**Statera, Gianni.**　　　　　　　　　**4.10109**
Death of a utopia: the development and decline of student movements in Europe / Gianni Statera. — New York: Oxford University Press, 1975. ix, 294 p.; 22 cm. 1. Student movements — Europe. 2. Youth — Europe — Political activity. I. T.
LA628.7.S7　　　322.4/4/094　　　*LC* 74-79634　　　*ISBN* 0195017951

### LA630 Britain. Ireland

**Dent, H. C. (Harold Collett), 1894-.**　　**4.10110**
Education in England and Wales / H. C. Dent. — [Hamden, Conn.]: Linnet Books, c1977. 171 p.: ill.; 24 cm. First-5th ed. published under title: The educational system of England and Wales. 1. Education — England — History. 2. Education — Wales — History. 3. Comparative education I. T.
LA631.D385 1977　　　370/.942　　　*LC* 77-12936　　　*ISBN* 0208017429

**Leach, Arthur Francis, 1851-1915.**　　• **4.10111**
Educational charters and documents 598 to 1909. Cambridge: The University Press, 1911. 582 p.; 20 cm. 1. Education — Great Britain — History. 2. Universities and colleges — Great Britain — History. I. T.
LA 631 L43 1911　　　*LC* 12-4367

**Maclure, Stuart.**　　　　　　　　　• **4.10112**
Educational documents: England and Wales 1816–1967 / [by] J. Stuart Maclure. — 2nd ed. — London: Chapman & Hall, 1968. ix, 323 p.; 25 cm. 1. Education — England — History — Sources. 2. Education — Wales — Addresses, essays, lectures. I. T.
LA631.M25 1968　　　370/.942 19　　　*LC* 68-119308

**Wardle, David.**　　　　　　　　　**4.10113**
The rise of the schooled society; the history of formal schooling in England. — London and Boston: Routledge & Kegan Paul, [1974] vii, 182 p.; 23 cm. 1. Education — Great Britain — History. I. T.
LA631.W37 1974　　　370/.942　　　*LC* 73-86578　　　*ISBN* 0710077173

**Orme, Nicholas.**　　　　　　　　　**4.10114**
English schools in the Middle Ages. — London: Methuen [distributed by Harper & Row, Barnes & Noble Import Division, New York, 1973] xiv, 369 p.: illus.; 24 cm. 1. Education, Medieval — England — History. I. T.
LA631.3.O75　　　370/.942　　　*LC* 73-178498　　　*ISBN* 0416160800

**Tompson, Richard S.**    **4.10115**
Classics or charity: the dilemma of the 18th century grammar school / [by] Richard S. Tompson. — Manchester: Manchester University Press, 1972 (c1971) viii, 168 p.: 1 ill.; 23 cm. 1. Public schools — England — History. I. T.
LA631.5.T45    373.42    *LC* 72-176268    *ISBN* 0719004683

**Digby, Anne.**    **4.10116**
Children, school, and society in nineteenth–century England / Anne Digby and Peter Searby. — London; New York: Macmillan, 1981. 258 p.; 23 cm. 1. Education — Great Britain — History — 19th century. 2. Educational sociology — Great Britain — History — 19th century — Sources. 3. England — Civilization — 19th century — Sources. 4. Great Britain — History — 19th century — Sources. I. Searby, Peter. II. T.
LA631.7.D53 1981    370.19/3/0942 19    *LC* 82-100863    *ISBN* 0333246780

**Silver, Harold.**    **4.10117**
Education as history: interpreting nineteenth–and twentieth–century education / Harold Silver; foreword by David B. Tyack. — London; New York: Methuen, 1983. xiii, 314 p.; 22 cm. 1. Education — Great Britain — History. 2. Education — United States — History. 3. Educational sociology — Great Britain — History. 4. Educational sociology — United States — History. I. T.
LA631.7.S44 1983    370/.941 19    *LC* 82-20853    *ISBN* 0416333109

**Rathbone, Charles H., comp.**    **4.10118**
Open education: the informal classroom; a selection of readings that examine the practices and principles of the British infant schools and their American counterparts. Selected and edited by Charles H. Rathbone. — New York: Citation Press, 1971. xiv, 207 p.: illus.; 21 cm. 1. Education, Elementary — Gt. Brit. — Addresses, essays, lectures. 2. Education, Elementary — U.S. — Addresses, essays, lectures. I. T.
LA633.R3    372.24/1    *LC* 73-173449    *ISBN* 0590095056

**Judge, Harry George.**    **4.10119**
A generation of schooling: English secondary schools since 1944 / Harry Judge. — Oxford; New York: Oxford University Press, 1984. 227 p.; 23 cm. Includes index. 1. Education, Secondary — England — History — 20th century. I. T.
LA634.J82 1984    372.942 19    *LC* 84-7939    *ISBN* 0192191756

**Great Britain. Central Advisory Council for Education**    • **4.10120**
**(England)**
Children and their primary schools: a report of the Central Advisory Council for Education (England). — London: H.M.S.O., 1967. 2 v.: illus. (forms) tables, diagrs., plates (part col.); 24 1/2 cm. 1. Education — Great Britain — 1945- I. T.
LA635.A45 1967    372.9/42    *LC* 67-77815

**Rutter, Michael.**    **4.10121**
Fifteen thousand hours: secondary schools and their effects on children / Michael Rutter ... [et al.]. — Cambridge, Mass.: Harvard University Press, 1979. viii, 285 p.: ill.; 22 cm. Includes indexes. 1. High schools — England — London. 2. High school students — England — London — Attitudes. I. T.
LA635.F5    373.421/2    *LC* 78-23382    *ISBN* 0674300254

**Berlak, Ann.**    **4.10122**
Dilemmas of schooling: teaching and social change / Ann & Harold Berlak. — London; New York: Methuen, 1981. x, 299 p.: ill.; 22 cm. Includes indexes. 1. Education, Elementary — Great Britain — Social aspects. I. Berlak, Harold. II. T.
LA637.B47 1981    372/.241/0942 19    *LC* 81-153638    *ISBN* 0416741401

**Akenson, Donald H.**    **4.10123**
A mirror to Kathleen's face: education in independent Ireland, 1922–1960 / Donald Harman Akenson. — Montreal: McGill-Queen's University Press, 1975. x, 224 p.; 23 cm. Includes index. 1. Education — Ireland — History. I. T.
LA641.8.A44    370/.9415    *LC* 76-356281    *ISBN* 0773502033

## LA670–1040 Other European Countries

**Chisick, Harvey, 1946-.**    **4.10124**
The limits of reform in the Enlightenment: attitudes toward the education of the lower classes in eighteenth–century France / Harvey Chisick. — Princeton, N.J.: Princeton University Press, c1981. xvi, 324 p.; 23 cm. Includes index. 1. Education — France — History — 18th century. 2. Enlightenment I. T.
LA691.5.C52    370/.944 19    *LC* 80-7512    *ISBN* 0691053057

**Palmer, R. R. (Robert Roswell), 1909-.**    **4.10125**
The improvement of humanity: education and the French Revolution / R.R. Palmer. — Princeton, N.J.: Princeton University Press, c1985. viii, 347 p.; 25 cm. 1. Education — France — History — 18th century. 2. France — History — Revolution, 1789-1799 — Education and the revolution. I. T.
LA691.5.P35 1985    370/.944 19    *LC* 84-15048    *ISBN* 0691054347

**Cohen, Habiba S.**    **4.10126**
Elusive reform: the French universities, 1968–1978 / Habiba S. Cohen. — Boulder, Colo.: Westview Press, 1978. xv, 280 p.: graphs; 24 cm. — (A Westview replica edition) 1. Universities and colleges — France — History. I. T.
LA699.C57    378.44    *LC* 78-19677    *ISBN* 0891581952

**Jarausch, Konrad Hugo.**    **4.10127**
Students, society, and politics in imperial Germany: the rise of academic illiberalism / Konrad H. Jarausch. — Princeton, N.J.: Princeton University Press, c1982. xvi, 448 p.: ill.; 24 cm. 1. Education, Higher — Germany — History — 19th century. 2. Students — Germany — Political activity — History — 19th century. I. T.
LA727.J36 1982    378/.1981/0943 19    *LC* 81-47926    *ISBN* 0691053456

**McClelland, Charles E.**    **4.10128**
State, society, and university in Germany, 1700–1914 / Charles E. McClelland. — Cambridge; New York: Cambridge University Press, 1980. ix, 381 p.; 24 cm. Includes index. 1. Universities and colleges — Germany — History. 2. Germany — Intellectual life — History. 3. Germany — History — 18th century I. T.
LA727.M32    378.43    *LC* 79-13575    *ISBN* 0521227429

**Ringer, Fritz K., 1934-.**    **4.10129**
The decline of the German mandarins; the German academic community, 1890–1933 [by] Fritz K. Ringer. Cambridge, Mass., Harvard University Press, 1969. 528 p. 24 cm. Based on the author's dissertation The German universities and the crisis of learning, 1918-1925, 1960. 1. Universities and colleges — Germany — History. 2. Germany — Intellectual life — 20th century I. T.
LA727.R47    001.2/0943    *LC* 68-54023

**Hans, Nicholas A., 1888-.**    • **4.10130**
The Russian tradition in education. — London: Routledge & K. Paul, [1963] 196 p. 1. Education — Russia — History. I. T.
LA831.H353    *LC* 63-25594

**Fitzpatrick, Sheila.**    **4.10131**
Education and social mobility in the Soviet Union, 1921–1934 / Sheila Fitzpatrick. — Cambridge, Eng.; New York: Cambridge University Press, 1979. x, 355 p.; 23 cm. (Soviet and East European studies.) (Studies of the Russian Institute, Columbia University) Includes index. 1. School management and organization — Russia — History. 2. Social mobility — Russia. 3. Russia — Politics and government — 1917-1936. I. T. II. Series.
LA831.8.F57    370/.947    *LC* 78-58788    *ISBN* 0521223253

**Matthews, Mervyn.**    **4.10132**
Education in the Soviet Union: policies and institutions since Stalin / Mervyn Matthews. — London; Boston: Allen & Unwin, 1982. xiv, 225 p.; 23 cm. Includes index. 1. Education — Soviet Union — History — 20th century. 2. Communism and education I. T.
LA831.82.M33 1982    370/.947 19    *LC* 82-6656    *ISBN* 0043701140

**Ablin, Fred, comp.**    • **4.10133**
Contemporary Soviet education: a collection of readings from Soviet journals / with an introd. by George S. Counts. — White Plains, N.Y.: International Arts and Sciences Press [1969] xiii, 295 p.: ill.; 29 cm. Translations of these readings first appeared in Soviet education. 1. Education — Soviet Union I. Soviet education. II. T.
LA832.A63    370/.947    *LC* 68-14428

**Jacoby, Susan.**    **4.10134**
Inside Soviet schools. New York, Hill and Wang [1974] 248 p. 21 cm. 1. Education — Soviet Union I. T.
LA832.J32    370/.947    *LC* 73-91173    *ISBN* 0809058464

**Soviet education in the 1980s** / edited by J.J. Tomiak.    **4.10135**
London: Croom Helm; New York: St. Martin's Press, 1983. x, 326 p.; 23 cm. 1. Education — Soviet Union — Congresses. I. Tomiak, J. J.
LA832.S735 1983    370/.947 19    *LC* 83-13845    *ISBN* 0312747772

## LA1045–1491 Asia. Islamic Countries

**Schooling in the ASEAN region: primary and secondary**    **4.10136**
**education in Indonesia, Malaysia, the Philippines, Singapore,**
**and Thailand** / edited by T. Neville Postlethwaite and R.
**Murray Thomas.**
Oxford; New York: Pergamon Press, 1980. xvii, 328 p.: ill.; 21 cm. 1. Education, Elementary — Asia, Southeastern. 2. Education, Secondary — Asia, Southeastern. 3. Comparative education I. Postlethwaite, T. Neville. II. Thomas, R. Murray (Robert Murray)
LA1059.S6 S3 1980    372.9/59 19    *LC* 79-41357    *ISBN* 0080242898

**Chen, Theodore Hsi-en, 1902-.**      4.10137
The Maoist educational revolution [by] Theodore Hsi-en Chen. New York, Praeger [1974] xv, 295 p. 25 cm. (Praeger special studies in international economics and development) 1. Mao, Tse-tung, 1893-1976. 2. Education — China — History — 1949-1976 I. T.
LA1131.C376    370/.951    LC 72-89643    ISBN 0275080408

**Toward a new world outlook: a documentary history of**      4.10138
**education in the People's Republic of China, 1949–1976 / edited by Shi Ming Hu and Eli Seifman.**
New York: AMS Press, 1977 (c1976). xx, 335 p.; 24 cm. — (Asian studies series; 2) 1. Education — China — History — 1949-1976 I. Hu, Shi Ming, 1927- II. Seifman, Eli.
LA1131.T64    370/.951    LC 76-23977    ISBN 0404154018

**Unger, Jonathan.**      4.10139
Education under Mao: class and competition in Canton schools, 1960–1980 / Jonathan Unger. — New York: Columbia University Press, 1982. xii, 308 p.; 24 cm. — (Studies of the East Asian Institute.) Includes index. 1. Education — China — Canton — History. I. T. II. Series.
LA1134.C35 U53 1982    370/.951/27 19    LC 81-15470    ISBN 0231052987

**Tsurumi, E. Patricia, 1938-.**      4.10140
Japanese colonial education in Taiwan, 1895–1945 / E. Patricia Tsurumi. — Cambridge, Mass.: Harvard University Press, 1977. xiii, 334 p.; 24 cm. — (Harvard East Asian series. 88) Includes index. 1. Education — Taiwan — History — To 1945 I. T. II. Series.
LA1136.T76    370/.951/249    LC 76-29628    ISBN 0674471873

**Schooling in East Asia: forces of change: formal and nonformal**      4.10141
**eduction in Japan, The Republic of China, The People's Republic of China, South Korea, North Korea, Hong Kong, and Macau / edited by R. Murray Thomas and T. Neville Postlethwaite.**
Oxford; New York: Pergamon Press, 1983. xiii, 350 p.: ill.; 22 cm. 1. Education — East Asia — Addresses, essays, lectures. 2. School management and organization — East Asia — Addresses, essays, lectures. 3. Education and state — East Asia — Addresses, essays, lectures. I. Thomas, R. Murray (Robert Murray), 1921- II. Postlethwaite, T. Neville.
LA1141.S36 1983    370/.95 19    LC 83-2275    ISBN 0080268048

**Rudolph, Susanne Hoeber.**      4.10142
Education and politics in India: studies in organzation, society, and policy / edited by Susanne Hoeber Rudolph and Lloyd I. Rudolph; contributors: Paul R. Brass [and others]. — Cambridge, Mass.: Harvard University Press, 1972. x, 470 p.; 25 cm. 1. Education — India. 2. Education and state — India. I. Rudolph, Lloyd I. joint author. II. Brass, Paul R. III. T.
LA1151.R82    370/.954    LC 71-186675    ISBN 0674238656

**Roden, Donald, 1944-.**      4.10143
Schooldays in Imperial Japan: a study in the culture of a student elite / Donald Roden. — Berkeley: University of California Press, c1980. xiii, 300 p.: ill.; 24 cm. Originally presented as the author's thesis, University of Wisconsin, 1975. 'Published under the auspices of the Center for Japanese and Korean Studies, University of California, Berkeley.' Includes index. 1. Education — Japan — History 2. Students — Japan — History. 3. Elite (Social sciences) — Japan — History. I. University of California, Berkeley. Center for Japanese and Korean Studies. II. T.
LA1311.R62 1980    370/.952    LC 79-64477    ISBN 0520039106

**Cummings, William K.**      4.10144
Education and equality in Japan / William K. Cummings. — Princeton, N.J.: Princeton University Press, c1980. xvi, 305 p.: ill.; 24 cm. Includes index. 1. Education — Japan — History — 1945- 2. Educational equalization — Japan — History — 20th century. I. T.
LA1311.82.C85    370/.952    LC 79-3199    ISBN 0691093857

**Duke, Benjamin C.**      4.10145
The Japanese school: lessons for industrial America / Benjamin Duke. — New York: Praeger, 1986. xx, 242 p.: ill.; 24 cm. 'Praeger special studies. Praeger scientific.' Includes index. 1. Education — Japan — Aims and objectives. 2. Education — United States — Aims and objectives. 3. Labor and laboring classes — Education — Japan. 4. Labor productivity — Japan. I. T.
LA1312.D85 1986    370/.952 19    LC 86-5002    ISBN 0275920534

**Smith, Henry DeWitt.**      4.10146
Japan's first student radicals [by] Henry DeWitt Smith, II. — Cambridge, Mass.: Harvard University Press, 1972. xv, 341 p.: illus., facsims.; 24 cm. — (Harvard East Asian series. 70) 1. Shinjinkai. 2. College students — Japan — Political activity. I. T. II. Series.
LA1318.7.S55    378.1/98/10952    LC 72-81276    ISBN 0674471857

**Tibawi, Abdul Latif.**      4.10147
Islamic education: its traditions and modernization into the Arab national systems [by] A. L. Tibawi. — London: Luzac, 1972. 256 p.: col. plate.; 22 cm.

Label mounted on t.p.: Distributed in the United States by Crane, Russak & Co., New York. 1. Education — Arab countries. 2. Islam — Education I. T.
LA1491.T5    370/.917/671    LC 73-159526    ISBN 0718901614

## LA1500–2090 Africa

**Education in Africa: a comparative survey / edited by A. Babs**      4.10148
**Fafunwa, J.U. Aisiku.**
London; Boston: G. Allen & Unwin, 1982. 270 p.: map; 22 cm. 1. Education — South Africa. 2. Comparative education I. Fafunwa, A. Babs, 1923- II. Aisiku, J. U.
LA1501.E364 1982    370/.968 19    LC 81-19129    ISBN 0043701132

**Thompson, A. R.**      4.10149
Education and development in Africa / A. R. Thompson. — New York: St. Martin's Press, 1981. viii, 358 p.; 22 cm. Includes index. 1. Education — Africa, Southern. 2. Education — Economic aspects — Africa, Southern. 3. Education — Developing countries I. T.
LA1501.T48 1981    370/.968 19    LC 80-24736    ISBN 0312237243

**The Future of the university in Southern Africa / edited by**      4.10150
**Hendrik W. van der Merwe and David Welsh, in association with the Centre for Intergroup Studies.**
New York: St. Martin's Press, 1978, c1977. xi, 302 p.; 22 cm. 1. Universities and colleges — Africa, Southern — Addresses, essays, lectures. I. Van der Merwe, Hendrik W. II. Welsh, David John. III. University of Cape Town. Centre for Intergroup Studies.
LA1503.F87 1978    378.68    LC 78-60638    ISBN 0312314841

**Wagaw, Teshome G., 1930-.**      4.10151
Education in Ethiopia: prospect and retrospect / Teshome G. Wagaw. — Ann Arbor: University of Michigan Press, 1979. xv, 256 p.: map; 24 cm. Includes index. 1. Education — Ethiopia — History. I. T.
LA1516.W33    370/.963 19    LC 79-274    ISBN 0472089455

**Sheffield, James R.**      4.10152
Education in Kenya: an historical study [by] James R. Sheffield. — New York: Teachers College Press, [1973] vii, 126 p.: map.; 24 cm. — (Publications of the Center for Education in Africa, Institute of International Studies) 1. Education — Kenya — History. I. T.
LA1561.S44    370/.9676/2    LC 72-88639

## LA2100–2189 Australia

**Macpherson, James, 1942-.**      4.10153
The feral classroom / James Macpherson. — Melbourne; Boston: Routledge & Kegan Paul, 1983. 239 p.: ill.; 22 cm. — (Routledge education books.) Includes indexes. 1. Parsons, Talcott, 1902- 2. Classroom environment — Australia — Case studies. 3. Social interaction — Australia — Case studies. 4. High school students — Australia. I. T. II. Series.
LA2106.7.M22 1983    373.18/0973 19    LC 83-13900    ISBN 0710095147

## LA2301–2397 Biography

**Directory of American scholars.**      • 4.10154
1st- ed.; 1942-. New York: Bowker. v. Irregular. 'A biographical directory.' (varies). 4th(1963)- issued in 4 vols. 1. Scholars — United States — Directories I. Cattell, Jaques, 1904-1960. II. Jaques Cattell Press.
LA2311.C32    LA2311.D59.

**Raphael, Ray.**      4.10155
The teacher's voice: a sense of who we are / Ray Raphael. — 1st ed. — Portsmouth, NH: Heinemann, c1985. 137 p.; 23 cm. 1. Teachers — United States — Interviews. 2. Teachers — United States — Biography. 3. Teaching — Vocational guidance — United States. 4. Teaching satisfaction I. T.
LA2311.R36 1985    371.1/0092/2 19    LC 85-5471    ISBN 0435082213

**Collins, Marva.**      4.10156
Marva Collins' way / Marva Collins and Civia Tamarkin. — 1st ed. — Los Angeles: J.P. Tarcher; Boston: Distributed by Houghton Mifflin, c1982. 228 p.: ill.; 22 cm. 1. Collins, Marva. 2. Teachers — Illinois — Chicago — Biography. I. Tamarkin, Civia. II. T.
LA2317.C62 A35 1982    372.11/092/4 19    LC 82-10516    ISBN 0874772354

**Kohl, Herbert R.** 4.10157
Growing minds: on becoming a teacher / Herbert Kohl; foreword by Joseph Featherstone. — 1st ed. — New York: Harper & Row, c1984. xviii, 163 p.: ill.; 22 cm. — (Harper & Row series on the professions.) 1. Kohl, Herbert R. 2. Elementary school teachers — United States — Biography. 3. Education — United States — Aims and objectives. 4. Teaching — Vocational guidance — United States. I. T. II. Series.
LA2317.K64 A33 1984    371.1/02 19    LC 82-48671    ISBN 0060152575

**Lutz, Alma.** • 4.10158
Emma Willard, pioneer educator of American women. Boston, Beacon Press [1964] viii, 143 p. 1. Willard, Emma (Hart) 1787-1870 2. Emma Willard School (Troy, N.Y.) I. T.
LA2317 W5 L82    LC 64-15364

# LB THEORY AND PRACTICE OF EDUCATION. TEACHING

## LB5–7 Collections

**National Society for the Study of Education.** • 4.10159
Yearbook of the National Society for the Study of Education. 1st- 1902-. Chicago: distributed by the University of Chicago Press. v. in    : ill., tables, diagrs.; 23-24 cm. Annual. List of preceding publications at end of each vol. Some vols. also have distinctive titles. 1. Education — United States I. T.
LB5.N3    LC 06-16938

**Barnett, Zolo George, 1914- ed.** • 4.10160
Philosophy and educational development / [by] Henry David Aiken [and others] Edited by George Barnett. — Boston: Houghton Mifflin, [1966] xv, 157 p.; 21 cm. 1. Education — Philosophy — Addresses, essays, lectures. I. Aiken, Henry David, 1912- II. T.
LB7.B35    370.12    LC 66-31837

**Eby, Frederick, 1874-1968, ed.** • 4.10161
Early Protestant educators: the educational writings of Martin Luther, John Calvin, and other leaders of Protestant thought. — New York: AMS Press, [1971] xiii, 312 p.; 18 cm. Reprint of the 1931 ed. 1. Education — History — Sources. I. Luther, Martin, 1483-1546. II. T.
LB7.E3 1971    370.1/08    LC 76-149656

**Philosophy of education: essays and commentaries / edited by** • 4.10162
**Hobert W. Burns, Charles J. Brauner; foreword by Robert H. Beck.**
New York: Ronald Press, c1962. xiii, 442 p. 1. Education — Philosophy — Collected works. I. Burns, Hobert W II. Brauner, Charles J
LB7.P48    LC 62-13710

**Scheffler, Israel. ed.** • 4.10163
Philosophy and education; modern readings. — 2d ed. — Boston: Allyn and Bacon, 1966. x, 387 p.; 22 cm. 1. Education — Philosophy — Collections. I. T.
LB7.S28 1966    370.1    LC 66-20642

## LB14–41 General Works

**Dejnozka, Edward L.** 4.10164
American educators' encyclopedia / Edward L. Dejnozka and David E. Kapel. — Westport, Conn.: Greenwood Press, 1982. xxvii, 634 p.; 29 cm. Includes index. 1. Education — Dictionaries. I. Kapel, David E. II. T.
LB15.D37 1982    370/.3 19    LC 81-6664    ISBN 0313209545

**Encyclopedia of educational research / sponsored by the** 4.10165
**American Educational Research Association; Harold E. Mitzel, editor–in–chief; associate editors, John Hardin Best and William Rabinowitz.**
5th ed. — New York: Free Press, c1982. 4 v.; 29 cm. 1. Education — Dictionaries. 2. Education — Bibliography I. Mitzel, Harold E. II. Best, John Hardin. III. Rabinowitz, William. IV. American Educational Research Association.
LB15.E48 1982    370/.7/8073 19    LC 82-2332    ISBN 0029004500

**Good, Carter Victor, 1897- ed.** 4.10166
Dictionary of education; prepared under the auspices of Phi Delta Kappa. Carter V. Good, editor. Winifred R. Merkel, assistant editor. — 3d ed. — New York: McGraw-Hill, [1973] xix, 681 p.; 23 cm. 1. Education — Dictionaries. I. Phi Delta Kappa. II. T.
LB15.G6 1973    370/.3    LC 73-4784    ISBN 0070237204

**The International encyclopedia of education: research and** 4.10167
**studies / editors–in–chief, Torsten Husén, T. Neville Postlethwaite.**
1st ed. — Oxford; New York: Pergamon Press, 1985. 10 v.: ill.; 26 cm. Vol. 10: Indexes. 1. Education — Dictionaries. 2. Education — Research — Dictionaries. I. Husén, Torsten, 1916- II. Postlethwaite, T. Neville.
LB15.I569 1985    370/.3/21 19    LC 84-20750    ISBN 0080281192

**The international encyclopedia of higher education / Asa S.** 4.10168
**Knowles, editor in chief.**
1st ed. — San Francisco: Jossey-Bass Publishers, 1977. 10 v. (5208 p.) 1. Education, Higher — Dictionaries. I. Knowles, Asa S. (Asa Smallidge), 1909-
LB15.I57    LB15 I57.    378/.003    LC 77-73647    ISBN 0875893236

**International handbook of education systems / editors, J.** 4.10169
**Cameron ... [et al.].**
Chichester [West Sussex]; New York: Wiley, c1983. 2 v.: ill.; 24 cm. 1. Education — Dictionaries. 2. Education — Europe — Handbooks, manuals, etc. 3. Education — Canada — Handbooks, manuals, etc. 4. Education — Africa — Handbooks, manuals, etc. I. Cameron, John, 1914-
LB15.I58 1983    370/.321 19    LC 82-17375    ISBN 0471900788

**Taxonomy of educational objectives; the classification of** 4.10170
**educational goals, by a committee of college and university examiners. Benjamin S. Bloom, editor [and others]**
1st ed.]. — New York: Longmans, Green, 1956-. v.    : illus.; 22 cm. Handbook 2- have imprint: New York, D. McKay Co. 1. Education — Aims and objectives I. Bloom, Benjamin Samuel, 1913- ed.
LB17.T3    370.1    LC 64-12369

**Goodlad, John I.** 4.10171
What schools are for / by John I. Goodlad. — [Bloomington, Ind.: Phi Delta Kappa Educational Foundation], c1979. viii, 127 p.; 23 cm. 'A publication of the Phi Delta Kappa Educational Foundation.' 1. Education — Aims and objectives 2. Education — Philosophy — History. 3. Educational sociology I. T.
LB41.G65    370.11    LC 79-54644    ISBN 0873674227

**Gross, Beatrice. comp.** • 4.10172
Radical school reform / edited by Beatrice and Ronald Gross. — New York: Simon and Schuster, [1970, c1969] 350 p.; 22 cm. 1. Education — Addresses, essays, lectures. I. Gross, Ronald. joint comp. II. T.
LB41.G84 1970    370/.8    LC 72-92188    ISBN 0671204122

**Hare, William F.** 4.10173
Open–mindedness and education / William Hare. — Montreal: McGill-Queen's University Press, c1979. xii, 166 p.; 21 cm. Includes index. 1. Education — Aims and objectives 2. Judgment 3. Reasoning I. T.
LB41.H285    370.1    LC 80-474068    ISBN 0773503455

**Hawkins, David, 1913-.** 4.10174
The informed vision; essays on learning and human nature. — New York: Agathon Press; distributed by Schocken books, [1974] viii, 246 p.; 22 cm. 1. Education — Addresses, essays, lectures. 2. Science — Study and teaching — Addresses, essays, lectures. I. T.
LB41.H34    370    LC 73-81796    ISBN 0875860419

**Henry, Jules, 1904-1969.** 4.10175
Essays on education. — Harmondsworth [Eng.]: Penguin, 1971. 183 p.; 19 cm. — (Penguin education specials) 1. Education — Addresses, essays, lectures. I. T.
LB41.H43 1971    370/.8    LC 70-884404    ISBN 0140806121

**Whitehead, Alfred North, 1861-1947.** • 4.10176
The organisation of thought, educational and scientific. — London: Williams and Norgate, 1917. vii, 228 p.; 22 cm. 1. Education — Addresses, essays, lectures. I. T.
LB41.W5    370/.8    LC e 18-79

# LB45 Educational Anthropology

**Brameld, Theodore Burghard Hurt, 1904-.**      • **4.10177**
Cultural foundations of education: an interdisciplinary exploration. Foreword by Clyde Kluckhohn. [1st ed.] New York, Harper [1957] 330 p. 1. Educational anthropology I. T.
LB45 B7      *LC* 57-10359

**Greene, Maxine.**      **4.10178**
Landscapes of learning / Maxine Greene. — New York: Teachers College Press, c1978. 255 p.; 23 cm. 1. Educational anthropology 2. Education — Philosophy 3. Educational sociology 4. Women — Education I. T.
LB45.G68      370.19/3      *LC* 78-6571      *ISBN* 080772534X

**Kimball, Solon Toothaker. comp.**      **4.10179**
Culture and the educative process: an anthropological perspective [compiled by] Solon T. Kimball. — New York: Teachers College Press, [1974] x, 285 p.; 24 cm. — (Anthropology & education) 1. Educational anthropology — Addresses, essays, lectures. I. T.
LB45.K5 1974      301.5/6      *LC* 73-21760      *ISBN* 080772422X

**Spindler, George Dearborn.**      **4.10180**
Education and cultural process; toward an anthropology of education. Edited by George D. Spindler. — New York: Holt, Rinehart and Winston, [1974] xii, 561 p.: illus.; 23 cm. 1. Educational anthropology — Addresses, essays, lectures. I. T.
LB45.S64      301.5/6      *LC* 74-1347      *ISBN* 0030851807

**Wax, Murray Lionel, 1922-.**      **4.10181**
Anthropological perspectives on education. Edited by Murray L. Wax, Stanley Diamond [and] Fred O. Gearing. — New York: Basic Books, [1971] xv, 392 p.; 25 cm. 1. Educational anthropology — Addresses, essays, lectures. I. Diamond, Stanley, 1922- II. Gearing, Fred O., 1922- III. T.
LB45.W33      370.19/3      *LC* 71-147020      *ISBN* 0465003419

**Weiss, Paul, 1901-.**      • **4.10182**
The making of men. — Carbondale: Southern Illinois University Press, [1967] 157 p.; 23 cm. 1. Educational anthropology I. T.
LB45.W36      370.19/3      *LC* 67-10046

# LB51–885 Systems of Individual Educators, by Period and Nationality

## LB51–375 ANCIENT TO 16TH CENTURY

**Barrow, Robin.**      **4.10183**
Plato and education / Robin Barrow. London; Boston: Routledge & K. Paul, 1976. vi, 83 p.; 23 cm. (Students library of education) 1. Plato. 2. Education — Philosophy 3. Education, Greek I. T.
LB85.P7 B35 1976      370.1      *LC* 76-367059      *ISBN* 0710083432

## LB472–575 16TH, 17TH, 18TH CENTURIES

**Comenius, Johann Amos, 1592-1670.**      • **4.10184**
The analytical didactic of Comenius / Jan Amos Komenský; translated from the Latin with introduction and notes by Vladimir Jelinek. — 1st English ed. — Chicago: University of Chicago Press, 1953. xvii, 239 p. Translation of chapter 10 of the author's Linguarum methodus novissima. 1. Education — Early works to 1800. 2. Teaching I. T.
LB475.C6 A54      *LC* 53-12896

**Locke, John, 1632-1704.**      **4.10185**
The educational writings of John Locke; a critical edition with introduction and notes, by James L. Axtell. London, Cambridge U.P., 1968. xiv, 442 p. 23 cm. 1. Education — Early works to 1800. I. Axtell, James. ed. II. T.
LB475.L6A2 1968      370.1/08      *LC* 68-18341      *ISBN* 0521407366

**Rousseau, Jean-Jacques, 1712-1778.**      • **4.10186**
Émile for today / selected, translated, and interpreted by William Boyd. — London: Heinemann, 1956. vi, 198 p. — (The Heinemann education series) 1. Education — Early works to 1800. I. Boyd, William, 1874-1962. II. T. III. Series.
LB512.E5 B6      *LC* 57-561      *ISBN* 0435801007

**Boyd, William, 1874-1962.**      • **4.10187**
The educational theory of Jean Jacques Rousseau / by William Boyd. — New York: Russell & Russell, 1963. xiii, 368 p. 1. Rousseau, Jean-Jacques, 1712-1778. 2. Education I. T.
LB518.B66 1963      *LC* 63-15150      *ISBN* 0846203596

**Franklin, Benjamin, 1706-1790.**      • **4.10188**
Educational views of Benjamin Franklin / edited by Thomas Woody. — New York; London: McGraw-Hill book company, inc., 1931. xvi, 270 p.: front. (port.) facsim.; 20 cm. 1. Education 2. Education — Pennsylvania. I. Woody, Thomas, 1891-1960, ed. II. T.
LB575.F723 1931      *LC* 31-12966

## LB621–695 19TH CENTURY (TO 1871)

## LB621–675 Foreign Educators

**Downs, Robert Bingham, 1903-.**      **4.10189**
Heinrich Pestalozzi, father of modern pedagogy, by Robert B. Downs. — Boston: Twayne Publishers, [1975] 147 p.: port.; 22 cm. — (Twayne's world leaders series) 1. Pestalozzi, Johann Heinrich, 1746-1827. I. T.
LB627.D68      370/.92/4 B      *LC* 74-14554      *ISBN* 0805735607

**Gutek, Gerald Lee.**      • **4.10190**
Pestalozzi & education. — New York: Random House, [1968] 178 p.; 19 cm. — (An Original Random House study in education, SED15) (Studies in the Western educational tradition.) 1. Pestalozzi, Johann Heinrich, 1746-1827. I. T.
LB628.G77      370.1/0924      *LC* 68-23001

**Downs, Robert Bingham, 1903-.**      **4.10191**
Friedrich Froebel / by Robert B. Downs. — Boston: Twayne Publishers, c1978. 126 p.: port.; 21 cm. — (Twayne's world leaders series: TWLS 74) Includes index. 1. Fröbel, Friedrich, 1782-1852. 2. Teachers — Germany — Biography. 3. Education — Philosophy I. T.
LB638.D68      370/.92/4 B      *LC* 77-13512      *ISBN* 0805776680

**Connell, William Fraser.**      • **4.10192**
The educational thought and influence of Matthew Arnold / William Fraser Connell; with an introduction by Sir Fred Clarke. — London: Routledge & K. Paul, c1950. xvi, 304 p.; 23 cm. — (International library of sociology and social reconstruction) 1. Arnold, Matthew, 1822-1888. I. T.
LB675 A82 C6      *LC* 51-6402

**Mackenzie, Hettie Millicent (Hughes) 1863-1942.**      • **4.10193**
Hegel's educational theory and practice. With an introductory note by J. S. Mackenzie. — New York: Haskell House Publishers, 1971. xxi, 192 p.; 22 cm. Reprint of the 1909 ed. 1. Hegel, Georg Wilhelm Friedrich, 1770-1831. I. T.
LB675.H4 M3 1971      370.1/0924      *LC* 79-122985      *ISBN* 0838311180

**Kant, Immanuel, 1724-1804.**      • **4.10194**
The educational theory of Immanuel Kant. Translated and edited, with an introd., by Edward Franklin Buchner. Philadelphia, Lippincott, 1904. — St. Clair Shores, Mich.: Scholarly Press, [196-?] 309 p.; 21 cm. — (Lippincott educational series) Translation of Kant's lecture notes for a course in education, which were first published in 1804 under title: Über Pädagogik, and selections on education from his other writings. 1. Education — Philosophy I. Buchner, Edward Franklin, 1868-1929, tr. II. T. III. Series.
LB675.K18513 1960z      370.1      *LC* 77-8271

**Mill, John Stuart, 1806-1873.**      • **4.10195**
John Stuart Mill on education / edited, with an introd. and notes, by Francis W. Garforth. — New York: Teachers College Press, Columbia University [1971] viii, 236 p.; 19 cm. (Classics in education, no. 43) 1. Education — Philosophy I. Garforth, F. W. (Francis William), 1917- ed. II. T.
LB675.M517      370.1      *LC* 75-155230

**Culler, A. Dwight (Arthur Dwight), 1917-.**      • **4.10196**
The imperial intellect; a study of Newman's educational ideal. New Haven, Yale University Press, 1955. xiii, 327 p. ill., ports., facsims. 1. Newman, John Henry, 1801-1890. I. T.
LB675 N45 C8      *LC* 55-8700

**Spencer, Herbert, 1820-1903.**　　　　　　　　　　● 4.10197
Education: intellectual, moral, and physical / by Herbert Spencer. — Totowa,
N.J.: Littlefield, Adams, 1963. vii, 22-283 p.; 21 cm. — (Classic essays on
education) 1. Education I. T.
LB675.S7 1963　　　*LC* 63-23957

**Spencer, Herbert, 1820-1903.**　　　　　　　　　　● 4.10198
Herbert Spencer on education / Edited with an introd. and notes by Andreas M.
Kazamias. — New York: Teachers College Press, Teachers College, Columbia
University, [1966] viii, 228 p.; 19 cm. — (Classics in education, no. 30)
1. Education — Philosophy I. Kazamias, Andreas M. ed. II. T.
LB675.S79 K3　　　370.12　　　*LC* 66-17068

# LB695 American Educators

**Jefferson, Thomas, President, United States, 1743-1826.**　　　● 4.10199
Crusade against ignorance: Thomas Jefferson on education / edited with an
introd. and notes, by Gordon C. Lee. — New York: Teachers College Press,
Columbia University, 1961. vi, 167 p. — (Classics in education; no. 6)
1. Education — Philosophy I. T.
LB695.J36 1961　　　*LC* 61-10961

**Conant, James Bryant, 1893-1978.**　　　　　　　　● 4.10200
Thomas Jefferson and the development of American public education.
Berkeley: University of California Press, 1962. x, 164 p.; 24 cm. (Jefferson
memorial lectures) 1. Jefferson, Thomas, 1743-1826. 2. Education — United
States — History. I. T. II. Series.
LB695.J4 C6　　　379.73　　　*LC* 61-12104

**Mann, Horace, 1796-1859.**　　　　　　　　　　● 4.10201
The republic and the school: the education of free men / edited by Lawrence A.
Cremin. — New York: Teachers College, Columbia University, 1957. 112 p.; 21
cm. — (Classics in education. no. 1) 1. Education — Addresses, essays,
lectures. I. Massachusetts. Board of Education. II. T. III. Series.
LB695.M235　　　*LC* 57-9102

**Messerli, Jonathan, 1926-.**　　　　　　　　　　● 4.10202
Horace Mann; a biography. — [1st ed.]. — New York: Knopf, 1972 [c1971]
xviii, 604, xxxvii p.: illus.; 25 cm. 1. Mann, Horace, 1796-1859. I. T.
LB695.M35 M4　　　370/.92/4 B　　　*LC* 78-154905　　　*ISBN* 0394429206

# LB775–875 1871–1950

## LB775 Foreign Educators, A–Z

**Fraser, Stewart.**　　　　　　　　　　　　　4.10203
Jullien's plan for comparative education, 1816–1817. [New York]: Bureau of
Publications, Teachers College, Columbia University, [1968] 147 p.; 19 cm.
(Teachers College. Columbia University. Comparative education studies)
Includes M. A. Jullien's Plan and preliminary views for a work on comparative
education, first published in 1817. 1. Comparative education I. Jullien, Marc
Antoine, 1775-1848 Plan and preliminary views for a work on comparative
education. II. T.
LB775.J773 F7　　　370.19

**Maritain, Jacques, 1882-1973.**　　　　　　　　● 4.10204
Education at the crossroads / by Jacques Maritain. — New Haven: Yale
University Press, 1943. x, 120 p. — (The Terry lectures) Includes index.
1. Education I. T.
LB775.M3565　　　*LC* a 43-2582

**Montessori, Maria, 1870-1952.**　　　　　　　　● 4.10205
[Metodo della pedagogia scientifica. English] The Montessori method.
[Translated from the Italian by Anne E. George] Introd. by J. McV. Hunt. New
York, Schocken Books [1964] xxxix, 376 p. illus. 21 cm. Translation of Il
metodo della pedagogia scientifica. 1. Montessori method of education I. T.
LB775.M7613 1964a　　　372　　　*LC* 64-24014

**Montessori, Maria, 1870-1952.**　　　　　　　　● 4.10206
[Metodo della pedagogia scientifica. English] The discovery of the child.
Translated by M. Joseph Costelloe. [1st American ed.] Notre Dame, Ind., Fides
Publishers [1967] x, 365 p. 22 cm. Translation of Il metodo della pedagogia
scientifica. 1. Montessori method of education I. T.
LB775.M7613 1967　　　371.9　　　*LC* 67-24813

**Montessori, Maria, 1870-1952.**　　　　　　　　● 4.10207
The secret of childhood. Notre Dame, Ind., Fides Publishers [1966] xxvi, 264 p.
20 cm. 1. Child study. 2. Education of children I. T.
LB775.M785 1966　　　*LC* 66-20175

**Montessori, Maria, 1870-1952.**　　　　　　　　● 4.10208
Spontaneous activity in education. Introd. by John J. McDermott. [Translated
from the Italian by Florence Simmonds]. — New York: Schocken Books,
[1965] xxviii, 355 p.: illus.; 21 cm. — (Schocken paperbacks, SB97) First
published in English in 1917 as v. 1 of the author's The advanced Montessori
method. 1. Montessori method of education I. T.
LB775.M7863　　　372　　　*LC* 65-18641

**Hainstock, Elizabeth G.**　　　　　　　　　　4.10209
The essential Montessori / Elizabeth G. Hainstock. — Updated ed. — New
York: New American Library, c1986. xii, 129 p.; 21 cm. 'A Plume book.'
1. Montessori method of education I. T.
LB775.M8 H26 1986　　　371.3/92 19　　　*LC* 85-29880　　　*ISBN*
0452258081

**Kramer, Rita.**　　　　　　　　　　　　　4.10210
Maria Montessori: a biography / by Rita Kramer. — New York: Putnam,
c1976. 410 p., [8] leaves of plates: ill.; 24 cm. 1. Montessori, Maria, 1870-1952.
I. T.
LB775.M8 K7 1976　　　370/.92/4 B 19　　　*LC* 75-37486　　　*ISBN*
0399113045

**Lillard, Paula Polk.**　　　　　　　　　　　4.10211
Montessori, a modern approach. — New York: Schocken Books, [1972] xvii,
174 p.: ill.; 21 cm. 1. Montessori method of education I. T.
LB775.M8 L54　　　371.3　　　*LC* 78-163334　　　*ISBN* 0805234233

**Piaget, Jean, 1896-.**　　　　　　　　　　　● 4.10212
[Psychologie et pédagogie. English] Science of education and the psychology of
the child / translated from the French by Derek Coltman. — New York: Orion
Press, 1970. 186 p.; 22 cm. Translation of Psychologie et pédagogie.
1. Education — Addresses, essays, lectures. 2. Educational psychology —
Addresses, essays, lectures. I. T.
LB775.P48713　　　370.15　　　*LC* 70-106302

**Elkind, David, 1931-.**　　　　　　　　　　　4.10213
Child development and education: a Piagetian perspective / David Elkind. New
York: Oxford University Press, c1976. xiii, 274 p.; 22 cm. Includes index.
1. Piaget, Jean, 1896- 2. Child development 3. Education — Philosophy I. T.
LB775.P49 E44　　　370.15/2　　　*LC* 75-46361　　　*ISBN* 0195020685

**Read, Herbert Edward, Sir, 1893-1968.**　　　　　● 4.10214
Education through art. [3d rev. ed.] New York, Pantheon Books [c1958] xxiv,
328 p. illus. (part. col.) 23 cm. 1. Education — Philosophy 2. Art —
Psychology 3. Art — Study and teaching I. T.
LB775.R372 1958　　　*LC* a 60-2803

**Russell, Bertrand, 1872-1970.**　　　　　　　　● 4.10215
Education and the good life. New York, Liveright [1970, c1926] 319 p. 21 cm.
(Liveright paperbound edition) 'Liveright L-12.' 1. Education 2. Moral
education 3. Educational psychology I. T.
LB775.R8 1970　　　370.1　　　*LC* 73-114378

**Russell, Bertrand, 1872-1970.**　　　　　　　　● 4.10216
Education and the social order / Bertrand Russell. — New ed. — London:
Unwin Books, 1967. 150 p. (Unwin books; 73) American ed. has title:
Education and the modern world. Includes index. 1. Education 2. Education
— Aims and objectives 3. Sociology I. T. II. Title: Education and the modern
world.
LB775.R83 1967　　　370.1

**Simon, Louis, 1908-.**　　　　　　　　　　　● 4.10217
Shaw on education / Louis Simon. — New York: Columbia University Press,
1958. xviii, 290 p.; 22 cm. 1. Shaw, Bernard, 1856-1950. 2. Education —
Philosophy I. T.
LB775.S6665 S5　　　370.1/092/4　　　*LC* 58-11678

# LB875 American Educators

## LB875 A–C

**Bestor, Arthur Eugene, 1908-.**　　　　　　　　4.10218
Educational wastelands: the retreat from learning in our public schools /
Arthur Bestor. — 2nd ed. / with retrospectives by Clarence J. Karier and
Foster McMurray. — Urbana: University of Illinois Press, c1985. xii, 292 p.; 24
cm. 'Publications of Arthur Bestor on educational questions': p. 289-292.
1. Bestor, Arthur Eugene, 1908- 2. Education — United States — Aims and
objectives. 3. Education — Philosophy I. Karier, Clarence J. II. McMurray,
Foster. III. T.
LB875.B345 1985　　　370/.973 19　　　*LC* 85-1014　　　*ISBN* 0252012267

**Bode, Boyd Henry, 1873-1953.**                           • **4.10219**
Progressive education at the crossroads / by Boyd H. Bode. — New York and
Chicago: Newson & company, [1938] 128 p.; 18 cm. 1. Education —
Experimental methods 2. Education of children 3. Educational psychology
I. T.
LB 875 B666 P        *LC* 38-13086

**Brameld, Theodore Burghard Hurt, 1904-.**                **4.10220**
Education for the emerging age: newer ends and stronger means. — New York,
Harper [1965] 244 p. 21 cm. 'Portions of this book were publihed previously
under the title, End and Means in Education—A Midcentury Appraisal.'
1. Education — Philosophy I. T.
LB875.B715        370.1        *LC* 60-15207

**Brameld, Theodore Burghard Hurt, 1904-.**                • **4.10221**
Philosophies of education in cultural perspective. — New York, Dryden Press
[1955] 446 p. illus. 24 cm. — (Dryden Press professional books in education)
'An extensive and intensive revision of the first half of ... [the author's] Patterns
of educational philosophy.' 1. Education — Philosophy I. T.
LB875.B723        370.1        *LC* 55-14599

**Brameld, Theodore Burghard Hurt, 1904-.**                • **4.10222**
Toward a reconstructed philosophy of education. — [New York]: Dryden
Press, [1956] 417 p. — (Dryden Press professional books in education)
1. Education — Philosophy I. Brameld, Theodore Burghard Hurt, 1904-
Patterns of educational philosophy. II. T.
LB875.B724        *LC* 56-13909

**Childs, John Lawrence, 1889-.**                          • **4.10223**
American pragmatism and education, an interpretation and criticism. — New
York: Holt, [1956] 373 p. 1. Pragmatism 2. Education — Philosophy I. T.
LB875.C47        *LC* 56-6061

## LB875 DEWEY
### (see also: B945.D4)

**Dewey, John, 1859-1952.**                                **4.10224**
The middle works, 1899–1924 / John Dewey; edited by Jo Ann Boydston; with
an introd. by Joe R. Burnett ... [et al.]. — Carbondale: Southern Illinois
University Press, c1976-c1983. 15 v.: ill.; 23 cm. Continues: The early works,
1882-1898. Continued by: The later works, 1925-1953. 1. Dewey, John,
1859-1952. 2. Education — Philosophy I. Boydston, Jo Ann, 1924- II. T.
LB875.D34 1976        370.1/092/4        *LC* 76-7231        *ISBN* 0809307537

**Dewey, John, 1859-1952.**                                • **4.10225**
Democracy and education: an introduction to the philosophy of education, by
John Dewey. — New York: The Macmillan company, 1916. xii, p., 1 l., 434 p.;
21 cm. — (Text-book series in education) 1. Education I. T. II. Series.
LB875.D35        *LC* 16-7522

**Horne, Herman Harrell, 1874-.**                          • **4.10226**
The democratic philosophy of education: companion to Dewey's Democracy
and education; exposition and comment / by Herman Harrell Horne. — New
York: Macmillan, 1932. xxiii, 547 p.: port.; 20 cm. 1. Dewey, John, 1859-1952.
Democracy and education. 2. Education — Philosophy I. T.
LB875.D365        *LC* 32-6631

**Dewey, John, 1859-1952.**                                • **4.10227**
Education today / by John Dewey; edited and with a foreword by Joseph
Ratner ... New York: G. P. Putnam's sons, [c1940] xix, 373 p.; 23 cm.
1. Education 2. Education — United States I. Ratner, Joseph, 1901- ed. II. T.
LB875.D39        370.81        *LC* 40-31507

**Dewey, John, 1859-1952.**                                • **4.10228**
Experience and education, by John Dewey. — New York: The Macmillan
company, 1938. xii, p., 2 l., 116 p.; 19 cm. — (The Kappa Delta Pi lecture series.
[no. 10]) 1. Experience 2. Education I. T. II. Series.
LB875.D3943        370.1        *LC* 38-8618

**Dewey, John, 1859-1952.**                                **4.10229**
The school and society; being three lectures by John Dewey ... [3d ed.] Chicago,
The University of Chicago press; New York, McClure, Phillips & company,
1900. 129 p., 1 l. incl. iv charts. 4 pl. 20 cm. 1. University of Chicago.
Elememtary school. 2. Education of children I. T.
LB875.D4        *LC* 00-4840

**Guide to the works of John Dewey. Edited by Jo Ann**     **4.10230**
**Boydston.**
Carbondale: Southern Illinois University Press, [1970] xv, 395 p.; 23 cm.
1. Dewey, John, 1859-1952 — Addresses, essays, lectures. I. Boydston, Jo
Ann, 1924- ed.
LB875.D5 G83        191        *LC* 70-112383        *ISBN* 0809304392

## LB875 H–Z

**Hook, Sidney, 1902-.**                                   • **4.10231**
Education for modern man: a new perspective. — New, enl. ed. — New York:
Knopf, 1963. 235 p.; 22 cm. — (Borzoi books in education) 1. Education —
Aims and objectives 2. Teaching I. T.
LB875.H72 1963        370.1        *LC* 62-15572

**Hutchins, Robert Maynard, 1899-.**                       • **4.10232**
The conflict in education in a democratic society, by Robert M. Hutchins. —
Westport, Conn.: Greenwood Press, [1972, c1953] 112 p.; 23 cm. 1. Education
— Philosophy 2. Education — United States I. T.
LB875.H96 1972        370.1        *LC* 77-138117        *ISBN* 0837156939

**Meiklejohn, Alexander, 1872-1964.**                      • **4.10233**
Education between two worlds / Alexander Meiklejohn. — New York:
Atherton Press, 1966 [c1965] xii, 303 p. — (An Atheling book; EP-104)
Reprinted from the 1942 edition with a new editor's foreword. 1. Education —
Philosophy I. T. II. Series.
LB875.M33 1966        *LC* 66-6409

**Redden, John D.**                                        • **4.10234**
A Catholic philosophy of education / by John D. Redden and Francis A. Ryan.
— Rev. ed. — Milwaukee: Bruce Pub. Co., c1956. xiii, 601 p. 1. Catholic
Church — Education 2. Education — Philosophy I. Ryan, Francis Aloysius,
1887- II. T.
LB875 R43 1956        *LC* 56-2706

**Whitehead, Alfred North, 1861-1947.**                    • **4.10235**
The aims of education & other essays, by A. N. Whitehead. — New York: The
Macmillan company, 1929. vi p., 1 l., 247 p.; 20 cm. 'Chapters I, IV, VI, XIII,
IX, and X have been published in my book, The organisation of thought ...
1917. Chapter II ... published [1922] as a separate pamphlet.'—Pref.
1. Education — Addresses, essays, lectures. 2. Education — Curricula I. T.
LB875.W48        *LC* 29-10164

# LB880–885 1951-

## LB880 Foreign Educators, A–Z

**Freire, Paulo, 1921-.**                                  **4.10236**
[Pedagogía del oprimido. English] Pedagogy of the oppressed / translated by
Myra Bergman Ramos. — [New York]: Herder and Herder [1970] 186 p.; 22
cm. Translation of Pedagogía del oprimido. 1. Education — Philosophy
2. Liberty. I. T.
LB880.F7313        370.1        *LC* 70-110074

**Nash, Paul, 1924-.**                                     • **4.10237**
Authority and freedom in education: an introduction to the philosophy of
education. — New York: Wiley, [1966] x, 342 p.; 24 cm. 1. Education —
Philosophy — 1965- I. T.
LB880.N29        370.1        *LC* 66-17624

**Peters, R. S. (Richard Stanley), 1919-.**                • **4.10238**
Authority, responsibility, and education. [1st American ed.] New York,
Eriksson-Taplinger Co. [1960, c1959] 137 p. 19 cm. 1. Authority 2. Education
— Philosophy I. T.
LB880.P4 1960        *LC* 60-8911

## LB885 American Educators, A–Z

**Bantock, G. H. (Geoffrey Herman), 1914-.**               • **4.10239**
Education and values: essays in the theory of education / G. H. Bantock. —
London: Faber and Faber, c1965. 182 p. 1. Education — Philosophy
2. Education — 1945- I. T.
LB885.B24        370.1        *LC* 66-35195

**Bruner, Jerome S. (Jerome Seymour)**                     • **4.10240**
The process of education. Cambridge: Harvard University Press, 1960. 97 p.; 21
cm. 1. Education — Aims and objectives I. T.
LB885.B78        370.1        *LC* 60-15235

**Bruner, Jerome S. (Jerome Seymour)**                     • **4.10241**
Toward a theory of instruction, by Jerome S. Bruner. — Cambridge, Mass.:
Belknap Press of Harvard University, 1966. x, 176 p.; 21 cm. 1. Education —
Philosophy — 1965- I. T.
LB885.B79        371.3        *LC* 66-13179

**Combs, Arthur Wright.**      **4.10242**
Myths in education: beliefs that hinder progress and their alternatives / Arthur W. Combs. — Boston: Allyn and Bacon, c1979. x, 240 p.: ill.; 22 cm. 1. Combs, Arthur Wright. 2. Education — Philosophy 3. Education — Aims and objectives I. T.
LB885.C525 M95     370.1     *LC* 78-17338     *ISBN* 0205060218

**Counts, George S. (George Sylvester), 1889-1974.**      **4.10243**
George S. Counts, educator for a new age / edited by Lawrence J. Dennis and William Edward Eaton. — Carbondale: Southern Illinois University Press; London: Feffer & Simons, c1980. ix, 155 p.: port.; 24 cm. Includes index. 1. Counts, George S. (George Sylvester), 1889-1974. 2. Education — United States — History. 3. National characteristics, American 4. United States — Civilization — 20th century I. Dennis, Lawrence J. II. Eaton, William Edward, 1943- III. T.
LB885.C66 1980     370/.092/4     *LC* 79-28182     *ISBN* 0809309548

**Greene, Maxine.**      **4.10244**
Teacher as stranger; educational philosophy for the modern age. — Belmont, Calif.: Wadsworth Pub. Co., [1973] 308 p.; 23 cm. 1. Education — Philosophy 2. Education — 1965- I. T.
LB885.G68     370.1     *LC* 72-87809     *ISBN* 0534002056

**Henry, Jules, 1904-1969.**      **4.10245**
Jules Henry on education. — [1st American ed.]. — New York: Random House, [1972] 183 p.; 22 cm. 1. Educational anthropology 2. Handicapped children — Education — United States. I. T. II. Title: On education.
LB885.H43 1972     370.19/3     *LC* 75-37047     *ISBN* 0394480309

**Holt, John Caldwell, 1923-.**      **4.10246**
Freedom and beyond [by] John Holt. — [1st ed.]. — New York: E. P. Dutton, 1972. 273 p.: illus.; 22 cm. 1. Education — Philosophy — 1965- 2. Educational innovations — United States. 3. Child rearing I. T.
LB885.H6394 1972     370.1     *LC* 76-179842     *ISBN* 0525109226

**Jones, Howard Mumford, 1892-.**      • **4.10247**
Reflections on learning. — Freeport. N.Y.: Books for Libraries Press, [1969. c1958] 97 p.; 22 cm. — (Essay index reprint series) 1. Education — Philosophy 2. Education — U.S. — 1945- I. T.
LB885.J6 1969     370.1     *LC* 69-17580     *ISBN* 0836900227

**Lerner, Max, 1902-.**      • **4.10248**
Education and a radical humanism; notes toward a theory of the educational crisis. Columbus, Ohio State University Press [1962] 63 p. 21 cm. ([The Kappa Delta Pi lecture series]) 1. Education — Philosophy 2. United States — Intellectual life I. T.
LB885.L422     370.10973     *LC* 62-3556

**McPeck, John E.**      **4.10249**
Critical thinking and education / John E. McPeck. — Oxford: Martin Robertson, 1981. 170 p.; 23 cm. Includes index. 1. McPeck, John E. 2. Education — Philosophy 3. Logic I. T.
LB885.M35 C74 1981     370/.1 19     *ISBN* 0855203846

**Montagu, Ashley, 1905-.**      • **4.10250**
Education and human relations. — New York: Grove Press, 1958. 191 p.; 21 cm. (Evergreen book. E-87) 1. Education — Philosophy 2. Interpersonal relations I. T. II. Series.
LB885.M6

**Conrad, David R., 1937-.**      **4.10251**
Education for transformation: implications in Lewis Mumford's ecohumanism / by David R. Conrad. — Palm Springs, Calif.: ETC Publications, c1976. 230 p.; 24 cm. Includes index. 1. Mumford, Lewis, 1895- 2. Education — Philosophy I. T.
LB885.M722 C66     370.1     *LC* 75-25867     *ISBN* 0882800302

**Phillips, Norman R.**      **4.10252**
The quest for excellence: the neo–conservative critique of educational mediocrity / by Norman R. Phillips. — New York: Philosophical Library, c1978. viii, 179 p.; 22 cm. 1. Education — Philosophy 2. Conservatism I. T.
LB885.P53 Q44 1978     370.1     *LC* 77-87940     *ISBN* 080222220X

**Rafferty, Max Lewis, 1917-.**      • **4.10253**
Max Rafferty on education, by Max Rafferty. — New York: Devin-Adair Co., 1968. 274 p.; 21 cm. 1. Education — Philosophy 2. Education — United States I. T.
LB885.R2716     370.1     *LC* 68-26083

**Carbone, Peter F.**      **4.10254**
The social and educational thought of Harold Rugg / Peter F. Carbone, Jr. — Durham, N.C.: Duke University Press, 1977. xi, 225 p.; 23 cm. A revision of the author's thesis, Harvard University, 1967. Includes index. 1. Rugg, Harold

Ordway, 1886-1960. 2. Education — Philosophy 3. Educational sociology I. T.
LB885.R73 C37 1977     370/.92/4 B     *LC* 75-36176     *ISBN* 0822303558

**Scheffler, Israel.**      • **4.10255**
Conditions of knowledge: an introduction to epistemology and education. — Chicago: Scott, Foresman [1965] 117 p.; 22 cm. — (Keystones of education series) Includes bibliographical references. 1. Education — Philosophy 2. Knowledge, Theory of I. T.
LB885.S34     121     *LC* 65-17733

**Smith, Philip L.**      **4.10256**
The problem of values in educational thought / Philip L. Smith. — 1st ed. — Ames: Iowa State University Press, 1982. x, 92 p.; 21 cm. 1. Smith, Philip L. 2. Education — Philosophy 3. Judgment I. T.
LB885.S5717 1982     370/.1 19     *LC* 81-23650     *ISBN* 0813818532

# LB1025–1050 Teaching

**Burton, William Henry, 1890-.**      • **4.10257**
The guidance of learning activities; a summary of the principles of teaching based on the growth of the learner. 3d ed. New York, Appleton-Century-Crofts [1962] 581 p. illus. 26 cm. 1. Teaching 2. Learning I. T.
LB1025.B982 1962     371.3     *LC* 62-8331

**Goodman, Paul, 1911-1972.**      • **4.10258**
Compulsory mis–education, and The community of scholars. — New York: Vintage Books, [1966, c1964] 339 p.; 19 cm. 1. Education of children 2. Education, Higher — 1945- 3. Universities and colleges — United States I. T. II. Title: The community of scholars.
LB1025.G496     370.110973     *LC* 66-13013

**Highet, Gilbert, 1906-1978.**      • **4.10259**
The art of teaching. — [1st ed.]. — New York: Knopf, 1950. xviii, 291, vii p.; 22 cm. 1. Teaching I. T.
LB1025.H63 1950     371.3     *LC* 50-9306

**Bennett, Neville.**      **4.10260**
Teaching styles and pupil progress / Neville Bennett, with Joyce Jordan, George Long, Barbara Wade; foreword by Jerome Bruner. Cambridge, Mass.: Harvard University Press, 1976. xv, 201 p.: ill.; 22 cm. Includes indexes. 1. Teaching 2. Open plan schools I. T.
LB1025.2.B448     372.1/1/02     *LC* 76-40500     *ISBN* 0674870956

**Almond, Brenda.**      **4.10261**
Means and ends in education / Brenda Cohen. — London; Boston: Allen & Unwin, 1983, c1982. xiv, 113 p.; 23 cm. — (Introductory studies in philosophy of education.) Includes index. 1. Education — Philosophy I. T. II. Series.
LB1025.2.C59 1983     370/.1 19     *LC* 82-11430     *ISBN* 0043701221

**Combs, Arthur Wright.**      **4.10262**
A personal approach to teaching: beliefs that make a difference / Arthur W. Combs. — Boston: Allyn and Bacon, c1982. x, 194 p.; 22 cm. 1. Teaching 2. Educational psychology I. T.
LB1025.2.C628     371.1/02 19     *LC* 81-10788     *ISBN* 0205076432

**Eble, Kenneth Eugene.**      **4.10263**
The craft of teaching: [a guide to mastering the professor's art] / Kenneth E. Eble. 1st ed. — San Francisco: Jossey-Bass Publishers, 1976. xiv, 179 p.; 24 cm. (The Jossey-Bass series in higher education) Includes index. 1. Teaching 2. Education, Humanistic I. T.
LB1025.2.E24     371.1/02     *LC* 76-11894     *ISBN* 0875892841

**Gage, N. L. (Nathaniel Lees), 1917-.**      **4.10264**
The scientific basis of the art of teaching / N. L. Gage. — New York: Teachers College Press, Teachers College, Columbia University, 1978. 122 p.; 23 cm. — (The Julius and Rosa Sachs memorial lectures) Delivered at Teachers College, Columbia University, April 1977. 1. Teaching 2. Education — Research I. T.
LB1025.2.G29     371.1/02     *LC* 78-6250     *ISBN* 0807725374

**Highet, Gilbert, 1906-1978.**      **4.10265**
The immortal profession: the joys of teaching and learning / Gilbert Highet. — New York: Weybright and Talley, c1976. vii, 223 p.; 21 cm. 1. Teaching I. T.
LB1025.2.H5     371.1/02     *LC* 76-5515     *ISBN* 067940130X

**Instructional design: principles and applications** / Leslie J.    **4.10266**
Briggs, editor; contributing authors, Amy S. Ackerman ... [et al.].
Englewood Cliffs, N.J.: Educational Technology Publications, c1977. xxx, 532 p.; 25 cm. 1. Teaching 2. Lesson planning I. Briggs, Leslie J. II. Ackerman, Amy S.
LB1025.2.I645     371.3     *LC* 77-23216     *ISBN* 0877780986

**Kohl, Herbert R.**      **4.10267**
On teaching / Herbert R. Kohl. New York: Schocken Books, 1976. 185 p.; 21 cm. Includes index. 1. Teaching I. T.
LB1025.2.K62     371.1/02     *LC* 76-9131     *ISBN* 0805236333

**O'Neill, William F.**      **4.10268**
Educational ideologies: contemporary expressions of educational philosophy / William F. O'Neill. — Santa Monica, Calif.: Goodyear Pub. Co., c1981. xxxvi, 410 p.: ill.; 24 cm. 1. Education — Philosophy I. T.
LB1025.2.O53     370/.1 19     *LC* 80-27816     *ISBN* 0830223053

**Berman, Louise M.**      **4.10269**
New priorities in the curriculum [by] Louise M. Berman. — Columbus, Ohio: C. E. Merrill, [1968] xii, 241 p.; 23 cm. — (Merrill's international series in education) 1. Curriculum planning 2. Educational innovations I. T.
LB1027.B474     375/.006     *LC* 68-28703

**Curriculum innovation: [readings]** / edited by Alan Harris,    **4.10270**
Martin Lawn, William Prescott.
New York: Wiley, [1975] 388 p.: ill.; 23 cm. 'A Halsted Press book.' To accompany the teaching materials for the course Curriculum design and development, prepared by the Curriculum Design and Development Course Team of the Faculty of Educational Studies at the Open University. 1. Curriculum planning — Addresses, essays, lectures. I. Harris, Alan Edward, 1936- II. Lawn, Martin. III. Prescott, William, 1939- IV. Open University. Curriculum Design and Development Course Team.
LB1027.C94     375/.001     *LC* 75-22488     *ISBN* 0470140860

**Flanders, Ned A.**      • **4.10271**
Analyzing teaching behavior [by] Ned A. Flanders. — Reading, Mass.: Addison-Wesley Pub. Co., [1970] xvi, 448 p.: illus.; 24 cm. — (Addison-Wesley series in education) 1. Interaction analysis in education 2. Teaching I. T.
LB1027.F555     371.1     *LC* 70-104967

**Gamson, Zelda F.**      **4.10272**
Liberating education / Zelda F. Gamson and associates, Nancy B. Black ... [et al.]; afterword by David Riesman. — 1st ed. — San Francisco, Calif.: Jossey-Bass, c1984. xxiii, 253 p.; 24 cm. — (Jossey-Bass higher education series.) Includes index. 1. Educational innovations — United States — Addresses, essays, lectures. 2. Education, Higher — United States — Addresses, essays, lectures. 3. Education, Humanistic — United States — Addresses, essays, lectures. 4. Academic freedom — United States — Addresses, essays, lectures. I. Black, Nancy B. II. T. III. Series.
LB1027.G286 1984     378.73 19     *LC* 83-49260     *ISBN* 0875896030

**Joyce, Bruce R.**      **4.10273**
The structure of school improvement / Bruce R. Joyce, Richard H. Hersh, Michael McKibbin. — New York: Longman, c1983. xiii, 290 p.; 24 cm. 1. School improvement programs 2. Curriculum planning 3. Teachers — Selection and appointment 4. Educational technology I. Hersh, Richard H., 1942- II. McKibbin, Michael. III. T.
LB1027.J647 1983     371 19     *LC* 82-17931     *ISBN* 0582280923

**Kilpatrick, William Heard, 1871-1965.**      **4.10274**
The project method; the use of the purposeful act in the educative process, by William Heard Kilpatrick. New York, Teachers college, Columbia university [c1919] 18 p. 23 cm. 1. Project method in education. I. T.
LB1027.K55     *LC* 21-7

**Mehan, Hugh, 1941-.**      **4.10275**
Learning lessons: social organization in the classroom / Hugh Mehan. — Cambridge, Mass.: Harvard University Press, 1979. xvii, 227 p.: ill.; 24 cm. Includes index. 1. Lesson planning 2. Students — Conduct of life 3. Educational sociology I. T.
LB1027.M276     372.13 19     *LC* 78-24298     *ISBN* 0674520157

**Rich, John Martin. comp.**      **4.10276**
Innovations in education: reformers and their critics / John Martin Rich. — 3d ed. — Boston: Allyn and Bacon, c1981. xii, 344 p.; 24 cm. 1. Educational innovations — Addresses, essays, lectures. 2. Education — Philosophy — Addresses, essays, lectures. I. T.
LB1027.R513 1981     370     *LC* 80-14904     *ISBN* 0205071414

## LB1027.5 Student Guidance and Counseling

**Belkin, Gary S.**      **4.10277**
Practical counseling in the schools / Gary S. Belkin. — 2nd ed. — Dubuque, Iowa: Brown, c1981. xvii, 519 p.: ill., ports; 24 cm. Includes indexes. 1. Personnel service in education 2. Counseling I. T.
LB1027.5.B38 1981     371.4 19     *LC* 80-66844     *ISBN* 0697060551

**Mental health and going to school: the Woodlawn program of**    **4.10278**
**assessment, early intervention, and evaluation** / Sheppard G.
**Kellam ... [et al.].**
Chicago: University of Chicago Press, 1975. xvi, 213 p.: ill.; 23 cm. Includes index. 1. Chicago. Woodlawn. 2. Personnel service in education — Illinois — Chicago. 3. Child mental health services — Illinois — Chicago. I. Kellam, Sheppard G.
LB1027.5.M443     372.1/7/10977311     *LC* 74-10341     *ISBN* 0226429687

**Miller, Theodore K.**      **4.10279**
The future of student affairs: [a guide to student development for tomorrow's higher education] / Theodore K. Miller, Judith S. Prince. — 1st ed. — San Francisco: Jossey-Bass Publishers, 1976. xviii, 220 p.; 24 cm. 'Sponsored by the American College Personnel Association.' Includes index. 1. College student development programs — United States. I. Prince, Judith Sosebee, joint author. II. American College Personnel Association. III. T.
LB1027.5.M5213     378.1/94     *LC* 76-19496     *ISBN* 0875892981

**The Utilization of classroom peers as behavior change agents** /    **4.10280**
**edited by Phillip S. Strain.**
New York: Plenum Press, c1981. xii, 366 p.; 23 cm. — (Applied clinical psychology.) 1. Peer counseling of students — Addresses, essays, lectures. 2. Peer-group tutoring of students — Addresses, essays, lectures. I. Strain, Phillip S. II. Series.
LB1027.5.U85     371.4/044 19     *LC* 81-1733     *ISBN* 0306406187

## LB1028 Educational Research

**Block, Alan W.**      **4.10281**
Effective schools: a summary of research / [prepared by Alan W. Block]. — Arlington, Va. (1800 N. Kent St., Arlington 22209): Educational Research Service, c1983. iii, 125 p.; 28 cm. — (Research brief / Educational Research Service, Inc.) 1. Education — Research — United States. 2. Educational surveys — United States I. Educational Research Service (Arlington, Va.) II. T.
LB1028.B53 1983     370/.7/8073 19     *LC* 84-119175

**Directory of ERIC microfiche collections** / prepared by the    **4.10282**
**Educational Resources Information Center (ERIC), ERIC**
**Processing and Reference Facility.**
Washington, D.C.: National Institute of Education, U.S. Dept. of Education. v.: 28 cm. Description based on: Sept. 1983. Vols. for <Sept. 1983-> distributed to depository libraries in microfiche. 1. Education — Research — Information services — Directories. I. ERIC Processing and Reference Facility (U.S.) II. National Institute of Education (U.S.)
LB1028.D56     *LC* sn 87-12229

**Feinberg, Walter, 1937-.**      **4.10283**
Understanding education: toward a reconstruction of educational inquiry / Walter Feinberg. — Cambridge [Cambridgeshire]; New York: Cambridge University Press, 1983. xi, 270 p.: ill.; 24 cm. 1. Education — Research I. T.
LB1028.F34 1983     370/.7/8 19     *LC* 82-12790     *ISBN* 0521248647

**Goetz, Judith Preissle.**      **4.10284**
Ethnography and qualitative design in educational research / Judith Preissle Goetz, Margaret Diane LeCompte. — Orlando, Fla.: Academic Press, 1984. xii, 292 p.: ill.; 24 cm. Includes indexes. 1. Education — Research 2. Ethnology — Methodology 3. Education — Evaluation — Methodology. I. LeCompte, Margaret Diane. II. T.
LB1028.G55 1984     370/.7/8 19     *LC* 83-15713     *ISBN* 0122874803

**Good, Carter Victor, 1897-.**      **4.10285**
Essentials of educational research; methodology and design [by] Carter V. Good. 2d ed. New York, Appleton-Century-Crofts [1971, c1972] x, 470 p. 24 cm. 1. Education — Research I. T.
LB1028.G58 1972     370/.78     *LC* 73-164362

**Handbook of research on teaching** / edited by Merlin C.    **4.10286**
**Wittrock.**
3rd ed. — New York: Macmillan; London: Collier Macmillan, 1985. xi, 1037 p.: ill.; 29 cm. 'A project of the American Educational Research Association.' Rev. ed. of: Second handbook of research on teaching. 1973. 1. Education — Research — United States. I. Wittrock, M. C. (Merlin C.),

1931- II. American Educational Research Association. III. Second handbook of research on teaching.
LB1028.H315 1985    371.1/07/072 19    *LC* 85-4866    *ISBN* 0029003105

**Kennedy, James R. (James Randolph), 1928-.**    **4.10287**
Library research guide to education: illustrated search strategy and sources / by James R. Kennedy, Jr. — Ann Arbor, Mich.: Pierian Press, 1979. x, 80 p. (p. 78-80 blank for 'Notes'): ill.; 29 cm. (Library research guides series; no. 3) Includes index. 1. Education — Research — Handbooks, manuals, etc. 2. Libraries — Handbooks, manuals, etc. 3. Libraries and students 4. Reference books — Education. 5. Education — Bibliography I. T.
LB1028.K38    025.5/8    *LC* 79-88940    *ISBN* 0876501153

**Review of research in education.**    **4.10288**
1- 1973-. Itasca, Ill., F. E. Peacock Publishers. v. 24 cm. Annual. 'A publication of the American Educational Research Association.' 1. Education — Research — United States — Periodicals. I. American Educational Research Association.
LB1028.R43    370/.78/073    *LC* 72-89719

## LB1028.3–1028.75 Educational Technology. Computers in Education

**Cuban, Larry.**    **4.10289**
Teachers and machines: the classroom use of technology since 1920 / Larry Cuban. — New York: Teachers College Press, c1986. x, 134 p.: ill.; 23 cm. Includes index. 1. Educational technology — History. 2. Educational broadcasting — History. I. T.
LB1028.3.C8 1986    371.3/07/8 19    *LC* 85-14789    *ISBN* 080772792X

**Educational media and technology yearbook.**    **4.10289a**
1985- . — Littleton, Co.: Libraries Unlimited, 1985-. v. Annual. 1. Educational technology — Yearbooks. 2. Instructional materials centers — Yearbooks. 3. Instructional materials personnel — Directories. I. Association for Educational Communications and Technology. II. American Society for Training and Development. Media Division.
LB1028.3.E37    *LC* sn 84-2352

**Heinich, Robert.**    **4.10290**
Instructional media and the new technologies of instruction / Robert Heinich, Michael Molenda, James D. Russell. — 2nd ed. — New York: Wiley, c1985. xiv, 414 p.: ill. (some col.); 29 cm. 1. Educational technology I. Molenda, Michael. II. Russell, James D. III. T. IV. Title: Instructional media.
LB1028.3.H45 1985    371.3/07/8 19    *LC* 84-20875    *ISBN* 0471878359

**The Computer in education: a critical perspective / Douglas**    **4.10291**
**Sloan, editor.**
New York: Teachers College Press, c1985. 129 p.: ill.; 23 cm. 1. Education — Data processing 2. Education — Aims and objectives I. Sloan, Douglas.
LB1028.43.C638 1985    370/.28/5 19    *LC* 85-4679    *ISBN* 0807727822

**Microcomputers in the schools / edited by James L. Thomas.**    **4.10292**
Phoenix, Ariz.: Oryx Press, 1981. xviii, 158 p.; 29 cm. Includes index. 1. Education — Data processing — Addresses, essays, lectures. 2. Computer-assisted instruction — Addresses, essays, lectures. 3. Microcomputers — Addresses, essays, lectures. I. Thomas, James L., 1945-
LB1028.43.M53    370/.28/52 19    *LC* 81-14087    *ISBN* 0897740017

**Pogrow, Stanley.**    **4.10293**
Education in the computer age: issues of policy, practice, and reform / Stanley Pogrow; foreword by Michael W. Kirst. — Beverly Hills, Calif.: Sage Publications, c1983. 231 p.: ill.; 23 cm. — (Managing information. v. 6) 1. Education — United States — Data processing. 2. Computer-assisted instruction — United States. 3. Education — Data processing — Government policy — United States. I. T. II. Series.
LB1028.43.P63 1983    370/.28/5 19    *LC* 83-11213    *ISBN* 0803919921

**Budoff, Milton, 1929-.**    **4.10294**
Microcomputers in special education: an introduction to instructional applications / Milton Budoff, Joan Thormann, Ann Gras. — Rev. ed. — Cambridge, MA: Brookline Books, c1985. xiii, 252 p.: ill.; 23 cm. Includes index. 1. Computer-assisted instruction 2. Handicapped children — Education — Data processing. 3. Microcomputers I. Thormann, Joan, 1945- II. Gras, Ann, 1926- III. T.
LB1028.5.B79 1985    371.9/043 19    *LC* 85-19524    *ISBN* 0914797182

**Maffei, Anthony C.**    **4.10295**
Classroom computers: a practical guide for effective teaching / Anthony C. Maffei. — New York, N.Y.: Human Sciences Press, c1986. 266 p.: ill.; 23 cm. Includes index. 1. Computer-assisted instruction 2. Education — Computer programs. 3. Computer literacy I. T.
LB1028.5.M19 1986    371.3/9445 19    *LC* 85-8206    *ISBN* 0898852552

**Mager, Robert Frank, 1923-.**    **4.10296**
Preparing instructional objectives / Robert F. Mager. — Rev. 2nd ed. — Belmont, Calif.: Pitman Management and Training, c1984. vi, 136 p.: ill.; 24 cm. 1. Programmed instruction I. T.
LB1028.5.M2 1984    371.3/9442 19    *LC* 83-60503    *ISBN* 0822443414

**Orwig, Gary W., 1945-.**    **4.10297**
Creating computer programs for learning: a guide for trainers, parents, and teachers / Gary W. Orwig. — Reston, Va.: Reston Pub. Co., c1983. xiv, 178 p.: ill.; 24 cm. — (A Reward book) Includes index. 1. Computer-assisted instruction 2. Programmed instruction 3. Computer managed instruction I. T.
LB1028.5.O72 1983    370/.28/5 19    *LC* 83-4597    *ISBN* 0835911683

**T.E.S.S.: the educational software selector.**    **4.10298**
1984 ed.-    . — New York: EPIE Institute & Teachers College Press, c1984-. v.: ill.; 29 cm. (Computers and education series.) Annual. 1. Education — Computer programs — Catalogs. 2. Computer-assisted instruction — Catalogs. I. EPIE Institute. II. Title: The Educational software selector. III. Title: TESS: the educational software selector. IV. Series.
LB1028.5.T18    371 11    *LC* sn 84-1735

**Truett, Carol, 1942-.**    **4.10299**
Choosing educational software: a buyer's guide / Carol Truett and Lori Gillespie. — Littleton, Colo.: Libraries Unlimited, 1984. xiii, 202 p.: ill.; 24 cm. Includes index. 1. Computer-assisted instruction — United States — Equipment and supplies — Evaluation. 2. Computer software — Evaluation. 3. Computer-assisted instruction — Information services — Directories. 4. Computer software — Information services — Directories. I. Gillespie, Lori, 1956- II. T.
LB1028.5.T69 1984    001.64/25/0687 19    *LC* 83-24906    *ISBN* 0872873889

**Williams, Frederick, 1933-.**    **4.10300**
Microcomputers in elementary education: perspectives on implementation / Frederick Williams and Victoria Williams; with a foreword by Everett M. Rogers. — Belmont, Calif.: Wadsworth Pub. Co., c1984. xvii, 174 p.: ill.; 25 cm. Includes index. 1. Computer-assisted instruction — United States — Evaluation. 2. Computer-assisted instruction — California — Los Angeles Metropolitan Area — Case studies. 3. Education, Elementary — California — Los Angeles Metropolitan Area — Audio-visual aids — Case studies. 4. Education — Data processing I. Williams, Victoria. II. T.
LB1028.5.W525 1984    372/.028/5 19    *LC* 83-23247    *ISBN* 0534032427

## LB1029 Other Special Topics, A–Z

**Knowles, Asa S. (Asa Smallidge), 1909-.**    **4.10301**
Handbook of cooperative education [by] Asa S. Knowles & associates. [1st ed.] San Francisco, Jossey-Bass, 1971. xxiii, 386 p. 24 cm. (The Jossey-Bass series in higher education) 1. Education, Cooperative — United States. I. T.
LB1029.C6 K6    378.1/04    *LC* 75-173854    *ISBN* 0875891128

**Graubard, Allen, 1938-.**    **4.10302**
Free the children; radical reform and the free school movement. — [1st ed.]. — New York: Pantheon Books, [c1972] xiii, 306 p.; 22 cm. 1. Free schools — United States. I. T.
LB1029.F7 G7 1972    371/.02    *LC* 72-3401    *ISBN* 0394471326

**Kozol, Jonathan.**    **4.10303**
Alternative schools: a guide for educators and parents / Jonathan Kozol. — New York: Continuum, 1982. x, 132 p.; 21 cm. Rev ed. of: Free schools. 1972. 1. Free schools — United States. I. T.
LB1029.F7 K6 1982    371/.04 19    *LC* 82-9765    *ISBN* 0826402267

**Belch, Jean.**    **4.10304**
Contemporary games; a directory and bibliography covering games and play situations or simulations used for instruction and training by schools, colleges and universities, government, business, and management. — Detroit: Gale Research Co., [1973-1974] 2 v.; 29 cm. 1. Educational games — Directories. 2. Educational games — Bibliography. 3. Management games — Directories. 4. Management games — Bibliography. I. T.
LB1029.G3 B44    016.3713    *LC* 72-6353

**Cratty, Bryant J.**    **4.10305**
Active learning: games to enhance academic abilities / Bryant J. Cratty. — 2nd ed. — Englewood Cliffs, N.J.: Prentice-Hall, c1985. xii, 163 p.: ill.; 25 cm. 1. Educational games I. T.
LB1029.G3 C7 1985    371.3/07/8 19    *LC* 84-22323    *ISBN* 0130034681

**Sprung, Barbara.**    **4.10306**
Non–sexist education for young children: a practical guide / Barbara Sprung; [photos. by Ann–Marie Mott]. New York: Citation Press, 1975. 115 p., [1] leaf of plates: ill.; 21 cm. Results of a project conducted by the Women's Action Alliance. 1. Educational games 2. Sex discrimination in education 3. Sexism I. Women's Action Alliance. II. T.
LB1029.G3 S67    372.1/3    *LC* 75-22490    *ISBN* 0590096052

**Devaney, Kathleen.**    **4.10307**
Developing open education in America: a review of theory and practice in the public schools / by Kathleen Devaney. — Washington: National Association for the Education of Young Children, c1974. xi, 191 p.: ill.; 26 cm. Includes index. 1. Open plan schools — United States. I. T.
LB1029.O6 D48    371.3    *LC* 74-78803

**The Philosophy of open education** / edited and with an introd.    **4.10308**
by David Nyberg.
London; Boston: Routledge & K. Paul, 1976 (c1975). xiii, 213 p.; 23 cm. (International library of the philosophy of education.) 1. Open plan schools I. Nyberg, David, 1943- II. Series.
LB1029.O6 P47    371.3    *LC* 75-332535    *ISBN* 0710082851

## LB1031–1032 Individual Instruction. Group Work

**Flanagan, John Clemans, 1906-.**    **4.10309**
Behavioral objectives: a guide to individualizing learning / John Clemans Flanagan, Robert Frank Mager, William Maurice Shanner. — Palo Alto, Ca.: Westinghouse Learning Press, 1971. 4 v. 1. Individualized instruction I. Mager, Robert Frank, 1923- II. Shanner, William Maurice, 1915- III. T.
LB1031.F635x

**Jackson, Philip W. (Philip Wesley), 1928-.**    **4.10310**
Life in classrooms / [by] Philip W. Jackson. — New York: Holt, Rinehart and Winston [1971] xi, 177 p.; 24 cm. 1. Education, Elementary — Aims and objectives 2. Teacher-student relationships 3. Achievement motivation in children I. T.
LB1032.J3    372    *LC* 68-12794

**Schmuck, Richard A.**    **4.10311**
Group processes in the classroom / Richard A. Schmuck, Patricia A. Schmuck. — 4th ed. — Dubuque, Iowa: W.C. Brown, c1983. xiii, 380 p.: ill.; 23 cm. Includes index. 1. Group work in education 2. Social groups I. Schmuck, Patricia A. II. T.
LB1032.S35 1983    371.2/5 19    *LC* 82-71508    *ISBN* 0697060934

**The Social context of instruction: group organization and group**    **4.10312**
**processes** / edited by Penelope L. Peterson, Louise Cherry Wilkinson, and Maureen Hallinan.
New York: Academic Press, 1984. xiv, 252 p.; 24 cm. — (Educational psychology.) 1. Group work in education — Addresses, essays, lectures. I. Peterson, Penelope L. II. Wilkinson, Louise Cherry. III. Hallinan, Maureen T. IV. Series.
LB1032.S64 1984    371.2/5 19    *LC* 83-9954    *ISBN* 0125522207

## LB1033 Teacher–Student Relationships

**Brophy, Jere E.**    **4.10313**
Teacher–student relationships: causes and consequences [by] Jere E. Brophy [and] Thomas L. Good. — New York: Holt, Rinehart and Winston, [1974] xvi, 400 p.; 23 cm. 1. Teacher-student relationships 2. Interaction analysis in education 3. Child psychology I. Good, Thomas L., 1943- joint author. II. T.
LB1033.B67    371.1/02    *LC* 73-14740    *ISBN* 003085749X

**Gorman, Alfred H.**    **4.10314**
Teachers and learners: the interactive process of education / [by] Alfred H. Gorman. — 2nd ed. — Boston: Allyn and Bacon, [1974] xi, 232 p.: ill.; 22 cm. 1. Teacher-student relationships 2. Interaction analysis in education I. T.
LB1033.G66 1974    371.1/02    *LC* 73-83199

**Raths, Louis Edward.**    • **4.10315**
Values and teaching: working with values in the classroom / [by] Louis E. Raths, Merrill Harmin [and] Sidney B. Simon. — Columbus, Ohio: C. E. Merrill Books [1966] ix, 275 p.; 22 cm. (Merrill's international education series)
1. Teaching 2. Values I. Harmin, Merrill. joint author. II. Simon, Sidney B. joint author. III. T.
LB1033.R37    370.19334    *LC* 66-13815

## LB1042 Stories. Storytelling

**Bauer, Caroline Feller.**    **4.10316**
Handbook for storytellers / Caroline Feller Bauer. — Chicago: American Library Association, 1977. xvi, 381 p.: ill.; 25 cm. 1. Storytelling — Handbooks, manuals, etc. I. T.
LB1042.B38    372.6/4    *LC* 76-56385    *ISBN* 0838902251

**Pellowski, Anne.**    **4.10317**
The story vine: a source book of unusual and easy–to–tell stories from around the world / Anne Pellowski; illustrated by Lynn Sweat. — New York: Macmillan; London: Collier Macmillan, c1984. ix, 116 p.: ill.; 24 cm. 1. Storytelling 2. Tales 3. Children's stories I. Sweat, Lynn. II. T.
LB1042.P43 1984b    372.6/4 19    *LC* 83-27307    *ISBN* 0027705900

**Ross, Ramon Royal.**    **4.10318**
Storyteller / Ramon Royal Ross; [cover photo by Rosalian Kaplan]. — 2d ed. — Columbus, Ohio: Merrill, c1980. xi, 226 p.: ill.; 23 cm. 1. Storytelling I. T.
LB1042.R67 1980    808.5/43 19    *LC* 79-92795    *ISBN* 0675081696

**Sawyer, Ruth, 1880-1970.**    **4.10319**
The way of the storyteller. — New York: Viking Press, [1962] 360 p.; 21 cm. 1. Storytelling I. T.
LB1042.S35 1962    372.214    *LC* 62-15697

**Shedlock, Marie L., 1854-1935.**    **4.10320**
The art of the story–teller; foreword by Anne Carroll Moore. 3d ed., rev. with a new bibliography by Eulalie Steinmetz. [New York] Dover Publications [1952, c1951] xxi, 290 p. 21 cm. 1. Storytelling 2. Children's stories 3. Children's literature — Bibliography I. T.
LB1042.S5 1952    372.214    *LC* 52-9976

## LB1042.5–1044 Audiovisual Education

**The Encyclopaedia of educational media communications and**    **4.10321**
**technology** / [edited by] Derick Unwin and Ray McAleese.
Westport, Conn.: Greenwood Press, 1978. xviii, 800 p.: ill.; 24 cm. 1. Audio-visual materials — Dictionaries. 2. Educational technology — Dictionaries. I. Unwin, Derick. II. McAleese, Ray. joint author.
LB1042.5.E52 1978b    371.3/078    *LC* 78-26988    *ISBN* 0313209219

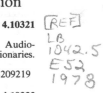

**Index to producers and distributors.**    **4.10322**
1st- ed.; 1971-. Los Angeles: National Information Center for Educational Media, University of Southern California, 1971-. v; 28 cm. Three times a month. 1. Audio-visual materials — Catalogs. I. National Information Center for Educational Media.
LB1043.A1 N26    011

**Audio video market place: AVMP.**    **4.10323**
1984- . — New York: R.R. Bowker Co., c1984-. v.; 28 cm. Annual. 'A multimedia guide.' 1. Audio-visual materials — Directories. 2. Educational broadcasting — Directories. 3. Video tape recorders and recording — Directories.
LB1043.A86    *LC* 85-651452

**Brown, James W. (James Wilson), 1913 Sept. 18-.**    **4.10324**
AV instruction: technology, media, and methods / James W. Brown, Richard B. Lewis, Fred F. Harcleroad. — 6th ed. — New York: McGraw-Hill, c1983. x, 528 p.: ill. (some col.); 24 cm. Includes index. 1. Audio-visual education I. Lewis, Richard Byrd, 1908- II. Harcleroad, Fred F. III. T. IV. Title: Audiovisual instruction. V. Title: A.V. instruction.
LB1043.B75 1983    371.3/3 19    *LC* 82-7801    *ISBN* 007008176X

**Kemp, Jerrold E.**    **4.10325**
Planning and producing instructional media / Jerrold E. Kemp, Deane K. Dayton; with the assistance of Ron Carraher and Richard F. Szumski. — 5th ed. — New York: Harper & Row, c1985. xvii, 292 p.: ill.; 29 cm. Rev. ed. of: Planning and producing audiovisual materials. 4th ed c1980. 1. Audio-visual materials 2. Audio-visual equipment I. Dayton, Deane K. II. Kemp, Jerrold E. Planning and producing audiovisual materials. III. T.
LB1043.K4 1985    371.3/3 19    *LC* 84-10909    *ISBN* 0060435887

**Educators guide to free audio and video materials.**    **4.10326**
24th- ed.; 1977-. Randolph, Wisc.: Educators' Progress Service. v. 28 cm. Annual. 1. Audio-visual materials — Catalogs. 2. Free material — Catalogs. 3. Audio-visual materials — Directories. 4. Free material — Directories. I. Educators' Progress Service.
LB1043.Z9 E34    371.3/07/8    *LC* 78-641014

**Media review digest.**    **4.10327**
1973/74-. Ann Arbor, Mich., Pierian Press. v. 29 cm. Annual. 'The only complete guide to reviews of non-book media.' Issued in two parts: Pt. 1. Films and filmstrips, miscellaneous media; Pt. 2. Records and tapes. Supplements issued quarterly. 1. Audio-visual materials — Catalogs — Periodicals. 2. Audio-visual materials — Reviews — Bibliography — Periodicals. I. Wall, C. Edward. ed.
LB1043.Z9 M4     011     LC 76-641245

**Educators' guide to free filmstrips.**    **4.10328**
1st- ed.; 1949-. Randolph, Wis., Educators' Progress Service. v. 29 cm. Annual. 1. Filmstrips — Catalogs. I. Horkheimer, Mary Foley, 1905- II. Educators' Progress Service, Randolph, Wis. III. Title: Educators' guide to free slidefilms.
LB1043.8.E4     LC 50-11650 rev

**Educators guide to free films / John C. Diffor and Mary F.**    **4.10329**
**Horkheimer, eds.**
46th ed. Randolph, Wis.: Educators Progress Service, 1986. 1 v. Began with 1941. Description based on: 29th ed. (1969). I. Educators' Progress Service.
LB1044.E24     371.335230838     LC 45-412

**Educational film/video locator of the Consortium of University**    **4.10330**
**Film Centers and R.R. Bowker.**
3rd. ed. (1986)-     . — New York: Bowker, 1986-. v.; 29 cm. Third ed.- issued in two volumes. 1. Motion pictures — Catalogs 2. Motion pictures in education 3. Motion pictures — Directories. 4. Video tapes — Catalogs 5. Video tapes in education — Catalogs. I. Consortium of University Film Centers. II. R.R. Bowker Company.
LB1044.Z9 E37     LC 86-644320

**Index to 16mm educational films / National Information Center**    **4.10331**
**for Educational Media, University of Southern California.**
[1st ed.]-     . — New York: McGraw-Hill, c1967-. v.; 28 cm. Issued in 4 vols., <1977->. 1. Motion pictures — Catalogs — Periodicals. 2. Motion pictures in education — Periodicals. I. National Information Center for Educational Media.
LB1044.Z9 I574     011 19     LC 82-642106

**Index to 35mm educational filmstrips / National Information**    **4.10332**
**Center for Educational Media, School of Performing Arts,**
**University of Southern California.**
[1st ed.]-     . — New York: McGraw-Hill, c1968-. v.; 28 cm. Issues for 1973-<1985> published in two or more volumes. 1. Filmstrips — Catalogs. 2. Filmstrips in education — Periodicals. I. National Information Center for Educational Media.
LB1044.Z9 I58     011/.37 19     LC 82-642276

**Index to educational audio tapes.**    **4.10333**
1st ed. (1971)-     . — Los Angeles, Calif.: National Information Center for Educational Media, University of Southern California, c1971-. v.; 28 cm. 1. Phonotapes — Periodicals. 2. Phonotapes in education — Periodicals. I. National Information Center for Educational Media.
LB1044.4.Z9 I53     011/.38 19     LC 82-642171

**Index to educational videotapes.**    **4.10334**
1st ed. (1971)-     . — Los Angeles: National Information Center for Educational Media, University of Southern California, 1971-. v.; 28 cm. Annual. Issues for <1985-> published in three volumes. 1. Video tapes — Catalogs 2. Video tapes in education — Periodicals. I. National Information Center for Educational Media.
LB1044.4.Z9 I54     011/.37 19     LC 82-642126

**Gattegno, Caleb.**    • **4.10335**
Towards a visual culture; educating through television. — [New York]: Outerbridge & Dienstfrey; distributed by Dutton, [1969] x, 117 p.: illus.; 23 cm. 1. Television in education I. T.
LB1044.7.G34 1969     371.33/58     LC 76-91461

**Devine, Thomas G., 1928-.**    **4.10336**
Teaching study skills: a guide for teachers / Thomas G. Devine. — 2nd ed. — Boston: Allyn and Bacon, c1987. xxi, 359 p.; 25 cm. 1. Study, Method of — Handbooks, manuals, etc. I. T.
LB1049.D48 1987     371.3/028/12 19     LC 86-14029     ISBN 0205089844

## LB1050 Reading

**Bettelheim, Bruno.**    **4.10337**
On learning to read: the child's fascination with meaning / Bruno Bettelheim & Karen Zelan. — 1st ed. — New York: Knopf, 1982. x, 306 p.; 22 cm. 1. Reading I. Zelan, Karen. II. T.
LB1050.B47 1982     372.4 19     LC 81-47492     ISBN 0394515927

**Downing, John A.**    **4.10338**
Comparative reading: cross–national studies of behavior and processes in reading and writing / [edited by] John Downing. — New York: Macmillan, [1973, c1973] xii, 595 p.: ill.; 24 cm. 1. Reading — Addresses, essays, lectures. 2. Comparative education — Addresses, essays, lectures. I. T.
LB1050.D67     418     LC 77-182447

**Hildreth, Gertrude Howell, 1898-1984.**    **4.10339**
Teaching reading: a guide to basic principles and modern practices / Gertrude Hildreth. — New York: Holt, 1958. 612 p.: ill. 1. Reading I. T.
LB1050.H5     LC 58-10430

**Kohl, Herbert R.**    **4.10340**
Reading, how to [by] Herbert Kohl. — [1st ed.]. — New York: Dutton, 1973. xiii, 224 p.: illus.; 22 cm. 1. Reading I. T.
LB1050.K6 1973     428/.4     LC 78-158608     ISBN 0525188959

**Meek, Margaret.**    **4.10341**
Learning to read / Margaret Meek. — London: Bodley Head, 1982. 254 p.; 23 cm. Includes index. 1. Reading I. T.
LB1050.M42 1982     428.4 19     LC 83-670127     ISBN 0370301544

**Mitchell, D. C. (Don C.)**    **4.10342**
The process of reading: a cognitive analysis of fluent reading and learning to read / D.C. Mitchell. — Chichester; New York: Wiley, c1982. xiii, 244 p.: ill.; 24 cm. Includes indexes. 1. Reading I. T.
LB1050.M56 1982     428.4 19     LC 81-21912     ISBN 0471101990

**Schank, Roger C., 1946-.**    **4.10343**
Reading and understanding: teaching from the perspective of artificial intelligence / Roger C. Schank. — Hillsdale, N.J.: L. Erlbaum Associates, 1982. xii, 196 p.; 24 cm. — (Psychology of reading.) 1. Reading 2. Reading comprehension 3. Artificial intelligence 4. Memory I. T. II. Series.
LB1050.S22 1982     372.4 19     LC 81-9915     ISBN 0898591694

**Vacca, Richard T.**    **4.10344**
Content area reading / Richard T. Vacca, Jo Anne L. Vacca. — 2nd ed. — Boston: Little, Brown, c1986. xvi, 480 p.: ill.; 25 cm. 1. Content area reading I. Vacca, Jo Anne L. II. T.
LB1050.455.V33 1986     428.4/3 19     LC 85-19807     ISBN 0316894907

## LB1050.5 Remedial Teaching

**Beech, John R.**    **4.10345**
Learning to read: a cognitive approach to reading and poor reading / John R. Beech. — London: Croom Helm; San Diego, CA: College-Hill Press, c1985. 147 p.: ill.; 23 cm. Includes indexes. 1. Reading disability 2. Reading — Remedial teaching I. T.
LB1050.5.B43 1985     372.4/3 19     LC 84-21421     ISBN 0887441106

**Harris, Albert Josiah.**    **4.10346**
How to increase reading ability: a guide to developmental and remedial methods / Albert J. Harris, Edward R. Sipay. — 8th ed. — New York: Longman, c1985. xxi, 825 p.: ill.; 25 cm. Includes indexes. 1. Developmental reading 2. Reading — Remedial teaching I. Sipay, Edward R. II. T.
LB1050.53.H37 1985     372.4/1 19     LC 84-28870     ISBN 0582285461

## LB1051–1091 Educational Psychology

**Arnold, Darlene Baden, 1948-.**    **4.10347**
Education/psychology journals: a scholar's guide / by Darlene Baden Arnold and Kenneth O. Doyle, Jr. — Metuchen, N.J.: Scarecrow Press, 1975. 143 p.; 22 cm. Includes index. 1. Educational psychology — Periodicals. I. Doyle, Kenneth O. joint author. II. T.
LB1051.A732     370.15/05     LC 74-23507     ISBN 0810807793

**Atkinson, Richard C.**    • **4.10348**
An introduction to mathematical learning theory [by] Richard C. Atkinson, Gordon H. Bower [and] Edward J. Crothers. New York, Wiley [1965] xiii, 429 p. ill. 1. Learning, Psychology of — Mathematical models I. Bower, Gordon H. jt. author II. Crothers, Edward J., jt. author III. T.
LB1051 A744     LC 65-24283

**Bloom, Benjamin Samuel, 1913-.**      **4.10349**
Human characteristics and school learning / Benjamin S. Bloom. — New York;
Toronto: McGraw-Hill, c1976. xii, 284 p.; 24 cm. 1. Learning, Psychology of
I. T.
LB1051.B4545      370.15/2      *LC* 76-4094      *ISBN* 0070061173

**Bode, Boyd Henry, 1873-1953.**      • **4.10350**
How we learn. — Westport, Conn.: Greenwood Press, [1971, c1940] 308 p.; 23
cm. 'This book began as a revision of ... Conflicting psychologies of learning ...
however, well over half of the present document consists of entirely new
material, and the rest was ... extensively revised and reorganized.' 1. Learning,
Psychology of 2. Intellect 3. Education — Philosophy I. T.
LB1051.B463 1971      370.15/2      *LC* 77-138204      *ISBN* 0837155622

**Bruner, Jerome S. (Jerome Seymour)**      • **4.10351**
The relevance of education / by Jerome S. Bruner. Edited by Anita Gil. — [1st
ed.]. — New York: Norton, [1971] xvi, 175 p.; 22 cm. 1. Educational
psychology 2. Child study. I. T.
LB1051.B74 1971      370.15      *LC* 74-139376      *ISBN* 0393043347

**Bugelski, B. R. (Bergen Richard), 1913-.**      • **4.10352**
The psychology of learning applied to teaching [by] B. R. Bugelski. 2d ed.
Indianapolis, Bobbs-Merrill [1971] xvi, 344 p. illus. 24 cm. 1. Learning,
Psychology of I. T.
LB1051.B783 1971      370.152      *LC* 79-149402

**Hilgard, Ernest Ropiequet, 1904-.**      • **4.10353**
Theories of learning / [by] Ernest R. Hilgard [and] Gordon H. Bower. — 3d ed.
— New York: Appleton-Century-Crofts, [1966] vii, 661 p.; ill.; 24 cm. —
(Century psychology series) 1. Learning, Psychology of I. Bower, Gordon H.
joint author. II. T.
LB1051.H52 1966      153.15      *LC* 66-16758

**Hill, Winfred F.**      **4.10354**
Learning: a survey of psychological interpretations / Winfred F. Hill. — 4th ed.
— New York: Harper & Row, c1985. xii, 242 p.: ill.; 24 cm. Includes index.
1. Learning, Psychology of I. T.
LB1051.H524 1985      153.1/5 19      *LC* 84-15679      *ISBN* 006042818X

**James, William, 1842-1910.**      • **4.10355**
Talks to teachers on psychology, and to students on some of life's ideals. Introd.
by Paul Woodring. New York, Norton [1958] 191 p. 19 cm. (The Norton
library, N7) 1. Educational psychology I. T.
LB1051.J34 1958      370.15      *LC* 58-11663

**Mowrer, Orval Hobart, 1907-.**      • **4.10356**
Learning theory and behavior. — New York: Wiley, [1960] 555 p.: illus.; 24 cm.
1. Learning, Psychology of 2. Behaviorism (Psychology) I. T.
LB1051.M737      370.15      *LC* 59-15671

**Mowrer, Orval Hobart, 1907-.**      • **4.10357**
Learning theory and the symbolic processes. New York, Wiley [1960] 473 p. ill.
1. Learning, Psychology of I. T.
LB1051 M75      *LC* 60-10320

**Novak, Joseph Donald.**      **4.10358**
A theory of education / by Joseph D. Novak; with a foreword by Ralph W.
Tyler. — Ithaca, N.Y.: Cornell University Press, 1977. 295 p.: ill.; 23 cm.
Includes index. 1. Learning, Psychology of 2. Education — Philosophy I. T.
LB1051.N68      370.1      *LC* 77-3123      *ISBN* 0801411041

**Rogers, Carl R. (Carl Ransom), 1902-.**      **4.10359**
Freedom to learn for the 80's / Carl R. Rogers; with special contributions by
Julie Ann Allender ... [et al.]. — Columbus, Ohio: C.E. Merrill Pub. Co., c1983.
viii, 312 p.; ill.; 25 cm. Rev. ed. of: Freedom to learn. 1969. 1. Learning,
Psychology of 2. Education — Experimental methods 3. Academic freedom
4. Educational innovations I. T.
LB1051.R636 1983      370.15 19      *LC* 82-61108      *ISBN* 0675200121

**Schooling and the acquisition of knowledge / edited by Richard**      **4.10360**
**C. Anderson, Rand J. Spiro, William E. Montague.**
Hillsdale, N.J.: Lawrence Erlbaum Associates; New York: distributed by the
Halsted Press Division of Wiley, 1977. x, 448 p.; ill.; 24 cm. 1. Learning,
Psychology of — Addresses, essays, lectures. 2. Cognition — Addresses,
essays, lectures. 3. Education — Aims and objectives — Addresses, essays,
lectures. I. Anderson, Richard C. (Richard Chase), 1934- II. Spiro, Rand J.
III. Montague, William Edward, 1931-
LB1051.S374      370.15      *LC* 77-22004      *ISBN* 047099293X

**Steinberg, Ira S.**      **4.10361**
Behaviorism and schooling / Ira S. Steinberg. — New York: St. Martin's, 1980.
ix, 126 p.; 23 cm. 1. Learning, Psychology of 2. Students — Psychology
3. Behaviorism (Psychology) I. T.
LB1051.S71256 1980      370.15      *LC* 80-13602      *ISBN* 0312072538

**Thorndike, Edward L. (Edward Lee), 1874-1949.**      • **4.10362**
Educational psychology. — Westport, Conn.: Greenwood Press [1970] 3 v.: ill.;
23 cm. Reprint of the 1913-14 ed. 1. Educational psychology I. T.
LB1051.T52 1970      370.15      *LC* 77-100848      *ISBN* 0837140412

**Thorndike, Edward L. (Edward Lee), 1874-1949.**      **4.10363**
The fundamentals of learning [by] Edward L. Thorndike [and the staff of the
Division of Psychology of the Institute of Educational Research of Teachers
College, Columbia University] New York, AMS Press [1971] xvii, 638 p. illus.
23 cm. Reprint of the 1932 ed. 1. Learning, Psychology of 2. Association of
ideas I. Columbia University. Teachers College. Institute of Psychological
Research. II. T.
LB1051.T53 1971      153.1/5      *LC* 72-137270      *ISBN* 0404064299

## LB1055 Addresses. Essays. Lectures

**Murphy, Gardner, 1895-.**      • **4.10364**
Freeing intelligence through teaching: a dialectic of the rational and the
personal / by Gardner Murphy; foreword by Arthur G. Wirth. — 1st ed. —
New York: Harper, c1961. 64 p. –. (The John Dewey Society lectureship series;
no.4) 1. Learning, Psychology of 2. Teaching I. T. II. Series.
LB1055.M8      *LC* 61-14838

## LB1057–1091 Special Aspects

**Holt, John Caldwell, 1923-.**      **4.10365**
How children learn / John Holt. — Rev. ed. — New York, N.Y.: Delacorte
Press/Seymour Lawrence, c1983. xii, 303 p.; 21 cm. 'A Merloyd Lawrence
book.' 1. Learning 2. Education of children 3. Cognition in children I. T.
LB1060.H64 1983      370.15/23 19      *LC* 82-17311      *ISBN* 0440038359

**Hullfish, Henry Gordon, 1894-.**      • **4.10366**
Reflective thinking: the method of education / H. Gordon Hullfish and Philip
G. Smith. — New York: Dodd, Mead, 1961. xii, 273 p. 1. Thought and
thinking I. Smith, Philip G. II. T.
LB1062.H8      *LC* 61-7307

**Massialas, Byron G., 1929-.**      • **4.10367**
Creative encounters in the classroom; teaching and learning through discovery
[by] Byron G. Massialas [and] Jack Zevin. — New York: Wiley, [1967] x,
274 p.: illus.; 22 cm. 1. Creative thinking (Education) 2. Learning by discovery
I. Zevin, Jack. joint author. II. T.
LB1062.M35      371.3      *LC* 67-13527

**Sanders, Donald A.**      **4.10368**
Teaching creativity through metaphor: an integrated brain approach / Donald
A. Sanders, Judith A. Sanders. — New York: Longman, c1984. xi, 319 p.: ill.;
23 cm. — (Contemporary topics for teachers series.) 1. Creative thinking
(Education) 2. Educational innovations 3. Motivation in education
4. Teaching 5. Brain — Research I. Sanders, Judith A. II. T. III. Series.
LB1062.S312 1984      370.15/7 19      *LC* 83-25604      *ISBN* 0582281857

**Mathematico deductive theory of rote learning: a study in**      • **4.10369**
**scientific methodology / by Clark L. Hull [and others].**
Westport, Conn.: Greenwood Press, [1970, c1940] xii, 329 p.: ill.; 23 cm.
1. Learning, Psychology of 2. Logic, Symbolic and mathematical I. Hull,
Clark Leonard, 1884-1952.
LB1063.M3 1970      153.1/522      *LC* 74-95126      *ISBN* 083713126X

**Motivation in education / edited by Samuel Ball.**      **4.10370**
New York: Academic Press, 1977. xiii, 204 p.; 24 cm. (Educational psychology)
1. Motivation in education I. Ball, Samuel.
LB1065.M67      370.15/4      *LC* 76-27432      *ISBN* 012077450X

**Cognitive learning in children: theories and strategies / edited**      **4.10371**
**by Joel R. Levin, Vernon L. Allen.**
New York: Academic Press, 1976. xvi, 297 p.: ill.; 24 cm. — (Educational
psychology) 'This book presents several programs of research and development
conducted at the Wisconsin Research and Development Center for Cognitive
Learning.' 1. Educational psychology 2. Cognition in children I. Levin, Joel
R. II. Allen, Vernon L., 1933- III. Wisconsin Research and Development
Center for Cognitive Learning.
LB1067.C56      370.15/2      *LC* 75-40610      *ISBN* 012444850X

**Jones, Richard Matthew, 1925-.**      • **4.10372**
Fantasy and feeling in education / by Richard M. Jones. — New York: New
York University Press, 1968. xi, 276 p.: ill.; 22 cm. 1. Perceptual learning
2. Interaction analysis in education I. T.
LB1067.J6 1968      370.15      *LC* 68-29430

**Miller, Neal E. (Neal Elgar), 1909-.** • 4.10373
Social learning and imitation, by Neal E. Miller and John Dollard. New Haven, Pub. for the Institute of human relations by Yale university press; London, H. Milford, Oxford university press, 1941. xiv, 341 p. illus., diagrs. 24 cm. 1. Learning, Psychology of 2. Imitation 3. Social psychology I. Dollard, John, 1900- joint author. II. Yale university. Institute of human relations. III. T.
LB1069.M5 1941          301.15          LC 41-23888

**Bandura, Albert, 1925-.** 4.10374
Social learning theory / Albert Bandura. — Englewood Cliffs, N.J.: Prentice Hall, c1977. viii, 247 p.; 24 cm. Includes indexes. 1. Social learning I. T.
LB1084.B357          153.1/5          LC 76-43024          ISBN 0138167516. ISBN 0138167443 pbk

**Cooper, Harris M.** 4.10375
Pygmalion grows up: studies in the expectation communication process / Harris M. Cooper, Thomas L. Good. — New York: Longman, c1983. xv, 173 p.; 24 cm. — (Research on teaching monograph series.) Includes index. 1. Interaction analysis in education 2. Expectation (Psychology) 3. Academic achievement 4. Classroom environment — Psychological aspects. I. Good, Thomas L., 1943- II. T. III. Series.
LB1084.C57 1983          370.15/3 19          LC 82-14876          ISBN 0582284015

**Cunningham, Ruth, 1907-.** • 4.10376
Understanding group behavior of boys and girls / by Ruth Cunningham and associates. — New York: Bureau of Publications, Teachers College, Columbia University, c1951. xviii, 446 p.: ill. 'Prepared for the Horace Mann-Lincoln Institute of School Experimentation, Teachers College, Columbia University.' 1. Social psychology I. Horace Mann-Lincoln Institute of School Experimentation. II. T.
LB1084.C8          LC 51-9636

# LB1101–1139 Child Study

**Donaldson, Margaret C.** 4.10377
Children's minds / Margaret Donaldson. — 1st American ed. — New York: Norton, 1979, c1978. x, 166 p.: ill.; 22 cm. 1. Child development 2. Child psychology I. T.
LB1115.D59 1979          370.15          LC 78-24211          ISBN 0393011852

**Goodwin, William Lawrence, 1935-.** 4.10378
Handbook for measurement and evaluation in early childhood education / William L. Goodwin, Laura A. Driscoll. — 1st ed. — San Francisco: Jossey-Bass Publishers, 1980. xviii, 632 p.; 26 cm. — (The Jossey-Bass social and behavioral science series) Includes indexes. 1. Child development — Evaluation. 2. Ability testing I. Driscoll, Laura A. joint author. II. T.
LB1115.G635          372.1/2/6 19          LC 79-88768          ISBN 0875894402

**Kraus, Philip E., 1908-.** 4.10379
Yesterday's children: a longitudinal study of children from kindergarten into the adult years [by] Philip E. Kraus. — New York: Wiley, [1973] xvi, 191 p.; 23 cm. 'A Wiley-Interscience publication.' 1. Child psychology — Longitudinal studies. 2. Exceptional children — Education — Longitudinal studies. 3. Problem children — Education — Longitudinal studies. I. T.
LB1115.K69 1973          370.15 19          LC 72-10125          ISBN 0471507229

**Wall, William Douglas.** 4.10380
Constructive education for children / by W. D. Wall; foreword by Jean Piaget. — London: Harrap, 1975. xv, 349 p.; 24 cm. (Studies and surveys in comparative education.) 'The first version of this work was written ... under the title: Education and mental health, and published ... in 1955.' 1. Child development 2. Education, Primary I. Wall, William Douglas. Education and mental health. II. T. III. Series.
LB1115.W217          372          LC 76-356490          ISBN 9231011952 pbk

**Foshay, Arthur Wellesley, 1912-.** • 4.10381
Children's social values; an action research study, by Arthur W. Foshay, Kenneth D. Wann, and associates. New York, Bureau of Publications, Teachers College, Columbia University, 1954. 323 p. 22 cm. 'A publication of the Horace Mann-Lincoln Institute of School Experimentation, Teachers College, Columbia University.' 1. Attitude (Psychology) 2. Education Research (Firm) I. Wann, Kenneth D., 1915- joint author. II. T.
LB1117.F6          LC 54-10094

**Jersild, Arthur Thomas, 1902-.** • 4.10382
In search of self: an exploration of the role of the school in promoting self-understanding. — New York: Bureau of Publications, Teachers College, Columbia University, 1952. xii, 141 p.; 22 cm. 'A publication of the Horace

Mann-Lincoln Institute of School Experimentation, Teachers College, Columbia University.' 1. Child study. I. T.
LB1117.J43          370.15          LC 52-12030

**Piaget, Jean, 1896-.** • 4.10383
[Jugement moral chez l'enfant. English] The moral judgement of the child [Translated by Marjorie Gabain. 1st American ed.] Glencoe, Ill., Free Press [1948] ix, 418 p. 22 cm. 1. Child study. 2. Character tests 3. Moral education I. T.
LB1117.P5 1948          136.7417          LC 48-7086

**Dewey, John, 1859-1952.** • 4.10384
The child and the curriculum / by John Dewey. — Chicago: University of Chicago, 1902. 40 p.; 19 cm. — (Contributions to education; no. 5) 1. Education of children I. T.
LB1119.D42 1902a

**Isaacs, Susan Sutherland Fairhurst, 1885-1948.** • 4.10385
Intellectual growth in young children / by Susan Isaacs; with an appendix on children's 'why' questions by Nathan Isaacs. — London: Routledge & K. Paul, [1930]. xi, 370 p.; 22 cm. (Her The behaviour of young children; 1) 1. Child study. 2. Educational psychology I. Isaacs, Nathan, 1895-1966. II. T. III. Series.
LB1131.I7 1966          LC 31-26531

**Rosenthal, Robert, 1933-.** • 4.10386
Pygmalion in the classroom; teacher expectation and pupils' intellectual development [by] Robert Rosenthal [and] Lenore Jacobson. New York, Holt, Rinehart and Winston [1968] xi, 240 p. illus. 23 cm. 1. Prediction of scholastic success 2. Children — Intelligence levels. I. Jacobson, Lenore. joint author. II. T.
LB1131.R585          372.12/64 19          LC 68-19667          ISBN 0030688051

## LB1137 Play. Play Therapy

**Axline, Virginia Mae, 1911-.** • 4.10387
Play therapy: the inner dynamics of childhood / [Under the editorship of Leonard Carmichael]; with an introduction by Carl R. Rogers. — Boston: Houghton Mifflin Co., [1947] xii, 379 p.: ill.; 22 cm. 1. Play therapy 2. Child study. I. Carmichael, Leonard, 1898- ed. II. T.
LB1137.A9          136.7          LC 47-5183

**Reilly, Mary.** 4.10388
Play as exploratory learning: studies of curiosity behavior / Mary Reilly, editor. — Beverly Hills [Calif.]: Sage Publications, [1974] 317 p.: ill.; 24 cm. 1. Play I. T.
LB1137.R44          153.1/52          LC 72-98044          ISBN 0803901593

**Sapora, Allen Victor Heimback, 1912-.** • 4.10389
The theory of play and recreation [by] Allen V. Sapora [and] Elmer D. Mitchell. — 3d ed. — New York, Ronald Press Co. [1961] 558 p. 21 cm. Previous editions, by Elmer D. Mitchell and Bernard S. Mason, published under title: The theory of play. 1. Play 2. Physical education and training I. Mitchell, Elmer Dayton, 1889- joint author. II. T.
LB1137.S24          790          LC 61-8420

## LB1139 Special Topics, A–Z

**Piaget, Jean, 1896-.** • 4.10390
The child's conception of geometry, by Jean Piaget, Bärbel Inhelder, and Alina Szeminska. Translated from the French by E. A. Lunzer. — New York: Basic Books, 1960. 411 p. illus. 22 cm. Translation of La géométrie spontanée de l'enfant. 1. Geometry concept I. T.
LB1139.G4P53          136.74513          LC 60-7177

**Bloom, Lois.** 4.10391
Language development and language disorders / Lois Bloom, Margaret Lahey. — New York: Wiley, c1978. xii, 685 p.: ill.; 24 cm. — (Wiley series on communication disorders) Includes indexes. 1. Children — Language 2. Language arts — Remedial teaching I. Lahey, Margaret, 1932- joint author. II. T. III. Series.
LB1139.L3 B578          371.9/14          LC 77-21482          ISBN 0471082201

**Elliot, Alison J.** 4.10392
Child language / Alison J. Elliot. — Cambridge [Eng.]; New York: Cambridge University Press, 1981. vi, 194 p.; 23 cm. — (Cambridge textbooks in linguistics.) Includes index. 1. Children — Language I. T.
LB1139.L3 E44 1981          401/.9 19          LC 80-41240          ISBN 0521295564

**Heath, Shirley Brice.** 4.10393
Ways with words: language, life, and work in communities and classrooms / Shirley Brice Heath. — Cambridge [Cambridgeshire]; New York: Cambridge

University Press, 1983. xiii, 421 p., [8] p. of plates: ill., map; 24 cm. Includes index. 1. Children — Language 2. Language arts 3. Interaction analysis in education 4. Community and school I. T.
LB1139.L3 H37 1983      372.6 19      LC 82-22062      *ISBN* 0521253349

**Lenneberg, Eric H. ed.**                                        • 4.10394
New directions in the study of language. Eric H. Lenneberg, editor. — Cambridge: M.I.T. Press, [1964] ix, 194 p.: illus.; 22 cm. 1. Children — Language I. T.
LB1139.L3 L4      158.8      *LC* 64-8088

**Miller, George Armitage, 1920-.**                              4.10395
Spontaneous apprentices: children and language / George A. Miller. — New York: Seabury Press, 1977. xxvii, 188 p.; 22 cm. — (The Tree of life) (A Continuum book) 1. Children — Language I. T. II. Series.
LB1139.L3 M56      372.6      *LC* 77-8677      *ISBN* 0816493308

**Moerk, Ernst L.**                                              4.10396
The mother of Eve—as a first language teacher / Ernst L. Moerk; with a commentary by Donald M. Baer. — Norwood, N.J.: Ablex Pub. Corp., c1983. x, 158 p.; 24 cm. — (Monographs on infancy.) Includes indexes. 1. Children — Language — Case studies. 2. Mother and child — Case studies. 3. Interpersonal relations — Case studies. I. T. II. Series.
LB1139.L3 M655 1983      372.6 19      *LC* 82-16358      *ISBN* 0893911623

**Piaget, Jean, 1896-.**                                         • 4.10397
[Langage et la pensée chez l'enfant. English] The language and thought of the child / Pref. by E. Claparède. 3d ed. [rev. and enl. Translated by Marjorie Gabain] New York: Humanities Press [1959] xxiv, 288 p.: ill.; 23 cm. (International library of psychology, philosophy, and scientific method.) 1. Child study. 2. Children — Language I. T. II. Series.
LB1139.L3 Px      *LC* a 60-3678

---

# LB1140–1489 Preschool Education. Nursery Schools. Kindergartens

**Beadle, Muriel.**                                              • 4.10398
A child's mind; how children learn during the critical years from birth to age five. Illustrated by E. John Pfiffner. — [1st ed.]. — Garden City, N.Y.: Doubleday, 1970. xxiii, 294 p.: illus.; 25 cm. 1. Education, Preschool 2. Learning, Psychology of I. T.
LB1140.B36      155.41/3      *LC* 75-89079

**Deasey, Denison.**                                             4.10399
Education under six / Denison Deasey. — New York: St. Martin's Press, 1978. 130 [i. e. 230] p.; 23 cm. 1. Education, Preschool — History. I. T.
LB1140.D37 1978      372/.21/09      *LC* 77-21081      *ISBN* 0312237480

**Austin, Gilbert R.**                                           4.10400
Early childhood education: an international perspective / Gilbert R. Austin. New York: Academic Press, 1976. xiii, 369 p.; 24 cm. (Educational psychology) 1. Education, Preschool 2. Compensatory education I. T.
LB1140.2.A87      372.21      *LC* 75-44761      *ISBN* 0120685507

**Biber, Barbara, 1903-.**                                       4.10401
Early education and psychological development / Barbara Biber. — New Haven: Yale University Press, c1984. xvi, 333 p.: ill.; 25 cm. Includes index. 1. Education, Preschool 2. Child psychology 3. Child development 4. Interaction analysis in education 5. Play I. T.
LB1140.2.B523 1984      372/.21 19      *LC* 84-40190      *ISBN* 0300028024

**Braun, Samuel J., 1934-.**                                     4.10402
History and theory of early childhood education [by] Samuel J. Braun [and] Esther P. Edwards. — Worthington, Ohio: C. A. Jones Pub. Co., [1972] x, 397 p.: illus.; 24 cm. 1. Education, Preschool I. Edwards. Esther P., joint author. II. T.
LB1140.2.B7      372.21/09      *LC* 79-181374      *ISBN* 0839600127

**Evans, Ellis D.**                                              4.10403
Contemporary influences in early childhood education [by] Ellis D. Evans. — 2d ed. — New York: Holt, Rinehart and Winston, [1975] v, 403 p.: illus.; 24 cm. 1. Education, Preschool — United States — 1945- I. T.
LB1140.2.E9 1975      372.21/0973      *LC* 74-16007      *ISBN* 0030895847

**Hess, Robert D.**                                              4.10404
Teachers of young children / Robert D. Hess, Doreen J. Croft. — 3rd ed. — Boston: Houghton Mifflin, c1981. ix, 437 p.: ill.; 24 cm. 1. Education, Preschool I. Croft, Doreen J. II. T.
LB1140.2.H48 1981      372/.21 19      *LC* 80-81928      *ISBN* 0395291720

**McGrew, William Clement, 1944-.**                              4.10405
An ethological study of children's behavior [by] W. C. McGrew. — New York: Academic Press, 1972. xiv, 257 p.: illus.; 24 cm. — (The Child psychology series) 1. Nursery schools 2. Behaviorism (Psychology) I. T.
LB1140.2.M3      155.4/18      *LC* 71-182617      *ISBN* 0124839509

**Weber, Lillian.**                                              4.10406
The English infant school and informal education. — Englewood Cliffs, N.J.: Prentice-Hall, [1971] xii, 276 p.; 24 cm. 'A Center for Urban Education book.' 1. Education, Preschool — Gt. Brit. I. T.
LB1140.2.W43      372.24/1/0942      *LC* 71-167910      *ISBN* 0132812959

**Yardley, Alice.**                                              4.10407
Structure in early learning / Alice Yardley. — Citation Press, 1975 (c1974) viii, 116 p. Includes index. 1. Education, Preschool I. T.
LB1140.2.Y34      *LC* 73-94155      *ISBN* 0590073958

**Ferreiro, Emilia.**                                            4.10408
[Sistemas de escritura en el desarrollo del niño. English] Literacy before schooling / Emilia Ferreiro and Ana Teberosky; translated by Karen Goodman Castro; preface by Yetta Goodman. — Exeter, N.H.: Heinemann Educational Books, 1982. xii, 289 p.: ill.; 22 cm. Translation of: Los sistemas de escritura en el desarrollo del niño. 1. Language arts (Preschool) 2. Language arts (Elementary) 3. Language arts — Latin America. I. Teberosky, Ana. II. T.
LB1140.5.L3 F4713 1982      372.6 19      *LC* 82-15839      *ISBN* 0435082027

**Larrick, Nancy.**                                              4.10409
A parent's guide to children's reading / by Nancy Larrick; illustrated with drawings from favorite children's books. — 5th ed., completely revised. — Philadelphia: Westminster Press, 1982. 271 p.: ill.; 24 cm. Includes index. 1. Reading (Preschool) — Handbooks, manuals, etc. 2. Language arts (Preschool) — Handbooks, manuals, etc. 3. Children — Books and reading — Handbooks, manuals, etc. I. T.
LB1140.5.R4 L37 1982      372.4 19      *LC* 82-24702      *ISBN* 0664327052

**Some persistent questions on beginning reading. Robert C.**    4.10410
**Aukerman, editor.**
Newark, Del.: International Reading Association, [1972] vi, 177 p.; 24 cm. A collection of papers presented at the International Reading Association convention at Atlantic City. 1. Reading (Preschool) 2. Reading readiness I. Aukerman, Robert C., 1910- ed. II. International Reading Association.
LB1140.5.R4 S64      372.4/14      *LC* 73-190454

**Rudolph, Marguerita.**                                         4.10411
Kindergarten and early schooling / Marguerita Rudolph, Dorothy H. Cohen. — 2nd ed. — Englewood Cliffs, N.J.: Prentice-Hall, c1984. xxi, 426 p.: ill.; 24 cm. Rev. ed. of: Kindergarten and early schooling / Dorothy H. Cohen, Marguerita Rudolph. c1977. 1. Kindergarten — Methods and manuals 2. Education, Preschool — Curricula. I. Cohen, Dorothy II. II. Cohen, Dorothy H. Kindergarten and early schooling. III. T.
LB1169.R75 1984      372/.218 19      *LC* 83-8684      *ISBN* 0135153387

**Paley, Vivian Gussin, 1929-.**                                 4.10412
Boys & girls: superheroes in the doll corner / Vivian Gussin Paley; with a foreword by Philip W. Jackson. — Chicago: University of Chicago Press, 1984. xii, 116 p.; 21 cm. 1. Kindergarten — United States — Case studies. 2. Child development — Case studies. 3. Play — Case studies. 4. Identity (Psychology) — Case studies. 5. Stereotype (Psychology) — Case studies. 6. Teaching — Case studies. I. T. II. Title: Boys and girls.
LB1195.P18 1984      372/.218/0973 19      *LC* 84-93      *ISBN* 0226644901

**Shapiro, Michael Steven.**                                     4.10413
Child's garden: the kindergarten movement from Froebel to Dewey / Michael Steven Shapiro. — University Park: Pennsylvania State University Press, c1983. xi, 223 p.: ill.; 24 cm. 1. Kindergarten facilities — History. I. T.
LB1199.S43 1983      372/.218/09 19      *LC* 82-42774      *ISBN* 0271003502

**Ross, Elizabeth Dale.**                                        4.10414
The kindergarten crusade: the establishment of preschool education in the United States / by Elizabeth Dale Ross. Athens: Ohio University Press, c1976. ix, 120 p.; 25 cm. Includes index. 1. Kindergarten facilities — United States — History. I. T.
LB1205.R67      372.21/8/0973      *LC* 75-36986      *ISBN* 0821402064

**Heilman, Arthur W.**    4.10460
Principles and practices of teaching reading / Arthur W. Heilman, Timothy R. Blair, William H. Rupley. — 6th ed. — Columbus: Merrill, c1986. xii, 583 p.: ill. (some col.); 25 cm. 1. Reading (Elementary) I. Blair, Timothy R. II. Rupley, William H. III. T.
LB1573.H325 1986    372.4/1 19    *LC* 85-71976    *ISBN* 0675203570

**McKim, Margaret Grace, 1914-.**    • 4.10461
Guiding growth in reading in the modern elementary school. — 2d ed. [by] Margaret G. McKim [and] Helen Caskey. — New York: Macmilan, [1963] 454 p.: illus.; 24 cm. 1. Reading (Elementary) I. Caskey, Helen, joint author. II. T.
LB1573.M177 1963    372.41    *LC* 63-8396

**Spache, George Daniel, 1909-.**    4.10462
Reading in the elementary school / George D. Spache, Evelyn B. Spache. — 5th ed. — Boston: Allyn and Bacon, c1986. xi, 609 p.: ill.; 24 cm. 1. Reading (Elementary) I. Spache, Evelyn B. II. T.
LB1573.S792 1986    372.4/1 19    *LC* 85-13501    *ISBN* 0205084222

**Tinker, Miles Albert, 1893-.**    4.10463
Teaching elementary reading / Miles A. Tinker, Constance M. McCullough. — 4th ed. — Englewood Cliffs, N.J.: Prentice-Hall, [1975] x, 661 p. Includes indexes. 1. Reading (Elementary) I. McCullough, Constance Mary, 1912- joint author. II. T.
LB1573.T55 1975    372.4/1    *LC* 74-23962    *ISBN* 0138920834

**Veatch, Jeannette, 1910-.**    4.10464
Reading in the elementary school / Jeannette Veatch, with the assistance of Philip J. Acinapuro. — 2d ed. — New York: Wiley, c1978. x, 628 p.: ill.; 24 cm. 1. Reading (Elementary) I. Acinapuro, Philip J. II. T.
LB1573.V44 1978    372.4    *LC* 78-14722    *ISBN* 0471068845

**Heilman, Arthur W.**    4.10465
Phonics in proper perspective / Arthur W. Heilman. — 5th ed. — Columbus: Merrill, c1985. vi, 117 p.: ill.; 25 cm. Includes index. 1. Reading (Elementary) — Phonetic method I. T.
LB1573.3.H44 1985    372.4/145 19    *LC* 84-60988    *ISBN* 0675203767

**Stauffer, Russell G.**    4.10466
The language–experience approach to the teaching of reading / Russell G. Stauffer. — 2d ed. — New York: Harper & Row, c1980. ix, 341 p.: ill.; 24 cm. 1. Reading (Elementary) — Language experience approach I. T.
LB1573.33.S72 1980    372.4/1    *LC* 79-17805    *ISBN* 0060464097

**Trelease, Jim.**    4.10467
The read–aloud handbook / by Jim Trelease; photographs by Joanne Rathe. — New York, N.Y., U.S.A.: Penguin Books, 1985. xix, 243 p.: ill.; 24 cm. (Penguin handbooks) Includes index. 1. Oral reading I. T.
LB1573.5.T68 1985    372.6 19    *LC* 85-217583    *ISBN* 0140467270

**Hildreth, Gertrude Howell, 1898-.**    • 4.10468
Teaching spelling; a guide to basic principles and practices. New York, H. Holt [1955] 346 p. 22 cm. 1. English language — Orthography and spelling I. T.
LB1574.H5    *372.42    *LC* 55-6055

## LB1575–1576 Literature. Language Arts

**Huck, Charlotte S.**    4.10469
Children's literature in the elementary school / Charlotte S. Huck, Susan Hepler, Janet Hickman. — 4th ed. — New York: Holt, Rinehart, and Winston, c1987. p. cm. Includes index. 1. Literature — Study and teaching (Elementary) — United States. 2. Children's literature — United States. I. Hepler, Susan Ingrid. II. Hickman, Janet. III. T.
LB1575.5.U5 H79 1987    372.6/4 19    *LC* 86-29467    *ISBN* 0030417708

**Lundsteen, Sara W.**    4.10470
Listening: its impact at all levels on reading and the other language arts / Sara W. Lundsteen. — Rev. ed. — Urbana, Ill.: ERIC Clearinghouse on Reading andCommunication Skills, National Institute of Education: National Council of Teachers of English, 1979. xvi, 170 p.: ill.; 23 cm. 1. Language arts 2. Reading 3. Listening I. National Council of Teachers of English. II. ERIC Clearinghouse on Reading and Communication Skills. III. T.
LB 1575.8 L96 1979    *LC* 79-14249    *ISBN* 0814129498

**Anderson, Paul S.**    4.10471
Language skills in elementary education / Paul S. Anderson, Diane Lapp. — 3d ed. — New York: Macmillan, c1979. xvii, 458 p.: ill.; 25 cm. 1. Language arts (Elementary) I. Lapp, Diane. joint author. II. T.
LB1576.A616 1979    372.6/044    *LC* 78-6498    *ISBN* 0023031409

**Applebee, Arthur N.**    4.10472
Tradition and reform in the teaching of English: a history / Arthur N. Applebee. — Urbana, Ill.: National Council of Teachers of English, [1974] xi, 298 p.; 24 cm. Includes index. 1. English language — Study and teaching I. T.
LB1576.A63    420/.7/1073    *LC* 74-82650

**Chomsky, Carol.**    4.10473
The acquisition of syntax in children from 5 to 10. — Cambridge, Mass.: M.I.T. Press, [c1969] 126 p.: illus.; 24 cm. — (M.I.T. research monograph, no. 57) Based on the author's thesis, Harvard University, 1968. 1. English language — Study and teaching (Elementary) 2. English language — Syntax I. T.
LB1576.C555    372.6/1    *LC* 70-87287    *ISBN* 0262030330

**Eight approaches to teaching composition / edited by Timothy**    4.10474
**R. Donovan, Ben W. McClelland.**
Urbana, Ill.: National Council of Teachers of English, c1980. xv, 160 p.; 23 cm. 1. English language — Composition and exercises I. Donovan, Timothy R., 1945- II. McClelland, Ben W., 1943-
LB1576.E34    808/.042/07 19    *LC* 80-20474    *ISBN* 0814113036

**Evans, Tricia.**    4.10475
Teaching English / Tricia Evans. — London: Croom Helm, c1982. 212 p.: ill.; 23 cm. 1. English language — Study and teaching I. T.
LB1576.E87 1982    420/.7/12 19    *LC* 82-121916    *ISBN* 0709909012

**Greene, Harry Andrew, 1889-.**    4.10476
Developing language skills in the elementary schools / Harry A. Greene, Walter T. Petty. — 5th ed. — Boston: Allyn and Bacon, [1975] xiv, 513 p.: ill.; 24 cm. 1. Language arts (Elementary) I. Petty, Walter Thomas, 1918- joint author. II. T.
LB1576.G743 1975    372.6/044    *LC* 74-28460    *ISBN* 0205046703

**Herrick, Virgil E., ed.**    • 4.10477
Children and the language arts / edited by Virgil E. Herrick [and] Leland B. Jacobs. — Englewood Cliffs [N.J.]: Prentice-Hall, 1955. 524 p.: illus.; 23 cm. — (Prentice-Hall education series) 1. English language — Study and teaching 2. Children — Language I. Jacobs, Leland B. (Leland Blair), 1907- joint ed. II. T.
LB1576.H34    372.61    *LC* 55-7957

**Howie, Sherry Hill, 1941-.**    4.10478
A guidebook for teaching writing in content areas / Sherry Hill Howie. — Boston: Allyn and Bacon, c1984. x, 238 p.: ill., forms; 28 cm. (Guidebook for teaching series.) 1. Language arts — Correlation with content subjects 2. English language — Study and teaching 3. English language — Composition and exercises I. T. II. Title: Writing in content areas. III. Series.
LB1576.H68 1984    808/.042/07 19    *LC* 83-13379    *ISBN* 0205080707

**Judy, Stephen N.**    4.10479
The ABCs of literacy: a guide for parents and educators / Stephen N. Judy. — New York: Oxford University Press, 1980. xvii, 361 p.; 22 cm. Includes index. 1. English language — Study and teaching — United States. 2. Language arts — United States. 3. Community and school — United States I. T.
LB1576.J82    428/.007/1073    *LC* 79-4475    *ISBN* 0195025873

**Language and thinking in school: a whole–language curriculum /**    4.10480
**Kenneth S. Goodman ... [et al.].**
3rd ed. — New York: R.C. Owen Publishers, 1986. xi, 417 p. Rev. ed. of: Language and thinking in school / E. Brooks Smith, Kenneth S. Goodman, Robert Meredith. 2nd ed. c1976. 1. Language arts 2. Thought and thinking 3. English language — Study and teaching 4. Children — Language I. Goodman, Kenneth S. II. Smith, E. Brooks, 1917- Language and thinking in school.
LB1576.L294 1986    372.6 19    *LC* 86-28601    *ISBN* 0913461814

## LB1584 Social Sciences

**Gollnick, Donna M.**    4.10481
Multicultural education in a pluralistic society / Donna M. Gollnick, Philip C. Chinn. — 2nd ed. — Columbus: C.E. Merrill, c1986. ix, 291 p.: ill.; 24 cm. 1. Social sciences — Study and teaching (Elementary) — United States. 2. Pluralism (Social sciences) — Study and teaching (Elementary) — United States. 3. Social sciences — Study and teaching (Secondary) — United States. 4. Pluralism (Social sciences) — Study and teaching (Secondary) — United States. 5. Intercultural education — United States. I. Chinn, Philip C., 1937- II. T.
LB1584.G62 1986    375/.0084 19    *LC* 85-28469    *ISBN* 0675205735

**Jarolimek, John. ed.**    4.10482
Readings for social studies in elementary education. Edited by John Jarolimek [and] Huber M. Walsh. — 3d ed. — New York: Macmillan, [1974] xi, 467 p.:

illus.; 24 cm. 1. Social sciences — Study and teaching (Elementary) I. Walsh, Huber M. joint ed. II. T.
LB1584.J29 1974      372.8/3/08      *LC* 73-3889      *ISBN* 0023604204

**Jarolimek, John.**      **4.10483**
Social studies in elementary education / John Jarolimek. — 7th ed. — New York: Macmillan; London: Collier Macmillan Publishers, c1986. x, 390 p.: ill.; 26 cm. 1. Social sciences — Study and teaching (Elementary) I. T.
LB1584.J3 1986      372.8/3044 19      *LC* 85-4927      *ISBN* 0023605405

**Michaelis, John Udell, 1912-.**      **4.10484**
Social studies for children: a guide to basic instruction / John U. Michaelis. — 8th ed. — Englewood Cliffs, N.J.: Prentice-Hall, c1985. xii, 428 p.: ill.; 24 cm. 1. Social sciences — Study and teaching (Elementary) I. T.
LB1584.M43 1985      372.8/3044 19      *LC* 84-9767      *ISBN* 0138188998

## LB1585 Science

**Carin, Arthur A.**      **4.10485**
Teaching science through discovery / Arthur A. Carin, Robert B. Sund. — 5th ed. — Columbus: Merrill, c1985. ix, 502 p.: [8] p. of plates: ill. (some col.); 27 cm. Includes index. 1. Science — Study and teaching (Elementary) I. Sund, Robert B. II. T.
LB1585.C28 1985      372.3/5044 19      *LC* 84-42912      *ISBN* 0675203872

**Friedl, Alfred E.**      **4.10486**
Teaching science to children: an integrated approach / Alfred E. Friedl. — 1st ed. — New York: Random House, c1986. vii, 301 p.: ill.; 28 cm. 1. Science — Study and teaching (Elementary) 2. Activity programs in education I. T.
LB1585.F69 1986      372.3/5044 19      *LC* 85-28157      *ISBN* 0394356411

**Friedl, Alfred E.**      **4.10487**
Teaching science to children: the inquiry approach applied [by] Alfred E. Friedl. — [1st ed.]. — New York: Random House, [1972] viii, 337 p.: illus.; 25 cm. 1. Science — Study and teaching (Elementary) I. T.
LB1585.F7      372.3/5/044      *LC* 76-159417      *ISBN* 0394313402

**Kuslan, Louis I.**      **4.10488**
Teaching children science: an inquiry approach / Louis I. Kuslan, A. Harris Stone. — 2d ed. — Belmont, Calif.: Wadsworth Pub. Co., c1972. viii, 533 p.: ill. 1. Science — Study and teaching (Elementary) 2. Learning by discovery I. Stone, A. Harris. II. T.
LB1585.K8 1972      *LC* 70-184482      *ISBN* 0534001319

**Victor, Edward, 1914-.**      **4.10489**
Science for the elementary school / Edward Victor. — 5th ed. — New York: Macmillan; London: Collier MacMillan, [1984], c1985. ix, 786 p.: ill.; 27 cm. 1. Science — Study and teaching (Elementary) I. T.
LB1585.V46 1985      372.3/5044 19      *LC* 83-26229      *ISBN* 0024228605

**Blough, Glenn Orlando.**      **4.10490**
Elementary school science and how to teach it / Glenn O. Blough, Julius Schwartz. — 7th ed. — New York: Holt, Rinehart, and Winston, c1984. xiii, 620 p.: ill.; 24 cm. Includes index. 1. Science — Study and teaching (Elementary) — United States. I. Schwartz, Julius, 1907- II. T.
LB1585.3.B55 1984      372.3/5044 19      *LC* 83-22537      *ISBN* 0030628660

**Greene, Walter H.**      **4.10491**
Health education in the elementary school: teaching for relevance / Walter H. Greene, Frank H. Jenne, Patricia M. Legos. — New York: Macmillan, c1978. xvii, 397 p.: ill.; 26 cm. 1. Health education (Elementary) I. Jenne, Frank H., 1920- joint author. II. Legos, Patricia M., joint author. III. T.
LB1587.A3 G73 1978      372.3/7      *LC* 77-5911      *ISBN* 0023465905

## LB1603–1695 Secondary Education

**Conant, James Bryant, 1893-1978.**      • **4.10492**
The American high school today: a first report to interested citizens. — [1st ed.] New York: McGraw-Hill [1959] xiii, 140 p.: ill.; 21 cm. (Carnegie series in American education, 1) 1. Education, Secondary — 1945- 2. High schools — United States. I. T. II. Series.
LB1607.C647      373.73      *LC* 59-8527

**Friedenberg, Edgar Zodiag, 1921-.**      • **4.10493**
Coming of age in America: growth and acquiescence [by] Edgar Z. Friedenberg. — New York: Random House, [1965] xii, 300 p.; 22 cm. 1. Adolescence 2. Education, Secondary — 1945- I. T.
LB1607.F78      301.431      *LC* 65-11250

**Hahn, Robert O.**      **4.10494**
Creative teachers: who wants them? [By] Robert O. Hahn. — New York: Wiley, [1973] x, 272 p.; 23 cm. 1. High school teaching 2. Creative thinking (Education) I. T.
LB1607.H16      373.1/1/02      *LC* 73-6592      *ISBN* 0471339059

**National Association of Secondary-School Principals.**      • **4.10495**
**Commission on the Experimental Study of the Utilization of the Staff in the Secondary School.**
Focus on change; guide to better schools, by J. Lloyd Trump [director, and] Dorsey Baynham. — Chicago: Rand McNally, [1961] 147 p.: illus., diagrs.; 21 cm. 1. High schools — United States. I. Trump, J. Lloyd, 1908- II. Baynham, Dorsey. III. T.
LB1607.N22      373.73      *LC* 61-10181

**Rivlin, Harry Nathaniel, 1904-.**      • **4.10496**
Teaching adolescents in secondary schools; the principles of effective teaching in junior and senior high schools. — 2d ed. — New York: Appleton-Century-Crofts, [1961] 479 p.: illus.; 24 cm. — (Textbooks in education) 1. Education, Secondary — 1945- I. T.
LB1607.R57 1961      373      *LC* 61-5357

**Sizer, Theodore R.**      • **4.10497**
Secondary schools at the turn of the century / [by] Theodore R. Sizer. — New Haven: Yale University Press, 1964. xiv, 304 p.; 23 cm. 'Report of the Commitee of Ten on Secondary School Studies, with the reports of the conferences arranged by the committee': p. 209-271. 1. Education, Secondary 2. Education — United States I. National Education Association of the United States. Committee of Ten on Secondary School Studies. Report II. T.
LB1607 S54      *LC* 64-20935

**Keller, Franklin Jefferson, 1887-.**      • **4.10498**
The double–purpose high school; closing the gap between vocational and academic preparation, by Franklin J. Keller. — Westport, Conn.: Greenwood Press, [1969, c1953] vi, 207 p.; 23 cm. 1. High schools — U.S. 2. Vocational education — U.S. 3. Education, Secondary — 1945- I. T.
LB1620.K43 1969      373.2/4      *LC* 72-98236      *ISBN* 0837128757

**Alexander, William Marvin, 1912-.**      **4.10499**
The exemplary middle school / William M. Alexander, Paul S. George. — New York: Holt, Rinehart and Winston, c1981. xii, 356 p.: ill.; 24 cm. 1. Middle schools I. George, Paul S. joint author. II. T.
LB1623.A43      373.2/36 19      *LC* 80-27086      *ISBN* 003052301X

**Briggs, Thomas Henry, 1877-.**      **4.10500**
The junior high school, by Thomas H. Briggs. Boston, Houghton [c1920] x, 350 p. illus. 19 cm. (Riverside textbooks in education ... Division of secondary education) 1. High schools — United States. I. T.
LB1623.B7      *LC* 20-13790

**Calhoun, Frederick S.**      **4.10501**
Organization of the middle grades: a summary of research / [prepared by Frederick S. Calhoun]. — Arlington, Va. (1800 N. Kent St., Arlington 22209): Educational Research Service, c1983. viii, 200 p.: ill.; 28 cm. — (Research brief / Educational Research Service, Inc.) Updates and expands: Summary of research on middle schools / Heather S. Doob. 1. Middle schools — United States. I. Doob, Heather S. Summary of research on middle schools. II. Educational Research Service (Arlington, Va.) III. T.
LB1623.C2 1983      373.2/36 19      *LC* 83-126087

**Eichhorn, Donald H.**      **4.10502**
The middle school [by] Donald H. Eichhorn. — New York: Center for Applied Research in Education, [1966] x, 116 p.: illus.; 24 cm. — (The Library of education) 1. Middle schools I. T.
LB1623.E35      373.2/36      *LC* 66-26052

**The Emergent middle school** [by] William M. Alexander [and others].      **4.10503**
New York: Holt, Rinehart and Winston, [1968] viii, 191 p.; 23 cm. 1. Middle schools I. Alexander, William Marvin, 1912-
LB1623.E37      373.2/36      *LC* 68-20642

**A Guide to an effective middle school** / [edited by] Nicholas P. Georgiady, James E. Heald, Louis G. Romano.      **4.10504**
New York, N.Y.: Irvington Publishers, 1984. 470 p.: ill. Includes index. 1. Middle schools — United States — Addresses, essays, lectures. I. Georgiady, Nicholas Peter, 1921- II. Heald, James E. III. Romano, Louis G.
LB1623.G84 1984      373.2/36 19      *LC* 84-8920      *ISBN* 0829015248

**Lipsitz, Joan.**      4.10505
Successful schools for young adolescents / Joan Lipsitz. — New Brunswick, N.J.: Transaction Books, c1984. xiii, 223 p.; 24 cm. Includes index. 1. Education, Secondary — United States — Aims and objectives. 2. Middle schools — United States — Evaluation. 3. Middle schools — United States — Case studies. I. T.
LB1623.L56 1984     373.73 19     *LC* 83-9139     *ISBN* 0878554874

**Moss, Theodore Crandall, 1922-.**      • 4.10506
Middle school [by] Theodore C. Moss. — Boston: Houghton Mifflin, [1969] xiv, 283 p.: illus., plans.; 21 cm. 1. Middle schools I. T.
LB1623.M65     373.2/36     *LC* 75-5022

**Perspectives: middle school education, 1964–1984 / John H.**      4.10507
**Lounsbury, editor.**
Columbus, Ohio (P.O. Box 14882, Columbus 43214): National Middle School Association, c1984. vii, 184 p.; 23 cm. 1. Middle schools — United States — History — 20th century — Addresses, essays, lectures. I. Lounsbury, John H. II. National Middle School Association.
LB1623.P39 1984     373.2/36 19     *LC* 85-112968

**Van Til, William.**      4.10508
Modern education for the junior high school years [by] William Van Til, Gordon F. Vars [and] John H. Lounsbury. — 2d ed. — Indianapolis: Bobbs-Merrill Co., [1967] xi, 592 p.: illus.; 24 cm. 1. Junior high schools I. Vars, Gordon F., joint author. II. Lounsbury, John H. joint author. III. T.
LB1623.V34 1967     373.2/36     *LC* 66-25826

**Powell, Arthur G., 1937-.**      4.10509
The shopping mall high school: winners and losers in the educational marketplace / Arthur G. Powell, Eleanor Farrar, and David K. Cohen. — Boston: Houghton Mifflin, 1985. 360 p.; 24 cm. 'The second report from A Study of High Schools, co-sponsored by the National Association of Secondary School Principals and the Commission on Educational Issues of the National Association of Independent Schools.' Includes index. 1. High schools — United States — Curricula. 2. Student activities — United States. 3. Personnel service in secondary education — United States. 4. Individualized instruction I. Farrar, Eleanor. II. Cohen, David K., 1934- III. National Association of Secondary School Principals (U.S.) IV. National Association of Independent Schools. Commission on Educational Issues. V. T.
LB1628.5.P68 1985     373.73 19     *LC* 85-7664     *ISBN* 0395379040

**Hook, J. N. (Julius Nicholas), 1913-.**      4.10510
The teaching of high school English / J.N. Hook, William H. Evans. — 5th ed. — New York: Wiley, c1982. xiii, 521 p.; 24 cm. 1. English language — Study and teaching (Secondary) I. Evans, William Howard, 1924- II. T.
LB1631.H56 1982     428/.007/12 19     *LC* 81-19682     *ISBN* 0471089230

**Mathieson, Margaret.**      4.10511
The preachers of culture: a study of English and its teachers / Margaret Mathieson. — Totowa, N.J.: Rowman and Littlefield, 1975. 231 p.; 23 cm. 1. English language — Study and teaching I. T.
LB1631.M39 1975     420/.7     *LC* 75-17992     *ISBN* 0874717523

**Robinson, H. Alan, 1921-.**      4.10512
Teaching reading, writing, and study strategies: the content areas / H. Alan Robinson. — 3rd ed. — Boston: Allyn and Bacon, 1983. xxii, 329 p.: ill.; 24 cm. Rev. ed. of: Teaching reading and study strategies, 2nd ed. c1978. 1. Language arts (Secondary) 2. Language arts — Correlation with content subjects 3. Education, Secondary — Curricula. I. T.
LB1631.R54 1983     428.4/07/12 19     *LC* 82-16359     *ISBN* 0205079385

**Simmons, John Stephen.**      4.10513
Decisions about the teaching of English / John S. Simmons, Robert E. Shafer, Gail B. West. — Boston: Allyn and Bacon, c1976. ix, 313 p.: ill.; 24 cm. 1. English language — Study and teaching (Secondary) 2. English philology — Study and teaching (Secondary) I. Shafer, Robert Eugene, 1925- joint author. II. West, Gail B., 1940- joint author. III. T.
LB1631.S498     808/.007/12     *LC* 75-25697     *ISBN* 0205045421

**Willinsky, John, 1950-.**      4.10514
The well-tempered tongue: the politics of standard English in the high school / John Willinsky; foreword by Edgar Friedenberg. — New York: P. Lang, c1984. xviii, 163 p.; 23 cm. (American university studies. Education. vol. 4) Includes index. 1. English language — Study and teaching (Secondary) — Nova Scotia — Case studies. 2. Language and education — Social aspects — Nova Scotia — Case studies. 3. Students — Nova Scotia — Language (New words, slang, etc.) — Case studies. I. T. II. Series.
LB1631.W44 1984     428/.007/12716 19     *LC* 84-47530     *ISBN* 0820401080

**Santeusanio, Richard P., 1942-.**      4.10515
A practical approach to content area reading / Richard P. Santeusanio. — Reading, Mass.: Addison-Wesley, c1983. xii, 388 p.: ill.; 25 cm. 1. Reading (Secondary education) 2. Content area reading I. T.
LB1632.S33 1983     428.4/3/0712 19     *LC* 82-6740     *ISBN* 0201074079

**Trent, James W.**      4.10516
Beyond high school; a psychosociological study of 10,000 high school graduates [by] James W. Trent and Leland L. Medsker. Foreword by Edward Joseph Shoben, Jr. — [1st ed.]. — San Francisco: Jossey-Bass, 1968. xxiv, 333 p.: illus.; 24 cm. 1. High school graduates — United States. I. Medsker, Leland L. joint author. II. T.
LB1695.T7 1968     373.1/8     *LC* 68-21318

# LB1705–2278 Teachers: Education, Training

**Borrowman, Merle L.**      • 4.10517
The liberal and technical in teacher education: a historical survey of American thought. — Teachers College: Columbia University, 1956. 247 p.; 24 cm. (Teachers College studies in education) 1. Teachers — Training of — United States 2. Education — Philosophy I. T. II. Series.
LB1715.B66     *LC* 56-7372

**Conant, James Bryant, 1893-1978.**      • 4.10518
The education of American teachers. New York, McGraw-Hill [1963] ix, 275 p. 22 cm. (Carnegie series in American education) 1. Teachers — Training of — United States 2. Teachers — Certification — United States. I. T. II. Series.
LB1715.C617 1963     370.7     *LC* 63-20444

**McCarty, Donald James, 1921-.**      4.10519
New perspectives on teacher education [by] Donald J. McCarty and associates. — [1st ed.]. — San Francisco: Jossey-Bass Publishers, 1973. xiv, 255 p.; 24 cm. — (The Jossey-Bass series in higher education) 1. Teachers — Training of I. T.
LB1715.M15     370/.71     *LC* 73-1852     *ISBN* 0875891713

**Mattingly, Paul H.**      4.10520
The classless profession: American schoolmen in the nineteenth century / by Paul H. Mattingly. — New York: New York University Press, 1975. xxiii, 235 p.: ill.; 24 cm. (New York University series in education and socialization in American history) Includes index. 1. Teachers — United States — History. 2. Teachers — Training of — United States — History. I. T.
LB1715.M343     371.1/00973     *LC* 74-29126     *ISBN* 0814754007

**Rugg, Harold Ordway, 1886-1960.**      • 4.10521
The teacher of teachers: frontiers of theory and practice in teacher education. — Westport Conn.: Greenwood Press, [1970, c1952] x, 308 p.; 23 cm. 1. Teachers — Training of I. T.
LB1715.R8 1970     370/.71     *LC* 73-98239     *ISBN* 0837128730

**Sarason, Seymour Bernard, 1919-.**      4.10522
The preparation of teachers: an unstudied problem in education / Seymour B. Sarason, Kenneth S. Davidson, Burton Blatt. — Rev. ed. — Cambridge, MA: Brookline Books, c1986. xx, vii-xv, 124 p.; 23 cm. 1. Teachers — Training of 2. Educational psychology I. Davidson, Kenneth S. II. Blatt, Burton, 1927- III. T.
LB1715.S25 1986     370/.7/1 19     *LC* 86-4171     *ISBN* 0914797263

**Smith, James A.**      • 4.10523
Setting conditions for creative teaching in the elementary school / [by] James A. Smith; foreword by E. Paul Torrance. — Boston: Allyn and Bacon, 1966. xviii, 207 p.: ill.; 22 cm. 1. Education, Elementary — 1965- 2. Elementary school teaching 3. Creative ability (Child psychology) I. T.
LB1715.S483     372.13     *LC* 66-14156

**Weaver, W. Timothy.**      4.10524
America's teacher quality problem: alternatives for reform / W. Timothy Weaver. — New York, NY: Praeger, 1983. xii, 270 p.: ill.; 25 cm. Includes index. 1. Teachers — Training of — United States 2. Teachers — United States — Rating of. I. T.
LB1715.W357 1983     371.1/44/0973 19     *LC* 83-13804     *ISBN* 0030687772

**Doll, Ronald C.**      4.10525
Supervision for staff development, ideas and application / Ronald C. Doll. — Boston: Allyn and Bacon, c1983. x, 399 p.; 24 cm. 1. Teachers — In-service training 2. School supervision I. T.
LB1731.D585 1983     371.1/46 19     *LC* 82-20604     *ISBN* 0205078540

**Woellmer, Elizabeth H.**      • 4.10526
Requirements for certification of teachers, counselors, librarians, administrators for elementary schools, secondary schools, junior colleges. [1935]-. Chicago: University of Chicago Press. v. maps. 28 cm. Annual. 1. Teachers — Certification — United States. 2. Teachers — United States. 3. Teachers — Legal status, laws, etc. 4. School superintendents I. T. II. Title: Requirements for certification of teachers, counselors, librarians, administrators.
LB1771.W6     *LC* a 43-1905

**Carnegie Forum on Education and the Economy. Task Force on**     4.10527
**Teaching as a Profession.**
A nation prepared: teachers for the 21st century: the report of the Task Force on Teaching as a Profession, Carnegie Forum on Education and the Economy, May 1986. — Washington, D.C.: The Forum, c1986. ix, 135 p.: ill. (some col.); 22 x 28 cm. 1. Teachers — United States. 2. Teachers — Training of — United States 3. Teachers' socio-economic status — United States. 4. Education and state — United States. I. T.
LB1775.C34 1986    371.1/00973 19    *LC* 86-11743    *ISBN* 0961668504

**Heck, Shirley F.**      4.10528
The complex roles of the teacher: an ecological perspective / Shirley F. Heck, C. Ray Williams; foreword by John I. Goodlad. — New York: Teachers College Press, Teachers College, Columbia University, 1984. xvii, 212 p.; 23 cm. Includes index. 1. Teaching 2. Interaction analysis in education 3. First year teachers — United States — Case studies. I. Williams, C. Ray. II. T.
LB1775.H42 1984    371.1/02 19    *LC* 83-17865    *ISBN* 0807727482

**Lieberman, Myron, 1919-.**      • 4.10529
Education as a profession. Englewood Cliffs, N.J.: Prentice-Hall, 1956. 540 p.; 24 cm. 1. Teaching — Vocational guidance I. T.
LB1775.L44    371.1069    *LC* 56-10901

**Lortie, Dan Clement, 1926-.**      4.10530
Schoolteacher; a sociological study [by] Dan C. Lortie. Chicago: University of Chicago Press, [1975] xii, 284 p.; 23 cm. 1. Teaching — Vocational guidance — United States. 2. Teachers — Social conditions — United States. 3. Teachers — Psychology. I. T.
LB1775.L56    371.1/02/023    *LC* 74-11428    *ISBN* 0226493512

**Livesey, Herbert B.**      4.10531
The professors: who they are, what they do, what they really want, and what they need / Herbert Livesey. — New York: Charterhouse, [1975] 343 p.; 22 cm. Includes index. 1. College teachers — United States 2. College teaching — Vocational guidance — United States. 3. United States — Intellectual life I. T.
LB1778.L58    378.1/2/0973    *LC* 74-25730    *ISBN* 0883270463

**Wilson, Logan, 1907-.**      4.10532
The academic man, a study in the sociology of a profession [by] Logan Wilson ... London, New York [etc.] Oxford University Press, 1942. vi p., 2 β., 3-248 p. incl. tables. 22 cm. 1. Teachers 2. Universities and colleges I. T.
LB1778.W5    *LC* 42-10217

**Wilson, Logan, 1907-.**      4.10533
American academics: then and now / Logan Wilson. — New York: Oxford University Press, 1979. 309 p.; 22 cm. Continues the author's earlier work, The academic man. 1. College teachers I. T.
LB1778.W52    378.1/2    *LC* 78-12118    *ISBN* 0195024826

**Shils, Edward Albert, 1911-.**      4.10534
The academic ethic / Edward Shils. — University of Chicago Press ed. — Chicago: University of Chicago Press, 1984, c1983. 104 p.; 24 cm. 'The report of a study group of the International Council on the Future of the University, Jeanne Hersch ... [et al.].' 'Reprinted from Minerva, vol. 20:1-2'—T.p. verso. 1. College teachers — Professional ethics I. International Council on the Future of the University. II. T.
LB1779.S44 1984    174/.9379 19    *LC* 84-6    *ISBN* 0226753301

**Heitzmann, William Ray. comp.**      4.10535
Student teaching, classroom management, and professionalism, edited by Wm. Ray Heitzmann and Charles Staropoli. — New York: MSS Information Corp., [1974] 196 p.; 24 cm. A collection of articles previously published in various journals. 1. Student teaching — Addresses, essays, lectures. 2. Classroom management — Addresses, essays, lectures. 3. Teaching — Vocational guidance — Addresses, essays, lectures. I. Staropoli, Charles, joint comp. II. T.
LB2157.A3 H38 1974    370/.733    *LC* 73-18119    *ISBN* 084225143X

**Hevener, Fillmer.**      4.10536
Successful student teaching: a handbook for elementary and secondary student teachers / by Fillmer Hevener Jr. — Sanatoga, Calif.: Century Twenty One Pub., 1981. vii, 133 [2] p.: ill.; 28 cm. 1. Student teaching — Handbooks, manuals, etc. 2. Student teachers — Handbooks, manuals, etc. I. T.
LB2157.A3H455    *LC* 80-69332    *ISBN* 0865480400

**Johnson, James Allen, 1932-.**      4.10537
A brief history of student teaching, by Jim Johnson. — De Kalb, Ill.: Creative Educational Materials, [1968] xiv, 222 p.; 23 cm. 1. Student teaching — United States — History. I. T.
LB2157.U5 J6    370/.733    *LC* 68-7109

**Brauner, Charles J.**      • 4.10538
The evolution of American educational theory / Charles J. Brauner. — Stanford, Calif.: Stanford University, 1962. v, 341, xviii, 192 p.: diagrs.; 28 cm. 1. Education — Study and teaching I. Brauner, Charles J. Evolution of American educational theory. II. T. III. Title: The evolution of American educational theory.
LB2165.B72    *LC* 64-12855

**Tomorrow's teachers: a report of the Holmes Group.**      4.10539
East Lansing, MI (501 Erickson Hall, East Lansing 48824-1034): Holmes Group, c1986. xi, 97 p.; 23 cm. 1. Teachers — Training of — United States 2. Universities and colleges — United States — Curricula — Planning. I. Holmes Group (U.S.)
LB2165.T65 1986    370/.7/32640973 19    *LC* 86-170613

**Teaching abroad / Barbara Cahn Connotillo, editor, with Walter**      4.10540
**Jackson.**
New expanded and revised ed. of 1976 publication. — New York: Institute of International Education, c1984. xiii, 128 p.; 22 cm. — (The learning traveler; v. 3) 1. Teachers, Foreign — Employment — Directories. I. Connotillo, Barbara Cahn. II. Cohen, Gail A. Teaching abroad. III. Institute of International Education (New York, N.Y.) IV. Series.
LB2283.B42    *ISBN* 0872061248

---

# LB2300–2411 Higher Education

**Yearbook of higher education.**      • 4.10541
1st-16th ed.; 1969-1984/85. Chicago [etc.]: Marquis Academic Media, Marquis Who's Who [etc.] v.; 24-29 cm. Annual. 1. Education, Higher — Yearbooks.
LB2300.Y4    378.73    *LC* 69-18308

**Higher education in tomorrow's world, edited by Algo D.**      4.10542
**Henderson.**
Ann Arbor, University of Michigan [1968] x, 189 p. 24 cm. 'A symposium of the international conference on higher education commemorating the sesquicentennial of The University of Michigan, April 26-29, 1967.' 1. Education, Higher — Congresses. I. Henderson, Algo Donmyer, 1897- II. University of Michigan.
LB2301.H52    378    *LC* 67-65596

**Becker, Gary Stanley, 1930-.**      4.10543
Human capital: a theoretical and empirical analysis, with special reference to education / by Gary S. Becker. — 2d ed. — New York: National Bureau of Economic Research: distributed by Columbia University Press, 1975. xvii, 268 p.: ill.; 24 cm. (Human behavior and social institutions; 5) 1. Education — Economic aspects 2. Vocational guidance I. T. II. Series.
LB2321.B27 1975    338.4/7/37    *LC* 74-83469    *ISBN* 0870145134

**Hutchins, Robert Maynard, 1899-.**      • 4.10544
The higher learning in America, by Robert Maynard Hutchins. — New Haven, Yale University Press; London, H. Milford, Oxford University Press, 1936. 4 p. l., 119 p. 21 cm. — ([Storrs lectures, Yale university]) 1. Education, Higher 2. Universities and colleges — U.S. I. T.
LB2321.M85    378.73    *LC* 36-27474

**Newman, John Henry, 1801-1890.**      4.10545
The idea of a university: defined and illustrated: I. In nine discourses delivered to the Catholics of Dublin. II. In occasional lectures and essays addressed to the members of the Catholic University / by John Henry Newman; edited with introd. and notes by I. T. Ker. — Oxford: Clarendon Press, 1976. lxxv, 684 p.; 23 cm. 1. Universities and colleges — Collected works. 2. Education, Higher — Collected works. I. Ker, I. T. (Ian Turnbull) II. T.
LB2321.N54 1976    378    *LC* 76-375677    *ISBN* 0198118961

## LB2322 1965–

**Chickering, Arthur W., 1927-.**      • 4.10546
Education and identity [by] Arthur W. Chickering. — [1st ed.]. — San Francisco: Jossey-Bass, 1969. xiv, 367 p.; 24 cm. — (The Jossey-Bass series in higher education) 1. Education, Higher 2. Educational sociology I. T.
LB2322.C45    378/.01    *LC* 70-75938    *ISBN* 0875890350

**Clark, Burton R.**        4.10547
The higher education system: academic organization in cross–national perspective / Burton R. Clark. — Berkeley: University of California Press, c1983. xiii, 315 p.; 24 cm. Includes index. 1. Education, Higher 2. Comparative education I. T.
LB2322.C57 1983     378 19     *LC* 82-13521     *ISBN* 0520048415

**Commission on Non-traditional Study.**        4.10548
Diversity by design. Samuel B. Gould, chairman. — [1st ed.]. — San Francisco: Jossey-Bass Publishers, 1973. xxvii, 178 p.; 24 cm. — (The Jossey-Bass series in higher education) 1. Education, Higher — 1965- 2. Self-culture I. Gould, Samuel B. II. T.
LB2322.C65 1973     378.1/7/9     *LC* 73-3772     *ISBN* 087589173X

**Habermas, Jürgen.**        4.10549
Toward a rational society: student protest, science and politics / translated [from the German] by Jeremy J. Shapiro. — London: Heinemann Educational, 1971. ix, 132 p.; 23 cm. 'The first three essays were published in 'Protestbewegung und Hochschulreform' (1969) by Suhrkamp Verlag. The first and third essays were abridged for the English edition by the author. The last three essays were published in 'Technik und Wissenschaft als 'Ideologie" by Suhrkamp Verlag in 1968.' - title page verso. 1. Education, Higher — 1965- 2. College students — Political activity I. T.
LB2322.H3 1971     378/.008     *LC* 76-582616     *ISBN* 0435823809

**Mood, Alexander McFarlane, 1913-.**        4.10550
The future of higher education: some speculations and suggestions, by Alexander M. Mood. A report prepared for the Carnegie Commission on Higher Education. — New York: McGraw-Hill, [1973] xvi, 166 p.; 24 cm. 1. Education, Higher — 1965- 2. Universities and colleges — Administration I. Carnegie Commission on Higher Education. II. T.
LB2322.M66     378.1     *LC* 73-6533     *ISBN* 0070100640

**Taylor, Harold, 1914-.**        4.10551
Students without teachers; the crisis in the university. — [1st ed.]. — New York: McGraw-Hill, [1969] xiv, 333 p.; 22 cm. 1. Education, Higher — 1965- 2. Intellectual life I. T.
LB2322.T3     378.1/001     *LC* 70-79499

## LB2324 Special Aspects

**Brubacher, John Seiler, 1898-.**        4.10552
On the philosophy of higher education / John S. Brubacher. — Rev. ed. — San Francisco: Jossey-Bass, 1982. xviii, 168 p.; 24 cm. — (Jossey-Bass series in higher education.) Includes index. 1. Education, Higher — Philosophy. I. T. II. Series.
LB2324.B78 1982     378/.001 19     *LC* 82-48076     *ISBN* 0875895360

**Smith, Bruce L. R.**        4.10553
The state of academic science: the universities in the nation's research effort / Bruce L.R. Smith and Joseph J. Karlesky. — New York: Change Magazine Press, c1977-78. 2 v.: graph.; 24 cm. 1. Education, Higher — Research 2. Research — United States I. Karlesky, Joseph J., 1943- II. T.
LB2324.S65     Q180.U5 S39.     507/.20973     *LC* 77-72979     *ISBN* 0915390094

## LB2325 Addresses. Essays. Lectures

**Issues in higher education and the professions in the 1980s /**        4.10554
[edited by] Martha Boaz.
Littleton, Colo.: Libraries Unlimited, 1981. 179 p.; 24 cm. 1. Education, Higher — United States — Addresses, essays, lectures. 2. Professional education — United States — Addresses, essays, lectures. I. Boaz, Martha Terosse, 1913-
LB2325.I84     378.73 19     *LC* 81-12357     *ISBN* 0872872602

**Kerr, Clark, 1911-.**        4.10555
The uses of the university / Clark Kerr. — 3rd ed. — Cambridge, Mass.: Harvard University Press, 1982. ix, 204 p.; 21 cm. 'The Godkin lectures on the essentials of free government and the duties of the citizen'–T.p. verso. 1. Education, Higher — Addresses, essays, lectures. I. T. II. Title: Godkin lectures.
LB2325.K43 1982     378 19     *LC* 82-3146     *ISBN* 0674931718

## LB2327 Junior Colleges (Private)

**Diener, Thomas.**        4.10556
Growth of an American invention: a documentary history of the junior and community college movement / Thomas Diener. — Westport, Conn.: Greenwood Press, [1985], 1986. xviii, 249 p.; 25 cm. (Contributions to the study of education. 0196-707X; no. 16) 1. Junior colleges — United States — History. 2. Community colleges — United States — History. I. T. II. Series.
LB2327.D53 1986     378/.1543 19     *LC* 85-9832     *ISBN* 0313249938

## LB2328–2329 Community Colleges. Junior Colleges (Public)

**Blocker, Clyde E.**        • 4.10557
The two–year college; a social synthesis [by] Clyde E. Blocker, Robert H. Plummer [and] Richard C. Richardson, Jr. — Englewood Cliffs, N.J.: Prentice-Hall, [1965] xii, 298 p.: illus.; 24 cm. — (Prentice-Hall series in education) 1. Junior colleges I. Plummer, Robert H., joint author. II. Richardson, Richard C. joint author. III. T.
LB2328.B53     378.1543     *LC* 65-19734

**Breneman, David W.**        4.10558
Financing community colleges: an economic perspective / David W. Breneman, Susan C. Nelson. — Washington, D.C.: Brookings Institution, c1981. xiii, 222 p.; 24 cm. — (Studies in higher education policy.) 1. Community colleges — United States — Finance. 2. Federal aid to higher education — United States. I. Nelson, Susan C. II. T. III. Series.
LB2328.B685     379.1/214/0973 19     *LC* 81-17042     *ISBN* 081571064X

**Bushnell, David S.**        4.10559
Organizing for change: new priorities for community colleges [by] David S. Bushnell. — New York: McGraw-Hill, [1973] xvi, 237 p.; 24 cm. Report of a study project, Project Focus, initiated by the American Association of Junior Colleges. 1. Community colleges — United States. I. American Association of Junior Colleges. II. T.
LB2328.B86     378.1/543     *LC* 72-10908     *ISBN* 0070093113

**Cohen, Arthur M.**        4.10560
The American community college / Arthur M. Cohen, Florence B. Brawer. — 1st ed. — San Francisco: Jossey-Bass, 1982. xxvi, 445 p.; 24 cm. — (Jossey-Bass series in higher education.) Includes index. 1. Community colleges — United States. I. Brawer, Florence B., 1922- II. T. III. Series.
LB2328.C55 1982     378/.052 19     *LC* 81-19319     *ISBN* 0875895115

**Deegan, William L.**        4.10561
Renewing the American community college: priorities and strategies for effective leadership / William L. Deegan, Dale Tillery, and associates; foreword by Clark Kerr. — 1st ed. — San Francisco: Jossey-Bass, 1985. xxvi, 340 p.; 24 cm. (Jossey-Bass higher education series.) 'Published in cooperation with ERIC Clearinghouse for Junior Colleges'–T.p. verso. 1. Community colleges — United States. 2. Leadership I. Tillery, Dale. II. ERIC Clearinghouse for Junior Colleges. III. T. IV. Series.
LB2328.D37 1985     378/.052 19     *LC* 85-45052     *ISBN* 0875896642

**Gleazer, Edmund J.**        4.10562
Project Focus: a forecast study of community colleges [by] Edmund J. Gleazer Jr. New York, McGraw-Hill [c1973.] 239 p. 24 cm. 1. Community colleges — United States. I. T.
LB 2328 G55 1973     *LC* 72-10558     *ISBN* 0070234353

**Vaughan, George B.**        4.10563
Issues for community college leaders in a new era / [edited by] George B. Vaughan and associates; foreword by Arthur M. Cohen. — 1st ed. — San Francisco: Jossey-Bass, 1983. xxi, 275 p.; 24 cm. — (Jossey-Bass higher education series.) 'Published in cooperation with ERIC Clearinghouse for Junior Colleges'–T.p. verso. Includes index. 1. Community colleges — United States — Administration — Addresses, essays, lectures. I. T. II. Series.
LB2328.I87 1983     378/.052 19     *LC* 83-48167     *ISBN* 0875895867

**London, Howard B.**        4.10564
The culture of a community college / Howard B. London. — New York: Praeger, 1978. xvii, 181 p.; 24 cm. 1. Community colleges — United States. 2. Education, Humanistic — United States. 3. College students' socio-economic status — United States. 4. United States — Intellectual life I. T.
LB2328.L58     378.1/543/0973     *LC* 78-8697     *ISBN* 0030447011

**Medsker, Leland L.**        4.10565
Breaking the access barriers: a profile of two–year colleges / by Leland L. Medsker and Dale Tillery; with a commentary by Joseph P. Cosand. — New York: McGraw-Hill, [1971] x, 183 p.: maps.; 23 cm. 1. Junior colleges — U.S. I. Tillery, Dale. joint author. II. T.
LB2328.M39     378.1/543/0973     *LC* 74-141305     *ISBN* 0070100233

**Medsker, Leland L.**        • 4.10566
The junior college: progress and prospect. — New York: McGraw-Hill, 1960. 367 p.: illus.; 22 cm. — (The Carnegie series in American education) 1. Junior colleges I. T.
LB2328.M4     378.154     *LC* 59-14459

**Monroe, Charles R.**      4.10567
Profile of the community college; [a handbook, by] Charles R. Monroe. — [1st ed.]. — San Francisco: Jossey-Bass, 1972. xiv, 435 p.; 24 cm. — (The Jossey-Bass series in higher education) 1. Community colleges I. T.
LB2328.M56    378/.052    LC 77-186576    ISBN 0875891241

**Zoglin, Mary Lou, 1928-.**      4.10568
Power and politics in the community college / Mary Lou Zoglin. — Palm Springs, Calif.: ETC Publications, 1976. x, 166 p.; 24 cm. 1. Community colleges — United States — History. 2. Community colleges — United States — Administration. I. T.
LB2328.Z63    378/.052/0973    LC 75-35618    ISBN 088280037X

**Zwerling, L. Steven.**      4.10569
Second best: the crisis of the community college / L. Steven Zwerling. — New York: McGraw-Hill, c1976. xxi, 382 p.: 22 cm. Includes index. 1. Community colleges — United States. 2. Students — Socioeconomic status — United States. I. T.
LB2328.Z93    378.1/543    LC 75-31735    ISBN 0070730903

## LB2331 Special Topics

**Barzun, Jacques, 1907-.**      • 4.10570
Teacher in America / by Jacques Barzun. — Boston: Little, Brown and company, [1945] vi, 321 p.; 21 cm. 'An Atlantic monthly press book.' 'First edition.' London edition (V. Gollancz ltd.) has title: We who teach. 1. College teaching — United States. 2. Education, Higher — United States. 3. United States — Intellectual life I. T.
LB2331.B374 1945    378/.12/0973 19    LC 45-1580

**Dressel, Paul Leroy, 1910-.**      4.10571
Higher education as a field of study: [the emergence of a profession] / Paul L. Dressel, Lewis B. Mayhew. — 1st ed — San Francisco: Jossey-Bass, 1974. xi, 214 p.; 24 cm. (The Jossey-Bass series in higher education) Includes index. 1. Education, Higher — Study and teaching. I. Mayhew, Lewis B. joint author. II. T.
LB2331.D69    378/.007/11    LC 73-21073    ISBN 0875892264

**Eble, Kenneth Eugene.**      4.10572
Professors as teachers [by] Kenneth E. Eble. — [1st ed.]. — San Francisco: Jossey-Bass, 1972. xiv, 202 p.; 24 cm. — (The Jossey-Bass series in higher education) 'A report of the Project to Improve College Teaching, sponsored from 1969 to 1971 by the American Association of University Professors and the Association of American Colleges.' 1. College teaching I. Project to Improve College Teaching. II. T.
LB2331.E33    378.1/2    LC 78-186579    ISBN 0875891187

**Wilson, Robert Charles, 1920-.**      4.10573
College professors and their impact on students / Robert C. Wilson, Jerry G. Gaff; [with] Evelyn R. Dienst, Lynn Wood, James L. Bavry. — New York: Wiley, [1975] xi, 220 p.: graphs; 24 cm. 'A Wiley-Interscience publication.' Includes index. 1. College teaching 2. Teacher-student relationships I. Gaff, Jerry G. joint author. II. T.
LB2331.W53    378.1/2    LC 74-26553    ISBN 0471949612

**Epstein, Leon D.**      4.10574
Governing the university; [the campus and the public interest, by] Leon D. Epstein. — [1st ed.]. — San Francisco: Jossey-Bass Publishers, 1974. xiv, 253 p.; 24 cm. — (The Jossey-Bass series in higher education) 1. University autonomy I. T.
LB2331.4.E67    378.1/01    LC 73-20967    ISBN 0875892159

**Bok, Derek Curtis.**      4.10575
Beyond the ivory tower: social responsibilities of the modern university / Derek Bok. — Cambridge, Mass.: Harvard University Press, 1982. 318 p.; 25 cm. 1. Education, Higher — United States — Aims and objectives. 2. Academic freedom — United States. I. T.
LB2331.72.B64 1982    378/.01/0973 19    LC 81-20278    ISBN 0674068998

**Bowen, Howard Rothmann, 1908-.**      4.10576
The state of the nation and the agenda for higher education / Howard R. Bowen. — 1st ed. — San Francisco: Jossey-Bass, 1982. xviii, 212 p.; 24 cm. (Jossey-Bass series in higher education.) Includes index. 1. Education, Higher — United States. 2. Education, Higher — Aims and objectives 3. United States — Social conditions — 1980- I. T. II. Series.
LB2331.72.B68 1982    378.73 19    LC 81-20746    ISBN 0875895158

## LB2332–2335 Teaching Personnel. Academic Freedom

**Beale, Howard K. (Howard Kennedy), 1899-1959.**      • 4.10577
A history of freedom of teaching in American schools / by Howard K. Beale. — New York: Octagon Books, 1966 [c1941] xviii, 343 p.: forms; 22 cm. 1. Teaching, Freedom of — United States. 2. Education — United States — History. 3. United States — Social conditions I. T.
LB2332.B3 1966    LC 66-17503

**Hook, Sidney, 1902- comp.**      • 4.10578
In defense of academic freedom. — New York: Pegasus, [1971] 266 p.; 21 cm. 1. Academic freedom — Addresses, essays, lectures. 2. Self-government (in education) — Addresses, essays, lectures. I. T.
LB2332.H58    378.1/21    LC 79-128666

**MacIver, Robert M. (Robert Morrison), 1882-1970.**      • 4.10579
Academic freedom in our time, by Robert M. MacIver. New York, Gordian Press, 1967 [c1955] xiv, 329 p. 24 cm. 'Prepared for the American Academic Freedom Project at Columbia University.' 1. Academic freedom I. T.
LB2332.M28 1967    378.1/21    LC 67-18441

**Farley, Jennie.**      4.10580
Academic women and employment discrimination: a critical annotated bibliography / Jennie Farley. — Ithaca, N.Y.: New York State School of Industrial and Labor Relations, Cornell University, c1982. 103 p.; 23 cm. — (Cornell industrial and labor relations bibliography series. no. 16) Includes indexes. 1. Women college teachers — United States — Abstracts. 2. Sex discrimination against women — United States — Abstracts. 3. Women college teachers — Employment — United States — Abstracts. I. T. II. Series.
LB2332.3.F37 1982    016.378/12/088042 19    LC 82-3570    ISBN 0875460925

**Simeone, Angela.**      4.10581
Academic women: working towards equality / Angela Simeone. — South Hadley, Mass.: Bergin & Garvey, 1987. xiv, 161 p.; 24 cm. Includes index. 1. Women college teachers — United States. 2. College teachers' socio-economic status — United States. 3. Sex discrimination in education — United States. I. T.
LB2332.3.S56 1987    378/.12/088042 19    LC 86-26436    ISBN 0897891112

**Garbarino, Joseph William, 1919-.**      4.10582
Faculty bargaining: change and conflict: a report prepared for the Carnegie Commission on Higher Education and the Ford Foundation / by Joseph W. Garbarino, in association with Bill Aussieker. — New York: McGraw-Hill, [1975] ix, 278 p.; 23 cm. Includes index. 1. Collective bargaining — College teachers I. Aussieker, Bill, joint author. II. Carnegie Commission on Higher Education. III. Ford Foundation. IV. T.
LB2334.G37    331.89/041/37812    LC 75-8661    ISBN 0070101116

## LB2336–2340 Scholarships. Grants

**Foundation grants to individuals / compiled by the Foundation Center.**      4.10583
[1st ed.]-      . — New York: Foundation Center, 1977-. v.; 28 cm. 1. Endowments — United States — Directories. 2. Scholarships — United States — Directories. 3. Student loan funds — United States — Directories. I. Foundation Center.
LB2336.F598    LC sn 87-27610

**Directory of financial aids for women.**      4.10584
1st ed. (1978)-      . — Santa Barbara, Calif.: Reference Service Press, 1978-. v.; 29 cm. 1. Women — Scholarships, fellowships, etc. — United States — Directories. 2. Student aid — United States — Directories. 3. Interns — United States — Directories. I. Schlachter, Gail A.
LB2338.D564    378.3/025/73 19    LC 85-648776

**Directory of research grants.**      4.10585
[Phoenix, Ariz., etc.] Oryx Press. v. 29 cm. Annual. Began with 1975. 1. Scholarships — United States — Directories. 2. Research grants — United States — Directories.
LB2338.D57    001.4/4/02573    LC 76-47074

**The Grants register.**      4.10586
1987-89-      . — New York: St. Martin's Press, 1986-. v.; 24 cm. Biennial. Biennial. 1. Scholarships — Directories.
LB2338.G764    378.34    ISBN 0312326939 1987-89

## LB2341–2342 Administration. Finance

**Astin, Alexander W.**      **4.10587**
Maximizing leadership effectiveness / Alexander W. Astin, Rita A. Scherrei. — 1st ed. — San Francisco: Jossey-Bass, 1980. xvi, 238 p.; 24 cm. — (The Jossey-Bass series in higher education) Includes index. 1. Universities and colleges — United States — Administration 2. Leadership 3. College presidents — United States. I. Scherrei, Rita A. joint author. II. T.
LB2341.A756    378.73    *LC* 79-9665    *ISBN* 0875894542

**Bénézet, Louis Tomlinson, 1915-.**      **4.10588**
Style and substance: leadership and the college presidency / Louis T. Benezet, Joseph Katz, Frances W. Magnusson. — Washington, D.C.: American Council on Education, c1981. vii, 121 p.; 23 cm. 1. College presidents — United States. 2. Leadership I. Katz, Joseph, 1920- II. Magnusson, Frances W. III. American Council on Education. IV. T.
LB2341.B439 1981    378/.111 19    *LC* 81-17679    *ISBN* 0826814565

**Cohen, Michael D.**      **4.10589**
Leadership and ambiguity: the American college president / Michael D. Cohen and James G. March. — 2nd ed. — Boston, Mass.: Harvard Business School Press, c1986. xxi, 298 p.: ill.; 25 cm. Includes index. 1. College presidents — United States. 2. Universities and colleges — United States — Administration I. March, James G. II. Carnegie Commission on Higher Education. III. T.
LB2341.C56 1986    378/.111 19    *LC* 85-27268    *ISBN* 0875841740

**Conrad, Clifton.**      **4.10590**
The undergraduate curriculum: a guide to innovation and reform / Clifton F. Conrad. — Boulder, Colo.: Westview Press, 1979 (c1978). xv, 213 p.; 24 cm. — (Westview special studies in higher education) 1. Universities and colleges — Administration 2. Universities and colleges — Curricula 3. Educational innovations I. T.
LB2341.C758    378.1/99    *LC* 78-19637    *ISBN* 0891581960

**Cowley, W. H. (William Harold), 1899-.**      **4.10591**
Presidents, professors, and trustees: [the evolution of American academic government] / by W. H. Cowley; edited by Donald T. Williams, Jr.. — 1st ed. — San Francisco, CA: Jossey-Bass, 1980. xviii, 260 p.; 24 cm. — (The Jossey-Bass series in higher education) Includes index. 1. Universities and colleges — United States — Administration — History. 2. College administrators — United States — History. I. Williams, Donald T. II. T.
LB2341.C83    378.73    *LC* 79-92461    *ISBN* 0875894488

**Dressel, Paul Leroy, 1910-.**      **4.10592**
Administrative leadership / Paul L. Dressel. — 1st ed. — San Francisco: Jossey-Bass, 1981. xviii, 243 p.; 24 cm. Includes index. 1. Universities and colleges — United States — Administration — Decision making. I. T.
LB2341.D688    378.73 19    *LC* 81-81962    *ISBN* 087589500X

**Martorana, S. V.**      **4.10593**
Managing academic change: [interactive forces and leadership in higher education] / S. V. Martorana, Eileen Kuhns; with a foreword by Fred F. Harcleroad. — 1st ed. — San Francisco: Jossey-Bass, 1975. xviii, 218 p,; 24 cm. (The Jossey-Bass series in higher education) Includes index. 1. Universities and colleges — United States — Administration — Addresses, essays, lectures. I. Kuhns, Eileen Pease, 1923- joint author. II. T.
LB2341.M32    378.73    *LC* 74-27909    *ISBN* 0875892531

**Mayhew, Lewis B.**      **4.10594**
Surviving the eighties / Lewis B. Mayhew. — 1st ed. — San Francisco: Jossey-Bass Publishers, 1979. xiv, 350 p.; 24 cm. (The Jossey-Bass series in higher education) Includes index. 1. Universities and colleges — United States — Planning. 2. Universities and colleges — United States — Finance. 3. College attendance — United States. I. T.
LB2341.M34    378.1/07/0973    *LC* 79-88773    *ISBN* 0875894283

**Millett, John David, 1912-.**      **4.10595**
New structures of campus power / John D. Millett. — 1st ed. — San Francisco: Jossey-Bass, c1978. xxii, 294 p.; 24 cm. — (The Jossey-Bass series in higher education) Includes index. 1. Universities and colleges — United States — Administration — Case studies. I. T.
LB2341.M4628    378.1/01/0973    *LC* 77-82911    *ISBN* 0875893503

**Policy making and effective leadership / J. Victor Baldridge ... [et al.].**      **4.10596**
1st ed. — San Francisco: Jossey-Bass Publishers, 1978. xxv, 290 p.; 24 cm. — (Jossey-Bass series in higher education) 'A national study of academic management.' Includes index. 1. Universities and colleges — United States — Administration 2. Leadership I. Baldridge, J. Victor.
LB2341.P62    378.73    *LC* 77-82909    *ISBN* 0875893511

**Bowen, Howard Rothmann, 1908-.**      **4.10597**
The costs of higher education: how much do colleges and universities spend per student and how much should they spend? / Howard R. Bowen. — 1st ed. — San Francisco: Jossey-Bass Publishers, 1980. xxiii, 287 p.; 24 cm. — (The

Carnegie Council series) Includes index. 1. College costs — United States. 2. Universities and colleges — United States — Finance. I. T.
LB2342.B63    379.1/18/0973 19    *LC* 80-8321    *ISBN* 0875894852

**Carnegie Commission on Higher Education.**      **4.10598**
Higher education: who pays? Who benefits? Who should pay?: A report and recommendations. — New York: McGraw-Hill, 1973. ix, 190 p.: ill.; 23 cm. 1. Universities and colleges — Finance I. T.
LB2342.C26    379/.1214    *LC* 73-8856    *ISBN* 0070100799

**The College cost book / College Scholarship Service.**      **4.10599**
New York: College Entrance Examination Board. v. 28 cm. Imprint varies. 1. College costs — United States. 2. Scholarships — United States I. College Entrance Examination Board. College Scholarship Service. II. Title: Student expenses at postsecondary institutions.
LB2342.C633a    378.3/0973    *LC* 80-648095

**Financial responsibilities of governing boards of colleges and universities.**      **4.10600**
2nd ed. — Washington, D.C.: Association of Governing Boards of Universities and Colleges: National Association of College and University Business Officers, c1985. p. cm. 1. Universities and colleges — United States — Finance. I. Association of Governing Boards of Universities and Colleges. II. National Association of College and University Business Officers.
LB2342.F49 1985    379.1/214/0973 19    *LC* 85-3926    *ISBN* 0915164175

**Finn, Chester E., 1944-.**      **4.10601**
Scholars, dollars, and bureaucrats / Chester E. Finn, Jr. — Washington: Brookings Institution, c1978. xiii, 238 p.; 24 cm. — (Studies in higher education policy.) 1. Federal aid to higher education — United States. 2. Higher education and state — United States. I. T. II. Series.
LB2342.F55    379/.1214/0973    *LC* 78-13363    *ISBN* 081572828X

**Gomberg, Irene L.**      **4.10602**
Trends in financial indicators of colleges and universities / by Irene L. Gomberg and Frank J. Atelsek. — Washington, D.C.: American Council on Education, 1981. iv, 40 p.: ill.; 28 cm. I. T.
LB2342.G6x

**Jones, Dennis P.**      **4.10603**
Higher–education budgeting at the state level: concepts and principles / Dennis P. Jones. — Boulder, Colo.: National Center for Higher Education Management Systems, 1984. xi, 113 p.: ill.; 23 cm. 1. Universities and colleges — United States — Finance 2. Universities and colleges — United States — Administration 3. Higher education and state 4. Education, Higher — Finance. I. National Center for Higher Education Management Systems. II. T.
LB2342.J654 1984

**Mecklenburger, James. comp.**      **4.10604**
Education vouchers: from theory to Alum Rock. Edited by James A. Mecklenburger [and] Richard W. Hostrop. — [Homewood, Ill.]: ETC Publication, 1972. 412 p.: illus.; 23 cm. 1. Alum Rock Union Elementary School District. 2. Educational vouchers I. Hostrop, Richard W. joint comp. II. T.
LB2342.M38    379/.13    *LC* 72-8872    *ISBN* 0882800027

**Gordon, Virginia N.**      **4.10605**
The undecided college student: an academic and career advising challenge / by Virginia N. Gordon. — Springfield, Ill., U.S.A.: C.C. Thomas, c1984. xiv, 125 p.; 24 cm. 1. Personnel service in higher education — United States. 2. Vocational guidance — United States. 3. College student orientation — United States. I. T.
LB2343.G64 1984    378/.19425/0973 19    *LC* 83-24364    *ISBN* 0398049890

**Voeks, Virginia.**      **4.10606**
On becoming an educated person: an orientation to college and life / Virginia Voeks. — 4th ed. — Philadelphia: Saunders, 1979. xv, 249 p.: ill.; 25 cm. — (Saunders survival series.) 1. College student orientation 2. Study, Method of 3. Student adjustment 4. Self-culture I. T. II. Series.
LB2343.3.V63 1979    378.1/8    *LC* 79-3931    *ISBN* 0721690696

## LB2350–2360 Choice of College. Entrance Requirements

**Aiken, Wilford Merton, 1882-.**      **4.10607**
The story of the eight–year study, with conclusions and recommendations. New York, Harper, c1942. 157 p. (Adventure in American education, v. 1) On half-title: Progressive Education Association publications. Commission on the Relation of School and College. 1. Articulation (Education) 2. Education,

Higher — United States — Aims and objectives. I. American Education Fellowship. II. T.
LB2350.A5    *LC* 42-36126

**The College handbook.**      **4.10608**
New York, College Entrance Examination Board. v. 25 cm. 1. Universities and colleges — United States — Entrance requirements I. College Entrance Examination Board.
LB2351.A1 C6

**Selective admissions in higher education: [comment and**    **4.10609**
**recommendations and two reports: a report of the Carnegie**
**Council on Policy Studies in Higher Education].**
1st ed. — San Francisco: Jossey-Bass Publishers, 1977. xiii, 256 p.: ill.; 24 cm. — (The Carnegie Council series) 1. Universities and colleges — United States — Admission. I. Manning, Winton Howard, 1930- Pursuit of fairness in admissions to higher education. 1977. II. Willingham, Warren W. Status of selective admissions. 1977. III. Carnegie Council on Policy Studies in Higher Education. Public policy and academic policy. 1977.
LB2351.S455    378.1/05/60973    *LC* 77-88501    *ISBN* 0875893619

**Wechsler, Harold S., 1946-.**      **4.10610**
The qualified student: a history of selective college admission in America / Harold S. Wechsler. New York: Wiley, c1977. xvii, 341 p.; 24 cm. 'A Wiley-Interscience publication.' Includes index. 1. Universities and colleges — United States — Admission. I. T.
LB2351.W36    378.1/05/60973    *LC* 76-47692    *ISBN* 0471924415

**Owen, David, 1955-.**      **4.10611**
None of the above: behind the myth of scholastic aptitude / David Owen. — Boston: Houghton Mifflin, 1985. xxi, 327 p.: ill.; 24 cm. Includes index. 1. Scholastic aptitude test 2. Prediction of scholastic success — Evaluation. I. T.
LB2353.57.O94 1985    378/.1664 19    *LC* 84-25262    *ISBN* 0395355400

## LB2361–2365 Curriculum

**Levine, Arthur.**      **4.10612**
Handbook on undergraduate curriculum / Arthur Levine. — 1st ed. — San Francisco: Jossey-Bass, c1978. xxxv, 662 p.; 24 cm. — (The Carnegie Council series) 'Prepared for the Carnegie Council on Policy Studies in Higher Education.' 1. Universities and colleges — Curricula I. Carnegie Council on Policy Studies in Higher Education. II. T.
LB2361.L45    378.1/99    *LC* 78-50893    *ISBN* 0875893767

**Carnegie Foundation for the Advancement of Teaching.**    **4.10613**
Missions of the college curriculum: a contemporary review with suggestions: a commentary of the Carnegie Foundation for the Advancement of Teaching. — 1st ed. — San Francisco: Jossey-Bass, 1977. xvii, 322 p.: ill.; 24 cm. — (The Carnegie Council series) Includes index. 1. Universities and colleges — United States — Curricula I. T.
LB2361.5.C37 1977    378.1/99/0973    *LC* 77-84320    *ISBN* 0875893600

**In opposition to core curriculum: alternative models for**    **4.10614**
**undergraduate education / edited by James W. Hall with**
**Barbara L. Kevles.**
Westport, Conn.: Greenwood, 1982. xxv, 235 p.: ill.; 22 cm. — (Contributions to the study of education. 0196-707X; no. 4) Includes index. 1. Universities and colleges — United States — Curricula — Planning. I. Hall, James W. II. Kevles, Barbara L. III. Series.
LB2361.5.I5 1982    378/.199/0973 19    *LC* 81-8125    *ISBN* 0313229023

**Mayhew, Lewis B.**      **4.10615**
Changing the curriculum [by] Lewis B. Mayhew [and] Patrick J. Ford. Foreword by Winfred I. Godwin. — [1st ed.]. — San Francisco: Jossey-Bass, 1971. xvi, 188 p.; 24 cm. — (The Jossey-Bass series in higher education) 1. Education, Higher — U.S. — Curricula. I. Ford, Patrick Joseph, 1941- joint author. II. T.
LB2361.5.M38    378.1/99/0973    *LC* 79-159265    *ISBN* 0875891047

**Rudolph, Frederick.**      • **4.10616**
Curriculum: a history of the American undergraduate course of study since 1636 / Frederick Rudolph; [prepared for the Carnegie Council on Policy Studies in Higher Education]. — 1st ed. — San Francisco: Jossey-Bass Publishers, 1977. xiii, 362 p.; 28 cm. — (The Carnegie Council series) Includes indexes. 1. Universities and colleges — United States — Curricula — History. I. Carnegie Council on Policy Studies in Higher Education. II. T.
LB2361.5.R8    378.1/99/0973    *LC* 77-84319    *ISBN* 0875893589

**Richardson, Richard C.**      **4.10617**
Literacy in the open–access college / Richard C. Richardson, Jr., Elizabeth C. Fisk, Morris A. Okun. — 1st ed. — San Francisco: Jossey-Bass, 1983. xviii, 187 p.; 24 cm. — (Jossey-Bass higher education series.) Includes index. 1. Language arts (Higher) — United States — Case studies. 2. Community colleges — United States — Open admission — Case studies. 3. Community colleges — United States — Curricula — Case studies. I. Fisk, Elizabeth C. II. Okun, Morris A. III. T. IV. Series.
LB2365.L38 R52 1983    378/.052 19    *LC* 83-11999    *ISBN* 0875895697

**Campbell, William Giles, 1902-.**      **4.10618**
Form and style: theses, reports, term papers / William Giles Campbell, Stephen Vaughan Ballou, Carole Slade. — 7th ed. — Boston: Houghton Mifflin, c1986. xii, 226 p.: ill.; 29 cm. Includes indexes. 1. Report writing 2. Dissertations, Academic 3. Abstracting I. Ballou, Stephen V. II. Slade, Carole. III. T.
LB2369.C3 1986    808/.02 19    *LC* 85-80771    *ISBN* 039535725X

**Turabian, Kate L.**      **4.10619**
A manual for writers of term papers, theses, and dissertations / Kate L. Turabian. — 5th ed. / revised and expanded by Bonnie Birtwistle Honigsblum. — Chicago: University of Chicago Press, 1987. ix, 300 p.; 23 cm. — (Chicago guides to writing, editing, and publishing.) Includes index. 1. Dissertations, Academic 2. Report writing I. Honigsblum, Bonnie Birtwistle. II. T. III. Series.
LB2369.T8 1987    808/.02 19    *LC* 86-19128    *ISBN* 0226816249

**Keeping graduate programs responsive to national needs /**    **4.10620**
**Michael J. Pelczar, Jr., Lewis C. Solmon, editors.**
San Francisco: Jossey-Bass, c1984. 126 p.; 23 cm. (New directions for higher education, 0271-0560; no. 46 (June 1984) (Paperback sourcebooks in the Jossey-Bass higher education series) 1. Universities and colleges — United States — Graduate work — Addresses, essays, lectures. 2. Industry and education — United States — Addresses, essays, lectures. I. Pelczar, Michael J. (Michael Joseph), 1916- II. Solmon, Lewis C.
LB2371.K44 1984    378/.1553/0973 19    *LC* 83-82811    *ISBN* 087589986X

**The Learning traveler. Vol.2, Vacation study abroad.**    **4.10621**
31st- ed.; 1980-. New York, N.Y., Institute of International Education. v. 23 cm. Annual. 1. Foreign study — Directories. I. Institute of International Education (New York, N.Y.)
LB2375.S8    370.19/6/025    *LC* 80-647933

**The Learning traveler. Vol. 1, Academic year abroad.**    **4.10622**
15th ed. (1986-87)-     . — New York, NY: Institute of International Education, c1986-. v.; 22 cm. Annual. 1. Foreign study — Periodicals. 2. Foreign study — Directories. I. Institute of International Education (New York, N.Y.)
LB2376.U46    370.19/6/05 19    *LC* 86-651558

## LB2381–2391 Academic Degrees

**Dore, Ronald Philip.**      **4.10623**
The diploma disease: education, qualification, and development / Ronald Dore. Berkeley: University of California Press, 1976. xiii, 214 p.; 23 cm. Includes index. 1. Degrees, Academic I. T.
LB2381.D67 1976    378/.24    *LC* 75-22653    *ISBN* 0520031075

**Sullivan, Eugene J.**      **4.10624**
Guide to external degree programs in the United States / edited by Eugene Sullivan. — 2nd ed. — New York: American Council on Education: Macmillan, c1983. xii, 124 p.; 24 cm. — (American Council on Education/Macmillan series in higher education.) Includes indexes. 1. Degrees, Academic — United States. 2. University extension — United States. 3. Correspondence schools and courses — United States. 4. College credits — United States. I. American Council on Education. II. T. III. Series.
LB2381.G84 1983    378/.24/0973 19    *LC* 83-7049    *ISBN* 0029323509

**Houle, Cyril Orvin, 1913-.**      **4.10625**
The external degree [by] Cyril O. Houle. Foreword by Samuel B. Gould. Epilogue by John Summerskill. — [1st ed.]. — San Francisco: Jossey-Bass Publishers, 1973. xxii, 214 p.; 24 cm. — (The Jossey-Bass series in higher education) 1. Degrees, Academic — United States. 2. Adult education — United States. I. T.
LB2381.H68    378.1/7/9    *LC* 73-3775    *ISBN* 0875891756

**Keeton, Morris T.**      **4.10626**
Experiential learning / Morris T. Keeton and associates; foreword by Virginia B. Smith. — 1st ed. — San Francisco: Jossey-Bass Publishers, 1976. xxviii, 265 p.; 24 cm. (The Jossey-Bass series in higher education) Consists of papers commissioned by CAEL (Cooperative Assessment of Experiential Learning) Includes index. 1. Degrees, Academic — United States. 2. College-level

examinations 3. Experiential learning I. Cooperative Assessment of Experiential Learning (Project) II. T.
LB2381.K43     378.1/554     LC 75-44884     ISBN 0875892779

**Who offers part–time degree programs? / Karen C. Hegener,**     **4.10627**
editor, Andrew T. Rowan, data editor, Amy J. Goldstein, assistant editor.
2nd ed. — Princeton, N.J.: Peterson's Guides, c1985. v, 417 p.; 28 cm. Cover title: Peterson's Who offers part-time degree programs? Includes index. 1. Degrees, Academic — United States. 2. Students, Part-time — United States. 3. Universities and colleges — United States — Directories. 4. Evening and continuation schools — United States — Directories. I. Hegener, Karen C. II. Rowan, Andrew T., 1962- III. Goldstein, Amy J. IV. Title: Peterson's Who offers part-time degree programs?
LB2381.W53 1984     378/.24/02573 19     LC 84-22744     ISBN 0878662855

**Sternberg, David Joel.**     **4.10628**
How to complete and survive a doctoral dissertation / by David Sternberg. — 1st ed. — New York: St. Martin's Press, c1981. 231 p.; 21 cm. 1. Doctor of philosophy degree 2. Report writing 3. Dissertations, Academic I. T.
LB2386.S74     808/.02 19     LC 81-161088     ISBN 0312396066

**Smith, Hugh, 18th cent.**     **4.10629**
Academic dress and insignia of the world; gowns, hats, chains of office, hoods, rings, medals and other degree insignia of universities & other institutions of learning, by Hugh Smith assisted by Kevin Sheard. — Cape Town: A. A. Balkema, 1970. 3 v. (xiii, 1843 p.): illus.; 26 cm. 1. Academic costume I. Sheard, Kevin. II. T.
LB2389.S6     LC 70-486324

## LB2523–2525 School Law
(see also: KF4101-4258)

**School law in changing times / edited by M.A. McGhehey.**     **4.10630**
Topeka, Kan.: National Organization on Legal Problems of Education, c1982. vi, 256 p.; 24 cm. Papers presented at the National Organization on Legal Problems of Education 1981 Annual Convention, 'The Law School of School Law'. 1. School law and legislation — United States — Congresses. I. McGhehey, M. A. II. National Organization on Legal Problems of Education.
LB 2523 S366 1982

**Peltason, J. W. (Jack Walter), 1923-.**     • **4.10631**
Fifty–eight lonely men: Southern Federal judges and school desegregation / introd. by Paul H. Douglas. — New York: Harcourt, Brace & World, [1961] 270 p. 1. Segregation in education — Law and legislation — United States. 2. Judges — Southern States. I. T.
LB2525.P45     LC 61-12350

## LB2801–3095 School Administration. Organization

**Association for Supervision and Curriculum Development.**     **4.10632**
Perceiving, behaving, becoming: a new focus for education / prepared by the ASCD 1962 Yearbook Committee; Arthur W. Combs, Chairman. — Washington, D. C. The Association, 1962. viii, 256 p.: ill.; 23 cm. — (Its Yearbook; 1962) 1. Educational psychology 2. Personality I. Combs, Arthur Wright. II. T. III. Series.
LB2804.A8 1962     LC 44-6213

**Alfonso, Robert J., 1928-.**     **4.10633**
Instructional supervision: a behavior system / Robert J. Alfonso, Gerald R. Firth, Richard F. Neville. — 2d ed. — Boston: Allyn and Bacon, c1981. xi, 488 p.: ill.; 25 cm. 1. School supervision — United States. I. Firth, Gerald R. joint author. II. Neville, Richard F., 1931- joint author. III. T.
LB2805.A448 1981     371.2/00973     LC 80-14749     ISBN 0205071422

**Campbell, Roald Fay, 1905-.**     **4.10634**
Introduction to educational administration. — 6th ed. / Roald F. Campbell, John E. Corbally, Raphael O. Nystrand. — Boston: Allyn and Bacon, c1983. x, 269 p.: ill.; 25 cm. 1. School management and organization I. Corbally, John E. (John Edward), 1924- II. Nystrand, Raphael O. III. T.
LB2805.C25 1983     371.2 19     LC 82-24475     ISBN 0205079830

**Coons, John E.**     **4.10635**
Education by choice: the case for family control / by John E. Coons and Stephen D. Sugarman. — Berkeley: University of California Press, 1982. xiv,

249 p.; 25 cm. 1. School management and organization — United States. 2. Home and school — United States. I. Sugarman, Stephen D., joint author. II. T.
LB2805.C657     379/.15     LC 77-20318     ISBN 0520036131

**Gross, Neal Crasilneck, 1920-.**     **4.10636**
Implementing organizational innovations: a sociological analysis of planned educational change / [by] Neal Gross, Joseph B. Giacquinta [and] Marilyn Bernstein. — New York: Basic Books, [1971] vi, 309 p.: ill.; 22 cm. 'Research ... was carried out under the auspices of the Center for Research and Development on Educational Differences and was performed pursuant to contract OE 5-10-239 with the Office of Education, U.S. Department of Health, Education, and Welfare.' 1. School management and organization 2. Educational sociology I. Giacquinta, Joseph B., 1937- joint author. II. Bernstein, Marilyn. joint author. III. T.
LB2805.G76     371.2/07     LC 76-47016     ISBN 0465032133

**Monahan, William G.**     **4.10637**
Theoretical dimensions of educational administration / William G. Monahan. — New York: Macmillan, [1975] xii, 481 p.; 24 cm. 1. School management and organization I. T.
LB2805.M635     371.2     LC 74-11749     ISBN 0023819405

**Morphet, Edgar Leroy, 1895-.**     **4.10638**
[Educational administration] Educational organization and administration: concepts, practices, and issues / Edgar L. Morphet, Roe L. Johns, Theodore L. Reller. — 4th ed. — Englewood Cliffs, N.J.: Prentice-Hall, c1982. x, 422 p.: ill.; 24 cm. First published in 1959 as: Educational administration / Edgar L. Morphet, Roe L. Johns, Theodore L. Reller. 1. School management and organization I. Johns, Roe Lyell, 1900- II. Reller, Theodore Lee. III. T.
LB2805.M68 1982     371.2 19     LC 81-10641     ISBN 0132367297

*[handwritten: LB 2805 M87 1947]*

**Sergiovanni, Thomas J.**     **4.10639**
Supervision: human perspectives / Thomas J. Sergiovanni, Robert J. Starratt. — 3rd ed. — New York: McGraw-Hill, c1983. 366 p.: ill.; 24 cm. 1. School supervision 2. School management and organization I. Starratt, Robert J. II. T.
LB2805.S52 1983     371.2/013 19     LC 82-10084     ISBN 0070563128

**Tyack, David B.**     **4.10640**
Managers of virtue: public school leadership in America, 1820–1980 / David Tyack & Elisabeth Hansot. — New York: Basic Books, c1982. vii, 312 p.; 24 cm. 1. School management and organization — United States — History. 2. Educational sociology — United States — History. 3. Leadership — History. I. Hansot, Elisabeth. II. T.
LB2805.T9 1982     371.2/00973 19     LC 81-22923     ISBN 0465043763

**Useem, Elizabeth L., 1943- comp.**     **4.10641**
The education establishment. Edited by Elizabeth L. and Michael Useem. — Englewood Cliffs, N.J.: Prentice-Hall, [1974] viii, 180 p.; 22 cm. — (The American establishments series) (A Spectrum book) 1. School management and organization — United States. I. Useem, Michael. joint comp. II. T.
LB2805.U83 1974     379/.15/0973     LC 74-1250     ISBN 0132365626

**Zeigler, L. Harmon (Luther Harmon), 1936-.**     **4.10642**
Governing American schools: political interaction in local school districts / L. Harmon Zeigler, M. Kent Jennings, with the assistance of G. Wayne Peak. — North Scituate, Mass.: Duxbury Press, [1974] xvi, 269 p.; 25 cm. 1. School management and organization — United States. 2. School districts — United States. I. Jennings, M. Kent. joint author. II. Peak, G. Wayne, joint author. III. T.
LB2805.Z44     379/.153/0973     LC 74-75716     ISBN 0878720677

**March, James G.**     **4.10643**
Ambiguity and choice in organizations / by James G. March and Johan P. Olsen, with contributions by Søren Christensen ... [et al.]. — 2d ed. — Bergen: Universitetsforlaget, c1979. 408 p.; 22 cm. Includes index. 1. School management and organization — Decision making 2. Associations, institutions, etc. 3. Decision-making 4. Uncertainty I. Olsen, Johan P. joint author. II. T.
LB2806.M353 1979     371.2 19     LC 80-504092     ISBN 8200019608

**Warren, Donald R., 1933-.**     **4.10644**
To enforce education: a history of the founding years of the United States Office of Education, by Donald R. Warren. — Detroit: Wayne State University Press, 1974. 239 p.: ports.; 24 cm. 1. United States. Office of Education — History. I. T.
LB2807.W33 1974     379.73     LC 73-8209

**Firestone, William A.**     **4.10645**
Great expectations for small schools: the limitations of Federal projects / William A. Firestone. — New York, N.Y.: Praeger, 1980. 212 p.; 24 cm. — (Praeger studies in ethnographic perspectives on American education.) Includes index. 1. School districts — South Dakota — Case studies. 2. Education, Rural — South Dakota — Case studies. 3. School size — Case

studies. 4. Federal aid to education — South Dakota — Case studies. I. T. II. Series.
LB2817.F57   370.19/346/09783 19   LC 80-23199   ISBN 0030573971

**Fantini, Mario D.**    4.10646
Decentralization: achieving reform [by] Mario Fantini and Marilyn Gittell. — New York: Praeger, [1973] v, 170 p.; 22 cm. 1. Schools — Decentralization 2. Community and school — United States I. Gittell, Marilyn. joint author. II. T.
LB2819.F34   379/.1535   LC 70-83335

# LB2822 High School and Elementary School Administration

**Glickman, Carl D.**    4.10647
Supervision of instruction: a developmental approach / Carl D. Glickman. — Boston: Allyn and Bacon, c1985. xx, 424 p.: ill.; 25 cm. 1. School supervision I. T.
LB2822.G57 1985   371.2 19   LC 84-29986   ISBN 0205034680

**Hampton, Bill R., 1934-.**    4.10648
Solving problems in secondary school administration: a human organization approach / Bill R. Hampton, Robert H. Lauer. — Boston: Allyn and Bacon, c1981. xii, 312 p.: ill.; 24 cm. 1. High schools — Administration I. Lauer, Robert H., 1933- joint author. II. T.
LB2822.H29   373.12   LC 80-18033   ISBN 0205069517

**Sergiovanni, Thomas J.**    4.10649
Handbook for effective department leadership: concepts and practices in today's secondary schools / Thomas J. Sergiovanni. — 2nd ed. — Boston: Allyn and Bacon, c1984. x, 506 p.: ill.; 25 cm. 1. Departmental chairmen (High schools) — Handbooks, manuals, etc. I. T.
LB2822.S44 1984   373.12/013 19   LC 83-19718   ISBN 0205081088

**Krajewski, Robert J.**    4.10650
The elementary school principalship: leadership for the 80s / Robert J. Krajewski, John S. Martin, John C. Walden. — New York: Holt, Rinehart and Winston, c1983. x, 310 p.; 25 cm. 1. Elementary school administration — United States. 2. Elementary school principals — United States. I. Martin, John S. (John Stokes), 1929- II. Walden, John C. III. T.
LB2822.5.K7 1983   372.12/012/0973 19   LC 82-18716   ISBN 0030567467

# LB2824–2830 School Finance

**Investment in education; the equity–efficiency quandary. Edited**    4.10651
**by Theodore W. Schultz.**
Chicago: University of Chicago Press, [1972] 292 p.: illus.; 24 cm. Papers prepared for the workshop held at the University of Chicago, June 7-10, 1971; sponsored by the Committee on Basic Research in Education. 'Published also as part 2 of volume 80, number 3, of the Journal of political economy, May/June 1972.' 1. Education — Finance — Addresses, essays, lectures. 2. Education — Economic aspects — Addresses, essays, lectures. I. Schultz, Theodore William, 1902- ed. II. Committee on Basic Research in Education.
LB2824.I55   338.4/7/378   LC 72-84408   ISBN 0226740803

**Reischauer, Robert D. (Robert Danton), 1941-.**    4.10652
Reforming school finance [by] Robert D. Reischauer and Robert W. Hartman, with the assistance of Daniel J. Sullivan. Washington, Brookings Institution [1973] xiii, 185 p. 23 cm. (Studies in social economics.) 1. Education — Finance I. Hartman, Robert W. joint author. II. T. III. Series.
LB2824.R37   379   LC 73-1080   ISBN 081577396X ISBN 0815773951

**Benson, Charles Scott.**    4.10653
The economics of public education / Charles S. Benson. — 3d ed. — Boston: Houghton Mifflin, c1978. xv, 413 p.: ill.; 25 cm. 1. Education — Finance I. T.
LB2825.B427 1978   379/.12/0973   LC 77-77670   ISBN 0395186196

**Burrup, Percy E., 1910-.**    4.10654
Financing education in a climate of change / Percy E. Burrup, Vern Brimley, Jr. — 3rd ed. — Boston: Allyn and Bacon, c1982. vii, 424 p.; 24 cm. 1. Education — United States — Finance. I. Brimley, Vern. II. T.
LB2825.B86 1982   379.1/21/0973 19   LC 81-12852   ISBN 020507748X

**Carroll, Stephen J., 1940-.**    4.10655
The search for equity in school finance / Stephen J. Carroll and Rolla Edward Park. — Cambridge, MA: Ballinger Pub. Co., 1983. xiv, 185 p. — (Rand educational policy study.) 1. Education — United States — Finance. I. Park, Rolla Edward. II. T. III. Series.
LB2825.C316 1982   379.1/22/0973 19   LC 82-11510   ISBN 0884108406

**The Changing politics of school finance / edited by Nelda H.**    4.10656
**Cambron–McCabe and Allan Odden.**
Cambridge, Mass.: Ballinger Pub. Co., c1982. xvi, 289 p.; 24 cm. — (Third annual yearbook of the American Education Finance Association) 1. Education — United States — Finance — Addresses, essays, lectures. I. Cambron-McCabe, Nelda H. II. Odden, Allan.
LB2825.C43 1983   379.1/21/0973 19   LC 82-13849   ISBN 0884108961

**Gurwitz, Aaron S.**    4.10657
The economics of public school finance / Aaron Samuel Gurwitz. — Cambridge, Mass.: Ballinger Pub. Co., 1982. xx, 205 p.: ill.; 24 cm. — (Rand educational policy study.) Includes index. 1. Education — United States — Finance. 2. Public schools — United States — Finance. I. T. II. Series.
LB2825.G86 1982   379.1/21/0973 19   LC 81-20552   ISBN 0884108597

**Johns, Roe Lyell, 1900-.**    4.10658
The economics and financing of education / Roe L. Johns, Edgar L. Morphet, Kern Alexander. — 4th ed. — Englewood Cliffs, N.J.: Prentice-Hall, c1983. x, 371 p.: ill.; 24 cm. 1. Education — United States — Finance. I. Morphet, Edgar Leroy, 1895- II. Alexander, Kern. III. T.
LB2825.J57 1983   379.1/21/0973 19   LC 82-9802   ISBN 0132251280

**LaNoue, George R. comp.**    4.10659
Educational vouchers; concepts and controversies, edited by George R. La Noue. — New York: Teachers College Press, [1972] viii, 176 p.; 23 cm. 1. Educational vouchers — United States — Addresses, essays, lectures. I. T.
LB2825.L16   379/.13   LC 78-187726

**School finance policies and practices: the 1980s, a decade of**    4.10660
**conflict / edited by James W. Guthrie.**
Cambridge, MA: Ballinger Pub. Co., c1980. xxvii, 277 p.: ill.; 24 cm. — (First annual yearbook of the American Education Finance Association) 1. Education — United States — Finance — Addresses, essays, lectures. 2. United States — Social policy — Addresses, essays, lectures. I. Guthrie, James W.
LB2825.S337   379.1/1/0973 19   LC 80-19707   ISBN 0884101959

**Thomas, Norman C.**    4.10661
Education in national politics / Norman C. Thomas. — New York: D. McKay Co., [1975] vii, 246 p.; 23 cm. (Educational policy, planning, and theory) 1. Federal aid to education — United States 2. United States — Politics and government I. T.
LB2825.T52   379/.121/0973   LC 74-83092   ISBN 0679302670

**Twentieth Century Fund. Task Force on Federal Elementary**    4.10662
**and Secondary Education Policy.**
Making the grade: report / of the Twentieth Century Fund Task Force on Federal Elementary and Secondary Education Policy; background paper by Paul E. Peterson. — New York: The Fund, 1983. x, 174 p.: ill.; 23 cm. 1. Federal aid to education — United States 2. Educational equalization — United States. I. Peterson, Paul E. II. T.
LB2825.T93 1983   379.1/212/0973 19   LC 83-184620   ISBN 0870781510

**Zeigler, L. Harmon (Luther Harmon), 1936-.**    • 4.10663
The politics of education in the States [by] Harmon Zeigler and Karl F. Johnson. Indianapolis, Bobbs-Merrill [1972] xviii, 246 p. 21 cm. (The Bobbs-Merrill policy analysis series) 1. Education — United States — Finance. I. Johnson, Karl F., joint author. II. T.
LB2825.Z45   379/.73   LC 70-175225

**Perspectives in state school support programs / edited by K.**    4.10664
**Forbis Jordan and Nelda H. Cambron–McCabe.**
Cambridge, Mass.: Ballinger Pub. Co., c1981. xxvii, 373 p.; 24 cm. — (Second annual yearbook of the American Education Finance Association) 1. State aid to education — United States — Addresses, essays, lectures. I. Jordan, K. Forbis (Kenneth Forbis) 1930- II. Cambron-McCabe, Nelda H.
LB2828.P47   379.1/22/0973 19   LC 81-8074   ISBN 0884101975

**Tidwell, Sam B.**    4.10665
Financial and managerial accounting for elementary and secondary school systems / by Sam B. Tidwell. — [3rd ed.]. — Chicago: Research Corporation, Association of School Business Officials, 1985. xx, 528 p.: forms; 24 cm. First ed. published in 1960 under title: Public school fund accounting. Includes

index. 1. Schools — Accounting I. T. II. Title: Financial and managerial accounting ...
LB2830.T48 1974     LB2830.T5 1985x.     657/.832

## LB2831 School Boards

**Bendiner, Robert.**     ● **4.10666**
The politics of schools; a crisis in self–government. — [1st ed.]. — New York: Harper & Row, [1969] xiii, 240 p.; 22 cm. 1. School boards — United States I. T.
LB2831.B42 1969     379/.1531/0973     *LC* 73-83585

**Understanding school boards: problems and prospects / edited**   **4.10667**
**by Peter J. Cistone.**
Lexington, Mass.: Lexington Books, c1975. xvii, 285 p.; 24 cm. (Lexington Books politics of education series) 'A National School Boards Association research study.' Results of papers presented at a symposium sponsored by the National School Boards Association and held April 16-18, 1975, in Miami Beach. 1. School boards — United States — Addresses, essays, lectures. 2. Community and school — United States — Addresses, essays, lectures. I. Cistone, Peter J. II. National School Boards Association.
LB2831.U52     379/.1531/0973     *LC* 75-24658     *ISBN* 0669002275

## LB2831.5 Personnel Management

**Personnel administration in education: leadership for**   **4.10668**
**instructional improvement / Ben M. Harris ... [et al.].**
2nd ed. — Boston: Allyn and Bacon, c1985. ix, 324 p.; 25 cm. 1. School personnel administration — United States. I. Harris, Ben M.
LB2831.5.P44 1985     371.2/01 19     *LC* 84-14457     *ISBN* 0205082009

**Blumberg, Arthur, 1923-.**     **4.10669**
The school superintendent: living with conflict / Arthur Blumberg with Phyllis Blumberg; foreword by Seymour Sarason. — New York: Teachers College, Columbia University, c1985. xv, 233 p.; 24 cm. Includes index. 1. School superintendents — United States. I. Blumberg, Phyllis, 1933- II. T.
LB2831.72.B55 1985     371.2/011/0973 19     *LC* 84-14953     *ISBN* 0807727644

## LB2831.9 Principals

**Gross, Neal Crasilneck, 1920-.**     **4.10670**
The sex factor and the management of schools / Neal Gross, Anne E. Trask. — New York: Wiley, c1976. vii, 279 p.: graphs; 24 cm. 'A Wiley-Interscience publication.' 1. School superintendents 2. Sex role I. Trask, Anne E., joint author. II. T.
LB2831.9.G76     372.1/2/012     *LC* 75-34337     *ISBN* 0471328006

**Wolcott, Harry F., 1929-.**     **4.10671**
The man in the principal's office; an ethnography [by] Harry F. Wolcott. — New York: Holt, Rinehart and Winston, [1973] xviii, 334 p.: illus.; 24 cm. — (Case studies in education and culture.) 1. School superintendents I. T. II. Series.
LB2831.9.W64     372.1/2/012     *LC* 72-81014     *ISBN* 0030912369

**Lipham, James M.**     **4.10672**
The principalship: concepts, competencies, and cases / James M. Lipham, Robb E. Rankin, James A. Hoeh, Jr. — New York, N.Y.: Longman, c1985. xv, 335 p.: ill.; 24 cm. Includes indexes. 1. School superintendents — United States. 2. School supervision — United States. I. Rankin, Robb. II. Hoeh, James A. III. T.
LB2831.92.L57 1985     371.2/012/0973 19     *LC* 84-21858     *ISBN* 058228581X

## LB2832–2844 Teaching Personnel

**Fiszman, Joseph R.**     **4.10673**
Revolution and tradition in people's Poland: education and socialization / by Joseph R. Fiszman. — [Princeton, N.J.]: Princeton University Press, 1973 (c1972) xxii, 382 p.; 23 cm. 1. Teachers — Poland. 2. Teachers — Social conditions — Poland. I. T.
LB2832.4.P6 F57     301.5/6     *LC* 70-166369     *ISBN* 0691051941

**Kaufman, Polly Welts, 1929-.**     **4.10674**
Women teachers on the frontier / Polly Welts Kaufman. — New Haven: Yale University Press, c1984. xxiii, 270 p.: ill.; 25 cm. Includes index. 1. Women teachers — United States — History — 19th century. 2. Education — United States — History — 19th century. 3. Women pioneers — United States — History — 19th century. I. T.
LB2837.K35 1984     371.1/0088042 19     *LC* 83-14699     *ISBN* 0300030436

**Woman's 'true' profession: voices from the history of teaching /**   **4.10675**
**Nancy Hoffman.**
Old Westbury, N.Y.: Feminist Press; New York: McGraw-Hill, c1981. xxiii, 327 p.: ill.; 24 cm. — (Women's lives, women's work.) Includes index. 1. Women teachers — United States — History. I. Hoffman, Nancy. II. Series.
LB2837.W65 1981     371.1/00973 19     *LC* 80-23329     *ISBN* 0912670932

**Teacher competence / Gayle C. Hall, editor.**     **4.10676**
Bloomington, IN: Phi Delta Kappa, Center on Evaluation, Development and Research, [1985]. [xvi], 284 p.; 28 cm. — (Hot topics series; no. 10) Cover title. 1. Teachers — Rating of 2. Teachers — Certification 3. Teachers — Training of I. Hall, Gayle C. II. Phi Delta Kappa. Center on Evaluation, Development, and Research. III. Series.
LB2838.T42x     371.144

**Tecker, Glenn H.**     **4.10677**
Merit, measurement, and money: establishing teacher performance evaluation and incentive programs / Glenn H. Tecker. — Alexandria, Va.: NSBA, c1985. 113 p.: ill.; 28 cm. 1. Teachers — Rating of — United States. 2. Teachers — Salaries, pensions, etc. — United States. 3. Performance awards — United States. I. T.
LB2838.T43 1985     371.1/44 19     *LC* 84-19052     *ISBN* 0883641011

**Grace, Gerald Rupert.**     **4.10678**
Role conflict and the teacher [by] Gerald R. Grace. — London; Boston: Routledge and Kegan Paul, 1972. x, 149 p.; 23 cm. — (International library of sociology.) 1. Teachers — Psychology. 2. Social role I. T.
LB2840.G65 1972     371.1/04     *LC* 72-172562     *ISBN* 0710073534

**Cedoline, Anthony J.**     **4.10679**
Job burnout in public education: symptoms, causes, and survival skills / Anthony J. Cedoline. — New York: Teachers College Press, 1982. xii, 256 p.; 24 cm. 1. Teachers — Job stress 2. School administrators — Psychology. 3. Burn out (Psychology) I. T.
LB2840.2.C425 1982     371.1/001/9 19     *LC* 81-23289     *ISBN* 080772694X

**Duke, Daniel Linden.**     **4.10680**
Teaching—the imperiled profession / Daniel Linden Duke. — Albany: State University of New York Press, c1984. v, 174 p.; 24 cm. Includes index. 1. Teachers — United States — Job stress. 2. Teachers — United States — Job satisfaction. 3. Teacher morale I. T.
LB2840.2.D85 1984     371.1/0023/73 19     *LC* 83-18181     *ISBN* 0873957881

**Zabalza, Antoni, 1946-.**     **4.10681**
The economics of teacher supply / Antoni Zabalza, Philip Turnbull, Gareth Williams. — Cambridge [Eng.]; New York: Cambridge University Press, 1979. xi, 280 p.: ill.; 24 cm. Includes index. 1. Teachers — Salaries, etc. 2. Teachers — Supply and demand I. Turnbull, Philip. joint author. II. Williams, Gareth L. joint author. III. T.
LB2842.2.Z3     331.1/26     *LC* 78-967     *ISBN* 0521220785

**Pronin, Barbara.**     **4.10682**
Substitute teaching: a handbook for hassle–free subbing / by Barbara Pronin. — 1st ed. — New York: St. Martin's Press, c1983. xi, 241 p.; 22 cm. Includes index. 1. Substitute teachers — Handbooks, manuals, etc. I. T.
LB2844.1.S8 P76 1983     371.1/4122 19     *LC* 82-16865     *ISBN* 0312774818

**Johnson, Susan Moore.**     **4.10683**
Teacher unions in schools / Susan Moore Johnson. — Philadelphia: Temple University Press, 1984. xii, 253 p.; 22 cm. Includes index. 1. Teachers' unions — United States. I. T.
LB2844.53.U6 J63 1984     331.88/11371100973 19     *LC* 83-18067     *ISBN* 0877223270

**Selden, David.**     **4.10684**
The teacher rebellion / David Selden. — Washington, D.C.: Howard University Press, 1985. x, 260 p.; 22 cm. Includes index. 1. Teachers' unions — United States — History — 20th century. I. T.
LB2844.53.U6 S44 1985     331.88/113711/00973 19     *LC* 83-4403     *ISBN* 088258099X

**Urban, Wayne J.**      4.10685
Why teachers organized / by Wayne J. Urban. — Detroit: Wayne State University Press, 1982. 202 p.; 24 cm. Includes index. 1. Teachers' unions — United States — History. I. T.
LB2844.53.U6 U7 1982      331.88/113711/00973 19      *LC* 82-11160
     *ISBN* 0814317146

**Eberts, Randall W.**      4.10686
Unions and public schools: the effect of collective bargaining on American education / Randall W. Eberts, Joe A. Stone. — Lexington, Mass.: Lexington Books, c1984. xvi, 195 p.: ill.; 24 cm. (Lexington Books politics of education series.) Includes index. 1. Collective bargaining — Teachers — United States. 2. Teachers' unions — United States. 3. School personnel management — United States. 4. Academic achievement I. Stone, Joe A. II. T. III. Series.
LB2844.59.U6 E23 1984      331.89/041371100973 19      *LC* 82-48862
     *ISBN* 066906372X

**Webster, William G. (William Gerald)**      4.10687
Effective collective bargaining in public education / William G. Webster, Sr. — 1st ed. — Ames: Iowa State University Press, 1985. x, 233 p.: ill.; 24 cm. Includes index. 1. Collective bargaining — Teachers — United States. I. T.
LB2844.59.U6 W43 1985      331.89/0413711/00973 19      *LC* 85-2516
     *ISBN* 0813805260

## LB2846 School Reports. Records

**Children, parents, and school records.** [Edited by J. William      4.10688
Rioux and Stuart A. Sandow.**
Columbia, Md.: National Committee for Citizens in Education, 1974] x, 313 p.; 23 cm. Cover title. Half title: Students, parents, and school records. 1. Schools — United States — Records and correspondence. 2. School reports — United States. I. Rioux, J. William. ed. II. Sandow, Stuart A. ed. III. National Committee for Citizens in Education. IV. Title: Students, parents, and school records.
LB2846.C48      371.4/042      *LC* 74-177203

## LB2890–2997 School Administration in Other Regions or Countries

**Loh, Philip Fook Seng.**      4.10689
Seeds of separatism: educational policy in Malaya, 1874–1940 / Philip Loh Fook Seng. Kuala Lumpur; New York: Oxford University Press, 1976 (c1975). x, 165 p.: graphs; 26 cm. (East Asian social science monographs) Includes index. 1. School management and organization — Malaya. 2. Education and state — Malaya. I. T.
LB2965.M4 L64      379/.152/095951      *LC* 76-375132      *ISBN* 0195802853

**McLaren, Ian A.**      4.10690
Education in a small democracy – New Zealand [by] Ian A. McLaren. — London; Boston: Routledge & K. Paul, 1974. xx, 172 p.: illus., map.; 23 cm. — (World education series) Includes index. 1. School management and organization — New Zealand. I. T.
LB2983.M33      370/.9931      *LC* 73-91035      *ISBN* 071007798X

## LB3011–3095 Classroom Management. Discipline

**Hymes, James L., 1913-.**      • 4.10691
Behavior and misbehavior; a teacher's guide to action. — New York: Prentice-Hall, 1955. 140 p.; 19 cm. 1. School discipline I. T.
LB3011.H95      371.5      *LC* 55-7777

**Alschuler, Alfred S., 1939-.**      4.10692
School discipline: a socially literate solution / Alfred S. Alschuler. — New York: McGraw-Hill, c1980. xi, 215 p.; 24 cm. Includes index. 1. Freire, Paulo, 1921- 2. School discipline 3. Education — Philosophy I. T.
LB3012.A47      371.5      *LC* 79-26621      *ISBN* 0070011273

**Bybee, Rodger W.**      4.10693
Violence, values, and justice in the schools / Rodger W. Bybee, E. Gordon Gee. — Boston, Mass.: Allyn and Bacon, c1982. x, 254 p.; 25 cm. 1. School discipline — United States. 2. School violence — United States. 3. School discipline — Law and legislation — United States. I. Gee, E. Gordon (Elwood Gordon), 1944- II. T.
LB3012.B9      371.5 19      *LC* 81-12710      *ISBN* 0205073875

**Charles, C. M.**      4.10694
Building classroom discipline: from models to practice / C.M. Charles; collaboration by Karen Blaine. — 2nd ed. — New York: Longman, c1985. vii, 247 p.; 23 cm. 1. School discipline I. Blaine, Karen. II. T.
LB3012.C46 1985      371.5 19      *LC* 84-5765      *ISBN* 0582285321

**Deitz, Samuel M.**      4.10695
Discipline in the schools: a guide to reducing misbehavior / Samuel M. Deitz, John H. Hummel. — Englewood Cliffs, N.J.: Educational Technology Publications, c1978. xiii, 270 p.: graphs; 25 cm. 1. School discipline I. Hummel, John H. joint author. II. T.
LB3012.D44      371.5      *LC* 78-18269      *ISBN* 0877781273

**Rich, John Martin.**      4.10696
Innovative school discipline / by John Martin Rich. — Springfield, Ill., U.S.A.: C.C.Thomas, c1985. viii, 109 p.; 27 cm. 1. School discipline I. T.
LB3012.R55 1985      371.5 19      *LC* 85-8052      *ISBN* 0398051526

**Carew, Jean V., 1936-.**      4.10697
Beyond bias: perspectives on classrooms / Jean V. Carew and Sara Lawrence Lightfoot. — Cambridge, Mass.: Harvard University Press, c1979. 291 p.; 24 cm. Includes index. 1. Classroom management 2. Teacher-student relationships 3. Interaction analysis in education I. Lightfoot, Sara Lawrence. joint author. II. T.
LB3013.C34      372.1/1/02      *LC* 78-20997      *ISBN* 0674068823

**Gordon, Thomas, 1918-.**      4.10698
T.E.T., teacher effectiveness training / by Thomas Gordon, with Noel Burch. — New York: P. H. Wyden, c1974. xvii, 366 p.: ill.; 22 cm. Includes index. 1. Classroom management 2. Child rearing I. Burch, Noel, joint author. II. T. III. Title: Teacher effectiveness training.
LB3013.G66      371.1/02      *LC* 74-17798      *ISBN* 0883260808

**Jones, Vernon F., 1945-.**      4.10699
Comprehensive classroom management: creating positive learning environments / Vernon F. Jones, Louise S. Jones. — 2nd ed. — Boston: Allyn and Bacon, c1986. xix, 459 p.: ill.; 24 cm. Rev. ed. of: Responsible classroom discipline. c1981. Includes indexes. 1. Classroom management 2. Interaction analysis in education 3. School discipline I. Jones, Louise S., 1949- II. Jones, Vernon F., 1945- Responsible classroom discipline. III. T.
LB3013.J66 1986      371.1/024 19      *LC* 85-9045      *ISBN* 0205085245

**Kerr, Mary Margaret.**      4.10700
Strategies for managing behavior problems in the classroom / Mary Margaret Kerr, C. Michael Nelson. — Columbus, Ohio: C.E. Merrill Pub. Co., c1983. xvi, 356 p.: ill.; 27 cm. Includes index. 1. Classroom management I. Nelson, C. Michael (Charles Michael), 1941- II. T.
LB3013.K47 1983      371.93 19      *LC* 82-62476      *ISBN* 0675200326

**Wolfgang, Charles H.**      4.10701
Solving discipline problems: strategies for classroom teachers / Charles H. Wolfgang, Carl D. Glickman. — 2nd ed. — Boston: Allyn and Bacon, c1986. xiii, 330 p.: ill.; 25 cm. 1. Classroom management 2. School discipline I. Glickman, Carl D. II. T.
LB3013.W62 1986      371.1/024 19      *LC* 85-19984      *ISBN* 0205086306

**School class size: research and policy** / Gene V. Glass ... [et      4.10702
al.].
Beverly Hills, Calif.: Sage Publications, c1982. 160 p.: graphs; 23 cm. Includes indexes. 1. Class size — Addresses, essays, lectures. I. Glass, Gene V., 1940-
LB3013.2.S36 1982      371.2/51 19      *LC* 81-23308      *ISBN* 0803918054

**Goldstein, Arnold P.**      4.10703
School violence / Arnold P. Goldstein, Steven J. Apter, Berj Haroutunian. — Englewood Cliffs, N.J.: Prentice-Hall, c1984. x, 246 p.: ill.; 24 cm. 1. School violence — United States. 2. Moral education — United States. 3. Behavior modification 4. Socialization I. Apter, Steven J. (Steven Jeffrey), 1945- II. Haroutunian, Berj. III. T.
LB3013.3.G64 1984      371.5/8/0973 19      *LC* 83-8670      *ISBN* 0137945450

**Winters, Wendy Glasgow.**      4.10704
The practice of social work in schools: an ecological perspective / Wendy Glasgow Winters, Freda Easton. — New York: Free Press, c1983. xiv, 176 p.; 25 cm. — (Fields of practice series.) Includes index. 1. School social work I. Easton, Freda. II. T. III. Series.
LB3013.4.W56 1983      371.4/6 19      *LC* 83-5537      *ISBN* 0029356601

**Reconstructing educational psychology** / edited by Bill Gillham.      4.10705
London: Croon Helm, c1978. 197 p.; 23 cm. Includes index. 1. School psychologists — Great Britain — Addresses, essays, lectures. I. Gillham, Bill.
LB3013.6.R38      371.2/02      *LC* 78-314388      *ISBN* 0856646318

**The School psychologist: an introduction / edited by George W. Hynd.**   **4.10706**
1st ed. — Syracuse, N.Y.: Syracuse University Press, 1983. xv, 332 p.: ill.; 21 cm. 1. School psychologists — Addresses, essays, lectures. I. Hynd, George W.
LB3013.6.S27 1983    371.2/022 19    *LC* 82-19337    *ISBN* 0815622899

**Corporal punishment in American education: readings in history, practice, and alternatives / edited by Irwin A. Hyman and James H. Wise; pref. by Nat Hentoff.**   **4.10707**
Philadelphia: Temple University Press, 1979. xv, 471 p.; 24 cm. 1. Corporal punishment — United States — History — Addresses, essays, lectures. I. Hyman, Irwin. II. Wise, James H.
LB3025.C67    371.5/4/0973    *LC* 79-17    *ISBN* 0877221472

## LB3045–3048 TEXTBOOKS
(see also: LT)

**Jenkinson, Edward B.**   **4.10708**
Censors in the classroom: the mind benders / by Edward B. Jenkinson. — Carbondale: Southern Illinois University Press, c1979. xix, 184 p.; 23 cm. 1. Textbooks — United States — Censorship. I. T.
LB3047.J46    379/.156    *LC* 79-17417    *ISBN* 0809309297

## LB3051–3060 EDUCATIONAL TESTS AND MEASUREMENTS

**Ability testing: uses, consequences, and controversies / Committee on Ability Testing, Assembly of Behavioral and Social Sciences, National Research Council; Alexandra K. Wigdor and Wendell R. Garner, editors.**   **4.10709**
Washington, D.C.: National Academy Press, 1982. 2 v.: ill.; 23 cm. 1. Educational tests and measurements — United States 2. Ability testing I. Wigdor, Alexandra K. II. Garner, Wendell R. III. Assembly of Behavioral and Social Sciences (U.S.). Committee on Ability Testing.
LB3051.A52    371.2/6/0973 19    *LC* 81-18870    *ISBN* 0309032288

**American Psychological Association.**   **4.10710**
Standards for educational and psychological testing / American Educational Research Association, American Psychological Association, National Council on Measurement in Education. — Washington, DC: American Psychological Association, c1985. viii, 100 p.; 26 cm. Rev. ed. of: Standards for educational & psychological tests. 1974. Includes index. 1. Educational tests and measurements — Standards — United States. 2. Psychological tests — Standards — United States. I. American Educational Research Association. II. National Council on Measurement in Education. III. American Psychological Association. Standards for educational & psychological tests. IV. T.
LB3051.A693 1985    371.2/6/0973 19    *LC* 85-71493    *ISBN* 0912704950

**Gay, L. R.**   **4.10711**
Educational evaluation & measurement: competencies for analysis and application / L.R. Gay. — Columbus: C.E. Merrill Pub Co., c1980. xvi, 543 p.: ill.; 26 cm. 1. Educational tests and measurements I. T. II. Title: Educational evaluation and measurement.
LB3051.G34    371.2/6 19    *LC* 79-90705    *ISBN* 0675081432

**Gronlund, Norman Edward, 1920-.**   **4.10712**
Measurement and evaluation in teaching / Norman E. Gronlund. — 5th ed. — New York: Macmillan; London: Collier Macmillan, c1985. xv, 540 p.: ill.; 25 cm. 1. Educational tests and measurements I. T.
LB3051.G74 1985    371.2/6 19    *LC* 84-866    *ISBN* 0023481102

**Hopkins, Charles D.**   **4.10713**
Classroom measurement & evaluation / Charles D. Hopkins, Richard L. Antes. — 2nd ed. — Itasca, Ill.: F. E. Peacock Publishers, c1985. xii, 527 p.: ill.; 25 cm. 1. Educational tests and measurements I. Antes, Richard L. II. T. III. Title: Classroom measurements and evaluations.
LB3051.H698 1985    371.2/6 19    *LC* 83-61761    *ISBN* 087581297X

**Nairn, Allan.**   **4.10714**
The reign of ETS: the corporation that makes up minds / by Allan Nairn and associates. — [Washington, D.C.]: Ralph Nader, 1980. xvii, 554 p.; 28 cm. — 'The Ralph Nader report on the Educational Testing Service.' Errata slip inserted. 1. Educational Testing Service. 2. Educational tests and measurements — United States I. Nader, Ralph. II. T.
LB3051.N25    371.26013    *LC* 80-107761

**The Rise and fall of national test scores / edited by Gilbert R. Austin, Herbert Garber.**   **4.10715**
New York: Academic Press, 1982. xvii, 270 p.; 24 cm. — (Educational psychology.) 1. Educational tests and measurements — United States —

Evaluation — Addresses, essays, lectures. 2. Academic achievement — Evaluation — Addresses, essays, lectures. I. Austin, Gilbert R. II. Garber, Herbert. III. Series.
LB3051.R56    371.2/6 19    *LC* 81-17668    *ISBN* 0120685809

## LB3061 CLASSIFICATION OF PUPILS

**Goodlad, John I.**   **• 4.10716**
The nongraded elementary school [by] John I. Goodlad [and] Robert H. Anderson. — Rev. ed. — New York: Harcourt, Brace & World, [1963] 248 p.: illus.; 23 cm. 1. Nongraded schools I. Anderson, Robert Henry, 1918- joint author. II. T.
LB3061.G6 1963    371.25    *LC* 63-13112

**Oakes, Jeannie.**   **4.10717**
Keeping track: how schools structure inequality / Jeannie Oakes. — New Haven: Yale University Press, c1985. xvi, 231 p.; 22 cm. Includes index. 1. Ability grouping in education I. T.
LB3061.O22 1985    371.2/54 19    *LC* 84-20931    *ISBN* 0300032927

**Bagwell, William, 1923-.**   **4.10718**
School desegregation in the Carolinas; two case studies. — [1st ed.]. — Columbia: University of South Carolina Press, [1972] xv, 341 p.; 23 cm. 1. Segregation in education — Greensboro, N.C. — Case studies. 2. Segregation in education — Greenville, S.C. — Case studies. I. T.
LB3062.B3    370.19/342    *LC* 71-166195    *ISBN* 0872492354

# LB3201–3325 School Buildings. Vandalism

**Council of Educational Facility Planners, International.**   **4.10719**
Guide for planning educational facilities: an authoritative and comprehensive guide to the planning of educational facilities from the conception of need through utilization of the facility. — Rev. 1985. — Columbus, Ohio: Council of Educational Facility Planners, International, c1985. 192 p. Includes index. 1. School buildings 2. School facilities — Planning I. Council of Educational Facility Planners. Guide for planning educational facilities. II. T.
LB3205.C65 1976    371.6    *LC* 76-17296

**Casserly, Michael D.**   **4.10720**
School vandalism: strategies for prevention / Michael D. Casserly, Scott A. Bass, John R. Garrett. — Lexington, Mass.: Lexington Books, c1980. x, 166 p.; 24 cm. Includes index. 1. School vandalism I. Bass, Scott A. joint author. II. Garrett, John R. joint author. III. T.
LB3249.C37    371.5/8 19    *LC* 80-8118    *ISBN* 066903956X

**School crime and disruption / Ernst Wenk and Nora Harlow, editors.**   **4.10721**
Davis, Calif.: Responsible Action, c1978. 238 p.; 22 cm. (Dialogue books) 1. School vandalism — Addresses, essays, lectures. 2. School violence — Addresses, essays, lectures. I. Wenk, Ernst A. II. Harlow, Nora.
LB3249.S36    364.1/64    *LC* 78-51102    *ISBN* 0931364043

# LB3602–3640 School Life

**Sale, Kirkpatrick.**   **4.10722**
SDS. — [1st ed.]. — New York: Random House, [1973] 752 p.; 25 cm. 1. Students for a Democratic Society (U.S.) — History. 2. Radicalism — United States. I. T.
LB3602.S8363 S24    322.4/2    *LC* 72-12647    *ISBN* 0394478894

**Heath, Douglas H.**   **4.10723**
Growing up in college; liberal education and maturity [by] Douglas H. Heath. — [1st ed.]. — San Francisco: Jossey-Bass, 1968. xvi, 326 p.; 24 cm. — (The Jossey-Bass series in higher education) 1. Education, Higher — Aims and objectives 2. Maturation (Psychology) I. T.
LB3605.H38    370/.01    *LC* 68-54946

**English, Earl, 1905-.**   **4.10724**
Scholastic journalism / Earl English, Clarence Hach. — 7th ed. — Ames: Iowa State University Press, 1984. xi, 331 p.: ill.; 29 cm. 1. Journalism, School 2. Journalism I. Hach, Clarence, 1917- II. T.
LB3621.E52 1984    373.18/97 19    *LC* 83-13027    *ISBN* 0813814006

## LC SPECIAL ASPECTS OF EDUCATION

**Powys, John Cowper, 1872-1963.**                                    **4.10725**
The meaning of culture. New York, W. W. Norton & company inc. [c1939] ix, 282 p. front. (port.) 23 cm. 1. Culture I. T.
LC31.P75 1939      *LC* 39-30754

**Gold, Martin, 1931-.**                                    **4.10726**
Expelled to a friendlier place: a study of effective alternative schools / Martin Gold and David W. Mann. — Ann Arbor: University of Michigan Press, c1984. xi, 174 p.: ill.; 23 cm. Includes index. 1. Non-formal education — United States — Case studies. 2. Problem children — Education — United States — Case studies. 3. Deviant behavior — Case studies. I. Mann, David W. II. T.
LC45.4.G64 1984      371/.04 19      *LC* 83-21792      *ISBN* 0472080466

**Kraushaar, Otto F.**                                    • **4.10727**
American nonpublic schools: patterns of diversity / [by] Otto F. Kraushaar. — Baltimore: Johns Hopkins University Press, [1972] xv, 387 p.; 24 cm. 1. Private schools — United States — History. I. T.
LC49.K7      371/.02/0973      *LC* 75-186475      *ISBN* 0801813840

## LC65–67 Economic Aspects

**Benson, Charles Scott.**                                    **4.10728**
Implementing the learning society; [new strategies for financing social objectives, by] Charles S. Benson [and] Harold L. Hodgkinson. With the assistance of Jessica S. Pers. — San Francisco: Jossey-Bass Publishers, 1974. xvii, 147 p.; 24 cm. — (The Jossey-Bass series in higher education) 1. Education, Higher — Economic aspects — United States. 2. Educational equalization — United States. I. Hodgkinson, Harold L. joint author. II. Pers, Jessica S., joint author. III. T.
LC66.B45      338.4/3      *LC* 73-21072      *ISBN* 0875892205

**Berg, Ivar E.**                                    **4.10729**
Education and jobs: the great training robbery / by Ivar Berg with the assistance of Sherry Gorelick; foreword by Eli Ginzberg. — New York: Published for the Center for Urban Education by Praeger Publishers, [1970] xx, 200 p.; 22 cm. 1. Education — Economic aspects — United States. 2. Employee morale — United States. 3. Labor turnover — United States. I. Gorelick, Sherry. joint author. II. T.
LC66.B47 1970      331.1/14      *LC* 74-99815

**Bowles, Samuel.**                                    **4.10730**
Schooling in capitalist America: educational reform and the contradictions of economic life / Samuel Bowles and Herbert Gintis. — New York: Basic Books, c1976. ix, 340 p.; 25 cm. 1. Education — Economic aspects — United States. 2. Education and state — United States. 3. Capitalism — United States. I. Gintis, Herbert. joint author. II. T.
LC66.B68      370/.973      *LC* 75-7267      *ISBN* 0465072305

**Does college matter? Some evidence on the impacts of higher**                                    **4.10731**
**education, edited by Lewis C. Solmon and Paul J. Taubman.**
New York: Academic Press, 1973. xvii, 415 p.; 24 cm. Conference held at Woods Hole, Mass., July 16-19, 1972, sponsored by the Panel on the Benefits of Higher Education. 1. Education — Economic aspects — United States — Congresses. 2. Education, Higher — Aims and objectives — Congresses. 3. Education, Higher — United States — 1965- — Congresses. 4. Universities and colleges — United States — Finance — Congresses. I. Solmon, Lewis C. ed. II. Taubman, Paul, 1939- ed. III. National Research Council. Office of Scientific Personnel. Board on Human Resources. Panel on the Benefits of Higher Education.
LC66.D63      301.5/6      *LC* 73-7443      *ISBN* 0126550506

## LC71–245 Social Aspects

### LC71–120 Education and State

**Conant, James Bryant, 1893-1978.**                                    • **4.10732**
Education and liberty; the role of the schools in a modern democracy. Cambridge, Harvard University Press, 1953. xii, 168 p. 22 cm. 'Based on lectures delivered at the University of Virginia under the Page-Barbour Foundation on February 12, 13 [and] 14, 1952.' 1. Education and state 2. Education — 1945- I. Page-Barbour Foundation. II. T.
LC71.C65      370.973      *LC* 52-9384

**Tesconi, Charles A.**                                    **4.10733**
The anti–man culture, bureautechnocracy and the schools / Charles A. Tesconi, Jr., with Van Cleve Morris. — Urbana, Ill.: University of Illinois Press, c1972. xiii, 232 p. 1. Education and state I. Morris, Van Cleve. II. T.
LC71.T43      *LC* 75-160385      *ISBN* 0252001893 939

**Arons, Stephen.**                                    **4.10734**
Compelling belief: the culture of American schooling / Stephen Arons. — New York: McGraw-Hill, c1983. xi, 228 p.; 24 cm. Includes index. 1. Academic freedom — United States. 2. Education — United States 3. Free schools — United States. 4. Education and state — United States. I. T.
LC72.2.A76 1983      379.73 19      *LC* 82-7798      *ISBN* 0070023263

**Henderson, John Cleaves.**                                    • **4.10735**
Thomas Jefferson's views on public education / by John C. Henderson. — New York: G. P. Putnam's Sons, 1890. viii, 387 p.: port.; 21 cm. Includes index. 1. Jefferson, Thomas, 1743-1826. 2. Education — United States I. T.
LC89.H4 1890a

**Powers, Richard H.**                                    **4.10736**
The dilemma of education in a democracy / Richard H. Powers. — Chicago: Regnery Gateway, c1984. 253 p.; 24 cm. 1. Education and state — United States. 2. Education — Philosophy I. T.
LC89.P69 1984      379.73 19      *LC* 81-85568      *ISBN* 0895266628

**Stickney, Benjamin D.**                                    **4.10737**
The great education debate: Washington and the schools / by Benjamin D. Stickney and Laurence R. Marcus. — Springfield, Ill., U.S.A.: C.C. Thomas, c1984. ix, 193 p.; 24 cm. 1. Education and state — United States. I. Marcus, Laurence R. II. T.
LC89.S67 1984      379.73 19      *LC* 83-24129      *ISBN* 0398049599

**Tyack, David B.**                                    **4.10738**
Public schools in hard times: the Great Depression and recent years / David Tyack, Robert Lowe, Elisabeth Hansot. — Cambridge, Mass.: Harvard University Press, 1984. 267 p.: ill.; 25 cm. Includes index. 1. Education and state — United States — History — 20th century. 2. Public schools — United States — History — 20th century. 3. Depressions — 1929 — United States 4. United States — Economic conditions — 1971- I. Lowe, Robert, 1947- II. Hansot, Elisabeth. III. T.
LC89.T93 1984      379.73 19      *LC* 83-22679      *ISBN* 0674738004

**Wiggin, Gladys Anna, 1907-.**                                    • **4.10739**
Education and nationalism; an historical interpretation of American education. New York, McGraw-Hill, 1962. 518 p. 24 cm. (Foundations in education) (McGraw-Hill series in education) 1. Nationalism and education — United States. I. T.
LC89.W5      *LC* 60-53357

**Wirt, Frederick M.**                                    **4.10740**
Schools in conflict: the politics of education / by Frederick M. Wirt, Michael W. Kirst. — Berkeley, Calif.: McCutchan Pub. Corp., c1982. xii, 322 p.: ill.; 24 cm. 1. Education and state — United States. 2. Politics and education — United States. I. Kirst, Michael W. II. T.
LC89.W577 1982      379.73 19      *LC* 81-83250      *ISBN* 0821122614

**Bildungswesen in der Bundesrepublik Deutschland. English.**                                    **4.10741**
Between elite and mass education: education in the Federal Republic of Germany / Max Planck Institute for Human Development and Education, Berlin, Federal Republic of Germany; with a foreword by James S. Coleman; translated by Raymond Meyer and Adriane Heinrichs–Goodwin. — Albany: State University of New York Press, [1983], c1979. xviii, 348 p.: ill.; 24 cm. Translation of: Das Bildungswesen in der Bundesrepublik Deutschland. Includes indexes. 1. Education and state — Germany (West.) 2. Education and state — United States. 3. Comparative education 4. Education — United

States 5. Education — Germany (West). I. Max-Planck-Institut für Bildungsforschung. II. T.
LC93.G4 B55313 1983     370/.943 19     *LC* 83-18314     *ISBN* 0873957091

**Tent, James F.**          **4.10742**
Mission on the Rhine: reeducation and denazification in American–occupied Germany / James F. Tent. — Chicago: University of Chicago Press, c1982. xvii, 369 p., [12] p. of plates: ill.; 24 cm. Includes index. 1. Education and state — Germany (West) — History. 2. Denazification 3. Germany — History — Allied occupation, 1945- I. T.
LC93.G4 T46 1982     379.43 19     *LC* 82-4896     *ISBN* 0226793575

**Löfstedt, Jan-Ingvar.**          **4.10743**
Chinese educational policy: changes and contradictions, 1949–79 / by Jan–Ingvar Löfstedt. — Stockholm: Almqvist & Wiksell International; Atlantic Highlands, N.J.: Humanities Press, c1980. 203 p.: map; 25 cm. 1. Education and state — China. I. T.
LC94.C5 L6     *ISBN* 9122004203

**Van den Berghe, Pierre L.**          **4.10744**
Power and privilege at an African university [by] Pierre L. van den Berghe. With the assistance of Paul Alabi [and others] Cambridge, Mass., Schenkman Pub. Co.; distributed by General Learning Press [Morristown, N.J., 1973] x, 273 p. 24 cm. 1. Education, Higher — Nigeria. 2. Nigeria — Intellectual life. 3. Nigeria — Social conditions — 1960- I. T.
LC95.N55 V36     378.669     *LC* 72-81519

**Boles, Donald E. (Donald Edward), 1926-.**          **4.10745**
The Bible, religion, and the public schools [by] Donald E. Boles. [3d ed.] Ames, Iowa State University Press, 1965. xii, 408 p. 23 cm. 1. Religion in the public schools I. T.
LC111.B55 1965     377.1     *LC* 65-16369

**McCarthy, Martha M.**          **4.10746**
A delicate balance: church, state, and the schools / Martha M. McCarthy. — Bloomington, Ind.: Phi Delta Kappan Educational Foundation, c1983. vi, 178 p.; 23 cm. 1. Church and education — United States 2. Church and state — United States 3. Church schools — Law and legislation — United States. 4. Education and state — United States. I. T.
LC111.M34 1983     377/.1/0973 19     *LC* 83-60797     *ISBN* 0873674278

## LC129–148 Attendance

**Keim, Albert N.**          **4.10747**
Compulsory education and the Amish: the right not to be modern / edited by Albert N. Keim. — Boston: Beacon Press, [1975] x, 211 p., [1] leaf of plates; 21 cm. Includes index. 1. Education, Compulsory — United States. 2. Amish — Education — United States. 3. Educational law and legislation — United States I. T.
LC131.K43 1975     379/.23     *LC* 74-16665     *ISBN* 0807005002

**Astin, Alexander W.**          **4.10748**
Preventing students from dropping out / Alexander W. Astin. — 1st ed. — San Francisco: Jossey-Bass, 1975. xv, 204 p.; 24 cm. (The Jossey-Bass series in higher education) Includes index. 1. Dropouts I. T.
LC142.A84     378.1/69/13     *LC* 74-28915     *ISBN* 0875892558

**Carnegie Council on Policy Studies in Higher Education.**          **4.10749**
Three thousand futures: the next twenty years for higher education: final report of the Carnegie Council on Policy Studies in Higher Education. — 1st ed. — San Francisco: Jossey-Bass, 1980. xxi, 439 p.: ill.; 24 cm. — (The Carnegie Council series) Includes index. 1. College attendance — United States. 2. Education, Higher — United States. I. T.
LC148.C29 1980     378/.1059/73 19     *LC* 79-9675     *ISBN* 0875894534

**Tinto, Vincent.**          **4.10750**
Leaving college: rethinking the causes and cures of student attrition / Vincent Tinto. — Chicago: University of Chicago Press, 1987. x, 246 p.: ill.; 24 cm. Includes index. 1. College dropouts — United States. 2. College attendance — United States. I. T.
LC148.T57 1987     378/.16913/0973 19     *LC* 86-11379     *ISBN* 0226804461

## LC149–160 Literacy. Illiteracy

**Cipolla, Carlo M.**          **4.10751**
Literacy and development in the West. by Carlo M. Cipolla. Baltimore, Md., Penguin Books [1969] 143 p. 18 cm. 1. Literacy I. T.
LC149.C5 1969b     379/.24     *LC* 73-5918

**Freire, Paulo, 1921-.**          **4.10752**
The politics of education: culture, power, and liberation / Paulo Freire; introduction by Henry A. Giroux; translated by Donaldo Macedo. — South Hadley, Mass.: Bergin & Garvey, 1985. xxvii, 209 p.: ill.; 24 cm. 1. Literacy 2. Education — Political aspects. 3. Education — Social aspects. 4. Education — Developing countries I. T.
LC149.F76 1985     370 19     *LC* 84-18572     *ISBN* 0897890426

**Literacy as a human problem / edited by James C. Raymond.**          **4.10753**
University, Ala.: University of Alabama Press, c1982. x, 206 p.; 22 cm. Papers presented at the 6th Alabama Symposium on English and American Literature held at the University of Alabama in 1979. 1. Literacy — Congresses. 2. English language — Study and teaching — Congresses. I. Raymond, James C., 1940- II. Alabama Symposium on English and American Literature. (6th: 1979: University of Alabama)
LC149.L498 1982     428.2/07/073 19     *LC* 81-19757     *ISBN* 0817301100

**Pattison, Robert.**          **4.10754**
On literacy: the politics of the word from Homer to the Age of Rock / Robert Pattison. — New York: Oxford University Press, 1982. xiii, 246 p.; 22 cm. Includes index. 1. Literacy I. T.
LC149.P33 1982     001.2 19     *LC* 82-3547     *ISBN* 0195031377

**Taylor, Denny, 1947-.**          **4.10755**
Family literacy: young children learning to read and write / Denny Taylor; foreword by Dorothy S. Strickland. — Exeter, N.H.: Heinemann Educational Books, 1983. 120 p.: ill.; 21 cm. 1. Literacy 2. Reading 3. English language — Composition and exercises 4. Family — Books and reading. I. T.
LC149.T37 1983     302.2 19     *LC* 82-21166     *ISBN* 0435082043

**Computers and literacy / edited by Daniel Chandler and Stephen Marcus.**          **4.10756**
Milton Keynes, England; Philadelphia: Open University Press, 1985. xi, 155 p.; 23 cm. Includes indexes. 1. Computers and literacy — Congresses — Computer-assisted instruction. 2. English language — Congresses. 3. Language arts — Computer-assisted instruction — Congresses. I. Chandler, Daniel. II. Marcus, Stephen.
LC149.5.C65 1985     428/.0028/5 19     *LC* 85-3109     *ISBN* 0335150314

**Kozol, Jonathan.**          **4.10757**
Illiterate America / Jonathan Kozol. — 1st ed. — Garden City, N.Y.: Anchor Press/Doubleday, 1985. xvii, 270 p.; 24 cm. 1. Literacy — United States. I. T.
LC151.K68 1985     370/.973 19     *LC* 84-20487     *ISBN* 0385195362

## LC165–182 Higher Education and State

**Carnegie Council on Policy Studies in Higher Education.**          **4.10758**
The Carnegie Council on Policy Studies in Higher Education: a summary of reports and recommendations. — San Francisco: Jossey-Bass Publishers, 1980. x, 489 p.; 26 cm. Includes index. 1. Higher education and state — United States — Addresses, essays, lectures. I. T.
LC173.C365 1980     378.73 19     *LC* 80-7999     *ISBN* 0875894747

**Carnegie Foundation for the Advancement of Teaching.**          **4.10759**
The States and higher education: a proud past and a vital future: a commentary of the Carnegie Foundation for the Advancement of Teaching. 1st ed. — San Francisco: Jossey-Bass Publishers, 1976. xvi, 94 p.: graphs; 24 cm. (The Carnegie Council series) 1. Higher education and state — United States. I. T.
LC173.C37 1976     379/.1214/0973     *LC* 76-11958     *ISBN* 0875892825

**Millett, John David, 1912-.**          **4.10760**
Conflict in higher education: state government coordination versus institutional independence / John D. Millett; with the assistance of Fred F. Harcleroad ... [et al.]. — 1st ed. — San Francisco: Jossey-Bass, 1984. xxii, 285 p.; 24 cm. Includes index. 1. Higher education and state — United States. 2. University autonomy — United States. I. Harcleroad, Fred F. II. T.
LC173.M54 1984     379.1/52 19     *LC* 83-24806     *ISBN* 0875895891

**Whitehead, John S.**          **4.10761**
The separation of college and state; Columbia, Dartmouth, Harvard, and Yale, 1776–1876, by John S. Whitehead. — New Haven: Yale University Press, 1973. x, 262 p.; 23 cm. — (Yale publications in history. Miscellany, 97) A revision of the author's thesis, Yale. 1. Higher education and state — United States — History. I. T.
LC173.W53 1973     379     *LC* 73-77170     *ISBN* 0300016069

# LC189–214 Educational Sociology

**Social psychology of education: theory and research / edited by**    **4.10762**
**Daniel Bar–Tal, Leonard Saxe.**
Washington: Hemisphere Pub. Corp.; New York: distributed solely by Halsted Press, c1978. xvi, 384 p.; 24 cm. 1. Educational sociology — Addresses, essays, lectures. 2. Social psychology — Addresses, essays, lectures. I. Bar-Tal, Daniel. II. Saxe, Leonard.
LC189.S669     370.19     *LC* 77-28746     *ISBN* 0470263067

**Apple, Michael W.**          **4.10763**
Ideology and curriculum / Michael W. Apple. — London; Boston: Routledge & K. Paul, 1979. viii, 203 p.; 23 cm. — (Routledge education books.) 1. Educational sociology 2. Education and state I. T. II. Series.
LC191.A67     370.19/3     *LC* 78-41238     *ISBN* 0710001363

**Carnoy, Martin. comp.**          **4.10764**
Schooling in a corporate society: the political economy of education in America / edited by Martin Carnoy. — 2d ed. — New York: McKay, [1975] x, 374 p.: ill.; 21 cm. (Educational policy, planning, and theory) 1. Educational sociology — United States — Addresses, essays, lectures. 2. Educational equalization — United States — Addresses, essays, lectures. I. T.
LC191.C315 1975     370.19/0973     *LC* 75-321521     *ISBN* 0679302743

**Davies, Bronwyn, 1945-.**          **4.10765**
Life in the classroom and playground: the accounts of primary school children / Bronwyn Davies; illustrated by Paul, Jacob, and Daniel Davies. — London; Boston: Routledge & K. Paul, 1982. x, 206 p.: ill.; 23 cm. — (Social worlds of childhood.) Includes indexes. 1. School children — Attitudes. 2. Socialization I. T. II. Series.
LC191.D354 1982     372.18/1 19     *LC* 82-11297     *ISBN* 0710092105

**Dreeben, Robert.**          **4.10766**
On what is learned in school. Reading, Mass.: Addison-Wesley Pub. Co. [1968] xv, 160 p.; 22 cm. (Addison-Wesley series in education) 1. Educational sociology 2. Social learning I. T.
LC191.D7     370.19     *LC* 68-25923

**Durkheim, Emile, 1858-1917.**          • **4.10767**
Education and sociology / translated, and with an introd., by Sherwood D. Fox; foreword by Talcott Parsons. — Glencoe, Ill.: Free Press [1956] 163 p.; 22 cm. 1. Educational sociology I. T.
LC191 D813     *LC* 55-11002

**Freire, Paulo, 1921-.**          • **4.10768**
[Educação como prática da liberdade. English] Education for critical consciousness. [1st American ed.] New York, Seabury Press [1973] xiv, 164 p. illus. 22 cm. (A Continuum book) Translation of Educação como prática da liberdade, and of Extensión y comunicación. 1. Educational sociology — Latin America. 2. Liberty. I. Freire, Paulo, 1921- Extensión y comunicación. English. 1973. II. T.
LC191.F7613 1973     370.19/098     *LC* 72-12830     *ISBN* 0816491135

**Havighurst, Robert James, 1900-.**          • **4.10769**
Society and education [by] Robert J. Havighurst and Bernice L. Neugarten. — 3d ed. — Boston: Allyn and Bacon, 1967. xiii, 538 p.: illus.; 24 cm. 1. Educational sociology I. Neugarten, Bernice Levin, 1916- joint author. II. T.
LC191.H33 1967     370.193     *LC* 66-27001

**Mead, Margaret, 1901-1978.**          • **4.10770**
The school in American culture. Cambridge, Harvard University Press, 1951. 48 p. 19 cm. (The Inglis lecture, 1950) 1. Educational psychology 2. Teachers — United States. I. T.
LC191.M52     371.11     *LC* 51-9913

**Power and ideology in education / edited, and with an introd.,**    **4.10771**
**by Jerome Karabel and A. H. Halsey.**
New York: Oxford University Press, 1977. xi, 670 p.: ill.; 25 cm. 1. Educational sociology — Addresses, essays, lectures. 2. Education — Economic aspects — Addresses, essays, lectures. 3. Education and state — Addresses, essays, lectures. I. Karabel, Jerome. II. Halsey, A. H.
LC191.P66     370.19     *LC* 76-56677     *ISBN* 019502138X

**Silver, Harold.**          **4.10772**
Education and the social condition / Harold Silver. — London; New York: Methuen, 1980. 213 p.; 23 cm. 1. Educational sociology I. T.
LC191 S587 1980     370.193     *LC* 80-40304     *ISBN* 0416740308

**Apple, Michael W.**          **4.10773**
Education and power / Michael W. Apple. — Boston: Routledge & Kegan Paul, 1982. vii, 218 p.; 25 cm. Includes index. 1. Educational sociology — United States. 2. Education and state — United States. I. T.
LC191.4.A65 1982     306 19     *LC* 81-19920     *ISBN* 0710009771

**Apple, Michael W.**          **4.10774**
Teachers and texts: a political economy of class and gender relations in education / Michael W. Apple. — New York: Routledge & Kegan Paul, 1986. viii, 259 p.; 23 cm. Includes index. 1. Education — Social aspects — United States. 2. Discrimination in education — United States. 3. Women teachers — United States — History. 4. Textbooks — Publication and distribution — Social aspects — United States. 5. Computer-assisted instruction — Social aspects — United States. 6. Social structure — United States. I. T.
LC191.4.A67 1986     370.19/0973 19     *LC* 86-13877     *ISBN* 0710207743

**Levine, Daniel U., 1935-.**          **4.10775**
Society and education / Daniel U. Levine, Robert J. Havighurst. — 6th ed. — Boston: Allyn and Bacon, c1984. xii, 593 p.: ill.; 25 cm. Previous ed. by Robert J. Havighurst and Daniel U. Levine. Includes index. 1. Educational sociology — United States. 2. Educational equalization — United States. 3. Minorities — Education — United States. 4. Pluralism (Social sciences) — United States. I. Havighurst, Robert James, 1900- II. T.
LC191.4.L48 1984     370.19/0973 19     *LC* 83-15689     *ISBN* 0205080847

**Shor, Ira, 1945-.**          **4.10776**
Culture wars: school and society in the conservative restoration, 1969–1984 / Ira Shor. — Boston: Routledge & K. Paul, 1985. xvii, 238 p.; 22 cm. (Critical social thought.) Includes index. 1. Educational sociology — United States. 2. Education — United States — Curricula. 3. Politics and education — United States. 4. Conservatism — United States. I. T. II. Series.
LC191.4.S54 1986     370.19 19     *LC* 85-2305     *ISBN* 0710206372

**Race, class, and education / [edited by] Len Barton and**    **4.10777**
**Stephen Walker.**
London: Croom Helm, c1983. 235 p.; 23 cm. Contains partial papers of the fifth Westhill Sociology of Education Conference, held at Westhill College, Jan. 1982. Remaining papers to be published under the title: Gender, class, and education. Includes bibliographies and index. 1. Educational sociology — Great Britain — Addresses, essays, lectures. 2. Minorities — Education — Great Britain — Addresses, essays, lectures. 3. Education and state — Great Britain — Addresses, essays, lectures. I. Barton, Len. II. Walker, Stephen, 1944- III. Westhill College. IV. Westhill Sociology of Education Conference. (5th: 1982: Westhill College)
LC191.8.G7 R33 1983     370.19/0941 19     *LC* 82-229657     *ISBN* 0709906838

# LC202–208 Education and Social Background

**Jencks, Christopher.**          • **4.10778**
Inequality; a reassessment of the effect of family and schooling in America [by] Christopher Jencks [and others]. — New York: Basic Books, [1972] xii, 399 p.: illus.; 25 cm. 1. Educational sociology — United States. I. T.
LC205.J46     370.19/3/0973     *LC* 72-89172     *ISBN* 0465032648

# LC212–214 Discrimination in Education

**Sedlacek, William E.**          **4.10779**
Racism in American education: a model for change / William E. Sedlacek, Glenwood C. Brooks, Jr. Chicago: Nelson-Hall, c1976. xii, 226 p.; 23 cm. Includes indexes. 1. Discrimination in education — United States. 2. Race discrimination — United States I. Brooks, Glenwood C., joint author. II. T.
LC212.2.S42     370.19/342/0973     *LC* 76-6909     *ISBN* 088229136X

**Sex bias in the schools: the research evidence / edited by Janice**    **4.10780**
**Pottker and Andrew Fishel.**
Rutherford [N.J.]: Fairleigh Dickinson University Press, c1977. 571 p.: ill.; 24 cm. 1. Sex differences in education — Addresses, essays, lectures. 2. Women — Education — United States — Addresses, essays, lectures. I. Pottker, Janice. II. Fishel, Andrew.
LC212.2.S48 1977     376     *LC* 74-200     *ISBN* 0838614647

**St. John, Nancy Hoyt.**          **4.10781**
School desegregation: outcomes for children / [by] Nancy H. St. John; with a foreword by Nathan Glazer. — New York: Wiley, [1975] xv, 236 p.; 23 cm. 'A Wiley-Interscience publication.' 1. School integration — United States I. T.
LC212.5.S25     370.19/342     *LC* 74-18492     *ISBN* 0471826332

**Brown, Les, 1914-.**          **4.10782**
Justice, morality, and education: a new focus in ethics in education / Les Brown. — New York: St. Martin's Press, 1985. xiv, 366 p.; 23 cm. Includes indexes. 1. Educational equalization — United States. 2. Right to education — United States. 3. Education — Moral and ethical aspects. I. T.
LC213.2.B76 1985     370.19/0973 19     *LC* 85-2457     *ISBN* 0312449488

**Coleman, James Samuel, 1926-.**  • **4.10783**
Equality of educational opportunity, by James S. Coleman [and others. — Washington]: U.S. Dept. of Health, Education, and Welfare, Office of Education; [for sale by the Superintendent of Documents, U.S. Govt. Print. Off., 1966] vi, 737, vii, 548 p.: illus.; 26 cm. 'OE-38001' and 'OE-38001 (Supplement)' 'A publication of the National Center for Educational Statistics.' Bound in 2 parts; the second part has special t. p.: Supplemental appendix to the survey; section 9.10/correlation tables. 1. Educational equalization — United States. 2. Minorities — Education (Secondary) — United States. I. United States. Office of Education. II. National Center for Education Statistics. III. T. IV. Title: Supplemental appendix to the survey on Equality of educational opportunity.
LC213.2.C64 1966    370.19/0973    *LC* hew66-127

**The 'Inequality' controversy: schooling and distributive justice /**    **4.10784**
**Donald M. Levine & Mary Jo Bane.**
New York: Basic Books, [1975] viii, 338 p.: ill.; 24 cm. 1. Educational equalization — United States. 2. Education — Economic aspects — United States. I. Levine, Donald M. II. Bane, Mary Jo.
LC213.2.I43    370.19    *LC* 74-25910    *ISBN* 0465032435

**Shapiro, June.**    **4.10785**
Equal their chances: children's activities for non–sexist learning / June Shapiro, Sylvia Kramer, Catherine Hunerberg. — Englewood Cliffs, N.J.: Prentice-Hall, c1981. x, 164 p.: ill.; 24 cm. 'A Spectrum book.' 1. Educational equalization — United States. 2. Sex discrimination in education — United States. 3. Sexism — United States. I. Kramer, Sylvia. II. Hunerberg, Catherine. III. T.
LC213.2.S5    370.19/345 19    *LC* 81-4826    *ISBN* 0132837625

**Grant, Carl A.**    **4.10786**
After the school bell rings / Carl A. Grant, Christine E. Sleeter. — Philadelphia: Falmer Press, 1986. ix, 294 p.; 24 cm. Includes indexes. 1. Educational equalization — Middle West — Case studies. 2. Junior high school students' socio-economic status — Middle West — Case studies. 3. Sex discrimination in education — Middle West — Case studies. 4. Children of minorities — Education (Secondary) — Middle West — Case studies. 5. Handicapped children — Education (Secondary) — Middle West — Case studies. I. Sleeter, Christine E., 1948- II. T.
LC213.22.M53 G73 1986    370.19/0977 19    *LC* 85-29404    *ISBN* 1850000859

**Crain, Robert L.**    **4.10787**
Making desegregation work: how schools create social climates / Robert L. Crain, Rita E. Mahard, and Ruth E. Narot. — Cambridge, Mass.: Ballinger Pub. Co., c1982. xvii, 286 p.; 24 cm. — (Rand educational policy study.) Includes index. 1. School integration — United States 2. School environment — United States. I. Mahard, Rita E. II. Narot, Ruth E. III. T. IV. Series.
LC214.2.C7    370.19/342 19    *LC* 81-10971    *ISBN* 0884101991

**Desegregated schools: appraisals of an American experiment /**    **4.10788**
**edited by Ray C. Rist.**
New York: Academic Press, 1979. xiii, 242 p.; 24 cm. Includes indexes. 1. School integration — United States — Addresses, essays, lectures. I. Rist, Ray C.
LC214.2.D46    370.19/342    *LC* 79-6958    *ISBN* 0125889801

**Hochschild, Jennifer L., 1950-.**    **4.10789**
The new American dilemma: liberal democracy and school desegregation / Jennifer L. Hochschild. — New Haven: Yale University Press, c1984. xvi, 263 p.; 22 cm. Includes index. 1. School integration — Government policy — United States — Citizen participation. I. T.
LC214.2.H63 1984    370.19/342 19    *LC* 84-40196    *ISBN* 0300031130

**Kirp, David L.**    **4.10790**
Just schools: the idea of racial equality in American education / David L. Kirp. — Berkeley: University of California Press, c1982. xiii, 374 p.; 24 cm. 1. School integration — United States — Case studies. 2. Educational equalization — United States — Case studies. I. T.
LC214.2.K57 1982    370.19/342 19    *LC* 81-16497    *ISBN* 0520045750

**Metcalf, George R., 1914-.**    **4.10791**
From Little Rock to Boston: the history of school desegregation / George R. Metcalf. — Westport, Conn.: Greenwood Press, 1983. x, 292 p.; 25 cm. — (Contributions to the study of education. 0196-707X; no. 8) Includes index. 1. School integration — United States — History. I. T. II. Series.
LC214.2.M46 1983    370.19/342 19    *LC* 82-15581    *ISBN* 0313234701

**Race and schooling in the city / edited by Adam Yarmolinsky,**    **4.10792**
**Lance Liebman, and Corinne S. Schelling.**
Cambridge, Mass.: Harvard University Press, 1981. ix, 279 p.; 25 cm. 1. School integration — United States 2. Discrimination in education — Law and legislation — United States. I. Yarmolinsky, Adam. II. Liebman, Lance. III. Schelling, Corinne Saposs.
LC214.2.R32    370.19/342 19    *LC* 80-20424    *ISBN* 0674745779

**School desegregation: past, present, and future / edited by**    **4.10793**
**Walter G. Stephan and Joe R. Feagin.**
New York: Plenum Press, c1980. xiv, 357 p.: ill.; 24 cm. — (Perspectives in social psychology) 1. School integration — United States — Addresses, essays, lectures. I. Stephan, Walter G. II. Feagin, Joe R.
LC214.2.S355    370.19/342 19    *LC* 79-23436    *ISBN* 0306403781

**Shades of Brown: new perspectives on school desegregation /**    **4.10794**
**edited by Derrick Bell.**
New York: Teachers College Press, Columbia University, 1980. x, 150 p.; 25 cm. 'Earlier versions of the essays ... were read at a symposium ... held at the Harvard Law School, in the Fall of 1978.' 1. School integration — United States — Addresses, essays, lectures. 2. Discrimination in education — Law and legislation — United States — Addresses, essays, lectures. I. Bell, Derrick, A.
LC214.2.S5    370.19/342/0973 19    *LC* 80-21877    *ISBN* 0807725951

**Weinberg, Meyer, 1920-.**    **4.10795**
The search for quality integrated education: policy and research on minority students in school and college / Meyer Weinberg. — Westport, Conn.: Greenwood Press, 1983. xv, 354 p.; 24 cm. — (Contributions to the study of education. 0196-707X; no. 7) Includes index. 1. School integration — United States 2. Educational equalization — United States. 3. Education, Urban — United States. 4. Minorities — Education — United States. I. T. II. Series.
LC214.2.W44 1983    370.19/342 19    *LC* 82-12016    *ISBN* 031323714X

**Willie, Charles Vert, 1927-.**    **4.10796**
Community politics and educational change: ten school systems under court order / Charles V. Willie, Susan L. Greenblatt. — New York: Longman, c1980. xvi, 351 p.: maps; 24 cm. 1. School integration — United States — Addresses, essays, lectures. 2. Education and state — United States — Addresses, essays, lectures. 3. Discrimination in education — Law and legislation — United States — Addresses, essays, lectures. I. Greenblatt, Susan L. joint author. II. T.
LC214.2.W53    370.19/342    *LC* 80-11076    *ISBN* 0582281474

**Willie, Charles Vert, 1927-.**    **4.10797**
The sociology of urban education: desegregation and integration / Charles Vert Willie. — Lexington, Mass.: Lexington Books, c1978. xv, 184 p.; 24 cm. 1. School integration — United States 2. Education, Urban — United States. I. T.
LC214.2.W54    370.19/348/0973    *LC* 78-4403    *ISBN* 0669023485

**Orfield, Gary.**    **4.10798**
Must we bus?: segregated schools and national policy / Gary Orfield. — Washington: Brookings Institution, c1978. xiv, 470 p.; 24 cm. 1. School integration — United States 2. School children — United States — Transportation. I. T.
LC214.5.O73    370.19/342    *LC* 77-91803    *ISBN* 0815766386

**Strategies for effective desegregation: lessons from research /**    **4.10799**
**Willis D. Hawley ... [et al.].**
Lexington, Mass.: Lexington Books, c1983. x, 210 p.; 24 cm. Includes index. 1. School integration — United States — Addresses, essays, lectures. I. Hawley, Willis D.
LC214.5.S73 1983    370.19/342 19    *LC* 82-47968    *ISBN* 0669057223

**Buell, Emmett H.**    **4.10800**
School desegregation and defended neighborhoods: the Boston controversy / Emmett H. Buell, Jr., with Richard A. Brisbin, Jr. — Lexington, Mass.: Lexington Books c1982. xiv, 202 p.: ill.; 24 cm. — (Lexington Books politics of education series.) 1. Busing for school integration — Massachusetts — Boston. I. Brisbin, Richard A. II. T. III. Series.
LC214.523.B67 B83    370.19/342 19    *LC* 78-19589    *ISBN* 0669026468

## LC215–238 Community and School

**Litwak, Eugene, 1925-.**    **4.10801**
School, family, and neighborhood: the theory and practice of school–community relations [by] Eugene Litwak and Henry J. Meyer. Cheryl Elise Mickelson, research associate. — New York: Columbia University Press, 1974. xiii, 300 p.; 24 cm. 1. Community and school 2. Home and school I. Meyer, Henry Joseph, 1913- joint author. II. T.
LC215.L52    370.19/31    *LC* 73-17274    *ISBN* 0231033540

**Fantini, Mario D.**     4.10802
Community control and the urban school [by] Mario Fantini, Marilyn Gittell [and] Richard Magat. Introd. by Kenneth B. Clark. — New York: Praeger Publishers, [1970] xix, 268 p.; 21 cm. — (Praeger paperbacks, P-281) 1. Community and school 2. Education, Urban I. Gittell, Marilyn. joint author. II. Magat, Richard. joint author. III. T.
LC219.F35 1970     370/.9173/2     *LC* 69-12706

**Lightfoot, Sara Lawrence.**     4.10803
Worlds apart: relationships between families and schools / Sara Lawrence Lightfoot. — New York: Basic Books, c1978. xiii, 257 p.; 22 cm. Includes index. 1. Home and school — United States. 2. Students — United States — Social conditions. I. T.
LC225.L53     370.19/31     *LC* 78-54506     *ISBN* 0465092446

**Universities in the urban crisis / Thomas P. Murphy, editor;**     4.10804
**foreword by Mancur Olson.**
New York: Dunellen Pub. Co.; Port Washington, N.Y.: distributed by Kennikat Press, c1975. xix, 418 p.; 23 cm. 1. Community and college — United States — Addresses, essays, lectures. 2. Education, Urban — United States — Addresses, essays, lectures. 3. Higher education and state — United States — Addresses, essays, lectures. I. Murphy, Thomas P., 1931-
LC238.U54     379     *LC* 73-89069     *ISBN* 0804670811

---

# LC251–291 Moral Education. Character Building

**Durkheim, Emile, 1858-1917.**     • 4.10805
Moral education: a study in the theory and application of the sociology of education / foreword by Paul Fauconnet; translated by Everett K. Wilson and Herman Schnurer; edited with an introd., by Everett K. Wilson. — [New York]: Free Press of Glencoe [1961] 288 p.; 22 cm. 1. Moral education I. T.
LC262 D813     *LC* 59-6815

**Howe, Leland W.**     4.10806
Personalizing education: values clarification and beyond / Leland W. Howe, Mary Martha Howe. — New York: Hart Pub. Co., [1975] 574 p.: ill.; 21 cm. Includes indexes. 1. Moral education I. Howe, Mary Martha, joint author. II. T.
LC268.H67     370.11/4     *LC* 74-27697     *ISBN* 0805511385

**Moral education ... it comes with the territory / edited by**     4.10807
**David Purpel & Kevin Ryan.**
Berkeley, Calif.: Distributed by McCutchan Pub. Corp., c1976. xix, 424 p.; 24 cm. 'A Phi Delta Kappa publication.' 1. Moral education — Addresses, essays, lectures. I. Purpel, David E. II. Ryan, Kevin.
LC268.M685     370.11/4     *LC* 76-18041     *ISBN* 0821115162

**Straughan, Roger.**     4.10808
Can we teach children to be good? / Roger Straughan. — London; Boston: Allen & Unwin, 1982. viii, 115 p.; 23 cm. — (Introductory studies in philosophy of education.) Includes index. 1. Moral education 2. Education — Philosophy 3. Education — Aims and objectives I. T. II. Series.
LC268.S8 1982     370.11/4 19     *LC* 82-11387     *ISBN* 0043701205

**The Hidden curriculum and moral education: deception or**     4.10809
**discovery? / edited by Henry Giroux and David Purpel.**
Berkeley, Calif.: McCutchan Pub. Corp., c1983. x, 425 p.; 24 cm. 1. Moral education — United States. 2. Education — United States — Curricula. I. Giroux, Henry A. II. Purpel, David E.
LC311.H5 1983     370.11/4/0973 19     *LC* 82-62034     *ISBN* 0821115197

**Donohue, John W., 1917-.**     4.10810
Catholicism and education / [by] John W. Donohue. — New York: Harper & Row, [1973] vii, 152 p.; 22 cm. 1. Catholic Church — Education I. T.
LC473.D64     377/.8/2     *LC* 73-1035

**Peshkin, Alan.**     4.10811
God's choice: the total world of a fundamentalist Christian school / Alan Peshkin. — Chicago: University of Chicago Press, 1986. x, 349 p.; 24 cm. Includes index. 1. Christian schools — United States — Case studies. 2. Fundamentalism — Case studies. I. T.
LC562.P47 1986     377/.0973 19     *LC* 85-24524     *ISBN* 0226661989

**Miller, Howard, 1941-.**     4.10812
The revolutionary college: American Presbyterian higher education, 1707–1837 / Howard Miller. New York: New York University Press, 1976. xxiii, 381 p.; ill.; 24 cm. (New York University series in education and socialization in

American history.) 1. Presbyterian Church in the U.S.A. — Education I. T. II. Series.
LC580.M48     377/.8/5     *LC* 75-27053     *ISBN* 0814754076

**Gartner, Lloyd P., 1927- comp.**     • 4.10813
Jewish education in the United States; a documentary history, edited, with an introd. and notes, by Lloyd P. Gartner. New York, Teachers College Press [c1969] xv, 224 p. 20 cm. (Classics in education, no. 41) 1. Jews — United States — Education — History — Sources. I. T.
LC741.G35     370/.973     *LC* 73-112708

**Gorelick, Sherry.**     4.10814
City College and the Jewish poor: education in New York, 1880–1924 / Sherry Gorelick. — New Brunswick, N.J.: Rutgers University Press, c1981. x, 269 p.: ill.; 24 cm. Includes index. 1. City University of New York. City College. 2. Jews — New York (N.Y.) — Education. 3. Jews — New York (N.Y.) — Economic conditions. 4. Occupational mobility — New York (N.Y.) I. T.
LC743.N5 G67     378/.00892407471 19     *LC* 80-22128     *ISBN* 081350905X

---

# LC1011–1021 Humanistic Education. Liberal Education

**Adler, Mortimer Jerome, 1902-.**     4.10815
Paideia problems and possibilities / Mortimer J. Adler, on behalf of the members of the Paideia Group. — New York: Macmillan; London: Collier Macmillan, 1983. xii, 113 p.; 22 cm. Second vol. of the author's trilogy; the 3rd of which is The Paideia program, and the 1st of which is The Paideia proposal. 1. Education, Humanistic — United States — Philosophy. 2. Education, Elementary — United States — Aims and objectives. 3. Education, Secondary — United States — Aims and objectives. I. T.
LC1011.A34 1983     370/.973 19     *LC* 83-12025     *ISBN* 0025002201

**Against mediocrity: the humanities in America's high schools /**     4.10816
**edited by Chester E. Finn, Jr., Diane Ravitch, Robert T.**
**Fancher; with a foreword by William Bennett.**
New York: Holmes & Meier, 1984. xi, 276 p.; 24 cm. 'A project of the Educational Excellence Network of Vanderbilt University's Institute for Public Policy Studies.' 1. Education, Humanistic — United States. 2. Humanities — Study and teaching (Secondary) — United States. I. Finn, Chester E., 1944- II. Ravitch, Diane. III. Fancher, Robert T. IV. Vanderbilt Institute for Public Policy Studies.
LC1011.A42 1984     373.19/8/0973 19     *LC* 83-22819     *ISBN* 084190944X

**Blanshard, Brand, 1892-1987.**     4.10817
The uses of a liberal education and other talks to students / edited by Eugene Freeman. — [1st ed.]. — La Salle, Ill.: Open Court Pub. Co., 1974 (c1973). xxi, 415 p.; 24 cm. 1. Education, Humanistic 2. Education — Philosophy I. T.
LC1011.B55     370.11/2     *LC* 73-76196     *ISBN* 0875481221

**Boyer, Ernest L.**     4.10818
A quest for common learning: the aims of general education / Ernest L. Boyer & Arthur Levine. — Washington, D.C.: Carnegie Foundation for the Advancement of Teaching, [1981] ix, 68 p.; 23 cm. — (Carnegie Foundation essay). 1. Education, Humanistic — United States. 2. Education — United States — Aims and objectives. I. Levine, Arthur. II. T. III. Series.
LC1011.B64     370.11/0973 19     *LC* 81-66307     *ISBN* 0931050189

**Carnegie Foundation for the Advancement of Teaching.**     4.10819
Common learning: a Carnegie colloquium on general education. — Washington, D.C.: Carnegie Foundation for the Advancement of Teaching, [c1981] x, 146 p.; 24 cm. 1. Education, Humanistic — United States — Congresses. 2. Education, Higher — United States — Congresses I. Colloquium on Common Learning (1981: University of Chicago) II. T.
LC 1011 C73 1981

**Hicks, David V.**     4.10820
Norms & nobility: a treatise on education / David V. Hicks. — New York: Praeger, 1981. vii, 167 p.; 24 cm. Includes index. 1. Classical education 2. Classical education — Philosophy. 3. Classical education — Curricula. I. T. II. Title: Norms and nobility.
LC1011.H525     370/.1 19     *LC* 81-2447     *ISBN* 0030592739

**Hutchins, Robert Maynard, 1899-.**     • 4.10821
Great books: the foundation of a liberal education. — New York: Simon and Schuster, 1954. 115 p.; 22 cm. 1. Education, Humanistic I. T.
LC1011.H85     *LC* 54-5466

**Kimball, Bruce A., 1951-.**      **4.10822**
Orators & philosophers: a history of the idea of liberal education / Bruce A. Kimball; with a foreword by Joseph L. Featherstone. — New York: Teachers College, Columbia University, c1986. xix, 293 p.; 24 cm. 1. Education, Humanistic — Philosophy — History. 2. Philosophy, Ancient 3. Philosophy, Medieval 4. Learning and scholarship I. T. II. Title: Orators and philosophers.
LC1011.K56 1986     370.11/2 19     LC 85-22272     ISBN 0807727903

**Roszak, Theodore, 1933-.**      **• 4.10823**
The dissenting academy, edited by Theodore Roszak. — New York: Pantheon Books, [1968] x, 304 p.; 22 cm. 1. Education, Humanistic — Addresses, essays, lectures. I. T.
LC1011.R7     378/.008     LC 68-10254

**Van Doren, Mark, 1894-1972.**      **• 4.10824**
Liberal education. With a new pref. by the author. — Boston: Beacon Press, [1959] 178 p.; 21 cm. — (Beacon paperback no. 86) 1. Education, Humanistic I. T.
LC1011.V3 1959     370.1     LC 59-10739

**Winter, David G., 1939-.**      **4.10825**
A new case for the liberal arts / David G. Winter, David C. McClelland, Abigail J. Stewart. — 1st ed. — San Francisco: Jossey-Bass, 1981. xxii, 247 p.: ill.; 24 cm. — (Jossey-Bass series in higher education.) Includes index. 1. Education, Humanistic I. McClelland, David Clarence. II. Stewart, Abigail J. III. T. IV. Series.
LC1011.W53     370.11/2 19     LC 81-81963     ISBN 0875895026

**Wirth, Arthur G.**      **4.10826**
Education in the technological society; the vocational–liberal studies controversy in the early twentieth century [by] Arthur G. Wirth. — Scranton [Pa.]: Intext Educational Publishers, [1971, c1972] xi, 259 p.; 23 cm. — (The Intext series in foundations of education) 1. Education, Humanistic — U.S. — 1965- 2. Vocational education — U.S. I. T.
LC1011.W55     370.11/2/0973     LC 78-177303     ISBN 0700224149

**Bennett, William John, 1943-.**      **4.10827**
To reclaim a legacy: a report on the humanities in higher education / William J. Bennett. — Washington, D.C.: National Endowment for the Humanities, [1984] iii, 32 p.; 23 cm. 'November 1984.' Item 831-B-1 1. Education, Humanistic — United States. 2. Humanities — Study and teaching (Higher) — United States. I. National Endowment for the Humanities. II. T.
LC1021.B46 1984     370.11/2/0973 19     LC 85-600999

# LC1030–1099 Other Special Types of Education

**Grant, Gerald.**      **4.10828**
On competence: a critical analysis of competence–based reforms in higher education / Gerald Grant ... [et al.]. — 1st ed. — San Francisco: Jossey-Bass Publishers, 1979. xxii, 592 p.; 24 cm. — (The Jossey-Bass series in higher education) Includes indexes. 1. Competency based education — United States. 2. Education, Higher — United States. I. T.
LC1032.O5     378.73     LC 79-83572     ISBN 0875894054

**Adler, Mortimer Jerome, 1902-.**      **4.10829**
The Paideia program: an educational syllabus / Mortimer J. Adler; essays by the Paideia Group; preface and introduction by Mortimer J. Adler. — 1st Macmillan paperbacks ed. — New York: Macmillan; London: Collier Macmillan, 1984. xii, 238 p.; 21 cm. Third vol. of the author's trilogy; the 1st of which is The Paideia proprosal, and the 2nd of which is Paideia problems and possibilities. 1. Basic education — United States — Curricula — Addresses, essays, lectures. I. Paideia Group. II. T.
LC1035.6.A35 1984     375/.00973 19     LC 84-14338     ISBN 0020130406

**Essays on career education and English, K–12 / edited by**      **4.10830**
**Marjorie M. Kaiser.**
Urbana, Ill.: Project on Career Education, National Council of Teachers of English: distributed by NCTE, 1980. xii, 132 p.; 23 cm. 1. Career education — United States — Addresses, essays, lectures. 2. English language — Study and teaching — United States — Addresses, essays, lectures. I. Kaiser, Marjorie M., 1933- II. National Council of Teachers of English. Project on Career Education.
LC1037.5.E83     370.11/3/0973     LC 79-21408     ISBN 0814115853

**Lazerson, Marvin. comp.**      **4.10831**
American education and vocationalism: a documentary history, 1870-1970. Edited, with an introd. and notes, by Marvin Lazerson and W. Norton Grubb. New York, Teachers College Press, Columbia University [1974] xii, 176 p. 19

cm. (Classics in education, no. 48) 1. Vocational education — United States — History — Addresses, essays, lectures. I. Grubb, W. Norton. joint comp. II. T.
LC1045.L36     370.11/3/0973     LC 73-87511

**Work, youth, and schooling: historical perspectives on**      **4.10832**
**vocationalism in American education / edited by Harvey Kantor**
**and David B. Tyack; [contributors, James D. Anderson ... et**
**al.].**
Stanford, Calif.: Stanford University Press, 1982. x, 367 p.; 23 cm. 'Product of a conference sponsored by the National Institute of Education ... and held at the Boys Town Center for the Study of Youth Development, Stanford University, on August 17-18, 1979'–P. v. 1. Vocational education — United States — Congresses. 2. Industry and education — United States — Congresses. I. Anderson, James D. II. Kantor, Harvey. III. Tyack, David B. IV. National Institute of Education (U.S.)
LC1045.W6 1982     370.11/3/0973 19     LC 81-50788     ISBN 0804711216

**Cheit, Earl Frank.**      **4.10833**
The useful arts and the liberal tradition / by Earl F. Cheit. — New York: McGraw-Hill, [1975] xviii, 166 p.: ill.; 23 cm. 'Sponsored by the Carnegie Commission on Higher Education.' Includes index. 1. Professional education — United States 2. Education, Humanistic — United States. I. T.
LC1059.C48     LC1059 C48.     378/.01/3     LC 74-23876     ISBN 0070101086

**Carnoy, Martin.**      **4.10834**
Schooling and work in the democratic state / Martin Carnoy and Henry M. Levin. — Stanford, Calif.: Stanford University Press, 1985. 307 p.; 23 cm. Includes index. 1. Industry and education — United States — Forecasting. 2. Educational equalization — United States. 3. High school graduates — Employment — United States. I. Levin, Henry M. II. T.
LC1085.C37 1985     370.19/3 19     LC 83-40697     ISBN 0804712425

**Wirtz, Willard, 1912-.**      **4.10835**
The boundless resource: a prospectus for an education–work policy / Willard Wirtz and the National Manpower Institute. — Washington: New Republic Book Co., 1975. xiii, 205 p.; 22 cm. 1. Industry and education — United States. 2. Adult education — United States. I. National Manpower Institute. II. T.
LC1085.W57     370.11/3     LC 75-30556     ISBN 0915220075

**Tiedt, Pamela L.**      **4.10836**
Multicultural teaching: a handbook of activities, information, and resources / Pamela L. Tiedt and Iris M. Tiedt. — Boston: Allyn and Bacon, c1979. x, 353 p.: ill.; 25 cm. 'Resources for multilingual/multicultural approaches to teaching': p. 277-323. Includes index. 1. Intercultural education — United States. 2. Language arts (Elementary) I. Tiedt, Iris M. joint author. II. T.
LC1099.T53     372.6/044     LC 78-25870     ISBN 0205064450

# LC1390–5163 Education of Special Classes of Persons

**Chandos, John.**      **4.10837**
Boys together: English public schools, 1800–1864 / John Chandos. — New Haven: Yale University Press, 1984. 411 p., [16] p. of plates: ill.; 24 cm. Includes index. 1. Boys — Education — England — History — 19th century. 2. Public schools, Endowed (Great Britain) — History — 19th century. I. T.
LC1390.C43 1984     373.2/22/0941 19     LC 84-40192     ISBN 0300032153

## LC1401–2571 Women

**Frazier, Nancy.**      **4.10838**
Sexism in school and society [by] Nancy Frazier [and] Myra Sadker. New York, Harper & Row [1973] xv, 215 p. illus. 21 cm. (Critical issues in education) 1. Women — Education 2. Sex differences in education 3. Sexism I. Sadker, Myra. joint author. II. T.
LC1481.F72     376     LC 72-11496     ISBN 006042172X

**Howe, Florence.**      **4.10839**
Myths of coeducation: selected essays, 1964–1983 / Florence Howe. — Bloomington: Indiana University Press, c1984. xii, 306 p.; 25 cm. 1. Women — Education — United States — Addresses, essays, lectures. 2. Women's studies — United States — Addresses, essays, lectures. 3. Feminism — United States — Addresses, essays, lectures. 4. Sex discrimination in education — United States — Addresses, essays, lectures. 5. Afro-Americans — Education — United States — Addresses, essays, lectures. I. T.
LC1752.H69 1984     376 19     LC 84-47702     ISBN 0253339669

Solomon, Barbara Miller.                                    4.10840
In the company of educated women: a history of women and higher education
in America / Barbara Miller Solomon. — New Haven: Yale University Press,
c1985. xxi, 298 p, [16] p. of plates: ports.; 24 cm. Includes index. 1. Women —
Education (Higher) — United States — History. 2. Women's colleges —
United States — History. 3. Women college students — United States —
History. I. T.
LC1752.S65 1985      376/.973 19      *LC* 84-19681      *ISBN* 0300033141

Dziech, Billie Wright, 1941-.                              4.10841
The lecherous professor: sexual harassment on campus / Billie Wright Dziech,
Linda Weiner. — Boston: Beacon Press, c1984. vii, 219 p.; 22 cm. Includes
index. 1. Women college students — United States. 2. Sexual harassment of
women — United States. 3. College teachers — United States 4. Sexual
harassment — Law and legislation — United States. I. Weiner, Linda. II. T.
LC1756.D97 1984      370.19/345 19      *LC* 82-73960      *ISBN*
0807031003

Feldman, Saul D.                                          4.10842
Escape from the doll's house: women in graduate and professional school
education / by Saul D. Feldman; a report prepared for the Carnegie
Commission on Higher Education. — New York: McGraw-Hill, [1974, c1973]
xvi, 208 p.: forms.; 24 cm. A revision of the author's thesis, University of
Washington. 1. Universities and colleges — United States — Graduate work of
women. 2. Professional education of women — United States. I. Carnegie
Commission on Higher Education. II. T. III. Title: Women in graduate and
professional school education.
LC1756.F44 1974      376/.65      *LC* 73-12829      *ISBN* 0070100691

Horowitz, Helen Lefkowitz.                                4.10843
Alma mater: design and experience in the women's colleges from their
nineteenth–century beginnings to the 1930s / Helen Lefkowitz Horowitz. — 1st
ed. — New York: Knopf, 1984. xxii, 420 p.: ill.; 25 cm. Includes index.
1. Women's colleges — United States — History. I. T.
LC1756.H67 1984      376/.973 19      *LC* 84-47506      *ISBN* 0394534395

Komarovsky, Mirra, 1906-.                                 4.10844
Women in college: shaping new feminine identities / Mirra Komarovsky. —
New York: Basic Books, c1985. x, 355 p.; 22 cm. Includes index. 1. Women —
Education (Higher) — Social aspects — United States — Case studies.
2. Women's colleges — Social aspects — United States — Case studies.
3. Vocational interests — United States — Case studies. 4. Sex role — United
States — Case studies. I. T.
LC1756.K65 1985      376/.65/0973 19      *LC* 84-45307      *ISBN*
0465091989

Fletcher, Sheila.                                         4.10845
Feminists and bureaucrats: a study in the development of girls' education in the
nineteenth century / Sheila Fletcher. — Cambridge; New York: Cambridge
University Press, 1980. viii, 249 p.; 24 cm. Includes index. 1. Women —
Education — England — History. 2. Public schools, Endowed (Great Britain)
3. Education and state — England — History. I. T.
LC2052.F56      376/.942 19      *LC* 79-20630      *ISBN* 0521228808

# LC2601–2611 Education in Developing Countries

Curle, Adam.                                              4.10846
Educational problems of developing societies, with case studies of Ghana,
Pakistan, and Nigeria. Expanded and updated ed. New York, Praeger [1973] ix,
200 p. 25 cm. (Praeger special studies in international economics and
development) First published in 1969 under title: Educational problems of
developing societies, with case studies of Ghana and Pakistan. 1. Education —
Developing countries — Case studies. 2. Education — Ghana — Case studies.
3. Education — Pakistan — Case studies. 4. Education — Nigeria — Case
studies. I. T.
LC2605.C86 1973      370/.9172/4      *LC* 72-90663

The Education dilemma: policy issues for developing countries in     4.10847
the 1980s / edited by John Simmons; with a foreword by
Torsten Husen.
1st ed. — Oxford; New York: Pergamon Press , 1980. xv, 262 p.; 22 cm.
(Pergamon international library of science, technology, engineering, and social
studies) 1. Educational planning — Developing countries. 2. Labor supply —
Developing countries 3. Migration, Internal — Developing countries
I. Simmons, John, 1938-
LC2605.E32 1980      379/.15/091724      *LC* 79-40071      *ISBN*
0080243045

## LC2667–2698 Hispanic Americans

Durán, Richard P.                                         4.10848
Hispanics' education and background: predictors of college achievement /
Richard P. Durán. — New York: College Entrance Examination Board: Copies
ordered from College Board Publications, 1983. x, 150 p.: ill.; 23 cm. Includes
index. 1. Hispanic Americans — Education (Secondary) — United States.
2. Hispanic Americans — United States — Social conditions. 3. Prediction of
scholastic success 4. Universities and colleges — United States — Entrance
examinations. I. T.
LC2670.4.D87 1983      373/.08968073 19      *LC* 83-70185      *ISBN*
0874471575

The Puerto Rican community and its children on the mainland:     4.10849
a source book for teachers, social workers, and other
professionals / [edited] by Francesco Cordasco and Eugene
Bucchioni.
3rd rev. ed. — Metuchen, N.J.: Scarecrow Press, 1982. xi, 457 p.: ill.; 23 cm.
Includes index. 1. Puerto Ricans — Education — United States.
2. Bilingualism 3. Students — United States — Socioeconomic status.
4. Education, Urban — United States. I. Cordasco, Francesco, 1920-
II. Bucchioni, Eugene.
LC2692.P8 1982      305.8/687295/073 19      *LC* 81-21250      *ISBN*
0810815060

## LC2701–2913 Afro–Americans

Ballard, Allen B.                                         4.10850
The education of Black folk; the Afro–American struggle for knowledge in
white America [by] Allen B. Ballard. [1st ed.] New York, Harper & Row [1973]
vi, 173 p. 22 cm. 'Portions of this work appeared in Change.' 1. Afro–
Americans — Education — History. I. T.
LC2741.B34 1973      378.73      *LC* 73-156504      *ISBN* 0060102225

Hale-Benson, Janice E., 1948-.                            4.10851
Black children: their roots, culture, and learning styles / Janice E. Hale. —
Provo, Utah: Brigham Young University Press, c1982. xv, 191 p.: ill.; 23 cm.
Includes index. 1. Afro-American children — Education. 2. Afro-Americans
— Social conditions I. T.
LC2771.H34 1982      371.8/2 19      *LC* 82-9627      *ISBN* 0842520929

Paley, Vivian Gussin, 1929-.                              4.10852
White teacher / Vivian Gussin Paley. — Cambridge: Harvard University Press,
1979. xvi, 140 p.; 22 cm. 1. Afro-Americans — Education 2. Kindergarten
3. Classroom management I. T.
LC2771.P34      371.9/7/96073      *LC* 78-9841      *ISBN* 0674951859

Rist, Ray C.                                              4.10853
The urban school: a factory for failure; a study of education in American society
[by] Ray C. Rist. Cambridge, Mass., MIT Press [1973] xv, 265 p. 24 cm.
1. Afro-Americans — Education 2. Education, Urban — United States. I. T.
LC2771.R57      372.9/73      *LC* 73-15580      *ISBN* 0262180642

Black dialects & reading. Edited by Bernice E. Cullinan.     4.10854
Margaret Kocher, linguistic consultant.
Urbana, Ill., ERIC Clearinghouse on Reading and Communication Skills
[1974] x, 198 p. illus. 24 cm. Papers presented at a conference held in May 1972
in New York and sponsored by the Language and Reading Commission, New
York University. 1. Afro-Americans — Education — Reading — Congresses.
2. Afro-Americans — Language — Congresses. 3. English language in the
United States — Dialects — Congresses. I. Cullinan, Bernice E. ed. II. New
York University. Language and Reading Commission.
LC2778.R4 B52      428/.4/2      *LC* 73-88933      *ISBN* 0814100572

Black colleges in America: challenge, development, survival /     4.10855
Charles V. Willie and Ronald R. Edmonds, editors.
New York: Teachers College Press, c1978. xii, 292 p.; 23 cm. 1. Afro-American
universities and colleges — Addresses, essays, lectures. I. Willie, Charles Vert,
1927- II. Edmonds, Ronald R., 1935-
LC2781.B44      378.73      *LC* 78-17147      *ISBN* 0807725285

Gurin, Patricia.                                          4.10856
Black consciousness, identity, and achievement: a study of students in
historically Black colleges / Patricia Gurin, Edgar Epps. — New York: Wiley,
[1975] xiv, 545 p.: ill.; 23 cm. Includes indexes. 1. Afro-American college
students 2. Afro-Americans — Race identity I. Epps, Edgar G., 1929- joint
author. II. T.
LC2781.G79      378.1/98/1      *LC* 75-5847      *ISBN* 047133670X

Howard University. Institute for the Study of Educational     4.10857
Policy.
Equal educational opportunity for Blacks in U.S. higher education: an
assessment / Institute for the Study of Educational Policy, Howard University.
— Washington: Published for ISEP by Howard University Press, 1976. xxxiii,

330 p.: ill.; 23 cm. 1. Afro-American college students — United States. 2. Educational equalization — United States. I. T.
LC2781.H68 1976     378     *LC* 75-43488     *ISBN* 0882580728

**Jones, Ann, 1937-.**       **4.10858**
Uncle Tom's campus. — New York: Praeger, [1973] ix, 225 p.; 22 cm. 1. Afro-Americans — Education (Higher) I. T.
LC2781.J65     378/.008996073 19     *LC* 72-83005

**Sowell, Thomas, 1930-.**       **4.10859**
Black education: myths and tragedies. New York, McKay [1972] x, 338 p. 22 cm. 1. Afro-Americans — Education (Higher) 2. Education, Higher — United States. I. T.
LC2781.S68     378.73     *LC* 70-188267

**Stikes, C. Scully, 1945-.**       **4.10860**
Black students in higher education / C. Scully Stikes. — Carbondale: Southern Illinois University Press, c1984. xiv, 180 p.; 23 cm. Includes index. 1. Afro-Americans — Education (Higher) 2. Afro-American college students — Attitudes. 3. Afro-American college students — Social conditions. I. T.
LC2781.S74 1984     378/.1982 19     *LC* 83-20154     *ISBN* 0809310953

**Thompson, Daniel C. (Daniel Calbert)**       **4.10861**
Private Black colleges at the crossroads / [by] Daniel C. Thompson. — Westport, Conn.: Greenwood Press [1973] xi, 308 p.; 21 cm. (Contributions in Afro-American and African studies. no. 13) 1. Afro-American universities and colleges 2. Private universities and colleges — United States. I. T. II. Series.
LC2781.T46     378.73     *LC* 72-841     *ISBN* 0837164109

**Blackwell, James Edward, 1925-.**       **4.10862**
Mainstreaming outsiders: the production of Black professionals / James E. Blackwell. — Bayside, N.Y.: General Hall, c1981. x, 345 p.; 24 cm. Includes 53 tables and 2 indexes. 1. Afro-Americans — Professional education 2. Afro-American college graduates — Employment. I. T.
LC2785.B55     378/.00896073 19     *LC* 81-82121     *ISBN* 0930390393

**Bullock, Henry Allen.**       **• 4.10863**
A history of Negro education in the South: from 1619 to the present. — Cambridge, Mass.: Harvard University Press, 1967. xi, 339 p.: ill.; 25 cm. 1. Afro-Americans — Education — Southern States I. T.
LC2801.B9     370/.975     *LC* 67-20873

**Clark, Reginald.**       **4.10864**
Family life and school achievement: why poor black children succeed or fail / Reginald Clark. — Chicago: University of Chicago Press, 1983. xiii, 249 p.; 24 cm. 1. Afro-Americans — Education 2. Home and school — United States. 3. Family — United States 4. Academic achievement. I. T.
LC2801.C56 1983     370/.890973 19     *LC* 83-3481     *ISBN* 0226107698

**Du Bois, W. E. B. (William Edward Burghardt), 1868-1963.**       **4.10865**
The education of Black people; ten critiques, 1906–1960. Edited by Herbert Aptheker. Amherst, University of Massachusetts Press, 1973. xii, 171 p. 24 cm. 1. Afro-Americans — Education — Addresses, essays, lectures. I. T.
LC2801.D79 1973     370.11/2     *LC* 72-90495

**Foner, Philip Sheldon, 1910-.**       **4.10866**
Three who dared: Prudence Crandall, Margaret Douglass, Myrtilla Miner: champions of antebellum Black education / Philip S. Foner and Josephine F. Pacheco. — Westport, Conn.: Greenwood Press, 1984. xviii, 234 p.: ports.; 22 cm. — (Contributions in women's studies. 0147-104X; no. 47) Includes index. 1. Crandall, Prudence, 1803-1890. 2. Douglass, Margaret. 3. Miner, Myrtilla, 1815-1864. 4. Afro-Americans — Education — History — 19th century. 5. Slavery — United States — Anti-slavery movements. 6. Women educators — United States — Biography. I. Pacheco, Josephine F. II. T. III. Series.
LC2801.F57 1984     370/.8996073 19     *LC* 83-12830     *ISBN* 0313235848

**Holmes, Dwight Oliver Wendell, 1877-.**       **• 4.10867**
The evolution of the Negro college. New York, AMS Press [1970] xi, 221 p. 23 cm. Reprint of the 1934 ed. 1. Afro-Americans — Education 2. Afro-American universities and colleges — United States. I. T.
LC2801.H57 1970     378.73     *LC* 74-128993     *ISBN* 0404001726

**Jones, Jacqueline, 1948-.**       **4.10868**
Soldiers of light and love: northern teachers and Georgia blacks, 1865–1873 / Jacqueline Jones. — Chapel Hill: University of North Carolina Press, c1980. xiii, 273 p.; 24 cm. (The Fred W. Morrison series in Southern studies) Includes index. 1. American Missionary Association — History — 19th century. 2. Freedmen in Georgia — Education — History — 19th century. 3. Teachers — Georgia — History — 19th century. 4. Reconstruction — Georgia. I. T.
LC2801.J645     975.8/041     *LC* 79-27129     *ISBN* 0807814350

**Mohraz, Judy Jolley.**       **4.10869**
The separate problem: case studies of Black education in the North, 1900–1930 / Judy Jolley Mohraz. — Westport, Conn.: Greenwood Press, 1979. xvi, 165 p.;

22 cm. — (Contributions in Afro-American and African studies. no. 42 0069-9624) Includes index. 1. Afro-Americans — Education — History. 2. Segregation in education — United States — History. I. T. II. Series.
LC2801.M6     370/.973     *LC* 78-4026     *ISBN* 031320411X

**Morris, Robert Charles, 1942-.**       **4.10870**
Reading, 'riting, and reconstruction: the education of freedmen in the South, 1861–1870 / Robert C. Morris. — Chicago: University of Chicago Press, 1982 (c1981). xv, 341, 9 p.: ill.; 22 cm. Includes index. 1. Afro-Americans — Education — History. 2. Freedmen — Education — History. 3. Reconstruction I. T.
LC2801.M64     371.97/96073 19     *LC* 80-25370     *ISBN* 0226539288

**Sarratt, Reed.**       **• 4.10871**
The ordeal of desegregation; the first decade. [1st ed.] New York, Harper and Row [1966] x, 374 p. 1. Segregation in education 2. Education — Southern States I. T.
LC2801 S26     *LC* 64-25152

**Sowell, Thomas, 1930-.**       **4.10872**
Education: assumptions versus history: collected papers / Thomas Sowell. — Stanford, Calif.: Hoover Institution Press, Stanford University, c1986. x, 203 p.; 23 cm. 1. Afro-Americans — Education — History — 20th century. 2. Discrimination in education — United States — History — 20th century. 3. College integration — United States — History — 20th century. I. T.
LC2801.S64 1986     370.19/34/0973 19     *LC* 85-18131     *ISBN* 0817981128

**Spivey, Donald.**       **4.10873**
Schooling for the new slavery: Black industrial education, 1868–1915 / Donald Spivey. — Westport, Conn.: Greenwood Press, 1978. xii, 162 p.; 22 cm. — (Contributions in Afro-American and African studies. no. 38 0069-9624) Includes index. 1. Afro-Americans — Education — History. 2. Manual training — United States — History. I. T. II. Series.
LC2801.S65     371.9/7/96073     *LC* 77-87974     *ISBN* 0313200513

**Weis, Lois.**       **4.10874**
Between two worlds: Black students in an urban community college / Lois Weis. — Boston: Routledge & Kegan Paul, 1985. p. cm. — (Critical social thought.) Includes index. 1. Afro-Americans — Education (Higher) — United States — Case studies. 2. Community colleges — United States — Case studies. 3. Education, Urban — United States — Case studies. 4. Culture conflict — United States — Case studies. I. T. II. Series.
LC2801.W36 1985     378/.1982 19     *LC* 84-24960     *ISBN* 0710099800

**Wolters, Raymond, 1938-.**       **4.10875**
The new Negro on campus: Black college rebellions of the 1920s / Raymond Wolters. — Princeton, N.J.: Princeton University Press, [1975] viii, 370 p.; 23 cm. 1. Afro-American universities and colleges — History. I. T.
LC2801.W57     378.73     *LC* 74-4662     *ISBN* 069104628X

**Franklin, Vincent P.**       **4.10876**
The education of Black Philadelphia: the social and educational history of a minority community, 1900–1950 / Vincent P. Franklin. — Philadelphia: University of Pennsylvania Press, 1979. xxi, 298 p.: ill.; 24 cm. Includes index. 1. Afro-Americans — Education — Pennsylvania — Philadelphia 2. Philadelphia (Pa.) — Race relations. I. T.
LC2802.P4 F72     370/.9748/11     *LC* 79-5045     *ISBN* 0812277694

**Vaughn, William Preston.**       **4.10877**
Schools for all; the Blacks & public education in the South, 1865–1877. [Lexington] University Press of Kentucky [1974] ix, 180 p. 24 cm. 'A Phi Alpha Theta award book.' 1. Afro-Americans — Education — Southern States — History. I. T.
LC2802.S9 V38     370/.975     *LC* 73-86408     *ISBN* 0813113121

**Homel, Michael W. (Michael Wallace), 1944-.**       **4.10878**
Down from equality: Black Chicagoans and the public schools, 1920–41 / Michael W. Homel. — Urbana: University of Illinois Press, c1984. xiii, 219 p.: ill.; 24 cm. — (Blacks in the New World.) Includes index. 1. Afro-American children — Education — Illinois — Chicago — History. 2. School integration — Illinois — Chicago — History. I. T. II. Series.
LC2803.C5 H65 1984     370/.9773/11 19     *LC* 83-6893     *ISBN* 0252009819

**Kohl, Herbert R.**       **• 4.10879**
36 children / [by] Herbert Kohl; illus. by Robert George Jackson, III. — [New York]: New American Library [1967] 227 p.: ill.; 22 cm. Includes letters, stories, etc. by the author's students in an East Harlem elementary school. 1. Afro-Americans — Education — New York (N.Y.) 2. Afro-American children's writings 3. Harlem (New York, N.Y.). I. T.
LC2803.H3 K6 1967     372.9/7471     *LC* 67-26240

Campbell, Robert, 1922-.    **4.10880**
The chasm; the life and death of a great experiment in ghetto education. With an introd. by James Baldwin. Boston, Houghton Mifflin, 1974. xx, 251 p. 22 cm. 1. Afro-Americans — Education — New York (N.Y.) 2. Socially handicapped children — Education — New York (City) 3. Education — Experimental methods I. T.
LC2803.N5 C35    370/.8996073 19    *LC* 74-3077    *ISBN* 0395185025

Richardson, Joe Martin.    **4.10881**
A history of Fisk University, 1865–1946 / Joe M. Richardson. — University: University of Alabama Press, c1980. 227 p.: ill.; 25 cm. Includes index. 1. Fisk University — History. I. T.
LC2851.F52 R5    378.768/55    *LC* 79-9736    *ISBN* 0817300155

Campbell, Clarice T.    **4.10882**
Mississippi, the view from Tougaloo / Clarice T. Campbell and Oscar Allan Rogers, Jr. — Jackson: University Press of Mississippi, c1979. xii, 276 p., [17] leaves of plates: ill.; 23 cm. Includes index. 1. Tougaloo College. I. Rogers, Oscar A., joint author. II. T.
LC2851.T6 C35    378.762/51    *LC* 78-10229    *ISBN* 0878050914

# LC3001–3501 Asian Americans. Other Asian Peoples

The Education of Asian and Pacific Americans: historical    **4.10883**
perspectives and prescriptions for the future / edited by Don T. Nakanishi and Marsha Hirano–Nakanishi.
Phoenix, AZ: Oryx Press, 1983. ix, 141 p.: ill.; 24 cm. 1. Asian Americans — Education — United States — Addresses, essays, lectures. 2. Hawaiians — Education — Hawaii — Addresses, essays, lectures. I. Nakanishi, Don T. II. Hirano-Nakanishi, Marsha.
LC3015.E38 1983    371.97/95/073 19    *LC* 82-22257    *ISBN* 0897740300

Low, Victor.    **4.10884**
The unimpressible race: a century of educational struggle by the Chinese in San Francisco / Victor Low. — San Francisco: East/West Pub. Co., c1982. xix, 236 p.: ill.; 23 cm. Includes indexes. 1. Chinese Americans — Education — California — San Francisco — History. I. T.
LC3075.S26 L68 1982    370/.899510794/61 19    *LC* 82-71121    *ISBN* 0934788049

Scott, Rachel.    **4.10885**
Wedding man is nicer than cats, Miss: a teacher at work with immigrant children. — New York: St. Martin's Press, 1972 (c1971) 192 p.; 23 cm. 1. Pakistanis — Great Britain — Education. 2. East Indians — Great Britain — Education. I. T.
LC3485.G7 S36 1971b    370.19/342    *LC* 73-177263

Ashton-Warner, Sylvia.    • **4.10886**
Teacher. New York: Simon and Schuster, 1963. 224 p.: ill.; 24 cm. Autobiographical. 1. Ashton-Warner, Sylvia. 2. Maoris — Education. 3. Education — Experimental methods 4. Teachers — New Zealand — Biography. I. T.
LC3501.M3 A8    371.9893    *LC* 63-8659

# LC3701–3743 Linguistic Minorities. Bilingual Schools

Education and colonialism / [edited by] Philip G. Altbach, Gail    **4.10887**
P. Kelly.
New York: Longman, c1978. viii, 372 p.; 21 cm. (Educational policy, planning, and theory) Includes index. 1. Minorities — Education — United States — History. 2. Women — Education — United States — History. 3. Education — Developing countries I. Altbach, Philip G. II. Kelly, Gail Paradise.
LC3719.E36    371.9/7    *LC* 77-22777    *ISBN* 0582280036

Miller, Jane, 1932-.    **4.10888**
Many voices: bilingualism, culture, and education / Jane Miller. — London; Boston: Routledge & Kegan Paul, 1983. xi, 212 p.; 23 cm. Includes index. 1. Education, Bilingual 2. Bilingualism I. T.
LC3719.M54 1983    371.97 19    *LC* 82-20433    *ISBN* 0710093314

Olivas, Michael A.    **4.10889**
The dilemma of access: minorities in two year colleges / Michael A. Olivas, with the assistance of Nan Alimba. — Washington: Published for ISEP by Howard University Press, 1979. xv, 259 p.; 23 cm. Includes index. 1. Minorities — Education, Higher — United States. 2. Junior colleges —

United States. I. Alimba, Nan. joint author. II. Howard University. Institute for the Study of Educational Policy. III. T.
LC3727.O43    378.1/543/0973    *LC* 79-2575    *ISBN* 0882580795

Ambert, Alba N., 1946-.    **4.10890**
Bilingual education: a sourcebook / Alba N. Ambert, Sarah E. Melendez. — New York: Garland Pub., 1985. xv, 340 p.; 23 cm. (Garland reference library of social science; vol. 197) 1. Education, Bilingual — United States. I. Melendez, Sarah E., 1941- II. T.
LC3731.A65 1985    371.97 19    *LC* 83-48211    *ISBN* 0824090551

Andersson, Theodore, 1903-.    **4.10891**
Bilingual schooling in the United States: history, rationale, implications, and planning / by Theodore Andersson and Mildred Boyer; with a new foreword and supplementary bibliography by Francesco Cordasco. — Detroit: B. Ethridge Books, 1976. 2 v.: ill.; 24 cm. 'The bilingual task was performed by the Southwest Educational Development Laboratory.' Reprint of the 1970 ed. published by Southwest Educational Development Laboratory, Austin, Tex. 1. Education, Bilingual — United States. 2. Bilingualism — Bibliography. I. Boyer, Mildred, 1926- II. Southwest Educational Development Laboratory. III. T.
LC3731.A75 1976    371.9/7    *LC* 76-5907    *ISBN* 0879170506

Astin, Alexander W.    **4.10892**
Minorities in American higher education / Alexander W. Astin. — 1st ed. — San Francisco: Jossey-Bass, 1982. xix, 263 p.; 24 cm. — (Jossey-Bass series in higher education.) Includes index. 1. Minorities — Education (Higher) — United States. I. T. II. Series.
LC3731.A83 1982    371.97/0973 19    *LC* 81-48663    *ISBN* 0875895239

Beyond desegregation: urgent issues in the education of    **4.10893**
minorities: papers from the series of seminars on critical problems and issues in the education of minorities / cosponsored by the College Board and Educational Testing Service; Will Antell ... [et al.].
New York: College Entrance Examination Board, 1978. x, 76 p.; 28 cm. 1. Minorities — Education — United States. I. Antell, Will. II. College Entrance Examination Board. III. Educational Testing Service.
LC3731.B49    371.9/7/0973    *LC* 77-95022

Bresnick, David.    **4.10894**
Black/white/green/red: the politics of education in ethnic America / David Bresnick, Murray Polner, Seymour Lachman. — New York: Longman, c1978. x, 166 p.; 21 cm. — (Educational policy, planning, and theory) Includes index. 1. Minorities — Education — United States. 2. Politics and education I. Lachman, Seymour. joint author. II. Polner, Murray. joint author. III. T.
LC3731.B67    370.19/342/0973    *LC* 77-18306    *ISBN* 0582280427

Cordasco, Francesco, 1920-.    **4.10895**
Bilingual schooling in the United States: a sourcebook for educational personnel / by Francesco Cordasco; with a foreword by A. Bruce Gaarder. New York: McGraw Hill, c1976. xxviii, 387 p.; 24 cm. Includes index. 1. Education, Bilingual — United States. I. T.
LC3731.C668    371.9/7    *LC* 76-29056    *ISBN* 0070131279

King, Edith W.    **4.10896**
Teaching ethnic awareness: methods and materials for the elementary school / Edith W. King. — Santa Monica, Calif.: Goodyear Pub. Co., c1980. x, 197 p.: ill.; 24 cm. 1. Minorities — Education (Elementary) — United States. 2. Intercultural education — United States. 3. Ethnic attitudes — United States. I. T.
LC3731.K56    371.9/7/0973 19    *LC* 79-20677    *ISBN* 083028866X

Krug, Mark M., 1915-.    **4.10897**
The melting of the ethnics: education of the immigrants, 1880–1914 / by Mark Krug. Bloomington, Ind.: Phi Delta Kappa Educational Foundation, c1976. v, 123 p.; 23 cm. (Perspectives in American education) Includes index. 1. Minorities — Education — United States. 2. Acculturation I. T. II. Series.
LC3731.K78    371.9/7    *LC* 75-26385    *ISBN* 087367409X

On equality of educational opportunity. Edited by Frederick    **4.10898**
Mosteller & Daniel P. Moynihan.
[1st ed.]. — New York: Random House, [1972] xiv, 570 p.; 21 cm. Papers deriving from the Harvard University faculty seminar on the Coleman report held during the academic year 1966-1967. 1. Coleman, James Samuel, 1926- Equality of educational opportunity — Addresses, essays, lectures. 2. Minorities — Education — United States. I. Mosteller, Frederick, 1916- ed. II. Moynihan, Daniel P. (Daniel Patrick), 1927- ed. III. Harvard University.
LC3731.O5    370/.973    *LC* 78-117653    *ISBN* 0394711548

Pialorsi, Frank. comp.    **4.10899**
Teaching the bilingual: new methods and old traditions / Frank Pialorsi, editor. — Tucson: University of Arizona Press, [1974] vii, 263 p.: 23 cm. 1. Education, Bilingual — United States — Addresses, essays, lectures. I. T.
LC3731.P52    371.9/7    *LC* 73-87717    *ISBN* 0816503729

**Watson, Bernard C.**     **4.10900**
In spite of the system: the individual and educational reform / [by] Bernard C. Watson. — Cambridge, Mass.: Ballinger Pub. Co., [c1974] xiv, 121 p.; 24 cm. 1. Minorities — Education — United States. 2. Public schools — United States. I. T.
LC3731.W37     370.19/34     *LC* 74-16370     *ISBN* 0884101592

**Weinberg, Meyer, 1920-.**     **4.10901**
A chance to learn: the history of race and education in the United States / Meyer Weinberg. — Cambridge; New York: Cambridge University Press, 1977. viii, 471 p. Includes index. 1. Minorities — Education — United States — History. 2. Discrimination in education — United States — History. I. T.
LC3731.W44    LC3731 W44.    370.19/342    *LC* 76-4235    *ISBN* 0521213037

**Weinberg, Meyer, 1920-.**     **4.10902**
Minority students: a research appraisal / Meyer Weinberg. Washington: U.S. Dept. of Health, Education, and Welfare, National Institute of Education: for sale by the Supt. of Docs., U.S. Govt. Print. Off., 1977. vi, 398 p.; 26 cm. Includes indexes. 1. Minorities — Education — United States. I. T.
LC3731.W444    371.9/7/0973    *LC* 77-601917

**Berrol, Selma Cantor.**     **4.10903**
Immigrants at school, New York City, 1898–1914 / Selma Cantor Berrol. — New York: Arno Press, 1978. ix, 423 p.: ill.; 24 cm. — (Bilingual-bicultural education in the United States) Originally presented as the author's thesis, City University of New York, 1967. 1. Minorities — Education — New York (City) I. T. II. Series.
LC3733.N5 B47 1978    371.9/7/097471    *LC* 77-90872    *ISBN* 0405110774

## LC3950–3990 Exceptional Children: General

**Ecology of exceptional children / James J. Gallagher, guest editor.**     **4.10904**
San Francisco: Jossey-Bass, 1980. ix, 109 p.; 24 cm. (New directions for exceptional children. no. 1) 1. Exceptional children — Education — Addresses, essays, lectures. 2. Home and school — Addresses, essays, lectures. 3. Mainstreaming in education — Addresses, essays, lectures. I. Gallagher, James John, 1926- II. Series.
LC3950.N48 no. 1 LC3969    371.9 19    *LC* 79-92038

**Language intervention with children / Diane Bricker, guest editor.**     **4.10905**
San Francisco (433 California St., San Francisco 94104): Jossey-Bass, 1980. viii, 99 p.: ill.; 24 cm. (New directions for exceptional children. no. 2) 1. Language disorders in children 2. Physically handicapped children — Rehabilitation. I. Bricker, Diane D. II. Series.
LC3950.N48 no. 2 RJ496.L35    618.92/855 19    *LC* 79-92039

**D'Zamko, Mary Elizabeth, 1927-.**     **4.10906**
Helping exceptional students succeed in the regular classroom / Mary Elizabeth D'Zamko and William D. Hedges. — West Nyack, N.Y.: Parker, c1985. xviii, 262 p.: ill.; 25 cm. 1. Special education 2. Mainstreaming in education 3. Remedial teaching 4. Activity programs in education I. Hedges, William D. II. T.
LC3965.D93 1985    371.9/046 19    *LC* 84-26437    *ISBN* 0133860469

**Gowan, John Curtis. ed.**     • **4.10907**
The guidance of exceptional children: a book of readings / edited by John Curtis Gowan, George D. Demos, and Charles J. Kokaska. — 2d ed. — New York: McKay, [1972] xi, 465 p.; 21 cm. 1. Exceptional children — Education — Addresses, essays, lectures. 2. Personnel service in education — Addresses, essays, lectures. I. Demos, George D. joint ed. II. Kokaska, Charles J. joint ed. III. T.
LC3965.G6 1972    371.9    *LC* 70-185135

**Graubard, Paul S.**     **4.10908**
Classrooms that work; prescriptions for change [by] Paul Graubard and Harry Rosenberg. — [1st ed.]. — New York: Dutton, 1974. x, 214 p.; 22 cm. 'A Sunrise book.' 1. Special education I. Rosenberg, Harry Ewing, 1932- joint author. II. T.
LC3965.G75 1974    371.9    *LC* 74-4157    *ISBN* 0876901313

**Handbook of special education / edited by James M. Kauffman & Daniel P. Hallahan, editors.**     **4.10909**
Englewood Cliffs, N.J.: Prentice-Hall, c1981. xv, 807 p.: ill.; 29 cm. 1. Exceptional children — Education — Addresses, essays, lectures. 2. Learning disabled children — Education — Addresses, essays, lectures. I. Kauffman, James M. II. Hallahan, Daniel P., 1944-
LC3965.H26    371.9    *LC* 80-17390    *ISBN* 0133817563

**Suran, Bernard G.**     **4.10910**
Special children: an integrative approach / Bernard G. Suran, Joseph V. Rizzo. — 2nd ed. — Glenview, Ill.: Scott, Foresman, c1983. 587 p.: ill.; 24 cm. — (Scott, Foresman series in special education.) Includes indexes. 1. Special education I. Rizzo, Joseph V., 1942- II. T. III. Series.
LC3965.S9 1983    371.9 19    *LC* 82-23039    *ISBN* 0673158063

**Taber, Florence M.**     **4.10911**
Microcomputers in special education: selection and decision making process / Florence M. Taber. — Reston, Va.: The Council for Exceptional Children, 1983. 102 p.: ill.; 23 cm. 'A product of the ERIC Clearinghouse on Handicapped and Gifted Children.' 1. Exceptional children — Education — Data processing. 2. Microcomputers I. ERIC Clearinghouse on Handicapped and Gifted Children. II. T.
LC3969.T3 1983    371.9/028/5 19    *LC* 82-23543    *ISBN* 0865861358

**Granger, Lori.**     **4.10912**
The magic feather: the truth about 'special education' / Lori Granger and Bill Granger. — 1st ed. — New York: Dutton, c1986. xii, 259 p.; 22 cm. Includes index. 1. Exceptional children — Education — United States. 2. Exceptional children — United States — Rating of — Evaluation. I. Granger, Bill. II. T.
LC3981.G73 1986    371.9/0973 19    *LC* 86-8973    *ISBN* 0525244514

## LC3991–4000 Gifted Children

**Davis, Gary A., 1938-.**     **4.10913**
Education of the gifted and talented / Gary A. Davis, Sylvia B. Rimm. — Englewood Cliffs, N.J.: Prentice-Hall, c1985. xiii, 448 p.; 24 cm. Includes indexes. 1. Gifted children — Education 2. Educational acceleration 3. Gifted children — Education — Curricula. I. Rimm, Sylvia B., 1935- II. T.
LC3993.D38 1985    371.95 19    *LC* 84-11476    *ISBN* 0132365979

**Tuttle, Frederick B.**     **4.10914**
Characteristics and identification of gifted and talented students / by Frederick B. Tuttle, Jr., Laurence A. Becker. — 2nd ed. — Washington, D.C.: NEA Professional Library, National Education Association, c1983. 143 p.: ill.; 23 cm. 1. Gifted children 2. Talented students 3. Students — Rating of I. Becker, Laurence A. II. T.
LC3993.T83 1983    371.95 19    *LC* 83-13132    *ISBN* 0810607328

**Learning–disabled/gifted children: identification and programming / edited by Lynn H. Fox, Linda Brody, Dianne Tobin.**     **4.10915**
Baltimore: University Park Press, c1983. xi, 297 p.: ill.; 24 cm. 1. Gifted children — Education — Evaluation — Addresses, essays, lectures. 2. Learning disabled children — Education — Addresses, essays, lectures. I. Fox, Lynn H., 1944- II. Brody, Linda. III. Tobin, Dianne.
LC3993.2.L43 1983    371.95/2 19    *LC* 83-5930    *ISBN* 0839118813

**A Practical guide to counseling the gifted in a school setting / Joyce VanTassel–Baska, editor.**     **4.10916**
Reston, Va.: Council for Exceptional Children, 1983. 59 p.; 23 cm. 'A product of the ERIC Clearinghouse on Handicapped and Gifted Children.' 1. Gifted children — Education — Addresses, essays, lectures. 2. Personnel service in education — Addresses, essays, lectures. I. VanTassel-Baska, Joyce. II. ERIC Clearinghouse on Handicapped and Gifted Children.
LC3993.2.P7 1983    371.95 19    *LC* 83-7256    *ISBN* 0865861463

**Clark, Gilbert.**     **4.10917**
Educating artistically talented students / Gilbert Clark, Enid Zimmerman. — 1st ed. — Syracuse, N.Y.: Syracuse University Press, 1984. xi, 199 p., [1] p. of plates: ill.; 24 cm. Includes indexes. 1. Gifted children — Education — United States — Art. 2. Art — Study and teaching — United States. 3. Gifted children — Education — United States — Art — Curricula. 4. Gifted children — Identification I. Zimmerman, Enid. II. T.
LC3993.265.C53 1984    371.95 19    *LC* 84-16368    *ISBN* 0815623208

**Cox, June, 1919-.**     **4.10918**
Educating able learners: programs and promising practices / by June Cox, Neil Daniel, and Bruce O. Boston. — 1st ed. — Austin: University of Texas Press, 1985. xv, 243 p.: ill.; 24 cm. 'A national study conducted by the Sid W. Richardson Foundation.' Includes index. 1. Gifted children — Education — United States. I. Daniel, Neil, 1932- II. Boston, Bruce O. III. T. IV. Title: Programs and promising practices.
LC3993.9.C68 1985    371.95/0973 19    *LC* 85-7405    *ISBN* 0292703864

**Defensible programs for the gifted** / edited by C. June Maker;    **4.10919**
contributors, David C. Berliner ... [et al.].
Rockville, Md.: Aspen Publishers, 1986. xix, 357 p.; 24 cm. — (Critical issues in gifted education.) 1. Gifted children — Education — United States. I. Maker, C. June. II. Berliner, David C. III. Series.
LC3993.9.D44 1986      371.9/5/0973 19      *LC 86-17345*      *ISBN* 0871893770

**Gallagher, James John, 1926-.**    **4.10920**
Teaching the gifted child / James J. Gallagher. — 3rd ed. — Boston: Allyn and Bacon, c1985. ix, 485 p.: ill.; 25 cm. 1. Gifted children — Education — United States. I. T.
LC3993.9.G35 1985      371.95 19      *LC 84-45685*      *ISBN* 0205084214

**Howley, Aimee.**    **4.10921**
Teaching gifted children: principles and strategies / Aimee Howley, Craig B. Howley, Edwina D. Pendarvis. — Boston: Little, Brown, c1986. xvi, 439 p.: ill.; 25 cm. Includes indexes. 1. Gifted children — Education — United States. 2. Gifted children — Education — Curricula. I. Howley, Craig B. II. Pendarvis, Edwina D. III. T.
LC3993.9.H68 1986      371.95/6/0973 19      *LC 85-19875*      *ISBN* 0316375853

**Whitmore, Joanne Rand, 1938-.**    **4.10922**
Intellectual giftedness in disabled persons / Joanne Rand Whitmore, C. June Maker. — Rockville, Md.: Aspen Systems Corp., 1985. xii, 331 p.; 24 cm. Includes index. 1. Gifted children — Education — United States. 2. Learning disabilities — United States. 3. Handicapped children — Education — United States. I. Maker, C. June. II. T.
LC3993.9.W45 1985      371.95 19      *LC 85-15039*      *ISBN* 0871892367

**Tempest, N. R.**    **4.10923**
Teaching clever children, 7–11 [by] N. R. Tempest. — London; Boston: Routledge and K. Paul, 1974. vii, 111 p.; 22 cm. Includes index. 1. Gifted children — Education — Great Britain. I. T.
LC3997.G7 T45      371.9/5/0942      *LC 73-91039*      *ISBN* 0710078056

## LC4001–4803 Handicapped Children

**The Directory for exceptional children.**    **4.10924**
[1st]- ed.; 1954-. Boston, P. Sargent. 19-23 cm. 1. Exceptional children — Directories. I. Hayes, Eugene Nelson, 1920- ed. II. Sargent, Porter.
LC4007.D5      371.92058      *LC 54-4975*

**Educating severely and profoundly handicapped students** /    **4.10925**
[edited by] Les Sternberg, Gary L. Adams.
Rockville, Md.: Aspen Systems Corp., 1982. xiii, 366 p.: ill.; 24 cm. 1. Handicapped children — Education — Addresses, essays, lectures. I. Sternberg, Les. II. Adams, Gary L.
LC4015.E37 1982      371.9 19      *LC 82-4102*      *ISBN* 0894436953

**Kirk, Samuel Alexander, 1904-.**    **4.10926**
Educating exceptional children / Samuel A. Kirk, James J. Gallagher. — 5th ed. — Boston: Houghton Mifflin, 1986. xv, 563 p.: ill.; 24 cm. 1. Handicapped children — Education 2. Special education I. T.
LC4015.K5 1972      *LC 85-81509*      *ISBN* 0395357748

**Larsen, Stephen C., 1943-.**    **4.10927**
Methods for educating the handicapped: an individualized education program approach / Stephen C. Larsen, Mary S. Poplin. — Boston: Allyn and Bacon, c1980. ix, 446 p.: ill.; 24 cm. 1. Handicapped children — Education 2. Individualized instruction I. Poplin, Mary S., 1951- II. T.
LC4015.L37      371.9      *LC 79-13924*      *ISBN* 020506678X

**Stephens, Thomas M.**    **4.10928**
Teaching mainstreamed students / Thomas M. Stephens, A. Edward Blackhurst, Larry A. Magliocca. — New York: Wiley, c1982. x, 380 p.: ill.; 24 cm. 1. Handicapped children — Education 2. Mainstreaming in education I. Blackhurst, A. Edward. II. Magliocca, Larry A. III. T.
LC4015.S73 1982      371.9 19      *LC 82-2593*      *ISBN* 0471024791

**Systematic instruction of persons with severe handicaps** /    **4.10929**
Martha E. Snell, editor.
3rd ed. — Columbus, Ohio: Charles E. Merrill, 1987. xi, 532 p.: ill.; 25 cm. Includes index. Previous editions titled Systematic instruction of the moderately and severely handicapped. 1. Handicapped children — Education — Addresses, essays, lectures. I. Snell, Martha E. II. Title: Systematic instruction of the moderately and severely handicapped.
LC4015.S95 1987      *LC 86-62348*      *ISBN* 0675204682

**Assessment in special education** / John T. Neisworth, editor.    **4.10930**
Rockville, Md.: Aspen Systems Corp., 1982. vi, 233 p.; 27 cm. 1. Handicapped children — Education — Evaluation — Addresses, essays, lectures. I. Neisworth, John T.
LC4019.A74 1982      371.9 19      *LC 82-11455*      *ISBN* 0894438085

**Attitudes and attitude change in special education: theory and**    **4.10931**
**practice** / edited by Reginald L. Jones.
Reston, Va.: Council for Exceptional Children, 1984. xi, 257 p.: ill.; 23 cm. 'A project of the ERIC Clearinghouse on Handicapped and Gifted Children.' 1. Handicapped children — Education — Addresses, essays, lectures. 2. Mainstreaming in education — Addresses, essays, lectures. 3. Attitude change — Addresses, essays, lectures. 4. Handicapped — Social conditions — Addresses, essays, lectures. 5. Teachers — Attitudes — Addresses, essays, lectures. 6. Public opinion — Addresses, essays, lectures. I. Jones, Reginald Lanier, 1931- II. Council for Exceptional Children. III. ERIC Clearinghouse on Handicapped and Gifted Children.
LC4019.A75 1984      371.9 19      *LC 84-12050*      *ISBN* 0865861374

**Bush, Clifford L., 1915-.**    **4.10932**
Dictionary of reading and learning disability / by Clifford L. Bush and Robert C. Andrews. — Los Angeles, Calif.: Western Psychological Services, 1980. iv, 179 p.; 23 cm. 1. Handicapped children — Education — Dictionaries. 2. Reading — Dictionaries. I. Andrews, Robert C. II. T.
LC4019.B88 1980      371.9/03      *LC 79-57293*

**The Present situation and trends of research in the field of**    **4.10933**
**special education, four studies: Sweden and other Scandinavian**
**countries, Union of Soviet Socialist Republics, United States of**
**America, Uruguay.**
Paris, Unesco, 1973. 306 p. 24 cm. 1. Handicapped children — Education — Case studies. I. Unesco.
LC4019.P73      371.9/07/2      *LC 74-162591*      *ISBN* 9231011065

**Nave, Gary.**    **4.10934**
Computer technology for the handicapped in special education and rehabilitation: a resource guide / Gary Nave, Philip Browning, Jeri Carter. — Eugene, Or: The International Council for Computers in Education, 1983. xxiv, 190 p.; 28 cm. 1. Computer-assisted instruction — Bibliography 2. Handicapped — Bibliography I. Browning, Philip L. II. Carter, Jeri. III. International Council for Computers in Education. IV. University of Oregon. Rehabilitation Research and Training Center in Mental Retardation. V. T.
LC 4023 N32 1983      *ISBN* 0871141426

**Microcomputers and exceptional children** / Randy Elliot    **4.10935**
**Bennett and Charles A. Maher, co–editors.**
New York: Haworth Press, c1984. 113 p.; 23 cm. 'Also published as Special services in the schools, Volume 1, Number 1, Fall 1984'—Verso t.p. 1. Handicapped children — Education — Data processing — Addresses, essays, lectures. 2. Computer-assisted instruction — Addresses, essays, lectures. 3. Microcomputers — Addresses, essays, lectures. I. Bennett, Randy Elliot, 1952- II. Maher, Charles A., 1944-
LC4024.M53 1984      371.9/043 19      *LC 84-10784*      *ISBN* 0866562974

**Cottle, Thomas J.**    **4.10936**
Barred from school, 2 million children! / Thomas J. Cottle. — Washington: New Republic Book Co., 1976. 186 p.; 24 cm. Includes index. 1. Handicapped children — Education — United States. 2. Children of minorities — Education — United States. I. T.
LC4031.C67      371.9/6      *LC 76-20607*      *ISBN* 0915220121

**Sage, Daniel D.**    **4.10937**
Policy and management in special education / Daniel D. Sage, Leonard C. Burrello. — Englewood Cliffs, N.J.: Prentice-Hall, c1986. xiv, 304 p.: ill.; 24 cm. 1. Handicapped children — Education — United States — Management. I. Burrello, Leonard C., 1942- II. T.
LC4031.S24 1986      371.9 19      *LC 85-12038*      *ISBN* 0136848044

**Spodek, Bernard.**    **4.10938**
Mainstreaming young children / Bernard Spodek, Olivia N. Saracho, Richard C. Lee. — Belmont, Calif.: Wadsworth Pub. Co., c1984. xv, 320 p.; 24 cm. 1. Handicapped children — Education — United States. 2. Mainstreaming in education — United States. 3. Education, Preschool — United States. 4. Education, Primary — United States. I. Saracho, Olivia N. II. Lee, Richard C., 1952- III. T.
LC4031.S75 1984      371.9/046 19      *LC 83-12544*      *ISBN* 0534028039

**Brickman, William W.**    **4.10939**
Education and the many faces of the disadvantaged: cultural and historical perspectives. Edited by William W. Brickman [and] Stanley Lehrer. — New York: Wiley, [1972] xvii, 435 p.; 23 cm. 1. Socially handicapped children — Education — U.S. — Addresses, essays, lectures. I. Lehrer, Stanley. joint author. II. T.
LC4091.B75      371.9/67/0973      *LC 74-37166*      *ISBN* 0471103500

**Ginsburg, Herbert.**     **4.10940**
The myth of the deprived child: poor children's intellect and education. — Englewood Cliffs, N.J.: Prentice-Hall, [c1972] xvi, 252 p.: ill.; 24 cm. 1. Socially handicapped children — Education — U.S. I. T.
LC4091.G5     371.9/67/0973     *LC* 76-166042     *ISBN* 0136091563

**Project Head Start: a legacy of the War on Poverty / edited by**     **4.10941**
**Edward Zigler, Jeanette Valentine.**
New York: Free Press, c1979. xxvi, 610 p.: ill.; 24 cm. Includes indexes. 1. Project Head Start. 2. Socially handicapped children — Education (Preschool) — United States I. Zigler, Edward, 1930- II. Valentine, Jeanette.
LC4091.P73     371.9/67     *LC* 78-24671     *ISBN* 0029358205

**Apter, Steven J. (Steven Jeffrey), 1945-.**     **4.10942**
Troubled children/troubled systems / Steven J. Apter. — New York: Pergamon Press, c1982. xvi, 267 p.: ill.; 23 cm. — (Pergamon general psychology series. 104) Includes indexes. 1. Mentally ill children — Education I. T. II. Series.
LC4165.A68 1982     371.94 19     *LC* 81-12026     *ISBN* 0080271677

**Calhoun, Mary Lynne.**     **4.10943**
Teaching and learning strategies for physically handicapped students / Mary Lynne Calhoun and Margaret F. Hawisher. — Baltimore: University Park Press, c1979. ix, 362 p.: ill.; 23 cm. 1. Physically handicapped children — Education I. Hawisher, Margaret F. joint author. II. T.
LC4215.C29     371.9/1     *LC* 79-12255     *ISBN* 0839113943

## LC4601–4821 MENTALLY HANDICAPPED CHILDREN

**Sailor, Wayne.**     **4.10944**
Severely handicapped students: an instructional design / Wayne Sailor, Doug Guess. — Boston: Houghton Mifflin Co., c1983. xiii, 386 p.: ill.; 25 cm. Includes index. 1. Mentally handicapped children — Education — Curricula. 2. Curriculum planning I. Guess, Doug. II. T.
LC4602.S18 1983     371.9 19     *LC* 82-83289     *ISBN* 0395327881

**Strategies for teaching retarded and special needs learners /**     **4.10945**
**Edward A. Polloway ... [et al.].**
3rd. — Columbus: C.E. Merrill Pub. Co., c1985. x, 516 p.: ill.; 24 cm. Includes indexes. Rev. ed. of: Strategies for teaching the mentally retarded / James S. Payne ... [et al.]. 2nd ed. c1981. 1. Mentally handicapped children — Education I. Polloway, Edward A. II. Strategies for teaching the mentally retarded.
LC4602.S87 1985     371.92/8 19     *LC* 84-61119     *ISBN* 0675202914

**Gillespie, Patricia H.**     **4.10946**
Teaching reading to the mildly retarded child [by] Patricia H. Gillespie [and] Lowell E. Johnson. — Columbus: Merrill, [1974] viii, 376 p.: illus.; 24 cm. 1. Mentally handicapped children — Education — Reading. I. Johnson. Lowell E., joint author. II. T.
LC4620.G54     371.9/282     *LC* 73-88245     *ISBN* 0675088593

**Langone, John, 1950-.**     **4.10947**
Teaching retarded learners: curriculum and methods for improving instruction / John Langone. — Boston: Allyn and Bacon, c1986. xiii, 464 p.: ill.; 24 cm. 1. Mentally handicapped children — Education — United States. 2. Mentally handicapped children — Education — United States — Curricula. I. T.
LC4631.L36 1986     371.92/8/0973 19     *LC* 85-23009     *ISBN* 0205086829

**Long, Nicholas James, 1929- ed.**     **4.10948**
Conflict in the classroom: the education of emotionally disturbed children / [edited by] Nicholas J. Long, William C. Morse, Ruth G. Newman. — 4th ed. — Belmont, Calif.: Wadsworth Pub. Co., c1980. xii, 447 p.: ill.; 24 cm. 1. Emotional problems of children 2. Mentally handicapped children — Education — United States. I. Morse, William Charles. II. Newman, Ruth G. III. T.
LC4631.L6 1980     371.9/4 19     *LC* 79-20955     *ISBN* 0534007910

**Severe mental retardation: from theory to practice / edited by**     **4.10949**
**Diane Bricker, John Filler.**
Reston, Va.: Division on Mental Retardation of the Council for Exceptional Children, c1985. — 293 p.; 24 cm. 1. Mentally handicapped — United States. 2. Mentally handicapped children — United States I. Bricker, Diane D. II. Filler, John. III. Council for Exceptional Children Division on Mental Retardation.
LC 4631 S498 1985

**Cratty, Bryant J.**     **4.10950**
Motor activity and the education of retardates [by] Bryant J. Cratty. — 2d ed. — Philadelphia: Lea & Febiger, 1974. xiii, 303 p.: illus.; 25 cm. — (Health education, physical education, and recreation series) 1. Mentally handicapped children — Education 2. Perceptual-motor learning I. T.
LC4661.C7 1974     371.9/28     *LC* 73-23008     *ISBN* 0812104269

**Hallahan, Daniel P., 1944-.**     **4.10951**
Psychoeducational foundations of learning disabilities [by] Daniel P. Hallahan [and] William M. Cruickshank. — Englewood Cliffs, N.J.: Prentice-Hall, [1973] xiv, 317 p.: illus.; 24 cm. — (Prentice-Hall series in special education) 1. Learning disabilities 2. Learning, Psychology of 3. Perceptual-motor learning I. Cruickshank, William M. joint author. II. T.
LC4661.H26     371.9/2     *LC* 72-10543     *ISBN* 0137342853

**Cruickshank, William M.**     **4.10952**
Learning disabilities: the struggle from adolescence toward adulthood / William M. Cruickshank, William C. Morse, Jeannie S. Johns. — 1st ed. — Syracuse, N.Y.: Syracuse University Press, 1980. xi, 285 p.: ill.; 24 cm. Includes index. 1. Learning disabilities 2. Adolescence I. Morse, William Charles. joint author. II. Johns, Jeannie S. joint author. III. T.
LC4704.C77     371.9/2     *LC* 79-23529     *ISBN* 0815622201

**Hammill, Donald D., 1934-.**     **4.10953**
Teaching students with learning and behavior problems / Donald D. Hammill, Nettie R. Bartel. — 4th ed. — Boston: Allyn and Bacon, c1986. xiii, 418 p.: ill.; 24 cm. Rev. ed. of: Teaching children with learning and behavior problems. Canadian ed. c1984. Includes indexes. 1. Learning disabilities — Addresses, essays, lectures. 2. Learning disabled children — Education — Canada — Addresses, essays, lectures. 3. Learning disabled children — Education — United States — Addresses, essays, lectures. I. Bartel, Nettie R. II. Hammill, Donald D., 1934- Teaching children with learning and behavior problems. III. T.
LC4704.H35 1986     371.9 19     *LC* 85-30803     *ISBN* 020508768X

**Lerner, Janet W.**     **4.10954**
Learning disabilities: theories, diagnosis, and teaching strategies / Janet W. Lerner. — 4th ed. — Boston: Houghton Mifflin Co., c1985. xiv, 581 p.: ill.; 24 cm. Includes indexes. 1. Learning disabilities I. T.
LC4704.L48 1985     371.9 19     *LC* 84-82413     *ISBN* 0395357756

**Myers, Patricia I., 1929-.**     **4.10955**
Learning disabilities: basic concepts, assessment practices, and instructional strategies / Patricia I. Myers, Donald D. Hammill. — Austin, Tex.: Pro-ED, c1982. viii, 481 p.: ill.; 23 cm. Includes indexes. 1. Learning disabilities 2. Learning disabled children — Education. I. Hammill, Donald D., 1934- II. T.
LC4704.M93 1982     371.9, 19     *LC* 82-444     *ISBN* 0936104228

**Ross, Alan O.**     **4.10956**
Psychological aspects of learning disabilities & reading disorders / Alan O. Ross. — New York: McGraw-Hill, c1976. xiii, 191 p.; 25 cm. (McGraw-Hill series in special education) Includes indexes. 1. Learning disabilities — Psychological aspects. 2. Child psychology 3. Reading disability — Psychological aspects. I. T.
LC4704.R68     371.9/2     *LC* 75-20254     *ISBN* 007053845X

## LC5001–5060 Working Class Education

**Goldstrom, J. M.**     **4.10957**
The social content of education, 1808–1870; a study of the working class school reader in England and Ireland [by] J. M. Goldstrom. — Shannon, Ireland: Irish University Press, [1972] xv, 226 p.; 25 cm. 1. Labor and laboring classes — Education — Great Britain — History. 2. Readers — Civilization. 3. Great Britain — Social conditions — 19th century I. T.
LC5056.G7 G64     301.5/6     *LC* 72-192453     *ISBN* 0716510049

## LC5101–5143 Urban Education

**Ornstein, Allan C.**     • **4.10958**
Urban education: student unrest, teacher behaviors, and Black power / [by] Allan C. Ornstein. — Columbus, Ohio: Merrill, [1972] ix, 198 p.; 23 cm. 1. Education, Urban — United States. I. T.
LC5101.O7     370/.973     *LC* 77-189271     *ISBN* 0675091063

**Education and the city: theory, history, and contemporary**     **4.10959**
**practice / edited by Gerald Grace.**
London; Boston: Routledge & K. Paul, 1984. xiii, 302 p. 1. Education, Urban — Addresses, essays, lectures. 2. Educational sociology — Addresses, essays, lectures. 3. Education, Urban — History — Addresses, essays, lectures. 4. Education, Urban — Great Britain — Addresses, essays, lectures. 5. Education, Urban — United States — Addresses, essays, lectures. I. Grace, Gerald Rupert.
LC5115.E38 1984     370.19/348 19     *LC* 83-22983     *ISBN* 0710099185

## LC5146–5148 Rural Education

**Coombs, Philip Hall, 1915–.**                                    **4.10970**
Attacking rural poverty; how nonformal education can help [by] Philip H. Coombs, with Manzoor Ahmed. A research report for the World Bank, prepared by the International Council for Educational Development. Edited by Barbara Baird Israel. Baltimore, Johns Hopkins University Press [1974] xvi, 292 p. 23 cm. 1. Education, Rural 2. Agricultural education — Developing countries. I. Ahmed, Manzoor, 1940- joint author. II. World Bank. III. International Council for Educational Development. IV. T.
LC5146.C65 1974        370.19/3        LC 73-19350        ISBN 0801816009
ISBN 0801816017

**Fuller, Wayne Edison, 1919–.**                                    **4.10971**
The old country school: the story of rural education in the Middle West / Wayne E. Fuller. — Chicago: University of Chicago Press, 1982. ix, 302 p., [16] p. of plates: ill.; 24 cm. 1. Education, Rural — Middle West — History. 2. Middle West — Rural conditions. I. T.
LC5147.M55 F84 1982        370.19/346/0977 19        LC 81-16069        ISBN 0226268829

**The Ripe harvest; educating migrant children. Edited by Arnold**        **4.10972**
**B. Cheyney.**
Coral Gables, Fla.: University of Miami Press, [1972] xi, 246 p.; 24 cm. 1. Children of migrant laborers — Education — United States — Addresses, essays, lectures. I. Cheyney, Arnold B. ed.
LC5151.R5        371.9/675/0973        LC 73-158927        ISBN 0870242067

## LC5201–6691 Education Extension. Adult Education

**Adult education and training in industrialized countries /**        **4.10973**
**Richard E. Peterson ... [et al.].**
New York: Praeger, 1982. 500 p.; 24 cm. — (Praeger special studies series in comparative education.) Includes indexes 1. Adult education I. Peterson, Richard E. II. Series.
LC5215.A34        LC 81-84672        ISBN 0030615518

**Andragogy in action / Malcolm S. Knowles and associates.**        **4.10974**
1st ed. — San Francisco: Jossey-Bass, 1984. xxiv, 444 p.: ill.; 24 cm. (Jossey-Bass management series.) (Jossey-Bass higher education series.) Includes index. 1. Adult education — Philosophy — Addresses, essays, lectures. 2. Continuing education — Addresses, essays, lectures. 3. Professional education — Addresses, essays, lectures. 4. Management — Study and teaching (Higher) — Addresses, essays, lectures. I. Knowles, Malcolm Shepherd, 1913- II. Series. III. Series: Jossey-Bass higher education series.
LC5215.A53 1984        374 19        LC 84-47989        ISBN 0875896219

**Charters, Alexander N.**        **4.10975**
Comparing adult education worldwide / Alexander N. Charters and associates. — 1st ed. — San Francisco: Jossey-Bass Publishers, 1981. xxi, 272 p.; 24 cm. — (AEA handbook series in adult education.) (Jossey-Bass series in higher education.) Includes indexes. 1. Adult education 2. Comparative education I. T. II. Series. III. Series: Jossey-Bass series in higher education.
LC5215.C5 1981        374 19        LC 80-8911        ISBN 0875894941

**Knowles, Malcolm Shepherd, 1913–.**        **4.10976**
The adult learner: a neglected species / Malcolm Knowles. — 3rd ed. — Houston: Gulf Pub. Co., Book Division, c1984. x, 292 p.: ill.; 24 cm. — (Building blocks of human potential series) Includes indexes. 1. Adult education I. T.
LC5215.K59 1984        374 19        LC 83-22642        ISBN 0872010058

**Argyris, Chris, 1923–.**        **4.10977**
Increasing leadership effectiveness / Chris Argyris. New York: Wiley, c1976. xvi, 286 p.; 24 cm. (Wiley series in behavior) 'A Wiley-Interscience publication.' Includes index. 1. Adult education 2. Leadership I. T.
LC5219.A7 1976        374        LC 76-12784        ISBN 0471016683

**Cross, K. Patricia (Kathryn Patricia), 1926–.**        **4.10978**
Adults as learners / K. Patricia Cross. — 1st ed. — San Francisco: Jossey-Bass, 1981. xxvi, 300 p.; 24 cm. — (The Jossey-Bass series in higher education) Includes index. 1. Adult education 2. Continuing education I. T.
LC5219.C744        374 19        LC 80-26985        ISBN 0875894917

**Providing continuing education by media and technology /**        **4.10979**
**Martin N. Chamberlain, guest editor.**
San Francisco: Jossey-Bass, 1980. ix, 104 p.; 24 cm. (New directions for continuing education. no. 5 0195-2242) 1. Continuing education — Audio-

---

**Gittell, Marilyn. comp.**        **4.10960**
The politics of urban education, edited by Marilyn Gittell and Alan G. Hevesi. — New York: F. A. Praeger, [1969] x, 386 p.; 24 cm. — (Praeger university series) 1. Education, Urban — U.S. I. Hevesi, Alan G., joint comp. II. T.
LC5131.G52        370.19/348        LC 69-15747

**Katz, Michael B.**        **4.10961**
Class, Bureaucracy, and schools: the illusion of educational change in America / Michael B. Katz. — Expanded ed. — New York: Praeger, 1975. xxiv, 208 p.; 20 cm. (Praeger university series) Includes index. 1. Education, Urban — United States — History. 2. Educational sociology — United States. 3. Education — Aims and objectives. I. T.
LC5131.K36 1975        370.19/348/0973        LC 74-9401        ISBN 0275525503

**Payne, Charles M.**        **4.10962**
Getting what we ask for: the ambiguity of success and failure in urban education / Charles M. Payne. — Westport, Conn.: Greenwood Press, 1984. vi, 206 p.; 24 cm. (Contributions to the study of education. 0196-707X; no. 12) Includes index. 1. Education, Urban — United States. 2. Education, Urban — Illinois — West Chicago. 3. Educational equalization — United States. 4. Socially handicapped children — Education — United States. I. T. II. Series.
LC5131.P39 1984        370.19/348/0973 19        LC 83-18623        ISBN 0313235201

**Rethinking urban education / Herbert J. Walberg [and] Andrew**        **4.10963**
**T. Kopan, editors.**
[1st ed.]. — San Francisco: Jossey-Bass, 1972. xv, 334 p.; 24 cm. 1. Education, Urban — United States. I. Walberg, Herbert J., 1937- ed. II. Kopan, Andrew T., ed.
LC5131.R49        370.19/348        LC 72-83962        ISBN 0875891403

**Schools in cities: consensus and conflict in American educational**        **4.10964**
**history / Ronald K. Goodenow and Diane Ravitch, editors.**
New York: Holmes & Meier, 1983. x, 326 p.: ill.; 24 cm. Selected essays from a conference on community studies in the history of education held at Teachers College, Columbia University, in New York, 1980. 1. Education, Urban — United States — History — 19th century — Addresses, essays, lectures. 2. Education, Urban — United States — History — 20th century — Addresses, essays, lectures. I. Goodenow, Ronald K. II. Ravitch, Diane.
LC5131.S373 1983        370.19/348/0973 19        LC 83-8374        ISBN 0841908508

**Tyack, David B.**        **4.10965**
The one best system: a history of American urban education / David B. Tyack. — Cambridge, Mass.: Harvard University Press, 1974. xii, 353 p.: 19 ill.; 24 cm. Includes index. 1. Education, Urban — United States. I. T.
LC5131.T92        370.19/348/0973        LC 74-77184        ISBN 0674637801

**Schrag, Peter.**        • **4.10966**
Village school downtown; politics and education; a Boston report. — Boston, Beacon Press [1967] 191 p. 21 cm. 1. Boston — Public schools. 2. Education, Urban 3. Politics and education I. T.
LC5133.B6S3        370/.9744/61        LC 67-14113

**Comer, James P.**        **4.10967**
School power: implications of an intervention project / James P. Comer; introd. by Albert J. Solnit and Samuel Nash. — New York: Free Press; London: Collier Macmillan, c1980. xvii, 285 p.; 24 cm. 1. Yale University. Child Study Center. 2. Education, Urban — Connecticut — New Haven. 3. Community and school — Connecticut — New Haven. 4. Motivation in education 5. Public schools — Connecticut — New Haven. I. T.
LC5133.N37 C65        370.19/31/097468        LC 80-757        ISBN 002906550X

**Fuchs, Estelle.**        **4.10968**
Teachers talk; views from inside city schools. [1st ed.] Garden City, N.Y., Anchor Books, 1969 [c1967] xiv, 224 p. 19 cm. 1. Education, Urban — New York (N.Y.) 2. Public schools — New York (N.Y.) I. T.
LC5133.N4 F8 1969        371.1/009173/2        LC 69-13701

**Foster, Herbert L.**        **4.10969**
Ribbin', jivin', and playin' the dozens: the persistent dilemma in our schools / Herbert L. Foster. — 2nd ed. — Cambridge, Mass.: Ballinger Pub. Co., c1986. xiii, 359 p.: port.; 23 cm. Spine title: Ribbin', jivin' & playin' the dozens. 1. Education, Urban — United States. 2. Afro-Americans — Education 3. School discipline — United States. 4. Afro-American students — Language (New words, slang, etc.) I. T. II. Title: Ribbin', jivin' & playin' the dozens.
LC5141.F67 1986        370.19/348/0973 19        LC 85-13392        ISBN 0884109828

visual aids — Addresses, essays, lectures. 2. Educational technology — Addresses, essays, lectures. I. Chamberlain, Martin Nichols, 1914- II. Series.
LC5219.P7x    374/.27 19    *LC* 79-89388

**Daloz, Laurent A.**    **4.10980**
Effective teaching and mentoring: realizing the transformational power of adult learning / Laurent A. Daloz. — 1st ed. — San Francisco, Calif.: Jossey-Bass, c1986. p. cm. (Jossey-Bass higher education series.) Includes index. 1. Mentors in education — United States. 2. Adult education — United States. 3. Motivation in adult education — United States. I. T. II. Series.
LC5225.M45 D35 1986    374/.973 19    *LC* 86-10317    *ISBN* 155542001X

**Apps, Jerold W., 1934-.**    **4.10981**
Improving practice in continuing education / Jerold W. Apps. — 1st ed. — San Francisco: Jossey-Bass, 1985. xviii, 227 p.; 24 cm. (Jossey-Bass higher education series.) Includes index. 1. Continuing education — United States — Case studies. I. T. II. Series.
LC5251.A869 1985    374/.973 19    *LC* 85-9871    *ISBN* 0875896545

**Aslanian, Carol B.**    **4.10982**
Americans in transition: life changes as reasons for adult learning / Carol B. Aslanian, Henry M. Brickell, with the assistance of Marsha Davis Ullman. — New York: College Entrance Examination Board, 1980. xvi, 172 p.: ill.; 23 cm. On cover: Future Directions for a Learning Society, the College Board. 1. Adult education — United States. 2. Continuing education — United States. I. Brickell, Henry M. II. Ullman, Marsha Davis. III. Future Directions for a Learning Society. IV. T.
LC5251.A895    374/.973 19    *LC* 80-154177    *ISBN* 0874471273

**Boone, Edgar John, 1930-.**    **4.10983**
Serving personal and community needs through adult education / [edited by] Edgar J. Boone, Ronald W. Shearon, Estelle E. White, and associates. — 1st ed. — San Francisco: Jossey-Bass, 1980. xx, 338 p.; 24 cm. — (The Adult Education Association handbook series in adult education) Includes index. 1. Adult education — United States — Addresses, essays, lectures. 2. Labor and laboring classes — Education — United States — Addresses, essays, lectures. I. Shearon, Ronald W. joint author. II. White, Estelle E. joint author. III. T.
LC5251.B64    374/.973    *LC* 79-9664    *ISBN* 0875894518

**Examining controversies in adult education / [edited by] Burton**    **4.10984**
**W. Kreitlow and associates.**
1st ed. — San Francisco: Jossey-Bass Publishers, 1981. xxiv, 290 p.; 24 cm. — (The AEA handbook series in adult education) (The Jossey-Bass series in higher education) Includes indexes. 1. Adult education — United States — Addresses, essays, lectures. I. Kreitlow, Burton W.
LC5251.E9    374/.973 19    *LC* 80-27058    *ISBN* 0875894895

**Newman, Michael, 1939-.**    **4.10985**
The poor cousin: a study of adult education / by Michael Newman. — London; Boston: Allen & Unwin, 1979. x, 249 p.; 23 cm. 1. Adult education — Great Britain. I. T.
LC5256.G7 N46    374.9/41    *LC* 78-40740    *ISBN* 0043740022

**Distance education: international perspectives / edited by David**    **4.10986**
**Sewart, Desmond Keegan, and Börje Holmberg.**
London: Croom Helm; New York: St. Martin's Press, 1983. xiii, 445 p.: ill.; 23 cm. 1. Distance education — Addresses, essays, lectures. I. Sewart, David. II. Keegan, Desmond. III. Holmberg, Börje.
LC5800.D57 1983    371.3 19    *LC* 83-4973    *ISBN* 0312213190

**Morrison, Theodore, 1901-.**    **4.10987**
Chautauqua: a center for education, religion, and the arts in America / Theodore Morrison; drawings by Jane E. Nelson. — Chicago: University of Chicago Press, 1974. viii, 351 p.: ill.; 21 x 22 cm. Includes index. 1. Chautauqua Institution. I. T.
LC6301.C5 M67    974.7/95    *LC* 74-75614    *ISBN* 0226540626

---

# LD–LG INDIVIDUAL INSTITUTIONS, A–Z

---

# LD United States

**Pentony, DeVere Edwin, 1924-.**    • **4.10988**
Unfinished rebellions / [by] DeVere Pentony, Robert Smith [and] Richard Axen. — [1st ed.] San Francisco: Jossey-Bass, 1971. xiv, 315 p.; 24 cm. (The

Jossey-Bass series in higher education) 1. San Francisco State College. 2. College students — California — San Francisco — Political activity. 3. College teachers — California — San Francisco — Political activity. I. Smith, Robert, 1916- joint author. II. Axen, Richard, joint author. III. T.
LD729.C975 P4    378.1/98/1    *LC* 72-148658    *ISBN* 0875890954

**McGill, William J. (William James), 1922-.**    **4.10989**
The year of the monkey: revolt on campus, 1968–69 / William J. McGill. — New York: McGraw-Hill, c1982. xii, 297 p., [8] p. of plates: ill.; 24 cm. Includes index. 1. University of California, San Diego. 2. Student strikes — California — San Diego. I. T.
LD729.6.S3 M33 1982    378/.1981/0979498 19    *LC* 82-67    *ISBN* 007044997X

**Storr, Richard J.**    • **4.10990**
Harper's university: the beginnings; a history of the University of Chicago / by Richard J. Storr; drawings by Virgil Burnett. — Chicago: University of Chicago Press [1966] xvi, 411 p.: ill., ports.; 24 cm. 1. Harper, William Rainey, 1856-1906. 2. University of Chicago — History. I. T.
LD924.5.H3 S8    *LC* 66-13890

**Humphrey, David C., 1937-.**    **4.10991**
From King's College to Columbia, 1746–1800 / David C. Humphrey. — New York: Columbia University Press, 1976. x, 413 p.: ill.; 24 cm. Includes index. 1. Columbia University — History. I. T.
LD1249.H85    378.747/1    *LC* 75-41351    *ISBN* 0231039425

**Tobias, Marilyn, 1942-.**    **4.10992**
Old Dartmouth on trial: the transformation of the academic community in nineteenth–century America / Marilyn Tobias. — New York: New York University Press, 1982. xii, 249 p.: ill.; 24 cm. — (New York University series in education and socialization in American history.) Revision of thesis (Ph.D.)— New York University. 1. Dartmouth College. I. T. II. Series.
LD1438.T6 1982    378.742/3 19    *LC* 81-18779    *ISBN* 0814781683

**Synnott, Marcia Graham.**    **4.10993**
The half–opened door: discrimination and admissions at Harvard, Yale, and Princeton, 1900–1970 / Marcia Graham Synnott. — Westport, Conn.: Greenwood Press, 1979. xxi, 310 p.; 25 cm. — (Contributions in American history; 80) Includes index. 1. Harvard University — Admission — History. 2. Yale University — Admission — History. 3. Princeton University — Admission — History. I. T.
LD2126.S9    378.744/4    *LC* 78-66714    *ISBN* 0313206171

**Langer, William L. (William Leonard), 1896-1977.**    **4.10994**
In and out of the ivory tower: the autobiography of William L. Langer. — New York: N. Watson Academic Publications, c1977. x, 268 p.: port; 24 cm. Includes index. 1. Langer, William L. (William Leonard), 1896-1977. 2. Harvard University — Faculty 3. College teachers — Massachusetts — Biography. I. T.
LD2137.L33 1977    378.1/2/0924 B    *LC* 77-20035    *ISBN* 088202177X

**James, Henry, 1879-1947.**    • **4.10995**
Charles W. Eliot, president of Harvard University, 1869–1909, by Henry James ... Boston, New York, Houghton Mifflin Company, 1930. 2 v. fronts., plates, ports., diagr. 23 cm. 1. Eliot, Charles William, 1834-1926. 2. Harvard University. I. T.
LD2148 1869 .J3    *LC* 30-29682

**Morison, Samuel Eliot, 1887-1976.**    • **4.10996**
Three centuries of Harvard, 1636–1936 / by Samuel Eliot Morison. — Cambridge, Mass.: Harvard Univ. Press, 1936. viii, 512 p.: maps. 1. Harvard University — History I. T.
LD2151. M65    378.744    *LC* 36-14160

**Hawkins, Hugh.**    • **4.10997**
Pioneer: a history of the Johns Hopkins University, 1874–1899. — Ithaca, N.Y.: Cornell University Press, [1960] xiv, 368 p.: port.; 24 cm. 1. Johns Hopkins University — History. I. T.
LD2628.3.H3    *LC* 61-245

**Warch, Richard, 1939-.**    **4.10998**
School of the prophets: Yale College, 1701–1740. New Haven, Yale University Press, 1973. xii, 339 p. illus. 25 cm. (Yale scene. University series. 2) 1. Yale University — History. I. T. II. Series.
LD6335.W34    378.746/8    *LC* 73-77169    *ISBN* 0300016050

**Pierson, George Wilson, 1904-.**    • **4.10999**
Yale College, an educational history, 1871–1921. New Haven, Yale University Press, 1952. xv, 773 p. ports. 24 cm. (His Yale: college and university, 1871-1937, v. 1) 1. Yale University — History. I. T.
LD6337.P5    378.744    *LC* 52-5356

**Pierson, George Wilson, 1904-.**                                    • **4.11000**
Yale: the University College, 1921–1937. — New Haven: Yale University Press, 1955. xviii, 740 p.: ill., ports., map; 24 cm. (His Yale: college and university, 1871-1937, v. 2) 1. Yale University — History. I. T.
LD6337.P52        378.746        *LC* 55-8709

**Clark, Burton R.**                                    • **4.11001**
The open door college: a case study. — New York: McGraw-Hill, 1960. 207 p.: illus.; 22 cm. — (The Carnegie series in American education) 1. San Jose Junior College, San Jose, Calif. 2. Junior colleges — United States — Case studies. I. T.
LD6501.S394 C55        378.79474        *LC* 59-14440

**Green, Elizabeth Alden, 1908-.**                                    **4.11002**
Mary Lyon and Mount Holyoke: opening the gates / Elizabeth Alden Green. — Hanover, N.H.: University Press of New England, 1979. xvii, 406 p.: ill.; 24 cm. Includes index. 1. Lyon, Mary, 1797-1849. 2. Mount Holyoke College — History. 3. Women — Education — United States — History. 4. College administrators — United States — Biography. I. T.
LD7092.65.L9 G73        378.744/23        *LC* 78-68857        *ISBN* 0874511720

**Holmes, Pauline.**                                    • **4.11003**
A tercentenary history of the Boston Public Latin School, 1635–1935. Westport, Conn.: Greenwood Press [1970] xxiv, 541 p.: ill., facsims., maps, ports.; 23 cm. First published 1935 as v. 25 of the Harvard studies in education. 1. Boston Latin School (Mass.) I. T.
LD7501.B7 L46 1970        373.744/61        *LC* 73-104278        *ISBN* 0837139503

**Mayhew, Katherine Camp.**                                    • **4.11004**
The Dewey School: The laboratory school of the University of Chicago, 1896–1903 / by Katherine Camp Mayhew and Anna Camp Edwards, introd. by John Dewey. — New York: Atherton Press, 1966, c1965. xvi, 489 p.: ports. — (An Atheling book, EP-103) 1. Chicago. University. University Elementary School. 2. Education — Experimental methods I. Edwards, Anna Camp. II. T. III. Title: The laboratory school of the University of Chicago, 1896-1903.
LD7501.C4 C625 1966        *LC* 66-6798

**Dennison, George, 1925-.**                                    • **4.11005**
The lives of children; the story of the First Street School. — New York: Random House, [1969] 308 p.; 22 cm. 1. First Street School. 2. Socially handicapped children — Education I. T.
LD7501.N5 F524        372.9/7471        *LC* 74-85566

## LE–LG Other Countries

**Lanning, John Tate, 1902-.**                                    **4.11006**
The eighteenth–century enlightenment in the University of San Carlos de Guatemala. — Ithaca, N.Y.: Cornell University Press, [1956] xxv, 372 p.: ill., ports., facsims.; 24 cm. 1. Universidad de San Carlos de Guatemala — History. 2. Enlightenment I. T.
LE11.G82 L3        *LC* 56-14315

**Hackett, M. B.**                                    • **4.11007**
The original statutes of Cambridge University; the text and its history, by M. B. Hackett. Cambridge, Cambridge [Eng.] University Press, 1970. xix, 398 p. 24 cm. 1. University of Cambridge. I. Cambridge. University. Constituciones Vniuersitatis Cantebrigiensis. II. T.
LF101.A735        378.425/9        *LC* 69-10217        *ISBN* 0521070767

**Mullinger, James Bass, 1834-1917.**                                    • **4.11008**
The University of Cambridge / by James Bass Mullinger. — Cambridge: University Press, 1873-1919. v. 1. University of Cambridge — History. I. T.
LF109.M82        *LC* 07-15052

**The History of the University of Oxford / general editor, T.H.**        **4.11009**
**Aston.**
Oxford [Oxfordshire]; New York: Oxford University Press, c1984. 1 v. 1. University of Oxford — History — Collected works. I. Aston, T. H. (Trevor Henry)
LF508.H57 1984        378.425/74 19        *LC* 83-17303

**Hemmings, Ray.**                                    **4.11010**
Children's freedom: A. S. Neill and the evolution of the Summerhill idea. — New York: Schocken Books, [1973, c1972] xiii, 218 p.: ill.; 21 cm. 1. Neill, Alexander Sutherland, 1883-1973. 2. Summerhill School. 3. Child rearing I. T.
LF795.L692953 H39        370.1/092/4        *LC* 72-94295        *ISBN* 0805234845

**Neill, Alexander Sutherland, 1883-1973.**                                    **4.11011**
Neill! Neill! Orange peel! An autobiography, by A. S. Neill. New York, Hart Pub. Co. [1972] 538 p. illus. 24 cm. 1. Neill, Alexander Sutherland, 1883-1973. 2. Summerhill School. I. T.
LF795.L692953 N38        371.2/012/0924        *LC* 76-180998        *ISBN* 0805510427

**Neill, Alexander Sutherland, 1883-1973.**                                    • **4.11012**
Summerhill: a radical approach to child rearing / with a foreword by Erich Fromm. — New York: Hart Pub. Co. [1960] 392 p.; 23 cm. 1. Summerhill School. I. T.
LF795.L692953 N4        372.94264        *LC* 60-7043

## LJ Student Fraternities and Societies

**Baird's manual of American college fraternities.**                                    • **4.11013**
[1st]- ed.; 1879-. Menasha, Wisc. [etc.] G. Banta Co. [etc.] v. ill. 15-24 cm. Supplements accompany some editions. 1. Greek letter societies
LJ31.B2        *LC* 49-4194

**Leemon, Thomas A.**                                    **4.11014**
The rites of passage in a student culture; a study of the dynamics of transition [by] Thomas A. Leemon. — New York: Teachers College Press, Columbia University, [1972] x, 215 p.; 23 cm. — (Anthropology & education series) 1. Greek letter societies 2. Hazing 3. Initiations (into trades, societies, etc.) I. T.
LJ31.L43        378.1/98/55        *LC* 72-81190

## LT Textbooks
(see also: LB3045-3048)

**Arnold, June, 1926- Charles H.**                                    • **4.11015**
History of American schoolbooks / by Charles Carpenter. — Philadelphia: University of Pennsylvania Press, [1963] 322 p.: ill., facsims., port.; 22 cm. 1. Textbooks — United States. I. T. II. Title: American schoolbooks.
LT23.C3 1963        371.320973        *LC* 62-10747

**Nietz, John Alfred, 1888-.**                                    • **4.11016**
Old textbooks: spelling, grammar, reading, arithmetic, geography, American history, civil government, physiology, penmanship, art, music, as taught in the common schools from colonial days to 1900 / John A. Nietz. — Pittsburgh: University of Pittsburgh Press, [1961] vii, 364 p.: ill., facsims., maps, port.; 24 cm. 1. Textbooks — United States — History. I. T.
LT23.N5        371.320973        *LC* 60-13851